41st

EDITION

CAMRA's **GOOD** **BEER** **GUIDE**

2014

Edited by Roger Protz

Project Co-ordinator **Emma Haines**
Assistant Editors **Ione Brown, Katie Hunt, Simon Tuite**
Head of Publishing **Simon Hall**

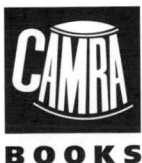

BOOKS

Contents

About the Good Beer Guide   4
It's far more than just a pub guide

Introduction   6
**Campaigning victory steels
the resolve to achieve more
to boost our national drink**

Pubs – Vital Community Hubs   8
Local action can save threatened pubs

CAMRA's Pub of the Year   10
Rochdale pub judged best in Britain

Beer Trends   11
**Back to the future: brewers are
digging deep into the archives to
revive renowned beer styles**

York Pub Crawl   12
**A wealth of history and real ale
options make for an ideal city
pub tour**

CAMRA Beer Festivals   16

It's Better Down the Pub...   20
**...so let's make sure we all use
and enjoy it!**
A word from our sponsor: It's Better
Down the Pub

All About Ale   22
The best beer comes naturally

How beer is brewed   23

Beer Appreciation   26
**Enhance your drinking experience
with this brief guide to beer tasting**

Britain's Classic Beer Styles   28

CAMRA's Beers of the Year   32

The Pubs

ENGLAND   **35**
Bedfordshire   36
Public transport information   **43**
Berkshire   44
Buckinghamshire   51
Cambridgeshire   59
Cheshire   68
Cornwall   78
Cumbria   88
Derbyshire   100
LocAle   **113**
Devon   114
Dorset   132
Durham   141
Essex   152
Gloucestershire & Bristol   167
Hampshire   181
Herefordshire   197
Hertfordshire   201
Isle of Wight   210
Kent   214
Lancashire   234
Leicestershire & Rutland   250
Lincolnshire   260
London index   **275**
Greater London   276
Greater Manchester   316
Merseyside   336
Norfolk   346
Northamptonshire   361
Northumberland   368
Nottinghamshire   374
Oxfordshire   384
Shropshire   394
Somerset   402
Staffordshire   416
Suffolk   428
Surrey   438
Sussex   448
Tyne & Wear   465
Warwickshire   473
West Midlands   480
Wiltshire   496
Worcestershire   505
Yorkshire   513
WALES   **565**
Glamorgan   566
Gwent   578
Mid-Wales   584
North-East Wales   589
North-West Wales   595
West Wales   601
SCOTLAND   **611**
Aberdeen & Grampian   612
Argyll & the Isles   618
Ayrshire & Arran   621
Borders   624
Dumfries & Galloway   627
Edinburgh & The Lothians   630
Greater Glasgow & Clyde Valley   636
Highlands & Western Isles   642
Kingdom of Fife   647
Loch Lomond, Stirling & The Trossachs   650
Northern Isles   653
Tayside   655
NORTHERN IRELAND   **660**
CHANNEL ISLANDS   **663**
ISLE OF MAN   **667**

The Breweries

The Power of One Voice 674
From individual potential... to collective achievement
A word from our sponsor: Society of Independent Brewers

How to use the   676
Breweries section

The breweries   677
Republic of Ireland breweries   889

Closed & future breweries   892

Indexes & Further Information

Places index   894

Beers index   905

Award winning pubs   933
Local CAMRA Pubs of the Year

Readers' recommendations   935

Have your say   936

National Brewery Centre 937

Books for beer lovers   939

Good Beer Guide digital editions   941

Join the Campaign!   944

Special thanks to 150,000 CAMRA members who carried out research for the pub entries; the Campaign's Regional Directors and Area Organisers, who co-ordinated the pub entries; the Campaign's Brewery Liaison Officers and Brewery Liaison Coordinators, who carried out research for and co-ordinated the brewery entries; Paul Moorhouse for assembling the beer tasting notes; Rick Pickup for advising on new breweries; John Duffy for updating Irish breweries information; Michael Slaughter for advising on heritage pubs; Alex Presland for technical support; the publicans, breweries and others who kindly contributed their photographs; and CAMRA's National Executive for their support.

Thanks also to the following at CAMRA head office: Lauren Anderson, Mike Benner, Steven Brooks, Claire Cain, Martin Clemmey, Caroline Clerembeaux, John Cottrell, Neil Cox, Gillian Dale, Catrin Davies, Aaron Dobbing, Robert Ferguson, Nick Forshaw, Gary Fowler, Anita Gibson, Karen Gorden, Sarah Hall, Tony Jerome, Chris Lewis, Jonathan Mail, Jay Norton, Marilyn O'Donoghue, Steve Powell, Gary Ranson, Emily Ryans, Gregory Rycroft, Nicky Shipp, Barnaby Smith, Tom Stainer, Ron Stocks, Claire-Michelle Taverner-Pearson, Neil Walker, Liz Wickham.

Photo credits: [Key: t = top; b = bottom; c=centre; l = left; r = right] p4: Bob Steel; p10(bc): Colin Bowling; p12-15: Cath Harries; p16: Alison Cross; p17: Ascot Racecourse; p19: Richard Brooks; p20: Punch Taverns; p22: Cath Harries; p23: beergenie.co.uk; p24(t) Tom Stainer; p24(b) beergenie.co.uk; p25(tl) Tom Stainer; p25(tr) Valentyn Volkov/shutterstock; p25(bl) photowind/shutterstock; p25(br) Tom Stainer; p26: Cath Harries; p31: Walter de Cantelupe; p34: Cath Harries; p671: Cath Harries; p674: Barclay Imaging 2013; p675: Jon Cartwright; p937-938: National Brewery Centre

Maps & illustrations: Cover illustrations (front & back), illustration p3: © Claire Rollet; map p15, illustration p25: Mark Walker, MW Digital Graphics; illustration p27: Stephen Bere; Pubs section maps: David and Morag Perrot, PerroCarto.

Production: Cover design: Hannah Moore; colour pages design: Keith Holmes, Thames Street Studio; database, typesetting and indexes: AMA Dataset; design assistance: Dale Tomlinson.

Printed and bound in the UK by William Clowes, Beccles, Suffolk.

Type set in Stag and Dax.

Published by the Campaign for Real Ale Ltd, 230 Hatfield Road, St Albans, Herts, AL1 4LW. www.camra.org.uk

© Campaign for Real Ale 2013/2014.
All rights reserved. ISBN 978-1-85249-312-7

All of the papers used in this book are recyclable and made from wood grown in managed, sustainable forests. They are manufactured at mills certified to ISO 14001 and/or EMAS.

About the Good Beer Guide
It's far more than just a pub guide
The Good Beer Guide is the lodestar pointing you to breweries, their ales and the essential outlets in towns and rural areas where you can enjoy them

For 41 years, the *Good Beer Guide* has celebrated two great British institutions: the pub and cask-conditioned real ale – cornerstones of our communities and our way of life. It's far more than a pub guide. Pubs are the central core, the essential outlets for real ale, but the *Good Beer Guide* has always walked tall on two feet, with its Breweries section complementing the pub listings by detailing all the producers of cask beer, and their ales.

Comprehensive Breweries section
As well as listing some 4,500 of the finest outlets for real ale, the *Good Beer Guide* is also a comprehensive listing of all British and Irish breweries and their core beers. Breweries are monitored on a regular basis, and each brewery is visited by CAMRA members, who speak to the brewer and check on the beers being produced before reporting to the Guide. The information is also available on a database for members running beer festivals or producing local guides. As soon as a new brewery comes on stream, a liaison officer will be appointed to make sure the breweries section of the Guide is updated every year and readers are aware of the increased choice available.

Democratically selected entries
The way in which pubs are chosen is equally meticulous and unique. The entire 150,000-plus membership of CAMRA is involved and those members who cannot be active or attend regular meetings are invited to recommend pubs via email or branch websites. Branch areas are broken down into regions so pubs can be monitored regularly. The quality of beer in each pub is checked using a meticulous 'beer scoring' system. Special branch meetings are convened once a year where members vote on the final selection for the Guide.

Regular inspections
The entries in most pub guides are chosen either by small editorial teams or by members of the public, whose recommendations are not necessarily checked. On the other hand, every pub that appears in this Guide has been visited regularly, often weekly, by CAMRA members. We offer full entries, with no unchecked 'lucky dip' sections of pubs sent in at random. Readers' recommendations for the Guide are passed to the local branch, who take this feedback on board during their surveying.

It's not only about quality beer
The key driving force of the *Good Beer Guide* – beer quality – has not changed over 41 years.

Land of Liberty, Peace & Plenty, Heronsgate, Hertfordshire

The Guide takes account of the history and architecture of pubs and such important aspects as food, family and disabled facilities, gardens, special events such as mini-beer festivals, and even the standard of the toilets. But it's always been our belief that if a publican looks after the real ales in the cellar then the care and attention paid to the rest of the pub, and the quality of the other facilities, will be of an equally high standard.

CAMRA volunteers are called on to be minor essayists, describing in detail all aspects of the pubs they choose. We know, from the feedback we receive, that users of the Guide need full information about pubs before embarking on journeys to visit them.

Town & country pubs

In addition, users want a good spread of pubs. Unlike some guides that concentrate on rural pubs, we recognise that most people live in towns and cities and expect a good selection of pubs in those areas. But we don't neglect suburban and country pubs: on the contrary, CAMRA campaigns for the survival of rural pubs that are often vital hubs of their isolated communities.

We are at pains to ensure that all areas of the country are covered. Each county or region has an allocation of pubs based on a scientific calculation of population, number of licensed premises and the level of 'tourist penetration'. As a result, the Guide's reach is unparalleled.

Still proudly independent

Unlike many of our competitors, **all of our pub entries are free**. CAMRA is a proudly independent organisation and we do not charge pub owners. There are no hidden costs of appearing in the *Good Beer Guide*. CAMRA is a broad church and the Guide reflects that by choosing pubs across a wide spectrum that will appeal to people from all walks of life, regardless of income and background.

Keeping up to date

The Campaign has more than 200 branches. Each branch surveys the pubs in its area and monitors not only the quality of the cask beer in each one but also watches for change of ownership or management that could affect the range of ale on offer and overall quality. The information gathered by members is compiled on a county-by-county basis by regional organisers and forwarded electronically to the Guide's editorial team, where entries are edited on screen and stored in a database. Together with the breweries database, CAMRA and the Guide share an unrivalled electronic storehouse of information about pubs and breweries.

There is a cynical saying in the publishing world that 'all guide books are out of date as soon as they appear'. That's not the case with the *Good Beer Guide*. Thanks to modern technology, the Guide is checked and re-checked many times before publication. Proofs are corrected at regional and branch level, and both pubs and breweries can be amended or even deleted at a late date. Checking doesn't stop there: both CAMRA's national website and its monthly newspaper *What's Brewing* publish regular information and updates about the Guide, including pubs that have closed or where beer quality has declined: yet another good reason for being a member of the Campaign.

Additional resources

There are limits to the size of the *Good Beer Guide*. We believe – thanks to our members' efforts and the recommendations sent in by readers – that we offer a choice of the very best pubs throughout the country. But the Guide is complemented by other resources, including local pub guides produced by CAMRA branches and available at beer festivals, local outlets and **www.camra.org.uk/books**, and the online **www.whatpub.com** – CAMRA's official guide to all known real ale outlets in the country.

Reader updates & feedback

CAMPAIGN FOR REAL ALE

- All CAMRA members can vote for the quality of beer in pubs by using the National Beer Scoring Scheme. The scheme uses a 0–5 scale that can be submitted online. For more information go to **www.beer-scoring.org.uk**.
- You can keep you copy of the Guide up to date by visiting the *Good Beer Guide* area of the CAMRA website: **www.camra.org.uk/gbg**. Click on 'Updates to GBG 2014' where you will find information about changes to pubs and breweries.
- The Guide is keen to hear from readers. If you wish to recommend a pub or feel that one you have visited fell below expectations, then we would like to know. Please use the Readers' Recommendations and Have Your Say forms at the back of the book or contact the editor at **camragbgeditor@camra.org.uk**.

Introduction

Campaigning victory steels the resolve to achieve more to boost our national drink

A sensational victory was achieved by beer drinkers in 2013 – one that will have a far-reaching impact on both the brewing industry and the country's hard-pressed pubs. It was a victory that proved that beer drinkers and pubgoers are a force to be reckoned with when they stand united.

The change was signalled in March when the Chancellor of the Exchequer, George Osborne, announced in his annual budget that he was reducing the duty on a pint of beer by a penny. At the same time, he scrapped the Beer Duty Escalator that had automatically increased beer duty every year in the budget since 2008.

If a penny off a pint seems – pardon the pun – small beer, it was a step in the right direction after years of seemingly inexorable price rises. And the axing of the Beer Duty Escalator has long-term implications for the health of brewing and pub-running. If the Escalator had not been axed in March 2013, the price of a pint would have risen by around 10p.

These two measures came about because Chancellor Osborne was put under enormous pressure by beer drinkers and the brewing industry. Marston's Wychwood brewery started the ball rolling by launching an industry backed e-petition to demand that the Escalator be scrapped. If 100,000 signatures can be secured for a petition, then a parliamentary debate is automatically triggered. Few petitions reach the required number, but with CAMRA's support the petition was successful and a four-hour parliamentary debate followed.

The petition was backed by a mass lobby of Parliament, supported by publicans and brewers from all parts of the country. The lobby was followed by a rally addressed by publicans, MPs – including Andrew Griffiths and Greg Mulholland, chairmen respectively of the Parliamentary Beer Group and Parliamentary Save the Pub Group – and CAMRA's national chairman Colin Valentine and chief executive Mike Benner. During the ensuing parliamentary debate, Minister of State for Business & Enterprise Sajid Javid provided his support. The message had clearly got through to the higher echelons of government.

The cuts in duty, however small, are welcome news for publicans and drinkers. But CAMRA is not resting on its laurels. Twenty-six pubs close every week and the *Good Beer Guide* is crucially aware of the fact that when pubs close outlets for cask beer will die with them. It's a simple equation: no pub = no real ale.

It's vital that pressure is maintained on the Government to support an industry – brewing and pub retailing – that gives employment to around one million people as well as pleasure to consumers. CAMRA will urge the chancellor to freeze duty in the 2014 budget and – to underline this – the Guide urges its readers to lobby their MPs to back the call for a duty freeze.

This edition of the Guide is devoted to the pub, a great British institution at the heart of communities in towns, cities and rural areas. When a pub is closed down, in many cases the communities they served wither and die. But help is at hand and in the following pages we report on community action in different parts of the country to rescue closed pubs.

The campaign to scrap the Beer Duty Escalator was taken to the heart of parliament

Two beers, my friend will pay: MPs Andrew Griffiths (left) and Greg Mulholland toast the end of the Beer Duty Escalator

CAMRA is throwing its considerable weight, with its 150,000 members, behind the pub. The aim is to get more people to use their locals on a regular basis. Busy pubs will not become closed pubs. To this end, the Campaign organises Community Pubs Month every April when local CAMRA branches are active in encouraging beer lovers to visit their locals.

One way to increase pub-going is to encourage locals to organise charity events. Research by CAMRA and PubAid shows that when pubs run charity events they draw in more people from their communities. Around 85 per cent of British pubs regularly stage charity events and in the year 2012–13, £100 million was raised for good causes. One splendid example is the Ship Victory in Chester that raised £105,000 for the breast care unit at the local hospital. Again, CAMRA has promotional packs available with help and advice on running charity events: **www.communitypubscampaign.org.uk/great-charity-pubs**.

CAMRA has been active on another front: the urgent need for reform of the way in which national pub companies – who own half the country's pubs – conduct their affairs. An announcement was due to be made in the autumn of 2013 by Business Secretary Vince Cable in response to demands from CAMRA and trade bodies that have called for a Fair Deal for the Local. One reason why pubs fail is because of the crippling burden of rents imposed on tenants and lessees by the pubcos. Dr Cable has been urged to bring in a Statutory Code for the pubcos, as self-regulation has all too clearly failed.

The Fair Deal for the Local campaign has called for independent arbitration to fix fair rents for licensees in order that tenants of national pubcos should not be worse off than publicans who run free trade pubs. There should also be a provision for licensees running national pub company outlets to pay a 'free of tie' rent that would enable them to source beers from other suppliers as well as the pub companies. This would allow publicans to offer a wider range of guest beers that will attract more customers.

In spite of all the problems besetting pubs, the beer outlook could not be more promising. Real ale continues to out-perform other types of beer and is the only area of growth in a sector that, overall, continues to decline. As the Guide's Breweries section shows, many new breweries have opened in the past year (a remarkable and record-breaking 187) and Britain can boast both that it has the biggest number of breweries since the 1930s and, per head of population, has more breweries than any other country on the planet.

At long last, beer is getting the promotion it deserves. CAMRA has given its support to a generic media campaign with the theme Let There Be Beer. Television commercials, funded by some of the country's biggest brewers, will run for the next three years. Shepherd Neame has joined Greene King and Wells & Young's in advertising real ale on television. But the success of good beer and good pubs requires constant vigilance. The Guide urges all its readers to throw their weight behind the campaigns to save and boost the Great British Pub, the key outlet for Great British Beer.

Cheers!

CAMRA's chief executive Mike Benner speaking at a central London rally to save the pub

CAMRA members throughout the country joined a mass lobby of parliament to scrap the Beer Duty Escalator. National chairman Colin Valentine is on the far left

Pubs – Vital Community Hubs
Local action can save threatened pubs

The British pub has a vital role to play in holding local communities together. In order to meet modern demands, many pubs offer not only good beer but also stage regular festivals, charity events and live entertainment. And when a pub is threatened with closure beer lovers can work together – using new legislation – to save it, often forming co-operatives to ensure local control.

Real beer and live music provide recipe for ongoing success

Ivy House, Nunhead, South London

When Tessa Blunden, a young solicitor, heard in autumn 2013 that pub giant Enterprise Inns planned to close the Ivy House and sell it to a property developer she was outraged and found that many other customers shared her anger. They banded together and used new government legislation to help save the pub. The Ivy House was due to re-open in late summer 2013 and it will once again become a vibrant part of the local community.

The pub has a large stage in the main room where the likes of Elvis Costello, Joe Beck, Dr Feelgood and Ian Dury once strutted their stuff and it will once more offer 'pub rock' to drinkers as well as real ale and good pub food.

Enterprise Inns gave its tenants five days' notice and said the property developer would turn it into flats. The local CAMRA branch immediately sprang in to action and began moves to get the Ivy House listed. Blunden used her skills as a lawyer specialising in real estate litigation to block the sale of the pub.

Blunden set up a steering group dedicated to saving the Ivy House and recruited other local people with specialist skills. They included an expert in land management and a town planner with knowledge of historic buildings.

The steering group was aided by the new Localism Act, introduced in November 2011 and designed to hand more power from central government to local authorities and local people. The act has a provision known as the Community Right to Bid that enables groups to list a building as 'an asset of community value'.

CAMRA had already won a Grade-II listing for the Ivy House from English Heritage. Using the Localism Act, the steering group then won a further listing from the local authority, the London Borough of Southwark, declaring the pub to be a community asset.

Enterprise Inns' plans to sell the pub were blocked. But the steering group now faced the daunting task of raising £810,000 to buy the pub, with more cash needed to refurbish the building and hire staff. The steering group was turned into the Ivy House Community Pub Ltd and the money was raised with a loan of £550,000 from the Architectural Heritage Fund, plus a grant of £450,000 from the Social Investment Business Group.

A further £100,000 was needed to finish the work on the pub. To find this additional investment, the limited company became a co-operative and called on all those who supported the Ivy House to become shareholders. The share offer closed on 31 May 2013 and the enthusiasm for the pub was measured by the fact that £144,500 was raised.

The pub will become a free house and will sell beers from local brewers.

Landlady passes the baton to her regulars

Fox & Goose, Hebden Bridge, West Yorkshire

When Julia Warren, publican at the Fox & Goose, was forced to retire on health grounds, she was determined the pub wouldn't be sold to a national pub company. The Fox & Goose has a long history as an ale house and Julia was keen to maintain the tradition of supplying beer from local breweries.

The pub became a legal ale house in the 17th century and flourished in modern times, winning several awards from the local branch of CAMRA, including its Pub of the Year in 2006.

When Julia announced her retirement, 100 local people packed in to the pub in January 2013 to discuss how to save it. The locals immediately offered to raise £8,200 towards buying the pub. A steering group, Friends of the Fox & Goose, was

Ivy House, Nunhead, South London

Locals at the Fox & Goose, Hebden Bridge, discuss how to buy it from retiring landlady

set up and they sought advice from the Plunkett Foundation, which advises people on how to save such local assets as village shops. Dave Hollings of Co-operative & Mutual Solutions also came to give his advice and experience. He has helped create several co-ops, including the first-ever pub to be owned and run by locals, the Old Crown at Hesket Newmarket in Cumbria.

The major breakthrough came when Calderdale Council listed the Fox & Goose as a community asset under the new Localism Act. This gave the steering group the right to make the first bid for the pub, with six months to raise the necessary money. It turned itself into the Fox & Goose (Hebden Bridge) Ltd, a co-operative or, in legal terms, an Industrial and Provident Society.

A share offer was launched on 1 May 2013 with the aim of raising £130,000. The share offer was due to close at the end of July. If successful, the co-op will own the building, not the business, and it will have to re-launch the pub.

Councillor Dave Young, who chairs Fox & Goose Ltd, said when the share offer was launched: 'The co-op is no longer a dream – it's a reality and an exciting opportunity. Friends of the Fox believe this is a viable proposition to save a well-loved local and retain it for the community.'

Last village survivor gains celebrity support

Bull, Great Milton, Oxfordshire

One pub that has been saved and re-opened as a co-operative is the Bull in the village of Great Milton in Oxfordshire. It was put up for

sale by Greene King in November 2012 and this prompted swift action by the 300 residents.

They were determined to save the Bull as they had lost three other pubs in the village, the Bell, the King's Head and the Red Lion. The Bull was the only remaining pub for the community. It's a Grade II-listed, thatched building, overlooking the village green. It dates from 1684, and has beams, a large inglenook and such traditional pub games as darts, cribbage and Aunt Sally. In 1918 it became part of the Wallingford Brewery pub estate and passed in 1947 to Morrells of Oxford, which was taken over by Greene King in 2002.

The residents include celebrity chef Raymond Blanc, whose Michelin-starred restaurant Le Manoir aux Quat' Saisons is based in Great Milton. Blanc is from northern France, likes British beer and pubs, and has a beer menu in his restaurant.

The Bull's loyal customers formed the Great Milton Community Pub Ltd – set up as an Industrial and Provident Society that received both a grant and support from the Plunkett Society.

£250,000 was raised – including a donation from Raymond Blanc – and the sale was completed in April 2013, just 145 days after Greene King had put it on the market.

Steve Harrod, the chairman of the co-operative, who ironically lives in the former Red Lion, said: 'Our motivation is to run the Bull as a traditional village pub with quality food. It will be retained as a community asset for future generations. It's also popular with guests at Le Manoir, who want a pint in a nice pub environment.'

The Bull sells cask beers from the local Vale Brewery in Brill.

The Bull, Great Milton, gained enormous local support which has helped save it

---

How to save your local

If your pub is threatened with closure, contact your local CAMRA branch: **www.camra.org.uk/branches**. Set up an action or steering group and speak to your local council and get them to list the pub as a community asset.

For full details of how to use the Localism Act, go to **www.gov.uk** and follow the link to 'A Plain English Guide to the Localism Act'.

Seek help, advice and possible funding from The Plunkett Foundation: **www.plunkett.co.uk**, Co-operative & Mutual Solutions: **www.cms.coop**, and Pub is the Hub: **www.pubisthehub.org.uk**.

CAMRA's Pub of the Year

Rochdale pub judged best in Britain

A pub with strong connections to the birth of the 19th-century co-operative movement was crowned CAMRA National Pub of the Year in 2013.

The Baum in Toad Lane, Rochdale, Greater Manchester (see p330), stands next door to the Pioneers Museum, which commemorates the work of industrial workers in 1844 who opened the first co-op store in the town. The Baum – pronounced 'borm' as in warm – has been a pub for only 30 years. It was converted from Morris's Hardware Store in the 1980s.

CAMRA's National Pub of the Year competition recognises all the criteria that make a great pub: atmosphere, decor, welcome, service, value for money, customer mix and – most importantly – the quality of the beer. The Baum has eight handpumps, with one reserved for cider, and specialises in serving beers from local microbreweries. Excellent food includes vegetarian dishes, with a tapas menu at weekends. There's an upstairs dining room and a large garden, conservatory and pétanque pitch.

Simon Crompton started work in the Baum in 1993 and became manager a year later. In 2005, Simon and his wife Heidi bought the pub just two days after the birth of their first child. Heidi Crompton said: 'We were ecstatic to hear that we'd been voted CAMRA's National Pub of the Year. We are very proud of the team that has played an important role in the Baum's success and it's a testament to their hard work that consumers have recognised our pub with this prestigious award.

'We are a family-run pub with our values influencing every aspect of the business. We are dedicated to the "buy local, shop local" initiative, always willing to support independent businesses.'

> CAMRA's National Pub of the Year competition analyses all the criteria that make up a good pub. The competition is judged by CAMRA's 150,000-plus members. Each branch selects its top pub. The branch winners are entered into 16 regional competitions, with the regional winners battling it out to reach the final stages of the competition. Look out for the ♥ symbol against pub entries in the Guide and see 'Award winning pubs' on pages 933-934 for the winning branch pubs.

The three other finalists in the 2013 competition were:

Bridge End Inn, Ruabon, North-East Wales (see p594)
Winner of the National Pub of the Year competition in 2012 the Bridge End Inn was the first Welsh winner of the award. It was taken over by the McGivern family in 2009 and sells five real ales.

Conqueror Alehouse, Ramsgate, Kent (see p228)
The town's smallest free house, where ale and cider are served straight from casks. It offers a quiet, music- and TV-free atmosphere in which to enjoy a pint or two.

Tom Cobley Tavern, Spreyton, Devon (see p128)
National Pub of the Year winner in 2006, it sells 14 different cask beers every week, plus 20 ciders in a pub that's 'part of community life'.

Beer Trends
Back to the future: brewers are digging deep into the archives to revive renowned beer styles

Innovation and history may seem odd bedfellows but brewers have dug deep into ancient recipe books to recreate great beer styles from the past – and in some cases they have given the beers a modern twist.

The buzz beer of the moment is India Pale Ale. It was a style developed in the 19th century for export from England to India and had only a brief life span. But brewers in Britain, the U.S., Australia, New Zealand and even Belgium and France have rekindled interest in IPA.

The Breweries section of the Guide has no shortage of modern interpretations of IPA – but what did the original beers taste like? The answer has come from Shepherd Neame, England's oldest brewery which traces its history back to 1698. Its new Classic Collection is the result of code-cracking that would bring applause from veterans of Bletchley Park in World War Two.

Brewer Stewart Main and company archivist John Owen discovered some old brewers' logs from the 19th century, with recipes written in code to prevent rival breweries copying them. Following months of patient work, Main and Owen broke the code and were able to present a series of recipes that enabled the brewery to launch its collection in cask, as well as stronger bottled versions. Along with India Pale Ale, Shepherd Neame has also produced Double Stout, Brilliant Ale, Mild and Porter.

India Pale Ale was brewed with pale malt and two classic English hops: Fuggles and East Kent Goldings. The hops were added three times during the copper boil to extract the maximum of aroma and bitterness. The beer enables drinkers to appreciate what the British 'Raj' drank when supplies reached Bombay and Calcutta in Victorian times. It has a rich juicy and biscuit malt character, with tart orange and lemon fruit from the hops along with a deep bitter note.

The beer was first brewed in 1870 and was preceded by several decades by the brewery's Brilliant Ale. Discovering the recipe came as a surprise, as pale ale was in its infancy in the early 19th century and was thought to be the reserve of Burton upon Trent. But in the 1820s Shepherd Neame brewed a beer with just pale malt and Goldings, with a honey malt and fruity hop character. The recreated version replaces Goldings with American Cascade hops that give a pronounced citrus kick to the beer.

Fuller's in West London has also been delving deep into old recipe books for its Past Masters series. The beers in the series include XX Strong Ale from 1891, Double Stout from 1893 and Old Burton Extra from 1931. They are available only in bottle-conditioned form but the Old Burton serves to remind us that Burton Ale, now largely forgotten, was once a brewing phenomenon, produced not only in its town of origin but in just about every brewery in the country. The point is emphasised by the fact that Young's Winter Warmer started life as the London brewery's version of Burton.

Burton Bridge Brewery offers its Bridge Bitter as a true local version of the style, while at the neighbouring Tower Brewery John Mills has two: Salt's Burton Ale, based on a recipe from one of the long-gone Burton brewers, and Gone for a Burton, with a shattered red triangle logo that is a sad reflection on the demise of mighty Bass.

Scottish brewing also has a foot in the camps of old and new. Black Isle with Oatmeal Stout and Cairngorm's Black Gold recall the hey-day of distinctive dark beers in Scotland while Highland Brewery has revived the fortunes of Mild ale with Dark Munro. Stewart Brewing at Loanhead pays homage to a great Scottish style with its malty 80/- and Fyne Ales, based near Loch Fyne in Argyll won the Champion Beer of Scotland award in 2013 for its golden ale Jarl.

Several breweries are producing what they call 'craft keg'. They should not be confused with the dreadful keg beers of the 1970s. In many cases they are thoughtfully produced beers and meet a demand from bars that can't handle cask ale. But as they are filtered and served by applied gas pressure, they are not included in this Guide.

York Pub Crawl
A wealth of history and real ale options make for an ideal city pub tour

Situated at the point where the East Coast Main Line from London to Edinburgh meets the Transpennine line from Manchester and Liverpool to Hull and Scarborough, the best way to reach York is by rail. And once there you need merely to step off the train and into the pub – what better way is there to start any city break!

York has a long history of welcoming visitors. The Romans founded the city as Eboracum, and the Saxons knew it as Eoforwic. Invading Vikings named the city Jorvik and made it their seat of power in Northumbria. The city now pays tribute to its Viking history with the annual week-long Jorvik festival in February which culminates in the burning of a Viking longship.

The large central bar at the York Tap

The York Tap welcomes visitors to the city

Modern-day visitors tend to arrive by train, rather than longship, but there's still a great deal to see. York has 12 pubs in this year's *Good Beer Guide* (see pages 536-537), and all are worth a visit, but few are as convenient for the rail traveller as our first port of call.

1 The **York Tap**, situated in the station, opened in 2011 and has won praise from both beer drinkers and lovers of architecture. The original bar closed after World War Two and for many years it was a model railway museum. It has been transformed by the Pivní Group, which also runs the Euston and Sheffield station taps as well as another pub in York. *Pivní* is the Czech word for bar and all the taps have a close relationship with the Czech brewer Bernard, whose pale and dark lagers are available on draught.

The York Tap, with its restored Edwardian design, is breathtaking. It's dominated by a large circular bar with a central gantry and has a marble floor, large windows that give views to left and right of the city walls and the station platforms, and comfortable leather chairs and chesterfields. There are many Art Nouveau touches, including lampshades and an impressive stained-glass cupola in the ceiling. The bar groans under the weight of no fewer than 20 pumps that dispense a range of Yorkshire brews, including Rooster's, Tapped Brew Co and Wold Top, along with Thornbridge Jaipur IPA from further south in Derbyshire. The Tap won the prestigious title of Best Cask Beer Pub in the 2012 awards from the trade paper the *Publican's Morning Advertiser*.

A quick saunter round the city walls ends in one of York's most historic areas, Micklegate, entered through the ancient entrance known as Micklegate Bar. The area is now a beer oasis, dominated by bars aimed at a younger crowd.

2 **Brigantes Bar & Brasserie** at 114 Micklegate bucks the trend, offering a fine range of cask beers in a modern and stylish setting that has a strong Belgian feel, with bare wooden floors, settles and wooden tables. The Low Countries character is underscored by a large

Brigantes Bar & Brasserie has a Belgian feel

range of Belgian beers, with further imports from Germany and the U.S.. The bar is split-level, with a small serving area at the front and a back room with walls decorated with brewery memorabilia.

Brigantes opened eight years ago and is run by the Market Town Taverns group. As the York Brewery is just behind Brigantes, expect to see its beers on the bar. Alongside them you will find Black Sheep Best Bitter, Taylor Landlord and beers from Great Heck.

Brigantes' bottled beers

The success of Brigantes has allowed Market Town to add a shop next door that has been turned into an area for serious dining. The food is excellent, ranging from full meals to sandwiches, paninis and light snacks. Don't be fooled by the modern feel of the place: it's a listed Georgian building, with a fine function room upstairs, and it was the birthplace of Joseph Aloysius Hansom, inventor of the Hansom cab.

York Brewery, with its Tap Room and visitor centre, at 12 Toft Green, is a minute's walk from Brigantes. The brewery dates from 1996 and was the first new brewery opened within the city walls for 40 years – and they take the status of the walls seriously here: you're either Within the Walls or Outside. The brewery is based in a building that used to be the city morgue: no jokes, please, about it being a good place for a stiff drink.

The brewery was taken over in 2008 by Mitchells of Lancaster, which closed its own brewery in 1999 to concentrate on its hotels and pubs on the other side of the Pennines but then had an itch to get back in to brewing. It hasn't done York Brewery any harm as it has added 52 Mitchell's pubs to its impressive total of 490 outlets supplied direct or via distributors.

Visitors can tour the compact brewery with its 20-barrel plant that includes an additional fermenting vessel – the installation of which required walls to be knocked down and Brigantes' kitchen to be moved. A clamber up narrow stairs leads into the surprisingly spacious Brewery Tap Room, with tables fashioned from wooden beer casks

and decorated with brewery memorabilia and a collection of beer books. The bar serves the three regular brewery beers, Guzzler, Yorkshire Terrier and Centurion's Ghost, as well as monthly specials. Prices are keen: Guzzler, for example, costs £2.56 a pint and all beers are less than £3. You can become a member for £3 a year and get a further 10% reduction on beer and items from the brewery shop.

A short walk back along Micklegate and over the River Ouse will take you to the heart of historic York, dominated by the Minster, one of the finest Gothic buildings in Europe, and certainly worth the detour if you have time, if only for the amazing views of York afforded by the climb to the top of the 230-foot tower.

The **Old White Swan**, 80 Goodramgate, is in the heart of the city, just a short saunter from the Minster. The inn is nicknamed the Mucky Duck and is a tribute to owners Nicholson's Inns, who have restored its glory from a sad period as a sports bar with limited beer. It dates from the 16th century and, not surprisingly, is rich in history: highwayman Dick Turpin was executed here while Guy Fawkes – who cynics say was the last man to enter parliament with honest intentions – was born nearby.

The Old White Swan, known as the Mucky Duck

The inn is built round a courtyard and has three heavily beamed bars with flagstones, settles, chesterfields, bare brick walls and an impressive inglenook in one room: watch out for the low beams as you enter the Stagecoach Bar, which has a vast array of pump clips from the many cask ales served over the years. The inn has a well that suggests it brewed its own ale centuries ago. There's a house beer, Nicholson's Pale Ale, along with offerings from Downton, Titanic and York and a rare sighting of John Smith's in cask.

The **Snickleway Inn** at 47 Goodramgate offers more history, and John Smith's Cask, just a few yards away. It has had many

The Snickleway Inn is named for York's snickets

names over the years and the lettering Anglers Arms above the bar indicates one of them: the pub is still called the Anglers by regulars. The side and back rooms of the pub have low ceilings but the front bar has a high one: it was once a jetty over the narrow road in medieval times when it was inadvisable to pass by in the early morning as chamber pots were unloaded.

The inn was previously known as the House of Tudor and during the Cromwell Revolution it was used as a Royalist outpost during the Siege of York in 1644. There's an impressive fireplace in the back room, which has bare brick walls. The Snickleway, which takes its current name from York's narrow passageways known as snickleways or snickets, is reputed to be the most haunted pub in the city. Resident spirits include a cat called Shamus and a young girl who was knocked down by a brewery dray.

As well as John Smith's Cask, visitors can enjoy beers from Rooster's, Rudgate and Saltaire and, appropriately, Jenning's Snecklifter. Male drinkers who want to feel seriously depressed can weigh themselves for 20p in the Gent's toilet.

6 **Pivní** at Patrick Pool, next to Newgate Market, takes you straight from Old York to Old Prague. Run by the owners of the York Tap, it's in a breathtaking half-timbered medieval building. Inside, the long bar and narrow seating area, with a tiled floor, and large porcelain founts dispensing Bernard lager, create a deliberate

Czech atmosphere. There's more space and comfortable seating one floor up in a large room with a beamed ceiling and half-timbered walls that stress the building's history. There are views over a verdant courtyard at the back and the ancient market to the front. There's an impressive range of cask beers for such a small pub, including Dark Star, Mallinsons, Tapped and Tyne Bank. There's also a large range of draught beers from many countries, including the Czech Republic and the U.S.. Food can be enjoyed in the upstairs rooms and don't miss the nostalgic old movie posters.

The Maltings

7 The **Maltings**, Tanners Moat, is one of the city's most popular cask beer pubs but it would never have got off the ground if owners Shaun and Maxine Collinge had listened to Shaun's mother, who worked in the pub trade. When Shaun told her he planned to concentrate on real ale, his mother said bluntly: 'You'll fail'. Shaun, Maxine and a legion of admirers have proved her wrong.

The pub is alongside the Lendal Bridge over the Ouse and it was called the Lendal Bridge Inn until 1993 when the Collinges took over. It has a bulging wooden ceiling, half-panelled walls, tiled floors and standing timbers. There's a vast range of old brewery metal advertising panels decorating the rambling bar that will bring a tear to the eye of any nostalgic beer lover mourning the loss of much-loved brews. But don't get carried away and curse, as swearing is banned and will lead to eviction from the premises.

the **Maltings**

7 Real Ales
4 Traditional Ciders
A FINE SELECTION OF
Bottled Beers
ALWAYS AVAILABLE

There's excellent lunchtime food and the beer range may include Black Sheep, Kirkstall, Portobello, Tapped and York but it's a range that changes daily if not hourly. The Maltings is halfway between the Minster and the railway station and is a fine place for a final beer if you're heading for a train.

And if you miss your train, there's always the option of settling in and waiting for another back at the York Tap...

Pivní serves traditional Bernard Czech lager

While in York, there are conducted tours of the city walls, and places to visit include the castle museum (**www.yorkcastlemuseum.org.uk**), the Jorvik Viking Centre, which traces the city's Viking roots (**www.jorvik-viking-centre.co.uk**), and the National Railway Museum, a short walk from the station (**www.nrm.org.uk**): the museum is having funding problems, so check before visiting. And, course, a visit to the spectacular

Minster is obligatory (**www.yorkminster.org**). See **www.visityork.org** for details of all of these and the many other attractions York has to offer.

The beers listed are liable to change. Thanks to Karl Smith and his colleagues in the York branch of CAMRA for their guided tour. Don't miss the branch's award-winning guide *Real Ale in York* (£3.99) from **www.camra.org.uk/books**.

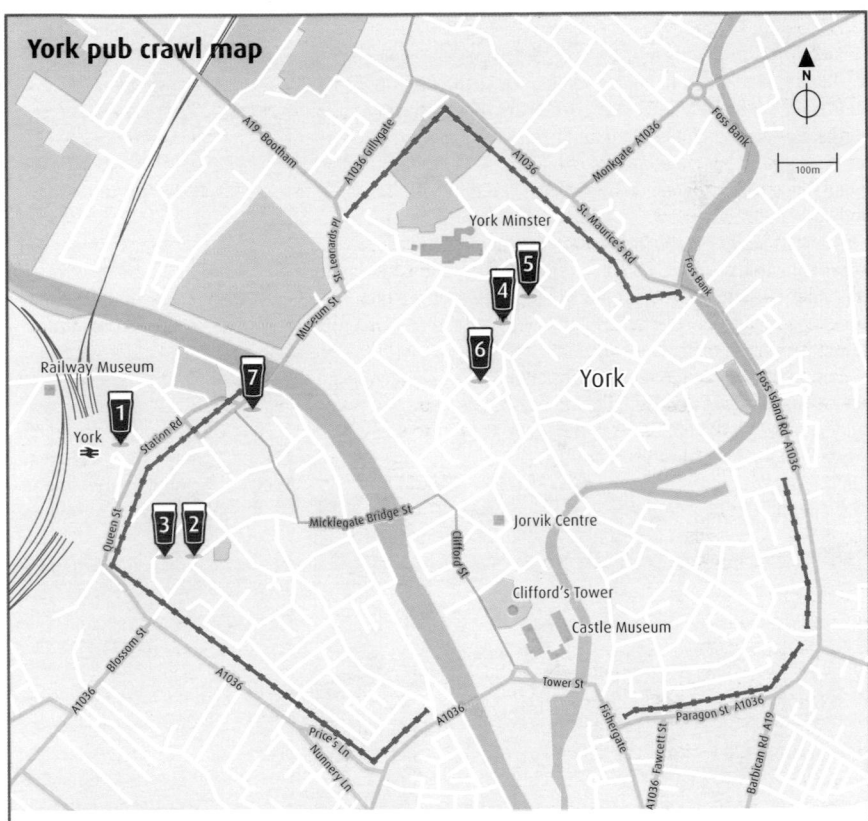

York pub crawl map

Pub information

1. York Tap
York Railway Station, YO1 1AB
❂ 9am-11pm Mon & Tue; 9am-midnight; 10am-11pm Sun
☎ (01904) 659009
⊕ www.yorktap.com

2. Brigantes Bar & Brasserie
114 Micklegate, YO1 6JX
❂ 12-11
☎ (01904) 675355

3. York Brewery & Tap Room
12 Toft Green, YO1 6JT
❂ Brewery tours: 12.30, 2, 3.30 and 5 Mon-Sat

❂ Visitor centre: 11-11; closed Sun
❂ Tap room: 12-8; closed Sun
☎ (01904) 621162
⊕ www.york-brewery.co.uk

4. Old White Swan
80 Goodramgate, YO1 7LF
❂ 10-midnight (1am Fri & Sat)
☎ (01904) 540911

5. Snickleway Inn
47 Goodramgate, YO1 7LS
❂ 12-11 (midnight Thu-Sat)
☎ (01904) 656138
⊕ www.thesnicklewayinn.co.uk

6. Pivní
6 Patrick Pool, YO1 8BB
❂ 11.30-11.30 (11.45 Fri & Sat); 12-11.30 Sun
☎ (01904) 635464
⊕ www.pivni.co.uk

7. Maltings
Tanners Moat, Lendal, YO1 1HU
❂ 11-11; 12-10.30 Sun
☎ (01904) 655387
⊕ www.maltings.co.uk

CAMRA Beer Festivals

THE CAMPAIGN FOR REAL ALE'S BEER FESTIVALS are shop windows for cask beer. They give drinkers throughout the country the opportunity to sample beers from independent brewers rare to particular localities. Some festivals specialise in particular styles, such as winter beers and dark beers or golden beers in summer, and many also offer traditional cider and perry, too.

Festivals can be major national events, such as the Great British in London in August and the National Winter Ales festival in Derby in February. On the other hand, many festivals are town or city events – but, regardless of size, they attempt to present a good range of beer, along with food, music and, where possible, family facilities.

Festivals are run entirely by volunteers and an enormous commitment is required. It's not a question of putting up the beer and then opening the doors to the public. Real ale is a living, breathing product. It needs careful handling and time to 'drop bright' before it's ready to serve.

But there are many aspects to consider: building the gantries and stillages to accommodate the beer casks, arranging for food and security... and then having to dismantle the entire operation as soon as the festival closes.

A volunteer mans the hand pulls at a CAMRA beer festival

Russ Gilbert is the organiser of the Derby beer festival, which has been running for 36 years and is one of the biggest events in the country. More than 250 beers are served, including one from every brewery in Derbyshire, with a City Bar offering beers from all the breweries in Derby itself.

The festival runs for five days in the middle of July. In 2013, as well as the main Assembly Rooms, a marquee was built on the market square: the two venues offered a capacity of 1,400 people. Planning the event starts many months before July. Russ convenes a meeting to set up a festival committee and all the roles – beer and food ordering, getting the equipment to house the beer, and stewarding, for example – are allocated. In total, 250 CAMRA members are involved in running the event, some for a few sessions, others for the entire festival.

Beer, naturally, is the main consideration. 'Drinkers want choice,' Russ says. Lists of beers are drawn up and then divided

JANUARY
Atherton – Bent & Bongs
Beer Bash
Cambridge – Winter
Colchester – Winter
Exeter – Winter
Manchester
Salisbury – Winter

FEBRUARY
National Winter Ales – Derby
Battersea
Chelmsford – Winter
Chesterfield
Darlington – Spring
Dorchester
Dover – White Cliffs Winter
Ely – Winter
Fleetwood
Gosport – Winter
Hucknall
Jersey – Winter
Liverpool
Luton
Pendle
Redditch
Stockton – Ale & Arty
Tewkesbury – Winter
Wigan

MARCH
Bradford
Bristol
Bromley
Burton
Chippenham
Hove – Sussex
Leeds
Leicester
London Drinker
Loughborough
St Neots – Booze on
the Ouse
Thanet
Walsall
Winchester

APRIL
Barnsley
Bexley
Bolton
Bury St Edmunds – East Anglian
Coventry
Doncaster
Farnham
Glenrothes – Kingdom of Fife
Larbert – Falkirk
Maldon

into which ones can be sourced directly and which need to be ordered from wholesalers. Brewers swap beers between them for ease of delivery, which means a particular brewery may have a large range of beers to offer, not just its own brands. Titanic Brewery in Stoke-on-Trent, which delivers to a substantial number of pubs in the Midlands, is one of the main suppliers of beer to the Derby festival. Local beers, on the other hand, will be picked up by CAMRA members in cars and vans.

The beer is set up three days before the festival opens. With such a large number of beers, they have to be arranged on gantries over two storeys. The gantries have to be erected – the work is done by volunteers who are trained professionals and can meet the strict requirements of Health & Safety: a collapsed gantry while the festival is open would be a disaster for both the beer and the volunteers behind the bar.

When the casks are in position they have to be 'tapped and spiled' to allow the beer to breathe and become clear. Most beers will be served by gravity straight from taps in the casks. If some are pulled by handpumps, lines will have to be attached to casks and beer engines. Beer has to be served cool and great attention is given to temperature in both the main building and the marquee: if air conditioning is not available, then chiller units will have to be hired. Special 'in-cask' cooling devices can be inserted through spile holes on top of casks: they circulate cold water through tubes.

FAMILY FRIENDLY FESTIVALS

◆ Ascot Racecourse Beer Festival in October is a fantastic event which combines an exciting day out at the races with top class refreshment from the CAMRA-run real ale bar. See: www.ascotbeerfest.seberkscamra.org.uk

◆ Minehead beer festival is held in September at the town railway station, one of 10 stations along a 20-mile stretch of track operating a steam railway. Beer is available on the trains as well as on the platform so, climb aboard for the most scenic beer festival around. See: www.west-somerset-railway.co.uk

◆ Nottingham Robin Hood Beer Festival in October is held in the grounds of Nottingham Castle. Along with a record selection of real ales, visitors can enjoy the impressive castle, underground tunnels, gardens and Medieval playground. See: www.beerfestival.nottinghamcamra.org

Visitors enjoying Ascot Racecourse Beer Festival

Mansfield
New Mills
Newcastle upon Tyne
Oldham
Paisley

MAY
Aberdeen
Banbury
Cambridge
Clitheroe
Colchester
Dewsbury
London – East Dulwich
Halifax
Kidderminster
Kingston
Lincoln
Macclesfield
Newark
Newport (Gwent)
Northampton – Delapre Abbey
Reading
Skipton
Southampton
Stockport
Stourbridge
Wolverhampton
Yapton

JUNE
Braintree
Bromsgrove
Cardiff – Great Welsh
Gibberd Garden – Harlow
Greater Manchester Cider
and Perry Festival
Hitchin
Lewes – South Downs
Rugby
Salisbury
St Ives (Cornwall)
Stratford-Upon-Avon
Tenterden – Kent & East
Sussex Railway
Thurrock

JULY
Ardingly
Bishops Stortford
Canterbury – Kent
Chelmsford
Chorlton
Derby
Devizes
Ealing
Edinburgh – Scottish
Hereford – Beer on the Wye

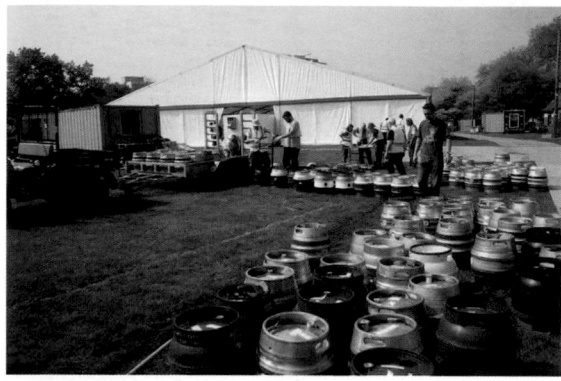

Running a beer festival is a big logistical challenge and CAMRA relies on the skills and experience of its volunteers

Russ and his committee use outside caterers to supply most of the food at the festival but some is organised by the Assembly Rooms staff and a local cheese supplier also provides his wares.

When the festival ends, there's still punishing hard work for the volunteers to carry out. The 'take down' starts on Sunday night and the Assembly Rooms and the marquee have to be cleared within two days. All the equipment that's been hired has to be returned while empty casks are either picked up by brewers or taken back by volunteers.

The power of beer festivals to attract drinkers and win them to CAMRA membership can be seen in Chippenham in Wiltshire. A few years ago, Gareth MacDonald and his wife had the choice of either going shopping or dropping into the festival. They wisely chose the latter and not only did they join the Campaign but Gareth is now the beer festival organiser.

It's a comparatively small local festival that celebrated its 21st anniversary in 2013 – but it still has to be organised in a professional manner. Gareth has a committee of 12 members of the North Wilts branch to help him run the event in the sports hall of the Olympiad Leisure Centre, a splendid venue that backs on to the River Avon.

NATIONAL BEER FESTIVALS

◆ The Great British Beer Festival (GBBF) is CAMRA's showcase event. The festival has been running sine 1977 and is held at Olympia in London each August. Billed as 'the biggest pub in the world' and staffed by over 1,000 volunteers, the festival offers more than 600 beers from Britain and around the world, music, games, food and much more. See: www.gbbf.org.uk

◆ The Scottish Real Ale Festival in June is in the fine city of Edinburgh and is three-day celebration of the revived and now thriving brewing scene in Scotland, from the Hebrides down to the Borders. See: www.sraf.org.uk

◆ The Great Welsh Beer & Cider Festival is held in Cardiff each June. Wales has also seen a real flourishing of inventive new brewers in recent years and this excellent variety is proudly represented. See: www.gwbcf.org.uk

Maidenhead
Plymouth
Rochford – South East Essex
Cider Festival
Stowmarket
Winchcombe – Cotswold
Woodcote – Steam Fair
Wykefest – Wyke Regis

AUGUST
Great British – London
Clacton
Darlington
Grantham
Harbury
Ipswich
Morecambe
Peterborough
Stafford
Swansea
Watnall – Moorgreen
Worcester

SEPTEMBER
Bridgnorth – Severn Valley
Burnley
Carmarthen
Chappel
Durham
East Malling (Kent)
Erewash Valley (Long Eaton)
Faversham – Hop
Hinckley
Jersey
Keighley
Lytham
Melton Mowbray
Minehead (West Somerset
Railway)
Nantwich
North Cotswolds –
Moreton-in-Marsh
Northwich
Portsmouth
Ripley – Derbyshire
St Albans
St Helens
Scunthorpe
St Ives (Cambs) – Booze
on the Ouse
Tamworth
Ulverston
Witham
York

OCTOBER
Alloa
Ascot

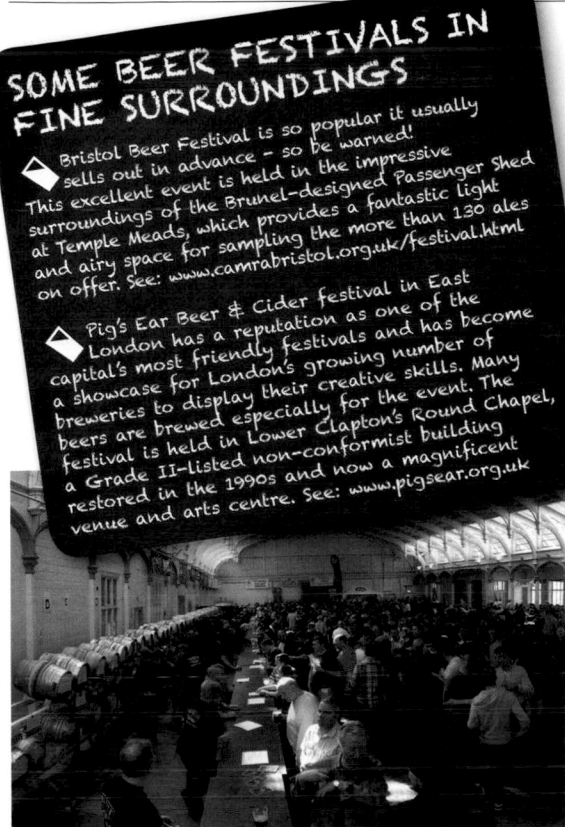

SOME BEER FESTIVALS IN FINE SURROUNDINGS

◆ Bristol Beer Festival is so popular it usually sells out in advance – so be warned! This excellent event is held in the impressive surroundings of the Brunel-designed Passenger Shed at Temple Meads, which provides a fantastic light and airy space for sampling the more than 130 ales on offer. See: www.camrabristol.org.uk/festival.html

◆ Pig's Ear Beer & Cider festival in East London has a reputation as one of the capital's most friendly festivals and has become a showcase for London's growing number of breweries to display their creative skills. Many beers are brewed especially for the event. The festival is held in Lower Clapton's Round Chapel, a Grade II-listed non-conformist building restored in the 1990s and now a magnificent venue and arts centre. See: www.pigsear.org.uk

Bristol Beer Festival, in Brunel's Passenger Shed

The event starts to be planned as soon as the Christmas and New Year holiday is over – even though the festival is held in April.

Gareth and his team source as much beer and cider as possible direct from local suppliers within a 60-70 mile radius. RCH and Mole breweries deliver beer from further afield. In total, the two-day event on Friday and Saturday offers 100 beers and 25 ciders and perries. The members supply their own security, while food comes direct from local suppliers, including a maker of renowned local pasties. Groups hired to perform live music, including a jazz combo on the Saturday night, are chosen by using local contacts – many of the groups also play regularly in pubs in the area.

Stillage is erected on Wednesday to allow the beer to settle for 48 hours. A forklift truck is hired to take the casks into the hall and then raise them on to the cradles. Signage is put up so visitors can easily spot where particular beers and ciders are available.

The best moment of the year, Gareth says, is when the doors of the hall open and he sees a queue disappearing round the corner of the building. But once the festival ends, there's still work to be done. The volunteers have to return at 9.30 am on Sunday morning and clear the hall by 12.30 as it's needed for sports events in the afternoon.

But it's worth the effort as CAMRA, through festivals large and small, is presenting to the drinking public a great choice of beers from all parts of the country. And festivals are a good way to recruit new members – including those who prefer a tasty beer to the chore of the weekly shop.

Barnsley
Basingstoke – Hampshire Octoberfest
Bath
Bedford
Birkenhead
Birmingham
Cambridge – Octoberfest
Carlisle
Chelmsford Cider Festival
Chester
Chesterfield – Market
Croydon & Sutton – Wallington
Eastbourne
Egremont, Cumbria
Falmouth
Gainsborough
Huddersfield – Oktoberfest
Kendal
Long Eaton
Louth
MIlton Keynes
Norwich
Nottingham
Oxford
Quorn Octoberfest
Redhill
Richmond (N Yorks.)
Sheffield
Solihull
South Woodham Ferrers – South Essex
Southport
Spa Valley Railway (West Kent)
Stoke-on-Trent – Potteries
Sunderland
Swindon
Troon – Ayrshire
Twickenham
Weymouth
Woolston – Southampton
Worthing

NOVEMBER
Belfast
Dudley
Heathrow
Poole
Rochford
Saltburn
Shrewsbury
Wakefield
Wantage
Watford
Woking

DECEMBER
Harwich
London – Pig's Ear

It's Better Down the Pub...
...so let's make sure we all use and enjoy it!

It's Better Down the Pub is a campaign launched in 2013 to bring people together to celebrate the great British pub and to encourage its use.

Here we all are enjoying the new 2014 *Good Beer Guide* and it is a safe bet that we all have at least two things in common: we all enjoy great British beer and we love drinking it in the pub. Perhaps there is also a third shared experience to add to these – we relish the opportunity to share our love of beer and pubs with each other and to evangelise with the, as yet, unconverted.

This is where the *It's Better Down the Pub* campaign comes in; with eight out of ten people counting themselves as 'pub goers' and over 15 million visiting a pub once a week, the campaign is inviting those who love the pub to share their best pub experiences while encouraging new or lapsed customers to visit their local. Following the success of launch events held across the UK the campaign has already captured the imagination of pub-goers and publicans who are showing fantastic support on the campaign's social media networks. With great stories being shared online, the campaign has kicked off to a superb start as it works to get the public talking about why *'It's Better Down the Pub'*.

What is IBDTP?

It's Better Down the Pub is a national campaign that celebrates our communal love for the great British pub and aims to focus attention on all the positive things about pubs and away from the backdrop of negative stories and pub closures which have dominated headlines in recent times. The campaign is the brainchild of a like-minded bunch of organisations and companies representing every aspect of Britain's 51,000 pubs.

The campaign is now attracting support from a raft of other leading brewers, pub businesses, industry organisations and pub support companies which represent the full range of activity involved in making the great British pub the institution we know and love.

The sponsors and partners make beer, spirits, wines and soft drinks; run pubs, bars and inns; campaign for beer, local brewers and rural pubs and provide entertainment, but most of all they love the pub and want to celebrate people's passion for pubs across the UK!

To get the ball rolling, a short film featuring real pubs and real people was created, which gave inspiration to share as many great pub moments as possible. The film highlights some of the reasons why the pub is such a fantastic place to be, and how the humble local is the bedrock of British life. You can see this film at **www.itsbetterdownthepub.com**

Why is IBDTP so important?

For sure we don't need to rehearse the arguments about why pubs are so important to us in Britain. We all know that the pub remains a central pillar of communities across Britain and is the original place for socialising, meeting new people and

talking about the role pubs play in so many people's lives, as the heartbeat of so many communities. The campaign seeks to remind those who have forgotten, nudge those who have lapsed and inform those who are not aware of why It's Better Down the Pub. **The campaign needs YOU to get involved.**

How you can help

Whether it is with family and friends, work colleagues or complete strangers, we have all had precious moments in pubs. They may be life-changing moments, regular get-togethers that bring great joys or even the simple pleasures of a fantastic pint and a moment or two of quiet contemplation on your own.

Whatever they may be we would like you to share your best times and favourite pub moments and to get all your friends to do the same! In fact, let's get the whole nation to share in those memories. *It's Better Down* the Pub wants to create a tidal wave of positivity about pubs, the people who work in them, the people who use them and the central role they play in everyday life.

If you agree, please take a picture, make your own film, or write a story about why you love the great British pub. Then upload onto our website (**www.itsbetterdownthepub.com**), tweet **@IBDTP** and have your say on Facebook (**www.facebook.com/ItsBetterDownThePub**). Help to create excitement and do it in the most creative way you think or simply give an example of why the pub has been, and always will be, a fantastic part of your life!

simply unwinding from a hard day at work. There are thousands of fantastic pubs across the UK and as CAMRA members know only too well the future of some of these is in serious doubt. Previously thriving classic town-centre bars, local pubs and roadside inns alike are suffering and face the threat of closure with reduced revenue and profits. *It's Better Down the Pub* does not seek to address the complex array of factors causing this difficulty but it is trying to add something positive to the situation by encouraging more people to take advantage of all the pub has to offer.

We are a proud and passionate pub-going nation who love our great British pubs and all that they stand for. Now is the time to start

SO WHAT'S IN IT FOR YOU?

We recognise that we all need a little incentive to share the good news every now and again so *It's Better Down the Pub* has an abundance of fantastic competitions, prizes and giveaways running throughout the campaign. There are lots of ways to win prizes on the website, Twitter and Facebook. Here's how...

★ **Website** – Bi-monthly competitions for the best photo, film and story, with the opportunity to win iPads, digital cameras and camcorders, will be run throughout the competition.

★ **Twitter and Facebook** – As well as weekly competitions for best entries, with prizes such as pub vouchers, match tickets and brewery tours, spot prizes are also given away frequently. Spot prizes including branded merchandise and *It's Better Down the Pub* t-shirts, will be awarded for top tweets, re-tweets, comments and contribution to the campaign.

★ **Pubs can win too!** – In addition to individuals winning prizes, the pub with the most entries on the website also has the chance to win – everyone's a winner! Entries can show the pub in its broadest context from a local boozer, gastro pub or to a city centre location that's a great music venue. Just get your punters to 'upvote' you on the website and the pub with the most votes wins!

So **it's now over to you!** Whatever way you enjoy pubs we want you to share what you most love about the great British pub. Tweet, post or upload a short video and get involved... it's simple!

Join in the conversation at www.facebook.com/ItsBetterDownThePub or @IBDTP and visit the website: www.itsbetterdownthepub.com

All About Ale
The best beer comes naturally

Real ale or cask-conditioned beer is the pinnacle of the brewing art. It's a beer produced with the finest raw materials, allowed to ferment and age naturally, and it's served from the cask without the need for gas pressure.

Most beer – lager as well as ale – is filtered, often pasteurised, and run into sealed containers called kegs in the brewery. When it reaches the pub, it's served by applied gas pressure, either carbon dioxide or nitrogen or a mix of both. The *Good Beer Guide* is dedicated – with unswerving passion and commitment – to real ale: unpasteurised beer served without artificial gas pressure.

CAMRA was founded in the early 1970s specifically to save and promote real ale. The style was threatened with extinction by the rise of large brewing groups hell-bent on foisting national keg and lager brands on the drinking public. As a result of mergers, takeovers and brewery closures, real ale faced extinction and the Campaign's pioneers set out to save it.

More than 40 years later, cask beer is a buoyant sector of the British beer market, the only type of beer showing growth rather than decline. There are other types of beer available and CAMRA is not hostile to them. For example, the Campaign for more than 20 years has supported the independence of the Czech Budweiser Budvar brewery and its struggle to remain free from takeover by its American namesake. Budvar is a lager beer and CAMRA has always recognised that genuine lagers – not the risible interpretations produced by global brewers in Britain – are part of the rich brewing heritage of central Europe. Across the North Sea, Belgium produces some of the most glorious beers known to person-kind – which are acclaimed in CAMRA's own publications.

But on home soil, the Campaign and the Guide remain dedicated to a style of beer that's unique to this country and is part of the warp and weft of our island's history and traditions.

To uphold that tradition in the 21st century is not to be backward-looking or to wallow in nostalgia. Real ale chimes with the time as drinkers seek out beers that are made naturally from the finest ingredients. It's possible to make something called 'beer' with rice, maize and corn syrup, and flavoured with juice squeezed from pulverised hops. The world's biggest beer brand even lists rice before barley malt on its label. But cask beer brewers turn their backs on such practices and prefer instead to use the finest malting barley along with hops left in their natural state. Real ale brewers may blend in other grains, such as wheat or oats, but they avoid the cheap adjuncts used by global brands.

Consumers are increasingly concerned by the way food and drink are made. They don't want products that are trunked half-way round the world and are stuffed with preservatives to keep them in edible or drinkable condition. Neither are they impressed by dubious advertising that masks the fact that a 'Belgian' lager is brewed in Wales and an 'Australian' one is manufactured in Manchester. The wine term 'terroir' has entered the beer world as drinkers seek confirmation that their beers are made locally from ingredients grown by farmers rooted in the finest forms of husbandry. Thanks to the work of such companies as Warminster Maltings in Wiltshire and Branthill Farm in Norfolk, it's now possible to trace where barley is grown, down to the precise fields where it's harvested. Hop growers are developing new varieties that require fewer agri-chemicals and allow natural predators such as ladybirds to kill the mites that attack the plants.

The finished product is a beer that's neither filtered nor pasteurised and is pulled to the pub bar without the use of applied gas pressure. In all its forms – from the palest pale ale to the blackest Stout – it's the pinnacle of the brewer's art and the best of British.

How beer is brewed

It's a long journey from the barley field to the pub cellar. Enormous skill is needed to turn grain and hops into a great pint of beer

Beer is a field of golden barley. Beer is an orchard of lush green hops. Beer is malt mixed with pure water, boiled with hops and fermented by carefully nurtured yeast cultures. It's the world's most complex alcoholic drink. Whether it's a summer refresher or a vintage ale designed for sipping, it deserves both respect and an understanding of the skill of the master brewers who make it.

Barley is beer's building block. Other grain can be used and many brewers blend in small amounts of wheat or oats and even rye, but barley is the preferred grain because it works in perfect harmony with hops and yeast. Brewers throughout the world recognise that maritime barley is the best variety to use and Britain is fortunate to have an abundance of maritime strains, many of them grown in rich alluvial soil reclaimed from the sea centuries ago.

But beer can't be made directly from barley in its harvested state. The barley has first to be taken to a specialist malster who allows it to partially germinate before kilning it to halt the process: turning it into malt so that the journey that creates beer can begin.

All beer, regardless of colour, is made mainly from pale malt as it has the highest level of enzymes – natural chemical catalysts – that are crucial to the brewing process. Higher temperatures produce brown, black and chocolate malts used for colour and flavour in darker beers. Roasted barley, which is not malted, is often featured in Stouts while a method similar to toffee making produces specialist crystal and caramalts which are used for colour and flavour. Depending on the mix of malts, the grain will give aromas and flavours similar to Horlicks, Ovaltine, oatmeal biscuits, Ryvita, almonds and other nuts, honey, butterscotch, caramel, tobacco and vanilla.

Pale malt that emerges from the kiln looks almost identical to barley but it has undergone an amazing transformation, with starch starting to turn into the sugar that is essential for fermentation.

The annual harvest has also produced beer's other key ingredient: hops. In common with grain, hops need good soil, in this case loamy or sandy soils that retain a good supply of water. Kent, Herefordshire and Worcestershire are the main hop-growing counties of England. Hops grow at great speed in the spring and summer and once harvested they are dried by warm air in special sheds or oast houses.

The brewing process

When malt reaches the brewery it's screened to clean it then ground in a mill into a powder called grist. Grist and pure treated hot water from the boiler – called 'liquor' by brewers – flow into the mash tun, where the porridge-like mixture of grain and water starts the brewing process. The mixture is left to stand in the mash tun for some two hours and during that time enzymes in the malt convert the remaining starch into fermentable sugar.

When starch conversion is complete, the brewer and his team will run the sweet extract, called wort, from the slotted base of the tun. The

A rolling field of English barley, ripening ready for harvest

wort is pumped to a second vessel, the copper, where it's vigorously boiled with hops. The hops are usually added in stages: at the start of the boil, half way through and just before the end in order to extract the maximum aroma and bitterness from the plants.

The copper boil lasts between 90 minutes and two hours. The used hops are strained off by the hop back, then the hopped wort is passed through a cooler to lower the temperature and is then pumped to fermenting vessels. These can be open or closed, upright or horizontal, but it's here that the liquid starts the conversion to alcohol with the aid of yeast.

Ale fermentation is rapid and lasts for a week – it's a method known as 'warm fermentation' to distinguish it from the cold fermentation method used to make genuine lager. Yeast converts malt sugar into alcohol and carbon dioxide and creates a dense, rocky blanket on top of the liquid. It also produces natural chemical compounds called esters that give off aromas reminiscent of apples, oranges, pear drops, banana, liquorice, molasses and, in especially strong beers, fresh leather. These add to the complexity of the finished beer.

Eventually the yeast will be overcome by the alcohol it has created and the yeast blanket is skimmed from the vessel. The brewer measures the density of the 'green' or unfinished beer with a hydrometer to ensure the transformation of sugar to alcohol is complete: depending on the style of beer being produced, fermentation may be stopped earlier to leave some sugar in the beer to avoid it tasting too dry or astringent. The beer will rest for several days in conditioning tanks to mature and to purge unwanted rough alcohols and esters.

Then comes the major divide in the world of brewing. One route leads to filtered, pasteurised and carbonated beer. The other creates Britain's great contribution to the world of beer: cask-conditioned ale. Cask ale is unique as it's not finished in the brewery but in the pub cellar. From conditioning tanks, it's racked into casks. Finings, a natural clarifying agent made from isinglass, is added to clear the beer. Additional hops may also be placed in the casks for extra aroma and

Hops & bitterness

Hops contain acids, oils and resins that deliver bitterness to beer along with fragrant aromas of spice, pepper, grass, cedar wood and citrus fruit. The oils and tannins in the plant help stabilise beer and prevent infection. Brewers often declare the units of bitterness – measured as IBUs or EBUs (International or European Bitterness Units) – as a useful guide to their drinks. A Mild ale will have IBUs in the low 20s whereas an IPA might have 80 IBUs or more.

flavour and brewing sugar may also be added to encourage a strong secondary fermentation.

The beer that reaches the pub cellar is said to be 'still working' as remaining yeast turns the final sugars into alcohol and CO_2. Casks, set up on a cradle known as the stillage, have to be vented to allow the natural gas to escape. A cask has two openings: a bung at the flat end where a tap is inserted to serve the beer; and a shive hole on top. A soft porous peg of wood, a spile, is knocked into the shive, enabling some of the CO_2 to escape. As fermentation dies down, the soft spile is replaced after 24 hours by a hard one that leaves some gas in the cask: this gives the beer its natural sparkle.

Inside the cask the isinglass sinks to the floor, attracting yeast in solution. The publican will draw off small samples of the beer and when he or she is satisfied is has 'dropped bright', plastic tubes or 'lines' are attached to the tap and the beer is drawn by a suction pump activated by a handpump on the bar. The recommended serving temperature for real ale is 11 or 12 degrees C. Some golden summer beers are served between 8 and 10 degrees and they may go through a special cooler below the bar.

It's a long journey, from grain to glass, but the end result is a natural beer, with low carbonation and bursting with the full flavours of malt and hops. It's beer at its best.

Types of malt

All beer, regardless of colour, is made predominantly from pale malt. Other types of malt include crystal, which adds a nutty or toffee note, and such dark malts as black and chocolate that give notes of coffee, chocolate, burnt fruit and tobacco. Roasted barley is often used in Porters and Stouts. The finest malting barley is widely considered to be Maris Otter. Although yielding less than more modern varieties, it is nonetheless becoming more widely grown to meet the demands of the increasing number of high-quality real ale breweries.

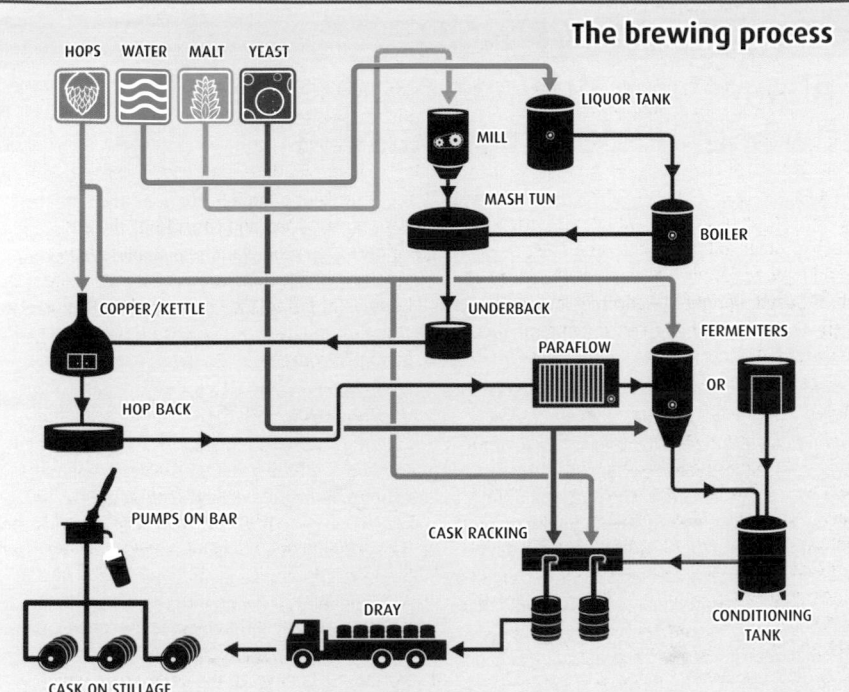

The brewing process

HOPS WATER MALT YEAST

LIQUOR TANK

MILL

MASH TUN

BOILER

COPPER/KETTLE

UNDERBACK

PARAFLOW

FERMENTERS

OR

HOP BACK

PUMPS ON BAR

CASK RACKING

DRAY

CONDITIONING TANK

CASK ON STILLAGE

No two breweries are identical. Some will use open fermenters, others more modern closed conical vessels. Yeast is added to the fermenter to turn malt sugar into alcohol and often to casks to encourage a secondary fermentation in the pub cellar. Hops are added during the copper boil but may also be added to the fermenter and even casks to ehance hop aroma.

Beer is made from just four key ingredients:

1

HOPS: There are around two dozen hop varieties in England, ranging from the Golding and the Fuggle, first grown in the 18th and 19th centuries, to more modern ones, such as Boadicea and Endeavour. Hops can be used in the brewery either as whole flowers or ground and compressed into pellets.

2

WATER: Pure water, called 'liquor' by brewers, can come from springs, bore holes or from the public supply. It will be thoroughly filtered and brewers often add such sulphates as gypsum and magnesium to enhance the flavours of malt and hops.

3

MALT: Malsters steep barley in water to absorb moisture, then spread it on heated floors or inside rotating drums where it starts to germinate. Once germination is under way, the grain is transferred to an oven known as a kiln. Heat dries the grain and, depending on the temperature, produces pale or darker malts.

4

YEAST: Yeast is a type of fungus that feeds on sugary liquids. Every brewery will have its own yeast culture that's carefully guarded and stored, as it gives its own important 'house character' to the beer.

Beer Appreciation
Enhance your drinking experience with this brief guide to beer tasting

Beer has begun to emerge from the giant shadow cast by wine. Often dismissed as a simple refresher, beer is now seen as a complex drink with its own vocabulary, due to a greater understanding of the ingredients used in its production.

The key role played by two quite different components – grain and hops – marks beer out from most other types of alcohol. While wine and cider, for example, are made by crushing fruit, barley first has to be turned into malt and then is boiled with hops that add bitterness to balance the biscuit character of the grain. Water, too, plays a crucial role in brewing and brewers will adapt their 'brewing liquor' to suit the type of beer they are making. Finally, special yeast cultures add their own aromas and flavours as they convert malt sugars into alcohol.

Appreciating beer
The previous section has shown the way in which real ale is made. We can now raise the level of our appreciation of the end product by sampling and tasting to pick out the different elements created by the brewing process. Gently swirl the liquid in the glass to release the aroma or the 'nose' and appreciate the malt, hop and fruit notes that emerge. Allow the beer to trickle over the tongue, which picks up bitterness, sweetness and salt, and enjoy the palate or 'mouthfeel' as the beer coats the cheeks. Finally, appreciate the 'finish' or aftertaste as the beer passes down the back of the throat.

On the nose you may find a rich biscuit or Ovaltine-like malt character. Hops will add their own distinctive note: depending on the variety used, hop notes may be resinous, citrus, spicy, peppery, floral or herbal – to name just a few. Fruit may be detected and this comes from both the hops and the yeast. A sulphur or salty note may be detected: this is derived from the water, which will have had sulphates added to replicate the famous salty waters of Burton upon Trent, home of classic pale ale brewing.

In the mouth, the malt may have a delicious juicy note while hop bitterness will build, balancing any fruitiness. Finally the finish, if the beer is well-balanced, will combine all the elements of malt, hops and fruit into a satisfying, dry finish. The flavour characteristics of a particular beer will depend on its style: see the Britain's Classic Beer Styles section that follows. Suffice it to say that a Mild ale will offer a pronounced malt and caramel note, with restrained bitterness, while Bitters and IPAs will have a robust hop character, Porters and Stouts a roasted and toasted grain note, while barley wines are fruity and vinous, and old ales will often have a slight hint of sourness allied to ripe malt, gentle hops and notes of leather and tobacco.

Holding a beer tasting
Tasting beer can be carried out in the home but greater appreciation and understanding will emerge if a group of people take part – and there's no better place to do it than in a pub.

Many pubs now stage regular beer festivals, with a wide choice of beers available. If festivals are not held in your local but it has a good range on the bar, ask whether a room or part of the bar could be set aside for a tasting event.

Glasses should be either half-pint beer glasses or the large ones used for red wine. You will need fresh water and a supply of crackers to allow tasters to clean their palates between beers. Scoring sheets add to the enjoyment of the event, especially if you want to name a 'best beer'. The sheets should be divided into marks out of 10 for appearance, aroma, palate and finish. Usually, not more than six beers are judged in a single event.

Depending on the availability of beer, you could base a tasting around just one style or related pair of styles, such as Mild, Bitter or Porter and Stout. However, it's unlikely that many pubs would have six versions of a single style, so it's best to have a mixed event. It's advisable to work up from the lowest strength: it would be difficult to judge a Mild after a barley wine.

Marks for appearance will be based on the clarity of the beer when the glass is held up to the light. Does it have a good head of foam, which indicates the beer has what brewers call 'condition'? The absence of foam means the beer is flat. Some beers, such as wheat beers, are designed to have a cloudy appearance, and this should be borne in mind when marking.

Marks for aroma will be based on the appeal of the beer as it's sniffed. Is there a good balance of malt, hops and fruit or is the beer overly malty or, conversely, too bitter? If you are judging bitter beers, including IPA, then expect to find the balance tilted toward hops and bitterness. Palate is based on the appeal of the beer in the mouth: you would mark down for cloying sweetness or harsh bitterness, and give higher marks when both characteristics are in balance. Finally, the finish: is the beer harmonious as it passes over the back of the tongue and down the throat, well-balanced between malt, hops and fruit, ending neither too malty nor too bitter. Again, marks in this section will be guided by the style of beer: you would expect a profound roasted grain character from a Stout or Porter.

If it's not possible to organise a tasting event of your own, bear in mind that many CAMRA festivals stage beer tastings, often hosted by experts in the field. Monitor the festivals listed in this Guide. The Great British Beer Festival, held in London every August, usually has beer tastings every day of the week: **www.gbbf.org.uk**.

Matching beer and food

The appreciation of beer is heightened if it's enjoyed with food. For too long, beer and food has meant lager and curry, and even in that context India Pale Ale would be a better and more logical companion. As many entries in the Guide make clear, more and more pub landlords are creating imaginative recipes that match beer with food and even use beer in the cooking process.

The pleasure of matching beer with food is often heightened by an element of surprise. Porters and Stouts, for example, are ideal companions for oysters and other shellfish, with the acidity of the beer cutting the salty nature of the food. In Cork in Ireland, where Stout is part of the furniture, an annual oyster and beer festival is staged. The same style of beer is also the perfect match for chocolate desserts, with the roasted grain and bitter character of the beer cutting the sweetness of the dish and complementing chocolate's bitter notes.

In the Czech Republic, a great brewing country, Pilsner is considered the perfect companion for carp, a traditional fish dish. Taking a leaf from the Czech book, a hoppy and spicy golden ale would be the perfect match for white fish. Roast beef and English pale ale are a famous duo in this country and there's no shortage of beers on offer: go for ales with a spicy and peppery hop character to match not just the beef but fiery English mustard.

Pale ale is also the perfect companion for cheese. Where Stilton is involved, hold the port wine – the world's greatest cheese deserves one of the world's greatest beer styles, IPA, with high hop bitterness to balance the creamy/tangy nature of the cheese.

With pasta dishes, much will depend on the sauces used. Spaghetti bolognese or carbonara cry out for a hoppy pale ale or best bitter while the heat of pasta arrabiatta demands a powerful kick of hops from a special or extra strong Bitter. Pale ale or Bitter stand up well to vegetable dishes, such as roasted squash or peppers, served with roast potatoes. And when the meal is finished, settle back and enjoy a 'snifter' in a brandy glass of barley wine, old ale or vintage ale.

Beer flavour chart

Example beer flavour profile

This chart is used by CAMRA tasting panels and others in order to produce distinct flavour profiles for individual beers. The chart indicates the aromas and flavours produced by different types of malt along with hop characteristics and beer faults. The flavour elements on the chart are some of the most commonly found but are by no means exhaustive. The blue 'spider' trace shows the profile of an example beer with the most pronounced flavour elements plotted towards the outer edge of the chart.

Britain's Classic Beer Styles

IN THE WORLD OF BEER, Britain is best known for the style known as Bitter which, in the 20th century, developed from the pale ales first brewed in Victorian times. But there is far more to British beer than Bitter. Older styles have reappeared while the likes of golden ale, fruit beer and wheat beer have been fashioned in recent years to give further choice to drinkers. In this briefing, **Roger Protz** gives an indication of some of the great beers available in British pubs and recommends some of his favourite versions of each style.

PORTER & STOUT

Porter was a London beer that created the first commercial brewing industry in the world in the early 18th century. Porter started life as a brown beer and became darker when new technology made it possible to roast grain at higher temperatures to obtain greater colour and flavour. The strongest version of Porter was dubbed Stout Porter or Stout for short. The name Porter was the result of the beer's popularity with the large number of porters working the streets, markets and docks of 18th-century London.

Porter and Stout were exported to the rest of the British Isles and, as a result, Arthur Guinness built his own Porter brewery in Dublin. During World War One, when the British government prevented brewers from using heavily-roasted malts in order to divert energy to the arms industry, Guinness and other Irish brewers came to dominate the market. In recent years, Porter and Stout have made a spirited comeback in both Britain and the United States, with brewers digging deep in to old recipe books to create genuine versions of the style from the 18th and 19th centuries.

Look for a jet-black colour with a hint of ruby around the edge of the glass. Expect a dark and roasted malt character, with raisin and sultana fruit, espresso or cappuccino coffee, liquorice and molasses. The beer should have deep hop bitterness to balance the richness of malt and fruit.

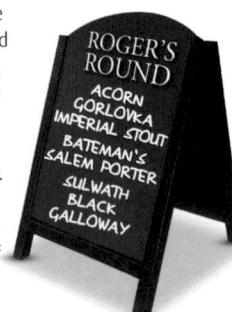

ROGER'S ROUND
ACORN GORLOVKA IMPERIAL STOUT
BATEMAN'S SALEM PORTER
SULWATH BLACK GALLOWAY

MILD

Mild was once the most popular style of beer in Britain but it was overtaken by Bitter in the 1950s. It was developed in the 18th and 19th centuries as a less aggressively bitter style of beer than Porter and Stout, and was primarily drunk by industrial and agricultural

workers to refresh them after long hours of arduous labour. Early Milds were much stronger that modern interpretations, which tend to fall in the 3% to 3.5% category, though Rudgate's Dark Ruby Mild at 4.4% is more in keeping with earlier strengths. Mild is usually dark brown in colour, due to the use of well-roasted malts or roasted barley, but there are paler versions such as Banks's Mild, Timothy Taylor's Golden Best and McMullen's AK. Look for rich malty aromas and flavours, with hints of dark fruit, chocolate, coffee and caramel, with a gentle underpinning of hop bitterness.

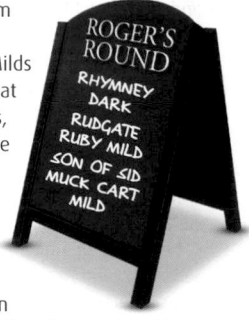

ROGER'S ROUND
RHYMNEY DARK
RUDGATE RUBY MILD
SON OF SID
MUCK CART MILD

OLD ALE

Old ale is another style from the 18th century, stored for months or even years in wooden vessels where the beer picked up some lactic sourness from wild yeasts and tannins in the wood. As a result of the sour taste, it was dubbed 'stale' by drinkers and the beer was one of the components of the early blended Porters. In recent years, old ale has made a return to popularity, primarily due to the popularity of Theakston's Old Peculier and Gale's Prize Old Ale. Contrary to expectation, old ales do not have to be especially strong and can be no more than 4% alcohol. Neither do they have to be dark: old ale can be pale and bursting with lush malt, tart fruit and spicy hops. Darker versions will have a more profound malt character, with powerful hints of roasted grain, dark fruit, polished leather and fresh tobacco. The hallmark of the style is a lengthy period of maturation, often in bottle rather than cask.

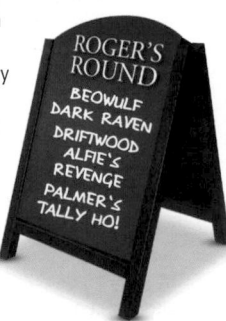

ROGER'S ROUND
BEOWULF DARK RAVEN
DRIFTWOOD ALFIE'S REVENGE
PALMER'S TALLY HO!

BARLEY WINE

Barley wine dates from the 18th and 19th centuries when England was often at war with France and it was the duty of patriots, usually from the upper classes, to drink ale rather that French claret. Barley wine had to be strong – often between 10% and 12% – and was stored for as long as 18 months or two years. The biggest-selling barley wine for many years was Whitbread's 10.9% Gold Label, now available only in cans. Fuller's Vintage Ale (8.5%) is a bottle-conditioned version of its Golden Pride and is brewed with different varieties of malts and hops every year.

Expect massive sweet malt and ripe fruit of the pear drop, orange and lemon type, with darker fruits, chocolate and coffee if darker malts are used. Hop rates are generous and produce bitterness and peppery, grassy and floral notes.

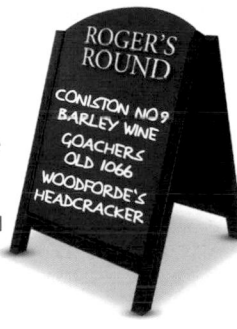

IPA

India Pale Ale changed the face of brewing in the 19th century. The new technologies of the industrial revolution enabled brewers to use pale malts to fashion beers that were pale bronze in colour. First brewed in London and Burton upon Trent for the colonial trade, IPAs were strong in alcohol and high in hops to keep them in good condition during long sea journeys. IPA's life span was brief, driven out of the colonies by German lager. But the style has made a spirited recovery in recent years, brewed with great passion in both Britain and the U.S.. In Chicago, Goose Island's IPA is arguably the finest American interpretation of the style while in Britain Marston's Old Empire and Meantime's IPA are just two modern versions of the style arousing new interest. Look for a big peppery hop aroma and palate balanced by juicy malt and tart citrus fruit.

BURTON ALE

As the name suggests, the origins of Burton Ale lie in Burton upon Trent, but the style became so popular in the 18th and 19th centuries that most brewers had 'a Burton' in their portfolio and the expression 'gone for a Burton' entered the English language. Bass at one time had six different versions of the beer, ranging from 6% to 11.5%: the stronger versions were exported to Russia and the Baltic States.

In the 20th century, Burton was overtaken in popularity by pale ale and Bitter but it was revived with great success in the late 1970s with the launch of Ind Coope Draught Burton Ale. But when Allied Breweries broke up, the beer moved first to Tetley's in Leeds and then J W Lees in Manchester, where it's brewed in small batches but is worth seeking out: it's based on the recipe for a once-famous bottled beer, Double Diamond Export. Other Burton Ales exist under different names today: Young's Winter Warmer was originally called Burton.

Bass No 1, brewed occasionally, is called a barley wine but is in fact the last remaining version of a Bass Burton Ale. Look for a bright amber colour, a rich malty and fruity character underscored by a solid resinous and piny hop note.

PALE ALE

The success of IPA in the colonial trade led to a demand for beer of a similar colour and character in Britain. IPA, with its heavy hopping, was considered too bitter for the domestic market, and brewers responded with a beer dubbed pale ale that was lower in both alcohol and hops. Pale ale was known as 'the beer of the railway age', transported round the country from Burton upon Trent by the new railway system. Brewers from London, Liverpool and Manchester built breweries in Burton to make use of the local, mineral-rich water to make their own versions of pale ale. From the early years of the 20th century, Bitter began to overtake pale ale in popularity and as a result pale ale became mainly a bottled product. A true pale ale should be different to Bitter, identical to IPA in colour and brewed without the addition of coloured malts.

It should have a spicy, resinous aroma and palate, with biscuity malt and tart citrus fruit. Many beers are called Bitter today but are in fact pale ale, Marston's Pedigree being a case in point.

ROGER'S ROUND
AN TEALLACH CROFTERS PALE ALE
B&T SHEFFORD PALE ALE
DARK STAR AMERICAN PALE ALE

BITTER

Towards the end of the 19th century, brewers built large estates of tied pubs and they moved away from beers stored for months or years and developed 'running beers' that could be served after a few days of conditioning in the pub cellar. Bitter was a new type of running beer: it was a member of the pale ale family but was generally deep bronze or copper in colour due to the use of slightly darker malts, such as crystal, that gave the beer fullness of palate. Best is a stronger version of Bitter but there is considerable crossover. Bitter falls into the 3.4% to 3.9% band, while Best Bitter is 4% upwards, though a number of brewers dub their ordinary Bitters 'best'. A further development of Bitter comes in the shape of extra or special strong Bitter of 5% or more: Fuller's ESB and Greene King Abbot being well-known examples. With ordinary Bitter, look for spicy, peppery and grassy hop character, a powerful bitterness, tangy fruit and juicy/nutty malt.

With Best and strong Bitters, malt and fruit character will tend to dominate but hop aroma and bitterness are still crucial to the style, often achieved by 'late hopping' in the brewery or by adding hops to casks before filling.

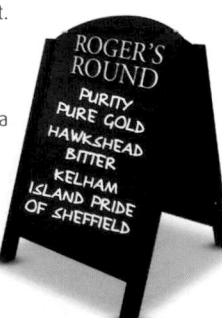

ROGER'S ROUND
PURITY PURE GOLD
HAWKSHEAD BITTER
KELHAM ISLAND PRIDE OF SHEFFIELD

GOLDEN ALE

Golden ales have become so popular, with brewers of all sizes producing them, that they now have their own category in the Champion Beer of Britain competition. Exmoor Gold and Hop Back Summer Lightning launched the trend in the early 1980s

and other brewers quickly followed suit in a rush to win younger drinkers away from mass-produced lagers to the pleasures of cask beer. The style is different to pale ale in two crucial ways: golden ale is paler, often brewed with lager malt or specially produced low temperature ale malt and, as a result, hops are allowed to give full expression, balancing sappy malt with luscious fruity, floral, herbal, spicy and resinous characteristics.

While brewers of pale ale tend to use such traditional English hops as Fuggles and Goldings, imported hops from North America, the Czech Republic, Germany, Slovenia and New Zealand give radically different hop notes to golden ale. As a result, golden ales offer a new and exciting drinking experience. They are often served colder than draught Bitter and some brewers, such as Fuller's, have installed special cooling devices attached to beer engines to ensure the beer reaches the glass at an acceptably refreshing temperature.

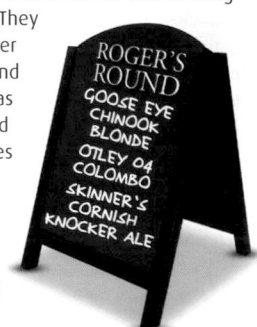

ROGER'S ROUND
GOOSE EYE CHINOOK BLONDE
OTLEY 04 COLOMBO
SKINNER'S CORNISH KNOCKER ALE

WHEAT BEER

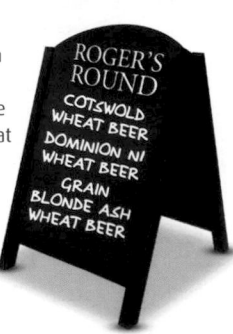

Wheat beer is a style closely associated with Bavaria and Belgium and the popularity of the style in Britain has encouraged many brewers to add wheat beer to the portfolios. The title is something of a misnomer as all 'wheat beers' are a blend of malted barley as well as wheat, as the latter grain is difficult to brew with and needs the addition of barley, which acts as a natural filter during the mashing stage. But wheat, if used with special strains of yeast developed for brewing the style, gives distinctive aromas and flavours, such as clove, banana and bubblegum that make it a complex and refreshing beer. The Belgian version of wheat beer often has the addition of herbs and spices, such as milled coriander seeds and orange peel – a habit that dates back to medieval times.

ROGER'S ROUND
COTSWOLD WHEAT BEER
DOMINION NI WHEAT BEER
GRAIN BLONDE ASH WHEAT BEER

FRUIT/SPECIALITY BEERS

Brewers have become restless in recent years in their quest for new flavours that will help them reach a wider and more appreciative audience for their beers. The popularity in Britain of Belgian fruit beers has not gone unnoticed and now many home-grown brewers are using fruit in their beer. Others have gone the extra mile and add honey, herbs, heather, spices, and even spirit – brandy and rum feature in a number of speciality beers.

It's important to dispel the belief that fruit and honey beers are sweet: both fruit and honey add new dimensions to the brewing process and are highly fermentable, with the result that beers that use the likes of cherries or raspberry are dry and quenching rather than cloying.

SCOTTISH BEERS

Historically, Scottish beers tend to be darker, sweeter and less heavily hopped that beers south of the border: a reflection of a colder climate where hops don't grow and beer needs to be nourishing. The classic traditional styles are Light, Heavy and Export, which are not dissimilar to Mild, Bitter and IPA. They are also often known as 60, 70 and 80 Shilling Ales from a 19th-century method of invoicing beers according to their strength. A 'Wee Heavy' or 90 Shilling Ale, now rare, is the Scottish equivalent of barley wine. Many of the newer brewers in Scotland produce beers that are lighter in colour and with more generous hop rates.

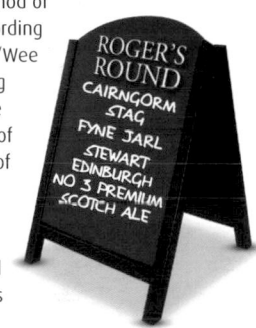

Only accept perfect pints

Remember, you're the consumer, forking out a high price for beer, so don't be afraid to take your pint back to the bar if:

- It's either too cold or too warm. Cask beer should be cool, not cold – but bear in mind that some golden ales are meant to be served at a lower temperature than Milds and Bitters. At the other end of the spectrum, it's a myth that real ale should be served at room temperature. Warm beer tastes bad, as the temperature creates unpleasant off flavours. If your beer smells of acetone, vinegar or stale bread, take it back.

- The pint has no head, is totally flat and out of condition.

- It's not only flat but hazy and has yeast particles or protein floating in the liquid.

If you get the response 'Real ale is meant to be warm and cloudy', invite the publican to join the 21st century. If the offending pub has a Cask Marque plaque, get in touch with Cask Marque. Otherwise, let us know at the *Good Beer Guide* – **camragbgeditor@camra.org.uk**.

And please go back to the bar if you are served a short measure – less than a pint (or half-pint) of liquid in the glass. Drinkers lose millions of pounds a year as a result of short measures. It's an outrageous rip-off. CAMRA beer festivals serve beer in over-size glasses that ensure drinkers always get the amount of beer they have paid for. Most pub owners refuse to use over-size glasses, preferring brim-measure glasses that allow them consistently to serve short measures. It's a scandal. Don't put up with it.

CAMRA's Beers of the Year

THE BEERS LISTED BELOW are CAMRA'S Beers of the Year. They were short-listed for the 2013 Champion Beer of Britain competition, held at the Great British Beer Festival in August, or the Champion Winter Beer of Britain Competition, held in January that year. Each beer was found by a panel of trained CAMRA judges to be consistently outstanding in its category and they all receive a 🍺 against their entry in the Breweries section. In the Champion Beer of Britain finals, the best beers from each category in both competitions are judged together to decide the overall national winner. For the full results, visit **www.camra.org.uk/cbob**.

BEST BITTERS
Barngates, Tag Lag
Batham, Best Bitter
Bowman, Quiver Bitter
Bryncelyn, Oh Boy
Castle Rock, Elsie Mo
Everards, Tiger Best Bitter
Fyne, Maverick
Hawkshead, Red
Ilkley, Best
Isle of Skye, Red Cuillin
Malvern Hills, Black Pear
Milton, Pegasus
Mordue, Workie Ticket
Purple Moose, Cwrw Glaslyn/
 Glaslyn Ale
Skinner's, Betty Stogs
Surrey Hills, Shere Drop
Uley, Bitter
Woodforde's, Nelson's
 Revenge

BITTERS
Acorn, Barnsley Bitter
An Teallach, Beinn Dearg Ale
Buntingford, Twitchell
Butcombe, Bitter
Cumbrian Legendary,
 Esthwaite Bitter
Fyne, Piper's Gold
Hawkshead, Windermere Pale
Hobsons, Best Bitter
Humpty Dumpty, Nord
 Atlantic
Kinver, Light Railway
Moor, Revival
Purple Moose, Cwrw Eryri/
 Snowdonia Ale
Rhymney, Hobby Horse
Surrey Hills, Ranmore Ale
Thornbridge, Wild Swan
Timothy Taylor, Boltmaker
Triple fff, Alton's Pride
Whim, Hartington Bitter

BARLEY WINES & STRONG OLD ALES
Darwin, Extinction Ale
Heart of Wales, High as a Kite
Hogs Back, A Over T/Aromas
 Over Tongham
Isle of Skye, Cuillin Beast
Kinver, Over the Edge
Ole Slewfoot, Friend of
 the Devil
Outstanding, Pushing Out
Parish, Baz's Bonce Blower
RCH, Santa Fe

GOLDEN ALES
Blue Monkey, BG Sips
Buntingford, Polar Star
Cumbrian Legendary,
 Loweswater Gold
Dark Star, American Pale Ale
Elland, Beyond the Pale
Fyne, Jarl
Otley, O2 Croeso
St Austell, Proper Job
Salopian, Oracle

MILDS
Bank Top, Dark Mild
Castle Rock, Black Gold
Cotswold Spring,
 Old Sodbury Mild
Elgood's, Black Dog
Fernandes, Malt Shovel Mild
Great Orme, Welsh Black
Harveys, Sussex XX Mild Ale
Holden's, Black Country Mild
Williams, Black

OLD ALES & STRONG MILDS
Adnams, Old Ale
Blue Anchor, Spingo Special
Brown Cow, Captain Oates Mild
Brunswick, Black Sabbath
Downton, Dark Delight
Jennings, Sneck Lifter
Kelburn, Dark Moor
Peakstones Rock, Black Hole
Purple Moose, Ochr Tywyll y
 Mws/Dark Side of the Moose

PORTERS
Ayr, Rabbie's Porter
Blythe, Johnsons
Derby, Penny's Porter
Elland, 1872 Porter
Growler, Old Growler
Hammerpot, Bottle
 Wreck Porter
Hawkshead, Brodie's Prime
RCH, Old Slug Porter

SPECIALITY BEERS
Bowman, Elderado
Cairngorm, Trade Winds
Conwy, Honey Fayre/Cwrw Mel
Growler, Umbel Magna
Marble, Ginger
Milestone, Raspberry
 Wheat Beer
Saltaire, Triple Chocoholic
Skinner's, Ginger Tosser
Titanic, Chocolate & Vanilla Stout

STOUTS
Bartrams, Comrade Bill
 Bartram's Egalitarian Anti
 Imperialist Soviet Stout
Deeside, Talorcan
Exeter, Darkness
Fulstow, Sledgehammer Stout
Heart of Wales, Welsh Black
Hop Back, Entire Stout
Jarrow, McConnells Irish Stout
Marble, Stouter Stout
Titanic, Stout

STRONG BITTERS
Beeston, On the Huh
Castle Rock, Screech Owl
Exmoor, Stag
Highland, St Magnus Ale
Hop Back, Summer Lightning
Kirkstall, Dissolution IPA
Marble, Dobber
Rhymney, Export Ale
Salopian, Golden Thread

REAL ALE IN A BOTTLE
Beowulf, Dragon Smoke Stout
Conwy, Clogwyn Gold
Fuller's, 1845
Harveys, Imperial Extra
 Double Stout
Hopshackle, Restoration
Marble, Chocolate Marble
Marble, Lagonda IPA
Neath, Black
O'Hanlon's, Port Stout
Old Bear, Black Mari'a
Samuel Smith, Yorkshire Stingo
Spire, Sgt Pepper Stout
Stewart, Embra
Stewart, St. Giles
Wells & Young's, Young's Special
 London Ale
Woodforde's, Nelson's Revenge
Worthington's, White Shield

CHAMPION WINTER BEER OF BRITAIN 2013
Elland, 1872 Porter

CHAMPION BEER OF BRITAIN 2013
Elland, 1872 Porter

The Pubs

England	**35**
Wales	**565**
Scotland	**611**
Northern Ireland, Channel Islands, Isle of Man	**659**

Fat Cat, Norwich (p353)

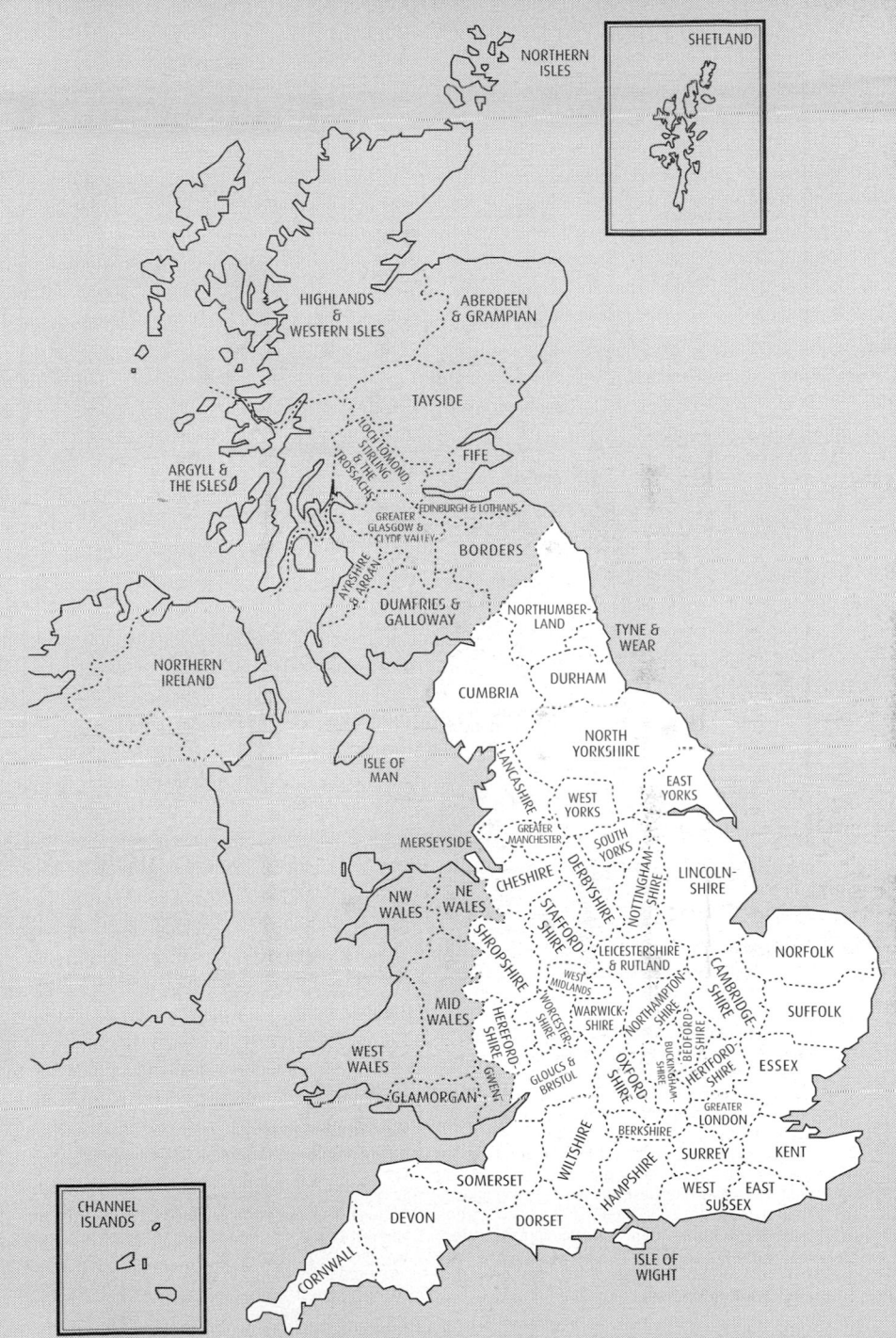

SHETLAND

NORTHERN
ISLES

HIGHLANDS
&
WESTERN ISLES

ABERDEEN
& GRAMPIAN

TAYSIDE

LOCH LOMOND
STIRLING
& THE
TROSSACHS

FIFE

ARGYLL &
THE ISLES

EDINBURGH & LOTHIANS

GREATER
GLASGOW &
CLYDE VALLEY

BORDERS

AYRSHIRE
& ARRAN

DUMFRIES &
GALLOWAY

NORTHERN
IRELAND

NORTHUMBER-
LAND

TYNE &
WEAR

DURHAM

CUMBRIA

ISLE OF
MAN

NORTH
YORKSHIRE

EAST
YORKS

LANCASHIRE

WEST
YORKS

MERSEYSIDE

GREATER
MANCHESTER

SOUTH
YORKS

LINCOLN-
SHIRE

NW
WALES

NE
WALES

CHESHIRE

DERBYSHIRE

NOTTINGHAM-
SHIRE

STAFFORD-
SHIRE

SHROPSHIRE

LEICESTERSHIRE
& RUTLAND

NORFOLK

WEST
MIDLANDS

WARWICK-
SHIRE

NORTHAMPTON-
SHIRE

CAMBRIDGE-
SHIRE

SUFFOLK

MID
WALES

WORCESTER-
SHIRE

HEREFORD-
SHIRE / GWENT

BEDFORD-
SHIRE

BUCKINGHAM-
SHIRE

HERTFORD-
SHIRE

ESSEX

WEST
WALES

GLOUCS &
BRISTOL

OXFORD-
SHIRE

GREATER
LONDON

GLAMORGAN

BERKSHIRE

SURREY

KENT

WILTSHIRE

SOMERSET

HAMPSHIRE

WEST
SUSSEX

EAST
SUSSEX

CHANNEL
ISLANDS

DEVON

DORSET

ISLE OF
WIGHT

CORNWALL

England

Ampthill

Albion 🏆 L

36 Dunstable Street, MK45 2JT TL033377
11.30-11 (midnight Fri & Sat); 12-10.30 Sun
☎ (01525) 634857
B&T Shefford Bitter, Golden Fox, Dragon Slayer; Everards Tiger Best Bitter; guest beers H
A proper narrow-fronted Victorian pub with one large bar. Twelve handpumps offer a range of local B&T beers, Everards Tiger and eight constantly changing ales mainly from microbreweries (available in a bat holding three third pints if you can't decide). Three real ciders or perries are also kept. Beer and cider festivals are held regularly. There is a snug meeting room and a patio garden. Dogs are welcome. English music night is hosted once a month. CAMRA Bedfordshire Pub of the Year 2012 and local CAMRA Pub of the Year 2012 and 2013. ⛬❀♣●⚲⊟

Arlesey

Vicars Inn L

68 Church Lane, SG15 6UX
12-3.30 (not Mon-Thu), 5-midnight; 12-4, 7-midnight Sat & Sun ☎ (01462) 731215
Wells Eagle IPA; guest beer H
Located close to the railway station and opposite the church, the Vicars offers well-kept and competitively priced ales, with the guest usually a lower-gravity session beer. The front bar is particularly cosy, and you are welcome to join in the friendly conversation whether you are a regular or an occasional visitor. Larger groups frequent the lounge bar at the rear. The Sunday afternoon quiz and dominoes evenings are popular. There is an enclosed garden and a function room for hosting events. Q❀⊟⇌♣P⊟(72,E7)

Bedford

Bedford Arms

2 Bromham Road, MK40 2QA (opp HM Prison)
12-midnight ☎ (01234) 214656
thebedfordarmsbedford.co.uk
Courage Directors; Wells Bombardier; Young's Bitter, Special; guest beers H
A Charles Wells Speciality Beer House offering three regularly changing guest beers and a changing guest cider as well as four regular Wells & Young's ales. Burgers, home-made chilli and Pieminister pies are available on Thursday and Friday evenings and noon-10pm at weekends. There is live jazz on Monday evening and Sunday afternoon, local bands on Sunday evening, traditional music on the first Thursday of the month and a book club on the second Thursday. ⛬❀◑♿⇌●⚲⊟

Burnaby Arms

66 Stanley Street, MK41 7RU (in Prime Ministers area N of town centre)

🕒 5 (12 Sat)-11; 12-10.30 Sun ☎ (01234) 330056
🌐 burnabyarmsbedford.co.uk
Courage Directors; Wells Eagle IPA; Young's London Gold; guest beers Ⓗ
Recently refurbished to give a fresh and inviting new look, with a marked improvement in beer choice. This street-corner community pub is run as a joint family business with the Devonshire Arms and has a warm welcome for everyone. Hot home-made pies are available throughout opening hours. Local CAMRA Most Improved Pub of the Year 2013. Q🌑🕮♣⊱⊟(10)

Cricketers Arms Ⓛ
35 Goldington Road, MK40 3LH (on A4280 near rugby ground)
🕒 5 (7 Sun)-11 ☎ (01234) 303958 🌐 cricketersarms.co.uk
Adnams Southwold Bitter; guest beers Ⓗ
Also known as the Welsh Embassy, this small, welcoming, one-bar pub near Bedford Blues rugby ground is popular with fans of the game and very busy on match days. It opens at noon on Saturdays for Blues home games. Live rugby is shown (terrestrial TV only) and the pub opens early for live Six Nations games. Guest beers include brews from local SIBA breweries. There is a covered, heated courtyard for smokers and drinkers. Local CAMRA Pub of the Year 2012. 🕮⊱⊟(5)

Devonshire Arms ▼ Ⓛ
32 Dudley Street, MK40 3TB (1 mile E of town centre S of A4280)
🕒 5 (4 Fri, 12 Sat)-11; 12-10.30 Sun ☎ (01234) 359329
🌐 devonshirearmsbedford.co.uk
Courage Directors; Wells Eagle IPA; Young's Special, London Gold; guest beers Ⓗ
Pleasant Victorian LocAle pub in a popular residential area. Guest and seasonal ales are mainly from Wells & Young's, the two ciders and perry are from Westons. Pub festivals are held each year. The front bar has bare floorboards and an open fire, while the carpeted rear bar is a traditional saloon. The rear garden has a heated gazebo for smokers, and a no-smoking paved area. A good range of wines is sold by the glass or bottle. Local CAMRA Pub of the Year 2013. ⌂Q🕮🗄🍴⊱⊟(4)

Three Cups Ⓛ
45 Newnham Street, MK40 3JR (200yds S of A4280 near rugby ground)
🕒 11-11 (midnight Fri & Sat); 12-10.30 Sun
☎ (01234) 352153
Greene King IPA, Abbot; Morland Old Speckled Hen; guest beers Ⓗ
Comfortable inn dating from the 1770s, rebadged as a Greene King Local Hero pub, offering five guest ales, often from local microbreweries. Tasting thirds are available for all beers. Locally sourced home-cooked food is served lunchtimes and evenings, including a speciality Scotch egg menu. The old wood panelling has survived refurbishment, helping to retain some of the pub's original character. Five minutes from the town centre and close to the Peacock Auction Rooms and Bedford Blues rugby ground. ⌂🌑🕮◖♣P⊱⊟(4,5,7)

Wellington Arms Ⓛ
40-42 Wellington Street, MK40 2JX (off A6 N of town centre)
🕒 12-11 (10.30 Sun) ☎ (01234) 308033

Adnams Southwold Bitter; B&T Two Brewers; guest beers Ⓗ
Award-winning, street-corner local operated by B&T Brewery, offering a wide range of regional and microbrewery beers, plus Westons cider (and perry in summer) from 14 handpumps. A selection of draught Belgian and Dutch beers plus a wide range of imported bottled beers is also available. There is a courtyard for drinkers and smokers. A friendly pub with a mixed clientele, it can get very busy on Friday and Saturday evenings. 🕮🍴⊱

White Horse Ⓛ
84 Newnham Avenue, MK41 9PX
🕒 11 (12 Sun)-11 ☎ (01234) 409306
🌐 whitehorsebedford.co.uk
Wells Eagle IPA, Bombardier; guest beers Ⓗ
This large, one-bar suburban pub is situated a mile east of the town centre. Good-value food is available, with a Sunday roast and regular themed and charity evenings. Monday is open mic night, Sunday and Tuesday are quiz nights, with an additional fundraising quiz most Wednesdays. The pub has won several brewery and local business awards. A May Day weekend local beer, food and talent festival, and a November beer and banger festival, are held each year. Check the website for monthly events. 🌑🕮◖♿P⊱⊟(4)

Biggleswade

Golden Pheasant Ⓛ
71 High Street, SG18 0JH
🕒 12 (11 Fri & Sat)-midnight; 1-midnight Sun
☎ (01767) 313653 🌐 goldenpheasantpub.co.uk
Courage Directors; Wells Eagle IPA; guest beers Ⓗ
This cosy town-centre pub is less than five minutes' walk from the bus and train stations. Customers enjoy excellent ales and partake in friendly banter and popular pub games evenings. There is a single bar with low ceilings and oak beams, plus a large patio area at the rear with sheltered seating. Four continually rotating guest ales cross the spectrum of beer styles and often come from microbreweries. The real cider range varies, sometimes featuring local producers. Q🕮≈♣🍴⊱⊟

Stratton House Hotel Ⓛ
London Road, SG18 8ED
🕒 10-midnight ☎ (01767) 312442
🌐 strattonhouse-hotel.com
St Austell Landlords Choice; guest beers Ⓗ
The front bar is popular with all ages and provides comfortable seating with tables for bar meals. Outside is a small patio area and the hotel has a separate restaurant. The St Austell-brewed house ale is always competitively priced while three rotating guest beers can vary in style and colour. A springtime beer and cider festival is held. There is a quiz every other Sunday evening, regular Tuesday evening poker and free Wi-Fi – password on request. 🕮⌂◖♿≈P⊱⊟

Wheatsheaf

5 Lawrence Road, SG18 0LS
✪ 11-4, 7-11.30; 11-midnight Fri & Sat; 12-11 Sun
☎ (01767) 222220
Greene King IPA; guest beer Ⓗ
The licensees have run this back-street pub for a quarter of a century and have received many awards for good cellarmanship from Greene King. Sport dominates the conversation and the TV in this friendly single-room pub, which also offers regular games of darts, cribbage and dominoes as well as occasional trips to the races. There is a very pleasant garden at the rear. ⌂≠♣⌐

Bolnhurst

Plough ⒧

Kimbolton Road, MK44 2EX (on B660 S of village)
TL088587
✪ closed Mon; 12-3, 6.30-11; 12-3 Sun ☎ (01234) 376274
⊕ bolnhurst.com
Beer range varies Ⓗ
Award-winning pub restaurant dating back to Tudor times, offering excellent food and beer, and good service. The main bar features a wood-burning stove, and a second room is set aside for diners and functions. Up to three real ales, often from local microbreweries, are selected to complement the food. Outside is a large garden with decking beside a small pond. The pub is closed from Christmas until the second week of January each year. ⌂Q⌐❀⊙⇪P

Carlton

Fox ⒧

High Street, MK43 7LA
✪ 12-3, 6-11; 12-11 Fri & Sat; 12-10.30 Sun
☎ (01234) 720235 ⊕ thefoxatcarlton.co.uk
St Austell Tribute; Wells Eagle IPA; guest beers Ⓗ
A charming thatched community pub with a warm welcome and an attractive garden popular with families. The two guest beers are often from local microbreweries. Home-cooked lunches (daily) and evening meals (Wed-Sat) are served in the restaurant, with a range of snacks available in the bar. Themed food evenings feature occasionally and there's an annual summer beer and cider festival, with a garden outhouse used as an additional bar. Q⌐❀⊙♣P⌐(25)

Clophill

Stone Jug

10 Back Street, MK45 4BY (500yds off A6 at N end of village) TL083381
✪ 12-3.30, 6-11; 12-11 Fri & Sat; 12-10.30 Sun
☎ (01525) 860526
B&T Shefford Bitter; guest beers Ⓗ
Originally three 16th-century cottages, this popular village local has an L-shaped bar that serves two drinking areas and a family/function room. Excellent home-made lunches are available Tuesday to Saturday. The four guest beers are often from local breweries, the cider is Westons. Picnic benches at the front and a rear patio garden offer space for outdoor drinking in fine weather. Parking can be difficult at busy times. A former CAMRA Bedfordshire Pub of the Year.
Q⌐❀⊙♣⌐P⌐(44, 81)

Cople

Five Bells

1 Northill Road, MK44 3TU
✪ 12-2.30, 4.30-11.30; 12-11.30 Thu; 12-midnight Fri & Sat; 12-10.30 Sun ☎ (01234) 831330 ⊕ fivebellscople.co.uk
Greene King XX Mild, IPA; guest beers Ⓗ
A 17th-century building with colour-washed rough cast walls over a timber frame, listed for its special architectural and historic interest. The main bar has low beams and a side room with an even lower ceiling. There is a second smaller bar which can be used for functions and a small room at the back for dining. A large garden opens onto fields at the rear. The guest beer is from Greene King. No food Sunday evening. ⌂⌐❀⊙⇪P⌐⌐(74)

Dunstable

Globe ⒧

43 Winfield Street, LU6 1LS (off High Street North opp old grammar school)
✪ 12-11 (midnight Fri & Sat); 12-10.30 Sun
☎ (01582) 512300 ⊕ globe-pub.co.uk
B&T Shefford Bitter, Shefford Dark Mild, Golden Fox, Edwin Taylor's Extra Stout; Everards Tiger Best Bitter; guest beers Ⓗ
Popular beer destination and community local where 13 handpumps boast a good range of regular B&T beers, five ever-changing microbrewery beers, real cider and perry. Over 20 Belgian beers are also available and regular beer festivals are hosted. Bare boards, bar stools, breweriana and a famous plank at the end of the bar create a traditional town pub atmosphere buzzing with conversation. Acoustic music night is Tuesday. ⌂Q❀⇪♣⌐⌐(31,61)

Pheasant ⒧

208 West Street, LU6 1NX
✪ 12-11; 10.30-midnight Fri & Sat ☎ (01582) 662706
Courage Directors; Sharp's Doom Bar; guest beers Ⓗ
Family-run free house a short walk west of the busier part of town. Six handpumps dispense the regular beers plus continually rotating guests, often from microbreweries. Flights of three third pints are available to enable full range tasting. The large rear sports bar has pool and darts, and doubles as a popular function room catering for up to 150 people. Live sporting events are screened here as well as in the more traditional front bar. There is a heated front patio for smokers. ❀⇔⊙♣P⌐⌐

Victoria ⒧

69 West Street, LU6 1ST
✪ 11-12.30am (1am Fri & Sat); 12-midnight Sun
☎ (01582) 662682 ⊕ victoriapub.co.uk
Tring Victoria Bitter; guest beers Ⓗ
This popular town-centre pub offers a very warm welcome. Four beers are on handpump – Victoria Bitter from Tring Brewery and three ever-changing guests from regional and microbreweries. Good-value food is served lunchtimes and the Sunday roast is highly recommended. Pub activities include darts, dominoes, crib, golf and a football team. Two beer festivals are held each year. There is a separate function room and a heated beer garden. Quiz night is the last Tuesday of the month. ❀⊙♣⌐⌐(34,61)

Dunton

March Hare 🍺 ⅃
34 High Street, SG18 8RN
☼ 6-11 (midnight Thu & Fri); 12-midnight Sat; 12-10.30 Sun
☎ (01767) 448093 ⊕ duntonvillage.org.uk/pub/home.htm
Beer range varies ⒣
Run by a CAMRA husband and wife team, this local Pub of the Year 2013 plays a key role in village life and will soon open a community shop. Three or four excellent varied ales are kept, one usually from Buntingford Brewery, plus local Dunton cider. Summer and winter festivals are a recent addition. Monthly themed food nights are very popular, with private parties catered for on request. Regular live events include folk music on the first Tuesday of the month and morris dancing. ⓶Q⊛♣●🍴(188)

Eversholt

Green Man
Church End, MK17 9DU SP984325
☼ 12-3.30, 6-11.30, 12-midnight Fri & Sat; 12-11.30 Sun
☎ (01525) 288111 ⊕ greenmaneversholt.com
Beer range varies ⒣
A genuine free house with three varying guest ales usually on offer. It features flagstone floors and exposed brick fireplaces and is conveniently located near the tourist attractions of Woburn. Freshly prepared, good-quality food, including an award-winning Sunday lunch, is served in the bar and the separate restaurant (not Sun eve). Live music features on the first Thursday of the month. Outside is a large patio and garden. Event news is posted on Twitter and Facebook. ⓶⊛⑴&P⁵

Everton

Thornton Arms
1 Potton Road, SG19 2LD
☼ 12-2, 5.30-11; 12-11 Sat; 12-9 Sun ☎ (01767) 681149
⊕ the-thornton-arms.co.uk
Wells Eagle IPA; guest beers ⒣
Friendly three-room village pub built in 1852 and located next to the Greensand Ridge Walk which crosses central Bedfordshire. The front entrance leads directly to the main bar area where there is comfortable seating. On the right is a restaurant space with very popular Sunday lunches (book ahead), fish nights and steak nights; at the rear is a games room with TV, gaming machines and darts, pool and cribbage. Guest beers usually come from regional and national breweries. ⊛♣P⁵🍴(188,190)

Flitton

Jolly Coopers ⅃
Wardhedges, MK45 5ED TL067358
☼ 12-3 (not Mon), 5.30-11.30; 12-midnight Sat; 12-10.30 Sun
☎ (01525) 860626
Wells Eagle IPA; guest beers ⒣
Situated in the quiet hamlet of Wardhedges at the east end of Flitton, the landlord and lady take obvious pride in this wonderful country community pub. Two ever-changing and varied guest ales are available alongside the regular Eagle. Traditional British food is served in the bar and separate restaurant, with a choice of menus. There is a large garden to the rear and a patio with spectacular floral displays in the summer months. Dogs are welcome in the flagstoned bar. ⓶⊛⑴&♣P⁵

Great Barford

Anchor Inn
High Street, MK44 3LF (by river bridge 1 mile S of village centre) TL134517
☼ 12-3, 6.30 (6 Fri)-11; 12-11 Sat; 12-10.30 Sun
☎ (01234) 870364 ⊕ anchorinngreatbarford.co.uk
Young's Bitter; guest beers ⒣
Busy local inn next to the church, overlooking the River Great Ouse. At least two guest beers are usually available from an extensive range offered by the pub company. Good home-cooked food is available in the bar and restaurant, as well as a fine selection of wines. The pub is popular with river users in the summer. Occasional themed nights are hosted, mainly during the winter months. Three rooms are available for B&B.
Q⊛🛏⑴&ΛP⁵🍴(27)

Harlington

Carpenters Arms
Sundon Road, LU5 6LS
☼ 12-3.30, 6-11.30; 12-midnight Fri & Sat; 12-11.30 Sun
☎ (01525) 872384
Greene King IPA; Woodforde's Wherry; guest beers ⒣
Situated in the heart of Harlington, this low-beamed 'watch your head' traditional village pub was first licensed in 1790 and has listings of landlords from then until the present. The current landlord is a local who has always lived in the village. Two regular beers and two changing guests are available. Food is reasonably priced with good helpings. The railway station and occasional bus service along with a range of country walks make this a popular stop-off. ⓶Q☙⊛⑴&⇌P🍴(X42)

Old Sun
34 Sundon Road, LU5 6LS TL037303
☼ 12-midnight (1am Fri-Sun) ☎ (01525) 877330
Harveys Sussex Best Bitter; St Austell Tribute; Thwaites Wainwright; guest beers ⒣
This half-timbered traditional building dates from the 1740s and has been an inn since 1785. The interior comprises two separate bars with log fires and a side room in this up and down pub. Up to two guest ales are available at weekends and food is served on some evenings – ring first to check. The pub is situated in a popular commuter village a short walk from the station, and is the perfect place to start or finish a walk in the surrounding Chilterns. ⓶Q⊛⑴⊟⇌♣P⁵🍴(20,X42)

Heath & Reach

Axe & Compass ⅃
Leighton Road, LU7 0AA
☼ 12-midnight ☎ (01525) 237394
⊕ theaxeandcompass.co.uk
Beer range varies ⒣
Run by a resourceful new landlord since 2011, this village community pub is now flourishing. The older front bar with its low wood beams serves as a lounge and dining area while the rear public bar has gaming machines, a pool table and TV screen. Local beers feature strongly from breweries such as Hopping Mad, Tring, White Park and Concrete Cow. The real ale loyalty card (buy six pints, get one free) is popular with regulars. Accommodation is available in a separate lodge. ⊛🛏⑴⊟♣P⁵🍴(150)

Henlow

Engineers Arms ⅃

68 High Street, SG16 6AA
☼ 12-midnight (1am Fri & Sat) ☎ (01462) 812284
⊕ engineersarms.co.uk
Beer range varies Ⓗ
Friendly and well-regarded pub with an ever-changing range of beer styles on up to 10 handpumps, plus five ciders and a perry. The main room features wide-screen TVs and sports-themed autographed pictures. The front bar has books, brewery memorabilia and local pictures. Occasional live music and disco evenings are held plus regular poker sessions. The October beer festival features over 100 real ales and in February there is a cider and country wine festival.
🏤⛪🍴🏕♣🍴♿⅃–🚐(71,188,190)

Kensworth

Farmer's Boy

216 Common Road, LU6 2PJ
☼ 12-midnight ☎ (01582) 872207
⊕ farmersboykensworth.co.uk
Fuller's London Pride, Bengal Lancer, ESB; Gale's HSB Ⓗ
Located on the main road between the A5 and Whipsnade, this 19th-century village pub has been under new management since mid-2011. It now has eight handpumps offering the usual Fuller's favourites plus three ever-changing guest ales. The interior is very much in keeping with a building of its era. If you like your steaks then this is the place to come, with every type and size available. Dog-friendly. 🏤Q🐾⛪🕽♿P⅃–🚐(X31)

Leighton Buzzard

Golden Bell

5 Church Square, LU7 1AE TL920250
☼ 10-11.30 (midnight Fri & Sat); 11-11 Sun
☎ (01525) 373330 ⊕ thegoldenbell.co.uk
Taylor Landlord; Tetley Golden Bell Bitter; guest beers Ⓗ
With its frontage dating from the 18th century and Grade II-listing, this lively and welcoming community local has a single bar with low-beamed ceilings and sofas at one end. Food features fresh produce from local suppliers and is served throughout opening hours. Guest beers often include Adnams Broadside, Sharp's Doom Bar or St Austell Tribute – one on gravity dispense. Sport is shown on four large screens and activities include a dominoes team and monthly themed quiz.
⛪🕽♣P⅃–🚐

Red Lion

1 North Street, LU7 1EF
☼ 10-11 (midnight Fri & Sat); 11-11 Sun ☎ (01525) 374350
Banks's Bitter; Greene King Abbot; guest beer Ⓗ
This 17th-century building is a town-centre institution. An old-fashioned pub with old-fashioned values, the manager of 20 years offers a warm welcome. The public bar has all the traditional pub games whilst the main bar resembles a living room with comfy chairs, a large fish tank, TV and the pub's dogs wandering around. As well as the range of well-kept ales there is a selection of Irish and Scottish malt whiskies.
Q⛪🍴♣⅃–🚐

Swan Hotel

50 High Street, LU7 1EA TL921250
☼ 7am-midnight (11.30 Sun); 7am-10 Sun
☎ (01525) 380170
Greene King Abbot; Ruddles Best Bitter; guest beers Ⓗ
Originally a coaching inn dating from the 17th century, the building was tastefully renovated by Wetherspoon in 2011. With good-value food and 39 guest rooms, the Swan is busy and bustling for much of the week. The friendly and efficient staff operate one long bar serving two rooms, a conservatory and a courtyard. Real cider is available and guest beers regularly come from local microbreweries such as Vale, Tring, Concrete Cow and Oxfordshire Ales. Events include occasional Meet the Brewer evenings.
🏤Q🍴🕽♿♣⅃–🚐

Luton

Bricklayers Arms

16-18 High Town Road, LU2 0DD TL093217
☼ 12-11 Mon; 12-2.30, 5-11 Tue-Thu; 12-midnight Fri & Sat; 12-10.30 Sun ☎ (01582) 611017
⊕ bricklayersarmsluton.co.uk
Batemans XB; guest beers Ⓗ
The five busy handpumps serve a choice of light, amber or dark beer from an ever-changing range of guest ales from local and national breweries, often including a mild and an Oakham brew, with draught Belgian beers also available. This quirky town-centre pub has been run by the same landlady for 26 years. It is popular with Hatters fans on match days, with TVs in both bars showing football and other sporting events. Quiz night is Monday. Lunchtime bar meals are served Monday to Saturday. ⛪🕽⇄♣P⅃

English Rose

46 Old Bedford Road, LU2 7PA TL090219
☼ 12-11 ☎ (01582) 723889
Beer range varies Ⓗ
Popular town local with a friendly village-pub atmosphere. Four frequently changing guest beers are chosen from a range of breweries nationwide, with hundreds of different ales served over recent years. An ever-changing cider or perry is also available. Quiz night is Tuesday. The pub garden is probably the best in town, catering for smokers and non-smokers in four specially designed heated huts. An annual beer festival is held each June, as well as a Christmas beer festival throughout December. ⛪🕽♿⇄♣⅃–🚐(24,25)

London Hatter

46 Park Street, LU1 3ET TL094210
☼ 8-midnight (1am Fri & Sat); 8-11.30 Sun
☎ (01582) 390920
Adnams Broadside; Greene King Abbot; Ruddles Best Bitter; guest beers Ⓗ
Wetherspoon's tasteful conversion of a former nightclub at the university end of town opened in 2011. Guest ales greet you on the first four handpumps, often including a local ale; the second four pumps dispense the regular beers. Real cider and perry are also usually available. The pub's smart interior caters more for dining than partying and local history, in pictures, adorns the walls.
🏤Q🐾⛪🕽♿⇄♣⅃

Wigmore Arms

Wigmore Lane, LU2 8AD TL121224
11-11 (1am Fri); 10-midnight Sat; 11-10.30 Sun
(01582) 417343
Greene King IPA; Wells Bombardier; guest beers H
Lively and large pub in a residential area of Luton next to Asda supermarket. The modern two-bar interior has a comfortable lounge with a dining area where food is served all day every day. The sports bar has two large HD screens and a 3D TV showing TV sports including the Luton Town channel. Live music features on the last Saturday of the month. Beer festivals are held in April and October each year. P

Potton

Rising Sun

11 Everton Road, SG19 2PA
12-3, 5-midnight; 12-midnight Sat; 12-11 Sun
(01767) 260231
Wells Eagle IPA, Bombardier; guest beers H
Popular open-plan community pub with wooden beams and a covered well. It has a snug area with comfortable seating and upstairs is a quiet function room and roof-top terrace. The eight well-kept ales include two more from the Wells & Young's range, one from Oakham and three guests from microbreweries. A real cider is also kept, often from a local producer. Beer festivals are held on the early May and late August bank holiday weekends. Good-value food is served daily until 9.30pm. P (188,190)

Renhold

Polhill Arms

25 Wilden Road, MK41 0JP (at Salph End) TL082527
12-3, 5-11; 12-11 Fri & Sat; 12-10.30 Sun
(01234) 771398 polhillarms.co.uk
Greene King IPA, Old Speckled Hen; guest beers H
One-bar, family-friendly village local with a welcoming atmosphere and a large garden, play area and restaurant. An interesting collection of pub and brewery artefacts is on view. Traditional pub food is served as well as fish and chips (not Sun or Mon eves). Live entertainment and quiz nights feature regularly, and darts and skittles are played. Three guest beers are usually available, with Olde Trip a popular choice.
A P (27,151)

Salford

Red Lion Hotel

Wavendon Road, MK17 8AZ (2 miles N of M1 jct 13) SP934389
11-2.30, 6.30-11; 12-2.30, 6-11 Sun (01908) 583117
redlionhotel.eu
Wells Eagle IPA, Bombardier H
Friendly, traditional country hotel serving a fine choice of home-cooked food in the bar and restaurant. The cosy bar is heated by an open fire in winter and offers a selection of interesting board games. The large garden includes a covered area and a secure children's playground. Six rooms are available for overnight accommodation.
Q P

Sandy

Sir William Peel

39 High Street, SG19 1AG (opp church)
12 (11 Sat)-midnight; 12-10.30 Sun (01767) 680607
sirwilliampeel.webs.com
Batemans XB; guest beers H
Popular open-plan free house a short walk from the railway station and bus stops. Alongside Batemans XB are three rotating guest ales and several real ciders. The spring beer and cider festival is held in the former stables at the rear, with outdoor seating nearby. No food is available except the Sunday afternoon cheeseboard, but you are welcome to bring in a take-away meal. Regular quizzes, live music and jam sessions are hosted. The pub sponsors its own football team. Dog-friendly – refreshments provided.
P (73,188,190)

Shefford

Brewery Tap

14 North Bridge Street, SG17 5DH
11.30-11; 12-10.30 Sun (01462) 628448
B&T Shefford Bitter, Dunstable Giant, Dragon Slayer; Everards Tiger Best Bitter; guest beers H
Renamed by the nearby B&T Brewery in 1996, the Tap is primarily a drinkers' pub, offering four regular beers and at least one guest. A breweriana display adorns the open-plan interior, which is divided into two distinct areas plus a family room at the rear, all served from a common bar. Lunchtime pies and rolls are available. Darts, dominoes and cribbage teams are actively supported. The rear patio garden is heated on cool evenings. Car park access is through an archway next to the pub. P (71,72)

Souldrop

Bedford Arms

High Street, MK44 1EY (½ mile W of A6) SP987617
closed Mon; 12-3, 6-11; 12-midnight Fri & Sat; 12-11 Sun
(01234) 781384
Black Sheep Best Bitter; Greene King IPA; Phipps NBC Red Star; guest beers H
Large village pub created partly from a 17th-century hop and ale house. Guest beers are often from local microbreweries, cider is from local producer Eversheds. The restaurant has a central, open fireplace and offers traditional pub favourites prepared to order, with daily specials and a roast on Sunday lunchtime. A games room with skittles runs off the main bar. The spacious garden with pétanque is popular with families in summer. Local CAMRA Country Pub of the Year 2013.
P (26)

Stevington

Royal George

8-10 Silver Street, MK43 7QP
12-2 (not Wed), 5-11; 12-11 Sat & Sun (01234) 822184
Wells Eagle IPA; guest beers H
A friendly community pub created from two old houses joined together. London commuters will appreciate the hanging straps over the bar. Two Westons real ciders or perries are served from the cellar. Good-value lunches (no lunch Sun or Wed) include bacon, egg and chips, sandwiches and baguettes. Live bands play occasionally at

weekends. A key to the 18th-century Stevington windmill east of the village centre may be borrowed for a small deposit. ⋈⊛ℂ♣🐾P⬥🚃(25)

Studham

Red Lion
Church Road, LU6 2QA TL022158
✪ 12-2.30, 5-11; 12-11 Fri & Sat; 12-10.30 Sun
☎ (01582) 872530 ⊕ theredlion-studham.co.uk
Adnams Southwold Bitter; Greene King IPA; Taylor Landlord; guest beers Ⓗ
Ideally situated in the centre of the village adjacent to a wildlife common and in the middle of a network of countryside footpaths, this pub is a focal point for the local community. With Whipsnade Zoo only a couple of miles away, this is the perfect place to rest for a pint and a bite to eat by the log fire after a long day trekking around the zoo. See the blackboard for current and upcoming guest ales. ⋈Q❅⊛ℂ⅊♣P⬥🚃(X31)

Tebworth

Queen's Head Ⓛ
The Lane, LU7 9QB TL991268
✪ closed Mon-Wed; 12-3, 6-11 Thu & Fri; 12-3.30, 7-11 Sat & Sun ☎ (01525) 874101
Adnams Broadside Ⓖ; Wells Eagle IPA Ⓗ, Bombardier Ⓖ
Marvellously traditional two-room village local, popular for darts and dominoes. The Eagle IPA is served from the bar; two varying ales are served on gravity direct from the cellar. Live music is a regular attraction on Friday. The pub has featured in this Guide more than 26 times under the current landlord – a TV, radio and stage actor who always has a joke to share and a tale to tell. A great example of a small village pub well supported by locals. ⋈Q❅⅊♣P⅊

Toddington

Oddfellows Arms
2 Conger Lane, LU5 6BP TL010289
✪ 5-11 (midnight Fri); 1-midnight Sat; 1-11 Sun
☎ (01525) 872021
Adnams Broadside; Fuller's London Pride; guest beers Ⓗ
Attractive 15th-century pub facing the village green with a heavily beamed ceiling, open fires in the bars and a brass-topped bar featuring a vast collection of pumpclips. There is a separate games room with a pool table. Westons Old Rosie is available often alongside a guest cider or perry. Beer festivals are held in the autumn. The patio garden is popular in summer and has a shelter for smokers. ⋈❅⅊♣🐾⅊🚃(142,244)

Totternhoe

Old Farm
16 Church Road, LU6 1RE SP988209
✪ 12-3, 5-11 (midnight Fri); 12-midnight Sat; 12-11 Sun
☎ (07536) 661294 ⊕ oldfarminn.co.uk
Fuller's ESB, London Pride; guest beer Ⓗ

Located in the conservation area of Church End, this charming village pub boasts two inglenooks. The public bar with its low-boarded ceiling is where you will find good conversation and traditional pub games. Dogs are welcome in the front bar and there is a large child-friendly garden. Monday is music night. Tasty home-cooked food is served including popular Sunday roasts (no food Sun and Mon eves). ⊛⅊⅊⅊♣P

Whipsnade

Old Hunters Lodge Ⓛ
The Crossroads, LU6 2LN TL014181
✪ 11.30-2.30 (3 Sat), 5.30-11; 12-11 Sun ☎ (01582) 872228
⊕ old-hunters.com
Greene King Abbot; Tring Brock Bitter; guest beers Ⓗ
Beautiful 15th-century thatched inn set on the outskirts of Whipsnade village and close to Whipsnade Zoo. The guest beer range at this free house always includes microbreweries. A log fire warms the cosy main bar where there is plenty of comfortable seating as well as traditional dining tables. Multiple separate restaurant areas can be used as function rooms. The colourful front garden makes a lovely area for summer dining and drinking. The six guest rooms include a bridal suite. ⋈Q⊛⅊ℂⅅP🚃(X31)

Wingfield

Plough
Tebworth Road, LU7 9QH TL002263
✪ 12-3, 5.30-midnight; 12-midnight Sat; 12-10.30 Sun
☎ (01525) 873077 ⊕ theploughinn.com
Fuller's London Pride, ESB; Gale's Seafarers Ale, HSB; guest beers Ⓗ
Charming thatched village inn dating from the 17th century, decorated with paintings of rural scenes and ploughs. Beware the low beams! Good home-cooked food is served daily except Sunday evening when a fortnightly quiz is held. There are tables outside at the front, and to the rear is a conservatory and prize-winning garden, illuminated at night in the summer. Heated umbrellas are provided for smokers. ⋈Q❅ℂⅅ♣P⬥🚃(68)

Wootton

Chequers Ⓛ
Hall End, MK43 9HP (NW edge of village) SP001457
✪ 12-3, 6-11; 12-11 Fri-Sun ☎ (01234) 765005
⊕ chequerswootton.co.uk
Wells Eagle IPA; guest beers Ⓗ
Originally a farmhouse, this handsome old free house retains a wealth of heavy wooden beams and period features. A wide range of guest beers is offered, often including local microbrewery ales. An interesting, quality menu is served in the restaurant and good-value bar food is available throughout the pub (not Sun eve). Monday is fish and chips night while three different pies feature on Tuesday evening. The large, pleasant garden is popular in fine weather. ⋈Q❅⊛ℂⅅ♣P⬥🚃(68)

A glass of bitter beer or pale ale, taken with the principal meal of the day, does more good and less harm than any medicine the physician can prescribe. **Dr Carpenter**, 1750

Public transport information
Leave the car behind and travel to the pub by bus, train or tram

Using public transport is an excellent way to get to the pub, but many people use it irregularly, and systems can be slightly different from place to place. So, below are some useful websites and phone numbers where you can find all the information you might need.

Combined information

The national **Traveline** system gives information on all rail and local bus services throughout England, Scotland and Wales. Calls are put through to a local call centre and if necessary your call will be switched through to a more relevant one. There are also services for mobiles, including a next-bus text service and smart-phone app. The website offers other services including timetables and a journey planner with mapping:

- 0871 200 22 33
  www.traveline.org.uk

The **Transport Direct** website uniquely offers information for door-to-door travel by public transport, bicycle and car around England, Scotland and Wales. The site provides street-level mapping of transport stops and stations, places and addresses and can generate route maps for various types of journeys:

- **www.transportdirect.info**

LONDON

In London use Traveline or **Transport for London (TfL)** travel services. TfL provides information and route planning for all of London's transport networks, including London Underground and Overground, Docklands Light Railway, National Rail, buses, River Buses, Tramlink, Barclays Cycles and cycle routes. Detailed ticketing information helps you find the most cost effective ways to travel in London. There are also live departure boards, service and traffic updates; mobile services and more:

- 020 7222 1234
  www.tfl.gov.uk

Trains

National Rail Enquiries covers the whole of Great Britain's rail network and provides service information, ticketing, online journey planning and other information.

- 08457 48 49 50
  www.nationalrail.co.uk

Coaches

The two main UK coach companies are **National Express** and **Scottish Citylink**. Between them, they serve everywhere from Cornwall to the Highlands. Their websites offer timetables, journey planning, ticketing and route mapping, along with other useful information.

- National Express. 08717 81 81 81
  www.nationalexpress.com

- Scottish Citylink: 08705 50 50 50
  www.citylink.co.uk

National Express has kindly teamed up with CAMRA to offer members a 15% discounted rate on coach travel until 1st June 2014. National Express coaches operate to more than 1,000 UK destinations and carry over 18 million customers a year. For further details and to take up this offer, simply sign in to your CAMRA account at **www.camra.org.uk**

Northern Ireland & islands

For travel outside mainland Britain but within the area of this Guide, information is available from the following companies:

NORTHERN IRELAND
- Translink: 028 9066 6630
  www.translink.co.uk

ISLE OF MAN
- Isle of Man Transport: 01624 662 525
  www.iombusandrail.info

JERSEY
- Liberty Bus: 01534 828 555
  www.libertybus.je

GUERNSEY
- Island Coachways: 01481 720 210
  www.buses.gg

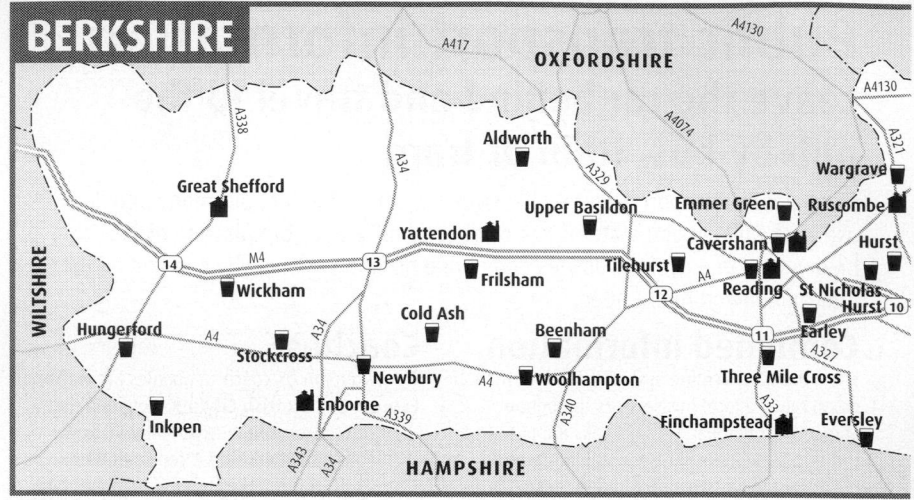

Aldworth

Bell Inn ▾ ★ 🄻
Bell Lane, RG8 9SE (off B4009) SU555796
❀ closed Mon; 11-3, 6-11; 12-3, 7-10.30 Sun
☎ (01635) 578272
Arkell's 3B, Kingsdown; West Berkshire Maggs' Mild, Old Tyler, seasonal beers 🄷
An enduring entry in the Guide and a classic rural gem, this venue features a timeless interior and a capacious garden for hot days. With 250 years of history, it is now in its fifth generation of ownership. A delicious variety of rolls, soups and puds is served. Old Tyler is a beer name unique to the Bell. Local draught ciders from Tutts Clump and Upton are very popular. ▲Q❀☀🄽♣●P

Beenham

Six Bells 🄻
The Green, RG7 5NX SU584689
❀ 12-2.30 (not Mon), 6-11; 12-3, 6.30-11 Sat; 12-3, 6.30-10.30 Sun ☎ (0118) 971 3368 ⊕ thesixbells.co.uk
West Berkshire Good Old Boy; guest beers 🄷
Lovely welcoming local village pub offering three ales from smaller breweries in Berks, Bucks and Hants, with West Berkshire normally represented. Settle down for a variety of games in either of the bars, against a backdrop of open fires and an eclectic mix of worldwide artefacts. The Wednesday pie and pudding club is deservedly popular, with home-cooked meals available throughout the week. ▲Q❀🚗🄽🄳♣P🖳(104)

Binfield

Jack o' Newbury ▾ 🄻
Terrace Road North, RG42 5PH SU845718
❀ 11-3, 5.30-11; 12-3, 7-10.30 Sun ☎ (01344) 454881
⊕ jackofnewbury.co.uk
Loddon Hoppit; West Berkshire Good Old Boy; Young's Special; guest beer 🄷
Traditional Victorian pub on the edge of the village, deservedly popular with locals and visitors. The house beer, Binfield Best (3.9%), of unknown provenance, is popular with the locals. This is one of the few remaining pubs in the area with a skittle alley, which can be hired for events. Good home-

cooked food is served (no food Sun and Mon eves). Multiple CAMRA Branch Pub of the Year award winner. ▲Q❀🄽♣P🖳(151)

Victoria Arms
Terrace Road North, RG42 5JA SU842713
❀ 11.30-11 (midnight Fri & Sat); 12-11 Sun
☎ (01344) 483856 ⊕ victoriaarmsbinfield.co.uk
Fuller's Chiswick Bitter, Discovery, London Pride, ESB, seasonal beers; Gale's HSB 🄷
Welcoming pub in Binfield village serving six Fuller's ales at peak times, including seasonals. Outside is a covered, heated terrace available for private functions, and a beer garden. Food includes regular specials, with hog roasts and barbecues in summer. Local CAMRA Community Pub of the Year, the Victoria Arms is a vibrant part of the local area and hosts charity events, quiz nights and occasional live music. ▲❀🄽🄳P🖳(53,153)

Bracknell

Cannie Man
Hanover Gardens, RG12 7PD
❀ 11-11 (10.30 Sun) ☎ (01344) 307620
Fuller's London Pride; Hogs Back TEA; guest beer 🄷
A well-maintained community pub with a welcoming atmosphere built in the style of the local estate, supporting thriving darts, pool and football teams. The spacious bar contains large screens showing TV sport and hosts live music at weekends. At least three well-kept beers are served. Microwave food is available. Children are welcome until early evening. Those with disability may need help negotiating two small steps into the pub. 🚗❀🄽♣P🖳(171,172)

Old Manor 🄻
Grenville Place, RG12 1BP (adjacent to Weather Way exit on Met Office/College roundabout)
❀ 8am-midnight (1am Fri & Sat) ☎ (01344) 304490
Greene King Abbot; Ruddles Best Bitter; guest beers 🄷
An attractive 17th-century brick manor house with two distinct themed bars separated by a half-timbered snug and the larger Monks Room popular for meals, meetings and private functions. A busy, vibrant community pub with a mixed clientele, this

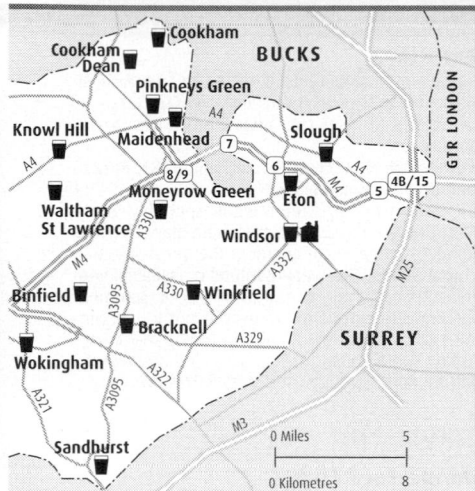

Wetherspoon's serves the company's usual beverage and menu range, with eight real ales, six of them varying, and two ciders/perries. Food is available until 10pm. Outside is a pleasant walled garden and two large terraces.
Q☼♨◐◑Ġ⇌♠P⌐🖵

Caversham

Baron Cadogan Ⓛ
22-24 Prospect Street, RG4 8JG
☼ 8am-11 (midnight Fri & Sat); 8am-10.30 Sun
☎ (0118) 948 1078
Fuller's ESB; Loddon Ferryman's Gold; Ruddles Best Bitter Ⓗ; guest beers Ⓗ/Ⓖ
A Wetherspoon hostelry on a more intimate scale than many, attracting a diverse crowd of customers since it first opened in 1997. (Baron Cadogan's family seat was nearby.) Paintings by local artists adorn the walls, and TV screens on mute show news and occasional sporting events. The house beer is from the local Loddon Brewery and other microbreweries are also represented. Real cider is also kept. Q◐Ġ♠⌐🖵(2,2a,22,24)

Fox & Hounds Ⓛ
51 Gosbrook Road, RG4 8BN
☼ 12-11 (10.30 Sun) ☎ (0118) 375 9205
Beer range varies Ⓗ
Recently refurbished and now run by Kevin and Kerri from Two Bridges Brewery, the pub offers its own beers alongside others from local microbreweries. Real cider and perry are also available, plus rolls and snacks. A popular quiz night is held on Thursday. Music nights reflect the pub's history – John Lennon and Paul McCartney played a gig here in 1960 as The Nerk Twins.
♨☼♣♠⌐🖵(2,2a)

Griffin
10-12 Church Road, RG4 7AD
☼ 11-11 (10.30 Sun) ☎ (0118) 947 5018
⊕ thegriffincaversham.co.uk
Adnams Broadside; Courage Best Bitter, Directors; Sharp's Doom Bar; guest beer Ⓗ
The current pub was built in 1916 and offers good food and ale. An extensive Chef & Brewer menu is available all day, with numerous specials on

chalkboards and regular themed-produce weeks. The spacious pub with a heated rear patio garden offers plenty of opportunity for a quiet drink or a big family meal. The guest ale changes weekly and is chosen from a variety of local and national breweries. ♨Q☼♨◐P⌐🖵

Cold Ash

Castle Inn Ⓛ
Cold Ash Hill, RG18 9PS SU511697
☼ 11.30-11.30 (midnight Fri & Sat); 12-11 Sun
☎ (01635) 863232 ⊕ thecastleatcoldash.co.uk
Courage Best Bitter; Fuller's London Pride; Sharp's Doom Bar; guest beers Ⓗ
A 19th-century inn, a favourite with villagers and visitors alike. Very popular with pensioners for the weekday lunch, it also gets busy for Sunday roasts. During the summer months cream teas are served on the colourful flowering patio. There is always a beer from West Berkshire brewery alongside the three regulars and two rotating guests. Wyatt's cider is sometimes available. A meat raffle is held on Fridays. ♨☼♨◐♣P⌐🖵(101)

Cookham

Bounty Ⓛ
Riverside, SL8 5RG (over railway bridge from Bourne End or walk along Cookham towpath) SU890872
☼ 12-11; 12-dusk Sat & Sun only winter ☎ (01628) 520056
⊕ thebountypub.com
Rebellion IPA, Mutiny; guest beer Ⓗ
Located on National Trust's Cockmarsh between Cookham village and Bourne End, this quirky, characterful pub is only accessible on foot or by boat. Dogs, walkers and children are made welcome. Bar billiards can be played while listening to '60s music. Live events feature throughout the summer, including theatre. Summer weekends can be very busy. Food is served until 8pm. Note the reduced winter opening hours. ♨☼♨◐⇌(Bourne End)⌐

Cookham Dean

Jolly Farmer Ⓛ
Church Road, SL6 9PD
☼ 11.30-11 (11.45 Fri); 12-10.30 Sun ☎ (01628) 482905
⊕ jollyfarmercookhamdean.co.uk
Brakspear Bitter; Courage Best Bitter; St Austell Trelawny; guest beers Ⓗ
Local pub owned by the village since 1987. The adults-only bar is cosy while the larger Dean bar accommodates families, diners and drinkers, with a real log fire in winter. The three guest ales always include a LocAle. Ideal for walkers, the pub is dog-friendly and has a large beer garden plus children's play area. Beer festivals are held throughout the year. ♨Q☼♨◐Ġ♠P⌐

Earley

Maiden Over ⓛ
Silverdale Road, RG6 7NG
✪ 10 (11.30 Sun)-11 ☎ (0118) 966 7575
⊕ themaidenover.com
Fuller's London Pride; guest beers Ⓗ
Locals Warwick and Rachel took over in late 2010 and have worked hard to put this estate pub at the heart of the community. You can play pool, darts, crib, dominoes or backgammon while watching TV sport. Good pub food includes the occasional special Ethiopian food event. An impressive range of 100 bottled beers from local breweries has been accrued. Family-friendly, dog-friendly and recently breastfeeding-friendly! Coffee from 7am, breakfast from 7.30am and ale from 10am.
🏚️☎⊛◑ ⊞⇌♣P⁵⃔⊒(20a)

Emmer Green

Black Horse
Kidmore End Road, RG4 8SE
✪ 11 (12 Sun)-11 ☎ (0118) 947 4111
Courage Best Bitter; Young's Bitter; guest beer Ⓗ
A traditional village local, now part of Reading's northern suburbs and one of two 'Horses' that face each other across the road. This pub is opposite the recreation ground and just off the village centre. Turn right when you go in for the busy public bar with pool and TV sport; turn left for the quieter lounge bar with a real fire. A decked outdoor drinking and smoking area is to the rear.
🏚️⊛⊞♣⁵⃔⊒(2,2a,23,24)

Eton

Watermans Arms ⓛ
Brocas Street, SL4 6BW
✪ 11-11.30 (midnight Fri & Sat); 11-11 Sun
☎ (01753) 861001 ⊕ watermans-eton.com
Beer range varies Ⓗ
A few yards from Eton Bridge, the interior of this inn features rowing memorabilia and murals, and there is a good selection of books on sale in aid of the local Swan Lifeline charity. A function room is available free of charge. Six beers are offered including two from local micros (Binghams and Windsor & Eton) and a house beer brewed by Caledonian. The Sunday carvery is recommended.
🏚️⊛◑⇌(Windsor & Eton Riverside)●⊒(60)

Eversley

Tally Ho ⓛ
Fleet Hill, RG27 0RR (On the A327 at the jct of B3348 Fleet Hill, just N of the river)
✪ 10.30-11 (midnight Fri & Sat; 10.30 Sun)
☎ (0118) 973 2134
Brunning & Price Original Bitter; guest beers Ⓗ
Tally Ho was formerly a Blubeckers Restaurant but is now a freehouse and part of Home Counties Pub Restaurants. Recently revamped following a major fire, it is laid out entirely as a food pub – at busy times most tables can often by taken by diners enjoying the high-quality food. Four handpumps are always in use with one beer from the Phoenix brewery and three guest beers including at least one LocAle. The large, attractive garden is perfect for summer drinking. ⊛◑P⊒

Frilsham

Pot Kiln ⓛ
Yattendon-Bucklebury Road, RG18 0XX (on unnamed road between Yattendon and Bucklebury) SU552730
✪ 12-2.30, 6-11; 12-11 Sat; 12-9.30 Sun ☎ (01635) 201366
⊕ potkiln.org
West Berkshire Mr Chubb's Lunchtime Bitter, Brick Kiln Bitter, seasonal beers Ⓗ
The seasonal beer is the monthly speciality from West Berks, but may occasionally be drawn from its standard range to complement the guest selection from a regional brewery. Bar food is available, with venison Scotch egg a local favourite. On summer Sundays the outdoor pizza oven is put to work in the enclosed garden. A cribbage group meets on Friday. The adjoining restaurant is led by TV chef and owner Mike Robinson. 🏚️Q⊛◑ ⊞♣P

Hungerford

Hungerford Club ⓛ
3 The Croft, RG17 0HY (on foot via Church Lane, by road via Church St and Croft Rd) SU336686
✪ 11-3, 7-11 (10.30 Sun) ☎ (01488) 682357
⊕ hungerford-club.co.uk
Fuller's Chiswick Bitter, London Pride; guest beer Ⓗ
A welcoming sports and social club with a comfortable lounge where you can enjoy friendly conversation with club members over a pint of beer. Fuller's provide the regular ales but guest beers are almost always also on offer. Quiz nights and curry nights are held once a month. Filled rolls are available Saturday lunchtimes. Show this Guide or CAMRA membership card for entry. ⊛⇌♣P⁵⃔⊒

Hurst

Castle Inn ⓛ
Church Hill, RG10 0SJ
✪ 12-2.30 (3 Sat), 5.30-11; 12-10.30 Sun
☎ (0118) 934 0034 ⊕ castlehurst.co.uk
Binghams Twyford Tipple; guest beers Ⓗ
A cosy local and a destination country pub. Outside, you can choose between the private garden, seating overlooking the village bowling green or tables with a view of the local church. Inside, the separate snug bar doubles as a family room; the small bar fronts the public area with an adjoining dining room. Leased from the church opposite, this free house serves local ales and good well-priced food, sourced locally whenever possible. Opening hours are reduced in winter.
🏚️Q⧖⊛◑ ⊞P⊒(129)

Inkpen

Crown & Garter ⓛ
Inkpen Common, RG17 9QR SU378639
✪ 12-3 (not Mon & Tue), 5.30-11; 12-5, 7-10.30 Sun
☎ (01488) 668325 ⊕ crownandgarter.co.uk
Two Cocks Gibbet Ale; West Berkshire Good Old Boy Ⓗ
This recently refurbished 17th-century former coaching inn is set in an area of outstanding natural beauty. Home-cooked food and local ales can be enjoyed in the dining area or in the bar, warmed by a wood-burning stove. Gibbet Ale is exclusively brewed for the pub. Real cider, from a local producer, is kept in summer. Outside at the front is a large, mature garden. Separate en-suite accommodation is available.
🏚️Q⧖⊛◑⊞◑♣⁵⃔⊟⊒(13)

Knowl Hill

Bird in Hand 🅛

Bath Road, RG10 9UP (on A4 between Reading and Maidenhead)

🌣 11-11; 12-10.30 Sun ☎ (01628) 826622

🌐 birdinhand.co.uk

Beer range varies 🄷

A pub with a 600-year history. The beer range normally includes something from the local Binghams Brewery. Excellent food is served all day. The lounge offers a relaxed atmosphere with oak panelling and a real fire, and in summer the lovely beer garden hosts barbecues. A discount on real ales is offered on production of a CAMRA membership card. Ample parking is available and there are full hotel facilities.

🏰Q🕭🕸🍴◑🗓♿P⁵⏴🚌(127,239)

Maidenhead

Bear

8-10 High Street, SL6 1QJ (near town hall)

🌣 8am-midnight (11 Sun) ☎ (01628) 763030

Greene King IPA, Abbot; guest beers 🄷

Large Wetherspoon pub, formerly a coaching inn, refurbished in 2009 and having an open plan bar with several different seating areas. A spiral staircase leads to an upper floor with an additional bar and comfy sofas. The 10 handpumps dispense up to five guest ales, including many from local breweries. Two or three ciders are often available, including Mr Whiteheads. ◑🗓≈🍴🚌

Greyhound 🅛

92-96 Queens Street, SL6 1HZ (near station)

🌣 8am-midnight (1am Fri & Sat) ☎ (01628) 779410

Fuller's London Pride; Greene King Abbot; Loddon Hoppit; guest beers 🄷

A large Wetherspoon's named after the original pub where King Charles I met his children the night before his execution. The large open-plan bar has a family area at the rear and a separate small room at the front. A quiet pub during the week, it has music on Friday and Saturday nights. Guest beers often include ales from local microbreweries. Real cider from Mr Whitehead's is served. ◑🗓≈🍴⁵⏴🚌

Maidenhead Conservative Club

32 York Road, SL6 1SF (close to station)

🌣 11-11 (11.45 Fri & Sat); 12-11 Sun ☎ (01628) 620579

🌐 maidenheadconclub.co.uk

Fuller's London Pride, seasonal beers; guest beers 🄷

The steward is a CAMRA member and the club was winner of the CAMRA Regional Club of the Year in 2012. Two guest ales from independent breweries are available, along with a selection of bottle-conditioned beers. Hot meals are served weekday lunchtimes. Crib and darts nights are held during the week. A public car park is close by. Show a CAMRA membership card for entry for a minimal fee. 🕭◑🗓≈♣⁵⏴🚌

Moneyrow Green

White Hart

SL6 2ND (½ mile S of village)

🌣 12-11 (10 Sun) ☎ (01628) 621460

🌐 thewhitehartolyport.com

Greene King IPA; Morland Old Speckled Hen; guest beers 🄷

TV and traditional pub games, including bar billiards, are available in the public bar, while the

smaller wood-panelled lounge bar has leather sofas and a real fire in winter. The guest ale range features non-Greene King beers. Food is available every day except Monday. Regular quiz and live music evenings are held, along with a summer beer festival. Outside is a large fenced beer garden with a children's play area and pétanque square. 🏰🕭🕸◑🗓♣P⁵⏴🚌(6)

Newbury

Lock, Stock & Barrel 🅛

104 Northbrook Street, RG14 1AA SU471672

🌣 11-11 (midnight Fri & Sat); 12-10.30 Sun

☎ (01635) 580550 🌐 lockstockandbarrelnewbury.co.uk

Fuller's Discovery, London Pride, ESB, seasonal beers 🄷

Stylish and comfortably furnished town-centre pub with a roof terrace and outside seating to take advantage of a fine day. Situated overlooking the lock on the Kennet and Avon Canal, this is a great place to view the canal activities including duck races and the annual crafty craft race on the May bank holiday Monday. Fresh home-cooked food is served along with Fuller's beers and local guest ales from either Butts or West Berkshire breweries. 🕭🕸◑🗓≈⁵⏴🚌

Pinkneys Green

Stag & Hounds 🅛

1 Lee Lane, SL6 6NU

🌣 11-3, 5.30-11; 11-11 Fri & Sat; 12-10.30 Sun

☎ (01628) 630268

Sharp's Doom Bar; guest beers 🄷

The pub, next to the National Trust-owned green, always offers one or two Rebellion ales and three other frequently changing guests. It has two rooms, one a dining room where good-value meals are served. Beer festivals take place in the function room, one on the second weekend of May when Carters Steam Fair visits the green. There is a large garden and a heated shelter for smokers. Wednesday is quiz night and two wide-screen TVs show sport. Well-behaved dogs are welcome. Q🕭🕸◑♣P⁵⏴🚌(5,8)

Reading

Alehouse 🅛

2 Broad Street, RG1 2BH

🌣 11-11; 12-10.30 Sun ☎ (0118) 950 8119

🌐 hobgoblinreading.co.uk

Beer range varies 🄷

The Alehouse, formerly the Hobgoblin, is the perfect antidote to town-centre bars. The pub champions many microbreweries (local and from further afield) and is the only bar in Reading that serves mead, as well as an excellent range of cider and perry. Not everyone will appreciate the unique character of this traditional pub, but those who do come back for more. 🕸≈🍴🎲🚌

Hop Leaf 🅛

163-165 Southampton Street, RG1 2QZ

🌣 12-11.30 (12.30am Fri & Sat) ☎ (0118) 931 4700

🌐 hopback.co.uk/our-pubs/the-hopleaf.html

Hop Back Golden Best, Redsells EKG, Crop Circle, Summer Lightning; guest beers 🄷

A recently refurbished traditional local with an impressive sporting pedigree - why not try your hand at one of the few bar billiards tables in

Reading, or play a game of crib or backgammon? Fans of classic rock will enjoy the landlord's choice in music. An interesting variety of pub snacks is served and dogs are welcome. A good range of daily newspapers is provided. ⏴♣️🐾(5,6)

Nag's Head ☶ 🄻
5 Russell Street, RG1 7XD
⏣ 12-11 (midnight Fri); 11-midnight Sat ☎ (0118) 957 4649
⊕ nagsheadreading.com
Beer range varies Ⓗ
In six years the Nag's has established itself as a premier ale and cider venue. Pies and baguettes are available during the week, with a roast on Sunday. An eclectic mix of bottled beers is stocked. Numerous board games are available above the (tuned and working) upright piano. Gets busy on Reading FC match days.
🏚⏴🕮🍴◖◗⇌(West)♣️🐾P⁵⏴

Retreat 🄻
8 St John's Street, RG1 4EH
⏣ 4.30-11; 12-11.30 Fri & Sat; 12-11 Sun ☎ (0118) 957 1593
Loddons Ferrymans Gold; Sharp's Cornish Coaster Ⓗ
Tucked in a terraced side street, this friendly community pub is well worth seeking out. A new licensee has taken over the reins but things remain pretty similar. A large range of real ale is skilfully squeezed into the small bar. Locally renowned for regular live music and hosting local events, this pub was one of the first in the country to be registered as a Community Asset under the new government Localism Act. Q♣️🐾⁵

Zerodegrees 🄻
9 Bridge Street, RG1 2LR
⏣ 12-midnight (11 Sun) ☎ (0118) 959 7959
⊕ zerodegrees.co.uk/reading/
Zerodegrees Wheat Ale, Black Lager, Pale Ale, Pilsner, seasonal beers Ⓟ
Microbrewery and restaurant specialising in wood-fired pizza/Italian food. It has a large bar with seating for around 50 people and many more standing, as well as an area upstairs. This is Reading's only brewery, with the brewing vessels on view in the bar. The beer in the German tradition is served live from tanks but may be a little cold for some drinkers' tastes – but you can always let it warm up a bit. Trendy, a great introduction to real beer for younger adults.
🕮◖◗🕎⇌🐾

St Nicholas Hurst

Wheelwrights Arms
Davis Way, RG10 0TR (on B3030, opp entrance to Dinton Pastures) SU790725
⏣ 11.30-3, 5.30-11; 11.30-11 Sat; 12-10.30 Sun
☎ (0118) 934 4100 ⊕ thewheelwrightsarms.co.uk
Wadworth Henry's IPA, Horizon, 6X, Bishops Tipple, seasonal beers; guest beers Ⓗ
A classic country pub with two bars with low beams, plus a dining area extension that can be booked for functions. Up to eight Wadworth beers and guest ales are provided. Good pub grub is served every lunchtime, and evenings except Sunday. Families are welcome, children until 8.30pm. The garden has heated, covered benches. Newspapers are provided. CAMRA members get a 10 per cent discount on Wadworth beers. One of a handful of pubs taking the Brewers' Creations range from Wadworth. 🏚🕮◖◗🕎🐾P⁵⏴(128)

Sandhurst

Rose & Crown 🄻
108 High Street, GU47 8HA (on main A321 W of railway station)
⏣ 12-11 (midnight Fri & Sat); 12-10 Sun ☎ (01252) 878938
⊕ roseandcrownsandhurst.info
Otter Bitter; guest beers Ⓗ
An 18th-century inn, the oldest of seven surviving pubs in Sandhurst, recently refurbished, providing an expanded bar area with additional seating for socialising, dining and watching TV. The large garden has a children's play area. There is decked seating front and rear, with designated smoking areas. The tenants take pride in their range of ales which includes five guests, one a LocAle, and personally prepare a variety of traditional pub-grub dishes with constantly changing specials. Sunday lunch is a real treat.
🏚🕮🍴◖◗⇌♣️🐾P⁵⏴(194)

Slough

Moon & Spoon 🄻
86 High Street, SL1 1EL
⏣ 8am-midnight ☎ (01753) 531650
Greene King Abbot; Ruddles Best Bitter; guest beers Ⓗ
Large Wetherspoon pub popular with a cross-section of the community. Inside is a long modern bar with zoned sections, including a family dining area and private booths. Regular steak and curry nights are hosted. Four interesting guest ales are usually on offer with a choice of real ciders. Food is served 8am-10pm, with a 20 per cent discount for CAMRA members. 🕮◖🕎⇌🐾

Stockcross

Lord Lyon 🄻
Ermin Street, RG20 8LL (3 miles W of Newbury town centre, 1 mile from A34/A4 jct) SU437685
⏣ 12-3, 5-11; 12-10.30 Sun ☎ (01488) 608366
⊕ lordlyon.co.uk
Arkell's Wiltshire Gold, Kingsdown Ⓗ
A rambling Victorian building originally built for workers on the nearby Benham estate. Now owned by Arkell's Brewery, it offers mainly locally sourced food including a recently introduced vegetarian menu. Five en-suite bedrooms are available. Voted CAMRA Community Pub of the Year for the branch in 2011, and for Berkshire in 2012. 🏚Q🕮🍴◖◗🏠♣️🐾P⁵⏴(4)

Rising Sun 🄻
Ermin Street, RG20 8LG SU433686
⏣ 12-3, 6-11 (closed Mon), 12-11 Sat & Sun
☎ (01488) 608131
West Berkshire Mr Chubb's Lunchtime Bitter, Good Old Boy, seasonal beers; guest beer Ⓗ
Traditional village pub located three miles to the west of Newbury. Acquired by West Berkshire Brewery in 2005, it is its only tied house. Recently refurbished, the pub has three separate drinking areas including a snug. Locally sourced and free-range food is served Tuesday to Sunday. One of the guest ales is also from West Berkshire.
🏚Q🕮◖◗♣️🐾P🐾(4)

Three Mile Cross

Swan ⓛ

Basingstoke Road, RG7 1AT
☼ 11-11; 12-3, 7-11 Sat; 12-4 Sun ☎ (0118) 988 3674
⊕ theswan-3mx.co.uk
Fuller's London Pride; Loddon Hoppit; Taylor Boltmaker, Landlord; Wadworth 6X; guest beer Ⓗ

A Grade II-listed 17th-century inn, which has been occupied by the current licensees for 30 years. The nearest pub to the Madejski Stadium, the Swan has a large sports crowd on match days. Locally produced and hearty home-cooked food is served. The outdoor drinking/barbecue area to the rear is home to Mr Doyle, gigantic Irish Wolfhound and mascot of London Irish RFC. Look out for the inglenook fireplace and the brass plaques in the loos, where famous visitors are recorded for posterity. ⏰⊛◑⅄P⸋▱(72,82,82k)

Tilehurst

Fox & Hounds

116 City Road, RG31 5SB
☼ 11.30-11; 12-10.30 Sun ☎ (0118) 942 2982
⊕ foxandhounds-tilehurst.co.uk
Courage Best Bitter; Sharp's Doom Bar Ⓗ**; guest beer** Ⓗ/Ⓖ

When the Fox & Hounds was built in the 1800s it would have been in the countryside and now, although surrounded by suburbia, it retains the feel of a country pub. The original bar with very low beams at the front contrasts with a modern conservatory adding family space and light at the rear. The garden has a large covered patio and enough room for a marquee in which to hold occasional beer festivals. CAMRA members receive a discount on beer. ▦⏰⊛◑⅄♣P⸋▱(33)

Royal Oak

69 Westwood Glen, RG31 5NW
☼ 2-11; 12-midnight Fri & Sat; 12-11 Sun ☎ (0118) 941 6056
⊕ theroyaloak-tilehurst.co.uk
Beer range varies Ⓗ

Perched at the summit of a steep driveway and predating most of the surrounding suburban housing, this charmingly quirky building has been frequently extended and lies close to an old drovers' route. The building is a traditional 'bitsa' with various phases of building, so one bar has you towering above the bar staff while the other bar is on the level. Show your CAMRA membership card for a discount on real ales. ⊛◑♣P⸋▱(33)

Upper Basildon

Red Lion ⓛ

Aldworth Road, RG8 8NG
☼ 11-3, 5-11; 12-10.30 Sun ☎ (01491) 671234
⊕ theredlionupperbasildon.co.uk
Brakspear Bitter; West Berkshire Good Old Boy; guest beers Ⓗ

Now the only pub in the village, the Red Lion is popular with locals and equally welcoming to drinkers and diners. There is a large garden to the rear for all to enjoy. The historic core has been sympathetically extended to include a separate restaurant area, and the good-quality food ranges from basic to posh. Three changing guest beers always offer a local brew. Pub games including cribbage and shut the box are available. The bus from Reading stops directly outside the pub. ▦⏰⊛◑♣P▱(132,133)

Waltham St Lawrence

Bell ⓛ

The Street, RG10 0JJ
☼ 12-3, 5-11; 12-11 Sat; 12-10.30 Sun ☎ (0118) 934 1788
⊕ thebellwalthamstlawrence.co.uk
Beer range varies Ⓗ

Dating back to the 14th century and originally a private dwelling, it was bequeathed to the village in 1608. A free house, it offers an ever-changing range of mostly local ales. Up to eight cask ciders and perries are also available, served directly from the cellar. Food is taken seriously here – from the home-made ketchup to freshly baked beer bread, hams and stocks, everything is made on site. ▦Q⏰⊛◑●⸋▱(4)

Wargrave

Wargrave & District Snooker Club

Woodclyffe Hostel, Church Street, RG10 8EP
☼ 7-11; closed Sat & Sun ☎ (0118) 940 1548
Beer range varies Ⓗ

The Victorian Woodclyffe Hostel, bequeathed to the village by a benefactor, houses the club and public library. At least one regularly changing ale from around the UK is always on handpump and you will find bar billiards, darts, cards, games and TV in the bar area. Show this Guide or CAMRA membership card to gain entry (£3 guest fee to use one of the three snooker tables in the adjoining hall). ⇌♣▱(850)

Wickham

Five Bells ⓛ

Baydon Road, RG20 8HH (follow B4000 from Newbury through Stockcross towards Lambourn)
☼ 11-3, 5-11; 11-11 Sat & Sun ☎ (01488) 657300
⊕ fivebellswickham.co.uk
Beer range varies Ⓗ

This traditional thatched free house has been completely transformed by the new owners into a thriving establishment. Thirteen handpumps dispense nine changing real ales from across the country and four real ciders. More than 30 Belgian beers, served in the correct glasses, are also kept, making this a real destination pub for beer lovers. Good home-cooked food is available, as well as five boutique bedrooms. ▦Q⏰⊛⌂◑⅄♣●⸋

Windsor

Acre ⓛ

Donnelly House, Victoria Street, SL4 1EN
☼ 11-11 (midnight Fri & Sat); 12-10.30 Sun ☎ (01753) 841083 ⊕ theacrewindsor.com
Windsor & Eton Windsor Knot; guest beers Ⓗ

Former social club, now open to non-members, serving three real ales – one from the local Windsor & Eton Brewery plus two ever-changing guests. Live music is hosted at weekends and an open mic night on Mondays. Live sporting events are shown regularly. Home-made Sunday roasts are served 1-4pm. Two function rooms are available for hire. There is a multi-storey car park across the road. ◑⇌(Windsor & Eton Central)▱(77)

Carpenters Arms 🏆

4 Market Street, SL4 1PB
☼ 11-11 (midnight Fri & Sat) ☎ (01753) 863739

Fuller's London Pride; Sharp's Doom Bar; guest beers ⊞

Situated on a narrow cobbled street, the pub's interior is on several levels with the lower drinking area housing what is reputedly an old passageway to Windsor Castle. The front windows feature etchings of the tools of the trade that gave the pub its name. The regular ales here are supplemented by another six beers, with details on a large blackboard. Real cider is also occasionally available. A former CAMRA branch Pub of the Year.
⊕➡(Windsor & Eton Central)🚌(71,702)

Two Brewers

34 Park Street, SL4 1LB
✪ 11.30-11 (11.30 Fri & Sat); 12-10.30 Sun
☎ (01753) 855426 ⊕ twobrewerswindsor.co.uk
Fuller's London Pride; St Austell Tribute; Sharp's Doom Bar; guest beer ⊞

Small, cosy, wood-panelled 17th-century inn, close to the Cambridge Gate entrance to Windsor Great Park and a great place to stop after viewing the Castle from the Long Walk. Popular with locals and tourists alike, it is advisable to book a table if intending to eat (no food on Fri and Sat eves). Dogs are welcome, but due to its size, children are not allowed inside the pub. However, there are seats at the front if weather permits.
Q❀⊕➡(Windsor & Eton Central)🚌(71,702)

Vansittart Arms ⓛ

105 Vansittart Road, SL4 5DD
✪ 12-11 (11.30 Thu; midnight Fri); 10.30-midnight Sat;
10.30-9.30 Sun ☎ (01753) 865988
Fuller's Discovery, London Pride, ESB; guest beer ⊞

Located a few minutes' walk west of the town centre, this popular Fuller's pub is a Guide regular. There are two distinct areas to the main bar and a pool room to the rear which contains a small library for book swaps. Sport is keenly followed, with rugby taking priority. The large garden is ideal for summer barbecues and there is also occasional live music. The ales often include a guest from outside the Fuller's range. Parking may be difficult.
🏨🌅❀⊕➡(Windsor & Eton Central)🗜🚌(71,702)

Windlesora ⓛ

11 William Street, SL4 1BB
✪ 9am-midnight (1am Fri & Sat) ☎ (01753) 754050
Greene King Abbot; Ruddles Best Bitter; guest beers ⊞

Tucked away just off the main shopping street, this Wetherspoon pub will not win any awards for its architecture, but the enthusiastic manager makes an effort to stock beers from local micros, including Windsor & Eton and Binghams, and even displays a map showing their location. Relatively quiet during the day, its proximity to nightclubs make it a handy stop-off for a younger crowd. ⊕➡🌅🗜🚌(77)

Winkfield

Duke of Edinburgh

Woodside Road, Woodside, SL4 2DP (off main road to Ascot from Windsor Great Park, through hamlet of Woodside) SU928709
✪ 11-11; 12-6.30 Sun ☎ (01344) 882736
⊕ thedukeofedinburgh.com
Arkell's 2B, 3B, Kingsdown, seasonal beer ⊞

This Arkell's tied house has received a number of CAMRA awards over the years. The restaurant serves a wide variety of excellent food both lunchtimes and evenings (no food Sun) and has a

friendly bar area. Charity football evenings are hosted throughout the year. Outside is a smoking shelter with heaters. Dogs are allowed in the bar (on a lead) and in the spacious beer garden.
🏨❀⊕◑🗜P🚌

Wokingham

Crispin

45 Denmark Street, RG40 2AY (near old town hall)
✪ 12-11.30 (12.30am Fri & Sat) ☎ (0118) 978 0309
⊕ crispinpub.co.uk
Beer range varies ⊞

Reputedly one of the oldest inns in Wokingham, this pub offers four constantly changing real ales including local brews from Vale, Binghams and Loddon. No food is served but in the evening you can bring in your own takeaway. Occasional live music events and beer festivals are held. There is a garden area, with seating and a smoking area. Free Wi-Fi. 🏨Q❀➡♣🌅🗜🚌(190)

Crooked Billet

Honey Hill, RG40 3BJ
✪ 12-11 (10.30 Sun) ☎ (0118) 978 0438
⊕ crookedbilletwokingham.co.uk
Brakspear Bitter; Wychwood Hobgoblin, seasonal beers ⊞

Traditional country pub with a variety of interesting walks close by. The bar area has an open fire and the ambience of a proper local. A snug is also available for small group meetings. Brakspear Bitter is the regular brew, with up to three other real ales available. A separate restaurant provides an extensive menu. To the rear is an attractive beer garden adjacent to farmland. Plenty of parking is available. 🏨Q🌅❀⊕🗜P

White Horse

Easthampstead Road, RG40 3AF (1 mile S of town centre)
✪ 12-11 (6 Sun) ☎ (0118) 979 7402
⊕ whitehorsewokingham.co.uk
Greene King IPA, Abbot; guest beers ⊞

One mile south of the town centre, this much-improved inn has views across fields and a rural feel. Tasty, home-made, traditional English food is served lunchtimes and evenings (until 4pm Sun). Outside there is a secluded beer garden for barbecues in the summer and a newly developed front garden plus plenty of parking. Q❀⊕◑🗜♣P🌅

Woolhampton

Rowbarge

Station Road, RG7 5SH (near station and main Reading-Newbury bus route)
✪ 11.30-11 (11.30 Fri & Sat); 11.30-10.30 Sun
☎ (0118) 971 2213 ⊕ rowbarge-woolhampton.co.uk
Brunning & Price Original Bitter; guest beer ⊞

A pub since the 18th century, the Rowbarge was extensively renovated in 2012. The large garden is on the banks of the River Kennet, with access to the towpath and moorings. Five of the six handpumps offer a varying range of ales, often from local breweries. Food is available all day and there is a separate restaurant area.
🌅❀⊕◑🗜➡(Midgham)P🗜🚌(1)

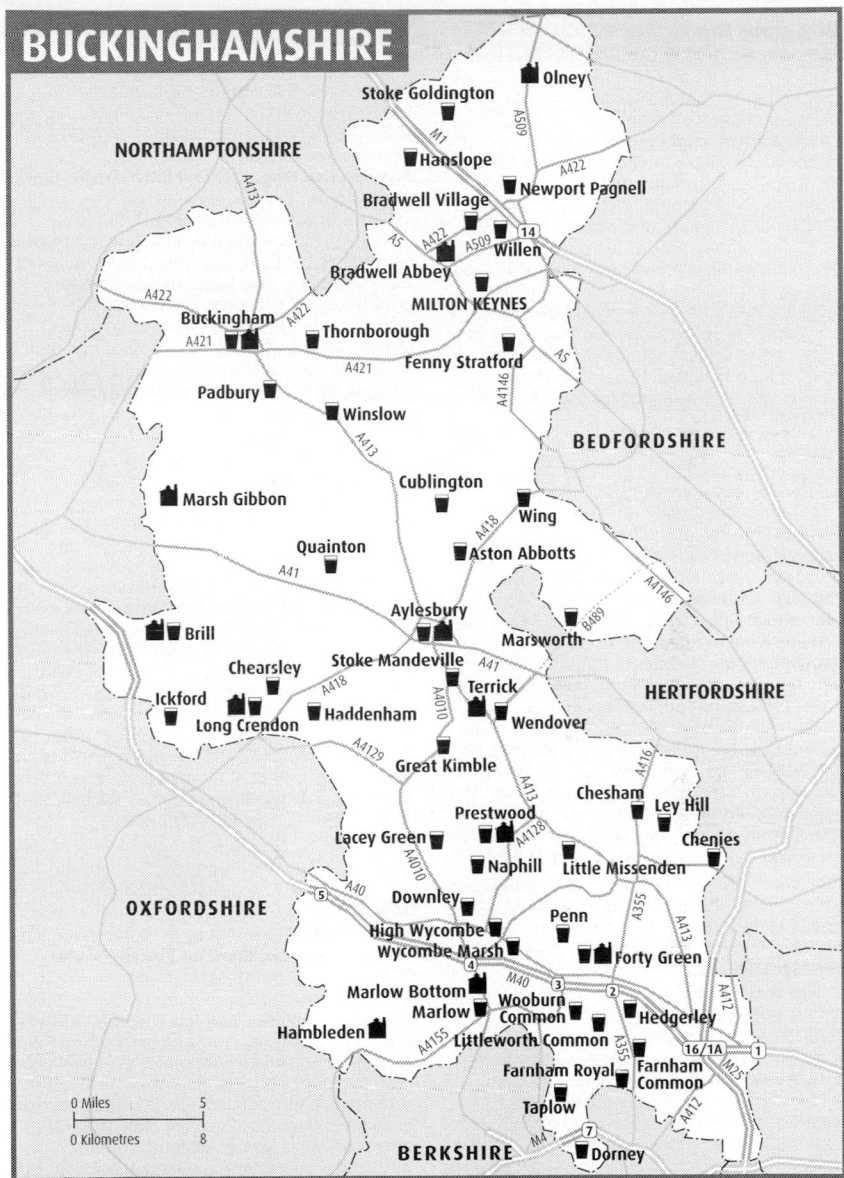

ENGLAND

BUCKINGHAMSHIRE

Aston Abbotts

Royal Oak Inn
Wingrave Road, HP22 4LT (close to A418)
☼ 12-2.30, 5-11; 12-10.30 Sun ☎ (01296) 681262
Fuller's London Pride; Sharp's Doom Bar; guest beers Ⓗ
A Grade II-listed, sixteenth-century half-thatched village inn with a lovely timbered interior. Dual fireplaces separate the dining area from the large bar area with its distinctive inglenook fireplace. In addition to the regular Doom Bar and London Pride, ales are sourced from smaller breweries, both local and further afield. A range of bottled ciders is also stocked and, occasionally, cider on draught.
᛭Q✿⇄◖P⌐

Aylesbury

Farmers' Bar at King's Head ♀ ⌊
King's Head Passage, Market Square, HP20 2RW
☼ 11-11; 12-10.30 Sun ☎ (01296) 718812
⊕ farmersbar.co.uk
Chiltern Beechwood Bitter, Cobblestones; guest beers Ⓗ
When Chiltern Brewery took over the running of the Farmers' Bar for the National Trust, it became the first bar in the country to be no-smoking and free of piped music. Dating from circa 1455, this is the oldest courtyard inn in England and was donated by the Rothschild family in 1924. Ales are often used in cooking and lunches are made from fresh, locally-sourced ingredients. ᛭Q✿◑↺⇄♦▱

Hop Pole Inn L

83 Bicester Road, HP19 9AZ (near Gatehouse Industrial Area)
✪ 12 (4 Mon)-11; 12-midnight Fri & Sat; 12-10.30 Sun
☎ (01296) 482129
Vale Best Bitter; guest beers H
'Aylesbury's Permanent Beer Festival' is home to the Aylesbury Brewhouse and shop, opened in December 2011 by Guide editor Roger Protz, bringing brewing back to the town after nearly 75 years. The individual brews feature regularly in the pub, but may not last very long! This is Vale's sister brewery and the Hop Pole is its main outlet, featuring Vale beers plus a myriad microbrewery ales. Two beer festivals are held every year at Easter and in October, when the choice more than doubles from the usual 10 beers available. A friendly welcome and good food add to the attraction. ✿●⬢-🖃

Brill

Pointer

27 Church Street, HP18 9RT
✪ 12-11 (midnight Fri & Sat); 12-10.30 Sun
☎ (01844) 238339 ⊕ thepointerbrill.co.uk
Vale Gravitas; guest beers H
Recently reopened, extensive refurbishment has transformed the character of this pub. It is now decorated in a modern style that complements the original structure of the building. Wonderful food is produced in the open kitchen and served in the separate vaulted dining room as well as the bar. The main bar has both tables and couches, with plenty of room for drinkers and diners alike. An outbuilding has been converted into a butcher's shop (limited opening times). The Pointer supports the Brill beer festival in August. ♨Q✿◑♣⬢

Buckingham

Woolpack

57 Well Street, MK18 1EP
✪ 11-11 (midnight Fri & Sat); 12-10.30 Sun
☎ (01280) 817972 ⊕ buckinghamwoolpack.co.uk
St Austell Tribute; Sharp's Doom Bar; guest beers H
Busy, nicely modernised pub with a pleasant riverside garden, just off the town centre. Four handpumps serve two regular beers and guest ales from the SIBA list. Freshly cooked food is good and varied, locally sourced where possible, and children are welcome in the large back room. Parking nearby can be awkward. The Woolpack holds beer festivals from time to time. ♨➤✿◑ 🍺&♣⬢-🖃

Chearsley

Bell

The Green, HP18 0DJ
✪ 12-3, 6-11; 10-4, 6-11 Sat; 10-4, 7-10.30 Sun
☎ (01844) 208077 ⊕ thebellchearsley.co.uk
Fuller's London Pride; Gale's HSB; guest beers H
Attractive 14th-century thatched inn on the edge of the village green, ideal for sunny summer days and cool winter evenings alike. The ales are well kept, and come from the Fuller's stable. Well known for both its ale and good, wholesome food, the pub also featured in Midsomer Murders. The pretty garden is child-friendly. ♨Q✿◑P🖃(110)

Chenies

Red Lion L

Latimer Road, WD3 6ED (off A404 between Chorleywood and Little Chalfont) TQ021982
✪ 11-2.30, 5.30-11; 12-10.30 Sun ☎ (01923) 282722
⊕ redlionchenies.co.uk
Rebellion Lion Pride; Vale Best Bitter; Wadworth 6X; guest beer H
Excellent, traditional village pub with a long-serving landlord. It has a homely front room with comfortable bench seating, and a dining room at the rear. High-quality home-cooked food is available every day. Dogs and walkers are welcome; the Chess Valley Walk and Chenies Manor – open to the public – are close by. There is an outside patio with seating and disabled access near the small car park at the rear. Q✿◑&P

Chesham

Black Cat

Lycrome Road, Lye Green, HP5 3LF (off A413) SP977034
✪ 11-2.30, 5 (7 Mon)-11; 11-11 Sat; 12-10.30 Sun
☎ (01494) 773966 ⊕ blackcatchesham.co.uk
Taylor Landlord; Young's Bitter; guest beer H
Cosy, welcoming pub with a relaxed atmosphere. The single-bar interior has much black cat memorabilia and includes a collection of pump clips. Generous portions of good food are served, both in the bar and in the back room which doubles as a dining area. Families with well-behaved children are welcome and the pub is dog-friendly. The spacious garden at the rear features a woodland walk for children. Games are popular here, with darts, crib and quiz nights. ♨Q➤✿◑&♣P⬢-🖃(353)

Black Horse L

Vale Road, HP5 3NS (at bottom of Nashleigh Hill, turn right into Vale Rd and follow for 1 mile) SP964046
✪ 12-3, 6-11; 12-6 Sun ☎ (01494) 784656
⊕ black-horse-inn.co.uk
Fuller's London Pride; Tring Side Pocket for a Toad; guest beers H
Situated in a beautiful valley, this traditional pub has something to offer all year round, with log fires to banish winter chills and a large garden pleasant for summer days. But the main draw is the beer – there are always four on offer, including two constantly changing guests. The pub holds a popular quiz on Mondays and occasional beer festivals – bonfire night is a particular highlight. Children and dogs are welcome. Runner-up local CAMRA Pub of the Year 2012. ♨Q➤✿◑&●P

INDEPENDENT BREWERIES

Aylesbury Aylesbury
Britannia Forty Green
Buckingham Buckingham
Chiltern Terrick
Concrete Cow Bradwell Abbey
Hopping Mad Olney
Malt Prestwood (NEW)
Old Luxters Hambleden
Oxfordshire Ales Marsh Gibbon
Rebellion Marlow Bottom
Vale Brill
XT Long Crendon

Queen's Head ⓛ

120 Church Street, HP5 1JD (in old town) SP956013
✪ 12-11 (midnight Thu-Sat); 12-10.30 Sun
☎ (01494) 778690 ⊕ queensheadchesham.co.uk
**Brakspear Bitter; Fuller's London Pride, ESB; guest
beer** Ⓗ

A traditional ale house and restaurant situated in
the old part of town. This is a lovely old pub with
the River Chess flowing past the entrance to its
yard and under the corner of the public bar. First
licensed in 1759, many of the building's original
features have remained intact. There are two real
fires. The Tour de Pednor charity cycle ride starts
here and is usually linked with one of the pub's
beer and cider festivals. ♨Q✿🕙🐕🍴🕭◗🟦⊖♣P'–🚃

Cublington

Unicorn

High Street, LU7 0LQ
✪ 10.30-11 (midnight Fri & Sat); 10.30-8.30 Sun
☎ (01296) 681261 ⊕ theunicornpub.co.uk
**Sharp's Doom Bar; Shepherd Neame Spitfire; guest
beers** Ⓗ

Village free house in a quiet location, recently
restored to provide first-class facilities in a 16th-
century building. It has a long, single bar with real
fires at both ends and an unobtrusive restaurant
which is always busy. A function room is also
available and many clubs and societies meet here
regularly, enjoying the ambience. Four ales are on
offer, including LocAle guests from Tring, Vale, XT
and others. Boules and Aunt Sally are played in the
large, secure garden. ♨✿◗🕭&♣P'–🚃(651)

Dorney

Palmer Arms

Village Road, SL4 6QW
✪ 11-11; 12-10.30 Sun ☎ (01628) 666612
⊕ thepalmerarms.com
Greene King IPA, Abbot; guest beer Ⓗ

Large pub in a conservation village close to Eton
Rowing Lake and the Jubilee River. The emphasis is
on food but there is a dedicated area for drinkers,
with comfy chairs and sofas. Families are welcome
and the large garden has an enclosed children's
play area. The publicans are keen on promoting
real ales and hold occasional beer festivals with
live music. The guest ale comes from the Greene
King list. ✿🕭◗&P'–

Downley

Le De Spencers Arms

The Common, HP13 5YQ (across common from village)
✪ 12-11 (midnight Fri & Sat); 12-10.30 Sun
☎ (01494) 535317 ⊕ ledespencersarms.co.uk
**Fuller's London Pride; Gale's Seafarers Ale; guest
beer** Ⓗ

A flint pub on Downley Common, accessible by car
and just half a mile by road or across the common
from the village hall bus stop. This inn has a
welcoming atmosphere, open fire, rustic beams
and stone-flagged floor. Serving home-cooked
food, excellent real ales and wines, it is popular
with walkers and cyclists (dog-friendly too).
Wednesday quiz nights, music nights, beer and
food events add to the attraction of this Fuller's
Master Cellarman pub serving four ales, including
one regularly changing guest. ♨✿🕭◗P'–🚃(31)

Farnham Common

Emperor ⓛ

Blackpond Lane, SL2 3EG SU959842
✪ 12-11 (midnight Fri & Sat); 12-10.30 Sun
☎ (01753) 643006 ⊕ theemperorpub.co.uk
Fuller's London Pride; guest beers Ⓗ

Country pub and restaurant with four handpumps
serving London Pride and an ever-changing
selection of beers including one or two LocAles.
The bar area features cosy seating and there is a
restaurant area to the rear serving quality food.
This old establishment, originally the Brickmakers,
was called the King of Prussia in 1906. In 1917 it
became the Emperor of India, then reverted back
to the King of Prussia before becoming just the
Emperor in recent years. ♨Q✿🕙🕭◗P'–🚃(X74)

Farnham Royal

Crown Inn

Crown Lane, SL2 3SQ SU955840
✪ 11-11 (midnight Fri & Sat); 12-10.30 Sun
☎ (01753) 647714 ⊕ crowninnpub.co.uk
Beer range varies Ⓗ

A truly picturesque gem near Burnham Beeches
which is home to the second oldest wisteria in the
country. Rambling and Tardis-like inside, it has a
traditional interior with a restaurant serving proper
home-made food – including home-grown veggies
and eggs from the pub's chickens – all day (until
6pm Sun). There is also a large function room. The
handpumps offer a varied range of three ales.
Watch out for chickens, or even a goat, to the rear
of the car park. Live music features monthly; phone
for details. ♨Q✿🕙🕭◗P'–

Forty Green

Royal Standard of England

Brindle Lane, HP9 1XT
✪ 11-11.30 (11 Sun) ☎ (01494) 673382 ⊕ rsoe.co.uk
**Brakspear Bitter; Britannia Pale Ale, Golden Ale;
Chiltern Ale; Rebellion IPA; Windsor & Eton
Conqueror** Ⓗ

This historic hostelry with its fascinating pedigree is
well worth a detour. A barrel-shaped wooden
partition wall/noticeboard leads to rooms
containing log fires or cast iron stoves. Architecture
and furniture is mixed rustic with hops adorning
bar areas. The food is of an exemplary standard
and bottled beers are sourced from craft breweries.
Orchard Pig farm-pressed cider is also served. This
area is a walkers' paradise. ♨Q✿🕭◗♣P

Great Kimble

Swan

Grove Lane, Smokey Row, HP17 9TR
✪ 12-3.30, 5.30 (5 Sat)-11; 12-3.30, 7-11.30 Sun
☎ (01844) 275288
Beer range varies Ⓗ

Facing the village green and on the ancient route
of the lower Icknield Way, the Swan is a
welcoming two-room pub, in countryside popular
with walkers. The tiled taproom has a real fire in
winter while the lounge bar opens onto an
enclosed beer garden, popular in summer. A
genuine free house, the pub features a changing
selection of well-kept ales, many from local
breweries. ♨Q✿🍴◗🕭🍴♣P🚃

Haddenham

Rising Sun
9 Thame Road, HP17 8EN
✪ 12-2.30, 5-11; 12-1am Fri & Sat; 12-10.30 Sun
☎ (01844) 291744
Beer range varies Ⓗ/Ⓖ
The Riser is a hive of activity throughout the year, with visiting pool and darts teams as well as Aunt Sally in the secluded garden in the summer months. Regular live music and nibbles on Tuesday evenings add to the pub's ever-expanding repertoire. Boasting Vale and XT ales straight from the cask and an ever-changing selection of guest ales, this local is a jewel in Haddenham's crown and a friendly haven for regulars and visitors alike.
🏵⇌(Haddenham & Thame Parkway)♣●🖾(280)

Hanslope

Watts Arms Ⓛ
Castlethorpe Road, MK19 7LG
✪ 12-11 (11.30 Thu; midnight Fri & Sat); 12-10.30 Sun
☎ (01908) 510246 ● thewattsarms.co.uk
Wells Eagle IPA; guest beers Ⓗ
The landlord is a real ale enthusiast and this shows in the consistently excellent quality of his beers. These come from Wells & Young's, plus an ever-changing guest choice. Freshly home-cooked dishes are served lunchtimes and evenings until 9pm (no food Tue all day and Sun eves). Local CAMRA Pub of the Year 2012.
🏚Q🏵❶♣P'–🖾(33)

Hedgerley

White Horse Ⓛ
Village Lane, SL2 3UY (in old village, near church)
✪ 11-2.30, 5-11; 11-11 Sat; 12-10.30 Sun ☎ (01753) 643225
Rebellion IPA; guest beers Ⓖ
Village inn that has won many local CAMRA awards, with an impressive range of up to eight real ales. Beers come from breweries all over the country, including those newly opened, making this a mecca for ale lovers. A draft Belgian beer is also available. Three real ciders complement the ales all year round. This classic pub has a well-tended garden which hosts regular bank holiday beer festivals, and the heated, covered patio provides additional seating at busy times.
🏚Q🏵❶🕀♣●P

High Wycombe

Belle Vue
45 Gordon Road, HP13 6EQ
✪ 12-2, 4.30-11; 12-1am Fri & Sat; 12-10.30 Sun
☎ (01494) 524728 ● thebv.co.uk
Adnams Broadside; Sharp's Doom Bar; guest beers Ⓗ
Situated a short walk from the railway station, this friendly community pub has featured in the Guide for the past 10 years. It keeps six ales and four ciders, and holds two beer festivals every year. Traditional inside with a real fire, live music is hosted at the weekends, plus regular quiz nights, a literary society, knitting circle, ukulele club, vinyl night, folk sessions and occasional charity events, film nights and even Christmas carol 'shouting'! It also has permanent art exhibitions.
🏚🏵🖾⇌♣●'–🖾(31,35)

Falcon
9 Cornmarket, HP11 2AX
✪ 7-midnight (1am Fri & Sat) ☎ (01494) 538610
Greene King Abbot; Ruddles County; guest beers Ⓗ
Located in the centre of High Wycombe, just outside the Eden shopping centre, this lively open-plan Wetherspoon pub offers a great range of real ales. A welcome commitment to local beers ensures there is always at least one ale from nearby to try. A separate area is reserved for diners, ensuring there is plenty of space for those who wish only to sample the excellent ale.
🏚Q🏵❶♿⇌●'–🖾

Ickford

Rising Sun
36 Worminghall Road, HP18 9JD
✪ 12-2.30, 4-11; 12-11 Sat & Sun ☎ (01844) 339238
● risingsunickford.com
Beer range varies Ⓗ
A short drive from junction 8A of the M40, the Rising Sun is a traditional thatched inn that dates back to the 15th century, with exposed oak beams and a real fire. The pub serves home-made food, sourcing ingredients locally, and has four regular ales and a rotating guest. Dog-friendly and popular with ramblers, it hosts live music, quizzes, crib and Aunt Sally. The large beer garden has a children's play area and smokers' shelter. 🏚Q🏵❶♣P'–🖾

Lacey Green

Black Horse
Main Road, HP27 0QU
✪ 11-3 (not Mon), 5-11; 11-11 Thu; 11-midnight Fri; 12-midnight Sat; 12-11 Sun ☎ (01844) 345195
● blackhorse-pub.co.uk
Brakspear Bitter; guest beers Ⓗ
This friendly village pub, located in the heart of the Chilterns, offers four ales, three changing regularly, plus a good selection of bottled beers and one varying real cider. Excellent home-cooked and freshly prepared food is available, including traditional Sunday lunch (children under six eat free). Walkers, cyclists and families are welcome and there is a play area in the garden. A full English breakfast is served Tuesday to Saturday and traditional pub games are a feature.
🏚Q🏵❶♿♣●P'–🖾(300)

Whip Inn
Pink Road, Loosely Row, HP27 0PG
✪ 11-11 (midnight Fri & Sat); 12-10.30 Sun
☎ (01494) 344060 ● thewhipinn.co.uk
Beer range varies Ⓗ
High in the Chilterns and popular with ale aficionados, ramblers and cyclists, this pub is renowned for its variety of ales. It has six handpumps, serving more than 900 beers per annum, featuring many local breweries as well as other micros and nationals. Two real ciders are also kept and the pub holds annual beer festivals in May and September. An excellent range of reasonably priced bar food is on offer. The attractive enclosed garden overlooks Lacey Green Windmill. 🏚Q🏵❶♣●P'–🖾(300)

Ley Hill

Swan 🅛
Blackwell Hall Lane, HP5 1UT (opp cricket pitch)
SP990018
✪ 12-2.30, 5.30-11 (not Mon eve); 12-10.30 Sun
☎ (01494) 783075 ⊕ swanleyhill.com
St Austell Tribute; Taylor Landlord; Tring Side Pocket
for a Toad; guest beer Ⓗ
Originally three 16th-century cottages, the Swan is
believed to be the oldest pub in the county and is
reputed to have provided the last ale for prisoners
en route to the nearby gallows. Clark Gable, James
Stewart and Glenn Miller were all frequent visitors
here. Snug, bar and restaurant areas feature
stripped wooden beams. The rear garden and
roadside seating area overlook the cricket club, golf
course and beacon. A summer music and beer
festival is held annually. Guest ales may not be
available in winter. Children are welcome but no
dogs. ♨Q❀◑●P⊒(73)

Little Missenden

Crown Inn
HP7 0RD (off A413, between Amersham & Gt
Missenden) SU924989
✪ 11-3, 6-11; 12-3, 7-10.30 Sun ☎ (01494) 862571
⊕ the-crown-little-missenden.co.uk
Adnams Southwold Bitter; Courage Directors;
Rebellion IPA; St Austell Tribute Ⓗ
This stalwart of the Guide never ceases to offer a
good pint and a warm welcome. The clientele
includes a good mix of regulars and those passing
through, perhaps enjoying some of the local walks.
The landlord is a real ale enthusiast and often
rotates his beers, so it is a good idea to check if you
are after a particular pint. The pub also has three
en-suite rooms available. ♨Q❀➟◑P⁵⊒(177)

Littleworth Common

Blackwood Arms
Common Lane, SL1 8PP SU937863
✪ closed Mon; 12-11; 12-9.30 (7 winter) Sun
☎ (01753) 645672
Brakspear Bitter, Oxford Gold; Wychwood Hobgoblin;
guest beers Ⓗ
A delightful Victorian country pub brought back to
life by an enthusiastic couple after a long period of
closure. Close to Burnham Beeches and popular
with walkers and diners, it has a roaring fire in
winter and an attractive garden with plenty of
seating for the summer. Guest ales include two
from the Marston's group plus one free of tie. Dog-
and horse-friendly, hay is provided.
♨Q➣❀◑P⁵

Long Crendon

Eight Bells
51 High Street, HP18 9AL
✪ 12-3 (not Mon), 5.30-11; 12-11 Sat & Sun
☎ (01844) 208244 ⊕ eightbellspub.com
XT Four Ⓗ; guest beers Ⓖ
Renowned for great real ale and Cask Marque-
accredited for all the years the current landlady has
been at the helm. Beer festivals are held annually
over the Easter weekend and the August bank
holiday. Unique ale Hel's Bells and XT Four are
regulars, with three changing guest ales on gravity
behind the bar. A welcoming and friendly local,

with good home-cooked food too. See the website
for details of live music events.
♨❀◑♣●P⊒(261)

Marlow

Duke of Cambridge
19 Queens Road, SL7 2PS
✪ 12-11 (12.30am Fri & Sat); 10-11 Sun ☎ (01628) 488555
Rebellion IPA, Mutiny; guest beer Ⓗ
The last remaining true locals' local in town, a short
stroll from the central High Street. A community
pub patronised by a colourful clientele, it hosts crib
and darts league teams, and sporadic feature
nights, plus annual sea fishing and horse racing
trips. Two Rebellion brews are supplemented by a
guest ale, often a stout or a porter. Sunday roast
lunches and Wednesday fish and chip suppers are
popular. It is the rendezvous for the Hashers
joggers at 10am every Sunday.
♨❀◑&♣⁵⊒(800,850)

Three Horseshoes 🅛
Burroughs Grove Hill, Little Marlow, SL7 3RA (on High
Wycombe-Marlow Bottom road)
✪ 11.30-3, 5-11; 11.30-11 Fri & Sat; 12-5, 7-10.30 Sun
☎ (01628) 483109
Rebellion Mild, IPA, Smuggler; guest beer Ⓗ
A large open-plan pub a short bus ride from High
Wycombe and Marlow. With an extensive specials
board, open fires and a pleasant garden, this pub is
popular with diners, drinkers and families. Close
proximity to the Rebellion Beer Company means
that the six Rebellion ales on offer are always in
great condition. ♨Q❀◑P⁵⊒(800,850)

Marsworth

Anglers Retreat 🅛
Startops End, HP23 4LJ (opp Startops Reservoir car park)
SP919141
✪ 11-11 (midnight Fri & Sat) ☎ (01442) 822250
St Austell Tribute; Tring Side Pocket for a Toad; guest
beers Ⓗ
Traditional one-bar local with a fish theme in
evidence and a parrot in the bar. A conservatory
and garden with an aviary provide extra space. The
four beers are a mixture of local and small national
brews, with Tring Brewery providing the LocAle
beer. A welcoming base when investigating the
Tring Reservoirs, B&B rooms are also available,
with good value food to complete your stay. A very
rural experience. ♨Q➣❀➟◑&♣P⁵⊒(164)

Red Lion 🍷 🅛
90 Vicarage Road, HP23 4LU (opp church) SP919147
✪ 11-3, 5-11; 11-11 Sat; 12-10.30 Sun ☎ (01296) 668366
Fuller's London Pride; guest beers Ⓗ
Genuine 17th-century village pub close to the
Grand Union Canal. A central bar serves three
areas: an upstairs lounge with comfortable sofas, a
small snug to the left of the entrance, and a public
bar with an open coal fire and separate games area
hosting bar billiards, darts and shove-ha'penny.
Five or more well-kept beers, some from local
breweries, are available, and the kitchen serves
generous portions of excellent home-cooked food.
Westons Traditional Scrumpy is kept.
♨Q➣❀◑🍴&♣●P⁵⊒(61)

Milton Keynes: Bradwell Village

Prince Albert
17 Vicarage Road, MK13 9AG
✪ 12-11 (midnight Fri & Sat) ☎ (01908) 226524
⊕ princealbertbradwell.co.uk
Wells Eagle IPA; guest beers Ⓗ
Now run by the former licensees of the Victoria across the road, this friendly Charles Wells' tenancy offers a selection of well-kept Wells and guest ales, and exceptional-value food. There is a pleasant garden at the back and, with its quiet location, it can still feel like the village pub it once was.
✿◑ⓖ P⁵─☐(33)

Milton Keynes: Central

Barn
800 Secklow Gate West, MK9 3BZ
✪ 12-11 (10.30 Sun) ☎ (01908) 663388
Beer range varies Ⓗ
Part of a Premier Inn, the Barn, formerly called the Old Barn, is ideally placed for Milton Keynes centre. It offers a changing selection of ales, often but not exclusively from the Marston's stable, and the usual Beefeater menu of reasonably priced food. Very family friendly. Daytime parking is on meter.
ᘔ✿╍◑ⓖ☐

Wetherspoon's
201 Midsummer Boulevard, MK9 1EA
✪ 7am-11 (midnight Fri & Sat) ☎ (01908) 606074
Greene King Abbot; Ruddles Best Bitter; guest beers Ⓗ
Unbeatable for price and beer choice, this cavernous 'Spoons' has been a local CAMRA Pub of the Year on two occasions. Food from the usual Wetherspoon menu is available, served until late. The pub can get extremely busy and service can be tardy at times, but with 12 handpumps it offers the biggest variety of ales in town.
Q✿◑ⓖ⇌(Central)🖶⁵─☐

Milton Keynes: Fenny Stratford

Red Lion
11 Lock View Lane, MK1 1BY (off Simpson Road)
✪ 12-11 (midnight Fri & Sat); 12-10.30 Sun
☎ (01908) 372317
Beer range varies Ⓗ
Tucked alongside a lock on the Grand Union Canal, this Grade II-listed gem promises friendly conversation and a rolling choice of up to three ales, selected to contrast in style and strength. There is a main bar with TV and pool, a quieter small lounge, and a lock-side garden and covered smoking area outside. ⚏✿ⓖ⇌♣🖶P⁵─☐(18)

Milton Keynes: Willen

Ship Ashore
Granville Square, Willen Local Centre, MK15 9JL
✪ 11.30-11 (midnight Fri & Sat) ☎ (01908) 694360
Greene King IPA; Purity Ubu; Woodforde's Wherry; guest beers Ⓗ
Large, smart estate pub, with eight handpumps dispensing a constantly changing range of ales. The pub is strongly food-oriented but drinkers are always made to feel welcome. It is located in a small local centre not far from Willen and Tongwell Lakes and their recreational facilities. Ample free parking is available. ⚏✿◑ⓖ♣P⁵─☐(1,2)

Naphill

Wheel
100 Main Road, HP14 4QA
✪ 12 (4.30 Mon)-11; 12-10.30 Sun ☎ (01494) 562210
⊕ thewheelnaphill.com
Greene King IPA Reserve; Ruddles Best Bitter; guest beers Ⓗ
This award-winning Chilterns village pub is popular with locals, walkers and cyclists, and is dog- and family-friendly too. Fantastic home-made food is served using local produce alongside four cask ales – two regulars and two regularly changing guests from both nationals and independent microbreweries. It has a traditional public bar, a snug bar and a large restaurant area. Outside is a large garden at the front and a quiet secluded courtyard at the rear. Two large beer festivals are held each year. ⚏✿╍◑ ⓖ♣P⁵─☐(300)

Newport Pagnell

Cannon Ⓛ
50 High Street, MK16 8AQ
✪ 11-11 (midnight Fri & Sat); 12-11 Sun ☎ (01908) 211495
Banks's Bitter; Marston's Pedigree; guest beers Ⓗ
This family-run town-centre free house, long a fixture in the Guide, is a true drinkers' local where keenly priced, excellently kept ales from Marston's and other often LocAle breweries are appreciated by loyal regulars. There is a heated smoking area, a large car park accessed from Union Street behind the pub, and bike racks at the front. ⚏Q✿P⁵─☐

Rose & Crown Ⓛ
61 Silver Street, MK16 0EG
✪ closed Mon; 11-11 ☎ (01908) 611685
⊕ roseandcrown.eu
Wells Eagle IPA; Young's Special; guest beer Ⓗ
In a residential back-street location, this Wells & Young's house is a true local. The traditional public bar has a pool table, and the lounge is cosy and comfortable with an impressive fireplace. Beers come mostly from Wells & Young's, but sometimes there is a guest ale. Live music, themed evenings and quiz nights all feature. ✿◑ⓖ♣⁵─☐

Padbury

New Inn
Winslow Road, MK18 2AW (on A413 Buckingham-Aylesbury road)
✪ 5-11; closed Wed; 12-2.30, 5-midnight Fri; 11-midnight Sat; 11-10 Sun ☎ (01280) 813173
Beer range varies Ⓗ
With three linked bars seamlessly blending old and new, a smart modern dining room and a pleasant garden, this pub is a fine example of an old inn that has undergone a sensitive modernisation while retaining genuine character. Ales, often local, come from three handpumps, and one bar doubles as the village shop. Run by the third generation of the same family. ⚏Q✿◑ⓖ♣P⁵─☐(60)

Penn

Horse & Jockey
Church Road, HP10 8EG (near top of Hammersley Lane)
✪ 12-3, 5-11; 12-midnight Fri-Sun ☎ (01494) 815963
⊕ horseandjockeytylersgreen.co.uk

Adnams Southwold Bitter; Black Sheep Best Bitter; Fuller's London Pride; Greene King Abbot; Sharp's Doom Bar; guest beer Ⓗ
Opened as an inn in 1821, this traditional pub is near the distinctive Tylers Green Church. The single bar is U-shaped with the larger left-hand side used for dining and the right-hand side featuring a dartboard. There are five regular ales and one guest. Food is available lunchtimes and evenings all week, with pensioners' specials Monday to Wednesday. There are two real ciders from Westons. ஜQ❀◑&♣♦P⌐₩(31)

Prestwood

Green Man
2 High Street, HP16 9EB (on A4128 near Great Missenden)
☀ 12-midnight (1am Fri & Sat); 12-10.30 Sun
☎ (01494) 890074
Greene King IPA; guest beer Ⓗ
Cosy local with two interconnecting bars. Darts, crib and dominoes players are among the clientele. There is seating outside on the front patio/smoking area and in the garden at the rear. Late afternoon customers regularly pop in to sample a varied selection of flavourful beers from the pub company's portfolio and indulge in friendly badinage. Dogs are welcome. Great Missenden, one mile away, is home to the Roald Dahl Museum and various eclectic shops are situated in the narrow high street. ஜ❀&P

Quainton

George & Dragon
32 The Green, HP22 4AR
☀ closed Mon; 12-2.30, 5-11; 12-11 Sat; 12-3, 6-10.30 Sun
☎ (01296) 655436 ⊕ georgeanddragonquainton.co.uk
Beer range varies Ⓗ
Free house offering a good range of beers including two LocAles – usually Vale and XT. The interior is divided between the public bar and saloon bar, with home-cooked food served in both bars but the latter offering more of a dining experience. Parts of the building date back to the 1700s with traditional English features such as inglenook fireplaces, beams and a quarry tiled floor. The public bar has a dartboard, jukebox and TV. Regular beer festivals feature in summer. ஜ◑✦&♣♦P⌐₩(16)

Stoke Goldington

Lamb 🏆 Ⓛ
16-20 High Street, MK16 8NR
☀ 12-2.30 (not Mon), 5-11; 12-11 Sat; 12-7 Sun
☎ (01908) 551233 ⊕ thelambatstokegoldington.co.uk
Tring Death or Glory; guest beers Ⓗ
The village is picture postcard-perfect and the Lamb is at its heart – a welcoming, friendly free house with a fine choice of unfailingly excellent ale, often including a LocAle, real cider and superb, generously portioned food. The pub has a cosy bar area, large separate restaurant, less formal dining

When you have lost your inns, drown your empty selves, for you will have lost the last of England.
Hilaire Belloc, The Four Men, 1912

room and a large garden with a stage area for live music. Local CAMRA Pub of the Year for 2013. ஜ❀◑✦&♦P⌐₩(37)

Stoke Mandeville

Bull
5 Risborough Road, HP22 5UP
☀ 12-11.30 (12.30am Sat) ☎ (01296) 613632
⊕ thebullstokemandeville.co.uk
Adnams Southwold Bitter; Brains SA; St Austell Tribute; Sharp's Doom Bar Ⓗ
Reopened in 2012, this small two-bar village pub, situated on a main road, is well served by buses and trains. The public bar at the front is popular with locals, especially those who gather to watch football and horse racing on TV. The comfortable lounge bar at the back tends to be quieter and leads to a large secure garden which is very popular, especially in summer. Q❀◑✦≒♣P⌐₩(300)

Taplow

Oak & Saw Ⓛ
Rectory Road, SL6 0ET
☀ 12-11 (midnight Fri); 12-10.30 Sun ☎ (01628) 604074
⊕ oakandsaw.co.uk
Brakspear Bitter; Fuller's London Pride; guest beer Ⓗ
Situated opposite the village green and church in an idyllic setting, the pub offers three real ales including a monthly beer from Rebellion. Good pub food is served all day, every day except Sunday and Monday evenings. Steak nights feature every Saturday, with a free bottle of wine for every two steaks purchased. There are quizzes on the second and fourth Sundays of the month. The small garden at the rear has a covered smoking area. Dogs are allowed but not in the dining area.
ஜ❀◑≒P⌐₩(53,75)

Thornborough

Two Brewers
Bridge Street, MK18 2DN (off A421 Milton Keynes-Buckingham road)
☀ 12-2 (Wed & Sat only), 6 (5 Sat)-midnight; 11.15-3, 7-10.30 Sun ☎ (01280) 812020
Beer range varies Ⓗ
Everyone's idea of a country pub, run by the same landlord for almost 30 years. Set in a tranquil village, it has a cosy snug with inglenook fireplace and a larger main bar with wood-burning stove, pool tables and darts. Closed weekday lunchtimes except Wednesday when pensioners get half-price drinks. ஜQ❀❀♣⌐

Wendover

Pack Horse
29 Tring Road, HP22 6NR
☀ 12-11 (midnight Fri & Sat); 12-10.30 Sun
☎ (01296) 622075
Fuller's London Pride; Gale's Seafarers Ale; guest beer Ⓗ
Small, friendly village pub dating from 1769, run by the same family for 49 years. It is situated at the end of a terrace of thatched cottages known as Anne Boleyn Cottages, reputedly given to Anne Boleyn as a wedding present from Henry VIII. The wall above the bar is decorated with RAF squadron badges, denoting connections with nearby RAF

Halton. The pub is home to men's and women's darts, dominoes and cribbage teams. The owners also run the White Swan, another Fuller's pub in the village worth a visit. ⇌♣'–🖬

Wing

Queen's Head 🅛
9 High Street, LU7 0NS
😊 closed Mon; 11.30-3, 5.30-11; 11.30-11 Fri & Sat; 12-10.30 Sun ☎ (01296) 688268 ⊕ thequeensheadwing.co.uk
Wells Bombardier; Young's Bitter; guest beers 🅗
A 16th-century village-centre free house with a comfortable public bar and restaurant. LocAle accredited, guest beers are from nearby Tring, Vale, Hopping Mad and other micros. The restaurant at the rear has a well-deserved reputation for quality food. Log fires in winter months complement the warmly welcoming atmosphere and the pub is TV-free. The large garden has a patio and a covered, heated smoking area. There is ample car parking. 🛏️❀ᗡ▷ ⬱ᗇP'–🖬(100,150)

Winslow

Nag's Head
39 Sheep Street, MK18 3HL
😊 6-11.30 (1.30am Fri & Sat); 12-4.30, 7-11 Sun
☎ (01296) 712037
Hook Norton Hooky Bitter; Shepherd Neame Spitfire; Tetley Bitter 🅗
The bar of this lively hostelry is adorned with a massive collection of souvenir spoons, and is watched over by Eric, a startlingly lifelike waxwork in the front window. The 18th-century pub has a traditional interior with prints of rural scenes ornamenting the walls and a pool table at the rear. Outside is a covered smoking area and beer garden. 🛏️❀♣P'–🖬(60)

Wooburn Common

Royal Standard
Wooburn Common Road, HP10 0JS (follow signs to Odds Farm) SU923876
😊 12-11 (10.30 Sun) ☎ (01628) 521121
⊕ theroyalstandard.biz
Caledonian Deuchars IPA 🅗**; Hop Back Summer Lightning** 🅖**; St Austell Tribute; guest beers** 🅗
Ever-popular semi-rural inn with a congenial ambience in the bar, catering for diners and discerning drinkers alike. Ten real ales, five direct from the cask, alongside many real ciders, make this venue an important flagship pub in the area. There is always at least one dark beer on offer, either a stout, porter or dark mild. Two beer festivals are held, one over the May Day weekend, the other on the last weekend in October. Quiz night is the second Monday of the month.
🛏️Q❀ᗡ▷ᗇ♣P'–

Wycombe Marsh

General Havelock
114 Kingsmead Road, HP11 1HZ
😊 12-2.30, 5.30-11; 12-11 Fri & Sat; 12-11.30 Sun
☎ (01494) 520391 ⊕ generalhavelock.co.uk
Fuller's London Pride, ESB; Gale's Seafarers Ale; guest beers 🅗
This imposing building used to be a farmhouse. It is now set between a ski slope and playing fields on the boundary between Wycombe Marsh and Loudwater. A family-run establishment for 25 years, it is very much a locals' pub, serving Fuller's beers. Lunches are available daily, evening meals Friday and Saturday. A Guide regular, it is full of charm with a big happy family atmosphere.
🛏️❀▷♣P'–🖬(35)

Watts Arms, Hanslope (Photo: Claire-Michelle Taverner-Pearson)

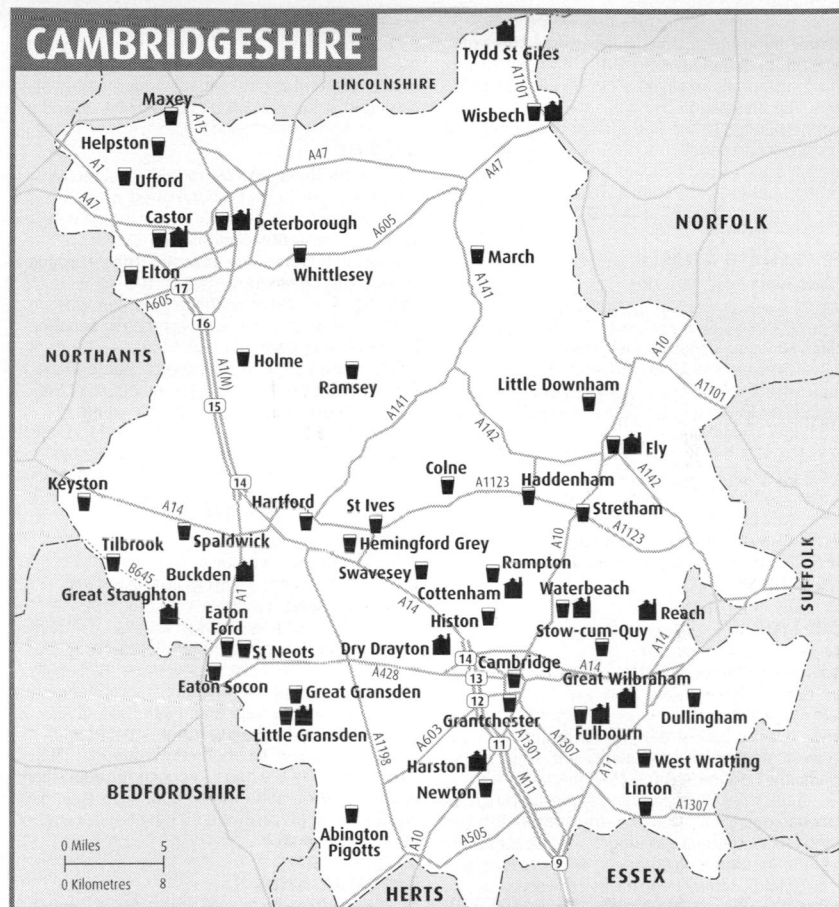

ENGLAND

Abington Pigotts

Pig & Abbot
High Street, SG8 0SD (off A505 through Litlington)
TL306444
🌣 12-3, 6-11; 12-11 Sat; 12-10.30 Sun ☎ (01763) 853515
⊕ pigandabbot.co.uk
Adnams Southwold Bitter; Fuller's London Pride; guest beers Ⓗ
Located in a remote part of the south Cambridgeshire countryside, this Queen Anne-period pub offers a warm welcome. The interior features exposed oak beams and two real fires, including a large inglenook with a wood-burning stove. A comfortable restaurant offers traditional home-made pub food. Two guest beers are kept, often from Woodforde's, Humpty Dumpty, Mighty Oak or Timothy Taylor. ♿Q❄️⊛◑♣P

Cambridge

Cambridge Blue Ⓛ
85 Gwydir Street, CB1 2LG
🌣 12-11 (10.30 Sun) ☎ (01223) 471680
⊕ the-cambridgeblue.co.uk
Beer range varies Ⓗ
Busy, recently extended community pub with a surprisingly large garden. The interior is decorated with breweriana and pump clips from the hundreds

of different beers served each year. A huge selection of bottled beers is on offer, with Belgian beers a speciality, plus several German and Belgian beers on draught. Ciders, perries and mead are also stocked. Impressive beer festivals are held in February, June, October and December. Wholesome home-cooked food is available all day. CAMRA Cambridge and Cambridgeshire Pub of the Year 2011. ♿Q❄️⊛◑🍴≉♣♥🚆(2)

Castle Inn
38 Castle Street, CB3 0AJ
🌣 11.30-3, 5-11; 11.30-11.30 Fri & Sat; 12-11 Sun
☎ (01223) 353194 ⊕ thecastleinncambridge.com
Adnams Southwold Bitter, Explorer, Broadside; Purity Mad Goose; guest beers Ⓗ
Adnams' most westerly tied house, the Castle offers a great selection of the brewery's own beers, including seasonals, plus a range of interesting changing guests. There is a wide range of drinking areas across two floors plus a suntrap garden next to the mound of the long-demolished castle. Excellent food is served every session – the Castleburgers are renowned. The landlord was Barry Wom in the Rutles. ♿⊛◑🚆

Champion of the Thames
68 King Street, CB1 1LN
🌣 11-11 (midnight Fri & Sat; 10.30 Sun) ☎ (01223) 352043
Greene King IPA, Abbot; guest beers Ⓗ

59

Small, two-room, city-centre pub with a truly friendly atmosphere. This is one of four remaining pubs on the infamous King Street Run pub crawl, which historically involved a pint in each of eight pubs. The oarsman in the pub's name is commemorated in the fine etched windows. Both bars are wood-panelled with Victorian counters and bar backs, fixed benches and a part-glazed partition between the rooms. Opening hours may vary in winter. ﾙQ✿♦⬛≢♣⌐▱

Devonshire Arms Ⓛ
1 Devonshire Road, CB1 2BH
✪ 11-11 (midnight Fri & Sat); 12-10.30 Sun
☎ (01223) 316610 ⊕ individualpubs.co.uk/devonshire
Milton Minotaur, Pegasus; guest beers Ⓗ
Milton Brewery's first pub in Cambridge and impressively renovated, it has front and rear drinking areas offering a mixture of wooden booths and larger tables. Up to five Milton beers are available plus three changing guests, a real cider and a selection of Belgian bottled beers. Good-quality food is on offer every session including pizzas cooked in the stone bake oven. A wood-burning stove warms the back room in winter. Local CAMRA Pub of the Year for 2012.
ﾙQ✿❶≢♦⬝⌐▱(2)

Elm Tree Ⓛ
16a Orchard Street, CB1 1JT
✪ 11-11; 12-10.30 Sun ☎ (01223) 502632
⊕ theelmtreecambridge.co.uk
Beer range varies Ⓗ
Quiet, relaxed back-street pub decorated with brewery memorabilia and quirky bric-a-brac. Ten handpumps dispense three changing ales from B&T, three from Wells & Young's, plus guests from a myriad micros. A cider or perry is also kept. To complement the draught ales there is a menu of over 100 bottled Belgian beers, with occasional beer tastings. Interesting snacks are served at lunchtimes. Music gigs – mainly folk and blues – and story-telling evenings feature occasionally.
❶⬝≢♣⬝⌐▱(2)

Flying Pig ♥
106 Hills Road, CB2 1LQ
✪ 12-11 (midnight Fri); 7-11 Sat & Sun ☎ (01223) 354623
Black Sheep Best Bitter; Crouch Vale Brewers Gold; guest beers Ⓗ
Cosy and friendly L-shaped pub, with a local feel despite being on a main road. The walls and ceilings are adorned with various posters and pig paraphernalia. Basic pub grub is served weekday lunchtimes only. In the evenings, the intimate lighting is enhanced by candles on the tables. Background music is usually jazz or blues, and is unobtrusive. As well as the regular real ales, two draught beers are offered from Freedom Brewery. Live acoustic music plays most Tuesday evenings.
✿❶≢▱

Free Press
7 Prospect Row, CB1 1DU
✪ 12-2, 6-11; 12-11 Fri & Sat; 12-2.30, 7-10.30 Sun
☎ (01223) 368337 ⊕ freepresspub.com
Greene King XX Mild, IPA, Abbot; guest beers Ⓗ
Cosy, friendly pub serving high-quality food and great beer, including the rare XX Mild. Guests are from Greene King's seasonal and guest lists. An inn for 120 years, it nearly closed as part of the Kite redevelopment in the 1970s, when the interior was reduced to a shell. Most of what you see now

is a loving reconstruction, though the tiny snug was part of the original pub. It was named (tongue in cheek) after a temperance movement newspaper that lasted for just one edition! An intimate walled garden is at the rear. ﾙQ⬝✿❶⬛♣⬝⌐▱(2)

Geldart
1 Ainsworth Street, CB1 2PF (off Mill Road via Kingston & Sturton streets)
✪ closed Mon; 5-11.30 (1am Fri); 12-1am Sat; 12-11.30 Sun
☎ (01223) 314264 ⊕ the-geldart.co.uk
Caledonian Deuchars IPA; St Austell Tribute; Young's Special; guest beers Ⓗ
This large back-street corner pub within walking distance of the railway station has two separate bar areas. Five changing guest beers come from Punch Finest Cask and SIBA Direct. Home-made food includes hot rock – where diners cook their own meat on a volcanic stone. Live music is hosted, from folk to jazz (see website for details). Functions can be catered for. The real ale bar also has a good selection of malt whiskies and rums. Free Wi-Fi access. ﾙ⬝✿❶⬛≢⬝

Hopbine Ⓛ
11-12 Fair Street, CB1 1HA
✪ 11-11.30 ☎ (01223) 367204 ⊕ thehopbine.co.uk
Beer range varies Ⓗ
Sold in early 2011 by Admiral Taverns and now leased to the tenants of the Portland Arms, the Hopbine is free of tie with seven ever-changing real ales, including offerings from local breweries. A real cider is also kept and a selection of continental bottled beers. To the left of the entrance is a bare-boarded area with pool table while the rest of the pub is more comfortable. Food concentrates on pub classics. Quiz night is Sunday. CAMRA members receive a 10 per cent discount on beer. ❶⬝≢♣⬝▱

Kingston Arms Ⓛ
33 Kingston Street, CB1 2NU
✪ 12-3, 5-11; 12-midnight Fri; 11-midnight Sat; 11-11 Sun
☎ (01223) 319414 ⊕ kingston-arms.co.uk
Crouch Vale Brewers Gold; Oakham Jeffrey Hudson Bitter; Thornbridge Jaipur IPA; Taylor Landlord; Woodforde's Wherry; guest beers Ⓗ
Classic side-street pub just off Mill Road. Eleven handpumps serve regular and changing guest beers plus a varying local cider and Broadoak Perry. A large selection of Belgian and other bottled beers is stocked and monthly beer festivals are held in the warmer months. Award-winning food is

available at all sessions. The walled garden has canopies and heaters and is popular all year round. CAMRA members receive a 20p discount per pint. A recession beer and food menu are offered at bargain prices. Free Wi-Fi and newspapers. 﨎Q✿❍❄♣♠'➖🖥(2)

Live & Let Live ⅃
40 Mawson Road, CB1 2EA
✪ 11.30-2.30, 5.30 (6 Sat)-11; 12-3, 7-11 Sun
☎ (01223) 460261 ⊕ the-live.co.uk
Nethergate Umbel Ale; guest beers 🅗
Wood panelling and railway and beer memorabilia add to the atmosphere at this discreet street-corner local just off Mill Road. Seven handpumps present a changing range of beer styles. The eighth handpump dispenses locally produced Cassells cider. There is an outstanding collection of rums from around the world, and occasional rum festivals. Food is restricted to snacks – the pork pies and Scotch eggs are excellent. Q❄♣♠🖥(2)

Maypole ⅃
20a Portugal Place, CB5 8AF
✪ 11.30-midnight (2am Fri & Sat); 12-11.30 Sun
☎ (01223) 352999 ⊕ maypolefreehouse.co.uk
Beer range varies 🅗
The Castiglione family, who have run this city-centre pub for over 30 years, bought the freehold from Punch Taverns in 2009. The Maypole is now a showcase for quality beers, with up to 16 ales on offer including a selection from local breweries. The interior comprises two rooms either side of the bar plus a large function room upstairs. A pleasant suntrap patio also provides covered space for smokers. Food focuses on home-cooked Italian dishes. ✿❍🍴♠'➖🖥(1,2)

Mill ⅃
14 Mill Lane, CB2 1RX
✪ 11-11 (midnight Thu-Sat) ☎ (01223) 311829
⊕ themillpubcambridge.co.uk
Beer range varies 🅗
A honeypot location next to the Mill Pond. The pub was refurbished in summer 2012 with improvements including an attractive, wood-panelled side room. The bar has a wood-block top with eight handpumps including one dispensing cider. There is a strong commitment to locally brewed beers – the likes of Milton, Fellows, BlackBar, Cambridge Moonshine and Lord Conrad's are frequently available. An Adnams beer is generally also available. A polypin of local cider often sits behind the bar. Q❍❍❄♠

St Radegund ⅃
127 King Street, CB1 1LD
✪ 5 (12 Sat)-11; 12-10.30 Sun ☎ (01223) 311794
Beer range varies 🅗
The smallest pub in Cambridge, this unique, traditional free house offers up to eight real ales, mostly from local breweries, including Milton, and four real ciders. The interior is packed with local sporting memorabilia and the ceiling covered in inscriptions. This is also the base of the infamous Hash House Harriers and has its own rowing and cricket teams. The rain check tree enables you to buy a drink for someone arriving later. Occasional background music is not intrusive. Q❄♠🖥

Castor

Prince of Wales Feathers ⅃
38 Peterborough Road, PE5 7AL
✪ 12-midnight (1am Fri & Sat) ☎ (01733) 380222
⊕ princeofwalesfeathers.co.uk
Adnams Broadside; Woodforde's Wherry 🅗; guest beers 🅗/🅖
This 17th-century stone-built inn has an open-plan layout divided into a number of areas including the bar and a TV area with leather sofas. Six real ales are available including one served from the cellar, always including a beer from the local Castor Ales. A real cider and a perry are kept at all times. Lunches are served daily with evening meals weekdays only. Live music is hosted every Saturday and a quiz night on Sunday. An annual beer festival is held in May. 﨎✿❍♣♠'➖🖥(9,404)

Colne

Green Man ⅃
East Street, PE28 3LZ
✪ 12-2.30 (not Mon), 5-11; 12-11 Fri-Sun ☎ (01487) 840368
⊕ greenmancolne.co.uk
Elgood's Cambridge Bitter; Oakham Inferno; Sharp's Doom Bar; guest beers 🅗
Picturesque 17th-century village local in an old Fenland fruit-growing area. This busy, friendly pub has a public bar with pool, darts and TV, and a warm, sociable lounge with a modern dining area extension serving good food. Quiz nights are held fortnightly. Outside, the garden has a children's play area and hosts barbecues in summer. There is camping nearby at Earith Lakes. ⌂✿❍🍴♿♣♠P'➖

Dullingham

Boot
18 Brinkley Road, CB8 9UW
✪ 11.30-2.30, 5-11; 11.30-11.30 Sat; 11.30-10.30 Sun
☎ (01638) 507327
Adnams Southwold Bitter; Fuller's London Pride; guest beer 🅗
Traditional village inn which Greene King tried to close. Rescued by a villager, it is now a vibrant and welcoming community local where something is always going on. The pub is home to darts, crib and pétanque teams, and hosts regular live music and beer festivals twice a year. Simple, good-value pub grub is served lunchtimes (no food Sun), and fish and chips on Wednesday evenings. Children are welcome until 8pm. 﨎✿❍❄♣P'➖

Eaton Ford

Barley Mow
27 Crosshall Road, PE19 7AB
✪ 11.30-11 (midnight Thu-Sat); 12-11 Sun
☎ (01480) 474435 ⊕ barleystneots.co.uk
Greene King IPA, Abbot; guest beer 🅗
Simple one-bar community pub with a wide variety of activities focused on the regulars, live music events and seasonal celebrations. A long service counter dominates the centre of the bar. Images of past pub social events adorn the walls, some dating back to the early part of the last century. There is a large beer garden with an extensive children's play area. ⌂✿❍♣P'➖🖥(X5)

Eaton Socon

Rivermill Tavern 🄻
School Lane, PE19 8GW
🔵 12-11 (midnight Fri) ☎ (01480) 219612
⊕ rivermilltavern.co.uk
Adnams Broadside; Greene King IPA; guest beers 🄷
This popular riverside pub on the River Great Ouse was converted from a flour mill and has a galleried area above the bar. There is an extensive, varied menu, served all day on Saturday and Sunday. Live music features on Tuesday, Wednesday and Friday evenings and a quiz is hosted on Sunday evening. Up to three guest beers are stocked from independent breweries. The patio offers splendid views of the river and marina. Moorings are available. ⑤❀◑▲♣♠Pˢ⎕(X5)

Waggon & Horses
184 Great North Road, PE19 8EF
🔵 12-3, 5-11; 12-11 Fri & Sat; 12-10 Sun ☎ (01480) 386373
Adnams Broadside; Woodforde's Wherry 🄷; guest beer 🄶
Traditional village pub, formerly a coaching inn, dating from the 1700s, with a large open inglenook fireplace and many exposed oak timbers and beams. The area close to the entrance functions as a bar, and the area beyond the fireplace as a dining area. ❦Q⑤❀◑Pˢ⎕(X5)

Elton

Crown Inn 🄻
8 Duck Street, PE8 6RQ (off B671 into Middle St, follow brown signs)
🔵 12-11 ☎ (01832) 280232 ⊕ thecrowninn.org
Grainstore Phipps IPA; Greene King IPA; guest beers 🄷
This 16th-century stone pub with thatched roof has one main bar, a small dining area to the front and a restaurant to the rear. Five ales are usually on offer via handpump including the house beer, Golden Crown Ale, brewed by Tydd Steam. There is a dedicated handpump for real cider. No bar food is served Saturday evening or Sunday. Five-star B&B accommodation is available. ❦❀⌂◑♠Pˢ⎕(X4,24)

Ely

Fountain
1 Silver Street, CB7 4JF
🔵 5-11; 12-2, 6-11 Sat; 12-3, 7-10.30 Sun ☎ (01353) 663122
Adnams Southwold Bitter; guest beers 🄷
Attractive street-corner pub opposite the Porta monastic gatehouse. Full of character inside, it has an eclectic mix of furnishings, local historic photographs and paintings on display. There is a large and welcoming open fireplace with a fire throughout the winter. Four or more beers are usually available, with three guests. ❦Q⇌

Townhouse Pub ♈ 🄻
60-64 Market Street, CB7 4LS (near Ely Museum)
TL5410680446
🔵 11-11 (1.30am Fri & Sat); 12-11 Sun ☎ (01353) 664338
⊕ thetownhousepub.co.uk
Beer range varies 🄷
Grade II-listed, renovated Georgian town house with a popular modern bar, airy conservatory and enclosed rear garden. An Oakham Ales Oakademy, it offers three changing ales and local Pickled Pig cider. At least one beer is always on offer at a

discounted price 5-7pm weekdays and 7-9pm weekends. Live music plays on Friday and Saturday evenings and a quiz is hosted on Sunday. An annual beer festival is held in July. Although the pub has a stepped main entrance, there is separate disabled access. ❀◑♠ᣠ

Fulbourn

Six Bells
9 High Street, CB21 5DH
🔵 11-3, 6-midnight; 11.30-midnight Fri-Sun
☎ (01223) 880244 ⊕ thesixbellsfulbourn.com
Adnams Southwold Bitter, Broadside; Greene King IPA; Woodforde's Wherry; guest beers 🄷
Gloriously traditional thatched village pub, previously a coaching inn. The main bar has low ceilings, a real fire and many cosy corners. Locally sourced and home-cooked food is served in the bar or the separate dining room (no food Sun or Mon eve). The function room hosts a trad jazz club on the first and third Wednesday of the month. ❦⑤❀◑⊟凸♣♠Pˢ⎕(1,3)

Grantchester

Blue Ball Inn
57 Broadway, CB3 9NQ
🔵 2-11; 12-midnight Sat; 12-7 Sun ☎ (01223) 840679
Adnams Southwold Bitter; guest beer 🄷
Small, authentic local built in 1893 and retaining its original two-bar layout and many old fittings (including the landlord). No lager, no TV, no children – good beer, good conversation and traditional pub games are the order of the day. The piano is still played and there is live music every Thursday. At the back is a small walled garden with a heated 'smokeatorium'. Try your hand at ringing the bull. Dogs welcome. The name commemorates a balloon flight. ❦Q❀♣ᣠ⎕(18)

Green Man 🄻
59 High Street, CB3 9NF
🔵 11-11 ☎ (01223) 844669
⊕ thegreenmangrantchester.co.uk
Beer range varies 🄶
Five-hundred-year-old building complete with oak beams. The single-bar pub has been under the current enthusiastic ownership since reopening in 2009. Beers are sourced from regionals and micros, including local breweries, and regular beer festivals are held. Good home-made food made with local ingredients is served lunchtimes and evenings, all day Saturday and Sunday. The extensive beer garden leads towards the River Cam. ❦Q⑤❀◑♠Pˢ⎕(18)

Great Gransden

Crown & Cushion 🄻
2 West Street, SG19 3AT
🔵 closed Mon; 3-11; 12-11 Sat; 12-10 Sun
☎ (01767) 677214 ⊕ crownandcushion.com
Beer range varies 🄷
Picture-postcard village pub with a thatched roof and oak beams, believed to date partly from the 16th century. The lounge and dining area features a large fireplace with wood-burning stove. This busy village pub has much to offer including live music on Wednesdays and Thursdays (see website for details). Two guest beers are usually from Milton and Oakham. An interesting menu focusing

on Indonesian cuisine is available Friday to Sunday and at other times by prior arrangement. ♨Q◑♣P⁵–₪(18)

Haddenham

Three Kings
1 Station Road, CB6 3XD (at crossroads on A1123 in village)
✪ 11-11; 12-10.30 Sun ☎ (01353) 749080
Greene King IPA, Abbot; Morland Old Speckled Hen Ⓗ
This 17th-century building has been updated over time, but retains its rustic framework and charm with plenty of exposed old beams, cosy areas and an inglenook fireplace. The village pub primarily specialises in food but is justifiably proud of its quality beer and is well supported by local drinkers. At the rear is a relaxing outside courtyard drinking area and a large car park. ♨⊛◑P⁵–

Hartford

King of the Belgians
27 Main Street, PE29 1XU
✪ 11-11 (midnight Fri & Sat); 12-10.30 Sun
☎ (01480) 52030 ⊕ kingofthebelgians.com
Beer range varies Ⓗ
A 16th-century pub offering an ever-changing selection of three real ales and good-value food every day, with a traditional roast on Sundays until 9pm. Solid oak beams and a copper-topped bar feature in the public bar and there is a welcoming separate dining area. Regular quizzes and pub games nights are held. ⤳⊛◑⊟♣P₪(1a)

Helpston

Blue Bell Ⓛ
10 Woodgate, PE6 7ED
✪ 11.30-2.30 (3 Sat), 5 (6 Sat)-11; 12-10 Sun
☎ (01733) 252394
Grainstore John Clare; guest beers Ⓗ
Quiet 17th-century stone village pub with the main entrance at the side. There are two wood-panelled bars, a number of dining areas, and a snug named after local poet John Clare. The local Grainstore Brewery supplies the house beer, and there are two further guest beers from breweries around the country. A traditional cider is added in the summer. Good-value food is served lunchtime and evenings. ♨Q⤳⊛◑⊟♣P⁵–₪(201)

Hemingford Grey

Cock Ⓛ
47 High Street, PE28 9BJ (off A14, SE of Huntingdon)
✪ 11.30-3, 6-11; 12-4, 6.30-10.30 Sun ☎ (01480) 463609
⊕ cambscuisine.com
Brewsters Hophead; Great Oakley Wot's Occurring; Nethergate IPA; guest beer Ⓗ
A winner of local, regional and national CAMRA awards, this pub has been in the Guide for more than 10 consecutive years. The cosy bar area is popular with locals and diners alike who enjoy the well-kept locally sourced beers and real Cromwell cider produced in the village. The separate restaurant (booking essential at all times) features an extensive fish board, meat, game and excellent home-made sausages. During the summer, occasional beer festivals are held in the garden. ♨Q⊛◑⊟▲♣P⁵–₪(5)

Histon

Red Lion
27 High Street, CB24 9JD
✪ 10.30-11 (midnight Fri); 12-11 Sun ☎ (01223) 564437
⊕ redlion-histon.com
Batemans XB; Oakham Bishops Farewell; Tring Blonde; guest beers Ⓗ
Two-bar free house with four changing guest beers, two Belgian and a German beer on draught, complemented by a huge range of bottled Belgian and German beers plus cider and perry from the cask. Food is served every lunchtime and monthly themed food nights are popular. Two beer festivals are held each year – an Easter aperitif then the main event in September. The guided bus stops within half a mile. ♨⤳⊛◑⊟♣♣P⁵–₪(8)

Holme

Admiral Wells Ⓛ
41 Station Road, PE7 3PH (jct of B660 and Yaxley Rd)
✪ 11-2.30, 5-11; 11-11 Sat; 11-10.30 Sun ☎ (01487) 800748
⊕ admiralwells.co.uk
Adnams Southwold Bitter, Broadside; Digfield Shacklebush; Oakham JHB; guest beers Ⓗ
Victorian inn named after one of Nelson's pall bearers and officially the lowest ground-level pub in the UK. It has two drinking areas in a modern contemporary style, and a function room at the rear. Next to the old Holme railway station, and the East Coast mainline, the walls are adorned with photographs from steam railway days. Up to seven real ales and a cider are usually available and the pub serves excellent food. Quiz night is Tuesday. ♨Q⤳⊛◑⊟♣♣P⁵–

Keyston

Pheasant Ⓛ
Village Loop, PE28 0RE (on B663, 1 mile S of A14, E of Thrapston)
✪ closed Mon; 12-3, 6-11; 12-11 Fri & Sat; 12-5 Sun
☎ (01832) 710241 ⊕ thepheasant-keyston.co.uk
Adnams Southwold Bitter, Broadside; guest beer Ⓗ
The village is named after Ketil's Stone, probably an Anglo-Saxon boundary marker. Created from a row of thatched cottages in an idyllic setting, the pub offers high-quality food, fine wines and well-kept cask ales. There is a splendid lounge bar and three dining areas. A regularly changing guest beer is offered, usually from Nene Valley Brewery. One of the few pubs included in the first issue of the Guide in 1972. ♨Q⤳⊛◑P

Linton

Crown Inn
11 High Street, CB21 4HS
✪ 12-2.30, 5.30-11; 12-11 Sat; 12-8 Sun ☎ (01223) 891759
⊕ crownatlinton.co.uk
H&H Bitter; guest beers Ⓗ
Family-owned and run, this former coaching inn has an interior divided by exposed beams and wooden posts into a number of comfortable seating areas. The main bar features an old lantern advertising Watney's Red Barrel. A large restaurant at the back provides plenty of seating for diners (no food Sun eve). Guest beers generally include some LocAles and occasional mini-beer festivals are held. Happy hour is 5.30-7pm. Five B&B rooms are available. ♨⤳⊛◖◑P₪(13)

Little Downham

Plough
106 Main Street, CB6 2SX (W end of village)
✪ 12-3 (not Mon), 6-11; 12-midnight Fri & Sat; 12-3, 6-10.30 Sun ☎ (01353) 698297
Greene King IPA; guest beers Ⓗ
This early Victorian Grade II-listed village pub retains much of its historic charm and character, attracting locals as well as visitors from further afield. Three cask beers are usually on offer and an occasional local cider. Thai food is served, with takeaways available. The pub stays open all day at weekends if busy. Children are welcome until 9pm.
Ⓜ☺❍♣☝♿━🚲(125)

Little Gransden

Chequers Ⓛ
71 Main Road, SG19 3DW
✪ 12-2, 7-11; 12-11 Fri & Sat; 12-6, 7-10.30 Sun
☎ (01767) 677348 ⊕ chequersgransden.co.uk
Beer range varies Ⓗ
Village pub, owned and run by the same family for more than 60 years. The unspoilt middle bar, with its wooden bench seating and roaring fire, is a favourite spot to catch up on the local gossip. The pub's Son of Sid brewhouse brews for the pub and local beer festivals. Fish and chips are a highlight on Friday night (booking essential). Real cider is usually available. Winner of numerous CAMRA awards. Ⓜ Q☺Ⓓ♣☝P♿━🖵🚲(18A)

March

Hippodrome Ⓛ
Dartford Road, PE15 8AQ
✪ 8-midnight (1am Fri & Sat) ☎ (01354) 602980
Greene King IPA; Ruddles Best Bitter; guest beers Ⓗ
Opened in 2011 as a Wetherspoon pub after a major refurbishment. Vintage cinema posters adorn the walls and a large, impressive work of art, The March Montage, is on the wall above the bar. Other interesting artefacts include an original Hunter Penrose process camera, film cans and a rogues' gallery of local figures. Ten handpumps serve the two regular beers plus changing guests. 🚲❍&≼☝P♿━🚲(33)

Rose & Crown Ⓛ
41 St Peters Road, PE15 9NA
✪ 12-11 (midnight Fri & Sat) ☎ (01354) 652077
⊕ the-rose-and-crown-march.co.uk
Oakham Jeffrey Hudson Bitter; guest beers Ⓗ
Traditional 150-year-old family-run free house. This is a community pub with low-beamed ceilings in both rooms and a real fire. Up to six handpumped real ales are offered, mainly from micros, plus a real cider and/or perry. The pub also holds an Easter beer festival. Good-quality food is served lunchtimes and evenings. Quiz night is Thursday and occasional live music features on Saturday.
Ⓜ Q☺❍Ⓓ♣☝P♿━🚲(X9,33)

Maxey

Blue Bell Ⓛ
High Street, PE6 9EE
✪ 5.30 (1 Sat)-11; 12-11 (12-4.30, 7.30-11 winter) Sun ☎ (01788) 348182
Abbeydale Absolution; Fuller's London Pride, ESB; guest beers Ⓗ

A 19th-century stone-built country pub with a narrow interior featuring the main bar at the front with a real fire. Nine handpumps dispense ales from large and small breweries from far and wide. The pub is a meeting place for several groups including birdwatchers and golfers. A former CAMRA Community Pub of the Year and local Pub of the Year. Ⓜ Q☝☺☀P♿━🚲(413)

Newton

Queen's Head
CB22 7PG
✪ 11.30-2.30, 6-11; 12-2.30, 7-10.30 Sun ☎ (01223) 870436
Adnams Southwold Bitter, Broadside; guest beers Ⓖ
This village local is one of a handful across the country to have appeared in every edition of the Guide. The list of landlords since 1729 has just 18 entries, with the names displayed on the wall in the simply furnished but timeless public bar. Also on display is Belinda, the stuffed goose in the case above the bar, who used to patrol the car park. The cosy lounge has a welcoming fire in the colder months. Simple but excellent food centres on soup and sandwiches. Guest beers are Adnams' seasonals. Ⓜ Q❍Ⓓ🗜A♣☝P🚲(31)

Peterborough

Palmerston Arms Ⓛ
82 Oundle Road, Woodston, PE2 9PA (on main A605 ½ mile from city centre)
✪ 3-11; 12-midnight Fri & Sat; 12-10.30 Sun
☎ (01733) 565865
Castle Rock Harvest Pale; Oakham Ales Citra Ⓗ/Ⓖ**; guest beers** Ⓖ
A welcome return to the Guide for this 400-year-old listed stone-built locals' pub. Owned by Batemans, three of its beers sit among nine or more ales, also including some from Oakham Ales. Traditional ciders, perries and an extensive range of malt whiskies are available. Most beers are served straight from the cellar which can be viewed through a large glass screen. Rolls and a variety of snacks tempt customers. Live music features on some nights. Busy on match days. Ⓜ☺♣☝♿━🚲(1)

Brewery Tap Ⓛ
80 Westgate, PE1 2AA
✪ 12-11 (late Fri & Sat) ☎ (01733) 358500
Oakham Jeffrey Hudson Bitter, Citra, Inferno, Bishops Farewell; guest beers Ⓗ
Housed in a former 1930s Labour Exchange, the Tap claims to be one of Europe's largest brewpubs. Up to 12 ales are on offer, mainly from the Oakham range. A mezzanine floor area with some brewing artefacts is incorporated in the pub's modern design. Authentic Thai food is served. Live music plays on Friday and Saturday nights. Close to bus and rail stations. ❍▶≼🚲

Charters Ⓛ
Town Bridge, PE1 1FP (down steps at Town Bridge)
✪ 12-11 (late Fri & Sat); 12-10.30 Sun ☎ (01733) 315700
Oakham Jeffrey Hudson Bitter, Citra, Inferno, Bishops Farewell; guest beers Ⓗ/Ⓖ
A converted Dutch grain barge from circa 1907, Charters sits on the River Nene near to the city centre. Up to 12 beers are on offer plus cider. An oriental restaurant is on the upper deck and food is also served in the bar. The large garden with a

marquee, bar and landing stage for boats is popular in summer. Live music plays some weekends inside and outside the pub. Very busy on football match days. Close to the Nene Valley Railway. ⊛⊙◗≢♣♠P'⊾⊟

Coalheavers Arms

5 Park Street, Woodston, PE2 9BH (just off main London Road)
✪ 12-2 (Thu only), 5-11; 12-11 Fri & Sat; 12-10.30 Sun
☎ (01733) 565664 ⊕ individualpubs.co.uk/coalheavers
Milton Bombers Drop, Justinian, Sparta; guest beers Ⓗ
This friendly one-roomed back-street community pub dates from the 1850s. Up to four guest ales are available alongside cider, Belgian bottled beers and an English unpasteurised lager. Bombers Drop is the house beer from Milton. Home-made jumbo Scotch eggs are available all week, and fresh rolls on Friday. Beer festivals are held in spring and autumn. A free quiz is hosted on Sunday night. The large garden is popular with families in the summer and the pub gets very busy on football match days. Q⊛♣♠'⊾⊟⊟(5,6,46)

Draper's Arms Ⓛ

29-31 Cowgate, PE1 1LZ
✪ 9-midnight (1am Fri & Sat) ☎ (01733) 847570
Courage Directors; Greene King Abbot; Ruddles Best Bitter; guest beers Ⓗ
A converted former draper's shop circa 1899, this is one of two Wetherspoon pubs in the city. The beer range, including many from local microbreweries, is dispensed through 10 handpumps. The interior is divided by wood panels, creating intimate spaces. Food is served all day and regular beer and wine festivals are held throughout the year. Quiz night is Wednesday. A regular local CAMRA top-10 real ale pub, and Wetherspoon Pub of the Year in 2012. Close to bus and rail stations. Q⊙◗&≢♠⊟

Hand & Heart ★ Ⓛ

12 Highbury Street, Millfield, PE1 3BE
✪ 3-11.30; 11.30-midnight Fri & Sat; 11-11.30 Sun
☎ (01733) 564653 ⊕ handandheart.peterboroughpubs.co.uk
Beer range varies Ⓗ
The unspoilt interior of this 1930s back-street pub means it is identified by CAMRA as one of Britain's Best Real Heritage Pubs. There is a main bar to the front and a quiet room to the rear connected by a drinking corridor. Five handpumps often feature some hard-to-find real ales. The garden has an outside bar and stage used for three annual beer festivals and live music events. On weekday evenings various pub teams and events are hosted including a monthly cheese club.
⋈Q⊛⊟♣'⊾⊟(1)

Ostrich Ⓛ

17 North Street, PE1 2RA
✪ 11-11 (1am Fri & Sat); 12-11 Sun ☎ (01733) 746370
Oakham Ales Jeffrey Hudson Bitter; guest beers Ⓗ
Refurbished in 2009 after a series of rebrands, this single-room pub reopened with its original name dating back to the '20s. The U-shaped bar features many pictures and posters of bygone breweries and famous acts who appeared in the city. Up to five regularly changing beers are on offer, many from local breweries, and a real cider. Live music plays most weekends. The small enclosed patio at the rear is a suntrap. A relaxing side-street pub off the main drag. ⊛&≢♣♠'⊾⊟

Ploughman Ⓛ

Staniland Way, Werrington, PE4 6NA (within shopping centre)
✪ 2-11; 12-midnight Fri & Sat; 12-11 Sun ☎ (01733) 327696
Beer range varies Ⓗ
This rejuvenated two-roomed community pub is now at the forefront of the city's real ale outlets. Five handpumps serve beers from breweries near and far. An annual beer festival is held early in July. Darts, pool and poker are popular, charity events are well supported and live music is hosted at weekends. The pub is under threat of demolition from redevelopment of the supermarket next door. ⊛⊟♣P'⊾⊟(1,406,413)

Rampton

Black Horse

6 High Street, CB24 8QE
✪ closed Mon; 6-11 (midnight Sat); 12-7 Sun
☎ (01954) 251867
Beer range varies Ⓗ
This former Greene King pub has been a free house for some time. At least one of the beers is likely to be a local ale and all are guaranteed to be interesting. Beers are available in third-pint glasses if you aren't sure which one to choose. The interior comprises two bars separated by an archway – both are smart and comfortable. Home-made food is available most evenings and Sunday lunchtime. ⋈Q⋟⊛◗&♣P'

Ramsey

Jolly Sailor Ⓛ

43 Great Whyte, PE26 1HH
✪ 11 (12 Sun)-midnight ☎ (01487) 813388
Adnams Southwold Bitter; Fuller's London Pride; Greene King Abbot; Wells Bombardier; Woodforde's Wherry; guest beer Ⓗ
More than 400 years old, this Grade II-listed building has been extended over the years. Its three linked rooms feature exposed wooden beams from various periods in its history. A welcoming, friendly pub, it attracts a mixed clientele of all ages and hosts occasional charity nights and acoustic music sessions. Guest beers are available at the weekend. Good-value home-cooked food is served. ⋈Q⊛⊙&⊟♣P'⊾⊟(31)

Railway

132 Great Whyte, PE26 1HS
✪ 12-midnight (2am Fri & Sat) ☎ (01487) 812597
Greene King Abbot; Thwaites Lancaster Bomber; Woodforde's Wherry; guest beer Ⓗ
Red brick 1930s community pub that is largely intact, with two rooms, each with a real fire, separated by a central bar. A friendly hostelry serving good-quality real ale, it was awarded a local CAMRA Gold Award in 2011. Live music features on Saturdays. Handy for the nearby marina in the summer months. ⋈Q⊛⊟&♣P⊟(31)

St Ives

Floods Tavern Ⓛ

27 The Broadway, PE27 5BX
✪ 12-11 (midnight Thu-Sun) ☎ (01480) 700676
⊕ floods-tavern.com
Elgood's Cambridge Bitter Ⓗ
Elgood's house benefitting from a stylish contemporary revamp and a new menu. Three of

its real ales are served. The bar area features a real fire and TV screens showing live football. The riverside garden provides free moorings, idyllic views of the historic St Ives Bridge and Holt Island Nature Reserve plus an outdoor cocktail bar, music stage and large outdoor screen for special sporting events. Live music features on some Fridays and Saturdays. ♨❀◖◗♣⌐☕

Royal Oak 🅛
13 Crown Street, PE27 5EB
✪ 10-11 (2am Fri & Sat); 12-midnight Sun ☎ (01480) 462586
Oakham Inferno; Sharp's Doom Bar; Wychwood Hobgoblin; guest beers 🅗
Busy mainly 18th-century town-centre pub, one of a number of historic listed inns in St Ives, whose most famous inhabitant was Oliver Cromwell. The interior layout and character were happily preserved in a sensitive renovation in the 1990s. A changing range of guest beers keeps the customers happy. Thursday quiz night, card nights, karaoke and live music are also provided. Traditional, freshly prepared food is served at lunchtime. ☕◖♿♠⌐

St Neots

Hog & Partridge 🅛
25 Russell Street, PE19 1BA
✪ 6-11 (midnight Thu); 4-midnight Fri; 12-midnight Sat; 12-11 Sun ☎ (01480) 406330
Beer range varies 🅗/🅖
A small, traditional back-street pub with the comfortable feel of a lounge bar. Up to five guest beers are offered, typically including two from Batemans, and often focusing on microbreweries. Also available are two real ciders and a good range of bottled ciders, Trappist beers, plus British and foreign bottled beers. Tapas are available Thursday-Saturday evenings. CAMRA members receive a discount. Q☕❀◗♠P♨⌐☕(X5)

Olde Sun 🍺 🅛
11 Huntingdon Street, PE19 1BL
✪ 12-11 ☎ (01480) 216863 ⊕ yeoldesun.moonfruit.com
Woodforde's Wherry; guest beers 🅗
Low-beamed, cosy, traditional town-centre pub with two large inglenook fireplaces, three bar areas, a dining area and a secluded patio. Five constantly changing guest beers come from various regional breweries including Adnams, Elgood's, Marston's, Thwaites and Woodforde's. A good range of home-cooked food is served, with a main menu of traditional pub fare plus blackboard specials (no food Sun and Mon eves). Shove-ha'penny and bar billiards are played. ♨❀◖◗♣♨⌐☕(X5)

Pig 'n' Falcon 🅛
9 New Street, PE19 1AE (behind Barretts department store)
✪ 10-midnight (1am Thu; 2am Fri & Sat); 11-midnight Sun ☎ (07951) 785678 ⊕ pignfalcon.co.uk
Greene King IPA 🅗**, Abbot** 🅖**; Oakham Inferno; Potbelly Best** 🅗**; guest beers** 🅖
This town-centre free house has up to 10 real ales and four real ciders, focusing on microbrews and unusual beers including milds, porters and stouts. A good range of bottled ciders, British and foreign bottled beers including Trappist ales is also kept. Four beer festivals are held each year. Live blues and rock nights are hosted on Wednesday, Friday, Saturday and Sunday. Outside is a large,

imaginatively created, covered and heated beer garden. CAMRA members receive a discount on beer. ☕❀≋♣●♨⌐☕(X5)

Spaldwick

George
5-7 High Street, PE28 0TD (off A14)
✪ 11.30-3, 5.30-11; 11.30-midnight Fri & Sat; 12-10.30 Sun
☎ (01480) 890293 ⊕ thegeorgespaldwick.co.uk
Taylor Landlord; Woodforde's Wherry; guest beer 🅗
A Grade II-listed former coaching inn, dating back to 1679, this smart pub-bistro is light and airy with large comfy sofas and a warm fire in winter months. An old barn has been converted into a stylish dining room. Food is available lunchtimes and evenings (all day until 7pm Sun). The menu varies and focuses on fresh and local ingredients. ♨Q☕❀◖◗♿P♨

Stow-cum-Quy

White Swan 🅛
9 Main Street, CB25 9AB
✪ 12-11 (10.30 Sun & Mon; 11.30 Fri & Sat)
☎ (01223) 811821 ⊕ whiteswanquy.co.uk
Adnams Broadside; Oakham Jeffrey Hudson Bitter; guest beer 🅗
A 17th-century timber-framed village pub that offers well-kept real ales, an extensive wine list and modern British cuisine while maintaining a welcoming community spirit. The right-hand bar is more oriented towards drinkers. Guest beers from local breweries including BlackBar, Fellows and Lord Conrad's often feature, a Woodforde's beer is always available, and sometimes a draught French beer. Beer festivals are held in August and November. ♨Q☕❀◖◗P♨⌐☕(10)

Stretham

Lazy Otter 🅛
Cambridge Road, CB6 3LU (just off A10 Cambridge/Ely Road S of Stretham)
✪ 10-11; 11-10 Sun ☎ (01353) 649780 ⊕ lazyotter.com
Greene King IPA; guest beers 🅗
Spacious free house on the banks of the River Great Ouse, conveniently linked by the riverbank footpath for walkers and cyclists. It has a modern feel with a large bar area and an extensive restaurant serving locally sourced food. The real ales usually number five and are constantly changing. Outside there is plenty of room to relax, and a play area for children. Five moorings are available if visiting by boat. Dogs are welcome. ♨☕❀◖◗●P♨

Swavesey

White Horse
1 Market Street, CB24 4QG
✪ 12-2.30 (not Mon), 6-11; 2-11 Sat; 12-10.30 Sun
☎ (01954) 232470
Beer range varies 🅗
The public bar is a true classic with a polished tiled floor, beamed ceiling, wood-panelling and elevated fireplace. The large lounge bar with dining area is in what was once a separate property and the pool and function rooms behind the public bar are also later additions. Beyond them is a large garden with childrens' play equipment. An annual regional pinball meet is

hosted and the bar boasts its own vintage machine. A beer festival is held every May bank holiday. ♨️🚲🕭🌑①❄️🍴☕🚆

Tilbrook

White Horse 🄻
High Street, PE28 0JP
🌑 12 (5.30 Mon)-11; 12-11 Sun ☎ (01480) 860764
🌐 whitehorsetilbrook.com
Wells Eagle IPA, Bombardier; Young's Bitter; guest beer 🄷
Two-roomed village pub dating in parts back to 1735 and surrounded by large gardens and open fields. The public bar is furnished with sofas and bar stools and provides darts and hood skittles. There is also a large lounge, dining area and bright conservatory with further seating. Traditional, locally sourced food is served (no food all day Mon and Sun eve). The garden has swings and slides for children and a petting zoo. 🚲🕭①❄️🍴P'☕🚆(150)

Ufford

White Hart 🄻
Main Street, PE9 3BH
🌑 12-11 (midnight Fri & Sat); 12-9 Sun ☎ (01780) 740250
🌐 whitehartufford.co.uk
Adnams Southwold Bitter; guest beers 🄷
Stone-built 16th-century local situated in the centre of the village across from the church. There is a public bar to the front, a restaurant to the rear and an orangery to the side, leading to a separate function room. To the rear is a patio, large garden with tables and children's play area. Six individually styled en-suite bedrooms are available. ♨️Q🕭🌑①❄️🍴P'☕

Waterbeach

Sun Inn
Chapel Street, CB25 9HR
🌑 5-11; 12-midnight Fri-Sun ☎ (01223) 861254
Woodforde's Wherry; guest beers 🄷
With a guiding philosophy of 'good beer, good food, good music', this village local goes from strength to strength. The small, cosy lounge is dominated by a huge fireplace while the simply appointed, wood-block-floored public is always lively. Behind the bar is a small meeting room and upstairs a function room where regular gigs are hosted. A changing guest beer comes from Punch's Finest Cask range. Beer and music festivals feature on May and August bank holiday weekends. No food Monday or Sunday evenings. ♨️🕭①❄️🍴🌿🍴☕🚆(9)

West Wratting

Chestnut Tree
1 Mill Road, CB21 5LT
🌑 12-3, 5.30-11; 12-midnight Fri & Sat; 12-10.30 Sun
☎ (01223) 290384 🌐 chestnuttreepub.co.uk
Greene King IPA, Abbot; guest beers 🄷
Two bar locals' pub on the edge of the village, acquired by the present owners from Greene King in 2012. Now free of tie, the guest beers are mainly from microbreweries including local suppliers. The two regular ales on offer change from time to time. The public bar is furnished in a simple style and has been extended to make space for a pool table, while the saloon bar is more

comfortable. Darts and pool teams play here and there is a small lending library. ♨️Q🕭①❄️🍴P'☕🚆(16)

Whittlesey

Boat 🄻
2 Ramsey Road, PE7 1DR
🌑 4 (11 Fri-Sun)-midnight ☎ (01733) 202488
🌐 theboatuk.com
Elgood's Black Dog, Cambridge Bitter, Golden Newt, seasonal beers; guest beers 🄶
This 11th-century inn is mentioned in the Domesday Book. The lounge has an unusual boat-shaped bar and hosts a whisky club that meets on the first Friday of every month. Up to five traditional ciders and perries supplement the real ales that are all served direct from the cask. Live music plays on Saturday evenings. Outside is a pétanque terrain. Good-value accommodation is offered. 🚲🕭🌑①❄️🌿🍴P'☕🚆(31,33)

George Hotel 🄻
10 Market Street, PE7 1AB
🌑 7-midnight (1am Fri & Sat) ☎ (01733) 359970
Courage Directors; Fuller's London Pride; Greene King Abbot; Ruddles Best Bitter; guest beers 🄷
Built in the late 1700s, the building was significantly altered in the mid-19th century before receiving a Grade II listing in 1974. It was closed and unloved until Wetherspoon refurbished and reopened it in 2010. Now a local favourite once again, it offers a large selection of real ales – up to 10 at any one time – and Wetherspoon's good-value food menu. ♨️Q🚲🕭🌑①❄️🌿🍴P'☕🚆(31,32,33)

Letter B 🄻
53-57 Church Street, PE7 1DE
🌑 5-11; 3.30-midnight Fri; 12-midnight Sat; 12-11 Sun
☎ (01733) 206975 🌐 theletterbpublichouse.co.uk
Tydd Steam Barn Ale; guest beers 🄷
This 200-year-old traditional pub near the town centre is popular with both locals and visitors. It is home to the Lions & the Gruftons – a group of local real ale enthusiasts. A small beer festival features on Straw Bear weekend and another in the spring. A good selection of mainly local real ales is offered, including a beer from Great Yarmouth Brewing, plus a range of ciders. Good value B&B accommodation is very popular. Local CAMRA Pub of the Year 2012. Q🕭🌿❄️🌿🍴☕🚆(31,33,701)

Wisbech

Red Lion 🄻
32 North Brink, PE13 1JR
🌑 11.30-3, 6-11; 11.30-3, 7-midnight Sat; 12-11 Sun
☎ (01945) 582022
Elgood's Black Dog, Cambridge Bitter 🄷
The nearest Elgood's pub to the brewery and often frequented by brewery staff, the Red Lion is a comfortable pub where discerning drinkers and diners alike are well catered for. The fine ales, which always include an Elgood's seasonal beer, are complemented by excellent home-cooked food served seven days a week. Children are welcome. Wheelchair access is from the rear, where the outdoor drinking area is popular on sunny days. Q🚲🕭🌑①❄️P'☕🚆(X1)

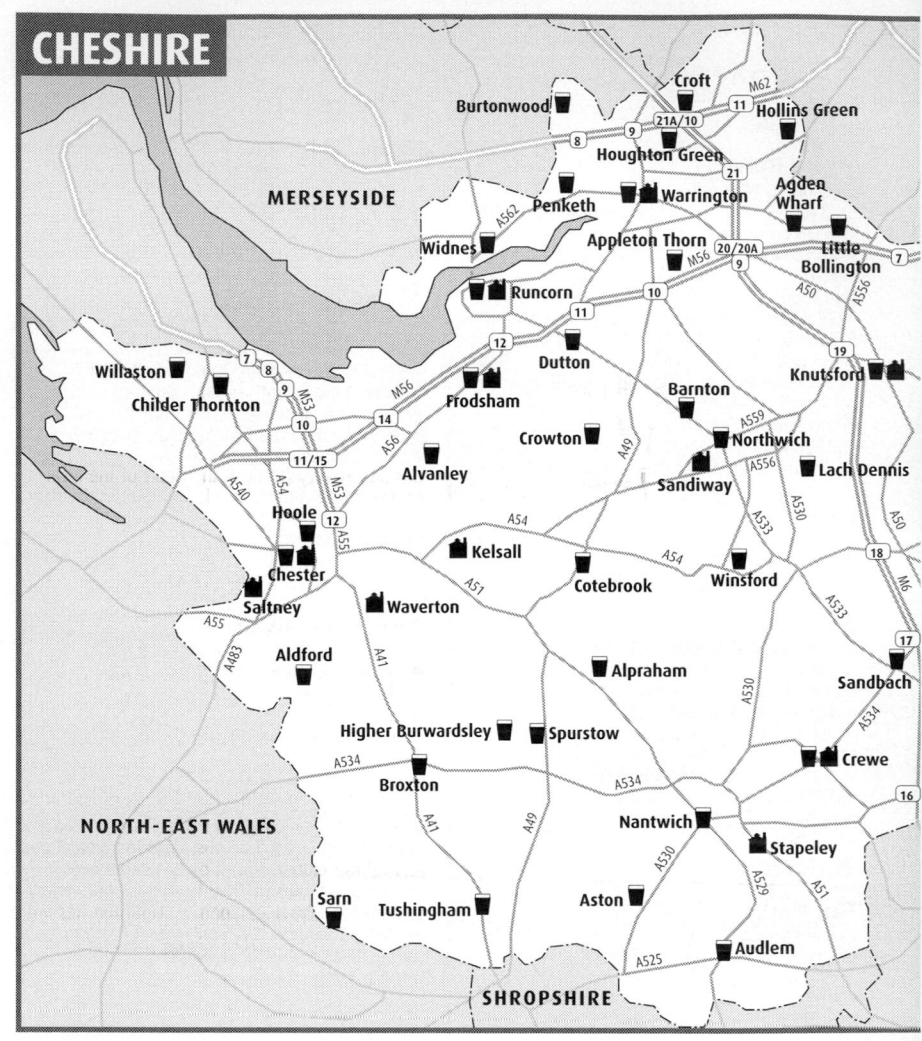

CHESHIRE

Croft · Burtonwood · Hollins Green · Houghton Green · Warrington · Agden Wharf · MERSEYSIDE · Penketh · Appleton Thorn · Little Bollington · Widnes · Runcorn · Dutton · Knutsford · Willaston · Barnton · Childer Thornton · Frodsham · Northwich · Crowton · Lach Dennis · Alvanley · Sandiway · Hoole · Chester · Kelsall · Cotebrook · Winsford · Saltney · Waverton · Aldford · Alpraham · Sandbach · Higher Burwardsley · Spurstow · Crewe · Broxton · NORTH-EAST WALES · Nantwich · Stapeley · Sarn · Tushingham · Aston · Audlem · SHROPSHIRE

Agden Wharf

Barn Owl 🗓
Warrington Lane, WA13 0SW (off A56) SJ707872
☼ 11-11 ☎ (01925) 752020 ⊕ thebarnowlinn.co.uk
**Thwaites Original, Wainwright, Lancaster Bomber;
guest beers** Ⓗ
The pub and its canalside patio enjoy fine views
across rolling countryside. Three regular Thwaites
beers are complemented by up to four guests,
sourced mainly from micros. Renowned for its
home-made food as well as its ale, the pub's
freshly cooked dishes made with mainly local
produce are very popular and it gets especially
busy at meal times. ⬢⬢⬢⬢⬢⬢⬢

Alderley Edge

Alderley Edge Sports & Social Club 🗓
Stevens Street, SK9 7NL
☼ 12-2.30, 6-midnight; 7-11 Sun ☎ (01625) 585506
Beer range varies Ⓗ
Four good-value real ales feature at this rare outlet
in the UK's champagne capital, including up to

three LocAles from within 15 miles. Real cider is
also available in season. A simple food menu is
offered and facilities include full-size snooker
tables, a county-class bowling green and television
sports. Beer festivals are held in July and
November. Visitors are welcome – buzz the buzzer
and show a copy of this Guide or CAMRA
membership card for entry. Non-members are
admitted for £1. ⬢⬢⬢⬢⬢⬢⬢⬢

Aldford

Grosvenor Arms
Chester Road, CH3 6HJ (on B5130)
☼ 11.30-11; 12-10.30 Sun ☎ (01244) 620228
⊕ grosvenorarms-aldford.co.uk
**Brunning & Price Original Bitter; Weetwood Eastgate;
guest beers** Ⓗ
A spacious, stylish and upmarket pub with a multi-
room interior and a pleasant conservatory leading
to an outside terrace and lawn with picnic tables.
Full of character, the decor could be described as
'modern-traditional', with lots of bare wood,
bookcases, pictures and chalkboards. Four ever-

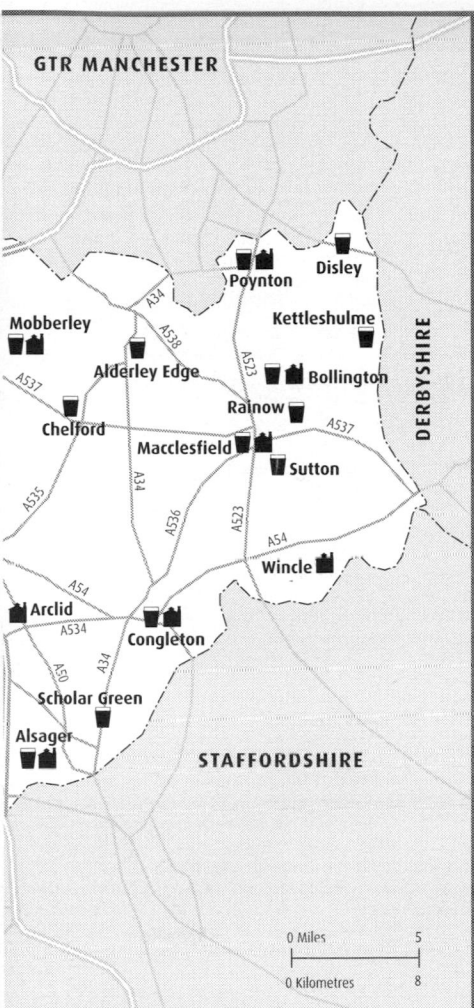

GTR MANCHESTER

Poynton • Disley

Mobberley

Kettleshulme

Alderley Edge • Bollington

Rainow

Chelford • Macclesfield

Sutton

Wincle

Arclid

Congleton

Scholar Green

Alsager

STAFFORDSHIRE

DERBYSHIRE

0 Miles 5

0 Kilometres 8

✪ 4 (3 Sun)-11; 1-midnight Fri & Sat ☎ (01270) 873669
Beer range varies Ⓗ
Large two-roomed pub offering a changing range
of beers, often sourced from microbreweries and
including ales from its own on-site brewery,
Goodall's. Three draught ciders and a selection of
bottled beers are also stocked, and a beer festival
is held at Easter. Baps and wraps are available at all
times. The garden is popular in summer. The pub is
well served by public transport, and there is a
public car park to the rear. ♨✿🕯◑👤♿🚲♣🚆(20)

Alvanley

White Lion Ⓛ
Manley Road, WA6 9DD (opp church) SJ497740
✪ 12-11 (10.30 Sun) ☎ (01928) 722949
🌐 whitelionalvanley.co.uk
Hartleys XB; Robinsons Dark 1892, seasonal beers Ⓗ
Refurbished and much improved in recent years,
this pub is very much at the heart of the local
community. Events are held throughout the year
supporting the village charity fund. Food plays a
major role here but the casual drinker is always
most welcome. The Broadoak Ale is rebadged
Robinsons 1892. ♨Q🕭✿◑👤♿P⅃

Appleton Thorn

Appleton Thorn Village Hall
Stretton Road, WA4 4RT SJ637838
✪ closed Mon-Wed; 7.30-11.30; 1 4, 7.30-10.30 Sun
☎ (01925) 261187 🌐 appletonthornvillagehall.co.uk
Beer range varies Ⓗ
The hub of the community, the village hall has a
comfortable, cosy lounge and a larger bar/function
room, both served from a central bar. The function
room host quizzes, live music and the annual beer
festival in October. Seven pumps serve ever-
changing real ales, mainly from microbreweries,
plus up to eight ciders/perries. Light lunches are
available Sundays 1-3pm only. Local CAMRA Club of
the Year 2012. Q🕭✿◑👤♿♣♠P🖥🚆

Aston

Bhurtpore Inn Ⓛ
Wrenbury Road, CW5 8DQ (¼ mile NW from A530
Nantwich-Whitchurch road) SJ610469
✪ 12-2.30, 6.30-11.30; 12-midnight Fri & Sat; 12-11 Sun
☎ (01270) 780917 🌐 bhurtpore.co.uk
Beer range varies Ⓗ
This popular, friendly, genuine free house at the
heart of the local community has featured in every
issue of the Guide since 1992. Eleven handpumps
deliver a wonderful choice, frequently including
LocAle. Three premium and three session beers,
one strong, and a mild or porter/stout, are always
on offer, including several ales from Shropshire
breweries such as Hobsons at Cleobury Mortimer.
An excellent range of home-cooked, locally
sourced food is available – curries a speciality.
♨Q✿◑♿▲🚃(Wrenbury)♣♠P⅃🚆(72)

Audlem

Lord Combermere Ⓛ
The Square, CW3 0AQ (opp St James' Church)
✪ 12-12.30am ☎ (01270) 812277
🌐 thelordcombermere.co.uk
Greene King IPA; Taylor Landlord; Wells Bombardier;
guest beers Ⓗ

---

changing guest beers complement the house beer
brewed by Phoenix. High-quality food from an
imaginative menu is very popular and served all
day until 10pm (9pm Sun). ♨Q🕭✿◑👤♿♣P⅃🚆

Alpraham

Travellers Rest ★ Ⓛ
Chester Road, CW6 9JA (on A51 at N end of village)
✪ 6.30-11; 12-5, 6-11 Sat; 12-3, 7-10.30 Sun
☎ (01829) 260523
Weetwood Eastgate; Tetley Bitter Ⓗ
A regular entry in the Guide, this is an unspoilt gem
of an inn, identified by CAMRA as one of Britain's
Best Real Heritage Pubs. Four rooms remind you of
a time when the pace of life was much slower.
Whether you are a regular or an occasional visitor
you will be made to feel welcome – good beer and
conversation being the priority. Q✿♣P⅃🚆(84)

Alsager

Lodge Ⓛ
88 Crewe Road, ST7 2LX

Friendly local with polite and helpful staff, situated in the middle of Audlem. Open plan with a central bar, vestiges of the pub's 18th-century origins remain. Entertainment includes a Tuesday quiz night and a beer festival over the August bank holiday. Good home-cooked food is served daily from a varied range, including a full gluten-free menu. Popular with ramblers and canal users.
🏚️⊛◑&🐾P⏚🚃(73)

Barnton

Barnton Cricket Club ⅃

Broomsedge, Townfield Lane, CW8 4QL (200yds from A533 via Stoneheyes Lane) SJ632757
⊛ 6.30-11.30 (11 Wed; 12.30am Thu; midnight Fri); 4-midnight Sat; 12-11 Sun ☎ (01606) 77702
⊕ barntoncc.co.uk
Theakston Best Bitter; Thwaites Nutty Black, Original; guest beers ⊞
This club remains as popular as ever. Multiple sports are played here – cricket, squash, poker, darts, dominoes, pool and ten-pin bowling. The bar offers three regular and up to four guest beers sourced from microbreweries, and a popular beer festival is held every November. Meals are available Thursday to Sunday evenings and Sunday lunchtimes. Local CAMRA Club of the Year 2013.
⊛◑&🐾P⏚🚃(4)

Bollington

Poachers Inn ⅃

95 Ingersley Road, SK10 5RE
⊛ 12-2 (not Mon), 5.30-11; 12-11 Sun ☎ (01625) 572086
⊕ thepoachers.org
Storm Brewing Desert Storm; Weetwood Old Dog; guest beers ⊞
Friendly and welcoming family-run free house near the Gritstone Way. The interior is divided into comfortable seating areas warmed by a coal fire in winter, and the garden is a suntrap in summer. The licensee enthusiastically supports local breweries including nearby Happy Valley. World beers are available in bottles. Well-regarded, good-value, home-prepared food is served, with pie night on Wednesday. Monthly quiz nights support local charities. The pub has featured in the Guide for 12 consecutive years. 🏚️🏃⊛◑🐾P⏚🚃

Vale Inn ⅃

29-31 Adlington Road, SK10 5JT
⊛ 12-2.30, 5-11; 12-11 Fri & Sat; 12-10.30 Sun
☎ (01625) 575147 ⊕ valeinn.co.uk
Beer range varies ⊞
The brewery tap for the nearby Bollington Brewing Company, it features three to five of its beers plus one or two guests, often from local breweries. Seasonal mini beer festivals are held and excellent home-cooked food is served. The pub is popular with the local community as well as walkers and bikers using the nearby canal and Middlewood Way footpath. It sponsors the local Bollington cricket team – games can be watched from the beer garden. 🏚️🏃⊛◑🐾P⏚🚃

Broxton

Sandstone

Nantwich Road, CH3 9JH (A534, E of A41)
⊛ 12-3, 6-11; 12-11 Sat; 12-10.30 Sun ☎ (01829) 782333
⊕ thesandstone.co.uk

Beer range varies ⊞
Popular yet peaceful rural inn with a relaxed, hospitable ambience and friendly staff. The landlord is knowledgeable and enthusiastic about the cask ales on offer, with local microbrews favoured, and takes great care to serve them correctly. The pub is ideally situated for walking the spectacular countryside around the Sandstone Trail. A quiz is held on Tuesday. Food is superb value and highly recommended – a traditional but eclectic menu features freshly prepared local ingredients. Well-behaved children and dogs welcome.
🏚️Q🏃⊛◑&P⏚

Burtonwood

Fiddle i' th' Bag

Alder Lane, WA5 4BJ SJ584929
⊛ 12-3, 5.30-11; 12-11 Sat & Sun ☎ (01925) 225442
Beer range varies ⊞
A notice promising purgatory for parking offenders sets the tone at this eccentric pub. Music from the 1920s to 1950s serenades customers as they try the eagerly proffered beer samples. Up to three constantly changing ales are chosen carefully by mine host, often including a mild, supped amidst a plethora of memorabilia guarded by two orang-utans in evening dress. Food is served lunchtimes and evenings. Well worth a visit. ⊛◑P🚃(329)

Chelford

Egerton Arms ⅃

Knutsford Road, SK11 9BB
⊛ 12-11 (10.30 Sun) ☎ (01625) 861366
⊕ chelfordegertonarms.co.uk
Copper Dragon Golden Pippin; Wells Bombardier; guest beers ⊞
This free house has an open plan bar and dining area with a small games room and a decked garden area at the rear. Four of the six handpumps

are normally dedicated to beers from local microbreweries. The pub is child- and dog friendly, and very popular for food (booking recommended at weekends). A traditional jazz group performs on the last Friday of the month. A high-class deli, opened in 2012, now adjoins the pub.
🏛️🍽️🕮🍴❤️🎵P🖐️🚪

Chester

Bear & Billet
94 Lower Bridge Street, CH1 1RU
🕐 12-11 (11.30 Thu; midnight Fri & Sat) ☎ (01244) 311886
🌐 bearandbillet.com
Okells Bitter; guest beers ℍ
Characterful building dating from 1664, retaining much of the original woodwork. The ground floor bar area has a wooden floor and fine real fire, and further back two separate spaces are set mainly for dining, with a large screen for TV sports. The first floor has a comfortable dining area for about 50 people, the second floor serves as a function room accommodating another 40. Outside is a small yard with tables. 🏛️🕮🍴❤️🍴🖐️🚪

Brewery Tap 🍷 🄻
52-54 Lower Bridge Street, CH1 1RU
🕐 12-11 (10.30 Sun) ☎ (01244) 340999 🌐 the-tap.co.uk
Beer range varies ℍ
Situated on the first floor of a former Jacobean banqueting hall, the pub is reached via steps from the street. The large room has stone floors, high ceilings and tapestries, creating a terrific ambience. A comprehensive, frequently changing list of real ales from micros, many local, complements the Spitting Feathers house beers. The real cider is usually from Wales. Inventive, freshly prepared food is served. Q🕮❤️🍴🚪

Cellar
19-21 City Road, CH1 3AE
🕐 4-midnight (2.30am Fri); 12-2.30am Sat; 12-midnight Sun ☎ (01244) 318950 🌐 thecellarchester.co.uk
Beer range varies ℍ
Modern, street-level bar with a cellar available to hire for private functions. Sparsely furnished with high tables and stools, there is plenty of room to stand on the busy nights when live music is hosted, usually Friday and Saturday. Two TV screens occasionally show sport. Four handpumps serve a changing range of ales mainly from micros such as RedWillow and Liverpool Organic, and there is also a wide selection of foreign beers. No food is served. ❤️🚪

Cross Keys
2 Duke Street, CH1 1RP
🕐 12-11 (11.30 Fri & Sat); 12-10.30 Sun ☎ (01244) 344460
Joule's Blonde, Pale Ale, Slumbering Monk; guest beer ℍ
Recently refurbished, this Victorian gem has a single room at ground floor level with leather seats, oak floors, wood panels and stained glass windows featuring other Joule's houses. A new function room is available for hire. Outside there is a small veranda area for enjoying the late afternoon sunshine. Classic pub food is served. 🏛️🕮🍴❤️🚪

Old Harkers Arms 🄻
1 Russell Street, CH3 5AL (down steps off City Road to canal towpath)

🕐 11.30-11; 12-10.30 Sun ☎ (01244) 344525
🌐 harkersarms-chester.co.uk
Brunning & Price Original Bitter; Weetwood Cheshire Cat; guest beers ℍ
Upmarket pub converted from the ground floor of a Victorian canalside warehouse. Timber flooring, traditional wooden furniture and cast iron pillars reflect its former use. Blackboards list the real ales, with tasting notes – nine beers are usually available, including a selection of bitters, stouts, milds and porters, many from local breweries. Ciders are listed separately and dispensed from the cellar. Food is served all day. There is outside seating with views of the canal. Q🕮🍴❤️🍴🚪

Olde Cottage Inn
34-36 Brook Street, CH1 3DZ
🕐 4 (2 Sat)-midnight; 2-11 Sun ☎ (01244) 324065
🌐 oldecottagechester.co.uk
Sharp's Cornish Coaster; Taylor Golden Best; guest beers ℍ
Traditional unspoilt alehouse that started life as three separate buildings in the early 19th century. This friendly and welcoming local is handily placed close to the railway station. A central bar area serves both a main room with cosy real fire and a side games room. The pub is home to 11 teams including darts, pool, dominoes and bagatelle. A small seating area to the rear leads to a surprisingly large courtyard hidden away from the bustle of Brook Street. 🏛️🍴❤️🍴🚪

Pied Bull 🄻
57 Northgate Street, CH1 2HQ
🕐 10-11 (midnight Fri & Sat) ☎ (01244) 325829
🌐 piedbull.co.uk
Beer range varies ℍ
This oak-beamed city-centre pub is the oldest continuously licensed premises in Chester and is reputed to be haunted. Home to the only microbrewery within Chester's walls, it produces a rapidly expanding range of house ales (including CAMRA award-winning beer Matador) to complement the varying guest beers. House ales can be taken away in bottles. Staff are knowledgeable, enthusiastic and friendly, and regular beer festivals are held. Traditional, high-quality pub meals made with locally sourced ingredients are available all day. Quiz night is Thursday. Q🛏️🕮🍴❤️🚪

Telford's Warehouse 🄻
Canal Basin, Tower Wharf, CH1 4EZ
🕐 12-11 (1am Wed; 12.30am Thu; 2am Fri & Sat); 12-1am Sun ☎ (01244) 390090 🌐 telfordswarehousechester.com
Thwaites Original; Weetwood Cheshire Cat; guest beers ℍ
Converted Georgian warehouse overlooking the canal basin with an outside drinking area next to the water. Friendly staff serve two house cask ales plus a varying range of guests, usually seasonal and often local. A major live music venue; check the website for details as admission charges may apply. The pub also hosts regular salsa and Latin dance classes, open mic sessions and an annual beer festival. Quality food is prepared from the finest and freshest ingredients and sourced locally where possible. Q🕮🍴P🖐️🚪

Childer Thornton

White Lion

New Road, CH66 5PU (off A41 between Great Sutton and Hooton)
⏲ 11.30-11.30 (11 Sun) ☎ (0151) 339 3402
Thwaites Original, Wainwright, Lancaster Bomber; guest beer Ⓗ
This friendly village inn has been a public house since 1724. The main bar features the original inglenook fireplace where the locals gather round on winter evenings. A small snug is located off the bar and there is a separate cosy room across the corridor, mostly used for dining. Home-cooked good-value meals are available all day until 8pm. There are pleasant outdoor drinking areas at the back and front of the pub. ⌂❀◐◑●P⊽

Congleton

Beartown Tap 𝕃

18 Willow Street, CW12 1RL
⏲ 4 (12 Fri & Sat)-11; 12-10.30 Sun ☎ 07858 728856
Beartown Kodiak Gold, Bearskinful, Honey Bear, Polar Eclipse, Ursa Major; guest beers Ⓗ
Famed Congleton real ale outlet, just yards from the Beartown Brewery. Five handpumps usually offer Beartown beers with a sixth for guest ales from other small breweries. The drinking area is divided into three rooms and warmed by a wood-burning stove, with a function room upstairs. Outside is a secluded patio for summer days. A former CAMRA regional Pub of the Year. ⌂❀●⚑–🚌

Queen's Head Hotel 𝕃

Park Lane, CW12 3DE
⏲ 12-midnight (1am Fri & Sat) ☎ (01260) 272546
🌐 queensheadpub.org.uk
Draught Bass; Joule's Bitter; guest beers Ⓗ
Probably the most improved privately-owned pub in town, with knowledgeable and friendly bar staff and eight handpumps providing a mix of regular ales and beers from microbreweries. The kitchen has been refurbished and meals are cooked to order lunchtimes and evenings. Darts and pool teams are flourishing and the gardens have been re-landscaped with the addition of a boules court. ⌂♞❀⛟◐◑⊟♿⇌♣●P⚑–🚌

Young Pretender 𝕃

30-34 Lawton Street, CW12 1RT
⏲ 12-midnight (1am Thu-Sat) ☎ (01260) 273277
Beer range varies Ⓗ
Having brought the Treacle Tap to Macclesfield, the owners' next venture was to convert this former toy shop into a bar offering an impressive range of real ales on handpump complemented by bottled European beers. Now developing into a major social venue for the town, the pub offers regular film, quiz and music nights plus Meet the Brewer and foreign language conversation sessions. Specialist pies are available. A superb addition to Congleton. ♞♿⇌P⚑–🚌

Cotebrook

Fox & Barrel 𝕃

Foxbank, CW6 9DZ SJ573659
⏲ 12-11 (10.30 Sun) ☎ (01829) 760529
🌐 foxandbarrel.co.uk
Caledonian Deuchars IPA; Weetwood Eastgate Ale; guest beers Ⓗ
Friendly country pub with a welcoming, relaxed atmosphere and helpful staff. Dating from 1730, it was sensitively refurbished in traditional style several years ago. A central bar serves a number of rooms and alcoves, with dining and drinking throughout. Guest beers come from local breweries as well as further afield. Food is served all day until 9.30pm (9pm Sun). Outside is a terraced area and beer garden. ⌂Q❀◐◑P

Crewe

Borough Arms 🏆 𝕃

33 Earle Street, CW1 2BG (on Earle Street Bridge) SJ707557
⏲ 5 (12 Fri & Sat)-11; 12-10.30 Sun ☎ (01270) 254999
🌐 borougharmscrewe.co.uk
Beer range varies Ⓗ
A split-level single bar serves three distinct drinking areas. The top bar has nine handpumps, the lower bar is home to a range of classic Belgian and continental beers. A further large room downstairs leads to a sheltered, walled beer garden. The absence of pool, music and gaming machines encourages earnest conversation, and dominoes matches are played. A wide range of ales is served, mainly from small and microbrewers. Home to the Borough Arms Brewery. Q♞❀♣⚑–⊽🚌(14)

Hop Pole 𝕃

Wistaston Road, CW2 7RQ
⏲ 12-11 (midnight Sat) ☎ (01270) 666730
Beer range varies Ⓗ
A classic Crewe pub not far from the town centre with many original fixtures and fittings, including most of the sash windows and alcove seating in the lounge. Three real ales are usually available. There is a great outdoor area to the rear with heating, seating and a bowling green. Friendly and welcoming, traditional pub games are played and live music is hosted. There is a large function room upstairs. ⌂♞❀⊟♣⚑–🚌

Hops 𝕃

8-10 Prince Albert Street, CW1 2DF
⏲ 11 (5 Mon)-11.30; 12-11.30 Sun ☎ (01270) 211100
Townhouse Enigma; guest beers Ⓗ
Friendly, family-run free house in a quiet part of the town centre. It has a comfortable downstairs bar, more seating on the first floor, and outside space for fine weather. The Townhouse house beer is joined by four guest ales, usually from local microbreweries. A comprehensive range of Belgian beers, bottled and draught, is always available. Lunchtime meals are served Wednesday-Saturday. CAMRA members receive a discount on real ale on Monday nights. Local CAMRA Pub of the Year 2011. Q❀◐♿⇌♣●P⚑–🚌

Croft

General Elliot

5 Lord Street, WA3 7DE
⏲ 12-11 (midnight Fri); 12-10.30 Sun ☎ (01925) 766900
🌐 thegeneralelliot.co.uk
Derwent Mild; guest beers Ⓗ
The General Elliot has been a pub or hotel since the 1700s, surrounded by country walks and historic attractions. It is steeped in history which the locals love to recount. A restaurant and public bar, it has retained its original character with a modern twist.

The patio overlooks verdant pastures and is a pleasant place to relax with a pint from one of the three handpumps while watching the sunset. A social centre in Croft with its own village store. ✪❶▶P🖩(19)

Crowton

Hare & Hounds

Station Road, CW8 2RN SJ578745
🟢 12-3 (not Tue), 5 (7 Sat)-11; 12 (5 Tue)-11 summer; 12-5, 7-11 (12-11 summer) Sun ☎ (01928) 788851
⊕ harenhounds.co.uk
Greene King IPA; guest beers 🅷
Quiet country pub and restaurant with three linked rooms. In winter there are open fires, with free toast and forks on Tuesday evenings. A variety of changing guest beers is on offer from the Punch list. The annual Easter duck race on the garden stream raises thousands of pounds for local charities. Joe the landlord can usually be spotted as he'll be wearing his chef's uniform. For the hardy smoker there is a covered table outside with space heating. No food (except toast!) Tuesdays.
🅰Q✪❶▶P⌐-🖩(48)

Disley

White Lion 🅛

135 Buxton Road, SK12 2HA
🟢 12 (6.30 Mon)-11 (12.30am Fri & Sat); 12-11 Sun
☎ (01663) 762800
Beer range varies 🅷
Large pub on the A6 towards the easterly end of the village. It offers eight constantly changing beers from SIBA-member microbreweries. The contemporary, largely open-plan interior has a separate dog room with blankets, water bowls and canine dinners. A comprehensive and varied food menu is served all day until 9pm (no food Mon). Quiz night is Thursday and live entertainment features on the last Saturday of the month. A short walk from Peak Forest Canal (bridge 26).
🅰✪❶≠P🖩(199)

Dutton

Tunnel Top 🅛

Northwich Road, WA4 4JY
🟢 12-11 (10 Sun) ☎ (01928) 718181 ⊕ tunneltop.co.uk
Beer range varies 🅷
This pub has gone from strength to strength thanks to the dedication of managers Moira and Kevin. Specialising in beers from local breweries, regulars include Coach House and Frodsham. Food is also sourced locally and served in the restaurant. Sports fans can watch their game on the giant 8-foot screen in the separate pavilion bar. The pub is an avid supporter of several local charities.
🅰✪❶▶P⌐

Frodsham

Helter Skelter 🍺 🅛

31 Church Street, WA6 6PN SJ518777
🟢 11-11 (11.30 Fri & Sat); 12-10.30 Sun ☎ (01928) 733361
⊕ helterskelter-frodsham.co.uk
Weetwood Best Bitter; guest beers 🅷
A haven for discerning real ale drinkers, this single-room bar with eight handpumps provides a comprehensive, ever-changing array of beers with prominent tasting notes and an emphasis on new

local and national micros. Settees, pews and stools surround a central standing space that fills at busy times. Food is served in the bar or upstairs restaurant. Parking is easy at the nearby station and shopping precinct. Local CAMRA Pub of the Year 2013. ❶▶≠●🖩🖩

Higher Burwardsley

Pheasant Inn 🅛

CH3 9PF
🟢 11-11; 12-10.30 Sun ☎ (01928) 770434
⊕ thepheasantinn.co.uk
Weetwood Best Bitter, Eastgate, Old Dog; guest beer 🅷
Charming country inn nestling among the Peckforton Hills and ideally situated for hikers walking the Sandstone Trail or visitors to the nearby Candle Workshops. Ales are mainly from the local Weetwood Brewery with a guest beer to add variety. Food is high quality and prepared from fresh, locally sourced products. The outside seating area offers magnificent views over the Cheshire Plain towards the Clwydian Hills. Accommodation is available in 12 en-suite rooms housed in old Cheshire sandstone buildings. 🅰Q✪🖙❶▶🕭P⌐

Hollins Green

Black Swan

Manchester Road, Rixton, WA3 6LA
🟢 11-11.30 (12.30am Fri & Sat); 12-11 Sun
☎ (0161) 222 4444 ⊕ theblackswan.co.uk
Beer range varies 🅷
Old coaching inn much enlarged in 2012. The emphasis is on dining but ample space remains for drinkers. Up to six changing beers include at least one from Thwaites or Robinsons, plus one from a local microbrewery. Quality food is served all day. The pub hosts a wide range of occasionally quirky community events for adults and children. The extensive garden has a duck pond and children's play area. There is a farmers' market on the second Saturday of the month. Local CAMRA Community Pub of the Year 2012.
🅰🐾✪🖙❶▶🕭Å≠(Glazebrook)♣P⌐-🖩(100)

Hoole

Lodge Bar

8-10 Hoole Road, CH2 3NH
🟢 11-11 (midnight Fri & Sat) ☎ (01244) 324971
⊕ lodgebar.co.uk
Beer range varies 🅷
Café-style bar at the Bawn Lodge Hotel situated half a mile from Chester railway station. Three handpumps serve a changing range of ales mostly from independents such as Abbeydale or Hornbeam at very competitive prices. Good-value food is available all day. The bar is one of the very few places where bagatelle can still be played. TV screens show terrestrial TV. The large garden area at the front is very popular in summer.
✪🖙❶▶🕭≠(Chester)♣P⌐-🖩

Houghton Green

Plough 🅛

Mill Lane, WA2 0SU (off Delph Lane) SJ622918
🟢 11.30-11.30 (midnight Fri); 12-11 Sun ☎ (01925) 815409
Sharp's Doom Bar; Thwaites Wainwright; Wells Bombardier 🅷

Although off the beaten track, the Plough is easy to find on Mill Lane. As a Flaming Grill pub it has a good choice of family meals and offers regular themed events such as steak and burger nights. There are usually six real ales on handpump, typically four or five changing, often from local breweries such as George Wright and Weetwood. A popular quiz night is held on Thursday. There is a large car park and outdoor drinking and dining area. ⟶☼❶&P'‑🍺(23,26)

Kettleshulme

Swan
Macclesfield Road, SK23 7QU (on B5470)
✪ 12-11 (midnight Fri & Sat); 12-10.30 Sun
☎ (01663) 732943 ⊕ verynicepubs.co.uk/swankettleshulme
Marston's Burton Bitter; guest beers Ⓗ
Small, idyllic, 15th-century stone building with a quaint interior featuring timber beams, stone fireplaces and an open fire in winter. Two changing guest beers, usually from quality micros, are always available, and a small beer festival takes place in early September. Food is of high quality from an interesting, ever-changing menu (booking advisable; no food Mon). Situated in the Peak District National Park, surrounded by good walking country, families and walkers are welcome. Outside there are two patios for warmer weather. ⋒Q☼☂❶P🍺(60,64)

Knutsford

Cross Keys Hotel Ⓛ
52 King Street, WA16 6DT
✪ 11.30-2.30, 5.30-11; 11.30-midnight Fri & Sat; 11.30-11 Sun ☎ (01565) 750404 ⊕ crosskeysknutsford.com
Copper Dragon Golden Pippin; Jennings Cumberland Ale; Taylor Landlord; guest beers Ⓗ
This former 18th-century coaching inn is now a friendly and lively town-centre pub with modern guest accommodation. The lounge and vault are separated by an unusual wood and glass partition, while the dining area, reached via steps from the lounge, has been converted from the old cellar. A wide choice of sandwiches and pub food is served Tuesday-Sunday lunchtime. Two guest beers are usually available, at least one from a Cheshire brewery. ⋒⟶☼☂❶⬚≒♣P🍺

Lach Dennis

Duke of Portland
Penny's Lane, CW9 7SY (on B5082 1¼ miles off A556)
SJ704720
✪ 12-11 (midnight Fri & Sat); 12-10 Sun ☎ (01606) 46264
⊕ dukeofportland.com
Brakspear Oxford Gold; Marston's Pedigree; guest beers Ⓗ
Popular with local foodies, this public house balances a good dining experience with decent ale provision. Marston's owned, it offers a choice of up to four beers, two regular and two guest. The interior features high ceilings, oak-effect panelling, plenty of comfy leather sofas and a couple of snugs away from the main dining area. With a large fire for the winter months, and a good-sized terrace for the summer, you may well stay for one more drink than you intended. ⋒Q⟶☼❶P'‑

Little Bollington

Swan with Two Nicks Ⓛ
Park Lane, WA14 4TJ (off A56)
✪ 12-11 (10.30 Sun) ☎ (0161) 928 2914
⊕ swanwithtwonicks.co.uk
Black Sheep Best Bitter; Greene King Abbot; Taylor Landlord; guest beers Ⓗ
Welcoming country pub on the fringes of the Dunham Massey National Trust property. The interior is rustic and comprises several rooms with a central bar. Local beers feature on the seven beer engines, up to four from Dunham Massey Brewery. The house beer, Swan With Two Nicks, is from Coach House. A varied food offering including gluten free dishes is available all day until 9pm (8pm Sun), served in the pub and restaurant. Handy for canal boaters, and dogs are welcome. ⋒⟶☼❶⬚P'‑🍺

Macclesfield

Park Tavern Ⓛ
158 Park Lane, SK11 6UB
✪ 4 (12 Sat & Sun)-11 ☎ (01625) 667846
⊕ park-tavern.co.uk
Beer range varies Ⓗ
Town-centre pub built in 1825 with a large bar area, a separate panelled room and an enclosed yard at the rear. It was renovated in a modern style in 2011 and reopened as a free house. An outlet for Bollington Brewery beers, five of its beers are on the bar plus one guest and two real ciders. This is a must-visit pub in Macclesfield and on the Real Ale Trail. Curry nights are Wednesday and Thursday, and roasts are served on Sunday. ⟶☼&≒♦'‑

The Macc Ⓛ
Mill Green, SK11 7PE
✪ 4-11.30 (midnight Thu); 12-midnight Fri & Sat; 11.30-midnight Sun ☎ (01625) 423704
RedWillow Macclesfield Bitter; guest beers Ⓗ
Situated on the route from central Macclesfield to the football ground, this large two-room pub has a lounge bar divided into smaller areas. An excellent free house, it features one house beer from the local RedWillow Brewery and five varying guests from the country's more innovative brewers. An extensive list of bottled world beers is also stocked. Food is available all day. ⋒⟶☼❶⬚≒♣♦'‑🍺

Treacle Tap Ⓛ
43 Sunderland Street, SK11 6JL
✪ 12-11 (midnight Thu-Sat) ☎ (01625) 615938
⊕ thetreacletap.co.uk
Beer range varies Ⓗ
A favourite with the local CAMRA branch. Originally a saddlery, the narrow building has a boarded floor, simple wooden tables and chairs, and a bar at the rear serving three rotating guest beers. One of the best pubs in town for local beer, where friendly bar staff will help you choose. A large selection of bottled Belgian, American and world beers is also available. Excellent pies, charcuterie and cheeses are served all day. Acoustic sessions are held on Sunday afternoons. Q⟶❶≒🍺

Waters Green Tavern Ⓛ
96 Waters Green, SK11 6LH
✪ 12-3, 5.30-11; 12-3, 7-11 Sat; 12-3, 7-10.30 Sun
☎ (01625) 422653
Beer range varies Ⓗ

The first of Macclesfield's free houses continues to delight real ale drinkers. The interior is open plan with two distinct seating areas and a pool room, and bar staff are knowledgeable about the great range of beers on offer. Ales are usually from northern brewers and number up to six, served alongside a real cider or perry. Great-value home-cooked fare is available at lunchtimes and is very popular. A regular in the Guide and a multi CAMRA award winner. ▲❀❁≈♣●'–⊟

Wharf ♈ 𝕃
107 Brook Street, SK11 7AW
❂ 12-midnight ☎ (01625) 261879 ⊕ thewharfmacc.co.uk
Beer range varies ⊞
Family-friendly community pub with a lounge area with comfortable seating, warmed by a real stove in the fireplace, with plenty of books and games on the shelves. Behind the bar is an open wood-floored area with space for darts, pool, live music (on Friday evening) and a TV. The four guests usually include a dark beer and a LocAle. Two ciders and a wide range of bottled British and foreign beers are also on offer. Local CAMRA Pub of the Year 2013. ▲➽❀❁♣●'–⊟

Mobberley
Bull's Head 𝕃
Mill Lane, WA16 7HX
❂ 12-11 (midnight Fri & Sat); 12-10.30 Sun
☎ (01565) 873395 ⊕ thebullsheadpub.co.uk
Weetwood 1812 Overture, Bull's Head Bitter, Mobberley Wobbly; guest beers ⊞
Excellent country inn that bills itself as 'A real pub - local and proud'. The cobbled frontage is a promise of the delights within - low beams, exposed Cheshire brick, stone floors, three open fires, candlelit tables and an old back-to-back fireplace. Six Cheshire beers are part of the pub's ethos, with the house beers brewed by Weetwood. Each handpump has tasting notes and tasters are provided to help you decide. Much of the good freshly cooked fare is locally sourced. ▲➽❀❁♣●P'–⊟

Nantwich
Black Lion 𝕃
29 Welsh Row, CW5 5ED
❂ 12-3 (not Mon), 5-11; 12-11 Sat; 12-10.30 Sun
☎ (01270) 628711 ⊕ blacklion-nantwich.co.uk
Weetwood Best Bitter, Cheshire Cat ⊞
Comfortable black and white timbered pub dating from the 17th century. Three beers from Cheshire brewers Weetwood are always available alongside three guests often from nearby microbreweries such as Phoenix and Northern. Real cider can be found in summer. Quality meals are served in the bar or upstairs restaurant (no food Mon). There are board games, a Monday night quiz and occasional live music. Local CAMRA Town Pub of the Year 2013. ▲❀❁●'–⊟

Crown Hotel 𝕃
24 High Street, CW5 5AS
❂ 10-11.15 (11 Tue) ☎ (01270) 625283
⊕ crownhotelnantwich.co.uk
Woodlands Crown Ale; guest beers ⊞
Grade II-listed building dating from 1583. The traditional bar offers a range of guest beers, often LocAle, and a house ale brewed by Woodlands. The

bar leads to an Italian restaurant. A pianist plays regularly throughout the week and entertainment upstairs includes a monthly film night and live music. The pub hosts an annual Easter jazz and blues festival. Television sports are screened. ▲❡❁❂♣≈P'–⊟(84)

Northwich
Penny Black 𝕃
110 Witton Street, CW9 5AB SJ661740
❂ 8-midnight (1am Fri & Sat) ☎ (01606) 42029
Greene King Abbot; Ruddles Best Bitter; guest beers ⊞
Wetherspoon has done an excellent job of bringing this Grade II-listed former post office, dating from 1914, back to life. Large and mainly open plan, it has TVs screening news channels with subtitles throughout the day. LocAle-accredited, Cheshire-brewed ales are often on the bar as well as at least one darker beer - a mild, stout or porter. The car park is behind the pub off Meadow Street immediately after the Royal Mail sorting office. A former local CAMRA Pub of the Year. Q❀❀❁♣≈●P'–⊟

Penketh
Ferry Tavern 𝕃
Station Road, WA5 2UJ (across railway and canal from end of Station Rd) SJ563866
❂ 12-3, 5.30-11; 12-11 Sat; 12-10.30 Sun ☎ (01925) 791117
⊕ theferrytavern.com
Greene King Abbot; Ruddles County; guest beers ⊞
The Ferry Tavern has been a favourite with CAMRA members, walkers, sailors, cyclists and music lovers for many years. Its enthusiastic young licensees and staff constantly provide new activities to entertain both locals and visitors. Up to three interesting guest ales are served. The scenic location between the River Mersey and St Helens Canal has had its drawbacks - check the high water marks on the bar. The large garden is usually packed in the summer and appeals to all age ranges. ▲❀♣P

Poynton
Poynton British Legion 𝕃
St George's Road West, SK12 1JY (off A523)
❂ 12-midnight (11 Mon-Thu); 12-10.30 Sun
☎ (01625) 873 120 ⊕ poyntonlegionclub.co.uk
Beer range varies ⊞
Spacious private members' club offering a minimum of four handpulled beers, two from the on-site Worth brewery and two from micros. A comfortable and quiet lounge drinking area is complemented by a public bar with two snooker tables and a large-screen TV. A function room and bowling green are available for hire. Monthly folk, quiz and jazz nights are hosted. For free entry show a CAMRA membership card or a copy of this Guide. Winner of several Greater Manchester Club of the Year awards. ❀❐♣≈♣●P'–⊟

Rainow
Robin Hood 𝕃
Chapel Brow, SK10 5XE
❂ 4.30-11 (midnight Wed); 12-midnight Thu-Sun
☎ (01625) 574060 ⊕ robinhood-rainow.co.uk
Black Sheep Best Bitter; guest beers ⊞

This pleasant rural pub has recently been refurbished and is situated on the left hand side of the B5470 in Rainow, just in the Peak district. It features a large car park and garden along with a covered smoking area. Food is served throughout the pub lunchtimes and evenings. Up to six beers are available according to the day of week, three of these being LocAle. Accomodation is available in three en-suite rooms in the adjacent barn.
⚄Q☼🏠🍴◑🅱P⌐🚐

Runcorn

Ferry Boat ℓ
Church Street, WA7 1LR
✪ 8-11 ☎ (01928) 583380
Greene King IPA; Marston's Pedigree; Ruddles County H
Named after the ferry service that used to ply between Runcorn and Widnes, the pub is located in the centre of Runcorn old town opposite the bus station. This ex-cinema, a typical Wetherspoon conversion, is spacious inside with a separate family area, and outside seating to the front and rear. Regular Meet the Brewer evenings are held.
☼🅰◑🅱🚐P⌐🚐

Lion
Greenway Road, WA7 5AG
✪ 12-11 (10.30 Sun)
Adnams Old Ale; Cains IPA H
Edge-of-town pub, about 200 yards from the railway station, whose recent refurbishment has given it a modern, fresh new look, with the bar the central focus in a bright, open room. The new owners' dedication to cask ale is reflected in the variety of different beers on offer during the short space of time since the pub reopened. ⇌🚐

Prospect 🏆 ℓ
Weston Road, Weston Village, WA7 4LD
✪ 12-11 (10.30 Sun) ☎ (01928) 561280
⊕ folkattheprospect.co.uk
Adnams Broadside; Taylor Landlord H
A traditional two-room pub on the outskirts of Weston village, serving a range of beers from three handpumps. This is the meeting place for a well-established local folk scene. The bar area has an unusual decor featuring vinyl 45s and LPs. No food is served on Sunday evening.
⚄🅰◑🅰🚐⇌♣P⌐🚐(3A,3C)

Sandbach

Lower Chequer ℓ
Crown Bank, CW11 1FW
✪ 12 (6 Mon-Wed; 5 Thu)-11 summer; 1 (6 Mon-Wed; 5 Thu)-11 winter; 12 (1 winter)-10.30 Sun ☎ 07932 943977
Wood Shropshire Lad; guest beers H
A warm welcome is assured from the award-winning licensees who have rejuvenated this black and white timbered pub set back on the cobbled square. Dating from 1570, the interior has two rooms and outside there is seating to the front and a marquee and patio to the rear. Six real ales are available, all from small breweries, with regulars plus local and regional ales. A porter, mild or stout is always on offer as well as a cider and a perry. A former CAMRA Champion Pub of Cheshire.
Q🅰♣P⌐🚐(38)

Old Hall ℓ
High Street, CW11 1Al
✪ 10.30-11; 12-10.30 Sun ☎ (01270) 758170
Brunning & Price Original Bitter; RedWillow Feckless; Three Tuns XXX; guest beers H
This magnificent 16th-century black and white timbered hall has been rescued after several years of deterioration by a high-quality restoration by the Brunning & Price chain. The original Tudor beamed walls, fireplace and wood panelling at the front of the building blend well with upmarket dining areas and a modern conservatory at the rear. A bar area as you enter displays the six beers on handpump, all from small breweries. ⚄Q☼🅰◑🅱P⌐

Sarn

Queen's Head
SY14 7LN (off B5069)
✪ closed Mon; 6-midnight; 12-11 Sun ☎ (01948) 770244
⊕ queensheadsarn.co.uk
Taylor Golden Best; guest beer H
This welcoming village inn, known locally as the Sarn, is adjacent to a converted water mill on Wych Brook that marks the boundary with Wales. Excellent-value home-cooked meals are served in the homely dining room while drinkers congregate in the convivial lounge. There is also a small games room. Up to two guest beers are on offer, one often from a local microbrewery, and the pub provides a rare outlet for Taylor's light mild.
⚄Q🅰◑🅰🅰♣P⌐

Scholar Green

Rising Sun
Station Road, ST7 3JT (off A34)
✪ 12-3, 5-11.30; 9.30-midnight Fri; 12-midnight Sat & Sun ☎ (01782) 776235 ⊕ risingsuncheshire.co.uk
Jennings Cocker Hoop; Marston's Burton Bitter, Pedigree H
Welcoming pub nestling next to fields on the edge of the village, with a fine view up to Mow Cop. There is a comfortable seating area with a real fire around a central bar, with a wood-beamed ceiling adding to the homely feel. The landlord makes good use of the Marston's range, with two seasonal guest ales, often one from Ringwood, always available. A full range of good-value meals is served in the bar and adjoining restaurant.
⚄🅰◑♣P⌐

Spurstow

Yew Tree ℓ
Long Lane, CW6 9RD
✪ 12-11; 11-10.30 Sun ☎ 01829 260074
⊕ theyewtreebunbury.com
Merlin Merlin's Gold; Stonehouse Station Bitter; guest beers H
Handsome, 19th-century village pub – the interior features real fires, old beams and a large circular bar. At least six real ales are on offer, including two house beers. An excellent food menu offers freshly made, locally sourced food from a seasonal menu. Numerous special events are hosted throughout the year. A well-maintained outdoor area is popular in the warmer months, and car parking is available. Well worth the effort to seek out this great pub. ⚄Q🅰◑🅰♣P⌐

Sutton

Church House
Church Lane, SK11 0DS
✪ 12-midnight ☎ (01260) 252436
Banks's Bitter; Robinsons Unicorn; guest beer Ⓗ
This is a popular locals' pub boosted in visitor numbers by walkers and cyclists. The menu provides good home-cooked food with plenty of variety. The drinks selection is also ample, with two permanent beers on offer plus three guest ales from local microbreweries. Outside, there is space for a smoking area and also the occasional summer beer festival held beside the car park. The pub is a lovely stroll uphill from a Camping Club site. Families and dogs are made welcome.
ᐃᗡ♨◑ᴧ♣P╘₋₪

Sutton Hall Ⓛ
Bullocks Lane, SK11 0HE
✪ 11.30-11; 12-10.30 Sun ☎ (01260) 253211
⊕ suttonhall.co.uk
Brunning & Price Original Bitter; Flowers Original; Wincle Lord Lucan; guest beers Ⓗ
Splendid 480-year-old manor house set in its own grounds, close to the Macclesfield Canal. Tastefully refurbished by Brunning & Price, the interior is notable for its many secluded spaces, snug, library and seven dining areas. While there is a strong food focus and an excellent menu, drinkers are most welcome to enjoy the five real ales on offer, often from local breweries. Complemented by lovely gardens, this is a real gem.
ᐃQᗡ♨◑ᴧP╘₋₪

Tushingham

Blue Bell Ⓛ
Bradley Farm Lane, SY13 4QS (signed Bell o' t' Hill from A41, 4 miles N of Whitchurch)
✪ closed Mon; 12-2, 6-11; 12-3, 7-11 Sun ☎ (01948) 662172
⊕ bluebellinn.net
Oakham JHB; Salopian Shropshire Gold; guest beer Ⓗ
Originally built around 1530 and extended in 1667, this magnificent timber-framed pub is Grade II-listed and retains many ancient features such as the cobblestones leading to a sturdy oak front door. One wall in the dining room reveals part of the original wattle and daub. Beers are mainly from local Cheshire and Shropshire breweries, and home-cooked food is served. Well-behaved dogs are welcome in the main bar. Four caravan pitches are available for hire in the paddock.
ᐃQᗡ♨◑ᴧ♣P

Warrington

Bull's Head
33 Church Street, WA1 2SX
✪ 12 (Tue 1)-11 (11.30 Thu-Sat) ☎ (01925) 575730
Beer range varies Ⓗ
A 17th-century inn with modern additions to the interior. A popular sport pub, it has TV screens in all public areas, a pool table and an excellent bowling green. A choice of three real ales is usually available, typically from Copper Dragon or Sharp's. Although very close to the town centre and handy for public transport, Church Street is relatively quiet, making for a relaxed atmosphere. The venue for a noted acoustic music night on Sundays.
Q➣⇌(Central)♣╘₋₪

Lower Angel Ⓛ
27 Buttermarket Street, WA1 2LY
✪ 11-11 (midnight Fri; 12.30am Sat); 12-10 Sun
☎ (01925) 653326 ⊕ lowerangel.co.uk
Tetley Bitter; Tipsy Angel Dark Mild; guest beers Ⓗ
Small Victorian gem in the town centre. The two-roomed pub has a traditional vault and lounge, and a beer garden overlooking the Tipsy Angel Brewery. The main outlet for Tipsy Angel brews, there are eight handpumps dispensing two regular beers and an ever-changing range of guests. The vault has a top shelf of more than 80 malt whiskies. ♨Ɽ⇌(Central)╘₋₪

Tavern Ⓛ
25 Church Street, WA1 2SS
✪ 2-11; 12-midnight Fri & Sat; 12-11 Sun ☎ (07789) 151610
Beer range varies Ⓗ
Celebrating 15 consecutive years in the Guide, the Tavern is the main outlet for 4T's Brewery. The Sports Bar offers eight beers mainly from microbreweries during the week, with four more beers added in the Music Bar at weekends. The two bars are connected by a covered beer garden. An range of whiskies, vodkas and brandy is stocked as well as bottled Belgian beers. Sport features on several large screens. A friendly welcome awaits you at this pub. ♨⇌(Central)♣╘₋₪

Widnes

Church View
Lunts Heath Road, WA8 5RY
✪ 12-11 (11.30 Fri & Sat); 12-10.30 Sun ☎ (0151) 424 3296
Wells Bombardier; Morland Old Speckled Hen Ⓗ
Large estate-side family pub on the edge of town with the emphasis on food. The open-plan split-level interior is tastefully decorated in pastel shades. Food is served until 10pm (9pm Sun). Live music plays most weekends and a weekly quiz night is held. Qᗡ♨◑ᴧP╘₋₪(6,7A)

Willaston

Nag's Head Ⓛ
Hooton Road, CH64 1SJ
✪ 11-11 (midnight Fri & Sat; 10.30 Sun) ☎ (0151) 328 0808
⊕ thenagswillaston.co.uk
Wells Bombardier; York Guzzler; guest beer Ⓗ
Nestled in historic Willaston village – famous for its mill and the preserved station of Hadlow Road – the Nag's Head has risen from obscurity to a friendly village local. Refurbished in 2011, the pub combines good food and good beer served in warm, relaxed surroundings. Food available all day ranges from light bites to full meals. Popular with locals, tourists and walkers. Qᗡ♨◑♣P₪

Winsford

Queen's Arms Ⓛ
Dene Drive, CW7 1AT
✪ 9-midnight ☎ (01606) 595350
Greene King Abbot; Ruddles Best Bitter; guest beers Ⓗ
Classic Wetherspoon establishment close to the Winsford Cross shopping centre. It has TV screens at both ends of the bar room with the sound usually muted. There are comfortable seating and dining areas, a patio to the front and a roof terrace providing fresh air in the summer and, for the more hardy, winter. ᗡ♨◑ᴧ♣P╘₋₪

CORNWALL

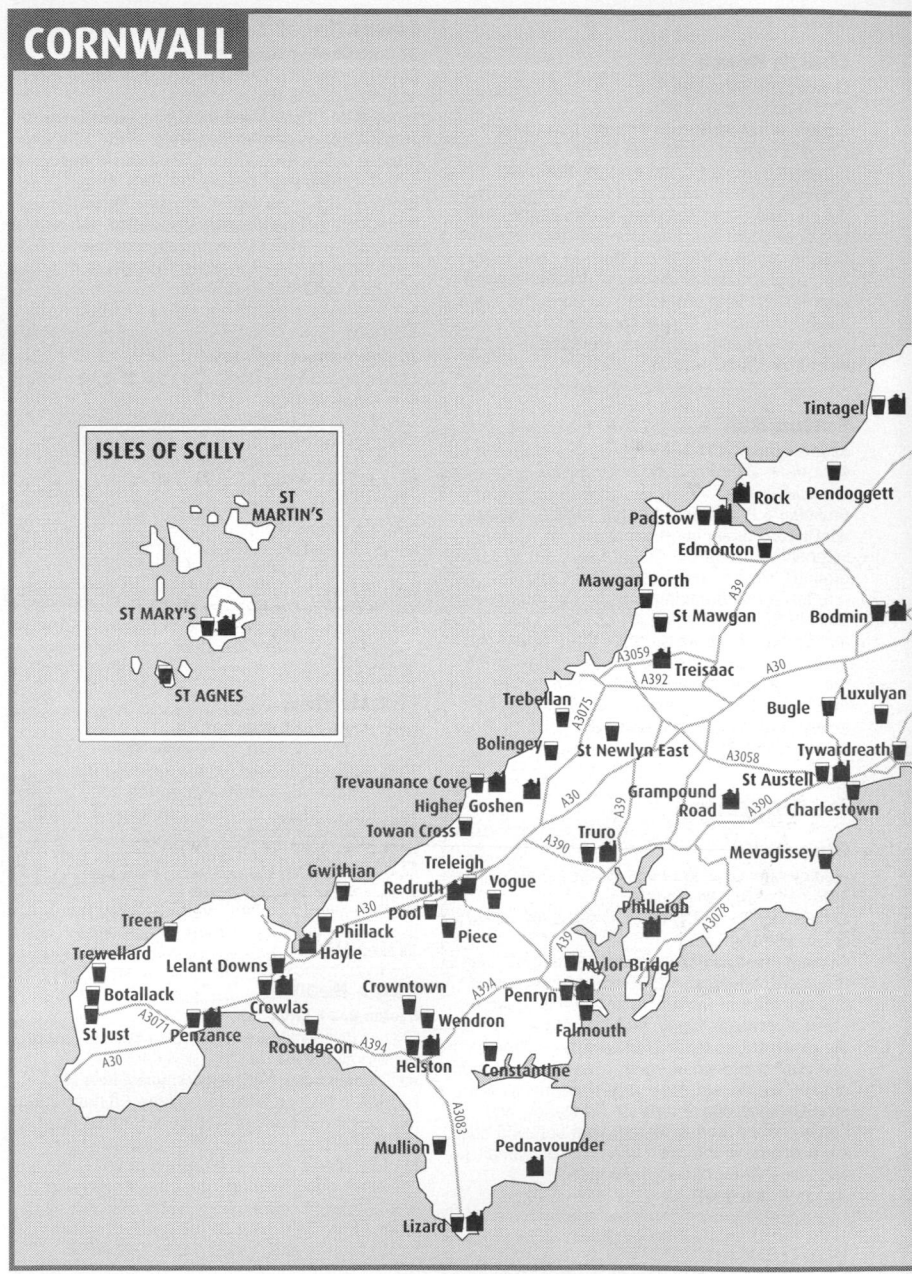

ISLES OF SCILLY

ST MARTIN'S

ST MARY'S

ST AGNES

Tintagel

Rock   Pendoggett

Padstow

Edmonton

Mawgan Porth

St Mawgan   Bodmin

Treisaac   Luxulyan

Trebellan   Bugle

Bolingey   St Newlyn East   Tywardreath

Trevaunance Cove   St Austell

Higher Goshen   Grampound   Charlestown

Towan Cross   Road

Truro   Mevagissey

Treleigh

Gwithian   Vogue

Redruth

Treen   Pool   Phlleigh

Trewellard   Phillack   Piece

Lelant Downs   Hayle

Botallack   Mylor Bridge

Crowlas   Crowntown   Penryn

St Just   Wendron   Falmouth

Penzance   Rosudgeon

Helston   Constantine

Mullion   Pednavounder

Lizard

Altarnun

Rising Sun Inn [L]

PL15 7SN (1 mile off A30, N of Five Lanes) SX216824

✪ 12-2.30, 5.30-11; 12-11 Sat; 12-10.30 Sun

☎ (01566) 86636 ⏏ therisingsuninn.co.uk

Penpont St Nonna's, Shipwreck Coast; Skinner's Betty Stogs; guest beers [H]

This characterful building on the outskirts of Altarnun has been a pub for 150 years, and always enjoys good community support. The interior is cosy and warm, with beamed ceilings, open fireplaces, and pictures and antique guns decorating the walls. Deceptively spacious, the pub offers ample seating in the bar area and a separate restaurant, although you can also eat in the bar. Food is prepared using locally-sourced produce where possible. The pub is family-friendly and dogs are welcome. ♨Q❄☎❀◗♿▲♣♠P☖🚲

Blisland

Blisland Inn [L]

The Green, PL30 4JF (off A30 N of Bodmin) SX100732

✪ 11.30-11; 12-10.30 Sun ☎ (01208) 850739

Beer range varies [H]/[G]

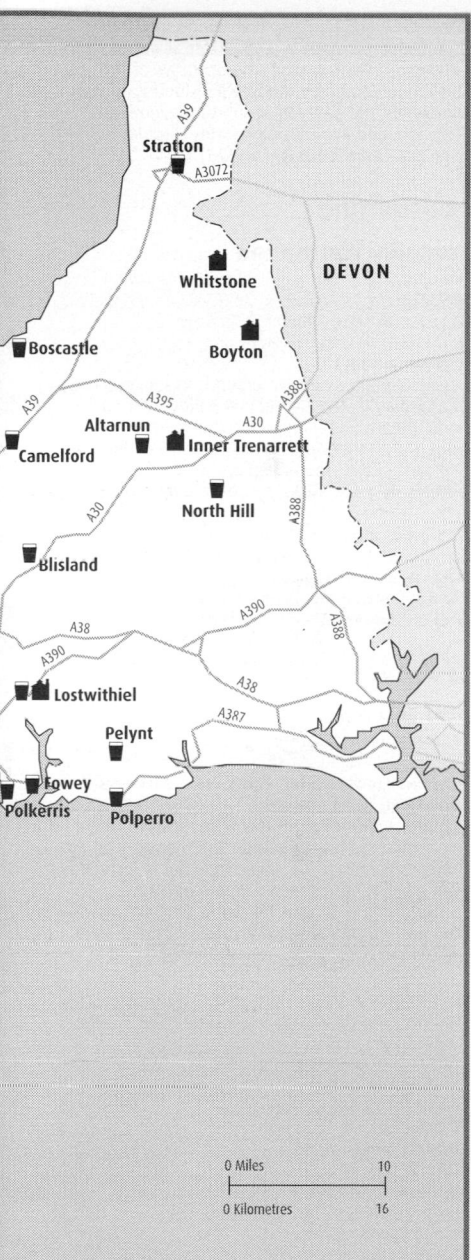

Friendly rural community pub sited in an idyllic location by the village green on the edge of Bodmin Moor that has long had a reputation as a real ale centre of excellence. More than 3,000 different real ales have been dispensed over the years, with six or seven usually available at any one time with at least two brewed locally. Real ciders, including more unusual and hard-to-find examples, are also offered. Good, freshly prepared food is served, often featuring locally-sourced ingredients. Popular with walkers and cyclists, well-behaved children and dogs are also welcome. Q❄☆⍟◑⌷▲♣⌑

Bodmin

Chapel an Gansblydhen 🄻
Fore Street, PL31 2HR SX068670
❄ 8am-midnight ☎ (01208) 261730
Greene King Abbot; Ruddles Best Bitter; guest beers 🄷
This town centre pub has been converted from a former Methodist chapel, with many original features restored or retained. Four real ales are on offer, mostly from Cornish microbreweries, with two draught ciders also available. The pub pioneered the Wetherspoon Ale Club which meets every Wednesday and includes events such as Meet the Brewer evenings, tutored tastings and beer quizzes. Two beer festivals and a real cider festival are held annually, and a popular quiz night on Sunday. ⌂Q❄☆◑⌷♿▲♣⌑'–🛏(529,555,593)

Masons Arms 🄻
5-7 Higher Bore Street, PL31 1JS (top of town centre)
❄ 12-11.30 (11 Sun) ☎ (01208) 77442
Sharp's Cornish Coaster; Tintagel Keystone; guest beers 🄷
A welcoming two-bar free house close to the town centre and near the Camel Trail. Three real ales are always on offer with the emphasis on local breweries. Two beer festivals are held annually. Entertainment includes a quiz night on Tuesday and Trigg Morris on Thursday; Bodmin Folk Club meet here every Friday. A beer garden with a grassed area is at the rear of the pub. Free Wi-Fi is available, and there is a large function room for hire. ⌂Q❄☆◑⌷♣P'–🛏(529,555)

Bolingey

Bolingey Inn 🄻
Penwartha Road, TR6 0DH SW763532
❄ 11-midnight (1am Fri & Sat); 12-11 Sun ☎ (01872) 571626
Sharp's Doom Bar; guest beers 🄷
There is always a warm welcome from the licensees at this quaint two-roomed village inn, with four beers on handpump from local breweries or further afield. Two annual beer festivals maintain the interest. Substantial home-cooked meals are available. Worth seeking out, the pub is a short but well-hidden distance from the brighter lights of Perranporth and its excellent golden beach. The car park is small, but daytime buses are a short (if a little hilly) walk away. ⌂Q☆◑▲♣P'–🛏(587)

Boscastle

Napoleon Inn
High Street, PL35 0BD (top of village on Tintagel side) SX099907
❄ 11-11 ☎ (01840) 250204 ⊕ napoleoninn.co.uk
St Austell Dartmoor Best Bitter, Trelawny, Tribute, HSD 🄶
Comfortable 16th-century inn in upper Boscastle, reputedly once a recruiting centre for press gangs. Tribute and HSD are always available, plus a lower strength beer in summer. Several drinking areas on different levels cluster around the central bar. One room is simply furnished with wooden settles, tables and chairs, and hosts the TV and dartboard. The larger beamed lounge is divided into three areas and a restaurant. Local singers perform on Tuesday nights, other live music plays on Fridays and summer Wednesdays. ⌂Q❄☆◑⌷♣P'–🛏(594,595)

Botallack

Queen's Arms 🄻

St Just, TR19 7QG (off B3306) SW368328
❂ 12-11.30 (12.30am Fri & Sat) ☎ (01736) 788318
⊕ queensarms-botallack.co.uk
Beer range varies 🄷
Deep in Penwith mining country, this is a charming, family-run and family-friendly free house in a granite village. A warm welcome is assured in the pub. Although a single bar, it has several distinct drinking and dining areas including a separate family room. The pleasant décor depicts mining scenes reflecting the once-dominant local industry. Up to four ales, usually from Cornish microbreweries, are offered, and imaginative meals are served. An annual beer festival is held in the spacious beer garden in September.
🏚Q⏰✹🍴◑ ⋏P⁵⊷⊟(10,507,300)

Bugle

Bugle Inn 🄻

57 Fore Street, PL26 8PB (on A391) SX015589
❂ 10-midnight ☎ (01726) 850307 ⊕ bugleinn.co.uk
St Austell Dartmoor Best Bitter, Tribute, Proper Job 🄷
This family-run village-centre pub is welcoming and lively, with plenty of local banter in the bar. Situated in the heart of china clay country, its comfortable and spacious interior accommodates a Z-shaped bar with several dining areas, open fires, and an interesting collection of carved coconuts and witch effigies. Hearty home-cooked meals, starting with breakfast, are served all day. With five en-suite rooms, this family-friendly pub provides an ideal base for visiting the nearby Eden Project and other local attractions.
🏚⏰✹🍴◑⋏≉♣P⁵⊷⊟(529)

Camelford

Masons Arms

11 Market Place, PL32 9PB (on A39) SX106837
❂ 11-midnight ☎ (01840) 213309
St Austell Trelawny, Tribute, Proper Job 🄷
Family-friendly, unpretentious two-room pub with stone walls and low beamed ceilings, over 300 years old and popular with locals; well-behaved children and dogs are welcome. The public bar has part-tiled, part-wood floors, and the separate lounge has a flagstone floor. Many interesting knick-knacks are on display such as long-vanished domestic products, old toys, and an eclectic collection of bottles, jugs and tankards suspended from the beams. The beer garden overlooks an early stage of the River Camel.
🏚Q⏰✹◑⊟⋏♣⁵⊷⊟(510,584,594)

Charlestown

Harbourside Inn 🄻

Charlestown Road, PL25 3NJ (on harbour front) SX029516
❂ 11-11 (midnight Fri & Sat); 12-11 Sun ☎ (01726) 68051
⊕ pierhousehotel.com/harbourside_inn_in_cornwall.htm
Draught Bass; St Austell Tribute; Sharp's Doom Bar; Skinner's Betty Stogs, Cornish Knocker; guest beer 🄷
With up to seven real ales available, this lively, sport-oriented pub beside the historic harbour is a popular watering hole, especially with television and film crews on location. Features of the single-bar interior include exposed stonework and mixed

slate and wood flooring, with wood furnishings throughout. Formerly a harbourside warehouse, its expansive glass frontage affords views of the tall ships moored nearby. Good-value food is served throughout the day. Major sporting events are screened, and live music plays on Saturday evenings. ✹🍴◑▸&⋏♣⁵⊷⊟(525)

Constantine

Trengilly Wartha Inn 🄻

Nancenoy, TR11 5RP (off B329 near Constantine) SW732283
❂ 11-3, 6-midnight; 12-midnight Sat & Sun
☎ (01326) 340332 ⊕ trengilly.co.uk
Beer range varies 🄷
Versatile inn in extensive grounds including a lake, in an isolated steeply wooded valley – the pub's name means 'settlement above the trees'. Originally a farmhouse, it has a variety of furniture and rooms, the wood-beamed bar displaying pictures by local artists. A conservatory extension serves as the family room. The three varied real ales are mainly from Cornish microbreweries. The Trengilly's other emphasis is on fresh food, with a wide-ranging and imaginative menu using mostly Cornish produce and presented with flair.
🏚Q⏰✹🍴◑♣P⁵⟋

Crowlas

Star Inn 🏆 🄻

TR20 8DX (on A30 just E of Penzance) SW516332
❂ 11.30-11; 12-10.30 Sun ☎ (01736) 740375
Penzance Crowlas Bitter, Potion No 9, Brisons Bitter, Scilly Stout; guest beers 🄷
Cornwall CAMRA Pub of the Year for 2013, this impressive red-brick roadside free house is an ale drinker's paradise. The single long bar is festooned with handpumps, dispensing an ever-changing range of real ales from the pub's own brewhouse plus beers from around the country. A real locals' pub where beer quality reigns supreme and

INDEPENDENT BREWERIES

Ales of Scilly St Mary's
Atlantic Treisaac
Blue Anchor Helston
Castle Lostwithiel
Coastal Redruth
Cornish Chough Lizard
Cornish Crown Penzance
Driftwood Trevaunance Cove
Fry's Boyton
Green Room Redruth
Harbour Bodmin
Hogswood Higher Goshen
Keltek Redruth
Lizard Pednavounder
Longhill Whitstone
Padstow Padstow (NEW)
Paradise Hayle
Penpont Inner Trenarrett
Penzance Crowlas
Rebel Penryn
Roseland Philleigh
Sharp's (Molson Coors) Rock
Skinner's Truro
St Austell St Austell
Tintagel Tintagel
Wooden Hand Grampound Road

conversation abounds – no music, TV or noisy machines. Best to come by bus (stop nearby), as you will stay a while. Q❀♣●P⁂–🚌(17,18)

Crowntown

Crown Inn

TR13 0AD (on B3303 between Camborne and Helston) SW637309

⏲ 5.30-11; 7-10.30 Sun ☎ (01326) 565538

🌐 crownlodges.co.uk

Beer range varies H

Spacious granite community pub, once a Trevarno estate hunting lodge and about 250 years old. There are several distinct drinking areas, a dining area (with an old Gothic arched doorway), and a separate space for the pool table. The varied choice of beers is mainly but not exclusively Cornish, dispensed straight from the cellar despite the array of four handpumps. Real cider is from Westons. An interesting collection of beer mats and tankards festoons the beams. Accommodation is in four en-suite lodges. ❀❀🛏◑♿♣●P⁂

Edmonton

Quarryman Inn L

PL27 7JA (off A39 near Royal Cornwall Showground) SW965727

⏲ 12-11 ☎ (01208) 816444 🌐 thequarryman.co.uk

St Austell Proper Job; guest beers H

A diversion to this ever-popular gem of a pub, close to the County Showground, well rewards the effort. Conversation and banter thrive in this characterful and convivial free house where mobile phone usage is prohibited. Frequented by locals and tourists alike, the quiet, comfortable interior divides into a public bar and larger lounge with dining area. Local art features among the somewhat eclectic decor. An ever-changing beer menu offers up to four quality ales, and the excellent cuisine is locally sourced. ♨Q❀🛏◐◑⊟Å♣P⁂–🚌(510,555,594)

Falmouth

'front L

Custom House Quay, TR11 3JT (behind Trago Mills) SW811325

⏲ 11-11.30 (midnight Fri & Sat); 11-11 Sun ☎ 07593 811734

Beer range varies H/G

This friendly cellar-style former CAMRA National Pub of the Year finalist offers a wide choice of frequently changing beers from near and far, always including some brews from Skinner's and other local micros. Porters and golden ales are usually represented along with a wide choice of ciders, foreign beers and locally produced ginger beer. It can be busy in the evenings, with musical entertainment sometimes provided. No food, but you can bring your own. ❀⇌(Town)●🚌

5 Degrees West

Grove Place, TR11 4AU SW812323

⏲ 11-midnight (1am Fri & Sat) ☎ (01326) 311288

🌐 5degreesfalmouth.co.uk

St Austell Tribute; Sharp's Special; Skinner's Porthleven H**; guest beers** H/G

Spacious, airy two-level pub/bistro bar on two floors, the more food-oriented section above street level and the pub proper down in the basement. The upstairs room offers views across the harbour, and leads to an outside patio for open-air drinking and barbecues in warmer weather. Three or four local ciders are offered alongside the ales. Downstairs, the bar has the feel of a student nightclub, opening at 9pm for late beer drinking and live entertainment. ♨❀❀◐◑⇌(Town)●⁂–🚌

Boathouse L

Trevethan Hill, TR11 2AG

⏲ 4 (12 Fri-Sun)-midnight ☎ (01326) 315425

Beer range varies H

Large, family-oriented pub on two floors, up a short but steep hill on the edge of the town centre. The interior is decorated like a wooden boat; there is also a decked balcony for outdoor drinking with impressive river views. The four beers vary but at least two are normally Cornish, and local brewery Rebel is usually represented. The cider is frequently varied and may be something unusual for the area. Food is served 12-2.30 Friday-Sunday and 6-9 all week. ♨❀❀◐◑⇌♣●⁂–🚌

Seven Stars ★ L

The Moor, TR11 3QA

⏲ 11-3, 6-11; 12-3, 7-10.30 Sun ☎ (01326) 312111

Draught Bass; Sharp's Special; Skinner's Cornish Knocker; guest beers G

Grade II-listed and unspoilt, this town-centre drinkers' pub has been run by the same family for several generations. The interior comprises a narrow taproom at the front, a quieter snug to the rear, and a passageway with the original bottle & jug hatch. Note the collection of key fobs from around the world, and mobile phones nailed to the wall as a warning – their use is discouraged. No food, but you can bring your own and eat it on benches outside. Q❀⊟⇌(Town)⁂–🚌

Fowey

Galleon Inn

12 Fore Street, PL23 1AQ

⏲ 10-11 (midnight summer); 11-11 Sun ☎ (01726) 833014

🌐 galleon-inn.co.uk

Sharp's Cornish Coaster, Doom Bar; Skinner's Betty Stogs; guest beers H

Riverside pub in the town centre dating back 400 years, now fully modernised. Reached off Fore Street through a glass-covered corridor with a colourful marine life mural, it is the only free house in Fowey. It features mainly Cornish ales and boasts delightful harbour views from the main bar and conservatory. Tables outside overlook the water and there is a heated, sheltered courtyard. A wide range of meals is available daily. Accommodation is en suite, some rooms affording river views. ♨Q❀🛏◐◑⁂–🚌(25,524,525)

Gwithian

Red River Inn L

1 Prosper Hill, TR27 5BW SW586411

⏲ closed Mon winter; 12-2, 5.30-11; 12-11 Sat & Sun

☎ (01736) 753223 🌐 red-river-inn.com

Sharp's Own; guest beers H

Worth seeking out near the dunes of Hayle Towans, this community-oriented, family-friendly free house named after the nearby river recently added a general store, now effectively the village shop. Its quiet, relaxing single-bar interior accommodates both drinking and dining. Wood dominates the furnishings, and a wood-burning

stove adds winter warmth. Besides Sharp's Own, up to four further ales are available, two generally from Cornish breweries. Freshly cooked meals using local produce are served daily. A beer festival is held every Easter.
🏚Q🛏🐕🍴◐🕭⚅Å♠P⚲🖳(515,547)

Helston

Blue Anchor
50 Coinagehall Street, TR13 8EU SW658274
✪ 10.30-midnight (11 Sun) ☎ (01326) 562821
🌐 spingoales.com
Blue Anchor Flora Daze, Jubilee IPA, Ben's Stout, Spingo Middle, Spingo Special, seasonal beer ℍ
More than 600 years old, this thatched former monks' hospice is one of the oldest brewpubs in Britain. It has changed little over the years, with its two small bars to the right and a sitting room to the left, all with well-worn granite floors. At the rear are a skittle alley and a partly covered garden where barbecues can be held, each with its own bar. Regular live entertainment, beer festivals and charity events are held throughout the year.
🏚Q🛏🐕🍴⚅🕭♣⚲🖳

Lelant Downs

Watermill Inn 🄻
Old Coach Road, TR27 6LQ (off A3074, on secondary St Ives road) SW541364
✪ 12-11 ☎ (01736) 757912 🌐 watermillincornwall.co.uk
Skinner's Betty Stogs; guest beers ℍ
Near Lelant Saltings station, this family-friendly two-storey free house stands in beautiful surroundings. A former 18th-century mill house, its original working watermill complete with millstones features downstairs in the single bar. The comfortable interior divides into separate drinking and dining areas, where bar meals are served. Upstairs, the former mill loft functions as a stylish evenings-only restaurant. An extensive beer garden, where beer festivals are held annually in June and November, straddles the mill stream. Live music plays on Friday evenings.
🏚Q🛏🐕🍴◐Å≉(Lelant Saltings)P⚲🖳(14,17)

Lizard

Witch Ball 🄻
TR12 7NJ SW704125
✪ 12 (5 Mon-Wed)-11; 12-midnight Sat winter; 12-11 (midnight Thu-Sat) summer; 12-11 Sun ☎ (01326) 290662
🌐 witchball.co.uk
Cornish Chough Kynance Blonde; St Austell Tribute; guest beer ℍ
Old farm cottage and former restaurant converted to a popular village pub – entrance is via a pathway through a large roadside seating area at the front. The small bar has a very low original black-beamed ceiling. A dining area is to the left, seating for drinkers to the right, and a stove by the centre wall warms proceedings in winter. A lively charity beer festival is held here every August with barbecue and live bands in attendance.
🏚🛏🐕🍴⚅Å♣⚲🖳(37)

Lostwithiel

Globe Inn 🄻
3 North Street, PL22 0EG SX105598

✪ 12-2.30, 6-11 (5-midnight Fri; 6-midnight Sat)
☎ (01208) 872501 🌐 globeinn.com
Sharp's Doom Bar; Skinner's Betty Stogs; guest beers ℍ
In the narrow streets of this ancient stannary town, close to the railway station, you will find this cosy 13th-century free house. An old, rambling building, it features a single bar with several drinking and dining areas, and to the rear an intimate restaurant and sheltered suntrap patio. The varying beer menu includes up to two guests, generally from microbreweries. Fish and game are specialities on an extensive menu of home-cooked food, prepared using seasonal local produce. All accommodation is en suite. 🏚Q🐕🛌◐Å≉♣⚲

Luxulyan

King's Arms
Bridges, PL30 5EF SX048580
✪ 10-midnight Mar-Oct; 11-11 (midnight Fri & Sat) Nov-Feb; 11.30-midnight Sun ☎ (01726) 850202
St Austell Trelawny, Tribute, Proper Job, HSD ℍ
Granite inn, known locally as Bridges, with one large bar divided into two areas, and a skittle alley in an outbuilding. The pub offers breakfast from 8.30am to noon in summer, takeaways and a Sunday roast. It has a PayPoint terminal and a defibrillator kit for heart attacks. Nearby are the beautiful Luxulyan Valley, famous for its wildlife and industrial archaeology, and the Eden Project. Luxulyan is a request stop on the Atlantic Coast Line Rail Ale Trail. Q🛏🐕🍴◐⚅Å≉♣P⚲🖳(523)

Mawgan Porth

Merrymoor 🄻
TR8 4BA (beside B3276 coast road)
✪ 10-11.30 ☎ (01637) 860258 🌐 merrymoorinn.com
St Austell Tribute; Sharp's Doom Bar, Own; guest beers ℍ
Atmospheric pub run by the same family since 1961. The spacious main bar with its picture windows overlooking the sandy beach just 50 yards away is supplemented by a separate family room and large beer garden. Locally sourced food is cooked on the premises, with a carvery on Sundays. This pub is at the heart of the local community and raises large sums for charity every year. There is ample parking, and accommodation in seven en-suite rooms.
Q🛏🐕🛌◐⚅Å P⚲🖳(556)

Mevagissey

Fountain Inn
3 Cliff Street, PL26 6QH
✪ 12-midnight ☎ (01726) 842320
St Austell Dartmoor Best Bitter, Tribute, HSD ℍ
Friendly two-bar 15th-century inn near the harbour, with slate floors, stone walls and low-beamed ceilings. The decor includes historic photographs and paintings of old Mevagissey. The Smugglers Bar once housed a pilchard press – a glass plate in the floor covers the pit where the fish oil was collected, which also served as a store for contraband. The varied menu offers a range of home-cooked dishes. Nearby buses connect with St Austell and the Lost Gardens of Heligan.
🏚Q🛌◐🕭♣🖳(524,525,526)

Mullion

Mounts Bay Inn
Churchtown, TR12 7HN
🌣 11-11 (midnight Fri & Sat); 12-10.30 Sun
☎ (01326) 240221 ⊕ mountsbaymullion.co.uk
Sharp's Doom Bar; guest beers Ⓗ
This light and airy pub with a modern wood interior is in the village centre. Intimate tables by the entrance lead to the main bar, with its plentiful seating beyond. One wall is mostly glass, overlooking the suntrap garden with its picnic tables and smoking area. A separate dining room is adorned with photographs of the village and surrounding area over the years. Up to three varying guest ales are usually Cornish. Draught cider is available in summer.
Ⓩ❀✿◖ዑ& ♣ ✿ ⌐ Ⓜ(37)

Mylor Bridge

Lemon Arms
Lemon Hill, TR11 5NA (off A393 at Penryn) SW804362
🌣 11-3, 6.30-11; 12-3, 7-11 Sun ☎ (01326) 373666
St Austell Trelawny, Tribute Ⓗ
There has been a hostelry on this site since 1765. Once called the Griffin Inn, it became the Red Lion in 1829 and took its present name in 1837. A friendly one-bar pub in the centre of the village, it is home to local sports teams. Good home-cooked food is available (booking for the popular Sunday lunches is advisable). Families with children are made most welcome. Daytime buses run from Falmouth and Truro during the week.
🏚Ⓩ❀◖ዑ♣PⒽ(500)

North Hill

Racehorse Inn
PL15 7PG (off B3254) SX273766
🌣 closed Mon winter; 12-3 (not Mon-Fri), 6-11; 12-3, 4-11 Sun ☎ (01566) 786916 ⊕ theracehorseinn.co.uk
Harbour Light Ale; Penpont Shipwreck Coast; St Austell Tribute; Sharp's Doom Bar Ⓗ
Delightfully situated at the foot of Hawk's Tor in the heart of beautiful Cornish countryside, the Racehorse is a welcoming community pub, popular with locals and walkers alike. Formerly the village school, it is believed to be over 300 years old. It has a large single bar with distinct drinking areas separated by a wooden screen, and a separate restaurant, or you can eat in the bar. Excellent home-cooked food features locally sourced ingredients. Winter opening hours vary.
🏚Q Ⓩ❀◖ዑ&♣PⒽ

Padstow

Golden Lion
Lanadwell Street, PL28 8AN
🌣 11 (12 Sun)-11 ☎ (01841) 532797
⊕ goldenlionpadstow.co.uk
Sharp's Doom Bar; Skinner's Betty Stogs; Tintagel Castle Gold Ⓗ
An old, unspoilt free house situated away from the busy harbour area, offering a friendly welcome to locals and tourists alike. Its cosy interior accommodates a public bar, partitioned to create a family and dining area, and a comfortable lounge bar/restaurant; outside is a seated patio. A selection of home-cooked meals is served daily. On 1 May, 'Obby 'Oss Day, the Red 'Oss is stabled at

the pub – energetically emerging and dancing through the streets of Padstow.
🏚Ⓩ❀◖ዑ Ⓔ&Å♣✿ ⌐ Ⓜ(555,556,557)

Pelynt

Jubilee Inn
Jubilee Hill, PL13 2JZ (on B3359) SX206549
🌣 11-11; 12-10.30 Sun ☎ (01503) 220312
⊕ jubilee-inn.co.uk
St Austell Trelawny, Tribute, Black Prince, Proper Job Ⓗ
Seventeenth-century village inn once called the Axe, renamed in 1887 to celebrate Queen Victoria's Golden Jubilee. Inside are oak-beamed ceilings, antique furniture, a Delabole slate floor and a wood-panelled bar with a huge burnished copper hood, plus a collection of royal jubilee and other memorabilia. An extensive restaurant menu features locally sourced produce. The beer range usually reduces in winter, while one of the regular brews may be replaced from time to time by a St Austell seasonal beer.
🏚Q❀◖ዑ Ⓔ&Å♣P✿ ⌐ Ⓜ(573)

Pendoggett

Cornish Arms Ⓛ
St Kew, PL30 3HH (on B3314) SX024794
🌣 11-11 (11-2.30, 5-midnight Mon-Fri winter)
☎ (01208) 880263 ⊕ cornisharms.com
Sharp's Doom Bar; guest beer Ⓗ
A 16th-century coaching inn, this picturesque family-run free house is family-friendly, welcoming and full of charm and character. Its flagstoned floors, open beams, wooden panels and partitions all reflect the pub's origins. The quiet, atmospheric interior accommodates a main bar, snug, two further drinking and dining areas and a restaurant. Caricatures of locals decorate the walls, and a collection of handbells hangs over the bar. Excellent English and Thai cuisine is offered, with a Thai banquet held monthly. The house beer is from Sharp's. Q Ⓩ❀◖ዑ Å♣P✿

Penryn

Seven Stars
73 The Terrace, TR10 8EL SW784344
🌣 11 (12 Sun)-11 ☎ (01326) 373573
Blue Anchor Ben's Stout, Spingo Middle; guest beers Ⓗ
The nearest Penryn has to an ale house, this single-bar pub is run by a jovial Dutchman. Decorated with foreign cash, postcards and beer-related clippings, its spacious interior has a raised drinking annexe at the rear, dominated by a large ship's wheel. The pub is home to Penryn Community Theatre, who entertain with plays and pantos, and a piano is available for competent pianists; live music features occasionally. Guest beers are usually from nearby brewery Rebel or other Cornish micros. 🏚❀⇌✿ ⌐ Ⓜ

Penzance

Admiral Benbow
46 Chapel Street, TR18 4AF SW474301
🌣 11-11; 12-10.30 Sun ☎ (01736) 363448
St Austell Proper Job; Sharp's Doom Bar; guest beer Ⓗ
Four-hundred-year-old town-centre pub, designed like a ship, with bars on both floors. The narrow

street frontage and bar area belie its Tardis-like interior, with its many nooks, crannies and separate drinking areas including the Wreck Bar upstairs. Themed on piratical/nautical lines, the pub is festooned with salvage from local wrecks to give added interest to a rambling maze of rooms on the two floors, worth a few minutes' exploration. A single Cornish guest beer is offered during the summer. ♨ ☎ ◖ ❱ ⏢ ≉ ⬚

Crown Inn L

Victoria Square, TR18 2EP SW474306
🌣 12-midnight (12.30am Fri & Sat) ☎ (01736) 351070
⊕ thecrownpenzance.co.uk
Cornish Crown Mousehole Bitter, Ale, SPA; guest beer Ⓗ

Proper locals' pub on the corner of a rare Victorian residential square in the town centre, and the tap for Cornish Crown Brewery. Essentially a one-room pub, it is tidily furnished with upholstered window bench seats and a huge mirror covering one wall, and a cosy two-table snug behind. Outside drinking is on a small patio overlooking the street. Food is available Thursday evening to Saturday only. The Cornish Crown beer selection varies according to availability; the single guest beer changes frequently. ♨ Q ❀ ◖ ❱ ⏢ ≉ ♣ ⬚ ⬚

Phillack

Bucket of Blood

14 Churchtown Road, TR27 5AE SW563383
🌣 11-2.30 (not Mon-Wed winter), 5.30-11 (midnight Sat summer); 12-4, 5.30 (7 winter)-11 Sun ☎ (01736) 752378
⊕ bucketofblood.co.uk
St Austell Dartmoor Best Bitter, Tribute, Proper Job, HSD Ⓗ

Close to Hayle Towans, this historic, reputedly haunted pub is both family- and dog-friendly. Named after a local gory legend, the single-bar interior separates into cosy drinking and dining areas. The (very) low-beamed ceiling, slate flooring and wooden furnishings, mainly settles, contribute to the character, an open fire adding warmth. A mural of St Ives Bay adorns one wall. The beer menu varies within St Austell Brewery's range with HSD always available. Quality meals are available April-October. ♨ Q ❀ ◖ ❱ ♣ ⬚ ⬚

Piece

Countryman Inn

Carnkie, TR16 6SG (on Four Lanes-Pool road) SW679398
🌣 11-11 (midnight Sat); 12-11 Sun ☎ (01209) 215960
Courage Best Bitter; Sharp's Doom Bar; Skinner's Betty Stogs, Heligan Honey; Theakston Old Peculier; guest beers Ⓗ

Once a grocery shop for local miners, this lively country pub near Carn Brea sits high among old copper mines in the Camborne district. A massive old cast-iron cooking range dominates the larger bar; families are welcome in the smaller bar. Live entertainment features most nights and a raffle in support of local charities is held on Sunday lunchtimes. The range of ales is largely unchanging although a guest may appear occasionally. Food is served all day. ♨ ❀ ◖ ⬚ ♣ ❱ ⬚ (442)

Polkerris

Rashleigh Inn L

PL24 2TL (off A3082 Par-Fowey road) SX094522

🌣 11-11; 12-10.30 Sun ☎ (01726) 813991
⊕ therashleighinnpolkerris.co.uk
Otter Bitter; Taylor Landlord; Young's Special; guest beers Ⓗ

Excellent family-run free house located near the Saints Way footpath beside a secluded beach. Formerly a pilchard boathouse dating from the 18th century, its cosy, atmospheric interior features exposed stonework, beamed ceilings, comfortable furnishings and a splendid slate-topped bar with up to six ales on offer. A sheltered terrace affords panoramic views of St Austell Bay. Piano-accompanied singalongs are held on Saturday evenings. Meals are served in the bar and split-level restaurant. Well-behaved dogs on leads are allowed in the bar only. ♨ Q ❀ ◖ ❱ ♣ P ⬚

Polperro

Blue Peter Inn L

Quay Road, PL13 2QZ SX210509
🌣 8.30-11 (10.30 Sun) ☎ (01503) 272743
⊕ thebluepeter.co.uk
Beer range varies Ⓗ

Named after the naval flag, this friendly inn is reached via a flight of steps near the quay, and is the only pub with a sea view in the village. It offers up to five real ales in summer, mainly from Cornwall or Devon, and a varied menu of home-cooked dishes including breakfast. Low beams and wooden floors are decorated with unusual souvenirs, breweriana and work by local artists. The pub is popular with visitors, locals, fishermen – and their dogs. ♨ ☎ ◖ ❱ ⬚ (572,573)

Crumplehorn Inn L

The Old Mill, PL13 2RJ (at end of A387) SX205515
🌣 11-11; 12-10.30 Sun ☎ (01503) 272348
⊕ crumplehorn-inn.co.uk
St Austell Tribute; guest beers Ⓗ

Once a mill and mentioned in the Domesday Book, this 14th-century inn at the village entrance has a fine working waterwheel outside. Inside, the split-level bar is divided into three comfortable areas with flagstone floors and low ceilings. Guest beers are mostly Cornish, and the menu features locally caught fish. A spacious patio by the millstream offers large umbrellas for protection from the sun. B&B and self-catering accommodation are available. In summer catch the milk float tram down to the harbour. ♨ Q ☎ ❀ ⬚ ◖ ❱ ♣ ⬚ (572,573)

Pool

Plume of Feathers

Fore Street, TR15 3PF (on A3047) SW669416
🌣 11.30-11.30; 12-midnight Sat; 11.30-10 Sun
☎ (01209) 713513
Beer range varies Ⓗ

Cosy old granite inn on the main road, with low beams and several drinking areas around a central bar. The ever-changing beer range comes mainly from Cornish and south-west microbreweries, with three brews always available. A beer festival is held in summer. Family-friendly, with an outdoor play area, it is also a meeting place for clubs and has a pool table. Once used as a mortuary for a local mining disaster, the pub is home to a sociable ghost called Lucy. No food Sunday evening. ♨ ☎ ❀ ◖ ♣ P ❱ ⬚ (14,18,41)

Rosudgeon

Falmouth Packet ⌊

TR20 9QE (on A394 Penzance-Helston road) SW558296
🌂 12-3, 5.30-11 (midnight Sat); 12-11 Fri & Sun
☎ (01736) 762240 ⊕ falmouthpacketinn.co.uk
Penzance Jolly Farmer, Tater Du; guest beers Ⓗ
Enjoying a worthy reputation for fine ales and
excellent cuisine, this vibrant family-run free house
is worth seeking out. The quiet single-bar interior
divides into drinking and dining areas. An adjoining
conservatory provides additional space, weather
permitting. Comfortable throughout, the pub's
open fire, exposed stonework, slate floors and
wooden furnishings add character. Up to two guest
ales are offered alongside the regular Penzance
ales. The imaginative menu features locally
sourced produce. A two-bedroom holiday let is
available. ⛤Q⛵❀🖼◑&♣P⁵⊟(2,2A,302)

St Agnes: Isles of Scilly

Turk's Head

TR22 0PL (close to landing stage) SV883085
🌂 11 (12 Sun)-11 Jul & Aug; 11-4.30, 7-11; 12-4.30, 7-10.30
Sun ☎ (01720) 422434
St Austell Tribute; guest beers Ⓗ
The only pub on the island, well-loved by locals
and visitors alike, with an outdoor drinking area
that can have few rivals for its scenic beauty.
Opening hours may vary slightly according to boat
times; the jetty is only a couple of minutes' walk
away and you can watch your boat approaching
from the bar. Evening boat trips run from St Mary's
in summer to sample the ale and food. Tribute is
sold as a house beer named Turk's Ale, while the
two guest ales are always selected from the Ales of
Scilly, Skinner's or Sharp's ranges. Order lunchtime
pasties early. ⛵❀◑▲♣⁵

St Austell

Rann Wartha ⌊

9 Biddick's Court, PL25 5EW
🌂 9am-midnight (1am Fri & Sat) ☎ (01726) 222940
**Greene King Abbot; Ruddles Best Bitter; Skinner's
Betty Stogs; guest beers** Ⓗ
Popular town-centre Wetherspoon appealing to all
ages and families, offering up to four varying guest
beers including at least two Cornish brews. The bar
is L-shaped, with an area for family meals. Walls
are decorated with portraits of local historic people
associated with the area's china clay industry. The
pub's Cornish name means Higher Quarter, relating
to its position in the town. An ale club is held on
Wednesday. Disabled access includes a ramp, lifts
and wide main door. ⛤Q⛵❀◑&⇌⁵⊟

St Just

Star Inn

1 Fore Street, TR19 7LL SW371314
🌂 11.30-midnight (11.30 Sun) ☎ (01736) 788767
⊕ thestarinn-stjust.co.uk
**St Austell Dartmoor Best Bitter, Tribute, Proper Job,
seasonal beer** Ⓗ
A proper drinkers' pub, this 18th-century granite
inn is a timeless place where the emphasis is on
good ale and conversation. The atmospheric single
bar's décor reflects long associations with mining
and maritime activities of yesteryear, with Celtic
flags adorning the beamed ceiling, while wooden

furnishings and an open fire enhance the
ambience. A separate snug functions as a family or
function room. Up to five St Austell ales are served,
but no food. Live music features on Monday and
Saturday nights. ⛤Q⛵❀&▲♣⁵⊟(10,300,504)

St Mary's: Isles of Scilly

Old Town Inn

Old Town, TR21 0NN (on A3112) SV914104
🌂 12 (5 Mon-Fri winter)-11; 12-10.30 Sun
☎ (01720) 422301 ⊕ oldtowninn.co.uk
**Ales of Scilly Scuppered; Sharp's Doom Bar; guest
beer** Ⓗ
Modern and roomy pub near the airport. Wood
panelling and flooring dominate the two bars, the
front room used mainly for day-to-day drinking,
while the side room is used for dining and
functions. The pub offers occasional live
entertainment and twice-yearly beer festivals,
usually in June and September. Doom Bar is always
available, Scuppered might be replaced with
another island brew, while the single guest beer
changes regularly. Accommodation is in three four-
star rooms. ⛵❀🖼◑&▲👤P

St Mawgan

Falcon Inn ⌊

TR8 4EP (near Newquay airport) SW873658
🌂 11-3, 5.30-11 (midnight Fri & Sat) winter; 11-11 (midnight
Fri & Sat) summer; 12-11 Sun ☎ (01637) 860225
⊕ thefalconinnstmawgan.co.uk
Beer range varies Ⓗ
Nestling in the unspoilt Lanherne Valley, this
charming, family-friendly, 16th-century free house
is a quiet retreat despite its proximity to Newquay
Airport. The popular, picturesque pub is a hub for
local events. Its peaceful, relaxed interior features
a cosy single bar with a large open hearth and
adjoining stylish restaurant. Four varying real ales,
at least one local, are always available. A high-
quality and comprehensive home-cooked menu is
served daily. For alfresco drinking/dining, the
extensive well-kept gardens are perfect in
summer. ⛤Q⛵❀🖼◑▲♣P⁵⊟(556)

St Newlyn East

Pheasant Inn

Churchtown, TR8 5LJ
🌂 12-3, 6-midnight winter; 12-midnight Fri, Sat & summer;
12-11 Sun ☎ (01872) 510237
**St Austell Trelawny; Sharp's Own; Skinner's Betty
Stogs; guest beer** Ⓗ
Stone-fronted village local opposite the church and
at the centre of the community – darts, euchre and
football teams are all supported. Two bar areas
supply mostly Cornish ales, and an annual beer
festival takes place in November. Popular for its
quality meals featuring local produce, the pub
takes its meat only from the village butcher. Dogs
are welcome. The car park to the rear is entered via
a narrow access. ⛤❀◑♣P⁵⊟(586)

Stratton

King's Arms ⌊

Howells Road, EX23 9BX (off A39) SS230064
🌂 12-11 ☎ (01288) 352396
**Sharp's Doom Bar; Tintagel Cornwall's Pride; guest
beers** Ⓗ

Popular 17th-century local in the heart of this ancient market town. The pub's name reflects the town's political loyalties after the Civil War – the battle of Stamford Hill took place near here in 1643. Many original features remain in the two simply furnished bars floored with a mix of well-worn Delabole slate and wood. The two guest beers are usually from West Country microbreweries, with draught cider available in summer. A must-visit if you are in the Bude area. ⚠Q🐕🏠🍴◑🍺♣♠P⅃-🚆

Tintagel

King Arthur's Arms

Fore Street, PL34 0DA SX056885
🕒 9am-midnight ☎ (01840) 770831
🌐 kingarthursarms.co.uk
St Austell Tribute; Sharp's Doom Bar; Tintagel Cornwall's Pride, Castle Gold Ⓗ
Comfortable 14th-century granite inn with beamed ceilings opposite the NT Old Post Office. You can start drinking early in this pub. Three additional beers are served in summer, usually from the Tintagel Brewery range. Food is offered until 9pm, with breakfast from 9am. It has good facilities for families of all ages, with an outside area and a large interior for the summer trade, offering various pub games. It has eight rooms for B&B accommodation. Parking is at the Pay & Display car park next door. ⚠🛏🐕🏠◑🍺♣A♣⅃-🚆(594)

Towan Cross

Victory Inn Ⓛ

Porthtowan, TR4 8BN SW706484
🕒 12-midnight ☎ (01209) 890359
🌐 thevictoryinncornwall.co.uk
St Austell Tribute; Skinner's Betty Stogs; guest beers Ⓗ
A traditional local, this large, convivial, family-run free house is situated on the cliffs above Porthtowan. The open-plan single bar accommodates separate dining areas and a pool table. An adjoining conservatory doubles as a family or dining room. Comfortably furnished throughout, the atmosphere is quiet and restful. Up to four ales are on offer, mainly from the Skinner's range, and an interesting good-value menu uses local produce. A large beer garden, ample parking and camping facilities are at the rear. Q🛏🐕🏠◑🍺A♣P⅃-🚆(304)

Trebellan

Smugglers' Den Inn Ⓛ

TR8 5PY (off Cubert road from A3075) SW783574
🕒 11-11 summer; 12-3, 6-11 Thu-Sat winter; 12-11 Sun
☎ (01637) 830209 🌐 thesmugglersden.co.uk
St Austell Tribute; Skinner's Smugglers Ale; guest beers Ⓗ
Picture-postcard thatched pub in an idyllic setting at the bottom of narrow country lanes -fortunately well signposted. Popular for dining winter or summer, its beer range is always interesting, mainly sourced from local breweries. Beams, paved yards and open fires add to the atmosphere. Folk or jazz evenings and quiz nights are held

> Beer: a high and mighty liquor.
> **Julius Caesar**

occasionally. There is a nearby caravan site, and local buses stop at the top of the (rather hilly) lane. A May Day weekend ale and pie festival is held. ⚠Q🐕🏠◑AP⅃-🚆(585,591,592)

Treen (Zennor)

Gurnard's Head Ⓛ

Zennor, TR26 3DE (on B3306 north coast road) SW436376
🕒 10-11.30 ☎ (01736) 796928 🌐 gurnardshead.co.uk
St Austell Tribute; Skinner's Betty Stogs; guest beers Ⓗ
Named after the nearby headland, this impressive, characterful free house with a well-earned reputation for fine ale and excellent cuisine draws custom from near and far. The expansive wood-floored interior accommodates a single bar, cosy snug and stylish dining room. Open fires, attractive decor, wood furnishings and comfy sofas help create a relaxed atmosphere; local art features throughout. An extensive menu changes daily, reflecting the availability of local produce. One or two guest ales are from Cornish microbreweries. ⚠Q🛏🐕🏠◑♿A♣P⅃-🚆(507,508,300)

Treleigh

Treleigh Arms Ⓛ

Basset Road, TR16 4AY (beside old Redruth bypass) SW703436
🕒 11-3, 5-11; 11-11 Fri-Sun ☎ (01209) 315095
🌐 treleigharms.org.uk/tarms
Draught Bass; Sharp's Doom Bar; Skinner's Betty Stogs; guest beer Ⓗ
Roadside free house, a popular stop-off for diners, with a good mix of locals drinking at the bar. The welcoming and comfortable interior features exposed stone walls and a wood-burning stove for winter; there is no intrusive TV or jukebox. The quality food menu is sometimes boosted when the Royle Treleigh Yacht Club holds a gastronomic evening (no boat required). Quiz night is Tuesday. The garden includes a pétanque pitch. Dogs are welcome. ⚠Q🐕◑♣P⅃-

Trevaunance Cove

Driftwood Spars Ⓛ

Quay Road, TR5 0RT (signed from St Agnes Peterville) SW721513
🕒 11-11 (1am Fri & Sat) ☎ (01872) 552428
🌐 driftwoodspars.com
Driftwood Bluehills Bitter, Red Mission, Montol, Lou's Brew; guest beers Ⓗ
Outstanding coastal free house and brewpub at the forefront of real ale promotion, with seven real ales always available, annual beer festivals in March and May, and tutored tasting sessions. Popular and vibrant, the nautically themed pub has three different bars, a sea view dining room and a sun terrace. An imaginative menu emphasises local seasonal produce. Entertainment includes live music and occasional live theatre. Outside are two separate beer gardens and ample parking. The pub is licensed for weddings. ⚠Q🛏🐕🏠◑🍺♿A♣P⅃-🚆(85,315,583)

Trewellard

Trewellard Arms 🅛
Trewellard Road, TR19 7TA (on B3318/B3306 jct) SW377338
✪ 12-midnight ☎ (01736) 788634
⊕ goodpubfoodlandsend.co.uk
Beer range varies Ⓗ
Formerly the nearby Geevor mine owner's residence, this is now a thriving family-run free house. Family friendly and welcoming, its cosy interior accommodates a spacious open-beamed single bar, a pleasant restaurant and a secluded cellar area. Open fires enhance the homely atmosphere. The ever-changing beer menu features up to six ales. An annual May beer festival is held. Home-cooked meals are good value. Outside is a patio beer garden. Ample parking is available, and the pub is easily accessible by bus.
🏚Q🐕☺◑ Å♣P⁵⃑🖩(10,300,507)

Truro

City Inn 🅛
Pydar Street, TR1 3SP SW822452
✪ 12-11.30 (12.30am Fri & Sat) ☎ (01872) 272623
⊕ thecityinntruro.co.uk
Courage Best Bitter; Sharp's Doom Bar; Skinner's Betty Stogs; guest beer Ⓗ
With the atmosphere of a village local, this two-bar pub is very community-focused. Near the city centre, by the railway viaduct, the welcoming building has a wood-beamed front bar with several drinking and dining areas and an impressive water jug collection; the more sports-oriented back bar has a large-screen TV. There is a suntrap beer garden to the rear. Good-value home-cooked meals are served daily. Regular charity events include annual conker and hogs pudding championships, and occasional beer festivals are held. Q🐕☺🖉◑ ⊟≷⁵⃑🖩

Wig & Pen
Frances Street, TR1 3DP
✪ 11-11 (midnight Fri & Sat); 11-8 Sun ☎ (01872) 273028
⊕ wigandpentruro.co.uk
Beer range varies Ⓗ
Convenient for the town and railway station, the Wig has a single L-shaped bar with a quiet, friendly atmosphere. Popular with locals, it also welcomes visitors. The beers sometimes vary within the St Austell range but HSD is always available. The basement restaurant opens in the evenings, with the emphasis on good-quality food cooked in-house and featuring local produce. Home-made crisps and pork scratchings are recommended. The pub's name reflects the law court nearby.
🏚Q🐕☺◑≷⁵⃑🖩

Tywardreath

New Inn
Fore Street, PL24 2QP SX086543
✪ 12-11 ☎ (01726) 813901
Draught Bass Ⓖ; St Austell Trelawny, Tribute, Proper Job Ⓗ, seasonal beer Ⓖ
The newest pub in the village when it was built in 1752, but now the only one remaining. A classic local, it is very much at the heart of the community, concentrating on good beer – and one of the few remaining Cornish pubs with no food on offer. Pub games, good conversation and local music are the themes here. It sells the only gravity-dispensed Draught Bass in the St Austell Brewery pub estate, and always offers St Austell's seasonal ales when available.
🏚Q🐕☺😀Ⓖ& Å≷(Par)♣P⁵⃑🖩(524,525,526)

Vogue

Star Inn 🅛
St Day, TR16 5NP (on Redruth-St Day road) SW724424
✪ 12-midnight (1am Fri & Sat); 11-11 Sun
☎ (01209) 820242 ⊕ starInnvogue.biz
Beer range varies Ⓗ
Community-oriented 19th-century traditional village local. Full of character, its homely interior includes a spacious single bar for drinking and dining, plus a quiet lounge area and a separate cosy dining room. An ever-changing beer menu always features a Skinner's ale. Popular, good-value home-cooked food is served daily. Entertainment includes traditional pub games, quiz nights, karaoke and live music. An annual June beer festival coincides with the local feast day. Outside are a boules court and camping area.
🏚🐕☺🖉◑ Å♣♣P⁵⃑🖩(43)

Wendron

New Inn 🅛
TR13 0EA (on B3297 Helston-Redruth road) SW310678
✪ closed Mon winter; 12-3, 6-11 (7-10.30 Sun)
☎ (01326) 572683
St Austell Tribute; Skinner's Betty Stogs; guest beers Ⓗ
The character of this welcoming family-run, single-bar village pub has changed little over the years. A free house, it offers up to four ales from an ever-changing beer menu, generally supplied by microbreweries. The eclectic décor of the cosy, homely bar is dominated by an interesting carving of the Four Horsemen of the Apocalypse. The adjoining dining room is attractively furnished. Good-value cuisine includes daily home-cooked specials prepared by the landlady and her daughter. Q☺◑♣P⁵⃑🖩(2A,34)

Choosing pubs

CAMRA members and branches choose the pubs listed in the Good Beer Guide. There is no payment for entry, and pubs are inspected on a regular basis by personal visits; publicans are not sent a questionnaire once a year, as is the case with some pub guides. CAMRA branches monitor all the pubs in their areas, and the choice of pubs for the guide is often the result of democratic vote at branch meetings. However, recommendations from readers are welcomed and will be passed on to the relevant branch: write to Good Beer Guide, CAMRA, 230 Hatfield Road, St Albans, Hertfordshire, AL1 4LW; or send an email to: **gbgeditor@camra.org.uk**

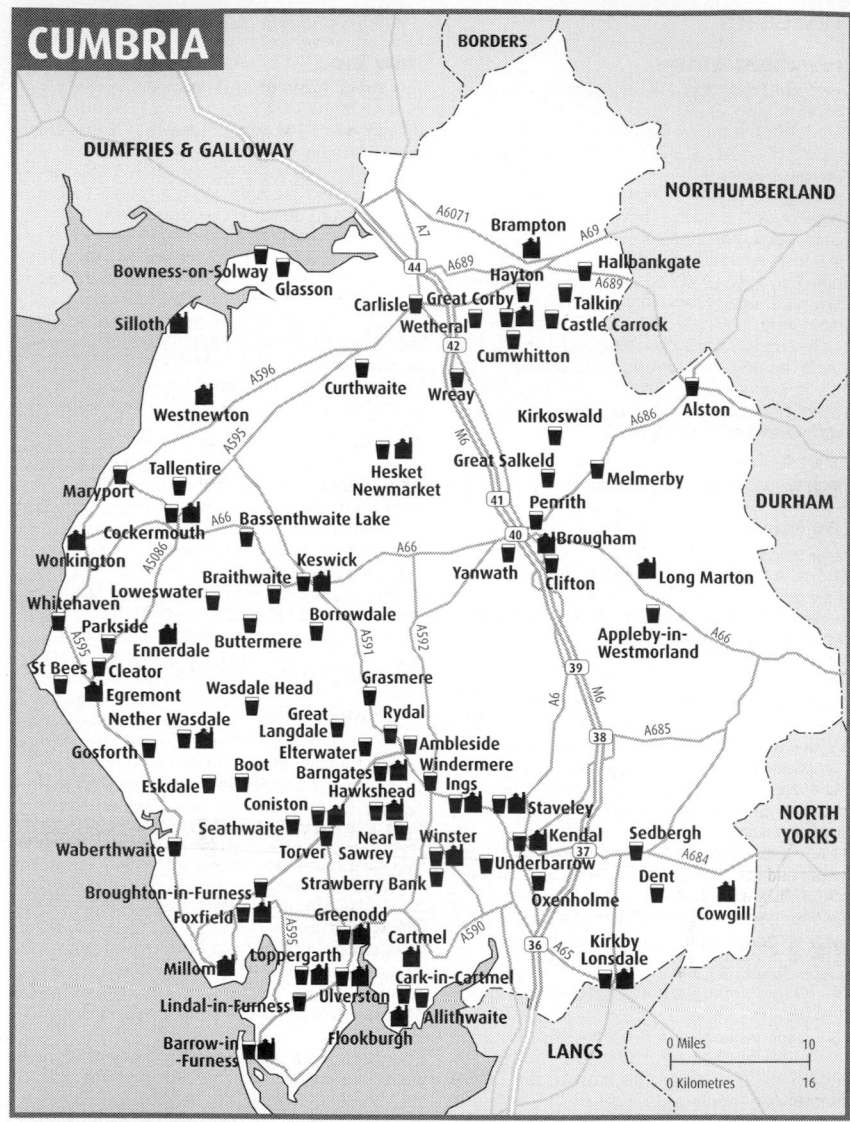

CUMBRIA

Allithwaite

Pheasant Inn ⓛ

Flookburgh Road, LA11 7RQ

☼ 12-11 (midnight Thu-Sat) ☎ (01539) 532239

🌐 thepheasantinnallithwaite.co.uk

Thwaites Original; guest beers ⒣

Free house catering to locals and tourists alike, extensively refurbished in 2011 and incorporating an extension with stunning views over Humphrey Head to Morecambe Bay. One of the walks described in CAMRA's Lake District Pub Walks starts at Kents Bank station and visits here. The four guest beers are from local breweries. The emphasis is on good-quality and good-value food, but there is a separate bar area with open fires, where dogs are welcome if on a lead. Quiz night is Thursday.
🕮🏵🕽🕭🖳⛟(Kents Bank)P╚➡(530,532)

Alston

Cumberland Inn ⓛ

Townfoot, CA9 3HX

☼ 12-11 ☎ (01434) 381875 🌐 cumberlandinnalston.com

Yates Bitter; guest beers ⒣

A family-run 19th-century inn overlooking the South Tyne River. Close to the Coast-to-Coast cycle route and Pennine Way, it is an ideal base for exploring the highest market town in England and enjoying fishing on the South Tyne. Popular pub food is enjoyed by locals and visitors alike. The house beer is Yates Bitter, with guest beers from Geltsdale, Hesket Newmarket, Allendale, High House Farm and Mordue breweries as well as from further afield. Old Rosie and occasional Cumbrian ciders and perry are stocked. Local Cider Pub of the Year 2013. 🕮Q🏵🕽🕭🖳➡(680)

Ambleside

Queen's Hotel

Market Place, LA22 9BU

🕓 10-11.45 (12.45am Fri & Sat); 11-11.45 Sun
☎ (015394) 32206 ⊕ queenshotelambleside.com
Coniston Bluebird; Cumbrian Legendary Loweswater Gold; Hawkshead Windermere Pale Ale; Jennings Cumberland Ale; Yates Bitter Ⓗ

Town-centre hotel with a large bar and dining area, a cellar bar beneath and the separate Victoria's Restaurant on the ground floor. It is popular with locals and visitors for the quality of the beers and its location in the centre of the Lake District. Buses run to several villages and towns with tourist attractions and fine walking opportunities.
🅰️🚪◑🌙'–🚭(555)

Appleby-in-Westmorland

Golden Ball

4 High Wiend, CA16 6RD (off Boroughgate)

🕓 11 (12 Sun)-midnight ☎ (01768) 351493
Marston's Burton Bitter; guest beers Ⓗ

A traditional side-street pub with a lounge and public bar, TV and excellent rock and blues jukebox in the bar. Both bars are served from a central back-to-back bar area offering up to six real ales on handpump. As well as a strong local following, the pub attracts visitors, including railway enthusiasts using the Settle to Carlisle Railway. The patio has a large covered area. 🅰️🚪🥨🍀'–🚭(563)

Midland Hotel 🍸

25 Clifford Street, CA16 6TS (opp railway station)

🕓 closed Mon; 11.30 (5 Tue & Wed)-11; 12-11 Sun
☎ (01768) 351524 ⊕ themidlandhotelappleby.co.uk
Beer range varies Ⓗ

Set in the beautiful Eden Valley between the Lake District and Yorkshire National Parks, and adjacent to Appleby station on the Settle to Carlisle Railway. The pub has been extensively refurbished and much improved, with a modern feel, and is a free house with up to three handpumps offering LocAles from Cumbria and microbreweries nationwide. Real cider and perry are regularly available. Excellent locally sourced food is on offer.
🏨🅰️🚪◑🥨🍀P'–🚭

Barngates

Drunken Duck Inn Ⓛ

LA22 0NG (signed off the B5286 Hawkshead to Ambleside road) NY351013

🕓 11.30-11; 12-10.30 Sun ☎ (01539) 436347
⊕ drunkenduckinn.co.uk
Beer range varies Ⓗ

Home of Barngates Brewery, the Duck always serves four of the 10 beers brewed here and brewery tours can be arranged. The bar has been extensively renovated to create a pleasing mix of local and modern styles. Lunchtime and evening meals are served, always of exceptionally high standard. The outside seating area at the front offers magnificent views of the fells to the north east. 🏨Q🅰️🚪◑P'–

Barrow-in-Furness

Furness Railway Ⓛ

76-80 Abbey Road, LA14 1PQ

🕓 8-midnight (1am Fri & Sat) ☎ (01229) 820818

Courage Directors; Greene King Abbot; Ruddles Best Bitter; guest beers Ⓗ
On the ground floor of the old central Co-op department store, divided into four distinct drinking areas, the pub is a fine example of early 20th-century commercial architecture and a credit to Wetherspoon who have given this building a new lease of life. It can be busy throughout the day but particularly at weekends, when it is a popular starting point for the town-centre circuit. Good-value food is served all day. 🌙◑🚪👍♿♻️🚭

Queen's Arms Ⓛ

Biggar Village, LA14 3YG

🕓 closed Mon; 6-11.30 Tue; 12-10.30 Wed & Thu; 12-midnight Fri & Sat; 12-10.30 Sun ☎ (01229) 471880
⊕ thequeensarmsbiggar.co.uk
Barngates Red Bull Terrier; Hawkshead Lakeland Gold; Ulverston Laughing Gravy Ⓗ

Nestled in the ancient village of Biggar, the Queen's Arms has risen like a phoenix from the ashes, sporting a substantial revamp while retaining its character and style. Several draught beers are served and there is always a warm welcome. The pub boasts a variety of events including arts and crafts, book clubs, and live music on Tuesday and Saturday. Beer festivals are planned. 🏨Q🅰️🚪◑●P🍴

Bassenthwaite Lake

Pheasant Hotel ★

Peil Wyke, CA13 9YE (signed off A66)

🕓 11.30-2.30, 5.30-10.30; 11-10.30 Fri & Sat; 12-2.30, 6-10.30 Sun ☎ (017687) 76234 ⊕ the-pheasant.co.uk

INDEPENDENT BREWERIES

Abraham Thompson's Barrow-in-Furness
Barngates Barngates
Beckstones Millom
Blackbeck Egremont
Bowness Bay Winster
Coniston Coniston
Cumberland Great Corby
Cumbrian Legendary Hawkshead
Dent Cowgill
Derwent Silloth
Eden Brougham
Ennerdale Ennerdale
Fell Flookburgh (NEW)
Foxfield Foxfield
Geltsdale Brampton
Great Gable Egremont
Greenodd Greenodd
Hardknott Millom
Hawkshead Staveley
Healey's Loppergarth (NEW)
Hesket Newmarket Hesket Newmarket
Jennings (Marston's) Cockermouth
Kendal Kendal
Keswick Keswick
Kirkby Lonsdale Kirkby Lonsdale
Mitchell Krause Workington
Strands Nether Wasdale
Stringers Ulverston
Tirril Long Marton
Ulverston Ulverston
Unsworth's Yard Cartmel (NEW)
Watermill Ings
Winster Valley Winster
Yates Westnewton

Coniston Bluebird; Corby Ale H
A well-established Lake District hotel that is more than 300 years old. The pub was frequented by John Peel, the legendary huntsman who was immortalised in song. The modern visitor will find a traditional cosy bar with leather sofas and settles, and walls adorned with hunting prints. Exceptional food is served in the separate restaurant.
Q ☞ ⊕ ⊙ ⊙ ⊟ & P ⊱ ⊟ (X5)

Boot

Brook House Inn L
CA19 1TG (200yds from Dalegarth station) SD176008
✪ 11-11 ☎ (01946) 723288 ⊕ brookhouseinn.co.uk
Cumbrian Legendary Langdale; Hawkshead Bitter; guest beers H
Very popular family-run pub offering high standards in food and drink. At least four handpumped beers of varying styles are sourced from local microbreweries. Additional beers and at least one draught cider are available during the main tourist season and school holidays. It participates in two beer festivals annually. The main Poacher Bar has a solid fuel stove lit during most of the year.
▲ Q ☞ ⊕ ⊙ ⊙ ⋏ ≋ (Dalegarth) ♣ ● P ⊱

Woolpack Inn L
Hardknott Pass, Eskdale, CA19 1TH (just over 1 mile from Dalegarth terminus of La'l Ratty)
✪ Hours vary; phone ahead to check ☎ (01946) 723230
Beer range varies H
Landmark Lakeland pub near Hardknott Pass and frequented by tourists throughout the year. Usually four handpumped beers are available, mostly sourced from local breweries and catering for a wide range of tastes, including fruit beers and ranging through traditional brown beers to dark milds. The main Walker's Bar successfully combines traditional decor with more current vogues. Wood-burning stoves are situated at each end of the bar and are lit for most of the year. The inn takes part in the annual Boot Beer Festival.
▲ Q ☞ ⊕ ⊙ ⊙ ⊟ & ⋏ ♣ ● P

Borrowdale

Riverside Bar at Scafell Hotel
Rosthwaite, CA12 5XB (on B5289)
✪ 12-11.30 (10.30 Sun) ☎ (017687) 77208 ⊕ scafell.co.uk
Copper Dragon Golden Pippin; Jennings Bitter, Cumberland Ale, Sneck Lifter H
Primarily a walkers' bar with slate flags and a coal fire. Six handpumps dispense a good variety of cask beers which are in consistently good condition; they enhance an impressive selection of bar meals and snacks. In good weather relax in the Riverside's garden with superb mountain views. In bad weather sit in the warmth of the bar and try to get a seat in the window looking directly over the river. ▲ ⊛ ⊕ ⊙ ⋏ P ⊟ (78)

Bowness-on-Solway

King's Arms
CA7 5AF
✪ 5 (3 summer)-midnight Mon-Fri; 12-midnight Sat & Sun
☎ (01697) 351426 ⊕ kingsarmsbowness.co.uk
Geltsdale Cold Fell, guest beers (summer) H
Situated in the centre of the village this pub is a popular stopping off point for visitors to the area

walking the Hadrian's Wall route. It's a community pub with a library, band practice every other Sunday and a regular quiz on Thursday. Set on the Solway coast in an area of outstanding natural beauty it is popular with bird-watchers and cyclists as well as the 'wall' walkers and locals. Meals are served every evening and weekend lunchtimes. Guest beers in the summer come from the Jennings or Marston's range. ▲ Q ⊛ ⊕ ⊙ ⊟ ♣ ⊟ (93)

Braithwaite

Middle Ruddings Country Inn ♥ L
CA12 5RY (just off A66 at Braithwaite)
✪ 10.30-11 ☎ (01768) 778436 ⊕ middle-ruddings.co.uk
Beer range varies H
Country inn close to the A66 with great views of Skiddaw. It has three handpumps and only sells Cumbrian beers, which constantly change. The pub hosts both a beer lovers' and a cider lovers' dinner as annual events, and usually has at least four ciders available with one on handpump and the others served from the cask. It is family run and family friendly, with children and dogs welcome. The restaurant promotes local produce, and the inn supports local events and has two quiz teams.
▲ Q ☞ ⊛ ⊕ ⊙ ⋏ ● P ⊱ ⊟ ⊟ (X5,74,74A)

Broughton-in-Furness

Manor Arms ♥ L
The Square, LA20 6HY
✪ 12-11.30 (midnight Fri & Sat); 12-11 Sun
☎ (01229) 716286 ⊕ manorarmsthesquare.co.uk
Cumberland Corby Blonde; Yates Bitter; guest beers H
An outstanding free house owned by the Varty family for 25 years; Scott has been in charge for over four years since the retirement of David and Christine. It is the winner of numerous CAMRA awards, including local CAMRA Pub of the Year 2013. A comprehensive, frequently changing choice of up to eight real ales is served – with a range to suit all tastes. Six traditional ciders and perries are also available. A mini beer festival is held – the place to sample real ales and ciders. There is free Wi-Fi, and families and dogs are welcome.
▲ Q ⊕ ♣ ● ⊟ ⊟ (7,7B)

Buttermere

Bridge Hotel
CA13 9UZ
✪ 8.30am-11 (10.30 Sun) ☎ (01768) 770252
⊕ bridge-hotel.com
Coniston Bluebird; Hawkshead Bitter; Jennings Cumberland Ale H
Nestled between Buttermere and Crummock on Millbeck, the site of a former mill, this hostelry has been selling ale since about 1734 – although not continuously. In 1850 Queen Victoria and Prince Albert visited the pub and today's visitor also receives a warm welcome. With a quiet lounge bar, four handpumps serve three local regulars and one changing ale from independent Lakeland breweries. Outside seating offers stunning views of Buttermere Fells, with the lake a five-minute stroll away. Q ☞ ⊛ ⊕ ⊙ ⊟ ⋏ P ⊟ (77,77a)

Cark-in-Cartmel

Engine Inn L
LA11 7NZ (3 miles W of Grange-over-Sands)

✪ 11.30-1am (midnight Sun) ☎ (01539) 558341
⊕ engineinn.co.uk
Beer range varies Ⓗ
Run by a family who are enthusiastic CAMRA members, this 17th-century inn, 300 yards from the railway station, is an excellent ending to the walk from Grange described in CAMRA's Lake District Pub Walks. Beers from the Punch Taverns range are supplemented by ales from local breweries. The pub (with five en-suite rooms) is named after a former mill engine in the village. It was extensively and tastefully refurbished in 2010, retaining the separate restaurant and games room. ﾑ۞ﾷ◖& A⇌♣♠P⪑–局(530,532)

Carlisle

Crown & Thistle
53 Church Street, Stanwix, CA3 9DS
✪ 10-midnight (11 Sun) ☎ (01228) 528191
Greene King IPA; guest beers Ⓗ
A real locals' old-fashioned boozer, refurbished and with a separate bar and lounge. Outside is a smoking area with further seating which is well used on hot summer days. Strong support for the city football team ensures it gets busy after a home game. Darts, dominoes, whist and, on Thursday, a popular quiz night attract a varied mix of customers. Horse racing and other sports feature on the TVs, which are not left on longer than necessary. ۞⊕♣⪑–局(76,62)

King's Head Ⓛ
Fisher Street, CA3 8RF (behind old town hall)
✪ 10-11 (midnight Fri); 11-midnight Sat; 12-11 Sun
☎ (01228) 533797 ⊕ kingsheadcarlisle.co.uk
Yates Bitter; guest beers Ⓗ
Winner of many CAMRA awards and one of the oldest pubs in Carlisle. Pictures of old Carlisle adorn the walls inside, and outside is an explanation of why the city is not in the Domesday Book. Local brews and takeaway beer cartons are available. The castle and cathedral are nearby. Good-value meals are served at lunchtime, and the covered smoking area has a large TV and barbecue for parties. Children are not allowed. Local CAMRA Pub of the Year 2012. ۞◖⇌♣⪑–局

Spinners Arms
Cummersdale Road, Cummersdale, CA2 6BD (2½ miles W of city centre off B5299)
✪ 6 (5 Fri)-midnight; 12-midnight Sat & Sun
☎ (01228) 532928 ⊕ thespinnersarms.org.uk
Beer range varies Ⓗ
Cosy family-friendly refurbished hostelry with unique animal-decorated gutters and a welcoming real fire. It is situated less than half a mile from Carlisle's south-western boundary, close to the Cumbrian Way and National Cycle Route 7, which run alongside the River Caldew. A good variety of guest ales from the Borders, Cumbria, Northumbria and northern microbreweries is stocked. There is regular live music, with Irish music sessions every second and fourth Wednesday. Evening bar meals are served (not Tue). Children are welcome until 9pm and well-behaved dogs permitted.
ﾑ۞◗&♣⪑–局(75)

William Rufus Ⓛ
10-16 Botchergate, CA1 1QS
✪ 8am-midnight (1am Tue-Thu; 2am Fri & Sat)
☎ (01228) 633160

Greene King Abbot; Jennings Sneck Lifter; Ruddles Best Bitter; guest beers Ⓗ
Typical Wetherspoon Lloyds No.1 bar open from breakfast until late, named after the designer and builder of Carlisle Castle. It is popular with shoppers and families but can get noisy at nights and weekends, and is the venue for watching sporting events on the pub's numerous TV screens. Food is served all day and there is a separate dining area. Children are welcome but with restrictions. It is two minutes from the railway station and on many bus routes. Outdoor facilities are at the planning stage. ㅎ◗&⇌局

Castle Carrock

Duke of Cumberland Ⓛ
CA8 9LU
✪ 12-11.30 (midnight Fri & Sat) ☎ (01228) 670341
⊕ thedukeofcumberlandinn.com
Geltsdale Cold Fell; guest beers Ⓗ
At the heart of this charming village, the Duke reopened in 2009 and is now successfully re-established, with a strong local following. The pub is the centre for the popular annual Music on the Marr folk festival in July. At the foot of the northern Pennines, it is also ideally located for outdoor activity enthusiasts, who can enjoy real ale from the local Geltsdale Brewery and sample the home-made food which has a growing reputation. The layout separates the games and TV area from the dining area. ﾑㅎ۞◖&♣P

Cleator

Brook Ⓛ
Trumpet Terrace, CA23 3DX (on A5086 between Cleator Moor and Egremont) NY021140
✪ 12-11 (1am Fri & Sat); 12-midnight Sun ☎ (01946) 811635
Ennerdale Liquidator; Hawkshead Lakeland Gold; Yates Golden Ale Ⓗ
Lighting provided by candles and fairy lights makes for a cosy but quirky feel here. While it is very community-centred – regulars' birthdays are chalked up on the noticeboard – it is not cliquey. The food is very popular and booking is advised. The beers are cherished by a young and knowledgeable cellarman. Meals are served Monday to Saturday evenings and Thursday to Saturday lunchtimes. Local CAMRA Pub of the Year 2012. ﾑ◗♣♠⪑–局(22,31)

Clifton

George & Dragon
CA10 2ER
✪ 11-midnight ☎ (01768) 865381
⊕ georgeanddragonclifton.co.uk
Cumberland Corby Ale; guest beers Ⓗ
Beautiful country estate inn situated on the main A6 road south of Penrith. This pub, with a restaurant and accommodation, specialises in serving fresh local produce from the Lowther estate. The inn is close to Lowther Castle, and Askham Hall, the site of the last battle fought on English soil in December 1745, is close by. Nearby Askham Fell has superb views of Ullswater.
ﾑQㅎ۞ﾷ◖⊟♣P⪑–局(106)

Cockermouth

Bush

53 Main Street, CA13 9JS
❂ 11-11 (midnight Fri & Sat) ☎ (01900) 822064
Jennings Bitter, Cumberland Ale, Cocker Hoop, Sneck Lifter Ⓗ
A traditional pub in historic Cockermouth. Wall plaques record the flood water level from November 2009 when the town's two rivers burst their banks. Sympathetic refurbishment has restored the original features. The pub has a warm, friendly atmosphere, with two bars with slate and wooden floors and stone fireplaces. Home-cooked food is available at lunchtimes, including Sundays. Sporting fixtures are screened in the back bar, while Thursday is acoustic night featuring local bands. Child- and dog-friendly. ᴹQ❀◖♿⌐-🖿

Castle Bar Ⓛ

14 Market Place, CA13 9NQ
❂ 11-11 (midnight Fri & Sat); 12-11 Sun ☎ (01900) 829904
⊕ cockermouth.org.uk/castlebar
Cumbrian Legendary Loweswater Gold; Jennings Bitter Ⓗ
Large pub overlooking the marketplace, spread over three floors with a terraced courtyard beer garden. Modern interior design retains many historic features within this fine old building. A restaurant on the first floor serves from a comprehensive menu throughout the building. Large TV screens show sporting events but there are rooms furnished with large sofas for quieter conversation. Private function rooms may be booked for family celebrations and receptions. ᴹ❀◖♿⌐♿●🖿

Coniston

Black Bull Inn Ⓛ

Yewdale Road, LA21 8DU
❂ 11-11 (10.30 Sun) ☎ (01539) 441335
⊕ blackbullconiston.co.uk
Coniston Oliver's Light Ale, Bluebird Bitter, Bluebird Premium XB, Old Man Ale, Special Oatmeal Stout, Blacksmiths Ale Ⓗ
A 16th-century coaching inn that serves good food in traditional and comfortable surroundings and is the tap house for the on-site Coniston brewery. The spacious bar and lounge, with beamed ceilings and tasteful decor, are always well frequented by tourists visiting this popular area. The outside seating area is perfect for the summer months, in this spectacular location near Coniston Old Man. ᴹQ🌲❀⌐◖♿Å●P⌐-🖿(X12,505)

Sun Hotel Ⓛ

LA21 8HQ (up the Walna Scar road from the village)
❂ 11-11.30 (11 Sun) ☎ (01539) 441248
⊕ thesunconiston.com
Coniston Bluebird; Copper Dragon Golden Pippin; Cumbria Legendary Loweswater Gold; Hawkshead Bitter; guest beers Ⓗ
Set above the village, the Sun has a large, comfortable bar area with slate floors and exposed beams. An open fire set into a traditional range makes for a cosy scene in the winter months. Upstairs there is a games room with darts, pool and a TV for sporting events. The large garden terrace overlooking the village catches the sun for most of the day. Eight handpumps offer mostly local ales. ᴹQ❀⌐◖♿Å♿P⌐-🖿(X12,505)

Cumwhitton

Pheasant Inn Ⓛ

CA8 9EX (4 miles SE of A69 at Warwick Bridge)
❂ closed Mon; 6-11 (10.30 Sun) ☎ (01228) 560102
⊕ pheasantinncumwhitton.co.uk
Geltsdale Pheasant Ale; guest beers Ⓗ
Partly dating from the 17th century, this pub has a well-deserved reputation for excellent food using fresh local ingredients, but retains that good pub welcome for the thirsty visitor in for a pint. There are three handpumps for real ale, including Pheasant Ale supplied by Geltsdale Brewery from nearby Brampton. The venue has won several CAMRA awards, proudly displayed in the bar alongside a water jug collection. Quiz nights are held every second week. ᴹ❀⌐◖♿Å♿P

Curthwaite

Royal Oak Ⓛ

CA7 8BG
❂ 12-2, 5-11.30; 12-10.30 Sun ☎ (01228) 710219
Beer range varies Ⓗ
Located in a quiet village off the beaten track, this traditional country pub sources three ales from Cumberland, Eden, Geltsdale, Hesket Newmarket or Jennings breweries. Local groups sometimes hold meetings here and, after the diners have finished, it is very much a place for a quiet drink. It has a well-deserved reputation for very good food using local seasonal produce, served in a large restaurant. An extensive takeaway menu is provided as a service to locals. 🌲❀◖♿♿P⌐-

Dent

George & Dragon Ⓛ

Main Street, LA10 5QL
❂ 11 (12 Sun)-11 ☎ (01539) 625256
⊕ thegeorgeanddragondent.co.uk
Dent Ale, Golden Fleece, Station Porter, Aviator, Rambrau, Ramsbottom Ⓗ
The Dent Brewery tap showcases all its own beers. Set in the cobbled main street of this attractive village, it is a friendly, two-bar local welcoming walkers, cyclists and dogs. A games room with pool table is off the front bar and a restaurant offering a good variety of meals is down a flight of stairs. Extensive mahogany panelling is adorned with brewery memorabilia and awards for the pub and brewery. Served by the local bus on Wednesday and Saturday. ᴹQ🌲❀⌐◖♿⌐Å♿●P🖿(564)

Elterwater

Britannia Inn

LA22 9HP
❂ 10.30 (12 Sun)-11 ☎ (01539) 437210 ⊕ britinn.co.uk
Coniston Bluebird; Eden Gold; guest beers Ⓗ
Attractive pub set next to a small triangular village green in a location with superb views. An entrance lobby with seating leads to a small bar area to the right. Guest beers are chosen from near and far and include a specially blended beer with a unique pumpclip from Coniston Brewery. There is a separate dining room and a back room with seating. See the pub's website for details of the annual Champion of Champions beer festival. ᴹQ❀⌐◖♿P⌐-🖿(516)

Eskdale

King George IV
Eskdale Green, CA19 1TS SD149998
☼ 11-1am ☎ (01946) 723470 ⊕ kinggeorge-eskdale.co.uk
Beer range varies Ⓗ
Popular Lakeland pub situated at the entrance to Eskdale Valley. It has an open fire in the main bar, oak beams and a slate floor. Four beers are on handpump in winter, increasing to 10 in season, supplied by microbreweries, local and national, covering a range of styles, both traditional and current. Food is served throughout the day, and two beer festivals are held a year. Opening times may vary. ⚏Q☞⬤⌂⏃◑ㅐよA⊒≈

Foxfield

Prince of Wales Ⓛ
LA20 6BX (opp station)
☼ closed Mon & Tue; 2.45-11 (midnight Fri & Sat); 12-10.30 Sun ☎ (01229) 716238 ⊕ princeofwalesfoxfield.co.uk
Beer range varies Ⓗ
Honoured among CAMRA's Top 40 campaigners, Stuart and Lynda are testament to what can be achieved through passion and hard work at this gem of a pub. The guest ales come from the pub's two house breweries – Foxfield and Tigertops – plus breweries throughout the country. Beers will always include a mild. Beer and cider festivals throughout the year are an added bonus (see website for details). A discount on B&B is offered to CAMRA members. Bus and rail stops are outside.
⚏Q⬤⌂よ≈ㅐ◑ ⊕P⸖ 日⊒(7)

Glasson

Highland Laddie Ⓛ
Water Street, CA7 5DT (9 miles NW of Carlisle off B5307)
☼ 12-midnight (1am Fri & Sat) ☎ (01697) 351839
⊕ highlandladdieinnglasson.co.uk
Jennings Dark Mild, Bitter, Cocker Hoop Ⓗ
Popular village local close to the Solway Firth and a bird reserve, and the only pub in the area open all day for people walking the Hadrian's Wall route. Meetings are held in the pub for the fishermen who follow the ancient occupation of haaf net fishing, unique to the Solway. The licensee has gained a reputation for providing excellent food, locally sourced, including delicacies such as sea salmon, sea bass and sea trout. Usually three LocAles are available. ⚏Q⬤◑ 日よA◆⊒(93)

Gosforth

Gosforth Hall Inn
Wasdale Road, CA20 1AZ (from A595 follow road signed to Wasdale. Adjacent to St Mary's church) NY071037
☼ 12 (3 Sun & Mon)-midnight ☎ (01946) 725322
⊕ gosforthhallinn.co.uk
Hawkshead Bitter; Keswick Thirst Run; Yates Golden Ale Ⓗ
Gosforth Hall is a mid-17th-century fortified farmhouse and is Grade II-listed. The original kitchen, now the lounge, features the widest spanning sandstone hearth in England; it also has a priest hole. This family- and dog-friendly inn, with boules pitch and large landscaped garden, serves meals lunchtimes and every evening. Rod's pies famously satisfy the heartiest of hungers acquired walking the Lakeland Fells. A beer festival is held in May. ⚏Q☞⬤⌂◑ 日よㅐP⸖ 日⊒(6,X6)

Horse & Groom
Eskdale Road, CA20 1JA NY073034
☼ 11-11; 12-10.30 Sun ☎ (01946) 725254
⊕ horsengroom.co.uk
Great Gable Burnmoor Pale Ale, Wastwater Gold, Yewbarrow Ⓗ
A recently and comfortably refurbished village pub, it is now the main outlet for the Great Gable Brewery and its CAMRA award-winning beers. Guest and seasonal beers can be interesting. Gosforth gives easy access to the spectacular Wasdale and Eskdale valleys, with great walking and climbing, and you can get lots of advice from the experienced landlord.
⚏Q☞⬤⌂◑ 日ㅐP⸖⊒(6,X6)

Grasmere

Dale Lodge Hotel (Tweedies Bar)
Langdale Road, LA22 9SW
☼ 12-11 (midnight Thu-Sat) ☎ (01539) 435300
⊕ dalelodgehotel.co.uk
Theakston Old Peculier; guest beers Ⓗ
A popular pub and hotel in the middle of the village, with a stone-flagged floor and a large wood-burning stove. The regular beers are complemented by a range of guest ales from far and wide. For those undecided on which to choose, you can get three third-pint samplers for the price of a pint. The large lawned grounds have ample seating. The Grasmere Guzzler beer festival, including a hog roast, is held each September.
⚏⬤⌂◑ ⊕P⸖⊒(555,599)

Great Corby

Corby Bridge Inn
CA4 8LL (2 miles S of the A69 at Warwick Bridge)
☼ 3-11 (midnight Sat & Sun) ☎ (01228) 560221
⊕ corbybridgeinn.org.uk
Thwaites Wainwright, Lancaster Bomber; guest beers Ⓗ
A short walk from Wetheral railway station across a spectacular viaduct over the River Eden leads to this lovely village pub. Set in a listed building but modernised a few years ago, it retains its original character. Four handpumps greet the visitor on entry, with an L-shaped room to the right and two further rooms to the left, all open plan. A back room contains a pool table and dartboard. Meals are available Thursday-Saturday evenings and Sunday lunchtime. ⚏⬤⌂◑ よ≈(Wetheral)ㅐP⸖

Great Langdale

Old Dungeon Ghyll Hotel
LA22 9JY (over bridge at end of B5343)
☼ 11-11 (10.30 Sun) ☎ (01539) 437272 ⊕ odg.co.uk
Black Sheep Ale; Cumbrian Legendary Esthwaite Bitter; Jennings Cumberland Ale; Theakston Old Peculier; Yates Bitter; guest beers Ⓗ
A haven for walkers and climbers, converted from a cowshed in the late 1940s, and offering a friendly welcome to those in muddy boots and wet waterproofs. The fire in the old range is much appreciated in winter, while impressive views of the surrounding fells can be enjoyed from the patio benches. An excellent range of Cumbrian beers is complemented by good home-cooked pub food. Meals in the hotel need to be booked in advance. ⚏Q☞⬤⌂◑ A⊕P⸖⊒(516)

Great Salkeld

Highland Drove ⓛ

CA11 9NA (off B6412 between A686 and Lazonby)
✪ 12-3 (not Mon), 6-midnight; 12-midnight Sat & Sun
☎ (01768) 898349 ⊕ kyloes.co.uk
Eden Kyloes; Theakston Black Bull Bitter; guest beers Ⓗ

Situated just off the main road through this attractive village, everything here is of a high standard. The exceptionally well-stocked bar has a lounge and a games room either side, with the award-winning Kyloes restaurant upstairs, all with well-chosen decor featuring exposed timber and brickwork embellished with Highland-style soft furnishings, brass and copper ornaments. Excellent food is available throughout and themed nights have recently been introduced. Watch out for the Highland cows! ♨⚘🛏◑🍴🛢♣P'–🚆(680)

Greenodd

Ship Inn ⓛ

Main Street, LA12 7QZ
✪ closed Mon; 5-11 (midnight Sat); 12-10.30 Sun
☎ (07782) 655294
Beer range varies Ⓗ

A traditional village inn and the tap house for Greenodd Brewery, the Ship was completely refurbished in 2012, opening up the bar area. A horseshoe bar serves the main open-plan area, which has slate floors, wooden beams and open fires. There is a quiet room through the back and a games room upstairs. A good mix of locals can usually be found putting the world to rights, and visitors are made most welcome. ♨♣P🛢🚆(X12)

Hallbankgate

Belted Will ⓛ

CA8 2NJ (on A689 Alston road 4 miles E of Brampton)
✪ 5 (12 Sat & Sun)-11 ☎ (01697) 746236 ⊕ beltedwill.co.uk
Caledonian Deuchars IPA; guest beers Ⓗ

The intriguing name (nickname of the 16th-century Lord William Howard from nearby Naworth Castle) is not all that attracts people here, as a warm welcome is assured from hosts Stephen and Alyson. Set in what was once an industrialised area, not now apparent, the pub has a strong local community spirit. Its peaceful location at the foot of the North Pennines lends itself to all manner of outdoor activities, including cycling, golfing, fishing, pony trekking, bird watching (RSPB) and walking. ♨⚘🛏◑🍴🛢♣'–🚆(680)

Hawkshead

King's Arms Hotel ⓛ

The Square, LA22 0NZ
✪ 11-midnight ☎ (01539) 436372
⊕ kingsarmshawkshead.co.uk
Cumbrian Legendary Loweswater Gold; Hawkshead Bitter; guest beers Ⓗ

Popular 500-year-old inn with an open fire and traditional beamed ceilings, one of which is held up by a life-size monarch, hand carved by local artist Jimmy (The Whistle) Whitworth. There is a separate dining room and bar area and the outside seating area fronts onto the village square. Occasional live music plays. Ales are predominantly sourced locally. ♨⚘🛏◑Ⓐ🚆(505)

Hayton

Stone Inn

CA8 9HR
✪ 12-2, 5.30-11; 12-midnight Sat; 12-11 Sun
☎ (01228) 670896
Thwaites Original; guest beer Ⓗ

A traditional family-run inn situated in the village of Hayton. The landlady provides a warm welcome to all at this community pub, also home to the local leek club. An upstairs dining room can be hired for small gatherings. Note the fine pair of 1904 Christ Church Boat Club oars adorning one wall and ask to see the CAMRA mirror. The guest ale is usually from a local brewery. ♨◖♣P

Hesket Newmarket

Old Crown ⓛ

Main Street, CA7 8JG
✪ 12-3 (not Mon-Thu), 5.30-11; 5.30-10.30 Sun
☎ (01697) 478288 ⊕ theoldcrownpub.co.uk
Hesket Newmarket Blencathra Bitter, Haystacks, Black Sail Stout, Scafell Blonde, Doris's 90th Birthday Ale, Catbells Pale Ale Ⓗ

Britain's first co-operatively owned pub, in a picturesque village on the edge of the northern Lakeland Fells. This thriving traditional inn is owned by more than 100 local people and supporters who are dedicated to maintaining its original character. It offers Hesket Newmarket beers from the brewery located in a barn at the rear, with new brews tried out in the pub. Brewery tours can be arranged in advance. A firm favourite of Prince Charles and Sir Chris Bonington. ♨Q⚘◑🛢Ⓐ♣'–

Ings

Watermill Inn ⓛ

LA8 9PY (turn off A591 by church)
✪ 11-11 (10.30 Sun) ☎ (01539) 821309
⊕ lakelandpub.co.uk
Theakston Old Peculier; Watermill Collie Wobbles, A Bit'er Ruff, Isle of Dogs, Wruff Night; guest beers Ⓗ

Friendly, family-owned inn and brewery that has deservedly won many local and national awards during its 22-year history. The excellent range and quality continue, now with eight Watermill beers brewed on site, and a new brewery and accommodation extension in progress. Two separate bars are served from a central counter, and viewing windows look into both the cellar and brewery. A wide selection of meals is served daily until 9pm, and dogs are provided with biscuits and water. ♨Q⚘◑🛢🍴🛢♣♠P'–🚆(555)

Kendal

Alexanders ⓛ

Castle Green Lane, LA9 6RG
✪ 12-11 ☎ (01539) 797017
Beer range varies Ⓗ

Set in the grounds of the Castle Green Hotel (a former electricity board regional headquarters), Alexanders occupies an older barn/stable block and, as a free house, offers up to four different Cumbrian beers, often including Bowness Bay, Kirkby Lonsdale and Hawkshead. A large conservatory provides comfortable seating, dining facilities and fine views over the extensive pub and hotel grounds, Kendal castle ruins and the distant fells. Q⚘🛏◑🛢♣P'–

Burgundy's Wine Bar

19 Lowther Street, LA9 4DH

✪ closed Mon; 11.30-3.30 (not Tue & Wed), 6.30-midnight; 11-midnight Sat; 7-11 Sun ☎ (01539) 733803

⊕ burgundyswinebar.co.uk

Beer range varies Ⓗ

Multi-level, town-centre bar, with a separate entrance to the brewhouse. It offers a fine selection of real ales – some brewed on site – as well as an above-average range of continental lagers, both draught and bottled. The street-level bar area has bench seating, upstairs is a mezzanine floor with tables and chairs and access to a patio, while downstairs is another room with access to the rear alleyway. The Cumbria Beer Challenge is hosted here prior to Easter each year.

❀⇌●'̲⊟(41,555)

Rifleman's Arms Ⓛ

4 Greenside, LA9 4LD

✪ 6.30 (4.30 Fri)-midnight; 12-midnight Sat & Sun ☎ (01539) 723224

Tetley Bitter; guest beers Ⓗ

A local community pub on the edge of town with the Vaux motif still etched on the windows. Numerous local groups meet here and it hosts a popular live folk music session on a Thursday evening. It is quiet and dog friendly, with a Sunday quiz and traditional pub games. There are always five real ales available – beers making regular appearances on the guest pumps include Abbot, Landlord and Doom Bar, along with many local ales. Q♣♣⊟(44,48)

Keswick

Dog & Gun Ⓛ

2 Lake Road, CA12 5BT (off Market Place)

✪ 12-11 ☎ (01768) 773463

Keswick Thirst Rescue; Theakston Old Peculier Ⓗ

Busy town-centre pub popular with locals and tourists. A changing selection of six real ales is on offer, including two from the nearby Keswick Brewing Company. The price list is clearly displayed at the bar and a chalkboard gives beer descriptions. The pub retains many original features, including the stone floor and low ceiling. Bar meals are served all day – Hungarian goulash is a house special. Food is also provided for well-behaved dogs. ⋈Q◖▲⊟(X4,X5,73)

Kirkby Lonsdale

Orange Tree Ⓛ

9 Fairbank, LA6 2BD

✪ 12-11 (midnight Fri & Sat) ☎ (01524) 271716

⊕ theorangetreehotel.co.uk

Kirkby Lonsdale Ruskin's Bitter, Radical Red, Monumental Blonde; guest beers Ⓗ

The Kirkby Lonsdale brewery tap is just up from the church in this lovely market town. Friendly, enthusiastic staff ensure a warm welcome here. The front bar has old photographs and rugby prints, and there is a separate cosy dining area to the rear of the bar where good wholesome meals are served, with most ingredients from local suppliers. Three Kirkby Lonsdale beers are always on, plus three guest ales from near and far.

⋈⅍≠◖▲♣●⊟(567)

Kirkoswald

Fetherston Arms

The Square, CA10 1DQ

✪ 12 (6 Tue)-11 ☎ (01768) 898284

Beer range varies Ⓗ

Comparatively new to the pub scene, the Fethers was once a small private hotel and then a restaurant, before incorporating the adjacent buildings to become a pub in its own right after the closure of the nearby Black Bull. Its commitment to real ale is borne out by the beer festival it regularly organises, bringing in enthusiasts from a wide area. It is situated in the centre of this historic village opposite the cobbled square where the market used to take place. ⋈❀≠◖▲♣●⊟

Lindal-in-Furness

Railway Inn Ⓛ

London Road, LA12 0LL

✪ 4-11 (midnight Fri & Sat); closed Tue; 12-7 Sun ☎ (01229) 462889

Yates Bitter; guest beers Ⓗ

A welcoming open-plan, single-room pub with a beamed ceiling and slate floor. At one end is a comfortable lounge area around a stone fireplace and open fire. Adding to the character is a centrally positioned bar made from old church pews, with up to five handpumps active, and a local beer always available. Food is served evenings (except Monday) and Sunday lunchtimes (booking advisable). Visitors are also welcome at the quiz night on Thursday. ⋈❀◖'̲⊟(6,6A)

Loppergarth

Wellington Ⓛ

Main Street, LA12 0JL (1 mile from A590 between Lindal and Pennington) SD260772

✪ 6-midnight (1am Fri & Sat) ☎ (01229) 582388

Beer range varies Ⓗ

Superb village local one mile from the A590. The pub has its own working microbrewery – a custom-made stainless steel plant which is viewable from the games room. Four handpumps primarily dispense beers brewed on the premises. These include a blonde, a golden bitter and a traditional darker best bitter. Wood-burning stoves make this a cosy pub, with games, books and good conversation. There is a quiz on alternate Saturdays. Dogs on leads are welcome. ⋈⅍❀♣●

Loweswater

Kirkstile Inn

CA13 0RU (off B5289, 5 miles from Cockermouth via Lorton) NY140210

✪ 10-11 ☎ (01900) 85219 ⊕ kirkstile.com

Cumbrian Legendary Gold, Grasmoor, Langdale, Esthwaite Ⓗ

A 17th-century inn with low ceilings and stone walls nestling between Loweswater and Crummock Water. It has a bar, two seating areas and a pleasant restaurant, and is the tap for Cumbrian Legendary Ales. With six handpumps, five beers are from its own brewery and one is a guest Cumbrian beer. Food is served lunchtimes and evenings and it can be busy with diners during peak times. An annual beer festival is held. Dogs are allowed but not between 6-10pm.

⋈Q⅍❀≠◖&P☰

Maryport

Lifeboat Inn
Shipping Brow, Senhouse Street, CA15 6AB
✪ 11 (12 Sun)-11 ☎ (01900) 814636
Cumbrian Legendary Langdale Bitter, Loweswater Gold; Jennings Bitter, Cocker Hoop 🅷
Small but cosy bar with a log fire and a large function room upstairs. From the outside seating there are stunning views across the harbour to Scotland. Four handpumps dispense local cask ales and both these and the good selection of meals are reasonably priced. An annual World's Biggest Vegetable competition is held here and there are weekly Mexican and curry nights. ⚄🏠🌸◑ À≈🗖🖳

Melmerby

Shepherds Inn 🄻
CA10 1HF (9 miles from Penrith on A686)
✪ 12-11 (midnight Fri & Sat) ☎ (01768) 881439
⊕ shepherdsinnmelmerby.co.uk
Beer range varies 🅷
A red sandstone pub dating from 1789 nestling at the foot of the Pennine Way Fells and on the edge of the village green. An adjacent barn has been incorporated, resulting in differing floor levels, with the main bar on the lowest level. Melmerby is an attractive village on one of the world's most scenic drives, the A686 from the North East to the Lakes. Food is locally sourced and available all day. A favourite with tourists, walkers, hikers, cyclists, drivers and bike enthusiasts. ⚄🏠🌸◑ 🖴À♣Pᴸ

Near Sawrey

Tower Bank Arms 🄻
LA22 0LF (on B5285 2 miles S of Hawkshead) SD370956
✪ 11-11; 12-10.30 Sun ☎ (01539) 436334
⊕ towerbankarms.co.uk
Barngates Cat Nap; Cumbrian Legendary Loweswater Gold; Hawkshead Bitter, Brodie's Prime; guest beers 🅷
All the features of a 17th-century Lakeland inn are to be found here: slate floor, oak beams and an open fire in the range. Its location next to Hill Top, the former home of Beatrix Potter, means it can become busy at peak holiday times. Food of a very high standard is served in the bar and the restaurant, and children and dogs are made most welcome. All beers are sourced locally. Afternoon opening in winter may be variable; phone to check. ⚄Q🌸🖾◑♣◑Pᴸ🖳

Nether Wasdale

Strands 🄻
CA20 1ET NY125039
✪ 11-11; 12-10.30 Sun ☎ (01946) 762237
⊕ strandshotel.co.uk
Strands Pied Piper, Errmmm..., T'Errmmm-inator, Bersteinale, Fruits de Lune 🅷
A hotel at the entrance to the Wasdale Valley voted as having Britain's Best View, with vistas of Wastwater and England's highest mountain. It was built around 1800 as a hotel and post house; the hotel has always been a centre of local life. It has its own microbrewery and holds an annual beer festival in May. Bottles of beers in a range of styles, all brewed and bottled on the premises, can be bought here. Free Wi-Fi is available. Dogs on leads are welcome. ⚄Q🌸🖾◑ Àᴾᴸ

Oxenholme

Station Inn
LA9 7RF
✪ 12-midnight (11 Sun) ☎ (01539) 724094
Black Sheep Best Bitter; Hawkshead Bitter; Moorhouse's Pride of Pendle, Blond Witch 🅷
Originally a farmhouse on the edge of Kendal, in a beautiful rural setting, it lies near the main line railway station. Outside there is a large garden complete with crazy golf and a large children's play area. The extensive menu has many locally sourced ingredients, along with daily specials. The inn is close to one of the Coast-to-Coast cycle routes and there is hard standing for caravans on site. ⚄Q🌸🖾◑ 🖴À≈♣Pᴸ🖳(108)

Parkside

Parkside Hotel
Parkside Road, CA25 5HF; 11.30-3 (only), 6-10.30 Sun
☎ (01946) 811001 ⊕ parksidehotelcumbria.co.uk
Beer range varies 🅷
Hotel with good cask ales well kept by an enthusiastic landlord. Quirky furnishing and decor abound, but there is always a warm welcome from the landlord's dog as well as the staff. Traditional food is served every evening, but lunches only on Sunday. Convenient for the Coast-to-Coast route, both for walkers and cyclists. Dogs are welcome on leads. 🌸🖾◑Pᴸ🖳(31,31A)

Penrith

Agricultural Hotel 🍺 🄻
Castlegate, CA11 7JE (close to railway station)
✪ 11-11; 12-10.30 Sun ☎ (01768) 862622
⊕ the-agricultural-hotel.co.uk
Jennings Bitter, Cumberland Ale, Sneck Lifter; guest beers 🅷
The hotel is built from local sandstone and the bar and dining room are open plan, with steps from one to the other. There is also a small reception area. It has a Victorian shuttered bar of sash screens with six handpumps selling Jennings and guest beers. Food is served in the large dining area, as well as in the bar at quiet times. Very convenient for the railway station and nearby bus stops. Local CAMRA Pub of the Year 2013. ⚄Q🌸🖾◑♿≈♣Pᴸ🖳

Royal 🄻
92 Wilson Row, CA11 7PZ
✪ 12-midnight; 11-1am Sat ☎ (01768) 862670
Beer range varies 🅷
Traditional pub on the edge of the town centre with tiled walls and lots of mellow wood. It has three separate areas served by one bar. Two handpumps offer beers from all over the UK, featuring LocAles and beers from Cumbrian brewers. It is home to darts, dominoes and pool teams, and there is full sports TV coverage. Live music sessions with a broad appeal are held on Sunday afternoons outwith the football season. Food is served Saturday and Sunday 12-5pm, Monday-Thursday 5-8.30pm (no food on Friday). ⚄◑♿≈♣ᴸ🖳(104)

Rydal

Glen Rothay Hotel (Badger Bar) 🄻
LA22 9LR

✪ 11-11 (10.30 Sun) ☎ (01539) 434500
⊕ theglenrothay.co.uk
Beer range varies Ⓗ
The roadside entrance leads into the bar area with its plinth-mounted handpumps serving beers from, mainly, Cumbrian brewers. The adjoining Oak Room has fine panelling and an elaborate fireplace with an impressive dated overmantel. This venue has won several awards for environmental awareness, with local suppliers used for most food purchases. Badgers can often be seen in the grounds of an evening.
🏚Q🕏🐾🍴◑♣P⌑🚆(555,599)

St Bees

Manor House
11-12 Main Street, CA27 0DE
✪ 11-11 (10.30 Sun) ☎ (01946) 820587
⊕ manorhousestbees.co.uk
Beer range varies Ⓗ
A dog-friendly and hospitable country inn in the heart of the beautiful seaside village of St Bees. It features a bar with pool table, dartboard, jukebox and TV. Food is served at lunchtimes and evenings in the adjacent lounge bar. To the rear is a private beer garden, outside to the front is a popular seating area. Four changing cask ales from all over the country are available all year. It is an ideal start to the Coast-to-Coast walk.
🕏🍴◑ 🛏🚆P🚆(20,X6)

Seathwaite

Newfield Inn Ⓛ
LA20 6ED (6 miles N of Broughton) SD228960
✪ 11-11 ☎ (01229) 716208 ⊕ newfieldinn.co.uk
Jennings Cumberland Ale; Cumberland Corby Ale; Cumbrian Legendary Esthwaite Bitter Ⓗ
A 17th-century free house in the Duddon Valley, Wordsworth's favourite area, and an oasis for fell walkers and travellers passing through. Note the unique banded slate floor in the bar. Good food is served all day and steaks are a speciality. The spacious beer garden has excellent views towards the Coniston Fells. The pub is a venue for the Broughton Festival of Beer held each autumn.
🏚Q🕏🍴◑ Å♣P⌑

Sedbergh

Red Lion
Finkle Street, LA10 5BZ
✪ 11.30-2, 6-11.30; 11.30-3, 6-12.30am Fri; 11.30-midnight Sat & Sun ☎ (015394) 620433 ⊕ theredlionsedbergh.co.uk
Jennings Cockle Warmer; guest beers Ⓗ
Town-centre pub popular with the locals, opposite the parish church of St Andrews, serving a wide range of beers from the Marston's group of breweries. The open-plan bar area has several quiet areas and an open fire, complete with free Wi-Fi. Fresh local produce is used in many of the items on the good-value menu (no food on Mon).
🏚🕏◑ Å♣⌑🚆

Staveley

Beer Hall Ⓛ
Mill Yard, LA8 9LR
✪ 12-6 (5 Mon); 12-11 Fri & Sat; 12-8 Sun ☎ (01539) 825260
⊕ hawksheadbrewery.co.uk

Hawkshead Bitter, Red, Lakeland Gold, Brodie's Prime, Windermere Pale, seasonal beers Ⓗ
The brewery tap to the next-door brewery, the building has two storeys; on both floors there is a mix of comfy sofas and solid wooden furniture. The food menu has been developed to complement Hawkshead beers. Spring and summer beer festivals are held, with up to 60 beers to sample. The beer shop has a fantastic display of bottled Hawkshead and foreign beers. CAMRA members and train users get a 10 per cent discount.
Q🕏◑🍴🐾♣P🚆(555)

Eagle & Child Ⓛ
Kendal Road, LA8 9LP
✪ 11.30 (11 Sat & Sun)-11.30 ☎ (01539) 821320
⊕ eaglechildinn.co.uk
Hawkshead Bitter; guest beers Ⓗ
In winter there are log fires to keep you warm and in summer riverside tables and a garden to enjoy. The pub has an interesting range of artefacts around the walls. Regular beer festivals are held in a marquee next to the River Kent, complementing the range of beers in the pub. There are great lunchtime food deals including a two course Sunday lunch, and an entertaining Thursday evening quiz, which make this a popular pub with locals and visitors alike. 🏚🕏🍴◑ 🛏♣P⌑🚆(555)

Strawberry Bank

Masons Arms Ⓛ
Cartmel Fell, LA11 6NW SD413895
✪ 11.30-11; 12-10.30 Sun ☎ (01539) 568486
⊕ strawberrybank.com
Hawkshead Bitter; Thwaites Wainwright; guest beers Ⓗ
Owned by the Individual Inns group, this picturesque pub is set on a hillside, with spectacular views across the Winster Valley. Two solid fuel ranges and three seating areas provide a cosy atmosphere in winter, while the outdoor seating and dining area is an idyllic location on a warm sunny day. Dogs are welcome in the garden only. The pub is popular with walkers and the local community alike. 🏚Q⛵🕏🍴◑♣P⌑

Talkin

Blacksmiths Arms Ⓛ
CA8 1LE
✪ 12-3, 6-11 ☎ (01697) 73452 ⊕ blacksmithstalkin.co.uk
Black Sheep Best Bitter; Cumberland Corby Bitter; Geltsdale Brampton Bitter; Yates Bitter Ⓗ
Since taking over in 1997, the present owners have made this probably the most popular pub in the vicinity. The winning formula includes four real ales, a superbly stocked bar, friendly efficient staff, no TV and meticulous attention to detail. With a golf course and country park within two miles and plenty of other outdoor activities available locally, being on the edge of an Area of Outstanding Natural Beauty, the pub attracts visitors from far outside the north Cumbria area.
🏚Q🕏🍴◑🛏Å♣P⌑

Tallentire

Bush Inn
CA13 0PT
✪ closed Mon; 5.30-11.30; 12-2, 7-11 Sun
☎ (01900) 823707

Beer range varies Ⓗ
Sympathetically decorated but airy and not over-fussy, this venue represents a good mix of the modern and traditional. It is noted for the quality of both its beer and its food. The interesting selection of guest beers is usually from the north of England and Scotland, often featuring the landlord's favoured styles of golden and pale ale, with at least one from any of the Cumbrian breweries. It is in a charming small village setting, with an unassuming exterior. ⚲Q🕭🌶♣P🖵(58)

Torver

Church House Inn Ⓛ

LA21 8AZ (2 miles SW of Coniston near jct of A593/A5084) SD285942
✪ 12-midnight ☎ (01539) 441282
⊕ churchhouseinntorver.com
Barngates Tag Lag; Coniston Bluebird; Cumbrian Legendary Loweswater Gold; guest beers Ⓗ
Offering good-quality food in the bar and dining room, and a friendly welcome, this unspoilt 14th-century inn features low beams, flagged floors and a magnificent open fire. It is a welcome sight whether you have just walked up Coniston Old Man or simply come in search of a fine pint (there are up to five to choose from) and a bit of craic with the locals. Occasional live folk music plays at weekends. The garden boasts a great view of the surrounding fells. ⚲Q🕭🛏🕭🖐🌶♣P🖵(X12)

Ulverston

Devonshire Arms Ⓛ

Braddyll Terrace, Victoria Road, LA12 0DH
✪ 4-11; 12-midnight Fri & Sat; 12-11 Sun ☎ (01229) 582537
Beer range varies Ⓗ
Situated between bus and train stations (adjacent to the railway bridge), the Dev is a large single-room pub. Distinct areas are formed by the use of comfortable bench seating. Two TVs show major sporting events, and there is a jukebox, as well as pool, darts and dominoes. This is a real locals' pub, where all are welcome. Six handpumps serve superb ales from near and far. A beer festival is held on the May Day weekend. ⏚🕭🖐🌶♣P🖵

Farmers Arms

Market Place, LA12 7BB
✪ 9.30am-11 (midnight Fri & Sat); 9.30am-10.30 Sun
☎ (01229) 584469 ⊕ thefarmers-ulverston.co.uk
Beer range varies Ⓗ
Smart, busy, centrally located pub with a heated, covered terrace at the front. Six beers are available along with a good selection of wines. This local opens early for breakfast and coffee, with quality meals served lunchtimes and evenings (see blackboards over the fireplace for daily specials). There is a raised area to the rear that is mainly for diners. Meals can be also taken in the comfortable bar, although this can get busy at weekends. Quiz night, Thursday, is always well attended. 🕭🖐🌶🖵

Mill Ⓛ

Mill Street, LA12 7EB
✪ 11-11 (1am Fri & Sat); 11-10.30 Sun ☎ (01229) 581384
⊕ mill-at-ulverston.co.uk
Lancaster Amber, Blonde, Black, Red; guest beers Ⓗ
With a town-centre location near the top end of King Street, the Mill has an interesting and

characterful layout over the various floors, centred around a restored original waterwheel. The main bar has 10 handpulls, dispensing six guest beers alongside the Lancaster Brewery range. There is a first floor outdoor patio area with seating, and picnic tables to the front. Quality food is popular, served in the bar and in an upstairs restaurant (booking recommended). Live music plays and the pub holds occasional beer festivals. 🕭🖐🖐🖐🌶♣🖵

Stan Laurel Inn Ⓛ

The Ellers, LA12 0AB
✪ 7-11 Mon; 12-2.30, 6-11 (midnight Thu-Sat); 12-11.30 Sun
☎ (01229) 582814 ⊕ thestanlaurel.co.uk
Thwaites Original; guest beers Ⓗ
Just off the centre of Stan Laurel's home town, the Stan offers a warm welcome to locals and visitors alike. Six handpulls serve a variety of mainly locally brewed beers. Excellent-value quality food is available throughout the week (no food Mon). Adjacent to the bar is a large room with pool and darts and a smaller room primarily used by diners. In winter a log-burning stove adds to the pub's comfortable ambience. Well-behaved dogs are welcome. 🕭🛏🖐🌶♣P🖵

Swan Inn Ⓛ

Swan Street, LA12 7JX
✪ 3.30-11; 12-midnight Fri & Sat; 12-11 Sun
☎ (01229) 582519
Beer range varies Ⓗ
Easily accessed, just off the town centre, the Swan offers up to 10 real ales, many rare for the area, sourced from near and far, encompassing all styles and strengths. There are always beers from both Hawkshead and Yates. A single bar serves three drinking areas, one with a real fire. Sunday is quiz night and there is poker on Wednesdays. Occasional beer festivals take place in a large marquee in the garden, with all beers on handpull. ⚲🕭🖐🌶♣●🖵(6,6A,X35)

Underbarrow

Punch Bowl Inn Ⓛ

LA8 8HQ
✪ 12-3, 4 (6 Thu)-11; 12-11 Sat & Sun ☎ (01539) 568234
⊕ the-punchbowl.co.uk
Beer range varies Ⓗ
Traditional village inn on a scenic route between Kendal and Windermere Lake. The flagstone-floored main bar includes big leather sofas around an inglenook fireplace. The pub is popular with locals, walkers and their dogs, and those who love good beer with food. There are separate dining and function rooms. Happy hour is 4-7pm each Wednesday, and a beer festival in a marquee in the grounds takes place in the early summer (see website for details). ⚲Q🌶🕭🖐🌶♣P

Waberthwaite

Brown Cow Ⓛ

LA19 5YJ (on A595) SD106932
✪ 11.30-1am; 12-midnight Sun ☎ (01229) 717243
⊕ thebrowncowinn.com
Hawkshead Bitter; Lancaster Amber; Moorhouse's Pride of Pendle Ⓗ
Popular 100-year-old Cumbrian village pub offering up to seven interesting and frequently changing real ales, usually from Cumbrian and north

Lancashire breweries, and always a cider. Meals use locally sourced food. There is occasional live music, regular quiz nights, and annual beer festivals in June and October. The Western Fells and Eskmeals Nature Reserve are close by. A former winner of local CAMRA branch awards.
ᴁᏝ✿╅◑▯♿Å♣♠P'─▯🖳(6X)

Wasdale Head

Wasdale Head Inn ᒻ

CA20 1EX (at head of Wasdale, 9 miles from A595) SD186087
✪ 10 (12 Sun)-11 ☎ (019467) 726229 ⊕ wasdale.com
Beer range varies Ⓗ
Used by travellers for 200 years, coming from Black Sail, Sty Head and Burnmoor passes to ply their trade, this pub lies in Wasdale Head, birthplace of climbing, famed for England's highest mountain, deepest lake, smallest church and biggest liar. Walkers, climbers, dirty boots and dogs are welcome in Ritson's Bar. A range of seven beers, mostly Cumbrian, is on sale. Drink in summer by the Mosedale Beck, or relax in winter by the log-burning stove. Hot drinks and pub food are available all day. ᴁQ✿╅◑▯⚓Å♣♠P'─

Wetheral

Wheatsheaf ᒻ

CA4 8HD
✪ 12-11 (midnight Fri & Sat) ☎ (01228) 560686
⊕ wheatsheafwetheral.co.uk
Cumberland Corby Bitter; guest beers Ⓗ
The Wheatsheaf is a short walk up the hill from the village green in this picturesque village near to the River Eden. This venue, originally three separate rooms now knocked into one, with a central bar, is very much a local and supported by those living nearby. It offers one regular beer from the nearest brewery and another, Wheatsheaf Ale, from a different local brewery. There is a beer garden and ample parking. ᴁ✿◑▯⇄♣P'─🖳(75)

Whitehaven

Globe

Main Street, Hensingham, CA28 8QX
✪ 5 (12 Sat & Sun)-11 ☎ (01946) 590772
⊕ theglobehensingham.co.uk
Beer range varies Ⓗ
A traditional local with a friendly, welcoming atmosphere. Two TVs show sports – mainly football – but they are not overly intrusive. Two handpumps serve a varied choice of beers, with Cumbrian breweries always well represented. Reasonably priced, traditional food is served each evening and Sunday lunchtime. The pub has recently been refurbished, creating a separate dining area upstairs. Customers can use the car park of sister pub the Lowther Arms, which is about 400 yards down the road. ᴁᏝ✿◑▯P'─🖳(30)

Windermere

Elleray Hotel

2-6 Cross Street, LA23 1AE
✪ 12-11 (midnight Fri & Sat) ☎ (01539) 488464
⊕ elleraywindermere.co.uk
Copper Dragon Golden Pippin; Cumbrian Legendary Loweswater Gold; Jennings Cumberland; guest beers Ⓗ
A friendly pub close to the town centre with a large main bar and separate restaurant. Four real ales are served throughout the year, with a stronger guest beer usually available during the winter months. Live music is performed most weekends, and an acoustic session is held on the first Tuesday of the month. The large beer garden is a suntrap during the summer months. Dogs are welcome in the bar. A member of the CAMRA discount scheme.
ᴁ✿╅◑▯⚓'─🖳

Winster

Brown Horse Inn ᒻ

LA23 3NR (on A5074)
✪ 12-11 ☎ (01539) 443443 ⊕ thebrownhorseinn.co.uk
Winster Valley Dark Horse, Chaser, Hurdler, Old School Bitter; guest beers Ⓗ
Traditional rural inn with its own microbrewery, where the four handpumps usually serve the pub's own beers. The interior comprises a main bar with open beams, large tables and a log fire, and a separate restaurant area, but meals are served throughout the day in both areas. Local eggs and potatoes are available to buy over the bar. Beware: the brewery's Lakes Lager is keg. The outside seating area offers spectacular views of the surrounding countryside. Q✿╅◑▯⚓P'─

Wreay

Plough Inn ᒻ

Wreay, CA4 0RL (5 miles S of Carlisle, W of A6, 3 miles from jct 42 of the M6) NY436490
✪ closed Mon & Tue; 12-2.30 (not Sun), 6-11
☎ (01697) 475770 ⊕ wreayplough.co.uk
Cumberland Corby Ale; guest beers Ⓗ
Five miles from the centre of Carlisle in a small, peaceful village, this pub is a real gem. Dating from 1786, the venue continues to be the traditional meeting place for the village guardians, the 12 men of Wreay – look for the display of their clay pipes. With a reputation for excellent food – locally sourced where possible – it is on two levels, with the main entrance and bar on the ground floor and dining tables down a few steps. Q✿◑▯⚓P

Yanwath

Gate Inn

CA10 2LF
✪ 12-11 (10.30 Sun) ☎ (01768) 862386
⊕ yanwathgate.com
Beer range varies Ⓗ
Cosy pub in a village three miles south of Penrith with an intimate bar, an open fire and candles on the tables. This Cumbrian dining pub affords a warm welcome to everyone and their dogs. Drinkers can sample three different local ales and some uncommon foreign beers on draught. A superb wine list includes 12 served by the glass. There is a lovely beer garden and a well-appointed self-catering cottage. ᴁᏝ✿◑▯♣♠P'─🖳(108)

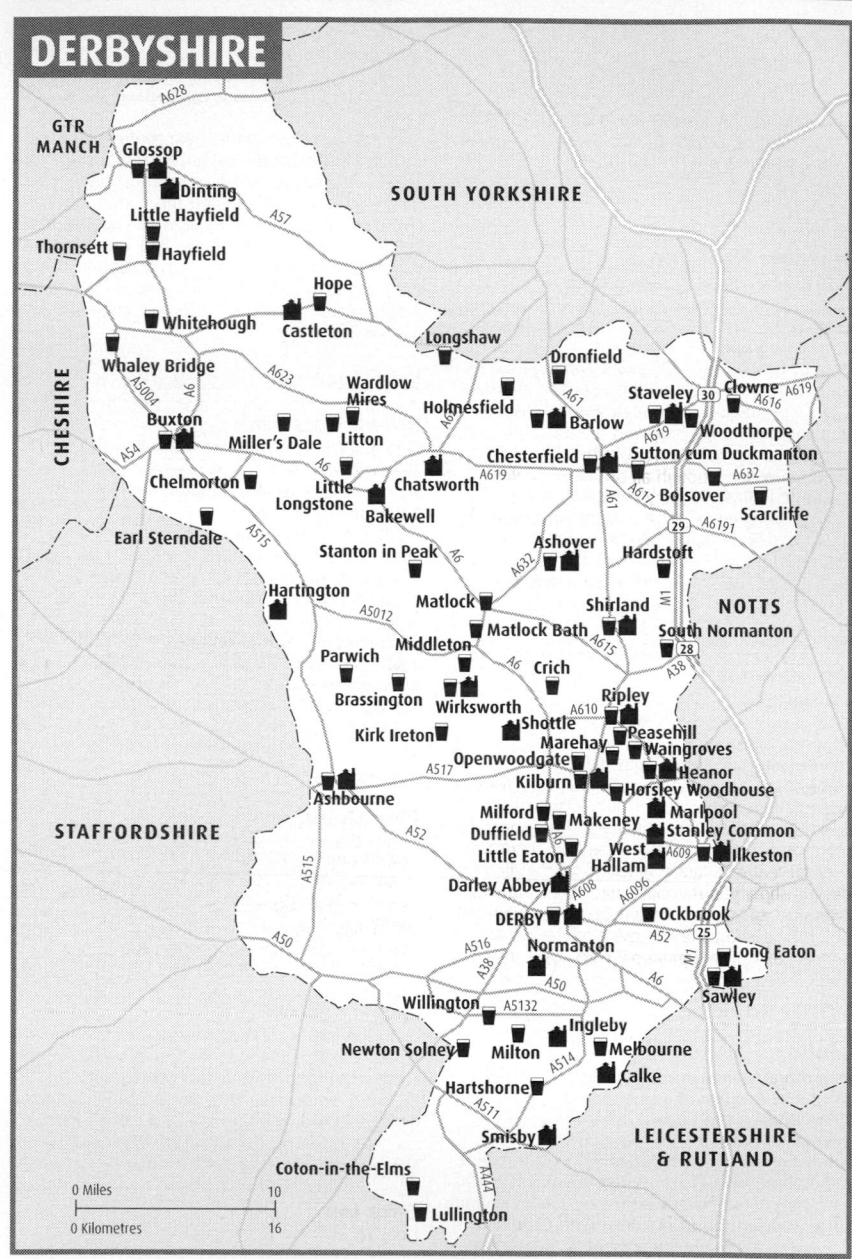

DERBYSHIRE

GTR MANCH

Glossop
Dinting
Little Hayfield
Thornsett
Hayfield

SOUTH YORKSHIRE

Hope
Whitehough
Castleton
Longshaw
Dronfield

CHESHIRE

Whaley Bridge
Wardlow Mires
Holmesfield
Staveley
Clowne
Buxton
Barlow
Woodthorpe
Miller's Dale
Litton
Chesterfield
Sutton cum Duckmanton
Chelmorton
Little Longstone
Chatsworth
Bolsover
Scarcliffe
Bakewell
Earl Sterndale
Stanton in Peak
Ashover
Hardstoft
Hartington
Matlock
Shirland
NOTTS
Matlock Bath
South Normanton
Middleton
Parwich
Crich
Brassington
Wirksworth
Ripley
Kirk Ireton
Shottle
Peasehill
Marehay
Waingroves
Openwoodgate
Heanor
Kilburn
Horsley Woodhouse
Ashbourne
Milford
Marlpool
STAFFORDSHIRE
Duffield
Makeney
Stanley Common
Little Eaton
West Hallam
Ilkeston
Darley Abbey
DERBY
Ockbrook
Normanton
Long Eaton
Willington
Sawley
Ingleby
Newton Solney
Milton
Melbourne
Hartshorne
Calke
Smisby
LEICESTERSHIRE & RUTLAND
Coton-in-the-Elms
Lullington

0 Miles 10
0 Kilometres 16

Ashbourne

Smith's Tavern ♀

36 St John's Sreet, DE6 1GH (on one-way section of A515 heading N through town) SK1806246737

✪ 12-midnight (11 Sun) ☎ (01335) 300809

Brakspear Oxford Gold; Jenning's Cumberland Ale; Marston's Pedigree; Ringwood Fortyniner Ⓗ
Pub with a narrow frontage, but with three rooms one behind the other, the rearmost of which can be used for meetings. It is especially popular for the range of carefully kept ales which includes a changing freely selected local ale as a guest at the weekend. It was local CAMRA Pub of the Year for

2013. Parking is in the town square opposite or in Shaw Croft car park behind the pub. (Access to the pub from front door only.) Q☒

Ashover

Old Poets' Corner ♀ Ⓛ

Butts Road, S45 0EW (downhill from church)
✪ 12-11 ☎ (01246) 590888 ⊕ oldpoets.co.uk

Ashover Light Rale, Poet's Tipple; guest beers Ⓗ
The home of Ashover Brewery, this mock-Tudor building has a warm, welcoming atmosphere, with open fires, candlelit tables and hop-strewn beams. Choose from 10 handpumps, including regular

Ashover beers, along with a range of guest ales, six traditional ciders, draught and bottled Belgian beers, and country wines. Entertainment includes live music, a weekly quiz, folk evenings and three beer festivals a year. Dogs are welcome. This winner of local CAMRA Pub of the Year 2013 is in a well-pubbed, highly attractive village.
ᴹᴬQ✿🛏🕩❑🖤♣♠Pᴸ⚷(63,64)

Barlow

Hare & Hounds 🅛
Commonside Road, S18 7SJ (from B6051, turn up hill at Commonside Rd)
☼1 (12 Sat & Sun)-11 ☎ (0114) 289 0464
Barlow Heath Robinson, Three Valleys IPA; guest beers 🅗
Friendly, traditional village pub with three rooms around a central bar, plus a separate games room. The tap for Barlow Brewery, this pub has a strong community feel, though all are made welcome. In summer, Barlow Brewery's Carnival Ale is very popular. Views over the village to the countryside can be enjoyed from the back room. A tiny terrace area with colourful window boxes and planters is to the front of the pub. The landlord has been here for over 30 years. ᴹᴬ✿🖫♣P⚷(89,89A)

Bolsover

Blue Bell
57 High Street, S44 6HF
☼12-3.30, 5-midnight; 12-3, 7-midnight Sun
☎ (01246) 823508 ⊕ bolsover.uk.com
Marston's Burton Bitter; Wychwood Hobgoblin; guest beers 🅗
Situated 200 yards from Bolsover Castle and built in 1749, this historic pub still retains many of its original features. Speak nicely to the landlord and he will show you the old stable and coachman's quarters. This venue is a traditional two-roomed pub where you can rediscover the art of conversation. The panoramic view from the beer garden is spectacular, and excellent food is served lunchtimes and evenings. Q⛵✿🕩🖫♣Pᴸ⚷

Fidlers Rest 🅛
Craggs Road, S44 6BQ (just off A632, Bolsover Hill)
☼5 (12 Sat & Sun)-11 ☎ (01246) 828300
Beer range varies 🅗
Built as a private residence in 1812 by Peter Fidler, the famous explorer who mapped the Canadian wilderness for the Hudson Bay Company. Guest beers are sourced mainly from local micros plus regular ales from Northumbria and Yorkshire. The modern interior has fine views over Bolsover Castle and the Peak District. Q✿♣ᴸ⚷

Brassington

Miner's Arms
Miner's Hill, DE4 4HJ
☼5-11 Mon; 12-3, 5-midnight; 12-midnight Fri-Sun
☎ (01629) 540222 ⊕ minersarmsbrassington.co.uk
Banks's Sunbeam; Marston's Pedigree; guest beers 🅗
Early 18th-century pub set in the centre of a pretty limestone village. A large open fire partially separates the bar area from the lounge in the low-beamed, long single room, and a warm welcome is extended to visitors and dogs. There is a small patio area to the rear with views across the rooftops and beyond. Up to four guest beers are available from the Marston's range. Good-value home-cooked food is served (no food Sun or Mon eves). ᴹᴬ✿🛏🕩♣🖤Pᴸ

Buxton

Ramsay's Bar
Buckingham Hotel, 1 Burlington Road, SK17 9AS
☼2 (4 Fri; 5 Mon-Thu)-11; 1-11 Sun ☎ (01298) 70481
⊕ buckinghamhotel.co.uk
Howard Town Longendale Lights; Thornbridge Kipling; guest beers 🅗
Public bar located within a hotel named after local artist George Ramsay and offering the widest selection of beers from microbreweries in Buxton. Selected ales are discounted daily during 'Hoppy Hour' (5-8pm but later on Sun & Mon). Occasional sports events are shown on TV. Well-behaved dogs are welcome in the bar. ✿🛏🕩🖫▲🚻P⚷(58,118)

Swan
40 High Street, SK17 6HB
☼11-1am ☎ (01298) 23278
Morland Old Speckled Hen; Tetley Bitter; guest beers 🅗

INDEPENDENT BREWERIES

Amber Ripley
Ashover Ashover
Barlow Barlow
Black Iris Derby
Bottle Brook Kilburn
Brampton Chesterfield
Brunswick Derby
Bumpmill Shirland (NEW)
Buxton Buxton
Coppice Side Heanor
Dancing Duck Derby
Derby Derby
Derventio Darley Abbey
Falstaff Derby: Normanton
Globe Glossop
Hartshorns Derby
Haywood Bad Ram Ashbourne
Hope Valley Castleton
Howard Town Glossop
John Thompson Ingleby
Leadmill Heanor
Leatherbritches Smisby
Marlpool Marlpool
Middle Earth Derby
Mouselow Farm Dinting (NEW)
Mr Grundy's Derby
Muirhouse Ilkeston
North Star Ilkeston
Nutbrook Stanley Common/West Hallam
Old Sawley Sawley (NEW)
Peak Ales Chatsworth
Raw Staveley
Rowditch Derby
Shiny Derby (NEW)
Shottle Farm Shottle
Spire Staveley
Tap House Smisby
Thornbridge Bakewell
Tollgate Calke
Townes Staveley
Wentwell Derby
Whim Hartington
Wirksworth Wirksworth

A hostelry that prides itself on being a drinkers' pub, with a friendly, welcoming atmosphere. The comfortable three rooms are served by a central bar; TVs in two rooms show major sports events. The seasonal Storm beer changes regularly and the pub is home to thriving darts and dominoes teams. There is a pub car park at the rear and also large public car parking nearby. ⬤≉♣P🖫

Wye Bridge House

Fairfield Road, SK17 7DJ
⬤ 8-midnight (1am Fri & Sat) ☎ (01298) 70932
Greene King Abbot; Ruddles Best Bitter; Wychwood Hobgoblin; guest beers Ⓗ
Wetherspoon pub in the former Midland Railway Hotel with a deserved reputation for serving an excellent selection of up to five guest beers in addition to two real ciders on draught. Occasional beer festivals and brewery trips are organised. The extensive outdoor patio area is popular in summer. The car park is small but a public car park is situated a short walk away. Q🕭⛄🕭⬤≉♦P🖫(199)

Chelmorton

Church Inn

Main Street, SK17 9SL
⬤ 12-3.30, 6-11; 12-midnight Fri-Sun ☎ (01298) 85319
Adnams Southwold Bitter; Marston's Burton Bitter, Pedigree; guest beers Ⓗ
Set in beautiful surroundings opposite the local church, this traditional village pub caters both for locals and walkers. The main room is laid out for dining and good home-cooked food is on offer; however, a cosy pub atmosphere is maintained, with a low ceiling and real fire. Guest beers are usually from local micros. Parking is available at the end of the road in front of the pub and there is a patio area outside. Monday is quiz night and accommodation is available. ⚑Q🕭🐾⬤♣♣

Chesterfield

Chesterfield Arms Ⓛ

Newbold Road, S41 7PH
⬤ 12-11 ☎ (01246) 236634
Everards Sunchaser; Fuller's London Pride; Leatherbritches CAD, Bounder; guest beers Ⓗ
A real ale emporium, this welcoming, family-run pub offers a selection of 10 beers, augmented by six ciders. Panelled walls, open fires and hop-strewn beams create a relaxing ambience. A log-burning stove heats the barn area, open weekends, serving additional ales. A large conservatory has just been added. Monday is pie and peas night, with a quiz on Wednesday and a curry night Thursday. Live music is on the last Thursday of the month. Highly placed in the East & West Midlands Best (GBPA) cellar award, and local CAMRA Pub of the Year 2012. ⚑🐾≉♦P꜒🖫(10)

Derby Tup Ⓛ

387 Sheffield Road, Whittington Moor, S41 8LS
⬤ 12-3 (not Wed), 5-11; 12-midnight Fri-Sun
☎ (01246) 454316
Castle Rock Harvest Pale, Screech Owl; guest beers Ⓗ
Ten handpumps offer beers from near and far with a stout or porter usually available, as well as Westons Old Rosie cider. The main bar has a real fire, a variety of wooden settles and etched glass windows dating from its original incarnation as the Brunswick Hotel. There is also a small snug. The pub is popular with followers of Chesterfield FC whose stadium is close by. Dogs are welcome, and quiz night is on Thursday. ⚑🐾♦🖫(43,50)

Rose & Crown Ⓛ

104 Old Road, Brampton, S40 2QT
⬤ 12-11 (midnight Fri & Sat) ☎ (01246) 563750
🌐 roseandcrownbrampton.co.uk
Brampton Golden Bud, Best, Wasp Nest, seasonal beers; Everards Tiger; guest beers Ⓗ
Everards' Project William's triumphant renovation of a run-down local enabled the Brampton Brewery to open its first tied house. A compact snug provides room for groups, while the main room has plenty of quiet corners. Memorabilia from the original brewery festoon the walls. Good-value food is served, including local award-winning produce. Quiz night is Tuesday, and jazz features on the first Sunday (afternoon), and a music quiz on the last Sunday of the month. A rear drinking area can be accessed through the pub. Free Wi-Fi is available. ⚑🐾🕭♣♦P꜒🖫(170)

Rutland Arms Ⓛ

16 Stephenson Place, S40 1XL
⬤ 11.30-11.30 (12.30am Thu-Sat); 12-11 Sun
☎ (01246) 205857
Greene King Abbot; Sharp's Doom Bar; Thornbridge Jaipur IPA; guest beers Ⓗ
In the shadow of the famous Crooked Spire parish church, the Rutland is a traditional pub in an area of clubs and bars. The pub is distinguishable by its castellated roof line and, inside, it has two areas divided by steps, with subdued lighting and wooden panelling. As well as the regular beers, there are five guests, including ales from local breweries. Westons Old Rosie is available, together with three other varying ciders. Families are welcome at meal times. ⚑🕭≉♦꜒🖫

Spa Lane Vaults

34 St Mary's Gate, S41 7TH
⬤ 8-11 (midnight Thu-Sat) ☎ (01246) 246300
Greene King Abbot; Ruddles Best Bitter; Wychwood Hobgoblin; guest beers Ⓗ
For many years known as the Phoenix Hotel, the building was converted by Wetherspoon 12 years ago. The interior is spacious and modern, divided into separate areas. There is air-conditioning and a patio area to the rear. Beers from near and far are available as well as a range of ciders. The pub is centrally located, close to the Crooked Spire parish church. Public parking is close by. 🕭🐾🕭≉♦꜒🖫

Tramway Tavern Ⓛ

192 Chatsworth Road, Brampton, S40 2AT
⬤ 4-11; 12-midnight Fri & Sat; 12-11 Sun ☎ (01246) 200111
Brampton Golden Bud, Best, seasonal beers; guest beers Ⓗ
Situated on the Brampton Mile, this is the Brampton Brewery tap. There are eight handpulls on the bar, four Brampton beers, one Everards and three changing guests. There is a bring your vinyl night every Wednesday, and a monthly music jam night on Sunday. A selection of Belgian and world beers is available, along with traditional ciders and perries. One area is dedicated to pictures and history of the old tram service that once passed by this hostelry's doorway. There is an outdoor courtyard to the rear. Free Wi-Fi available. ⚑🐾♦꜒🖫

White Swan Ⓛ

St Mary's Gate, S41 7TJ

✪ 12-midnight (1am Fri & Sat) ☎ (01246) 229570

Raw Mucky Duck; guest beers Ⓗ

The White Swan is a contemporary twist on a traditional pub. This Raw Brewing Company tied house opened in 2012 offering 12 cask ales, including house beer Mucky Duck and a wide range of local and national guest beers. There is an impressive bottled beer selection as well as real ciders. A large screen can be found upstairs in the function room. Great-tasting home-made food is available all day Monday to Saturday and Sunday lunchtimes, including a roast. Sit, relax and enjoy.

🐕◑♿⇌●ᴸ

Clowne

Clowne Community Centre Ⓛ

Recreation Close, Villa Park, S43 4PL

✪ 7-11 ☎ (01246) 819546

Beer range varies Ⓗ

A council-run community centre widely used by the locals for functions. The Rock & Blues Club has live bands every Sunday and there is a popular quiz night on Tuesday, with free food. The place is well cared for, with a relaxed and friendly atmosphere, and it has a beer festival in May. There is a Timothy Taylor changing house beer, plus guests. Ample car parking is available. Q🐃🐕🍴🚪♿Pᴸ–☐🚐(53,77,79)

Coton-in-the-Elms

Black Horse

17 Burton Road, DE12 8HJ SK246152

✪ 4-11 (midnight Fri); 1-midnight Sat; 12-10.30 Sun

☎ (01283) 762947 ⊕ theblackhorsederbyshire.co.uk

Draught Bass; Joule's Original Pale Ale; Marston's Pedigree; guest beer Ⓗ

A 19th-century village pub, this Guide regular of some 30 years ago was revived in 2009 as a lively free house, after more than a decade of neglect. Tastefully renovated, the bright and airy main room is divided by glass-topped wood partitions. A separate small snug, served through a hatch, features a bar billiards table. The guest beer is often sourced from a local microbrewery, and real cider is Woody's. Quiz night is Tuesday and there is occasional live music on Sunday. Mini beer festivals are sometimes held on bank holiday weekends; check website for details. 🏚🐕♣●Pᴸ–🚐(22)

Crich

Cliff Inn Ⓛ

Town End, DE4 5DP

✪ 5 (7 Mon)-11; 12-11 Sat & Sun ☎ (01773) 852444

Buxton Moor Top; Sharp's Doom Bar; guest beers Ⓗ

Traditional gritstone-built free house at the top of the village near the Crich Tramway Museum. Built in about 1800, its two compact rooms are largely unchanged since the 1960s. The five handpumps normally dispense up to four LocAles. Home-made food is served Tuesday-Friday evenings and weekend lunchtimes. Walker- and dog-friendly. 🏚Q🐃🐕◑🍴Pᴸ–🚐(140,144)

Derby

Alexandra Hotel Ⓛ

203 Siddals Road, DE1 2QE

✪ 12-11 (midnight Fri); 11-midnight Sat ☎ (01332) 293993

⊕ alexandrahotelderby.co.uk

Castle Rock Harvest Pale, seasonal beers; guest beers Ⓗ

The Alex was originally called the Midland Coffee House. Long a Shipstones house and now with Castle Rock, it serves a range of six to eight guest ales, usually including a mild and a stout or porter, with a focus on local Amber Ales and, farther afield, Dark Star. The bar is adorned with railway memorabilia, the lounge with breweriana, both linked by a central servery. The pub was the birthplace of Derby CAMRA in 1974.

🏚Q🐕🛏🚪♿⇌♣●Pᴸ–🚐

Babington Arms Ⓛ

11-13 Babington Lane, DE1 1TA

✪ 8-11 (midnight Fri & Sat) ☎ (01332) 383647

Greene King Abbot; Marston's Burton Bitter, Pedigree; Ruddles Best Bitter; Theakston Old Peculier; guest beers Ⓗ

Probably the best Wetherspoon in the country, the pub has won the company's prestigious Cask Ale Pub of the Year and local CAMRA City Pub of the Year twice. It showcases an amazing range of 16 beers on handpump, listed on a TV screen, and holds regular themed brewery weekends. The pub stands in the former grounds of Babington House, whose owner's plot led to the downfall of Mary Queen of Scots. Displays feature the former Grand Theatre that stands next door. Q◑♿●🚐

Brewery Tap – Derby's Royal Standard Ⓛ

1 Derwent Street, DE1 2ED

✪ 11-11 (midnight Thu; 1am Fri & Sat) ☎ (01332) 366283

⊕ brewerytap-dbc.co.uk

Derby Triple Hop, Business As Usual, Dashingly Dark, Double Mash, Old Intentional; guest beers Ⓗ

Situated on the banks of the River Derwent, two sizeable bars sit either side of the entrance of this flat-iron-shaped pub, thankfully rescued from demolition. Exposed brickwork and wooden flooring give a contemporary feel, added to by modern and eclectic food choices. Patrons may choose from 10 handpumps and numerous foreign bottled beers. A rack of ale, accompanied by local cheese, is also available. There is live music on Sunday, a music quiz on Monday and open mic on Tuesday. 🐕◑♿ᴸ–🚐

Coach & Horses

Mansfield Road, DE1 3RF

✪ 12-midnight (1am Sat) ☎ (01332) 258901

Draught Bass; guest beers Ⓗ

Attractive Arts and Crafts Edwardian-style corner house in Little Chester, the oldest part of Derby, dating back to Roman times. Focused on the local community, there is a games room for pool and darts, and events include popular Sunday night quizzes, support for local charities and a book exchange. Draught Bass is served, plus two SIBA cask ales. Live music is featured on bank holidays with a larger range of beers. A discount is available for CAMRA members. 🐕🚪♣Pᴸ–🚐(H1)

Exeter Arms 🍽 Ⓛ

13 Exeter Place, DE1 2EU

✪ 11-11 (11.30 Wed & Thu; midnight Fri & Sat); 12-10.30 Sun

☎ (01332) 605323 ⊕ exeterarms.co.uk

Dancing Duck Ay Up, Nice Weather, Dark Drake, Gold; Marston's Pedigree; guest beers Ⓗ

A remarkable transformation in recent times by Dancing Duck brewery and the licensees have earned the pub local CAMRA Pub of the Year 2013. The Ex simply oozes old world charm and features a small bar with open fire, partitioned lounges and a wooden-settled snug with an old-fashioned range. The adjoining atmospheric cottage dating from about 1815 has been incorporated into the pub and the rear garden houses a stable-type bar which opens for beer festivals. Live music is a feature. ⋈❀❁◑♣●'-

Falstaff 🅛

74 Silverhill Road, DE23 6UJ
✪ 12-11 (midnight Fri & Sat) ☎ (01332) 342902
⊕ falstaffbrewery.co.uk
Falstaff Fist Full of Hops, Phoenix, Smiling Assassin, seasonal beer Ⓗ
A 20-minute walk from the city centre rewards you with this atmospheric and reputedly haunted free house. Originally a coaching inn before the surrounding area was built up, it is now the Falstaff brewery tap, making it the best real ale house in the Normanton area of Derby. The curved bar has a small lounge on one side where Offiler's Brewery memorabilia is displayed. Other collectables can be viewed throughout the games room and second bar room. ⋈❀❁♣●'-🖛

Five Lamps 🅛

25 Duffield Road, DE1 3BH
✪ 12-11 (midnight Fri & Sat) ☎ (01332) 348730
⊕ fivelampsderby.co.uk
Buxton Blonde; Derby Five Lamps; Everards Tiger; Peak Ales Chatsworth Gold; Whim Hartington Bitter; guest beers Ⓗ
Since it reopened in 2010, the pub has gone from strength to strength thanks to the dedication of the licensees and staff, which culminated in local CAMRA Pub of the Year 2012. Fourteen handpumps showcase many local ales from breweries such as Peak, Buxton, Muirhouse and Whim. The Lamps is essentially open plan but with many little nooks and crannies to give it a homely feel. It has been tastefully refurbished with wood panelling and leather seating in a traditional style.
Q❀❁&●P'-🖛

Flowerpot 🅛

23-25 King Street, DE1 3DZ
✪ 11-11 (midnight Fri & Sat); 12-11 Sun ☎ (01332) 204955
Black Iris Sunflower; Blue Monkey BG Sips, seasonal beers; Oakham Bishops Farewell; Whim Hartington IPA; guest beers Ⓗ/Ⓖ
Dating from around 1800 but much expanded from its original premises, this pub reaches back from the small, roadside frontage and divides into several interlinking rooms. One room provides the stage for regular live bands and another has a glass cellar wall, revealing rows of stillaged firkins, which can be seen from the bar and from the road outside. Eight real ales are usually available and it is now the home of the Black Iris Brewery. Gurkha curries are a speciality on Tuesday evenings.
❀❁&●'-🖛

Furnace Inn 🅛

Duke Street, DE1 3BX
✪ 4 (12 Fri & Sat)-midnight; 12-11 Sun ☎ (01332) 331563
Blue Monkey Infinity; Draught Bass; Shiny Launch Pad, Golden Man, Reflection IPA; guest beers Ⓗ
Former Hardys & Hansons pub given a new lease of life by the Shiny Brewing Company whose brewery

resides at the rear and whose beers are featured. The pub has been smartly refurbished with two distinct sides off a central bar, and serves up to eight real ales and two real ciders/perries, with guest ales sourced from all over the country. Cheese, open mic and comedy nights are regular features and a beer festival is held over Halloween. ❀♣●'-

Horse & Groom

48 Elms Street, DE1 3HN
✪ 12-11 ⊕ horseandgroomderby.co.uk
Draught Bass; guest beers Ⓗ
Situated in the city's old West End, the pub dates from around 1850. A complete refurbishment has restored the building back to a thriving community local, with ladies' and gents' darts teams and two pool teams. The regular Bass is accompanied by three changing guests, often from Thornbridge, Ossett or Whim. There is regular live music at the weekend, jazz on the last Wednesday of the month, and a folk and blue-grass jamming session most Sunday evenings. ❀♣'-🖛

New Zealand Arms 🅛

2 Langley Street, DE22 3GL
✪ 12-midnight ☎ (01332) 384945 ⊕ newzealandarms.com
Dancing Duck Ay Up, Nice Weather, Dark Drake, 22; guest beer Ⓗ
The popular brewery tap for Dancing Duck is a 15-minute walk from the city centre, and features six of its ales plus guests and draught ciders. Comfortable surroundings, pleasant staff and a good choice of home-cooked food have helped to re-establish the pub after a period of closure. Also, the Dancing Duck beers are very reasonably priced. Wednesday is quiz night, with music nights Monday, Thursday and Saturday. Food is served Wednesday to Friday evenings and Saturday and Sunday lunchtimes. ❀❁◑♣●'-🖛(28,29)

Old Silk Mill 🅛

19 Full Street, DE1 3AF
✪ 11-midnight (11.30 Mon); 12-11 Sun ☎ (07943) 142924
Castle Rock Harvest Pale Ⓗ**; Draught Bass** Ⓖ**; Kelham Island Pale Rider; Oakham Bishops Farewell; Thornbridge Jaipur IPA** Ⓗ**; guest beers** Ⓗ/Ⓖ
Built in 1928 to replace the original pub, the inn is close to the silk mill which was the first factory in the world, now a museum. A warm welcome awaits, especially in the winter with real fires. There is live music on a Tuesday, Thursday and Sunday. The pub serves at least nine real ales and one real cider. At weekends the rear bar offers beers straight from the cask. ⋈❀❁●

Peacock Inn 🅛

87 Nottingham Road, DE1 3QS
✪ 11-11 (midnight Thu-Sat); 12-10.30 Sun
☎ (01332) 583308
Leatherbritches Peacock Pale Ale; Marston's Pedigree; Oakham Bishops Farewell Ⓗ**; Sarah Hughes Dark Ruby** Ⓖ**; Whim Arbor Light** Ⓗ**; guest beers** Ⓗ/Ⓖ
Attractive 18th-century stone-built pub that used to be a staging post on the main coach road out of Derby, which ran alongside the now filled-in old Derby Canal. Two rooms on different levels are divided by a central bar and have wooden floors, stove burners, photos of old Derby and Derby County memorabilia. Up to nine real ales and two ciders and/or perries feature; beer festivals are held in the large, covered garden area to the rear. ⋈Q❀❁❁●'-

Rowditch Inn

246 Uttoxeter New Road, DE22 3LL

✪ 12-2 (Sat & Sun only), 7-11 ☎ (01332) 343123

Marston's Pedigree; guest beers Ⓗ

This plain-fronted but warmly welcoming roadside hostelry has an unexpectedly deep interior, which divides into two drinking areas and a small snug. The rear garden is a positive haven in warmer weather. Pumpclips adorning the walls of the bar are evidence of myriad guest ales. The output of the pub's brewery is almost exclusively consumed on the premises. Worth the walk or the 10-minute bus ride out of the city centre. ⚒❀♣'–🖵

Station Inn

12 Midland Road, DE1 2SN

✪ 11.30-2.30, 6-11; 11.30-11 Fri & Sat; 12-3, 7-10.30 Sun

☎ (01332) 608014

Caledonian Deuchars IPA Ⓗ; **Draught Bass** Ⓖ; **Marston's Pedigree; Wells Bombardier; guest beer** Ⓗ

Immaculately kept city pub with an ornate frontage by Charrington & Co, convenient for the railway station and some of Derby's best Indian restaurants. Behind the bar and pool room is a large function room used by various organisations including CAMRA. The landlord chairs the local Pub Watch scheme, and is renowned for his award-winning cellar and excellent Bass from the jug. Opening hours may be restricted when Derby County are playing at home. ⇌🖵

Dronfield

Coach & Horses Ⓛ

Sheffield Road, S18 2GD

✪ 5-10 Mon; 12-11 (midnight Fri & Sat); 12-10.30 Sun

☎ (01246) 413269

Thornbridge Jaipur IPA, seasonal beers Ⓗ

Roadside pub north of the town centre, with one comfortably furnished open-plan room. It is owned by Sheffield FC, the world's oldest football club, founded in 1857, whose ground is adjacent, but operated by Thornbridge Brewery. There are up to five Thornbridge beers available on a rotating basis, usually including the latest specials. Bar snacks are served every day until late. Regular live music takes place, including an acoustic night every Monday. Q❀◖⇌♣♠P'–🖵(43,43A)

Three Tuns ♥ Ⓛ

135 Cemetery Road, S18 1XX

✪ 12-11 (midnight Fri & Sat) ☎ (01246) 410556

Spire Whiter Shade of Pale, Dark Side of the Moon, seasonal beers; guest beers Ⓗ

Built in 1938 by Stones Brewery as one of several Brewers' Tudor roadhouses in the area; in 2011 it was acquired by Spire Brewery, refurbished and renamed. The 14 handpumps showcase a changing range of six Spire beers, together with six guest beers and two real ciders. The menu features simple, good-value food with quality ingredients, available Tuesday to Saturday until 7pm and until 5pm Sundays. Home-made pizzas cooked in a wood-fired oven in the outdoor drinking area are sometimes available. ❀◖⇌🚲♠P'–🖵(43,44)

Duffield

Pattenmakers Arms Ⓛ

4 Crown Street, DE56 4EY

✪ 12-2, 5-midnight; 12-midnight Fri-Sun ☎ (01332) 842844

⊕ pattenmakersarms.co.uk

Draught Bass Ⓖ; **Marston's Pedigree; Taylor Landlord; guest beers** Ⓗ

A classic Edwardian pub, tucked away behind the main road but well worth seeking out. It is a traditional, very welcoming local that has dedicated and attentive staff. It retains much of its original character, with quarry and parquet floors and stained, etched glass windows. Good-value wholesome food is served at lunchtimes; children eat for free. There is live entertainment some weekends, and skittles, darts, dominoes and quiz teams, with Sunday evening quizzes and weekend meat raffles. The Ecclesbourne Heritage Railway is close by. ❀◖⇌♣♠P'–🖵

Earl Sterndale

Quiet Woman

SK17 0BU (off B5053)

✪ 12-3 (4 Sat; 5 Sun), 7-11 ☎ (01298) 83211

Jennings Dark Mild; Marston's Burton Bitter; guest beer Ⓗ

Unspoilt, basic local with an unusual name and pub sign set in the heart of the Peak District National Park, opposite the church and village green. Inside, a low-beamed room has a real fire on the left and a small bar to the right. There is a separate games room with a pool table. Local fresh eggs and traditional pork pies can be purchased at the bar. The pub offers a selection of naturally conditioned bottled beers brewed by Leek Brewery. ⚒Q🕭❀Å♣P🖵(442)

Glossop

Bull's Head

102 Church Street, Old Glossop, SK13 7RN

✪ 4-midnight; 1-1am Sat & Sun ☎ (01457) 853291

Robinsons 1892, Unicorn, seasonal beers Ⓗ

Acquired by Robinsons from Bass in 1992, the pub is one of the oldest in the area. Inside, oak beams and a flagged taproom floor are interesting features, but for many the excellent reputation of the authentic Indian cuisine is the major attraction (served from 5pm Tue-Sun). Under the same management for 10 years, the pub is handy for a well-earned pint after walking on nearby Bleaklow. There is a daytime bus service from the town centre every 30 minutes Monday-Saturday. ⚒Q❀🚲◖P🖵(390)

Crown Inn ★

142 Victoria Street, SK13 8JF (on Hayfield Rd out of town centre)

✪ 12 (5 Mon-Thu)-11; 12-10.30 Sun ☎ (01457) 862824

Samuel Smith OBB Ⓗ

End-of-terrace local, a few minutes from the town centre and railway station, built in 1846 and the only Smith's house in the High Peak area since its acquisition by the brewery in 1977. An attractive curved bar serves two side snugs, both with real fires in winter, and a pool/games room. Pictures of bygone Glossop add to the traditional character. Prices are keen and the brewery's bottled beers are also available. An enclosed outdoor drinking area is provided in the rear yard. ⚒Q❀&⇌♣'–🖵

Star Inn Ⓛ

2 Howard Street, SK13 7DD (next to railway station)

✪ 2 (4 Mon & Tue)-11; 2-midnight Fri; 12-midnight Sat; 12-10.30 Sun ☎ (01457) 853072

Taylor Landlord; guest beers Ⓗ

This highly popular town-centre pub run by a dedicated CAMRA member is situated adjacent to the railway station. Guest beers are sourced from SIBA breweries and Old Rosie cider is a regular - all available on handpump. Regular beer and cider festivals are held throughout the year. The town is ideally situated for walking within the Dark Peak area. Q❤️✦P⁵⌐☐(61,236,397)

Hardstoft

Shoulder at Hardstoft 🄻
S45 8AE
☼ 11-11 ☎ (01246) 850276 ⊕ thefamousshoulder.co.uk
Greene King Abbot; Peak Ales Bakewell Best; Thornbridge Brewery Jaipur IPA; guest beers Ⓗ
Friendly, welcoming staff greet you at this 300-year-old local country pub only 10 minutes from junction 29 of the M1. Log fires and relaxing surroundings are provided for you to enjoy one of five local real ales on the bar, with food sourced locally as well. Located on the Five Pits Trail (from Tibshelf to Grassmoor), it welcomes walkers, cyclists and dogs, with four letting rooms and an excellent beer garden.
🏨Q🐕☺️🍴🕪 🍽️🚭ÅP⁵⌐☐☐

Hartshorne

Admiral Rodney Inn
65 Main Street, DE11 7ES (on A514) SK325211
☼ 6-11.30; 5.30-midnight Fri; 12-2, 4-11.30 Sat; 12-midnight Sun ☎ (01283) 216482
Marston's Pedigree; guest beers Ⓗ
Traditional 19th-century village pub substantially rebuilt in 1959, and extended in 1998 to provide an open-plan L-shaped drinking area, retaining the original oak beams in the former snug. A small raised area behind the bar is served through a hatch. Up to four guest beers are available, usually from SIBA members. The cheese society meets here monthly on a Monday evening. Quiz night is Friday. The grounds include a cricket pitch, the pub remaining open during Saturday afternoon matches. 🏨Q🕪🚭♣P⁵⌐☐(61)

Hayfield

George
14 Church Street, SK22 2JE
☼ 11.45-11 (11.30 Fri & Sat); 12-11 Sun ☎ (01663) 743 691
⊕ georgehotelhayfield.co.uk
Banks's Bitter; Marston's Single Hop; Ringwood 4X Porter Ⓗ
Rambling stone-built 16th-century pub in the centre of the village, originally a mail house. The Derby Militia was formed here in 1808. In addition to the handpulled ales, Thatchers Heritage cider is available. The interesting interior includes stained glass mullioned windows and a magnificent cast iron range fireplace incorporating a real fire in winter. Two comfortable lounges, a cosy bar area and a separate dining room are complemented by a function room. Hikers and cyclists are welcome. A short walk from Hayfield bus station.
🏨🕪🍴🕪Å🍽️P⁵⌐☐(358,61)

Heanor

Red Lion 🄻
2 Derby Road, DE75 7QG
☼ 8am-11 (midnight Thu-Sat) ☎ (01773) 533767

Greene King Abbot; Ruddles Best Bitter; guest beers Ⓗ
A Grade II-listed building, this Wetherspoon pub is in a good location just off the town centre and near the main bus routes. It is Cask Marque accredited, with friendly, helpful staff serving up to four rapidly changing guest beers, usually from local microbreweries, alongside the two regulars and one real cider. The large, open-plan layout has three distinct drinking sections including a designated family area where food is served all day. There is good disabled access and outside is a patio, with a covered, heated smoking area.
🐕🕪🕪🍴♣🍽️⁵⌐☐(1A,138,R1)

Holmesfield

Rutland Arms 🏆
96 Main Road, S18 7WT
☼ 12-11.30 ☎ (0114) 289 0374
Black Sheep Best Bitter; Castle Rock Harvest Pale; guest beers Ⓗ
Friendly and welcoming old country pub in a dormitory village on the edge of Sheffield. Renowned for its good atmosphere and real fires, the pub comprises a cosy main bar area on two levels and a small conservatory. Up to four guest beers are available from local and national breweries. Simple food is served lunchtimes, including soup and sandwiches. 🏨🕪🕪♣P⁵⌐☐

Hope

Cheshire Cheese 🄻
Edale Road, S33 6ZF SK170841
☼ closed Mon; 12-3, 6-midnight; 12-midnight Sat; 12-10.30 (7 winter) Sun ☎ (01433) 620381
⊕ thecheshirecheeseinn.co.uk
Bradfield Farmers Blonde; Castle Rock Harvest Pale; Peak Ales Swift Nick; guest beers Ⓗ
Cosy inn dating from 1578 with an open-plan bar area and a smaller room at a lower level that was probably originally used to house animals, but nowadays is a dining area (no food Mon eve). It is situated in walking country but parking is limited and the road outside narrow. Outdoor activities can be arranged by the pub. There are four double/twin rooms for B&B. 🏨Q🕪🕪🍴🕪ÅP⁵⌐

Horsley Woodhouse

Old Oak Inn
176 Main Street, DE7 6AW (on A609)
☼ 4 (3 Thu & Fri)-11; 12-11 Sat; 12-10.30 Sun ☎ (01332) 881299
Beer range varies Ⓗ
Flagship of the Leadmill and Bottle Brook breweries, featuring a wide range of beers from both, plus rotating guest ales. This traditional pub boasts four rooms of differing character including a family room and two with open fires. At weekends and bank holidays drinkers can enjoy the RURAD bar, a mini beer festival with 10 beers from Leadmill, Bottle Brook and breweries near and far. There is occasional live music in this homely, dog-friendly and good-value pub. 🏨Q🕪🕪🍴♣✦P☐

Ilkeston

Dewdrop Inn 🏆 🄻
24 Station Street, DE7 5TE (50yds from A6096 by railway bridge)

✪ 4 (3 Fri)-11; 12-11 Sat; 12-10.30 Sun ☎ (0115) 9329684
Castle Rock Harvest Pale; Oakham Bishops Farewell; guest beers Ⓗ
Multi-award-winning local CAMRA Pub of the Year 2012 which has just undergone some recent sympathetic refurbishment. The enthusiastic landlords of this classic, multi-room Victorian pub serve six changing guest beers from microbreweries, often including a dark beer, alongside at least two ciders. There is a warm, comfy lounge with a real fire, and a bar with a pool table and a classic jukebox. The third family room can be reserved for meetings and functions. Hearty cobs are made to order. The rear yard includes a covered, heated smokers' area.
ಈ▷⊛⊟♣●ᴸ–⊟(27)

Spanish Bar Ⓛ
76 South Street, DE7 5QJ
✪ 10-11; 11-midnight Fri & Sat; 11-11 Sun
☎ (0115) 9308666
Lincoln Green Hood; Whim Hartington IPA; guest beers Ⓗ
Friendly town-centre free house run by the Elms family since opening in 1999, which has won numerous CAMRA awards. It offers five real ales including three guests often from Castle Rock and Blue Monkey, complemented by two real ciders. The main bar has a comfy seating area with a logburner. A second room, with a large screen for showing sport, is open at busy times including for Tuesday quizzes, darts and dominoes nights. The pretty rear garden, with skittle alley, hosts an annual beer festival. There is also a covered, heated, smoking area. ಈ⊛♣●ᴸ–⊟

Kilburn

Hunter Arms Ⓛ
Church Street, DE56 0LU
✪ 12-11 (midnight Fri & Sat) ☎ (01332) 781518
Blue Monkey Infinity; Oakham Bishops Farewell; guest beers Ⓗ
Twice the local CAMRA Pub of the Year, winning in both 2011 and 2012, this Victorian pub was named after the owners of the nearby Kilburn Hall. Rejuvenated as a free house by the current owner in 2009, the Hunters is a single-roomed pub but with several distinct drinking areas and a large upstairs function room. Curry nights, barbecues, beer and cider festivals all feature occasionally at this attractive, tastefully-decorated village local, along with TV and free Wi-Fi. ಈ⊛◑♣P ᴸ–⊟

Kirk Ireton

Barley Mow Inn
Main Street, DE6 3JP (off B5023) SK266501
✪ 12-2, 7-11 (10.30 Sun) ☎ (01335) 370306
Whim Hartington IPA; guest beers Ⓖ
Set in a charming village overlooking the Ecclesbourne Valley, this tall, gabled Jacobean building houses an old-fashioned down-to-earth pub, of the type that is increasingly hard to find. Several interconnecting rooms of different character have low beams, mullioned windows and well-worn woodwork, and there is a welcoming open fire in the main bar. A small serving hatch reveals a stillage with up to six gravity beers. Local breweries such as Blue Monkey, Dancing Duck, Burton Bridge, Thornbridge and Peak Ales often feature. ಈQ⊛➳⊟♣●

Little Eaton

Queen's Head Ⓛ
131 Alfreton Road, DE21 5DF
✪ 11-11 (midnight Fri & Sat) ☎ (01332) 986065
⊕ queenshead-dbc.co.uk
Derby Hop Till You Drop, Business As Usual, Double Mash, Dashingly Dark, Old Intentional; guest beers Ⓗ
A historic Derbyshire stone village inn, boasting some original features including low beamed ceilings. The original main entrance has been renovated and the bar relocated to create a welcoming and stylish interior. There is an attractive patio garden to one side for warmer summer days. Nine real ales are usually available, five from Derby Brewing Company, who rescued the pub from oblivion. A range of good, home-made, locally sourced food is offered, all prepared and cooked on site. ⊛◑&♣Pᴸ–⊟

Little Hayfield

Lantern Pike
45 Glossop Road, SK22 2NG
✪ 12-3 (not Mon), 5-11; 12-11 Sat & Sun ☎ (01663) 747590
⊕ lanternpikeinn.co.uk
Taylor Landlord; guest beer Ⓗ
Picturesque ivy-clad pub nestling in a small hamlet within the Dark Peak area. The comfortable, traditional lounge bar, with a real fire in winter, connects to separate dining areas. Coronation Street originator Tony Warren once lived nearby and wrote some of the first episodes of the soap while in the pub (see photos and letter on display). There are superb views from the rear patio. Hikers are welcome. Approximately 10 minutes' walk from Hayfield. ಈ⊛➳◑Pᴸ–⊟(61)

Little Longstone

Packhorse Inn Ⓛ
Main Street, DE45 1NN SK191718
✪ 12-3, 4.45-11; 12-11 Sat & Sun ☎ (01629) 640471
⊕ packhorselongstone.co.uk
Black Sheep Best Bitter; Thornbridge Wild Swan, Kipling, Jaipur IPA; guest beers Ⓗ
A small pub that began life as two miners' cottages, which has been welcoming drinkers since 1787. Situated just a short walk from stunning views of Monsal Head, dogs and walkers are welcome. Fresh local produce is a passion, an ethos also extended to the beers, which include at least two from the nearby Thornbridge Brewery. To the rear is a large beer garden which features a barbecue in the summer months. Meals are available all day on Saturday and Sunday.
ಈ▷⊛◑⊟Å♣ᴸ–⊟(173)

Litton

Red Lion Ⓛ
Church Lane, SK17 8QU SK163753
✪ 12-11 (midnight Fri & Sat); 12-10.30 Sun
☎ (01298) 871458 ⊕ theredlionlitton.co.uk
Abbeydale Absolution; Bradfield Farmers Blonde; Oakwell Barnsley Bitter; guest beers Ⓗ
Nestling on the green and the only pub in the village, the Red Lion is a welcome refuge for locals and visitors alike. There is a large fireplace serving several rooms off a central passageway, and the guest beers are often LocAle. Not to be missed is the annual Wakes Week at the end of June, with

events including well dressing on the village green. Food is available all day every day. ♨Q❀⇆◑◐♣⁵–⊟(65)

Long Eaton

Barge Inn Ⓛ

177 Tamworth Road, NG10 1DH

⏲ 12-11.30 (1am Fri & Sat) ☎ (0115) 9725559

Beer range varies Ⓗ

Spacious, open-plan pub with a central bar and six handpumps serving changing beers of all styles from microbreweries, usually including Copper Dragon Golden Pippin. There is a separate darts and pool area, two TV screens, an outside skittle alley and a large, upstairs function room which hosts regular live bands. This friendly, family-run local has good transport links, with a bus stop outside and a railway station 15 minutes' walk away. The tree-lined Erewash Canal, with moorings available, is overlooked from the front patio. Dogs are welcome. ❀⇌♣●P⁵–⊟(15)

Hole in the Wall Ⓛ

6 Regent Street, NG10 1JX

⏲ 11-11.30 ☎ (0115) 9734920

Draught Bass; Nottingham EPA; guest beers Ⓗ

The landlord of this free house has been in place for 27 years, serving an excellent range of beers. Guests usually come from Oakham or local microbreweries. Situated just off the town centre, this 125-year-old pub has a quiet lounge and a main bar with pool table where breweriana and local CAMRA awards are displayed. The decked garden area has an enclosed skittle alley and barbecue area. Dogs are welcome. A Pay & Display car park is opposite. ❀⊞♣●⁵–⊟

Longshaw

Grouse Inn

S11 7TZ (on A625) SK258779

⏲ 12-3, 6-11; 12-11 Sat & Sun ☎ (01433) 630423

🌐 thegrouseinn-derbyshire.co.uk

Banks's Bitter, Fine Fettle; Marston's EPA, Pedigree; guest beer Ⓗ

In the same family since 1965, this free house stands in isolation on bleak moorland south west of Sheffield, and is deservedly popular with walkers and climbers. There are some fine photographs of nearby gritstone edges, as well as a collection of international bank notes on display. The comfortable lounge is situated at the front, with a smaller room to the rear separated off. Food is served lunchtimes and evenings (not Mon eve), all day on Sunday. A self-catering holiday flat can be hired. ♨Q♉❀⇆◑◐P⁵–⊡

Lullington

Colvile Arms

Main Street, DE12 8EG SK249131

⏲ 6-11; 12-3, 7-10.30 Sun ☎ (01827) 373212

Draught Bass; Marston's Pedigree; guest beer Ⓗ

Popular free house at the heart of an attractive hamlet at the southern tip of the county, leased from the Lullington Estate, once the seat of the Colvile family. The pub is believed to date back to the 18th century. Inside, the public bar includes an adjoining hallway and snug, each featuring high-backed settles with wood panelling. The bar and a comfortable lounge are on opposite sides of a central serving area. A second lounge/function room overlooks the beer garden and lawn. Food is limited to filled cobs. ❀⊞♣P⁵–

Makeney

Holly Bush Inn ★

Holly Bush Lane, DE56 0RX (off A6 at Milford Makeney Road)

⏲ 12-11 ☎ (01332) 841729 🌐 hollybushinnmakeney.co.uk

Fuller's London Pride; Greene King Abbot Ⓗ**; Marston's Pedigree; Ruddles County** Ⓖ**; Taylor Landlord** Ⓗ

This late 17th-century Grade II-listed pub oozing character has stood on the Derby turnpike since before the new road was opened in 1818 – Dick Turpin drank here. The pub has been identified by CAMRA as one of Britain's Best Real Heritage Pubs and its interior features an enclosed wooden snug sandwiched between two bars with real fires. The regular beer range is supplemented by three changing guests, with Westons Old Rosie cider and Bee Sting perry. Beer festivals are held in March and October. ♨Q♉❀◑⊞♣●P⁵–

Marehay

Holly Bush Inn

51 Brook Lane, DE5 8JA

⏲ 12-11 ☎ (01773) 570830

Greene King Abbot; Marston's Pedigree; guest beers Ⓗ

Single-roomed, former Shipstones pub that reopened in late 2011 after being bought by the current licensee, which has become a popular venue, particularly at weekends when entertainment is provided. Situated in a village just outside Ripley, the centrally located bar servery always has five real ales, occasionally supplemented by a real cider. Good-value food, quizzes and occasional beer festivals make the Bush a worthwhile destination for visitors to the area. ♨Q♉❀◑♿♣P⁵–⊟(148)

Matlock

MoCa 🏆 Ⓛ

77 Dale Road, DE4 3LT

⏲ 11-10.30 (11 Fri & Sat) ☎ (01629) 258084

Beer range varies Ⓗ

On the main A6 through Matlock, this single-room, modern bar hosts six handpulls featuring ales from six dedicated breweries – Abbeydale, Blue Monkey, Brampton, Dancing Duck, Kelham Island and Oakham. There is a raised seating area by the front window, street side of the bar, together with an outside decked area to the rear. Popular music memorabilia adorns the walls. Local CAMRA Pub of the Year 2013. ❀◑⇌⊟

Thorntree Inn

48 Jackson Road, DE4 3JQ

⏲ 12-2 (not Mon), 6-11; 12-2.30, 5-midnight Fri; 12-midnight Sat; 12-11 Sun ☎ (01623) 580295

🌐 thorntreeatmatlock.co.uk

Draught Bass; Ruddles Best Bitter; Taylor Landlord; guest beers Ⓗ

Perched high on the hill on the north side of Matlock, this two-roomed tavern is little altered and enjoys beautiful, far-reaching views from the delightful patio, over the town and along the Derwent Valley. It is a compact pub, popular with office workers at lunchtime and locals at night. It has free Wi-Fi and is dog friendly. Home-made food is served Tuesday-Friday lunchtime, pie night is Wednesday 6-8pm and a choice of two roasts/ veg option is served 5-6pm on Sunday. Q✿🅓♣'–🖭(M1)

Matlock Bath

Fishpond
204 South Parade, DE4 3NR
✪ 11-11 (midnight Fri & Sat) ☎ (01629) 581529
⊕ thefishpondmatlockbath.co.uk
Beer range varies Ⓗ
Located at the southern end of the unique promenade, this spacious, open-plan pub, with a large central bar, features ales from local breweries including Thornbridge, Blue Monkey and Navigation. Regular guests come from Kelham Island and Oakham. Live entertainment features Thursday to Saturday, and there are front and rear drinking areas outside. All meals are made from fresh produce, and an artisan bakery on site sells its fresh bread to all. 🅰🏮✿🅓♿❄'–🖭

Melbourne

Blue Bell Inn
53 Church Street, DE73 8EJ
✪ 11-11; 11.30-10.30 Sun ☎ (01332) 865764
⊕ thebluebellinnmelbourne.co.uk
Shardlow Golden Eye, Reverend Eaton; guest beers Ⓗ
The tap for Shardlow Brewery is close to Melbourne Hall and the 12th-century Norman church. Run on traditional lines, the bar has a sporting emphasis and the restaurant has an Italian-themed menu. A range of beers from Shardlow is on offer including the popular Reverend Eaton, with guests mainly from local breweries. Real cider is available all year and beer festivals are held twice yearly in March and October. ✿🅓🅮♣❄'–🖭(61)

Middleton

Nelson Arms
The Green, Main Street, DE4 4LU
✪ 5 (12 Sat)-midnight; 12-11 Sun ☎ (01629) 825154
⊕ nelsonarmsmiddleton.co.uk
Marston's Pedigree; guest beers Ⓗ
Friendly, family-owned free house located at the top of the village. A small, comfortable bar is to the left as you enter; a large beamed room to the right has a welcoming fire and an interesting array of pictures, artefacts and curious ornaments adorning the walls. A separate pool/function/family room is to the rear of the pub, as is an outdoor drinking area. Real cider complements the choice of up to three guest ales. 🅰🏮✿🅮♿♣❄P'–🖭(6.1)

Milford

King William IV
The Bridge, DE56 0RR
✪ 5 (12 Sat)-11.30; 12.30-11 Sun ☎ (01332) 840842
Greene King Abbot; Sharp's Doom Bar; Taylor Landlord; guest beers Ⓗ
Heading north on the A6, this stone-built Georgian inn, dramatically situated at the foot of sandstone cliffs, hoves into view. The elongated bar contains period furniture and a magnificent open fire at one end. The regular beers are supplemented by an imaginative choice of two rotating guest beers. Old

Rosie cider is also served. Music nights are held twice a week, along with a weekly quiz night. Street parking is available on the adjacent Makeney Road. 🅰🅓♣❄🖭(61,62,63)

Miller's Dale

Angler's Rest Ⓛ
SK17 8SN (on B6049) SK142734
✪ 12-3, 6.30-11; 12-11 Sat; 12-9 Sun ☎ (01298) 871323
⊕ theanglersrest.co.uk
Adnams Southwold Bitter; Storm Silk of Amnesia; guest beers Ⓗ
This ivy-clad inn dating from 1753 on the banks of the River Wye is handy for the spectacular walk along the Monsal Trail. It is a multi-room pub including a cosy lounge with a real fire and a comfortable dining room. Walking boots and dogs are welcome in the hikers' bar. Good, traditional pub food is served daily, and the guest beers are mostly LocAle. A self-catering apartment is available to rent. 🅰Q✿🅮🅓🅓A♣❄P🖭(65)

Milton

Swan Inn
Main Street, DE65 6EF
✪ 11-3 (5 Thu), 6-11; 11-5, 6-midnight Fri & Sat; 12-10.30 Sun ☎ (01283) 703188
Marston's Pedigree; Sharp's Doom Bar; guest beer Ⓗ
Free house run since 2001 by licensees Stella and Roger, who serve highly praised ale including at least one guest beer, often from a local microbrewery. Excellent home-cooked food is on offer and the pub has mini beer festivals. There is a fine display of railway memorabilia in the bar. The pub, situated 1½ miles east of Repton – its nearest village and bus route – is well worth seeking out. The Cygnets tea room operates during the day. 🅰✿🅮🅓♿P'–

Newton Solney

Brickmakers Arms
9 Main Street, DE15 0SJ (on B5008, opp junction with Trent Lane) SK281256
✪ 5 (4 Fri; 12 Sat)-11; 12-11 Sun ☎ (01283) 703170
Burton Bridge Golden Delicious, Bridge Bitter, Burton Porter, Stairway to Heaven; guest beer Ⓗ
Bought by the Burton Bridge Brewery in 2011 in its first foray into Derbyshire, this comfortable, cosy local is at the end of an 18th-century terrace of cottages. Internally, it features a narrow central bar with a small room at one end served through a hatch, and an impressive oak-panelled room at the other. A good selection of Belgian bottled beers, English fruit wines and malt whiskies is also stocked. Quiz night is Monday, bingo Tuesday. An interesting range of books is available. 🅰Q🏮✿♣❄P'–🖭(V3)

Ockbrook

Royal Oak ▼ Ⓛ
55 Green Lane, DE72 3SE
✪ 11.30-2.30, 5.30-11 (11.30 Fri); 11.30-3, 6-11.30 Sat; 12-4, 6-11 Sun ☎ (01332) 662378 ⊕ royaloakockbrook.com
Draught Bass; guest beers Ⓗ
Very attractive 18th-century pub with a number of small rooms. Run by the Wilson family since Coronation year, many improvements have been made while retaining all of the original character

and features. Excellent home-cooked food is served every lunchtime and Monday to Friday evenings (no food Tue eve). A large function room hosts many community and public events including live music and open mic nights. Outside there are two pleasant gardens, one with a play area for children. Q✿🕪🕭♣🕭P¹⁄₂☐(9,9A)

Openwoodgate

Black Bull's Head 🍺
2 Kilburn Lane, DE56 0SF
☼ 12-11 (10.30 Sun) ☎ (07860) 757741
Greene King Abbot; Oakham Bishops Farewell; guest beers Ⓗ
Former Greene King house built in the mid-19th century and later remodelled in handsome Edwardian style, with far-reaching views over Belper. Now thriving as a free house, it was local CAMRA Pub of the Year in 2013. Eight real ales and two ciders are available, with four ales and four ciders in the Bedlam Bar, which opens Friday to Sunday. Well-behaved dogs and children are welcome in this pub, which has two rooms but three distinct seating areas around a central bar. 🏠Q🍴✿🕭♣🕭¹⁄₂☐(7.1,6X)

Parwich

Sycamore
Main Street, DE6 1QL (next to village church)
SK1882854310
☼ 12-11 (10.30 Sun) ☎ (01335) 390212
Robinsons Unicorn, Double Hop Ⓗ
A true village hub in the centre of a very picturesque and remote-feeling village, although only 15 minutes' drive from Ashbourne. The landlady took on the village store a few years back and runs it from a side room off the bar corridor as well as serving very well-kept beers from Robinsons, including Old Tom when available. Local CAMRA Rural Pub of the Year for 2013. Opening hours may vary in winter. 🏠Q🍴✿🕪🕭P¹⁄₂☐

Peasehill

Beehive Inn
151 Peasehill Road, DE5 3JN
☼ 6 (4 Sun)-midnight ☎ (07896) 832141
Beer range varies Ⓗ
Former Home Ales pub whose sign still adorns the gable end, owned by the same licensee for over 20 years. A two-roomed tavern with a central bar, it features beers from Dancing Duck, Oakham and Blue Monkey breweries. The Honeypot, situated at the top of the large garden, offers a selection of beers and ciders served on gravity, along with foreign beers on draught. The Honeypot is open every lunchtime and Friday, Saturday and Sunday afternoons until 10pm. Beer festivals regularly feature. 🏠✿🕭♣🕭P¹⁄₂☐(147)

Ripley

Pear Tree
4 Derby Road, DE5 3HR
☼ 11 (12 Sun)-midnight ☎ (01773) 742468
Greene King XX Mild, IPA, Abbot; guest beer Ⓗ
Victorian in appearance but late Georgian in origin, this former Hardy's Ales pub is probably the best remaining example of a traditional local in Ripley, now owned by Greene King and kept by the same

licensee for 18 years. It is two-roomed, the front bar almost occupying the width of the pub, with a delightful back snug, unchanged in over half a century. Dogs and children are welcome here, and open fires add warmth to both the front bar and rear snug in winter. 🏠✿🕪🕭♣🕭P¹⁄₂☐(9,6)

Talbot Taphouse Ⓛ
1 Butterley Hill, DE5 3LT
☼ 5-11; 12-11.30 Fri & Sat; 12-11 Sun ☎ (01773) 742626
Amber Blonde, Barnes Wallis, Imperial IPA, Original Stout, seasonal beers; guest beers Ⓗ
The eye-catching Amber Ales brewery tap occupies a flat-iron site, and is handily situated between the town centre and the Midland Railway heritage centre. Renovated in 2009, the Victorian former Shipstones house is blissfully free of electronic accoutrements, with the traditional games of bar billiards and table skittles holding sway. Innovation in brewing is the name of the game here, with experimental brews frequently featured, and beer safaris are organised by the nearby brewery. CAMRA members enjoy discounted prices on Amber Ales products. 🏠Q♣🕭P☐(9)

Sawley

Nag's Head
Wilne Road, NG10 3AL
☼ 11-11.30 (midnight Fri & Sat); 12-11 Sun
☎ (0115) 9732983
Marston's Burton Bitter, Pedigree, seasonal beers Ⓗ
Early 19th-century inn located close to Sawley marina in the historic area of Old Sawley, with friendly staff serving handpumped ales from the Marston's range. A flagstone floor and low ceilings help to create a lively atmosphere in the rustic, dog-friendly bar, with a quieter ambience in the intimate lounge. Good-value home-cooked food is served lunchtimes and early evenings Monday-Saturday. Q✿🕪🕭♣P¹⁄₂☐

White Lion Ⓛ
352 Tamworth Road, NG10 3AT
☼ 2-midnight (1am Fri & Sat); 12-midnight Sun
☎ (0115) 9463061
Draught Bass; Blue Monkey BG Sips; Castle Rock Black Gold; guest beers Ⓗ
This 18th-century pub was reopened as a free house in 2011. Extensively refurbished to a high standard, it is a traditional two-room pub with a central bar, and serves up to six draught beers, some from microbreweries. Close to the thriving Sawley marina and historic church, the pub boasts a large rear garden and boules pitch. Open fires add warmth during the winter months. There are no gaming machines or jukebox. Bar billiards is popular at this busy, friendly local. 🏠Q🍴✿🕭♣🕭P¹⁄₂☐

Scarcliffe

Horse & Groom
Rotherham Road, S44 6ST (B6417 Bolsover-Shirebrook road) SK490687
☼ 12-midnight ☎ (01246) 823152
Black Sheep Best Bitter; Greene King Abbot; Sharp's Doom Bar; Stones Bitter; Wells Bombardier; guest beers Ⓗ
Over 500 years old and managed by the daughter of the owner, this genuine, family-run free house offers up to seven real ales. The pub has featured

in this Guide for 15 years and an impressive array of CAMRA awards indicates the care and attention the family gives to the real ales. The lounge bar is mobile free, with a large open fire. No hot food is served, but locally made pork pies must be tried. Accommodation is available, but booking is essential. ♨Q❀✦↩🕭👌А♣P⌐🖳(53,82)

Shirland

Shoulder of Mutton

Hallfieldgate Lane, DE55 6AA (on B6013, Wessington-Shirland crossroads) SK393582

✪5 (7 Tue; 4.30 Thu)-11; 11-11.30 Fri & Sat; 11-10.30 Sun
☎ (01773) 834992
Beer range varies Ⓗ

Eclectic, 16th-century traditional drinking den, nestling on the edge of Amber Valley. The beer garden offers spectacular views and sunsets. It is a true free house where real people enjoy real ale from small breweries; there is no beer list on the wall because the ales change daily. The regular customers are drawn from far and wide, fuelling the unique, easy atmosphere created by the irrepressible landlord and landlady. Dogs and hikers are welcome. Check out the teacups.
♨Q❀🕭👌А♣P⌐

South Normanton

Clock Inn

107 Market Street, DE55 2AA

✪4-11 (midnight Fri); 12-midnight Sat; 12-11 Sun
☎ (01773) 811396 ⊕ theclockinn.co.uk
Jennings Cumberland Ale; guest beers Ⓗ

Multiple-roomed pub served from a single bar, with lounge and public bar areas. Two guest beers are usually on offer, with a mixture of national and regional brewers supported. Bar snacks are available at all times, and a barbecue is usually held on bank holidays. Large-screen TVs show sport, with different events available on request. Outside is a very nice beer garden with a seating area. Dogs are welcome in one room.
ॐ❀🕭👌♣P⌐🖳

Devonshire Arms ♥ Ⓛ

137 Market Street, DE55 2AA

✪12-midnight ☎ (01773) 810748
Sarah Hughes Dark Ruby; guest beers Ⓗ

A genuine family-managed free house offering four reasonably priced real ales and one real cider. Regulars can suggest their favourite beers, which the landlord will try to order. Home-cooked meals are served every day except Sunday, when a very popular carvery is available – booking is strongly advised. Vegetarians, vegans and coeliacs are all catered for, and daily specials are offered. Most live sports are shown on four large-screen TVs. Local CAMRA Pub of the Year 2008-2013.
ॐ❀🕦👌♣👌P⌐🖳(9.1,9.2,331)

Stanton in Peak

Flying Childers

Main Road, DE4 2LW (off B6056 Bakewell-Ashbourne road) SK240643

✪12-2 (not Mon & Tue), 7-11; 12-3, 7-11 Sat & Sun
☎ (01629) 636333
Wells Bombardier; guest beers Ⓗ

Four cottages knocked into one during the 18th century, this is an unspoilt village pub named after

a famous racehorse owned by the Duke of Devonshire. It is located near the historic Stanton Moor and Nine Ladies stone circle, and is popular with tourists, walkers and locals alike. Both rooms are welcoming, with real fires, and there is a pleasant beer garden outside. Hearty home-made soups and snacks are available at lunchtime. The guest beers change regularly. Dogs are welcome.
♨Q❀🕦🕭👌А♣P🖳

Staveley

All Inn Ⓛ

Lowgates, S43 3TX (on A619)

✪4.30-11.30 (1am Fri); 1-1am Sat; 1-11.30 Sun
☎ (01246) 473303
Beer range varies Ⓗ

Family-run, friendly, well-maintained pub which has deservedly become very popular with the local community. It has a central bar flanked by a smart lounge area to the left, and to the right and towards the back, a larger sports bar where pub games are played. These include dominoes, pool, darts and poker, while widescreen TVs feature sports events. Usually there are two beers from the nearby Raw Brewing Company on the bar, plus two guests from other micros, often unusual for the area. ❀👌♣👌P⌐🖳

Sutton cum Duckmanton

Arkwright Arms Ⓛ

Chesterfield Road, S44 5JG (A632 between Chesterfield and Bolsover)

✪11-11 (midnight Fri & Sat) ☎ (01246) 232053
⊕ arkwrightarms.co.uk
Beer range varies Ⓗ

Brewers' Tudor-fronted free house, with three rooms all made cosy by open fires. An ever-changing range of 10 guest ales, many from local micros, is complemented by 12 ciders and four perries. Beer festivals are held at Easter and on bank holidays, with mini events throughout the year. Quality food is served until 8pm Monday to Saturday, and until 3pm Sunday. The spacious beer garden has play equipment for children. A winner of numerous CAMRA awards, including East Midlands Cider Pub of the Year 2011 and 2012, and local Pub of the Year 2011.
♨❀🕦👌♣👌P⌐🖳(81,82,83)

Thornsett

Printers Arms

Birch Vale, SK22 1AZ

✪4.30-11; 12-midnight Sat; 12-7.30 Sun ☎ (01663) 744650
Beer range varies Ⓗ

Small stone-built pub substantially refurbished in 2010 resulting in a significantly enlarged open-plan interior with flag floors throughout. Three handpumps usually serve two varying beers from Storm Brewery and a further guest beer, often from one of the local micros. A small pool and darts area sits adjacent to the lounge bar, and TVs provide sports coverage in all areas. The front patio offers views across the Sett Valley and there is a children's play area opposite. ♨❀🖳(62)

Waingroves

Thorn Tree Inn

161 Church Street, DE5 9TE

⊙ 5-11; 3-11.30 Fri; 12-11.30 Sat; 12-10.30 Sun
☎ (01773) 513351 ⊕ thorntreewaingroves.co.uk
Beer range varies ℍ
Owned by Punch Taverns before being bought and turned into a free house by the current owner in 2010, this is now the only pub in a village that used to boast several. The interior comprises a main bar area, snug, restaurant and function room. Six real ales, constantly changing, and a couple of ciders, guarantee an excellent choice for even the most discerning drinker. All are very welcome here, including children and dogs, who appreciate the open fire in winter. Regular quiz nights and an annual beer festival also feature.
ᗰᏁᛤᛁᏜᏱᏝᏠᏜᏢᑊ–ᗐ(1A)

Wardlow Mires

Three Stags' Heads ★
SK17 8RW (A623/B6465 jct) SK180756
⊙ closed Mon-Thu; 7-11 Fri; 11-11 Sat; 12-10.30 Sun
☎ (01298) 872268
Abbeydale Brimstone, Deception, Absolution, Black Lurcher ℍ
A quaint 300-year-old pub with two small rooms, stone-flagged floors and low ceilings. Unspoilt, it is one of the few pubs in the area identified by CAMRA as one of Britain's Best Real Heritage Pubs. An ancient range warms the bar and the house dogs – the house beer, Black Lurcher, is named after a former resident. The food is locally sourced, with game a speciality. A severe rebuke awaits those wanting draught lager, but imported bottled lagers are available. ᗰQᛤᏜᏜᏜᏢᑊ–ᗐ

Whaley Bridge

Shepherds Arms
7 Old Road, SK23 7HR
⊙ 3 (12 Sat; 2 Sun)-midnight ☎ (01663) 732384
Marston's Burton Bitter, Pedigree; guest beers ℍ
Little gem of a pub nestling close to the centre of the village. Attractive, whitewashed and stone-built, this hostelry has been preserved unspoilt, conveying the feel of the farmhouse it once was. The unchanged taproom is a delight, with open fire, flagged floor and scrubbed table tops. Additionally, there is a comfortable lounge also with an open fire in winter. The changing guest beers are selected from the Marston's range.
ᗰQᛤᏱᏜᏜᏢᑊ–ᗐ(199,60)

Whitehough

Old Hall Inn ℒ
SK23 6EJ (⅓ mile off B6062)
⊙ 12-midnight ☎ (01663) 750529 ⊕ old-hall-inn.co.uk
Marston's Burton Bitter; guest beers ℍ
Nestling in an attractive hamlet, this 16th-century family-run inn was winner of best cask pub in the East & West Midlands in the Great British Pub Awards for the past three years. Eight handpulled local ales, with regulars from Thornbridge, are served, and local produce is used throughout the popular menu. The adjacent 14th-century

Whitehough Hall, with minstrels' gallery, is used for dining and is accessed directly from the inn. Popular beer festivals take place on the third weekend in September and the last weekend in February.
ᗯᛤᏜᏜᏜᏜᏜ≈(Chinley)ᏜᏢᑊ–ᗐ(189,190)

Willington

Green Man
1 Canal Bridge, DE65 6BQ
⊙ 11.30-11 (11.30 Wed & Thu; midnight Fri & Sat); 12-11 Sun
☎ (01283) 702377
Draught Bass; Marston's Pedigree; Taylor Landlord; guest beer ℍ
An attractive two-roomed pub at the heart of the village and near the canal, dating back to the start of the 18th century. The pub features oak beams throughout, along with traditional bench seating. A large rear garden is complemented by tables and chairs at the front during the summer months. Live music sessions are held regularly and good home-cooked food is served daily. Live sports fixtures are screened. ᛤᏜᏱᏜ≈ᏜᏢᑊ–ᗐ(V3)

Wirksworth

Royal Oak ℒ
North End, DE4 4FG (off B5035)
⊙ 8-11.30 (midnight Fri & Sat); 12-3, 8-11 Sun
☎ (01629) 823000
Draught Bass; Taylor Landlord; Whim Hartington IPA; guest beers ℍ
Excellent, ultra-traditional local situated near the marketplace, highlighted at night by rows of fairy lights. The bar features old pictures of local interest and there is also a pool room and smoking grotto. The Oak enjoys a long-standing reputation for quality Draught Bass, and always has five ales on handpump to choose from, including a LocAle. The Ecclesbourne Valley Railway visitor attraction is close by, and this former lead mining town is an architectural gem with much to interest the historian. Qᛤᑊ–ᗐ(6.1)

Woodthorpe

Albert Inn
Woodthorpe Road, S43 3BZ
⊙ 5-11; 12-10.30 Sun ☎ (01246) 472634
⊕ thealbertinn.com
Wells Bombardier; guest beers ℍ
Friendly and welcoming community pub with a relaxed atmosphere and roaring log fire in the spacious and comfortable main room. Three changing guest beers are on handpump sourced from micro and national breweries. A small range of bottled Belgian beers is also available. Delicious food with vegetarian options, made with locally sourced produce, is prepared and cooked by the landlady, and served in generous proportions Wednesday-Friday evenings, plus popular Sunday lunches. Well-behaved dogs on a lead are welcome. A separate function room is available for hire. ᗰᛤᏜᏜᏢᑊ–ᗐ

A number of entries in the Guide refer to the pubs' support for the LocAle scheme. The aim of the scheme is to get publicans to stock at least one cask beer that comes from a local brewery no further than 20 miles away. It also encourages publicans to use the Direct Delivery Scheme run by SIBA, the Society of Independent Brewers (see p609). SIBA members deliver direct to pubs in their localities instead of going through the central warehouses of pub-owning companies.

The aim is a simple one: to cut down on 'beer miles'. Research by CAMRA shows that food and drink transport accounts for 25 per cent of all HGV vehicle miles in Britain. Taking into account the miles that ingredients have travelled on top of distribution journeys, an imported lager produced by a multi-national brewery could have notched up more than 24,000 'beer miles' by the time it reaches a pub.

Supporters of LocAle point out that £10 spent on locally-supplied goods generates £25 for the local economy. Keeping trade local helps enterprises, creates more economic activity and jobs, and makes other services more viable. The scheme also generates consumer support for local breweries.

Support for LocAle has grown at a rapid pace. It's been embraced by pubs and CAMRA branches throughout England and has now crossed the borders into Scotland and Wales.

For more information, see the CAMRA website www. camra.org.uk and type 'locale' into the search window.

What is CAMRA LocAle?

- An initiative that promotes pubs which sell locally-brewed real ale.
- The scheme builds on a growing consumer demand for quality local produce and an increased awareness of 'green' issues.
- The LocAle scheme was created in 2007 by CAMRA's Nottingham branch which wanted to help support the tradition of brewing within Nottinghamshire, following the demise of local brewer Hardys & Hansons.

Everyone benefits from local pubs stocking locally brewed real ale...

- Public houses, as stocking local real ales can increase pub visits
- Consumers, who enjoy greater beer choice and locally brewed beer
- Local brewers, who gain from increased sales and get better feedback from consumers
- The local economy, because more money is spent and retained in the local economy
- The environment, due to fewer 'beer miles' resulting in less road congestion and pollution
- Tourism, due to an increased sense of local identity and pride – let's celebrate what makes our locality different.

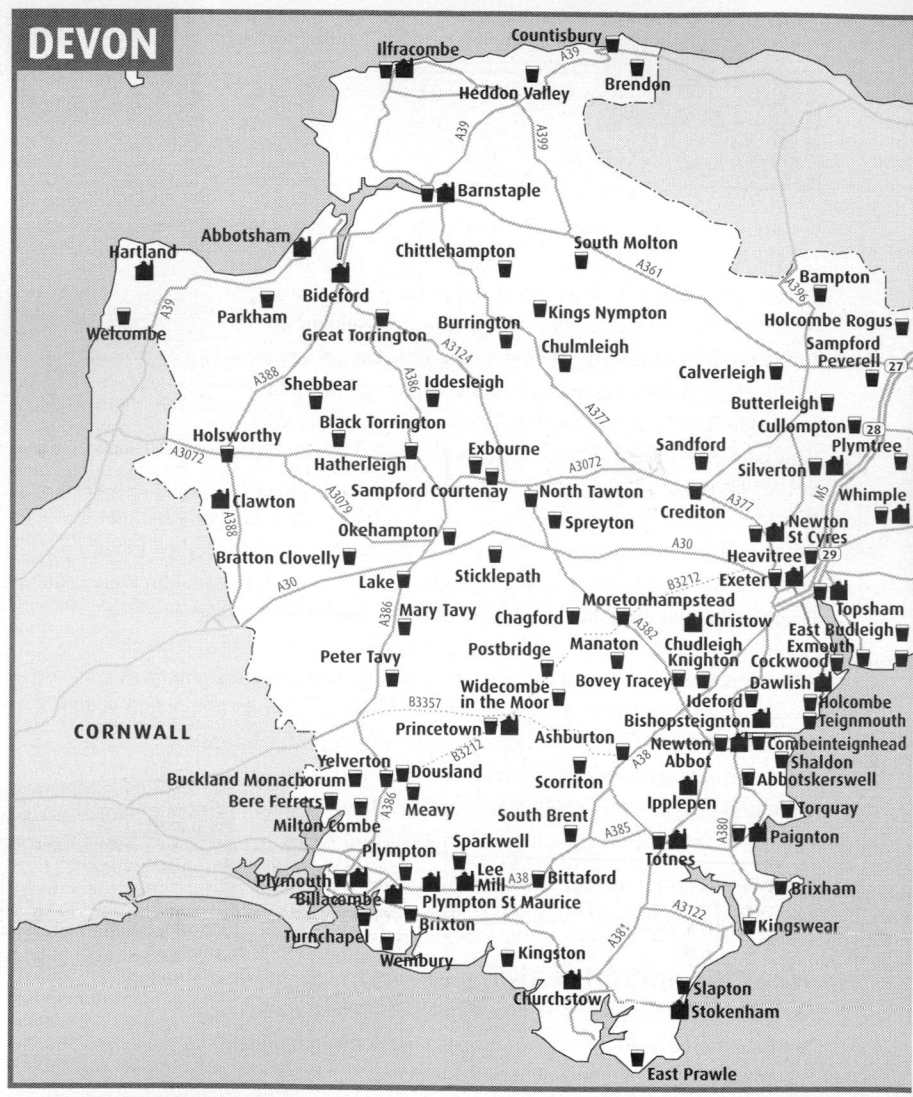

DEVON

Ilfracombe
Countisbury
Heddon Valley
Brendon
Barnstaple
Abbotsham
Hartland
Chittlehampton
South Molton
Bampton
Bideford
Kings Nympton
Holcombe Rogus
Parkham
Burrington
Sampford
Welcombe
Great Torrington
Chulmleigh
Peverell
Calverleigh
Shebbear
Iddesleigh
Butterleigh
Black Torrington
Cullompton
Holsworthy
Exbourne
Sandford
Plymtree
Hatherleigh
Silverton
Clawton
Sampford Courtenay
North Tawton
Whimple
Crediton
Newton
Okehampton
Spreyton
St Cyres
Bratton Clovelly
Heavitree
Exeter
Lake
Sticklepath
Topsham
Mary Tavy
Chagford
Moretonhampstead
Christow
East Budleigh
Peter Tavy
Postbridge
Manaton
Chudleigh
Exmouth
Knighton
Cockwood
Widecombe
Bovey Tracey
Dawlish
in the Moor
Ideford
Holcombe
CORNWALL
Princetown
Bishopsteignton
Teignmouth
Ashburton
Newton
Combeinteignhead
Yelverton
Abbot
Shaldon
Dousland
Scorriton
Abbotskerswell
Buckland Monachorum
Ipplepen
Torquay
Bere Ferrers
Meavy
South Brent
Milton Combe
Sparkwell
Paignton
Plympton
Totnes
Lee
Plymouth
Mill
Bittaford
Brixham
Billacombe
Plympton St Maurice
Turnchapel
Brixton
Kingswear
Wembury
Kingston
Churchstow
Slapton
Stokenham
East Prawle

Abbotskerswell

Court Farm Inn

Wilton Way, TQ12 5PG (next to the parish church)
🕐 11 (12 Sun)-midnight ☎ (01626) 361866
🌐 courtfarminn.net
Draught Bass; Otter Ale; guest beers Ⓗ
This 17th-century Devon longhouse caters for both drinkers and diners, with the four real ales complemented by an extensive food menu. The interior has flagged floors and beamed ceilings, and an upper room is used as an additional dining area and function room. Food is served all day Thursday-Sunday. Darts and pool are played in the bar. The garden is very popular in summer and has a heated smoking area. 🌟🕮🕭🍴🅿🚲🚃(177)

Ashburton

Dartmoor Lodge Ⓛ

Peartree Cross, TQ13 7JW (just off A38 at Peartee jct)

🕐 11-11; 12-10.30 Sun ☎ (01364) 652232
🌐 dartmoorlodge.co.uk
Butcombe Bitter; Dartmoor Jail Ale; guest beers Ⓗ
A good selection of local real ales is served at this roadside hotel on the edge of the Dartmoor National Park and the town of Ashburton. There is a friendly, comfortable atmosphere in the oak-beamed bar and restaurant area which, in winter, has a welcoming log fire. Good-quality local food is served all day every day. The location makes it an ideal base for walkers, cyclists and canoeists. Ashton Still cider is sold.
🛏Q🌟🕭🕮🍴🅿🚲🚃(X38,88)

Exeter Inn Ⓛ

26 West Street, TQ13 7DU (on main road through Ashburton opp church)
🕐 11-2.30, 5-11 (midnight Fri & Sat); 12-3, 7-10.30 Sun
☎ (01364) 652013
Dartmoor IPA, Legend Ⓗ
The oldest pub in Ashburton, built in 1131, with additions in the 17th century. A friendly local that

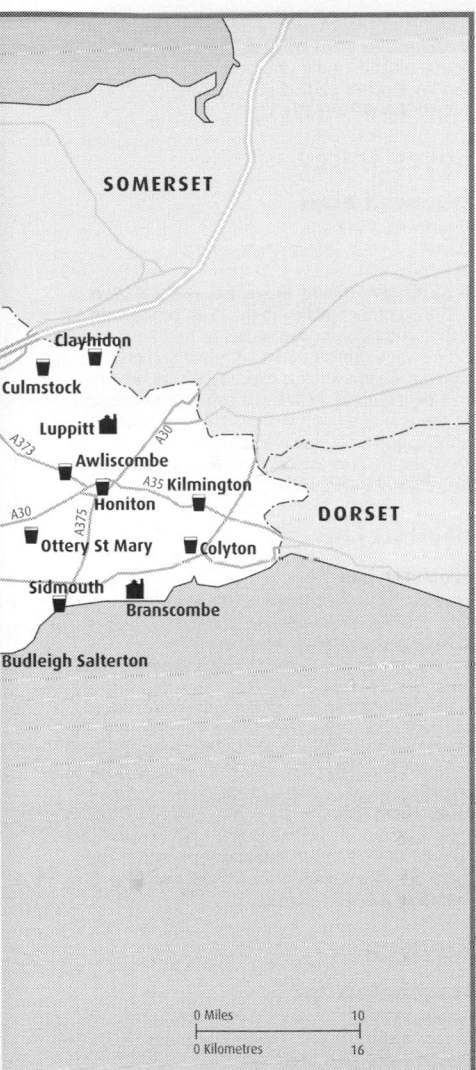

from West Country breweries, and good value food is served lunchtimes and evenings. There is a garden, a large car park, and a limited bus service. Live music features on the last Friday of the month, and there is a regular monthly quiz night. Two en-suite letting bedrooms are available.
🏠🕭🕙💷◑♣P↻▪🖵 (694,368)

Bampton

Swan
Station Road, EX16 9NG
🟢 8am-11 (10.30 Sun); 10.30-midnight Fri & Sat
☎ (01398) 332248 ⊕ theswan.co
Beer range varies Ⓗ
The oldest pub in Bampton, and the original lodgings for the masons and craftsmen who were hired to enlarge the nearby church. The pub has recently been renovated, with solid oak fittings, polished wood tables and boarded flooring, to give it a wine bar feel. The large fireplace contains the original bread oven from 1450. A large public car park, on the site of the old railway station, is close by. The two guest beers are always from South West breweries. ♨Q🕭🕙💷◑Ġ♣P↻▪🖵 (398)

Barnstaple

Panniers Ⓛ
33-34 Boutport Street, EX31 1RX (opp Queen's Theatre and 200yds from bus terminus)
🟢 7-11 (midnight Fri & Sat) ☎ (01271) 329720
Greene King Abbot; Ruddles Best Bitter; guest beers Ⓗ
Popular Wetherspoon pub close to the historic Pannier Market with an unrivalled selection of real ales in the area, many from local microbreweries, plus cider from Westons. The split-level interior offers several distinct seating areas including a

originally housed the workers constructing the nearby church, it was used by Sir Francis Drake on his journeys to London. There are drinking areas either side of the entrance hallway in the main bar, which is L-shaped, rustic and wood-panelled, with a canopy. A smaller bar at the rear is served via a small hatch and counter. Local Thompstone's Cider is on sale. Q🕙◑♣●↻▪🖵 (X38,88)

Awliscombe

Honiton Inn
EX14 3PJ (in centre of village on A373 2 miles from Honiton)
🟢 11.30-2.30, 5.30 (5 Fri & Sat)-11; 12-5 Sun
☎ (01404) 46161 ⊕ thehonitoninn.com
Otter Bitter; guest beers Ⓗ
A traditional village pub two miles from Honiton which has recently been modernised and refurbished, creating a warm welcome and a friendly atmosphere. Most of the beers are sourced

INDEPENDENT BREWERIES
Barum Barnstaple
Bays Paignton
Beer Engine Newton St Cyres
Branscombe Vale Branscombe
Bridgetown Totnes
Clearwater Bideford
Country Life Abbotsham
Dartmoor Princetown
Devon Earth Paignton
Exe Valley Silverton
Exeter Exeter
Forge Hartland
Garage Plympton St Maurice
Holsworthy Clawton
Hunter's Ipplepen
Isca Dawlish
Jollyboat Bideford
Noss Beer Works Lee Mill (NEW)
O'Hanlon's Whimple
Otter Luppitt
Platform 5 Newton Abbot (NEW)
Plymouth Plymouth
Quercus Churchstow
Red Rock Bishopsteignton
South Hams Stokenham
Summerskills Billacombe
Tavy Plymouth (NEW)
Teignworthy Newton Abbot
Topsham Topsham
Wizard Ilfracombe

small space for families. An exclusive beer festival for CAMRA Devon branches is held every February/ March. There are several framed prints hanging around the pub depicting local historic scenes and characters. The rear garden area has covered and heated seating and is a suntrap in summer. ኤ⊛ΦᏰ╚╣ᝌ╌⊟

Reform Inn 🗓
Reform Street, Pilton, EX31 1PD
✪ 11.30-11 (midnight Fri & Sat); 12-11 Sun
☎ (01271) 323164
Barum Breakfast, EPA, Original Ⓗ
Well-established, popular community local and brewery tap for Barum Brewery, whose beers dominate here. From the main road, look above roof level for the pub sign to locate it. The skittle alley is the setting for the annual Green Man beer festival in July, and other regular beer festivals are held during the year. Music is played in the public bar, with open mic sessions every Monday and bands on alternate Fridays. The lounge bar is quieter. ⊛⊟♣╚╌⊟(1,2,3)

Bere Ferrers

Olde Plough Inn
Fore Street, PL20 7JG (close to church and river)
✪ 11-3, 6-11; 11-11 Sat; 12-11 Sun ☎ (01822) 840358
Sharp's Doom Bar; guest beers Ⓗ
A 16th-century village inn with outstanding views over the River Tavy from the beer garden and only a 15-minute walk from the station on the picturesque Tamar Valley line. Inside, there are flagstones, exposed stonework, beams, real fires and a welcoming atmosphere that attracts both locals and visitors. Live music, acoustic and jam sessions feature, along with fish and chip suppers and curry nights. Up to three guest beers come from local and popular nationals. Real cider is available in summer. ₳ኤ⊛Φ⇌♣ᝌ╚

Bittaford

Horse & Groom 🗓
Exeter Road, PL21 0EL SX667569
✪ 12-11 (midnight Fri & Sat) ☎ (01752) 892358
Hunter's Albion Ale; guest beers Ⓗ
Very much a 1930s community village pub, it offers three varying beers from Devon and Cornwall, plus a house beer brewed by Hunter's. The large open-plan bar has a central fireplace. The pub is decorated with historic photos of the area taken from the former Moorhaven Hospital which overlooked the village. Local charities are supported by regular beer and cider festivals. Excellent food is served, and dogs are welcome in the bar area. ₳⊛Φ⊟▲♣ᝌᏢ╚⊟(X38,X80)

Black Torrington

Torridge Inn
Broad Street, EX21 5PT SS465055
✪ 12-3 (not Tue or winter), 6.30-11; 12-11 Sat; 12-10.30 Sun
☎ (01409) 231243 ⊕ thetorridgeinn.co.uk
St Austell Tribute; guest beers Ⓗ
Friendly village local dating from the 18th century and close to both the Tarka Trail and the Ruby Trail walks. A large log fire welcomes in winter, while in summer the pleasant beer garden affords attractive views of the Torridge Valley. At least two real ales are always available (with a discount

scheme for CAMRA members), together with Sam's Medium cider from Winkleigh. A good selection of home-cooked locally sourced food is served, with Sunday lunches particularly popular. ₳Q⊛Φ♣ᝌᏢ⊟(639,642)

Bovey Tracey

Cromwell Arms
Fore Street, TQ13 9AE
✪ 11-11; 12-10.30 Sun ☎ (01626) 833473
⊕ thecromwellarms.co.uk
St Austell IPA, Tribute, Proper Job, seasonal beers Ⓗ
A 17th-century building in the town centre with 12 letting rooms and good access to Dartmoor. There is one large drinking area with two sections showing beams and exposed stonework, as well as two dining areas including a separate restaurant. At the rear is a large wisteria-covered smokers' retreat, and a pagoda where occasional barbecues are held. Quizzes are on Tuesdays and Sundays. ₳Q⊛≈Φ╚♣Ᏸ╚⊟(39)

Bratton Clovelly

Clovelly Inn 🗓
EX20 4JZ (between A30 and A3079) SX464919
✪ 12-3, 6-midnight; 12-midnight Sat & Sun
☎ (01837) 871447 ⊕ clovellyinn.co.uk
Dartmoor Legend, Jail Ale; St Austell Dartmoor Best Bitter Ⓗ
Traditional village pub on the edge of Dartmoor National Park dating back to the 18th century. The cosy main bar, with a large wood-burning stove, is complemented by two separate dining areas (book ahead for meals in the evenings) and a games room. Three real ales are kept and Sam's Medium cider is also available in summer. Jazz sessions are held on the second Monday of each month and there are also regular acoustic/folk evenings. ₳ኤ⊛Φ▲♣ᝌᏢ╚⊟(633)

Brendon

Staghunters Inn 🗓
Lynton, EX35 6PS (1 mile S of A39) SS767481
✪ 12-11 ☎ (01598) 741222 ⊕ staghunters.com
Exmoor Gold; guest beers Ⓗ
Family-run hotel on the River Lyn set in a picturesque valley. Built on the site of an old abbey, it was also once a coaching inn. Up to five regularly changing real ales are served, with the emphasis on West Country brewers. Cider is mainly from Palmerhayes. A wide range of traditional, locally sourced food is available to suit all pockets. Dogs are welcome in the bar and in overnight accommodation for a nominal charge. ⊛≈ΦᝌᏢ╚

Brixham

Queen's Arms
31 Station Hill, TQ5 8BN
✪ 4-11; 12-midnight Fri & Sat; 12-11 Sun ☎ (01803) 852074
Beer range varies Ⓗ
Reopened just two years ago, this end-of-terrace back-street local (previously associated with the now defunct railway station) has become the heart of the local community. It has a small one-room bar with a wood-burning stove, and serves six changing ales, two of which are supplied by Hunter's Brewery. One is always priced at £2.50.

The pub has live music on Saturdays, hosts ale events throughout the year and holds an annual beer festival. ▲△❀♣☻⚊

Brixton

Foxhound Inn L

PL8 2AH SX554522
🌑 11-11 (midnight Fri & Sat); 12-11 Sun ☎ (01752) 880271
⊕ foxhoundinn.co.uk
Courage Best Bitter; guest beers Ⓗ
An 18th-century former coaching house in a rural village just east of Plymouth, well served by a frequent daytime bus service. The pub has two separate bars and a small restaurant. Traditional English meals are made using locally sourced ingredients from a nearby National Trust farm. Look out for Red Coat, an ale crafted by the landlord, among the four guest ales. A monthly quiz night is held, as are curry nights. Local CAMRA Country Pub of the Year 2013.
▲Q☎❀◑⬠▲♣☻P⚊◻(93,94)

Buckland Monachorum

Drake Manor Inn L

The Village, PL20 7NA
🌑 11.30-2.30, 6.30-11; 11.30-11.30 Fri & Sat; 12-11 Sun
☎ (01822) 853892 ⊕ drakemanorinn.co.uk
Dartmoor Jail Ale; Otter Ale; Sharp's Doom Bar Ⓗ
Cosy and friendly pub dating from the 16th century, located in a pleasant village on the edge of Dartmoor. It attracts a regular clientele who are happy to be assisted with the daily crossword. The inviting traditional interior features an intimate meeting area, a public bar and a restaurant area in which to sample the good food. The garden, with a stream, is an enjoyable suntrap. Good-value food is served at both lunch and evening times.
▲Q☎❀◑⬠⚊◻(55,56)

Budleigh Salterton

Salterton Arms

22 Chapel Street, EX9 6LX
🌑 11-11.30; 12-11 Sun ☎ (01395) 445048
Otter Ale; St Austell Dartmoor Best Bitter; guest beers Ⓗ
A very friendly, traditional local pub, clean and tidy with a new decor of wooden and Cotswold stone floors. There is a good choice of two regular ales from the Otter and St Austell breweries, plus two guest ales. Good-value food is served downstairs, as well as in a separate restaurant upstairs. Children and dogs, darts and euchre players are all warmly welcomed. ▲◑⬠♣☻◻(157,357)

Burrington

Portsmouth Arms Hotel

Umberleigh, EX37 9ND (on A377 about 4 miles S of Umberleigh)
🌑 12 (4 winter)-11 ☎ (01769) 561117
Otter Bitter; Skinner's Betty Stogs Ⓗ
Featuring a cob structure some 600 years old at the entrance to the front bar area, there are also original oak beams and a woodburner with a print of the Earl of Portsmouth above the fire. The horseshoe-shaped bar has three handpumps and links the front area to the public bar towards the back, where pool and darts are played. Quality freshly cooked food using locally sourced produce

is served every day until 9pm. Well-behaved children and dogs welcome.
▲Q❀☎◑⬠▲≈P⚊

Butterleigh

Butterleigh Inn 🏆 L

The Green, EX15 1PN (opp church)
🌑 6-11 Mon; 12-2.30, 6-11 (midnight Fri & Sat); 12-3 Sun
☎ (01884) 855433 ⊕ butterleighinn.co.uk
Cotleigh Tawny Owl; Dartmoor Dartmoor IPA; Otter Ale; guest beer Ⓗ
An excellent country pub in a small, quaint village, this is a splendid 17th-century Devon cob building. Lunchtimes tend to be quiet. It is busier evenings and weekends, when a mix of generations creates a great atmosphere with diverse conversation. A choice of three real ales is always on offer, two of which are LocAle, and ciders. There is a main bar, lounge and a modern dining room. Drink inside or outside, with lovely surroundings either way. Local CAMRA Pub of the Year 2013.
▲Q☎❀☎◑⬠♣☻P⚊

Calverleigh

Rose & Crown L

EX16 8BA (on the old Rackenford road)
🌑 12-midnight ☎ (01884) 256301
⊕ roseandcrowncalverleigh.co.uk
Butcombe Bitter; Otter Ale; guest beers Ⓗ
A traditional 18th-century country pub with beamed ceilings and exposed stone walls, just a mile from Tiverton town centre, with a restaurant, secluded beer garden and a skittle alley that doubles as a function room. Excellent home-cooked food (made with local produce where possible) is available noon to 9.30pm, together with local cider from Palmerhayes across the road. One guest beer is usually on offer, and occasionally two. Q❀◑⬠♣☻P

Chagford

Globe L

9 High Street, TQ13 8AJ
🌑 11-11 (10.30 Sun) ☎ (01647) 433485
⊕ theglobeinnchagford.co.uk
Dartmoor IPA; Otter Ale, Bitter Ⓗ
Overlooking the parish church, this attractive pub was formerly a coaching inn and cooperage which has evolved into a focal point for the village. Serving good food, it additionally offers music evenings and a cinema club plus myriad other events and functions. It has two separate bars, one a splendid, traditional public bar, and both warmed by large open fires. A small courtyard garden is at the rear and a car park is close by. The cider is Westons Old Rosie. ▲❀☎◑⬠☻◻(173,178)

Sandy Park Inn L

Sandy Park, TQ13 8JW (on A382 Moretonhampstead-Whiddon Down road)
🌑 11-11 (10.30 Sun) ☎ (01647) 433267
⊕ sandyparkinn.co.uk
Dartmoor IPA; Jail Ale; Otter Bitter Ⓗ**; guest beers** Ⓗ/Ⓖ
Thatched free house, thought to be 17th century. The main bar has a large open fireplace, ancient beams, a stone floor and high-backed wooden bench seating. Beyond is a small snug. There is a separate dining room serving home-cooked food

(all day Sun; no food Mon winter). Castle Drogo (NT), Fingle Bridge and Chagford Village are nearby. A large garden is reached via steps at the rear and there is a small car park at the front of the pub. ♨❀⇆❶▶P🛏(173,178)

Chittlehampton

Bell Inn ⏃
The Square, EX37 9QL (opp church) SS636254
✪ 11-3, 6-midnight; 11-midnight Sat; 12-11 Sun
☎ (01769) 540368 ⏛ thebellatchittlehampton.co.uk
Beer range varies ⒣/Ⓖ
Large, comfortable and homely village local which has been in the same family since 1975. Four handpumps feature a constantly changing selection of ales, supplemented by a further choice on gravity listed near the bar. The cider is Cheddar Valley from Thatchers. The conservatory offers views of the garden and there is a children's outdoor play area next to the orchard which is home to several alpacas. Look for the etched window commemorating its local CAMRA Pub of the Year award. ❀⇆❶♿♣●⁀🛏(658,859)

Chudleigh Knighton

Anchor ⏃
Plymouth Road, TQ13 0EN
✪ 3 (12 Sat)-11; 12-10.30 Sun ☎ (01626) 852366
Beer range varies ⒣
A 15th-century coaching inn on the old Plymouth turnpike with the stables now used as a skittle alley. A small, mainly unspoilt public bar contrasts with a larger area that was once a vet's surgery, with both leading out to a hidden garden and smoker's gazebo. The three handpumps show a strong emphasis towards local breweries, especially Dartmoor and Teignworthy. Unusually, curries can ordered for delivery to the pub.
♨Q❀❶◫⁀🛏(39,182)

Chulmleigh

Old Court House
South Molton Street, EX18 7BW (200yds N of town centre)
✪ 11-11 ☎ (01769) 580045 ⏛ oldcourthouseinn.co.uk
Butcombe Bitter; Exmoor Ale; guest beers ⒣
Grade II historic local with three real ales and Thatchers Traditional Dry cider always available. The fire adds to the warm welcome in the bar, with the restaurant situated to the rear. A wall in one of the bedrooms still bears the coat of arms that marks the time Charles I stayed here in 1634. A quiz night each Thursday supports local charities and a discount of 10p per pint is available to CAMRA members. ♨❀⇆❶♣●⁀🛏(377)

Clayhidon

Half Moon Inn
EX15 3TJ
✪ closed Mon; 12-3, 6-11 (closed Sun eve winter)
☎ (01823) 680291 ⏛ halfmoondevon.co.uk
Otter Bitter; guest beers ⒣
The Half Moon is well known for its traditional food, presented with style in warm, welcoming surroundings. Quality local produce is freshly and carefully prepared in the kitchens, including the famous home-made desserts. The pub has a fascinating history, an amazing view over the

beautiful Culm Valley, a lovely log fire, a function room for parties or meetings and a great selection of frequently changing real ales. It has a 5-star food hygiene rating. ♨Q❄❀❶▲♣●P⁀

Cockwood

Anchor Inn ⏃
EX6 8RA (just off the A379, outside Starcross, next to Cockwood harbour) SX976807
✪ 11-11; 11.30-10.30 Sun ☎ (01626) 890203
⏛ anchorinncockwood.com
Otter Ale; St Austell Tribute; guest beers ⒣
On picturesque Cockwood harbour, this 450-year-old inn and former seaman's mission has many old settles, timber panelling, low beams and snugs, with an impressive display of old nautical memorabilia all around. Live music is an occasional feature. It has an award-winning, extensive seafood menu, especially mussels. Haunted by a friendly short and his dog, this is a really atmospheric Devon gem. Being close to the main GWR line, it is also a steam train spotters' paradise. Guest ales are all LocAle. ♨Q❀❶♿♣●P⁀🛏(2)

Ship Inn
Church Road, EX6 8NU (just off A379, outside Starcross, close to Cockwood harbour) SX975806
✪ 11-11; 12-10.30 Sun ☎ (01626) 890373
⏛ shipinncockwood.co.uk
Dartmoor Jail Ale; Exmoor Ale; St Austell Tribute; Sharp's Doom Bar; guest beers ⒣
A very busy family-run pub, close to the picturesque harbour at Cockwood, with a large beer garden with views of the estuary, and a roaring log fire for the winter. The pub is popular with drinkers and diners alike, offering a choice of four regular ales and three rotating ciders, and an excellent food menu. Meals are made with local produce where possible, including a varied choice of locally caught fish. ♨Q❀❶▲♣●🛏(2)

Colyton

Kingfisher Inn
Dolphin Street, EX24 6NA
✪ 11-3, 6-11 (midnight Fri); 11-midnight Sat; 12-10.30 (6 winter) Sun ☎ (01297) 552476 ⏛ kingfisherinn.co.uk
Sharp's Doom Bar; Skinner's Betty Stogs; guest beers ⒣
A traditional 16th-century stone and timber pub close to the centre of the town, with a public car park nearby, and a tram that connects to Seaton. A separate restaurant at the rear serves locally sourced good-value food. Themed food events take place once a month, and skittles, darts, crib and boules are regularly played at this friendly pub. Families and dogs are welcome. One or two guest beers are served, usually from the West Country. A beer festival is held over the spring bank holiday. ❄❀❶▲♣⁀🛏(20,885)

Combeinteignhead

Wild Goose ⏃
Shaldon Road, TQ12 4RA
✪ 11-3, 5.30-11 (midnight Thu & Fri); 12-3, 7-11 Sun
☎ (01626) 872241
Hunter's Black Jack; Sharp's Doom Bar; guest beers ⒣
Charming 17th-century beamed pub and restaurant with a cosy, welcoming atmosphere. A changing range of ales is offered, as is a good selection of

bottled continental beers. The real cider comes from various producers, mainly from the South West. Food is sourced locally. Friday night music is eclectic but good while the Saturday night quiz is popular. An attractive garden at the rear abuts a 14th-century red sandstone church. Two holiday cottages are available to rent. ᵂQ✿🏚◑♣🐕P⚐

Countisbury

Blue Ball Inn Ⓛ
Countisbury Hill, EX35 6NE (1 mile E of Lynmouth) SS747496
✪ 9-11 ☎ (01598) 741263 ⊕ blueballinn.com
Clearwater Real Smiler; Exmoor Stag; St Austell Tribute; guest beers Ⓗ
Old coaching inn open every day of the year, with low ceilings, blackened beams and a large 13th-century inglenook fire near the bar. Four real ales are available including one guest. Food is served all day from an extensive menu either in the bar or the large dining area. Outside there is a spacious patio area with the car park opposite. It is ideal for walking and other outdoor pursuits and very dog-friendly. A beer festival is held every November. ᵂQ✿🏚◑P⚐(300,401)

Crediton

Crediton Inn Ⓛ
28a Mill Street, EX17 1EZ (near A377 and station)
✪ 10-11; 12-3, 7-10.30 Sun ☎ (01363) 772882
⊕ crediton-inn.co.uk
O'Hanlon's Yellowhammer; guest beers Ⓗ
The framed deeds date this inn to 1878, and its windows are etched with the ancient town seal. This genuine free house is well supported by the locals. The handpumps have increased to 10, serving beers from local breweries, with an ale festival in November. The skittle alley doubles as a function room. Good home-cooked food is served at weekends, with snacks and renowned Scotch eggs available at other times. The bubbly owner is the longest-serving landlady in Crediton, with 33 years behind the bar. ᵂ✿◑≒♣P⚐(50,51,315)

Cullompton

Pony & Trap Ⓛ
10 Exeter Hill, EX15 1DJ (on B3181 S of town)
✪ 12-2, 5-11.30; 12-5, 8-11 Sun ☎ (01884) 34182
⊕ ponyandtrapcullompton.co.uk
Butcombe Bitter; Dartmoor IPA, Jail Ale; Otter Bitter; guest beers Ⓗ
Traditional local with a good atmosphere and a mixed clientele. The smart interior features a logburner, making it cosy in winter, while flowers and ornaments give a homely feel. There are always six real ales on in the week and seven at weekends; food is available Tuesday to Sunday lunchtimes, and evenings on request in advance. There is a seating area and garden outside. Live music plays once a month and games include darts, skittles, shove ha'penny and shut the box. ᵂQ✿◑♣⚐(1)

Culmstock

Culm Valley Inn
EX15 3JJ

✪ 12-3, 6-11; 11-11 Fri & Sat; 12-10.30 Sun
☎ (01884) 840354 ⊕ culmvalleyinn.co.uk
Beer range varies Ⓖ
A 300-year-old village inn by a medieval bridge on the River Culm, with at least six changing real ales from small breweries at any one time, rising to 10 at weekends, all served by gravity from the cellar room behind the bar. Bollhayes and Tricky ciders are also on sale. A rustic bar leads to another room, then to the restaurant. A beer festival is held every end of May bank holiday. The car park at the front of the pub has a recently installed totem pole. Dogs are welcome. ᵂQ✿🏚◑♣🐕P

Dousland

Burrator Inn Ⓛ
PL20 6NP
✪ 11-11 (12.30am Sat); 12-11 Sun ☎ (01822) 853121
⊕ theburratorinn.com
Dartmoor IPA, Jail Ale; St Austell Tribute; Sharp's Doom Bar Ⓗ
Substantial pub on the road between Yelverton and Princetown, close to the picturesque Burrator Reservoir. The interior comprises several rooms, including a separate dining room, offering a pool table and two dartboards. Home-made food and pies are produced from locally sourced suppliers, and are served throughout the day. There is ample parking, and a large enclosed beer garden incorporating a children's play area. A beer festival is held annually in September; a Sunday quiz night, live music and other entertainment also feature. ᵂQ🐕✿🏚◑♿♣P⚐(55,98)

East Budleigh

Sir Walter Raleigh Inn Ⓛ
22 High Street, EX9 7ED (off B3178 opp Hayes Lane)
✪ 12-2.30, 6-11; 12-2.30, 7-10.30 Sun ☎ (01395) 442510
⊕ sirwalterraleighinn.co.uk
Otter Ale; Sharp's Doom Bar; guest beers Ⓗ
Set in the middle of the delightful village of East Budleigh, the birthplace of Sir Walter Raleigh, this is a truly welcoming 16th-century free house country pub. Good-quality pub food is served lunchtimes and evenings, and normally there are four real ales to choose from. Originally two cottages, it was then converted into a Jacobean-style pub. There are original wooden beams throughout the two different areas. This gem is well worth a visit for good-quality real ale. Q✿◑⚐(157)

East Prawle

Pig's Nose Inn ♉ Ⓛ
TQ7 2BY SX781365
✪ 12-2.30, 6-11; 12-3, 6-11 (closed winter) Sun
☎ (01548) 511209 ⊕ pigsnoseinn.co.uk
Otter Bitter; South Hams Eddystone Ⓖ; guest beers Ⓗ
An old three-roomed smugglers' inn on the village green in an area that attracts birdwatchers and coastal walkers. Gravity beers are stored on a specially made rack behind the bar. Home-cooked, locally sourced food is served. Children and dogs are welcome and even have their own menus. The maritime-themed interior is cluttered with objects, children's games and knitting for adults. There are occasional live music events in a hall adjoining the pub. Current local CAMRA Pub of the Year. ᵂ🐕✿◑▲♣🐕⚐

Exbourne

Red Lion Inn 🄻
High Street, EX20 3RY (200yds N of jct with A386)
SS602018
⊕ 12-11 ☎ (01837) 851551
Dartmoor Legend; St Austell Tribute; guest beers 🄖
A 16th-century village local that has no draught lager, only bottles. Casks are placed at one end of the bar along with Sam's Dry and Medium ciders from Winkleigh. Good-value locally sourced food is served all day until 9.30pm in the adjacent dining areas. An offset room contains a pool table and TV, and well-behaved children and dogs are welcome. Charity beer festivals are held three times a year, including one with a pantomime after Christmas.
🏚Q🕸🕪♣🐾P🖼(318)

Exeter

George's Meeting House
38 South Street, EX1 1ED
⊕ 8-midnight ☎ (01392) 454250
Dartmoor Jail Ale; Greene King Abbot; guest beers 🄗
Formerly George's Meeting, listed as having special interest as an unaltered 18th-century building that was a Unitarian chapel dating from 1760 and named after King George III. There are lovely stained glass windows, upstairs galleries and even a pulpit in situ. Nicely converted by Wetherspoon, the pub opened in January 2005. It is very popular both lunchtimes and evenings. Food is served all day, and there is a good range of real ales always available. The real cider is Sandford Orchards.
Q🕭🕸🕪≒(Central)🐾♨🖼

Great Western Hotel 🄻
St David's Station, EX4 4NU
⊕ 10-midnight (1am Fri & Sat) ☎ (01392) 274039
⊕ greatwesternhotel.co.uk
Branscombe Vale Branoc; Dartmoor Jail Ale 🄗/🄖; RCH PG Steam 🄗/🄖, Pitchfork; guest beers 🄗
Traditional railway hotel that features one of the largest ranges of real ales in the city (at least eight at any one time). It has a good community spirit, and has twice been winner of local CAMRA Pub of the Year. Meals are served in the bars and Brunel restaurant. To impress diners, the Great Western offers fairly priced home-cooked food that comes from a varied menu, with curry night on Wednesday and a roast on Sunday. Children and dogs are welcome.
Q🕸🕪🕭🕪≒(St David's)♣P🖼(H)

Hour Glass Inn
21 Melbourne Street, EX2 4AU (approx 300yds from Quayside)
⊕ 12-3, 5-11 (midnight Sat); 12-10.30 Sun
☎ (01392) 258722
Beer range varies 🄗
A traditional pub in the back streets of Exeter, in the hub of the local area close to the Quay and about five minutes' walk from the main city centre. The pub has two restaurants and a bar, serving contemporary and continental food. It is very traditional in its features, with a mixture of live entertainment including light theatre and music, which has proved popular with its eclectic group of customers. 🏚Q🕪🕭♣♨🖼(S,T)

Imperial 🄻
New North Road, EX4 4AH
⊕ 8am-midnight (1am Fri & Sat) ☎ (01392) 434050

Greene King Abbot; Ruddles Best Bitter; guest beers 🄗
Large Wetherspoon pub near the university, with public transport close by. Its large sunny garden offers plenty of tables and seating. Ten beers are usually available, plus guest ales, often from local breweries. Good-value food is served all day. Built in 1810 as Elmfield House, then changed to the Imperial Hotel in 1923, its attractive architecture and orangery are still there to be enjoyed. Beer festivals are regularly held throughout the year, with some showcasing local breweries.
Q🕭🕸🕪🕭≒(St David's)P🖼(D,50)

Mill on the Exe
Bonhay Road, EX4 3AB
⊕ 10.30-11 ☎ (01392) 214464 ⊕ millontheexe.co.uk
St Austell Dartmoor Best Bitter, Tribute, Proper Job; guest beer 🄗
Beautiful riverside pub, formerly a paper mill, with a welcoming and vibrant atmosphere. It has two bars over two floors, each boasting four handpumps with St Austell brews, seasonal and guest ales. It also stocks a selection of bottled ales, including Clouded Yellow, with more guest brewery ales in the future. Quality home-cooked food is served from noon to 9pm daily. The large garden has stunning views of Blackaller Weir. Children and dogs are welcome.
🏚🕸🕪🕭≒(St Thomas)P♨🖼

Exmouth

First & Last Inn 🄻
10 Church Street, EX8 1PE (off B3178 Rolle Street)
⊕ 11-11 (11.30 Sat); 12-10.30 Sun ☎ (01395) 263275
⊕ members.multimania.co.uk/fnlpub
Courage Directors; Otter Ale 🄗; guest beers 🄗/🄖
Victorian pub near the town centre, with a public car park opposite, a genuine free house, much enlarged by the present owners. It provides three distinct drinking areas, and an outside patio area with heated awnings. Games include pool and darts, and there is a skittle alley. Televised sport is prominent in the pub. Well-behaved dogs are welcome. Two or three guest beers are sold, usually from the West Country, and the cider is Thatchers Dry. The pub has air conditioning.
🕸🕭≒🐾♨🖼(57,157)

Grapevine
2 Victoria Road, EX8 1DL
⊕ 9-11 (midnight Fri & Sat); 9-5 Sun ☎ (01395) 222208
⊕ grapevineexmouth.com
Beer range varies 🄗
The Grapevine, which opened in November 2010 as a bistro pub, is located centrally just off the pedestrianised Strand area, and has gained a reputation for being the place to go in Exmouth for eating and drinking. The excellent food with regularly changing plat du jour and the selection of real ales, mainly from local breweries, plus ciders and continental beers, make this venue the ideal place for people looking for something special. Live music is regularly featured. 🕸🕪🕭≒🐾♨🖼(57,97)

Holly Tree
161 Withycombe Village Road, EX8 3AN (leave A376 at Gipsy Lane lights, then turn left)
⊕ 11 (12 Sun)-midnight ☎ (01395) 273440
Draught Bass; Greene King Abbot; St Austell Dartmoor Best Bitter, Proper Job; Wells Bombardier; guest beers 🄗

A very popular traditional pub that concentrates on serving good beer. There are two darts, four pool and two euchre teams, and Sunday is quiz night. It is a pub much supported by the local community, where beer and conversation predominate. Dogs are welcome at all times, and families until 7pm. There is a covered smoking area outside, plus two separate areas to sit outside. This is a warm, comfortable and friendly local. ❀&♣P⁵⌐⌂(97)

Powder Monkey L

2-2a The Parade, EX8 1RJ
❂ 8am-midnight (1am Fri & Sat) ☎ (01395) 280090
Greene King Abbot; Ruddles Best Bitter; guest beers Ⓗ
A Wetherspoon pub named after Nancy Perriam, whose sewing skills earned her a berth in the navy where she also acted as a powder monkey. Nancy lived in nearby Tower Street. A powder monkey was naval slang for boys and girls who filled shells and cartridges with gunpowder on board ships of war. The building was converted from local newspaper offices. The bar is adjacent to the central seating areas, with a number of rooms off it. ♨Q❀❸⅃&≈☙⁵⌐⌂(57)

Great Torrington

Black Horse Inn

High Street, EX38 8HN
❂ 11-11 (11.30 Fri & Sat); 12-11 Sun ☎ (01805) 622121
⊕ blackhorsedevon.co.uk
Courage Best Bitter; guest beers Ⓗ
Dating back to the 16th-century, this coaching inn was used by Hopton and Fairfax during the Civil War Battle of Torrington in 1646. It is run by a local family and has a distinctive frontage, with its white wall and dark framed leaded light windows. The interior is rich with traditional oak beams and panels, and purports to have a resident ghost. Up to four real ales are available along with great-value bar food or a full dining experience in the restaurant. Q⊟⅃❸

Hatherleigh

Tally Ho! L

14 Market Street, EX20 3JN (opp church)
❂ 12-11 (1am Fri & Sat); 11-11 Tue ☎ (01837) 810306
⊕ tallyhohatherleigh.co.uk
Clearwater Devon Dympsy; St Austell Tribute; guest beers Ⓗ
Oak-beamed 15th-century inn with a single bar which has two wood-burning fires. The real ale prices are significantly reduced on Tuesday market day from 11am to 3pm. Happy hour runs from 3pm to 6pm weekdays, when selected drinks are again reduced in price. Good-quality food made with local produce is served in the bar or separate dining room. A chess group meets every first Saturday and a mah jong group every last Sunday, both at 3pm. ♨Q❀⊟❸♣⁵⌐⌂(51,118)

Heavitree

Royal Oak L

79-81 Fore Street, EX1 2RN
❂ 11.30-11 (midnight Fri & Sat); 12-11 Sun
☎ (01392) 254121 ⊕ heavitreeroyaloak.co.uk
Adnams Broadside; Otter Amber, Ale; Young's Bitter; guest beers Ⓗ

A traditional family-run town pub on several regular bus routes, with plenty of parking nearby. Four regular ales plus two guests are on offer at any one time. Good-value pub food is served lunchtimes, with a traditional roast on Sunday; no food is served evenings except for a steak/fish night on Thursday. With a large comfortable main bar and a smaller side room, the pub has a real community feel, while remaining welcoming to visitors. It has front and rear beer gardens with a covered smoking area. ☾❀❸⅃⊟♣⁵⌐⌂

Heddon Valley

Hunters Inn L

EX31 4PY (signed from A399) SS655481
❂ 10-11 ☎ (01598) 763230 ⊕ thehuntersinn.net
Exmoor Ale, Stag, Gold; Hunters Dr Heale, Miss Loosemore, Mr Sluggett Ⓗ
Popular, large renovated inn in a picturesque valley where peacocks are allowed to wander freely. Several real ales are on offer, including up to three brewed for the pub by Country Life Brewery. The cider is Sam's Medium from Winkleigh. It is easy to see why walkers, hikers, cyclists, families with children and dog owners are all attracted here. A three-day beer and music festival in early September is well supported by locals and held in the rear garden area. ♨Q❀⊟❸&▲♣☙P

Holcombe

Smugglers Inn L

27 Teignmouth Road, EX7 0LA (on A379 between Dawlish and Teignmouth)
❂ 11-11 ☎ (01626) 862301 ⊕ thesmugglersinn.net
Dartmoor Legend; Teignworthy Reel Ale; guest beer Ⓗ
With splendid coastal views, this roadside free house has an excellent reputation. Good food is served lunchtimes and evenings, the carvery being a particular attraction. There are two regular ales and one varying guest. The bar area has a wood-burning stove. The outside area is popular throughout the seasons, with a separate smokers' canopy. A mini beer festival is held towards the end of January, usually featuring around 14 ales, and regular entertainment is hosted. There is a car park and buses pass the door. ♨❀❸&AP⁵⌐⌂(2)

Holcombe Rogus

Prince of Wales Inn

TA21 0PN
❂ 5.30-11 Mon; 12-3, 5.30-11 (midnight Fri); 12-midnight Sat; 12-10 Sun ☎ (01823) 672070
Otter Bitter; Sharp's Doom Bar; guest beers Ⓗ
A 17th-century country pub, lying close to the Grand Western Canal and the Somerset border. The area is popular with walkers and cyclists. Inside, the bar features unusual cash register handpumps. Home-cooked food, including vegetarian options and a carvery on Sundays, is served, and there are regular food-themed nights. A large log-burning stove warms the pub in winter. There is a darts area, shove ha'penny and dominoes, plus occasional live music. The attractive walled garden is popular in summer. ♨☾❀❸♣P

Holsworthy

Old Market Inn 🆛

Chapel Street, EX22 6AY (on A388 S of town square)
✪ 11-midnight (1am Fri & Sat); 12-11 Sun
☎ (01409) 253941 ⊕ oldmarketinn.co.uk
Bays Gold; Holsworthy Muck 'n' Straw, Sunshine;
Skinner's Betty Stogs 🅷
Friendly, family-run free house in an historic
market town mentioned in the Domesday Book. Up
to six beers are served on gravity as well as four
from handpumps. Most of the beers are from
Devon and Cornwall breweries and the cider is
Autumn Scrumpy from Winkleigh. During St Peter's
Fair week in July a mini beer festival is held. Home
of the Holsworthy Comedy Club where local acts
appear regularly. Local CAMRA Pub of the Year
2012. ✿⇔◀⑴&♣🐾P½⌹(X9)

Honiton

Holt 🆛

178 High Street, EX14 1LA
✪ 11-3, 5.30-11 (midnight Sat); closed Sun & Mon
☎ (01404) 47707 ⊕ theholt-honiton.com
Otter Bitter, Amber, Bright, Ale, Head; guest beer 🅷
The Holt has a slate floor and ochre walls, which
makes for a smart decor, with lots of exposed
wood. The kitchen is fully open, allowing you to
watch the chefs preparing their delicious award-
winning main meals and tapas. The pub is the first
to be opened by Otter Brewery and is also the
brewery tap; this is reflected in the five
handpumps and the innovative taster racks – third-
pint measures are also available.
⑴▶⇌⌹(20,52B,367)

Iddesleigh

Duke of York

EX19 8BG (off B3217 next to church) SS569082
✪ 11-11; 12-10.30 Sun ☎ (01837) 810253
Adnams Broadside; Cotleigh Tawny; guest beers 🅶
A 15th-century inn where village resident Michael
Morpurgo was inspired to write his famous book,
War Horse, which went on to become a successful
film. The bar is simply furnished, with old beams,
an inglenook fire, rocking chair and 1970s photos
of locals. At least three real ales are served straight
from the cask, plus Sam's Medium and Dry cider
from Winkleigh. Food is available every day from
noon to 9.30pm (9pm Sun). Well-behaved dogs are
welcome. Accommodation is available in seven en-
suite rooms. 🏨Q✿⇔◀⑴Å♣🐾

Ideford

Royal Oak

TQ13 0AY
✪ 12-2.30 (not Mon), 6-11.15; 12-3, 7-11 Sun
☎ (01626) 852274
Courage Directors; guest beers 🅷
A charming, traditional 17th-century inn with
flagstone floor and beamed ceilings. The small,
cosy single bar is festooned with historic
memorabilia, mainly concerning Nelson and
Trafalgar. At the rear is a small sheltered patio,
with more tables across the road by the pub car
park. Children and dogs are welcome. The hostelry
is in the village centre and is popular with locals,
hashers, cyclists, walkers and morris dancers.
🏨✿◀⑴&♣P½

Ilfracombe

George & Dragon

4 Fore Street, EX34 9ED
✪ 10 (12 Sun)-midnight ☎ (01271) 863851
⊕ georgeanddragonilfracombe.co.uk
Exmoor Ale; St Austell Tribute; Shepherd Neame
Spitfire 🅷
Dating from 1360, the oldest pub in Ilfracombe and
one of the town's earliest buildings is handily close
to the harbour and pier. Three real ales are on offer
in an atmosphere of wooden beams and large
fireplaces. Fresh local produce, including
vegetables and herbs from the pub's garden, is
sourced for the wide range of bar snacks and
home-cooked meals available every day
lunchtimes and evenings. There is out-front seating
and dogs are welcome. Q⑴▶♣⌹(3,21A,30)

Ship & Pilot ♈ 🆛

10 Broad Street, EX34 9EE
✪ 11-midnight; 12-11 Sun ☎ (01271) 863562
Draught Bass 🅶; St Austell Trelawny; Wizard Druid's
Fluid 🅷
With a front painted a distinctive bright yellow, this
thriving and friendly local has been transformed in
recent years by its enterprising licensee. Six real
ales are usually available, together with at least
three real ciders and a perry. Food-wise, only bar
snacks are served, but the licensee allows food to
be brought in and consumed on the premises
provided a drink is purchased to accompany the
meal. Local CAMRA Pub of the Year 2013.
✿♣🐾⌹(3,30,301)

Kilmington

New Inn 🆛

The Hill, EX13 7SF (in village, S of A35)
✪ 11.30-2.30, 6-11; 12-3, 7-10.30 Sun ☎ (01297) 33376
Palmers Copper Ale, Best Bitter, Dorset Gold, Tally
Ho!; guest beer 🅷
Thatched Devon longhouse that became a pub in
the early 1800s, appearing in every issue of the
Guide (one of the magnificent seven) for 22 of
those years with the current landlord. It was rebuilt
after a major fire in 2004, retaining a welcoming
atmosphere and gaining excellent toilets with
disabled access. There is a large, safe garden, and a
well-used skittle alley. A quiz night is held monthly
with other events that maintain this pub's position
as an important part of village life.
Q✿⑴&♣P⌹(380)

Old Inn 🆛

EX13 7RB
✪ 11-3, 6-11; 12-3, 7-10.30 Sun ☎ (01297) 32096
⊕ oldinnkilmington.co.uk
Branscombe Vale Branoc, BVB Best Bitter; Otter
Bitter; guest beer 🅷
Thatched 16th-century inn on the A35. The
Cricketers' bar, a lounge with a log fire, and a
restaurant area are complemented by a suntrap
patio and a raised lawn. Food, served lunchtimes
and evenings (not Sun eve), is sourced locally,
including good mussels, and the many specials are
changed daily. See the website for more about
beer fests held at the end of May, August, bonfire
night in November, and regular themed nights. A
loyalty card system operates, earning points
towards meal vouchers. 🏨Q✿⑴⊞Å P½⌹(380)

Kings Nympton

Grove Inn L

EX37 9ST SS684195

✪ 12-3 (not Mon winter), 6-11; 12-4, 7-10.30 (not eve winter) Sun ☎ (01769) 580406 ⊕ thegroveinn.co.uk

Exmoor Ale; guest beers H

A 17th-century Grade II-listed thatched pub, its single bar has low beams with bookmarks hanging from them and the adjacent dining area has an open fire in winter. Four real ales are available plus Sam's Dry cider from Winkleigh. Award-winning food is served, with Tuesday's fish & chips in Exmoor Ale batter being popular (booking recommended). Children and dogs are welcome in the pub and the self-catering cottage nearby.
▲Q❀⇦❍❹♣♠᠁

Kingston

Dolphin Inn

Kingston, TQ7 4QE (next to the church) SX634478
✪ 12-3, 6-11; 12-3, 7-10.30 Sun ☎ (01548) 810314
⊕ dolphin-inn.co.uk

Beer range varies H

Very much a pub of two halves: the main building was converted from three 16th-century cottages, while the family room, gents toilet and large beer garden are on the opposite side of the road. Up to four West Country ales are served. Open inglenook fires give a cosy, intimate feel in winter. This pub is a community focal point, and is popular with tourists in summer. Excellent home-cooked food with locally sourced ingredients is also on offer. Dogs are welcome. ▲Q☎❀⇦❍♣♠P᠁

Kingswear

Ship Inn

Higher Street, TQ6 0AG
✪ 12-3, 6-midnight; 12-midnight Sat & Sun
☎ (01803) 752348 ⊕ shipinnforecast.com

Adnams Southwold Bitter; Otter Ale, Bitter; guest beers H

A 15th-century building next to the church, with lovely views overlooking the River Dart. This popular village pub has a well-deserved reputation for food and real ale. Up to six beers are available in the summer. Beer festivals are held in conjunction with Dartmouth festivals (food, sailing). The horseshoe-shaped bar is themed with naval memorabilia while two real fires make it cosy in winter. ▲Q❀❍⇌᠁⇦🚲(22,24,120)

Lake

Bearslake Inn L

EX20 4HQ (on A386) SX528888
✪ 11-11; 12-10.30 Sun ☎ (01837) 861334
⊕ bearslakeinn.com

Dartmoor Jail Ale, Legend; Otter Bitter H**; guest beers** H/G

Grade II-listed thatched Devon longhouse dating back to the 13th century and originally a working farm. The single bar serves up to four real ales, primarily from West Country brewers. There is a lounge area with log fires that is ideal for families. Views of Dartmoor can be enjoyed from the large riverside garden and the Granite Way path is close by. Excellent food is served in the bar or restaurant, prepared from local ingredients.
▲Q☎❀⇦❍♣᠁⇌🚲(118)

Manaton

Kestor Inn L

TQ13 9UF (on main road through village)
✪ 11-11 ☎ (01647) 221626 ⊕ kestorinn.com

Dartmoor Legend; Otter Bitter; guest beers H

Spacious village inn on Dartmoor with an open-plan L-shaped bar and plenty of seating. There is also a separate pool room and a long dining room, which can be used for functions. It has a friendly atmosphere, and a good selection of local real ales on offer. The lobby area of the pub has been turned into a small shop selling basic items, and a book exchange scheme is in operation. Sam's Medium cider is sold. ▲Q❀❍♣♠P

Mary Tavy

Mary Tavy Inn L

Lane Head, PL19 9PN
✪ 12-2.30, 6-11; 12-2.30, 5-midnight Fri; 12-midnight Sat; 12-11 Sun ☎ (01822) 810326 ⊕ themarytavyinn.co.uk

Dartmoor Jail Ale; guest beers H

A traditional roadside inn where families and dogs are welcome, with up to four varying real ales available. The popular bar accommodates pool, darts, TV and a large fire. This is complemented by a spacious restaurant and beer garden, with views up to Dartmoor. Music nights, charity events, quizzes, a Sunday carvery and a Whitsun bank holiday beer festival feature on the pub's programme. Modern B&B accommodation is available in the adjacent building. The pub closes Saturday and Sunday lunchtimes and Monday in winter. ▲Q☎❀⇦❍⊟♣P

Meavy

Royal Oak L

PL20 6PJ (on the village green) SX541672
✪ 11-3, 5-11 (11-11 Fri & Sat summer); 11-3, 6-9 (12-11 summer) Sun ☎ (01822) 852944 ⊕ royaloakinn.org.uk

Dartmoor IPA, Jail Ale; guest beers H

An iconic English village inn, dating from the 16th century, next to the church and overlooking the green where the eponymous tree stands. The lounge has a restaurant serving home-cooked food, complemented by an eclectic wine list. Up to four local ales figure prominently. The public bar provides a return to its history and agricultural roots: flagstone floor, large open fire, photos of times past. There is a good cider range.
▲Q❀❍⊟▲♣♠⇌🚲(56)

Milton Combe

Who'd Have Thought It? L

PL20 6HP SX489661
✪ 12-3, 6-11 (10.30 Sun) winter; 12-11 summer
☎ (01822) 853313 ⊕ whodhavethoughtitdevon.co.uk

Beer range varies H

A cosy old village pub that continues to improve. The three rooms are tastefully decorated with a traditional feel. The cosy bar area has a fine old fireplace with a wood-burning stove and low-level lighting, which creates a wonderful ambience. Despite the many diners, drinkers are well catered for. Four handpumps feature three constantly changing West Country ales, plus the pub's very own Itchy Pig cider. There is a covered outside drinking area next to the fast-running stream.
▲Q❀⇦❍⊟▲♣♠P᠁⇌🚲(55)

Moretonhampstead

Union Inn 🄻
10 Ford Street, TQ13 8LN
🕓 11-11; 12-10.30 Sun ☎ (01647) 440199
🌐 theunioninn.co.uk
Fuller's London Pride; Red Rock Breakwater, Lighthouse, Red Rock 🄷
A 16-century village-centre free house. The beamed bar and adjoining pool room display old photographs of the village. The function room – with its own bar and skittle alley – is reached via a corridor displaying many artefacts relating to the inn's history. Value-for-money Red Rock beers are given house names. The good home-cooked food is served all day on Sunday. There is outside seating on a decking area next to the small rear car park. 🔥❀◖◗♿P🚌(173,359)

Newton Abbot

Richard Hopkins
34-42 Queen Street, TQ12 2EW
🕓 8am-midnight ☎ (01626) 323930
Greene King Abbot; Ruddles Best Bitter; guest beers 🄷
A popular town-centre Wetherspoon pub offering up to 10 real ales, with several from South-West brewers plus ciders from the West Country and Wales. The spacious interior is divided into separate seating areas, with prints depicting local people and historic events adorning the wood-panelled walls. A covered area at the front of the pub is available for smokers and serves as additional space for dining and drinking. A festival of Devon beers is hosted each spring. 🐴❀◖◗♿🚆🍎🚬🚌

Newton St Cyres

Beer Engine 🄻
EX5 5AX (beside railway station N of A377)
🕓 11-11; 12-10.30 Sun ☎ (01392) 851282
🌐 thebeerengine.co.uk
Beer Engine Rail Ale, Silver Bullet, Piston Bitter, Sleeper Heavy; guest beer 🄷
A Georgian pub, built in 1850, on the Exeter to Barnstaple Tarka Line. Popular with drinkers and diners alike, it is well frequented by locals, visitors and the cricket team. The dining area adjoining the bar serves its own bread made with beer yeast, along with locally sourced food, available lunchtimes and evenings. The pub brews its own ales which, like the pictures and old pub signs, reflect a railway theme. 🔥Q🐴❀◖◗♿🚆P🚬🍺

North Tawton

Railway Inn 🄻
Whiddon Down Road, EX20 2BE (1 mile S of town off A3124) SS666000
🕓 12-3 (not Mon-Thu), 6-11 ☎ (01837) 82789
Teignworthy Reel Ale; guest beers 🄷
Next to the former North Tawton station and with numerous old station photos and memorabilia adorning the walls, this friendly local is part of a working farm. The always-welcoming landlord has a translation of his Devon dialect displayed in the bar area to help confused visitors. Guest ales, usually from the West Country, change regularly and real cider is available in summer. The dining room is popular in the evening (no food Thu). Guide dogs only. 🔥Q◖◗♣🍎P

Okehampton

Plymouth Inn 🄻
26 West Street, EX20 1HH (W end of town)
🕓 11-midnight ☎ (01837) 53633
Beer range varies 🄶
A friendly village-style local situated at the west edge of town. Constantly changing ales are served on gravity from stillage behind the bar, plus Winkleigh Sam's cider in summer months. Two popular beer festivals are held every year, one coinciding with the Ten Tors Challenge in May. The venue is popular with Dartmoor visitors and walkers. Reasonably priced, locally sourced food and snacks are sold. A quiz night is held every month. Children and dogs welcome. 🐴❀◖◗⛺♣🍎🚬🚌(X9,510)

Ottery St Mary

Lamb & Flag 🄻
Batts Lane, EX11 1EY (off Yonder St)
🕓 10.30-11 (midnight Thu-Sat); 12-10.30 Sun
☎ (01404) 812616
Otter Bitter, Ale; guest beers 🄷
The pub has undergone extensive refurbishment during the past three years. It now provides a warm and welcoming atmosphere for customers wishing to dine in the newly completed 30-seater restaurant, or for those simply enjoying a peaceful drink in the main bar. The facilities include free Wi-Fi, a multi-function room for celebrations, live music and conferencing. Traditional pub games are played, and there is a pool table, dartboard and skittles. A Sunday carvery is served from midday to 6pm. 🐴◖◗🛏♿♣🚌(60A,380)

Paignton

Henry's Bar 🄻
TQ4 6AJ
🕓 11-11 ☎ (01803) 551190
Dartmoor IPA; Sharp's Doom Bar; Skinner's Betty Stoggs; guest beers 🄷
A splendid traditional-style pub nicely situated between gift shops and arcades. It is also close to the railway, bus stations and the beach. The venue is warm and welcoming, and the beers very reasonably priced. A good range of draught and bottled ciders is available. Home-cooked, wholesome and fairly priced food is served all day until 9pm, with a highly regarded roast on Sunday. Families are welcome until 10pm. Wi-Fi is free and the place is dog-friendly. ❀◖◗🚆🍎🚬🚌

Isaac Merritt 🄻
54-58 Torquay Road, TQ3 3AA
🕓 8am-midnight ☎ (01803) 556066
Courage Directors; Greene King Abbot; Ruddles Best Bitter; guest beers 🄷
Busy town-centre Wetherspoon themed around the inventor of the Singer sewing machine. Its comfortable, friendly atmosphere with cosy seated alcoves makes it popular with all ages. This superb establishment has a deserved reputation for beer quality and choice. Guest beers are usually from West Country breweries. At the rear is a covered, heated seating area for smokers. There is a separate family dining area, with meals served all day. The pub is fully accessible to wheelchair users, with a designated ground floor toilet. ❀◖◗♿🚆🍎🚬🚌(12)

Waterside Inn L

128 Dartmouth Road, Goodrington, TQ4 6ND
✪ 11.30 (11 Sat)-11; 12-10.30 Sun ☎ (01803) 551113
Courage Best Bitter; guest beers Ⓗ

A welcoming, friendly family pub with a single, large, open-plan bar featuring several TV screens and a dining area with carvery. Food is served all day. A small garden and patio are at the rear, with additional picnic tables around the building. The smoking area is covered. Books and videos are sold on behalf of a local hospice, and free Wi-Fi is available. Guest beers are usually from South-West breweries. CAMRA members receive a 20p per pint discount. ⚲❀◑&♠♣P⁵⁻⊟(12,120)

Parkham

Bell Inn L

Rectory Lane, EX39 5PL (1 mile S of A39 at Horns Cross)
SS387212
✪ 12-2, 5.30-11; 5-midnight Fri; 5.30-midnight Sat; 12-3, 6-midnight Sun ☎ (01237) 451201
⊕ thebellinnparkham.co.uk
Sharp's Doom Bar; guest beers Ⓗ

Originally a forge and two cottages, this historic 13th-century thatched inn with its stone walls, oak beams and open fires still retains a rustic charm. No stranger to these pages in recent years, the single bar serves up to five ales; one is normally a local guest, and there is a beer festival each year in early June. The menu is large and varied, with locally produced food served both lunchtimes and evenings. ♨❀◑♣P⁵⁻⊟(372)

Peter Tavy

Peter Tavy Inn

Lane Head, PL19 9PN
✪ 12-11 (10.30 Sun) ☎ (01822) 810348
⊕ petertavyinn.com
Dartmoor Jail Ale; guest beers Ⓗ

In a quiet village on the edge of Dartmoor, a varying range of up to five local beers can be found in the pub's small central bar. Traditionally attired throughout, there are also two larger rooms, one for families. A patio and hidden garden are added attractions. The pub is renowned for its food, but drinkers are made welcome. Summer hours are extended. The inn is situated on the No. 27 cycle route, near a caravan and camping site. ♨Q⚲❀◑AP⁵⁻

Plymouth

Artillery Arms L

6 Pound Street, Stonehouse, PL1 3RH (behind Stonehouse Barracks and Millbay Docks)
✪ 11 (4 Mon & Tue)-midnight; 12-midnight Sun
☎ (01752) 262515
Dartmoor Jail Ale; Draught Bass; guest beer Ⓗ

Cracking back-street local tucked away in the old quarter of Stonehouse, close to the magnificent Grade I-listed Royal William Yard, and maintaining the area's military connections. Good home-cooked food is served (no food Sun). Two South-West guest beers and Thatchers Heritage cider are normally available. An out of season beach party takes place on the last weekend of February, and charity monkey racing also features. This place is a real find and is popular with hockey teams, who use the nearby pitches. ♨Q❀◑⇌(Devonport) ●⁵⁻⊟(34)

Brass Monkey L

12-14 Royal Parade, PL1 1DS
✪ 9am-11 (midnight Wed & Thu; 1am Fri & Sat); 9am-7 Sun
☎ (01752) 260442 ⊕ thebrassmonkeyplymouth.co.uk
Hunter's Half Bore, Black Jack; guest beers Ⓗ

A modern, bustling city-centre pub with a wide clientele. It serves up to eight real ales and two real ciders, including two house beers brewed by Hunter's. It is very conveniently situated for shopping, buses, the Hoe and the Barbican. Several TVs are dotted around, balanced by photographs of pre-war Plymouth. Good-value family meals are served by friendly and efficient staff. Several ale festivals are held each year, with a generous discount offered to CAMRA members. ⚲◑&⇌●⊟

Dolphin Hotel

14 The Barbican, Barbican, PL1 2LS
✪ 10-11 (midnight Thu-Sat); 11-11 Sun ☎ (01752) 660876
Draught Bass; St Austell Tribute; guest beers Ⓖ

An unpretentious hostelry steeped in history, the Dolphin is a Plymouth institution. A recent make-under has left the character thankfully untouched, with tiled floors, well-used wooden benches, together with a real open fire, all adding to the ambience. The walls are adorned with paintings by local artist the late Beryl Cook, who painted many of the characters she encountered in the Dolphin. The best Bass in the West Country is served straight from the cask behind the bar, with up to seven guest ales available. ♨Q⇌⁵⁻⊟(25)

Fawn Private Members Club L

39 Prospect Street, Greenbank, PL4 8NY
✪ 3 (2 Fri; 12 Sat & Sun)-11 ☎ (01752) 226385
Bays Topsail; St Austell Proper Job; guest beers Ⓗ

The club is named after the now-scrapped HMS Fawn. CAMRA members are welcome with a membership card; regular visitors will be required to join. The club is popular for rugby and other televised sports, and supports multiple darts and euchre teams. Three guest ales from the local area are generally on sale, as well as a rotating range of local ciders. A covered smoking area is on the patio. Local CAMRA Club of the Year 2013. ❀&⇌♣●⁵⁻⊟

Ferry House Inn

888 Wolseley Road, Saltash Passage, PL5 1LA
✪ 12-midnight ☎ (01752) 361063
Dartmoor Jail Ale; Draught Bass; Sharp's Doom Bar Ⓗ

Picturesque riverside pub on the River Tamar, which separates Devon from Cornwall. There is a decking area outside, giving spectacular views of Brunel's iconic 1859 railway bridge. Good home-cooked food is served daily, and uses locally sourced ingredients, with a daily specials board also featuring. The bars display photos of Brunel's bridge dating back to the turn of the 20th century, as well as photos of the pub and the Saltash foot ferry, after which it was named. ♨⚲❀◑&⇌(Saltash) ●⁵⁻⊟(13)

Fortescue Hotel ♈ L

37 Mutley Plain, PL4 6JQ
✪ 11-11 (midnight Thu-Sat); 12-10.30 Sun
☎ (01752) 660673
Bays Devon Dumpling; St Austell Proper Job; Skinner's Betty Stogs; guest beers Ⓗ

The landlord is a real ale enthusiast and the bar has nine handpumps; one is dedicated to a real cider, the rest serve the regular beers and a range of guests. Several local ales are always available, and up to four real ciders/perries. There is a long main bar, a cellar bar and a beer garden, covered and heated in winter. Lunchtime meals are served on Sundays only. Local CAMRA Pub of the Year 2013. ⓩ⍟◖⎚♣♠⇆🖳

Lord High Admiral
33 Stonehouse Street, Stonehouse, PL1 3PE
🌣 8am-11; 9am-10.30 Sun ☎ (01752) 256881
St Austell Tribute, HSD; guest beer Ⓗ
Excellent back-street pub set among industrial units, close to Millbay Docks. This friendly community pub has been revitalised over the past couple of years. Good-value food is served from breakfast time until 2pm, and again in the early evening. Free tapas accompany the well-kept St Austell ales – one guest ale may also be available. It has a large-screen TV for sporting enthusiasts. The real fire adds to the ambience in winter. ♨ⓩ⍟◖⇆(Devonport)♣⇆🖳

Minerva Inn Ⓛ
31 Looe Street, Barbican, PL4 0EA
🌣 11.30-11 (midnight Fri & Sat); 1.30-10.30 Sun
☎ (01752) 223047 ⊕ minervainn.co.uk
St Austell Tribute, HSD; guest beers Ⓗ
Plymouth's oldest pub, dating from circa 1540, and within easy walking distance of the city centre and the historic Barbican. The pub has a long, narrow bar, leading through to a cosy seating area at the rear. Two guest beers during the week are supplemented by spring and autumn beer festivals, where beer comes from all over the country. Live music takes place Thursday-Saturday evenings, and Sunday lunchtimes. The pub benefits from a varied clientele. ♨Qⓩ⍟⇆♣♠⇆🖳

Thistle Park Tavern Ⓛ
32 Commercial Road, Coxside, PL4 0LE
🌣 12-midnight (2am Fri & Sat) ☎ (01752) 204890
⊕ thistlepark.com
St Austell Tribute; South Hams XSB, Eddystone, seasonal beer Ⓗ
Brewery tap for the South Hams Brewery which, as Sutton, was located next door. There is a roof garden and an excellent Thai restaurant upstairs. Biltong is available at the bar. Cheddar Valley cider and Dortmunder lager are on offer alongside up to four South Hams beers. The pub can be accessed across the swing bridge from the Barbican (which shuts at 9.30pm) and is close to the National Marine Aquarium. Live music and late opening hours feature at the weekend. ♨⍟⊟⇆♣♠⇆🖳

Plympton

George Inn
191 Ridgeway, PL7 2HJ SX545562
🌣 11.30-11 (midnight Fri & Sat); 12-11 Sun
☎ (01752) 342674 ⊕ thegeorgeplympton.co.uk
St Austell Dartmoor Best Bitter, Tribute, HSD, seasonal beer Ⓗ
A 17th-century former coaching house on the old Plymouth-Exeter road. The flagstone bar is complemented by a spacious dining room, and the florally bedecked patio is especially popular during fine weather. There is a large function room available upstairs. A specials board supplements an extensive menu and booking is advisable at weekends. A popular quiz is held monthly on the second Sunday. Dogs on leads are welcome in the bar area. ♨Qⓩ⍟◖⊟♣♠P⇆🖳(22)

London Inn Ⓛ
8 Church Road, Plympton St Maurice, PL7 1NH
🌣 12-11 (midnight Fri & Sat) ☎ (01752) 657045
Beer range varies Ⓗ
A very friendly 16th-century pub, next to the church, and the epitome of a typical village inn. The cosy lounge bar is adorned with a large collection of Royal Naval memorabilia, while the public bar boasts a pool table, a dartboard and TVs for sports enthusiasts. It is the brewery tap for the Garage Brewery, whose ale is supplemented by up to three other ales and several ciders. The pub is allegedly haunted, by Captain Hinds. Dogs welcome. ♨Q⍟⊟♣♠P⇆🖳(20,22)

Union Inn Ⓛ
17 Underwood Road, PL7 1SY
🌣 4-11 (11.30 Fri); 12-midnight Sat; 12-11 Sun
☎ (01752) 336756 ⊕ unioninnplympton.com
Beer range varies Ⓗ
Family-run community hostelry that offers a warm welcome to all who enter this traditional, cosy, 19th-century pub. The landlord's passion for ale is evident, with up to four changing beers providing a year-round beer festival. There are also four real ciders served on gravity. All meals are freshly prepared using local produce (booking is advisable). Lunchtime meals are only available at weekends. Dogs on leads are welcome. CAMRA branch Cider Pub of the Year 2013 runner-up. ♨Q⍟⍟◖⊟♣♠P⇆🖳(20,22)

Plymtree

Blacksmith's Arms Ⓛ
EX15 2JU
🌣 closed Mon; 6 (12 Sat)-midnight; 12-5 Sun
☎ (01884) 277474 ⊕ blacksmiths.wordpress.com
St Austell Trelawny; Sharp's Doom Bar; guest beers Ⓗ
Nestled in beautiful countryside in an attractive village and sought after by locals, ramblers and visitors, this traditional pub embraces the atmosphere of true village life. It features a range of 14 local ales, with three on handpump at any one time. The wine cellar is extensive, and quality food in generous portions with punchy flavours is served Tuesday to Saturday evenings and weekend lunchtimes. The Blacksmith's Arms now offers a 10 per cent discount on food and drink to CAMRA members. ♨⍟⍟◖Å♣⇆

Postbridge

Warren House Inn Ⓛ
PL20 6TA (on B3212 between Postbridge and Bennett's Cross) SX674809
🌣 11-10 (5 Mon & Tue; 11 Fri & Sat) winter; 11-11 (10.30 Sun) summer ☎ (01822) 880208 ⊕ warrenhouseinn.co.uk
Otter Ale; guest beers Ⓗ
Isolated and exposed at 1425 feet above sea level, this is one of the highest pubs in England. The interior features exposed beams, wood panelling, rustic benches and tables, and a famous fire. Daytime and evening menus offer home-cooked dishes made with locally sourced ingredients. There is a large family room, and tables outside give breathtaking views over the moors. Countryman cider is available, and guest beers vary with the seasons, with one strong ale usually featured. ♨Q⍟⍟◖▶Å♠P⇆🖳(82,98)

Princetown

Plume of Feathers ⍓

The Square, PL20 6QQ

✪ 10.30-11 (midnight Fri & Sat) ☎ (01822) 890240
⊕ theplumeoffeathersdartmoor.co.uk

St Austell Tribute, Proper Job, HSD; guest beers ⊞
Princetown's oldest building, dating from 1785, features granite walls, slate floors and slate-topped tables. A later addition is the large family/function room with its own bar. Food is served all day, with a carvery in the family room on weekend lunchtimes. Ample outdoor seating is available on the spacious patio, alongside a children's play area. There is also a large car park, campsite and camping barn on site. Three local ales complement the three regulars. The pub is served by an infrequent bus service from Tavistock.
ॾQ✿⍓⌂⊕⌃⟊♣⟊♣P⌐-⊟(98)

Sampford Courtenay

New Inn

EX20 2TB (on A3072 Hatherleigh-Crediton Road) SS633009

✪ 12-11 (11.30 Fri-Sun) ☎ (01837) 82247

Otter Ale; Skinner's Betty Stogs; guest beers ⒢
A 16th-century coaching house with original low beams and a real fire at both ends of the bar. Three beers are usually available in summer, as are Sampford Courtenay Ravenswood cider and Devon cream teas. Quality food is served daily lunchtimes and evenings, with fish dishes a speciality. Behind the pub is a pleasant beer garden which is the location for a charity beer festival in May. Dogs and children are welcome.
ॾQ✿⍓⌃♣P⌐-⊟(51,51A)

Sampford Peverell

Globe Inn ⍓

16 Lower Town, EX16 7BJ

✪ 11-midnight ☎ (01884) 821214 ⊕ the-globeinn.co.uk

Otter Bitter; Sharp's Doom Bar; guest beers ⊞
Traditional Devon village inn backing onto the Grand Western Canal, which runs between Tiverton and the Somerset border. The large car park at the rear of the pub also has access to the canal towpath. An early breakfast can be booked 8-11am daily. A sheltered courtyard and large garden with children's play area is also towards the rear. There are two function rooms and seven guest rooms available. The real cider on sale is Sheppy's Farmhouse. ॾ⍓⌂⊕⌃⟊♣⟊♣P⌐-⊟(1)

Sandford

Lamb Inn

The Square, EX17 4LW

✪ 10.30-11 ☎ (01363) 773676 ⊕ lambinnsandford.co.uk

Otter Bitter; guest beers ⊞
A traditional 16th-century free house in the village centre, with a warm, welcoming atmosphere. It is well supported by locals and visitors alike, enjoying mainly award-winning food, West Country ales, and Sandford Orchards cider. Skittles is played four nights a week in the alley-cum-cinema-cum-conference venue. There are open mic music and comedy evenings. Six B&B rooms are available. Children and dogs are welcome. It is frequented by the village football, squash and cricket teams.
ॾQ✿⍓⌂⊕⌃♣⌐-⊟(369)

Scorriton

Tradesman's Arms ⍓

TQ11 0JB (near Buckfastleigh, about 3 miles from A38)

✪ 12-2.30, 6-11.30; 12-11 Sun ☎ (01364) 631206
⊕ thetradesmansarms.co.uk

Dartmoor IPA; guest beers ⊞
On the edge of Dartmoor, this pub reopened after it was bought by four locals who drank at the pub prior to its demise. It was renovated and updated, and has an L-shaped main bar with plenty of seating in a long alcove to one side, with a conservatory open to the pub at the other. There is a friendly atmosphere, and good local food is served together with local Thompstones cider. One of the guest beers is from Hunter's. Accommodation is available.
ॾQ✿⍓⌂⊕⌃♣⟊♣P

Shaldon

Clifford Arms ⍓

34 Fore Street, TQ14 0DE

✪ 11-2.30, 5-11 (11.30 Fri & Sat); 11.30-3, 5.30-10.30 Sun ☎ (01626) 872311

Dartmoor IPA, Jail Ale; guest beers ⊞
In the centre of a pretty coastal village, this pub has an attractive, modern interior, and a warming log fire in winter. The guest and seasonal beers are sourced mainly from West Country breweries. The restaurant area at the rear serves good-quality food every day, and leads out onto a sunny, decked patio. Special menus are offered alongside modern jazz evenings on Monday and monthly Sunday lunchtime trad jazz sessions. The cider is Westons scrumpy. ॾ✿⍓♣⌐-⊟(11)

Shaldon Conservative Club ⍓

Dagmar Street, TQ14 0DU

✪ 12-3, 5-11; 12-11 Sat & Sun ☎ (01626) 873667

Teignworthy Reel Ale; guest beers ⊞
A friendly, welcoming club in the centre of this coastal village and recently refurbished. It offers two real ales and a real cider at very reasonable prices. The single bar is comfortable and cosy and is home to snooker, darts and euchre teams. At the hub of the community, it hosts charity events, wakes and private parties. Live music features regularly and includes a well-supported open mic night. Televised Rugby Union is also popular. CAMRA members are welcome. ⌃♣⟊

Shebbear

Devil's Stone Inn

EX21 5RU (in village square) SS438094

✪ 12-3, 6-11; 11-11 Fri-Sun ☎ (01409) 281210
⊕ devilsstoneinn.com

Beer range varies ⊞
Reputed to be one of the 12 most haunted pubs in Britain, this 17th-century former coaching inn takes its name from the Devil's Stone located in the church opposite. A special evening of entertainment is held on 5 November each year when the stone is ceremonially turned to ward off evil spirits. This cosy venue, with flagstone floors, open fireplaces and wood beams, has four handpumps serving a range of ales, mainly from the West Country, plus local cider in summer.
ॾQ✿⍓⌂⊕⌃♣⟊♣P⌐-⊟(72)

Sidmouth

Marine
The Esplanade, EX10 8BB
✪ 11 (12 Sun)-midnight ☎ (01395) 513145
Branscombe Vale Branoc; guest beers ⊞
The only pub on the seafront in Sidmouth, with a small drinking area outside with tables and chairs for customers to enjoy the lovely view. Well-behaved dogs are welcome inside. There is a large room on two levels, with one bar. Sports fans are well catered for with several screens around the room. This is a family-run pub (a rarity these days, unfortunately), and this is reflected in the friendly atmosphere that attracts an eclectic clientele of all ages. ⤳❀◖◗&ᵗ-⊟

Swan Inn
37 York Street, EX10 8BY
✪ 11 (12 Sun)-11 ☎ (01395) 512849
Young's Bitter, Special; guest beer ⊞
Traditional and quiet back-street inn, established around 1770, which lies just off the centre of this quaint town, a short walk from the seafront and bus terminus. An old-style wood-panelled bar with an open fire leads to a dedicated dining area serving good food, attracting a strong local trade. Three beers, all from the Wells & Young's range, are normally available. Dogs, but not children, are welcome indoors. Find out about the King of Chit – a traditional competition.
🅿Q❀◗&♣ᵗ-⊟(52,157)

Silverton

Lamb Inn ⃝
Fore Street, EX5 4HZ
✪ 11.30-3, 6-11.30; 11.30-11.30 Sat & Sun
☎ (01392) 860272 ⊕ thelambinnsilverton.co.uk
Exe Valley Dob's Best Bitter; Otter Ale; guest beer Ⓖ
Popular family-run pub in the centre of Silverton, with stone floors, stripped timber and old pine furniture, as well as good comfy bar stools. A fine display of old pumpclips jogs the memory of ales long gone. At least three beers are served by gravity from a temperature-controlled stillage behind the bar at very competitive prices. There is a well-used function room and skittles alley. Good-value home-cooked food is available lunchtimes and evenings, plus a popular Sunday roast.
🅿Q⤳❀◖◗&♣⊟(55B)

Slapton

Queen's Arms ⃝
TQ7 2PN
✪ 12-3, 6-11; 7-10.30 Sun ☎ (01548) 580800
⊕ queensarmsslapton.co.uk
Dartmoor Jail Ale; Otter Ale, Bright; guest beer ⊞
A hearty welcome awaits at this 14th-century village-centre pub. Numerous photographs depicting the WWII evacuation adorn the walls. A flower-filled garden with patios is at the rear, and children and dogs are welcome. An extensive menu is available with daily specials; the chef is particularly known for his home-made pies. During winter, Sunday roasts are served (booking advisable). A takeaway food service is offered and an open fire warms you in the colder weather.
🅿⤳❀◖◗Åᵗ♣Pᵗ-⊟(93)

South Brent

Oak ⃝
Station Road, TQ10 9BE (near old railway station)
✪ 12-2, 4-11; 12-11 Sat & Sun ☎ (01364) 72133
⊕ oakonline.net
Dartmoor IPA; Otter Ale; Teignworthy Gun Dog; guest beers ⊞
Village-centre pub on the edge of Dartmoor. The wood-panelled, L-shaped bar is surrounded by a large open-plan area with plenty of seating. An excellent range of real ales is available. At the rear a restaurant serves good-quality food, and a new function room can be found upstairs, which is available for meetings. There is a no-smoking courtyard outside and accommodation is offered. Occasional beer festivals are held, with a discount on real ales for CAMRA members. Varying real ciders are sold. Q❀🏠◗&Å♣

South Molton

Town Arms Hotel ⃝
124 East Street, EX36 3BU
✪ 11 (12 Sun)-midnight ☎ (01769) 572531
Draught Bass; Exmoor Ale; Sharp's Doom Bar ⊞
Main-street local in this historic market town, an ideal location for exploring Exmoor and north Devon. The main bar has a pool table and open fire, with interesting old photographs on the walls. A quieter back room can be used by families. The pub is popular with locals and can get very lively at times, particularly Thursday market day. There is a strong commitment to real ale and CAMRA members receive a discount of 10p per pint. Well-behaved dogs are welcome.
🅿⤳❀🏠♣Pᵗ-⊟(X7,155)

Sparkwell

Treby Arms
PL7 5DD
✪ 11-11 summer; 11-3, 6-11 (not Mon); 11-11 Sat & Sun winter ☎ (01752) 837363 ⊕ thetrebyarms.co.uk
Dartmoor Jail Ale; St Austell Tribute ⊞
Built in 1812, the Treby is an archetypal country pub, set in the centre of the village, close to a golf course and zoological park. It is very popular both with local and city folk. The excellent food menu is varied, with special deals frequently offered, and is highly recommended. There is an outside seating area for warm days, and a large children's play area across the road. Winner of Masterchef: The Professionals 2012. 🅿⤳❀◖◗&♣Pᵗ-⊟(59)

Spreyton

Tom Cobley Tavern ⃝
EX17 5AL (off A3124 in village)
✪ 6.30-11 Mon; 12-3, 6-11 (1am Fri & Sat); 12-4, 7-11 Sun
☎ (01647) 231314 ⊕ tomcobleytavern.co.uk
Beer range varies ⊞/Ⓖ
A choice of 14 real ales all from West Country brewers together with 16 real ciders and delicious home-cooked food make this a gem of a pub. It was a finalist for CAMRA National Pub of the Year in 2012, testifying that this is a true community pub. Children and dogs are welcome in the bar, and the garden is a delight on warm sunny days. Six comfortable guest rooms are available for night stops. Best of all is the warm and friendly greeting from the family and staff. 🅿Q❀🏠◗♣P

Sticklepath

Taw River Inn

EX20 2NW (on main road through village) SX642941
☼ 12-midnight (11 Sun) ☎ (01837) 840377
⊕ tawriver.co.uk
Dartmoor Legend; St Austell Tribute; Sharp's Doom Bar; guest beers Ⓗ
A former 17th-century manor house, this oak-beamed pub is popular with locals and visitors alike. Set in an active village on the edge of Dartmoor, it is ideally situated for exploring the area or visiting the Finch Foundry Museum (National Trust) opposite. The varied real ales, together with the local Sticklepath cider, are attractively priced, and good-value pub food is served in both the bar area and adjacent dining room. Well-behaved children and dogs are welcome. ♨&⏾Ⓓ&♣●P'–⊟(X9)

Teignmouth

Blue Anchor Ⓛ

Teign Street, TQ14 8EG
☼ 12-11.30 (midnight Fri-Sun) ☎ (01626) 772741
Beer range varies Ⓗ
A pub since the Napoleonic period and a former Devenish outlet, the Blue Anchor is now a genuine free house. Situated in a preservation area close to the docks, it has a narrow front entrance into a single bar that features stained glass windows and a wood-burning stove. Six beers are normally sold, with a strong emphasis on local brews. The bar has a jukebox and can be very lively at weekends, especially when rugby is televised.
♨&⏾≠♣●P'–⊟(2,11)

Brass Monkey

Hollands Road, TQ14 8SR
☼ 11 (12 Sun)-midnight ☎ (01626) 773961
St Austell Tribute, HSD Ⓗ
Town-centre community oriented pub with a warm welcome from the long-serving and award-winning licensees. Ideally situated between the railway station and the town bus stops, it makes a perfect waiting room for travellers. Regular sporting events feature on TV, and it offers a Tuesday quiz night, weekend karaoke, free Wi-Fi and an early-evening happy hour. A splendid retreat from the busy town centre. Sunday lunch is available. &≠♣⊟(2,11)

Topsham

Bridge Inn ★ Ⓛ

Bridge Hill, EX3 0QQ
☼ 12-2, 6-10.30 (11 Fri & Sat); 12-2, 7-10.30 Sun
☎ (01392) 873862 ⊕ cheffers.co.uk
Branscombe Vale Branoc; guest beers Ⓖ
Historic, cosy, 16th-century inn run by six generations of the same family since 1897, with a varying range of ales from local breweries and further afield. This inn is a delight for fans of real ale, in a traditional setting overlooking the banks of the River Clyst. The inn was visited by the Queen in 1998. Nine beers are usually available, all dispensed by gravity straight from the cellar.
♨Q&⏾Ⓓ⊟≠P⊟(57,T)

Exeter Inn Ⓛ

68 High Street, EX3 0DY
☼ 11-11 (midnight Fri & Sat); 12-10.30 Sun
☎ (01392) 873131

Teignworthy Beachcomber; guest beers Ⓗ
A welcoming and genuine community pub run by an enthusiastic and friendly couple who are SIBA members. It was originally a coaching house and dates from the 17th century; part of the building is thatched. The pub offers one regular ale and six varying guest ales of local and national origin. Traditional pub games are played, and three large-screen TVs show sporting events. The real cider comes from Green Valley. ♨&⏾≠♣●'–⊟(57,T)

Torquay

Buccaneer Inn

41-43 Babbacombe Downs Road, Babbacombe, TQ1 3LN
☼ 12-11 (midnight Fri-Sun) ☎ (01803) 312661
⊕ thebuccaneerinn.co.uk
St Austell Tribute, Proper Job, HSD Ⓗ
Located atop the highest clifftop promenade in England, this warm and welcoming pub has spectacular views across Lyme Bay from both the lounge bar and patio. An extensive and varied menu is served, with local seafood specials in the summer and a popular Sunday lunch. Winner of the 2012 St Austell Estates Cask Ale Pub of the Year award. Tribute and HSD are always available.
⏽&⏾Ⓓ&♣⊟(32)

Hole in the Wall Ⓛ

6 Park Lane, TQ1 2AU
☼ 12-midnight ☎ (01803) 200755
⊕ holeinthewalltorquay.co.uk
Bays Topsail; Butcombe Bitter; Dartmoor Jail Ale; Otter Bitter; Sharp's Doom Bar; guest beers Ⓗ
Close to but tucked away from the harbour, this is Torquay's oldest inn (circa 1540). A real ale haven with beamed ceilings and cobbled floors, it is popular with holidaymakers and seafarers as well as businessmen and locals. A narrow passageway outside is adorned with floral displays and makes a very pleasant alfresco drinking area. A busy and roomy restaurant serves highly regarded food. Dogs on leads are welcome. ⏾Ⓓ&●⊟(11,12)

Totnes

Bay Horse Inn Ⓛ

8 Cistern Street, TQ9 5SP
☼ 12-midnight ☎ (01803) 862088
Dartmoor Jail Ale; Otter Bitter; guest beers Ⓗ
A 15th-century coaching inn at the top of the picturesque town of Totnes, serving a minimum of four local real ales including one on gravity. Live jazz features on Sunday night, with folk and acoustic sessions on Monday and Thursday. Beer festivals are held at Easter, during the Totnes festival in September, and during the winter months. At the rear is a large, attractive garden with a heated patio and disabled access.
♨&⏾Ⓓ≠♣●'–⊟(93)

Turnchapel

Boringdon Arms Ⓛ

13 Boringdon Terrace, PL9 9TQ
☼ 11-midnight (1am Fri & Sat); 12-midnight Sun
☎ (01752) 402053 ⊕ boringdonarms.co.uk
St Austell Tribute, Proper Job; Sharp's Doom Bar Ⓗ
A former regional CAMRA Pub of the Year, the pub sits in a waterside village site, and benefits from a regular bus service from Plymouth. You can also

get here by water taxi from the Barbican to Mount Batten, followed by a short waterside walk. The pub has a deserved reputation for good ale and excellent home-cooked food, including the popular value-for-money lunch menu. Photographs of past rail lines adorn the walls.
🏚Q🍽🐕🏨🌳🍺◑🔌♿🚪(2)

Clovelly Bay Inn L
1 Boringdon Road, PL9 9TB
❂ 11-3 (not winter), 6-11; 12-11 Sat; 12-3, 6-11 Fri & Sat summer; 12-4, 7-10.30 Sun ☎ (01752) 402765
⊕ clovellybayinn.co.uk
Beer range varies H/G
Family-run free house nestled in a picturesque village on the South West Coast Path. It has an enthusiastic landlord with a passion for real ales and ciders, with up to 10 available. The pub holds a variety of festivals throughout the year, with an emphasis on local produce and a willingness to source beers and ciders from further afield. It is also renowned for its wonderful food. Local CAMRA Pub of the Year 2011, and runner-up 2012.
🏚Q🌳🍽◑🍺🚻♿♣🚪(2)

Welcome

Old Smithy Inn L
EX39 6HG (2 miles W of A39 at Welcome Cross) SS231178
❂ 12-midnight ☎ (01288) 331305 ⊕ theoldsmithyinn.co.uk
Beer range varies H
What looks from the outside like a traditional thatched inn turns out to be something quite different when you step through the door. The surprisingly funky decor adds a unique charm and character to the welcoming and cosy interior, and the choice of three constantly changing ales is complemented by a range of ciders, all mainly from the West Country. Regular events include quiz and folk nights. A 14th-century outbuilding has now been converted into a lodge for backpackers.
🏚🌳◑♣P

Wembury

Odd Wheel L
Knighton Road, PL9 0JD
❂ 12-3, 5-midnight; 12-midnight Fri-Sun ☎ (01752) 863052
⊕ theoddwheel.co.uk
Dartmoor Jail Ale; St Austell Tribute; Sharp's Doom Bar; guest beers H
Friendly country pub at the northern end of this picturesque village, refurbished in 2010. Many walking routes are close by, including the South West Coast Path. Three regular beers are supplemented by up to three guests, mainly from Devon and Cornwall, and regular beer festivals are

held. Food is served daily, with ingredients from locally sourced suppliers. There is a terraced garden and play area for children. Dogs are welcome.
🏚🌳❀◑🍺🚻♣P♿🚪(48)

Whimple

New Fountain Inn L
Church Road, EX5 2TA
❂ 6.30-11 Mon; 12-2 (3 Sat), 6.30-11; 12-3, 7-10.30 Sun
☎ (01404) 822350
Teignworthy Reel Ale; guest beers G
Converted from cottages in about 1890, this pub has changed little over the years, although modern toilets were added in an extension to one of the bars in 2009. The other bar retains many original features including a real fire in winter. A genuine free house, the handpumps are not in use – ale is fetched from the cellar. Good-value home-cooked food is served. The village heritage centre in the car park is worth visiting. Opening hours may change; it is advisable to phone. 🏚Q◑🍺🚻♣P🚪

Widecombe in the Moor

Rugglestone Inn
TQ13 7TF (¼ mile from village centre) SX721760
❂ 11.30-3, 6-midnight; 11.30-midnight Sat; 12-11 Sun
☎ (01364) 621327 ⊕ rugglestoneinn.co.uk
Dartmoor Legend; guest beer G
Unspoilt pub in a splendid Dartmoor setting. This Grade II-listed building was converted to an inn back in 1832. The stone-flagged bar area has seating, with beer also served through a hatch in the passageway, and an open fire warms the lounge. A wide selection of home-cooked food is available. Across the stream is a large grassed seating area. Local farm cider is sold; the house beer is from Teignworthy. Local CAMRA Pub of the Year 2012. 🏚Q🌳❀◑🍺🚻▲♣P🍴

Yelverton

Rock Inn
PL20 6DS
❂ 11-11 (12.30am Fri & Sat); 12-10.30 Sun
☎ (01822) 852022 ⊕ rockinndartmoor.co.uk
Dartmoor Jail Ale, seasonal beer; St Austell Tribute; Sharp's Doom Bar H
This large pub with three bars is extremely popular with locals and tourists alike. The lounge bar has low-level piped music and features old photos of the area, while the cosy and relaxed Farmer's Bar is where conversation flourishes. The back bar, with pool tables and louder music, attracts a younger clientele. Top quality beer is served with care. Live music features on some weekends.
🏚Q❀◑🍺♣P🔌🚪

Cask breather

Where an entry states that some beers in a pub are served with the aid of cask breathers, this means that demand valves are connected to both casks and cylinders of gas; as beer is drawn off, it is replaced by applied gas (either carbon dioxide, nitrogen or both) to prevent oxidation. The method is not acceptable to CAMRA as it does not allow beer to condition and mature naturally. The Campaign believes brewers and publicans should use the size of casks best suited to the turnover of beer in order to avoid oxidation. If a pub in the Good Beer Guide uses cask breathers, we list only those beers that are free of the device.

Britain's Best Real Heritage Pubs

Geoff Brandwood

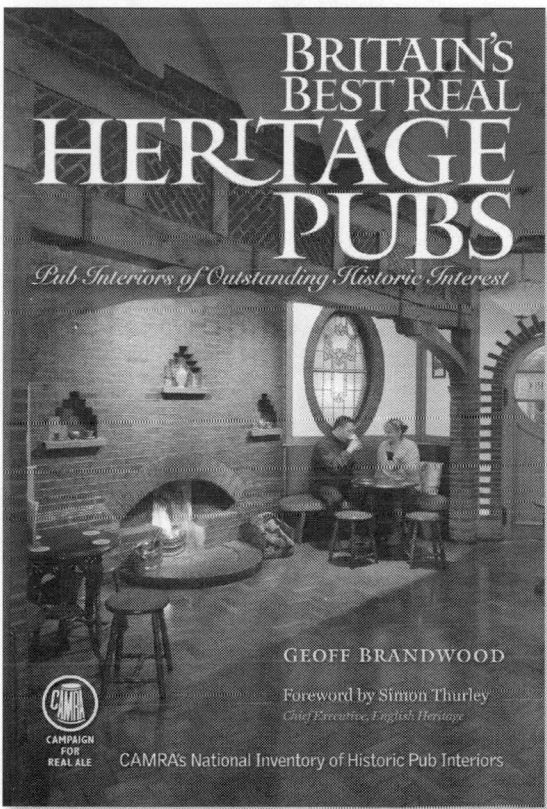

This new full-colour guide lists 270 pubs throughout the UK that have interiors of real historic significance – some over a century old. Illustrated with high quality photography, the book's extensive listings are the product of years of surveying and research by CAMRA's Pub Heritage Group, which is dedicated to preserving and protecting our rich pub heritage. The book features a forward by Simon Thurley, Chief Executive of English Heritage.

For more information about heritage pubs and the work of CAMRA's Pub Heritage Group, please visit **www.heritagepubs.org.uk**

£9.99 ISBN 978-1-85249-304-2 CAMRA members' price £7.99 288 pages

For this and other books on beer and pubs visit CAMRA's online bookshop at **www.camra.org.uk/books** or call **01727 867201**

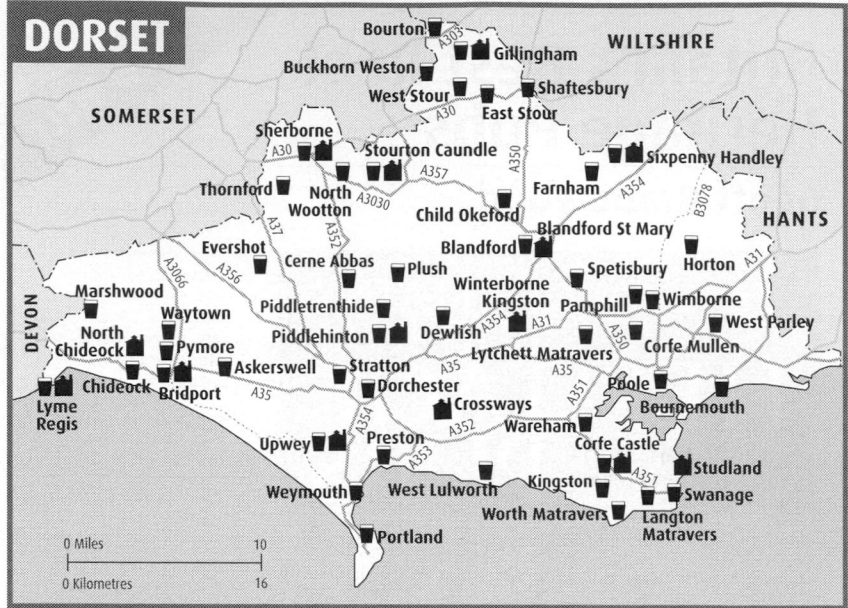

Askerswell

Spyway Inn Ⓛ
DT2 9EP SY528933
✪ 12-3, 6-11 ☎ (01308) 485250 ⊕ spyway-inn.co.uk
Otter Bitter, Ale; guest beer Ⓖ
Family-friendly 16th-century smugglers' inn
perched on a hill outside Askerswell on the road to
Eggardon Hill fort. From March to October there is
usually a guest beer and a local cider on draught as
well as the Otter beers on gravity. The small lounge
bar has beams and a woodburner; a further bar has
tables for dining. The food menu features dishes
made with locally produced ingredients. Popular
with locals and walkers, the sunny garden enjoys a
fine view and the play area attracts families. Dogs
are welcome in the garden. ▣Q✿♠✦◖ Å♠P↳

Blandford

Dolphin Ⓛ
42 East Street, DT11 7DR
✪ 11.30-11.30 (midnight Fri & Sat) ☎ (01258) 456813
⊕ thedolphinblandford.co.uk
**Dorset Piddle Piddle, seasonal beers; Taylor Landlord;
guest beers** Ⓗ
Friendly locals' pub retaining many original
features including wood panelling. Owned by
Piddle Brewery, two or three of its beers are
always available on the seven handpumps.
Traditional cider and a large whisky selection are
also offered. The good-value food menu and
seasonal specials board are popular (booking
recommended for Sunday lunch). Board games and
newspapers are available. Live music is hosted
regularly and a quiz night on Sunday. ▣◖♠➡(X8)

Bournemouth

Cricketers Arms
41 Windham Road, Springbourne, BH1 4RN
✪ 11-11 (10.30 Sun) ☎ (01202) 551589
Fuller's London Pride; guest beers Ⓗ

This unspoilt Victorian gem dating back to 1847 is
the oldest pub in Bournemouth and retains many
original features including internal stained glass
windows and superb gents toilets. The vaulted
upper section of the lounge was converted from a
gym many years ago, and was where legendary
boxer Freddie Mills trained. Mounted posters from
historic rock gigs of the '70s hang on the walls.
Various entertainment includes live folk music, card
bingo and an annual beer festival.
✿◖♠≈♣♠P↳

Goat & Tricycle
27-29 West Hill Road, BH2 5PF
✪ 12-11 (11.30 Fri & Sat) ☎ (01202) 314220
⊕ goatandtricycle.co.uk
**Wadworth Henry's IPA, Horizon, 6X, seasonal beers;
guest beers** Ⓗ
A hidden gem in the back streets of Bournemouth,
about 400 yards from the town centre in an area
known as The Triangle. This popular and award-
winning split-level bar offers comfortable
surroundings for drinkers and diners alike. Eleven
handpumps dispense Wadworth beers, one
draught cider plus rotating guest ales. Good-value
food is available daily until 9pm. A partially
covered courtyard caters for smokers and alfresco
drinkers. ▣✿◖♠♣♠↳➡(M1,M2)

Porterhouse Ⓛ
113 Poole Road, Westbourne, BH4 9BG
✪ 11-11 (midnight Fri & Sat); 12-11 Sun ☎ (01202) 768586
**Marston's seasonal beers; Ringwood Best Bitter,
Fortyniner, Old Thumper** Ⓗ
Previously known as the Old Thumper, this ever-
popular Ringwood house offers the full range plus
beers from other Marston's breweries. The
welcoming, oak-panelled pub is popular with locals
and visitors alike. Board games and cards are
played and the sound of conversation dominates
the friendly atmosphere. Sandwiches are available
at lunchtimes plus home-made roasts on Sunday.
Dogs are welcome outside food-service hours.
Q◖≈(Bransome)♣♠↳➡

Bourton

White Lion Inn
High Street, SP8 5AT ST77863093
✪ 12-2.30, 5-11; 12-11 Fri & Sat; 12-10.30 Sun
☎ (01747) 840866 ⊕ whitelionbourton.co.uk
Otter Amber; Sharp's Doom Bar; guest beer ⊞
The White Lion is a traditional inn dating from
1763. Originally separate rooms, the cosy
flagstoned bar has been opened out but there is
always a quiet corner to be found. The real cider is
Thatchers. There is a comfortable, intimate
restaurant and, to the rear, a large beer garden.
The pub is set back from the B3081 with plenty of
parking. ♨Q✿⊷❶●P☷(158)

Bridport

George Hotel ℏ
4 South Street, DT6 3NQ
✪ 11-11 (midnight Fri & Sat); 12-10.30 Sun
☎ (01308) 423187
Palmers Copper Ale, IPA, 200, Tally Ho! ⊞
Fine, traditional and cheerful Palmers pub at the
centre of this busy market town. The long main bar
has a warm, comfortable feel and there is a
peaceful family room across the passageway with
service through a hatch to the corridor. With the
thatched Palmers Brewery less than a mile away,
the real ales have few beer miles on the clock.
Palmers Dorset Gold replaces the 200 in summer.
There is no parking but several public car parks
nearby. Dog-friendly. ♨Q♒❶⎙☷(31,X53)

Ropemakers ℏ
36 West Street, DT6 3QP
✪ 11-11 (12.30am Fri); 10-12.30am Sat; 12-3 (later in
summer) Sun ☎ (01308) 421255 ⊕ theropemakers.com
Palmers Copper Ale, Best Bitter, 200, seasonal beer ⊞
Deceptively large pub about 10 minutes' walk from
the Old Brewery, serving the full Palmer's range of
ales with Dorset Gold in summer and Tally Ho! in
winter. Inside, it has lots of separate themed areas
decorated with memorabilia and local history. At
the rear is a large partially covered courtyard;
disabled access is via the back door. Quality home-
cooked food, sourced from local suppliers, is
available lunchtimes and evenings, with traditional
roasts on Sunday and breakfasts on Saturday
morning. Live music plays on Friday and Saturday
evenings. ♒✿❶⎙☷

Tiger Inn ℏ
14-16 Barrack Street, DT6 3LY
✪ 12-11 (midnight Fri & Sat) ☎ (01308) 427543
⊕ tigerinnbridport.co.uk
Sharp's Doom Bar; guest beers ⊞
Bright and cheerful Victorian ale house offering a
frequently changing beer list with three guests
mainly from West Country breweries, plus cider.
The single split-level bar has TV for major sporting
events, plus pub games including a skittle alley.
Children are allowed in the top bar. There is a
pretty garden and a heated courtyard. Close to the
town centre and shops, the Tiger is a well-hidden
secret worth seeking out. A beer festival is held
annually. CAMRA members receive a discount.
Local CAMRA Town Pub of the Year 2012.
♨✿⊷♣●'⎙☷(31,X53)

Buckhorn Weston

Stapleton Arms
Church Hill, SP8 5HS (between A303 and A30) ST757246
✪ 11-3, 6-11; 11-11 Sat & Sun ☎ (01963) 370396
⊕ thestapletonarms.com
Butcombe Bitter; Moor Revival; guest beers ⊞
Imposing village pub with a large car park and
secluded garden. The two guest beers often reflect
the seasons, including milds in May, winter brews
and summer ales – frequently from local breweries.
Real ciders and a wide selection of draught and
bottled foreign beers are always available.
Excellent food is served as well as classic bar snacks
such as hand-made pork pies, Scotch eggs and
chutney. Children, dogs and muddy boots are
welcome. Modern en-suite accommodation
completes the Drink, Eat, Sleep motto.
♨Q♒✿⊷❶●P

Cerne Abbas

Royal Oak
23 Long Street, DT2 7JG
✪ 11-3, 6-11 ☎ (01300) 341797
Badger First Gold, Tanglefoot, seasonal beer ⊞
A delightful thatched pub in the heart of the
village, built in 1540 using stone and other building
materials from the abbey, which was largely
destroyed following the Dissolution of the
Monasteries. The recently refurbished interior has
kept its cosy feel and is made up of three
interconnecting rooms. Good wholesome food is
served lunchtimes and evenings with daily
specials. The pub may open all day during the
summer; please ring the pub for details.
♨Q♒✿⊷❶▲♣'⎙☷(216)

Chideock

George Inn ℏ
Main Street, DT6 6JD
✪ 12-3, 6-11 ☎ (01297) 489419 ⊕ georgeinnchideock.co.uk
Palmers Copper Ale, Best Bitter, Dorset Gold, 200,
Tally Ho! ⊞
Traditional Dorset thatched pub, popular with locals
and visitors alike. Real ales and ciders are served in
a welcoming, friendly atmosphere by one of the
log fires during the winter or on the sun terrace in
the summer (where you will also find a wood-fired
oven cooking pizzas on Thursday nights). A local,
seasonal, award-winning menu is available seven
days a week lunchtimes and evenings.
♨Q♒✿⊷❶⊟♣●P'⎙☷(31,X53)

INDEPENDENT BREWERIES

Art Brew North Chideock
Blackmore Stourton Caundle
Corfe Castle Corfe Castle
Dorset (DBC) Crossways
DT Upwey
Hall & Woodhouse (Badger) Blandford St Mary
Isle of Purbeck Studland
Mighty Hop Lyme Regis
Palmers Bridport
Piddle Piddlehinton
Sherborne Sherborne
Sixpenny Sixpenny Handley
Small Paul's Gillingham
Sunny Republic Winterborne Kingston
Town Mill Lyme Regis

Child Okeford

Saxon Inn

Gold Hill, DT11 8HD (along narrow lane N of village)
ST829135

✪ 12-3, 6-11 ☎ (01258) 860310 ⊕ saxoninn.co.uk

Butcombe Bitter; Otter Bitter; guest beers Ⓗ

Friendly inn close to the Hambledon Hill fort with spectacular views across the Blackmore Vale. This inn was converted from three farm cottages in the 1950s but feels older, with low-beamed ceilings and settles. The bar serves two rooms plus a lounge/dining room with panelled walls and a wood-burning stove. Excellent food is available daily. Outside is a large, quiet garden with a sheltered area to the rear. ♨✿❀◑♿♣P⁵⁻

Corfe Castle

Royal British Legion Club

East Street, BH20 5EQ (on A351)

✪ 12-2.30, 6-11; 12-11 Sat & Sun ☎ (01929) 480591

Ringwood Best Bitter; Taylor Landlord; guest beer Ⓗ

Built in Purbeck stone, this friendly club has a bar area with upholstered bench seating, wooden tables and chairs. Major sporting events are shown on TV; darts, shove-ha'penny and occasional live music are played. Filled rolls are available at lunchtimes and an upstairs meeting room can be hired. A lovely garden has a boules court and views over the Purbecks. Show a CAMRA membership card or a copy of this Guide for entry.
✿♿≈(Swanage Steam Railway)♣P⁵⁻◱(40)

Corfe Mullen

Lambs Green Inn

Lambs Green Lane, BH21 3DN (500yds S of A31)

✪ 11-11 (10.30 Sun) ☎ (01202) 881974

Ringwood Best Bitter; St Austell Tribute; Sharp's Doom Bar; guest beers Ⓗ

Part-thatched former farmhouse with a lovely rustic atmosphere, retaining its original beamed ceilings and small rooms. Up to three guest beers are available from the Vintage Inns selection. Excellent food is served all day in the bar or in the separate, pleasant dining area. The extensive rear garden is a gem with views over Wimborne Minster. ♨❧✿◑♿♣P⁵⁻◱(3,4)

Dewlish

Oak at Dewlish

DT2 7ND SY774981

✪ 11.30-2.30, 6-11; 12-2.30, 7-11 Sun ☎ (01258) 837352
⊕ oakpub.co.uk

Beer range varies Ⓗ

Unpretentious village inn with two or three ever-changing ales, mainly from West Country breweries such as Cotleigh, Isle of Purbeck and Dartmoor. The horseshoe-shaped bar has a dining area and opens on to a patio and large garden. To the rear is a separate room with a pool table. A varied food menu offers good home-cooked dishes made using local produce. B&B and self-catering accommodation is available in a converted coach house next door. Dogs and children are welcome. ♨Q❧✿❀◑♣●♿P⁵⁻◱(311)

Dorchester

Blue Raddle Ⓛ

9 Church Street, DT1 1JN

✪ 11.30-3 (not Mon), 6.30-11; 12-3, 7-10.30 Sun
☎ (01305) 267762

Butcombe Bitter; Fuller's London Pride; Otter Bitter; St Austell Tribute; Sixpenny Gold; guest beer Ⓗ

Popular, genuine, town-centre free house with friendly staff and an enthusiastic landlord. In addition to the regular beers, guest ales and local ciders are also on offer. Good locally sourced food is served lunchtimes (not Sun) and Thursday-Saturday evenings. The pub takes part in local events and hosts regular folk music sessions. Piped comedy shows and Private Eye are available in the conveniences. No children, but dogs are welcome. Q◑♿≈(South)♣●◱

Colliton Club

Colliton House, Colliton Park, DT1 1XJ (opp County Hall and Crown Court)

✪ 9-3, 6-11.30; 10-3.30, 7-midnight Sat; closed Sun
☎ (01305) 224503 ⊕ collitonclub.co.uk

Dartmoor Best; Greene King Abbot; St Austell Tribute; guest beers Ⓗ

Thriving club opposite County Council HQ with at least six real ales always available including a changing range of guests often from Flack Manor, Hop Back and Hall & Woodhouse. The club is housed in the mainly 17th-century Grade II-listed Colliton House and welcomes CAMRA members – just show your membership card. Busy in and out of office hours, this is a popular meeting place for a number of local associations. Evening snacks are served. Dogs and children are allowed. A regular winner of CAMRA Wessex Region Club of the Year. Q❀◑≈(South/West)♣⁵⁻◱

Tom Browns Ⓛ

47 High East Street, DT1 1LU

✪ 11-11 (2am Fri & Sat); 12-11 Sun ☎ (01305) 264020

Dorset Tom Browns Bitter, Flashman's Clout, seasonal beers; guest beers Ⓗ

Previously home to the Goldfinch Brewery, this is now the Dorset Brewing Company tap. The full range of Goldfinch (now brewed by DBC), DBC and interesting guest ales rotates round the eight handpumps, plus a local cider. Refurbished but retaining the feel of a town-centre ale house, the pub hosts mini beer festivals, live music and other events. Food includes award-winning pies. The large riverside garden is ideal for lazy pints in the sun. There is a fully functional skittle alley. Dog-friendly. ♨Q❧❀◑≈(West/South)♣●⁵⁻◱

East Stour

King's Arms

East Stour Common, SP8 5NB (on A30, 3½ miles W of Shaftesbury) ST813231

✪ 12-3, 5.30-11; 12-midnight Sat; 12-10.30 Sun
☎ (01747) 838325 ⊕ kingsarmseaststour.com

Greene King IPA; St Austell Tribute; Sharp's Doom Bar; guest beers Ⓗ

This imposing roadside pub is a multi-roomed establishment served by a single bar, with many areas for diners. The bar is popular with locals, who have a say in the selection of the guest beers. The Scottish-influenced food is excellent, made with locally sourced ingredients where possible, and the all-day Sunday carvery can be very busy. The patio and enclosed garden are a welcome addition in

summer, and there is accommodation all year round. Dogs and muddy boots welcome.
🏨🅟🍴◑ᕯ🅿🏵

Evershot

Acorn Inn 🅛
28 Fore Street, DT2 0JW
☼ 11-11 (10.30 Sun) ☎ (01935) 83228 ⊕ acorn-inn.co.uk
Beer range varies Ⓗ
Small 16th-century hotel with a fine pillared porch. A large flagstoned room at the back is known as the village bar, adorned with local photographs – a smaller bar and restaurant are at the front. Two ales are always available, usually from Dorset Brewing Company, Yeovil Ales or Otter Brewery. A third real ale and local cider are added in summer. The skittle alley can be hired for functions. This is the coaching inn mentioned in Thomas Hardy's Tess of the d'Urbervilles as the Sow & Acorn.
🏨Q🍴🏵◑♣🅿ᕯ🏵(212,X37,D11)

Farnham

Museum Inn 🅛
DT11 8DE (off A354)
☼ 12-11 ☎ (01725) 516261 ⊕ museuminn.co.uk
Fuller's London Pride; Sixpenny 6d Best; guest beer Ⓗ
Set in the tranquil Dorset countryside, this 17th-century inn has a cosy, intimate feel. Refurbished in 2012, the interior is open plan but divided into four distinct areas. Some original features have been retained including the flagstone floor in the bar area, large inglenook and window seat. The pub is predominantly food oriented but welcoming to those who just want a drink. Food is served all day with a good, varied menu including a vegetarian option. At least one local ale is available. Dog-friendly. 🏨Q🍴🏵◑🅿ᕯ

Gillingham

Phoenix
High Street, SP8 4AW ST80632653
☼ 10-3, 6-11 (not Mon); 10-11 Fri; 11-midnight Sat; 12-3, 6-11 Sun ☎ (01747) 823277
St Austell Tribute; Sharp's Doom Bar Ⓗ
First built in the 15th century as a coaching inn, with its own brewery and stables, the pub was rebuilt in the 17th century following a fire, hence the Phoenix. It has a single-bar open-plan layout with a dining area to one side. There are two public car parks within walking distance. It can be boisterous on busy evenings. ◑🍴🏵(158)

Horton

Drusilla's Inn 🅛
Horton Road, Wigbeth, BH21 7JH SU046070
☼ 10-11 ☎ (01258) 840297 ⊕ drusillasinn.co.uk
Flack Manor Double Drop; Ringwood Best Bitter; guest beer Ⓗ
Attractive thatched pub with views over the rolling Dorset countryside. Although a restaurant has been added to the back of the building, the bar still has a traditional feel, warmed by a real fire in winter. Staff and locals are very friendly. A wide variety of food is available from bar snacks to à la carte meals. The two- or three-course meals are exceptional value for money. Numerous special events are held during the year – see the website for details. 🏨🏵◑♣🅿ᕯ🏵

Kingston

Scott Arms
West Street, BH20 5LH SY957796
☼ 11-11 ☎ (01929) 480270 ⊕ thescottarms.com
Dorset Jurassic; Ringwood Best Bitter; guest beers Ⓗ
This imposing Virginia creeper-covered corner pub has an upper and lower bar, the upper part a series of cosy interconnected rooms, and a garden with unrivalled views across Corfe Castle to Poole Harbour. Two guest beers are kept, often from Butcombe or Otter, and the pub serves local real cider produced just down the hill. Good home-cooked food including some exotic dishes is available lunchtimes and evenings.
🏨🍴🏵◑♣🅿🏵(40,44)

Langton Matravers

Ship Inn 🅛
Coombe Hill, BH19 3EU
☼ 12-3, 5.30-11; 12-11 Fri-Sun ☎ (01929) 426910
⊕ shipinnlangton.co.uk
Isle of Purbeck Best Bitter; Palmers Copper Ale, Dorset Gold; guest beer Ⓗ
Founded in 1765, this attractive inn is situated in the heart of the village in the centre of the Purbecks. It has a flagstone-floored main bar with perimeter benches. Restaurant-style seating dominates the rear. The beer garden is a suntrap in summer. Live music plays every Friday in summer and quiz night is Wednesday. Ever-changing riddles above the bar provide an interesting sobriety test. Children and dogs are welcome.
🏨Q🍴🏵◑♣A♣🅿ᕯ🏵(40)

Lyme Regis

Royal Standard 🅛
25 Marine Parade, DT7 3JF
☼ 10-11 ☎ (01297) 442637
⊕ theroyalstandardlymeregis.co.uk
Palmers Copper Ale, Best, Dorset Gold, 200 Ⓗ
Popular 400-year-old pub with a restaurant and beach-side terrace. Interior stained glass, originally from the Three Cups Hotel, depicts the the Duke of Monmouth landing on the nearby beach in the 1685 rebellion. Palmers Tally Ho! is available in the winter. Home-cooked meals feature local produce and freshly caught fish, with vegetarian dishes also on the menu. Ideal for families, the pub can be busy in the summer, and usually stays open late at weekends. 🏨🏵◑A♣ᕯ🏵(31,X53)

Volunteer 🅛
31 Broad Street, DT7 3QE
☼ 11-11; 12-10.30 Sun ☎ (01297) 442214
Branscombe Vale Donegal Ⓖ**; St Austell Tribute; guest beers** Ⓗ
Old two-room pub in the heart of this historic seaside town, a few steps from the seafront, with a lovely olde-worlde atmosphere. Popular with locals, the main bar buzzes with jolly banter and conversation. The house beer, Donegal, is Branscombe Vale Best and is stillaged behind the bar. A rotating choice of two West Country guest ales is on offer. Food is served at weekends only in the winter. Dogs are welcome, and children in the refurbished family room. 🏨🍴◑♣🏵(31,X53)

Lytchett Matravers

Rose & Crown
178 Wareham Road, BH16 6DT
✪ 12-11 (2am Fri & Sat); 12-10.30 Sun ☎ (01202) 625325
⊕ roseandcrownlytchett.co.uk
Sharp's Doom Bar; guest beers Ⓗ
This former Badger pub is now a welcoming two-bar free house. The Doom Bar is served alongside up to three guest beers, often from local breweries. Real cider is available in the public bar, where there is a dartboard and real fire. Good-quality home-cooked food is popular – Sunday lunch is highly recommended. Outside is a covered smoking area and a separate garden. The pub hosts comedy and music on-site and at the village hall, plus a beer festival. ♨🏠🌐⊅🅰♣🍴P⌐❋⊟(387,X8)

Marshwood

Bottle Inn Ⓛ
DT6 5QJ (on B3165) SY376997
✪ 12-11 ☎ (01297) 678484 ⊕ bottle-inn.net
Sunny Republic Huna Red; Yeovil POSH IPA; guest beers Ⓗ
Remotely situated on the Dorset/Devon border, a single bar serves two small rooms, with a family room and skittle alley at the rear, leading to a large garden overlooking Marshwood Vale. Six local ales are served from Sunny Republic, Exe Valley, Art Brew, Yeovil and others alongside six ciders and perries from Sandford and Cornish Orchard. The pub holds a beer festival in July incorporating a nettle-eating competition. Bar food is available. Closing time is flexible if the pub is busy. ♨Q🏠🌐⊅🅰♣P

North Wootton

Three Elms Inn ♈
DT9 5JW (on A3030)
✪ 11-11; 12-10.30 Sun ☎ (01935) 812881
⊕ thethreeelmsinn.co.uk
Beer range varies Ⓗ
This enterprising rural free house is not only a thriving pub but is also the village shop and post office. The comfortable L-shaped bar is popular with drinkers and diners alike who come to enjoy the two real ales and traditional pub fare (no food Mon). The beers change every week and are rarely repeated, although they are not over 5% ABV. Outside is a large garden with children's playground. Local CAMRA Rural Pub of the Year 2013. ♨Q🏠🌐⊅🅰P

Pamphill

Vine Inn ★
Vine Hill, BH21 4EE (off B3082) ST994003
✪ 11 (12 Sun)-3, 7-10.30 ☎ (01202) 882259
Fuller's London Pride Ⓗ; guest beer Ⓖ
Identified by CAMRA as one of Britain's Best Real Heritage Pubs, with a warm and homely ambience in two small rooms either side of the bar and a further seating area upstairs accessible from the public bar. The hedge-lined garden, a suntrap in summer, provides a lovely little haven. The guest beer is often from a local brewery and real ciders are also stocked. Sandwiches and ploughman's are available at lunchtimes. A must-visit pub when in the area. Winner of many local CAMRA awards. Q🏠🌐🅱♣🍴P⌐⊟

Piddlehinton

Thimble Inn Ⓛ
14 High Street, DT2 7TD
✪ closed Mon; 11.30-3, 6-11 ☎ (01300) 348270
⊕ thethimbleinnpiddlehinton.co.uk
Palmers Copper Ale, Best Bitter, 200, Tally Ho! Ⓗ
Large partly thatched village pub on the River Piddle with cheery, welcoming staff. The spacious low-beamed bar has two attractive brick fireplaces and plenty of nooks and crannies for cosy twosomes and larger groups. A well-kept range of Palmer's ales is available, along with Dorset Gold in the summer, and food is served lunchtimes and evenings. The river runs through the large garden, and there is plenty of parking. A two-bedroom apartment is a new addition. Dogs are welcome. ♨🏠🌐🛏🌐⊅🅶P⌐❋⊟(307)

Piddletrenthide

Poacher's Inn
DT2 7QX
✪ 8am-midnight ☎ (01300) 348358
⊕ thepoachersinn.co.uk
Butcombe Bitter; St Austell Tribute; Sharp's Doom Bar Ⓗ
A quiet family pub with a friendly welcome and three permanent real ales, renowned for its good food featuring ingredients sourced from local suppliers. It has a 17th-century restaurant, riverside garden and 21-room accommodation arranged around a central courtyard, with a swimming pool for use during the summer months. Q🏠🌐🛏🌐🅶🅰♣P⌐⊟❋⊟(307)

Plush

Brace of Pheasants
DT2 7RQ
✪ 12-3, 7-11 ☎ (01300) 348357 ⊕ braceofpheasants.co.uk
Sharp's Doom Bar; guest beer Ⓖ
Cosy village pub with a friendly welcome for all (including dogs). The main bar, with a real fire in winter, serves ales direct from the casks, with a guest from the likes of Flack Manor, Sunny Republic or Cottage. Superb food is served in the bar and restaurant areas. A large sloping cottage garden to the rear has tables and a covered, heated area for smokers. Widely renowned for well-kept ales and good food, the pub can get busy and booking is a must for meals. Four comfortable bedrooms are available. ♨Q🏠🌐🛏🌐⊅P⌐

Poole

Bermuda Triangle
10 Parr Street, Lower Parkstone, BH14 0JY
✪ 12-3, 5-11 (midnight Fri); 12-midnight Sat; 12-11 Sun
☎ (01202) 748087
Beer range varies Ⓗ
As the name suggests, this bustling, multi-award-winning pub explores the mystery of the Triangle and carries a nautical theme. The single-room bar has a split-level interior and is bedecked with an intriguing range of curios, maps, newspaper cuttings and even part of an aircraft wing. Run by the same owner for 23 years, the bar has four handpumps offering an ever-changing range of ales sourced from far and wide alongside speciality German lagers and foreign beers. 🌐⇌(Parkstone)⊟(M1)

Blue Boar

29 Market Close, BH15 1NE
🕒 12-11 (midnight Fri & Sat) ☎ (01202) 682247
🌐 blueboarpoole.co.uk
Fuller's London Pride, ESB; Gale's Seafarers Ale; guest beer Ⓗ
Situated in the heart of Poole, this large, creeper-covered pub boasts an array of military and diving artefacts and has three distinctive bars over three floors. At ground level is an L-shaped bar with a large fireplace as its centrepiece. The rustic cellar bar hosts weekly jazz nights on a Thursday and occasional music nights. The first floor has a function room with conference facilities and is available to hire. An extensive locally sourced home-cooked food menu is offered. ♒️❀◑≠🖥

Branksome Railway Hotel Ⓛ

429 Poole Road, Branksome, BH12 1DQ (opp train station)
🕒 11-11; 12-10.30 Sun ☎ (01202) 769555
🌐 branksomerailwayhotel.co.uk
Hop Back Summer Lightning; Otter Ale; Sharp's Doom Bar; guest beer Ⓗ
Dating from 1894, this Victorian station hotel has been recently decorated inside and out. The large, open-plan interior is divided into two areas served by one bar. The front space has a pool table, cosy seating area and a large gas fire. The rear is carpeted with more comfortable seats and views of passing trains. A DJ and occasional live music play at weekends. En-suite accommodation is offered and a function room is available for hire. Local CAMRA Pub of the Year winner 2012.
🖙❀≠(Branksome)♣P🖥(M1,M2)

Brewhouse

68 High Street, BH15 1DA
🕒 11-11; 12-10.30 Sun ☎ (01202) 685288
Milk Street Mermaid, Beer, seasonal beers; guest beer Ⓗ
Popular local owned by the Milk Street Brewery of Frome, Somerset. Mermaid is almost exclusively brewed for the people of Poole. The split-level interior has a bar at street level with two pool tables at the rear. Seating is available outside at the front on the High Street to watch the world go by, and on the patio area at the rear. On Sunday there is a meat draw. Two real ciders are usually available. ❀≠♣♠♨🖥

Bricklayers Arms Ⓛ

41 Parr Street, Lower Parkstone, BH14 0JX
🕒 12-2.30, 5-11 (midnight Fri); 12-midnight Sat; 12-11 Sun ☎ (01202) 740304
Hop Back Summer Lightning; Ringwood Best Bitter, Fortyniner; Sharp's Doom Bar Ⓗ
Attractive pub with a clean, light and airy decor, fresh flowers and an open fire. Popular with locals, the L-shaped bar has plenty of seating at tables, creating a relaxed, friendly environment. There is decking to the front with more seating and a garden to the rear, with a modern rustic style. Children are permitted in outside areas but not after 8pm. Free Wi-Fi is available.
♒️Q❀≠(Parkstone)♨🖥(M1,1b)

La Cruz

73-75 Commercial Road, Parkstone, BH14 0JB
🕒 closed Mon; 3 (5 Fri-Sun)-midnight ☎ (01202) 710661
🌐 la-cruz.co.uk
Beer range varies Ⓗ

Essentially a restaurant bar, but also another place to find interesting ales in bustling Ashley Cross. The two ever-changing ales are always 4.5% ABV or higher; do ask for recommendations to accompany food prepared by Tim the chef from his range of home-cooked locally sourced dishes. Offering something for everyone, the comfortable bar area welcomes drinkers and diners alike, the restaurant provides a venue for couples or parties and you can relax in the cosy astroturfed beer garden at the rear. Q❀❀◑Ⓖ≠(Parkstone)🖥

Poole Ex-Servicemen's Club

66 North Road, BH14 0LY
🕒 6-11 Mon & Tue; 12-3, 6-midnight Wed & Thu; 12-midnight Fri-Sun ☎ (01202) 744515
Beer range varies Ⓗ
A social club affiliated to the Royal British Legion, visitors are welcome with a CAMRA membership card or a copy of this Guide. Three ever-changing ales from breweries across the country are available as well as a real cider, and two annual beer festivals are held in summer and winter. The club has a large main room with side meeting room, pool room, upstairs snooker room and rear beer garden. There are eight dartboards and free Wi-Fi. ❀❀♿≠(Parkstone)♠P♨🖥(M2)

Portland

George Inn

133 Reforne, DT5 2AP
🕒 12-midnight (11 Sun) ☎ (01305) 820011
🌐 thegeorgeinn.org
Beer range varies Ⓗ
A friendly, family-oriented local dating from the mid-18th century with four separate bar and dining areas and a large enclosed beer garden. Food is available every day and the substantial Sunday roasts are very popular. There are usually three ales on offer on both handpump and gravity – typically Black Sheep Best Bitter, St Austell Tribute and a local beer. A well-attended beer festival is held annually around St George's Day. ❀❀◑🖥(1)

Royal Portland Arms Ⓛ

40 Fortuneswell, DT5 1LZ
🕒 11-midnight (11.30 weekdays winter); 11-1.30am Fri & Sat; 12-midnight Sun ☎ (01305) 862255
Beer range varies Ⓗ/Ⓖ
Dating back 200 years, this Portland-stone pub stands on the main road with public car parks nearby. George III is reputed to have stopped here for a drink and a plate of Portland mutton on a visit to the island. A basic one-bar pub, it offers a choice of local ales from breweries including Dorset, Yeovil and Isle of Purbeck, and ciders plus bar snacks. Live music plays on Fridays and Sunday afternoons in winter. Popular foodie events include a cheese club every Wednesday. CAMRA members receive a discount on beer. Q♣♠♨🖥(1)

Preston

Spiceship

240 Preston Road, DT3 6BJ
🕒 11.30-midnight summer; 12-11 Sun & winter ☎ (01305) 834651 🌐 spiceship.co.uk
Ringwood Best Bitter; Sharp's Doom Bar; Taylor Landlord; guest beer Ⓗ
Large Grade II-listed coaching house pub with a friendly atmosphere and rotating guest beer

GOOD BEER GUIDE 2014

(Butcombe Bitter, Dartmoor Jail Ale or Dorset Jurassic). The separate dining area serves quality food lunchtimes and evenings with vegetarian and vegan options and daily specials. Thursday is curry night. A number of screens show televised events and live music plays on Fridays. Teams are fielded in the local darts leagues and there is a golf society. Outside is a large grassed area with tables and a children's play area. Overnight accommodation is available. Children and pets most welcome. ⛄🕮🛏🕮⬛♣P⌐🖳(4,X53)

Pymore

Pymore Inn
DT6 5PN
🟢 closed Mon; 12-3, 6-11; 12-4, 7-11 (closed eve winter) Sun
☎ (01308) 422625
St Austell Trelawny, Tribute 🄷
Attractive Georgian ivy-clad free house about a mile north of Bridport. A cosy village local with a warm welcome, it offers a sensibly priced food menu and specials board featuring locally sourced ingredients. A third local beer is added in summer as well as real cider. Children and dogs are allowed in the large grassy garden. A function room is available for small parties. 🕮Q⛄🕮🕮♣P

Shaftesbury

Two Brewers
24 St James Street, St James, SP7 8HE ST86162270
🟢 12-3, 5-11; 11-midnight Fri & Sat; 12-10.30 Sun
☎ (01747) 852210 🌐 yeoldetwobrewers.co.uk
Ringwood Best Bitter, Sharp's Doom Bar 🄷
A traditional 18th-century pub sitting at the foot of the famous Gold Hill in an area once bustling with tanneries and laundries using the abundant local water supply. This is probably the reason the original landlords, two brothers, chose to brew their own beer here. A single bar, that usually has two guest beers, caters for a number of discreet areas including an adjacent skittle alley and a separate restaurant. The large beer garden has fine views and is host to an annual beer festival. 🕮Q⛄🕮🕮P⌐🖳

Sherborne

Digby Tap
Cooks Lane, DT9 3NS
🟢 11 (12 Sun)-11 ☎ (01935) 813148 🌐 digbytap.co.uk
Beer range varies 🄷
The Digby Tap is an institution in west Dorset. Hidden away between the railway station and the abbey, it is worth seeking out for the building alone, which dates back to the 16th century. It was once the parish workhouse and many features of the original building remain. The interior feels like stepping back in time, yet the pub remains popular with all ages. Four or five ales from across the West Country are always available. Bought by the pint or jug, they offer superb value. 🕮Q🕮🕮🕮🖳

Sixpenny Handley

Sixpenny Tap
The Dairy Building, Manor Farm, SP5 5NU (turn off B3018 onto unclassified road ¼ mile S of village, signed behind farm buildings) ST99811663
🟢 closed Sun-Tue; 4.30-6 (6.30 Fri); 11-1pm Sat
☎ (01725) 762006 🌐 sixpennybrewery.co.uk

Waylands Sixpenny 6d Best, 106 Jack FM, 6d Gold, Man in the Wall, IPA 🄷
The bar/brewery shop is attached to the brewhouse, situated in the main farmyard. Five real ales are regularly on tap but often an occasional or seasonal ale will be added on gravity. Due to complex leasing arrangements with the farm, opening hours are restricted, but when open the pub is extremely busy and very popular. At about 100 sq ft the bar is one of the smallest in the country, but outdoor seating (covered in winter) is also available. 🕮Å♣P⌐🖳(184)

Spetisbury

Woodpecker 🏆
High Street, DT11 9DJ
🟢 12-3, 6-11 (7-10.30 Sun) ☎ (01258) 452658
Beer range varies 🄷
An imposing free house situated on the A350 in the heart of the picturesque village of Spetisbury. This comfortable open-plan pub offers four ever-changing ales from the surrounding areas, two real ciders and two perries. Good-quality food is available at every session. Bar billiards and shove-ha'penny are played. The spacious garden is home to an annual cider festival and the perfect place for whiling away an afternoon. Winner of local CAMRA Rural Pub of the Year 2012. 🕮🕮♣🕮P🖳(X8)

Stourton Caundle

Trooper Inn 🏆
Golden Hill, DT10 2JW (1½ miles E of A357) ST715149
🟢 closed Mon; 12-2.30 (3.30 Sun), 7-11 ☎ (01963) 362405
🌐 thetrooperinn.co.uk
Sharp's Cornish Coaster; guest beers 🄷
Stone-built, single-room community pub with a separate function room/skittle alley. There is an attached camping and caravan site and a children's play area next to the beer garden. Good food is available lunchtimes and early evenings, with a popular Friday fish and chips night. Two guest beers are often on tap, one from the pub's own microbrewery, the other from elsewhere in the region, plus a farmhouse cider. An annual beer festival is held in the spring. Dogs and walkers are welcome. Q🕮🕮⅄Å♣P

Stratton

Saxon Arms
20 The Square, DT2 9WG
🟢 11-3, 5.15-11; 11-11 Fri-Sun ☎ (01305) 260020
🌐 thesaxon-stratton.co.uk
Ringwood Best Bitter; Taylor Landlord; guest beers 🄷
Newly built in 2001, this flint and thatch pub has the feel of a country inn. Outside, a patio area overlooks the green and village hall. The bar divides into three areas including a dining space serving quality food from locally sourced producers. Two guest beers are available in addition to the two regular beers. This busy pub with helpful staff is an integral part of the local community. Dog friendly. 🕮Q🕮🕮P⌐🖳(212)

Swanage

Red Lion
63 High Street, BH19 2LY
🟢 11-11.30; 12-11 Sun ☎ (01929) 423533
🌐 redlionswanage.co.uk

Palmers Copper Ale; Ringwood Best Bitter; Sharp's Doom Bar; Taylor Landlord Ⓗ; guest beers Ⓖ
A 17th-century hostelry, centrally located for the beach, steam railway and coastal path. An impressive range of up to 24 ciders is available alongside a wide choice of ales. There is also an excellent variety of food on offer, served in the bar and dining room. Outside there are covered and heated smoking areas in the large garden. Luxury accommodation is available in a separate coach house. A real gem for locals and visitors alike.
ᛘQ✿⌂⌖◑⬒≷(Swanage Steam Railway)♣●P⁵⎕(40,50)

Thornford

Lime Tree
Pound Road, DT9 6QD
✪ 12-2.30 (not Mon), 6-11 (not Mon summer); 12-2.30, 6-10.30 (closed eve winter) Sun ☎ (01935) 872294
⊕ thelimetreethornford.co.uk
Beer range varies Ⓗ
A traditional free house in the centre of the village with up to four handpumps dispensing Otter, Butcombe and other local and national beers. Offering a warm welcome to drinkers and diners, it has a traditional bar area and a contemporary restaurant providing excellent food including a take-away service (no food Mon). A coffee morning is hosted on Tuesday 10am-noon. Local CAMRA Rural Pub of the Year 2012.
ᛘ✿◑≷♣P⁵⎕(74)

Upwey

Royal Standard
700 Dorchester Road, DT3 5LA
✪ 12-3, 6-midnight; 12-midnight Sat; 12-11 Sun
☎ (01305) 812558 ⊕ theroyalstandardupwey.co.uk
Royal Standard DT3; Yeovil Star Gazer; guest beers Ⓗ
Comfortable and homely two-roomed pub on the outskirts of Weymouth, popular with locals and visitors alike. The wood-panelled public bar is complemented by a lounge bar/restaurant area, all recently refurbished. The pub has two ever-changing guest beers and was winner of a Best Cellar Award for the South West area in 2011. The on-site microbrewery brews DT3 and DT4 ales, and the pub hosts an annual beer festival and sausage & cider festival.
ᛘQ✿✿◑⬒≷♣●P⎕(10,31)

Wareham

King's Arms
41 North Street, BH20 4AD
✪ 11-11; 12-10.30 Sun ☎ (01929) 552503
Ringwood Best Bitter; guest beers Ⓗ
A traditional thatched inn that has its roots in the 1500s and survived the great fire of 1762. This multi-roomed establishment has a flagstone-floored public bar, real fire, a drinking corridor and two rooms exclusively for dining. To the rear is a large garden with a covered area for smokers. A good range of reasonably priced home-cooked food and three guest beers from the southern counties are on offer alongside the Best Bitter. Dogs are welcome.
ᛘQ✿◑⬒≷♣●P⁵⎕(40,X53)

Waytown

Hare & Hounds Ⓛ
DT6 5LQ SY470978
✪ 12-3, 6.30 (6 summer)-11 ☎ (01308) 488203
Palmers Copper Ale, Best Bitter, 200, seasonal beer Ⓗ
Hidden down winding lanes, this rural gem is an unspoilt village local and well worth seeking out. The garden, with stunning views across the Brit Valley, is a major attraction in summer with a play area and grassy expanse for children to let off steam. Bridge Farm cider is a regular and the attractive food menu features home-cooked meals and fresh local produce. A quiz replaces food on Sunday evenings in winter. Palmers Dorset Gold is available in summer and Tally Ho! in winter. Closing time may vary if the pub is busy.
ᛘQ➳✿◑⬒♣●P⁵

West Lulworth

Castle Inn Ⓛ
Main Road, BH20 5RN
✪ 12-2, 7-11; 12-3, 6-11 Sat; 12-3, 7-10.30 Sun
☎ (01929) 400311 ⊕ lulworthinn.com
Palmers Best Bitter; guest beers Ⓖ
Winner of local CAMRA Rural Pub of the Year in 2011, this enchanting 16th-century thatched inn close to Lulworth Cove has two comfortable bars, one with a low ceiling, both beamed. Six mostly local ales and around 19 traditional ciders/perries are served alongside an extensive food menu offering good-value, home-made dishes in generous portions. At the rear is a tiered garden with a giant chess set. Board games are available inside. The inn has 15 bedrooms, 14 en suite. Very dog-friendly. Q✿➳◑⬒Å♣●P⁵

West Parley

Owl's Nest Ⓛ
196 Christchurch Road, BH22 8SS
✪ 11.30-3 (not Mon), 5 (6 Sat)-11.30; 12-3 Sun
☎ (01202) 572793 ⊕ theowlsnest-westparley.com
Otter Bitter, Ale; Ringwood Best Bitter; guest beer Ⓗ
Tudor-style building with beamed ceilings and an open fire providing a welcoming and comfortable ambience. The pub is decorated with a number of collections - toby jugs hanging from the ceiling, military hats above the bar and many owls strategically positioned around the walls of the two rooms. Four handpumps serve a selection of locally sourced beers. The pub offers a range of excellent home-cooked food, pies a speciality, and there is a monthly live Irish music night.
ᛘ✿◑P⁵⎕(13,37)

West Stour

Ship Inn
SP8 5RP (on A30) ST78492257
✪ 12-3, 6-11; 12-11 (7 Nov-Feb) Sun ☎ (01747) 838640
⊕ shipinn-dorset.com
Beer range varies Ⓗ
Once a coaching inn, this popular roadside pub has fine views across the Blackmore Vale. The public bar features a flagstone floor and low ceiling; the separate restaurant area is light and airy with stripped oak floorboards and farmhouse furniture. There is a patio and large garden to the rear. This friendly pub is renowned for superb home-cooked food (no meals Sun eve) and comfortable

accommodation. Three beers and three ciders are usually available with a beer festival held in July. Dogs are welcome in the bar. ▲Q❀⇔◁❁♣♠P'⌐

Weymouth

Boot Inn
High West Street, DT4 8JH
❂ 11-11 (midnight Fri & Sat); 12-10.30 Sun
☎ (01305) 770327 ⊕ bootweymouth.co.uk
Ringwood Best Bitter, Fortyniner, Old Thumper; guest beers Ⓗ
Weymouth's oldest pub has a single bar area leading to comfortable rooms at both ends. The Ringwood beer range is supplemented by ales from the Marston's group and Cheddar Valley cider. No meals are served except large pork pies but there may be an impromptu banquet on Sundays when the fare is provided by both landlord and customers, especially game. It's a conversation-dominated venue with customers spilling outside when the weather is clement. Live music is hosted on Tuesdays, a quiz on Wednesdays.
▲Q❀&⬤≑♣♠⌐

Globe Inn
24 East Street, DT4 8BN
❂ 11-1am; 12-midnight Sun ☎ (01305) 786061
⊕ theglobeweymouth.co.uk
Dartmoor Jail Ale; Ringwood Old Thumper; St Austell Tribute; Sharp's Doom Bar; guest beers Ⓗ
Welcoming street-corner free house near Weymouth harbour and the town bridge, within walking distance of the town centre, main beach and esplanade. Up to six handpumps serve four regular beers plus two guests and a real cider. The separate games room has a pool table and pub games. Accommodation is available in four letting rooms. The local scooter club and local branch of the Royal Marine Association meet here every week. Q⇔≑♣♠'⌐

Swan Inn Ⓛ
41 St Thomas Street, DT4 8EH
❂ 7am-midnight (1am Fri & Sat) ☎ (01305) 750231
Courage Directors; Dorset Tom Browns; Greene King Abbot; Ringwood Old Thumper; guest beers Ⓗ
Single-bar Wetherspoon town-centre pub close to Weymouth harbour and town bridge. Food is served all day, with breakfasts from 7am. Extremely popular, it can get very busy at weekends and is often noisy due to the low ceiling. It has a child-free zone. Five or six changing guest beers are always available. The small enclosed garden at the rear is used as a smoking area.
❀◁&≑'⌐

Wellington Arms
13 St Albans Street, DT4 8PY
❂ 10-11 (or later); 12-11 Sun ☎ (07810) 574924
Ringwood Best Bitter, Fortyniner; guest beer Ⓗ
You are assured of a warm welcome from the friendly landlord and his family at this peaceful and homely family-run oasis in the centre of Weymouth. A Grade II-listed green faience tile frontage dates from 1850 and the wood-panelled interior and mirrors are essential features of this former Eldridge Pope town pub. Good home-cooked food is served daily until 7pm (9pm Fri and Sat). In summer additional beers from the Marston's range are available. ▲➢◁♣♠⌐

Wimborne

Green Man
1 Victoria Road, BH21 1EN
❂ 10-11.30 (12.30am Fri & Sat) ☎ (01202) 881021
⊕ greenmanwimborne.com
Wadworth Henry's IPA, 6X, Bishops Tipple Ⓗ
Note the green man in the floor when entering this traditional 18th-century one-bar inn. The vibrant community pub is divided into separate areas, including a family room, and dogs are welcome. Live entertainment features at the weekend (check website). Westons Scrumpy cider is on handpump. The award-winning flower displays in the front garden make this a very popular attraction in summer. A great base for exploring the historic town and model village.
▲➢❀◁♣♠'⌐(3,4,13)

Worth Matravers

Square & Compass ★
BH19 3LF (off B3069) SY974777
❂ 12-3, 6-11; 12-11 Fri-Sun ☎ (01929) 439229
⊕ squareandcompasspub.co.uk
Hattie Brown's Mustang Sally, seasonal beers; guest beers Ⓖ
One of only seven pubs to feature in every edition of this Guide, this iconic, multi-award-winning inn is perched on top of the Jurassic coast. It has two distinct rooms, one with a large real fire, a sea-facing garden and a fossil museum with exhibits collected locally. A single serving hatch offers beers from near and far. The pub is now producing its own beers nearby as well as making its own cider. Regular live music and various festivals are hosted – see the website for details. Truly a pub for all seasons. ▲Q❀♣⌐P⌐(44)

The soul of beer

Brewers call barley malt the 'soul of beer'. While a great deal of attention has been rightly paid to hops in recent years, the role of malt in brewing must not be ignored. Malt contains starch that is converted to a special form of sugar known as maltose during the brewing process. It is maltose that is attacked by yeast during fermentation and turned into alcohol and carbon dioxide. Other grains can be used in brewing, notably wheat. But barley malt is the preferred grain as it gives a delightful biscuity / cracker / Ovaltine note to beer. Unlike wheat, barley has a husk that works as a natural filter during the first stage of brewing, known as the mash. Cereals such as rice and corn / maize are widely used by global producers of mass-market lagers, but brewers of hand-crafted beer avoid them.

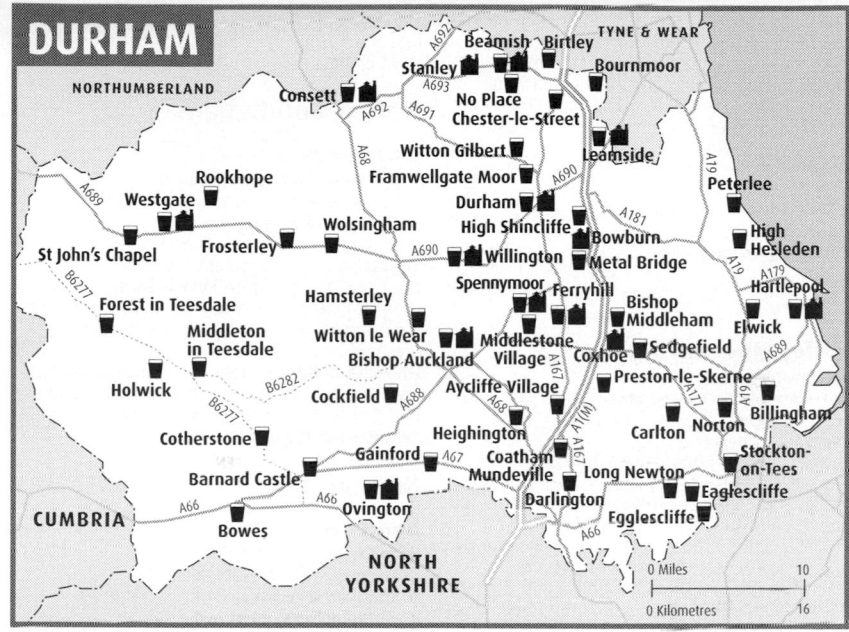

Co Durham incorporates part of the former county of Cleveland

Aycliffe Village

County
13 The Green, DL5 6LX
☼ 11.30-3, 5-midnight; 12-11 Sun ☎ (01325) 312273
⊕ thecountyaycliffevillage.com
Beer range varies ℍ
Overlooking the award-winning green in a picturesque village, this attractive free house was originally three 17th-century cottages. Although some original features remain it is now open plan, with the bar and three dining areas unified by bright modern decor, complemented by older beams and log fireplaces. Up to four guests come from local micros including Just A Minute and Yard of Ale, and from breweries further afield such as Hawkshead and Yorkshire Dales. Sunday is quiz night. ♨Q☻☆❀✍❶P↲⊟

Barnard Castle

Old Well Inn ℓ
21 The Bank, DL12 8PH
☼ 12-11 ☎ (01833) 690130 ⊕ theoldwellinn.co.uk
Courage Directors; Taylor Landlord; guest beers ℍ
The boundary of this 17th-century town centre CAMRA award-winning inn incorporates part of the medieval castle wall. The pub has a cosy front bar and a comfortable lounge, a separate restaurant and an airy conservatory, plus an enclosed beer garden. At least five well-kept beers are available including three guests from local micros. Excellent food is served every day. A 10-day beer festival is held at Easter. Thursday is acoustic night, with guests from Barnard Castle Folk Club on the last Thursday of the month. Q❀✍❶⊟↲⊟(75,76)

Beamish

Black Horse ℓ
Red Row, DH9 0RW
☼ 11-11.30 (midnight Sat); 11-11 Sun ☎ (01207) 232569
⊕ blackhorsebeamish.co.uk
Consett Aleworks White Hot, Red Dust; Wells Bombardier ℍ
The pub building was originally the first and largest in a row of cottages and has been beautifully restored, retaining all of its 300-year-old charm and atmosphere, with the bar featuring flagstone flooring and open fires. The spacious restaurant offers a seasonal menu using fresh ingredients sourced from over 10 acres of on-site vegetable gardens and orchards. Outside there is extensive seating with views over the Beamish Valley. ♨Q☻☆❀✍❶⅋P↲⊟

Stables Bar & Restaurant ℓ
Beamish Hall Country House Hotel, DH9 0YB (behind main hall in Stables courtyard)
☼ 11-11 (midnight Fri & Sat); 12-10.30 Sun
☎ (01207) 288750 ⊕ beamish-hall.co.uk/stables
Beer range varies ℍ
The Stables is attached to Beamish Hall Country House Hotel, and has its own microbrewery. Stone floors, old beams, solid furniture and crackling log fires in winter help to create a relaxing environment. Outside is a courtyard seating area and, behind the pub, an excellent play area for children. Beer festivals are hosted in September and January. The pub is also a popular live music venue. An extensive menu of locally produced food is served. ♨☻☆❀✍❶&♥P↲

Billingham

Greenholme Catholic Club
37 Wolviston Road, TS23 2RU (on E side of old A19, just S of Roseberry Rd roundabout, next to bus stop)
☼ 7-11 (midnight Fri); 12-midnight Sat; 12-10.30 Sun
☎ (07561) 192557
Beer range varies ℍ

Teesside's best-kept secret, this Victorian mansion and former school is now a friendly private members' club, with a genuine welcome for CAMRA members. Dedicated and enthusiastic volunteers ensure that the club's reputation for serving 150 different beers annually continues. Five ales and a cider are usually offered, with up to 10 beers during regular beer festivals held over each of the bank holiday weekends. The club is also renowned for its vibrant R&B/rock scene, with guest bands performing most weekends. ⌕⊛&♣⦿P'–⊟(36)

Birtley

Barley Mow Inn Ⓛ
Durham Road, DH3 2AG
✪ 11-midnight; 10-11.30 Sun ☎ (0191) 410 45044
⊕ barleymowinn.co.uk
Beer range varies Ⓗ
The Barley Mow offers a tremendous range of 13 real ales at any one time and actively promotes real ales through beer festivals, supporting local breweries and CAMRA. A full food menu is available lunchtimes and evenings. Good weekly entertainment features on Thursdays and Saturdays. This welcoming, spacious pub is family oriented and home to several darts and dominoes teams. ⌕⊛⦅D⊞♣⦿P'–⊟

Bishop Auckland

Bay Horse
Bondgate, DL14 7PE (50 yds N of bus station)
✪ 11-11 (1am Fri & Sat); 12-11 Sun ☎ (01388) 609765
Taylor Landlord; guest beer Ⓗ
At the heart of Bishop Auckland's pub scene since 1530, this welcoming hostelry is a haven from shopping during the week, and a joyfully boisterous place on a weekend, with Friday live bands and Saturday night karaoke. It retains its roots as a long-established, proper pub. ㎡⊛⊞♣⦿⊟

Pollards
104 Etherley Lane, DL14 6TW
✪ 7-11 Mon; 12-2, 5-11.30; 12-2, 7-10.30 Sun
☎ (01388) 603539
Beer range varies Ⓗ
The pub has a reputation for good food as well as five well-kept ales and good conversation. Four separate but linked drinking areas form the main part of this bright and comfortable establishment on the edge of town, with a large restaurant to the rear. A popular quiz is held on Sunday evenings with supper included. Food is served lunchtimes and evenings, including a renowned carvery on Sunday. ㎡Q⊛⦅D⊞&≈♣P'–⊟⊟(94)

Stanley Jefferson
5 Market Place, DL14 7NJ
✪ 9am-midnight (1am Fri & Sat) ☎ (01388) 452836
Greene King Abbot; Ruddles Best Bitter; guest beers Ⓗ
This interesting conversion of former solicitors' offices offers all the facilities you would expect from a Wetherspoon establishment. Several separate but linked drinking areas and a glass-roofed bar area provide the opportunity for privacy or company. Close to the Bishop of Durham's palace and park, the pub takes its name from locally schooled Mr Jefferson – better known as

Stan Laurel. There is a large walled garden to the rear and a small pavement patio to the front. Quiz night is Wednesday. ⊛⦅D&≈⦿'–⊟

Bishop Middleham

Cross Keys
9 High Street, DL17 9AR (1 mile from A177)
✪ 12 (2.30 Mon)-11; 12-10.30 Sun ☎ (01740) 651231
Wells Bombardier; guest beer Ⓗ
Busy family-run village pub with a friendly atmosphere and a reputation for excellent meals. The spacious, open-plan lounge bar is complemented by a large restaurant and function room serving an extensive menu of freshly-prepared meals. Situated in excellent wildlife and walking country, a three-mile circular walk starts opposite. Quiz night is Tuesday, Teesside Tornadoes Bike Club meets on Wednesday and the pub has its own football team. ㎡⊛⦅D⊟

Bournmoor

Dun Cow Ⓛ
Primrose Hill, DH4 6DY
✪ 12-midnight ☎ (0191) 385 2631
⊕ theduncowbournmoor.co.uk
Maxim Lambton's; guest beer Ⓗ
Welcoming 18th-century country pub with an often-sighted 'grey lady' ghost. Traditional English pub fare is served in the lounge and bar, and à la carte in the conservatory restaurant. There's a function room for up to 100 people and a marquee for up to 400. Family-friendly with extensive gardens, it has beer festivals in March and October offering local ales, and live music festivals (first Saturday in June, last in September). ㎡⊛⦅D&♣⦿P'–⊟⊟

Bowes

Bowes Club (CIU)
Arch House, The Street, DL12 9HR
✪ 7 (5 Sat & Sun)-midnight ☎ 07716 191446
Beer range varies Ⓗ
Previously the village lock-up, this 18th-century stone building is now a small, thriving club that hosts many community events. There are two downstairs rooms – one with pool and darts, the other with a cosy fire in the fine old fireplace – and a meeting room upstairs. The single handpump features a changing guest beer, often sourced locally. Guests including CAMRA members are welcome – if in the area you must experience this gem. Opening hours may vary. ㎡⊛⊞♣

Carlton

Smiths Arms

Carlton Village, TS21 1EA (3 miles NW of Stockton centre)
☼ 12-3, 5-11; 12-midnight Fri & Sat; 12-10.30 Sun
☎ (01740) 630471
Taylor Landlord; guest beer Ⓗ

Situated at the centre of a rural village, where a strong community spirit continues to prevail, this typical late-Victorian family-run pub manages to satisfy drinkers and diners alike. The pub is one of the few in the local area to have retained a public bar, where the convivial host serves a regular beer and a guest. The restaurant, converted from the next-door blacksmith's workshop, offers good-value, quality food, including early-bird specials. There are real fires throughout.
🏚❀❀◑ ☖ఉ♣P⁴↦(6)

Chester-le-Street

Butcher's Arms

Middle Chare, DH3 3QD (off Front Street on left from Market Place)
☼ 11-11 ☎ (0191) 386 3605
Jennings Cumberland Ale; Marston's Pedigree; guest beers Ⓗ

A cosy pub in the centre of town acknowledged for the quality and quantity of its beers. The pub is also noted for its food, with the landlady's home cooking a speciality – Sunday lunches are popular and good value for money. Teas and coffees are also available. Convenient for the railway station and all buses through the town. Q❀❀◑⇌♣⁴↦🖼

Chester-le-Street Cricket Club 🄻

Ropery Lane, DH3 3PF
☼ 11-11 (midnight Fri-Sun) ☎ (0191) 388 3684
⊕ chesterlestreet-cc.com
Consett Red Dust; Cumberland Corby Ale; guest beer Ⓗ

A welcoming club house with two main rooms downstairs and an area outside for warm-weather drinking – all with fine views over the cricket ground. Sandwiches and pies are available from the bar on most days. Functions for up to 100 people (including wheelchair users) can be accommodated in the well-appointed function room on the first floor. Local CAMRA Club of the Year for the past five years, runner up in 2013.
❀☖ఉ⇌♦P⁴↦🖼

Pelaw Grange Greyhound Stadium

Drum Road, DH3 2AF (signed from Barley Mow roundabout on A167)
☼ 6.30-11 (closed Mon, Wed & Thu); 12-4 Sun
☎ (0191) 410 2141 ⊕ pelawgrange.co.uk
Beer range varies Ⓗ

The bar is managed by a CAMRA member – this is the only greyhound stadium in Britain with real ales. The large open bar, Panorama restaurant and concert room all overlook the track. There is a lively atmosphere on race nights (Tue, Fri & Sat) – CAMRA members are admitted free. An annual beer festival is hosted on the Easter weekend and trips to local microbreweries are organised. The trackside terrace is available for smokers. Children are welcome. ❀◑ఉP⁴↦🖼(21,22,50)

Smith's Arms 🄻

Castle Drive, Castle Dene, DH3 4HE NZ299507
☼ 4 (12 Sat)-11.30; 12-10.30 Sun ☎ (0191) 385 6915

Black Sheep Best Bitter; Jarrow Rivet Catcher; guest beer Ⓗ

A little off the beaten track, this traditional inn with well-kept bar has a small, cosy bar with a log-burning stove, a room with a pool table and a larger lounge with an open fire. The pub is reputed to be haunted. 🏚Q☖♣P⁴↦

Coatham Mundeville

Foresters Arms

Brafferton Lane, DL1 3LU (on A167 ¼ mile S of A1M jct 59)
☼ 12 (4 Mon)-midnight, closed Tue; 12-10.30 Sun
☎ (01325) 320565
Black Sheep Best Bitter; guest beers Ⓗ

You can be assured of a warm welcome at this Grade II-listed historic stone-built roadside pub with a main bar and an adjoining restaurant/function room. A hub of the local community, it is home to many clubs including a ukulele club and reptile club. A quiz is held every Thursday and there are live music events at weekends. To the rear is a large car park and garden which features the Foresters Farm (chickens, ducks, sheep). Beware – the pub is reputedly haunted and mysterious happenings occur. 🏚❀◑ఉ🅰♣P⁴↦🖼

Cockfield

Queen's Head

106 Front Street, DL13 5AA
☼ 5 (11 Sat)-11; 12-11 Sun ☎ (01388) 710981
Beer range varies Ⓗ

Towards the north end of the village, this cosy, welcoming and popular pub serves two constantly changing beers from the Marston's range. It has an open-plan interior and various seating areas and tables outside at the front of the building. A proper community local, it is very handy for the historic Cockfield Fell and associated industrial archaeology. Well worth a visit. ❀◑♣P🖼(6,8)

Consett

Company Row 🄻

Victoria Road, DH8 5BQ (near bus station)
☼ 8-11 (midnight Thu; 1am Fri & Sat) ☎ (01207) 585600
Greene King Abbot Ⓗ

Named after the rows of houses built by the Derwent Iron Company for its workers, this Wetherspoon establishment is a real asset to Consett town centre. Good beer and good food make this social pub popular with a wide clientele of all ages. The award-winning manager and team are welcoming and enthusiastic about selling real ale. ఉ◑ఉ♦🖼

Grey Horse 🄻

115 Sherburn Terrace, DH8 6NE (A692, then right along Sherburn Terrace)
☼ 12-12.30am (midnight Sun) ☎ (01207) 502585
⊕ thegreyhorse.co.uk
Consett Ale Works Steel Town Bitter, White Hot, Red Dust, Cast Iron, Black Bob, Men of Steel Ⓗ

Traditional pub dating back to 1848. The interior comprises a lounge and L-shaped bar, with a wood-beamed ceiling. Consett Ale Works Brewery is located at the rear. Beer festivals are held twice a year, live entertainment is hosted on Thursday and a quiz on Wednesday. The coast-to-coast cycle route is close by. 🏚Q❀☖ఉ♣♦

Cotherstone

Red Lion
Main Street, DL12 9QE
✪ 12-3 (not Mon-Fri), 7-11; 12-4, 7-10.30 Sun
☎ (01833) 650236
Yorkshire Dales Best Bitter; guest beers Ⓗ
Eighteenth-century Grade II-listed coaching inn, built in stone and set in the idyllic village of Cotherstone. Simply furnished, this homely local with two open fires has changed little since the '60s. You won't find a TV, jukebox or bandit, just good beer and conversation. Children, dogs and clean boots are welcome. The venue is used by local clubs and has a free-to-play pool room. The small garden is a suntrap. A guest beer often comes from local brewery Mithril Ales at Aldbrough St John. ⚒Q�ွ֍♣Å♣P

Darlington

Darlington Snooker Club Ⓛ
1 Corporation Road, DL3 6AE (corner of Northgate)
✪ 11-midnight (late Fri & Sat); 12-midnight Sun
☎ (01325) 241388
Beer range varies Ⓗ
First-floor, family-run and family-oriented private snooker club offering a friendly welcome. Four guest beers from micros countrywide and a small range of real ales in bottles are stocked. A comfortable TV lounge is available for those not playing on one of the 10 snooker tables. Twice yearly, the club plays host to a professional celebrity, and two beer festivals are held annually. Frequently voted CAMRA Regional Club of the Year and a finalist National Club in 2012, guests are welcome – show a CAMRA membership card or copy of this Guide for entry. Q☞≈(North Rd)♣🖳

Number Twenty 2 Ⓛ
22 Coniscliffe Road, DL3 7RG
✪ 12-11 (9 Mon); closed Sun ☎ (01325) 354590
⊕ villagebrewer.co.uk/our-pubs/number-twenty-2
Burton Bridge Bitter; Village Brewer White Boar, Old Raby; guest beers Ⓗ
Town-centre ale house with a passion for cask beer and winner of many CAMRA awards. Ales are dispensed from up to 13 handpumps, including a stout or porter, and regularly come from local micros, along with nine draught European beers. Huge curved windows, stained glass panels and a high ceiling give the interior an airy, spacious feel. To the rear, the Canteen serves upmarket home-cooked lunches and early evening meals. This is the home of Village Brewer beers, commissioned from Hambleton by the licensee. Q◑占≈🖳

Old Yard Tapas Bar
98 Bondgate, DL3 7JY
✪ 11-11; 12-10.30 Sun ☎ (01325) 467385 ⊕ tapasbar.co.uk
John Smith's Bitter; Theakston Old Peculier; guest beers Ⓗ
Interesting mixture of a town-centre bar and Mediterranean-style taverna offering a range of real ales alongside a fascinating blend of international wines and spirits in a friendly setting. Five guest beers from micros local and countrywide are stocked, with an extra three at the weekend. Although this is a thriving restaurant, you are more than welcome to pop in for a pint, and maybe a tapa or two (Greek and Spanish). The excellent south-facing pavement café is popular in good weather. The TV is for sport only. ֍◑≈՚🖳

Quakerhouse ▼ Ⓛ
2 Mechanics Yard, DL3 7QF (off High Row)
✪ 11 (12 Sun)-midnight ☎ 07783 960105
⊕ quakerhouse.net
Beer range varies Ⓗ
Ten times local CAMRA Town Pub of the Year, this bar is the first point of call for CAMRA members visiting Darlington. The lively award-winning free house opened in 1998 in the former Quaker Coffee House in one of the old yards just off the pedestrianised town centre. The drinking establishment has the feel of a cellar bar, offering 10 guests from regional and microbreweries countrywide, and Old Rosie cider. A popular music venue, it caters for all tastes from acoustic to rock – on Wednesday there is a door charge after 7.30pm. ֍占≈♣◑🖵🖳

Voodoo Café
84 Skinnergate, DL3 7LX
✪ 10-4, 5-10; 11-9 Sun ☎ (01325) 467555
⊕ voodoocafe.co.uk
Beer range varies Ⓗ
A Mexican/South American-themed continental-style café/bar. Downstairs is an atmospheric, colourful bar area, simply furnished, serving handpulled beers from microbreweries such as Mallinsons and Mithril Ales. The bar specialises in an impressive range of bottled beer from North and South American microbreweries. Upstairs is the vibrant main restaurant. During the warmer months outdoor seating in the street is provided. A popular Latin dance venue, there are salsa lessons on Tuesday evenings. ☞◑占≈🖳

Durham

Bishops' Mill Ⓛ
Walkergate, DH1 1HA (within Walkergate complex opp Gala)
✪ 8-midnight (11 Sun) ☎ (0191) 370 8510
Greene King Abbot Ⓗ
A Wetherspoon Lloyds No.1 Bar, it takes its name from the historic mill that stood for centuries adjacent to this site. First recorded in the Boldon Book of 1183, the Bishops' Mill was the place where the freemen of Durham went to grind their corn. The corn mill was rebuilt in the 17th century, and stood here until 1972. The mill race was later used to power the adjacent ice rink. The pub hosts regular beer festivals and Meet the Brewer events. A modern pub with an energetic approach to real ales and food, it can get busy at weekends. ☞◑占՚🖳

Castle Eden Inn Ⓛ
Stockton Road, Castle Eden, TS27 4SD
✪ 11 (12 Sun)-11 ☎ (01429) 835137 ⊕ castleedeninn.com
Durham Magus; Hambleton Nightmare Ⓗ
Situated in a village famous for the Castle Eden Brewery, this former coaching inn has a comfortable lounge, bar and restaurant. With friendly staff and a convivial atmosphere, it welcomes all, including families. The Michelin award-winning restaurant serves high-quality food made with the best of local ingredients. Regular events and entertainment are hosted. ⚒Q☞֍◑⊟占P

Colpitts Hotel
Colpitts Terrace, DH1 4EL
✪ 2 (12 Thu-Sat)-11; 12-10.30 Sun ☎ (0191) 386 9913

Samuel Smith OBB Ⓗ

Set in a perfect location, this unspoilt late-Victorian pub has changed little since it was first built. Occupying a corner site, the building has an unusual A-shape with three rooms: a small lounge, a snug used as a pool room and the comfortable main bar partially divided by a fireplace. Like all Sam Smith's pubs, the noise comes from conversation not jukebox or games machines. A must-visit hostelry for anyone who appreciates pubs and a landlady who enjoys her job.
🏚Q🕭🛏🍴🚋♿🚆

Dun Cow

37 Old Elvet, DH1 3HN (between Royal County Hotel & Durham Prison)

🌣 11-11.30; 12-10.30 Sun ☎ (0191) 386 9219

Black Sheep Best Bitter; Camerons Castle Eden Ale; Jennings Cumberland Ale Ⓗ

As the legend tells, in 995AD Lindisfarne monks were searching for a resting place for the body of St Cuthbert when they came across a milkmaid looking for her lost cow. She directed them to Dun Holm (Durham). This Grade II-listed pub, dating back to the 16th century in parts, is named after the historic animal. At the front of the building is a friendly snug and to the rear is a larger lounge. The story of the monks' journey is told on the wall of the corridor alongside the two rooms. Pies and snacks are available. 🏚Q🕭🕯◑🍴♿🚋♿🚆

Durham City Rugby Football Club

Hollow Drift, Green Lane, DH1 3JU (heading along Old Elvet, go past Durham Prison along Green Lane 300yds then turn right)

🌣 12-11 (2 Mon & Wed); 10-6 Sun ☎ (0191) 386 1172

Black Sheep Best Bitter; Taylor Landlord Ⓗ

Set in the great vista of Hollow Drift, the club offers a warm welcome from staff and members. It is open every lunchtime for tasty meals, and most evenings depending on sporting activity. Local CAMRA Club of the Year 2013 winner. Two permanent cask ales are available. 🚋🕭◑P🍴

Fox Cub

Durham Gate, Spennymoor, DH6 5JY (near Thinford in Durham Gate)

🌣 11 (12 Sun)-11 ☎ (01388) 819140

⊕ foxcubpubsspennymoor.co.uk

Marston's Old Empire Ⓗ

Spacious pub restaurant, built in 2011 in the Durham Gate regeneration area. The Marston's beer range is available and a wide range of pub food. There is a play area at the front and good family facilities. A quiz is held on Sunday evenings. 🚋🕭◑P🍴

Half Moon Ⓛ

86 New Elvet, DH1 3AQ (opp Royal County Hotel)

🌣 11-11 (midnight Fri & Sat); 12-11 Sun ☎ (0191) 383 6981

Draught Bass; Fuller's London Pride; Taylor Landlord Ⓗ

City-centre pub named after the crescent-shaped bar that runs from the front room through to the lounge area. Now run by the son of the landlord who ran it for 30 years, the interior is largely unchanged with traditional decor throughout and interesting photos of the pub at the beginning of the 20th century on the walls. Attracting a lively crowd on Friday and Saturday evenings, it has a large back yard next to the river which is popular in summer. Football is regularly screened on TV. 🕭🚋🍴🚆(21)

Head of Steam Ⓛ

Reform Place, DH1 4RZ (through archway from North Rd)

🌣 11-midnight (2am Fri & Sat); 11-11 Sun

⊕ theheadofsteam.co.uk

Beer range varies Ⓗ

Large, open-plan, modern pub over two floors. In addition to real ale, the pub offers an extensive range of bottled European beers, alongside a selection of real ciders – it was awarded Durham City Cider Pub of the Year 2013. High-quality food is prepared on the premises, and the pub often holds special events, all featuring a special or themed selection of ales and ciders. During the day, the pub is family-friendly. One floor can be reserved for private functions. 🕭◑♿🍴

John Duck Ⓛ

91-91a Claypath, DH1 1QS (opp Gala theatre, Walkergate)

🌣 12-midnight (11 Sun) ☎ 07508 221451

Durham John Duck Ⓗ

This pub was named after Sir John Duck of Haswell, a mayor of Durham. An attractive, good-sized venue over several levels, with an elevated rear terrace, it stocks at least five real ales and two ciders. Live bands play at weekends and live sport is regularly screened. 🕭♥🍴🚆

Market Tavern

27 Market Place, DH1 3NJ

🌣 11-11 (midnight Thu; 1am Fri & Sat); 12-11 Sun ☎ (0191) 386 2069

Beer range varies Ⓗ

Situated in Durham's historic market place, this recently refurbished, single-roomed, L-shaped bar offers an array of six ales from all over Britain. The management makes full use of its guest list and has featured Mordue, Hydes, Beartown and Oakleaf breweries, to name a few. One of the most-improved venues in town, it serves good food up to 9pm, with friendly staff who offer a warm welcome to both the regular and casual visitor. ◑♿🚋

Olde Elm Tree Ⓛ

12 Crossgate, DH1 4PS (up cobbled hill from Fighting Cocks)

🌣 12-11; 11-midnight Fri & Sat; 12-10.30 Sun ☎ (0191) 386 4621

Wychwood Hobgoblin; guest beers Ⓗ

One of Durham's oldest and most popular pubs, dating back to at least 1600. As befits its age, it is reputed to have two ghosts. The interior comprises an L-shaped bar room and a top room linked by a set of stairs. It attracts a good mix including students, locals and bikers. Enjoy excellent home-cooked food, the Wednesday quiz (arrive early) and a folk group on Monday and Tuesday. Sport can be watched regularly. 🕭◑♿🚋♣♥P🍴🚆

Shakespeare Tavern

63 Saddler Street, DH1 3NU (100yds from Market Place)

🌣 11-11 (1am Fri & Sat) ☎ (0191) 384 3261

Caledonian Deuchars IPA; Fuller's London Pride; guest beers Ⓗ

Located in the city centre close to the Cathedral, this pub has a small bar, a recently spruced up side snug and a back lounge that was enlarged in 2008. The inn was originally a haunt for 19th-century theatre actors and patrons, hence the name. Despite recent alterations and other ill-judged attempts at change over the years, it has largely maintained its character, except in the eyes of the purists. Popular with locals and students, when busy it can be a sociable squeeze. Q🚲🕾♿

Victoria Inn ★ 🅛
86 Hallgarth Street, DH1 3AS
✪ 11.45-3, 7-11.30 ☎ (0191) 386 5269
⊕ victoriainn-durhamcity.co.uk
Big Lamp Bitter; guest beers Ⓗ
Grade II-listed three-room Victorian pub that remains almost unaltered since it was built in 1899. A warm welcome mixed with quaint decor, coal fires, a tiny snug and a genuine Victorian cash drawer help create an olde-worlde feel. Ales are mainly from local breweries and a wide selection of single malt whiskies is on display. No meals are served but toasties are available. Voted local CAMRA Pub of the Year for the seventh time in 2012 and runner up in 2013.
🏚Q🏚🖰🚲♣🕯🚲(21)

Water House 🅛
65 North Road, DH1 4SQ
✪ 8am-11.45 ☎ (0191) 370 6540
Greene King Abbot; Ruddles Best Bitter; guest beers Ⓗ
Situated in former water board offices and a short distance from the bus station, this pub is popular with young and old alike and extremely busy at weekends. A selection of beers from regional and microbrewers awaits, with single brewery weekends now a feature. The modern decor is complemented by coal-effect open fires. Good-value food is served. An excellent Wetherspoon establishment. ◑♿🚲🚲

Eaglescliffe

Cleveland Bay
718 Yarm Road, TS16 0JE (jct of A67 and A135)
✪ 11-1am ☎ (01642) 780275
Beer range varies Ⓗ
This busy locals' pub and previous CAMRA branch award winner is under the stewardship of an enthusiastic licensee who has established an enviable reputation for serving a fine range of premium best bitters, in over-sized glasses, as well as a free Sunday roast lunch buffet. The main bar, with four handpumps, has two sports TVs, and there is a quieter lounge and a function room where live bands play on Friday evenings. Third-pint glasses and tasting notes are available.
🕯🚲🚲P⅃🖰🚲(7)

Egglescliffe

Pot & Glass
Church Road, TS16 9DQ (300yds E of A135, opp church)
✪ 12-2 (not Mon), 6-11; 12-2, 5.30-midnight Fri; 12-2, 6-midnight Sat; 12-11 Sun ☎ (01642) 651009
Draught Bass; Black Sheep Best Bitter; Caledonian Deuchars IPA; guest beers Ⓗ
A classic and ever-popular multi-roomed village local situated in a quiet cul-de-sac opposite the parish church. Former licensee and cabinet maker Charlie Abbey, whose last resting place overlooks the pub, fashioned the ornate bar fronts from old country furniture. Tasting notes are available for the seven beers on handpump. Outside is a large south-facing garden. Themed food evenings support the good-value home-cooked menu.
Q🕸🏚◑🚲🚲P⅃🖰🚲(7)

Elwick

McOrville Inn
34 The Green, TS27 3EF (300yds E of A19)
✪ 11-11; 12-10.30 Sun ☎ (01429) 273344 ⊕ mcorville.co.uk
Black Sheep Best Bitter; guest beers Ⓗ
A welcome return to the Guide for this ancient 16th-century traditional inn, situated on the village green and named after a local horse who won the 1802 St Leger. One regular beer together with two guests from Consett Ale Works, Hadrian Border or Ossett are served. A quality food menu that supports local suppliers and farmers, and includes real home-made chips, is served all day every day and offers very good value. A secret secluded garden and a more extensive beer garden are both south facing. 🏚Q🕸◑P⅃

Ferryhill

Surtees Arms 🅛
Chilton Lane, DL17 0DH
✪ 4 (12 Sun)-11; 12-midnight Sat ☎ (01740) 655724
⊕ thesurteesarms.co.uk
Yard of Ale One Foot in the Yard, Surtees Gold; guest beers Ⓗ
This traditional multi-roomed pub was Durham Pub of the Year 2011 and runner-up 2012 and 2013. Locally and nationally sourced ales and ciders are on offer here as well as beers from the on-site Yard of Ale Brewery (est 2008). Annual beer festivals are held in the summer and at Halloween. Live music and charity nights are regular events. A large function room is available for private gatherings. Lunches are served on Sunday only.
🏚Q🕸🏚◑🚲♣🕯⅃🚲

Forest in Teesdale

Langdon Beck Hotel
DL12 0XP (on B6277, 8 miles NW of Middleton in Teesdale) NY853312
✪ 11-10.30 (closed Mon Oct-Easter); 12-10.30 Sun ☎ (01833) 622267 ⊕ langdonbeckhotel.com
Black Sheep Best Bitter; Jarrow Rivet Catcher Ⓗ
Known as the Sportsman's Rest in the early 1800s, this pub nestles in the North Pennines, three miles from the Pennine Way and the River Tees. It is popular with walkers, fishermen and those seeking hospitality in scenic and peaceful surroundings. Meals are provided at lunchtimes and evenings. The lounge restaurant offers scenic views of the Pennine hills. A beer festival is held over the late May bank holiday weekend. 🏚Q🕸🕸🖰◑🏚♿🖰

Framwellgate Moor

Tap & Spile 🍺 🅛
Front Street, DH1 5EE (off A167 bypass)
✪ 12-3 (Fri & Sat only), 6 (5 Fri)-11; 12-3, 7-10.30 Sun ☎ (0191) 386 5451
Beer range varies Ⓗ
One of the last survivors of the old Cameron's chain, the inn has two front bars and a large back room which can be partitioned into two. Families are welcome in the back room until 9pm. A former local CAMRA award winner and Pub of the Year 2013, it has a varied selection of ales from near and far, with eight constantly changing beers on handpump. The pub has a very welcoming atmosphere with friendly bar staff. Folk music nights are a weekly event. Q🕸🏚🕯🚲(21)

Frosterley

Black Bull

Bridge End, DL13 2SL (100yds S of A689 at W end of village)

☼ closed Mon & Tue; 10.30-11; 10.30-5.30 Sun

☎ (01388) 527784

Beer range varies Ⓗ

A truly unique family-run pub next to the Weardale Railway and river, with four guest ales usually from local brewers, and up to four ciders and perries. Bare boards, stone flags, all manner of artefacts and antique furniture create a wonderful ambience, with music, plays and story-telling the regular entertainment. The outbuilding houses a peal of bells, visited by enthusiasts from far and wide. Good food is made using high-quality, locally sourced produce. Local CAMRA Cider Pub of the Year 2012. Winter hours may vary.

ᛗQ❀◐Å♣●P☷(101)

Gainford

Cross Keys Ⓛ

High Row, DL2 3DN (on A67 between Darlington & Barnard Castle)

☼ 3-midnight Mon; 12-1am Sat; 12-midnight Sun

☎ (01325) 730237

Sharp's Doom Bar; guest beer Ⓗ

Attractive pub built in 1759 overlooking the village green. The exterior has won Northumbria in Bloom awards on several occasions. Inside, there is a split-level bar, pool room and lounge/restaurant – landlord Ian's curries on a Wednesday night are legendary, also his Sunday lunches. A beer from local Mithril Ales is always on offer. Thursday is games night, Sunday is quiz night and there is monthly entertainment on a Saturday. The picturesque beer garden has a smoking shelter. Santa's sleigh sets off from here every Christmas Eve. ᛗ❧❀◐&♣'☷(75,76)

Hamsterley

Cross Keys

DL13 3PX (2 miles S of A68) NZ115311

☼ 12-3, 5-11; 12-11 Sat & Sun ☎ (01388) 488457

⊕ thecrosskeyshamsterley.com

Beer range varies Ⓗ

Comfortable, family-run pub in the centre of a pretty village, handy for Hamsterley Forest. Popular with locals and holidaymakers alike, the Keys hosts regular community events and is very much a part of village life. The bar across the front of the building has a huge fireplace and joins the dining area. There is a separate dog-friendly snug at the rear, and a restaurant to the side. The emphasis is on local produce in the cooking.

ᛗQ❧❀◐Å♣'

Hartlepool

Brewery Tap

Stockton Street, TS24 7QS (on A689 in front of Camerons Brewery)

☼ 11-4; closed Sun ☎ (01429) 868686

⊕ cameronsbrewery.com

Camerons Strongarm Ⓗ

When Camerons Brewery discovered that it owned a somewhat derelict pub next to the brewery, the old Stranton's future was secured – it was converted into the brewery tap, museum and visitors' centre. Strongarm, Cameron's flagship brand, is always available, together with the brewery's monthly specials. The brewery tap also acts as the starting point for brewery tours, for which there is a small charge. Conferences, evening opening and social events can be arranged. Q&≈P☷☷(36)

Causeway

Vicarage Gardens, Stranton, TS24 7QT (beside Camerons Brewery)

☼ 12-11 (11.30 Thu; midnight Fri & Sat) ☎ (01429) 273954

Banks's Bitter; Camerons Strongarm; guest beers Ⓗ

Marvellous multi-roomed, red-brick Victorian building and Cameron's unofficial brewery tap for more than a century, the Causeway is now owned by Marston's, though the sales of banked Strongarm remain huge. A CAMRA multi-award-winning pub, it even gets a mention in Hansard for the quality of its Strongarm. Three guest beers are sourced from the Marston's range. Good-value bar snacks are available. The licensee hosts an eclectic mix of live music most evenings, while Tuesday is quiz night. ᛗ❀◐&≈♣'☷(36)

Fishermans Arms

Southgate, TS24 0JJ (on headland close to Fish Quay)

☼ 5-11.30; 3-midnight Fri & Sat; 3-11.30 Sun

☎ (01429) 266029 ⊕ thefishermans.co.uk

Black Sheep Best Bitter; Jennings Cumberland Ale; guest beer Ⓗ

The Fish is a friendly, family-run, one-room community pub close to the Fish Quay, the town wall and the site of the Anglo Saxon monastery founded by St Aidan in 640AD. Three handpumps include a guest from the Punch Taverns list. Quizzes are held on Tuesday and Sunday, and the pub supports darts, with the women's team generally outperforming the men. Details of regular live bands and two annual beer festivals (showcasing up to 20 beers) can be found on the pub's website. Q♣'☷(7)

Globe

26 Northgate, TS24 0LJ (on headland, towards Fish Quay)

☼ 11-11 ☎ (01429) 860097

Camerons Strongarm Ⓗ

Opposite the port that was once bustling with fishing boats, coal staithes and pit props, this friendly family-run community pub is under the stewardship of licensees celebrating 28 years of service to the trade. The interior comprises a main public bar and a smaller, quieter lounge with a centrepiece Victorian fireplace and exposed brickwork. The price of the Strongarm (ask for a Hartlepool Head) reflects the pub's freehold status – savings negotiated with Camerons have been passed on to the customer.

ᛗQ❧❀&♣'☷☷(7)

Rat Race Ale House ♥

Station Approach, TS24 7ED (on platform 1 of railway station)

☼ 12.02-2.15, 4.02-8.15; 12.02-9 Sat; closed Sun & Mon

☎ (07889) 828648 ⊕ ratracealehouse.co.uk

Beer range varies Ⓗ/Ⓖ

The station's former newsagent's is now an ale lovers' paradise, with 200 different ales featured annually. CAMRA Regional Cider Pub of the Year 2012 and Branch Pub of the Year, its opening/closing times coincide with the arrival/departure of the coast trains. No fizzy lager, beer or cider, no spirits or alcopops, no food, no TV, no jukebox, no one-arm bandit, no quiz machine, no bar! Just four ever-changing real ales, cider and perry, served in over-sized glasses at reasonable prices. Perfect. Q🔌≈♣♿⬜🚋

Heighington

Bay Horse

28 West Green, DL5 6PE

✪ 12-10 ☎ (01325) 312312

Black Sheep Best Bitter; Taylor Landlord Ⓗ

Picturesque, historic, 300-year-old pub overlooking the award-winning village's largest green. Its traditional interior with exposed beams and stone walls is partitioned into distinct drinking and dining areas, with a large restaurant extending from the lounge. Food plays a prominent role, with bar snacks and full home-cooked meals served. However, drinkers are welcome to enjoy the good range of beers on offer in the bar. ✿◑🍴🔌P🚋(1,16)

George & Dragon

4 East Green, DL5 6PP

✪ 12-11 (midnight Fri & Sat); 12-10.30 Sun

☎ (01325) 313152

Black Sheep Best Bitter; guest beers Ⓗ

A warm and welcoming pub in a picturesque village, in a fine position on the smaller green. An old coaching inn, it has been refurbished in a modern style. The main bar, with real log fire, serves a regular real ale, up to four guests and a real cider, ensuring its popularity with lovers of good beer. A separate bar has a large-screen TV for sporting events. Excellent food is served daily in the lounge and conservatory-style restaurant area. 🏨Q✿◑🍴🔌♣♿🚋(1,16)

High Hesleden

Ship Inn

TS27 4QD (signed from B1281, between A19 and Blackhall) NZ454382

✪ closed Mon; 12-3 (Sat only), 6-11; 12-9 Sun

☎ (01429) 836453 ⊕ theshipinn.net

Beer range varies Ⓗ

Now in its 13th year of continual family ownership, complete satisfaction is guaranteed at this nautically-themed rural gem. The landlord serves seven ever-changing real beers sourced mainly from local microbreweries, and real cider, while his wife runs the superb restaurant offering top-quality food at reasonable prices, including mid-week 'early doors' two-course specials. Six chalets and the Crow's Nest flat provide good-value accommodation. There are stupendous coastal views from the well-kept gardens. CAMRA Regional Pub of the Year 2012. 🏨Q✿🍴◑🍴♿♣♣P🚋(206)

High Shincliffe

Avenue Inn

Avenue Street, DH1 2PT (150yds from A177)

✪ 12-11 ☎ (0191) 386 5954 ⊕ theavenue.biz

Black Sheep Best Bitter; guest beers Ⓗ

A friendly out-of-town pub offering decent B&B facilities, providing a handy base for walkers exploring the attractive countryside. The Monday night quiz and Thursday night dominoes knockout are popular with the regulars. The evening menu

offers quality food at modest prices and the pub serves traditional Sunday lunches. Regular bus services stop just outside, providing easy access to historic Durham City nearby. ✿🍴◑♣P🍴🚋

Holwick

Strathmore Arms

DL12 0NJ (just outside Middleton in Teesdale)

✪ closed Tue; 12-late ☎ (01833) 640362

Allendale Golden Plover; guest beers Ⓗ

Three miles off the B6277 at Middleton in Teesdale and on the Pennine Way, this 17th-century stone and buttressed roadside pub has a welcoming bar with a stone flag floor, beams and a real fire, and a separate lounge with a tiled floor and pool table. Guest ales are usually from Allendale. A beer festival is held at the end of July, live music every Friday. Food is served at all sessions. Outside is a beer garden and camping field, and four en-suite letting rooms are available. Dogs are welcome. 🏨Q☎✿🍴◑🐾♣P

Leamside

Three Horseshoes Ⓛ

Pit House Lane, DH4 6QQ (½ mile N of A690 at West Rainton)

✪ 11-11 (midnight Fri & Sat) ☎ (0191) 584 2394

⊕ threehorseshoesleamside.co.uk

Jennings Cumberland Ale; Taylor Landlord Ⓗ

A significant country pub, extended to provide a thriving restaurant, with a spacious garden area. The landlord is a past winner of local CAMRA and regional Pub of the Year competitions with previous pubs. The comfortable and well-maintained bar has an open fire in winter and offers a varied choice of real ales, a large range of whiskies and real cider from Westons. Food is served daily (booking advisable) including hot bar snacks. The pub is home to local cycle and clay pigeon clubs. Leamside Brewery is now set up on site. 🏨✿◑🍴♿♣♣P🍴

Long Newton

Vane Arms

Darlington Road, TS21 1DB (W end of village, close to A66)

✪ 12-2 (not Mon), 5-11 (midnight Fri & Sat); 12-11 Sun

☎ (01642) 580401 ⊕ vanearms.com

Beer range varies Ⓗ

This lovely village pub, comprising a public bar and restaurant, was left abandoned for 898 days before a local couple, new to the trade, bought the freehold. They quickly established an enviable reputation for serving four microbrewery-sourced beers, together with home-made and reasonably priced top-quality restaurant meals. The licensees celebrated their second '898 day' period of tenure with the opening of four newly refurbished en-suite letting bedrooms. A quarterly newsletter details various community events organised by the licensees. 🏨Q✿🍴◑🍴♿♣P🍴🚋(87A)

Metal Bridge

Old Mill Hotel

Thinford Road, DH6 5NX (off A1M jct 61, follow signs on A177 for 1¼ miles) NZ303351

✪ 12-11 (10.30 Sun) ☎ (01740) 652928

⊕ oldmilldurham.co.uk

Beer range varies Ⓗ
Originally built as a paper mill in 1813, this spacious inn is now the venue of choice for discerning locals and visitors alike. Offering good-quality food and well-kept ales, three handpumps serve an ever-changing range, with the nearby Durham Brewery often supplying one of the beers. The food menu is extensive with daily specials written up on a board above the bar. Larger groups are welcome – including CAMRA every Christmas in the conservatory. Accommodation is of a high standard, with all rooms en suite. ᕼ❀🖂🕮❶◗♿P⚊

Middlestone Village

Ship Inn

Low Road, DL14 8AB (on B6287)
❸ 4 (12 Fri-Sun)-11 ☎ (01388) 810904
⊕ shipinnmiddlestone.co.uk
Beer range varies Ⓗ
At the heart of a small village, the Ship draws its regulars from far and wide. It has a three-part bar with an open fire and various pieces of Vaux brewery memorabilia on display, and a large function room upstairs which hosts twice-yearly beer festivals. The rooftop patio has spectacular views, and there is always an event either in the offing or taking place. Sunday lunches are popular. ᕼ❀◗♿♣P🖾(2,3)

Middleton in Teesdale

Teesdale Hotel

Market Place, DL12 0QG
❸ 11 (12 Sun)-11 ☎ (01833) 640264 ⊕ teesdalehotel.co.uk
Black Sheep Best Bitter; guest beers Ⓗ
A fine 18th-century coaching inn with a stone-built exterior and covered archway to the patio area and car park. This is a popular village local as well as providing accommodation and food for visitors. It is also a stop-off for tourists and Pennine walkers – Middleton in Teesdale is often referred to as 'the capital of Upper Teesdale', with High Force and Cauldron Snout nearby. Up to two guest beers from local micros may be found in the newly refurbished bar, especially in summer. Meals can be enjoyed in the main bar or the quieter restaurant. ᕼQ❀🖂🕮◗P⚊🖾(95,96)

No Place

Beamish Mary 𝕃

DH9 0QH (follow signs to No Place off A693 from Chester-le-Street to Stanley)
❸ 12-11.20 (10.50 Sun) ☎ (0191) 370 0237
Beer range varies Ⓗ
This pub has returned to something like its former glory under new ownership, now tenanted. Full of character, it is well respected for its warm welcome, generously portioned pub grub and ample ranges of well-kept real ale and real cider. The location is handy for visitors to the nearby world-renowned Beamish Open Air Museum. A former local CAMRA Pub of the Year, it holds an annual beer festival. ᕼ❀🖂🕮◗🖰♿♣🖱P⚊🖾(8,78)

Norton

George & Dragon

109 High Street, TS20 1AA (100yds S of duck pond)
❸ 12-11 (midnight Wed-Sun) ☎ (01642) 554150

Greene King Abbot; guest beer Ⓗ
Traditional community pub, described by one regular as 'how pubs used to be and how pubs ought to be'. The George comprises a bar, where drinkers sit on leather benches and photographs of yesteryear adorn the walls, a large lounge and a games room. The guest beer, always a premium bitter, is chosen by customers. Excellent-value home-made pub grub, including a whopping breakfast, is served. Going home thirsty or hungry is not an option. ᕼ❀◗◗🖰♿♣⚊🖾(35,37,38)

Ovington

Four Alls 𝕃

The Green, DL11 7BP (2 miles south of Winston & A67)
❸ 7 (6 Fri; 4 Sat)-11; 7-10.30 Sun ☎ (01833) 627302
⊕ thefouralls-teesdale.co.uk
Beer range varies Ⓗ
Friendly 18th-century inn opposite the village green in what is known as the Maypole Village. A Victorian sign denotes the Four Alls: 'I Govern All (Queen), I Fight For All (Soldier), I Pray For All (Parson), I Pay For All (Farmer).' The pub has a bar, games room and restaurant serving excellent-value food. Home of the Four Alls Brewery, brewing just for the pub, two guest beers include one brewed in the pub and one from the local Mithril Ales. Comfortable country-inn accommodation is available in six rooms in a lovely setting. ᕼQ❀🖂🕮◗♿♣P⚊

Peterlee

Five Quarter

Units 3b-3c Hailsham Place, SR8 1AB (near St Cuthberts Church)
❸ 8-11 ☎ (0191) 518 58880
Greene King Abbot; Hook Norton Cotswold Lion; Shepherd Neame Red Sail Ⓗ
This well-presented Wetherspoon bar is an oasis of real ale in this area. Good food is available and a TV shows sport. The pub is named after the nearby Horden Colliery which at one time was the biggest pit in Britain, where miners worked the High Main, Five Quarter and Yard seams. ᕼ❀◗♿🖱P⚊🖾

Preston-le-Skerne

Blacksmiths Arms

Ricknall Lane, DL5 6JH (1 mile E of A167 at Gretna Green)
❸ closed Mon; 11.30-2, 6-11; 12-10.30 Sun
☎ (01325) 314873 ⊕ blacksmithsarms-pls.co.uk
Beer range varies Ⓗ
Welcoming free house known locally as the Hammers, situated in a rural location near Newton Aycliffe. A long corridor separates the cosy bar (adorned with pump clips of previous beers), restaurant and beamed lounge furnished in farmhouse style. The pub has an excellent reputation for home-cooked food, and up to three guest beers are available, sourced mainly from local micros. A regular local CAMRA award winner, it even has a helicopter landing pad. Q⚊❀◗🖰♿♣P⚊

Rookhope

Rookhope Inn

Rear Hogarth Terrace, DL13 2BG
❸ 12-midnight ☎ (01388) 517215

Beer range varies ℍ

In a quiet valley in Upper Weardale, this is an ideal base for exploration of this old lead mining area. The lounge has a pool table and TV, with comfy settees to sink into after a hard day's walking or cycling – the coast-to-coast route passes the door and the pub is a favourite staging point. The bar has a welcoming open fire, while the restaurant is popular for a more formal meal. Tables to the front of the building are busy in summer.
ꂦQ🌣✎◑ ⊞♣P🖪(101)

St John's Chapel

Blue Bell

12 Hood Street, DL13 1QJ

☼ 5 (12 Sat & Sun)-1am ☎ (01388) 537256

Beer range varies ℍ

Originally a pair of cottages, the Blue Bell is a friendly, cosy pub with a bar across the front of the building leading to a small pool room, and a garden to the rear. Right on the A689, it serves the local community and those who holiday in Upper Weardale. Pub games are popular and there are plenty of books to choose from.
ꂦ🌣♣◖P⅃–🖪(101)

Sedgefield

Nag's Head

8 West End, TS21 2BS

☼ 6 (5 Fri & Sat)-midnight; 12-3, 7-11 Sun
☎ (01740) 620234

Taylor Landlord; guest beers ℍ

Situated at the centre of the village, close to Sedgefield Racecourse, this free house attracts all age groups – families with well-behaved children are welcome. There is a comfortable bar, a smaller lounge and a restaurant offering traditional Sunday lunch prepared with fresh local produce. Meals are also served in the bar (no food Sun and Mon eve). The landlord and landlady both come from the village. ꂦ🌣◑⊞&♣🖪

Spennymoor

Frog & Ferret

Coulson Street, DL16 7RS

☼ 3 (12 Fri & Sat)-11; 12-10.30 Sun ☎ (01388) 818312

Beer range varies ℍ

Friendly, family-run free house offering four constantly changing real ales sourced locally and from far and wide. A welcoming atmosphere greets you on arrival at the three-sided bar in the comfortably furnished lounge, with brick, stone and wood cladding. Darts and dominoes are played and bar snacks are available. Well-behaved children are permitted until 4pm. The pub hosts a quiz on Sunday evening, and a music quiz on the first Wednesday evening of the month.
ꂦ🌣&♣P⅃

Stockton-on-Tees

Sun Inn

Knowles Street, TS18 1SU

☼ 11-11; 12-10.30 Sun ☎ (01642) 611461

Draught Bass; guest beers ℍ

This very popular town-centre drinkers' pub, reputed to sell more Draught Bass than any other pub in the country, has now introduced a couple of guests. The pub was rescued from an uncertain

future 10 years ago by a regular who became the licensee and very quickly established record sales of banked Bass. The pub supports darts, football teams and various charitable causes. On Monday evenings the function room is home to the famous Stockton Folk Club. ⇌(Stockton/Thornaby)♣⅃–🖪

Thomas Sheraton

4 Bridge Road, TS18 1BH (at S end of High St)

☼ 8-midnight (11 Sun) ☎ (01642) 606134

Greene King Abbot; Ruddles Best Bitter; guest beers ℍ

This previous local CAMRA Branch Pub of the Year is a fine Wetherspoon conversion of the Victorian law courts and named after one of the country's great Georgian cabinet makers, born in the town in 1751. It comprises several dining and drinking areas, together with a balcony and sunny patio upstairs. Eight guest beers are mainly sourced locally, and real cider is kept. Meet the Brewer events, beer festivals and celebrations of Saints' days are all supported. CAMRA members receive a 20 per cent discount on the food menu.
⌣🌣◑&⇌(Stockton/Thornaby)♦⅃–🖪

Westgate

Hare & Hounds

24 Front Street, DL13 1RX (on A689)

☼ 12-2.30 (Sat only), 6.30-11; 12-3, 6.30-9.30 Sun
☎ (01388) 517212

Black Sheep Best Bitter; Hare & Hounds Hare of the Dog ℍ

Situated on the main road up Weardale, with the river at the bottom of the garden. The spacious stone-flagged bar is fitted out with furniture and other items salvaged from the former village chapel, and the restaurant has a patio overlooking the Wear. Catch up on the local news over a pint brewed only a few feet below you, while watching the pub's poultry in the rear garden. Food is locally sourced, including the famous Sunday carvery.
ꂦQ🌣◑&⅄♣P🖪(101)

Willington

Black Horse

42 Low Willington, DL15 0BD (on A690 at N end of village) NZ205349

☼ 6 (12 Sat & Sun)-11 ☎ 07727 280196

Beer range varies ℍ

A tasteful refurbishment a couple of years ago created a spacious, open-plan pub while maintaining separate drinking areas. Beers are mostly from local brewers, pub games are regularly played, and sport is popular on the large screens. Local car clubs use the Black Horse as a base, and the pub enthusiastically supports the local ladies' football team. Handily placed between Durham and Weardale. ꂦ🌣&P⅃

Witton Gilbert

Glendenning Arms

Front Street, DH7 6SY (off A691 bypass)

☼ 4 (12 Sun)-11; 3-midnight Fri; 12-midnight Sat
☎ (0191) 371 0316

Black Sheep Best Bitter, Ale ℍ

A typical village community local and Guide regular with a small, comfortable lounge and a lively and welcoming bar with the original Vaux 1970s red and white handpulls. The bar is attractively decorated in a contemporary style while the lounge remains more traditional. The pub runs darts, dominoes and football teams. Situated on the village's main road, there is ample car parking. ᗰ❀🏠♣P🏠➖🗔(15)

Travellers Rest

Front Street, DH7 6TQ (off A691 bypass 3 miles from city centre)
✪ 11-11; 12-10.30 Sun ☎ (0191) 371 0458
Beer range varies Ⓗ
Open-plan country-style pub, popular with diners. The bar area is split into three sections with a conservatory off to the side where families are welcome. There is also a more private dining room. Now owned by TR Leisure Partnership, an extensive food menu suits all tastes, with dining throughout the pub. Quiz nights are Tuesday and Sunday. Q➤❀🏵♣P🏠➖🗔(15)

Witton le Wear

Dun Cow

19 High Street, DL14 0AY
✪ 6 (1 Sat; 12 Sun)-11 ☎ (01388) 448294
Black Sheep Best Bitter; Jennings Cumberland Ale; Wells Bombardier Ⓗ
Dating from 1799, this comfortable and welcoming pub is set back from the road through the village, close to the A68. The single room has an open fire at both ends, one guarded by a sleeping fox who always seems to have just closed its eyes, the other by an impressive set of horns. A seated area to the front offers pleasant views, and the area to the left of the bar is fitted with bench seats. Some interesting football memorabilia completes the decor. ᗰQ❀♣P🏠

Victoria Ⓛ

School Street, DL14 0AS
✪ Closed Tue; 6-11 Mon, Wed & Thu; 12-midnight Fri & Sat; 12-10.30 Sun ☎ 07779 128204
Wychwood Hobgoblin; guest beers Ⓗ

This pleasant village pub has a central bar serving a small pool room and split-level bar, including a raised dining area. The bar has great views over the Wear Valley from the rear and the church from the front. Beers come from the Marstons range and local independent breweries, with Thursday being beer discussion night. Food is available Friday-Sunday. There is a car park to the rear, overlooked by the patio. ➤❀🏵♣P🏠

Wolsingham

Black Bull

27 Market Place, DL13 3AB
✪ 12-11 (11.30 Sun) ☎ (01388) 527332
Caledonian Deuchars IPA; guest beer Ⓗ
A recent refurbishment has not diminished the appeal of this welcoming Weardale institution. Situated on the A689 opposite the town hall, it has a snug bar, lounge and a formal dining room offering good food. To the rear is a south-facing garden, and there are tables to the front. Close to the Weardale Way, the pub is the base for the local cricket team and hosts social events. County Cider Pub of the Year 2013.
ᗰQ❀🏠🏵🏠♣Å➤♣🏠➖🗔(101)

Black Lion

21 Meadhope Street, DL13 3EN (50yds N of market place)
✪ 6.30 (6 Fri; 12 Sat)-11; 12-10.30 Sun ☎ (01388) 527772
Beer range varies Ⓗ
Hidden away a minute from the Market Place, this friendly and comfortable gem is a great place to relax. The open fire is the focus in the single, open-plan room, with a pool table to the rear and the bar plus a TV showing sport to the front. Regular beer festivals often feature. Local charities benefit from the pub's fundraising efforts. Outside is a suntrap garden. Ask for the cider menu, as there are up to six on offer. ᗰQ❀♣●🗔(101)

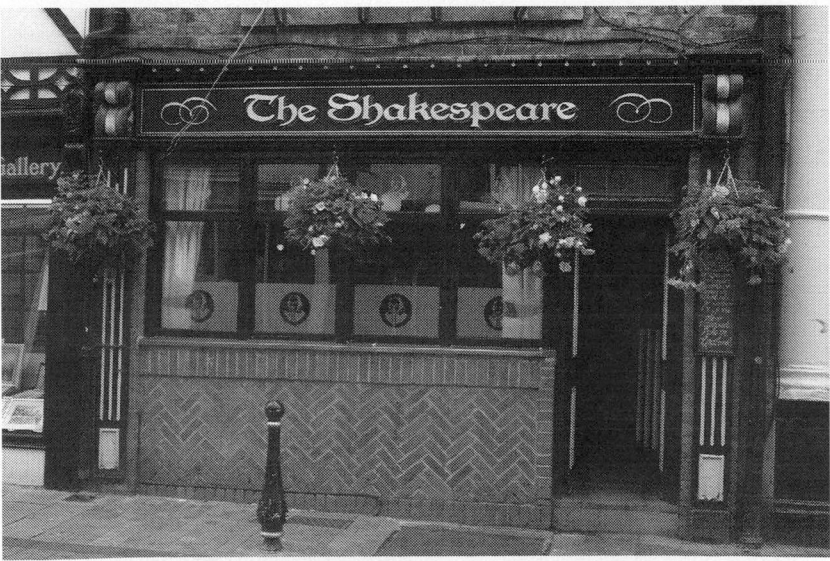

Shakespeare Tavern, Durham (Photo: Adam Bruderer)

Aythorpe Roding

Axe & Compasses 🄻

Dunmow Road, CM6 1PP (on B1845 5 miles SW of Dunmow) TL594154
🕓 12-11 (midnight Fri & Sat); 12-10.30 Sun
☎ (01279) 876648 🌐 theaxeandcompasses.co.uk
Colchester No.1; Sharp's Doom Bar 🄷**; guest beers** 🄷/🄶
An attractive thatched pub in open countryside south of Dunmow. It is frequented by a mixed clientele of diners, drinkers, walkers and farming folk. Good beer and good food are always available, with friendly and efficient service. Bar snacks are served and fine dining is in a separate restaurant. In winter there are log fires and in summer a pleasant garden, with views to the windmill. Quiz and curry nights and other themed evenings are hosted, with seasonal food offers.
🏚Q🕸🄽🅿🗝🚃(7,18,346)

Ballards Gore (Stambridge)

Shepherd & Dog 🄻

Gore Road, SS4 2DA (between Rochford and Paglesham) TQ904927
🕓 12-3, 6-11; 12-11 Sat & Sun ☎ (01702) 258279
Beer range varies 🄷

Local CAMRA Country Pub of the Year in 2013, this excellent hostelry offers a warm welcome. No TV, music or fruit machines make this a great pub for conversationalists. Up to four real ales generally come from local microbreweries such as Wibblers and Mighty Oak. During the summer there is also a real cider on handpump. The locally sourced, freshly prepared food is popular, so booking is advised for meals. Walkers, cyclists and coach groups are welcome. Open mic night is held fortnightly on Thursday evening. 🕸🄽🅰🅿🚃(60)

Belchamp Otten

Red Lion

Fowes Lane, CO10 7BQ (on a very small single track lane, signed by the duck pond) TL799415
🕓 closed Tue; 12-3, 5.30-11 Mon, Wed & Thu; 12-11 Fri & Sat; 12-7 Sun ☎ (01787) 278301 🌐 ottenredlion.co.uk
Adnams Southwold Bitter; guest beers 🄷
Lovely local pub hidden away in the smallest of the Belchamps. The owners provide a warm welcome, with an open fire in winter. There is local artwork here for sale. Pub games include bar billiards and darts, while live music is scheduled on the last Saturday of the month in summertime. Reasonably priced, wholesome, home-cooked food is available at lunchtimes and evenings (no food Mon and Tue)

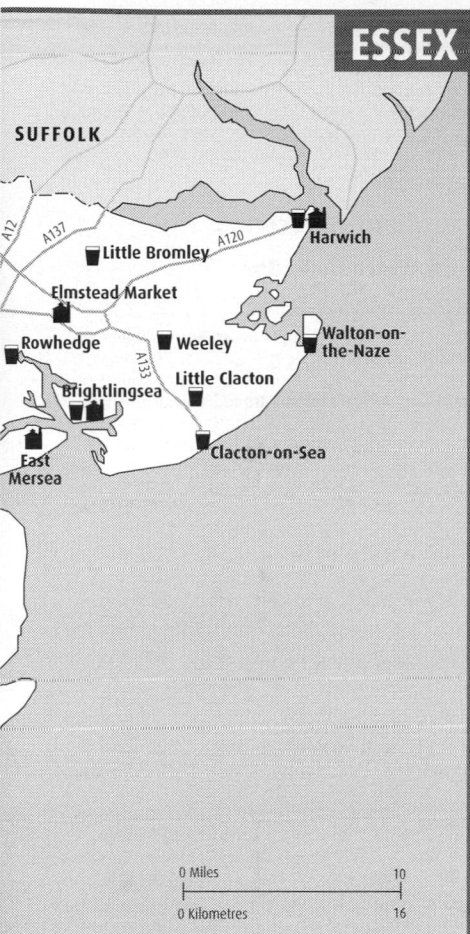

Popular Wetherspoon venue, especially at weekends, with the usual suspects on handpump, plus guest beers often from Essex breweries. Four draught ciders are sold. Breakfast is available until noon, other meals until 10pm. There is no music, but there are fruit machines and muted TVs, and an outside area at the rear for drinking and smoking. The car park at the rear is Pay & Display but arriving here by public transport is easy, with the station and bus stops close by. Q✿◑&≠♠⊷☐(100)

Coach & Horses

36 Chapel Street, CM12 9LU (near Waitrose)
✿ 10-11; 12-10.30 Sun ☎ (01277) 622873
⊕ thecoachandhorses.org
Adnams Southwold Bitter; Greene King IPA, Abbot; Sharp's Doom Bar; guest beer Ⓗ
Close to the High Street, this popular one-bar pub – a long-standing Guide entry – has a welcoming and friendly atmosphere. Usually there are five beers; the guest is often a golden ale and is likely to be sourced from a local brewery. The decor includes an interesting jug collection, numerous plates and pictures. The food is described as restaurant quality and is served lunchtimes and evenings Monday to Saturday, 12-7pm on Sunday (booking recommended). Wednesday is curry night.
♨✿◑≠P☐(100)

Blackmore

Leather Bottle

Horsefayre Green, CM4 0RL
✿ 11-11 (midnight Fri & Sat); 12-11 Sun ☎ (01277) 821891
⊕ theleatherbottle.net
Adnams Southwold Bitter; Sharp's Doom Bar Ⓗ**; guest beers** Ⓗ/Ⓖ
Large village pub with a small flagstone-floored bar area. Most of the interior is taken up by a good-quality restaurant. Two guest beers are generally available on handpump, with maybe a third on gravity at weekends in the summer, usually including a beer of around 5% ABV or higher. Westons Old Rosie cider is also sold. An annexe to the bar has a silent fruit machine.
♨✿◑⊟♠P☐(32)

and to takeaway, too. There are excellent views, good walks and cycle rides from here.
♨Q✿◑♣♠P

Belchamp St Paul

Half Moon

Cole Green, CO10 7DP TL792423
✿ 12-3, 6-midnight; 12-midnight Sat & Sun
☎ (01787) 277402 ⊕ halfmoonbelchamp.co.uk
Greene King IPA; guest beers Ⓗ
Warm and friendly rural pub with a thatched roof, dating from about 1685 and opposite the village green. Three beers are on sale and guest beers change regularly. The pub is popular with locals and has an excellent choice of bar and restaurant meals (no food Sun eve). There are chickens in the back garden. The pub provided one of the locations for the first Lovejoy TV series. Outside there is a separate smoking area. ♨Q➳✿◑♣P⊷

Billericay

Blue Boar

39 High Street, CM12 9BA
✿ 9am-11.30 ☎ (01277) 655552
Greene King Abbot; Marston's Pedigree; Ruddles Best Bitter; guest beers Ⓗ

Braintree

King William IV Ⓛ

114 London Road, CM77 7PU (on B1053) TL749492
✿ 3-midnight; 12-1am Fri & Sat; 12-11 Sun
☎ (01376) 567755
Beer range varies Ⓖ
Cosy 19th-century traditional free house with a main bar and a walk-through leading to a small back bar with a dartboard. The pub reopened in 2009, having been closed for two years. A range of four or five ales is served by gravity from a side cellar, usually featuring a Sharp's beer and Essex microbreweries. Three or four ciders include Westons and other selections. Beer festivals are held twice a year in a marquee in the large garden. Friendly dogs are welcome. ✿♣♠P☐(70,352)

Wagon & Horses Ⓛ

53 South Street, CM7 3QD
✿ 12-11.30 (6 Sun) ☎ (01376) 552388
Beer range varies Ⓗ
The Wagon is the first of Greene King's Local Heroes pubs and the landlord is free to source beers out of tie as well as from the brewery.

Sixteen handpumps generally have eight beers on tap, three or four from Greene King and four or five others, often local. Occasionally, mini beer festivals are held in which 16 different beers are offered. Note the unusual glass-topped well inside. A beer garden can be enjoyed in the summer. Q✪⊛≈P⅃⊶

Brentwood

Rising Sun ⌶

144 Ongar Road, CM15 9DJ (on A128, at Western Rd jct)
✪ 3-11.30 (midnight Fri); 12-midnight Sat; 12-10.30 Sun
☎ (01277) 213749
Fuller's London Pride; Sharp's Cornish Coaster; Taylor Landlord; guest beers Ⓗ
Very pleasant, friendly local with five real ales, in an area not renowned for choice. This is a splendid community local, with a charity quiz on Monday evening and frequent darts matches in the public bar. Five handpumps in the saloon bar dispense three regular ales plus a beer from Brentwood Brewery and a guest from anywhere. Framed prints of the local area decorate the walls. Outside is a covered, heated smokers' area and patio.
♨✿⊕♿♣P⅃⊶(71,72,73)

Brightlingsea

Railway Tavern ⌶

58 Station Road, CO7 0DT
✪ 5-10; 3-11 Fri; 12-11 Sat; 12-3, 7-10.30 Sun
Crouch Vale Best; guest beers Ⓗ
A simple, basic pub which always has three real ales and at most times includes one from the on-site brewery, the Famous Railway Tavern brewery. There is also at least one changing cider and the pub hosts a cider festival on the first weekend in May. Live music events happen throughout the year. There is a strong community sense in the pub and the regulars are always on the lookout for football or cricket opponents. There are several interesting railway posters on display.
♨Q✿♠⅃⊶(78)

Broads Green

Walnut Tree

CM3 1DT (¾ mile S of Great Waltham village) TL694125
✪ 12-midnight ☎ (01245) 360222
Greene King IPA; Morland Original Bitter; Ruddles Best Bitter; guest beer Ⓖ
Handsome Victorian brick-built pub overlooking a large green. The front door opens directly into a small snug. To the left is the wood-panelled public bar, little changed since it was built; to the right is the more modern lounge. Outside is a garden and seating in front of the pub. There is no food – the landlord prefers to concentrate on his beers (served on gravity from a half-cellar) and to maintain a traditional atmosphere. An outside Gents is still in use. ♨Q✿♣P⅃⊶(33,52)

Broxted

Prince of Wales ⌶

Brick End, CM6 2BJ TL573259
✪ closed Mon; 11.30-11; 12-11 Sun ☎ (01279) 850256
Greene King IPA; guest beers Ⓗ
In the southern part of Broxted, this former Charrington's pub, for many years in the doldrums, has been transformed into a welcoming community venue after the ownership changed in

late 2011. It has a comfortable split-level bar, an adjoining room with two woodburners and a conservatory seating up to 50. Generously portioned pub grub, the majority locally sourced, will satisfy the most demanding appetite. A small garden is to the rear. Four beers are always available, with LocAle from Bishop Nick.
♨Q⊛✿⊕P⅃⊶(5)

Burnham-on-Crouch

New Welcome Sailor

Station Road, CM0 8HF
✪ 12-11 ☎ (01621) 784778
Dark Star Hophead; Sharp's Doom Bar; Wibblers IPA; guest beers Ⓗ
This comfortable community local was winner of the local CAMRA Most Improved Pub of the Year award in 2013. Within the large, single-room, L-shaped interior there are traditional pub games plus Sky TV. A function room is available for special events. No food is served. The guest beer may well come from Farmer's Ales. ♨✿≈♣⊕P⅃⊶(31X)

Queen's Head ⌶

26 Providence, CM0 8JU (opp clock tower)
✪ 2 (5 Mon)-11; 12-11 Fri-Sun ☎ (01621) 784825
Dark Star Hophead; Wibblers Providence IPA; guest beers Ⓗ
Tucked away behind the High Street, this busy local recently won CAMRA's Joe Goodwin award following a tasteful refurbishment in 2009. Four cask beers are available, in a variety of styles, mostly from local microbreweries. Traditional home-made Essex huffers can be ordered, or try the curried goat for a taste of the Caribbean. There are monthly live music evenings, and the annual beer festival takes place over the August bank holiday. ♨✿⊕≈♣⊕⅃⊟⊶(31X)

Castle Hedingham

Bell ⌶

10 St James Street, CO9 3EJ TL784356

INDEPENDENT BREWERIES	
Bishop Nick Braintree	
Brentwood Brentwood	
Brightlingsea Brightlingsea (NEW)	
Colchester Wakes Colne	
Crouch Vale South Woodham Ferrers	
Deverell's Grays	
Dominion Moreton (NEW)	
Farmer's Maldon	
Felstar Felsted	
Growler Pentlow	
Hart of Stebbing Stebbing	
Harwich Town Harwich	
Highwood Chelmsford	
Hop Monster/George's Great Wakering	
Indian Summer Saffron Walden	
Mersea Island East Mersea	
Mighty Oak Maldon	
Railway Tavern Brightlingsea	
Red Fox Coggeshall	
Round Tower Chelmsford (NEW)	
Saffron Henham	
Shalford Shalford	
Sticklegs Elmstead Market	
Vens Rawreth	
Wibblers Mayland	

✪ 11.45-3, 6-11; 12-midnight Fri & Sat; 12-11 Sun
☎ (01787) 460350 ⊕ hedinghambell.co.uk
**Adnams Southwold Bitter; Mighty Oak IPA, Maldon
Gold; guest beer** Ⓖ
Fifteenth-century Gray's-owned coaching inn with
small rooms for drinking and dining alongside two
main bars. Beer is dispensed from the cask, and
summer and winter beer festivals are held. Jazz is
played lunchtimes on the last Sunday of the
month, local musicians play on Friday evenings and
Sunday is quiz night. Locally sourced food includes
Turkish specials prepared in a wood-fired stone
oven, and Monday evening features a barbecued
fish menu. Local CAMRA Pub of the Year 2011.
🏨Q🛏🌣✪🍴🍽🅿︎💷🚆(89)

Chelmsford

Ale House Ⓛ
24-26 Viaduct Road, CM1 1TS
✪ 11-11 (midnight Fri & Sat); 12-11 Sun ☎ (01245) 359964
Beer range varies Ⓗ
A newly opened conversion of three railway arches
facing the side of Chelmsford bus station. Twelve
handpumps dispense continually changing beers,
often from Adnams, Sharp's and Black Sheep, with
the rest from anywhere, always including dark
beers and stronger beers. The manager is a fan of
more hoppy beers so one or two of these always
feature. Five or six varied real ciders are sold. Food
is baguettes, soup and pizzas lunchtimes, and
pizzas and cheese/meat plates evenings (no food
Sun). A microbrewery is planned. 🌣🍴🖐♿🚆🍴

Barista Ⓛ
44-45 Duke Street, CM1 1JA
✪ 11.30-11 (midnight Wed & Thu; 2am Fri & Sat); closed Sun
☎ (01245) 493333 ⊕ baristachelmsford.com
Beer range varies Ⓖ
New, modern bar with comfortable leather
furniture and subdued lighting close to the railway
and bus stations. Three varied, often local, gravity-
fed beers change weekly and are dispensed
from an upstairs cellar. Popular beer festivals are
held at least twice a year. Food is served weekday
lunchtimes. Over-21s are welcomed. 🌣🍴♿🚆🍴💷🚆

Cricketers Ⓛ
143 Moulsham Street, CM2 0JT
✪ 11-11 (midnight Fri & Sat); 12-11 Sun ☎ (01245) 268211
⊕ thecricketers.biz
Bishop Nick Ridley's Rite Ⓗ**; Greene King Abbot** Ⓖ**;
guest beers** Ⓗ
Friendly street-corner pub at the southern end of
the main shopping area, recently taken over by a
new landlord and refurbished. The front bar has a
pool table, and live sport TV at certain times. The
back bar is quieter. Three guest ales are offered,
with an emphasis on Essex breweries. It has a
covered outdoor patio area for smokers. Live music
is on the first Saturday of the month and there is a
soul music DJ on the third Saturday. No food
Sunday evening. 🌣🍴🍴🍴💷🚆(100,42)

Oddfellows Arms Ⓛ
195 Springfield Road, CM2 6JP
✪ 12-11 (midnight Fri & Sat) ☎ (01245) 490514
⊕ theoddfellowsarms.com
**Adnams Broadside; Black Sheep Best Bitter; Growler
IPA; Mighty Oak Maldon Gold; Sharp's Doom Bar** Ⓗ
Newly refurbished, this pub has a modern wood
interior but maintains a local feel. There is a large
U-shaped bar area, with a back room containing a

pool table, leading out to the garden/smoking
area. Beer festivals are hosted in mid-February and
late July. There is monthly live music and poker
nights are held Tuesdays and Thursdays. Food is
served lunchtimes and evenings weekdays, and all
day at weekends. 🌣🍴♿🍴🍽💷🚆(54,71,73)

Orange Tree Ⓛ
6 Lower Anchor Street, CM2 0AS
✪ 12-11 (11.30 Fri & Sat) ☎ (01245) 262664 ⊕ the-ot.com
Black Sheep Best Bitter Ⓗ**; Dark Star Hophead** Ⓖ**;
Mighty Oak Oscar Wilde** Ⓗ**; guest beers** Ⓗ/Ⓖ
The Orange Tree is one of the best real ale pubs in
Chelmsford and was runner-up local CAMRA Pub of
the Year 2012 and 2013. There are three
permanent beers plus at least five guests (often
including stouts or porters). Guests are from the
Gray's listing and the cider is from the Westons
range. There is a charity quiz every Tuesday, and
rock/blues bands play one Saturday a month.
Lunchtime food is served, including Sunday roasts,
with a curry night on Thursday evening.
Q🌣🍴🖐♿🍴💷🚆

Queen's Head Ⓛ
30 Lower Anchor Street, CM2 0AS
✪ 12-11 (11.30 Fri & Sat) ☎ (01245) 265181
⊕ queensheadchelmsford.co.uk
**Crouch Vale Essex Boys Best Bitter, Brewer's Gold,
Yakima Gold; guest beers** Ⓗ
Crouch Vale Brewery's only pub, the Queen's Head
sells three of its beers permanently, with a fourth
Crouch Vale pump varying between a seasonal
beer and Amarillo. The four guest ales vary from far
and wide, but always include a dark beer. The
cider, not always available in the winter, is from
the Westons range. This popular local can be busy
when there is a cricket match at the county ground,
or when clubs and societies (such as the Essex
Beard Club) meet. 🏨Q🌣🍴🖐♿🍴💷🚆

Woolpack
23 Mildmay Road, CM2 0DN (S of main road into town)
✪ 12-11 (midnight Fri & Sat) ☎ (01245) 259295
H&H Bitter; guest beers Ⓗ
Local CAMRA Pub of the Year 2011, it offers six
Greene King-supplied guest ales plus one guest
free of tie. The small public bar has darts and a pool
table. The large main lounge leads to an annexe
with a large-screen TV. There is a quiz on Tuesday,
monthly folk music, and beer festivals at Easter and
in September. An ever-changing range of speciality
sausages and spicy pickled eggs complements the
food menu, which is available Monday to Friday
and Sunday lunchtime. 🌣🍴🍴🍴💷🚆

Clacton-on-Sea

Moon & Starfish
1 Marine Parade East, CO15 1PU
✪ 8am-11 (12.30am Fri & Sat) ☎ (01255) 222998
**Greene King Abbot; Ruddles Best Bitter; guest
beers** Ⓗ
A large, busy but welcoming Wetherspoon pub
with friendly staff right on the seafront, opposite
the local pleasure pier and close to the town centre
shops. It is readily accessible, being only a short
walk from the railway station and bus stops. Well
used by locals and holidaymakers, it has an area
away from the bar that is set up for the use of
diners, and there is an outside seating area
overlooking the sea. Q🛏🌣🍴♿🍴🍴💷🚆

Old Lifeboat House 🍷
39 Marine Parade East, CO15 6AD
⏲ 11-11; 12-10.30 Sun ☎ (01255) 476799
St Austell Proper Job; guest beers Ⓗ
This family-run pub has gone from strength to strength and has been voted CAMRA branch Pub of the Year for two years running. It consistently serves beers from all over the country, which means there are different ales to try weekly. Up to six real ciders/perries are also on offer. Each Wednesday the beers are sold at discounted prices, with a selection of meals served lunchtime and evening. Beer festivals are held during the last weekends of April and October. ❀♿⇌♣●P⊱

Coggeshall

Chapel Inn 𝕃
4 Market Hill, CO6 1TS
⏲ 12-11 (1am Fri & Sat) ☎ (01376) 561655
🌐 thechapelinn.com
Adnams Ghost Ship; Red Fox Bitter, seasonal beers; Sharp's Doom Bar Ⓗ
Legally licensed since 1554 and built in place of a chapel in the market square, the building is said at one point to have been home to the high sheriff of Essex, and boasts remains of a Roman road with its drainage aqueducts in the beer cellar. This is a LocAle pub selling beers from the nearby Red Fox Brewery. The pub is a reasonable size but remains cosy, its beams separating areas for people to eat or drink in. ♨❀◑◐♣P⊱🚌(70)

Colchester

Ale House 𝕃
82 Butt Road, CO3 3DA
⏲ 3-11; 12-midnight Thu & Fri; 12-11 Sat; 12-10 Sun
☎ (01206) 573464
Ale House Best; guest beers Ⓗ
Formerly an Adnams pub, the Dragoon, but now free of tie, it has been saved from closure by a previous landlord and lovingly restored, much improved both inside and out with a lovely garden. It showcases a good selection of real ales, many from local microbreweries, usually including a dark ale. The interior is heavily beamed, with comfortable seating. Darts is popular in the pub, plus it boasts a rare bar billiards table.
❀◑⇌(Town)♣⊱🚌(1,64,68)

Bricklayers
27 Bergholt Road, CO4 5AA (jct A134/B1508)
⏲ 11-3, 5.30-11; 11-midnight Fri; 11-11 Sat; 12-7 Sun
☎ (01206) 852008
Adnams Southwold Bitter, Explorer, Broadside, seasonal beers; guest beers Ⓗ
Close to Colchester North station, this Adnams' house offers up to nine ales with a wide variety of guests, as well as Crone's cider. It comprises a large lounge bar and conservatory, plus a busy public bar with pool table and dartboard. The Brick is a friendly, lively pub popular with locals and commuters. Run by a multi CAMRA-award-winning family, it offers good-value home-made food at lunchtimes and a recommended Sunday roast.
❀◑⊟⇌(North)♣●P⊱🚌

British Grenadier
67 Military Road, CO1 2AP (½ mile SE of Town station)
⏲ 12-2.30 (not Tue-Thu), 5-11.30; 5-midnight Fri; 11-midnight Sat; 12-3, 7-11.30 Sun ☎ (07832) 215118
Adnams Southwold Bitter, seasonal beers; guest beers Ⓗ
Welcoming, traditional corner pub with a main bar and a smaller bar serving a room with a pool table. An ever-changing range of beers is offered from the Adnams' list – the many pumpclips on display testament to the wide range of ales previously dispensed. An open fire warms the main bar in winter. Darts and pool are played regularly and there is a quiz night every Sunday evening.
♨❀♿⇌(Town)♣⊱🗑🚌(6,61,66)

Fat Cat 𝕃
65 Butt Road, CO3 3BZ (on B1026 near police station)
⏲ 12-11 (midnight Fri & Sat) ☎ (01206) 577990
Crouch Vale Brewers Gold; Farmer's Puck's Folly, Golden Boar; Fat Cat Honey Ⓗ**; Woodforde's Wherry; guest beers** Ⓖ
Choice is a priority at this friendly local. Up to 12 real ales, Belgian and Pitfield bottled beers plus real cider are dispensed from the taproom. Colchester, Dark Star, Green Jack and Mauldons beers usually make the guest list. Lunchtime meals can be had Thursday to Sunday, but pork pies, pasties and Scotch eggs are always available. It is ideal for a pint when Colchester United are at home, with a bus leaving the pub an hour before kick-off for the game.
♨❀◑⇌(Town)●⊱🚌(1,64,68)

Hole in the Wall
2 Balkerne Hill, CO3 3AA (near Mercury Theatre)
⏲ 11-11 (midnight Thu-Sat); 12.30-10.30 Sun
☎ (01206) 579897
St Austell Tribute; Wychwood Hobgoblin; guest beers Ⓗ
Standing next to Colchester's ancient Roman gateway and just a few yards from the Mercury Theatre, this traditional pub offers a balanced selection of ales. Food at lunchtime is locally sourced and home cooked, to be enjoyed in the cosy bar areas or outside on the sunny balcony. Well known for live music, this is a friendly pub for all drinkers, completed by its black baize pool table and interior Roman wall and, if he is about, Harry the Cat. ♨❀◑⊱🚌

Live & Let Live 𝕃
12 Millers Lane, Stanway, CO3 0PS (off A1124)
TL955247
⏲ 12-11 (midnight Sat & Sun) ☎ (01206) 574071
Sticklegs Isla Rose; guest beers Ⓗ
The only pub in Stanway and at the heart of the community, the Live comprises a public bar with pool table, dartboard and a large-screen TV for sport, plus a quiet homely saloon bar. Local breweries are well supported with the changing list of guest ales. A good range of bottled beers is also available, along with some excellent home-cooked pub grub. Sausage & Beer festivals are held every summer and winter, and the pub regularly hosts a classic motorcycle club. ♨❀◑◐⊟♣P⊱🚌(65)

New Inn 𝕃
36 Chapel Street South, CO2 7AX
⏲ 12-11 (midnight Fri & Sat) ☎ (01206) 575277
Wells Eagle IPA; guest beers Ⓗ
Traditional street-corner two-bar pub offering a changing ale selection. A fine choice of malt whiskies is also on offer. There are open fires in both public and saloon bars, and a room is available for functions. Darts and pool are played plus there is live music every Friday evening, with

a jam night on Tuesday. The pub has an outdoor area with garden furniture. Satellite sport and Wi-Fi are available and dogs are welcome.
🏚Q🍺😺❄️🍴🚃(Town)♣P⁵⌐

Odd One Out 🅛
28 Mersea Road, CO2 7ET (on B1025)
🌑 4.30 (12 Fri & Sat)-11; 12-10.30 Sun ☎ (01206) 513958
Mauldons Silver Adder; guest beers Ⓗ
Winner of many CAMRA awards, the Oddie offers up to seven real ales including one dark and one strong ale, plus real ciders and perry and a fabulous range of whiskies. This is one of Colchester's best-loved pubs and has a character all of its own. Nourishing cheese rolls sustain the customers, who enjoy local, familiar and unusual ales in a unique atmosphere of almost nostalgic calm. Dog-friendly.
🏚Q😺🚃(Town)🍴⁵⌐🚭(8A,67,68)

Purple Dog
42 Eld Lane, CO1 1LS
🌑 11-11 (1am Thu & Fri); 10-1.30am Sat; 11-10.30 Sun
☎ (01206) 564995
Adnams Broadside; Crouch Vale Brewers Gold; Sharp's Doom Bar; Woodforde's Wherry; guest beers Ⓗ
Large timber-framed pub right in the town centre. Known as The Clarence until 2006, this is the first appearance in the Guide for this busy pub. Up to six real ales are on offer, primarily from East Anglia, and regular beer festivals are also held. This hostelry comprises a modern interior with distinct areas set aside for drinking. Good home-cooked food is available daily. It can be lively in the evenings and especially at weekends, when it is very popular with a younger clientele.
😺🍴🚃(Town)⁵⌐

Victoria Inn 🏆 🅛
10 North Station Road, CO1 1RB (opp Causton Rd)
🌑 12-11 (midnight Fri & Sat); 2-10.30 Sun
☎ (01206) 514510 ⊕ victoriainncolchester.co.uk
Beer range varies Ⓗ
Local CAMRA 2013 Real Ale and Cider Pub of the Year, where northern hospitality comes as standard. With a comfy cider bar and a public bar selling up to six real ales, this is a proper pub, complete with sheltered courtyard and function room. Beer and cider festivals, locally brewed ales, plus imports from Yorkshire, are all worth looking out for. Board games including shove ha'penny are freely available and there is live music at weekends. 🏚😺🚃(North)♣🍴⁵⌐🚭

Cold Norton

Norton 🅛
54 Latchingdon Road, CM3 6JB (near B1010 and B1012)
🌑 4.30 (11.30 Wed & Thu)-11; 11.30-midnight Fri & Sat; 11.30-11 Sun ☎ (01621) 826948 ⊕ savethenorton.org
Beer range varies Ⓗ
Welcoming, community-owned pub that has secured its long-term future by organising a successful share sale in 2012; planned refurbishment includes a new restaurant. There are usually two beers from local microbreweries on offer, with others sourced from far and near; the website details which beers are on and coming next. The pub plays a vital role in the local community, with events such as an annual beer festival, organised walks, live music and darts nights. Home-cooked food is available Wednesday to Sunday. 🍺😺🍴⌐🚭🚭(D1,D2,D5)

Colne Engaine

Five Bells 🅛
7 Mill Lane, CO6 2HY (2 miles E of Halstead) TL851303
🌑 12-3, 6-11; 12-11 Thu-Sun ☎ (01787) 224166
⊕ fivebells.net
Adnams Southwold Bitter; guest beers Ⓗ
A 16th-century free house on the Essex-Suffolk border in the heart of the village, with fine views over the Colne valley. It offers a range of ales from local breweries, with Adnams a permanent feature. The pub has both dining and drinking areas, with a separate restaurant. Outside there is a terrace with a covered and heated area for smokers. There is an annual beer festival and live music regularly features. 🏚Q😺🍺🍴🍺♣P⁵⌐

Copford

Alma 🅛
Copford Green, CO6 1BZ TL928226
🌑 12-3, 5-11.30 (midnight Fri); 12-midnight Sat; 12-11 Sun
☎ (01206) 210607 ⊕ thealma.org.uk
Greene King IPA, Abbot; Red Fox Hunter's Gold Ⓗ
Picturesque country pub set next to a small village green at the heart of the community. Popular with locals and visitors alike, it offers Greene King ales plus a guest from the local Red Fox Brewery. An annual beer festival takes place every spring bank holiday. Lunchtime meals are served daily, there is a roast on Sunday, and evening meals are served Thursday to Saturday. Free Wi-Fi is available, with TV sport in the main bar. Local classic car and motorcycle enthusiasts meet here.
🏚Q😺🍺🍴P⁵⌐

Cornish Hall End

Horse & Groom
CM7 4HF (on B1057, nr Finchingfield) TL683366
🌑 closed Mon; 12-midnight ☎ (01799) 586306
⊕ thehorseandgroom.org
Greene King IPA; guest beers Ⓗ
A pleasant village pub opposite the parish church with a restaurant and garden. It runs beer festivals and events and is a warm and friendly place, with beers that change frequently. The pub is the social centre of this village, supporting many charities too, and good food is offered. Special lunches, carveries and fish and chip nights are held regularly – these are very popular so book ahead. Poker is played every Friday evening. 🏚Q🍺😺🍺P⁵⌐

Coxtie Green

White Horse 🅛
173 Coxtie Green Road, CM14 5PX (1 mile W of A128, at jct with Mores Lane) TQ564959
🌑 11.30-11 (midnight Fri & Sat); 12-11 Sun
☎ (01277) 372410
Beer range varies Ⓗ
Splendid country free house with a very relaxed, friendly atmosphere. There is a large, comfortable saloon bar that leads through to an extended public bar with satellite TV and a dartboard. Ten handpumps are now in constant use, with six guest beers and four changing brews from Brentwood (the pub is now badged as the Brentwood Brewery tap). There is a large rear garden where a beer festival is held each July, plus occasional small events. The bus service is limited but reliable.
😺🍺♣🍴P⁵⌐🚭(71,72)

Duton Hill

Three Horseshoes ⅃
CM6 2DX (1 mile W of B184) TL606268
✪ 12-2.30 (not Mon-Thu), 6-11; 12-3, 6-11 Sat; 12-3, 7-10.30 Sun ☎ (01371) 870681
Mighty Oak Captain Bob; guest beers ⒣
Cosy village local with a garden, wildlife pond and terrace overlooking the Chelmer Valley and farmland. The landlord hosts a weekend of open-air theatre in July. A millennium beacon in the garden, breweriana and a remarkable collection of Butlin's memorabilia are features. A beer festival is held on the late spring bank holiday in the Dutton Hill Den. Look for the pub sign depicting a famous painting, Our Blacksmith, by a former local resident, Sir George Clausen.
🏚️🏵️&♣️P¹⁄₂🚍(313)

Epping

Forest Gate
111 Bell Common, CM16 4DZ (opp Bell Hotel) TL450011
✪ 10-2.30, 5-11; 12-3, 7-10.30 Sun ☎ (01992) 572312
Adnams Southwold Bitter, Broadside; Growler IPA ⒣; **guest beers** ⒣/⒢
A gem of an old-fashioned free house on the edge of Epping Forest and Epping town. The building is 17th century, with low ceilings and flag floors. It is frequented both by locals and walkers and is dog-friendly. Sandwiches and soups are usually available but the emphasis is on serving real ale in a traditional setting. There are no TVs or games machines; it is just a peaceful place with a large outdoor seating area on the front lawn.
🏚️Q🏵️◑♣️P🚍(213,214,575)

Fordham

Three Horseshoes
74 Church Road, CO6 3NJ TL927281
✪ closed Mon winter; 12-3, 5-11; 12-11 Sat; 12-8 Sun
☎ (01206) 240195 ⊕ threehorseshoes-fordham.co.uk
Beer range varies ⒣
Comprising two welcoming bars, both with real fires to offer a cosy atmosphere, where local brewery beers are always on offer. Quiz nights are on the last Thursday of every month and a traditional folk evening is held on the first Tuesday, with other events taking place regularly. There are separate rooms for drinking and dining and a good quality menu is available. Another area is available for those just requiring coffee or tea. 🏚️Q🏵️◑P¹⁄₂

Fuller Street

Square & Compasses ⅃
Fairstead, CM3 2BB (1½ miles E off the A131 at Gt Leighs, St Anne's Castle) TL748161
✪ 11.30-3, 5.30-11; 12-midnight Sat; 12-11 Sun
☎ (01245) 361477 ⊕ thesquareandcompasses.co.uk
Growler Stoker's IPA; guest beers ⒢
Known locally as the Stokehole, this is a 17th-century three-roomed free house with a first-floor private dining room. There are exposed beams throughout and two inglenook fireplaces with woodburners. Old local woodworking tools adorn the Taproom Bar. Up to four beers and Westons cider and perry are sold. Food is prepared from locally sourced produce including game from the surrounding estates (but no food Sun eve).
🏚️🏵️◑♣️P¹⁄₂

Goldhanger

Chequers
The Square, CM9 8AS (500yds from B1026) TL904088
✪ 11-11; 12-10.30 Sun ☎ (01621) 788203
⊕ thechequersgoldhanger.co.uk
Adnams Broadside; Crouch Vale Brewers Gold; Sharp's Doom Bar; Taylor Landlord; Young's Bitter; guest beers ⒣
Multi-roomed 15th-century Essex village pub with timber ceilings where a warm welcome greets you. A good selection of beers, including guests, is served along with bar snacks and a wide range of home-cooked main meals. It has a games room with bar billiards and a courtyard beer garden. Beer festivals take place twice a year, in March and September. The pub has a very limited bus service and the parking is on the opposite side of the road.
🏚️🏵️◑ 🗐&♣️P¹⁄₂

Grays

Theobald Arms
141 Argent Street, RM17 6HR
✪ 11-11 (midnight Fri & Sat); 12-11 Sun ☎ (01375) 372253
⊕ theobaldarms.com
Beer range varies ⒣
Genuine, traditional pub with a public bar that has an unusual hexagonal pool table. The changing selection of four guest beers features local independent breweries, and a range of British bottled beers is also stocked. Regular St George's weekend and summer beer festivals are held in the old stables and on the rear enclosed patio. Lunchtime meals are served Monday to Friday, and darts and cards are played. A former local CAMRA Pub of the Year. 🏵️◑🗐&➡️♣️P¹⁄₂

White Hart
Kings Walk, Argent Street, RM17 6HR
✪ 12-11.30 (midnight Fri & Sat); 12-11 Sun
☎ (01375) 373319 ⊕ whitehartgrays.co.uk
Crouch Vale Brewers Gold; Sharp's White Hart Ale; guest beers ⒣
Traditional local outside the town centre, rejuvenated since it was taken over in 2006. The regular ales, including the house beer, are supplemented by three guests (one usually dark) and a selection of bottled Belgian beers. There is a meeting/function room and a beer garden. The pub supports pool and darts teams, and sport is screened on the TVs. Live blues bands play on alternate Thursdays, and a beer festival is held in February/March. Local CAMRA Pub of the Year 2011. 🏚️🏵️🖃◑🗐➡️♣️P¹⁄₂🚍

Great Dunmow

Angel & Harp ⅃
Church End, CM6 2AD TL628228
✪ 9am-11 (11.30 Fri & Sat); 9am-10.30 Sun
☎ (01371) 859259 ⊕ angelandharp.co.uk
Growler IPA; guest beers ⒣
A pub that has refurbished its building and its restaurant to increase business. There is a substantial garden area, a patio and a large car park. The pub also has a function room and runs occasional beer festivals. Local ales regularly feature as guest beers alongside the Growler IPA which is always available. This pub is on the north-east side of Great Dunmow and accommodates families and large parties although the drinking area is small. Q🏚️🏵️◑&P¹⁄₂

Great Easton

Swan
The Endway, CM6 2HG (off B184) TL606255
✪ 12-3 (not Mon), 6-11; 12-3, 7-10.30 (not eve winter) Sun
☎ (01371) 870359 ⊕ swangreateaston.co.uk
Adnams Southwold Bitter; guest beer H
A warm welcome is assured at this 15th-century free house in an attractive village. A log-burning stove, exposed beams and comfortable sofas feature in the lounge, while pool and darts are played in the public bar. All meals are prepared to order from fresh local produce, including the chips. The chef looks after the beers, chosen to complement the food. Accommodation is now available in four superb double rooms.
ᴁQ♿☕🍴◑⬕♣P

Harwich

Alma Inn
25 Kings Head Street, CO12 3EE
✪ 12-11 (midnight Fri & Sat) ☎ (01255) 318681
⊕ almaharwich.co.uk
Adnams Southwold Bitter, Broadside; guest beers H
Just a short walk from the quay, this unspoilt 16th-century building has been trading as an inn since 1873. A good selection of ales is always available, with the Adnams' beers as regulars, and guests from local and national breweries, complemented by bottled beers and ciders. Food is served lunchtimes and evenings, made with locally sourced produce when possible and cooked fresh on site. This is a must-visit venue whether arriving by sea, rail or road, with accommodation soon to be available.
ᴁ♿☕◑≈(Town)🍴⬕➖🚆(102,103,104)

New Bell Inn
Outpart Eastward, CO12 3EN
✪ 11-3, 7-11 (midnight Fri & Sat); 12-4, 7-11 (12-11 summer) Sun ☎ (01255) 503545
Mighty Oak Oscar Wilde; guest beers H
Excellent community local that makes a great base to explore the history of Old Harwich. A good range of ever-changing ales is looked after by the knowledgeable staff, and the hearty, home-cooked lunchtime food is very popular. Three drinking areas and a walled garden make the pub cosy in the winter and airy in the summer. The pub is used by many local groups, becoming Sausage HQ during the Harwich Sausage Festival in November.
Q☕◑⬕≈(Town)P🚆(102,103,104)

Hatfield Broad Oak

Cock Inn
High Street, CM22 7HF TL546164
✪ 12-11 (12.30am Fri & Sat); 12-10.30 Sun
☎ (01279) 718306
Adnams Southwold Bitter; Woodforde's Wherry; guest beers H
A friendly village local, close to Hatfield Forest; walkers and dogs are welcome. The building is a 16th-century Grade II-listed old coaching inn, decorated in a sympathetic yet elegant style. Sensibly priced but generous meals are cooked to order using local produce, and unusual home-made desserts also feature on the menu. Meals are served until 9pm daily (5pm on Sun). A second bar has a dartboard and satellite sport viewing, while the third room is a quiet area. Free Wi-Fi available.
ᴁQ♿☕◑♣P🚆(5,347)

Hempstead

Bluebell Inn
High Street, CB10 2PD (on B1054) TL633380
✪ closed Mon; 11-3, 6-11; 11.30-11 Sat; 12-7 Sun
☎ (01799) 599199 ⊕ thebluebellinn.co.uk
Adnams Sole Star, Southwold Bitter, Broadside; Woodforde's Wherry; guest beers H
Late 16th-century village pub with 18th-century additions, reputed to be the birthplace of Dick Turpin; the bar displays posters about his life. Six beers are usually available. The restaurant serves excellent meals from an extensive menu and the large bar has a log fire. Ample seating is provided outside, plus a children's play area. A folk evening is hosted on a Tuesday. ᴁQ☕◑♿♣P➖🚆(18)

Henham

Cock Inn L
Church Street, CM22 6AL (1 mile off B1051) TL545286
✪ 12-3, 5-11; 12-midnight Thu-Sun ☎ (01279) 850347
⊕ thecockinnhenham.co.uk
Greene King IPA; Sharp's Doom Bar; guest beers H
Traditional village pub in residential surroundings with outdoor seating at the front and a garden at the rear. The main and snug bars both have open fires, and the snug has a large TV where major sporting events are screened. A large separate dining room is next to the bar. The Saffron Brewery is 100 yards away and one of its beers is normally available here. There are regular quiz nights. No food Sunday evenings. ᴁQ☕◑P🚆(7,7a)

Herongate Tye

Olde Dog Inn L
129 Billericay Road, CM13 3SD (E of A128) TQ641909
✪ 11.30 (12 Sat)-11; 12-10.30 Sun ☎ (01277) 810337
⊕ theoldedoginn.co.uk
Crouch Vale Brewers Gold G**; Greene King Abbot** H**; guest beers** G
Owned and run by one family, this free house with beer garden dates from the 17th century. Six real ales are always on handpump, including three regularly changing guest beers of varying styles from countryside microbreweries and nationals, plus its own Olde Dog IPA brewed by the local Crouch Vale Brewery. It has period decor, and a variety of beer mats and oddities adorns the walls and ceilings. Food is available at the bar or separate restaurant area lunchtimes and evenings.
ᴁ☕◑♿P➖

Hockley

White Hart
274 Main Road, SS5 4NS
✪ 11-11; 12-10.30 Sun ☎ (01702) 203438
⊕ whitepharthockley.co.uk
Beer range varies H
A friendly local, dating from the 18th century and facing the village green. This pub is community-oriented and supportive of local charities through its quiz nights and music events. Up to three changing guest ales are served. Lunchtime food is available all week, including roasts on Sunday, with evening meals served Tuesday-Saturday. Sporting events are shown in the separate function room. There is a large rear garden plus picnic tables at the front. A beer festival is held at Easter.
ᴁQ☕◑≈P➖(7,8)

Horndon-on-the-Hill

Bell Inn

High Road, SS17 8LD (near centre of village, almost opp Woolmarket) TQ642463

✪ 11-11; 12-10.30 Sun ☎ (01375) 642463 ⊕ bell-inn.co.uk

Crouch Vale Brewers Gold; Greene King IPA; guest beers Ⓗ

Popular 15th-century coaching inn, run by the same family since 1938, with beamed bars featuring wood panelling and carvings. Note the unusual hot cross bun collection – a bun has been added every Good Friday for more than 100 years. Two regular beers plus two guests are served, including ales from Essex breweries. The award-winning restaurant is open daily, lunchtimes and evenings, but it can get busy, so booking is advisable. Gourmet nights are held. Accommodation is available in 15 bedrooms.
🏚Q🌤🍴◑👶♣Pˡ–🚪(374)

Lamarsh

Lamarsh Lion

Bures Road, CO8 5EP (1¼ miles NW of Bures) TL892355

✪ 12-11 (10.30 Sun) ☎ (01787) 227918

Adnams Southwold Bitter Ⓗ/Ⓖ**; Greene King IPA; guest beers** Ⓗ

Rural 14th-century pub with fine views across the Stour Valley. The pub comprises a mixture of both stone flooring and carpeted areas, and comfortable seating is available throughout. A separate dining area offers a varied menu combined with regular specials. There is also a games room with a large-screen TV and sofa seating. Cyclists and ramblers are welcome and there is a large open fire to relax by. The large garden area includes a Wendy house to keep the children entertained.
🏚🕒🌤◑👶♣Pˡ

Layer Breton

Hare & Hounds

Crayes Green, CO2 0PN TL943188

✪ 11.30-midnight (11 Sun) ☎ (01206) 330459

⊕ thehareandhound.co.uk

Greene King IPA, Abbot; Mighty Oak Oscar Wilde Ⓗ

Community pub with an L-shaped bar serving various seating areas. A large real fire warms the place in winter and makes for a pleasant atmosphere. Monthly quiz nights and live music take place. Up to five real ales are served with some from local breweries. Annual beer festivals are held in summer and winter and also for St George's Day. The restaurant offers a good-quality varying menu and this area is also available to hire.
🏚Q🌤🍴◑Pˡ

Layer-de-la-Haye

Layer Fox Ⓛ

2 Malting Green Road, CO2 0JH (on B1026) TL968200

✪ 9am-11.30 (midnight Fri & Sat); 9am-10.30 Sun

☎ (01206) 738723 ⊕ thelayerfox.co.uk

Red Fox Bitter; guest beers Ⓗ

Friendly single-bar pub at the heart of the community, with comfortable seating in various areas and on different levels. Usually four beers are offered, mainly from local breweries. A varied and good-quality menu is on offer, along with Sunday roasts and a monthly curry night. This venue is open daily from 9am, with a delicatessen counter,

PayPoint and cash machine. Accommodation is available in the Sleepy Fox B&B chalets.
🏚Q🕒🌤🍴◑👶♣Pˡ–🚪(50)

Leigh-on-Sea

Crooked Billet

51 High Street, SS9 2EP (½ mile E of Leigh station)

✪ 12-11 (10.30 Sun) ☎ (01702) 480289

Adnams Southwold Bitter; Ha'penny London Stone; Nicholson's Pale Ale; Sharp's Doom Bar; guest beers Ⓗ

Classic historic pub at the heart of Old Leigh, a fishing village overlooking the Thames Estuary. Local CAMRA Pub of the Year 2012, it has two bars with bare floorboards and beamed ceilings. The walls are adorned with local fishing pictures. Beer tasting evenings are held occasionally. Traditional pub food is served daily. A small garden to the side is complemented by a large shared waterside seating area. The venue is popular in the summer, as is the Thornbridge Jaipur IPA when available.
Q🌤◑🚪ˡ

Elms

1060 London Road, SS9 3ND (on A13)

✪ 8am-midnight (1am Fri & Sat); 8am-11 Sun

☎ (01702) 474687

Greene King Abbot; Ruddles Best Bitter; guest beers Ⓗ

Old coaching inn converted by Wetherspoon into a large, open pub decorated with old photos of the local area. Breakfast is available until noon, plus main meals and snacks until 10pm. Children are admitted until 9pm. Six changing guest ales and up to three real ciders are served. There is no music but there are fruit machines and muted TVs. Outside is a paved, heated and covered area for smokers and the pub also has a hedged front garden. 🌤◑👶♣Pˡ–🚪

Mayflower Ⓛ

5-6 High Street, SS9 2EN

✪ 11-9; 12-11 Thu-Sun; 11-11 summer ☎ (01702) 478535

⊕ mayfloweroldleigh.com

Crouch Vale Yakima Gold; Fuller's London Pride; guest beers Ⓗ

A recent addition to Leigh old town pubs, this small single-bar hostelry is unusual in that it adjoins a fish and chip restaurant. The popular food menu consists mainly, unsurprisingly, of fish dishes. Four ales are served, with the guest ales usually from East Anglia. One of the walls depicts the passenger manifest of the Mayflower who sailed on the Mayflower. The pub has a drinking/smoking terrace. Music nights are held, with jazz on Sundays. Bell Wharf beach is nearby.
🕒🌤◑👶≈ˡ

Little Bromley

Haywain Ⓛ

Bentley Road, CO11 2PL

✪ closed Mon; 12-2.30 (not Tue), 6-10.30; 12-5 Sun

☎ (01206) 390004 ⊕ thehaywain.co.uk

Adnams Southwold Bitter; guest beers Ⓗ

Traditional 18th-century inn, reopened in 2007, with exposed beams and real fires, representing a true community pub. There is an additional reception room with a self-contained bar. Landlady Dawn provides a good menu of home-made, locally sourced food, including a number of vegetarian dishes. There are always three to four real ales available, with Adnams Southwold Bitter on permanently. Landlord Andy sources his beer from local breweries and ensures it is in good condition. ₳Q❁☺❁◑♣P↕🖿(2)

Little Clacton

Blacksmiths Arms
20 The Street, CO16 9LQ
❂ 12-11 ☎ (01255) 860888
Beer range varies Ⓗ
Nice village community local with a traditional two-bar layout, a real fire and a lovely garden with a covered patio. The pub dates back at least 200 years. It has a restaurant that doubles as a function room and a separate games room, home to pool and darts teams. Live music plays occasionally on Saturday evenings. In the main bar there is an unobtrusive TV, mainly used for sporting events. ₳❁☺❁◑❶♣P↕🖿(2,3,4)

Little Thurrock

Traitor's Gate
40-42 Broadway, RM17 6EW (on A126)
❂ 3 (1 Fri)-11; 12-11 Sat; 12-10.30 Sun ☎ (01375) 372628
Beer range varies Ⓗ
A variety of four guest beers is on offer, with forthcoming beers displayed on a blackboard above the bar, as well as two ciders on draught. This friendly hostelry has a wide and varied clientele, mostly local. Look out for the rare bar billiards table. Sport is shown on large-screen TVs. Two beer festivals are held annually in April and August. The beer garden has won Thurrock in Bloom awards in recent years.
❁♿♣●↕🖿(22A,66)

Little Walden

Crown
High Street, CB10 1XA (on B1052) TL546415
❂ 11.30-2.30, 6-11; 12-10.30 Sun ☎ (01799) 522475
⊕ thecrownlittlewalden.co.uk/index.html
Adnams Broadside; Greene King Abbot; Woodforde's Wherry; guest beer Ⓖ
Charming 18th-century beamed pub in a quiet hamlet. The pub is popular with diners, especially at weekends, when booking is advisable. Evening meals are served Tuesday to Saturday. An excellent range of beers is dispensed direct from the cask, which can be enjoyed on the covered patio area. The pub hosts traditional jazz on Wednesday evenings and has a function room for club meetings and private parties. ₳Q❁☺❁◑♿P↕

Littley Green

Compasses ▼ Ⓛ
CM3 1BU (turn off B1417 at former Ridley's Brewery, Hartford End) TL699172
❂ 12-3, 5.30-11.30; 12-11.30 Thu-Sun ☎ (01245) 362308
⊕ compasseslittleygreen.co.uk
Adnams Southwold Bitter; guest beers Ⓖ
Local CAMRA Pub of the Year and East Anglian Pub of the Year 2012. Formerly Ridley's brewery tap, it is a picturesque Victorian country pub in a quiet hamlet. Beers are drawn direct from the cask in the half-cellar. Renowned filled huffers (giant baps) are available lunchtimes and evenings. There are

seats and tables outside and in the large gardens. Two or three guest beers are from local breweries, usually including one from Bishop Nick, and real ciders and perries are available. A folk evening is held monthly. ₳Q❁❁◑♣●P

Loughton

Victoria Tavern
165 Smarts Lane, IG10 4BP (off A121 at edge of forest)
❂ 11-3, 5-11; 11-11 Sat; 12-10.30 Sun ☎ (020) 8508 1779
Adnams Southwold Bitter; Greene King IPA; Taylor Landlord Ⓗ
A traditional pub on the edge of Epping Forest and Loughton. There is one big bar, with a raised dining area. It has a large garden area and the pub is used both by locals and walkers. Well-behaved dogs are welcome inside and in the garden. It is a family-friendly pub, serving generous portions of well-cooked pub food daily. There is occasionally a real fire, and it has a lively atmosphere, with charity events, quizzes and music.
Q❁❁◑♿⊖P↕🖿(20,167)

Maldon

Queen Victoria Ⓛ
Spital Road, CM9 6ED
❂ 11-midnight; 11.30-11 Sun ☎ (01621) 852923
Farmer's Puck's Folly; Wibblers Dengie IPA; guest beers Ⓗ
A friendly, family run Victorian local five minutes' walk from Maldon High Street. Guest beers always include a local ale. The pub is divided into three areas: a public bar, lounge bar and a dining area. It offers hearty home-cooked food with a changing specials board. It is a popular meeting place for local groups and has several darts and dominoes teams. There is a monthly quiz, and you can make use of free Wi-Fi. Note the wonderful hanging baskets. On the 31 bus route from Chelmsford. ❁☺❁◑♿♣P↕🖿(31,31X)

Queen's Head Ⓛ
The Hythe, CM9 5HN
❂ 11-11 (midnight Fri & Sat); 11-10.30 Sun
☎ (01621) 854112 ⊕ thequeensheadmaldon.co.uk
Adnams Southwold Bitter; Bishop Nick Ridley's Rite; Farmer's Puck's Folly; Greene King IPA; Sharp's Doom Bar; guest beers Ⓗ
Maldon's internationally-renowned annual Mud Race originated in the mid-1970s as a bet in this historic riverside pub. Up to 10 beers are on tap during the summer months. The spacious outdoor seating area affords fine views of the River Blackwater and the town's flotilla of Thames barges. There is a focus on fresh local produce in the food menu, which is available all day in the two bars and the separate restaurant. Well-behaved children and dogs are welcome.
₳Q❁☺◑♿♣↕

Margaretting Tye

White Hart Inn Ⓛ
Swan Lane, CM4 9JX TL684011
❂ 11.30-3, 6-midnight (1am Fri); 11.30-1am Sat; 12-midnight Sun ☎ (01277) 840478 ⊕ thewhitehart.uk.com
Adnams Southwold Bitter, Broadside; Mighty Oak IPA, Oscar Wilde; Red Fox Hunter's Gold; guest beers Ⓖ
Slightly off the beaten track, this fine pub has origins in the 17th century. Known for good

traditional home-cooked food and good ale, it generally offers at least two or three guest beers, all on gravity. Regular club meetings are held here for cyclists, car owners, ramblers and young farmers. Very much community focused, a book stall raises money for charities, and beer festivals are held in July and November. Children are however confined to the conservatory. Accommodation is also available.
ᛗᚫQ♻️🕮🏚️🌑🕕🚃♣️P♨️⊑

Monk Street

Farmhouse Inn ⌹

CM6 2NR (off B184, 2 miles S of Thaxted) TL614288
✪ 11-midnight (11 Sun) ☎ (01371) 830864
⊕ farmhouseinn.org
Greene King IPA; Mighty Oak Maldon Gold; guest beer ⊞
Built in the 16th century, this former Dunmow Brewery pub has been enlarged to incorporate a restaurant and accommodation; the bar is in the original part of the building. The quiet hamlet of Monk Street overlooks the Chelmer Valley, two miles from historic Thaxted. A disused well in the garden supplied the hamlet with water during World War II. The pub has a rear patio, front garden and a top field. Draught cider from Westons is usually sold in summer.
Q♻️🕮🏚️🕕🌑🚃P♨️⊑🚌(313)

Mount Bures

Thatchers Arms ⌹

Hall Road, CO8 5AT TL905319
✪ closed Mon; 12-3, 6-11; 12-11 Sat & Sun
☎ (01787) 227460 ⊕ thatchersarms.co.uk
Adnams Southwold Bitter; Crouch Vale Brewers Gold; guest beers ⊞
Family- and dog-friendly country pub on the Essex-Suffolk border, with exceptional views over the Stour Valley. It was 2013 local CAMRA Rural Pub of the Year and offers up to five real ales – Adnams Southwold Bitter and Crouch Vale Brewers Gold permanently – plus a range of bottled English beers. Excellent locally sourced home-made food is available daily. Beer festivals are held each spring and autumn. The Thatchers also boasts a bar billiards table, piano and a cinema! ♻️🕮🌑🕖Å♣️P♨️⊑

Old Harlow

Queen's Head ⌹

26 Churchgate Street, Churchgate Street, CM17 0JT
TL483114
✪ 11.45-11; 12-10.30 Sun ☎ (01279) 427266
Adnams Southwold Bitter, Broadside; Crouch Vale Essex Boys, Brewers Gold; guest beer ⊞
Originally an early Tudor building (with solid beams spanning a spacious interior), beer has been sold since 1750 on these premises. The setting is a pretty village on the edge of Harlow. The smaller side bar has a fire in the winter and a full range of food is served lunchtimes and evenings. There are regular quizzes, charity events and cocktail evenings. The outside area looks over fields, and barbecues are held in the summer.
ᛗᚫQ🌑🕕⊟P♨️⊑🚃(7,59)

Ongar

Cock Tavern

218 High Street, CM5 9AB
✪ 11-midnight ☎ (01277) 632615 ⊕ cocktavernongar.co.uk
Adnams Southwold Bitter; guest beers ⊞
Located at the north end of the High Street near the preserved railway station, next to the library and close to public car parks. The Grade II-listed building is constructed with timber frames, part plasterboard and part weatherboard. Three rotating guest ales are on tap, normally from local breweries. Live music plays every Saturday night. A spacious function room is available.
ᛗᚫ♻️🌑🕕♣️♨️⊑🚃(20,32,46)

Paglesham

Punch Bowl

Church End, SS4 2DP (signed from Rochford)
✪ 11.30-3 (2.30 Mon), 6.30-11 (10 Mon); 12-10.30 Sun
☎ (01702) 258376
Adnams Southwold Bitter; guest beers ⊞
A 16th-century, south-facing building clad in white Essex weatherboard, formerly a baker's and sailmaker's. Situated in a quiet one-street village, it has been an ale house since the mid-1800s and was reputedly used by smugglers. The low-beamed single bar is adorned with a large collection of mugs, old local pictures and brassware. The small cosy restaurant next to the bar serves excellent reasonably priced food. Picnic tables are to the front of the pub. Q🌑🕕🕖♣️P♨️⊑

Purleigh

Bell ⌹

The Street, CM3 6QJ
✪ closed Mon; 11.30 (12 Sat)-3, 6-11; 12-4 Sun
☎ (01621) 828348 ⊕ purleighbell.co.uk
Adnams Southwold Bitter; Mighty Oak Captain Bob; guest beers ⊞
Traditional village pub dating back to the 14th century, standing on a hill with far-reaching views over the Blackwater Estuary. The interior includes an open fire in a large inglenook, three heavily beamed dining areas and a hop-decorated bar. Up to four ales are offered, with guests often from local microbreweries. The Bell has a reputation for good food, with a strong emphasis on seafood. Allegedly, it was once the home of George Washington's great-great-great grandfather.
ᛗᚫQ🌑🕕♣️P♨️⊑

Rayleigh

Roebuck

138 High Street, SS6 7BU (close to library)
✪ 9am-midnight ☎ (01268) 748430
Courage Directors; Greene King Abbot; Ruddles Best Bitter; guest beers ⊞
Friendly Wetherspoon pub in the High Street with a varied selection of guest beers from around the UK, as well as Westons Old Rosie and Wyld Wood cider on draught. Families are welcome in a sectioned-off area. Breakfast is served 8am-midday, with the main menu served till 10pm. There are outside areas to the front and side for smoking and drinking, with heaters for when it is cold. Wi-Fi is available. Rayleigh is served by many buses and a railway station. ♻️🌑🕕🏚️🚃🍴♨️⊑🚃(1,7,8)

Ridgewell

White Horse Inn L
Mill Road, CO9 4SG (on A1017) TL735408
☼ 12 (5 Mon & Tue)-11 ☎ (01440) 785532
⊕ ridgewellwhitehorse.com
Mighty Oak Oscar Wilde; Shortts Farm Strummer; guest beers G
A CAMRA award-winning real ale pub set in a pretty village which was home to the American 381st Heavy Bomb Group during World War II. At least one dark beer is always available. Annual beer festivals are held in March and August on the patio behind the pub. As well as a choice of excellent real ale, the pub offers a selection of good-quality wines, plus 4-star accommodation.
🏨🕮🏮🍴🌓🖥♿♣🚬P♿─🕎

Rochford

Golden Lion L
35 North Street, SS4 1AB (200yds N of town square)
☼ 11-midnight (1am Fri & Sat) ☎ (01702) 545487
⊕ goldenlionrochford.co.uk
Adnams Southwold Bitter; Greene King Abbot; Mighty Oak Maldon Gold; guest beers H
Multi-award-winning pub situated within the town-centre conservation area. This is a small, 16th-century, traditional Essex weatherboarded free house with stained glass windows and a pretty patio garden to the rear – look for the vintage petrol pump water feature. The decor includes hops above the bar and a fireplace with a traditional logburner. Six ales are always available including three changing guests (one usually a dark beer) from local micros – and a real cider. A true community local with its own cricket team.
🏨🕮🚆♿─🕎(7,8,60)

Horse & Groom L
1 Southend Road, SS4 1HA
☼ 11.30-11; 12-10.30 Sun ☎ (01702) 544015
⊕ horseandgroomrochford.co.uk
Mighty Oak Maldon Gold; guest beers H
A Guide regular and deservedly frequent winner of local CAMRA awards. This traditional and friendly pub is a few minutes' walk from the town centre and railway station. The guest ales include a selection from Essex breweries as well as further afield, and a real cider is always available. The restaurant is run by award-winning Harrisons of Hockley, offering first-class cuisine. Food is served most lunchtimes, and Thursday to Saturday evenings. 🕮🍴🚆♿P🖥(7,8,60)

Rowhedge

Olde Albion
High Street, CO5 7ES (3 miles SE of Colchester) TM031215
☼ 12-3 (not Mon), 5-11; 12-11 Thu-Sat; 12-10.30 Sun
☎ (01206) 728972
Beer range varies H/G
Friendly pub overlooking the River Colne, with riverside seating available in summer. The split-level interior comprises one bar and various seating areas. Beer festivals are held for St George's Day and the summer regatta, plus a mini festival each October. A varied beer range is offered from handpump and occasionally from gravity. There is live music on the last Saturday of each month. Biff, the friendliest pub dog, looks forward to welcoming you. 🏨♣─🕎(66)

Saffron Walden

King's Arms
10 Market Hill, CB10 1HQ TL537386
☼ 12-midnight (11 Mon); 12-12.30am Fri & Sat; 12-11 Sun
☎ (01799) 522768
Sharp's Doom Bar; Woodforde's Wherry; guest beers H
Venerable multi-roomed pub, just off the market square (market days are Tuesday and Saturday). Five handpumps feature Wherry, Doom Bar and one Adnams' ale, augmented by a Saffron Brewery beer and a mild. There is live music at weekends, acoustic music on Thursdays and a monthly quiz. Welcoming log fires in the winter and a pleasant patio for alfresco eating and drinking are particular features. Food is served at lunchtimes and on some evenings. 🕮Q🕮🏮🍴🖥P♿─🕎(5,301,59)

Old English Gentleman
11 Gold Street, CB10 1EJ (E of B184/B1052 jct) TL537383
☼ 11-11 (midnight Tue-Thu; 1am Fri & Sat)
☎ (01799) 523595 ⊕ oldenglishgentleman.com
Adnams Southwold Bitter; Woodforde's Wherry; guest beers H
An 18th-century town-centre pub with log fires and a welcoming atmosphere. It serves a selection of guest ales and an extensive menu of bar food and sandwiches that changes regularly. Traditional roasts and chef's specials are available on Sunday in the bar or dining area, where a variety of works of art is displayed. Saffron Walden is busy on Tuesday and Saturday market days. There is a heated patio at the rear. Local CAMRA Pub of the Year 2012. 🏨🕮🖥♿─🕎(5,7,301)

Temeraire L
55 High Street, CB10 1AA TL536383
☼ 9am-midnight (1am Fri) ☎ (01799) 516975
Greene King IPA; Ruddles Best Bitter; guest beers H
Fine Georgian building that was once a working men's club. Local management have agreed to stock either a Growler or Shalford beer at all times. In addition to the regular Wetherspoon beer festivals, the pub hosts occasional Meet the Brewer sessions and beer tastings. It was the winner of a regional Wetherspoon food award, hosts a Monday quiz night, and its real cider is usually Westons. Families are welcome and there is a large garden and a covered smoking area.
🕮🏮🖥♿♣🚬P♿─🕎(5,7,301)

Shalford

George Inn L
The Street, CM7 5HH TL721292
☼ 6-11 Mon; 12-3 (4 Sat), 6-11; 12-6 Sun ☎ (01371) 850207
⊕ thegeorgeinnshalford.co.uk
Fuller's London Pride; Shalford 1319 Mild, Stoneley Bitter; Young's Bitter; guest beers H
Attractively beamed 15th-century inn, at the centre of village life. In summer it is pleasant to sit outside on the patio, while in winter the roaring log fire draws you inside. A true local, it attracts both drinkers and diners, and has a separate dining area. Various clubs and social events feature throughout the year including a summer beer festival. Shalford Brewery beers are always available.
🏨Q🕮🏮🖥♿♣P♿─🕎(9,10)

Southend-on-Sea

Borough Hotel
10-12 Marine Parade, SS1 2EJ (on seafront, opp Adventure Island)
✪ 10-midnight (2am Fri & Sat) ☎ (01702) 466936
Courage Best Bitter; guest beers Ⓗ
Welcoming, spacious and comfortable pub close to Southend's famous pier. The venue features up to five cask ales and is especially popular on sunny summer days. It has a jukebox and satellite TV, with a sports area at the rear for pool and darts matches. Live music plays most weekends. There are seating areas on the pavement to the front and to the rear. A short walk from Southend bus station. ⓑ☸⌂≠≈(Central)♣⚊⚐

Last Post
Weston Road, SS1 1AS
✪ 8am-midnight (1am Fri & Sat) ☎ (01702) 431682
Greene King Abbot; Ruddles Best Bitter; guest beers Ⓗ
A huge and popular Wetherspoon pub in the town centre, run by a well-managed and knowledgeable team. There are two bar areas serving an extensive beer range that changes regularly; Essex brewers Brentwood and Growler are particularly supported. Also on offer are at least four ciders and one perry. Just off the high street, the pub is close to public transport. It can get busy at evenings or weekends, and for some live televised football matches or other sporting events.
ⓑ◖◗&≈(Central/Victoria)●⚊⚐

Olde Trout Tavern ♈ Ⓛ
56 London Road, SS1 1NX (opp Sainsbury's)
✪ 11-11 (midnight Fri & Sat); 12-11 Sun ☎ (01702) 337000
⊕ theoldtrout.webs.com
George's Trout Ale; guest beers Ⓗ
Local CAMRA Pub of the Year 2013, this modern town-centre hostelry is within walking distance of Southend high street and both mainline railway stations. The house beer, George's Trout Ale, is from the local brewery – with three other changing guests, often from other Essex breweries, while Westons Traditional Scrumpy is served on handpump. Strong bottled beer is also available. Hot meals and snacks are served 12-7pm (to 4pm Sun). A quiz night is held fortnightly on Sundays. An interesting selection of clocks adorns the walls.
◖◗≈(Victoria/Central)●

Southminster

Station Arms Ⓛ
39 Station Road, CM0 7EW (near B1021)
✪ 12-2.30, 6 (5.30 Fri)-11; 2-11 Sat; 12-4, 7-10.30 Sun
☎ (01621) 772225 ⊕ thestationarms.co.uk
Adnams Southwold Bitter; George's Broadsword; Mighty Oak Oscar Wilde; guest beers Ⓗ
This is a classic among Essex weatherboarded pubs. Two beer festivals are held in January and May in an adjoining outbuilding to the rear, and a courtyard provides a pleasant place to enjoy the excellent and varied range of ales throughout the seasons – weather permitting. Music nights showcase blues on the third Saturday and folk on the first Friday of the month, and a darts team plays on Wednesday evening. There is a weekly meat raffle. The pub has featured in the Guide for 23 consecutive years. ⚏Q☸☀♣●⚊⚐(31X)

Stanford-le-Hope

Rising Sun ♈ Ⓛ
Church Hill, SS17 0EU (opp church and near A1014)
✪ 3-10.30; 12-midnight Thu-Sun ☎ (01375) 671097
Beer range varies Ⓗ
Much-improved single-bar town pub in the shadow of the church. The five guest beers are mainly from independent breweries, including LocAles, and up to three ciders or perries are stocked. Freshly prepared, locally sourced food is served Sunday lunchtime in a dining area at one end of the bar. Fortnightly quiz nights are held to raise money for a local charity, and beer festivals are hosted three times a year. Local CAMRA Pub of the Year 2013. ☸◖≈♣●P⚊⚐(100,200,374)

Stansted Mountfitchet

Rose & Crown
31 Bentfield Green, CM24 8HX (1 mile W of B1383)
TL505256
✪ 12-3, 6-midnight; 12-midnight Sat; 12-10 Sun
☎ (01279) 812107
Beer range varies Ⓗ
Family-run Victorian pub near a duckpond on the edge of a small hamlet. This free house has been modernised to provide one large bar but retains the atmosphere of a village inn and is well used by locals. The front of the pub is brightened by floral displays. Food is traditional and good value, made from locally sourced produce (no meals Sun eve). Guest beers are from local breweries. The smoking area is covered and heated. Children and dogs are welcome. ⚏ⓑ☸◖♣P⚊⚐(7,7a)

Stapleford Tawney

Moletrap
Tawney Common, CM16 7PU TL500013
✪ 11.30-2.30, 6-11; 12-3, 7-11 Sun ☎ (01992) 522394
⊕ themoletrap.co.uk
Fuller's London Pride; guest beers Ⓗ
This 200-year-old family-run pub, set in beautiful countryside and reached by leafy lanes, is in a very remote location. It offers a good selection of varying guest ales, usually including at least one dark ale, and serves good-value home-cooked food (no food Sun or Mon eves). There is a very cosy bar with a real fire. Well-behaved children are allowed, but no dogs inside. For warmer weather there is plenty of outside seating and an extensive beer garden with amazing views of the nearby countryside. Though difficult to locate, it is well worth the effort. ⚏Q☸◖&P⚊

Stebbing

White Hart Ⓛ
High Street, CM6 3SQ TL660244
✪ 11-3, 5-11; 11-11 Sat; 12-10.30 Sun ☎ (01371) 856383
Hart of Stebbing IPA; Wells Eagle IPA; guest beer Ⓗ
Friendly 15th-century timbered inn in a picturesque village, featuring exposed beams, an open fire, eclectic collections from chamber pots to cigarette cards, an old red post box on an interior wall, and a selection of exposed lath and plaster wall behind a glass screen. The Hart of Stebbing microbrewery is in the garage, producing beers currently only available here and at beer festivals. Good-value food is served daily. There is a patio and a covered heated gazebo. ⚏Q☸◖♣P⚊⚐(16)

Steeple Bumpstead

Fox & Hounds

3 Chapel Street, CB9 7DQ TL679412
✪ 12-3, 5-11; 12-midnight Fri & Sat; 12-11 Sun
☎ (01440) 731810 ⊕ foxinsteeple.co.uk
Greene King IPA; guest beers Ⓗ
A 500-year-old former coaching inn with a main
bar warmed by an open fire. There is a rear
courtyard garden, and two other rooms used
mainly for dining. Four beers are from local and
national breweries. The locally sourced food ranges
from bar snacks to a full à la carte menu. Live music
plays on occasional Friday evenings and quiz nights
are hosted on some Sundays. Reduced price beer,
wine and free cheese are on offer on Wednesday
evenings, with steak night on Thursdays.
⚫Q♿🏠🕑◑♿♣Pᴸ-🚆(18)

Stock

Hoop

High Street, CM4 9BD (on B1007)
✪ 11 (12 Sun)-11 ☎ (01277) 841137 ⊕ thehoop.co.uk
Adnams Southwold Bitter Ⓗ; **guest beers** Ⓗ/Ⓖ
Traditional weatherboarded pub with a heavily
beamed interior and lots of character that
welcomes drinkers and diners alike. A long-
standing Guide entry, it serves three guest beers –
some from local micros – and a cider or perry is
usually available. Home-made food is served in the
bar, or upstairs in the AA rosette Oak Room – at
lunchtimes, evenings and all day Saturday. There is
no music, no TV, it is dog-friendly, and there is free
Wi-Fi. A beer festival is held over the May bank
holiday. Q🏠◑♿♣❀ᴸ-🚆(100)

Stow Maries

Prince of Wales ♈ Ⓛ

Woodham Road, CM3 6SA (near B1012) TL830993
✪ 11-11 (midnight Fri & Sat); 12-10.30 Sun
☎ (01621) 828971 ⊕ prince-stowmaries.net
Crouch Vale Brewers Gold; Elgood's Black Dog Ⓗ;
guest beers Ⓗ/Ⓖ
Very attractive weatherboarded pub, originally two
cottages, which housed a bakery and a beer house.
There are five cosy drinking areas, most with open
fires. For the warmer months the pub boasts a
delightful rear garden terrace and courtyard. The
home-cooked food is prepared using mainly locally
sourced produce. As well as the guest ales from all
over the country, a good range of unusual Belgian
and German bottled beers is on offer. Local CAMRA
Pub of the Year for 2012 and 2013.
⚫Q♿🏠🕑◑♿♿A❀Pᴸ-🚆

Waltham Abbey

Woodbine Inn Ⓛ

Honey Lane, EN9 3QT (near M25 jct 26)
✪ 11-11 (2am Fri & Sat) ☎ (01992) 713050
⊕ thewoodbine.co.uk
**Crouch Vale Brewers Gold; Greene King Abbot; Mighty
Oak Oscar Wilde; Sharp's Doom Bar; guest beers** Ⓗ
On the edge of Epping Forest and close to junction
26 of the M25, this traditional pub is frequented by
walkers and cyclists, and is also horse rider- and
dog-friendly. It is popular with beer drinkers who
enjoy ales from both local and distant breweries.
Pub food is freshly made from local ingredients,
with home-cooked ham and local sausages as

specialities. The Ale Sampling Society meets here
on the first Sunday of the month, with guest
brewers speaking and presenting their beers.
♿🏠🕑◑♣❀P🚆(250,255)

Walton-on-the-Naze

Victory

Suffolk Street, CO14 8AR
✪ 11-11 (11.30 Fri & Sat); 12-10.30 Sun ☎ (01255) 677857
Greene King IPA, Abbot; guest beers Ⓗ
A traditional pub, run by father and son, well-
supported by the local community and visitors to
this seaside resort. It is in the town but close to the
pier and beach. Always welcoming, the Victory has
a characterful interior, with upper and lower bars
and a separate dining area. The pub hosts regular
varied live music evenings and is home to the
world-famous Bah Humbug Club, whose members
raise money for charity. A true guest ale is always
available. ⚫🏠🕑◑A⇄♣ᴸ-🚆

Warley

Brave Nelson

138 Woodman Road, CM14 5AL (½ mile E of B186)
✪ 11-11; 12-10.30 Sun ☎ (01277) 211690
Beer range varies Ⓗ
Cosy local featuring wood-panelled bars, with
understated nautical memorabilia including
pictures, drawings and plates. Saved from closure
in 2012 by a strong local campaign, its new guv'nor
has renewed the handpumps and beer lines and
improved the cellar. The beer range varies, but
includes ales from Brentwood, Cottage or Adnams.
There is a fortnightly Sunday evening charity quiz,
and darts, pool and crib are played, while
widescreen TVs often show sport. Pig racing is
planned. Food is served 11-3pm Monday-Friday
and 11-5pm Saturday. The garden has a sheltered
smoking area. ⚫🏠🕑◑♿♣Pᴸ-

Weeley

White Hart

Clacton Road, Weeley Heath, CO16 9ED (on B1441)
✪ 12-2.30, 4-11 (10 Mon); 12-11 Fri & Sat; 12-10.30 Sun
☎ (01255) 830384
Beer range varies Ⓗ
Typical single-roomed village local. The friendly
landlord and landlady serve consistently good-
quality beer, hence the White Hart is a regular
entry in the Guide. The pub hosts pool and darts
teams. There is a garden with a covered patio for
smokers. This is a great sportsman's pub; different
sporting events can be shown on various TV
screens. It is community focused, hosting regular
quizzes, and the Real Ale Club puts on a Christmas
carol concert. 🏠A♣❀Pᴸ-🚆(76)

Wendens Ambo

Bell ♈

Royston Road, CB11 4JY (on B1039) TL511364
✪ 11.30-11 (12.30am Fri & Sat); 12-10.30 Sun
☎ (01799) 540382 ⊕ thebellatwenden.co.uk
Oakham JHB; Woodforde's Wherry; guest beers Ⓗ
Classic country pub in a picturesque village. A
charity fundraising event, the Bell Bash, is held on
the August bank holiday weekend, with beer
festivals hosted throughout the year serving cask
beers outside. A chalkboard features forthcoming

guest ales. Traditional pub food is served at lunchtimes, main meals in the evenings and weekends (no food Mon). The large garden has a pétanque pitch and children's play equipment. Quiz night is Thursday and Tuesday is games night. Local CAMRA Pub of the Year 2013.
⚌🍷😊🌓 ≷(Audley End)♣🍴P⌑−🚪(59,301)

Westcliff-on-Sea

Cricketers
228 London Road, SS0 7JG (on A13)
🌓 11.30-midnight (2am Fri & Sat); 12-11 Sun
☎ (01702) 343168
Dark Star Hophead; Greene King Abbot; Sharp's Doom Bar; guest beers Ⓗ
A large street-corner Gray & Sons hostelry, close to Southend. It houses a Thai restaurant, separate from the main bar. Up to eight ales can be found including the three regulars – the guests are mainly from local breweries. A large selection of foreign beers is sold (mostly bottled, although some are available on draught), together with a varied wine selection. Club Riga adjoins the premises, so this popular pub can get busy on music nights.
😊🌓≷(Victoria)⌑−🚪(2,24)

White Notley

Cross Keys Ⓛ
1 The Street, CM8 1RQ
🌓 12-3, 5-midnight; 12-midnight Fri-Sun ☎ (01376) 583297
Beer range varies Ⓗ
Two-bar ex-Ridley's village local that was closed for some months after Greene King gave up on it, but which has now been revitalised by new local owners. Three continuously changing Essex beers are sold and food is available Wednesday-Sunday lunchtimes and Wednesday-Saturday evenings.
⚌Q🍷😊🌓🍴🚪≷♣P⌑−

Widdington

Fleur de Lys
High Street, CB11 3SG TL538316
🌓 12-3 (not Mon), 6-11; 12-11.30 Fri & Sat; 12-10.30 Sun
☎ (01799) 543280 ⊕ thefleurdelys.co.uk
Adnams Southwold Bitter; Sharp's Doom Bar; guest beers Ⓗ
Rumours of a ghost abound at this welcoming 400-year-old village local. The games room has a full-sized pool table, fuzzball table and dartboard. This was the first pub to be saved from closure by the local branch of CAMRA after the branch's formation. Quality meals are offered made with fresh local ingredients. The source of the River Cam and Prior's Hall Barn, an English Heritage site, are both nearby.
⚌Q😊🌓&♣P🚪(301)

Witham

Battesford Court
100-102 Newland Street, CM8 1AH
🌓 8am-midnight (1am Fri & Sat); 8am-11 Sun
☎ (01376) 504080
Greene King Abbot; Ruddles Best Bitter; guest beers Ⓗ
Large Wetherspoon conversion of a former hotel of the same name. It has distinct areas, with wood panelling or oak beams. There is a family area, and smoking is permitted outside at the rear. Five guest beers are served, usually including something local, plus Westons cider. The usual Wetherspoon food offering is available. The 16th-century building was previously the courthouse of the manor of Battesford. Q😊🌓≷🍴⌑−

Woodham Mortimer

Hurdlemakers Arms Ⓛ
Post Office Road, CM9 6ST (off A414)
🌓 12-11 (9 Sun) ☎ (01245) 225169
⊕ hurdlemakersarms.co.uk
Farmer's Golden Boar; Mighty Oak Kings; Wibblers Apprentice; guest beers Ⓗ
A 400-year-old Gray's country pub popular with walkers, cyclists, locals and families. Five handpumps mainly dispense beers from local microbreweries, often featuring monthly specials. There is a very substantial beer garden with children's play equipment and a barbecue area, while a quaint wooden barn and a modern marquee cater for functions. An annual beer festival is held on the last weekend of June. The pub is noted for its home-cooked food, available daily. ⚌Q🍷😊🌓&♣🍴P⌑−🚪(D2,31)

Writtle

Wheatsheaf Ⓛ
70 The Green, CM1 3DU (S of A1060)
🌓 11 2.30, 5.30 11, 11 midnight Fri & Sat, 12 11 Sun
☎ (01245) 420695
Adnams Southwold Bitter; Farmer's Drop of Nelson's Blood; Mighty Oak Oscar Wilde, Maldon Gold; Sharp's Doom Bar; Wibblers Apprentice Ⓗ
Traditional village pub with a small public bar, an equally compact lounge, and a covered patio for smokers by the road. It serves two guest beers from the wide Gray's list on gravity. The atmosphere is generally quiet, with televisions switched on only for occasional sporting events. A folk night is held on the third Friday of each month. Note the Gray's sign in the public bar.
Q🚪♣P⌑−🚪(45)

Pub opening hours

The Licensing Act of November 2005 for England and Wales gave pub owners the ability to apply for more flexible and extended opening hours from the licensing authorities. The most obvious change has been that many pubs now stay open until midnight or later at weekends. The experience has been that some pubs scaled down their opening hours where they found there was insufficient demand to remain open until midnight or later. The opening hours for pubs listed in the Guide have been checked before going to press, but readers planning to make journeys to pubs are advised to phone and check current hours.

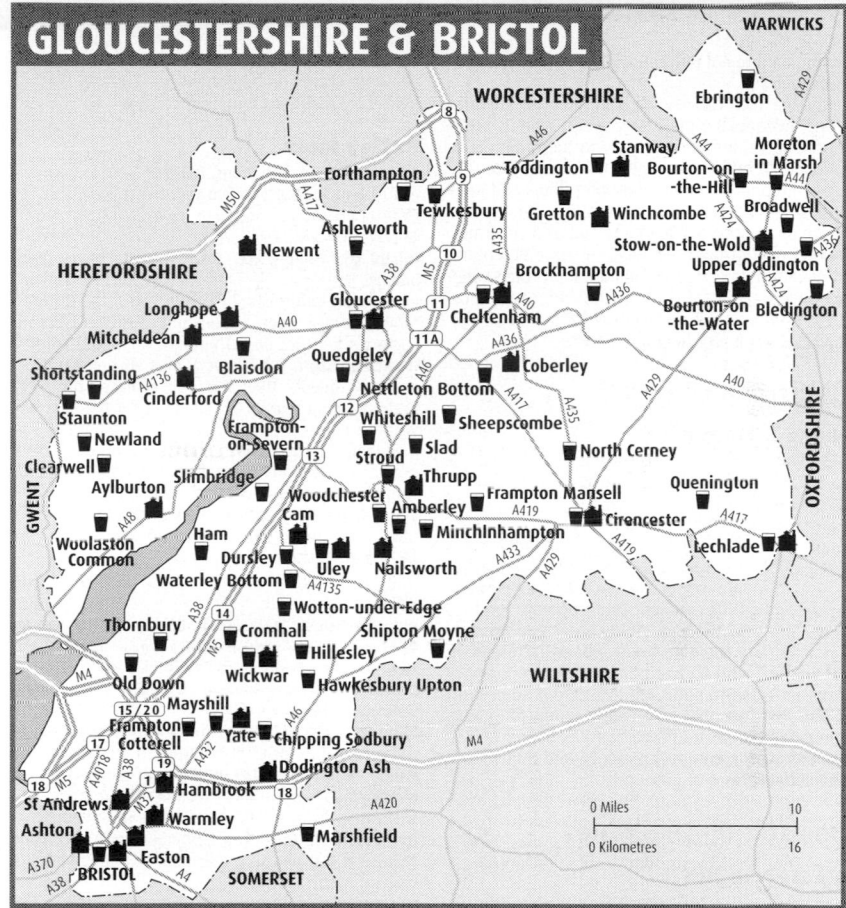

GLOUCESTERSHIRE & BRISTOL

Amberley

Amberley Inn L
Culver Hill, GL5 5AF
✪ 11-11 ☎ (01453) 872565 ⊕ theamberleyinn.co.uk
**Fuller's London Pride; Stroud Tom Long, Budding;
guest beers** Ⓗ
Gabled and mullioned hotel built of Cotswold stone
and situated on the edge of Minchinhampton
Common, from where it commands magnificent
views over the Woodchester Valley. It was rebuilt
in 1926 in Arts and Crafts style, with distinctive
door and window ironwork by Alfred Bucknell,
Ernest Gimson's blacksmith, and has two oak-
panelled bars with leaded glass, parquet floors and
log fires. The lounge is a tranquil haven, the public
bar popular with locals, and there is a small snug
across the corridor. Dogs and walkers welcome.
ﾑQ৲❀⏱⏱❶⏱⏱(28,127)

Ashleworth

Boat Inn L
The Quay, GL19 4HZ SO819251
✪ closed Mon; 11.30-3 (not Wed & Thu winter), 6.30-11.30;
12-11.30 Sun ☎ (01452) 700272 ⊕ boatinn.wordpress.com/
Beer range varies Ⓖ
This tranquil haven on the banks of the River
Severn is a real gem. Owned by the same family

for over 450 years, it serves microbrewery beers by
gravity along with eight ciders. The fireplace has a
bread oven in it. There is a covered courtyard with
tables and a grass area on the river edge with
more tables. Soup and rolls are available at
lunchtime. The pub has its own moorings and is
very popular in the summer. Q❀♣●P'–

Blaisdon

Red Hart L
GL17 0AH (middle of village)
✪ 12-3, 6 (7 Sun)-11 ☎ (01452) 830477 ⊕ redhartinn.co.uk
Young's Bitter; guest beers Ⓗ
A charming old pub with flagstone floors, low
beams and an open fire which, allied to chatty staff
and regulars, provides a welcoming atmosphere.
The guest beers are sourced from a wide area in a
variety of strengths, but local breweries always
feature, particularly Bespoke, with either a perry or
cider also available. A selection of good-value,
quality food sometimes proves so popular that
dining spreads into the bar area. There is a large,
family-friendly garden. ﾑ৲❀❶●P

Bledington

King's Head L
The Green, OX7 6XQ (on village green) SP243228

�🌑 11.30-11; 12-10.30 Sun ☎ (01608) 658365
🌐 kingsheadinn.net
Butcombe Original Bitter; Hook Norton Hooky Bitter; guest beers 🅗
Delightful 16th-century inn built in honey-coloured stone, overlooking the village green with its pretty brook, ducks and pet bantams. In the main bar original old beams, an inglenook with military brasses, open wood fire, flagstone floors and high-back settles create a cosy atmosphere. Quality food is served in both public rooms and in a separate, quieter dining room, while 12 en-suite bedrooms offer charming luxury accommodation. Guest ales are varied, often from Gloucestershire. Good local walks to nearby villages start close by.
🏚Q🌠🕏🏠🕪 🖼🗢(Kingham)♣P⅄⎯

Bourton-on-the-Hill

Horse & Groom 🏠

GL56 9AQ (at top of hill on main road)
🌑 11-2.30 (3 Sat), 6-11; 12-3.30 Sun ☎ (01386) 700413
🌐 horseandgroom.info
Goff's Jouster; guest beers 🅗
Grade II-listed Georgian stone inn serving three good-value local real ales. This is a family-run free house in private ownership since 2005, winning many awards for excellent contemporary food served in two attractive dining areas and the bar. The light, airy separate bar has been tastefully refurbished with an open fire. Two miles from Moreton in Marsh and close to Batsford Arboretum, it offers five refurbished en-suite rooms for guests. The delightful sheltered garden has plenty of seating, with views over the Cotswold countryside.
🏚Q🕏🏠🕪P🖼

Bourton-on-the-Water

Mousetrap Inn 🏠

Lansdowne, GL54 2AR (300yds W of village centre)
🌑 11.30-3, 6-11; 12-3, 6-10.30 Sun ☎ (01451) 820579
🌐 mousetrap-inn.co.uk
Butcombe Rare Breed; Hook Norton Old Hooky; guest beer 🅗
Attractive, traditional Cotswold-stone pub which is a family-run free house, in the quieter Lansdowne part of Bourton. It is popular with the local community as well as offering 10 comfortable en-suite letting rooms. The pub is known for its friendly service, carefully selected real ales and excellent home-cooked meals. A welcoming, cosy atmosphere is created with a feature fireplace and coal-effect fire. The patio area in front with tables and hanging baskets provides a sheltered suntrap in summer. Q🕏🏠🕪♣P🖼(801,855)

Bristol: Central

Bank

8 John Street, BS1 2HR (take lane by arcade in All Saints Lane)
🌑 12-midnight (1am Thu-Sat) ☎ (0117) 930 4691
🌐 banktavern.com
Beer range varies 🅗
Popular with a mixed crowd, this compact one-bar pub is right in the centre yet well hidden. A strong supporter of South West microbrewers, it offers three or four constantly varying ales, including dark or strong options, plus varying guest ciders. Food is served 12-4pm daily, with popular roasts on Sunday. Many live events and party nights take

place – including a summer fair and a Christmas party featuring live reindeer. Expect quirky humour, and ask about CAMRA discounts. Dogs allowed. Closes on bank holidays. Free Wi-Fi is available. 🏚🕮🕭🗢(Temple Meads)🍴⅄⎯🖼

Barley Mow

39 Barton Road, The Dings, BS2 0LP (400yds from rear exit of Temple Meads station over footbridge)
🌑 12-11 (11.30 Fri & Sat); 12-10 Sun ☎ (0117) 930 4709
🌐 barleymowbristol.com
Bristol Beer Factory Acer, No.7, seasonal beers; guest beer 🅗
Completely refurbished in early 2013, the Barley Mow has now been relaunched as Bristol Beer Factory's flagship pub. The eight handpulls offer two beers from the brewery plus six constantly changing guests. Beer menus are placed on every table. Regular events are planned for the second Wednesday of the month – all beer related including Tap Takeover nights featuring a different brewer every time. A small range of quality food changes frequently, with traditional roasts on Sunday. There are a few seats at the front and a patio to the rear, where dogs are welcome.
🏚🕮🕭🗢(Temple Meads)⅄⎯🖼

Bell

Hillgrove Street, Stokes Croft, BS2 8JT (off Jamaica St)
🌑 12-midnight (1am Fri); 4-1am Sat; 1-midnight Sun
☎ (0117) 909 6612 🌐 bell.butcombe.com
Bristol Beer Factory Sunrise; Butcombe Bitter, Gold, seasonal beer 🅗
Pleasant, eclectic, two-roomed pub where DJs often spin their discs from 10pm in the back room. Friday evenings attract drinkers on their way to nearby clubs, while local workers are regular customers for the lunchtime and early evening food. Sunday lunches are popular, too. A surprising feature is the pleasant rear garden with a patio,

INDEPENDENT BREWERIES

Arbor Bristol
Ashley Down Bristol: St Andrews
Bath Ales Bristol: Warmley
Battledown Cheltenham
Bespoke Mitcheldean
Bristol Beer Factory Bristol: Ashton
Ciren Cirencester (NEW)
Corinium Cirencester (NEW)
Cotswold Bourton on the Water
Cotswold Lion Coberley
Cotswold Spring Dodington Ash
Donnington Stow-on-the-Wold
Freeminer Cinderford
Gloucester Gloucester
Goff's Winchcombe
Great Western Bristol: Hambrook
Halfpenny Lechlade
May Hill Longhope
Nailsworth Nailsworth
Prescott Cheltenham
Rocket Science Yate (NEW)
Severn Vale Cam
Stanway Stanway
Stroud Thrupp
Terrace Aylburton (NEW)
Towles' Bristol: Easton
Uley Uley
Whittingtons Newent
Wickwar Wickwar
Zerodegrees Bristol

which is heated in colder weather. Local art on the wood-panelled walls adds a bohemian feel. There is a dartboard in the back room. ❀◐◑♣–🚌

Bridge Inn

16 Passage Street, BS2 0JF
⏲ 12-11.30 (midnight Fri & Sat); 6-11.30 Sun
☎ (0117) 929 0942
Bath Ales Gem; Dark Star Hophead; guest beers Ⓗ
Tiny pub close to the station, yet only a short walk from the city centre. Music industry memorabilia features and a collection of vinyl records is available to play. There is free Wi-Fi and occasional live music. Guest beers are adventurous, with two from high-quality microbreweries. Lunch is served weekdays, with just the curry of the week in the evenings until 10pm, except Sunday which is cheese night. Outside tables increase capacity in good weather. It now stocks a range of UK and US bottled beers. ❀◐⇌(Temple Meads)♣▯🚌

Colston Yard

Colston Street, BS1 5BD
⏲ 11-midnight (1am Fri); 12-1am Sat; 12-11 Sun
☎ (0117) 376 3232 🌐 colstonyard.butcombe.com
Butcombe Bitter, Gold, seasonal beers; guest beers Ⓗ
Impressive renovation of the old defunct Smiles Brewery and tap site, reopened by Butcombe in late 2007. The pub has a pleasant contemporary and airy feel. In addition to the Butcombe range there are always several guest ales (sometimes as many as six) and a number of interesting foreign draught and bottled beers. An extensive bar and restaurant menu features local produce, served lunchtimes and evenings. It's handy for the Colston Hall and Bristol Royal Infirmary. Outside tables are available in better weather. ❀◐◑♿🚌(20)

Cornubia

142 Temple Street, BS1 6EN (opp fire station)
⏲ 12-11 (11.30 Thu-Sat); closed Sun ☎ (0117) 925 4415
🌐 thecornubia.co.uk
Beer range varies Ⓗ
Genuine free house much developed over the past few years. A great selection of guest beers of all styles from all over is offered across the 10 handpumps – including a house beer brewed by Arbor and a changing real cider. The atmosphere is convivial, with a real fire, subtle lighting, pictures, patriotic flags and numerous pumpclips on the walls, and a turtle tank too. The bench seating outside is now surrounded by new wooden fencing. A must-visit pub where dogs are welcome. A CAMRA discount is offered.
🔥❀⇌(Temple Meads)🍎–🚌

Eldon House

6 Lower Clifton Hill, BS8 1BT (off top of Jacobs Wells Rd)
⏲ 12-3, 5-midnight; 12-1am Fri & Sat; 12-11 Sun
☎ (0117) 922 1271 🌐 theeldonhouse.com
Bath Ales Spa, Gem; guest beers Ⓗ
A tasteful extension in 2009 has not detracted from the traditional look and feel of this cosy end-of-terrace pub, which lies close to the busy Clifton Triangle area. Get off a bus at the top of Park Street and head a short way down Jacobs Wells Road. The four or five beers include guests from well-chosen independent brewers, often including one from Bristol Beer Factory. Good-quality food is served daily and Sunday roasts are popular. There is free Wi-Fi and many events are hosted. ◐◑🚌

Green Man

21 Alfred Place, Kingsdown, BS2 8HD
⏲ 4 (2 Sat)-11; 12-10.30 Sun ☎ (0117) 930 4824
Beer range varies Ⓗ
Small, dimly-lit Dawkins' pub, formerly known as the Bell, offering a selection of four or five independent guest beers, plus some from the Dawkins range. Home-cooked food comes from a small but interesting changing menu, and is mainly organic or ethically produced (served Fri and Sat eves and Sun afternoon). Organic ciders are offered too. The pub hosts two beer festivals per year, and morris men appear sometimes. There is a small patio to the rear for smokers. ◐◑🍎🚌(20)

Gryphon

41 Colston Street, BS1 5AP
⏲ 1-11 (1.30am Fri & Sat); 6-11 Sun ☎ 07894 239567
🌐 gryphonbristol.co.uk
Beer range varies Ⓗ
This pub is a shrine to dark beer and great rock/heavy metal music. Posters and guitars vie for space on the walls with many pumpclips for featured beers. Triangular in shape due to its corner plot and just a few yards uphill from Colston Hall, up to six handpumps dispense rapidly changing brews from all over, mostly dark and often strong. Live bands sometimes play upstairs and there are beer festivals in March and September. A CAMRA discount is offered. It may open earlier than shown.
◐◑🚌

Highbury Vaults

164 St Michaels Hill, Kingsdown, BS2 8DE
⏲ 12-midnight (11 Sun) ☎ (0117) 973 3203
🌐 highburyvaults.com
Bath Ales Spa; St Austell Tribute; Young's Bitter, Gold, Special; guest beers Ⓗ
In the same hands, and in this Guide, for many years, the pub is popular with students and hospital staff. Dating from the mid-19th century, its interior is dark and dimly lit, with a small front snug bar, main drinking area and a bar billiards table. Outside is a large heated patio and garden. Good-quality food is served every lunchtime and weekday evenings. Owned by Young's, the establishment is allowed some freedom with the beer range. Toilets are down steep stairs.
Q❀◐◑⇌(Clifton Down)♣–🚌(8,9)

Hillgrove Porter Stores

53 Hillgrove Street North, Kingsdown, BS2 8LT
⏲ 4-midnight (1am Fri); 2-1am Sat; 2-midnight Sun
☎ (0117) 924 9818
Dawkins Brassknocker, Bristol Best, seasonal beers; guest beers Ⓗ
The first of the Dawkins Taverns, the brainchild of a local entrepreneur who also bought Matthews Brewery in 2009. An excellent community pub, it usually dispenses up to seven guest ales, including dark beers and rare styles, plus Ashridge cider. The interior is horseshoe shaped, with a wonderfully comfortable lounge area hidden behind the bar, and there is a pleasant patio outside. Mini beer festivals are held in conjunction with the other Dawkins' pubs. Food is served 6-9pm, with – unusually – Sunday roasts 5-9pm. ❀◑♣🍎–🚌

Horse & Groom

17 St Georges Road, BS1 5UU (behind Council House)
⏲ 12-11; 1.30-7 Sun ☎ 07585 122581
St Austell Tribute, Proper Job; guest beers Ⓗ

Cosy city-centre pub directly behind the Council House on College Green and opposite a large car park – but do not expect change for it unless you stop for a drink. It acts as St Austell's showcase in Bristol but also features up to three guest beers. You may take drinks into the neighbouring Siam Angel Café or bring in food from there – symbiosis in action! The internet jukebox can play almost any music on demand. Sunday hours may extend as trade develops. Thatchers Heritage cider is served. ᴍ❀♣♠'ᐨ➡

King's Head ★
60 Victoria Street, BS1 6DE
❂ 11 (12 Sat)-11.30; 12-2.30, 6.30-11.30 Sun
☎ (0117) 929 2338
Butcombe Gold; Fuller's London Pride; Hogs Back TEA; Sharp's Doom Bar Ⓗ
Classic small pub, dating from at least 1660 and identified by CAMRA as one of Britain's Best Real Heritage Pubs. A narrow area around the bar leads to the tramcar snug at the rear. Pictures of old Bristol make fascinating viewing. An earlier landlady is reputed to haunt the pub. Popular food is served, weekday lunchtimes only. There are tables outside for summer drinking. A monthly quiz takes place on the third Thursday. The beer range changes occasionally. It's close to Temple Meads station and well served by buses. Q❀⑴≋(Temple Meads)➡

Old Fish Market
59-63 Baldwin Street, BS1 1QZ (200yds from city centre)
❂ 12-11 (midnight Fri & Sat); 12-10 Sun ☎ (0117) 921 1515
Butcombe Bitter; Fuller's London Pride, ESB, seasonal beers Ⓗ
Spacious Fuller's pub, once a fish market, that has become the main venue for a great pint and TV sport – all big events are screened, when it can get extremely busy. It has a large front bar and an indoor patio to the side, as well as several discreet seating booths behind the bar for those wishing to avoid the sport. Thai and English meals are served lunchtimes and evenings Monday to Friday and all day at weekends. Children are allowed until 9pm but no dogs. ⑴▶க≋(Temple Meads)➡

Orchard Inn
12 Hanover Place, Spike Island, BS1 6XT (off Cumberland Rd near SS Great Britain)
❂ 12 (11 Sat & Sun)-11 ☎ (0117) 926 2678
Fuller's London Pride; Otter Bitter Ⓗ**; guest beers** Ⓖ
Popular one-bar, street-corner local, close to the SS Great Britain and a 10-minute walk from the centre along the harbourside. It serves up to six guest beers on gravity, and up to 24 different ciders. Pies and rolls are served lunchtimes, with snacks at most other times. It's popular with Bristol City fans before home games. Live music is played some Saturday evenings and there is a big screen for sport. A real wood-burning stove is a new addition. ❀⑴♣♠'ᐨ➡(500)

Seven Stars
1 Thomas Lane, Redcliffe, BS1 6JG (just off Victoria St)
❂ 12-11 (10.30 Sun) ☎ (0117) 927 2845
Beer range varies Ⓗ
Small free house that was local CAMRA Pub of the Year 2011. Generous discounts for CAMRA members apply at all times, and for others in happy hour. Features are a pool table, a rock-oriented jukebox and outdoor seating. Eight

changing pumps dispense a full range of styles and strengths, plus ciders and perries. Quality live acoustic acts play on weekend afternoons. Beeriodicals are held on the first Monday to Thursday of every month, with 20 beers from a different county each time. Many who live miles away call this their local. Dogs welcome. ❀≋(Temple Meads)♣♠'ᐨ➡(1,54,X39)

Three Tuns
78 St Georges Road, Hotwells, BS1 5UR (300yds from cathedral towards Hotwells)
❂ 12-2.30, 4-11; 12-11 Thu (midnight Fri & Sat); 4-10.30 Sun
☎ (0117) 907 0689
Arbor Ales Brigstow, seasonal beers; guest beers Ⓗ
Run by Arbor Ales, this is independent beer nirvana. Seven pumps dispense the full range of beer styles, with two or three from Arbor and the rest from top-rated British brewers, plus many unusual bottled beers and several ciders. A CAMRA discount applies. The L-shaped interior has scrubbed wooden tables and mixed seating, plus a covered, heated rear patio. Food is limited to rolls and bar snacks. Unmissable beer festivals take place twice per year. Free Wi-Fi is available and dogs are allowed. Local CAMRA Pub of the Year 2012. ᴍ❀♠'ᐨ➡

Volunteer Tavern
9 New Street, BS2 9DX (very close to main Cabot Circus car park across carriageway from shops)
❂ 12-11 ☎ (0117) 955 8498 ⊕ volunteertavern.co.uk
Beer range varies Ⓗ
Tucked away in a side street but extremely close to Cabot Circus shops and convenient for Old Market and its bus interchange. Dating from 1670 and listed, it reopened in 2011 after being closed for six months. It has quickly become a popular fixture on the local scene, always with four changing beers including at least one dark one plus changing ciders. Regular beer festivals with 25-plus ales are held, and live music events. Food is served every day and is hugely popular on Sundays – book ahead. Dogs are welcome and there is free Wi-Fi. ❀⑴▶≋(Temple Meads)♠'ᐨ➡

Bristol: East

Chelsea Inn
60-62 Chelsea Road, Easton, BS5 6AU
❂ 1-midnight ☎ (0117) 329 1316 ⊕ thechelseabs5.co.uk
Beer range varies Ⓗ
Street-corner community local with one large room and a collection of vintage sofas, armchairs and other furniture. Pictures from local artists are for sale or commission. In a cosmopolitan area, it attracts a varied crowd, many relatively young. Free Wi-Fi and a small exchange library are available. Up to four changing beers are served and two ciders. Live music features, with jazz on Tuesday and eclectic choices on Wednesday and Saturday. Look for the interesting graffiti in the garden. Dog-friendly. ❀≋(Stapleton Rd)♣♠'ᐨ➡(6,7)

St Georges Hall
203 Church Road, Redfield, BS5 9HL (on A420)
❂ 9am-midnight ☎ (0117) 955 1488
Greene King Abbot; Ruddles Best Bitter; Sharp's Doom Bar; guest beers Ⓗ
Bustling suburban Wetherspoon establishment popular with the locals, located on the main A420 towards the east of the city. Up to seven guest ales

are sold, with a leaning towards stronger ones – Thornbridge Jaipur is a frequent visitor. A suggested guest beer list is on the bar and drinkers are encouraged to participate. Several ciders, including Westons, add to the appeal. Every Wednesday all real ale is discounted. There is a small patio area outside to the right as you enter.
Q✿🕭◑♿⬲(Lawrence Hill)●ᴸ–🚃(42,43,44)

Bristol: North

Annexe

Seymour Road, Bishopston, BS7 9EQ (directly behind Sportsman pub near county cricket ground)
🟠 11.30-3, 5-11.30; 11.30-11.30 Sat; 12-11 Sun
☎ (0117) 949 3931 ⏥ the-annexe.co.uk
St Austell Tribute; Sharp's Doom Bar; Taylor Landlord; Wye Valley HPA; guest beers Ⓗ
Community pub not far from the Memorial Stadium. Inside is a converted skittle alley and a large conservatory/family room to one side. Several TVs show live sport, including one out on the partially covered patio outside. Good wholesome food, including quality pizzas, is served, and a pool table is available. Monday is quiz night in this continuously improving pub, which is now quite adventurous with guest beers too. No dogs allowed. Q⬳✿🕭◑♿♣ᴸ–🚃(75,76)

Duke of York

2 Jubilee Road, St Werburghs, BS2 9RS
🟠 5-11; 4 (3 Sat)-midnight Fri; 3-11 Sun ☎ (0117) 941 3677
Beer range varies Ⓗ
Well-hidden free house serving an eclectic clientele. Visit in daylight for the enchanted forest mural exterior, then at night experience the warm glow of the grotto-like interior. The decor comprises fairy lights, odd memorabilia, wooden floors, a rare refurbished skittle alley, local art and more. There are two rooms, with an extra bar upstairs offering a quite different feel. Four handpumps serve unusual beers, plus real ciders from polypins and a good range of bottled ales.
🏚✿⬲(Montpelier)♣●ᴸ–🚃(5,25)

Miners Arms

136 Mina Road, St Werburghs, BS2 9YQ (400yds from M32 jct 3)
🟠 4-11 (midnight Fri); 2-midnight Sat; 12-11 Sun
☎ (0117) 907 9874
St Austell Tribute; Taylor Landlord; guest beers Ⓗ
Close to St Werburghs city farm and Bristol Climbing Centre, this is an excellent three-roomed street-corner local, part of the local Dawkins' chain and free of previous beer ties, with a split-level interior. Usually two guest beers and two from Dawkins join the regulars, along with Westons cider. Another small, quiet bar lies to the side, and a larger pool room to the rear. Children and dogs are welcome. The function room can be booked. Thursday is quiz night. Note the antique cigarette machine.
🏚✿🕰⬲(Montpelier)♣●ᴸ–🚃(5,25)

Bristol: South

Star & Dove

75-78 St Lukes Road, Totterdown, BS3 4RY (400yds from A37 in Totterdown)
🟠 12 (5 Mon)-midnight ☎ (0117) 933 2892
⏥ staranddove.co.uk
Beer range varies Ⓗ

Very large red brick street-corner pub, previously known as the Cumberland. Reopened a few years ago, it is now a thriving food and drink emporium with a strong local following. Three separate areas include one suitable for functions and there is also an à la carte restaurant upstairs. Up to six changing real ales are sold ranging from the common national brands to almost anything – as witnessed by the many pumpclips on show. Expect some surprises on the bottled beer list too.
🏚⬳✿🕭◑🕰⬲(Bedminster)ᴸ–🚃(20,512)

Victoria Park

66 Raymend Road, Bedminster, BS3 4QW (250yds off St Johns Lane)
🟠 11-11 (11.30 Fri & Sat); 11-10.30 Sun ☎ (0117) 330 6043
⏥ thevictoriapark.co.uk
Wye Valley Butty Bach; guest beers Ⓗ
Previously known as the Raymend, this red-brick building lies in a residential area, and is evidence that a failing suburban pub can be transformed into a thriving business. The interior has something of a gastro-pub feel but drinkers are most welcome. There is a large garden/patio area to the rear. Three pumps serve quality beers, usually including a dark offering. The interesting all-day menu is displayed on a chalkboard and a large drop-down screen shows major sports events.
⬳✿🕭◑⬲(Bedminster)♣ᴸ–🚃(20,90,91)

Windmill

14 Windmill Hill, Bedminster, BS3 4LU (100yds uphill from Bedminster station)
🟠 12-11 (midnight Fri & Sat); 12-10.30 Sun
☎ (0117) 963 5440 ⏥ thewindmillbristol.com
Bath Ales Gem; Bristol Beer Factory Sunrise; guest beer Ⓗ
With pastel colours and wooden flooring throughout, the pub is on two levels, with a family room on the lower area where children are welcome until 8pm. One beer from the nearby Bristol Beer Factory is always on offer, plus one or two guests, as well as real cider and foreign bottled beers. Good food is served all day until 10pm and Sunday roasts too. There is free Wi-Fi and an old 1970s jukebox. Outside is a small patio area to the front.
🏚⬳✿🕭◑⬲(Bedminster)●ᴸ–🚃(75,76,77)

Bristol: West

Hophouse

16 Kings Road, Clifton, BS8 4AB
🟠 12-11 (1am Fri-Sat); 12-10.30 Sun ☎ (0117) 923 7390
Beer range varies Ⓗ
A free house since 2011, this large open-plan pub is on two levels and adjoins the Victorian Clifton Arcade. The upstairs serves as the restaurant. Five regularly changing real ales are served, almost always from South West brewers – Moor is a particular favourite. In addition there are usually a couple of ciders from small producers. TV screens are used only for major rugby, golf or tennis events. The décor is predominantly wood and muted green tones, with tri-fold doors that open out at the front in summer. ✿◑♿●🚃(8,9)

Portcullis

3 Wellington Terrace, Clifton, BS8 4LE (close to Clifton side of suspension bridge)
🟠 4.30 (12 Sat)-11; 12-10.30 Sun ☎ (0117) 908 5536
Dawkins Bristol Best; guest beers Ⓗ

A pub since 1821 and rescued by Dawkins in 2008, with a downstairs bar and a quieter upstairs lounge that can be used for functions and events, with a supply of board games. Seven handpumps dispense two to four Dawkins' beers and a range of interesting guests from other micros in all styles and strengths. Real ciders and good value tapas-style nibbles are usually served. Several mini beer and cider festivals take place. The pub is dog friendly and offers free Wi-Fi. The rear garden is accessed from upstairs. ✪●🖾(8,9)

Prince of Wales

84 Stoke Lane, Westbury on Trym, BS9 3SP (off A4018, 5 mins walk from Westbury centre)
✪ 11-11 (midnight Fri); 12-10.30 Sun ☎ (0117) 962 3715
⊕ princeofwales.butcombe.com
Butcombe Bitter, Gold, seasonal beers; Fuller's London Pride; guest beers Ⓗ
Busy Butcombe-owned pub on the edge of Westbury village, with a magnificent exterior and a friendly, welcoming feel inside, with a number of drinking areas. Up to seven real ales are served including Butcombe seasonal beers and some from larger regional brewers. Meals are served lunchtimes only Monday to Saturday. Conversation dominates except when major rugby fixtures are shown on a drop-down large screen. You can escape to the large garden and patio at the rear in summer. Kids are welcome until 7pm.
Q✪◑‰🖾(1,20)

RAFA Club

Carlton Lodge, 38 Eastfield, Westbury on Trym, BS9 4BE (between Eastfield Rd and Grange Park)
✪ 12-2.30 (3 Fri & Sat), 7-11; 7.30-midnight Sat; 12-5 Sun
☎ (0117) 940 5300
Palmers Copper Ⓖ**, Dorset Gold; Wadworth 6X; Wye Valley Butty Bach; guest beers** Ⓗ
Run entirely by unpaid volunteers, this ex-RAF social club, based in a Georgian country house, offers up to two guest ales plus the regulars. Show your CAMRA card to gain entry. The bar features RAF memorabilia, pictures and models. A pool table is downstairs, and a skittles alley in an outbuilding, plus darts. The club hosts themed evenings on saints' days, and an annual beer and cider festival. Live music plays on Saturday evening. Q✪&♣P‰🖾(1,20,54)

Victoria

20 Chock Lane, Westbury on Trym, BS9 3EX (in small lane behind churchyard)
✪ 12-2.30, 6-11; 12-3, 7-10.30 Sun ☎ (0117) 950 0441
⊕ thevictoriapub.co.uk
Butcombe Bitter; Wadworth Henry's Original IPA, 6X, seasonal beer; guest beer Ⓗ
Once a courthouse, this traditional, relaxed and welcoming Wadworth-owned pub has been in this Guide for many years. A raised garden to the rear is a suntrap in summer. Pictures of Westbury as a village adorn the walls. Popular home-cooked food is available lunchtimes and evenings (no food Sun eve). Entertainment includes quizzes, themed meals and regular pub outings. Various societies meet here. Bonus card offers are now available if you provide your email address.
Q✪◑‰🖾(1,20,54)

Victoria

2 Southleigh Road, Clifton, BS8 2BH (off St Pauls Rd)
✪ 4 (12 Sat)-11; 12-10.30 Sun ☎ (0117) 974 5675
Dawkins Brassknocker, Bristol Best; guest beers Ⓗ

Grade II-listed, 19th-century Dawkins' tavern, tucked away just off the bottom of Whiteladies Road and next to the Clifton Lido. Six pumps offer a changing selection of independent beers and ciders, always including two or more from Dawkins Brewery. The walls are adorned with pumpclips and brewery mirrors, plus an amusing collection of obsolete keg fonts on a mantelpiece. Regular events including beer festivals and quizzes are held. An ever-increasing stock of bottled Belgian beers is available. Parking close by is difficult. Dog-friendly. ♨Q≋(Clifton Down)●🖾(1,40,54)

White Lion

Passage Road, Westbury on Trym, BS9 3HW
✪ 11.30-11 ☎ (0117) 959 2897
Bath Ales Gem; Butcombe Bitter; Sharp's Doom Bar; guest beers Ⓗ
Sprawling, smart Ember Inns pub just a short stroll from the Westbury village centre. The long curved bar serves several large areas, made more homely by partitioning that leaves plenty of secluded nooks and crannies. While very big on food service there is also plenty for the drinker. Up to three guest beers are served from the seasonal Ember list and are often from breweries not often seen locally. Suggestions for future guests are welcome. Quizzes are Wednesdays and Sundays and there is free Wi-Fi. ♨Q☎✪◑&P‰🖾(1,20)

Broadwell

Fox Inn Ⓛ

The Green, GL56 0UF (off A429 in village centre) SP202276
✪ 11-2.30, 6-11; 12-3, 7-10.30 Sun ☎ (01451) 870909
Donnington BB, SBA Ⓗ
Attractive stone-built hostelry overlooking the village green, one of the best Donnington pubs. The beers are good value, brewed only a few miles away, and popular with visitors. A friendly local, it offers good company and quality home-cooked food. Features include original flagstone flooring in the bar area, jugs hanging from beams and Aunt Sally played in the garden. At the back is a camping and caravan site with local walks. A special experience is assured at this family-run pub.
♨Q✪◑▲♣P‰🖾

Brockhampton

Craven Arms Ⓛ

Kingsbury Street, GL54 5XQ (off A436 in centre of village) SP035224
✪ closed Mon; 12-3, 6-11; 12-11 Sat; 12-5 Sun
☎ (01242) 820410 ⊕ thecravenarms.co.uk
Cotswold Spring Stunner; Otter Bitter; guest beers Ⓗ
Spacious 17th-century pub, with carefully kept and selected beers. Set in an attractive hillside village with truly outstanding views and walks, it has a bar area with an open fire and an excellent dining room separated by church-style stone windows. A beer festival is held on the second weekend in July in the garden. Handy for nearby Sudeley Castle, this is a well-managed gem, run by a really enthusiastic, friendly family who also organise functions for locals each month. Local CAMRA 2012 Pub of the Year. ♨Q☎✪⌂♨◑⊞&▲♣P

Cheltenham

Cheltenham Motor Club ⓛ

Upper Park Street, GL52 6SA (access from A40 London Rd via Crown Passage)

✪ 6 (12 Sat)-midnight; 7-midnight Sun ☎ (01242) 522590
⊕ cheltmc.com

Stroud Tom Long; guest beers Ⓗ

CAMRA members are very welcome at this friendly club, National Club of the Year winner for 2013 and a multiple winner of Gloucestershire and South West Regional Club of the Year. Three regularly changing ales – four at weekends and busy times – from breweries throughout the country feature alongside Stroud Tom Long and Thatchers cider. The Club hosts two beer festivals annually (one in September for charity, one on New Year's Eve/Day), and is home to local league quiz, darts and pool teams. Q✆♣♠P'-₪(B)

Jolly Brewmaster ⓛ

39 Painswick Road, GL50 2EZ

✪ 3-11; 12-10.30 Sun ☎ (01242) 772261

Beer range varies Ⓗ

Local CAMRA Pub of the Year and runner-up 2012 South West Regional Cider Pub of the Year. Seven handpumps feature a changing range of ales from Gloucestershire and beyond, alongside Black Rat cider and perry and a choice of Gwynt y Ddraig ciders. Relaxed and friendly, this busy pub features original etched windows, a horseshoe bar and an open fire. The attractive beer garden serves as an extra room in the summer and offers winter warmth for smokers. ஜQ❀♠'-₪(10)

Moon Under Water ⓛ

16-28 Bath Road, GL53 7HA

✪ 9am-midnight (1am Fri & Sat) ☎ (01242) 583945

Greene King Abbot; Ruddles Best Bitter; guest beers Ⓗ

An open-plan Lloyds No.1 near the east end of the pedestrianised high street, once a car showroom. The decked area at the rear overlooks the River Chelt and Sandford Park, and there is a municipal car park within 100 yards. Some five changing guest ales from a wide range of microbreweries supplement the standard beers, with Westons Marcle Hill and Old Rosie ciders to boot. The dance floor is used only Friday and Saturday from 8pm. Food is served 8am-10pm. ➳❀◑⅘♠'-₪

Moran's Eating House

123-129 Bath Road, GL53 7LS (approx ½ mile from centre at town end of Bath Road shopping area)

✪ 10-11; closed Sun ☎ (01242) 581411
⊕ moranseatinghouse.co.uk

Taylor Landlord; guest beer Ⓗ

Highly regarded as a restaurant, the separate impressive bar has evolved into a superb ale and wine bar for general socialising, and now serves two ales, usually Timothy Taylor Landlord and another changing guest, typically from Wye Valley, Purity, Box Steam or Bespoke. The interesting bar menu including tapas, platters, speciality sandwiches and hand-made cakes is worth contemplating. There is a pleasant conservatory to the rear and outdoor seating in a covered courtyard to the front. ➳❀◑'-₪(F,46)

Royal Oak ⓛ

43 The Burgage, Prestbury, GL52 3DL

✪ 11.30-11; 12-10.30 Sun ☎ (01242) 522344
⊕ royal-oak-prestbury.co.uk

Taylor Landlord; guest beers Ⓗ

Attractive 16th-century village free house, the closest pub to Prestbury Park racecourse. The quiet public bar features oak beams, parquet flooring, equine prints and a logburner. Good-quality food is served in the lounge bar with daily specials (booking advised). Two changing guest beers feature alongside Thatchers cider. A large garden hosts an annual beer festival in May and cider festival in August, and is home to the Pavilion skittle alley and function room. Parking is limited. ஜQ❀◑♠P'-₪(A)

Royal Union Bar & Grill ⓛ

37 Hatherley Street, GL50 2TT

✪ 12-11 (midnight Fri & Sat) ☎ 07957 577450

Sharp's Doom Bar; guest beers Ⓗ

At least four changing guest ales from near and far supplement the four regulars (at least one of which is local) in this pub, which has been brought into the 21st century. A Belgian beer festival is hosted annually. Over 20 single malts are also available, as well as a great range of good-value wines. Food is normally served all day, ranging from snacks lunchtime to speciality sharing menus in the evening (no food Mon & Tue eves). On Sundays only brunch is served. ஜQ➳❀◑♣♠'-₪(94)

Strand ⓛ

40-42 High Street, GL50 1EE

✪ 12-11; 10-midnight Sat; 12-10.30 Sun ☎ (01242) 511848
⊕ strandpub.co.uk

Beer range varies Ⓗ

Modern, comfortable pub at the east end of the High Street, offering five beers including at least one from the featured brewery of the month, plus a cider. Good-value food is served daily (12-2.30pm, 6-9pm Mon-Fri; 12-8pm Sat; 12-4pm Sun), with a gourmet burger night on Wednesday. An upstairs function room is available for hire, along with a cellar bar that is home to live comedy on the last Thursday of the month and music most Friday nights. A large garden and patio provide a pleasant outdoor drinking venue. ❀◑♠'-₪

Chipping Sodbury

Grapes

45 Rounceval Street, BS37 6AS

✪ 12-midnight (11 Sun) ☎ (01454) 312145
⊕ thegrapeschippingsodbury.com

Beer range varies Ⓗ

After seven years as part of the neighbouring Indian restaurant, and still sharing its toilets, the Grapes re-emerged as a community pub in its own right in 2009. It has since gone from strength to strength and now features up to six changing guest beers from all over the UK, including dark and/or strong brews. The interior features an open fireplace with a logburner and various bits of furniture and knick-knacks – some donated by locals. Darts and crib teams play here and board games are available. ஜ❀♣♠'-₪(342,581)

Cirencester

Corinium Hotel ⓛ

12 Gloucester Street, GL7 2DG (off A435 N of town centre)

✪ 11-11 (10.30 Sun) ☎ (01285) 659711
⊕ coriniumhotel.co.uk

Beer range varies Ⓗ

Agreeable 2-star hotel with a discreet frontage entered via an attractive, narrow courtyard; this leads into a slightly idiosyncratic interior, with a comfortable lounge area complete with woodburner. The varying thickness and layout of the walls hint at the building's heritage as an Elizabethan wool merchant's house. Three guest ales usually include at least one LocAle. A modern vestibule goes through to a smart dining room and the pleasant suntrap of a garden at the rear.
⚄☸☏⬥⏣⬥P🍽

Drillmans Arms
34 Gloucester Road, Stratton, GL7 2JY (on old A417 N of jct with A435)
☸ 11-2.30, 5.30-midnight; 11-midnight Sat; 12-4.30, 7-11 Sun ☎ (01285) 653892
Sharp's Doom Bar; guest beers Ⓗ
This busy roadside hostelry is a great community hub, its interior featuring low-beamed ceilings and a wood-burning stove, creating a warm and welcoming atmosphere. Current local CAMRA Pub of the Year again, three beers change regularly for those who welcome something different to sample. The lunchtime menu is popular and there is a smaller rear bar adjacent to the skittle alley/function room that regularly fills with darts, pool and skittles teams. A beer festival is hosted on the August bank holiday weekend. ⚄☸🅟⬥P⛟🚃

Waggon & Horses Ⓛ
11 London Road, GL7 2PU (on road to centre from A435 roundabout)
☸ closed Sun & Mon; 5-11 ☎ (01285) 652022
⬡ thewaggonandhorses.co.uk
Beer range varies Ⓗ
With the bar counter in front of the entrance, the eye is drawn to the vast array of alcoholic beverages offered beyond the usual five guest beers (Arbor Ales are popular) and Thatchers cider on handpump. A fine balance between the Thai cuisine and drinking sides of this modern pub has been achieved, with a more formal dining area and separate function room at the rear. A real fire and some subtle decorating make this a cracking location to spend an evening. ⚄☸⬥●⛟🚃

Clearwell

Lamb Ⓛ
High Street, GL16 8JU SO570081
☸ closed Mon & Tue; 6-11 Wed & Thu; 12-3, 6-11 Fri & Sat; 12-4, 7-10.30 Sun ☎ (01594) 835441
Wye Valley Bitter; guest beers Ⓖ
A village local with two bars: a tidy snug with a woodburner and a main bar with an open fire. The main room has large, attractive settles alongside long tables flanking the fireplace, making an ideal setting for family or group occasions. The beer selection is indicated on the defunct handpumps, as all the ales are poured straight from the cask in the cellar directly behind the bar. Most of the ales are sourced from local brewers. ⚄Q☸⬥⬥P⛟

Cromhall

Royal Oak Ⓛ
Bibstone, GL12 8AD (3 miles E of jct 14 of M5 on B4058)
☸ 11 (4 Mon)-11 ☎ (01454) 261638
GWB Maiden Voyage; guest beers Ⓗ
Built in 1674, this spacious single-bar pub is situated in the hamlet of Bibstone. It has a

separate games room and a dining area with an impressive Jacobean inglenook fireplace (the restaurant is shut Mondays). The main bar area has a well and a splendid stained glass window behind the bar. Children are welcome until 9pm and there is disabled access. Dogs are not allowed in the pub.
⚄Q☸⬥⬥P

Dursley

Old Spot Ⓨ Ⓛ
2 Hill Road, GL11 4JQ (next to bus station)
☸ 11 (12 Sun)-11 ☎ (01453) 542870 ⬡ oldspotinn.co.uk
Uley Old Ric; guest beers Ⓗ
Current county CAMRA Pub of the Year, this award-winning free house dates from 1776, serving up to eight independent ales. Named after the Gloucestershire Old Spot pig, a porcine theme blends with the extensive brewery memorabilia, low ceilings and log fires to create a convivial atmosphere. The pretty garden has a heated, covered area. Wholesome, freshly prepared dishes complement the pub's enthusiasm for real ale. On the Cotswold Way, it hosts regular beer festivals, and is adjacent to ample free parking.
⚄Q☸⬥⛟⬥●⛟🚃

Ebrington

Ebrington Arms Ⓛ
GL55 6NH (centre of village by green) SP186399
☸ 12-11 ☎ (01386) 593223 ⬡ theebringtonarms.co.uk
Prescott Hill Climb; Stroud Budding; Uley Bitter; guest beers Ⓗ
Local CAMRA Pub of the Year 2009-11 and runner-up in 2012, this 17th-century Cotswold-stone free house serves five selected beers, mainly from Gloucestershire. It has an attractive low-beamed bar with three cosy separate dining rooms, all with open fires. The family-run inn serves high-quality food – its varied menu recently gained two AA rosettes. Two miles from Chipping Campden and popular with the local community, it has five en-suite letting rooms. On fine days you can sit in a beautiful walled garden. ⚄Q☸⬥⏣Å⬥P

Forthampton

Lower Lode Inn Ⓛ
GL19 4RE (follow sign to Forthampton from A438 Tewkesbury-Ledbury road) SO878317
☸ 12-midnight (2am Fri & Sat) ☎ (01684) 293224
⬡ lowerlodeinn.co.uk
Donnington BB; Malvern Hills Black Pear; Sharp's Doom Bar; guest beers Ⓗ
An attractive brick-built 15th-century coaching inn. Note the stained glass before admiring the three acres of lawned frontage looking across the River Severn to Tewkesbury Abbey, complete with moorings and a private slipway. This is a licensed touring park site, with en-suite accommodation, day fishing licences and a separate function room available. Regular ales are complemented by changing guests (two in winter, three in summer). An annual beer festival takes place in September. A ferry operates Easter to October.
⚄Q⛟☸⬥⏣⬥Å⬥P⛟

Frampton Cotterell

Globe
366 Church Rd, BS36 2AB

✪ 12-11 (10.30 Sun) ☎ (01454) 778286
⊕ theglobeframptoncotterell.co.uk
**Butcombe Bitter; Fuller's London Pride; Uley Pigs Ear;
guest beers** Ⓗ
Independent free house situated on the Frome Valley walkway, which links the Cotswolds with the Avon Valley walkway. An open-plan pub with a separate pavillion that can be hired for functions, it specialises in home-made food using local produce. The pub has an active golf society, a Tuesday quiz and caters for children with an excellent play area. Three guest beers are normally available and include many local brews. Moles Black Rat cider is served. ▲▷☼◖◗➡P⌐🖳(581)

Rising Sun
43 Ryecroft Road, BS36 2HN
✪ 11.30-11.30 (midnight Fri & Sat); 12-11 Sun
☎ (01454) 772330
Butcombe Bitter; Draught Bass; Great Western Maiden Voyage, Classic Gold, seasonal beers; guest beer Ⓗ
The brewery tap for the Great Western Brewery, owned by the same family that has run this excellent free house for many years. At least two Great Western beers and at least one guest are available. The three-roomed interior comprises the main bar, a small snug, and a conservatory/restaurant. Food is served all day (until 8pm Sun). There is also a skittle alley/function room, a covered smoking area, an enclosed child-safe beer garden and free Wi-Fi.The pub has featured in almost every edition of this Guide.
Q☼◖◗♣P⌐🖳(581)

Frampton Mansell

Crown Inn Ⓛ
GL6 8JG (off A419 Cirencester to Stroud road opp petrol station)
✪ 12-midnight ☎ (01285) 760601
⊕ thecrowninn-cotswolds.co.uk
Butcombe Bitter; Stroud Organic Ale; Uley Laurie Lee's Bitter; guest beer Ⓗ
A thriving village local dating back to 1633, when it was a cider house with a slaughterhouse next to it. The three rooms feature exposed stone walls and wooden beams, all with an open fire. In summer the fires are replaced by lighted candles and the suntrap front garden offers fine views over the Golden Valley. Children are welcome and there are even children's books available. The pub has a modern 12-bedroom hotel annexe with ample car parking. ▲Q▷☼🚃◖◗🍴&P⌐🖳(54,54A)

Frampton-on-Severn

Bell Inn
The Green, GL2 7EP
✪ 11-11 ☎ (01452) 740346 ⊕ thebellatframpton.co.uk
Butcombe Bitter; Mole's Elmo's Fire, Rucking Mole; guest beer Ⓗ
Imposing three-storey Georgian inn overlooking the longest village green in England, where cricket is regularly played in summer. A former barn alongside is used for meetings and skittles; a second barn delights children with its farm animal collection. High-quality home-cooked food is served until 9pm (8pm Sun), and there are themed evenings. Thatchers cider is available. Accommodation comprises two suites and two double rooms. It is on national cycle route 41, close to both the canal and M5. ▲Q☼🚃◖◗♣➡P⌐

Gloucester

Dick Whittington Ⓛ
100 Westgate Street, GL1 2PE
✪ 11-11 (midnight Thu-Sat); 12-midnight Sun
☎ (01452) 502039
Butcombe Bitter; Wells Bombardier; guest beers Ⓗ
The imposing 18th-century brick frontage of this Grade I-listed building masks a 15th-century structure that was the Whittington family's town house until 1546. Offering up to five guest ales and three ciders, the Victorian-style bar blends well with the spacious medieval interior. Home-cooked food is served 12-9pm (until 6pm Sun). There are occasional themed evenings, musical events and Meet the Brewer nights. A spacious cellar bar hosts private functions, with a patio/garden for smokers. Q☼◖◗➡🕭⌐

Fountain Inn Ⓛ
53 Westgate Street, GL1 2NW
✪ 11-11 (midnight Fri & Sat); 12-11 Sun ☎ (01452) 522562
Hook Norton Hooky Mild; Purity Pure Gold; St Austell Tribute; guest beers Ⓗ
Seventeenth-century inn on a site where ale was almost certainly being served in 1216. The main entrance leads from Westgate Street into a courtyard ablaze with flowers in summer. The Cathedral Bar has a panelled ceiling, a carved stone fireplace and log fire. A modernised ground floor function room doubles as a bar overflow, while an upstairs room hosts meetings and Victorian music hall evenings. Four guest ales include a local offering. ▲Q☼◖◗&🕭♣⌐

Linden Tree
73-75 Bristol Road, GL1 5SN (on A430 S of docks)
✪ 11.30-2.30, 6-11; 11.30-11.30 Fri & Sat; 12-11 Sun
☎ (01452) 527869 ⊕ lindentreegloucester.co.uk
Wadworth Henry's Original IPA, Horizon, 6X, Bishops Tipple, seasonal beer Ⓗ; **guest beers** Ⓖ
Part of a Grade II-listed Georgian terrace, this is a very popular community pub. Its modest entrance masks an interior not untypical of a Cotswold pub. The open fire, warm colour scheme and somewhat eccentric decorative features contribute to a homely atmosphere. The skittle alley opens up to provide extra space when needed. Up to three guest beers are available from family brewers. Substantial home-cooked meals are offered (no food Sat/Sun eves). Accommodation is reasonably priced. ▲Q☼🚃◖◗♣⌐🖳(12)

Pelican Inn Ⓛ
4 St Mary's Street, GL1 2QR
✪ 11-midnight ☎ (01452) 387877
Wye Valley Bitter, HPA, Butty Bach, Dorothy Goodbody's Wholesome Stout Ⓗ
Licensed as an alehouse in the 17th-century, it is thought that some of its beams could have come from Drake's Golden Hind, which began life as the Pelican. Rescued and refurbished by Wye Valley Brewery in 2012, the pub rapidly gained popularity among the city's ale drinkers. The single bar is dominated by conversation; there is a smaller room to the side and an attractive outdoor area. Ciders and perry come from Westons and Severn Cider. No food is served. ▲Q☼&🕭♣🕭⌐

Gretton

Royal Oak L

Gretton Road, GL54 5EP (at E end of village, 1½ miles from Winchcombe)
🌣 12-11 (10.30 Sun) ☎ (01242) 604999
⊕ royaloakgretton.co.uk
Brakspear Oxford Gold; Jennings Cockerhoop; Wye Valley HPA; guest beers Ⓗ
Re-entry of a Guide regular following a major refurbishment, now with six handpumps, including some beers from Marston's. The Royal Oak was voted most-improved North Cotswold Pub in 2013, serving home-cooked food in two areas and boasting a stunning conservatory with superb views over the local GWR steam railway and distant hills. There are excellent walks nearby and a tennis court for hire in the garden, which has new furniture and chickens. It is advisable to book at weekends. Local owners have established a fresh treasure in an outstanding location.
🏠❄🕯🌜🕔🛏♣P▸

Ham

Salutation L

Ham Green, Berkeley, GL13 9QH (from Berkeley take road signed Jenner Museum) ST681984
🌣 12-2.30 (not Mon), 5-11; 11-11 Sat; 12-10.30 Sun
☎ (01453) 810284 ⊕ salutationinn.biz
Cotswold Spring Stunner; Severn Vale Dursley Steam Bitter; guest beers Ⓗ
An attractive, welcoming hostelry that has won several CAMRA awards recently. A proper rural free house, it sources its beers and ciders from local producers where possible and is popular with walkers and cyclists. It is situated in the Severn Valley, within walking distance of the Jenner Museum, Berkeley Castle and Deer Park. There are two cosy bars with a log fire and a skittle alley/function room. Food is served lunchtimes and early evening. A pretty, child-friendly garden adorns the front. 🏠Q🕯🌜🕔🛏♣🕯P

Hawkesbury Upton

Beaufort Arms L

High Street, GL9 1AU (off A46, 6 miles N of M4 jct 18)
🌣 12-11 (10.30 Sun) ☎ (01454) 238217
⊕ beaufortarms.com
Bath Spa; Bristol Beer Factory No.7; guest beers Ⓗ
Built in 1602, this Grade II-listed Cotswold stone free house is close to the historic Somerset Monument. It has separate public and lounge bars, a dining room and a skittle alley/function room. Up to five ales and a traditional cider are on handpump. The pub contains an ever-increasing amount of ancient brewery and local memorabilia. Outside is an attractive garden (complete with barbecue). This warm, welcoming pub is at the centre of most local community activities.
🏠Q🕯🌜🕔🛏♣A♣🕯P▸

Hillesley

Fleece Inn L

Chapel Lane, GL12 7RD (Between Wotton-Under-Edge and Hawkesbury-Upton)
🌣 11-11 (midnight Fri & Sat) ☎ (01453) 520003
⊕ thefleeceinnhillesley.com
Butcombe Bitter; guest beers Ⓗ
An attractive 17th-century community-owned pub with a single bar with a separate lounge/dining room and a snug area. The extensive menu is mainly sourced from local produce. The pub operates a 10% discount for CAMRA members on the real ales, which are mainly sourced from local micros. Thatcher's Heritage cider is available on handpump. Children and dogs are welcome and the garden has a safe play area with limited access to the large car park. 🏠Q🕯🌜🕔🛏♣🕯P▸

Lechlade

Crown Inn L

High Street, GL7 3AE (opp traffic lights at A417/A361 jct)
🌣 12-midnight (11 Sun) ☎ (01367) 252198
⊕ crownlechlade.co.uk
Halfpenny Ha'penny Ale, Thames Tickler, Four Seasons, Old Lech, seasonal beers Ⓗ
The centre of the expanding Halfpenny Brewery empire, this twin-roomed, wooden-floored brewpub flourishes, with up to six Halfpenny ales available. Renowned for its parties, friendly clientele and unusual choice of games (including Aunt Sally), this enthusiastic establishment makes for a memorable drinking experience. Two fireplaces flank the front room, and an eclectic array of paraphernalia adorns the walls. A beer festival is hosted on the August bank holiday weekend. 🏠🕯🌜🕔♣A♣🕯P▸

Marshfield

Catherine Wheel L

High Street, SN14 8LR (off A420 between Chippenham and Bristol)
🌣 12-11 ☎ (01225) 892220 ⊕ thecatherinewheel.co.uk
Butcombe Bitter; Cotswold Spring Stunner; Sharp's Doom Bar Ⓗ
Attractively restored Georgian-fronted pub on the village High Street. From the front door lies a pretty dining room to the left and an L-shaped bar off to the right with a log-burning stove, in turn leading to quieter rooms to the rear. Three regular beers are complemented by an occasional guest for special events. Curry night is on the first Thursday and music night on the last Thursday of every month. It is a very friendly local where dogs are also welcome. 🏠Q🕯🌜🕔🛏♣P▸(635)

Mayshill

New Inn

Badminton Road, BS36 2NT (on A432 between Coalpit Heath and Nibley)
🌣 11.45-3, 5.30-11 (10 Mon; 10.30 Tue); 11.45-11 Fri & Sat; 12-10 Sun ☎ (01454) 773161
Beer range varies Ⓗ
A 17th-century inn hugely popular for its food (including gluten-free options), so book ahead. Expect three changing guest beers from far and wide – one of them likely to be dark – plus a changing cider. The main bar is warmed by a real fire in winter, and the rear area is more of a restaurant. Children are welcome until 8.45pm. The garden, with play area, is pleasant in summer. Generous beer discounts are available to CAMRA members on Sunday and Monday evenings. The pub offers free Wi-Fi.
🏠Q🕯🌜🕔🕯P▸(X42,342,581)

Minchinhampton

Weighbridge Inn Ⓛ

Longfords, GL6 9AL (on road from Nailsworth to Avening near Longford Mill)

✪ 12-11 (10.30 Sun) ☎ (01453) 832520 ⊕ 2in1pub.co.uk

Uley Old Spot; Wadworth 6X; guest beer Ⓗ

Whitewashed and imposing, the Weighbridge stands beside the original packhorse trail to Bristol (now a bridleway). The road in front became a turnpike in 1822 and there was a public weighbridge next to the pub. Inside are stone walls decorated with agricultural artefacts and exposed beams hung with a large collection of keys from neighbouring mills. Log fires provide winter warmth. The Wadworth 6X is particularly highly regarded and the guest beer is often from a local micro. ᴹQ🍴🛏️◐🍺🅿️⟲

Moreton in Marsh

Inn on the Marsh

Stow Road, GL56 0DW (on A429 at S end of town)

✪ 12-2.30 (3 Sun), 7-11; 11-3, 6-11 Thu-Sat & summer ☎ (01608) 650709

Marston's Pedigree; Ringwood Best Bitter; guest beers Ⓗ

A charming Marston's pub offering two interesting house guest ales from the group's range. Next to a duck pond, this former bakery features woven hanging baskets on display. The bar area has a cosy, dedicated locals' section, and a welcoming lounge area with an open fire and comfortable seating. The charming large conservatory serves good-value food with a Dutch East Indies influence, and is ideal for parties. One of the very best pubs in Moreton, it holds small beer festivals at intervals throughout the year. ᴹQ🛏️◐⛿Å⟲♣🍺🅿️⟲🚆

Nettleton Bottom

Golden Heart Ⓛ

GL4 8LA (on A417)

✪ 10.30-3, 5-11; 10.30-11 Fri & Sat; 10-11 Sun ☎ (01242) 870261 ⊕ thegoldenheart.co.uk

Brakspear Bitter; Cotswold Lion Best in Show; Otter Bitter; guest beer Ⓗ

Four-hundred-year-old Cotswold free house beside the single carriageway section of the Swindon to Gloucester road. Its large log fire, bare stone walls, mixed furniture and assorted mementos ooze rustic charm. The finest locally sourced produce contributes to the national award-winning food (served all day Sat & Sun). Children are fully catered for. To the rear, a large stone-paved patio and lawn abut a cow pasture. Two en-suite bedrooms are available, and caravan parking is permitted. ᴹQ🛏️🍴◐🅿️⟲

Newland

Ostrich Inn

GL16 8NP

✪ 12-3, 7-11 ☎ (01594) 833260 ⊕ theostrichinn.com

Beer range varies Ⓗ

A charming, largely unspoilt pub on the western edge of the Forest of Dean, adjoining the Wye Valley. This fine hostelry has a wealth of flagstones, beams and period features to admire, and offers up to eight ales depending on the season. A wide-ranging menu usually features some more unusual items. The church opposite the

pub is known as the Cathedral of the Forest, where the deceased from the Royal Forest of Dean were brought for their final resting place. ᴹQ🛏️◐Å

North Cerney

Bathurst Arms Ⓛ

GL7 7BZ (on A435)

✪ 12-11 ☎ (01285) 831281 ⊕ bathurstarms.com

Wickwar Coopers IPA, seasonal beers; guest beers Ⓗ

Built in 1699, this old wheelwright's house (an original template still adorns the attractive garden) has been selling ale since the Beer Act of 1830. Bordering the River Churn, the spacious hostelry has two main areas: the left-hand side of the building for LocAle-seeking drinkers, featuring flagstone floors and an inglenook fireplace, the other half given over to the restaurant and dining areas. Several small beer festivals are hosted each year to slake the thirsts of the pub's rowing club. ᴹ🛏️♣◐🅿️🚆(151)

Old Down

Fox Inn

Inner Down, BS32 4PR

✪ 12-3, 6-11; 12-11 Sun ☎ (01454) 412507

Butcombe Bitter; Draught Bass; Sharp's Doom Bar; guest beers Ⓗ

Tucked away in the small hamlet of Old Down, this is a cosy 18th-century inn with an L-shaped bar and low wooden beams. Old prints of the pub and of Bristol adorn the walls. A wide choice of high-quality food is served. There is a small children's room as well as a play area in the pleasant garden. The well-lit veranda outside is covered by a grapevine. Six pumps dispense the regulars plus guests, mainly sourced from regional brewers. Moles Black Rat cider is also served. Q🛏️◐🍺🅿️⟲

Quedgeley

Haywain

Bristol Road, GL2 4PE

✪ 11.30-11; 12-10.30 Sun ☎ (01452) 720124 ⊕ haywainpubquedgeley.co.uk

Banks's Bitter; Marston's Pedigree; Wychwood Hobgoblin; guest beer Ⓗ

Spacious, modern estate pub built in 1985, but already with its third name. A reproduction of the Constable masterpiece greets customers on entry, and a portrait of the artist complements framed pictures throughout. A horseshoe bar takes centre stage, and prominent pillars help to create some discrete seating areas, with table service for food. A quality two-for-one menu is available. It is ideal for families, with its internal and external children's play area and large outdoor seating space. 🛏️◐🅿️

Quenington

Keepers Arms

Church Road, GL7 5BL

✪ 12-3 (not Mon & Tue), 7-11 ☎ (01285) 750349 ⊕ thekeepersarms.co.uk

Beer range varies Ⓗ

A proper community hub, its young, enthusiastic owners have modernised even more of this once-dour village free house. Dogs, children and cricketers are welcome in the refurbished oak bar with its three changing ales. With a great reputation for unpretentious food (no food Mon and Tue), there are food theme nights, quizzes and occasional live music. The small front garden of this picturesque hostelry is popular with cyclists and ramblers in summer. Three en-suite rooms are now available. ▲↻🏠✲◑♣P'🔚

Sheepscombe

Butchers Arms

GL6 7RH SO893105
✪ 11.30-3, 6.30 (6 Fri)-11; 11.30-11 Sat; 12-10.30 Sun
☎ (01452) 812113 ⊕ butchers-arms.co.uk
Butcombe Rare Breed; Moles Bitter; guest beer Ⓗ
Popular 17th-century Cotswold-stone pub basking in a picturesque village in one of the combes north of Stroud. Its inn sign, a painted three-dimensional carving of a butcher and a pig, is world famous. Inside, the pub benefits from a high-quality inter-war refurbishment, including generous bay windows, leaded panes and parquet flooring. A wood-burning stove provides warmth in winter and the pub's orientation means the forecourt tables and steeply sloping side garden are suntraps in summer. ▲Q✲◑♣P'🔚(15,23)

Shipton Moyne

Cat & Custard Pot Ⓛ

The Street, GL8 8PN (on Tetbury road)
✪ 11-3, 6-11.30; 11.30-3, 6-11 Sun ☎ (01666) 880249
Bath Ales Gem; Wadworth Henry's Original IPA, 6X; Wickwar BOB; guest beer Ⓗ
Blessed with an attractive, unique pub sign, this handsome village inn is largely open plan, the rooms opened out to cope with the demand for its popular menu. On sunny days the front garden turns into the focal point for the local dog-walking society, with the (usually) quiet snug behind the main bar popular with families and social groups. There is an equestrian element to the memorabilia adorning the walls, including an explanation of the unusual pub name. ▲Q✲◑♣P

Shortstanding

New Inn Ⓛ

Ross Road, GL16 7NT (just N of Berry Hill)
✪ 12-midnight (10 Sun) ☎ (01594) 836857
Sharp's Doom Bar; Wye Valley Bitter; guest beers Ⓗ
Set on the edge of the Forest of Dean with views across open countryside, and within easy reach of the Wye Valley at Symonds Yat, this large and welcoming single-bar pub has flagstones, alcoves and log fires. LocAle beers are available and the enthusiastic staff delight in serving generous portions from their well-priced food menu. A large TV at one end of the bar discreetly displays many sporting events with the sound turned down low. ▲↻✲◑🅿AP'🔚

Slad

Woolpack Ⓛ

GL6 7QA (on B4070)
✪ 12-midnight ☎ (01452) 813929
⊕ thewoolpackinn-slad.com
Butcombe Gold; Stroud Budding; Uley Bitter, Old Spot, Pigs Ear; guest beer Ⓗ
Local CAMRA Pub of the Year, this is a very popular 17th-century inn made famous by Cider with Rosie

(author Laurie Lee was a regular all his life). Only one room deep, the pub offers superb views over the Slad Valley, and has been thoughtfully restored – the built-in dark wooden settles in the end rooms are recent. The bar runs the length of the building, extending into all four rooms. Wilces Cider and Westons Country Perry are available. Dogs and walkers are welcome. ▲Q↻✲◑ ⊟♣ 🍺P'🔚

Slimbridge

Tudor Arms Ⓛ

Shepherds Patch, GL2 7BP
✪ 11-11; 12-10.30 Sun ☎ (01453) 890306
⊕ thetudorarms.co.uk
Uley Bitter, Pigs Ear; Wadworth 6X; guest beers Ⓗ
Winner of local CAMRA awards for seven consecutive years, this large family-owned and operated free house is near the Wildfowl and Wetlands Trust site. Two bars and five dining areas are constantly being improved, and excellent home-cooked food is available all day. Children are welcome. High-class accommodation is available in the modern lodge alongside, and a separately owned caravan and camping park is immediately behind. Two guest ales from local brewers complement up to nine ciders and perries. Q✲◑ ⊟♿Å♣🍺P'🔚

Staunton

White Horse Ⓛ

GL16 8PA (on A4136)
✪ 12-3, 6-11 Tue-Sat; 12-11 Sun ☎ (01594) 834001
⊕ whitehorseinnstaunton.co.uk
Beer Range Varies Ⓗ
'The last pub in England' is situated in the centre of the small village of Staunton close to the Welsh Border. At least one local ale is served with up to four during the summer months. Home-cooked food is available and is made from fresh, locally-sourced ingredients where possible. ▲Q↻✲◑♿P'🔚

Stroud

Crown & Sceptre Ⓛ

98 Horns Road, GL5 1EG
✪ 3 (12 Fri & Sat)-11; 12-10.30 Sun ☎ (01453) 762588
⊕ crownandsceptrestroud.com
Stroud Budding; Uley Bitter, Pigs Ear; guest beer Ⓗ
Lively back-street pub that is the beating heart of the local community. A genuine free house, the regular guest beer comes from Blue Anchor. An eclectic selection of framed prints and posters graces the walls. A large oak table is popular with local groups, including a knitting circle, and the pub also has its own motorcycle society. Satellite sport is screened in the back bar, which has a rare bar billiards table. A terrace at the back offers panoramic views over Stroud. ▲↻✲◑⇄♣🍺P'🔚(8,227)

Queen Vic Ⓛ

5 Gloucester Street, GL5 1QG
✪ 10-11 (1am Fri; 2am Sat); 12-11 Sun ☎ (01453) 762396
Beer range varies Ⓗ
Cavernous, single-room town-centre pub/sports bar with two pool tables and regular live bands. Satellite sport is screened throughout the pub and even outside – there is a screen in the covered smoking area in the front yard. One rebadged

house beer (Dangerfield) is sold alongside an imaginative and varied range of three ales from microbreweries up and down the country, including the likes of Blindmans, Kelham Island, Otley, Skinner's and Salopian. Beer festivals are held at Easter and in September. Black Rat cider is sold. ✿❧✿♨⌐▦

Tewkesbury

Nottingham Arms Ⓛ
129 High Street, GL20 5JU
✪ 11-11 (midnight Thu-Sat); 12-midnight Sun
☎ (01684) 276346
Adnams Broadside; Greene King IPA; guest beers Ⓗ
Fourteenth-century town-centre pub with two welcoming rooms, a public bar at the front and the restaurant behind, both mostly timber-framed. Photographs of old Tewkesbury adorn the walls. Five real ales are now offered, one from a local brewer, plus Westons Old Rosie cider. The pub is noted for its excellent, well-priced contemporary cuisine, served lunchtimes and evenings. Knowledgeable staff will happily tell you about the resident ghosts. Live music features most Sunday evenings and Thursday is quiz night. ♨◑▮♨⌐▦

Olde Black Bear
68 High Street, GL20 5BJ
✪ 11-11; 12-10.30 Sun ☎ (01684) 292202
Adnams Broadside; Wells Bombardier; guest beers Ⓗ
Built in 1308 and originally a coaching house, it is reputedly the oldest inn in Gloucestershire. As might be expected in such a historic building, the interior is rich in timber, both frames and beams. It is allegedly haunted by three ghosts, including a cavalier and an old lady, and was used as a hospital during the Wars of the Roses. Quiz nights are Sunday and Wednesday, with satellite TV screened inside and out. Private moorings and fishing are available. ♨Q➹✿◑▮♨⌐▦

Royal Hop Pole Ⓛ
94 Church Street, GL20 5RS (between Abbey and Cross)
✪ 7am (8am Sun)-11 ☎ (01684) 274039
Greene King Abbot; Ruddles Best Bitter; guest beers Ⓗ
Town-centre landmark that is an amalgamation of historic buildings dating from the 15th and 18th centuries. Known as the Royal Hop Pole since a visit from Princess Mary of Teck (Queen Mary, Royal Consort of George V) in September 1891, it was mentioned in The Pickwick Papers. Not short of interior space, wood panelling graces swathes of this popular, multi-roomed drinking establishment, complete with an attractive patio and garden at the rear. A couple of LocAle beers are usually available. Q➹✿➡◑♨P♨⌐▦

Theoc House Ⓛ
85 Barton Street, GL20 5PY
✪ 8.30am-11 ☎ (01684) 296562 ∰ theochouse.co.uk
Severn Vale Severn Sins Stout; guest beers Ⓗ
A fully refurbished town-centre hostelry that is a blend of pub, café and coffee lounge. The owners have succeeded in creating a relaxed atmosphere, and they compete with a certain national pub chain by opening all day to serve good-value breakfast, brunch and evening meals. Only two real ales are regularly available, usually a bitter and a stout, but there are plans to offer more. Quiz night is Sunday, while jazz evenings are the second and fourth Wednesdays of the month. Q➹◑▮

White Bear Ⓛ
Bredon Road, GL20 5BU
✪ 10.30-midnight ☎ (01684) 296614
Draught Bass; guest beers Ⓗ
On the north-western edge of the town centre, this good-value, family-run pub attracts a varied clientele. Handily situated close to the marina, it is popular with river users. The open-plan L-shaped bar offers room to play pool, cribbage and darts; there is also a skittle alley. Live music features every Sunday evening. The three guest beers change frequently and usually include offerings from smaller breweries, while a range of three traditional Thatchers ciders is also offered. ♣♨▦

Thornbury

Anchor Ⓛ
Gloucester Road, Lower Morton, BS35 1JY
✪ 11-11 ☎ (01454) 281375 ∰ theanchorthornbury.co.uk
Draught Bass; guest beers Ⓗ
Licensed since 1695 and the second-oldest pub in Thornbury, this friendly, traditional inn serves good home-cooked food, five changing guest beers, often local, and a real cider. Dogs are welcome in the public bar, which was the original pub, and is home to darts, crib and dominoes teams. The pub also has its own cricket team and angling syndicate. The garden includes a boules piste and children's play area. The inn is the base for the local CAMRA branch; new members welcome – ask at the bar. ✿◑▮➡♣♨P♨⌐▦(309,310)

Toddington

Pheasant Inn Ⓛ
The Roundabout, GL54 5DT (jct of B4632 and B4077)
✪ 11-11 ☎ (01242) 621271
Stanway Stanney Bitter, seasonal beer Ⓗ
A friendly, independently owned pub serving several local villages, with four letting rooms. Parts of the large bar have hunting, racing and railway themes. The pub is handy for the Gloucestershire-Warwickshire railway, the Cotswold Way and Hailes Abbey, and is the brewery tap for Stanway Brewery located in the nearby Jacobean brewhouse of Stanway House. The quality of the beer is assured, often by the presence of the brewer. Breakfast and good-value Thai food is served and it also offers a convenience store and post office. ♨➹✿➡◑♨▲♣P♨⌐▦(606)

Uley

Old Crown Ⓛ
17 The Green, GL11 5SN (at top end of village)
✪ 12-11 ☎ (01453) 860502 ∰ theoldcrownuley.co.uk
Uley Bitter, Pigs Ear; guest beers Ⓗ
Attractive 17th-century whitewashed coaching inn in the picturesque village of Uley on the edge of the Cotswold Way. The pub serves as the village local as well as attracting passing walkers. The low-beamed single bar has a welcoming fire. Beers are mainly sourced from microbreweries. Four en-suite double bedrooms are available and food is served lunchtimes and evenings. There is a covered smoking area and a pleasant walled garden. ♨Q✿➡◑♣P♨⌐

Upper Oddington

Horse & Groom ⊻ 🗓

GL56 0XH (top of village signed off A436 E of Stow)
🌑 12-3, 5.30-11 (6-10.30 Sun) ☎ (01451) 830584
⊕ horseandgroom.uk.com
Wye Valley Bitter, Hereford Pale Ale 🎔
You are assured of a warm welcome at this
attractive, privately owned, 16th-century inn run
by dedicated licensees, achieving many awards
including local CAMRA branch Pub of the Year
2013. It has an extended bar area for locals, with a
sitting room linked via a real open log fire in an
inglenook setting. Good-value Wye Valley beers
are always available, with guests changing weekly,
usually from a Gloucestershire brewer. There is a
large car park and an attractive garden and patio
area. ♨️ ⧗ 🏨 🍴◑ ⅋P🛒

Waterley Bottom

New Inn 🗓

GL11 6EF (signed from North Nibley) ST758964
🌑 12-2.30 (not Mon), 6 (5 Fri)-11; 12-11 Sat, Sun & bank hols;
closed winter Mon ☎ (01451) 543659
Beer range varies 🎔
Free house nestling in a tiny hamlet in a scenic
valley surrounded by steep hills. During the 19th
century it was a cider house frequented by mill
workers taking the footpath to Dursley. It has a
cosy lounge/dining area with a pair of ancient beer
engines on display and a smaller public bar. The
child-friendly garden has a terraced area with a
pool table. It offers an imaginative menu, and
Thatchers and Westons cider and perry are sold.
♨️Q🏨🍴◑ ⧗⅋ ⧫P⅃

Whiteshill

Star Inn 🗓

Star Green, GL6 6AE
🌑 5-11; 12-11.30 Fri & Sat; 12-11 Sun ☎ (01453) 765321
⊕ stroud-starinn.co.uk
Bath Ales Gem; Otter Amber; Purity Ubu; guest
beer 🇬
A welcoming village inn with at least three real
ales served straight from casks racked directly
behind the bar. Extensively renovated in 2010, the
main bar features a large inglenook fireplace with
a wood-burning stove, slate floors and two oak
drinking counters dividing the space. The TV
prioritises rugby. Themed food nights (including
curry and quiz), occasional live music and an
annual beer festival take place. They offer B&B
accommodation in adjacent cottages, and fresh
Cornish pasties on Fridays. ♨️🏨🍴◑⧗⅋P⅃🛒(93)

Wickwar

Wickwar Social Club 🗓

35 High Street, GL12 8NP
🌑 12-1.30, 5-11; 12-2, 4-midnight Sat; 12-6 Sun
☎ (01454) 294221
Beer range varies 🎔

Comfortable, friendly two-bar social club that is
gaining a reputation for its ales. There is a walled
outside drinking area at the rear which is suitable
for children and has a covered smoking area. The
main bar has a pool table at one end and a
widescreen TV usually used for sports coverage.
Just inside the front entrance there is a quiet snug.
CAMRA members and holders of a current Guide
are welcome on an occasional basis. ⧗⅋⧫⅃🛒

Woodchester

Royal Oak 🗓

Church Road, North Woodchester, GL5 5PQ (signed
from A46)
🌑 5 (3.30 Fri)-11; 12-3, 5-11 Sat; 12-4, 7-11 Sun
☎ (01453) 872735
Stroud Budding; Uley Hogshead, Bitter; guest beer 🎔
Whitewashed, refurbished, 17th-century inn, a free
house again after being rescued from a pubco.
Inside there are bare Cotswold-stone walls,
exposed beams and a flagstone floor. The bar front
incorporates mahogany doors from a Gloucester
bank. The elegant lounge bar has a magnificent
open fireplace with a log fire, the public bar a
woodburner. This lively, friendly local attracts
people from miles around. The pub has a patio
garden with views over the Woodchester Valley.
♨️Q⧗🏨🍴◑ ⧗P🛒(46,40)

Woolaston Common

Rising Sun

GL15 6NU (1 mile off A48 at Woolaston) SO590009
🌑 12-2.30, 6.30-11.30; 12-3, 6.30-midnight Sat; 12-3,
6.30-11 Sun ☎ (01594) 529282
Butcombe Bitter; Wye Valley Bitter; guest beer 🎔
Off the beaten track, this 350-year-old stone-built
hostelry is well worth seeking out. It is featured in
the circular pub walks of the Forest as it is popular
with walkers who admire the spectacular views
here. There is a large main bar and a well-liked
snug. The food is home-cooked, using local
produce where possible (no food lunchtimes
Monday & Tuesday). The guest ale is usually a local
brew. The cribbage league meets here on
Tuesdays. ♨️⧗🍴◑ ⅄⧫P⅃

Wotton-under-Edge

Star Inn 🗓

21 Market Street, GL12 7AE
🌑 12-11 (midnight Fri & Sat) ☎ (01453) 844651
Wickwar Coopers; guest beers 🎔
At the top of this historic town on the Cotswold
Way, this comfortable 16th-century two-bar pub
has an exposed Cotswold-stone interior and
contains memorabilia of the White Star Line,
famous as operators of the ill-fated Titanic; John
Cambridge, who started the company, was born on
the premises in 1784. Major sporting events can be
watched in the public bar or a quiet pint enjoyed in
the lounge. A function room is used by the wider
community. Q⧗🏨🍴◑⧗⅋⧫⅃🛒

What is your best – your very best – ale a glass?' 'Twopence-halfpenny,' says the landlord,
'is the price of the genuine Stunning Ale.' 'Then,' says I, producing the money, 'Just draw
me a glass of the Genuine Stunning, if you please, with a good head to it.'
Charles Dickens, David Copperfield

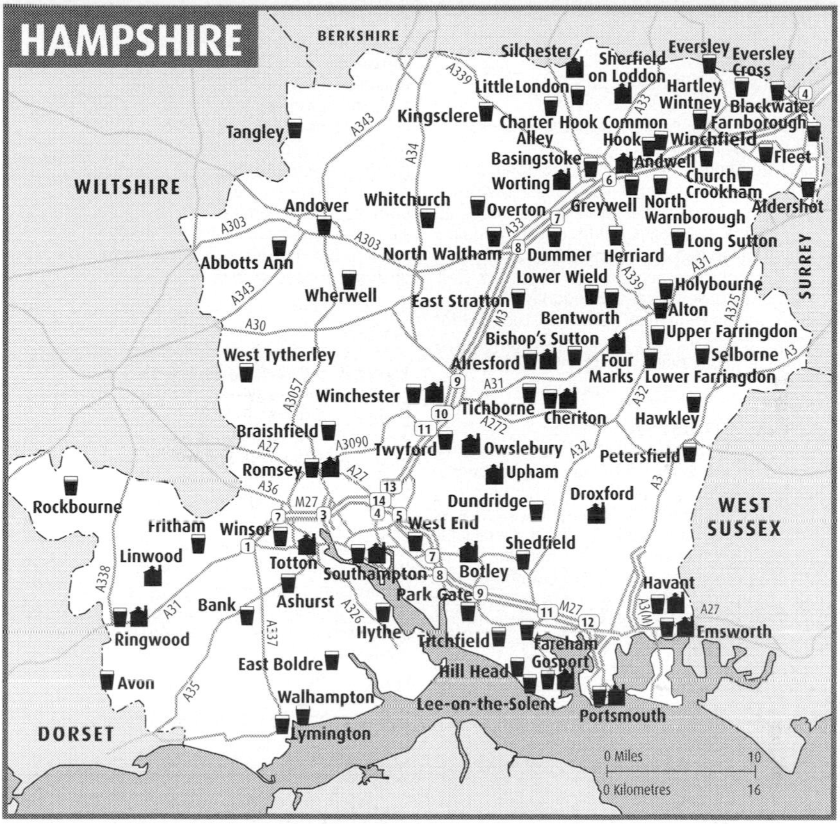

Abbotts Ann

Eagle 𝕃

High Street, SP11 7BG SU328435
⏲ 11.30-11; 12-10.30 Sun ☎ (01264) 710339
🌐 eagleabbottsann.co.uk
Skinner's Betty Stogs; guest beers Ⓗ
Located in a picturesque village, this pub is at the heart of the community. Friendly conversation and banter rule the house. The regular Betty Stogs is supplemented by three changing beers, often from local breweries, plus up to four real ciders. Locally sourced food is available (no food Tue and Sun eves). A popular beer festival with live music is held each summer. The public bar features pool and there is a skittle alley at the rear.
⛰Q❀◐◑⊟♣♠P⁚–⊟(77,87)

Aldershot

Garden Gate

Church Lane East, GU11 3BT
⏲ 5-midnight (11 Mon); 4-1am Fri; 12.30-1am Sat; 12-10.30 Sun ☎ (01252) 321051
Greene King IPA; guest beers Ⓗ
A small, friendly local just south-west of the town centre. A cosy single bar serves two distinct drinking areas, with a separate room leading to a small patio and smoking area to the rear. Two guest beers are available, tending to be a Greene King seasonal or a beer from the brewery guest list. Lots of events are held, such as regular live music, poker on Wednesday, and a quiz on Thursday.
❀⇶♣P⁚–⊟

White Lion 𝕃

20 Lower Farnham Road, GU12 4EA
⏲ 1-11 (10.30 Mon; midnight Fri); 12-midnight Sat; 12-10.30 Sun ☎ (01252) 323832
Triple fff Alton's Pride, Pressed Rat & Warthog, Moondance, seasonal beers; guest beers Ⓗ
A genuine two-bar pub, one of two owned by Triple fff Brewery. It is popular with locals, visitors and vintage scooter enthusiasts – the landlord's passion. Three Triple fff beers are usually available, including the award-winning Alton's Pride. Dark beers are also featured. The pub is only 15-minutes' walk from the football ground and visiting fans are always made welcome. Pizzas are available at all times. ⛰❀⊟♣⁚–⊟(3,20)

Alresford

Running Horse Inn 𝕃

22 Pound Hill, SO24 9BW
⏲ 11-3, 6-11; 12-11 Sat; 12-8 Sun ☎ (01962) 734782
🌐 runninghorseinn.com
Flowerpots Bitter; guest beers Ⓗ
Grade II-listed pub, just west of Alresford's centre. The main bar has a certain old charm with an unusual cribbage board set into a table and recently reintroduced bar billiards. To the left, the other bar has now become a restaurant area. The pub sources much of its food and drink from local suppliers. Beer drinkers are enticed with three third-pint samplers and a CAMRA members' discount. Closed Tuesday lunchtime and all day Monday. ⛰♘❀◐◑♣P⊟(64,67)

Alton

Eight Bells
33 Church Street, GU34 2DA
✪ 11-11; 12-10.30 Sun ☎ (01420) 82417
Bowman Swift One; Palmers Copper Ale; Sharp's Doom Bar; guest beer Ⓗ
Popular free house, dating from circa 1640, just outside the town centre. Opposite lies St Lawrence Church, site of the Civil War Battle of Alton. The pub has an original oak-beamed interior with a main bar and smaller drinking area, plus a restored listed smoking shelter incorporating a 17th-century well in a secluded paved garden. Filled rolls are available Monday-Saturday from noon. Look out for Phil's famous secret beer festival, following the late summer bank holiday. ▲Q✿✖ᕐ-➾(38,64)

George
Butts Road, GU34 1LH
✪ 11-11 (10 Sun) ☎ (01420) 82331 ⊕ thegeorgealton.co.uk
Dartmoor Jail Ale; St Austell Tribute; Sharp's Doom Bar; guest beer Ⓗ
A huge improvement in ale quality has followed the return of previous landlords. The three regular beers are supplemented by a guest from the Punch list. A varied food menu is offered lunchtimes and evenings, plus an extensive wine list. The clientele is mixed – families at lunchtimes with ale fans and diners in the evening. Previously the Duke's Head, it was the courthouse where the murderer of Sweet Fanny Adams was tried and convicted. Live music plays monthly. CAMRA members receive a 20p per pint discount. ▲➲✿✪◑⬥P⌐-➾(64)

Railway Arms Ⓛ
26 Anstey Road, GU34 2RB
✪ 12-11 (midnight Fri & Sat) ☎ (01420) 82218
Triple fff Alton's Pride, Pressed Rat & Warthog, Moondance, seasonal beers; guest beers Ⓗ
Friendly pub close to the Watercress Line and mainline station, owned by Triple fff Brewery, whose own beers are supplemented by ales from a host of micros. Bottled cider is from Mr Whitehead's. A rear function room, with its own bar, is available for hire. The patio area, designed with a traditional railway theme, incorporates a covered smoking area. There are tables outside at the front under a striking sculpture of a steam locomotive. Well-behaved dogs and CAMRA members are welcome. ✿♣⌐-➾(64,65)

Andover

Wyke Down Country Pub
Picket Piece, SP11 6LX
✪ 11-2.30; 6 (5 Fri)-11; 12-2.30, 5-11 Sat; 12-3.30, 6-10.30 Sun ☎ (01264) 352048 ⊕ wykedown.co.uk
Fuller's London Pride; guest beers Ⓗ
A family-run pub and restaurant in a 19th-century barn overlooking its own spacious campsite and the scenic north Hampshire countryside. The main bar is adorned with farming implements and signs from its early era, while there is an ample conservatory. Outside is a small swimming pool, and the pub runs a 300-yard golf driving range and a small farm. Special events are often arranged, including a vehicle meet. ➲✿◑⬥P⌐

Ashurst

Forest Inn Ⓛ
Lyndhurst Road, SO40 7DU (on A35 at E end of village)

✪ 11.30-11.30; 12-10.30 Sun ☎ (023) 8029 3071
Flack Manor Double Drop; Ringwood Best Bitter, Fortyniner; guest beers Ⓗ
A single-storey building on the south side of the A35, some way east of Ashurst. The interior is split by a large brick double fireplace, with a lounge bar on the right and an adjoining dining room. The pub is run by a young couple with young, friendly staff. A varied menu (some dishes available in half portions), good home-cooked food, interesting specials and reasonable prices all make this a good place to eat. There is live music on Fridays and a quiz on Sundays. ▲➲✿◑⬥P⌐-➾(6)

Avon

Tyrrell's Ford Country Inn Ⓛ
Ringwood Road, BH23 7BQ (on B3347, halfway between Ringwood and Christchurch)
✪ 10.30-11 ☎ (01425) 672646 ⊕ tyrrellsford.co.uk
Ringwood Best Bitter; guest beers Ⓗ
An 18th-century manor house that was the residence of Lord and Lady Manners, set in eight acres of grounds with a sweeping driveway, just 100 yards from the Avon Valley Path. Named after William Rufus's killer, this 3-star inn has a comfortably furnished lounge bar overlooking the garden, a candlelit restaurant, open fires, a mural and a minstrels' gallery. Two guest ales from Wadworth, Flack Manor, Goddards or others are always available. Family, dog, horse and walker friendly, with many board games, bagatelle and bar billiards. ▲Q➲✿◑⬥♣P⌐

Bank

Oak Inn
Pinkney Lane, SO43 7FD (turn S from A35, 1 mile W of Lyndhurst)
✪ 11.30-3, 6-11; 11.30-11 Sat; 12-10.30 Sun
☎ (023) 8028 2350 ⊕ oakinnlyndhurst.co.uk
Fuller's London Pride, seasonal beers; Gale's Seafarers Ale, HSB; guest beer Ⓟ
The Oak is in a hamlet, just south of the A35 and one mile to the west of Lyndhurst. It is popular with walkers, cyclists and horse riders. The pub serves high-quality locally sourced food,

INDEPENDENT BREWERIES

Alfred's Winchester (NEW)
Andwell Andwell
Botley Botley
Bowman Droxford
Dancing Man Southampton
Emsworth Emsworth
Flack Manor Romsey
Flowerpots Cheriton
Fulflood Arms Winchester
Havant Havant
Hensting Owslebury
Irving Portsmouth
Itchen Valley New Alresford
Longdog Worting
Oakleaf Gosport
Red Shoot Linwood
Ringwood (Marston's) Ringwood
Sherfield Village Sherfield on Loddon
Triple fff Four Marks
Upham Upham
Vibrant Forest Totton
Wild Weather Silchester (NEW)

specialising in game and seafood, and booking is highly recommended. The ales are dispensed from taps in wooden cask-ends, propelled by gas-driven pumps in the cellar. The garden's tranquility is a delight in summer. A red K6 telephone box adds to the pub's character. ⚞🗝️❀◑P⚟

Basingstoke

Lloyds No.1
Unit R6, Festival Place, RG21 7BB (follow the signs to Festival Place; opposite Vue)
✪ 8am-12.30am (2am Fri & Sat) ☎ (01256) 854800
Greene King Abbot; Ruddles Best Bitter; guest beers H
Family-focused part of the JD Wetherspoon chain with four guest beers that change daily, in addition to the regular ales. This venue is spacious and relaxed. Food is served all day from an extensive and well-priced menu, with daily offers and meal deals. The bar hosts two world real ale and cider festivals per year. 🗝️❀◑&⚞P⚟🍴

Queens Arms
Bunnian Place, RG21 7JE (100yds E of railway station)
✪ 11-11 (midnight Fri & Sat) ☎ (01256) 465488
Courage Best Bitter; Sharp's Doom Bar; guest beers H
Just outside the main shopping area, this cosy pub is handy for all transport links. It attracts a wide-ranging clientele of all ages from all walks of life, and is a regular port of call for rail commuters. The choice of up to four guest beers is imaginative and the turnaround can be swift. Good-value home-cooked food is served lunchtimes and evenings. During warmer weather the shady courtyard garden at the rear is a popular attraction. Q❀◑⚞P⚟🍴

Way Inn
Chapel Hill, RG21 5TB (opp Holy Ghost church)
✪ 12-11 (10.30 Sun) ☎ (01256) 321520
Caledonian Deuchars IPA; Greene King Abbot; Taylor Landlord; guest beers H
Previously the Rising Sun, this pub, just north of the rail station, provides a comfortable environment for all age groups. It has a spacious, discreetly lit bar area at the front, with the rear bar area available for group reservations as well as occasional live music. There is a large car park, an outside patio and a south-facing garden. There are no TVs or bar games but there is an online jukebox. The menu offers home-cooked traditional food, available lunchtimes and evenings (no food Sun eve), with a good vegetarian range. ⚞❀◑&⚞P⚟🍴

Bentworth

Star Inn L
Village Street, GU34 5RB (opp village crossroads)
✪ 12-3, 5-11.30; 12-11 Fri-Sun ☎ (01420) 561224
⊕ star-inn.com
Fuller's London Pride; Palmers Copper Ale; Triple fff Moondance; guest beer H
Located at the crossroads in the centre of Bentworth, this pub is a real hub for the local community but equally welcoming to visitors. As well as the four well-kept real ales and excellent food, this pub provides quiz nights, regular live music with a blues theme on Friday nights, and a jam session on Sundays. At other times there is unobtrusive music in the bar and a separate quiet

dining area. Regular cinema events and a popular annual blues festival are also hosted. ⚞Q🗝️❀◑&P⚟

Bishop's Sutton

Ship Inn
SO24 0AQ (on B3047)
✪ 12-2.30 (not Mon), 6-11; 12-3, 7-10.30 Sun
☎ (01962) 732863
Palmers Copper Ale; guest beers H
Comfortable, genuine family-run free house with a split-level bar and a log fire providing a cosy, relaxing atmosphere. There are separate areas for pub games, families and dining, plus a restaurant. The food is home-cooked, with daily specials on the board (no food Mon lunchtime). Popular with walkers from the nearby St Swithun's Way, this pub is the hub of the village. The regular bus between Winchester and Alton stops outside, and the Watercress Line preserved steam railway is nearby. ⚞Q🗝️❀◑♣P⚟🍴(64)

Blackwater

Mr Bumble
19 London Road, GU17 9AP
✪ 12-11 (midnight Fri); 11-midnight Sat; 12-10.30 Sun
☎ (01276) 32691
Fuller's London Pride; guest beers H
Formerly the Red Lion, this large pub is split up into several areas served by a central, L-shaped bar. Fully carpeted and comfortably furnished, it has a homely feel despite its size. The pub is free of tie and the landlady of 19 years, Philippa, supplements the regular London Pride with three guest beers, usually including at least one LocAle. Pool is a popular pastime here, with three tables provided, as are darts and cribbage. Live bands play on Saturdays. ❀⚞♣P⚟(3)

Braishfield

Newport Inn
Newport Lane, SO51 0PL SU373250
✪ 12-2.30 (not Mon), 6-11; 7-10.30 Sun ☎ (01794) 368225
Fuller's London Pride, seasonal beers; Gale's Seafarers Ale, HSB H
Two-bar former Gale's pub, found down a narrow lane, run by the same family since 1941. Ham or cheese sandwiches or ploughman's are the only food available, but their quality and value are legendary. The decor, inside and out, has changed little since the 1970s. Traditional singalongs round the piano are held on Saturday evenings and local folk musicians often play on Thursday evenings. Darts and other traditional pub games such as dominoes and cribbage are played in the public bar. ⚞Q❀🍺♣P

Charter Alley

White Hart
White Hart Lane, RG26 5QA (1 mile W of A340, opp turning for Little London) SU593577
✪ 12-2.30 (3 Sat), 7 (5.30 Thu-Sat)-11; 12-4, 7-10.30 Sun
☎ (01256) 850048 ⊕ whitehartcharteralley.com
Triple fff Moondance; guest beers H
Cosy inn, built in 1819, the epicentre of this rural village, where all comers are assured of a friendly greeting. Welcoming features include log fires, oak beams and a capacious restaurant, serving a

variety of quality food and home-made pies. The breweriana-decorated main bar has six pumps dispensing an array of ales that changes so frequently that an email notification service is available by subscription. It has been a stalwart Guide entry for over 20 years. No food Sunday and Monday evenings. ⚑Q☺🅿🚲🕭🌙🍴🛏🅿≈☗

Cheriton

Flowerpots Inn Ⓛ
Brandy Mount, SO24 0QQ (½ mile N of A272 between Winchester and Petersfield) SU581283
☼ 12-2.30 (3 Sat), 6-11; 12-3, 7-10.30 Sun
☎ (01962) 771318 ⊕ flowerpots.f2s.com
Flowerpots Perridge Pale, Bitter, Goodens Gold, seasonal beers Ⓖ
Excellent two-bar village pub with its own brewery. The public bar boasts a 19th-century 30-foot well, and a large log fire in winter. The lounge is small and cosy. There is an attractive garden and a large marquee that provides welcome overflow space on busy days. Good home-cooked food is available daily (no food Sun eve). The Watercress steam railway is three miles away. There are good walks nearby so the pub is popular with walkers and cyclists. Three B&B rooms are available. ⚑Q☺🍴🕭🌙🍴🛏🅿≈🚲(67)

Hinton Arms
Petersfield Road, SO24 0NH (on A272 nr B3046 jct)
☼ 10-3, 6-11; 10-11 Sun ☎ (01962) 771252
⊕ hintonarms.co.uk
Bowman Elderado, Swift One, Wallops Wood, Quiver Bitter Ⓗ
Welcoming food-based pub with wooden beams decorated with tankards and a hunting theme. The L-shaped bar serves four beers under house names, which are all rebadged Bowman Ales (Hinton's Own: Swift One; Hinton's Crest: Quiver). Two wood-burning stoves keep the pub cosy in winter, while the garden provides extra seating in summer. Traditional English pub food is served, with game and fish specials. The pub is also the base for a walk celebrating the Battle of Cheriton in 1664. ⚑Q☺🌙🍴🅿🚲(67)

Church Crookham

Tweseldown
Beacon Hill Road, GU52 8DY SU819518
☼ 11-11.30 (midnight Fri & Sat); 12-11 Sun
☎ (01252) 613976 ⊕ thetweseldown.co.uk
Courage Best Bitter; Fuller's London Pride; Triple fff Alton's Pride; guest beer Ⓗ
Close to Tweseldown racecourse, which hosted the 1948 Olympics equestrian events, there has been a pub here since around 1840. This incarnation has a lively public bar with music, dartboard and pool table, a quiet saloon bar, 60-seat Barn function room and a garden. Friendly staff serve three permanent ales and a changing guest beer. Genuine home-made food (main menu plus specials) is available. The decor is horse-racing themed and there are real log fires. Dogs are welcome. Free Wi-Fi on request. ⚑Q☺🌙🕭🚲🅿≈🚲(70,71)

Dummer

Sun Inn Ⓛ
Winchester Road, RG25 2DJ (on A30 1 mile S of jct 7 on M3) SU577465
☼ 12-11 (midnight Sat); 12-10.30 Sun ☎ (01256) 397234
⊕ suninndummer.com
Sharp's Doom Bar; Triple fff Alton's Pride, Moondance Ⓗ
Formerly a coaching inn on the main London-Winchester road, the Sun has had a recent makeover and now provides a smart, clean and comfortable environment in which to enjoy the two local real ales and the locally sourced food from the stylish, well-presented menu. Big comfy sofas and tables grace the bar area, and there is a separate, more formal dining area. Conference facilities are available. There is a large garden to the rear with a children's play area. Q☺🌙🅿≈

Dundridge

Hampshire Bowman Ⓛ
Dundridge Lane, SO32 1GD (1½ miles E of B3035) SU578184
☼ 12-11 (midnight Fri); 12-10.30 Sun ☎ (01489) 892940
⊕ hampshirebowman.com
Bowman Swift One, Wallops Wood; guest beers Ⓖ
A classic country pub down a narrow winding lane in an idyllic spot and catering for almost everyone. There are two bars – the old bar has a mix of wood and brick flooring with a woodburner and is used mainly by diners enjoying the excellent food. The pub is dog friendly but fines (for charity) mobile phone users. It is very popular with walkers. Outside, there is a large covered patio and large garden. Quiz night is Monday. ⚑Q☺🌙🕭🍴🅿≈

East Boldre

Turfcutters Arms Ⓛ
Main Road, SO42 7WL (¾ mile SE of B3054 Hatchet Pond)
☼ 11-11 (10.30 Sun) ☎ (01590) 612331
⊕ the-turfcutters-new-forest.co.uk
Ringwood Best Bitter, Fortyniner; guest beers Ⓗ
Lovely brick-built, bay-windowed pub, on the edge of Bagshot Moor, just a couple of miles from Beaulieu village. Its name derives from commoners' turbary rights; the old irons for this hang on the walls. The interior is cosy and rustic with beams, stone floors, scrubbed tables and fireplaces. The bar, normally alive with conversation, dispenses four ales. Two side rooms provide more seating. Food is from midday until 9pm in summer and from 2.30pm in winter. Accommodation is in three en-suite rooms in converted stables. ⚑Q☺🌙🕭🍴🅿≈🚲(112)

East Stratton

Northbrook Arms
Stratton Lane, SO21 3DU SU542398
☼ 11.30-11 (11.30 Fri & Sat); 11.30-10.30 Sun
☎ (01932) 774150 ⊕ thenorthbrookarms.com
Cotleigh Barn Owl; Tawny Owl; Dorset Piddle Jimmy Riddle; guest beers Ⓗ
Just minutes off the A33 between Basingstoke and Winchester, this hostelry is in the idyllic village of East Stratton. It is a friendly 19th-century village pub with three separate rooms – a bar, snug and

large dining room serving excellent home-cooked meals. There are six handpumps dispensing real ales including local guest beers. Accommodation is available and there is also a skittle alley. A beer festival is hosted in May. This gem of a country pub has been owned by Lord Northbrook and his family for many generations. ⚲Q⚲⚲⚲⚲⚫⚫P⚲

Emsworth

Coal Exchange
21 South Street, PO10 7EG
⚙ 10.30-3, 5.30-11; 10.30-midnight Fri & Sat; 12-11 Sun
☎ (01243) 375866 ⚫ thecoalexchange.co.uk
Fuller's London Pride, seasonal beers; Gale's Seafarers Ale, HSB; guest beers Ⓗ
A comfortable single-bar pub a short distance from Emsworth Harbour, popular as a yachting venue and for walks along the shoreline. The harbour helped give the pub its name as it was the place where local farmers traded their produce for coal delivered by sea. As well as award-winning lunchtime meals, the Tuesday curry and Thursday international nights are very popular – so an early arrival is vital. No entry after 10.30pm Friday and Saturday. Live music takes place on Wednesday and Saturday. ⚲⚲⚲⚲⚲⚲⚲(700)

Eversley

Golden Pot Ⓛ
Reading Road, RG27 0NB SU78861/
⚙ 11.30-3, 5.30-11; 12-3.30 Sun ☎ (0118) 973 2104
⚫ golden-pot.co.uk
Beer range varies Ⓗ
A cosy red-brick cottage with creepers on the wall and attractive plants amid the front seating. The pub is supplied by 13 breweries, seven being LocAle, with three ales on at any time. The bar has a striking stained-glass feature and wood-burning stoves. The focus is on food, the tables arranged for dining, and quality ale to complement the meal. A delightful feature is the Vineyard garden at the rear. Opening hours may vary in the evening, so check before you pop along. Q⚲⚲⚫P⚲(82)

Eversley Cross

Frog & Wicket
The Green, RG27 0NS SU796616
⚙ 11-11 (midnight Fri & Sat); 12-10.30 Sun
☎ (0118) 973 1126 ⚫ thefrogandwicket.co.uk
Fuller's London Pride, seasonal beers; Gale's Seafarers Ale, HSB; guest beer Ⓗ
A spacious double-fronted pub opposite the cricket green. As its name suggests, the interior displays an array of both froggy and sporting memorabilia and you can play Put the Ring on the Bull's Nose in the bar. A wood stove is in the separate dining room, adjacent to the main bar. There is also a skittle alley, and special food and music nights are held regularly. See the website for up to date information on regular live music.
⚲⚲⚲⚫⚫⚲P⚲⚲(82)

Fareham

Crown
40 West Street, PO16 0JW
⚙ 7am-midnight ☎ (01329) 241750
Greene King Abbot; Ruddles Best Bitter; guest beers Ⓗ

A delightful, cosy, Wetherspoon town-centre pub with character and some history. From 1841 to 1911 this was the home of the Crown Brewery. After that it became the Crown Inn, and in 2009 Wetherspoon took it over. Two regular ales are offered with three changing guest beers, focusing on small local independents. Beer choice increases during occasional beer festivals. The usual Wetherspoon range of food is available all day, including breakfasts. Q⚲⚫⚫⚲⚲⚲⚲

Golden Lion
28 High Street, PO16 7AE
⚙ 11.30-11 (9 Mon); 12-3.30 Sun ☎ (01329) 234061
⚫ thegoldenlionfareham.info
Fuller's London Pride; Gale's Seafarers Ale, HSB Ⓗ
A Grade II-listed pub in the High Street conservation area, a short walk from the town centre. It has a traditional layout with a fresh and bright décor. The licensee holds the Fuller's Master Cellarman accolade. Home-cooked traditional food is sourced through local suppliers. Book ahead for Sunday lunch and for the popular steak night on Saturday. Thursday is quiz night and a folk band plays on the last Tuesday of every month.
Q⚲⚫P⚲⚲

Lord Arthur Lee Ⓛ
100-108 West Street, PO16 0EP
⚙ 8am-11 (midnight Fri & Sat) ☎ (01329) 280447
Greene King Abbot; Ruddles Best Bitter; guest beers Ⓗ
Popular with office workers and shoppers, this spacious Wetherspoon pub is near the town centre, bus and train stations. The walls are lined with photographs and historic details of the pub's namesake and other local figures. The family area is often popular at lunchtimes. Three regular ales and up to five guest beers are offered, mainly selected from small independent breweries; occasional beer festivals offer increased choice. The usual Wetherspoon range of food is available all day including breakfasts. ⚲⚫⚲⚲⚲⚲

Farnborough

Prince of Wales ⚲ Ⓛ
184 Rectory Road, GU14 8AL
⚙ 11.30-2.30, 5.30-11; 11.30-11 Fri & Sat; 12-10.30 Sun
☎ (01252) 545578
Dark Star Hophead; Fuller's London Pride; Hop Back Summer Lightning; Ringwood Fortyniner; Young's Bitter; guest beers Ⓗ
With a well-earned reputation for maintaining 10 cask ales in prime condition, it is little wonder that this cosy freehold pub has featured in the Guide for many years. Current CAMRA branch Pub of the Year, an award it has won numerous times, it was voted among the top 16 pubs in the country in 2011. The five guest beers include a monthly special at a reduced price. Good lunches are served throughout the week, and an annual beer festival takes place in October. ⚲⚫⚲(North)P⚲⚲(73)

Fleet

Prince Arthur
238 Fleet Road, GU51 4BX
⚙ 8-11 (midnight Thu; 1am Fri & Sat) ☎ (01252) 622660
Greene King Abbot; Ruddles Best Bitter; guest beers Ⓗ

A relatively small Wetherspoon pub named after Prince Arthur, Duke of Connaught, who was commander of the nearby Aldershot garrison. It has a couple of more intimate seating areas and a small patio area to the rear. It is to the southern end of Fleet's high street, around a mile from the railway station. It offers up to five guest ales, often from Hampshire and neighbouring counties, and has regular mini beer festivals. Q✿❶▶●⬩–🖵

Fritham

Royal Oak L

SO43 7HJ (W end of village) SU232141
✪ 11.30-2.30 (3 summer), 6-11; 11-11 Sat; 12-10.30 Sun
☎ (023) 8081 2606
Bowman Wallops Wood; Flack Manor Double Drop; Ringwood Best Bitter; guest beers Ⓖ
Thatched gem at the end of a New Forest track. The main bar leads to several interconnected areas featuring low beams and doors, colourwashed walls, log fires and wooden floors, all served via a hatchway. Guest ales are from small local brewers – the house beer, Royal Oak, is Wallops Wood. Simple but excellent lunches include local cheeses. The vast garden has plenty of picnic tables and hosts barbecues and hog roasts. A warm welcome awaits walkers, cyclists and equestrians (facilities provided); dogs abound. ⛺Q🕭✿⬩Å

Gosport

Junction Tavern

Leesland Road, PO12 3ND
✪ 11-midnight (1am Fri & Sat); 12-midnight Sun
☎ (023) 9258 5140 ⊕ junctiontavern.com
Hammerpot Red Hunter; guest beers Ⓗ
For many years a keg-only pub, situated next to the railway line that finally closed in the 1960s. In 2010 the new licensee, Deana Geary, introduced real ale, and the premises became free of tie in 2011. Normally two guest beers are on offer, with up to four real ciders and a real perry from Lilley's and Mr Whitehead's. Beer festivals are a regular event over the Easter and August bank holiday weekends. ✿♣●⬩–🖵(E1)

Middlecroft L

Middlecroft Lane, PO12 3DH
✪ 11-midnight (1am Fri & Sat); 12-11.30 Sun
☎ (023) 9258 2477
Oakleaf Nuptuale Ⓗ
Relatively unspoilt 1930s pub in the middle of a housing estate, with two separate bars, one of which is usually quiet. The public bar on the right as you go in has a games area with darts and pool, and the lounge bar on the left has a dance floor and is sometimes used for functions. There is an acoustic music session on Wednesday evenings, karaoke on Thursday evenings and live music most Saturday evenings. Q✿🖴♣P⬩–

Queen's Hotel L

143 Queen's Road, PO12 1LG
✪ 11.30-2.30 (Fri only), 5-11; 11.30-11 Sat; 12-3, 7-10.30 Sun
☎ (07974) 031671
Ringwood Fortyniner; Young's Bitter; guest beers Ⓗ
This locals' pub is hidden away in the back streets, yet it enjoys a nationwide reputation. The licensee has been here for almost 30 years, and has won many CAMRA awards. Normally three guest beers and a real cider are available. An Oakleaf beer is

served regularly, and the guest beer range often includes porters and stouts. An annual beer festival takes place in October. Snacks are served Friday lunchtime, and hours are often extended at weekends. ⛺✿♣●⬩–🖵

Greywell

Fox & Goose

The Street, RG29 1BY
✪ 11-11 (8 Mon & Tue; 9 Sun) ☎ (01256) 702062
⊕ foxandgoosegreywell.co.uk
Dorset Jurassic; Sharp's Doom Bar; Taylor Landlord; guest beers Ⓗ
A popular 16th-century family-run pub set in the tranquil village of Greywell. It is backed by a large field that is available for camping. There are several good walks nearby including part of the Basingstoke Canal and its Greywell Tunnel with its population of bats and the ruin of King John's castle. The pub is child friendly and customers may take well-behaved dogs inside. Food is available midday Tuesday-Sunday and evenings Monday-Saturday. ⛺Q✿❶🖴🕭Å P⬩–

Hartley Wintney

Waggon & Horses 🏆

High Street, RG27 8NY
✪ 11-11 (midnight Fri & Sat); 12-11 Sun ☎ (01252) 842119
Courage Best Bitter Ⓗ; **Gale's HSB** Ⓖ; **guest beers** Ⓗ/Ⓖ
A village pub whose landlord of 30 years has won several local CAMRA awards. HSB and Courage Best are regularly served alongside changing guest beers. The pub's lively public bar contrasts with a quieter lounge. Tables outside on the pavement enable guests to enjoy the atmosphere of the village, renowned for its antique shops. At the rear is a pleasant courtyard garden and a heated, covered smokers' area. Food is served lunchtimes only, not Sundays. ⛺Q✿❶🖴🕭●⬩–🖵(100,72)

Havant

Robin Hood

6 Homewell, PO9 1EE
✪ 11-11 (midnight Fri); 12-11 Sun ☎ (023) 9248 2779
Fuller's London Pride, seasonal beers; Gale's Seafarers Ale, HSB; guest beers Ⓗ
A single-bar pub that started life as two Georgian cottages and now blends in well with the later Victorian houses on either side. Inside, the front part of the bar has a stone floor, changing to wood and then carpet as you move towards the rear, which gives access to a small garden and smoking area. The open fireplaces and low beams add to the charm of this comfortable town-centre pub. ⛺✿❶≈⬩–

Hawkley

Hawkley Inn

Pococks Lane, GU33 6NE SU747291
✪ 12-3, 5.30-11; 12-11 Sat; 12-10.30 Sun ☎ (01730) 827205
⊕ hawkleyinn.co.uk
Bowman Wallops Wood; Dark Star Hophead; guest beers Ⓗ
A genuine free 'hoose' with a large veranda at the front and a large secure garden to the rear. Seven ales greet the drinker, all sourced direct from small brewers. Five further handpumps in the rear bar

serve ciders and perry. The interior is rustic in nature; the long-suffering moose's head can be relied upon to reflect the mood of the season and the whims of the locals. ♨Q☻☼◖●

Herriard

Fur & Feathers Ⓛ
Back Lane, RG25 2PN (on the old Basingstoke-Alton road, parallel to the A339) SU671447
☺ closed Mon; 12-3, 5-11; 12-11 Fri & Sat; 12-6 Sun
☎ (01256) 384170 ⊕ franskitchen.co.uk
Sharp's Doom Bar; guest beers Ⓗ
Victorian alehouse built for local farmworkers in 1880, now open plan with a central bar area. The two guest beers are often from local breweries including Hogs Back, Flack Manor and Andwell. The two dining areas either side of the bar area provide a pleasant atmosphere in which to enjoy the mouthwatering menu that utilises the very best and most local ingredients available. A small, quality selection of whisky and brandy is available to complete your pub/dining experience, as is a selection of Havana cigars from the humidor.
♨Q☼◖&P⁴-₩(13)

Hill Head

Crofton Ⓛ
48 Crofton Lane, PO14 3QF
☺ 11-11; 12-10.30 Sun ☎ (01329) 314222
Oakleaf Hole Hearted; Sharp's Doom Bar; guest beers Ⓗ
This modern estate pub is one of the more successful Punch Taverns outlets. The premises comprise a public bar and a large lounge and dining area which was extended in 2012. Normally four guest beers are available from the Punch range plus two casks of SIBA beer a week and Westons scrumpy cider. The separate function room with skittle alley also hosts special events including a beer festival in November. Meals are available all day Friday to Sunday.
♨Q☼◖☒&♣●P⁴-₩(5A)

Holybourne

Queen's Head
20 London Road, GU34 4EG
☺ 12-11 (11.30 Thu; 12.30am Fri & Sat); 12-10.30 Sun
☎ (01420) 86331
Greene King IPA; guest beers Ⓗ
Traditional and friendly pub offering an interesting selection of local and guest ales. The Queen's comprises three recently refurbished rooms plus a covered and heated smoking area. Home-made hearty food is served daily featuring the pub's infamous pies. There is regular live music throughout the year, with the charity music and beer event, Altonbury, on the first Saturday in July. The extensive beer garden features a children's play area and dogs are permitted on a short lead. Happy hour is 4.30-6pm Monday-Friday.
Q☼◖☒≈(Alton)♣P⁴-₩(65)

Hook

White Hart Hotel Ⓛ
London Road, RG27 9DZ (5 mins from M3 jct 5, next to Hook Texaco garage) SU732548
☺ 11-11; 12-10.30 Sun ☎ (01256) 762462
Sharp's Doom Bar; guest beers Ⓗ

You will always get a warm welcome at the White Hart, a 16th-century coaching inn. Recently refurbished, it has a spacious bar area, oak beams and some nooks where you can sit. The bar area is busy and has softly piped music and TVs showing sport; the opposite end is much quieter and ideal for enjoying a meal. One or two – usually local – guests are served. There is an extensive beer garden to the side and a large car park behind.
♨☼☒◖&≈P⁴-₩(10,211)

Hook Common

Crooked Billet
London Road, RG27 9EH (A30 E of Hook) SU736549
☺ 11.30-3, 6-midnight; 11.30-midnight Sat; 12-11 Sun
☎ (01256) 762118 ⊕ thecrookedbilletpub.co.uk
Courage Best Bitter; guest beers Ⓗ
The Crooked Billet is on the London Road just outside Hook and has been a free house under the same ownership for 27 years. Three guest beers are sold. In the summer you can enjoy the pleasant riverside garden or the air-conditioned bars, restaurant or snug. In winter, warm up around one of the traditional log fires. Good food and ales are always available here. ♨Q☼☒◖⊟P

Hythe

Ebenezers Ⓛ
18a Pylewell Road, SO45 6AR (a few yards SW of pier)
☺ 11-2.30, 5.30-11; 11-11.30 Fri & Sat; 12-11 Sun
☎ (023) 8020 7799
Flack Manor Double Drop; Greene King Abbot; guest beer Ⓗ
Delightful little pub, built in 1845 as a Baptist chapel, which has been a school and a store for flour and furniture, but now serves some of the best local ales in the area. The open-plan bar is modern but with a traditional feel that attracts seekers of conversation. Home-made pub food is available lunchtimes and evenings. Outside is a large covered smoking area. Nearby is the world's oldest pier railway, connecting with the Southampton ferry. Q☼☒◖&⁴-₩(8,9)

Kingsclere

Swan Hotel Ⓛ
Swan Street, RG20 5PP
☺ 11-3, 5.30-11 (11.30 Fri & Sat); 12-3.30, 7-10.30 Sun ☎ (01635) 298314 ⊕ swankingsclere.co.uk
Theakston XB; Young's Bitter; guest beers Ⓗ
Welcoming inn frequented by an eclectic mix of customers, serving five beers including three changing local guests. The pub is one of the county's oldest coaching inns, dating from 1449 and close to the Watership Down beauty spot, and a Grade II-listed building recently gently refurbished in accordance with its age. It retains original oak beams and fireplaces, and offers nine en-suite bedrooms. Good food is served in both the dining room and the bar (no food Sun).
♨Q☒◖♣P⁴-₩

Lee-on-the-Solent

Bun Penny
36 Manor Way, PO13 9JH
☺ 11-11 (midnight Fri & Sat); 12-10 Sun ☎ (023) 9255 0214
⊕ bunpenny.co.uk
Otter Bitter Ⓖ; guest beers Ⓗ

Originally a farmhouse and then a coaching inn, the Bun Penny is just a short walk from local shops, buses and the beach. There is a bar area with a stone floor and a separate restaurant that can also cater for groups. Normally three guest beers are available, often from local breweries, with two real ciders from Westons. Live music often takes place on Friday evenings, and occasionally Sunday afternoons. Food is available until 7pm on Sundays.
ᗰQ⊛❶❺⬤P⭢⊟

Little London

Plough Inn ℒ

Silchester Road, RG26 5EP SU621596
❀ 12-3, 5.30 (6 Sat)-11; 12-3, 7-10.30 Sun
☎ (01256) 850628
Palmers Dorset Gold; Ringwood Best Bitter ⬢; guest beers Ⓖ

Wonderful village pub and recent CAMRA Regional Pub of the Year, where in winter you can enjoy a glass of beer in front of one of the log fires or play a game of bar billiards. A good range of baguettes is available (no food Sun eve). There is a secluded garden at the side of the pub. It is ideal for ramblers and cyclists visiting Pamber Wood or the extensive Roman ruins at nearby Silchester. CAMRA branch Pub of the Year 2011. ᗰQ❺⊛♣P⭢⊟(14)

Long Sutton

Four Horseshoes

The Street, RG29 1TA (follow brown signs from B3349 Odiham to Alton Rd) SU748471
❀ 12-3 (not Mon & Tue), 6.30-11; 12-5 Sun
☎ (01256) 862488 ⊕ fourhorseshoes.com
Beer range varies ⬢

Cosy rural pub providing a welcome respite from the nearby Blackwater Valley urban area, with wooden beams and real fires. Two or three beers are served, from a range of breweries often including Palmers and Slater's, with takeaway beer keenly priced. Jazz is played on the second and fourth Tuesdays of the month, and classic motorbike clubs meet here. Home-cooked food is available lunchtimes and evenings.
ᗰQ⊛❹❶ ᐱP

Lower Farringdon

Golden Pheasant

Fareham Road, GU34 3DJ (at Farringdon crossroads on A32)
❀ 12-11 (10.30 Sun) ☎ (01420) 588255
Sharp's Doom Bar; guest beers ⬢

Located three miles south of Alton on the A32, this privately owned free house serves an excellent selection of up to four cask ales, often including one from Cheriton Brewery. The publican is renowned in the local area for his excellent food. Candlelit dining with piano accompaniment is hosted every third Friday (booking required). Fresh fish is available daily as part of a menu combining old favourites and contemporary dishes. There is a large bar area and a quiet, separate dining room. The pub has ample parking. The cider is bottled Legless. Live music plays occasionally.
ᗰQ❺⊛❶♣P⭢

Lower Wield

Yew Tree ℒ

SO24 9RX SU636398
❀ closed Mon; 12-3, 6-11; 12-10.30 Sun ☎ (01256) 389224
⊕ the-yewtree.org.uk
Triple fff Alton's Pride; guest beer ⬢

Out-of-the-way rural local set in picturesque rolling Hampshire countryside, with an old yew tree growing outside (hence the name), situated on a quiet country lane opposite the local cricket pitch. The house beer is Triple fff Alton's Pride and the guest comes from a local brewery. All beers are sold at bargain-basement prices. The pub has a separate dining area where locally renowned and reasonably priced food is served. The nearest bus stop is Medstead, 1½ miles away. ᗰQ⊛❶P

Lymington

Borough Arms

39 Avenue Road, SO41 9GP (on B3054 at N edge of town centre)
❀ 4-10.30 Mon; 5-10.30 Tue; 5-7 Wed; 12-2, 4-10.30 Thu; 12-2, 4-11.30 Fri; 12-11.30 Sat; 12-10.30 Sun
☎ (01590) 672814
Ringwood Best Bitter, Fortyniner; guest beer ⬢

Lively, single-bar community pub with darts, pool, jukebox and selective sports TV. An adjoining carpeted lounge area with seating is suitable for conversation. The pub is a former post house, built in 1855 and in the Jolliffe family for three generations. Guest ales are from both local and countrywide sources, with rapidly changing ciders primarily from Lilley's Cider Barn and Burley Cider Farm. Bar snacks are crisps, nuts and sweets, generally available throughout the day. Handy for St Barbe Museum, library and town centre.
ᗰQ⊛➪♣⬤P⭢⊟

North Waltham

Fox ℒ

Popham Lane, RG25 2BE (off Frog Lane, between village and A30, M3 jct 7) SU563458
❀ 11-11 (midnight Fri & Sat); 12-10.30 Sun
☎ (01256) 397288 ⊕ thefox.org
Brakspear Bitter; Sharp's Doom Bar; West Berkshire Good Old Boy; guest beer ⬢

Lovely country pub overlooking farmland. The interior is divided into two – a popular restaurant and a public bar with woodburner where food is also served (booking advisable). Outside there is an extensive beer garden and a children's play area. Once a year the pub holds a charity oyster festival with a beer tent and many other stalls and attractions. There is ample parking to the rear.
ᗰQ⊛❶ ⊟❺P⭢⊟

North Warnborough

Mill House ℒ

Hook Road, RG29 1ET (M3 jct 5; head towards Odiham) SU731521
❀ 11-11 ☎ (01256) 702953 ⊕ millhouse-hook.co.uk
Andwell King John; Brunning & Price Original Bitter; Three Castles Saxon Archer; guest beers ⬢

Listed as one of eight mills of Odiham in the Domesday Book, current sections are 17th-century additions, and it was last used as a corn mill in 1895. Now under Brunning & Price ownership, with a pleasant central bar area with eight handpumps.

It has separate dining areas and a lower level view of the waterwheel and restaurant. The area surrounding the millpond fed from the Whitewater provides a pleasant outdoor seating area linking the function barn and parking. Disabled access by request. ♨Q✿❍◑🍴P↲🏚(10)

Overton

Greyhound
46 Winchester Street, RG25 3HS SU516494
✪ 5-11 (11.30 Fri); 12-3, 6-11.30 Sat; 12-3, 7-11.30 Sun
☎ (01256) 770241
Greene King IPA, Abbot; Skinner's Betty Stogs Ⓗ
This venue is near the village centre and bus stops. It is a typical village pub with a welcoming bar between a TV lounge and a games area that has a pool table and a dartboard. An integral part of village life, it supports the cricket team and several pub games including cribbage and quizzes. At the back is a well-lit courtyard area with seating and floral displays. ♨Q✿P↲🏚(74,76,86)

Red Lion Ⓛ
37 High Street, RG25 3HQ SU514497
✪ 11.30-3, 6-11 (midnight Fri & Sat); 12-10 Sun
☎ (01256) 773363 ⊕ redlion-overton.co.uk
Flowerpots Bitter; guest beer Ⓗ
Close to the village centre, this pub styles itself as a gastro-pub turned from boozie to foodie. The main menu includes a vegetarian dish and there are daily specials with a contemporary flair and dash. Three smartly decorated areas include a restaurant, main bar and snug with upholstered bench settees. The one or two guest ales are usually from local Hampshire breweries. There is a car park at the rear and a partially covered patio area. A recently refurbished separate function room is available for corporate events and private parties. The skittle alley has been retained. ♨Q✿❍◑P↲🏚(76,86)

Park Gate

Village Inn
67 Botley Road, SO31 1AZ
✪ 11.30-11 (midnight Fri & Sat) ☎ (01489) 573223
⊕ emberpubanddining.co.uk/thevillageinnsouthampton/
Ringwood Best Bitter; Sharp's Doom Bar; guest beers Ⓗ
The Village Inn is part of Ember Inns, who continue to promote their commitment to serving good real ale. It is a popular gastro-pub with a modern layout, less than five minutes' walk from Swanwick railway station. It generally serves at least six different real ales in a relaxed, comfortable lounge setting that encourages conversation. The range of ales is regularly changing and will appeal to CAMRA members who enjoy seeking out rare, less mainstream brands. Q🚶✿❍◑↲≂(Swanwick)P↲🏚(26,28)

Petersfield

George
28 The Square, GU32 3HH
✪ 9am-11 (1am Fri & Sat); 9am-10.30 Sun
☎ (01730) 233343 ⊕ thegeorgepetersfield.co.uk
Beer range varies Ⓗ
A cosy bistro bar with a tasteful old-fashioned feel. The decoration includes a large clock and a collection of tea and coffee pots. There is a small drinking area at the front and a larger seated area

to the rear which gives access to a large patio garden. Three real ales are offered, usually one locally produced. In addition to the beer you can partake of breakfast and afternoon tea as well as the usual lunch and evening meals. Live acoustic music plays on Friday evenings. 🚶✿◑≂↲🏚

Good Intent
40 College Street, GU31 4AF
✪ 11-3, 5 (5.30 Sat)-11 (11.30 Fri); 12-3, 7-11 Sun
☎ (01730) 263838 ⊕ goodintentpetersfield.co.uk
Fuller's London Pride, seasonal beers; Gale's Seafarers Ale, HSB; guest beers Ⓗ
A 16th-century coaching inn on the old route from London to Portsmouth, the pub now has a single bar and restaurant. Although in the middle of town, the attractive building has a country pub atmosphere. Many of the oak beams used to build it were taken from the ship it is named after. There is live music every Sunday featuring local artists, and folk music every second Tuesday of the month. Look out for the unusual swear box on the bar! ✿🍴❍≂P🏚

Square Brewery
7 The Square, GU32 3HJ
✪ 10-11 ☎ (01730) 264291 ⊕ thesquarebrewery.com
Fuller's London Pride, seasonal beers; Gale's HSB; guest beers Ⓗ
A substantial tiled building in the centre of town, this single-bar pub has a modern feel inside. It is a popular venue for live music, with bands playing on Saturday evenings and jazz on Sunday afternoon. Excellent food, freshly prepared from local ingredients, is on offer, with breakfast from 10am and lunchtime meals daily. The pub may stay open later in the evening. A house beer (brewery unnamed) is also available. ◑↲🏚

Portsmouth

Artillery Arms Ⓛ
Hester Road, PO4 8HB
✪ 12-11.30 (midnight Fri & Sat) ☎ (023) 9273 3610
Bowman Swift One; Oakleaf IPA; Ringwood Fortyniner; guest beers Ⓗ
Tucked away from the main road, this two-bar free house offers a range of quality local ales alongside changing guest beers. There is a good-sized outside area with children's play equipment. Sunday lunches are renowned for their quality and the pub is a pre-match meeting place for football fans heading for Fratton Park. It is very popular with the locals and supports both darts and pool teams, offering a warm welcome to everyone. ✿❑♣↲🏚(1,2,17)

Barley Mow
39 Castle Road, Southsea, PO5 3DE
✪ 12 (11 Sat)-midnight; 12-11 Sun ☎ (023) 9282 3492
⊕ barleymowsouthsea.com
Fuller's London Pride; Gale's HSB; guest beers Ⓗ
Opposite the striking Clock Tower, this friendly two-bar community pub offers a selection of seven ales including a mild, stout or porter. It hosts an impressive array of events including live music, meat raffles, quizzes, theme nights, pool, darts, golf and cricket teams, bar billiards, chess league, and monthly druid moots – all listed on the pub website. The garden is worth checking out – it is colourful, with some hidden treasures, and has won awards in its own right. ✿❑≂(Portsmouth & Southsea)♣🏚(1,7,15)

Eastfield Hotel
124 Prince Albert Road, Southsea, PO4 9HT
✪ 11-11 (12.30 Fri & Sat) ☎ (07894) 154488
Fuller's London Pride; Skinner's Cornish Knocker; guest beers Ⓗ
Traditionally tiled outside, this two-bar pub has been refurbished recently but retains its wood panelling in the quiet lounge bar. The livelier public bar shows live football and welcomes away fans when Pompey are playing. It is a community pub with pool and darts teams, Sunday quiz, barbecues and kids' events. Regular ale Cornish Knocker, a local rarity, was chosen as it shared the landlord's name, but remains popular – guest ales are also often chosen for quirky names.
Ⓩ✿Ⓓ♣●🖫(2,16,17)

Hole in the Wall ♈ Ⓛ
36 Great Southsea Street, Southsea, PO5 3BY
✪ 4-11; 12-midnight Fri; 4-midnight Sat; 2-11 Sun
☎ (023) 9229 8085 ⊕ theholeinthewallpub.co.uk
Oakleaf Hole Hearted Ⓖ; guest beers Ⓗ/Ⓖ
The Hole is probably the smallest pub in Portsmouth, but as a genuine free house it has one of the best ranges of beer from microbreweries. The current beer selection is shown on the website. Hole Hearted, originally brewed just for this pub, is on gravity. Real cider is always available. It is open Saturdays 12-2pm for Pompey home games. Food, in the form of quality sausages and suet puddings, is available 5-8pm Tuesday-Saturday. No admittance after 11pm. CAMRA branch Pub of the Year 2013.
Q◗≢(Portsmouth & Southsea)●🖫🖫(7,15)

Isambard Kingdom Brunel
2 Guildhall Walk, PO1 2DD
✪ 7-midnight (1am Fri & Sat) ☎ (023) 9229 5112
Greene King Abbot; Ringwood Old Thumper; Ruddles Best Bitter; Shepherd Neame Spitfire; guest beers Ⓗ
Previously a gas showroom, the Isambard Kingdom Brunel, named after the famous engineer born nearby, was Wetherspoon's first pub in Portsmouth. Its grand entrance, which includes a gasworkers' war memorial, complements the Guildhall opposite; this proximity makes the pub busy on event nights. Inside, it is spacious and airy, with 12 handpumps (not usually all in use), including one local guest, and Westons ciders. It features the chain's usual all-day menu and seasonal beer festivals, plus a regional summer festival.
Q▷✿Ⓓ◗&≢(Portsmouth & Southsea)●🖫

Lawrence Arms Ⓛ
63 Lawrence Road, Southsea, PO5 1NU
✪ 2-11.30 (12.30am Fri); 11-12.30am Sat; 11-11 Sun
☎ (023) 9282 1280 ⊕ lawrence-arms-portsmouth.co.uk
Hop Back Summer Lightning; Sharp's Doom Bar; guest beer Ⓗ
Proud of its heritage since 1887, this street-corner pub's exterior retains some traditional tiles and lanterns. Inside, the L-shaped bar faces a large lounge area. Pub games are down the side leading to the garden, which includes a playhouse against a mural-painted wall. Very much a friendly community pub, there are darts, pool, and football teams, weekly meat draws, quizzes and themed days. Guest ales are Irving seasonals plus one other, and Westons cider (including boxes). Food includes tasty gourmet toasties.
Ⓩ✿&♣●'–🖫(2,17,18)

Leopold Tavern Ⓛ
154 Albert Road, Southsea, PO4 0JT
✪ 11-midnight; 12-11 Sun ☎ (023) 9282 9748
Bowman Swift One; Hop Back Summer Lightning; guest beers Ⓗ
A former Portsmouth & Brighton United Breweries pub, this has become a real beer drinkers' mecca. In addition to the two regular beers there are eight changing real ales, a number of ciders and perries, and up to 110 bottled beers from various countries. Regular beer festivals are held with well over 50 real ales passing through the handpumps. The pub is popular with football fans and gig-goers on the way to the nearby Wedgewood Rooms.
✿●'–🖫(2,17,18)

Marmion Tavern
20 Marmion Road, PO5 2BA
✪ 12-11 (midnight Thu-Sat); 12-10.30 Sun
☎ (023) 9273 7765
Courage Directors; Fuller's London Pride; Hop Back Summer Lightning Ⓗ
Just off the main shopping precinct of Southsea, this is a small pub with the bar area in a horseshoe shape. On one side at the end is a dartboard, with comfortable furnishings down the left and tables and chairs on the right. There is more room at the front and down the right side of the bar. Food is served daily at lunchtime; the menu choice is small but good. As you walk in there is an intriguing painting on the ceiling of the Battle of Trafalgar.
◗♣🖫(1,7,17)

Northcote Hotel Ⓛ
35 Francis Avenue, Southsea, PO4 0HL (just off Albert Rd, left hand side going N)
✪ 11-midnight (1am Fri & Sat) ☎ (023) 9278 9888
⊕ northcotehotel.co.uk
Hop Back Summer Lightning; Irving Invincible; Taylor Landlord; Wadworth 6X Ⓗ
The Northcote stands on a large corner plot with a heated seating area outside. The public bar is of good size and supports darts and pool teams, while the carpeted lounge is smaller and cosy. Throughout the pub there is plenty of memorabilia, ranging from a replica RMS Titanic to Sherlock Holmes mementos, plus many pictures of stars who have called in. This pub has a warm atmosphere with welcoming staff.
✿Ⓓ♣'–🖫(2,17,18)

Old Customs House
Vernon Building, Gunwharf Quay, PO1 3TY
✪ 9-midnight (10.30 winter; 2am Fri & Sat); 12-midnight Sun
☎ (023) 9283 2333 ⊕ theoldcustomshouse.com
Fuller's London Pride, ESB, seasonal beers; Gale's Seafarers Ale, HSB Ⓗ
Formerly HMS Vernon, the original layout of these naval offices in the Gunwharf Quays retail complex is retained, with the entrance and many separate rooms highlighting the Grade II-listed building's history. Outside there is a heated rear patio and seating at the front which is ideal for people watching. Beer-wise, in addition to the seasonal ales there are a couple of beer festivals including a regular Easter event, and a number of the food dishes include local ales in their recipes.
Q▷✿Ⓓ◗&≢(Harbour)🖫

Old House at Home Ⓛ
104 Locksway Road, Milton, PO4 8JR
✪ 12-11.30 (1am Fri & Sat) ☎ (023) 9273 2606
Beer range varies Ⓗ

Large two-bar community local with a varied range of three beers on offer during the week, and up to six at the weekend, including two Hampshire ales. The pub holds an annual Easter beer and music festival in its large enclosed garden. It is the current CAMRA branch Cider Pub of the Year, with up 20 available. It has warming real fires in the winter, and supports several darts and pool teams.
🏚🕭⊛♣🍴P🕳🖵(15,16)

Phoenix
13 Duncan Road, Southsea, PO5 2QU
✪ 10-midnight (1am Fri & Sat); 12-midnight Sun
☎ (023) 9278 1055
Beer range varies Ⓗ
A cosy two-bar locals' pub a short walk from Albert Road. The three changing beers come from far and wide. The public bar has a large-screen TV for sports events and hosts live music. The walls of the lounge are covered with photos of people who have appeared in the Goons – including three Goons. It also has table billiards and a table-top Space Invaders machine. Next to the lounge is a quirky patio garden and separate games room, part of the former Dock End brewery.
⊛⊟♣🍴🕳🖵(2)

Rose in June
102 Milton Road, PO3 6AR
✪ 12-midnight (1am Fri & Sat) ☎ (023) 9282 4191
⊕ theroseinjune.co.uk
Ballard's Midhurst Mild; Gale's HSB; Irving Invincible; Ringwood Best Bitter; guest beers Ⓗ
Just under a mile from Fratton Park, this two-bar pub is popular with football fans. There is plenty going on, with a curry night on the first Wednesday of the month, Tuesday quizzes, pool and darts teams, and occasional comedy nights, the events split between the two distinct bars. The extensive garden has a play area and is used for barbecues and the summer beer festival. Ciders include Cheddar Valley, Old Rosie and Black Rat, and there is a perry and a regular mild.
⊛⊟♣🍴🕳🖵(2,17,18)

Sir Loin of Beef Ⓛ
152 Highland Road, Southsea, PO4 9NH
✪ 11-11.30 (midnight Fri & Sat); 12-11.30 Sun
☎ (023) 9282 0115
Gale's HSB; Irving Frigate; Titanic Plum Porter; guest beers Ⓗ
Brightly decorated one-bar free house enjoying a warm Mediterranean feel, especially with the painted hops and colourful umbrellas on the ceiling. There are eight beers, a mix of light and dark, mostly from Southern independent breweries, plus a good selection of bottled ales (also available to take out) and boxed cider. One of the beers is offered at a value price. Entertainment includes Thursday quizzes, Sunday jazz most weeks, jukebox, pinball and bar billiards, plus plenty of submarine paraphernalia.
👤♣🍴🖵(1,2,17)

Winchester Arms Ⓛ
99 Winchester Road, Buckland, PO2 7PS
✪ 3 (4 Mon)-11; 12-11 Sat & Sun ☎ (023) 9266 2443
⊕ thewinchpub.co.uk
Oakleaf Hole Hearted; Sharp's Doom Bar; guest beer Ⓗ
A proper back-street local, this friendly two-bar pub offers two regular beers and a varying guest. The local science fiction group meets here on the

second Tuesday of the month, and there is live music every Sunday evening. A beer festival is held over the spring bank holiday weekend. The garden has a covered smoking area. It may stay open until midnight on Fridays and Saturdays if busy. Dogs are welcome, but beware of the cat. ⊛⊟♣🍴🕳

Ringwood

Inn on the Furlong
12 Meeting House Lane, BH24 1EY (by bus terminus and main car park)
✪ 9.30-11 (midnight Fri & Sat); 10-11 Sun
☎ (01425) 475139 ⊕ innonthefurlong.co.uk
Jennings Cocker Hoop; Ringwood Best Bitter, Fortyniner, Old Thumper Ⓗ
A cream-painted Victorian house, conveniently located between the bus station and the town centre. Popular breakfasts start at 9.30am, lunch is available until 3pm, and themed food is served on Wednesday to Friday evenings (curries, fine dining, and tapas respectively). A slightly raised bar serves several interlinked rooms, including a family area and a conservatory. Outside are two small patios, one with its own bar (in fine weather) and a weatherproofed TV. There is a games room for members of the pub's games club only.
🏚Q🕭⊛◑🚃♿A🍴🖵

Railway Hotel
35 Hightown Road, BH24 1NQ (off Christchurch Road) SU152048
✪ 11-11.30 ☎ (01425) 473701
⊕ therailwayhotel-ringwood.co.uk
Beer range varies Ⓗ
A very modest, traditional two-bar pub, opposite where the railway station used to be. The public bar on the right usually has a good mixture of friendly locals; the smaller left-hand bar is mostly used for dining, families and impromptu meetings. Accommodation is offered in two twin rooms and the pub provides very reasonably priced traditional English food, including a Sunday roast. The four beers are mainly from Admiral's list, and there is a slight bias towards traditional ales.
Q🕭⊛🚃◑⊟A♣P🕳🖵

Rockbourne

Rose & Thistle
SP6 3NL
✪ 11-3, 6-10.30; 11-11 Sat; 12-10.30 (8 winter) Sun
☎ (01725) 518236 ⊕ roseandthistle.co.uk
Butcombe Gold; Ringwood Best Bitter; Sharp's Doom Bar; guest beer Ⓗ
Delightful 16th-century thatched gem with beamed ceilings, two log fires and a cottage garden, in a pretty village with a Roman villa. Food includes local game and fish, and home-made sorbets and ice cream (no food Sun eve). The cosy restaurant has a collection of Simon Drew animal caricatures, and the stone-floored bar has numerous Vanity Fair prints. A guest ale appears in summer and occasionally at other times. There is live music on the last Sunday in May (the anniversary of the owner taking over).
🏚⊛◑♣🍴P🕳

Romsey

Old House at Home
62 Love Lane, SO51 8DE (NE of town centre, adjoining Waitrose car park)
🕒 11-11 (11.30 Fri and Sat); 12-10.30 Sun
☎ (01794) 513175 ⊕ theoldhouseathomeromsey.co.uk
Fuller's London Pride, seasonal beers; Gale's Seafarers Ale, HSB; guest beer Ⓗ
The interior of this part-thatched pub is divided into a carpeted and part wood-panelled bar with beams and booths, a cosy restaurant, and a wood-floored bar-cum-dining area; outside are a heated patio and a gravelled and planted garden. The all-day menu is augmented by lunchtime specials and an evening à la carte choice. Entertainment includes folk music on Mondays, a quiz on alternate Sundays, and televised major sporting events (terrestrial channels only). Under-18s are not permitted in the pub after 9pm. 🕮🌢❶◗≠P⁵-ₘ

Romsey Beer Emporium
15 Bell Street, SO51 8GY (S of Market Place, opp W entrance to Bradbeers)
🕒 9.15am-6; 12-4 1st Sun of month ☎ (01794) 517764
⊕ romseybeeremporium.co.uk
Beer range varies Ⓖ
A mecca for lovers of beer, cider and perry in Romsey and for miles around, the Beer Emporium opened in 2011. This attractive and welcoming shop always stocks one draught beer and one draught cider or perry, and its bottled selection comprises more than 200 beers, principally from UK, Belgium, Germany and the US, and about 30 ciders and perries. Other offerings include home-brew kits, books, glasses and T-shirts. ≈●ₘ

Selborne

Selborne Arms
High Street, GU34 3JR
🕒 11-3, 6-11; 11-11 Sat summer; 12-11 Sun
☎ (01420) 511247 ⊕ selbornearms.co.uk
Courage Best Bitter; Oakleaf Suthwyk Old Dick; Ringwood Fortyniner; guest beers Ⓗ
A traditional award-winning village pub with real fires and a friendly atmosphere, located at the foot of the zig-zag path carved by famous naturalist Gilbert White. Extensive menus showcase local and home-made produce. Up to four guest beers come from local microbreweries, and Mr Whitehead's ciders are always available. A play area in the huge garden is popular with children and parents. No bus service Sundays and bank holidays. 🕮Q🕮◗❣♣●P⁵-ₘ(38)

Shedfield

Wheatsheaf Inn Ⓛ
Botley Road, SO32 2JG (on A334)
🕒 12-11 (10.30 Sun) ☎ (01329) 833024
Flowerpots Perridge Pale, Bitter, Goodens Gold, seasonal beer; guest beers Ⓖ
Traditional, popular roadside inn with two bars. There are no frills here, just good beer and banter. The lively public bar has a woodburner in winter and the small lounge is quieter. The daily home-cooked food is excellent (evening meals Tue and Wed only). The small garden is a delight in summer. Live blues, jazz or folk is played most Saturday evenings. A beer festival is held on the late spring bank holiday weekend. 🕮Q🕮≠♣●P⁵-ₘ(69)

Southampton

Bitter Virtue Off-Licence Ⓛ
70 Cambridge Road, SO14 6US (jct with Alma Rd)
🕒 closed Mon; 10.30-8.30 (2 Sun) ☎ (023) 8055 4881
⊕ bittervirtue.co.uk
Beer range varies Ⓖ
This off-licence is a utopia for bottled beer from around the world, including Belgium, Germany, US and the UK. It stocks over 550 different bottles at all times, in a diverse range of styles. At least two of the four real ale casks stillaged to the rear of the shop, and draught real cider, are available for carry-out. Branded glasses, brewery T-shirts, books and memorabilia are also available. The staff are always willing to advise from their extensive experience. ❶●ₘ

Guide Dog Ⓛ
38 Earl's Road, SO14 6SF
🕒 12-11 (10.30 Sun) ☎ (023) 8022 5642
⊕ theguidedogsouthampton.co.uk
Flowerpots Goodens Gold; Fuller's ESB; guest beers Ⓗ
Single-roomed back-street local that is a former CAMRA Wessex Pub of the Year. Up to six guest beers, with a wide range of strengths, are mainly from local breweries and can be purchased in thirds. Good-value rolls are served at lunchtimes (no food Sun). Within walking distance of St Mary's Stadium, it is busy on match days. Other attractions include the Friday meat draw, October beer festival and charity events that maintain the tradition that led to the pub's name. ♣⁵-ₘ(7,U6)

Hop Inn Ⓛ
Woodmill Lane, SO18 2PH
🕒 12 (11 Sat)-11; 12-10.30 Sun ☎ (023) 8055 7723
Bowman Swift One; Gale's HSB; guest beers Ⓗ
By Riverside Park in Bitterne, the unassuming Hop Inn could easily be overlooked, but step inside the lounge bar and it instantly feels like home. A long L-shaped bar sits one side with seating on the other. The public bar is reached though a separate entrance and houses bar games and a jukebox. Six handpumps offer a selection of ales and cider. A quiz is held on the first Sunday of the month; competitors receive complimentary cheese and biscuits. 🕮🌢🕮❣◗≠P⁵-ₘ(2,7)

Junction Inn Ⓛ
21 Priory Road, SO17 2JZ
🕒 12-11 (midnight Fri & Sat) ☎ (023) 8058 4486
⊕ thejunction-inn.co.uk
Greene King XX Mild, IPA, Abbot; guest beers Ⓗ
Refurbished after a serious fire in 2012, this is a Greene King 'local hero' beer house, which means landlord Martin can select four tied real ales and four free-of-tie LocAle varieties. Since reopening there have been 70 ales from two dozen local breweries plus local ciders and bottled beer. It has a new improved menu with excellent vegetarian choices, plus a fast food menu for football days. Live music plays monthly, there is a quiz every Friday and karaoke on the last Saturday. Dog-friendly, it has three darts and two crib teams, and a bar billiards table. 🕮Q🕮🕮◗≠(St Denys)♣●P⁵-

Key & Anchor Ⓛ
90 Millbrook Road East, SO15 1JQ (jct of Cracknore Rd)
🕒 12-11 (midnight Fri & Sat); 12-10.30 Sun
☎ (023) 8090 0747
Ringwood Fortyniner, Old Thumper; guest beer Ⓗ

A friendly street-corner local dating back to 1862. Three handpumps serve two regular beers and one occasional guest. The open-hearth fires and comfortable leather sofas, combined with excellent real ale, make for enjoyable visits. Bar stools and tables and chairs will suit the more traditional pubgoer. Karaoke is featured on Saturday nights. Summer barbecues are held in the spacious garden, and there is a terrace at the front. Be careful not to trip over the large, friendly pub dogs. ⚲✿♿≠(Central)♣ᵔᵓ–🚅

Park Inn

37 Carlisle Road, SO16 4FN (frontage in Shirley Park Rd)
🌑 11.30-11.30; 12-11.30 Sat & Sun ☎ (023) 8078 7835
Wadworth Henry's IPA, 6X, Old Timer, seasonal beers; guest beer Ⓗ
Early Victorian local that became a Wadworth house in the 1980s. It is a single-bar pub but retains two entrances and its two-bar feeling; many brewery-themed mirrors adorn the walls. Six handpumps serve the Wadworth range, including seasonal beers, and a guest beer. There is a paved area with seating for outside drinkers/smokers. Sundays are busy, with a lunchtime meat draw and a popular evening quiz. There are two annual beer festivals, free Wi-Fi, and dogs are welcomed. Lunchtime sandwiches/snacks are served Mondays and Wednesday-Saturday. Q✿♣●ᵔᵓ–🚅

Platform Tavern

Town Quay, SO14 2NY (rear entrance in Winkle Street)
🌑 12-11 (midnight Thu-Sat) ☎ (023) 8033 7232
⊕ platformtavern.com
Fuller's London Pride; Gale's Seafarers Ale; guest beers Ⓗ
With unusual decor, its African art and leather sofas provide a comfortable contrast to the old Town Wall and more usual dark pub furniture. The Dancing Man Brewery provides three of the beers in a range of sometimes experimental styles. Live music plays on Thursday and Friday evenings and Sunday lunchtimes. Food is good quality, good value and popular. Several beer festivals are held during the year. Outside tables provide a venue for pavement drinking in summer as well as for smoking. ◑●ᵔᵓ–🚅(U1,U6,Citylink)

Richmond Inn

108 Portswood Road, SO17 2FW
🌑 11-11 (midnight Fri & Sat) ☎ (023) 8067 1383
⊕ richmondsouthampton.co.uk
Greene King IPA, Abbot; Morland Old Golden Hen; guest beers Ⓗ
A welcoming local, built in 1878 as a one-bar pub, converted to two bars in the 1960s, and now with an archway connecting the two. Otherwise it is little changed and still has the striking Richmond Inn etched windows. The walls are decorated with many prints and photos of Southampton's history, mostly with a maritime theme. A function room hosts Southampton's weekly folk club, The Fo'c'sle, on Friday nights. There is a quiz and curry night every Tuesday. ✿◑🖩♣ᵔᵓ–🚅

Rockstone Ⓛ

63 Onslow Road, SO14 0JL (on main Bevois Valley strip)
🌑 11-midnight (1am Fri & Sat) ☎ (023) 8033 0350
⊕ therockstone.co.uk
Beer range varies Ⓗ
One of the best new pubs in central Southampton, run by husband and wife team Max and Aimee. High-quality home-cooked food features alongside

six changing guest ales, mostly Hampshire brewed – some may have house names. LocAle accredited, the landlord is also a local cider enthusiast. Ale festivals in March and October are complemented by themed nights throughout the year, with a free quiz every Monday. First-time and regular visitors are always welcomed with a convivial greeting. ⚲Q✿◑●ᵔᵓ–🚅🖩(U6,7)

South Western Arms

38-40 Adelaide Road, SO17 2HW
🌑 12-11 (midnight Fri-Sun) ☎ (023) 8032 4542
⊕ southwesternarms.com
Sunny Republic Beach Blonde; guest beers Ⓗ
The South Western has a single bar with a raised seating area on the ground floor; there is more seating and a pool table in the gallery upstairs. At the rear is a walled garden with a covered smoking area which is an oasis in the summer, although the trains passing beyond the wall regularly remind you that you are in town. Two mini beer festivals are held each year. There are normally nine real ales and up to 20 foreign bottled beers available. ✿≠(St Denys)♣●Pᵔᵓ–🚅(7)

Talking Heads

320 Portswood Road, SO17 2TD
🌑 4-1am (3am Fri); 2-3am Sat; 2-1am Sun
☎ (023) 8067 8446 ⊕ thetalkingheads.co.uk
Andwell King John; Longdog Lamplight Porter; guest beers Ⓗ
Formerly the Red Lion, now a popular combined pub and late-closing music and comedy venue (which also claims to be haunted). It is a popular meeting place for university societies and motorcycle enthusiasts. The music venue may be hired for private functions. The main bar has notable original pub windows. Lady Libby house beer is Andwell's King John. Food purchased from the nearby chippie can be consumed on the premises. Entrance charges may apply for entertainment. ♿✿🖩♣●Pᵔᵓ–🚅(2,5,U6)

Wellington Arms Ⓛ

56 Park Road, SO15 3DE (on the corner of Park Rd and Mansion Rd)
🌑 12-11.30 (12.30am Fri & Sat) ☎ (023) 8022 0356
⊕ wellingtonarmssouthampton.co.uk
Fuller's London Pride, ESB; Ringwood Old Thumper; guest beers Ⓗ
A proper traditional pub with two bars supporting a total of 11 real ale handpumps, the Welly is hidden away in residential streets but also close to the main road and transport links. The beer range includes many local guests. The building dates from the 1860s, is the consulate of Redonda, and its interior is adorned with pewter tankards and Wellingtonian memorabilia. The Thursday night quiz is highly popular. The garden is paved and has a heated smoking area. ⚲✿🖩ᵔᵓ–🚅

Tangley

Cricketers Arms Ⓛ

SP11 0SH (towards Lower Chute) SU327528
🌑 11-3 (not Mon & Thu), 6-11; 12-3, 7-10.30 Sun
☎ (01264) 730283 ⊕ thecricketers.eu
Bowman Swift One, Wallops Wood Ⓖ
In attractive countryside, this 16th-century drovers' inn sits below the Berkshire Downs. The two Bowman ales, served from stillage behind the bar, may be supplemented by a local guest in summer months. The front bar, with its huge inglenook

fireplace, is used mainly for drinking, while traditional home-cooked food is available in the flagstoned dining area at the rear.
ᴍᴬQ❦☜☺☙⟐⏚⇘P⅃⬚(C6)

Tichborne

Tichborne Arms
SO24 0NA (on road N out of Tichborne) SU571304
❂ 11.45-3, 6-11 (midnight Fri); 12-11.30 Sat; 12-4 Sun
☎ (01962) 733760 ⊕ tichbornearms.co.uk
Palmers Copper Ale; guest beers ⑤
Thatched country pub with a compact wood-panelled public bar with open fire and piano, and a larger rustic lounge with a woodburner and antiques. The bar serves ales direct from the cask, with at least two guest beers, and real cider during the summer. A continually changing menu features home-cooked, locally sourced, seasonal food. Outside is a large, comfortable, covered patio and garden which hosts a three-day beer festival every August. Dogs are welcomed by the four resident canines. ᴍᴬQ❦☺☙⟐⏚♣♦P⅃

Titchfield

Queen's Head ⅃
High Street, PO14 4AQ (100yds N of village square)
❂ 11-11 ☎ (01329) 842154 ⊕ queenshead-titchfield.co.uk
Beer range varies ⒣
A handsome, listed pub dating from the 17th century, with a homely bar and central fireplace. Four regularly rotated ales are predominantly from local breweries, including Irving and Oakleaf. It has a separate restaurant, and upstairs is a function room catering for events such as theatre nights. Outside, a patio area leads to a rear car park. Home-made, locally sourced food is served lunchtimes and evenings (lunchtime only Sun) and a quiz and meat raffle are held every Sunday evening. Q❦☺☙P⅃⬚(4,4A,X4)

Wheatsheaf ⅃
1 East Street, PO14 4AD (E end of East Street)
❂ 12-3, 6-11 Mon; 12-11 (midnight Fri & Sat)
☎ (01329) 842965 ⊕ wheatsheaftitchfield.co.uk
Flowerpots Bitter; Palmers IPA; guest beers ⒣
A compact 17th-century free house with a good reputation for ale and food quality. The cosy bar has a real fire and the separate snug is ideal for quiet conversation. Guest beers often come from local breweries and beer festivals are held summer and winter. Food is available in the bar or separate restaurant every day except Monday including traditional Sunday lunches and popular steak nights on Tuesdays. Beyond the restaurant a covered area leads to the car park.
ᴍᴬQ❦☺☙⏚♦P⅃⬚(4,4A,X4)

Twyford

Bugle Inn ⅃
Park Lane, SO21 1QT (jct of High St and Park Lane)
❂ 12-11 (10.30 Sun) ☎ (01962) 714888
⊕ bugleinntwyford.co.uk
Beer range varies ⒣
Attractive, modernised pub, reopened in 2008 after closure and a battle with property developers. There is one long, open bar with plush sofas at one end and a restaurant area at the other; the central bar has stools for casual drinkers. Quality food is the big feature, focusing on local, often organic,

produce, with suppliers including Overton's Laverstoke Farm. Table booking is advisable. A beer from each of the LocAle breweries – Bowman, Flowerpots and Upham – is frequently accompanied by a guest. Free Wi-Fi.
ᴍᴬQ☺☙P⅃⬚(69)

Phoenix Inn ⅃
High Street, SO21 1RF
❂ 11.30-2.30, 6-11; 11.30-11 Fri & Sat; 12-10.30 Sun
☎ (01962) 713322 ⊕ thephoenixinn.co.uk
Flowerpots Bitter; Greene King IPA; Morland Old Speckled Hen; guest beers ⒣
The Phoenix was originally a 17th-century inn on the old Winchester to Portsmouth turnpike. The large, long bar is multi-level and there is a popular skittle alley and function room to the rear. An impressive bank of eight handpumps dispenses four Greene King beers and four LocAle guests. Traditional pub food is served, and there are themed nights: pizzas on Wednesdays and fish and chips on Thursdays. There is a large-screen TV for major sporting events. Occasional live music and quiz nights take place – check the website.
ᴍᴬQ☺☙♣P⅃⬚(69)

Upper Farringdon

Rose & Crown ⅃
Crows Lane, GU34 3ED (signed off A32) SU715351
❂ 12-3, 5.30-11; 12-11 Sat; 12-10.30 Sun ☎ (01420) 588231
⊕ roseandcrownfarringdon.co.uk
Sharp's Doom Bar; guest beers ⒣
Built in 1810 by the Knight family of Chawton, this hostelry is off the beaten track but worth seeking out. Enter this friendly pub to find a welcoming L-shaped bar with a seating area warmed by a log fire, a dining area and a modern restaurant. An imaginative menu is supplemented by lunchtime bar snacks. Food is served lunchtimes and evenings, all day on Sunday. Three guest beers include one from Triple fff. Families, walkers and dogs are welcome and there is a spacious garden.
ᴍᴬQ☺☙P⅃

Walhampton

Waggon & Horses
Undershore Road, SO41 5SB (100yds W of Lymington ferry terminal)
❂ 12-11 (10 Sun) ☎ (01590) 672517
Wadworth Henry's IPA, 6X, seasonal beers ⒣
Former thatched pub, rebuilt in 1908, close to the Isle of Wight ferry terminal, used until 1731 as a resting point for donkeys and carts before the ferry to town was replaced by a toll bridge. It has been tastefully refurbished with atmospheric lighting, alcoves and cushions. Quality locally sourced food is served lunchtimes and evenings, with booking advised. Up to four ales are available from the Wadworth range. Dogs are allowed in the bar area only. Chess and board games are available for entertainment. ᴍᴬQ☺☙⇌(Lymington Pier)♣P⅃

West End

Master Builder
Swaythling Road, SO30 3AH
❂ 11.30-11 (11.30 Fri & Sat); 12-11 Sun ☎ (023) 8047 2426
⊕ masterbuildersouthampton.co.uk
Wadworth Henry's IPA, 6X, Bishops Tipple, seasonal beers ⒣

A single-bar pub with three distinct parts: a raised dining area, a bar area, and a games and sports bar through an archway. The dining area can be reached by an outside ramp, although the pub does not have full disabled facilities. There is also a conservatory and garden with a covered smoking area. Conservatory and dining areas are bookable for private functions. Two mini beer festivals are held each year. The real fire is in the games and sports bar. ⛫❀◐◑♣P⁴–🚌(A,8,8A)

West Tytherley

Black Horse 🏆 L

North Lane, SP5 1NF

⏲ 7-10.30 Mon; 12-3 (not Tue), 6-11; 12-8 (4.30 winter) Sun ☎ (01794) 340308 🌐 theblackhorsepublichouse.co.uk

Hop Back GFB; guest beers H

A welcoming, traditional village free house. The main bar with old farming paraphernalia is complemented by a dining room plus function room and skittle alley. The pub has its own football team and helped with the restoration of the village church bell – believed to be the oldest in the world. Locally sourced produce, including buffalo, features on the menu (no food Mon eve). The guest beer range always includes Bowman and Flowerpots plus one other local brewery. Local CAMRA Pub of the Year 2013. ⛫Q❀◐◑⊞♣●P⁴–🚌(37)

Wherwell

White Lion

Winchester Road, SP11 7JF (B3420 S of A303 at Andover) SU389409

⏲ 7.30 (8 Sat & Sun)-11 ☎ (01264) 860317

🌐 thewhitelionwherwell.co.uk

Ringwood Best Bitter; Sharp's Doom Bar; Taylor Landlord; guest beers H

Pleasant former coaching inn at the centre of a historic thatched village alongside the famous trout fishing haven of the River Test. This venue was built in 1611 and hit by a cannonball in the Civil War, which still hangs on the bar. Today the pub is used by the village community and by walkers on the Test Valley Way. It is open for breakfasts to non-residents and lunch hampers are also available. No food Sunday evening. Q❀🛏◐◑P⁴–

Whitchurch

Bell Inn

Bell Street, RG28 7DD

⏲ 10-11; 12-10.30 Sun ☎ (01256) 893120

🌐 thebellwhitchurch.co.uk

Courage Best Bitter; Fuller's London Pride; Gale's Seafarers Ale H

The 15th-century, half-timbered, family-run Bell just oozes the character of a traditional pub. Sea-going pictures predominate while a separate area off the lounge provides space for enjoying a quiet pint or a meeting for a club or society. Conversation and local gossip rules in both bars and quiz evenings are very popular. There is a pool table and a small library that raises funds for charity. Outside is a small pleasant patio. The pub has an electric car charging point. Q❀🛏◐⊞♣P🚌(76,86)

> Bread is the staff of life, but beer is life itself. **Traditional**

Prince Regent L

104 London Road, RG28 7LT SU469483

⏲ 12-11 (10.30 Sun) ☎ (01256) 895525

Fuller's London Pride; Hop Back Summer Lightning; Wells Bombardier H

The pub up the hill is a single-bar local free house on the edge of this historic country town, overlooking the higher reaches of the Test Valley. It is a locals' pub where conversation is difficult to avoid while you enjoy some of the best real ale prices in the area. There is a keen interest in sporting events, with a pool table and sports TV, and an emphasis on football matches. It has an excellent jukebox. ♣P🚌(76,86)

White Hart Hotel

The Square, RG28 7DN

⏲ 11-11; 12-10.30 Sun ☎ (01256) 892900

🌐 whiteharthotelwhitchurch.co.uk

Arkell's 3B, Moonlight Ale, Kingsdown Ale H

This 15th-century coaching inn is a centre of community life, with a lively public bar, pleasant dining area and a quiet restaurant to the rear, also used for private functions and meetings. Live music, discos and quizzes all feature. Breakfasts and teas are served and it is a popular cyclists' stop. One of the decorated bollards outside commemorates the author Charles Kingsley, who stayed in the hotel. In the square, the right to demonstrate was won for the country in the 19th century, and Lord Denning, former Master of the Rolls, was born in the building across the road. ⛫Q❀🛏◐◑⊞♿P⁴–🚌(76,86)

Winchester

Albion

2 Stockbridge Road, SO23 7BZ

⏲ 12-11 (midnight Fri & Sat); 12-10.30 Sun

☎ (01962) 864259

Beer range varies H

Small, cosy pub opposite the bottom of Station Hill, thus the closest pub to Winchester rail station. The street-corner location at a busy intersection gives it an unusual shape, and makes it an ideal place from which to watch the world go by. Food is served weekday lunchtimes, and evenings except Friday. The three changing ales often include one from Dark Star, and there is an interesting foreign beer selection both on handpump and bottled. ⛫◐◑⇌🚌

Bishop on the Bridge

1 High Street, SO23 9JX

⏲ 11-11 (midnight Fri & Sat; 10.30 Sun) ☎ (01962) 855111

🌐 bishoponthebridge.co.uk

Fuller's London Pride, ESB, seasonal beers H

Large, spacious L-shaped pub with a mixed clientele, from families to circuit drinkers. The side of the building and the patio area overlook part of the River Itchen as it flows out of the City Mill. Two changing beers are from the Fuller's brewery and are supplemented by a selection of its bottled ales. There is a monthly live music evening and a pub quiz every Tuesday. Disabled access is via the rear entrance on Colebrook Street. ⛫❀◐◑♿–🚌

Black Boy L

1 Wharf Hill, SO23 9NQ (just off Chesil St B3404)

⏲ 12-11 (midnight Fri & Sat; 10.30 Sun) ☎ (01962) 861754

🌐 theblackboypub.com

Bowman Swift One; Flowerpots Bitter; Itchen Valley Pure Gold; Ringwood Best Bitter; guest beer Ⓗ
A centuries-old rambling building with many interconnected rooms, resembling an over-stocked folk museum. Serviced from a central bar, one room is themed as a country kitchen complete with working Aga, another a butcher's, with papier mache joints, while other areas are tradesmen's workshops. Taxidermy surprises come at every turn. Pub food is served daily except Mondays and Sunday evenings. A guest beer usually comes from another local brewery. A splendid medieval-style smoking shelter graces the patio/garden. The Black Rat restaurant, opposite, is under the same ownership. ≜Q✿⏣◑➽◑⌐⊐(4)

Hyde Tavern Ⓛ
57 Hyde Street, SO23 7DY
✪ 12.30-2.30 (not Mon-Wed), 5-11.30 (12.30am Fri); 12-midnight Sat; 12-11 Sun ☎ (01962) 862592
⊕ hydetavern.com
Flowerpots Bitter Ⓗ; guest beers Ⓖ
An imposing double gable dominates the exterior of this small, medieval, timber-framed building. The two-roomed interior is below street level – beware of low ceilings and undulating floors. A cellar room is used for regular events. Up to seven beers from small local breweries feature, always including a mild or stout, and real ciders are available. There is no regular road, but customers may order takeaways and a barbecue can be hired. Outside is a delightful, secluded garden.
≜Q✿⏣⏣≈♣◑⌐⊐

St James Tavern
3 Romsey Road, SO22 5BE
✪ 12-11 (midnight Fri & Sat); 12-10.30 Sun
☎ (01962) 861288
Wadworth Henry's IPA, Horizon, 6X, Bishops Tipple; guest beer Ⓗ
An unusual acutely-angled end-of-terrace pub on the steep Romsey Road hill. Inside is a single split-level L-shaped bar, with lots of wood and dark walls, giving a restful feel. Outside at the rear is a smart patio. The food menu has interesting specials and themes: curry on Monday, pie & pint on Wednesday and Saturday brunch. There is a quiz on Tuesday and live acoustic music on the second and last Sunday in the month. The cider is Westons Old Rosie. ➽✿◑≈♣◑⌐⊐(4,5,66)

Wykeham Arms
75 Kingsgate Street, SO23 9PE (immediately outside the city's ancient Kingsgate)

✪ 11-11 ☎ (01962) 853834
⊕ wykehamarmswinchester.co.uk
Flowerpots Goodens Gold; Fuller's London Pride, seasonal beers; Gale's Seafarers Ale, HSB Ⓗ
Dating from 1755, this is a Georgian inn in historic streets between the Cathedral Close and the college. Many interlinked rooms are crammed with memorabilia, much Nelsonian; old school desks masquerade as bar tables. It can become crowded but never loses its civilised, conversational atmosphere; booking for meals is advisable at busy times. Although a Fuller's house, a Flowerpots beer is always offered but the variety may vary. The accommodation, comprising 14 rooms, is highly rated. ≜Q⏣◑⌐⊐(1,69)

Winchfield

Barley Mow
The Hurst, RG27 8DE SU777538
✪ 12-3, 5.30-11 (10 Mon); 12-3.30, 5.30-11.30 Fri & Sat; 12-10.30 Sun ☎ (01252) 617490 ⊕ barley-mow.com
Fuller's London Pride; Sharp's Doom Bar; guest beer Ⓗ
An attractive modernised country pub in a pleasant location close to the Basingstoke Canal and ideal for walkers, with a real log fire and comfortable seating. It offers a good range of pub food, including a takeaway menu. A range of traditional pub games and board games is available on request. Three real ales are served, including a rotating guest, often Brakspear Bitter or Hogs Back TEA. The first Monday of the month is quiz night and there is an annual beer and music festival.
≜Q➽✿◑♣◑P⌐

Winsor

Compass Inn
Winsor Road, SO40 2HE
✪ 12-11 ☎ (023) 8081 2237 ⊕ compassinn.co.uk
Flack Manor Double Drop; Gale's HSB; Sharp's Doom Bar; Young's Bitter Ⓗ
Easily found at the east end of Winsor village, the Compass is a cosy wood-floored three-roomed pub, seeming larger inside than out. There is a public bar with a pool table, a lounge with bare brick walls, plenty of polished brass and a woodburner, plus an adjoining dining room. Outside is a colourful garden with lots of shelter, ideal for the pub's beer festivals. It is very dog-friendly: there are organised dog walks every month with food before and after. ≜Q➽✿◑⏣Å♣P⌐⊐(11,T3)

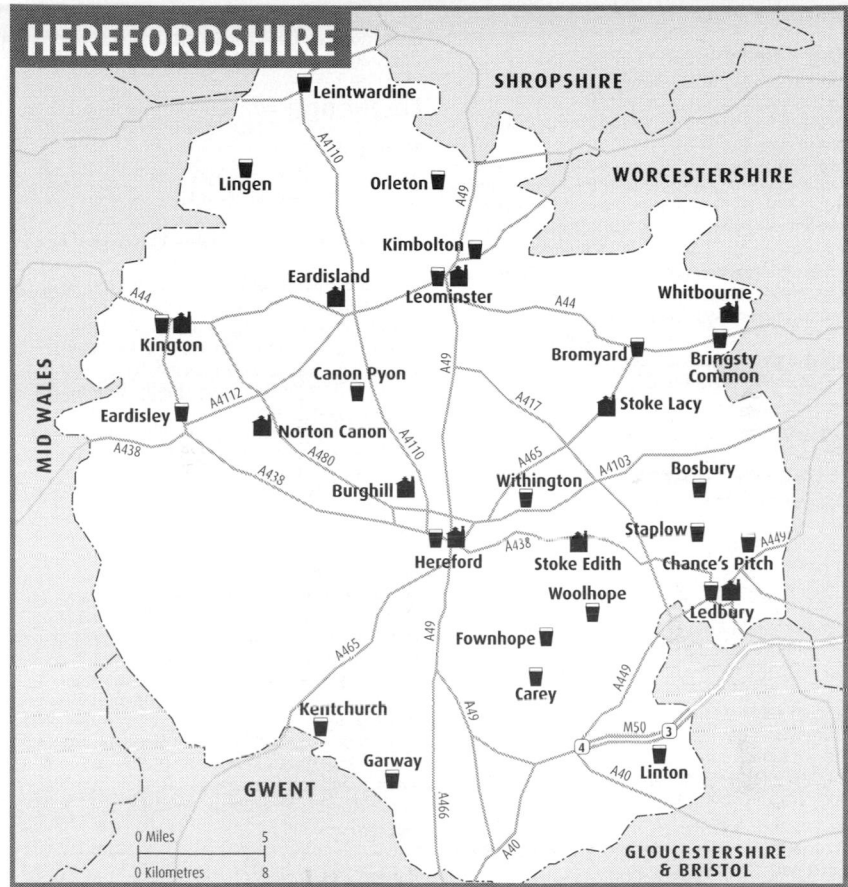

Bosbury

Bell Inn

HR8 1PX (on B4220, in village)

☼ 12-2.30 (not Mon & Tue), 5-11; 12-2.30, 5-midnight Fri; 12-midnight Sat; 12-10.30 Sun ☎ (01531) 640285

⊕ thebellatbosbury.com

Ledbury Gold; Otter Bitter; Wye Valley HPA Ⓗ

This black and white timbered terraced inn gets its name from the bells of the imposing village church that stands opposite. The traditional two-bar interior includes a restaurant area (no food Mon or Sun eve) contrasting with a basic yet comfortable public bar, replete with grand fireplace, alcoves, books and newspapers. Friendly and welcoming, this pub lies at the heart of its community. A large, attractive garden features at the rear. Plenty of on-street parking is usually available.

🏰Q❀◑ ⊟➡ 🚲(417)

Bringsty Common

Live & Let Live Ⓛ

WR6 5UW (off A44, at Cat & Mouse sign follow right-hand track down onto common) SO699547

☼ closed Mon; 12-11 (12-2.30, 6-11 Tue-Thu winter); 12-10.30 Sun ☎ (01886) 821462

⊕ liveandletlive-bringsty.co.uk

Malvern Hills Black Pear; Wye Valley Butty Bach; guest beer Ⓗ

This isolated and cosy 16th century Grade-II listed ex-cider house is Herefordshire's only thatched pub. It can be accessed via a short track across the common. The owners have lovingly renovated the pub to an extraordinarily high standard: downstairs is much exposed timber, flagstone floors, settles and a fine fireplace with oak overmantle; upstairs is the Thatch Restaurant. Quality locally sourced food (including Bringsty lamb) can be enjoyed both in the bar and the restaurant. A beer festival is held in the garden each Easter.

🏰Q🐾❀◑ ▲P⁵⊟🚲(420)

Bromyard

Rose & Lion Ⓛ

5 New Road, HR7 4AJ

☼ 11-11 (midnight Fri & Sat) ☎ (01885) 482381

Wye Valley Bitter, HPA, Butty Bach Ⓗ

One of the expanding Wye Valley Brewery estate, the Rosie enjoys a loyal following by locals, and is never anything but friendly. The two small original rooms are complemented by a further bar to the rear plus an annexe with fully equipped disabled toilets and a pleasant garden. Furnished in a modern but appropriate style, it acts as a venue for live folk music on Sunday nights – there is always a real buzz about the place. No food is served.

Q❀⊟&♣P⁵⊟🚲(420)

Canon Pyon

Nag's Head 🅛
HR4 8NY (on A4110, in village)
✪ closed Tue; 12-3 (not Mon), 5-11; 12-3, 5-midnight Thu; 12-3, 5-1am Fri; 12-1am Sat; 12-11 Sun ☎ (01432) 830725
⊕ thenags.co.uk
Otter Amber; Wye Valley Butty Bach Ⓗ
Refitted in contemporary style, the large single bar in this 17th-century building has original timbers and a flagstone floor, and feels very cosy with its real fire. The bar and separate restaurant offer a range of home-prepared food (no food Mon or Sun eves) from bar snacks to a full à la carte menu and a roast on Sundays. Outside is a large adventure playground. This pub was the first home of the Wye Valley Brewery, whose beers still feature.
⚏Q⮂⚛◑⊟♣P⁵⊸⊟(501)

Carey

Cottage of Content 🅛
HR2 6NG (in village)
✪ closed Mon & winter Tue; 12-2, 6-10.30 summer Tue & Wed; 12-2, 6.30-10.30 Thu; 12-2, 6.30-11 Fri & Sat; 12-3 Sun ☎ (01432) 840242 ⊕ cottageofcontent.co.uk
Hobsons Best Bitter; Wye Valley Butty Bach; guest beer Ⓗ
A truly beautiful old black and white building in delightful surroundings, with parts dating from 1485. There are two bars and a separate restaurant. Although food of high quality predominates, drinkers are welcome. Booking is advised at most times for the freshly prepared bar meals at lunchtime and à la carte in the evening. There is a large garden on the hillside to the rear. Dogs are allowed in the bar only. The pub may close for short breaks in winter. ⚏Q⚛⮐◑⚛P⁵⁻

Chance's Pitch

Wellington Inn 🅛
WR13 6HW (on A449, near B4218 jct)
✪ closed Mon; 12-3, 6.30-11; 12-4 Sun ☎ (01684) 540269
⊕ thewellingtoninnmalvern.co.uk
Goff's Tournament; guest beers Ⓗ
Located on the main Ledbury-Malvern road, this is a traditional, dog- and child-friendly pub in an extended multi-level building, enjoying good views across open country. There is a drinkers-only area in the middle with a real fire plus reading material, a restaurant above and a drinking/dining area below. An extensive menu is offered, ranging from sandwiches and snacks to full à la carte, all ingredients from local suppliers. ⚏Q⮂⚛◑⚛P⁵⁻

Eardisley

Tram Inn 🅛
HR3 6PG (on A4111, in village)
✪ closed Mon; 12-3, 6-midnight (12.30am Fri & Sat); 12-3, 7-10.30 Sun ☎ (01544) 327251 ⊕ thetraminn.co.uk
Hobsons Best Bitter; Wye Valley Butty Bach; guest beer Ⓗ
The name of this fine black and white inn alludes to a horse-operated plateway that once passed nearby – a preserved plate section is on view. The much-altered 16th-century building has a public bar and a lounge with exposed beams and cosy corners, plus an informal dining room and a games room to the rear. Traditional, locally sourced, freshly made pub meals are served including

Sunday roasts (no food Sun eve). Draught Dunkertons and bottled Orgasmic and Gwatkins ciders are stocked. ⚏Q⚛◑▲♣⚛P⁵⁻⊟(446,462)

Fownhope

New Inn 🅛
HR1 4PE (on B4224, in village)
✪ 12-3, 6 (5 Fri)-midnight; 11-midnight Sat; 12-midnight Sun ☎ (01432) 860350 ⊕ thenewinnfownhope.co.uk
Hobsons Best Bitter; Wye Valley Bitter; guest beer Ⓗ
This locals' pub at the heart of a thriving two-pub village has two pleasant seating areas served by a single bar, one with large-screen TV. Fownhope football team use the pub as a base. Home-prepared pub-style food is served weekday lunchtimes with weekly themed evenings such as fish and chips, pies or curry. There are also jam sessions, singalongs and quizzes. Dates vary, so ring or check the website for all evening events. The guest beer is sourced locally.
⚏⮂⚛⚛▲♣P⁵⁻⊟(453)

Garway

Garway Moon 🅛
Garway Common, HR2 8RQ SO465227
✪ 12-3 (not Mon & Wed), 6-midnight; closed Tue; 12-midnight Sat & Sun ☎ (01600) 750270
⊕ garwaymooninn.co.uk
Wye Valley HPA, Butty Bach; guest beers Ⓗ
A remote but popular and welcoming pub overlooking the delightful village green and cricket pitch, with a lounge and public bar plus a separate snug/family room and garden. Beers are from regional and local breweries including Wye Valley and Butcombe. Traditional, good-value, home-prepared bar and restaurant meals are served with vegetarian options. Pizza night is Wednesday, curry night Thursday, roasts on Sunday.
⚏⮂⚛◑⊟▲♣⚛P⊟(412)

Hereford

Barrels ▼ 🅛
69 St Owen Street, HR1 2JQ
✪ 11-11.30 (midnight Fri & Sat); 12-11.30 Sun ☎ (01432) 274968
Wye Valley Bitter, HPA, Dorothy Goodbody's Golden Ale, Butty Bach; guest beers Ⓗ
CAMRA Herefordshire Pub of the Year for the sixth time, this was once home to Wye Valley Brewery and now enjoys a cult following in the city and beyond. Four distinct rooms cater for all age groups; a pool table occupies one, another has a large-screen TV (only for major sporting events), otherwise conversation rules. The cobbled and decked courtyard and adjacent brewery bar are

INDEPENDENT BREWERIES
Arrow Kington
Brew On Whitbourne
Hereford Hereford
Ledbury Ledbury (NEW)
Mayfields Leominster
Mulberry Duck Burghill (NEW)
Saxon City Stoke Edith (brewing suspended)
Shoes Norton Canon
Simpsons Eardisland (NEW)
Wobbly Hereford (NEW)
Wye Valley Stoke Lacy

home to an annual charity beer and music festival held each August bank holiday weekend.
😊🍴🈂🚻🚗♿💪🍺🚉

King's Fee 🅛
49-53 Commercial Road, HR1 2BJ
😊 8am-midnight ☎ (01432) 373240
Greene King Abbot; Ruddles Best Bitter; guest beers 🅗
Award-winning Wetherspoon conversion of an old supermarket. A large, light and airy open-plan main bar with numerous alcoves leads to an elevated family seating area (children welcome up to 7pm) and a courtyard. The decor is contemporary in style, and features local history panels and woodcut prints by a local artist. Good-value food is served all day. Five local ciders on handpump are complemented by the usual offer from Westons. Opens at 7am for breakfast.
Q🈂😊🍴♿🈂🈂🚻🚗♿🍺🚉

Volunteer Inn
21 Harold Street, HR1 2QU
😊 11-11 (midnight Fri & Sat); 12-11 Sun ☎ (01432) 276189
Greene King Abbot; Otter Bitter; guest beers 🅗
A lively and friendly atmosphere is assured at this contemporary community pub, with two bars, a skittle alley and a great little snug. The home-cooked food, including vegetarian and vegan options, is available until 5pm (7pm Fri). Events include a quiz on Monday, curry and a pint on Wednesday, and a local farmers' vegetable sale on Thursday (6-8pm). The two guest beers come mainly from national breweries.
🏰Q🈂😊🍴🈂🈂🚻♿🚗🚉(76)

Kentchurch

Bridge Inn
HR2 0BY (on B4347)
😊 6-11 Mon; closed Tue; 12-2.30, 6-11 (12-11 Sat summer); 12-5 (midnight summer) Sun ☎ (01981) 240408
⊕ bridgeinnkentchurch.co.uk
Otter Bitter; guest beers 🅗
Situated close to the Welsh border on the banks of the River Monnow, the building probably dates from the 14th century. It has a welcoming single front bar and a restaurant with excellent views, and boasts riverside gardens and a pétanque piste for summer days. The freshly prepared food ranges from bar snacks to full à la carte (no food Sun eve). Guest beers are from regional and local breweries, usually including Wye Valley. A beer festival is held in May. 🏰Q😊🈂🈂♿🚐P🚉

Kimbolton

Stockton Cross 🅛
HR6 0HD (on A4112, W of village)
😊 closed Mon; 12-3, 7-11 (not Sun eve) ☎ (01568) 612509
Wye Valley HPA, Butty Bach; guest beer 🅗
Prominently situated at the edge of the village, this single-bar black and white pub dates from the 16th century and has some interesting features. The long, narrow bar and its two cosy alcoves set either side of the large fireplace accommodate both drinkers and diners. The interesting menu, including a good vegetarian choice, is mainly sourced locally and freshly prepared. Regular events include an open mic night on the second Wednesday of the month and a curry and quiz night on the last Wednesday. 🏰🚐😊🈂🍴P🚉

Kington

Olde Tavern ★ 🅛
22 Victoria Road, HR5 3BX
😊 6.30-10.30 (midnight Wed & Thu); 3.30-midnight Fri; 12-midnight Sat & Sun ☎ (01544) 239033
Hobsons Mild; Ludlow Best; Wye Valley Butty Bach; guest beer 🅗
Diminutive Grade II-listed two-room time warp with an entrance lobby, still with its off-sales hatch, leading to a main bar with many original features, alcove seating and fascinating curios. The old smoke room to the right has a flagstone floor and bench seating, plus a serving hatch to the bar. The Tavern offers a warm welcome from staff and locals alike. Regulars take pride in the pub-based activities, including the annual beer festival on the spring bank holiday. Q😊😊🍴🈂🚗🚉

Ledbury

Prince of Wales 🅛
Church Lane, HR8 1DL
😊 11-11 (10.30 Sun) ☎ (01531) 632250 ⊕ powledbury.com
Butcombe Bitter; Hobsons Best Bitter; Ledbury Dark; Otter Bitter; Wye Valley HPA, Butty Bach; guest beer 🅗
Set in a delightful cobbled alley leading up to the imposing church, this 16th-century timber-framed pub boasts two bars, one with a discrete alcove where a folk jam session is held each Wednesday evening and alternate Sunday afternoons. This is a true community pub, bustling with locals and visitors. Draught cider from Westons is stocked, together with an extensive range of foreign beers – both draught and bottled. The bar meals are excellent value, including the Sunday roasts.
🚐😊🈂🍴🚗🈂🈂🚻♿🚉

Talbot Hotel 🅛
14 New Street, HR8 2DX
😊 11-11 (midnight Fri & Sat) ☎ (01531) 632963
⊕ talbotledbury.co.uk
Wadworth Henry's IPA, 6X; Wye Valley Butty Bach; guest beer 🅗
An outstanding black and white half-timbered hotel and bar dating back to the 1590s, with direct links to the Civil War. Various comfortably furnished seating areas, with discreet nooks and corners, surround an island servery facing a splendid fireplace. The restaurant, with its superb wood panelling, offers affordable fine cuisine using locally sourced ingredients, while conventional bar snacks are also available in the bar. The guest beer is from Wadworth's seasonal range or Red Shoot subsidiary. 🏰😊🈂🍴🈂🚗♿🚉

Leintwardine

Sun Inn ★ 🅛
Rosemary Lane, SY7 0LP (off A4113, in village)
😊 11 (5.30 Mon)-11; 11-10.30 Sun ☎ (01547) 540705
⊕ suninn-leintwardine.co.uk
Hobsons Mild, Twisted Spire, Best Bitter; guest beers 🅗
One of Britain's last remaining parlour pubs, the inn owes its survival to the Herefordshire CAMRA-led Save the Sun campaign of 2009. The public bar features bench furniture, a simple fireplace and gentle conversation. The other front room is the parlour where ex-landlady of 74 years, Flossie, once held court. To the rear, a new pavilion-style extension overlooks the garden. A beer festival is

held annually on the August bank holiday Sunday. Some beers are served straight from the cask on request. ⚠Q🍴🕿🌁🍴🎯▲♣♠🖾(738,740)

Leominster

Bell Inn 🅛
39 Etnam Street, HR6 8AE
🌣 12-midnight 🕿 (01568) 612818
Purple Moose Cwrw Eryri (Snowdonia Ale); Wye Valley HPA; guest beers 🎛
A welcome return to the Guide under enthusiastic new licensees. This terraced pub features a U-shaped island bar with recently refreshed light, modern decor, plus a pleasant garden to the rear. The Bell is a premier venue for live music on Thursday nights. The guest beers are generally from local breweries. There is free on-street parking nearby and a Pay & Display car park to the rear. ⚠🕿🎯🌁♣🖾

Grape Vaults 🅛
2-4 Broad Street, HR6 8BS
🌣 11-11 🕿 (01568) 611404 🌐 thegrapevaults.co.uk
Ludlow Best, Gold; guest beers 🎛
A plain façade conceals a real gem of a pub with fireplace, bench seating and much original woodwork. The pull-down TV screen is only used for important sports fixtures. A small snug is tucked away behind a part-glazed screen and the Gents is probably the smallest in the country. English pub food is served at reasonable prices (not Sun eve). Live music plays on Sunday afternoons. Guest beers are local. A beer festival is held alongside the annual Victorian market in December. ⚠Q🎯🌁≈🖾

Lingen

Royal George 🅛
SY7 0DY (on minor road N of B4362 and S of A4113) SO366669
🌣 closed Mon; 6-11; 12-3, 6-11 Sat; 12-3 Sun
🕿 (01544) 267322
Wye Valley Butty Bach; guest beer 🎛
A remote pub set in beautiful surroundings known as Mortimer Country – the Mortimer Trail passes nearby and there is a variety of local walks. Boasting its own spacious and very pleasant garden, the pub has one large bar warmed by two wood-burning stoves. Traditional pub meals are available at all sessions. This was the original home of the Dunn Plowman Brewery back in the mid-1980s. ⚠Q🕿🎯♦P▄─🖾

Linton

Alma Inn 🅛
HR9 7RY (off B4221, W of M50 jct 3) SO659255
🌣 6-11; 12-3, 6-11 Sat; 12-3, 7-10.30 Sun 🕿 (01989) 720355
🌐 lintonfestival.org/about/the-alma-inn
Butcombe Bitter; Ludlow Gold; Malvern Hills Black Pear; Oakham JHB 🎛
CAMRA Herefordshire Pub of the Year runner-up in 2012, and winner outright on two previous occasions, the Alma is testament to the fact village pubs do not have to sell food to thrive. Run with real passion, the free house has a conventional front bar with a real fire and a pool room to the rear. Events include a major music festival in June and summer sessions in August, both held in the extensive grounds, with accompanying beer festivals. ⚠Q🍴🕿🎯🌁▲♣P▄─

Orleton

Boot Inn 🅛
SY8 4HN (off B4361, in village)
🌣 12-3, 5.30-11; 12-11.30 Sat; 12-11 Sun 🕿 (01568) 780228
🌐 thebootinnorleton.co.uk
Hobsons Best Bitter; Wye Valley HPA; guest beer 🎛
A comfortable and welcoming 16th-century black and white village pub with a large inglenook fireplace and original oak beams. A charity quiz is held monthly on a Tuesday in winter and a beer and cider festival in July in the large beer garden, which includes a children's play area. The home-prepared food ranges from bar snacks to interesting gourmet meals. The Wye Valley HPA may alternate with Butty Bach. The bus stops right outside. ⚠Q🍴🕿🎯🌁P▄─🖾(492)

Staplow

Oak Inn 🅛
HR8 1NP (on B4214)
🌣 12-11 (10.30 Sun) 🕿 (01531) 640954
🌐 oakinnstaplow.co.uk
Bathams Best Bitter; Wye Valley Bitter; guest beers 🎛
The focus is on dining at this stylishly refurbished rural inn, which enjoys a county-wide reputation for first-class affordable food, but drinkers are also welcome. The front bar divides into three areas: one with sofas and low tables, a snug, and a dining room featuring an open kitchen. At the rear is a further room with scrubbed tables. Booking is essential for meals. Quality accommodation boasts bucolic views across nearby orchards. ⚠Q🍴🕿🎯🌁🍴♦P▄─🖾(417)

Withington

Cross Keys 🅛
HR1 3NN (on A465 in Withington Marsh)
🌣 5 (12 Sat)-11; 12-10.30 Sun 🕿 (01432) 820616
Otter Ale; Wye Valley Butty Bach; guest beer 🎛
Conversation rules at this traditional local, run by the same landlord for over 30 years. At the heart of the community, it is a favourite for its atmosphere. A long and narrow single bar divides into two drinking areas, both with original beams, exposed stonework, real fires and basic bench seating. A folk jam session is held on the last Thursday of the month. Filled rolls are available on Saturdays. The house beer is from Wye Valley. ⚠Q🍴🎯▲♣P▄─🖾(420)

Woolhope

Crown Inn 🅛
HR1 4QP SO611357
🌣 12-3, 6-11 (midnight Fri); 12-midnight Sat; 12-11 Sun
🕿 (01432) 860468 🌐 crowninnwoolhope.co.uk
Hobsons Best Bitter; Wye Valley HPA; guest beer 🎛
Situated next to the church, the Crown has a large bar complemented by a restaurant and a public bar area in the conservatory by the front door. Sandwiches and meals are all home prepared using locally sourced ingredients. Curries feature on Monday evening and gourmet nights are held monthly on the third Thursday. The bar also hosts darts and quoits teams. A wide range of local bottled ciders and perries is stocked including the pub's own home brew, and the guest beer is local. ⚠Q🕿🎯🌁🍴♣♠P▄─🖾(453,454)

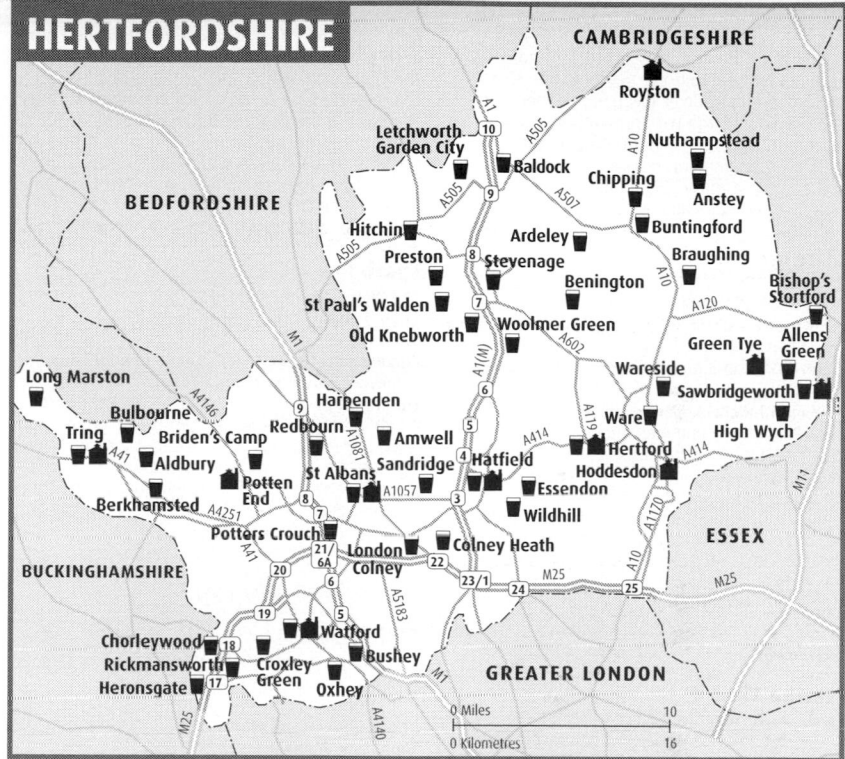

HERTFORDSHIRE

Aldbury

Valiant Trooper L
Trooper Road, HP23 5RW SP964123
✪ 11-11 (10.30 Sun) ☎ (01442) 851203
⊕ valianttrooper.co.uk
Fuller's London Pride; Tring Ridgeway, Side Pocket for a Toad; guest beers Ⓗ
Edge-of-village local dating from the 17th century in a popular walking area. The beamed bar gives way to a spacious food area but beer is the most important ingredient here. Six ales are available with well-known larger micros and LocAle breweries represented. Good food made with locally sourced ingredients is served in the bar and garden in warmer weather. A regular in the Guide for many years with an enthusiastic landlord and staff, this is a must-visit for beer lovers. Dogs are welcome. ♨Q🐾🏵️🌓🌗&♣🅿🚃(30,31)

Allens Green

Queen's Head L
CM21 0LS TL455170
✪ 12-2.30 (not Mon & Tue), 5-11; 12-10.30 Sun
☎ (01279) 723393 ⊕ shirevillageinns.co.uk
Fuller's London Pride; Mighty Oak Maldon Gold Ⓗ; guest beers Ⓖ
Popular with locals, cyclists, walkers and their dogs, this is a small traditional village inn with a large lawn for summer relaxation. Honest and simple food is served but the emphasis is on an interesting and varied beer range. Festivals are held every third weekend of the month and on bank holiday weekends, when beers are served by gravity from a self-service bar. Q🏵️🌓&♣🅿

Amwell

Elephant & Castle
Amwell Lane, AL4 8EA TL167131
✪ 12-2.30, 5.30-11; 12-11 Sat; 12-10.30 Sun
☎ (01582) 832175
Greene King IPA, Abbot; H&H Bitter; guest beer Ⓗ
Hidden away in an attractive and peaceful setting, this popular, successful rural community pub dates from 1714 and has never forsaken real ale. Terracotta tiles in the front bar, a 200-foot well in the back, two real fires and two large gardens (one for adults only) complete the picture. Lunches are served daily and evening meals Tuesday-Saturday. The pub hosts Amwell Day, a local charity fundraising event, in June each year. ♨Q🏵️🌓🅿🚃

Anstey

Blind Fiddler
Anstey Village, SG9 0BW TL405330
✪ 12-11 (7 Mon) ☎ (01763) 848000

Buntingford Twitchell; Fuller's London Pride; guest beer H

Named after the local legend Fiddler George who disappeared exploring the tunnel under Anstey Castle, the Blind Fiddler has been opened out to create a single large bar area with a separate restaurant. Beers come from Buntingford and Fuller's. Entertainment includes monthly quiz nights and live music. Pétanque is popular, and there is a rare bar billiards table. ♿🍴♿♿🚲♻️P

Ardeley

Jolly Waggoner

Ardeley, SG2 7AH (off B1037 between Walkern and Cottered) TL311271
🕐 12-11.30 (12.30am Fri & Sat) ☎ (01438) 861350
🌐 thejollywaggoner.co.uk
Buntingford Highwayman; guest beers H

This 16th-century pub was once farmworkers' cottages. Now managed by the nearby Church Farm, the Jolly Waggoner has a reputation for fine food, most of it sourced from the farm itself or local suppliers. Real ale is sourced locally too, from Buntingford, Red Squirrel and Nethergate. Regular events include speciality food evenings, guest landlords and a beer festival in August.
♿🍴♿♿♻️P♻️

Baldock

Orange Tree 🏆 L

Norton Road, SG7 5AW TL242339
🕐 12-2.30, 4.30-11; 12-midnight Thu-Sat; 12-10.30 Sun
☎ (01462) 892341 🌐 theorangetreebaldock.com
Greene King XX Mild, IPA, Abbot; guest beers H

A very friendly, 300-year-old cosmopolitan local where intellectual banter is always welcome. The pub has two bars, a function room, a games room with bar billiards, a large garden and a shelter for smokers with sofas and a real fire. Five guest beers always include a Buntingford Brewery LocAle, alongside the local Apple Cottage Cider. Good home-made food featuring meat from the local butcher is served. Entertainment includes regular live music, a quiz night on Tuesday and a quarterly beer festival. ♿🍴♿♿♿♻️P♻️🚲(94)

Benington

Lordship Arms

42 Whempstead Road, SG2 7BX TL307228
🕐 12-3, 6 (7 Sun)-11 ☎ (01438) 869665
🌐 lordshiparms.co.uk
Black Sheep Best Bitter; Crouch Vale Brewers Gold; Taylor Landlord; guest beers H

Single-bar pub situated at the village's southern end and run by the same husband and wife team for the past 20 years. A very tidy bar is decorated with telephone memorabilia – even some of the handpumps are modelled on telephones. Good-quality sandwiches and snacks are available at lunchtimes. The well-maintained garden sports superb floral displays. Classic car club meetings are held here in the summer. A repeat winner of local and county CAMRA Pub of the Year.
♿Q♿♻️P🚲🚲(384)

Berkhamsted

Crown L

145 High Street, HP4 3HH SP992077

🕐 8-midnight (1am Fri & Sat) ☎ (01442) 863993
Fuller's London Pride; Greene King IPA, Abbot; guest beers H

This multi-area Wetherspoons pub spreads its beer choice perfectly between local breweries such as Tring and Red Squirrel and larger brewers with at least six ales always available along with two real ciders. A friendly place with a village feel in this historic town linked with Graham Greene and other literary luminaries. Its inexpensive food is, as always, an added draw. Q♿♿♿♿🚲♻️♻️🚲

Lamb L

277 High Street, HP4 1AJ SP987080
🕐 11-11 (midnight Fri & Sat); 12-10.30 Sun
☎ (01442) 862615
Adnams Ghost Ship; Fuller's London Pride; Tring Ridgeway, Side Pocket for a Toad H

The future of real ale in town seems safe in the hands of the landlord of the Lamb. His commitment is evident as he continues to serve top-condition beers in this pub and another pub in town he has recently taken over, also serving four beers. The clientele at this compact high street local are a mixed, friendly bunch, usually willing to chat. Floral hanging baskets make for a colourful welcome in the spring and summer. No food at weekends.
♿Q♿♿🚲♻️♻️🚲(500,501)

Rising Sun L

1 Canalside, George Street, HP4 2EG (at lock 55 on Grand Union Canal) SP997077
🕐 3-11 (midnight Thu); 12-midnight Fri & Sat; 12-10.30 Sun
☎ (01442) 864913 🌐 theriser.co.uk
Tring Riser; guest beers H

Well-loved community pub serving five ales, 10 ciders and draught Belgian and American beer. A previous CAMRA branch and Cider Pub of the Year, it holds four festivals a year. Well known for its ploughman's, it offers free bar nibbles on Friday evenings and hosts a cheese club on the third Saturday of the month. Its canalside location makes it very popular in fine weather. The bus stop is five minutes' walk. CAMRA discounts are available on ales, ciders and perries.
Q♿♿🚲♻️♻️🚲(500,501)

Bishop's Stortford

Bricklayers Arms L

61 Hadham Road, CM23 2QY TL482214
🕐 12-11 Mon (midnight Tue-Thu; 1.30am Fri & Sat; 11.30 Sun) ☎ (01279) 657803
Beer range varies H

The Bricklayers is committed to showcasing local beers – the four handpumps continually rotate, offering a good selection of East Anglian and London ales. Built on the site of a former brickworks, this popular pub has served the local community for 150 years. Once a Benskin's house, it is now an independent free house. There is a quiet, comfortable lounge and a lively sports-oriented public bar and pool room with several TV screens. Outside there is a covered, heated smokers' patio and a large, secluded deck. Dogs are welcome throughout the pub. ♿♿♿♻️🚲

Cock Inn

2 Stansted Road, CM23 2DX (at jct of Hockerill St and Stansted Rd) TL493213
🕐 12-midnight (11 Sun) ☎ (01279) 652386
Adnams Southwold Bitter, Ghost Ship; Shepherd Neame Spitfire; Taylor Landlord; guest beers H

This timber-framed coaching inn has been serving ales since 1620 and was reputedly frequented by Dick Turpin. The beer range has an East Anglian theme including two rotating guest ales. Popular with locals for its lively atmosphere, the pub is a haven for sports lovers, offering satellite TV, darts and a pool table. ♠️🏵️🍺🍴🚌(308,510)

Jolly Brewers
170 South Street, CM23 3BG TL488207
✪ 12-midnight ☎ (01279) 836055
⊕ stansted-hotels-jollybrewers.com
Greene King IPA; Taylor Landlord; guest beers ⊞
Community-based pub on the edge of the main town centre. Originally called the Teetotalers, it still retains two bars, one used for pool and darts, with a large sports TV. Several darts and pool teams as well as a local golf society are based here. Food is available weekday lunchtimes only. The accommodation (bed only, no breakfast) is ideal for Stansted Airport, with 24-hour buses to the airport. 🛏️🚃🍴🚌(308,510,511)

Braughing

Golden Fleece
20 Green End, SG11 2PG
✪ 11.30-3, 5.30-11; 11.30-midnight Sat; 12-10.30 Sun
☎ (01920) 823555 ⊕ goldenfleecebraughing.co.uk
Adnams Southwold Bitter; guest beers ⊞
A large rural pub built in the early 1700s, with wooden floors, beams and a large fireplace. It was closed as a pub in 2003 but reopened in 2010 after extensive remodelling of the interior layout. Guest ales come from local breweries such as Buntingford, Nethergate and Saffron. The food is all gluten-free, and includes a changing range of daily specials, monthly tapas nights and themed food evenings. ♠️Q🏵️🍴🅿️🚌(331,386)

Briden's Camp

Crown & Sceptre 🄻
Red Lion Lane, HP2 6EY (from A4146 at Water End take Red Lion Lane opp Red Lion up hill for ½ mile) TL044111
✪ 12-3, 5.30-11; 12-11 Sat & Sun ☎ (01442) 234660
⊕ crownandsceptrepub.co.uk
Greene King IPA, Abbot; guest beers ⊞
This friendly country pub dates from 1839. The handpumps are on two sides of the U-shaped bar, so remember there's more available than first meets the eye – mind the beams if you are tall. It has a patio and beer garden and holds its own beer festivals using an outside bar (also available for functions). On the Chiltern Way, it is popular with walkers and cyclists. Great Gaddesden Cricket Club is opposite. No food on Sunday evenings. Dogs are not permitted inside. ♠️Q🏵️🍴🅿️🚌(X31)

Bulbourne

Grand Junction Arms
Bulbourne Road, HP23 5QE (next to Grand Union canal bridge 138) SP932135
✪ 12-11 (10.30 Sun) ☎ (01442) 891400
⊕ grandjunctionarms.co.uk
Sharp's Doom Bar; Tring Side Pocket for a Toad; guest beers ⊞
Impressive canalside pub with a large garden and wild flower orchard, children's play area and bicycle park. The modern interior is divided into several areas, with wooden/flagstone floors and mixed seating including stools at the bar. Due to the popularity of the food, booking is advisable for diners. A curry and quiz night is held on Sunday. Artwork for sale is displayed throughout the pub. Children are welcome until 7pm, but no dogs inside. Wi-Fi available. ♠️🏵️🍴🅿️🚌(61)

Buntingford

Brambles 🄻
117 High Street, SG9 9AF TL360298
✪ 12-11 (10.30 Sun) ☎ (01763) 273158
Fuller's London Pride, ESB; guest beers ⊞
Brambles has two bars, both warmed by real fires, and eight handpumps dispensing the ales. Fuller's London Pride and ESB are always available, with other regular beers from Buntingford or Church End breweries. The clientele is very varied and can get exuberant at weekends. Unusually, the pub has no sign outside. ♠️🏵️🍺🍴🚌(331,700)

Bushey

Swan
25 Park Road, WD23 3EE TQ132954
✪ 11-11; 12-10.30 Sun ☎ (020) 8950 2256
Greene King Abbot; Sharp's Doom Bar; Taylor Landlord; Young's Bitter ⊞
Single bar in a residential street off Bushey High Street offering four regular ales. Two real fireplaces add to a homely and welcoming feel. Bar snacks are available all day including sausage rolls and toasties. Regular events are held to celebrate traditional dates such as Burns Night and Valentine's Day. There are three TV screens, allowing multiple sports to be shown simultaneously. The Ladies is in the back garden. Free Wi-Fi. ♠️🏵️🍴🚌

Chipping

Countryman
Ermine Street, SG9 0PG TL356319
✪ closed Mon-Thu; 12-11 Fri & Sat; 12-10.30 Sun
☎ (01763) 272721
Beer range varies ⊞
Built in 1663 and a pub since 1760, the Countryman has a one-bar, split-level interior. The room boasts some well executed carvings on the bar front, an impressive fireplace and some obscure agricultural implements. Two real ales are usually available. The beer itself will vary, but tends to be brown and around 4-4.5% ABV. Note the restricted opening hours. ♠️Q🏵️🅿️🚌(331)

Chorleywood

Rose & Crown 🄻
Common Road, WD3 5LW TQ027963
✪ 11.30-3, 5.30-11 (midnight Fri); 11.30-11.30 Sat; 12-10 Sun ☎ (01923) 283841 ⊕ roseandcrownchorleywood.co.uk
Fuller's London Pride; Young's Bitter; guest beers ⊞
A warm welcome awaits both regulars and visitors at this one-bar pub. The back bar was converted to a popular restaurant 17 years ago, and offers regular food deals such as a Monday lunch club. Large wall clocks indicate London and Florida time. Guest beers usually come from fairly local breweries such as Rebellion and Tring. The drinking area can be crowded, but is relaxing and homely. Dog-friendly. ♠️🏵️🍺🍴🅿️🚌(336)

Colney Heath

Crooked Billet L
88 High Street, AL4 0NP TL202060
☼ 11-2.30, 4.30-11; 11.30-11 Sat; 12-10.30 Sun
☎ (01727) 822128
Tring Side Pocket for a Toad; guest beers H
Popular and friendly cottage-style village pub
dating back over 200 years. A genuine free house,
it stocks three to five guest beers from national,
regional and microbreweries. A wide selection of
good-value home-made food is served lunchtimes
and Friday and Saturday evenings. Summer
barbecues and Saturday events are held
occasionally. This is a favourite stop-off for walkers
on the many local footpaths. Families are welcome
in the large garden (which has play equipment)
and in the bar until 9pm.
ᴍ🌫⊛◑◐⬛♣♠Pᵇ⊟(304)

Croxley Green

Sportsman ♈ L
2 Scots Hill, WD3 3AD TQ069953
☼ 12-11 (10.30 Sun) ☎ (01923) 443360
⊕ thesportsmanpub.co.uk
Beer range varies H
Award-winning, family-run, genuine pub with a
real ale focus. Up to eight handpumps dispense an
ever-changing selection of ales to suit a variety of
tastes. A further handpump serves real cider. The
beers are sourced from around the country with a
focus on local and London breweries. A real ale
tasting rack is available. A popular weekly quiz,
regular live music on a Saturday and other social
events add to the community feel. ⊛♣♠Pᵇ⊟

Essendon

Candlestick L
West End Lane, AL9 6BA TL262083
☼ closed Mon; 12-11 (8 Sun) ☎ (01707) 261322
⊕ thecandlestickpub.co.uk
Greene King IPA; guest beers H
A remote country pub/restaurant where good food
features strongly lunchtimes and evenings. It is a
popular destination for walkers and cyclists, who
are rewarded with two guest ales from
Hertfordshire brewers. Originally called the
Chequers, the pub became known as the
Candlestick because of the habit of a previous
landlord who took the sole candle to the cellar
when collecting the beer, leaving customers in the
dark. Now a friendly, well-lit free house with a
beer festival held in June. ᴍ🌫⊛◑Pᵇ

Harpenden

Cross Keys L
39 High Street, AL5 2SD (opp war memorial) TL133144
☼ 11-11; 12-10.30 Sun ☎ (01582) 763989
⊕ cross-keys-harpenden.co.uk
Rebellion IPA; Taylor Landlord; Tring Jack o'Legs H
Tucked in among the shops in the town centre, this
two-bar pub has retained its traditional charm with
a fine pewter bar top and flagstone floors. The
original oak-beamed ceiling has tankards from past
and present customers hanging from it. When
weather permits enjoy your pint in the secluded,
attractive rear garden. Traditional home-cooked
lunches are served Monday to Saturday. Quiet
conversation is preferred over electronic

entertainment although a radio may be produced
when a major rugby match is being played.
Q🌫⊛◑♣⬛≠♣ᵇ⊟

White Horse L
Redbourn Lane, Hatching Green, AL5 2JP TL134130
☼ 9.30am-11 (midnight Sat & Sun) ☎ (01582) 469290
⊕ thewhitehorseharpenden.co.uk
**Sharp's Doom Bar; Tring Side Pocket for a Toad; guest
beer** H
Located in Hatching Green a few minutes' walk
from Harpenden town centre, this fine old pub was
given a contemporary makeover and restaurant
extension several years ago. The bar is warm and
cosy, the dining room light and airy, and there is a
room upstairs for private functions. Outside, the
large, leafy garden has barbecues when the
weather allows. Opening at 9.30am for breakfast,
food is served all day until 9pm.
ᴍ🌫⊛◑◐⬛P⊟(321,620)

Hatfield

Horse & Groom
21 Park Street, AL9 5AT (in Old Hatfield) TL233086
☼ 11.30-11 (midnight Fri & Sat); 12-10.30 Sun
☎ (01707) 264765
**Black Sheep Best Bitter; Greene King Abbot; guest
beers** H
One of two pubs in Old Hatfield, this allegedly
haunted, 16th-century, Grade II-listed building,
formerly timber-framed and now brick clad, is
thought to house a priest hole. Up to five real ales
are served and occasional beer festivals held.
Tuesday is bangers and mash night – purchase an
ale for a free helping. Lunches are available daily
except Sunday. The railway and bus station are a
few minutes' walk away via Blood & Guts Alley.
ᴍQ🌫⊛◑≠♣ᵇ⊟

Heronsgate

Land of Liberty, Peace & Plenty L
Long Lane, WD3 5BS TQ023949
☼ 12-11 (midnight Fri & Sat); 12-10.30 Sun
☎ (01923) 282226 ⊕ landoflibertypub.com
Beer range varies H
Welcoming pub close to the M25 with historic
connections to the Chartists who had a short-lived
rural community nearby. Popular with walkers,
cyclists, locals and real ale enthusiasts, six or more
beers are usually offered, including LocAles, all
from microbreweries and covering a range of
styles. Ciders, perries and malt whiskies are always
stocked. Beer festivals, tastings and other regular
events are held throughout the year. Bar snacks are
available all day. There is a large outside pavilion
for families. A regular CAMRA award winner.
ᴍ⊛♣♠Pᵇ⊟(R4)

Hertford

Black Horse
29-31 West Street, SG13 8EZ TL324123
☼ 12-11 (midnight Fri & Sat); 12-10.30 Sun
☎ (01992) 583630 ⊕ theblackhorse.biz
Beer range varies H
Timbered free house dating from 1642 with a
country-pub feel. Situated in one of Hertford's most
attractive streets, it is near the start of the Cole
Green Way. Handy on match days for Hertford
Town FC supporters and one of the only pubs in

Britain with a rugby team affiliated to the RFU. The large well-kept garden has a separate children's area and is suitable for dogs on leads. CAMRA members enjoy a discount on real ales. Children welcome until 8pm. ᴁㄱ֍◑♣●ᇦ

Hertford Club
Lombard House, Bull Plain, SG14 1DT
🌑 12-3 (not Mon & Tue), 5-11; 12-11 Fri-Sun
☎ (01992) 421422 ∰ hertfordclub.co.uk
Beer range varies Ⓗ
Dating from the 15th century with later additions, Lombard House on the River Lea was built as an English Hall House and is one of the oldest buildings in Hertford. It has been the home of this private members' club since 1897. CAMRA members may be signed in on production of a membership card. You will find three ever-changing beers and real cider, which in summer can be enjoyed in the delightful walled garden. A well-supported open acoustic club is hosted on Sunday evening. ㄱ֍◑≈(East)♣●

Old Barge
2 The Folly, SG14 1QD (ask for Folly Island and you'll find the Old Barge) TL326128
🌑 11-11 (midnight Fri & Sat); 12-11 Sun ☎ (01992) 581871
∰ theoldbarge.co.uk
Dark Star Hophead; St Austell Tribute; Sharp's Doom Bar; guest beers Ⓗ
A free house pleasantly situated canalside on Folly Island offering both ale and real cider together with locally sourced home-cooked food. The pub hosts regular beer festivals, a popular quiz night every Sunday and a jazz night every second Thursday of the month. Look out for the children's crayfish festival in August and Folly at the Folly – music and fun supporting charity.
ᴁㄱ֍◑≈(East)♣●ᵉᴸᇦ

Old Cross Tavern Ⓛ
8 St Andrew Street, SG14 1JA TL323126
🌑 12 (4.30 Mon-Thu)-11; 12-10.30 Sun ☎ (01992) 583133
Old Cross Tavern Gertcha!; Taylor Landlord; guest beers Ⓗ
Superb town free house offering a friendly welcome. Up to eight real ales, usually including a dark beer of some distinction, come from brewers large and small, including the pub's own microbrewery, and there is a fine choice of Belgian bottle-conditioned beers. Two beer festivals are held every year – one over the spring bank holiday, the other in October. No TV or music here, just good old-fashioned conversation. Home-made pork pies are available. ᴁQ֍≈(North)♣ᇦ

High Wych

Rising Sun Ⓨ
High Wych Road, CM21 0HZ TL463141
🌑 12-2.30 (not Tue; 2 Wed), 5.30-11; 12-3, 7-10.30 Sun
☎ (01279) 724099
Courage Best Bitter; guest beers Ⓖ
A regular in the Guide for many years, this small village pub has been refurbished but retains its simple, rustic character, with a blazing real fire the centrepiece in winter. Popular with walkers and friendly locals, it holds a monthly quiz and an annual vegetable competition. The pub has never used handpumps – all beers are served by gravity. Two or three guest ales usually come from small independent breweries. Parking is in the village hall car park opposite. ᴁQ֍♣Pᇦ(347)

Hitchin

Half Moon Ⓛ
57 Queen Street, SG4 9TZ TL186288
🌑 12-2.30 (2 Wed), 5-midnight; 12-1am Fri & Sat; 12-11 Sun
☎ (01462) 452448 ∰ thehalfmoonhitchin.co.uk
Adnams Southwold Bitter; Young's Special; guest beers Ⓗ
This split-level one-bar pub dates from 1748 and was once owned by Hitchin brewer W&S Lucas. It sells two regular and six guest beers, often from local breweries, plus two regular ciders, a perry and four guests. Home-prepared food and tapas are served daily. Monthly quiz and speciality food nights are popular in this friendly community local. Cribbage is played during the summer. A former CAMRA Hertfordshire Pub of the Year.
ᴁㄱ֍◑♣●Pᴸ

Radcliffe Arms Ⓛ
31 Walsworth Road, SG4 9ST TL190295
🌑 8-11; 9-11 Sat; 9-4 Sun ☎ (01462) 456111
∰ radcliffearms.com
Buntingford Twitchell; guest beer Ⓗ
A popular gastro-pub with a clean and open modern interior. While the majority of the space is laid out for dining there is a public bar area to the right which has increased in size in the last year. The bar is open to drinkers all day, every day and sports two handpumps which will usually be found supplying LocAle beers from north Hertfordshire's Buntingford Brewery. As well as a large conservatory there are also several tables under umbrellas outside. ㄱ֍◑と≈Pᴸᵉᵈ

Letchworth Garden City

Three Magnets Ⓛ
18-20 Leys Avenue, SG6 3EW TL219326
🌑 8am-midnight (1am Fri & Sat) ☎ (01462) 681093
Greene King Abbot; Ruddles Best Bitter; guest beers Ⓗ
The Wetherspoon chain aims to be all things to all people and this pub succeeds very well. A conversion of a 1924 furniture shop, the Three Magnets is a family venue during the day and early evening, a social club later, a quiet pub except during major national and international sports events (with TVs silenced at other times), and a restaurant serving competitively priced food all day. The walls are decorated with many old photographs of early Letchworth. Qㄱ֍◑とᇦ

London Colney

Bull
Barnet Road, AL2 1QU TL182037
🌑 12-11 (midnight Fri & Sat) ☎ (01727) 823160
∰ thebullatlondoncolney.co.uk
Black Sheep Best Bitter; Greene King IPA Ⓗ; **guest beers** Ⓖ
Lovely old 17th-century timbered building near the River Colne with a cosy lounge and original fireplace, offering a range of real ales. The large public bar features darts, pool and TV. Outside there is a children's play area. Evening events include a quiz on Sunday and live music on Saturday. Good-value home-made meals are served Monday to Saturday lunchtimes. Wednesday is food night and curry evenings are held monthly. ֍◑ᕊ♣●Pᇦ

Long Marston

Queen's Head
38 Tring Road, HP23 4QL SP899155
☼ 12-11 ☎ (01296) 668368 ⊕ qhlm.co.uk
Fuller's London Pride; guest beers Ⓗ
The Queen's Head is a traditional pub with low ceilings, oak beams and open fires creating a cosy country feel. Sympathetically refurbished, it offers a warm welcome and serves Fuller's beer, locally sourced food seven days a week, and coffee from 10am weekdays. Themed evenings such as a curry night and Tuesday quiz night ensure this is a vibrant, bustling place to visit. There is B&B accommodation for the weary tourist or business traveller. ♨️⊛�;⊃🍴⬤⬆️♣P⁵⬅🚌(164)

Nuthampstead

Woodman
Stocking Lane, SG8 8NB TL412344
☼ 4-8 Mon; 11-11; 12-7 Sun ☎ (01763) 848328
⊕ thewoodman-inn.co.uk
Adnams Southwold Bitter; Greene King IPA; guest beer Ⓖ
Seventeenth-century free house with an L-shaped bar and a wonderful open fire. The restaurant offers à la carte meals as well as house specials and snacks (no food Sun eve). Beer is dispensed by gravity from casks behind the bar. The TV is restricted to major sports events. Functions are catered for in a marquee in the garden. During WWII the USAF 398th Bomber Group was based nearby and much memorabilia is displayed here. Ideally located for visiting local attractions such as Duxford Imperial War Museum. ♨️Q⊛🚲⊃🍴⬤♣P

Old Knebworth

Lytton Arms
Park Lane, SG3 6QB TL230203
☼ 11-11 (midnight Fri & Sat); 12-10.30 Sun
☎ (01438) 812312 ⊕ lyttonarms.co.uk
Adnams Southwold Bitter; Dark Star Hophead; Mighty Oak Maldon Gold; Sharp's Doom Bar; guest beers Ⓗ
Nineteenth-century pub adjacent to the Knebworth House estate, built for Hawkes & Company of Bishop's Stortford whose original logo may still be seen in the wrought ironwork of the pub sign. Four house beers are supplemented by a changing mix from regional and microbrewers. Good home-made food is available every day. Outside is an attractive decked patio and garden. Live music is a feature of Friday evenings.
♨️🚲⊛⊃🍴⬤♣P⁵⬅🚌(44,45)

Oxhey

Villiers Arms
108 Villiers Road, WD19 4AJ TQ121950
☼ 4 (3 Sat)-11.30; 3-10.30 Sun ☎ (01923) 221556
⊕ thevilliersarms.co.uk
Beer range varies Ⓗ
Single room, street corner inn dating from the late 19th century. Up to three changing ales are offered, with Welsh beers particularly popular. The bar is decorated with beer and drinks memorabilia, boxing magazine covers and sheet music covers. There is a fire in the winter. Live rugby is shown regularly and dogs are very welcome.
♨️Q⊛≈(Bushey)♣🚌

Potters Crouch

Holly Bush
Bedmond Lane, AL2 3NN (at jct of Potters Crouch Lane and Ragged Hall Lane) TL116052
☼ 12-2.30 (3 Sat), 6-11; 12-3, 7-10 Sun ☎ (01727) 851792
⊕ thehollybushpub.co.uk
Fuller's London Pride, ESB; Gale's Seafarers Ale Ⓗ
An attractive early 17th-century pub in rural surroundings, beautifully and tastefully furnished to a high standard and boasting large oak tables and period chairs. Spotless throughout, there is no jukebox, slot machine or TV to disturb the drinker in any of the three separate areas. The food menu is not extensive but is of high quality. The garden is lovely in summer and children are welcome, but not in the bar. ♨️Q⊛🚲⊃⬆️P⁵⬅🚌(300, 301)

Preston

Red Lion Ⓛ
The Green, SG4 7UD TL180247
☼ 12-2.30 (3.30 Sat), 5.30-11; 12-3.30, 7-10.30 Sun
☎ (01462) 459585 ⊕ theredlionpreston.co.uk
Fuller's London Pride; Young's Bitter; guest beers Ⓗ
This attractive Queen Anne free house stands on the village green and 30 years ago it was the first community-owned pub in Great Britain. An ever-changing list of beers is offered, many from small breweries. Ray and Jo prepare the fresh home-made food, sourcing many of the ingredients locally (no food Sun eve or all day Mon). The pub hosts the village cricket teams and fundraises for charity. A regular beer festival is held around November the 5th every year. Local CAMRA Pub of the Year 2012. ♨️Q🚲⊛🚲⊃♣⬤P⁵⬅🚌(88)

Redbourn

Cricketers Ⓛ
East Common, AL3 7ND TL104119
☼ 12-11 (midnight Fri & Sat); 12-10.30 Sun
☎ (01582) 620612 ⊕ thecricketersofredbourn.co.uk
Greene King IPA; guest beers Ⓗ
Redbourn's only free house dates back to 1725. Five real ales and a cider are always available and the food is excellent. The pub is opposite Redbourn common and the historic cricket pitch, making it a perfect setting for a summer's day drink. In winter a wood-burning stove makes for a cosy atmosphere. Additional parking is available on the common. The pub is now hosting summer beer festivals with local beers - all under marquees in the car park. Dog-friendly.
♨️Q🚲⊛🚲⊃⬆️P⁵⬅🚌(34,46,620)

Rickmansworth

Feathers
Church Street, WD3 1DJ TQ060942
☼ 12-11 (midnight Fri & Sat); 12-10.30 Sun
☎ (01923) 770081 ⊕ thefeathers.co.uk
Castle Rock Harvest Pale; Fuller's London Pride; guest beers Ⓗ
This comfortable, rambling building has been a pub for over 200 years. Now more upmarket under new management, with a pleasant candlelit atmosphere in the evening, it is quite food oriented, with table service also available for drink orders. The pricing reflects this, but the beer quality is consistently high. Two carefully chosen guests supplement the regular beers and the pub is

noteworthy for being the only one in the area to serve Harvest Pale as a permanent beer. Quiz evenings are held weekly and occasional beer festivals are staged. ⮂🅯🕮◗P⅃🖿🍺🍴

St Albans

Blacksmiths Arms

56 St Peter's Street, AL1 3HG TL150075
❂ 10 (11 Mon)-11 (12.30am Fri & Sat); 12-10.30 Sun
☎ (01727) 868845
Wells Bombardier; guest beers Ⓗ
A large, welcoming high-street pub with an open-plan bar and extensive beer garden. The pub is recovering well from its previous incarnation as a Hogshead bar. Two regular ales along with up to seven guest beers and a handpumped cider are offered. Good-quality reasonably priced pub grub is served and real ale festivals are a regular feature in the main and garden bars. A loyalty promotion is offered for real ale – buy seven, get one free.
🏨⮂🅯◗&🍴🍺⅃🖿🍴

Boot Inn

4 Market Place, AL3 5DG TL147072
❂ 12-midnight (12.45am Fri & Sat); 12-11.30 Sun
☎ (01727) 857533 ⊕ thebootstalbans.com
Beer range varies Ⓗ
City-centre, one-bar pub dating back to 1420 with a warm and welcoming atmosphere. It can be busy weekend evenings and on Wednesday and Saturday market days. The Clock Tower and Abbey are nearby. The bar features a real fire, exposed beams, a low ceiling and wood flooring. Families are welcome until 6pm. Cider is on handpump in summer. Bands play on Sunday afternoons and occasional weekday evenings.
🏨⮂◗⮂(Abbey)🍺🖿

Farmer's Boy Ⓛ

134 London Road, AL1 1PQ TL152068
❂ 12-11 (midnight Wed & Thu; 1.30am Fri & Sat)
☎ (01727) 860535 ⊕ farmersboy.co.uk
Oakham Scarlet Macaw; guest beers Ⓗ
Cosy, cottage-style pub, home of the Verulam Brewery. Three other breweries – Alecraft, Private Brewery of Bob and That Little Place – also brew using the same equipment. Three regular beers and three guests, one a dark beer, and an extensive selection of Belgian and bottled beers, as well as two traditional ciders, are offered. Beer festivals are held in spring, summer and autumn. A music quiz features on Tuesday night and live music on Thursday night. Sport is screened on TV. Outside is an enclosed drinking area.
🏨⮂🅯◗⮂(City)🍺🍴⅃🖿(724)

Garibaldi

61 Albert Street, AL1 1RT TL149068
❂ 12-11.30 (midnight Fri & Sat); 12-11 Sun
☎ (01727) 894745 ⊕ garibaldistalbans.co.uk
Fuller's Chiswick Bitter, London Pride, ESB; Gale's Seafarers Ale, HSB; guest beer Ⓗ
A classic example of a quality back-street local in the heart of Sopwell. Larger inside than its frontage suggests, it is like the Tardis with beer. Named after the 19th-century Italian patriot, the Garibaldi has an extensive, if expensive, range of Fuller's ales and serves excellent home-cooked food, with a fine Sunday roast. Regular live music, quizzes, darts, monthly karaoke and charity events, combined with hospitable staff, give the place a community feel. 🏨⮂🅯◗&⮂(Abbey)🍺⅃

Lower Red Lion

34-36 Fishpool Street, AL3 4RX TL143072
❂ 12-11 (10.30 Sun) ☎ (01727) 855669
⊕ thelowerredlion.co.uk
Oakham JHB; St Austell Tribute; guest beers Ⓗ
This is the sort of quintessentially British pub that expatriates probably dream about. It has two bars full of character. Set in a conservation area, the city centre is 10 minutes' walk and the site of Roman Verulamium close by. One handpump is reserved for cider and perry. Now under new management.
🏨Q🅯🍺🍴🍺P⅃

Mermaid

98 Hatfield Road, AL1 3RL TL152074
❂ 12-11 (midnight Wed, Fri & Sat); 12-10.30 Sun
☎ (01727) 568912
Oakham Citra; guest beers Ⓗ
Handy for both the main railway station and the city centre, this friendly free house features seven real ales usually from microbreweries, plus a range of ciders, perries and foreign bottled beers. Try the six thirds of cider or ale if you can't decide. Occasional themed evenings are held throughout the year plus live music and occasional beer and cider festivals. There is step-free access from the car park and level access throughout. A must-visit on any trip to the city. ⮂🅯◗&⮂(City)🍺🍴P⅃🖿

Six Bells Ⓛ

16-18 St Michael's Street, AL3 4SH TL137074
❂ 12-11 (midnight Fri & Sat); 12-10.30 Sun
☎ (01727) 856945 ⊕ the-six-bells.com
Oakham JHB; Taylor Landlord; Tring Ridgeway; guest beers Ⓗ
This 16th-century free house is a traditional ale drinkers' haven with three regular beers and two changing guests, at least one from a Hertfordshire brewer. It is the only licensed premises within the walls of Roman Verulamium and within walking distance of the city centre, cathedral, park and museum. Occasional quiz nights and live music feature. Good home-cooked food is served lunchtimes and evenings (no food Sun eve). The pleasant patio area makes a visit here compulsory in summer. 🏨⮂🅯◗🍺🍴P⅃🖿(300,301)

White Hart Tap

4 Keyfield Terrace, AL1 1QJ TL150069
❂ 12-11 ☎ (01727) 860974 ⊕ whitehearttap.co.uk
Castle Rock Harvest Pale; Fuller's London Pride; Sharp's Doom Bar; Taylor Landlord; guest beers Ⓗ
Welcoming, one-bar, back-street local offering guest beers from the Punch Taverns range. Good-value, home-cooked food, featuring fresh vegetables from the pub's own allotment, is served every lunchtime and Monday-Saturday evenings, with curries on Monday, fish and chips on Friday and roasts on Sunday. Quiz night is Wednesday and live music plays occasionally on Saturday. There is a heated, covered smoking area outside and barbecues are held in summer. Regular beer festivals are hosted including one over the August bank holiday weekend. A public car park is opposite the pub. 🏨⮂🅯◗⮂(Abbey/City)🍺⅃🖿

St Paul's Walden

Strathmore Arms Ⓛ

London Road, SG4 8BT TL193222
❂ 6-11 Mon; 12-2.30, 5-11; 12-11 Fri & Sat; 12-10.30 Sun
☎ (01438) 871654 ⊕ thestrathmorearms.co.uk

Buntingford Strathmore Bitter; guest beers H
The pub is on the Bowes-Lyon estate and caters for drinkers, diners and those wishing to play pub games, including bar billiards. It hosts several beer festivals, obscure breweries a speciality, and 'tickers' are welcome to try the ever-changing rota of guest beers. Unusual bottled beers are also available along with a cider and a perry. The pub is well known for raising funds around the local area. A former local CAMRA Pub of the Year and Community Pub of the Year.
Q☺❀❍🄳 🄶👗♣👜P🖳(304)

Sandridge

Green Man
31 High Street, AL4 9DD TL169104
❀ 11-11 (midnight Fri & Sat); 12-11 Sun ☎ (01727) 854845
Black Sheep Best Bitter G**; Greene King IPA** H**, Abbot; guest beer** G
Located in the centre of Sandridge, this family-run pub extends a warm welcome to all ale and cider drinkers alike. The landlord has been in residence for over 25 years. Up to three ales are available straight from the cask, and up to six real ciders from Westons and Millwhites are also kept. The pub is on the doorstep of the newly established 850 acre Heartwood Forest, making it the ideal place for refreshment after a stroll in the woods.
🚶Q☺❀❍🄳👗♣👜P🖳(304,620)

Sawbridgeworth

Gate L
81 London Road, CM21 9JJ TL481150
❀ 11.30-2.30 (2 Wed), 5.30-11; 11.30-11 Fri & Sat; 12-11 Sun ☎ (01279) 722313 ⊕ thegatepub.com
Beer range varies H
A lively pub particularly popular with sports fans as there are satellite screens in all bars. The small Sawbridgeworth Brewery at the back provides house beers. Large beer festivals are held over the Easter and August bank holiday weekends. The pub is home to several sports teams. No dogs are allowed inside. ❀🄳👗≒P🖳(510,511)

Old Bell
38 Bell Street, CM21 9AN TL484148
❀ 11-11 (1am Fri & Sat); 12-11 Sun ☎ (01279) 721050 ⊕ theoldbellpublichouse.co.uk
Adnams Broadside; Woodforde's Wherry; guest beers H
The Old Bell is a Grade II-listed timber-framed coaching inn dating from the 16th century. Exposed beams enhance the cosy main bar; there is also an adjoining lounge and dining area. The spacious courtyard offers an attractive setting to enjoy in warmer weather. There is live music on Friday nights, with Monday evening alternating between a jam session and a ukulele club.
❀≒P🖳(510,511)

Stevenage

Our Mutual Friend
Broadwater Crescent, SG2 8EH TL249226
❀ 12-11 (11.30 Fri & Sat) ☎ (01438) 312282
⊕ omfpub.co.uk
Beer range varies H
Thriving community pub on the southern side of Stevenage serving an ever-changing selection of cask beer. It has appeared in every issue of the Guide since being brought back from the cask ale graveyard in 2002. Eight or more real ciders and perries are also offered. Regular beer festivals are held throughout the year. Winner of many local CAMRA awards including Pub of the Year. Can be very busy on Stevenage FC match days. The original pub was owned by Lord Lytton, a friend of Charles Dickens. The writer allowed Lytton to use the name of his novel. Q☺❀🄳👗♣👜P🖳(4,5)

Standing Order
33 High Street, SG1 3AU TL233250
❀ 8-midnight (11 Sun) ☎ (01438) 316972
Greene King Abbot; Ruddles Best Bitter; guest beers H
There is a keen focus on cask ale at this establishment, with many beers sourced from microbreweries far and wide. Situated at the northern end of Stevenage Old Town, the pub's name reflects the building's past history as a bank from the early '60s to the late '90s – it was converted to a pub by Wetherspoon in 2000.
Q☺❀🄳👗👜P🖳

Tring

Anchor L
73 Western Road, HP23 4BH SP919111
❀ 12-11 ☎ (01442) 823280
Greene King IPA, Abbot; Morland Old Speckled Hen; Tring Side Pocket for a Toad; guest beer H
Located a short walk from Tring town centre, the Anchor is entered through a small front terrace that leads to a deceptively spacious bar. The front bar area has quirky wall decoration, with wine crates and pictures of local interest, and TVs for sporting events. Beyond the bar is a more formal dining area where food is served until 6pm every day. A warm welcome is offered by the management and bar staff in this family friendly establishment.
🚶❀❀🄳♣≒🖳

King's Arms
King Street, HP23 6BE SP921111
❀ 12-2.30 (3 Fri), 7-11; 11.30-3, 7-11 Sat; 12-4, 7-10.30 Sun ☎ (01442) 823318 ⊕ kingsarmstring.co.uk
Wadworth 6X; guest beers H
Situated in the historic Tring triangle, this Victorian pub has deservedly featured in the Guide for over 30 years. The pink exterior walls distinguish it as independent from any brewery ties. Inside, it has a retro feel with green paint, wood panelling, open fires and walls adorned with much beer paraphernalia. The seasonal, home-cooked menu features interesting, high-quality, worldwide cuisine. A frequent CAMRA branch and regional Pub of the Year. 🚶Q❀🄳♣👜≒🖳(61,500,501)

Robin Hood L
1 Brook Street, HP23 5ED SP925116
❀ 11-3, 5.30-11; 11.30-11.30 Fri; 12-11.30 Sat; 12-11 Sun ☎ (01442) 824912 ⊕ therobinhoodtring.co.uk
Fuller's Chiswick, Discovery, London Pride, ESB; Gale's Seafarers Ale; guest beer H
Situated on the edge of Tring town centre, this welcoming 17th-century Fuller's pub has log-burners, beams and low ceilings, giving it a warm, friendly feel. There is a light and airy conservatory to the rear and further back is a covered smoking area. The menu is based mostly on good pub food with speciality evenings including sausage night. Fish features frequently on the specials board. 🚶Q❀🄳♣👜≒🖳(61,500,501)

Ware

Crooked Billet

140 Musley Hill, SG12 7NL TL362150
5.30-11 (midnight Fri); 12-midnight Sat; 12-11.30 Sun
(01920) 462516
Hook Norton Hooky Bitter; guest beers H
Stuart and Sue have presided over the Billet for 19 years, with full use of the local SIBA Direct Delivery scheme resulting in over 350 different ales being sold. Three handpumps offer ever-changing ales, always including a mild, porter or stout. A fourth ale is sometimes available from the cellar. An annual beer festival is hosted. Two small bars feature two real fires, TV sport, pool and darts. Carlisle United and Ware FC fans are always assured a warm welcome. (395)

Wareside

Chequers

Ware Road, SG12 7QY TL395156
12-3 (3.15 Wed), 6-11; 12-4, 6-10.30 Sun
(01920) 467010
Adnams Southwold Bitter; Buntingford Highwayman IPA; guest beers H
A traditional free house run by the same family for 17 years. Dating from the 15th century, it was originally a coaching inn and has three distinct bar areas and a restaurant. One guest beer is usually from a small brewery. All food is home made, with vegetarian options. Walkers and cyclists are welcome, making this a good base for a country ramble. No machines or music, and swearing is banned. Q P (M3,M4)

Watford

West Herts Sports Club

8 Park Avenue, WD18 7HP TQ103964
4 (10 Sat)-11; 12-11.30 Fri; 12-10.30 Sun
(01923) 229239 westhertssports.co.uk
Fuller's London Pride; Young's Bitter; guest beers H
Multiple winner of CAMRA East Anglian Club of the Year, up to three guest beers are available, usually from small independent breweries such as Growler. The clubhouse has a modern bar decorated with sporting photographs and memorabilia. A separate function room, home of the Watford Beer Festival, is available to hire, and major sporting events are screened. Rolls are usually on offer. Non-members carrying a CAMRA membership card or this Guide may enter up to four times a year. P

Wildhill

Woodman

45 Wildhill Road, AL9 6EA (between A1000 and B158) TL264068
11.30-2.30, 5.30-11; 12-2.30, 7-10.30 Sun
(01707) 642618
Greene King IPA, Abbot; guest beers H
An all-round superb boozer! This excellent, friendly village pub extends a warm welcome to a varied clientele of all ages. Six beers are available including four guests – usually including one from a Hertfordshire brewery. Good pub grub is served at lunchtime (no food Sun). The large garden is ideal in summer. The Woodmanstick beer festival takes place in September. It's a pleasant three-mile walk from Welham Green station. Winner of local CAMRA branch Pub of the Year a record nine times. P

Woolmer Green

Chequers

16 London Road, SG3 6JP TL253185
12 (4 Mon)-11; 12-8.30 Sun (01438) 813216
benicksatthechequers.co.uk
Young's Bitter; guest beers H
Large inn on the Great North Road at the southern end of the village. It has an open-plan bar with a central fireplace sporting a real fire during the cooler months. Cask ale is very popular, with high quality compensating for a limited range. Good home-cooked food featuring fresh ingredients is served (no food Mon), including fantastic-value pies on Wednesday and Saturday. Take time to look at the secret zoo featuring interesting birds and animals. P (300,301)

Six Bells, St Albans (Photo: Katie Hunt)

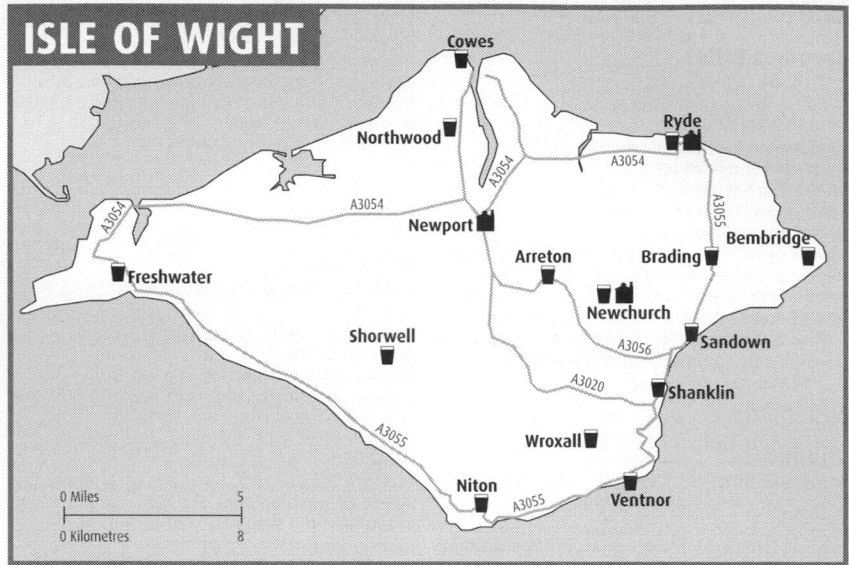

ISLE OF WIGHT

Cowes
Northwood
Ryde
A3054
A3054
A3054
Newport
Bembridge
Arreton
Brading
Freshwater
Newchurch
Shorwell
A3056
Sandown
A3020
Shanklin
Wroxall
Niton
A3055
Ventnor

0 Miles 5
0 Kilometres 8

Arreton

Dairyman's Daughter 🅛
Main Road, PO30 3AA (main road into Arreton from Newport) SZ53258680
☼ 10-11; 12-10.30 Sun ☎ (01983) 539361
⊕ thedairymansdaughter.com
Beer range varies Ⓗ
A hugely popular museum, gift, craft and pub experience on the site of the once massive Arreton Barn. As well as a range of eight beers there is a large selection of Island bottled beers in the old brewery. The full menu starts at 6pm but there is plenty to tempt the palate throughout the day, from creams tea to snacks. Adjacent is the 11th-century church of St George, the carp pond, the Maritime Museum and the dairyman's daughter's grave. ⋟🏕🕪&P⁵⁻🚇(8)

Bembridge

Old Village Inn 🍷 🅛
61 High Street, PO35 5SF
☼ 12-11 ☎ (01983) 872616 ⊕ yeoldevillageinn.co.uk
Beer range varies Ⓗ
The Old Village Steak and Ale House is the latest addition to the Bembridge scene, offering quality beer and food in a refined and relaxed atmosphere. It specialises in local meat and fish dishes from around the Island served alongside a fine choice of real ales and selected wines. Live music plays on occasional Fridays and a popular quiz is held on the first Saturday of the month. There is a patio area and pétanque terrain to the rear. 🏚⋟🏕🕪&▲♣🐾P⁵⁻🚇(8)

Brading

Dark Horse 🅛
10 High Street, PO36 0DG
☼ 11-3, 6-11; 12-10.30 Sun ☎ (01983) 407985
⊕ darkhorseisleofwight.co.uk
Goddards Fuggle-Dee-Dum; guest beers Ⓗ
An atmospheric 17th-century coaching and posting inn with an open fire, beamed ceilings and stone

walls. It offers an extensive menu, specials board, wine list and a choice of three real ales. Well-behaved children are welcome. A holiday apartment is available to rent above the pub for short breaks or full holidays. This pub presents an ideal base for walkers, cyclists and bird watchers as it is close to the station with direct links to the Haven Street Steam Railway.
🏚Q⋟🏕🕪&▲⇌P⁵⁻🚇(2,3)

Cowes

Anchor Inn 🅛
1 High Street, PO31 7SA (opp Sainsbury's)
☼ 11-11 (midnight Fri & Sat); 12-10.30 Sun
☎ (01983) 292823 ⊕ theanchorcowes.co.uk
Draught Bass; Goddards Fuggle-Dee-Dum; guest beers Ⓗ
Close to the marina, tempting visiting yachtsmen for their first pint ashore. A recent conversion has integrated the stables and created a pleasant beer garden. A good selection of beer is on offer, with one Island ale and two guests always available. A varied food menu is served in prodigious quantities. Frequent live entertainment is provided. Accommodation is in seven comfortable rooms.
🏚⋟🏕🕪⬛⁵⁻🚇(1)

Union Inn
Watch House Lane, PO31 7QH (just off the Parade)
☼ 11-midnight; 12-10.30 Sun ☎ (01983) 293163
⊕ unioninncowes.co.uk
Fuller's London Pride, seasonal beers; Gale's Seafarers Ale, HSB Ⓗ
A haven for yachting enthusiasts, locals and holidaymakers, one three-sided bar serves the lounge, snug, dining area and airy conservatory. A roaring fire in winter adds to the cosy atmosphere. Delicious family meals are available with portions

for children and ingredients sourced from local suppliers. The pub may close at 11pm but frequently stays open later. ⚫Q♒⊟◑▶♣⤴–🖵(1)

Freshwater

Prince of Wales 🅛
Princes Road, PO40 9ED
⚫ 3 (12 Sun)-11; 12-11.30 Fri & Sat ☎ (01983) 753535
Beer range varies Ⓗ
Fine, unspoilt gem of a town pub run by possibly the longest-serving landlord on the Isle of Wight. Just off the main Freshwater shopping centre, it has a large garden and pleasant public and lounge bars. The four frequently changing beers always include one from Yates'.
Q♒⚫🅴Å♣P⤴–🗝🖵(7,12)

Newchurch

Pointer Inn
High Street, PO36 0NN (next to church)
⚫ 11-11; 12-10.30 Sun ☎ (01983) 865202
🌐 pointerinn.com
Fuller's London Pride, seasonal beers; Gale's HSB; guest beer Ⓗ
Ancient village local with a warm welcome for families. The home-cooked food is prepared by a chef with a vast experience of Island trade (booking is essential). Food is served until 9.30pm (9pm Sun). Outside, the large garden has a pétanque terrain and there is a covered area for smokers. Awards include Fuller's Best Country/Village Pub 2012. ⚫Q♒⚫◑Å♣P⤴–🖵(23)

Niton

Buddle 🅛
St Catherine's Road, Niton Undercliff, PO38 2NE (follow signs to St Catherine's Lighthouse) SZ50207580
⚫ 11-11 (midnight Fri & Sat); 12-10.30 Sun
☎ (01983) 730243 🌐 buddleinn.co.uk
Beer range varies Ⓗ
Originally a farmhouse dating from the 16th century, the Buddle was reputedly a smugglers' inn during the 18th century. Extensively refurbished, it retains its ancient flagstones and beams, inglenook fireplace and many interesting photographs. A popular destination dining pub, serving good locally sourced food, it also has a strong real ale following, with a choice of six beers. Situated near the lighthouse, it has many links to Trinity House.
⚫Q♒⚫◑♣♦P🖵(6)

White Lion 🅛
High Street, PO38 2AT
⚫ 11-midnight; 12-9 Sun ☎ (01983) 730293
🌐 whitelionniton.co.uk
Otter Bitter; Sharp's Doom Bar; Yates' Undercliff Experience; guest beer Ⓗ
A very picturesque pub of some character, at the centre of the village, opposite the local store and bus stop. It has a popular public bar with extended drinking and dining areas as well as a separate formal area/function room. No one quite knows when the building became an inn but it almost certainly was when it was leased to John Clark in 1744. The garden encompasses a large family dining area along with a climbing area and bouncy castle. ⚫♒⚫◑🅶♣P⤴–🖵(6)

Northwood

Travellers Joy 🅛
85 Pallance Road, PO31 8LS (on Northwood-Porchfield road) SZ48009360
⚫ 12-2.30, 5-11; 11-11 Thu-Sat; 12-11 Sun
☎ (01983) 298024 🌐 tjoy.co.uk
Island Wight Gold; guest beers Ⓗ
Offering one of the best choices of cask ale on the island, this long-standing old country inn was the Island's first beer exhibition house. Seven carefully chosen, varied and interesting ales rotate to supplement the Wight Gold, always including Island beers. A real cider is sometimes also available. A good range of home-cooked food is served lunchtimes and evenings. The pub is a popular venue for real ale followers, the local community and visitors seeking a friendly and amenable base. ⚫Q♒⚫◑Å♣♦P⤴–🖵(1)

Ryde

Lake Huron 🅛
51 Upton Road, PO33 3HR (on Ryde-Havenstreet road)
⚫ 12-11 ☎ (01983) 508125
Beer range varies Ⓗ
This delightful pub on the outskirts of Ryde is the only survivor from the six-strong George Lake estate, founded in the 19th century. Previously a wine and spirits shop called the Eclipse, it was taken over by the Lake family in 1878 and became a staging post for the Newport-Ryde coach. Surprisingly large inside with many rooms and plenty of character, it remains a back-street local with a friendly, lively atmosphere. The beers regularly come from Ringwood, Hook Norton and Young's breweries. Well worth a visit.
Q♒⚫🅶Å⇌(St Johns)♣⤴–🖵(33,37)

S Fowler & Co 🅛
41-43 Union Street, PO33 2LF
⚫ 7am-midnight (1am Fri & Sat) ☎ (01983) 812112
Courage Directors; Greene King IPA; Ruddles Best Bitter; guest beers Ⓗ
Although not the most charismatic pub in the Wetherspoon chain, this converted drapery store offers a varied range of up to 12 well-kept beers. Situated in the centre of town, there is a bus stop conveniently outside. The pub's name was at the suggestion of the local CAMRA branch; not only is it the name of the former store, but also that of the first local CAMRA chairman and revered early campaigner. The upstairs restaurant is family-friendly. Q♒◑🅶⇌(Esplanade)♦🖵(3,4,9)

Simeon Arms 🅛
21 Simeon Street, PO33 1JG (short walk from Canoe Lake)
⚫ 11-11 (11.30 Mon; 11.45 Thu-Sat); 12-11.30 Sun
☎ (01983) 614954 🌐 simeonarms.co.uk
Courage Best Bitter; Goddards Ale of Wight; guest beer Ⓗ
Thriving yet unlikely gem tucked away in a Ryde back street with a large interior and annexed function hall. The pub is immensely popular with the local community who come to participate in various leagues including shove-ha'penny, darts, crib and pool, and pétanque on the enormous floodlit terrain in summer. You can always expect to find a local ale. Live music plays on Saturday and Sunday nights. The smoking area outside is heated and covered. ♒⚫◑⇌(St John's Road)♣⤴–🖵

Solent Inn Ⓛ
7 Monkton Street, PO33 1JW (behind Ryde Castle Hotel on seafront)
☼ 12-11 ☎ (01983) 563546
Beer range varies Ⓗ
Excellent street-corner local with a warm, welcoming atmosphere and four ales, at least one from the Island. Live music is hosted at least twice a week, and shove-ha'penny is played – Ryde is one of the few places where a local league can be found. Parts of this handsome pub are ancient, going back to medieval times, and it originally fronted the sea before reclamation of land, hence the name. Beware – the public bar slopes downhill alarmingly! Closing time may vary in winter.
Q❄❀≉(Esplanade)♣⬱⊟

Sandown

Castle Inn Ⓛ
12-14 Fitzroy Street, PO36 8HY (off High Street)
☼ 11-11 (midnight Fri); 10.30-1am Sat; 12-10.30 Sun
☎ (01983) 403169 ⊕ sandowncastle.co.uk
Young's Special; guest beers Ⓗ
The Castle is an excellent town free house and locals' pub with four darts teams, crib and a pétanque terrain. Six real ales are on offer including the best from local breweries. There is a children's room at the back and a patio for warm weather. The TV is not allowed to intrude, but is turned on for special occasions. Happy hour is popular, as is the Sunday quiz. Beer festivals are held several times a year, usually featuring local ales. ∰Q❄❀&≉♣♥⬱⊟(3,8)

Shanklin

Chine Inn Ⓛ
Chine Hill, PO37 6BW
☼ 12-11 ☎ (01983) 865880
Sharp's Doom Bar; guest beers Ⓗ
This inn with magnificent views of the bay is a classic – the building, which has stood since 1621, must be one of the oldest pubs with a licence on the Island. Live music plays on Saturday nights and Sunday afternoons. The Chine Inn ghosts – a girl in blue and an old man in the corner – have been seen by small children. Winter opening hours may vary. ∰Q❄❀❸≉♥⊟(2,3)

King Harry's Bar
Glenbrook Hotel, 8 Church Road, PO37 6NU (on edge of Old Village)
☼ 11 (12 winter)-11; 12-10.30 Sun ☎ (01983) 863119
⊕ kingharrysbar.moonfruit.com
Fuller's ESB; guest beers Ⓗ
Charming 19th-century thatched property with two established Tudor bars, restaurants, decked gardens and the Chine walk, plus car parking front and rear. Up to three guest beers are offered, chosen for their originality. Food is served in the summer months commencing at Easter – the long-established Henry VIII kitchen specialises in steaks to die for. Function facilities and live entertainment are provided. Q❄❀⊯❸Ⓖ▲≉♣♥⬱⊟⊟(2,3)

Waterfront Inn Ⓛ
19 Esplanade, PO37 6BN
☼ 11-11; 12-10.30 Sun ⊕ waterfront-inn.co.uk
Goddards Fuggle-Dee-Dum; guest beer Ⓖ
A delightful bar and hotel situated right on the seafront with panoramic sea views and just a stone's throw from the sandy beach. Previously known as the Norfolk Hotel, it was here that Charles Darwin stayed for a few weeks during 1858 while writing on the Origin of Species, and praised both the hotel and the seaside town of Shanklin. Bring your family here to enjoy a sunny meal on the terrace with a beer in summer. Winter hours may vary. Q❄❀⊯❸▲≉♥P⬱⊟(2,3)

Shorwell

Crown Inn Ⓛ
Walkers Lane, PO30 3JZ
☼ 10.30 (11.30 Sun)-11 ☎ (01983) 740293
⊕ crowninnshorwell.co.uk
Adnams Broadside; Goddards Fuggle-Dee-Dum; St Austell Tribute; Sharp's Doom Bar; guest beers Ⓗ
This 300-year-old hostelry has a central multi-sided bar and traditional bar areas offering a range of four to six beers and a good home-cooked pub menu all day prepared by head chef Paul Hayward. The pub has a trout stream running through the garden, ducks in abundance to keep the children amused, and plenty of car parking.
∰Q❄❀❸&▲♣P⊟(12)

Ventnor

Perks Ⓛ
46 High Street, PO38 1LT (next to Tesco Express)
☼ 9-11 ☎ (01983) 562653 ⊕ perksofventnor.com
Draught Bass Ⓗ
Perks is one of those gems that happen infrequently – good service, sensible prices, quality beer, plenty of wine and home-cooked food. The decor is Best of British, with a great collection of memorabilia. Owner Graham Perks has spent 25 years running a succession of bars in Ventnor and knows what the customer wants: pleasant surroundings, good company and a tipple to suit the most discerning palate. Q❀❸&♥⊟(3,6)

Volunteer Ⓛ
30 Victoria Street, PO38 1ES (50yds from bus terminal)
☼ 11 (12 Fri-Sun)-midnight ☎ (01983) 852537
⊕ volunteer-inn.co.uk
Courage Best Bitter; guest beers Ⓗ
Built in 1866, the Volunteer is one of the smallest pubs on the island. A past winner of local CAMRA Pub of the Year, up to six beers are available including a local brew. No chips, no children, no fruit machines, no video games – just a pure adult drinking house and one of the few places where you can still play Rings and enjoy a traditional games night. Live music is hosted on Sunday afternoon. Westons Old Rosie cider is available. Q❄&♣♥⊟(3,6)

Wroxall

Four Seasons Ⓛ
2 Clarence Road, PO38 3BY
☼ 11-12.30am ☎ (01983) 854701
⊕ the-fourseasons-inn.co.uk
Beer range varies Ⓗ
Formerly known as the Star, this pub was brought back to life after a fire. Now a successful village pub, it has an Island-wide reputation for good food, with all produce sourced locally and cooked fresh to order. Meals are served all day and under-10s eat free. Three changing ales usually include one from Yates'. ∰Q❄❀❸&▲♣P⊟(3)

101 Beer Days Out

Tim Hampson

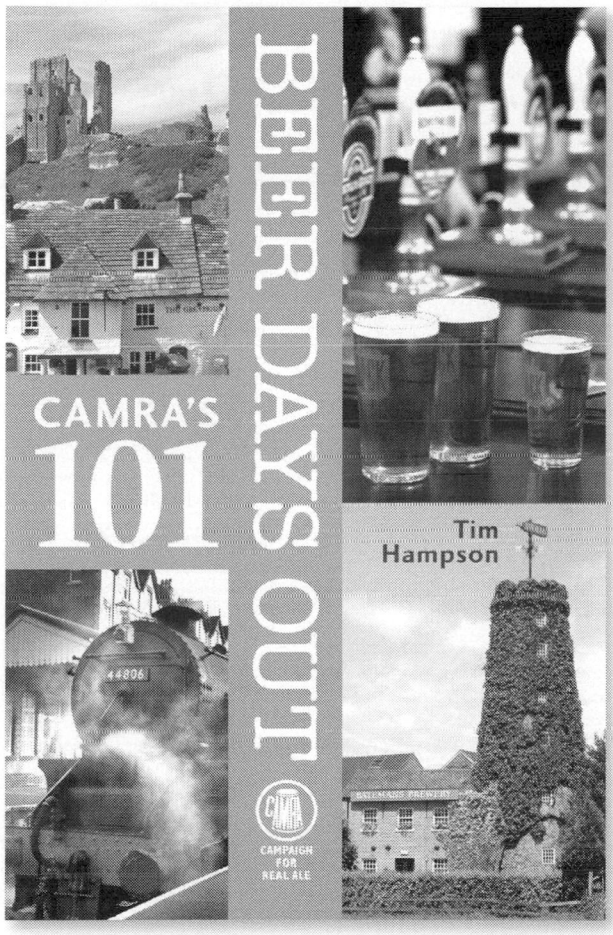

101 Beer Days Out is the perfect handbook for the beer tourist wanting to explore beer and brewing culture in their local area and around the UK. From historic city pubs to beer festivals; idyllic country pub walks to rail ale trails; tourist brewery tours to serious brewing courses – Britain has beer and brewing experiences to rival any in the world. *101 Beer Days Out* brings together for the first time the best of these experiences, ordered geographically and with full visitor information, maps and colour photography – the perfect way to celebrate Britain's national drink.

£12.99   ISBN 978-1-85249-288-5   CAMRA members' price £10.99   224 pages

For this and other books on beer and pubs visit CAMRA's online bookshop at **www.camra.org.uk/books** or call **01727 867201**

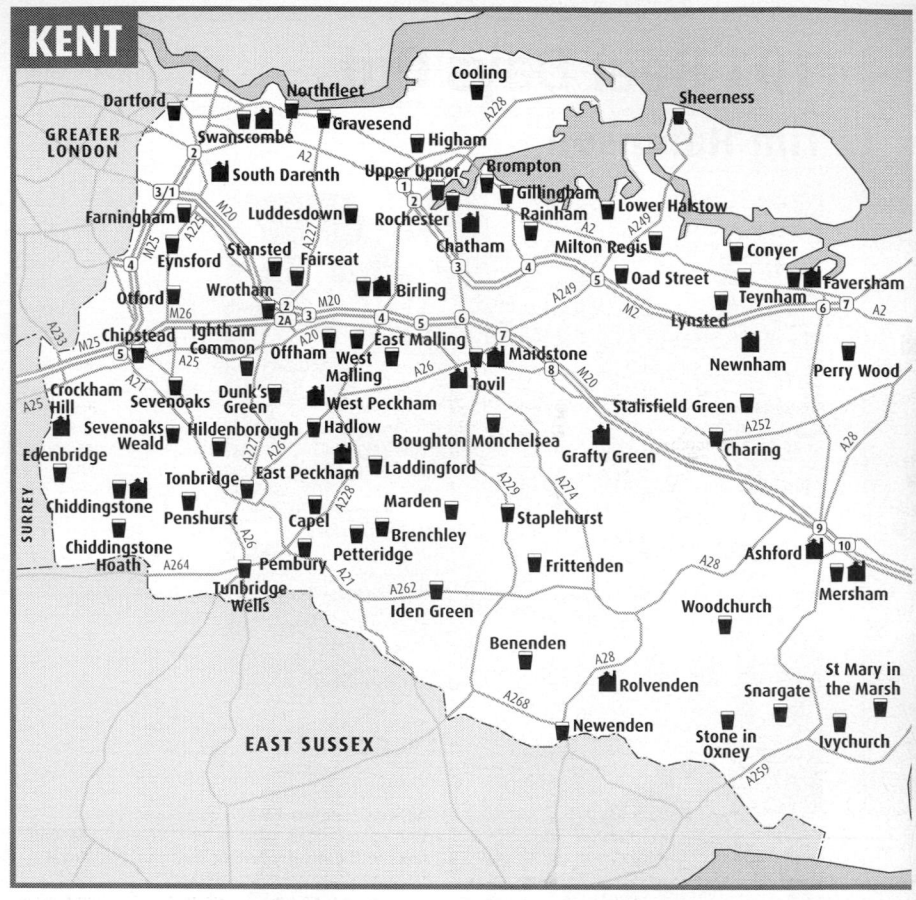

KENT

Dartford
GREATER LONDON
Swanscombe
South Darenth
Farningham
Eynsford
Stansted
Wrotham
Otford
Chipstead
Ightham Common
Crockham Hill
Sevenoaks
Sevenoaks Weald
Edenbridge
Chiddingstone
Chiddingstone Hoath
Tonbridge
Penshurst
Tunbridge Wells
Northfleet
Gravesend
Luddesdown
Fairseat
Offham
Dunk's Green
Hildenborough
East Peckham
Pembury
Cooling
Higham
Upper Upnor
Rochester
Chatham
Birling
East Malling
West Malling
West Peckham
Hadlow
Laddingford
Capel
Petteridge
Iden Green
Brompton
Gillingham
Rainham
Milton Regis
Maidstone
Tovil
Boughton Monchelsea
Marden
Brenchley
Frittenden
Benenden
Newenden
Sheerness
Lower Halstow
Conyer
Oad Street
Teynham
Lynsted
Newnham
Stalisfield Green
Grafty Green
Staplehurst
Woodchurch
Rolvenden
Stone in Oxney
Faversham
Perry Wood
Charing
Ashford
Mersham
Snargate
St Mary in the Marsh
Ivychurch

SURREY

EAST SUSSEX

Benenden

Bull 🅛
The Street, TN17 4DE
✪ 12-midnight ☎ (01580) 240054
⊕ thebullatbenenden.co.uk
Dark Star Hophead; Harveys Sussex Best Bitter; Larkins Traditional; guest beer Ⓗ
Genuine free house overlooking the village green where you can watch the local cricket team. The building dates from the 17th century and features wooden floors, oak beams and an inglenook fireplace. Meals may be consumed in the separate restaurant or in the public bar (no food Sun eves). Booking is advisable for the Friday fish and chips evening and Sunday lunchtime carvery (two sessions). An acoustic music club is held monthly on a Thursday and there is live music most Sunday afternoons. ♨Q❀◑♣♠P⌐━⊟(297)

Birling

Nevill Bull 🅛
1 Ryarsh Road, ME19 5JW
✪ 11-3, 6-11; 12-11 Fri & Sat; 12-5 Sun ☎ (01732) 843193
⊕ nevillbull.co.uk
Beer range varies Ⓗ
This village-centre pub was named in memory of Lt Michael Nevill who was killed in World War II.

Inside, the pub is full of character and quirkiness, with wood beams, comfortable sofas, a log fire and old table games. It is popular for its locally sourced food, including a hog roast on Sundays. Events include a jazz band on the third Thursday of the month with a good-value set meal. This is the closest pub to the Kent Brewery and a selection of its beers feature. The pub holds a beer festival at Easter. ♨Q❀◑♣P⌐━⊟(58)

Bishopsbourne

Mermaid 🅛
The Street, CT4 5HX
✪ 12-3.30, 6-11; 12-11 Sat; 12-3.30, 7-11 Sun
☎ (01227) 830581
Shepherd Neame Master Brew, seasonal beer Ⓗ
Charming red-brick pub, built in 1865 as a tap house for estate workers, nestling in a pretty valley and well worth the short detour from the A2. The two bars are a good place for a chat or a game of darts. Home-cooked meals are served lunchtimes (no food Sun). There is live music monthly, occasional quizzes and summer barbecues. A heated and covered area is provided for smokers. Walkers and dogs are welcome, but children are allowed only in the attractive enclosed garden. A ramp is available for wheelchair users. ♨❀◑★♣⌐

Traditional games include darts and bat and trap. There is a Monday quiz night and crib on Wednesday evenings. One of the two guest beers is usually from a Kent brewery, and an annual beer festival is hosted over the spring bank holiday weekend in a marquee in the attractive garden. Excellent home-cooked food, using local produce, is served (no food Mon). ▲Q❀⏻◗♣P⁵▬⊟(13,14)

0 Miles 5
0 Kilometres 8

Brenchley

Halfway House ♥ 🄻
Horsmonden Road, TN12 7AX (½ mile SE of village) TQ682413
❂ 12-11.30 (10.30 Sun) ☎ (01892) 722526
Goacher's Fine Light Ale; Rother Valley Smild; guest beers Ⓖ
Tucked away in a valley beyond the village church, this CAMRA award-winning late 18th-century coaching inn with a rustic, beamed interior and large garden is an essential destination. About 10 ales are always available, dispensed direct from cooled casks, along with real Kentish Chiddingstone cider. This range is supplemented at Whitsun and August bank holiday beer festivals by at least 50 more ales. There is also a good selection of food (no food Sun eve), and three en suite rooms. ▲Q❍❀⏃◗♣●P⁵▬⊟(297)

Brompton

King George V
1 Prospect Row, ME7 5AL TQ761687
❂ 11.45-11.30; 12-10.30 Sun ☎ (01634) 842418
⊕ kgvpub.com
Adnams Southwold Bitter; guest beers Ⓗ
One of the oldest pubs in the Medway area, with links to the nearby historic dockyard and Royal Engineers' barracks. Known locally as the KG Five, it consists of a single bar with three connected areas as well as a covered and heated smoking part to the rear. A wide selection of bottled Belgian beers, whiskies, rums and real cider is offered. Food is

Boughton Monchelsea

Cock Inn 🄻
Heath Road, ME17 4JD
❂ 12-11; 12-6 (10.30 summer) Sun ☎ (01622) 743166
⊕ cockinnmaidstone.co.uk
Shepherd Neame Master Brew, Spitfire, seasonal beers Ⓗ
Dating from the 16th century, this former coaching inn offers all the Shepherd Neame seasonal and pilot brewery beers. Low ceilings, oak beams and a large inglenook fireplace with a log fire in the winter all feature. Excellent food is served in both the bar and good-sized restaurant (no food Sun eves). Outside there is an extensive patio. Shove-ha'penny and board games are available and canine visitors are welcome. There is a bus service but it is infrequent. ▲❀⏻◗&♣P⁵▬(59)

Bramling

Haywain 🄻
Canterbury Road, CT3 1NB (on A257)
❂ 7-11 Mon; 12-3, 6-11; 12-4 Sun ☎ (01227) 720676
Fuller's London Pride; Wells Bombardier; guest beers Ⓗ
Classic and friendly country pub which features hanging hop bines and assorted curios. The cosy snug is mainly used for diners and meetings.

INDEPENDENT BREWERIES

Canterbury Ales Chartham
Canterbury Brewers Canterbury
Caveman Swanscombe (NEW)
Farriers Arms Mersham
Goacher's Tovil
Goody Ales Herne
Hop Fuzz West Hythe
Hopdaemon Newnham
Kent Birling
Larkins Chiddingstone
Mad Cat Faversham (NEW)
Millis South Darenth
Nelson Chatham
Old Dairy Rolvenden
Ramsgate (Gadds) Broadstairs
Ripple Steam Sutton
Rockin' Robin Maidstone
Shepherd Neame Faversham
Spencer's Ashford (NEW)
Swan West Peckham
Tír Dhá Ghlas Dover
Tonbridge East Peckham
Wantsum Hersden
Westerham Crockham Hill
Whitstable Grafty Green

served lunchtimes through the week and also evenings from Tuesday to Saturday. Four rooms are available for accommodation.
Q✿✿🏠🍴🕭🍽🚆(101,182)

Canterbury

Bottle Shop
The Goods Shed, Station Road West, CT2 8AN (adjacent to Canterbury West station)
✪ closed Mon; 12 (11 Sat)-10.30; 11-4 Sun
☎ (01227) 656280 ⊕ bottle-shop.co.uk
Beer range varies Ⓖ
Located in the Goods Shed, a permanent farmers' market and food hall acclaimed in the national press, the shop specialises in bottled beers from the UK and all over the world. Choose from over 400 beers, many of them rarely found in the UK, either to take home or enjoy on the premises in unforgettable surroundings. A selection of ales is also served from mini casks. Bottled cider – and occasionally draught – is also sold. The website has details of regular tasting events and the monthly board game club. Q✿✿&≈(West)P🕭🍽🚆(4,6)

City Arms Ⓛ
7 Butchery Lane, CT1 2JR
✪ 10.30-11 (12.30am Fri & Sat) ☎ (01227) 458081
⊕ thecityarmspub.co.uk
Canterbury Brewery Engenious Stout, Foundry Torpedo, Foundry Black; Ramsgate Seasider Ⓗ
One of the oldest pubs in Canterbury, this 15th-century inn was known as the Angel & Castle until 1892. A sister pub of the nearby Foundry brewpub, it serves a changing range of its beers, plus guest ales. CAMRA members receive a 10 per cent discount. The pub is popular with younger drinkers at weekends. There is limited seating on the pavement outside, giving a view of the cathedral entrance. Ciders from Kent Cider and Kentish Pip are served, and food is available noon to 5pm. ✿◐≈(East/West)🍴🚆

Dolphin Ⓛ
17 St Radigunds, CT1 2AA (off Northgate, next to St Radigunds car park)
✪ 12-12.30am ☎ (01227) 455963
⊕ thedolphincanterbury.co.uk
Sharp's Doom Bar; Taylor Landlord; guest beers Ⓗ
Friendly local decorated with 1950s-1970s memorabilia and free of TV screens. Good pub food in generous portions is served daily, with roasts on Sunday. It has a comprehensive collection of board games and free internet access. A pianist plays every Sunday evening, and the infamous Dolphin Goat quiz rears its head on the first Monday of the month. The attractive enclosed veranda is popular with diners, and there is a large garden. Westons cider is served and guest beers from Kent microbreweries. 🚃✿◐≈(West)🍴🕭

Eight Bells
34 London Road, CT2 8LN
✪ 12-11 (midnight Thu-Sat); 12-10.30 Sun
☎ (01227) 454794
Sharp's Doom Bar; Young's Bitter Ⓗ
Small, traditional local dating from 1708 and rebuilt in 1902, retaining original embossed windows and decorated with memorabilia. Live music takes place fortnightly on Fridays, and a quiz, usually on the last Wednesday of the month. Five darts teams play every week and their trophies are on display.

Roast lunches are served on Sunday, and a simple menu at other times. There is an attractive, small walled garden. ✿◐≈(West)♣🕭🍽🚆(3,22)

Foundry Brew Pub 🍷 Ⓛ
White Horse Lane, CT1 2RU (just off High St)
✪ 12-midnight (3am Fri & Sat); 12-11 Sun
☎ (01227) 455899 ⊕ thefoundrycanterbury.co.uk
Canterbury Brewers Foundryman's Gold, Loco, GB, Torpedo, seasonal beers; guest beers Ⓗ
The home of Canterbury Brewers and once part of a foundry. The brewery is visible from the main bar, which usually offers seven ales, including one Kent guest beer, plus three local ciders. The brewery's bottled real ale is on sale to take away. Good-value pub food is available 12-6pm. A barbecue takes place every Friday night on the small patio, and a DJ plays upstairs on Friday and Saturday nights. CAMRA members receive a 10 per cent discount on food and handpump beers. Local Branch Pub of the Year 2013. ✿◐&≈(East/West)🍴🕭🚆

King's Head Ⓛ
204 Wincheap, CT1 3RY (on A28 S of city centre)
✪ 12-2.30, 4.45-midnight; 12-midnight Fri & Sat; 12-11.30 Sun ☎ (01227) 462885
Greene King IPA; Harveys Sussex Best Bitter; guest beers Ⓗ
Traditional, friendly, community local, 15 minutes' walk from the city centre. Bar billiards and darts are played in this 15th-century inn and, in summer, bat and trap league matches are held in the garden. There is a monthly Sunday quiz from September to April. Two guest beers are sold, one usually from a local microbrewery, plus Kentish Pip cider and Westons perry. Lunchtime food is Saturday and Sunday only, but evening food is every day, with a curry night every Thursday. Three-star B&B is available, with parking for residents only. 🚃✿🏠◐≈(East)♣🕭🍽(1,28)

New Inn
19 Havelock Street, CT1 1NP (off ring road near St Augustine's Abbey)
✪ 12-2, 6-11; 12 midnight Fri & Sat ☎ (01227) 464584
Adnams Ghost Ship; Greene King IPA; guest beers Ⓗ
Victorian back-street terraced house close to the cathedral, St Augustine's Abbey and the bus station. The main bar has red walls, a wooden floor and a jukebox. At the back is a long conservatory with two cosy alcoves, one known as the library. Usually three guest beers from Kent breweries and Dark Star plus Biddenden cider are on sale. Beer festivals are held on Whitsun and August bank holiday weekends. Disabled access is through the garden and conservatory via Old Ruttington Lane. No food Mondays. 🚃✿◐&♣🕭🍽🚆

Unicorn Inn Ⓛ
61 St Dunstan's Street, CT2 8BS
✪ 11.30-11 (midnight Fri & Sat) ☎ (01227) 463187
⊕ unicorninn.com
Sharp's Doom Bar; Shepherd Neame Master Brew; guest beers Ⓗ
Comfortable 1604 pub near the historic Westgate boasting a very attractive suntrap garden and one of the only pubs in Canterbury to still have a bar billiards table. A quiz, set by regular customers, is held every Sunday evening. One guest beer is usually from a Kent microbrewery (see Twitter for beer updates). Kentish Pip cider is served on draught. The food is excellent value, with a two meals for £10 offer (no food Sun evening). Sporting

ENGLAND

events are televised unobtrusively, and there is occasional acoustic music.
₳❀◑▶≋(West)♣♠‡–₪(3,4,6)

Capel

Dovecote Inn
Alders Road, TN12 6SU (½ mile W of A228 towards Tudeley) TQ643441
❁ 5.30-9.30 Mon; 12-3, 5.30-11; 12-9.30 Sun
☎ (01892) 835966
Harveys Sussex Best Bitter; guest beers Ⓖ
In orchard and hop countryside, though accessible by a few minutes' walk from a main bus route, the Dovecote is an ideal escape from busy town life. Westons Old Rosie cider and a varied range of ale, including a stronger beer, are served direct from the cask and can be enjoyed in the cosy, hop-strewn interior or outside on the shaded patio. Good home-cooked meals are served (not Sun or Mon eves). Book ahead for Sunday lunch.
₳Q❀◑▶♣♠P‡–₪(6A)

Charing

Bowl Inn
Egg Hill Road, TN27 0HG TQ950514
❁ 4-11.30; 12-midnight Fri & Sat; 12-11 Sun
☎ (01233) 712256 ⊕ bowl-inn.co.uk
Fuller's London Pride; guest beers ⒣
Sixteenth-century free house located on top of the North Downs in an area of outstanding natural beauty, signposted from the A20 and A251. A large inglenook fire warms the bar, and an octagonal pool table is partly situated in another fireplace. A popular stop-off for walkers and cyclists, and the large garden is an attraction in summer. Camping is available (booking essential). ₳❀❀⌂◑Å♣P‡–

Chiddingstone

Castle Inn 🄻
TN8 7AH
❁ 10-11; 12-10.30 Sun ⊕ castleinn-kent.co.uk
Harveys Sussex Best Bitter; Larkins Traditional Ale, seasonal beer ⒣
Impressive hostelry adjacent to Chiddingstone Castle grounds and facing the church in this pretty village. The building dates from the early 15th century and incorporates a rare unspoilt public bar and a secluded courtyard garden. The extensive menu is served throughout the bar and restaurant areas (not Sun eve). Visitors come from near and far and include Bob the brewer sampling his own Larkins ales, which are a must-try for anyone when in the area. Nearby attractions include Hever Castle and Penshurst Place. A function room is available for hire. ₳Q❀◑▶🄴♣–

Chiddingstone Hoath

Rock 🄻
Hoath Corner, TN8 7BS TQ497431
❁ 12-11 (10.30 Sun) ☎ (01892) 870296
Larkins Traditional Ale, seasonal beers; guest beers ⒣
The hamlet of Hoath Corner is just 1½ miles south of Chiddingstone and the brewery that supplies its regular ales. Named after the local rocky sandstone outcrops, this early 16th-century drovers' inn

retains its agrarian character in decor and patronage. Dogs loll in front of the woodburning stove on the time-worn brick floor. Try your hand at the rare ring the bull game. Guest beers from the West Country often feature. Food is popular (available Wed-Sun) but space is at a premium, so please pre-book. ₳Q❀◑▶♣P

Chipstead

Bricklayers Arms
39 Chevening Road, TN13 2RZ
❁ 11-midnight (10.30 Sun) ☎ (01732) 743424
⊕ the-bricklayers-arms.co.uk
Harveys Sussex Best Bitter ⒢, seasonal beer ⒣
Vibrant community pub, converted from a terrace of cottages and facing the sailing lake. It has a diverse clientele, including locals and dog walkers in the stone-flagged bar area, with diners mainly congregating in the restaurant, where popular speciality food nights are held (no food Sun eve). The Bricks also opens from 10am for tea, coffee and cakes. Other draws include monthly live music and a Tuesday quiz night. Harveys seasonal brews supplement the Sussex Best served from the cask. Note Churchill's bricklaying skills on the pub sign.
₳⅗❀◑▶‡–₪(401)

Coldred

Carpenter's Arms 🄻
The Green, CT15 5AJ
❁ 6 (7 Sun)-11 ☎ (01304) 830190
Beer range varies ⒣/Ⓖ
Overlooking the village green, this 18th-century two-roomed pub is a real gem and well worth seeking out. It has been in the same family for over 100 years and is one of CAMRA's Real Heritage Pubs, a true community pub and a haven for good conversation. Two real ales are offered from microbreweries alongside Westons First Quality cider. The pub hosts regular community events, including an annual maggot race. May open in the afternoon for groups. ₳⅗❀🄴♣♠P₪(88A,89A)

Conyer

Ship Inn
The Quay, ME9 9HR TQ962648
❁ 12-3, 6-11 (midnight Fri); 11-11.30 Sat; 11-9.30 Sun
☎ (01795) 520881 ⊕ shipinnconyer.co.uk
Adnams Southwold Bitter; Shepherd Neame Master Brew; guest beers ⒣
This pub, once the haunt of smugglers, is on the quayside at Conyer Creek, the only pub left in this village. A popular destination for locals as well as walkers, cyclists and birdwatchers, it has strong links with the local yacht club. Food is of a high standard (it makes its own bread and sausages). Guest beers are sometimes from local microbreweries such as Old Dairy.
₳Q❀◑▶P‡–₪(344,345,346)

Cooling

Horseshoe & Castle 🄻
Main Road, ME3 8DJ TQ759761
❁ 11.30-3 (not Mon), 5.45-11; 11.30-11 Wed-Sat; 12-10.30 Sun ☎ (01634) 221691 ⊕ horseshoeandcastle.co.uk

Shepherd Neame Master Brew; guest beer Ⓗ
Welcoming free house in a quiet village on the Hoo
Peninsula. The restaurant specialises in seafood
(closed on Mon). Accommodation of a high
standard is available for those who wish to explore
the area. The village has two main points of
interest – the local graveyard, which was used in a
film version of Great Expectations, where young
Pip met the convict Magwitch, and the ruined
castle nearby. ♨Q❀🍴⊕◖♿●P⌂⁔

Dartford

Ivy Leaf Ⓛ
72 Darenth Road, DA1 1LS
✪ 11-11; 12-10.30 Sun ☎ (01322) 220993
Sharp's Doom Bar; Wells Bombardier; guest beers Ⓗ
Medium-sized pub with a single U-shaped bar with
wood/coal fires at each end. Four guest ales are on
offer, with at least one brewed locally. Home-
made food and sandwiches are served at
lunchtimes. Outside is a covered smoking area and
a grassed beer garden. Live music takes place on
Thursday and Saturday evenings. Situated halfway
between East Hill and Princes Road, there is a
Fastrack B bus stop by the pub and it is a five-
minute walk from Dartford football ground.
♨❀◖P⌂⁔🚃(B)

Malt Shovel
3 Darenth Road, DA1 1LP
✪ 12 (2 Mon)-11 ☎ (01322) 224381
St Austell Tribute; Young's Bitter; guest beer Ⓗ
Two-bar pub just off East Hill dating from 1673 and
still maintaining its rural charm, especially in the
low-ceilinged taproom which has an original
Dartford Brewery mirror. The main bar has a
spacious conservatory attached, leading to a large
grassed beer garden overlooking the parish church.
Food is served lunchtimes and evenings, except
Monday when the pub hosts a quiz in the evening.
❀◖◭≈♣P⌂⁔🚃

Paper Moon Ⓛ
55 High Street, DA1 1DS
✪ 8am-11 ☎ (01322) 281127
**Adnams Broadside; Greene King Abbot; Kent Boss's
Brew; Ruddles Best Bitter; guest beers** Ⓗ
Town-centre corner pub, part of the Wetherspoon
chain. Formerly Lloyds Bank, the name reflects the
town's historic connection with the papermaking
industry and is decorated with memorabilia
recalling Dartford's past. The bar offers eight beers
– four regulars including a house beer from Kent
Brewery and four guests – plus a draught cider. The
pub conducts frequent brewery promotions and
charity events. A community venue, it features
regular darts competitions. ➷◖♿≈♣●🚃

Deal

Deal Hoy Ⓛ
16 Duke Street, CT14 6DU
✪ 11.30 (12 Sun)-midnight ☎ (01304) 363972
Shepherd Neame Master Brew, seasonal beers Ⓗ
Situated just off the High Street, this lively local is
well worth a visit. The Victorian exterior gives way
to a comfortable modern interior, the bar
decorated with hops. Shepherd Neame beers are
offered alongside Thatchers Heritage cider.
Features include live music every Wednesday and

regular curry and quiz nights. Burgers are served on
Wednesday and Friday in the evenings. An
attractive patio beckons in the summer, with a
heated area for smokers. Free Wi-Fi.
❀◖≈♦⌂⁔🚃(15A)

Just Reproach Ⓛ
14 King Street, CT14 6HX
✪ 12-2, 5-9 (11 Fri & Sat); 12-2 Sun ⊕ thejustreproach.co.uk
Beer range varies Ⓖ
In this micropub you will not find a bar, keg beer,
spirits, food, music, TV or fruit machines, and using
mobile phones will lead to a fine. However, the
welcoming ambience and quality of real ale more
than compensate. High benches and table service
make for friendly interaction and the notice on the
wall explaining the pub's name is a guaranteed
conversation starter. Kentish breweries regularly
feature among the four real ales, and cider is from
a Kentish cider maker. Close to bus station.
Q≈♦🚃

Mill Inn
78 Mill Hill, CT14 9ER
✪ 12-midnight (10 Sun)
**Brains The Rev James; St Austell Tribute; guest
beers** Ⓗ
Large housing estate establishment, situated on
the outskirts of Deal, with a friendly community
spirit. The pub has a substantial main bar and a
smaller side bar. It supports pool and darts teams
and sponsors Deal Town Rangers football team.
Live music events are held every Saturday plus a
weekly meat raffle. It has a good-sized garden
with a bouncy castle in the summer. Families and
dogs are made welcome. ➷❀♿◭♿♣⌂⁔🚃(14,15)

Prince Albert
187-189 Middle Street, CT14 6LW
✪ 6 (12 Sun)-11 ☎ (01304) 375425
Beer range varies Ⓗ
Behind the Fremlins windows and inviting curved
doors lies an exceptionally well-kept Victorian
street-corner pub, situated just off the seafront, a
10-minute walk north of the town centre and
railway station. The well-dressed landlord serves a
changing range of three real ales from smaller,
often local, breweries in the cosy bar. Evening
meals are available Wednesday to Saturday, with
roast lunches on Sunday. The small, sheltered
courtyard is ideal in summer.
♨➷❀◖≈⌂⁔🚃(15A)

Ship Ⓛ
141 Middle Street, CT14 6JZ
✪ 11 (12 Sun)-11 ☎ (01304) 372222
**Caledonian Deuchars IPA; Dark Star Hophead; Fuller's
London Pride; Ramsgate Gadds' No.7; guest beers** Ⓗ
A good-value traditional pub just off the seafront in
Deal's historic conservation area, 10 minutes' walk
from the town centre. The dark wooden floors and
subdued lighting give it a warm, comfortable,
almost nautical feel. Four regular real ales are
offered alongside a changing guest ale, often from
the Ramsgate Brewery. The pub has a cosy rear bar
overlooking a large patio garden, accessed by a
staircase. Live music is hosted every other
Thursday. ♨❀≈⌂⁔🚃(15A)

Dover

Eight Bells 🅛
19 Cannon Street, CT16 1BZ
😊 8-11 (midnight Fri & Sat) ☎ (01304) 205030
Greene King Abbot; Ruddles Best Bitter; Shepherd
Neame Spitfire; guest beers ⊞
Popular, bustling Wetherspoon on Dover's main
shopping street, opposite St Mary's church.
Converted from a cinema, it is reputedly haunted
by a lady singer. A large split-level L-shaped bar
has a lift giving disabled access to the main dining
area and toilets. Outdoor seating overlooks the
pedestrian precinct. Twelve handpumps adorn the
bar, with 10 normally in use, including one or more
real ales from Kent breweries. Close to bus and
railway stations. 🛏🕦&≠(Priory)🌑'–🖾

Louis Armstrong 🅛
58 Maison Dieu Road, CT16 1RA
😊 2 (7 Sun)-11 ☎ (01304) 204759
Hopdaemon Skrimshander IPA; guest beers ⊞
An important local music venue for many years
where the landlady has just celebrated 50 years'
service. The pub has an L-shaped bar with stage,
mirrored wall and old music posters, and a fine
garden at the rear. Up to four real ales are served,
mainly from Kent microbreweries. There is a late
summer beer festival in September. Good-value
food is served on Wednesday evening. It is on
Dover's ring road, with a large public car park
opposite and many local bus services close by.
🕦🌑♦'–🖾

Red Lion
54 Charlton Green, CT16 2PS
😊 11-midnight (1am Fri & Sat); 12-midnight Sun
☎ (01304) 202899
Wells Bombardier; guest beer ⊞
Welcoming two-bar local with a cosy public bar and
open fire, and a short corridor leading to the larger
split-level saloon bar. It has a large, attractive
walled garden with a skittle alley and covered
smoking area. A sport-oriented pub, it supports
darts, football and skittles teams and TV sports.
There is also occasional live entertainment. Food is
available lunchtimes. The pub is in a cul-de-sac off
Dover's one-way system and is easily accessible by
bus. 🅜🕦🅗&♦'–🖾

Dunk's Green

Kentish Rifleman 🅛
Roughway Lane, TN11 9RU (4 miles N of Tonbridge off
A227)
😊 11.30-3, 6-11; 11.30-11 Sat; 12-11 Sun ☎ (01732) 810727
⊕ thekentishrifleman.co.uk
Harveys Sussex Best Bitter; Whitstable Native; guest
beers ⊞
Attractively appointed mid-16th century inn
nestling in a quiet hamlet. The small cosy front bar
belies the spacious rooms beyond, tastefully
decorated in warm colours and with real fires to
dispel the chill in winter. Extensive lunchtime and
evening menus are available (no food Sun and
Mon eves). Local ales from Tonbridge or
Westerham breweries are seen often, along with
real Biddenden cider. The large, pretty garden,
overlooking fields, attracts walkers and cyclists
seeking refreshment on warm days. Twin room
B&B is available. 🅜Q🌑🕦&P🖾(222)

East Brabourne

Five Bells Inn 🅛
The Street, TN25 5LP (sat nav recommended; in the
lanes from A20 via Smeeth and Brabourne Lees or via
Stowting from the B2068)
😊 11.30-11.30 ☎ (01303) 813334
⊕ fivebellsinnbrabourne.com
Beer range varies ⊞
A 16th-century inn at the foot of the North Downs,
convenient for walkers on the North Downs Way
and specialising in Kentish beers, ciders, wines and
food. Breakfasts, lunches, and evening meals are
all served using local ingredients. Families are
welcome, and there is a beer garden and live
music Tuesday evenings. 🅜Q🛏🌑🕦&♦P'–🖾

East Malling

Rising Sun 🅛
125 Mill Street, ME19 6BX
😊 12-11 (10.30 Sun) ☎ (01732) 843284
Goacher's Fine Light; Theakston Best Bitter; guest
beer ⊞
Community free house run by the same family for
over 23 years, whose low prices and good quality
are greatly appreciated. Guest beers may be local
or national. Food is served weekday lunchtimes.
There is a large patio garden to the rear for
summer drinking. Sport is popular here and all
major football matches and other sports events are
shown on large TVs, while the pub is home to
several teams including darts, football and cricket.
A lunchtime meat raffle is held on Sundays.
🌑🕦≠♦'–🖾(58)

Eastry

Five Bells
The Cross, CT13 0HX
😊 11-11.30 (1am Fri & Sat) ☎ (01304) 611188
⊕ thefivebellseastry.com
Greene King IPA; guest beer ⊞
During her five years in charge, Mary has worked
hard to build up a good community-led pub
featuring live music, quiz nights and poker
evenings. This venue has a comfortable lounge bar
where good-value food is served all day, and pool,
darts and TV are played in the public bar. The
adjacent old fire station, with historic memorabilia,
can be used as a function room, and also hosts a
beer festival in April. The rear patio has a children's
play area and pétanque pitch.
🅜🌑🛏🕦🅗&♦P'–🖾(14,87,88)

Edenbridge

Old Eden 🅛
121 High Street, TN8 5AX (by roundabout just S of river)
😊 12-11 (midnight Fri & Sat); 11-10 Sun ☎ (01732) 862398
⊕ theoldeden.com
Taylor Landlord; Westerham 1965; guest beers ⊞
Brick and wooden beam partitions create an
interesting and homely pub interior and reflect the
building's history as a row of cottages. Regular
beers are supplemented by a house beer from
Westerham Brewery and two guests, with a
preference for local brews. Westons Old Rosie real
cider may also be available. Good-quality home-

cooked meals focusing on local ingredients are served (no food Sun eve), with booking advisable at weekends.
🏚🐾🏵🌜🍺(Town)♣🐾P⅄🖿(231,233,236)

Elham

King's Arms 🄻
The Square, CT4 6TJ (in village square near church, just off main road) TR176438
✪ 11-11.30; 12-10.30 Sun ☎ (01303) 840242
⊕ kingsarmselham.com
Harveys Sussex Best Bitter; Hopdaemon Golden Braid, Skrimshander IPA 🄷
Overlooking the village square and the fine medieval church, the hostelry is the focal point for social activities across the area, providing a friendly atmosphere for regulars, visitors and walkers from the Elham Valley. Customers are always guaranteed a good pint of Kentish ale and a hearty meal, with discounted food available to senior citizens Monday to Friday lunchtimes. Parking is in the square. 🏚🐾🏵🌜🍺🐾🖿(17)

Eynsford

Five Bells
High Street, DA4 0AB
✪ 4 (12 Sat)-11; 12-10.30 Sun ☎ (01322) 863135
Harveys Sussex Best Bitter; Long Man Long Blonde; Sharp's Doom Bar; guest beer 🄷
Pleasant traditional pub in a very attractive village. Separate public and saloon bars are retained, as is the dartboard, which is becoming a rarity in the area. Old wooden tables and a display of pressure gauges feature in the public bar. The interior was recently refurbished without changing the character of the pub. The pub quiz is the third Thursday each month. Q🏵🌜♣P⅄🖿(421,478)

Fairseat

Vigo 🄻
Gravesend Road, TN15 7JL (on A227)
✪ 6-11 (12.30am Fri); 12-12.30am Sat; 12-5, 7-11 Sun
☎ (01732) 822465 ⊕ vigoinn.co.uk
Beer range varies 🄷
A classic ale drinkers' haven, this was a former drovers' inn on the North Downs between Gravesend and Wrotham. It retains a traditional, quiet bar with a large open fireplace at one end. Daddlums, a rare form of Kentish table skittles, is still played here. This pub specialises in beers from local Kent microbreweries such as Goacher's, Old Dairy, Goody Ales and others. Acoustic music sessions are held nightly Wednesday to Saturday evenings and Sunday lunchtime. Sunday lunches are served. 🏚Q🌂🌜🏵🐾P🖿(308)

Farningham

Chequers
87 High Street, DA4 0DT (250yds from A20/jct 3 M25)
✪ 12-11.30 ☎ (01322) 865222
Fuller's London Pride, ESB; Harveys Sussex Best Bitter; Taylor Landlord; guest beers 🄷
Popular, cosy, one-bar corner local in an attractive riverside village. The unusual decor includes murals depicting local scenes, two large decorative

candelabra and a life-size model waiter. Ten handpumps dispense four regular beers and up to six guests. Food is served Monday to Saturday lunchtimes. Regular live music takes place on Sundays from 6pm and monthly quiz nights on Tuesdays. Visitors to the pub can use community parking in the Lion Hotel car park.
🏚🌜♣🖿(421,478)

Faversham

Bear Inn
3 Market Place, ME13 7AG
✪ 10.30-11; 12-10.30 Sun ☎ (01795) 532668
Shepherd Neame Master Brew, seasonal beers 🄷
Located centrally on the historic market square, this quaint but attractive pub dates from the 16th century. Inside is appealing, with its series of small cosy snugs running the length of the building. The lunchtime menu is popular with regulars and visitors. A general knowledge quiz is held on the last Monday of the month. The pub often features seasonal ales as well as beers from the Shepherd Neame pilot brewery. 🏚Q🌜🍺⅄🖿

Elephant 🄻
31 The Mall, ME13 8JN
✪ closed Mon; 3 (12 Sat)-11; 12-7 Sun ☎ (01795) 590157
Hopdaemon On the Hop; guest beers 🄷
Local CAMRA Pub of the Year for seven consecutive years to 2012. This is a traditional ale house featuring five real ales, often including a mild. The house beer is a mixture provided by Hopdaemon for the pub, and the real cider on handpump is often local. Beers are mainly sourced from local microbreweries and there are two beer festivals during the year. An open log fire blazes in winter, and there is a well-tended walled garden for the summer. Regular music nights feature local artists. 🏚🌂🍺♣🐾⅄🖿

Leading Light
20-22 Preston Street, ME13 8NZ
✪ 8am-11 ☎ (01795) 535075
Greene King Abbot; Ruddles Best Bitter; guest beers 🄷
A Wetherspoon pub that gets its name from Henry Wreight, a leading light in 19th-century Faversham. This hostelry is a nice example of the pub chain offering the usual fare and beer festivals throughout the year. East Kent microbrewery beers often feature. 🐾🌂🌜🐾🍺🐾⅄🖿

Phoenix Tavern
98-99 Abbey Street, ME13 7BH
✪ 12-11 (midnight Fri & Sat) ☎ (01795) 591462
⊕ thephoenixtavernfaversham.co.uk
Harveys Sussex Best Bitter; guest beers 🄷
A 14th-century traditional English pub set in the heart of Faversham on one of England's longest medieval streets. A warm welcome is extended to all, including well-behaved dogs. Fresh food is prepared daily using locally sourced ingredients. A varied events calendar includes meetings of the Timothy Taylor appreciation society and a real ale advisory board that assists with real ale selection. Usually, guest beers are from Otter, Ringwood, Timothy Taylor or Gadds'. Live jazz plays on Sunday afternoons. A secluded walled garden is at the rear. 🏚Q🐾🌂🏵🌜🍺♣P⅄🖿

Shipwright's Arms Ⓛ

Ham Road, Hollowshore, ME13 7TU (1½ miles north of Faversham) TR017636

✪ closed Mon eve winter; 11-3 (4 Sat), 6-10 (11 summer); 12-4, 6-10 Sun ☎ (01795) 590088

Goacher's Real Mild Ale, Shipwrecked; Whitstable EIPA; guest beer Ⓖ

Remote 300-year-old family-run free house, a good reward after a 45-minute walk across the marshes from Faversham. The wooden-clad building's interior reflects its nautical heritage, with many associated ornaments and pictures on display or tucked into nooks and crannies. It is popular with walkers off the Saxon Shore Way and boat owners from the adjacent boatyard. The large garden at the rear is open spring-autumn, with outside seating at the front all seasons. In severe winter weather telephone to check opening times. Dog-friendly. ⚲Q✿❀❍▶P⌐

Swan & Harlequin

Conduit Street, ME13 7DF

✪ 12-11 (10.30 Sun) ☎ (01795) 532341

Dark Star American Pale Ale; Shepherd Neame Master Brew Ⓗ**; guest beers** Ⓖ

Just north of the Shepherd Neame Brewery, sitting very close to Faversham Creek, this two-bar pub offers a friendly welcome to real ale drinkers, with competitive prices and a change in policy that saw an expansion of the range of ales to reflect customers' choice. Beer is either dispensed on handpump or fetched from the adjacent cellar. Food is available on Sunday afternoons only. Sport is shown on a big screen and well-behaved dogs are welcome. There is limited parking. ⚲☙✿❀⇔❀▣P⌐

Finglesham

Crown Inn Ⓛ

The Street, CT14 0NA

✪ 12-11 ☎ (01304) 612555 ⊕ thecrownatfinglesham.co.uk

Canterbury Wife of Bath; guest beers Ⓗ

Traditional rural pub with a welcoming atmosphere, wooden floors and real fires. Three to four real ales, many from local breweries, and Biddenden cider are on sale. Good home-made food is served lunchtimes and evenings, all day Friday and Saturday. The restaurant opens out on to the garden, which has a large children's play area. Community and charity events, live music, bat and trap, quiz nights and food and drink offers all keep the pub busy throughout the year. Dogs are welcome in the bar. ⚲☙✿❍Ⅰ❀❀❍P⌐▣(13,14)

Folkestone

East Cliff Tavern

13-15 East Cliff, CT19 6BU (from harbour, up hill straight on past lifeboat and second right; from Dover Road looking south, turn left at Raglan, first left, down hill, footpath across railway – no trains)

✪ 5 (12 Sat & Sun)-11 ☎ (01303) 251132

Beer range varies Ⓗ

Friendly terraced back-street pub, near a footpath across the railway line, a short walk from the harbour. The main bar is to the right and there are usually two beers, often from local breweries, with Biddenden cider on gravity behind the bar. Old photographs of Folkestone decorate the walls and community events include weekly raffles. A TV is in

the saloon bar. Opening hours may vary at quiet times; check if making a special visit. Q✿❀Ⅰ❀❀❍⌐

Guildhall

42 The Bayle, CT20 1SQ (off pedestrian part of Sandgate Rd, near Old High St)

✪ 12-11 (midnight Fri & Sat); 12-10.30 Sun ☎ (01303) 251393

Greene King IPA; Harveys Sussex Best Bitter; guest beers Ⓗ

A welcoming, traditional single-bar pub, close to the town centre. Large windows give the interior a light, airy feel. This is an ideal place to take a break from the hustle and bustle and enjoy good beer. Two guest ales are normally stocked from the Punch Taverns Finest Cask selection. A real cider may be sold in the summer. Good-value food is served at lunchtimes, and occasionally evenings if pre-booked. ✿❍❀❀P⌐▣

Pullman

7-9 Church Street, CT20 1SE (off Rendezvous St in pedestrian zone)

✪ 12-10 (11 Fri & Sat); 12-6 Sun ☎ (01303) 240538

Beer range varies Ⓗ

A smart, comfortable pub with background classical music near the town-centre shopping area. The three distinct bar areas are wood panelled, with prints of old Folkestone, and there is an exotic walled garden. Four beers from regional and local breweries are on sale. There is a beer festival in October, and good-value food is served every day. The venue may close early on Mondays in January and February. At weekends in December you can enjoy classical jazz on the piano. ⚲✿❍❀❀⌐▣

Fordwich

Fordwich Arms Ⓛ

King Street, CT2 0DB

✪ 11-midnight (1am Fri & Sat); 12-11 Sun ☎ (01227) 710444 ⊕ fordwicharms.co.uk

Flowers Original; Sharp's Doom Bar; Shepherd Neame Master Brew; Wadworth 6X Ⓗ

Classic 1930s building opposite the town hall in England's smallest town, overlooking the River Stour. The large bar has a lovely fireplace and there is a separate dining room. Meals are served in both areas (no food Sun eve). The pub hosts themed evenings, including a popular pudding night on the second Wednesday of the month (booking essential). A folk club meets every second and fourth Sunday night, and live jazz features in the garden once a month on summer Sunday afternoons. ⚲Q✿❍❀⏚⇌(Sturry)P⌐▣(4,6,8)

George & Dragon Ⓛ

64 King Street, CT2 0DB

✪ 11.30-11 (10.30 Sun) ☎ (01227) 710661

Brunning & Price Original Bitter; guest beers Ⓗ

Attractive pub, parts of which date back to the 15th century. In 1944 it was a set for the film A Canterbury Tale. Next to the River Stour, the pub has been tastefully refurbished, and has a large drinking area with comfortable furniture and wooden beams, a popular restaurant and a pretty, sheltered garden. Five varying guest beers generally include some from Kentish microbreweries. Drinks are at a reduced price 5-7pm Monday to Friday. ⚲Q☙✿❍⏚⇌(Sturry)❀P⌐▣(4,6,8)

Frittenden

Bell & Jorrocks
Biddenden Road, TN17 2EJ TQ815412
🌣 12 (11 Sat)-11; 12-10.30 Sun ☎ (01580) 852415
⊕ thebellandjorrocks.co.uk
Harveys Sussex Best Bitter; Woodforde's Wherry; guest beers Ⓗ
The only pub in the village, this is very much the centre of the local community, providing good pub-grub meals, including menus for kids, as well as a more gourmet specials board. A TV and a pool table are kept to the sides. Behind the pub are old stables, often used for annual beer festivals, with a function room available above. The fireplace is dominated by a Heinkel 111 propeller from a German World War II bomber shot down locally.
🏰⍤🐴❶♿🍴♣🚬

Gillingham

Frog & Toad
38 Burnt Oak Terrace, ME7 1DR TQ774688
🌣 1 (2 Mon)-11; 12-11 Fri & Sat; 12-10.30 Sun
☎ (01634) 852231
Fuller's London Pride; guest beers Ⓗ
A former three times Pub of the Year winner, this back-street local is well worth a visit. Guest brews are mostly sourced from the Cottage Brewery and are supplemented at its three annual beer festivals held during bank holidays. Sunday lunches are served (bookings advisable), and occasional weekend entertainment is also catered for. The landlord prides himself on not having any gaming machines in the pub. Q🌣≠♣🌭🚬🚍(176)

Marquis of Lorne Ⓛ
9 Mill Road, ME7 1HL (from Gillingham rail station walk to the western end of the High Street and turn right; proceed for 50yds) TQ769966
🌣 11-11; 12-10.30 Sun ☎ (01634) 577790
Wells Bombardier; guest beers Ⓗ
A local that has five beers, one usually from a Kent brewery, plus a mild, up to four ciders and three imported German beers. The landlord has an interest in the military and it is not unusual to see customers dressed in old uniforms. There is one fruit machine but no jukebox. Q♿≠🌭🚍

Will Adams
73 Saxton Street, ME7 5EG TQ770683
🌣 7-11; 12.30-4 Sat; 12-3, 8-11 Sun ☎ (01634) 575902
⊕ thewilladams.co.uk
Beer range varies Ⓗ
Single-bar pub named after the local navigator and adventurer – the interior is painted with scenes depicting his life and times. Three or four beers are on offer from breweries and micros across the country, plus three ciders and a perry. Good-value food is available when Gillingham FC are playing at home; the opening times may vary. Twice local CAMRA Pub of the Year. ≠♣🌭🚍

Gravesend

Jolly Drayman
1 Love Lane, Wellington Street, DA12 1JA
🌣 12-11.30 (midnight Fri & Sat); 12-11 Sun
☎ (01474) 352355 ⊕ jollydrayman.com

Dark Star Hophead; St Austell Tribute; guest beers Ⓗ
Comfortable pub with original low ceilings just outside the town centre. The entrance is via what used to be the back of the pub, which looks out onto the alleyway opposite. It was once part of Walkers Brewery. This pub hosts men's and women's darts teams, and daddlums (Kentish skittles) is played on alternate Sundays. Four ales are available. Beer festivals take place twice yearly in May and November. Q🌣🏰♿≠♣P🍴🚍

Rum Puncheon Ⓛ
87 West Street, DA11 0BL (on one-way system, next to Tilbury Ferry)
🌣 11 (12 Sat)-11; 12-10.30 Sun ☎ (01474) 353434
⊕ rumpuncheon.co.uk
Beer range varies Ⓗ
Large riverside building between the ferry and town pier. The L-shaped bar has a log fire and chandeliers, while upstairs a function room opens onto a balcony with river views. A rear terrace also enjoys the same outlook. Eight ales rotate regularly including some from Kent micros. There is a quiz night on the last Wednesday of each month. Home-cooked meals are available lunchtimes. Note the Russell's Brewery windows.
🏰Q🌣♿≠🍴🚍

Ship & Lobster
Mark Lane, Denton, DA12 2QB (E of town; follow Ordnance Rd then Norfolk Rd into Mark Lane)
🌣 11-11 ☎ (01474) 324571 ⊕ shipandlobster.co.uk
Beer range varies Ⓗ
In an industrial area, the pub is reputed to be the Ship in Dickens' Great Expectations. It is on the Saxon Shore Way and popular with walkers and anglers. Internally there is a nautical theme, with pictures of ships and shipping. The pub can be busy when there are angling competitions. There is an outside drinking area on the sea wall with views of the Thames. Three ales are usually available, including one from a Kent brewery. ❶🌭P

Hadlow

Two Brewers
Maidstone Road, TN11 0NJ (on A26)
🌣 12-3, 5-midnight; 12-midnight Wed & Thu; 12-1am Fri & Sat; 12-11.30 Sun ☎ (01732) 850267
⊕ thetwobrewershadlow.co.uk
Harveys Sussex XX Mild Ale, Hadlow Bitter, Sussex Best Bitter, seasonal beers Ⓗ
Genuine community local that has been improving for a while, especially under new tenants, which attracts many visitors passing through town, including walkers and cyclists. It has been nicely decorated by the brewery, with wooden floors and etched glass screening. A range of pub games is available, such as shove-ha'penny, cribbage and shut the box. It is popular with diners, particularly when special events are held (no food Sun eve or Mon). The fine range of Harveys ales is justifiably popular. Handily, a late night bus stops nearby. 🌣❶♿♣P🍴🚍(7,77)

Hastingleigh

Bowl Inn Ⓛ
The Street, TN25 5HU TR095449
🌣 closed Mon; 5 (12 Sat)-11.30; 12-10.30 Sun
☎ (01233) 750354 ⊕ thebowlonline.co.uk

Beer range varies Ⓗ
A lovingly restored listed village pub that retains many period features including a taproom used for playing pool, and free from jukebox and games machines. It was local CAMRA Pub of the Year in 2012. Quiz night is Tuesday. The lovely garden is home to a tame European eagle owl. A beer festival is held on August bank holiday Monday. Excellent sandwiches and baguettes are available at the weekend. ⋈Q✿✿◖♣🖤P⌐

Herne

Butcher's Arms Ⓛ
29A Herne Street, CT6 7HL (opp church)
✪ closed Mon; 12-2, 6-9; 12-3 Sun ☎ (01227) 371000
⊕ micropub.co.uk
Adnams Broadside; Dark Star Hophead; Fuller's ESB; Hopdaemon Incubus; guest beers Ⓖ
Britain's first micropub, opened in 2005, is a real ale gem and the inspiration for other micropubs. Once a butcher's shop, it still has the original chopping tables. It has seating for 12 customers and standing room for about 20 – the compact drinking area ensuring lively banter. Customers can also buy beer to drink at home. Snack food includes local Ashmore cheeses, and the local cider, Broomfield, is available in bottles. The pub has won five CAMRA awards, and the landlord was voted one of CAMRA's top 40 campaigners. Q🖾(4,6)

Herne Bay

Prince of Wales Ⓛ
173 Mortimer Street, CT6 5DS (at E end of town, between seafront and High St)
✪ 10 (12 Sun)-midnight ☎ (01227) 374205
⊕ princeofwaleshernebay.co.uk
Shepherd Neame Master Brew, Kent's Best, Spitfire, seasonal beers Ⓗ
Splendid Victorian pub, reflecting the heyday of this seaside town. The stylish woodwork, tiled fireplaces, marble mantelpieces and etched glass are not overwhelmed by discreet TV screens for sporting events. It displays a unique collection of water jugs. Only 100 yards from the seafront, the four bars include a large games room with pool and darts and a small, beautifully decorated back bar. There is a patio with seating. Shepherd Neame's microbrewery beers, and guest ales, are occasionally available. ⋈✿🖾◖♣⌐🖾(4,6)

Higham

Stone Horse
Dillywood Lane, ME3 8EN (off B2000 Cliffe Rd)
TQ732713
✪ 12-3, 6-11; 12-11 Fri & Sat; 12-3.30, 7-10.30 Sun
☎ (01634) 722046
Courage Best Bitter; guest beers Ⓗ
Friendly country pub just outside the edge of Strood. It is surrounded by fields and is a short walk from the edge of the Medway Towns. The unspoilt public bar has a wood-burning range. Good-value food is served throughout the week (but no food Sun eves) and daily specials are on offer. Up to three guest beers are usually available, with Harveys Sussex Best Bitter served most of the time. ⋈Q✿◖◖ 🖾♣P⌐🖾(133)

Hildenborough

Plough Ⓛ
Leigh Road, TN11 9AJ (½ mile S of Hildenborough at Powdermills) TQ568469
✪ closed Mon; 12-3, 6-11; 12-5 Sun ☎ (01732) 832149
⊕ theploughatleigh.com
Harveys Sussex Best Bitter; guest beers Ⓗ
A 16th-century inn that features exposed brickwork, hop-clad beams and an unusual and impressive open-sided fireplace. The extensive stream-side grounds contain mature weeping willow trees, ample picnic bench seating, a children's play area and even a wishing well. The pub is an assured outlet for those seeking local Tonbridge and Westerham beers. Good food can be eaten in the bar, restaurant or garden. The popular Sunday carvery is served in the adjacent Great Barn (no food Sun eve). ⋈Q✿✿P⌐🖾(210)

Hythe

Three Mariners Ⓛ
37 Windmill Street, CT21 6BH
✪ 4-10 Mon; 12-11; 12-midnight Fri & Sat; 12-11 Sun
☎ (01303) 260406
Young's Bitter; guest beers Ⓗ
Hidden away down a side street not far from the Royal Military Canal, this refurbished traditional pub is well worth visiting. Friendly staff and locals are always happy to have a chat with you. With no food available, it attracts customers for the quality and selection of real ales on offer, which can be enjoyed in either of the two bars, or in the partly heated outside area that is popular with smokers. ⋈✿✿🖾♣🖤⌐🖾

Iden Green

Peacock
Goudhurst Road, TN17 2PB (1½ miles E of Goudhurst at A262/B2085 jct 1) TQ747374
✪ 12-11 (6 Sun) ☎ (01580) 211233
⊕ peacockidengreen.co.uk
Shepherd Neame Master Brew, Kent's Best, Bishops Finger, seasonal beer Ⓗ
Quintessentially English traditional country pub with an exterior of weatherboard cladding and a tile-hung façade. Inside there are low oak-beamed ceilings ('duck or grouse'), tiled floors and a wonderful inglenook fireplace in which logs are burning on chilly days. There are three distinct areas in a U shape around a central bar. The rear left area is principally for diners, although the good-value food, encompassing vegetarian choices, can be eaten anywhere, including in a large secluded garden on warmer days. ⋈Q✿◖◖ 🖾♣P⌐🖾(297)

Ightham Common

Old House ★
Redwell Lane, TN15 9EE (½ mile SW of Ightham village, between A25 and A227) TQ590558
✪ 7-9 (11 Wed-Fri); 12-3, 7-11 Sat & Sun ☎ (01732) 886077
Beer range varies Ⓖ
Rescued from Watneys in 1970, this gem has remained in the same family ever since. Located down a secluded country lane, it is a Grade II-listed

building comprising an entrance lobby and two separate bars. The public bar features a Victorian wood-panelled counter, parquet flooring and a massive inglenook fireplace. The lounge has a chaise longue. Up to six beers are served on gravity from the taproom, selected by the landlord from a good range of breweries. ﹏Q❀⊞Å♣P⅃

Ivychurch

Bell Inn ▼
Ashford Road, TN29 0AL (signed from the A2070 between Brenzett and Hamstreet, 1 mile from A259/A2070 roundabout) TR028275
❂ 12-11 (10.30 Sun) ☎ (01797) 344355
⊕ thebellinnromneymarsh.co.uk
St Austell Trelawney; Sharp's Doom Bar; Wadworth Henry's IPA; guest beers ℍ
Like many marsh pubs, this house is adjacent to the church. A warm welcome awaits at this hostelry, popular for its excellent ales and ciders as well as the selection of food. The current licensees have achieved an enviable reputation for the establishment, gaining the honour of local CAMRA Pub of the Year in 2010, 2011 and 2013. Well worth finding, it was once the centre of the Romney Marsh Owlers (Smugglers).
﹏⅀❀①⊞৬♣❁P⅃

Laddingford

Chequers
The Street, ME18 6BP (1 mile SW of Yalding) TQ689481
❂ 12-3, 5-11; 12-11 Sat & Sun ☎ (01622) 871266
⊕ chequersladdingford.co.uk
Adnams Southwold Bitter; guest beers ℍ
A community-focused, 15th-century pub with colourful window boxes and hanging baskets. The oak-beamed bar with split-level dining area has numerous artefacts throughout. The large rear garden with children's play equipment is popular during the April beer festival. Good-quality food is served (snacks only on Mon), with home-made sausages on Thursday, and regular themed food nights. One double bedroom is available for letting. A bus stops outside or there is a train to Beltring Halt, with a 20-minute walk.
﹏Q❀☏①♣P⅃➡(23,26)

Lower Halstow

Three Tuns ℒ
The Street, ME9 7DY TQ859672
❂ 12-11 (midnight Fri & Sat); 12-10.30 Sun
☎ (01795) 842840 ⊕ thethreetunsrestaurant.co.uk
Goacher's Mild; Millis Kentish Best; guest beers ℍ
True family village pub with a friendly, cheerful atmosphere and lively conversation. A range of mainly local Kentish ales and a local cider on handpump is on offer, plus another on draught. It does a quirky range of bar snacks, has an award for best pub chips, and a local reputation for good food. Events are held throughout the year (see the website). A function room, games room, log fires, sofa seating, brick walls and beams add character. It has a large garden with streamside decking.
﹏⅀❀①⊞♣❁P⅃➡(327)

Luddesdown

Cock Inn ℒ
Henley Street, DA13 0XB (1 mile SE of Sole St station) TQ664672
❂ 12-11 (10.30 Sun) ☎ (01474) 814208
⊕ cockluddesdowne.com
Adnams Southwold Bitter, Lighthouse, Broadside; Goacher's Mild; Shepherd Neame Master Brew; guest beers ℍ
Ultra-traditional rural free house dating from 1713 and under the same ownership since 1984, with two bars, a large conservatory, a function room and a very comfortable heated smoking area. It is the meeting place for a number of local clubs and societies. Traditional pub games are played including pétanque, bar billiards and several forms of darts. The free quiz on a Tuesday evening hosted by the landlord is not for the faint-hearted. No children allowed in the bars or garden.
﹏Q❀①⊞♣P⅃☷

Lynsted

Black Lion ℒ
Lynsted Lane, ME9 0RJ (close to church) TQ943609
❂ 11-3, 6-11; 12-3, 7-10.30 Sun ☎ (01795) 521229
Goacher's Mild, Light, Dark, seasonal beers ℍ
Village local sought out by the discerning drinker as three or four Goacher's ales are always available. In the main bar warming fires greet you in winter, while a bar billiards table sits in the small adjoining bar. The characterful landlord holds court and still uses Arkwright's till. Home-cooked food is available daily. It has a large garden and three separate letting rooms. Home-made political cartoons adorn the entrance hall.
﹏Q❀☏①⊞♣P⅃➡(345)

Maidstone

Flower Pot ▼ ℒ
96 Sandling Road, ME14 2RJ (off A229 N of town centre)
❂ 12 (11 Sat)-11; 12-10.30 Sun ☎ (01622) 757705
⊕ flowerpotpub.com
Goacher's Gold Star; Kent Brewery Pale; guest beers ℍ
This split-level street-corner free house, close to the football stadium, is a real-ale lovers' paradise. The lower bar houses a pool table while nine handpumps adorn the upper bar, dispensing ales mainly from micros. Four ciders are served straight from the cask. TV screens show the beers on offer along with the strength and price. Music nights are held every other Saturday and jam nights every Tuesday. Beer festivals take place in May and August. ﹏Q❀◖≈(East)♣❁⅃➡(101,155)

Pilot
25 Upper Stone Street, ME15 6EU (on A229)
❂ 12-3 (not Mon), 6-11; 12-midnight Fri & Sat; 12-11 Sun
☎ (01622) 691162 ⊕ thepilotpub.com
Harveys Sussex XX Mild, Sussex Best Bitter, Armada Ale, seasonal beers ℍ
Maidstone's country pub in the town, the welcoming 16th-century, Grade II-listed building features a beamed interior and inglenook fireplaces. Excellent Sunday roasts are served 12-3pm followed by live music and a fun quiz in the

evening. Jam nights are held monthly on a Wednesday. No food Monday, Tuesday or Sunday evening. Darts can be played, and at the rear there is a pétanque piste and two covered smoking areas. Westons Old Rosie cider is sold.
⛫❀◐≋(West)♣●⁼–🚌

Rifle Volunteers [L]

28 Wyatt Street, ME14 1EU
⊙ 11-3, 6 (7 Sat)-11; 12-3, 7-10.30 Sun ☎ (01622) 758891
Goacher's Real Mild, Fine Light, Crown Imperial Stout [H]
Quiet street-corner single-bar pub owned by the local Goacher's Brewery. It retains most of its original features and has featured regularly in this Guide. The pub fields a quiz team in the local league. A short walk from the shopping district, this is an oasis of calm where conversation can be enjoyed unhindered by music or fruit machines.
Q❀≋(East)♣⁼–

Society Rooms

Brenchley House, Week Street, ME14 1RF
⊙ 7-midnight ☎ (01622) 350910
Courage Directors; Greene King Abbot; Ruddles Best Bitter; guest beers [H]
A light and airy Wetherspoon's opposite Maidstone East station, which occupies the site of a former newspaper printing works. The pub is named after William Shipley, founder of the Royal Society of Arts and the Maidstone Society for Promoting Useful Knowledge. There is a large outside drinking/smoking area, and food is available all day. ❀◐♿≋(East)⁼–🚌

Swan [L]

2 County Road, ME14 1UY (opp prison, near County Hall)
⊙ 12-11 ☎ (01622) 751264 🌐 theswaninnmaidstone.co.uk
Shepherd Neame Master Brew, Kent's Best, seasonal beers [H]
Community-oriented pub that runs two teams in the local quiz league and hosts popular card games. Coach trips are organised to various events, and sometimes live music takes place at weekends. It is just a little away from the shops and near the East station. The prison gates nearby featured in the movie Porridge and the TV sitcom Birds of a Feather. Shepherd Neame's seasonal and pilot microbrewery ales regularly appear, and mini beer festivals are held during the year.
⛫❀≋(East)♣⁼–

Wheatsheaf

301 Loose Road, ME15 9PY (S of Maidstone at A229/A274 jct)
⊙ 4-11; 12-11.30 Fri & Sat; 12-10.30 Sun ☎ (01622) 752624
🌐 thewheatsheaf-maidstone.co.uk
Courage Best Bitter; guest beers [H]
There has been an inn here since the 1600s, the current pub having been built in 1830. It is a free house, owned by the same family for 29 years. There are usually at least two guest beers including Caledonian seasonal brews, and occasional beer festivals. One long spacious bar shows live football and rugby, and the community pub hosts two darts teams and a golf society. Excellent food is served Friday to Sunday lunchtimes and Friday to Saturday evenings. ❀◐♣⁼–🚌(5,82,89)

Marden

Stile Bridge [L]

Staplehurst Road, TN12 9BH (on A229 at foot of Linton Hill by jct with B2079)
⊙ 11-11; 12-7 Sun ☎ (01622) 831236
🌐 thestilebridge.co.uk
Dark Star Hophead; Shepherd Neame Master Brew; guest beers [H]
Five real ales and three ciders await visitors to this large roadside pub. There is a welcoming atmosphere with a good mixture of drinking and dining areas, all with pub and drinking memorabilia on the walls. Local microbreweries are supported alongside a good selection of genuine continental beers and lagers. Spring and summer bank holidays feature beer and music festivals, while live music is hosted at other times.
⛫❀◐⊟●P⁼–▯🚌(5)

Margate

Lifeboat Ale & Cider House

1 Market Street, CT9 1EU
⊙ 12-1am (2am Thu-Sat) ☎ (07837) 024259
🌐 thelifeboat-margate.com
Beer range varies [G]
Small hostelry in the old town district of Margate within walking distance of the Turner Contemporary Art Centre. A wooden stillage divides this excellent pub into a front and back room. Up to six real ales, mainly from Kent breweries, are served direct from the cask, along with a wider selection of Kentish ciders and perries – it is a former Kent CAMRA Cider Pub of the Year winner. All food is sourced from local suppliers. Live music is a feature on Thursdays.
⛫◐≋●🚌(8,34)

Mechanical Elephant

28-30 Marine Terrace, CT9 1XJ
⊙ 8am-11 (1am Fri & Sat) ☎ (01843) 234100
Greene King Abbot; Ruddles Best Bitter; guest beers [H]
Ideally located opposite the main beach, with a flower-bedecked summer balcony offering the famous sunset views. This newly refurbished Wetherspoon is a quiet daytime pub. On Friday and Saturday evenings it becomes a Lloyds No.1 bar with recorded music. Good-value food and a good selection of well-kept ales is on sale, including Kent and regional guest beers. The staff are friendly and accommodating. Its name derives from a large roving mechanical elephant that gave rides along the sea front in the 1950s.
❀◐♿≋●⁼–🚌

Northern Belle

4 Mansion Street, CT9 1HE
⊙ 11-11; 12-10.30 Sun ☎ (07810) 088347
Shepherd Neame Master Brew, Kent's Best, seasonal beers [H]
Margate's oldest pub is situated down a tiny road opposite the pier and Turner Contemporary Art Centre. This hostelry was built in 1680 from two fishermen's cottages and was previously called the Waterman's Arms and then Aurora Borealis. Its present name derives from the wreck of an American cargo ship in 1857 where local men rescued the crew. Timbers from the wreck can still be seen in the bar. Newly refurbished, it has a cosy

maritime theme. Live music takes place on Sunday afternoons. An ideal place to catch up on local gossip. ♿❤✦–☷(8,34)

Mersham

Farriers Arms Ⓛ

The Forstal, TN25 6NU (from jct 10 on M20 towards Sellinge A20 turn right towards Mersham village; through village turn right into Church Rd; pub on left approx ½ mile)

✪ 11-midnight (1am Fri; 1.30am Sat); 11-11.30 Sun
☎ (01233) 720444 ⊕ thefarriersarms.com
Old Forge Brewery Farriers 1606; guest beers Ⓗ
Community-owned Grade II-listed pub dating back to 1606. The pub's adjacent five-barrel microbrewery produces Farriers 1606 and seasonal ales. An annual beer festival takes place in late July, as well as many other events throughout the year. Food is served in the bar or the pub's Anvil restaurant, lunchtimes and evenings Monday to Thursday and all day Friday to Sunday. The 125 bus runs Monday to Friday. ♨Q♿✿◑♿♣P–☷(125)

Milton Regis

Three Hats ▼

93 High Street, ME10 2AR
✪ 11-11 ☎ (01795) 427645
Shepherd Neame Master Brew; guest beers Ⓗ
Popular and friendly local in the medieval High Street, the focal point for many local social activities. The open-plan interior has low beams to the front rising just enough at the rear to accommodate a dartboard, with a large patio area beyond. Occasional live music and karaoke take place, with a meat raffle on Sundays. The enthusiastic landlord features beers from many areas ranging from the West Country to Scotland, particularly during his twice-yearly beer festivals. Local CAMRA Pub of the Year 2013.
♨✿◑❤(Sittingbourne)♣●–☷(347)

Minster-in-Thanet

Minster & Monkton Royal British Legion Club

61 Augustine Road, CT12 4DH
✪ 11-11 (midnight Fri & Sat); 12-11 Sun ☎ (01843) 821471
⊕ rblminster.org
Courage Best Bitter; guest beers Ⓗ
Friendly British Legion club that has plenty of room, with its main bar, side room and separate bar full of naval memorabilia for all to enjoy. Darts and pool can be played, with bingo, quizzes and other social events regularly planned. Guest beers are often from the local Ramsgate Brewery, Caledonian Brewery, and occasionally from Sharp's and Shepherd Neame. The beer is well kept and sells quickly. Entry is permitted on production of a current Guide or the phone app. ♿✿♿❤♣–☷

Newenden

White Hart Ⓛ

Rye Road, TN18 5PN (on A268 in centre of village)
TQ834273
✪ 11 (12 Sun)-11 ☎ (01797) 252166
⊕ thewhitehartnewenden.co.uk

Harveys Sussex Best Bitter; Rother Valley Level Best; guest beers Ⓗ
Historic 16th-century weatherboarded building that includes old oak-beamed bars and an inglenook fireplace. The pub provides good-quality home-cooked food and has six en-suite rooms. Conveniently situated for the Kent & East Sussex Railway and several National Trust properties, it is an ideal base for exploring the Rother Valley. ♨♿✿◑♿▲♣P–☷(340,341)

Northfleet

Earl Grey

177 Vale Road, DA11 8BP
✪ 12-midnight ☎ (01474) 365240
Shepherd Neame Master Brew, Spitfire, seasonal beers Ⓗ
Distinctive late 18th-century cottage-style building with a Kentish brick and flint exterior that is rarely seen in this area. The interior consists of an L-shaped bar with a raised seating area at one end, and the place exudes a homely and convivial atmosphere. Darts and pool are played and the pub also hosts several football teams.
✿♿♣P–☷(495,499)

Oad Street

Plough & Harrow

Oad Street, Borden, ME9 8LB (opp craft centre)
TQ870620
✪ 12-11 ☎ (01795) 843351
⊕ theploughandharrowpub.co.uk
Shepherd Neame Master Brew; guest beers Ⓗ
Village free house with old world charm, on a main road. It has a small bar area, which can become crowded, with well-used furniture, an open fire, low ceilings, wood beams and a friendly atmosphere. The beer can sometimes be all from Shepherd Neame, but microbrewery guests such as Dark Star Hophead are increasingly available and proving popular. Regular live music plays, and there is a beer garden. Pub food ranges from light bites to main meals (no food Sun eve).
♨✿◑♿♣P–

Offham

King's Arms

Teston Road, ME19 5NR
✪ 12-midnight ☎ (01732) 845208
⊕ kingsarmsoffham.co.uk
Kent Pale; Shepherd Neame Master Brew; guest beers Ⓗ
The village's only remaining pub, it was originally two 16th-century farm cottages. The name shows loyalty to Richard I. There are two bar areas, one for darts and major sports viewing on a large (terrestrial) TV. A third room at the rear has more tables and chairs. A warm atmosphere and well-kept ales provide a welcome retreat from the world's cares. Lunches and evening meals are available including Thai food on Friday evenings and Sunday roasts 12-4pm. ♨✿◑♣P–☷(70)

Otford

Crown L

10 High Street, TN14 5PQ (next to village duck pond)
🟢 12-11 (11.30 Fri Sat) ☎ (01959) 522847
🌐 crownpubotford.co.uk
Tonbridge Three in a Bed; Westerham Otford Crown Ale; guest beers Ⓗ
Partly 16th-century whitewashed cottage-style pub hosting many community activities, with several darts teams. Entertainment includes live music, quiz nights and comedy evenings. Excellent home-cooked meals are served every lunchtime (Sunday roasts until 4.30pm) and Thursday-Saturday evenings. Westerham Otford Crown Ale is the house beer, a blend of Finchcocks and Freedom Ales. Beer festivals are held in the garden in July and October. ﾐQ✿Ⓒ▮Å≒♣♥≞☐(431,432)

Pembury

King William IV

87 Hastings Road, TN2 4JS
🟢 12-11 (midnight Fri & Sat); 12-10.30 Sun
☎ (01892) 825460 🌐 thekingwill.co.uk
Greene King IPA, Abbot; guest beers Ⓗ
The King Will continues to thrive as a genuine village local. The open-plan layout has a main area for diners, and stools clustered around the bar for drinkers. The nearby fire encourages conversation between villagers and visitors, such as thawing walkers. Good food served by friendly staff is available at Sunday lunchtime. Bar billiards, other pub games and live music provide the entertainment. Major events in the calendar are celebrated, and in summer the large garden is sometimes given over to barbecues.
ﾐ⑤✿Ⓒ♣♣P≞☐(6,208)

Penshurst

Spotted Dog L

Smart's Hill, TN11 8EE (turn off B2188 S of Penshurst) TQ523418
🟢 11.30-11 (3 Mon); 12-9 Sun ☎ (01892) 870253
🌐 thespotteddogpub.co.uk
Black Cat Original; Harveys Sussex Best Bitter; Larkins Traditional Ale; guest beer Ⓗ
Charming 15th-century cottage-style inn offering an attractive front patio and a rear tiered terrace affording fine views over the High Weald. The rambling, beamed interior is especially cosy in winter when warmed by its open fires. The pub is a strong supporter of local Larkins and Black Cat breweries, where a seasonal ale may alternate with the regular beer. Families, walkers and dogs are welcome and private functions are catered for. Classic car owners meet here regularly. Booking for Sunday lunch is advisable.
ﾐ⑤✿Ⓒ♣♥≞☐(231)

Perry Wood

Rose & Crown

Crown Hill, ME13 9RY TR042552
🟢 11.30-3, 6.30-11 (not Mon eve); 12-10.30 Sun
☎ (01227) 752214 🌐 roseandcrownperrywood.co.uk
Adnams Southwold Bitter; Harveys Sussex Best Bitter; guest beers Ⓗ

Historic 16th-century free house in an area of outstanding natural beauty, popular with walkers (remove muddy boots though) and cyclists. Exposed beams are decorated with old woodcutting tools and local hops. Warmed in winter by a large inglenook fireplace, well-behaved dogs and children are always welcome here, and it has an extensive garden with a children's play area. The food menu is produced using, wherever possible, locally sourced ingredients and served in the bar or separate restaurant (no food Mon eve). ﾐQ⑤✿Ⓒ▮♣P

Petham

Chequers L

Stone Street, CT4 5PW (on B2068)
🟢 12-3 (not Mon), 6-11; 12-4, 7-10.30 Sun
☎ (01227) 700734
Dark Star Hophead, Partridge Best Bitter; Sharp's Doom Bar Ⓗ**; Whitstable East India Pale Ale** Ⓖ**, Winkle Picker** Ⓗ
On the Roman road from Canterbury to Hythe, the Chequers was built around 1830. The bar area has comfortable leather sofas. A spacious dining area and restaurant is at the back, with a tempting menu including a popular Sunday carvery (no food Sun and Mon eves). Darts and pool are played in the small side bar. Up to six beers are on sale at busy times. A green hop beer festival is planned for October. Local CAMRA Pub of the Year 2011.
ﾐ✿Ⓒ▮Å♣P≞☐(18,620)

Petteridge

Hopbine

Petteridge Lane, TN12 7NE TQ668413
🟢 12-2.30, 6-11; 12-3, 7-10.30 Sun ☎ (01892) 722561
Hall & Woodhouse K&B Sussex Bitter, Badger First Gold, seasonal beers Ⓗ
Attractive weatherboarded building perched on a hilly corner in a quiet hamlet, though accessible by a nearby bus route. The central log fire adds to the homely atmosphere within. Popular home-prepared food is served daily except Wednesday. This is the most easterly Hall & Woodhouse pub, selling its Dorset Badger beers. It has the distinction of being both under the same licensees for 29 years and in this Guide for more than 25. Seating is available in the garden and by the entrance. ﾐQ✿Ⓒ▮♣P☐(297)

Rainham

Mackland Arms L

Station Road, ME8 7PS (from Rainham rail station walk N along Station Rd for 400yds) TQ820664
🟢 10-midnight (1am Fri & Sat); 12-10.30 Sun
☎ (01634) 232178
Shepherd Neame Master Brew; guest beers Ⓗ
Small but recently enlarged pub in an old part of Rainham and only a few minutes' walk north from the rail station. It offers a friendly welcome and good quality ales, including some guests from other breweries. The garden/patio area is a suntrap in the summer and can be very busy.
Q✿≒♣≞☐(120,121,327)

Ramsgate

Artillery Arms L

36 Westcliff Road, CT11 9JS
🔵 12-11 (midnight Fri-Sun) ☎ (07833) 383914
Sharp's Doom Bar; guest beers Ⓗ
Celebrated small alehouse a short walk up the hill
from Waitrose, deservedly popular and attracting a
diverse clientele. The lower bar area with stairs
leads to an upper area with more seating. The
present landlord maintains a long tradition of
stocking a carefully considered range of real ales.
Doom Bar is the house bitter but five other
handpumps serve a varying selection of beers from
Kent and beyond. Interesting old painted windows
depict battle scenes and the theme is continued
with displays of other militaria. 🚃(9,Loop)

Churchill Tavern

19-22 The Paragon, CT11 9JX
🔵 12-11 (1am Fri & Sat) ☎ (01843) 587862
🌐 churchilltavern.co.uk
Greene King IPA; guest beers Ⓗ
Spacious yet cosy pub overlooking the Royal
Marina, with superb views across the English
channel. Built as the Paragon Hotel in 1816, the
building has seen a number of changes through the
centuries. It offers a variety of guest ales in a
warm, welcoming atmosphere. You can get a good
selection of meals in the pub or separate dining
area. It has a small outdoor roof terrace. Live bands
play most Saturday evenings and Sunday
afternoons, and a popular quiz night is held on
Monday evenings. 🏚🕲🕩🍴🚃(34,88)

Comfort Inn (San Clu)

Victoria Parade, CT11 8DT
🔵 11-11; 12-10.30 Sun ☎ (01843) 592345
🌐 comfortinnramsgate.co.uk
Courage Best Bitter, Directors; Ramsgate Gadds'
No.3 Ⓗ
Victorian listed building on the town's East Cliff. The
still impressive frontage used to be even more so
until a fire in the 1920s completely destroyed one
wing, where the garden now stands. With stunning
views across the sea, it is particularly popular in
fine weather. The hotel's public area has been
revamped in a jarringly modern style, with the bar
immediately adjacent to the restaurant. The well-
kept beers make the hotel a useful drinking option
for this under-represented part of town.
🕲🕲🍴🕩♿P🚃(9,Loop)

Conqueror Alehouse L

4C Grange Road, CT11 9LR
🔵 closed Mon; 11.30-2.30, 5.30-9.30; 12-3 Sun
☎ (07890) 203282 🌐 conqueror-alehouse.co.uk
Beer range varies Ⓖ
Welcoming micropub with room for about 20
customers, offering a cosy and pleasant music- and
TV-free environment. Opened in a former retail
outlet in 2010 by an ex-local CAMRA chairman, it
offers three constantly changing real ales, served
straight from the cask, as well as the local
Broomfield cider and a perry. It is named after a
two-funnelled paddle steamer that operated
excursions from the town in the early 1900s,
pictures of which adorn the walls. It was a finalist
in CAMRA National Pub of the Year 2013.
Q🚲♿🚃(Loop,34)

Montefiore Arms 🍺 L

1 Trinity Place, CT11 7HJ
🔵 12-2.30 (not Wed; 4.30 Sat), 7-11; 12-3, 7-10.30 Sun
☎ (01843) 593265 🌐 montefiorearms.co.uk
Ramsgate Gadds' No.7; guest beers Ⓗ
A long-established regular in this Guide, the Monte
enjoys a good reputation with real ale drinkers in
the Thanet area. Most shifts at this friendly back-
street local just off Hereson Road are presided over
by the consummately professional landlord,
serving an excellent and competitively priced
Gadds' bitter, two changing guest ales and
Biddenden cider. Sunday lunchtimes are
particularly well patronised, with a popular high-
rolling meat raffle as the climax. During the week
quiz and darts teams play league matches.
Q♿🚆(Dumpton Park)🐕●🍴🚃(9,9X,Loop)

Sir Stanley Gray L

Pegwell Bay Hotel, 81 Pegwell Road, CT11 0NJ
🔵 11-11 (midnight Fri & Sat); 11.30-10.30 Sun
☎ (01843) 599590 🌐 pegwellbayhotel.co.uk
Ramsgate Gadds' No.5; guest beers Ⓗ
Welcoming pub in the village of Pegwell, with
scenic views over Pegwell Bay and across the
Channel. Connected to the Pegwell Bay Hotel via a
tunnel, the atmosphere is warm and friendly, with
low beams and an intimate feel. There is a
separate games area, and a full pub food menu
supplemented by home-cooked daily specials. The
bar offers four real ales including regionals and
independents. Although part of a hotel, the pub
retains a good local following. A smoking terrace is
outside. 🏚👥🕲🍴🕩♿P🍴

Rochester

Britannia Bar Café L

376 High Street, ME1 1DJ
🔵 10-11 (2am Fri & Sat); 12-11 Sun ☎ (01634) 815204
🌐 britannia-bar-cafe.co.uk
Goacher's Fine Light; guest beers Ⓗ
Three handpumps adorn the bar in this very
friendly town house, an entry in the Guide
continuously since 2002. One of the guest ales is
likely to be from Scotland. Excellent-quality food is
served, with a monthly themed dinner evening
being very popular. The walled garden is a suntrap
in summer months. Within easy reach of both
Chatham and Rochester rail stations and on various
bus routes. Q🕲🕩🚆🍴🚃

Eagle Tavern

124 High Street, ME1 1JT TQ743684
🔵 12-9 (11 Tue & Wed; midnight Thu & Sat); 12-8 Sun
☎ (01634) 409040 🌐 theeagletavern.org.uk
St Austell Tribute; Sharp's Doom Bar; Wells
Bombardier Ⓗ
Friendly local in the middle of the historic
Rochester High Street, with plenty of parking
nearby. Various events, such as live bands and
quizzes, are held in the evenings, with jazz at
Sunday lunchtimes when the pub gets very busy.
The garden at the back gives a good view of the
old city wall. A varied food menu is provided at
lunchtimes (but no food Sun). 🕲🕩♿🍴🚃

Good Intent

83 John Street, ME1 1YL
🔵 12-midnight ☎ (01634) 843118
Beer range varies Ⓖ

A back-street pub for real ale enthusiasts, with a gravity-fed system for dispensing up to three beers. The casks can be seen clearly in the public bar, which has a pool table and a large-screen TV for major sports fixtures. The back bar is accessed via a garden gate and has a much quieter atmosphere. A monthly quiz is held in this bar, as well as live music events. There are regular beer festivals. Q✿❀☺⚹≢♣♠P¹⊷⛾

Man of Kent ⌊

6-8 John Street, ME1 1YN (200yds left off A2 from bottom of Star Hill)
✪ 2-11; 12-midnight Fri & Sat; 12-11 Sun ☎ (07772) 214315
Goacher's Fine Light, Gold Star; guest beers Ⓗ
All the draught ales served from the 11 handpumps on the bar come from Kent breweries only. An extensive range of Kent wines and ciders is also served, while a number of German and Belgian ales are offered on draught and in bottles. Live music is played on Thursday evenings. An enclosed garden allows for pleasant drinking in summer months. ⚹✿≢♠¹⊷⛾⛾

Two Brewers

113 Rochester High Street, ME1 1JS
✪ 11-11 (midnight Sat); 12-10.30 Sun ☎ (01634) 812448
⊕ twobrewersrochester.com
Shepherd Neame Master Brew, Spitfire, Bishops Finger Ⓗ
Long and narrow traditional building reputed to be the smallest pub in Rochester. Built in 1683, the present façade was erected in 1775. The classic sign depicts two draymen carrying a barrel of beer between them on a pole from the brewery to the inn. Photos of old Rochester adorn the walls. There is live music on Sunday from 4pm and a Blues night on the first Thursday of each month. No food is served, except a Sunday lunchtime roast. A large-screen TV shows major sporting events. ≢⛾

Who'd Ha' Thought It

9 Baker Street, ME1 3DN
✪ 12-11.30 (midnight Fri & Sat) ☎ (01634) 830144
⊕ whodha.co.uk
Beer range varies Ⓗ
A charming back-street local off Rochester's Maidstone Road, offering three rotating ales. This is a friendly free house with a wood-panelled bar, log fire, a large TV with satellite sport and a snug bar to the rear. A range of events is held, including live music and monthly charity quiz evenings. There is a well-maintained family- and dog-friendly garden where barbecues and beer festivals are held. Bar snacks including rolls and pizzas are on sale. ⚹✿♣¹⊷⛾(134,155)

St Mary in the Marsh

Star Inn

TN29 0BX (from New Romney turn by the Plough into St Mary's Rd; after 1¼ miles bear left at signpost for ½ mile then turn right at end of road; the Star is on right opp church) TR065279
✪ 12-11 (11.30 Fri-Sun) ☎ (01797) 362139
⊕ thestarinn-themarsh.co.uk
Young's Bitter; guest beers Ⓗ
Warm, traditional pub with an open fire and a bar billiard table to accompany the excellent beer and good food. Built in the reign of Edward IV, Noel Coward used to live in an adjacent cottage, and his first play was written there. Edith Nesbitt, author of

the Railway Children, is buried in the church graveyard of St Mary the Virgin opposite.
⚹✿❀☺⛐⚹♣♠P¹⊷⛾(11A)

Sandgate

Ship Inn ⌊

65 Sandgate High Street, CT20 3AH (on A259)
✪ 11-11.30 (12.30am Fri & Sat) ☎ (01303) 248525
Dark Star Hophead; Greene King IPA, Abbot; Hop Back Summer Lightning; Hopdaemon Incubus Ⓗ**; guest beers** Ⓖ
Narrow pub on the corner fronting on to the High Street, parts of it dating from 1798. It has a front bar and a back room, plus a restaurant with sea views and an upstairs top deck for drinkers, both added in 2010. Nautical maps and pictures featured on the walls reflect the landlord's naval interests. Biddenden ciders are always available and an August bank holiday beer festival is held. No food is served Sunday evenings.
⚹✿⛐⊲Ⓓ⊞♣♠¹⊷⛾(10,16,101)

Sandwich

Crispin Inn ⌊

4 High Street, CT13 9EA
✪ 11-11 (midnight Fri & Sat); 12-10.30 Sun
☎ (01304) 621967 ⊕ sandwichpubs.co.uk
Adnams Broadside; Sharp's Doom Bar; guest beers Ⓗ
A 15th-century pub by Sandwich's old toll bridge. Low ceilings, wooden beams and hops create an old-world feel, providing a congenial ambience for locals and tourists alike. In winter the snug beckons with comfy chairs; in summer sit in the riverside courtyard. Beers from across the UK, always including one from a Kent brewery, are on offer. The home-cooked food has a Caribbean twist, and there is occasional live music. The pub is only a short walk from public transport. Dog-friendly.
⚹✿❀☺Ⓓ⊲Ⓐ≢♣♠¹⊷⛾

George & Dragon ⌊

24 Fisher Street, CT13 9EJ
✪ 11-3, 6-11; 11-11 Sat; 11-4.30 Sun ☎ (01304) 613106
⊕ georgeanddragon-sandwich.co.uk
Shepherd Neame Master Brew; guest beers Ⓗ
Tucked away in a quiet side street, close to the historic quayside of this Cinque Port, this is a 15th-century pub and restaurant. The welcoming and relaxed bar atmosphere is helped by wooden flooring, beamed ceilings and a real fire. Superb home-cooked bar snacks complement the restaurant's menu. Guest ales vary, with Kentish breweries featured, including Wantsum and Hopdaemon. An attractive suntrap courtyard is at the back. Dogs are welcome in the bar. It is a short walk from bus and railway services.
⚹✿❀☺Ⓓ⊲Ⓐ≢¹⊷⛾

Market Inn ⌊

7 Cattle Market, CT13 9AE
✪ 10 (12 Sun)-11 ☎ (01304) 447182
Shepherd Neame Master Brew, Spitfire, seasonal beers Ⓗ
Nestling in the heart of Sandwich, this venue offers a warm and friendly welcome. It is a large, one-bar Shepherd Neame pub serving its typical beer range including occasional beers from its microbrewery. Entertainment includes darts, bar billiards, a weekly quiz, a meat raffle and occasional folk

music on Sunday afternoons. Home-cooked food is available, including the pub's award-winning Market Sandwich. Afternoon tea can be taken in the 16th-century tea room. A handy place for a drink while waiting for your bus. ♨🍽🕽👌🅰🜚♿🚆🖵

Sevenoaks

Anchor
32 London Road, TN13 1AS
🕒 11-3, 6-11; 10.30-11 Fri; 10.30-4.30, 7-11 Sat; 12-11 Sun
☎ (01732) 454898 ⊕ anchorsevenoaks.co.uk
Harveys Sussex Best Bitter; Sharp's Doom Bar; guest beer 🅷
Community local run for many years by effervescent landlord Barry, who organises numerous entertaining events including bi-monthly live blues gigs on Wednesdays, poker and open-mic nights. There are resident men's and women's darts teams. The guest beer is often a local ale from, for example, Old Dairy or Tonbridge breweries. Quality pub food is served Monday-Saturday lunchtimes, and is particularly noted at Christmas. A regular Guide entry. (🍴🚆🖵

Chequers
73 High Street, TN13 1LD
🕒 12-10.30 (11 Tue-Thu); 12-midnight Fri & Sat
☎ (01732) 450144 ⊕ chequerssevenoaks.co.uk
Black Sheep Best Bitter; Harveys Sussex Best Bitter; St Austell Tribute; guest beers 🅷
A 16th-century Grade II-listed building that retains many of the original features, and is supposedly haunted by the ghost of a woman. Up to half a dozen real ales are available, often including local Tonbridge and Westerham brews, with Westons Old Rosie for cider lovers. There is a cask ale price reduction on Monday evening. Lunchtime meals are served throughout the week, with evening meals Monday, Wednesday and Thursday. Live music frequently takes place on Saturday night and there are quizzes on Wednesday. ♨🍲🕽🍴🍽🖵

White Hart 🅛
Tonbridge Road, TN13 1SG (on top of hill 1 mile S of town centre on A225)
🕒 11-11; 12-10.30 Sun ☎ (01732) 452022
⊕ whitehart-sevenoaks.co.uk
Fuller's London Pride; Harveys Sussex Best Bitter; guest beers 🅷
Smart whitewashed coaching inn that sits facing the grounds of Knole Park, which has been providing sustenance since the early 17th century. The spacious, rambling interior provides snug areas to drink or dine. The charming patio, garden and conservatory are suntraps in summer. The guest beer range always includes a local brew and a house beer from Manchester's Phoenix Brewery. Real cider comes from nearby Chiddingstone. Excellent food is available until 10pm. Check the website for regular beer, cider and food events.
♨Q🍽🅿🖵(401,402)

Sevenoaks Weald

Windmill
Windmill Road, TN14 6PN
🕒 12 (3 Mon)-11; 12-10.30 Sun ☎ (01732) 463330
⊕ wealdwindmill.co.uk
Beer range varies 🅷

A fine example of a failing Victorian pub revitalised by the efforts of a new and enthusiastic owner. A full refurbishment, featuring wooden settles, candlelit tables and a heavily hop-strewn bar, has produced a smart yet homely atmosphere. Between five and six superbly kept ales, with an emphasis on local brews, are supplemented by three Kentish ciders. A weekday afternoon (3-6pm) Cask Club promotion features reduced-price beers. Imaginative, quality food is served (no food Mon or Sun eve). Live acoustic music plays every Sunday evening. ♨Q🍽🕽🍴🚆🖵(401,402)

Sheerness

Red Lion
61 High Street, Blue Town, ME12 1RW TQ911750
🕒 11-midnight (1am Thu-Sat); 12-midnight Sun
☎ (01795) 664354
Beer range varies 🅷
Popular and traditional locals' pub in the historic Blue Town area opposite the former naval dockyard wall. A recent makeover has created a light, bright and more contemporary look. Where possible the landlord tries to accommodate customers' preferences for real ale, and beer is often from microbreweries. Smokers are catered for in the enclosed heated courtyard, tables provided. ♨🍽🕽🚆🍴🖵

Snargate

Red Lion ★ 🅛
TN29 9UQ (on B2080, 1 mile NW of Brenzett)
🕒 12-3, 7-11 (10.30 Sun) ☎ (01797) 344648
Beer range varies 🅶
Superb unspoilt 16th-century pub, in the same family for 100 years and universally known as Doris's. It is on the road that separates Walland Marsh from Romney Marsh. Identified by CAMRA as one of Britain's Best Real Heritage Pubs, the inside is decorated with posters from the 1940s and the Women's Land Army. Beers from small breweries are served, including Goacher's. A beer festival is held in June and a mini festival in October.
♨Q🍽🍴🖵P

Stalisfield Green

Plough Inn 🅛
ME13 0HY TQ955529
🕒 closed Mon; 12-3, 6-11; 12-11.30 Sat; 12-6 Sun
☎ (01795) 890256 ⊕ stalisfieldgreen.com
Beer range varies 🅷
A country inn on the North Downs, justifiably proud of its local ales sourced from Kentish microbrewers, and of the locally supplied produce used in the seasonal and constantly changing menu. The pub makes its own tomato sauce and sausages. It has a large family-friendly garden where chickens may often run wild. The 660 bus from Faversham is infrequent, but may be of use.
♨Q🍽🕽🅰🍴🖵P🖵(660)

Stansted

Black Horse 🅛
Tumblefield Road, TN15 7PR (1 mile N of A20 jct 2)
TQ606620

✪ 12-11 (10.30 Sun) ☎ (01732) 822355
⊕ theblackhorsestansted.co.uk
Larkins Traditional; guest beers ⊞
Situated in the heart of the North Downs, this
village free house is surrounded by rolling hills and
woodlands, attracting ramblers and cyclists.
Traditional English meals are served Tuesday to
Sunday until 9.30pm. Recently refurbished, the pub
hosts regular live music, card games and quizzes.
Three real ales are offered, normally from Larkins,
with guests from other breweries. An extensive
range of wines and bottled beers is also available.
ᴍᏐ❀🍴❶♣P⅃

Staplehurst

Lord Raglan ⅃
Chart Hill Road, TN12 0DE (½ mile N of A229) TQ786472
✪ 12-3, 6.30-11; closed Sun ☎ (01622) 843747
**Goacher's Fine Light; Harveys Sussex Best Bitter;
guest beer** ⊞
A delightful, traditional free house in a rural
setting, named after an English General born in
1788, and 10 minutes' walk from the Cross at Hand
bus stop on the A229. There are log fires at each
end of the hop-decorated bar, which has no noisy
distractions, allowing conversation. Two regular
beers and an occasional guest and Double Vision
cider are on tap. Excellent snacks and full meals are
always available and there is a separate dining
area. It has a large garden for the summer.
ᴍQ❀❶♣P☒(5)

Stone in Oxney

Ferry Inn
Appledore Road, TN30 7JY
✪ 12-11 ☎ (01233) 758246 ⊕ oxneyferry.com
**Harveys Sussex Best Bitter; Sharp's Doom Bar;
Westerham Oxney Ale; guest beer** ⊞
Both this 17th-century brick and peg tile inn and
associated cottages are under a strict preservation
order. Set in rural countryside on the Saxon Shore
Way beside a river which, centuries ago, was over
200 yards wide, it was from the pub that a ferry
once operated to Appledore. The ferry also had a
long association with smuggling operations, and
during the Napoleonic Wars troops were billeted
here. May close early on winter evenings if quiet.
ᴍQᏐ❀🍴❶ዿ♣P⅃

Stourmouth

Rising Sun
The Street, CT3 1HY
✪ 11-11; 12-10.30 Sun ☎ (01227) 721364
⊕ therisingsunstourmouth.co.uk
Beer range varies ⊞
Set in the middle of the countryside, this extensive,
modern-style country public house and restaurant
maintain the traditional values of excellent
customer service. The beer range includes a session
beer and often something unexpected, alongside
Westons cider. The Rising Sun prides itself on its
freshly prepared food. It has a patio to the front
and a pleasant garden, and hosts quiz, pool,
pétanque and bat and trap teams. The summer
brings hog roasts and occasional live music in the
garden. The pub is dog-friendly.
ᴍᏐ❀🍴❶ዿ🅰♣P☒(11)

Stowting

Tiger Inn ⅃
Main Street, TN25 6BA (2½ miles N of M20 jct 11,
village signed off B2068)
✪ 12 (4 Mon)-11; closed Tue; 12-10.30 Sun
☎ (01303) 862130 ⊕ tigerinn.co.uk
Shepherd Neame Master Brew; guest beers ⊞
A remote rural retreat that lies in the scattered
hamlet of Stowting, nestling in some beautiful
countryside at the foot of the North Downs. Food is
provided all day. Parts of the inn date back to the
16th century and it still advertises Mackesons
Hythe Ales on its frontage. Despite changes to the
interior over the years it has lost none of its
character and is still a warm local pub that feels like
a farmhouse kitchen. ᴍQᏐ❀🍴❶ዿ♣●P⅃

Swanscombe

George & Dragon ♥ ⅃
1 London Road, DA10 0LQ
✪ 12 (4 Mon & Tue)-11; 12-10.30 Sun ☎ (01322) 386440
⊕ georgedragonswanscombe.co.uk
Caveman Citra; guest beers ⊞
Chosen as CAMRA branch Pub of the Year 2013, this
enterprising former Victorian coaching inn has a
horseshoe-shaped bar supporting 15 handpumps,
three for locally produced ciders. It has an
interesting whisky cabinet and chilled bottle bar,
and is home of the Caveman microbrewery. The
restaurant is open Wednesday-Saturday lunchtimes
and evenings, and Sunday lunchtime for traditional
roasts. Regular entertainment and charity quiz
nights are held. It is handy for Ebbsfleet United
Football Club and Ebbsfleet International station.
Accommodation comprises five rooms.
ᴍ🍴❶ዿ≉♣●P⅃☒(480,490,B)

Teynham

Swan ⅃
78 London Road, ME9 9QH
✪ 12 (4 Mon)-midnight ☎ (01795) 521218
Beer range varies ⊞
A 1930s roadside inn with one large open bar, free
from tie, which offers a choice of good beers in
Teynham. The enthusiastic landlord is keen on real
ale and regularly sources a beer from Wantsum
Brewery on one pump and a local microbrewery
guest for the other. Beers and real cider – Dudda's
Tun from a local farm – are sold at reasonable
prices. Pub games include shut the box. Food is
available lunchtimes and evenings (lunch only
Sun). A function room is available.
ᴍ❶ዿ≉♣●P⅃☒(7,333,335)

Tonbridge

Humphrey Bean
94 High Street, TN9 1AP (near castle and river)
✪ 9am-midnight (1am Fri & Sat) ☎ (01732) 773850
**Adnams Broadside; Greene King Abbot; Ruddles Best
Bitter; Thornbridge Jaipur IPA, seasonal beers** ⊞
A large former post office, this Wetherspoon pub is
an essential destination for Tonbridge beer-
seekers. It usually serves in excess of eight quality
ales, ranging from brews from small independents
to large regional breweries. Additionally, the

manager has organised several brewery showcase events, making the venue a veritable beer-topia. A choice of real ciders is also available – ask at the bar. The rear garden, bedecked with floral displays in summer, overlooks the river and castle. The pub opens at 7am for breakfast. ⏰✿⑴♿⇆☕P⬗⊟

Tunbridge Wells

Bedford
21 High Street, TN1 1UX
✪ 12-11 (midnight Fri & Sat); 12-10.30 Sun
☎ (01892) 544662 ⊕ thebedfordtw.co.uk
Greene King IPA, IPA Gold, Abbot; guest beers Ⓗ
After being taken over and refurbished by Greene King, this corner pub, a few paces from the railway station, has settled into a classic ale house. Eight to 10 handpumps dispense regular beers and guests, usually from Kent or adjacent counties (there is a tiered pricing system by strength, and reduced prices Wed from 6pm). A local real cider is also available. The atmosphere goes from contemplative to lively, with live music, TV sport and quizzes. No meals are served, but quality snacks are available. ⇆♣●⊟

Duke of York
17 The Pantiles, TN2 5TD
✪ 11-11 (10.30 Sun) ☎ (01892) 517619
Fuller's London Pride, seasonal beers; Gale's Seafarers Ale, HSB; guest beers Ⓗ
This early 18th-century corner hostelry is centrally located in the historic Pantiles and close to the Chalybeate Spring that established this Royal spa town. Inside, a warm ambience is created by the wooden floor, ceiling and assorted seating, including church pews opposite the bar. It was recently acquired by Fuller's Brewery of Chiswick, London, increasing the variety of ales available to drinkers in west Kent. Hearty pub lunches are served (no food Fri or Sat). Children and dogs are welcome. ✿⑴⇆⊟

Grove Tavern Ⓛ
19 Berkeley Road, TN1 1YR (up Frog Lane off High St)
✪ 12-11 ☎ (01892) 526549 ⊕ grovetavern.co.uk
Harveys Sussex Best Bitter; Taylor Landlord; guest beers Ⓗ
A traditional town pub offering a warm welcome, friendly atmosphere, great banter and great beer. One of the contenders for the oldest hostelry in the Wells, the Grove is set down a quiet lane in the old village area, easy to miss but is well worth tracking down. It is renowned for its well-kept beers, including two changing guests. Food is not served, but the locals will often take in snacks to share. Children and dogs are allowed, with pool and darts providing entertainment. ♨⇆♣●⊟

Ragged Trousers
44 The Pantiles, TN2 5TN
✪ 12-11 ☎ (01892) 542715 ⊕ raggedtrousers.co.uk
Beer range varies Ⓗ
Lively and quirky pub located in the famous Georgian Pantiles area of the town. Café-style outdoor seating overlooks the bustling pedestrianised central piazza, where the local traders' market is regularly held. It has a relaxing, intimate atmosphere inside aided by low lighting, candles and music. Three handpumps dispense a rotating selection of ales, often including those from Larkins, Longman and Dark Star breweries.

Food covers the full gamut of fare from trad to artisan, all at reasonable prices (lunchtimes and Wed-Thu eves). ⏰✿⑴⇆♣⬗⊟

Royal Oak Ⓛ
92 Prospect Road, TN2 4SY
✪ 12-11 (10.30 Sun) ☎ (01892) 542546
Harveys Sussex Best Bitter; Larkins Traditional Ale; guest beers Ⓗ
A quiet retreat from the bustle of the town's shopping centre, where good cellarmanship, home-cooked food and popular beer and cider festivals have rightly earned the Royal Oak many local CAMRA accolades. The interior features an island bar, wood-panelled walls, diverse seating areas including a TV corner, drinking booths and a lounge with sofas and assorted magazines. The venue has quiz nights, and regular live music takes place at weekends. Food is available Wednesday to Sunday. ⏰✿⑴♣P⬗⊟(285)

Upper Upnor

King's Arms
2 High Street, ME2 4XG TQ757704
✪ 11.30 (12 Sun)-11 ☎ (01634) 717490
⊕ kingsarmsupnor.co.uk
Adnams Southwold Bitter; guest beers Ⓗ
The pub is set at one end of the scenic cobbled High Street, which leads to the River Medway and an historic castle. This village local is known for its food, which varies from home-cooked pub fare to an à la carte menu. There are usually at least four guest ales, including a mild, and a fine range of European bottled beers. Real cider and perry are sold and in the summer the pub has a beer festival in the large garden area. Q⏰✿⑴⊞●⬗⊟(197)

Walmer

Berry � Ⓛ
23 Canada Road, CT14 7EQ
✪ 11 (5.30 Tue; 12 Thu)-11, 11.30-11 Sun
☎ (01304) 362411 ⊕ theberrywalmer.co.uk
Dark Star American Pale Ale; Harveys Sussex Best Bitter; guest beers Ⓗ
Far from an ordinary pub, with its 10 handpumps alongside two ciders and a perry. This family-run, friendly, unfussy hostelry celebrates awards and certificates going back to 2008, including CAMRA branch Pub of the Year six years running, and East Kent Pub of the Year 2011. Entertainment includes darts, pool, a monthly quiz and live music on some Saturdays. There is a real ale festival in February, a cider festival in May, and a continental flavour is assured at the Oktoberfest. It is close to main bus routes. ♨✿♣●⬗⊟(12,13,14)

West Malling

Bull Ⓛ
1 High Street, ME19 6QH
✪ 12-2.30, 4-11; 12-11 Fri & Sat; 12-10.30 Sun
☎ (01732) 842753 ⊕ thebullinnwestmalling.com
Taylor Landlord; Young's Bitter; guest beers Ⓗ
A convivial two-room pub that is now a free house, at the north end of the village by the railway line. Considerable renovation and decoration has been undertaken by the owner, although he has been careful to preserve the character of the main bar

with its wood-panelling, hops on the beams and log fire. Since the buyout there are now six beers – two regular and four changing guest ales plus a local cider on handpump. Evening meals are served Friday and Saturday only.
🏨🛏️❄️🍴◑⇌♣♿💧—🚆(72,151)

Westgate-on-Sea

Bake & Alehouse 🗒️
21 St Mildred's Road, CT8 8RE (behind Carlton cinema)
🟢 closed Mon; 12-2, 5.30-9; 12-2 Sun ☎ (07581) 468797
🌐 bakeandalehouse.com
Beer range varies 🅖
One of the earliest of a burgeoning number of micropubs (small converted premises, defiantly mega-keg free) in this part of east Kent. This former baker's shop, down an alleyway next to the Carlton cinema, has room for around 20 people and has been sensitively managed to create an intimate and friendly community atmosphere. Four predominantly Kentish ales and real cider are normally available. Food comprises local pork pies and cheese, which seems to keep regulars and visitors alike satisfied. Q⇌♦🚆(8,8A)

Whitstable

Ship Centurion 🗒️
111 High Street, CT5 1AY
🟢 11-11; 12-7 Sun ☎ (01227) 264740
Adnams Southwold Bitter; Elgood's Black Dog; Young's Special; guest beer 🅗
A friendly and traditional town-centre pub, which gets very busy at weekends. Colourful hanging baskets add to its charm in summer. Pictures of old Whitstable hang in the main bar. A mild is always served, while home-cooked bar food often features authentic German dishes, and there is always a schnitzel on the menu on Saturday (no food Sun). Live music plays on Thursday evenings (except in January) and Friday lunchtimes. There is a summer cider festival and an October beer fest.
◑▶⇌♿—🚆(4,5,6)

Woodchurch

Six Bells
Bethersden Road, TN26 3QQ (close to village green opp church) TQ942349
🟢 12-midnight ☎ (01233) 860246 🌐 6-bells.co.uk

Fuller's London Pride; Harveys Sussex Best Bitter; Hopdaemon Golden Braid; Taylor Landlord; guest beers 🅗
Dogs are welcome in this unspoilt and friendly village local, which has a separate public bar and a saloon bar with a dining area, but with plenty of space for drinkers. Beer festivals are held several times throughout the year. A good range of freshly prepared meals is available seven days a week – all day on Sunday. There are gardens to the front and rear of the pub; the large enclosed garden at the rear is ideal for families.
🏨Q🛏️❄️◑⊟♿♣P♿—🚆(2A)

Worth

Blue Pigeons 🗒️
The Street, CT14 0DS
🟢 12-11 (10 Sun) ☎ (01304) 613233
🌐 thebluepigeons.co.uk
Fuller's London Pride; guest beers 🅗
The service in this pub is welcoming and the decor comfortable and relaxing. The large wood-floored main bar leads through to a smaller snug and vaulted restaurant. Up to four real ales are available including beers from Wantsum Brewery and Canterbury Ales. A wide variety of good-quality and good-value home-made food is available. At the back, an enclosed patio overlooks the large garden, and there is plenty of seating at the front. Food events are held throughout the year.
🏨🛏️❄️🍴◑P♿—🚆(13)

Wrotham

Bull Hotel
Bull Lane, TN15 7RF
🟢 12-3, 6-11; 12-11 Sat & Sun ☎ (01732) 789800
🌐 thebullhotel.com
Dark Star Hophead, Partridge Best Bitter; guest beers 🅗
Well-appointed historic hotel, partly dating from the 14th century. The guest beer is often a Dark Star seasonal, although other small breweries are represented. It has a good reputation for food, served lunchtimes and evenings, with curry night on Thursday and fish night on Friday. Jazz features every last Wednesday evening of the month. The separate Buttery, once the village bakery, hosts corporate events, wedding receptions and birthday parties. 🏨Q❄️🍴◑P♿—🚆(306,308)

Fishing for beer

Ah! My beloved brother of the rod, do you know the taste of beer – of bitter beer – cooled in the flowing river? Take your bottle of beer, sink it deep, deep in the shady water, where the cooling springs and fishes are. Then, the day being very hot and bright, and the sun blazing on your devoted head, consider it a matter of duty to have to fish that long, wide stream. An hour or so of good hammering will bring you to the end of it, and then – let me ask you avec impressement – how about that beer? Is it cool? Is it refreshing? Does it gurgle, gurgle and 'go down glug' as they say in Devonshire? Is it heavenly? Is it Paradise and all the Peris to boot? Ah! If you have never tasted beer under these or similar circumstance, you have, believe me, never tasted it at all.
Francis Francis, By Lake and River, 16th century

LANCASHIRE

CUMBRIA

NORTH YORKSHIRE

WEST YORKSHIRE

GREATER MANCHESTER

MERSEYSIDE

Silverdale
Warton
Carnforth 35
Wennington
Wray
Morecambe
Heysham
Lancaster
Lancaster University
Dolphinholme
Slaidburn
Winmarleigh
Fleetwood
Cleveleys
Chipping
Waddington
Barnoldswick
Bispham
Great Eccleston
Clitheroe
Pendleton
Blacko
Black Lane Ends
Poulton-le-Fylde
Barton
Goosnargh
Old Langho
Whalley
Fence
Colne
BLACKPOOL
Longridge
Great Harwood
Clayton le Moors
Nelson
St Annes on the Sea
Salwick
Lea Town
Preston
Samlesbury
Wilpshire
Burnley
Worsthorne
St Annes
Penwortham
Blackburn
Cliviger
Lytham
Bamber Bridge
Cherry Tree
Accrington
Rawtenstall
Lostock Hall
Higher Wheelton
Tockholes
Waterfoot
Walmer Bridge
Leyland
Wheelton
Darwen
Haslingden
Whitworth
Croston
Euxton
Rufford
Eccleston
Chorley
Edgworth
Mawdesley
Coppull
Bispham Green
Wrightington
Adlington
Burscough
Parbold
Ormskirk
Haskayne
Aughton Park
Aughton
Tontine

0 Miles 5
0 Kilometres 8

Accrington

Commercial L
1 Church Street, BB5 2EN
⚙ 9-11.45 (12.45am Fri & Sat) ☎ (01254) 300140
Greene King Abbot; Ruddles Best Bitter; guest beers Ⓗ
Open plan in typical Wetherspoon tradition, this venue contains many local features with more than a nod to the local Tiffany glass collection. It is adjacent to the bus station and markets, and only a short walk to the railway station. The pub supports LocAle, with six of the 10 handpumps given over to guest beers alongside two ciders. Q❀◑ⓓ⇌Pↆ⤵

Grants L
1 Manchester Road, BB5 2BQ
⚙ 12-11 (midnight Thu-Sat) ☎ (01254) 393938
Beer range varies Ⓗ
A large imposing building on the edge of the town centre, thoroughly modern and something of a place to be seen at weekends. A true free house, it sells up to seven beers. LocAle is supported, with many beers sourced within Lancashire. Third-pints are served and, for a treat, a wooden tray of third-pint samplers of all seven beers may be purchased. An eighth pump serves real cider and others are often available from polypins behind the bar. ❀⇌●ↆ⤵(464,484,X41)

Peel Park L
Turkey Street, BB5 6EW (200yds from A679, adj to Peel Park school)
⚙ 12-11.30 ☎ (01254) 235830
Tetley Bitter; guest beers Ⓗ
A true free house opposite the site of the old Stanley football ground. Six beers are sold, mainly from micros such as Three B's and Slaters, and regional brewers like Robinsons. The main bar is a

large open front room which is split into two sections. There is a separate small pool room and a rear room used for functions and meetings. An annual beer festival is held over the spring bank holiday weekend. ▲⚙♦❶⌕♣P↳☐(23,263)

Adlington

Spinners Arms ⓛ
23 Church Street, PR7 4EX
✪ 12-11 (midnight Fri & Sat) ☎ (01257) 483331
Rudgate Mild; Taylor Landlord; Thwaites Wainwright; guest beers Ⓗ
The pub is known as the Bottom Spinners to differentiate it from the other Spinners Arms in the village. Welcoming and friendly, a single bar serves three seating areas and there is a pleasant outdoor drinking area to the front. It has no pool table or gaming machine, just an open log fire. The bar menu offers home-cooked food with weekend specials. Four alternating guest beers, often sourced from local breweries, always include a mild. Small functions are catered for.
▲Q⚙❶⌕P↳☐

Aughton

Derby Arms
Prescot Road, Bowker's Green, L39 6TA (at Bowker's Green on B5197, S of Ormskirk) SD407043
✪ 11.30-midnight (1am Fri & Sat); 12-midnight Sun
☎ (01695) 422237
Tetley Dark Mild, Bitter; guest beers Ⓗ
Friendly country pub with a long award-winning heritage – one wall proudly displays over 20 CAMRA awards. The interior is both atmospheric and intimate, with locals and staff giving a warm welcome to all. Five handpumps serve two Tetley beers and an interesting range of guests. Quiz nights are Tuesday and Thursday, and regular charity events are hosted. Excellent-value food is served throughout the day, while a popular pub breakfast is available from 9am till late on Saturdays. ▲⚙❶ ⊟♣P

Stanley Arms
St Michael Road, L39 6SA (off A59 at Aughton Springs) SD391055
✪ 12-11 (11.30 Thu & Sat; midnight Fri) ☎ (01695) 432241
Taylor Landlord; Tetley Dark Mild, Bitter; guest beers Ⓗ
Beside a historic Norman church, the Stanley Arms has distinctive 18th-century architecture and was originally a coaching stop for postal deliveries. Decorated throughout with Tudor-style woodwork, there are several side rooms containing brewing memorabilia around the centrally placed bar, which dispenses from five handpumps. Immaculately kept both inside and out, the pub is exceptionally popular for its excellent home-cooked and locally sourced food. Beer and jazz festivals are held twice-yearly, with proceeds going to kidney research. Wi-Fi enabled.
▲⚙❶P↳☐(311)

Aughton Park

Dog & Gun
233 Long Lane, L39 5BU (near railway station) SD413064
✪ 4 (12 Sat & Sun)-midnight ☎ (01695) 423303

Banks's Bitter; Marston's Pedigree; Ringwood Boondoggle; guest beers Ⓗ
A genuine community pub dating from 1891, featuring an unspoilt interior. Two rooms, one with a real fire, are set around the central bar, with ales served from six handpulls. The pub supports football, darts, quiz and bowling teams, and is also frequented by cycling and archery clubs. There are outside drinking areas to the front and rear, an award-winning floral display, and an impressive menagerie of animals including ducks, chickens, geese and pigs. Look out for Shirley the parrot.
▲Q⌕⚙⊛❶♣P↳

Bamber Bridge

Withy Arms ⓛ
122 Station Road, PR5 6QP
✪ 11-midnight (1am Fri & Sat); 12-11 Sun
☎ (01772) 697706 ⊕ withyarms.com
Marston's Pedigree; Wychwood Hobgoblin; guest beers Ⓗ
On the main crossroads in Bamber Bridge and 10 minutes' walk from the railway station, the pub was reopened after being bought by a local business for the office space. The new owners are real ale enthusiasts and they decided to refurbish the pub and now it has six handpumps. The house bitter is brewed by Thwaites and the guest beers are usually from local micros. There is a separate small room on the right. It serves food at weekends and has a quiz night on Tuesday.
▲⌕⚙❶P↳☐(113,125)

Barnoldswick

Fountain
14 Church Street, BB18 5UT
✪ 12-11 (12.30am Fri & Sat); 12-10.30 Sun
☎ (01282) 813412 ⊕ thefountaininnbarnoldswick.co.uk/
Dark Horse Hetton Pale; Tetley Bitter; Thwaites Wainwright; Wychwood Hobgoblin Ⓗ
A free house that has become very popular since it was bought from a pubco chain. The landlady has transformed the pub into a real ale haven in the centre of the town, and has kept to a policy of offering a rotating guest beer and a real cider (usually Thatchers). It has a relaxing bar/lounge area with logburner, and a separate dining area.

INDEPENDENT BREWERIES
Arkwright's Preston
Barlick Barnoldswick (NEW)
Bluestone Whitworth (NEW)
Bowland Clitheroe
Burscough Burscough
Cross Bay Morecambe
Fuzzy Duck Poulton-le-Fylde
Goosnargh Goosnargh (NEW)
Hart of Preston Preston
Hopstar Darwen
Lancaster Lancaster
Lytham St Annes
Moonstone Burnley
Moorhouse's Burnley
Old School Warton (NEW)
Reedley Hallows Burnley
Rossendale Haslingden
Three B's Blackburn
Thwaites Blackburn
Worsthorne Burnley

Live music plays on Thursdays. Food is served lunchtimes and evenings.
🅼🌜⛫🍴◑🍺🚻(29,215)

Barton

Boar's Head 🅛
724 Garstang Road, PR3 5DR (on the A6, next to St Lawrence parish church)
✪ 12-11 (midnight Thu-Sat) ☎ (01772) 864330
⊕ boarsheadbarton.co.uk
Beer range varies ℍ
On the A6 north of Preston, this Mitchells house is split into a spacious dining area, a games room and a small lounge adjacent to the bar. Four real ales are normally on sale, with one each from York Brewery and Lancaster Brewery, plus two guests. It is a family-friendly pub with a large children's play area and a patio to the rear alongside a large car park. Quiz night is Thursday, which is also curry night. Food is served till 9pm except Sunday, when there is a carvery till 8pm.
Q🌜⛫◑🍴♣Pᵗ🚻(40,41)

Bispham Green

Eagle & Child 🅛
Malt Kiln Lane, L40 3SG (off B5246)
✪ 12-3, 5.30-11; 12-11 Sat; 12-10.30 Sun ☎ (01257) 462297
Beer range varies ℍ
An 18th-century pub with cheerful staff and eight handpumps with local ales showcased. Southport Carousel is always available and a variety of guest ales from the likes of Allgates, Prospect and Moorhouse's. This busy, classic country inn is the Lancashire Dining Pub of the Year for the fifth time, so book early for a table. The beer garden, with its wildlife area and great views, hosts a beer festival on the May bank holiday. Quiz night is every Monday. 🅼Q⛫◑Pᵗ

Black Lane Ends

Black Lane Ends
Skipton Old Road, BB8 7EP (off A56, 3 miles E of Colne golf club)
✪ 12-11 ☎ (01282) 863070
Taylor Landlord; guest beers ℍ
Once known as the Hare & Hounds, stunning views await you at this isolated country pub in between Colne and Skipton. The regular beer is usually Taylor Landlord, but you will also find other Taylor's beers on, along with a guest from the likes of Ossett or Black Sheep. The pub is well known for its high-quality food. A central bar area also serves the two dining rooms at either side. 🅼🌜⛫◑P

Blackburn

Black Bull 🅛
Brokenstone Road, BB3 0LL (Heys Lane/Bog Height Rd crossroads)
✪ 4-11 (midnight Fri); 12-midnight Sat; 12-10.30 Sun ☎ (01254) 581381 ⊕ threebsbrewery.co.uk
Three B's Stokers Slake, Bobbins Bitter, Black Bull Bitter, Pinch Noggin, Knocker Up ℍ
Originally a Thwaites outlet, it was purchased by Three B's Brewery as its first tied house. It serves the complete range of Three B's beers, along with its seasonal beers, and is the only place where you can try Black Bull Bitter. Those wishing to sample several beers can try the three-third-pints offer.

The occasional guest or cider is on one of the handpumps. The pub enjoys great views looking west and south, but is only a few miles from Blackburn town centre. 🅼Q⛫♿◑Pᵗ

Blacko

Rising Sun 🅛
330 Gisburn Road, BB9 6LS (on A682)
✪ 12-2 (not Mon-Wed), 5-11; 12-midnight Fri & Sat; 12-11 Sun ☎ (01282) 612173
Moorhouse's Premier Bitter, Pride of Pendle, Blond Witch; guest beers ℍ
Run by a CAMRA member, the Rising Sun is the only tied Moorhouse's pub in Pendle, and overlooks the famous old hill. In addition to Moorhouse's brews, it has served over 200 different guest beers since the current licensee took over, with guests sourced from both regional and microbreweries from all around Britain. Dogs and walkers are made welcome. Bar snacks and meals are served daily (all day until 7pm at weekends). The local Pendleside delicacy of Stew 'n' Hard is popular. 🅼Q⛫◑⛲♣P🚻(P70,P71)

Blackpool: Bispham

Bispham Hotel
70 Red Bank Road, FY2 9HY (300yds from promenade)
✪ 12 (11 Sat)-11; 12-10.30 Sun ☎ (01253) 351752
Samuel Smith OBB ℍ
Well-maintained, mid-1930s Art Deco pub. A popular two-bar local, it is well known for its low-priced ale drawn from oak casks. With no music, food, TV or children, it is a haven for a pint and a chat, and is only a four-minute walk from the promenade, seafront and the Blackpool-Fleetwood tramway. The pub sign features an old tram, a reminder that there used to be a tram depot behind the pub. Quizzes are on Thursday and Sunday. An upstairs meeting room is available. Q⛫♿🚻ᵗ🚻(3,4)

Blackpool: Town Centre

Auctioneer 🅛
235-237 Lytham Road, FY1 6ET (on B5262)
✪ 8am-12.30am ☎ (01253) 346412
Greene King Abbot; Ruddles Best Bitter; guest beers ℍ
The first Wetherspoon's to be opened on the Fylde, in 1999. In the South Shore area of Blackpool, it is handy for the Blackpool South railway, as well as Bloomfield Road football ground. The walls feature many pictures of old Blackpool. There is an outside drinking area to the rear and a few tables out front in the summer months. This community pub is close to the Waterloo Road shopping area, and gets very busy in summer with trade from the nearby hotels. Up to six different guest beers are served. ⛫◑♿🚃(South)🚻ᵗ🚻

Blackpool Cricket Club 🅛
Barlow Crescent, West Park Drive, FY3 9EQ (follow brown signs to Stanley Park)
✪ 7-11; 12-midnight Fri & Sat; 12-11 Sun ☎ (01253) 393347
⊕ blackpoolcricket.co.uk
Thwaites Wainwright; guest beers ℍ
The club is part of Stanley Park and home to numerous teams that take part in local leagues. County cricket matches are occasionally played here, there are squash courts, and hockey and

rugby teams from the Stanley Park pitches use the club's facilities. Large-screen TVs show all sports events. Quiz nights and live entertainment are held in the lounge. Local CAMRA branch Club of the Year for the past three years. ☎⊛❶⅃P⅄⊟(4,16,61)

Gillespies
87-89 Topping Street, FY1 3AA (off Church St and close to Winter Gardens)
⊛ 10-11 (midnight Fri & Sat); 11-11 Sun ☎ (01253) 627882
Beer range varies ⊞
Near to the Winter Gardens, this smart and popular town-centre pub sells four ales from the Greene King portfolio. It has prominent TV screens and comfortable seating, usually feeling like a café bar during the day and a sports bar in the evenings. Good-value food is available until 7pm, with children welcome up until that time. A discount on real ale is available to CAMRA members.
☎❶⇌(North)⅄⊟

Layton Rakes ⅃
17-25 Market Street, FY1 1EZ (off Talbot Square close to Town Hall)
⊛ 8am-midnight (1am Fri & Sat) ☎ (01253) 743710
Greene King Abbot; Ruddles Best Bitter; guest beers ⊞
Opened in November 2011, this three-storey pub includes a roof terrace and two bars. Three beers are available on the first-floor bar. Tastefully decorated, it features snippets of the resort's heritage including a carousel horse sculpture, a waltzer car, and a wall artwork immortalising one of Blackpool's adopted sons, Charlie Cairoli, the famous Blackpool circus clown. A total of 11 handpumps offer three regular beers and up to eight different guests. ☎⊛❶⅄⇌(North)⊟⊟

Ramsden Arms ⅃
204 Talbot Road, FY1 3AZ (on A586 close to Blackpool North railway station)
⊛ 10.30-midnight (1am Sat); 12-midnight Sun
☎ (01253) 291713
Fuller's London Pride; guest beers ⊞
Tudor-fronted Tetley heritage pub to the east of Blackpool North station on the main Talbot Road. It serves three cask ales – generally London Pride and two guest beers. The styling is traditional, with memorabilia adorning the walls and a vast collection of jugs and tankards. TVs show live sport, and there are two snooker tables plus dominoes and poker. The pub is frequented by locals but visitors are made welcome. Bar snacks are served 11-7pm daily and Wi-Fi is available.
☎⊛⇌(North)⊟♣P⅄⊟

Saddle Inn ⅃
286 Whitegate Drive, FY3 9PH (at Preston Old Rd jct on A583)
⊛ 10.30-11 (midnight Fri & Sat); 12-11 Sun
☎ (01253) 767827
Draught Bass; Greene King IPA; guest beers ⊞
Blackpool's oldest pub, established in 1770, the Saddle comprises a main bar and two side rooms, plus a large patio outside for drinking and dining during the summer months. Guest beers (up to four of them) are generally from local breweries, and a good range of food is served all day at at this friendly locals' pub. ☎⊛❶⅃P⅄⊟(4,16,61)

Burnley

Bridge Bier Huis ⅃
2 Bank Parade, BB11 1UH (behind shopping centre)
⊛ closed Mon & Tue; 12-midnight (1am Fri & Sat); 12-11 Sun
☎ (01282) 411304 ⊕ thebridgebierhuis.co.uk
Moorhouse's Premier; guest beers ⊞
West Pennines Pub of the Year 2012, this is a free house with a large open-plan bar area and a small snug. It offers up to two Moorhouse's beers and three changing guests, mainly from microbreweries, alongside a real cider. More than 60 foreign bottled beers are available; seven foreign beers are on tap, usually including two rare German beers. Wednesday is quiz night; on some weekends live music is hosted. It opens at 5pm on a Tuesday evening if Burnley FC are at home. ☎⊛❶⇌(Central)♣●⊟

Brun Lea ⅃
31-39 Manchester Road, BB11 1HG
⊛ 8-midnight (1am Fri-Sun) ☎ (01282) 463700
Moorhouse's Pendle Witches Brew; Ruddles Best Bitter; guest beers ⊞
A Lloyds No.1 bar, this large modern pub just off the town centre has up to eight ales on offer; guests can be from breweries such as Kelham Island, Exmoor, Ringwood and Goose Eye, along with more local brews. Two TVs show major sporting events as well as rolling news. Friday and Saturday nights can be lively when a band has been playing, and it gets very busy when Burnley FC are at home. ❶⅄⇌(Manchester Rd)●⊟(X43)

Talbot Hotel ⅃
65 Church Street, BB11 2RS (on A56 close to town centre)
⊛ 5-midnight; 4-1am Fri; 12-1am Sat; 12-midnight Sun
☎ (01282) 412074 ⊕ talbotburnley.co.uk
Holt Bitter; Moorhouse's Premier; Taylor Landlord; Thwaites Wainwright; guest beers ⊞
A warm welcome awaits at this free house, which dates back to the 1800s. The landlord is a real ale enthusiast and offers four guest beers in addition to the four regulars. These guests are frequently from east Lancashire breweries, with others from further afield including Scotland. Live bands feature every weekend plus one Wednesday per month. There are two pool tables and a widescreen TV for sports fans. Four en-suite rooms are available for guests. ☎⊛⇌(Central)♣P⅄⊟(4,X43,X44)

Burscough

Hop Vine ♈ ⅃
Liverpool Road North, L40 4BY (on A59, near Burscough Bridge rail/bus interchange)
⊛ 10.30-midnight (12.30am Fri & Sat) ☎ (01704) 893799
⊕ thehopvine.co.uk
Burscough Priory Gold, Mere Blonde, seasonal beers; guest beers ⊞
This spacious former coaching house is now a thriving community brewpub renowned for its friendly atmosphere and popular for its exceptional ale and food. The classic country pub interior has wood panelling and wood and tile flooring throughout, and is decorated with historic local maps, photographs and vintage bottled ales. The award-winning Burscough Brewery operates from the attractive floral courtyard at the rear. Catering for all age groups, it offers great-value meals, live music, twice-yearly beer festivals and other seasonal events. ☎⊛❶⅄⇌(Bridge)P⅄⊟(2A,2B)

Ring o' Bells 🄻

Ring o' Bells Lane, Lathom, L40 5TF (take A5209 from Burscough, turn left at Ring o' Bells crossroads) SD459110
11-11 (midnight Fri & Sat) ☎ (01704) 893157
Liverpool Organic Higsons Bitter; Thwaites Langdale Tup, Wainwright; guest beers 🄷
Impressive country pub in large rural grounds only 20 minutes' walk along the Leeds-to-Liverpool canal from Burscough village. Reopened in 2011 by a local pubco, the huge split-level interior boasts stone and wood floors and offers a separate locals' area and family area with playpen. Six handpumps serve Thwaites and local microbrewery beers. The outstanding food is well priced and locally sourced (beef is company farmed and slaughtered). Dog-friendly, the pub also offers an upstairs private function room and 24-hour canal moorings. ⚐Q⚐⚐⚐⚐♿⇌(Hoscar)♣P⚐⚐(3A,337)

Ship Inn (Blood Tub) 🄻

4 Wheat Lane, Lathom, L40 4BX (take School Lane from Burscough; turn right after humpbacked bridge) SD452116
12-midnight ☎ (01704) 893117 🌐 shipatlathom.co.uk
Moorhouse's Ship's Special, seasonal beers; guest beers 🄷
A traditional country pub set in an idyllic canalside location. The cosy central bar with real fire separates the two dining areas, which serve pub classics through to interesting and changing specials. There is a dog-friendly boot room complete with logburner. The pub is exceptionally popular in summer, with the large beer garden often packed out. A highlight of the year is the September Beer, Pie & Sausage festival, with over 40 hand-pulled ales on offer. ⚐⚐⚐⚐⚐⚐♿⇌(Bridge)P⚐⚐(754)

Carnforth

Snug 🏆

Unit 6, Carnforth Gateway Building, LA5 9TR (at the N end of former mainline up platform)
closed Sun & Mon; 12-2, 5-9 ☎ (01524) 396861
Beer range varies 🄷
A micropub that is very small as well as minimalist. Ale, cider, wine and a few soft drinks are the only beverages, light snacks the only food, conversation and passing trains the only sounds. The decor is simple – just painted walls, bare floorboards and chunky tall tables. The eye is drawn to a beautiful glazed wooden cabinet, floor to ceiling, where the drinks are stored. Parking is on the station car park, where there is a charge. Q⇌♣⚐⚐(5,55,55A)

Cherry Tree

Station 🄻

391 Preston Old Road, BB2 5LW
3-12.30am; 11-1.30am Fri & Sat; 11-12.30am Sun
☎ (01254) 201643
Thwaites Nutty Black, Original, Wainwright, Lancaster Bomber; guest beers 🄷
Located right next to the railway station, this is not the quietest of pubs but it is a must-visit establishment for those seeking the full range of Thwaite's beers. Patrons are a mixture of young and old, enjoying games of darts, dominoes and pool. Satellite sport is shown on three TVs and via a large projector screen. ⚐♿⇌P⚐⚐(152,124)

Chipping

Tillotsons Arms 🄻

18 Talbot Street, PR3 2QE
12-3 (not Mon), 5-midnight; 12-midnight Sat; 12-11 Sun
☎ (01995) 61568
Beer range varies 🄷
In a picturesque village in the Trough of Bowland, this two-roomed, beamed pub built in 1836 has three real ales from local micros, always including at least one from Bowland or Hawkshead. Child- and dog-friendly, it has two real fires and a beer garden to the rear. Locally sourced home-cooked food is available lunchtimes and evenings, and all day Saturday and Sunday. The pub is on the SIBA direct delivery scheme. ⚐Q⚐⚐⚐♣⚐⚐(4)

Chorley

Malt 'n' Hops 🄻

50-52 Friday Street, PR6 0AH (behind railway station)
12.30-11; 12-10.30 Sun ☎ (01257) 260967
Holt Bitter; guest beers 🄷
Originally converted from an old shop in 1989, it is handily situated for both the railway and bus stations. It has a single L- shaped bar on two levels, and the decor is very much of the Edwardian period. The friendly chat of the locals is complemented by the noise of the very vocal parrot. Now a genuine free house, there are up to four guest ales usually sourced from local micros, and a cider. Home-made hot pot is provided on Wednesday quiz nights. ⚐⚐⇌⚐⚐⚐

Potters Arms 🄻

42 Brooke Street, PR7 3BY (next to Morrisons)
3-11.30 (midnight Fri); 12-4, 7-midnight Sat; 12-5, 7-11 Sun ☎ (01257) 267954
Black Sheep Best Bitter; Three B's Doff Cocker; guest beer 🄷
Small, friendly free house named after the owners, at the bottom of Brooke Street alongside the railway bridge. The central bar serves two games areas, while two comfortable lounges are popular with locals and visitors alike. The pub displays a fine selection of photographs from the world of music, as well as vintage local scenes. Regular darts and dominoes nights are well attended and the chip butties go down a treat. The smoking area is covered. ⚐⇌♣P⚐⚐(1,1A,2)

Railway Inn

20 Steeley Lane, PR6 0RD (under subway from train station)
12-midnight (1am Fri & Sat) ☎ (01257) 411449
Beer range varies 🄷
Adjacent to the railway station and 100 yards from the bus station, this is a community local that offers a changing range of up to four real ales from the Marston's portfolio. Darts, dominoes, pool and pinball are popular with the locals, along with seasonal music festivals and Saturday night concerts. Open mic sessions on Sunday evening are successful, with the pub providing its own instruments and PA system to make participation easier. ⚐⚐⇌♣⚐⚐

Rose & Crown 🄻

15 St Thomas's Road, PR7 1HP
12-11 (midnight Fri & Sat) ☎ (01257) 368022
Jennings Cumberland Ale; Thwaites Wainwright; guest beers 🄷

Stone-built pub, opposite the police station, with a central bar covering two drinking areas along with the former stables to the rear of the pub courtyard. There is a mixed age range, with youth in the majority at weekends when it is busy and lively, but there are plenty of bar staff. All major sporting events are shown on wall-mounted TV screens and there are occasional live music nights. Good-value food is served at lunchtime Monday to Friday. Dogs and children are welcome. ⊛◑⇌♣ᵎᐧᐧ⊟

White Bull Ⓛ

135 Market Street, PR7 2SG (S end of Market St near Big Lamp)
✪ 12-11 (1am Fri & Sat) ☎ (01257) 232745
Bank Top Flat Cap; Thwaites Wainwright; Wells Bombardier; guest beer Ⓗ
Single-bar pub that is a beacon for real ale in an area where so many pubs around it are closing. The games room is partitioned to the right of the comfortable L-shaped lounge. The walls are adorned with memorabilia from the landlord's favourite football team, Preston North End. Pies are served all day. Children are permitted in the beer garden if supervised. ⊛⇌♣ᵎᐧ⊟

Clayton le Moors

Forts Arms Ⓛ

1 Lower Barnes Street, BB5 5TA
✪ 4-midnight (1am Thu); 12-2am Fri & Sat; 12-midnight Sun
☎ (01254) 433713
Bowland Hen Harrier; guest beers Ⓗ
Partially opened out in a modern style, the pub boasts a large function suite. A regular bus service stops at the end of Sparth Road, 300 yards from the building. On the beer front there are normally three ales from local breweries and two other guests from further afield. ⊛♣ᵎᐧ⊟(6,7)

Cleveleys

Jolly Tars Ⓛ

154-158 Victoria Road West, FY5 3NE (on B5412)
✪ 8-11 (11.30 Thu-Sat) ☎ (01253) 856042
Greene King Abbot; Ruddles Best Bitter; guest beers Ⓗ
A Wetherspoon pub with up to eight guest beers, usually including a selection of George Wright and Hawkshead brewery offerings. The pub theme is Cleveleys between the two world wars. The staff are friendly and efficient, and while the pub is open plan it includes several secluded booths. The venue is handy for the tram service and a number of bus routes. ⋈⊛◑よ⊟ᵎᐧ⊟

Victoria Hotel

183 Victoria Road West, FY5 3PZ (approx ½ mile from town centre, on B5412)
✪ 11-11; 12-10.30 Sun ☎ (01253) 853306
Samuel Smith OBB Ⓗ
Large corner main-road pub in a residential area, a short walk from the shopping centre, the Blackpool-Fleetwood tramway and various bus routes. Wooden beams, leaded windows and two open fires feature in the comfortable, spacious lounge. The popular Vaults has a separate entrance. This local is well known for low-priced ale drawn from oak casks. There is no music, TV or food to distract from conversation in this relaxing venue. A separate meeting room is available. ⋈Q⊛⊟よ⊟Pᵎᐧ⊟(9,11,74)

Cliviger

Queen Ⓛ

412 Burnley Road, BB10 4SU (on A646 4 miles from Burnley)
✪ 5 (4 Tue; 1 Wed & Thu)-11; 12-11 Fri- Sun
☎ (01282) 436712
Thwaites Original; guest beers Ⓗ
A true free house, this roadside local has just undergone a complete refurbishment but still retains two separate rooms. Both rooms have real fires with a widescreen TV in one room for sports fans. The other room is for conversation only. Two of the three guest handpumps are mainly for local brews, with the third having beers from further afield. Pie and peas, and snacks, are served during opening hours, and walkers with their dogs are welcome. ⋈Q⊛⊟よPᵎᐧ⊟(589,592)

Colne

Wallace Hartley

35-37 Church Street, BB8 0EB
✪ 8am-11 (midnight Thu; 1am Fri & Sat) ☎ (01282) 857790
Greene King Abbot; Ruddles Best Bitter; guest beers Ⓗ
A Wetherspoon house that opened in 2008, and was named after the bandmaster from the Titanic, who was born in Colne. In keeping with most Wetherspoon pubs, there can be anything up to 10 real ales on offer, some of them from local breweries. The venue has several distinct seating areas, some with dark oak panelling. In addition to the exhibits associated with Wallace Hartley and the Titanic, photographs of old Colne can be found. ⊛◑よ⇌Pᵎᐧ⊟

Coppull

Red Herring

Mill Lane, PR7 5AN (off B5251 next to Coppull Mill)
✪ 3-11; 12-11.30 Fri & Sat; 12-11 Sun ☎ (01257) 470130
Beer range varies Ⓗ
Real ale pub in the former offices of the next-door mill. It was converted to a pub some years ago; the bar area comprises a large single room plus an extension, with up to three microbrew beers available, usually from northern micros. TV sports fans are catered for, as are anglers, who use the pond opposite. The pub hosts regular music nights and barbecues, and has a large first-floor function room. Train spotters will enjoy its close proximity to the West Coast main line. ⊛♣ᵎᐧ⊟(1,2,362)

Croston

Wheatsheaf

Town Road, PR26 9RA
✪ 12-11 (midnight Fri); 10-midnight Sat; 10-10.30 Sun
☎ (01772) 600370 ⊕ wheatsheaf-croston.com
Beer range varies Ⓗ
On the main road down from the station and overlooking the village green, this recently refurbished pub has a contemporary feel. It has a distinct area for dining as well as a comfortable drinking area with sofa and chairs. The large outdoor drinking space to the front is also used to hold an annual beer festival during October. Four varying ales are sold (see website for current list), with Windemere Pale frequently retaining house status. Children welcome. ⋈⇌⊛◑⇌♦Pᵎᐧ⊟(7,112)

Darwen

Number 39 ⓛ

39 Bridge Street, BB3 2AA (in pedestrianised street just off town centre)

✪ 12-11 ☎ (01254) 704305

Hopstar Dizzy Danny, Lancashire Gold, JC; guest beers Ⓗ

A good LocAle bar in the centre of town, formerly a Thai restaurant and now the brewery tap for Hopstar, with new brews tried out here first. Three beers from Hopstar and a guest are on sale, as well as real cider, with a large variety of continental and world bottled beers and also draught Timmermans from Belgium. Live music night is every Thursday, featuring jazz and bands. ≈♣👜

Dolphinholme

Fleece

LA2 9AQ

✪ 4-10 Mon; 3-11 (midnight Fri & Sat); 12-10 Sun

☎ (01524) 791233 ⊕ thefleeceinndolphinholme.co.uk

Beer range varies Ⓗ

Former farmhouse in the middle of nowhere, but as the nearby village and the country beyond have no pubs, it is the local for quite a lot of people. Strangers are welcomed, too. The main entrance gives onto a hall with loads of old prints; the main bar, oak-beamed with pews and (usually) a fire, is to the right; the dining room, opened in 2004, is to the left. There are two rooms – one designated a family room – and a permanent marquee for functions. ⋓≳❀🖼🄾🌢🅰♣P⁵–₪(147)

Eccleston

Original Farmers Arms ⓛ

Towngate, PR7 5QS (on B5250)

✪ 12-midnight (11.30 Sun) ☎ (01257) 451594

Black Sheep Best Bitter; Tetley Bitter; Thwaites Wainwright; Wells Bombardier; guest beers Ⓗ

White-painted village pub that has expanded over the years into the cottage next door, adding a substantial dining area. However, the original part of the pub is still used mainly for drinking. The three rotating guest beers are predominantly sourced from local breweries large and small. Meals are available throughout the day seven days a week, and there is accommodation in four good-value guest rooms. ❀🄾🌢P⁵–₪(113,347)

Edgworth

White Horse ⓛ

2-4 Bury Road, BL7 0AY SD742168

✪ 5-11 Mon & Tue; 12-3, 5-midnight; 12-midnight Fri & Sat; 12-11 Sun ☎ (01204) 852929

Bank Top Flat Cap; Moorhouse's Pendle Witches Brew; Taylor Landlord; Thwaites Wainwright; guest beers Ⓗ

This particular White Horse has heraldic origins, dating back to the 18th century - white being the colour of peace and the horse representing stead - readiness for all events in the name of the king. (A wall plaque outside explains more.) Situated prominently at the Bolton-Bury crossroads, this local is a large corner building. The impressively decorated interior has dining for locals and tourists, who come to enjoy exquisite cuisine. The range of real ales on five handpumps includes some from LocAle breweries. ⋓❀🄾🌢P⁵–₪(537)

Euxton

Bay Horse

Wigan Road, PR7 6JH (at jct of Euxton Lane and close to Buckshaw Village)

✪ 11-11 (midnight Thu-Sat); 12-midnight Sun

☎ (01257) 266398 ⊕ thebayhorseeuxton.co.uk

Greene King IPA; guest beers Ⓗ

The pub consists of a large, comfortable, L-shaped lounge bar mostly used for dining and a smaller area used solely for drinking. Well appointed and pleasantly decorated, it can cater for functions. It has a beer garden and a covered outdoor area for smokers. A Stonegate pub, four changing guest ales are usually on sale, often from micros. Food is served all day from noon with last orders at 8.30pm.

≳❀🄾≈(Buckshaw Parkway)P⁵–₪(109)

Fence

White Swan ⓛ

300 Wheatley Lane Road, BB12 9QA (off A6068)

✪ 5-10.30 Mon; 12-11 (midnight Fri); 10-midnight Sat; 10-10.30 Sun ☎ (01282) 611773 ⊕ whiteswanatfence.co.uk

Taylor Golden Best, Boltmaker, Landlord Ⓗ

Large, traditional, stone-built pub at the eastern edge of Fence village. Completely refurbished in 2007, it still has a superb atmosphere. Good, wholesome food made with fresh local ingredients is served throughout the day (though no food Mon). It is open for brunch at weekends. Quiz night is Wednesday and satellite TV shows football and Six Nations rugby in the bar area. Two open fires heat the small pub during the winter months. ⋓Q🄾🌢P⁵–₪(65)

Fleetwood

Strawberry Gardens ♈ ⓛ

Poulton Road, FY7 6TF (on A587)

✪ 12-12.30am (1am Fri & Sat) ☎ (01253) 771991

Beer range varies Ⓗ

Free house with a choice of 12 beers alongside Old Rosie and three other ciders. It is home to Fleetwood Folk Club, two racing pigeon clubs and crown green bowling teams. A beer festival is held at the end of May, and it was local CAMRA Pub of the Year 2013 and local Cider Pub of the Year 2012. CAMRA members receive a discount and food is served daily until 8pm. Hosted by TV celebrity Syd Little, away fans are welcome when playing Fleetwood Town FC. 🄾🌢₪🎄👜P⁵–₪(7,14,80)

Thomas Drummond

London Street, FY7 6JY (between Lord St and Dock St)

✪ 8am-11 (midnight Thu-Sat) ☎ (01253) 775020

Greene King Abbot; Ruddles Best Bitter; guest beers Ⓗ

A Wetherspoon pub named after a builder who helped construct the town. It also displays details of the town's founder, Sir Peter Hesketh Fleetwood, and architect Decimus Burton. It was a church hall and a furniture warehouse in a former life. Food is served 8am-10pm daily, and children are welcome until 9pm. Cider is on sale here and there is on-road parking outside. Free Wi-Fi. ❀🄾🌢₪👜–₪(1,14)

Goosnargh

Horns Inn ★ Ⓛ

Horns Lane, PR3 2FJ (corner of Inglewhite Rd, 2 miles NE of village) SD575391

☼ 11.30-3 (not Mon), 6-11; 12-9 Sun ☎ (01772) 865230

⊕ hornsinn.co.uk

Beer range varies Ⓗ

Country pub dating from 1782 close to the Forest of Bowland, with five rooms including a rare snug where customers sit behind the bar counter while staff serve from the same area – one of only three in the country. Although marked private, it is open to all. A five-barrel brewery, Goosnargh Brewing Company, has recently been installed. The pub has at least one beer brewed on site and one from a local micro. It serves good food using locally sourced ingredients. Accommodation is in a converted barn at the rear. ᴹQ✿❋⊕ ÅP

Great Eccleston

Black Bull

The Square, PR3 0YB (on main street)

☼ 12-11 ☎ (01995) 670224

Black Sheep Best Bitter; Moorhouse's Pride of Pendle; Thwaites Wainwright; guest beers Ⓗ

The pub is on the south side of the village square diagonally opposite the White Bull. In past times the square was used for bull-baiting. A good choice of well-kept beers from the SIBA list is available. The pub recently underwent a subtle and stylish refurbishment, resulting in a comfortable, well-liked hostelry. It has teams in all the local sports leagues. A popular venue for locals and visitors alike. ᴹQ❧✿❋⊕Åᴾ♣Pᴸ➶(42,76,82)

White Bull

The Square, PR3 0ZB (in village square)

☼ 11-midnight; 12-11.30 Sun ☎ (01995) 670203

Black Sheep Best Bitter; guest beers Ⓗ

On the north side of the village square diagonally opposite the Black Bull. The White Bull is an old coaching inn with stone floors, real fires and other unspoiled period features. It is very popular for its well-kept beers and locally sourced and home-cooked food. Guest beers come from the SIBA list. A real local, with pool, darts and other pub teams. ᴹQ❧✿⊕Å♣ᴸ➶(42,76,82)

Great Harwood

Victoria ★ Ⓛ

St John's Street, BB6 7EP

☼ 3-11 (midnight Fri & Sat); 12-10.30 Sun ☎ (01254) 885210

Black Sheep Best Bitter; Bowland Gold; Taylor Landlord; guest beers Ⓗ

Cosy, welcoming pub built in 1905 by Alfred Nuttall, featuring much fine woodwork, cream and green Art Nouveau tiling and etched internal windows. The local name, Butcher Brig, refers to the railway bridge that once stood nearby. The three regular beers are joined on the bar by another five handpumps, dispensing a varying range of beers, with local Lancashire and Yorkshire brewers well represented. There is a popular weekly quiz night and an annual beer festival in autumn. Q❧✿Å♣♦ᴸ

Haskayne

Ship Inn

6 Rosemary Lane, L39 7JP (signed off A5147 between Maghull and Southport) SD364082

☼ 12-midnight ☎ (01704) 840077

Holt Bitter; guest beers Ⓗ

The Ship was constructed in 1787 and claims to be the first pub built beside a canal. Nowadays, passing trade is more likely to come from the nearby M57/M58 interchange, the pub being just off the A5147. Guest beers tend to come from breweries such as Burscough, Saltaire and Phoenix, with more available in summer. A previous winner of the local CAMRA Pub of the Year award, the venue has a beer garden with play area. ᴹQ❧✿⊕⊕Å♣Pᴸ➶(300,315)

Haslingden

Green Squirrel

148 Manchester Road, BB4 6NP

☼ 4 (2 Mon)-midnight; 2-2am Fri; 12-2am Sat; 12-midnight Sun

Moorhouse's Premier, Blond Witch Ⓗ

Large, stone-built pub close to Haslingden centre. This is a very friendly local, named after the cricket team that the co-owners all once played for (the pub was previously named the Crown). Beers are usually from Moorhouse's, although there may be the occasional guest beer as well. Live music events take place on Sunday evenings. It lies on the main road from Accrington to Rochdale. ᴹ♣ᴸ➶(464)

Heysham

Royal

7 Main Street, LA3 2RN (70yds towards St Patrick's chapel from Heysham village bus stop)

☼ 12-11.30 (midnight Fri & Sat); 12-11 Sun

☎ (01524) 859298

Thwaites Lancaster Bomber; guest beers Ⓗ

The Royal is a 15th-century inn in the heart of the village. As you enter, a tiny locals' bar is on the right and a restaurant is on the left. The main bar is accessed via a winding passage and opens onto a large landscaped garden (open until 11pm). Six handpumps provide the beers, often including ales from York and Cross Bay. Forthcoming guest beers are usually listed on the website. Outside is a covered and heated smoking area. ᴹQ❧✿⊕⊕Pᴸ➶(4,5)

Higher Wheelton

Golden Lion Ⓛ

369 Blackburn Road, PR6 8HP (on A674)

☼ 11-1am ☎ (01254) 830855 ⊕ goldenlionwheelton.net

Thwaites Nutty Black, Original, Wainwright, Lancaster Bomber, seasonal beers; guest beers Ⓗ

In the centre of the village, this stone-built single-bar pub has a comfortable bar/lounge with a partitioned-off games area. The walls are adorned with old photographs of the area, and TV sports fans are well catered for. Outside drinking areas are to the front and rear, and good-value meals are served all day. Guest beers are from the Thwaites 1807 Cask Club range. Late opening is subject to demand. ᴹQ✿⊕♣Pᴸ➶(124)

Lancaster

Borough L

3 Dalton Square, LA1 1PP (near town hall)
✪ 9am-11.30 (12.30am Fri & Sat) ☎ (01524) 64170
⊕ theboroughlancaster.co.uk
Lancaster Amber; guest beers H

An upmarket town house built in 1824 but with a Victorian frontage, it is now a pub that succeeds in appealing both to food lovers and ale aficionados. The front area resembles a gentlemen's club, with deep-buttoned chairs and chandeliers, while the large back room is a restaurant and the bar is in a passage between them. Outside is a sheltered patio with covered smoking area. A comedy club is hosted on Sunday evenings. ❀➊⬤&≠ᴸ-🖃

Sun

63 Church Street, LA1 1ET
✪ 10-midnight ☎ (01524) 66006
⊕ thesunhotelandbar.co.uk
Lancaster Blonde, seasonal beers; Thwaites Wainwright; guest beers H

Quality is the name of the game here. The decor combines a mixture of exposed stonework, wood panelling and solid furniture, with ambient candlelight in the evenings. Some original features remain, including stone fireplaces and a well. The pub is the primary outlet for Lancaster Brewery in the city, as well as offering up to four guest beers. Wi-Fi internet access is available. Outside is a peaceful courtyard with a heated and covered smoking area. ➳❀🏨➊⬤&≠ᴸ-🖃

Three Mariners

Bridge Lane, LA1 1EE (near Parksafe car park entrance)
✪ 12-2 Mon-Wed winter; 12-midnight Thu-Sat; 12-11 Sun
☎ (01524) 388957
York Guzzler; guest beers H

Claimed to be the oldest pub in Lancaster, it is built into the side of Castle Hill. The narrow strip of cobbles at the front has tables for drinkers and is what is left of Bridge Lane, once the link between the town and its port. The pub is a popular watering hole and is involved with the maritime section of the Lancaster Music Festival. Home-cooked, reasonably priced food is available (no food Mon-Wed in winter). Music takes place on the first Sunday of the month. Limited parking. ⋒Q❀⬤&≠♣🖃

Water Witch

Tow Path, Aldcliffe Road, LA1 1SU (on canal towpath near Penny St bridge)
✪ 11-midnight (11 Sun) ☎ (01524) 63828
⊕ thewaterwitch.co.uk
Beer range varies H

The Water Witch was a passenger packet boat that once plied the Lancaster Canal. The pub, originally a canal company stable block, assumed the name in 1978 – the first true canalside pub on this stretch of water. Wedged between the towpath and a retaining wall, it is long and narrow, with bare stone walls and floors. A mezzanine floor and the space underneath it are used mainly for dining. There are seats on the towpath. Quiz night is Thursday. ⋒❀➊≠ᴸ-🖃

White Cross L

Quarry Road, LA1 4XT (behind town hall, on canal towpath)
✪ 11.30-11 (12.30am Fri & Sat); 12-11 Sun ☎ (01524) 33999
⊕ thewhitecross.co.uk

Caledonian Deuchars IPA; Sharp's Doom Bar; Theakston Old Peculier; Tirril Old Faithful; guest beers H

A modern renovation of an old canalside mill building with an open-plan interior and a light, airy feel. Double doors open onto extensive canalside seating, making this a popular location for summer afternoons and evenings. The 14 ales available, including Tirril's, concentrate on Lancastrian, Cumbrian and Pennine brewers, and there is a choice of real ciders. Meals are served throughout the week, including a Sunday roast. There is a popular Tuesday night quiz, and a beer and pie festival each April. ❀➊&≠♣⬤P ᴸ-🖃

Lancaster University

Graduate College Bar

Bailrigg, LA1 4ZA (on pedestrian square in Alexandra Park; Graduate College is signposted)
✪ 7-11; 5-11.30 Fri & Sat (term time); 8-11 Sun
☎ (01524) 592824
Beer range varies H

The Graduate College Bar is much pubbier and attracts a higher age range than the usual student watering hole. The choice of beer is good, with eight handpumps. There is a beer fest in June and a cider fest in October. Curry night is Friday, while open mic night alternates with live bands on Thursday. ❀&♣⬤P ᴸ-🖃(3)

Lea Town

Smith's Arms L

Lea Lane, PR4 0RP (rear of BNFL Salwick) SD476311
✪ 12-midnight ☎ (01772) 760555
Thwaites Original, Wainwright, Lancaster Bomber, seasonal beers; guest beers H

Open-plan country pub with a main bar and a lower level specifically for food. A Thwaite's tied house, it is near the Preston-Lancaster Canal and on route 62 of the national cycle network. This hostelry offers guest beers alternating with seasonal beers from the 1807 Cask Club range. It regularly wins awards for its food and beer and can get busy, particularly on Sundays when meals are served all day. It has a covered smoking area with a real log fire and leather sofas. ⋒❀➊&P ᴸ-

Leyland

Leyland Lion ♟ L

60 Hough Lane, PR25 2SA
✪ 9am-11.30 (12.30am Fri & Sat) ☎ (01772) 643990
Moorhouse's Leyland Lion; Ruddles Best Bitter; guest beers H

Opened in 2010, this conversion of a town-centre post office is smaller than most Wetherspoon pubs. A central log fire feature is also unusual for this operator. The pub's name commemorates the buses that made this town famous throughout the world, which were built a few yards up the road. Six guest beers are usually available, often sourced from local breweries, plus a real cider. Handy for the Commercial Vehicle Museum. ⋒➳❀➊&≠⬤ᴸ-🖃

Railway at Leyland

1 Preston Road, PR25 4NT
✪ 4-11.30 (midnight Wed & Thu); 12-2am Fri; 12-1.30am Sat); 12-midnight Sun ☎ (01772) 458427
⊕ therailwayatleyland.co.uk

Black Sheep Best Bitter; guest beers Ⓗ
Since it was refurbished in 2007, this pub has led the way as Leyland has been transformed into a town much more attractive to the real ale drinker. The bright and airy interior makes it a welcoming hostelry, with four cask ales always available including three changing guest beers. Although a large pub, it can get extremely busy on weekend evenings when there is live entertainment. A first-floor function room was added in 2012, which can accommodate up to 100 people.
❀◑ㅑ&≉♣P⁵－🖫(111)

Longridge

Corporation Arms Ⓛ
Lower Road, PR3 2YJ (nr B6243/B6245 jct)
❀ 11-11; 12-10.30 Sun ☎ (01772) 782644
⊕ corporationarms.com
Beer range varies Ⓗ
Eighteenth-century inn close to the Longridge reservoirs on the road to Ribchester, handy for local walks. This free house has a reputation for excellent ale, food, service and accommodation (booking advised). Four handpumps serve beers sourced from local breweries – Bowland, Copper Dragon and Phoenix are some of the favourites. Real cider is available during summer months. There is an annual beer festival on the spring bank holiday weekend. Note the horse trough outside, reputedly used by Oliver Cromwell to water his horse on his way to the Battle of Preston.
🏚Q❀🍴◑&♣P⁵－🖫(3,3A)

Lostock Hall

Anchor
43 Croston Road, PR5 5LA (300yds from B5254)
❀ 4.30-11.30; 4-midnight Fri; 11-midnight Sat; 12-midnight Sun ☎ (01772) 335637
Beer range varies Ⓗ
Just a short distance from the Tardy Gate shopping area and alongside the Preston to Blackburn railway line, this friendly community pub offers five changing cask ales from the Heineken Cellarman's Reserve list, with LocAle beers often available. In May and September a beer festival is held in marquees on a large grassy area adjacent to the pub. To the rear is a boules pitch used in summer. Meals are served Sunday only, 3-5pm.
🏚❀≉♣P⁵－🖫

Lytham

County Hotel Ⓛ
1 Church Road, FY8 5LH
❀ 12-11 (midnight Fri & Sat) ☎ (01253) 795128
Lytham Trinity; Moorhouse's Pendle Witches Brew; guest beers Ⓗ
A comfortable hotel dating from the 1800s in the centre of town, offering popular local ales. The large lounge is divided into two areas: sport viewing on plasma TV, and small quiet bays. At least two beers from the Lytham Brewery plus two to four changing guests are on sale. Good-value, appetising food is served until 10pm (9pm Sun), and Wednesday is curry night. Quiz night is Thursday. Accommodation comprises 22 en-suite rooms. ❀🍴◑&≉♣P🖫

Queen's Hotel
Central Beach, FY8 5LB (on promenade almost opp windmill)
❀ 12-11 (10.30 Sun) ☎ (01253) 737316
⊕ queenslytham.co.uk
Caledonian Deuchars IPA; Theakston Old Peculier; guest beers Ⓗ
A comfortable pub with views over the Ribble Estuary, built in 1854 as the Neptune. It still retains many of its original Victorian features. A well-liked and sophisticated venue, the pub and its guest rooms have a certain elegance, matched by the top-quality, locally sourced food including a very popular Saturday oyster bar. The well-kept cask beers are soon to total five. The pub is very dog-friendly. Q🌟❀🍴◑&≉⁵－🖫

Railway Hotel Ⓛ
Station Road, FY8 5DH (next to fire station on B5259)
❀ 8am-midnight ☎ (01253) 797250
Greene King Abbot; Ruddles Best Bitter; guest beers Ⓗ
The latest acquisition by the JD Wetherspoon chain on the Fylde coast. Converted from a pub, it has a new-look interior, a large beer garden at the front and a novel no-smoking beer garden at the side. Three distinct themed drinking areas feature golfing memorabilia, railway signage and old seaside photos from the '50s depicting Lytham's halcyon days. Three regular beers are supplemented by four changing guest ales, as well as a replica beer from a defunct local brewery, now brewed at Moorhouse's. 🏚❀◑&≉⁵－🖫

Taps Ⓛ
12 Henry Street, FY8 5LE (between West Beach and Market Square)
❀ 11-11 (midnight Fri & Sat) ☎ (01253) 736226
Greene King IPA; guest beers Ⓗ
A multi award-winning landlord is now at the helm in this red-bricked, wood-floored pub, which is small, cosy and often crowded. You are greeted with warm and friendly service from very knowledgeable staff. Quiz nights are every Monday, and locally sourced home-made dishes are served daily 11-4pm. A real fire burns in winter months, dogs are permitted outside, and 11 handpumps serve changing beers from all over the country, including one cider. Heated outdoor smoking/no-smoking areas are to the side and rear. 🏚❀◑&Å≉♣●⁵－🖫(7,11,68)

Mawdesley

Red Lion
68-70 New Street, L40 2QP
❀ 12-11 (midnight Fri & Sat) ☎ (01704) 822208
⊕ redlionmawdesley.com
Copper Dragon Golden Pippin; guest beers Ⓗ
This small white-painted pub is at the centre of the village and has a growing reputation for food, which is served in the attractive conservatory at the rear. Meals are also served in the lounge bar at the front and there is a small public bar where sport can be watched on TV. The two guest beers are from the Enterprise list and include ales from local breweries. No food Monday.
🏚❀◑🎏♣P🖫(337,347)

Morecambe

Palatine

The Crescent, LA4 5BZ (overlooking promenade opp clock tower)
🌣 10.30-midnight (1am Fri & Sat); 10.30-11.30 Sun
☎ (01524) 410503 ⊕ thepalatine.co.uk
Lancaster Amber, Blonde, Black, Red; guest beers Ⓗ
An Edwardian mid-terrace pub on the seafront. The ground floor was completely transformed in late 2008, featuring much bare stone and woodwork. The bar room is quite small, with some intimate corners. An upstairs room is rather different; it is cosy and carpeted, and many of the fittings such as leaded lights, shelving and the fireplace appear to be original. Enjoy the spectacular views across the bay, especially at sunset. There are seats on the pavement in front. 🏵🍺🕪🕹🗲🍴🛏🚃

Smuggler's Den

56 Poulton Road, LA4 5HB
🌣 3-11; 1-midnight Fri-Sun ☎ (01524) 421684
Beer range varies Ⓗ
The oldest pub in Morecambe, dating from circa 1640. It acquired its current name and look in the 1960s, when the stained glass windows were put in, and some interesting maritime artefacts and brass shell cases are on display. An impressive open fire warms the bar during the colder months. There are ladies' and gents' darts teams, and a pub quiz is held. A bike rack is available for customers. 🏯🏵🗲♣🍴P🛏🚃(5,430)

Nelson

Shooters

Southfield Lane, BB10 3RJ
🌣 3 (4 Mon)-midnight; 12-midnight Fri-Sun
☎ (01282) 614153
Thwaites Original, Wainwright Ⓗ
Welcoming country pub well away from the centre of Nelson. In addition to the two regular beers, you may occasionally find one of Thwaite's range of seasonal beers. Food is served Thursday-Sunday only. From the front of the pub there are spectacular views over the surrounding countryside. Occasional live bands play here. 🏯🏵🍺🗲P🚃(93)

Old Langho

Black Bull

Old Langho Road, BB6 8AW (off A59, just W of jct with A666)
🌣 12-11 (midnight Fri); 11-midnight Sat & Sun
☎ (01254) 248801 ⊕ theblackbullinnlancs.co.uk
Marston's Old Empire Ⓗ
Visitors can be sure of a warm welcome at this (allegedly) haunted pub, dating back to 1554, whether dining or enjoying one of the five real ales. As a Marston's house you can expect to see beers from Jennings and Brakspear as well. Try the three third-pints option if you can't decide. Quiz night is Tuesday, poker on Sunday. Excellent food is served from an extensive menu, including brunch at weekends. As it is close to Blackburn Rovers training ground you may even bump into some of the players. 🏯🏵🍺🍺🕹🗲P🚃(25)

Ormskirk

Farmers Club

65 Burscough Street, L39 2EL
🌣 12-11.30 ☎ (01695) 572172
Black Sheep Best Bitter; Tetley Bitter Ⓗ
Housed in a former Georgian dispensary, the club's grand portico entrance leads into an impressive interior containing a full-sized snooker table and darts facilities. Live football matches are screened. The club has been voted local CAMRA Club of the Year for the last two years and has also won the regional award. Visitors are asked to present a CAMRA membership card or a copy of this Guide to gain entry. 🏵🍺♣🛏🚃(3A)

Parbold

Stocks Tavern Ⓛ

16 Alder Lane, WN8 7NN (on A5209)
🌣 12-11.30 (midnight Sat); 12-11 Sun ☎ (01257) 462874
⊕ thestockstavern.co.uk
Beer range varies Ⓗ
Charming local village pub built in 1810 and refurbished summer 2012. It has low-beamed ceilings, wood floor and panelling, and offers two real fires. The taproom boasts two TVs showing sporting events. The pub attracts canal enthusiasts, walkers, cyclists and locals. Excellent good-value food is served lunchtimes Monday to Friday, and all day Saturday and Sunday. Five handpumps dispense mainly local beers. There is a discount on drinks for CAMRA members. 🏯🍽🕪🗲🍺♣P🚃

Wayfarer Ⓛ

1-3 Alder Lane, WN8 7NL (on A5209)
🌣 12-3, 5-11; 12-midnight Fri & Sat; 12-11 Sun
☎ (01257) 464600 ⊕ wayfarerparbold.co.uk
Tetley Bitter; guest beers Ⓗ
With up to six guest beers, including at least one LocAle, and an extensive food menu, there is something here that will tickle your tastebuds. Converted from cottages built in the 18th century, the Wayfarer has panoramic views outside and a variety of styles on the inside – including a thoroughly modern restaurant, a bar with nooks and crannies, and a sophisticated dining area. It is close to the Leeds and Liverpool Canal, Parbold Hill, and welcomes walkers. 🏯🏵🕪🕹🗲P🛏🚃

Pendleton

Swan with Two Necks Ⓛ

Main Street, BB7 1PT (½ mile E of A59 turn-off)
🌣 12-2.30 (not Mon); 6-11; 12-11 Sun ☎ (01200) 423112
⊕ swanwithtwonecks.co.uk
Copper Dragon Golden Pippin; guest beers Ⓗ
A pub that was in the final four of CAMRA's national Pub of the Year competition in 2012. Guest beers are often from micros such as Phoenix, Dark Star and Salamander, and there is always a real cider. A discount is offered for CAMRA members. The home-made food here comes in portions ideal for hungry walkers. There is outdoor seating in the garden and in front of the pub, looking out onto a small stream running through the beautifully kept village. Cosy open fires blaze in the winter months. An amazing collection of teapots is on display. 🏯Q🏵🕪🗲🍴P🛏

Penwortham

Black Bull ⃝

83 Pope Lane, PR1 9BA
❀ 11-11 (midnight Fri & Sat); 12-11 Sun ☎ (01772) 752953
⊕ blackbull-penwortham.co.uk
Greene King IPA; Thwaites Wainwright; guest beers ⃝
Attractive cottage-style inn dating back to the
1800s, which has managed to retain a village pub
atmosphere despite its location in a well-populated
area. On entering, a narrow passageway leads
through to a central bar serving a number of
drinking areas including a separate public bar. A
friendly community pub, the many social events
include a popular Thursday quiz, while local
charities are actively supported. Two guest beers
are always available. The pub is a Beautiful Beer
gold award winner. Q❀⊕♣P⃝-⃝ (3,3A)

Poulton-le-Fylde

Castle Gardens

Poulton Road, FY6 7NII (on Carleton crossroads)
❀ 11.30-11 (midnight Fri & Sat) ☎ (01253) 890015
**Moorhouse's Pendle Witches Brew; Taylor Landlord;
Thwaites Original; guest beers** ⃝
A Victorian pub that was once the centre of a huge
pleasure gardens. Good food, popular with diners,
is served, but the emphasis is still on the pub. It
holds an annual summer beer festival and there is
a varied choice of well-kept beers. The Tuesday
quiz night regularly attracts more than 100
participants. This is a venue that is popular, warm,
comfortable and family-friendly.
♨⤚❀⊕◗⃝♣P⃝-⃝ (14,16)

Grapevine (Café Bar) ⃝

19-21 Market Place, FY6 7AS (just off B5267, between
Ball St and Blackpool Rd)
❀ closed Mon; 6-midnight (1am Fri & Sat); 6-11 Sun
☎ (01253) 896700
Thwaites Original, Wainwright; guest beers ⃝
The Grapevine café/wine bar is situated in the
heart of historic Poulton-le-Fylde. Formerly an
ironmongers and hardware shop, it is thought to
date back to 1754. Today the building serves as a
popular venue and meeting place for all ages.
During the day it opens as an upmarket café with a
selection of coffees, teas and home-cooked food.
By night it becomes a pleasant, informal wine bar
with several quality cask ales on offer. ◗⥰⃝

Old Town Hall

5 Church Street, FY6 7AP
❀ 11.30-11 (11.30 Thu & Fri); 11-11.30 Sat; 12-11 Sun
☎ (01253) 892257
Beer range varies ⃝
Originally built as a pub but used as council offices
for most of the 20th century, a recent beneficial
refurbishment moved the bar across the
downstairs drinking area. This community locals'
pub, much used by racing aficionados and football
fans, is a popular call on the small but busy Poulton
circuit. Live music features most weekends, and a
folk club meets on the last Thursday of each month
in the upstairs function room/wine bar, where
further changes are planned. ⃝⥰⃝ (2,42,84)

Thatched House ⃝

30 Ball Street, FY6 7BQ (on B5267)
❀ 11.30-11 (11.30 Thu; midnight Fri & Sat); 12-11 Sun
☎ (01253) 891063
Lytham Thatched House Bitter; guest beers ⃝

Placed in the middle of Poulton centre next to a
Norman church since 1885, with slot machines and
sport TV, this is a very busy weekend pub. It serves
six different guest beers and also holds beer
festivals at various times of the year. The pub has
four open-plan rooms and standing facilities
around the bar area. It's handy for the buses and
the railway station. Pictures of sporting heroes
decorate the wood-panelled walls.
♨❀⊕♣⥰⃝-⃝⃝ (2,42,84)

Preston

Bitter Suite

53 Fylde Road, PR1 2XQ
❀ 12-3, 6-11 (not Mon eve); 12-midnight Fri & Sat; 7-11 Sun
☎ (01772) 827007 ⊕ bittersuitepreston.co.uk
Beer range varies ⃝
A free house serving six guest beers from
microbreweries, with an emphasis on Yorkshire
brewers. Guests change almost hourly, and it hosts
at least four mini festivals each year. It has a
single-room bar set back from Fylde Road at the
side of the unrelated Mad Ferret. Simple home-
cooked lunches including pies and burgers are
served weekdays. Although surrounded by
university buildings, it is not primarily a student
bar. Live music plays on Wednesday and Saturday,
and an upstairs room is available for hire. Twice
winner of local CAMRA Pub of the Year.
❀◗♣⃝ (31,35,61)

Black Horse ★

166 Friargate, PR1 2EJ
❀ 10.30-11 (midnight Fri & Sat); 12-10.30 Sun
☎ (01772) 204855 ⊕ blackhorse-preston.co.uk
**Robinsons 1892, Dizzy Blond, Unicorn, Double Hop,
Old Tom, seasonal beers** ⃝
Classic Grade II-listed inn in the main shopping area
close to the historic open market. With its tiled bar
and walls and mosaic floor, it is identified by
CAMRA as one of Britain's Best Real Heritage Pubs.
The two front rooms with real log fires bear photos
of old Preston; the famous hall of mirrors seating
area is to the rear, and memorabilia of a previous
landlord is displayed. Up to eight Robinsons beers
are regularly on sale. A covered smoking area is
upstairs, as is the Graze and Grog café, serving
home-made food during the day (no food Sun).
♨◗⥰⃝

Continental

South Meadow Lane, PR1 8JP (off Fishergate Hill)
❀ 12-midnight (1am Fri & Sat); 12-11.30 Sun
☎ (01772) 499425 ⊕ newcontinental.net
Beer range varies ⃝
Beside the Ribble, the main railway line and Miller
Park. A two-times winner of local CAMRA Pub of
the Year, it has a main bar area, a lounge with a
real fire in winter and conservatories overlooking
the garden. Live music and theatre feature
regularly in a separate arts/events space also used
for beer festivals. Seven microbrewery beers are
on offer including the house ale from Marble, a
beer from Pictish and a dark beer. Freshly cooked
meals are served lunchtimes and evenings (no
food Mon). ♨Q❀⊕◗⃝♣P⃝-⃝ (3A)

Grey Friar

144 Friargate, PR1 2EJ (jct of Ringway)
❀ 9am-midnight (1am Fri & Sat) ☎ (01772) 558542
**Greene King Abbot; Ruddles Best Bitter; guest
beers** ⃝

Modern open-plan Wetherspoon pub with raised areas to the side and rear, in a fine real ale drinking part of the city. Formerly a carpet store, Preston's students and citizens, both young and old, appreciate the range of ales and food at good prices, with up to seven guests beers on sale. The social mix creates a bustling atmosphere and the bar can get extremely busy at weekends. The pub plays an active role in local CAMRA recruiting. ⏵🏠♿🕿🍴🚲

Market Tavern

33-35 Market Street, PR1 2ES
✪ 10.30-9 (11 Thu; midnight Fri & Sat); 12-9 Sun
☎ (01772) 254425
Beer range varies Ⓗ
Three handpumps serve guest beers from all over the country, usually from micros but with no particular emphasis. This is a small, popular, city-centre local in a pedestrianised area overlooking the historic Victorian outdoor market. A selection of imported bottled beers is also on offer, plus German Weisse on draught. Outside seating is available in summer. With two intimate seating booths, conversation rules in this former local CAMRA Pub of the Year. No food is served, but you are welcome to bring your own. Q🕏🍴

Old Black Bull

35 Friargate, PR1 2AT
✪ 10.30-11 (midnight Fri & Sat); 12-10.30 Sun
☎ (01772) 823397
Beer range varies Ⓗ
Mock-Tudor city-centre pub now completely free of tie. A small front vault, a main bar with distinctive black and white floor tiles, two comfortable lounge areas (one recently extended) all combine to make a popular venue. There is also a patio to the rear. Live music plays on Saturday evenings, and TV sport is shown. Nine guest beers come from micros or small independents sourced from all over Britain. The house beer is supplied by Joshua Tetley. Three times winner of local CAMRA Pub of the Year. 🕏⏵🏠🍴🚲

Old Vic Ⓛ

78 Fishergate, PR1 2UH
✪ 11.30-11 (midnight Fri; 1am Sat); 12-midnight Sun
☎ (01772) 254690
Courage Directors; guest beers Ⓗ
Opposite the railway station and on bus routes into the city, this is a popular pub that can get busy at weekends. Seven handpumps offer the widest range of LocAle beers in the area, with Moorhouse's and several smaller microbreweries usually represented. A number of TVs show sports events while the pub hosts thriving pool and darts teams. Meals are served 12-5pm (1-4pm Sun). To the rear is an outdoor decked smoking area and a car park that is only available Sundays and evenings. 🕏⏵🏠🍴🚲

Olde Dog & Partridge

44 Friargate, PR1 2AT
✪ 11-3, 5-11.30; 11-1am Sat; 12-midnight Sun
☎ (01772) 252217
Holt Bitter; Taylor Landlord; Tetley Dark Mild; guest beers Ⓗ
Down-to-earth city-centre pub that specialises in rock music. The landlord has worked here for more than 30 years and offers five real ales including two guest beers from the SIBA direct delivery scheme, plus a real cider. There is a monthly live music night, a weekly quiz on Thursday and a rock DJ on Sunday evening. Excellent-value pub lunches are served (no food Sun) and a covered Smokey-O-Joes smoking area is provided at the rear. 🕏⏵🍴🚲🏠

Wheatsheaf Ⓛ

50 Water Lane, PR2 2NL (on A583)
✪ 11-11 (11.30 Fri & Sat); 12-10.30 Sun ☎ (01772) 725917
Beer range varies Ⓗ
A Victorian local on the way to Preston Marina, a mile from the city centre, owned by Amber Taverns. Five attractively priced guest beers include at least one from Moorhouse's and often Courage Directors, otherwise they come from anywhere in the country. Third-of-a-pint tasting racks are available. At least two beer festivals are held a year in a marquee at the rear. The pub is big on TV sport, and live music plays Friday and Saturday nights. Daytime snacks are served. There is disabled access through the courtyard. 🕏♿🍴🚲🏠(68,35)

Rawtenstall

Craven Heifer Ⓛ

264-266 Burnley Road, BB4 8LA (on A682, N of Rawtenstall)
✪ 4-midnight; 1-1am Sat & Sun ☎ (01706) 214757
Moorhouse's Black Cat, Premier, Witch Hunt, Blond Witch, Pendle Witches Brew Ⓗ
One of Moorhouse's tied pubs – the only one in Rossendale. The six handpumps offer the full range of Moorhouse's beers, including seasonal ones, and there is a surprisingly good selection of malt whiskies as well. This is a friendly local with a spacious lounge bar that extends over the river, warmed by a large open fire in winter. There is some form of entertainment at most weekends. At Easter the pub hosts the Pendle Witches Vintage Velo cycle race. 🚃🚌🕏🚲🏠(X43)

White Lion Ⓛ

72 Burnley Road, BB4 8EW
✪ 4.30-midnight (2am Fri); 12-midnight Sun
☎ (01706) 213117
Black Sheep Best Bitter; Copper Dragon Golden Pippin; Moorhouse's Pride of Pendle; guest beers Ⓗ
Originally a row of cottages, combined to become a pub in 1816 (the front of the building is listed). It is a large, friendly place with four handpumps, one offering a regularly changing guest beer which may come from a local brewery or from further afield. Quiz night is Tuesday, entertainment features on Friday and Saturday evenings. Rossendale ski slope and the East Lancs steam railway are not far away. 🕏🚲P🍴🏠(X43)

Rufford

Hesketh Arms

81 Liverpool Road, L40 1SB (on A59 at jct with B5246)
✪ 12-11 (midnight Fri & Sat) ☎ (01704) 821002
Moorhouse's Pride of Pendle; Tetley Bitter; guest beers Ⓗ
A spacious former Greenall's inn on the A59, the Hesketh is now a free house serving up to six ales, mostly from local microbreweries. Set in the charming village of Rufford, it is near to the National Trust property of Rufford Old Hall, the delightful St Mary's Marina, and the popular Mere Sands nature reserve. A large split-level pub with

several dining areas, it serves good-quality food throughout the day. Monthly live entertainment and a Tuesday quiz attract a mixed clientele. ⑄⬥◑◗⊟⬥⇌P⊾⊟(2A,347)

St Annes on the Sea

Fifteens of St Annes ⓛ
42 St Annes Road West, FY8 1RF (in St Annes Square)
✪ 11-11 (11.30 Fri; midnight Sat); 12-11 Sun
☎ (01253) 725852 ⊕ fifteensstannes.com
Hawkshead 15's Stout; Moorhouse's 15's Ale; guest beers ⊞
Situated in the heart of St Annes Square, this real gem of a pub has lit up and added to the real ale scene in the area. A Lloyds bank in a previous life, this watering hole has its own unique style and its vault is definitely a must-see. Awarded CAMRA branch Pub of the Year 2012, Martin and his team continue to provide a delightful selection of wonderfully kept beers. Live sport and occasional live music/DJ enhance this pub's appeal.
⬥⇌◗⊾⊟(11,68)

Trawl Boat Inn ⓛ
36-38 Wood Street, FY8 1QR (in side street off St Annes Square)
✪ 8am-midnight (1am Fri & Sat) ☎ (01253) 783080
Greene King Abbot; Ruddles Best Bitter; guest beers ⊞
This Wetherspoon pub was originally a solicitor's office, situated about 400 yards from the seafront. Its tasteful decor with natural fire creates a good, warm atmosphere; it has eight guest beers on at any one time, supporting local breweries. Located just off the square, the name comes from an old pub closed many years ago. It is handy for the shops and railway station and caters for young and old alike, with a designated area for families.
⩜⑄◑◗⬥⇌⊾⊟

Salwick

Windmill Tavern
Clifton Lane, PR4 0YE (off A583 via Clifton village, at BNFL Salwick works)
✪ closed Mon; 12-3, 5-11; 12-midnight Fri & Sat; 12-10.30 Sun ☎ (01772) 687203 ⊕ windmilltavern.com
York Yorkshire Terrier; guest beers ⊞
A semi-rural pub in an 18th-century windmill on the edge of the village of Salwick, with a large beer garden overlooking the nearby nuclear fuel production facility. The emphasis is on good locally sourced food, with most of the former mill outbuildings occupied by a large dining area. The mill itself is next to the unusual circular drinking area in the ground floor of the mill tower. Not all trains stop at Salwick station. Q⑄◑◗⇌♣P⊾

Samlesbury

New Hall Tavern ⓛ
Cuerdale Lane, PR5 0XA (on B6230)
✪ 12-11 (midnight Thu-Sat) ☎ (01772) 877942
Shepherd Neame Spitfire; guest beers ⊞
On a crossroads just off junction 31 of the M6, close to the InBev brewery, this pub has a large car park and a heated outdoor smoking area. Indoors it is divided up by wood and glass panels, providing separate areas for dining. Up to six real ales are served, the guests often from local micros. Home-cooked food is sourced from local produce where

possible. Old photos and prints give an insight into the history of the area, which includes the nearby Samlesbury Hall. ⩜⬥◑◗⬥♣P⊾

Silverdale

Woodlands
Woodlands Drive, LA5 0RU
✪ 6-11; 12-midnight Sat; 12-11.30 Sun ☎ (01524) 701655
Beer range varies ⊞
Large country house on an elevated site, converted circa 1878 to a pub with only minimal alterations. The bar has a large fireplace as big as the counter and great views across Morecambe Bay. Beer pumps are in another room with a list of the four ales available on the wall facing the bar. Home-made sandwiches are served at weekends. The smoking area is covered and sheltered. There is a beer festival of 30 ales in October, and a quiz on the last Sunday of the month.
⩜Q⑄⬥♣♣P⊾⊟(33)

Slaidburn

Hark to Bounty
Townend, BB7 3EP SD710524
✪ 11 (12 Sun)-11 ☎ (01200) 446746 ⊕ harktobounty.co.uk
Theakston Best Bitter, Old Peculier; guest beers ⊞
The pub is reputed to date back to the 1300s, although most of the existing fabric of the building dates from the 16th century. Upstairs is the Courtroom, used as the local court from the early 19th century until the mid-1930s. This was originally the Manorial or Moot Court which dealt with local miscreants. Guest beers can be from breweries such as Tirril, Moorhouse's, Caledonian and Brains. Excellent traditional home-cooked food is served, with a daily specials board. It is convenient for walkers in the Ribble Valley.
⩜Q⬥◖◑◗P⊾⊟(10,10a)

Tockholes

Royal Arms ⓛ
Tockholes Road, BB3 0PA (3 miles W of Darwen)
✪ 12-11 (6 Mon); 12-10.30 Sun ☎ (01254) 705373
Beer range varies ⊞
An old, traditional free house formed from two cottages, small but with a great atmosphere in its four back-to-back rooms. Original stone walls have been retained, with flagged and wooden floors and three real fires. Beers are from LocAle microbreweries such as Chorley or Rossendale. On the edge of the West Pennine Moors, it is close to Darwen Tower and overlooking Roddlesworth Woods. The pub welcomes walkers with dogs and offers good meals Wednesday to Sunday. A beer festival is held yearly. ⩜Q⬥◑P⊟(223,535)

Tontine

Delph ⓛ
Sefton Road, WN5 8UJ (off B5206)
✪ 12-midnight (1am Fri & Sat); 12-11.30 Sun ☎ (01695) 622239
Beer range varies ⊞
A warm welcome and a friendly atmosphere greet you here. The pub retains a separate vault with a pool table and TV. Good-value meals complement the various real ales served in a relaxed environment. Popular with all age groups, children are welcome. Darts, dominoes and pool are played

in the local league and a quiz night is held on Wednesdays. Winner of several local CAMRA awards. ✿⦿▶❄(Orrell)♣P'–

Waddington

Waddington Arms
West View, BB7 3HP (in village centre)
✿ 11-11 (midnight Sat) ☎ (01200) 423262
⊕ waddingtonarms.co.uk
Moorhouse's Waddy Ale; Theakston Best Bitter; Thwaites Wainwright; guest beers ⊞
Situated in the centre of the village, this old pub has two 17th-century fireplaces and other important architectural features adding to the ambience. Primarily food-led, it offers an extensive menu, often featuring locally sourced produce. Moorhouse's brews the Waddy Ale specially for the pub. There is a small beer garden at the rear and outdoor seating at the front of the pub overlooking the brook and the Coronation Gardens. Six en-suite bedrooms are available.
🚷Q✿❀⏿⦿ ఈ♣P'–🖳(7,7A,10A)

Walmer Bridge

Walmer Bridge Inn
65 Liverpool Old Road, PR4 5QE
✿ 4-midnight (1am Fri); 12-1am Sat; 12-midnight Sun
☎ (01772) 612296 ⊕ thewalmerbridge.co.uk
Robinsons Unicorn; guest beers ⊞
Village local comprising two rooms, both requiring you to go through four doors to reach the bar. The comfortable lounge contains photographs of bygone Walmer Bridge and Longton. The Vault is popular with the sporting fraternity, while outside there is a large garden with a children's play area. The keen landlord usually has two changing guest beers on offer, and he also supplies cask ales for functions at the nearby village hall. ✿⦿♣P'–🖳(2)

Waterfoot

Jolly Sailor
Booth Place, BB4 9BD
✿ 12-midnight ☎ (01706) 226340 ⊕ jolly-sailor.co.uk
Copper Dragon Golden Pippin; Moorhouse's Pride of Pendle; guest beers ⊞
A friendly local and deservedly popular with all age groups, the Jolly Sailor always has four handpumps in use, serving the two regular beers along with two changing guests. It received a Punch Taverns quality service award in 2012. There is live music every Saturday evening, and food is served 12-8pm during the week, 12-6pm at weekends.
🌣✿⦿'–🖳(483)

Roebuck
482 Burnley Rd East, BB4 9JR
✿ 4-11; 2.30-midnight Fri; 12-midnight Sat; 12.30-10.30 Sun
☎ (01706) 223550
Bowland Gold; Thwaites Original; guest beers ⊞
Large stone-built pub on the Bacup-Rawtenstall main road. The original stone-flagged floor is still to be seen. The central bar area has a large number of coins inserted into the woodwor. The Roebuck is a free house; along with the regular beer from Bowland there is usually another changing Bowland beer, in addition to a guest beer on the fourth handpump. This hostelry is a fine example of a village local, with a large garden at the rear.
🚷✿P'–🖳

Wennington

Bridge
Tatham, LA2 8NL (on B6480 S of Wennington)
✿ 12-11; 12-2.30, 5-11 Wed & Thu; 12-10.30 Sun
☎ (01524) 221326
Black Sheep Best Bitter; Everards Beacon; York Guzzler; guest beer ⊞
Two linked buildings, one dating from 1642, the other from 1744, make up a small bar, cosy and low-beamed with two dining rooms. The pub is set in an isolated spot south of Wennington, but attracts a large number of local customers, as well as walkers in the summer months. It offers good, well-priced food and features in a Turner painting. Quiz night is Friday. There is an associated caravan park and helipad. 🚷Q✿⦿▶ Å❄♣P'–🖳(80,81b)

Whalley

Dog Inn 🅛
55 King Street, BB7 9SP
✿ 11-11 (midnight Fri & Sat); 12-10.30 Sun
☎ (01254) 823009 ⊕ dog-innwhalley.co.uk
Beer range varies ⊞
One of four pubs at the crossroads in Whalley village. The six handpumps feature ales from northern England, with guest beers from as far afield as Orkney and Cornwall. The whiteboard behind the bar tempts with a constantly changing selection of brews, all sold at one price and usually including a porter or a mild. Bottled cider is also available from Lancaster and Dove Syke. The pub has three distinct seating areas, with pool and darts in a separate room. ✿⦿❄'–🖳(26,27,225)

Wheelton

Red Lion
196 Blackburn Road, PR6 8EU
✿ 12-2, 4-1am; 12-1am Fri-Sun ☎ (01254) 830241
Hawkshead Bitter; guest beers ⊞
Built around 1826, this authentic village pub reflects the former mill village it used to serve. Close to the West Pennine Moors, many local walks pass by. It is a free house, and four guest beers are usually available, sourced from far and wide. Thursday features the famous curry night and there is a Sunday roast. Quiz night is Wednesday and there is live music on alternate weekends. Dog-and family-friendly, and the local branch of the Royal British Legion meets here monthly.
🚷✿♣P'–🖳(124)

Whitworth

Sportsman
464 Market Street, OL12 8QN
✿ 12-midnight ☎ (01706) 854402
⊕ sportsmanpubandguesthousewhitworth.com
Copper Dragon Golden Pippin; Taylor Landlord; Tetley Bitter; guest beers ⊞
A friendly, family-run pub with a good selection of real ales, which reopened after refurbishment by the current landlord in 2010. A welcoming open fire greets you in winter. It has ties with Whitworth Spartans Rugby League team, along with pool and boules teams. An AA 3-star award was given in 2012 for the quality of its accommodation. The location is very handy for the Healey Dell Nature Reserve. 🚷🌣❀⦿'–🖳(464)

Wilpshire

Rising Sun

797 Whalley New Road, BB1 9BE (on A666)

🌣 12-11.30 ☎ (01254) 247379

Theakston Best Bitter; guest beers Ⓗ

Situated about two miles from Blackburn town centre, the pub was once a Matthew Brown house and was built at the end of the 1800s. The changing guest ale is likely to be from Thwaites, Three B's (both Blackburn) or Theakston. In the lounge a real fire is great on cold winter nights and a piano encourages a Saturday night song or two. There is a separate bar for cards and dominoes players, and photos of old Blackburn pubs are displayed on the walls. ♨Q⊞⇌♣℄–🖳(225)

Winmarleigh

Patten Arms

Park Lane, PR3 0JU (on B5272 3 miles N of Garstang)

🌣 4-11 (midnight Sat); 12-10 Sun ☎ (01524) 791484

Jennings Cumberland Ale; Tetley Bitter; guest beers Ⓗ

Genuine, isolated free house situated away from villages on a minor road, yet enjoying regular local custom. This early 19th-century Grade II-listed building has a single bar with a country-pub feel, high-backed bench seats, cream-painted walls and open fires. There is a separate restaurant, and terraced seating overlooking a bowling green. ♨🕸🕭▲♣℄–

Worsthorne

Crooked Billet 🅛

1 Smith Square, BB10 3NQ

🌣 7 (5 Thu)-midnight; 4-1am Fri; 12-1am Sat; 12-12.30am Sun ☎ (07766) 230175

Taylor Golden Best, Landlord; Tetley Bitter; Worsthorne Gold, Packhorse Ⓗ

A true free house, this village local retains its tiling, along with a superb wood- and glass-panelled bar. A warm and welcoming pub, it makes a return to the Guide after many years of pubco mismanagement. Regular music nights are held, along with a quiz night on Wednesday and a special Thai night once a month. It is very handy for walking on the nearby moors. Q🕸🕭P℄–

Wray

George & Dragon

Main Street, LA2 8QG (off B6480)

🌣 6-11 Mon; 12-2.30, 5-midnight; 12-midnight Sat; 12-11 Sun ☎ (01524) 221403

Everards Beacon; guest beers Ⓗ

A genuine village local that also has an excellent reputation for its food. Inside, there are two bar rooms of quite different sizes, and a restaurant. Unusual pub games are available, as is Wi-Fi broadband, and there is a Wednesday night quiz. The extensive beer garden has an aviary, as well as an unheated but covered smoking area. Wray hosts a popular scarecrow festival in May. ♨Q🕸🕭♣℄–🖳(80,81B)

Wrightington

White Lion

117 Mossy Lea Road, WN6 9RE (on B5250 approx 1 mile from jct 27 of M6)

🌣 10.30-10.30; 12-midnight Thu-Sat; 12-10.30 Sun ☎ (01257) 425977 ⊕ thewhitelionlancs.co.uk

Beer range varies Ⓗ

Extremely popular country pub, with a good mix of drinkers and diners. Eight handpumps are in constant use, serving beers from the Marston's range. There is a weekly quiz on Tuesday and a poker league on Thursday. Themed evenings are held in the restaurant. The pub is family-friendly, with a large garden area. It is reputed to be haunted by the ghost of an old lady who used to inhabit one of the cottages now making up the restaurant. 🕸🕭⊞🦽P℄–🖳(113)

Swan with Two Necks, Pendleton

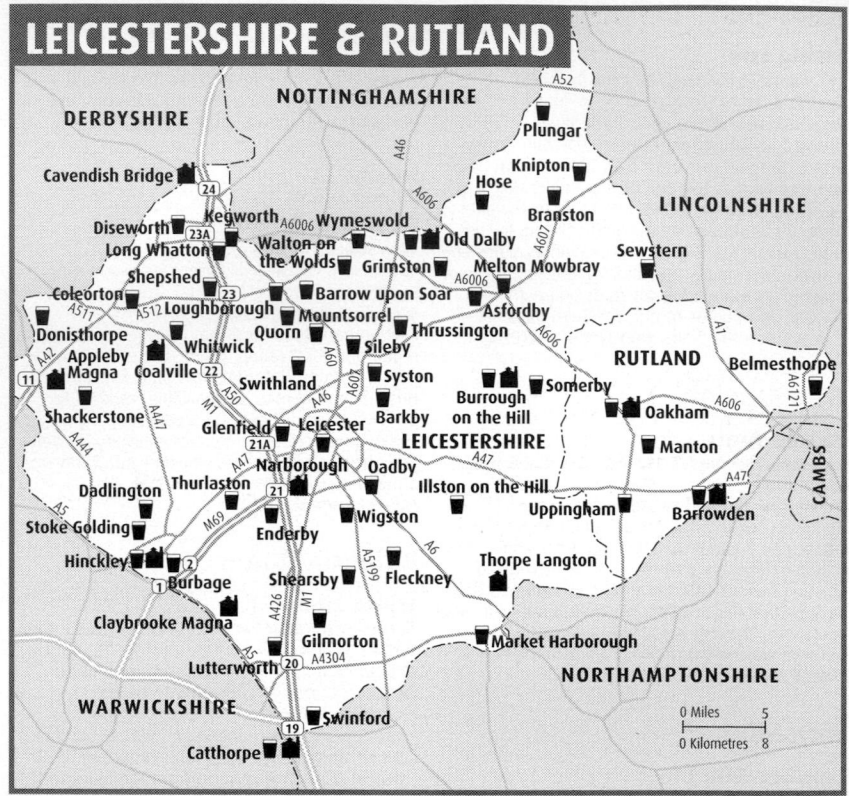

LEICESTERSHIRE & RUTLAND

Asfordby

Horseshoes
128 Main Street, LE14 3SA
✪ 12-4, 7-11 Mon, Wed & Thu; 12-11.30 Tue, Fri-Sun
☎ (01664) 813392
Batemans Dark Mild, XB, seasonal beers Ⓗ
A single-roomed pub at the heart of the village, it compensates for its plain and simple decor with a warm welcome for all. This community inn is home to darts teams and has a skittle alley. This is the only Bateman's house within the CAMRA branch area with at least two of the brewery's real ales available plus a seasonal beer. ♨🍴♣︎🚌(5)

Barkby

Malt Shovel Ⓛ
27 Main Street, LE7 3QG
✪ 11.30-3, 5-11.30 (midnight Fri); 11.30-midnight Sat & Sun
☎ (0116) 269 2558
Thwaites Nutty Black, Original, Wainwright, Lancaster Bomber, seasonal beer; guest beer Ⓗ
Family-friendly village pub serving good-value home-cooked food in the bar and restaurant, while offering drinkers a warm welcome. A beer festival is held on the first weekend in August. There is a large garden area for the summer months, including a pétanque court. ♨🛏🕮🍴🅟🚌

Barrow upon Soar

Soar Bridge Inn
29 Bridge Street, LE12 8PN

✪ 12-11 (10.30 Sun) ☎ (01509) 412686
Everards Tiger, Original; guest beer Ⓗ
Situated next to the bridge that gave it its name, this pub is popular with walkers, boaters and drinkers. The large single-room interior divides into distinct areas, with a separate restaurant, function room and skittle alley. Outside there is a floodlit pétanque court, beer terrace and garden. Well-behaved dogs and children are welcome. Home-made food is available Tuesday to Sunday. The first Monday of the month is Grand Union Folk Club night and a weekly quiz is held on Thursday. ♨🍴🕮🅟🚌(2,27)

Barrowden

Exeter Arms Ⓛ
28 Main Street, LE15 8EQ (1 mile S of A47)

INDEPENDENT BREWERIES

Barrowden Barrowden
Belvoir Old Dalby
Dow Bridge Catthorpe
Elliswood Hinckley (NEW)
Everards Narborough
Gas Dog Burrough on the Hill (NEW)
Golden Duck Appleby Magna
Grainstore Oakham
Langton Thorpe Langton
Long Lane Coalville
Parish Burrough on the Hill
Pig Pub Claybrooke Magna (NEW)
Shardlow Cavendish Bridge

✪ 12-2.30 (not Mon), 6-11; 12-3.30, 6-11 Sat; 12-5 Sun
☎ (01572) 747247
Barrowden Beech, Pilot, Hop Gear, Own Gear, seasonal ales Ⓗ
Collyweston slate-roofed pub with a fine view over the valley and village duck pond. It offers a warm welcome and serves highly regarded food. Pétanque is played here in the summer and dominoes in the winter. Folk music and quiz nights are hosted on alternate Mondays. The patio area is the place to spend a sunny day. Barrowden Brewery is situated in a barn to the rear. CAMRA award-winning ale Pilot won Beer of the Festival in Rugby. ᴍQⓈ✿➠◖◗➎♣P⁵–🖳(12)

Belmesthorpe

Blue Bell ☗ Ⓛ
Shepherds Walk, PE9 4JG TF042102
✪ 12-2 (not Mon), 6-11 (5-11.30 Fri); 12-11.30 Sat; 12-10 30 Sun ☎ (01780) 753081
Draught Bass; guest beers Ⓗ
The Blue Bell is a historic village pub. Low ceilings, a roaring fire and stone walls are part of its charm. Six handpulls offer a wide range of well-kept guest beers, including at least one LocAle and real cider. Dogs on leads are welcome in the bar area. Good honest home-made pub food is available Tuesday to Sunday lunchtimes (booking advisable). Local CAMRA Pub of the Year 2013. ᴍQⓈ♣🐾P⁵–

Branston

Wheel Ⓛ
Main Street, NG32 1RU
✪ closed Mon; 11-11; 12-10.30 Sun ☎ (01476) 870376
⊕ thewheelinnbranston.co.uk
Batemans XB; guest beers Ⓗ
This attractive stone-built 18th-century pub has a small bar with some seating and a larger restaurant area, sympathetically renovated. The deceptively large outdoor space is quiet and relaxing in the summer months, with traditional outbuildings used to host festivals and regular live music. The Wheel boasts an extensive lunch and evening food menu using locally sourced ingredients where possible, including produce from the nearby Belvoir Estate. Cask cider is often on the bar in summer. Local CAMRA Pub of the Year 2012. ᴍQⓈ◖◗🐶&P⁵–

Burbage

Lime Kilns
Watling Street, LE10 3ED (on A5 between M69 jct and A47 Dodwells roundabout)
✪ 12-3, 5.30-11; 12-11 Sat; 12-10.30 Sun ☎ (01455) 631158
⊕ limekilnsinn.co.uk
Jennings Cocker Hoop; Marston's Burton Bitter, Pedigree; guest beers Ⓗ
Situated alongside the Ashby Canal, the pub was originally an 18th-century coaching inn. It offers free moorings, a large beer garden by the canal, a children's play area and free Wi-Fi. The first floor lounge has canal views and an open fire in winter. Guest beers change regularly and real ciders include Thatchers Traditional, Cheddar Valley and Heritage. Traditional food is served, with special deals including Monday Curry Night and Pie and a Pint on Wednesday. ᴍQⓈ◖◗🐾P

Burrough on the Hill

Grant's Free House Ⓛ
4 Main Street, LE14 2JQ
✪ 5-11; 12-midnight Sat; 12-11 Sun ☎ (01664) 452141
Parish PSB, Farm Gold, Burrough Bitter, Baz's Bonce Blower Ⓗ
A 16th-century inn formerly known as the Stag & Hounds, Grant's Free House is firmly established as the home of the Parish Brewery which is located in an adjacent outbuilding. The bar is on two levels surrounding a central servery on three sides and is warmed by a real fire. Evening meals are served in the bar and restaurant to the rear which doubles as a function room. A beer festival is held annually on the late May bank holiday. ᴍQⓈ◖◗🍴P⁵–🖳(113)

Catthorpe

Cherry Tree
Main Street, LE17 6DB
✪ 12-2.30, 5-11.30 (12.30am Fri); 12-12.30am Sat; 12-11.30 Sun ☎ (01788) 860430 ⊕ cherrytree-pub.co.uk
Jennings Bitter; guest beers Ⓗ
Community free house, popular with villagers and townsfolk. Locally sourced food is served and there are changing guest beers, sometimes from the nearby Dow Bridge Brewery. Railway and aviation memorabilia adorn the walls, including a jet fighter ejection seat in the corner. The small south-facing garden overlooks the River Avon. Regular beer festivals are held. A true traditional village local. ᴍQⓈ◖◗▲♣P⁵–

Coleorton

King's Arms
187 The Moor, LE67 8GD
✪ 12-11 ☎ (01530) 815435 ⊕ kingsarmscoleorton.co.uk
Draught Bass; guest beers Ⓗ
Lively yet cosy family-run free house set in the heart of the National Forest. The manager's father owns the Tap House Brewery and a range of Tap House beers is always available. Home-made, traditional food is served daily (no meals Sun and Mon eve). Outside there is a large car park, beer garden, secure children's play area and pétanque pitch. Regular events and beer festivals are publicised on the website. ᴍQⓈ◖◗&P⁵–

Dadlington

Dog & Hedgehog Ⓛ
2 The Green, CV13 6JB (just off the green)
✪ 12-11 (4 Sun) ☎ (01455) 213151
Battlefield Henry Tudor Red Ale; Byatt's Phoenix Gold; Quartz Dadlington Hamlet Ⓗ
This friendly free house continues to build on its reputation for good ales, as well as serving the best in locally produced food in its fine restaurant. Situated in a picturesque location, the terrace and beer garden overlook the Ashby Canal and famous site of the Battle of Bosworth (1485). The bar boasts three LocAles, two rebadged for the pub – Henry Tudor is Tunnel Nelson's Column and Dadlington Hamlet is Quartz Crystal. ᴍQⓈ◖◗P🖳(86)

Diseworth

Plough Inn
33 Hall Gate, DE74 2QJ

✪ 11.30-3, 5-11; 11.30-11 Fri & Sat; 12-10.30 Sun
☎ (01332) 810333 ⊕ theploughdiseworth.com
Draught Bass; Greene King Abbot; Marston's Pedigree; guest beers Ⓗ
Situated in a village with many half-timbered buildings, this is a cosy, multi-roomed pub with parts dating back to the 13th century. Low-beamed ceilings and exposed brickwork are just some of the original features discovered during renovation work in the 1990s. There is an interesting display of old photographs of the area. Tasty home-made food is served. The spacious, well-presented beer garden is popular in summer. Joint local CAMRA Village Pub of the Year 2011. ⚙✿◑♿♣♠P↙☒

Donisthorpe

Halfway House
65 Church Street, DE12 7PX
✪ 12-11 ☎ (01530) 588783
⊕ halfwayhousedonisthorpe.com
Beer range varies Ⓗ
Traditional village inn set in the heart of Donisthorpe. One of the three oldest buildings in the village, the pub dates back hundreds of years. Recently refurbished to a high standard, it now has a public bar, lounge bar and a separate dining room, with beamed ceilings and a wood-burning fire. Home-made food is served Tuesday to Saturday. Three guest beers are available, one usually from Burton Bridge, and can be served in a taster selection of three one-third pints. Dogs are welcome. ⚙Q✿◑ ⊟P↙

Enderby

New Inn
51 High Street, LE19 4AG
✪ 12-2.30 (not Mon), 6 (5.30 Fri)-11.30; 12-3, 7-10.30 Sun
☎ (0116) 286 3126
Everards Beacon, Sunchaser, Tiger, Original, seasonal beers; guest beer Ⓗ
Friendly thatched village local dating from 1549 tucked away at the top of the High Street. Everard's first tied house, the pub is well known locally for the quality of its beer and is frequented by Everard's brewery staff. Three rooms are served by a central bar, with long-alley skittles and a snooker room to the rear. Outside there is a patio area and garden. Lunches are served Tuesday to Saturday. Q✿◑♣P↙

Fleckney

Golden Shield Ⓛ
46 Main Street, LE8 8AN
✪ 12-2.30 (not Mon & Tue), 4-11; 12-midnight Fri & Sat; 11.30-11 Sun ☎ (0116) 240 2366
Banks's Bitter; Greene King IPA, Abbot; Taylor Landlord; guest beers Ⓗ
Village pub in the heart of Leicestershire serving six real ales, including ever-changing LocAles and microbrewery beers. Home-cooked and à la carte meals are available lunchtimes Wednesday to Sunday and evenings Tuesday to Saturday – Sunday lunches are always popular. ✿◑ ⊟♣P↙☒(49B)

Gilmorton

Red Lion
Main Street, LE17 5LT

✪ 12-2 (not Mon), 5-11; 12-10.30 Sun ☎ (01455) 203564
⊕ theredliongilmorton.co.uk
Banks's Mild; Marston's Pedigree; guest beers Ⓗ
Marston's National Cask Ale Pub of the Year in 2012, this village bistro is popular with both locals and visiting diners. It is open plan, bright and spacious, with a friendly and modern feel. Two regular beers are usually available alongside up to three guest ales from the Marston's list. Food is prepared and cooked on the premises and made from local produce where possible, with herbs from the garden, home-made bread and flavoured ice creams. ⚙✿◑♿P↙

Glenfield

Forge Ⓛ
Main Street, LE3 8DG
✪ 11 (12 Sat)-11; 12-10.30 Sun ☎ (0116) 287 1702
⊕ theforgeinn.co.uk
Everards Beacon, Tiger, Original; guest beers Ⓗ
A village pub on the edge of Leicester with a warm, welcoming atmosphere. Modern British food is served in the restaurant and snacks in the bar. One or two guest beers are available, plus a changing cider, usually from a local producer. Quiz night is Sunday and there is live music on the last Friday of the month. A charity music festival is held in May. The pub has launched a Bring Back Jugs campaign. ✿◑♿♠P↙☒

Grimston

Black Horse
3 Main Street, LE14 3BZ
✪ 12-3, 6-11; 12-6 Sun ☎ (01664) 812358
⊕ theblackhorsegrimston.co.uk
Adnams Southwold Bitter; Marston's Pedigree; guest beers Ⓗ
The pub overlooks the village green and is busy both lunchtimes and evenings with a reputation for good food and ale. The cosy single-room interior is divided into three areas on two separate levels, warmed by a real fire. The garden has patio heaters and a pétanque court where local teams play. Two regular and two guest real ales are usually available. CAMRA branch Pub of the Year 2011. ⚙✿◑♣↙☒(23)

Hinckley

Ashby Road Sports & Social Club Ⓛ
Hangmans Lane, LE10 3DA (on N edge of town off B4667 Ashby Rd) SP429959
✪ 7 (5 Fri)-11; 12-11.30 Sat; 12-11 Sun ☎ (01455) 615159
Sharp's Doom Bar; guest beers Ⓗ
A regular in the Guide since 2008 and frequent winner of branch Club of the Year, this private members' club welcomes CAMRA members. The stewardess has 10 years' service. Sharp's Doom Bar is always available plus two changing guest ales, local and national, from Wednesday to Sunday. Facilities include free Wi-Fi, satellite TV for sporting fixtures, traditional games, camping, caravanning and large function rooms for hire. Easily accessible, the club has a large car park and is on three bus routes. ⛄✿♿♠P↙☒(48,81A,158)

Queen's Head Inn ♥
40 Upper Bond Street, LE10 1RJ (just beyond police station and courts)

⊘ 5-11 (midnight Fri & Sat); 12-7 Sun ☎ (01455) 632018
⊕ thequeensheadinn.co.uk
Beer range varies Ⓗ
Family-run free house serving three ever-changing real ales from national brewers. Near the town centre, on a bus route and 10 minutes' walk from the railway station, the modernised building retains many Victorian features in its four rooms. It has log fires in winter, weekly pub games, live music most weekends, big-screen TV sport and a monthly charity quiz. Current local CAMRA Pub of the Year, it offers a discount to CAMRA members.
ﯼ☺♣🖤—🖼(48,158)

Hose

Rose & Crown ♈ Ⓛ
Bolton Lane, LE14 4JE
⊘ 12-3 (not Mon & Tue), 6-10 (11 Wed & Thu; midnight Fri);
12-midnight Sat; 12-10 Sun ☎ (01949) 869458
⊕ theroseandcrownhose.co.uk
Tetley Bitter; guest beers Ⓗ
Set in the heart of the Vale of Belvoir, this 200-year-old country pub has undergone a new lease of life over the past couple of years. Six cask ales are offered, with no keg beer, and a wide-ranging food menu. The pub is a large, comfortable bar and seating area, and a separate restaurant. Outside is an attractive and spacious deck plus a paddock. Regular live music events are held through the year. Local CAMRA Pub of the Year 2013.
ﯼ☺🕦♣P

Illston on the Hill

Fox & Goose
Main Street, LE7 9EG
⊘ 6 (11 Sat)-midnight; 11-midnight (9 winter) Sun
☎ (0116) 259 6340
Everards Beacon, Tiger, seasonal beers; guest beers Ⓗ
Unique gem of a pub unscathed by the passing of time, with many artefacts including pictures of hunting scenes, McLachlan cartoons, animal traps, farming implements and various taxidermy exhibits. In 1997, when major structural work was undertaken, photographs were taken before work began to ensure that each item could be put back in exactly the same place. A conkers contest and an onion-growing competition are held annually to raise funds for charities. Evening meals are served Thursday to Saturday. Cider is available in summer.
ﯼQ☺🕦🍴♣🖤—

Kegworth

Red Lion
24 High Street, DE74 2DA
⊘ 11.30-11; 12-10.30 Sun ☎ (01509) 672466
⊕ redlionkegworth.com
**Adnams Southwold Bitter; Castle Rock Harvest Pale;
Draught Bass; Gale's HSB; Nutbrook The Mild Side** Ⓗ
Georgian building standing on the 19th-century route of the A6, with four rooms served from one bar. There are bench seats and original features including coal fires. Eight cask ales and real cider are available plus a good selection of malt whiskies. Food is served every lunchtime and weekday evenings. Outside is a large car park and garden plus a pétanque court and children's play area. En-suite accommodation is available. Local CAMRA Village Pub 2012.
ﯼQ🚌☺🖤🕦🍴♣🖤P—🖼

Knipton

Manners Arms Ⓛ
Croxton Road, NG32 1RH
⊘ 11-11; 12-10.30 Sun ☎ (01476) 879222
⊕ mannersarms.com
Batemans XXB; Fuller's London Pride; guest beer Ⓗ
Impressive former Georgian hunting lodge set in the heart of the Vale of Belvoir. The bar and lounge, with tall bookshelves and comfortable seating, are warmed by an inviting open fireplace. One long bar serves four cask ales including a mild. Light meals are available in the bar and a wide range of interesting food made with local produce is served in the restaurant. A wonderful patio and garden are ideal for lazing on a hot summer's day.
ﯼQ☺🍴🕦🍴♿P

Leicester

Ale Wagon
27 Rutland Street, LE1 1RE
⊘ 11-11; 7-10.30 Sun ☎ (0116) 262 3330 ⊕ alewagon.co.uk
Hoskins HOB, IPA Ⓗ**, Old Navigation** Ⓟ**; guest beers** Ⓗ
Run by the Hoskins family, this city-centre pub with a 1930s interior, including an original oak staircase, has two rooms with tiled and parquet floors and a central bar. There is always a selection of Hoskins Brothers ales and guests available. The pub is popular with visiting rugby fans and real ale drinkers. A function room is available to hire. Handy for the nearby Curve Theatre. ﯼ≢♣🖤🖼

Black Horse Ⓛ
65 Narrow Lane, Aylestone, LE2 8NA (400yds from St Andrew's Church)
⊘ 12-11 (midnight Fri & Sat) ☎ (0116) 283 7225
Everards Beacon, Tiger, Original; guest beers Ⓗ
A welcoming, traditional four-roomed Victorian pub in Aylestone Village Conservation Area with a distinctive bar servery. Eight real ales are always available and home-cooked food is served lunchtimes and evenings Monday to Friday, all day Saturday and Sunday. There is a large beer garden and children's play area. The skittle alley and function room are available for hire. Live music and a comedy club feature regularly plus a quiz every Sunday. Beer festivals are held and community events hosted. ﯼQ☺🕦🍴🍴♣🖤—🖼

Black Horse
1 Foxon Street, Braunstone Gate, LE3 5LT
⊘ 12-midnight ☎ (0116) 254 0046
Everards Beacon, Sunchaser, Tiger, Original; guest beers Ⓗ
The only remaining traditional pub in a street of youth-oriented bars. It has two rooms separated by a central bar, wood-panelled walls and practical furniture, providing a comfortable ambience. A real community pub, there is live music four nights a week and a quiz night on Wednesday. The guest beers are sourced through Everards and the cider is Westons Old Rosie. A large selection of whiskies and other rare spirits is available. ☺🍴♣🖤—🖼

Criterion
44 Millstone Lane, LE1 5JN
⊘ 12-11 (10.30 Sun) ☎ (0116) 262 5418
Beer range varies Ⓗ
Two-roomed 1960s city-centre pub offering up to 12 guest ales from micros and regionals at weekends. Beer festivals are held regularly, with many beers on gravity from the cellar. More than

100 international bottled beers are stocked. Darts and dominoes are played in the bar. A pop quiz is hosted on Tuesday, general knowledge quiz on Wednesday, live music on Thursday and Saturday, and it is a venue for the Leicester Comedy Festival. Pub food is available Sunday and Monday, with Italian-style pizzas Tuesday to Saturday.
&④▶♣🌢⁵⌐

King's Head
36 King Street, LE1 6RL
✪ 12-11 (midnight Fri & Sat) ☎ (0116) 254 8240
⏚ thekingsleicester.co.uk
Black Country Bradley's Finest Golden, Pig on the Wall, Fireside; guest beers Ⓗ
Small split-level one-roomed city centre local, recently bought by Black Country Ales. It is popular with real ale enthusiasts and football and rugby supporters on match days – the pub is close to the grounds. It holds regular beer festivals and has up to five regularly changing guest beers and two varying ciders. Cobs and hot snacks are available. Smokers can use the roof terrace. Access can also be gained from New Walk. ⍩&⩩⪥♣🌢⁵⌐

Old Horse
198 London Road, LE2 1NE
✪ 11-11.30 (midnight Fri & Sat; 11 Sun) ☎ (0116) 254 8384
⏚ oldhorseleicester.co.uk
Everards Beacon, Sunchaser, Tiger, Original, seasonal beers; guest beers Ⓗ
Nineteenth-century coaching inn immortalised by Michael Green in The Art of Coarse Rugby. It is popular with all sections of the community including students and the local church choir. Lots of interesting bric-a-brac hang from the ceilings. Weekly quiz nights and karaoke are held. The large garden features a children's play area, pétanque pitch, owls and a Tardis. CAMRA members receive a 10 per cent discount on beer.
&④▶&♣🌢P⁵⌐(31,31A)

Pub
12 New Walk, LE1 6TF (opp council offices)
✪ 12-11 (midnight Fri & Sat); 2-10 Sun
⏚ thepubleicester.co.uk
Beowulf Dragon Smoke Stout; Oakham Inferno; guest beers Ⓗ
Behind the small frontage lies a warm, welcoming interior with a modern bar offering a wide range of microbrewery ales and continental draught and bottled beers. The Pub is home to Leicester Morris Men and a firm favourite with rugby and football fans. LocAle breweries often feature among the 15 handpulls, supporting up to 12 changing guests. Food is served lunchtimes Monday to Saturday and evenings Tuesday to Saturday. ④▶&⪥

Salmon �
19 Butt Close Lane, LE1 4QA
✪ 12-11 (8 Mon; midnight Fri & Sat); closed Sun
☎ (0116) 253 2301
Beer range varies Ⓗ
Victorian corner back-street free house, with a friendly, welcoming atmosphere. It has a strong sports following, especially for rugby. The large, open U-shaped bar offers a selection of beers from six handpumps, mainly from microbreweries. Cellar runs are offered. One mild is usually available along with a cider. St Margaret's bus station is nearby. Local CAMRA Pub of the Year 2013.
&④🌢⁵⌐

Slug & Lettuce Ⓛ
27 Market Street, LE1 6DP
✪ 10-11 (1am Fri & Sat) ☎ (0116) 255 5370
⏚ slugandlettuce.co.uk/leicester
Oakham Inferno; Wells Bombardier; guest beers Ⓗ
A real ale establishment for everyone – young and old, families and football fans. The pub is passionate about promoting LocAle and supporting microbreweries, with three guest beers usually available. Regular beer festivals have helped the Slug cement its reputation in Leicester and beyond as a real ale pub for all who enjoy good honest beer. There is an extensive food menu with many special offers. &④▶&⪥⌐

Swan & Rushes
19 Infirmary Square, LE1 5WR
✪ 12-11 (midnight Thu-Sat; 11.30 Sun) ☎ (0116) 233 9167
⏚ swanandrushes.co.uk
Batemans XB; Oakham JHB, Bishops Farewell, seasonal beers; guest beers Ⓗ
Comfortable, triangular, two-roomed pub in the city centre with a relaxed atmosphere, filled with breweriana and framed photos on the wall. Up to nine real ales are available and a changing real cider, and the bottled beer menu features more than 100 international classics. Home-made pizzas are served. Several food-linked beer festivals are held each year plus cider and cheese events. Thursday is quiz night, open mic is the second Wednesday of the month and live gigs take place on some Saturdays. &④▶⊞♣🌢⁵⌐

Tom Hoskins
131 Beaumanor Road, LE4 5QE
✪ 12-11.30 (midnight Fri); 10.30-midnight Sat; 10.30-11.30 Sun ☎ (0116) 266 9659
Banks's Mild; Brains Bitter; Greene King IPA; guest beers Ⓗ
Hospitable, two-room, city-suburbs pub catering for the mature drinker. Between four and six ales are always available, including a mild and changing guest beers. If you are hungry there are freshly made cobs. Darts is played in the bar and the pub is popular with local football and rugby teams. Regular Sunday evening quiz nights are held. A barber is available Thursday and Friday afternoons and Saturday and Sunday mornings. &⊞&♣P⁵⌐

Western
70 Western Road, LE3 0GA
✪ 12-midnight (1am Fri & Sat) ☎ (0116) 254 5287
Steamin' Billy Tipsy Fisherman, Bitter, Skydiver Ⓗ; **guest beers** Ⓗ/Ⓖ
Traditional local in a residential location with a bar and lounge, popular with a good mixed clientele of all ages. Up to five guest beers are available, mainly from microbreweries. Old pub signs decorate the walls. The pub gets busy on football match days. ⍩&④⊞♣🌢⁵⌐

Long Whatton

Royal Oak
26 The Green, LE12 5DB
✪ 12-11 (midnight Fri & Sat) ☎ (01509) 843694
⏚ theroyaloaklongwhatton.co.uk
Draught Bass; St Austell Tribute; Sharp's Doom Bar; guest beers Ⓗ
Tastefully modernised, award-winning gastro-pub welcoming real ale drinkers and diners alike.

Regularly changing guest beers usually include one from Blue Monkey. The owners are passionate about their ale and hold two beer festivals a year. Local produce is used to create an interesting menu including 'nip & tuck' – four nips of beer and locally-produced nibbles on a platter. Convenient for East Midlands airport and Donington race circuit, accommodation is available in a separate building. Local CAMRA Village Pub 2011. ⬤✿🏮◗🔥🅿️⸗🚻

Loughborough

Generous Briton
85 Ashby Road, LE11 3AB
⬤ 12-11 (midnight Fri & Sat) ☎ (01509) 263565
🌐 bogiespubs.co.uk
Black Sheep Best Bitter; Castle Rock Harvest Pale; Oakham Citra; Taylor Landlord; guest beers Ⓗ
Reopened in 2011 as a genuine free house, the GB is ideally situated between the town centre and university. The traditional bar has a dartboard and features old local photographs; the lounge has a pool table and jukebox. Satellite sport is shown throughout. A limited food menu is available but customers are welcome to bring their own food. There is an enclosed beer garden to the rear and families are welcome until 7.45pm. Joint local CAMRA Most Improved Pub 2011, Town Pub 2011 and 2012, and Pub of the Year 2012.
⬤✿🏮♣🔥⸗🚻(126)

Organ Grinder 🍷
4 Woodgate, LE11 2TY
⬤ 12-11 ☎ (01509) 264008
Blue Monkey BG Sips, Guerilla, Infinity; guest beers Ⓗ
Previously known as the Pack Horse, bought by Blue Monkey in 2012, the pub has received a top-to-bottom renovation, uncovering lots of interesting original features. There is a new stable bar at the back, reflecting the pub's past life as a coaching inn. Eight cask ales are always available – seven rotating Blue Monkey beers and one from Batemans. There is also a choice of two real ciders and a perry, as well as Belgian bottled beers. CAMRA branch Most Improved Pub 2012 and Pub of the Year 2013. ⬤✿🔥🅿️⸗🚻

Paget Arms
41 Oxford Street, LE11 5DP
⬤ 12-midnight ☎ (01509) 266216
Steamin' Billy Bitter, Skydiver; guest beers Ⓗ/Ⓖ
Located on a corner at the end of a row of terraced houses, this former Everard's pub has been refurbished and is now one of Steamin' Billy's locals. Six real ales include at least two from Steamin' Billy. It is a popular student pub but attracts a mix of drinkers. Home-cooked food includes pizzas and doorstep sandwiches. There are two attractive rooms with ample seating, and a large, enclosed garden with a heated, covered area for smokers. ⬤✿◗🟦♣🔥⸗

Tap & Mallet
36 Nottingham Road, LE11 1EU
⬤ 7 (5 Tue & Thu; 12 Sat; 3.30 Sun)-2am ☎ (01509) 210028
Abbeydale Deception; Batemans Dark Mild, XB; guest beers Ⓗ
Genuine free house specialising in beers from microbreweries not commonly found in the Loughborough area, plus seasonal brews from Abbeydale and Oakham. The large single-room interior is divided into two distinct drinking areas – a public bar with pool table, darts and boxed

games, and a quieter lounge area that can be partitioned off for functions. Outside there is a large, secluded lawned garden and patio area with children's play equipment and pets' corner. Westons cider is available. ⬤✿≷♣🔥⸗🚻

Lutterworth

Fox
34 Rugby Road, LE17 4BN
⬤ 12 (5 Mon)-midnight (1am Fri & Sat) ☎ (01455) 550935
Draught Bass; Sharp's Doom Bar; guest beers Ⓗ
Situated half a mile from the M1 and close to the replica Sir Frank Whittle jet aircraft, this popular pub offers a warm welcome. The L-shaped open-plan interior is warmed by real fires. Four beers are available including two regularly changing guests. Food is served lunchtimes – the Sunday roasts are excellent. A function room hosts bands and private parties. A big attraction is the award-winning landscaped garden and outside drinking area. ⬤✿◗🅿️⸗🚻

Greyhound
High Street, LE17 4EJ
⬤ 6.30-11 ☎ (01455) 553307 🌐 greyhoundinn.co.uk
Beer range varies Ⓗ
Situated on the main thoroughfare, this Grade II-listed coach house hotel dates from 1758. You can be sure of a warm welcome on entering the smart reception lounge, with period-style furnishings, nautical pictures, old clocks and original features. The bar area has a wood block floor. Food is served in the plush restaurant and there is an outside paved courtyard for summer drinks. The beer range includes three frequently changing microbrews. A popular venue for private parties and weddings. Q✿🏮◗🟦⸗🚻

Unicorn
29 Church Street, LE17 4AE
⬤ 10.30-11 (midnight Thu-Sat); 12-11 Sun
☎ (01455) 552486
Adnams Broadside; Draught Bass; Greene King IPA; guest beer Ⓗ
Traditional street-corner local built in 1919 on the site of an 18th-century coach house. A busy and friendly community pub, it supports a number of league teams and games are played in the bar including table skittles. The small, comfortable lounge has photographs of old Lutterworth and doubles as a family-friendly dining area for good inexpensive lunchtime food including vegetarian and children's options. There is a small car park at the rear. ⬤🛏️◗🟦♣🅿️⸗🚻

Manton

Horse & Jockey Ⓛ
St Marys Road, LE15 8SU
⬤ 11 (12 Sun)-11 ☎ (01572) 737335
🌐 horseandjockeyrutland.co.uk
Grainstore Fall at the First; Greene King IPA Ⓗ
A warm welcome to this lovely traditional pub new to the Guide. It gets very busy in the summer with a great position near Rutland Water and on the Rutland Water Cycle Route. Good-quality home-cooked food is available every day. The pub is home to Rutland Morris and Jason, the landlord, is a tourism representative for the county. Dominoes and quiz nights feature regularly.
⬤🛏️✿🏮◗🟦♣🅿️⸗🚻(1)

Market Harborough

Admiral Nelson
49 Nelson Street, LE16 9AX
❸ 5 (3 Fri; 12 Sat)-midnight; 12-11 Sun ☎ (01858) 433173
Wells Eagle IPA, Bombardier; guest beers ⊞
Welcoming, friendly locals' pub, built in 1900, a
short stroll from the centre of the historic market
town. Just off the beaten track, this pub is the
town's best-kept secret, offering a lounge with TV
(where they like their rugby) and bar with darts,
pool, jukebox and another TV. A function room is
available. Outside is a heated and covered smoking
area with seating. Dogs are welcome. ⊛🖺♣🅿🚾

Cherry Tree
Church Walk, Kettering Road, Little Bowden, LE16 8AE
❸ 12-2.30, 5-11; 12-11.30 Fri & Sat; 12-10.30 Sun
☎ (01858) 463525
Everards Beacon, Sunchaser, Tiger, Original; guest
beers ⊞
Although this pub is situated in Little Bowden, it is
very much part of the Market Harborough
community. A spacious building with low beams
and a thatched roof, it has many alcoves and
seating areas for drinkers and diners to choose
from. Outside is a large garden with children's play
area. A beer festival is held over the August bank
holiday. Guest beers are from the Everard's list. No
food Sunday or Monday evenings. 🐕⊛🕪🚲♣🚾

Sugar Loaf
18 High Street, LE16 7NJ
❸ 8-11 (midnight Tue-Thu; 1am Fri & Sat) ☎ (01858) 469231
Greene King Abbot; Ruddles Best Bitter; Shepherd
Neame Spitfire; guest beers ⊞
Originally a grocery store, the old grocer's chair
remains at this Wetherspoon establishment. Guest
beers are from near and far, including
microbreweries. The choice of cider varies from
time to time. Quiz nights are held on the first,
second and third Wednesday of the month. The
pub acts as an agent for local musical theatre.
Families are welcome until 9pm. 🐕🕪♿🌭🚲

Melton Mowbray

Anne of Cleves Ⓛ
12 Burton Street, LE13 1AE (just S of St Mary's Church)
❸ 11-11 (midnight Fri & Sat); 12-10.30 Sun
☎ (01664) 481336 ⊕ theanneofcleves.co.uk
Everards Tiger, Original; guest beers ⊞
One of Melton Mowbray and Everard's most
historic pubs and an icon for the town. Part of the
property dates back to 1327 when it was home to
monks. The house was gifted to Anne of Cleves by
Henry VIII as part of her divorce settlement. It is
now a popular hostelry following a sympathetic
restoration in 1996. It has stone-flagged floors,
exposed timber beams and tapestries throughout.
The beer garden recently won an East Midlands in
Bloom award. ᄴQ⊛🕪🚲🌭🅿🚾(5)

Boat ⚑
57 Burton Street, LE13 1AF
❸ 11-3 (not Mon), 5-midnight; 11-midnight Thu-Sat;
12-midnight Sun ☎ (01664) 500969
Draught Bass; Theakston Best Bitter; Wells
Bombardier; guest beer ⊞
A classic single-roomed pub that takes its name
from a canal basin that was once adjacent. The
walls are decorated with old pictures of the town
and a map of the old Melton-Oakham canal whose

workers this establishment once served. The pub is
always busy with mature drinkers and local darts
teams who enjoy good conversation with their
pint. A range-style open fire gives plenty of
warmth in winter. ᄴ🚲🚾(5)

Mountsorrel

Swan Inn
10 Loughborough Road, LE12 7AT
❸ 12-2.30, 5.30-11; 12-11 Sat; 12-10.30 Sun
☎ (0116) 230 2340 ⊕ the-swan-inn.eu
Black Sheep Best Bitter; Ruddles County; Theakston
XB, Old Peculier; guest beers ⊞
Traditional 17th-century, Grade II-listed coaching
inn. The split-level interior has open fires, stone
floors and low ceilings, and includes a small dining
area with a polished wood floor. Good quality,
interesting food is cooked to order, with the menu
changing weekly, and monthly themed nights.
Outside is a secluded riverside garden with
moorings. ᄴ⊛🕪🅿🚾

Oadby

Cow & Plough
Gartree Road, LE2 2FB
❸ 11-11 ☎ (0116) 271 2616
Fuller's London Pride; Steamin' Billy Bitter, Skydiver;
guest beers ⊞
Situated in a converted farm building with a
conservatory, the pub is decked out with
breweriana. It is home to Steamin' Billy beers
named after the owner's now departed Jack Russell
who features on the logo and pump clips. A mild
and cider are always available. A restaurant has
been added in the former dairy buildings.
🐕⊛🕪🖺♿♣🌭🅿🚾

Lord Keeper of the Great Seal
96-100 The Parade, LE2 5BF
❸ 7am-midnight ☎ (0116) 272 0957
Greene King Abbot; Ruddles Best Bitter; guest
beers ⊞
Named after Sir Nathan Wright, a local landowner
who held this position in the 17th century, this
typical Wetherspoon conversion of a row of shops
stands on the site of Sandhurst Infants School. It
features pictures of old buildings and industries of
Oadby and a varied library of books. Regular beer
festivals and charity events are held. Families are
welcome until 9pm. 🐕⊛🕪♿🌭🚾(31,31A)

Oakham

Grainstore Ⓛ
Station Approach, LE15 6RE (next to station)
❸ 11-11 (midnight Fri & Sat) ☎ (01572) 770065
⊕ grainstorebrewery.com
Grainstore Rutland Panther, Cooking, Rutland Bitter,
Triple B, 1050, seasonal beers ⊞
A pub and brewery in a cleverly converted small
warehouse over four floors, retaining some original
features. Brewery tours are available but must be
booked in advance. The beer range always includes
a mild, and a range of bottle-conditioned Belgian
beers is also stocked. Home-made food is served at
lunchtime. Live bands feature regularly during the
month. An annual beer festival is held over the
August bank holiday. Dog- and walker-friendly.
Q⊛🕪♿🚲♣🅿🚾

Lord Nelson L

11 Market Place, LE15 6DT

✪ 9am (11 Sun)-11 ☎ (01572) 868340

⊕ thelordnelsonoakham.com

Castle Rock Harvest Pale; guest beers Ⓗ

A sympathetic refurbishment of Nick's Restaurant in the corner of the marketplace. Part of the Thurlby Group of pubs, the Lord Nelson is a traditional-looking example of a pub in a traditional town. It serves good quality beer and has become a new addition to the county's real ale circuit. Good-quality home-cooked food is available daily. A regular quiz night is hosted. ⚌Q❶❀₤≠⊟(1)

White Lion Hotel

30 Melton Road, LE15 6AY

✪ 12-3 (not Mon), 6-midnight ☎ (01572) 724844

Fuller's London Pride; guest beers Ⓗ

A repeat entry in the Guide confirms that standards, choice and hospitality have been maintained at the White Lion. A must-visit inn for home-made traditional food – make sure you are hungry as one size fits all. Beer is always of top quality and the guests change regularly, often from Blue Monkey or Ossett breweries. Old-fashioned standards are upheld, with the landlord in collar and tie and Bruce, the peanut-eating pet, giving you a smile. ⚌❀❦❶≒♣P≟⊟

Old Dalby

Sample Cellar L

Belvoir Brewery, Station Road, LE14 3NQ

✪ 12-10 (8 Sun) ☎ (01664) 823455 ⊕ belvoirbrewery.co.uk

Belvoir Dark Horse, Beaver Bitter, seasonal beers Ⓗ

The brick-fronted Sample Cellar on the outskirts of the village incorporates a bar, function room and visitors' centre, with brewery tours available by arrangement. The comfortable, spacious interior, filled with brewing artefacts, has a traditional bar area, with room for long-alley skittles and a bar billiards table. Two large internal windows provide views into the brewery. A full menu is served daily, with the focus on good wholesome food made with local produce. Local CAMRA Pub of the Year 2011. ❀❶❀♣P≟

Plungar

Anchor L

Granby Lane, NG13 0JJ

✪ 12-3 (not Mon-Fri), 6-11 Sat; 12-10.30 Sun

☎ (01949) 860589

Welbeck Abbey Red Feather; guest beers Ⓗ

This brick building in the middle of a small Leicestershire village dates from 1774. At one time the local courtroom, the interior now comprises a large bar and lounge area, a separate restaurant and a pool room. Outside is an attractive beer garden and seating area. The Anchor has developed a reputation for serving a good variety of food, using locally sourced ingredients. The range of quality ales includes at least one and sometimes all local brewery beers. ⚌Q❀❶≒♣P

Quorn

Manor House

Woodhouse Road, LE12 8AL

✪ 12-11 (midnight Sat; 10 Sun) ☎ (01509) 413416

⊕ themanorhouseatquorn.co.uk

Batemans XB; Draught Bass; Taylor Landlord; guest beers Ⓗ

Built in 1899 by the Great Central Railway, the Manor House was designed to serve passengers arriving at Quorn & Woodhouse Station, which it still does today – the preserved steam- and diesel-hauled trains pass by 200 yards from the door. The building was refurbished in 2005 and now has an open-plan bar and award-winning restaurant with a separate function/meeting room available to hire. A free house, two guest beers are available during the week and three at weekends. CAMRA members receive a discount. ❀❶❦≒⇌P⊟

Sewstern

Blue Dog

46 Main Street, NG33 5RQ

✪ 11-11; 12-10.30 Sun ☎ (01476) 860097

Black Sheep Best Bitter; guest beers Ⓗ

Friendly and welcoming pub west of the village, handy for walkers at the southern end of the Viking Way. The unusual name reflects the tradition of local farm workers on the Tollemache estate being paid partly in blue tokens. The 300-year-old building was once a war hospital and has a ghost – a drummer boy called Albert. Microbreweries are often represented among the guest ales, and a beer festival is held in May. Wednesday is fish and chips night. ⚌Q❂❀❶⊞♣P≟⊟(55,56)

Shackerstone

Rising Sun L

Church Road, CV13 6NN SK374066

✪ 11-2.30, 6-midnight; 11.30-midnight Sat & Sun

☎ (01827) 880215 ⊕ risingsunpub.com

Grays Celtic Gold; Marston's Pedigree; Taylor Landlord; guest beers Ⓗ

Traditional family-owned free house in the heart of Shackerstone village near the Ashby Canal and the preserved Battlefield Railway. It has a wood-panelled bar serving traditional ales, restaurant, pool room with Sky Sports, family-friendly conservatory and an attractive garden. The pub, popular with locals and visitors alike, is renowned for the quality and variety of its ales and serves good pub food – the ideal hub for visiting this rural part of Leicestershire. ⚌Q❂❀❶⊞❦♣●P≟

Shearsby

Chandlers Arms ♥ L

Fenny Lane, LE17 6PL (close to A5199)

✪ 12-3 (not Mon), 7 (6 Fri)-11; 12-4, 6-11 Sat; 12-4, 7-10.30 Sun ☎ (0116) 247 8384 ⊕ chandlersatshearsby.co.uk

Dow Bridge Acris; guest beers Ⓗ

Classic, quaint old country pub overlooking the village green. Popular with walkers, cyclists, diners and visitors from the city, it also has strong local support. It was the first pub in CAMRA's Leicester branch to be accredited to the LocAle scheme. Microbrewery beers are always on the bar, often locally sourced. Draught cider is available in summer. No food is served Sunday evening or Monday. Local CAMRA County Pub of the Year 2013 – for the fifth year in succession. ❀❶♣●P≟

Shepshed

Black Swan

21 Loughborough Road, LE12 9DL

✪ 6 (5.30 Tue-Thu; 4 Fri; 1.30 Sat; 12 Sun)-1.30am
☎ (01509) 502659
Adnams Broadside; Draught Bass; Taylor Landlord; guest beers Ⓗ
Multi-roomed pub situated in a prominent position close to the town centre, offering two guest beers alongside the regulars. The main room has two drinking areas, both with comfortable seating. A further small room can be used by families. The upstairs restaurant serves good-quality food. Shepshed Dynamo football ground is nearby.
ᴀᴀQ✿⊛◖◐P⁵⌐⊟

Sileby

Horse & Trumpet
4 Barrow Road, LE12 7LP
✪ 12-midnight (11 Sun) ☎ (01509) 812549
Belvoir Dark Horse; Steamin' Billy Tipsy Fisherman, Bitter, Skydiver; guest beers Ⓗ
This multi-room pub with open fires has undergone a huge transformation since becoming part of the Steamin' Billy chain. Two guest beers are on offer plus a real cider and perry. No hot food is served but cobs are available and there is a monthly curry club. Open mic nights feature weekly and jazz nights monthly. Well-behaved dogs are welcome in the bar and seating area outside.
ᴀᴀ⊛≈♣◖P⁵⌐⊟(2)

Somerby

Stilton Cheese Ⓛ
High Street, LE14 2QB
✪ 12-3, 6 (7 Sun)-11 ☎ (01664) 454394
⊕ stiltoncheeseinn.co.uk
Grainstore Ten Fifty; Marston's Burton Bitter; guest beers Ⓗ
Late 16th-century pub built in local ironstone, like most of the buildings in the village. The interior comprises two bars and a function room. Five ales are usually served up, with local breweries well represented. On purchasing their drinks, tall customers should take care not to bump their heads on the low beam adorned with a wide range of pump clips. Look out for the large stuffed pike mounted on the wall. An ideal place to stop off for lunch while walking the Leicestershire Round.
ᴀᴀQ✿⊛◖P⊟(113)

Stoke Golding

George & Dragon Ⓛ
Station Road, CV13 6EZ SP396971
✪ closed Mon; 12-3, 6-11; 12-11 Fri & Sat; 12-10.30 Sun
☎ (01455) 213268
Church End Gravediggers Ale, What The Fox's Hat, Stout Coffin, Fallen Angel; guest beer Ⓗ
The Church End Brewery chose this Georgian building for its first pub in 2011. Following refurbishment, the interior is traditional with a snug and small library. The bar boasts a spread of Church End ales with four regular beers, three more chosen from the brewery's extensive range and

> Not all chemicals are bad. Without chemicals such as hydrogen and oxygen, for example, there would be no way to make water, a vital ingredient in beer.
> **Dave Barry**

one guest. Excellent locally sourced bar food is served at lunchtimes Tuesday-Saturday, including Leicestershire's famous pork pies and cheeses.
ᴀᴀQ✿⊛◖⊞♣◖P⁵⌐⊟(86)

Swinford

Chequers
High Street, LE17 6BL
✪ 12-2.30 (not Mon), 7-midnight; 12-3, 7-11 Sun
☎ (01788) 860318 ⊕ chequersswinford.co.uk
Adnams Southwold Bitter; guest beers Ⓗ
Open-plan village local, popular with families. The bar has wooden floors, a woodburner for winter and a skittles table at one end, with pictures of the village on the walls throughout. The large garden is popular in the summer and hosts the annual worm-charming championship. A large marquee in the car park is used for events during the year. The 16th-century Stanford Hall is nearby.
ᴀᴀ✿⊛◖♣P⁵⌐⊟

Swithland

Griffin Inn
174 Main Street, LE12 8TJ
✪ 9-11.30 (11 Sun) ☎ (01509) 890535
⊕ griffininnswithland.co.uk
Everards Beacon, Tiger, Original; guest beers Ⓗ
Welcoming local with three comfortable rooms. Set in the heart of Charnwood Forest, there are many walking and cycling routes nearby. Swithland Reservoir, Bradgate Park and the preserved Great Central Railway are also close. Alongside the regular food menu, light snacks are available every afternoon including Melton Mowbray pork pies. Guest ales are chosen from Everard's Old English Ale Club, with three frequently stocked in addition to the regulars. ᴀᴀQ⊛◖⅃Ⴋ⅄♣P⁵⌐⊟

Syston

Syston & District Social Club Ⓛ
36 High Street, LE7 1GP
✪ 7.30-11; 12-2.30, 5.30-midnight Fri; 12-midnight Sat; 12-4, 7-11 Sun ☎ (0116) 260 9086 ⊕ systonsocial.co.uk
Banks's Mild, Bitter; guest beers Ⓗ
Formerly the Bull's Head, this club is home to many local societies and sports teams including darts, crib, skittles and chess. It has a large function room, available to hire. The range of six beers includes four regularly changing guests, often from microbreweries or from the Marston's list. An annual beer festival is held in June. Show your CAMRA membership card or a copy of this Guide for entry. ⊛Ⴋ≈♣⊟(5A)

Thrussington

Blue Lion
5 Rearsby Road, LE7 4UD
✪ 12-2.30 (not Wed; 4 Sat), 5.30-11; 12-5, 7-10.30 Sun
☎ (01664) 424266
Marston's Burton Bitter, Pedigree, seasonal beers; guest beers Ⓗ
This late 18th-century rural inn was once two cottages. Good-value pub grub, featuring meat supplied by the local butcher, is served in the comfortable lounge. However, the bar is the heart of the hostelry, where locals meet for darts and dominoes matches, kept under control by licensees Mandy and Bob. ᴀᴀQ◖◐⊞Ⴋ⅄♣P⊟

Thurlaston

Elephant & Castle 🅛

26 Main Street, LE9 7TP SP502990
☼ 12-2.30 (not Mon & Tue), 6-11; 12-3, 7-10.30 Sun
☎ (01455) 888213
Everards Beacon, Tiger, Original; guest beers 🅗
A regular in the Guide, this friendly local inn is set
in the heart of the village. The pub's ales benefit
from the landlord's national awards in
cellarmanship. It offers three Everard's beers and
two rotating guests, plus a real cider. Beer festivals
are held twice a year. The refurbished front lounge
has a logburner, and to the rear is a restaurant/
lounge. Outside is a children's play area, patio and
car park. Walking and cycle routes pass the pub.
The landlady's speciality home-made pies and
good-value Sunday lunches are a treat.
Q✆🏵🕔🅲👶♣👜P⅄-🖼(148)

Uppingham

Crown Inn 🅛

19 High Street East, LE15 9PY
☼ 11-11; 11.30-10.30 Sun ☎ (01572) 822302
⊕ thecrownrutland.co.uk
Everards Tiger, Original, seasonal beers; guest beer 🅗
A warm welcome is assured at this traditional
market-town pub dating from 1739. Recently
refurbished, it offers up to seven ales and good-
quality, home-cooked food in the bar and
restaurant. Live music plays monthly or more often
and a beer festival is held every April over St
George's Day. The pub is home to a local dominoes
team. En-suite accommodation is available. Winner
of seven CAMRA awards including local CAMRA Pub
of the Year 2011 and runner-up 2013.
🏵🕔🅲👶♣👜P⅄-🖼(1,12,747)

Walton on the Wolds

Anchor Inn

2 Loughborough Road, LE12 8HT
☼ 12-3 (not Mon), 7-11; 12-10.30 Sun ☎ (01509) 880018
Adnams Southwold Bitter; Black Sheep Best Bitter;
Fuller's London Pride; Taylor Landlord; guest beer 🅗
The pub is situated in the centre of a small village
within easy reach of Leicester and Nottingham. It's
a popular venue for walkers who stop for a well-
earned home-cooked lunch in front of the log fire.
There is a food menu to suit all tastes alongside an
extensive specials board. Outside is an elevated

seating area to the front and a garden and large car
park to the rear. En-suite B&B accommodation is
available. 🏵🕔🅲🕕P🖼

Whitwick

Three Horseshoes ★

11 Leicester Road, LE67 5GN
☼ 11-3, 6.30-11; 12-2, 7-10.30 Sun ☎ (01530) 837311
Draught Bass; Marston's Pedigree 🅗
Identified by CAMRA as one of Britain's Best Real
Heritage Pubs, the Three Horseshoes is nicknamed
'Polly's' after a former landlady, Polly Burton. The
pub was originally two separate buildings but now
has two rooms. To the left is a long bar with a
quarry-tiled floor and open fires, wooden bench
seating and pre-war fittings; to the right is a
similarly furnished small snug. 🏵Q🅲♣🖼

Wigston

William Wygston

84 Leicester Road, LE18 1DR
☼ 9am-midnight ☎ (0116) 288 8397
Greene King Abbot; Ruddles Best Bitter; guest
beers 🅗
Classic Wetherspoon establishment named after
William Wygston (1456-1536), an extremely
wealthy wool merchant, philanthropist, MP, and
twice mayor of Leicester. Staffed by an efficient,
friendly and helpful team of employees, it offers an
ever-changing array of guest beers, often from
local breweries Grainstore, Langton and Shardlow.
Interesting pictures depicting bygone Wigston and
Leicester adorn the walls. ✆🕕🕔👜🖼

Wymeswold

Three Crowns 🅛

45 Far Street, LE12 6TZ
☼ 12-11 ☎ (01509) 880153
Adnams Southwold Bitter; Marston's Pedigree; guest
beers 🅗
Late 18th-century pub standing opposite the
church. This friendly village local features a
beamed ceiling in the bar and a split-level snug/
lounge. Guest beers are usually from local
breweries including Castle Rock, Belvoir or
Nottingham. Regular quiz nights and live music are
hosted. A function room is available to hire. There
is a daytime bus service. 🏵Q✆🏵🕕👶♣P⅄-🖼

The sign of the Bell

Mr Jones and Partridge travelled on to Gloucester. Being arrived here, they chose for
their house of entertainment the sign of the Bell; an excellent house, and which I do most
seriously recommend to every reader who shall visit this ancient city. The master of it is
brother to the great preacher, Whitfield, but is absolutely untainted with the pernicious
principles of Methodism, or of any other heretical sect. He is indeed a very honest, plain
man, and in my opinion not likely to create any disturbance either in Church or State. His
wife hath, I believe, had much pretension to beauty, and is still a very fine woman. Her
person and deportment might have made a shining figure in the politest assemblies; but
though she must be conscious of this and many other perfections, she seems perfectly
contented with, and resigned to the state of life to which she is called – To be concise,
she is a very friendly, good-natured woman; and so industrious to oblige that the guests
must be of a very morose disposition who are not extremely well satisfied in her house.
Henry Fielding (1707-54), The History of Tom Jones, 1749

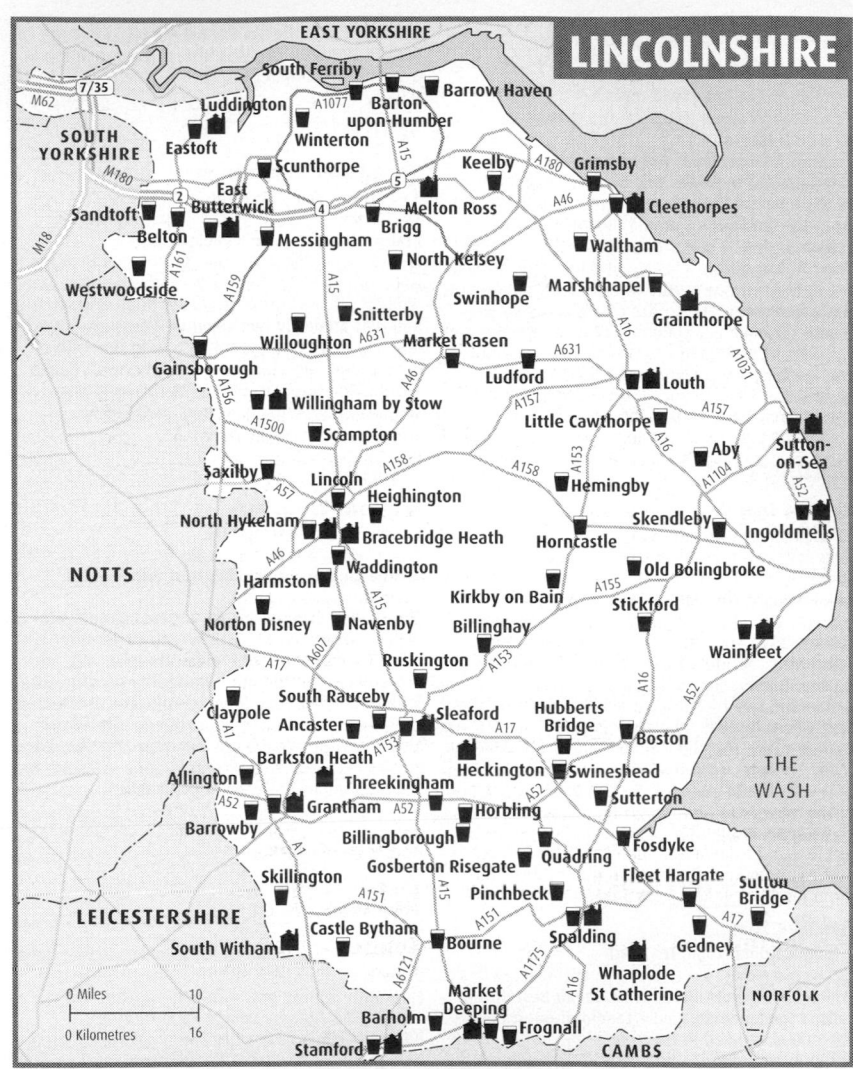

LINCOLNSHIRE

EAST YORKSHIRE

South Ferriby
7/35
M62
Luddington A1077 Barton-upon-Humber Barrow Haven
SOUTH YORKSHIRE
Eastoft Winterton
M180
Scunthorpe A15 Keelby A180 Grimsby
East Butterwick
Sandtoft A46 Cleethorpes
Belton Messingham Brigg Melton Ross
M18 North Kelsey Waltham
Westwoodside A161 A159 A15 Swinhope Marshchapel
Snitterby Grainthorpe
Willoughton A631 Market Rasen A631 A1031
Gainsborough A156 Ludford Louth
Willingham by Stow A157 Little Cawthorpe A157 Aby Sutton-on-Sea
A1500 Scampton A52
Saxilby A57 A158 A158 A153 Hemingby A1104
Lincoln Heighington A16
North Hykeham Skendleby Ingoldmells
Bracebridge Heath Horncastle
NOTTS A46 Waddington Old Bolingbroke
Harmston A15 Kirkby on Bain A155 Stickford
Norton Disney Navenby Billinghay
A17 A607 Ruskington A153 Wainfleet
South Rauceby A16 A52
Claypole Sleaford Hubberts Bridge
Ancaster A17 Boston
Barkston Heath A153 THE WASH
Allington Heckington Swineshead
A52 Threekingham A52 Sutterton
Barrowby Grantham A52 Horbling
Billingborough Fosdyke
Skillington Gosberton Risegate Quadring Fleet Hargate Sutton Bridge
A151 A15 Pinchbeck A151 A17
LEICESTERSHIRE Castle Bytham
South Witham Bourne Spalding Gedney
A6121 Whaplode
0 Miles 10 Market Deeping A16 St Catherine NORFOLK
0 Kilometres 16 Barholm Frognall
Stamford CAMBS

Aby

Railway Tavern
Main Road, LN13 0DR (off A16 via S Thoresby)
☼ 12-midnight (closed Tue winter) ☎ (01507) 480676
Beer range varies ⒣
Cosy village pub worth searching out for its varied beer list and excellent food. A real community pub with a warm welcome for all, it has an open fire and a Wednesday quiz night. Dogs are permitted and there are plenty of good walks close by. Food is home-made with locally sourced ingredients to the Taste of Lincolnshire standard, and is usually available until 8.30pm. ♨Q☼⒤♿🅰♣P⅃

Allington

Welby Arms
The Green, NG32 2EA (1 mile from A1 Gonerby Moor jct or A52)
☼ 12-2.30, 6-11; 12-10.30 Sun ☎ (01400) 281361
⊕ thewelbyarmsallington.com

Jennings Cumberland Ale; John Smith's Bitter; Taylor Landlord; guest beers ⒣
By the village green, this welcoming, cosy village pub is the ideal base from which to explore the local attractions of Belvoir Castle and Belton House. The en-suite accommodation overlooks the enclosed rear patio area, while the bar serving six real ales has guest ales listed on the blackboard. The bar is split into three areas, with a separate restaurant. The pub holds a quiz on the third Monday of the month. ♨Q☼🛏⒤♿P⅃

Ancaster

Ancaster Sports & Social Club
Ermine Street, NG32 3PW
☼ 7 (12 Sat)-11; 12-10.30 Sun ☎ (01400) 230896
John Smith's Bitter; guest beer ⒣
Voted local CAMRA Club of the Year 2012 and 2013 and 2012 Lincolnshire Club of the Year, this village venue is home to numerous sporting teams and hosts local cup finals. The excellent well-kept John Smith's is supplemented by different guest beers.

There is an airy conservatory and an outside seating area overlooking the sports pitches. 🕹♣P⅄

Barholm

Five Horseshoes Ⓛ
Main Street, PE9 4RA
🟢 4 (1 Sat)-11; 12-10.30 Sun ☎ (01778) 560238
Adnams Southwold Bitter; Oakham JHB; guest beers Ⓗ
A limestone cottage pub with a traditional atmosphere (and no jukebox), comprising two bars, two side rooms and a TV/pool room. An open fire burns throughout the winter and there are stuffed birds on display. Outside there is a garden, a kids' play area and a car park. Barbecues and music events are held in the summer. Six handpumps dispense a regularly changing range of beers by local and regional microbreweries.
🏚Q🕹🕹♣P⅄

Barrow Haven

Haven Inn Ⓛ
Ferry Road, DN19 7EX (approx 1½ miles E of Barrow-upon-Humber) TA063230
🟢 11.30-11.30 ☎ (01469) 530247 🌐 thehaveninn.co.uk
Black Sheep Best Bitter; Taylor Landlord; guest beers Ⓗ
Built in 1730 as a coaching inn for travellers using the nearby ferry, it has remained a place renowned for hospitality, good food and comfortable lodgings ever since. Full of character, the bars have traditional beamed ceilings, with a warm welcome by the open fire in the lounge. Themed food events, such as pie and steak nights, are popular. A great pub for dining and drinking, with quality wine and good beer including guest ales often from local breweries. 🏚🕹🕹🕹♣P⅄

Barrowby

White Swan
High Road, NG32 1BH
🟢 12-midnight (1am Fri & Sat) ☎ (01476) 562735
Adnams Southwold Bitter; Sharp's Doom Bar; guest beer Ⓗ
The landlord is a CAMRA member who has just celebrated 20 years as licensee at this traditional village inn, a former local CAMRA Pub of the Year. It has separate bar and lounge areas and a large beer garden. The pub plays host to local cribbage, darts, football and cricket teams. Many local groups meet here including folk (on the second Thursday of the month) and astronomy (Friday). Quiz night is on the first Sunday of the month. 🏚🕹🕹♣P⅄

Barton-upon-Humber

Stables
6A Holydyke, DN18 5PS
🟢 12-2, 5-9; 12-11 Sat & Sun ☎ (01652) 660789
🌐 stablesinbarton.co.uk
Beer range varies Ⓗ
Predominantly a dining establishment, but definitely worth a visit to sample the well-kept and interesting ales. The enthusiastic manager sources beers locally, with a Wold Top ale often one of the two draught beers on offer. The upper level here is dedicated to relaxed dining, but the lower level has some seating just for drinking. Be warned:

weekend evenings are busy and standing may be the only option. However there are plans to create more seating. 🕹🕹🕹🕹(350)

Belton

Crown
Church Lane, Churchtown, DN9 1PA (off A161, behind church)
🟢 12-midnight (1.30am Fri & Sat) ☎ (01427) 872834
Batemans XB; Bradfield Farmer's Blonde; Jennings Cocker Hoop; guest beers Ⓗ
Difficult to find but well worth the effort, this hidden gem is a haven for the discerning drinker. Six cask ales are always on offer, including a rotating guest beer from the nearby Glentworth Brewery. Quizzes, live music and pub games are enjoyed at this friendly local, which also holds occasional beer festivals. Winner of local CAMRA District Pub of the Year for 2013. 🏚🕹🕹♣P⅄(399)

Billingborough

Fortescue Arms
27 High Street, NG34 0QB
🟢 12-3, 5.30-11; 12-11 Sat & Sun ☎ (01529) 240228
🌐 fortescuearms.co.uk
Greene King Abbot; guest beers Ⓗ
Fine, Grade II-listed inn with an interesting multi-roomed interior and a rustic feel, popular with diners and with a large patio to the rear. Nearby is the site of Sempringham Priory and its monument to Gwenllian, daughter of the Prince of Wales, who was confined to the priory in the 12th century. Stone from the priory was used to build part of the inn. Guest beers are usually from micros.
🏚Q🕹🕹🕹♣P⅄🕹

Billinghay

Coach & Horses
Tattershall Road, LN4 4DD
🟢 12-3 (not Mon & Tue), 6-11; 6-10.30 Sun
☎ (01526) 860250 🌐 coachandhorsesbillinghay.co.uk
Everards Tiger; Wells Bombardier; guest beer Ⓗ

INDEPENDENT BREWERIES
8 Sail Heckington
Austendyke Spalding (NEW)
Axholme Luddington
Bacchus Sutton-on-Sea
Batemans Wainfleet
Black Horse Grainthorpe (NEW)
Blue Bell Whaplode St Catherine
Blue Cow South Witham
Brewster's Grantham
Cathedral Heights Bracebridge Heath
DarkTribe East Butterwick
Fulstow Louth
Grafters Willingham by Stow
Hopshackle Market Deeping
Leila Cottage Ingoldmells
Melbourn Stamford
Newby Wyke Grantham
Oldershaw Barkston Heath
Poachers North Hykeham
Riverside Wainfleet
Sleaford (Hop Me Up) Sleaford
Tom Wood's Melton Ross
Willy's Cleethorpes

Traditional public house situated on the main A153 route to the coast. A large parking area accommodates motorhome and caravan stopovers. For the hungry, there is an extensive home-cooked range of meals available (no food Mon and Tue). Events and rallies take place in the adjacent two-acre field. The Wolds Bikers meet on the first and third Monday of the month. ▲Q⛄❄☀❶⊞♿⅄♣P

Boston

Carpenters Arms
20 Witham Street, PE21 6PU (near marketplace)
❂ 12-midnight (1am Fri); 11-1am Sat ☎ (01205) 362840
Batemans XB, XXXB; guest beer Ⓗ
Multi-roomed low-ceilinged traditional local hidden in the maze of side streets off the medieval Wormgate and overlooked by the magnificent Boston Stump. Although a Bateman's house, the Carpenters always has a guest beer on handpump. There is a patio area outside for sunny days. The pub is close to the town centre but you may need to ask for directions more than once to find it. Food is available at lunchtimes Friday to Sunday only. ▲☀❶⊞♿≢♣⅃⊟

Eagle
144 West Street, PE21 8RE
❂ 11 (11.30 Thu)-11; 11-midnight Fri & Sat
☎ (01205) 361116
Banks's Bitter; Castle Rock Black Gold, Harvest Pale; Fuller's London Pride; guest beers Ⓗ
Part of the Castle Rock chain, the Eagle is known as the real ale pub of Boston. This two-roomed, friendly hostelry has an L-shaped bar with a large TV screen for big sporting events. The small cosy lounge has an open fire. The pub stocks a wide range of guest ales, usually including one or more Castle Rock beers, and at least one cider. A function room upstairs is home to Boston Folk Club. Thursday is quiz night – allegedly the hardest in town. ▲Q☀❶♿≢♣🐾⅃⊟

Golden Lion
46 High Street, PE21 8SP
❂ 6 (12 Fri-Sun)-midnight ☎ (01205) 352745
Draught Bass; Wells Bombardier; guest beer Ⓗ
Low-beamed ceilings and wood panelling mark out this pub on the old High Street, away from the main shopping thoroughfares. Recently reopened and serving a good range of beers, it is home to active traditional games teams. Old fishing boat nameplates hang above the bar as a reminder of the history of Boston as a fishing port. ☀≢♣⅃

Moon Under Water
6 High Street, PE21 8SH
❂ 9am-midnight (1am Fri & Sat) ☎ (01205) 311911
Greene King Abbot; Ruddles Best Bitter; guest beers Ⓗ
A large, lively town-centre Wetherspoon pub near the tidal section of the River Witham. Formerly a Government building, an imposing staircase leads from the lounge up to the toilets. A spacious conservatory-style dining area is supplemented by a second child-friendly dining room adjacent to the lounge. The pub offers a good number of guest ales and a large range of continental bottled beers. Local history photographs and information boards highlight important people associated with Boston. ☀❶♿≢🐾⅃⊟

Bourne

Smith's of Bourne Ⓛ
25 North Street, PE10 9AE
❂ 9am-11 (midnight Fri & Sat) ☎ (01778) 426819
⊕ smithsofbourne.co.uk
Adnams Southwold Bitter; Castle Rock Harvest Pale; guest beers Ⓗ
A CAMRA/English Heritage award winner for the successful and imaginative conversion to a public house from an old grocers. There is a main bar in the front serving six beers from – mainly – independent brewers via handpump. This bar serves a maze of interconnecting rooms over a further two floors. Outside to the side there is a well-equipped patio leading to a large beer garden at the rear. There is an annual beer festival in July. ▲Q☀❶♿⅃⊟(101,102)

Brigg

Black Bull
3 Wrawby Street, DN20 8JH
❂ 11-3, 7-11; 11-11 Wed-Sat; 12-11 Sun ☎ (01652) 652153
Everards Tiger; John Smith's Bitter; guest beer Ⓗ
Popular, cosy, town-centre public house, with a large open-plan seating/drinking area and a TV at one end. Home-cooked pub meals can be eaten here or in the separate, raised dining area every lunchtime, and Wednesday to Sunday evenings until 7pm. Quiz night is Wednesday. A changing guest beer supplements the two regular beers. A smoking area is provided at the rear of the building, and the pub operates a no-swearing policy. ☀❶♣P⅃⊟(909)

Yarborough Hunt Ⓛ
49 Bridge Street, DN20 8NS
❂ 11-11 (midnight Fri); 10-midnight Thu & Sat
☎ (01652) 658333
Tom Wood's Best Bitter, Lincoln Gold, Bomber County, Imp Stout; guest beers Ⓗ
This former Sergeants Brewery tap was built in the 1700s and retains original rustic features. Simply furnished, it has warm, welcoming open fires in three of its four rooms, lit when cold outside. Wood and flagstone floors feature throughout, and an outside smoking area is covered and heated. The full range of Tom Wood's beers is supplemented by three varying guest beers and draught Westons Old Rosie cider. A good selection of bottled beers and ciders is stocked plus a wide range of malt whiskies and wines. ▲Q☀♿≢♣🐾⅃⊟

Castle Bytham

Castle Inn Ⓛ
High Street, NG33 4RZ
❂ 10-3 (Sun only), 6-11 ☎ (01780) 410504
Newby Wyke Bear Island; Woodforde's Wherry; guest beers Ⓗ
A 17th-century village gem with Newby Wyke beers featuring permanently on the bar, along with regularly changing guest ales sourced both locally and nationally. A traditional cider and perry are also on offer. Folk nights are a regular feature. An excellent food menu is available every evening and Sunday lunchtime. ▲Q☀❶🐾P⅃⊟

Fox & Hounds Ⓛ
6 High Street, NG33 4RZ
❂ 12.30-2.30 (not Mon-Wed), 6 (5 Sat)-11.30; 12.30-2.30, 6-10.30 Sun ☎ (01780) 410336

Marston's Pedigree; Oakham Ales Bishops Farewell; guest beers ⊞
Welcoming, friendly village local which has been in the same family for the past 16 years. The beers on the bar are Marston's Pedigree and Oakham Bishops Farewell, plus guests. A regular quiz night is held on the first Sunday of the month. The excellent home-cooked food is supplemented by a curry night on the first Thursday of the month, the curries sourced from the award-winning Bengal Clipper in Stamford. ⛺✿◑▮◗P⸻

Claypole

Five Bells ♈ 𝕃
95 Main Street, NG23 5BJ
✪ 11 (4 Mon)-11; 12-10.30 Sun ☎ (01636) 626561
⊕ thefivebellsclaypole.co.uk
Greene King IPA; guest beers ⊞
Popular and very well-supported village pub that was local CAMRA Pub of the Year 2012 and 2013. Four beers and two ciders are always available at the bar and the guest ales are sourced predominantly from local micros. The pub holds an annual beer festival in June. There is a large public bar, a small lounge, and a restaurant serving home-cooked food. Outside there is a spacious beer garden and children's play area. Four en-suite rooms are available. ✿🛏◑🚗⧗♣◗P⸻

Cleethorpes

No. 2 Refreshment Room
Station Approach, DN35 8AX (on station)
✪ 7.30am-midnight ☎ (07905) 375587
Hancock's HB; M&B Mild; Sharp's Doom Bar; Worthington's Bitter; guest beers ⊞
This is a little treasure, a small and cosy pub with a reputation for good beer quality, serving four regular beers plus two guests from both national and independent breweries. Its location on the station ensures a flow of customers enjoying a drink before or after their journeys. A free buffet is provided on Sunday evenings. Smokers may use a covered and heated area on the station concourse. Buses stop within 200 yards. ✿➥⸻🚞

Nottingham House Hotel
5-7 Seaview Street, DN35 8EU
✪ 12-11 (midnight Thu; 1am Fri & Sat) ☎ (01472) 505150
Tetley Mild, Bitter; Wychwood Hobgoblin; guest beers ⊞
Located at the highest point in town and very much a traditional-style local, with two contrasting front rooms and a rear snug that has been restored to its original look, with fittings to match. The restaurant is upstairs, serving fresh, locally-sourced food Wednesday to Saturday and Sunday lunches, but meals can also be served in any of the bars. Three beer festivals are held annually. ⛺Q👗🛏◑🚗⧗➥♣◗🚞(9,14)

Willy's
17 High Cliff Road, DN35 8RQ
✪ 11-11 (2am Fri & Sat) ☎ (01472) 602145
Draught Bass; Willy's Original; guest beers ⊞
Willy's overlooks the River Humber and beach through a glass frontage, giving spectacular views while enjoying the beers. Willy's Original is brewed on the premises and the brewery can be seen from the bar. Food is served lunchtimes, and supper clubs are hosted on Tuesday and Thursday

evenings. Extensive camping facilities are available at Meridian Park. Two real ciders are served and can include Moles Black Rat and Gwynt y Ddraig Black Dragon. There is a covered smoking area at the rear. ✿◑▮➥◗⸻🚞(9,46)

East Butterwick

Dog & Gun 𝕃
High Street, DN17 3AJ (off A18 at Keadby Bridge E bank) SE837058
✪ 5 (12 Sat & Sun)-11 ☎ (01724) 782324
DarkTribe Three Point Six, Captain Floyd, Old Gaffer; John Smith's Bitter ⊞
Traditional cosy village local nestling alongside the River Trent. Three separate drinking areas are linked around a polished wood bar; the bar area is simply decorated and furnished, with a warming real fire. Home to the DarkTribe microbrewery, the pub features three of its own beers – Three Point Six is permanent, the other two are rotated from the range. Darts is popular, and the pub hosts monthly Wheels vehicle nights in summer. Bench tables are set up on the riverbank during the warmer months. ⛺✿🛏⧗♣P⸻🚞(12)

Eastoft

River Don Tavern 𝕃
Sampson Street, DN17 4PQ (on A161 Goole-Gainsborough road)
✪ 3.30 (12 Sun)-11 ☎ (01724) 798040
⊕ riverdontavernandlodge.co.uk
Batemans Yella Belly Gold; guest beers ⊞
Traditional village local, open plan in design but with two discrete drinking areas. Recently refurbished, it now includes four accommodation lodges at the rear, all en suite. Two real ales (three in summer) are always on offer, usually sourced from Lincolnshire and Yorkshire micros, plus a real cider. It is also the main outlet for the local Axholme Brewing Co. Tasty pub food is served Monday-Saturday evenings plus an excellent carvery on Sunday. The summer beer festival includes live music. ⛺✿🛏◑♣◗P⸻🚞(356)

Fleet Hargate

Rose & Crown
Old Main Road, PE12 8LH
✪ 12-3, 6-11; 12-midnight Fri & Sat; 12-4, 7-11 Sun ☎ (01406) 422165
Elgood's Cambridge Bitter; Tetley Bitter; guest beer ⊞
A friendly welcome awaits at this village local as you step down into its U-shaped bar/lounge. The beamed ceiling and bay windows suit the building and the neat rear garden has an attractive summer house. The pub engages in various activities supporting the community. The landlord is keen on Elgood's beers and often has one of its seasonal or special ales available as a guest. ⛺Q👗✿◗▮♣P⸻

Fosdyke

Ship Inn
Moulton Washway, PE12 6LH
✪ 12-3, 6-11 (10 Sun) ☎ (01205) 260764
⊕ maritimecruises.co.uk/ship inn.html
Adnams Southwold Bitter; Batemans XB; guest beer ⊞

The pub is located just outside Fosdyke when travelling from Boston on the main A17 next to the bridge. As its name suggests, this former Bateman's hostelry is dedicated to all things maritime – maps, photographs, charts and model ships of every description are in plentiful supply. The inn is near to the busy Fosdyke Marina and both boaters and landlubbers are well catered for with excellent home-cooked food and a welcome cheer. ♨Q⛟◑♿P

Frognall

Goat L

155 Spalding Road, PE6 8SA

12-3, 6-11; 12-11 Fri & Sat; 12-10.30 Sun

☎ (01778) 347629 🌐 thegoatfrognall.com

Beer range varies [H]/[G]

A large pub with a single bar and a number of dining and restaurant areas. There are six handpumps with one dedicated to a real cider. In addition to the ales on handpump, a number of stronger beers are served straight from the cellar. Beers come mostly from micros and independents, often including local Hopshackle beers. A popular beer festival is held in June. ♨Q⛟❀◑♿●P☐

Gainsborough

Blues Club

Northolme, North Street, DN21 2QW (adjacent to Gainsborough Trinity football ground)

7-midnight; 5-1am Fri; 12-1am Sat; 12-midnight Sun

☎ (01427) 613688

Beer range varies [H]

The club has a bar area with several TVs showing sport, a quieter lounge and a large function room that hosts regular live entertainment (admission charges may apply). Two changing real ales are usually available, and details of forthcoming beers can be emailed to customers on request. CAMRA guests are always welcome on production of a membership card or a copy of the Guide. ⊟♿♣

Canute L

14-18 Silver Street, DN21 2DP (50yds S of marketplace)

9am-midnight ☎ (01427) 678715

Wells Bombardier; guest beers [H]

A typical lively town-centre pub where Charles Wells Bombardier is a permanent feature. Landlord Neil is keen to provide a varying range of other beers – there are usually at least five real ales available. Tasting notes are provided, which is a rarity for the area. Good-quality food is served and live sport is shown. The pub can be busy on Friday and Saturday nights. ⛟❀◑♿P⚌🚌

Eight Jolly Brewers L

Ship Court, Silver Street, DN21 2DW (behind the Canute, facing Riverside Gardens)

11 (12 Sun)-midnight ☎ (07767) 638806

Glentworth Lightyear; guest beers [H]

In the Guide for 19 years, this real ale haven is based in a 300-year-old Grade II-listed building and offers eight varying beers in the recently refurbished bar. Many are sourced from northern micros, but new breweries from all areas also feature. Real cider and a wide selection of continental bottled beers are also available. Quality live music can be heard on Thursday night. On Sunday lunchtimes customers bring in food to share. The pub is near the bus station. Q♿●P⚌🚌

R Bar

3 Lord Street, DN21 2DD (400yds W of market square)

2-midnight (1am Fri); 11-1am Sat; 12-midnight Sun

☎ (01427) 611265

Beer range varies [H]

Records show that this building was the Old Boar's Head in 1821, although it may have been a pub before then. It was the Hickman Arms until about 1930 and then a Rechabite hall until 2006. Up to three beers are available, with Ossett Brewery featuring regularly. Poker night is held on Monday, and sport is screened on satellite TV. The jukebox has a wide selection of music. Discounts on real ales are available to CAMRA members. ❀●

Ship Inn

Dog and Duck Lane, Morton, DN21 3BB

4-11; 12-11 Sat; 12-10.30 Sun ☎ (01427) 613298

Beer range varies [H]

Friendly, easy-to-find pub, on a main road not far from the River Trent and recently refurbished to a high standard inside and out. It sells one real ale from a regional brewer, sometimes two at weekends. Bingo is on Monday and a quiz on Thursday. Lunchtime food is served weekends, as well as evening meals (not Wed or Sun). There are TVs at both ends of the pub and occasional unobtrusive music. The 100 Lincoln to Scunthorpe bus runs nearby. ❀◐♣⚌🚌(100)

Gedney

Old Black Lion

Chapelgate, PE12 0BW

closed Mon; 12-3 (4 Sat), 6-11; 12-4, 7-10.30 Sun

☎ (01406) 362465

Oldershaw Newton's Drop; guest beers [H]

A Grade II-listed village pub dating from around 1700 with a welcoming atmosphere, low beamed ceilings and a series of small rooms. Note the two black lions standing guard at the front door. The beers are usually from microbreweries, often from local sources, and a good choice of home-made food is served. The pub is located near to the A17 (eastbound) and on a quiet minor road running parallel to it. ♨⛟❀◑⊟♿Ⅹ♣●P⚌🚌

Gosberton Risegate

Duke of York L

105 Risegate Road, PE11 4EY

12 (6.30 Mon)-11; 11-3, 7-10.30 Sun ☎ (01775) 840193

Batemans XB; St Austell Tribute; guest beers [H]

A friendly pub and a long-standing entry in the Guide which has a deserved reputation for value-for-money beers and food. As well as regular beers, guests come from a range of independent brewers. A wide choice of cooked food is available with portions to suit the largest appetite. Local community life is supported through charities, sports teams and other social events. Visitors can expect an enthusiastic welcome from the two pub dogs. ♨❀◑⊟♿♣P⚌

Grantham

Black Dog

19 Watergate, NG31 6NS

12-11 (midnight Sat) ☎ (01476) 978507

Mansfield Cask Ale; Marston's Pedigree; guest beer [H]

With a large, welcoming and friendly interior, this Marston's pub has four handpulls serving beers from the Marston's portfolio. Quality food is available daily – look out for the daily specials board. Quiz night is Thursday. Three big screens show live sporting events, with a fourth in the beer garden for the sports addicts. ❀◑▶♣℄⊟(1,3A)

Nobody Inn ⓛ
9 North Street, NG31 6NU (opp Asda car park)
❀ 12-11 (10.30 Sun) ☎ (01476) 565288 ⊕ nobodyinn.com
Wells Bombardier; guest beers Ⓗ
A superb example of a well-run independent town pub, selling a range of six beers featuring LocAle from Newby Wyke. Grantham Gold is brewed exclusively for the pub. Popular with drinkers and sports fans alike, it has five screens around the bar showing different sporting events at a volume conducive to normal conversation. Allow time to find the hidden entrance to the toilets and watch out for the spider. ❀&♣℄⊟

Grimsby

Barge
Riverhead, DN31 1NH
❀ 10-11 (2am Tue, Fri & Sat); 7-11 Sun ☎ (01472) 340911
⊕ thebargegrimsby.co.uk
Wells Bombardier; Wychwood Hobgoblin Ⓗ
The Barge is an old converted grain barge moored in the town centre. In the afternoon the custom is quieter and tends towards food and beer, while in the evening the jukebox is turned up and the bar takes on a rock/student feel. A quiz is held on Mondays and various bizarre eating challenges are occasionally held. The cider is from Skidbrooke. ❀◑≈♣♨℄⊟

Rose & Crown
Louth Road, DN33 2HR (2 miles from town on A16)
❀ 11-11 (midnight Fri & Sat); 11.30-11 Sun
☎ (01472) 278517
Abbeydale Moonshine; Tetley Bitter; guest beers Ⓗ
Part of the Ember Inns chain, this well-appointed and friendly pub has an emphasis on good, reasonably priced food but is rightly proud of its five real ales. One large bar serves several seating areas. Quiz nights are Monday and Wednesday, Tuesday is grill night, Wednesday is fish night, while Thursday is curry night. There is a seated and heated patio out front and a grassed seating area to the side. ❀⛶❀◑&P℄⊟(8,51)

Spider's Web
180 Carr Lane, DN32 8LN
❀ 12-11 (midnight Fri & Sat) ☎ (01472) 692065
⊕ thespiderswebgy.co.uk
John Smith's Bitter; Taylor Landlord; guest beers Ⓗ
Three-roomed and built in the '50s, this popular community pub holds regular music nights of various genres, with live music enjoyed most weekends. In the bar, games such as poker, darts and pool are played, and there is a weekly quiz night. The lounge has plenty of seating, while the music room with a stage has a naval theme reflecting ties with the Naval Association. ❀⛁♣P℄⊟(14)

Wheatsheaf
47 Bargate, DN34 5AD
❀ 11-11 (midnight Thu-Sat); 12-11 Sun ☎ (01472) 246821
Abbeydale Moonshine; Everards Tiger; Taylor Landlord; guest beers Ⓗ
A well-used chain pub, the Wheatsheaf provides an emphasis on a good, affordable range of food, in

addition to regular beers and two guest ales. Two bars serve a split-level layout in a contemporary style; there are various seating areas on the upper floor while the lower level is more intimate. An outdoor space at the rear incorporates a heated patio for smokers plus a raised patio with a grassed area to the front. Quiz nights are Thursday and Sunday. ❀◑⛁&≈(Town)P℄⊟

Yarborough Hotel ♈
29 Bethlehem Street, DN31 1JN
❀ 8-midnight (1am Fri & Sat) ☎ (01472) 268283
Greene King Abbot; Ruddles Best Bitter; guest beers Ⓗ
Three-times CAMRA local Pub of the Year, this spacious Wetherspoon utilises the ground floor of what used to be an imposing Victorian railway hotel. Comprising two large bar areas, it also has a front and rear snug plus a seated patio area. It is always busy, particularly at weekends. Good-value meals are served from opening until late. Up to eight guest beers are available, together with cider. Located in the town centre, it is on most bus routes and adjacent to the railway station. Q⛶❀◑&≈(Town)♨℄⊟

Harmston

Thorold Arms
High Street, LN5 9SN
❀ 12-3 (not Mon & Tue), 6-11; 12-3, 7-11 Sun
☎ (01522) 720358 ⊕ thoroldarms.co.uk
Beer range varies Ⓗ
In the heart of the village, this community pub, built in the 17th century, offers a comfortable bar with open fire, sofas and traditional tables and chairs. A separate dining room serves home-cooked meals. Four handpumps deliver a variety of cask ales, some sourced from Lincolnshire brewers. A changing cider is offered on an additional handpump. Regular events take place together with the annual Harmstock music and beer festival held over the August bank holiday weekend. ♨Q❀◑♣♨P℄⊟(1)

Heighington

Butcher & Beast
High Street, LN4 1JS
❀ 12-11 (10.30 Sun) ☎ (01522) 790386
⊕ butcherandbeast.co.uk
Batemans XB, Yella Belly Gold, XXXB; Everards Original; guest beers Ⓗ
Opened up, but retaining distinct areas, the pub features photos of the village through the years. Pub games, quizzes and raffles are popular. Guest beers are from the Bateman's list; Westons, Thatchers and/or guest ciders are sold; monthly special foreign bottled beers also feature. Meals, using local produce, are available at all times except Sunday evening. ♨Q⛶❀◑♣♨P℄⊟(2)

Hemingby

Coach & Horses ⓛ
Church Lane, LN9 5QF (1 mile from A158 at Baumber)
❀ 12-2 (not Mon & Tue), 6 (7 Sat)-11; 12-3, 7-10.30 Sun
☎ (01507) 578280
Riverside Dixon's Major; guest beers Ⓗ
Opposite the church in a quiet village, this free house and former coaching inn has been owned by the same couple for 20 years and is an established

part of the local community. With its low beams, decorative china and horse brasses, the traditionally furnished interior hosts darts, pool and dominoes teams, plus quiz teams in summer. The three ales always include one from Riverside, and a mild. Modestly-priced, home-cooked food is served. ⚙Q♿❄️◑♿Å♣P⁵⊖(6)

Horbling

Plough Inn
4 Spring Lane, NG34 0PF
🌀 11.30-2.30, 6.30 (6 Wed)-11 (11.30 Thu); 11.30-2.30, 4-midnight Fri; 11.30-midnight Sat; 12-10.30 Sun
☎ (01529) 240263
Beer range varies Ⓗ
Low-beamed true community pub, built in 1832 and owned by the parish council, in a quiet village. In addition to the lounge and bar, its snug is surely one of the smallest and most intimate of its kind. Beers are often from microbreweries, and change regularly. Home-cooked meals are served in the bar and restaurant. Spring wells are a feature just a few yards down the lane. ⚙❄️♿❄️◑♿♣P⁵⊖

Horncastle

Red Lion
Bull Ring, LN9 5HT
🌀 12-11 Mon & Sun; 11-11 (midnight Fri & Sat)
☎ (01507) 523338
Oakwell Barnsley Bitter, Senior; guest beer Ⓗ
Typical market-town pub with a large bar/lounge with old bay windows, overlooking the Bull Ring town centre. Above the bar a collection of 1,000 assorted keyrings hangs on display, while framed photographs of Lion Theatre productions from 1988 adorn the walls. The theatre is part of the pub premises, located at the rear, and run by the Horncastle Theatre Company – productions sometimes star the landlord. A snug and a dining room also feature. No food on Monday. ❄️♿❄️◑♿♣⁵⊖

Hubberts Bridge

Wheatsheaf Inn
Station Road, PE20 3QR
🌀 12-2.30 (2 Mon), 5-10.30; 12-2, 5-9 Sun
☎ (01205) 290347 ⊕ thewheatsheafinn.org
Batemans XB; Sharp's Doom Bar; guest beer Ⓗ
A pleasant rural free house that has been a pub for well over 100 years and is now run by a family partnership. It stands on the banks of the South Forty Foot Navigation, with moorings nearby. Eventually it is planned that this waterway will link with the entire Midland canal system, with access currently available via the River Witham at Boston. The pub holds an annual beer festival in August and regular live music events throughout the year. Food is sourced locally. ⚙Q♿❄️◑Å≈♣P⁵

Ingoldmells

Countryman Ⓛ
Chapel Road, PE25 1ND
🌀 12-midnight summer (winter times vary)
☎ (01754) 872268 ⊕ countryman-ingoldmells.co.uk
Leila Cottage Leila's Lazy Days, Ace Ale, Lincolnshire Life; guest beer Ⓗ
The privately-owned Countryman appears to be a modern building but it incorporates the early 19th-

century Leila Cottage, which gives its name to the brewery behind the pub. A notorious smuggler, James Waite, used to reside here when Ingoldmells was a wild and lonely place, but he certainly would not recognise the current holiday coast, with Skegness, Butlins and Fantasy Island nearby. Information boards give brewery, pub and beer notes for visitors. The pub is on northern bus routes from Skegness. ❄️♿❄️◑♿ÅP⁵⊖⊖

Keelby

Nag's Head
8 Manor Street, DN41 8EF
🌀 12-midnight (10.30 Sun) ☎ (01469) 560660
Batemans XB; Theakston Mild; guest beers Ⓗ
Small two-roomed village pub opposite the school. It is one of the last regional pubs with a regular mild, and the two guest beers often come from northern English breweries. A small beer garden includes a play area and a covered, illuminated and heated smoking area. Tuesday is quiz night, bingo is on Wednesday and there is live music at weekends. Food is not provided except for the occasional summer weekend barbecue. The Cleethorpes-Hull bus passes close by. ⚙❄️♿P⁵⊖(X1)

Kirkby on Bain

Ebrington Arms
Main Street, LN10 6YT
🌀 12-2 (not Mon), 6-11 ☎ (01526) 354560
⊕ ebringtonarms.com
Adnams Broadside; Batemans XB; Black Sheep Golden Sheep; Castle Rock Harvest Pale; Sharp's Doom Bar; guest beers Ⓗ
Attractive country pub close to the River Bain and dating from 1610. World War II airmen used to slot coins into the ceiling beams to pay for beer when they returned from missions over Germany. Many of these coins are still in situ and make a unique memorial to the dead. The popular restaurant offers good food made with local produce (booking advised). There is a convenient caravan site within a mile of the pub. This year sees the introduction of a 42-whisky menu. ⚙Q♿◑♿Å♣P⁵

Lincoln

Adam & Eve Tavern
25 Lindum Road, LN2 1NT
🌀 12-11 (11.30 Thu; midnight Fri & Sat) ☎ (01522) 537108
⊕ adamandevelincoln.co.uk
Caledonian Deuchars IPA; Greene King Abbot; guest beer Ⓗ
A whitewashed, stone-built free house situated prominently at the top of Lindum Hill in the shadow of the cathedral. Reputedly the oldest tavern in Lincoln, dating back as far as 1701, it consists of a front lounge bar (also used for private functions) and a spacious main bar with a variety of seating areas. The two guest beers change frequently. Occasional music nights and regular Sunday quizzes take place, and food is served until 7pm. ⚙❄️◑❄️♣P⁵⊖

Golden Eagle
21 High Street, LN5 8BD
🌀 11-11 (11.30 Fri & Sat); 12-11 Sun ☎ (01522) 521058
Batemans XB; Castle Rock Harvest Pale; guest beers Ⓗ

This former coachhouse, close to Lincoln City FC, has much to offer, with 10 handpumps and a cider in the two bars, one a traditional lounge with open fire, the other showing televised sports. The pub is welcoming to children and well-behaved dogs. The large beer garden has been renovated and is now one of the best in Lincoln, with plenty of covered, heated seating and, in the summer, a beer festival and barbecues. ᛗᏱᏱᏱᏱᏱᏱᏱᏱᏱᏱᏱ

Jolly Brewer ♥ 🍸
27 Broadgate, LN2 5AQ
🌣 2-10 Mon; 4-11 Tue & Thu; 4-midnight Wed; 12-midnight Fri & Sat; 12-6 Sun ☎ (01522) 528583
Idle Black Abbot; Oldershaw Mowbray's Mash; Tom Wood's Lincoln Gold; guest beers Ⓗ
Near the Drill Hall, the Art Deco-style interior gives this free house a distinctive ambience. The single bar area has beers mostly from small brewers not too far away, with Westons perry and ciders from smaller producers on gravity. The corridor link has art displays and is the family area. Regular live music, open mic nights and quizzes are supported by a good jukebox and lively conversation. The rear courtyard has a partially covered area for wet weather smokers. ᛗᏱᏱᏱᏱᏱᏱᏱᏱᏱ

Morning Star
11 Greetwell Gate, LN2 4AW
🌣 11-midnight; 12-11 Sun ☎ (01522) 527079
⊕ morningstarlincoln.co.uk
Caledonian Deuchars IPA; Draught Bass; Greene King Abbot; Ruddles Best Bitter; Taylor Golden Best; Wells Bombardier; guest beer Ⓗ
A cosy traditional pub close to the cathedral in the uphill part of the city. Reputedly dating from the 18th century, it was refurbished in early 2013 retaining the character of the pub. The main bar has an L-shaped tiled area plus a TV room and a nice snug with a small library. There is good craic in the bar from regulars, plus live music occasionally during the year. ᛗQᏱᏱᏱᏱᏱᏱᏱ

Ritz 🍸
143-147 High Street, LN5 7PJ
🌣 8am-midnight (1am Fri & Sat) ☎ (01522) 512103
Greene King Abbot; Ruddles Best Bitter; guest beers Ⓗ
For 60 years the Ritz was the city's entertainment hub, hosting films and live shows. The cinema closed in 1996, and the foyer and stalls were converted by JD Wetherspoon. The interior celebrates past glories, with numerous signed photos of the top-line acts that performed here. The beer range includes plenty of brews from local micros. Westons Old Rosie cider is ever-present. The pub gets particularly busy when there is a match at nearby Sincil Bank. QᏱᏱᏱᏱᏱᏱᏱᏱᏱ

Strugglers Inn 🍸
83 Westgate, LN1 3BG
🌣 12-11 (midnight Wed & Thu; 1am Fri); 11-1am Sat ☎ (01522) 535023
Draught Bass; Taylor Landlord; guest beers Ⓗ
Small, basic and popular pub near the castle and cathedral, which has won many awards. Two real fires make it snug in winter. In summer the rear sunken terrace is a lunchtime suntrap. Plenty of guest beers feature on the nine handpumps, frequently from Lincolnshire, Nottinghamshire and Yorkshire, and occasional beer festivals are hosted. Pumpclips adorn the walls. Live acoustic music sometimes features on Sunday teatimes but the main source of entertainment is conversation. Snacks such as pork pies are usually available. ᛗQᏱᏱᏱᏱᏱ

Treaty of Commerce
173 High Street, LN5 7AF
🌣 11-11 (1am Fri & Sat); 12-10.30 Sun ☎ (01522) 262940
⊕ treatyofcommerce.co.uk
Batemans XB, Yella Belly Gold, XXXB; guest beers Ⓗ
This old High Street pub, close to the railway and bus station, was tastefully refurbished in 2011, with a new bar including six handpumps and a seating area as you enter. Towards the rear is an open fireplace and extra drinking and dining areas. Good-quality food is served all week, with a special offer on match days – pie and a free pint. The large beer garden has an award-winning floral display. A friendly, welcoming place to socialise. ᛗᏱᏱᏱᏱᏱᏱᏱ

Victoria
6 Union Road, LN1 3BJ
🌣 11-midnight (1am Fri-Sat); 12-midnight Sun ☎ (01522) 541000
Batemans XB; Castle Rock Harvest Pale; Taylor Landlord; guest beers Ⓗ
Now in its 30th consecutive year in this Guide, this small, welcoming Victorian pub has two bars with up to five guest beers, and a real cider or perry in the cellar. The outdoor seating area is heated and sheltered in the colder months and sits by the west wall of the castle, creating a pleasant suntrap in the summer. Meals are served at lunchtimes; sandwiches and snacks are available all day. Live music events are held most Saturday evenings plus an occasional pub quiz. QᏱᏱᏱᏱᏱᏱ

Wig & Mitre
30 Steep Hill, LN2 1LU
🌣 8.30am-11 ☎ (01522) 535190 ⊕ wigandmitre.com
Black Sheep Best Bitter; Everards Tiger; Oakham JHB; guest beer Ⓗ
A welcome rest for drinkers who have tackled the famous Steep Hill. This 14th-century building covers two floors and has a reputation for excellent food. Those seeking a quiet pint are just as welcome. The venue holds regular food and beer tasting events – check the website for details. Family and dog friendly. ᛗQᏱ

Little Cawthorpe

Royal Oak Inn (Splash) 🍸
Watery Lane, LN11 8LZ (right off main road to Legbourne then left onto Buston Lane through ford and turn left)
🌣 11-midnight ☎ (01507) 600750 ⊕ royaloaksplash.co.uk
Black Sheep Best Bitter; Greene King IPA, Abbot; Morland Old Speckled Hen; guest beer Ⓗ
Known locally as the Splash because of the picturesque ford nearby, this 400-year-old inn is situated in its own large lawned gardens on the edge of the Lincolnshire Wolds near Louth. Four beers are regularly available, plus a guest ale often from a local brewery. Three restaurants cover most culinary requirements and themed evenings are popular. The en-suite rooms are often used by visitors to Cadwell Park race track three miles away, and to explore the Wolds. ᛗᏱᏱᏱᏱᏱᏱᏱᏱᏱ

Louth

Boar's Head 🄻

12 Newmarket, LN11 9HH (next to cattle market)
✪ closed Mon; 12 (9.30am Thu)-2.30, 6 (7 Wed & Thu)-11; 12-3, 6-11 Sun ☎ (01507) 603561
Batemans XB, XXXB; guest beers Ⓗ
A Bateman's pub a short walk from the town centre, with a good guest beer list. The interior includes two main rooms plus the old snug, warmed by real fires in the winter, and there is always a friendly welcome. Pub games include darts, dominoes and pool. Thursday is cattle market day, which is why the pub opens earlier. Lunches are served daily except Monday, depending on the season; Sunday lunch is worth booking.
🏚Q🄰▶🄳♣🔑

Brown Cow

133 Newmarket, LN11 9EG
✪ 12-3 (Fri only), 5-midnight; 12-midnight Sat & Sun ☎ (01507) 605146
Adnams Southwold Bitter; Black Sheep Best Bitter; Castle Rock Harvest Pale; guest beer Ⓗ
Formerly the Newmarket Inn, this family-run, classically decorated free house is only five minutes' walk from the town centre. A free quiz is held every Sunday night and the local folk club meets here on a Tuesday evening. The popular bistro serves traditional home-cooked food made with locally sourced produce (booking is recommended). Food is available Wednesday to Saturday lunchtimes and evenings, 12-3pm only on Sunday. Q🏵🄰P

Cobbles Bar

2 New Street, LN11 9PU (off Cornmarket)
✪ 10-midnight (2am Fri & Sat); 12-10 Sun ☎ 07736 275262
Black Sheep Best Bitter; guest beer Ⓗ
Traditional pub-style bar based in the centre of town, with friendly staff at all times. This small but accommodating venue has multiple personalities, from bustling coffee shop serving light lunches to a busy pre-club local with DJs and live music at the weekend. It has a good beer trade, with two contrasting cask ales, as well as a huge selection of exotic spirits. Disabled access is right through the front doors. 🏵🄰🕭🖫

Gas Lamp Lounge 🍺 🄻

13 Thames Street, LN11 7AD
✪ 5 (12 Sat & Sun)-11 ☎ (01507) 607661
Fulstow Marsh Mild, Fulstow Common, Northway IPA, Pride of Fulstow; guest beer Ⓗ
The tap for Fulstow Brewery, this recently converted building is a warm and welcoming venue, with four regular beers from the upstairs brewery and a guest beer. Quality ales can be enjoyed in the bar without the bother of noisy TVs and loud music. Benches are set along the canalside for enjoying a drink in the summer, and inside is a roaring logburner to sit beside in the winter months. Dogs are welcome. 🏚Q🕭♣P

Joseph Morton 🄻

Pawnshop Passage, LN11 9EZ (in small alleyway off Mercer Row)
✪ 9am-11 (midnight Fri & Sat) ☎ (01507) 353700
Greene King Abbot; Ruddles Best Bitter; guest beers Ⓗ
Wetherspoon pub opened in 2011 and comprising several combined properties, the tallest of which is a former warehouse built between 1808 and 1834,

with cast-iron wall plates bearing the name of local ironmonger Joseph Morton. There is also a smaller warehouse facing Kidgate, rebuilt in 1818 along with two 19th-century houses in Pawnshop Passage. Some cast-iron gears were found in the renovation and are part of a ceiling decoration.
🏵🄰🕭♣🔑

Olde Whyte Swanne

45 Eastgate, LN11 9NP
✪ 11-3, 5-11; 11-11 Sat; 12-4 Sun ☎ (01507) 601312
Theakston Best Bitter; Wadworth 6X; guest beer Ⓗ
The Olde Whyte Swanne is Louth's oldest public house, established in the early 1600s. Upon entering this Grade II-listed building you are met by traditional low-beamed ceilings and a real fire. Beyond this is another more modern room which is used for dining. The bar offers a variety of beers and a cider on handpump. Outside is a pleasant beer garden area which has recently been spruced up. 🏚Q🏵🄰🕭♣🔑🖫

Ludford

White Hart Inn

Magna Mile, LN8 6AD
✪ closed Mon; 12-2 (not Tue-Thu), 6-11; 12-3.30, 7-11 Sun ☎ (01507) 313489 ⊕ whitehartludford.blogspot.co.uk
Beer range varies Ⓗ
Former coaching house dating from the 18th-century, now a two-roomed rural village inn. It is close to the Viking Way, popular with hikers and ramblers. Four different guest beers are offered – the licensees pride themselves on serving real ale from microbreweries. All food is home made, using ingredients from local suppliers, and meals are available lunchtimes and evenings. There is guest accommodation separate from the pub.
🏚Q🏵🚲🄰P

Market Deeping

Vine 🄻

19 Church Street, PE6 8AN
✪ 5 (12 Fri & Sat)-11; 12-10.30 Sun ☎ (01778) 218622
Sharp's Doom Bar; Wells Vine Ale; guest beers Ⓗ
A free house since 2011, this small and friendly two-bar pub was once a Victorian school. The old limestone building features oak beams and stone floors, with a large patio at the rear. Five handpumps dispense two regular beers and a constantly changing range of guests including local Hopshackle brewery beers. No food is served but free nibbles are provided Sunday lunchtime and early during the week. The TV in the main bar is only turned on for major sporting events.
🏵🔑🖫(101)

Market Rasen

Aston Arms

18 Market Place, LN8 3HL
✪ 11-11 (11.30 Fri & Sat); 12-10.30 Sun ☎ (01637) 842313
Theakston Best Bitter; Wells Bombardier; guest beer Ⓗ
Large, popular pub on the market square; to the side is a covered, heated, smoking area with wheelchair access to the bar. Inside, a central bar serves a games area with pool and shove-ha'penny, a family area and a lounge with a real fire. Excellent-value food is served daily which is popular with families, racegoers and walking

groups (the Viking Way passes nearby). There are TVs for sport in the lounge and games areas.
P (3,23)

Marshchapel

White Horse

Sea Dyke Way, DN36 5SX
4 (12 Sun)-midnight; 12-1am Fri & Sat ☎ (01472) 388280
Beer range varies H
Two-roomed coaching inn, formerly a Hewitt's Brewery pub, now an Enterprise Inn, whose landlord is the second generation of the family to be its licensee. Real ales outsell lager considerably, with two guest beers coming from the likes of Theakston, Black Sheep, Caledonian and St Austell. Cider is regularly available. Locally sourced food is served lunchtimes Friday-Sunday and evenings Wednesday-Saturday. There is bingo on the last Saturday of the month, a Friday free quiz and a regular open night for musicians.
P (50)

Messingham

Bird in the Barley

Northfield Road, DN17 3SQ (½ mile from Messingham on A159)
closed Mon; 11-3, 5-11 ☎ (01724) 764744
Jennings Sneck Lifter; guest beers H
A country-style pub with a mix of traditional and modern design. The interior features oak beams, wooden flooring and a dining conservatory. A seated drinkers' area includes leather sofas and armchairs around a large open fire. There are two beer gardens, one with a large canopy and heater. Good home-cooked food is made from locally sourced ingredients. The single regular real ale is supplemented by one or two guest beers, usually from the Jenning's range. Cyclops tasting notes are displayed on the handpumps.
Q P (100,353)

Pooleys

46 High Street, DN17 3NT
closed Mon; 6 (7 Sun)-11 ☎ (01724) 762220
Batemans XB; guest beers H
Pooleys is an attractive, well-appointed licensed village tea room by day, serving food and cream teas, and by evening a popular village pub. It comprises three separate drinking areas with rustic furniture and fittings, including a bar area with a real fire in a large chimney breast. Batemans XB is a stock beer and three rotating guest beers are also offered, often from the likes of Batemans, Everards, Oakham, St Austell and Timothy Taylor. Unusual foreign beers and lagers are also served.
Q (100)

Navenby

Lion & Royal

57 High Street, LN5 0DZ
12-11 (midnight Fri & Sat); 12-10.30 Sun
☎ (01522) 810368
Greene King Abbot; Tetley Bitter; guest beers H
Formerly known as the Lion, a visit in 1870 from the Prince of Wales, Edward VII, prompted the addition of Royal in the title. Dambusters Wing Commander Guy Gibson also honeymooned here. Good-value food is served until 8pm (4pm Sun and Mon). Live local music features on the second and fourth Saturday of every month. The hourly Lincoln-Grantham bus stops just outside.
P (1)

North Hykeham

Centurion

Newark Road, LN6 8LB
11.30-11 (midnight Thu-Sat) ☎ (01522) 509814
Abbeydale Moonshine; Tetley Bitter; York Yorkshire Terrier; guest beers H
A 20-minute bus ride from Lincoln city centre takes you to this modern Ember Inn, where the food is reasonably priced and children are welcome when eating. Three regular beers and two guest beers are usually available. Prices, and future guest beers, are prominently displayed. It is very handy for a beer after shopping at the superstore next door. P (27,46)

North Kelsey

Butchers Arms L

Middle Street, LN7 6EH (off main road through village)
4-midnight (1.30am Fri); 12-1.30am Sat; 12-midnight Sun
☎ (01652) 678002
Tom Wood's Best Bitter, Lincoln Gold; guest beer H
Traditional village local, open plan in design. The main bar area is simply but comfortably furnished in rustic style around a polished wood bar, and has a real fire. A games area for darts is located in one corner. The two regular beers are supplemented by a guest beer or a seasonal or core beer from the Tom Wood's range. Weekly quiz nights are popular. An attractive beer garden is available for alfresco drinking. The pub's great strength is that it does not change from year to year. P

Norton Disney

Green Man L

Main Street, LN6 9JU
12-2, 5.30-11; 12-11 Sat & Sun ☎ (01522) 789804
Black Sheep Ale; guest beers H
In the heart of the village, with a large garden and parking area, this is a cosy bar with TV, fire and doubles dartboard, and a separate restaurant serving excellent food. The pub is gaining a reputation for unusual guest beers and a good range of real ciders. Quiz night is every second Friday and poker night every Thursday.
P

Old Bolingbroke

Black Horse Inn

Moat Lane, PE23 4HH
closed Mon; 8.30-11 Tue; 12-3, 7-11 ☎ (01790) 763388
Milestone Black Pearl; Young's Bitter; guest beers H
In a splendid walking area, this fine old country inn has early origins from the 14th century but was largely rebuilt in 1930. Henry IV was born at nearby Bolingbroke Castle, which was also besieged during the Civil War. The battle of Winceby, which was fought a few miles from Bolingbroke in 1643, witnessed the first nationally important victory for Oliver Cromwell's cavalry. Still part of the Duchy of Lancaster, the Black Horse is a great place to visit when exploring the Lincolnshire Wolds.
Q P

Pinchbeck

Bull Inn

1 Knight Street, PE11 3RA

✪ 12-11 (midnight Fri & Sat) ☎ (01775) 723022

John Smith's Bitter; guest beers Ⓗ

Welcoming, friendly village pub opposite the green, which still has the old stocks. The Bull has two comfortable bars: the public bar with a log fire, and the lounge, used mainly for dining. A carved bull's head features on the long bar front, with the bar rail representing its horns. The pub has a reputation for good food, from bar snacks to meals in the upstairs restaurant. Guest beers change regularly, often coming from local micros.

🏚️🕭🅭🖰🖧P💺🖳🖳

Quadring

White Hart

7 Town Drove, PE11 4PU

✪ 12-2.30 (Mon only), 6.30-11; 12-3, 6.30-11 Sat & Sun

☎ (01775) 822178

Batemans XXXB; guest beer Ⓗ

Friendly, small village pub, very popular with locals. It serves only one, occasionally changing, real ale at a time, always in excellent condition. Buses from Boston and Spalding stop at the nearby crossroads (not eves or Sun). Pool and darts are offered in the bar – the landlord often joins in the pool. 🏚️🖙🕭🅖🖧P💺🖳(59)

Ruskington

Shoulder of Mutton

11 Church Street, NG34 9DU

✪ 12-11 ☎ (01526) 832220

John Smith's Bitter; Sharp's Doom Bar; Wells Bombardier; guest beer Ⓗ

A popular and thriving pub in the heart of the village which attracts a clientele of all ages. It is probably one of the oldest buildings in Ruskington and has low wooden ceilings in its two main rooms. Reputedly, it once housed a butcher's shop, hence the name. Although additions have been made in recent years they have not spoilt the essential character. There is a separate pool room. 🕭🖙🖧P💺🖳

Sandtoft

Reindeer

Thorne Road, DN8 5SZ (follow signs for Sandtoft from A18)

✪ 12-midnight ☎ (01724) 710774 ⊕ thereindeerinn.com

Black Sheep Best Bitter; Taylor Landlord; guest beers Ⓗ

Popular village pub with a reputation for good food as well as cask ale. At least one guest beer sourced from a local brewery is always available. The venue has recently undergone extensive refurbishment and caters for a wide clientele, hosting a variety of events. Sandtoft Transport Museum is nearby. 🏚️🖙🕭🖰🖙🅖🖖P💺

Saxilby

Anglers

65 High Street, LN1 2HA

✪ 11.30-12.30am; 12-midnight Sun ☎ (01522) 702200

Caledonian Deuchars IPA; Theakston XB; guest beers Ⓗ

Where other pubs are closed or constantly changing hands, the Anglers has had the same landlord behind the bar for 20 years. The two guest beers are from the pubco list, with pleasant surprises at times. Various local sports teams are run from the pub, making for a vibrant bar, and there is a quieter lounge. No food is served but there is a splendid chip shop outside. It's close to bus stops and the railway station, with good moorings on the Fossdyke nearby. 🕭🖧A🖙🖧P💺🖳(100,105)

Scampton

Dambusters Inn Ⓛ

23 High Street, LN1 2SD

✪ 12-3 (not Mon), 5-9.30 (10 Wed; 11 Thu; midnight Fri); 12-midnight Sat; 12-6 Sun ☎ (01522) 731333

⊕ dambustersinn.co.uk

Poachers Shy Talk Bitter; Thwaites Lancaster Bomber; Tom Wood's Best Bitter; guest beers Ⓗ

Named after nearby RAF Scampton's famous 617 Squadron, this Edwardian former post office has only been an inn for 15 years. Increasingly good food, and even better beer, has elevated its local popularity. The open fire and lofty beams suit the atmosphere of its World War II artefacts and memorabilia. Its cosy tranquility is lessened on the weekend nearest 17 May, when 617's mettle is celebrated with an ale festival (repeated in the autumn). Thornbridge Jaipur IPA is served on the last weekend of each month. 🕭Q🖙🕭🖰🅖🖧P💺🖳(103)

Scunthorpe

Berkeley ★

Doncaster Road, DN15 7DS (½ mile from end of M181)

✪ 11.30-2.30, 5-11; 12-11 Fri & Sat; 12-10.30 Sun

☎ (01724) 842333

Samuel Smith OBB Ⓗ

Roadhouse-style pub dating from 1940, identified by CAMRA as one of Britain's Best Real Heritage Pubs, with original features and Art Deco details. It comprises three bars (one a dining area), with seven guest rooms and a beer garden. Evening meals are served Monday-Saturday, plus a carvery on Sunday. It is a bus ride or a 25-minute downhill walk from the town centre or train station, and a five-minute walk to Glanford Park football ground. It may occasionally close when SUFC play local rivals. The car park is large. 🕭Q🕭🖰🖙🅖P💺🖳(31,32)

Blue Bell

1-7 Oswald Road, DN15 7PU (at town centre crossroads)

✪ 8am-11 (midnight Fri; 1am Sat) ☎ (01724) 863921

Greene King Abbot; Ruddles Best Bitter; Wychwood Hobgoblin; guest beers Ⓗ

Popular Wetherspoon conversion of former shop units in the town centre, now a large, single L-shaped room. Open plan in design, it is on two levels, with tables for drinking and dining. The beer garden at the rear has a heated patio for smokers. Meals are available lunchtimes until 10pm. It offers three regular real ales, guest beers and real ciders on draught. Beer festivals are staged in spring and autumn, plus mini beer festivals and occasional Meet the Brewer evenings. A CAMRA member discount is offered on beer/food on Wednesdays. Q🕭🖰🅖🖙🖳🖳

Chancel

Cambridge Avenue, Bottesford, DN16 3LG
🌣 11-11 (midnight Thu-Sun) ☎ (01724) 840913
Beer range varies Ⓗ
Large community pub comprising two rooms – one is a public bar with pool and TV, the other an open-plan, spacious lounge that is attractively decorated and comfortably furnished. Meals are served in the lounge Wednesday-Friday lunchtimes and evenings, plus Sunday lunchtime (booking advisable). A partly grassed patio area with bench seats can be accessed from the lounge. Two or three rotating guest beers are offered, plus one or two real ciders. **Q🌣🕏❀◑母&♣●P╵~₪**(32A)

Malt Shovel Ⓛ

219 Ashby High Street, Ashby, DN16 2JP (in Ashby Broadway shopping area)
🌣 10-11 (midnight Fri & Sat); 12-11 Sun ☎ (01724) 843318
Exmoor Gold; Tom Wood's Best Bitter, Lincoln Gold; guest beers Ⓗ
Offering the widest real ale and cider choice in the area, this is one of only a handful of pubs elevated to the prestigious Oakademy of Excellence, awarded for perfectly served, permanent Oakham ales. Twice-yearly week-long beer festivals are held in spring and autumn. The pub is busy lunch and teatimes for good-value home-cooked food. Magazines, newspapers, book swap and members-only snooker facilities are available. Quizzes take place Tuesdays and Thursdays, with live music alternate Saturdays, and a monthly folk night on Sundays. Handy for the local shops.
🌣🕏❀◑&●╵~₪(6,31,32)

Skendleby

Blacksmiths Arms

Main Road, PE23 4QE
🌣 12-3 (not Mon), 5.30-11 (not Sun eve winter)
☎ (01754) 890662
Batemans XB; guest beers Ⓗ
Dating back to the 18th century, this attractive pub nestles on the south-east edge of the Lincolnshire Wolds and offers panoramic views. Ducking beneath the low door lintel, fortunately well padded, you discover a cosy, friendly atmosphere in the small quarry-tiled snug bar, complete with range and settles. The cellar is visible through a glass panel behind the bar. The dining room at the rear incorporates the building's old well. It is an ideal base for walking and cycling.
🕰Q🕏❀母♣P╵~₪

Skillington

Cross Swords Inn Ⓛ

The Square, NG33 5HB (2 miles from A1)
🌣 7-11 Mon; 12-2, 6-11 (not Sun eve) ☎ (01476) 861132
🌐 thecross-swordsinn.co.uk
Grainstore Phipps IPA; guest beers Ⓗ
Impressive stone-built pub dating from the early to mid-1800s. The current hosts, Francis and Linda, have owned the inn since 1991. The ales on the bar are from Grainstore and other LocAle brewers. Quality pub food is available daily. The pub boasts three letting cottages. **🕰🌣🕏❀◑&P╵**

Sleaford

Packhorse Inn

7 Northgate, NG34 7BH

🌣 8am-midnight ☎ (01529) 308730
Courage Directors; Greene King Abbot; Ruddles Best Bitter; guest beers Ⓗ
An 18th-century coaching inn on the London to Lincoln road which has had several names during its lifetime, reverting to the original name when taken over by Wetherspoon a few years ago. Despite being remodelled as partly open plan, it retains an intimate atmosphere. As the Lion Hotel it hosted the opening dinner for the Sleaford Railway, an event that marked the start of the decline in coaching trade. **Q🌣🕏❀◑&~●╵~₪**

Snitterby

Royal Oak 🍷

High Street, DN21 4TP (½ mile off A15)
🌣 5 (12 Sat)-11; 12-9 Sun ☎ (01673) 818273
Batemans Yella Belly Gold; Greene King IPA; Thwaites Original; guest beers Ⓗ
Traditional pub gem in a sleepy village, rustic in style with wooden fixtures and fittings and a wood-panelled bar. The bar is simply but comfortably furnished, and there is a small snug with a TV, both having real fires. The beer garden has wooden bench tables and overlooks a stream. Three regular real ales are supplemented by up to four guest beers from all over the UK. Mini beer festivals are staged on bank holidays. Evening meals featuring locally sourced produce are served Thursday to Saturday. **🕰Q🕏◑ÅP╵**

South Ferriby

Nelthorpe Arms

School Lane, DN18 6HW (off A1077 Scunthorpe to Barton road)
🌣 3-11 Mon; 12-11 (midnight Sat) ☎ (01652) 635235
Tetley Bitter; guest beers Ⓗ
This two-room village local is well worth seeking out, tucked away off the main road. The bar is wood-panelled, with bench seating and sofas at one end, and has a pool table. The restaurant offers a wide range of home-cooked quality meals. Two guest real ales are served. An annual music and beer festival is held, there is live music on Saturday evening, and the pub hosts a monthly open mic night. Comfortable accommodation is available in four en-suite rooms. **🕏~◑母&♣P╵~₪**(350,450)

South Rauceby

Bustard Inn Ⓛ

44 Main Street, NG34 8QG
🌣 closed Mon; 12-2.30, 5-30-11; 12-4 Sun
☎ (01529) 488250 🌐 thebustardinn.co.uk
Batemans XB; Riverside Cheeky Bustard; guest beers Ⓗ
Attractive Grade II-listed inn built in 1860 by the Rauceby Estate. Local legend has it that the last Great Bustard was shot on the hill behind the pub. The pub has had several Royal visitors – King George VI and Prince Charles when they were stationed at nearby RAF Cranwell. The beers on the bar include Cheeky Bustard, brewed by Riverside (Wainfleet) for the pub. Excellent food is served lunchtimes and evenings, and there are regular live jazz nights. **🕏◑P**

Spalding

Ivy Wall
18-19 New Road, PE11 1DQ
✪ 9-midnight (1am Fri & Sat) ☎ (01775) 719770
Greene King Abbot; Ruddles Best Bitter; Wychwood
Hobgoblin; guest beers Ⓗ
The town-centre site on which this spacious
modern pub now stands has had a variety of uses
over the years, and used to be on the bank of the
former Westlode river. Excavations during the
rebuild in 2005 discovered an undercroft and cellar
from the late medieval period. Photographs and
archaeological finds are displayed on the wall.
Changing guest ales are normally sourced from
local breweries, and there is a guest cider
dispensed by gravity. Food is served all day.
⚇❂◑⚘⛵ᵈ⌐

Lincoln Arms
4 Bridge Street, PE11 1XA
✪ 11-12.30am (6 Sun) ☎ (01775) 710017
Mansfield Cask Ale; guest beer Ⓗ
Overlooking the picturesque River Welland and a
stone's throw from Ayscoughfee Hall, this town
local has the relaxed feel and atmosphere of a
village pub, with a regular clientele, where lively
conversation and pub games prevail. Regular
changing guest ales are from the Marston's stable.
Every second Thursday of the month Spalding Folk
Club holds a jam session. No meals are served, but
a selection of rolls is available Monday to Saturday
lunchtimes. ⚇❂&⚞⚘ᵈ⌐

Red Lion Hotel
Market Place, PE11 1SU
✪ 10-midnight ☎ (01775) 722869
⊕ redlionhotel-spalding.co.uk
Draught Bass; Fuller's London Pride; Greene King
Abbot; Wells Bombardier; guest beer Ⓗ
A cosy and welcoming one-room traditional hotel
bar popular with locals and visitors, overlooking the
marketplace, with tables and chairs outside in fine
weather. The bar is a regular entry in the Guide due
to its consistently well-kept range of cask ales,
which the bar staff take great pride in serving in
top condition. It is a rare outlet for Bass in the
locality. The restaurant serves a range of Indian
cuisine. ❂⚞⚘≉

Stamford

Green Man Ⓛ
29 Scotgate, PE9 2YQ
✪ 11 (12 Sun)-midnight ☎ (01780) 753598
Castle Rock Harvest Pale; guest beers Ⓗ
Dating from 1796, this stone-built former coaching
inn has an L-shaped split-level bar, and is warmed
by a real fire. Up to eight ales and seven ciders,
complemented by a good range of European
bottled beers, are on offer. Two beer festivals are
held, at Easter and September, on the secluded
patio, which has one of only five stepping stones
from the inn's coaching days. A regular entry in the
Guide, the pub has much beer memorabilia
adorning the walls. ⚇❂⚞◑≉⚘⛵ᵈᵘ⌐(201)

Jolly Brewer Ⓛ
1 Foundry Road, PE9 2PP
✪ 11-midnight; 12-11.30 Sun ☎ (01780) 755141
⊕ jollybrewer.com
Oakham JHB; Sharp's Doom Bar; guest beers Ⓗ

With a stone-built exterior and an L-shaped room
around the bar, the pub dates back to 1830. An
adjoining small room serves as a dining area.
Home-cooked food made with locally sourced
ingredients is served daily. The pub is home to
pool, darts, crib and dominoes teams from the local
community. Beers from six handpumps come from
local and countrywide brewers; another handpump
serves traditional cider. A good range of malt
whiskies is also available. Plans have been made
for a small microbrewery to be built on site.
⚇❂◑≉⚘⛵ᵈᵘ⌐(9)

Tobie Norris Ⓛ
12 St Paul's Street, PE9 2BE
✪ 11.30-11; 12-10.30 Sun ☎ (01780) 753800
⊕ tobienorris.com
Adnams Southwold Bitter; Castle Rock Harvest Pale;
guest beers Ⓗ
The building, parts of which date back to 1280, was
bought by Tobie Norris in 1617 and used as a bell
foundry. A conversion from the former RAFA Club
gained it CAMRA's Conversion to Pub Use award in
2007. Split into many small rooms with real fires, it
has stone floors and low beams. Five handpumps
serve beers from local and countrywide brewers.
Specialities of the house include pizzas with
unusual toppings. Two beer festivals are held each
year. ⚇Q❂◑≉⚘⛵ᵈᵘ⌐(202,203)

Stickford

Red Lion Inn Ⓛ
Church Road, PE22 8EP
✪ closed Mon & Tue; 7-11 Wed & Thu; 4-11.30 Fri; 1.30-11.30
Sat; 12-10.30 Sun ☎ (01205) 480395
⊕ redlionstickford.co.uk
Batemans XB; guest beer Ⓗ
The pub name Red Lion, the most common in
England, is frequently found hereabouts because it
was a heraldic emblem of the 14th-century John of
Gaunt, Earl of Lancaster and Lord of the Manor at
nearby Bolingbroke Castle. This friendly, cosy, two-
bar pub has a small room used as a restaurant and
for private functions. Food is served evenings and
Sunday lunchtime, featuring local produce, such as
rabbit pie. Beer festivals are held. There are two
en-suite letting bedrooms. ⚇Q❂⚞◑⊟⚘Pᵈ⌐

Sutterton

Thatched Cottage
Pools Lane, PE20 2EZ
✪ 11.30-11.30 ☎ (01205) 460870
⊕ thatchedcottagerestaurant.co.uk
Beer range varies Ⓗ
Thatched 17th-century listed building, a rarity in
fen country, a private house until 1985. Although
extended and modernised to the rear, the bar and
separate dining room exhibit a wealth of ancient
timbers and inglenook fireplaces. Tall people
beware! Behind the pub is a country farm store,
and meat is butchered and cured on the premises.
A country park with arboretum is being developed,
with an area for pétanque and quoits. Up to four
real ales are dispensed. Q❂◑⊟&Pᵈ⌐

Sutton Bridge

Gathering
46 Bridge Road, PE12 9UA

closed Mon & Tue; 5.30-10.30 Wed & Thu; 1-midnight Fri; 12-midnight Sat; 1-10.30 Sun ☎ (01406) 359909 ⊕ thegatheringrockpub.com

Sharp's Doom Bar; Wychwood Hobgoblin; guest beer Ⓗ

A rock and metal-themed pub that features up-and-coming live bands. You will also find open mic nights, monthly quiz nights and occasional charity auctions. There is a quieter ambience at other times. The owners are proud of their well-kept pub and keen on their real ales, and there is a guest beer from time to time. The building, now nicely renovated, dates from 1733 and is reputedly home to five ghosts, including a former landlord. The bar front is constructed from Victorian cast-iron fireplaces. ♨❀ᕕ♣☀≟

Sutton-on-Sea

Bacchus Hotel Ⓛ

17 High Street, LN12 2EY (on main A52 through town)
10-midnight (1am Fri & Sat) ☎ (01507) 441204 ⊕ bacchushotel.co.uk

Bacchus Bittermans, Sutton Pride; Courage Directors; Ruddles County; Sharp's Doom Bar; guest beers Ⓗ

A long-established hotel selling a varied range of beers, including several from local breweries and the hotel's microbrewery. Well-attended beer festivals are held over the late spring and autumn bank holiday weekends. The pub is used regularly by local clubs and societies and is also popular with tourists. A wide range of food is available, from bar snacks to restaurant meals. There is a large garden and patio area, and it is on the bus route between Skegness and Mablethorpe.
♨Q☎❀⇔Ⓞ🖰👪♣P≟ᕹ(9)

Swineshead

Pig & Whistle

Market Place, PE20 3LJ
5.30 (12 Sat)-11; 12-4, 7.30-11 Sun ☎ (01205) 821381 ⊕ pig-and-whistle-real-ale.co.uk

Banks's Mild; Fuller's London Pride; guest beers Ⓗ

Years ago the pub was called the Green Dragon. Its fortunes gradually declined; it became run down and, despite a change of name, it eventually closed. Now the current owners have brought it back to life as a vibrant and thriving village local, successfully blending old and new to recreate a genuine community pub with an emphasis on beer and traditional pub games. Guest beers come from a wide range of breweries and the food comprises home-made pizzas and bar snacks. ♨❀♣☀P≟

Swinhope

Click 'em Inn

LN8 6BS (2 miles N of Binbrook on B1203) TF222973
12-3 (not Mon-Wed), 5-11; 12-11.30 Fri & Sat; 12-10.30 Sun ☎ (01472) 398253 ⊕ clickeminn-marketrasen.co.uk

Batemans XXXB; Taylor Landlord; guest beers Ⓗ

Country pub set in the picturesque Lincolnshire Wolds, and a good stopping place for walkers and cyclists. The unusual name originates from the

For we could not now take time for further search (to land our ship) our victuals being much spent especially our beer. **Log of the Mayflower**

counting of sheep through a nearby clicking gate. Good home-cooked food is available in the bar and conservatory. Two guest beers are offered alongside the house beer, Terry's Tipple (from Batemans). An outside covered but unheated area is available to smokers. Local CAMRA Country Pub of the Year 2012. ❀Ⓞ▸♣P≟

Threekingham

Three Kings Inn

Saltersway, NG34 0AU
closed Mon; 12-3, 6-11 (10.30 Sun) ☎ (01529) 240249 ⊕ thethreekingsinn.com

Draught Bass; Taylor Landlord; guest beer Ⓗ

A fine country inn displaying charm and character. Its bright and comfortable lounge bar, with attractive rural prints, and panelled dining room serving locally-sourced food, are deservedly popular with locals and visitors. Guest beers are usually from independent brewers. There is a pleasant beer terrace and garden for summer months and a large function room. The pub's name refers to the slaying, by the Saxons, of three Danish chieftains in battle in 870 at nearby Stow; look for the effigies above the entrance. ♨❀Ⓞ▸AP≟

Waddington

Three Horseshoes

High Street, LN5 9RF
12 (3 Mon; 11 Sat)-midnight; 12-11 Sun ☎ (01522) 720448

John Smith's Bitter; guest beers Ⓗ

A small community pub located in the centre of the village just a short bus journey from Lincoln. The four frequently changing guest beers are mainly sourced from microbreweries. The main bar area is the heart of the pub and is complemented by a smaller lounge with a real fire in winter. Various sports teams make the pub their home, which gives the bar area a lively ambience.
♨☎❀🖰♣≟ᕹ(1,13)

Wainfleet

Batemans Brewery Visitor Centre

Salem Bridge Brewery, Mill Lane, PE24 4JE
closed Mon, Tue & Jan; 11.30-4 Feb-Dec ☎ (01754) 882009 ⊕ bateman.co.uk

Batemans Dark Mild, XB, Yella Belly Gold, XXXB, seasonal beer; guest beer Ⓗ

A visit to the brewery offers the chance to experience the Bateman's blend of proud tradition with forward-looking outlook. Mr George's Bar, within the iconic windmill, is an ideal venue to sample those Good Honest Ales. Further entertainment is to be found with brewery tours featuring the Theatre of Beers, traditional pub games and the pleasant beer garden. A good range of bar snacks is served 12-2pm. Tours are 12.30pm and 2.30pm in summer, 2.30pm winter. Two holiday cottages are available to hire.
♨Q❀Ⓞ🖰👪A⇌♣P≟ᕹ

Waltham

Tilted Barrel

2 Kirkgate, DN37 0LS
11-11 (midnight Thu-Sat) ☎ (01472) 826887

Morland Old Speckled Hen; Tetley Bitter; Theakston Bitter; guest beers Ⓗ

Set in the heart of the village of Waltham, adjacent to the town of Grimsby, the pub has a three-sided bar where the background music level allows for conversation, and a separate dining-area-cum-lounge which can be used for functions. The bar can get crowded – surely the sign of a decent hostelry. Meals are served Sunday lunchtime and all day Tuesday-Saturday. If you wish to linger, en-suite accommodation is available. ⚫️🅷🐸🕭🕪🅿🐾➖🆀(9)

Westwoodside

Carpenters Arms
Newbigg, DN9 2AT (on B1396 in centre of village)
❀ 4 (2 Sat)-11.30; 12-11.30 Sun ☎ (01427) 752416
Black Sheep Best Bitter; Brains The Rev James; Caledonian Deuchars IPA; guest beers 🅷
Popular village local that takes an active part in local community life and has raised significant sums of money each year for charities. Under the present licensees the beer range has increased – five are frequently on offer, including at least two sourced from microbreweries. Traditional games are a feature here, and the pub participates in the annual Haxey Hood contest. 🕭🕪🐾🅿➖🆀(391,399)

Willingham by Stow

Half Moon ▼ 🅛
23 High Street, DN21 5JZ (200yds from B1241 jct)
❀ 12-2 (not Mon), 6-11; 12-11 Sat; 12-10.30 Sun
☎ (01427) 788340
Grafters Traditional, Moonlight; guest beers 🅷
Home to Grafters Brewery, this popular village pub goes from strength to strength. It offers four permanent Grafters ales, and four additional pumps serve a Bateman's beer and three rotating guests, mostly from micros. Seasonal Grafters beers are also sold when brewed. The renowned home-cooked fish and chips are a must, available

lunchtimes and evenings Tuesday-Friday, all day Saturday, and Sunday lunchtime (booking recommended). Brewery tours including food and a tasting session can be arranged by appointment. 🅼🆀🐾🕭🕪🕭🐾🐾➖🆀(100)

Willoughton

Stirrup Inn 🅛
1 Templefield Road, DN21 5RZ
❀ 5 (3 Sat)-11.30; 12-11 Sun ☎ (01427) 668270
Black Sheep Best Bitter; guest beers 🅷
Built from local Lincolnshire limestone, this hidden gem in an out-of-the-way location is well worth seeking out, and you can be sure of a warm welcome. The pub just oozes character, with a roaring log fire in winter, and is popular with locals and folk from further afield. A choice of ales is always available, with Black Sheep Best Bitter a permanent fixture and two changing guests. Pub quizzes are well supported and traditional pub games are played. 🅼🆀🐸🐾🐾🅿➖

Winterton

George Hogg 🅛
Market Street, DN15 9PT
❀ 9.30am (1 Mon & Tue)-11 ☎ (01724) 732270
⊕ thegeorgehogg.co.uk
Tom Wood's Best Bitter; York Guzzler; guest beer 🅷
Popular Grade II-listed marketplace pub and local CAMRA award winner. There is a large lounge dining area and separate public bar, both with real fires. Good-value, locally sourced food is served, plus home-made snacks, and it opens for Sunday breakfast from 9.30am. The guest beer is generally sourced from a local brewery. The pub has an annual beer festival, and is a popular meeting place for football teams and the local supporters' club. An upstairs restaurant plus tea and coffee are also available. 🅼🆀🐸🕭🕭🐾🅿➖🆀(350)

Thorold Arms, Harmston

London index

Central London	**278**	Southgate: N14	289	Barnes: SW13	304
Bishopsgate: EC2*	280	Stoke Newington: N16	289	Battersea: SW11	304
Bloomsbury: WC1*	281	Stroud Green: N4	288	Belgravia: SW1*	301
Chancery Lane: WC2*	281	Winchmore Hill: N21	290	Brixton: SW2	302
Charing Cross: WC2*	281			Brixton: SW9	303
Clerkenwell: EC1*	278	**North West London**	**291**	Carshalton	306
Covent Garden: WC2*	282	Camden Town: NW1	291	Cheam	306
Finsbury: EC1*	279	Euston: NW1*	291	Clapham: SW4	303
Fleet Street: EC4*	280	Hampstead: NW3	291	Earl's Court: SW5*	303
Hatton Garden: EC1*	279	Harefield	292	Gloucester Road: SW7*	303
Holborn: WC1*	281	Harrow	292	Kew	306
Holborn: WC2*	282	Hendon: NW4	292	Kingston upon Thames	306
Old Street: EC1*	279	Kentish Town: NW5	292	Lambeth, South: SW8	303
Smithfield: EC1*	279	Kenton, South	293	New Malden	307
St Pancras: WC1*	281	Rayners Lane	293	Parsons Green: SW6	303
Temple: WC2*	282	Ruislip Common	293	Pimlico: SW1*	301
Tower Hill: EC3*	280	Ruislip Manor	293	Putney: SW15	304
		St John's Wood: NW8	292	Richmond	307
East London	**282**	South Kenton	293	St James: SW1*	302
Aldgate: E1*	282			South Lambeth: SW8	303
Barking	286	**South East London**	**293**	South Wimbledon: SW19	305
Bethnal Green: E2	283	Addiscombe	298	Streatham: SW16	305
Bow: E3	283	Beckenham	298	Streatham Hill: SW2	303
Chadwell Heath	286	Bermondsey: SE1*	293	Surbiton	308
Chingford: E4	284	Bexley	298	Sutton	308
Clapton: E5	284	Bexleyheath	298	Tooting: SW17	305
Collier Row	286	Blackfen	298	Victoria: SW1*	302
Hackney: E8	284	Blackheath: SE3	294	Wallington	308
Hackney, South: E8	284	Borough: SE1*	293	Wandsworth: SW18	305
Hackney Wick: E9	284	Brockley: SE4	294	Westminster: SW1*	302
Haggerston: E2*	283	Bromley	298	Whitehall: SW1*	302
Hornchurch	286	Camberwell: SE5	294	Wimbledon: SW19	306
Leyton: E10	285	Catford: SE6	295	Wimbledon, South: SW19	305
Leytonstone: E11	285	Chelsfield	299		
Plaistow: E13	285	Croydon	299	**West London:**	**308**
Rainham	286	Crystal Palace: SE19	296	Acton: W3	310
Romford	286	Denmark Hill: SE5	295	Brentford	312
Spitalfields: E1*	283	Deptford: SE8	295	Chiswick: W4	310
South Hackney: E8	284	Downe	300	Ealing: W5	310
Upper Walthamstow: E17	285	Dulwich, East: SE22	297	Ealing, West: W13	312
Walthamstow: E17	285	East Dulwich: SE22	297	Feltham	312
Walthamstow, Upper: E17	285	East Greenwich: SE10	295	Greenford	312
Westfield Stratford City: E20	286	Eltham: SE9	295	Hammersmith: W6	311
Woodford Green	286	Farnborough	300	Hampton	312
		Forest Hill: SE23	297	Hampton Hill	313
North London	**287**	Greenwich, East: SE10	295	Hanwell: W7	311
Archway: N19	290	Greenwich, North: SE10	295	Harlington	313
Barnet, High	290	Herne Hill: SE24	297	Hayes	313
Barnet, New	291	Lewisham: SE13	296	Hayes End	313
Canonbury: N5	288	London Bridge: SE1*	294	Hounslow	313
Cockfosters	290	New Cross: SE14	296	Isleworth	313
East Finchley: N2	288	North Greenwich: SE10	295	Maida Hill: W9*	311
Edmonton, Lower: N9	289	Orpington	300	Marylebone: W1*	308
Enfield	290	Peckham: SE15	296	Mayfair: W1*	308
Finchley, East: N2	288	Penge: SE20	297	Norwood Green	313
Finchley, North: N12	289	Petts Wood	300	Notting Hill: W11*	312
High Barnet	290	Plumstead: SE18	296	Notting Hill Gate: W8*	311
Highgate: N6	288	Rotherhithe: SE16	296	Paddington: W2*	309
Holloway: N7	288	Sidcup	300	Shepherd's Bush: W12	312
Hornsey: N8	289	Southwark: SE1*	294	Soho: W1*	309
Hoxton: N1*	287	Upper Belvedere	301	Southall	314
Islington: N1*	287	Waterloo: SE1*	294	Teddington	314
King's Cross: N1*	287	Welling	301	Twickenham	314
Kingsland: N1	288	West Norwood: SE27	298	Uxbridge	314
Lower Edmonton: N9	289	West Wickham	301	West Ealing: W13	312
Muswell Hill: N10	289	Woolwich: SE18	296	Whitton	314
New Barnet	291				
North Finchley: N12	289	**South West London:**	**301**		
Ponders End	291	Balham: SW12	304	*Shown on Inner London map	

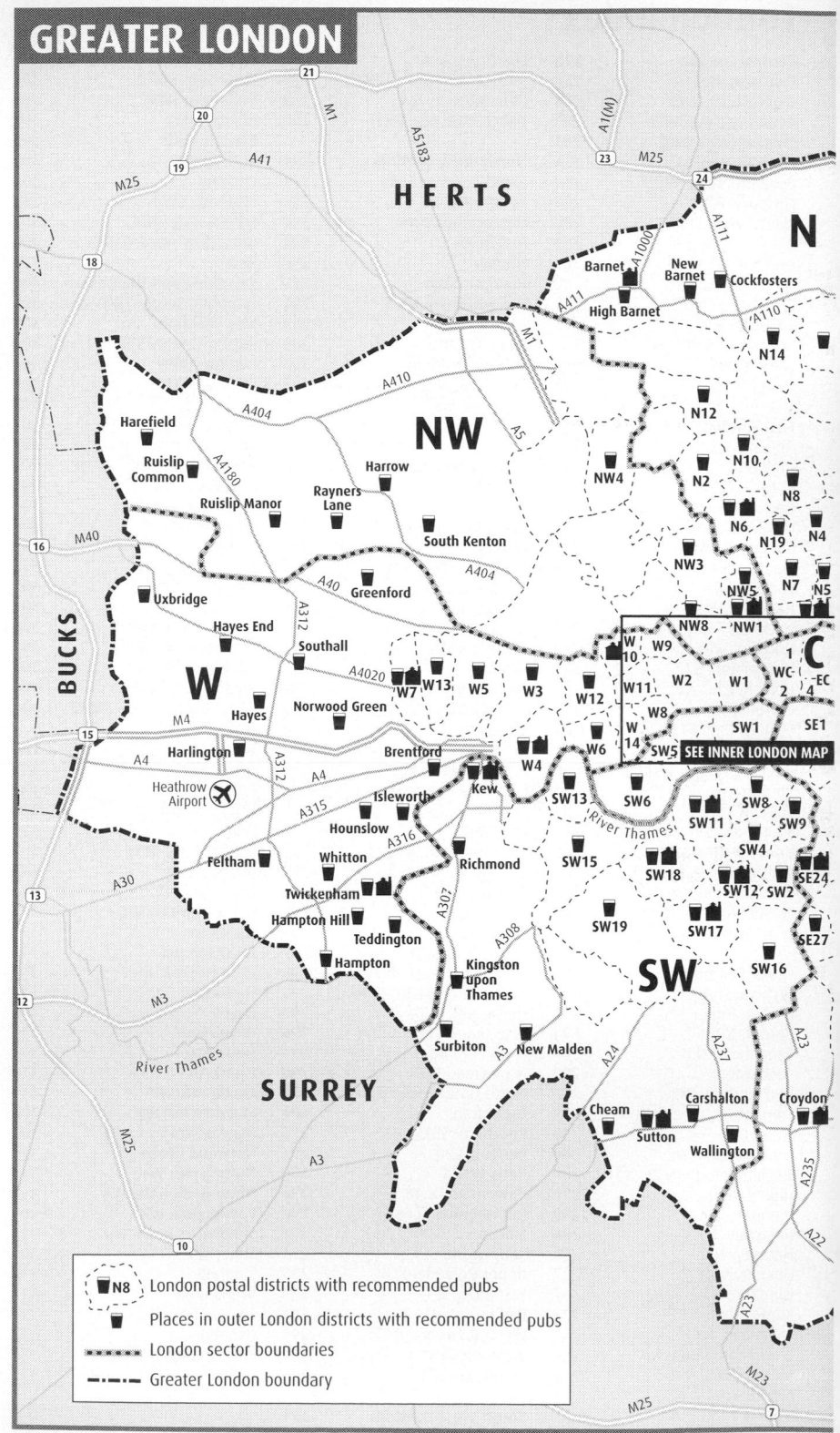

ENGLAND

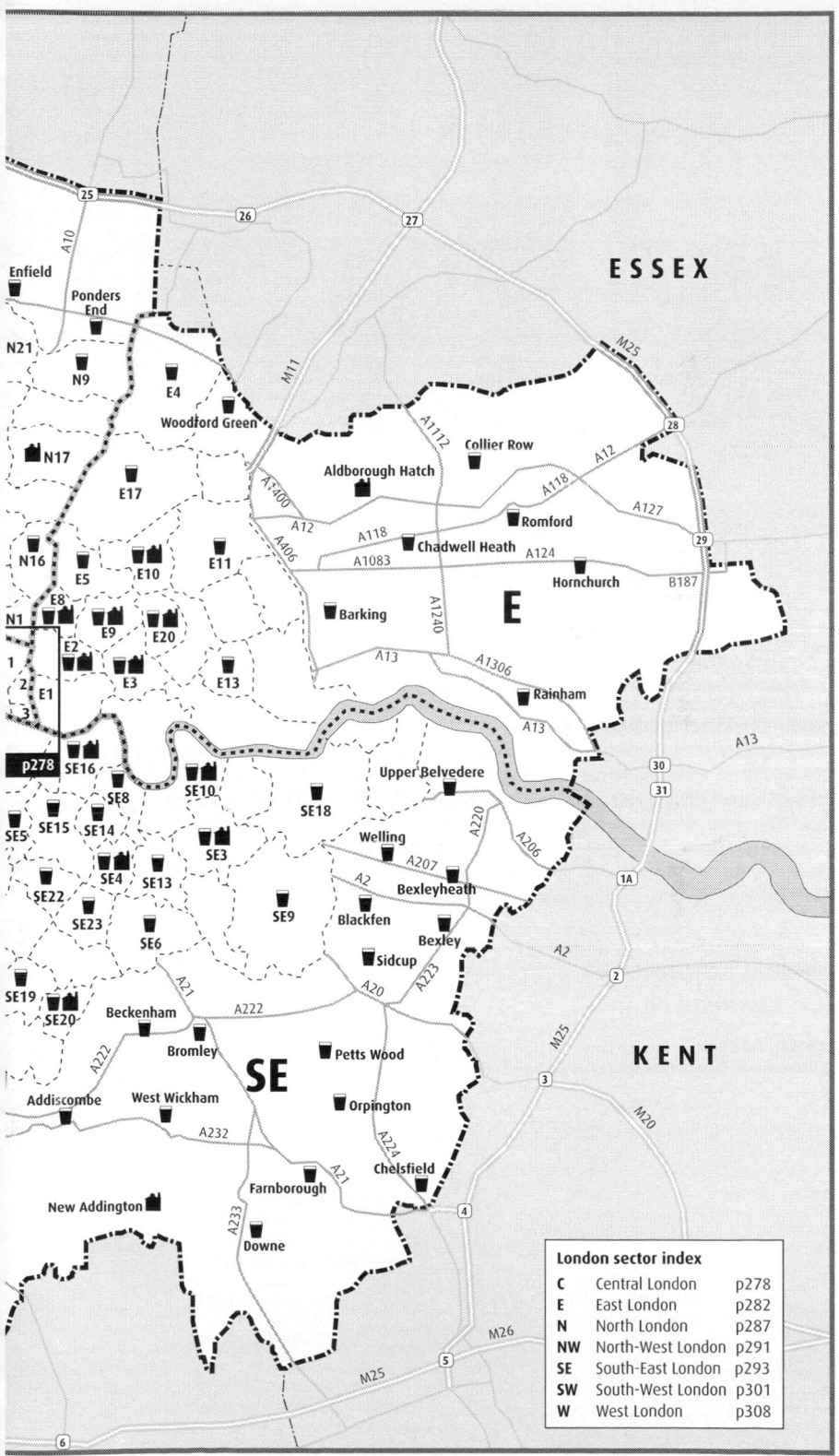

London sector index

C	Central London	p278
E	East London	p282
N	North London	p287
NW	North-West London	p291
SE	South-East London	p293
SW	South-West London	p301
W	West London	p308

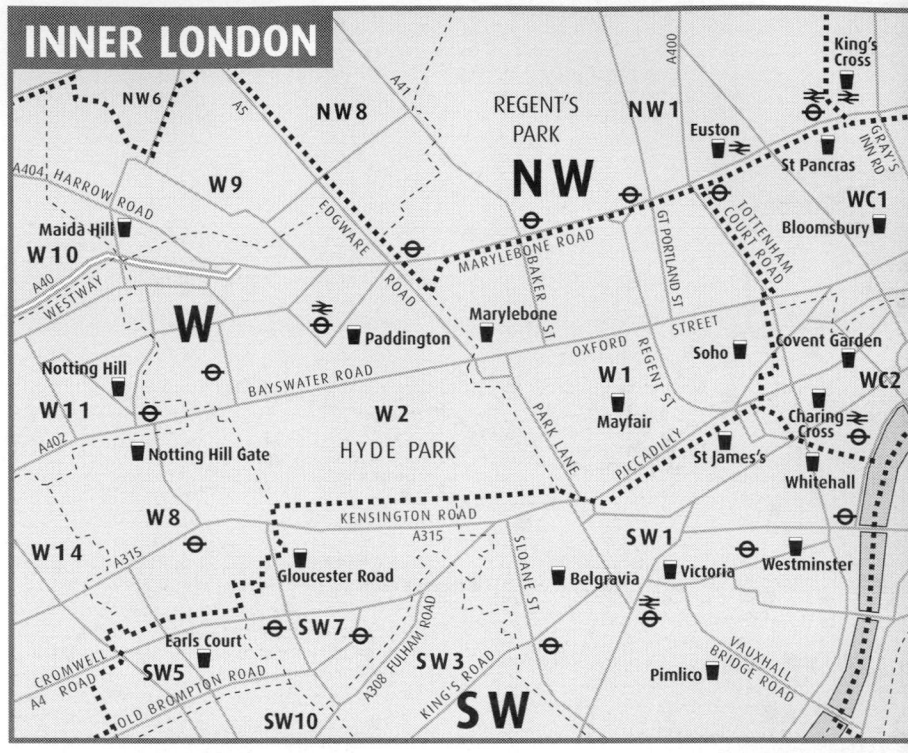

How to find London pubs

Greater London is divided into seven sectors: Central, East, North, North-West, South-East, South-West and West, reflecting postal boundaries. The Central sector includes the City (EC1 to EC4) and Holborn, Covent Garden and The Strand (WC1/2), where pubs are listed in postal district order. In each of the other six sectors the pubs with London postcodes are listed first in postal district order (E1, E2 etc), followed by those in outer London districts, which are listed in alphabetical order (Barking, Chadwell Heath etc) – see Greater London map. Postal district numbers can be found on every street name plate in the London postcode area.

CENTRAL LONDON
EC1: Clerkenwell

Crown Tavern Ⓛ
42 Clerkenwell Green, EC1R 0EG
✪ 12 (9am Sat)-11 ☎ (020) 7523 4973
⊕ thecrowntavernec1.co.uk
Beer range varies Ⓗ
The original 18th-century building included the Apollo Concert Room on the first floor, which is now a bar and function room, while the downstairs bar is divided into a number of attractive drinking areas. Five changing real ales are served, and an extensive à la carte and set menu is available throughout the day, with roasts on Sundays. The beer garden continues out onto the Green, with a view of the Old Sessions House and the Marx Memorial Library. ✿◑≢❸(Farringdon)↤⊠

Gunmakers Ⓛ
13 Eyre Street Hill, EC1R 5ET
✪ 12-11; closed Sat & Sun ☎ (020) 7278 1022
⊕ thegunmakers.co.uk
Beer range varies Ⓗ

Just off Clerkenwell Road, this small pub is usually busy and drinkers often spread out onto the pavement. A Punch tenancy, it is free of tie for real ales and serves a diverse choice of five from a wide range, including beers from microbreweries within 35 miles and mostly delivered direct. Food is served lunchtimes and evenings until 9.30pm. A quiet pub with no music, TV or machines.
Q◑≢(Farringdon)❸(Chancery Lane/Farringdon)⊠

Jerusalem Tavern
55 Britton Street, EC1M 5UQ
✪ 11-11; closed Sat & Sun ☎ (020) 7490 4281
St Peter's Mild, Best Bitter, Golden Ale, seasonal beers Ⓐ
St Peter's Brewery's only pub in London, opened in 1996 as a re-creation of an 18th-century tavern. Up to six beers, including the regular Mild and Golden Ale, are served by air pressure from the fake cask ends on the wall behind the bar. The decor is bare wooden floors and bare walls, with a mixture of wooden chairs and tables. The menu is basic, with two or three specials at lunchtime and bar snacks in the evening. ▲Q◑≢❸(Farringdon)⊠

Olde Mitre ★ 🖫

1 Ely Court, Ely Place, EC1N 6SJ

🕒 11-11; closed Sat & Sun ☎ (020) 7405 4751

Fuller's Discovery, London Pride; guest beers Ⓗ

Identified by CAMRA as one of Britain's Best Real Heritage Pubs, it is hidden in the alley between Hatton Garden and Ely Place. It has extensive wood panelling in the two bars and the snug. A small function room upstairs is available for special occasions. There has been a pub on this site since 1546; the current building is from the 18th century. Fuller's took over in 2009, but Scotty and Kathy still hold their special festivals (Scottish week, mild month, etc). Food is bar snacks including toasties.

Q🏠🍴🖫🌳(Farringdon)⊖(Chancery Lane)🚶🚲♿

EC1: Old Street

Artillery Arms 🖫

102 Bunhill Row, EC1Y 8ND

🕒 12-11 (10.30 Sun) ☎ (020) 7253 4683

🌐 artilleryarms.co.uk

Fuller's Chiswick Bitter, Discovery, London Pride, ESB, seasonal beers Ⓗ

Small single-room pub with a central bar. Some of the servery has stained glass panels, there are also two screens at the window overlooking Bunhill Row, and the venue has a bare wooden floor throughout. Walls at the rear display military prints and a framed collection of cigarette cards. Upstairs is a dining room with a comprehensive menu. There are occasional guest ales and a mini festival is staged in the autumn.

Q🍴🌳⊖(Moorgate/Old St)♿🚲

EC1: Finsbury

Exmouth Arms 🖫

23 Exmouth Market, EC1R 4QL

🕒 10-midnight (1.30am Fri); 12-1.30am Sat; 12-10.30 Sun

☎ (020) 3551 4772 🌐 exmoutharms.com

Beer range varies Ⓗ

Four – typically local – ales are constantly changing alongside a wide range of bottled beers and a dozen keg beers. Food ranges from main meals to sliders (mini-burgers with unusual fillings) to Sunday roasts (served until 10pm, 9pm Sun). Recent rebuilding was in 1915 (see date stone); the exterior shows former ownership by Courage. The inside has however been totally reconstructed in a minimalist fashion. The small bar upstairs is now a cocktail bar and used for overflow on busy nights. 🌳🌳(Farringdon)⊖(Angel/Farringdon)🚲

Old Fountain 🍺 🖫

3 Baldwin Street, EC1V 9NU

🕒 11 (12 Sat)-11; 12-10 Sun ☎ (020) 7253 2970

🌐 oldfountain.co.uk

Fuller's London Pride; guest beers Ⓗ

Privately owned free house split into two: one bar has a dartboard and the other a large fish tank. Relax upstairs on the roof garden, with two large parasols and heating. The comprehensive beer range comes mainly from local and microbreweries; the pub is noted for new brews and an extensive range of local bottled beers. The lunchtime menu is served 12-2.30pm; evening menu 5-10pm. Check Twitter and the website for beer festivals. Local CAMRA Pub of the Year 2013.

🏠🏠🌳🌳⊖🚶🚲♿🚲

EC1: Hatton Garden

Craft Beer Co 🖫

82 Leather Lane, EC1N 7TR

🕒 12-11 (10.30 Sun) ☎ 07502 337339

🌐 thecraftbeerco.com

Beer range varies Ⓗ

A pub that will not disappoint. Two handpumps dispense the specially brewed house beer and a real cider, and 14 more offer guest beers from independent microbreweries. With over 100 international bottled beers besides, you may find it difficult to leave. You can either relax with the real ales in the bar downstairs and admire the clock-faced mirrored ceiling, or go upstairs where there is extra seating. Bar snacks include good-quality Scotch eggs and pork pies.

Q⊖(Chancery Lane)🚶🚲

EC1: Smithfield

Old Red Cow 🖫

71-72 Long Lane, EC1A 9EJ

🕒 12-11 (midnight Fri & Sat) ☎ (020) 7726 2595

🌐 theoldredcow.com

Beer range varies Ⓗ

Small but lively pub near Smithfield Market. Four handpumps serve a changing range of beers, often from local breweries such as Redemption and Windsor & Eton. In addition, 60-70 different bottled beers are also on sale. Good British tapas-style food is served all day. Special events include beer and food pairings, beer tastings, brewery beer festivals and Meet the Brewer nights. An upstairs room can be hired for functions.

🌳🌳🌳(Farringdon)⊖(Barbican)🚶🚲

EC2: Bishopsgate

Hamilton Hall

Unit 32, The Concourse, Liverpool Street Station, EC2M 7PY
☼ 9am-11.30 ☎ (020) 7247 3579
Fuller's London Pride; Greene King Abbot; guest beers Ⓗ

Once a ballroom, now a Wetherspoon pub, with 10 handpumps serving a wide range of brews, including local ales. It is a friendly place inside a beautiful building, where children are welcome. Real ale is dispensed from the entrance-level and upstairs bars. Enjoy service with a smile as this station pub can get very busy. TV screens show train departures and arrivals. Breakfasts are served from 7am on weekdays.
Q❂♿≢⊖(Liverpool St)♨᛫₋⊟

Magpie

12 New Street, EC2M 4TP
✿ 10-11.30; closed Sat & Sun ☎ (020) 7929 3889
Fuller's London Pride; St Austell Nicholson's Pale Ale; Sharp's Doom Bar; guest beers Ⓗ

A long-established inn on the edge of the City, now one of M&B's flagship Nicholson's real ale pubs and very handy for Liverpool Street Station. It can become very crowded in the evening rush hour, when the roadway outside is often pressed into service as an overspill, although many do not notice there is also an upstairs bar that may be available. Up to seven guest beers come from Nicholson's seasonal list.
❂≢⊖(Liverpool St)♨᛫₋⊟

EC3: Tower Hill

Chamberlain Ⓛ

130-135 Minories, EC3N 1NU
✿ 11-11 (midnight Thu & Fri); 12-11 Sat; 12-10.30 Sun
☎ (020) 7680 1500
Fuller's London Pride, ESB, seasonal beers; Gale's Seafarers Ale Ⓗ

One of the few pubs open seven days a week in the City of London. On the right-hand side of the ground floor of the Chamberlain Hotel, close to the Tower of London and Leadenhall covered market, it has entrances from the Minories and from within the hotel. The bar has a granite top and there is plenty of wood and brass to give a quality atmosphere. Food is served until 10pm (9.30pm Sun).
⥿🛏❂♿≢(Fenchurch St)⊖(Tower Gateway/Tower Hill)₋⊟

Hung Drawn & Quartered

26-27 Great Tower Street, EC3R 5AQ
✿ 11-11 (midnight Sat); 11-6 Sun ☎ (020) 7626 6123
⊕ hung-drawn-and-quartered.co.uk
Fuller's Chiswick Bitter, Discovery, London Pride, Bengal Lancer, ESB, seasonal beers Ⓗ

A Fuller's Ale & Pie pub near the Tower of London, in a listed building that was a bank and before that a part of Christ's Hospital, a school founded in 1552 to educate poor children (now in Sussex). The interior boasts high ceilings and wood panelling, and pictures of former monarchs adorn the walls. Food is served until 9pm (5pm Sun). Periodic beer festivals feature other London breweries. The TV is usually mute. Note the gallows.
❂≢(Fenchurch St)⊖(Monument/Tower Gateway/Tower Hill)⊟

Liberty Bounds

15 Trinity Square, EC3N 4AA
☼ 9am-midnight (2am Fri & Sat) ☎ (020) 7481 0513
Fuller's London Pride; Greene King IPA, Abbot; guest beers Ⓗ

A large Wetherspoon pub in a grand building close to the Tower of London, converted to pub use in 1998. Seating is available on two levels in the main bar, with a quieter lounge area upstairs via a wide, grand staircase. This pub attracts a good mix of City workers and tourists, and is one of few in the area to open at weekends. It has the chain's two major beer festivals during the year. Breakfasts are served from 8am.
Q❂♿≢(Fenchurch St)⊖(Tower Gateway/Tower Hill)♨⊟

EC4: Fleet Street

Castle

26 Furnival Street, EC4A 1JS
✿ 11-11; closed Sat & Sun ☎ (020) 7405 5470
Growler Red Car Best Bitter; guest beers Ⓗ

Small Red Car pub with eight handpumps dispensing various guest ales (check the chalkboard for those now serving and what is next). The dark wood panelling is offset by a

INDEPENDENT BREWERIES

Adventure Sutton (NEW)
Barnet Barnet (NEW)
Beavertown E3: Hackney Wick
Belleville SW12: Wandsworth Common (NEW)
Botanist Kew
Brüpond E10: Leyton (NEW)
Brew By Numbers SE16: Southwark (NEW)
Brew Wharf SE1: Borough
Brockley SE4: Brockley (NEW)
Brodie's E10: Leyton
By the Horns SW17: Summerstown
Clarence & Fredericks Croydon (NEW)
Crate E9: Hackney Wick (NEW)
Cronx New Addington (NEW)
Earls N1: Islington (NEW)
East London E10: Leyton
Ellenberg's/Weird Beard W7: Hanwell (NEW)
Five Points E8: Hackney Downs (NEW)
Florence (Head in a Hat) SE24: Herne Hill
Fuller's W4: Chiswick
Ha'penny Aldborough Hatch
Hackney E2: Haggerston
Howling Hops E5: Hackney (NEW)
Kernel SE16: Bermondsey
Lamb W4: Chiswick (NEW)
Late Knights/Shamblemoose SE20: Penge (NEW)
Little Brew NW1: Camden
London Brewing N6: Highgate
London Fields E8: Hackney
Meantime SE10: Greenwich
Moncada W10: Kensal Town
Partizan SE16: South Bermondsey (NEW)
Portobello W10: North Kensington (NEW)
Pressure Drop E8: Hackney (NEW)
Redchurch E2: Bethnal Green
Redemption N17: Tottenham
Rocky Head SW18: Southfields (NEW)
Sambrook's SW11: Battersea
Tap East E20: Stratford
Truman's E2: Hackney Wick
Twickenham Twickenham
Zerodegrees SE3: Blackheath

selection of mirrors, including the mirrored bar back, to brighten the atmosphere, and the long windowshelf bar is divided by two small screens. Upstairs is mainly for lunchtime trade and private functions. The menu is sourced fresh from Borough Market and Smithfield Market (full menu 12-3pm, snacks only eves).
🏔◀🕮🚆(Farringdon)⊖(Chancery Lane/Farringdon) 🚇

WC1: Bloomsbury

Calthorpe Arms
252 Grays Inn Road, WC1X 8JR
✪ 11-11.30 (midnight Fri & Sat); 12-10.30 Sun
☎ (020) 7278 4732
Young's Bitter, Special, seasonal beer; guest beer Ⓗ
Unusual double doors lead into this single-bar corner local. With no music and an unobtrusive corner TV, it is easy either to strike up a conversation at the bar or to take one of the tables along the sides for more privacy. The upstairs dining room opens for lunch (12-2.30pm) but can be booked at other times. Evening meals are served 6-9.30pm. Young's bottle-conditioned beers are stocked. There is pavement seating outside.
🏛◀🕮🚆(King's Cross)⊖(Russell Sq)🍴–🚇

Lamb Ⓛ
94 Lambs Conduit Street, WC1N 3LZ
✪ 12-11 (midnight Thu-Sat); 12-10.30 Sun
☎ (020) 7405 0713
St Austell Tribute; Young's Bitter, Special, seasonal beers; guest beers Ⓗ
Beautifully preserved, Grade II-listed and one of London's Real Heritage pubs, with a small snug and etched glass snob screens in place above the bar. The Empire Bar and restaurant are upstairs. The glorious Victorian history of the pub and area is commemorated by a working polyphon (predecessor to the gramophone). Among nine handpumps, three or four guest beers usually include one from Sambrook's, with a real cider in summer. At the back is a small walled garden.
Q🏛◀🕮⊖(Russell Sq)🍴🚇

WC1: Holborn

Penderel's Oak
286-288 High Holborn, WC1V 7HJ
✪ 9am-11 (midnight Thu; 1am Fri & Sat); 10-11 Sun
☎ (020) 7242 5669
Adnams Broadside; Fuller's London Pride; Greene King IPA, Abbot; guest beers Ⓗ
Large, busy Wetherspoon pub on High Holborn in the direction of Chancery Lane. Tables at the front lead to the bar and to a raised seating area. There is also a back room, and various settees and high stools; low-key lighting adds to the atmosphere. Pavement seating is provided outside and a cellar bar, available for hire, is popular with younger visitors. Food is served from 7am until 10pm and children are welcome during the day.
Q🏛◀🕮♿⊖(Chancery Lane/Holborn)🍴–🚇

WC1: St Pancras

Mabel's Tavern
9 Mabledon Place, WC1H 9AZ
✪ 11-11 (midnight Thu-Sat); 12-10.30 Sun
☎ (020) 7387 7739

Shepherd Neame Master Brew, Kent's Best, Spitfire, Bishops Finger, seasonal beers Ⓗ
Originally owned by Whitbread and called the Kentish Arms (note the plaque on the outside wall), the pub was renamed for landlady Mabel Macinelly, who is said to haunt these cosy premises. Up to the left of the bar is a snug, and a raised area at the back has a traditional fireplace with a large TV screen above it. Various prints and old photos adorn the walls. Food is served until 10pm (9pm Fri-Sun). Handy for the British Library.
🏛◀🕮🚆⊖(Kings Cross/St Pancras)🍴–🚇

Queen's Head
66 Acton Street, WC1X 9NB
✪ 12 (4 Sat)-midnight; 12-11 Sun ☎ (020) 7713 5772
🌐 queensheadlondon.com
Dark Star Hophead; guest beers Ⓗ
Narrow late-Georgian premises with a single bar, a smoking patio at the rear and benches out front. The piano is used for jazz and blues on Thursdays. Guest beers are from microbreweries and include one dark beer. One handpump serves cider, with three more real ciders and a range of keg and bottled beers. Sharing platters of pub snacks are available at this comfortable locals' pub, with occasional tourists, off the Grays Inn Road. May close later weekdays.
🏛◀🕮🚆⊖(Kings Cross/St Pancras)🍺🍴–🚇

WC2: Chancery Lane

Seven Stars
53-54 Carey Street, WC2A 2JB
✪ 11-11; 12-11.30 Sat; 12-10.30 Sun ☎ (020) 7242 8521
Adnams Southwold Bitter, Gunhill, Broadside; guest beers Ⓗ
One of London's Real Heritage Pubs and Grade II-listed, the building is claimed to date from 1602. The bar, with its decorative Victorian bar-back, is in the narrow central space between two other distinctive drinking areas. Impressive mirrors advertise breweries and drinks. The pub is popular with the legal profession and features caricatures with a legal theme and classic film posters. Cat lovers will admire Ray Brown, the resident pub cat. Two guest beers come from smaller regional brewers.
Q◀🕮⊖(Chancery Lane/Holborn/Temple)🚇

WC2: Charing Cross

Harp Ⓛ
47 Chandos Place, WC2N 4HS
✪ 10.30-11.30 (11 Mon); 12-10.30 Sun ☎ (020) 7836 0291
🌐 harpcoventgarden.com
Dark Star Hophead; Harveys Sussex Best Bitter; Sambrook's Wandle, Junction; guest beers Ⓗ
Small, friendly, independent free house that has become a haven for beer choice, generally including a mild or porter and London microbrewery seasonals. A fine range of real ciders is also offered. The narrow bar is adorned with mirrors and portraits. There is no intrusive music or TV and a cosy upstairs room provides a refuge from the busy throng. Numerous past awards culminated in the ultimate accolade, CAMRA National Pub of the Year in 2011.
Q🚆⊖(Charing Cross/Leicester Sq)🍺🚇

WC2: Covent Garden

Coach & Horses
42 Wellington Street, WC2E 7BD
◯ 11-11; 12-10.30 Sun ☎ (020) 7240 0553
Courage Best Bitter; Shepherd Neame Spitfire ℍ
A small independent pub with a lot of Irish
influence, very much a locals' pub but also
welcoming to tourists. A fantastic collection of
about 70 Irish whiskeys and Scotch whiskies is
stocked. Food is served 11-3.30pm Monday to
Saturday and may also be offered at Sunday
lunchtime. There are photos of Gaelic football
teams, and the sport of hurling also features, plus
theatre posters. When you visit, say hello to the bar
team: Jodie, Michael and Sean. Q◖◗Θ☷

Cross Keys ⒧
31 Endell Street, WC2H 9BA
◯ 11-11; 12-10.30 Sun ☎ (020) 7836 5185
⊕ crosskeyscoventgarden.com
Brodie's Mild, London Fields, Jamaican Stout,
seasonal beers; guest beer ℍ
The pub was built in the mid-1840s when Endell
(formerly Belton) Street was widened as part of
clearing the St Giles' Rookery. An ornate façade
reveals a long, welcoming bar, subdued lighting,
comfortable banquette seating and tables and
chairs, and a mix of copper kettles, pans, street
signs, stuffed fish, framed pictures and photos,
Beatles memorabilia and a fine Truman, Hanbury &
Buxton mirror. Families are welcome (over 12s
only) until 7pm unless it is busy. ⟓◖◗Θ♠☷

Nell of Old Drury
29 Catherine Street, WC2B 5JS
◯ 12-2.30, 5-11.30 (midnight Fri); 12-midnight Sat; closed
Sun ☎ (020) 7836 5328 ⊕ nellofolddrury.com
Adnams Broadside; Sambrook's Wandle ℍ
Originally licensed as the Lamb, and known as the
Sir John Falstaff in 1835, this pub was a location in
Hitchcock's film Frenzy. The cosy small bar, decked
with theatre bills and photographs, is a popular
haunt for theatregoers who pre-order interval
drinks. The large bay window with cushion-strewn
ledge gives a good view of the Drury Lane Theatre.
Upstairs there is additional seating. Dogs are
allowed, but no children, and no food is served.
Θ☷

Sun
21 Drury Lane, WC2B 5RH
◯ 12-11.30 (11.45 Fri & Sat; 7 Sun) ☎ (020) 7240 2789
Flowers Original; Greene King IPA ℍ
A locals' pub attracting mainly office workers and
residents from the nearby flats, this Enterprise,
formerly Whitbread, house is an end-of-terrace bar
rebuilt in the 1880s. Regular groups and classes use
the first-floor room and bar. Three TV screens are
available for football and it does get busy in the
evening. Poker night is Tuesday. Dogs are welcome
and children until 7pm. Pizzas and sandwiches are
served until 9pm (4pm Sun).
Θ(Covent Garden/Holborn)☷

White Swan
14 New Row, WC2N 4LF
◯ 10-11 (11.30 Fri & Sat); 12-10.30 Sun ☎ (020) 3077 1129
Fuller's London Pride; St Austell Nicholson's Pale Ale;
Windsor & Eton Knight of the Garter; guest beers ℍ
Once owned by the famous London banking firm
Hoare & Co and formerly an O'Neills outlet, it is
now an M&B Nicholson's pub with eight

handpumps. Just a stone's throw from Covent
Garden, it is popular with tourists. It has been
tastefully refurbished with a small bar; there
is limited seating in the bar area but with more
room past a partition. The first-floor dining room
can be booked for functions.
◖◗⇌(Charing Cross)Θ(Leicester Sq)☷

WC2: Holborn

Ship Tavern
12 Gate Street, WC2A 3HP
◯ 11-11 (midnight Thu-Sat); 11-10.30 Sun
☎ (020) 7405 1992 ⊕ theshiptavern.co.uk
Caledonian Deuchars IPA, 1549; St Austell Tribute;
Wells Bombardier; guest beers ℍ
In a passage behind Holborn Station, a pub has
been on this site since 1549. It used to be one of
the few Younger's pubs in London. Decor is a mix
of alcoves and stools, with mahogany-coloured
walls and prints of early 20th-century ships. Six
handpumps serve regional beers, including two
guests. Food is served all day and regular pie
promotions are held. The Oakroom restaurant
upstairs is available for private dining and there is
live jazz every Sunday. ◖◗Θ☷

WC2: Temple

Devereux
20 Devereux Court, WC2R 3JJ
◯ 12-11; closed Sat & Sun ☎ (020) 7583 4562
Greene King IPA; Marston's EPA; Sambrook's Wandle;
Sharp's Doom Bar; guest beers ℍ
Attractive Grade II-listed pub built in 1844; part of
the site used to be the Grecian Coffee House. The
comfortable lounge with wood panelling has a bar
with five handpumps. Prints on the walls show
local places of interest and historic figures, the
judges and wigs reflecting proximity to the law
courts. Upstairs is a restaurant available for hire.
Ale drinkers can enjoy changing guest beers from
brewers such as Hop Back. ◖◗Θ☷

Edgar Wallace
40 Essex Street, WC2R 3JF
◯ 10.30-11; closed Sat & Sun ☎ (020) 7353 3120
Crouch Vale Brewers Gold; Growler Edgar's Pale Ale;
guest beers ℍ
There has been a pub on this site since 1777. Now
leased from Enterprise, this one has so far collected
about 140 of the 170 or so books written by Edgar
Wallace. The comfortable downstairs room has a
fine wooden bar with seven handpumps and there
is also seating upstairs. The pub operates a try-
before-you-buy policy but, to compensate for this,
half pints are charged at a premium rate. Look out
for beer festivals. Q◖◗Θ☷

EAST LONDON
E1: Aldgate

Dispensary
19A Leman Street, E1 8EN
◯ 12-11; closed Sat & Sun ☎ (020) 7977 0486
⊕ thedispensarylondon.co.uk
Growler Florence NightingAle; guest beers ℍ
Grade II-listed former hospital that started a new
life as a pub and dining house in 2006. There are
five handpumps to choose from, with up to four
guest ales selected from local and regional
breweries alongside the house beer; on Monday

there will be one or two leading to a full house on Thursday and Friday. There is plenty of seating for eating and drinking, including on a balcony above the bar, and also a function room that can be hired. Q◑▶✆(Aldgate East)●½–🖿

Goodman's Field
87-91 Mansell Street, E1 8AN
✪ 9am-11 ☎ (020) 7680 2850
Fuller's London Pride; Greene King IPA, Abbot; guest beers H
Modern Wetherspoon pub not far from Tower Bridge and the Tower of London. The spacious L-shaped bar is comfortably furnished. The TVs are muted except for major sporting events, and are confined to one area. Breakfast is available from 7.30am (8.30am weekends). The three regular beers are accompanied by three guests and a real cider (usually Westons). This pub is usually less busy than those nearer the Tower and is fully accessible by wheelchair. Q♿🐕◑▶♿✆(Fenchurch St)✆(Tower Gateway/Tower Hill)●🖿

E1: Spitalfields
Pride of Spitalfields L
3 Heneage Street, E1 5LJ
✪ 11-midnight (2am Fri & Sat); 12-midnight Sun
☎ (020) 7247 8933
Crouch Vale Brewers Gold; Fuller's London Pride, ESB; Sharp's Doom Bar; guest beer H
A Guide regular just off Brick Lane with its numerous curry houses, and a short walk from Liverpool Street Station and the City. A small free house, it is always busy, with an excellent atmosphere. Lenny the resident cat normally bags a comfortable seat by the radiator. Pub food is available weekday lunchtimes. The piano is there for customers to play and music fans can play their own discs on Monday nights. ◀≠(Liverpool St)✆(Aldgate East/Shoreditch High St)½–🖿

E2: Bethnal Green
Camel L
277 Globe Road, E2 0JD
✪ 4 (12 Fri & Sat)-11; 12-10.30 Sun ☎ (020) 8983 9888
Crouch Vale Brewers Gold; Sambrook's Wandle, Junction; guest beers H
An updated version of a tile-fronted East End back-street boozer, close to famous boxing venue York Hall and the Bethnal Green Museum of Childhood. Now candlelit and filled with a predominantly young crowd, with quiet background music, the pub is popular for its food, especially the pies, as well as its beer. Two or three real ciders complement the ales from many local brewers. There are tables on the street outside. Regular quiz nights are held. ✪◑▶≠(Bethnal Green/Cambridge Heath)✆●🖿

Carpenter's Arms
73 Cheshire Street, E2 6EG
✪ 4-11.30; 12-11 Thu; 12-12.30am Fri & Sat; 12-11 Sun
☎ (020) 7739 6342 ⊕ carpentersarmsfreehouse.com
Taylor Landlord; guest beers H
Former Truman's street-corner pub, tastefully refurbished and popular with the young Whitechapel crowd. Pictures on the wall show historic views of the pub and local area. An

opening at the rear of the front bar leads to two back rooms, the garden and smoking area, and the toilets. An extensive selection of world and UK bottled beers is available, plus bar meals including cured meats, cheese and pâté, and lunchtime specials such as tagliatelle or mussels. ✪◑≠✆(Shoreditch High St)½–🖿

E2: Haggerston
Albion in Goldsmith's Row L
94 Goldsmith's Row, E2 8QY
✪ 12-11 (1am Fri & Sat); 12-midnight Sun
☎ (020) 7739 0185 ⊕ thealbioningoldsmithsrow.co.uk
Adnams Ghost Ship; Caledonian Deuchars IPA; Taylor Landlord; guest beer H
A rarity in East London, this free house is operated by the owner, who has been running the pub since 1998. It was built by West's Brewery in the 1920s and was the Duke of Sussex until renamed by the present landlord after his favourite football team, West Bromwich Albion. The guest beer is chosen from a micro or regional brewery. Bar snacks are served. Situated between Broadway Market and Columbia Flower Market, it attracts a cosmopolitan clientele. 🐕✪≠(Cambridge Heath)½–🖿

Sebright Arms
31-35 Coate Street, E2 9AG
✪ 5 11 (midnight Thu-Sat); 12-10.30 Sun
☎ (020) 7729 0937 ⊕ sebrightarms.co.uk
Beer range varies H
Previously a pub with a chequered history, the Sebright is now a very busy establishment serving up to four real ales and bottle-conditioned beer, including beers from London microbreweries, along with real cider. The interior comprises two wood-panelled rooms. Food (run separately from the bar) is available from a varying menu and includes Sunday roasts. Bi-annual beer festivals are held, and various entertainment is staged in The Venue downstairs. Otherwise there is music but no TVs. ✪▶≠(Cambridge Heath)●🖿

E3: Bow
Eleanor Arms
460 Old Ford Road, E3 5JP
✪ 12 (4 Mon-Thu)-11; 12-10.30 Sun ☎ (020) 8980 6992
⊕ eleanorarms.co.uk
Shepherd Neame Kent's Best, seasonal beers H
Built in 1879, this pub off the beaten track is definitely worth a visit. The rear area was once a separate bar, and there is 1930s wood panelling. Quiz night is the first Thursday of the month and there is a jazz jam on Sundays. Friday and Saturday evenings feature music played from the landlord's gigantic collection, from Fairport to the Pogues. This is the No.1 pub in London according to a recent Danish pub guide. ✪✆(Bow Church/Bow Rd)●½–🖿(8)

Palm Tree
127 Grove Road, E3 5RP (in Mile End Park; road access via Haverfield Rd)
✪ 12.30-midnight (2am Sun); 12-midnight Sun
☎ (020) 8980 2918
Beer range varies H
Stepping inside this pub is like stepping back in time. Rebuilt by Truman's and now one of London's Real Heritage Pubs, it was marooned when surrounding buildings were demolished to create

Mile End Park. Run by the same family for over 35 years, it gives you a real East End welcome, serving a varied range of beers from two handpumps. Live music at weekends, no fruit machines and no widescreen TVs make for the right atmosphere. Real cider is usually available.
&⊕&⊖(Mile End)♦P⁵–⊟

E4: Chingford

King's Ford ⎩
250-252 Chingford Mount Road, E4 8JL
✪ 9am-midnight (1am Fri & Sat) ☎ (020) 8523 9365
Courage Directors; Greene King Abbot; Ruddles Best Bitter; guest beer Ⓗ
A spacious Wetherspoon conversion, the long single room has the bar halfway down on the right-hand side. There are 10 handpumps, four on the front serving regular ales and six serving the cider and guest ales, including at least one from a local brewery. As well as the two main Wetherspoon beer festivals, it also holds local beer festivals and Meet the Brewer nights. Two large screens are mute except for major sporting events. Breakfasts are served from 8am. ⅁⊕&♦⁵–⊟

King's Head ⎩
2B Kings Head Hill, E4 7EA
✪ 12-11 (midnight Fri & Sat) ☎ (020) 8529 6283
⊕ thekingsheadchingford.co.uk
Courage Best Bitter; Fuller's London Pride; Taylor Landlord; Young's Bitter; guest beers Ⓗ
A popular and welcoming Stonegate pub located in leafy North Chingford. It is very roomy, with various seating areas, a small garden and a car park. The number of handpumps has recently increased to 10, to include one real cider, five regular beers (selected by customer vote) and four guest ales, often with one from a local brewery. Food is available all day from a wide-ranging menu. Quiz nights are Sunday and Wednesday evenings.
&Q⊕⊕&⇌♦P⁵–⊟

Station House
134-138 Station Road, E4 6AN
✪ 12-11 (1am Fri & Sat) ☎ (020) 8529 8576
Banks's Mild; Marston's Pedigree, seasonal beer; guest beer Ⓗ
A free house opposite Chingford Station and very close to popular Epping Forest – walkers and cyclists are welcome. Its roomy interior attracts a wide mix of customers during the day but it targets a younger crowd on Friday and Saturday evenings, when there is a DJ. Beers from five handpumps include three guests, and a good, all-round food menu is available. Quiz night is Thursday.
⊕⊕&&⇌♣P⁵–⊟

E5: Clapton

Anchor & Hope ⎩
15 High Hill Ferry, E5 9HG (800yds N of Lea Bridge Rd, along river path)
✪ 1-11 (midnight Fri & Sat); 12-11 Sun ☎ (020) 8806 1730
Fuller's London Pride, ESB; guest beers Ⓗ
One of Fuller's smallest pubs, on the bank of the River Lea and dating from about 1850. Refurbished a couple of years ago, it has one bar with wood panelling and a dartboard at the rear, with a wood fire and bar at the front. Drinkers include wildlife enthusiasts and bird watchers, boaters and locals. Guest beers are from the Fuller's seasonal range.

With occasional live music and pub quizzes, and barbecues in summer, it is worth seeking out.
&&♣⁵–⊟(393)

Clapton Hart ⎩
231 Lower Clapton Road, E5 8EG
✪ 4-11 Mon-Wed; 12-midnight; 12-11 Sun
☎ (020) 8985 8124 ⊕ claptonhart.com
Beer range varies Ⓗ
This multi-roomed Antic pub is a real oasis. Eight handpumps serve a changing range of ales, mostly from small breweries. Staff are helpful, with tasters readily offered. The interior could be described as shabby chic, with an assortment of furniture and bric-a-brac. Food is served Monday to Friday 5-9.30pm, Saturday 12-9.30pm and Sunday 12-4pm for roasts and 6-9pm. Children are permitted until 9pm. Music is played, but there are no TVs.
&⅁⊕⊕⊖⊟

E8: Hackney

Cock Tavern ⎩
315 Mare Street, E8 1EJ
✪ 12-11 (1am Fri & Sat); 12-11.30 Sun ☎ (020) 8533 6369
Beer range varies Ⓗ
There has been a Cock Tavern in central Hackney since the 1650s, this latest incarnation having been built by Truman's in the 1930s. It is a bustling, town-centre, single-roomed pub which boasts Hackney's smallest pub garden. The Howling Hops brewery is located in the cellar and four home-brewed beers are usually on sale, alongside varying guest beers and a good selection of real ciders. Basic but high-quality bar snacks are served.
⇌(Hackney Downs)⊖(Hackney Central)♦⁵–⊟

E8: South Hackney

Dove ⎩
24-28 Broadway Market, E8 4QJ
✪ 12-11 (midnight Fri & Sat) ☎ (020) 7275 7617
Crouch Vale Brewers Gold; Taylor Landlord; guest beers Ⓗ
At the bottom of Broadway Market, this street-corner pub always has a vibrant atmosphere. The single bar has a good-size drinking area, with more seating to the rear. At least one local beer and another from a microbrewery are available on the six handpumps; there is also a wide selection of European (especially Belgian) bottled and draught beers. Food choices include Thai curry, game pie, wild boar burgers and four different sausages to accompany onion gravy and mash.
Q⊕⊕&⊖(London Fields)⊟(236,394)

E9: Hackney Wick

Crate Brewery & Pizzeria ⎩
Unit 7, White Building, Queen's Yard, White Post Lane, E9 5EN (down steps by canal bridge)
✪ 12-10.30 ☎ 07834 275687 ⊕ cratebrewery.com
Crate Golden, Best Bitter; guest beers Ⓗ
Four varying cask ales, bottle-conditioned and keg beers are produced at this canalside brewpub in a former printworks. Up to 50 other bottled beers are also on offer. The bar and furnishings were designed and built by local people using reclaimed materials. Brunch is served 9am-noon and pizzas 12-10pm. Children are welcome. Music is played, but there are no TV screens.
⅁⊕⊕&⊖⁵–⊟(276,488)

E10: Leyton

Drum L
557-559 Lea Bridge Road, E10 7EQ
✪ 9am-midnight (1am Fri & Sat) ☎ (020) 8539 9845
Greene King Abbot; Ruddles Best Bitter; guest beers H
This is one of the original pubs in the Wetherspoon chain. Along one long single bar in front of the main seating area are 10 handpumps, one usually serving a locally brewed beer and one a real cider. To the rear is additional seating and a family area, with an enclosed garden at the back. The central TV screen is mute except for major sporting events.
✿◗⊖(Leyton Midland Rd)●'-⊞

King William the Fourth L
816 High Road Leyton, E10 6AE
✪ 11-midnight (1am Fri & Sat); 12-midnight Sun
☎ (020) 8556 2460 ⊕ williamthefourth.net
Beer range varies H
Large Victorian corner pub with many original features. Brodie's brews its beers at the rear behind the garden. Two Brodie's beer festivals are yearly attractions. The single bar is to the right of a large seating area, with extra seating in the rear non-serving bar. Sporting events are shown on a large screen at the front and a smaller one in the rear bar area. Live music features at weekends. B&B is also available.
✿⇌◗⊖(Leyton Midland Rd)♣⊞

Leyton Orient Supporters Club L
Matchroom Stadium, Oliver Road, E10 5NF
✪ from 12.30 Sat match days; 5.30 weekdays (not during game) ☎ (020) 8988 8288 ⊕ orientsupporters.org
Mighty Oak Oscar Wilde G; guest beers H
This may be the best clubhouse in the Football League. Serving real ale since 1995, it now usually offers a range of seven, and one or two ciders or perries, with bar snacks and rolls available. Closed during matches, it reopens afterwards. Two beer festivals are held each season, plus special brewery-themed nights. Free entry is permitted with a CAMRA membership card or a copy of the Guide. It has previously shared the national CAMRA Club of the Year award. ♿⊖●'-⊞

E11: Leytonstone

Red Lion L
640 High Road Leytonstone, E11 3AA
✪ 12-11 (midnight Thu; 2am Fri & Sat) ☎ (020) 8988 2929
⊕ theredlionleytonstone.com
Beer range varies H
Large Victorian pub in the heart of Leytonstone which has become very popular since its reopening by Antic. It has 10 handpumps with a changing selection from small breweries such as Redemption and Thornbridge. A varied menu offers quality food at pub prices. You will find a quiz night on Mondays, DJs on Fridays and Saturdays, and live music on Sundays.
✿◗⊖(Leytonstone/Leytonstone High Rd)
♣●'-⊞(257,W14)

E13: Plaistow

Black Lion
59-61 High Street, E13 0AD
✪ 11-11; 12-10.30 Sun ☎ (020) 8472 2351
⊕ blacklionplaistow.co.uk
Beer range varies H
An old coaching inn with beams and wood panelling, rebuilt in 1747. The smaller back bar is accessible by a separate door or through the end of the main bar. Next to the original cobbled courtyard, stables and outbuildings have been converted to a function room for hire and another room used by West Ham Boys Amateur Boxing Club. Up to six beers often feature Courage Best Bitter, Sharp's and Mighty Oak. The landlord has been here for 27 years. ✿◗⇌⊖P'-⊞

E17: Upper Walthamstow

Duke's Head
112 Wood Street, E17 3HX
✪ 12-11 (midnight Fri); 11-11 Sat; 12-10.30 Sun
☎ (020) 8521 9347
Greene King IPA; Wychwood Hobgoblin; guest beer H
There has been a pub on this site since 1722; the current establishment dates from 1837. Now an Enterprise tenancy, it has a single L-shaped bar, with plenty of tables and chairs (moved when entertainment is on) at the front, and a pool table towards the back. It is renowned for its music nights, which are usually on a Friday or Saturday. The bands are mainly rock or heavy metal with the occasional tribute act. ✿⇌(Wood St)P'-⊞(W16)

E17: Walthamstow

Bell L
617 Forest Road, E17 4NE
✪ 12-11 (midnight Wed & Thu; 1am Fri & Sat)
☎ (020) 8523 2277 ⊕ belle17.com
Beer range varies H
Large Victorian pub refurbished and reopened in 2012. The interior is open plan but has two distinct areas. It is comfortably furnished and often very busy. Eight handpumps serve a range of ales from regional, micro and local breweries. Tuesday is quiz night, DJs provide entertainment Fridays and Saturday evening, and live jazz is performed on Sunday evening. Food is available all day. Children are allowed until 8pm. The smoking area is spacious. There are no TV screens.
♿⤳✿◗♿⇌⊖(Walthamstow Central)'-⊞

Nag's Head L
9 Orford Road, E17 9LP
✪ 12-11 (10.30 Sun) ☎ (020) 8520 9709
⊕ thenagshead17.com
Mighty Oak Oscar Wilde; St Austell Tribute; Taylor Landlord; guest beers H
A cat-friendly pub in the heart of Walthamstow Village conservation area; look out for Tetley Tales, for sale behind the bar, written in honour of Tetley, the legendary Walthamstow Village cat. Seven handpumps serve a varied range of ales. There are wine tastings and pilates upstairs and on Fridays and Saturdays an extra quiet bar serves spirits and bottled beers. Outside seating is at the front and a covered patio at the rear. Food is served all day.
✿◗⇌⊖(Walthamstow Central)'-⊞(W12)

Olde Rose & Crown L
53-55 Hoe Street, E17 4SA
✪ 12-11 (midnight Fri & Sat) ☎ (020) 8509 3880
⊕ yeolderoseandcrowntheatrepub.co.uk
Beer range varies H
A large and friendly Victorian pub. Six handpumps serve beers from SIBA and local breweries alongside one cider pump and two cider boxes on

the back bar. The theatre upstairs has regular productions and hosts the Walthamstow folk club, quiz nights and comedy club nights. Also held in the bar are live music events and a monthly 78s disco. Food on Wednesday, Friday and Saturday evenings comes from an outside concession on the forecourt. Sunday roast is served 1-5pm. Look out for special beer festivals.
🕏◁≢⊖(Walthamstow Central)♠⁺–🖾

E20: Westfield Stratford City

Tap East 🗓
7 International Square, Montfichet Road, E20 1ET
🕏 11-11; 12-10 Sun ☎ (020) 8555 4467
Tap East East End Mild, James Wilson Bitter, guest beers 🖽
A brewpub opened in 2011 in Europe's largest shopping centre, located in the Great Eastern Market at the far end of the lower mall. You can see the brewery from outside through a glass door and windows. Three house beers, three guests and a real cider are served, and over 100 international bottled beers are also available. Traditional pub food is served until 10pm. Just the place to relax and escape the shops.
🕏◁▲≢⊖(Stratford/Stratford International)⁺–🖾

Barking

Barking Dog
61 Station Parade, IG11 8TU
🕏 9am-11 (10.30 Sun) ☎ (020) 8507 9109
Greene King Abbot; Ruddles Best Bitter; guest beers 🖽
A Wetherspoon pub close to Barking Station and numerous bus routes, popular with locals and passing commuters alike. It can be boisterous, and has less impressive decor than some pubs in this chain, but there are 12 handpumps serving up to six different guest beers of varying types and strengths, plus four periodically changing regular beers and two real ciders from Westons. Food is served all day (breakfasts from 8am) and muted TV screens show rolling news. ⭢◁▲≢⊖♠⁺–🖾

Chadwell Heath

Eva Hart ▼
1128 High Road, RM6 4AH (on A118)
🕏 9am-midnight ☎ (020) 8597 1069
Courage Directors; Greene King Abbot; Ruddles Best Bitter; Wychwood Hobgoblin; guest beers 🖽
Large, comfortable Wetherspoon pub in a building that used to be the local police station. It is named after a local singer and music teacher who was one of the longest-living survivors of the Titanic disaster; photographs and memorabilia are on display. A great choice of four or more guest ales is normally available on handpump, usually including at least one stout or porter. Good-value food is served 8am-10pm. Local CAMRA Pub of the Year 2013. ⭢🕏◁▲≢P⁺–🖾

Collier Row

Colley Rowe Inn
54-56 Collier Row Road, RM5 3PA (on B174)
🕏 9am-midnight (1am Wed & Thu; 2am Fri & Sat)
☎ (01708) 760633
Greene King Abbot; Ruddles Best Bitter; guest beers 🖽

Pleasant Wetherspoon pub, with some cosy alcoves, which provides some of the best real ale in the Romford area and is managed by a CAMRA member. Three or four guest beers are normally available, plus three real ciders from Westons, or sometimes a perry. Food is served all day every day. The Colley is a 10-minute bus ride from Romford railway station (on three bus routes, near three other routes). There is a segregated smoking area on the pavement. Q◁▲♠⁺–🖾(247,252,294)

Hornchurch

JJ Moons
48-52 High Street, RM12 4UN (on A124)
🕏 9am-11.30 (12.30am Fri) ☎ (01708) 478410
Greene King Abbot; Ruddles Best Bitter; Thornbridge Jaipur IPA; Wychwood Hobgoblin; guest beers 🖽
Busy Wetherspoon high-street pub, popular with all age groups, featuring a changing selection of ales with an emphasis on breweries from London and the South East. The Jaipur IPA alternates with Hobgoblin. Watercolour paintings of local scenes provide the main decoration, with the usual local-interest panels to the rear of the pub. A family area is available until 6pm.
Q◁▲≢(Emerson Park)⁺–🖾

Rainham

Phoenix 🗓
Broadway, RM13 9YW (on B1335, near clock tower)
🕏 11-11; 12-3, 7-11 Sun ☎ (01708) 553700
Courage Directors; Fuller's London Pride; Greene King Abbot; John Smith's Bitter; guest beers 🖽
Busy, spacious town pub close to Rainham Station and convenient for the RSPB Rainham Marshes nature reserve. It has two bars: a public bar with dartboard, and a saloon for dining. Poker is played on Wednesday, quizzes and live performances alternate on Thursday and Saturday, and Sunday offers more entertainment. The large garden has five aviaries and a barbecue area. A family fun day is held every bank holiday Monday. Accommodation comprises seven twin rooms and one single. 🕏🛏◁🍴≢♣P⁺–🖾

Romford

Moon & Stars
99-103 South Street, RM1 1NX
🕏 9am-midnight (1am Fri & Sat) ☎ (01708) 730117
Courage Directors; Greene King Abbot; Ruddles Best Bitter; guest beers 🖽
Popular Wetherspoon pub, handy for Romford railway station and buses. Five rotating guest beers range in strength from session bitters to strong ales, catering for all tastes. Friday and Saturday evenings are busy, which makes for an exciting atmosphere, although finding a table may be difficult. Breakfast is available from 8am to noon, and good-value coffees are served. The full menu is available until 10pm. Real ciders come from the Westons range. Q◁▲≢♠⁺–🖾

Woodford Green

Cricketers 🗓
299-301 High Road, IG8 9HQ (on A1099)
🕏 11.30-11 (midnight Fri & Sat); 12-11 Sun
☎ (020) 8504 2734
McMullen AK, Cask Ale, Country Bitter 🖽

A warm and comfortable two-bar local with a dartboard in the public bar and plaques in the saloon for all 18 first-class cricket counties, together with photographs of former local MP Sir Winston Churchill, whose statue stands on the green almost opposite. Good-value food is served Monday to Saturday lunchtimes. There are picnic tables on the front patio, and a covered smoking area with seating at the rear. Boules is played on a pitch behind the pub. ✿◗🍺♣P¹⁻🚃(179,W13)

Travellers Friend
496-498 High Road, IG8 0PN (on slip road off A104)
✿ 12-11 ☎ (020) 8504 2435
Adnams Broadside; Courage Best Bitter; Greene King IPA Gold; Morland Original Bitter; Wells Bombardier; guest beer Ⓗ
One of London's Real Heritage Pubs, this gem of a friendly, comfortable local features oak-panelled walls and rare original snob screens. Five beers are served by handpump, including a guest ale. As far as is known, the pub has never sold keg bitter. A comfortable heated patio and smoking area is at the rear, picnic tables are at the front and there is a small car park. Q✿◗P¹⁻🚃(20,179,W13)

NORTH LONDON
N1: Hoxton

Baring Ⓛ
55 Baring Street, N1 3DS
✿ 12-11 (10.30 Sun) ☎ (020) 7359 5785
Adnams Broadside; Taylor Landlord; guest beers Ⓗ
A corner pub just off New North Road, offering welcome seating with settees in the corner. An interesting selection of books is available, along with board games, and a big-screen TV shows sports. Westons Old Rosie cider is served and lunchtime and evening meals are provided. There is a garden to the rear. The pub has its own football and cricket teams. 🏠✿◗⇌(Essex Rd)♣🐾¹⁻🚃

Howl at the Moon Ⓛ
178 Hoxton Street, N1 5LH
✿ 12-11 (1am Fri & Sat) ☎ (020) 3341 2525
⊕ hoxtonhowl.com
Hackney Best Bitter; guest beers Ⓗ
A pleasant conversion of a disused pub in a once run-down but now revived area. Five real ales are served, with one real cider on tap plus two cider boxes behind the bar. A superb selection of music is played. Mixed seating consists of sofas and chairs around the bar, and numerous interesting items adorn the walls. The pleasant staff offer tastings. Real English food is served lunchtimes and evenings at a reasonable price. Live blues features on Friday. ✿◗🍺♣🐾¹⁻🚃

Prince Arthur
49 Brunswick Place, N1 6EB
✿ 11.30-midnight; 12-6 Sat & Sun ☎ (020) 7253 3187
Shepherd Neame Master Brew, Spitfire, seasonal beers Ⓗ
This corner pub with traditionally glazed windows is a Shepherd Neame tied house. Situated near the new Tech City development on Old Street, it attracts two sets of clientèle: local residents and IT workers. As the landlord used to be a boxer, the walls are adorned with photographs of the sport. Sandwiches are available, though not main meals. There is also a dartboard, and a small seating area outside for smokers. ✿◗😀(Old St)♣¹⁻🚃

N1: Islington

Barnsbury Ⓛ
209-211 Liverpool Road, N1 1LX
✿ 12-11 (10.30 Sun) ☎ (020) 7607 5519
⊕ thebarnsbury.co.uk
Beer range varies Ⓗ
Large, traditional, friendly local with a separate dining area and rear garden terrace. A free house, it offers up to four changing real ales ranging from light to dark. There are regular pub favourites on the menu as well as more modern food; the various Sunday roasts are popular with locals. Recent refurbishment has subtly lifted the interior, which is comfortable and bright, with an interesting take on chandeliers. It is a relaxing oasis half a mile from the Angel. ✿◗😀(Angel)¹⁻🚃

Charles Lamb
16 Elia Street, N1 8DE
✿ 12 (4 Mon & Tue)-11; 12-10.30 Sun ☎ (020) 7837 5040
⊕ thecharleslambpub.com
Dark Star Hophead; Windsor & Eton Windsor Knot; guest beers Ⓗ
Charming, deservedly busy little pub serving four real ales, all from independent brewers and always in perfect condition, as well as occasional cask cider. Service is fast, friendly and efficient. There is also a worthwhile range of bottle-conditioned ales. Food is a point of pride, but all seating is available to non-diners. The decor is traditional with bare floorboards. There is some outside seating in a quiet street. ✿◗😀(Angel)♣¹⁻🚃

New Rose Ⓛ
84-86 Essex Road, N1 8LU
✿ 12-11 (midnight Thu; 2am Fri & Sat); 12-10.30 Sun
☎ (020) 7226 1082 ⊕ thenewrose.co.uk
Beer range varies Ⓗ
Spacious and friendly pub, traditional but quirky, in the heart of Islington. A changing range of four quality real ales, light through dark, is sold. A tempting menu of pub favourites, made from locally sourced ingredients, features home-cooked pizzas as a speciality. Enjoy a pint in the small rear garden or on a bench at the front, catch the big game on screen, or chill with DJ sounds on late nights. 🏠✿◗⇌(Essex Rd)😀(Angel)¹⁻🚃

N1: King's Cross

Parcel Yard
Unit M8, Northern Entrance, King's Cross Station, N1C 4AH
✿ 8am-11; 9am-10.30 Sun ☎ (020) 7713 7258
⊕ parcelyard.co.uk
Fuller's Chiswick Bitter, Discovery, London Pride, seasonal beers; Gale's Seafarers Ale; guest beers Ⓗ
Large pub approached by stairs at the end of a new concourse. Used by local workers, commuters and for meetings, as well as bars on two levels there are semi-private rooms converted from offices (which can be booked) and an indoor balcony. The lower bar has 12 handpumps, the upstairs bar fewer. There is no music and the interior consists of minimal decor and rescued furniture. Breakfast is served until 11.45am, main meals 12-10pm. Disabled access is by lift. There are no smoking facilities. Q◗♿⇌😀🚃

N1: Kingsland

Duke of Wellington Ⓛ
119 Balls Pond Road, N1 4BL
✪ 3-midnight (1am Thu & Fri); 12-1am Sat; 12-11.30 Sun
☎ (020) 7275 7640 ⊕ thedukeofwellingtonN1.com
Sambrook's Wandle; guest beers Ⓗ
The Duke has rightly become a very popular local
for young and old alike, with a small island bar
offering a range of four ales and at least two ciders.
Good food is available at all times, including home-
made Scotch eggs, and Sunday lunch is served until
8pm. Tables are provided for smokers on the
pavement outside. Comedy club night is the last
Thursday of the month. Beer festivals are held
several times each year.
🏚🍴➍❷(Dalston Jct/Dalston Kingsland)♿⌐♨

N2: East Finchley

Bald Faced Stag Ⓛ
69 High Road, N2 8AB
✪ 12-11 (midnight Fri); 11-midnight Sat ☎ (020) 8442 1201
⊕ thebaldfacedstagn2.co.uk
Beer range varies Ⓗ
A short walk from East Finchley Underground
station, this large and busy open-plan pub with a
three-sided bar affords a friendly welcome. As well
as a regular house beer from the Greene King
stable, it often features beers from smaller
independent breweries. Bar meals are served, with
a large, busy restaurant area to the rear. Quiz night
is Wednesday. Popular with patrons from the
nearby Phoenix cinema, it holds beer festivals
twice a year. Over-21s only. ⊛➍❷P♿⌐♨

N4: Stroud Green

Old Dairy
1-3 Crouch Hill, N4 4AP
✪ 12-11 (midnight Thu; 1am Fri & Sat); 12-10.30 Sun
☎ (020) 7263 3337 ⊕ theolddairyn4.co.uk
Greene King Stroud Green Hobbler; guest beers Ⓗ
Very popular in the evenings, this Greene King
Realpubs outlet was built as a dairy and the outer
walls on Crouch Hill feature decorations showing all
of its previous dairy activities. The cavernous space
is divided between a restaurant at one end and
two large rooms served by the bar. The menu of
British standards is common to both. Four or five
ales are available, including a house beer from
Greene King. A real cider is served in summer.
➍❷&❷(Crouch Hill)♨(W3,W7,210)

N5: Canonbury

Snooty Fox Ⓛ
75 Grosvenor Avenue, N5 2NN
✪ 4-11.30 (1am Fri); 12-1am Sat; 12-10.30 Sun
☎ (020) 7354 9532 ⊕ snootyfoxlondon.co.uk
Hackney Best; St Austell Tribute; guest beers Ⓗ
Vibrant, spacious pub with 1960s icons depicted
throughout and a 45rpm jukebox giving a retro
feel. The light, airy lounge leads to a small patio, a
pleasant spot to enjoy some of up to five real ales
and watch the world go by. It has an occasional DJ
for music and several seasonal beer festivals
featuring around 30 beers. Good modern British
food is cooked to order, Sunday roasts are served
and table bookings are welcome. ⊛➍❷♿⌐♨

N6: Highgate

Bull Ⓛ
13 North Hill, N6 4AB
✪ 12-10.30 (midnight Fri & Sat) ☎ (020) 8341 0510
⊕ thebullhighgate.co.uk
London Brewing Company Beer Street, seasonal
beers; guest beers Ⓗ
Home to the London Brewing Company, this
brewpub has three of its beers available, another
three guest beers from microbreweries and a cider
on handpump. Rescued after 15 years as a
restaurant, it still has a very foodie vibe but attracts
an increasing number of local drinkers. The bar
area is currently small although there are plans to
extend it. There is a garden area at the front.
🏚🍴⊛➍❷&❷♣♿P♿⌐♨(143,603)

Gatehouse
1 North Road, N6 4BD
✪ 9am-11 (midnight Fri & Sat) ☎ (020) 8340 8054
Fuller's London Pride; Greene King Abbot; guest
beers Ⓗ
Large, well-kept Tudor-style Wetherspoon pub that
was once a toll house, on a busy corner in Highgate
Village, offering five or more rotating guest beers.
With numerous booths and a separate 42-cover
restaurant, it is panelled throughout and hung with
photos depicting historic local views. It has a fair-
sized enclosed garden with heaters, and two
screens for terrestrial TV sport. Upstairs, a variety
theatre ranges from opera to modern drama, with
combined meal and ticket deals sometimes
available. Q⊛➍❷&❷♿⌐♨

Prince of Wales
53 Highgate High Street, N6 5JX
✪ 12-11 (midnight Fri & Sat) ☎ (020) 8340 0445
Butcombe Bitter; guest beers Ⓗ
Situated in the centre of the village at the top of
the High Street, this traditional pub serves three
guest ales, often from West Country brewers. A
Thai menu is available lunchtimes, evenings and all
day at weekends, along with Sunday roasts. The
pub holds a challenging quiz on Tuesday and also
sponsors a cricket team, whose highest scores are
celebrated on bats displayed in the bar. A rear
outdoor area offers smoking and drinking
overlooking Pond Square. 🏚Q⊛➍❷♣♿⌐♨

Red Lion & Sun
25 North Road, N6 4BE
✪ 12-midnight (11 Sun) ☎ (020) 8340 1780
⊕ theredlionandsun.com
Greene King IPA, Abbot; guest beers Ⓗ
Rebuilt in 1926, although there has been a pub on
this site since the 1500s. Two guest beers rotate
regularly. A large front garden with a heated
smoking area leads to a single room with separate
drinking areas around the bar. Pews, chairs and
dining tables and two real fires provide an informal
drinking and dining atmosphere. Food is served all
day every day, with hog roasts on the rear patio
and front garden barbecues in summer. Dogs,
children and walkers welcome. 🏚⊛➍❷&❷♿⌐♨

N7: Holloway

Coronet
338-346 Holloway Road, N7 6NJ
✪ 9am-11 (10.30 Sun) ☎ (020) 7609 5014
Fuller's London Pride; Greene King Abbot; Ruddles
Best Bitter; guest beers Ⓗ

Impressive Wetherspoon conversion of an old cinema. Originally the Savoy, designed by William Glen, it showed its last film in 1983 and is now adorned with large prints of movie stars and former local entertainers, with an old projector the centrepiece of a raised dais towards the rear. Popular with all age groups, it frequently has up to six guest ales available, with single brewery festivals at times. Expect plastic glasses and higher prices when Arsenal are playing at home. Q🌡️⚪️♿️⊖(Holloway Rd)🍴⊷⊟

N8: Hornsey

Three Compasses 🅛
62 High Street, N8 7NX
⊕ 11-11 (midnight Fri & Sat); 12-11 Sun ☎ (020) 8340 2729
⊕ threecompasses.com
Fuller's London Pride; Redemption Pale Ale; Taylor Landlord; guest beers 🅗
Large front windows contribute to an airy, bright feel in the front bar of this award-winning community pub, a popular after-work venue for local young professionals and those heading for events at nearby Alexandra Palace. The rear bar is much larger, with daylight from a skylight roof, a pool table, two dartboards, a large-screen TV at the end and occasional live music. Three changing guest ales are served on the front bar.
⚪️♿️⇌♣️⊟(41,144,W3)

N9: Lower Edmonton

Beehive
24 Little Bury Street, N9 9JZ
⊕ 12-11.30 (1am Fri & Sat); 12-11 Sun ☎ (020) 8360 4358
Greene King IPA; Morland Old Speckled Hen; Sharp's Doom Bar; guest beer 🅗
Community one-bar pub with a pool table. The licensee has recently joined the SIBA direct delivery scheme to offer a wider range of guest ales. Fresh daily specials as well as traditional pub grub are available lunch and evening. Every second Tuesday of the month there is a jam session. It recently won gold in the Enfield in Bloom Pub of the Year competition. No admittance nor outside drinking after 11pm, to keep local residents happy.
🌡️⚪️♣️P⊷⊟(329,W8)

Stag & Hounds 🅛
371 Bury Street West, N9 9JW
⊕ 12-midnight (11 Mon; 10.30 Sun) ☎ (020) 8360 7412
Beer range varies 🅗
A spacious M&B Ember Inns pub run by a landlady with a great enthusiasm for real ale, consulting customers before deciding on which seasonal ales to pick from the company list. Predominantly an eating house, it has a cosy section primarily for drinkers. The TV is mute, showing news with subtitles. Tuesday is quiz night. The garden is gated, and therefore child-friendly.
🐕🌡️⚪️♿️P⊟(192,329,W8)

N10: Muswell Hill

John Baird 🅛
122 Fortis Green Road, N10 3HN
⊕ 11-11 (midnight Fri & Sat); 12-10.30 Sun
☎ (020) 8444 8830 ⊕ thejohnbaird.co.uk
Brakspear Bitter; Sharp's Doom Bar; guest beers 🅗
The Baird has become a mecca for real ale and cider fans in this part of North London, sporting up

to six ales and a couple of ciders. One wing of this large pub is home to an excellent Thai restaurant and the other provides ample space for drinkers and those wanting to watch major sporting events in comfort. A sizeable outside smoking and drinking area is provided at the rear. A quiz night is held on Tuesday. 🏛️🌡️⚪️♿️🍴⊷⊟(102,234)

N12: North Finchley

Bohemia 🅛
762-764 High Road, N12 9QH
⊕ 4-11 Mon; 12-11 (midnight Thu; 1am Fri & Sat); 12-10.30 Sun ☎ (020) 8446 6661 ⊕ thebohemia.com
Beer range varies 🅗
Part of the Gregarious (ex-Antic) pub chain, this bar is located in a busy high street and is handy for the shops. It is large and open-plan with a barn-like structure. The beers include a wide range of Belgian and American bottles. In the middle of the pub is an old-fashioned football table. Prices can be expensive for the area. Food is available 12-3pm and 5-10pm. ⚪️♿️⊖(Woodside Park)⊟

Elephant Inn 🅛
283 Ballards Lane, N12 8NR
⊕ 11-11 (midnight Fri & Sat); 12-10.30 Sun
☎ (020) 8343 6110 ⊕ elephantinnfinchley.co.uk
Fuller's London Pride, ESB, seasonal beer 🅗
Long-established Fuller's pub serving a varied clientele. The large U-shaped bar is split into three distinctive drinking areas, including a sports bar showing most major TV sports events. Meals focus on Thai food and an upstairs restaurant is open 6-10.30pm. Well-behaved dogs are welcome. Numerous pub games are available including darts and dominoes. There is a large patio at the front. 🌡️⚪️⊖(West Finchley)♣️⊷⊟

N14: Southgate

New Crown
80-84 Chase Side, N14 5PH
⊕ 9am-12.30am (1am Fri & Sat) ☎ (020) 8882 8758
Greene King Abbot; Ruddles Best Bitter; guest beers 🅗
A large Wetherspoon pub converted from a supermarket in the 1990s. Close to the shops, it is often busy but the staff generally cope well and many have an interest in the ales. As well as the twice-yearly national beer festivals, the pub hosts its own, often with a specific brewery theme. Ciders, often from Westons, are available. Sparklers may be used; if you are concerned, please ask for them to be removed. Breakfasts are served from 8am. ⚪️♿️⊖🍴⊟

N16: Stoke Newington

Jolly Butchers 🅛
204 Stoke Newington High Street, N16 7HU
⊕ 4-midnight (1am Fri); 12-1am Sat; 12-11 Sun
☎ (020) 7241 2185 ⊕ jollybutchers.co.uk
Beer range varies 🅗
A classic Art Deco-style bar boasting elaborate ironwork and glass, with a lively modern feel and the enviable status of being a true free house. Nine handpumps offer six different real ales, usually from microbreweries, and three ciders or perries. The beer is complemented by great food on weekday evenings and at lunchtime, and in the evening at weekends. 🐕🌡️⇌🍴⊷⊟

Railway Tavern Ⓛ

2 St Jude's Street, N16 8JT
✪ 4-11 (midnight Fri); 12-midnight Sat; 12-10.30 Sun
☎ (020) 0011 1195
Beer range varies Ⓗ
A gem of a pub a stone's throw from busy Kingsland High Street. It has six varied and interesting cask ales to suit all tastes, including one from Adnams and a LocAle. A tasty Thai menu and Sunday roasts complete the offering. It is full of quirky character, friendly, and a perfect venue to relax away from the sports crowd, with good beer and good company.
Ⓓ⊖(Dalston Jct/Dalston Kingsland)⊟

N19: Archway

Charlotte Despard Ⓛ

17 Archway Road, N19 3TX
✪ 4 (5 Mon)-1am; 3-midnight Sun ☎ (020) 7272 7878
⊕ thecharlottedespard.co.uk
Beer range varies Ⓗ
Popular community local in a former co-operative store and named after the Irish nationalist and suffragette. Four real ales are served, all from London breweries (usually East London Brewing, Redemption and Sambrook's) and there is one handpump for real cider. A very large selection of bottled beers and spirits is also available. Evening meals are served and there is a quiz on Tuesday nights. Ⓓ⊖(Archway/Upper Holloway)♣♠⊟

N21: Winchmore Hill

Dog & Duck

74 Hoppers Road, N21 3LH
✪ 12-11 (10.30 Sun) ☎ (020) 8886 1987
⊕ dogandduckwinchmorehill.co.uk
Fuller's London Pride; Greene King IPA; Taylor Landlord; Young's Bitter; guest beer Ⓗ
Small, friendly pub with one bar, popular with locals and welcoming to visitors. A large-screen TV shows sporting events. Local football teams meet here and there is a golf society. The walls are adorned with local history photographs and a Victorian map of the area. The patio-style walled garden at the rear welcomes dogs at quiet times. ✿⇄⚡-⊟(W9)

Orange Tree Ⓛ

18 Highfield Road, N21 3HA
✪ 12-midnight (12.30am Fri & Sat) ☎ (020) 8360 4853
⊕ orangetreepub.com
Greene King IPA; Morland Old Speckled Hen; guest beers Ⓗ
This old-fashioned, original back-street local has been in the Guide for 20 consecutive years. Originally a Taylor Walker house with the signs still outside, it has been a free house for many years. Always welcoming, with friendly bar staff, it has two darts teams, a fortnightly quiz and summer barbecues in the prize-winning garden. Just a few yards from the New River Walk, it is close to Green Lanes for pedestrians but with no direct vehicular access. ⛟✿⇄♣P⚡-⊟(329)

Cockfosters

Cock & Dragon

14 Chalk Lane, EN4 9HU TQ277967
✪ 11-11 (11.30 Fri & Sat; 10.30 Sun) ☎ (020) 8449 7160
⊕ cockanddragon-cockfosters.co.uk

Greene King IPA, seasonal beer; Sharp's Doom Bar; guest beer Ⓗ
A pub within 10 minutes' walk of Cockfosters Underground station. The London Loop passes close by and Trent Park is not far. The main bar has several alcoves and nice areas to sit. Thai food is served in the bar and in the restaurant at the back, with an English menu option at lunchtime. There is a pleasant secluded rear garden with a heated, decked area for smokers. Disabled access is via a side entrance. ✿Ⓓ♿⊖P⚡-⊟(298)

Enfield

Moon Under Water

115-117 Chase Side, EN2 6NN
✪ 9am-11 (10.30 Sun) ☎ (020) 8366 9855
Courage Directors; Greene King Abbot; Ruddles Best Bitter; guest beers Ⓗ
A Wetherspoon conversion of a former dairy. The building has a church-like appearance and light floods in from windows on three sides. There is a dedicated area for families until 8.30pm in a side extension of the main bar. Westons Old Rosie is invariably one of two real ciders. Breakfast is served until noon and meals until 10pm. Sparklers may be used; if you are concerned, please ask for them to be removed. ✿Ⓓ♿⇄(Gordon Hill)♠P⚡-⊟(191,W9)

Wonder Ⓛ

1 Batley Road, EN2 0JG
✪ 11-11; 12-10.30 Sun ☎ (020) 8363 0202
McMullen AK, Cask Ale, Country Bitter, seasonal beer Ⓗ
A friendly local back-street pub. Neither of the two bars has a TV, and so it is football-free. There is a dartboard plus cards and cribbage on request. Sessions on the piano take place on Saturday and Sunday nights. A selection of hot pies is available all day, with mushy peas if you like. ♨Q✿⊕⇄(Gordon Hill)♣P⚡-⊟(191,W8)

High Barnet

Lord Nelson

14 West End Lane, EN5 2SA
✪ 12-11 (midnight Fri & Sat; 10.30 Sun) ☎ (020) 8449 7249
⊕ thelordnelsonph.co.uk
Wells Bombardier; Young's Bitter, Special, seasonal beer; guest beer Ⓗ
Homely, dog-friendly pub on the outskirts of High Barnet, served by several bus routes. In keeping with its name, there are several maritime artefacts, although a vast collection of cruet sets predominates. Good-value, home-cooked food is served until 8.30pm. Cribbage, dominoes and scrabble sets are available. Look for the autographs of Richard Burton and Liz Taylor on the wall. There is one TV, used sparingly. A guest beer is available occasionally. ✿Ⓓ♣⚡-⊟

Olde Mitre Inne ♛

58 High Street, EN5 5SJ
✪ 12-11 (1am Fri & Sat) ☎ (020) 8449 5701
Adnams Southwold Bitter; Black Sheep Best Bitter; guest beers Ⓗ
Extensive wood panels and wood flooring, basic seating and tables feature in this popular pub, whose history goes back to the 16th century as a coaching inn. The lower rear area leads out to a large patio garden with two further rooms known

as Stable and Carriage. There are four, frequently changing guest beers. Winner of local CAMRA Pub of the Year four years in a row. Q❀◑⊖♣●⁻⊟

New Barnet

Builders Arms

3 Albert Road, EN4 9SH
⚙ 12-midnight (1am Fri & Sat) ☎ (020) 8216 5678
Greene King IPA, Abbot, seasonal beer; guest beer Ⓗ
A popular real ale outlet since the 1970s, hidden away in a side street off the East Barnet Road. The quiet saloon bar is a contrast to the lively public bar, which has a pool table and TV. There is a garden at the back where you can watch the trains go by. Look for the imitation blue plaque above the entrance. Thai food is served 12-10pm.
Q❀◑⊟≹♣⁻⊟

Ponders End

Picture Palace 𝕃

Howard's Hall, Lincoln Road, EN3 4AQ (jct with High St)
⚙ 9am-11 (midnight Fri & Sat) ☎ (020) 8344 9690
Greene King Abbot; Ruddles Best Bitter; guest beers Ⓗ
A Wetherspoon conversion of a 1920s cinema with some architectural features preserved in the main hall and bar area. Also notice the film murals above the bar. A huge screen is available for showing sport or films in silent mode. There is an outside patio to the left-hand side. The nearby Redemption Brewery sometimes supplies a LocAle. Sparklers may be used; if you are concerned, please ask for them to be removed.
❀◑♿≹(Ponders End/Southbury)●P⁻⊟

NORTH-WEST LONDON
NW1: Camden Town

Prince Albert 𝕃

163 Royal College Street, NW1 0SG
⚙ 12-11 (10 Sun) ☎ (020) 7485 0270
🌐 princealbertcamden.com
Beer range varies Ⓗ
A sensitive refurbishment of an old Charrington's pub by private owners. The leaded Toby windows and wooden floors have been tastefully restored. The outside tiling is striking but the main reason for visiting is the beer range. Guest beers change monthly and include LocAles from Sambrook's and occasionally others. Upstairs is a restaurant and the garden is one of the most pleasant in Camden.
♘❀◑♿⊖(Camden Rd/Town)⁻⊟

Tapping the Admiral 🏆 𝕃

77 Castle Road, NW1 8SU
⚙ 12-11 (midnight Wed-Sat); 12-10.30 Sun
☎ (020) 7267 6118 🌐 tappingtheadmiral.co.uk
Dark Star Hophead; London Fields Hackney Hopster; Redemption Big Chief; Twickenham Naked Ladies; Windsor & Eton Knight of the Garter; guest beers Ⓗ
A community pub to enjoy, where friendly and knowledgeable staff offer a warm welcome. Eight handpumps dispense high-quality guest ales, mainly from local breweries. A British food menu boasts awesome home-made pies, fresh fish and home-made chips, fab salads, sandwiches and wraps. The beer garden is well designed. There is a Wednesday quiz and live music on Saturday nights. Local CAMRA Pub of the Year 2013.
♘❀◑⊖(Kentish Town West)●⁻⊟

NW1: Euston

Bree Louise 𝕃

69 Cobourg Street, NW1 2HH
⚙ 11.30-11; 12-10.30 Sun ☎ (020) 7681 4930
🌐 thebreelouise.com
Windsor & Eton Knight of the Garter, Windsor Knot, Conqueror Ⓗ**; guest beers** Ⓗ/Ⓖ
One-bar corner pub, busy with locals and Euston commuters. A cooled gravity stillage complemented by handpumps (beers change but usually include LocAles) provide a large range, alongside up to 11 ciders. Regular beer festivals are held. Pumpclips festoon the walls. There is no music, just conversation, but TVs show sport occasionally at the weekend. Pavement seating is available. The pub may close later on weekdays.
❀◑≹⊖(Euston/Euston Sq)●⁻⊟

Doric Arch

1 Eversholt Street, NW1 1DN
⚙ 10-11 (10.30 Sun) ☎ (020) 7383 3359
Fuller's Discovery, London Pride, ESB, seasonal beer; Kelham Island Pale Rider; guest beers Ⓗ
Formerly the Head of Steam, this pub has been in the Guide for nearly 20 years. Up a flight of stairs, the window allows for a view of the busy urban world below. The pub is right next to Euston Station and is used extensively by commuters. The excellent staff are very helpful and informative about ale. Toilets are downstairs, but be warned: you need a code from the bar. Brewery and railway memorabilia adorn the walls. ◑≹⊖●⊟

Euston Tap

West Lodge, 190 Euston Road, NW1 2EF
⚙ 12-11.30 (10.30 Sun) ☎ (020) 3137 8837
🌐 eustontap.com
Fyne Ales Jarl; Marble Draft, Best; guest beers Ⓟ
At the front of the main station building, the Tap occupies an impressive Grade II-listed Portland stone lodge, one of the few relics from the original 1830s station. Up to eight changing beers are pumped up to taps behind the bar. Space is rather limited although there is a large outside drinking area as well as seating up a wrought-iron spiral staircase, where you will also find the toilets. The opposite lodge, the Cider Tap, opening at 3.30pm (not Sun), features six real ciders.
❀≹⊖(Euston/Euston Sq)●⁻⊟

NW3: Hampstead

Duke of Hamilton

23-25 New End, NW3 1JD
⚙ 11-11.30; 12-10.30 Sun ☎ (020) 7794 0258
🌐 thedukeofhamilton.com
Fuller's London Pride; guest beers Ⓗ
An old favourite, recently saved from conversion into flats, this back-street pub continues to serve a wide range of ales. Ale Club is Monday and Tuesday, curry night is Tuesday (no food on Monday). The cellar bar is being developed for dining and football viewing, while the main bar is more rugby-oriented. There are outside areas front and rear. Live music is performed on the first Friday of the month.
❀◑⊖(Hampstead/Hampstead Heath)
♣⁻⊟(268,603)

Holly Bush

22 Holly Mount, NW3 6SG (up Holly Bush Steps from Heath St)

✪ 12-11 (10.30 Sun) ☎ (020) 7435 2892
⊕ hollybushhampstead.co.uk
Butcombe Bitter; Fuller's London Pride, ESB, seasonal beer; Gale's Seafarers Ale Ⓗ
Handsome pub with a fine wood-panelled interior and several rooms of different sizes at different levels. A Grade II-listed building, originally the stables of artist George Romney's house, it retains many historic features and is one of London's Real Heritage Pubs. Food is good and unpretentious. A small smoking and seating area is at the front. At nearly the highest point in Hampstead (and one of the highest in London), this makes an excellent destination pub. ⋈⛱❀◗☺⌁–☒(46,268,603)

NW4: Hendon

Greyhound
52 Church End, NW4 4JT
✪ 12-midnight (1am Fri & Sat); 12-11 Sun
☎ (020) 8457 9730
Courage Best Bitter; Wells Bombardier; Young's Bitter, Special; guest beers Ⓗ
Traditional cask ale pub in an historic area, with a village feel about it. Three drinking areas include one that is wood panelled and used for dining. There is a large TV showing sporting events. Mondays and Wednesdays have quiz nights starting at 9pm and the last Thursday in the month is a jazz evening. There is an extensive view westward from outside the pub.
⋈◗☺–☒(143,183,326)

NW5: Kentish Town

Pineapple Ⓛ
51 Leverton Street, NW5 2NX
✪ 12-11 (10.30 Sun) ☎ (020) 7284 4631
Adnams Broadside; McMullen AK; Sharp's Doom Bar; guest beer Ⓗ
A real community pub, saved from closure by the locals, Grade II-listed and one of London's Real Heritage Pubs, notable for its mirrors and splendid bar-back. The front bar with comfortable seating around tables leads through to an informal conservatory overlooking the patio garden. It has a Thai kitchen with traditional Sunday roasts. LocAles can include beers from across London and, the pub being free of tie, the overall range changes regularly. Local CAMRA Pub of the Year 2012.
Q⛱◗≈☺♣–☒

Southampton Arms
139 Highgate Road, NW5 1LE
✪ 12-11 (midnight Fri & Sat); 12-10.30 Sun
☎ (020) 7485 1511 ⊕ thesouthamptonarms.co.uk
Hackney Best Bitter; Howling Hops Duchess Single Hop; Kent Twelfth Night; guest beers Ⓗ
The 2011 CAMRA London Pub of the Year and a former London Cider Pub of the Year, this pub does what it says on the sign outside – Ale, Cider, Meat. On and behind the bar, 18 handpumps serve almost equal amounts of cider and varied beers from microbreweries across the UK. Snacks include pork pies, cheese and meat baps. Music on vinyl is played and the piano is in regular use. At the rear is a secluded patio.
⋈◗≈☺(Gospel Oak/Kentish Town)
♣☺–☒(214,C2,C11)

NW8: St John's Wood

Clifton Ⓛ
96 Clifton Hill, NW8 0JT
✪ 12-11 (10.30 Sun) ☎ (020) 7372 3427
⊕ cliftonstjohnswood.com
Sambrook's Wandle; guest beers Ⓗ
A hunting lodge 200 years ago before gaining a licence, this pub was given hotel status by King Edward VII so that he could visit Lily Langtry here, as royalty could not visit pubs. A pleasant terrace with mature trees leads into a small front room with a decorative wooden island bar, with bronze inserts. To the rear, dropping a level, is a larger room (once two) leading into a conservatory reserved for dining. There is a wide choice of board games.
⋈⛱◗☺(Kilburn High Rd/Kilburn Park)–☒(U9)

Harefield

Old Orchard Ⓛ
Jacks Lane, off Park Lane, UB9 6HJ
✪ 12-11 (10.30 Sun) ☎ (01895) 822631
⊕ oldorchard-harefield.co.uk
Brunning & Price Original Bitter; Mighty Oak Oscar Wilde; Tring Side Pocket for a Toad; guest beers Ⓗ
Brunning & Price establishment that was once a country house before becoming a restaurant. Refurbished in 2010, the pub is lined with bookcases and pictures and has an unfussy array of mismatched tables and chairs and three welcoming real fires in the colder months. Three guest beers are usually available, mostly from local breweries. There are commanding views from the Colne Valley from the terrace and beer garden.
⋈Q⛱⛱❀◗♿♣☝P–☒(331,U9)

Harrow

Castle ★
30 West Street, HA1 3EF
✪ 12-11 (midnight Fri & Sat) ☎ (020) 8422 3155
⊕ castle-harrow.co.uk
Fuller's Discovery, London Pride, ESB; Gale's HSB; guest beer Ⓗ
Situated in the heart of historic Harrow-on-the-Hill, this is a popular and friendly Fuller's house. Built in 1901 and Grade II-listed, it is one of Britain's Best Real Heritage Pubs. Food is served until 9pm every day; reservations are recommended for Sunday lunchtime. Three real coal fires help to keep the pub warm and cosy in the colder months and a secluded beer garden is popular during the summer. ⋈Q⛱❀◗♿♣–☒(258,H17)

Moon on the Hill
373-375 Station Road, HA1 2AW
✪ 9am-midnight (12.30am Fri & Sat) ☎ (020) 8863 3670
Greene King Abbot; Ruddles Best Bitter; guest beers Ⓗ
Small, busy Wetherspoon pub close to Harrow-on-the-Hill station and served by numerous bus routes. Serving food all day, it is popular with price-conscious regulars, office workers and students from the nearby University of Westminster. The pub gets extremely busy when there are sporting events on at nearby Wembley Stadium and plastic glasses may be used on these occasions. Breakfasts are served from 8am. ☺◗♿≈☺(Harrow-on-the-Hill)☝☒

White Horse

50 Middle Road, HA2 0HL

✪ 12-11 (midnight Wed-Sat) ☎ (020) 8422 1215

⊕ thewhitehorseharrow.co.uk

Fuller's London Pride, ESB; Gale's Seafarers Ale; guest beer ℍ

The landlord of this large pub takes pride in the good service that all his customers receive, and in the high standards he sets for his staff and for everything that is sold. There is a quiz every Thursday and a dinner-dance on the last Saturday of every month. The home-cooked food is sold all day except on Sunday, when last food orders are at 6pm. ♨✿☼◖Θ(South Harrow)P⁺⊟

Rayners Lane

Village Inn

402-408 Rayners Lane, HA5 5DY

✪ 9am-11 (midnight Thu; 12.30am Fri & Sat)

☎ (020) 8868 8551

Greene King Abbot; Ruddles Best Bitter; Thornbridge Jaipur IPA; Wychwood Hobgoblin; guest beers ℍ

Another split-level, double-fronted shop conversion. The rear of the pub, accessed down a few steps, sports the traditional Wetherspoon booths with a row of tables down the centre. A terraced area behind has a variety of large potted plants among the picnic tables. The front pavement has a few tables and chairs for that alfresco moment. The pub's clientele is a good cross-section who mingle quite happily together. Breakfasts are served from 8am. Q✿✿☼◖&Θ♣✿⁺⊟

Ruislip Common

Woodman

Breakspear Road, HA4 7SE

✪ 11-midnight; 12-11 Sun ☎ (01895) 635763

⊕ thewoodmanruislip.co.uk

Courage Best Bitter; Otter Ale; guest beer ℍ

A cheerful and welcoming two-bar local in the northern area of Ruislip close to Ruislip Lido and the woods, and opposite Hillingdon Borough football club. The cosy lounge bar is traditional in atmosphere with no intrusive electronic machines, although the TV may be on for sports matches. Note the collection of bottled beers on display. There is also a good selection of single malt whiskies. The public bar is friendly and comfortable, with a dartboard and other pub games. Q✿✿☼◖&Θ♣P⁺⊟(331)

Ruislip Manor

J J Moons 🅛

12 Victoria Road, HA4 0AA

✪ 9am-midnight (1am Fri & Sat); 9am-11 Sun

☎ (01895) 622373

Courage Directors; Fuller's London Pride; Greene King Abbot; Ruddles Best Bitter; Wychwood Hobgoblin; guest beers ℍ

Opened in 1990 in a former Woolworths and still with the same licensee, this busy Wetherspoon pub has two ciders on draught alongside the beers. A real ale club meets on Wednesday evenings, offering suggestions on which guest beers to stock and participating in a cellar dash when up to 16 ales can be tried. Additional beer festivals are held throughout the year as well as the chain's regular bi-annual events. Breakfasts are served from 8am. Q✿✿☼◖&Θ✿⁺⊟(114,398,H13)

South Kenton

Windermere ★

Windermere Avenue, HA9 8QT

✪ 11-11.30 (12.30am Thu-Sat) ☎ (020) 8904 7484

⊕ windermerepub.com

Courage Best Bitter; Young's Special ℍ

A genuine community pub and identified by CAMRA as one of Britain's Best Real Heritage Pubs, next to South Kenton Station. Built in 1938 or 1939 with three bars, the public is now only used for functions. The saloon and lounge have many original features including the large inner porches, bar counters, back-fittings, wall panelling and fireplaces. A quiz night is held on alternate Thursdays and live entertainment takes place on a regular basis. A guest ale is usually available on special occasions. ✿✿☼&Θ♣P⁺⊟(223)

SOUTH-EAST LONDON
SE1: Bermondsey

Simon the Tanner

231 Long Lane, SE1 4PR

✪ 12 (5 Mon)-11; 12-10.30 Sun ☎ (020) 7357 8740

⊕ simonthetanner.co.uk

Beer range varies ℍ

A mid-terrace modestly sized pub which is Grade II-listed, mainly for its exterior. Inside are bare floorboards and a nice mix of traditional and contemporary decor. Glazed only along its short frontage and with no outdoor drinking areas, it benefits from air conditioning to the rear. The upright piano is put through its paces every Wednesday. Food is a quality take on standard dishes like pies, burgers and soups. Three regularly changing real ales often come from London breweries. ◖⇌(London Bridge)Θ(Borough)✿⊟

SE1: Borough

Market Porter

9 Stoney Street, SE1 9AA

✪ 6-9am, 11 (12 Sat)-11; 12-10.30 Sun ☎ (020) 7407 2495

Harveys Sussex Best Bitter; guest beers ℍ

Iconic pub that is a mecca for beer lovers all over the world. Situated on the western edge of Borough Market, you will find a staggering array of beers dispensed from the 12 pumps. The central bar does a good job of serving the dozens of customers that are here at any given time, and there is a tucked-away area at the back, warmed by a real fire. The upstairs restaurant satisfies those that require sustenance with their ale. ♨◖⇌Θ(London Bridge)✿⊟

Rake

14 Winchester Walk, SE1 9AG

✪ 12 (10 Sat)-11; 12-8 Sun ☎ (020) 7407 0557

Beer range varies ℍ

This small bar is operated by Utobeer of Borough Market and offers three cask ales. Dark Star and Oakham ales appear regularly, with others being sourced from independent breweries, Utobeer's own Tap East brewpub, or from other London breweries. The heated patio doubles the area available, with overspill into the market when busy. Bar snacks are available. Regular beer festivals and Meet the Brewer events are held. Q✿&⇌Θ(London Bridge)⊟

Royal Oak

44 Tabard Street, SE1 4JU
✪ 11 (12 Sat)-11.30; 12-9 Sun ☎ (020) 7357 7173
Harveys Sussex XX Mild, Pale, Sussex Best Bitter, Armada, seasonal beers Ⓗ
A back-to-basics drinkers' pub with charm and history, separated into two sections by the bar. You cannot help but fall in love with the quaintness of the book and games library, or the friendliness of the staff. Once inside, you could be forgiven for thinking you are in an old country pub, and the high ceilings and quirky decorations add to the atmosphere. Many regulars come from miles away to spend time here, as should you.
Q❀❁≹(London Bridge)⊖❀⊟

Ship

68 Borough Road, SE1 1DX
✪ 11-11 (midnight Fri & Sat); 12-10.30 Sun
☎ (020) 7403 7059 ⊕ shipborough.co.uk
Fuller's Discovery, London Pride, seasonal beers Ⓗ
Halfway between Borough and Elephant & Castle, this is a great example of a pub that brilliantly combines good beer, good food, sport and music. As part of the local Victorian landscape, the pub is long and thin, and the bar runs most of its length along one side, with larger spaces at the front and rear. As with all Fuller's pubs, the menu is hearty and a pie is always the perfect accompaniment to a pint. ❀❁≹(London Bridge)⊖❀'⊟

SE1: London Bridge

Shipwrights Arms

88 Tooley Street, SE1 2TF
✪ 11-midnight (1am Fri & Sat); 12-11 Sun
☎ (020) 7378 1486 ⊕ shipwrightsarms.co.uk
Black Sheep Ale; Caledonian Deuchars IPA, Flying Scotsman; Sharp's Doom Bar; Shepherd Neame Spitfire; Wells Bombardier Ⓗ
Grade II-listed pub built in 1884 with an original tiled mural of shipwrights at work. A traditional style has been retained, including the rare central island bar. Up to six real ales are served by efficient and friendly staff. Near to London Bridge public transport links and with numerous buses passing by, and with the river, Tower Bridge and City also close, the pub is popular with commuters, tourists and locals alike. Good home-made food is available lunchtimes and evenings. ❀❁≹⊖'⊟

SE1: Southwark

Charles Dickens

160 Union Street, SE1 0LH
✪ 12-11 (6 Sun) ☎ (020) 7401 3744
⊕ thecharlesdickens.co.uk
Beer range varies Ⓗ
A classic back-street boozer, tucked away between Borough High Street and Blackfriars Road. Do not be fooled by its out-of-the-way location, though, as it boasts a lively atmosphere in the evenings, two screens for sport, a partially covered beer garden and an unpretentious local quality. Sunday afternoons are a more chilled affair with a roast available. Up to six constantly changing real ales, often from Adnams plus interesting microbreweries, are advertised on a blackboard. The pub quiz is on Wednesday at 8.30pm.
Q❀❁≹(Waterloo East)⊖(Borough/Southwark)'⊟

SE1: Waterloo

King's Arms

25 Roupell Street, SE1 8TB
✪ 11 (12 Sat)-11; 12-10.30 Sun ☎ (020) 7207 0784
Adnams Southwold Bitter; Jennings Cumberland Ale; Ringwood Boondoggle; guest beers Ⓗ
On a corner in a back street, here is a treasure worth seeking out. Seating is at a premium, however, and it is not unusual to find as many people drinking and chatting in the street as inside. Ten pumps provide a varied beer range, and the two separate sides of the bar allow you to change your scene (and beer selection) without changing pub. There is a long room at the back, given over to dining. ❀❁≹(Waterloo/Waterloo East)⊖⊟⊟

SE3: Blackheath

Princess of Wales

1a Montpelier Row, SE3 0RL
✪ 12-11 (10.30 Sun) ☎ (020) 8852 5784
⊕ princessofwalespub.co.uk
Fuller's London Pride; Sambrook's Junction; Sharp's Doom Bar; guest beers Ⓗ
Historic pub on the edge of Blackheath village, overlooking the open expanse of the heath itself. It is well patronised, especially during the summer months, with a wide mix of clientele. Cosy and welcoming, it has an L-shaped bar that leads around to a conservatory and walled garden area. Complementing the regular beers are up to three guests from varied breweries, which have included Red Squirrel, Moles and Adnams. The food is deservedly popular, especially the Sunday roasts. ❀❁❁⬧≹❀⊟

Royal Standard

44 Vanbrugh Park, SE3 7JQ
✪ 11 (12 Sun)-11 ☎ (020) 8858 1533
Fuller's London Pride; guest beers Ⓗ
This Orchid venue attracts a mixed crowd in a good-natured atmosphere and gives its name to the local centre as a whole. Up to four guest beers change weekly; it claims to have served 300 different real ales since May 2008. The pub hosts monthly Meet the Brewer events, occasional live music, a poker evening on Monday and a Sunday night pub quiz. ❀❁⬧≹(Westcombe Park)P⊟

SE4: Brockley

Talbot

2 Tyrwhitt Road, SE4 1QG
✪ 12-11 (midnight Fri & Sat) ☎ (020) 8692 2665
Fuller's London Pride; Harveys Sussex Best Bitter; guest beers Ⓗ
A fine Victorian suburban pub on two floors which has built up a good reputation since reopening a few years ago. The decor has a nice balance between old and new, and the pub is popular with all ages. There are usually two or three guest beers on offer, plus a tasty food menu. It also has a large outdoor seating area. Events include quiz nights and live music, plus the occasional beer festival.
Q❀❁≹(St Johns)'⊟

SE5: Camberwell

Bear

296a Camberwell New Road, SE5 0RP

✪ 4-11 (midnight Fri & Sat); 12-11 Sun ☎ (020) 7274 7037
⊕ thebear-freehouse.co.uk
Beer range varies Ⓗ
A renovated Victorian pub with a tiled exterior, a lovely bar with cut-glass mirrors, and stained glass in some doors. Up to four real ales come free-of-tie from breweries such as Cottage, Redemption and Westerham. The menu offers mainly traditional English and French food. The pub attracts a varied and discerning clientele. The front bar has piped music, while the rear bar is quieter. The upstairs room, available for hire, hosts swing dancing on Wednesday evenings. Sport is shown occasionally. ⓓ♣ℒ⊟

Hermits Cave Ⓛ
28 Camberwell Church Street, SE5 8QU
✪ 12-midnight (2am Fri & Sat) ☎ (020) 7703 3188
Loddon Gravesend Shrimpers; guest beers Ⓗ
Run by the same family for 25 years, this corner pub has remained essentially unchanged. Etched windows and wooden floors add to the traditional feel, popular with a cross-section of local residents and art college students. A corner TV provides the only distraction to convivial conversation. Up to three guest beers come from independent breweries. Three real ciders on handpump increase to five during summer months. An impressive range of whiskies includes examples from Wales and Japan. Q⇌⊖(Denmark Hill)●⊟

SE5: Denmark Hill

Fox on the Hill
149 Denmark Hill, SE5 8EH
✪ 9am-midnight (12.30am Fri & Sat) ☎ (020) 7738 4756
Greene King Abbot; Morland Old Speckled Hen; Ruddles Best Bitter; guest beers Ⓗ
Spacious and welcoming Wetherspoon pub at the top of a steep hill. Inside are a number of cosy, low-screened booths, while outside is a spacious garden, smokers' terrace and front lawn with picnic tables. Wall displays depict the history of the local area, including former resident John Ruskin, after whom the nearby park is named. Up to seven guest beers are usually available and the pub hosts regular Meet the Brewer events. Breakfasts are served from 8am. ⓑ☆ⓓ⅙⇌⊖●P⅄⊟

SE6: Catford

Catford Bridge Tavern ⓨ
Station Approach, Catford Bridge, SE6 4RE
✪ 4-midnight (1am Fri & Sat); 12-midnight Sun
☎ (020) 3066 2060 ⊕ catfordbridgetavern.com
Beer range varies Ⓗ
Outcry in 2012 prevented this mock-Tudor pub from conversion to flats and a supermarket. Saloon and public bar areas remain, with a central island, though bar service is only to the front. Part of the rear has tables for diners only, typical meals being sea bass, duck or steak. There are bare floors, eclectic furniture, dark wood and painted panelling throughout. The four real ales usually come from small independent breweries. Local CAMRA Pub of the Year 2013. ⓓ⇌(Catford/Catford Bridge)●⅄⊟

SE8: Deptford

Dog & Bell Ⓛ
116 Prince Street, SE8 3JD
✪ 12-11.30 (midnight Sat); 12-11 Sun ☎ (020) 8692 5664

Fuller's London Pride, ESB; guest beers Ⓗ
Traditional back-street pub offering four or five excellent beers and simple, tasty meals. It has a good mixture of clientele, a lively bar and a real fire in winter. Charlie and Eileen have run the pub since 1988 and know their business, as is attested by the many awards and citations the pub has had over the years. Whether they are walkers along the Thames Path, cycling clubs, locals or visitors from further away, all agree this pub rings their bell. ⚞Q☆ⓓ⇌♣ℒ⊟(47,188,199)

SE9: Eltham

Howerd Club
447 Rochester Way, SE9 6PH
✪ 12-4 (Sat & Sun only), 7.30-11 ☎ (020) 8856 7212
Fuller's London Pride; guest beers Ⓗ
A warm welcome awaits at this tiny social club tucked away at the back of a community hall. A former CAMRA National Club of the Year, it serves London Pride and two other changing ales: one Fuller's and one usually from Shepherd Neame. Children are welcome until 8.30pm. Decor includes memorabilia linked to former local celebrity Frankie Howerd, and a copy of every Guide since 1996 is also to hand. ⓑ☆⅙⇌⊟(132,286)

Park Tavern
45 Passey Place, SE9 5DA
✪ 12-11 ☎ (020) 8850 8919 ⊕ parktaverneltham.co.uk
Young's Bitter; guest beers Ⓗ
Handsome Victorian pub with historic Truman signage to the front and side. Owned by the Proper Little Pub Company, it has no TV or pool table, just jazz or light classical background music, creating a relaxed atmosphere. The beautiful interior and furnishings are in keeping with the period of the building, with a real log fire and newspapers. A good choice of up to seven real ales is available. As well as seating at the front and side, there is a rear garden with heating. ⚞Q☆ⓓ⇌♣ℒ⊟

SE10: East Greenwich

Pelton Arms
23-25 Pelton Road, SE10 9PQ
✪ 12-midnight (1am Fri & Sat); 12-11 Sun
☎ (020) 8858 0572 ⊕ peltonarmspub.com
Greene King IPA; Wells Bombardier; guest beers Ⓗ
If you visit Greenwich it is well worth the 10-minute walk from the town centre to experience this gem of a community pub. It has an L-shaped bar and an eclectic mix of furnishings and soft lighting, giving the place a cosy and welcoming feel. There are usually seven different guest ales. Regular events include the Tuesday night quiz, live bands each weekend, and not forgetting the Wednesday night knitting club. ⚞☆ⓓ⅙⇌(Maze Hill)♣ℒ⊟

SE10: North Greenwich

Pilot Inn
68 River Way, SE10 0BE
✪ 11-11 ☎ (020) 8858 5910 ⊕ pilotgreenwich.co.uk
Fuller's Discovery, London Pride, seasonal beer Ⓗ
Expect a great range of Fuller's beers in this pub, which used to be at the centre of intense industrial activity and is now one of the oldest buildings on the North Greenwich Peninsula. Although built in 1801, the pub has been substantially altered inside

and out so that almost nothing obviously old remains. A three-level Tudor farmhouse-style interior is bedecked with various nautical paraphernalia. The garden to the rear is perfect for summer days. 🕷🏳◑ᵃ🚳❂P⅃─🚍

SE13: Lewisham

Ravensbourne Arms
323 Lewisham High Street, SE13 6NR
✪ 4 (12 Thu)-midnight; 12-1am Fri & Sat; 12-midnight Sun
☎ (020) 8613 7070 ⊕ ravensbournearms.com
Beer range varies Ⓗ
An adventurous Antic pub renovation, this one (formerly the Coach & Horses) typifies shabby chic, with retro furniture, kitsch ornaments, a range of seating areas, bar billiards and table football. A rotating range of up to five guest beers, often from microbreweries including those local to London, complements a good menu of foreign bottled beers. Cask cider is always available, and good food is served until 10pm every day. There is occasional live music. 🕷◑ᵃ⇌(Ladywell)♣🏳⅃─🚍

SE14: New Cross

Royal Albert
460 New Cross Road, SE14 6TJ
✪ 4-midnight; 12-1am Fri & Sat; 12-midnight Sun
☎ (020) 8692 3737 ⊕ royalalbertpub.com
Beer range varies Ⓗ
A gregarious pub with a moustache as its logo, providing a relaxed, homely ambience – almost romantic come the evening – for a mixed clientele of local academics, musicians and people out for an enjoyable time. Its L-shaped bar leads to a conservatory and an open-to-view kitchen. Guest beers come mainly from microbreweries, with local beers well represented. The menu includes steaks, chops, pies and game. A front patio offers outside drinking. There is a disabled toilet but no regular step-free access. 🕷◑⇌❂♣🏳⅃─🚍

SE15: Peckham

Kentish Drovers
71-79 Peckham High Street, SE15 5RS
✪ 9am-midnight (1am Wed & Thu; 2am Fri & Sat)
☎ (020) 7277 4283
Ruddles Best Bitter; Young's Special; guest beers Ⓗ
In the heart of Peckham near the prize-winning contemporary library, this converted bank is a popular Wetherspoon pub whose customers reflect a multicultural locality. It is split into two areas, one opposite the bar and another to the rear that leads to a small courtyard. Look for the lovely mosaic floor at the front. The pub takes its name from the old practice of driving livestock to London. Alongside several guest beers there is a range of ciders on handpump. Breakfasts are served from 8am. Q🕷◑ᵃ⇌❂(Peckham Rye)🏳⅃─🚍

SE16: Rotherhithe

Surrey Docks
185 Lower Road, SE16 2LW
✪ 9am-midnight (1am Fri & Sat) ☎ (020) 7394 2832
Fuller's London Pride; Greene King Abbot; Ruddles Best Bitter; guest beers Ⓗ
Modern Wetherspoon pub that commemorates the Surrey Commercial Docks, which operated here from 1807 to 1970. Information panels on the walls chart the history of the area and some of its more famous residents. Up to six real ales and at least one real cider make this pub a must, as do the friendly and helpful staff and characterful local clientele. The pub is well served by public transport, including the London Overground station opposite. Breakfasts are served from 8am. 🕷◑ᵃ❂(Surrey Quays)🏳⅃─🚍

SE18: Plumstead

Star Inn
158 Plumstead Common Road, SE18 2UL
✪ 11-11 (midnight Fri & Sat); 12-11 Sun ☎ (020) 8854 1524
Courage Best Bitter; Harveys Sussex Best Bitter; Sharp's Doom Bar Ⓗ
Close to Plumstead Common, this friendly pub is an uphill climb from the town centre. It is one of London's Real Heritage Pubs; inside are Victorian features from its predecessor and a rare surviving example of a compartmentalised interior in this part of London. The saloon bar on the left is contemporary with its inter-war rebuilding. In bygone days, when Woolwich Arsenal played their football matches on the common, the team used the Star as their changing room. ♣🚍

SE18: Woolwich

Prince Albert (Rose's)
49 Hare Street, SE18 6NE
✪ 11-11; 12-6 Sun ☎ (020) 8854 1538
Beer range varies Ⓗ
The nearest real ale pub to Woolwich Ferry, this friendly pub was rebuilt in 1928 with 12-foot high ceilings giving space without it feeling like a cavern. A long single bar with a narrow frontage, its interior is traditional and uncluttered, with wooden panelling, banquette seating and matching furniture. There are two or three varying ales on at a time from the likes of Brains, Ilkley, Adnams and Fuller's, and occasional beer festivals. Its dual name echoes its 1850s predecessor, Rose's Wine House. Q⇌❂(Woolwich Arsenal)♣🚍

SE19: Crystal Palace

Grape & Grain 🍷 Ⅼ
2 Anerley Hill, SE19 2AA
✪ 12-11 (midnight Fri & Sat; 10.30 Sun) ☎ (020) 8778 4109
⊕ thegrapeandgrainse19.co.uk
Purity Pure Gold; Westerham Finchcocks Original; guest beers Ⓗ
One of the most impressive pubs in the south-east of London for real ale, with up to 12 choices available, plus five ciders and a perry. Licensees Rick and Angela have ensured LocAle accreditation, with ales coming from many of the 40 qualifying local breweries. There are occasional beer festivals and Meet the Brewer events, free jazz every Sunday and a 17-piece swing band on Monday evenings. Local CAMRA Pub of the Year 2013. 🕷◑ᵃ⇌❂♣🏳⅃─🍴🚍

Westow House
79 Westow Hill, SE19 1TX
✪ 12 (Mon 5.30)-midnight; 12-2am Fri & Sat; 12-11 Sun
☎ (020) 8670 0654 ⊕ westowhouse.com
Beer range varies Ⓗ
A popular Antic pub with a quirky mix of furniture and artwork, situated within the vibrant Crystal Palace triangle. The pub has a changing selection

of seven real ales drawn mostly from microbreweries, often including those from the Greater London area. Occasional Meet the Brewer events are also held. Lunchtime and evening meals are served daily. There is regular live music, especially on Thursdays, and a quiz night on Tuesdays. At the front is a large outside drinking area. ⊛⊕❃❂♦⌐₩

SE20: Penge

Moon & Stars
164-166 High Street, SE20 7QS
✪ 9am-11 (10.30 Sun) ☎ (020) 8776 5680
Greene King Abbot; Ruddles Best Bitter; Thornbridge Jaipur IPA; Wychwood Hobgoblin; guest beers ℍ
At one end of Penge High Street, this popular one-bar Wetherspoon pub opened on the site of a 1930s cinema in 1994. It has a wide front area, alcoves for small groups down one side, and a raised dining area at the back. Six or seven guest ales and a cider are generally available. There is scope to request particular new beers via a suggestion system. An outdoor seating area is at the back. Breakfasts are served from 8am. ⊛⊕&❃(Kent House)₩♦⌐₩

SE22: East Dulwich

East Dulwich Tavern
1 Lordship Lane, SE22 8EW
✪ 12-midnight (1am Fri & Sat; 11 Sun) ☎ (020) 8693 1316
∰ eastdulwichtavern.com
Adnams Lighthouse; Black Sheep Best Bitter; guest beers ℍ
Attractive Victorian corner pub with an amazing tiled floor in the main bar and a first-floor function room. Operated by Antic, the EDT has this chain's trademark eclectically furnished interior. Up to five real ales are on offer. In addition, there is a good-quality menu, live music, jazz nights, a monthly film club and occasional craft fairs. Outside seating is available on the pub forecourt. ⚄⊕❃♣⌐₩

SE23: Forest Hill

All Inn One
53 Perry Vale, SE23 2NE
✪ 12 (3 Mon)-11.30; 12-1.30am Fri & Sat
☎ (020) 8699 3311 ∰ allinnone.org.uk
Brains SA; Caledonian Deuchars IPA; guest beers ℍ
Also known as the Foresters, this large red-brick pub is located behind Forest Hill station, reached by a subway. Welcoming staff, good food and ample seating make the roomy, open-plan bar warm and comfortable, while the separate wood-panelled dining room adds a touch of grandeur. A spacious garden with children's play equipment and smoking area is an oasis in the summer. Live acoustic music takes place on Mondays and once a month there is traditional Irish music.
✆⊛⊕&❃❂♦⌐₩(122,185,356)

Blythe Hill Tavern ★
319 Stanstead Road, SE23 1JB
✪ 11-11.30 (midnight Thu-Sun) ☎ (020) 8690 5176
Courage Best Bitter; Dark Star Hophead; Fuller's London Pride; Harveys Sussex Best Bitter; guest beer ℍ
An imposing Victorian corner pub and identified by CAMRA as one of Britain's Best Real Heritage Pubs, with an interesting three-room interior and 1920s

panelling. Here is a friendly local where landlord and barmen uphold the tradition of serving customers in collar and tie. There is something for everyone: sport on TV (never too loud), quiz nights (Mondays, September to April), traditional Irish music on Thursday nights, real cider and an attractive beer garden with children's play area. Local CAMRA Pub of the Year 2012.
⚄Q⊛⊟❃(Catford/Catford Bridge)
♦P⌐₩(171,185)

Capitol
11-21 London Road, SE23 3TW
✪ 9am-midnight (1am Fri & Sat) ☎ (020) 8291 8920
Fuller's London Pride; Greene King Abbot; Ruddles Best Bitter; guest beers ℍ
Originally a cinema (1929-1973) and then a bingo hall (1978-1996), this Wetherspoon pub is a classic example of Art Deco, designed by the architect J. Stanley Beard, and still bears its original name. There were plans to convert and even demolish the building while it remained closed from 1973 to 1978. Tours of the circle and other parts of the reputedly haunted building can be arranged for groups, particularly during the very popular open house weekend in September.
✆⊛⊕&❃❂♦⌐₩

Sylvan Post
24-28 Dartmouth Road, SE23 3XU
✪ 4-11 (midnight Fri); 12-midnight Sat; 12-11 Sun
☎ (020) 8291 5712 ∰ sylvanpost.com
Beer range varies ℍ
Minimalist conversion by Antic of a former 1960s post office which retains all the character of the original building, including a strong room transformed into a snug and ample postal memorabilia to remind you of its former use. There are board games as well as vintage table football. As well as a varying range of microbrewery ales and an interesting food menu, real cider on handpump is normally available. ✆⊕&❃❂♦₩

SE24: Herne Hill

Florence 𝕃
131-133 Dulwich Road, SE24 0NG
✪ 11.30-midnight (1am Fri); 11-1am Sat; 11-midnight Sun
☎ (020) 7326 4987 ∰ florencehernehill.com
Florence Bonobo, Weasel, Beaver; guest beer ℍ
Spacious and airy brewpub close to Herne Hill Station and Brockwell Park. The main front area surrounds a central island bar and leads to a rear area with an open view into the kitchen. The brewing activity can be seen through a glass partition. Three house beers are normally on offer plus one guest beer, usually from Greene King. Outside is a pleasant garden and a well-equipped children's playroom. There is also table football.
✆⊛⊕&❃⌐₩

Half Moon ★
10 Half Moon Lane, SE24 9HU
✪ 12-midnight (1am Fri & Sat); 12-10.30 Sun
☎ (020) 7274 2733
Caledonian Deuchars IPA; Fuller's London Pride; Sambrook's Wandle ℍ
Dating from 1896, this pub has been identified by CAMRA as one of Britain's Best Real Heritage Pubs. The L-shaped bar serves two main rooms; there is also a large function room and a lovely snug. The well-preserved interior features wood panelling, a chandelier, engraved mirrors and leaded windows.

At the front is a spacious terrace. Live music is performed on Friday and Saturday nights; there is an MC on Tuesdays, a quiz on Thursdays and a monthly comedy evening. ✿🅳≢ఓ⌐🖼

SE27: West Norwood

Hope
49 Norwood High Street, SE27 9JS
✪ 11-11.30 (midnight Fri & Sat); 12-11 Sun
☎ (020) 8670 2035
Young's Bitter, Special, seasonal beer; guest beer Ⓗ
One of Young's older pubs, dating back to the 1840s, close to West Norwood Cemetery and the South London Theatre. A central bar and, in winter, a cosy open fire help to create a relaxed and welcoming atmosphere. Outside is a terraced beer garden with lighting and a covered, heated seating area, together with an attractive fish pond. Barbecues are held during the warmer months and a beer festival takes place in the autumn. Children and dogs are welcome. 🚶🐕✿≢ఓ⌐🖼

Addiscombe

Claret Free House
5A Bingham Corner, Lower Addiscombe Road, CR0 7AA
✪ 11.30-11 (11.30 Thu; midnight Fri & Sat); 12-11 Sun
☎ (020) 8656 7452
Palmers Best Bitter; guest beers Ⓗ
Nestling in a row of shops, this family-owned free house has featured in this Guide for over 25 years continuously. The popularity of the house beer, Palmers Best Bitter, was marked in 2012 by the issue of a brewery certificate commemorating one million pints sold – look for it on the wall. Five further handpumps serve a changing range of guest beers from local micros and smaller breweries. The pub is conveniently located close to the Tramlink stop. 🅁🚲🖼(130,289,367)

Beckenham

Jolly Woodman
9 Chancery Lane, BR3 6NR
✪ 12 (4 Mon)-11 ☎ (020) 8663 1031
Harveys Sussex Best Bitter; Taylor Landlord; guest beers Ⓗ
Family-run traditional back-street local with welcoming and efficient staff and a cosy, cheerful atmosphere, popular with a mixed clientele of all ages. It comprises a single L-shaped room with a small front-of-bar area, a stove lit in winter, and a larger seating area to the rear. Outside are benches at the front in a quiet street, and a flower-filled rear courtyard – pretty in summer. Home-made hot meals and sandwiches are served at lunchtimes. Dog and morris dancer friendly.
Q✿🅳≢ఓ⌐🖼(227,367)

Bexley

Railway Tavern
38 Bexley High Street, DA5 1AH
✪ 11-11 (midnight Fri & Sat); 12-11 Sun ☎ (01322) 522779
Courage Best Bitter; guest beers Ⓗ
Wonderfully unspoilt old High Street local with one long bar, offering a welcome refuge from the trendy bars up the road. Guest beers have been from many smaller independent breweries not often seen in this area. The pub hosts live music on

Friday evenings and Sunday afternoons, and poker and karaoke evenings during the week. ✿≢ఓ⌐🖼

Bexleyheath

Furze Wren
Broadway Square, 6 Market Place, DA6 7DY
✪ 9am-midnight ☎ (020) 8298 2590
Greene King Abbot; Ruddles Best Bitter; Shepherd Neame Spitfire; Wychwood Hobgoblin; guest beers Ⓗ
Spacious Wetherspoon pub named after a local bird, the Dartford Warbler. Its location in the Market Place puts it at the heart of the shopping area, with a full mix of clientele. The large windows make this a great place to eat, drink and people-watch. The toilets are at bar level, which is a rarity for this chain of pubs. There are information panels on local characters. Breakfasts are served from 8am. 🚲✿🅳ఓ⌐🖼

Robin Hood & Little John 🍺 Ⓛ
78 Lion Road, DA6 8PF
✪ 11-3, 5.30 (7 Sat)-11; 12-4, 7-10.30 Sun
☎ (020) 8303 1128
Adnams Southwold Bitter, Broadside; Brains The Rev James; Brakspear Bitter; Fuller's London Pride; Sharp's Doom Bar; guest beers Ⓗ
Back-street pub dating from the 1830s when it was surrounded by fields. Eight real ales include guests from small independent breweries. It has a reputation for home-cooked food at lunchtimes and evenings (Mon-Thu until 8.30pm), with Italian specials, which can be eaten at tables made from old Singer sewing machines (no food Sun). A regular local CAMRA Pub of the Year, it has won the London Regional Pub of the Year award three times. Over-21s only. Q✿🅳⌐

Blackfen

George Staples
273 Blackfen Road, DA15 8PR
✪ 12-11 (10.30 Sun) ☎ (020) 8850 3181
Morland Old Speckled Hen; guest beer Ⓗ
Originally the Woodman Inn, built in 1845 and one of the first buildings in Blackfen, this pub was demolished and rebuilt in 1931 when large-scale building began in the area. Recently refurbished and renamed after the original landlord, it is now a comfortable and pleasant pub. Mirrors along one wall give the impression of a much larger space. Food is served until 9pm. 🚲🅳ఓ⌐🖼(51,132)

Bromley

Barrel & Horn
204-206 High Street, BR1 1PW
✪ 12-11 (11.30 Fri & Sat; 10.30 Sun) ☎ (020) 8290 2039
🌐 barrelandhorn.com
Beer range varies Ⓗ
Owned by Fuller's, though not presented in the usual Fuller's style and best described as a nod towards 1950s chic, this family-friendly pub serves a changing range of ales, all of which can be regarded as guests. Beers from local Bromley brewer Late Knights are regularly featured and real cider is available on handpump. Home-cooked food has a distinctly American twist. Staff are friendly, knowledgeable and enthusiastic. Quiz night is Monday and there is live music Thursdays to Saturdays. 🅳ఓ≢(Bromley North/South)🚲⌐🖼

Red Lion

10 North Road, BR1 3LG
🟢 11 (12 Sun)-11 ☎ (020) 8460 2691
Greene King IPA, Abbot; Harveys Sussex Best Bitter;
guest beers Ⓗ
A popular back-street local and a long-standing
regular entry in this Guide. The two guest ales
change frequently and the large display of
pumpclips above the bar is testimony to the
number of consistently well-kept beers served by
Chris, Siobhan and staff over the years. This small
pub, noted for its original tiling and bookshelves,
has a friendly, welcoming atmosphere. Darts is
played and football matches shown. Local CAMRA
2012 Pub of the Year.
ﾑＱ🏵️🚷◑≹(Bromley North)♣⁵-🚐(314)

Chelsfield

Five Bells

Church Road, BR6 7RE
🟢 11.30-11; 12-10.30 Sun ☎ (01689) 821044
⊕ thefivebells-chelsfieldvillage.co.uk
Courage Best Bitter; Sharp's Doom Bar; guest beers Ⓗ
In an unspoilt 17th-century village, this is a
welcoming two-bar pub. Small local breweries
usually feature among the guest beers, which
include a cask on gravity in the public bar. A
quarterly guide lists events, including a weekly
charity quiz and monthly live jazz. Beer festivals
are held at Easter and in October. Snacks are
always available but check for evening restaurant
service. 🏵️◑🅱️♣P⁵-🚐(R3)

Croydon

Builders Arms

65 Leslie Park Road, CRO 6TP
🟢 12-11 (midnight Fri & Sat; 10.30 Sun) ☎ (020) 8654 1803
Fuller's Chiswick Bitter, London Pride, seasonal beers;
Gale's HSB Ⓗ
An attractive, detached pub in a back street in the
east of the town. The two bars differ in character:
one has the feel of a public bar and the other has
comfortable seating extending to a pleasant
secluded garden at the rear. There are TVs for sport
in both bars. Food is served until 9pm (8pm at
weekends), including curries on Monday evenings.
Children are welcome in the bars until 8pm.
Occasional live music performances are held.
ﾑﾗ🏵️◑🅱️≹(East)🚐(Lebanon Rd)♣⁵-🚐

Dog & Bull

24 Surrey Street, CRO 1RG
🟢 11.30-11 (midnight Thu-Sat); 12-10.30 Sun
☎ (020) 8667 9718
Young's Bitter, Special, seasonal beers; guest beers Ⓗ
Situated in the street market, this is Croydon's
oldest pub. The Young's connection dates back to
1832, the building being Grade II-listed. There is a
main room with an island bar, plus two adjoining
drinking areas at the side and back; the latter has a
TV screen for sporting events. Spring and autumn
beer festivals are held. The pub has an excellent
outdoor drinking area at the rear and a function
room upstairs.
Ｑ🏵️◑≹(East/West)🚐(George St/Reeves Corner)
⊖(West)⁵-🚐

George

17-21 George Street, CRO 1LA
🟢 9-midnight (1am Fri & Sat) ☎ (020) 8649 9077

Greene King Abbot; Marston's Pedigree; Ruddles Best
Bitter; guest beers Ⓗ
Popular Wetherspoon pub in the main shopping
area of central Croydon. There is a single large
room with two bars and it can be difficult to get
served at busy times. Guest beers include many
from local breweries and Dark Star, Thornbridge
and Oakham beers are regularly present. There is
always a good selection too at the mini beer
festivals and Meet the Brewer events which are
held periodically. Breakfasts are served from 8am.
ﾗ◑👶≹(East/West)🚐(George St/Reeves Corner)
⊖(West)♠🚐

Glamorgan

81 Cherry Orchard Road, CRO 6BE
🟢 12-11 (midnight Fri); 4-midnight Sat; closed Sun
☎ (020) 8688 6333 ⊕ theglamorgan.co.uk
Fuller's London Pride; Harveys Sussex Best Bitter;
guest beers Ⓗ
A modern Punch Taverns pub, just five minutes'
walk from East Croydon station. It provides an
above-average range and quality of food. There are
three rooms and an outdoor patio area which also
caters for smokers. One room has a dartboard and
pool table, another is reserved for diners. The pub
can get busy at times with weekday trade from
local offices. Bookings are taken for private
functions, especially on Sundays when the pub is
otherwise closed. 🏵️◑≹🚐(East)⁵-🚐

Green Dragon Ⓛ

58-60 High Street, CRO 1NA
🟢 10-midnight (1am Fri & Sat); 12-10.30 Sun
☎ (020) 8667 0684 ⊕ greendragoncroydon.co.uk
Beer range varies Ⓗ/Ⓖ
A lively Stonegate pub near Croydon's historic
market, popular with a wide section of the
community and run by enthusiastic staff with a
keen interest in ale. Six handpumps and two
gravity casks dispense a constantly changing range
of beers, including those from Croydon breweries
and other local brewers. A real cider is also served.
A wide variety of music and other events takes
place upstairs, including live jazz on Sunday
afternoons. Local CAMRA Pub of the Year 2012 and
2013.
◑🅶≹(East/West)🚐(George St/Reeves Corner)
⊖(West)♠🚐

Half & Half Ⓛ

282 High Street, CRO 1NG
🟢 4-11 (midnight Thu); 12-midnight Fri; 1-midnight Sat; 3-11
Sun ☎ (020) 8726 0080 ⊕ halfandhalf.uk.com
Dark Star Hophead; guest beer Ⓗ
Street-corner bar between the town centre and the
South End restaurant area. The guest beer is usually
sourced from a local microbrewery, possibly one of
Croydon's. A range of mainly Czech, Belgian and
German bottled beers is also available. Food is
limited to interesting nibbles. A variety of events
takes place including Meet the Brewer sessions
and beer tastings. The downstairs room can be
booked for functions. Over-21s only.
🚐(George St)🚐

Royal Standard

1 Sheldon Street, CRO 1SS
🟢 12-midnight (11 Sun) ☎ (020) 8688 9749
⊕ royalstandard-croydon.co.uk
Fuller's Chiswick Bitter, London Pride, ESB, seasonal
beers; Gale's HSB Ⓗ

A street-corner local dwarfed by the adjacent Croydon flyover and multi-storey car park. This quiet retreat just south of the town centre offers a single bar with three different drinking areas, each with its own character. Do not miss the tucked-away area behind the bar, which has a two-seat misericord and a Dunville's Royal Irish Distillery wall mirror. As well as tables beside the pavement, there is a small separate enclosed garden across the road nestling under the flyover.
Q✿₪(George St/Reeves Corner)♣⊟

Skylark

34-36 South End, CRO 1DP

✪ 9am-midnight (1am Fri & Sat) ☎ (020) 8649 9909

Courage Best Bitter; Greene King Abbot; Marston's Pedigree; guest beers ⊞

South of the town centre in the restaurant quarter, this Wetherspoon pub is often quiet at weekends and late evening. The large open-plan layout of what had been a Green Shield Stamp building includes an interesting balcony. Local microbrewery beers often feature in mini festivals and events and are regularly on the bar. The name and some internal decoration reflect Croydon's aviation history. The upstairs bar area can be booked for weddings and other celebrations.
➲✿◑♿≢(South)♦⅃⊟

Spreadeagle

39-41 Katharine Street, CRO 1NX

✪ 11-11 (midnight Fri & Sat); 12-10.30 Sun
☎ (020) 8781 1134

Fuller's Chiswick Bitter, London Pride, ESB, seasonal beers; Gale's HSB; guest beer ⊞

Spacious Fuller's Ale & Pie house in the town centre with a separate upstairs bar and well served by local transport – George Street tram stop is nearby. As well as the wide selection of handpumped ales, an extensive range of Fuller's bottled beers is available. Guest beer policy is to feature an ale from a local brewery. The manager holds Fuller's Master Cellarman accreditation. Sport can be viewed comfortably on several TV screens throughout the pub.
◑♿≢(East/West)₪(George St/Reeves Corner)
⊖(West)⅃⊟

Downe

Queen's Head ⅃

25 High Street, BR6 7US

✪ 12-11 (11.30 Fri & Sat; 10.30 Sun) ☎ (01689) 852145
⊕ queensheaddowne.com

Harveys Sussex Best Bitter; Sharp's Doom Bar; guest beers ⊞

Attractive pub, dating from 1565, in the centre of an historic village just 17 minutes by bus from Bromley South or Orpington. Charles Darwin, a regular patron, lived at Downe House less than a mile away. Traditional and comfortable, with three fireplaces and several dining areas, it is popular with walkers all year round. Guest beers regularly include those from the nearby Westerham Brewery. The menu includes vegetarian soups, daily home-cooked specials, pies and baguettes (12-9pm Mon-Sat, lunchtime only Sun).
ᨓ✿◑⛃P⅃⊟(146,R8)

Farnborough

Woodman

50 High Street, BR6 7BA

✪ 12-11 (10.30 Sun) ☎ (01689) 852663 ⊕ thewoody.co.uk

Shepherd Neame Master Brew, Kent's Best, Spitfire, seasonal beers ⊞

A welcoming community pub whose landlord is a real ale enthusiast, regularly featuring Shepherd Neame's seasonal and pilot microbrewery beers. The good-value food is made from locally sourced ingredients where possible. A quiz night is held on Thursdays with food available (booking necessary); there are also charity bingo nights and live music events. Summer barbecues are an added attraction in the large garden of this dog-friendly pub.
✿◑♦P⅃⊟(358,402)

Orpington

Orpington Liberal Club ⅃

7 Station Road, BR6 0RZ

✪ 1-3 (not Mon-Thu), 8-11; 12-3, 7-11 Sat; 12-3, 8-10.30 Sun
☎ (01689) 01689 820882 ⊕ orpingtonliberalclub.co.uk

Beer range varies ⊞

Recently refurbished, this club is free of tie and is run by a real ale enthusiast who does not serve national brands, but focuses purely on LocAles and microbrewery beers. Well over 100 different real ales were served in 2012 and prices are extremely competitive. The club has regular live music, runs occasional beer festivals and has a large rear garden. CAMRA or Liberal Party membership cards are required for entry. Local CAMRA Club of the Year 2013. Q✿₪≢♣⅃⊟

Petts Wood

Sovereign of the Seas ⅃

109-111 Queensway, BR5 1DG

✪ 9am-11.30 ☎ (01689) 891606

Adnams Broadside, Explorer; Greene King Abbot; Ruddles Best Bitter; guest beers ⊞

Large, popular Wetherspoon pub boasting 12 handpumps, six offering a changing range of guest beers, ciders and perries. The long, narrow layout gives the pub a cosy atmosphere, an impression enhanced by the varied seating styles, including a couple of snug alcoves. Themed panels refer to the ship after which the pub is named, and to former local resident, William Willett, the daylight saving campaigner. There is also a community noticeboard. ✿◑♿≢♦⅃⊟(208,K7,R3)

Sidcup

Tailor's Chalk

47-49 Sidcup High Street, DA14 6ED

✪ 9am-11 ☎ (020) 8308 6880

Courage Best Bitter; Greene King Abbot; Ruddles Best Bitter; guest beers ⊞

More compact than a usual Wetherspoon pub, with lots of nooks and crannies, the building was once a bespoke tailor's (hence the name) and also a former Hogshead chain pub. The large internal pillars can make it seem more full than it actually is. There is the usual changing range of guest beers, often from local breweries. News is always on the large TV screen by the door, and breakfasts are served from 8am. ➲◑♿⊟

Upper Belvedere

Prince of Wales Ⓛ
13a Woolwich Road, DA17 5EE
☼ 2-10.30 Mon & Tue; 12-11 (midnight Fri & Sat)
☎ (01322) 433737
Dark Star Hophead; Westerham British Bulldog; Young's Bitter; guest beers Ⓗ
Built around 1863, this small cosy pub with a horseshoe-shaped bar stands on what was once Lessness Heath. Westerham and Dark Star beers are normally on offer, and the beers sold are generally under 4.5% ABV. Sports fans can watch the large-screen TVs. Made-to-order snacks and meals are available, with a Sunday roast (1-6pm) and also a well-priced Thursday meal deal. There is entertainment on Saturday nights and quiz night on Sunday. Free Wi-Fi is available.
❀◑⁂–⊟(99,401)

Welling

New Cross Turnpike Ⓛ
55 Bellegrove Road, DA16 3PB
☼ 9am-midnight ☎ (020) 8304 1600
Courage Best Bitter, Directors; Greene King Abbot; Shepherd Neame Spitfire; guest beers Ⓗ
The pub takes its name from its location on what was the New Cross Turnpike, one of many old private toll roads. It is a good Wetherspoon with an attractive layout on four levels, including a gallery and patio. Opened in 1998, it was previously a NatWest bank. Up to eight guest ales are dispensed by the helpful staff. Breakfasts are served from 8am. Disabled access includes two wheelchair lifts, and it has a ground-floor toilet. ❀◑♿⇌●⁂–⊟

West Wickham

Railway Hotel
Red Lodge Road, BR4 0EW
☼ 11.30-11; 12-10.30 Sun ☎ (020) 8776 0043
Fuller's London Pride; Harveys Sussex Best Bitter; Young's Bitter; guest beers Ⓗ
A good-sized Ember Inns establishment, conveniently served by three bus routes and a railway station. Its three regular ales, three guest ales and plentiful choice of food all day make it an attractive local venue. Several events through the year showcase particular beer styles including, on a small scale, an Oktoberfest and a winter ales collection. The management are responsive to beer requests from discerning customers. Quiz nights are held on Tuesdays and Sundays.
♨❀◑♿⇌P⊟(119,194,352)

SOUTH-WEST LONDON
SW1: Belgravia

Antelope
22-24 Eaton Terrace, SW1W 8EZ
☼ 12-11 (11.30 Fri; 10 Sun) ☎ (020) 7824 8512
⊕ antelope-eaton-terrace.co.uk
Fuller's London Pride, ESB, London Porter, seasonal beer; Gale's Seafarers Ale Ⓗ
Claimed to date back to the 17th century, this pub is now operated by Fuller's. Preserved original features include etched glass windows, a side room used as a snug and a central bar. Sporting and other photos/prints are displayed, as well as a very interesting map of the area in 1836. This is an upmarket house frequented mainly by local professionals. The pub plays cricket against the Churchill Arms (Notting Hill). The upstairs bar and side room can be hired for functions.
⏧◑⊖(Sloane Sq)⊟

Horse & Groom
7 Groom Place, SW1X 7BA
☼ 11-11; closed Sat & Sun ☎ (020) 7235 6980
⊕ thehorseandgroombelgravia.com
Shepherd Neame Master Brew, Spitfire, seasonal beers Ⓗ
Excellent pub that has been a Guide regular for many years. It dates back to the 1850s and its beautiful mews setting is close to Buckingham Palace and Belgrave Square, surrounded by embassies, upmarket houses and offices. Food includes fabulous fish and chips, pies and curries, all home-cooked. The pub is available for private use at weekends and the function room may be booked for events with catering for up to 50.
❀◑⊖(Hyde Park Corner)⊟

Star Tavern Ⓛ
6 Belgrave Mews West, SW1X 8HT
☼ 11 (12 Sat)-11; 12-10.30 Sun ☎ (020) 7235 3019
⊕ star-tavern-belgravia.co.uk
Fuller's London Pride, ESB, seasonal beer; Gale's Seafarers Ale Ⓗ
Situated in a mews close to embassies, the Star is rich in the history of the powerful, famous and infamous – it is rumoured that the Great Train Robbery was planned here. Now a popular Fuller's pub, local residents, business people and embassy staff rub shoulders with casual visitors. Sometimes a special Fuller's beer can be found. Upstairs is a dining room, bookable for functions. This pub has featured in every edition of this Guide.
♨Q◑⊖(Hyde Park Corner/Knightsbridge)⊟

SW1: Pimlico

Cask Pub & Kitchen Ⓛ
6 Charlwood Street, SW1V 2EE
☼ 12-11 (10.30 Sun) ☎ (020) 7630 7225
⊕ caskpubandkitchen.com
Beer range varies Ⓗ
Formerly the Pimlico Tram and converted to a beer destination pub by Martin Hayes, who has since acquired and converted three more premises in London and one in Brighton. Ten handpumps serve real ales from many microbreweries such as Arbor Ales and Dark Star, and there is a vast range of bottled beers. Meet the Brewer events are held regularly. Burgers feature strongly on the menu, with Sunday roasts until late afternoon.
◑⇌(Victoria)⊖(Pimlico/Victoria)Ⓤ⊟

Jugged Hare
172 Vauxhall Bridge Road, SW1V 1DX
☼ 11-11 (11.30 Thu & Fri); 12-10.30 Sun ☎ (020) 7828 1543
⊕ juggedharevictoria.co.uk
Fuller's London Pride, ESB, seasonal beers; Gale's Seafarers Ale Ⓗ
Formerly a NatWest bank that was converted in 1996 to a Fuller's Ale & Pie House with the hallmark mahogany decor and chandeliers. The pub is supported by a loyal band of regulars, plus office workers and tourists enjoying the all-day food; jugged hare pie is on the menu. Both the back room and the balcony can be booked for functions. ◑⇌(Victoria)⊖(Pimlico/Victoria)⁂–⊟

SW1: St James's

Red Lion ★

2 Duke of York Street, SW1Y 6JP
✪ 11.30-11; closed Sun ☎ (020) 7321 0782
⊕ redlionmayfair.co.uk
Fuller's Chiswick Bitter, Discovery, London Pride, ESB, seasonal beers; guest beers ⊞

Close to the upmarket shops in Jermyn Street, this is a justifiably celebrated little gem, worth visiting just for its spectacular Victorian interior of etched mirrors and glass. The Grade II-listed building dates from 1821 and was given a new frontage in 1871; it has been identified by CAMRA as one of Britain's Best Real Heritage Pubs. The interior is tiny and visitors often spill onto the pavement outside. Mind the precipitous steps down to the toilets. Food is served 12-3pm (4pm Sat).
Q◖Θ(Green Park/Piccadilly Circus)🚻

SW1: Victoria

Cask & Glass

39 Palace Street, SW1E 5HN
✪ 11-11; 12-8 Sat; closed Sun ☎ (020) 7834 7630
Shepherd Neame Master Brew, Kent's Best, Spitfire, seasonal beers ⊞

First licensed in 1862 as the Duke of Cambridge, this attractive one-room pub on the route between Buckingham Palace and Westminster Cathedral, adorned with flowers in summer, is a haven for tourists, office workers and local residents. The wood-panelled bar has pictures of local scenes and politicians. Look out for the bull's-eye windows and the two paintings of the pub on the way to the toilets. A cosy place for a pint after (or instead of) visiting the sights. Q✿◖◖⇌Θ⌐🚻

Wetherspoon's

Unit 5, 1st Floor, Main Concourse, Victoria Station, SW1V 1JT
✪ 9am-midnight (10.30 Sun) ☎ (020) 7931 0445
Fuller's London Pride; Greene King IPA, Abbot; guest beers ⊞

Attractive, modern glass-fronted bar above WH Smith, between the two sides of the Victoria Station concourse, accessed mainly by escalators. The clientèle includes tourists, office workers and weekend football supporters enjoying a drink on arrival in London or before their train leaves. TV screens show times of train departures. A choice of guest beers and two Westons ciders is available. Breakfasts are served from 7.30am. A good place perhaps for a Brief Encounter. Q🐾◖⇌Θ🚻

SW1: Westminster

Buckingham Arms

62 Petty France, SW1H 9EU
✪ 11-11 (6 Sat); closed Sun ☎ (020) 7222 3386
⊕ buckinghamarms.com
Sambrook's Wandle; Wells Bombardier; Young's Bitter, Special; guest beer ⊞

Said to have once been a hat shop, this pub was opened in the 1720s as the Bell, renamed the Black Horse in the 1740s, rebuilt in 1898 and renamed the Buckingham Arms in 1901. Substantially renovated in recent years, it has appeared in every edition of this Guide. A mix of modern and traditional seats and tables, high and low, draws civil servants and visitors alike.
🐾◖Θ(St James's Park)🚻

Sanctuary House Hotel

33 Tothill Street, SW1H 9LA
✪ 10-11; 12-10.30 Sun ☎ (020) 7799 4044
⊕ sanctuaryhousehotel.co.uk
Fuller's Chiswick Bitter, Discovery, London Pride, ESB, seasonal beer ⊞

A Fuller's Ale & Pie House and hotel, mainly drawing office workers and visitors to Westminster Abbey and other nearby attractions. This converted early 20th-century office building has housed publishers and politicians and is on ancient marshland and Tothill Fields, scene of trials by combat and 18th-century duels. Now in quieter times it offers warmth and hospitality. The fields were within the limits of sanctuary at the Abbey, hence perhaps the medieval-style mural on the back wall. 🐾🛏◖◖ᵔΘ(St James's Park)🚻

Speaker ℂ

46 Great Peter Street, SW1P 2HA
✪ 12-11; closed Sat, Sun & bank holidays ☎ (020) 7222 1749
Taylor Landlord; Young's Bitter; guest beers ⊞

Comfortable wood-panelled and parliamentary caricature-decorated one-bar local that dates from at least 1729 when it was the Castle, renamed Elephant & Castle around 1800, and The Speaker in 1999. This was the Devil's Acre, a notorious slum and next to the world's first public gasworks. The pub now welcomes residents from local estates, workers from government offices and Channel 4, who enjoy the range of five beers and home-made food – no music, TV or children.
Q◖◖ᵔΘ(St James's Park)🚻

SW1: Whitehall

Lord Moon of the Mall

16-18 Whitehall, SW1A 2DY
✪ 9am-11.30 (midnight Fri & Sat; 11 Sun)
☎ (020) 7839 7701
Fuller's London Pride; Greene King IPA; Wychwood Hobgoblin; guest beers ⊞

A 1995 Wetherspoon conversion, formerly the premises of Cocks Biddulph Ltd from 1759 at 43 Charing Cross; the building was designed by Richard Coad and built 1870-3. The pale pink sandstone, dark-wood panelling, high ceilings and arched windows would still be recognisable to the Victorian bank clerks. It is entirely open plan, with a family dining area to the rear where children are welcome until 9.30pm. There are up to seven rotating guest beers.
🐾◖⇌(Charing Cross)Θ(Charing Cross/Westminster)👶🚻

SW2: Brixton

Elm Park Tavern ℂ

76 Elm Park, SW2 2UB
✪ 4 (12 Sat)-midnight; 12-11 Sun ☎ 07852 345974
Belleville Commonside Pale Ale, Brownstone, Thames Surfer; Purity Pure Gold, Pure Ubu ⊞

Comfortable two-bar free house, the last pub on the estate, which showcases beers from the local Belleville Brewery alongside a couple of guests, usually from Purity. Satellite TV sport is shown if requested, preferably in advance. Thursday is quiz night. A unique portrait of 18th-century stage mimic Samuel Foote dominates the front bar and both rooms have some interesting stained glass. Note the restricted weekday opening hours.
✿⌐🚻

SW2: Streatham Hill

Crown & Sceptre ⦿
2A Streatham Hill, SW2 4AH
✪ 9am-midnight (1am Fri & Sat) ☎ (020) 8671 0843
Greene King Abbot; Ruddles Best Bitter; Sambrook's Wandle, Junction; guest beers Ⓗ
A landmark building at the junction of the South Circular and the A23, this ex-Truman's pub was the earliest Wetherspoon conversion in south-west London. Still superbly run by the same young manager of many years standing, it remains an oasis for quality beer. As well as the original Truman's façade and tiling outside, it has kept a pub atmosphere and is decorated with unusual framed floral artwork on the walls. The TVs are muted except for major sporting events.
⊛⦿≉●P⪦–⊟

SW4: Clapham

Windmill on the Common
Clapham Common South Side, SW4 9DE
✪ 11-midnight; 12-11 Sun ☎ (020) 8673 4578
⊕ windmillclapham.co.uk
Wells Bombardier; Young's Bitter, Special; guest beer Ⓗ
Large landmark public house since 1665, although most parts date from the 18th and 19th centuries. Among several distinct drinking areas is the domed room that has a whispering gallery effect to rival that of St Paul's Cathedral. Conversations from across the opposite side of the room can be heard as if spoken right next to you – which may help during quiz night on Sunday. The 29-bedroom hotel entrance is around the corner in Holly Lodge.
▦⊛⊷⦿⦵⊖(Clapham Common/South)P⪦–⊟

SW5: Earl's Court

Blackbird
209 Earl's Court Road, SW5 9AN
✪ 8.30-11 (11.30 Thu-Sat; 10.30 Sun) ☎ (020) 7835 1855
⊕ blackbirdearlscourt.co.uk
Fuller's Discovery, London Pride, ESB, seasonal beers Ⓗ
Typical Fuller's Ale & Pie House, formerly a branch of the Midland Bank and sympathetically converted in 1993, occupying a large corner site over the road from Earl's Court Underground station and within walking distance of major tourist attractions such as the South Kensington museums. Large windows create a pleasant and airy atmosphere, throwing into relief the dark panelling and impressive central column adorning the attractive horseshoe-shaped bar. Breakfast is served from 8.30am.
⦿≉(West Brompton)⊖⊟

King's Head
17 Hogarth Place, SW5 0QT
✪ 11 (10 Sat & Sun)-11; 11-10.30 Sun ☎ (020) 7373 5239
Westerham Puddledock Porter; guest beers Ⓗ
A friendly corner pub off the busy Earl's Court Road, recently refurbished in a modern style with a wooden floor and coloured tiling around the bar. There is comfortable sofa seating, plus high stools around tall tables. Quiz night is Monday and as well as live music on Wednesday evenings there may be a string quartet evening on the first Sunday in the month. ⌂⦿⦵⊟

SW6: Parsons Green

White Horse ⦿
1-3 Parsons Green, SW6 4UL
✪ 11-11.30 (midnight Fri & Sat) ☎ (020) 7736 2115
⊕ whitehorsesw6.com
Harveys Sussex Best Bitter; Oakham JHB; guest beers Ⓗ
Destination M&B pub which normally boasts six guest beers. Regular beer and food matching events take place as well as beer festivals, including the not to be missed Old Ale Festival in November, where the Coach House, which is normally reserved for dining, has a stillage. The pub can get busy when Chelsea FC are playing at home, but the upstairs area is a good place to escape the crowds. ▦Q⊛⦿⊖●⪦–⊟(22)

SW7: Gloucester Road

Queen's Arms
30 Queens Gate Mews, SW7 5QL
✪ 12-11 (10.30 Sun) ☎ (020) 7823 9293
⊕ thequeensarmskensington.co.uk
Fuller's London Pride; Sharp's Doom Bar; guest beers Ⓗ
Lovely corner mews pub that is well worth seeking out for its real ales and its large range of interesting bottled beers, malt whiskies and other spirits. Note the very unusual curved doors. The L-shaped room features wood floors and panelling. The clientèle reflects the location: well-heeled locals, students from Imperial College and musicians from, and visitors to, the nearby Albert Hall. The food menu and specials are of superior quality. Q⦿⦵●⊟

SW8: South Lambeth

Canton Arms
177 South Lambeth Road, SW8 1XP
✪ 11 (5 Mon)-11; 11-10.30 Sun ☎ (020) 7582 8710
⊕ cantonarms.com
Skinner's Betty Stogs; Taylor Golden Best; guest beers Ⓗ
Very much a gastro-pub but with four handpumps, this local has an airy, open-plan interior with bare wooden floors and basic furniture around a central bar. Mirrors and pumpclips adorn the walls and low-level lighting provides a moody atmosphere. Blackboards show real ales, wines and food available. To the rear is a restaurant area and at the front an outside drinking area faces the main road. Bar snacks are served all day Monday-Saturday. Sport is shown on terrestrial TV channels.
⊛⦿⊖(Stockwell)⊟

SW9: Brixton

Crown & Anchor
246 Brixton Road, SW9 6AQ
✪ 4.30 (12 Sat)-midnight; 12-10.30 Sun ☎ (020) 7737 0060
⊕ crownandanchorbrixton.co.uk
Beer range varies Ⓗ
Recently reinvented to bring real ale to something of a pub desert, this modernised gastro-pub offers six changing real ales, sometimes from London micros, as well as three ciders and a perry from Sandford. Meals are available every evening and also at lunchtime on Saturdays and Sundays. There are tables outside, but no shelter for smokers.
⌂⊛⦿≉⊖●⊟

Trinity Arms

45 Trinity Gardens, SW9 8DR

⏺ 11-11 (midnight Fri); 12-midnight Sat; 12-11 Sun

☎ (020) 7274 4544 ⊕ trinityarms.co.uk

Young's Bitter, Special, London Gold, seasonal beer Ⓗ

A friendly, comfortable, traditional pub tucked away in a quiet square off the busy Acre Lane and Brixton High Road, named after an ancient asylum nearby. With drinking areas around three sides of a horseshoe-shaped bar and front and back patios outside, it is popular in the evening with office workers and locals, and busy on Brixton Academy nights. Well-kept real ale is a big attraction. Families are welcome until 7.30pm and food is available until 10pm. ⏺◑≒⊖≒⊟

SW11: Battersea

Beehive

197 St John's Hill, SW11 1TH

⏺ 12-midnight ☎ (020) 7450 1756

⊕ beehivestjohnshill.co.uk

Fuller's London Pride, Bengal Lancer, ESB; guest beers Ⓗ

Cosy local and one of the few traditional pubs remaining on this thoroughfare. What you see is what you get: a friendly atmosphere and well-kept Fuller's ales. Classic pub decor includes old prints of Wandsworth as well as more recent cycling photographs. There are two large-screen TVs showing most major sporting events. On sunny days, watch the world and his dog go by from the pavement drinking area. Expect a friendly welcome from Cheddar, the pub dog.

⏺◑≒⊖(Clapham Jct)♣≒⊟

Eagle Ale House ▼ Ⓛ

104 Chatham Road, SW11 6HG

⏺ 3 (12 Sat)-11; 12-10.30 Sun ☎ (020) 7228 2328

⊕ eaglealehouse.co.uk

Beer range varies Ⓗ

Just off the busy Northcote Road, this charming local with leather sofas, old bottles and books is a bastion for beers from microbreweries from London, Surrey and further afield. Everyone and their dog are welcome, with a choice of six or seven ales typically on offer. A heated marquee in the garden is used for special occasions such as beer festivals. The large-screen TV shows major sporting events. Local CAMRA Pub of the Year 2012 after three years as runner-up.

🏚⏺◑♣≒⊟(319,G1)

Falcon ★ Ⓛ

2 St John's Hill, SW11 1RU

⏺ 10-11 (midnight Fri & Sat; 10.30 Sun) ☎ (020) 7228 2076

Beer range varies Ⓗ

On the corner, close to Clapham Junction station, this flagship M&B Nicholson's pub continues to be run by the same enthusiastic manager. Gravity dispense from casks at his popular beer festivals can double the regular 20 or so real ales available round the vast central bar. A late-Victorian gem and identified by CAMRA as one of Britain's Best Real Heritage pubs, it retains its partitions and etched and stained glass. The back half is usually reserved for diners. Q◑◐&≒⊖(Clapham Jct)♠⊟

Fox & Hounds

66 Latchmere Road, SW11 2JU

⏺ 11-3 (not Mon), 5-11; 12-11 Fri & Sat; 12-10.30 Sun

☎ (020) 7924 5483 ⊕ thefoxandhoundspub.co.uk

St Austell Tribute; Sambrook's Wandle; guest beers Ⓗ

A prominent street-corner pub that sits well among the Victorian streets down from Lavender Hill. Like its surroundings, the pub has undergone gentrification and is justifiably popular for its food, especially with families. The decor features brewery mirrors, art prints and Orlando the Marmalade Cat. You may also catch sight of Charlie and Melton, the resident pub cats. Guest beers usually include one from Dark Star. No food weekday lunchtimes. The yard at the rear has a heated and covered area.

⏺⊛◑≒⊖(Clapham Jct)≒⊟

Powder Keg Diplomacy

147 St John's Hill, SW11 1TQ

⏺ 4-11; 12-midnight Thu & Fri; 10-midnight Sat; 10-10.30 Sun

☎ (020) 7450 6457 ⊕ powderkegdiplomacy.co.uk

Beer range varies Ⓗ

A new and immensely popular gastro-pub kitted out in colonial style. Three handpumps dispense real ale from innovative micros like Head in a Hat, Oakham and Windsor & Eton, and it also features around 50 expertly chosen bottled beers from around the world. It has a high-class yet reasonably priced restaurant with immaculate service. Meet the Brewer events are held every six weeks or so.

⏺◑≒⊖(Clapham Jct)≒⊟

SW12: Balham

Nightingale Ⓛ

97 Nightingale Lane, SW12 8NX

⏺ 11 (12 Sun)-midnight ☎ (020) 8673 1637

Sambrook's Wandle; Sharp's Doom Bar; Young's Bitter, Special; guest beer Ⓗ

The Bird, as it is known, is a haven for a quiet and rewarding drink, a real pub welcoming visitors and locals alike. Outside, the Grade II-listed building has a popular garden and heated patio for families. Its annual charity walk is now in its 34th year and there is a craft fair on the last Sunday of each month, with 10 tables in the garden selling local produce. A guess the beer competition is held every Friday.

🏚Q⏺⊛◑&≒(Wandsworth Common) ⊖(Clapham South)♣≒⊟(G1)

SW13: Barnes

Red Lion

2 Castelnau, SW13 9RU

⏺ 11-11; 12-10.30 Sun ☎ (020) 8748 2984

⊕ red-lion-barnes.co.uk

Fuller's Chiswick Bitter, London Pride, ESB; seasonal beer Ⓗ

Large Victorian landmark pub at the entrance to the Wetland Centre. It has been opened out in recent years although the back room, with its ornate fireplace, chandelier, dark wood panelling and pillars, still has a more exclusive feel. Beyond is a decked patio and a spacious no-smoking garden. The landlord has won the Fuller's Cellarman of the Year award three times. Excellent food is available from a varied, modern menu, and children are welcome during the day. 🏚⊛◑&P≒⊟

SW15: Putney

Bricklayer's Arms

32 Waterman Street, SW15 1DD

✪ 12-11 (10.30 Sun) ☎ (020) 8789 0222
⊕ bricklayers-arms.co.uk
Beer range varies Ⓗ
Small, welcoming, family-owned free house usually featuring a rotating range of beers from microbreweries, often with several from just one brewery, complemented by a real cider or perry. Shove-ha'penny and bar skittles are played, and there is a pub cricket team. Regular beer festivals grace the patio outside. Its popularity with Fulham FC supporters tends to reduce the beer range after home matches. A regular local CAMRA Pub of the Year and twice regional winner.
🏨❀≠⊖(Putney Bridge)♣●ⁱ–🖾

Green Man
Wildcroft Road, Putney Heath, SW15 3NG
✪ 11-11 (midnight Fri & Sat); 12-10.30 Sun
☎ (020) 8788 8096 ⊕ greenmanputney.co.uk
Young's Bitter, Special, seasonal beer Ⓗ
On the edge of the heath opposite the bus terminus up Putney Hill, this charming, warm and welcoming Young's pub dates back to around 1700 and retains an intimate atmosphere. Outside are a sheltered front patio and a large, split-level back garden ideal for families in summer. Quiz night is Tuesday, poker night Wednesday, and you can use the pub's board games. Meals are served lunchtimes and evenings Monday to Thursday and all day Friday to Sunday. 🏨❀🕩&♣ⁱ–🖾

SW16: Streatham
Pied Bull
498 Streatham High Road, SW16 3QB
✪ 12-11 (midnight Fri & Sat) ☎ (020) 8764 4003
⊕ thepiedbullstreatham.com
Young's Bitter, Special, seasonal beers Ⓗ
Landmark three-bar pub opposite Streatham Common. The open-plan lounge bar welcomes children, the dog-friendly public bar to the left features a skylight and attractive etched screens, and a panelled games room to the rear has three pool tables. The paved garden is popular during warmer weather and smokers have a heated, covered area with a TV screen. Meals and bar snacks are sold. Terrestrial TV sport is shown, especially rugby. 🏨❀🕩⊟&≠(Streatham/Streatham Common)♣ⁱ–🖾

Railway Ⓛ
2 Greyhound Lane, SW16 5SD
✪ 12-11 (midnight Thu; 1am Fri & Sat) ☎ (020) 8769 9448
⊕ therailwaySW16.co.uk
Sambrook's Wandle, Junction; guest beers Ⓗ
Four handpumps serve only London-brewed ales in this much-improved pub. The spacious front bar with its high ceiling and large windows has a wine-bar atmosphere, with tasteful low-level lighting. The back bar hosts comedy shows on the last Monday of the month and can be hired at other times. A concrete area to the rear is used for dining in warm weather and a twice-monthly farmers' market. There are quiz nights, food nights and craft workshops – no TV here. Dogs and children welcome. ❀🕩&≠(Streatham Common)ⁱ–🖾

SW17: Tooting
Antelope
76 Mitcham Road, SW17 9NG

✪ 4-11 (midnight Fri); 12-midnight Sat; 12-11 Sun
☎ (020) 8672 3888 ⊕ theantelopepub.com
Adnams Lighthouse; Purity Pure Ubu; guest beers Ⓗ
A large Victorian pub serving a changing variety of ales and food all day, with Sunday roasts especially recommended. Wood panelling, candles and a real fire give a cosy feel to this friendly, welcoming pub, rescued from oblivion, refurbished and revived by Antic. It hosts a weekly quiz, occasional comedy nights and other special events. At the back is a huge separate room and there is also seating outside. You may find an unusual real cider here. 🏨🏠❀🕩&⊖(Tooting Broadway)ⁱ–🗗🖾

SW18: Wandsworth
Grapes
39 Fairfield Street, SW18 1DX
✪ 12-11 (midnight Fri & Sat; 10.30 Sun) ☎ (020) 8874 3414
Young's Bitter, Special Ⓗ
A gem of a street-corner local providing an oasis of calm from the traffic on the manic Wandsworth one-way system. Always friendly and welcoming, the well-decorated bar offers unobtrusive TV sport and there is both a heated patio for smokers and a suntrap secret garden for everyone. A former local CAMRA Pub of the Year, this hostelry serves excellent beer as well as good-value lunches during the week. A seasonal ale is occasionally available. ❀🕩≠(Town)ⁱ–🖾

Le Gothique
Royal Victoria Patriotic Building, John Archer Way, SW18 3SX
✪ 12-3, 6-11; closed Sat & Sun ☎ (020) 8870 6567
⊕ legothique.co.uk
Beer range varies Ⓗ
Well-established free house, French restaurant and wedding venue hidden within a vast, haunted, 1857 orphanage building, used by intelligence services in World War II and now housing apartments and studios. Wall panels illustrate its rich history. Three real ales are on offer, usually from Downton, Sambrook's and Shepherd Neame, although other small breweries may feature. Beer festivals are held the last weekends in March and October (Halloween). It is usually booked for weddings at weekends. ❀🕩&P ⁱ–🖾(77,219)

Old Sergeant Ⓛ
104 Garratt Lane, SW18 4DJ
✪ 12-11 (midnight Fri & Sat) ☎ (020) 8874 4099
Sambrook's Wandle; Young's Bitter, Special; guest beers Ⓗ
Awarded Best Community Pub of 2012, this friendly and impressively refurbished local has also been voted the best place to bring your dog for a drink. Table menus for the excellent food include an informative beer list. The John Young Room upstairs displays treasured memorabilia of the late chairman and the Wandsworth brewery. Quiz night is Monday. The regular newsletter is now titled The Grumpy Pub Company but you will not feel grumpy here. Enjoy! ❀🕩&ⁱ–🖾(44,270)

SW19: South Wimbledon
Sultan
78 Norman Road, SW19 1BT
✪ 12-11 (midnight Fri & Sat) ☎ (020) 8544 9323
Hop Back GFB, Entire Stout, Summer Lightning; guest beer Ⓗ

A traditional and well-run corner local that can get lively at times. It offers a warm welcome to those seeking Hop Back beers in the brewery's only tied house in London. There is a smaller bar, usually open in the evenings, with a dartboard. A beer club with reduced prices operates Wednesday 6-9pm, and there is a weekend beer festival every autumn. The guest beer is usually a Hop Back seasonal or from the Downton Brewery. The cat prefers to be left alone.
🏚🏠♿⊖(Colliers Wood)♣¹⁻🚌(200)

Trafalgar ⃝
23 High Path, SW19 2JY
❸ 3 (12 Fri-Sun)-11 ☎ (020) 8542 5342 ⊕ thetraf.com
Beer range varies Ⓗ
A small, hidden gem with darts and cricket teams, popular with locals and visitors alike. The house beer, Market Ale, is from Ascot Brewery and there are up to three other beers, often including a dark one and frequently from local breweries. There is regular live music, including trad jazz on Sunday afternoons, and Thursday is curry night. Three times local CAMRA Pub of the Year.
🏚🚇(Morden Rd)⊖♣🚌🚌

SW19: Wimbledon

Hand in Hand ⃝
6 Crooked Billet, SW19 4RQ
❸ 11 (12 Sun)-11 ☎ (020) 8946 5720
⊕ thehandinhandwimbledon.co.uk
Courage Directors; Wells Bombardier; Young's Bitter, Special; guest beers Ⓗ
This celebrated ale house and community hub, on the edge of Wimbledon Common and dating back to the early 19th century, is also a great place to eat, with beer featuring in several recipes. The licensee runs an educational programme on cellar management and beer tasting. The family room at the front is used by various local groups and societies on weekday evenings. During warm weather drinkers spill out onto the grassy area in front of the pub. One guest beer is often from Sambrook's. 🏚Q🏠🏚🍴♣¹⁻🚌(200)

Carshalton

Hope ♈ ⃝
48 West Street, SM5 2PR
❸ 12-11 (10.30 Sun) ☎ (020) 8240 1255
⊕ hopecarshalton.co.uk
Downton New Forest Ale; Windsor & Eton Knight of the Garter; guest beers Ⓗ
CAMRA Greater London Pub of the Year 2012 and local Pub of the Year 2013, this pub is owned by members of the local community. The seven handpumps dispense beers from microbreweries, including a dark ale, and a good range of British and foreign bottled beers is stocked. Real cider is also always available. Regular themed festivals are held, and many other community events. A conservatory has been added to help make room for the many customers from near and far.
🏚Q🏠🍴⇌♣🍴P¹⁻🅿🚌

Sun ⃝
4 North Street, SM5 2HU
❸ 12 (5 Mon winter)-11 (midnight Fri & Sat); 12-10.30 Sun ☎ (020) 8773 4549 ⊕ thesuncarshalton.com
Sharp's Doom Bar; guest beers Ⓗ

With the ponds, Honeywood Museum and Sutton Ecology Centre nearby, this is a family-friendly watering hole, proud of its beer and food. Contemporary decor complements the older architecture. Four guest beers are available, usually including one that is locally brewed. The menu offers a good range of fairly priced meals. Children are welcome until 7pm, with plenty to entertain them indoors and in the garden. An acoustic night is held on the first Sunday of the month.
🏚🚌🏠🍴⊖♣¹⁻🚌

Windsor Castle
378 Carshalton Road, SM5 3PT
❸ 11-11 (11.30 Fri & Sat); 12-10.30 Sun ☎ (020) 8669 1191
⊕ windsorcastlepub.com
Shepherd Neame Master Brew, Kent's Best, Spitfire, Bishops Finger; guest beers Ⓗ
This popular corner pub serves three changing Shepherd Neame beers and four guests from regional and microbreweries. A beer festival is held in May. A regular quiz on Tuesdays and live music events on Saturdays feature all year round. The restaurant area serves lunches daily and evening meals Tuesday to Saturday. Outside is a covered courtyard and smoking area, leading to both a spacious garden and a function room.
🏚🍴⇌(Carlshaton Beeches)♣P¹⁻🚌

Cheam

Railway
32 Station Way, SM3 8SQ
❸ 12-11 (midnight Thu-Sat) ☎ (020) 8395 5393
Courage Best Bitter, Directors; guest beers Ⓗ
A local landmark for over 200 years, this cosy drinkers' pub is located in Cheam Village, near the station. The pub changed management in 2012 and has since enjoyed a steady programme of tasteful redecoration and refurbishment while retaining its warmth and charm. The friendly staff are happy to offer ale tasters. Regular events include quiz and poker nights, the occasional evening of live music and very popular open mic nights. Well-behaved dogs are welcome. 🏚⇌🚌

Kew

Botanist Brewery & Kitchen
3-5 Kew Green, TW9 3AA
❸ 12-11 (midnight Fri & Sat; 10.30 Sun) ☎ (020) 8948 4838
⊕ thebotanistkew.com
Botanist 65 Mild, 391, Humulus Lupulus, OK Bitter, Nemophila Stout, Queen Charlotte Ⓗ
A lively pub-restaurant with its own microbrewery, the Botanist is favoured by local drinkers and diners. Originally a row of shops, its internal space divides into different areas, each with its own character. Pavement tables fronting Kew Green are popular in the summer while a small rear yard provides a refuge for smokers. Kew Gardens are only five minutes' walk away and a takeaway beer service is available.
Q🏠🏚🍴⇌(Kew Bridge)⊖(Kew Gardens)¹⁻🚌(65,391)

Kingston upon Thames

Boaters Inn ⃝
Canbury Gardens, Lower Ham Road, KT2 5AU (off A307 via Woodside Rd)
❸ 11-11 ☎ (020) 8541 4672 ⊕ boaterskingston.com

Greene King Boaters; guest beers Ⓗ

The pub is in a former council tea room beside the River Thames with boat mooring (check in advance). The five changing guest beers come mainly from local breweries. One open area curves round the bar with views of the river and gardens. The food is popular, especially on Sundays when jazz is played in the evening. Quiz night is Tuesday. The outside tables get filled up in good weather when customers spill out into the gardens.
ᴥ✿◑&●¹–⊟(65)

Druid's Head

2 Market Place, KT1 1JT

✪ 11-11 (midnight Thu-Sat); 12-11 Sun ☎ (020) 8546 0723

Greene King IPA, Abbot; guest beers Ⓗ

Classic, Grade II-listed marketplace pub, dating from the 17th century. Note the mews and interesting glasswork. The older public bar has a cosy feel while the split-level main bar tends to be busier. Guest beers change on a regular basis and are supplied by Greene King, but can be from other brewers. Food is available all day until 10pm and includes traditional Sunday roasts. Live sport is shown. Upstairs rooms are available to hire.
Q✿◑⊟≒¹–⊟

King's Tun 🅛

153-157 Clarence Street, KT1 1QT

✪ 9-midnight (1am Fri & Sat) ☎ (020) 8547 3827

Fuller's London Pride; Greene King IPA, Abbot; Sharp's Doom Bar; Thornbridge Jaipur IPA; guest beers Ⓗ

The former Kingston Empire Music Hall, dating back to 1910, offers two large bars on separate floors and can get busy in the evenings, particularly at weekends. Wetherspoon's wide-ranging menu includes steak night on Tuesday, curry night on Thursday and Sunday roasts. Guest beers change every few days and include those from local micros. Westons Marcle Hill and Old Rosie ciders are available. The upstairs bar can be hired for functions. Q◑&≒●⊟

Willoughby Arms 🏆 🅛

47 Willoughby Road, KT2 6LN

✪ 10.30 (12 Sun)-midnight ☎ (020) 8546 4236

⊕ thewilloughbyarms.com

Fuller's London Pride; guest beers Ⓗ

Friendly Victorian back-street local, divided into a sports bar with games and a big-screen TV, and a comfortable lounge bar. Beer festivals are held around Valentine's Day, St George's Day and Halloween. Guest beers always include something from Twickenham Fine Ales and often another local brewery beer. An upstairs function room can be hired for events. Pizzas and pies are available, cooked on the premises. The garden includes a covered, heated and lit smoking area with another large TV screen. Q✿⊟&♣●¹–⊟(371,K5)

Wych Elm 🅛

93 Elm Road, KT2 6HT

✪ 11-3, 5-midnight; 11-midnight Sat; 12-11 Sun

☎ (020) 8546 3271 ⊕ thewychelm.co.uk

Fuller's Chiswick Bitter, London Pride, ESB, seasonal beers Ⓗ

Welcoming and friendly back-street local and a long-standing Guide entry, where high beer quality has been maintained for more than 25 years. The comfortable saloon leads to an award-winning garden, and the basic but tidy public bar has a TV showing sport. Excellent home-cooked lunches are

served daily (no food Mon). Live jazz features on the last Saturday of the month, and there are occasional barbecues. Q✿◑⊟≒♣¹–⊟(K5)

New Malden

Woodies

Thetford Road, KT3 5DX

✪ 11-11; 12-10.30 Sun ☎ (020) 8949 5824

⊕ woodiesfreehouse.co.uk

Adnams Broadside; Fuller's London Pride, ESB; Young's Bitter; guest beers Ⓗ

A former sports pavilion, this free house is festooned with sporting and theatrical memorabilia. Three changing guest ales mainly come directly from small breweries; forthcoming beers are listed on the website. Westons 1st Quality cider, home-cooked lunches, a Sunday carvery and summer weekend barbecues are also on offer, with a beer festival every August. The large patio outside has a covered and heated area for smokers. Local CAMRA Pub of the Year for 2011 and four of the previous five years.
▦✿◑&●P¹–⊟(265)

Richmond

Prince's Head

28 The Green, TW9 1LX

✪ 11 (12 Sun)-11 ☎ (020) 8940 1572 ⊕ princeshead.co.uk

Fuller's Chiswick Bitter, London Pride, ESB, seasonal beer Ⓗ

Friendly, traditional pub with a deceptively spacious interior, on the corner of Richmond Green. It attracts a slightly older crowd than the neighbouring Cricketers. Sports fans can watch matches on TV but it is easy to escape around the back where there are cosy separate seating areas with subdued lighting and gilt-edged mirrors on the walls. Outside are benches to sit and view the idyllic Green. A good range of pub grub is served until 9pm. ◑≒Θ¹–⊟

Red Cow

59 Sheen Road, TW9 1YJ

✪ 11-11.30 (11 Sun & Mon; midnight Fri & Sat)

☎ (020) 8940 2511 ⊕ redcowpub.com

St Austell Tribute; Young's Bitter, Special; guest beers Ⓗ

Dating back at least 200 years, this popular community local maintains a traditional atmosphere despite extensive changes over the years. The Victorian painted glass panels can still be seen behind the bar. A changing menu of home-cooked food is served until 10pm (no food Sun eve). Tuesday is quiz night and live music is performed regularly. There is a front patio area and free Wi-Fi. Guest beers are often from Twickenham. The first floor has four en-suite bedrooms providing B&B accommodation. ✿⋈◑≒Θ¹–⊟

Roebuck

130 Richmond Hill, TW10 6RN

✪ 12-11 (midnight Fri & Sat; 10.30 Sun) ☎ (020) 8948 2329

Fuller's London Pride; guest beers Ⓗ

Former local CAMRA Pub of the Year returning to the Guide both refreshed and rejuvenated, it now serves eight guest beers from independent breweries and one real cider on tap, which are regularly rotated. The terrace and upstairs bar (open at weekends) offer stunning views across Petersham Meadows and the River Thames. Well-priced drinks and excellent meals can be enjoyed, and a large function room is available for local groups. 🏃🏠🌭📶(65,371)

Surbiton

Lamb 🅛
73 Brighton Road, KT6 5NF
🟢 12-11 (midnight Thu-Sat) ☎ (020) 8390 9229
Surrey Hills Ranmore Ale; guest beers 🅗
Small, cosy, family-run pub, built in 1850 and formerly divided into four separate rooms; it also had a small brewery in Victorian times. It retains its original horseshoe-shaped bar. Under its current management it has evolved into a thriving community local, a free house offering LocAles. Specialist cheeses are always available. Music and other events are regularly held. Local CAMRA Pub of the Year 2012. 🏠🚂🌭📶

New Prince 🅛
117 Ewell Road, KT6 6AL
🟢 11-11 (midnight Fri & Sat) ☎ (020) 8296 0265
Fuller's London Pride; Gale's Seafarers Ale, HSB; guest beer 🅗
Excellent example of a small, comfortable and welcoming community pub. It was built as a Charrington's house, the Prince of Wales, more than 150 years ago, and the beamed ceiling and photos of bygone local scenes give a traditional feel. The main bar is light and airy and a side room with dartboard leads off towards the surprisingly large garden. Disabled access is via the garden. The guest beer is supplied by Fuller's but can be from other brewers. 🏠🌭♿🅿🌳📶

Sutton

Little Windsor
13 Greyhound Road, SM1 4BY
🟢 12-11.30 (midnight Fri & Sat; 11 Sun) ☎ (020) 8643 2574
Fuller's Chiswick Bitter, Discovery, London Pride, ESB, seasonal beers 🅗
Small street-corner local in the New Town area, east of the town centre. It is popular with locals, especially in the evening and at weekends for sport on TV. The L-shaped bar leads to a heated, covered terrace and garden. Bridge nights are held on Mondays and quiz nights on Thursdays. An extensive menu is offered lunchtime and evening, and children are welcome until 9pm. Discounts are available on four-pint jugs of beer purchased at the bar. 🚂🏠🌭📶

Moon on the Hill
5-9 Hill Road, SM1 1DZ
🟢 9am-midnight (1am Fri & Sat) ☎ (020) 8643 1202
Adnams Broadside; Greene King Abbot; Ruddles Best Bitter; guest beers 🅗
Formerly the furniture section of a department store, this is a popular and well-established Wetherspoon conveniently close to Sutton's main shopping area. Bars on three levels provide plenty of seating and there is a garden for those preferring to eat and drink alfresco. An ever-changing range of guest beers is locally sourced whenever possible and the pub holds mini beer festivals throughout the year. Occasional Meet the Brewer sessions are also held. Breakfasts are served from 8am. 🚂🏠🌭♿🍴📶

Robin Hood
52 West Street, SM1 1SH
🟢 11-11 (midnight Fri & Sat) ☎ (020) 8643 7584
🌐 robinhoodsutton.com
Young's Bitter, Special; guest beers 🅗
A traditional English local where the food is home-cooked; Sunday roasts, daily curries, vegetarian lasagne and burgers are all available. There are baby-changing facilities, a large, recently refurbished function room, a piano, books and a variety of historic photographs. Live music events featuring different styles are held on the last Saturday of each month, with quiz nights on Mondays and cribbage nights on Tuesdays. Charity and other events include parties, golf, darts, and Halloween and St George's Day functions. 🏃🚂🏠🌭♿🍴🚉(W Sutton)♣🅿📶

Wallington

Whispering Moon
25 Ross Parade, SM6 8QF
🟢 9am-midnight (1am Fri & Sat) ☎ (020) 8647 7020
Adnams Broadside; Greene King Abbot; Ruddles Best Bitter; guest beers 🅗
This friendly Wetherspoon pub occupies the former Odeon cinema premises on the high street, near the station and convenient for the local CAMRA October beer festival in Wallington Hall. The pub is L-shaped, with a raised dining section where regular meal deals are offered. The decor includes historic photographs of the local area. Customers can use the book provided to express their preferences for guest ales and the manager is keen to source these from the local area. 🌭♿🚉📶

WEST LONDON
W1: Marylebone

Carpenters Arms
12 Seymour Place, W1H 7NE
🟢 11-11; 12-10.30 Sun ☎ (020) 7723 1050
Harveys Sussex Best Bitter; guest beers 🅗
A sister pub to the Market Porter in SE1, but with a smaller range of guest beers, this establishment is a haven from the bustle of Edgware Road. Many local people enjoy watching TV sport, and playing darts in the rear alcove. It has had a sensitive refurbishment, preserving the mosaics, and on the side wall is a display of facsimiles of woodworking tools. The upstairs function room is available for hire. 🏠🚉(Marble Arch)♣📶

W1: Mayfair

Coach & Horses
5 Bruton Street, W1J 6PT
🟢 11.30 (12 Sat)-11.30; closed Sun ☎ (020) 7629 4123
Brains SA Gold; Fuller's London Pride; guest beer 🅗
An excellent refuge from the nearby Bond Street shopping area. First licensed in 1738, it was rebuilt in 1933 and has an imposing mock-Tudor exterior. Inside, the atmosphere is traditional, with wooden beams and panelling. Pictures on the walls feature caricatures of 19th-century politicians and clerics. Four handpumps include a changing series of guest ales. The small dining room with bar upstairs is available for private functions.
🌭🚉(Bond St/Green Park/Oxford Circus)📶

Windmill
6-8 Mill Street, W1S 2AZ
☼ 11-11; 12-4.30 Sat; closed Sun ☎ (020) 7491 8050
⊕ windmillmayfair.co.uk
Meantime London Pale Ale; Young's Bitter, Special; guest beers Ⓗ
In adjoining buildings previously housing a nightclub, this pub has a well-furnished lounge bar with wood panelling, decorative ceilings and frieze, with a quieter lower area at the rear that is available for private functions. There is a restaurant on the first floor. Pies are a speciality; the Pie Club claims 6,000 members who enjoy changing monthly specials. A roof garden bar and restaurant has recently opened. Q❀◑⊖(Oxford Circus)⍟

W1: Soho

Argyll Arms ★
18 Argyll Street, W1F 7TP
☼ 10-11 (11.30 Fri & Sat; 10.30 Sun) ☎ (020) 7734 6117
Brains SA Gold; Fuller's London Pride; St Austell Nicholson's Pale Ale; Windsor & Eton Knight of the Garter; guest beers Ⓗ
This Victorian M&B Nicholson's house is identified by CAMRA as one of Britain's Best Real Heritage Pubs and Grade II*-listed. Three snugs are separated by etched glass partitions; note the remarkable decorated Bass mirror. The bar-back is impressive, and adjacent is a rare survivor, a manager's office with etched glazing. The magnificent saloon is decorated with ornate mirrors. With eight of the 16 handpumps in regular use, enjoy guest ales from brewers such as Green Jack, Leeds and Thornbridge. Food is served all day.
❀◑⊖(Oxford Circus)⍟

Dog & Duck ★
18 Bateman Street, W1D 3AJ
☼ 11-11 (11.30 Fri & Sat); 12-10.30 Sun ☎ (020) 7494 0697
Fuller's London Pride; St Austell Nicholson's Pale Ale; guest beers Ⓗ
In the heart of Soho, this Grade II-listed M&B Nicholson's outlet was built in 1897. An elaborate mosaic depicts dogs and ducks, and wonderful advertising mirrors adorn the walls. Changing guest beers may include Sambrook's Wandle and Orkney Dark Island. The upstairs Orwell Bar can be hired for functions. The pub is small and popular, especially with media people, so that its not just smokers who have to drink outside.
◑⊖(Tottenham Ct Rd)⍟

Nellie Dean of Soho
89 Dean Street, W1D 3SU
☼ 11-11 (midnight Fri & Sat; 10.30 Sun) ☎ (020) 7734 2572
Fuller's London Pride; Sharp's Doom Bar; Taylor Landlord; guest beers Ⓗ
Replacing premises originally licensed in 1683 as the Dolphin, the current Grade II-listed building dates from 1900. The pub now offers up to five real ales and reasonably priced food. The name was changed to Nellie Dean of Soho in 1967 – Nellie Dean was a character in a sentimental ballad dating from 1905. The upstairs bar has a pool table and jukebox and can be hired for functions.
◑⊖(Tottenham Ct Rd)⍟

Queen's Head Ⓛ
15 Denman Street, W1D 7HN
☼ 11-11.30 (midnight Fri & Sat); 12-10.30 Sun
☎ (020) 7437 1540 ⊕ queensheadpiccadilly.com

Fuller's London Pride; Moncada Blonde; Sambrook's Wandle; guest beers Ⓗ
This pub dates from 1738, taking its name from Queen's Street, renamed Denman Street in 1862 in honour of a Lord Chief Justice born here. In the 1840s it was known as the Courier's Club, trading in wine, brandy and coal. Later, reduced in size, it became part of the Piccadilly Theatre site. With the main bar on the ground floor and more accommodation upstairs, it is a rare free house in central London for pre-theatre dining and drinking.
◑⊖(Piccadilly Circus)⍟

Three Greyhounds
25 Greek Street, W1D 5DD
☼ 11-11.30 (midnight Fri & Sat); 12-10.30 Sun
☎ (020) 7494 0953
Fuller's London Pride; St Austell Nicholson's Pale Ale; guest beers Ⓗ
Popular M&B Nicholson's pub, just off Shaftesbury Avenue and full of tourists and wanderers through Soho, first licensed as a beer house in 1846 and rebuilt in 1925. Plaques inside and out describe its interesting history. It was refurbished in 2012 and given a fresh coat of paint, a new bar and handpumps. Recent guest beers have included Thornbridge Jaipur IPA and Red Squirrel London Porter. It makes a comfortable break from the Soho streets, but can become rather crowded.
◑⊖(Leicester Sq/Tottenham Ct Rd)♣⍟

W2: Paddington

Cleveland Arms
28 Chilworth Street, W2 6DT
☼ 11-11.30 (midnight Fri & Sat); 12-10.50 Sun
☎ (020) 7706 1759
Greene King IPA; Harveys Sussex Best Bitter; Taylor Landlord; guest beers Ⓗ
A few minutes' walk from Paddington Station, this 1852 Grade II-listed pub, named after the first Duke of Cleveland, is a friendly free house serving mainly locals. Guest beers often include an ale rare for London. The rear games room can be hired for functions. Quiz night is Tuesday, and there are free bar snacks Sunday lunchtime. Children and dogs are welcome. Pop music may be rather loud in the evenings. Local CAMRA Pub of the Year runner-up in 2012. ◑⇌⊖♣⍟

Mad Bishop & Bear
Upper Level, Paddington Station, W2 1HB
☼ 8am-11 (11.30 Fri); 10-10.30 Sun ☎ (020) 7402 2441
⊕ madbishopandbear.co.uk
Fuller's Chiswick Bitter, Discovery, London Pride, ESB, seasonal beer; guest beer Ⓗ
Above the shopping complex just behind the station concourse, the traditional pub interior features a long bar, mirrors, good prints and a rather grand chandelier, with train information screens and two TVs for sport. The raised area can be hired for events. It does not get too crowded, even in the rush hour. Note that the bar may close early if there are football crowds passing through.
❀◑⇌⊖⍟

Victoria ★
10a Strathearn Place, W2 2NH
☼ 11-11; 12-10.30 Sun ☎ (020) 7724 1191
⊕ victoriapaddington.co.uk
Fuller's Chiswick Bitter, Discovery, London Pride, ESB, seasonal beers Ⓗ

There is plenty to admire in this Grade II-listed mid-Victorian inn, identified by CAMRA as one of Britain's Best Real Heritage Pubs, including ornately gilded mirrors above a crescent-shaped bar, painted tiles in wall niches and numerous portraits of Queen Victoria. The walls display cartoons, paperweights and a Silver Jubilee plate. A recessed area at the back is furnished with a leather bench seat. Upstairs, via a spiral staircase, there is a library and theatre bar available for public use. Tuesday is quiz night.
Q✿❀♦❋❍(Lancaster Gate/Paddington)≛–⊟

W3: Acton

Red Lion & Pineapple
281 High Street, W3 9BP
◎ 9am-midnight (1am Fri & Sat) ☎ (020) 8896 2248
Greene King IPA, Abbot; guest beers Ⓗ
A Wetherspoon pub formerly owned by Fuller's, it was originally two pubs which then combined, hence the unusual name and layout. The larger room is home to the circular bar, surrounded by red and black tiles. The windows are large, with etched and stained tops, and the walls are decorated with photographs of old Acton. The smaller room is mainly for diners and families. Customers can vote on the choice of up to six guest beers. Breakfasts are served from 8am.
Q⧖✿❀♦❍(Acton Town)●≛–⊟

W4: Chiswick

Fox & Hounds/Mawson Arms
110 Chiswick Lane South, W4 2QA
◎ 10.30-8; closed Sat & Sun ☎ (020) 8994 2936
⊕ mawsonarmschiswick.co.uk
Fuller's Chiswick Bitter, Discovery, London Pride, ESB, seasonal beers Ⓗ
On the corner of the Griffin Brewery and its de facto brewery tap, this listed pub is the start for the Fuller's brewery tour. The unusual double naming is an historical relic of separate licences needed for beer and spirits. Hot food is available until 7pm and the pub is well known for its sausages and pies. Brewery memorabilia on the walls include ancestral portraits of the Fuller, Smith and Turner families. It opens at weekends for functions only.
♨Q♦♦⊟(190)

Old Pack Horse
434 Chiswick High Road, W4 5TF
◎ 11-midnight (1am Thu; 2am Fri & Sat); 12-midnight Sun
☎ (020) 8994 2872 ⊕ oldpackhorsechiswick.co.uk
Fuller's London Pride, Bengal Lancer, ESB, seasonal beers; guest beers Ⓗ
A Grade II-listed corner pub last rebuilt in 1910 but claimed to date back to 1747. Sensitively refurbished recently, it has a beautiful frontage often featured in local photographs, and a view across Turnham Green. With ornate woodwork and glasswork including some stained glass panels, it is one of London's Real Heritage Pubs. Five drinking areas include a snug and a Thai restaurant at the back. A bar name refers to the long-gone Chiswick Empire, and walls display theatre memorabilia.
⧖✿❀♦⊞❍(Chiswick Park/Gunnersbury)●≛–⊟

Tabard Ⓛ
2 Bath Road, W4 1LW
◎ 12-11 (midnight Thu-Sat) ☎ (020) 8994 3492
Beer range varies Ⓗ

The pub dates back to 1880 and was built as part of the Bedford Park estate, the first London garden suburb. Notable features include the swing sign painted by TM Rooke, original tiling by William de Morgan and Walter Crane, and Arts & Crafts mirrors and pictures. Ten handpumps serve two ciders and eight changing guest ales, a virtual permanent beer festival always including local beers. The first-floor intimate fringe theatre has hosted the likes of Al Murray and Russell Brand.
⧖✿❀♦♦❋❍(Turnham Green)●≛–⊟

W5: Ealing

Questors (Grapevine Bar) Ⓛ
12 Mattock Lane, W5 5BQ
◎ 7-11; 12-2.30, 7-10.30 Sun ☎ (020) 8567 0011
⊕ questors.org.uk
Fuller's London Pride; guest beers Ⓗ
Friendly theatre bar set opposite Walpole Park just south of the centre of Ealing. It regularly serves guest beers, usually including one from a local brewery, and also runs CAMRA-themed festivals twice a year. Books are available, as are Belgian beers and obscure whiskies. The club is run by enthusiastic volunteers and was the 2012 national CAMRA Club of the Year.
Q⧖✿❀≛❍(Ealing Broadway)♣P≛–⊟

Red Lion
13 St Marys Road, W5 5RA
◎ 12-11 (midnight Thu & Fri); 11-midnight Sat
☎ (020) 8567 2541 ⊕ redlionealing.co.uk
Fuller's Chiswick Bitter, London Pride, ESB, seasonal beer; guest beer Ⓗ
A popular local, affectionately known as Stage 6, opposite Ealing Studios. Photographs of TV and film stars who have been associated with the studios are on display alongside other memorabilia of the films that made them famous. The pub has gained its own reputation for home-made food in recent years and is unusual in the area for not having a TV or jukebox. The covered patio at the back now has braziers and hosts occasional beer festivals.
Q⧖✿❀♦≛(Ealing Broadway)❍(Ealing Broadway/South Ealing)≛–⊟(65)

Sir Michael Balcon
46-47 The Mall, W5 3TJ
◎ 9am-11.30 ☎ (020) 8799 2850
Adnams Broadside; Fuller's London Pride; Greene King IPA, Abbot; guest beers Ⓗ
Located on the Uxbridge Road east of Ealing town centre, this became a Wetherspoon pub in 2008, named after the legendary film producer whose life and films form the basis of many of the wall displays. It is split level, with a raised area at the rear and a glass-covered area at the front for smokers. Guest ales are often from Adnams or Hogs Back. Breakfasts are served from 8am.
♨Q⧖✿❀♦♦≛❍(Ealing Broadway)●≛–⊟

Wheatsheaf
41 Haven Lane, W5 2HZ
◎ 11-11; 12-10.30 Sun ☎ (020) 8997 5240
⊕ wheatsheaf-ealing.co.uk
Fuller's Chiswick Bitter, London Pride, ESB; guest beer Ⓗ
Tucked away up a side street just north of Ealing town centre, the interior is deceptively large and appears to have been constructed almost entirely of wood. The main saloon connects to an open-plan area at the rear. There is also a small area at

the front, Rugby Corner, which is frequented by devotees of the oval ball. Several screens show televised sport and a quiz night is held on Monday. ♨️👥❄️◑➡️⊖(Ealing Broadway)⭧🖼️

W6: Hammersmith

Andover Arms
57 Aldensley Road, W6 0DL
❂ 12-midnight (11 Sun) ☎ (020) 8748 2155
⊕ theandoverarms.com
Fuller's Chiswick Bitter, London Pride, seasonal beer; guest beers Ⓗ
A frequent entry in this Guide, tucked away in the side streets of Hammersmith, this popular local is an enduring real ale champion. The kitchen offers a wide range of lunchtime and evening meals. There is a TV for major sporting events, traditional pub games such as dominoes are available, and the pub holds regular quiz and live music nights. Two guest ales are a recent innovation and drinkers can sup beers from brewers such as Brains or Long Man. ♨️◑⊖(Ravenscourt Park)♣️🖼️

Dove
19 Upper Mall, W6 9TA
❂ 11-11; 12-10.30 Sun ☎ (020) 8748 9474
⊕ dovehammersmith.co.uk
Fuller's London Pride, ESB, seasonal beer; Gale's Seafarers Ale Ⓗ
Traditional Fuller's pub, a Grade II-listed building overlooking the Thames and hence often crowded in summer. One of London's Real Heritage Pubs, it holds the Guinness world record for the smallest bar area. Classic food with a twist is served every day; meals can take a little time to arrive at busy times but are worth the wait. The likes of Dylan Thomas, Ernest Hemingway and Alec Guinness have reputedly enjoyed a pint or two here. ♨️Q❄️◑⊖(Ravenscourt Park)♣️⭧🖼️

Swan
46 Hammersmith Broadway, W6 0DZ
❂ 10-11 (midnight Fri & Sat; 10.30 Sun) ☎ (020) 8748 1043
Fuller's London Pride; St Austell Nicholson's Pale Ale; Windsor & Eton Knight of the Garter; guest beers Ⓗ
Wood predominates in this bustling M&B Nicholson's pub, handily placed opposite Hammersmith Broadway. Ornate stairs lead to a first-floor restaurant and bar, and to the toilets. Guest beers are from regional brewers such as Red Squirrel, Sambrook's and Thornbridge. Note the fine tessellated gables. ◑⊖🖼️

W7: Hanwell

Fox ♈
Green Lane, W7 2PJ
❂ 11-11; 12-10.30 Sun ☎ (020) 8567 4021
⊕ thefoxpub.co.uk
Fuller's London Pride; Sharp's Cornish Coaster; Taylor Landlord; guest beers Ⓗ
Wonderful back-street free house, as popular with walkers, cyclists and other nearby canal users as with locals. A good range of beers, with changing guest ales from independent breweries, is complemented by excellent, inexpensive food, including a popular Sunday lunch (booking recommended). Add in beer festivals and occasional jazz, and it is no surprise that the Fox has been the local CAMRA Pub of the Year since 2010. ♨️👥❄️◑🚲♣️P⭧🖼️(195,E8)

Viaduct
221 Uxbridge Road, W7 3TD
❂ 12-11 (midnight Fri; 10.30 Sun) ☎ (020) 8810 0815
⊕ viaducthanwell.co.uk
Fuller's Chiswick Bitter, London Pride, ESB; Gale's HSB; guest beer Ⓗ
Rebuilt by Fuller's after years of neglect, this historic pub (circa 1700), renamed around 1838 after the famous Wharncliffe Viaduct, has a larger bar with a restaurant serving daily specials, and a smaller one with a widescreen TV for sport. Lounge and saloon are split by a low head-level partition with the warning 'Duck or Grouse', which is often spotted too late. A traditional pub with plenty of character and a friendly atmosphere – well worth a visit. ♨️Q👥❄️◑🚲♿❄️♣️P⭧🖼️

W8: Notting Hill Gate

Churchill Arms ♈
119 Kensington Church Street, W8 7LN
❂ 11-11 (midnight Thu-Sat); 12-10.30 Sun
☎ (020) 7727 4242 ⊕ churchillarmskensington.co.uk
Fuller's Chiswick Bitter, Discovery, London Pride, ESB, seasonal beers Ⓗ
Gerry, the long-serving landlord, keeps standards high at this multi-award-winning London Real Heritage pub. Churchillian and Irish memorabilia hang from the panelled ceiling, and plaques at the bar commemorate former drinkers. There is a Thai restaurant at the rear, one of the first in a London pub; traditional Sunday roasts are also served. It is often very busy, both inside and on the pavement, with drinkers standing below the hanging flower baskets which create a visual landmark in the street. Q👥◑⊖🖼️

Uxbridge Arms
13 Uxbridge Street, W8 7TQ
❂ 12-11 (10.30 Sun) ☎ (020) 7727 7326
Fuller's London Pride; Harveys Sussex Best Bitter; St Austell Tribute Ⓗ
The manager, Linda, and her team run a great hostelry, which is part of the Enterprise estate. The pub dates from 1836, starting as a beer house. Wood panelled and carpeted throughout, the bar has a welcoming appeal. The Lt Colonel's tunic has been part of the fabric, together with the plates, for a number of years now. Introduce yourself to Debs when you arrive – she has got to be one of the best barmaids in the business. Q❄️⊖⭧🖼️

W9: Maida Hill

Union Tavern Ⓛ
45 Woodfield Road, W9 2BA
❂ 12-11 (midnight Fri & Sat; 10.30 Sun) ☎ (020) 7286 1886
⊕ union-tavern.co.uk
Beer range varies Ⓗ
A radical departure by Fuller's – this is an unbranded beer house offering cask ales produced only within 30 miles and, with one brewery exception, from London. The mainly young crowd enjoys reduced beer prices on Monday, a weekly quiz, and Meet the Brewer events on the last Thursday of the month. Good-value food is another plus, with traditional Sunday lunch a feature. The canalside terrace comes into its own on a warm, sunny day. 👥❄️◑⊖(Westbourne Park)🚲⭧🖼️

W11: Notting Hill

Duke of Wellington
179-181 Portobello Road, W11 2ED
✪ 11 (10.30 Sat)-midnight; 11-11 Sun ☎ (020) 7727 6727
⊕ thedukeofwellingtonpub.com
Purity Pure Gold; Young's Bitter, Special, London Gold Ⓗ
Located on a corner of Portobello Road, this Young's pub, dating back to the 1850s, is at the heart of the present-day market and attracts many visitors as well as locals. The interior features an impressive island bar with a tall bar-back, surrounded by partitioned recesses in dark wood topped with etched glass. Pavement tables are particularly in demand during the summer months. ⛵✿◑ዼ⊖(Ladbroke Grove/Notting Hill Gate) ⅊₋₪(23,52,452)

W12: Shepherd's Bush

Defector's Weld Ⓛ
170 Uxbridge Road, W12 8AA
✪ 12-midnight (2am Fri & Sat; 11 Sun) ☎ (020) 8749 0008
⊕ defectors-weld.com
Adnams Southwold Bitter; guest beers Ⓗ
Downstairs, the large horseshoe-shaped main bar has five handpumps. Frequently rotating guest beers include at least one from Moncada, Redemption, Sambrook's or Twickenham. An upstairs bar is available for hire. DJs play music Thursday to Sunday evenings (no admission after midnight Fri & Sat). On Queens Park Rangers match days the pub is for home fans only, but CAMRA members not wearing team colours are welcome. ﾑ◑ዼ⊖(Shepherd's Bush/Shepherd's Bush Market)⅊₋₪

W13: West Ealing

Forester ★ Ⓛ
2 Leighton Road, W13 9EP
✪ 10-11.30 (midnight Thu-Sat); 12-11 Sun
☎ (020) 8567 1654 ⊕ theforesterealing.com
Fuller's London Pride, ESB, seasonal beers; guest beers Ⓗ
This pub was built in 1909 from designs by Nowell Parr for the Royal Brewery of Brentford and bought by Fuller's in 2012. Thai and English food are available daily except Sunday, when a traditional carvery is served until 6pm. Wednesday is quiz night and on Thursday there are poker tournaments. Two guest beers are supplemented by two more Fuller's beers. Several beer festivals a year are held. ﾑ⛵✿⊠◑⊞ዼ⊖(Northfields)●⅊₋₪(E2,E3)

Brentford

Magpie & Crown Ⓛ
128 High Street, TW8 8EW
✪ 12-midnight (1am Thu-Sat) ☎ (020) 8560 4570
Twickenham Grandstand Bitter; guest beers Ⓗ
This mock-Tudor free house is a popular haunt for beer lovers, with five eclectic guest ales, a cider and a perry, three Belgian beers on draught and an extensive range of Belgian and German bottled beers, all served by enthusiastic and knowledgeable staff. There are tables and a cycle rack at the front, and a rear patio. Food is available lunchtimes and evenings daily, with roasts on Sunday. ✿◑⊜●₋₪

Feltham

Moon on the Square
Unit 30, The Centre, High Street, TW13 4AU
✪ 9am-midnight (10.30 Sun) ☎ (020) 8893 1293
Courage Best Bitter; Greene King Abbot; Ruddles Best Bitter; guest beers Ⓗ
A real ale oasis that continues to flourish in Feltham. The interior is early Wetherspoon: wood panels and glass-partitioned booths, with pictures and local history panels. Eight real ales include varying guests including local brews, with a bar-top gravity cask on tap during beer festivals in April and October. Westons cider is available. Food is served all day, with breakfasts from 8am. Families welcome until 6pm. ⛵◑ዼⅺ●₪(117,235)

Greenford

Black Horse
425 Oldfield Lane North, UB6 0AS
✪ 11.30-11 (midnight Thu-Sat); 12-11 Sun
☎ (020) 8578 1384 ⊕ blackhorsegreenford.co.uk
Fuller's London Pride, ESB; guest beer Ⓗ
Large split-level pub very close to mainline rail, tube and bus routes, tastefully refurbished, with a large landscaped garden overlooking the Grand Union Canal. Beer used to be delivered here by canal barge, and bargees and walkers are frequent visitors. Good food includes special deals on Tuesdays and Wednesdays. There is TV, music – karaoke or jam night on Wednesday and a monthly live band on Saturday – and a quiz on Thursday night. Q⛵✿◑ ⊞ዼⅺ⊖♣⅊₋₪(92,395)

Hampton

Jolly Coopers
16 High Street, TW12 2SJ
✪ 11-11 (12.30am Fri & Sat); 12-10.30 Sun
☎ (020) 8979 3384
Caledonian Deuchars IPA; Courage Best Bitter; Hop Back Summer Lightning; guest beers Ⓗ
A popular, traditional community pub proud of its heritage; a wooden wall panel lists landlords from 1727 to the present owners (since 1986). The horseshoe bar features five handpumps. Customers can vote from a list of possible guest beers for the following month. Walls are adorned with 257 water jugs, old pictures and bric-a-brac of interest. Excellent traditional bar food, tapas, paella and Sunday lunches are served; Squiffy's Restaurant is located beyond the bar (no food on Mon). ﾑ⛵✿◑ዼⅺ♣⅊₋₪

Railway Bell
Station Road, TW12 2AP
✪ 11-11; 12-10.30 Sun ☎ (020) 8979 1897
⊕ therailwaybell.ph
Adnams Southwold Bitter; Courage Best Bitter; Skinner's Betty Stogs; guest beers Ⓗ
Down a driveway beside the Tudor Road bridge over the railway, this small cottage-style pub, known locally as the Dip, has a large, comfortable front terrace. Two separate bars are simply furnished and one is decorated with old photographs of the locality. Five ales on handpump are normally available. Good food is available most lunchtimes and evenings including a substantial Sunday lunch (no food Sat eve). ﾑQ⛵✿◑ⅺ♣⅊₋₪(111,216)

Hampton Hill

Roebuck
72 Hampton Road, TW12 1JN
☼ 11-11 (11.30 Fri & Sat); 12-4, 7-10.30 Sun
☎ (020) 8255 8133
St Austell Tribute; Sambrook's Junction; Young's Bitter; guest beers ⊞
One cannot do justice in a few words to the extensive and eclectic collection that fills this comfortable Victorian local. The wickerwork Harley-Davidson hanging from the ceiling is most notable but do not miss the vintage fruit machines or the bank notes. Traffic lights in the bar and award-winning garden (with gazebo for smokers) mark closing time. There is a summer house for cooler evenings, available for hire. Two guest beers change regularly. ᴙ✿╬◖╪(Fulwell)♣╘▬

Harlington

White Hart
158 High Street, UB3 5DP
☼ 11-11 (11.30 Thu; midnight Fri & Sat); 12-11 Sun
☎ (020) 8759 9608 ⊕ whitehartharlington.co.uk
Fuller's London Pride, ESB; guest beer ⊞
Large Grade II-listed Fuller's pub standing proud at the north end of the village. The bar provides access to an open-plan area with sport on large TV screens and a seated area favoured by diners. The pub was refurbished in 2009 to improve facilities and create an open interior. Local history is the theme of the wall displays enjoyed by locals and visitors from nearby Heathrow Airport. Quiz night is Thursday. ✿✿◖♣P╘▬(90,140,H98)

Hayes

Botwell Inn
25-29 Coldharbour Lane, UB3 3EB
☼ 9am-midnight ☎ (020) 8848 3112
Greene King Abbot; Ruddles Best Bitter; Wychwood Hobgoblin; guest beers ⊞
A large Wetherspoon pub opened in 2000 following a shop conversion of furnishers S Moore & Son, with several areas for dining and drinking. There is a fenced, paved area to the front and a patio at the rear with large parasols with heaters. Guest beers are usually from Adnams, Itchen Valley, Weltons and Windsor & Eton, and at least one Westons cider is available. Beer festivals are held annually. Breakfasts are served from 8am. Q✿✿◖╬(Hayes & Harlington)♣╘▬

Hayes End

Angel
697 Uxbridge Road, UB4 8HX
☼ 11-midnight (1am Fri & Sat) ☎ (020) 8848 8020
⊕ angelpub.net
Fuller's Chiswick Bitter, London Pride; Gale's HSB; guest beer ⊞
A real community local with three bars, although the large rear bar is mostly used for functions. The small saloon bar is quiet and the traditional atmosphere is maintained in the larger public bar, which has a pool table annexe. The pub has teams in both darts and pool leagues and sponsors Hayes Angels football team. Regular events include jazz, film, jam, comedy nights and Sunday bingo. ᴙQ✿✿◖♣P╘▬(427,607,H98)

Hounslow

Moon under Water
84-88 Staines Road, TW3 3LF (W end of High St)
☼ 9am-12.30am ☎ (020) 8572 7506
Greene King Abbot; Ruddles Best Bitter; guest beers ⊞
Early Wetherspoon shop conversion in original style, still displaying many local history panels and photos. Very popular, it has a diverse customer base. Up to five guest ales are often locally sourced, with many more at festival times when all 12 handpumps are put to work. The cider is usually Westons Old Rosie, again with others during festivals. Children are welcome until 8.30pm; the rear is the family area and there is a patio outside. Q✿✿◖♣⊖(Hounslow Central)♣╘▬

Isleworth

London Apprentice
62 Church Street, TW7 6BG
☼ 11-11 (midnight Fri & Sat) ☎ (020) 8560 1915
⊕ thelondonapprentice.co.uk
Fuller's London Pride; Sharp's Doom Bar; guest beers ⊞
Famous Grade II*-listed former Isleworth Brewery riverside pub in old Isleworth, with a unique name and interesting history. The interior is classic traditional, although opened out, with an upstairs Riverview Room. The large patio has many tables, with more seating on the riverbank. Four guest ales are regularly on offer, as well as excellent food. With acoustic music on Monday, board games on Wednesday, Thursday poker and a Sunday quiz, it is well worth the short walk from the bus stop. ✿◖♣╘▬(H37)

Red Lion Ⓛ
92-94 Linkfield Road, TW7 6QJ
☼ 12-11.30 (11 Tue; midnight Fri & Sat); 12-11 Sun
☎ (020) 8560 1457 ⊕ red-lion.info
H&H Olde Trip; Sharp's Cornish Coaster; guest beers ⊞
Spacious two-bar free house with a strong community focus and always something going on: a performance by its own theatre group, the Thursday quiz, and live music throughout the week. Up to eight guest beers complement the regular bitter, and up to four ciders or perries. Twice-yearly beer festivals feature champion beers; weekend festivals have regional themes. Lunches are Wednesday-Sunday, evening meals Tuesday-Saturday. ✿◖╬╪♣╘▬

Norwood Green

Plough
Tentelow Lane, UB2 4LG
☼ 11 (12 Sun)-midnight ☎ (020) 8574 7473
⊕ ploughinnnorwoodgreen.co.uk
Fuller's London Pride; Gale's Seafarers Ale; guest beer ⊞
This 17th-century Grade II-listed building, with exposed wooden beams and low ceilings, is Fuller's oldest pub. It was acquired in 1816 and is now run by a splendid landlord who takes pride in friendly service. At weekends, food is available in the afternoons, handy for the many ramblers who visit (no food Sun eve). Folk and country music plays on Tuesdays, with more live music on Fridays. ᴙ✿✿◖♣╘▬(120)

Southall

Southall Conservative & Unionist Club

Fairlawn, High Street, UB1 3HB

☼ 11.30-2.30 (3 Fri & Sat), 7 (6 Fri & Sat)-11; 12-3, 7-10.30 Sun ☎ (020) 8574 0261

Rebellion IPA, seasonal beer Ⓗ

Virtually the last real ale outlet in this historic market town, situated behind the former town hall. Show a copy of this Guide or a CAMRA membership card for entry. A selection of beers from the Rebellion range is to be found inside. Meals are served some lunchtimes and various events are held most evenings. An ideal meeting place before enjoying a curry in one of the many local restaurants. ☸◖⇌♣P🖳

Teddington

Clock House

69 High Street, TW11 8HA

☼ 11-11.30 (midnight Fri & Sat); 11-11 Sun
☎ (020) 8977 3909 ⊕ theclockhousepub.com

Fuller's London Pride; Sharp's Cornish Coaster, Doom Bar; Twickenham Naked Ladies Ⓗ

This popular and friendly pub, previously the King's Arms, underwent a major refurbishment and change of name in 2008. The bar area features a traditional fireplace, comfortable seating to the right and a small side dining room. To the rear are a function room and an outside paved patio area with a covered space. A good selection of food is offered. A small car park can be reached via a side road. ♨☸◖⇌P🢒🖳

Masons Arms

41 Walpole Road, TW11 8PJ

☼ 12-11 (11.30 Fri & Sat; 10.30 Sun) ☎ (020) 8977 6521
⊕ the-masons-arms.co.uk

Downton Quadhop; Sambrook's Junction; guest beers Ⓗ

Traditional back-street community pub dating from 1860, retaining many period features but with a contemporary feel. The four handpumps have bespoke handles which are a tribute to the woodturner's skill, and wall decorations display the publican's interest in beer. Westons Traditional Scrumpy is served alongside two changing guest beers. The digital jukebox is confined to the old public bar area. Quiz and cribbage nights are held occasionally. There is a small rear patio. ♨☸&⇌♣🢒🖳

Twickenham

Rifleman

7 Fourth Cross Road, TW2 5EL

☼ 12-11 (10.30 Sun) ☎ (020) 8893 3836
⊕ theriflemantwickenham.co.uk

Butcombe Bitter; Ringwood Bitter; Twickenham Naked Ladies; guest beers Ⓗ

Small, cosy and friendly, this is a traditional late-Victorian local. Very much a community hub with board games, darts, TV sport and free Wi-Fi, it is located in a side road not far from Twickenham stadium and Harlequins rugby club. Monday is quiz night and Thursday hosts a lively open mic evening. There is a small front patio and a beer garden at the back. Toasted sandwiches are available until 7pm.
☸⇌(Fulwell/Strawberry Hill)♣🢒🖳

Sussex Arms ▼

15 Staines Road, TW2 5BG

☼ 12-11 (10.30 Sun) ☎ (020) 8894 7468
⊕ thesussexarmstwickenham.co.uk

Beer range varies Ⓗ

Excellent ale and cider house. Eighteen handpumps dispense beers from independent breweries, including Twickenham, plus ciders and perries. Get your 10th pint free with the pub's loyalty card. The kitchen serves Anthea's world-famous pies and much more. Acoustic blues and Irish music feature on a regular basis. It has a huge, well-equipped garden including a boules pitch. Local CAMRA Pub of the Year and London Cider Pub of the Year 2012. ♨☸◖⇌(Strawberry Hill)🍲🢒🖳

William Webb Ellis

24 London Road, TW1 3RR

☼ 9am-11 ☎ (020) 8744 4300

Beer range varies Ⓗ

A Wetherspoon pub in the centre of the home town of English rugby, named after the alleged inventor of the game. It is large and spacious, with live news and sport on silent screens. Twelve handpumps are in constant use. The rear patio is open until 9pm, food is served all day and children are welcome until 8pm. A Monday ale club offers reduced prices and third of a pint glasses. Free Wi-Fi. ➶☸◖&⇌🢒🖳

Uxbridge

Three Tuns

24 High Street, UB8 1JN

☼ 11-11 (1am Fri & Sat); 12-11 Sun ☎ (01895) 233960

Black Sheep Best Bitter; Greene King IPA; Tetley Bitter; guest beer Ⓗ

A traditional high-street pub in a 350-year-old, Grade II-listed building. There is a front area with a hot food counter and, down a few steps to the rear, a stone-flagged bar area, with a conservatory to one side, a small, covered patio at the back, and tables to the front on the pedestrianised high street. Good-quality food is served at lunchtimes and evenings, with the bar and food service attentive and friendly. ♨➶☸◖&Ө🢒🖳

Whitton

Admiral Nelson

123 Nelson Road, TW2 7BB

☼ 11-11 (midnight Fri & Sat); 12-10.30 Sun
☎ (020) 8894 9998 ⊕ admiral-nelson-whitton.co.uk

Fuller's Chiswick Bitter, London Pride, ESB, seasonal beers; guest beer Ⓗ

A former beer house fully licensed in 1861 and rebuilt in the 1930s. This large landmark pub, with a small side patio, stands in a prominent position at the end of the high street. The interior has both Nelsonian and rugby themes. Near to Twickenham Stadium and Twickenham Stoop, it is a haven for rugby fans on match days. Large TVs provide sport coverage. Sunday is quiz night. ♨☸◖&⇌🢒🖳(281,481,H22)

Well coude he know a draught of London ale. **Geoffrey Chaucer**

London Pub Walks – 2nd Edition

Bob Steel

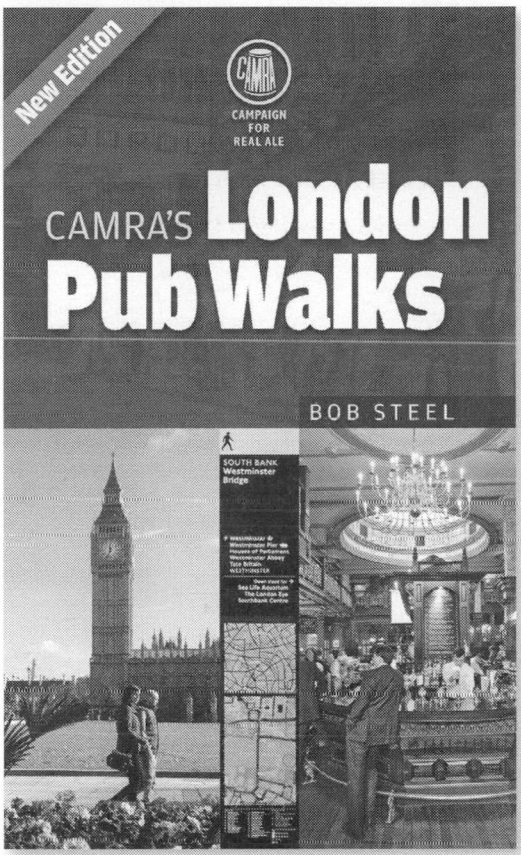

CAMRA's pocket-size walking guide to London is back. This fantastic second edition is packed with interesting new routes, fully updated classic routes from the first edition, new pubs and a special selection of routes that take full advantage of London's public transport network. With 30 walks around more than 190 pubs, **CAMRA's London Pub Walks** enables you to explore the entire city while never being far from a decent pint.

£9.99 ISBN 978-1-85249-310-3 CAMRA members' price £7.99 192 pages

For this and other books on beer and pubs visit CAMRA's online bookshop at **www.camra.org.uk/books** or call **01727 867201**

GREATER MANCHESTER

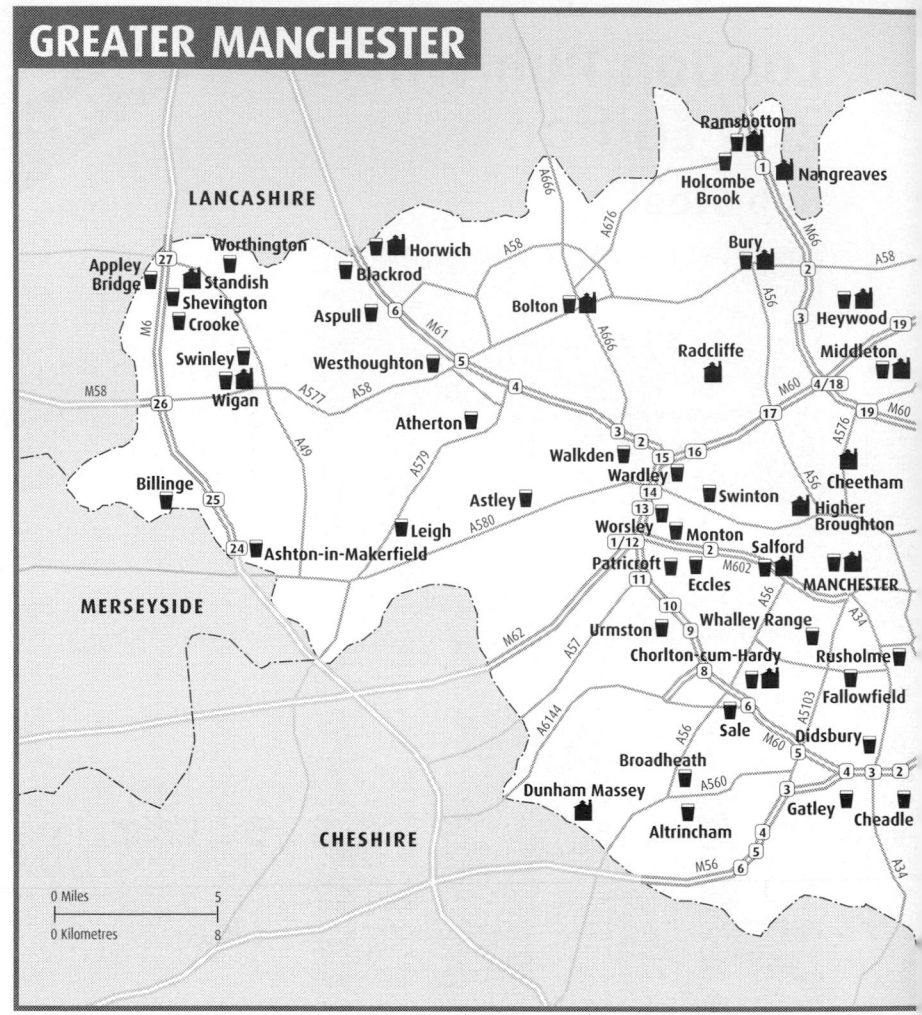

0 Miles 5
0 Kilometres 8

Altrincham

Costello's Bar 🍺 Ⓛ
18 Goose Green, WA14 1DW (down pedestrian road opp jct of Stamford New Rd & Regent Rd)
🕐 12-11 (midnight Fri & Sat); 12-10.30 Sun
☎ (0161) 929 0903 ⊕ costellosbar.co.uk
Dunham Massey Big Tree Bitter; guest beers Ⓗ
The Dunham Massey Brewing Company's only pub and its brewery tap. Costello's opened in late 2010 and is situated in Altrincham's Goose Green. The bar has a modern feel and attracts locals and visitors alike. Do not get too attached to any one beer as the brewery has over 25 different recipes and showcases them all here. ⑳&⩫🖿➤🖿

Old Market Tavern Ⓛ
Old Market Place, WA14 4DN (on A56)
🕐 12-11 (midnight Wed-Sat) ☎ (0161) 927 7062
⊕ omt123.co.uk
Caledonian Deuchars IPA; George Wright Drunken Duck, Northern Lights; Phoenix Arizona; guest beers Ⓗ
Entertainment is always on offer – Monday is open mic jam night, Wednesday quiz night (with a free

buffet), Thursday open acoustic session and rock bands on Friday, Saturday and Sunday evenings. Eleven handpumps are almost always in use, with seven guests coming from local microbreweries. A whiteboard lists what is available, including a real cider. Meals are served until 4pm and children are welcome. ⑳Q⩫🖿➤🖿

Appley Bridge

Wheatsheaf
287 Miles Lane, WN6 9DQ (on B5375 Shevington-Appley Bridge road)
🕐 11.30-11; 12-10.30 Sun ☎ (01257) 252299
⊕ thewheatsheafatappleybridge.co.uk
Tetley Bitter; guest beers Ⓗ
Suburban pub within half a mile's walk of the Leeds/Liverpool Canal and railway station. It has been revitalised by the current licensees since taking over in 2009 and now has five handpumps, with one real cider, Tetley Cask Bitter and three rotating guests, always including a blonde beer. The interior includes a lounge bar area and homely quiet area divided by a fish tank, and a vault with TV sport. Outside there are several drinking areas,

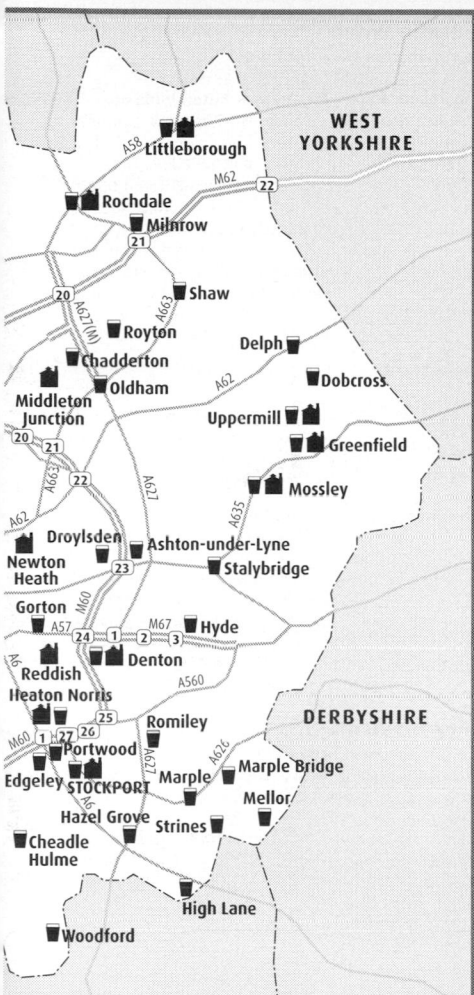

Greene King Abbot; Ruddles Best Bitter; guest beers Ⓗ
Directly facing the fine Victorian Market Hall and square, this Wetherspoon outlet is easily accessible by bus and train. Families are welcome in the lower level; above are the bar and lounge/dining area which lead to the rear entrance and outdoor patio/smoking area. Wetherspoon's usual good value applies to the beers and food. Two real ale festivals are run each year. TVs have no volume. Q❅❀◑&≍₨╘⊟(206,350)

Dog & Pheasant
528 Oldham Road, OL7 9PQ
❂ 12-11 (11.30 Fri & Sat); 12-10.30 Sun ☎ (0161) 330 4894
Banks's Mild, Sunbeam; Marston's Burton Bitter, Pedigree; guest beers Ⓗ
Known as the Top Dog, this popular, friendly local near the Medlock Valley Country Park has been a regular Guide entry since 1992. It has a large bar serving three areas, plus another room at the front. The beer range is supplemented by two guests from the Marston's portfolio. A menu of good-value food includes vegetarian options. Quiz night is Thursday. The pub is home to a local hiking group called the Bog Trotters. ⌂❀◑╘⊟(409,419)

Aspull

Gerrard Arms Hotel Ⓛ
615 Bolton Road, WN2 1PZ (on B5239)
❂ 12 (4 Mon & Tue)-11; 12-midnight Fri & Sat
☎ (01942) 832346 ⊕ thegerrard.com
Prospect Silver Tally; Tetley Mild, Bitter; guest beer Ⓗ

one with a TV. Home-made pizzas and a limited range of bar snacks are available evenings and weekends. Q❀🍴≍♣♠P╘⊟(611,612,635)

Ashton-in-Makerfield

Sir Thomas Gerard Ⓛ
2 Gerard Street, WN4 9AN (on A58)
❂ 8am-midnight (2am Fri & Sat) ☎ (01942) 713519
Greene King Abbot; Ruddles County; guest beers Ⓗ
CAMRA award-winning Wetherspoon pub close to Haydock Park Racecourse. It offers 12 handpumps with local ales from Coach House, George Wright and Phoenix among others. As well as the national beer festivals, other themed festivals are held during the year. There is a beer garden for the hot summer months and during the winter the pub has a cosy atmosphere. ❀◑&♠P╘⊟(320,600,601)

Ashton-under-Lyne

Ash Tree Ⓛ
9-11 Wellington Road, OL6 6DA
❂ 8am-midnight ☎ (0161) 339 9670

One-room, open-plan, cosy pub with a light and airy interior. Tetley and Prospect beers feature regularly alongside varying guests. Locally sourced food is served and entertainment includes a quiz night with supper on Thursday. Two TVs screen sport, usually with the volume off. No under-16s allowed. The pub is adjacent to Borsdane Wood, a local nature reserve. ☮️◑▶P⅄

Astley

Boathouse Inn
Higher Green Lane, M29 7JB
☀️ 12-midnight (11 Sun) ☎ (01942) 883300
Ruddles County; Taylor Landlord Ⓗ
Situated on the towpath of the Bridgewater Canal, the pub is off Higher Green Lane. It was originally built with stabling for the horses that pulled the barges on the canal. There is an old-fashioned taproom with pictures of the area past and present, and a spacious lounge with wood decor and big tables where you can spread out with the newspapers. Live music features most weekends. ☮️◑▶P

Bull's Head
504 Manchester Road, M29 7BP
☀️ 11.30-11 (midnight Fri-Sun) ☎ (01942) 887109
Black Sheep Ale; Thwaites Original, Wainwright Ⓗ
A large, comfortable pub offering a good range of beers – you can even try before you buy. Outside there are various seating areas, some with heaters for when it is chilly, plus lawns for sun worshippers. Quiz nights are held on Sunday, Monday and Wednesday. The pub welcomes children over 14 when dining with an adult in the evening. Occasional beer festivals are held. ♨️☮️◑▶&P⅄🖥

Atherton

Atherton Arms
6 Tyldesley Road, M46 9DD
☀️ 11-11.30; 11.30-1am Fri & Sat; 12-12.30am Sun
☎ (01942) 875996 ⊕ athertonarms.co.uk
Holts Mild, Bitter Ⓗ
Traditional public house with a great atmosphere and facilities, including a full-sized snooker table and function room. The pub is known for its superb beer garden, which has TV screens and heaters. The beer is competitively priced and promotions change on a monthly basis, with happy days Monday to Friday. Midweek, the pub offers a wide range of entertainment. Friday and Saturday is Steve's karaoke and there is live entertainment every Sunday. ☮️🗑⅄🖥

Jolly Nailor ☗ Ⓛ
20-22 Market Street, M46 0DN
☀️ 12-11 (midnight Sat & Sun) ☎ (01942) 792640
⊕ thejollynailor.com
AllGates California, seasonal beers Ⓗ
The Jolly Nailor is a revitalised local situated on the main Market Street in Atherton. The pub was purchased by AllGates in early 2010 and refurbished with the addition of six handpumps selling a range of cask beers plus draught cider. The interior is divided into three areas for live music, TV sport and the weekly quiz. There is still space for the ladies' and men's darts teams. Local CAMRA Pub of the Year 2013. ♨️☮️◑♣️🖥

Pendle Witch Ⓛ
2-4 Warburton Place, M46 0EQ
☀️ 11 (12 Sun)-midnight ☎ (01942) 884537
Moorhouse's Black Cat, Premier Bitter, Pride of Pendle, Blond Witch, Pendle Witches Brew, seasonal beers Ⓗ
A real gem hidden down a narrow alley. The entrance, part of a conservatory, leads to an open-plan bar that serves the full range of Moorhouse's beers plus up to two guests. The games area has a pool table and large-screen TV. Regular rock nights are hosted and occasional beer festivals are held. Food is served during the day, with a cheese night on Thursday. There is a well-kept garden for summer. The pub is close to town-centre parking. ☮️◑&♣️⅄

Billinge

Hare & Hounds Ⓛ
142 Upholland Road, WN5 7JH
☀️ 4-11 (midnight Fri); 12-midnight Sat; 12-11 Sun
Thwaites Wainwright; guest beers Ⓗ
Friendly, welcoming, red-brick pub divided into a lounge and taproom (once the smoking room). Five handpumps dispense one regular beer and three guests. TVs in both rooms show live sport, especially rugby, and local league darts is played. Entertainment is provided on Saturday evenings. Local pies are available. Local CAMRA Best New Cask Outlet 2011. ☮️🗑&♣️P⅄🖥(197,352)

Masons Arms Ⓛ
99 Carr Mill Road, WN5 7TY (off A571)
☀️ 2-11 (midnight Thu & Fri); 12-midnight Sat; 12-10.30 Sun
☎ (01744) 603572 ⊕ masonsarmsbillinge.co.uk
Beer range varies Ⓗ
Built of local stone in 1779, the pub has been run by the same family for over 200 years. It is well placed for walking and cycling the local area. Five handpumps offer regularly changing guest beers. Midweek sees folk and quiz nights. There is a luxurious smoking shelter with a bison's head and logburner, and the beer garden overlooks fields to the rear. The pub is just the place for a quiet chat as the TV is usually silent. Free Wi-Fi. ♨️☮️▶P⅄

Blackrod

Poacher
Scot Lane, BL6 5SG
☀️ 12-12.30am (1.30am Fri & Sat); 12-midnight Sun
☎ (01942) 832203
Jennings Dark Mild, Bitter, Cumberland Ale; Marston's Pedigree; guest beer Ⓗ
A traditional inn catering for the older, discerning drinker. Up to five guest beers are served from the Marston's range, plus more than 60 single malts. Entertainment is hosted on the last Saturday of the month. The pub has its own mini market with milk, bread and other groceries available. Q☮️◑≠P⅄🖥(575)

Bolton

Bank Top Brewery Tap Ⓛ
68-70 Belmont Road, BL1 7AN (400yds from A666/A58 jct)
☀️ 12-11 (11.30 Fri & Sat) ☎ (01204) 302837
Beer range varies Ⓗ
Local CAMRA Pub of the Year 2011, this is the brewery tap for Bank Top. It serves the complete

range of Bank Top beers rotating on nine handpulls plus a guest. Beers are competitively priced and the brewery owner is often on site. A warm, comfortable pub on the edge of the West Pennine Moors, it is popular with walkers and their dogs. The large outdoor drinking area is busy in summer. Q❀⊟♿♣⁻–🚌(537)

Barristers
7 Bradshawgate, BL1 1HJ (on A575, near Market Cross)
⏲ 12-1am (2am Fri & Sat) ☎ (01204) 365174
Black Sheep Best Bitter; Moorhouse's Blond Witch; Tetley Bitter; guest beers 🄷
Barristers Bar is part of the Swan Hotel, a listed building dating from 1845. The wood-panelled interior has been retained and tastefully decorated to recreate a traditional pub atmosphere. The regular range of real ales is supplemented by six guests usually including some from local independent breweries. A heated courtyard with tables is used as a smoking area, and disabled toilet facilities are available. A pianist or guitarist plays live music most evenings. ❀⇌⁻–

Bob's Smithy Inn 🄻
1448 Chorley Old Road, BL1 7PX (on B6226 uphill from A58 ring road) SD674111
⏲ 4-11 (midnight Fri); 12-midnight Sat; 12-11 Sun
☎ (01204) 842622
Bank Top Flat Cap; Taylor Best Bitter; Tetley Bitter; guest beers 🄷
An intimate stone-built hostelry on the edge of the moors, now boasting its own restaurant, handy for walkers and visitors to the Reebok Stadium. The inn is some 200 years old and is named after a blacksmith who allegedly spent more time here than he did at his smithy across the road. This is a genuine free house, offering guest beers from small independent breweries. Dogs are welcome and there is a covered smoking area at the side of the pub. ♨Q❀◐P⁻–🚌(125,126)

Bolton Ukranian Club 🄻
99 Castle Street, BL2 1JP
⏲ 3.30 (12 Fri-Sun)-11.30 ☎ (01204) 526038
Beer range varies 🄷
Large, imposing building to the north-east of town with a comfortable and well-laid-out two-room bar. Two of its three handpulls generally showcase beers from Bolton breweries Bank Top and Blackedge. Guest beers from further afield feature on the third. The Bolton CAMRA beer festival is held here in April, and the pub is home to societies including brass band and bagpipes. Show a CAMRA membership card or this Guide for entry. Q⇌♣P

Dog & Partridge 🄻
22 Manor Street, BL1 1TU
⏲ 7-3am; 4-4am Sat ☎ (01204) 388596
Bank Top Flat Cap, Port O Call; Prospect Silver Tally; Thwaites Wainwright 🄷
Small, traditional free house just off Bolton town centre, popular with both young and old. Bands play every weekend, and there is an excellent outdoor staged area that hosts popular summer gigs. Beers are very competitively priced for a town-centre pub. A large selection of board games is available. ❀⇌♣⁻

Hope & Anchor
147 Chorley Old Road, BL1 5QH (on B6226)
⏲ 12-midnight (1am Fri & Sat) ☎ (01204) 842650
Lees Bitter; Taylor Landlord; Tetley Bitter 🄷
Situated less than two miles from Bolton town centre, near Doffcocker Lodge, a well-known nature reserve, this traditional local dating from the late Victorian era attracts walkers and bird watchers. A central bar serves two distinct snugs used for different functions, such as quiz nights. A new extension with disabled access and a pool room does not affect the original pub layout. TV sport is shown. Sandwiches are always available. Q🐎❀♣P⁻–🚌(125,519)

House Without a Name 🄻
75-77 Lea Gate, Harwood, BL2 3ET
⏲ 2-11.30 (midnight Fri); 12-midnight Sat; 12-11.30 Sun
☎ (01204) 433568
Courage Best Bitter; Holt Bitter; Lancaster Amber; guest beers 🄷
A welcome return to this Guide, a traditional village pub dating from 1810 which has recently been refurbished. Memorabilia from the local Trafalgar Society is on display and the pub is awash with poignant old local pictures. The terrace is a suntrap in the evenings. This pub is popular with walkers and their dogs. The three guest beers are often from local breweries Bank Top, Dunscar Bridge and Prospect. Quizzes are held on Monday evenings. Bar food is served every day. ❀◐⊟♣⁻–🚌(507)

Spinning Mule
Unit 2, Nelson Square, BL1 1JT (just off Bradshawgate)
⏲ 9-midnight (1am Fri & Sat) ☎ (01204) 533339
Greene King Abbot; Ruddles Best Bitter; guest beers 🄷
Newly built in 1998, this town-centre pub is an open-plan split-level building with a comfortable dining area in a modern Wetherspoon style. It is named after Samuel Crompton's Mule, a revolutionary invention in cotton spinning that made Bolton famous throughout the world. The Mule supports Moorhouse's and other local breweries, with up to six handpumped beers generally available. Q◐♿⇌

Broadheath

Railway ★
153 Manchester Road, WA14 5NT (on A56 adjacent to retail park)
⏲ 12-11 (midnight Fri & Sat); 12-9.30 Sun
☎ (0161) 941 3383
Holt Mild, IPA, Bitter 🄷
Grade II-listed Victorian pub identified by CAMRA as one of Britain's Best Real Heritage Pubs. Once a row of terraced cottages running alongside the local railway, it has retained multiple rooms with a taproom and parlour either side of a hallway leading to the bar. To the rear of the bar are a further two rooms. The drinking area outside features a gas lampost and an original red telephone box. ♨Q🐎❀⊟⇌🚊♣⁻–🚌

Bury

Art Picture House 🄻
36 Haymarket Street, BL9 0AY (opp Interchange)
⏲ 8am-midnight (2am Fri; 3am Sat) ☎ (0161) 705 4040
Greene King Abbot; Ruddles Best Bitter; guest beers 🄷
A Wetherspoon Lloyds No.1, this beautifully restored former 1920s cinema, tastefully decorated with stills of black and white films and historic local photos, is located opposite the bus and tram

ENGLAND

Interchange. It features eight handpumps offering an ever-changing range that regularly includes Moorhouse's and Phoenix beers, plus ales from other local breweries. One handpump is reserved for cider – often from Gwynt y Ddraig. Quiet during the day, but music plays at night. A £2 entry charge applies after 11pm Saturday. ኤᏇ❺♿⚞♨Ɽ♦㊊

Automatic Café & Malt Real Ale Bar 🄻

The Met, Market Street, BL9 0BW (500yds N of Interchange)
❻ 10am-11 (midnight Fri & Sat); 12-10.30 Sun
☎ (0161) 763 9399 ∰ automaticcafe.com
Outstanding Silver Fox; guest beers Ⓗ
This welcoming independent bar and restaurant shares The Met with two theatres. The Malt Bar, to the left of the entrance, is open for service for theatregoers on Friday and Saturday evenings and daytime Saturday. Four handpumped ales are available at both bars. Silver Fox, the house beer, is also available in the upstairs Theatre Bar. Chess, backgammon and draughts are played. Popular with market day shoppers, families and parties as well as discerning real ale enthusiasts.
Q ኤᏇ❺♿⚞(Bolton St)Ɽ♣㊊㊐

Black Bull

8 Lowercroft Road, BL8 2EY (on B6196)
❻ 12-midnight (1am Fri & Sat) ☎ (0161) 761 5961
∰ theblackbullbury.co.uk
Thwaites Nutty Black, Original, Wainwright, Lancaster Bomber, seasonal beers Ⓗ
A family-run local with a warm and friendly atmosphere enjoyed by drinkers and diners alike. Guest beers are from Thwaites 1807 Cask Club range. Excellent meals, served daily, are prepared mainly from locally sourced top-quality produce. Diners are advised to book as the pub's reputation creates high demand. 🚶❀❺♿㊊㊐(486,510)

Lamb Inn 🄻

533 Tottington Road, BL8 1UB (on B6123)
❻ 4.30-11 (midnight Fri); 1-1am Sat; 1-midnight Sun
☎ (0161) 764 2714
Beer range varies Ⓗ
Originally a coaching house built in 1831, this is a popular family-run local with a pleasant atmosphere. The landlord is enthusiastic about real ales with local breweries Deeply Vale, Phoenix, George Wright and Moorhouse's the regulars. Other breweries from near and far are also represented. A good selection of malt whiskies is stocked. Excellent home-cooked food is served at weekends. Sky Sports screens on four TVs. Free Wi-Fi available. 🚶ኤ❀❺♣㊊㊐(468,469)

Robert Peel 🄻

5-8 Market Street, BL9 0LD
❻ 8am-midnight (1am Fri & Sat) ☎ (0161) 764 7287
Greene King Abbot; Ruddles Best Bitter; guest beers Ⓗ
Situated in Bury's cultural quarter, the Robert Peel is a popular establishment – its mixture of tables and booths making it the largest open public area in Bury. This Wetherspoon pub is named after a local mill owner and MP, whose son became prime minister and founded the modern police force. The decor celebrates other local worthies including Richmal Crompton, author of the Just William books. Local Cider Pub of the Year 2012, with up to six available from makers including Gwynt y Ddraig and Westons. Q ኤᏇ❺♿⚞(Bolton St)Ɽ♦㊐

Trackside 🄻

Platform 2, East Lancashire Railway, Bolton Street Station, BL9 0EY
❻ 12 (9am Wed & Thu)-midnight; 9am-12.30am Fri & Sat; 9am-11.30 Sun ☎ (0161) 764 6461
∰ eastlancsrailway.org.uk
Beer range varies Ⓗ
Renowned for its widely sourced and ever-changing range of nine cask ales and outstanding selection of ciders, perries, foreign bottled beers and malt whiskies, this is a great venue in which to relive the days of steam. Food is served Wednesday-Sunday. A folk night is held on the last Thursday of the month. There is ample extra seating on the platform. The house beer Piston Broke is brewed by Outstanding. Note: parking is Pay & Display. ኤ❀❺♿⚞(Bolton St)Ɽ♦㊊㊐

Two Tubs

19 The Wylde, BL9 0LA (opp parish church)
❻ 12 (11am Wed)-11 (1am Thu; 2am Fri & Sat); 5-midnight Sun ☎ (0161) 764 2206
Thwaites Original, Lancaster Bomber, seasonal beer Ⓗ
This historic pub, centrally located in the culture quarter, is a 400-year-old Grade II-listed building. The interior features lath and plaster panels, with a bar in the vault to the left as you enter the front door. To the rear is a modern extension, with a separate bar that only opens at peak times. A popular venue for food on weekday lunchtimes, it also gets very busy at weekends. ❀❺♿⚞(Bolton St)Ɽ㊊

Chadderton

Rose of Lancaster

7 Haigh Lane, OL1 2TQ
❻ 11.30-11 (11.30 Fri & Sat); 12-11 Sun ☎ (0161) 624 3031
∰ roseoflancaster.co.uk
Lees Brewer's Dark, Bitter, seasonal beers Ⓗ
This large, extended, recently renovated inn overlooks Rochdale Canal and open farmland. It has a separate lounge and vault, plus a conservatory-style area for dining. The pub is astonishingly popular with a broad clientele, attracting a mix of locals, walkers, boaters and diners. Food is a big draw and well priced. A large range of Lees beers is complemented by quick and cheerful service. There is a large outdoor drinking area for good weather. Buses and trains are nearby. ❀❺❐♿⚞(Mills Hill)♣㊊㊐(59,64)

Cheadle

Crown

81 High Street, SK8 1AA (on A560, opp parish church)
❻ 11-11 (11.30 Thu; midnight Fri; 12.30am Sat); 12-10.30 Sun ☎ (0161) 493 5837
Hydes Owd Oak, Original Bitter, seasonal beers; guest beers Ⓗ
Some years ago Hydes converted this former fish shop into a pub. It has a narrow interior that broadens out towards the rear, a bar accommodating seven handpumps and a raised seating area. A new arrangement of seating has been added to give more room at the front. The pub is popular with drinkers and those who enjoy the weekly quizzes. Occasional beer festivals are hosted. ❺♿㊊㊐(X57,310)

Cheadle Hulme

Cheadle Hulme
47 Station Road, SK8 7AA (on A5149 by railway station)
✪ 12-11 (midnight Fri & Sat); 12-10.30 Sun
☎ (0161) 485 4706
Holt Mild, IPA, Bitter, seasonal beers; guest beers Ⓗ
This well-managed Holt house has an extensive bar serving four comfortably furnished spaces separated by half-glazed screens. The pub maintains a traditional feel with friendly staff and efficient service, and serves excellent food, with meals from the carvery available until 8.30pm daily. The regular Holt range is supplemented by up to four guests. Thursday is quiz night, live entertainment features monthly on a Saturday night. A split-level terrace provides extra space. There are plans to add a small brewing plant to the premises. ✪◖◗❦⛱≋♣P⅄–🖩(X57,313)

Chorlton-cum-Hardy

Bar Ⓛ
533 Wilbraham Road, M21 0UE (opp Morrisons)
✪ 12-11.30 (1am Thu; 12.30am Fri); 11.30-12.30am Sat; 11.30-11.30 Sun ☎ (0161) 861 7576
Castle Rock Harvest Pale; Hardknott Cool Fusion; guest beers Ⓗ
The first of Chorlton's modern café bars in the late '90s and still going strong more than 15 years later. The emphasis is on real ale and good-quality food made with locally sourced ingredients. Seven handpumps are tucked away on the bar furthest from the door, serving the two regular beers and up to five guests focusing on local breweries. Quiz night is Monday. ⅄❦◖◗🖩♣⅄–🖩

Beech Inn
72 Beech Road, M21 9EG
✪ 4-11; 12-midnight Fri & Sat; 12-11 Sun
Black Sheep Best Bitter; Copper Dragon Golden Pippin; Taylor Golden Best, Landlord; guest beer Ⓗ
The Beech is a traditional three-room pub with the bar placed centrally and a snug to the side. It is home to a wide range of community groups including Irish and Cajun music, a weekly folk club that takes over the whole of the back room, and a monthly free comedy night. Big bay windows let in plenty of light in the front room while the back room has more of a traditional public-bar feel, complete with dartboard. Refurbished in early 2013. ♒Q⅄❦⛱♣⅄–🖩

Electrik
559 Wilbraham Road, M21 0AE
✪ 12 (1 Mon)-12.30am (1.30am Fri); 11-1.30am Sat; 11-12.30 Sun ☎ (0161) 881 3315 ⊕ electrikbar.co.uk
Thwaites Wainwright; guest beers Ⓗ
A modern bar, Electrik is a favourite on the Chorlton pub scene. It has four handpumps dispensing one regular beer, two guests including its own Electric Ale Experience beers, plus one cider. American beers also feature. The food menu is based around locally sourced pub grub and light snacks, with roasts on Sundays. Although quiet during the day, the bar can be very lively towards the weekend, assisted by a free jukebox and guest DJs. Quiz night is Tuesday. ⅄❦◖◗⛱🖩♣♥–

Marble Beer House Ⓛ
57 Manchester Road, M21 9PW (50yds N of library)
✪ 12-11 (midnight Thu-Sat) ☎ (0161) 881 9206

Marble Pint, Manchester Bitter, Ginger, seasonal beers; guest beers Ⓗ
A rarity in the Chorlton area, this one-room pub specialises only in beer – food is limited to snacks and there are no themed evenings, DJs or other distractions. The return of former managers Helen and Vicky has created a settled team with a warm welcome for all. The beer range and quality, with five Marble Brewery beers and two guests – Hawkshead, Pictish, RedWillow and Oakham all feature regularly – are second to none.
Q⅄❦◖⛱♥⅄–🖩

Parlour Ⓛ
60 Beech Road, M21 9EG
✪ 12-11 (1am Fri & Sat) ☎ (0161) 881 4871
⊕ theparlour.info
Beer range varies Ⓗ
A street corner hostelry with a difference, successfully treading the line between beer haven and dining pub. There is plenty of comfortable seating for drinkers, who are offered five guest ales dominated by local microbreweries such as RedWillow, plus two ciders/perries. Visitors to the dining area can select from an interesting menu featuring the finest ingredients from local suppliers. The Parlour's owners also run the Castle in Manchester and Eagle Inn in Salford.
⅄❦◖◗⛱♥⅄–🖩

Pi (Chorlton) Ⓛ
99 Manchester Road, M21 9GA (500yds from B5217/A6010 jct)
✪ 11-11 (midnight Wed & Thu; 12.30am Fri); 12-11 Sat & Sun
☎ (0161) 882 0000 ⊕ pi-chorlton.co.uk
Tatton Gold; guest beers Ⓗ
Popular café bar to the north of Chorlton's main street. Five handpumps serve four real ales and a guest cider or perry alongside a selection of 10 world beers on draught – no mainstream brands here. An impressive menu of 80 bottled beers from around the world is also kept. Gourmet Pieminister pies with trimmings are served until 11pm daily. The service is always friendly —it is the little touches like complementary peanuts and blankets for those sitting outside that make Pi stand out from the crowd. Q⅄❦◖◗⛱♥⅄–🖩

Sedge Lynn Ⓛ
21a Manchester Road, M21 9PN (next to library)
✪ 9-11 (midnight Fri & Sat) ☎ (0161) 860 0141
Greene King Abbot; Moorhouse's Blond Witch; Phoenix Wobbly Bob; Ruddles Best Bitter; guest beers Ⓗ
The high barrelled ceiling of this large Wetherspoon pub gives a hint of its past as a temperance movement billiard hall, but raised areas break up the open-plan interior well. With four permanent ales and four to five changing guest ales from northern brewers including Acorn, Moorhouse's, Ossett and Thwaites, as well as real cider from Westons, there is plenty of choice. The clientele is varied and eclectic across the age range, which makes this an interesting place to drink. Q⅄❦◖◗⛱🖩♥⅄–🖩

Crooke

Crooke Hall Inn Ⓛ
Crooke Road, WN6 8LR (signed off B5375)
✪ 12-midnight ☎ (01942) 204451
Beer range varies Ⓗ

Refurbished by AllGates Brewery in 2011, this village pub is popular with locals, walkers and bargees along the Leeds & Liverpool Canal. Inside, there are three rooms with two real fires plus a cellar room available for functions. Regular folk nights are held. The pub hosts a darts team which meets on Monday evenings. Pool is played and sport is shown on screens. Food is not currently available. Outside is a large beer garden with children's play area. ♨️☙🏵️🗘♣P⅃🚌

Delph

Royal Oak (Th' Heights)
Broad Lane, Heights, OL3 5TX (via Thame Lane, off main Delph-Denshaw road) SD982090
🌣 closed Mon; 7 (5 Thu & Fri)-11; 12-midnight Sun
☎ (01457) 874460
Black Sheep Best Bitter; guest beers 🅗
Isolated 250-year-old stone pub on a packhorse route overlooking the Tame Valley. In a popular walking area, this quintessential moorland inn has outstanding views. The building comprises a cosy bar and three rooms, each with an open fire. The comfortable snug has exposed beams and old photos of the inn. A Millstone beer is always available; the house beer is from Moorhouse's. The pub has featured in the Guide for 22 years. ♨️Q🏵️P

Denton

Lowes Arms
301 Hyde Road, M34 3FF
🌣 12-3, 5-midnight; 12-midnight Fri-Sun ☎ (0161) 336 3064
Beer range varies 🅗
Built in 1824 to serve the new Manchester Road, this thriving local has a reputation for quality beers and good-value food. Beers from Hornbeam and Phoenix breweries feature regularly among the range of frequently changing guest beers on offer. The comfortable lounge and separate spacious games room cater for all tastes and provide a friendly and relaxing atmosphere.
🏵️🗘🖪≈(Hyde Central)♣P⅃🚌

Didsbury

Fletcher Moss
1 William Street, M20 6RQ (off Wilmslow Rd, A5145 via Albert Hill St)
🌣 12-11 (midnight Fri-Sat) ☎ (0161) 438 0073
Hydes Manchester's Finest, Original Bitter, seasonal beers; guest beers 🅗
Named after the alderman who donated the nearby botanical gardens to Manchester, this thriving community local attracts people of all ages. This is a pub for lively conversation, with no piped music. The front encompasses two traditional snugs, full of Hydes' memorabilia, while the rear opens up into a large, bright conservatory area. There is a quiz every Tuesday and live acoustic music on alternate Mondays. Board games are available. The cider is Gwynt y Ddraig Farmhouse Scrumpy. Q🏵️&🖪(Village)♣P⅃🚌(42,142)

Gateway
882 Wilmslow Road, M20 5PG (jct Kingsway)
🌣 8-11 ☎ (0161) 438 1700
Greene King Abbot; Hawkshead Gateway to the Lakes; Ruddles Best Bitter; guest beers 🅗
Acquired by Wetherspoon in 2011, this large late-1930s roadhouse was built near the site of an old

toll bar. The company has done an excellent job in improving the comfort within. Although often busy, there are sufficient distinct separate areas to enable visitors to have a quiet drink and chat if they wish. The location is very handy for the popular Parrs Wood leisure complex opposite and its public transport terminus, which features in the pub's decor. ♨️🏵️🗘≈(East)🖪(East)♣P⅃🚌(42,142)

Royal Oak
729 Wilmslow Road, M20 6WF (on A5145, jct Old Oak St)
🌣 11-11 (midnight Fri-Sat) ☎ (0161) 434 4788
⊕ royaloakpubmanchester.co.uk
Marston's Burton Bitter, Pedigree, seasonal beers; guest beers 🅗
Built around 1850, this multi-roomed pub is akin to the community centre of the village. The pub is famous for its award-winning cheese and pâté lunches (served Mon-Fri) which many have tried to copy but none has been able to surpass for choice or value. The pub is especially busy when Manchester City are playing at home. Four guest beers per month are served.
🏵️🗘🖪(Village)⅃🚌(42,142)

Dobcross

Navigation Inn 🅛
21-23 Wool Road, OL3 5NS
🌣 12-2.30, 5-11 (midnight Fri); 12-11 Sat; 12-10.30 Sun
☎ (01457) 872418
Millstone Tiger Rut; Taylor Landlord; Thwaites Wainwright; guest beers 🅗
Close to Huddersfield Narrow Canal with good transport connections from Oldham and Huddersfield, this family-run pub welcomes families, walkers and dogs. The traditional open-plan stone-built property has a curved centralised bar and ample seating for diners and drinkers. Five handpulled beers are regularly available from both local and national breweries. Home-made food is served seven days a week sourced from the local area. Themed food evenings are held throughout the year. Q♨️🏵️🖾🗘&P⅃🚌(184,350)

Swan Inn (Top House)
The Square, OL3 5AA
🌣 12-2 (not Mon), 5-11 (midnight Fri); 12-midnight Sat; 12-11 Sun ☎ (01457) 873451 ⊕ theswandobcross.com
Banks's Sunbeam; Jennings Cumberland Ale; Marston's Pedigree; guest beer 🅗
A focal point for the local community, this rejuvenated stone pub overlooks the attractive village square. Built in 1765, the pub has been tastefully renovated with flagged floors and three rooms, each with an open fire. The historical function room hosts entertainment including theatre, poetry reading and music. Annual events such as the Whit Friday Brass Band Contest, Rushcart Festival and Yanks Weekend are popular. A home-cooked menu features dishes from around the world (no food Sun eve).
♨️🏵️🖪(184,353,354)

Droylsden

King's Head
169 Market Street, M43 7AY
🌣 11.30-midnight; 12-11 Sun ☎ (01298) 277193
Holt Bitter, seasonal beers 🅗

Large, busy pub standing at the junction of Greenside Lane, a few minutes' walk from the crossroads in the centre of Droylsden and the Metrolink line from Manchester to Ashton-under-Lyne. Droylsden FC ground is close by. Attracting a mixed clientele, there is a choice of two lounges and a large public bar. This often unsung local is doing an excellent job – the use of 36-gallon barrels in the cellar is an indication of its popularity. ◑▶◁⑤⬥P⬱⊟

Eccles

Lamb Hotel ★

33 Regent Street, M30 0BP (opp Metrolink station)
✪ 11.30-11 (11.30 Sat); 12-11.30 Sun ☎ (0161) 787 7297
Holt Mild, Bitter, IPA ⊞
This is a fine red brick and terracotta Joseph Holt pub built in 1906. Immediately to the right on entering is the comparatively spartan vault. Straight on is the lobby leading to the central bar, two comfortable lounges and, rarely seen nowadays, a billiard room with full-size table in regular use. Splendid woodwork and tiling is a feature of this Grade II-listed pub. It's a large and friendly local that tends to attract a more mature clientele. ◁⊟⬱⊟⬥P⊟

Fallowfield

Friendship

353 Wilmslow Road, M14 6XS (B5093, jct Egerton Rd)
✪ 12-11 (midnight Fri & Sat) ☎ (0161) 224 5758
Hydes 1863, Original Bitter, Manchester's Finest, seasonal beers; guest beers ⊞
Impressive Victorian mansion in a busy student area. This is not purely the domain of the young, however, as it attracts a good mix of folk. A large horseshoe bar serves a variety of areas – some quiet. The rear extension completed a few years ago has created space for the provision of interesting and popular oriental food, including takeaways. The many TV screens provide for sports fans. Nine handpumps offer the Hydes' range, as well as varying guest ales. ✪◑▶◁⑤●P⬱⊟(42,43)

Gatley

Horse & Farrier

144 Gatley Road, SK8 4AB (jct Church Rd)
✪ 11-11 (midnight Fri & Sat); 12-10.30 Sun
☎ (0161) 428 2080
Hydes 1863, Original Bitter, seasonal beers; guest beers ⊞
Formed from three cottages, this Hydes Heritage house has a central bar and a food bar at the rear. Meals are served until 3pm (5pm Sat & Sun). A couple of seats are set cosily under the stairs that lead up to the Martingale function room. There is an outside smoking area past rooms on the left. Quarterly beer festivals are held, with real cider also available. Q✪◑◁⬱●P⬱⊟(11A,44)

Gorton

Vale Cottage

Kirk Street, M18 8UE (off Hyde Rd A57, E of jct Chapman St)
✪ 12-4, 7-11 ☎ (0161) 230 7347 ● valecottage-inn.co.uk
Taylor Landlord; guest beers ⊞

Well hidden in the Gore Brook conservation area, Vale Cottage has the feel of a country pub. Parts date from the 17th century, hence the low-beamed ceilings, multiple drinking areas and reputed ghost. It has a relaxed atmosphere, where conversation predominates. Popular lively quizzes are held on Tuesday (general knowledge) and Thursday (music). Excellent home-cooked meals (lunchtimes Sun-Fri, evenings Mon-Thu) can be enjoyed in the garden in warmer weather. A real gem not to be missed. Q✪◑⬱(Ryder Brow)P⬱⊟(201,203)

Greenfield

Railway ⅃

11 Shaw Hall Bank Road, OL3 7JZ (opp station)
✪ 12-midnight (1am Thu & Fri); 11.30-1am Sat
☎ (01457) 872307
Copper Dragon Golden Pippin; Millstone Tiger Rut; Moorhouse's Blond Witch; Theakston Lightfoot, Old Peculier; Wells Bombardier ⊞
Unspoilt pub comprising a central bar, games area and taproom, decorated with old photos of Saddleworth. The Railway is a popular venue for live music on Thursday, Friday (unplugged night) and Sunday. It is also a stop-off on the Transpennine Real Ale Trail. Various ciders are served on gravity. A good base for outdoor pursuits, it affords beautiful views across the Chew Valley. ✪◁▲⬱●P⬱⊟(180,350)

Wellington ⅃

29 Chew Valley Road, OL3 7AF (100yds past Tesco)
✪ 2-11 (10 Mon); 12-11.20 Fri & Sat; 12-10.30 Sun
Thwaites Nutty Black, Original, Wainwright; guest beers ⊞
Friendly village free house on the end of a terrace. The pub comprises a small bar area, open-plan dining room and a separate sports room with Sky TV, cribbage and a dartboard. Good home-made food includes pies, puddings and real chips, served Thursday and Friday evenings and throughout the day at weekends. Up to five guest beers are available, and real cider in summer. There are roadside picnic tables for alfresco drinking. ✪◑▶⬱⬥●⬱⊟(180,350)

Hazel Grove

Grapes

196 London Road, SK7 4DQ (on A6, jct Hatherlow Lane)
✪ 11.30-11; 11-midnight Fri & Sat; 12-10.30 Sun
☎ (0161) 483 4479
Robinsons 1892, Unicorn ⊞
This charming pub is one of the oldest in Hazel Grove. It retains its classic town pub layout – the central bar separates the large vault on the left from the three-roomed lounge on the right, which still has some original-looking wooden beams. The back room displays images of old Hazel Grove, and to the rear is a small beer garden. Mild is offered at two different temperatures according to taste. ✪◁⬱⬥P⬱⊟(192,199)

Wilfred Wood

204 London Road, SK7 4DQ (on A6, jct Hatherlow Lane)
✪ 11-midnight (1am Fri & Sat) ☎ (0161) 419 2440
Greene King Abbot; Ruddles Best Bitter; guest beers ⊞
A spacious open-plan house where clever design has made the interior appear more intimate. Large

wooden pillars break up open areas and there are a few panelled booths at the back. Occupying former shop premises, the pub's name commemorates the town's heroic Victoria Cross winner. Ten handpumps serve a good choice of locally sourced beers alongside Wetherspoon regulars. Traditional cider is available from polypins stored in bar-side cool cabinets. A smoking area is to the rear. Wi-Fi available. Q❀☺◑&⇌❤⁌⊟(192,199)

Heywood

Edwin Waugh 🅛
10-12 Market Street, OL10 4LY
❀9am-midnight (1am Fri & Sat) ☎ (01706) 621480
Greene King Abbot; Ruddles Best Bitter; guest beers Ⓗ
This Wetherspoon establishment has large windows to the front and one side. Open plan with some booths, it is furnished with a mix of easy chairs, stools and dining chairs and tables. Outside there is a small patio to the rear. The pub is named after the dialect poet Edwin Waugh, known as the Burns of Lancashire, who died in 1890. His memorabilia features on the walls. Beers from Phoenix, Greenfield and Moorhouse's are among the guests alongside Westons and Gwynt y Ddraig ciders. Q❀☺◑&❤⁌⊟(163)

High Lane

Royal Oak
Buxton Road, SK6 8AY
❀12-midnight ☎ (01663) 766827
Marston's Burton Bitter, Pedigree; guest beers Ⓗ
On the main A6 as it ascends from Stockport towards the Peak District and Lyme Park, this traditional inn offers four guest beers from the Marston's portfolio in addition to the two regulars. A dog-friendly room is available and families are also welcome. Food is served lunchtimes during the week and all day until 6pm at weekends. The pub is home to crib, darts and pool league teams. ⋈Q❀☺◑⇌(Middlewood)♣P⊟(199)

Holcombe Brook

Hare & Hounds 🅛
400 Bolton Road West, BL0 9RY (on A676 at jct with Longsight Rd)
❀12-11 (midnight Thu-Sat) ☎ (01706) 822107
🌐 hareandhoundsbury.com
Beer range varies Ⓗ
There has been an inn on this site for over 100 years. This multi-award-winning pub is currently local CAMRA Area Pub of the Year 2013. You can view the 10 or more ever-changing beers currently available on the website's ale cam. Beer festivals are held throughout the year when the landlord sources ales from all around the country, especially from new breweries. Excellent food is served until 9pm. The pub has its own pool and quiz teams. Free Wi-Fi. ⋈❀☺◑&♣P⁌⊟(472,474)

Horwich

Bowling Green
175 Lee Lane, BL6 7JD
❀4 (12 Fri-Sun)-midnight ☎ (01204) 460308
Beer range varies Ⓗ
A welcome new entry to the Guide, this former Tetley Walker house, now free of tie with five handpulls, offers ever-changing beers from around the country. The original tiles feature in the long narrow vault. Rock bands play at least once a week, usually Friday. CAMRA members receive a small discount on production of a membership card. ♣⊟(125)

Crown
1 Chorley New Road, BL6 7QJ (jct A673/B6226)
❀11-11 (midnight Fri & Sat); 12-11.30 Sun
☎ (01204) 693109
Holt Mild, Bitter, seasonal beers Ⓗ
A grand local landmark, handy for the Reebok Stadium, Rivington Pike and the West Pennine Moors. Lever Park across the road was a gift from Lord Leverhulme, the soap magnate and great benefactor to his home town. Darts and dominoes teams play on Tuesday and Thursday evenings and there is a vault and games room at the rear. Various artists provide entertainment on Sunday evenings. Children are welcome at lunchtime when dining. ❀☺◑&♣P⁌⊟(125,575)

Original Bay Horse
206 Lee Lane, BL6 7JF (on B6226, 200yds from A673)
❀1-midnight; 12-12.30am Fri & Sat; 12-midnight Sun
☎ (01204) 696231
Bank Top Flat Cap; Coach House Gunpowder Mild; Lees Bitter; guest beers Ⓗ
Dating from 1777, this stone-built pub has been run by the same family for many years and is locally known as the Long Pull. In the lounge, pool and darts are played and live sports coverage on TV is popular, while the cosy, traditional vault has some interesting football memorabilia. A Moorhouse's beer is usually available, as is Westons Old Rosie cider. ❀☺♣❤⁌⊟(125,575)

Victoria & Albert ▼
114 Lee Lane, BL6 7AF (on B6226)
❀12-11 (midnight Fri & Sat) ☎ (01204) 770837
🌐 vicandalbert.co.uk
Holt Bitter; guest beers Ⓗ
Formerly the Albert Arms, the pub is situated opposite Horwich Public Hall. Recently refurbished, it is now a modern and comfortable lounge-style pub with three separate seating areas. Two guest beers are offered, one usually from Moorhouse's. Outside is a beer garden and the toilets have disabled access. It is handy for the West Pennine Moors and walkers are always welcome. Over-21s only. Local CAMRA Pub of the Year 2012. ⁌⊟(125)

Hyde

Cheshire Ring
72 Manchester Road, SK14 2BJ
❀12 (4 Mon & Tue; 1 Wed; 3.30 Thu & Fri)-11; 12-10.30 Sun
☎ (07917) 055629
Beartown Kodiak Gold, Bearskinful, seasonal beers; guest beers Ⓗ
One of the oldest pubs in Hyde and comprehensively overhauled several years ago by Beartown. Seven handpumps offer a range of Beartown ales and guests from micros in addition to ciders, perries and continental beers. A selection of bottled beers is also stocked and occasional beer festivals offer additional drinking choice. Gentle background music plays and live bands perform upstairs. Food includes home-made curries on Thursday evenings and Sunday lunches. Opening hours vary with the season. ⌛❀▣⇌(Central)❤⁌⊟

Godley Hall

Godley Hill Road, Godley Hill, SK14 3BL (signed from jct of Mottram Rd and Station Rd)

✪ 4-10.30 Mon; 12-11.30 ☎ (0161) 368 4415

Morland Old Speckled Hen; Theakston Best Bitter; guest beer ⊞

The pub is an 18th-century building with some original features. Friendly staff offer a warm welcome to all including families and dogs. Food is served Monday, Tuesday and Thursday 5-7pm and Friday-Sunday 12-5pm. The guest beer changes weekly. The pub is home to the Godley Golfing Society and hosts an acoustic music night on Monday. Outside seating is available.

🚶✿⊙◐⇌(Godley)P⅊–₪(201, 202)

Queen's Inn

23 Clarendon Place, SK14 2ND

✪ 11-11 ☎ (0161) 368 2230

Holt Mild, Bitter, seasonal beers ⊞

A town-centre community pub with a warm welcome. Home to several sports teams, the interior is divided into four distinct areas to cater for all needs, including a large function room that is a favourite for wedding receptions. Close to Hyde bus station and the market, the Queen's is popular with shoppers during the day. A late licence is available for special events.

🕭✿⊞占⇌(Central/Newton for Hyde)♣⅊–₪

Sportsman ⓛ

57 Mottram Road, SK14 2NN

✪ 11 (12 Sun)-midnight ☎ (0161) 368 5000

Rossendale Floral Dance, Pitch Porter, Sunshine; guest beers ⊞

Rossendale Brewery tied house offering the full range of its Pennine Ales plus up to three guests from micros. Bar snacks are served and there is a restaurant upstairs specialising in genuine home-cooked Cuban food and tapas. This former CAMRA Pub of the Region retains its character. The rear patio includes a covered and heated smoking area.

🚶Q✿⊙◐⊞⇌(Central/Newton for Hyde)●P⅊–₪

Leigh

Leigh Rugby Union Club

Round Ash Park, Hand Lane, WN7 3NA (off Beech Walk)

✪ 7 (12 Sat & Sun)-11 ☎ (01942) 673526

Coach House Round Ash Bitter, seasonal beers ⊞

A true community club with men's and ladies' rugby teams plus crown green bowls, darts and dominoes. Put all that together with an enthusiastic, hard-working bar team and a friendly crowd of locals and you can't go wrong. The Annual Scrumdown beer festival is held in May, with more than 30 real ales and ciders. Well worth the 10-minute walk from Leigh bus station. Regional CAMRA Club of the Year 2007-2011. ✿P⅊–

Thomas Burke ⓛ

20A Leigh Road, WN7 1QR

✪ 9am-midnight (1am Fri & Sat) ☎ (01942) 685640

Greene King Abbot; Ruddles County ⊞

Popular with all ages, this Wetherspoon pub is named after a renowned Leigh tenor, known as the Lancashire Caruso. The pub divides into three areas: the main long bar, a raised dining area and, in what was once a cinema foyer, lounge-style seating. Ten handpumps offer a changing range of beers from local to distant breweries. ◐占–

White Lion ⓛ

6A Leigh Road, WN7 1QL

✪ 12-midnight (1am Fri) ☎ (07510) 905995

AllGates California, seasonal beers ⊞

Fully refurbished and reopened in 2011, the White Lion is situated opposite Leigh's historic parish church just a few minutes' walk from Leigh's centre. A friendly town-centre pub, you can choose whether to enjoy the comfort of the main bar, bar games in the vault, or the quiet of the snug. Six handpumps dispense a selection of AllGates real ales plus guests, and draught Gwynt y Ddraig cider. Local CAMRA Pub of the Year 2012. ♣●⅊–₪

Littleborough

Red Lion ⓛ

6 Halifax Road, OL15 0HB (on A58 adjacent to railway bridge)

✪ 2 (12.30 Fri & Sat)-midnight; 1-midnight Sun ☎ (01706) 378195

Lees Bitter; Taylor Landlord; guest beers ⊞

Detached stone-built pub on a main road with four distinct rooms, each different in character. Beer and conversation dominate throughout the premises, with two rooms for games and TV sport. The main room is large and homely, the adjacent snug room has comfortable high-back chairs. Up to five guest beers supplement the two regulars and the house beer from Phoenix. Two German/Belgian beers are also available and one handpump supplies real cider from Thatchers or Westons. A proper community pub.

Q⊞⇌♣●P₪(528,590)

White House

Blackstone Edge, Halifax Road, OL15 0LG (on A58 to Halifax)

✪ 12-2, 6.30-9.30; 12-9 Sun ☎ (01706) 378456

⊕ thewhitehousepub.co.uk

Holt Bitter; Theakston Best Bitter; guest beers ⊞

The Pennine Way passes this 17th-century coaching house, a landmark at 1,300 feet that benefits from outstanding views. A family-run inn for the last 29 years, it extends a warm and friendly welcome to all. There are two bars, both with log fires. Four handpumps serve two regular and two guest beers, often from local breweries. A good selection of bottled beers, cider and wine complements the excellent food menu and daily specials (food served all day Sun).

🚶Q🕭✿⊙◐⊞占●P⅊–₪(528)

Manchester: City Centre

Angel

6 Angel Street, M4 4BQ (off Rochdale Rd)

✪ 12-11 ☎ (0161) 833 4786 ⊕ theangelmanchester.com

Bob's White Lion; guest beers ⊞

Beers change as regularly as the wind at this pub, now with 10 handpumps available. The landlord offers a local and countrywide variety, with Hawkshead, Hornbeam Liverpool, Organic and Pictish beers included – it is a mini festival each week. Cider is also on draught, usually Hecks. The food menu has an excellent range to appeal to all, with home-made fare served lunchtimes and evenings (no food Sun eve). Frequently visited by locals, office workers and visitors, the Angel goes from strength to strength.

🚶Q✿⊙◐⇌(Victoria)₪♣●P⅊–₪

Bar Fringe

8 Swan Street, M4 5JN (near Oldham Rd/Oldham St jct)
❂ 12-11.30 (midnight Fri & Sat) ☎ (0161) 835 3815
Beer range varies Ⓗ
This Belgian-style bar with welcoming and friendly staff is situated above the elusive River Tib. It has five handpumps offering a great range of beers – Phoenix and Cottage ales regularly feature, with guests and seasonals always available. Belgian and continental beers are on draught and in bottles too. Thatchers Cheddar Valley and a guest cider are served from the cask. The interior features a motorbike hung above the door, quirky ornamental rats and a fantastic jukebox.
🌞◖⇌(Victoria)🚃●'–🖵

Cask Bar

29 Liverpool Road, M3 4NQ
❂ 12-11 (10.30 Sun) ☎ (0161) 819 2527 ⊕ caskmanc.co.uk
Beer range varies Ⓗ
Despite the name, this bar specialises in continental beers, with a massive selection both on tap and in bottles. Four guest handpumps showcase breweries including Phoenix, Pictish, RedWillow, Abbeydale and Facers. An extremely narrow entrance brings you into a small seated area. A larger back room with soft furnishings leads to the patio garden. No food is available, however 'you are welcome to bring your own as long as you take your rubbish with you'!
🌞⇌(Deansgate)🚃'–🖵

Castle Hotel

66 Oldham Street, M4 1LE (near Warwick St)
❂ 12-1am (2am Fri & Sat) ☎ (0161) 237 9485
⊕ thecastlehotel.info
Robinsons Dizzy Blonde, Cumbria Way, Unicorn, seasonal beers; guest beers Ⓗ
This well-managed pub is Robinsons' only hostelry in the city centre. It usually serves four guest ales and a cider alongside five beers from the brewery's own range. A Grade II-listed building, it retains many original features following a recent renovation. Enter into a small vault with the bar opposite. Behind the bar is a dimly lit snug and a larger room for music and arts events. A recent addition is an upstairs room, used when busy.
🌞⇌(Victoria/Piccadilly)🚃●'–🖵

City Arms Ⓛ

46-48 Kennedy Street, M2 4BQ
❂ 12-11 (midnight Fri & Sat); 12-8 Sun ☎ (0161) 236 4610
Moorhouse's Pride of Pendle; Thwaites Original; guest beers Ⓗ
Busy little two-roomed city-centre hostelry tucked away on a back street close to Albert Square. Eight real ales are on offer including six ever-changing guests plus real cider in a box. It can be hectic during lunchtimes and weekend evenings. Pies are always available along with a selection of at least seven malt whiskies. Northern soul features on Saturday nights. A popular pub with a friendly feel and lots of regular customers – a local in the city centre. 🌞◖⇌(Oxford Rd)🚃♣●'–🖵

Crown & Kettle

2 Oldham Road, M4 5FE (jct Oldham Rd/Great Ancoats St)
❂ 12-11 (midnight Fri & Sat) ☎ (0161) 236 2923
Beer range varies Ⓗ
Listed building on a busy road junction. One central bar serves three rooms including a smart modern snug at the rear. Three beers from the Ossett

Brewery are complemented by two guest ales, a changing real cider and a small selection of foreign bottles. Note the particularly ornate ceiling and chandeliers. A fixture on the Northern Quarter real ale circuit. 🌞◖●'–🖵

Font

7-9 New Wakefield Street, M1 5NP (off Oxford Rd by railway viaduct)
❂ 11-1am (12.30am Sun) ☎ (0161) 236 0944
⊕ fontbar.com
Beer range varies Ⓗ
Split level café-bar with four handpumps showcasing beers from local and northern micros. Three ciders are always available as well as bottled beers from the UK, Belgium and the US among others. A wide selection of freshly cooked food is available until 8pm. In the evenings DJs provide the beats. Regularly changing art is on display. CAMRA members receive a 25 per cent discount on ales and cider on production of membership card. CAMRA branch Cider Pub of the Year 2012.
🌞◖◖⇌(Oxford Rd)🚃●🖵

Joshua Brooks

106 Princess Street, M1 6NG (jct Charles St)
❂ 12 (4 Mon; 11 Sat & Sun)-late ☎ (0161) 273 7336
⊕ joshuabrooks.co.uk
Beer range varies Ⓗ
Lively urban bar popular with students which has seen the beer range transformed over the past two years. Five ever-changing guest ales (often from very new micros) are accompanied by an excellent bottled selection and cider from the Westons range. Downstairs is a more clubby entertainment space which features everything from live music to theatre. Food is served daily until 7pm (5pm weekends). Joshua Brooks club membership includes a discount on cask beers (pints only). 🌞◖⇌(Oxford Rd)🚃(St Peter's Sq)●'–🖵(50,147)

Knott Bar Ⓛ

374 Deansgate, M3 4LY
❂ 12-11.30 (midnight Thu; 12.30am Fri & Sat)
☎ (0161) 839 9229
Castle Rock Harvest Pale; Hardknott Cool Fusion; Marble Manchester Bitter; guest beers Ⓗ
One of the city's premier beer houses with 10 consecutive entries in the Guide. A former CAMRA Regional Pub of the Year, it offers three regular ales complemented by four ever-changing guests from leading microbreweries such as RedWillow, Magic Rock and Summer Wine. Real cider is always available from a box on the back bar. The venue has an excellent reputation for quality meals, served until 8pm daily. Well served by rail and tram stations opposite and frequent free Metroshuttle buses until 7pm. 🌞🌞◖◖⇌(Deansgate)🚃●'–🖵

Marble Arch ★

73 Rochdale Road, M4 4HY (on A664, 200yds from A665 jct)
❂ 12-11 (midnight Fri & Sat) ☎ (0161) 832 5914
Marble Draft, Pint, Best, Ginger, seasonal beers; guest beers Ⓗ
A showcase for the award-winning Marble Brewery, this famous pub, just outside the city centre, celebrated 125 years in 2013. Two guest ales usually supplement the Marble range. The pub is listed and displays many interesting architectural features, from the imposing entrance to the sloping mosaic floor and the drinking frieze. A more modern back room is used primarily for

dining. The food is justifiably popular and served until 8.45pm (7.45pm Sun).
☜❀❄➊⊜≉(Victoria)🚇♿'–🚐

Micro Bar

Unit FC11, Manchester Arndale, 49 High Street, M4 3AH (inside Arndale Food Market, Upper High St entrance)
❀ 11-6; 12-5 Sun ☎ (0161) 277 9666
Boggart Hole Clough Meme, Cascade, Rum Porter; guest beers Ⓗ
A small kiosk bar, perched between fruit and veg and cheese stalls. Up to five handpumps dispense Boggart and guest beers from far and wide. One pump is reserved for cider/perry. Many bottled beers are offered. The bar is surrounded by food outlets from many nations, so a pint and a meal can be enjoyed at one of the amply provided tables, or on a stool at the raised shelf, with views of shoppers and trams outside. ≉(Victoria)🚇♿🚲🚐

Molly House

26 Richmond Street, M1 3NB (jct Sackville St)
❀ 12-midnight (Wed, Thu & Sun 1am; Fri & Sat 2am)
☎ (0161) 237 9329 ∰ themollyhouse.com
Beartown Kodiak Gold; guest beers Ⓗ
This comfortable yet modern pub set in the heart of Manchester's gay village has fast become a destination for more discerning/older village devotees. The welcoming ground floor has a bar and a small restaurant (tapas a speciality) as well as the papers and a small library. The larger upper floor has another bar, comfy sofas and a terrace smoking area. The house beer range comes from Beartown plus Hornbeam, Dunham Massey, RedWillow and other local brewers.
❀➊≉(Oxford Rd)🚇(St Peter's Sq)♿'–🚐(1,3)

Paramount

33-35 Oxford Street, M1 4BH
❀ 7-midnight (1am Fri-Sun) ☎ (0161) 233 1820
Elland Paramount Porter; Greene King Abbot; Moorhouse's Pendle Witches Ale; Robinsons Build a Rocket Boys; Thwaites Wainwright; guest beers Ⓗ
This large and extremely popular Wetherspoon pub has a very lively yet pleasant atmosphere. What really sets it apart, however, is the enthusiasm of the management team for its wide and interesting range of cask beer. Located in Manchester's old theatreland – hence the name – photos of closed theatres and cinemas adorn the walls. Nowadays it is very handy for a pint when visiting one of the many venues nearby, including the Bridgewater Hall, Palace Theatre and Manchester Central.
➊♿≉(Oxford Rd)🚇(St Peter's Sq)♿🚐(1,3)

Port Street Beer House

39-41 Port Street, M1 2EQ (opp Brewer St)
❀ closed Mon; 4 (2 Fri)-midnight; 12-1am Sat; 12-midnight Sun ☎ (0161) 237 9949 ∰ portstreetbeerhouse.co.uk
Beer range varies Ⓗ
A vast selection of ever-changing diverse ales and ciders, both UK and international, served by friendly and knowledgeable bar staff, is on offer at this beer house. Some beers are expensive, so it is advisable to check the prominently displayed price list first. However, quality well-exceeds prices, and the pub is popular with all sectors of the community. The bar area can get crowded, but there is ample space in the large room upstairs.
Q♿≉(Piccadilly)🚇'–🚐

Rising Sun

22 Queen Street, M2 5HX
❀ 12-10.30 (11.20 Fri & Sat); 1-7 Sun ☎ (0161) 834 1193
Beer range varies Ⓗ
Traditional historic city-centre pub, off Deansgate, with entrances on Queen Street and Lloyd Street (one of only three pubs in Manchester with two entrances). Eight handpumps dispense a range of ever-changing beers and regular real cider. Food is served lunchtimes Monday to Friday, and it hosts regular Meet the Brewer events and beer festivals. An impressive refurbishment in early 2012 has made a huge difference to this friendly locals' and visitors' pub. ➊≉(Deansgate)🚇♿🚐

Sandbar

120-122 Grosvenor Street, M1 7HL (off Oxford Rd A34/B5117 jct)
❀ 12-midnight (1am Thu; 2am Fri & Sat) ☎ (0161) 273 1552
∰ sandbaronline.net
Phoenix All Saints, Arizona; guest beers Ⓗ
An excellent conversion of 18th-century town houses, this quirky and bohemian bar is set in the heart of Manchester's student land, attracting students and university staff alike. Exhibitions of photographs and paintings adorn the walls and DJs do their thing at weekends. A good range of foreign beers complements the eight handpulled cask ales and the changing guest cider, which often comes from a smaller producer. Free Wi-fi available. ❀➊≉(Oxford Rd)♿'–🚐(42,43)

Waterhouse ⅃

67-71 Princess Street, M2 4EG (opp town hall)
❀ 9-midnight ☎ (0161) 200 5380
Phoenix Wobbly Bob; Rooster's Buckeye; Thwaites Wainwright; guest beers Ⓗ
This former row of three Georgian town houses was refurbished in 2012 and has been transformed into a multi-roomed Wetherspoon pub. The company's national beers have been replaced by three family and microbrewer regulars and joined by a daily changing range of five guest ales. Black Dragon cider is on handpump. Regular Meet The Brewer evenings are held and occasionally the pub features special beers brewed by members of the cellar team in collaboration with local microbrewers. Q☜❀➊♿≉(Oxford Rd)🚇♿'–🚐

Wharf ⅃

6 Slate Wharf, Castlefield, M15 4ST
❀ 11-11 (midnight Fri & Sat); 11-10.30 Sun
☎ (0161) 220 2960
Brunning & Price Original Bitter; Taylor Landlord; Weetwood Cheshire Cat; guest beers Ⓗ
Large pub in an impressive location sitting on the Castlefield Basin where the Bridgewater and Rochdale canals meet. A popular mooring point for leisure boaters, there is a large outside seating area overlooking the waterways. Food is major here, with a restaurant upstairs. The bar boasts 10 handpumps, eight serving real ale and the others real cider. Knowledgeable staff can also advise on the pub's large range of whiskies and wines.
🍴Q☜❀➊♿≉(Deansgate)🚇♣♿P'–🚐

Marple

Hare & Hounds

Dooley Lane, Otterspool, SK6 7EJ
❀ 11.30-11; 12-10.30 Sun ☎ (0161) 427 0293
∰ hareandhoundsmarple.co.uk

Hydes 1863, Original Bitter; guest beers ⊞
Attractive hostelry by the River Goyt on the Marple to Romiley road. The Hydes' beers provide some welcome variety in the area. The interior is open plan with a separate dining area and conservatory plus an improved and pleasant outdoor space. The pub offers something for everyone including good-value food. Seasonal beer festivals are held – see the website for details. Q ❀ ◑ ● P ⁵ ⌐

Railway

223 Stockport Road, SK6 6EN
❁ 12-11 (11.30 Fri & Sat); 12-10.30 Sun ☎ (0161) 427 2146
Robinsons Hatters, Unicorn, seasonal beers ⊞
First opened in 1878, this impressive pub has two open-plan, airy and relaxing rooms, complemented by an outside veranda and drinking area. Located alongside Rose Hill Station, many rail commuters still number among its customers; it is also handy for walkers and cyclists on the nearby Middlewood Way. A deservedly popular pub.
❀ ◑ ₺ ≷ (Rose Hill) P ⁵ ⌐

Marple Bridge

Hare & Hounds

19 Mill Brow, SK6 5LW (from A626 Lane Ends along Ley Lane for ¾ mile) SJ980896
❁ 12-3 (Fri only), 5-midnight (10 Mon & Tue); 12-midnight Sat; 12-10 Sun ☎ (0161) 427 4042
Robinsons Hatters, Dizzy Blonde, Unicorn ⊞, Old Tom ⌐, seasonal beers ⊞
Winner of the 2010 Robinsons Unicorn Shield for best-kept cellar, this is a hidden gem in the beautiful hamlet of Mill Brow. Extensively refurbished in 2008 to a high standard, this excellent country pub with a great atmosphere and a roaring fire in winter is the perfect place for both discerning drinkers and diners. Meals are freshly prepared and food is locally sourced. A genuine local that caters for everyone, including walkers, with some of the best views in the area.
♨ ❀ ◑ ₺ ♣ P ⁵ ⌐ (394)

Mellor

Oddfellows

Moor End Road, SK6 5PT
❁ closed Mon; 5-11 Tue; 12-midnight; 12-6 Sun
☎ (0161) 449 7826 ⊕ oddfellowsmellor.com
Marston's Pedigree; guest beers ⊞
This elegant stone-built pub is tucked away in a dip in the road in the old part of the village. The smart but traditional interior is enhanced by beams and flagged floors, with blazing real fires in winter. Guest beers are often sourced from micros such as Marble and Bollington, plus a house special from Moorhouse's. Sought-after food comes from a realistic menu with a gourmet twist. The 375 bus service passes the door but runs only infrequently.
♨ ❀ ◑ ₺ ⚔ P ⁵ ⌐ (375)

Middleton

Ring o' Bells

St Leonard's Square, M24 6DJ (up New Lane from Long St)
❁ 5-midnight; 12-1am Fri & Sat; 12-midnight Sun
☎ (0161) 654 9245 ⊕ ringobellsmiddleton.co.uk
Lees Bitter, seasonal beers ⊞
Opposite the 600-year-old St Leonard's Church, the inn dates from 1807. This friendly hostelry boasts

regular live music, a quiz night every second Sunday and a poetry night on the fourth Sunday of the month. Premier League football is screened. The upstairs function room features collages created from butterfly mosaics. A unique Pace Egg Play is held on Easter Monday and a Maypole event on the May bank holiday. ❀ ♣ P ⁵ ⌐ (17)

Tandle Hill Tavern

14 Thornham Lane, M24 2SD (1 mile along unmetalled road off A664 and A627) SD907094
❁ closed Mon; 5 (12 Sat & Sun)-11 ☎ (07775) 788042
Lees Bitter, seasonal beers ⊞
Remote two-roomed gem reached by a severely potholed lane from either Middleton (A664) or Royton (A627). The pub is popular with its many regulars, the local farming community and walkers from the nearby country park. Dogs are very welcome, with water and dog biscuits provided. Limited home-cooked food is offered on Sundays and toasties are usually available at other times. The house beer, Bumpy Lane, is a dry-hopped version of Lees Bitter. ♨ ❀

Milnrow

Waggon Inn

35 Butterworth Hall, OL16 3PE
❁ 12 (4 Mon)-midnight; 12-11 Sun ☎ (01706) 648313
Banks's Bitter; Brakspear Oxford Gold ⊞
A true family hostelry welcoming young and old, the Waggon dates back to 1782 and with its mullioned windows has the appearance of a real village pub. The beer range, supplied by Marston's, changes monthly, with a Wychwood beer usually included. A broad variety of live musical acts features at weekends which always draws a crowd. The pub is now within walking distance of the new Manchester tramline. ♨ ⛵ ❀ ₺ ⊞ P ⁵ ⌐ (181,182)

Monton

Park Hotel ☝

142 Monton Road, M30 9QD (B5229, corner of Hawthorne Ave)
❁ 11-11 (11.30 Thu; midnight Fri & Sat); 12-10.30 Sun
☎ (0161) 787 8608
Holt Mild, Bitter, IPA, seasonal beers; guest beer ⊞
Built in the 1970s, replacing an 1867 pub, then extended in the 1990s, the Park is a busy, well-run community pub. A central bar serves a large vault, an enormous lounge and the secluded Bridgewater room. The latter features a fish tank, a canal mural and a dartboard for ladies' matches on Tuesdays. The vault has two more boards for a 501 league on Thursdays and for 'log end' Holt's matches on Mondays. Entertainment is hosted on Saturdays, a quiz on Sundays, and an angling club meets here.
Q ❀ ⊞ ♣ P ⁵ ⌐

Mossley

Britannia Inn

217 Manchester Road, OL5 9AJ
❁ 2.45-11 Mon-Wed; 11.45-11 (midnight Fri & Sat); 12-midnight Sun ☎ (01457) 832799
⊕ britanniamossley.co.uk
Marston's Burton Bitter; guest beers ⊞
Imposing gritstone building yards from Mossley station, this former Marston's house offers a continually changing range of five guest beers, often including Mossley Brew from the local

Millstone brewery. Food is served from opening time until 7.30pm (5pm Sun). Smokers use the covered patio area in front of the pub.
🏠🌓🍴♣🚺—🚇(343,350)

Commercial

58 Manchester Road, OL5 0AA
🌓 12-11 (midnight Fri & Sat) ☎ 07849 186285
Millstone Tiger Rut; guest beers Ⓗ
Opened in 1831 to cater for travellers using the recently completed turnpike road (Manchester Rd). The 'Commi' is a boisterous semi-open-plan pub with bar areas, pool room and a low stage. Entertainment includes karaoke on Fridays and disco or live music on Saturdays in addition to darts on Tuesdays and poker on Thursdays. The pub is also home to a local Sunday League football team. Dog-friendly. 🏠🍴♣🚺—🚇(343,350)

Dysarts Arms

Huddersfield Road, OL5 9BT (on B6175 ½ mile S of A635)
🌓 12-midnight (1am Fri & Sat) ☎ (01457) 832103
Robinsons 1892, Unicorn, seasonal beers Ⓗ
Located outside the town, bordering open farmland and close to the pre-1974 Lancashire/ Yorkshire boundary, this pub was acquired by Robinsons when it took over Schofield's of Ashton-under-Lyne in 1926. The interior comprises a spacious, comfortable bar area, a cosy lounge with a real fire in winter and a tiny snug. A partially covered patio to the side allows for outdoor drinking and smoking. Caravans are welcome in the car park. 🚐🏠👤♣🅿🚺—🚇(350)

Rising Sun

235 Stockport Road, OL5 0RQ
🌓 12-midnight ☎ (01457) 238236 ⊕ risingsunmossley.co.uk
Black Sheep Best Bitter; Millstone Tiger Rut, Rising Sunsation, Stout Ⓗ
In a bracing location, the pub is well named due to its excellent views eastwards over the Tame Valley towards Saddleworth Moor. Four regular beers are augmented by an ever-changing selection of six guest ales and Pure North Rising Sun cider. The interior is semi open plan and has a games room used by the local Blue Grass Boys on Tuesdays and a folk club on alternate Wednesdays. Food is available Thursday-Sunday lunchtimes only. An outdoor patio and covered areas are available for smokers. 🚐🏠🌓♣🍴🅿—🚇(353)

Oldham

Ashton Arms 🄻

28-30 Clegg Street, OL1 1PL (rear of town square)
🌓 11.30-11 (11.30 Fri & Sat); 12-7.30 Sun
☎ (0161) 630 9709
Beer range varies Ⓗ
Extremely popular town-centre free house overlooking the old Town Hall, serving an excellent choice of four to six rotating beers from both new and long-established breweries. It specialises in local micros and LocAles with themed beer festivals throughout the year. Traditional cider and perry are sold all year round and the pub stocks a good selection of Belgian and German beers. Good-value food is available weekdays until 6pm (3pm Friday). Note the impressive stone fireplace.
🚐🏠🌓♣🍴—🚇

Carrion Crow

271 Huddersfield Road, OL4 2RJ (on A62 ¾ mile from town centre)
🌓 12-midnight ☎ (0161) 633 4490
Beer range varies Ⓗ
A busy, well-run local dating from 1705. The licensee is highly knowledgeable and offers four handpulls drawing widely from the Marston's range including the monthly guest beers. Cask ales are discounted on Mondays. Locally sourced produce is used in the food menu, with Sunday roasts always popular. Wholesome bar snacks are available until 7pm. Quiz night is Thursday and the pub hosts quiz and football teams. Charity events include an inter-pub beer walk. A marquee outside has picnic tables for up to 40 people and a market is held at Christmas. 🏠🌓♿♣🅿—🚇(81A,83)

Royal Oak ★

178 Union Street, OL1 1EN (400yds from Mumps Metrolink)
🌓 11 (12 Sun)-1am ☎ (0161) 633 2642
Robinsons Dizzy Blonde, Frederic's 175, Unicorn Bitter, Old Tom, seasonal beer Ⓗ
An excellent, friendly boozer handily placed for Mumps Metrolink station, the pub dates from 1823 and has a unique quadrant-shaped bar with stained glass windows and dark wood panelling from a quality refitting in 1928. The landlord is an avid cask beer enthusiast and offers four handpumps from the Robinsons' range including Old Tom in winter. Bar snacks are available at any hour. Quiz night is Wednesday and the Go-Go club features live bands on the last Saturday of month. British Legion ex-paratroopers meet monthly. 🍺🚇♣—

Patricroft

Bird in Hand

304 Liverpool Road, M30 0RY (adjacent to Eccles Fire Station)
🌓 11-11.30 (12.30am Fri & Sat) ☎ (0161) 789 3807
Holt Mild, IPA, Bitter; guest beer Ⓗ
The Bird in Hand is a traditional, friendly, multi-roomed pub. A short corridor leads to a central lobby, which provides access to the vault, snug, pool room and lounge. The bar to the right of the lobby also serves the vault and lounge. There are TVs throughout, although the one in the snug is not always turned on if you want somewhere quiet. There are live turns on a Sunday night. Many interesting local prints adorn the walls. 🏠🍺🌓♣🅿—🚇

Ramsbottom

First Chop 🄻

43 Bolton Street, BL0 9HU
🌓 closed Mon; 12 (4 Tue)-midnight; 12-1am Thu-Sat
☎ (01706) 827722 ⊕ thefirstchop.co.uk
Beer range varies Ⓗ
The pub is in a former shop premises on the main Ramsbottom shopping street. The owner has recently started brewing and one of his beers is usually on offer among the four ever-changing real ales. Up to six varying ciders are also kept. A loyalty card ensures CAMRA members receive every sixth pint free, plus a 20 per cent discount on food. The menu offers locally sourced and home-cooked fare. Live music features on Thursdays with a jam session on Sundays. 🌓♿🍴♣🚇(472,474)

Irwell Works Brewery Tap

Irwell Works Brewery, BL0 9YQ (opp Morrisons)
✪ closed Mon & Tue; 11-11 ☎ (01706) 825019
⊕ irwellworksbrewery.co.uk
Irwell Works Tin Plate, Copper Plate, Richard Mason 1888, Steam Plate, Iron Plate, seasonal beers ⊞
A fairly recent addition to the real ale scene in Ramsbottom, the bar is on the first floor above the brewery of the same name. The building was formerly the Irwell Steam, Tin, Copper and Iron Works. Ten or more of the brewery's ales are on sale, plus a real cider, and light lunchtime snacks are now available. Live music features occasionally. The pub runs a regular charity beer festival at the nearby Civic Hall. Ribble Valley Gold cider is sold. Dogs are welcome. ≈⊕🕆

Major Hotel ⌶

158-160 Bolton Street, BL0 9JA
✪ 3.30-midnight Mon & Tue; 12-midnight ☎ (01706) 826777
Bank Top Flat Cap; Lancaster Blonde; St Austell Tribute; guest beers ⊞
Now in its eighth year under the current owners, the Major prides itself on being a traditional local pub. The lounge houses a large logburner, while the bar is perfectly suited to pool, darts and Sky TV. Four real ales are always available from local micros as well as countrywide favourites. Unpretentious and reasonably priced food ranges from snacks to full meals. Just a short walk from the local steam railway.
⋓⊛◖⊡⇌♣P⊵⊟(472,474)

Rochdale

Baum ♈ ⌶

33-37 Toad Lane, OL12 0NU (follow signs for Museum and Conservation Area)
✪ 11.30-11 (midnight Fri & Sat); 11.30-10.30 Sun
☎ (01706) 352186 ⊕ thebaum.co.uk
Beer range varies ⊞
Fabulous pub with a relaxed and friendly atmosphere set within a conservation area and joined to the original Pioneer building that houses the first ever Co-op. A single bar with eight handpumps, one dedicated to cider, caters for two levels and a conservatory. Local beers are always available alongside others from far and wide. Excellent fresh food is sourced locally. Outside, there is a large beer garden and two boules pistes. Greater Manchester and National CAMRA Pub of the Year 2012. Not to be missed.
⋓⊛◖⇌⊟♣⊕P⊵⊟

Cemetery Hotel ★

470 Bury Road, OL11 5EU (on B6122)
✪ 12-midnight (1.30am Fri & Sat) ☎ (01706) 645635
Black Sheep Best Bitter; Copper Dragon Golden Pippin; Moorhouse's Pride of Pendle; Taylor Landlord ⊞
The Cemetery is an historic Grade II-listed Victorian pub with three separate rooms and a bar area, all with original fittings. It features a selection of real ales alongside an extensive menu, with steak and pint night on Tuesday and chicken and pint night on Thursday. The pub has a long association with Rochdale FC, with a room dedicated to the club. The large function room caters for all events, including band nights. A real cider weekend is held at the end of every month. ⋓⊛◖⊕P⊟(468)

Flying Horse Hotel ⌶

37 Packer Street, OL16 1NJ (opp town hall)
✪ 11.30-11 (12.30am Thu; 1.30am Fri & Sat); 12-12.30am Sun ☎ (01706) 646412 ⊕ theflyinghorsehotel.co.uk
Taylor Boltmaker, Landlord; guest beers ⊞
Set in a convenient town-centre location, handy for the bus station, the Flying Horse is a lively stone-built Edwardian pub boasting two real log fires. The friendly and efficient staff dispense up to seven real ales and one cask cider. Traditional home-made food is served daily. Live music is hosted on Friday and Saturday, plus jam night on Thursday. All major sporting events are shown on TV. A proud member of CAMRA's LocAle scheme.
⋓⊱⊄◖⊡⇌⊟P⊵⊟

Healey Hotel

172 Shawclough Road, OL12 6LW
✪ 11.30-11.30 (midnight Fri & Sat); 12-11.30 Sun
☎ (01706) 645453
Robinsons Dizzy Blonde, Unicorn, seasonal beers ⊞
Attractive old-world stone-built end of terrace pub with multiple rooms retaining many original features including tiles and woodwork. The Train Room contains a collection of original photos of the Rochdale to Bacup Railway. A large beer garden at the side of building has two boules pistes. The pub is a popular stop-off for walkers, with a bridle path to the rear and Healey Dell Nature Reserve nearby. Excellent home-cooked food is available.
⋓⊛◖♣⊕P⊵⊟(446)

Regal Moon ⌶

The Butts, OL16 1HB (next to bus station)
✪ 9am-midnight (1am Fri & Sat) ☎ (01706) 657434
Greene King Abbot; Ruddles Best Bitter; Thwaites Wainwright; guest beers ⊞
Imposing former cinema next to the main bus station retaining many original features including massive columns. Note the organ-playing mannequin above the bar. Up to 18 handpumps dispense quality beers from near and far, with local brews featuring regularly. The cider is usually from Westons with an occasional guest. The standard Wetherspoon range of meals and snacks is available. There is a patio to the rear for smokers. Wetherspoon Cask Ale Pub 2011. ⊛◖♿⊕⊵⊟

Romiley

Duke of York

Stockport Road, SK6 3AN (on B6104, 100yds from bridge 14 on Peak Forest Canal)
✪ 12-midnight (12.30am Fri & Sat) ☎ (0161) 406 9988
Black Sheep Best Bitter; John Smith's Bitter; Thwaites Wainwright; Wells Bombardier; guest beer ⊞
Built in 1786 and extensively refurbished, this traditional village pub retains its character and historic feel. Good-quality food is served in both the main bar and the upstairs restaurant. A free-to-enter quiz is held every Wednesday evening with each team winning a prize at the end. Beer festivals are hosted throughout the year.
⋓Q⊛◖⊡⇌P⊵⊟

Platform 1

6 Stockport Road, SK6 4BN
✪ 12-11 (midnight Thu-Sat) ☎ (0161) 406 8686
Beer range varies ⊞
The pub is adjacent to Romiley railway station. It opened in 2012 following complete refurbishment, and is now a free house and wine bar. The large

bar down the side of the mainly open-plan lower floor offers six real ales, with local micros such as Hornbeam and RedWillow often represented. A separate restaurant area on the first floor (Platform 2) serves food 12-8pm. 🐱❍▶️≠⌐☐

Royton

Puckersley Inn
22 Narrowgate Brow, OL2 6YD (off A671 via Dogford Rd and Fir Lane)
❂ 12-midnight ☎ (0161) 284 5370
Lees Brewer's Dark, Bitter, seasonal beers Ⓗ
Popular, detached, stone-fronted pub situated on the edge of the green belt, with panoramic views over Royton, Shaw and Oldham. This welcoming local has a traditional vault and a comfortable lounge. The dining extension serves an excellent range of well-prepared meals lunchtimes and evenings until 9pm. Cosy corners provide plenty of space to chat and chill out over a pint or two. A garden area is available for warmer weather.
🏚️🐱❍🍴♣P⌐☐(408)

Rusholme

Ford Madox Brown
Unit 3, Wilmslow Park, Oxford Road, M13 9NG (jct Hathersage Rd)
❂ 8am-midnight ☎ (0161) 256 6660
Greene King Abbot; Ruddles Best Bitter; guest beers Ⓗ
This very modern Wetherspoon pub is named after the eminent Victorian Pre-Raphaelite painter who lived nearby in Victoria Park, and built on the site of the old Rusholme Hall. Handy for the Curry Mile, MRI Hospital, Whitworth Gallery and University, it is popular with students but attracts a real cross section of people. Although an open-plan pub it has a warmer feeling than you might expect, with charity and community events held regularly.
Q🐱❍🚹⌐☐(42,43)

Sale

J P Joule Ⓛ
2A Northenden Road, M33 3BR
❂ 9-midnight (1am Fri & Sat) ☎ (0161) 928 9889
Greene King Abbot; Morland Old Speckled Hen; Phoenix Wobbly Bob; Ruddles Best Bitter; guest beers Ⓗ
Situated yards from Sale Metrolink station and on several major bus routes, this is an extremely popular Wetherspoon establishment named after the famous physicist, frequented by people of all ages from near and far. The pub is spread over two floors connected by a stunning staircase, each floor with its own extensive bar hosting a total of 14 handpumps. Look for the CAMRA noticeboard on the ground floor at the far end of the bar.
🚶🐱❍🚹⌐☐

Volunteer Hotel Ⓛ
81 Cross Street, M33 7HJ
❂ 12-midnight (11 Sun) ☎ (0161) 973 5503
Holt Mild, Bitter, seasonal beers Ⓗ
Large late-Victorian establishment on the main road with friendly and welcoming staff. The ground floor has been opened out to create one large room with pool tables and darts on one side and seating on two levels on the other. Up a flight of stairs behind the bar is a Grade II-listed wood-

panelled room used for functions and meetings. A quiz is held every Thursday in the main lounge. Free Wi-Fi. 🐱♿🚹P⌐☐

Salford

Eagle Inn
18-19 Collier Street, M3 7DW (near jct Blackfriars Rd/ Trinity Way)
❂ 12.30 (3 Mon)-midnight; 12.30-3am Sat & Sun
☎ (0161) 819 5002
Holt IPA, Bitter; guest beers Ⓗ
Known locally as the Lamp Oil, this traditional Salford pub was once home to a shop where oil was sold. It has recently been refurbished without destroying its traditional features, and drinkers have a choice of three rooms, plus a heated outdoor smoking area. The tenant provides her own choice of quality popular music, and there are plans for a live music venue in the tied cottage next door. Local CAMRA branch Most Improved Pub 2012. 🖫≠(Victoria)☐♣🍴⌐☐(92,98)

King's Arms
11 Bloom Street, M3 6AN (off Chapel Street)
❂ 12-11 ☎ (0161) 839 8726 🌐 kingsarmssalford.com
Beer range varies Ⓗ/Ⓖ
This is a pub, music venue, theatre and artists' studios. A sterling ale range often includes locally brewed beers from Robinsons and Phoenix, and there is usually a cask of something on gravity dispense. Entering the pub, the snug is to the left, the bar and main room to the right. There is always a play on or club night taking place, including knitting/crafting evenings. Not just for students, you are made to feel welcome as part of the wider Salford art community. The Sunday lunches are popular with the locals. 🐱❍≠(Central)🍴⌐☐

Mark Addy
Stanley Street, M3 5EJ (off New Bailey St, by river)
❂ 11.30-11 (8 Sun) ☎ (0161) 832 4080 🌐 markaddy.co.uk
RedWillow Mark Addy Fearless, Mark Addy Headless; guest beers Ⓗ
An ingenious conversion from old premises, set into the bank of the River Irwell but above water level. Tables by the windows give good views of the river and waterfowl. A barrel-vaulted ceiling is supported by six massive cast iron pillars. Food is a major feature, prepared by chef Robert Owen Brown, and six handpumps dispense beers from local microbrewers. Real cider is sold from the box in summer. There is an extended beer garden further along the riverside, with inset arches.
🏚️🚶🐱❍≠(Central)🍴P⌐☐

New Oxford
11 Bexley Square, M3 6DB (off Chapel St)
❂ 12-midnight ☎ (0161) 832 7082 🌐 thenewoxford.com
Beer range varies Ⓗ
This pub is a true gem, with both staff and locals offering a warm welcome. The cask ales are exceptional with at least eight available at any one time from Acorn, Black Edge, Phoenix, Star and others. The bar's selection of bottled Belgian beers would rival a European bar, and with a matching interior. Draught Belgian beers and cask ciders are also offered. The New Oxford has been given a Community Pub Award in 2011 and was voted Cider Pub of the Year 2012. 🐱❍≠(Central)🍴⌐☐

Shaw

Black Horse

203A Rochdale Road, OL2 7JD

✪ 1 (4 Tue)-midnight; 12-midnight Sat & Sun

☎ (01706) 847173

Lees Bitter Ⓗ

A traditional and friendly two-roomed stone-built local on the main road between Shaw and High Crompton. The lounge bar has a cosy snug area with beams, a wooden ceiling and stained glass windows – the larger part of the room was once a stable block. The separate vault hosts darts, dominoes and TV sport, with access to the rear garden and smoking area. An ideal pub for a quiet drink. Well-behaved dogs on a lead are welcome. Q❀⊟♣Pᐟ–⊟(408,435)

Shevington

Silver Tally

41 Shevington Moor, WN6 0SQ

✪ 12-11 ☎ (01257) 472733 ∰ silvertally.co.uk

Prospect Silver Tally; guest beers Ⓗ

The first pub to be opened by Prospect Brewery and its brewery tap, as well as the brewery bar. It has three main areas for games, dining and drinking. The pub has been totally refurbished with a modern yet traditional feel to it. High-quality food is available from a real pub menu. Q⅏❀⊕☖♣♦Pᐟ–⊟(641)

Stalybridge

Society Rooms Ⓛ

49 Grosvenor Street, SK15 2JN

✪ 8-midnight ☎ (0161) 338 9740

Greene King Abbot; Ruddles Best Bitter; guest beers Ⓗ

This split-level Wetherspoon pub is named after the former Co-op store premises it now occupies in the town centre. Enthusiastic management and a strong focus on real ales, plus 10 handpumps, have made this a favourite destination for local drinkers. Beer-oriented events such as Meet the Brewer nights and ale requests by customers have helped to boost the pub's reputation. Real ciders are always available. ⅏❀⊕☖⇌♦–⊟

Stalybridge Labour Club

Acres Lane, SK15 2JR

✪ 12-midnight; closed Tue & Wed ☎ (0161) 303 9477

Thwaites Wainwright; guest beers Ⓗ

This large club boasts a welcoming lounge, a spacious function room (available for hire) and a games room with full-sized billiard table. The rotating guest beers – at least two are always on offer – are sourced from the Thwaites list. Catering is available on request. Entry to the club can be gained by production of this Guide or a CAMRA membership card. ☖⇌Pᐟ–⊟

Stalybridge Station Refreshment Rooms (Buffet Bar) ♀ ★ Ⓛ

Rassbottom Street, SK15 1RF (access from station platform)

✪ 10-11; 12-10.30 Sun ☎ (0161) 303 0007 ∰ buffetbar.org

Taylor Landlord; guest beers Ⓗ

Featured in many beer publications and even TV programmes, this enduring Victorian gem is worth missing a train for. The recent sympathetic refurbishment has allowed expansion of the food menu which now includes home-cooked meals. Nine handpumps dispense a variety of ever-changing beers, most locally sourced, plus at least one real cider or perry. A good range of interesting bottled beers is also available. A function room is used for events including live music and Meet the Brewer nights. Monday is quiz night. ⅏Q❀⊕☖⇌♣♦Pᐟ–⊟

White House Ⓛ

1 Water Street, SK15 2AG

✪ 12-11 (midnight Sat) ☎ (0161) 303 2154

Hydes Owd Oak, Original Bitter; guest beers Ⓗ

This popular pub close to both bus and rail stations is semi open plan but retains four distinct drinking areas and a quiet corner can usually be found even at busy times. Up to four ever-changing guest beers from micros complement the regulars from Hydes, and up to three real ciders are on offer. Quiz night is Sunday and live music features every Friday with a folk night every Thursday. Sunday lunches, including roasts, are served 12-6pm. ⇌♣♦⊟

Stockport: Central

Arden Arms ★

23 Millgate, SK1 2LX (jct Corporation St)

✪ 12-11 ☎ (0161) 480 2185 ∰ arden-arms.co.uk

Robinsons 1892, Dizzy Blonde, Double Hop, Unicorn Ⓗ, Old Tom Ⓖ, seasonal beer Ⓗ

This Grade II-listed building close to Stockport market is identified by CAMRA as one of Britain's Best Real Heritage Pubs. A multi-roomed pub that centres around one main serving area, the rear snug is an interesting feature as you have to walk through the bar to reach it. It is said that the cellars acted as a mortuary and they retain body niches in their walls. Many Victorian features remain, making this an unmissable gem. Evening meals are served Wednesday-Sunday 5.30-8pm. ⅏⅌❀⊕⊟♣ᐟ–⊟(300,384)

Boar's Head

2 Vernon Street, Market Place, SK1 1TY

✪ 11-11; 12-6.30 Sun ☎ (0161) 480 3978

Samuel Smith OBB Ⓗ

A multi-roomed pub with a cosy town-centre feel. Owners Samuel Smith spent a fair sum restoring this pub to what it may once have looked like. The front room is divided into a spartan public lounge to the right and a more substantial, comfortable room on the left furnished with cushioned pews, high-back chairs and stools. To the rear is a second lounge that was once a music room, and there is a decked area outside. ⅏Q❀ᐟ–

Crown Inn

154 Heaton Lane, SK4 1AR (jct with King St W under viaduct)

✪ 12-11 (10.30 Sun) ☎ (0161) 480 5850

∰ thecrowninn.110mb.com

Beer range varies Ⓗ

A busy hostelry, especially in the evenings. Around 16 ever-changing beers are available, with helpful and knowledgeable staff to advise those confused by the choice. Pictish and Bollington beers are regulars, and there is usually a mild, stout/porter and a cider. Four rooms radiate from the busy bar. Food is served until 3pm weekdays. Live music is a feature, with the rear yard and attractive outdoor seating area showcasing local bands at weekends. A real gem. ⅏Q❀⊕⇌♦ᐟ–⊟

ENGLAND

Pineapple

159 Heaton Lane, SK4 1AQ (off A6, near viaduct)
☼ 12-11 ☎ (0161) 480 3221
Robinsons 1892, Cumbria Way, Unicorn, seasonal beer Ⓗ

This three-roomed pub in the shadow of Stockport's famously impressive viaduct can be justly described as a community local in the town centre. The current licensee has been welcoming her locals, shoppers, office workers and visitors to the nearby Hat Works and Plaza Theatre alike into the pub for more than 25 years. The walls of the two comfortable lounges are adorned with numerous plates brought back by the regulars. To the rear is a games room. No lunches Sunday.
🕮◑⌺⬚≉♣⸏–꣒

Stockport: Edgeley

Armoury

31 Shaw Heath, SK3 8BD (on B5465, jct Greek St)
☼ 11-midnight (1am Fri & Sat) ☎ (0161) 477 3711
Robinsons 1892, Unicorn, seasonal beer Ⓗ
Comfortable, recently refurbished, multi-roomed local with a strong community involvement. It caters for a varied clientele from TV sports viewers to darts teams (with two leagues often playing on the same night) to quiet bookworms alike. Excellent well-priced food is available from a varied menu until 5pm, with efficient friendly service. There is a pleasant suntrap of a beer garden. Handy for the train station and football ground. A former CAMRA local branch Pub of the Year runner-up. **Q**🕮◑⌺♿≉♣⸏–꣒(310,369)

Olde Vic

1 Chatham Street, SK3 9ED (jct Shaw Heath)
☼ closed Mon; 5 (7 Sat)-late (last entry 10.50); 7-late (last entry 10.30) Sun ☎ (0161) 480 2410 ⊕ yeoldevic.com
Beer range varies Ⓗ
Once visited, never forgotten. This genuine local, containing a fascinating array of bric-a-brac and reading matter, hides behind an unkempt exterior. However a friendly and sometimes surprising welcome awaits. Landlord Steve will tease you given the chance, while you can be sure of a warm and cheerful greeting from Jo. Four handpumps dispense a changing variety from micros far and near, building on the Olde Vic's reputation as Stockport's first pub to offer a continuous rotation.
🛏🕮≉♣♥⸏–꣒(310,369)

Stockport: Heaton Norris

Magnet

51 Wellington Road North, SK4 1HJ (jct Duke St)
☼ 4 (12 Fri-Sun)-11 ☎ (0161) 429 6287
⊕ themagnetfreehouse.co.uk
Beer range varies Ⓗ
Within two years of being rescued from failure, the rejuvenated Magnet won acclaim as both CAMRA regional and local Pub of the Year 2011. The bar boasts 14 handpumps for beers sourced from all over the UK plus a draught cider. There is a bustling vault to the left, leading to a lower pool room, and a series of rooms separated by arched magnet doorways on the right. There is an upstairs beer terrace and function room, which are popular, as are the Monday cheese nights.
🛏Q🕮⌺♣♥P⸏–꣒(22,192)

Railway

74-76 Wellington Road North, SK4 1HF (jct Georges Rd)
☼ 12-midnight ☎ (0161) 477 3680
Holt Bitter; guest beers Ⓗ
A friendly pub with two lounges to the front, one with a feature fireplace with photos of old Stockport, the other more contemporary in decor with a raised stage area. A popular venue on the local darts league circuit, the games room houses a pool table and dartboard. Live music includes open-mic nights and jazz on a Sunday evening. This former CAMRA branch Pub of the Year serves four guest ales, often from local microbreweries, alongside the permanent Holt Bitter.
🕮⌺♣⸏–꣒(22,192)

Stockport: Portwood

Railway

1 Avenue Street, SK1 2BZ (jct Gt Portwood St A560)
☼ 12-11 (10.30 Sun) ☎ (0161) 429 6062
Outstanding Blond, seasonal beers; Pennine Floral Dance, Porter; Pictish Brewers Gold; guest beers Ⓗ
Bustling street-corner house with 15 handpumps showcasing the ranges of Pennine, Outstanding and Pictish breweries, plus guests. A changing mild and a real cider are also stocked, plus a selection of Belgian, German and other bottled beers. Occasional beer and cider festivals take place. Note the model railway atop the bar canopy, and the well-used bar billiards table. A development proposal that threatened the pub has now been dropped. A former local CAMRA Pub of the Year.
Q🕮♣♥⸏–꣒(325,330)

Strines

Sportsman

105 Strines Road, SK6 7GE (on B6101)
☼ 12-3, 5-11; 12-11 Sat & Sun ☎ (0161) 427 2888
⊕ the-sportsman-pub.co.uk
Beer range varies Ⓗ
Splendid white pub standing alone on the edge of the Goyt Valley, popular with local drinkers and diners. The comfortable lounge has large picture windows giving superb views over the wooded countryside, a monumental fireplace accommodates log fires in winter, and there is a separate taproom. Five guest beers, mainly from micros, are available and the landlord welcomes beer suggestions. Outside, a terrace and balcony are popular in summer and the pub is close to the Peak Forest Canal.
🛏🕮◑⌺♿▲≉♣P⸏–꣒(62,358)

Swinley

Fifteens Swinley

15 Upper Dicconson Street, WN1 2AD
☼ 12-11 (1am Fri & Sat) ☎ (01942) 820912
Beer range varies Ⓗ
Fifteens is a cosy pub spread over three levels with a pleasant drinking area outside at the front. It benefits from a homely environment and friendly, welcoming staff. The bar usually offers three real ales and a cider. The walls are decorated with memorabilia. With five comfortable rooms on offer, the pub makes an ideal base for anyone wanting to explore the area. 🚲♥

Swinton

Park Inn

135 Worsley Road, M27 5SP (on A572 just 200yds N of A580)

⏲ 11-11 ☎ (0161) 793 1568

Holt IPA, Bitter, seasonal beers [H]

A traditional local pub serving Holt ales since 1878. There is a vault to the left of the entrance where traditional pub games are enjoyed. To the right of the central bar is a lounge area and darts can be played here also. A small but cosy snug is to the rear, offering a quiet sanctuary without music or TV. Bitter is the most popular ale, but IPA, an occasional guest and seasonal ales are available too. Q⊟♿⇌♣⚐🚌

Uppermill

Cross Keys

off Running Hill Gate, OL3 6LW (off A670, up Church Rd)

⏲ 12-11.30 (midnight Fri & Sat) ☎ (01457) 874626

🌐 crosskeysuppermill.com

Lees Brewer's Dark, Bitter, seasonal beers [H]

Attractive 18th-century stone building with exposed beams throughout and a public bar featuring a stone-flagged floor. The pub is the centre for Mountain Rescue and the Saddleworth Runners. Folk nights take place on Wednesday and Sunday and annual events such as the Rushcart Festival and Wartime Weekend are popular. Home-cooked food features pies and puddings (food served all day Sat & Sun). Outside is a children's play area and covered, heated smoking area.
♨Q❀◑⊟P⚐

Waggon Inn

34 High Street, OL3 6HR

⏲ 11.30-11 (1am Fri & Sat); 11.45-11 Sun ☎ (01457) 872376

🌐 thewaggoninn.co.uk

Robinsons Unicorn, Dizzy Blond [H]**, Old Tom** [G]**, seasonal beer** [H]

Robinsons' pub in the centre of Uppermill featuring three beers from the Stockport brewery. Old Tom is served on gravity in December. Good-value home-cooked food includes senior specials and themed events (no eve meals Sun or Mon) – Thursday is steak night. There is a separate dining room, central bar, snug, lounge and pool/TV room. Annual events include the Whit Friday Brass Band Contest, Wartime Weekend and Rushcart Festival. Free Wi-Fi and high-quality B&B are available.
Q☋❀🛏◑▲⇌(Greenfield)♣P⚐🚌(184,350)

Urmston

Steamhouse

Station Road, M41 9SB

⏲ 12-11 (midnight Fri-Sun) ☎ (0161) 748 6487

🌐 thesteamhouse.co.uk

Beer range varies [H]

This multi-roomed pub is Urmston railway station's old waiting room and has retained a number of original features. The station itself is still operational so getting to and from here is very easy. The Sunday carvery (1-6pm) is very busy (advance booking required). There is an excellent choice of continental bottled beers and the cask ale range changes regularly, with Dunham Massey, Hydes, Thwaites, Hornbeam and Prospect among the brewers. Live music features on Thursday and Sunday, a quiz night on Monday and poker on Tuesday. ♨Q☋❀◑♿⇌♣P⚐🚌

Walkden

Bull's Head

12 High Street, M28 3NJ

⏲ 8am-midnight ☎ (0161) 702 5350

Greene King Abbot; Ruddles Best Bitter; guest beers [H]

This large pub reopened as a Wetherspoon outlet in 2012, and has gone from strength to strength. The spacious single-room interior has tables for dining and socialising, and a long bar with 10 handpumps in use. Real cider is available alongside the beers. The very large beer garden is excellent in summertime. Food is served all day, from 8am onwards. ♨Q☋❀◑♿⇌●⚐🚌

Wardley

Morning Star

520 Manchester Road, M27 9QW (opp Bagot St)

⏲ 12-11 (midnight Fri & Sat) ☎ (0161) 794 4927

Holt Mild, IPA, Bitter [H]

A smart red-brick Joseph Holt pub, built in its own grounds, set back from the main road. The front porch leads to a snug on the right and entry to the vault is to the left. Just beyond the snug are the central bar and a large, comfortable lounge. There is live entertainment on a Friday in this well-run community local.
❀⊟⇌(Moorside)♣P⚐🚌(36,37)

Westhoughton

Robert Shaw

34-40 Market Street, BL5 3AN (200yds from town hall)

⏲ 8-midnight (1am Fri & Sat) ☎ (01942) 844110

Greene King Abbot; Ruddles Best Bitter; guest beers [H]

Large open-plan public house, formerly the Co-op. It is named after the actor, who was born in Westhoughton. Wood panelling and bare brick dominate the decor in this modern Wetherspoon pub. Old photographs of the local Pretoria Pit Mine disaster that happened 100 years ago feature on the walls. The usual good-value Wetherspoon menu is served all day. The pub hosts four beer festivals a year. Q☋◑♿●P⚐🚌(540)

Whalley Range

Hillary Step [L]

199 Upper Chorlton Road, M16 0BH

⏲ 4-11.30; 3-12.30am Fri; 12-12.30am Sat; 12-11.30 Sun

☎ (0161) 881 1978 🌐 thehillarystep.co.uk

Beer range varies [H]

Modern bar in a small strip of shops and bars just north of Chorlton centre. Three handpumps are dedicated to Thwaites, Phoenix and Thornbridge breweries, with two more serving other guest ales. A good range of draught and bottled continental beers plus malt whiskies is also available. Cheese boards and charcuterie snacks are popular, with a large selection of other nibbles (olives, salami, nuts) also on offer. Live jazz plays on Sunday evening and a quiz is held on the first Tuesday of the month. Children are not permitted. ❀⊟♣⚐🚌

Wigan

Anvil [L]

Dorning Street, WN1 1ND (next to bus station)

⏲ 11-11 (10.30 Sun) ☎ (01942) 239444

AllGates Mild; Hydes Bitter; guest beers Ⓗ
Popular town-centre pub close to the bus station, winner of many local CAMRA awards (see the certificate wall). Seven handpumps dispense a selection of AllGates beers plus guests. A regular mild and a traditional cider as well as a range of continental draught and bottled beers are also available. Sport is shown on two TV screens. Outside is a covered, heated smoking shelter and drinking area. 🐾≈(Wallgate/N Western)●ⁱ-�

Berkeley ♈ Ⓛ
27-29 Wallgate, WN1 1LD
❂ 11.30-11 (midnight Fri & Sat); 12-10.30 Sun
☎ (01942) 242041
Beer range varies Ⓗ
The Berkeley is a former coaching house opposite Wallgate rail station and three minutes from Wigan North Western. The large bar hosts a range of rotating guests and food is served daily until 7pm. Watch your favourite sporting event on one of the eight large flat-screen TVs and the massive projector screen. A first-floor function room is available for hire. ◑≈(Wallgate/N Western)��

Boulevard
Wallgate, WN1 1LD
❂ 4-2am (2.30am Fri & Sat); 4-midnight Sun
☎ (01942) 497165 ⊕ boulevard-wigan.co.uk
Moorhouse's Pie Maker; guest beers Ⓗ
It is easy to miss the entrance to this surprisingly spacious basement pub. A long flight of stairs leads you down to the bar room which has a TV for sporting events, gaming machines and a jukebox. From the bar you enter a large back room where regular live music is played. Local beers and a cider are available. ≈(Wallgate/North Western)♣●🚍

Brocket Arms Ⓛ
Mesnes Road, Swinley, WN1 2DD
❂ 7am-midnight (1am Fri & Sat) ☎ (01942) 403500
Greene King Abbot; Marston's Pedigree; Ruddles County; guest beers Ⓗ
This pub is in a residential area a 15-minute walk from the town centre. The interior is large and open plan with two bars. Two conference rooms are available for private hire. Guest beers always feature. In addition to the usual Wetherspoon menu, the Sunday carvery is popular. There is a patio area to the front with benches and cover for smokers. Fundraising events are held for various charities. ➳🌂◑&●P-🚍

Royal Oak Ⓛ
Standishgate, WN1 1XL (on A49 N of town centre)
❂ 4 (12 Sun)-midnight; 12-1am Fri & Sat ☎ (01942) 323137
Beer range varies Ⓗ
Built in the early 17th century and close to Wigan centre on the A49, the Grade II-listed Royal Oak has always been a landmark pub on the Wigan Lane crawl. The multi-room interior is served by a long bar stocking an excellent range of real ales, plus foreign draught and bottled beers. Live music and food festivals are hosted. The pleasant beer garden is ideal in summer. 🌂&ⁱ-

Standish Unity Club Ⓛ
Cross Street, Standish, WN6 0HQ (opp library)
❂ 7.30-11 (midnight Fri & Sat) ☎ (01257) 424007
⊕ standishunityclub.com

Prospect Unity Gold; guest beers Ⓗ
Established for 12 years, this is an independent, non-profit-making club open to all. It has a comfortably furnished bar and function room with a separate pool/snooker room. It is also a music venue and available for private functions. There are quiz nights and the club has its own pool team. Prospect Unity Gold is a permanent beer, with many local breweries also showcased. The club hosts its own beer festival annually and CAMRA members are welcome at all times. Local CAMRA Club of the Year 2011. Q🌂&P🚍(113,362)

Woodford

Davenport Arms (Thief's Neck)
550 Chester Road, SK7 1PS (on A5102, jct Church La)
❂ 11-11; 12-10.30 Sun ☎ (0161) 439 2435
Robinsons 1892, Unicorn Ⓗ, **Old Tom** Ⓟ, **seasonal beer** Ⓗ
The Thief's Neck has long had a reputation for serving Robinsons' ales in peak condition. It has been run by the same family for 81 years – this is its 27th consecutive Guide listing. There is a traditional vault to the left where the furniture remains unchanged in 60 years, and a cosy snug to the right where children are permitted at lunchtime. The main bar and lounge are warmly welcoming. Excellent home-made lunches are served until 2.30pm (3pm Sat & Sun). 🏚Q🌂🍴◑Ḡ&♣P-🚍(X57,157)

Worsley

Bridgewater Hotel
23 Barton Road, M28 2PD (on B5211, 200yds S of M60 jct 13)
❂ 11-11 ☎ (0161) 794 6206
Greene King IPA; guest beers Ⓗ
This is where the Industrial Revolution really started. It is just across from the world's first commercial canal basin, first underground canal complex – giving access to the eponymous Duke's coal mines – and the first packet boat service. Sadly, no ghosts of former miners or boatmen will be found in this busy 20th century mock-Tudor pub. Previously a Boddington's house, this pub makes full use of the SIBA Direct Delivery Scheme and offers up to six real ales. ➳◑&P-🚍(33,68)

Worthington

Crown Hotel Ⓛ
Platt Lane, WN1 2XF (off A5106 Chorley to Wigan)
❂ 12-11 (10.30 Sun) ☎ (08000) 686678
⊕ thecrownatworthington.co.uk
Beer range varies Ⓗ
Privately owned free house in a country location with 10 en-suite bedrooms and function rooms. High-quality, home-cooked food is served in the bar and conservatory restaurant, and outside on the decked sun terrace at the rear. Up to 10 ales are offered and two or three ciders, with up to 16 different beers weekly. The pub hosts a cider festival in August and beer festivals throughout the year. An extensive selection of bottled beers is also stocked. Winner of six CAMRA awards. Q🌂🌂🍴◑●P-🚍(640,641)

I never drink water. I'm afraid it will become habit-forming. **W C Fields**

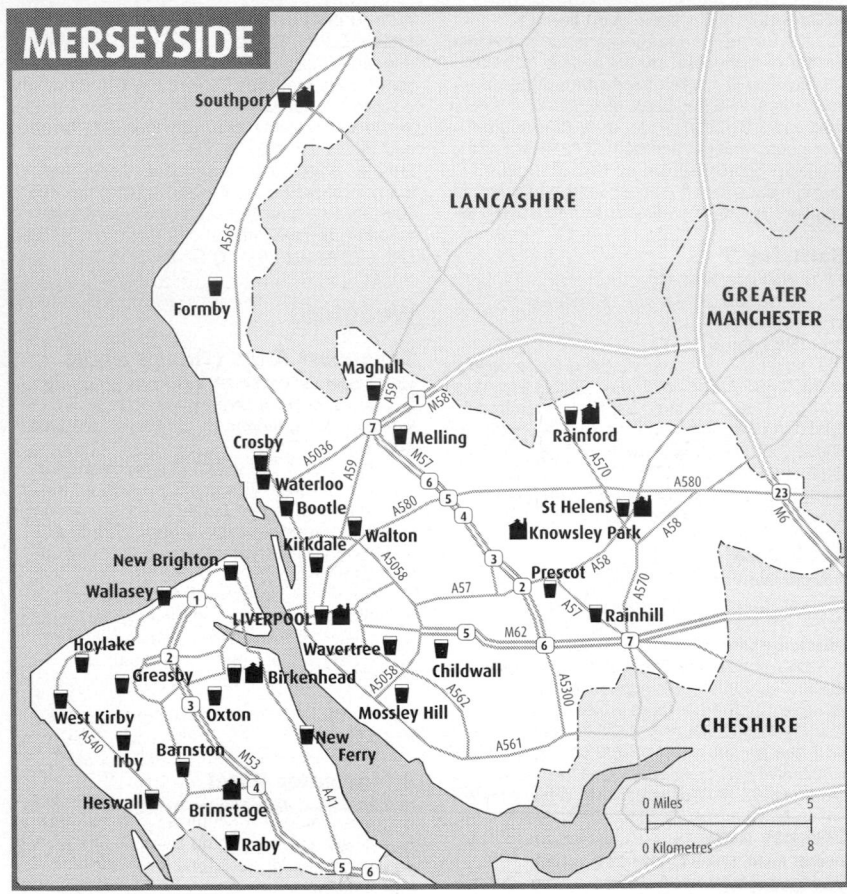

Barnston

Fox & Hounds L

107 Barnston Road, CH61 1BW (on A551)
⊕ 11-11; 12-10.30 Sun ☎ (0151) 648 7685
⊕ the-fox-hounds.co.uk
Brimstage Trappers Hat Bitter; Theakston Best Bitter, Old Peculier; guest beers Ⓗ
Village pub with bar, lounge and snug full of bric-a-brac, local photos and other memorabilia. The lounge, converted from tea rooms, is quiet with no music or games machines. The pub retains its original character including real fires in the bar and snug. The stone courtyard is a profusion of colour in the summer. Popular for its cask ales and real lunchtime food, it offers a fish dish of the day, daily specials and traditional Sunday roasts.
ᵐQこⓈ◑日と♣Pˡᵇ딜

Birkenhead

Gallaghers Pub & Barber's ☻ L

20 Chester Street, CH41 5DQ
⊕ 12-11.30 (midnight Fri-Sun) ☎ (0151) 649 9095
⊕ gallagherspubandbarbers.com
Brimstage Trappers Hat Bitter; guest beers Ⓗ
Genuine free house close to the famous Mersey ferries, resurrected after closure and refurbished in 2010 by a former Irish Guardsman as a unique pub and barber's shop. Six handpumps offer guest

beers, often from Rat, Salopian and Hawkshead, plus a real cider and perry in summer. A fascinating range of memorabilia includes military hats, photographs and a collection of Mersey shipping images. CAMRA Merseyside Pub of the Year 2011 and 2012. May close on Monday in winter.
✿₹(Hamilton Sq)●ˡ딜

Bootle

Merton Inn L

42 Merton Road, L20 3BW
⊕ 8am-midnight (1am Fri & Sat) ☎ (0151) 934 7790
Beer range varies Ⓗ

INDEPENDENT BREWERIES

Brimstage Brimstage
Evening Star St Helens (NEW)
George Wright Rainford
Liverpool Craft Liverpool
Liverpool One Liverpool
Liverpool Organic Liverpool
Mad Hatter Liverpool (NEW)
Melwood Knowsley Park (NEW)
Peerless Birkenhead
Southport Southport
Stamps Liverpool (NEW)
Wapping Liverpool

The Merton Inn was formerly two villas, combined to become a hotel in the 1930s. Used as a hospital during World War II, it was converted to a pub in the 1970s. This spacious multi-level venue, with wood panelling and subdued lighting, retains some of the character of its villa origins. The pub also boasts some specially commissioned abstract paintings depicting the local landscape. Up to 10 handpumps are available, often dispensing local and regional beers. ᏰᏪᴅᏦ(Oriel Rd)

Childwall

Childwall Fiveways Ⓛ
179 Queens Drive, L15 6XS
✪ 8-11.30 ☎ (0151) 738 2100
Greene King Abbot; guest beers Ⓗ
A former Higsons tied house, this large single-roomed pub opened as a Wetherspoon in 2010. Located in a leafy suburb, it has good motorway and public transport links. The refurbished interior is decorated with wood panelling, and outside there is a beer garden. A popular establishment, it can get busy, especially at weekends.
ᏰᏪᏅᏦP᛫ᗺ(79,81)

Crosby

Stamps Bar Ⓛ
5 Crown Buildings, L23 5SR
✪ 12-11 (midnight Fri & Sat) ☎ (0151) 286 2662
Beer range varies Ⓗ
'Real ale, real food, real music' is the Stamps motto and a visit will not disappoint. Five beers are available with local brewers well represented. One handpump offers real cider. Home-produced food is available Thursday to Saturday until early evening. Local musicians play live on Friday to Sunday. There is a quieter upstairs lounge area away from the bustle of the main bar. Free internet access and Wi-Fi is available. CAMRA members receive a 10 per cent discount on all Stamps Brewery beers. Ꮹ♨ᗺ

Formby

Freshfield Hotel ♟ Ⓛ
1a Massams Lane, Freshfield, L37 7EU
✪ 11-11 (midnight Fri & Sat) ☎ (01704) 874871
Greene King IPA, Abbot; Morland Original; Ruddles County Ⓗ
Following refurbishment the pub has increased its range of beers to 14. Due to a CAMRA-led campaign the extended bar area was retained, even though the refurbishment had been driven by a food-based agenda. The enlightened licensees have maintained the pub's usual consistency in beer quality and range, with Liverpool Organic beers featuring regularly. This dog-friendly pub set in a residential area has maintained its community focus, and is an example of how a Greene King pub should operate. ᎷᏪᏅᏦ(Freshfield)♣♨P᛫ᗺ(162,165)

Greasby

Coach & Horses
Greasby Road, CH49 3NG
✪ 11.30-11 (midnight Fri & Sat); 12-11 Sun
☎ (0151) 677 1656
Taylor Landlord Ⓗ

Charming whitewashed traditional street corner local dating back nearly 300 years. It became a pub in 1832 but was formerly a farmhouse where ale was brewed and sold from 1725. Two main rooms with matching snugs lie either side of the compact bar. A good selection of whiskies is stocked. Ex-Tranmere Rovers footballer Barrie Mitchell is an amiable licensee and football memorabilia adorn the wall of one of the snugs. Q♨ᏅᏦ♣P᛫ᗺ(437)

Greave Dunning
73 Greasby Road, CH49 3NF
✪ 11.30-midnight ☎ (0151) 606 1061
Greene King IPA; Liverpool Organic 24 Carat; Thwaites Wainwright; guest beers Ⓗ
Large and attractively decorated in a modern style but with comforts such as gas fires during the colder months, the pub maintains a comfortable, warm and welcoming feel. This Ember Inn has done much for the community, providing five handpumps offering three regular and two guest beers. Good food and a wonderful garden area attract visitors in summer. The pub is often busy at weekends. ᏰᏪᏪᏅᏦP᛫ᗺ(437)

Irby Mill
Mill Lane, CH49 3NT (on roundabout between Greasby and Irby)
✪ 12-11 (midnight Fri & Sat) ☎ (0151) 694 0194
⊕ irbymill.co.uk
Greene King Abbot; Wells Bombardier; guest beers Ⓗ
Formerly Lumsdens Café, the pub sits on the site of a former mill. With its thick sandstone walls and low beams, it transports you back to the good old days of country pubs. It has a small, L-shaped, stone-floored bar and a lounge used mainly by diners – the pub has an excellent reputation for home-made food. Passing hikers from the nearby Royden Park and Thurstaston Common and visiting CAMRA parties add to a strong local following. ᎷQ♨ᏪᏅᏦP᛫ᗺ

Heswall

Dee View Inn Ⓛ
Dee View Road, CH60 0DH
✪ 12-midnight (11 Sun) ☎ (0151) 342 2320
Brimstage Trappers Hat Bitter; Fuller's London Pride; Taylor Landlord; Wells Bombardier; guest beers Ⓗ
Homely, traditional local built in the late 1800s offering a warm welcome. Redecorated in 2008, it has retained its character and friendly atmosphere. It sits on a hairpin bend by the war memorial and famous mirror, with views over the Dee Estuary and close to the Wirral Way path. A popular and entertaining quiz night is held on Tuesday and live music is a frequent attraction. Traditional home-cooked food is served and children are welcome if dining. Ꮹ♣P᛫ᗺ

Hoylake

Ship Inn Ⓛ
Market Street, CH47 3BB
✪ 12-11.30 (12.30am Fri & Sat) ☎ (0151) 632 4319
Brimstage Trappers Hat Bitter; Caledonian Deuchars IPA; Greene King Abbot; Wells Bombardier; guest beer Ⓗ
Popular town-centre pub, first licensed in 1754 (recent testing has dated the building to 1730). Although modernised in recent years, with a single L-shaped bar area, old beams have been retained

in the back lounge. Good-value bar meals are served every lunchtime and weekday evenings. The large, secluded garden has a pond. ❀◗⇌P🖫

Irby

Shippons
6 Thingwall Road, CH61 3UA
❀ 12-11.30 (12.30am Fri & Sat) ☎ (0151) 648 0449
Thwaites Nutty Black, Original, Wainwright, Lancaster Bomber; guest beers Ⓗ
A welcoming focal point for the community, this sandstone village pub was converted from old farm buildings. With up to seven quality real ales, including a mild and frequently a porter or stout, a range of beer styles is guaranteed. A good choice of interesting guests comes from the Thwaite's beer club. The sheltered garden is a suntrap in summer, an ideal spot to relax and enjoy a few pints. Live music and sport on TV add to the enjoyment. ⅏❀◗⅃&P⅃⇌🖫(71)

Kirkdale

Thomas Frost Ⓛ
177-187 Walton Road, L4 4AJ
❀ 8-11.30 ☎ (0151) 207 8210
Greene King Abbot; guest beers Ⓗ
Formerly the Thomas Frost Drapery Store (1885), this Wetherspoon pub occupies the ground floor of a Grade II-listed building. The pub is near both Everton and Liverpool grounds and gets very busy on match days. It has a spacious open-plan layout with a large family area. Food is served 8am-10pm. ◗⇌🖫(20,21)

Liverpool: City Centre

Augustus John Ⓛ
Peach Street, L3 5TX (off Brownlow Hill)
❀ 11.30 (12 Sat)-1, 2-11; closed Sun ☎ (0151) 794 5507
Tetley Bitter; guest beers Ⓗ
Opened in 1901 and run by the University of Liverpool, the Augustus John is an open-plan pub popular with students, lecturers and locals. Up to four guest beers are available. A number of ciders are also on offer, and the pub was named local CAMRA Cider Pub of the Year 2011 and regional winner 2013. Pizza is served at all times, sport is shown and there is also a jukebox. Closed over Christmas and the New Year. ◗❀🖫

Baltic Fleet Ⓛ
33 Wapping, L1 8DQ
❀ 12-11 (midnight Fri & Sat) ☎ (0151) 709 3116
⊕ balticfleetpubliverpool.com
Wapping Baltic Gold, Bow Sprit, Stout; guest beers Ⓗ
Located near the Albert Dock, Liverpool's only brewpub is in a Grade II-listed building based on the 'flat iron' principle, with interior decoration on a nautical theme. Six handpumps serve beer from the Wapping Brewery in the cellar plus occasional guests. Pies and home-cooked scouse are regularly available. Tunnels in the cellar have led to some speculation of a dark period in the pub's history involving smuggling and press gangs. ◗⇌(James St)❀🖫

Belvedere Ⓛ
8 Sugnall Street, L7 7EB (off Falkener St)
❀ 12-11 (10.30 Sun) ☎ (0151) 709 0303
Beer range varies Ⓗ

Hidden in the Georgian area of the inner city, this small two-roomed community pub is a free house serving four rotating beers usually from local microbreweries. Rescued in 2006 from closure for housing development, this Grade II-listed building retains many original fixtures and interesting etched glass features. Attracting a mixed local clientele, including thirsty members of the Royal Liverpool Philharmonic Orchestra, this is a pub that offers a warm welcome and good conversation. ᐧᐧQ❀🖫🖫

Bridewell Ⓛ
1 Campbell Square, L1 5FB
❀ 12-11 (midnight Fri & Sat) ☎ (0151) 709 7000
⊕ liverpoolonebridewell.com
Beer range varies Ⓗ
Grade II-listed building dating from the mid-19th century when it was a police bridewell. The original cells provide unusual seating areas. Changing beers from Liverpool One and Lancaster breweries are available, together with Lees The Governor. Three handpumps are in regular use, plus two more in busy periods, with a selection of continental bottled beers also on offer. An upstairs function room hosts music and cultural events and is available for hire. Food is served daily (not Mon). There is a small outdoor patio area at the front. Q◗❀⇌(Central)⅃🖫

Caledonia Ⓛ
22 Caledonia Street, L7 7DX (behind Philharmonic Hall)
❀ 12-midnight (1am Fri & Sat) ☎ (0151) 708 0235
Taylor Golden Best; guest beers Ⓗ
Situated in the Georgian quarter of the city, this street-corner pub, popular with students, comprises one room on two levels and a small function room upstairs. The enterprising licensee has developed a programme of live music events and on these occasions the pub, which can be a haven for quiet conversation in the day, buzzes with atmosphere. Food is served 5-9pm Monday-Friday and 12-6pm Saturday and Sunday, with vegetarians and vegans catered for. ◗🖫

Clove Hitch Ⓛ
23 Hope Street, L1 9BQ
❀ 11-11 (midnight Fri & Sat; 10 Sun) ☎ (0151) 709 6574
⊕ theclovehitch.com
Beer range varies Ⓗ
The ground floor restaurant has two handpumps and downstairs in the 23 Club basement bar (open daily from 4.30pm) there are four handpumps usually serving one or two real ales from Liverpool Craft Brewery plus foreign bottled beers and eight keg beers on taps at the back of bar. The restaurant offers good-value meals all day and has a pleasant garden area for drinks and food. Popular with theatregoers. ◗⇌(Central)

Crown Hotel ★
43 Lime Street, L1 1JQ
❀ 9-11 (midnight Fri & Sat); 10-midnight Sun
☎ (0151) 707 6027 ⊕ thecrownliverpool.co.uk
Greene King IPA; guest beers Ⓗ
Just a few seconds' walk from Lime Street station, this Grade II-listed building boasts an Art Nouveau-style interior with ornate plasterwork ceilings. Many of the original features are retained in the two downstairs rooms, including some impressive wood panelling and original push bells. There is also an ornate glass dome above the staircase. Food is served until 10pm including breakfast until

noon. The outside of the pub is adorned with a stucco Walkers Ales Warrington frieze.
🏠🍺◑🐾(Lime St)🚇(Lime St)●🍴🚐

Dispensary 𝕃
87 Renshaw Street, L1 2SP
✪ 12-11 (midnight Fri & Sat) ☎ (0151) 709 2160
Cains Bitter; George Wright Mild; guest beers Ⓗ
This lively local in the city is a haven for real ale drinkers of all ages. The licensee's impeccable attention to beer quality shines through, and there is an ever-changing and imaginative choice of local and other interesting microbrewery beers, offering a good range in terms of both style and strength. Mark's Mild is dedicated to a much-loved barman who passed away in 2012. The attractive bar area has Victorian features, and to the rear is a raised wood-panelled area. ⯮(Central)🚐

Excelsior
121-123 Dale Street, L2 2JH (close to Birkenhead Tunnel entrance)
✪ 12-11 ☎ (0151) 236 0079
Adnams Broadside; Caledonian Deuchars IPA; guest beers Ⓗ
Large corner pub adjacent to what were Higsons 1962 brewery offices. A tastefully decorated and comfortable pub, it appeals to both a business and leisure clientele. The main room has a three-sided bar and an attractive area at the rear that can be used for meetings and functions. Six handpumps offer four changing beers from regional breweries, and two permanent beers from Adnams and Caledonian. Food includes award-winning pies, traditional dishes and tasty snacks. Local football is shown on three screens. Live music plays on Saturday night. ☀◑🍴⯮(Moorfields)🚐

Fall Well 𝕃
St Johns Way, L1 1LS
✪ 8am-11.30 (midnight Fri & Sat) ☎ (0151) 705 2050
Greene King Abbot; Ruddles County; guest beers Ⓗ
Often referred to as the Pet Shop by those who can remember its former use, this Wetherspoon pub is situated in a pedestrianised shopping area handy for the Playhouse, Royal Court and bus stops. The Fall Well was once an important source of water for the area and fed the fountain and garden of William Roe, a merchant who gave his name to Roe Street. The well stood on the site of the neighbouring Royal Court.
🍺◑♿⯮(Lime Street)↳🚐

Fly in the Loaf
Hardman Street, L1 9AS
✪ 12-11 (midnight Fri & Sat) ☎ (0151) 708 0817
Okells Bitter; guest beers Ⓗ
A former bakery, the pub's name comes from the slogan 'no flies in the loaf'. Owned by Isle of Man brewer Okells, it serves four of its beers alongside a changing range of four guests, and a good selection of foreign beers. The spacious interior has interesting raised seating areas, some adorned with ecclesiastical fittings. The pub attracts a range of customers and good-quality food is served, with Sunday roasts especially popular. There is a function room upstairs. ◑♿⯮(Central)🚐(86)

Globe
17 Cases Street, L1 1HW (opp Central station)
✪ 11 (10 Sat)-11; 12-10.30 Sun ☎ (0151) 707 0067
Black Sheep Best Bitter; Robinsons Unicorn; Sharp's Doom Bar; guest beers Ⓗ

This cosy two-roomed city centre pub won the local CAMRA branch's Community Pub award in 2012. Recently tastefully refurbished, its traditional, lively, conversational atmosphere remains unspoilt and it attracts regulars from across the city, as well as visitors. Photographs and newspaper articles lend insight into the pub's history and past local characters. A brass plaque in the back room commemorates the inaugural meeting of Merseyside CAMRA, held in 1974. Watch out for the sloping floor in the bar area. ⯮(Central)🚐

Grapes 𝕃
60 Roscoe Street, L1 9DW
✪ 12-1, 2-1am (2am Thu-Sat) ☎ (0151) 709 3977
⊕ thegrapesliverpool.co.uk
Caledonian Deuchars IPA; Jennings Cumberland Ale; guest beers Ⓗ
This corner local dates back to 1804 and has the original Mellors signage outside. Many of the nine handpumped beers are from local microbreweries such as Liverpool Organic and Liverpool Craft. There is a cosy beer garden at the rear popular with smokers. Live jazz plays every Sunday night from 9pm. ☀🍴⯮(Central)🚇↳🚐(82,84,C1)

Hub 𝕃
12 Hanover Street, L1 1AA
✪ 10-11 (midnight Thu); 9-midnight Fri & Sat
☎ (0151) 709 2410 ⊕ thehub-liverpool.com
Lancaster Amber; Liverpool Organic 24 Carat; guest beer Ⓗ
Serving interesting European-style food and good real ales, this Grade II-listed ale house and kitchen occupies the Casartelli Building, built in 1760. Initially an Italian family-run scientific manufacturing business, it was latterly a wine warehouse. A period of decay led to dismantling in 2001. A campaign to Stop the Rot led to reconstruction using as many original materials as possible. The house beer is Liverpool Organic 24 Carat and a rotating Lancaster Brewery beer is also offered. ◑⯮(Lime Street)🚇(Central)🚐(1)

Lady of Mann
19 Dale Street, L2 2EZ (behind Thomas Rigby's)
✪ 12-11 (7 Sun) ☎ (0151) 236 5556
Okells Bitter; guest beers Ⓗ
The Lady of Mann adjoins Thomas Rigby's and the two share a courtyard for open-air drinking. Named after the eponymous Manx ferry, this is an open-plan pub where exposed beams and woodwork lend an almost rustic feel. Owned by the Isle of Man brewery Okells, three handpumps dispense Okells Bitter and two guests. Cold food and snacks are served at all times and there is a large rear room that can be booked for events.
Q◑⯮(Moorfields)↳

Lime Kiln 𝕃
Fleet Street, L1 4NR
✪ 10-2am (1am Tue & Wed) ☎ (0151) 702 6810
Greene King Abbot; Ruddles County; guest beers Ⓗ
As a Lloyds No.1 bar, the decor and layout may not appear to offer much for the real ale drinker, but looks can be deceiving. Thanks to significant commitment by management, real ale is well catered for with at least one local beer usually available. Situated in the trendy Concert Square area, the bar is a peaceful haven during the day. A Victorian warehouse, home to manufacturing chemists, occupied this site from the early 1900s to the 1950s. 🍺◑♿⯮(Central)🚇(Central)↳🚐

Lion Tavern ★ Ⓛ

67 Moorfields, L2 2BP
☼ 11 (12 Sun)-midnight ☎ (0151) 236 1734
⊕ liontavern.com
Caledonian Deuchars IPA; Young's Bitter; guest beers Ⓗ
Named after the locomotive that worked the Liverpool to Manchester railway, the Lion features exquisite artwork plus intricately etched and stained glass that bear testimony to its Grade II-listed status. Regular society meetings and occasional Meet the Brewer events take place. Lunchtime food is served and speciality pork pies are available at all times. The house beer, brewed by George Wright, is called The Lion Returns, and the real cider comes from Westons.
⇌(Moorfields)●➡

Peter Kavanagh's ★

2-6 Egerton Street, L8 7LY (off Catherine St)
☼ 12-midnight (1am Fri & Sat) ☎ (0151) 709 3443
Greene King Abbot; guests beers Ⓗ
A splendid back-street local, this gem is situated in the Georgian area of Liverpool and has been identified by CAMRA as one of Britain's Best Real Heritage Pubs. Murals by Eric Robinson adorn the walls, thought to have been commissioned to cover a debt. There are fine stained glass windows with wooden shutters and two snugs with wooden benches – note the carved armrests, allegedly caricatures of the politically incorrect Peter Kavanagh. Up to four rotating guest beers are available. ▲Q◖➡(86)

Philharmonic ★

36 Hope Street, L1 9BX
☼ 11-midnight ☎ (0151) 707 2837
Beer range varies Ⓗ
Part of the Nicholson's group, this magnificent Grade II-listed establishment with stained glass windows, wood panelling and stucco ceilings is popular with locals, students and tourists alike. Each of the ornate rooms has its own character; this is the most spectacular pub interior in England and has a rare mosaic bar counter front. Notable for its marvellous marble-tiled Gents, ladies are welcome to visit but it is polite to ask first.
◖●⇌(Central)➡(86)

Richard John Blackler Ⓛ

Units 1 & 2 Charlotte Row, L1 1HU
☼ 8am-midnight (11 Mon & Tue); 10-midnight Sun
☎ (0151) 709 4802
Greene King Abbot; Ruddles County; guest beers Ⓗ
This Wetherspoon establishment is the ground floor of the former Blacklers department store that opened in 1908 and finally shut in April 1988, where the Beatles' George Harrison served his electrician's apprenticeship. Close to the bus station, St John's Shopping Centre and Liverpool One, it is always busy, but a good place to take a break. The rocking horse is a replica of one ridden by children who visited the store. The original is at Liverpool's Alder Hey Children's Hospital.
➠◖Å⇌(Central)➡

Richmond Hotel Ⓛ

32 Williamson Street, L1 1EB
☼ 10-11; 11-midnight Fri-Sun ☎ (0151) 709 2614
Southport Golden Sands; guest beers Ⓗ
Lively family-run pub in a pedestrianised shopping area, offering up to three guest ales from local and regional breweries. Formally a Bass house, the original Bass mirror remains. More than 50 malt whiskies are usually available, and there are occasional beer festivals and Meet the Brewer events. Sports fixtures are shown on TV. The pub sign, simply saying 'Richmond Pub', depicts World War II veteran Paddy Golden, a much-missed regular and one of the first to land on the Normandy beaches. Å⇌(Central)⸦➡

Roscoe Head Ⓛ

24 Roscoe Street, L1 2SX
☼ 11.30 (12 Sun)-midnight ☎ (0151) 709 4365
Jennings Cumberland Ale; Tetley Bitter; guest beers Ⓗ
One of the Magnificent Seven pubs that have been in every edition of the Guide, and local CAMRA Pub of the Year in 2012. This is a cosy four-roomed pub where conversation and the appreciation of real ale rule. Run by members of the same family for over 30 years, the name commemorates William Roscoe, a leading campaigner against the slave trade. Six handpumps feature two regular beers plus four changing guests, mostly from microbreweries. Food is served Monday to Friday lunchtimes. Q◖⇌(Central)♣➡

Swan

86 Wood Street, L1 4DQ
☼ 12-11 (2am Thu-Sat); 1-10.30 Sun ☎ (0151) 709 5081
Hydes Original; guest beers Ⓗ
Famous for its rock jukebox, the Swan, with its distinctive blue-tiled façade and stained glass windows, has changed little over the years. The walls are adorned with various pieces of artwork depicting swans and there is a striking and unusual mural on the stairs leading to the loos. Eight handpumps serve a selection of beer from national and microbreweries as well as Rosie's Triple D cider. The seating is a combination of wooden pews and traditional bar stools, and the back room is lit with red lightbulbs. ⇌(Central)●

Thomas Rigby's

23-25 Dale Street, L2 2EZ
☼ 11.30-11 (10.30 Sun) ☎ (0151) 236 3269
Okells Bitter, Olaf, Dr Okell's IPA; guest beers Ⓗ
This multi-roomed, Grade II-listed building, bearing the name of wine and spirit dealer Thomas Rigby, now supplies an extensive world beer range on draught and in bottles. Three ales on handpump come from the pub's owners Okells, another three are regularly changing guests. Good-value food is served until early evening, including specials, with one room providing a friendly and efficient table service. There is a courtyard for outdoor drinking. ◖●⇌(Moorfields)

Vernon Arms Ⓛ

69 Dale Street, L2 2HJ
☼ 11.45-11.30 (12.30am Fri & Sat) ☎ (0151) 236 6132
⊕ vernonarms.co.uk
Boggart Hole Clough Rum Porter; Brains The Rev James Ⓗ
Situated close to the business district, the Vernon retains the feel of a street-corner local. The single long-roomed bar serves three drinking areas including a back room with frosted glass windows advertising the Liverpool Brewing Company that used to serve the pub. The main bar has wood panelling, several large columns and a small snug area. The regular Boggart Rum Porter is popular with many and real cider on handpull is unusual for the city centre. ◖⇌(Moorfields)●➡

Victoria Cross ⓛ
1-3 Sir Thomas Street, L1 6BW
✪ 11-11 (midnight Sat) ☎ (0151) 277 2265
Beer range varies 🅷
As the name suggests, the theme of this corner pub is the highest military decoration awarded for valour in the face of the enemy, and the pub displays a commemorative board celebrating the achievements of those bestowed with the honour from Liverpool regiments. The bar room offers some very comfortable leather seating which is at a premium during busy evenings, especially if there is a live match on. The management prides itself on ensuring there is at least one local beer available. ⇌(Moorfields)🖼

Welkin ⓛ
7 Whitechapel, L1 6DS
✪ 8-11.15 (1am Fri & Sat) ☎ (0151) 243 1080
Greene King Abbot; Ruddles County; guest beers 🅷
Wetherspoon's Welkin is situated in the city centre, close to the popular Cavern Walks. Very much a café/bar rather than a traditional pub, it has two rooms: one large and L-shaped on the ground floor, and a smaller room with a dining area upstairs. Often busy with shoppers, it has recently benefited from a refurbishment. The pub takes its name from the old English word for sky, and commemorates Jeremiah Horrocks, one of Liverpool's greatest sons and the father of English astronomy.
🌀🕒♿⇌(Moorfields)🛒🖼

White Star
2-4 Rainford Gardens, L2 6PT
✪ 11.30-11 ☎ (0151) 231 6861 ⊕ thewhitestar.co.uk
Caledonian Deuchars IPA; guest beers 🅷
This characterful two-roomed pub is a traditional gem, situated close to the lively Mathew Street area. Memorabilia adorn the walls including, unsurprisingly, pictures of White Star shipping liners and photographs of the Beatles. A favourite with Liverpool locals, and particularly popular when live football matches are shown, it also attracts visitors from many parts of the world and is twinned with bars in both the Czech Republic and Norway. Guest beers are often from Bowland microbrewery in Lancashire. Pork pies and cob sandwiches are available. ⇌(Moorfields)🖼

Maghull

Frank Hornby ⓛ
38 Eastway, L31 6BR
✪ 8am-11.30 (midnight Fri & Sat) ☎ (0151) 520 4010
Beer range varies 🅷
Opened in 2012, this Wetherspoon pub is named after local man Frank Hornby, famous inventor of the Hornby train set, and unsurprisingly some examples of his work can be found displayed in the pub. In a suburban street, there is a decked area for outside drinking, while inside is spacious and light. A changing selection of guest ales includes beers from local breweries. 🌀🕒🕞

Hare & Hounds
53 Liverpool Road North, L31 2HF
✪ 11.30-midnight ☎ (0151) 526 1447
Beer range varies 🅷
Part of the Ember Inns estate, the Hare & Hounds is a spacious open-plan establishment where the emphasis is largely on dining – food is served 11.30-10pm every day. However, there is plenty

for ale lovers with between five and 10 beers on handpump at any one time. You can order three thirds for the price of a pint, and Ember beer menus are readily available, with an emphasis on seasonal ales. 🌀🕞♿P

Melling

Bootle Arms
Rock Lane, L31 1EN
✪ 11.30 (12 Sun)-11 ☎ (0151) 526 2886
⊕ bootlearmspub.co.uk
Beer range varies 🅷
Stone-built village pub, extended over the years into the adjoining cottages, in the heart of Melling village. The emphasis is on food with a large area inside given over to a dining area on three levels, but visitors dropping in for a pint can find many comfortable places to sit and enjoy a drink. There is outdoor seating and a large children's play area. The pub is on bus routes 133 and 236 Monday-Saturday daytime. 🏚🌀🕞🕞♿P⌚🖼(133,236)

Mossley Hill

Pi ⓛ
106 Rose Lane, L18 8AG
✪ 11-11 (11.30 Fri & Sat) ☎ (0151) 222 0443
⊕ pi-roselane.co.uk
Tatton Blonde; guest beers 🅷
A café-style bar in premises that was previously a shop, near to Mossley Hill railway station. The guest beer range always includes a LocAle. The bar also has a number of foreign beers on tap and stocks dozens of bottled beers. A simple hot food menu – real pies with sides – is available all day. There are plans for an extension into the property next door. 🕞⇌♦🖼(61,80)

New Brighton

Magazine Hotel ⓛ
7 Magazine Brow, CH45 1HP (above Egremont Promenade)
✪ 12-11 (11.30 Fri & Sat) ☎ (0151) 630 3169
⊕ the-magazine-hotel.co.uk
Draught Bass; Liverpool Organic Josephine Butler; guest beers 🅷
This multi-roomed, low-beamed pub, dating from 1759, suffered from a fire in 2010 but has been restored without losing its unique character. Three rooms lead off the main central bar area. Overlooking Egremont Promenade, the pub has fine views of the River Mersey. Renowned for its Draught Bass, it also offers three guest ales usually including a beer from a local brewery. Good-value lunchtime bar meals are served.
🏚Q🌀♿🕞♣P⌚🖼

Queen's Royal ⓛ
Marine Promenade, CH45 2JT
✪ 10.30-11 (10.30 Sun) ☎ (0151) 691 0101
⊕ thequeensroyal.com
Brimstage Trappers Hat Bitter; Hawkshead Windermere Pale; guest beers 🅷
An airy, modern bar in an imposing Victorian building, close to the Floral Hall Theatre and overlooking Marine Promenade, Marine Lake and Fort Perch Rock. A strong supporter of local ales, among the favourites are beers from Brimstage and Weetwood. The drinking area outside affords superb views over Liverpool Bay. Good-value,

hearty meals are served in the bar; the adjoining restaurant offers excellent quality food including a popular Sunday carvery. ⊛☕◀🕽&⇌🚲‑🚃

Stanley's Cask
212 Rake Lane, CH45 1JP
🟢 11-midnight (11 Mon & Wed) ☎ (0151) 691 1093
Beer range varies Ⓗ
This ever-popular local continues to thrive, due in no small part to the landlady who has a track record of serving good beer. Up to four guest ales are offered, mainly from national and regional breweries. A traditional, single-roomed community local, it hosts various sports teams, quiz nights and regular live music. ⊛&♣‑🚃(410)

New Ferry

Freddie's Club Ⓛ
36 Stanley Road, CH62 5AS
🟢 7 (5 Fri & Sat; 12 Sun)-11
Brimstage Trappers Hat Bitter; guest beer Ⓗ
A popular social club, formerly a Conservative Club, situated in a residential street a short walk from New Ferry shopping centre. Now converted into a comfortable lounge bar with adjoining snooker room with two full-size tables, it has two handpumps serving mainly local beers and offers regular live entertainment. A former local CAMRA Club of the Year, show a current copy of the Guide or CAMRA membership card for entry.
&⇌(Bebington)♣P‑🚃(401)

John Masefield
70-72 New Chester Road, CH62 5AD
🟢 8-11 (11.30 Fri & Sat) ☎ (0151) 644 4250
Greene King Abbot; Ruddles Best Bitter; guest beers Ⓗ
Comfortable open-plan Wetherspoon pub in a former bicycle shop. Named after a former poet laureate with local links, controversy surrounded the opening when locals suggested that the portrait on the pub's sign looked more like Adolf Hitler – judge for yourself. Two banks of handpumps include beers from local microbreweries and further afield, and cask ale significantly outsells the other beers on the bar. The pub features Wetherspoon's meal deals, a Wednesday night quiz and regular vintage bus pub trips. ⊛◀🕽&⇌(Bebington)‑🚃(1,41,401)

Oxton

Cock & Pullet Ⓛ
100 Woodchurch Road, CH42 9LP
🟢 12-midnight (1am Fri & Sat) ☎ (0151) 652 5437
Beer range varies Ⓗ
Revitalised genuine locals' pub, formerly the Royal, situated in hillside residential streets where Birkenhead merges into Oxton. Decorated with photographs of old Wirral, the central bar serves the main room and adjoining games area. This is a welcome true free house with six rotating guest beers, often including local brews from Brimstage and Liverpool Organic. A popular pub with football fans visiting Tranmere Rovers, it screens live sport on TV and hosts regular quiz nights and live music on Sunday evenings. ♣♠‑🚃(83,495)

Prescot

Clock Face Ⓨ Ⓛ
Derby Street, L34 3LL
🟢 11-11; 12-10.30 Sun ☎ (0151) 292 4121
Thwaites Original, Lancaster Bomber, seasonal beers; guest beers Ⓗ
An imposing sandstone town house that was converted into a pub in the late 1970s. The drinking area is divided into three comfortable areas with a real fire in the main lounge. The beers comes from the Thwaite's range, usually including three seasonal specials as well as two regular beers. Excellent home-cooked food is served offering good value for money. ♨Q◀🕽P🚃(10,10A)

Raby

Wheatsheaf Inn Ⓛ
Raby Mere Road, CH63 4JH SJ311798
🟢 11.30-11 (midnight Fri & Sat); 12-10.30 Sun
☎ (0151) 336 3416 ⊕ wheatsheaf-cowshed.co.uk
Brimstage Trappers Hat Bitter; Taylor Landlord; Tetley Bitter; Thwaites Original, Wainwright; guest beers Ⓗ
An inn for 350 years, this is Wirral's oldest pub. The thatched building was rebuilt following a fire in 1611 and is reputed to be haunted by Charlotte, who died here. The walls are decorated with old photographs of Raby. The bar has nine handpumps serving two rooms and a restaurant in a converted cowshed. Four guest beers are often from local breweries. Food is served in the bar until 5pm and in the restaurant every evening except Sunday and Monday. ♨Q✿⊛◀&P‑🚃(85)

Rainford

Star Inn Ⓛ
Church Road, WA11 8PX
🟢 11-11; 12-10.30 Sun ☎ (01744) 882639
Coach House Postlethwaite; guest beers Ⓗ
Comfortable pub towards the edge of the village of Rainford. It has a cosy lounge and a restaurant to the rear. Beers are sourced from local microbreweries, always including a dark brew. Meals are served Wednesday to Sunday. ✿⊛◀🕽P‑🚃

Rainhill

Ship Inn Ⓛ
804 Warrington Road, L35 6PE (on A57, 400yds W of jct 7 M62)
🟢 12-11 (10.30 Sun) ☎ (0151) 426 4165
Beer range varies Ⓗ
Large 1930s roadhouse in a semi-rural location. There is a small, quiet front bar and a large rear lounge featuring live sport on TV and occasional live bands and charity nights. Four handpumps offer beers from microbreweries. A large restaurant serves both locals and the lodge behind the pub. There are outside drinking areas to the front and rear. The pub is dog-friendly away from dining areas. Free Wi-Fi is available.
♨⊛☕◀🕽 ⊟&P‑🚃(61,137,138)

St Helens

Counting House Ⓛ
Hardshaw Street, WA10 1RE
🟢 11-11; 12-10.30 Sun ☎ (01744) 739562

George Wright Bank Job; Moorhouse's Saints Not Sinners; guest beers Ⓗ
This large, imposing pub was once the town's NatWest Bank. It boasts three pool tables and a large screen showing sporting events. Quiet during the day, it is livelier in the evening and attracts a younger clientele. The number of handpumps has recently increased to eight, featuring local microbreweries and a real cider. ◐&♣♠'–☱

Duke of Cambridge
Duke Street, WA10 2JE
✪ 11-11 (1am Fri & Sat); 12-11 Sun ☎ (01744) 733340
Moorhouse's Blond Witch; guest beers Ⓗ
A small local pub on the edge of the town centre, the Duke of Cambridge is a welcome real ale outlet among the many keg-only bars on Duke Street. Two handpulls feature a Moorhouse's beer and guest ales often from local micros. Entertainment is high on the list of attractions, with live bands at the weekend and a jam night on Wednesday. CAMRA branch Pub of the Year 2012. ☱

Phoenix Hotel Ⓛ
34 Canal Street, WA10 3LL
✪ 2-11; 12-1am Fri & Sat; 12-midnight Sun
☎ (01744) 751890
Beer range varies Ⓗ
Built in 1903, the pub has its name in mosaic tiles on an outer wall, and a mosaic tile floor. A community local, it offers up to six beers mostly from local microbreweries. The small bar is home to pool, darts and dominoes, and the spacious lounge is comfortable. Sky Sports is shown on numerous TVs. Music dominates, with karaoke on Friday nights and live Irish bands on Saturdays. A yard at the back has been converted into a heated smoking area. ❀🏠&♣♠'–

Sportsman's Inn Ⓛ
Duke Street, WA10 2JG
✪ 5-11; 2-midnight Sat; 12-10.30 Sun ☎ (01744) 738838
Marston's Pedigree; Wells Bombardier; guest beers Ⓗ
Friendly town-centre venue with pictures of St Helens RFC on the wall reflecting the town's sporting heritage. The pub is divided into two areas, a public bar and a comfortable lounge. It has recently become free of tie and offers a growing range of cask beers. At the weekends the focus is on entertainment, in line with many of the other pubs on Duke Street. 🏠♣'–☱

Turk's Head Ⓛ
49-51 Morley Street, WA10 2DQ
✪ 2-11.30 (12.30am Fri); 12-12.30am Sat; 12-11.30 Sun
☎ (01744) 751289
Beer range varies Ⓗ
A short distance from town, this popular pub was a previous CAMRA National Pub of the Year runner-up. Half-timbered, with etched glass windows, it was built in the 1870s by Ellis Warde Brewery, and features a distinctive turret inset with the brewery logo. It offers a constantly changing beer range, with 12 handpulls in use over the weekend, six at other times. Draught and bottled continental beers are also stocked. Thursday is curry and jazz night, and on Tuesday night there is a free quiz. Darts and dominoes are played. 🅼🏠◐🍴🕭♣♠'–🍴☱

Southport

Barons Bar (Scarisbrick Hotel) Ⓛ
239 Lord Street, PR8 1NZ (on A565, opp A570 Eastbank St)
✪ 11-11 (midnight Fri & Sat); 12-midnight Sun
☎ (01704) 543000
Moorhouse's Pride of Pendle; Tetley Bitter, Flag & Turret; guest beers Ⓗ
Set within the Scarisbrick Hotel, the Britannia Hotels' No.1 real ale bar provides the best range of local beers in town. The 10 handpumps (one serving real cider) are well-priced and regularly feature beers from the Southport, George Wright, Moorhouse's and Copper Dragon breweries. SIBA formerly held its northern heats tasting panels at the venue, and mini-festivals are still occasionally held. Britannia is to be congratulated for retaining the bar's award-winning heritage. Q❀🏠&🕭♠P'–☱

Fishermen's Rest Ⓛ
2 Weld Road, Birkdale, PR8 2AZ
✪ 12-11 (midnight Fri & Sat) ☎ (01704) 569986
Caledonian Deuchars IPA; Theakston Best Bitter; Thwaites Wainwright; guest beers Ⓗ
The Fishermen's Rest gets its name from the infamous 'Mexico' disaster of 1886. The event is still commemorated every 10th December by crews from the local Southport Lifeboat station. The pub was originally part of the Palace Hotel and was renamed after the bodies of the brave sailors and lifeboat crews were laid out in the building. Home to two teams in the local Southport & Formby Quiz League, the pub is also close to the Sefton Coastal Footpath. 🏃❀◐&🕭(Birkdale)P'–☱(X2,49)

Guest House Ⓛ
16 Union Street, PR9 0QE
✪ 11.30-11 (11.30 Fri & Sat); 12-10.30 Sun
☎ (01704) 537660 ⊕ guesthouse-southport.blogspot.com
Adnams Southwold Bitter; Caledonian Deuchars IPA; Jennings Cumberland Ale; Ruddles Best Bitter; Theakston Mild, Best Bitter Ⓗ
Close to fashionable Lord Street, the pub boasts an impressive half-timbered Edwardian frontage and an unspoilt wood-panelled interior with three separate drinking areas. Southport Brewery beers are often sold, and a good range of malt whiskies is stocked. A Thursday quiz night and acoustic folk club on the first and third Monday evenings of the month attract a mixed clientele. Morris dancers perform on special occasions. There is outdoor seating to the front and a pleasant courtyard to the rear. Q❀◐🏠🕭'–☱

Inn Beer Shop Ⓛ
657 Lord Street, PR9 0AW (on A565, N end of Lord St)
✪ 11-10.30 ☎ (01704) 533054
Beer range varies Ⓗ
Friendly café bar offering a huge selection of local, national and foreign bottled beers for takeaway or consumption on the premises. The long interior is lined with bottles and continental-style seating, leading to a comfy snug area complete with games. The bar serves foreign lagers, a Southport Brewery beer and two real ciders. Snacks and a tea/coffee service with cakes are available throughout the day. Outside seating is on fashionable Lord Street. Dog-friendly, it can get busy at weekends. ❀🕭♣♠'–☱

Lakeside Inn

The Promenade, PR9 0EA (200yds from Lord St overlooking Marine Lake)

☼ 11-11; 12-10.30 Sun ☎ (01704) 530173

Fuller's London Pride; guest beers Ⓗ

The Lakeside once featured in the Guinness Book of World Records as Britain's smallest pub. Run by one of Southport's longest-serving landlords, it is exceptionally friendly and stars appearing at the nearby Southport Theatre and Conference Centre often pop in. Rowers practising on the marine lake behind the pub are also regulars. Several awards have been presented to the licensees including local CAMRA Pub of the Year. Q❀❄✦⊸🖨

Sir Henry Segrave Ⓛ

93-97 Lord Street, PR8 1RH (on A565, S end of Lord Street)

☼ 8am-midnight (1am Fri & Sat) ☎ (01704) 530217

Greene King Abbot; Moorhouse's Pendle Witches Brew; Phoenix Wobbly Henry; Ruddles Best Bitter; Thwaites Wainwright Ⓗ

Named after the former land speed world record holder who used to race on Southport flats, this is a spacious Wetherspoon pub with an attractive 19th-century exterior. The manager is a strong supporter of real ale and runs regular brewery and beer festival trips, and occasional Meet the Brewer evenings. The 12 handpumps offer the best all-round choice of microbrewery beers in Southport – regular orders are placed with Phoenix, Saltaire, Titanic and Hawkshead. There is outside seating on the famous Lord Street. ⏁❀◖&⇌✦⊸🖨

Volunteer Arms Ⓛ

57-59 Eastbank Street, PR8 1DY

☼ 11 (12 Sun)-midnight ☎ (01704) 543794

Thwaites Lancaster Bomber, Wainwright Ⓗ

A tidy refurbished Thwaite's pub just off Lord Street in the heart of town. Ably run by Alan and staff, the two Thwaite's beers are always in top condition. Despite its proximity to shopping areas, the Volunteer is very much a community pub. The atmosphere is always friendly, especially on singalong Sunday. Photographs of old Southport adorn the walls. Lunches are served daily, from light snacks to hearty meals. ❀◖⇌✦⊸🖨

Willow Grove

387-389 Lord Street, PR9 0AG

☼ 8am-midnight (1am Fri; 2am Sat) ☎ (01704) 517830

Greene King Abbot; Phoenix Wobbly Bob; Ruddles Best Bitter; guest beers Ⓗ

Lloyds No.1 bar situated on the town's famous Victorian Lord Street opposite the impressive 1920s war memorial. The large L-shaped interior leads to a brightly-lit bar, furnished with a mixture of tall buffet chairs, restaurant tables and comfy sofas. The manager is a keen supporter of real ale and the nine handpumps serve a good selection of microbrewery beers, both local and from further afield. The pub can get very busy on Friday and Saturday nights. ⏁❀◖&⇌✦⊸🖨

Zetland Hotel

53 Zetland Street, PR9 0RH

☼ 12-midnight (10.30 Sun) ☎ (01704) 808404

Jennings Cumberland Ale; guest beers Ⓗ

Situated in a residential area just 10 minutes from Lord Street, the Zetland is a community pub offering excellent-value home-cooked food in a friendly atmosphere. The pub has Sky Sports and ESPN, and supports many bowling competitions

with one of the finest crown green facilities in the north-west. A large pub with several side rooms, it can cater for parties of up to 100. 🏚❀◖◗❆⇌✦P⊸🖨

Wallasey

Cheshire Cheese Ⓛ

2 Wallasey Village, CH44 2DH

☼ 12-11 (midnight Fri & Sat) ☎ (0151) 638 3641

⊕ thecheesewallasey.com

Theakston Best Bitter; Wells Bombardier; guest beers Ⓗ

Friendly local, Wallasey's oldest licensed premises, with a separate bar, snug and lounge. Outside is a walled garden where regular beer festivals are held. The handpumps are located in the lounge, with guest beers usually including a local ale, often from Liverpool Organic Brewery. Excellent home-cooked meals are served until early evening (no food Thu). Quiz nights are Monday and Wednesday, and the pub hosts a golf society and football, darts and bowls teams. Q❀◖◗❆⇌(Village)✦⊸🖨

Walton

Raven Ⓛ

72-74 Walton Vale, L9 2BU

☼ 8-midnight (1am Fri & Sat) ☎ (0151) 524 1255

Greene King Abbot; Ruddles County; guest beers Ⓗ

This open-plan Wetherspoon pub is busy with a local crowd most days but particularly at weekends. It is themed on Edgar Allan Poe's The Raven after a local, James William Carling, produced illustrations for the famous poem in the late 19th century. Born in 1857, Carling became a pavement artist when just five years old; he later went to America and is buried in Walton Cemetery. Aintree, the home of the world-famous Grand National, is less than a mile away. Q⏁◖◗&⇌(Orrell Park)⊸

Waterloo

Old Bank Ⓛ

34 South Road, L22 5PE

☼ 11-11.30; 12-12.30am Fri & Sat ☎ (0151) 928 7020

⊕ theoldbankwaterloo.co.uk

Beer range varies Ⓗ

Four handpumps dispense a range of beers, both local and from across the North West. A quiet oasis on weekday afternoons, the pub is a hive of activity most evenings and weekends with a strong commitment to live music and football. Music memorabilia adorn the walls, and a book-swap library and games are available. A courtyard at the back provides an outdoor drinking area for warmer days, and the marina and beach are nearby. ❀🖂⊸🖨(53)

Queen's Picture House Ⓛ

47-79 South Road, L22 5PE

☼ 9-11 (11.30 Fri & Sat) ☎ (0151) 949 2070

Greene King Abbot; Ruddles Best Bitter; guest beers Ⓗ

The pub takes its name from a cinema that once stood on the site, although the current building is a converted furniture store. The bright and functional main room and bar area are furnished with high tables and chairs, with some lower seating around the edge of the room and sofas close to the fireplace. To the right is a long room ideal for dining. The decor reflects the site's former use as a cinema, but also pays homage to local shipping and aviation links. ♿✿❶❹⌖✿ℓ–🍴(53,53A,133)

Stamps Too ⑨ ℒ
99 South Road, L22 0LR (opp Waterloo Station)
✪ 12-11 (11.45 Fri & Sat) ☎ (0151) 280 0035
Beer range varies Ⓗ
In this friendly, continental-style bar its six handpumps still dispense 90 per cent LocAle. The beers are largely from Liverpool Organic, Southport, Brimstage and AllGates, with a smattering of visitors from further afield. The walls are adorned with pump clips from beers that have come and gone. With café-style seating at the front, this one-room establishment is a popular live music and comedy venue. Lively banter can often be heard at the bar. Local CAMRA branch Pub of the Year.
♿⌖🍴(53)

Wavertree

Edinburgh
4 Sandown Lane, L15 8HY
✪ 2 (12 Fri-Sun)-midnight ☎ (0151) 733 3533
Beer range varies Ⓗ

A cosy Cain's pub at the end of a Victorian terrace with a small bar area and a separate 'front room'. The cask beer range usually includes local brews and beers from other small breweries, but not usually from the pub's owner. The Irish music night on Monday is popular and there is a Tuesday quiz.
✿⌖♣ℓ–🍴

West Kirby

White Lion
51 Grange Road, CH48 4EE
✪ 12-11 (10.30 Sun) ☎ (0151) 625 9037
Black Sheep Best Bitter; Courage Best Bitter; guest beers Ⓗ
Traditional local free house in a 200-year-old sandstone building close to West Kirby centre. The White Lion is a five-minute walk from fine views of the Welsh hills, and Marine Lake, the Promenade and beach are also within easy walking distance. The pub is a warm, welcoming retreat, especially in the colder months with a real fire by the bar – perfect after that Wirral Way ramble. An ever-changing range of guest beers is on offer. Quiz night is Monday. No food on Sunday.
🏚Q✿❶⌖ℓ–🍴(22,437)

Roscoe Head, Liverpool (Photo: Adrian Tierney-Jones)

NORFOLK

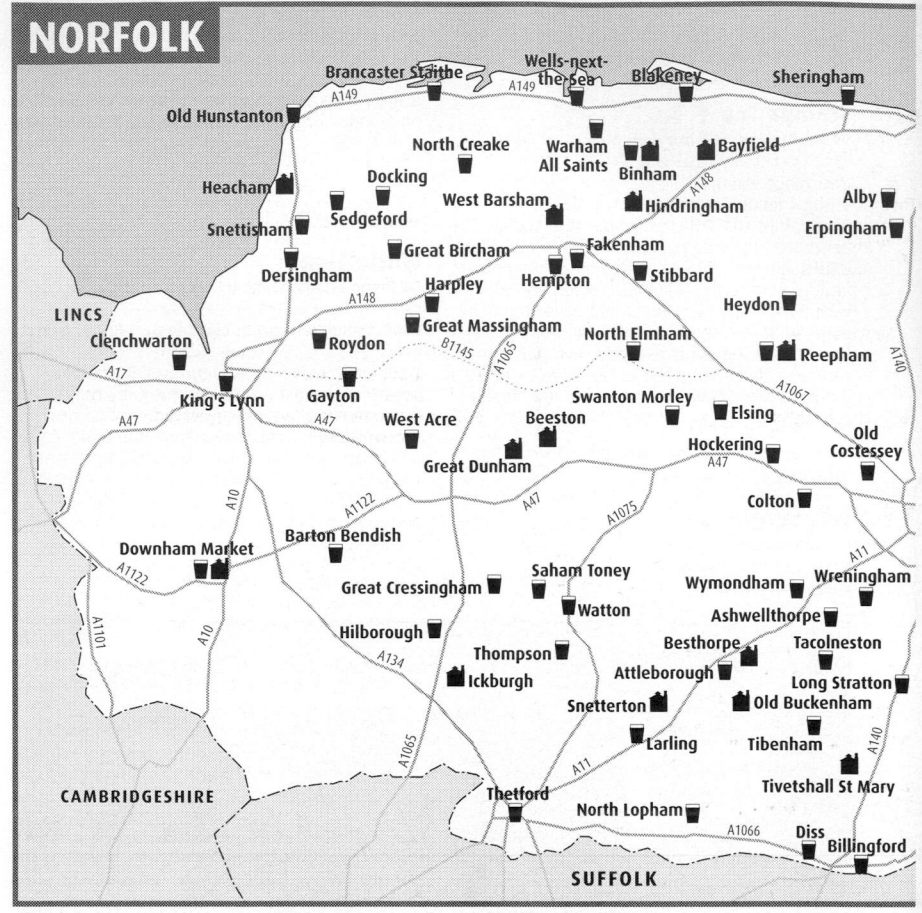

Brancaster Staithe   Wells-next-the-Sea   Blakeney   Sheringham
A149   A149

Old Hunstanton

North Creake   Warham   Bayfield
All Saints   Binham

Docking

Heacham   West Barsham   Hindringham   Alby
A148

Snettisham   Sedgeford   Erpingham

Great Bircham   Fakenham

Dersingham   Harpley   Hempton   Stibbard
A148

LINCS   Heydon

Clenchwarton   Roydon   Great Massingham   North Elmham   Reepham
A17   B1145   A1065   A1067   A140

King's Lynn   Gayton   Swanton Morley   Elsing
A47   A47   West Acre   Beeston   Hockering   Old Costessey
A47

Great Dunham

A10   A1122   A47   A1075   Colton

Barton Bendish   A11

Downham Market
A1122   Great Cressingham   Saham Toney   Wymondham   Wreningham

A10   Watton   Ashwellthorpe
A1101   Hilborough   Besthorpe   Tacolneston
A134   Thompson   Attleborough   Long Stratton
Ickburgh   Snetterton   Old Buckenham

A1065   Larling   Tibenham   A140

CAMBRIDGESHIRE   Thetford   Tivetshall St Mary
North Lopham   A1066   Diss   Billingford

SUFFOLK

Alby

Horseshoes 🅛
Cromer Road, NR11 7QE (on A140 halfway between
Cromer and Aylsham, next to Alby Crafts) TG208324
✪ closed Mon; 12-2.30 (3 Fri & Sat), 6.30-11; 12-4.30 Sun
☎ (01263) 761378 ⊕ albyhorseshoes.co.uk
Adnams Southwold Bitter; Woodforde's Wherry 🅷
A 19th-century inn that offers four real ales, always
from local breweries. There are two bars – one with
an unusually low counter – a wood-burning stove,
and a separate dining room. Traditional games of
Ring the Bull and Twister are located in the ceiling.
Pictures of old cars adorn the walls, the landlord
being a classic car enthusiast. Live music is '50s,
'60s and traditional country, with a touch of local
folk. Locally sourced home-cooked food is served.
Outside is a patio area and garden with tables and
umbrellas. ⌂Q✿⊞◑&♣P'🖵(2,44)

Ashwellthorpe

King's Head
The Turnpike, Norwich Road, NR16 1EL
✪ 12-11 (10.30 Sun-Tue) ☎ (01508) 489419
⊕ kingsheadashwellthorpe.co.uk
Woodforde's Wherry; guest beer 🅷
Family-run pub with a spacious open-plan interior
and a dining area to one side. On one side of the
main bar, overlooking the large back garden, is a
games area with a pool table and dartboard which
is guarded by a parrot. One interesting rotating
guest beer is always available. Good-quality home-
cooked food is offered at very reasonable prices.
⌂✿⊞◑♣P🖵(10A)

Attleborough

London Tavern 🅛
Church Street, NR17 2AH
✪ 11-11 (1.30am Fri & Sat) ☎ (01953) 457415
Wolf London Werewolf; guest beers 🅷
Family and dog friendly pub in the town centre,
opposite the main bus stops and 10 minutes' walk
from the railway station. The range of four guest
beers, normally from microbreweries, comes from
all over the UK. The pub has a dining room and
serves breakfast and lunch every day. Outside is a
covered smoking area and garden. A beer festival
takes place over the August bank holiday
weekend. CAMRA members receive a discount and
free Wi-Fi is available. ⌂⛵✿⊛&⇌P'🖵(6,6A,13)

Banningham

Crown Inn
Church Road, NR11 7DY (adjacent to village green, just
off B1145 or E of A140) TG217294

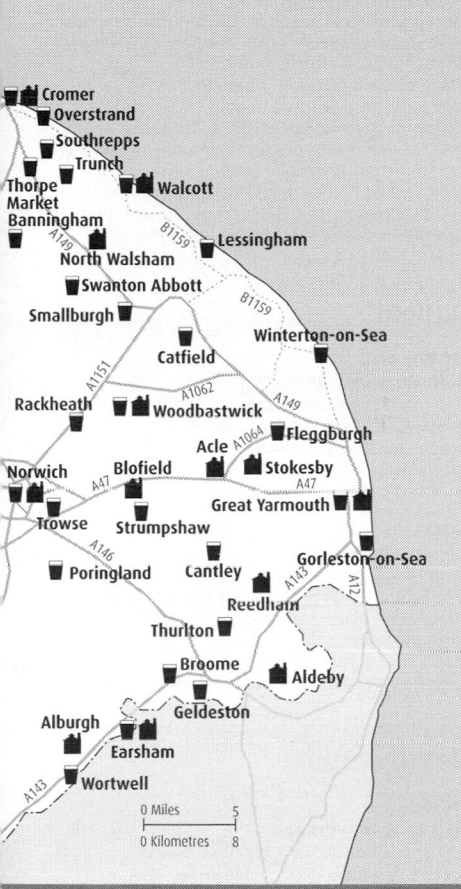

stable block and there is an extensive garden. Look out for the interesting pictures in the bar.
🅰Q🏵🍽🌓P

Billingford

Horseshoes

Lower Street, IP21 4HL
🟠 11-11; 12-10 Sun ☎ (0379) 740414
Adnams Southwold Bitter; guest beers 🅖
On the A143 Diss to Lowestoft road, this is an old hostelry that relies on passing trade but attracts locals for its beers. Handpumps advertise the ales on offer but all are dispensed straight from the casks in the taproom. Adnams Southwold Bitter is ever-present, with one or two guest beers depending on the season. Open long hours, with breakfast served 7-11am and meals from lunchtimes through to the evenings.
Q🏵🍽🌓♿♣P♐〓🗖(580)

Binham

Chequers Inn 🅛

Front Street, NR21 0AL TF983396
🟠 11.30-2.30, 6-11 (11.30 Fri & Sat); 12-2.30, 6-11 Sun
☎ (01328) 830297 ⊕ binhamchequers.info
Front Street Binham Cheer, Callum's Ale; guest beers 🅗
In the centre of the village and close to English Heritage's historic and picturesque Binham Priory, the Chequers is a single-room bar with welcoming roaring fires in winter. The pub is the home of the Front Street microbrewery, with three of its ales usually available, plus occasional guest beers from

🟠 12-2.30, 6.30-11 (12.30am Fri & Sat); 12-11 Sun
☎ (01263) 733534 ⊕ banninghamcrown.co.uk
Greene King IPA, Abbot; guest beers 🅗
Traditional, friendly free house in the heart of the village, opposite the parish church and village green, which has been run by the same family since 1991. Interior features include beams and a large working fireplace, in a building that has housed an inn since the 17th century. There is a patio with a covered smoking shelter, garden and barbecue area. Quality food, often made with locally sourced produce, is available lunchtimes and evenings. Monthly quiz nights and other special events are held regularly – see the website for details. 🅰🏵🌓♿♣P♐〓(18)

Barton Bendish

Berney Arms

Church Road, PE33 9GF
🟠 12-11 (10 Sun) ☎ (01366) 347995
⊕ theberneyarms.co.uk
Adnams Southwold Bitter, Broadside; guest beer 🅗
A good example of how a village local can adapt to modern times. There is beer from Adnams for the drinkers and fine food in both the dining room and bar for those who are hungry. The weekday lunchtime specials are great value and afternoon tea is a real treat. Accommodation is in the old

INDEPENDENT BREWERIES

Bees Walcott
Beeston Beeston
Buffy's Tivetshall St Mary
Chalk Hill Norwich
Elmtree Snetterton
Fakir Norwich
Fat Cat Norwich
Fox Heacham
Front Street Binham
Golden Triangle Norwich
Grain Alburgh
Humpty Dumpty Reedham
Iceni Ickburgh
Jo C's West Barsham (NEW)
Lacons Great Yarmouth (NEW)
Norfolk Hindringham
Norfolk Square Stokesby
Norwich Bear Norwich
Ole Slewfoot North Walsham
Opa Hay's Aldeby
Panther Reepham
Poppyland Cromer (NEW)
Stumptail Great Dunham (NEW)
Tipples Acle
Two Rivers Downham Market (NEW)
Uncle Stuarts Blofield
Wagtail Old Buckenham
Waveney Earsham
Why Not Norwich
Winter's Norwich
Wissey Valley Downham Market
Wolf Besthorpe
Woodforde's Woodbastwick
Yetman's Bayfield

other breweries. There is also an extensive range of Belgian beers, bottled as well as on draught. Excellent meals are served at all sessions. ﹣❀❁❂❃❄P❅﹣☷(46)

Blakeney

King's Arms
Westgate Street, NR25 7NQ (nr Blakeney harbour) TG026440
❂ 9.30-11; 12-10.30 Sun ☎ (01263) 740341
⊕ blakeneykingsarms.co.uk
Adnams Southwold Bitter; Marston's Pedigree; Morland Old Speckled Hen Ⓗ; guest beers Ⓗ/Ⓖ
Situated close to the harbour in one of Norfolk's most picturesque coastal villages, this old building was originally three fishermen's cottages. The interior comprises a series of interconnecting rooms, and there is a large garden to one side. Around five to six real ales are available, dispensed either by handpump or gravity, including at least one from Woodforde's. Cooked breakfasts are now available 9.30-11.30am, which is handy for campers and walkers. Children and dogs are welcome and en-suite accommodation is offered. ﹣Q❀❁❂❃❄P☷(Coasthopper)

Brancaster Staithe

Jolly Sailors
Main Road, PE31 8BJ
❂ 12-11 (12-3, 6-11 winter); 12-10.30 (12-3, 6-10.30 winter) Sun ☎ (01485) 210314 ⊕ jollysailorsbrancaster.co.uk
Adnams Broadside; Woodforde's Wherry; guest beers Ⓗ
A cosy inn with several small drinking areas and two dining rooms. It has a garden and play area, is family and dog friendly and has a new ice cream hut. Brancaster beers are produced by a local brewery to the pub's recipes and at least one is always available. Food offerings include local seafood and stone-baked pizza, with the oven visible from the bar. Brancaster harbour and the Norfolk coast path are just a short walk away. Coasthopper buses stop outside. ﹣❀❁❂❃❄P☷(Coasthopper)

Broome

Artichoke Ⓛ
162 Yarmouth Road, NR35 2NZ (just off A143, on main road through village) TM352915
❂ closed Mon; 12-11 (midnight Fri & Sat) ☎ (01986) 893325 ⊕ theartichokeatbroome.co.uk
Adnams Southwold Bitter Ⓗ, Broadside Ⓖ; Elgood's Black Dog Ⓗ; guest beers Ⓗ/Ⓖ
A community oriented village local made special by the people who run it. Delicious home-cooked food is served lunchtimes and evenings, which can be eaten either in the separate dining area, the main bar near a roaring log fire in winter, or in the garden in summer. A range of up to eight beers is offered, with emphasis on local ales dispensed either by handpump in the bar or by gravity from the tap room. There is a good frequent bus service from here to central Norwich. ﹣Q❀❁❂❃P❄☷(580,588)

Cantley

Cock
Manor Road, NR13 3JQ

❂ 11-3, 6-11; 12-11 Sun ☎ (01493) 700895
Adnams Southwold Bitter, Broadside; Fuller's London Pride; Wadworth Henry's IPA; Woodforde's Wherry Ⓗ
Old roadside inn situated a little way from the village of Cantley. It has a rambling interior with several rooms and some original beams visible. Although fairly food-oriented it sells a range of five cask ales with prices displayed prominently on the pumpclips. The restaurant is open seven days a week serving home-cooked food with bargain specials including fish and chips on Fridays. Quiz nights are on selected Mondays. ❀❁❂P

Catfield

Crown Inn Ⓛ
The Street, NR29 5AA TG387218
❂ 12-2.30, 7-11; 12-3, 7-midnight Sat; 12-3, 7-10.30 Sun ☎ (01692) 580128 ⊕ catfieldcrown.co.uk
Greene King IPA; guest beer Ⓗ
Tastefully furnished 300-year-old traditional village inn with a real fire in winter. The guest beer range, usually from local micros, changes regularly. A varied menu includes Italian dishes, which are a speciality. Fresh local ingredients are used where possible. Takeaway fish and chips are available from 5pm on Fridays. There is a separate function/dining room and a secluded garden for summer. Accommodation is in a detached building that was once a doctor's surgery. Close to the Broads and north Norfolk coast. ﹣Q❀❁❂❃P❄☷(12,12A)

Clenchwarton

Victory Ⓛ
245 Main Road, PE34 4AQ
❂ 12-11 (midnight Fri & Sat) ☎ (01553) 660682
Elgood's Cambridge Bitter, Pageant Ⓗ
A thriving Elgood's tied house which serves the occasional guest beer, the Victory has seen a lot of investment in the past couple of years. A new kitchen has made it possible to expand the food operation (look out for the themed nights). There is an outside drinking area and a garden for those who tire of the bar with its quirky games on the tables. Small beer festivals are sometimes held, with the casks on stillage in the bar. ❀❁❂❃P❄☷(55,505)

Colton

Ugly Bug Inn
High House Farm Lane, NR9 5DG (2 miles S of A47; turn off on roundabout on Honingham Rd) TG104908
❂ 12-2.30 (not Tue), 6-11; 12-3, 6-10.30 Sun ☎ (01603) 880794 ⊕ uglybuginn.co.uk
Beeston Worth the Wait; Humpty Dumpty Swallow Tail Ⓗ
This pub is well worth finding, a short drive off the A47 in Colton. It is large and has a beer garden, with a very friendly and relaxing atmosphere. Good-quality food is served in the dining room, and there are monthly jazz evenings. The landlord cellars his beers very well, and always has at least two beers on handpump, from local Beeston and Humpty Dumpty breweries. The pub is closed on Tuesday lunchtimes. Eight en-suite bedrooms are available. ❀❁❂❃P

Cromer

Red Lion Ⓛ
Brook Street, NR27 9HD (on top of cliffs above pier and lifeboat station near parish church)
✪ 11-11 (10.30 Sun) ☎ (01263) 514964
⊕ redlion-cromer.co.uk
Adnams Southwold Bitter; Woodforde's Wherry; guest beers Ⓗ
Splendidly situated with views of Cromer pier and the sea, the 19th-century Red Lion has retained many of its original features including panelling, a Victorian tiled floor and open wood fires. The work of local artists decorates the walls of the two bar areas. Up to four guest ales are usually available, often from local breweries such as Humpty Dumpty and Wolf. Beer festivals are held in the summer. The award-winning restaurant offers an extensive menu. Dogs are welcome and there is free Wi-Fi.
🅼🖚🅾Ⓓ🕭♣🅿⅄🖳(Coasthopper, X44)

Dersingham

Coach & Horses
77 Manor Road, PE31 6LN
✪ 12-11 ☎ (01485) 540391
Woodforde's Wherry; guest beers Ⓗ
Busy 19th-century carrstone pub close to Sandringham. It typically provides three guest ales, one constant. Entertainment includes quiz nights, bingo, poker games and live music on Friday nights and some Sundays. It is a popular pub for traditional food (check for winter availability). There is a large beer garden including a children's play area, music stand and heated smoking shelter. Three en-suite rooms are offered. A beer festival takes place in September, with around 20 real ales plus cider. Dog-friendly. 🅼Q🕭🖚Ⓓ🅲🅰🅿⅄🖳(11)

Diss

Cock Inn
Lower Denmark Street, IP22 4BE
✪ 12-11 (midnight Fri & Sat); 12-10.30 Sun
☎ (01379) 643633 ⊕ cockinndiss.co.uk
Adnams Southwold Bitter; guest beers Ⓗ
Popular edge-of-town pub in a pleasant location opposite Fair Green. It has been sympathetically restored and extended to provide four comfortable seating/drinking areas grouped around a U-shaped bar. It has a heavily beamed interior with a logburner and lots of character. Three ales (usually two session bitters and a best bitter) are always on handpump, with Adnams Southwold Bitter always available. Food is served 12-2pm and 6.30-9pm Wednesday-Sunday. Outside, there is plenty of seating for those warmer days and for watching the world go by. 🅼🕭Ⓓ🕭🅿⅄🖳

Docking

Railway Inn
Station Road, PE31 8LY
✪ 12-11 ☎ (01485) 518620
Buffy's Bitter; guest beers Ⓗ
Traditional locals' pub close to the old railway house and disused railway line. The theme continues in the bar, with railway pictures and a high-level working model train. The main bar boasts three handpumps which include two for guest beers, usually Woodforde's Wherry and Sharp's Doom Bar. Another smaller bar has lounge

settees and a small dining area. The main restaurant is in a large conservatory where locally produced food is served. Dogs are welcome in the bar. 🅼Q🕭🕭Ⓓ🅲🕭♣🅿⅄

Downham Market

Railway Arms
Downham Market Railway Station, PE38 9EN
✪ 10-12.10, 3.30-5.30 (9 Thu); 10-10.30 Fri; 10-12, 6-10.30 Sat; 12-2.30 day Sun ☎ (01366) 386636
⊕ railway-arms.co.uk
Beer range varies Ⓗ
Small cosy bar on the platform at Downham railway station selling two real ales, including beers from around the country that are not generally found in the area. At least two real ciders are also available, one of them from the local Pickled Pig. Look out for the model railway which travels round the ceiling. The library is also worth a visit. If you are travelling here from a long way away, call ahead to check opening hours. East Anglia Cider Pub of the Year. 🅼Q🕭♣🕭🖪🖳(61)

White Hart Ⓛ
58 Bridge Street, PE38 9DH
✪ 12-midnight (1am Fri & Sat); 12-10.30 Sun
☎ (01366) 387720
Beer range varies Ⓗ
A good no-nonsense drinkers' pub. The White Hart is an 18th-century building, featuring a pool table in one of its two bars. The other is for chatting! Elgood's ales are usually on, particularly the brewery's seasonal specials. You can find Elgood's Black Dog Mild here too, and other ales from all over the UK. There is a TV that shows occasional sport but this doesn't distract from a good discussion and a quality pint. 🅼🕭🕭♣🅿⅄🖳

Earsham

Queen's Head Ⓛ
Station Road, NR35 2TS (turn left off A143 signed to Earsham) TM321891
✪ 12-11 (10.30 Sun) ☎ (01986) 892623
Waveney East Coast Mild, Lightweight, seasonal beer; guest beer Ⓗ
Situated on the Norfolk-Suffolk border, near the Suffolk town of Bungay, this busy 17th-century locals' pub has a large front garden overlooking the village green. The main bar has a flagstone floor, wooden beams and a large fireplace with a roaring fire in winter. It is home to the Waveney Brewing Co, selling a range of – usually – four beers with at least one guest from another brewer. There is a separate dining area serving food at lunchtimes (not Mon and Tue). 🅼🕭Ⓓ♣🕭🅿⅄🖳(580)

Elsing

Mermaid Inn
Church Street, NR20 3EA (opp church) TG053165
✪ 12-3, 7 (6 Sat)-11; 12-3, 6.30-10.30 Sun
☎ (01362) 637640 ⊕ elsingmermaidinn.co.uk
Adnams Broadside; Woodforde's Wherry; guest beers Ⓖ
A 17th-century pub opposite the village church. The large single room has a log-burning fire at one end and a pool table at the other. There is also a restaurant. Cask ales sold here are mainly, though not exclusively, from local brewers, typically Humpty Dumpty and Batemans, which are

dispensed by gravity. Food is served every lunchtime and evening except Monday. The pub menu features curries, steaks and pie specials. A selection of books and pub games is available for patrons' use. ▲▲❀◑&▲P⅃

Erpingham

Erpingham Arms
Eagle Lane, NR11 7QA (1 mile from main A140 Aylsham-Cromer road) TG191319
✪ 12-3, 5-11; 12-11.30 Fri; 10-11.30 Sat; 12-10.30 Sun
☎ (01263) 761591 ⊕ erpinghamarms.com
Woodforde's Wherry, Nelson's Revenge; guest beers ⊞
Newly refurbished pub tracing its history back to the 1720s. It features a cosy main bar with wood-burning stoves, a small restaurant and a function room. The food champions the best of Norfolk and is locally sourced where possible. Choices include recipes that historically have a strong Norfolk connection. Guest ales are usually from Norfolk brewers. Beer festivals are held annually and also feature beers from Norfolk. There are quiz nights monthly and other themed events throughout the year. ▲▲Q⛱❀&◑P⅃❀(18)

Fakenham

Gallery Bistro
37 Market Place, NR21 9DN
✪ 8am-11pm ☎ (01328) 855000
Beer range varies ⊞
Situated in the town centre and originally called the Red Lion in the 17th century, the building was reconverted to a pub/bistro in 2000 after 30 years of use as council offices. The venue has a modern interior and café-style seating outside. It is popular with lunchtime drinkers and younger drinkers at the weekend, but caters for all. A large-screen TV attracts sports fans and there is occasional live music. A well-kept, regularly changing guest beer is offered. ❀◑⅃

Fleggburgh

King's Arms
Main Road, NR29 3AG
✪ 12-11 winter; closed Mon; 4.30-11.30 Tue; 12-11.30 (12.30am Fri & Sat) summer; 12-10.30 Sun
☎ (01493) 368463 ⊕ kingsfleggburgh.com
Winter's Fleggburgh Flyer; guest beers ⊞
Spacious one-room village inn, recently refurbished, which has bucked the trend of rundown and closure that has affected many local pubs by offering up to six interesting guest ales, plus cider available on gravity in summer. Food is from local sources, served lunchtimes and evenings, 12-7pm Sundays. Outside there are paved and grassed seating areas and a separate covered and heated smoking section. ▲▲❀◑&▲♣❀P⅃❀(6,730)

Gayton

Crown Inn
Lynn Road, PE32 1PA
✪ 12-11 ☎ (01553) 636252 ⊕ gaytoncrown.com
Greene King XX Mild, IPA, Abbot; guest beer ⊞
The Crown originates from the 16th century and has retained a charming historic atmosphere. It is a rare outlet for XX dark mild as well as an occasional

interesting guest beer. There are several drinking areas including a very cosy snug bar and an outside patio area for the summer with attractive flower beds. The large restaurant serves locally sourced food including game dishes and a popular Sunday carvery. ▲▲Q⛱❀❀◑❀⊞❀(48)

Geldeston

Locks Inn ❣ ⅃
Locks Lane, NR34 0HW (through village centre, turn left into Station Rd; after 300yds turn left onto track across marshes) TM390908
✪ 12 (9 Sat)-11 (closed Mon-Wed winter); 9-11 (7 winter) Sun ☎ (01508) 518414 ⊕ geldestonlocks.co.uk
Green Jack Excelsior, Orange Wheat Beer, Trawler Boys, Gone Fishing, seasonal beers; guest beers ⊞
On the north bank of the River Waveney, the pub is accessed by a long meandering track between dykes and marshes. The small main bar, with low ceiling beams and clay floor, retains an authentic feel, with candlelight adding atmosphere. The pub is owned by Green Jack Brewery, whose beers are supplemented by guest ales, real ciders and perries. Live music features on Thursday evening and Sunday afternoon. Local CAMRA branch Pub of the Year 2013. Sat nav users should use postcode NR34 0HS. ▲▲Q⛱❀◑♣❀P

Gorleston-on-Sea

Mariners Compass ⅃
21 Middleton Road, NR31 7AJ
✪ 10-12.30am (3am Sat); 10-11.30 Sun ☎ (01493) 659494
Woodforde's Wherry; guest beers ⊞
Ex-Steward & Patteson's house opened in the 1930s and fitted out in Brewers' Tudor style, retaining many of its original fittings inside. It is in the same hands as former CAMRA branch Pub of the Year winner the Mariners Tavern in Great Yarmouth, and has become one of the major real ale venues for the area. The pub has two drinking areas, the real ale bar occupying the old saloon space. Beers change regularly. Good-value bar snacks are always available. It has a fancy smoking area. ❀◑⊞&♣❀P⅃❀❀

New Entertainer
80 Pier Plain, NR31 6PG (off Englands Lane, on main road from town centre to harbour mouth)
✪ 3-11 (midnight Sat); 12-11 Sun ☎ (01493) 441643
⊕ newentertainer.co.uk
Greene King IPA; guest beers ⊞
Fairly close to the north end of the seafront, this traditional street-corner local with a curved frontage has an interesting design and layout. Traditional games are played here. There is always a fine choice of beers on offer, including up to eight guests, many locally brewed, and draught cider on handpump. The customers are as widely varied as the beer. The main entrance is at what appears to be the back. This dedicated free house is well worth seeking out. Q♣❀⅃❀(X1,8,5)

Great Bircham

King's Head
Lynn Road, PE31 7RJ (5 miles N of A148, 7 miles E of A149) TF773327
✪ 11-11; 12-10.30 Sun ☎ (01485) 578265
⊕ the-kings-head-bircham.co.uk
Woodforde's Wherry; guest beer ⊞

A modern bar within a Grade II-listed building in rural Norfolk. It achieves multiple ambitions of boutique hotel, friendly pub offering four ales in summer (three in winter) and quality restaurant serving seasonal local dishes such as hare or mussels along with fish and chips and cream teas. Themed evenings and quiz nights are popular with the local community, and for visitors it provides a fine base close to the Sandringham Estate, walking trails and other memorable west Norfolk attractions. ⚏Q☞✿☎◖◗⚘P⌐

Great Cressingham

Windmill Inn
Water End, IP25 6NN (off A1065 S of Swaffham)
TF846019
✪ 11.30-11 ☎ (01760) 756232 ⊕ oldewindmillinn.co.uk
Adnams Southwold Bitter, Broadside; Greene King IPA; Hancock's Windy Miller ℍ; guest beers ℍ/ⅿ
The Windmill is a perennial fixture in the Guide, and covers a multitude of rooms and a conservatory. Guest beers are drawn from a rolling list, with occasional surprises. Real cider is stocked and continues to be popular. There is plenty of accommodation and a range of games and music nights. The food covers all tastes from superb ham, egg and chips to more sophisticated fare. Opposite is a small caravan site.
⚏Q☞✿☎◖◗⚘⚘▲♣⚘P⌐

Great Massingham

Dabbling Duck ⌈
11 Abbey Road, PE32 2HN
✪ 12-11 (10.30 Sun) ☎ (01485) 520827
⊕ thedabblingduck.co.uk
Adnams Broadside; Beeston Worth the Wait; Greene King IPA; Woodforde's Wherry; guest beers ℍ
In an attractive village, the pub features bar areas with a roaring fire in winter and an extensive garden in summer. There is a separate restaurant for the many customers attracted by the excellent food, but also ample room for those who just wish to try one of the five or six beers on offer. Accommodation from which to enjoy this popular part of Norfolk is available and a wall map and guides from behind the bar feature details of local walks. Norfolk CAMRA Pub of the Year for 2011.
⚏✿☎◖◗⚘♣P⌐⚏(48)

Great Yarmouth

Barking Smack ⌈
16 Marine Parade, NR30 3AH (on seafront)
✪ 11-11 (midnight Fri); 11-10.30 Sun ☎ (01493) 859752
⊕ barkingsmack.com
Grain Best, Oak ℍ
Tastefully refurbished in 2012, this seafront pub stocks mostly Grain beers but is independently run. The L-shaped single bar has large windows giving access onto a patio area where barbecues are held in summer. Real cider and a range of international beers are also available. Check opening times out of season. Q✿◖◗⚘⚘

Mariners Tavern ⌈
69 Howard Street South, NR30 1LN (between harbour and marketplace, behind Palmers)
✪ 11 (12 Sun)-11; 12-11.30 Sun ☎ (01493) 332299
Greene King Abbot; guest beers ℍ

Traditional two-bar pub in the town centre, winner of local CAMRA Pub of the Year 2010. With up to 10 ales and eight real ciders/perries on offer, visitors could be excused for thinking that a beer festival is always in progress, given the range and choice from all over the country. Regular beer festivals are in fact held throughout the year, doubling the selection available, including one at Easter – a particular highlight – and when the town's maritime festival is held in early September. Most local buses stop nearby. ⚏☞✿◖◗⚏⚞⚘♣⚘⌐⚏⚏

St John's Head ⌈
58 North Quay, NR30 1JB
✪ 12-midnight; 11-11 Sun ☎ (01493) 843443
⊕ stjohnsheadrealalepub.co.uk
Elgood's Cambridge Bitter; guest beers ℍ
In one of the oldest areas of the town, this former Lacons Brewery pub is reputed to be built on land confiscated from monks of the Carmelite order. A single bar houses a large TV screen for live sport, and the pub is busy on match days. There is a pool table in one area, plus a smoking shelter which is minimalist but heated on a pay-per-use basis.
✿♿⚞(Vauxhall)♣⌐⚏

Harpley

Rose & Crown
Nethergate Street, PE31 6TW
✪ closed Mon; 12-3.30 (not Tue), 6.30-11 ☎ (01485) 521807
Adnams Broadside; Woodforde's Wherry; Nelson's Revenge ℍ
An attractive 17th-century pub in the centre of an unspoilt village close to Houghton Hall. It features open bar areas with a stylish and comfortable feel, and has log fires in winter. Welcoming to families and dogs, there is an extensive menu serving good food. Outside is a beer garden along with a barn area selling an eclectic mix of gifts, furniture and homewares. ⚏Q☞✿◖◗P⌐

Hempton

Bell
Front Green, NR21 7LG (turn by the Fakenham Garden Centre off the A1065) TF913293
✪ 11 2.30 (not Tue), 5 midnight; 11-midnight Sat; 12-4, 7-midnight Sun ☎ (01328) 864579 ⊕ hemptonbell.co.uk
Caledonian Flying Scotsman; Woodforde's Wherry; guest beers ℍ
A popular family-run traditional village pub with a relaxed, friendly atmosphere. It retains a two-bar layout little altered since the early 1970s. Pub games including dominoes, cribbage and poker dice are popular – you will be welcome to get involved. Changing guest beers are from micros or independent breweries and are typically over 4% ABV. Open mic folk sessions take place on the second Tuesday and trad jazz sessions on the last Thursday of the month. Q☞✿♣P⌐⚞

Heydon

Earle Arms ⌈
The Green, NR11 6AD (just off the B1149, 5 miles from Aylsham and only 20 minutes from Norwich, opp village green) TG113273
✪ closed Mon; 12-3, 6-11; 12-10.30 Sun ☎ (01263) 587376
⊕ theearlearms.com
Adnams Southwold Bitter; guest beer ℍ

Lovely 16th-century former coaching inn opposite the green, in the centre of a privately owned picture-postcard village that has often been used as a film location. The bar is mainly candlelit, with a welcoming atmosphere and a log fire in winter; it also has an interesting collection of horse racing memorabilia. The food is seasonal and locally sourced, cooked to order and of the highest quality. The restaurant is separate and booking is advisable. Real cider is available in the summer. The guest beer is from Woodforde's. ᴘQ❀◑☷❦P❧

Hilborough

Swan Inn ᴸ
Brandon Road, IP26 5BW (on A1065)
✪ 11-11; 12-10.30 Sun ☎ (01760) 756380
⊕ hilboroughswan.com
Beer range varies Ⓗ
The 17th-century Swan is directly on the A1065 at the heart of the small village of Hilborough. The landlady comes from a local family of gamekeepers and has generated a friendly atmosphere in which to enjoy both the ales (mainly from Elmtree, Humpty Dumpty and Beeston) and the home-made food prepared by her husband, who is the chef. There is a very popular carvery on Sundays. Accommodation is available. An excellent Breckland stopover.
ᴘ❀☷◑Å♣❦P❧

Hockering

Victoria
The Street, NR20 3HL (just off A47) TF863355
✪ 1 (12 Sat)-3, 6-11; 12-6 Sun ☎ (01603) 880507
Mighty Oak Oscar Wilde; Sharp's Doom Bar; guest beer Ⓗ
Located just north of the A47 Norwich-Dereham road and conveniently opposite the X1 bus stop, this friendly pub offers a warm welcome – and a real fire in winter. The guest beer varies but is normally a golden ale. The large single bar has a dartboard and also offers shut-the-box and cribbage. Beer festivals are held in summer and at Christmas. Live music plays occasionally.
ᴘ❀&♣P❧☷(X1)

King's Lynn

Crown & Mitre
Ferry Street, PE30 1LJ (off Tuesday Market Place)
✪ 12-2.30, 6-11 ☎ (01553) 774669
Beer range varies Ⓗ
As you sample one of the five or six guest beers in this riverside pub you can admire the many interesting objects that decorate the bar, most of which have a maritime or railway connection. When you tire of this, head up to the gallery and look out over the water. Do not come when the Mart is on (opens on February 14th for two weeks) as the pub will probably be closed. There is no pub car park, but plenty of public ones close by.
ᴘQ❀◑

Lattice House
Chapel Street, PE30 1EG
✪ 9am-11 (1am Fri & Sat) ☎ (01553) 769585
Greene King Abbot; Ruddles Best Bitter; guest beers Ⓗ
Unusually for a Wetherspoon establishment, this 15th-century building has been a pub since the

early 18th century, and many of the original features can still be seen. There are lots of rooms and three bars, with around 10 beers on offer. Public car parks can be found close by, or it is half a mile from the railway station. ᴘQ☷❀◑❦

Stuart House Hotel
35 Goodwins Road, PE30 5QX
✪ 6-11 (10.30 Sun) ☎ (01553) 772169
⊕ stuart-house-hotel.co.uk
Beer range varies Ⓗ
A long-standing entry in the Guide, this hotel bar is found tucked away down a gravel drive not far from the Walks park and football ground. There is often live music on the last Friday of the month and a beer festival during the last week in July. Check the website for special events and offers. It is about a half-mile walk from the station through the park. Note that it is only open evenings except by arrangement. ᴘQ❀✉◑≠P

Larling

Angel Inn ♛
NR16 2QU (off A11 between Thetford and Norwich, signed by B1111 East Harling) TL983890
✪ 10-midnight; 11-11 Sun ☎ (01953) 717963
⊕ angel-larling.co.uk
Adnams Southwold Bitter; guest beers Ⓗ
A popular pub run by the same family since 1913, recognised as the local CAMRA Pub of the Year for 2010 and 2013. Five real ales are always on handpump, including a mild. There is superb food, over 100 whiskies, and both the lounge and bar have open fires. The bar is enjoyed by friendly locals, passers-by and campers who make use of the Angel's campsite. A summer beer festival features more than 70 ales and the pub also hosts a whisky week.
ᴘQ❀✉◑🛏&Å≠(Harling Rd)P❧

Lessingham

Star Inn ᴸ
School Road, NR12 0DN (300yds off B1159 coast road) TG388283
✪ 12-3 (not Mon), 6-11 ☎ (01692) 580510
⊕ thestarlessingham.co.uk
Adnams Southwold Bitter; Buffy's Bitter; Greene King IPA; Woodforde's Wherry; guest beer Ⓗ
Excellent village local that serves well-kept beers to regulars from near and far, and has a relaxed, welcoming atmosphere. Situated near the north-east Norfolk coast, it is convenient for those visiting nearby East Ruston Old Vicarage Garden. The large beer garden is perfect for summer drinking. The cider is Westons Old Rosie. Dogs are welcome in the bar. Bar snacks and freshly prepared high-quality lunches and dinners are available daily (but no food Mon, and Sun eve).
ᴘQ❀✉◑Å♣❦P☷(34,36)

Long Stratton

Swan Hotel ᴸ
The Street, NR15 2XG (in centre of village on A140) TM197926
✪ 11-2.30 (3 Fri), 6-11; 12-10.30 Sun ☎ (01508) 530200
Adnams Southwold Bitter; Fuller's London Pride Ⓗ
Large former coaching inn on the busy A140. It has two bars serving two regular ales plus two changing guest ales, including at least one from a

local brewery. The pub has a wheelchair ramp and a separate disabled WC. Crib and whist are played. ♨ ♿ ◖◐ ⌂ ♿ ♣ P ⊒ (18)

North Creake

Jolly Farmers
1 Burnham Road, NR21 9JW
✪ closed Mon & Tue; 12-2.30, 7-11 (10.30 Sun)
☎ (01328) 738185 ⊕ jollyfarmers-northcreake.co.uk
Adnams Southwold Bitter ⊞; Woodforde's Wherry; guest beers Ⓖ
Comfortable chairs, open fires and excellent food from the finest local ingredients combine to create a great atmosphere in this unchanging local pub. You are as likely to meet locals as tourists straying from the nearby north Norfolk coast. Dogs and walkers are welcome. The very friendly landlords make this a lovely establishment – but note that it is closed Mondays and Tuesdays and in the afternoon. ♨ ♿ ⊛ ◖◐ ⌂ P ⌐

North Elmham

Railway Ⓛ
40 Station Road, NR20 5HH TF995202
✪ 11-midnight; 12-10:30 Sun ☎ (01362) 668300
Beer range varies ⊞/Ⓖ
A fine example of a rural community pub, set in central Norfolk. A rotating choice of ales is available, with beers dispensed either by handpump or gravity. The range tends to favour local brewers such as Wolf, Woodforde's and Elgood's, but beers from Somerset brewer Cottage also feature regularly. There is an adjacent function room that hosts many music events. Home-cooked meals using mainly locally sourced ingredients are available. The pub now offers B&B and has a campsite at the rear. ♨ ⊛ ⊠ ◖◐ ⚑ P ⊒ (21)

North Lopham

King's Head
The Street, IP22 2NE (2 miles N of A1066) TM037834
✪ 11.30-3 (not Mon), 5-11; 11.30-midnight Fri & Sat; 12-10.30 Sun ☎ (01379) 688007 ⊕ lophamkingshead.co.uk
Adnams Southwold Bitter; Woodforde's Wherry; guest beer ⊞
Two-bar timber-framed pub dating from the 16th century and set back from the main road through the village. The public bar has an inglenook fireplace and a pool table, while the comfortable saloon and dining area have a woodburner. The guest beer varies but is normally over 4%. Food is served lunchtimes and evenings Wednesday to Saturday, and Sunday lunchtimes. The pub has its own crazy golf course; clubs can be borrowed free of charge. Dog-friendly. ♨ ♿ ⊛ ◖◐ ⌂ ♣ P

Norwich

Alexandra Tavern
16 Stafford Street, NR2 3BB
✪ 12-11 (midnight Thu); 10.30-midnight Fri & Sat
☎ (01603) 627772 ⊕ alexandratavern.co.uk
Chalk Hill Tap, CHB, Gold; guest beers ⊞
Popular, bustling and very friendly, this pub is a little gem found just outside the city centre. The interior is brightly decorated, with the walls featuring pictures and articles about the landlord's charity achievements. The bar regularly serves three Chalk Hill Brewery beers as well as guest

ales, along with a good variety of food including a soup menu. There is a pool table, dartboard and board games. ♨ Q ⊛ ◖◐ ⌂ ♿ ♣ ⌐ ⊒ (19,20)

Beehive Ⓛ
30 Leopold Road, NR4 7PJ (between Newmarket and Unthank roads)
✪ 12 (4 Mon)-11; 12-midnight Fri & Sat ☎ (01603) 451628
⊕ beehivepubnorwich.co.uk
Fuller's London Pride; Green Jack Golden Best; guest beers ⊞
The pub is home to three darts, football and korfball teams and serves up to five guest ales, mainly from East Anglia. The venue is popular with the local community and has a weekly quiz on Wednesday and a monthly folk night. Free Wi-Fi and pub games are also available. The beer festival, held in the first week of July, is very popular, as are regular charity barbecues, also hosted during the summer months. Food is served lunchtimes only. ⊛ ◖ ♣ ● ⌐ ⊒

Cottage Ⓛ
9 Silver Road, NR3 4TB (N of city within easy walking distance of rail station and city centre)
✪ 12-11 (10.30-11 Sat) ☎ (01603) 665535
⊕ thecottagenorwich.co.uk
Crouch Vale Brewers Gold; Mauldons Blackberry Porter, Christies Golden; guest beers ⊞
A Mauldon's public house which offers a warm and friendly welcome, with quality ales from the brewery's range and up to 10 varied guests. Events include a St George's beer festival, a summer cider festival in August, monthly quiz nights, plus live music on Friday evening and Sunday afternoon, and Monday jazz jams. Excellent home-cooked food is served on a regular basis along with monthly themed food evenings. A beer garden is situated to the rear of the premises and is popular in sunny weather. ⊛ ◖ ⇌ ♣ ● ⌐ ⊒ (999)

Duke of Wellington Ⓛ
91-93 Waterloo Road, NR3 1EG
✪ 12-11 (midnight Fri & Sat); 12-10.30 Sun
☎ (01603) 441182 ⊕ dukeofwellingtonnorwich.co.uk
Elgood's Black Dog; Fuller's London Pride; Oakham Bishop's Farewell; Wells Bombardier; Wolf Golden Jackal, Straw Dog; guest beers ⊞/Ⓖ
This regular Guide entry offers a range of ales from around the country, with many served from the small taproom, which can be seen from the bar area. The back patio/garden area holds the pub's annual beer festival during the late summer bank holiday and is picturesque in the sunshine. There is no food available but customers may bring their own; plates, cutlery and condiments will be supplied by the friendly staff. Live folk music features every Tuesday. ♨ ⊛ ♣ ● P ⌐ ⊒ (9A,16)

Fat Cat Ⓛ
49 West End Street, NR2 4NA (off Dereham Rd/Nelson St jct)
✪ 12-11 (midnight Thu-Sat) ☎ (01603) 624364
⊕ fatcatpub.co.uk
Adnams Southwold Bitter; Fat Cat Best Bitter ⊞, Honey Cat ⊞/Ⓖ; Oakham Bishops Farewell Ⓖ; guest beers ⊞/Ⓖ
Excellent service is to be found here, with quality ales from the Fat Cat Brewery plus a selection of almost 30 guest ales from all over the UK, including many stouts, porters and dark milds. These complement the large amount of brewery memorabilia around the pub. Food is limited to

good-value rolls (still only 60p) and pies. A beer lover's paradise that no visitor to Norwich should miss, this is an outstanding example of what a real ale pub should be like. Q❀♣♠'–♐(21,22,23A,B)

Fat Cat & Canary ⬓

101 Thorpe Road, NR1 1TR (along Thorpe Rd from the station, the pub is about 1½ miles on the right)
❂ 12-11 (midnight Fri); 11-midnight Sat ☎ (01603) 436925
⊕ fatcatcanary.co.uk
Fat Cat Bitter, Cat & Canary, Honey Ale, Wild Cat, seasonal beers ⒣
New, third member of the Norwich-based Fat Cat mini-chain, about 1½ miles from the centre of the city, serving most of the brewery's ales and different guests from around the UK, together with continental beers. It has a second bar, only opened for occasions such as match days. There is a small TV to the rear of the main bar, a large car park and terraces to the front and rear, the latter being heated. Food is limited to home-made rolls, crisps and other snacks. Q❀♦≈♠P'–♐(14,14A,15)

Fat Cat Brewery Tap ⬓

98-100 Lawson Road, NR3 4LF (along Sprowston Rd, about 15 mins' walk from Anglia Sq)
❂ 12-11 (midnight Fri); 11-midnight Sat; 11-10.30 Sun
☎ (01603) 413153 ⊕ fatcattap.co.uk
Adnams Southwold Bitter; Fat Cat Bitter, Marmalade Cat; Harviestoun Bitter & Twisted; Oakham Bishops Farewell; guest beers ⒣/⒢
Once a 1970s estate pub dropped unsympathetically into Victorian suburbs, the Tap has blossomed since becoming the northernmost of the city's three 'Cats' and home of the Fat Cat Brewery. The large drinking area showcases extensive breweriana while the impressive bar hosts a generous selection of beers and ciders on gravity and handpump, complemented by a worldwide selection of bottled beers. Live music takes place twice a week and a challenging quiz fortnightly. Closing time is indicated by a set of traffic lights suspended from the ceiling. Don't miss! Q❀♦♣♠P'–♐(11,11A)

King's Arms

22 Hall Road, NR1 3HQ (about 10 mins' walk from the bus station)
❂ 11-11 (11.30 Fri & Sat); 12-11 Sun ☎ (01603) 766361
⊕ kingsarmsnorwich.co.uk
Batemans XB, XXXB; Beeston Worth the Wait; Hop Back Summer Lightning; guest beers ⒣
A friendly Bateman's house serving an extensive range of guest ales to complement the brewery's beers, usually including a stout or porter. It is to the south of the city centre. The only food served is Sunday roast, but the pub allows customers to bring their own food from various nearby takeaways (plates and condiments provided). The pub has monthly quiz nights, poker evenings and live music, and Westons Old Rosie cider is often available. Very busy on match days. ❀♦♣♠♠'

King's Head ⬓

42 Magdalen Street, NR3 1JE (a few yards from Anglia Square shopping area and buses)
❂ 12-midnight (11 Sun) ☎ (01603) 620468
⊕ kingsheadnorwich.co.uk
Winter's Kings Head Bitter; Woodforde's Nelson's Revenge; guest beers ⒣
Award-winning pub that offers a friendly welcome to all, with many of the beers sourced from Norfolk breweries and the smaller East Anglian

microbrewers, with a smattering from outside East Anglia. The house beer, KHB, is brewed by Winter's. No keg beers of any sort are sold, but a range of continental bottled beers is stocked, plus draught Kingfisher cider. The pub plays host to the Norwich bar billiard league, with the table situated in the rear drinking area. Q❀♦♣♠'–♐♐

Plough

58 St Benedicts, NR2 4AR
❂ 12-11 (midnight Fri & Sat); 12-10:30 Sun
☎ (01603) 661384 ⊕ theploughnorwich.co.uk
Grain Best, Oak ⒣
Popular pub in one of the city's oldest areas near the Norwich Arts Centre. As the Grain Brewery tap, it offers the full range of ales. The two-bar interior is fairly small, with wooden chairs and tables, and a roaring log fire in winter. The large Mediterranean-style courtyard garden is a fine place to while away a summer's evening. Excellent cocktails and spirits are also available, along with Vicky's special sausage pie, and barbecues in summer. ☖❀⬓'–♐(19,20,21)

Ribs of Beef ⬓

24 Wensum Street, NR3 1HY
❂ 11-12.30am (1am Fri & Sat); 10.30-11 Sun
☎ (01603) 619517 ⊕ ribsofbeef.co.uk
Adnams Southwold Bitter; Fuller's London Pride; Wolf Golden Jackal; Woodforde's Wherry ⒣
Traditional and well-decorated pub overlooking the River Wensum. A welcoming row of nine handpumps dispenses a large selection of local ales, with foreign beers and real cider also available. The pub is popular with visitors and the kitchen offers a great selection of meals made with locally sourced ingredients. The atmosphere is relaxed and friendly, with a room downstairs as well as a big screen that regularly shows major sporting events. Just the place to watch the boats go by. ⬓♦≈♠'–♐(21,22)

Take 5 ⬓

17 Tombland, NR3 1HF TG233088
❂ 11-11 (midnight Fri & Sat); closed Sun ☎ (01603) 763099
Beer range varies ⒣
Take 5 is a Grade II-listed building, dating in parts from the 15th century. A range of around five real ales is available, from Norfolk and Suffolk breweries. Real cider is served plus a selection of bottled beers and organic wines. Quality home-cooked food is sold all day, all sourced locally. A function room with a small terrace is upstairs, plus a cellar downstairs. Prior to 2004 it was named the Louis Marchesi, after the founder of the Round Table. Q⬓≈♠♐

Trafford Arms ⬓

61 Grove Road, NR1 3RL
❂ 11-11 (11.30 Fri & Sat); 12-10.30 Sun ☎ (01603) 628466
⊕ traffordarms.co.uk
Adnams Southwold Bitter; Tetley Bitter; Woodforde's Wherry; guest beers ⒣
Close to the city centre, a very warm welcome is assured at this public house run by the same licensees for over 20 years. It offers a wide range of beers, usually including a mild. Kingfisher Farm cider is available throughout the year. Excellent home-cooked food includes pie, curry and fish evenings each week. Monthly quiz nights are very popular. The annual Valentine's beer festival is one of the biggest in the country, with 70-plus ales. ☖⬓♦♣♠P'–♐(36,39)

Vine 🛏

7 Dove Street, NR2 1DE (close to Norwich Provision Market and Guildhall)

🌣 11-11; closed Sun ☎ (01603) 627362 🌐 vinethai.co.uk

Oakham JHB; guest beers Ⓗ

Norwich's smallest pub is a gem in the heart of the city, serving four quality ales and traditional Thai cuisine in a winning combination that is hard to beat. Located just off the marketplace, the restaurant is upstairs, although some customers prefer to eat downstairs in the bar area. In summer, tables and chairs are set out in the pedestrianised street where customers can while away their time watching shoppers go by. Beer festivals are held in January and late June.
Q🌣🕦♣🖾

White Lion

73 Oak Street, NR3 3AQ (just within the inner link road, near Barn Rd roundabout and the Marriotts Way Cycle Path, National cycle route 1)

🌣 12-11 (10.30 Sun) ☎ (01603) 632333
🌐 individualpubs.co.uk/whitelion

Milton Dionysus, Justinian, Nero, Pegasus, Sparta; guest beers Ⓗ

CAMRA East Anglia Cider Pub of the Year 2012, it serves an extensive range of over 20 ciders and perries, plus beers from the Milton brewery range and interesting guests. An annual beer festival is held in the autumn. There are a number of pub games on offer including bar billiards. Historic details of the surrounding area, and the many pubs that existed, adorn the walls. The food is varied and of good value, with many cider-based recipes on the menu. 🚶Q🌣🕦🖫♣🍴♀-🖾(28)

Wig & Pen 🛏

6 St Martin-at-Palace Plain, NR3 1RN (near Anglican Cathedral)

🌣 11.30-11 (midnight Thu-Sat); 11.30-6 Sun
☎ (01603) 625891 🌐 thewigandpen.com

Adnams Southwold Bitter; Fuller's London Pride; Oakham JHB; guest beers Ⓗ

Friendly 17th-century free house with a spacious patio immediately opposite the Bishop's Palace and with an impressive view of Norwich Cathedral spire. Three permanent ales and three guests are always available, usually including two local beers. The small back room can be used for meetings. Major sporting events are shown on two TVs. Good-quality food is available lunchtimes and evenings. The pub is a short walk from Tombland, where there are bus stands for several bus routes.
🚶🌣🕦🖫♀-🖾(11,13,36)

Old Costessey

Bush 🛏

58 The Street, NR8 5DD TG174119

🌣 11 (12 Sun)-11 ☎ (01603) 747227

Courage Best Bitter; Woodforde's Wherry; Young's Bitter Ⓗ

Village pub dating back to the 19th century and once frequented by the artist Alfred Munnings. Inside, it has been modernised yet retains a wood-beamed ceiling. The interior is divided into two bars, one with a dartboard – the pub has its own darts team – the other with a large open fire. Outside there is a large beer garden leading down to the river. 🚶Q🌣🖫♣P♀-

Old Hunstanton

Ancient Mariner

6 Golf Course Road, PE36 6JJ

🌣 11 (12 Sun)-11 ☎ (01485) 534411

Adnams Southwold Bitter, Broadside; guest beers Ⓗ

A popular pub adjoining the Le Strange Arms Hotel, with a large beer garden that has access to the beach. The inn consists of old barns and stables and includes a family room and restaurants. At least four ales are available. Live music nights are held every month. Old Hunstanton is the only village on the east coast to face west and the pub offers superb views of spectacular sunsets over the sea from the decking at the rear.
🚶Q🌣🖘🖫🕦🖫🖼AP🖾(36)

Overstrand

White Horse

34 High Street, NR27 0AB

🌣 11-11 ☎ (01263) 579237 🌐 whitehorseoverstrand.co.uk

Woodforde's Wherry; guest beers Ⓗ

In the centre of the coastal village of Overstrand just 460 yards from a sandy beach. Behind the White Horse's Edwardian exterior lies a recently refurbished pub offering excellent beer as well as outstanding food and accommodation. A spacious modern bar serves up to four guest ales, usually from local Norfolk breweries such as Humpty Dumpty, Grain, Buffy's and Wolf. Outside is a large beer garden with play equipment which also hosts occasional beer festivals in the summer. Dogs are welcome. Free Wi-Fi. 🌣🌣🖘🕦🖫♀-🖾(5,35)

Poringland

Royal Oak 🛏

44 The Street, NR14 7JT (on B1332) TG267023

🌣 12-11 (midnight Fri & Sat) ☎ (01508) 493734
🌐 poringlandroyaloak.com

Sharp's Doom Bar; Woodforde's Wherry Ⓗ

Former local CAMRA Pub of the Year, this is an unashamedly beer-oriented hostelry that offers a large range of beers both from brewers locally and across the UK, together with up to three real ciders from Westons. It has an open plan interior invitingly laid out, with numerous nooks and small seating areas, including a games area with a pool table and dartboard. No food is served but there is a fish and chip shop next door.
🚶🌣🖫♣♀P♀-🖵🖾(587,588)

Rackheath

Sole & Heel

2 Salhouse Road, NR13 6QH

🌣 12 (5 Mon)-11; 12-10 Sun ☎ (01603) 720146
🌐 soleandheel.co.uk

Hancock's Rackheath Liberator; guest beers Ⓖ

A warm and welcoming single-bar pub, with two restaurant areas for about 25 diners in each. Rackheath Liberator is the house ale, served on gravity from the cellar alongside three or four guest beers, split between local and national brews, and one or more real ciders. The restaurant has a large choice of fresh home-cooked and locally sourced food, including seasonal evening specials. There is a pleasant garden with decking, a children's play area and regular live music and events. 🌣🌣🕦🖫♀P♀-🖾(123,14,14A)

Reepham

King's Arms Ⓛ
Market Place, NR10 4JJ TG099231
❸ 11.30-3, 5.30-11; 11-11 Sat; 12-10.30 Sun
☎ (01603) 870345
Adnams Southwold Bitter; Greene King Abbot;
Panther Kings; Woodforde's Wherry; guest beers Ⓗ
A former coaching inn dating back to 1667,
situated in the picturesque square of this small
market town. Extended sympathetically in the
1990s, original beams, Norfolk brickwork and open
fires have been retained, providing several
drinking and dining areas. At least one ale from the
local Panther Brewery is always on handpump. The
comprehensive menu includes food sourced from
nearby butchers and bakers. Jazz bands play in the
rear courtyard on summer Sunday afternoons, and
a bar billiards table is available. Dogs are welcome.
ꩰQ✿❶&♣P⁵–₩(25)

Roydon

Union Jack
30 Station Road, PE32 1AW
❸ 12 (4 Tue-Thu)-midnight ☎ (01485) 601347
Beer range varies Ⓗ
Voted local CAMRA Pub of the Year in 2012, this is a
traditional village drinking pub, dating back to
1884. Four handpumps dispense a variety of ales,
mostly chosen from microbreweries. Beer festivals
are held over the Easter and August bank holidays
and usually feature local breweries. There is live
music each month, regular bingo and quizzes, and
weekly support for darts, crib and dominoes. Dogs
are welcome. ꩰ✿♣₩(48)

Saham Toney

Old Bell
1 Bell Lane, IP25 7HD
❸ 11-11 (10.30 Sun) ☎ (01953) 884934
⊕ theoldbellsaham.co.uk
Beer range varies Ⓗ
Immediately off the main street in Saham, the Bell
has improved a great deal in the past year and now
offers four guest beers of good quality. The lovely
old building comprises a long bar room and a
restaurant. Food is available daily from 11am
(noon on Sun). The pub sits next to the large
Saham mere, which you may not notice if you
arrive after dark. Have a look at the aerial photo in
the bar – it is very close to the pub.
ꩰQ🜚✿❶&♣P₩(1)

Sedgeford

King William
Heacham Road, PE36 5LU (on B1454)
❸ 11 (6 Mon)-11; 12-10.30 Sun ☎ (01485) 571765
⊕ thekingwilliamsedgeford.co.uk
Adnams Southwold Bitter; Greene King Abbot;
Woodforde's Wherry; guest beer Ⓗ
A large, well-appointed village pub, popular for the
locally produced food. Known by the locals as the
King Willie, it has an excellent reputation for
quality food but still retains a pub atmosphere that
attracts local drinkers. There are two bars and a
restaurant divided into four areas. A large garden
at the rear has a superb outdoor covered drinking/
dining area. Nine luxury rooms are available. Dog-
friendly bars. ꩰQ✿🛏❶⊟P⁵–

Sheringham

Crown Inn
East Cliff, NR26 8BQ (on promenade)
❸ 10-11 (midnight Fri & Sat); 11-11 Sun ☎ (01263) 823213
⊕ crown-sheringham.co.uk
Black Sheep Ale; Fuller's London Pride; Greene King
IPA, Abbot; Woodforde's Wherry Ⓗ
This spacious pub next to the Sheringham Museum
(The Mo) overlooks the beach and has fine sea
views. Two lounge bars and a central bar serve
up to five real ales and an extensive range of food,
which is available throughout the day. An outside
seating area facing the sea is popular in summer.
The Crown hosts a number of events including live
music on Saturday nights and a quiz on Monday
evenings. 🜚✿❶&ᴬ⇌♣P⁵–₩(Coasthopper,X44)

Lobster Ⓛ
13 High Street, NR26 8JP (bottom of High St towards
the sea)
❸ 11.30-midnight (1am Sat); 11.30-11.30 Sun
☎ (01263) 822716 ⊕ the-lobster.com
Adnams Southwold Bitter; Greene King Abbot;
Sharp's Doom Bar; Woodforde's Wherry Ⓗ
Large pub on the High Street close to the sea with a
nautical feel and marine artefacts adorning the
lounge bar. Four real ales are offered regularly and
up to 10 in the holiday season. Beer festivals are
held in the pub's large garden on most bank
holiday weekends. An annual classic car rally is
hosted along with other events linked to the Poppy
Line railway galas. A varied food menu is offered,
and there is free Wi-Fi. Dogs welcome.
ꩰQ🜚✿❶⊟&⇌♣🌢⁵–₩(Coasthopper,X44)

Windham Arms Ⓛ
15-17 Wyndham Street, NR26 8BA (Wyndham St is off
the bottom of the High St towards the sea) TG159434
❸ 12-11 (10.30 Sun) ☎ (01263) 822609
⊕ thewindhamarms.co.uk
Woodforde's Wherry; guest beers Ⓗ
CAMRA branch Pub of the Year for 2011. Close to
the beach and promenade, this cosy local is just
behind the main street, comprising two bars, one
incorporating the restaurant. Outside is a partly
covered drinking area with sea views in summer.
At least four Norfolk real ales are regularly on offer.
Greek food is a pub speciality. Meals are served
lunchtimes (summer only) and evenings. Beer
festivals are held to support local events such as
the Potty Festival.
Q🜚✿❶⊟ᴬ⇌🌢P⁵–₩(Coasthopper,5,9)

Smallburgh

Crown
North Walsham Road, NR12 9AD (on main A149 road
between North Walsham and Stalham) TG330245
❸ 7-11 Mon; 12-3, 5.30 (7 Sat)-11; 12-4 Sun
☎ (01692) 536314 ⊕ smallburghcrown.co.uk
Adnams Southwold Bitter; Greene King IPA;
Woodforde's Wherry; guest beers Ⓗ
Cosy wayside former coaching inn, with a
restaurant. A good range of ales is always
available, including a guest beer. The interior is
characterful and comfortable, with a large fire in
winter. Unlike many such pubs in this part of the
world, it has not suffered any corporate
makeovers, and retains an authentic pub
atmosphere. ꩰQ✿🛏❶&♣P⁵–₩(11A,6,34)

Snettisham

Rose & Crown
Old Church Road, PE31 7LX
🕭 11-11; 12-10.30 Sun ☎ (01485) 541382
⊕ roseandcrownsnettisham.co.uk
Adnams Southwold Bitter, Broadside; Woodforde's Wherry; guest beer ⊞
A popular traditional village inn with cosy bars, exposed beams, a real fire and a dining room. Head through the narrow passage to find a larger bar and dining areas with a contemporary feel. Well known for quality traditional and exciting local seasonal fare, the bars also remain popular with local drinkers. The garden and play area make it appealing to families. Accommodation is available for those who wish to spend longer in this beautiful area. ⚙Q❀☺➝◑ ⬜♿P⁵⊟(10,11)

Southrepps

Vernon Arms
2 Church Street, NR11 8NP (on A149 from North Walsham to Cromer; after Thorpe Market turn right at crossroads; continue into Southrepps and pub is on left past post office) TG2563636583
🕭 11 (12 Sun)-11 ☎ (01263) 833355 ⊕ vernonarms.com
Adnams Southwold Bitter; Black Sheep Best Bitter; Greene King Abbot; guest beers ⊞
Traditional Norfolk brick and flint free house set in the heart of a vibrant village community. Regular ales are augmented by a variety of guest beers. It is very popular with diners who appreciate fine food, locally sourced ingredients (where possible), the variety of dining areas, candlelit tables and excellent service. Fish and chips are available to take away 6-8pm Tuesday-Saturday. The pub has a log fire in winter and a heated smoking area, and there is a July beer festival with music (request your favourite beer in June). ⚙Q❀◑ ⬜♿P⁵⊟(33)

Stibbard

Ordnance Arms
Guist Bottom, NR20 5PF (on A1067) TF987267
🕭 5 (12 Sun)-11 ☎ (01328) 829471
Beer range varies ⊞
A roadside pub with a small but comfortable front bar, a larger back bar with hatch service, stone flooring and simple wooden furnishing, and a pool room between the two. Both bars have real fires. The pub is named after its use as a base for the first ordnance survey of Norfolk, and a number of maps adorn the walls. Adjacent to the pub is a popular Thai restaurant (open Tue-Sat eves), food from which may be eaten in the bar. ⚙❀➝P⁵⊟(X29)

Strumpshaw

Shoulder of Mutton
Norwich Road, NR13 4NT (on Brundall to Lingwood road S of A47) TG349078
🕭 10.30-11; 12-10.30 Sun ☎ (01603) 712274
Adnams Southwold Bitter, Broadside; guest beers ⊞
Traditional hub-of-the-community village local, deservedly popular. Most guest beers are from local Norfolk micros plus a few from further afield. Quality wine is from a local importer. An extensive choice of freshly prepared meals using local produce is served in the separate restaurant – booking is advisable, particularly on themed

evenings. The public bar has pool, darts, crib, Sky Sports and Wi-Fi, and pétanque is played. There is a covered, heated smoking area. It is close to the RSPB reserve with nature walks, as well as the boating centre of Brundall. Ramblers welcome. ❀❀◑ ⬜♿P⁵⊟(15A)

Swanton Abbott

Jolly Farmers
North Walsham Road, NR10 5DW (on small country lane off B1150)
🕭 12-2, 4.30-11; 12-11 Fri-Sun ☎ (01692) 538863
Adnams Southwold Bitter; Woodforde's Wherry; guest beer ⊞
Located in a rural north Norfolk village, this old inn reopened about two years ago after a short period of closure. The interior is largely open plan with different drinking areas, including a main bar with a small stage for occasional live performances and a pool area adjacent to the bar. This community local is very pub games oriented, supporting three darts teams and a pool team. There is a separate dining function/room and a large beer garden to the rear. ⚙❀◑♣P⁵⊟(210)

Swanton Morley

Angel
66 Greengate, NR20 4LX (on B1147 towards S edge of village) TG012162
🕭 12-11; 12-10 (6 winter) Sun ☎ (01362) 637407
⊕ theangelpub.co.uk
Hop Back Summer Lightning; Mighty Oak Oscar Wilde; Woodforde's Wherry; guest beer ⊞
Dating back to 1610, this inn boasts a connection with Abraham Lincoln's family. The owners are keen CAMRA members. There is a spacious main bar with a real fire and hop-draped ceilings, and a dining room serving food lunchtimes and evenings (not Sun eve). There are also themed food nights. A live folk group plays on the first Monday of each month. Four beers are usually available. The garden includes a bowling green. See the website for details of the annual beer festival. ⚙Q❀◑♿♣●P⊟(4)

Tacolneston

Pelican Inn Ⓛ
136 Norwich Road, NR16 1PZ (on B1113)
🕭 5-11; 12-2, 6-11 Sat; 12-4 Sun ☎ (01508) 489521
⊕ the-pelican-inn.co.uk
Beer range varies ⊞
Former roadside coaching inn dating from the 17th century, with an old rambling interior with lots of different drinking areas, and a separate restaurant at the rear. There is a large garden which hosts periodic beer festivals. A rotating range of real ales is usually available, mostly from local brewers. Regular events such as live music and quiz nights take place (see website for details). The pub has a bottle shop selling more than 100 different beers, mostly from local micros. En-suite rooms are available. ⚙Q❀❀➝◑♿♣P⁵⊟(10A)

Thetford

Albion
93-95 Castle Street, IP24 2DN (opp Castle Hill)
🕭 12-11 (11.30 Thu; 12.30am Fri); 11-12.30am Sat
☎ (01842) 752796

Greene King IPA, Abbot H
Although still run by the same family, the Albion has undergone a dramatic redesign internally with more of a Greene King house style, but it still offers very reasonable beer prices. Opposite is the Norman castle mound which is built on an Iceni hill fort 1,000 years older. Food is available by ordering out to surrounding restaurants. ▲⊛⋝♣ᵇ⌐

Black Horse
64 Magdalen Street, IP24 2BP
✪ 12-11; 11-1am Fri; 11-midnight Sat ☎ (01842) 762717
Greene King IPA; Woodforde's Wherry; guest beers H
The Horse is just a few yards from the centre of Thetford and offers two guest ales plus the regulars. It is divided into three areas: the bar, a dining area and a darts zone – very important to the teams it supports. There is a menu of good hearty food, so you will not go hungry. Run by a husband and wife team, the Black Horse continues to provide a supply of real ale in Thetford. ⊛◁⋝♣Pᵇ⌐

Thompson

Chequers
Griston Road, IP24 1PX (signed in village on big tree)
✪ 11-3, 6.30-11; 12-3, 7-10.30 Sun ☎ (01953) 483360
⊕ thompsonchequers.co.uk
Beer range varies H
Situated in the tiny village of Thompson, outside Watton, the 16th-century inn has a steep thatched roof and timber-framed interior. When approaching the bar it helps to be 16th-century height to clear the beam. There are two main rooms laid out for dining and a small area and one small room in which to drink. In the summer it is preferable to drink outside. The food is excellent. Wolf guest beers are a feature. Modern accommodation is available. ▲Q⊛⇌◁♣P

Thorpe Market

Gunton Arms Ⅱ
Cromer Road, NR11 8TZ (on A149 N Walsham/Cromer Rd ½ mile S of Thorpe Market; hanging sign on W side of road, pub at end of drive) TG2442434158
✪ 12-11 (10.30 Sun) ☎ (01263) 832010
⊕ theguntonarms.co.uk
Adnams Southwold Bitter, Broadside; Woodforde's Wherry; guest beer H
Award-winning inn situated in the beautiful grounds of Gunton Park with its deer herd, featuring tasteful decor, comfortable furnishings and log fires in winter. East Anglian ales predominate, with regular guests. The first-class restaurant features some dishes cooked in the vaulted main dining room. Accommodation is sumptuous and cosy; most rooms overlook the restored parklands and the deer. Interesting art and artefacts abound for the connoisseur. A high-quality pub worthy of an early visit. ▲Q⊛⇌◁⊟&♣Pᵇ⌐

Thurlton

Queen's Head Ⅱ
Beccles Road, NR14 6RJ (1 mile N of B1136 and 3 miles E of A146) TM414984
✪ 6-11; 5-midnight Fri; 12-midnight Sat; 12-9 Sun
☎ (01508) 548667 ⊕ thurlton-queenshead.co.uk
Beer range varies H

In the village centre, the pub was saved from closure seven years ago when purchased by members of the community and is run by locals Jem and Kathy. Four real ales are usually on offer, mainly from local brewers such as Green Jack, Humpty Dumpty, Buffy's and Grain. The pub is family friendly, with children allowed in the bar, while the village play area is to the rear. There are pool and darts teams and regular live music on Saturdays. ▲⊛&Pᵇ⌐

Tibenham

Greyhound
The Street, NR16 1PZ (300yds from church) TM136895
✪ 12-3 (not Tue), 6-30 (6 Sat)-midnight; 12-11 Sun
☎ (01379) 677676 ⊕ the-greyhound-tibenham.co.uk
Adnams Southwold Bitter; Fuller's London Pride H**; guest beers** H/G
Friendly local community pub in the heart of the south Norfolk countryside offering beers from Adnams and Fuller's plus rotating guests. The interior has many old beams and comprises a lounge, bar area and a small games room with pool table. There is a large car park, and a four-acre field at the rear which hosts many transport-themed events throughout the summer season. The field provides an ideal base for campers and caravanners, complete with electric hook-ups. Walkers may use the car park. ▲⊛◁⊟Å♣Pᵇ⌐

Trowse

White Horse
The Street, NR14 8ST
✪ 11.30-3.30, 5.30-11; 11.30-11 Fri & Sat; 11.30-10 Sun
☎ (01603) 622341 ⊕ whitehorsepub.co.uk
Crouch Vale Brewers Gold; Woodforde's Wherry H
First mentioned in 1836, this ex-Watney's pub was formerly on the busy Norwich-Lowestoft main road. Since Trowse Newton was bypassed, the pub now commands a central position in this quiet village, overlooking the green, which has a children's playground. With a comfortable carpeted dark-wood interior, split into three areas, the pub has a contemporary feel. Popular with office staff at lunchtimes and locals in the evening, there is also a separate function room for hire. ▲⊛◁&♣Pᵇ⌐🚌(587)

Trunch

Crown
Front Street, NR28 0AH (opp church) TG287348
✪ 12-3 (not Mon), 5.30-11 (11.30 Fri & Sat); 12-7 Sun
☎ (01263) 722341
Batemans XB, Yella Belly Gold; Greene King IPA; guest beers H
Set in the middle of a charming north Norfolk village with fine old flint cottages, close to the north Norfolk coast, the Crown, Bateman's only pub in the area, offers an excellent choice of beers and a friendly atmosphere. One of the guest beers is often a Bateman's seasonal beer; the cider is from Westons. Bar snacks are available at all times. A quiz night is held on the second Wednesday in the month; beer festivals and other events are on the pub's Facebook page. Dogs are welcome in the bar. ▲Q⊛🍺Pᵇ⌐🚌(5,34)

Walcott

Lighthouse Inn
Coast Road, NR12 0PE (on B1159) TG359319
☼ 11-11 ☎ (01692) 650371 ⊕ lighthouseinn.co.uk
Beer range varies Ⓗ
A spacious multi-roomed family-oriented pub with a large garden on the coast road between Cromer and Great Yarmouth. Owned and run by the same landlord for over 20 years and Cask Marque-accredited since 1999, the pub supplies a rotating range of real ales; up to four in summer but fewer in winter, usually from Adnams, Wolf, Woodforde's, and nearby local microbrewer Bees Brewery. Quality home-made food using locally sourced ingredients is available all day, including a children's menu and vegetarian options. A discount is available to CAMRA members. ⌂Ᏹ☺◑⏃♣P

Warham All Saints

Three Horseshoes
69 The Street, NR23 1NL (2 miles SE of Wells) TF948417
☼ 12-2.30, 6-11 ☎ (01328) 710547
Woodforde's Wherry; guest beers Ⓗ/Ⓖ
A real pub in every sense of the word, it has a perfect atmosphere for a quiet drink and conversation. The interior comprises three connected rooms that are filled with a fascinating collection of antiques and pictures, including the traditional game of Norfolk Twister. In winter months customers can warm themselves by a log fire in the main bar. The beer garden provides a quiet haven in the summer. The pub is renowned for good traditional cooking, featuring soups, pies and puddings. ⌂Q Ᏹ☺☺◑ よ A♣●P½

Watton

Willow House Ⓛ
2 High Street, IP25 6AE
☼ 10.30-11 (midnight Thu; 12.30am Fri & Sat); 10.30-7 Sun
☎ (01953) 881181 ⊕ thewillowhouse.co.uk
Greene King IPA, St Edmunds; guest beers Ⓗ
A black and white, thatched, 16th-century inn, the interior features cosy low-ceilinged rooms with a separate restaurant. It offers four real ales with two changing guests from good local sources. You can choose from pub food in the bars or a restaurant-only menu. A nice no-nonsense family-run atmosphere pervades. Seven en-suite rooms are available. The front bar features possibly the smallest toilet facilities you will find. Don't worry – there are more in the back bar. ☺☺◑P½ ₩

Wells-next-the-Sea

Albatros
The Quay, NR23 1AT (moored on quayside)
☼ 12-11 (10.30 Sun) ☎ 07979 087228 ⊕ albatros.eu.com
Woodforde's Wherry, Nelson's Revenge; guest beer Ⓖ
Possibly one of the Guide's most unusual entries, the Albatros is a Dutch North Sea clipper that is moored on the quayside of Wells harbour. The bar is in the hold of the ship and is adorned with nautical memorabilia, including shipping maps. It sells up to four Woodforde's beers by gravity. Dutch pancakes, savoury and sweet, are a speciality here.

Live bands perform regularly each Friday and Saturday night, as well as Sunday afternoons in high season. Being a 19th-century vessel, it is not disabled-friendly. ☺◑₩(Coasthopper)

Crown Hotel
The Buttlands, NR23 1EX (SE corner of The Buttlands)
☼ 8am-11 ☎ (01328) 710209 ⊕ thecrownhotelwells.co.uk
Beer range varies Ⓗ
A former coaching inn whose interior has been much modernised, overlooking the picturesque Buttlands Green. Inside are a bar and two restaurants, one of which looks out on the rear garden. Despite the light, airy, modern feel, a sense of history remains about the place, and old photographs of the hotel are all around the bar. There are usually up to two beers from local West Barsham-based Jo C's brewery, plus up to two rotating guest ales.
⌂Q Ᏹ☺☺◑ よ♣P🅟₩(Coasthopper)

West Acre

Stag Ⓛ
Low Road, PE32 1TR
☼ closed Mon; 12-3, 6.30-11 ☎ (01760) 755395
⊕ westacrestag.co.uk
Beer range varies Ⓗ
The pub, popular with walkers, cyclists and riders (there is a water trough for horses in the large car park) can be found at the east end of picturesque West Acre. This is a village renowned for its historic ruins and features occasional military re-enactments. A supporter of LocAle, the Stag maintains a high standard, with three varying beers, and also hosts excellent beer festivals. The popular restaurant offers a wide choice of food and there is a monthly quiz on a Sunday night.
⌂Q☺◑ ᕰよ A♣P₩

Winterton-on-Sea

Fisherman's Return
The Lane, NR29 4BN (off B1159) TG495194
☼ 11-2.30, 5.30 -10.30; 11-11 Sat; 11.30 -10.30 Sun
☎ (01493) 393305 ⊕ fishermansreturn.com
Greene King Skipper; Woodforde's Wherry Ⓗ
A large upmarket inn, over 300 years old, which retains many of its original features. There is a strong emphasis on food, and local ingredients are used where possible. In the 1920s the pub was a popular destination for day trippers from Great Yarmouth. The building to the rear, known as the Tinho, is a survivor of this period. The house ale is from Greene King. Three en-suite bedrooms are available. ⌂Ᏹ☺☺◑ ᕰよ♣●P½₩(1A)

Woodbastwick

Fur & Feather Inn
Slad Lane, NR13 6HQ (just off B1140) TG328151
☼ 10-10 (11 Fri & Sat); 10-9.30 Sun ☎ (01603) 720003
⊕ thefurandfeatherinn.co.uk
Woodforde's Mardlers, Wherry, Once Bittern, Sundew, Nelson's Revenge, Norfolk Nog Ⓖ
Converted from a row of three cottages, this large open-plan pub is largely food-oriented while offering customers the full range of beers from the adjoining Woodforde's Brewery. A tour of the brewery can be arranged in advance and combined with a meal. In summer the large garden provides an excellent area for a drink. The rare Norfolk Nip is

occasionally available, usually as a bottle-conditioned strong ale, which is much prized locally. Q☎❀◑ઠP⇐

Wortwell

Bell

52 High Street, IP20 0HH (off A143)
❂ 12-2.30 (not Mon), 5-11; 12-11 Fri & Sat; 12-10.30 Sun
☎ (01986) 788025 ⊕ wortwellbell.co.uk
Adnams Southwold Bitter; guest beers ⊞
A charming village inn just off the A143, voted South Norfolk Community Pub of the Year 2010. Adnams bitter is supplemented by one or two guest beers which are often based on customer requests. There are separate dining areas where good home-cooked food is served. The pub is family and dog friendly, with a room at the rear available for small functions. Two campsites are within easy reach. ᄊQ☎❀◑Å♣P⇐➡(580)

Wreningham

Bird in Hand

Church Road, NR16 1BJ (7 miles from Norwich on B1113) TM166988
❂ 12-11 ☎ (01508) 489438 ⊕ birdinhandwreningham.com
Adnams Southwold Bitter; Woodforde's Wherry; guest beers ⊞
The original bar of this roadside pub has been converted into the Victorian Dining Room and large extensions have been made to the side and rear of the building to make this a very spacious, if somewhat food-oriented, pub. There is a drinking area adorned with interesting old photos depicting scenes of local village life. Occasional quiz nights are held. Access to the pub is via the car park to the rear of the building. Q❀◑P⇐

Wymondham

Feathers Inn

13 Town Green, NR18 0PN (just off bottom end of marketplace)
❂ 11-2.30, 7-11; 6-midnight Fri; 7-11.30 Sat; 12-2.30, 7-10.30 Sun ☎ (01953) 605675
Adnams Southwold Bitter; Elgood's Feathers Tickler; Fuller's London Pride; Greene King Abbot; guest beers ⊞
The Feathers is an excellent local pub that dates from the early 18th century. It has a cosy bar with alcoves, and the walls are adorned with farming and other memorabilia, including an old bike. The real ale range includes two guest beers and a house beer, Feathers Tickler, brewed by Elgood's. A folk music night is held in the upstairs function room on the last Sunday of the month. Disabled access is through the rear door. Well served by buses. ᄊ❀◑ઠ⇌♣P⇐➡(6,6A,9)

Green Dragon 🅛

6 Church Street, NR18 0PH (close by Wymondham Abbey)
❂ 12-11 (midnight Fri & Sat); 12-10.30 Sun
☎ (01953) 607907 ⊕ greendragonnorfolk.co.uk
Beer range varies ⊞
A remarkable box construction half-timbered inn, formerly a medieval merchant's shop converted in the 16th century. The interior has two bars and a snug that retain many of their original beamed timbers. The medieval carved figures in the mantelpiece serve to emphasise its history. The rotating beer range of four real ales includes brews from Green Jack, Nethergate, Wolf and Humpty Dumpty. A good mix of locals and tourists gives a vibrant feel; quality food is also on offer. ᄊQ❀◑ઠ♣⇐➡(13,14)

Fat Cat, Norwich (Photo: Cath Harries)

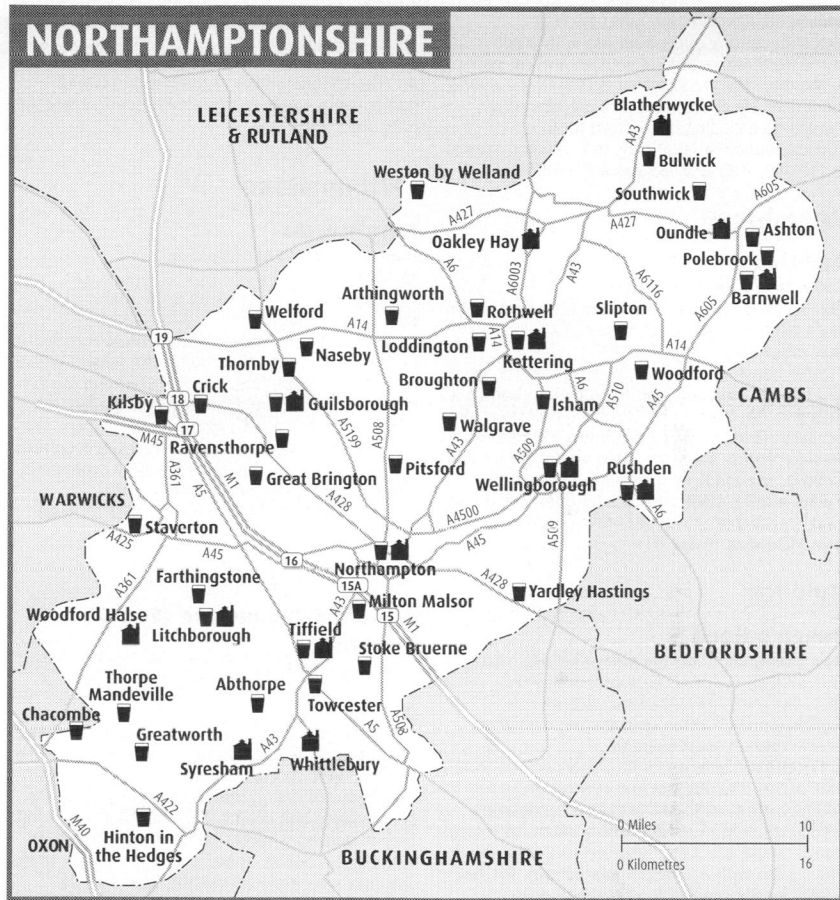

Abthorpe

New Inn 🄻
Silver Street, NN12 8QR SP648465
☼ 12-3 (not Mon & Tue), 6-11; 12-midnight Fri & Sat; 12-10.30 Sun ☎ (01327) 857306 ⊕ newinnabthorpe.co.uk
Hook Norton Hooky Bitter; seasonal beers 🄷
A tranquil country hostelry, hidden up a cul-de-sac off the corner of the village green. This mellow sandstone local with its inglenook fireplace and low-beamed ceilings is well worth searching out. Welcoming to visitors and locals alike, it offers high-quality meals cooked to order and served from the open kitchen, with much of the food locally sourced, including meat from the owner's farm. 🅰🆀🕮🍴🛆🌲Pˡ🚲

Arthingworth

Bull's Head
Kelmarsh Road, LE16 8JZ (off A508)
☼ 12-3, 6-11; 12-11 Sat & Sun ☎ (01858) 525637
⊕ thebullsheadonline.co.uk
Adnams Broadside; Sharp's Doom Bar; Thwaites Original; Wadworth 6X 🄷
A 19th-century former farmhouse situated in rolling countryside. It has several drinking areas on different levels and a restaurant to the front serving home-cooked food from local producers. Ideal for ramblers and cyclists, this is the perfect place to finish a walk or ride in the local area, or to stay over in one of the annexe rooms. A beer festival is held over the August bank holiday on the patio, with more than 30 beers. Sparklers can be removed on request. 🅰🆀🕮🍴🛆🌲Pˡ

Ashton

Chequered Skipper 🄻
The Green, PE8 5LD
☼ 11.30-3, 6-11; 11.30-11 Sat & Sun ☎ (01832) 273494
⊕ chequeredskipper.co.uk
Brewster's Hophead 🄷; **guest beers** 🄷/🄶
The centrepiece of the Rothschild's model village of Ashton, this thatched stone-built pub was rearranged internally in 1997 following a fire. There have been recent extensions to the side adding a coffee bar and a large function room. Regular events include at least two beer festivals each year. Up to four real ales are on offer, with regularly changing guests from local microbreweries. 🆀🕮🍴🌲Pˡ

Barnwell

Montagu Arms 🄻
PE8 5PH
☼ 12-3 (not Mon), 6-11; 12-11 Sat; 12-10.30 Sun
☎ (01832) 273726

Adnams Southwold Bitter; guest beers Ⓗ
Sixteenth-century stone-built inn with a public bar at the front and a large restaurant and car parking to the rear. There is disabled access to the dining room only. Up to four real ales are served via handpump including many from local microbreweries. A large play and camping area is to the rear. ₳Q⊛⏀▣₷▲♣♿P⌐♨(24)

Broughton

Red Lion Ⓛ

7 High Street, NN14 1NF (off A43)
⊛ 12-2.30 (not Mon), 5-11; 12-midnight Fri & Sat; 12-11 Sun
☎ (01536) 790239 ⊕ redlionbroughton.co.uk
Beer range varies Ⓗ
Popular ironstone locals' pub with three rooms: a bar, lounge and semi open-plan dining room. Six changing ales are served, including one from local lad Julian Church and another from a Northants brewery. Future beers are listed on the bar and the website. The landlady likes dark beers, so there is always a mild, stout or porter on offer. Good local food is available. A recent CAMRA award winner.
Q⊛⏀▣₷♣♿P⌐♨(39)

Bulwick

Queen's Head ♟ Ⓛ

Main Street, NN17 3DY (on main street opp church)
⊛ closed Mon; 12-3, 6-11; 12-10.30 Sun
☎ (01780) 450272 ⊕ thequeensheadbulwick.co.uk
Digfield Barnwell Bitter; Oakham JHB; Shepherd Neame Spitfire; guest beers Ⓗ
A 17-century stone pub with a Collyweston slate roof. Inside, the pub has low ceilings and exposed beams with a single bar with five handpumps serving a range of varying beers, often from local micros. There are three separate rooms for diners and a patio with a leafy pergola outside. The high-quality locally sourced food is thoroughly recommended. CAMRA local branch Pub of the Year 2013. ₳Q⊛⏀▣♣♿P⌐

Chacombe

George & Dragon

1 Silver Street, OX17 2JR (between A361 and B4525 near Banbury)
⊛ 12-midnight ☎ (01295) 711500 ⊕ georgeanddragon.org
Everards Beacon, Tiger; guest beers Ⓗ
A traditional stone-built pub in front of the small village green. The bar area has a stone-flagged floor and wooden beams, and the bar itself features a glass top revealing a 26ft well. This Everard's pub has two regular beers and two changing guests. There are three small rooms for diners along with three impressive fireplaces. Outside is a pretty patio terrace and Aunt Sally is played in the garden. Cider is stocked in summer only. ₳Q♿⊛⏀♣P⌐♨(500)

Crick

Royal Oak

22 Church Street, NN6 7TP (200yds from A428 past the church)
⊛ 4-11; 3-10.30 Sun ☎ (01788) 822340
Oakham JHB, Bishop's Farewell; guest beers Ⓗ
Friendly village local, hidden from the main A428 near the church. The wood-beamed cottage-style free house has pictures and brasses hanging from the walls. Open fires warm the two main drinking areas, giving the pub a cosy feel. Northants skittles and darts matches are played in the games room. An ever-changing beer range features 10-12 guests every week. Snacks are limited to crisps and nuts. ₳⏀⊛♣P⌐♨

Farthingstone

King's Arms

Main Street, NN12 8EZ (opp church)
⊛ closed Mon; 7-11 Tue-Thu; 6.30-midnight Fri; 12-4, 7-midnight Sat; 12-4, 9-11 Sun ☎ (01327) 361604
Beer range varies Ⓗ
A quintessentially English 18th-century free house in the heart of the countryside. The listed building with its inglenook fireplace and warming log fires has a unique and fascinating secret garden. A separate games room has Northants skittles. The pub is a retail outlet for fine cheeses and Cornish fish. Lunchtime food is served only at weekends, although speciality food evenings with entertainment are held regularly. ₳Q⊛⏀♣♿P

Great Brington

Althorp Coaching Inn (Fox & Hounds)

Main Street, NN7 4JA
⊛ 11-midnight; 12-11 Sun ☎ (01604) 770651
⊕ althorp-coaching-inn.co.uk
Fuller's London Pride; Greene King IPA; Hook Norton Old Hooky; St Austell Tribute; guest beers Ⓗ
A listed stone coaching inn in a small village with a thatched roof dating from the 16th century. The pub features oak beams, flagstone floors and log fires in winter. It serves good quality food along with eight real ales. There is a large car park to the rear and a separate restaurant area, outside courtyard and garden with a smoking area.
₳Q⊛⏀♣P⌐

Greatworth

Inn Ⓛ

Capel Road, OX17 2DT
⊛ 12-2.30 (not Mon), 6-11; 12-11 Sat & Sun
☎ (01295) 710976

Hook Norton Hooky Bitter, seasonal beer; guest beer Ⓗ
An enthusiastically run hostelry situated in the centre of this small village serving local real ales and good home-cooked food. The lovely cosy bar area has a large fireplace and low-beamed ceiling. On either side is a stepped restaurant and a small snug with games. Outside is a patio, garden and family room, and the local game of Aunt Sally. Real cider is available in summer. ♨️➪🏵️◑♣️P'–

Guilsborough

Ward Arms Ⓛ
High Street, NN6 8PY SP6813271096
🕐 12-2.30 (not Mon), 5-11; 12-midnight Fri-Sun
☎ (01604) 740265 ⊕ thewardarms.webs.com
Nobby's Best, Guilsborough Gold; guest beers Ⓗ
A 17th-century pub in the heart of a historic rural village, built from ironstone, with white rendering and a thatched roof. The old stables have been converted into Nobby's Brewery and visitor centre. Nobby's beers, including seasonals, feature heavily on the bar along with guests that increase in number in the summer. Traditional home-cooked locally-sourced food is served (not Mon lunch). Northants skittles and pool are played.
♨️Q🏵️◑◙♣️●P'–🗍🚃(60)

Hinton in the Hedges

Crewe Arms Ⓛ
Sparrow Corner, NN13 5NF (off A43/A422)
🕐 6 (12 Sat & Sun)-11 ☎ (01280) 705801
⊕ thecrewearms.com
Hook Norton Hooky Bitter; guest beers Ⓗ
Stone-built local tucked away in the village and well worth seeking out. Inside there are four rooms – a traditional bar, lounge, relaxing snug and garden room. Comfortable furnishings blend well with the original and newer parts of the building. Good-quality traditional home-cooked food is served (no food Mon). The two guest beers are from national, regional and, more often, microbreweries. CAMRA members receive a 10 per cent discount on accommodation.
♨️Q🏵️🛏️◑◙♿●P'–

Isham

Lilacs
39 Church Street, NN14 1HD (off A509 at church)
🕐 12-midnight ☎ (01536) 723948
Greene King IPA, Abbot; H&H Olde Trip; guest beer Ⓗ
A very warm welcome is assured from the landlord and his staff who are passionate about keeping and serving quality real ale. The pub has an interesting layout with a quiet snug room, a lounge to the front and an open, almost hall-like games and entertainment room to the rear. The U-shaped bar serves as wide a range of ales as possible from the Greene King list. Pool and Northants skittles are played. ♨️Q🏵️◑◙♣️P'–🚃(X4)

Kettering

Alexandra Arms Ⓛ
39 Victoria Street, NN16 0BU (400yds from bus station)
🕐 2-11; 12-midnight Fri & Sat; 12-11 Sun ☎ (01536) 522730
Beer range varies Ⓗ
Traditional town-centre street-corner local where you will always find a beer from an unknown

brewery. The landlord takes great pride in searching out new ales, with over 8,000 different beers from over 800 breweries served over a 10-year period. The front bar serves two opened-out rooms, with the walls covered in breweriana. The rear bar has a TV and Northants skittles table. The cellar is home to the Julian Church Brewery, with at least one of its beers always on the bar. Often voted Northamptonshire CAMRA Pub of the Year. Q🏵️◙➪♣️♿–🚃

Cherry Tree Ⓛ
Sheep Street, NN16 0AN (opp church)
🕐 12-midnight (6 Mon; 7 Wed; 1am Fri & Sat)
☎ (01536) 514706
Potbelly Best, Crazy Daze, Hedonism; Wells Bombardier; guest beers Ⓗ
The oldest hostelry in town, this green-tiled low-ceilinged building has the feel of a traditional village inn. Three Potbelly beers always feature and one from Oakham. The interior was opened out a few years ago and is served by a central L-shaped bar. The pub focuses on live music, with rock bands on Friday and Saturday nights and jam sessions on other nights. Music starts from 9.30pm, and the volume is loud. ♿➪●🚃

Three Cocks
48 Lower Street, NN16 8DJ
🕐 12-11.30 (11 Sun)
Beer range varies Ⓗ/Ⓖ
The pub has been refurbished to provide a warm and relaxing environment. The L-shaped servery is at the centre, supplying two bar areas furnished with comfortable armchairs and high-backed stools. On an upper level is a games area featuring Northants skittles and darts, and a shove-ha'penny board is available. Beers are often from Mighty Oak, Brentwood and George's. Well-filled cobs are on offer for the peckish. Q♿➪♣️●'–🚃

Kilsby

George
Watling Street, CV23 8YE
🕐 11.30-3, 5 30-11; 12-5, 6-11 Sun ☎ (01788) 822229
⊕ thegeorgeatkilsby.co.uk
Adnams Southwold Bitter; Fuller's London Pride; Taylor Landlord; guest beer Ⓗ
The George was rebuilt in the 1840s on the site of an old coaching inn using bricks from Kilsby railway tunnel. Ample car parking, a beer garden, dining room, lounge and function room plus accommodation make this a popular venue for events and private functions. A quiz night every Sunday, themed food nights midweek and jazz on the first Sunday of the month all add to the community spirit. Q🏵️🛏️◑◙♣️P'–🚃

Litchborough

Old Red Lion Ⓛ
4 Banbury Road, NN12 8JF
🕐 12-11 (10.30 Sun) ☎ (01327) 830064
Phipps Red Star; guest beers Ⓗ
The bar area here has flagstone flooring and a large inglenook with seats inside. A small passage leads to two further cosy rooms, one with a pool table. Near the Knightly Way footpath, the pub is popular with walkers and cyclists, and incorporates a mini shop selling local farm produce. A wide range of locally brewed bottled beers is stocked, with

Hoggleys Brewery a short distance away. Northants skittles is played in the new extension. ♨Q♿❄◐&♣P⊱

Loddington

Hare Ⓛ

5 Main Street, NN14 1LA
☼ 12-3, 5.30-11; 12-11 Sat & Sun ☎ (01536) 710337
⊕ thehareatloddington.co.uk
Sharp's Doom Bar; Wells Bombardier; guest beers Ⓗ
The Hare at Loddington is a listed building in the conservation area of this picturesque village. Built from local ironstone, it stands in the middle of Main Street surrounded by listed houses. The pub is open plan with four separate areas – one a dining area serving good home-cooked food made using local produce. Local ales come mainly from Julian Church and Langton breweries. ♨Q❄◐●P⊱

Milton Malsor

Compass Ⓛ

61 Green Street, NN7 3AT (follow signs for school)
☼ 5-11 (midnight Fri); 12-11 Sat & Sun ☎ (01604) 858365
Potbelly Best; guest beer Ⓗ
Two changing beers are available, usually local, often from Hoggleys Brewery. The long L-shaped interior has darts at one end and Northants skittles at the other, with four pub teams. Two beer festivals are held in outbuildings on the May and August bank holidays, and live music features occasionally. Well-behaved children are welcome until 8pm. ♨❄♣P⊱🚃(8,89)

Naseby

Royal Oak

Church Street, NN6 6DA (on B4036)
☼ 12-2 (not Tue), 5-11; 12-midnight Sat; 12-7 Sun
☎ (01604) 743310
Fuller's London Pride; Oakham Bishops Farewell; guest beers Ⓗ
A popular pub with walkers and Northants skittles players alike, the L-shaped single room is divided into three areas with a real fire in the wall between the main bar and games room. Four guest ales are served, always including one from Oakham Ales and usually another from a local brewery. A recent addition is home-cooked food (no lunch Tue). An annual beer festival is held on the St George's weekend in an adjoining barn. ♨Q♿❄◐&♣●P⊱

Northampton

Eastgate

98-100 Abington Street, NN1 2BP (E end of pedestrianised zone)
☼ 7am-11 ☎ (01604) 633535
Greene King Abbot; Ruddles Best Bitter; guest beers Ⓗ
Popular Wetherspoon pub boasting two banks of four handpumps, with one pump dedicated to a dark beer. Local microbreweries are supported and beer festivals feature international beers in racked casks served by gravity. Spread over two floors, there is a keg-only bar and smokers' balcony upstairs. The sound is usually muted on the TVs and there is no music. Q❄◐&●⊱🚃

Lamplighter Ⓛ

66 Overstone Road, NN1 3JS
☼ 12-midnight; 10-1am Fri & Sat; 10-11 Sun
☎ (01604) 631125
Phipps IPA; Vale Pale Ale; guest beers Ⓗ
A friendly locals' pub just outside the town centre and much the better for it. Open mic sessions are held on Monday and regular gigs and music nights on other nights. A good selection of bottled and continental beers is available. Home-cooked food is served until 8pm, and children are welcome during meal times. There is a roaring fire in the bar and an outside courtyard heated in the colder seasons. ♨❄◐&♣⊱🚃

Malt Shovel Tavern Ⓛ

121 Bridge Street, NN1 1QF (opp Carlsberg brewery)
☼ 11.30-3, 5-11; 11.30-11 Fri & Sat; 12-10.30 Sun
☎ (01604) 234212 ⊕ maltshoveltavern.com
Fuller's London Pride; Great Oakley Wot's Occurring, Harpers, Gobble; Oakham Bishops Farewell; guest beers Ⓗ
Just off the town centre, this popular pub is a former local CAMRA Pub of the Year. The tap for the Great Oakley Brewery, its beers always feature among the 14 handpumps. A real cider and Belgian draught and bottled beers are also available. At least two beer festivals are held each year, usually over bank holidays. Blues bands play on Wednesday nights. The pub has a strong rugby following. Home-made lunches are served Monday to Saturday. Well worth visiting. Q❄◐&⇌♣●⊱🚃(12,14)

Moon on the Square

6 The Parade, NN1 2EA
☼ 8am-11 (midnight Thu-Sun) ☎ (01604) 634062
Greene King Abbot; Ruddles Best Bitter; guest beers Ⓗ
Situated in the town centre opposite the largest historic market place in the country, this large, open-plan pub is on two levels (lift provided), with a quiet conservatory to the rear. It offers a good selection of ales and cider, and holds beer festivals several times a year. Food is served all day, every day. There are TV screens with the volume turned down and free Wi-Fi is provided. ♿◐&⇌●⊱🚃

Olde England Ⓛ

199 Kettering Road, NN1 4BP (near racecourse)
☼ 11-11 (midnight Fri & Sat); 12-11 Sun ☎ 07741 069768
⊕ theoldeengland.com
Great Oakley Wagtail Ⓖ; **Jennings Sneck Lifter; Marston's Old Empire** Ⓗ; **Potbelly Beijing Black** Ⓖ; **guest beers** Ⓗ/Ⓖ
A unique welcoming pub on three floors in a converted Victorian corner shop. The ground and first floors have a medieval theme and solid fuel burners. The cellar bar is in a contemporary style and is more intimate. Games include cards, dominoes, chess and various board games. More than 20 beers are available from local micros and regional breweries. There are also over 20 ciders from producers including Gwynt y Ddraig and Millwhites. ♨Q❄◐♣●⊱

Queen Adelaide Ⓛ

50 Manor Road, Kingsthorpe, NN2 6QJ (off A5199)
☼ 11.30-11.30; 12-10.30 Sun ☎ (01604) 714524
⊕ queenadelaide.com
Adnams Southwold Bitter, Broadside; Copper Dragon Golden Pippin; guest beers Ⓗ

This fine establishment has twice been local CAMRA Pub of the Year runner-up and is a regular Guide entry. An 18th-century listed stone-built local, it has low beams and an uneven floor in the bar. Run by a real ale and cider enthusiast, this friendly pub is known for high-quality beers and generous servings of good food. Up to four guest ales are often from local microbreweries. The Sunday roasts are exceptional (booking advised). A popular pub with rugby followers.
❀❍❶ 🖵🚶♣ 🚰P⁵–🚌(4,4A)

Road to Morocco

Bridgewater Drive, Abington Vale, NN3 3AG (off A4500, near Abington Park)
✪ 12-11 (midnight Fri & Sat); 12-10.30 Sun
☎ (01604) 632899
Greene King IPA, Abbot; Theakston Old Peculier; guest beers 🅷
This pub in the Abington Vale area of Northampton is well worth seeking out. Run by an enthusiastic landlord, eight real ales are usually served, with Theakston Old Peculier a regular favourite. The five guest beers are sourced from smaller and regional breweries, often including Cornish brews. It's a two-roomed pub with a pool table and live sport on TV. ❀🖵🚶♣🚰P⁵–🚌(5)

Wheatsheaf

126 Dallington Road, Dallington, NN5 7HN
✪ 11-11 (11.30 Fri & Sat); 12-10.30 Sun ☎ (01604) 758871
⊕ wheatsheafdallington.co.uk
Everards Sunchaser, Tiger; guest beers 🅷
Attractive stone and thatch two-roomed pub with an unspoilt frontage, tucked away in the conservation area of Dallington opposite the 13th-century village church. The bar has a partly flagstoned floor and hosts live music on Saturday nights and open mic on Tuesdays. The lounge/dining room is a large, quiet area with many photos of old Dallington on the walls. A veterans' lunch is served on Tuesday. Up to four guest ales and one real cider complement the regular beers.
🚌❀❍❶🖵🚶♣🚰P⁵–🚌

Wig & Pen 🍷 🕼

19 St Giles Street, NN1 1JA
✪ 12-11 (10.30 Sun) ☎ (01604) 622178
⊕ wigandpennorthampton.co.uk
Fuller's London Pride; Greene King IPA; Morland Old Speckled Hen; guest beers 🅷
The frontage of this pub is over 300 years old, while the long L-shaped bar was added 150 years ago. The oak-beamed bar offers six frequently changing guest beers including a mild and a local microbrewery beer. A guest cider and a wide range of bottled beers are also available. Jazz bands play on Tuesday nights and live bands perform in the beer garden on summer evenings. Good home-cooked food features local ingredients. CAMRA members receive a 10 per cent discount on beer. Local CAMRA Pub of The Year 2012.
❀❶🚶⚲♣🚰♂–🚌

Pitsford

Griffin Inn 🕼

25 High Street, NN6 9AD (between A43 and A508)
✪ 6-midnight; 12-4, 7-midnight Sun ☎ (01604) 880346
⊕ griffinpitsford.co.uk
Greene King Abbot; Potbelly Best; guest beers 🅷
Formerly cottages, this Grade II-listed 17th-century ironstone pub is family run and owned. It has

retained most of its original character and is festooned with fascinating artefacts in both the cosy bar room and larger comfortable lounges to the rear. Good, reasonably priced food is available in the restaurant. On Sunday there are quizzes at lunchtime and in the evening, while food-themed nights feature regularly. The two guest beers are often from Potbelly. Open all day on bank holidays.
🚌Q❀❶🖵🚶♣🚰P⁵–🚌(X7,62)

Polebrook

King's Arms 🕼

Kings Arms Lane, PE8 5LW
✪ 12-3, 6-11 (midnight Fri); 12-11.30 Sat; 12-11 Sun
☎ (01832) 272363 ⊕ thekingsarms-polebrook.co.uk
Beer range varies 🅷
Situated in the centre of the village, this traditional stone-built thatched inn has a main bar, three areas for diners and a small garden. Five real ales are on offer at weekends including two from the nearby Digfield Brewery. Third-pint glasses are available to allow customers to try a wide variety of beer. There is an annual themed beer festival mid-September and regular food and beer pairing evenings. 🚌Q❀❶❍🚶♣🚰P⁵–🚌(25)

Ravensthorpe

Chequers

Chequers Lane, NN6 8ER (between A428 and A5199)
✪ 12-3, 6-11; 12-11 Sat & Sun ☎ (01604) 770379
Fuller's London Pride; Oakham JHB; Thwaites Original; guest beers 🅷
The hosts have been welcoming visitors to this pub for more than 20 years. The brick-built Grade II-listed free house is popular with locals, walkers and fishermen alike. It has an L-shaped bar and a restaurant serving excellent home-cooked food. Outside is a children's play area and a separate building for Northants skittles.
Q❀❶🚶♣🚰P⁵–🚌(96)

Rothwell

Rowell Charter 🕼

Sun Hill, NN14 6AB (on old A6)
✪ 12-11 (10.30 Sun) ☎ (01536) 710453
Fuller's London Pride; Sharp's Doom Bar; guest beers 🅷
The Rowell Charter dates from 1642 and is built from Northants ironstone, with new rooms added to provide three split levels, with low door lintels and ceilings. The name commemorates the granting of the charter by King John in 1204 when the town was officially permitted to hold the annual fair and market. A proclamation is held every year on the first Monday after Trinity Sunday when the pub opens at 6am and holds a beer festival during the week. Five guest ales are offered, plus two ciders. 🚌Q❀❶🖵♣🚰P⁵–🚌(19)

Rushden

Rushden Historical Transport Society 🕼

Station Approach, NN10 0AW (on ring road)
✪ 7.30 (6 Wed & Thu; 4.30 Fri)-11, 12-11 Sat & Sun
☎ (01933) 318988 ⊕ rhts.co.uk
Grainstore Phipps IPA; Oakham Bishops Farewell; guest beers 🅷

Former Midland Railway station now a mecca for real ale. A real gem, the bar occupies the former ladies' waiting room, with gas lighting and walls adorned with enamel advertising panels and railway photos plus many CAMRA awards. On the platform, carriages including a Royal Mail postal van are used for meetings and skittles. Open weekends are held during the summer with steam- and diesel-hauled train rides. A beer festival is hosted in September. Day membership is £1 except on open days.
ᴹᴬQ☺&♣●'ᵗ⊟(X46,M50)

Slipton

Samuel Pepys Ⓛ
Slipton Lane, NN14 3AR (off A6116)
✪ 12-3, 5-11; 12-5 Sat; 12-5 (10.30 Easter-New Year) Sun
☎ (01832) 731739 ∰ samuel-pepys.com
Digfield Fools Nook Ⓗ; guest beers Ⓗ/Ⓖ
Set in a lovely thatched village, this ironstone pub has been modernised although it has retained the traditional low-beamed and brick-floored bar to the front where locals and visitors can chat or relax in cosy armchairs in front of a real fire. To the side is a dining/lounge bar while for more special occasions there is a conservatory restaurant decorated and furnished in a smart modern style. There are five guest beers, some on gravity, often come from local micros. ᴹᴬQ☺◑⊞Pᵗ

Southwick

Shuckburgh Arms Ⓛ
Main Street, PE8 5BL
✪ 10 (9 Sat & Sun)-11 ☎ (01832) 272044
∰ shuckburghpub.co.uk
Brewster's Hophead; Nene Valley Bitter; guest beer Ⓗ
Adjacent to the village hall and cricket pitch, this thatched stone pub has a front bar and side room. The main bar has five handpumps selling mostly local ales from microbreweries. Outside is a covered patio area with its own bar and handpump. A three-day music festival is hosted in July and the pub cricket team plays throughout the summer. ᴹᴬQ☺◑⊞&Å●Pᵗ

Staverton

Countryman
Daventry Road, NN11 6JH (on A425)
✪ 12-3, 6-11; 12-11 Sun ☎ (01327) 311815
∰ thecountrymanstaverton.co.uk
Fuller's London Pride; guest beers Ⓗ
Formerly the New Inn, the Countryman is the last of three pubs remaining in this lovely village. The L-shaped bar, with wood beams throughout, serves four areas, some set aside for diners, and an open hearth fire between the spaces provides some seclusion. With an enthusiastic landlord at the helm, a wide choice of reasonably priced food, sourced locally whenever possible, is served along with two changing guest beers, often from local breweries. ᴹᴬ☺◑&P⊟(65,66)

Stoke Bruerne

Boat Inn
Bridge Road, NN12 7SB (opp canal museum)
✪ 11-11; 12-10.30 Sun ☎ (01604) 862428 ∰ boatinn.co.uk
Banks's Bitter; Jennings Cumberland Ale; Marston's Old Empire; Wychwood Hobgoblin; guest beer Ⓗ

Situated on the banks of the Grand Union Canal, the Boat Inn has been run by the same family since 1877. The delightful Tap Bar with interconnecting rooms has open fires, original stone floors, window seats and views overlooking the canal and National Museum, while an adjoining room has Northants skittles. Popular with diners, a large extension houses the lounge, restaurant and bistro. Additional beers are sold in the summer. A canal boat is available to hire for parties. The cider is Thatchers Heritage. ᴹᴬQ➳☺◑⊞&♣●Pᵗ⊟(86)

Thornby

Red Lion
Welford Road, NN6 8SJ (on A5199)
✪ 10-2.30 (not Mon), 5-11; 12-11 Sat & Sun
☎ (01604) 740238 ∰ redlionthornby.co.uk
Beer range varies Ⓗ
Situated on the old A50, this traditional village pub dates back to 1719. The compact bar has two drinking areas with a wood-burning open fire in the lounge. To the rear is the restaurant, which occupies two linked rooms, one heavily beamed (no food Mon). There is always a guest beer from Adnams and Grainstore, with five to choose from. During the summer, classic car meetings are held along with pig roasts. ᴹᴬQ☺◑⊞&Pᵗ

Thorpe Mandeville

Three Conies Ⓛ
Banbury Lane, OX17 2EX
✪ 10-midnight ☎ (01295) 711025 ∰ threeconiesinn.co.uk
Hook Norton Hooky Bitter, Gold, Old Hooky, seasonal beers; guest beer Ⓗ
Located in a picturesque, untouched village, this popular pub dates from the 17th century when it was a drovers' inn. The beamed bars have open fires at both ends, and the restaurant has a vaulted ceiling and woodburner. A Northants skittles team plays here; they are rewarded with an annual beer festival in the summer and a cider festival in April. The pub opens at 10am for coffee. ᴹᴬ☺◑&♣Pᵗ

Tiffield

George Inn Ⓛ
21 High Street, NN12 8AD (off A43)
✪ 12-3 (not Tue), 6-midnight; 12-1am Sat; 12-7 Sun
☎ (01327) 350587 ∰ thegeorgeattiffield.co.uk
Great Oakley Wot's Occurring; Vale VPA; guest beers Ⓗ
Popular and welcoming village pub dating back to the 16th century with Victorian and more modern additions. It has three rooms – a cosy bar, games room with Northants skittles and a back room for dining which can also be booked for club and group meetings. Two ever-changing guest beers and Old Rosie cider complement the regular ales. Wednesday is live music night, with open mic sessions held every other week. Two annual beer festivals are hosted. Northamptonshire Rural Community Pub of the Year 2012/13.
ᴹᴬQ➳☺◑⊞Å♣●Pᵗ⊟(8,89)

Towcester

Plough
96 Watling Street, NN12 6BT
✪ 11-11 ☎ (01327) 350738 ∰ theploughinn.biz
Wells Bombardier; Young's Bitter; guest beers Ⓗ

The Plough has a cosy front bar with stone floors and a large bay window overlooking the main street, and a larger lounge bar/restaurant to the rear. A wide corridor runs from the front to the back of the pub, leading to a small drinking area outside. Two constantly changing guest beers are available. Just behind the building stands Bury Mount, on which the town's Roman fort once stood. No food is available on Monday. ◑▣P⁵⌐🖾(8,89)

Walgrave

Royal Oak

Zion Hill, NN6 9PN (2 miles N of A43)
❂ 11.30-2.30, 5.30 (5 Fri & Sat)-11; 12-10.30 Sun
☎ (01604) 781248
Adnams Southwold Bitter; Greene King Abbot; guest beers Ⓗ
A mid-19th century ironstone-built pub set back and high up from the main road. The wood-beamed front bar is semi open plan with a drinking area to the left of the bar and dining on either side, warmed by a log fire in a stone inglenook. To the rear is a small bar, cosy lounge and a function area. Outside, there is a room for Northants skittles and children's play equipment in the garden. Three changing guest beers are available.
Q⭹❀◑▣⅙♣P⁵⌐🖾(39)

Welford

Wharf Inn

NN6 6JQ (on A5199 N of village)
❂ 12-11 (midnight Sun) ☎ (01858) 575075
⊕ wharfinn.co.uk
Marston's Pedigree; guest beers Ⓗ
Situated on the Leicestershire border, this brick-built inn lies at the end of the Welford arm of the Grand Union Canal and is popular with narrowboat travellers, locals and tourists alike. Inside, the main bar and dining area are separated by a large open fire. A smaller bar is on a lower level to the front. A beer festival is hosted in the summer and themed events are held regularly. Four guest beers always include an Oakham ale. Well-behaved children and dogs are welcome. ♨Q⭹❀🚃◑▣⅙▲♣●P⁵⌐🖾

Wellingborough

Coach & Horses Ⓛ

17 Oxford Street, NN8 4HY
❂ 12-11 (9 Mon; 6 Sun) ☎ (01933) 441242
Beer range varies Ⓗ
Town-centre local with an enthusiastic landlord who is fully committed to offering a good choice of up to 14 beers and ciders, including two changing local microbrews, often from Great Oakley and Potbelly. A former CAMRA East Midlands Regional Pub of the Year runner-up, the Victorian pub has a single L-shaped room with cosy corners. Lots of breweriana adorn the front bar area, which is warmed by a real fire. Traditional home-cooked food is served lunchtimes and evenings (no food Sun eve, Mon and Tue). ♨Q❀◑⅙♣●⁵⌐🖾

Locomotive Ⓛ

111 Finedon Road, NN8 4AL (on A510)
❂ 12-11 ☎ (01933) 276600

Grainstore Phipps IPA; Sharp's Doom Bar; guest beers Ⓗ
A popular locals' pub on the outskirts of the town with a railway theme literally running throughout, with a display of classic 00-gauge locomotives behind the bar and a railway running above the servery. There are three rooms, the front bar with armchairs and a piano for a relaxing ambience. Bar billiards and skittles are played. A large selection of beers is served from Oakham, Great Oakley and other micros. No food on Sunday.
♨Q❀◑♣●⁵⌐🖾(45)

Weston by Welland

Wheel & Compass

Valley Road, LE16 8HZ (off B664)
❂ 12-11 (10.30 Sun) ☎ (01858) 565864
⊕ thewheelandcompass.co.uk
Greene King Abbot; Marston's Burton Bitter, Pedigree; guest beer Ⓗ
The Wheel has a small, cosy bar and lounge and a large dining room. An outside drinking area offers good views and is an ideal playground for children. The pub is one of the original five founders of the Welland Valley Beerfest, which attracts beer fans from all over the country in June. It is also a favourite stop-off for walkers on the Jurassic Way which runs close by. ♨Q❀🚃◑⅙P⁵⌐🖾(167)

Woodford

Duke's Arms Ⓛ

83 High Street, NN14 4HE (off A14/A510)
❂ 12-11 ☎ (01832) 732224
Digfield Fool's Nook; Greene King IPA, Abbot; guest beers Ⓗ
Now the only pub in the village, the Duke's overlooks the village green and is named after the Duke of Wellington who was a frequent visitor to Woodford. It has a main bar, dining room and games room with Northants skittles, darts and pool, and a new 3D TV. Home-cooked meals using local produce are served daily (no food Sun & Mon eve). Events include a beer festival on the Whitsun bank holiday and a music festival on the August bank holiday. Five guest beers often come from Oakham and Elgood's.
♨⭹❀◑▣⅙♣●P⁵⌐🖾(16)

Yardley Hastings

Rose & Crown Ⓛ

4 Northampton Road, NN7 1EX
❂ 12-3 (not Mon), 5-11; 12-midnight Fri & Sat; 12-10.30 Sun
☎ (01604) 696276 ⊕ roseandcrownbistro.co.uk
Phipps IPA; Greene King IPA, Abbot; guest beers Ⓗ
Hidden in the village, this ironstone pub has a large single room in olde-worlde style. It retains stone-flagged floors and beamed ceilings, and has a small drinking area in the bay window. The emphasis is on traditional home cooking, with a menu that changes daily, offering some tempting dishes and good service. Regular live music ranges from jazz to rock to blues. The landscaped gardens are wonderful in summer, now with a new boules court. ❀◑P⁵⌐🖾(P1)

Good ale is the true and proper drink of Englishmen. He is not deserving of the name of Englishman who speaketh against ale, that is good ale. **George Borrow**, Lavengro

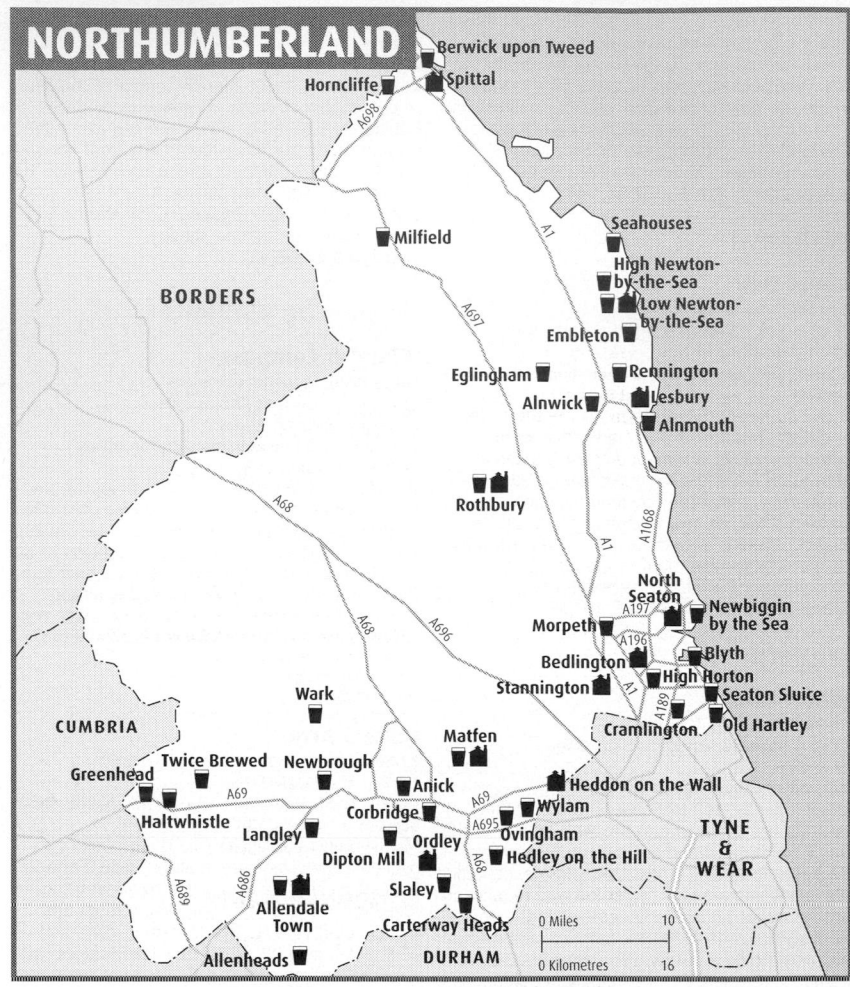

NORTHUMBERLAND

Berwick upon Tweed
Horncliffe
Spittal
BORDERS
Milfield
Seahouses
High Newton-by-the-Sea
Low Newton-by-the-Sea
Embleton
Eglingham
Rennington
Alnwick
Lesbury
Alnmouth
Rothbury
North Seaton
Newbiggin by the Sea
Morpeth
Bedlington
Blyth
High Horton
Wark
Stannington
Seaton Sluice
CUMBRIA
Matfen
Cramlington
Old Hartley
Twice Brewed Newbrough
Greenhead
Anick
Heddon on the Wall
Haltwhistle
Corbridge
Wylam
Langley
Ovingham
TYNE & WEAR
Dipton Mill
Ordley
Hedley on the Hill
Slaley
Allendale Town
Carterway Heads
0 Miles 10
Allenheads
DURHAM
0 Kilometres 16

Allendale Town

Golden Lion Hotel L
Market Place, NE47 9BD
☼ 12-1.30am (1am Wed; 2.30am Fri-Sun)
☎ (01434) 683225 ⊕ goldenlionhotel.net
Taylor Landlord; Wylam Gold Tankard; guest beers Ⓗ
A friendly and hospitable pub in the market place, home to sociable locals and their dogs. The walls are adorned with photographs of the annual tar barrel procession, an experience in itself. The pub has a late licence at the weekend. The local choir practises here on Tuesday evening, and there is live Irish music on the last Wednesday of the month. ▲✿🏠◐ ⑤🍴(688)

King's Head
Market Place, NE47 9BD (market place square, opp Co-Op)
☼ 12-11 ☎ (01434) 683681
Jennings Cumberland Ale; guest beers Ⓗ
A welcoming, upmarket inn situated in the town square next to the Golden Lion, popular with locals, tourists, ramblers and day trippers. The refurbished bar retains original features such as an open log fire. Traditional pub food is served all day. Rail and bus links to Allendale are good, and it is well worth

seeking out this small market town. The area is renowned for countryside walks. Handy for the PlusBus via Hexham rail station.
▲Q✿🏠◐ ⑤🍴(688)

Allenheads

Allenheads Inn L
NE47 9HJ
☼ 4 (12 Sat)-11; 12-10.30 Sun ☎ (01434) 685200
⊕ allenheadsinn.co.uk
Black Sheep Best Bitter; guest beers Ⓗ

INDEPENDENT BREWERIES
Allendale Allendale Town
Anarchy Stannington
Bear Claw Spittal (NEW)
Coquetdale Rothbury (NEW)
Gundog North Seaton
Hexhamshire Ordley
High House Farm Matfen
Northumberland Bedlington
Ship Inn Low Newton by the Sea
VIP Lesbury
Wylam Heddon on the Wall

Superb 18th-century rural inn with a public bar with log fire, games room and dining room. It is on the Coast-to-Coast cycle route and very popular with cyclists, ramblers and tourists. Good bar meals are available at a decent price. Originally the home of Sir Thomas Wentworth, the premises are bedecked with memorabilia and knick-knacks from a bygone age. Take care (and skis) in the winter. The pub will open early on request for coach parties and rambling groups. 🏚🌣🍴🍺◑👜♣P🍴(688)

Alnmouth

Red Lion Inn

22 Northumberland Street, NE66 2RJ
✪ 11-midnight ☎ (01665) 830584 ⊕ redlionalnmouth.com
Black Sheep Best Bitter; guest beers ⒣
Charming family-run 18th-century coaching inn with a cosy lounge bar with attractive woodwork. Panoramic views across the Aln estuary can be enjoyed from the decked area at the bottom of the garden. Occasional live music plays – open air in summer. An annual beer festival is held in October. The pub opens for breakfast from 9am and is well-patronised by tourists and locals. Dogs are welcome and there are excellent en-suite B&B facilities. 🏚Q🌣🍴🌣◑👜♣P🍴(501,518)

Alnwick

John Bull Inn

12 Howick Street, NE66 1UY
✪ 12-3 (not Mon-Fri), 7-11; 12-3, 7-10.30 Sun
☎ (01665) 602055 ⊕ john-bull-inn.co.uk
Beer range varies ⒣
Many times CAMRA North Northumberland Pub of the Year winner, this 180-year-old inn thrives on its reputation as a back-street local. The passionate landlord offers a wide range of cask-conditioned ales at varying ABVs, real cider, the widest range of bottled Belgian beers in the county and over 120 different single malt whiskies. A darts team competes in the local league, on Saturday night there is a cheese competition and the pub upholds the North-East tradition of an annual leek show. Q🌣♣🍴🍴(505)

Anick

Rat Inn

NE46 4LN (signed from Hexham A69 roundabout)
✪ 12-11 (10.30 Sun) ☎ (01434) 602814 ⊕ theratinn.com
Taylor Landlord; guest beers ⒣
Superb 1750 country inn with spectacular views across the Tyne Valley. It has a welcoming and friendly feel to it with an open log fire and chamber pots hanging from the ceiling. The Rat has an excellent reputation for good food prepared with locally sourced ingredients and appears in several food guides – in 2013 it was voted among the top 50 gastro-pubs in the country. Half portions are available for children. Well worth the short taxi ride from Hexham rail station. 🏚Q🌣🌣◑👜♣P🍴

Berwick upon Tweed

Barrels Ale House

59-61 Bridge Street, TD15 1ES (at town end of original bridge)
✪ 12-midnight ☎ (01289) 308013
Stewart Pentland IPA; guest beers ⒣

There is an Old Curiosity Shop-ambience to this pub, located in the old part of Berwick next to the original road bridge over the Tweed. The excellent real ale no doubt helps customers brave the 'dentist's chair' at the side of the bar. A downstairs bar is used by DJs and bands at weekends. Outside is a unique open drinking area surrounded by very high walls. A former winner of CAMRA Pub of the Year awards. 🌣👜🍴🍴

Pilot

31 Low Greens, TD15 1LZ
✪ 12 (11 Sat)-midnight ☎ (01289) 304214
Caledonian Deuchars IPA; guest beers ⒣
Well patronised by locals and sought out by train trippers who have heard about this gem, this stone-built end-of-terrace pub dates from the 19th century. It retains the original small room layout and boasts several nautical artefacts over 100 years old. The pub runs darts and quoits teams and hosts music nights. The bar staff are welcoming and friendly. 🏚🌣🍴🌣◑👜🌣🎐♣🍺

Blyth

Olivers

60 Bridge Street, NE24 2AP
✪ 3-11; 12-11.30 Sat; 12-10.30 Sun ☎ (01670) 368346
Anarchy Blonde Star; Black Sheep Best Bitter; Caledonian Deuchars IPA; guest beers ⒣
This warm and friendly one-roomed hostelry was converted from a former newsagent's and is a welcome real ale outlet within a beer desert. Well supported by locals, it is close to the regenerated quayside. Three real ales are available, one usually locally sourced. Complementary food is served on Saturday afternoons. Bus 308 passes outside and the bus station for other services to Blyth is a five-minute walk. ◑♣🍴(308)

Carterway Heads

Manor House Inn

DH8 9LX (on A68 S of Corbridge)
✪ 11-11; 12-10.30 Sun ☎ (01207) 255268
⊕ themanorhouseinn.com
Beer range varies ⒣
Warm and hospitable country inn with three open fires and many rooms, situated just off the A68 10 miles south of Corbridge. A double-glazed window in the bar wall allows customers to view the well-maintained cellar. Proper home-cooked food is freshly prepared on the premises and popular with tourists and locals. Excellent accommodation is available. Derwent Reservoir is nearby. 🏚🌣🌣🍴◑👜🌣♣🍴🍴

Corbridge

Angel Inn

Main Street, NE45 5LA
✪ 11 (12 Sun)-11 ☎ (01434) 632119
⊕ angelofcorbridge.co.uk
Cumberland Corby Ale; Hadrian Border Tyneside Blonde; guest beers ⒣
Superb former 1726 coaching inn located on the main road with good transport links. Seven handpulls offer a range of ales and it also keeps a wonderful selection of malt whiskies. Family-friendly with a reputation for good food, it is popular with tourists, ramblers and locals. A separate lounge area has comfy leather seating

and outside is a relaxed seating area. The town has strong links with the Romans and Hadrian's Wall is nearby. ♨Q☺☎🛏🕪◑🍴⇌P🚽(10,685)

Cramlington

Plough
Middle Farm Buildings, NE23 1DN
✪ 11-11 (midnight Fri & Sat); 12-11 Sun ☎ (01670) 737633
Allendale Wolf; Cullercoats Jack the Devil; Harviestoun Bitter & Twisted; guest beers H
This Sir John Fitzgerald outlet in the old village was originally farm buildings and has separate bar and lounge areas in the style of a traditional pub. With a commitment to sourcing the best ales from across the UK, the pub offers an excellent range of local microbrews on continual rotation to supplement the core beer range. A function room is available upstairs where children are welcome — under-18s are only permitted in bar areas during the day. ☺🍴⇌♣♠P🚽(X5,X10,X11)

Dipton Mill

Dipton Mill Inn L
Dipton Mill Road, NE46 1YA
✪ 12-2.30, 6-11; 12-3 Sun ☎ (01434) 606577
🌐 diptonmill.co.uk
Hexhamshire Devil's Elbow, Shire Bitter, Blackhall English Stout, Devil's Water, Whapweasel, Old Humbug H
The tap for Hexhamshire Brewery, this small inn is run by a keen landlord who brews his own excellent beers – Blackhall English Stout has proved so popular among drinkers that it has ousted the Guinness. To complement the ales there is great home-cooked food – Saturday is curry night. A cosy atmosphere and warm welcome make this pub well worth seeking out. The large garden has a stream running through it and there is plenty of countryside to explore. ♨Q☺◑♠P

Eglingham

Tankerville Arms L
15 The Village, NE66 2TX
✪ 12-11 (12.30am Fri & Sat); 12-10.30 Sun
☎ (01665) 578444 🌐 tankervillearms.com
Hadrian Border Tyneside Blonde; guest beers H
Well-appointed, traditional country pub dating from 1851. The bar serves three locally sourced beers and has several framed pictures that enhance the surroundings. An excellent open-beam restaurant complements this establishment. The beer garden at the rear is very tranquil with superb rural views. The pub hosts meetings for the local golf and cricket clubs and is popular with tourists and ramblers – families and dogs are welcome. Accommodation is en suite.
♨Q☺🛏◑🍴AP

Embleton

Greys Inn
Stanley Terrace, NE66 3UY
✪ 12-11 (10.30 Sun) ☎ (01665) 576983
Daleside Alnwick Amber, Alnwick IPA; guest beers H
Pleasant traditional pub located at the rear of this lovely seaside hamlet, just a short walk from a wonderful beach. The pub has three open fires and a framed 1904 grocery list hangs on the wall. This is an excellent venue to enjoy a bite to eat washed

down with a locally sourced real ale, sitting outside on the superb patio. It is home to a ladies' darts team, clay pigeon club and golf club.
♨☺☺◑🍴♣🚽(501)

Greenhead

Greenhead Hotel
CA8 7HB
✪ 11-11 ☎ (016977) 47411
🌐 greenheadhotelandhostel.co.uk
Beer range varies H
Despite the Brampton postcode, this establishment is well within the Northumberland border. Real ale has been introduced here by new owners after an absence of several years. The welcoming family hotel near the Roman wall is patronised by locals, tourists and ramblers. Many a walker has been comforted by the roaring log fire lit as soon as the weather gets cooler. A separate function room is available. ♨☺🛏◑🍴P🚽(185)

Haltwhistle

Black Bull
Black Bull Lane, Market Square, NE49 0BL (down cobbled lane)
✪ 12-11 (midnight Fri & Sat); 12-10.30 Sun
☎ (01434) 320463
Caledonian Deuchars IPA; guest beers H
Warm, welcoming, two-room pub close to Hadrian's Wall, located just off the marketplace down a cobbled lane. A low-beamed timber ceiling, open fire and horse brasses contribute to the traditional ambience. With six handpulls, the pub is popular with locals as well as ramblers. The friendly licensee treats customers as people not as a source of income. Regular themed nights are held. Ring to check winter hours – meal times can vary. ♨Q☺◑🚽(685)

Milecastle Inn L
North Road, NE49 9NN (on B6318 Military Road)
✪ 12-11 ☎ (01434) 321372 🌐 milecastle-inn.co.uk
Big Lamp Bitter, Prince Bishop, Sunny Daze H
This 1600s pub adjacent to Hadrian's Wall only sells ale from Newburn-based Big Lamp Brewery. Located a mile and a half north of Haltwhistle, the rural pub has a homely feel, attracting ramblers and tourists. Food is locally sourced and customers travel from as far as Newcastle and Carlisle. Two comfy holiday cottages are available. Check opening times from November to Easter. The Hadrian's Wall bus stops outside April-October.
♨Q☺☺◑🍴P🚽(122)

Hedley on the Hill

Feathers
NE43 7SW
✪ 12 (6 Mon)-11 ☎ (01661) 843607 🌐 thefeathers.net
Beer range varies H
Much-acclaimed country pub set in a pleasant hamlet with superb views over three counties. It has a comfortable feel with exposed stone walls and beams. The young and welcoming staff serve high-quality home-cooked food that complements the real ales. The pub has won awards for its food – book ahead for Sunday lunch. A beer festival is held at Easter with an uphill barrel race on Easter Monday. ♨Q☺☺◑P♣

High Horton

Three Horse Shoes

Hathery Lane, NE24 4HF (off A189 N of Cramlington, follow A192)

🟢 11-11 (midnight Fri & Sat); 12-11 Sun ☎ (01670) 822410
🌐 threehorseshoes-horton.co.uk

Greene King Abbot; Tetley Bitter; guest beers Ⓗ
Extended former coaching inn at the highest point in the Blyth Valley, with views of the Northumberland coast. The pub is open plan with distinct bar and dining areas plus a conservatory. Dedicated to real ale, there are regular beer festivals. A house beer is brewed by Carlsberg and guest ales are sourced from all over the country, often from local microbreweries. Two-pint carryouts are available. An extensive range of meals and snacks is available lunchtimes and evenings, all day Friday-Sunday.
Q🕸🕙🏠P🍴🖥(X5)

High Newton-by-the-Sea

Joiners Arms

Town Square, NE66 3EA (on B1340)

🟢 12-11 (10.30 Sun) ☎ (01665) 576112 🌐 joiners-arms.com

Anarchy St Marys; Hadrian Border Tyneside Blonde; guest beer Ⓗ
Eighteenth-century former manor house tastefully restored and refurbished following closure for two years. The house ale, St Marys, is named after the local church – for every pint sold a donation is made towards the church's upkeep. Set in a pleasant Northumbrian hamlet, the pub's seating area at the front overlooks a small picturesque green. Five en-suite bedrooms are fitted out to a high standard. ♨🛏🕸🏠🕙🍴♿AP🍴🖥(X18)

Horncliffe

Fishers Arms

Main Street, TD15 2XW

🟢 12-3 (3.15 Wed), 6-10.30; closed Tue; 12-3, 6-11 Fri & Sat; 12-2, 6-10.30 Sun ☎ (01289) 386866

Beer range varies Ⓗ
Traditional family-run inn dating from 1760 at the heart of Horncliffe life. It hosts monthly buskers' sessions, food theme nights, quiz nights, an OAP lunch every Thursday, and on Wednesday the Hooky Mats club. Part of a terrace in the village centre, the pub has separate dining and drinking areas. Reasonably priced home-cooked food is popular. The Tweed Cycle Way is nearby. B&B includes en-suite facilities. Arguably the best community pub in Northumberland.
Q🕸🛏🕙♿🖥(67)

Langley

Carts Bog Inn Ⓛ

NE47 5NW (3 miles off A69 on A686 to Alston)

🟢 12-2.30 (not Mon; 2 Wed), 5-11; 12-11 Sat; 12-10.30 Sun ☎ (01434) 684338 🌐 cartsbog.co.uk

Beer range varies Ⓗ
Excellent rural pub serving the Langley community and tourists. The building dates from 1730 and was built on the site of an ancient brewery (circa 1521). Carts really did get bogged down here. A large open fire divides the two-room interior and the walls proudly display pictures of bygone days. Good locally sourced food including meat from a nearby farm is served (booking essential for

Sunday lunch). Home to three quoits teams and a darts team, the pub hosts occasional live bands and a barbecue with marquees in the garden.
♨Q🕸🕙♿♣P🍴🖥(688)

Low Newton-by-the-Sea

Ship Inn

Newton Square, NE66 3EL (off B1340 between Seahouses and Craster)

🟢 11-11; 12-10.30 Sun ☎ (01665) 576262
🌐 shipinnnewton.co.uk

Ship Inn Sea Coal, Sea Wheat, White Horses, Pilgrim Ⓗ
Nestling in the corner of a three-sided arrangement of former fishermen's cottages and graced by a small village green virtually on the beach, this pub's location is unique. It is a short walk from the car park, with fine sea views. The pub offers an excellent food menu using fresh locally sourced ingredients, and does get busy. It sells its own beer from the brewery next door – please note that it is served colder than normal. Opening times may vary in winter so phone to check first. ♨Q🕸🕙♿🍴

Matfen

High House Farm Visitor Centre Ⓛ

Corbridge, NE20 0RG

🟢 10.30-9 (5 Mon & Tue); closed Wed ☎ (01661) 886192
🌐 highhousefarmbrewery.co.uk

High House Farm Auld Hemp, Nels's Best, Matfen Magic, seasonal beers Ⓗ
Visitor centre in the same converted Grade II-listed farm premises as the brewery. All real ales are sourced from the brewery, with tours available (book ahead). It has an award-winning restaurant offering a daytime menu, evening meals and Sunday lunches. A barn tearoom complements the traditional ambience. There is a children's play area outside. Situated one and a half miles from the Military Road and not far from the Roman wall, caravans are welcome. It is licensed for weddings and popular for wedding receptions.
Q🕸🕙♿P🍴

Milfield

Red Lion Inn

Main Road, NE71 6JD (E of A697)

🟢 11-2, 5-11; 11-midnight Sat & Sun ☎ (01668) 216224
🌐 redlionmilfield.co.uk

Black Sheep Best Bitter; guest beers Ⓗ
A true local pub at the heart of the village, just eight miles inside the border, dating back to the mid-1700s. Rescued by the current licensee from the tight grip of S&N, the Red Lion is a proper free house, with many varied guest beers served from the third handpump. Freshly prepared food is available, with blackboards proudly displaying where the local produce is sourced. Home to the local leek-growing club.
Q🕸🕙♿A♣♠P🍴🖥(267)

Morpeth

Tap & Spile Ⓛ

23 Manchester Street, NE61 1BH

🟢 12-2.30, 4.30-11; 12-11 Fri & Sat; 12-10.30 Sun ☎ (01670) 513894

Everards Tiger; Greene King Abbot; Hadrian Border Tyneside Blonde; Mordue Workie Ticket; Taylor Landlord; guest beers Ⓗ
Cosy, popular local, welcoming to all and handy for the nearby bus station. It has a busy, narrow bar to the front and quieter lounge to rear. A good choice of ales is on offer with local brews often available. Westons Old Rosie cider is stocked as well as a selection of fruit wines from Lindisfarne Winery. A traditional folk group plays on Sunday lunchtimes. Winner of local CAMRA awards. ⚌Q✿◑♣♠♦⌐

Newbiggin by the Sea

Queen's Head
7 High Street, NE64 6AT
✪ 10-midnight ☎ (01670) 817293
Beer range varies Ⓗ
Single-room pub with the bar, lounge and snug all together. Rebuilt in 1909, some Edwardian features remain including the curved bar counter. The owner and landlord sells competitively priced real ales and displays an ever-growing, impressive collection of guest beer pump clips on the walls. With advantageous opening times, this no-nonsense pub is popular with locals and visitors alike. All Newbiggin buses pass the door. ✿♣♠

Newbrough

Red Lion
Stanegate Road, NE47 5AR
✪ 12-11 (10.30 Sun) ☎ (01434) 674226
⚭ redlionnewbrough.co.uk
Beer range varies Ⓗ
Although the road outside was first laid by the Romans back in 71AD, long before Hadrian's Wall was built, this building's origins reputedly only date back to the early 13th century. There are many flagstones and beams plus much old stonework and impressive large fireplaces. Cyclists are welcome here – Route 72 of the National Cycle Network runs alongside and the pub operates a pick-up, drop-off luggage service. Opening times and food hours are liable to change in winter. ⚌✿♠◑♣♦⌐➡(683)

Old Hartley

Delaval Arms
NE26 4RL (jct of A193/B1325 S of Seaton Sluice)
✪ 12-11 (10.30 Sun) ☎ (0191) 237 0489
Beer range varies Ⓗ
Multi-roomed Grade II-listed building dating from 1748, with a listed WWI water storage tower behind the beer garden. Good-quality, affordable meals complement the beer, with guest ales coming from local micros. To the left as you enter is a room served through a hatch from the bar and to the right a room where children are welcome. Q✿✿◑♣P⌐

Ovingham

Bridge End Inn
West Road, NE42 6BN
✪ 4 (12 Sat)-11.30; 12-3.30, 7-10.30 Sun ☎ (01661) 832219
⚭ thebridgeendinn.co.uk
Taylor Landlord; Tetley Bitter; Wylam Gold Tankard, Collingwood; guest beer Ⓗ
Superb traditional family-run pub with the same licensee for 36 years. The back door opens onto the

village green where the Goosefair is held annually on the third Saturday in June, supported by the whole village. The pub hosts monthly music nights —blues, rock, '60s —a sailing club and an allotment club. Visitors are warmly welcomed by the friendly regulars and children are permitted until 9pm. Access is gained from Prudhoe over the bridge by pedestrian walkway. ⚌Q✿♣◑♣♠Å♦P➡(684,686,687)

Rennington

Horse Shoes Inn
6 Rennington Village, NE66 3RS
✪ 12-3 (not Mon; 3.15 Wed), 7 (6 Sat)-11 ☎ (01665) 577665
⚭ thehorseshoesrennington.co.uk
Hadrian Border Farne Island; guest beer Ⓗ
Superb traditional family-run village pub dating from 1851. The bar is warm and friendly with hops hanging over the serving area. There is a large restaurant serving good food made with locally sourced ingredients. The pub is home to two darts teams and hosts a scarecrow competition every August bank holiday Saturday and a leek show. Outside at the front is a pleasant beer garden. ⚌Q✿✿◑◑♣♠P⌐

Rothbury

Queen's Head
Townfoot, NE65 7SR
✪ 11-1am (midnight Sun) ☎ (01669) 620470
⚭ queensheadrothbury.com
Beer range varies Ⓗ
Friendly hotel dating from 1756 on the main street, very popular with locals, tourists and ramblers. Live folk music plays on the first Tuesday and last Thursday of the month (there is a charge and they often sell out). The hotel has pool and darts teams who compete in local leagues. All bedrooms are en suite. There is an hourly bus service. ✿✿◑◑♣♠P➡(X14,144)

Seahouses

Olde Ship Hotel
7-9 Main Street, NE68 7RD
✪ 11 (12 Sun)-11 ☎ (01665) 720200 ⚭ seahouses.co.uk
Black Sheep Best Bitter; Courage Directors; Hadrian Border Farne Island; Morland Old Speckled Hen; Ruddles County; Theakston Best Bitter; guest beers Ⓗ
This 1745 farmhouse was converted to the licensed trade in 1812 and has been family owned since 1910. Three quality bars are adorned with a veritable treasure trove of 19th and 20th century maritime memorabilia. Fully residential, the pub offers a unique menu of fish, fresh crab meals and snacks (no chips served). ⚌Q✿✿◑◑♣♠P⌐➡(501)

Seaton Sluice

Melton Constable
Beresford Road, NE26 4DA
✪ 12-11 (10.30 Sun) ☎ (0191) 237 7741
Black Sheep Best Bitter; Morland Old Speckled Hen; Thwaites Wainwright; guest beers Ⓗ
Large roadside inn a few minutes' walk from the beach and local history sights. The pub is named after the southern seat of Lord Hastings, a member of the Delaval family – Delaval Hall is close by. Tuesday is steak night, Wednesday is quiz night

and on Sunday evening live music plays. The pub also hosts a fishing club and BSA owners club. ⏴❀◖⏸⏤P⊟(308,309)

Slaley

Travellers Rest

NE46 1TT (on B6306 1 mile N of village)
❂ 12-11 (10.30 Sun) ☎ (01434) 673231
⏀ travellersrestslaley.com
Black Sheep Best Bitter; Caledonian Deuchars IPA; guest beer Ⓗ
Former farmhouse from the 16th century, licensed for over 150 years. The pub has an excellent reputation for good food and accommodation. The bar has a large open fire, stone flag floor, comfortable furniture and a beautiful wine rack carved from a large piece of wood. Children are welcome and there is a safe play area outside.
⏤Q⏴❀⏸◖⏀♣♠P

Twice Brewed

Twice Brewed Inn

Miltary Road, Bardon Mill, NE47 7AN (on B6318)
❂ 11-11 (10.30 Sun) ☎ (01434) 344534
⏀ twicebrewedinn.co.uk
Yates Twice Brewed Bitter; guest beers Ⓗ
Superb remote inn, close to Hadrian's Wall and patronised by tourists and ramblers. It offers a range of bottled beers named Beers of the World. Outside, the pub has its own well for water, and excellent views from the rear garden, which hosts a marquee in summer and is home to two quoits teams. The inn acts as a rural transport interchange and has 16 bedrooms, seven en suite. It has full disabled access and an IT suite with internet connection. ⏤Q⏴❀⏸◖⏸⏀ＡP

Wark

Battlesteads Hotel

NE48 3LS
❂ 11-11; 12-10.30 Sun ☎ (01434) 230209
⏀ battlesteadshotel.com
Black Sheep Best Bitter; Durham Magus; guest beers Ⓗ
Well-appointed 1747 former farmhouse with a superb walled garden to the rear, restaurant and large conservatory. Five handpulls provide an excellent choice of beer with up to three guests. Ingredients for the quality food menu are sourced within a 25-mile radius. With excellent accommodation including ground-floor rooms with disabled access, this family-friendly pub near Hadrian's Wall offers something for everyone. Future developments include a walking book based around the pub. Handy for the PlusBus via Hexham Rail Station. ⏤⏴❀⏸◖⏸⏀P⏴⊟(880)

Wylam

Black Bull

Main Street, NE41 8AB
❂ 4-11; 12-midnight Fri & Sat; 12-11 Sun ☎ (01661) 853112
⏀ blackbull-wylam.co.uk
Wylam Gold Tankard; guest beers Ⓗ
Very popular with the locals, this cheerful pub with a friendly landlord and staff is on the main street in Wylam. Real ale is now available on six handpulls, with beers mainly sourced from the nearby Wylam Brewery. Local home-cooked specialities include a steak night on Wednesday, fish night on Friday and curry night on the last Thursday of the month. Regular themed nights are hosted, many in support of charities. Wylam Waggonway is nearby, a popular walk that passes George Stephenson's cottage. ⏸◖⏸⏴♣⏴

Boathouse Inn ❢ Ⓛ

Station Road, NE41 8HR
❂ 11-11 (midnight Sat); 12-10.30 Sun ☎ (01661) 853431
⏀ boathousewylam.info
Beer range varies Ⓗ
Superb two-roomed pub with 15 handpulls, three dedicated to cider, with more ciders served from the cellar. Beers are sourced locally and nationwide, and on bank holidays themed beer festivals are held. Sunday roasts are popular, with lunchtime and early evening meals available throughout the week. The pub is a popular stopping-off point for Whistle Stops II travellers. Fifteen CAMRA awards cover a wall, including North East Regional Pub of the Year 2011. Saturday afternoons and the first Wednesday evening in the month are for buskers. ⏤Q⏴❀⏸◖⏴♣♠P

What is real ale?

Real ale is also known as cask-conditioned beer or simply cask beer. In the brewery, the beer is neither filtered nor pasteurised. It still contains sufficient yeast and sugar for it to continue to ferment and mature in the cask. Once it has reached the pub cellar, it has to be laid down for maturation to continue, and for yeast and protein to settle at the bottom of the cask. Some real ale also has extra hops added as the cask is filled, a process known as 'dry hopping' for increased flavour and aroma. Cask beer is best served at a cellar temperature of 11-12 degrees C, although some stronger ales can benefit from being served a little warmer.

Each cask has two holes, in one of which a tap is inserted and is connected to tubes or 'lines' that enable the beer to be drawn to the bar. The other hole, on top of the cask, enables some carbon dioxide produced during secondary fermentation to escape. It is vital that some gas, which gives the beer its natural sparkle or condition, is kept within the cask: the escape of gas is controlled by inserting porous wooden pegs called spiles into the spile hole. Real ale is a living product and must be consumed within three or four days of a cask being tapped as oxidation develops.

NOTTINGHAMSHIRE

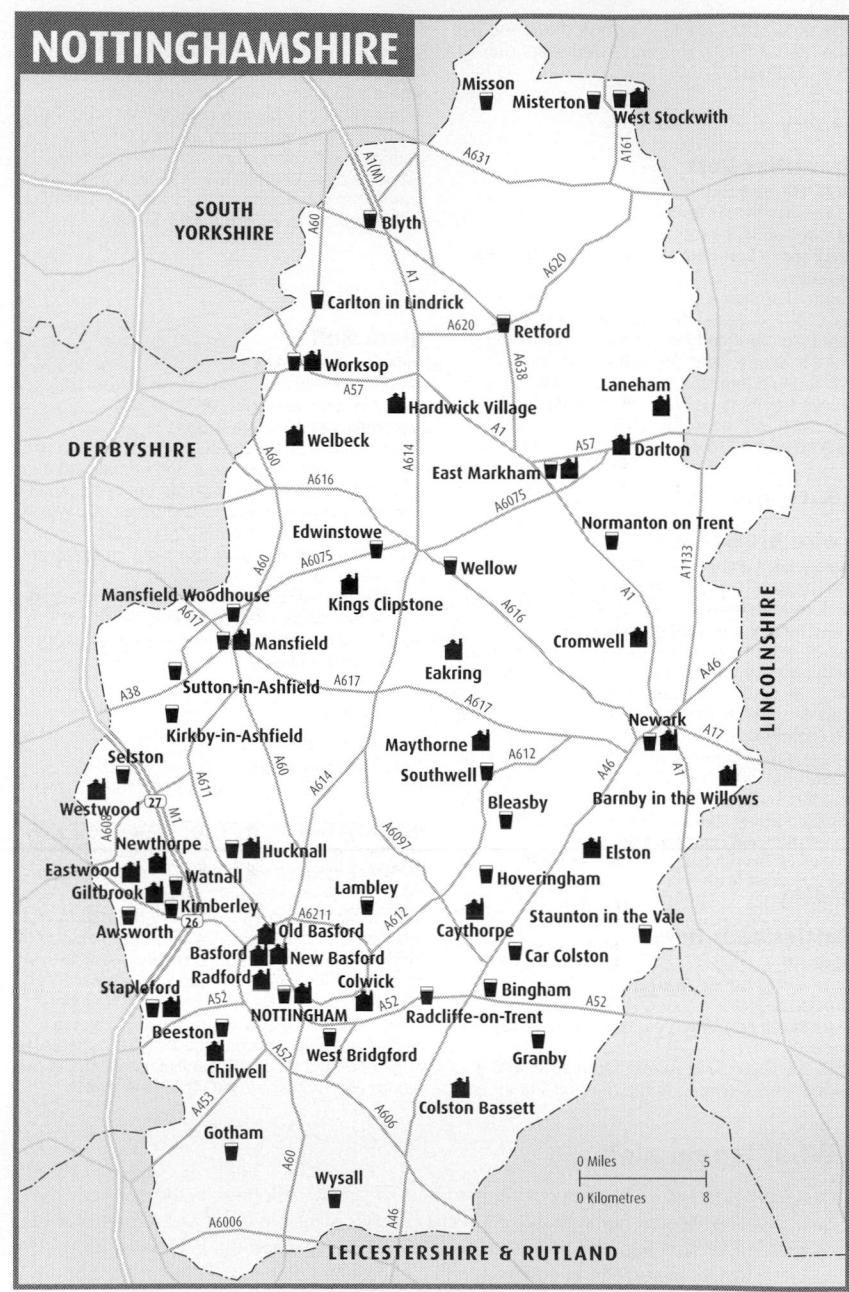

Misson
Misterton
West Stockwith

A631

A1(M)

A161

SOUTH
YORKSHIRE

A60

Blyth

A620

A1

Carlton in Lindrick

A620

Retford

Worksop

A638

A57

Laneham

Hardwick Village

A57

DERBYSHIRE

A60

Welbeck

A614

A1

Darlton

A616

East Markham

A6075

Edwinstowe

Normanton on Trent

A6075

A614

Wellow

A1133

Mansfield Woodhouse

A617

Kings Clipstone

A616

Cromwell

A46

Mansfield

Eakring

Sutton-in-Ashfield

A617

A38

A617

Kirkby-in-Ashfield

Maythorne

A612

Newark

A17

Selston

A614

A60

Southwell

A46

A1

Westwood

A611

M1

Bleasby

Barnby in the Willows

LINCOLNSHIRE

Newthorpe

A6097

Hucknall

Elston

Eastwood

Watnall

Lambley

Hoveringham

Giltbrook

Kimberley

A6211

A612

Awsworth

26

Old Basford

Caythorpe

Staunton in the Vale

Basford

New Basford

Car Colston

Stapleford

Radford

Colwick

Bingham

A52

A52

A52

NOTTINGHAM

Beeston

West Bridgford

Radcliffe-on-Trent

Granby

Chilwell

A52

Colston Bassett

A453

A606

Gotham

A60

Wysall

A46

A6006

0 Miles   5

0 Kilometres   8

LEICESTERSHIRE & RUTLAND

Awsworth

Gate Inn L

Main Street, NG16 2RN

☼ 12-midnight ☎ (0115) 932 9821

Burton Bridge XL; Muirhouse Forty Bridges; guest
beers ⊞

Deemed to be unviable and sold by the pub's
former owners, the Gate Inn reopened in 2010 as a
free house, and has quickly established itself as a
quality real ale outlet, winning Nottingham
CAMRA's Pub of Excellence award in 2011. A truly
welcoming and friendly local, this late 19th-
century pub has a bar, a lounge and a separate
room with a pool table. The current owners are
gradually renovating the pub and have now added
a skittle alley. ₩ Q ⑤ ♣ ● P ⊞ (R1)

Beeston

Crown L

Church Street, NG9 1FY

☼ 12-11.30 (11 Sun) ☎ (0115) 925 4738

⊕ crowninnbeeston.co.uk

Everards Sunchaser, Tiger; Fuller's London Pride; Leatherbritches Bounder, Cad, Scoundrel ⊞ An alehouse has stood on this Grade-II listed site since 1830. Since restoration by Everards, the Crown's range of ales has expanded to 14, plus real cider, and it was CAMRA East Midlands Pub of the Year in 2011. It has a cosy atmosphere created by five distinct drinking areas including a snug and three-seat 'confessional', which was originally used for off sales. The beer garden regularly hosts events. Snacks are available daily.
Q ♿ ✿ ⊞ & ≒ ♠ P ╘ ⊞

Victoria Hotel ⓛ

85 Dovecote Lane, NG9 1JG (off A6005 by station)
✪ 10.30 (12 Sun)-11 ☎ (0115) 925 4049
⊕ victoriabeeston.co.uk
Castle Rock Harvest Pale; Everards Tiger; Kelham Island Best Bitter; guest beers ⊞
Restored after years of neglect, this Victorian masterpiece appeals to all including ale and cider drinkers and diners. Handpumps dispense up to 16 ales – a taster tray of three thirds is offered if you cannot make up your mind – and there are around 110 whiskies behind the bar. The high quality food includes vegan and vegetarian options. Outside, a large non-smoking heated seating area is provided in the beer garden, which is home to the VicFest in July and beer festivals throughout the year. CAMRA and NUS discounts are offered Sunday-Thursday.
🔍 Q ✿ ⓓ ⊞ & ≒ ♠ P ⊞

Bingham

Horse & Plough

25 Long Acre, NG13 8AF
✪ 11-11 (11.30 Fri & Sat); 12-11 Sun ☎ (01949) 839313
⊕ horseandploughbingham.com
Caledonian Deuchars IPA; Thwaites Lancaster Bomber; guest beers ⊞
Situated in the heart of a busy market town, this warm, friendly, one-room free house is a former Methodist chapel and has a cottage-style interior and flagstone floor. Six cask ales are served including four guests, with a 'try before you buy' policy, and a cider from Westons. Freshly prepared food is served weekday lunchtimes and evenings in the bar, and the first floor à la carte restaurant offers a varied seasonal menu. Local CAMRA Pub of the Year 2012. ⓓ & ≒ ♠ ⊞

White Lion

Nottingham Road, NG13 8AT
✪ 11 (11.30 Sun)-11 ☎ (01949) 875541
Theakston Best Bitter; guest beers ⊞
The White Lion is your typical local pub, with a loyal following of regulars. Recently refurbished in both the bar and cellar, it now serves up to four cask ales. Basic good-value meals are available lunchtimes and evenings. The pub is home to pool and darts teams and runs a popular quiz night on Sunday. The bar houses a large screen showing all major games on Sky Sports. There is a good-sized decked area for outdoor drinking and a car park.
✿ ⓓ ⊞ & ≒ ♣ P ╘ ⊞

Bleasby

Waggon & Horses ⓛ

Gipsy Lane, NG14 7BE
✪ 12-2 (not Mon-Wed), 5-11; 12-midnight Sat; 12-11 Sun
☎ (01636) 830283

Beer range varies ⊞
Thriving village free house offering six real ales including brews from the award-winning Blue Monkey Brewery, and a cider. This is a true local pub overlooking the church and green with no gimmicks or electronic games, just good conversation and banter. It is well worth finding, in a lovely Trent Valley village close to Southwell Minster and races. Walkers with muddy boots and dogs with muddy paws are welcome.
🔍 Q ✿ ⓓ ⊞ & ≒ ♣ ♠ P ╘ ⊞

Blyth

Red Hart

Bawtry Road, S81 8HG
✪ 12-11.30 ☎ (01909) 591221 ⊕ redhart.co.uk
Beer range varies ⊞
An attractive village pub situated in the centre of Blyth with separate lounge and bar areas and a reasonably sized dining room. The walls in the lounge are decorated with photographs and paintings of various locations around the village. Guest ales change regularly, with beers from microbreweries usually available. Restaurant-quality food at pub prices is served daily. The pub hosts an annual beer festival during the late spring bank holiday. 🔍 ✿ ⓓ ⊞ P ╘ ⊞

Car Colston

Royal Oak

The Green, NG13 8JE

Alcazar Nottingham: Old Basford
Blue Monkey Giltbrook
Castle Rock Nottingham
Caythorpe Caythorpe
Copthorne Darlton
Double Top Worksop
Dukeries Worksop (NEW)
Flipside Colwick
Full Mash Stapleford
Funfair Elston
Grafton Worksop
Handley's Barnby in the Willows
Idle West Stockwith
Justice Mansfield (NEW)
Kings Clipstone Kings Clipstone (NEW)
Lincoln Green Hucknall
Magpie Nottingham
Mallard Maythorne
Maypole Eakring
Medieval Colston Bassett
Milestone Cromwell
Naked Westwood
Navigation Nottingham
Newark Newark (NEW)
Nomad Newthorpe (NEW)
Nottingham Nottingham: Radford
Pheasantry East Markham
Prior's Well Hardwick Village
Reality Nottingham: Chilwell
Robin Hood Nottingham: New Basford (NEW)
Springhead Laneham
Welbeck Abbey Welbeck
White Dog Eastwood (NEW)
Wollaton Nottingham: Basford (NEW)

✪ 11.30-3 (not Mon), 5.30-midnight; 11.30-midnight Fri & Sat; 12-10.30 Sun ☎ (01949) 20247 ⊕ brilliantpubs.co.uk/royaloaknotts

Marston's Burton Bitter; Ringwood Best Bitter; guest beers Ⓗ

Impressive country inn situated on one of England's largest village greens. The two-room interior includes a lounge and restaurant on one side and bar with comfortable seating on the other. Note the bar's vaulted brickwork ceiling – a legacy from the building's previous life as a hosiery factory. Good-quality, traditional food is served lunchtimes and evenings. There is a skittle alley to the rear. The landlord maintains his 100 per cent record for entries in the Guide. ⚞⌘◑⧄⚅⚞Α♣Pᶜ⊟

Carlton in Lindrick

Grey Horses Ⓛ

The Cross, S81 9EW SK593845

✪ 12-11.30 ☎ (01909) 730252

Welbeck Abbey Carlton Knight; guest beers Ⓗ

The Grey Horses is situated in the heart of the village. As the tap for the Welbeck Abbey Brewery, it serves two of its beers plus a brew unique to the pub. Other guest beers are also available. It has a front bar accessible from the street and a large lounge bar area. Meals are served until 8pm (4pm Sat and Sun). There is a function room upstairs. ⚞Q⌘◑⧄⚅♣Pᶜ⊟(21,22)

East Markham

Queen's Hotel

High Street, NG22 0RE SK741732

✪ 12 (2 Mon)-11 ☎ (01777) 870288

⊕ queenshoteleastmarkham.co.uk

Adnams Southwold Bitter; Everards Beacon, Tiger; guest beers Ⓗ

Situated on the village main street, this cosy Everard's public house has a warmly welcoming atmosphere enhanced by an open fire in winter. A single bar serves the lounge, pool room and dining area. Food ranges from hot and cold snacks to full home-cooked meals. There is a large garden area at the rear where you can enjoy a drink on a warm summer's day. The pub is a former winner of local CAMRA awards. ⚞Q❧⌘◑⧄♣Pᶜ⊟(36,37)

Edwinstowe

Forest Lodge Hotel ♈ Ⓛ

2-4 Church Street, NG21 9QA (by traffic lights on A6075 Mansfield-Ollerton road)

✪ 11.30-3, 5.30 (5 Fri)-11; 12-3, 6-10.30 Sun

☎ (01623) 824443 ⊕ forestlodgehotel.co.uk

Welbeck Abbey Forest Lodge EPA; Wells Bombardier; guest beers Ⓗ

A busy family-owned free house, this former coaching inn dating back to 1770 is located close to the 800-year-old Major Oak in Sherwood Forest. The central bar dispenses up to five real ales, including the house beer from Welbeck Abbey, plus a LocAle. Refurbished to high standards, it retains a traditional feel and has a large impressive function room available for private hire plus 12 en-suite rooms. A local CAMRA Branch Pub of the Year winner. ⚞Q⌘⧄◑⚅Pᶜ⊟(14,15)

Gotham

Sun Inn

1 The Square, NG11 0HX (opp church)

✪ 12-11 ☎ (0115) 878 9047 ⊕ suninngotham.co.uk

Everards Beacon, Tiger, Original; guest beers Ⓗ

A traditional two-roomed village pub opposite St Lawrence's church. Pub games such as darts and dominoes are played in the public bar, while the lounge is used for dining. Food is prepared by a Michelin-trained chef, and is available daily. Nine handpumps serve at least five real ales and three ciders from Westons. In the summer, the bright and colourful garden area is a popular place to while away the hours. Q⌘◑⧄♣●Pᶜ⊟(1)

Granby

Marquis of Granby

Dragon Street, NG13 9PN

✪ 4-11 (midnight Fri); 12-midnight Sat; 12-11 Sun

☎ (01949) 859517

Brewster's Hophead, Marquis; guest beers Ⓗ

Believed to be the original Marquis of Granby, dating back to 1760 or earlier, this small two-roomed pub is now the brewery tap for Brewster's. York stone floors complement the yew bar tops and wood-beamed rooms, period wallpaper features throughout and the lounge has a welcoming open fire in winter months. Guest beers served alongside the Brewster's range usually come from micros, and include a mild, stout or porter. Fish and chips night is Friday. ⚞⌘⧄◑♣P

Hoveringham

Reindeer Inn Ⓛ

Main Street, NG14 7JR SK699469

✪ 12-2 (not Mon & Tue), 5-11.30; 12-11.30 Thu-Sun

☎ (0115) 966 3629 ⊕ thereindeerinn.com

Black Sheep Best Bitter; Castle Rock Harvest Pale; guest beers Ⓗ

Genuine free house in a pleasant country village with traditional beams and a log fire for cold winter nights. A central servery divides the bar and restaurant areas. Well-kept ales are served alongside a good range of home-cooked food including vegetarian and vegan choices. The outside drinking area is served through the pub window and overlooks the village cricket pitch for those who like the sound of leather on willow as they drink. Dog-friendly. ⚞Q⌘◑⇌(Thurgaton)♣Pᶜ⊟

Hucknall

Green Dragon Ⓛ

Watnall Road, NG15 7JW

✪ 12-11 ☎ (0115) 964 0941

Beer range varies Ⓗ

Tastefully renovated in 2012, the pub retains separate bar and lounge areas although open plan. The bar has a pool table and dartboard while the lounge is split level and comfortably furnished. A number of pictures depicting Hucknall's past adorn the walls. At the front is a tarmacked patio area and at the side a separate family/function room. Wednesday is quiz night, Sunday a music quiz. ❧⌘⧄⇌⊟♣Pᶜ⊟

Kimberley

Nelson & Railway
12 Station Road, NG16 2NR
✪ 11-midnight; 12-11.30 Sun ☎ (0115) 938 2177
⊕ nelsonandrailway.co.uk
H&H Bitter; guest beers Ⓗ
Run by the same family for more than 40 years, this popular Victorian pub lies in the shadow of the defunct Kimberley Brewery buildings. Beers are usually from the Greene King portfolio but guests also appear, including a local ale at weekends. This multi-roomed pub has plenty of seating throughout and is renowned for its quality food and accommodation, with 11 rooms available. There are attractive gardens at the front and rear plus ample car parking. ❀⇔➀❶❙♣P⁵⊸⊟(R1)

Stag Inn Ⓛ
67 Nottingham Road, NG16 2NB
✪ 5 (1.30 Sat)-11; 12-10.30 Sun ☎ (0115) 938 3151
Adnams Southwold Bitter; Taylor Landlord; guest beers Ⓗ
This wattle-and-daub Tudor-style house dates from 1737 and is situated 200 yards from the town centre. Inside, there are two rooms linked by a central bar furnished with an eclectic mix of seating, including wooden settles. Table skittles and dominoes are played, but at most times conversation reigns. The spacious rear garden includes a children's play area and ample seating. An annual beer festival, held in late May, raises money for charity. The guest beers always include a brew from a lesser-known local brewery. Q❀❙♣P⁵⊸⊟(R1)

Kirkby-in-Ashfield

Duke of Wellington
Church Street, NG17 8LA
✪ 12-midnight (11 Sun) ☎ (01623) 753044
Marston's EPA; Wychwood Hobgoblin; guest beer Ⓗ
A friendly community pub situated in a 1600s building between Kirkby Cross and St Wilfrid's Church. The bar shows sport and there is a separate large L-shaped lounge. Outside are a skittles alley and children's play area. Meals, including vegetarian options, are popular, served lunchtimes and evenings. Quiz nights are Tuesday, Thursday and Saturday, and a folk club meets on the last Wednesday of the month. ♨Q❀➀❶❙⇌♣P⁵⊸⊟(9.3)

Lambley

Woodlark Inn Ⓛ
Church Street, NG4 4QB
✪ 11-11; 12-midnight Sun ☎ (0115) 931 2535
Castle Rock Harvest Pale; Samuel Smith OBB; Taylor Landlord; guest beer Ⓗ
Tucked away on the edge of the village just past the church, this delightful red-brick local is a quiet pub mercifully free of electronic machines, making the art of conversation a delight. A roaring coal fire greets you on cold winter nights. The bare brick and beamed bar is welcoming and dog-friendly while the comfortable lounge has a justifiable reputation for home cooking (booking recommended, even at lunchtime). The downstairs steak bar opens Friday and Saturday from 7pm. ♨Q❀➀❶♣●P⁵⊸⊟(47)

Mansfield

Bold Forester Ⓛ
Botany Avenue, NG18 5NF
✪ 11-11 (midnight Fri & Sat); 12-11.30 Sun
☎ (01623) 623970
Greene King IPA, London Glory, Abbot; Morland Old Speckled Hen; guest beers Ⓗ
A Hungry Horse-branded pub restaurant with an unusual range of up to 12 real ales, four from Greene King, two from Nottingham and up to six guests, plus real cider. The spacious open-plan pub features several large-screen TVs showing all major sport. Food is served every day until 9pm. Run by the same landlord for 15 years, the pub is a regular winner of local CAMRA branch Pub of the Year awards. ⏱❀➀❶❙⇌♣●P⁵⊸⊟

Court House
Market Place, NG18 1HX (next to town hall)
✪ 9am-11 (midnight Fri & Sat) ☎ (01623) 412720
Greene King Abbot; Mansfield Cask; Ruddles Best Bitter; guest beers Ⓗ
This friendly community pub in the town centre gets busy, especially at weekends. It offers a comprehensive range of at least five beers, often from local breweries including Springhead and Milestone, plus two traditional ciders. Food service is until 10pm every day, offering the typical excellent value and quality associated with Wetherspoon. Families are welcome. A regular local CAMRA branch award winner. Q⏱➀❶❙●⁵⊸⊟

Nell Gwyn Ⓛ
117 Sutton Road, NG18 5EX
✪ 2-midnight; 12-2am Fri & Sat; 12-midnight Sun
☎ (01623) 659850 ⊕ nell-gwyn.com
Copthorne Nell Gwyn; guest beers Ⓗ
One of the first buildings on Sutton Road and over 100 years old, this pub was originally a farmhouse, then a gentlemen's club in the early 1900s. It now claims to be Mansfield's best-kept secret – a little pub with a big heart. This welcoming community establishment is home to darts, dominoes and football teams, holds numerous charity events and has a customer loyalty card scheme. Up to three real ales are offered including the house beer brewed by Copthorne Brewery. ♨❀♣⁵⊸⊟

Railway Inn Ⓛ
9 Station Street, NG18 1EF
✪ 11-11 ☎ (01623) 623086
Beer range varies Ⓗ
Traditional real ale gem, close to the town centre, with a strong community focus. There are two small front rooms and the main bar at the rear serving three constantly changing real ales, at least one a LocAle. Double Top, Blue Monkey and Abbeydale beers feature regularly, plus a real cider and a range of bottled beers. Excellent, reasonably priced meals are served weekdays until 8pm (5.30pm Sun). Outside is a small walled garden and heated smoking area. Dogs are welcome. Q⏱❀➀❶⇌●⁵⊸⊟

Redgate Ⓛ
189 Westfield Lane, NG19 6EH
✪ 12-11 ☎ (01623) 624406 ⊕ redgateinn.co.uk
Justice Gold Digger; guest beers Ⓗ
This thriving community-based pub offers a friendly welcome. It has a large public bar with separate darts and pool areas, an indoor skittles

alley, plus an enclosed illuminated garden and smoking area. Up to five real ales are available – one from the pub's own brewery, Justice, and usually at least one other LocAle. Excellent-quality food is available in the restaurant or bar on request (no food Tue). Colliery plates and sporting photographs feature on the bar room walls. Dogs are welcome. ✿🌢🕽🍴♣P⁵–🚲🖳(6,23B)

Stag & Pheasant
Unit 4 Clumber Street, NG18 1NU
❋ 8am-midnight (12.30am Thu; 2am Fri; 3am Sat)
☎ (01623) 412890
Greene King Abbot; Ruddles Best Bitter; guest beers Ⓗ
Spacious Lloyds No.1 bar not far from the town centre. It gets busy at weekends, with music after 6pm and a DJ after 9pm on Friday and Saturday, when an entry charge applies. Two regular beers and three guests are usually on offer, plus two real ciders. The pub also serves Wetherspoon's excellent-value meals until 10pm every day.
🌢🕽🕭≉●⁵–🖳(1,11,14)

Widow Frost
41 Leeming Street, NG18 1NB (200yds from Market Place)
❋ 8am-midnight (1am Fri & Sat) ☎ (01623) 666790
Greene King Abbot; Ruddles Best Bitter; guest beers Ⓗ
Spacious pub situated close to the town centre. It gets busy, especially at weekends, but it is still possible to find a quiet corner. The full range of excellent-value Wetherspoon meals is served until 10pm every day, with a separate family dining area. Up to six beers are available plus two real ciders, served by friendly staff from a large bar. Regular Meet the Brewer events are held on weekdays. The pub is a local CAMRA award winner on numerous occasions.
Q🌢🕽🕭≉●⁵–🖳(1,10,16)

Mansfield Woodhouse

Greyhound
82 High Street, NG19 8BD
❋ 12-11 (midnight Fri & Sat); 12-10.30 Sun
☎ (01623) 464403
Adnams Broadside; Caledonian Deuchars IPA; McMullen AK; Theakston Old Peculier; guest beers Ⓗ
The original building dates back more than 400 years as a coaching stop. A regular entry in the Guide for the past 20 years, with the same licensee for 30 years, the pub is tied to the Heineken group, but offers a variety of real ales plus Westons Old Rosie cider. Two mini beer festivals are held each year. No hot food is available but there are some bar snacks. Quiz nights are Monday and Wednesday. Dogs are welcome in the public bar where pool, darts and dominoes are played.
Q✿🕽≉♣●P⁵–🖳(1,10)

New Inn Ⓛ
Station Street, NG19 8AB
❋ 12-11 (midnight Thu-Sat) ☎ (01623) 629663
Brampton Best, Golden Bud; Fuller's London Pride; Shepherd Neame Spitfire Ⓗ
Originally a coaching house on the main route north from Nottingham, this Grade II-listed family-run pub offers a warm welcome. It serves LocAle from Brampton Brewery and all food is home-cooked to order including an all-day breakfast from midday and bar snacks. Locals advise the pub dates

back to the 1700s and many pictures on the walls show trams running past in the 1800s.
🏚Q🌢✿🕽🕽🕭≉♣●P⁵–🖳(1,9,10)

Misson

Angel Inn
Dame Lane, DN10 6EB (opp church) SK690949
❋ 4-11 (midnight Fri); 12-midnight Sat; 12-11 Sun
☎ (01302) 711761 ⊕ angel-misson.co.uk
Beer range varies Ⓗ
A 200-year-old traditional village pub which has developed over many years into both a popular local and a venue for good food. An ideal place for quiet respite, there are pleasant walks through the countryside and along the river nearby. Accommodation has been recently refurbished. It's ideally located for Robin Hood Airport.
🏚Q🌢✿🕲🕽🕭P⁵–

Misterton

Haxey Gate Inn
Haxey Road, DN10 4BA SK765962
❋ 12-11 ☎ (01427) 890746 ⊕ haxeygate.co.uk
Batemans XB; guest beers Ⓗ
Occupying an idyllic position beside an ancient bridge over the River Idle, the Haxey Gate is a friendly local specialising in good, wholesome, reasonably priced food and well-kept beer. Diners can enjoy their refreshments throughout the inn, but the front-facing conservatory is popular, with plenty of seating. A choice of four real ales is available. 🏚✿🕽🕭P⁵–

Newark

Fox & Crown Ⓛ
4-6 Appletongate, NG24 1JY
❋ 10.30-11 (1am Fri & Sat); 10-11 Sun ☎ (01636) 605820
Castle Rock Sheriff's Tipple, Harvest Pale, Preservation, Elsie Mo; Everards Tiger; guest beers Ⓗ
Recently renovated, this open-plan Castle Rock pub now offers up to 10 cask beers often sourced from micros, real ciders and imported bottled beers. Seasonal ales and LocAles are always available from a varied beer menu. The pub holds 'new brew' nights and participates in local beer festivals. Quality traditional pub meals are served and theme nights feature throughout the season. Live bands play most weekends and quizzes are regular events. Disabled access is good.
🕽🕭≉(Castle/Northgate)

Just Beer Micropub 🍸 Ⓛ
Swan & Salmon Yard, 32A Castlegate, NG24 1BG
❋ 1-11; 11-midnight Fri & Sat; 12-10 Sun ☎ 07983 993747
⊕ justbeermicropub.biz
Beer range varies Ⓗ
Multi award-winning micropub situated in the historic heart of Newark. Since opening in 2010, many different beers have been served, supporting the microbrewery revolution, and rare beers are often available. Traditional values ensure a warm welcome and a vibrant customer mix, with varied local and UK beers, all served in oversized glasses. Traditional ciders and fine English perry are also on offer – no lagers or spirits. Local CAMRA Pub of the Year 2012 and 2013. Q🕭🏃≉(Castle)♣●P🖳🖳

Prince Rupert ⅃

46 Stodman Street, NG24 1AW (between Castlegate and market place)
🌣 11-midnight (1am Fri & Sat); 12-midnight Sun
☎ (01636) 918121 ⊕ theprincerupert.co.uk
Beer range varies Ⓗ

A lovingly restored historic building dating back to around 1452, winner of the CAMRA/English Heritage Conservation Award. It retains several rooms over two floors, with original features and a drinking area in the courtyard. Six handpumps dispense beers from breweries all over the UK, and real cider is always available. The pub participates in the Newark Beermuda Triangle Festival, held in January, and other festivals from time to time. High-quality pub food is available including speciality pizzas. Live music is a regular feature.
⋈Q🌣🜚⇌(Castle)♠🖳

Sir John Arderne ⅃

1-3 Church Street, NG24 1DT (corner of marketplace)
🌣 11-midnight ☎ (01636) 671334
Beer range varies Ⓗ

Large open-plan Wetherspoon pub named for 'the first true English surgeon', who lived locally, looking out on to the marketplace. The manager is committed to real ale and provides a constantly changing beer choice featuring new and local breweries. Meet the Brewer events are held occasionally. Value-for-money food is available daily. An interesting mixed clientele makes this a somewhat lively place at times. 🜚🜚&⇌⅄

Normanton on Trent

Crown ⅃

South Street, NG23 6RQ (exit A1 at B1164, follow signs to Normanton) SK792688
🌣 12-11 (10 Sun) ☎ (01636) 821973
Beer range varies Ⓗ

The Crown is rhe brewery tap for Milestone, who brew in the nearby village of Cromwell. The building has been sympathetically extended and renovated with a clear division between the dining area and the bar. Although very much a community pub, a friendly welcome is extended to all visitors. The beer is always in great condition and the pub also enjoys a good reputation for food including the legendary Sunday roasts (served until 8pm). There is a safe play area for children and a car park. ⋈🌣🜚&♣P⅄🖳(39)

Nottingham: Central

Canalhouse ⅃

48-52 Canal Street, NG1 7EH
🌣 11-11 (midnight Thu; 1am Fri & Sat); 11-10.30 Sun
☎ (0115) 955 5060 ⊕ thecanalhouse.co.uk
Castle Rock Harvest Pale; guest beers Ⓗ

Uniquely converted from an old Waterways Warehouse with the adjacent canal running through the pub and resident narrowboats moored inside. The venue is quiet and relaxed during the day, offering good home-made food and a range of Castle Rock beers, ciders and perries. Also check out the fridges housing over 120 bottled world beers. Outside is a generous seated patio overlooking the canal which gets busy on warm, sunny days. A CAMRA discount and other offers are available. Q🌣🜚⇌🖳♠P⅄🖳

Dragon ⅃

67 Long Row, NG1 6JE (opp Central Library)
🌣 12-11 (midnight Thu; 1am Fri & Sat); 11-11 Sun
☎ (0115) 941 7080 ⊕ the-dragon.co.uk
Adnams Southwold Bitter, Broadside; Castle Rock Harvest Pale Ⓗ

Small and welcoming unspoilt pub with a long, split-level interior and a laid-back ambience. Seating is a combination of bar stools and comfortable benches. There is a delightful enclosed beer garden at the back. An extensive menu of fresh home-cooked food is available until 9pm (5pm weekends). Check out the Scalextric room with a scale model of Market Square to drive round (phone for opening times). 🌣🜚🖳⅄🖳

Hand & Heart ⅃

65 Derby Road, NG1 5BA
🌣 12-midnight (11 Mon; 1am Fri & Sat); 12-11 Sun
☎ (0115) 958 2456 ⊕ thehandandheart.co.uk
Dancing Duck Roundheart, guests Ⓗ

Not apparent from the outside, or even from the front bar decorated in plush dark woods, but part of this pub is sunk deep into sandstone caves, creating a unique ambience. Eight beers are available, more during beer festivals, as are real ciders and perries, and for diners there is a high-quality food menu. Upstairs is a glass conservatory, built in the 1980s but converted to include an open balcony in 2012. Live music plays every Thursday. 🜚🜚♠⅄🖳

Kean's Head ⅃

46 St Mary's Gate, NG1 1QA (opp St Mary's Church)
🌣 11.30-11 (12.30am Fri & Sat); 12-10.30 Sun
☎ (0115) 947 4052
Castle Rock Harvest Pale, Preservation, Screech Owl; guest beers Ⓗ

Cosy one-room pub opposite the imposing St Mary's Church in the historic Lace Market district – the building was once a lace factory. Named in honour of the 19th-century actor Edmund Kean, it is busy at weekends and attracts a diverse and varied clientele. Owned by the Castle Rock group, it serves inventive, freshly-prepared traditional English and European food from an ever-changing menu. Three guest beers are usually available, often including a dark beer. 🜚&⇌🖳🖳

King William IV

6 Eyre Street, Sneinton, NG2 4PB
🌣 12 (11 Fri & Sat)-11; 12-10.30 Sun ☎ (0115) 958 9864
Oakham Bishops Farewell; guest beers Ⓗ

Nicknamed the King Billy, this cosy Victorian gem nestling on the edge of town is just a stone's throw from the Capital FM Arena. A family-run free house that oozes charm and character, it is a haven for real ale drinkers, with a choice of seven microbrewery ales from near and far, as well as a cider. Occasional live music and televised sport feature. A fine selection of rolls is available. Not to be missed on a visit to Nottingham.
Q⇌🖳♣♠⅄🖳(43)

Langtry's ⅃

4 South Sherwood Street, NG1 4BY
🌣 11-11; 12-10.30 Sun ☎ (0115) 947 2124
Flowers IPA; guest beers Ⓗ

Long known as the Peach Tree, Langtry's took on its current name in 1981 in honour of the famed Victorian starlet Lillie Langtry. Photographs and playbills from her career adorn the walls and delight pre-theatre patrons of the Theatre Royal and Royal Concert Hall. The selection of ciders is among the best in Nottingham with up to seven in summer, and a three-thirds cider tapas to help you make up your mind. Quality food is available all week featuring local ingredients. ▲▲&❀◖▷&☷●♪┗▭

Lincolnshire Poacher L
161-163 Mansfield Road, NG1 3FR
❂ 11-11 (midnight Thu-Sat); 12-11 Sun ☎ (0115) 941 1584
Castle Rock Harvest Pale; guest beers Ⓗ
Former local CAMRA Pub of the Year with 13 handpumps offering a wide selection of guest ales, mainly from microbreweries. A mild, stout or porter is always available along with real cider, continental bottled beers and a fine selection of whiskies. Meals are made with locally sourced ingredients. The pub features artwork celebrating its twinning with In de Wildeman bar in Amsterdam. Live music is showcased on Sundays. Q❀◖&☷♣●♪┗▭

Major Oak L
24-26 Pelham Street, NG1 2EG
❂ 10-midnight (1am Fri & Sat) ☎ (0115) 958 4825
Amber Barnes Wallis; guest beers Ⓗ
This modern real ale pub, formerly a Hogshead, serves a wide variety of ales often unusual for Nottingham. Running between two roads either side of Market Square, it has a narrow split-level interior with a long bar running down one side. You cannot escape the sport screened on many TVs. Food is served daily 10am-10pm. There is a pool table in the middle of the pub. ◖&☷♣●▭

Malt Cross L
16 St James's Street, NG1 6FE
❂ 11-11 (1am Fri & Sat); 11-6 Sun ☎ (0115) 941 1048
⏛ maltcross.com
Beer range varies Ⓗ
This Grade II-listed former Victorian music hall, built by Edwin Hill in 1877, is owned by a charitable trust. An upstairs gallery overlooks the ground floor area from all sides. The guest beers often include a Glastonbury ale, alongside others from local microbreweries. Monday is quiz night and live music plays on Tuesday evenings. Food is served until 8pm (5pm Sun). ◖☷♣▭

Organ Grinder L
21 Alfreton Road, Canning Circus, NG7 3JE
❂ 12-11 (11.30 Thu; midnight Sat & Sun) ☎ (0115) 970 0630
Batemans XB; Blue Monkey BG Sips, Guerrilla, seasonal beers; guest beers Ⓗ
Previously the Red Lion, this pub was bought and refurbished by Blue Monkey Brewery and is its first brewery tap. The split-level single-roomed pub boasts a wood-burning fire and outside is a decked garden leading to a terrace and small first-floor function room. The guest beers are usually from other microbreweries and two real ciders and a perry are always available. No meals, but bar snacks such as pork pies are sold. ▲▲❀♣●┗▭

VAT & Fiddle L
12-14 Queen's Bridge Road, NG2 1NB
❂ 11-11 (midnight Fri & Sat); 12-11 Sun ☎ (0115) 985 0611
Castle Rock Sheriff's Tipple, Black Gold, Harvest Pale, Preservation Fine Ale, Elsie Mo, Screech Owl Ⓗ
Brewery tap for the adjacent Castle Rock Brewery, a minute's walk from the station. Tours are available Monday to Saturday (book in advance), ending in Golding's Room which opened in 2011. Once in the pub, 12 handpumps mostly serve the Castle Rock range, with guests from local and new breweries completing the selection. A seated area outside at the front allows visitors to admire the Art Deco frontage and floral displays in summer. Hot food is served all week, with roasts on Sundays. Q☷❀◖&☷♣●♪┗▭

Nottingham: North

Gladstone L
45 Loscoe Road, Carrington, NG5 2AW (off A60)
❂ 5 (4 Fri, 12 Sat)-11 (midnight Thu-Sat); 12-11 Sun
☎ (0115) 912 9994
Castle Rock Harvest Pale; Fuller's London Pride; Nottingham EPA; Oakham Scarlet Macaw; Taylor Landlord; guest beer Ⓗ
This friendly back-street local sits in the middle of a Victorian terrace, just north of Nottingham, with traditional games in the bar and memorabilia decorating the walls. The lounge features a large collection of books – with customers encouraged to browse – old brasswork, ornaments and pictures. Outside, the secluded garden offers a haven in summer, winning many a Nottingham in Bloom award. The function room has hosted the Carrington Folk Club every Wednesday for 25 years. ❀⊞♣┗▭

Horse & Groom L
462 Radford Road, New Basford, NG7 7EA
❂ 12 (4 Mon)-11; 12-11.30 Fri; 11-11.30 Sat
☎ (0115) 970 3777 ⏛ horseandgroombasford.com
Castle Rock Harvest Pale; Nottingham Legend; guest beers Ⓗ
Friendly and popular pub sitting in the shadow of the defunct Shipstones Brewery. There are steps up to the front door but wheelchair access to the function room via a ramp is available on request. The pub has a cosy lounge with a real fire and a separate open taproom area. Nine handpumps serve mainly microbrewery beers including a mild and at least one local guest, and a real cider. ▲▲Q☷●▭

Hotel Deux L
2 Pelham Road, Sherwood Rise, NG5 1AP
❂ 5-11 (11.30 Thu & Fri); 6-11.30 Sat; 6-11 Sun
☎ (0115) 985 6724 ⏛ theguitarbar.co.uk
Blue Monkey BG Sips; guest beers Ⓗ
Formerly a hotel, now a friendly pub with a comfortably furnished main bar overlooking the front garden. The range of four beers varies, but usually includes a brew from Whim and Blue Monkey. Off the main bar is the Guitar Bar, featuring live entertainment at weekends from local, national and sometimes international artists (see website for details). A separate function room is much used by the local community. Board games are available. ❀P┗▭

Nottingham: South

Trent Navigation L
Meadow Lane, NG2 3HS
❂ 12-11 (midnight Fri); 11-midnight Sat; 11-10.30 Sun
☎ (0115) 986 5658 ⏛ trentnavigation.com
Navigation Traditional, Pale Ale, Golden, Classic IPA; guest beers Ⓗ
Once a Victorian canalside inn, the building was fully restored in 2011. The Navigation Brewery was installed in the old watering stables for canal horses at the rear, with a large screened patio area

separating the brewery and pub. Navigation beers dominate the bar but another five handpumps dispense guests and real cider. A good range of food complements the ales. Live music features most nights on a small raised area at one end of the pub. ⌖❶❺⇌🐾P¹-❋(2-10)

Nottingham: West

Johnson Arms Ⓛ
59 Abbey Street, Lenton, NG7 2NZ
✪ 12 (4 Sat)-11 ☎ (0115) 978 6355 ⊕ johnsonarms.co.uk
Adnams Southwold Bitter; guest beers Ⓗ
Popular two-room pub due to its proximity to the University of Nottingham and QMC hospital, this former Shipstones house retains the original etched windows, complemented by a green-tiled frontage. In 2012 the pub celebrated its 100th anniversary on the site. Annual highlights include quarterly beer festivals, Johnsonbury music festival, Eurovision night and the Mild Trail walks in May. Traditional home-cooked food includes JA burgers. The magnificent beer garden, with a pétanque court, is not to be missed. ⌖❶🐾🐾P¹-❋

Plough Inn Ⓛ
17 St Peter's Street, Radford, NG7 3EN
✪ 12-11 (midnight Thu-Sat) ☎ (0115) 970 2615
Nottingham Rock Ale Bitter Beer, Rock Ale Mild Beer, Legend, Extra Pale Ale, seasonal beer; guest beer Ⓗ
Linked with the old Nottingham Brewery since 1887, the Plough is now the brewery tap for the revived company. A full range of Nottingham beers is served, four regular and four rotating. The present building, a 1932 two-room house with a central servery, is largely unchanged. Attracting regulars from a wide area, this 'village pub in the city' has retained its local feel in a period of rapid change, offering real fires, an outside skittle alley and a popular quiz night. ⌗Q⌖❺🐾🐾P¹-❋

Radcliffe-on-Trent

Horse Chestnut Ⓛ
49 Main Road, NG12 2BE
✪ 12 (5 Mon & Tue)-11; 12-11.30 Fri & Sat
☎ (0115) 933 1994 ⊕ horsechestnutradcliffe.com
Black Sheep Best Bitter; Castle Rock Harvest Pale; Fuller's London Pride; guest beers Ⓗ
Previously known as the Cliffe Inn, this LocAle-accredited pub was totally refurbished in 2006 with 1920s-style decor. Very much a smart local pub that serves food, rather than a restaurant that serves beer, it offers six real ales including three ever-changing guests. Italian food includes freshly made pasta dishes and stone-baked pizzas from the in-house pizza oven. ⌖❶❺⇌🐾P¹-❋

Retford

Brick & Tile Inn
81 Moorgate, DN22 6RS SK709817
✪ 12-3 (5 Sat; 4 Sun), 7-11 ☎ (01777) 703681
Beer range varies Ⓗ
A quiet pub situated on the main road between Retford and Gainsborough. There is always a choice of two real ales available here – one a light beer and the other dark – usually from local breweries including Idle, Springhead and Milestone. Accommodation is available in two twin rooms and two single rooms. ⌖⇌P¹-❋

Dominie Cross
38 Grove Street, DN22 6JR SK706311
✪ 8am-11 ☎ (01777) 861150
Greene King IPA, Abbot; Morland Old Speckled Hen; guest beers Ⓗ
Named after the stone cross that marked Retford's southern boundary in medieval times, this Wetherspoon pub is tastefully decorated making good use of old Retford photographs. It offers a choice of seating areas from quiet corners to a raised space with a good view of the bar. Outside is a heated area where smoking is permitted. The pub is 200 yards from the market square and 50 yards from the bus station. ⍨⌖❶❺-❋

Turk's Head
Grove Street, DN22 6LE SK708811
✪ 11-2.30, 5-11; 11-11 Sat; 12-11 Sun ☎ (01777) 702742
Beer range varies Ⓗ
Situated close to the main market square, entry to this pub is via two large oak doors which both lead to an open-plan area served by an L-shaped bar. The room features plenty of oak panelling and has a large warming open fire. At the far end is a pool table. Four real ales are served. ⌗🐾¹-❋

Selston

Horse & Jockey Ⓛ
Church Lane, NG16 6FB SK459535
✪ 12-3.30, 5-1am; 12-4, 7-1am Sun ☎ (01773) 781012
Greene King Abbot Ⓖ**; Rudgate Ruby Mild** Ⓗ**; Taylor Landlord** Ⓖ**; Wychwood Hobgoblin; guest beers** Ⓗ
A drinking man's pub dating back to 1664 with large open fires and old flagstone floors. Up to six real ales are available, two served from the jug plus changing guests including a LocAle. A real cider or perry is always available. A quiz is held on Sunday evening and a folk night every Wednesday. No hot food is served. A winner of many CAMRA awards including local Pub of the Year 2012. ⌗Q⍨⌖❺🐾🐾P¹-❋

Southwell

Final Whistle Ⓛ
Station Street, NG25 0ET
✪ 12-11.30 (11 Sun) ☎ (01636) 814953
⊕ finalwhistlepub.co.uk
Everards Tiger; Fuller's London Pride; Leatherbritches Bounder; guest beers Ⓗ
Brilliant Everard's renovation at the terminus of the Southwell Trail, formerly the Beeching-cut rail line. A superb reconstruction of a 1920s railway station, it is full of railway memorabilia with booking offices, fireplaces and an open waiting room. The beer garden is styled as the platform, with seating and the old railway track alongside. Ten real ales plus six real ciders are always available in tip-top condition. Filled rolls, pies and cheeseboard snacks are served. Occasional live music plays. ⌗Q⌖❺🐾🐾P¹-❋(100)

Old Coach House Ⓛ
69 Easthorpe, NG25 0HY
✪ 5 (4 Fri; 2 Sat; 12 Sun)-midnight ☎ (01636) 813289
Black Sheep Best Bitter; guest beers Ⓗ
Genuine old-fashioned public house on the edge of the village built in the 17th century. It features five distinct areas, with an original fireplace and traditional furniture giving a feeling of age. Five varying guest beers, including a LocAle, are always

available. There is live jazz one Sunday a month, and a beer garden with a large heated smoking area. CAMRA discount is given with a valid membership card. ⚌⛄🏠♣♨'–⊟(100)

Stapleford

Horse & Jockey 🍷 Ⓛ
20 Nottingham Road, NG9 8AA
🌐 12-11 (midnight Fri & Sat) ☎ (0115) 875 9655
⊕ horseandjockeystapleford.co.uk
Full Mash Horse & Jockey; guest beers Ⓗ
Known locally as simply 'the Jockey', this pub is situated close to the main crossroads in the centre of town. Refurbished and turned into a traditional ale house in 2012, it offers a choice of ten ever-changing real ales, plus local ciders. It has two rooms; a main bar and a slightly raised function room behind. There are no fruit machines, pool tables or televisions. Local CAMRA Pub of the Year 2013. Q⛄♨'–⊟

Staunton in the Vale

Staunton Arms 🍷 Ⓛ
NG13 9PE
🌐 12-11 (midnight Fri & Sat); 11-10 Sun ☎ (01400) 281218
⊕ stauntonarms.co.uk
Castle Rock Harvest Pale; Draught Bass; guest beer Ⓗ
Two hundred-year-old listed pub in the far north of the Vale of Belvoir, carefully restored to retain its original character. The large bar offers comfortable seating for drinkers and diners, with a further separate raised restaurant area. The pub serves freshly prepared meals lunchtimes and evenings, and three cask beers, one always a LocAle. Mini-festivals are held occasionally, with upcoming events publicised on the website. CAMRA branch Pub of The Year 2013. ⚌Q⛄🏠♨⊟♨P

Sutton-in-Ashfield

Masons Arms Ⓛ
Unwin Road, NG17 4NB
🌐 12-11 ☎ (01623) 472704
Beer range varies Ⓗ
Easily recognisable with its solar panels on the roof, this is a thriving community pub with a friendly atmosphere. It has a comfortable lounge and spacious bar where darts and dominoes are played, both rooms served from a central bar. A conservatory to the rear leads to the smoking area and beer garden. Two ever-changing real ales and one real cider are available, with beers from Blue Monkey, Welbeck Abbey, Bradfield and Abbeydale featuring regularly. The pub holds a mini beer festival twice a year. Dogs welcome.
Q⛄🏠⊞♣♨P'–⊟(17)

Picture House
Fox Street, NG17 1DA
🌐 8am-midnight (1am Fri & Sat) ☎ (01623) 554627
Greene King Abbot; Ruddles Best Bitter; guest beers Ⓗ
An open-plan Wetherspoon pub housed in a former 1920s cinema, situated close to the bus station. The interior is Art Deco in style with a high ceiling and wood panels, with ample seating throughout. The usual good-value range of Wetherspoon meals is served every day until 10pm. Live sport is shown on a large screen above the front entrance. Free Wi-Fi available. ⛄⊕♨⊟

Watnall

Queen's Head
40 Main Road, NG16 1HT
🌐 12-11; 11.30-midnight Thu-Sat ☎ (0115) 938 6774
⊕ queensheadwatnall.com
Adnams Broadside; Everards Tiger, Original; Morland Old Speckled Hen; Wells Bombardier; guest beer Ⓗ
A 17th-century rural gem with a lounge/dining space, a small snug hidden behind the bar and an unusual locals' area with a grandfather clock. The internal fittings around the bar are original, and photos of locals adorn the walls. Home-cooked English food is served all day from lunchtime into the evening. The pub is reputedly haunted. Occasional beer festivals and live music feature. The extensive garden has children's play equipment and a marquee. ⚌Q⛄🏠⊕⊞P'–⊟

Wellow

Olde Red Lion Ⓛ
Eakring Road, NG22 0EG (opp maypole) SK669660
🌐 12-11 ☎ (01623) 861000
Beer range varies Ⓗ
This 400-year-old village pub is situated opposite the village green with its maypole and participates in a large event on May Day. The traditional wood-beamed interior includes a restaurant, lounge and bar areas with photographs and maps depicting the history of the village. Three real ales are available from local breweries. Sherwood Forest and Clumber Park are both nearby.
Q⛄🏠⊕⊞P⊟⊟(31,32)

West Bridgford

Poppy & Pint Ⓛ
Pierrepont Road, Lady Bay, NG2 5DX
🌐 9.30 (10 Sun)-11 ☎ (0115) 981 9995
Castle Rock Sheriff's Tipple, Black Gold, Harvest Pale, Preservation, Screech Owl; guest beers Ⓗ
A former British Legion Club converted in 2011 to become Castle Rock's largest pub. It has a large main bar with a raised area and a family area with a café bar (children welcome until 9pm), all with a homely, welcoming feel. Look for the old snooker table ends on one wall. A large function room is upstairs and the beer garden overlooks a bowling green. Twelve handpumps dispense the Castle Rock beers plus ales from new breweries. There are usually two real ciders and excellent food is served. The pub is motorhome-friendly.
Q⛄🏠⊕⊞♨P'–⊟

Stratford Haven Ⓛ
2 Stratford Road, NG2 6BA (behind Co-op)
🌐 11-11 (midnight Fri-Sat); 12-11 Sun ☎ (0115) 982 5981
Adnams Broadside; Batemans XB; Castle Rock Harvest Pale, Elsie Mo, Screech Owl; Everards Tiger Ⓗ
A former pet shop, the pub has a single narrow bar with a larger seating area at the back and a secluded snug to one side. Up to 12 cask ales plus a cider are available at any one time, including LocAles from owner Castle Rock's portfolio. A wide range of food includes a curry night on Monday and pie night on Tuesday. Sunday is silent quiz night and new brew day is the first Thursday of the month. Q🏠⊕⊞♨'–⊟

Trent Bridge Inn Ⓛ
2 Radcliffe Road, NG2 6AA
🌐 9-midnight ☎ (0115) 977 8940

Batemans XXXB; Greene King Abbot; Marston's Pedigree; Nottingham Rock Ale Mild Beer, Trent Bridge Inn Ale; Theakston Best Bitter; guest beers Ⓗ This prominent 1885 Victorian corner pub reopened in 2011 to much acclaim, and received a CAMRA branch award in 2012. A number of inter-connected, wood-panelled rooms are fitted with cosy booths, comfy sofas, an open fireplace and an array of mainly cricket-themed sporting memorabilia. Pleasant staff, led by an enthusiastic manager, are happy to let you sample any of the 12 real ales and two real ciders are usually available from several bars, including those in the function rooms. ▲▲🌑🏵️🄌🕭👆P🗢—🖵

West Stockwith

White Hart ♈ Ⓛ
Main Street, DN10 4ET SK787947
✪ 12-11 ☎ (01427) 890176
Idle Landlord; guest beers Ⓗ
Small country pub with a little garden overlooking the River Trent, Chesterfield Canal and West Stockwith Marina. One bar serves the recently refurbished bar, lounge and dining area. The Idle Brewery is situated in outbuildings at the side of the pub and the range of five real ales usually includes three from Idle. The area is especially busy during the summer, due to the canal and river traffic. Q🖢🏵️🄌🕭🅰️♣P🖵(97)

Worksop

Grafton Hotel Ⓛ
157-161 Gateford Road, S80 1UJ SK583798
✪ 3 (12 Sat & Sun)-11.30 ☎ (01909) 768089
Grafton Blondie; guest beers Ⓗ
This is the brewery tap for the Grafton Brewing Company, with 12 handpulls. At least three Grafton beers are always available at reasonable prices as well as guests from other breweries. A lively community pub, it has a spacious bar area and restaurant serving good-value food. Close to the railway station and Worksop Town Football Club, it also offers good accommodation. ▲▲🚌🄌🍴🗢♣—🖵

Mallard
Station Approach, S81 7AG (on railway platform) SK586797
✪ 12 (5 Mon; 11 Fri & Sat)-11; 12-10.30
Sun ☎ 07973 521824
Beer range varies Ⓗ
Formerly the Worksop station buffet, the Mallard is situated within the railway station buildings, with access from the car park. The pub offers a warm welcome as well as four real ales usually including

one from the Double Top Brewery and at least one traditional cider, a selection of foreign bottled beers and country fruit wines. A further room is available downstairs for special occasions – such as the four beer festivals the pub holds each year. Q🗢👆P🖵

Shireoaks Inn
Westgate, S80 1LT SK582788
✪ 11.30-11; 12-10.30 Sun ☎ (01909) 472118
⊕ shireoaksinn.co.uk
Beer range varies Ⓗ
A warm, friendly pub converted from cottages, the public bar houses a pool table and large-screen TV. The comfortable lounge bar has a separate dining area. Tasty home-cooked food is good value for money. The two handpulls dispense regularly changing guest ales. A small outside area with tables is available in the summer. Q🖢🏵️🄌🕭🅰️♣—🖵

Station Hotel
Carlton Road, S81 7AG (opp railway station) SK586797
✪ 11 (12 Sun)-11 ☎ (01909) 474108
⊕ thestationhotelworksop.co.uk
Beer range varies Ⓗ
Situated opposite Worksop railway station on the edge of the town centre, at least four regularly changing real ales are available. One long bar serves a large bar area with a separate dining room, and there is a further small room suitable for functions and meetings. Food is available lunchtimes and evenings and accommodation is offered. 🏵️🚌🄌 🝗🕭🗢P—🖵

Wysall

Plough Ⓛ
Main Street, Keyworth Road, NG12 5QQ
✪ 12-midnight ☎ (01509) 880339
Draught Bass; Greene King Abbot; Taylor Landlord; guest beer Ⓗ
A busy country pub in existence for more than 150 years, and for the last 14 years owned by the same family. This pleasantly updated village free house retains many period features and much original character, with an attractive beer garden at the front. A sensibly priced menu of traditional home-cooked pub favourites is available at lunchtime. Dogs are welcome after 3pm when food service is over. There is a separate area for pool, and a quiz is hosted on Tuesday. ▲▲Q🏵️🄌♣P—🖵(63)

One hundred years old

I met the other day an old man, who asked me to drink. 'I am not thirsty,' said I, 'and I will not drink with you.' 'Yes, you will,' said the old man, 'for I am this day one hundred years old; and you will never again have the opportunity of drinking the health of a man on his hundredth birthday.' So I broke my word and drank. 'How have you passed your time?' said I. 'As well as I could,' said the old man, 'always enjoying a good thing when it came honestly within my reach; not forgetting to praise God for putting it there'. 'I suppose you were fond of a glass of good ale when you were young'. 'Yes,' said the old man, 'I was, and so, thank God, I am still'. And he drank off a glass of ale.

George Barrow, 1857

ENGLAND

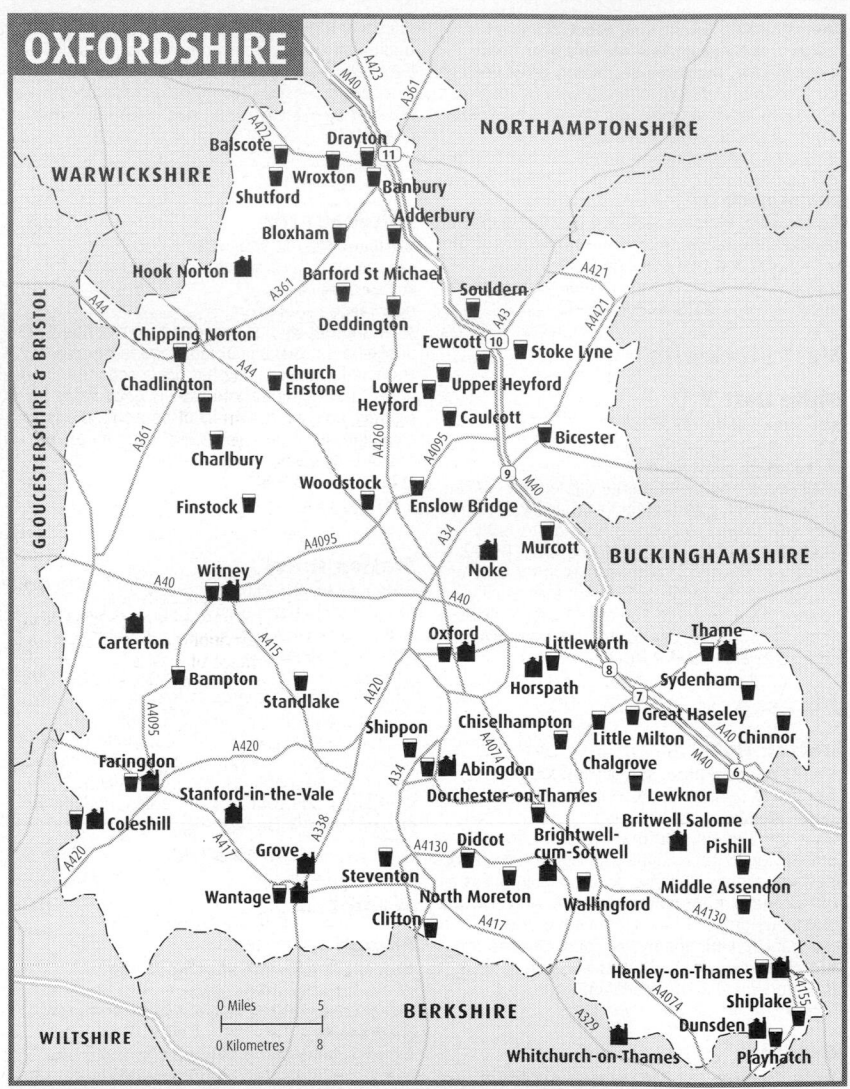

OXFORDSHIRE

Map showing towns and villages across Oxfordshire including:

NORTHAMPTONSHIRE

WARWICKSHIRE

Balscote · Drayton · Wroxton · Shutford · Banbury · Adderbury · Bloxham · Hook Norton · Barford St Michael · Souldern · Chipping Norton · Deddington · Fewcott · Stoke Lyne · Chadlington · Church Enstone · Lower Heyford · Upper Heyford · Caulcott · Bicester · Charlbury · Woodstock · Finstock · Enslow Bridge · Witney · Murcott · Noke · BUCKINGHAMSHIRE · Carterton · Oxford · Littleworth · Thame · Bampton · Standlake · Horspath · Sydenham · Shippon · Chiselhampton · Great Haseley · Little Milton · Chinnor · Faringdon · Abingdon · Chalgrove · Lewknor · Stanford-in-the-Vale · Dorchester-on-Thames · Britwell Salome · Coleshill · Grove · Didcot · Brightwell-cum-Sotwell · Pishill · Wantage · Steventon · North Moreton · Wallingford · Middle Assendon · Clifton · Henley-on-Thames · Shiplake · Dunsden · Whitchurch-on-Thames · Playhatch

GLOUCESTERSHIRE & BRISTOL

WILTSHIRE

BERKSHIRE

0 Miles 5
0 Kilometres 8

Abingdon

Brewery Tap ▼ Ⓛ

40-42 Ock Street, OX14 5BZ
✪ 11-11.30 (1am Fri & Sat); 12-11 Sun ☎ (01235) 521655
⊕ thebrewerytap.net
Loose Cannon Abingdon Bridge; Morland Original; guest beers Ⓗ
Morland created a tap for its brewery in 1993 by converting three Grade II-listed town houses. The brewery closed and its site was redeveloped in 2000, following a takeover by Greene King, but the pub, run by the same family since it opened, has thrived. There are usually four regularly changing guest beers, including local ales not from the Greene King list. The pub holds three beer festivals a year. ▯Q✿✐Ⓓ&♣Ᵽᷝ⊟

Nag's Head on the Thames Ⓛ

The Bridge, OX14 3HX
✪ 11-11 (midnight Fri & Sat); 12-10.30 Sun
☎ (01235) 524516 ⊕ thenagsheadonthethames.co.uk

Beer range varies Ⓗ
On an island right on Abingdon Bridge and split over two levels, with a large garden area next to the river, the pub has lovely views of the countryside and the town's historic buildings. A free house, it has eight regularly changing local beers, always including offerings from Loose Cannon and XT. Good food is available all day. Live music features at weekends and some weekdays. The Salter's Steamers cruises from Oxford pass by twice a day in summer. ▯➣✿Ⓓ&♣Ᵽᷝ⊟

Adderbury

Pickled Ploughman

Aynho Road, OX17 3NL (on B4100 Aynho Rd) SP477358
✪ 10.30-11 (10.30 Sun) ☎ (01295) 810327
⊕ thepickledploughman.co.uk
Hook Norton Hooky Bitter; guest beers Ⓗ
Following a tasteful and extensive refurbishment in 2012, this free house has built a reputation not only for its extensive menu of locally sourced

dishes but also for its four well-kept ales on handpump. A decked patio area to the rear offers an attractive area in the summer. The nearby camping and caravan site provides a pleasant base for exploring this picturesque ironstone village with its morris dancing heritage.
🏕Q🚲🏠🕽🕭🚹♿AP¼–�(S4)

Balscote

Butchers Arms
Shutford Road, OX15 6JQ (just off A422)
❂6-11; 12-3, 6-11 Sat; 12-11 Sun ☎ (01295) 730750
Hook Norton Hooky Bitter, Lion, Old Hooky; guest beer Ⓖ
This cosy parlour pub serves Hooky ales plus a monthly guest, straight from casks behind the bar. A traditional village inn with an open fire, it has been a Hook Norton pub since 1878, was once an abattoir and still has an icehouse in the garden. Home-made traditional pub grub is available, including weekly themed curry and steak nights. The pretty, spacious, family-friendly garden has Aunt Sally and children's activities. Walkers, muddy boots and dogs on leads are always welcome.
🏕Q🚲🏠🕽🕭♣🖈P¼–🕯

Bampton

Morris Clown
High Street, OX18 2JW
❂5 (1 Sat)-11; 12-10.30 Sun ☎ (01993) 850217
Beer range varies Ⓗ
A regular in the Guide, this former Courage inn has been run by the same family for two generations. Three guest ales, often local, are kept, and real cider is available in the summer months. The single-bar, simply furnished free house is heated in the winter by a huge log fire. Bar billiards is played, while Aunt Sally features in the sprawling rear garden. 🏕Q🏠♣🖈P¼–�(18)

Banbury

Bell Inn
12 Middleton Road, OX16 4QJ (on Middleton Rd out of town, past railway station)
❂12.30-3 (not Mon & Tue), 7-11; 12.30-11 Fri & Sat; 12-5.30, 8-10.30 Sun ☎ (01295) 253169
Adnams Southwold Bitter; guest beers Ⓗ
A long-time Guide entry, this is a straightforward two-bar pub. Situated handily for railway and bus stations, and near the town centre, it is nevertheless a true local, with loyal regulars and a warm welcome for visitors. The buzz of convivial conversation mixes with the sounds of pub games most weekday evenings – the Bell hosts darts, dominoes, pool, Aunt Sally and quiz teams. Adnams Southwold is supplemented by guest beers from Punch's Finest Cask list. 🏠🖳🚆♣P¼–�

Mill Arts Centre
Spiceball Park Road, OX16 5QE (on canalside near bus station and Castle Quay shopping centre)
❂12-11 (midnight Fri & Sat); hours vary Sun
☎ (01295) 279002 ⊕ themillartscentre.co.uk
Hook Norton Hooky Bitter; guest beers Ⓗ
The Millstream Bar, in Banbury's premier theatre and live music venue, has all the attributes of a good pub – welcoming staff, good-value snacks, pleasant decor and, above all, good beer. Hook Norton Hooky is the regular, with a well-chosen

range of guests. The bar is on the ground floor, with level access, next to an exhibition space showcasing local artists. There are tables outside by the lock gates of the Oxford Canal.
🚲🏠🕽🚹♿🚆P¼–�

White Horse
50-52 North Bar Street, OX16 0TH (N of Banbury Cross)
❂12-11 ☎ (01295) 277484 ⊕ whitehorsebanbury.co.uk
White Horse Bitter, Village Idiot, Wayland Smithy; guest beers Ⓗ
A warm and welcoming traditional ale house in the heart of Banbury, the White Horse serves an extensive range of quality cask-conditioned ales and a selection of home-made dishes, based on locally sourced ingredients. Outside is a courtyard area with patio furniture for warm-weather drinking. 🏕🚲🏠🕽🚹♿🚆🖈¼–�

Barford St Michael

George Inn
Lower Street, OX15 0RH (off B4031)
❂7-11; 12-4 Sun ☎ (01869) 338226
Beer range varies Ⓗ
Charming thatched free house dating from 1672. Landlord Martin, ably assisted by Dillon the Labrador, provides a warm welcome and a changing range of ales plus cider and perry from Westons and other makers. A beer festival is usually held in summer. No food is served, but customers can bring in food or order takeaways. Weddings and functions are catered for in a marquee in the garden. Opening hours can be extended to suit visitors on request.
Q🏠🖳▲♣🖈P¼–�

Bicester

Penny Black
Sheep Street, OX26 6JW (in pedestrianised area)
❂8am-midnight (1am Fri & Sat) ☎ (01869) 321535
Hook Norton Hooky Bitter, Old Hooky; Greene King Abbot; Ruddles Best Bitter; guest beers Ⓗ
This popular Wetherspoon outlet, formerly Bicester's main post office, opened in 1997. It is situated in the town's pedestrianised area, within walking distance of Bicester Town and Bicester

INDEPENDENT BREWERIES

Adkin Wantage
Appleford Brightwell-cum-Sotwell
Bell Street Henley-on-Thames (NEW)
Bellinger's Grove
Betjeman Wantage
Brakspear (Marston's) Witney
Compass Carterton
Complete Pig Britwell Salome
Faringdon Faringdon
Fisher Noke (NEW)
Hen House Whitchurch-on-Thames
Henley Henley-on-Thames (NEW)
Hook Norton Hook Norton
Loddon Dunsden
Loose Cannon Abingdon
Old Bog Oxford
Old Forge Coleshill
Shotover Horspath
Thame Thame
White Horse Stanford-in-the-Vale
Wychwood (Marston's) Witney

North railway stations and Bicester bus station. Up to 12 ales are on offer. The management aims to promote local breweries and two Hook Norton ales are now a permanent feature. Occasional Meet the Brewer evenings are held and 'request a guest' has also proved a hit with the regulars.
Q ⚞❀⏅◑ ⅃ ⚞(Town/North)🍴⚑⏚

Bloxham

Elephant & Castle ⅃
Humber Street, OX15 4LZ (off A361)
✪ 10-3, 6 (5 Fri)-11; 10-11 Sat; 12-10.30 Sun
☎ (01295) 720383 ⊕ bloxhampub.co.uk
Hook Norton Hooky Bitter, seasonal beer; guest beer Ⓗ
This 17th-century coaching inn now seems to face the wrong way as the old turnpike once ran through the current car park and its carriage entrance. More historic features, including a bread oven and photographs of old Bloxham, lie within. The pub has been in the hands of the same family for 40 years and extends a warm welcome to all. Food is served lunchtimes, except Sundays. Six ciders and perries from Westons are also kept. Dogs on leads are permitted. ⚞❀🚲◑⏥♣🍴P⚑⏚(488)

Caulcott

Horse & Groom
Lower Heyford Road, OX25 4ND (on B4030 between Middleton Stoney and Lower Heyford)
✪ 12-3, 6-11 (closed Mon eve); 12-3, 7-10.30 Sun
☎ (01869) 343257 ⊕ horseandgroomcaulcott.co.uk
White Horse Bitter; guest beers Ⓗ
A small pub with a big welcome, this genuine free house offers three guest ales, often from local micros and Cornish brewers. The French landlord/chef serves excellent food (booking advised, especially Sun lunch). The Bastille Day beer festival is not to be missed, and real cider is kept in summer. No dogs or under-sevens permitted inside. The good-sized beer garden is popular in warmer weather. Car parking is available nearby. Local CAMRA Pub of the Year 2010. ⚞Q❀◑⅃⚑

Chadlington

Tite Inn
Mill End, OX7 3NY
✪ 11-11 (closed Mon Jan to mid-March); 12-10.30 Sun
☎ (01608) 676910 ⊕ thetiteinn.co.uk
Sharp's Doom Bar; guest beers Ⓗ
A welcome return for this Guide regular. Bought by Ann and David in 2012, it now serves one regular and three ever-changing guests, plus Westons Old Rosie cider on handpump. The name derives from the old Oxfordshire dialect for the spring that runs under the pub and through the attractive hillside garden. Quality, affordable food is served in the bar or restaurant. A dog-friendly and thriving community pub, David Cameron has been known to drop in. ⚞Q⚞❀◑⏦🍴P⚑⏚(X9,S3)

Chalgrove

Red Lion
115 High Street, OX44 7SS SU635970
✪ 11.30-3, 6-midnight; 12-11.30 Sun ☎ (01865) 890625
⊕ redlionchalgrove.co.uk
Butcombe Bitter; Fuller's London Pride; Rebellion Mild; guest beers Ⓗ

Church-owned village local run by a friendly husband and wife team, both trained chefs. Good food is a speciality at this picturesque 16th-century pub. The two guest beers are from local breweries such as Rebellion and XT. The interior is divided into several distinct areas and the pub is used by a wide cross-section of the community. You can drink outside in both front and rear gardens, while a real fire awaits inside in the winter months.
⚞❀◑⅃♣🍴⚑⏚(101,106)

Charlbury

Rose & Crown
Market Street, OX7 3PL
✪ 12-11 (1am Fri); 11-1am Sat ☎ (01608) 810103
⊕ roseandcrown.charlbury.com
Ramsbury Bitter; guest beers Ⓗ
Twenty seven years in the Guide, this traditional wet-sales-only pub offers an impressive range of real ales, with one regular and six guests from micros all over the UK, many rare to the area. Choose from the main bar or the quieter, comfortable bottom bar where pool is played. A true community pub with an eclectic clientele, families and dogs are welcome. Fortnightly live music is hugely popular, along with the annual beer festival over the last weekend of January.
⚞⚞❀⏶⚞♣🍴⚑⏚(X9,S3)

Chinnor

Red Lion
3 High Street, OX39 4DL
✪ 12-2, 5-11.30; 12-2, 4.30-12.30am Fri; 12-midnight Sat; 12-11 Sun ☎ (01844) 353468 ⊕ redlionchinnor.co.uk
Beer range varies Ⓗ
Dating back approximately 400 years and originally three cottages, the Red Lion is a traditional, welcoming pub at the foot of the Chilterns in an area popular with hikers and cyclists. A changing range of four real ales is available, including many from local breweries. The separate public bar shows sporting events on Sky TV. A bouncy castle features in the garden for summer.
⚞❀◑⏦⅃P⚑⏚

Chipping Norton

Chequers 🏆
Goddards Lane, OX7 5NP (next to theatre, on corner of Spring St)
✪ 11-11 (midnight Fri & Sat); 11.30-11 Sun
☎ (01608) 644717 ⊕ chequers-pub.com
Fuller's Chiswick Bitter, Discovery, London Pride, ESB; Gale's HSB; guest beers Ⓗ
A traditional English pub with an emphasis on real ale – the landlord is a Master Cellarman – and home-cooked food. The beer range includes up to eight real ales from Fuller's plus guests, alongside bottled ales. The pub is a popular meeting place for discerning drinkers and also convenient for theatre-goers. The bar has four separate areas and there is an airy restaurant and function room to the rear. CAMRA members receive a 5 per cent discount Sunday to Wednesday. ⚞Q⚞◑⏚

Red Lion
Albion Street, OX7 5BJ
✪ 10-11.30 (midnight Fri & Sat); 10-11 Sun
☎ (01608) 644641
Hook Norton Hooky Bitter; guest beer Ⓗ

The smallest pub in Chipping Norton, dating back to 1684, is an ideal place to visit for a pint of Hook Norton beer and some good conversation. There are no jukeboxes or machines. The pub has a roaring fire in winter and a beer garden for the summer, and a giant vegetable competition is held each year. Pub lunches are served. A real community pub, much fundraising for charities is supported. Wi-Fi available. ⛄Q☺☜☕Ⓖ♣♠Pↆ₋🚾

Chiselhampton

Coach & Horses 🅛

Watlington Road, OX44 7UX (on B480)
❀ 11-11; 11-3.30, 7-10.30 Sun ☎ (01865) 890255
⊕ coachhorsesinn.co.uk
Hook Norton Old Hooky; guest beers Ⓗ
This 16th-century hotel and restaurant provides visitors with good-quality ales and an à la carte menu. There are several dining areas and a dedicated bar. The large patio area has ample room for those who like their alfresco summer drinking. The River Thame is only 200 yards away, providing excellent local fishing and walking. For those looking to stay, there are nine en-suite bedrooms and free Wi-Fi. ⛄☺☜☕Ⓖ&P🚾(101,106)

Church Enstone

Crown

Mill Lane, OX7 4NN (off A44, on B4030)
❀ 12-3, 6-11; 12-4 Sun ☎ (01608) 677262
Hook Norton Hooky Bitter; guest beers Ⓗ
A 17th-century Cotswold stone pub in an enchanting part of the village. Inside, wooden beams and flagstone floors add character, as do photographs of the locality. An inglenook fireplace is in use in the winter months. Following a walk in the countryside, the Crown is an ideal place to relax with a pint and a meal from the award-winning menu of locally sourced produce. The absence of a jukebox and games machines encourages conversation. Well-behaved dogs and children welcome. ⛄Q☜☕Ⓖ☕P🚾(S3)

Clifton

Duke of Cumberland's Head

Main Street, OX15 0PE (on B4031 between Aynho and Deddington)
❀ 12-11 ☎ (01869) 338534 ⊕ cliftonduke.com
Hook Norton Hooky Bitter; Sharp's Doom Bar Ⓗ
In the same family for 18 years, this well-managed low-beamed free house, in a quiet village beside the River Cherwell, offers a range of four ales on handpump. The monthly changing menu attracts diners from far and wide. For winter there is a log fire, in summer a pleasant garden where Aunt Sally is played. Dogs are welcome in the pub and the accommodation. There is a large car park to the rear. ⛄Q☜☺☕Ⓖ&♣P

Coleshill

Radnor Arms 🅛

32 Coleshill, SN6 7PR (on B4019)
❀ 11-11; 12-10.30 Sun ☎ (01793) 861515
⊕ radnorarmscoleshill.co.uk
Old Forge Anvil Ale, Blacksmiths Gold, Hammer & Tongs, Sledgehammer Ⓗ/🅖
Set in a beautiful National Trust village, the 18th-century building was the former smithy to the Coleshill estate. Old blacksmith's tools are displayed in the split-level two-room interior; one room has its own snug. This is the brewery tap for the on-site Old Forge Brewery. The beers are dispensed by gravity and handpump to be enjoyed with the traditional home-cooked pub fare. Walkers, children and well-behaved dogs are welcome. Local, county and regional CAMRA Pub of the Year 2011. ⛄Q☺☕Ⓓ♣♠Pↆ₋🚾(64)

Deddington

Crown & Tuns

New Street, OX15 0SP (on A4260)
❀ 12-3 (not Mon), 5-11; 12-6 Sun ☎ (01869) 337371
⊕ puddingface.com
Hook Norton Hooky Bitter, Old Hooky Ⓗ
Known affectionately as Puddingface – the Pie Place because it has a wide range of pies on the menu, this award-winning Hook Norton pub offers most of the beers in the range. Originally a 16th-century coaching inn overlooking the main Oxford to Banbury road, the peaceful rear patio area has been tastefully refurbished with terraced decking in keeping with the split-level interior. Aunt Sally is played in summer. ⛄Q☜☺☕Ⓓ&♣₋🚾

Didcot

Wheatsheaf

Wantage Road, OX11 0BS (on B4493)
❀ 11-midnight (12.30am Thu; 1am Fri & Sat); 12-11 Sun
☎ (01235) 519114
Beer range varies Ⓗ
There has been a Wheatsheaf on this site since the 17th century – the present pub was built in 1909. This tie-free town hostelry has recently gained a well-deserved reputation for the quality and variety of its beers, with up to six ales on offer at any time. The main bar features darts and a pool table, with a quieter room off to the side. There is a large garden and children's play area, and Aunt Sally is played in the summer. Live music features every Saturday with open-mic on Wednesdays. ⛄☺Ⓖ&🚋(Parkway)♣Pↆ₋🚾(32,X32)

Dorchester-on-Thames

George Hotel

High Street, OX10 7HH (opp Dorchester Abbey church lychgate)
❀ 11-11.30 (11 Sun) ☎ (01865) 340404
⊕ thegeorgedorchester.co.uk
Brakspear Bitter; Butcombe Bitter; Wadworth 6X; guest beer Ⓗ
The George combines the beauty of a historic building, complete with oak beams and inglenook fireplaces, with the facilities of a modern hotel. A striking 15th-century coaching inn, it is one of the oldest in the country. Liaan, the landlord, is passionate about serving real ale as perfectly as is possible. In the friendly front bar there are three regular ales and one complementary guest. CAMRA members receive a 50p per pint discount on ales. ⛄Q☜☺☕Ⓓ Ⓖↆ₋🚾(X39,X40)

Drayton

Roebuck Inn

Stratford Road, OX15 6EN
❀ 11-3, 6-11 ☎ (01295) 730542
⊕ roebuckinn-banbury.co.uk

Hook Norton Hooky Bitter, Old Hooky Ⓗ
Nestling alongside the Banbury to Stratford road, this charming inn has a chef patron who boasts several signature dishes. His home-made potato crisps are spectacular, the perfect accompaniment to the two award-winning Hooky ales. The split-level interior is heated during the winter months by a wood-burning stove; there is an out-front patio area for warmer times. The restaurant hosts themed evenings and doubles as a function room. Sunday lunches and regular quiz nights are popular. ♨❀◐◑♿P⁵–

Enslow Bridge

Rock of Gibraltar

Enslow Wharf, OX5 3AY
✪ 11 (4 Tue)-midnight; 12-10.30 Sun ☎ (01869) 331373
🌐 therockofgibraltar.co.uk
Beer range varies Ⓗ
This is a large canalside free house dating to the 1780s. Up to three beers are kept, mainly from local brewers, with Wye Valley Butty Bach and beers from XT regular visitors. A beer festival is held in June. The large garden attracts drinkers in good weather and narrowboaters make use of the moorings to enjoy this popular pub. Good home-cooked food is served in the restaurant, with Greek nights a speciality (no food Sun eve or Tue). Thursday is folk music night. ♨❀◐◑♣P🚌(25,25a)

Faringdon

Swan 🄻

1 Park Road, SN7 7BP
✪ 12 (4.30 Mon)-midnight; 12-2am Fri & Sat
☎ (01367) 241480
Faringdon Folly Ale; guest beers Ⓗ
The Swan was completely renovated in 2010. With up to six real ales available from the on-site Faringdon brewery and local Old Forge and Halfpenny breweries, there is always a wide choice available. Live music and folk jamming sessions keep the ever-increasing regular clientele entertained. Pub games include bar billiards, table skittles, bagatelle and many more.
Q❀♣●⁵–🚌(66)

Fewcott

White Lion

Fritwell Road, OX27 7NZ (1 mile from jct 10 M40)
✪ 7 (5.30 Fri)-11; 12-11 Sat; 12-6.30 Sun ☎ (01869) 346639
Beer range varies Ⓗ
A true free house and hub of the community, offering a constantly changing selection of four ales, mainly from micros, with a stout, porter or mild nearly always on offer. This popular village pub is ideal for enjoying conversation and watching sport on TV, though it can get busy on darts and quiz nights. The large garden is popular in summer; closed in winter. Accommodation is a single en-suite room (early booking recommended). Local CAMRA Pub of the Year 2011. ♨♉❀🛏♿♣P⁵–

Finstock

Plough Inn

The Bottom, High Street, OX7 3BY (off B4022)
✪ closed Mon; 12-2.30 (3 Sat), 6-11; 12-3 Sun
☎ (01993) 868333 🌐 theplough-inn.co.uk
Adnams Broadside; St Austell Trelawney; guest beer Ⓗ
A traditional 18th-century thatched pub with a front bar/dining room, inglenook fireplace, back bar and billiards room, and a patio and garden to the rear. The atmosphere is convivial, with three ales and scrumpy always on handpump. Popular with locals and walkers, this is a cosy dining venue and well-behaved children are welcome. Bella the mellow golden Lab is unobtrusive but likes a pat on the head (and handouts). Midweek meal deals include special offer fish and chips on Tuppence Tuesday. ♨Q❀◐◑🅳♣●P🚌(X9,53,69)

Great Haseley

Plough

Rectory Road, OX44 7JQ
✪ 12-3, 5-11; 12-11 Sat & Sun ☎ (01844) 279283
🌐 ploughpub.com
Beer range varies Ⓗ
Purchased from Punch Taverns by a collective of 120 villagers, and now restored to a thriving community pub, the Plough should serve as a model for other such ventures. This traditional, cosy and friendly two-bar pub, with a thatched roof and lots of exposed original stonework, offers at least two beers from local microbreweries, with XT and Vale often featured. Westons Traditional Scrumpy is also on handpump. One bar has a separate dining room serving a regularly changing and interesting menu, featuring much locally sourced produce (booking advisable Sat & Sun).
♨Q♉❀◐◑♿♣●P⁵–🚌(103)

Henley-on-Thames

Bird in Hand

61 Greys Road, RG9 1SB SU760824
✪ 12-2, 5-11; 12-11 Sat; 12-10.30 Sun ☎ (01491) 575775
Brakspear Bitter; Fuller's London Pride; Hook Norton Mild; guest beers Ⓗ
The Bird is a frequent winner of local CAMRA Pub of the Year and a Guide regular. Run by the same couple for 20 years, two ever-changing guest beers, often from local micros, complement the three regulars. The pub hosts darts and cribbage teams. The family room leads onto a delightful rear garden with a pond and aviary. Various events are held here, including mini beer festivals in May and September. TVs show sporting events. Dogs on leads are welcome. ♉❀▲⇌♣⁵–🚌(151,154)

Lewknor

Leathern Bottle

1 High Street, OX49 5TW (off B4009 nr M40 jct 6) SU716976
✪ 11-2.30 (3 Sat), 5.30-11; 12-3, 7-10.30 Sun
☎ (01844) 351482 🌐 theleathernbottle.co.uk
Brakspear Bitter; Marston's Pedigree; guest beer Ⓗ
This classic 17th-century inn has featured in all but one edition of the Guide. The pub has a reputation for great ale, good home-cooked pub food featuring locally sourced meats, log fires, a warm welcome and a garden that is child- and pet-friendly. Popular with walkers from the nearby Ridgeway, it is easily reached by car, or a short walk from the Oxford Tube coach stop at junction 6. The guest beer comes from the Brakspear Pub Co approved list. ♨♉❀◐◑🅳♿♣P⁵–🚌(W1)

ENGLAND

Little Milton

Lamb Inn
High Street, OX44 7PU (on A329)
☼ 12-3, 6.30-close; 12-10.30 Sun ☎ (01844) 279527
Brakspear Bitter; guest beers ⒣
A thatched 16th-century stone pub situated on the main road through the village. The attractive, welcoming split-level bar features plenty of original beams, with seating areas for those who just want a drink, as well as for diners enjoying the high-quality pub food. To the rear is a patio and a quiet garden where a beer festival is held in July. Brakspear Bitter is the regular ale, plus two changing guests. ᨏ⊛◑♣Pᵗᐟ⊟(103,104)

Littleworth

Cricketer's Arms ⓛ
38 Littleworth, OX33 1TR
☼ 12-3 (not Wed & Thu), 6-11; 12-11 Fri; 12-3, 7-10.30 Sun
☎ (01865) 872738 ⊕ cricketers-arms.co.uk
Hook Norton Hooky Bitter; Shotover Prospect; guest beers ⒣
A friendly, family-run free house, offering four cask ales from local breweries including frequent dark ales. A huge range of local bottled beers is also available as well as real cider. Great-value home-cooked food is served, and beer and sausage festivals are held in February and September. Popular with walkers – dogs and children are welcome. Local CAMRA Town and Village Pub of the Year in 2011. Q⧖⊛◑♣♿Pᵗᐟ⊟(104,280)

Lower Heyford

Bell Inn
21 Market Square, OX25 5NY
☼ 12-3, 5-11; 12-11 Fri & Sat; 12-10.30 Sun
☎ (01869) 347176
Beer range varies ⒣
Large multi-roomed pub in the centre of the village, close to the Oxford Canal and railway station at Heyford. Three guest ales change regularly and micros from near and far feature, with a real cider or perry always on offer. Good home cooked food is available lunchtimes and evenings. Regular music nights promote local bands. A large garden is popular in summer and Aunt Sally is played. A beer festival is held early in September. ᨏ⊛◑⇌(Heyford)♣♿Pᵗᐟ⊟(25A)

Middle Assendon

Rainbow
Stonor Road, RG9 6AU (on B480) SU738858
☼ 12-3, 6-11 (not Mon eve winter); 12-3, 7-10.30 Sun
☎ (01491) 574879 ⊕ rainbowinnhenley.co.uk
Brakspear Bitter ⒣
An exceptional 17th-century public house situated within the Stonor Valley. A warm and friendly welcome always awaits, along with a wet nose (Brian the pub dog). Traditional home-cooked fresh food is served in the cosy snug (mind your head) and a larger lounge. Ideally situated for cycling and circular walks around the Chilterns, the pub is also only a short drive from the regatta town of Henley-on-Thames. A lively local and the hub of the village, it hosts special events throughout the year. Q⊛◑⊟♣P

Murcott

Nut Tree
Main Street, OX5 2RE
☼ closed Mon; 12-midnight (7 Sun) ☎ (01865) 331253
⊕ nuttreeinn.co.uk
Vale Best Bitter; guest beers ⒣
Idyllic thatched pub complete with a pond in the front garden and spacious suntrap patio to the rear. This Michelin-starred inn serves stunning food but drinkers are also warmly welcomed and bar snacks are available. The three beers are mostly sourced from local breweries and the food is also sourced locally where possible, with rare-breed pigs reared in the back garden. The bus service is infrequent but it is worth finding a way to get here. ᨏQ⊛◑P⊟

North Moreton

Bear at Home ♥ ⓛ
High Street, OX11 9AT (off A4130) SU561894
☼ 12-3, 6-11; 12-11 Sat & summer Sun; closed eves
Jan-March Sun ☎ (01235) 811311 ⊕ bear-at-home.co.uk
Taylor Landlord; West Berkshire Bear Beer; guest beers ⒣
Friendly village local dating back to the 15th century. The main bar features sofas, an open fire and plenty of tables for diners to enjoy the excellent pub food. The four handpumps deliver a range of mostly local ales, including Bear Beer, brewed exclusively for the pub by West Berkshire. The Bear adjoins the village cricket ground where cricket matches are played most summer weekends. A four-day beer and cricket festival is held at the end of July. Local CAMRA Pub of the Year 2011. ᨏ⊛◑♣P⊟(95,131)

Oxford

Angel & Greyhound
30 St Clement's Street, OX4 1AB
☼ 11-11.30 (midnight Fri & Sat); 12-11 Sun
☎ (01865) 242660 ⊕ angelandgreyhound.com
Young's Bitter, Special, London Gold, seasonal beer; guest beer ⒣
A classic Young's alehouse once called the Oranges and Lemons. The current name derives from the names of two meadows to the rear, which in turn were named after pubs at one time in the High Street. A comfortable pub with conversation and traditional games, and a rare bar billiards table. There is outdoor seating to the front on the busy road and much quieter seating at the back. Before you go out check the weather forecast on the board. Q⊛◑♣ᵗᐟ⊟

Chequers
131 High Street, OX1 4DH
☼ 11 (12 Sun)-11 ☎ (01865) 727463
Brakspear Bitter, Oxford Gold; guest beers ⒣
Down a narrow medieval passageway off the High Street, the Chequers is a fine old inn, much of it dating back to the 16th century when it was converted from a money lender's tenement to a tavern. Note the fine carvings and the ceiling in the lower bar. Up to five frequently changing guest beers are available, with tasting notes provided, and interesting food is served. A cobbled courtyard provides alfresco drinking, dining and smoking facilities. ⊛◑⇌♥ᵗᐟ⊟

389

Grapes

7 George Street, OX1 2AT

✪ 11-11.30 (12.30am Fri & Sat) ☎ (01865) 793380

Bath Spa, Gem, Barnsey, seasonal beer Ⓗ

First built in 1820 and rebuilt in 1879, this is a rare Victorian pub in the city centre – the traditional exterior stands out from the surrounding chain bars and restaurants. The single narrow, panelled room has the bar on one side and there is some original tiling in the entrance. Opposite the New Theatre, this is the only outlet for Bath Ales in Oxfordshire. Q❶➡●🖳

Lamb & Flag

12 St Giles, OX1 3JS

✪ 12-11 (10.30 Sun) ☎ (01865) 515787

Palmers IPA; Shepherd Neame Spitfire; Skinner's Betty Stoggs; Theakston Old Peculier; guest beers Ⓗ

Grade II-listed building run by St John's College as a free house. Some of the profits from the pub support student scholarships. Beers from the South West feature – the house beer Lamb & Flag Gold is brewed by Palmers of Bridport. Two real ciders or perries are always available and beer festivals are held three or four times a year. Believed to be the setting for the inn in Thomas Hardy's novel Jude the Obscure, it has other literary links. Q❶➡●🖳

Masons Arms Ⓛ

2 Quarry School Place, Headington Quarry, OX3 8LH

✪ 5 (7 Mon; 11 Sat)-11; 12-4, 7-10.30 Sun

☎ (01865) 764579 ⊕ themasonsarmshq.co.uk

Harviestoun Bitter & Twisted; Rebellion Mutiny; West Berkshire Good Old Boy; guest beers Ⓗ

Family-run community pub full of character, hosting many pub games leagues, including bar billiards and Aunt Sally. The guest ales are varied and regularly come from the Old Bog Brewery (named after the original purpose of the building behind the pub where it is located). A range of local and foreign bottled beers is stocked. The pub is home to the Headington beer festival in September. A heated decking area and garden lead to the function room. Events include twice-monthly music nights. ❀♣●P≟🖳(H2)

Prince of Wales

73 Church Way, Iffley, OX4 4EF

✪ 10-midnight (1am Fri & Sat); 12-11 Sun ☎ (01865) 778554

Wadworth Henry's IPA, 6X, seasonal beers; guest beers Ⓗ

Attractive pub with a wood-panelled interior and modern art prints hanging on the walls, located in the suburb of Iffley a couple of miles from central Oxford and 400 yards from Iffley Lock if you are walking the Thames. Six real ales include ever-changing Wadworth seasonal and guest beers. Westons Old Rosie cider is available on draught. The pub is active in fundraising, and holds a charity quiz on Wednesday evenings. Live music frequently features, and there are darts and Aunt Sally teams. ❀❶♣●P

Rose & Crown Ⓛ

14 North Parade Avenue, OX2 6LX (½ mile N of city centre, off Banbury Road)

✪ 11-midnight ☎ (01865) 510551 ⊕ rose-n-crown.com

Adnams Southwold Bitter; Hook Norton Hooky Bitter; Shotover Prospect; guest beers Ⓗ

Now a free house, this popular Victorian local on a vibrant north Oxford street is a time capsule with two small rooms and many original features. No intrusive music, mobile phones or children are permitted but you can get a pickled egg or a home-made Scotch egg. A friendly community pub, there are books and local business cards to peruse. Landlords Andrew and Debbie celebrated 30 years here in 2013 and the pub's fame has even spread to Everest – see the photo on the wall. Outside is a heated, covered patio. Q❀❶♣≟🖳(2)

Royal Blenheim Ⓛ

13 St Ebbe's Street, OX1 1PT

✪ 11-11 (11.30 Wed, Thu & Sun; midnight Fri & Sat)

☎ (01865) 242355 ⊕ royalblenheim.co.uk

White Horse Bitter, Village Idiot, Wayland Smithy, seasonal beers; guest beers Ⓗ

Street-corner single-room Victorian pub with a bright, airy interior, next to the Museum of Modern Art. The pub is owned by Everards but leased to the White Horse Brewery. Ten handpumps dispense a full range of White Horse beers, plus guests (including one from Everards) and a real cider. Several TVs are usually on but not always with sound and never football, just rugby and various American sports. The quirky Wednesday quiz is very popular. ❶➡♣●🖳

White Hart

12 St Andrew's Street, Headington, OX3 9DL (3 miles E of city centre)

✪ 12-11.30 (12.30am Fri & Sat) ☎ (01865) 761737

Everards Sunchaser, Tiger; guest beers Ⓗ

This 17th-century establishment is located in the picturesque, Cotswold-stone area of Old Headington opposite a 12th-century church. In the 16th century it was an alehouse/brothel run by the notorious Joan of Headington. The decor includes wooden flooring and furniture. To the rear is one of the loveliest walled gardens in the Oxfordshire area. A good selection of guest beers changes weekly and the food is traditional and home made, with pies a speciality. An annual beer festival is held in spring. ❀❶ 🍴≟🖳

Pishill

Crown Inn

Stonor Road, RG9 6HH (on B480) SU718902

✪ 12-2.30, 6-11; 12-10 Sun ☎ (01491) 638364

⊕ thecrowninnpishill.co.uk

Brakspear Bitter; guest beers Ⓗ

This picturesque 15th-century pub in the Stonor Valley boasts magnificent scenery, walks and cycling. Diners and drinkers come for the freshly cooked food and great beer. The garden is popular during the warm months of the year, with a log fire the attraction during the winter ones. A beautifully renovated 400-year-old barn is available for weddings and parties. The venue also holds a licence for civil services. 🏨Q❀🍴❶ 🍴P

Playhatch

Flowing Spring

Henley Road, RG4 9RB (on A4155) SU745766

✪ closed Mon; 12-midnight (11.30 Sun) ☎ (0118) 969 9878

⊕ theflowingspringpub.co.uk

Fuller's London Pride, ESB; Gale's Seafarers Ale; guest beer Ⓗ

Popular 18th-century country pub hosting Fuller's ales plus occasional guests. The large stream-side garden has two slides and is overlooked by an unusual covered balcony. The pub serves home-made food, with gluten free, dairy free, vegetarian and vegan options. Events are held all year round including astronomy nights, comedy nights, murder mysteries, an annual ferret show, and a beer festival with live music in summer. Check out Quirky Corner and its collection of weird and wonderful artefacts. ▲🕯️🕸️🌀▶️🏠P⬳🚐(800)

Shiplake

Baskerville 🇱
7 Station Road, Lower Shiplake, RG9 3NY
🕓 11-11; 12-10.30 Sun ☎ (0118) 940 3332
🌐 thebaskerville.com
Fuller's London Pride; Loddon Hoppit; Sharp's Doom Bar; guest beer 🅷
Located at the heart of a riverside village, this thriving pub is easily reached by train and an ideal stop on the Thames Path to Henley. Very popular with villagers and diners who come for the excellent food, the pet-friendly bars have a sporting theme and real fires. The enclosed garden has a children's play area and hosts regular summer barbecues. Four en-suite rooms are available for those wanting to extend their stay. ▲🅾️🛏️🕸️🌀▶️♿⬅️P⬳🚐(800)

Shippon

Prince of Wales 🇱
60 Barrow Road, OX13 6JQ (off A415, NW of Abingdon)
🕓 12-3 (not Mon), 5-11; 12-11 Fri-Sun ☎ (01235) 538546
Loose Cannon Abingdon Bridge; Shotover Prospect; Skinner's Betty Stogs; Taylor Landlord; guest beers 🅷
At the centre of the village, this traditional country pub is rumoured to be haunted. It has two large rooms, both with log fires – one dominating the lounge – and a separate function room. An ever-changing menu of English food is available alongside a large selection of malt whiskies and ciders. The pub hosts regular beer and cider festivals and traditional jazz and folk music evenings. All visitors are welcome including walkers, cyclists and dogs. ▲Q🕸️🌀▶️🔌♿♣️👣P⬳🚐(4)

Shutford

George & Dragon
Church Lane, OX15 6PG (3 miles off A422, next to church)
🕓 12-2.30 (not Mon-Thu), 6-11, 12-11 Sat; 12-10.30 Sun
☎ (01295) 780320 🌐 thegeoranddragon.com
Hook Norton Hooky Bitter; guest beers 🅷
A traditional 13th-century listed building in the heart of the village, nestling in the hillside beside the church. The popular free house has a lively bar with an inglenook fireplace, tiled floor and a well-stocked bar with Hooky ale and four guest beers, plus a restaurant serving British food that is home-cooked from scratch and uses local ingredients. The pub hosts traditional games including darts and Aunt Sally. There is a separate TV room with Sky and ESPN for sport. ▲Q🛏️🕸️🌀▶️🔌♣️👣⬳🚙

Souldern

Fox Inn
Fox Lane, OX27 7JW
🕓 12-3, 5-11; 12-11 Sat; 12-4, 6-10.30 (closed winter eve) Sun ☎ (01869) 345284 🌐 thefoxatsouldern.co.uk
Hook Norton Hooky Bitter; guest beers 🅷

Free house situated at the centre of the village, a cul-de-sac off the B4100. Two guest beers come from local micros and a good mix of brewers: expect to see something from Yorkshire. A beer festival is held on the fourth weekend in July when northern micros feature strongly. The large garden is busy in good weather and Aunt Sally is played. The car park is small, but on-road parking is available nearby. Accommodation is in four en-suite rooms. ▲🕸️🛏️🌀▶️♣️P⬳

Standlake

Black Horse
81 High Street, OX29 7RH
🕓 11-3, 5-11; 11-11 Sat & Sun ☎ (01865) 300307
🌐 blackhorsestandlake.co.uk
Hook Norton Hooky Bitter; guest beers 🅷
The Black Horse has been here since 1672 – the building, once owned by Lincoln College, is a low-beamed stone inn typical of the period. There is a small bar with dining room adjoining, and a separate back room. In summer a marquee in the garden gives more covered space. The pub has built a reputation for good beer and good food – a mix of pub classics with a specials board and fresh fish daily from the Really Interesting Crab Company. ▲Q🕸️▶️♿♣️🚐(18,X15)

Steventon

Cherry Tree Inn
33 High Street, OX13 6RS
🕓 11.30 (12 Sat)-11.30; 12-11 Sun ☎ (01235) 831222
🌐 cherrytreesteventon.co.uk
Wadworth Horizon, Henry's IPA, JCB, 6X, seasonal beers; guest beers 🅷
The building dates back to the 17th century, becoming a pub in the mid-1800s with the coming of the GWR. This friendly Wadworth-managed house has two bars, a dining room and patio area. It is popular with villagers and attracts a busy lunchtime trade from the nearby trading estate. Two beer festivals are held in May and October and there are regular music nights. Families, walkers and well-behaved dogs are welcome. ▲Q🕸️🛏️🌀▶️♿♿♣️P⬳🚐(32C,36,X2)

North Star ★ 🇱
2 Stocks Lane, OX13 6SG (end of the Causeway off B4017)
🕓 5 (3 Fri)-11; 12-11.30 Sat; 12-11 Sun
Morland Original; guest beers 🇬
Identified by CAMRA as one of Britain's Best Real Heritage Pubs and situated next to the Causeway, a listed ancient monument, this wonderful unspoilt village inn has been run by the same family for 160 years. Popular with locals and visitors, it hosts many village clubs and social events. Inside it has a function/games room and two additional rooms, one with a snug space with three settles around an open fireplace. There is no bar counter – beers are served through a stable door or hatch. An ideal stop-off for walkers and their dogs. ▲Q🕸️♿♣️👣P⬳🚐(32C,X2,36)

Stoke Lyne

Peyton Arms
Main Street, OX27 8SD (¾ mile off B4100) SP567284
🕓 closed Mon; 12-2, 5-11; 12-7 Sat; 12-6
Sun ☎ 07546 066160

Hook Norton Hooky Bitter, Old Hooky Ⓖ
Situated in a rural farming community, within easy reach of junction 10 of the M40, this pub has no handpumps – two local Hook Norton Brewery ales are served direct from the cask. The hosts are local legends, very much a part of the character of the pub. A good old-fashioned hostelry for great conversation in a warm, friendly environment, the bar area is adults only – but children are welcome in the garden. No food but simple rolls are available. Phone ahead for weekday opening hours. ▲Ⓠ❀P

Sydenham

Inn at Emmington
Sydenham Road, OX39 4LD
❂ 12-2 (not Mon & Tue), 4-11; 12-11 Fri & Sat; 12-9 Sun
☎ (01844) 351367 ⊕ theinnatemmington.co.uk
Brakspear Bitter; Fuller's London Pride; guest beer Ⓗ
Situated with a view of the Chiltern Hills, the inn is popular with locals, walkers, cyclists and all who come to enjoy the cask ales, convivial atmosphere and excellent food. The interior comprises a bar and a small restaurant area with an open gas fireplace, and outside is a large well-kept garden featuring a 150-year-old walnut tree. There are seven bedrooms providing guests with a comfortable base to enjoy the inn and its rural surroundings. ❀🛏◑♣🐕P½🚆

Thame

Cross Keys
1 Park Street, OX9 3JS
❂ 12-2, 5-11; 12-11 Sat; 12-10.30 Sun ☎ (01844) 218202
Vale Best Bitter; guest beers Ⓗ
Transformed from a failing keg-only dive, this fantastic pub serves plentiful ales to discerning drinkers. Usually busy, the bar will see at least two beers change every day over the weekend, and more during the week. Keep a close eye on Twitter for unusual ales, especially those from the Thame Brewery at the back of the pub – but be warned, they will go quickly. With cribbage and other bar games available, you can easily idle an afternoon and evening away. Ⓠ❀🐕½🚆(280)

Upper Heyford

Barley Mow
Somerton Road, OX25 5LB
❂ 12-2.30, 5-11; 12-11 Sat; 12-4, 7-10.30 Sun
☎ (01869) 232300
Fuller's Chiswick Bitter, London Pride; guest beer Ⓗ
A warm welcome is assured at this community focused local, sited not far from the end of the runway of a now defunct RAF base. The landlord is a Fuller's Master Cellarman and his guest beer could be a Fuller's seasonal or come from a regional brewer. There is a large open bar and a separate dining area where home-made food is cooked to order. Aunt Sally can be played in the garden. ▲❀◑♣P½🚆(25)

> Beer is proof that God loves us and wants us to be happy. **Benjamin Franklin**

Wallingford

Dolphin
2 St Marys Street, OX10 0EL
❂ 10-midnight (2am Fri & Sat); 10-11.30 Sun
☎ (01491) 837377 ⊕ thedollyinwally.co.uk
Greene King IPA; Morland Original Bitter; guest beers Ⓗ
Recently refurbished with the addition of a new dining area and situated in the centre of a market town, this establishment features live music, karaoke, disco and sports TV. Traditional pub food is served all day until 9pm (not Sun eve or after 7pm Mon) and the breakfasts are said to be the best in the area. Entry on Friday and Saturday is only allowed before before 11.15pm – after this time the landlord acts as his own bouncer.
❂❀🛏◑👌♣P½🚆

George Hotel
25 High Street, OX10 0BS
❂ 11-11; 12-10.30 Sun ☎ (01491) 836665
⊕ georgehotelwallingford.co.uk
Rebellion IPA, seasonal beers Ⓗ
Probably the oldest continually occupied establishment in Wallingford and believed to have first opened in 1517. The cask ales, exclusively from the Rebellion Brewery, are available in the Tavern Bar and light bar meals are also offered. In summer months the hotel courtyard is an ideal suntrap in which to eat and drink alfresco, and more formal dining is available in Wealh's Restaurant & Bistro. Food is served all day in summer, lunchtimes and evenings in winter. The hotel hosts functions and is licensed for civil wedding ceremonies. ▲🛏❀🛏◑👌♣P½🚆

Wantage

Royal Oak Inn Ⓛ
Newbury Street, OX12 8DF (S of Market Sq)
❂ 5.30-11; 12-2.30, 7-11 Sat; 12-2, 7-10.30 Sun
☎ (01235) 763129 ⊕ royaloakwantage.co.uk
Wadworth 6X; West Berkshire Maggs Mild, Old Father Thames, Dr Hexter's Wedding Ale, Dr Hexter's Healer; guest beers Ⓖ
This multi-award-winning street-corner pub is a mecca for the discerning drinker and is a meeting place for many local clubs. Photographs of ships bearing the pub's name adorn the walls. The lounge bar features wrought-iron trelliswork covered in pump clips. The pub is the primary outlet for West Berkshire ales in the area – two beers carry the landlord's name – and also offers an extensive changing range of ciders and perries. CAMRA local, county, regional and national finalist Pub of the Year 2010. National Cider and Perry Pub of the Year in 2012. 🍺♣👌🚆

Shoulder of Mutton ♈ Ⓛ
38 Wallingford Street, OX12 8AX (E of market square)
❂ 11.30-11 ☎ 07870 577742 ⊕ themutton.co.uk
Beer range varies Ⓗ
A corner pub recently renovated by an enthusiastic landlord, renowned for its friendly atmosphere. The 10 beers are constantly changing, with a strong emphasis on LocAle – it is the main outlet for Betjeman beers brewed by the landlord. The interior comprises public and lounge bars with traditional decor and furnishings, a small, cosy snug and a 'lay-by' – the corridor leading to the outdoor patio and function room. It also has a vegetarian restaurant. Regular folk music evenings are hosted

and there is a weekly raffle. Local, county and regional Pub of the Year 2012, and branch Pub of the Year 2013. ⚔Q🍺🐕🚲🕪◑🍴🎵↪🚃

Witney

Eagle Tavern 🄻
22 Corn Street, OX28 6BL
🕐 11-3, 5-midnight (2am Fri); 11-2am Sat; 12-midnight Sun
☎ (01993) 700121
Hook Norton Hooky Bitter, Lion, Old Hooky, seasonal beers; Wychwood Hobgoblin Ⓗ
Following an excellent refurbishment by Hook Norton Brewery, this wood-panelled and stone-floored building has won a number of awards including Hook Norton Best-Kept Cellar and local CAMRA Town & Country Pub of the Year. The landlord has been running pubs in Corn Street for 20-odd years. An unobtrusive jukebox, friendly locals, welcoming staff and quality beer all add up to a must-visit pub. Wychwood Brewery is just around the corner. ⚔🍺◑👌🎵↪🚃(S1,S2)

New Inn 🄻
111 Corn Street, OX28 6AU
🕐 5-midnight (1am Fri); 12-1am Sat; 12-midnight Sun
☎ (01993) 703807
Black Sheep Best Bitter; Sharp's Doom Bar; Taylor Landlord; Tring Side Pocket for a Toad; guest beers Ⓗ
Traditional old pub with a great selection of beers. Just out of the town centre, it can be quiet midweek but is always busy when major rugby tournaments are televised. There is live music every Saturday night and the local knitting group meets here most Thursday evenings. Take a seat at the bar, where you will be welcome to engage in a full and frank exchange of views with the friendly regulars. The jukebox has an eclectic mix of music. ⚔🍺👌♣P↪🚃(S1,S2)

Woodstock

Black Prince
2 Manor Road, OX20 1XJ
🕐 12-11 ☎ (01993) 811530
St Austell Tribute; Sharp's Doom Bar; guest beer Ⓗ
Historic and pleasant 16th-century pub with an attractive riverside setting by the River Glyme, opposite Blenheim Palace. It has a modern interior where you can enjoy the ever-changing ales and fresh well-cooked snacks and meals at reasonable prices. There is a terrace to sit out on warmer days. The service is friendly and prompt. Well worth a visit. ⚔🐕🍺◑👌♣👍P🚃(S3)

Wroxton

White Horse
Stratford Road, OX15 6PZ
🕐 11-11; 12-10.30 Sun ☎ (01295) 675264
🌐 thewhitehorsewroxton.co.uk
Hook Norton Hooky Bitter; Sharp's Doom Bar; White Horse Bitter Ⓗ
Situated in a prominent position on the Banbury to Stratford road with a large car park to the side. The interior has been refurbished to create a comfortable, relaxed bar area at one end and a dining area at the other. An open fire provides warmth in winter. Outside on the patio there are picnic tables and a covered area for smokers; in the garden there is an Aunt Sally pitch and a climbing frame for children. ⚔🐕🍺◑👌P↪🚃(270)

Lamb & Flag, Oxford (Photo: Katie Hunt)

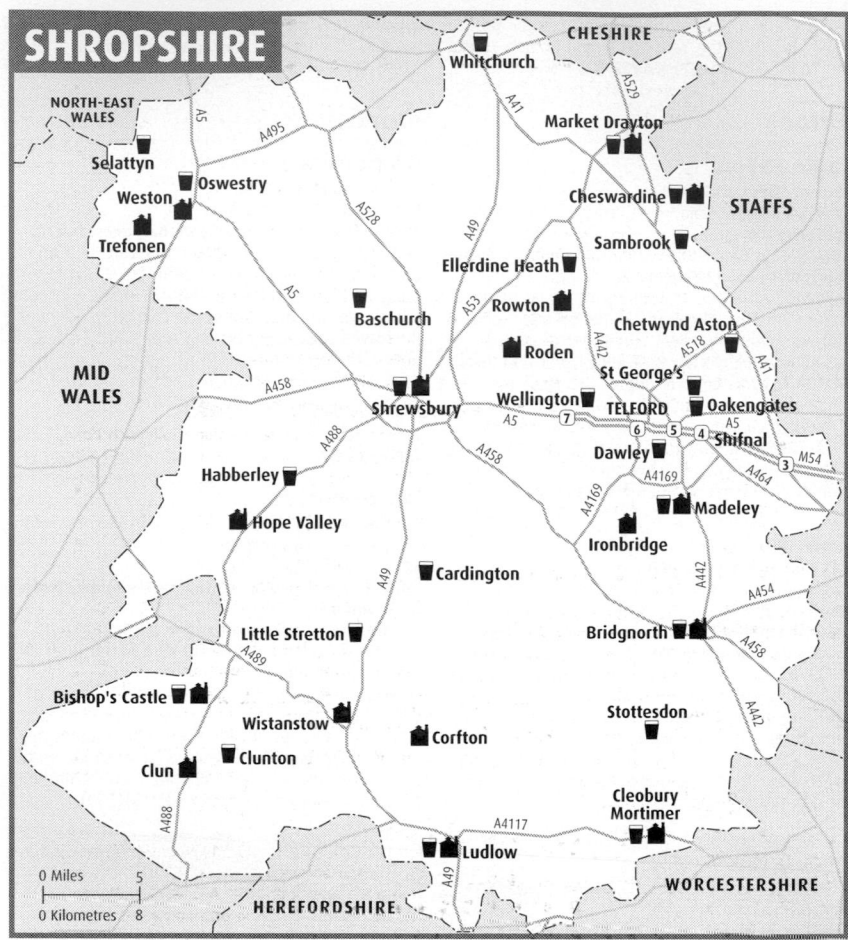

Baschurch

New Inn L

Church Road, SY4 2EF (off B5067 opp church)
☼ closed Mon; 11-3, 6-11; 11-11 Sat; 12-6 Sun
☎ (01939) 260335 ⊕ thenewinnbaschurch.co.uk
**Banks's Bitter; Hobsons Best Bitter; Stonehouse
Station Bitter; guest beer** Ⓗ
Sixteenth-century former post office and inn, first
granted a licence by Wrexham Brewery in 1850.
Refurbished in 2005, the pub has an open-plan
layout with three distinct areas – the modern bar
area has half-wood flooring and comfortable
seating, with exposed beams and an inglenook
fireplace adding character. Food and drink are
sourced as locally as possible. Dogs, walkers and
cyclists are all welcome. Real cider is stocked in
summer. Bus 576 stops in the village.
ฅQ꒰꒱(576)

Bishop's Castle

Crown & Anchor Vaults

High Street, SY9 5BQ
☼ 4-11 (10.30 Sun)
⊕ spitandsawdustproductions.blogspot.com
**Ludlow Gold; Monty's Sunshine; Wye Valley HPA;
guest beer** Ⓗ

Known locally as the Vaults, this no-frills local has
had extensive alterations to the interior, which has
created an open space around the central bar (and
the yard weatherproofed) so that customers can
appreciate the pub's regular music sessions. It
relies entirely on wet sales to survive so that, while
customers bringing in their own food are not
frowned upon, it is always best to ask first. Dogs
are most welcome. Beers from the Ludlow and
Monty's range are sold. ꒰꒱

Six Bells L

Church Street, SY9 5AA
☼ 12-2.30 (not Mon), 5-11; 12-11 Sat & Sun
☎ (01588) 638930 ⊕ sixbellsbrewery.co.uk
Six Bells Big Nev's, Ow Do!, Cloud Nine; guest beer Ⓗ
Brewery tap for the on-site Six Bells Brewery, re-
established on the site of the original one which
closed in the early 1900s. A friendly pub, it remains
full of character with a wood-beamed and stone-
walled bar. Three regular beers and one seasonal
special are available, plus cider in summer. The
lounge doubles as a dining room (no food all day
Mon and Sun and Tue eves). The pub participates in
the town's beer festival in July, with around 20 ales
available. Sunday hours may vary.
ฅQ꒰꒱(553)

Three Tuns ㋖

Salop Street, SY9 5BW
✪ 12-11 (10.30 Sun) ☎ (01588) 638797
⊕ thethreetunsinn.co.uk
Three Tuns 1642 Bitter, XXX, Cleric's Cure; guest beer Ⓗ
A truly historic pub, the Three Tuns is one of the Famous Four who were brewing in the early 1970s. Together with the adjoining, but separately owned, Three Tuns Brewery, from where it gets its beers, it has been on this site since 1640. It has four rooms – a dining lounge, a popular front bar, a snug and an extended timber-framed dining room. Good food is made with locally sourced, fresh ingredients from award-winning suppliers. Regular music sessions are hosted in the top room.
🚶Q🕏◑🍴🚲♿Å♣●⁺㋖ (443,745)

Bridgnorth

Golden Lion ㋖

83 High Street, High Town, WV16 4DS
✪ 11.30-2.30, 5-11; 11-11 Fri & Sat; 12-10.30 Sun
☎ (01746) 762016 ⊕ goldenlionbridgnorth.co.uk
Greene King IPA; Hobsons Town Crier; Wye Valley HPA; guest beers Ⓗ
This 17th-century coaching inn is a traditional town-centre hostelry with separate public and lounge bars. The two lounge bars are decorated with pictures recording the pub's history. The public bar is a regular haunt for sports fans. A fine collection of pump clips adorns the beams throughout. There is a car park to the rear along with an outdoor drinking area and a covered smoking area. Accommodation is en-suite with freeview TV. Q🕏🛏◑🍴🚲♣P⁺㋖

Hare & Hounds ㋖

8 Bernards Hill, Low Town, WV15 5AX (200yds up Bernards Hill off A442)
✪ 5 (3 Sun)-midnight; 3-1am Sat ☎ (01746) 768819
⊕ hareandhounds.biz/index.php
Hobsons Mild, Town Crier; guest beers Ⓗ
Family-friendly community pub with roaring open fires and a large sunny beer garden at the rear, with stunning views of Bridgnorth and the Severn Valley Railway. The pub welcomes regulars and visitors alike, including children and well-behaved dogs from the nearby Stanmore and Riverside Caravan Parks. Although a quiet pub in the week, it provides regular entertainment at the weekends. An annual beer festival is held on the last weekend in July. A great free house offering great local beers. 🚶Q🕏🕏🍴Å🚲♣●⁺㋖ (101,114)

King's Head ㋖

3 Whitburn Street, High Town, WV16 4QN
✪ 11-11 (midnight Fri & Sat); 12-10.30 Sun
☎ (01746) 762141 ⊕ kingsheadbridgnorth.co.uk
Hobsons Twisted Spire, Town Crier; guest beers Ⓗ
A Grade II-listed 16th-century coaching inn complete with timber beams, flagstone floor, leaded windows and roaring log fires in winter. Two regular and two guest beers are offered. The menu includes a pub grub section and daily blackboard specials featuring locally sourced produce. To the rear, the stable bar, open in the evenings and when the pub is busy, has four handpulls and hosts live music on Fridays. The courtyard has a pleasant seated area.
🚶Q🕏◑♿🚲⁺㋖

Old Castle ㋖

10/11 West Castle Street, WV16 4AB (between town centre and Severn Valley Railway)
✪ 11-11 ☎ (01746) 711420 ⊕ oldcastlebridgnorth.co.uk
Hobsons Town Crier; Sharp's Doom Bar; Taylor Landlord; Wye Valley HPA; guest beer Ⓗ
Situated a short walk from the railway, this lovely pub, dating from the 1600s, is very popular. It has a dining area to the front serving good tasty meals lunchtimes and evenings. The bar area has four handpumps offering a range of local and regional real ales. To the rear is a conservatory/games room with pool table and dartboard, and a small function room. The garden has lovely views over Bridgnorth and is an ideal spot for dining in the summer. 🚶🕏🕏◑♿🚲♣●⁺㋖

Railwayman's Arms ㋖

Severn Valley Railway Station, Hollybush Road, WV16 5DT (follow signs for SVR, pub is on Platform 1)
✪ 11.30 (11 Sat)-11; 12-10.30 Sun ☎ (01746) 764361
⊕ svr.co.uk
Bathams Best Bitter; Hobsons Mild, Best Bitter, Town Crier; guest beers Ⓗ
This popular venue has been a licensed refreshment room since 1861, and attracts locals and visitors. There are eight handpumps dispensing a selection of beers, one serving cider and one serving perry in summer. The landlord is proud of his cellarmanship. A CAMRA beer festival is held here every September. The bars are full of railway memorabilia and the platform is perfect for soaking up the atmosphere of the steam railway era.
🚶Q🕏🕏🚋(SVR)●P⁺㋖ (125,890)

White Lion ㋖

3 West Castle Street, WV16 4AB
✪ 11 (10.30 Fri & Sat)-11; 12-10.30 Sun ☎ (01746) 763962
⊕ whitelionbridgnorth.co.uk
Hop & Stagger High Town Ale, Golden Wander; Ludlow Gold; Olde Swan Original; guest beers Ⓗ
A warm welcome awaits locals and visitors to this 18th-century inn, with six handpumps offering local and national beers. Sam and Bob have converted a room into their own Hop & Stagger brewery, producing a good selection of beers that have proved very popular. A wide range of snacks is available including home-made Scotch eggs. A folk club, quizzes and music all feature here. A local artist has adorned the walls with murals depicting Bridgnorth scenes. 🚶Q🕏🕏◑🍴🚲♣●⁺㋖

INDEPENDENT BREWERIES

Clun Clun
Corvedale Corfton
Dickensian Roden
Hobsons Cleobury Mortimer
Hop & Stagger Bridgnorth
Ironbridge Ironbridge
Joule's Market Drayton
Lion's Tale Cheswardine
Ludlow Ludlow
Offa's Dyke Trefonen
Rowton Rowton
Salopian Shrewsbury
Shires Madeley
Six Bells Bishop's Castle
Stonehouse Weston
Three Tuns Bishop's Castle
Tunnfield Hope Valley (NEW)
Wood Wistanstow

Cardington

Royal Oak
SY6 7JZ
❂ closed Mon; 12-2.30, 6.30-midnight (11 Tue & Wed);
12-3.30, 7-11 Sun ☎ (01694) 771266 ⊕ at-the-oak.com
Ludlow Best; Sharp's Doom Bar; guest beers ℍ
Reputedly the oldest continuously licensed pub in
Shropshire, this ancient 15th-century free house in
a conservation village retains the character of a
country pub. The low-beamed bar has a roaring fire
in winter in a vast inglenook fireplace. The dining
room has exposed old beams and studwork. Guest
beers come mainly from local breweries. The menu
includes Fidget Pie made to a Shropshire recipe
that has been handed down from landlord to
landlord. Dog-friendly, and free Wi-Fi is available.
🏨Q❀◑Å♣P⁵⁻

Cheswardine

Red Lion
High Street, TF9 2RS
❂ 7-10.30 Mon; 4 (5 Thu & Fri)-11; 12-3, 7-10.30 Sun
☎ (01630) 662234
Lion's Tale Blooming Blonde, Lionbru,
Chesbrewnette; Marston's Burton Bitter ℍ
Home of the Lion's Tale brewery, with three of its
beers always on sale. This village pub also boasts
over 130 whiskies, which the landlord will be
happy to advise on. A music session night is held
on the second Tuesday of every month showcasing
local talent but, with its quieter corners and old-
time charms, the Red Lion is ideal whatever mood
you are in. 🏨Q❀⊞&P⁵⁻

Chetwynd Aston

Fox
Pave Lane, TF10 9LQ (½ mile W of A41)
❂ 12-11 (10.30 Sun) ☎ (01952) 815940
⊕ fox-newport.co.uk
Three Tuns XXX; Wood Shropshire Lad; guest beers ℍ
An open plan pub close to the National Sports
Centre near Lilleshall, this is a popular dining and
drinking venue attracting a clientele from near and
far. There is a spacious garden with outstanding
countryside views to enjoy in the summer and a
large original fireplace to warm up beside during
the winter. Note the vintage maps, bills of sale,
pictures and other artefacts around the walls. The
pub holds an occasional mini beer festival.
🏨Q❀◑&P⁵⁻

Cleobury Mortimer

King's Arms 🗓
6 Church Street, DY14 8BS
❂ 10-11 (midnight Thu-Sat); 10-10.30 Sun
☎ (01299) 271954 ⊕ kingsarms-cleobury.co.uk
Hobsons Mild, Twisted Spire, Best Bitter, Town Crier;
guest beer ℍ
This cosy pub situated opposite the church is the
brewery tap for Hobsons' award-winning ales. A
favourite with shoppers and locals, it has seating
on one side and a dining area on the other, with
original beams and a central log-burning fire. The
excellent menu includes locally sourced ingredients
wherever possible. Breakfast is available from
10am. Dogs are welcome. The perfect place to sink
into a comfy sofa with the daily newspaper and a
pint of Hobson's. 🏨☞◑⊞◑&Å⁵⁻(292)

Clunton

Crown Inn
SY7 0HU (on B4368)
❂ 4 (5 Tue; 12 Fri & Sat)-midnight; 12-11 Sun
☎ (01588) 660265 ⊕ crowninnclunton.co.uk
Hobsons Best Bitter; Stonehouse Station Bitter; guest
beer ℍ
This community-owned inn is now run by a local
family. It is set in the Clun Valley in a designated
area of outstanding natural beauty. A genuine pub,
it has three rooms, one a smart restaurant. A very
popular fish and chips night is held every
Wednesday (including takeaway) and a monthly
acoustic folk night on the third Wednesday. The
pub takes part in the annual Clun Valley Beer
Festival. 🏨Q❀◑⊞Å♣💧P⁵⁻🗺

Ellerdine Heath

Royal Oak 🗓
Hazles Road, TF6 6RL (2 miles off A442 towards A53)
SJ603226
❂ 12-11 ☎ (01939) 250300
Hobsons Best Bitter; Salopian Shropshire Gold; Wye
Valley HPA; guest beers ℍ
Also known as 'The Tiddly', this friendly rural
community pub welcomes locals, visitors, families
and dogs alike. Six handpulls dispense three
regular beers and up to three guests. Real cider is
usually available. A separate cosy dining room
offers locally sourced food and caters for parties.
Entertainment includes a folk night every third
Tuesday of the month plus seasonal music
evenings. A weekly Tuesday French conversation
group meets here. The pub holds a cider festival on
the last Saturday in July and an annual charity dog-
walking day. 🏨Q❀❀◑⊞&Å♣💧P⁵⁻

Habberley

Mytton Arms 🗓
SY5 0TP (S of Pontesbury off A488) SH398035
❂ 4 (12 Fri-Sun)-11 ☎ (01743) 792490
Hobsons Best Bitter; Three Tuns XXX; guest beers ℍ
Although off the beaten track, this popular village
pub, which has been rescued from the brink of
oblivion, is well worth seeking out. Its three
comfortable low-beamed rooms, together with a
friendly rustic atmosphere, make it a tempting
place to linger. Outside, there are seats to the front
and a paved area with a vine-covered pergola to
the side. Guest beers come from local and national
breweries. It's accessible in summer by the
Shropshire Hills shuttle bus. 🏨Q❀⊞♣P⁵⁻🗺

Little Stretton

Green Dragon 🗓
SY6 6RE
❂ 11.30-3, 6-midnight ☎ (01694) 722925
Wye Valley Butty Bach; guest beers ℍ
Situated on the B5477 south of Church Stretton
near the junction with the A49, the pub is in a
picturesque location with the Long Mynd behind
and Ragleth Hill in front. The L-shaped interior has
a comfortable drinking area with a wood-burning
stove at one end and a dedicated restaurant at the
other. Three guests beers are on offer and one
handpump is dedicated to cask cider or perry. The
Shrewsbury-Ludlow bus stops outside. A popular
stop-off for walkers. 🏨Q❀◑Å♣💧P🗺(435)

Ludlow

Charlton Arms 🅛

Ludford Bridge, SY8 1PJ (by Ludford Bridge)
🌣 11-midnight (1am Fri & Sat); 12-11 Sun
☎ (01584) 872813 🌐 thecharltonarms.co.uk
Hobsons Best Bitter; Ludlow Gold, Stairway; Wye Valley Butty Bach; guest beers 🅗
Now extensively refurbished, this fine building is situated to the south, overlooking the River Teme and across the historic Ludford Bridge up towards Ludlow's last remaining fortified gate and the town centre. It has an attractive bar and spacious lounge leading to a separate dining room with a terrace. The impressive function suite and roof bar offer fine views across the river towards the town. Accommodation is in 10 en-suite rooms. Dogs are allowed in the bar.
🅰️Q🌣🛏🏮🍽️🅙🦽🛗🅐🚲♿P⁵⁻🖦(492)

Church Inn 🅛

The Buttercross, SY8 1AW
🌣 10-11.30 (midnight Fri & Sat); 11-11.30 Sun
☎ (01584) 872174 🌐 thechurchinn.com
Hobsons Best Bitter, Town Crier; Ludlow Gold, Black Knight; Wye Valley Bitter; guest beers 🅗
Situated in the centre of Ludlow, close to the castle and market square, the Church is the only free house within the town walls and now has a residential ale conner to ensure the quality of the beer. The landlord, a former mayor of Ludlow, is a great advocate of real ale and also owns the Charlton Arms. Guest ales are usually from national microbreweries. Nine guest and family rooms are available for overnight stays. Dogs are welcome.
🅰️Q🌣🛏🍽️🚲🛗🖦(292,435)

Queens 🅛

113 Lower Galdeford, SY8 1RU
🌣 12-11 (midnight Fri & Sat); 12-10.30 Sun
☎ (01584) 879177 🌐 thequeensludlow.com
Hobsons Best Bitter; Ludlow Gold; Wye Valley Butty Bach; guest beer 🅗
Popular pub/cafe bar with a decent range of local ales. The light and airy L-shaped bar has two distinct areas, with dining down a short flight of steps. Good-value quality meals are freshly cooked from locally sourced ingredients (booking advised at weekends). Home of the Ludlow venison pie, the pub is a regular award winner at the Ludlow Festival. Live music features regularly. The large enclosed patio garden has views over Ludford. A family-run, friendly local. Dogs allowed.
🏮🍽️🅙🚲♿⁵⁻🖦(192)

Railway Shed 🅛

Station Drive, SY8 2PQ (150yds N of train station)
🌣 10-5 (6 Fri; 4 Sat); closed Sun ☎ (01564) 873291
🌐 theludlowbrewingcompany.co.uk
Ludlow Best, Gold, Black Knight, Boiling Well, Stairway 🅗
Brewery and bar/lounge located in a converted railway shed, with brewery visits welcome. Handy for the railway station, the venue is open during the day, offering five house beers as well as extensive off-sales. Ample comfortable seating is provided on two levels overlooking a modern brewing plant. State-of-the-art underfloor heating, recycling of rainwater, low energy lighting and solar panels make for super energy efficiency. The spacious premises is a venue for beer festivals, live music and private functions. Q🌣🚲♿🏮⁵⁻🖦

Market Drayton

Red Lion

Great Hales Street, TF9 1JP
🌣 11-11 (midnight Fri & Sat) ☎ (01630) 652602
🌐 joulesbrewery.co.uk
Joule's Blonde, Original Pale Ale, Slumbering Monk 🅗
Winner of the CAMRA/English Heritage Pub Design Awards 2011, this Joule's brewery tap is a former coaching inn built in 1623. Unique features include an illuminated well in the main bar and the mouse room – a Robert Thompson-inspired function room decorated with carved mice. Log fires and oak beams create a comfortable atmosphere in the bar where locally sourced food can be enjoyed from an extensive menu along with the Joule's range of beers produced in the adjacent brewery.
🅰️Q🌣🛏🍽️🚲♿P⁵⁻🖦

Oswestry

Griffin 🅛

Albion Hill, Leg Street, SY11 2NL
🌣 12-3, 5-midnight; 11-midnight Fri & Sat; 12-11 Sun
☎ (01691) 650156
Stonehouse Station Bitter; guest beers 🅗
This old, town-centre traditional pub has a cosy four-roomed layout with a really snug snug! The licensee is from the black country and sources an interesting variety of quality well-kept ales. Note the sculptural installation above the door entitled 'Three Skinny Drinkers', conjured up by a local artist as an original new pub sign. 🅰️🌣🛏🍽️🚲♿

Oak Inn 🅛

47 Church Street, SY11 2SZ
🌣 12-11 ☎ (01691) 659254
Stonehouse Station Bitter, Cambrian Gold; guest beer 🅗
An early 18th-century listed building opposite the parish church, formerly the coach house of the hotel next door. This unspoilt pub is close to the town centre and is one of Oswestry's many free houses. It has a public bar at the front and a larger, comfortable lounge to the rear with TV screens for sports events. A passage running down the side provides access to the lounge and also a covered area outside. 🚲♿⁵⁻🖦

Sambrook

Three Horseshoes

TF10 8AP (½ mile E of A41)
🌣 12-2 (not Mon), 4.30-11; 11-11 Sat & Sun
☎ (01952) 551133 🌐 theshoes-sambrook.co.uk
Hobsons Mild; St Austell Tribute; Salopian Shropshire Gold; guest beers 🅗
Eight years in the Guide for this traditional pub with a cosy dining room, lounge and quarry-tiled bar with woodburner. Visitors travel some distance to savour the ambience of this friendly local, frequented by young farmers, music groups, darts teams and occasionally dominoes match players. In warmer weather the excellent patio area is a pleasant place to relax after enjoying a meal of locally sourced fine food. One of the guest beers is normally from Joule's. 🅰️Q🏮🍽️🚲♿🙭⁵⁻

Selattyn

Cross Keys ♈ ★

Glyn Road, SY10 7DH (on B4579 Oswestry-Glyn Ceiriog road)
☼ closed Mon & Tue; 7 (6 Fri)-11; 12-5, 7-11 Sun
☎ (01691) 650247
Stonehouse Station Bitter; guest beers ℍ
Dating from the 17th century, this building has been an inn since 1840 and is identified by CAMRA as one of Britain's Best Real Heritage Pubs. It is situated next to the church in a village close to the Welsh border and Offa's Dyke. The small bar with a quarry-tiled floor has a large topical cartoon above the fireplace. There are two further rooms and a function room. The pub opens Monday-Saturday lunchtimes by arrangement. Accommodation is available in a self-catering cottage. The landlord is a keen campanologist. ▲Q☼✿⌂▲♣P

Shifnal

Odfellows Wine Bar

Market Place, TF11 9AU
☼ 11-11 ☎ (01952) 461517 ⊕ odleyinns.co.uk/odfellows
Salopian Shropshire Gold, Oracle; guest beers ℍ
Set in a town whose buildings many believe were the basis for Dickens' The Old Curiosity Shop, this popular gastro-pub overlooks Market Place and is handy for the railway station. As well as serving a range of mainly local beers, the pub has now started brewing its own beers, and has two dedicated handpumps for this. The owner also stages two beer festivals each year, in May and September. Food is of good quality and locally sourced whenever possible.
▲☎☼✿⌂◖◗♿≒P'–₪

Plough

26 Broadway, TF11 8AZ
☼ 12-11 (midnight Thu-Sat) ☎ (01952) 463118
⊕ artybars.co.uk
Hobsons Mild, Best Bitter; Shires Best Bitter; Three Tuns 1642 Bitter; guest beers ℍ
A family-run pub in a cosy 17th-century Grade II-listed building. It serves a range of eight real ales including many local guests from breweries such as Broughs, Three Tuns and Rowton, and two draught ciders. The traditional interior features exposed beams and tiled floors, with local artists' work adorning the walls. An extensive covered area outside has a stage for regular music events and the large rear garden is popular in summer. Traditional pub food is served daily lunchtimes and evenings. ✿◖◗≒♣'–₪(891,892)

White Hart ℟

High Street, TF11 8BH
☼ 12-11 ☎ (01952) 461161
Enville Ale; Greene King Abbot; Holden's Black Country Bitter; Salopian Shropshire Gold; Wye Valley HPA; Butty Bach; guest beers ℍ
Historic timber-framed two-room free house offering something for everyone. A recipient of numerous CAMRA awards – proudly displayed on the wall – it offers eight handpulls dispensing superbly kept ales at competitive prices. The landlord has consistently achieved top marks for Cask Marque inspections. Delicious home-made food is available lunchtimes Monday to Saturday. There is a suntrap patio to the rear and a separate beer garden where families are welcome. The pub hosts fundraising events. Q✿☼✿⌐≒♣P'–₪

Shrewsbury

Admiral Benbow ℟

24 Swan Hill, SY1 1NF (just off main square)
☼ 5 (12 Sat)-11; 7-10.30 Sun ☎ (01743) 244423
Ironbridge Gold; Ludlow Gold; Monty's Sunshine; Six Bells Cloud Nine; Titanic Iceberg; Wye Valley HPA; guest beers ℍ
Spacious free house offering a range of local beers plus a selection of ciders from Rosie's including Black Bart, Wicked Wasp, Triple D and Perfect Pear. A good range of Belgian beers is also available. Children are not permitted and under-30s are served at the management's discretion. An outside seating and smoking area is available at the rear. A small room off the bar can be used for functions. The Titanic beer may vary. ▲Q☼✿⌐≒♣♦'–

Coach & Horses

Swan Hill, SY1 1NP
☼ 11.30-midnight (12.30am Fri & Sat); 12-11.30 Sun
☎ (01743) 365661 ⊕ odleyinns.co.uk/coach-horses/
Salopian Shropshire Gold, Oracle; Stonehouse Station Bitter; guest beers ℍ
Set in a quiet street off the main shopping area, the pub provides a peaceful haven, with magnificent floral displays in summer. Victorian in style, it has a wood-panelled bar, a small side snug area and a large lounge where meals are served lunchtimes and evenings. Cheddar Valley cider is available on handpull. Q◖◗⌐♿≒♦'–₪

Loggerheads ★

1 Church Street, SY1 1UG (off St Marys St)
☼ 11-11.30 (1.30am Thu-Sat); 12-11.30 Sun
☎ (01743) 360275 ⊕ loggerheads.weebly.com
Banks's Bitter; Jennings Dark Mild, Bitter; Marston's Pedigree; guest beers ℍ
Classic 18th-century Grade-II listed pub in the town centre, identified by CAMRA as one of Britain's Best Real Heritage Pubs. The interior comprises a small bar, servery and three further rooms. The bar to the left has scrubbed tables and a shove-ha'penny board, and was 'gents only' until 1975. Good-value quality food is available including the speciality sausage and mash as well as a regular Tuesday steak night and Sunday roasts. Folk music plays on Sunday and Thursday evenings. Q◖◗≒♣₪

Nag's Head ℟

Wyle Cop, SY1 1XB (on RH side of Wyle Cop)
☼ 11.30-midnight (1am Fri & Sat); 12-midnight Sun
☎ (01743) 362455
Caledonian Deuchars IPA; Hobsons Best Bitter; Town Crier; Sharp's Doom Bar; Taylor Landlord; Wye Valley HPA; guest beer ℍ
The main features of this timber-framed building are best appreciated externally, in particular the upper storey jettying and to the rear the timber remnants of a 14th-century hall house including a screened passage that provided protection from draughts (and now provides shelter for smokers). The interior has remained unaltered for many years. The building is reputed to be haunted and is on the Shrewsbury Ghost Trail. ✿⌐≒♣'–₪

Prince of Wales ℟

Bynner Street, Belle Vue, SY3 7NZ
☼ 5 (12 Fri-Sun)-midnight ☎ (01743) 343301
⊕ princeofwaleshotel.co.uk
Greene King IPA; M&B Mild; St Austell Tribute; Salopian Golden Thread; Thwaites Wainwright; guest beers ℍ

Welcoming two-roomed community pub with a large decked suntrap garden adjoining a bowling green and heated smoking shelter. The green is overlooked by a 19th-century maltings. Darts, dominoes and bowls teams abound. Two beer festivals take place each year in February and May and popular themed nights are held. Food is available Friday-Sunday lunchtimes, plus regular special dining evenings. Shrewsbury Town FC memorabilia adorn the building inside and out, with some of the seating from the old Gay Meadow ground skirting the bowling green.
🏛🌃🕮🌐🍴♣P²⏱🚌

Salopian Bar 🅛
Smithfield Road, SY1 1PW (close to bus station)
🌑 11-11 (midnight Wed, Fri & Sat) ☎ (01743) 351505
🌐 thesalopianbar.co.uk
Salopian Oracle; Stonehouse Station Bitter; guest beers 🇭
The bar's dedicated management strives to increase the beer, cider and perry range to satisfy demand. An impressive range of bottled beer from Belgium and America is available and regular cider and perry are provided by Westons and Thatchers. Major sports events are shown on large-screen TV and local artwork on display is for sale. Winner of local CAMRA branch Pub of the Year 2011 and 2012 and Town Pub of the Year 2013. ♿🚲♣🚌

Three Fishes 🅛
Fish Street, SY1 1UR
🌑 11.30-3, 5-11; 11.30-11.30 Fri & Sat; 12-4, 7-10.30 Sun
☎ (01743) 344793
Sharp's Doom Bar; Stonehouse Station Bitter; Taylor Landlord; guest beers 🇭
Fifteenth-century building standing in the shadow of two churches, St Alkmunds and St Julians, within the maze of streets and passageways in the town's medieval quarter. Freshly prepared food is available lunchtimes and early evenings Monday to Saturday. The pub offers a range of up to six local and national beers, with some dark beers featuring regularly. A range of real ciders and perries is also available. Q🕮🚲♣🚌

Woodman Inn
Coton Hill, SY1 2DZ (by train station on Ellesmere Rd)
🌑 4 (12 Sat & Sun)-midnight ☎ (01743) 351007
Greene King Abbot; Salopian Shropshire Gold; Wye Valley Butty Bach; guest beers 🇭
Half-brick and half-timbered black and white corner pub originally built in the 1800s but destroyed by fire in 1923 and rebuilt in 1925. The pub is reputedly haunted by an ex-landlady who died when the pub burnt down. It has a wonderful oak-panelled lounge with two real log fires and traditional settles. The bar has the original stone-tiled flooring, wooden seating, log fire and listed leaded windows. The courtyard seating area doubles as a heated smoking area. Real cider is usually available in summer.
🏛Q🌃🕮🌐♿🚲♣🚌²⏱🚌

Stottesdon

Fighting Cocks 🍷 🅛
1 High Street, DY14 8TZ
🌑 6 (12 Sat)-midnight; 5-1am Fri; 12-10.30 Sun
☎ (01746) 718270
Hobsons Mild, Twisted Spire, Best Bitter; guest beers 🇭

A traditional pub in the heart of south Shropshire, first licensed in 1830. A hub for the community, it offers facilities for meetings and serves as a local shop. Alongside the locally brewed Hobson's beers, two guest beers are available. The traditional bar with log fire leads to two dining rooms. Live music is hosted most Saturday nights and an open mic night monthly. An apple day features in October and a beer festival in November. Local CAMRA Rural Pub and Marches Pub of the Year 2012.
🏛🌃🕮A♣🍴P²⏱

Telford: Dawley

Elephant & Castle
1 High Street, TF4 2ET
🌑 5 (4 Fri-Sun)-11 ☎ (01952) 610888
🌐 elephantdawley.net
Hobsons Mild; Joule's Original Pale Ale; Purple Moose Cwrw Madog/Madog's Ale; Wood Quaff; guest beers 🇭
Extensive Grade-II listed free house, recently restored to exacting standards. Notable features include 16th-century beams, oak bars, a conservatory and expansive suntrap garden. Beers are dispensed from 12 cooled handpulls, plus two more in a separate large function room. A comedy night is held on the last Friday of the month. The pub is half a mile from the Telford Steam Railway and three miles from Ironbridge Gorge. The sister inn to the Crown Inn in Oakengates, joint beer festivals are held the first weekends in May and October. 🏛Q🌃🕮🌐♿♣🍴P²⏱🚌

Telford: Madeley

All Nations 🅛
20 Coalport Road, TF7 5DP (off Legges Way opp Blists Hill Museum)
🌑 12-midnight ☎ (01952) 585747
Shires Best Bitter, Dabley Gold; guest beers 🇭
Small, friendly and locally renowned institution untouched by modern fads. One of the Famous Four last brewpubs, Shires brewery is at the back. Perry is sometimes available. Fresh rolls are made to order. A TV is set up in the bar for major rugby matches only. Browse the newspapers or bring and swap books. The garden has hens (eggs sold). On a quiet wooded hillside, just on the edge of the World Heritage Site, there are paths and a footbridge to nearby Blists Hill museum. Dog- and child-friendly. 🏛Q🌃🕮🍴A♣🍴P²⏱

Telford: Oakengates

Crown Inn 🅛
Market Street, TF2 6EA
🌑 12-11 ☎ (01952) 610888 🌐 crown@oakengates.net
Hobsons Best Bitter; guest beers 🇭
Dating from 1835, this pub has three distinct drinking areas and a suntrap courtyard. A wide range of beers is served from 14 cooled handpulls. Entertainment includes an acoustic club on Wednesday, quality live music on Thursday and a quiz night on the last Sunday of the month. Joint ale festivals are held with sister pub the Elephant & Castle in Dawley on the first weekends in May and October, with around 12,000 different ales offered since 1993. A large free car park is to the rear. Bus and railway stations are nearby.
🏛🌃🕮🌐♿🚲♣🍴P²⏱🚌

Old Fighting Cocks ♥ Ⅼ

48 Market Street, TF2 6DU
🌣 12-11 ☎ (01952) 615607
Everards Tiger; Ironbridge IPA, Gold; guest beers Ⓗ
This cosy, centrally situated pub has rapidly
become a firm favourite with ale drinkers, locals
and those participating in the Rail Ale Trail. Its
coach house roots are clearly visible, with original
stained-glass windows and a feeding hatch for
horses visible in the disabled toilet. The pub has a
bring-your-own-food policy and provides cutlery
and plates. An ale festival is held in winter. It also
boasts a 32-seat cinema upstairs for hire.
🏚Q🍴🕸️📇&⇌♣♨️ℒ–🚆

Station Hotel

42 Market Street, TF2 6DU
🌣 10-11; 10.30-3.30, 7-11 Sun ☎ (01952) 612949
Salopian Shropshire Gold; guest beers Ⓗ
Expect a warm welcome at this traditional multi-
roomed local pub. The ale range specialises in local
beers and those from the Yorkshire region.
Excellent home-made rolls, pies and cheeses are
usually available. Food events include home-made
burger night on Monday and curry on a
Wednesday. Two beer festivals are usually hosted
each year, one over the late May bank holiday and
another in late November in conjunction with the
Fighting Cocks. 🏚🕸️📇⇌♣♨️ℒ–🚆

Telford: St George's

St George's Sports & Social Club

Church Road, TF2 9LU
🌣 7-11; 6-midnight Fri; 12-12.15am Sat; 12-10.30 Sun
☎ (01952) 612911 ⊕ stgeorgesclub.co.uk
Banks's Mild, Bitter; Jennings Bitter; guest beers Ⓗ
Just a short 33 or 481 bus ride from Oakengates
railway station, this community club has been
CAMRA local branch Club of the Year numerous
times. Guest beers are mostly from the local area
and an extensive food menu is served until 9pm.
Renowned for its sports facilities, some floodlit, it is
popular with families. CAMRA members are always
welcome. A large function room and catering
service is available for hire.
🍴🕸️◑♣♨️P🚆(33,481)

Telford: Wellington

Cock Hotel Ⅼ

148 Hollyhead Road, TF1 2DL
🌣 4 (12 Thu)-11.30; 12-midnight Fri & Sat; 12-4, 7-11 Sun
☎ (01952) 244954 ⊕ cockhotel.co.uk
Hobsons Mild, Best Bitter; guest beers Ⓗ
This 18th-century coaching inn offers a warm
welcome and boasts an outstanding reputation for
quality beer. The main bar has seven handpulls,
one with a real cider. The Brasserie De Haan in a
separate room is home to over 80 Belgian beers
(both draught and bottled). There is a covered
smoking area at the rear. B&B accommodation is
available and has recently been refurbished to a
very high standard. 🏚Q🕸️🛌📇⇌♣♨️ℒ–🚆

William Withering

43-45 New Street, TF1 1LU
🌣 8am-midnight ☎ (01952) 642800
**Greene King Abbot; Ruddles Best Bitter; Salopian
Shropshire Gold; guest beers** Ⓗ
Named after a local physician and geologist, this
large open-plan Wetherspoon pub mixes period

1700s features with a typical modern bar. The 10
handpulls provide three house beers and seven
constantly changing ales from up and down the
country but focus on ales from the local area. Good-
value food is available until 10pm in a relaxed
atmosphere. 🍴🕸️◑&⇌♣♨️ℒ–🚆

Wrekin Inn Ⅼ

26 Wrekin Road, TF1 1RH (just off ring road)
🌣 4-11.30; 2-midnight Fri; 12-midnight Sat; 12-10.30 Sun
☎ (01952) 244865
**Hobsons Town Crier; Ludlow Gold; Three Tuns Cleric's
Cure; guest beers** Ⓗ
A short walk from the civic and leisure centres, this
is a popular live music venue. Between four and six
beers vary on rotation, always including LocAles
and often Oakham and Abbeydale brews. The cider
range also varies. The L-shaped bar has separate
drinking areas and live music and open mic nights
are held two or three nights a week. There is a
decked seating area outside. Beer and cider
festivals are held four times a year. Winter opening
hours may vary. 🏚🕸️📇&⇌♣♨️P℈–🚆

Whitchurch

Anchor Ⅼ

7 Pepper Street, SY13 1BG (off High Street)
🌣 11 (10 Fri)-11; 12-10.30 Sun ☎ (01948) 663806
⊕ theanchorbarandrestaurant.co.uk
Titanic Anchor Bitter; guest beers Ⓗ
Located just off the High Street, this tastefully
restored Victorian former hotel is separated into
four areas and still retains the original floorboards
in the public bar. Comfortable chairs are provided
in the lounge area around the island bar, which has
seven handpulls offering a varying range of mainly
local beers. The pub has a separate dining room
serving a range of locally sourced home-cooked
food with a daily specials board. Q◑📇&⇌♣♨️ℒ–🚆

Black Bear Ⅼ

49 High Street, SY13 1AZ
🌣 12-3, 6-11; 12-11 Sat & Sun ☎ (01948) 663800
⊕ blackbearpub.co.uk
Phoenix Monkeytown Mild; guest beers Ⓗ
Attractively renovated black and white corner pub
situated opposite the historic St Alkmund's church.
The ornate bar has six handpulls dispensing a
varying range of guest beers from both local and
lesser-known national microbreweries, with pump
clips adorning the walls, ceiling and bar area. Cider
is available on gravity. The pub has two separate
dining areas serving locally sourced home-cooked
food from an ever-changing menu. Q🕸️◑⇌♣

Whitchurch Cricket Club Ⅼ

SY13 3JG (via Greenfoot Lane off Tilstock Road or Cycle
Route 45)
🌣 6 (10 Sat; 6.30 Sun)-11 summer; 6.30-11 winter
☎ (01948) 663923 ⊕ whitchurchcc.play-cricket.com
**Thwaites Nutty Black; Woodlands Midnight Stout;
guest beers** Ⓗ
This current West Midlands CAMRA Club of the Year
goes from strength to strength. The bar has nine
handpulls serving a range of Shropshire and
Cheshire LocAle microbrewery beers. Two beer
festivals are held in February and July with 26
handpulls. Show your CAMRA membership card for
a discount. Dogs are welcome. Note that the club is
sometimes hired out for private functions so ring
ahead prior to travelling.
🕸️&Å⇌♣♨️P℈–🚆🚆(511)

300 More Beers to Try Before You Die!

Roger Protz

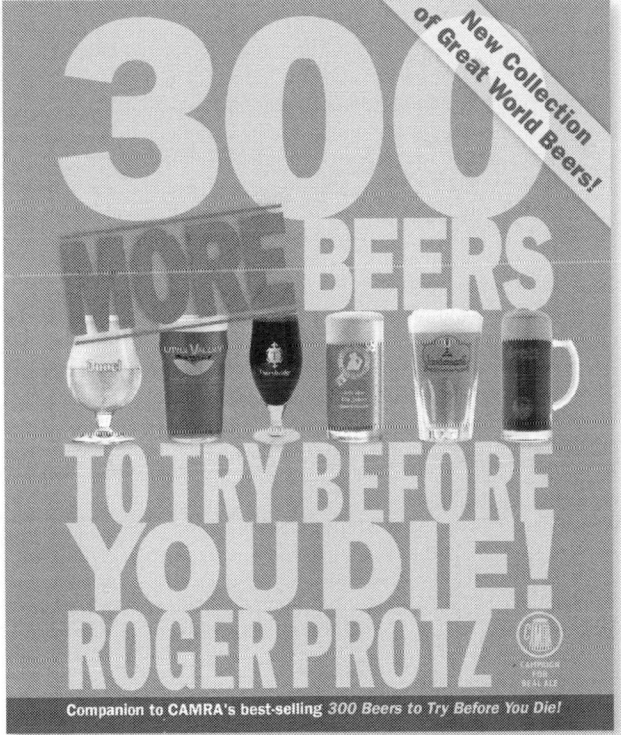

Companion to CAMRA's best-selling *300 Beers to Try Before You Die!*

300 More Beers to Try Before You Die! takes beer lovers on an exciting new odyssey through 300 of the best beers from around the world. A companion volume to the best-selling *300 Beers to Try Before You Die!*, award-winning beer writer Roger Protz selects 300 more beers that represent the very best and most interesting products of the brewer's art available today. The book charts the world-wide beer revival and features new ales from America, rediscovered classics like English abbey beer and inventive new twists on age-old recipes from experimental brewers in Europe and beyond, plus much, much more...

£14.99 ISBN 978-1-85249-295-3 CAMRA members' price £12.99 332 pages

For this and other books on beer and pubs visit CAMRA's online bookshop at **www.camra.org.uk/books** or call **01727 867201**

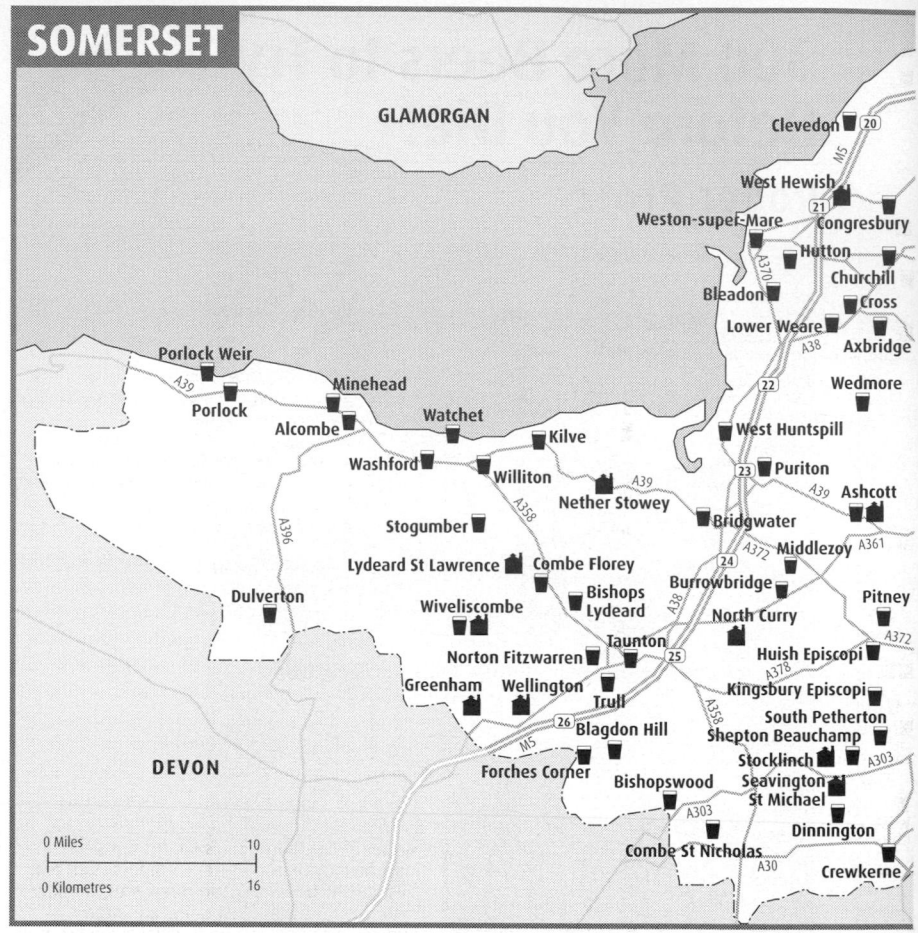

SOMERSET

GLAMORGAN

Clevedon 20

West Hewish

Weston-super-Mare 21 Congresbury

Hutton

Churchill

Bleadon Cross

Lower Weare

A38 Axbridge

Porlock Weir

Minehead

Wedmore

22

Porlock

Watchet

West Huntspill

Alcombe

Kilve

Washford

Williton

A39

23 Puriton

Nether Stowey

A39 Ashcott

Stogumber

Bridgwater

Middlezoy A361

A377

Lydeard St Lawrence

Combe Florey

24

Dulverton

Bishops
Lydeard

Burrowbridge

Pitney

Wiveliscombe

North Curry

A372

Norton Fitzwarren

Taunton 25

Huish Episcopi

Greenham

Wellington

Kingsbury Episcopi

Trull

26 Blagdon Hill

South Petherton

Shepton Beauchamp

DEVON

Forches Corner

Bishopswood

Stocklinch A303

Seavington
St Michael

A303

Dinnington

Combe St Nicholas

A30

Crewkerne

0 Miles 10

0 Kilometres 16

Alcombe

Britannia Inn

1 Manor Road, TA24 6EH

☼ 10.30-11 (midnight Fri & Sat); 12-11 Sun

☎ (01643) 702384 ⊕ britanniaalcombe.co.uk

Courage Best Bitter; guest beers Ⓗ

One of the oldest pubs in the Minehead area, the Britannia offers a comfortable public bar and saloon, plus a safe and secluded walled garden. There is also a skittle alley and private function room with cocktail bar. The traditional bar food menu is extensive, with daily specials, and a function room caters for either a set menu or à la carte lunches and dinners. The medieval village of Dunster, the Quantock Hills and Exmoor National Park are close by. Accommodation is en suite.

✿🛏🜚🕀🗄🗄🏕♣🗅🚃(18,28)

Ash

Bell Inn Ⓛ

3 Main Street, TA12 6NS

☼ 12-11 (midnight Sat); 12-10.30 Sun ☎ (01935) 822727

⊕ thebellinnash.co.uk

Beer range varies Ⓗ

The Bell continues to be a warm, welcoming, traditional pub, with up to four handpulls delivering ales, mostly from Somerset breweries. Locally sourced home-cooked meals are served up six days a week (no food on Mon) with an excellent roast dinner on Sundays and many daily specials. Popular live music nights take place as well as a Sunday evening quiz. Many unusual old church belfry items adorn the bar and walls.

🛏Q🜚🕀🗄🗄♣🗅🚃(N9A)

Ashcott

Ring o' Bells

High Street, TA7 9PZ

☼ 12-2.30, 7-11; 7-10.30 Sun ☎ (01458) 210232

⊕ ringobells.com

Beer range varies Ⓗ

Former winner of Somerset CAMRA awards, this family-run free house in the village has three bars on split levels separated by steps. Old fireplaces and beams enhance the separate dining area and modern skittle alley/function room. There is an enclosed garden and families are welcome. Two or three ales from micros near and far are served, as well as Wilkins cider, and they serve good home-cooked food. Meals and ales are available to take away. Ham Wall and Shapwick Heath nature reserves are nearby.

Q🜚🕀🗄♣🗅🚃(29,37,375)

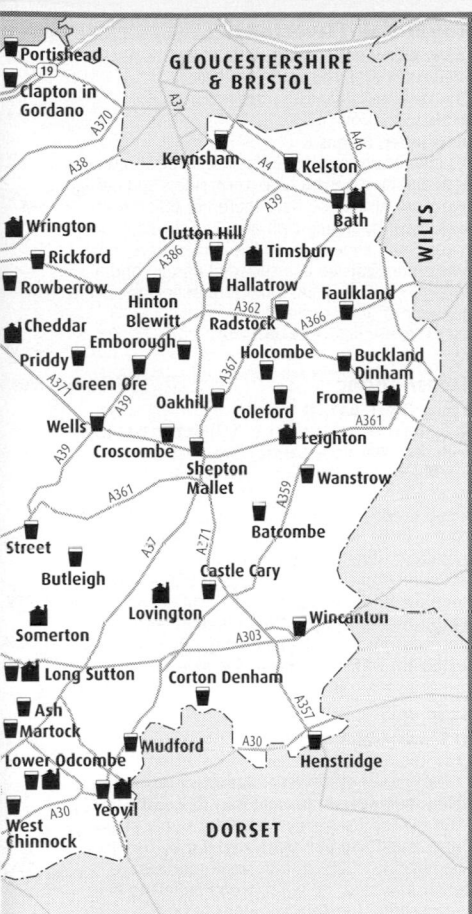

The Three Horseshoes is a 400-year-old country pub which has a spacious bar with an inglenook fireplace and beamed ceiling, a stunning dining room with a vaulted ceiling, and a lawned garden overlooked by the church tower. Open to all, it welcomes drinkers, foodies, walkers and dogs, as well as children – who get colouring books and games to keep them entertained. Comfortable accommodation is available. ⅏Q⅗⊛✍ⅎ⧗♿P⅄⊷

Bath

Bell

103 Walcot Street, BA1 5BW

🕑 11.30-11; 12-10.30 Sun ☎ (01225) 460426

🌐 thebellinbath.co.uk

Abbey Bellringer; Bath Ales Gem; Butcombe Bitter; Hop Back Summer Lightning; Otter Ale; RCH Pitchfork; Stonehenge Danish Dynamite Ⓗ

The Bell features bands on Monday and Wednesday evenings and Sunday lunchtimes. There is a long main bar and a number of seating areas. The wall space inside is taken up with posters for local events. A computer is available for free internet access and Wi-Fi. At the back of the pub is a garden with covered seating, behind which is the Love Lounge (open mic on Thursday nights) and a launderettette (sic). ⊛⧗≠(Spa)♣♿⅄⊷₪

Garrick's Head

7-8 St John's Place, Sawclose, BA1 1ET (next to Theatre Royal)

🕑 11-11 (midnight Thu-Sat); 12-10.30 Sun

☎ (01225) 318368 🌐 garricksheadpub.com

Beer range varies Ⓗ

A theatre pub for over 200 years, but originally the town house of Beau Nash, Bath's 18th-century Master of Ceremonies, this local is reputedly the most haunted pub in the city. Three or four real ales, mostly from local microbreweries, include some rarities, while local ciders are often complemented by a perry. Traditional food sourced from local ingredients is served lunchtimes and evenings. Tables in the pedestrianised area outside are ideally placed for watching the world go by. ⊛⧗≠(Spa)♿⅄⊷

Hop Pole

7 Albion Buildings, Upper Bristol Road, BA1 3AR

🕑 12-11 (midnight Fri & Sat) ☎ (01225) 446327

Bath Ales SPA, Gem, Barnsey; guest beers Ⓗ

A Bath Ales pub half a mile west of the city centre, close to Royal Victoria Park and the River Avon. Five or six real ales are available, including four from Bath Ales, plus a range of bottled foreign beers. The enclosed and spacious beer garden is popular with families. Food is served lunchtimes and evenings Monday to Friday, all day on Saturday and till 4pm on Sunday. Home-made bar snacks – nuts, pork scratchings and Scotch eggs – are also on offer. ⅏⊛⧗♿⅄⊷₪(14,17)

King of Wessex

5-10 James Street West, BA1 2BX (between Green Park Station and city centre, part of the Odeon cinema complex) ST747647

🕑 7-11 ☎ (01225) 303380

Greene King Abbot; Ruddles Best Bitter; guest beers Ⓗ

The only JD Wetherspoon establishment in Bath, it offers the best value for real ale in the city. The pub was newly built and opened in 2004, and is part of

Axbridge

Lamb

The Square, BS26 2AP

🕑 11.30-3, 6-11; 11.30-11 Thu; 11.30-11.30 Fri & Sat; 12-10.30 Sun ☎ (01934) 732253 🌐 lamb.butcombe.com

Butcombe Bitter, Gold, seasonal beers; Fuller's London Pride Ⓗ

Butcombe-owned Grade II-listed coaching house in the village square. The National Trust's medieval King John's Hunting Lodge lies directly opposite. There is a large low-beamed bar area and several smaller, quieter areas leading off from it. Outside drinking areas are to the front and rear via the courtyard. Lunchtime and evening meals are served (no food Sun eve). Butcombe seasonals are occasionally replaced by a guest beer, and the cider is Thatchers. The Weston to Wells 126 bus stops in the main square during the day. ⅏Q⊛⧗♣♿⅄⊷₪(126)

Batcombe

Three Horseshoes Inn

Off Back Lane, BA4 6HE (next to church) ST69023908

🕑 11-3, 6-11; 11-11 Sat; 12-10.30 Sun ☎ (01749) 850359

🌐 thethreehorseshoesinn.co.uk

Butcombe Bitter Ⓗ

a cinema and restaurant complex close to the city centre. It is heavily used, especially at weekends, and there is a wide clientele, with family groups very welcome. Seating is comfortable with an extensive mix of sofas and tables. Two beer festivals are held every year, together with special promotions. ♨️🍴🚮👃🍽️⇌(Spa)🍴☗(14,17,319)

Old Green Tree ★
12 Green Street, BA1 2JZ
☼ 11-11; 12-3 Sun ☎ (01225) 448259
Blindmans Green Tree Bitter; Butcombe Bitter; RCH Pitchfork; guest beers Ⓗ
Classic, unspoilt pub in a 300-year-old building. The three oak-panelled rooms include a superb northern-style drinking lobby, where it is nigh impossible not to strike up a conversation. Although it can get crowded, there is often space in the comfortable back bar. Beers are generally sourced from local microbreweries, with a stout or porter usually on offer in the winter months. A local farmhouse cider is also available, along with a range of fine wines and malt whiskies. Winter Sunday hours may be longer. Q◖◗➄⇌(Spa)🍴☗

Pig & Fiddle
2 Saracen Street, BA1 5BR
☼ 12-11.30 (midnight Fri); 11-11.30 Sat; 12-11 Sun
☎ (01225) 460868
Bristol Sunrise; Butcombe Bitter; Fuller's London Pride; guest beers Ⓗ
A large and busy town-centre pub with a varied clientele and a friendly atmosphere. One end is an old shop front, the other a courtyard with drinking benches and covered heaters. The decor is an esoteric collection of art displays and sports memorabilia. Up to three guest beers come from local breweries. Table football is played, and there are regular live music and open mic nights. The pub is popular with rugby fans and has several large TV screens. ♒️👃◖◗➄⇌(Spa)♣🍴☗⚑☗

Pulteney Arms
37 Daniel Street, BA2 6ND
☼ 12-3, 5-11 (midnight Thu); 12-midnight Fri & Sat; 12-10.30 Sun ☎ (01225) 463923 ⊕ thepulteneyarms.co.uk
Fuller's London Pride; Otter Bitter; Taylor Landlord; guest beers Ⓗ
Tucked away at the end of Great Pulteney Street, the Pulteney Arms has been open since 1792. There are five gas light fittings (now sadly condemned) above the bar. The decor shows an emphasis on sport, particularly rugby. The cat symbol on the pub sign refers to the Pulteney coat of arms. A wood-burning stove has now replaced the gas fire in the bar. The food menu is extensive and deservedly popular. No food Sunday evenings. ♨️Q♒️👃◖◗⇌(Spa)♣🍴☗⚑☗

Raven ♟
6-7 Queen Street, BA1 1HE
☼ 11.30-11 (midnight Fri & Sat); 12-10.30 Sun
☎ (01225) 425045 ⊕ theravenofbath.co.uk
Blindmans Raven, Ravens Gold; guest beers Ⓗ
Busy 18th-century free house in the heart of Bath. The six ales include two brewed exclusively by Blindmans. Guest ales come from far and wide, with several mini beer festivals a year. The main bar and the quieter first-floor bar serve the same range of ales. Famous for its sausages and Pieminister pies, the Raven is one of the few pubs in Bath serving food on Sunday evening. The pub is on several bus routes. ◖◗⇌(Spa)🍴☖

Royal Oak (Twerton)
Lower Bristol Road, Twerton, BA2 3BW (on A36 at intersection with road to Windsor Bridge)
☼ 4-11; 12-midnight Fri & Sat ☎ (01225) 481409
⊕ theroyaloak-bath.co.uk
Butts Jester, Barbus Ⓗ
A range of up to seven beers from microbreweries near and far is served here. Local ciders and bottled beers are also to be had. There are folk music sessions (alternating Irish and English) on Wednesday evenings and live music plays most weekends. Outside is a secluded garden and a small on-site car park. CAMRA members receive a discount of 50p per pint. ♨️Q👃⇌(Oldfield Park)🍴P⚑☗

Salamander
3 John Street, BA1 2JL
☼ 10-midnight (1am Fri & Sat); 10-11 Sun ☎ (01225) 428889
Bath Ales SPA, Gem, Barnsey, seasonal beer Ⓗ
An 18th-century building, tucked away in a side street, that opened as a coffee bar in 1957 and got a pub licence five years later. Taken over by Bath Ales 13 years ago and revamped in the company's inimitable style, it looks and feels like a pub that has been there for a century or more. Wooden floorboards, wood panelling and subdued lighting add to the ambience of the ground-floor bar, created from several small rooms. A popular restaurant is upstairs. ◖◗⇌(Spa)🍴☗

Star ★
23 The Vineyards, BA1 5NA
☼ 12-2.30, 5.30-midnight (1am Fri); 12-1am Sat;
12-midnight Sun ☎ (01225) 425072 ⊕ star-inn-bath.co.uk
Abbey Bellringer Ⓗ**; Draught Bass** Ⓖ**; guest beers** Ⓗ
Now the tap for Abbey Ales, Bath's only brewery, this classic town pub was fitted out by Gaskell & Chambers in 1928. Its four small rooms have benches around the walls, wood panelling and roaring fires. The smallest room has just a single bench, called Death Row, while the pub, which dates from around 1760, is coffin-shaped. Bass is served from the cask and complementary snuff is available. There is a Friday night folk session and a monthly quiz. ♨️Q➄⇌(Spa)♣🍴☗

INDEPENDENT BREWERIES
Abbey Bath
Blindmans Leighton
Butcombe Wrington
Cheddar Cheddar
Cotleigh Wiveliscombe
Cottage Lovington
Dawkins Timsbury
Exmoor Wiveliscombe
Glastonbury Somerton
Kubla Lydeard St Lawrence (NEW)
Masters Greenham
Milk Street Frome
Moor Long Sutton
North Curry North Curry
Odcombe Lower Odcombe
Ordnance City Ashcott (NEW)
Quantock Wellington
RCH West Hewish
Stocklinch Stocklinch (NEW)
Stowey Nether Stowey
Twisted Oak Wrington (NEW)
Windy Seavington St Michael
Yeovil Yeovil

Bishops Lydeard

Bird in Hand 🄛
34 Mount Street, TA4 3LH
🌑 12-11 (10 Sun) ☎ (01823) 432090
⊕ thebirdinhand34.com
Cotleigh Tawny; Exmoor Gold; guest beers ⊞
Very much a community pub, set at the centre of the village and 10 minutes' walk from West Somerset Railway. A free house, it serves four ales, mainly from local and south-west breweries. The slate-floored bar is warmed by an open fire in winter. Good locally produced and home-cooked food is served in the refurbished dining room, while the skittle alley accommodates functions. Families and dogs are welcome in the large garden. Weekly quiz nights and frequent mini beer festivals are hosted. ₳Q⊛◑♣P¹-🖳(17,28)

Bishopswood

Candlelight Inn
TA20 3RS (off A303 between Newton and Marsh)
🌑 12-2.30 (3 Sat & Sun), 6-11 ☎ (01460) 234476
⊕ candlelight-inn.co.uk
Otter Bitter; guest beers ⊞
Friendly country pub set in a pretty village in the Blackdown Hills. Features include flint walls, wooden floors and open fires as well as a lovely garden for summer days. Good food is served lunchtimes and evenings using local ingredients wherever possible. Beers come mainly from West Country breweries and there is usually a good selection of real ciders. A dining room is available for functions and large parties. ₳Q⊛◑♣P¹-

Blagdon Hill

Lamb & Flag 🄛
TA3 7SL (4 miles S of Taunton)
🌑 11-2.30, 5-11; 11-midnight Fri; 11-11 Sat; 12-10 (6 winter) Sun ☎ (01823) 421736 ⊕ lambandflag.co.uk
Beer range varies ⊞
Welcoming 16th-century free house with frequently changing ales, on the northern slopes of the Blackdown Hills. The main bar has the original flagstone floor and there is a candlelit dining area. Food is locally sourced and home made. There is a skittle alley and function room. The large garden, where the Oxford Shakespeare Co performs each August, has panoramic views. Folk music and quiz nights are held fortnightly. The pub also houses the local shop and post office. ₳Q⊛◑♣P¹-

Bleadon

Queen's Arms
Celtic Way, BS24 0NF (off A370)
🌑 11.30-11; 12-10.30 Sun ☎ (01934) 812080
⊕ queensarms.butcombe.com
Butcombe Bitter, Gold, seasonal beer ⊞
Seventeenth-century stone-built pub in the centre of the village. Three rooms converge on the bar; the largest is the main dining area. Food sales are strong, but not at the expense of ale drinkers – the pub is owned by the local Butcombe Brewery. Thatchers cider is also sold. Two real fires and exposed beams add to the cosy atmosphere. There is also a garden/patio with a sales hatch, and families are welcome. Regular number 83 buses serve the village from Weston. Free Wi-Fi. ₳Q⊛◑♣P¹-🖳(83)

Bridgwater

Carnival Inn
37 St Mary Street, TA6 3LX
🌑 8am-midnight (1am Fri & Sat) ☎ (01278) 726180
Greene King Abbot; Ruddles Best Bitter; guest beers ⊞
A town-centre Wetherspoon pub that takes its name from Bridgwater's famous carnival and which prides itself on the range and quality of its ales, often featuring beers from Somerset breweries. There is a large bar area with another large room off to one side. At the back up two steps is a family area and there is space in the garden at the rear for those who wish to smoke. Beer festivals are held twice a year. Q⊛◑&≠⊛¹-🖳

Fountain Inn 🄛
1 West Quay, TA6 3HL (corner of Town Bridge and Fore Street)
🌑 11-11 ☎ (01278) 444951
Butcombe Bitter; Wadworth 6X; guest beers ⊞
Traditional pub in a town-centre location next to the River Parrett, with a wood-burning stove that gives it a cosy feel. It has a large, friendly open bar with a library containing many books, comfortable seating and background music. This locally owned free house offers excellent value real ales, and Black Rat cider is also served. You can expect a warm welcome from the landlord and landlady, and a selection of newspapers is available every day. ₳⊛≠♣⊛¹-🖳

Buckland Dinham

Bell
High Street, BA11 2QT (on A362 Frome-Radstock road) ST752512
🌑 12-3 (not Mon & Tue), 6-midnight; 12-2.30, 7-11 Sun
☎ (01373) 462956 ⊕ bellatbuckland.co.uk
Butcombe Bitter; Sharp's Doom Bar; guest beers ⊞
A warm and cosy local pub that takes part in community activities – it has produced a village recipe book and holds film nights. It also offers a facility to order and pay for beer online. A three-day summer beer festival with live music is run in August and a cider festival in October. Local beers feature in home-prepared dishes. The pub has its own large campsite (featuring a collection of bikes), attracting CAMRA members from all over the UK. ₳Q🝙⊛◑🍴&A♣⊛P¹-🖳

Burrowbridge

King Alfred Inn 🄛
TA7 0RB (on A361)
🌑 12-2.30 Mon; 12-3, 5.30 (6 Sat)-11; 12-9 Sun
☎ (01823) 698379 ⊕ kingalfredinn.com
Butcombe Bitter; Otter Amber; guest beers ⊞
Traditional, unspoilt Grade II-listed country pub full of warmth and character, featuring live music on the first and third Sunday afternoons and a quiz on the first Tuesday evening each month. Most menu ingredients are sourced locally, many from the landlord's family farm (no food Sun eve or Mon). A beer festival is held over the August bank holiday weekend. Self-catering cottages are available in the pub grounds. CAMRA members receive a discount on real ale. ₳⊛🏠◑A♣⊛P¹-🖳(29)

Butleigh

Rose & Portcullis
Sub Road, BA6 8TQ
☼ 12-2.30, 5.30-11; 12-2.30, 7-10.30 Sun ☎ (01458) 850287
⊕ rose-and-portcullis.co.uk
Beer range varies Ⓗ
The village nestles in the hills south of Glastonbury and the building's blue lias stonework is typical of the area. Reopened in late 2011 after some months of closure, an extensive, sympathetic renovation has enhanced the interior. The first 15 months of trading saw close to 200 different beers on offer, which bodes well for the future. Food is very good quality and the establishment has gained an enviable reputation throughout the local area. Dogs and children are welcome.
ⓂQ☼◑♣P

Castle Cary

George Hotel
Market Place, BA7 7AH ST64113236
☼ 10-11 ☎ (01963) 350761
Greene King Abbot; Taylor Landlord; Wadworth 6X Ⓗ
The George is a family-run, thatched, 15th-century, country town hotel, situated in the centre of historic Castle Cary. The main bar has an original inglenook fireplace with an elm beam, said to date back to the 10th century. There is a small patio to the rear; parking is for residents only. The hotel has pleasant and comfortable discrete dining areas.
ⓂQ❧☼⇔◑ᵇ–ₘ(667)

Churchill

Crown Inn
The Batch, Skinners Lane, BS25 5PP (off A38, ¼ mile S of A368 jct)
☼ 11.30-11 (midnight Fri & Sat); 12-10.30 Sun
☎ (01934) 852995
Cotleigh Batch; Draught Bass; Palmers IPA; RCH Hewish IPA, PG Steam; St Austell Tribute; guest beers Ⓖ
Long-time Guide regular and winner of many CAMRA awards, the Crown suffered the sad loss of owner Tim Rogers in 2012, but remains under the same family. It is tucked away down a small lane yet close to the village centre. Several small rooms with stone-flagged floors are warmed by two log fires and offer an assortment of seating. Excellent food is provided (lunchtimes only) using local ingredients. Up to eight beers, usually local, are served on gravity. There are outside drinking areas. Dog-friendly. ⓂQ☼◑AP⁵–ₘ(121)

Clapton in Gordano

Black Horse
Clevedon Lane, BS20 7RH (2 miles from M5 jct 19) ST473739
☼ 11-11; 12-10 Sun ☎ (01275) 842105 ⊕ thekicker.co.uk
Butcombe Bitter; Courage Best Bitter; Exmoor Gold Ⓖ; Otter Bitter; Wadworth 6X; guest beer Ⓗ
Excellent 14th-century pub hidden away down a small lane. The snug was once the village lock-up. A large fireplace with a display of old rifles dominates the main bar. Beers are served from a small serving hatch - some on gravity. The games room doubles as a family room, with a children's play area in the pleasant garden. The Gordano Valley cycle route is nearby. Dogs are welcome.

Thatchers Dry and Heritage ciders are sold. Bar meals are served 12-2pm Monday to Saturday.
ⓂQ❧☼◑A♣♠P⁵⇐

Clevedon

Royal Oak
35 Copse Road, BS21 7QN (behind ice cream parlour near pier) ST402717
☼ 12-11 (midnight Fri & Sat) ☎ (01275) 790420
⊕ royaloakclevedon.com
Butcombe Bitter; Fuller's London Pride; Sharp's Doom Bar; guest beer Ⓗ
Lively, friendly, mid-terrace pub close to the seafront and connected via an alley. It has a large front window and a Tardis-like interior of many rooms. This community pub is home to darts, cribbage and cricket teams. The winner of various awards, it hosts many events, including cooking competitions and dancing ranging from morris men through belly dance to real Zulus. There is a quiz on Monday and folk music on Wednesday. Thatchers cider is sold. ⓂQ⊞♣♠⇐

Clutton Hill

Hunters Rest
King Lane, BS39 6HB (from A39 near Farmborough turn off by disused pub sign and drive one mile)
☼ 11.30-11 ☎ (01761) 452303 ⊕ huntersrest.co.uk
Bath Ales Gem; Butcombe Bitter; Otter Ale Ⓗ
Isolated, rambling pub built around 1750 as a hunting lodge. These days folk come to visit a grand country pub with award-winning food, served all day. The interior is enormous with lots of areas, including a comfy snug bar for non-diners. Children and dogs are welcome, and the garden offers fine views. Quality accommodation also features on the first floor. It can be approached from several routes but via the A39 is recommended for larger vehicles. Free Wi-Fi.
ⓂQ❧☼⇔◑⅄P⁵–

Coleford

King's Head
Underhill, BA3 5LU
☼ 2-midnight (1am Fri & Sat); 12-midnight Sun
☎ (01373) 812346 ⊕ kings-head-inn.com
Blindman's Buff; Butcombe Bitter Ⓗ
In the heart of the old part of the village, the King's Head was rebuilt after a fire in 1830. This rambling old inn offers a welcome for walkers and regulars. The flagstone-floored main bar has a roaring fire and there is a separate games room. The weekend after August bank holiday is the busiest of the year, when the pub plays host to an Irish music festival, with up to eight different beers. The cider is Thatchers Cheddar Valley. Ⓜ☼⊞⅄A♣♠P⁵–

Combe Florey

Farmers Arms Ⓛ
TA4 3HZ (on A358 between Bishops Lydeard and Williton)
☼ 11-11.30; 12-10.30 Sun ☎ (01823) 432267
⊕ farmersarmsatcombeflorey.co.uk
Exmoor Ale, Gold; St Austell Tribute, HSD Ⓗ
Old thatched inn with a small public bar, a large log fire and a restaurant area. The pub overlooks a scenic garden and stream. The West Somerset Steam Railway passes on an embankment at the

rear. While the inn is deservedly known for its food, the four regular ales have national recognition as the pub has been awarded the regional prize for Best Cellar by Innserve for the past two years. ᴹᴬQ☀❶ⓓP⅟☕(18,28)

Combe St Nicholas

Green Dragon 🅛
TA20 3NG
🌑 12-2.30 (not Mon), 6-midnight; 12-midnight Sat; 12-4 Sun
☎ (01460) 63311 ⊕ greendragon-combe.co.uk
Otter Bitter; guest beer Ⓗ
You cannot miss the large green dragon carved by the landlord when you visit this friendly free house, with origins in the 17th century. More woodcarvings can be found in both bars. Beers are sourced mainly from West Country breweries and there is a varied menu of good-value, home-cooked food served at lunchtimes (no food Mon lunch) and Tuesday to Saturday evenings. Local ingredients are used where possible and there is a popular Pie and a Pint night on Wednesdays. Live music features on alternate Fridays.
Q❶♣A♣P⅟☕(99,99A)

Congresbury

Plough ♟
High Street, BS49 5JA (off A370 at B3133 jct)
🌑 11.30-2.30, 4.30-11; 11.30-midnight Fri; 12-3, 7-11 Sun
☎ (01934) 877402 ⊕ the-plough-inn.net
Butcombe Bitter; St Austell Tribute; guest beers Ⓗ
Characterful village pub with flagstone floors and many original features, decorated with interesting local artefacts. Three or four guest beers are served from a row of old cask heads behind the bar, sourced mainly from local breweries. Thatchers cider is also stocked. Food is served daily lunchtimes and evenings, except Sunday evening, which is quiz night. The pub has real fires, no TV, and dogs are welcome. Mendip morris men meet here. CAMRA Bristol & District Pub of the Year 2013.
ᴹᴬQ☀❶♣♠P⅟☕(X1,353)

Corton Denham

Queen's Arms 🅛
DT9 4LR (3 miles S of A303)
🌑 10-11 (midnight Fri & Sat); 12-10.30 Sun
☎ (01963) 220317 ⊕ thequeensarms.com
Moor Queen's Revival; guest beers Ⓗ
Cosy, friendly, 18th-century pub in a secluded village. Moor Brewery beers are regulars, some of them pioneered here, and Queen's Revival is the house beer. Various local ciders are also served – the Queen's was Somerset CAMRA cider pub in 2012. Food ranges from local pork pies with mustard and pickles to main meals of good quality. The accommodation is highly rated and the garden has lovely views over rolling countryside. Dogs and muddy boots are welcome in the bar.
ᴹᴬQ☀❶♿♠P⅟

Crewkerne

King William
Barn Street, TA18 8BP (take last turning on left off A30 towards Chard)
🌑 5 (12 Sat)-midnight; 12-4 Sun ☎ (01460) 74492
Butcombe Bitter; guest beers Ⓗ

Hidden hostelry well patronised by locals where an enjoyable Saturday can be spent watching the racing. The pub is family and dog friendly and local music is supported on Saturdays, with an acoustic night on the last Wednesday of the month. There is a raised area with a pool table. Perry's local cider is served. ᴹᴬ☀♣♠P⅟☕(99,99A)

Croscombe

George Inn
Long Street, BA5 3QH (on A371 between Wells and Shepton Mallet) ST589443
🌑 12-3, 6-11 ☎ (01749) 342306 ⊕ thegeorgeinn.co.uk
Blindmans King George Ⓖ; Butcombe Bitter Ⓗ; guest beers Ⓗ/Ⓖ
A 17th-century inn, refurbished by the landlord, serving at least two guest ales and hosting two beer festivals a year, at Whitsun and in late October. There is a large main bar, a snug with a fireplace, a family room and a separate dining room. Food is home-cooked using locally sourced ingredients. To the rear is a skittle alley and a garden with a covered terrace. Guest beers are from West Country independents. The Blindmans King George is exclusively brewed for the pub.
ᴹᴬQ☀🛏❶♿♣♠P⅟☕(371)

Cross

New Inn
Old Coach Road, BS26 2EE (on A38/A361 jct)
🌑 12-11 (midnight Fri & Sat) ☎ (01934) 732455
⊕ newinncross.co.uk
Otter Ale; guest beers Ⓗ
Roadside inn on the A38, close to the historic medieval town of Axbridge. Popular for its extensive food menu served all day until 9pm (8pm Sun) and twice-yearly beer festivals, it usually has three guest beers that can often be adventurous. There is a function room on the first floor. A large hillside garden with children's play facilities offers a fine view of the Mendip Hills and Somerset Levels. Families are welcome – dogs too. There is a small car park opposite. Ale is discounted on Thursdays. ☀❶♣♠P⅟☕(126)

Dinnington

Dinnington Docks
TA17 8SX (approx 3 miles E of Ilminster off Crewkerne road)
🌑 11.30-3.30, 6-midnight; 11-midnight Sat; 12-10.30 Sun
☎ (01460) 52397
Butcombe Bitter; guest beers Ⓗ
Friendly locals' pub serving a selection of beers from West Country breweries, always including brews from Butcombe and Teignworthy and at least one guest beer. The varied food menu features fresh fish on Fridays and a carvery on Sunday lunchtimes. The pub has a railway theme and is adorned with old transport pictures and signs. Haircuts are available on the last Tuesday of the month and there is a vintage car meeting on the first Wednesday. ᴹᴬ☀❶♿♣♠P⅟

Dulverton

Bridge Inn 🅛
20 Bridge Street, TA22 9HJ

✪ 12-11 summer; 12-3, 6-11 (not Mon); 12-11 Fri & Sat winter; 12-11 Sun ☎ (01398) 324130
⊕ thebridgeinndulverton.com
Exmoor Ale; guest beers Ⓗ
Close to the River Barle, this warm, welcoming pub dating from 1845 has a cosy single-room bar with a wood-burning stove. Surrounding memorabilia is a reminder that the pub is set on the edge of Exmoor with walking and country pursuits nearby. A wide range of excellent food is available lunchtimes and evenings. The Bridge holds a Green Tourism Award in recognition of the environmentally-friendly way it is run. An annual beer festival coincides with the local folk festival over the Whitsun holiday.
🅼Q✿⏻Å♣⁵—🖷(25,398)

Rock House Inn Ⓛ
1 Jury Road, TA22 9DU
✪ 12-11 ☎ (01398) 323131 ⊕ rockhouseinndulverton.com
Sharp's Doom Bar; guest beers Ⓗ
Lively free house at the top of this attractive Exmoor town. Built on the side of a rock face, the pub was first licensed in 1837, although part of the property, which included a saddlery and a hayloft, is said to be much older. The locals congregate in the single bar and there is an adjoining dining room where food is served daily except Sunday evening and Monday lunchtime.
🅼✿⏻Å♣♠⁵—🖷(25,398)

Emborough

Old Down Inn Ⓛ
BA3 4SA ST628513
✪ 12-2, 6.30-11.30; 12-10.30 Sun ☎ (01761) 232398
Butcombe Bitter; Draught Bass Ⓖ
A free house first licensed in 1640, this establishment was once an important coaching inn. The spirit of the past lives on in the main bar, where beer is served straight from the cask. Two guests from local breweries are generally available. The bar snacks are excellent value, and likewise the main meals. This friendly and popular hostelry is a classic example of a traditional Somerset inn and is the centre of many local community activities. Q🏮✿🎗⏻🏵Å♠⁵—🖷

Faulkland

Tucker's Grave ★
BA3 5XF (on A366 1 mile E of village) ST751551
✪ 11.30-3, 6-11; 12-3, 7-10.30 Sun ☎ (01373) 834230
Butcombe Bitter, Rare Breed Ⓖ
A gem from a bygone age and identified by CAMRA as one of Britain's Best Real Heritage Pubs, this place was built in the mid-17th century and has changed very little since. It was named after Tucker, who hanged himself and was buried at the crossroads outside, and featured in a song by the 1970s punk band The Stranglers. There is no bar, and beers and Thatchers cider are served from an alcove. Shove-ha'penny is played and there is a skittle alley. Camping is available in the grounds.
🅼Q✿Å♣♠P⁵

Forches Corner

Merry Harriers
EX15 3TR (3 miles SE of Wellington)
✪ 12-3 (not Mon), 6.30-11; 12-3 Sun ☎ (01823) 421270
⊕ merryharriers.co.uk
Otter Head; guest beers Ⓗ

Friendly, family-owned and award-winning free house on the Blackdown Hills bordering Somerset and Devon. The bar separates the lounge from the dining area, where excellent meals using fresh fish, meat and game are served. Guest beers are normally from local breweries, with Exmoor beers featuring regularly. Locally made Bollhayes cider is also served. Although in a somewhat remote location, the pub has a thriving trade. There is a large, pleasant garden in which to enjoy the warm summer sunshine. 🅼Q🏮✿🎗⏻🏵&♣♠P⁵—

Frome

Griffin Inn
Milk Street, BA11 3DB
✪ 5-11; 4-1am Fri & Sat; 1-9 Sun ☎ (01373) 467766
Milk Street Usual, Funkey Monkey, Beer Ⓗ
Situated in the older part of Frome, known as Trinity or Chinatown, the Griffin is owned by Milk Street Brewery, with the small brewhouse at the back. It produces a wide range of ales served alongside seasonal beers. The single bar retains original features including open fires, etched windows and wooden floors, and a stained glass griffin is behind the bar. Monday is pub quiz night and live music plays regularly. A small garden opens all year. Food is limited to summer barbecues and Sunday lunches. 🏮≈♣P⁵—🖷

Green Ore

Ploughboy Inn
BA5 3ET (on A39/B3135 crossroads)
✪ closed Mon; 11-2.30, 5.30-10; 12-2.30, 7-11 Sat; 12-3, 7-10 Sun ☎ (01761) 241375 ⊕ ploughboyinn.com
Butcombe Bitter; Otter Ale; guest beers Ⓗ
In the same safe hands for over 25 years, this substantial stone free house to the north of Wells occupies a corner plot by the traffic lights in the hamlet of Green Ore. The 376 Wells to Bristol bus runs nearby and there is a large car park and pleasant beer garden to the rear. A single good-sized L-shaped bar is warmed by a real fire, and reasonably priced, excellent food is available 12-2pm and 7-9.30pm (9pm Sun). A guest beer is offered at busier times. No dogs.
🅼Q🏮⏻P⁵—🖷(376)

Hallatrow

Old Station
Wells Road, BS39 6EN
✪ 12-3, 5-11; 12-11 Fri & Sat; 12-10.30 Sun
☎ (01761) 452228 ⊕ theoldstationandcarriage.co.uk
Brains The Rev James, seasonal beer; Butcombe Bitter; guest beer Ⓗ
Unusual eclectic pub noted for its high-quality food at reasonable prices as well as its totally eccentric décor. A bewildering array of unexpected items appears throughout. An old GWR railway carriage serves as a dining room and the pub has its own crazy golf course. Owned by Brains, it often serves the small batch one-off beers from its in-house microbrewery. Book ahead to dine at weekends. Children are welcome, and there are five ground floor en-suite rooms available.
🏮≈⏻♣P⁵—🖷(376)

Henstridge

Bird in Hand
2 Ash Walk, BA8 0QD (100yds S of A30/A357 jct)
ST72331992
☼ 11-2.30, 5.30-11; 11-11 Sat; 12-3, 7.30-10.30 Sun
☎ (01963) 362255
Beer range varies Ⓗ
Old stone village pub with low ceilings, beams, a fireplace at each end of an attractive long bar, and a games room housing a TV. There is an adjoining skittle alley. Excellent quality rotating guest ales and good-value snacks make a visit to this friendly pub well worth while. ᴹQ✿◑ⓓ⑃♣♠P☲(58,58A)

Hinton Blewitt

Ring o' Bells
Upper Road, BS39 5AN (2 miles W of Temple Cloud from A37) ST594569
☼ 12-3, 5-11 (midnight Fri); 12-midnight Sat; 12-11 Sun
☎ (01761) 452239
Butcombe Bitter, seasonal beer; Fuller's London Pride; guest beer Ⓗ
Butcombe pub dating from the 19th century. A dining/function room with its own garden was added more recently, and blends nicely with the cosy bar and snug. Quality food is served, using local produce when possible. Local sports clubs meet here and much memorabilia is on show, particularly cricket-related. Cyclists, walkers, children and dogs are all most welcome. Ashton Still cider is served. ᴹQ✿◑♣♠⑃

Holcombe

Duke of Cumberland Ⓛ
Edford Hill, BA3 5HQ
☼ 10 (9 Sat & Sun)-midnight ☎ (01761) 233731
∰ thedukeholcombe.co.uk
Butcombe Bitter; Wadworth Swordfish Ⓗ
The landlord here has a good knowledge of and interest in real ale, and local activities are supported. Refurbished to a high standard prior to reopening, the pub is on the edge of the Mendip Hills in a fine walking area, with a beer garden on the banks of the river. Excellent bar and restaurant food are available at all times. There is a skittle alley and the cider is Thatchers Cheddar Valley. ᴹ✿◑⑃♣♠P⑃☲

Huish Episcopi

Rose & Crown (Eli's) ★
Wincanton Road, TA10 9QT (on A372)
☼ 10-3, 5.30-11; 11.30-11 Fri & Sat; 12-10.30 Sun
☎ (01458) 250494
Butcombe Bitter; Teignworthy Reel Ale; guest beers Ⓗ
Known locally as Eli's, this quaint free house is unusual in having no bar counter in the flagstoned taproom. Generations of the same family have served patrons with good food and ale to be consumed at leisure in the various small rooms; to rush in such a relaxed atmosphere would amount to sacrilege and there always seem to be locals willing to while away a little time with enchanting reminiscences. Buses 54 and 38 stop a 20-minute walk away. ᴥ✿◑♣♠P⑃☲(38,54)

Hutton

Old Inn
Main Road, BS24 9QQ
☼ 11.30-11 (midnight Fri & Sat); 12-11 Sun
☎ (01934) 812336
Butcombe Gold; Fuller's London Pride; Otter Head; St Austell Tribute Ⓗ
A genuine free house owned by a long-standing Guide landlord and now a thriving local, the Old Inn is right at the heart of the local community. The pub is extremely popular for its excellent and great-value food, particularly the Sunday carvery. Dogs are welcome. The car park behind the pub is accessed by narrow one-way lanes either side. Food is served all lunchtimes and evenings except Sunday, which is quiz night. The beer range may change occasionally and plans exist for two more pumps. ᴹⓉ✿◑⑃P⑃☲(4,4A)

Kelston

Old Crown
Bath Road, BA1 9AQ (3 miles from Bath on A431)
☼ 11.30-11; 12-10.30 Sun ☎ (01225) 423032
∰ oldcrown.butcombe.com
Butcombe Bitter, Gold, seasonal beer; Draught Bass; guest beer Ⓗ
Attractive multi-roomed 18th-century coaching inn owned by Butcombe Brewery. The rare cash register handpumps, flagstone floors, open fires and settles all help create a friendly atmosphere. On Monday evenings the landlord and regular customers contribute tapas dishes. In summertime, barbecues and live musical events are occasionally held in the large, attractive garden. Sunday is quiz night. Butcombe's own Ashton Still cider is sold. Take care crossing the busy road. ᴹQ✿◑⑃♠P☲(319,332)

Keynsham

Lock Keeper
Keynsham Road, BS31 2DD (on A4175)
☼ 11-midnight; 12-11 Sun ☎ (0117) 986 2383
∰ lockkeeperbristol.com
Bath Ales Gem; Young's Bitter, Special, seasonal beers Ⓗ
Multi-roomed Young's pub, noted for its food, by Keynsham lock on the River Avon. The original 17th-century cottage once brewed its own beer and was named the White Hart. It divides into two parts, with the older bar facing the canal, while the large conservatory and heated veranda overlook the river, pétanque pitches and the popular garden. Families are welcome and dogs are allowed in the bar area. Occasional live music features in summer. The pub may stay open later when busy. ✿◑⥵P⑃☲(318)

Kilve

Hood Arms Ⓛ
TA5 1EA (on A39)
☼ 11-11 ☎ (01278) 741210 ∰ thehoodarms.com
Exmoor Ale; Otter Head; guest beers Ⓗ
Former 17th-century coaching inn set beside the main road. It has oak beams, an open fireplace, a comfortable bar and a separate restaurant. Outside is a landscaped walled garden where boules is played in summer. The pub also has a bar billiards table. Special events for charities are held

regularly. There are 12 en-suite rooms and a lodge available to rent. It is an ideal base for walkers and fossil hunters at the nearby beach. Well-behaved dogs are welcome. ♨️✍️🅿️🚲♿🅰️♣♿P⅃🚱(14)

Kingsbury Episcopi

Wyndham Arms 🅛
TA12 6AT
🌣 12-midnght (1am Fri & Sat) ☎ (01935) 823239
⊕ wyndhamarms.com
Butcombe Bitter; Otter Ale; guest beers 🅗
Most of this large old pub is believed to be over 400 years old. It has a dining area off the bar which has an open log fire; there are antique settles in the bar itself and another log fire. Outside is a skittle alley/function room and another upstairs function room sometimes used for live music nights or meetings. The pub is justifiably proud of its outdoor smoking area with patio heaters and a pool table. Local charities are actively supported. Well worth a visit. ♨️Q🕏🅓♣♿P⅃

Long Sutton

Devonshire Arms
TA10 9LP
🌣 12-3, 6-11 (10.30 Sun) ☎ (01458) 241271
⊕ thedevonshirearms.com
Beer range varies 🅗
A fine old Grade II-listed building opposite the village green which houses a well-appointed contemporary bar and restaurant furnished with comfy chairs and glass-topped tables near a real log fire. The bar serves real ale mostly from Somerset breweries, and always offers beers from Moor Beer, which is only a couple of minutes from the pub. Drinkers can use the walled garden, the courtyard or the terrace overlooking the village green. En-suite accommodation is available. ♨️Q🕏✍️🅓♿♿P⅃

Lower Odcombe

Masons Arms
41 Lower Odcombe, BA22 8TX (off Yeovil to Montacute road)
🌣 12-2.30, 6-midnight ☎ (01935) 862591
⊕ masonsarmsodcombe.co.uk
Odcombe No.1, Spring, seasonal beers 🅗
A picturesque thatched free house in the main street of an attractive village. A small microbrewery at the rear of the pub brews for the Masons Arms only. Good food is served using local produce and booking is advisable for the restaurant. Well-behaved children and dogs are welcome. Local events are held on the pub field. B&B accommodation is offered and at the back of the pub is a caravan site with hook-ups, showers and a laundry room. 🕏✍️🅓🅰️♿P⅃🚱(81)

Lower Weare

Lamb Inn
Turnpike Road, BS26 2JF (on A38)
🌣 12-3, 6-11; 12-11 Sat; 12-7 Sun ☎ (01934) 732384
⊕ thelambatweare.co.uk
Butcombe Bitter; Cheddar Potholer; Sharp's Doom Bar 🅗
Traditional roadside village free house located on the A38 about a mile south of Cross and Axbridge. Three ales and Thatchers cider are offered plus

good-value food both lunchtimes and evenings (no food Sun eve). The large, comfortable interior leads out into a pleasant garden area with its own smokers' cabin. There is also a function room and skittle alley. Bus 619 passes close by.
Q🕏🕏🅓♿P⅃🚱(619)

Martock

White Hart Hotel 🅛
East Street, TA12 6JQ
🌣 12-2.30 (not Mon; 3 Sat), 5.30-11; 12-3 Sun
☎ (01935) 822005 ⊕ whiteharthotelmartock.co.uk
Otter Bitter; guest beers 🅗
A friendly family-run hotel built in 1735 and now a Grade II-listed building. Everyone is made welcome and the food is excellent, with a comprehensive menu plus a specials and bistro board. The owner and the chef continually look for new recipes. The cellar is well stocked with local and national beers. There are 10 excellent guest rooms and a skittle alley which can be used as a function room.
Q🕏🕏✍️🅓♣P⅃🚱(N9,N10)

Middlezoy

George Inn 🅛
42 Main Street, TA7 0NN (off A372, 1 mile NW of Othery)
🌣 closed Mon; 12-3, 7 (6.30 Fri & Sat)-midnight; 12-3, 7-11 Sun ☎ (01823) 698215 ⊕ thegeorgeinnmiddlezoy.co.uk
Butcombe Bitter; guest beers 🅗
Middlezoy is to be found surrounded by the sparsely populated wetland area known as the Somerset Levels. Its pub provides a welcoming haven for walkers and birdwatchers as well as the cheerful locals. The – unmistakably – South African landlord offers mainly local beer and cider, and tempts many to visit at Easter when the annual beer festival is held featuring ales from throughout the country. Food is available Wednesday to Saturday and includes excellent international game dishes, some of the more exotic being very popular. ♨️Q🕏🅓🅰️♣♿P⅃🚱(16)

Minehead

Kildare Lodge Hotel
Townsend Road, TA24 5RQ
🌣 11-3, 6.30-11; 12-5 Sun ☎ (01643) 702009
⊕ kildarelodge.co.uk
St Austell Trelawney, Dartmoor Best; guest beers 🅗
Situated just two minutes from Minehead town centre, this Grade II-listed building in the Arts and Crafts style retains many interesting features. It is an ideal base for exploring the Exmoor countryside, and medieval Dunster is also nearby. Accommodation includes 12 en-suite rooms and a bridal suite with four-poster bed. There is a small bar, two separate lounges and a dining room. The beers are very reasonably priced for the area. ♨️Q✍️🅓🅒♿♿P⅃🚱(18,28,398)

Queen's Head 🅛
Holloway Street, TA24 5NR (off the Parade)
🌣 11-11 (midnight Wed-Sat) ☎ (01643) 702940
Exmoor Gold; St Austell Tribute; Sharp's Doom Bar; guest beers 🅗
In a side street just off the Parade, this popular town pub sells up to eight ales, including house beer Queen's Head, at a very reasonable price. The spacious single bar has a raised seating area for

dining and families. There is a games room at the rear and a skittle alley. Good-value food is served daily with a carvery on Tuesday, Wednesday, Thursday and Sunday lunchtimes. There are twice-yearly beer festivals and live music features on some weekends. ⊕▲⇌♣⁌₋➗(18,28,398)

Mudford

Half Moon
Main Street, BA21 5TF (on A359 between Yeovil and Sparkford)
✪ 12-11 (10.30 Sun) ☎ (01935) 850289
⊕ thehalfmooninn.co.uk
Beer range varies Ⓖ
Welcoming 17th-century village roadside inn, extensively restored, with a good food and drink trade. The single bar is divided into several cosy areas. A comprehensive menu is displayed on blackboards with daily specials. Two regular West Country ales, usually from RCH, are on stillage behind the bar, together with two Westons ciders. There are also reduced-price takeaways. An outside courtyard is pleasant on warmer days. Accommodation is in the pub and the former skittle alley. Guide dogs are welcome.
Q❀⌂⊕&➗P⁌₋➗(1)

Norton Fitzwarren

Cross Keys Ⓛ
TA2 6NR (at A358/B3227 jct W of Taunton)
✪ 11-11; 12-10.30 Sun ☎ (01823) 333062
Beer range varies Ⓗ
Busy 19th-century former coaching inn and stables converted into a pub and restaurant, comprising several separate seating areas with open fires, exposed beams and timber floors. There is a large garden to the rear and a car park to the side. Four constantly changing real ales from local, regional and national breweries are usually available, as well as Westons Old Rosie cider. A large menu, offering traditional pub food, is served all day, and there is a skittle alley and regular live music.
⌂❀⊕&➗P⁌₋➗(18,25,28)

Oakhill

Oakhill Inn
Fosse Road, BA3 5HU (on A367 between Radstock and Shepton Mallet) ST635472
✪ 12-3, 5-11 (midnight Fri); 12-midnight Sat & Sun
☎ (01749) 840442 ⊕ theoakhillinn.com
Butcombe Bitter; guest beers Ⓗ
Large village-centre pub that is both a popular local and a family-friendly gastro-pub, with a strong emphasis on organic and locally sourced food. The bar serves two areas with an open feel. Regular quiz nights are held. Up to three changing guest ales, normally sourced from local micros, are on offer. There is a garden at the rear and the car park is 20 yards up the road in the Shepton Mallet direction. Accommodation is in five 4-star rooms.
⌂❀⌂⊕➗P➗

Pitney

Halfway House Ⓛ
Pitney Hill, TA10 9AB (on B3153 between Langport and Somerton)
✪ 11.30-3, 5.30-11 (midnight Fri & Sat); 12-11 Sun
☎ (01458) 252513 ⊕ thehalfwayhouse.co.uk

Butcombe Bitter; Hop Back Summer Lightning; Otter Bright; Teignworthy Reel Ale; guest beers Ⓖ
Serving eight to 10 local ales on gravity alongside many international bottled beers, this basic but buzzing pub deserves its many accolades, most recently Somerset CAMRA Pub of the Year 2011, as well as the distinction of featuring in the Guide continuously for 21 years. Superb home-cooked food is based on local produce, with good-sized portions, and a roast lunch is served on Sunday (no food Sun eve). Local ciders are from Wilkins and Gold Rush. There is a beer festival in March.
⌂Q❀⊕♣➗P⁌₋➗(38,54)

Porlock

Ship Inn Ⓛ
High Street, TA24 8QD
✪ 11 (12 Sun)-midnight ☎ (01643) 862507
⊕ shipinnporlock.co.uk
Exmoor Beast; Otter Bitter; guest beers Ⓗ
Known locally as the Top Ship, this 13th-century inn was in RD Blackmore's Lorna Doone. The bar appears not to have changed much since then, with flagstoned floors and inglenook fireplaces. A selection of real ales and Cheddar Valley cider is served. At the bottom of the notorious Porlock Hill, it offers home-cooked food, a three-tiered patio garden, a skittle alley and four en-suite bedrooms. Dogs and well-behaved children are welcome. A joint beer festival with the Ship at Porlock Weir is held annually. ⌂Q✆❀⌂⊕⌂&▲♣➗P⁌₋➗(39)

Porlock Weir

Ship Inn Ⓛ
TA24 8PB (take B3225 from Porlock)
✪ 11-11; 12-10.30 Sun ☎ (01643) 863288
⊕ thebottomship.co.uk
Exmoor Ale, Stag; St Austell Tribute, Proper Job; guest beers Ⓗ
Situated in the Exmoor National Park, and more than 400 years old, the Ship has possibly the best view from any pub in Somerset, overlooking the harbour and Bristol Channel towards South Wales. Good-value food is served by friendly staff. It is ideal for walkers, and close to Porlock village and the famous hill. The large nearby Pay & Display car park can be busy during holiday periods. A joint beer festival with the Ship at Porlock is held annually. ⌂❀⊕&▲♣➗⁌₋➗(39)

Portishead

Windmill Inn
58 Nore Road, BS20 6JZ (next to municipal golf course above coastal path)
✪ 11-11; 12-10.30 Sun ☎ (01275) 843677
⊕ thewindmillinn.org
Butcombe Bitter, Gold; Courage Best Bitter; Draught Bass; guest beers Ⓗ
Large split-level free house with a spacious patio to the rear, plus a recent extension enjoying panoramic views. Above the coastal path on the edge of town, the Severn Estuary and both Severn bridges can be seen on clear days. A varied menu is served all day and is enormously popular. One large area is set aside for families. The two guest ales are often locally sourced, and Thatchers cider is stocked. Q✆❀⊕&➗⁌₋➗(359)

Priddy

Hunters Lodge

BA5 3AR (isolated crossroads 1 mile from A39 close to TV mast) ST549500

✪ 11.30-2.30, 6.30-11; 12-2, 7-11 Sun ☎ (01749) 672275

Butcombe Bitter; Cheddar Potholer; guest beers Ⓖ

Timeless, classic roadside inn near Priddy, the highest village in Somerset, popular with cavers and walkers. The landlord has been in charge for well over 40 years. Three rooms include one with a flagged floor, and all beer is direct from casks behind the bar. Local cider is served. The simple home-cooked food is excellent and exceptional value. A folk musicians' drop-in session is held on Tuesday evening in the back room. The garden is pleasant and secluded. Mobile phones are not welcome but dogs are. ♨Q☎❀◑✿ੳ♣♠P

Queen Victoria Inn

Pelting Drove, BA5 3BA

✪ 12-11 ☎ (01749) 676385 ⊕ queenvictoria.butcombe.com

Butcombe Bitter, seasonal beer; Fuller's London Pride Ⓗ

Creeper-clad inn, a pub since 1851, with four rooms that feature low ceilings, flagged floors and three log fires. A wonderfully warm and relaxing haven on cold winter nights, it is popular during the Priddy Folk Festival in July and the annual fair in August. Reasonably priced home-cooked food is a speciality. Children and dogs are allowed and there is a play area by the car park. Cheddar Valley and Ashton Still ciders are sold. May close briefly on some afternoons. ♨Q❀◑ A♣♠P'–

Puriton

37 Club Ⓛ

1 West Approach, Woolavington Road, TA7 8AD (between Puriton and Woolavington)

✪ 6-11; 5-midnight Fri; 12-midnight Sat; 12-11 Sun ☎ (01278) 685190 ⊕ 37club.co.uk

Butcombe Bitter; Quantock Ale; guest beers Ⓗ

Formerly the social club of The Royal Ordnance Factory whose allocated number was 37, this is now a thriving club with two bars, a large function room, two skittle alleys, a football pitch with changing facilities and a private fishing lake. A varied menu is served Wednesday to Saturday evenings and booking is advised for the Sunday carvery lunch. There are also five snooker tables, pool and darts. Somerset CAMRA Club of the Year 2013. ☎❀◑♣♠P'–₪(102,375)

Radstock

Fromeway

Frome Road, BA3 3LG (¾ mile from Radstock centre on A362 Frome Road) ST697547

✪ closed Mon; 12-3, 6-11; 12-11 Sun ☎ (01761) 432116 ⊕ fromeway.co.uk

Butcombe Bitter; Wadworth 6X; guest beers Ⓗ

This friendly free house has been in the same family for five generations. The present landlord has been in charge for more than 36 years and produces his own sausages, faggots and home-cured hams for the excellent bar and restaurant meals. Popular with locals, the Fromeway has a warm and relaxing atmosphere. A single bar serves three regular ales, and there are weekly guest beers. The pub organises many functions, quizzes and walks for charity. Three charming bedrooms are available. Q☎❀◿◑&P'–₪

Rickford

Plume of Feathers

Leg Lane, BS40 7AH (off A368 2 miles from A38 jct; if approaching from Churchill, the left U-turn into Leg Lane is extremely tricky)

✪ 12-11 ☎ (01761) 462682 ⊕ theplumeoffeathers.com

Butcombe Bitter; Cheddar Potholer; guest beers Ⓗ

A 17th-century building that has been a pub since the 1800s. The interior is divided into a bar, restaurant and family room. The pub provides a pleasant and convenient base from which to walk, fish or explore the Mendips. It has a garden at the rear and a stream running along the front, leading to a ford. Butcombe seasonal beers often feature among the two guests. Dogs are welcome. A popular charity duck race occurs in July. Parking is limited. ♨Q☎❀◿◑♣P

Rowberrow

Swan Inn

Rowberrow Lane, BS25 1QL

✪ 12-3, 6-11; 12-11 Fri & Sat; 12-10.30 Sun ☎ (01934) 852371

Butcombe Bitter, Rare Breed, seasonal beer; guest beer Ⓗ

Believed to date from around the late 17th century, this Butcombe Brewery-owned country pub enjoys an attractive setting, nestling beneath the Dolebury Iron Age hill fort. A convenient stop for walkers on the Mendip Hills, the emphasis is on home-cooked food with unusual specials, but customers who just want a drink are welcome. There is a collection of artefacts around the walls and a grandfather clock. The large, attractive beer garden and car park are opposite. ♨Q❀◑P'–

Shepton Beauchamp

Duke of York Ⓛ

North Street, TA19 0LW

✪ 5.30-11 Mon; 12-midnight, 12-10.30 Sun ☎ (01460) 240314 ⊕ thedukeshepton.co.uk

Otter Ale; Teignworthy Reel Ale; guest beers Ⓗ

A charming pub in the centre of a pretty village, the Duke has four pumps dispensing West Country ales. The tables on the raised pavement in front allow patrons to observe the leisurely life of south Somerset. Very good food is served both in the bar and the restaurant (no food Sun eve or Mon), attracting visitors from the surrounding villages as well as the immediate locals. Dogs and children are welcome. ♨☎❀◿◑♣♠P'–

Shepton Mallet

Swan Inn

27 Town Street, BA4 5BE (N of town centre) ST618437

✪ 11-midnight ☎ (01749) 344995 ⊕ swanatshepton.co.uk

Dawkins Bob Wall; guest beer Ⓗ

A pub in a terrace of small shops. Inside, the front area is arranged mainly for diners (no meals Mon afternoon or Sun and Mon eves), with chairs and tables extending out on to the pavement. The bar area at the rear offers darts and shove-ha'penny, and live music features once or twice a month. Guest ales are chosen from local small brewers, and cider is from Thatchers. The car park is at the rear. ♨◿◑&A♣♠P'–₪

South Petherton

Brewers Arms 🅛
18 St James Street, TA13 5BW (½ mile off A303)
✪ 11.30-2.30, 6-11; 11.30-midnight Fri & Sat; 12-11 Sun
☎ (01460) 241887
Otter Bitter; guest beers Ⓗ
Travellers using the A303 in Somerset are advised that should they exit towards South Petherton, where they will find the ideal village pub. Frequently a finalist in the local CAMRA branch's Pub of the Year competitions, this free house has real cider and five ales, with excellent food to soak it up. The friendly staff and locals are welcoming to all, whether they are accompanied by dogs (on leads please), children or both. Beer festivals are held on the late May and August holidays.
🏛️🏵️◑🅰️♣🐾🕊️☒(81)

Stogumber

White Horse
High Street, TA4 3TA (turn left off A358 at Crowcombe)
✪ 12-11 ☎ (01984) 656277 ⊕ whitehorsestogumber.co.uk
Otter Bitter; St Austell Tribute, Proper Job; guest beers Ⓗ
Traditional free house opposite the church in this picturesque village lying between the Quantock and Brendon Hills, popular with ramblers, railway enthusiasts and locals alike. Locally produced food is served in the lounge and restaurant and most ales are sourced from West Country breweries. Activities include pool and skittles, with pétanque being played in summer. B&B is provided. The West Somerset Railway is about a mile away.
🏛️🏵️🛏️◑🚲♣🐾P🕊️

Street

Two Brewers
38 Leigh Road, BA16 0HB
✪ 11-2.30, 6-11; 11.30-2.30, 6-10.30 Sun ☎ (01458) 442421
⊕ thetwobrewers.co.uk
Courage Best Bitter; St Austell Tribute; guest beers Ⓗ
A friendly and traditional local on the edge of the town centre but with several buses stopping outside. There is a single bar, and a raised area for diners. Excellent, good-value food is served at all sessions. The relaxed atmosphere is helped by the absence of music and fruit machines. Guest beers are usually from the West Country. Accommodation is in three en-suite rooms in an old stable block. Clarks Village retail outlet and other attractions are nearby. Q🏵️🛏️◑♣P🕊️☒(29,375,377)

Taunton

Grove 🅛
40 Kingston Road, TA2 7SE
✪ 2-midnight; 12-11 Sat ☎ (01823) 283444
⊕ thegrovetaunton.co.uk
Exmoor Ale; St Austell Proper Job; guest beers Ⓗ
True community local, near the railway station, serving a selection of local ales plus cider in summer. It is home to football, skittles, darts and pool teams, and has a lively atmosphere, especially on football and music nights, but is quieter at the back where the old stable yard has been converted to a patio. Food is served on Wednesday quiz nights and Sunday lunchtimes, when the pub can be busy. CAMRA members receive a discount on real ale. 🏵️🚲♣🕊️☒(25,28)

Racehorse
157 East Reach, TA1 3HT
✪ 12-4, 6-11 (midnight Thu); 12-12.30am Fri & Sat; 12-11 Sun ☎ (01823) 327513
St Austell Trelawney, Tribute, Proper Job Ⓗ
Friendly pub close to the town centre at the top of East Reach. Multi-roomed with front and rear bars, as well as a small lounge with comfortable seating, it has two further drinking areas and a large walled beer garden. It is a popular meeting place and is good for conversation and atmosphere. The walls are adorned with various pieces of memorabilia such as old tin signs and musical instruments. No food is served, but there is regular live music.
🏵️🍴♣🕊️☒

Wyvern Club 🅛
Mountfields Road, TA1 3BJ (off South Road, approx 1 mile from town centre)
✪ 6.30 (5.30 Sat)-11; 12-3, 7-10.30 Sun ☎ (01823) 284591
⊕ wyvernclub.co.uk
Exmoor Ale; guest beers Ⓗ
Large, busy sport and social club, home to cricket, rugby and squash teams. It offers a variety of West Country beers, with guest ales changing frequently – beers from three different breweries are usually on offer, at club prices. Meals are served each evening until 9pm, plus Sunday lunchtime. The premises are available for daytime meetings and evening functions. Show this Guide or your CAMRA membership card to be signed in as a guest. A real ale festival is held in October. Children welcome.
🏵️🏵️◑🚲♣P☒(1A,99)

Trull

Winchester Arms
Church Road, TA3 7LG
✪ 12-3, 6.30-11 (10.30 Sun) ☎ (01823) 284723
⊕ winchesterarmstrull.co.uk
St Austell Tribute; guest beers Ⓗ
Thriving family-run community pub on the outskirts of Taunton near the Blackdown Hills. The comfortable bar area is separated from the long dining area by an impressive coal-effect fireplace. Three ales are mainly from South West breweries. Real cider is served in summer only. The locally sourced home-cooked food is excellent (booking is advised at popular times). The streamside gardens, perfect for family and dogs, are the venue for entertainment and barbecues. The pub offers good-value accommodation.
Q🏵️🛏️◑♣P🕊️☒(97)

Wanstrow

Pub
Station Road, BA4 4SZ ST711416
✪ 6.30-11 Mon; 12-2.30, 6-11; 12-2.30, 7-11 Sun ☎ (01749) 850455
Draught Bass; Blindman's Golden Spring; guest beers Ⓗ
An absolute gem, this friendly village local has a lounge bar with an open fire and flagstone floors that leads to a small restaurant. The pub serves two regular and two guest beers, sourced from almost anywhere, along with ciders from Thatchers and Rich's. Games include skittles, bar billiards and ring the bull. A small but imaginative menu is offered and all food is home cooked. The pub is not open Monday lunchtimes. 🏛️Q🏵️◑🍴♣🐾P

Washford

White Horse Inn
TA23 0JZ (off A39)
✪ 12-11 ☎ (01984) 640415 ⊕ exmoorpubs.co.uk
Beer range varies Ⓗ
Riverside free house only 500 yards from the ruins of Cleve Abbey, an ideal base for visits to the coast, Exmoor National Park, Quantock Hills and the nearby Torre Cider Farm. The inn dates back to 1709 and you can relax on the riverside balcony in summer or by roaring log fires in winter. The food includes locally sourced produce where possible. There is en-suite accommodation available. Voted Pub of the Year by the local press in 2012.
≙Q⊛⇆◖ᐧ♿♣♠P⌂-⊟(18,28)

Watchet

Esplanade Club Ⓛ
The Esplanade, TA23 0AJ (opp marina)
✪ 12-3 (Sun only), 7-midnight ☎ (01984) 634518
Beer range varies Ⓗ
Somerset CAMRA Club of the Year 2011 and 2012, with splendid views over the marina and Bristol Channel. Displaying old photographs and memorabilia, it was built in the 1860s as a sail-making factory but has been a club since the 1930s. Live entertainment features every weekend, with folk and open mic nights during the week. It is a short walk from the West Somerset Railway. Visitors showing this Guide or a CAMRA membership card are welcome. Also home to the boat-owners' club. ♿▲⇚♣♠⌂-⊟(14,18,28)

Star Inn Ⓛ
Mill Lane, TA23 0BZ
✪ 12-3.30 (4 Sun), 6.30-midnight ☎ (01984) 631367
⊕ thestarinnwatchet.co.uk
Beer range varies Ⓗ
Twice Somerset CAMRA Pub of the Year, the Star offers four changing beers from local and regional breweries in a cosy main bar, with small side rooms and a large garden. Mouthwatering food, including seafood, is locally sourced. There are quiz, darts and boules teams and the infamous Sunday Bad Boys Club. Port and cheese nights and beer trips are run. The Star is near the marina and the West Somerset Railway, and handy for the Quantock Hills. Dogs welcome.
≙⊛◖▲⇚♣♠⌂-⊟(14,18,28)

Wedmore

New Inn Ⓛ
Combe Batch, BS28 4DU
✪ 12-2.30 (not Mon), 5-midnight; 12-2am Fri; 12-1am Sat; 12-10.30 Sun ☎ (01934) 712099
Butcombe Bitter; guest beers Ⓗ
This traditional village inn is the centre for many local events including the famous annual turnip prize, conkers, spoof, penny chuffin' and apple bobbin'. The public bar, lounge and dining areas are complemented by beer gardens to the front and rear. A chalkboard lists forthcoming ales, mainly from the West Country, all served from three handpumps. Traditional, good-value, home-cooked food is served. There is a skittle alley/function room, and darts and skittles teams compete in the winter months.
Q⊛◖▲♣P⌂-⊟(668,670)

Wells

Full Moon
42 Southover, BA5 1UH ST5445
✪ 11-11 (midnight Fri & Sat); 12-10.30 Sun
☎ (01749) 675592
Cheddar Potholer; Moles Best; guest beers Ⓗ
Friendly locals' free house, reopened in 2012 following major refurbishment by its new landlords. The interior of the pub comprises a public bar with TV sport and jukebox and a quieter lounge area, which is divided between the bar, a snug-like area and a section suitable for dining. Out back is the city's largest pub courtyard and a beer garden beyond. The two guest beers are mainly sourced from local micros. Thatchers Traditional cider is served. Family and dog friendly.
≙⊛◖⇆♿▲♣♠⌂-⊟

West Chinnock

Muddled Man Ⓛ
Lower Street, TA18 7PT
✪ 11-2.30, 7-midnight; 11-midnight Fri & Sat; 12-11 Sun
☎ (01935) 881235
Beer range varies Ⓗ
Well worth seeking out, this cosy free house has been run by the same friendly family for over 13 years, serving a good range of West Country ales via three handpulls. Reasonably priced and locally sourced home-cooked food is on offer. Sunday lunch should be booked in advance due to demand. Dogs are welcome and the skittle alley can be booked for meetings or functions. Local charities are well supported. Many lager drinkers have been converted to real ale at this establishment. ≙Q⊱⊛◖♿♣♠⌂-

West Huntspill

Crossways Inn ♛ Ⓛ
Withy Road, TA9 3RA (on A38)
✪ 12-midnight (11.30 Sun) ☎ (01278) 783756
⊕ crosswaysinn.com
Exmoor Ale; RCH PG Steam; guest beers Ⓗ
Somerset CAMRA Pub of the Year 2013, this 17th-century inn offers up to six real ales including guest beers. It has several bar areas, two fireplaces with log fires during the winter, and an outside fireplace to keep smokers warm. There is also a dining room and skittle alley that can be used as a function room, plus outside areas front and back. An extensive food menu is offered plus a specials board, and breakfast is served 7.30-11am. Seven en-suite rooms are available.
≙⊛⇆◖♿▲♣♠P⌂-⊟(15,21)

Weston-super-Mare

Cabot Court Hotel
Knightstone Road, BS23 2AH (on seafront)
✪ 9am-midnight (1am Fri; 2am Sat) ☎ (01934) 427930
Greene King Abbot; Ruddles Best Bitter; guest beers Ⓗ
Large Wetherspoon conversion on the seafront between the Grand Pier and the Winter Gardens, opened in 2011. On four levels, each has a distinctive style. There are bars on the ground and second floors – note that different guest ales appear in each. The first floor Winter Gardens room is particularly comfortable, with sofas and a real fire in winter, and is a haven from the TVs and

speakers in the other rooms. Local breweries are supported, with Exmoor and Great Western breweries often featured. It has 21 letting rooms. ▲▲Q⛅☆⌂◑⅊⚞≒●²─₪

Criterion

45 Upper Church Road, BS23 2DY

✪ 12-midnight (1am Fri & Sat); 12-10.30 Sun ☎ 07527 425795

Courage Directors; St Austell Tribute; guest beers Ⓗ

Genuine free house and traditional community pub, just off the seafront in the Knightstone area. Believed to be one of the oldest pubs in town, it has interesting local photos on the walls. Pub games feature strongly, with darts, bar billiards and table skittles, plus a quiz on Tuesday. Bar snacks are served, with filled rolls at lunchtime. Two guest beers are offered, with all beer styles and local breweries well supported. Thatchers cider is often served, but is sometimes replaced by another. ▲▲♣●₪(1)

Off the Rails

Station Approach, BS23 1XY (on station concourse)

✪ 7am (9am Sun)-11 ☎ (01934) 415109

Beer range varies Ⓗ

A genuine free house, conveniently situated at the railway station, which is also the station buffet. Two changing beers are served, often – but not always – from West Country microbreweries, plus two local ciders from Rich's and Thatchers. The landlord is happy to receive suggestions from his regulars on which beers to stock. Two-pint carry-out containers are a handy feature for train travellers. Three TVs show sporting events, often silently. Quiz night is Tuesday and there is a free jukebox. Dogs are welcome. ▲≒♣●₪(112,126)

Waverley

69 Severn Road, BS23 1DR

✪ 12-11

Greene King Abbot; St Austell Tribute; guest beers Ⓗ

Genuine old-fashioned community free house in an area with few pubs, to the south of the town centre but walkable from the station. Two guest beers are usually on, including some of the more unusual ales. Thatchers ciders are served. A weekly quiz features, as does live music some weekends in what is known as the Brig, a former air raid shelter (and chapel of rest) to the rear. It also stages a regular farmers' market. Food is limited to basic snacks. ☆≒●²─₪(7)

Williton

Mason's Arms

2 North Road, TA4 4SN

✪ 11-2.30, 6-11; 12-3, 7-10.30 Sun ☎ (01984) 639200 ⊕ themasonsarms.com

Sharp's Doom Bar; Skinner's Betty Stogs; guest beers Ⓗ

Thatched 16th-century pub with oak beams throughout, with a reputation for good real ales, cider and locally sourced food. The pub hosts quiz teams and is in the local boules league. It has a pleasant beer garden where locals and visitors alike sit and relax. Rich's draught cider is always available and the beers tend to be from Devon or Cornwall breweries. Accommodation is in an outside annexe with five en-suite rooms. ☆⌂◑⅊≒●²─₪(14,18,28)

Wincanton

Nog Inn

South Street, BA9 9DL (50yds from market square)

✪ 10.30-11 (midnight Fri & Sat); 12-11 Sun ☎ (01963) 32998 ⊕ thenoginn.com

Otter Bitter; Sharp's Own; guest beers Ⓗ

Tucked away a short distance from the market square, this attractive listed pub with a striking Georgian façade fronts a long, narrow building, with parts dating back to the 16th century. A secluded sunny garden with covered seating is at the rear of the property. Regular open mic and comedy nights take place. The guest ales are often seasonal, with continental draught beers and real ciders always available. CAMRA members receive a discount on real ale. CAMRA Regional Pub of the Year 2011. ▲▲Q☆◑⅊♣●²─₪(58)

Wiveliscombe

Bear Inn Ⓛ

10 North Street, TA4 2JY

✪ 11-11 (midnight Thu-Sat); 12-11 Sun ☎ (01984) 623537 ⊕ thebearwiveliscombe.co.uk

Otter Amber; Sharp's Doom Bar; guest beers Ⓗ

Family-run community pub in the centre of town. Wiveliscombe has a long tradition of brewing and currently boasts two breweries, Cotleigh and Exmoor, both of which are within walking distance of the Bear, and their beers feature regularly as guest ales. An extensive menu offers good-value meals using local produce where possible. Located on the edge of the Brendon Hills and within easy reach of Exmoor, the pub is a good base for exploring these scenic areas. ▲▲⛅☆⌂◑⅊♣P²─₪(25)

Yeovil

Butchers Arms

13 Hendford, BA20 1TQ

✪ 11 (12 Sun)-midnight ☎ (01935) 476576

Beer range varies Ⓗ

Pleasant, friendly local on the fringe of the town centre, recently revitalised by experienced licensees after a difficult few years. The single L-shaped bar has a real fire. The beers are supplied by Dorset Brewing Company and include its own range plus guests from around the country. Good-value, simple pub grub is available at all sessions. Live music plays every Friday night. The cider is Westons Old Rosie. A welcome addition to Yeovil's real ale scene. ▲▲☆◑♣●²─₪

Quicksilver Mail

168 Hendford Hill, BA20 2RG (at jct of A30 and A37)

✪ 11-midnight; 12-11 Sun ☎ (01935) 424721 ⊕ quicksilvermail.com

Adnams Broadside; Butcombe Bitter; St Austell Tribute Ⓗ

A friendly, comfortable 18th-century hostelry beside a roundabout. The pub's name, unique in Britain, commemorates a high-speed mail coach. There is a large single bar and a separate lower-level dining area. Interesting photographs of the building and sporting memorabilia decorate the walls, and an old pub sign is also on display. Excellent food is served including the home-cooked Sunday lunch, and curry and steak nights are popular. The large function room hosts regular live music. ☆⌂◑♣●²─₪(47,99)

STAFFORDSHIRE

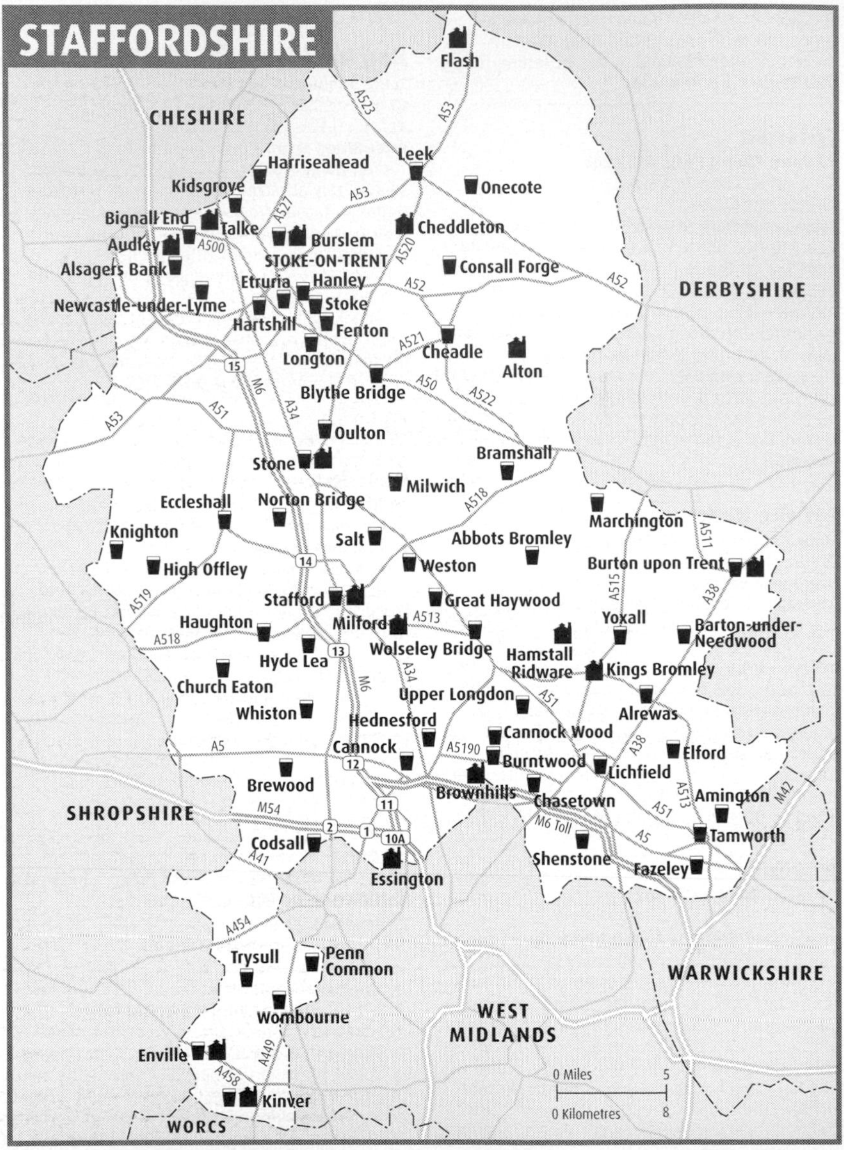
CHESHIRE
DERBYSHIRE
SHROPSHIRE
WARWICKSHIRE
WEST MIDLANDS
WORCS
Flash
Leek
Onecote
Harriseahead
Kidsgrove
Bignall End
Talke
Audley
Alsagers Bank
Burslem
STOKE-ON-TRENT
Cheddleton
Consall Forge
Etruria
Hanley
Newcastle-under-Lyme
Stoke
Hartshill
Fenton
Longton
Cheadle
Alton
Blythe Bridge
Oulton
Bramshall
Stone
Milwich
Eccleshall
Norton Bridge
Marchington
Knighton
Salt
Abbots Bromley
High Offley
Weston
Burton upon Trent
Stafford
Great Haywood
Yoxall
Haughton
Milford
Barton-under-Needwood
Wolseley Bridge
Hamstall Ridware
Hyde Lea
Kings Bromley
Church Eaton
Upper Longdon
Whiston
Alrewas
Hednesford
Cannock Wood
Cannock
Elford
Burntwood
Lichfield
Brewood
Brownhills
Chasetown
Amington
Tamworth
Codsall
Shenstone
Fazeley
Essington
Trysull
Penn Common
Wombourne
Enville
Kinver
A523
A53
A527
A500
A520
A52
A521
A50
A522
A34
A51
M6
A518
A519
A513
A515
A511
A38
A5
A5190
M54
A41
M6 Toll
M42
A454
A449
A458
15
14
13
12
11
10A
2
1
0 Miles 5
0 Kilometres 8

Abbots Bromley

Coach & Horses

High Street, WS15 3BN (on B5014, at E end of village)
12-2.30 (not Mon), 5.30-midnight; 12-midnight Sun
☎ (01283) 840256 coachandhorsesabbotsbromley.co.uk
Marston's Pedigree; St Austell Tribute; guest beer Ⓗ
Grade II-listed coaching inn dating back to 1745, although the building is even older, with links to Burton Abbey. The interior has recently been substantially refurbished, the extended bar retaining some old wooden beams and an assortment of memorabilia. Beyond the bar is a large dining area; the pub is gaining a reputation for fine home-cooked food. Occasional live music can be enjoyed. Abbots Bromley is famous for its annual Horn Dance, an ancient ritual that takes place every year in September, attracting visitors from around the world. Q❀◑♣P(428)

Alrewas

George & Dragon

120 Main Street, DE13 7AE (centre of village)
11 (12 Sun)-11 ☎ (01283) 791476
georgeanddragonalrewas.co.uk
Banks's Bitter; Jennings Cumberland Ale; Marston's Burton Bitter, Pedigree; guest beer Ⓗ
Imposing three-storey village local, thought to be a former coaching inn and dating back to the early 1700s. The comfortable main bar area is split into three distinct sections, and there is a separate lounge/dining room to one side (no meals served Sun eve). There is monthly live musical entertainment (check website). The Trent & Mersey Canal runs along the edge of the village, about 300 yards distant, and the National Memorial Arboretum is a mile to the east.
❀◑♿▲♣P(7,7E)

Alsagers Bank

Gresley Arms ⌊
High Street, ST7 8BQ (on B5367)
✪ 12 (3 Mon-Wed)-11 ☎ (01782) 722469
⊕ gresleyarms.co.uk
Beer range varies Ⓗ
Sat at the top of Alsagers Bank, with breathtaking views from the garden and dining room, the pub is perfect for a well-earned pint after a walk in the nearby Bateswood or Apedale country parks. The pub has four rooms, with 200-year-old beams and a real fire in the bar. Eight real ales and four real ciders, plus a range of imported bottled beers, are served. Bass, Three Tuns and Abbeydale beers appear regularly.
🏔🛏🏠◑⌟🅑🚻♣♠🅟⌐🚲(94,94A)

Amington

Gate Inn
Tamworth Road, B77 3BY
✪ 11-11 ☎ (01827) 63189 ⊕ gatepubtamworth.co.uk
Marston's Pedigree; guest beers Ⓗ
Pleasant multi-level canalside alehouse, popular with locals all year round and with boaters during the summer. Five or more guest beers from the Marston's list are served. The small bar room is accessed from the bottom of the lounge. Outside are a raised beer terrace and children's play area. A good-value lunchtime and evening menu is offered. It can get busy at weekends, with karaoke every second and fourth Sunday of the month, and open mic every first Sunday. Tuesday is quiz night.
🛏🏠◑⌟🅑🅟🚲(5,785)

Barton-under-Needwood

Royal Oak ♈
74 The Green, DE13 8JD (½ mile from B5016)
✪ 12-midnight (1am Fri & Sat; 11 Sun) ☎ (01283) 713852
Marston's Pedigree; guest beers Ⓗ/🄶
Bustling community local on the southern edge of the village, home to many traditional pub games teams and an over-40s football team. While parts of the building date back to the 16th century, the pub has existed only since the mid-1800s. Public bar and lounge customers are served from a central sunken bar, its floor being below the level of the rest of the ground floor. Beers are available on handpump, or by gravity direct from the cask, on request. 🏔Q🛏🏠🚻♣🅟⌐🚲(7,7A,7E)

Bignall End

Bignall End Cricket Club
Boon Hill, ST7 8LA (400yds from B5500)
✪ 7 (12 Fri-Sun)-midnight ☎ (01782) 720514
⊕ bignallend.play-cricket.com
Beer range varies Ⓗ
Friendly club now run like a pub, with everybody welcome. It has lovely views over the Cheshire Plain, where you can easily see Wales on a good day. The lively bar has sport on TV and there is a snooker room, plus an upstairs function room where excellent summer and winter beer festivals are held. The club has several cricket teams, plus two football teams. The bar serves three or four varying beers, usually from small, interesting brewers. There is outside sheltered seating overlooking the cricket pitch. ♿🅟⌐🚲(34)

Swan
58 Chapel Street, ST7 8QD (just off B5500 ½ mile E of Audley)
✪ 12-11 (10.30 Sun) ☎ (01782) 720622
⊕ theswaninn-stoke.co.uk
Draught Bass; Marston's Pedigree; Oakham Citra; guest beers Ⓗ
Good two-room local down a side street in the sleepy village of Bignall End, with a traditional bar and quiet lounge, plus a pleasant garden area complete with barbecue at the rear. Darts and dominoes teams, TV and real fires all feature here; good-quality food is also available. Paul and Linda continue to maintain the reputation of this award-winning pub, which offers four varied guest beers and four real ciders, all served in a convivial atmosphere. 🏔🏠🚻♣♠⌐🚲(34)

Blythe Bridge

One Legged Shunter ⌊
Caverswall Road, ST11 9BG (from Blythe Bridge follow directions to Foxfield Railway)
✪ closed Mon-Thu; 6.30-11 Fri; 11 (6.30 Oct-Easter)-11 Sat & Sun ⊕ foxfieldrailway.co.uk
Titanic Plum Porter; guest beers Ⓗ
The pub is part of Caverswall station on the Foxfield Light Railway (see website for details of train season), a small one-roomed affair with a traditional pot-bellied stove roaring away in winter. Three guest beers are available, sourced from local breweries. The pub also has its own train-themed labelled bottled beers. There is always a friendly welcome at the One Legged Shunter (children permitted until 9pm). Meals are available at the Railway café next door.
Q🛏♿🚂♠🅟⌐🚲(6B,6C,X50)

Bramshall

Old Bramshall Inn ⌊
Stone Road, ST14 5BG
✪ 12-midnight ☎ (01889) 565566 ⊕ bramshallinn.co.uk
Marston's Pedigree; Sharp's Doom Bar; Taylor Landlord; guest beers Ⓗ
Whether it be a drink with friends (and everyone at the pub is a friend), a light snack at lunchtime or a

INDEPENDENT BREWERIES
Beowulf Brownhills
Black Hole Burton upon Trent
Blythe Hamstall Ridware
Burton Bridge Burton upon Trent
Burton Old Cottage Burton upon Trent
Enville Enville
Flash Flash
Gates Burton Burton upon Trent
Kinver Kinver
Lymestone Stone
Marston's Burton upon Trent
Morton Essington
Peakstones Rock Alton
Quartz Kings Bromley
Shugborough Milford
Slater's Stafford
Staffordshire Cheddleton
Talke O' Th' Hill Talke (NEW)
Titanic Burslem
Tower Burton upon Trent
Townhouse Audley
Worthington's (Molson Coors) Burton upon Trent

full evening à la carte meal, the Old Bramshall Inn provides it all with warmth and friendliness. There are five handpumps on the bar, with beers from local breweries like Slater's and Titanic always available. Food is high quality and locally sourced wherever possible, served lunchtimes and evenings (12-6pm Sun). A Titanic Pub of Excellence. ♨ᕼ⑂⑂❶◗ᵬ♣P'⊟

Brewood

Swan Hotel ⓛ
15 Market Place, ST19 9BS
⊛ 11.45-midnight ☎ (01902) 850330
Caledonian Deuchars IPA; Courage Directors;
Theakston Black Bull Bitter; Wye Valley HPA; guest
beers ⊞
A regular CAMRA award winner, this old central village coaching inn, with low-beamed ceilings and seasonal log fires, is five minutes' walk from the Shropshire Union Canal and the Staffordshire Way. Cosy snugs displaying early prints of the area flank the central bar and there is a traditional skittle alley upstairs. Three of the six handpumps feature LocAles and there is a selection of over 70 malt whiskies. Baguettes are available lunchtimes and afternoons. ♨Q⑂ᵬ♣P'⊟(76,878)

Burntwood

Drill Inn
33 Springlestyche Lane, WS7 9HD (left off northbound Rugeley Road out of Burntwood) SK061101
⊛ 12-midnight (10.30 Sun) ☎ (01543) 675799
⊕ drillinnburntwood.co.uk
Beer range varies ⊞
Vibrant and friendly pub, tucked away down a country lane. The homely, sprawling main room is partnered by a snug. Three constantly changing ales are offered, plus occasional beer festivals. There is a large elevated beer garden to the rear, plus a children's play area; well-behaved children are welcome at all times. Good food is a draw here, supplemented by themed dining nights (no food Mon). There is live music on Friday evenings, usually a solo singer. ♨Qᕼ⑂❶◗ A♣P'⊟

White Swan
2 Cannock Road, WS7 0BJ
⊛ 4.30-11; 4-11.30 Fri; 12-11.30 Sat; 12-11 Sun
☎ (01543) 670555
Adnams Southwold Bitter; Greene King Abbot; Taylor
Landlord; guest beers ⊞
Busy ale-led community pub with a predominantly local clientele, but visitors and passing trade get a friendly welcome. The main room is a comfortable lounge, with a smaller room to the rear for games and meetings. Two changing guest beers are usually on offer, mostly through the SIBA list. A regular bus service from Lichfield stops a few yards from the pub. ᕼ⑂♣●P'⊟(60)

Burton upon Trent

Albion
245 Shobnall Road, DE14 2BE (on B5017)
⊛ 11-11; 11.30-10.30 Sun ☎ (01283) 568197
⊕ albionpubburtonontrent.co.uk
Marston's Pedigree; guest beers ⊞
Imposing, multi-gabled, 19th-century pub, formerly a hotel, named after the nearby Marston's Albion Brewery. The smartly furnished interior is

open plan, with several linked areas featuring numerous framed pictures, old local photographs, posters and advertisements. There is a large function room upstairs, plus a conservatory overlooking the garden which incorporates a children's play area. An extensive menu of hot meals and snacks, with 2-for-1 offers, is available all day; traditional roasts are served Sunday lunchtime. Quiz night is Wednesday.
ᕼ⑂❶◗ᵬP'⊟(10)

Burton Bridge Inn
24 Bridge Street, DE14 1SY (town end of Trent Bridge)
⊛ 12-2.30, 5-11; 11.30-11.30 Fri & Sat; 12-3, 7-11 Sun
☎ (01283) 536596 ⊕ burtonbridgeinn.co.uk
Burton Bridge Golden Delicious, Sovereign Gold,
Bridge Bitter, Burton Porter, Festival Ale, seasonal
beer; guest beer ⊞
This 17th-century pub is the flagship of the Burton Bridge Brewery estate and fronts the brewery itself. It incorporates two rooms served from a central bar: a smaller front room, with wooden pews and displaying many awards and brewery memorabilia, and a back room featuring oak beams and panels. The beer range is supplemented by a selection of malt whiskies and fruit wines. A small dining/function room and a skittle alley are upstairs and available for hire. No lunches Sunday. ♨Qᕼ❶♣'⊟

Coopers Tavern ★
43 Cross Street, DE14 1EG (off Station St)
⊛ 5 (12 Thu)-11; 12-11.30 Fri & Sat; 12-11 Sun
☎ (01283) 532551 ⊕ cooperstavern.co.uk
Draught Bass ⑤; Joule's Blonde, Original Pale Ale,
Slumbering Monk ⊞; guest beers ⊞/⑤
Classic, unspoilt 19th-century ale house, once the Bass Brewery tap and now part of the Joule's estate. The intimate inner taproom has barrel tables and bench seating, where the beer is served from a small counter by the cask stillage. The more comfortable lounge leads to a third small room. CAMRA regional Cider Pub of the Year in 2011, up to four varying ciders/perries are sold, plus fruit wines. Local folk musicians meet here on Tuesday evenings, and live music features some weekends.
♨Qᕼ⑁∗●'⊟

Devonshire Arms
86 Station Street, DE14 1BT
⊛ 12-3 (not Mon), 5-11; 12-11 Fri & Sat; 12-3, 7-11 Sun
☎ (01283) 562392 ⊕ thedevonshire.co.uk
Burton Bridge Golden Delicious, Bridge Bitter,
Damson Porter, Stairway to Heaven, Festival Ale;
guest beer ⊞
Popular old pub, dating from the 19th-century and Grade II-listed, and one of the six Burton Bridge Brewery hostelries in the area. It comprises a public bar at the front, and a larger, more comfortable, split-level lounge to the rear. Note the 1853 map of Burton, old photographs, and unusual arched wooden ceilings. An enclosed rear patio features flower borders and hanging baskets. Some continental bottled beers and English fruit wines are also stocked. Lunches are served Tuesday-Saturday only. ♨ᕼ❶⑁≉♣P'⊟

Elms Inn
36 Stapenhill Road, DE15 9AE (on A444)
⊛ 12-11.30 (midnight Fri & Sat); 12-11 Sun
☎ (01283) 535505 ⊕ the-elms-burton.co.uk
Draught Bass; Marston's Pedigree; guest beers ⊞

Lively local on the opposite bank of the River Trent from the town centre. Built as a private house in the late 19th century, this is one of Burton's original parlour pubs. With sensitive renovation, the small public bar and snug on either side of the bar, plus a side room served through a hatch, are largely unchanged. In contrast, the lounge to the rear has been extended and renovated in a more modern style. Meals are available until 7pm (3pm Sun). ▲Q✿◑🍴♣✱–🖵(18)

National Brewery Centre (Brewery Tap)

Horninglow Street, DE14 1NG (on A511, at Guild St jct)
✿ 11-11 (6 Mon & Tue); 12-6 Sun ☎ (01283) 532880
⊕ nationalbrewerycentre.co.uk
Sharp's Doom Bar; Worthington's Red Shield, E, White Shield, seasonal beer; guest beer Ⓗ
Formerly the Bass Museum/Coors Visitor Centre, the associated Brewery Tap showcases beers from the new William Worthington's Brewery, including the seasonal Shield beers. While the comfortable single-room bar still features an illuminated ice-block-look bar counter with chrome fonts and handpumps, the decor was toned down in a 2007 refurbishment. Food is served in the bar and the adjacent restaurant, while an L-shaped conservatory overlooks the garden and children's play area. The NBC organises numerous events – details on website. ☜✿◑🚃♿P'–🖵(1)

Old Cottage Tavern

36 Byrkley Street, DE14 2EG (behind town hall)
✿ 12 (11.30 Sun)-11 ☎ (01283) 511615
Burton Old Cottage Oak Ale, Stout, Halcyon Daze; guest beers Ⓗ
No longer owned by the brewery but leased from the Tadcaster Pub Company, this traditional local continues to operate as the Burton Old Cottage Brewery tap. The public bar at the front, with a cosy snug to one side, and the wood-panelled lounge to the rear, are served from a central bar. There is also a games/function room (with demountable skittle alley) upstairs. Guest beers are usually from other SIBA members. The Brewtown Folk Club and Spoken Word events are held here. ▲Q☜✿🚃◑🍴♣✱–🖵

Roebuck Inn

101 Station Street, DE14 1BT (corner of jct with Mosley St)
✿ 12-midnight (1am Fri & Sat) ☎ (01283) 511213
Draught Bass; Draught Burton Ale; Greene King Abbot; Marston's Pedigree; guest beer Ⓗ
Friendly Victorian corner-terrace pub near the railway station, once the Ind Coope Brewery tap, situated opposite the former brewery. Draught Burton Ale was launched here in 1976. Inside, there is a long narrow single room with dark wood panelling and the bar counter down one side. A small patio at the rear is available for outdoor drinking, plus a few tables and chairs outside at the front in summer. Live music is played early Sunday evenings. ▲✿🚃🚃♣✱–🖵

Cannock

Crystal Fountain ★

35 St Johns Road, WS11 0AL (jct of Avon Rd)
✿ 12-midnight ☎ (01543) 574812
Black Country Bradley's Finest Golden, Pig on the Wall, Fireside; guest beers Ⓗ

Neo-Georgian-style pub reopened in 2012 by Black Country Inns, serving its beers and guests alongside a real cider. Identified by CAMRA as one of Britain's Best Real Heritage Pubs, it is well worth a visit for its Art Deco interior. Look out for the dumb waiter behind the bar. Regular open mic nights take place along with entertainment on the last Saturday of the month. Family and pet friendly, there is a garden at the rear. ▲☜✿🚃◑🍴P

Linford Arms

79 High Street, WS11 1BN (near main bus station)
✿ 8-midnight (1am Fri & Sat) ☎ (01543) 469360
Greene King Abbot; Ruddles Best Bitter; guest beers Ⓗ
A Wetherspoon pub on two levels in an ideal town-centre location and handy for the main bus station. Up to eight real ales are sold including guests from local breweries. Historic photographs and prints of local interest decorate the walls. The pub's name comes from the builders' merchants who formerly occupied the premises. It can get very lively and bustling at weekends although there are some quieter areas away from the main bar. ☜◑♿🚃♣'–🖵

Cannock Wood

Park Gate Inn

Park Gate Road, WS15 4RN SK045126
✿ 11-11 (midnight Fri & Sat) ☎ (01543) 682223
⊕ theparkgate.co.uk
Holden's Golden Glow; St Austell Tribute; Sharp's Doom Bar; guest beer Ⓗ
Sitting on the southern edge of Cannock Chase forest, the Park Gate satisfies both drinkers and diners. The rustic bar is popular with walkers and often has a friendly dog population. A central wood-burning stove has two cosy alcoves either side. The separate dining rooms enjoy pleasant garden views, with reasonably priced food served. The garden features a well and a children's play area. The nearby Castle Ring, an Iron Age hill fort, offers excellent views. ▲☜✿◑🍴P

Chasetown

Uxbridge Arms

2 Church Street, WS7 3QL SK045080
✿ 12-midnight (1am Fri & Sat) ☎ (01543) 677852
Beer range varies Ⓗ
The five ales are forever changing in this Guide regular, as evidenced by the carefully categorised pumpclip collection. A wide range of country wines and malt whiskies is available, plus a constantly changing real cider. Sport is popular here, with bowls, darts and football teams. Chasewater Country Park and the associated heritage railway are close by. Good food is available in the lounge and upstairs restaurant (no food Sun eve). Dogs are welcome in the bar. Q✿◑🍴♣🐾P'–🖵

Cheadle

Huntsman 🅛

The Green, ST10 1XS
✿ 12-midnight ☎ (01538) 750502
⊕ thehuntsmancheadle.com
Joule's Slumbering Monk; Marston's Pedigree; Titanic Iceberg; guest beers Ⓗ
A 15-minute walk from Cheadle town centre, this is an excellent, friendly pub run by two local CAMRA

members. The three regular beers are complemented by three guest ales, one of which will always come from the local Peakstones Rock brewery. A beer festival is staged at the end of May in a tent in the beer garden, and the pub has hosted archaeological digs.
🏚🐕🍴🛏🍺&♣☕P⌐🖳(7A)

Church Eaton

Royal Oak ℓ
High Street, ST20 0AJ (centre of village signed from A518 at Haughton) SJ932019
✪ 5 (12 Sat)-11; 12-9 Sun ☎ (01785) 823078
⊕ theroyaloakchurcheaton.co.uk
Banks's Bitter; guest beers ℍ
Once threatened with closure, but saved by a local consortium, the Royal Oak is now a thriving pub at the centre of the community. The interior is split into a lounge area, a restaurant and an area with a dartboard, pool table and TV. Many of the guest beers are sourced from local breweries, and the restaurant is noted for its good food. The pub is about a mile north-east of the Shropshire Union Canal at High Onn Bridge.
🏚Q🐕🍴🛏&🅰♣P⌐🖳(482)

Codsall

Codsall Station ☗ ℓ
Chapel Lane, WV8 2EJ
✪ 11.30-2.30, 5-11; 11.30-11.30 Fri & Sat; 12-10.30 Sun
☎ (01902) 847061
Holden's Black Country Mild, Black Country Bitter, Golden Glow, Special; guest beers ℍ
Sensitively converted from the waiting room, offices and stationmaster's house, the Grade II-listed building now comprises a bar, lounge, snug and conservatory and displays worldwide railway memorabilia. A raised terrace overlooks the working platforms. Bar meals are available all week except Sunday, when sandwiches only are served until 5pm. Two guest beers are available and the mild is often replaced by Holden's Old Ale in winter. Beer festivals are held in May and the weekend after the August bank holiday.
🏚Q🍴🛏&⇌P⌐🖳(5,88)

Firs Club ℓ
Station Road, WV8 1BX (entrance along drive from shared Co-op car park)
✪ 7.30-11 (midnight Fri); 12-5, 7.30-midnight Sat; 12-5, 7.30-11 Sun ☎ (01902) 844674 ⊕ firsatcodsall.co.uk
Banks's Mild, Bitter ℙ; guest beers ℍ
Formerly the Conservative Club, it has a bar area, lounge and a sports lounge with a pool table, dartboard and card table. Interesting photos of old Codsall and surrounding areas are displayed around the club. Up to three guest ales are served, often from local breweries, and a beer festival is held in November. A large function room is available for hire. Show this Guide or a CAMRA membership card to be signed in. Q🍴&⇌♣P⌐🖳(5,88)

Consall Forge

Black Lion ℓ
ST9 0AJ (off A522 follow signs to Consall Gardens then Nature Reserve on hairpin bend, go straight on, ignore no vehicular access sign, bottom of hill, left along track to car park)

✪ 12-11 (10.30 Sun) ☎ (01782) 550294
⊕ blacklionpub.co.uk
Peakstones Rock Black Hole; guest beers ℍ
By foot, car, boat or steam train, seek out this rural gem in the Churnet Valley, a genuine free house with nine handpumps, complete with a varied and extensive range of beers and ciders. There is a good-sized beer garden outside which can get quite busy at times. The pub grub comes in ample portions and beer festivals are held every February and July, plus regular hog roasts and live entertainment. Not the easiest pub to find, but worth it. 🏚Q🐕🍴🛏🅰⇌♣☕P⌐

Eccleshall

Bell Inn ℓ
16 High Street, ST21 6BZ
✪ 11-12.30am; 12-midnight Sun ☎ (01785) 850378
⊕ thebelleccleshall.com
Banks's Bitter; Black Sheep Best Bitter; Brakspear Bitter; Holden's Black Country Mild, Black Country Bitter; Marston's Pedigree; guest beers ℍ
A busy pub in the centre of this small market town, now a firm favourite with regulars from far and wide. This former coaching inn has a multi-room layout. The number of handpulls has increased with an alteration of the bar layout. The pub hosts regular beer festivals throughout the year together with Thursday night quizzes and live music, mainly on Sundays. 🏚🐕🍴🛏🍺&♣P⌐🖳(350,432)

Royal Oak ℓ
25 High Street, ST21 6BW
✪ 11-11 (midnight Fri & Sat); 12-11 Sun ☎ (01785) 859065
⊕ royaloakeccleshall.co.uk
Joule's Blonde, Original Pale Ale, Slumbering Monk ℍ
Fully refurbished by Joule's of Market Drayton, featuring light oak and specially commissioned stained glass windows and panels. Portraits of past generations of the Joule's family adorn the walls together with old brewery advertisements. Sir Geoff Hurst, of the 1966 World Cup winning team, ran the pub when he retired from football. The first-floor upgrading to meeting and function rooms has now been completed. A welcome addition to the local real ale scene.
🏚Q🐕🍴🍺&P⌐🖳(350,432)

Star Inn ℓ
Copmere End, ST21 6EW (leave Eccleshall on the B5026, turn left at the sign for Copmere End and follow the road, pub is on crossroads)
✪ closed Mon; 12-3, 6-11; 12-11 Sat & Sun
☎ (01785) 850279 ⊕ thestarinn-eccleshall.co.uk
Draught Bass; Joule's Original Pale Ale; Titanic Anchor Bitter; Wells Bombardier; guest beer ℍ
A thriving 100-year-old pub in the heart of the beautiful Staffordshire countryside, adjacent to Copmere Lake. There are numerous walks around the area. The pub has become an integral part of this rural community, holding charity auctions and events. The extensive garden with play area is ideal for families. An excellent selection of bar meals and an à la carte menu are offered lunchtimes and evenings. The beer complements the award-winning, locally sourced food.
🏚Q🐕🍴🛏&🅰P⌐🖳(436)

Elford

Crown Inn ♥ ⓛ

The Square, B79 9DB (600yds E of A513) SK189106
☼ 6 (12 Sun)-11; 12-midnight Fri & Sat ☎ (01827) 383602
Burton Bridge Sovereign Gold; Draught Bass; guest
beer Ⓗ
Welcoming, cosy village pub, comprising a bar,
lounge and dining room. In the 18th century the
upstairs rooms were used as a courthouse, and
today's dining room once served as the cells.
Beamed ceilings feature throughout, with real fires
in the bar and lounge. Food is served 6-9pm
Wednesday-Thursday, 12-9pm Friday-Saturday, 12-
4pm Sunday. Bar snacks are available at all times.
The pub now hosts a village shop, open daily. No
evening bus service. ⚏⬤▶️🍴🅿︎🚇

Enville

Cat Inn ♥ ⓛ

Bridgnorth Road, DY7 5HA (on A458)
☼ 12-3 (not Mon), 5-11; 12-11 Fri & Sat; 12-6 Sun
☎ (01384) 872209 ⊕ thecatinn.com
Enville Ale, Ginger Beer; guest beers Ⓗ
Parts of this traditional country pub date back to
the 16th century. It has three oak-beamed rooms,
two with real fires. The Garden Room has been
refurbished and there is also a function room
upstairs. Hanging baskets adorn the beer garden
and courtyard during summer months. Regular
Enville beers are served plus two guest ales,
usually from local breweries. Home-made dishes
and daily specials, using local produce whenever
possible, are served. Local CAMRA Pub of the Year
2013. ⚏Q🐾⚘⬤▶️🍴🅿️🚇(585,588)

Fazeley

Three Horseshoes

New Street, B78 3RD (near jct of A4091 and B5404)
☼ 12-3, 6.30-11; 12-11 Fri-Sun ☎ (01827) 289754
Adnams Southwold Bitter; Draught Bass; Marston's
Pedigree Ⓗ
Welcoming red brick local situated in the back
streets of Fazeley, with the same landlady for 17
years. The single main room features a central bar
of wood and tilework, with a quarry-tiled floor. A
garden to the rear proves popular in the summer.
Drayton Manor Park is nearby and the pub sits near
the junction of the Coventry and Birmingham &
Fazeley canals. Car parking is possible on
surrounding streets. ⚘🍴🚇(110,780)

Great Haywood

Clifford Arms

Main Road, ST18 0SR (off A51 4 miles NW of Rugeley)
☼ 12-11.30 (midnight Fri & Sat); 12-11 Sun
☎ (01889) 881321 ⊕ thecliffordarms.co.uk
Adnams Broadside; Draught Bass; Morland Old
Speckled Hen; guest beers Ⓗ
Village centre inn with a large bar providing plenty
of seating and a restaurant adorned with past
photos of the pub. It is a popular local, home to
cribbage, dominoes and quiz teams, and to a tug o'
war team. It is also popular with walkers, cyclists,
boaters and visitors to the nearby Shugborough
Estate (NT). The Staffordshire Way and bridge 73 of
the Trent & Mersey Canal are 200 yards along Trent
Lane. The pub is very dog-friendly.
⚏Q🐾⚘⬤▶️🍴🅿️🚇(841)

Harriseahead

Royal Oak

42 High Steeet, ST7 4JT
☼ 7 (5 Fri; 2 Sat)-11; 12-11 Sun ☎ (01782) 513362
⊕ royaloak-harriseahead.com
Fuller's London Pride; Joule's Original Pale Ale;
Samuel Smith OBB; guest beers Ⓗ
A free house, and in the same family since 1984,
this is a two-roomed village pub with a welcoming
atmosphere. Six cask beers, including three guests
(always one from Oakham) are served, plus a good
selection of Belgian bottled beers. Old Rosie cider is
available in summer. Children, ramblers and dogs
are welcome. There is good walking country round
about including Cheshire's mountain, Mow Cop.
Monthly quizzes are held for local charities, and
there are pork pies and baps for the hungry.
⚏Q🐾⚘⬤▶️🍴🅿️🚇

Haughton

Bell Inn

Newport Road, ST18 9EX (on A518)
☼ 12-3, 5-midnight; 12-midnight Fri-Sun ☎ (01785) 780301
⊕ thebellhaughton.co.uk
Banks's Mild; Marston's EPA, Pedigree; Taylor
Landlord; guest beer Ⓗ
The L-shaped interior has a restaurant at the rear
that serves really good, locally sourced food. At the
front is a small, well-run and friendly bar that
serves snacks. As well as hosting charity events,
the pub has six dominoes teams. The guest beer
changes regularly and comes from the SIBA list,
often from a local brewer. Booking is
recommended for dining.
⚏🐾⚘⬤▶️🍴♿A♣️🚇(481)

Hednesford

Cross Keys Hotel ♥ ⓛ

42 Hill Street, WS12 2DN
☼ 12-midnight ☎ (01543) 879534
Brains The Rev James; Draught Bass; Holden's Golden
Glow; Morland Old Speckled Hen; Skinner's Betty
Stogs; guest beers Ⓗ
Former coaching inn, dating back to 1746, serving
up to eight real ales including several changing
guests. Hednesford Town football club was
originally based behind the pub and strong
connections remain, as the licensee is an ex-player
and now assistant manager. Sport is shown on TV
screens. Historic and sport photographs decorate
the walls. Monthly quiz nights are held. It is
rumoured that highwayman Dick Turpin stopped
here on his famous ride to York. Local CAMRA Pub
of the Year 2011 and 2012.
⚘🍴⬤♣️🅿️🚇(33A,60,62)

High Offley

Anchor Inn ★

Peggs Lane, Old Lea, ST20 0NG (by bridge 42 of
Shropshire Union Canal) SJ775256
☼ 12-3, 7-11 ☎ (01785) 284569
Wadworth 6X Ⓗ
On the Shropshire Union Canal, this Victorian two-
bar inn is a rare example of an unspoilt country
pub, and has a lovely award-winning garden. It has
been run by the same family since 1870, when it
was called the Sebastopol. About two miles from
the A519, the pub is not easily found but is well

worth the journey. Winter hours and Monday to Thursday lunchtime opening may vary so it is recommended to ring first. ≜Q❀⊕Å♠P¹–

Hyde Lea

Crown Inn Ⓛ
Hyde Lea, ST18 9BG
☺ 4 (12 Fri-Sun)-11 ☎ (01785) 253332
⊕ thecrowninnhydelea.net
Banks's Bitter; Greene King Abbot; Holden's Golden Glow; guest beers Ⓗ
Welcoming traditional country pub dedicated to quality real ale. The pleasant garden and play area give views of Stafford Castle. The guest beers come from the Enterprise list and feature local breweries, and the pub runs its own beer festivals. Good-value meals relying on local produce are served Friday and Saturday plus Sunday lunchtime. The pub also sells local produce as the village has no shop. The lounge/restaurant is available for functions mid-week. ≜Q➳❀⏀⊟Ġ♣♠P¹–

Kidsgrove

Blue Bell Ⓛ
25 Hardingswood, ST7 1EG (off A50 near Tesco)
☺ closed Mon; 1-4 (Sat only), 7.30-11; 12-10.30 Sun
☎ (01782) 774052 ⊕ bluebellkidsgrove.co.uk
Beer range varies Ⓗ
Genuine free house with the same owners for 15 years and in every Guide since 2000. There are no TV or games machines, just lively conversation. Occasional impromptu folk music takes place on Sunday evenings. The pub attracts customers from a wide area (it is easily reached by bus or train, or by boat on the Trent & Mersey and Macclesfield canals, which meet a few yards away). Six handpumps offer beers from microbreweries, plus Belgian and German ales, with Thatchers Cheddar Valley cider and Westons perry.
Q❀➳♠P¹–➡(20,20A,34A)

Kinver

Cross Inn Ⓛ
Church Hill, DY7 6HZ
☺ 12-11 (10.30 Sun) ☎ (01384) 872435
Black Country Bradley's Finest Golden, Pig on the Wall, Fireside; guest beers Ⓗ
Recently refurbished 19th-century pub situated a few hundred yards from the Staffs & Worcester canal. It brewed its own beers in the 19th century and still retains a strong community feel. It has a large L-shaped room with a log-burning fire at one end. The adjacent Tudor house is of particular architectural note as it has been faithfully restored and has won awards. Note: the 228 bus does not run evenings or Sunday. ≜➳Ġ♣♠P¹–➡(228)

Kinver Constitutional Club Ⓛ
119 High Street, DY7 6HL
☺ 5 (12 Wed & Thu)-11; 12-midnight Fri; 11.30-midnight Sat;
12-10.30 Sun ☎ (01384) 872044
⊕ kinverconstitutionalclub.co.uk
Enville Ale; Hobsons Best Bitter, Town Crier; Kinver Brewery Edge; Olde Swan Bumble Hole Bitter; Wye Valley HPA; guest beers Ⓗ
Built in 1902 on the site of an old pub, this converted hotel has three main areas and the bar always dispenses eight or 10 real ales, with as many as 18 for special events. The club enjoys an

enviable sporting reputation. CAMRA members are welcome but must be signed in; groups should book ahead. Buses run from Stourbridge, but there is no service after 7pm or on Sunday. It has frequently been voted CAMRA Club of the Year locally, and was National Club of the Year 2011.
≜❀⏀Ġ♣P¹–➡(228)

Knighton

Haberdashers Arms
Knighton, ST20 0QH (between Adbaston and Knighton) SJ753275
☺ 12.30 (7 Wed & Thu)-midnight; 12.30-1am Fri & Sat
☎ (01785) 280650 ⊕ haberdashersarms.com
Banks's Mild; guest beers Ⓗ
Traditional country pub, built about 1840, offering a warm, friendly welcome. It has four compact rooms, all served from a central bar. The extensive collection of oil lamps is not just for decoration; on monthly Lamp Nights the electric lights are switched off and the lamps are lit, creating a very special relaxed atmosphere. The pub hosts a range of events in its large garden, including the annual Potato Club Show and music festivals.
≜Q➳❀⊟Å♣P¹–

Leek

Cock Inn Ⓛ
19 Derby Street, ST13 6HN (near Market Square)
☺ 10-11 (10.30 Sun) ☎ (01538) 388013
Joule's Blonde, Original Pale Ale, Slumbering Monk; guest beer Ⓗ
Tastefully refurbished town-centre, split-level pub, with a lower bar area plus a raised area that is mainly reserved for diners. The neat garden at the rear leads to the car park and Leek Market. There are extensive lunch and evening food menus. Owned by Joule's of Market Drayton, its beer range is enhanced by a stronger seasonal beer selected by the knowledgeable licensee, plus a Westons cider which will be either Old Rosie or Traditional.
≜Q❀⏀♣♠P¹ ➡

Den Engel Ⓛ
11-13 Stanley Street, ST13 5HG (off Market Square)
☺ 4 (11 Sat)-11; 12-11 Sun ☎ (01538) 373751
Beer range varies Ⓗ
Free house, established in 1996, with around 100 Belgian bottled beers (Trappist, Abbey, etc), plus 11 Belgian draught beers on fonts. Four handpumps are in action, one always with a rotating Titanic beer, plus three changing guests from independents and microbreweries. An upstairs restaurant offers European cuisine with a Flemish influence (some dishes are cooked in beer), open Wednesday-Saturday evenings. On the first Sunday in the month tapas are served, and on the last Sunday a traditional Sunday lunch.
Q❀⏀♠¹–➡

Roebuck
18 Derby Street, ST13 5AB
☺ 10-11 (midnight Fri & Sat); 12-11 Sun ☎ (01538) 385602
Everards Tiger; Titanic Steerage, Anchor Bitter, Iceberg, White Star, Captain Smith's Strong Ale; guest beers Ⓗ
Splendid 17th-century black and white building, formerly a coaching inn, well refurbished two years ago by Titanic Brewery. There are a lounge, two snugs and a bar area with a striking quarter-circle

bar, sporting 10 handpumps. A stylish brass back-plate houses the cider taps (Westons Old Rosie plus one other) and lagers (a more adventurous selection than usual, including Freedom Organic). Nine Gale's English country wines are also on offer. Fresh, locally produced, traditional English food is served. A function room is available.
AAQ🕮😀🕮🍺▸P⁵—☒(16,18,P60)

Wilkes Head Ⓛ
15 St Edward Street, ST13 5DS
✪ 12 (3 Mon)-midnight; 12-11 Sun
Whim Arbor Light, Hartington Bitter, Hartington IPA, Flower Power; guest beers Ⓗ
A must-visit in a town full of good pubs. The second oldest hostelry in Leek, the multi-roomed Wilkes is renowned for live music – the landlord is a professional musician and regular gigs are held in the pub garden, which features a permanent stage. There are also folk nights, and the jukebox is brilliant. This venue is the Whim Brewery tap and sells its seasonal beers, plus a choice of guest beers and real ciders. Q😀♣🍺⁵—☒(18)

Lichfield

Duke of Wellington Ⓛ
Birmingham Road, WS14 9BJ
✪ 4-11; 12-11.30 Sat; 12-10.30 Sun ☎ (01543) 256584
Fuller's London Pride; Holden's Golden Glow; Marston's Pedigree; Wye Valley HPA Ⓗ
Former canalside pub, noted for good ale quality, that is well worth the 15-minute trek from the city centre. Next to the car park is the tell-tale hump and parapet of an old canal bridge. The open plan interior comprises three distinct drinking areas, one with a real fire. Live sports are shown on three separate screens. The pub is dog-friendly and during the summer months the large back garden is very popular. AA😀🕮♣🍺P⁵—☒(112)

Duke of York
23-25 Greenhill, WS13 6DY
✪ 12-11 (midnight Fri & Sat) ☎ (01543) 300386
Joule's Blonde, Original Pale Ale, Slumbering Monk; guest beers Ⓗ
Tastefully restored Grade II-listed pub with a split-level bar and a separate lounge, both with woodburners. There is also a multi-purpose room called the Courtyard. Good-quality food is served lunchtimes Monday-Saturday. A dark ale is often included as a guest beer, and a comprehensive malt whisky and country wine selection is also offered. Dogs are welcome except in the lounge. An annual beer festival is held in April, with around 30 ales served straight from the cask.
AAQ😀🕮🍺🚂(City)♣🍺P⁵—☒

George & Dragon
28 Beacon Street, WS13 7AJ
✪ 11-midnight (1am Fri & Sat); 12-11.30 Sun
☎ (01543) 254854 ⊕ brilliantpubs.co.uk/georgedragonstaffordshire
Banks's Mild, Bitter; Brakspear Oxford Gold; Marston's Pedigree; Wychwood Hobgoblin; guest beers Ⓗ
A friendly atmosphere greets all at this traditional local, a short walk beyond the historic Erasmus Darwin house. The interior comprises a public bar and cosy lounge where a small but tempting menu of bar snacks is available during all sessions. Outside is a large beer garden offering spectacular views of the cathedral. Darts, dominoes and board

games are played, and a silent quiz is staged on Thursday night and a raffle on Friday night, both for charity. The pub is dog-friendly. 😀🕮🐕A♣P⁵—☒

Horse & Jockey Ⓛ
8-10 Sandford Street, WS13 6QA
✪ 12-11 (midnight Fri & Sat); 12-10.30 Sun
☎ (01543) 410033
Fuller's London Pride; Holden's Golden Glow; Marston's Pedigree; Taylor Landlord; Wye Valley HPA; guest beers Ⓗ
A genuine free house that is deservedly one of the most popular pubs on Lichfield's real ale circuit. Up to three guests, mainly from micros, complement the regular ales. There is a cosy snug and a separate games room at the back of the large open-plan bar. Home-cooked food is served Monday to Saturday lunchtimes and a selection of bar snacks is always available. The over-21s and well-behaved dogs are welcome.
AA😀🕮🚂(City)♣P⁵—☒

Marchington

Bull's Head
Bag Lane, ST14 8LB
✪ 5 (12 Sat)-11; 12-3, 6-10.30 Sun ☎ (01283) 820358
⊕ bullsheadmarchington.co.uk
Marston's Pedigree; guest beer Ⓗ
Marchington is a small village approximately four miles west of Uttoxeter. The Bull's Head is a real country community pub; both bar and lounge have welcoming log fires in winter, while the rear patio is a summer suntrap. Parts of the bar retain traditional features from when the building was a Victorian coaching inn. Various sports and games teams meet here and there are regular quiz and music nights. AAQ😀🕮🍺♣P⁵—☒(402)

Milwich

Green Man
Sandon Lane, ST18 0EG (on B5027)
✪ 12-2 (not Mon-Wed), 5-11; 12-11 Fri & Sat; 12-10.30 Sun
☎ (01889) 505310 ⊕ greenmanmilwich.com
Adnams Southwold Bitter; Courage Directors; Draught Bass; Exmoor Gold; Sharp's Doom Bar; guest beer Ⓗ
A pub since 1775, this free house offers guest beers from regional brewers and microbreweries nationwide, and hosts regular beer festivals. The long-serving licensee has been here over 20 years, and there are historical records of previous landlords dating back to 1792. A popular resting place with walkers and cyclists, there is a small restaurant area off the bar. Westons or Thatchers cider is served. AAQ😀🕮🍺A♣🍺P⁵—

Newcastle-under-Lyme

Castle Mona
4 Victoria Street, ST5 1NT
✪ 4 (12 Sat)-midnight; 12-11.30 Sun ☎ (01782) 244142
Castle Rock Harvest Pale; Sharp's Doom Bar; Skinner's Cornish Knocker Ale; Wells Bombardier; guest beers Ⓗ
Situated only five minutes' walk along the A34 from Newcastle town centre, the pub features a wood-panelled lounge, complete with a woodburner, plus a traditional bar area where the regulars provide their own entertainment, with hours of chatter, banter and games of bar skittles and pool. Outside, there is a lovely well-kept beer

garden for the summer evenings. A real English pub that always offers a warm welcome and a sense of community spirit. ♨✿🅑♣●'-🖳(101)

Norton Bridge

Railway Inn
Station Road, ST15 0NT
✪ 5 (12 Sat)-11; 12-10.30 Sun ☎ (01785) 760289
Thwaites Original, Lancaster Bomber; guest beer 🅷
A thriving and popular village community pub that plays host to traditional pub games, and also to bi-monthly meetings of the North Staffordshire BSA Motorcycle Owners Club. A good range of home-cooked meals is available Monday to Saturday evenings, excellent value and not to be missed. Guest beers are from a variety of sources. A varied diary of weekend entertainment is available on the pub's Facebook page together with information on forthcoming guest beers.
♨Q🏷✿🅑 🅑🅑♣P'-🖳(490)

Onecote

Jervis Arms 🅛
ST13 7RU (on B5053 N of A53 Leek-Ashbourne road)
✪ 12-3, 7-midnight; 12-midnight Sun ☎ (01538) 304206
Titanic Steerage, Iceberg; Wadworth 6X; guest beers 🅷
A regular in this Guide, the pub has shown a long-term commitment to the real ale scene. Situated in the Peak District National Park, it is close to Alton Towers. Family-friendly, the beer garden has a river running through it and a good children's playground. There is a large car park just beyond. The landlord is fanatical about real ale, sourcing his guest beers from breweries near and far. Dogs are permitted in the bar. ♨🏷✿🅓🅑♣●P'-

Oulton

Brushmakers Arms
8 Kibblestone Road, ST15 8UW (500yds W of A520, 1 mile NE of Stone)
✪ 12-midnight (1am Fri & Sat) ☎ (01785) 812062
Thwaites Original, Wainwright, Lancaster Bomber; guest beer 🅷
Named after a local cottage industry, the Brush is a pub where time stands still. It has a traditional quarry-tiled floor to the bar and a small ornate lounge. Pictures and postcards adorn the walls, reflecting a bygone era. The small rear paved garden is a real suntrap and doubles as the smoking area. With no games machines or jukebox, conversation rules in this excellent village local. Well-behaved dogs welcome.
♨Q🏷✿🅑🅑🅐≉(Stone)♣P'-🖳(250)

Penn Common

Barley Mow
Pennwood Lane, WV4 5JN (follow signs to Penn Golf Club from A449) SO901949
✪ 12-2.30, 6-11 (midnight Thu & Fri); 12-midnight Sat; 12-10.30 Sun ☎ (01902) 333510 ⊕ barleymowpenn.co.uk
Greene King Abbot; Hobsons Town Crier; Taylor Landlord; guest beers 🅷
On the edge of Penn Common and sharing an access driveway with Penn Golf Club, this charming pub is worth seeking out. Built around 1630, it has low-beamed ceilings and steps leading down to the drinking and dining areas. It is rightly

renowned for its steaks. The compact single bar has a display of drip mats and foreign banknotes. The selection of six quality real ales is accompanied by Thatchers Heritage cider. Q🏷✿🅓🅑●P'-

Salt

Holly Bush Inn
ST18 0BX (turn W off A518 opp Weston Hall) SJ959277
✪ 12-11 (10.30 Sun) ☎ (01889) 508234
⊕ hollybushinn.co.uk
Adnams Southwold Bitter; Marston's Pedigree; guest beers 🅷
The pub claims to have origins as far back as 1190 and is reputedly the second-oldest inn to be granted a licence. The oldest part of the building retains a thatched roof. Extensions and alterations over the centuries means there are three distinct areas: a bar area, dining room and snug. Many awards have been won for the superb-quality meals. Guest beers come from the SIBA range.
♨Q🏷✿🅓🅑P'-🖳

Shenstone

Fox & Hounds
44 Main Street, WS14 0NB
✪ 12-11 (midnight Thu-Sat) ☎ (01543) 480257
⊕ foxandhoundsshenstone.com
Castle Rock Harvest Pale; Greene King IPA; Marston's Pedigree; guest beer 🅷
Distinctive white-painted village pub, Grade II-listed and dating from the 18th century. A cosy multi-level snug is towards the front, while the rear features a large comfy lounge and homely dining area. It has gas fires throughout - do not be fooled by the log stacks. Outside, there are a beer terrace, lawned beer garden and smokers' den. The guest beer is usually from a microbrewery. No evening meals on Sundays. Q✿🅓🅑≉P'-🖳(112)

Stafford

Greyhound 🅛
12 County Road, ST16 2PU (off A34, opp prison)
✪ 4-11.30; 3-midnight Fri & Sat; 12-11 Sun
☎ (01785) 222432 ⊕ greyhoundfreehousestafford.co.uk
Wells Bombardier; guest beers 🅷
A short walk from the centre of Stafford, this two-room free house is well worth a visit. The pub dates from 1831 and a newspaper article from the day it opened can be seen above the bar. Today the pub offers a changing range of eight ales, often from breweries in Yorkshire, and a range of bottled ciders. The Greyhound has won several CAMRA branch awards including Pub of the Year.
♨Q✿🅑🅑≉♣●P'-🖳(5,10,11)

Joxer Bradys
4 St Martin's Place, ST16 2LA (in the corner of Market Square)
✪ 11.30-11 (midnight Thu-Sat); 12-11 Sun
☎ (01785) 228183
Banks's Bitter; Jennings Cocker Hoop; Wychwood Hobgoblin; guest beers 🅷
A very welcoming multi-roomed pub in the corner of Stafford's Market Square. It offers a selection of five well-kept ales alongside Thatchers Heritage traditional cider, plus Stafford's best whisky menu. The pub was formerly known as the Chains and is reputed to have an underground tunnel leading to the dungeons of the Crown Court that used to be

nearby. Regular live music and comedy events are hosted. Guest beers come from Marston's breweries. ⌂&≠♣♠¹─⊟

Olde Rose & Crown
10 Market Street, ST16 2JZ
🌣 12-11 (midnight Fri & Sat); 12-10 Sun ☎ (01785) 251343
Joule's Blonde, Original Pale Ale, Slumbering Monk Ⓗ
Extensively refurbished at the end of 2011, this Joule's house is a fantastic pub right in the heart of Stafford. Three handpumps serve Joule's ales alongside a cider. Lunches are served Monday to Saturday and bar snacks are available all day, using locally sourced ingredients. Situated next door to the Gatehouse Theatre, the pub is a favourite of theatregoers and is often frequented by cast members enjoying an after-show pint. An acoustic night is held every Wednesday.
₳❀⊙&≠♠¹─⊟(X1,1,2)

Sun Ⓛ
7 Lichfield Road, ST17 4JX
🌣 11.30-11 (midnight Fri & Sat); 12-11 Sun
☎ (01785) 248361 ⊕ thesunstafford.co.uk
Everards Tiger; Titanic Steerage, Anchor Bitter, Iceberg, White Star, Captain Smith's; guest beers Ⓗ
One of Titanic Brewery's fleet, it has been clear sailing for this popular pub following an extensive refurbishment in 2010, and it was winner of the local CAMRA branch Pub of the Year in 2012. Twelve handpumps offer a constant choice of beers from Titanic, as well as a changing range of guest ales and cider. Food is served throughout the day, using ingredients sourced as locally to the pub as possible. Keep an eye out for the original pub sign now hanging inside.
₳Q☎❀⊙❶≠♣♠P¹─⊟(1,2,3)

Stoke-on-Trent: Burslem

Bull's Head Ⓛ
14 St John's Square, ST6 3AJ
🌣 3-11 (11.30 Wed & Thu); 12-midnight Fri & Sat; 12-11 Sun
☎ (01782) 834153
Titanic Steerage, Anchor Bitter, Iceberg, White Star, Plum Porter; guest beers Ⓗ
Titanic's two-roomed brewery tap in the centre of Burslem, only 10 minutes' walk from Port Vale's ground and welcoming to all supporters, home and away. The pub's island bar has up to 10 real ales on handpump and seven or more real ciders and perries, alongside malt whiskies, fruit wines and draught and bottled Belgian beers. Bar billiards, table skittles and an old vinyl jukebox are in the public bar. CAMRA regional Cider Pub of the Year 2012. ₳❀⌂♣♠¹─⊟

Duke William Ⓛ
2 St Johns Square, ST6 3AJ
🌣 11.30-11 (midnight Fri & Sat); 12-10.30 Sun
☎ (01782) 814809 ⊕ dukewilliamburslem.com
Joule's Slumbering Monk; Oakham Citra; Sharp's Doom Bar; Springhead Roaring Meg; guest beers Ⓗ
An imposing pub that has undergone a sympathetic restoration, with most of the original features intact, including the horseshoe-shaped bar and its heated foot rail, bell pushes in the lounge, serving hatch and leaded windows. Eight handpumps serve the house beers, three guest ales and a guest real cider. There is also a smoking area to the rear and a restaurant upstairs with its own bar and an English food menu. A beer festival is held annually. ₳⊙⌂&¹─⊟(98)

Post Office Vaults Ⓛ
3 Market Place, ST6 3AA
🌣 10-10.45 (12.45am Fri & Sat); 10-10.30 Sun
☎ (01782) 811027
Fuller's London Pride; Greene King Abbot; Wye Valley Butty Bach; guest beers Ⓗ
A small one-roomed pub in the centre of Burslem, popular with the local football club and community. The handpumps dispense three house beers and two rotating guest ales from a variety of microbreweries. Real cider is also available. Sport and live music feature on the array of TV screens, and there is a heated and lit smoking area to the rear with its own TV. Post Office memorabilia adorn the walls, including a factory clocking-in machine. Dogs welcome. &≠(Longport)❶¹─⊟(20,21,98)

Stoke-on-Trent: Etruria

Holy Inadequate ♈ Ⓛ
67 Etruria Old Road, ST1 5PE
🌣 4-11; 12-midnight Fri-Sun
Joule's Original Pale Ale; guest beers Ⓗ
Continuing its meteoric rise, the Holy is the current CAMRA branch Pub of the Year, and now serves seven real ales and three ciders. The pub's fervent support of microbrewers means it also now stocks an extensive range of British bottled beers, and hosts beer festivals on all bank holidays, with up to 26 beers on offer. A warm and friendly atmosphere always pervades, and dogs are welcome. Locally sourced bar snacks are available. A pub to cherish.
₳Q❀❶¹─⊟(17,34,34A)

Stoke-on-Trent: Fenton

Malt 'n' Hops
295 King Street, ST4 3EJ
🌣 12-4, 7-11; 12-midnight Fri & Sat; 12-11 Sun
☎ (01782) 313406 ⊕ maltnhops.com
Greene King Abbot; guest beers Ⓗ
A true free house, run by the same family for many years. The interior is open plan, however the split level gives the impression of a separate traditional bar and more comfortable lounge. The house beer is brewed by Tower, and up to five rotating guest ales and a real cider are available. There is also a large selection of bottled Belgian beers and at least one on draught. Sport is regularly shown on TV in the bar area. ♣♠¹─⊟(6,26)

Stoke-on-Trent: Hanley

Coachmakers Arms ★
Lichfield Street, ST1 3EA (off A5008)
🌣 12-11.30 (midnight Fri & Sat); 12-10.30 Sun
☎ (01782) 262158
Draught Bass; guest beers Ⓗ
A warm atmosphere and friendly character welcome you to the Coachmakers Arms, situated near Hanley bus station. This pub, recently refurbished and redecorated, provides five different guest beers including a mild and stout, along with cider from a cask box. The pub is popular with local drinkers as well as having many fans from outside Stoke-on-Trent. Possible renovation for the area has put this pub in jeopardy, so do not miss the opportunity to visit a gem.
₳Q☎❀≠♣♠¹─⊟

Stoke-on-Trent: Hartshill

Greyhound ⃟

67 George Street, ST5 1JT
✪ 12-11.30 (midnight Wed & Thu; 12.30am Fri & Sat)
☎ (01782) 635814
Everards Tiger; Titanic Steerage, Iceberg, White Star, Plum Porter; guest beers ⃟
Just 10 minutes' walk away from Newcastle town centre, on the Newcastle/Stoke-on-Trent border area known locally as Top of Castle. There are nine handpulls serving at least four of the Titanic fleet, Everards Tiger and a range of guest ales from breweries across the country. Two further handpulls dispense ciders and perries; bottled Belgian beers are also offered. Hot and cold snacks are available including local oatcakes, and a monthly sausage and mash evening is popular.
▨Q⃟♣♨⃠–⃟(25,26,101)

Stoke-on-Trent: Longton

Congress Inn ⃟

14 Sutherland Road, ST3 1HJ
✪ 12-11 (midnight Fri-Sun) ☎ (01782) 763667
⊕ thecongressinn.co.uk
Wadworth Henry's IPA, 6X; guest beers ⃟
Spacious two-roomed community pub drawing a loyal clientele from a wide area. It won first place in the 2011 local CAMRA Pub of the Year and 2012 Staffordshire CAMRA Pub of the Year competitions. Up to nine beers are on handpump, four of them regular; three real ciders are on gravity and there is a large selection of bottled Belgian beers. A beer festival is held every May, with 30 beers plus ciders on gravity. Traditional pub games include tabletop skittles. ⇌♨⃠–⃟

Stoke-on-Trent: Stoke

Glebe ⃟

35 Glebe Street, ST4 1HG
✪ 12-11 (11.30 Fri & Sat); 12-10.30 Sun ☎ (01782) 844600
Joule's Blonde, Original Pale Ale, Slumbering Monk ⃟
An equally short walk from both the rail station and Stoke town centre, this flagship pub for the reinvigorated Joule's Brewery is a beautifully restored corner tavern, the very impressive main features being the stained glass windows and wood panelling, plus an open fire that adds to the welcoming feeling on entering. Three Joule's beers are accompanied by a cider. Home-made food is served lunchtimes and evenings, with Staffs organic cheeses and pork pies available all day.
▨⃟⇌♨⃟(21,21A,F10)

Wheatsheaf ⃟

84-92 Church Street, ST4 1BU
✪ 8am-midnight (1am Fri & Sat) ☎ (01782) 747462
Greene King Abbot; Ruddles Best Bitter; guest beers ⃟
In Stoke town centre, this regular entry in the Guide has a well-earned reputation as one of the best real ale outlets in the Wetherspoon chain. It is a true community pub that actively supports the LocAle scheme, so much so that Lymestone has a permanent ale featuring in the range of up to five guest beers. Breakfast and beer are served from 8am. Meet the Brewer nights are an occasional feature, while the usual Wetherspoon food nights are always popular. Q▵⃟&⇌♣–⃟

White Star ⃟

63 Kingsway, ST4 1JB (off Church St)
✪ 11-midnight; 12-11 Sun ☎ (01782) 848732
Everards Tiger; Titanic Steerage, Anchor Bitter, Iceberg, White Star, Plum Porter; guest beers ⃟
One of the Titanic Brewery fleet, this award-winning pub has a convenient town-centre location and is a very popular local. With handpumps dispensing six from Titanic's superb range, plus Everards Tiger and four well-sourced guest ales, it is easy to see why. A comfortable, split-level bar is festooned with remembrances of the ill-fated Titanic voyage of 1912; delicious home-made food is served lunchtimes and evenings, and there is an upstairs function room with handpumps. Q⃟&⇌♣–⃟(23,25,26)

Stone

Royal Exchange ♟ ⃟

Radford Street, ST15 8DA
✪ 12-11 (midnight Fri & Sat) ☎ (01785) 812685
Everards Tiger; Titanic Mild, Steerage, Iceberg, White Star ⃟**, Plum Porter** ⃟/⃟**; guest beers** ⃟
Although one-roomed, there are four distinct drinking areas in this 2008 refurbishment by Everards and Titanic. Beers from both breweries are always available, together with up to four guest ales, mainly from micros, and a real cider. There are nights with acoustic music, and Stone Jazz Club meets here. The ingredients in the expanding food range are mainly locally sourced. Well-behaved dogs are welcome, and children until 9pm. There is a town car park opposite.
▨Q▵⃟⃟&⇌♣♨–⃟⃟(101,250,400)

Swan Inn ⃟

18 Stafford Street, ST15 8QW (on A520 by Trent & Mersey Canal)
✪ 12-midnight (11 Mon; 12.30am Tue); 11-1am Fri & Sat; 12-11 Sun ☎ (01785) 815570 ⊕ swaninnstone.co.uk
Blythe Ridware Pale; Holden's Golden Glow; Lymestone Stone Cutter, Eln Stein; Wincle Under Taker; guest beers ⃟
A carefully renovated Grade II-listed building, this thriving free house has served beers from over 700 breweries so far. Regular beers are from Blythe, Holden's, Joule's and Lymestone, with others from anywhere. There is an increasing range of real ciders – the pub was CAMRA branch Cider Pub of the Year in 2012. This venue hosts quiz nights and live music, and a beer festival in early July. Over-18s only. ▨⃟⃟&⇌♣♨–⃟(101,250,490)

Tamworth

Globe Inn

Lower Gungate, B79 7AT
✪ 11-11; 12-10.30 Sun ☎ (01827) 60455
⊕ theglobetamworth.com
Draught Bass; Holden's Black Country Mild; Worthington's Bitter; guest beer ⃟
One-roomed hotel bar, split into three areas including a raised dining space. A separate function room is available for hire. The mild is keenly priced, and the changing guest is sometimes from a local microbrewery. Karaoke nights are held on Thursday and Sunday – beware if you want a quiet drink. The bar has two large-screen TVs and can get very busy when sporting events, especially rugby, are shown. There is a Pay & Display car park next door.
⃟⃟⇌♣⃟

Sir Robert Peel 🗓

13-15 Lower Gungate, B79 7BA

🌑 2-11 (midnight Fri); 12-midnight Sat; 12-11 Sun

☎ (01827) 300910

Sharp's Doom Bar Ⓗ; guest beers Ⓗ/Ⓖ

Featuring in the Guide continuously for the last 10 years, this is a popular family-run free house. Up to seven ales are served, including two straight from the cask. The pub is a member of the Oakademy of Excellence and Oakham's beers, including one-off specials, make a regular appearance. Situated in the town centre, it can get busy at weekends, but Mondays and Wednesdays are ideal if you want a quiet pint. ≈●₩

Trysull

Bell Inn 🗓

Bell Road, WV5 7JB SO852940

🌑 11.30-3, 5-11.30; 11.30-midnight Sat; 12-11.30 Sun

☎ (01902) 892871 ⊕ thebellinntrysull.co.uk

Bathams Best Bitter; Holden's Black Country Mild, Black Country Bitter, Golden Glow, Special; guest beer Ⓗ

A fine 18th-century building next to the village church, comprising a smallish but cosy bar, a pleasant lounge and a large restaurant/dining room (lunchtime and Early Bird deals are very popular). As well as the Holden's range, Bathams Best Bitter is a regular together with changing guests, often sourced from microbreweries. A patio area is to the front of the pub. Popular with walkers – the Staffordshire & Worcestershire canal is a 15-minute walk away.
Q🕭🕮❊❶🔌🕭♣P₩(584,585,588)

Upper Longdon

Chetwynd Arms

57 Upper Way, WS15 1QB SK060146

🌑 12 (5 Mon)-11; 12-midnight Fri-Sun ☎ (01543) 490266

Holden's Golden Glow; Marston's Pedigree; guest beers Ⓗ

A village local close to Cannock Chase forest, this pub gives equal emphasis to beer in the bar and food in the adjoining dining room. Two guest ales are the norm, one of which is often Bass, the other usually from Bathams or Enville breweries. The favoured pub game here is dominoes, unless TV sport kicks in. There is plenty of car parking, and a large garden to the rear offers a peaceful summer retreat. ₩❊❶♣P₁₋₩(14)

Weston

Woolpack Inn

The Green, ST18 0JH (off A518)

🌑 11-11 (midnight Fri & Sat); 11.30-11 Sun

☎ (01889) 270238 ⊕ woolpackpubweston.co.uk

Banks's Bitter; Marston's Pedigree; Ringwood Old Thumper; guest beers Ⓗ

Known locally as the Inn on the Green, this welcoming village local has an extensive dining area, while another area of the pub hosts dominoes and darts. Over the years the low-ceilinged pub has been thoughtfully extended while retaining the original bar area. Four bays inside reflect the building's origins as a row of cottages and blacksmith's shop. The property is recorded as being owned by the Bagot family in the 1730s. Guest beers come from the Marston's family. ₩Q🕭🕮❊❶🔌🕭♣▲♣●P₁₋₩(X1)

Whiston

Swan Inn 🗓

Whiston Road, ST19 5QH SJ895144

🌑 12-3 (not Mon), 5-11; 12-11 Sun ☎ (01785) 716200

⊕ swanwhiston.co.uk

Holden's Black Country Mild, Black Country Bitter; guest beers Ⓗ

Although remotely situated, high-quality, well-kept ales and superb food make this a thriving pub. Built in 1593, burnt down and rebuilt in 1711, the oldest part today is the small bar housing an inglenook fireplace. The lounge features an intriguing central double-sided log fire. Six acres of grounds include a children's obstacle course, an aviary, rabbits and so on. A discount on ales is available to CAMRA members. Branch Pub of the Year 2011 and Cider Pub of the Year 2011.
₩Q🕭🕮❊❶🔌🕭▲♣●P₁₋₩(88,88A)

Wolseley Bridge

Wolseley Arms

ST17 0XS (on jct of A51 and A513)

🌑 12-11 (10.30 Sun) ☎ (01889) 883179

Everards Tiger; Marston's Pedigree; guest beer Ⓗ

With three real fires and an outdoor patio area, this country pub is a great place to enjoy a pint in winter or summer. Mainly food-focused, it keeps three great ales from regional breweries. It is the perfect place to enjoy the delights of Cannock Chase on its doorstep. Close by are an unusual craft centre and the Trent & Mersey canal.
₩🕭❊❶🔌P₁₋₩(825)

Wombourne

New Inn 🗓

1 Station Road, WV5 9EY

🌑 12-11 (11.30 Thu; midnight Fri & Sat) ☎ (01902) 892037

⊕ newinnpubwolverhampton.co.uk

Banks's Mild, Bitter Ⓗ/ℙ, Sunbeam; Jennings Cocker Hoop; guest beer Ⓗ

Comfortable open-plan pub with good-quality food at reasonable prices, mainly served in the lounge. Drinkers use the bar area, but both are served from the central horseshoe-shaped bar. The landlord is a real ale enthusiast and serves up guests from the Marston's stable. A small TV in the bar area is occasionally switched on for sport. Outside, there is a patio at the front and a large garden at the rear. A CAMRA discount is given from 6pm on Mondays.
Q🕭🕮❊❶🔌P₁₋₩(255,256)

Yoxall

Golden Cup

Main Street, DE13 8NQ (on A515)

🌑 12-3, 5-midnight; 12-1am Fri & Sat; 12-midnight Sun

☎ (01543) 472295 ⊕ goldencupyoxall.co.uk

Marston's Pedigree; guest beer Ⓗ

Impressive family-run 300-year-old inn at the centre of the village, opposite St Peter's Church, bedecked with attractive floral displays for much of the year. The pub features a smart L-shaped lounge with a beamed ceiling, primarily catering for diners, and a plainer public bar with a pool table and TVs. Colourful murals with a classical theme enhance the ladies' and men's toilets. The award-winning gardens stretch down to the River Swarbourn. ₩Q❊🕮❶🔌🕭▲♣●P₁₋₩(7,7E)

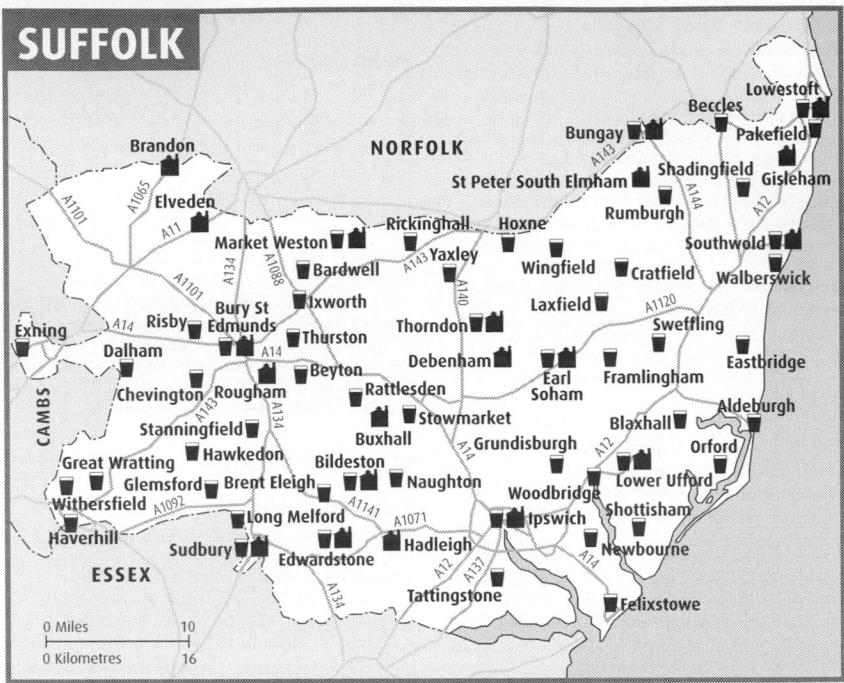

SUFFOLK

0 Miles 10
0 Kilometres 16

Aldeburgh

White Hart Ⓛ
222 High Street, IP15 5AJ
✪ 11.30-11; 12-10.30 Sun ☎ (01728) 453205
Adnams Sole Star, Southwold Bitter, Ghost Ship, Broadside; guest beers Ⓗ
Classic drinkers' pub adjacent to the town's renowned fish and chip shop. A popular meeting place for locals and visitors alike, families are welcome in the garden in summer. The single bar was formerly a public reading room. It has a high ceiling and stained glass windows and is decorated with nautical pictures. Salads, sandwiches and pizzas are available in summer or you can buy your fish and chips from next door and eat them in the garden with your pint. ♨Q❀◗☾ఊ℄☐(64,165)

Bardwell

Dun Cow
Up Street, IP31 1AA (off A143 at Stanton)
✪ 11.30-2, 5-midnight; 12-midnight Sat; 12-10.30 Sun
☎ (01359) 250806
Greene King IPA, seasonal ales; Morland Old Golden Hen Ⓗ
A traditional pub in a pleasant village set in the Suffolk countryside. The pub has two bars and offers speciality food nights. Party bookings are taken and coaches are welcome if booked in advance. The landlord offers a 'Dun Cow Special' from Greene King most of the time. The recently restored village windmill makes for some attractive photos and has occasional threshing open days. ♨Q❀◗☐♣P⇐

Beccles

Caxton Club Ⓛ
Gaol Lane, NR34 9SJ (next to supermarket car park)

✪ 12-1.30 (not Tue), 7-11; 12-2, 6.30-11 Fri; 12-11 Sat; 12-10.30 Sun ☎ (01502) 712829
Theakston Black Bull; guest beers Ⓗ
In 1890 this was a club for gentlemen only. Today all members and their guests are welcome – CAMRA members can be signed in for a small charge. Four beers and a cider (usually Westons) are available, some locally sourced. Situated close to the town centre and a short walk from the train and bus stations, this spacious club has a central bar, TV and darts room, and snooker room. There is also a large function room where live music is hosted on Friday and Saturday evenings. No dogs. ⇆❀ఊ⇆♣♠℄☐

Beyton

Bear Inn
Tostock Road, IP30 9AG
✪ 12-2, 5-11; 12-4, 7-10.30 Sun ☎ (01359) 270249
⊕ thebearinnbeyton.co.uk
Adnams Broadside; Woodforde's Wherry; guest beers Ⓗ
Rebuilt in 1900 after the original thatched premises burned down in a July thunderstorm – you can read a full account of this traumatic event in the bar. The pub has been run by the same family since 1922. Although recently updated, it is still very much a traditional inn and retains a separate public bar. A further bar/restaurant serves excellent food (Fri-Sun lunchtimes, Fri & Sat eves). The Bear was originally on the main Ipswich to Cambridge road and there is easy access from the A14. ♨Q❀◗℄A♣P℄☐

Bildeston

King's Head
132 High Street, IP7 7ED

closed Mon & Tue; 6 (4 Fri, Sat)-midnight; 12-10.30 Sun
☎ (01449) 741434 ⊕ bildestonkingshead.co.uk
King's Head Bildeston Best, seasonal beers; guest beers H
Home of the King's Head Brewery since 1996, this former coaching inn dates from around 1530. It has a single bar and retains exposed carved timbers and an inglenook fireplace. A friendly drinking-house atmosphere has evolved, with food available at the weekend only (lunchtimes Sat & Sun, eve meals Fri & Sat). There is a fully enclosed rear garden with a covered patio area, lawns and play equipment. The summer bank holiday beer festival is well established and popular. ▦⊛⊙❶

Blaxhall

Ship L
School Road, IP12 2DY TM367569
12-3, 6-midnight; 12-midnight Sat & Sun
☎ (01728) 688316 ⊕ blaxhallshipinn.co.uk
Adnams Southwold Bitter; Greene King Tolly English Ale; Woodforde's Wherry; guest beers H
A cosy two-roomed 16th-century pub on the edge of Suffolk Sandlings with a long-established reputation for traditional singing in the bar. It is also renowned for good food, the menu offering a wide choice of home-made dishes featuring locally sourced ingredients. Live music plays at least once a week including regular folk music sessions, especially on bank holiday weekends. Letting chalets beside the pub provide B&B accommodation. Dogs are welcome.
▦Q⅚⊛♿❶P

Brent Eleigh

Cock Inn ★
Lavenham Road, CO10 9PB
12-4, 6-11; 12-11 Fri & Sat; 12-10.30 Sun
☎ (01787) 247371
Adnams Southwold Bitter; Greene King Abbot; guest beers H
Unspoilt gem identified by CAMRA as one of Britain's Best Real Heritage Pubs. In winter both bars are snug and warm; in summer with the doors open, the bar is at one with its surroundings. The Bitch & Stitch knitting club meets here weekly. Hungry walkers and cyclists exploring the area will be pleased to know that landlady Deborah is a great cook and that food is available at all times. Real cider is generally Castling's Heath Cottage.
▦Q⊛♿❶⊟♣♿P

Bungay

Green Dragon L
29 Broad Street, NR35 1EE TM334899
11 (12 Sat)-midnight; 12-5 Sun ☎ (01986) 892681
Green Dragon Chaucer Ale, Gold, Bridge Street, seasonal beers H
Originally called the Horse & Groom, this is the home of the Green Dragon brewery. Bungay's only brewpub, it is a regular entry in the Guide. Ales are brewed in outbuildings next to the car park at the rear of the property. Brewery tours are available by appointment. This town pub has two good-sized bar areas and a small side garden. Bottle-conditioned and seasonal beers are often available. Wednesday is curry night (booking advisable).
▦⅚⊛⊟♿♣P⅃⊟(580,588)

Bury St Edmunds

Beerhouse L
1 Tayfen Road, IP32 6BH
5 (12 Sat)-11; 12-3, 6-10.30 Sun ☎ (01284) 766415
⊕ burybeerhouse.co.uk
Brewshed Pale Ale, Best Bitter, American Blonde, seasonal beers; guest beers H
Unique quarter-circular (gables at each end are 90 degrees to each other), brick-built Victorian building quite close to the railway station. Previously the Ipswich Arms, it was refurbished in 2010 prior to reopening in 2010 as an ale-focused traditional pub. A new microbrewery in the yard was established soon after, trading as the Brewshed brewery. Eight handpumps provide a varied selection of well-kept real ales and four ciders. Q⊛⧖♣♿⅃⊟

Dove ♥ L
68 Hospital Road, IP33 3JU
5-11; 12-3, 6-11 Sat; 12-3, 6-10.30 Sun ☎ (01284) 702787
⊕ thedovepub.co.uk
Woodforde's Wherry, seasonal beers; guest beers H
A traditional Victorian alehouse just five minutes' walk from the historic town centre. The Dove has six handpumps and real ciders but no music, TV, gaming machines or lager. A no-frills main bar has scrubbed floorboards, alongside the carpeted parlour. The staff offer a warm and friendly welcome and are knowledgeable about the beers they sell – a varied, ever-changing range from East Anglia and established regional brewers. CAMRA Regional Pub of the Year 2010/11. Q⊛♣♿P⅃⊟

Old Cannon L
86 Cannon Street, IP33 1JR
12-11 (10.30 Sun) ☎ (01284) 768769
⊕ oldcannonbrewery.co.uk
Adnams Southwold Bitter; Old Cannon Best Bitter, Gunner's Daughter, seasonal beers; guest beers H
Formerly the St Edmund's Head, this brewpub is on the site of the original Cannon Brewery. The brewing vessels are in clear view in an area in the bar, although no brewing takes place while the pub is open. As well as its own real ales and guests, a wide range of foreign beer is also offered. Good food is always available featuring locally

INDEPENDENT BREWERIES

Adnams Southwold
Bartrams Rougham
Brandon Brandon
Brewshed Bury St Edmunds
Cliff Quay Debenham
Cox & Holbrook Buxhall
Dove Street Ipswich
Earl Soham Earl Soham
Elveden Elveden
Green Dragon Bungay
Green Jack Lowestoft
Greene King Bury St Edmunds
Hellhound Hadleigh
Kings Head Bildeston
Mauldons Sudbury
Mill Green Edwardstone
Old Cannon Bury St Edmunds
Old Chimneys Market Weston
Shortts Farm Thorndon (NEW)
St Peter's St Peter South Elmham
Trinity Gisleham
Uffa Lower Ufford

sourced ingredients, including popular dishes made with the pub's own beers. Accommodation is available but parking is limited.
🏨Q☺🍴🍺◑≈P⁵–🖭

Rose & Crown
48 Whiting Street, IP33 1NP
✪ 11.30-11.30; 11.30-3, 7-11.30 Sat; 12-2.30, 7.30-11.30 Sun
☎ (01284) 755934
Greene King XX Mild, IPA, Abbot, seasonal beers; guest beers 🅗
In sight of Greene King's Westgate Brewery and offering the rare XX Mild, this is a very traditional pub with two bars and a separate off-sales hatch in between – an old layout now very seldom seen. The present tenants have run this house for 25 years, succeeding the landlady's father. Wholesome good-value lunches are served Monday to Saturday. The pub is listed – note the hanging tiles – and within a conservation area among many fine buildings. Children are welcome in the garden only. Q☺◑🍴🍺⁵–

Chevington

Greyhound
2 Chedburgh Road, IP29 5QS
✪ 12-2.30, 7 (6 Fri & Sat)-11; 12-2.30, 7-10.30 Sun
☎ (01284) 850765 🌐 chevingtongreyhound.co.uk
Adnams Southwold Bitter; guest beers 🅗
Run by the same owners for almost 25 years, this ordinary-looking free house has established an enviable reputation for authentic Asian cuisine, with a customer base far and wide. Good English food is just as available. Still very much a village pub, it retains a traditional bar, open fire, pool table and games. The large garden is well stocked with child-friendly features. The guest beer is often from Mersea Island Brewery, thanks to a family connection. 🏨🐶☺◑P⁵–

Cratfield

Poacher 🅛
Bell Green, IP19 0BL TM312751
✪ closed Mon; 12-2.30 (not Tue-Thu), 6-midnight; 12-midnight Sat & Sun ☎ (01986) 798206
Adnams Southwold Bitter 🅗**; guest beers** 🅗/🅖
A comfortable and rural inn that can be difficult to find in this dispersed village, but well worth the effort. The rustic building is timber framed and set back from the road. The pub offers a warm and friendly welcome coupled with a good selection of beers (up to eight at weekends) including some from local microbrewers, though not exclusively. The choice of cider varies. There is a separate dining area where food is served at weekends until 8.30pm. Live music features occasionally. 🏨Q🐶☺◑🍺🍴P⁵–

Dalham

Affleck Arms
1 Brookside, CB8 8TG
✪ 12-2 (not Mon), 5-11; 12-11 Sun ☎ (01638) 500306
Black Sheep Best Bitter; guest beers 🅗
The brook in front of the pub is in fact the River Kennet and it can come in through the front door sometimes – as it did in 1968, rising to bar level. Situated in a mainly thatched 16th-century village, this pub has a cosy restaurant and a bar with a prominent inglenook fireplace. Ales are from

microbreweries and an annual beer festival is hosted. The home-cooked food is exceptional and well priced. Outside overlooking the river is a rear patio and garden for diners and drinkers. 🏨Q☺🍴◑🚹P⁵–

Earl Soham

Victoria 🅛
The Street, IP13 7RL (on A1120)
✪ 11.30-3, 5.30-11 (11.30 Fri & Sat); 12-10.30 Sun
☎ (01728) 685758
Earl Soham Victoria Bitter, Sir Roger's Porter, Brandeston Gold, seasonal beers 🅗
Popular, traditional Victorian pub with two small bars and a large fire in winter months, which has changed little over the years – it even has an outside loo. An ever-changing food menu with daily specials is offered lunchtimes and evenings, all home cooked. The pub gets busy at weekends, especially on sunny days when even a seat in the garden can be hard to find. Dogs and children are welcome. The Earl Soham Brewery is just 150 yards away. 🏨Q🚶☺◑🍴P🖭

Eastbridge

Eels Foot 🅛
Leiston Road, IP16 4SN (close to entrance to Minsmere nature reserve) TM452661
✪ 11.30-3, 6-11; 11.30-11.30 Fri- Sun ☎ (01728) 830154
🌐 theeelsfootinn.co.uk
Adnams Southwold Bitter, Ghost Ship, Broadside, seasonal beer 🅗
Located adjacent to the famous nature reserve where avocets and otters are local success stories, the pub is very popular with ramblers and bird watchers. It has a good reputation for locally sourced home-cooked food, with a small restaurant area leading to a new large terraced seating area for alfresco drinking and dining on warmer days. There is also an outdoor play area for children. Traditional music sessions are held on Thursday evenings and live bands play monthly. En-suite accommodation is available for visitors exploring the heritage coastline. 🏨Q🚶☺🍴◑🚹AP⁵–

Edwardstone

White Horse
Mill Green, CO10 5PX TL951426
✪ 12-3, 5-11; 12-midnight Fri & Sat; 12-11 Sun
☎ (01787) 211211 🌐 edwardstonewhitehorse.co.uk
Adnams Southwold Bitter; Mill Green Mawkin Mild, White Horse Bitter, Loveleys Fair, seasonal beers 🅗
Well off the beaten track, this lovely rural free house has been recently extended. Alongside the pub and the Mill Green Eco Brewery there is a campsite and two self-catering chalets, all supplied with power from the site's own wind generator. Delicious home-made food uses locally sourced organic ingredients where possible. Beer and music festivals are held and the pub has a late licence when trade demands. Castling's Heath Cottage ciders are stocked. 🏨Q☺🍴◑🍺A🍴🚹P🖂

Exning

White Horse
23 Church Street, CB8 7EH

🌑 12-11 ☎ (01638) 577323
Beer range varies Ⓗ
Mentioned in the Domesday Book, this fine free house has been run by the same family since 1923. With a public bar, cosy lounge and a separate restaurant, it has a comfortable authenticity. An excellent menu of home-cooked food includes seafood, steaks and classic British dishes (booking advisable). Happy hour is 5.30-6.30pm, extended to 7pm on Friday. A private room is available for hire. ᴹ❀◐▯ ◳♣Pᵇ⌐

Felixstowe

Ferry Boat Ⓛ
The Ferry, IP11 9RZ TM328375
🌑 11-3, 5.30-11; 11-11 Sat; 12-10 Sun ☎ (01394) 284203
⊕ ferryboatinn.org.uk
Adnams Southwold Bitter; Woodforde's Wherry; guest beer Ⓗ
Very popular coastal pub set in a small hamlet north of the main town. The main bar has old stone-flagged flooring and traditional seating around a large fireplace. Food is mostly locally sourced and freshly prepared on the premises, with fish from the nearby fishermen's huts. Daily specials, gluten-free dishes and vegetarian options are available lunchtimes and evenings. A new garden room to the rear can cater for parties and functions, while the large garden at the front is busy in summer months. ᴹ⏁❀◐▯Pᵇ⌐

Framlingham

Station Hotel Ⓛ
Station Road, IP13 9EE (on B1116) TM284630
🌑 12-3, 5-11; 10-3, 7-10.30 Sun ☎ (01728) 723455
⊕ thestationhotel.net
Earl Soham Gannet Mild, Victoria Bitter, Brandeston Gold, seasonal beers Ⓗ
Cosy three-bar pub set in a former station buffet built in 1859 (the branch line closed in 1963). The pub enjoys a good reputation for food, all locally sourced and prepared on the premises, with the ever-changing menu displayed on chalkboards. Beers and a guest cider are dispensed from a set of Edwardian German silver handpumps. A beer festival is held at the end of July. The garden bar has a new wood-fired pizza oven. On Sunday, brunch and beer are available from 10am. Child- and dog-friendly. ᴹQ⏁❀◐♣ ♠Pᵇ⌐⊟(64,118,119)

Glemsford

Cherry Tree Inn
Tye Green, CO10 7RG
🌑 11-11 (midnight Fri & Sat); 12-10 Sun ☎ (01787) 281812
Beer range varies Ⓗ
Single bar local, beautifully situated overlooking the Tye Green in the centre of this long, straggling village which rises from Stour Valley in the south and descends north to the River Glem, from which the village takes its name. Family run and comfortable, the pub offers three beers, generally including a Growler ale from the nearby village of Pentlow. Worth a visit to photograph the pretty swinging cherry blossom sign as well as the beer. Dog-friendly. ❀◐▮

Great Wratting

Red Lion
School Road, CB9 7HA
🌑 11-2.30, 5-11; 11-1.30am Sat; 12-3, 7-10 Sun
☎ (01440) 783237
Adnams Southwold Bitter, Broadside, seasonal beers Ⓗ
The doorway to this village local is framed by whale's jawbones, making an unusual and amusing entrance. An Adnams' tied house dating from the 17th-18th century, it offers good beer, food and conversation as its mainstay. Locals love this pub and are passionate supporters of the entertainment and activities here, overseen by an enthusiastic landlord of long experience. Quiz nights and a darts league thrive. ᴹ❀◐♣P

Grundisburgh

Dog Ⓛ
The Green, IP13 6TA TM224509
🌑 closed Mon; 12-3, 5.30-11; 12-11 Fri-Sun
☎ (01473) 735267 ⊕ grundisburghdog.co.uk
Adnams Southwold Bitter; Earl Soham Victoria Bitter; Woodforde's Wherry; guest beer Ⓗ
Traditional two-room pub serving good beer and fine food. The public bar has a timber-beamed ceiling, flagstone flooring and comfortable seating, and offers a selection of pub games including darts and dominoes. The lounge bar is set for dining, with a varied menu of home-cooked meals and snacks made with locally sourced ingredients and including gluten-free options. Monthly themed food evenings are a highlight. Outside are seating areas to the front and rear and a children's play area. ᴹQ⏁❀◐▯ ◳♣P⊟(30,30A)

Haverhill

Royal Exchange
69-71 High Street, CB9 8HA
🌑 11-11; 12-10.30 Sun ☎ (01440) 702155
⊕ theroyalexchangepub.co.uk
Greene King IPA, Abbot, seasonal ales; Morland Original Bitter, Old Speckled Hen Ⓗ
Town-centre local with a classic street corner location. This Greene King-managed house has had the full refurbishment treatment, with scrubbed floors and old-style furniture. It can be boisterous with sports fans watching games on five TVs including 3D – free glasses supplied. The turnover on beer is rapid, ensuring high quality. ⏁❀♣⊟

Hawkedon

Queen's Head
Rede Road, IP29 4NN TL799530
🌑 5-11; 12-12.30am Fri, 12-midnight Sat; 12-11 Sun
☎ (01284) 789218 ⊕ hawkedonqueen.co.uk
Adnams Southwold Bitter; Woodforde's Wherry; guest beers Ⓗ/Ⓖ
Fifteenth-century free house off the beaten track with an unspoilt interior. In the bar is a huge fireplace with a stove. Real cider, perry and Belgian beer on tap are available. Locally sourced home-cooked food of very high quality is available Friday-Sunday. The pub holds a beer festival in July, and is a meeting place for classic car clubs. A butcher's shop on the premises is another string to its bow. A rural gem. ᴹQ❀◐♠♣Pᵇ⌐

Hoxne

Swan
Low Street, IP21 5AS TM179771
✪ 12-3, 6-11; 12-10.30 Sun ☎ (01379) 668275
Adnams Southwold bitter, Broadside ⑤; **Woodforde's Wherry; guest beers** Ⓗ
Good food made with fresh, seasonal, locally sourced ingredients is served alongside a selection of fine real ales. The timber-framed Grade II country pub was built in 1480 by the Bishop of Norwich and is full of history. It has three main rooms including a front bar with a large fireplace and high-beamed ceiling. The spacious garden backs onto the river and is close to where King Edmund, last Saxon king of East Anglia, was killed by the invading Danes. A beer festival is held in summer. ♨☞☸◑Pᵂ–⊟

Ipswich

Brewery Tap Ⓛ
Cliff Quay, IP3 0AT
✪ 11-3, 6-11; 11-11 Sat; 11-10.30 Sun ☎ (01473) 225501
⊕ thebrewerytap.org
Cliff Quay Bitter, Tolly Roger, seasonal beers; Earl Soham Victoria Bitter; guest beers Ⓗ
Old brewer's house located close to the former historic Tolly Cobbold brewery with a large main bar area and various more intimate spaces. Alongside beers that are mainly brewed locally is an extensive food menu with home-produced fare. Themed food nights, home-made pickled eggs and bar snacks are offered. There are great views of the River Orwell through a bay window in the bar, despite new sea defences being added. Regular live music plays. Two private function rooms are available and there is a secluded garden.
♨☞☸◑&♣Pᵂ–⊟(1,6)

Dove Street Inn Ⓛ
76 St Helens Street, IP4 2LA TM170445
✪ 12-midnight (10.30 Sun) ☎ (01473) 211270
⊕ dovestreetinn.co.uk
Adnams Broadside; Crouch Vale Brewers Gold; Fuller's London Pride Ⓗ; **guest beers** Ⓗ/⑤
A popular multi-roomed pub serving a large selection of real ales – including milds and traditional ciders – plus a choice of continental beers. Various ales from the nearby house brewery are also on handpump and there is a new beer shop next door. Home-cooked food and bar snacks are served at all times. Well-behaved dogs and children are welcome during the day. Three beer festivals are held annually, each with more than 60 cask ales. Letting rooms are available above the brewery. Q☞☸◑◐&♣Pᵂ–⊟⊟(66)

Fat Cat ♈ Ⓛ
288 Spring Road, IP4 5NL TM181448
✪ 12-11 (midnight Fri & Sat) ☎ (01473) 726524
⊕ fatcatipswich.co.uk
Crouch Vale Brewers Gold; Fuller's London Pride; Woodforde's Wherry; guest beers ⑤
This cosy drinking pub is a joy to visit with no background music or games machines. The walls display a selection of original enamel signs, posters and brewery artefacts. Up to 16 beers are dispensed from a taproom behind the bar, and a changing real cider is now kept. The secluded garden and patio provide extra space for occasional barbecues on summer afternoons. Snacks are available and plates provided for customers who

order in takeaways (not Fri or Sat eve). No children or dogs. Local CAMRA Branch Pub of the Year 2012 and 2013. Q☸≈(Derby Rd)♣●ᵂ–⊟(2,75)

Greyhound Ⓛ
9 Henley Road, IP1 3SE
✪ 11.30-11 (midnight Fri; 11.30 Sat); 10-10.30 Sun
☎ (01473) 252862 ⊕ thegreyhoundipswich.co.uk
Adnams Southwold Bitter, Ghost Ship, Broadside, seasonal beers; guest beer Ⓗ
The Greyhound has a cosy, traditional, small public bar at the front and a larger, more modern drinking and dining room to the side and rear. The outside drinking space can be busy in the summer months. Freshly prepared food from the menu and a daily specials board is served daily, with vegetarian options. Quiz nights are held twice a month on Sunday evenings. TVs are only used for sporting events. On Sunday, brunch is available 10-11.30am. Free Wi-Fi. Q☞☸◑◐&≈♣Pᵂ–⊟

Lord Nelson Ⓛ
81 Fore Street, IP4 1JZ
✪ 12-midnight (1.30am Fri & Sat); 12-11 Sun
☎ (01473) 407510 ⊕ lord-nelson.co.uk
Adnams Southwold Bitter, Ghost Ship, Broadside, seasonal beers ⑤
Dating from the 17th century, this pub is steeped in history. Situated a short walk from the waterfront, it is nautically themed with a half-timbered frontage and dormer windows. An unusual gravity dispense system incorporates a row of wooden casks to good effect and guarantees temperature-controlled real ales. The pub is also popular for locally prepared food including daily specials. Families and dogs are welcome and there is an enclosed patio area outside. Quiz nights are held twice a month. The public car park to the rear (off Star Lane) is free after 8pm. ☞☸◑≈ᵂ–⊟

Mulberry Tree Ⓛ
5 Woodbridge Road, IP4 2EA TM166447
✪ 12-11 (1am Fri & Sat) ☎ (01473) 225 776
Adnams Southwold Bitter Ⓗ; **guest beers** Ⓗ/⑤
Built in 1928, this imposing large bar close to the town centre was bought in 2012 by the current owner and refurbished as a free house after several years of neglect. It now has woodblock flooring throughout and a large open fire in the main bar area. There are plans for a new kitchen and outdoor seating to provide alfresco drinking and dining. Beers are served in oversized glasses. Live music plays on Friday and Saturday evenings and every other Sunday. Dogs and children are welcome. ♨☞☸◑≈●⊟(66)

St Jude's Brewery Tavern Ⓛ
69 St Matthew's Street, IP1 1EW
✪ closed Sun-Tue; 4-11 Wed; 12-midnight Thu-Sat; 12-11 Sun ☎ 07787 468514 ⊕ stjudestavern.com
Beer range varies ⑤
Small, friendly, gothic bar close to the town centre with sawdust on the floor and quirky artefacts on display. Formerly a photographic studio, it opened in 2011 as a tribute to a 19th-century back-street beer house. The only pub owned by the former St Jude's Brewery (which may be resurrected), up to 20 changing beers and four ciders are served from a gravity stillage. Some imported lagers are also kept. Occasional acoustic music plays and there is a TV for sport only. Themed nights include fancy dress halloween and pirate nights. A function room is available upstairs. &≈♣●⊟

Thomas Wolsey Ⓛ

9-13 St Peters Street, IP1 1XF (300yds from bus station)
✪ 4.30-midnight (closed Sun) ☎ (01473) 210055
**Adnams Ghost Ship; Crouch Vale Brewers Gold;
Woodforde's Wherry; guest beer** Ⓗ
Large single-room lounge bar set in a historic Grade
II-listed building. It has a patio area to the side and
two nicely furnished function rooms upstairs used
for a wide variety of events including story-telling
nights, charity quiz matches and meetings. Jazz and
R&B feature twice a month on Thursday evenings.
Over 40 quality wines are stocked (20 sold by the
glass). Games are available including darts. Home
supporters only on football match days.
ᗐ⊛≠♣'–⊟

Ixworth

Greyhound

49 High Street, IP31 2HJ
✪ 11-3, 6-11; 12-3, 7-11 Sun ☎ (01359) 230887
**Greene King XX Mild, IPA, Abbot, seasonal beers;
Ruddles Best Bitter** Ⓗ
Situated on the town's pretty High Street, this
traditional inn has three bars, one a lovely central
snug. The heart of the building dates back to Tudor
times. The pub is a rare outlet for XX Mild. Good-
value lunches and early evening meals are served
in the restaurant. Dominoes, crib, darts and pool
are played in leagues and for charity fundraising.
There is an area outside for camping and
caravanning. ⊛⊕⊟▲♣P⊟

Laxfield

King's Head (Low House) ★ Ⓛ

Gorams Mill Lane, IP13 8DW (behind churchyard)
TM296724
✪ 12-3, 6-11; 12-midnight Sat; 12-8 Sun ☎ (01986) 798395
⊕ laxfieldkingshead.co.uk
**Adnams Sole Star, Southwold Bitter, Ghost Ship,
Broadside, seasonal beers; guest beer** Ⓖ
A warren of small rooms, low ceilings, high-back
settles and beers served straight from their casks in
a taproom with no bar counter make this a special
and unique pub. Dating from about 1560, it has
changed little over the years. Traditional home-
cooked food features local ingredients, with special
themed evenings. A large garden to the rear has
croquet and pétanque, and an annual beer festival
is hosted. B&B, camping and self-catering
accommodation are available by arrangement.
Dog-friendly. ᵐQᗐ⊛♣⊕⊟▲♣P'–

Long Melford

Crown

Hall Street, CO10 9JL
✪ 11.30-11; 12-10.30 Sun ☎ (01787) 377666
⊕ thecrownhotelmelford.co.uk
Adnams Southwold Bitter, Ghost Ship; guest beers Ⓗ
This historic coaching inn dating from 1610 is a
traditional family run free house in the centre of a
long village, originally near the Mill Ford or Melford
as it has become known. A central servery provides
access to the bar, lounge and restaurant. Outside is
a large patio/garden area for summer drinking and
dining. As well as two regular beers there are two
ever-changing guests (Humpty Dumpty ales are
favoured) and an excellent bar and restaurant food
menu. Accommodation is in 12 guest rooms.
Q⊛⊭⊕♿P'–⊟

Lower Ufford

White Lion Ⓛ

Lower Street, IP13 6DW
✪ closed Mon; 11.30-2.30, 6-11; 11.30-2.30 Sun
☎ (01394) 460770 ⊕ uffordwhitelion.co.uk
**Adnams Southwold Bitter; Uffa Tipple, Gold; guest
beers** Ⓖ
Cosy, small, single-bar pub with a quarry-tiled floor
offering various home-brewed beers on gravity
stillage. Food is all locally sourced and freshly
prepared on the premises. The large garden leads
to the River Deben and includes a substantial
marquee that is used for entertainment on summer
days. Many special events are held including car
rallies, an annual beer festival over the August
bank holiday, themed balls, food evenings
including hog roasts and other private events.
ᵐQᗐ⊛⊕▲♣P

Lowestoft

Mariners Rest

60-62 Rotterdam Road, NR32 2HA
✪ 11-midnight (2am Fri & Sat); 12-11.30 Sun
☎ (01502) 218077
Beer range varies Ⓗ/Ⓖ
This welcoming local is called the Rest due to the
nearby cemetery and is part of the Mariners pub
chain. The comfortable open-plan interior has a
unique darts alley and a central bar serving a vast
array of ever-changing real ales and ciders,
dispensed on both handpump and gravity. It has a
good-sized enclosed garden with a heated
smoking area. The pub hosts a lot of community
fundraising events on behalf of local charities.
⊛≠♣●'–⊟

Norman Warrior Ⓛ

Fir Lane, NR32 2RB
✪ 11-midnight (12.30am Fri & Sat); 12-10.30 Sun
☎ (01502) 561982 ⊕ thenormanwarrior.co.uk
Greene King IPA; guest beers Ⓗ
Large estate pub situated between Lowestoft town
and Oulton Broad North railway stations. It has a
public bar with pool table and dartboard, leading to
a spacious beer garden and terrace where a well-
attended beer and cider festival with live music is
held over the August bank holiday weekend. The
comfortable lounge leads to a spacious restaurant.
CAMRA members receive a discount on real ales.
⊛⊕≠(Oulton Broad North)♣●P'–⊟

Oak Tavern Ⓛ

Crown Street West, NR32 1SQ
✪ 10.30-11; 12-10.30 Sun ☎ (01502) 537246
**Adnams Southwold Bitter; Greene King Abbot; guest
beers** Ⓗ
Popular with all ages, this lively drinkers' back-
street local has an open-plan bar divided into two
areas with a patio and car park to the rear. Four
real ales are always available, often including a
dark beer in the winter months. An annual beer
festival takes place during the summer and various
events are held throughout the year to raise
money for local charities. ⊛≠♣P'–⊟

Stanford Arms Ⓛ

94 Stanford Street, NR32 2DD
✪ 12-midnight (1am Fri & Sat); 12-11 Sun
☎ (01502) 587444 ⊕ stanfordarms.co.uk
**Green Jack Golden Best, Orange Wheat, Trawlerboys,
Rising Sun, Gone Fishing, seasonal beers** Ⓗ

This Green Jack Brewery tap is ideally situated five minutes' walk from the brewery, close to Lowestoft FC and a short walk from the town railway station. The spacious open-plan bar offers up to six Green Jack beers plus a guest and a real cider. To the rear is a large courtyard garden with its own wood-fired pizza oven (available for hire) – Friday is pizza night. Home-made snacks are available lunchtimes. Curries and quiz nights alternate on Wednesday evenings. ⋈😊≷♣♠≟

Triangle Tavern 🅛

29 St Peters Street, NR32 1QA

✪ 11-11 (midnight Thu; 1am Fri & Sat); 12-10.30 Sun
☎ (01502) 582711 ⊕ thetriangletavern.co.uk

Green Jack Golden Best, Orange Wheat, Trawlerboys, Rising Sun, seasonal beers; guest beers Ⓗ/Ⓖ

Popular town centre tavern located close to Triangle market place and 10 minutes' walk from train and bus stations. It has contrasting bars – the cosy front bar, adorned with many awards for fine ales brewed by Green Jack Brewery, hosts live music most Friday evenings. The back bar is more popular with a younger clientele, has a central pool table and stages lively DJ nights. The full range of Green Jack beers is available, plus guests and a changing real cider. 😊⊟≷♠≟🖼

Market Weston

Mill Inn 🅛

Bury Road, IP22 2PD TL979776

✪ 11-3 (not Mon), 5-11; 12-3, 7-11 Sun ☎ (01359) 221018
⊕ millinn-marketweston.co.uk

Old Chimneys Military Mild, Scarlet Tiger; guest beers Ⓗ

Striking white brick and flint-faced inn standing at a crossroads. It is the closest outlet for the Old Chimneys Brewery, located on the other side of the village. Run by the same landlady for more than 17 years, it offers an excellent choice of beers complemented by a good menu of home-cooked meals (no food Mon eve). ⋈Q⊙◐♣P

Naughton

Wheelhouse

Whatfield Road, IP7 7BS (450yds off B1078)

✪ 5-11 (9 Mon; 8 Tue); 6-11 Sat; 12-10.30 Sun
☎ (01449) 740496

Beer range varies Ⓗ

Please mind your head when entering this small rural thatched pub with very low beams in the main bar. The traditionally tiled floor is a foot lower than it once was and is now below ground level. The bar has a welcoming fire on cold nights. A larger public bar is brighter and more modern, and leads to a games room with pool table and darts. Opening times may vary to suit demand. A delightful, friendly pub, well worth seeking out. Dogs are welcome. ⋈Q😊&♣P🖼

Newbourne

Fox 🅛

The Street, IP12 4NY (close to village church) TM273431

✪ 11-11; 12-10.30 Sun ☎ (01473) 736307
⊕ debeninns.co.uk/fox

Adnams Southwold Bitter; guest beers Ⓗ

This 13th-century timber-framed inn has quaint old-world charm and is popular with families, ramblers and locals alike. Reputedly, some of the

timber used in its construction came from wrecked sailing ships. Good food served all day includes a full à la carte menu, gluten-free options and daily specials. The garden has a pond with fish and wildfowl. George Page, the Suffolk giant who stood 7ft 7in tall and died in 1870, is buried nearby. ⋈Q≷😊⊙◐&P≟🖼

Orford

Jolly Sailor

Quay Street, IP12 2NU TM424496

✪ 12-3, 5.30-11; 12-11 Sat; 12-10.30 Sun ☎ (01394) 450243
⊕ jollysailororford.co.uk

Adnams Southwold Bitter, Ghost Ship, Broadside, seasonal beers Ⓗ

Situated close to the modern quay, this 16th-century building is constructed in part from old ship's timbers and was formerly six fishermen's cottages. Sympathetically refurbished, it retains much character. The main bar is a wonderful drinking space with real local characters, while a tiny snug and three further rooms are used for dining, offering fresh fish dishes and plenty of local produce. Take-away fish and chips is available 6-7pm every Friday. ⋈Q≷😊⊟⊙◐&⅄P≟🖼

Pakefield

Oddfellows 🍷 🅛

6 Nightingale Road, NR33 7AU

✪ 11-11 ☎ (01502) 538415

Adnams Southwold Bitter, seasonal beers; guest beers Ⓗ

Popular inn situated near Pakefield's cliffs and just a stone's throw from the sea. A small, cosy pub with three open-plan areas, it has wooden flooring and panelling throughout. One area is reserved for diners (booking advised). The walls are festooned with pictures of old Pakefield. Up to four beers are available, usually including one or two from Green Jack Brewery. The pub hosts two beer festivals, one in the summer and the other showcasing dark beer in the winter. 😊⊙◐🖼

Rattlesden

Five Bells

High Street, IP30 0RA

✪ 12-12.30am (11.30 Sun) ☎ (01449) 737373

Beer range varies Ⓗ

Set on the high road through a picturesque village, this is a good old Suffolk drinking house – few of its kind still survive. Three well-chosen ales on the bar are usually sourced direct from the breweries. The cosy single-room interior has a games area on a lower level and there is occasional live music. Pub games include shut the box and shove-ha'penny, plus pétanque and croquet in the garden in summer. A dog-friendly pub. ⋈Q😊♣≟

Rickinghall

Bell Inn 🅛

The Street, IP22 1BN (adjacent to Botesdale)

✪ 11-11 (midnight Fri & Sat) ☎ (01379) 898445
⊕ thebellrickinghall.co.uk

Adnams Southwold Bitter, Broadside Ⓗ

Dating back to the 17th century, this inn was once used by travellers going from Great Yarmouth to Bury St Edmunds and London. It was a popular stop-off because of its extensive stabling, accommodation and lively bar. More recently, it has become the focal point of the village, popular with locals as well as visitors. The lounge has a log fire and beamed ceilings. Food is available seven days a week. Children and dogs are welcome. ▨✿🖂◑🐾P¼🖥🖥

Risby

Crown & Castle
South Street, IP28 6QU
✪ 12-3, 5 (6.30 Sat)-11; 12-3, 7-11 Sun ☎ (01284) 810398
🌐 crownandcastle.com
Greene King IPA, seasonal beers Ⓗ
This attractive flint-faced building opened as a pub and shop in the late 1800s. A 120ft well was discovered during alterations in recent times and is now a feature beneath a grille in the entrance lobby. The pub has classic back and front bars, with good food served in both. The back bar is the public, with games and conversation predominating – dogs are allowed in here outside food service times. ▨Q☎◑🖾P¼

Rumburgh

Buck Ⓛ
Mill Road, IP19 0NS
✪ 11.45-3, 6.30-11; 12-3, 7-10.30 Sun ☎ (01986) 785257
Adnams Southwold Bitter, seasonal beers; guest beers Ⓗ
This inn and the parish church were once part of a Benedictine priory. The traditional village pub now features a number of interlinked rooms on various levels, with stone floors, oak beams, wood-panelled walls and bench seating. Outside is a small garden. Guest beers and ciders are often locally sourced and occasional mini beer festivals are held. Home to the famous Old Glory morris dancers, this is a gem of a pub and at the heart of village life. Suffolk CAMRA Pub of the Year in 2012. ☎🖾◑🖾🍴🐾P¼

Shadingfield

Fox
London Road, NR34 8DD (on A145) TM434850
✪ closed Mon; 12-3, 6-11; 12-11 Sun ☎ (01502) 575100
🌐 shadingfieldfox.co.uk
Black Sheep Best Bitter; guest beers Ⓗ
Situated in a tiny village on the edge of Sotterley Park, this inn dates back to the 16th century. The original arched doors and carved fox heads have been retained. The interior comprises a bar, lounge/dining area and conservatory. Outside, a patio and small garden are popular in summer months, and there is a heated area for smokers. Beer festivals are held twice yearly, one on Father's Day weekend and the other close to Guy Fawkes night. Live music every Friday evening features local artists. ▨Q☎◑P¼🖥(524 - not Sun)

Shottisham

Sorrel Horse Ⓛ
Hollesley Road, IP12 3HD (in village just off B1083) TM320446
✪ 12-3, 6-11; 12-midnight Sat; 12-10.30 Sun
☎ (01394) 411617 🌐 thesorrelhorse-shottisham.co.uk
Adnams Southwold Bitter; Woodforde's Wherry; guest beers Ⓗ

Formerly a smugglers' inn dating back to the 15th century, this picturesque thatched two-bar pub retains a gravity stillage for its beers. Local villagers helped raise the funds to keep the pub open by buying shares in it a year or two back. The pub hosts regular music nights every other Monday and a weekly quiz night on Wednesday evening. The food menu offers various locally sourced dishes prepared on the premises, and special themed evenings also feature. The bar has an original bar billiards table. Seats in the garden are popular on sunny days. ▨Q🖾◑🐾P🖥

Southwold

Lord Nelson Ⓛ
42 East Street, IP18 6EJ
✪ 10.30-11; 12-10.30 Sun ☎ (01502) 722079
Adnams Southwold Bitter, Explorer, Broadside, seasonal beers Ⓗ
A regular entry in the Guide, this pub is situated near the Sailors' Reading Room Museum and just a stone's throw from the sea cliff. A busy and lively hostelry, it is popular with locals and visitors alike. It offers three drinking areas, with children welcome in the side room and the partly covered and heated patio area to the rear. The main bar is flagstoned and has an open fire. Much Nelson and other naval memorabilia adorns the walls. ▨🖾◑A¼🖥

Stanningfield

Red House
Bury Road, IP29 4RR
✪ 5 (12 Sat)-11.30; closed Wed; 12-11 Sun
☎ (01284) 828330
Greene King IPA; guest beers Ⓗ
Built in 1866 in Victorian red brick, the building may once have been a beer house but was a cobbler's around 1900 with possibly some beer sold on the side. Now a free house, rescued from closure by a vociferous local and CAMRA campaign, it has been sympathetically extended with extra bars and accommodation. Well supported, the pub fields teams in local leagues for cribbage, darts and bar billiards. Close to Lavenham, and surrounded by beautiful countryside, it is handy for places of interest. ▨Q🖾◑⬡P¼🖥

Stowmarket

King's Arms
Station Road, IP14 1RQ
✪ 11-11
Woodforde's Wherry; guest beers Ⓗ
Lively and friendly multi-roomed hostelry, just a short walk from the railway station and town centre. Pub games are popular here, and the pub hosts occasional live music and barbecues. Food is available until 4pm including snacks, stews, hotpots, chilli and omelettes. The patio to the rear leads to a smoking room plus various other function rooms used for live music and private parties. Dogs are welcome when the pub is not busy. An annual beer festival is held in July. The cider is usually Old Rosie. Q🖾◑≈🐾P¼🖥(88,88A)

Royal William
53 Union Street, IP14 1HP (off Stowupland St)
✪ 11 (12 Sun)-11 ☎ (01449) 674553

Greene King IPA; Oakham JHB; Woodforde's Wherry; guest beers Ⓖ
Tucked away down a side street and just a short walk from the town centre, this is a real gem of a pub. An end-of-terrace back-street bar, it is well supported by locals and visitors alike. Regular dominoes, darts and crib matches are played and sport is shown on TV. Ales are served by gravity dispense from the cellar behind the bar. Occasional live entertainment includes traditional music once a month. Food is served all day and includes various snacks and occasional specials at the weekend. ❀◖◗⥱♣⊱–🚌

Sudbury

Brewery Tap

21 East Street, CO10 2TP (200yds from Market Place)
⚙ 11-11 (midnight Fri & Sat); 12-10 Sun ☎ (01787) 370876
🌐 blackaddertap.co.uk
Mauldons Mole Trap, Silver Adder, Suffolk Pride Ⓗ**, seasonal beers; guest beers** Ⓗ/Ⓖ
The tap for the local Mauldons Brewery – all the brewery's ales can be found here off and on, and up to five guests are also made welcome. Food is limited to sandwiches, pies and soups, but takeaways can be ordered in. Beer festivals are held in April and October and regular jazz/music sessions and a monthly Sunday breakfast club also feature; however, conversation is the main entertainment in this traditional pub. Local CAMRA Pub of the Year 2012. Q❀♿⥱♣⊱–🗑🚌

Sweffling

White Horse 𝕃

Low Road, IP17 2BB (on B1119 between Framlingham and Saxmundham) TM344642
⚙ 7-11 Fri to Mon only ☎ (01728) 664178
🌐 swefflingwhitehorse.co.uk
Beer range varies Ⓖ
Recently reopened after a long period of closure, this building has been refurbished by the owners in a green and environmentally-friendly manner. A cosy, traditional two-room pub, it is warmed by a woodburner and wood-fired range. Gravity-dispensed beers from local brewers are served through a taproom door. A range of Fairtrade, organic and local Adnams' spirits is also available, and bar snacks are served. Live music plays monthly, there is a piano and various pub games are offered including bar billiards, darts, crib and board games. Horse and trap rides are often available in summer. ⛰Q🚸🛏♣🍎P🚌

Tattingstone

White Horse 𝕃

White Horse Hill, IP9 2NU TM136382
⚙ 12-3, 6-11; 12-11 Fri & Sat; 12-10 Sun ☎ (01473) 328060
🌐 whitehorsetattingstone.co.uk
Adnams Southwold Bitter; Crouch Vale Blackwater Mild, Brewers Gold; guest beers Ⓗ
A heavily beamed ceiling and log-burning stove dominate the main bar of this Grade II-listed 17th-century inn. Beers include a changing mild – the real cider is often from Westons. Excellent home-cooked food is available, and a curry night is held in conjunction with a local restaurant on the last Thursday of the month. The pub also hosts summer barbecues and other events including blue grass each month and various music nights. Dogs and bikers are welcome, and there are outside toilets and a caravan and campsite to the rear.
⛰Q🚸❀◖◗⛺♣🍎P🚌(96,96a)

Thorndon

Black Horse

The Street, IP23 7JR
⚙ 12-3, 5 (6 Sat)-11; 12-10.30 Sun ☎ (01379) 678523
🌐 theblackhorsethorndon.co.uk
Adnams Southwold Bitter; Greene King IPA; guest beers Ⓗ
Traditional country pub in the heart of a pretty village. Dating back to the 1600s and full of character, it has many historic photos of the village on display. The central bar has a log fire and two adjoining restaurant areas. Two guest ales are usually on offer, typically local and often from Brandon, Grain or Woodforde's breweries. At lunchtime there is a carvery and evening meals are served daily. Dogs on a lead are welcome in the main bar. ⛰Q❀◖◗P⊱–

Thurston

Fox & Hounds

Barton Road, IP31 3QT
⚙ 12-2.30, 5-11; 12-midnight Fri & Sat; 12-10.30 Sun
☎ (01359) 232228 🌐 thurstonfoxandhounds.co.uk
Adnams Southwold Bitter; Greene King IPA; guest beers Ⓗ
A listed building, this busy local pub sits in the middle of the village and is at the centre of local life. The restaurant, serving good home-cooked food, is within the public bar area but separated by uprights from an original wall. There is a separate bar for pool, darts and Sky TV. On bank holidays and special occasions live music is performed. Conker competitions are a feature in autumn. B&B accommodation is available.
❀🛏◖◗⛺⥱♣🍎P⊱–🚌

Walberswick

Anchor 𝕃

Main Street, IP18 6UA
⚙ 11-4, 6-11; 11-11 Sat; 12-11 Sun ☎ (01502) 722112
🌐 anchoratwalberswick.com
Adnams Southwold Bitter, Broadside, seasonal beers Ⓗ
In a picturesque coastal village, the Anchor is a classic example of Brewer's Tudor and caters for holidaymakers and locals alike. The open front bar is bright and comfortable, with oak flooring, wood panels and a smattering of local scenes on the walls. A large restaurant to the rear serves high-quality local produce. Apart from the perfect Adnams' ales, there is a generous selection of global bottled beers. Accommodation comes in the shape of four bedrooms in the main building and six additional garden chalet rooms.
⛰Q🚸❀🛏◖◗⊞♿⛺P⊱–

Wingfield

De La Pole Arms

Church Road, IP21 5RA (follow brown tourist signs to Wingfield Barns)
⚙ 12-3 (11 Sat); 12-10.30 Sun ☎ (01379) 384545
Adnams Southwold Bitter; Black Sheep Best Bitter Ⓗ
Traditional village pub in a lovely setting opposite the church where Elizabeth of York is buried.

Wingfield College stands next to the church with Wingfield Barns arts centre alongside. Extensively and lovingly restored in the mid-1990s, the pub is full of character, with oak beams and log fires in both bars. Dogs are welcome in the public bar and food is served in both the saloon bar and the restaurant area with its vaulted ceiling.
♨☎🐕🛏️🍽️🅿️🚃

Withersfield

White Horse
Hollow Hill, CB9 7SH
🌐 11-11; 12-10.30 Sun ☎ (01440) 706081
⊕ whitehorsewithersfield.co.uk
Greene King IPA; guest beers ⓗ
Withersfield village is on a Roman road traversing the country from Cambridge south-eastwards. The White Horse originates from the 1600s and probably once served as a coaching inn for this ancient route. It now has a public bar with a huge fire in winter, a separate restaurant and a large garden popular with families in summer. Cricket buffs will be interested in the pub's connection with Sir Donald Bradman. There are five B&B rooms. ♨Q☎🍽️🛏️🅿️🚃

Woodbridge

Angel
2 Theatre Street, IP12 4NE TM270491
🌐 12-3, 5-11 (midnight Fri); 12-midnight Sat; 12-10.30 Sun
☎ (01394) 383808 ⊕ theangelwoodbridge.co.uk
Adnams Southwold Bitter; guest beers ⓗ
A wide range of changing beers and a massive selection of gin are on offer at this popular and lively 16th-century inn, just off the market square. One bar is used for dining or private hire (by arrangement), with home-made food on offer and occasional themed food evenings. Bar areas are furnished in a homely style with additional outside covered seating areas. The pub hosts monthly gin tasting evenings, live music every other Monday and monthly open mic nights. Child- and dog-friendly. ♨☎🐕🅿️🚃

Cherry Tree Inn Ⓛ
73 Cumberland Street, IP12 4AG
🌐 10.30-11 ☎ (01394) 384627 ⊕ thecherrytreepub.co.uk

Adnams Southwold Bitter, Ghost Ship, Broadside, seasonal beers; Elgood's Black Dog Mild; guest beers ⓗ
Spacious bar with a large central counter and several distinct seating areas. Eight beers are usually on offer and two annual beer festivals are hosted. All food is locally sourced and home cooked, including gluten-free options, and served all day. Board games are available to play. The large garden has play equipment to the rear. Accommodation is offered in a converted barn beside the garden and car park. Wheelchair, child and dog friendly. ♨☎🐕🍽️🛏️🅿️🚃

Old Bell & Steelyard
103 New Street, IP12 1DZ
🌐 12-3, 6-11.30 (12.30am Fri & Sat); 12-3, 7-11 Sun
☎ (01394) 382933 ⊕ yeoldebellandsteelyard.co.uk
Greene King IPA, seasonal beers; guest beers ⓗ
Large multi-roomed pub with oak beams in two bars and a separate function room. The steelyard – a former cart weighbridge that still works – dates from 1650 and was on show at the Great Exhibition in 1851. Traditional games include bar billiards, chess and bar skittles. Occasional Hungarian dishes feature on a good home-cooked food menu. To the rear of the building is a large heated and covered patio area. An annual beer and cheese festival is held in July. Dog- and family-friendly.
♨☎🐕🛏️🍽️🚃

Yaxley

Cherry Tree Ⓨ Ⓛ
Old Norwich Road, IP23 8BH TM121743
🌐 closed Mon; 12-3, 6-midnight; 12-7 Sun
☎ (01379) 788050 ⊕ yaxleycherrytree.co.uk
Adnams Southwold Bitter; Earl Soham Victoria Bitter; Woodforde's Wherry; guest beers ⓗ
Unusual community village local incorporating a post office and shop, with a large enclosed garden to the rear. Four handpumps feature three rotating ales from East Anglia and one 'foreign' beer from outside the area. Beer festivals are held twice a year and barbecues every bank holiday Monday. The pub displays numerous historic photos of the village in the front bar and a vast display of pump clips in the back bar. The games room has pool and darts. A covered and heated area is provided outside for smokers. ♨☎🐕🛏️🅿️🚃

Spores for thought

Yeast is a fungus, a single cell plant that can convert a sugary liquid into equal proportions of alcohol and carbon dioxide. There are two basic types of yeast used in brewing, one for ale and one for lager. (The yeasts used to make the Belgian beers known as gueuze and lambic are wild spores in the atmosphere). It is often said that ale is produced by 'top fermentation' and lager by 'bottom fermentation'. While it is true that during ale fermentation a thick blanket of yeast head and protein is created on top of the liquid while only a thin slick appears on top of fermenting lager, the descriptions are seriously misleading. Yeast works at all levels of the sugar-rich liquid in order to turn malt sugars into alcohol. If yeast worked only at the top or bottom of the liquid, a substantial proportion of sugar would not be fermented. Ale is fermented at a high temperature, lager at a much lower one. The furious speed of ale fermentation creates the yeast head and with it the rich, fruity aromas and flavours that are typical of the style. It is more accurate to describe the ale method as 'warm fermentation' and the lager one as 'cold fermentation'.

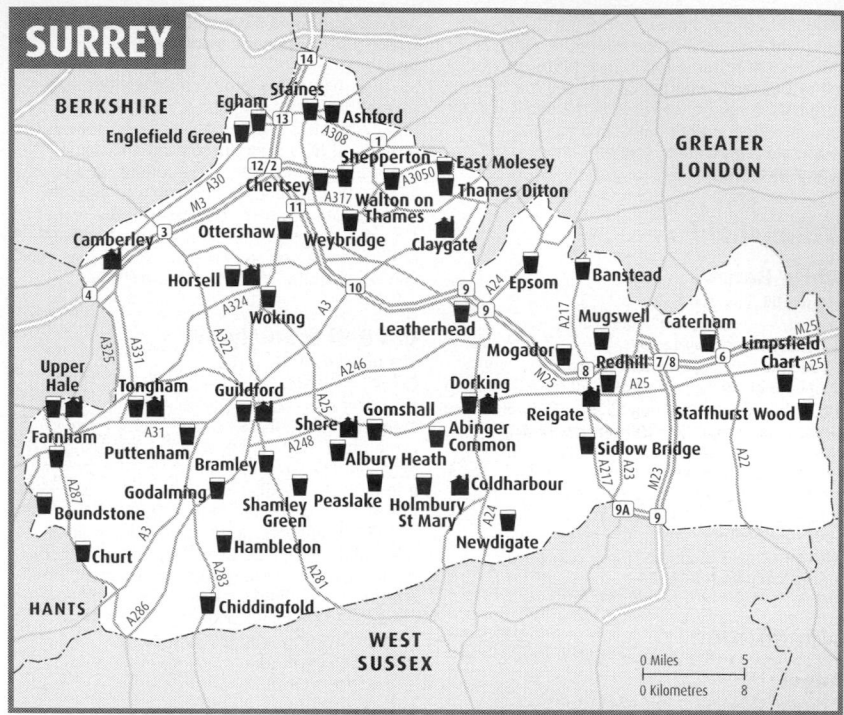

SURREY

BERKSHIRE

Egham
Staines
Ashford
Englefield Green
Shepperton — East Molesey
Chertsey — Thames Ditton
Walton on Thames
Ottershaw — Weybridge — Claygate
Camberley
Horsell
Woking
Leatherhead
Epsom
Banstead
Mugswell
Caterham
Limpsfield
Chart
Upper Hale
Tongham
Guildford
Dorking
Redhill
Mogador
Reigate
Staffhurst Wood
Farnham
Puttenham
Bramley
Shere
Gomshall
Abinger Common
Sidlow Bridge
Albury Heath
Godalming
Shamley Green
Peaslake
Holmbury St Mary
Coldharbour
Boundstone
Churt
Hambledon
Newdigate
HANTS
Chiddingfold
WEST SUSSEX

GREATER LONDON

0 Miles 5
0 Kilometres 8

Abinger Common

Abinger Hatch
Abinger Lane, RH5 6HZ TQ 115459
11-11.30; 12-10.30 Sun ☎ (01306) 730737
⊕ theabingerhatch.com
Beer range varies ⓗ
Very attractive 17th-century inn opposite the church. The interior rambles over three levels, all served from a beautiful bar constructed of English oak. The lowest part has large flagstones, with the other areas having bare boards. Good food is a feature, with a varied menu on offer. There are usually four or five beers available, mainly from regional brewers, often including one or two from Ringwood plus, sometimes, a local one. There are large gardens. ⚶Q♿😋🕩P⸺🚌

Albury Heath

William IV ⓛ
Dark Lane, Little London, GU5 9DG TQ066467
11-3, 5.30-11; 11-11 Sat; 12-10.30 Sun ☎ (01483) 202685
⊕ williamivalbury.com
Hogs Back TEA; Surrey Hills Ranmore Ale, Shere Drop; Young's Bitter ⓗ
Part 16th-century building set on a quiet lane adjoining extensive woodland in an area popular with walkers. The interior features beams, flagstones and a large fireplace where a welcoming wood fire burns brightly in winter. There are two traditional bars with a dining room up a few steps. Excellent home-made meals are served (no food Sun eve). Dishes include Gloucester Old Spot pork from the pigs kept in the field behind the pub. Shove-ha'penny can be played. ⚶Q😋🕩♣P⸺

Ashford

King's Fairway ⓛ
91 Fordbridge Road, TW15 2SS (on B377)
11.30-11 (midnight Fri & Sat) ☎ (01784) 423575
Fuller's London Pride; Sharp's Doom Bar; guest beers ⓗ
Large family-friendly pub in a cosy, traditional style. Six handpumps dispense two regular guest ales and frequently changing value-for-money guests, usually including one from Windsor & Eton. Food is also reasonably priced and served in a family dining area. Gas fires provide comfort in the winter months. Quiz nights are Wednesday and Sunday and curry night is Thursday, with additional themed food evenings and roasts on Sunday. There is soft music and a small TV area for news and sport. Alongside the seated patio is a heated smokers' refuge. Q😋😋🕩🚌P⸺🚌(290)

Banstead

Woolpack
186 High Street, SM7 2NZ (on B2217)
11-11; 12-10.30 Sun ☎ (01737) 354560
⊕ thewoolpackbanstead.co.uk
Shepherd Neame Master Brew, Spitfire, Bishops Finger; guest beers ⓗ
Although this pub is tied to Shepherd Neame it offers two ever-changing guest beers from smaller independent breweries. To the right of the bar is a wood-burning stove and some sofas. Behind the main bar seating area is a separate restaurant where good food is available all day (not Sun eve). There is a garden at the back and a patio to the front. Live jazz plays on the first Tuesday afternoon of the month. A beer festival is held in the summer. ⚶😋🕩🚌P⸺🚌

Boundstone

Bat & Ball
Bat and Ball Lane, GU10 4SA (off Sandrock Hill Road via Upper Bourne Lane) SU833444
✪ 11-11; 12-10.30 Sun ☎ (01252) 792108
⊕ thebatandball.co.uk
Bowman Swift One; Hogs Back TEA; guest beers H
Once a tallyman's office where hop-pickers received (and spent) their earnings, this is now a genuine free house offering six interesting beers mainly from adjoining counties, alongside excellent food. The beer range is clearly displayed with strengths and prices. A family-friendly front room complements the beamed, panelled and log-fired bar – a cosy inner sanctum for adults. The garden, with children's playground, hosts an annual beer festival. The last Thursday of the month is open mic night and other live music features occasionally. ᨏQ♨❀☸❍◗♿P⁵⊖🚋(16,17)

Bramley

Jolly Farmer L
High Street, GU5 0HB TQ008448
✪ 11 (12 Sun)-11 ☎ (01483) 893355 ⊕ jollyfarmer.co.uk
King Horsham Best Bitter; Young's Bitter; guest beers H
A privately owned free house, this traditional pub in the village centre is full of character with oak beams and heavy decoration, and has a cosy, welcoming atmosphere. High-quality food is served in the bar and a separate dining area lunchtimes and evenings. Three to six guest beers are from small breweries both local and further afield, with a dark beer usually available. The only lagers are interesting continental imports. Families and dogs are welcome.
Q❀☸❍◗♿♣♠P⁵⊖🚋(53,63)

Caterham

King & Queen L
34 High Street, CR3 5UA (on B2030)
✪ 11-11 (midnight Fri & Sat); 12-11 Sun ☎ (01883) 345438
⊕ kingandqueencaterham.co.uk
Fuller's Chiswick Bitter, London Pride, ESB, seasonal beers; guest beers H
Thanks to its outstanding beer quality, this pub has featured in the past 20 issues of the Guide. Originally three 17th-century cottages, the friendly hostelry has been serving the local community for around 170 years. It retains three distinct areas – the front room has the character of a public bar, the back room is used for darts, and the central area is welcoming with a log fire. Good food and snacks are available at most times. The smoking area is covered and heated. ᨏQ❀❍◗▣♣P⁵⊖🚋(400,409)

Chertsey

Coach & Horses L
14 St Ann's Road, KT16 9DG (on B375)
✪ 12-11 (8 Sun) ☎ (01932) 563085
⊕ coachandhorseschertsey.co.uk
Fuller's London Pride, ESB; Gale's Seafarers Ale H
Rambling, tile-hung, one-bar pub with interesting nooks and crannies situated on the edge of town. A perennial Guide entry, it is dedicated to serving regularly available Fuller's ales in superb condition. Good-value English food is available at lunchtimes and weekday evenings (no food Mon eve). League

darts is played. There is seating with an awning for smokers at the front. Close to the town's cricket and football grounds, frequent buses to Staines and Woking stop nearby. Free Wi-Fi available.
ᨏ❀☸❍◗♣P⁵⊖🚋(51,446)

Thyme at the Tavern L
20 London Street, KT16 8AA (jct of London St and Heriot Rd)
✪ 5-midnight Mon; 12-midnight (1am Fri & Sat)
☎ (01932) 429667 ⊕ thymeatthetavern.co.uk
Courage Best Bitter; Marston's Pedigree; guest beers H
This free house was local CAMRA Pub of the Year 2012. Alongside the two regular cask beers, two guests, usually from local or neighbouring county microbreweries, are available. Bottle-conditioned ales and continental bottled beers are also stocked. Occasional beer festivals are held. The pub is noted for its food (served Tue-Fri), particularly its Sunday lunches, but diners have to fit in with drinkers. Regular Friday night live music is hosted and the pub is heavily involved in local charity fundraising. It has a comfortable marquee smoking refuge. Dog friendly. ᨏ♨❀☸❍◗ᡱ♣⁵⊖🚋

Chiddingfold

Swan Inn L
Petworth Road, GU8 4TY SU960353
✪ 11-11 ☎ (01428) 684688 ⊕ theswaninnchiddingfold.com
Beer range varies H
A friendly welcome greets you at this hotel bar. The interior mixes modern and traditional with a feature fireplace, logburner, wooden beams and pictures adorning the walls. It has a separate bistro-style dining area. A varying range of beers is served, usually including an Adnams' ale and two guests, at least one local. Outside is a terraced garden for warmer days and plenty of parking across the road. An annual beer festival is held in a marquee. ᨏ❀☸❍◗♿P⁵⊖🚋(71)

Churt

Crossways L
Churt Road, GU10 2JS SU855382
✪ 11-3, 5-11; 11-11 Fri & Sat; 12-11 Sun ☎ (0871) 951100
⊕ weydonian.net/crossways/
Bowman Warbler; Courage Best Bitter; Hop Back Crop Circle H; **guest beers** G
A wide clientele of all ages and backgrounds mixes easily in the comfy saloon bar and old-fashioned quarry-tiled public with its small serving hatch and dartboard. The absence of gaming machines and jukebox ensures that the emphasis is on conversation. Four real ciders from makers such as Hecks and Burrow Hill are usually available

INDEPENDENT BREWERIES

Ascot Camberley
Brightwater Claygate (NEW)
Dorking Dorking
Farnham Upper Hale
Hogs Back Tongham
Leith Hill Coldharbour
Little Beer Guildford (NEW)
Pilgrim Reigate
Surrey Hills Dorking
Thurstons Horsell (NEW)
Tillingbourne Shere

alongside up to five guest beers from far and wide, but mainly Hampshire and Sussex micros. Handy for walks on local heathlands. No food on Sunday, evening meals on Wednesday only. Q✿❀⊕♣♠P❜⊱➼(19)

Dorking

Cobbett's L
23 West Street, RH4 1BY (on A25 eastbound)
✪ closed Mon; 12 (10am Fri & Sat)-8; 12-6 Sun
☎ (01306) 879877 ⊕ cobbettsrealales.co.uk
Beer range varies G
Excellent off-licence offering cask beer and cider at very fair prices. Two beers are usually available at the beginning of the week with five at the end, plus one or two on key-keg. LocAle breweries are always represented, often Dark Star, along with some from further away. There is usually a 'hop-monster' on tap towards the weekend, and perry is available in summer. Many bottled beers from the UK and overseas are also stocked. CAMRA members receive a five per cent discount (10 per cent discount for all on Tue). Q❧⇌(West)♠➼

Cricketers L
81 South Street, RH4 2JU (on A25 westbound)
✪ 12-11 (midnight Thu & Sat; 12.30am Fri)
☎ (01306) 889938 ⊕ cricketersdorking.co.uk
Fuller's Chiswick Bitter, London Pride, ESB; guest beer H
A traditional small town pub with bare brick walls decorated with old photographs and Fuller's beer adverts. A large screen shows major sporting events on terrestrial TV, especially rugby. Hidden away at the back of the pub is one its best features – a split-level walled Georgian garden, where spring and autumn beer festivals are held. There is also a TV in the garden. Children are welcome until early evening. Basic lunches are sold weekdays. ✿⊕♣❜⊱➼

Red Bar & Lounge L
45 Dene Street, RH4 2DW (off A25 High Street)
✪ 12-11 (midnight Fri & Sat); 12-10.30 Sun
☎ (01306) 882222
Dark Star Hophead; Surrey Hills Shere Drop; guest beer H
Situated just a short distance from the High Street, this food-oriented pub is a welcome respite for shoppers. Inside there are bare boards along with comfortable seating throughout the various areas; outside is some covered decking and a pleasant patio garden with tables and umbrellas for smokers. Wi-Fi and newspapers are available and dogs are welcome. Monthly comedy and music nights are hosted. A blackboard lists freshly prepared home-made specials (no food Sun eve). The guest beer is often local. ✿⊕♠P❜⊱➼

East Molesey

Albion
34 Bridge Road, KT8 9HA (off B3379)
✪ 11.30-midnight (11.30 Sun) ☎ (020) 8783 9342
Fuller's London Pride; Young's Bitter; guest beers H
Open-plan locals' pub, part of the Ember Inns estate. The central bar serves separate drinking and dining areas, with comfortable seating throughout. Reasonably priced food including vegetarian options is available from opening time until 9pm each day, with roasts on Sundays. The pub is a

short walk from Hampton Court Palace and the River Thames. Guest beers come from regional and larger microbreweries. Various deals are available on beer and food. ♿✿⊕♣⇌(Hampton Court)➼

Europa
171 Walton Road, KT8 0DX (on B369)
✪ 11.30 (11 Sun)-11 ☎ (020) 8979 8838
Fuller's London Pride; Sharp's Doom Bar; guest beer H
A relatively unspoilt three-room pub, popular for its support of the local music scene with bands playing several evenings a week. The public bar has a TV, dartboard and pool table, while the saloon has a comfortable feel with stained glass signs and skylights. There is a large garden with a children's play area. The Cabin bar features photographic memories of Hurst Park racecourse, which closed in 1962. Guest beers are usually from the larger breweries. ⌂✿⊕♣❀♠P❜⊱➼(411)

Egham

United Services Club L
111 Spring Rise, TW20 9PE (close to A30 Egham Hill)
✪ 12-11 (midnight Fri & Sat) ☎ (01784) 435120
⊕ eusc.co.uk
Rebellion IPA; Surrey Hills Ranmore Ale; guest beers H
Discerning real ale and cider drinkers' mecca strongly supporting local breweries. Ten handpumps serve a constantly changing range of guest ales and three ciders (plus more from the cellar). Three hugely popular beer and cider festivals a year attracting visitors from far and wide offer an eclectic range of ales, mostly from very new breweries. Satellite TV and free Wi-Fi are available and live music features most Saturday evenings. A copy of this Guide or a CAMRA membership card secures entry. ✿♿⇌❀♠P❜➼❐(71, 441)

Englefield Green

Beehive L
34 Middle Hill, TW20 0JQ (200yds N of A30 Egham Hill)
✪ 12-11 (midnight Fri & Sat); 12-10.30 Sun
☎ (01784) 431621 ⊕ beehiveegham.co.uk
Fuller's London Pride; Gale's Seafarers Ale, HSB, seasonal beers H
This small pub dating from the 1870s is now open plan with a light and airy feel. It passed through the hands of a number of local breweries including Ashby's before becoming an outlier of the Gale's estate before the Fuller's takeover. It now hosts an interesting variety of Fuller's ales including those under the Gale's badge and the occasional guest from elsewhere. Freshly cooked food is available throughout the day. Events include regular quiz nights and occasional live music. ⌂✿⊕P❜⊱➼(71,441)

Happy Man ♈
12 Harvest Road, TW20 0QS (200yds from A30 Egham Hill)
✪ 12-11.30 (midnight Fri & Sat); 12-10.30 Sun
☎ (01784) 433265
Hop Back Summer Lightning; guest beers H
Originally two Victorian cottages, the building was converted to a pub to serve the workers building Royal Holloway College. Recently refurbished but virtually unchanged, it is now a popular haunt of

students and locals. Four handpumps dispense Summer Lightning and three changing guest ales from microbreweries around the country, and sometimes additional beers on gravity from the cellar. Food is available all day. Darts and quiz nights are regular events. Local CAMRA Pub of the Year 2013. ❀❀❸❹❺❻➐✎⊟(71,441)

Epsom

Barley Mow ⓁL
12 Pikes Hill, KT17 4EA (off A2022)
❀ 12-11 (midnight Fri & Sat); 12-10.30 Sun
☎ (01372) 721044 ⊕ barley-mow-epsom.co.uk
Fuller's London Pride, ESB; guest beer Ⓗ
Large pub with various alcoves and seating areas around a central bar, popular with both diners and drinkers. Originally three cottages, the building is tucked away down a narrow side road. Old-style wooden furnishings and ornate leaded windows add to the ambience indoors and there is a secluded beer garden. An alleyway from the garden leads to the Upper High Street public car park. Guest beers are typically either Fuller's seasonal ales or from other family brewers. ❀❀❸❹❺❻✎⊟

Jolly Coopers ⓁL
84 Wheelers Lane, KT18 7SD (off B280 via Stamford Green Road)
❀ 12-11 (midnight Fri-Sat); 12-10.30 Sun ☎ (01372) 723222 ⊕ jollycoopers.co.uk
Beer range varies Ⓗ
More than 200 years old, this is an independently run, traditional pub in a residential area. It has a quiet lounge bar, a sports bar where darts is played and a snug space between the two. Outside is a heated smoking area and garden where barbecues are held. Beers are generally from microbreweries in Surrey and Sussex. An extensive food menu is available – roasts are served on Sundays and a curry night is held on Tuesday. Local CAMRA Pub of the Year 2011 and 2012. ❀Q❀❸❹❺❻P✎⊟(E9)

Rising Sun
14 Heathcote Road, KT18 5DX (off B290)
❀ 11-11 (midnight Fri & Sat); 12-10.30 Sun
☎ (01372) 740809 ⊕ therisingsunepsom.com
St Austell Tribute; Young's Bitter, Special; guest beer Ⓗ
Back street pub that is food led but retains a traditional bar area at the front. It has a covered patio and large garden to the rear, which hosts barbecues in summer, and a separate function room. The guest beer is from the Wells & Young's portfolio. Food is prepared on the premises using locally sourced ingredients. Public parking is available nearby in Church Street. The pub was the birthplace of the Society for Preservation of Beers from the Wood in 1963. ❀❀❸❹❺❻✎⊟

Farnham

Farnham Conservative Club ⓁL
Ivy Lane, GU9 7PQ (off Downing St)
❀ 11-3 (3.30 Fri), 5-11; 11-11 Sat; 12-3 Sun
☎ (01252) 723712 ⊕ farnhamconservativeclub.org.uk
Fuller's London Pride; guest beers Ⓗ
This is a private club situated in a wonderful Georgian house in the centre of Farnham. CAMRA members can be signed in upon arrival – please show your membership card at the bar. Popular

with diners and snooker players, it boasts a large and elegant function room with its own bar. There is a delightful patio area at the rear, a superb suntrap in summer. Parking is Pay & Display with a refund available. Q❀❸❹❺❻P⊟

Hop Blossom
Long Garden Walk, GU9 7HX (between Waitrose and Castle Street)
❀ 12-3, 5-11; 12-midnight Fri & Sat; 12-11 Sun
☎ (01252) 710770 ⊕ hopblossom.co.uk
Fuller's Chiswick Bitter, Discovery, London Pride, ESB; guest beer Ⓗ
Visitors are assured of a warm welcome from friendly staff at this cosy little pub. It is a convenient place to enjoy a well-kept Fuller's beer, and a log fire makes it an inviting place in winter. The main bar is fairly compact with a larger seating area at the back. Although there is no beer garden, in summer customers often spill out onto the pavement to enjoy the sunshine. ❀Q❀❸❹❺⊟

Nelson Arms
50 Castle Street, GU9 7JQ
❀ 12-11 (midnight Fri & Sat); 12-10.30 Sun
☎ (01252) 712554 ⊕ nelson-arms.co.uk
Andwell Gold Muddler; Sharp's Doom Bar; Taylor Landlord; guest beer Ⓗ
An inn for over 250 years, set in the shadow of Farnham Castle, the pub has a low-beamed, atmospheric bar and offers good food. The tenants have turned this into a great place to enjoy a pint or a meal at reasonable prices. The bar staff are friendly and efficient with a warm welcome whether the pub is busy or quiet. A good range of wine is available for those who prefer the grape to the grain. There is a small courtyard at the rear for smokers. ❀❸❹❺❻⊟

Queen's Head
9 The Borough, GU9 7NA
❀ 10-11 (midnight Fri & Sat); 10am-10.30 Sun
☎ (01252) 726524 ⊕ queensheadfarnham.co.uk
Fuller's London Pride, seasonal beers; Gale's HSB; guest beer Ⓗ
A friendly pub conveniently situated in central Farnham, with a bus stop right outside. The Queens Head is a cosy place to enjoy a beer and watch the world go by. A delicious range of food is available daily at lunchtime, and evening meals twice a week – pie night on Monday and steak night on Wednesday. Thursdays alternate between an open mic night and a quiz night. A range of Fuller's beers including a seasonal and a guest ale is available. ❀❀❸❹❺❻✎⊟

Shepherd & Flock
22 Moor Park Lane, GU9 9JB (centre of A325/A31 roundabout) SU854474
❀ 12-11 (11.30 Thu-Sat) ☎ (01252) 716675
⊕ shepherdandflock.co.uk
Hogs Back TEA; guest beers Ⓗ
'The great little pub on the great big roundabout,' this welcoming establishment has a friendly atmosphere and an excellent selection of beers on its eight handpumps. The Hogs Back TEA is complemented by a range of usually fairly local guest beers. Excellent food is available at lunchtimes and in the evenings. There are two outside spaces: a secluded beer garden to the rear and a large lawned area to the front, excellent for viewing the bustling traffic and the amusing signs opposite. ❀Q❀❀❸❹P✎⊟(46,65)

William Cobbett

4 Bridge Square, GU9 7QR

✪ 11-11.30 (12.30am Fri); 11.30-12.30am Sat; 12-10.30 Sun ☎ (01252) 726281

Fuller's London Pride; guest beers Ⓗ

Situated between the town centre and the railway station, this popular pub has a wonderfully dark interior with a number of drinking areas and a large outside space – mostly covered. It is full of eclectic memorabilia and has a good '60s/'70s jukebox. Live bands play occasionally on Wednesday evenings. The four guest beers are often from local microbreweries. Good-value pub food is served at lunchtimes and burgers on Friday and Saturday evenings. A favourite with younger drinkers, it has an upstairs pool room.
ﾑ⑈◑≈Pᵗ⊸曰

Godalming

Jack Phillips Ⓛ

48-56 High Street, GU7 1DY

✪ 7am-11 (midnight Thu; 1am Fri & Sat) ☎ (01483) 521750

Greene King Abbot; Ruddles Best Bitter; guest beers Ⓗ

Set in a modern building on the historic High Street, the light, airy decor of the Jack Phillips hints at an Art Deco passenger saloon of an ocean liner. Up to seven guest ales are available, usually including several LocAles to complement the current Wetherspoon selection. At least two real ciders are also on offer. Families are welcome in an area to the rear of the pub. The usual good-value Wetherspoon food menu is available.
Qぴ◑&≈⊛曰

Star

17 Church Street, GU7 1EL

✪ 11-midnight; 12-11 Sun & Mon ☎ (01483) 417717 ⊕ thestargodalming.co.uk

Greene King St Edmunds; H&H Olde Trip Ⓗ; guest beers Ⓗ/Ⓖ

The Star became a beer house soon after 1830, but parts of the building are older. Between the dark oak ceiling beams hang hundreds of pumpclips. Beyond the narrow bar is a patio with smoking area and a separate lounge with deep sofas. Up to eight real ales and four ciders are available, and regular beer festivals are held at Easter and Halloween. Sunday is quiz night. Folk music, knitting, chess and more feature on other nights.
⑈◑≈⊛ᵗ⊸曰

Gomshall

Compasses Ⓛ

50 Station Road, GU5 9LA (on A25)

✪ 11-11; 12-10.30 Sun ☎ (01483) 202506

Surrey Hills Ranmore Ale, Shere Drop, seasonal beers Ⓗ

This 19th-century roadside pub, standing between the A25 and the River Tillingbourne, has a traditional bar with three handpumps, decorated with old farming and other tools on its wooden pillars and beams. Home-made meals are served in the bar and the separate dining room (no food Sun eve). There is a garden and seating beside the stream. Live music plays every Friday, with a music festival over the August bank holiday. B&B is in two en-suite rooms. ⑈⇄◑≈Pᵗ⊸曰(32)

Gomshall Mill Ⓛ

52 Station Road, GU5 9LB (on A25)

✪ 12-11 (10.30 Sun) ☎ (01483) 203060 ⊕ gomshallmill.hcpr.co.uk

Beer range varies Ⓗ

Set astride the River Tillingbourne, the pub is within a 17th-century timber-framed and clad watermill. Dining areas are set on several levels and outside is a pleasant garden. The two water wheels, formerly used to produce flour, are open to view from the centre of the pub, with the mill-race running beneath your feet. While the emphasis is on excellent dining, the bar, with real fire, features four handpumps serving constantly changing brews, usually including two LocAles, one from Tillingbourne. ﾑぴ⑈◑&≈⊛P曰(32)

Guildford

King's Head

27 King's Road, GU1 4JW (on A320 Stoke Rd) SU855382

✪ 11-midnight (1am Fri & Sat); 12-11 Sun

☎ (01483) 568957 ⊕ kingsheadguildford.co.uk

Fuller's Chiswick Bitter, London Pride, ESB, seasonal beers; guest beers Ⓗ

Located off the edge of the town centre, this well-established pub attracts a well-mannered mix of discerning locals and office types in the know. The full range of Fuller's beers including seasonals is available as well as a local guest usually from Surrey Hills, and cider on draught. Multiple drinking areas and a dedicated dining lounge surround the island bar. A TV is turned on for important sporting events but mostly the background noise is conversation. Dogs are welcome.
ﾑ⑈◑&≈(London Rd)⊛Pᵗ⊸曰(3,34)

Rodboro Buildings

1-10 Bridge Street, GU1 4SB (opp Friary Centre)

✪ 9-1am (midnight Tue & Wed; 1.45am Fri & Sat) ☎ (01483) 306366

Greene King Abbot; Ruddles Best Bitter; guest beers Ⓗ

Constructed in 1900 as the Dennis Car Factory, this prominent listed building was converted in 1998 to a Wetherspoon pub, now branded as a Lloyds No.1. The upstairs bar is quieter and reserved for diners, while the main bar, which can be noisy in the evening, includes a dance floor at a lower level. Several of the guest beers are local, from Surrey, Sussex and Hampshire, but some are from further afield. Children are welcome, if dining, until 8pm.
◑&≈⊛曰

Royal Oak

Trinity Churchyard, GU1 3RR

✪ 11-11 (11.30 Thu; 1am Fri & Sat); 12-10.30 Sun

☎ (01483) 459023 ⊕ royaloakguildford.co.uk

Fuller's London Pride, seasonal beers; Gale's HSB; guest beers Ⓗ

Part of an early 17th-century terrace of houses converted to a pub around 1870, the pub is tucked away behind Holy Trinity graveyard, at the top of the cobbled High Street. The single bar often features live music including ukulele jams and open mic nights. Home-made food centres on traditional British classics – the Sunday roasts are especially popular. A now renowned beer festival is held the week before Christmas, one of several during the year. ⑈◑≈♣ᵗ⊸曰

Three Pigeons

169 High Street, GU1 3AJ
✪ 11-11; 10-midnight Fri & Sat; 10-10.30 Sun
☎ (01483) 575728 ⊕ threepigeonsguildford.co.uk
Sharp's Doom Bar; Taylor Landlord; guest beers Ⓗ
The downstairs bar with its snazzy uplighting has four, mostly local, guest ales, often including Fuller's London Pride, but otherwise frequently changing. The upstairs bar has just two handpumps and is popular with families escaping the more boisterous aspects of other town centre pubs. This bar may be reserved for parties and other functions. A small area out back is used mostly for smoking. ⊛⊙♣✦⧸–⊟

Hambledon

Merry Harriers Ⓛ

Hambledon Road, GU8 4DR SU967391
✪ 11-2.30, 5.30-11; 11-11 Sat; 11-8 Sun ☎ (01428) 682883
⊕ merryharriers.com
Pilgrim Progress; Surrey Hills Shere Drop; Tillingbourne Falls Gold; guest beers Ⓗ
An extremely warm welcome is assured at this traditional country pub. The main bar has an inglenook fireplace and is flanked by a small side room and a restaurant area/function room. Two frequently changing guest beers accompany the three regulars. Excellent food is served. Accommodation is in a converted barn in the garden, and the Surrey Hills Llamas are based next door offering treks round the local countryside. ⨳Q⟋⊛⊟⊙⅄♣Pᴸ–

Holmbury St Mary

King's Head Ⓛ

Pitland Street, RH5 6NP (off B2126) TQ112442
✪ closed Mon; 12-11 (10 Sun) ☎ (01306) 730282
⊕ kingsheadholmbury.co.uk
Dark Star Hophead; Otter Bitter; guest beers Ⓗ
This wonderfully unspoilt 17th-century pub is hidden away from the village centre and is popular with ramblers and cyclists exploring the lovely Surrey Hills countryside. The wooden-floored bar has some interesting old shooting photographs on the walls. Home-made meals include a selection of stews (no food Sun eve). Beer festivals are held on the late spring and August bank holidays. Otter Bitter is sold as Binyon's Quaffer. Two changing guest beers and a guest cider are available. The pub closes between 3 and 5 Tuesday-Thursday in winter. ⨳Q⟋⊛⊙♣✦Pᴸ⊟(22,25)

Horsell

Crown

104 High Street, GU21 4ST
✪ 12-11; 11-midnight Sat ☎ (01483) 771719
⊕ thecrownhorsell.co.uk
Beer range varies Ⓗ
A classic community local with a weekly quiz night on Wednesday and terrestrial sporting events on TV. Two handpumps dispense beers from the Punch range, while the third serves an ever-changing guest, sometimes from Thurstons, the Horsell brewing company. There is an annual beer festival, usually at Easter. Pizzas are available at any time to eat in or take away. The garden has a climbing frame for younger customers and a pétanque piste. ⨳⊛⊟♣Pᴸ–⊟(48)

Leatherhead

Edmund Tylney

30-34 High Street, KT22 8AW
✪ 8-11 (midnight Thu; 1am Fri & Sat) ☎ (01372) 362715
Greene King Abbot; Ruddles Best Bitter; Young's Bitter; guest beers Ⓗ
Formerly a Woolworths store, this Wetherspoon pub has a single bar serving multiple levels, one quieter and more secluded, with a large staircase separating the different areas. Friendly and efficient staff serve a choice of six guest ales including a local brew and three varying real ciders. Disabled access is only to the bar and lower level, including a WC. Children are allowed until 9pm. Edmund Tylney, a Leatherhead man, was Master of the Revels to Queen Elizabeth I. ⟋⊛⊙♿⧸✦ᴸ–⊟

Running Horse ♈

38 Bridge Street, KT22 8BZ (off B2122)
✪ 11.30-11; 12-10.30 Sun ☎ (01372) 372081
Shepherd Neame Master Brew, Kent's Best, Spitfire, Bishops Finger, seasonal beers; guest beer Ⓗ
Grade II*-listed pub dating from the 15th century with two bars. John Skelton (Poet Laureate to Henry VIII) wrote about Elinour Rumming brewing 'Nappy Ale' here. The lounge has low ceilings and exposed beams, the public has TV, pool and darts. Both have a real fire. Home-made meals use many local products. The guest beer is from Surrey Hills Brewery. Live bands play monthly, with a charity event on May Day. There are two areas outside with heating and shelter. Children are allowed until 9pm. Local CAMRA Pub of the Year 2013. ⨳Q⟋⊛⊙♿⧸✦Pᴸ–⊟

Limpsfield Chart

Carpenters Arms Ⓛ

12 Tally Road, RH8 0TG TQ424518
✪ 11-3, 5-11; 11-11 Sat; 12-10.30 Sun ☎ (01883) 722209
Westerham Finchcocks Original, British Bulldog, 1965 Special Bitter, seasonal beers Ⓗ
This Westerham Brewery tied house features the full range of its beers. The L-shaped bar has parquet flooring and provides ample room for both drinkers and diners. One side of the bar retains a dartboard. Good home-made food is served daily (no food Sun eve). The dog-friendly pub is situated on the National Trust's Limpsfield Common and is popular with walkers and horse riders. ⨳⟋⊛⊙♣Pᴸ–⊟(594)

Mogador

Sportsman

Mogador Road, KT20 7ES (W of A217 at Lower Kingswood) TQ239531
✪ 12-11 (10.30 Sun) ☎ (01737) 246655
⊕ timewellspent.info
Sharp's Doom Bar; Young's Bitter; guest beers Ⓗ
Food-oriented pub situated on the edge of Walton Heath and in good walking countryside. Originally built as a royal hunting lodge, parts date from the 16th century, although most of the building is of later construction, possibly early Victorian. Guest ales may be from large or small brewers, so could be anything from Greene King to Clarence & Fredericks. The pub can get very busy, especially at warm weekends when the garden comes into its own. ⨳⊛⊙Pᴸ–

Mugswell

Well House Inn L

Chipstead Lane, CR5 3SQ (off A217) TQ259552

✪ 12-11 (10.30 Sun) ☎ (01737) 830640

⊕ wellhouseinn.co.uk

Adnams Southwold Bitter; Fuller's London Pride; Surrey Hills Shere Drop; guest beers ⊞

The ghost of Harry the Monk is said to be a regular visitor at this Grade II-listed 16th-century pub. There are three bars, each with a log fire, and a conservatory. The two guest beers change frequently and are usually from local microbreweries; the cider is from Millwhites. The Domesday Book mentions the well outside – known as Mag's Well, hence the area's name. Good food is served (no food Sun or Mon eves). Families are welcome until 9pm. ᴍᴏ❀❶♣♦P

Newdigate

Surrey Oaks ♈ L

Parkgate Road, Parkgate, RH5 5DZ TQ205436

✪ 11.30-2.30 (3 Sat), 5.30 (6 Sat)-11; 12-9 Sun

☎ (01306) 631200 ⊕ surreyoaks.co.uk

Harveys Sussex Best Bitter; Surrey Hills Ranmore Ale; guest beers ⊞

Great 16th-century pub offering an excellent and ever-changing selection of ales from microbreweries (hoppy beers and dark ales popular), plus cider. Third-pint glasses are available. Good home-made food is served in the bar and restaurant (no food Sun or Mon eves). Low beams, flagstones and an inglenook feature; outside are two boules pitches in the large garden and a skittle alley in the barn. Beer festivals are held on the late spring and August bank holidays. Local CAMRA Pub of the Year 2003-2013. ᴍᴏ❀❶♣♦P

Ottershaw

Castle L

220 Brox Road, KT16 0LW (signed off A320 S of village) TQ 022631

✪ 11-11; 12-10.30 Sun ☎ (01932) 872373

⊕ the-castle-ottershaw.co.uk

Harveys Sussex Best Bitter; Hogs Back TEA; Sharp's Doom Bar; Taylor Landlord; guest beers ⊞

This attractive 19th-century pub on the southern fringe of the village has retained a two-bar layout – the Castle bar is essentially the public bar (dogs allowed) while the Tower, with a recently built conservatory, caters for diners. However, there is room for drinkers in both bars and the emphasis throughout is on conversation rather than video games or TV sport. Welcoming open fires warm both bars in winter. Outside is a heated wooden smokers' refuge built by the locals. Free Wi-Fi available. ᴍᴏ❀❶❶⊟P❧⊟(557)

Peaslake

Hurtwood Inn L

Walking Bottom, GU5 9RR TQ086446

✪ 12-11 (midnight Fri); 12-10.30 Sun ☎ (01306) 730851

⊕ hurtwoodinnhotel.com

Fuller's London Pride; Hogs Back TEA; Surrey Hills Shere Drop; guest beer ⊞

Dating from 1920, this three-star privately owned hotel has a bright and contemporary bar offering a wide range of bar snacks and meals as well as mostly LocAle beers. Furnishings include easy chairs and sofas, and there is a modern open fireplace and artwork featuring classic cars. The hotel's location at the heart of the beautiful Surrey Hills makes it a welcome stop-off for weary ramblers and cyclists. There is a separate restaurant and 21 en-suite rooms. ᴍᴦ❀❶⊟P⊟(25)

Puttenham

Good Intent

60-62 The Street, GU3 1AR SU931478

✪ 12-3, 6-11.30 (11 Mon); 12-11.30 Sat; 12-10.30 Sun

☎ (01483) 810387 ⊕ thegoodintentpub.co.uk

Otter Bitter; Sharp's Doom Bar; Taylor Landlord; guest beers ⊞

A 16th-century inn situated in an attractive village with the North Downs Way long distance path passing the front door. The cosy bar with oak beams and an inglenook fireplace is decorated with hops and hop-growing equipment which serves as a reminder that the last hop field in Surrey is just 500 yards along The Street. Three guest beers are normally available. Food is served every session except Sunday and Monday evenings, fish and chips night is Wednesday. ᴍᴏ❀❶▲♦P❧

Redhill

Garland

5 Brighton Road, RH1 6PP (on A23)

✪ 12-11 (midnight Fri & Sat) ☎ (01737) 760377

Harveys Sussex XX Mild, Hadlow Bitter, Sussex Best Bitter, Armada Ale, seasonal beers ⊞

Situated just south of the town centre, this classic town pub usually has six Harvey's beers available, sometimes including Surrey Hop Garland Ale, a beer brewed for the pub using Surrey hops. As well as attracting beer drinkers from afar, this is a locals' pub and is home to a number of darts, bar billiards and quiz teams. Food is served lunchtimes Monday to Friday and all day Sunday until 9.30pm. Dogs and children are welcome until 7.30pm. ᴦ❀❶❧♣P❧⊟

Hatch

44 Hatchlands Road, Shaws Corner, RH1 6AT (on A25)

✪ 11-midnight (12.30am Fri & Sat); 12-midnight Sun

☎ (01737) 765104 ⊕ thehatchpub.co.uk

Shepherd Neame Master Brew, Spitfire, Bishops Finger, seasonal beer ⊞

Dating from the 17th century, this comfortable pub was once a workhouse with a hayloft for horses. The L-shaped bar has eight handpumps, with beers from the Shepherd Neame microplant often available. There are two further rooms hidden away. Good-value meals are served (not eves Sun or Mon) and an extensive wine range is stocked. The bar area is decorated with a large collection of pictures of Spitfires. Thatchers Heritage cider sold. ᴍ❀❶❧♣♦❧⊟(420,460)

Jolly Brickmakers

58-60 Frenches Road, RH1 2HP

✪ 12-11 (midnight Fri & Sat) ☎ (01737) 789388

⊕ jollybrickmakers.co.uk

Brakspear Bitter; Marston's Pedigree; Ringwood Fortyniner; guest beer ⊞

North of the town centre and run by an enthusiastic and jovial landlord, this basic but friendly pub is very much part of the local community. There are two bars – the public containing some unusual moulded heraldic wall badges and the saloon with a bar billiards table, a paperback library and an impressive Bass mirror. Occasional beer festivals are held. The guest beer is from the Marston's list. No meals, but cutlery and plates are provided for takeaways. A proper pub! 🏵♣️⌐–🚃(430,435)

Shamley Green

Bricklayers Arms

The Green, GU5 0UA TQ033437
🌑 11-11 (10.30 Sun) ☎ (01483) 898377
⊕ bricklayersarmspub.co.uk
Exmoor Ale; Fuller's London Pride; Sharp's Doom Bar; guest beers Ⓗ

This Georgian pub is an ideal place to stop off while exploring the Surrey Hills. It has been extended over the years – the bar opened out to create space for different seating and games areas, with sofas around the fire. Two guest beers are usually available, one from the local area. Meals are all home made (no food Sun eve) and occasional themed menus are offered including a curry night and fresh fish specials. Dogs and families are welcome. 🏵🌫🏵🌓🕭♣️P⌐–🚃(53,63)

Shepperton

Barley Mow 🏛

67 Watersplash Road, TW17 0EE (off B376 in Shepperton Green)
🌑 12-11 (10.30 Sun) ☎ (01932) 225326 ⊕ themow.co.uk
Hogs Back TEA; Hop Back Summer Lightning; guest beers Ⓗ

Friendly side-street local in Shepperton Green to the west of the main village centre. Five handpumps adorn the horseshoe bar serving beers from the likes of Hogs Back, Windsor & Eton, WJ King and more local or more distant microbreweries. Past CAMRA awards are displayed on one of the beams along with a mass of pumpclips. Live rock 'n' roll or R&B plays on Friday and Saturday, jazz on Wednesday, and quiz night is Thursday. A covered and heated patio area is available for smokers. 🏵♣️🕭P⌐–🚃(438,458)

Sidlow Bridge

Three Horseshoes 🏛

Ironsbottom, RH2 8PT (off A217) TQ249462
🌑 12-11 (9.30 Sun) ☎ (01293) 862315
⊕ thethreehorseshoes-pub.co.uk
Dark Star Hophead; Fuller's London Pride, ESB; Pilgrim Surrey Bitter; Surrey Hills Shere Drop; guest beers Ⓗ

The 'Shoes was once home to a forge, hence the name, and is now a fine old-fashioned country pub – parts of the building date back 300 years. For a time it was a coaching inn on the London to Brighton route. A beer festival is held on the first May bank holiday. Very good food, including daily specials, is available lunchtimes and evenings, with barbecues held in the large garden. Two guest beers are on offer along with a varying cider. Q🏵🌓🕭P⌐–

Staffhurst Wood

Royal Oak 🏛

Caterfield Lane, RH8 0RR TQ407485

🌑 11-3, 5-11; 11-midnight Fri & Sat; 12-10 Sun
☎ (01883) 722207 ⊕ theroyaloakoxted.co.uk
Adnams Southwold Bitter; Harveys Sussex Best Bitter; Larkins Traditional Ⓗ; guest beers Ⓗ/Ⓖ

A rural free house well worth seeking out for both beer and food. Quality meals feature ingredients often sourced from local farms and are highly recommended (no food Sun eve). The pub welcomes walkers and their dogs. There is a log fire in winter and the large garden with extensive views is popular in summer. Children are permitted until 8pm. Discounts on beer and bar food are available for CAMRA members. Branch Cider Pub of the Year 2011-13, the pub offers a good choice of cider and perry. 🏵Q🌫🏵🕭🕭♣️🕭P⌐–

Staines

Bells

124 Church Street, TW18 4ZB (off B376)
🌑 12-3, 5-11; 12-midnight Fri & Sat; 12-11 Sun
☎ (01784) 454240
Young's Bitter, Special, seasonal beers; guest beers Ⓗ

Friendly, comfortable, 18th-century pub opposite St Mary's Church close to the Thames Path and within easy walking distance of the town centre. Regular beers and seasonals from Wells and Young's are available plus up to two guests from microbreweries around the country. Noted locally for the quality of its food, it is often busy in the evenings. The pleasant rear patio garden, with a large heated smokers' canopy, is especially popular in summer, attracting local workers and shoppers. Q🏵🕭♣️⌐–🚃(305)

George

2-8 High Street, TW18 4EE (on A308, opp old town hall)
🌑 8-11 (midnight Fri & Sat) ☎ (01784) 462181
Courage Best Bitter; Greene King Abbot; Ruddles Best Bitter; guest beers Ⓗ

Ever-popular, two-storey, town-centre Wetherspoon pub built in the 1990s. The spacious downstairs bar with its mixture of tables and intimate booths is always busy but a quieter bar can be reached via a spiral staircase. Up to six guest ales are dispensed from one bank of handpumps, with the national brands and two real ciders from Westons on the rear bank. A varied selection of foreign bottled beers and ciders is also stocked. Value-for-money pub food is served all day. 🕭♣️≒🕭🚃

Wheatsheaf & Pigeon

Penton Road, TW18 2LL (corner of Wheatsheaf Lane and Penton Rd)
🌑 12-11 (10.30 Sun) ☎ (01784) 452922
⊕ thewheatsheafandpigeon.co.uk
Courage Best Bitter; Sharp's Doom Bar; guest beers Ⓗ

Welcoming and friendly community local between Staines and Laleham, just a short walk from the Thames Path and from Staines Town FC. Well-kept ales often include West Country guests and good-value food is served every day (not Sun eve). Child- and dog-friendly, there is seating outside for the warmer months plus a covered smoking area. Quiz night is Sunday and beer festivals are held. The pub is particularly busy on football match days. The bus stops in Laleham Road. 🏵🕭P⌐–🚃(458)

Thames Ditton

George & Dragon
High Street, KT7 0RY (Off B364)
🟢 11 (12 Sun)-11 ☎ (020) 8398 2206
⊕ georgeanddragonthamesditton.co.uk
Shepherd Neame Master Brew Bitter, Spitfire, seasonal beer Ⓗ
Set back from the road this pub has the feel of a country pub but sits in the middle of the village of Thames Ditton. It has an open-plan layout around a central bar, with plenty of dark wood and comfortable leather seating. The landlord acts as quizmaster on most Thursday evenings. Regular jazz evenings are hosted on a Tuesday and there is an active golf society. Outside is a patio along with two outdoor smoking areas, one heated with a TV.
Q❀❀◖◗&⇌P⌐➖⊟(514,515)

Olde Swan
Summer Road, KT7 0QQ
🟢 11-11; 12-10.30 Sun ☎ (020) 8398 1814
⊕ yeoldeswan-thames-ditton.co.uk
Greene King IPA, Abbot; Morland Old Speckled Hen; guest beers Ⓗ
Although much altered, this pub backing onto the Thames can trace its history back to the 13th century and was once used as a hunting lodge by Henry VIII. The multi-roomed interior has a stylish yet traditional feel with stone walls, black flagstones around the bar areas and wooden floors in the seating areas. Guest beers are supplied by Greene King, but can be from other brewers. Access is from the riverside, not the street.
🚶❀❀◖◗&P⌐➖⊟(514,515)

Red Lion
85 High Street, KT7 0SF
🟢 11-11 (midnight Fri & Sat); 12-11 Sun ☎ (020) 8398 8662
Beer range varies Ⓗ
In new hands since autumn 2012, this quirkily decorated pub, divided into distinct areas, is situated close to the river and just away from the village centre. Colanders are used as lampshades and old doors, some retaining their locks, make up the front of the bar. There are two handpumps with local beers often available – Surrey Hills and Twickenham Fine Ales are among the regular brewers. ❀❀◖◗P⌐⊟(514,515)

Tongham

White Hart Ⓛ
76 The Street, GU10 1DH SU 886489
🟢 11-11 (midnight Fri & Sat); 12-10.30 Sun
☎ (01252) 782419 ⊕ thewhitehartongham.co.uk
Hogs Back TEA; guest beers Ⓗ
A friendly family-run pub with a central bar area serving three rooms: the lounge bar with a relaxed atmosphere and wood fire, the quiet saloon bar suitable for dining, and the sports bar, with the usual activities. Home-made food is served Tuesday to Sunday, plus bar snacks. The beer garden has decking and a covered smoking area. A live band features monthly and quiz night is Tuesday. Two beer festivals are held each year. Children and dogs are welcome.
🚶❀◖◗➕♣P⌐➖⊟(3,20)

Upper Hale

Alfred Free House
9 Bishops Road, GU9 0JA SU837490

🟢 5-11; 12-10.30 Sun ☎ (01252) 820385
⊕ thealfredfreehouse.co.uk
Ringwood Best Bitter; guest beers Ⓗ
A family run pub, the Alfred is a great place to enjoy a pint and a chat. The staff are very friendly and the home-cooked food, including Sunday lunches, is delicious. Beer festivals are held twice a year in May and October, as well as a host of themed evenings. Up to six guest ales are served.
🚶Q❀◖P⌐(4,5)

Walton on Thames

Ashley Park
Ashley Park Road, KT12 1JP (off B365)
🟢 11 (11.30 Sun)-midnight ☎ (01932) 220196
Fuller's London Pride; Sambrook's Junction; Sharp's Doom Bar; guest beers Ⓗ
Conveniently situated opposite the railway station, this large pub has several drinking and dining areas served from a central bar. Part of the Ember chain, it supports the company's real ale promotions with guest beers supplied from its list. The decor is simple, modern and smart, with high and low seating and a mixture of carpet and wood flooring. Monday is cask club day with reduced prices. There is a Travelodge next door.
🚶🚶❀❀◖◗&⇌P⌐➖⊟(458,555)

Bear
30 Bridge Street, KT12 1AH (off A3050)
🟢 10-11.30 (1am Fri-Sun) ☎ (01932) 253420
Fuller's London Pride; guest beer Ⓗ
Friendly one-bar community local in central Walton. This is a traditional family pub and has a play area with children welcome until 7pm. The pleasant patio garden also has a play area. The guest beer is normally from the Fuller's range. The pub opens at 10am for locally renowned reasonably priced breakfasts. Pool and darts are popular. 🚶🚶❀◖♣P⌐➖⊟

Regent
19 Church Street, KT12 2QP (on A3050)
🟢 9am-midnight (1am Fri & Sat) ☎ (01932) 243980
Greene King Abbot; Ruddles Best Bitter; guest beers Ⓗ
This pub opened in 1994 and is a conversion from a 1920s Art Deco cinema originally known as the Palace. The wood-panelled main bar, with reflecting lights hanging from the long curved ceiling, is on the ground level with a raised seating area at the rear. There are both cubicle areas and open drinking spaces. This Wetherspoon pub supports the company's national and local festivals. Westons and Gwynt y Ddraig cider are sold. Conveniently placed for the nearby shopping area.
Q❀◖◗&♣➖⊟

Weybridge

Old Crown
83 Thames Street, KT13 8LP (off A317)
🟢 11-11 ☎ (01932) 842844 ⊕ theoldcrownweybridge.co.uk
Courage Best Bitter, Directors; Young's Bitter; guest beer Ⓗ
Weatherboarded, Grade II-listed building dating back to at least 1729 at the confluence of the rivers Thames and Wey. The same family has been running this pub for over 50 years, now in their third generation. Wood-panelled drinking areas include a snug, public bar and dining room, with a

conservatory to the rear. There are two gardens, one running to the waterside with access for small boats. Food is available lunchtimes and Wednesday to Saturday evenings. Q⚜☻◑P⁵⧆

Woking

Herbert Wells ⓛ

51-57 Chertsey Road, GU21 5AJ
☼ 8am-midnight (1am Fri & Sat) ☎ (01483) 722818
Courage Best Bitter, Directors; Greene King Abbot; Hogs Back TEA; guest beers Ⓗ
A very popular town-centre Wetherspoon pub, this large, single-storey premises has various drinking and dining areas. Up to four guest ales are sourced from the local area as well as from further afield. Real cider features prominently, often from local producer Mr Whiteheads. While you are here, see if you can spot the many decorative pieces designed to celebrate the great HG Wells himself.
Q☻◑占≑♠⁵⧆

Sovereigns

Guildford Road, GU22 7QQ
☼ 11.30-midnight ☎ (01483) 751426
Adnams Broadside; Ringwood Best Bitter; Sharp's Doom Bar; guest beers Ⓗ

One of the older pubs in Woking, the Sovereigns was refurbished a few years ago and has a retro-'60s feel. Serving one of the widest ranges of real ales in the Ember Inns estate, five guest beers are usually on offer alongside the regulars. Food is served noon to 10pm each day. Children have their own menu and are welcome until 9pm. A charge is made for the car park, refundable at the bar.
☞☻◑占≑P⁵⧆

Woking Railway Athletic Club

Goldsworth Road, GU21 6JT
☼ 10.30-11 (11.30 Fri & Sat); 12-10.30 Sun
☎ (01483) 598499
Beer range varies Ⓗ
Friendly and lively social club tucked away near Victoria Arch, serving two ever-changing ales, often from local breweries. One side of the bar is sport oriented, with darts, free-to-play pool and TV sport, while the other side is quieter. Children are welcome at all times. Filled rolls are available on Saturday afternoon. Free Wi-Fi. For entry show a CAMRA membership card or a copy of this Guide. Local CAMRA Club of the Year 2010 and 2011.
≑♠⁵⧆

Crown, Horsell (Photo: Tim Griffiths)

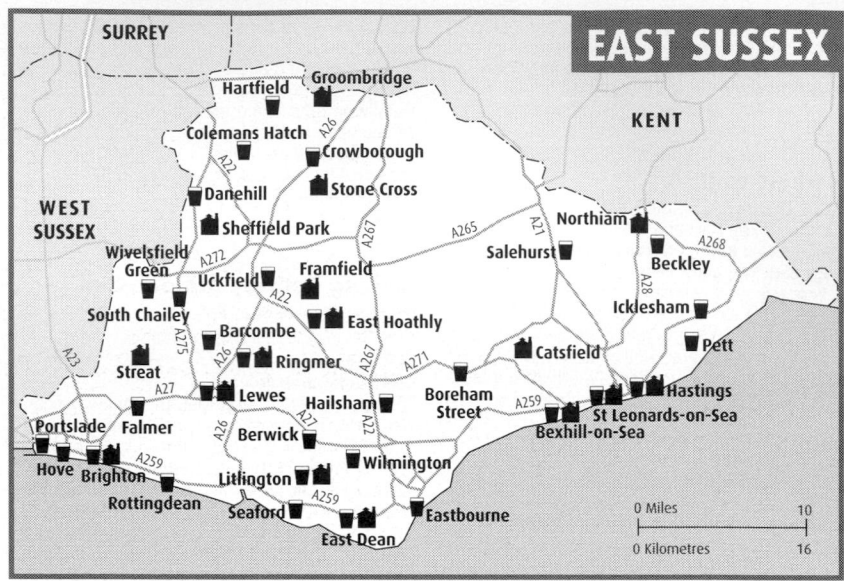

SUSSEX (EAST)

Barcombe

Royal Oak ℒ
High Street, BN8 5BA
🌣 10 (12 Sun)-11 ☎ (01273) 400418
⊕ royaloakbarcombe.co.uk
Harveys Sussex XX Mild, IPA, Sussex Best Bitter,
seasonal beers Ⓗ
Welcoming pub right in the heart of the village,
easily accessed from the main road. There is
parking outside or in the village car park 50 yards
away. The long front bar has wooden flooring and
wooden tables and chairs, and there is a separate
dining room. A skittle alley is attached to the
building. Three permanent Harvey's beers are on
plus a seasonal one. Good-value pub food is
served. ⌂Q⍩⍟⬤◗₤♣₤⊟(125)

Beckley

Rose & Crown ℒ
Northiam Road, TN31 6SE (N end of village)
🌣 12-midnight (11.30 Sun) ☎ (01797) 252161
Harveys Sussex Best Bitter; Taylor Landlord; guest
beers Ⓗ
Spacious free house with a welcoming ambience
and up to five cask beers on offer, some from local
breweries including Hastings, Old Dairy and Rother
Valley. The pub is popular with walkers, and dogs
and families are welcome. The main bar area has
two real fires. There is a separate dining area next
to it and good-value home-cooked food is available
(no food Sun eves). The garden enjoys fine views.
Sporting events on TV are shown.
⌂Q⍩⍟⬤◗₤♣P₤⊟(344)

Berwick

Cricketers' Arms ℒ
Berwick Village, BN26 6SP (S of A27)
🌣 11-3, 6-11; 11-11 Sat & summer; 12-10.30 Sun
☎ (01323) 870469 ⊕ cricketersberwick.co.uk

Harveys Sussex Best Bitter, Armada Ale, seasonal
beers Ⓖ
Nestled in a beautiful location just off the South
Downs Way, this Harvey's tied house is a traditional
country pub. Two regular ales and a seasonal guest
are available, served from a cellar room behind the
bar. The well-maintained gardens make this a
great place to stop in the summer, with real fires
keeping it cosy in the winter. Good-quality locally
produced food is available all day. ⌂Q⍟⬤◗₤♣P

Bexhill-on-Sea

Albatross Club
15 Marine Parade, TN40 1JS
🌣 11.30-2.30, 7-11 (closed Thu eve); 12-2.30 Sun
☎ (01424) 212916 ⊕ bexhillrafa.co.uk
Beer range varies Ⓗ
Local CAMRA branch Club of the Year 2012 and
2013. An extremely friendly, popular club dating
from the 1940s, with a comprehensive collection of
flying and RAF memorabilia. The constantly
changing beers are from local and national
microbreweries. In a small, separate TV room major
sporting events are shown. The club holds a twice-
yearly beer festival, and a live jazz band performs
on the fourth Tuesday of the month. Handy for
refreshments when attending the nearby De La
Warr Pavilion. Show a CAMRA membership card for
entry. Q◗₤⇌⊟⊟

Boreham Street

Bull's Head ℒ
BN27 4SG
🌣 12-3, 6-11; 12-11 Fri & Sat; 12-10.30 (6 winter) Sun
☎ (01323) 831981 ⊕ bullsheadborehamstreet.co.uk
Harveys Sussex Best Bitter, seasonal beers Ⓗ
An 18th-century building in six acres of land that
was Harvey's first tied house. There is wood
panelling throughout the large bar area and two
smaller dining rooms. The main bar real fire and
the dining room woodburner give a cosy feel.
Camping is available; there is a large, well-kept
garden in which regular summer events are held.

Three Harvey's ales are sold all year. Excellent locally sourced food is served lunchtimes and evenings (no food Mon lunch or Sun eve). ⌂Q☺Ⓓ♣♠P꙼ᱼ꙰(98)

Brighton

Basketmakers Arms
12 Gloucester Road, BN1 4AD
✪ 11-11 (midnight Fri & Sat); 12-11 Sun ☎ (01273) 689006
⊕ basket-makers-brighton.co.uk
Fuller's Discovery, London Pride, seasonal beers; Gale's Seafarers Ale, HSB; guest beers Ⓗ
A two-room street-corner pub, on the edge of Brighton's famous bohemian North Laine district. Eight handpumps serve the Fuller's range plus guests. Locally sourced home-made food is available every day including very popular traditional Sunday roasts. Real ale in a bottle is available to take away. The walls are adorned with old metal signs and tobacco tins containing messages, secrets and codes written by customers over the years. Around 100 whiskies are stocked. ⒶⒹ≍ᱼ꙰

Battle of Trafalgar
34 Guildford Road, BN1 3LW
✪ 12-11 (midnight Fri & Sat) ☎ (01273) 327997
Fuller's London Pride; Harveys Sussex Best Bitter; guest beers Ⓗ
Quirky locals' pub only a minute from Brighton railway station. A long narrow room next to the bar leads down to a beer garden; another room is behind the bar. Some of the prints on the walls are sea-themed appropriate to the pub's name. If you operate the Engine Room Telegraph (it is difficult not to if you don't know otherwise) you will be expected to make a donation to the RNLI. A monthly lesbian and gay real ale drinkers meeting takes place in the room behind the bar. ☺ⒶⒹ≍♣ᱼ꙰

Constant Service
96 Islingword Road, BN2 9SJ
✪ 3-midnight (1am Fri); 12-1am Sat; 12-midnight Sun ☎ (01273) 607058
Harveys Sussex Best Bitter, seasonal beers Ⓗ
A friendly one-bar locals' pub in the residential Hanover district of Brighton. This Harvey's tied house usually stocks three ales. There is a deck behind the bar playing a wide variety of vinyl LPs but it is quiet enough for good conversation. Two TVs show sport and there is live music every Thursday. Good-quality good-value food is served every evening as well as weekend lunchtimes. A small but lovely garden is at the rear. ⌂⛱☺Ⓓᱼ꙰(37B,81)

Craft Beer Co
22-23 Upper North Street, BN1 3FG
✪ 12-11 (11.30 Thu; midnight Fri; 1am Sat); 12-10.30 Sun ☎ (01273) 735799 ⊕ thecraftbeerco.com
Kent The Craft Pale; guest beers Ⓗ
A new pub selling traditional ales. Its range covers nine cask beers and there is also an extensive bottled beer range from around the world. The pub, as its name implies, prides itself on its handcrafted beer offering and the quality of its ales is celebrated by the local cognoscenti. This place can get busy in the evening at the weekend. ⌂Ⓓ≍ᵭ꙰

Evening Star Ⓛ
55-56 Surrey Street, BN1 3PB (150yds S of station)
✪ 12-11 (midnight Fri); 11.30-midnight Sat ☎ (01273) 328931 ⊕ eveningstarbrighton.co.uk
Dark Star Hophead, seasonal beers; guest beers Ⓗ
The flagship Dark Star pub with four of its beers always available, plus three from other microbreweries. Real cider and sometimes a perry are available on handpump. A varied selection of bottled beers and worldwide beers on draught is also available. A Guide regular, this small pub is popular with a mixed clientele of all ages from all over the country and can get very busy. Occasional beer festivals and live music are staged. There is patio seating at the front. ☺≍●ᱼ꙰

Lord Nelson Inn
36 Trafalgar Street, BN1 4ED
✪ 11.30-11; 12-10.30 Sun ☎ (01273) 695872
⊕ thelordnelsoninn.co.uk
Harveys Sussex XX Mild, IPA, Sussex Best Bitter, Armada Ale, seasonal beers Ⓗ
A no-frills old-fashioned pub close to the station, this Harvey's tied house is a Guide regular serving the full range of the brewery's beers, plus seasonal ales. Popular with all age groups, conversation rules with background music kept low. Theatre posters and old photos adorn the main bars and modern local photographs feature in the conservatory which is available for hire. Quiz night is Tuesday and occasional live music is hosted. A pull-down screen shows live sport. ☺Ⓓ≍ᱼ꙰

Mitre Tavern
13 Baker Street, BN1 4JN
✪ 10.30-11.30 (midnight Fri & Sat); 12-10.30 Sun ☎ (01273) 683173 ⊕ mitretavern.co.uk
Harveys Sussex XX Mild, Sussex Best Bitter, Armada Ale, seasonal beers Ⓗ
Time in the Mitre does not come after last orders; it is what this place is out of. More fitted to 1950 than 2014, this two-bar, cosy corner house is Wi-Fi-free and technology-light. Its back-street setting, chintzy wallpaper and never-busy feel give space for people to talk and to enjoy the Harvey's beers in peace. The full range of Harvey's from Best to Old is generally on offer and is always well kept and well served. ☺Ⓓ♿≍♣●ᱼ꙰

Prestonville Arms
64 Hamilton Road, BN1 5DN (in back street E of Seven Dials)

INDEPENDENT BREWERIES

1648 East Hoathly
Beachy Head East Dean
Black Cat Groombridge
FILO Hastings
Franklins Bexhill-on-Sea
Full Moon Catsfield
Harveys Lewes
Hastings St Leonards-on-Sea
Isfield Framfield
Kemptown Brighton
Kitchen Garden Sheffield Park
Long Man Litlington
North Laine Brighton (NEW)
Pin-Up Stone Cross
Rectory Streat
Rother Valley Northiam
Turners Ringmer

⚙ 5-11; 12-midnight Fri & Sat; 12-11 Sun ☎ (01273) 701007
⊕ theprestonvillearms.co.uk
Fuller's London Pride, seasonal beers; Gale's Seafarers Ale, HSB; guest beers Ⓗ
Friendly, popular locals' pub in a back-street residential area on a narrow and steeply sloping corner site – not a location you would pass by chance but worth seeking out. It has a large horseshoe-shaped bar with a wooden floor. Changing displays by local artists adorn the mezzanine floor level, while other half-panelled walls feature prints of old Brighton. Quiz nights are on Sundays and Tuesdays, while Wednesdays are curry nights. Live music is sometimes staged at the weekend. ⏰❀◑≈⁵⌐

Prince George
5 Trafalgar Street, BN1 4EQ
⚙ 12-midnight ☎ (01273) 681055
⊕ princegeorgebrighton.co.uk
Beer range varies Ⓗ
Close to many London Road bus routes, this pub has several cosy drinking areas off the main bar, which serves up to six real ales from Sussex microbreweries such as 1648, Ballard's, Dark Star and Langham. CAMRA members and students are offered a discount on selected beers. Award-winning vegetarian food is served until 9pm every day. The outside area at the rear is heated and covered. Families are welcome until 7pm. Quiz night is Sunday and a DJ plays on Thursday. ⏰❀◑≈⁵➟

Pump House Ⓛ
46 Market Street, BN1 1HH (in the Lanes)
⚙ 11-11 (midnight Fri & Sat); 11-10.30 Sun
☎ (01273) 827421 ⊕ nicholsonspubs.co.uk/ thepumphousebrighton
Harveys Sussex Best Bitter; Sharp's Doom Bar; guest beers Ⓗ
Historic pub in the Lanes area and part of the Nicholson's chain. A board in the bar reveals that the building was bought by a Miss Elliot in 1766 and was first recorded as a pub in 1776. The name derives from an old timber pier with a pump house used to pump seawater ashore for bathing in the 18th century. Three guest beers are drawn from a seasonal selection of about 30. The cider is Westons Old Rosie. A separate restaurant/function room is upstairs. ⏩◑➤≈♠⁵➟

Reservoir
1 Howard Road, BN2 9TP
⚙ 3-11 (midnight Fri); 12-11 Sun ☎ (01273) 692484
⊕ reservoirbrighton.co.uk
Beer range varies Ⓗ
The ground-floor bar is open plan with plenty of seating and the kitchen open to view in one corner. The downstairs bar is smaller, with several sofas, and gives access to a large garden patio. Sunday lunches are traditional, however Thai food is served 5-10pm Monday to Saturday. Beers are changed regularly – there are usually four real ales available, all from Sussex breweries, and at reasonable prices for the Brighton area. ❀➤⁵➟

Colemans Hatch

Hatch Inn Ⓛ
Kidds Hill, TN7 4EJ
⚙ 11.30-3, 5.30-11; 11-11 Sat; 12-11 Sun ☎ (01342) 822363
⊕ hatchinn.co.uk

Harveys Sussex Best Bitter; Larkins Traditional Ale; guest beer Ⓗ
A 15th-century pub located in the heart of Ashdown Forest. This venue, popular with walkers and diners, has low-beamed ceilings decorated with hop fronds, and two garden areas and picnic tables on the forecourt, ideal for summer drinking and dining. The daily food menu includes locally sourced food. The pub has featured in TV dramas and numerous advertisements. The Ashdown Forest visitor centre is nearby and Poohsticks Bridge is five minutes away in Upper Hartfield. ⏩Q❀◑P➟(291)

Crowborough

Cooper's Arms Ⓛ
Coopers Lane, TN6 1SN
⚙ 12-2.30 (not Mon), 6-11; 12-11 Sat; 12-10.30 Sun
☎ (01892) 654796
Dark Star Hophead, Partridge Best Bitter; guest beers Ⓗ
Very friendly ale house offering two changing guest beers from Sussex and beyond and real cider in the summer. Beer festivals are normally held at Easter and late in the winter, with all beers served from the 12 handpumps on the bar. A selection of bottled beers is also kept. A classic long bar forms the main drinking area, with a separate restaurant and side bar for games. Food is served at all times. Q❀◑♣P➟

Wheatsheaf Ⓛ
Mount Pleasant, Jarvis Brook, TN6 2NF
⚙ 12-11 (10.30 Sun) ☎ (01892) 663756
⊕ wheatsheafcrowborough.co.uk
Harveys Sussex XX Mild, IPA, Sussex Best Bitter, Armada Ale, seasonal beers Ⓗ
Unspoilt early-Victorian beer house with a large car park and a very unusual three-sided bar on two levels. This tied house always has a good range of Harvey's beers on hand which can be enjoyed in any of the three distinct drinking areas or the outside garden. Two beer festivals are normally held, in May and October. The lower bar area has an unusual copper fireplace originally designed for a yacht. ⏩❀✉◑≈♣P⁵➟

Danehill

Coach & Horses Ⓛ
School Lane, RH17 7JF
⚙ 12-3, 5.30-11; 12-11 Sat; 12-10.30 Sun ☎ (01825) 740369
⊕ coachandhorses.danehill.biz
Harveys Sussex Best Bitter; guest beers Ⓗ
A traditional country pub built in 1847 and retaining many original features. The former adjoining stables have been converted to a restaurant serving high-quality locally sourced food. There are separate public and saloon bars with real fires and simple farmhouse-style furniture. It has a large garden to the front with a children's play area and a rear patio with extensive farmland views. Black Pig cider is seasonally sold as well as a perry from the same source. Dog-friendly. ⏩Q❀◑➤♣➤P⁵➟(270)

East Dean

Tiger Inn Ⓛ
The Green, BN20 0DA TV557978

✪ 11-11 ☎ (01323) 423209 ⊕ beachyhead.org.uk/ the_tiger_inn
Beachy Head Original, Legless Rambler, seasonal beer; Harveys Sussex Best Bitter Ⓗ
Quaint 15th-century smugglers' inn on the village green, close to the South Downs Way, making it a haven for walkers, hikers and cyclists. The main bar boasts beams, an inglenook and a woodburner, and two smaller rooms provide further dining areas for the freshly cooked food served daily. The pub is the brewery tap for the nearby Beachy Head Brewery. Well-appointed accommodation is available. ⋈Q⏱⚲⊛⇋⍅⓪⅄♣P¹⊷⊟(12,12A)

East Hoathly

King's Head Ⓛ
1 High Street, BN8 6DR
✪ 11-11 (midnight Fri & Sat); 12-10.30 Sun
☎ (01825) 840238
Harveys Sussex Best Bitter; 1648 Triple Champion, Signature, seasonal beers Ⓗ
Five handpumps feature beers primarily from the adjacent 1648 Brewery in this 17th-century village local. The U-shaped bar is decorated with old prints of the pub and photographs of local sports clubs and events. There are function rooms and a dining area. Locally sourced home-cooked food is served at all sessions (12-9pm at weekends), and takeouts are available. Special Saturday food events are held monthly. Outdoor seating is in a walled rear garden and on a front patio. ⋈Q⏱⚲⊛⓪♣P¹⊷⊟(54)

Eastbourne

Buccaneer Ⓛ
Compton Street, BN21 4BW
✪ 11-11; 12-10.30 Sun ☎ (01323) 732829
Arundel Buccaneer Ale; Harveys Sussex Best Bitter; guest beers Ⓗ
Well situated for the theatres and seafront, there is one large L-shaped bar with partitioned seating which is decorated with old theatre posters. A raised area to the rear overlooks the tennis courts of Devonshire Park. Five ales are offered including three changing guests; a discount is offered to CAMRA members. The house beer is from Arundel Brewery, with 10p donated to the pub's charity, Canine Partners, for every pint sold. Good-value food is available all day, every day. ⓪⇋⊟⊟(3)

Counting House Ⓛ
Star Road, BN21 1NB
✪ 12-11 (midnight Fri & Sat); 12-10.30 Sun
☎ (01323) 731158
Wells Bombardier; guest beers Ⓗ
Attractive 16th-century Grade II-listed building, with the feel of a country pub in town. Its large garden makes it popular in summer. The part-panelled main bar has beams, an inglenook and a woodburner. There are two smaller rooms, one set for diners during service times when good, freshly cooked food is served. Popular with all ages, entertainment includes jam nights, film nights and a pool table. Seasonal beer festivals are held. The two guests are usually from local microbreweries. ⋈Q⏱⚲⊛⓪⇋P¹⊷⊟

Dew Drop Inn
37-39 South Street, BN21 4UP
✪ 12-midnight (1am Fri & Sat) ☎ (01323) 723313
Beer range varies Ⓗ

This Greene King pub, popular with drinkers of all ages, carries two guest beers, one of which is usually from Dark Star. Evenings attract a mainly younger crowd, and there are occasional special events, DJ nights and sometimes live bands. The horseshoe-shaped bar area is divided in two, with ample comfortable seating, and there is a small rear garden. Beer and cider festivals are held. A range of pub food, including speciality burgers, is served until 9pm. CAMRA members are offered a discount. ⋈⊛⓪⅄⇋¹⊷⊟

Dolphin
14 South Street, BN21 4XF
✪ 11-11 (midnight Fri & Sat); 12-10.30 Sun
☎ (01323) 746622
Brakspear Oxford Gold; Harveys Sussex Best Bitter; guest beer Ⓗ
Friendly pub with a relaxed atmosphere situated in the Little Chelsea area. Now part of the Brakspear estate, it still has Kemptown Brewery stained glass logos in the front windows. The main bar has an open fire, and there is plenty of seating with two separate rear rooms and a patio at the side. The regular guest ales come from Dark Star or Hastings breweries. Individually cooked food is served, with locally caught fish a speciality. Themed food nights feature regularly. ⋈⊛⓪⅄⇋¹⊷⊟

Eagle Ⓛ
57 South Street, BN21 4UT
✪ 11-11 (12.30am Fri & Sat) ☎ (01323) 417799
Harveys Sussex Best Bitter; guest beers Ⓗ
Up to five changing beers from local breweries and Westons Old Rosie cider are offered here alongside an excellent range of pub food, served until 9pm. This former Kemptown Brewery pub features some fine restored internal decoration in its single bar. TVs, including a 100-inch HD projection screen, show popular sports, and a pool table and dartboard are available. There is a small roof terrace. Regular beer and cider festivals are held. CAMRA members receive a discount.
⋈⊛⓪⇋♣⍅¹⊷⊟

London & County
46 Terminus Road, BN21 3LX
✪ 8am-midnight (1am Fri & Sat) ☎ (01323) 746310
Greene King Abbot; Ruddles Best Bitter; guest beers Ⓗ
A Wetherspoon Lloyds No.1 bar, originally the London County Bank in 1880 and arranged over two floors, located in the town centre, close to the railway station and all local bus routes. The smaller upper room is available for functions. Five varying guest beers and one real cider are on offer alongside the regular ales, and good-value food is served all day. Muted TV screens display news daily and music is played in the evenings. ⓪⅄⇋⍅⊟

Ship Inn Ⓛ
33-35 Meads Street, BN20 7RH
✪ 10-11 (midnight Fri); 10-10.30 Sun ☎ (01323) 733815
Beachy Head Original, Legless Rambler; Harveys Sussex Best Bitter; guest beer Ⓗ
Large welcoming venue that offers a relaxed atmosphere for visitors to enjoy quality ales and excellent food. Its regular beers are from local breweries plus a guest beer from further afield. The bar has armchairs, two dining areas and a large decked garden. The pub is within easy reach of local shops, the beach and the South Downs. ⋈Q⊛⓪¹⊷⊟(3)

Victoria Hotel 🅛

27 Latimer Road, BN22 7BU (behind TAVR Centre)
🌣 11-11 (midnight Fri & Sat); 12-10.30 Sun
☎ (01323) 722673 ⊕ victoriaeastbourne.co.uk
Harveys Sussex Best Bitter, Armada Ale, seasonal beers 🅗
Friendly, family-run local, serving all Harvey's seasonal ales. A large front bar features brewery memorabilia and prints of Victorian portraits, a smaller back bar has darts, pool and toad in the hole, and there is a rear suntrap garden for alfresco dining. TVs show major sporting events. Good-value home-made food is available lunchtimes (Thu-Sun) and evenings (Thu-Sat). The cider is Westons Old Rosie. A beer festival is held over the Easter weekend. 🏠🍴◑♣🐾↾–🚇(99,1,1A)

Falmer

Swan Inn

Middle Street, BN1 9PD (just off A27 N of village)
🌣 12-11 (4 Mon); 12-10.30 Sun ☎ (01273) 681842
⊕ theswanfalmer.co.uk
Gale's Seafarers Ale; Palmers Best, Tally Ho; guest beers 🅗
Cosy, traditional, family-run free house in a village close to the universities. There are three bars including a narrow public bar. The pub is over 100 years old and the walls are adorned with antique adverts and pictures of the village in days past. Food is available at lunchtimes. Being close to the Amex Stadium, the pub is very busy on Brighton match days when only home fans are admitted and there is no parking available. 🏠Q🏠◑🍴🐾⇌♣P↾–🚇(28,29)

Hailsham

King's Head 🅛

146 South Road, BN27 3NJ
🌣 5-11; 12.30-3, 4.30-11 Fri; 12-3, 6-11 Sat; 12-4, 7-10.30 Sun ☎ (01323) 440447
Harveys Sussex Best Bitter, seasonal beers 🅗
CAMRA branch Pub of the Year 2011 and a tied Harvey's house since 1841, the King's Head dates from 1700. There are two separate bars, exposed beams, open fireplaces and a quiet snug, plus a large beer garden. A friendly welcome awaits from the staff, locals and Benson the dog. This community local has several darts teams, a pool team, a knitting club, a weekly Sunday quiz and an annual summer beer festival. Traditional pub games include toad in the hole and shove-ha'penny. 🏠🏠🍴♣P↾–🚇(51,54,98)

Hartfield

Anchor Inn 🅛

Church Street, TN7 4AG
🌣 11-11.30; 12-11 Sun ☎ (01892) 770424
⊕ anchorinnhartfield.co.uk
Harveys Sussex Best Bitter; Larkins Traditional Ale; guest beers 🅗
The Anchor was built in 1465 as a manor house. In the early 1800s it was a workhouse but changed to selling beer in the 1860s. It is located in the centre of this Ashdown Forest village fronting Church Street. The interior has two bars, the front heated by a wood-burning stove with an inglenook in the rear cosy bar. The restaurant is used during busy periods. The wood-beamed front bar is decorated with old photographs. 🏠Q🏠🏠◑🏠🍴♣P↾–🚇

Hastings

Dolphin 🍷

11-12 Rock-a-Nore Road, TN34 3DW
🌣 11-11 (midnight Sat) ☎ (01424) 431197
Dark Star Hophead; Harveys Sussex Best Bitter; Young's Special; guest beers 🅗
Local CAMRA Branch Pub of the Year 2013. Overlooking the unique Hastings fishermen's huts at Rock-a-Nore, this old town pub is at the heart of the fishing community. It is decorated with fishing memorabilia and is particularly busy at weekends and holidays. Good food includes the speciality fish platter (no eve meals at weekends). Live music is on Friday and Saturday evenings and occasionally on other weekdays, quiz night is Thursday. 🏠Q🏠◑↾–🚇(20,100)

First In Last Out 🅛

14-15 High Street, TN34 3EY (in old town, near Stables Theatre)
🌣 12-11 (midnight Fri); 11-midnight Sat ☎ (01424) 425079
⊕ thefilo.co.uk
FILO Mike's Mild, Crofters, Old Town Tom, Cardinal, Churches Pale Ale; guest beer 🅗
Located in the picturesque old town area, this building has been an inn since 1896, but dates back to the 1500s. Formerly home to the FILO Brewery, now 300 yards away, the popular pub has a large bar warmed by a central open fire. Five beers are usually available. Fresh home-cooked food is served Monday to Saturday lunchtimes and some evenings, while Monday features a tapas night. Beer festivals are held over most bank holiday weekends, with real cider also on offer. 🏠Q🏠♣🐾🚇(20,100)

Stag Inn

14 All Saints Street, TN34 3BJ
🌣 12-midnight (11 Sun) ☎ (01424) 425734
⊕ staghastings.co.uk
Shepherd Neame Kent's Best, Spitfire, Bishops Finger, seasonal beers 🅗
Probably the oldest surviving pub in Hastings, in its present form it dates from 1547 and has many interesting and quirky features, including mummified cats on display. As a tied house, it is one of a few pubs to take beers from Shepherd Neame's microbrewery, and these are often available to complement the regular ales. Food is usually on offer (check first in winter months). Monday is quiz night, Tuesday folk night, Wednesday blue grass and Thursday singers. 🏠Q🏠◑♣↾–🚇(20,100)

White Rock Hotel 🅛

1-10 White Rock, TN34 1JU (opp pier)
🌣 10 (12 Sun)-11 ☎ (01424) 422240
⊕ thewhiterockhotel.com
Beer range varies 🅗
Large, friendly hotel adjacent to the theatre of the same name, featuring a stylish, contemporary bar with ample seating and a terrace overlooking the seafront and Hastings Pier, which is due for reconstruction in 2014. Four beers on offer are always from independent Sussex breweries; a good range of freshly prepared food is available until 10pm. Guest rooms are en-suite and many have sea views; the best are on the first floor with a balcony. The strict no smoking policy includes outdoor areas. Q🏠🏠🏠🍴⇌🐾🅟🍴

ENGLAND

Hove

Cliftonville Inn
98-101 George Street, BN3 3YE
✪ 8-11 (midnight Fri & Sat) ☎ (01273) 726969
Courage Directors; Greene King Abbot; Ruddles Best Bitter; guest beers Ⓗ
Located in the busy George Street shopping area, there are no prizes for the building or decor (a former furniture store), but full marks for the pub's well-kept real ales, which include several from local microbreweries, and for the number of real ciders available. There are the usual Wetherspoon promotional nights, and a good range of ales on at festivals. Locally relevant history panels adorn the walls, revealing that the pub's name refers to an old area of Hove. Q⏀⏦⇌♠⊟

Neptune Inn Ⓛ
10 Victoria Terrace, Kingsway, BN3 2WB
✪ 12-1am (2am Fri & Sat); 12-midnight Sun
☎ (01273) 736390 ⊕ theneptunelivemusicbar.co.uk
Greene King Abbot; Harveys Sussex Best Bitter; guest beers Ⓗ
Five handpumps serve regular favourites plus frequently changing guest ales, always in good condition. This traditional single-bar pub is frequented by a regular local clientele. Live music is strongly supported, with blues and rock every Friday and jazz on Sunday, together with monthly open mic, and vinyl nights on the second and fourth Mondays. This pub is situated on the Brighton to Shoreham coast road near central Hove. ⌐⊟(700)

Icklesham

Queen's Head
Parsonage Lane, TN36 4BL (opp village hall)
✪ 11-11; 12-10.30 Sun ☎ (01424) 814552
⊕ queenshead.com
Greene King IPA, Abbot; Harveys Sussex Best Bitter; guest beers Ⓗ
Early 17th-century inn, featuring in the Guide for its 30th consecutive year, serving rotating guest beers often from Dark Star, as well as from a number of local brewers and further afield. It stocks five beers, up to eight at weekends, and a real cider. Three log fires warm the five interior areas in the winter and a spacious garden offers fine views towards Winchelsea and Rye. There is live music 4-6pm on Sundays, and affordable food. A regular autumn beer festival offers Sussex and Kent beers. ♨Q⏦♣♠P⌐☐⊟(100)

Robin Hood Ⓛ
Main Road, TN36 4BD
✪ 11-3, 6-11; 11-11 Fri & Sat; 12-4, 7-10.30 Sun
☎ (01424) 814277
Beer range varies Ⓗ
Local CAMRA branch Pub of the Year 2012, this 17th-century inn offers six or seven beers, usually from local brewers, as well as at least two ciders, including local Battle Pink cider. The ale strength is wide-ranging, always including a low ABV beer. A separate dining area serves home-cooked food, and log fires warm two bar areas. Each July a successful village beer festival is held in an adjacent field. There is a pool table and a large rear garden. ♨Q⏦⏦⊞♣♠P⌐☐⊟(100)

Lewes

Brewers Arms ♥ Ⓛ
91 High Street, BN7 1XN (near castle)
✪ 10-11; 12-10.30 Sun ☎ (01273) 475524
⊕ brewersarmslewes.co.uk
Harveys Sussex Best Bitter; guest beers Ⓗ
Genuine family-run free house catering for most tastes in its two bars. At the front, the comfortable saloon offers a range of seating with books and games available. The rear bar has a pool table and two TVs show sporting events. It is popular on match days with both Lewes FC and Brighton & Hove Albion and visiting away fans. Food, including traditional breakfasts, is served until 7pm. The exterior proclaims the former owners, Page & Overtons, Brewers of Croydon. Q⏦⏦⊞⇌♣♠⌐⊟(28,29)

Elephant & Castle Ⓛ
White Hill, BN7 2DJ (off Fisher St, near old police station)
✪ 11.30-11 (midnight Fri & Sat); 12-11 Sun
☎ (01273) 473797 ⊕ elephantandcastlelewes.co.uk
Harveys Sussex Best Bitter; Taylor Landlord; guest beers Ⓗ
Built in 1838 to provide accommodation and stabling for a new road into the town, the Ellie is a spacious community-based pub, home to one of the famous Lewes bonfire societies and a Saturday folk club. Major sporting events including the Rugby Six Nations are shown on a large-screen TV. The pub has a big function room available for hire. The changing guest beer is usually from a Sussex brewer and the food is locally sourced. ♨⏦⏦⇌♣♠⌐⊟(127)

Gardener's Arms Ⓛ
46 Cliffe High Street, BN7 2AN
✪ 11-11; 12-10.30 Sun ☎ (01273) 474808
Harveys Sussex Best Bitter; guest beers Ⓗ
Small, genuine free house in the heart of Lewes, near Harvey's brewery. Five changing guest ales are on handpump, usually from small breweries all over the country. Harvey's seasonal ales and one-off brews often feature, and bottled and draught cider is available. Food consists of locally made pies and pasties. A Guide and ale trail regular, it is popular with Brighton and Lewes FC fans on match days. Customers' canine friends are made very welcome with water and dog treats. No children allowed. ⇌♣♠⌐⊟(28,29)

John Harvey Tavern Ⓛ
Bear Yard, Cliffe High Street, BN7 2AN (opp Harveys Brewery)
✪ 11-11; 12-10.30 Sun ☎ (01273) 479880
⊕ johnharveytavern.co.uk
Harveys IPA Ⓗ, Sussex Best Bitter Ⓖ, Armada Ale, seasonal beers Ⓗ
Harvey's tied house opposite the brewery shop dispensing beers on handpump and gravity. A warm welcome is assured in this modern pub, built in a former stable block close to the river. The venue has three separate areas: a main bar, a quieter room on the same level, and an upstairs restaurant/function room. It stages regular folk nights every Monday, jazz every second and third Wednesday, and live music every Saturday. Children are allowed only in the restaurant. The pub is dog-friendly (on leads please). ♨Q⏦⏦⇌⌐⊟(28,29)

Lewes Arms

1 Mount Place, BN7 1YH

❂ 11-11 (midnight Fri & Sat); 12-11 Sun ☎ (01273) 473152
⊕ thelewesarms.co.uk

Fuller's London Pride, seasonal beers; Gale's HSB; Harveys Sussex Best Bitter; guest beers ⊞

In the heart of the county town, the pub is a traditional alehouse popular with visitors and locals alike. Fuller's beers are served plus Harveys Best and a guest. It is home to the world pea-throwing championship, dwyle flunking, spaniel racing and other unusual events. A three-day music festival is hosted in August, with an annual pantomime in March in the upstairs function room in aid of a local charity. Home-made food is available every day; times vary. ▲Q🕸🌺❂◑⬚⬅♣'—⊟(28,29)

Lewes Constitutional Club ⓛ

139 High Street, BN7 1XS

❂ 4.30-10; 12-midnight Fri & Sat; 12-8 Sun
☎ (01273) 473076 ⊕ lewesconclub.co.uk

Harveys Sussex Best Bitter, seasonal beers; guest beers ⊞

Known locally as the Con Club, it has Harveys Old available in winter, usually outselling all others. For entry, show your CAMRA membership card or a copy of this Guide, and remember to sign the visitors' book. Live music events are held regularly, when a small admission charge is payable. Toad in the hole and darts are played and occasional beer festivals are held. 🌺⬅♣'—⊟(28,29)

Snowdrop Inn

119 South Street, BN7 2BU

❂ 12-midnight (11 Sun) ☎ (01273) 471018
⊕ thesnowdropinn.com

Dark Star Hophead, seasonal beers; Harveys Sussex Best Bitter, seasonal beers; guest beers ⊞

Very popular free house offering a range of up to six real ales, usually including two from Harveys and two from Dark Star, and one real cider. They do a daily changing menu of home-cooked food from fresh locally sourced produce, including a good selection for vegetarians. A full and varied programme of music is staged, usually four nights each week. There is a beer garden on either side of the pub and a large upstairs room if the bar is full. Children and dog friendly. 🕸🌺◑♣🐕'—⊟(28,29)

Litlington

Plough & Harrow ⓛ

The Street, BN26 5RE

❂ 11 (12 Sun)-11 ☎ (01323) 870632 ⊕ thepandh.co.uk

Dark Star American Pale Ale; Harveys Sussex Best Bitter; Long Man Best Bitter, Long Blonde; guest beer ⊞

With parts dating from the 16th century, this pretty village free house offers a variety of comfortable seating, including cut-down beer casks. As well as the main bar area, there is a separate dining area and an unusual snug with an inglenook fireplace. To the rear is an attractive garden with seating and barbecue. Food is cooked to order from an extensive range of locally sourced produce and features home-made desserts. The pub is the tap for the local Long Man Brewery. ▲Q🕸🌺◑♣P'—⬚⊟

Pett

Royal Oak

Pett Road, TN35 4HG

❂ 11-11; 12-10.30 Sun ☎ (01424) 812515
⊕ royaloakpett.com

Beer range varies ⊞

Village free house refurbished by the new owner in 2011, serving up to four real ales (always including one from Harveys) in two bar areas, one featuring a large open fireplace. Food is served in a separate dining area with an emphasis on local produce. The highlight of an excellent selection of traditional pub games is an antique bagatelle board, the forerunner of modern bar billiards. Events include a quiz and occasional live music. ▲🕸◑♣P⬚⊟(347)

Two Sawyers

TN35 4HB

❂ 12-11 (10.30 Sun) ☎ (01424) 812255
⊕ twosawyers.co.uk

Harveys Sussex Best Bitter; Ringwood Fortyniner; guest beers ⊞

Welcoming 17th-century village inn comprising two main bars, a separate restaurant and smaller dining areas. Four real ales are generally on offer plus a real cider. There is an interesting carved timber pub sign and a collection of antique saws which both reflect the pub's name. Food is served from an extensive menu each session and all day Sundays. Popular both with drinkers and diners, tourists are attracted by three en-suite rooms. ▲Q🕸🚐◑⬚&▲♣●P'—⊟(347)

Portslade

Stanley Arms ⓛ

47 Wolseley Road, BN41 1SS

❂ 4 (3 Wed-Fri)-11; 12-11 Sat; 12-10.30 Sun
☎ (01273) 430234 ⊕ thestanley.com

Beer range varies ⊞

A genuine family-run free house. Beer festivals are held in spring, summer and autumn. Reduced price cellar nights with free nibbles take place every second Monday. The pub has a football team and shows matches on HDTV. Quiz and crib evenings are organised plus occasional live music and talks by sports personalities. A meeting room is available. ▲Q🕸⬅(Fishersgate)♣●'—⬚⊟(2,2A,46)

Ringmer

Anchor Inn

Lewes Road, BN8 5QE

❂ 11-midnight; 11.30-11 Sun ☎ (01273) 812370
⊕ anchorinnringmer.co.uk

Harveys Sussex Best Bitter; guest beers ⊞

Situated opposite the village green, this family-run free house dates back to 1742 and occupies a prominent position in the centre of Ringmer. Food is served 12-2.30pm and 6-9pm weekdays, all day Saturday and 12-4pm Sunday. The two guest ales usually come from local Sussex breweries, and Westons Old Rosie cider is available in summer. Two large garden areas adjoin the building, and the separate small terrace garden has seating and a heated, covered smoking area. ▲🕸◑P'—⊟(28,29B,143)

Cock Inn 🅛

Uckfield Road, BN8 5RX (1 mile from village on slip road off A26)
🌑 11-3, 6-11; 11-11 Sun ☎ (01273) 812040
🌐 cockpub.co.uk
Harveys Sussex Best Bitter, seasonal beers; guest beers 🅗

A traditional family-run pub offering an extensive menu of quality food with vegetarian, vegan and gluten-free options. Harveys Sussex Best Bitter is always served plus two seasonal local ales (including Harveys, Hammerpot, WJ King, Isfield and Dark Star). It also sells a comprehensive range of Harvey's bottled beers. The bar has a large inglenook fireplace, exposed beams and a flagstone floor. There is a spacious dining area, a well-furnished beer garden and plenty of car parking space. ♨Q✿❀❂▲P⅃₋➴(29)

Rottingdean

Queen Victoria 🅛

54 High Street, BN2 7HF
🌑 12-11 (midnight Fri & Sat); 12-10.30 Sun
☎ (01273) 302121
Harveys Sussex Best Bitter; Long Man Long Blonde; guest beers 🅗

One-bar pub with a mock-Tudor frontage, originally built in the 1930s replacing an original pub that was situated opposite – the site is now the public car park. Among the former licensees were local folk singers the Copper Family. Note the chandelier over the bar, the harmonium by the front entrance, and the photographs of old Rottingdean on the back wall. ➴✿❀❂♧♣❂P➴

St Leonards-on-Sea

Horse & Groom 🅛

4 Mercatoria, TN38 0EB
🌑 11-11; 12-10.30 Sun ☎ (01424) 420612
Adnams Broadside; Fuller's London Pride; Harveys Sussex Best Bitter; guest beer 🅗

A pleasant back-street free house, well worth finding at the heart of old St Leonards. The outside gives no clue to the unusual horseshoe-shaped bar, with a separate, narrow, quieter room at the rear. Food is not served in the pub, but there is an adjoining restaurant open Tuesday to Saturday evenings and Sunday lunchtimes. The pub is a short walk from the seafront and Warrior Square. A quiet, atmospheric, dog-friendly hostelry where you can enjoy good conversation. ♨Q✿♣≋(Warrior Square)♣⅃₋➴

North Star Inn

Clarence Road, TN37 6SD
🌑 11-midnight (1am Fri); 12-midnight Sun
☎ (01424) 436576
Harveys Sussex Best Bitter; Taylor Landlord; guest beers 🅗

This friendly local is hidden away in a back street in the Bohemia area. Decorated with railway memorabilia, the large U-shaped bar room with an open fire offers a good range of up to three changing guest beers, often from local microbreweries. Although food is not usually available, there is a popular curry evening on Wednesdays. ♨Q✿♣≋(Warrior Square)♣⅃₋➴(99,100,341)

Tower

251 London Road, TN37 6NB
🌑 11-11.30; 12-11 Sun ☎ (01424) 721773
Dark Star Hophead, American Pale Ale; guest beers 🅗

The Tower is a free house offering very reasonably priced real ales, with two guest beers changing all the time. A variety of entertainment includes live sporting events on HDTV, themed events, a well-stocked jukebox and monthly meat raffles. The décor is not flash, but the wood-burning stove generates a warm atmosphere, as do the friendly staff. For those who knew the pub before its conversion to four real ales, a pleasant surprise awaits you. ♨≋(Warrior Square)♣➴

Salehurst

Halt 🅛

Church Lane, TN32 5PH (by church)
🌑 closed Mon; 12-3, 6-11 Tue & Wed; 12-11
☎ (01580) 880620 🌐 salehursthalt.co.uk
Harveys Sussex Best Bitter; guest beers 🅗

Visitors will find a warm welcome at this dog-friendly, traditional family-run pub which was originally a railway stop on a hop-picking line. Two guest beers are often from local microbreweries. In the summer three ciders are served, one in the winter. Good food is on the menu, locally sourced. From the garden, which has a pizza oven, there is a view over the beautiful Rother Valley. Inside there is a selection of board games and live music every second Sunday of the month. ♨Q✿❀❂♣♧♣⅃

Seaford

Old Plough

20 Church Street, BN25 1HG
🌑 11-11 (midnight Fri & Sat); 12-11 Sun ☎ (01323) 872921
🌐 theoldploughseaford.co.uk
Harveys Sussex Best Bitter; guest beers 🅗

Situated next to the ancient St Leonards Church (circa 1090), just off the town centre, this welcoming pub has several rooms leading off from the main bar area, giving the hostelry a lot of character. A good-value menu features many food and drink offers. Breakfast is served between 11am and noon. Five handpumps deliver beers mainly from Sussex breweries. The large patio area is an ideal place to relax during the summer. ✿❀❂≋(Lewes)⅃₋➴(12,12A,13X)

South Chailey

Horns Lodge 🅛

South Street, BN8 4BD (on A275)
🌑 11.30-2.30 (not Tue), 5.30-11; 11.30-11 Sat; 12-10.30 Sun
☎ (01273) 400422 🌐 hornslodge.com
Harveys Sussex Best Bitter; guest beers 🅗

Roadside pub that was originally a coaching inn on the London to Brighton postal service route. The bar has a games area for bar billiards, darts and toad in the hole. Home-cooked food is available lunchtimes and evenings (no food Tue). The pub has a beautiful, recently renovated garden with a covered and heated smoking area. There are annual beer, cider and sausage festivals and a Mr & Mrs contest. A charity quiz is held on the last Tuesday of each month. ♨✿❀❂♣♧♣P⅃₋➴(121)

Uckfield

Alma
65 Framfield Road, TN22 5AJ (on B2102)
☼ 11-11 (11.30 Fri & Sat); 12-10.30 Sun ☎ (01825) 762232
⊕ alma-arms.co.uk
Harveys Sussex XX Mild, Sussex Best Bitter, seasonal
beers ⊞
A Harvey's pub about five minutes' walk from the
town centre, station and buses. The large main bar
has smaller seating areas and there are
independent meeting/function rooms. A separate
area houses a number of traditional games
including toad in the hole. No food is served
Monday or Tuesday. Thai food is available on
Saturday evening and a carvery 12-4pm on Sunday.
Sussex XX Mild is served all year round and the
cider is Thatchers Heritage.
爲①▶ 凸よ⇄♣☀P'-局(318)

Wilmington

Giant's Rest ⌶
The Street, BN26 5SQ (off A27)
☼ 11-3, 6-11; 11.30-11 Sat; 12-10.30 Sun ☎ (01323) 870207
⊕ giantsrest.co.uk
Long Man Long Blonde, Best Bitter, seasonal beer ⊞
This Victorian building can be seen from the main
road; the interior is wooden, with wooden table
games distributed round the pub. A varied and
interesting menu is offered, featuring mainly local
produce. The outside seating area is ideal for
walkers visiting the Long Man, a nearby chalk
figure cut into the Downs, from which the pub gets
its name. 爲愛⇌①▶♣P局(126)

Wivelsfield Green

Cock Inn ⌶
North Common Road, RH17 7RH (900yds E of B2112)
☼ 12-11 (10.30 Sun) ☎ (01444) 471668
⊕ cockinn-wivelsfield.co.uk
Downlands Slugwash; Harveys Sussex Best Bitter,
seasonal beers; guest beers ⊞
The pub is on the eastern edge of the village and is
popular with walkers, cyclists and locals alike. A
more frequent bus service is available at the other
end of the village on routes 40/40X. Two guest
beers supplement the Harveys Sussex Best; in
winter one of these is always Harveys Old Ale. In
summer there is real cider. Darts, pool and bar
billiards are played in the public bar and a portable
skittle alley can be hired.
爲Q愛①凸♣P'-局(166,824)

SUSSEX (WEST)

Alfold Bars

Sir Roger Tichborne ⌶
Loxwood Road, RH14 0QS
☼ 11.30-11 ☎ (01403) 751873 ⊕ thetichborne.co.uk
Beer range varies ⊞
Familiar to all those who once completed the King
& Barnes Ale Trail, this small country pub, whose
origins date back to medieval times, was
completely refurbished and reopened in 2009 after
a period of closure. The restaurant enjoys extensive
views of the surrounding countryside. It is now an
attractive free house selling a variety of guest ales,
mostly local ones. Happily much of its original
rustic rural charm remains. 爲Q愛①P'-局(63)

456

Arundel

Red Lion ⌶
45 High Street, BN18 9AG
☼ 11-11 (midnight Thu-Sat); 12-11 Sun ☎ (01903) 882214
⊕ redlionarundel.com
Arundel Sussex Gold; Fuller's London Pride; guest
beers ⊞
Reputed to be over 200 years old, this handsome
red-brick building occupies a prominent position in
the main street of a historic and characterful castle
town, and is well placed for the castle, cathedral,
river and Wildfowl Trust. Two changing guest beers
always include at least one LocAle. Excellent food is
served all day and there is a quieter restaurant area
to the rear of the pub. Thatchers Traditional cider is
served. Music plays every Saturday, and Wi-Fi is
available. 爲⌂愛①⇄☀'-局(85,700)

Barnham

Murrell Arms
Yapton Road, PO22 0AS (300yds E of railway station,
under bridge) SU961042
☼ 11-11; 12-10.30 Sun ☎ (01243) 553320
⊕ murrellarms.co.uk
Fuller's London Pride, Bengal Lancer, seasonal beer;
Gale's HSB ⊞
An 1866 village pub still retaining its original two
bars, the Murrell has an atmosphere of antiquity.
Walls and ceilings are decorated with old pictures,
craft tools and local memorabilia, many of which
relate to former landlord and local historian Mervyn
Cutten. In the right-hand public bar the rare game
of ring the bull can still be played, while in the
smaller Stable Bar an upright piano remains. There
is a pleasant rear garden. Home-cooked meals
feature meat from the traditional butchers across
the road. 爲Q愛①凸A⇄♣P'-局(66,85A)

Bosham

White Swan ⌶
Station Road, PO18 8NG (beside A259 roundabout)
SU812053
☼ 12-11; 11.30-11.15 Fri & Sat; 11.30-10 Sun
☎ (01243) 578917 ⊕ thewhiteswanbosham.com
Beer range varies ⊞
Cosy Grade II-listed free house that reopened in
2011 after extensive refurbishment, with tasteful
use of stone flags on the bar floor and much
reclaimed timber. The restaurant area serves
reasonably priced home-cooked food and has the
old bread oven in the wall from its days as the
village bakery. Dark Star Hophead, Sharp's Doom
Bar and Hop Back Summer Lightning are usually on
offer, but may be replaced by others. Locally
sourced wines are also available. In fine weather
outside seating to the front can be used.
Q愛①凸⇄♣P'-局(700,56)

Burgess Hill

Quench Bar ⌶
2-4 Church Road, RH15 9AE
☼ 9-11 (12.30am Thu & Fri; 1am Sat); 10-10.30 Sun
☎ (01444) 253332 ⊕ quenchbar.co.uk
Harveys Sussex Best Bitter; guest beers ⊞
Although this popular modernised venue is a bar, it
conveys a pub-like atmosphere. Look out for the
beer map which plots the taste and characteristics
of beers, both real and keg. Up to three guest beers

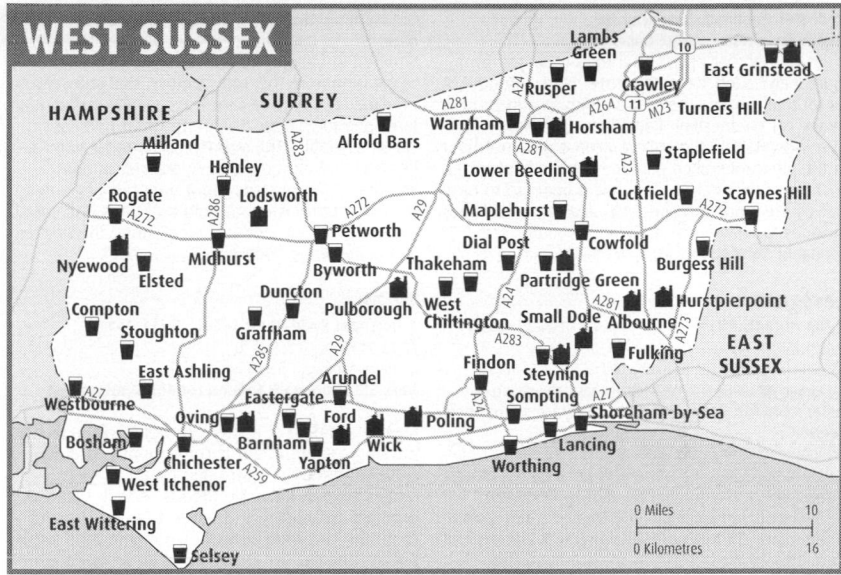

are mostly but not exclusively from Sussex independent brewers and often include Dark Star seasonals and beers from Downlands. A limited number of outside tables and chairs are provided. Sunday lunches are served from noon. All buses that serve Burgess Hill pass the door. ◑▶☒

Byworth

Black Horse 🅛
GU28 0HL (just off A283, 1 mile E of Petworth)
✪ 12-11 ☎ (01798) 342424 ⊕ theblackhorsebyworth.com
Flowerpots Bitter; Young's Bitter; guest beers Ⓗ
Friendly and welcoming old-style village pub, dating from the 16th century. The cosy bar area has a large open log fire, wood floors throughout, wattle and daub walls and large beams. It serves good real ales, and guest beers are LocAle. Excellent locally sourced seasonal food is available, with secluded dining areas overlooking the large steeply terraced garden at the back with stunning views. An iron staircase leads to an upstairs function room. Regular darts and quiz nights take place. Dog-friendly. ⍩Q☒☸◑➔日✚P☒(1,99)

Chichester

Bell Inn
3 Broyle Road, PO19 6AT (on A286 just N of Northgate)
SU860055
✪ 11.30-2.30, 5-midnight; 12-3, 7-11 Sun ☎ (01243) 783388
Beer range varies Ⓗ
Cosy city local with a traditional ambience enhanced by exposed brickwork, wood panelling and beams. A rear suntrap garden has a covered smoking area heated by a coal stove in winter. The pub tends to become busy after 10pm, when the nearby Festival Theatre empties out. The beer selection usually comprises two from the Enterprise range and one from a local micro, complemented by an extensive food menu (no food Sun eve). The parking area is small but a large public car park is nearby. ⍩Q☸◑➔✚P♿☒(60)

Bull Inn 🅛
4-5 Market Road, PO19 1JW (at Eastgate opp market)
SU864046
✪ 11.30 (11 Wed & Sat)-11; 11.30-midnight Fri & Sat; 12-10 Sun ☎ (01243) 792432
Beer range varies Ⓗ
Opposite the Market car park at Eastgate, this airy and friendly city local sells up to seven beers, mostly from local microbreweries. Look up to see the largest display of potato mashers in Sussex. The famous O'Hagans sausages are always available either as a bar meal or to take away. A meeting room is available and there is a covered garden and smoking area behind the pub. ⍩Q☸◑⇌日☒(51,700)

Chichester Inn 🅛
38 West Street, PO19 1RP (at Westgate roundabout)
SU858048
✪ 12-11.30 (midnight Fri & Sat); closed 2.30-5.30 Mon-Thu Jan-Apr; 12-10.30 Sun ☎ (01243) 783185
⊕ chichesterinn.co.uk

INDEPENDENT BREWERIES

Adur Steyning
Anchor Springs Wick
Arundel Ford
Baldy Pulborough (NEW)
Ballard's Nyewood
Baseline Small Dole
Bedlam Albourne
Dark Star Partridge Green
Downlands Small Dole (NEW)
Goldmark Poling (NEW)
Gribble Oving
Hammerpot Poling
Hepworth Horsham
High Weald East Grinstead (NEW)
Hurst Hurstpierpoint (NEW)
King Horsham
Kissingate Lower Beeding
Langham Lodsworth
Weltons Horsham

457

Dark Star Hophead, American Pale Ale; Harveys Sussex Best Bitter; guest beers Ⓗ
Pleasant two-bar pub with a high-ceilinged front lounge and a log fire with comfy chairs around it. A larger public bar to the rear doubles as a live music venue on Wednesday, Friday and Saturday evenings. Behind the pub you can enjoy your beer in the pleasant walled garden or in the heated and covered smoking area. Two guest beers from local micros are stocked, especially at weekends. Food includes Sunday lunches. Two B&B rooms are available. ᴹ☆ẞⰀⰀⰀⰀ P⁻◻

Eastgate

4 The Hornet, PO19 7JG (500yds E of Market Cross) SU865048
�",12 (11 Wed)-11.30; 10-midnight Fri; 10-12.30am Sat; 11-11 Sun ☎ (01243) 774877 ⊕ theeastgatepub.org.uk
Fuller's London Pride, ESB; Gale's Seafarers Ale; guest beers Ⓗ
Welcoming town pub with an attractive open-plan bar, a wood-burning stove and an area for diners. Good-quality traditional pub meals are home cooked and served daily. The heated patio garden is the venue for a beer festival in July featuring four local ales as well as others from around the country. The pub attracts locals, holidaymakers and shoppers from the nearby market with its warm welcome and traditional pub games such as darts, cribbage and pool. Music is turned up on Friday and Saturday late evenings. ᴹ☆ⰀⰀⰀ⁻◻(51,700)

Compton

Coach & Horses Ⓛ

The Square, PO18 9HA (on B2146) SU776148
🌐 12-3, 6-11; 12-4, 7-10.30 Sun ☎ (02392) 631228
⊕ coachandhorsescompton.com
Ballards Coach & Horses; guest beers Ⓗ
Sixteenth-century pub in a remote but charming village, popular with walkers and cyclists. The front bar is warm and welcoming, with an open fire and a wood-burning stove. This connects to the oldest part of the pub, now the restaurant. An adventurous menu of high-quality food is served every day, all sourced locally. Up to five beers are on offer from independent breweries, while Coach & Horses is a dry-hopped version of Ballards Best Bitter. There is a bar billiards table, and seats outside in the village square. ᴹQ☆ⰀⰀ◻(54)

Cowfold

Hare & Hounds Ⓛ

Henfield Road, RH13 8DR
🌐 11-3, 5-11; 11-11 Sat; 12-11 Sun ☎ (01403) 865354
Harveys Sussex Best Bitter; guest beers Ⓗ
Convivial village local where you can be sure of a warm welcome. It has a large stone-flagged bar area, a separate carpeted dining space, and an adjacent area for drinking. The log fire is the main focal point in winter. This free house frequently offers Dark Star beers along with other local ales, as well as milds and dark beers. An annual beer festival is held in July. Food is served during all sessions. ᴹQ♋☆ⰀⰀⰀ P⁻◻(17,86,100)

Crawley

Brewery Shades Ⓛ

85 High Street, RH10 1BA
🌐 10-11.30 (1am Sat; 10.30 Sun) ☎ (01293) 514105

Greene King Abbot; Morland Old Speckled Hen; guest beers Ⓗ
Situated in Crawley High Street and probably originating from the 14th century, this pub sells an imaginative range of cask ales, usually including at least one local beer. There are often two cask ciders available. The pub is very popular with ale drinkers and extremely busy on Fridays and Saturdays. The upstairs room, reputedly haunted, has been refurbished to hold meetings and social events. Excellent food is served during the day and in the evenings. ☆ⰀⰀⰀ◻

Swan Ⓛ

1 Horsham Road, West Green, RH11 7AY
🌐 12-11 (1am Fri & Sat) ☎ (01293) 527447
⊕ theswanpubcrawley.co.uk
Dark Star Hophead; Fuller's London Pride; guest beers Ⓗ
Superb example of a street-corner locals' pub. This bustling establishment is conveniently located close to the town centre and on a bus route with good transport links. No food is served; this is a drinkers' pub, but you are free to bring your own grub. The changing beers frequently include strong brews. Regular live music and two to three beer festivals annually are held. The pub supports CAMRA's Mild Day in May with up to 12 milds being available. ᴹ☆♋ⰀⰀⰀ⁻◻(23)

Cuckfield

Ship Inn Ⓛ

Whitemans Green, RH17 5BY (at B2115/B2036 jct)
🌐 12-2.30 (not Wed), 5.30-11; 12-11 Sat; 12-4 Sun
☎ (01444) 413219
Harveys Sussex Best Bitter; guest beers Ⓖ
A traditional family-run free house with four handpumps, although the beer is poured direct from the cask in a cool room behind the bar. The landlocked Ship is so called as it was a stopping point for convicted prisoners being deported to Australia. There is a comfortable lounge area and a pleasant garden to the rear. Food is served at all sessions. The pub was voted most popular by the Sussex-wide Bus to the Pub group in 2012. ᴹQ☆ⰀⰀⰀ P⁻◻(39,40,271)

Dial Post

Crown Inn Ⓛ

Worthing Road, RH13 8NH (leave A24 at Dial Post turn, pub is in centre of village)
🌐 11.30-3, 6 (5.30 Fri & Sat)-11; 11.30-4 Sun
☎ (01403) 710902 ⊕ floatingcrown.co.uk
Harveys Sussex Best Bitter; guest beers Ⓗ
Charming family-run 16th-century pub keen to support local breweries. Its superb home-cooked food is also sourced locally wherever possible. The cosy bar area has kept its traditional style, with oak beams and a woodburner. There is a choice of three dining areas, each with a different feel: the conservatory, the restaurant and the snug. This is a dog and walker friendly pub. No food Sunday evening. ᴹQ☆♋ⰀⰀⰀ P⁻◻(23)

Duncton

Cricketers Ⓛ

High Street, GU28 0LB (on A285 3 miles S of Petworth)
🌐 11 (12 Sun)-11 ☎ (01798) 342473
⊕ thecricketersduncton.co.uk

King Horsham Best Bitter; Triple fff Moondance; guest beers H
Welcoming family-run 16th-century coaching inn, said to be haunted, in the heart of the West Sussex countryside and close to Goodwood Racecourse. It has wooden beams throughout, with a solid oak wooden bar and a large inglenook fireplace. Good real ales and Thatchers draught cider are served. The excellent menu has locally sourced, seasonal, home-cooked food, including fish and game whenever possible. A separate function room is available for hire and a large secluded garden is to the rear. Children and dogs welcome.
🏚Q🕭🛏🍴🌡👌🍂🛇P⁵⁻🚆(99)

East Ashling

Horse & Groom L
PO18 9AX (on B2178 in village) SU820078
🌀 12-3, 6-11; 12-11 Sat; 12-6 Sun ☎ (01243) 575339
🌐 thehorseandgroomchichester.co.uk
Dark Star Hophead; Hop Back Summer Lightning; Sharp's Doom Bar; Young's Bitter; guest beers H
An inn for over 200 years, this fine village free house has a compact bar featuring flagstones, settles, half-panelled walls and a fine old range. Sympathetically extended, it remains unspoilt. The beers are meticulously presented and are sold at consistently good-value prices. A blackboard reveals the diverse, high-quality menu of home-made dishes, all sourced locally (no food Sun eve). En-suite accommodation is dog-friendly, some in a converted 17th-century oak-beamed flint barn.
🏚Q🕭🛏🍴👌🛡🚶≠(Bosham)🍂P⁵⁻🛢🚆(54)

East Grinstead

Old Dunnings Mill
Dunnings Road, RH19 4AT
🌀 9am-11.30 (midnight Fri & Sat; 11 Sun) ☎ (01342) 326341
🌐 theolddunningsmill.co.uk
Harveys Hadlow Bitter, Sussex Best Bitter, seasonal beers; guest beer H
Large pub on the edge of town based on an old water mill. Separate bar and restaurant areas are on various levels but the main areas are disabled-friendly. A heated, covered area to the rear has a working water wheel. Two beer festivals a year are planned. It is basically a quiet pub, although music is played on appropriate occasions. Families and pets welcome. 🏚Q🕭🛏🍴👌P⁵⁻🚆(84)

East Wittering

Shore L
Shore Road, PO20 8DZ (50yds from the sea) SZ794969
🌀 11-11 (10.30 Sun) ☎ (01243) 674454
🌐 theshorepub.co.uk
Dark Star Hophead; Fuller's London Pride; Palmers Copper Ale, Dorset Gold; Sharp's Doom Bar; guest beer H
Town pub welcoming both to locals and visitors, of which there are many in the summer months due to its close proximity to the sea. There are two main bars, a separate area for families, and a fair-sized decked area outside for drinking or smoking. A good lunchtime food menu can be enjoyed either in the bar or restaurant. Note that evening meals are only available on Thursday evening, when there is a special locals' night. Occasional live music is hosted. Q🕭🛏🍴🍂P⁵⁻🚆(52,53)

Eastergate

Wilkes' Head ♈ L
Church Lane, PO20 3UT (300yds S of A29 bus stops near B2233 roundabout, 1¼ miles W of Barnham station) SU943053
🌀 12-11 ☎ (01243) 543380 🌐 wilkesheadeastergate.co.uk
Adnams Southwold Bitter; guest beers H
Named after 18th-century radical John Wilkes, this small Grade II-listed red-brick pub dates from 1803. There is a cosy lounge to the left of the central bar and a larger main bar with inglenook fireplace, flagstones and low beams, plus a separate restaurant. The large garden houses a comfortable, heated smokers' shelter. Four guest beers come from Punch's Finest Cask Range or SIBA Local Direct Delivery. Regular beer festivals are held. CAMRA Regional Pub of the Year 2012 and local Pub of the Year 2013.
🏚Q🕭🍴🛏≠(Barnham)🍂🍂P⁵⁻🚆(66,85,85A)

Elsted

Three Horseshoes
Elsted Road, GU29 0JY (E end of village) SU819197
🌀 11-2.30, 6-11; 12-3, 7-10.30 Sun ☎ (01730) 825746
Bowman Wallops Wood; Flowerpots Bitter; Young's Bitter; guest beers G
Old and cosy rural inn divided into small rooms, including one reserved for dining and one with a blazing log fire in winter. Outside, the large, pleasant garden enjoys superb views of the South Downs. In summer there are five beers (mainly from local micros), and three in winter, all served by gravity from a stillage alongside the bar. Meals are substantial and of high quality. This is a popular and homely pub that you will be reluctant to leave.
🏚Q🕭🍴P

Findon

Gun Inn
High Street, BN14 0TA (in centre of village)
🌀 12-11.30 (9 Sun) ☎ (01903) 873206
🌐 thegunfindon.co.uk
Marston's Pedigree; Ringwood Best, Fortyniner; guest beers H
A 500-year-old village pub with a main bar and extra dining rooms. Award-winning cuisine is served lunchtimes and evenings, and Tuesday is French food night (no food Mon eve – open mic night). The landlady and her partner, who is the chef, have been at the pub for over three years. The garden features an unusual barbecue which is used in the summer. The pub is popular with walkers exploring the South Downs. A music festival is held annually in August.
🏚Q🕭🛏🍴🍂P🚆(1,23)

Fulking

Shepherd & Dog L
The Street, BN5 9LU
🌀 11-10.30; 12-8 Sun ☎ (01273) 857382
🌐 shepherdanddogpub.co.uk
Downlands Ruskins Ram Best Bitter, Truleigh Gold, seasonal beers; guest beers H
Situated in a picturesque location at the foot of the South Downs, with a small stream flowing through the spacious garden, the pub comprises a large traditionally styled room with low beams, plenty of tables and a patio area. This is the main outlet for

the excellent Downlands Brewery and at least three of its beers are usually available. Good, locally sourced food is served up daily. Walkers and dogs are welcome. ♨Q☺❂◐⬥Å♣P¹﹣

Graffham

Foresters Arms
The Street, GU28 0QA (3 miles W of A285; 99 bus will divert if booked ahead) SU930177
✪ 12-3, 6-11 (closed Mon winter); 12-3, 6-10.30 (not eve winter) Sun ☎ (01798) 867202 ⊕ forestersgraffham.co.uk
Dark Star Hophead; Harveys Sussex Best Bitter; guest beers Ⓗ
Fine Grade II-listed country pub built in 1609 and extended in Victorian times. An attractive garden and an impressive inglenook with blazing logs in winter make this a popular venue, as does its proximity to the South Downs Way and other fine walking country. Up to two guest beers are sourced from local independent breweries. There are three cosy en-suite rooms in the adjoining converted stables. An extensive food menu is available in the restaurant (booking recommended).
♨Q☺✿◐Å♣P¹﹣➼(99)

Henley

Duke of Cumberland Arms Ⓛ
Henley Village, GU27 3HQ (off A286, 3 miles N of Midhurst) SU894258
✪ 11-11; 12-10.30 Sun ☎ (01428) 652280
⊕ dukeofcumberland.com
Harveys Sussex Best Bitter; Langham Hip Hop, Sundowner, Best Bitter Ⓖ
Stunning 15th-century inn nestling against the hillside and set in 3½ acres of terraced gardens with extensive views. The rustic front bar has scrubbed-top tables and benches, plus a log fire at both ends, while to the rear is a new extension that blends in perfectly with the original pub and offers much-needed additional space, particularly for diners. Outside is a smokers' shelter with its own woodburner. A former local CAMRA Pub of the Year, this is a rural gem. ♨Q☺❂◐♣P¹﹣➼(70)

Horsham

Anchor Hotel Ⓛ
3 Market Square, RH12 1EU
✪ 11-11 (midnight Fri & Sat); 12-10.30 Sun
☎ (01403) 250640
Harveys Sussex Best Bitter; guest beers Ⓗ
This former Taylor Walker pub is an impressive Victorian building in the heart of the town, comprising a large ground-floor room and balcony room, plus a heated courtyard to the rear. Freshly prepared great British pub food is served daily. There is an emphasis on local ales, complemented by the occasional festival featuring beers from around the country. CAMRA members receive a 10 per cent discount on ales. The Anchor hosts a variety of entertainment including live music, comedy, DJs and quizzes. ➼☺◐⬥❖≠●¹﹣➼

Beer Essentials Ⓛ
30a East Street, RH12 1HL
✪ closed Mon; 10-6 (7 Fri & Sat); closed Sun
☎ (01403) 218890 ⊕ thebeeressentials.co.uk
Arundel Sussex Gold; guest beers Ⓖ
Specialist beer shop in a building that partly dates back to 1380, when it was used as staff

accommodation for the monastery at Steyning. There are always at least six ales drawn straight from the cask, and an extensive range of bottled beers from around the UK and abroad. JB medium cider is available along with a range of bottled ciders and lagers. Draught products can be taken away in minipins, polypins or two- to eight-pint containers. The proprietor runs an autumn beer festival in a local hall. ≠●➼

Black Jug
31 North Street, RH12 1RJ
✪ 11.30-11; 12-10.30 Sun ☎ (01403) 253526
⊕ blackjug-horsham.co.uk
Caledonian Deuchars IPA; Harveys Sussex Best Bitter; guest beers Ⓗ
Large, bustling, town-centre pub, the Jug is something of a Horsham institution. It has a welcoming interior with bookshelves, pictures, a fire and friendly, efficient staff. Two regular ales are available, with rotating guests and a cider. Excellent food is served all day and the pub is equally popular as a venue to meet and chat, with no intrusive music. It is close to the railway station and arts complex. It also has an extensive range of malt whiskies. ♨Q☺◐⬥≠●¹﹣➼

Piries Bar Ⓛ
Piries Alley – The Carfax, RH12 1EH
✪ 11 (12 Sun)-midnight ☎ (01403) 267846
⊕ piriesbar.co.uk
Dark Star Hophead; Long Man Sussex Pride; guest beer Ⓗ
In a building dating from the 15th century with exposed original timber beams, the pub is tucked away down a narrow alley adjoining Horsham's Carfax. It comprises a cosy downstairs room, an upstairs lounge bar and a small modern extension in character with the building. Regular charity events are organised. Evenings here can be lively, with karaoke on Sundays, late opening until midnight and occasional live music. With two cask ales always available, this bar is well worth a visit. ➼◐≠➼

Lambs Green

Lamb Ⓛ
RH12 4RG (2 miles N of A264)
✪ 11.30-3, 5.30-11; 11.30-11 Fri & Sat; 12-10.30 Sun
☎ (01293) 871336 ⊕ thelambinn.org
Dark Star Hophead; guest beers Ⓗ
Lovely old pub with a mixture of flagstones and wood floors interspersed with wrought-iron work, low-beamed ceilings and exposed brick walls. Furnishings include high-backed settles and soft sofas, and a real fire adds warmth in winter. The landlords and staff are committed to LocAle – all beers come from within 25 miles, and customers are canvassed on what to stock. The cider is from Biddenden. Both landlords are chefs, serving quality home-made locally sourced food. The conservatory can be hired for functions and the pub can provide outside catering.
♨Q➼☺◐♣●P¹﹣➼

Lancing

Crabtree Inn
140 Crabtree Lane, BN15 9NQ
✪ 12-11 (11.30 Thu; 12.30am Fri & Sat); 12-11.30 Sun
☎ (01903) 755514

Fuller's London Pride; guest beers ⊞
Traditional Kemp Town house that offers a wide-ranging selection of real ales. The large public bar has darts, pool and table football; the recently refurbished lounge bar offers a quieter, more relaxed experience. It can also be booked for functions. Live music is featured monthly. The garden is spacious, child and dog friendly, and includes a covered smoking area. The menu features home-made pies and a Sunday carvery. Recent investment has modernised the pub without sacrificing its traditional ambience.
▲Q❀◑⑪⬛♿≒♣P⌴☗⊞(7,16)

Maplehurst

White Horse ⅃
Park Lane, RH13 6LL
❀ 12-2.30 (not Mon), 6-11 (11.30 Fri & Sat); 12-3, 7.30-11 Sun ☎ (01403) 891208
Harveys Sussex Best Bitter; Weltons Pride 'n' Joy; guest beers ⊞
With 31 years under the same ownership, this splendid and welcoming country pub has featured in this Guide no fewer than 28 times. Popular with locals, cyclists and walkers, the cosy interior with its unusually large wooden bar boasts real fires and many interesting artefacts and bric-a-bac. While good honest pub fare is provided, the emphasis is on beer and conversation. Many local beers feature including a good selection of dark ales. Local JB cider is also stocked. ▲Q❀◑⑪⬛♣♣P⌴

Midhurst

Swan Inn ⅃
1 Red Lion Street, GU29 9PB (opp church in Old Town) SU88652150
❀ 11-11 (midnight Fri); 12-midnight Sat; 12-11 Sun
☎ (01730) 812853 ⊕ theswaninnmidhurst.co.uk
Harveys Sussex Best Bitter, seasonal beers ⊞
Historic split-level town pub with a lower section featuring a dartboard and TVs showing sport. The upper section is quieter and cosier with armchairs and a woodburner, wooden beams and more TVs in silent mode. Old Ale or Olympia is available according to season, plus other Harvey's seasonal beers. To the right of the side door is a small area used mainly for dining, offering a good menu of seasonal and local dishes, and roast lunches on Sundays. Accommodation is in three en-suite rooms. There is limited public parking nearby.
▲❀☒⇦◑⬛♣⌴☗⊞(1,60)

Milland

Black Fox Inn ⅃
Portsmouth Road, GU30 7JJ (on B2070) SU829291
❀ 12-2 (not Mon), 6-11; 12-3 Sun ☎ (01428) 723218
⊕ theblackfoxinn.co.uk
Bowman Swift One; Young's Special; guest beers ⊞
Situated on the B2070 and the West Sussex Border Path, this remote, comfortable free house has an air of spaciousness about its L-shaped bar, high ceilings and brick arches. Food from an extensive menu can be enjoyed in the restaurant which overlooks the patio and the enclosed garden with a playhouse for children. There is also a skittle alley for hire, four B&B rooms and a covered smoking area to the rear. Up to two guest beers usually come from Hants and Sussex micros. ❀⇦◑♣P⌴

Oving

Gribble Inn ⅃
Gribble Lane, PO20 2BP (W end of village) SU900050
❀ 11 (12 Sun)-11 ☎ (01243) 786893 ⊕ gribbleinn.co.uk
Gribble Ale, Fuzzy Duck, Reg's Tipple, Plucking Pheasant, Pig's Ear, Mokka Mild ⊞
Once home to a Miss Gribble, this attractive thatched cottage has been a traditional village pub for over 30 years and houses the Gribble Brewery. It now also incorporates the village shop. A wide range of Gribble draught beers is always on offer, complemented by seasonal brews throughout the year. Always cosy, with open log fires in winter, home-made food is served in the bar/restaurant. In summer a large, attractive garden offers occasional weekend barbecues and the skittle alley is also available for functions.
▲Q❀☒◑⬛♣P⌴☗(85,85A)

Partridge Green

Partridge ⅃
Church Road, RH13 8JS
❀ 12-11 ☎ (01403) 710391
Dark Star Partridge Best, Hophead, seasonal beers ⊞
The Dark Star Brewery tap – a former railway hotel – is near the brewery and adjacent to the popular Downs Link Trail that follows the old Guildford to Shoreham line. The spacious wood-panelled family lounge leads out into a pleasant patio and garden with playground, while the smaller front bar has a display of local photographs and offers darts and pool. The menu features locally sourced produce (no food Sun and Mon eves). Daily buses run from Brighton and Horsham. ▲❀◑P☗⊞(17,108)

Petworth

Angel Inn ⅃
Angel Street, GU28 0BG
❀ 10.30-11; 12-10.30 Sun ☎ (01798) 344445
⊕ angelinnpetworth.co.uk
Andwell King John; Langham Best Bitter; guest beer ⊞
Steps lead from the main road to this handsome part timber-framed building in a small market town, possibly dating back to the 14th century, which has been lovingly restored to reveal its past glories. A large single bar with various nooks and crannies gives a welcoming, homely feel and a large sunny courtyard is very popular in the summer months. Six en-suite bedrooms make the pub an excellent base for exploring Petworth House, Cowdray Park and the surrounding countryside. ▲Q❀☒⇦◑♣P⌴☗(1,99)

Rogate

White Horse Inn ⅃
East Street, GU31 5EA (on A272) SU808239
❀ 11-midnight (1am Fri & Sat); 12-midnight Sun
☎ (01730) 821333
Harveys IPA, Sussex Best Bitter, Armada Ale, seasonal beers ⊞
Dating from the 16th century, this old coaching inn has oak beams, flagstone floors and a huge log fire. A Harvey's tied house, you can expect up to five of its draught beers, including Olympia or Old Ale depending on season, plus other seasonal brews. Half the pub is used for dining – a large range of meals using local ingredients includes

vegetarian choices (no food Sun eve). The car park overlooks the village sports field behind the pub, where camping can be arranged.
♨✿◐♪▲♣P↳⌂(54,92)

Rusper

Royal Oak
Friday Street, RH12 4QA (on Langhurstwood Rd off A264 N of Horsham)
✿ 12-3, 5-9; 12-3, 6-11 Sat; 12-7 Sun ☎ (01293) 871393
⊕ theroyaloakrusper.webs.com
Surrey Hills Ranmore Ale; guest beers Ⓗ
The Royal Oak is a little gem set in the heart of the West Sussex countryside between Horsham and Dorking and within easy reach of the A24. The pub has two bars where you can enjoy your pint in front of a log fire in winter. Seven real ales from microbreweries, three ciders and two perries are always on offer. Children are not allowed inside but there is ample seating outside. Well worth a visit.
♨Q✿◐⇦♣P

Scaynes Hill

Sloop Inn
Sloop Lane, RH17 7NP
✿ 12-3, 5.30-11; 12-11 Sat & Sun ☎ (01444) 831219
⊕ thesloopinn.com
Dark Star American Pale Ale; Harveys Sussex Best Bitter; guest beers Ⓗ
A free house about 1½ miles from the village, it's a former Beards pub. There is an extensive garden area which is popular with families during the summer months. The timber-panelled bar has six handpumps which dispense up to four guest beers from local or microbreweries. Various events are held including folk music (open mic), live music, themed food nights, regular quiz nights and an annual steam rally. Look out for the glass case displaying LMS memorabilia. ♨⇘✿◐♪P↳

Selsey

Seal Hotel Ⓛ
6 Hillfield Road, PO20 0JX (on B2145, 600yds from sea) SZ851928
✿ 10.30-midnight; 12-11 Sun ☎ (01243) 602461
⊕ the-seal.com
Dark Star Hophead; Greene King Abbot; Young's Bitter; guest beers Ⓗ
A real community hub, family-run for 42 years. The spacious public bar has a pool table at one end. The comfortable lounge with restaurant offers quality home-cooked food including locally caught fish (booking advised). A good variety of guest beers is available, mostly from local micros. Acoustic live music often features on Sunday. The patio has seating and umbrellas to cater for smokers. Camping is available nearby at West Sands Caravan Park, and the 12 en-suite B&B rooms are popular.
Q✿⇦◐♿▲♣P↳⌂(51)

Shoreham-by-Sea

Duke of Wellington Ⓛ
368 Brighton Road, BN43 6RE (on A259)
✿ 12-midnight (1.30am Fri & Sat); 12-11 Sun
☎ (01273) 389818
Dark Star Hophead, seasonal beers; guest beers Ⓗ
On the eastern side of town, the pub is easily identified by the large Wellington boot sign. The

old leaded windows show that this was once a Kemptown Brewery house. There is frequent live music, mostly at weekends, held on a small platform. Pies and pasties are on offer, and there is a barbecue in the summer months in the large rear garden. A beer festival is held every three months. Thatchers cider is available all year.
♨✿⇗♣♥↳⌂(2,2A,700)

Red Lion
Old Shoreham Road, BN43 5TE
✿ 11.30-11; 12-10.30 Sun ☎ (01273) 453171
⊕ redlionshoreham.co.uk
Harveys Sussex Best Bitter; guest beers Ⓗ
A former 16th-century coaching inn well situated at the end of the Downslink Cycle Trail. The drinking area at the front has great views over the Downs and Lancing College. A raised dining area caters for good food. The Adur Beer Festival is held at Easter, and the pub is very popular when the Shoreham airshow is held in September. Guest beers come from local micros and beyond. Real cider is served in the summer, mainly Cheddar Valley.
♨Q✿◐♣P↳⌂(2A,9)

Sompting

Gardeners Arms ♈ Ⓛ
West Street, BN15 0AR (on S side of West Street)
✿ 11-11; 12-midnight Fri & Sat; 12-11 Sun
☎ (01903) 233666
Draught Bass; Harveys Sussex Best Bitter; Sharp's Doom Bar; guest beers Ⓗ
The Gardeners Arms is a vibrant, friendly 19th-century free house in the original village main street. A unique feature is the 1962 British Rail passenger carriage built onto the side of the building. The name of the pub remains unchanged since 1858, when market gardens were the main local employer. Five handpumps feature the regulars, plus a mild and a guest ale. Tuesday is quiz night. Quality home-cooked food is served daily; the amazing Sunday roasts are renowned.
♨✿◐⇦♿♣P↳⌂(7,7A)

Staplefield

Jolly Tanners ♈ Ⓛ
Handcross Road, RH17 6EF
✿ 11-3, 5.30-11; 11-11 Fri & Sat; 11-10.30 Sun
☎ (01444) 400335 ⊕ jollytanners.com
Fuller's London Pride; Harveys Sussex Best Bitter; guest beers Ⓗ
Independently run free house on the north corner of the cricket green. The pub takes great pride in providing a wide selection of real ales and ciders, as well as tasty food made using local ingredients where possible. This is a very friendly place and well worth a visit. Beer festivals are held regularly during the year, with an excellent range of beer to be enjoyed. Local CAMRA Pub of the Year 2011.
♨Q⇘✿◐⇦♿▲♣♥P↳⌂(271)

Steyning

Chequer Inn Ⓛ
41 High Street, BN44 3RE
✿ 10-11 (midnight Fri & Sat) ☎ (01903) 814437
⊕ chequerinnsteyning.co.uk
Dark Star Hophead; Gale's HSB; guest beers Ⓗ
An ever-popular 15th-century coaching inn in a pretty market town. The public bar has a sporty

feel, with TVs and a 100-year-old snooker table, and is dog-friendly, while the saloon bar is more cosy and food-oriented. The three guest beers often include LocAles and seasonals. There is a covered courtyard outside. Home-cooked traditional food using locally sourced ingredients is available, with the breakfast particularly recommended. ⚏Q✿⌕✍◑ ⊟♣P'⊸⊞(2A,100)

Stoughton

Hare & Hounds ℕ

PO18 9JQ (1 mile from B2146 bus stops, through Walderton) SU803115
✪ 11-3, 6-11; 11-11 Fri & Sat; 12-10.30 Sun
☎ (02392) 631433 🌐 hareandhoundspub.co.uk
Dark Star Hophead; Harveys Sussex Best Bitter; Otter Amber; guest beer Ⓗ
An ideal base for walking, this is a traditional country pub in a beautiful setting. A large dining room serves fresh local produce while the public bar, with pictures of vintage racing cars and its own open fire, is the locals' choice. Three open fires, along with stone-flagged floors and simple furniture, create a wonderful atmosphere. Outside is a paved drinking area and a garden at the back. The cider is Westons First Quality.
⚏Q✿◑ ⊟Å♣⬤P⊞(54)

Thakeham

White Lion Inn ℕ

The Street, RH20 3EP (just off B2139) TQ108174
✪ 11-11; 12-10.30 Sun ☎ (01798) 813141
🌐 whitelion-thakeham.co.uk
Fuller's London Pride; Harveys Sussex Best Bitter; Skinner's Betty Stogs; guest beers Ⓗ
An ivy-clad 15th-century pub with stone steps leading up from the street. Previously a coaching house, there are three separate bar areas and a restaurant serving top-quality food, with an open fire smoking the locally sourced hams. Four real ales are available, one a changing guest. With monthly music and quiz nights, the White Lion is a perfect example of an English country pub with a lovely nostalgic ambience. Dog-friendly.
⚏Q➳✿◑ ⊟♣P'

Turners Hill

Crown

East Street, RH10 4PT
✪ 9am-3, 6-11 (midnight Fri & Sat); 12-11 Sun
☎ (01342) 715218 🌐 thecrownatturnershill.co.uk
Harveys Sussex Best Bitter; Morland Old Speckled Hen; St Austell Tribute; guest beer Ⓗ
A 16th-century farmhouse and a 17th-century barn with Jacobean oak beams go to make up this venue, which converted to an inn in 1706. It holds a St George's Day celebration, a beer festival to coincide with the London to Brighton cycle ride, and a 30-ale festival in October. Leather settees surround a large open fire in the bar area, with another open fire in the restaurant, serving traditional English dishes. The pub has recently had a very tasteful redecoration.
⚏➳✿◑ &P'⊸⊞(82,84,291)

Red Lion ℕ

Lion Lane, RH10 4NU
✪ 11-3, 5-11; 11-11 Sat; 12-10.30 Sun ☎ (01342) 715416
🌐 redlionturnershill.com

Harveys Sussex XX Mild, IPA, Sussex Best Bitter, Armada Ale, seasonal beer; guest beer Ⓗ
Still very much a proper village local, offering a warm welcome to all who enter, it is a split-level pub, with a large inglenook fireplace. Good-value and high-quality lunches are served. There is a fortnightly quiz, and the recent conversion of an outside building allows space for occasional beer festivals. Children and dogs are welcome. North Sussex CAMRA held its first meeting here in 1974.
⚏Q➳✿◑♣⬤P'⊸⊞(82,84)

Warnham

Sussex Oak ℕ

2 Church Street, RH12 3QW
✪ 11-11 (10.30 Sun) ☎ (01403) 265028
🌐 thesussexoak.co.uk
Fuller's London Pride; Harveys Sussex Best Bitter; Taylor Landlord; guest beers Ⓗ
Popular village pub with a separate dining area. Six handpumps dispense three regular beers and two to three guests, usually local – LocAle is actively supported. Two handpumps offer real cider and perry in the summer months. An extensive menu of high-quality, reasonably priced food is available. There is a large garden with plenty of seating and dogs are welcome. Jazz nights are hosted twice a month on Thursdays and beer festivals are held over bank holidays. This pub has been in the Guide for the past 10 years. ⚏Q➳✿◑&♣⬤P'⊸⊞

West Chiltington

Five Bells ℕ

Smock Alley, RH20 2QX (1 mile SE of village) TQ091170
✪ 12-3, 6-11; 7-10.30 Sun ☎ (01798) 812143
🌐 thefivebellsinn.com
Harveys Sussex Best Bitter; Palmers Copper Ale; guest beers Ⓗ
Bill and Joan have been welcoming drinkers, diners, walkers and dog lovers to this charming family-run village free house since 1983. It has a cheery, spacious bar with a big, open copper-hooded fireplace, and large conservatory dining areas. Excellent ales, including LocAles, are served, with draught Kentish cider and nearly always a mild on handpump. Fantastic locally sourced home-cooked food is available every day (no food Sun eve). The accommodation is dog-friendly.
⚏Q➳✿◑♣⬤P⊞(1,74)

West Itchenor

Ship Inn

The Street, PO20 7AH SU799014
✪ 11-11; 12-10.30 Sun ☎ (01243) 512284
🌐 theshipinnitchenor.co.uk
Arundel Castle; Ballards Best Bitter; King Horsham Best Bitter; guest beer Ⓗ
Popular pub in the main street of an attractive village on the shore of picturesque Chichester harbour. Cosy bars decorated with yachting memorabilia add to the pub's character and are complemented by a pleasant patio, a suntrap in summer. Two of the bars have dining facilities, offering a wide range of traditional meals, often including locally landed fish. Three West Sussex ales are normally available, with one guest usually from a local brewery. Accommodation includes a four-bed family apartment.
⚏Q✿✍◑ ⊟&♣P'⊸⊞(52,53,150)

Westbourne

Stag's Head ⓛ
The Square, PO10 8UE (in village centre) SU757074
☼ 12-midnight (12.30am Fri & Sat); 12-11 Sun
☎ (01243) 372393 ⊕ stagsheadwestbourne.co.uk
Exmoor Gold; Harveys Sussex Best Bitter; Irving Invincible; Oakleaf Hole Hearted; Wychwood Hobgoblin Ⓗ
Early 19th-century pub built on the site of the village market and subsequently extended into a neighbouring shop. The newer area is mainly used for dining (no food Sun eves or Mon Sept-Apr), leaving the remainder of the L-shaped bar with its real fire for drinkers. There is an outside bar in the yard that comes into its own during beer festivals, when the usual diet of local microbrews is supplemented by beers from far and wide. Occasional cider festivals are also held.
🏚️✿◑⇌(Emsworth)♣⚲–🚲🚌(27,36,54)

Worthing

Castle ⓛ
1 Newland Road, BN11 1JR
☼ 5-11 (midnight Fri); 6-midnight Sat; closed Sun
☎ (01903) 230888
Beer range varies Ⓗ
A short walk from Worthing town centre or station, this imposing corner pub is now a genuine free house. The L-shaped bar has games at one end, while the other is a comfortable candlelit area in which to relax. A changing range of six beers along with a menu of proper pub food is available. On Saturday evenings the bar has a growing selection of chilli products for the unsuspecting to sample, watched over by the knowledgeable landlord and locals. ✿◑⇌♣🚲🚌

North Star ⓛ
Littlehampton Road, Durrington, BN13 1QY (on A2032, ½ mile N of Durrington station) TQ126046
☼ 11-midnight ☎ (01903) 247973
Arundel Gold; Fuller's London Pride; Ringwood Best; Taylor Landlord; guest beers Ⓗ
Spacious and deservedly popular 1930s roadhouse – now an M&B Ember Pub & Dining venue – with wide appeal. A pleasant interior features one long central bar, with various nooks and crannies leading off where drinkers can enjoy an always-interesting selection of well-kept ales, including changing guests from the Seasonal Cask Club. There are separate areas of varying size for dining and a south-west facing garden for alfresco drinking and eating. Occasional live music is staged. ↗✿◑♿⇌(Durrington)P⚲–🚌(5,6)

Parsonage Bar & Restaurant ⓛ
6-10 Tarring High Street, BN14 7NN
☼ 12-7 (11 Tue-Thu; midnight Fri & Sat) ☎ (01903) 820140
⊕ theparsonage.co.uk
Dark Star Hophead; Harveys Sussex Best Bitter Ⓗ; guest beers Ⓗ/Ⓖ
A welcome addition to Worthing's real ale scene, this 15th-century establishment was originally three cottages, saved from demolition in 1927 when bought by a local resident for £900. Once the Museum of Sussex Folklore, this Grade II-listed building has been a restaurant for 26 years, serving up food of the highest quality and now offering beers of similar distinction. At least two guest LocAles are available, served by gravity from an outside cold store. Q✿◑⇌(West)🚌(6,16)

Richard Cobden
2 Cobden Road, BN11 4BD
☼ 11 (12 Tue & Thu)-11; 12-10.30 Sun ☎ (01903) 236856
⊕ therichardcobden.co.uk
Adnams Southwold Bitter; Ringwood Best; guest beers Ⓗ
Welcoming traditional street-corner local and one with a strong sense of community spirit. It has an L-shaped bar with a real fire, wood panelling at one end, a dartboard at the other and a bijou patio garden. A very popular meat raffle is held on Sundays plus occasional live music and charity events. Slate shove-ha'penny is available to play. A local morris side perform a traditional mummers' play on New Year's Day. Dog-friendly. The Pulse bus stops nearby. 🏚️✿⇌♣⚲–🚌(9)

Selden Arms ⓛ
41 Lyndhurst Road, BN11 2DB (near Worthing hospital)
☼ 11-11 (11.30 Fri); 12-11.30 Sat; 12-10.30 Sun
Beer range varies Ⓗ
A regular in the Guide, this 19th-century dog-friendly free house has a small, single bar with six handpumps, at least one of which dispenses a dark ale. Belgian and German draught and bottled beers are also available. A beer festival is held at the end of January and there is occasional live music. The pub supports a darts team. Photographs of old Worthing hostelries adorn the walls, as well as a chalkboard displaying a list of forthcoming ales. No food served on Sunday. 🏚️◑⇌🚌(9,16)

Swan Inn ⓛ
79 High Street, BN11 1DN
☼ 11-11 (midnight Fri & Sat); 12-11 Sun ☎ (01903) 232923
Harveys Sussex Best Bitter; guest beers Ⓗ
A town-centre pub with a village feel to it. A long, attractive U-shaped bar dominates the single room, and various regimental badges adorn the frontage immediately above. A large collection of copper and brasses hangs from the beamed ceiling. Bar billiards, darts and cribbage are all played here. Music is a regular attraction, with blues every Wednesday, an open mic session on Sunday, and DJs at the weekend. The final Tuesday of each month features a folk music sing around. 🏚️✿◑⇌♣⚲–🚌(9,16)

Yapton

Maypole Inn ⓛ
Maypole Lane, BN18 0DP (pedestrian access across railway from Lake Lane, 1¼ miles E of Barnham station) SU978042
☼ 11.30-11 (midnight Fri & Sat); 12-11 Sun
☎ (01243) 551417
Dark Star Hophead; guest beers Ⓗ
Small flint-built free house down a narrow lane ending in a pedestrian crossing over the railway. The cosy lounge boasts two open fires and a row of eight handpumps, dispensing up to four guest beers and real cider. There is a traditional public bar and a skittle alley/function room with a bar billiards table. Bar meals are served lunchtimes with roasts on Sunday. Dogs are welcome. Local CAMRA Pub of the Year 2011. The 66 bus stops close by; the 700 in the village three quarters of a mile away. 🏚️Q✿◑♿👣⇌(Barnham/Ford)♣🐾P⚲–🚌(66,700)

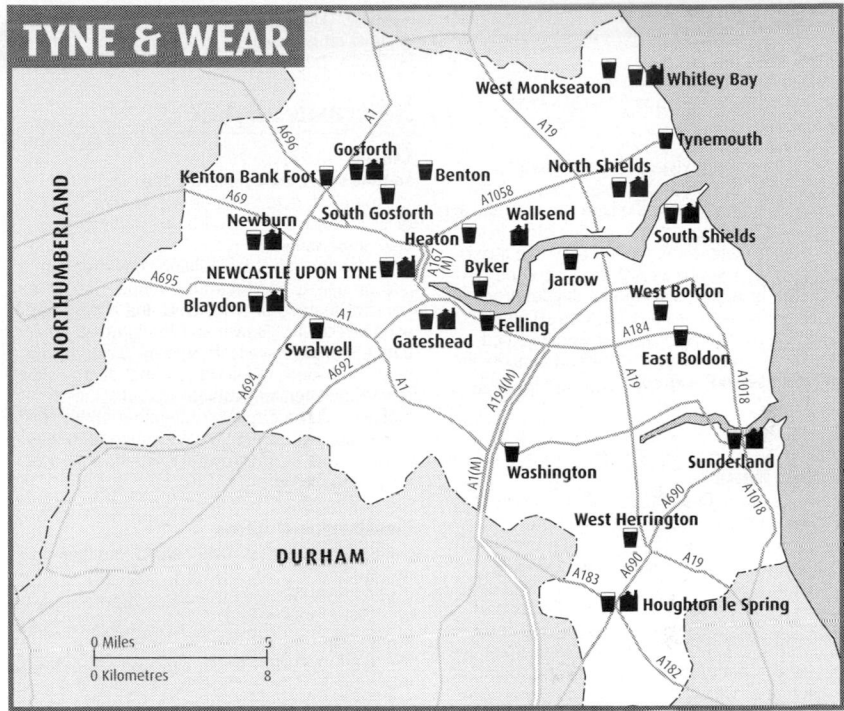

Map labels: West Monkseaton, Whitley Bay, Tynemouth, Gosforth, Benton, North Shields, Kenton Bank Foot, Newburn, South Gosforth, Wallsend, Heaton, South Shields, NEWCASTLE UPON TYNE, Byker, Jarrow, Blaydon, West Boldon, Swalwell, Gateshead, Felling, East Boldon, Washington, Sunderland, West Herrington, DURHAM, Houghton le Spring, NORTHUMBERLAND

0 Miles 5
0 Kilometres 8

Blaydon

Black Bull

Bridge Street, NE21 4JJ

☼ 2-11; 12-midnight Fri & Sat; 12-11 Sun ☎ (0191) 414 2846
⊕ blackbull-blaydon.co.uk

Black Sheep Best Bitter; Caledonian Deuchars IPA;
Morland Old Speckled Hen Ⓗ

Two-roomed pub with traditional values – 'No pool
table, no jukebox, no bandit' boasts the proud
landlord. There has been a pub on this site since
the 1800s, and the bar displays photographs of old
Blaydon. Two folk nights are held weekly, plus a
buskers' night, quiz night and live bands once a
month. Barbecues feature in the superb rear beer
garden during the summer months. The pub enjoys
excellent views of the River Tyne and Tyne Valley,
and dogs are welcome. The premises are
patronised by the local blind club.
ᴍQ৬⌨❀⊞♣●P⊞(10,602)

East Boldon

Grey Horse

Front Street, NE36 0SJ

☼ 11-11 (midnight Fri & Sat); 12-11 Sun ☎ (0191) 519 1796

Wells Bombardier Ⓗ

Large, pleasant, comfortably furnished two-room
pub on the main A184 road through the village,
with bus stops outside in both directions. Meals are
served throughout the day until mid-evening and
children are welcome when dining. The
enthusiastic manageress dispenses Wells
Bombardier and a changing range of five guest
beers, one always at a special-offer price. Level
access is available through a front entrance.
৬❀⍟⍾⊞P'-⊞(9,30,558)

Felling

Wheat Sheaf Ⓛ

26 Carlisle Street, NE10 0HQ

☼ 5 (12 Fri & Sat)-11; 12-10.30 Sun ☎ (0191) 420 0659
⊕ wheatsheaf-felling.co.uk

Big Lamp Sunny Daze, Bitter, Prince Bishop Ale; guest
beer Ⓗ

Welcoming street-corner pub owned by Big Lamp
Brewery, popular with a loyal band of regulars who
often travel quite a distance to drink here. The pub
features some original details, mismatched
furniture and, when needed, real coal fires, and
outdoor toilets have original Victorian urinals. There
is a fortnightly Monday night quiz, traditional folk
music featuring keen local musicians on Tuesday
nights and Wednesday is dominoes night. An
original CAMRA clock keeps time behind the bar.
ᴍ৬⊟⊞♣●'-⊞(27,93,94)

Gateshead

Central ★ Ⓛ

Half Moon Lane, NE8 2AN

☼ 12-midnight (1am Fri & Sat) ☎ (0191) 478 2543
⊕ theheadofsteam.co.uk/gateshead

Harviestoun Bitter & Twisted; guest beers Ⓗ

Marvellous mid-19th century Grade II-listed four-
storey wedge-shaped building very impressively
revived by the Head of Steam group and identified
by CAMRA as one of Britain's Best Real Heritage
Pubs. It has a revamped public bar, two function
rooms for live music and a rooftop terrace. The
main attraction is the quite magnificently restored
Buffet. It is fitted out circa 1900 with a carved U-
shaped counter and bar back, plasterwork frieze
and panelling. There is also a triangular snug with
dartboard. The 14 handpumps dispense many local
microbrewery beers. ❀⍾⊟⍺⊞♣●'-⊞

Houghton le Spring

Copt Hill L
Seaham Road, DH5 8LU (on B1404)
☼ 11-11 (midnight Thu-Sat) ☎ (0191) 584 4485
⊕ thecopthill.co.uk
Beer range varies Ⓗ
With a spectacular vista over the Houghton countryside, this former Vaux pub has a close connection with the local Maxim Brewery and acts as its unofficial tap, so at least one of its beers is always available, complemented by five guest ales, usually sourced locally. Excellent food including breakfast is served all day from an extensive menu – booking for the restaurant is advisable as it can get busy at evenings and weekends. Live music plays every Sunday night.
🏛🕏🏠◖🍴⑯🍴🅿♿🚋(20)

Jarrow

Robin Hood L
Primrose Hill, NE32 5UB (on old road parallel to A194)
☼ 12-11 (11.30 Fri & Sat) ☎ (0191) 428 5454
⊕ jarrowbrewery.co.uk
Jarrow Bitter, Rivetcatcher, Joblings Swinging Gibbet Ⓗ
The Robin Hood, original home of the Jarrow Brewery, recently celebrated 10 years in the Guide, and well merits its inclusion. This welcoming pub has a bar, lounge, conservatory and function room, as well as an attractive beer garden and a covered and heated smoking area. Four handpumps are dedicated to ales from the Jarrow Brewery, and two offer a choice of real ciders. Live entertainment is provided on Friday and Sunday evenings. A poker evening is held on Thursday and a quiz on Sunday afternoon. 🏛Q🕏⑯🍴♿🍴⑯🍴🅿♿🚋

Newburn

Keelman
Grange Road, NE15 8NL
☼ 11-11; 12-10.30 Sun ☎ (0191) 267 1689
⊕ keelmanslodge.co.uk
Big Lamp Sunny Daze, Bitter, Summerhill Stout, Prince Bishop, seasonal beers Ⓗ
This pub is the tap for Big Lamp Brewery alongside, set in a tastefully converted Grade II-listed former pumping station. The conservatory restaurant serves excellent food and quality accommodation is provided in the adjacent Keelman's Lodge and Salmon Cottage. Attractively situated by Tyne Riverside Country Park, the Coast-to-Coast cycleway and Hadrian's Wall National Trail.
🕏🕏🏠◖⑯🍴🅿♿🚋(22)

Newcastle: Benton

Benton Ale House
Front Street, NE7 7XE
☼ 11-11 (midnight Fri & Sat); 12-11 Sun ☎ (0191) 266 1512
Banks's Bitter; Jennings Cumberland Ale; Ringwood Boondoggle, Fortyniner; guest beers Ⓗ
Traditional, well-appointed pub with a horseshoe bar, run by a friendly manager and staff. Large bay windows give a light and airy feel to the lounge at the front, and the public bar is to the rear. Reasonably priced good-quality food is served – the food menu proudly announces 'fresh meat in home made dishes and Sunday lunches supplied by Lemington butchers' (booking essential for Sunday lunches). Quiz night is Wednesday. Interesting abstract art is displayed in the back bar. Families welcome. 🕏◖⑯🚋(Four Lane Ends)♣🅿♿🚋(1)

Newcastle: Byker

Cluny
36 Lime Street, Ouseburn, NE1 2PQ
☼ 11.30-11; 12-10.30 Sun ☎ (0191) 230 4474
⊕ thecluny.com
Beer range varies Ⓗ
Large former industrial building converted into a pub, art gallery and live music venue. The pub runs frequent themed beer festivals and always has a good selection of British and foreign draught and bottled products available. The art gallery shows work of all kinds ranging from final degree shows to local independent established artists in all media, with the displays changing monthly. Live music sessions are held most evenings and feature a wide range of British, European and American musicians. ◖♿⑯

Cumberland Arms L
James Place Street (off Byker Bank), Ouseburn, NE6 1LD
☼ 4.30 (12.30 Sat)-11; 12.30-10.30 Sun ☎ (0191) 265 6151
⊕ thecumberlandarms.co.uk
Wylam Rapper; guest beers Ⓗ
Three-storey venue rebuilt over 100 years ago and relatively little changed since. It stands in a prominent position overlooking the lower Ouseburn Valley. The pub is home to dance and music groups and its house beer, Wylam Rapper, is named after the traditional rapper sword dance. A multiple winner of regional Cider Pub of the Year awards, it generally offers up to six ciders and perries. Winter and summer beer festivals are held each year. 🏛Q🕏🏠⑯♣⑯🅿

Free Trade Inn ♥ L
St Lawrence Road, Ouseburn, NE6 1AP
☼ 11-11 (midnight Fri & Sat); 12-10.30 Sun
☎ (0191) 265 5764
Mordue IPA; guest beers Ⓗ
Often described as basic, this pub, full of character and characters, looks upstream with wonderful views of the bridges over the Tyne, and the Newcastle and Gateshead quaysides. Interesting beers come from far and wide – up to nine ales and two ciders are available on the bar, with cellar runs willingly offered. Service is with a smile, friendly

INDEPENDENT BREWERIES

Big Lamp Newburn
Cullercoats Wallsend
Darwin Sunderland
Delavals Whitley Bay
Firebrick Blaydon (NEW)
George N Porter Whitley Bay (NEW)
Hadrian Border Newburn
Jarrow South Shields
Maxim Houghton le Spring
Mordue North Shields
Northern FC Newcastle: Gosforth (NEW)
Ouseburn Valley Newcastle upon Tyne
Out There Newcastle upon Tyne (NEW)
Rail Ale Gateshead (NEW)
Temptation Houghton le Spring (NEW)
Three Kings North Shields
Tyne Bank Newcastle upon Tyne

and knowledgeable. Tasty sandwiches are supplied by a long-established local delicatessen. The jukebox is classic and free. ㎙Q☜☸➄🖳(Q2,106)

Newcastle: City Centre

Bacchus L
42-48 High Bridge, NE1 6BX
✪ 11.30-midnight; 12-11 Sun ☎ (0191) 261 1008
Jarrow Rivet Catcher; guest beers H
Local CAMRA Pub of the Year four years running, this smart, comfortable city-centre pub boasts nine handpumps offering a wide range of rapidly changing guest beers, with one pump dedicated to cider and another to beer from Orkney's Highland Brewing Company. A seasonal house beer is brewed by Yorkshire Dales, and a large range of draught and bottled foreign beers is available. Regular beer and food matching events are held. Photographs and posters showing the industries in which this region used to lead the world cover the walls. ☜◖☖🖳(Monument)◗●

Bodega L
125 Westgate Road, NE1 6BX
✪ 11-11 (midnight Fri & Sat); 12-10.30 Sun
☎ (0191) 221 1552
Big Lamp Prince Bishop; Durham Magus; guest beers H
Two fine stained-glass domes are the architectural highlights of the pub, which stands next to the Tyne Theatre and is popular with football and music fans. Televisions show sporting events and the pub can be busy on match days. The interior offers a number of standing and seating areas with separate booths for more intimate drinking. Several old brewery mirrors adorn the walls. A good selection of foreign bottled and draught beers is available. ◖☞(Central)🖳(Central)●

Bridge Hotel L
Castle Garth, NE1 1RQ
✪ 11.30-11 (midnight Fri & Sat); 11.30-10.30 Sun
☎ (0191) 232 6400
Black Sheep Best Bitter; Caledonian Deuchars IPA; guest beers H
This large Fitzgerald pub is situated next to Stephenson's spectacular High Level Bridge, the rear windows and the patio have views of the city walls, River Tyne and Gateshead Quays. The main bar area, adorned with many stained-glass windows, is divided into a number of seating areas with a raised section at the rear. Several guest beers come from far and wide. Among the live music events held in the upstairs function room is what is claimed to be the oldest folk club in the country. ☸◖☞(Central)🖳(Central)●☜

Broad Chare L
25 Broad Chare, Quayside, NE1 3DQ
✪ 11-11 (10 Mon) ☎ (0191) 211 2144
⊕ thebroadchare.co.uk
Wylam The Writer's Block; guest beers H
A warm welcome awaits in this cosy bar just off Newcastle's historic, bustling Quayside. Stripped floors and exposed brickwork make this a comfortable, quiet bar to relax in and enjoy a pint. Bar food is served all day and there is a restaurant upstairs if you wish to dine in style.
◖▶🖳(Monument)●🖳(Q2)

Centurion L
Central Station, Neville Street, NE1 5DG (At E side of the station, opp ticket office)
✪ 10-11 (midnight Fri & Sat) ☎ (0191) 261 6611
⊕ centurion-newcastle.co.uk/bar.asp
Black Sheep Best Bitter; Caledonian Deuchars IPA; Jarrow Rivet Catcher; guest beers H
This beautiful bar was built in 1893 as a sumptuous waiting lounge for first class passengers, featuring exquisite tiles and murals. It was closed in the 1960s, when the Transport Police used it as cells. Since restoration to its former glory, and further enhancement with improved lighting, the grandeur of the John Dobson-designed interior is now enjoyed by thousands of customers, locals, and visitors to Newcastle. A popular starting point for Whistle Stops II real ale outings.
☜☸◖◖◖☖☞(Central)🖳(Central)♣●🖳

Crown Posada ★ L
33 Side, NE1 3JE
✪ 12-11 (1am Fri); 12-4.30, 7-10.30 Sun ☎ (0191) 232 1269
Beer range varies H
An architecturally fine establishment, identified by CAMRA as one of Britain's Best Real Heritage Pubs. Behind the narrow street frontage with two impressive stained-glass windows lie a small snug, bar counter and a longer seating area. There is an interesting coffered ceiling, as well as local photographs and cartoons of long-gone customers and staff on the walls. Small brewers are enthusiastically supported, with three regular local ales. The pub has been sympathetically refurbished over the years and is an oasis of calm near the busy Quayside drinking, dining and clubbing circuit.
Q☞(Central)🖳(Central)☜-🖳(Q1,Q2)

Five Swans
14 St Mary's Place, NE1 7PG
✪ 8am-midnight (1am Fri & Sat) ☎ (0191) 232 3893
Greene King Abbot; Ruddles Best Bitter; guest beers H
Multi-roomed Wetherspoon pub opposite Newcastle Civic Centre and close to the main shopping areas. The beer range includes guests from all the local brewers as well as from further afield. Food is served all day. There is an outside drinking area to the front of the pub and a secret courtyard through the maze of rooms. Children are welcome until 9pm.
Q☜☸◖◖☖☞(Manors)🖳(Haymarket)●☜-🖳

Forth
Pink Lane, NE1 5DW
✪ 12-11 (midnight Thu & Fri); 11-midnight Sat
☎ (0191) 232 6478 ⊕ theforthnewcastle.co.uk
Harviestoun Blonde; Sharp's Doom Bar; guest beers H
A vibrant recently refurbished city-centre pub within easy walking distance of public transport. The interior features comfy sofas and a real fire, with the work of local artists decorating the walls. Sharp's and Harviestoun beers are complemented by three changing ales from local and national brewers. Upstairs there is a smoking area in the terraced garden.
☜☸◖◖☖☞(Central)🖳(Central)●☜-🖳

Hotspur
103 Percy Street, NE1 7RY (opp Haymarket metro and bus station)
✪ 12-11 Mon; 11-11am Tue; 11-11 Wed & Thu; 11-midnight Fri & Sat; 12-11 Sun ☎ (0191) 232 4352
Beer range varies H

Traditional double-fronted city-centre pub opposite Haymarket bus station and Eldon Square, with the universities close by. The Hotspur is a very popular pub and especially busy on match days. Newcastle University Folk Club plays on Tuesday nights. The interior has recently been refurbished and is much enhanced without losing character. Eight handpulls adorn the bar, six serving guest beers including one from a local microbrewery, and two serving real cider, typically from Westons.
≢(Central)🚊(Haymarket)●'—

Lady Grey's 🛗
20 Shakespeare Street, NE1 6AQ (opp Theatre Royal stage doors)
🌣 12-11 ☎ (0191) 232 3606 ⊕ ladygreys.co.uk
Mordue Northumbrian Blonde; guest beers Ⓗ
Close to the historic Theatre Royal and busy shopping areas, this pub, formerly the Adelphi, is a welcome addition to the city-centre real ale scene. Beers are mainly from local brewers Mordue, Hadrian & Border, Allendale and Wylam, with guests from all over the country. Food is served all day. ◑🌣🚊(Monument)●

Mile Castle
Westgate Road, NE1 5XU
🌣 7-midnight (1am Thu-Sat) ☎ (0191) 211 1160
Greene King Abbot; Ruddles Best Bitter; guest beers Ⓗ
Opened in 2009, this highly-thought-of Lloyds No.1 bar boasts 20 handpulls across three floors. Impressively redecorated, there are booths for diners on the second floor although meals are served to all areas throughout the day and evening. The name refers to the Roman forts that were built a mile apart and there is one reputed to be situated nearby. Transport links are excellent with rail and metro stations nearby and a bus stop outside the front door.
⤳⊙◑♿≢(Central)🚊(Central/Monument)●🚌

New Bridge 🛗
2 Argyle Street, NE1 6PF
🌣 11-11 (11.30 Thu & Fri); 12-10.30 Sun ☎ (0191) 232 1020
Tyne Bank Monument Bitter; guest beers Ⓗ
Just east of Newcastle city centre, well-served by buses and the metro, this establishment has no regular beers but offers an ever-changing choice from independent brewers. Although very much a locals' pub, all are made welcome. The building is next to a business park and facing a large extension to Northumbria University, so attracts a mixed lunchtime and early evening crowd enjoying the beer and home-made food.
🌣◑🚊(Manors)●🚌

Trent House
1-2 Leazes Lane, NE1 4QT
🌣 12 (6 Sun)-11 ☎ (0191) 261 2154
Beer range varies Ⓗ
The world-famous Trent House is situated by Leazes Park, Newcastle University and the RVI. Friendly and laid back, the pub is very popular with students. The Trent is home to the best jukebox in town, featuring an eclectic mix of classic rock, jazz and electronica. Retro video games are dotted around the ground floor bar area, and there is an upstairs room with a pool table. Board games are available from the bar. 🌣♣

Newcastle: Gosforth

County 🛗
High Street, NE3 1HB
🌣 12-11 (10.30 Sun) ☎ (0191) 285 6919
Caledonian Deuchars IPA; Fuller's London Pride; Jarrow Rivet Catcher; Wells Bombardier; Wylam Bitter; guest beers Ⓗ
The large L-shaped bar attracts a variety of visitors, from office workers to students, and can get very busy, especially at weekends. A separate quiet room at the back offers respite from the hustle and bustle of the main bar, and doubles as a small meeting or function room. Several guest beers are available. 🌣🚊(Regent Centre)P

Gosforth Hotel
High Street, NE3 1HB
🌣 11 (12 Sun)-11 ☎ (0191) 285 6617
Caledonian Deuchars IPA; Fuller's London Pride; Mordue Northumbrian Blonde, Workie Ticket; Taylor Landlord; guest beers Ⓗ
On the corner of a busy junction at the top of the High Street, this is a stalwart of the Gosforth pub scene. Three ales are regularly available along with an occasional guest beer. Popular with a wide clientele, from nearby office workers to locals and students, the pub often gets very busy. A quieter adjoining bar opens occasionally at busier times and also serves as a function room. ◑♿♣

Job Bulman 🛗
St Nicholas Avenue, NE3 1AA
🌣 8am-11 ☎ (0191) 223 6230
Greene King Abbot; Ruddles Best Bitter; guest beers Ⓗ
Popular Wetherspoon pub located near the High Street, striving to serve a wide range of real ales. Aside from the two core beers, up to six guests may be available, often from local established breweries and micros. The bar room has a number of booths around the walls and quieter seating at the back. There is a raised area to the right set aside for families and diners.
🏨⤳🌣◑♿🚊(Regent Centre)●'—🚌

Queen Victoria 🛗
206 High Street, NE3 1HD
🌣 12-11 (midnight Fri); 11-midnight Sat ☎ (0191) 285 8060
Copper Dragon Golden Pippin; Mordue Workie Ticket; guest beers Ⓗ
Popular High-Street pub located on a busy corner of Gosforth. Part of the Leopard Leisure group, the premises have benefited from major refurbishment. Meals and snacks are reasonably priced and the pub does a decent cheeseboard. Guest ales are sourced from the Punch list. Sunday is buskers' night, Wednesday evening folk night and Thursday quiz night.
◑♿🚊(Regent Centre)●

Newcastle: Heaton

Chillingham 🛗
Chillingham Road, NE6 5XN
🌣 11-11 (midnight Fri & Sat); 12-11 Sun ☎ (0191) 265 5915
⊕ thechillinghamnewcastle.co.uk
Black Sheep Best Bitter; Jarrow Rivet Catcher; Mordue Workie Ticket; guest beers Ⓗ
A large two-roomed pub with contrasting styles – the public bar in traditional dark wood with panelling and a historic mirror recalling the past glories of nearby Wallsend, and the lounge with a

contemporary feel, flat-screen sports TVs and artwork depicting the sights of Newcastle. The upstairs function room hosts live music and comedy nights. Appealing to the widest possible customer base, it offers an excellent choice of local microbrewery beers, as well as a bottled beer, whisky and wine of the month.
❀◑⬚🝖(Chillingham Rd)♣♦P🝖(62,63)

Newcastle: Kenton Bank Foot

Twin Farms
22 Main Road, NE13 8AB
✪ 11-11 (11.30 Fri); 12-10.30 Sun ☎ (0191) 286 1263
Black Sheep Best Bitter; Caledonian Deuchars IPA; guest beers Ⓗ
Large stone-built farmhouse standing in its own grounds. Very comfortable throughout, it has separate bar and family areas and space outside to sit and enjoy the extensive selection of beers on offer. Quiz night is Monday and an Early Bird menu is offered on Thursday. Barbecues are held in summer. The pub aims to reduce food miles and the ingredients used in meals are locally sourced from named suppliers.
🍴Q❧❀◑⬚🝖(Bank Foot)P🝖(X77,X78)

Newcastle: South Gosforth

Brandling Villa
Haddricks Mill Road, NE3 1QL
✪ 12-11 (midnight Fri & Sat) ☎ (0191) 284 0490
⊕ brandlingvilla.co.uk
Harvistoun Bitter & Twisted; Taylor Landlord; guest beers Ⓗ
Large double-fronted pub with keen, enthusiastic staff. The pub offers a constantly changing selection of 10 beers, available in third-pint glasses on request, plus two ciders on handpump. The imaginative manager organises various well-attended beer-related events including beer festivals, brewery takeovers, local sausage and pie festivals, music and cinema. 🍴❧❀◑⬚♣♦P🕭

Millstone
Haddricks Mill Road, NE3 1QL
✪ 11-11; 12-10.30 Sun ☎ (0191) 285 3429
Draught Bass; Hadrian Border Tyneside Blonde; guest beers Ⓗ
Refurbished by a new entrepreneurial pub group, this is a modern, stylish, two-roomed pub with a lounge to the front and small public bar to the rear. The enthusiastic CAMRA licensee sources beers from local microbreweries as well as national favourites. Bass has been the regulars' top choice for many years. The function room upstairs hosts CAMRA events. ❧❀◑⬚🝖P🕭

North Shields

Magnesia Bank
1 Camden Street, NE30 1NH
✪ 12-11 ☎ (0191) 257 8392
Beer range varies Ⓗ
The Maggy Bank is so called due to its former days as a bank before conversion to a social club and then a pub. Now a popular music venue, it hosts free live music every Friday and Saturday night and late Sunday afternoon. Tuesday is poker night. A former CAMRA Pub of the Year, it is now owned by Jarrow Brewery and features its beers. The name Magnesia comes from the Magnesia Stair, one of

the crowded streets of houses that led down to the riverside south of the current pub near the present-day stairs. ◑❶

Oddfellows Ⓛ
7 Albion Road, NE30 2RJ
✪ 11 (12 Sun)-11 ☎ (0191) 257 4288
⊕ oddfellowspub.co.uk
Beer range varies Ⓖ
Historic maps and photographs of pre-war North Shields cover the walls of this small, friendly, single-room lounge bar, and are also shown on a large flat-screen TV and relayed to the outside smoking area. The pub has strong sporting links with past boxing champions and current national darts players. Home to football and darts teams, the pub fundraises for charity and holds a beer festival annually in May. ❧❀◑⬚🝖♦🕭🝖(306)

South Shields

Alum Ale House
Ferry Street, NE33 1JR (next to ferry landing)
✪ 11-11 (midnight Fri & Sat); 12-11 Sun
Jennings Cumberland Ale, Sneck Lifter; Marston's Pedigree Ⓗ; **Ringwood Boondoggle** Ⓗ/Ⓟ; **Wychwood Hobgoblin** Ⓗ
A small traditional pub adjacent to the market place and River Tyne. The Alum is a firm favourite with local ale drinkers and a haven for good beers. The pub has a main bar, side room and cellar bar/function room. Wooden floors and low ceilings help to create a comfortable warm feel. There is a total of 12 handpumps, seven dispensing guest ales. A lively Irish music session takes place on the first Sunday of the month. 🍴Q❀◑⬚🝖♣♦P🕭🝖

Maltings Ⓛ
Claypath Lane, NE33 4PG (off Westoe Rd)
✪ 12-11.30 (10.30 Sun) ☎ (0191) 427 7147
Jarrow Bitter, Isis; guest beers Ⓗ
Situated on the first floor above the former home of the Jarrow Brewery, now used only for seasonal and special brews. The 13 handpumps carry a range of Jarrow and guest beers. Real cider is also available. The well-stocked U-shaped bar serves a comfortable L-shaped lounge and small bar room. Entertainment features regularly. This is a popular early evening meeting place for drinkers before moving on to the town centre. Q◑⬚🝖♦🕭🝖

Stag's Head ★
45 Fowler Street, NE33 1NS
✪ 12-11 (midnight Fri-Sun)
Draught Bass; Taylor Landlord; guest beer Ⓗ
Traditional, single-room, town-centre pub dominated by an attractive alcove back bar and an open fire with a stag's head above. Identified by CAMRA as one of Britain's Best Real Heritage Pubs, many original design features remain, including colourful tilework at the entrance and an acid-etched bay window at the front. Upstairs is an extra room with its own small bar, available for private hire. Three handpumped beers are usually available, always including Bass. 🍴🝖♣🝖

Steamboat
Coronation Street, Mill Dam, NE33 1EQ (follow signs for Customs House)
✪ 12-11 (midnight Thu-Sat); 12-11.30 Sun
☎ (0191) 454 0134
Beer range varies Ⓗ

A traditional hostelry in the historic Mill Dam area, this is one of the oldest pubs in South Shields. Extended in the '70s to incorporate the old Post Office, it now has a raised lounge area and a nautical and industrial theme throughout. Eight constantly changing real ales and a cider are available. A meeting place for many clubs and societies including CAMRA, it has been a CAMRA Pub of the Year winner or runner-up many times. ⊞♣♠⊟

Wouldhave ⓛ
16 Mile End Road, NE33 1TA
✪ 8am-midnight ☎ (0191) 427 6014
Greene King Abbot; Ruddles Best Bitter Ⓗ
The Wouldhave is a town-centre pub, part of the Wetherspoon chain, providing customers with well-priced bar meals and a selection of real ales. Downstairs is a bar with ample seating and tables and upstairs a family-friendly area. Six handpumps serve the two regular beers and a rotation of guest ales from around the country. The pub hosts beer festivals and Wetherspoon's cider and perry festival. ⓢⓘⓓ&⊞♠⊟

Sunderland

Avenue ⓛ
26 Zetland Street, Roker, SR6 0EQ (just off Roker Avenue)
✪ 11-11 (midnight Fri & Sat); 12-11 Sun ☎ (0191) 567 7412
⊕ theavenuepub.com
Beer range varies Ⓗ
Just a short walk from the Stadium of Light, this local pub hosts various themed nights throughout the week including music, bingo, football and a popular Thursday night quiz, often followed by a live band. The bar area has a pool table and there is a full-size snooker table and two dartboards in the upstairs games room. A function room provides extra space during busier periods and can be hired. ⊛⊞♣ᵘ⊟(E1,18,19)

Blue Bell
Fulwell Road, Fulwell, SR6 9AD
✪ 11-11 (midnight Sat); 12-11 Sun ☎ (0191) 5494020
Beer range varies Ⓗ
Large, popular, community pub with a traditional interior which attracts people of all ages. Five handpumps offer a range of guest ales, a sixth pump is dedicated to cider. Sports fixtures are shown on large-screen TV, and quiz nights are held on Tuesday and Wednesday nights. Food is served until 9pm with a carvery noon-5.30pm on Sunday. A function room is available upstairs. ⓢ⊛ⓘ&⊞♠Pᵘ⊟

Fitzgerald's ⓛ
10-12 Green Terrace, SR1 3PZ
✪ 11-11 (1am Fri & Sat); 12-10.30 Sun ☎ (0191) 567 0852
⊕ fitzgeraldssunderland.co.uk
Big Lamp Prince Bishop; Fyne Jarl; Jarrow Rivet Catcher; Orkney Red MacGregor; Taylor Boltmaker Ⓗ
A busy city-centre pub owned by the Sir John Fitzgerald group serving an excellent range of real ales including offerings from North-East microbreweries. A supporter of CAMRA's LocAle campaign, Fitzgerald's was last year's local branch Pub of the Year. It has a large main room and a smaller side room. Meet the Brewer nights and quiz nights are held regularly. ⊛ⓘ⇌⊞♠ᵘ⊟

Harbour View ⓛ
Benedict Road, Roker, SR6 0NU
✪ 10.30-11.30 (midnight Fri & Sat) ☎ (0191) 567 1402
Jarrow Rivet Catcher Ⓗ
Modern open-plan lounge bar close to Roker beach. The first floor Benedict's Bar, open at weekends, offers fine views across the nearby marina. Five guest beers from local microbreweries and from further afield are on offer. Although Sunderland AFC moved to their new home 16 years ago, the pub is still popular with both home and away fans on match days and it can get very busy. ⊛&ᵘ⊟(E1,18,19)

Isis ♈ ⓛ
26 Silksworth Row, SR1 3QJ
✪ 12-11.30 (midnight Fri & Sat) ☎ (0191) 514 7684
Jarrow Red Ellen, Caulker, Rivet Catcher Ⓗ
Situated on the edge of the city centre, this Grade II-listed building dating from 1885 was bought and refurbished in 2011 by Jarrow Brewery. The long bar, decorated with wood and brass, has an impressive selection of ales including three from Jarrow Brewery, six from local and national breweries plus three ciders. There is a double room snug/lounge parallel to the bar and two further rooms on the first floor that can be used for private functions. ⓢ⊕⇌⊞♠⊟(10,11)

King's Arms ⓛ
Beach Street, Deptford, SR4 6BU
✪ 12-11 (midnight Fri & Sat); 12-10.30 Sun
☎ (0191) 567 9804
Taylor Landlord; guest beers Ⓗ
One of Sunderland's oldest public houses dating back to 1834, this pub is adjacent to the industrial area of Deptford, next to the River Wear. The traditional interior is arranged around a central bar with wood panels and bare boards. Seven handpulls feature Leamside beers and a good Yorkshire selection. Regular beer festivals, live music and barbecues are held in a marquee to the rear. A former CAMRA local Pub of the Year and North East award winner. 益⊛⊞♠ᵘ⊟(10,11)

Museum Vaults ⓛ
33 Silksworth Row, Millfield, SR1 3QJ
✪ 12-11 (3 Tue; midnight Thu-Sat); 12-10.30 Sun
☎ (0191) 565 9443
Beer range varies Ⓗ
The last beer house in Sunderland until 1978, this gem of a local has been run by the same family for over 40 years. The small single-room pub has two open fires that brighten up the room in winter. A number of local clubs including anarchists use the Vaults as their base and the pub hosts small book fairs. Up to three beers, mainly from local micros, are usually on offer at below-average prices for the area. Packed with Sunderland football club memorabilia, this former Vaux pub sits opposite the site of the much-missed Vaux brewery. 益⊛⊞♠Pᵘ⊟(10,11)

Saltgrass ⓛ
Hanover Place, SR4 6BY (behind B&Q)
✪ 11.30-11 (midnight Fri & Sat); 12-10.30 Sun
☎ (0191) 567 0202
Black Sheep Ale; Maxim Swedish Blonde, Double Maxim; Sharp's Doom Bar Ⓗ
An old-style two-room pub with a friendly, warm welcome. It is situated at the bottom of a hill next to a once-bustling shipyard and is named after the tough saltgrass that used to dominate the area. The

interior has an open fire, polished wooden floors and beamed ceilings. Food is available lunchtimes and evenings. Live music is hosted on a Friday and Saturday evening. ⚐⚘◐❒P⊞(10)

TJ Doyles 🝆

Hanover Place, Deptford, SR4 6BY
🕒 4-11 (midnight Fri); 12-midnight Sat; 12-11 Sun
☎ (0191) 510 1554 ⊕ tjdoyles.com
Beer range varies Ⓗ
A friendly authentic Irish pub with three handpulls serving ales from the local Maxim Brewery. Memorabilia around the walls celebrate Gaelic and local sports as well as Irish culture and a large screen shows live sport. A raised area at one end is used for live bands on Thursday, Friday and Saturday nights. There is a smoking area and a decked beer garden to the rear. No food is available. ⚐⚘⛶❒⬤P⅃➖⊞(11,36A/C)

William Jameson 🝆

30-32 Fawcett Street, SR1 1RH (opposite Winter Gardens & Museum)
🕒 8am-midnight ☎ (0191) 514 5016
Greene King Abbot; Ruddles Best Bitter; Wychwood Hobgoblin Ⓗ
Large open-plan, single-storey pub centrally located near the shops and amenities. It offers one of the largest ranges of handpulled beers in the area, including several local brews, as well as a choice of ciders and lager. Polite and friendly staff serve a good selection of reasonably priced foods. ⛴◐⛶⛟❒⬤⊞

Swalwell

Sun Inn

Market Lane, NE16 3AL (just off roundabout at the end of Front St)
🕒 11 (12 Sun)-11 ☎ (0191) 488 7783
Brakspear Oxford Gold; Jennings Cocker Hoop; Ringwood Boondoggle Ⓗ
Situated in the heart of the historic village that spawned many internationally renowned engineers and industrialists, and of course the famous Swalwell cabbage. This truly no-nonsense, welcoming community pub has been providing good company for locals and strangers alike for more than 100 years. Sword dancers, darts, domino handicaps, a monthly pie competition and buskers' nights all feature. The enthusiastic licensees have increased the handpulls from one to four and also keep real cider on draught. Bar food and snacks are served, free on Sundays. ⛴⚘⛁♣⬤⅃➖⊞

Tynemouth

Hugos at the Coast

29 Front Street, NE30 4DZ
🕒 11-11 (midnight Fri & Sat) ☎ (0191) 257 8956
Beer range varies Ⓗ
A tasteful conversion of a former restaurant with pleasing décor – the walls are adorned with local photographs of yesteryear, Tynemouth beach and pony rides. Very popular with locals and tourists, the weekends are extremely busy. The men's darts team plays on Tuesday night, quiz night is Wednesday and live music plays on the last Thursday of the month. ⛴⚘◐⛁⛃❒♣⬤⊞(306)

Tynemouth Lodge Hotel

Tynemouth Road, NE30 4AA
🕒 11-11; 12-10.30 Sun ☎ (0191) 257 7565
⊕ tynemouthlodgehotel.co.uk
Caledonian Deuchars IPA; Draught Bass; Mordue Northumbrian Blonde; guest beers Ⓗ
This attractive externally tiled free house was built in 1799 and has featured in every issue of the Guide since 1983 when the current owner took over – he is now approaching his 30th anniversary. The comfortable U-shaped lounge with the bar on one side and the hatch on the other is noted in the area for reputedly selling the highest volume of Draught Bass on Tyneside. Three regular ales and one guest are usually available. The pub is next to Northumberland Park and near the Coast-to-Coast cycle route. ⚐Q⚘⛁❒P⊞(1)

Washington

Courtyard 🝆

Arts Centre, Biddick Lane, Fatfield, NE38 8AB
🕒 11-11 (midnight Fri & Sat); 12-11 Sun ☎ (0191) 417 0445
⊕ artscentrewashington.co.uk/courtyard.aspx
Taylor Landlord; guest beers Ⓗ
This café-style bar attached to the Washington Arts Centre boasts eight cask ales, real cider and perry, as well as a range of Belgian bottled beers. Ales from Leamside Brewery, owned by the licensee, are frequently on offer. Excellent-quality home-cooked food is served throughout the day. The pub hosts a weekly quiz and buskers' evenings. Outdoor seating is within the spacious courtyard. Biannual beer festivals are held on the Easter and August bank holiday weekends. Q⚘◐⛁♣⬤P⊞(M1)

Sir William de Wessyngton 🝆

2-3 Victoria Road, Concord, NE37 2SY (opp bus station)
🕒 8am-11pm ☎ (0191) 418 0100
Greene King Abbot; Ruddles Best Bitter; guest beers Ⓗ
A welcome oasis in the town, this establishment recently celebrated its 10th year as the only real ale outlet in Concord. Situated in a former snooker club, it is a typical Wetherspoon and offers the usual facilities and good-value beer and food. Frequent beer festivals and real ale promotions feature. The pub is named after a local land owner and distant relative of George Washington. Q⛴◐⛁⬤⅃➖⊞

West Boldon

Black Horse 🝆

Rectory Bank, NE36 0QQ (off A184)
🕒 11-11 (11.30 Fri & Sat); 12-11.30 Sun ☎ (0191) 536 1814
⊕ blackhorsewestboldon.co.uk
Jennings Cumberland Ale; guest beer Ⓗ
Old-fashioned two-roomed pub with one room predominantly a restaurant and the other an L-shaped bar. The walls and ceilings are decorated with bric-a-brac such as photographs, vinyl discs, old typewriters and sporting equipment. There is an eclectic mix of furniture with leather settees, wooden pews and wooden boxes used as tables.

A fine beer may be judged with only a sip, but it's better to be thoroughly sure.
Czech proverb

The pub can get busy in the evenings and at weekends, and usually has two handpull beers on sale – the Jennings and a guest. ✿❻▶P⁼–🚐(9)

West Herrington

Stables

McLaren Way, DH4 4ND (off B1286)
✪ 12-11 (midnight Fri & Sat) ☎ (0191) 584 9226
Black Sheep Best Bitter; Taylor Landlord; guest beer Ⓗ

The Stables may not look much like a pub from the outside, but this old barn conversion is well worth a visit. Warm and welcoming, it retains the original beams and wooden furnishings. It is deceptively large – you can choose to sit either in the main bar/restaurant area or the cosy snug behind the bar where a relaxing atmosphere awaits you. Quality food is served until 3pm. Dog-friendly. ᙏQ✿❻&P🚐(35)

West Monkseaton

Beacon Hotel

Earsdon Road, NE25 9PT
✪ 11.30-11 (midnight Fri & Sat) ☎ (0191) 253 6911
Caledonian Deuchars IPA; guest beers Ⓗ

A superb modern pub set back from the main road, popular with locals. The cellar has dedicated lines so the ale is served at the right temperature. The manager likes to source a wide-ranging variety of ales and there is a quick turnover. Customers can order a rack of ale with three third pints for variety. Excellent food is served, with theme nights

Monday to Thursday and chef's specials Friday and Saturday. Quiz nights are Sunday and Wednesday. CAMRA members receive a 20p discount on a pint. ᙏQ✿❻&🖬P

Whitley Bay

Briar Dene

71 The Links, NE26 1UE
✪ 11-11; 12-10.30 Sun ☎ (0191) 252 0926
Black Sheep Best Bitter; guest beers Ⓗ

This Fitzgerald pub has a large, attractive lounge with sea views to the links and St Mary's lighthouse, and a more compact rear bar with widescreen TV, pool and darts. The pub is known for its food, with local fish and chips a speciality. Thursday is grill night. Guest beers change regularly and are well advertised on chalkboards. Children are welcome in a family area in the lounge. There is seating outside at the front of the pub. Q🏃✿❻ ❑&♣♣P🚐(308,309)

Rockcliffe Arms

Algernon Place, NE26 2DT
✪ 11-11 (11.15 Fri & Sat); 12-11 Sun ☎ (0191) 253 1299
Beer range varies Ⓗ

Outstanding back-street Fitzgerald pub, a few minutes' walk from the Metro station. This one-room establishment has distinct bar and lounge areas with a snug in between. There are four constantly changing guest beers, with tasting notes on notices above the dividing arch. Regular darts and dominoes matches are held in the snug. A popular pub with real ale drinkers. ✿❑🚐♣⅃–

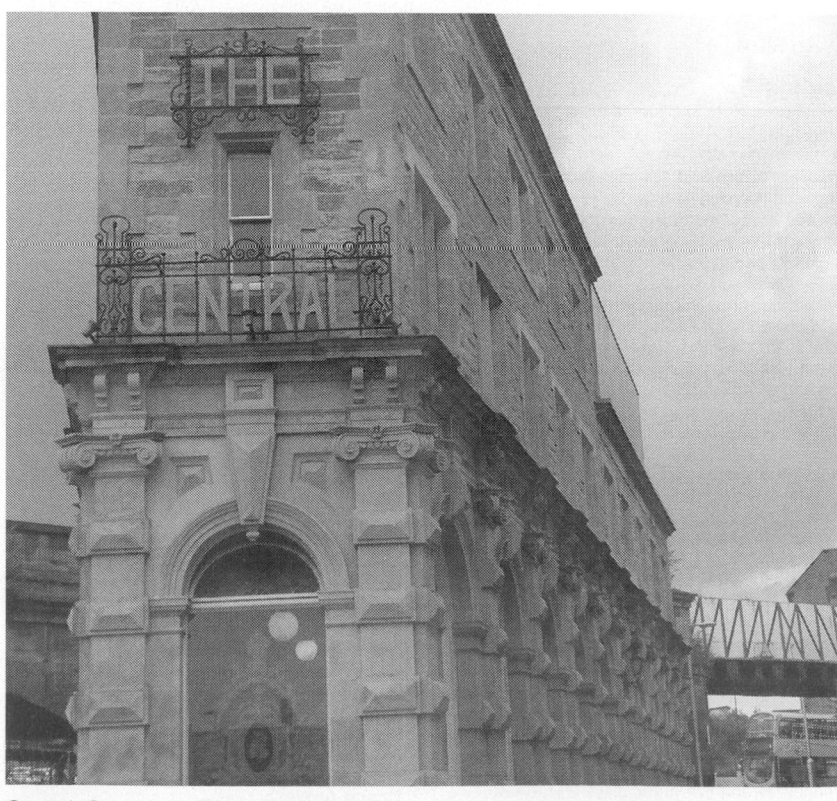

Central, Gateshead (Photo: Cat Button)

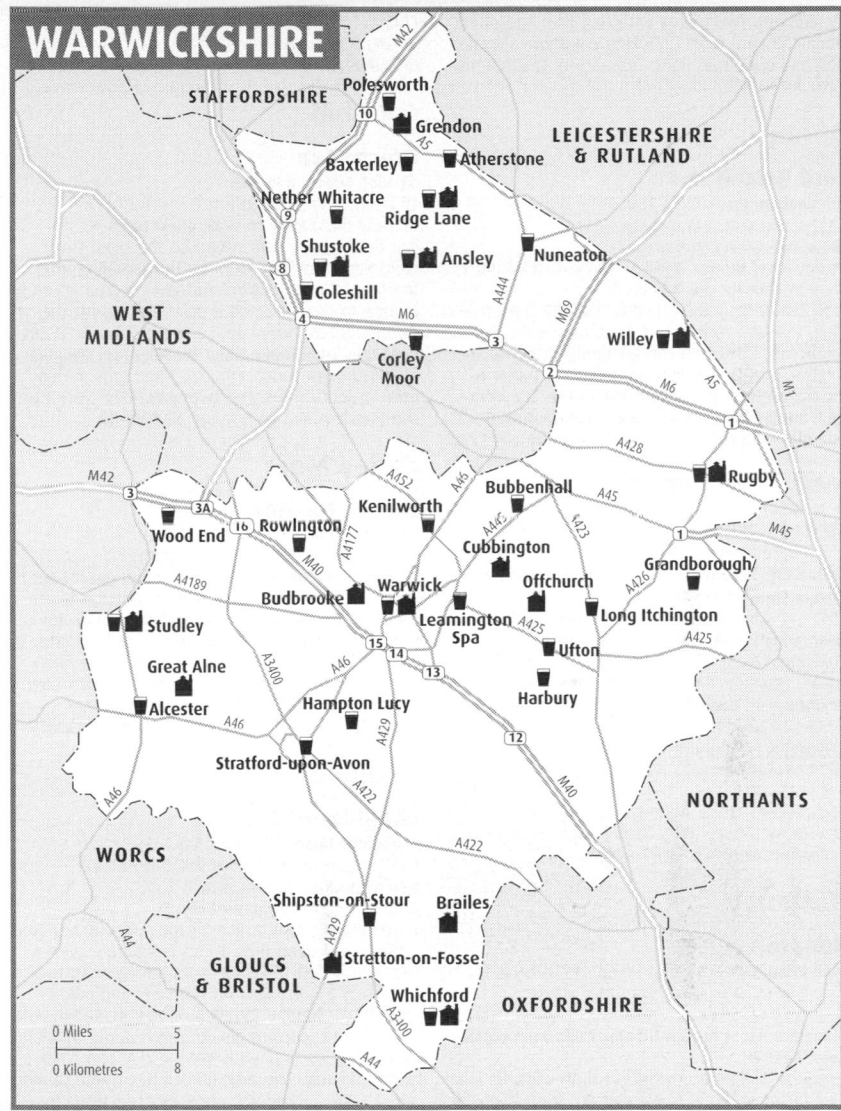

WARWICKSHIRE

STAFFORDSHIRE

Polesworth 10
Grendon
LEICESTERSHIRE & RUTLAND
Baxterley
Atherstone
Nether Whitacre 9
Ridge Lane
Shustoke 8
Ansley
Nuneaton
Coleshill

WEST MIDLANDS 4
Corley Moor
3
Willey

M42 3 3A
Wood End 16 Rowington
Kenilworth
Bubbenhall
Rugby
Cubbington
Grandborough
Budbrooke
Warwick
Offchurch
Long Itchington
Studley
Leamington Spa
Ufton
Great Alne
Hampton Lucy
Harbury
Alcester
13 12
Stratford-upon-Avon

NORTHANTS

WORCS

Shipston-on-Stour
Brailes
GLOUCS & BRISTOL
Stretton-on-Fosse
Whichford
OXFORDSHIRE

0 Miles 5
0 Kilometres 8

Alcester

Holly Bush
37 Henley Street, B49 5QX (behind church)
☼ 12-11 ☎ (01789) 762482 ⊕ thehollybushalcester.co.uk
Black Sheep Best Bitter; Hobsons Town Crier; Purity Pure Gold; Sharp's Doom Bar; guest beers ⓗ
This traditional 17th-century local has many original features. There is a function room and a walled garden at the rear. Four regular ales and four guests are on handpump and a beer festival is held in June. Traditional English and à la carte menus are available (not Sun eve). Folk sessions are held monthly and music may strike up at any time. ▲⚘⚙◗⊟♿♣↕–⊟(26,246,247)

Three Tuns
34 High Street, B49 5AB (next to post office)
☼ 12-2, 5.30 (6 Mon & Tue)-11; 12-11 Sat & Sun
☎ (01789) 762626

Butcombe Bitter; Hobsons Best Bitter; guest beers ⓗ
This local CAMRA award-winning pub is a must visit; no music, no pool and no food – how a real pub should be. The single-room interior has low beams, a stone-flagged floor and an exposed area of wattle and daub. Up to six ales from micros and independents provide a permanent yet ever-changing mini beer festival. Q♣⊟(26,246,247)

Turk's Head
4 High Street, B49 5AD (near church)
☼ 12-11 ☎ (01789) 765948 ⊕ theturkshead.net
Wye Valley Bitter, HPA; guest beers ⓗ
A central location makes this a popular place. The publican is a cask enthusiast and stages beer festivals during the summer months. Beers are sourced as locally as possible, served via four regular handpulls. A good range of changing bottled beers is available with the most popular making it to draught on occasion. The pub is

divided into two rooms with real fires and offers traditional pub food – booking advisable. Regular quiz and open mic nights are hosted. Worth a visit. 🏚🌣🕽🍽🍴⌂(26,246,247)

Ansley

Lord Nelson Inn ⓛ

Birmingham Road, CV10 9PQ
✪ 12-11 (10.30 Sun) ☎ (024) 7639 2305
⊕ thelordnelsoninnansley.co.uk
Victory Head Hunter, Band of Brothers, Third Party, Thick as Thieves; guest beers Ⓗ
Now featuring in the Guide for its 20th consecutive year, the Lord Nelson has been run by the Sperrin family since 1974. Seven handpulls dispense the family's own Sperrin brews under the name of Victory Brewery plus beers from other breweries local and not so local. The pub has a nautical theme and offers an extensive food menu. The courtyard garden can be a suntrap and is the venue for beer festivals and barbecues. 🌣🕽🍴P🍽⌂

Atherstone

Market Tavern ⓛ

Market Street, CV9 1ET
✪ 12-11 (midnight Fri & Sat); 12-10.30 Sun
Beer range varies Ⓗ
Traditional ale house overlooking the pretty market square (markets days are Tuesday and Friday). Two or three ales from the owning Warwickshire Beer Co are usually on offer, and two varying guests. In winter the focal point is the cosy open fire. In summertime the café-style seating to the front is popular, and the rear beer garden features patios and covered areas. Ale discounts are available for CAMRA members, and a free beer draw is held every Tuesday. 🏚🌣🍴🚲🍽⌂(48,765)

Baxterley

Rose Inn

Main Road, CV9 2LE (off B4116, W of Atherstone)
✪ 12-3, 6-11; 12-11 Fri-Sun ☎ (01827) 713939
⊕ roseinnbaxterley.com
Draught Bass; St Austell Tribute; Wells Bombardier; guest beer Ⓗ
Convivial village local where real ale outsells lager by a factor of three. Guest ales are from the Wells portfolio. The peaceful setting includes a duck pond and large gardens. The bar has an open coal fire, and welcomes dogs. There are three further intimate areas, a restaurant with a scenic view, and a skittle alley. Though at heart a community drinkers' pub, the Rose has a growing reputation for its excellent food. 🏚🌣🕽🍴🍽🍴P🍽⌂(766)

Bubbenhall

Malt Shovel ⓛ

Lower End, CV8 3BW
✪ 12-11 ☎ (024) 7630 1141
Greene King Abbot; Wells Bombardier; guest beers Ⓗ
Friendly village free house in a 17th-century Grade II-listed building with a large L-shaped lounge bar at the front and a small public bar to the rear. Outside is a small front patio and behind the spacious car park lies a large walled garden and adjacent bowling green, with access to woods in the summer. Home-cooked food is available. The two guest beers are usually LocAles, often from

Church End. A LocAle beer festival is held at the village hall every autumn. Q🌣🕽🍴🍴🌢🍴P🍽⌂(539)

Coleshill

Green Man

68 High Street, B46 3AH
✪ 11-11; 12-10.30 Sun ☎ (01675) 463376
Draught Bass; M&B Brew XI; guest beers Ⓗ
Tall three-storey pub sitting on the main town crossroads and hard to miss. The rambling interior features a boisterous bar and servery area, a comfy lounge to the rear, and a quiet side room. The decor is pleasantly dated, and a display of 1980s beermats may make older drinkers feel nostalgic. No jukebox or food, although filled rolls are on offer at lunchtimes. The two guest beers are from the Punch Finest Cask range. 🍴🍴P🍽⌂

Corley Moor

Bull & Butcher

Common Lane, CV7 8AQ SP279850
✪ 9 (11 Sun)-midnight ☎ (01676) 540241
Draught Bass; Greene King IPA, Abbot; guest beer Ⓗ
This family-friendly inn remains a popular locals' haunt while maintaining its fine reputation for food. The public bar at the front is divided into three cosy rooms, all warmed by fires in winter. The well-maintained garden with children's play area is busy in summer. Breakfast is served every day until 11am (10.30am Sun). 🏚Q🌣🕽🍴🍴P🍽

Grandborough

Shoulder of Mutton

Sawbridge Road, CV23 8DN (off A45)
✪ 12-3, 6-11; 12-11 Sat & Sun ☎ (01788) 814306
⊕ shoulderofmutton-grandborough.co.uk
Greene King Abbot; guest beers Ⓗ
A friendly and welcoming village pub with beamed ceilings and open fires. It has a separate games room with darts and Northamptonshire skittles, and hosts a quiz night on Thursday and poker evening on Sunday. Excellent food is served in both the pub and spacious dining conservatory (booking advisable). Curry night is Wednesday and steak night Thursday. The large garden has ample seating and a well-stocked fish pond. Beer festivals in summer feature live music and a hog roast. Cyclists and walkers are welcome. 🏚Q🌣🌣🕽🍴🍴🌢P

Hampton Lucy

Boar's Head ⓛ
Church Street, CV35 8BE
☼ 12-10; 11.30-11.30 Fri & Sat; 12-10 (6 winter) Sun
☎ (01789) 840533 ⊕ theboarsheadhamptonlucy.co.uk
Beer range varies ⊞
A deservedly popular village pub dating back to the 17th century. Situated on a Sustrans route and close to the River Avon, it is popular with cyclists, walkers and visitors to nearby Charlecote Park. At least five ales are served including one LocAle, often from the Church Farm Brewery. The menu offers fresh home-made food with daily specials, occasionally including squirrel. Outside is a sheltered rear garden. An annual themed beer festival is held. ▲Q❀◑⊞♣P⁵⌐

Harbury

Old New Inn ⓛ
Farm Sreet, CV33 9LS (SW side of village)
☼ 3.30 (12 Fri & Sat)-midnight; 12-11 Sun ☎ (01926) 614023
Church End Goat's Milk; guest beers ⊞
This stone pub on the edge of the village was once a farmhouse and a bakery. It has a splendid family garden at the rear. Inside, the two rooms have low ceilings reflecting the age of the building. The beer range changes regularly but brews from Purity and Wye Valley often feature. Sport is popular here with the TV screening major fixtures. The pub's darts, dominoes and pool teams are well supported. There is plenty of space in the car park. ▲☎❀⊞▲♣P⁵⌐(64A,65,66)

Kenilworth

Clarendon Arms
44 Castle Hill, CV8 1NB
☼ 11.30-3, 5.30-11.30; 11.30-12.30am Fri & Sat; 12-11.30 Sun ☎ (01926) 852017 ⊕ clarendonarmspub.co.uk
Wye Valley Butty Bach; guest beers ⊞
Just an arrow's throw from Kenilworth Castle, this multi-roomed restaurant and bar is a popular venue for its excellent range of food, available all day. Drinkers are not neglected, with Wye Valley and Hook Norton beers featuring prominently. To the rear there is a paved patio area with tables and umbrellas for fine weather while indoors there is a welcoming log-burning stove. A function room is available upstairs. Weekly and monthly themed promotions are held and special events celebrated. ▲❀◑⁵⌐

Famous Virgins & Castle
7 High Street, CV8 1LY (A429/A452 jct)
☼ 11-midnight (11 Sun) ☎ (01926) 853737
⊕ virginsandcastle.co.uk
Everards Beacon Bitter, Sunchaser Blonde, Tiger, Original; guest beer ⊞
The only Everards pub in Kenilworth. It was here that the original Coventry & Warwickshire branch of CAMRA was formed in 1974. The pub dates back to 1563 when it was called the Two Virgins Inn. By 1777 it was called the Sign of the Two Virgins. It merged with the Castle Tavern in 1828, to become the Virgins & Castle. ▲☎❀◑&●⁵⌐(11)

Old Bakery
12 High Street, CV8 1LZ (near A429/A452 jct)
☼ 5.30 (5 Fri & Sat)-11; 5-10.30 Sun ☎ (01926) 864111
⊕ theoldbakery.eu

St Austell Tribute; Wye Valley Bitter, HPA; guest beer ⊞
Located in the picturesque High Street, a 15-minute walk from Kenilworth Castle, this two-roomed hostelry offers ales in tip-top condition for the discerning drinker. Hop-festooned beams and rustic furniture add to an ambience where convivial banter thrives. Monday is fish and chips night (until 7.30pm) supplied by locally famous Alfie Grimshaw. A range of unusual nuts and snacks is offered. Accommodation is in 14 en-suite rooms. Free Wi-Fi. A golf society welcomes all players. Q❀⊨&P⌐(11)

Royal Oak ♈
New Street, CV8 2EZ (250yds from A429/A452 jct)
☼ 4 (12 Sat)-11; 12-10.30 Sun ☎ (01926) 856906
Adnams Southwold Bitter; Black Sheep Ale; Castle Rock Harvest Pale; guest beer ⊞
This traditional Grade II-listed pub close to the crossroads at the heart of old Kenilworth welcomes all sectors of the community and attracts a diverse clientele. Darts, pool, poker and chess are played. Karaoke is hosted on Saturday and acoustic music on Sunday twice a month. Live sport is shown and families and dogs are welcome. The number 11 Coventry-Leamington bus stops right outside the front door. A pleasant patio and garden are to the rear. Free Wi-Fi available. ☎❀♣⁵⌐(11)

Leamington Spa

Benjamin Satchwell
112-114 The Parade, CV32 4AQ (almost opp town hall)
☼ 7-midnight (1am Fri & Sat) ☎ (01926) 883733
Greene King Abbot; Ruddles Best Bitter; guest beers ⊞
Typical town-centre Wetherspoon's pub converted from two shops and stretching from The Parade right through to Bedford Street at the rear. The pub is named after a former Leamington notable who discovered the second of the springs that made the town a popular spa in Regency times. On the walls are panels depicting the history of Leamington and its benefactors. The impressively long bar has 12 handpumps, two of which are used for guest ciders. ☎◑&⇌♣●⌐

Jug & Jester ⓛ
11 Bath Street, CV31 3AF
☼ 8am-midnight (1am Fri & Sat) ☎ (01926) 331820
Greene King Abbot; Ruddles Best Bitter; guest beers ⊞
This pub was once the Theatre Royal. Today it is an interesting town pub with four distinct drinking areas on varying levels reflecting the original rooms. Pictures depicting the heritage of the town together with an eclectic mix of furniture help to create a comfortable ambience that attracts a mixed clientele of all ages. Look for the unusual collection of stoneware vats on the high shelf in the middle room. Convenient for a beer before a gig at the nearby Assembly. ▲Q☎❀◑&⇌●⁵⌐

Somerville Arms
4 Campion Terrace, CV32 4SX
☼ 12-2, 5.30-11; 12-11 Sat; 12-10.30 Sun ☎ (01926) 426746
⊕ somervillearms.co.uk
Adnams Southwold Bitter, Broadside; Everards Beacon, Sunchaser Blonde, Tiger, Original; guest beer ⊞

This friendly, traditional Victorian local hosts regular music nights and a monthly quiz. Always good humoured with a relaxed, welcoming atmosphere, the busy public bar at the front and the cosy lounge at the rear both feature their own drinking motto – 'Real ale for your health' and 'Abound in hops all ye who enter here'. The fine set of seven matching handpumps on the bar makes quite an impressive sight. Local CAMRA Pub of the Year 2012.
Q❀❄❤●ᵗ♫(67)

Talbot Inn
34 Rushmore Street, CV31 1JA
❂ 12-11 (midnight Fri & Sat) ☎ 07933 855377
Oakham JHB, Bishops Farewell; Wye Valley Bitter, Butty Bach; guest beers Ⓗ
Friendly free house standing at the end of a Victorian terrace between St Marys and Clapham Terrace canal bridges. The converted Victorian building is noted for the large wall mural painted on the side nearest the Grand Union Canal. The pub is popular with locals, canal users and walkers. Two changing guest beers augment the two regular ales and a Byatt's Brewery beer often features. In summer cider on gravity is usually available.
➰❀❄❤●ᵗ♫

Woodland Tavern Ⓛ
3 Regent Street, CV32 5HW
❂ 12-midnight (1am Fri & Sat); 12-11.30 Sun
☎ (01926) 425868
Slaughterhouse Saddleback Best Bitter; Wychwood Hobgoblin; guest beer Ⓗ
A traditional Victorian street-corner drinkers' pub, handy for the town centre, with a separate lounge and public bar. The cosy rooms and friendly mixed clientele help to create a lively atmosphere. The pub has a small walled beer garden featuring murals with local references and jokes. Part of the garden is sheltered in the old covered entrance. The only regular outlet for Slaughterhouse beer in Leamington Spa. ❀❄❄❄❄♫

Long Itchington

Green Man
Church Road, CV47 9PW
❂ 5-11 (midnight Fri); 12-midnight Sat; 12-10.30 Sun
☎ (01926) 812208 ⊕ greenmanlongitchington.co.uk
Black Sheep Best Bitter; Fuller's London Pride; Purity Mad Goose; St Austell Tribute; guest beers Ⓗ
Parts of this fine country inn date back to the 1700s, notably the original beams and low ceilings. The building has a number of linked drinking areas and a function room. It is home to several pub teams and holds an annual beer festival in May. There are benches on the front courtyard and a good-sized garden. The landlord is rumoured to be so passionate about real ale that he sings to his beer each morning to help it condition.
➰➰❀❄❄♣●Pᵗ♫(64)

Harvester Ⓛ
6 Church Road, CV47 9PE (off A423 at village pond, then first left)
❂ 12-2.30, 6-11; 12-3, 7-10.30 Sun ☎ (01926) 812698
⊕ theharvesterinn.co.uk
Hook Norton Hooky Bitter; guest beers Ⓗ
Simon and the Mills family have presided over this wholly unpretentious pub since 1984, set in a Warwickshire village boasting six hostelries. A regular Guide entry, the Harvester is central to the May bank holiday beer festival supported by all the

village pubs. Two guest ales are offered alongside the Hook Norton beer. In the separate restaurant, the steaks are highly recommended. A free Wi-Fi hotspot. Q❄●❄❄Pᵗ♫(64)

Nether Whitacre

Gate Inn
Gate Lane, B46 2DS SP232930
❂ 12-11 (10.30 Sun) ☎ (01675) 481292
Banks's Mild, Bitter; Marston's Pedigree; Ringwood Fortyniner; guest beers Ⓗ
Convivial rural alehouse with a variety of rooms, beers and food, topped off with a warm welcome. Diners tend to favour the conservatory and large lounge while drinkers gravitate to the quarry-tiled bar. Both main rooms feature wood-burning stoves. The pool table is in a small separate room. The guest ale is from the Marston's portfolio. To the rear is a large, child-friendly garden, plus a separate beer garden for adults. Local eggs are sold at the bar. ➰❀❄❤♣Pᵗ

Nuneaton

Crown
10 Bond Street, CV11 4BX (between rail and bus stations)
❂ 12-11 (midnight Fri & Sat) ☎ (024) 7637 3343
Oakham JHB; guest beers Ⓗ
Close to the railway and bus stations, this Guide regular boasts 10 handpulls dispensing seven real ales and three ciders. A large selection of malt whiskies and foreign bottled beers is also stocked. Live music plays on Saturday nights. A function room is available for hire and there is a large garden at the rear. Beer festivals are held in June and December. Food is served 4-9pm Friday, noon-6pm Saturday and popular Sunday lunches noon-4pm. CAMRA members receive a discount.
➰❀❄❄●Pᵗ♫

Felix Holt Ⓛ
3 Stratford Street, CV11 5BS
❂ 8am-midnight (1am Fri & Sat) ☎ (024) 7634 7785
Greene King Abbot; Ruddles Best Bitter; Thornbridge Jaipur IPA; guest beers Ⓗ
Large Wetherspoon outlet in the town centre. The pub takes its name from the George Eliot novel and the literary theme is reflected in the decor, with books and pictures illustrating local history. Alongside the regular beers a further six handpulls provide an interesting range of both local and guest ales. A discount is available for CAMRA members. Food is served 8am-10pm. Outside is a heated area for smokers. Q❄❄ᵗ

Horseshoes Ⓛ
2 Heath End Road, CV10 7JQ
❂ 12-11 (1am Fri & Sat) ☎ (024) 7767 5066
⊕ thehorseshoesbrewerytap.co.uk
Everards Tiger; Tunnel Late Ott, Trade Winds, Nelson's Column; guest beers Ⓗ
Traditional Edwardian-style English inn refurbished under Everard's Project William Scheme to transform struggling pubs into thriving alehouses. Two coal fires add to a welcoming ambience. Ten handpulls are complemented by a varied selection of bottled beer. Quiz nights are held weekly and regular festivals feature in the beer garden with live music. Excellent home-cooked food is served including speciality themed evenings and a popular

Sunday carvery. The snug is available for private functions. This is a family-friendly pub close to the Coventry Canal. ⚌Q⚌⚌⚌⚌⚌⚌P⚌⚌

Royal Oak
The Square, CV11 4JY
✪ 12 (4.30 Mon-Thu winter)-midnight; 12-11 Sun
☎ (024) 7638 2977
Draught Bass; Greene King Abbot; Morland Old Speckled Hen; guest beers Ⓗ
A popular locals' pub with a red-tile-floored bar and a separate lounge. The lounge is accessed by a passage and steps, with service via a hatch to the bar where there are six handpulls serving top-quality beers. Situated in a lively square away from the main road, the pub retains a village feel. Beer festivals are held in the pleasant garden to the rear. ⚌⚌⚌⚌⚌⚌

Polesworth
Bull's Head
Tamworth Road, B78 1JH (by canal bridge on B5000)
✪ 11-midnight (11 Sun) ☎ 07796 538415
Sharp's Doom Bar; Wood Shropshire Lad; guest beers Ⓗ
Simple canalside local with keenly priced ales and a strong local following. Now in its second year in the Guide, the pub has added extra handpumps. One or two guest ales are the norm, generally from interesting microbreweries. The L-shaped bar is usually busy, with the arched lounge a quieter place for conversation. The pub is home to several teams including cribbage and bowls. No food, but the independent Indian restaurant upstairs (open every evening) will fetch ale for you from downstairs. ⚌⚌P⚌(765,785)

Ridge Lane
Church End Brewery Tap Ⓛ
CV10 0RD (2 miles SW of Atherstone)
✪ 6 (12 Fri & Sat)-11; 12-10.30 Sun ☎ (01827) 713080
⊕ churchendbrewery.co.uk
Church End Gravediggers Ale, What the Fox's Hat, seasonal beers Ⓗ
Hard to spot from the road, access to this brewery tap is signposted by an 'A' board positioned at the entrance. The brewery can be seen through a large window in the bar area. Eight handpulls serve the bar and vestry. The beer menu can change quickly over four days although the mild is always on. Ever-changing ciders are dispensed direct from the cask. Children are not allowed inside but there is a large meadow garden with plenty of seating. Q⚌⚌A⚌⚌P⚌(41)

Rowington
Rowington Club Ⓛ
Rowington Green, CV35 7DB (just E of B4439, opp village hall) SP1988070150
✪ 2 (12 Sat & Sun)-11 ☎ (01564) 782087 ⊕ rowington.org/Rowington/rowington_club.html
Greene King IPA; Wye Valley HPA; guest beers Ⓗ
Busy and thriving community club, popular with locals, also open to non-member visitors (free entry for CAMRA members). Frequent entertainment is provided plus seasonal events such as Ladies' Day, August beer and music festival, Marrow Sunday and game fair. Four real ales are on offer at all times plus traditional ciders.

Bar snacks are available but no meals. The large beer garden overlooks the village cricket ground and the club is handy for local walking and cycling. Always friendly, it is well worth seeking out. ⚌⚌⚌⚌⚌(Lapworth)⚌⚌P⚌

Rugby
Lawrence Sheriff Ⓛ
28-29 High Street, CV21 3BW
✪ 8am-midnight (3am Thu-Sat) ☎ (01788) 517640
Greene King Abbot; Oakham Bishops Farewell; Ruddles Best Bitter; Saltaire Cascade Pale Ale; Tom Wood Lincoln Gold; guest beers Ⓗ
Built in Art Deco style during the 1930s for Boots the Chemist, this is now a Wetherspoon Lloyds No.1 bar named after the founder of Rugby School. Ten handpumps offer guest ales alongside the regular Wetherspoon's range. Breakfast is served from 8am, with food available all day until 9pm. Frequented by all age groups, the weekends are especially popular with the younger set – the music gets loud after 9pm. Show your CAMRA membership card for a discount on real ale. ⚌⚌⚌⚌⚌⚌

Merchants Inn Ⓛ
5-6 Little Church Street, CV21 3AW (behind Marks & Spencer)
✪ 12-midnight (1am Fri & Sat) ☎ (01788) 571119
⊕ merchantsinn.co.uk
Batemans XB Ⓗ; Oakham Bishops Farewell Ⓖ; Purity Mad Goose; guest beers Ⓗ
Dedicated to real ale, this gem of a pub is a must visit. A previous winner of Rugby & Warwickshire CAMRA and Cider Pub of the Year, it offers nine real ales, Belgian beers, six ciders and perry. It has a warm, cosy atmosphere, wooden seating, comfortable sofas, flagstone floors, an open fireplace and an abundance of brewery memorabilia. Good home-cooked food is popular. Beer festivals are held in spring and autumn plus other themed events. Live music is hosted on Tuesday. ⚌⚌⚌⚌⚌⚌⚌

Raglan Arms
50 Dunchurch Road, CV22 6AD
✪ 4-midnight (1am Fri); 12-1am Sat; 12-midnight Sun
☎ (01788) 544441
Fuller's London Pride; Greene King Abbot; guest beers Ⓗ
Opposite Rugby School playing fields, the Raglan Arms is a long-time Guide entry and has won many CAMRA awards. The cosy interior includes the bar, darts lounge and a small snug popular for meetings. Beers vary, with brews from Abbeydale and Oakham always popular. Raglan Bitter is a house beer. Major sporting events are shown on TV. Snacks are available at all times – try the pork pies and sausage rolls. Q⚌⚌⚌P⚌⚌

Seven Stars ⚌
40 Albert Square, CV21 2SH
✪ 12-11 (12.30am Fri & Sat); 12-10.30 Sun
☎ (01788) 546611
B&T Shefford Bitter, Golden Fox, Dragon Slayer; Everards Tiger; guest beers Ⓗ
Family brewers Everards of Leicestershire teamed with Banks and Taylor's of Bedfordshire to create their 24th Project William pub. Following refurbishment, the Seven Stars now has a smart traditional bar area, comfortable lounge, snug and small conservatory. Full of charm and character, it

is free of electronic games and music, making conversation a delight. The bar boasts 14 handpumps serving a range of beers including a mild and two ciders. Winner of local CAMRA Most Improved Pub and Pub of the Year 2012 awards.
⚲Q👥🐕🏠🍴♿🚆♣●♿🚃

Squirrel Inn 🅛
33 Church Street, CV21 3PU
🟢 12-11; 4-10.30 Sun ☎ (01788) 544154
Marston's Pedigree; guest beers Ⓗ
A warm welcome awaits all at this fine real ale emporium where an eclectic mixed clientele makes lively bar banter unavoidable. The guest ales change regularly but always include a LocAle, and Westons Old Rosie cider is also on handpump. Home-made jams and chutney are on sale along with bar snacks. Live acoustic music is a highlight on Wednesday and Saturday evenings. A wide selection of table-top games is available.
⚲Q🚆♣●🚃

Victoria Inn 🅛
1 Lower Hillmorton Road, CV21 3ST
🟢 12 (4 Mon-Wed)-midnight ☎ (01788) 544374
⊕ downthevic.com
Atomic Strike, Fission, Half Life, Bomb; Hook Norton Old Hooky; guest beers Ⓗ
The Victoria Inn is a traditional Victorian real ale pub, owned by the Atomic Brewery. It boasts 14 handpumps for real ale and Westons Old Rosie cider, served in a period lounge and traditional bar that doubles as a games room for darts and pool. Two further snugs and a courtyard garden provide additional space. A selection of foreign beers is available and Sky Sports is shown in both bars. Themed beer festivals are held twice a year. Rugby CAMRA Pub of the Year 2011. Q👥🐕🏠🚆♣●♿🚃

Shipston-on-Stour

Black Horse 🅛
Station Road, CV36 4BT (120yds from A3400 via Watery Lane)
🟢 12-3 (not Mon); 6-11; 12-11 Thu-Sat; 12-10.30 Sun
☎ (01608) 238489 ⊕ blackhorseshipston.com
Butcombe Bitter; Purity Mad Goose; Wye Valley Bitter; guest beer Ⓗ
This ancient stone-built 16th-century pub is the oldest inn and the only thatched building in Shipston, with a licence dating back to 1540. The pub has two rooms – a cosy and welcoming main bar with a large inglenook log fireplace and a second bar with a log fire, wooden beams and a dartboard. Thai food is served and available to take away. Free Wi-Fi available. CAMRA members receive a 10p discount on a pint.
⚲Q👥🐕🍴🏠♿♣●♿🚃

Shustoke

Griffin Inn 🍺 🅛
Church Road, B46 2LB (on B4116 on sharp bend)
🟢 12-2.30, 7-11; 12-10.30 Sun ☎ (01675) 481205
Hook Norton Old Hooky; Jennings Dark Mild; Marston's Pedigree; RCH Pitchfork; Theakston Old Peculier; guest beers Ⓗ
Thriving family-run Guide regular with its own brewery next door. A Griffin Inn beer usually features alongside the regular ales and four guests. One real cider is also available. Occasional beer festivals are overwhelmingly popular. The low-

beamed interior is blessedly music- and TV-free. In winter it is superbly cosy with the log-burning stoves roaring away. Children are welcome in the conservatory. No food served Sunday. Local eggs and sausages are sold at the bar.
⚲Q👥🐕🏠Ⓐ●P♿

Stratford-upon-Avon

Bear at the Swan's Nest Hotel 🍺 🅛
Swan's Nest Lane, CV37 7LT (S end of Clopton Bridge)
🟢 12-11 (midnight Fri & Sat) ☎ (01789) 265540
⊕ thebearfreehouse.co.uk
Castle Rock Harvest Pale; Hook Norton Old Hooky; North Cotswold Windrush Ale; Wye Valley Butty Bach; guest beers Ⓗ
Historic pub in a waterside location, five minutes' walk from the town centre, serving seven real ales. The focus tends to be on local and regional brewers such as Wye Valley, Hook Norton, Hobsons and Warwickshire Brewing Co, with seasonal beers available. The Bear is decked out with wood panelling, a pewter bar and picnic tables for riverside drinking. Excellent, home-made bar meals are served in a warm, friendly, welcoming atmosphere. Board games and newspapers are always available. ⚲👥🐕🏠🍴Ⓓ♿🚆♣●P🚃(23)

New Bull's Head 🅛
9 Bull Street, CV37 6DT (on SW side of town, 400yds from council offices)
🟢 11.30-11; 12-10.30 Sun ☎ (01789) 268832
⊕ thenewbullshead.co.uk
Hook Norton Lion; Sharp's Doom Bar; Taylor Landlord; guest beers Ⓗ
Formerly the West End, this family-run community local was rebranded and refurbished in early 2013. It serves a range of beers including a local ale, and at least three ales from around the UK. A wide range of strengths and a broad spectrum of styles are available. Lunchtime, evening and Sunday lunchtime menus change regularly, with vegetarian options available. Themed food nights are popular. A community shop provides groceries.
Q🏠Ⓓ🚆♿

Studley

Little Lark
108 Alcester Road, B80 7NP (Tom's Town Lane jct with A435) SP075632
🟢 12-3, 6-11; 12-midnight Fri & Sat; 12-10.30 Sun
☎ (01527) 853105
Sharp's Doom Bar; Taylor Landlord; Wye Valley HPA; guest beer Ⓗ
This popular village local has become a regular entry in the Guide. Formerly a Mad O'Rourke pub, it still maintains a link to its quirky past with front pages from its own newspaper adorning the walls. As well as real ale, a great selection of traditional fruit wines and single malt whiskies is always available. Good-quality reasonably priced meals cooked by the licensee are served seven days a week – the Desperate Dan Cow Pie is a house speciality. ⚲Q👥Ⓓ🏠♿♣●♿🚃(26,143,247)

Victoria Works 🅛
33 Redditch Road, B80 7AU
🟢 12 (4 Mon)-11 ☎ (0121) 445 4411
⊕ the-victoria-works.co.uk

ENGLAND

Weatheroak St Udley Mild, Light Oak, Weatheroak Ale, Victoria Works, Redwood, Keystone Hops; guest beer Ⓗ
Formerly the Nags Head, this pub has become the tap for the Weatheroak brewery. The horseshoe-shaped interior has separate comfortable seating areas on different levels. The full range of the brewery's superb beers is always available, with a changing guest ale and a real cider. Food is not currently available but you are welcome to bring your own. Live music evenings and open mic nights feature occasionally. ⊞●P⅙–⊟(143,247)

Ufton

White Hart
White Hart Lane, CV33 9PJ SP378622
✿ 11.30-3, 6-11; 11.30-4 Sun ☎ (01926) 612976
⊕ thewhitehartufton.com
Purity Mad Goose; Slaughterhouse Saddleback Best Bitter; guest beer Ⓗ
A 16th-century coaching inn featuring oak beams throughout. The free house offers a warm welcome, with historic photos of the pub and the village on display in the hallway. The garden has magnificent views over Warwickshire, and the Malvern Hills can be seen on a clear day. Pétanque is played next to the car park. The pub is an ideal starting or finishing point for a number of fine walks. Ufton Fields Nature Reserve is nearby.
⨺⌂⊛⟨➍P⅙–⊟⊟(63)

Warwick

Wild Boar ⟰ Ⓛ
27 Lakin Road, CV34 5BU
✿ 12-11.30 (12.30am Fri & Sat); 12-10.30 Sun
☎ (01926) 499968 ⊕ thewildboarwarwick.co.uk
Everards Sunchaser Blonde; Slaughterhouse Saddleback Best Bitter; guest beers Ⓗ
The Wild Boar is a friendly, traditional pub with a separate cosy snug. It is the brewery tap for Slaughterhouse with the microbrewery on site. Ten handpumps are on the bar offering four house beers, five varying guests and a cider. Good-quality lunchtime meals are served, including Sunday roasts. A large function room at the rear screens international rugby matches. Hops grow in pots in the patio garden. Current local CAMRA Pub of the Year. ⨺Q⌂⊛⟨⇌●⅙–⊟(X17)

Whichford

Norman Knight Ⓛ
CV36 5PE (opp village green)
✿ 7-11 Mon, 12-3, 6-11 winter; 11-11 summer; 12-midnight Sun ☎ (01608) 684621 ⊕ thenormanknight.co.uk
Hook Norton Hooky; Patriot Morris, Kiwi; guest beers Ⓗ
A traditional pub in the centre of Whichford overlooking the green. Very much a community pub at the heart of village life, it has won many local and regional awards for the quality of its beers, food and facilities. Music nights are held frequently and every third Thursday owners of classic cars and bikes meet here. It is also a popular pub for walkers who enjoy the delicious home-cooked meals. The Patriot Brewery is behind the pub. ⨺Q⌂⊛⟨➍⌂A♣●P⅙–⊟

Willey

Wood Farm Brewery Tap Ⓛ
Coalpit Lane, CV23 0SL
✿ 12-10 (9 Sun) ☎ (01788) 833469
⊕ woodfarmbrewery.co.uk
Wood Farm 1823 Mild, Webb Ellis Ale, Best Bitter, Victorious, Union, No. 8; guest beers Ⓗ
Wood Farm Visitors Centre is a converted barn situated over two floors and open all year round. The brewery can be viewed through large windows in the bar. Beer festivals are held in marquees in the garden. Home-cooked food is available, with a carvery during festivals. The brewery owners are big Leicester Tigers fans and the beer names all have a rugby theme. A lovely place to enjoy a good pint, set in 36 acres of countryside. ⨺⌂⊛⟨⌂●P

Wood End

Warwickshire Lad
Broad Lane, B94 5DP (on main B4101 road)
✿ 12 (11.30 Sun)-11 ☎ (01564) 742346
⊕ thewarwickshirelad.co.uk
St Austell Tribute; Whitworth Lad, Sobriety; guest beer Ⓗ
Country pub offering excellent freshly prepared food featuring local produce. Several beers come from the local Whitworth Brewing Company including The Lad – a beer commissioned by the pub. Children and well-behaved dogs on leads are welcome, and there is a garden and outside decking area. A log fire blazes in winter months. ⨺⌂⊛⟨⌂⇌P⅙

Beers suitable for vegetarians and vegans

A number of cask and bottle-fermented beers in the Good Beer Guide are listed as suitable for vegetarians and vegans. The main ingredients used in cask beer production are malted grain, hops, yeast and water, and these present no problems for drinkers who wish to avoid animal products. But most brewers of cask beer use isinglass as a clearing agent: isinglass is derived from the bladders of certain fish, including the sturgeon. Isinglass is added to a cask when it leaves the brewery and attracts yeast cells and protein, which fall to the bottom of the container. Other clearing agents – notably Irish moss, derived from seaweed – can be used in place of isinglass and the Guide feels that brewers should take a serious look at replacing isinglass with plant-derived finings, especially as the sturgeon is an endangered species.

Vegans avoid dairy products: lactose, a bi-product of cheese making, is used in milk stout, of which Mackeson is the best-known example.

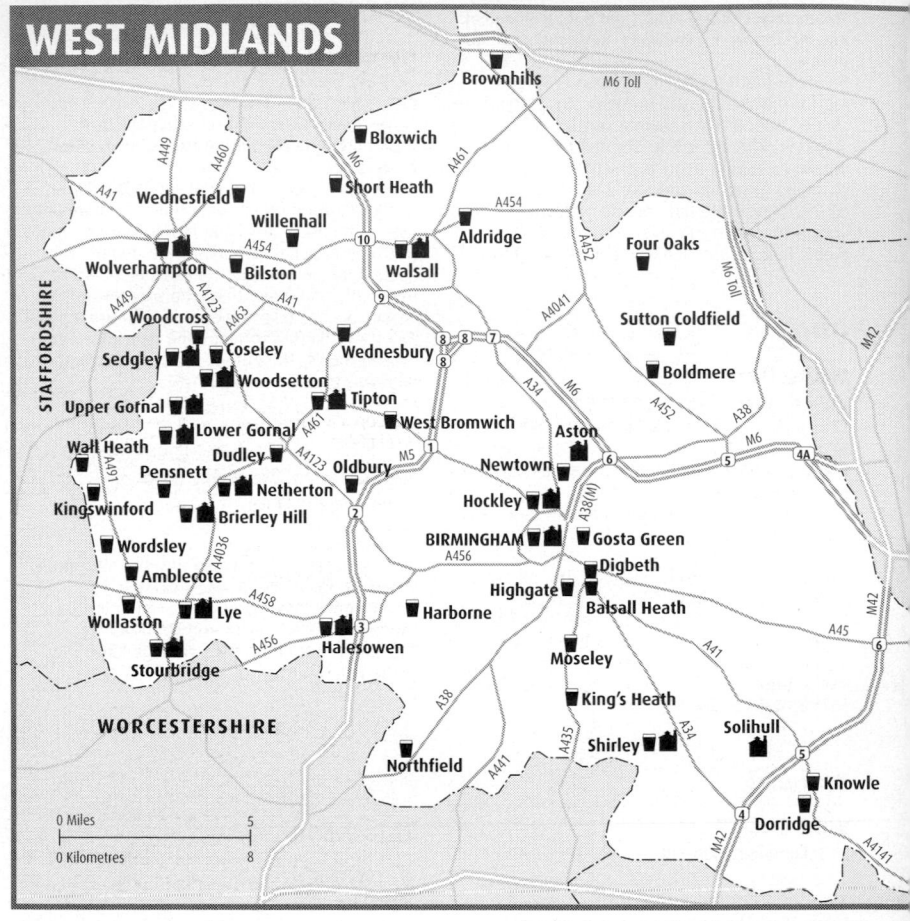

WEST MIDLANDS

Aldridge

Lazy Hill Tavern 🛈
196 Walsall Wood Road, WS9 8HB
☼ 6-11; 12-2.30, 7-10.30 Sun ☎ (01922) 452040
Blythe Staffie; Greene King IPA, Abbot; Holden's Black Country Mild, Golden Glow; Wye Valley Butty Bach Ⓗ
Large and welcoming family-run free house that has had the same licensee for 30 years. Originally a farmhouse, it first became a country club before becoming a pub in 1986. Four separate rooms are all similarly and comfortably furnished, with logburners in two. The large 160-seater function room is used mid-week by local sports/community organisations and can be booked for weddings and other functions. ♨️QP🖳(7,35,56)

Amblecote

Maverick 🛈
Brettell Lane, DY8 4BA (on A491 and A461 jct)
☼ 12-midnight (1am Wed, Fri & Sat; 11 Sun)
☎ (01384) 824099
Jennings Cumberland Ale; guest beers Ⓗ
A large corner establishment, a former CAMRA branch Pub of the Year. The pub has a Wild West theme and is a live music venue for blues, folk, rock and more. There are permanently four beers

on handpump, with three guests – two from local breweries. Sky Sports is screened in a separate area when no music is on. There is a covered, heated smoking area and a small garden. An occasional beer festival is held. Q♨️&♣️🍴💷🖳(256,257,246)

Robin Hood 🛈
196 Collis Street, DY8 4EQ (on A4102 one-way street off Brettell Lane A461)
☼ 12-3 (not Mon & Tue), 5-11; 12-midnight Fri & Sat; 12-11 Sun ☎ (01384) 821120
Bathams Best Bitter; Enville Ginger Beer; Holden's Golden Glow; Salopian Oracle; guest beers Ⓗ
Fine ales, high-quality food and a warm welcome – what more could you ask for from a Black Country local? Recent enhancements and the pub's forward-looking approach have strengthened its grasp on traditional values. The front rooms house a wonderful beer bottle collection, including international as well as historic brews. The pub hosts a popular beer and music festival in October. ♨️🌰♿🍴🕕♿P💷🖳(246,256,257)

Starving Rascal 🍷 🛈
1 Brettell Lane, DY8 4BN
☼ 4 (12 Sat & Sun)-11 ⊕ starvingrascal.co.uk
Enville White, Ale; Holden's Golden Glow; guest beers Ⓗ
With an expansion in the real ale range on offer during 2012, this pub continues to go from strength

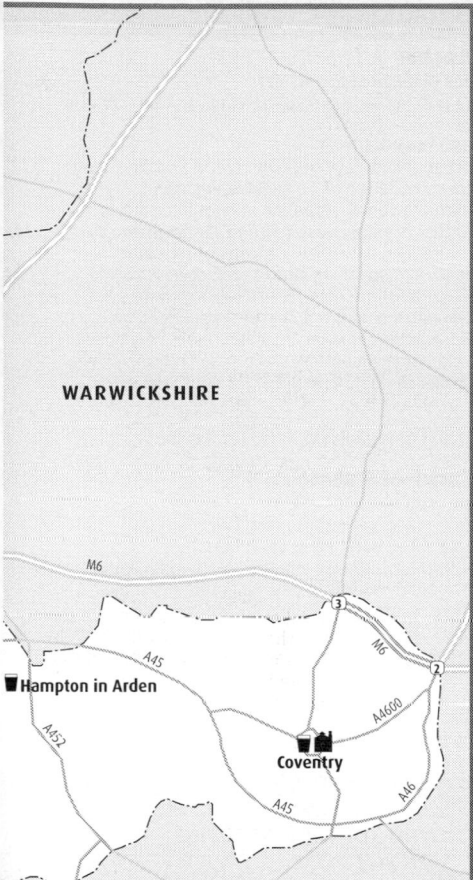

WARWICKSHIRE

M6

A45

M6

3

2

A4600

▼Hampton in Arden

A452

A45

A46

Coventry

🏚🏛

🌣 12-11 (midnight Fri & Sat) ☎ (0121) 440 1954
Enville Ale; Wye Valley Bitter; guest beers Ⓗ
Very traditional 19th-century multi-roomed inn,
well worth seeking out. Four real ales are always
on handpump. The two regular beers are
supplemented by a rotating Wye Valley beer plus a
further guest ale. Beer festivals are held four times
a year. The pub is well known for the good-value
Indian food that can be enjoyed every evening (no
food served Wed). The rear patio has recently been
enhanced by the addition of a log fire.
🏚🌣🅾◗🖪♣✣←🖪(50)

Birmingham: City Centre

Old Contemptibles Ⓛ
176 Edmund Street, B3 2HB (100yds from Snow Hill
station)
🌣 10 (12 Sat)-11; 12-6 Sun ☎ (0121) 200 3310
**Purity Pure Ubu; Sharp's Doom Bar; Thornbridge Lord
Marples; guest beers** Ⓗ
A welcome return to the Guide since this pub
became part of the Nicholson's chain. Named after
the famous World War I soldiers, this pub is very
popular with local office workers. The place
resembles a Victorian bar with its chandeliers and
leather settees. Good-quality food is served until
well into the evening and there is an impressive
wine list too. It has been known to close early if
there is not much custom.
◗▶➡(Snow Hill/New St)🖪(Snow Hill)♣🖪

Old Joint Stock Ⓛ
4 Temple Row West, B2 5NY (opp St Philip's Cathedral)
🌣 11-11; 12-5 Sun ☎ (0121) 200 1892
🌐 oldjointstocktheatre.co.uk
**Fuller's Chiswick Bitter, Discovery, London Pride, ESB;
Gale's HSB; guest beers** Ⓗ
Formerly the Old Joint Stock Bank, this imposing
Victorian Grade II-listed building boasts elaborate
features both externally and internally. Aside from
regular and seasonal Fuller's beers, the
management supports the LocAle scheme with
two or three guests. The theatre hosts
performances throughout the year and also
showcases local comedians and live jazz. Good-
quality food is served, with many pies on the
menu. There is a stairlift by the paved area at the
back down Wellington Passage.
🅾🌣◗♿➡(New St/Snow Hill)🖪(Snow Hill)←🖪

Post Office Vaults Ⓛ
84 New Street, B2 4BA (entrances are on both New St
and Pinfold St)
🌣 11-11 (midnight Fri & Sat); 12-11 Sun ☎ (0121) 643 7354
🌐 postofficevaults.co.uk
Hobsons Mild; Salopian Oracle; guest beers Ⓗ
This subterranean pub is a great place to visit for
connoisseurs of beer. Just minutes from New Street
station on the main pedestrianised shopping
street, its offerings more than make up for its
intimate size – an excellent range of eight real ales,
10 or more real ciders and perries and over 300
bottled beers from around the world is available.
The walls are adorned with pictures of old
Birmingham and the atmosphere is always
comfortable and friendly, with knowledgeable
staff.
Q➡(Moor St/New St/Snow Hill)🖪(Snow Hill)
♣●🖪

to strength. Two guest ales, sourced through the
SIBA direct delivery scheme, supplement the
regular beers; local ales, generally lighter in style,
are the order of the day. Sports TV is screened in
the front bar, with a quieter area in the rear
lounge. The pub stocks a large range of single malt
whiskies. 🏚♣🅿🖪(246)

Bilston

Trumpet Ⓛ
58 High Street, WV14 0EP
🌣 12-4, 7.30-11.30 ☎ (01902) 493723 🌐 trumpetjazz.org.uk
**Holden's Black Country Mild, Black Country Bitter,
Golden Glow, Special; guest beer** Ⓗ
Welcoming one-room local with jazz the main
feature seven nights per week and also Sunday
lunchtimes. The award-winning ales and the live
music draw in customers from around the area.
Music memorabilia of all styles and eras lines the
walls. A collection plate for donations is handed
around when the bands are playing. The venue is a
five- to 10-minute walk from the bus and Metro
stations. 🌣🖪(Central)←🖪

Birmingham: Balsall Heath

Old Moseley Arms Ⓛ
53 Tindal Street, B12 9QU (400yds off Moseley Road)

Prince Of Wales Ⓛ

84 Cambridge Street, B1 2NP (behind ICC/NIA and Rep Theatre)
✪ 11-11 (1am Thu; 2am Fri & Sat); 12-11 Sun
☎ (0121) 643 9460 ⊕ theprinceofwalesbirmingham.co.uk
Caledonian Deuchars IPA; Enville Ale; Purity Mad Goose; St Austell Tribute; Taylor Landlord; Tetley Mild; guest beers Ⓗ
Tastefully restored Victorian back-street pub that is always popular with the locals, visitors to the Symphony Hall, and anyone who loves live music. The one-roomed interior is a quirky blend of modern and traditional, with an L-shaped bar where eight handpulls take prominence. The toilets are interesting too. Freshly cooked pub favourites grace the menu, with a curry night on Wednesdays. Live music takes place every Sunday 4-7pm, with open-mic on Thursdays, when the pub can get very busy. ◖Ⅾ&⇌(New St)⊟

Square Peg Ⓛ

115 Corporation Street, B4 6PH
✪ 7am-midnight (1am Fri & Sat) ☎ (0121) 236 6530
Greene King Abbot; Marston's Pedigree; Ruddles Best Bitter; guest beers Ⓗ
Much-improved Wetherspoon outlet in the heart of the central drinking circuit. Sited in the former Lewis's department store, it boasts the longest bar in Birmingham at 82½ feet. It can get very crowded after work, and on Friday and Saturday evenings. Consistently improving beer quality enables this pub to make its Guide debut. A community noticeboard is on display. The food is typical Wetherspoon's fayre.
◖Ⅾ&⇌(Snow Hill)⊟(Snow Hill)●⊟

Victoria

48 John Bright Street, B1 1BN (next to stage door of Alexandra Theatre)
✪ 12-midnight (2am Fri & Sat) ☎ (0121) 633 9439
⊕ thevictoriabirmingham.co.uk
Wye Valley Butty Bach; guest beers Ⓗ
A theatre pub dating back to the 19th century, decorated with an eclectic mix of modern art and Victoriana. It also has its own ghost. Part of the Birmingham-based Bitters & Twisted mini-chain, it offers four ales including Wye Valley, Thornbridge and Dark Star. It serves excellent good-value food by the Soul Food Project, inspired by America's deep south, as well as a quirky twist on the classic British roast. It has live bands, DJs and quiz nights, and gets very busy on weekend nights.
◖Ⅾ⇌(New St/Moor St)⊟⊟

Wellington 🍺 Ⓛ

37 Bennetts Hill, B2 5SN (5 mins from New St and Snow Hill stations)
✪ 10-midnight ☎ (0121) 200 3115
⊕ thewellingtonrealale.co.uk
Black Country Bradley's Finest Golden, Pig on the Wall; Oakham Citra; Purity Mad Goose; Wye Valley HPA; guest beers Ⓗ
Highly successful pub voted local CAMRA Pub of the Year many times – it is like a permanent beer festival, with 16 ales and three ciders always on sale. The Wellie attracts a diverse customer base and is always friendly. Cheese nights, quiz nights and beer festivals are held throughout the year. The former offices above the pub have been acquired for additional bar space plus a meeting room. The pub does not sell food but customers are welcome to bring their own.
Q⇌(New St/Snow Hill)⊟(Snow Hill)♣●⊱⊟

Birmingham: Digbeth

Anchor ★ Ⓛ

308 Bradford Street, B5 6ET
✪ 11-11 (midnight Fri & Sat); 12-11 Sun ☎ (0121) 622 4516
⊕ anchorinndigbeth.co.uk
Beer range varies Ⓗ
Always a firm favourite with real ale drinkers for its changing range of 13 guest beers from microbreweries, alongside at least three ciders, the Anchor is within easy reach of Birmingham city centre, and extremely convenient for Digbeth coach station, being almost next door. A traditional Grade II-listed venue, it has been identified by CAMRA as one of Britain's Best Real Heritage Pubs. Close to Birmingham City ground, it is very popular with home supporters and can be particularly busy on match days. ⊞⇌(New St/Moor St)♣●⊱⊟

Birmingham: Gosta Green

Sacks of Potatoes Ⓛ

10 Gosta Green, B4 7ER
✪ 11 (12 Sun)-11 ☎ (0121) 503 5811
Wye Valley Butty Bach; guest beers Ⓗ
A lively pub run by a real ale enthusiast on the Aston University campus. Alongside guest ales there is always a rotating LocAle and a real cider/perry. The pub is popular with students and local office staff. The U-shaped counter has ample room and plenty of stools, with seating areas all around. Tables outside offer views overlooking the campus. Silent TV screens feature sport, and you can get good-value food at reasonable prices. The landlady hosts beer festivals throughout the year.
❀◖Ⅾ&⇌(Snow Hill)⊟(Snow Hill)♣●P⊱⊟(66)

Birmingham: Harborne

Bell

11 Old Church Road, B17 0BB
✪ 11.30-midnight ☎ (0121) 428 4609
Beer range varies Ⓗ
Tucked away off the beaten track by St Peter's, a Norman-style church, this is a small, scenic pub with a small bar and serving hatch to the snug at the back, and a through lounge. It is very pleasant

INDEPENDENT BREWERIES

Angel Halesowen
Backyard Walsall
Banks's (Marston's) Wolverhampton
Batham Brierley Hill
Beer Geek Birmingham: Aston
Black Country Lower Gornal
Broughs Wolverhampton
Byatt's Coventry
Craddock's Stourbridge
Fownes Upper Gornal (NEW)
Green Duck Stourbridge
Hearsall Coventry (NEW)
Holden's Woodsetton
Olde Swan Netherton
Rainbow Coventry (NEW)
Rock & Roll Birmingham
Sadler's Lye
Sarah Hughes Sedgley
Shed Solihull (NEW)
Toll End Tipton
Two Towers Birmingham: Hockley
Whitworth Shirley

to sit outside on those rare warm summer nights. A picturesque, unusual-shaped bowling green at the rear is now back in use. It has a small but changing beer range and popular food, including grill night on Thursdays. A quiz night is held every Sunday. ⏳🕮🌠🅑♣🅿♨

Green Man L
2 High Street, B17 9NE
✪ 11.30-11 (1am Fri & Sat) ☎ (0121) 428 3581
Purity Pure Ubu; guest beers 🅗
A M&B community pub furnished like other Ember Inns, which usually has a full range of ales. Busy and bustling due to its convenient situation on the High Street, it boasts a good-value food menu served daily until 10pm. There is a heated smoking area in the rear car park. The patio at the front can be pleasant in summer. Quiz nights are held every Sunday and Wednesday. It is ideally placed for the start of a pub crawl. ♨⏳🕮🅒🅑🦽♨🚃(22,23,24)

Harborne Club L
39 Albany Road, B17 9JX (200yds down road, last house on left)
✪ 12.30-3.30 (not Mon-Fri), 5.30-midnight (not Sun)
☎ (0121) 427 1638 ⊕ theharborneclub.co.uk
Beer range varies 🅗
Beneath its inconspicuous exterior lies a friendly interior with a small bar and comfortable, homely decor. A snooker room is upstairs. Two excellent-quality LocAles are always on and the support of CAMRA members is always appreciated by this private club tucked away off the main High Street. It is worth noting that the club does not open until 5.30pm on weekday evenings. TVs can show major sporting events. The Harborne Club welcomes CAMRA members – sign the attendance book for entry. ♣🚃(22,23,24)

Junction
212 High Street, B17 9PT
✪ 12-11; 11-midnight Thu & Fri; 10-midnight Sat; 11-11 Sun
☎ (0121) 428 2635 ⊕ thejunctionharborne.co.uk
Purity Mad Goose; guest beers 🅗
A distinctive Edwardian building that dominates the High Street. Inside there is a sophisticated feel to the decor – it has a tiled bar area with seating leading to a further main dining area. A changing beer range of up to six ales is offered, and quality food is served from an open-plan kitchen, with home-cooked roasts on Sundays. A pleasant, secluded beer garden is at the rear. Quiz night is every Monday. ♨🕮🅒🦽♨🚃(22,23,24)

White Horse L
2 York Street, B17 0HG
✪ 11 (12 Mon)-11.30; 11-12.30am Fri & Sat; 12-11.30 Sun
☎ (0121) 427 8004 ⊕ whitehorseharborne.com
Greene King Abbot; Wye Valley HPA; guest beers 🅗
A free house that has been much improved and extended over recent years. The emphasis is on real ale, complete with an electronic beer board linked to its website. There is an island bar with a front snug and a heated area at the rear. Regular live music nights are Friday and Saturday, sport is shown on TV, and quiz nights are every Tuesday and Thursday. The artwork on the walls is by local artists (some by the landlord) and is for sale. 🅑♨♨🚃(22,23,24)

Birmingham: Highgate

Lamp L
157 Barford Street, B5 6AH (500yds from A441 Pershore Rd near bottom of Hurst St)
✪ 12-11 ☎ (0121) 688 1220
Everards Tiger; Stanway Stanney Bitter; guest beers 🅗
Brewery tap and home to the Rock and Roll Brewery which was opened on the pub roof in 2012, with at least one house beer always available. This single-roomed pub is a vintage regular Guide entry, and Eddie the landlord has chalked up more than 20 years at the bar. A warm welcome awaits at this sadly rare example of the kind of small local pub that once graced every Birmingham street corner. ⇌(New St)🚃(35,45,47)

Birmingham: Hockley

Black Eagle L
16 Factory Road, B18 5JU (turn right out of Soho Benson Rd Metro station, cross road and walk 200yds)
✪ 11-3, 5.30-11; 11-11 Fri; 12-3, 7-11 Sat; 12-3 Sun
☎ (0121) 523 4008 ⊕ blackeaglepub.co.uk
Bathams Best Bitter; Holden's Golden Glow; Marston's Pedigree; Taylor Landlord; guest beers 🅗
Multi award-winning traditional pub that is an oasis in a desert, run by the same landlord for 23 years. The excellent restaurant at the rear serves traditional, home-cooked, good-value food. The beer garden is very popular in the summer, and hosts an annual beer festival in July. A changing range of two real ciders is available. As well as the regular beers, three guest ales are on handpump. ♨⏳🕮🅒🅑🚃(Soho Benson Rd)🍴♨🚃(74,75)

Lord Clifden
34 Great Hampton Street, B18 6AA
✪ 10-midnight ☎ (0121) 523 7515
Wye Valley HPA; guest beers 🅗
Its simple exterior belies what this pub has to offer. The interior is eclectic but comfortable, with walls adorned with urban art by Banksy. The large suntrap garden has table football and table tennis, and holds a beer festival in July. Sport is shown on a number of screens in the front bar and garden. Good-quality food, especially an interesting selection of burgers, is served all day. 🕮🅒🅑🦽⇌(Jewellery Quarter)🚃(Jewellery Quarter)♣🍴♨🚃

Red Lion L
94-95 Warstone Lane, B18 6NG
✪ 10-midnight (2am Fri & Sat) ☎ (0121) 233 9144
⊕ theredlionbirmingham.com
Bathams Best Bitter; guest beers 🅗
Traditional two-roomed pub close to the heart of the Jewellery Quarter with a smart, quirky feel, a lively front bar and a cosy, secluded back lounge. Excellent fresh food is served all day, with the Cow Club on Monday a highlight. There are three changing guest beers and two regularly changing ciders. A good-sized function room is available and there is a very well-appointed patio and smoking area to the rear. Regular quiz nights are held. 🕮🅒🅑⇌(Jewellery Quarter)🚃(Jewellery Quarter)🍴♨🚃(8,101)

Birmingham: King's Heath

King's Heath Cricket & Sports Club
Charlton House, 247 Alcester Road South, B14 6DT

✪ 12-midnight ☎ (0121) 444 1913
⊕ kingsheathsportsclub.co.uk
Greene King IPA; Wye Valley HPA, Butty Bach; guest beers ⊞
Welcoming sports club with two rooms: the comfortable lounge for relaxed drinking, the large room for watching sporting events on wide screens and also housing two full-size snooker tables. Beer festivals are held in April and December as well as other social events, including live music. CAMRA members are welcome on production of a membership card (maximum 10 visits a year). The beer range always includes a rotating guest ale, with a minimum of five real ales available.
✪⬤⬤🍴♣P¹⊟(18,50)

Pear Tree ℒ

25-27 Alcester Road South, B14 7JQ
✪ 9-11.30 (midnight Thu; 1am Fri & Sat) ☎ (0121) 441 6710
Greene King Abbot; Ruddles County; guest beers ⊞
An excellent Wetherspoon outlet run by an enthusiastic manager who is a keen CAMRA member. At least four guest ales are available, plus a selection of real ciders/perries. The guest beers are highly driven by the LocAle policy and many local beers feature. The building is a former bank and very accessible by local transport. In winter months a large gas fire in the middle of the pub gives an open-fire impression. Food is the standard Wetherspoon fayre. ⤳⬤♿♣⬤⊟

Red Lion ℒ

229 Vicarage Road, B14 7LY
✪ 11.30-11 (midnight Thu-Sat); 11-11 Sun
☎ (0121) 444 2803
M&B Brew XI; guest beers ⊞
Grade II-listed imposing neo-Gothic pub built in 1908 with a comfortable open-plan design and a central bar decorated to the Ember Inns style. The upstairs function room hosts a Wednesday folk club and regular bands throughout the year. Quizzes are held Sundays and Thursdays, and a poker night on Mondays. Pub meals dominate the usual Ember Inns menu. ⤳✪⬤♿P⊟(11,35)

Birmingham: Moseley

Prince of Wales ℒ

118 Alcester Road, B13 8EE
✪ 12-11.30 (1am Fri & Sat) ☎ (0121) 449 4198
⊕ theprincemoseley.co.uk
Castle Rock Harvest Pale; Oakham Bishops Farewell; Purity Mad Goose; St Austell Tribute; Sharp's Doom Bar; Taylor Landlord; guest beers ⊞
A traditional pub with a few surprises. A large, welcoming bar greets visitors on entering, warmed by a roaring fire in winter. As well as the extensive listed beer range, two further house beers plus two real ciders are also on sale, along with a range of around 30 bottled Belgian beers. The pub features three rooms in total and, to the rear, a large covered and heated beer garden with a dedicated cigar room. ♨Q✪⬤⬤¹⊟(50)

Birmingham: Newtown

Bartons Arms ★

144 High Street, B6 4UP (at A34/B4144 jct, opposite Newtown Baths)
✪ 12-11 ☎ (0121) 333 5988 ⊕ bartons-arms.co.uk
Oakham JHB, Inferno, Citra, Bishops Farewell; guest beer ⊞
Oakham Brewery's only pub in the West Midlands, the Bartons Arms is a truly beautiful building with original Jacobean styling and Minton Hollins tiles throughout. Identified by CAMRA as one of Britain's Best Real Heritage pubs the 1901 interior is Grade II-listed. Features include a central tiled staircase and a rare tile painting. Superb Thai food is served all week and families are welcome to dine in the lounge. A range of Oakham ales and one guest ale are available. Ciders are from Westons.
♨Q⤳⬤🖳(St Paul's)⬤P⊟(33,51)

Birmingham: Northfield

Black Horse ★ ℒ

Bristol Road South, B31 2QT (opp Sainsbury's)
✪ 8am-11 (1am Fri & Sat; midnight Sun) ☎ (0121) 477 1800
Greene King Abbot; Purity Pure Ubu; Ruddles Best Bitter; guest beers ⊞
Identified by CAMRA as one of Britain's Best Real Heritage Pubs this was a failing local, which many people felt was unfriendly, until it was rescued by a £2.5 million refurbishment by Wetherspoon. It is a welcome outlet for real ale in a poorly served area of the city. The beer quality has consistently improved. Unusually for a Wetherspoon establishment, it has a multi-room interior with bars on two levels. A magnificent 1929 'Brewers Tudor' roadhouse, it has an outdoor smoking area and a bowling green to the rear.
✪⬤♿⇋♣⬤P⊟

Bloxwich

Turf Tavern ★

13 Wolverhampton Road, WS3 2EZ (opp Bloxwich Park)
✪ 7-11 (10 Mon); 12-2.30, 7-11 Fri & Sat; 12-2.30, 7-10.30 Sun ☎ (01922) 407745
Holden's Black Country Mild; Oakham Bishops Farewell; Otter Bright; guest beers ⊞
A Grade II-listed building, this unspoilt gem is known locally as Tinky's after a former licensee, and has been in the same family since around 1875. A tiled floor is a feature of the bar, while the other two rooms are steeped in nostalgia and offer a haven for those who enjoy a quiet drink and the art of conversation. An outside courtyard serves as a pleasant summer drinking area. Not to be missed. ♨Q⤳✪⬤♿⇋¹⊟(301)

Boldmere

Bishop Vesey ♥ ℒ

63 Boldmere Road, B73 5UY
✪ 8-11 (midnight Fri & Sat) ☎ (0121) 355 5077
Backyard Blonde; Greene King Abbot; Purity Mad Goose; Ruddles Best Bitter; guest beers ⊞
Boasting 13 consecutive years in the Guide and local CAMRA Pub of the Year 2012 and 2013, this busy Wetherspoon pub has a loyal local clientele and a thriving darts team. It comprises an open-plan layout with upstairs seating and an outside patio/smokers' area. Children are welcome in the family area until 9pm. Up to five guest beers, many from local micros, together with regular beer festivals, make this a JDW not to miss.
⤳✪⬤♿¹⊟

Brierley Hill

Vine

10 Delph Road, DY5 2TN

✪ 12-11 (10.30 Sun) ☎ (01384) 78293
Bathams Mild Ale, Best Bitter Ⓗ
Classic, unspoilt brewery tap with an ornately
decorated façade proclaiming the Shakespearian
quotation: 'Blessing of your heart, you brew good
ale'. Step inside and you enter an elongated pub
with a labyrinthine feel. The rooms have
contrasting characters. The front bar is small and
staunchly traditional, while the larger rear bar with
its own servery and leather seating houses the
dartboard. On the other side of the central
passageway is a homely lounge partly converted
from former brewery offices.
🏚Q🕏⭐◖🝖♣P'–🖵(X96)

Brownhills

Royal Oak Ⓛ
68 Chester Road, WS8 6DU (on A452 approx 500yds
from Anchor Bridge towards Shire Oak)
✪ 12-11 (midnight Thu-Sun) ☎ (01543) 452089
⊕ theroyaloakpub.co.uk
Purity Mad Goose; Taylor Landlord; guest beers Ⓗ
Known locally as the Middle Oak, this 1937 Art
Deco-style pub is set back from the main road. The
traditional bar plays host to darts and dominoes
teams while the very comfortable lounge provides
a more relaxed atmosphere. The pub also boasts its
own skittle alley, a separate dining room and a
patio drinking area leading to a large garden. Food
is served lunchtimes and evenings (except Sun
eve). 🏚🕏⭐◖🝖♣'–🖵(10,33,56)

Swan
Pelsall Road, WS8 7DL
✪ 4 (2 Fri; 12 Sat & Sun)-midnight ☎ (01543) 820628
Holden's Golden Glow; guest beer Ⓗ
Reopened in 2011 after a spell of closure, this is a
two-roomed community focused pub served by a
central bar. It has a larger bar area and a small
lounge divided into two separate areas, the smaller
of which houses a pool table. There is an outside
drinking area at the front of the pub. The Swan has
been refurbished throughout and is a very
welcoming venue attracting both locals and
visitors. 🕏⭐🝖♣P

Coseley

Old Chainyard Ⓛ
63 Castle Street, WV14 9DW
✪ 11-2.30, 5-11; 12-4, 7-11 Sat; 12-4 Sun ☎ (01902) 256359
Beer range varies Ⓗ
Single-roomed community pub brought back from
the brink by enterprising young tenants. There is an
open mic night every other Monday and things get
livelier and louder on Friday and Saturday
evenings. Beer festivals are held twice yearly. The
house beer, Anvil Ale, is from Kinver Brewery.
🕏⭐≂♣●P'–🖵(81)

Coventry

Boat Ⓛ
31 Shilton Lane, Walsgrave, CV2 2AB
✪ 11 (12 Sun)-midnight ☎ (024) 7661 2191
Draught Bass; Thwaites Original; guest beers Ⓗ
Charming Victorian pub sympathetically
refurbished eight years ago. Two regular and
between two and five guest ales are available in
the public bar and lounge. There are two additional
rooms: one was once used for smoking meat (the

meat hooks are still visible), the other is a quiet
snug. Pictures adorn the walls which add to the
Victorian character. The pub hosts darts and
dominoes teams in local leagues. Children are
welcome when dining until 9.30pm (no food Sun
eves). Free Wi-Fi is available. ⭐◖🝖♣P'–🖵(30)

Broomfield Tavern Ⓛ
14-16 Broomfield Place, Spon End, CV5 6GY (adjacent
to the rugby ground)
✪ 12-11 (1am Fri; 2am Sat; 10.30 Sun) ☎ (024) 7663 0969
Draught Bass; guest beers Ⓗ
In a quiet area adjacent to the main road, with car
parking, overlooking the park. An increasing
number of handpumps dispense the unusual
Church End Low Rider and guest beers (often Sarah
Hughes Dark Ruby) along with three traditional
ciders/perries from small producers. Regular
festivals feature more beers on additional
handpumps. Live blues/rock music is on Fridays,
karaoke on Saturdays, acoustic folk on Mondays,
bluegrass on Thursdays, and a quiz on Wednesdays.
On Sundays good-value lunches are normally
available up to 3.30pm. 🏚🕏⭐♣●'–🖵(6,6Λ,10)

City Arms Ⓛ
1 Earlsdon Street, Earlsdon, CV5 6EP (on roundabout at
centre of Earlsdon)
✪ 8-midnight (1am Fri & Sat) ☎ (024) 7671 8170
**Greene King Abbot; Ruddles Best Bitter; guest
beers** Ⓗ
Large open-plan mock Tudor-style pub located on a
prominent site in the centre of Earlsdon. Plenty of
seating is available, and there is a partly covered
outdoor area. It attracts a varied clientele and is
very busy at weekends. Part of the Wetherspoon
chain, it sells more real ale than its three sister
pubs in the city. Recent improvements to the cellar
have enabled the pub to cope better with the
turnover of ales. ⭐◖🖐●P'–🖵(5,12)

Establishment Ⓛ
51 Bayley Lane, CV1 5RN (between cathedral and Holy
Trinity church)
✪ 11-11 (midnight Thu; 2am Fri & Sat); 10-11 Sun
☎ (024) 7622 2727 ⊕ establishmentbars.co.uk
**Byatt's Coventry Bitter; Sharp's Doom Bar; guest
beers** Ⓗ
Situated in the cobbled streets of the cathedral
quarter, it is set in the Old County Hall which dates
back to 1783 and used to be the main court in
Coventry. The building is infamous as the place
where the last public hanging took place. Features
from the old courtroom have been beautifully
restored, including the judge's seat and the crown
crest along with the viewing gallery and the dock.
The cells have been transformed into a dining area.
🕏⭐◖🖐'–🖵

Gatehouse Tavern Ⓛ
46 Hill Street, CV1 4AN (close to Belgrade Theatre and
Spon St, near jct 8 of ring road)
✪ 11-11 (midnight Thu-Sat); 12-10.30 Sun
☎ (024) 7663 0140 ⊕ gatehousetavern.com
Beer range varies Ⓗ
A pub reconstructed by the landlord in the '90s
from the long-disused gatehouse of textile
company Leigh Mills. It is now a thriving free house
serving a changing range of six real ales, including
LocAles. There is a large garden, unusual for a city-
centre pub, which is popular in summer. The
stained glass windows, depicting the Six Nations,
are an indication of the sporting leanings of this

pub, with major events being shown, especially rugby and speedway plus the ubiquitous football. ⊛◑☙⌐☖

Greyhound Inn ♀

Sutton Stop, Hawkesbury Junction, CV6 6DF (off Grange Rd at jct of Coventry and Oxford canals)
✪ 11-11; 12-10.30 Sun ☎ (024) 7636 3046
⊕ greyhoundinn.org
Draught Bass; Marston's Pedigree; guest beers Ⓗ
Voted local CAMRA Pub of the Year consecutively 2010-2013, it is also a four-times winner of the Godiva Award for the best pub in Coventry & Warwickshire. Dating from circa 1930, it has a terrace overlooking the junction of two canals. An extensive menu of freshly cooked food is available. A separate beer garden bar serves two real ales. Two beer festivals are staged a year. It is a pleasant 25-minute canalside walk from the Ricoh Arena. ⋈Q⊛◑♣☙P⌐

Hearsall Inn Ⓛ

45 Craven Street, Chapelfields, CV5 8DS (1 mile W of city centre, off Allesley Old Road)
✪ 11.30 (11 Sun)-11 ☎ (024) 7671 5729 ⊕ hearsallinn.com
Church End Goats Milk; Draught Bass; Hearsall Chapelfields Bitter; guest beer Ⓗ
Popular and dynamic community local situated in the historic watchmaking area. The pub is home to darts and football teams, and hosts traditional Irish music including tuition sessions on Tuesday evenings. One of the few free houses in Coventry, it has four handpumps with a tendency towards locally produced beers, one of which is brewed on the premises. ⋈☎⊛⊟♣☙⌐☖(6,6A,10)

Nursery Tavern

38-39 Lord Street, Chapelfields, CV5 8DA (1 mile W of city centre, off Allesley Old Road)
✪ 12-11.30 (midnight Fri & Sat; 11 Sun) ☎ (024) 7667 4530
Courage Best Bitter; Fuller's London Pride; Hook Norton Hooky Mild, Hooky Bitter; guest beers Ⓗ
Community pub in the old watchmaking quarter which stocks seven beers and has interesting rugby union and Formula 1 paraphernalia. It has two front rooms served by a central bar. Free-to-enter music nights feature regularly in the third room at the rear, which also hosts monthly quizzes and doubles as a restaurant on Sunday lunchtime, offering great-value roasts. Beer festivals have been held in the rear garden every June and December for over 20 years. Q☎⊛◑♣☙⌐☖(6,6A,10)

Old Windmill

22-23 Spon Street, CV1 3BA (in mediaeval Spon St, behind IKEA)
✪ 3-11 Mon; 11-1am; 12-midnight Sun ☎ (024) 7625 1717
Morland Old Speckled Hen; Purity Mad Goose; Sharp's Doom Bar; Taylor Landlord; Theakston Old Peculier; Wychwood Hobgoblin; guest beer Ⓗ
Beers include one from the local brewery, Purity; these are supplemented by two traditional ciders and a perry. Regular beer festivals add to the range. Built in the late-15th century on this site, the pub now stands among many other historic buildings moved to this street. It was sympathetically modified in the 1980s to increase the public spaces, enlarge the bar, and to incorporate an external brewhouse inside the pub; it retains a lot of the characteristic separate areas of the original building. ⋈◑☙⌐☖

Rose & Woodbine

40 North Street, Stoke Heath, CV2 3FW (Stoke area of city)
✪ 12-11 (11.30 Fri-Sun) ☎ (024) 7645 1480
⊕ roseandwoodbine.co.uk
Beer range varies Ⓗ
A friendly local community pub that allows children up until 7pm and permits well-behaved dogs. Good-value food is served 12-4pm Tuesday to Saturday. Events including a disco night, quiz nights and bingo are held weekly. Originally a butcher's shop, it is now owned by the Northampton Brewing Company. ⋈☞⊛◑⊟♣☙⌐☖(6,6A,10)

Town Wall Tavern

Bond Street, CV1 4AH (behind Belgrade Theatre)
✪ 12-11 (midnight Fri & Sat; 6.30 Sun) ☎ (024) 7622 0963
⊕ townwalltavern.co.uk
Adnams Southwold Bitter, Broadside; Caledonian Deuchars IPA; Draught Bass; guest beer Ⓗ
Traditional pub inside the city ring road serving a fine selection of ales, Old Rosie cider, and up to three guest beers in different styles. Good home-cooked food is available; it is convenient for early pre-theatre supper, but only does lunch on Mondays and traditional roasts on Sundays. There are discreet smaller areas for eating and drinking in the lounge, while the public bar is popular with regulars. Both have real fires. Note the donkey box snug and Atkinsons window within the lounge. There is a small smoking patio. No under-18s. ⋈☎◑⊟☙⌐☖

Whitefriars Olde Ale House

114-115 Gosford Street, CV1 5DL
✪ 12-midnight (1am Fri & Sat; 11 Sun) ☎ (024) 7625 1655
Sharp's Doom Bar; guest beers Ⓗ
A 14th-century building once part of the Whitefriars monastery, subsequently a butcher's shop before being renovated and made into a pub. The small front room used to be the friars' kitchen, now with a welcoming fire in the winter months. Eight frequently changing guest ales are available. Beer festivals offering cider and perry and featuring live music are held regularly. Live music also plays on some Saturday evenings and can be rather loud. No food on Sundays. ⋈☎◑♣☙⌐☖(8,9)

Dorridge

Forest Hotel

25 Station Approach, B93 8JA (in centre of Dorridge, opp railway station)
✪ 11-11 (midnight Thu-Sat; 10.30 Sun) ☎ (01564) 772120
⊕ forest-hotel.com
Hook Norton Hooky Bitter; Wye Valley HPA; guest beer Ⓗ
Victorian hotel with a bar room decorated in a contemporary, eclectic style with polished wooden tables, armchairs and sofas. The restaurant specialises in fine dining and meals are also served in the bar. There is a large, partly-covered outdoor seating area with several patio heaters. A cider and ale festival is held in July and a real ale festival in November. Free Wi-Fi is available. Voted Most Improved Pub 2012 by the local CAMRA branch. ⊛⇔◑⌖♣⇌P⌐☖(S2,S3)

Dudley

Court House [L]

30 New Street, DY1 1LP (a short walk from bus station towards police station)

☼ 12-11 (10.30 Sun) ☎ (01384) 240062

Black Country Bradley's Finest Golden, Pig on the Wall, Fireside; guest beers [H]

Run by Black Country Traditional Inns as a specialist real ale pub, the regular beers come from the company's own brewery alongside a large selection of guest ales from across the country. The pub has developed a reputation for regularly offering a dark beer. Cider drinkers are well catered for with a choice of four ciders. The small snug and the large upstairs function room complement the facilities. CAMRA Cider Pub of the Year 2012 and 2013. Q⌂&♣♠🖵(1)

Fellows

1 The Broadway, DY1 4QD

☼ 12-11 (midnight Fri & Sat; 10 Sun) ☎ (01384) 243600

⊕ thefellowsdudley.co.uk

Holden's Black Country Bitter, Golden Glow, Special [H]

Grade II-listed building close to the centre of Dudley, the bus station and Dudley Zoo. It has a modern café-style bar with a separate restaurant area. Most of Holden's Brewery beers are on draught, with Black Country Mild available in bottles. Meals are served 12-8pm Monday-Wednesday, 12-9pm Thursday-Saturday and 12-6pm Sunday. ♨⌂⛵❶&P⅃🖵(1,126)

Lamp Tavern [L]

116 High Street, DY1 1QT

☼ 12-11 (10.30 Sun) ☎ (01384) 254129

Bathams Mild Ale, Best Bitter [H]

Classic Batham's pub with a large front bar with traditional games and a cosy back room with a more relaxed feel. The old Queen's Cross Brewery has been converted into a large function room available for hire and staging music nights. An outside area for drinking overlooks the southern area of the Black Country to the Clent Hills beyond. B&B accommodation is in the adjacent Lamp Cottage (CAMRA members are offered a discount – ring for details). ♨⌂⛵❶&♣P⅃🖵

Four Oaks

Butlers Arms

444 Lichfield Road, B74 4BL (near corner with Butlers Lane)

☼ 12-11 (midnight Fri & Sat; 10.30 Sun) ☎ (0121) 308 0765

⊕ butlersarms.co.uk

Beer range varies [H]

A spacious car park, nearby bus stop and train station at Butlers Lane attract the voyagers. The interior is an eclectic mix of styles with lamps, mirrors and curiosities reflecting the landlord's inimitable taste. Four guest beers vary but include a beer from Caledonian and Greene King Abbot. The succulent food comes by way of a chalkboard full of fish specials and a menu with meat and vegetarian alternatives at great prices. This is a family-run pub with great staff and a comfortable feel. Q⌂⛵❶&≈(Butlers Lane)P⅃🖵(112,966,905)

Crown

66 Walsall Road, B74 4RA

☼ 11.30-midnight ☎ (0121) 323 2715

Greene King IPA; Taylor Landlord; Thornbridge Lord Marples; guest beers [H]

Welcoming Ember Inn with up to six real ales from far and wide, all tasting tip-top. This imposing pub with a large car park is fronted by flower borders, shrubs and heated patio areas. Inside it is spacious but with a warm, friendly atmosphere. Good food for all tastes is served until 10pm by attentive staff. A great community spirit is cemented by local events such as beer and wine tasting and charity fundraisers. ♨⌂⛵❶&≈(Butlers Lane)♣P⅃🖵(366)

Halesowen

Coombs Wood Sports & Social Club

Stewarts Road, B62 8NA (just off A4034 Long Lane, towards Blackheath)

☼ 6.30-midnight (11 Mon); 4-midnight Fri; 12.30-1am Sat; 12-midnight Sun ☎ (0121) 561 1932 ⊕ coombswood.co.uk

Beer range varies [H]

This members' club has moved from its pavilion into a brand new purpose-built club house. It is a thriving, welcoming, family-friendly club that also hosts bowls and darts teams, and for the spectator the mega-TV shows Premier League football. Up to seven beers are available, often from small brewers, growing to 12 during the beer festival in late January when more than 30 beers are served over the weekend. You can get bar snacks at the weekends. Current CAMRA branch Club of the Year – show a CAMRA membership card or this Guide for entry. ⌂⛵❶&≈(Rowley Regis)♣♠P⅃🖵(140,241)

Hawne Tavern [L]

76 Attwood Street, B63 3UG (just off Stourbridge Rd, down Short St opp Tesco Express)

☼ 4.30 (12 Sat)-11; 12-10.30 Sun ☎ (0121) 602 2601

Banks's Bitter; Bathams Best Bitter; Bob's White Lion; guest beers [H]

A back-street locals' pub just off the main bus route. The large bar has a pool table and TV showing sport, and separate seating areas. The lounge is smaller and cosier. There are three regular and up to six guest ales, many of which are from microbreweries, with northern beers a speciality. Baguettes are served in the evenings; hot sandwiches and chips are available at weekends. The enclosed rear garden is ideal for smokers and sun worshippers. Q⌂⛵❶♣⅃🖵(9)

Somers Sports & Social Club

2 Grange Hill, B62 0JH (at A456/B4551 jct)

☼ 12-2.30, 6-11; 12-11 Sat & Sun ☎ (0121) 550 1645

⊕ somersclub.co.uk

Bathams Best Bitter; Enville Ale; Holden's Black Country Bitter; Olde Swan Original; Wye Valley HPA; guest beers [H]

Grade II*-listed building set in acres of landscaped grounds. The long bar features 11 beers including six guests, many local, usually with one from Oakham. The lounge overlooks the large garden, which has a children's play area and a crown green bowling green. Three times winner of CAMRA's national Club of the Year, CAMRA members are welcome to visit – large groups should phone ahead. Lunchtime pub food is served (not Sun). See the website for details of the regular evening entertainment. ♨Q⌂⛵&♣P⅃🖵(9,241)

Waggon & Horses 𝕃

21 Stourbridge Road, B63 3TU (on main A458, ½ mile from bus station)
⏲ 12-11.30 (12.30am Fri & Sat) ☎ (0121) 550 4989
🌐 waggonales.co.uk
Bathams Best Bitter; Bob's White Lion; Holden's Golden Glow; Nottingham Extra Pale Ale; Oakham Inferno; guest beers Ⓗ
A thoroughly welcoming pub with an enviable reputation for a wide selection of expertly kept beers. Fourteen ales are always available, usually including a stout or a mild, plus real cider and draught Belgian beers. The traditional interior comprises a long bar flanked by quieter seating areas at both ends. Top-quality home-made hot and cold food is now served Monday to Saturday 12-6.30pm – later on Monday and Wednesday – with regular steak and curry nights on Mondays. Q◑◐⊟●⊟(9)

Hampton in Arden

White Lion

10 High Street, B92 0AA (opp church) SP2025080820
⏲ 12-11 (midnight Thu-Sat); 12-10.30 Sun
☎ (01675) 442833 🌐 thewhitelioninn.com
Banks's Sunbeam; Hobsons Best Bitter; M&B Brew XI; Sharp's Doom Bar; Wychwood Hobgoblin Ⓗ
A charming 17th-century timber-framed building with Grade II status, the White Lion has been licensed since 1838. It has an L-shaped lounge and dining area with a separate public bar, with lovely real fires. The dining area is light, airy and open plan. Quality pub food with a French accent is served lunchtimes and evenings. The quantity and quality of real ales have improved since the current tenant took over in 2010, and it was voted Most Improved Pub 2011 by the local CAMRA branch. ♨Q❀⊨◑◐⊟♿⇌P⁵–⊟(82)

Kingswinford

Park Tavern 𝕃

182 Cot Lane, DY6 9QG (on corner of Cot Lane and Broad St)
⏲ 11-11 (1am Fri & Sat) ☎ (01384) 287178
Bathams Best Bitter; Enville Ale, Ginger Beer; Taylor Landlord; guest beers Ⓗ
Popular and lively old pub in the back streets of Kingswinford, currently serving six real ales. Opened as the Brickmakers Arms in 1855, it became the Park Tavern in 1859. The bar and lounge both have their own feel, but the TV does dominate when there are sporting events on. For the peckish try the selection of cobs. There is a patio at the rear for smokers and sports enthusiasts alike. A CAMRA discount applies for members. ❀⊟♣P⁵–⊟(226)

Knowle

Red Lion

1672 High Street, B93 0LY (in centre of Knowle, opp church)
⏲ 11.30-11 (midnight Fri & Sat) ☎ (01564) 771522
Greene King IPA; Purity Pure Ubu; guest beers Ⓗ
Large 17th-century Grade II-listed building with a single bar servicing a number of secluded areas within the pub. The interior has been extensively modernised while still retaining some of the original character, including exposed beams and a cast-iron fireplace dating from 1779. Three coal-effect gas fires add to the ambience. Up to four regularly changing guest ales are on offer along with standard Ember Inns food, available until 10pm daily. Q❀◑◐♿P⁵–⊟(S2,S3,88)

Vaults 🏆

St John's Close, B93 0JU (off High Street, A4141)
⏲ 12-2.30, 5-11; 12-11.30 Fri & Sat; 12-11 Sun
☎ (01564) 773656
Adnams Lighthouse; St Austell Tribute; Sharp's Doom Bar; Tetley Bitter; guest beers Ⓗ
Traditional pub that can be relied on for a wide range of quality real ales, as well as real cider from the Weston's range. In recent years it has been a regular winner of the local CAMRA branch Pub of the Year, and is a popular meeting place for those visiting the many local restaurants. Wi-Fi is available, and major sporting events are shown on ESPN Sports TV. Light meals are served 12-2pm Monday-Saturday. ◑●P⁵–⊟(S2,S3,88)

Lower Gornal

Black Bear

86 Deepdale Lane, DY3 2AE
⏲ 5 (4 Fri; 12 Sat)-11; 12-10.30 Sun ☎ (01384) 253333
Beer range varies Ⓗ
Once a farmhouse and now a traditional Black Country pub, serving at least four guest beers. The house beer is from Kinver. Subsidence has taken its toll and there is a distinct slope to the split-level interior; a large buttress supports the downhill exterior walls. Inside, the walls feature interesting local history prints. Views from the garden are stunning and dogs are welcome here. There are bus stops close by or you could choose to walk uphill from the Gornal Wood bus station. ♨❀♣⊟(27,257)

Five Ways Inn

375 Himley Road, DY3 2PZ (jct of B4176/4175, 3 mins from Gornal Wood bus station)
⏲ 9am-midnight (1am Fri & Sat) ☎ (01384) 252968
Bathams Best Bitter; guest beer Ⓗ
Family-friendly Gornal Wood corner house. It has one J-shaped room dividing the bar into two distinctive areas. The pub has a cottage-like feeling with a carpeted floor and mugs hanging from the ceiling. There is a raised concrete decking area overlooking the car park at the back. Buses 257 and 297 pass close by and Gornal Wood bus station is a short walk away. It opens at 9am for home-cooked breakfasts seven days a week. ♨♿♣P⊟(257,297)

Fountain

8 Temple Street, DY3 2PE (on B4157 5 mins from Gornal Wood bus station)
⏲ 12-11 (10.30 Sun) ☎ (01384) 242777
🌐 fountaininnrealale.co.uk
Greene King Abbot; Hobsons Town Crier; Morland Old Speckled Hen; RCH Pitchfork; guest beers Ⓗ
Serial Guide entry and twice winner of local CAMRA Pub of the Year. This excellent free house serves eight real ales accompanied by draught Belgian beers, a real cider and 12 fruit wines. The busy, vibrant bar is complemented by an elevated dining area serving excellent food weekday lunchtimes and evenings, all day Saturday, and Sunday lunches until 5pm. During the summer months the rear garden is a suntrap and a pleasant area to while away an hour or two. ♉❀◑◐♿♣●⊟(27,297)

Red Cow ▼ 🗓

84 Grosvenor Road, DY3 2PR (five mins' walk from bus stop in Corncrake Rd)
✪ 4 (12 Sat & Sun)-midnight
Holden's Golden Glow; Wye Valley Butty Bach; guest beers 🖽

An early 19th-century hostelry in a cul-de-sac that is part of Grosvenor Road. This community pub supports numerous pub games teams. The narrow bar is to the left. The cosy lounge to the right is divided into two areas by a large chimney breast, which has openings either side to afford passage between them. A large garden is at the rear. The pub serves a real cider and six beers. CAMRA branch Pub of the Year 2013.
⚒️🕭🏠🖾&♣🍺P≟₪(257)

Lye

Windsor Castle Inn 🗓

7 Stourbridge Road, DY9 7DG (at Lye Cross)
✪ 12-11 ☎ (01384) 89/809 ∰ sadlersales.co.uk
Sadler's Red House Mild, Mellow Yellow, Worcester Sorcerer, Thin Ice, Hop Bomb, Mud City Stout; guest beers 🖽

Tap house for the family-owned Sadler's Ales since 2004, showcasing its full range of regular beers along with monthly specials. The modern yet cosy interior creates an atmosphere that is relaxed and laid-back during the week, livening up at weekends. Tasty home-made food is served daily from a varied award-winning menu or, alternatively, purchase a two-pint carry-out container if you are frequenting one of the many local curry houses for which Lye is famed.
Q🖾🕭&🍺🍺P≟₪(9,276)

Netherton

Olde Swan ★ 🗓

89 Halesowen Road, DY2 9PY (in town centre on A459 Dudley-Old Hill road)
✪ 11-11; 12-4, 7-11 Sun ☎ (01384) 253075
Olde Swan Original, Dark Swan, Entire, Bumble Hole Bitter 🖽

One of the last four remaining English home-brew pubs from 1974, deservedly identified by CAMRA as one of Britain's Best Real Heritage Pubs and home to the Olde Swan Brewery, resurrected in 2000. The front bar is an unspoilt treasure and there is a cosy rear snug. Food is served in the lounge Monday-Saturday lunchtimes and Monday evenings. The upstairs restaurant is highly regarded for its à la carte menu (open Tue-Sat). Sunday lunches are also served, with booking essential.
⚒️Q🖾🕭&♣P≟₪(243,244,81)

Oldbury

Court of Requests

Church Street, B69 3AF (close to town centre)
✪ 7am-midnight (1am Fri & Sat) ☎ (0121) 543 6970
Greene King Abbot; Ruddles Best Bitter; guest beers 🖽

A deceptively large building, built as a court but more recently used as a library, this Wetherspoon outlet has more character than most. The bar area reflects its library heritage, while moving down a level to the smartly decorated restaurant area reveals its origins as a courthouse, with photos of the judiciary and legal documents adorning the walls. The absence of TVs or piped music allows the

art of conversation to flourish. The beer range varies, and good-value food is served.
⚒️Q🖾🕭🕭&≈(Sandwell & Dudley)
🍺P≟₪(87,120,4)

Pensnett

Lenches Bridge 🗓

2 High Street, DY6 8XD
✪ 12-11; 11-midnight Fri & Sat; 11-11 Sun
☎ (01384) 830900
Enville Ale, Ginger Beer; guest beers 🖽

Refurbished roadside pub close to Pensnett trading estate which changed its name from the Talbot in 2012. It has a separate traditional bar, sells up to eight real ales, a real cider and continental beers, and offers a selection of food, including breakfast from 9am Friday-Sunday. It is part of a pub group that includes the Park Tavern, Kingswinford and the Wallheath Tavern. A CAMRA discount applies on production of a membership card. ⚒️🖾🕭≈🕭&🍺P≟₪(205)

Sedgley

Beacon Hotel ★ 🗓

129 Bilston Street, DY3 1JE (A463)
✪ 12-2.30 (3 Fri), 5.30-11; 12-3, 6-11 Sat; 12-3, 7-10.30 Sun
☎ (01902) 883380 ∰ sarahhughesbrewery.co.uk
Sarah Hughes Pale Amber, Sedgley Surprise, Dark Ruby Mild; guest beers 🖽

In the shadow of the ancient Sedgley Beacon, this old hotel has sat virtually unchanged for decades. It is a Grade II-listed building and is identified by CAMRA as one of Britain's Best Real Heritage Pubs where time has stood still, but make no mistake, it is vibrant. At its heart is a unique servery with hatches for service. There are four rooms including a family room. The Sarah Hughes Brewery lives in a tower out the back and supplies the pub.
Q🖾🕭P≟₪(229,223,224)

Bull's Head

27 Bilston Street, DY3 1JA (A463)
✪ 10 (9am Sat & Sun)-11 ☎ (01902) 661676
Holden's Black Country Mild, Black Country Bitter 🖽, **Golden Glow** 🖽/🅿, **Special** 🖽

This listed building is not far from the centre of Sedgley village. The bar area extends across the front of the pub and into the two bay windows. More drinking space is available further back in a raised area to the side. Beyond that is now housed a Thai restaurant which also serves takeaways and English breakfasts. A warm welcome ensures regulars and visitors alike. Holden's seasonal beers are often available. ⚒️🖾🕭🕭♣≟🗓₪(1,27,223)

Mount Pleasant

144 High Street, DY3 1RH (A459)
✪ 6.30 (7 Mon & Tue)-11; 12-3, 7-10.30 Sun
Beer range varies 🖽

Known locally as the Stump by its many regulars, this friendly, popular free house serves an interesting selection of eight beers. It possesses a Tardis-like interior and a mock-Tudor frontage. The front bar has a convivially warm atmosphere while the lounge has an intimate feel, with its two rooms on different levels housing various nooks and crannies to hide away in, and its two real coal stoves. Food is limited to ham or cheese cobs. Dog-friendly, it is five minutes' walk from Sedgley.
⚒️Q🖾🕭♣P≟₪(1)

Shirley

Bernie's Real Ale Off-Licence 🗒

266 Cranmore Boulevard, B90 4PX (off A34, opp TRW research site)
✪ 11.30-2, 4-10; 11.30-10 Fri & Sat; closed Sun
☎ (0121) 744 2827
Taylor Landlord; guest beers ⊞
Long-standing Guide entry proudly displaying a wide choice of real ale pumps as though it were a pub. The changing guest beers offer a range of styles from mainly small or microbreweries from the north of England; some newer local breweries are proving popular too. Traditional Rich's cider is always available. Various takeaway containers are supplied for draught ale and complement the huge range of bottled ales, ciders and continental beers.
🕭●🖾(76,6,5)

Short Heath

Duke of Cambridge 🍷

82 Coltham Road, WV12 5QD
✪ 12-11 ☎ (01922) 712038
Black Country Bradley's Finest Golden, Pig on the Wall, Fireside; guest beers ⊞
A traditional welcoming pub converted from 17th-century cottages about 200 years ago. There are three comfortable rooms, including a tastefully refurbished family lounge/family room with a pool table. The public bar has a solid fuel burner, and original beams feature in the further room. A quiz is held every other Wednesday. Local CAMRA Pub of the Year 2013. ♨Q🕭🕸🔁♣●🕭🖾(341,369)

Whimsey 🗒

13 High Road, WV12 4JR
✪ 1-midnight; 12-1am Fri & Sat; 1-1am Sun
☎ (01902) 630634
Enville Ale; Exmoor Gold; Taylor Landlord; guest beer ⊞
A popular 19th-century street-corner local with two rooms where staff and customers are friendly and welcoming. There is a beer garden at the side of the pub. The guest beer is normally Olde Swan Bumble Hole, but it occasionally changes. Bar snacks are served, and pork and stuffing sandwiches are very popular on Friday nights.
♨🕭🕸♣P🕭🖾(326)

Stourbridge

Royal Exchange 🗒

75 Enville Street, DY8 1XW (on A458 just off ring road)
✪ 12-11 (10.30 Sun) ☎ (01384) 396726
Bathams Mild Ale, Best Bitter, Bathams XXX ⊞
This venue has a busy basic bar to the front and a small cosy lounge to the rear, accessed through a side passage. The bar is decorated with a mixed bag of whisky bottles and boxes, pewter tankards and foreign bank notes. The beer is very good value, and served in glass mugs on request. There is a public car park directly opposite, a covered and heated smoking area to the rear, and a function room upstairs which can be booked without charge. Q🕸🔁≈(Town)♣P🕭🖾(X96,227,228)

Sutton Coldfield

Horse & Jockey

90 Birmingham Road, B72 1LY
✪ 11.30-midnight ☎ (0121) 321 2412

M&B Brew XI; Marston's Pedigree; Purity Pure Ubu; guest beers ⊞
Prominent multi-gabled Ember Inn on a street corner. The mock-Tudor exterior features deep bay windows and elaborate hanging lamps. The well-decorated cosy interior is warmed by three flaming gas fires, and displays pictures of old Sutton. Two interesting guest beers feature, changing about once a week, and ale prices are keen for the area. Good pub grub is offered, with an dining area where children are permitted until 9pm. Car parking is Pay & Display. 🕭🕸🕼🕭≈(Wylde Green)P🕭🖾

Station

Station Street, Sutton Coldfield, B73 6AT (near Sutton station southbound platform)
✪ 12-11 (midnight Fri & Sat); 12-10.30 Sun
☎ (0121) 362 4961 ⊕ thestationsuttoncoldfield.co.uk
Black Sheep Best Bitter; Holden's Golden Glow; guest beer ⊞
Busy mixed clientele pub with a spacious lounge and bar plus an upstairs function room. The pub hosts a Monday night quiz, live music on Tuesday evening and a comedy night on the last Thursday in the month. The outdoor drinking area plays host to DJs and live music in the summer. The guest ale is sometimes rebadged Holden's Bitter. Good home-cooked food is served all day. Children are welcome until 6pm. Car parking is Pay & Display. ♨🕭🕸🕭≈🕭🖾

Three Tuns

19 High Street, B72 1XS (uphill N from town centre)
✪ 11.30-midnight (11 Mon; 11.30 Tue; 1am Fri & Sat); 11.30-11 Sun ☎ (0121) 355 2996 ⊕ threetuns.net
Thwaites Original, Wainwright, Lancaster Bomber; guest beer ⊞
A 16th-century coaching inn with a central glazed canopy to envelop both sides of the pub and shield the courtyard from the weather. The interior has four rooms: one for quiet contemplation, a bar for chat, a lounge for food and regular live music, and a Sky Sports and games room. Sometimes the guest ale is a special from Thwaites. Food is served noon-9pm (8pm Sun & Mon) and children are welcome until 9pm. Q🕭🕸🔁🕼🕭≈♣P🖾

Tipton

Tamebridge

45 Tame Road, DY4 7JA (off A461)
✪ 12-11 ☎ (0121) 557 2496
RCH Pitchfork; Wye Valley HPA; guest beers ⊞
Alongside the Oldbury arm of the River Tame, the Tamebridge stands out with its bright-red painted brickwork. The bar, which has a large coal fire, leads onto a small cosy snug area. There is also a family room, all rooms having large-screen TVs. Outside is a covered, heated smoking area and garden. The pub has a separate toilet for wheelchair users. It usually serves four real ales including two regularly changing guests. ♨🕭🕸🔁🕼≈(Dudley Port)🖾(Black Lake) P🕭🖾(74)

Upper Gornal

Britannia ★ 🗒

109 Kent Street, DY3 1UX (on A459)
✪ 12-11 (10.30 Sun) ☎ (01902) 883253
Bathams Mild Ale, Best Bitter ⊞

The Britannia has been identified by CAMRA as one of Britain's Best Real Heritage Pubs thanks to the taproom at the rear with its wall-mounted handpumps. Named Sally's by locals after the legendary former landlady Sally Perry, service can be obtained from the main front bar, itself a very comfortable place to be, with both areas warmed with a roaring open fire. There is also a family/ games room with a TV. Behind the pub is the former brewhouse, and a delightful garden with a smoking shelter. Bar snacks are available. ⚌Q⎈⬠❀⊟⚬♣♒⊟(1)

Jolly Crispin
25 Clarence Street, DY3 1UL (A459)
✪ 4 (12 Fri & Sat)-11; 12-10.30 Sun ☎ (01902) 672220
⊕ thejollycrispin.co.uk
Beer range varies ⏣
Lively pub on the main route from Dudley to Sedgley, a shoemaker's house in the 18th century, staging a festival of beer every day. The locals are friendly and the fires glow. The pub features regular beers from the on-site Fownes Brewing and up to eight guest ales, complemented by a real cider. A twice yearly cider festival is held in the garden. The no.1 bus from Dudley to Wolverhampton stops outside. ⚌⬠⊟♣♦P♒⊟(1)

Wall Heath

Wall Heath Tavern ⏣
14 High street, DY6 0HA (on A449)
✪ 12-midnight (1am Thu-Sat) ☎ (01384) 287319
Enville Ale, Ginger Beer; Holden's Golden Glow; Sharp's Doom Bar; Taylor Landlord; guest beers ⏣
After a long period spent under different names, this former Ansells pub has been reinstated as the Wall Heath Tavern. Serving up to 10 real ales, with a major emphasis on Enville Ales, it can get busy, particularly at weekends. The lounge is predominantly for food, especially in the evenings, serving good-value cooking. There is a large patio area at the rear, which is busy in the summer months. A CAMRA discount applies on production of a membership card.
⚌⎈⬠◖⊟♣P♒⊟(205,255,256)

Walsall

Black Country Arms ⏣
High Street, WS1 1QW (in market, opp Asda)
✪ 11-11 (midnight Fri); 12-midnight Sat; 12-11 Sun
☎ (01922) 640588 ⊕ blackcountryarms.co.uk
Black Country Bradley's Finest Golden, Pig on the Wall, Fireside; guest beers ⏣
Large, imposing three-level pub, part of which was originally the Green Dragon Inn dating back to at least the 18th century. It lay empty for 70 years until extensive refurbishment in 1986-7, incorporating a former music shop next door. The impressive mahogany bar boasts 16 handpulls serving up to 11 microbrewery guest beers from all over the UK, and two real ciders. Live music features on the last Friday of the month and regular quiz nights are held. ⎈⬠◖⇌♣♦P♒⊟

Butts Tavern
44 Butts Street, WS4 2BJ (200yds from Arboretum's Lichfield St entrance)
✪ 12-midnight ☎ (01922) 629332 ⊕ buttstavern.co.uk
Greene King Abbot; Holden's Golden Glow; Wye Valley Butty Bach; guest beers ⏣

A community-based local comprising a large main bar with a small stage and Sky TV and a smaller bar at the rear with a pool table and darts facilities. The six handpulls often feature guest beers. The pub hosts a weekly quiz night on Tuesday and entertainment on Friday and Saturday evenings. There is an outside patio and smoking area. Dominoes and crib teams are based here. A friendly welcome is assured. Lydia's PMT is a house beer. ⎈⬠⊟⚬⇌♣♒⊟(22,394,977)

Longhorn
255 Sutton Road, WS5 3AR
✪ 11-midnight ☎ (01922) 625065
Greene King IPA; Purity Pure Ubu; guest beers ⏣
A large 1930s roadside inn, the rear of the pub is given over to diners while drinkers tend to occupy the front area. The Longhorn hosts many charity events throughout the year and has a real community feel. There are quiz nights on Sundays and Wednesdays. Regular food and drinks deals are offered, and CAMRA members benefit from 20p off a pint of real ale, with up to five guest ales on handpump. There is a function area available free to hire. ⚌⎈⬠◖♣P♒

Lyndon House Hotel ⏣
9-10 Upper Rushall Street, WS1 2HA (between market and St Matthew's Church)
✪ 11.30-11 (1am Fri & Sat); 12-11 Sun ☎ (01922) 612511
⊕ lyndonhousehotel.co.uk
Bathams Best Bitter; Burton Bridge Golden Delicious; Greene King Abbot; Holden's Golden Glow; Theakston Best Bitter; guest beer ⏣
The pub is part of a hotel complex and the bar (formerly The Royal Exchange) was converted in the '80s. It incorporates old brick and many old timbers to warm and cosy effect. The luxurious hotel was formerly a Salvation Army hostel. Popular with business people, its clientele is drawn from all over the town, representing a slice of Walsall life. Occasional live entertainment takes place. Lunchtime meals are served all week, with a carvery on Sunday, evening meals are available Monday-Thursday only.
⚌Q⬠⊟◖⊡♒P♒⊟(51,377)

Pretty Bricks ⏣
5 John Street, WS2 8AF (near magistrates court, off B4210)
✪ 12-11 (midnight Fri & Sat) ☎ (01922) 612553
Black Country Bradley's Finest Golden, Pig on the Wall, Fireside; guest beers ⏣
A friendly and cosy Victorian pub dating from 1845. There are two downstairs rooms and a large upstairs function room. The Bricks has a place in CAMRA history – it is one of the pubs from where CAMRA was launched nationally in 1972 and where Walsall CAMRA was founded in that same year. Up to five guest beers are on offer. A quiz night is held on the first Wednesday of the month and a cheese and tapas night at the end of each month.
⚌Q⎈⬠◖⊟⇌♣♦♒⊟(301)

St Matthew's Hall
Lichfield Street, WS1 1SX
✪ 8am-midnight (2am Fri & Sat) ☎ (01922) 700820
Greene King Abbot; Ruddles Best Bitter; guest beers ⏣
A lively Wetherspoon outlet with two log fires and music playing daily from noon onwards. There are large beer gardens with sheltered areas located to the front and rear of the building. A selection of

local and national guest ales supplements the two regular offerings. There is a DJ every Friday and Saturday till 2am. 🏚🛏🕮🕮🍴👍🚶🍽🚪

Walsall Cricket Club

Gorway Road, WS1 3BE (off A34, by university campus)
🕘 8-10.30; 12-11 (4-10.30 winter) Sat; 12-11 (8 winter) Sun
☎ (01922) 622094 ⊕ walsallcricketclub.com
Wye Valley HPA; guest beers Ⓗ
Established in 1812, the club held a major celebration in 2012 to mark its 200-year history. There is a comfortable single-roomed lounge displaying cricket memorabilia, and two large screens for sporting events. The bar is manned by members. On match days the cricket can be viewed through panoramic windows, although in good weather the lounge is opened onto the patio area. It's an ideal summer evening retreat in the heart of town. Show a CAMRA membership card for entry. 🏚👍♣🚪(51)

White Lion

150 Sandwell Street, WS1 3EQ (at jct of Sandwell St and Little London)
🕘 12-11 (midnight Thu-Sun) ☎ (01922) 628542
Adnams Southwold Bitter; Greene King IPA; Taylor Landlord; Wye Valley HPA; guest beers Ⓗ
Imposing late-Victorian street-corner local. Its large sloping bar, with its deep and shallow ends, sits in the curve of the building and is a great community melting pot. There is also a comfortable lounge and a small walled garden. Food is served on Saturday evening and Sunday lunchtime, plus a steak night on Tuesday. Live bands play every Friday, jazz night is the first Monday of the month, open mic night is Thursday, the darts team meets on Wednesday, and dominoes is played on Thursday. The pub is child-friendly until 8.30pm.
🏚🛏🕮🍴👍🚶🚪(404)

Wednesbury

Cottage Spring

106 Franchise Street, WS10 9RG
🕘 2-11.30; 12-12.30am Fri & Sat; 12-11.30 Sun
☎ (0121) 526 6354
Holden's Black Country Bitter; guest beer Ⓗ
An 18th-century two-room inn. Photographs of the pub from the '50s and '60s adorn the walls. The public bar features one of the early versions of the red telephone box. The L-shaped lounge has old-fashioned advertisements on the walls. Karaoke takes place on Friday and Saturday nights, and Sunday lunches are served. Q🕮🍴🍴♣P

Old Blue Ball Ⓛ

19 Hall End, WS10 9ED (just off B4200 Whitley St; buses 311A and 313 pass by)
🕘 12-3, 5-11; 12-11 Fri-Sun ☎ (0121) 556 0197
Everards Original; Morland Old Speckled Hen; Olde Swan Original; Wye Valley Butty Bach; guest beers Ⓗ
The small bar has chamber pots, jugs and advertising mirrors as decoration. Darts is played in the lounge, where there are old canal maps and a history of cockfights on the walls. The small snug has a sketch of the pub plus paintings on display. The popular stand-up passage contains artists' impressions of old Wednesbury. The large split-level garden includes an outside TV and children's play area. Q🛏🕮🍴♣🚶🚪(311A,313)

Olde Leathern Bottel

40 Vicarage Road, WS10 9DW (just off A461; bus 311 from Walsall is 5 mins' walk)
🕘 6-11 Mon; 12-2.30, 6-11 (11.30 Fri); 11-11.30 Sat; 12-4, 7-11 Sun ☎ (0121) 505 0230
Beer range varies Ⓗ
The Bottel is set in cottages dating from 1510. It has four rooms adorned with old photos, including a snug that is also used as a function room. At the rear is a pleasant benched area with plant pots. Two beers are on handpump (three at weekends), with Wye Valley HPA often making an appearance. There is a quiz on Sunday evenings and the occasional beer festivals have proved to be very popular. Closed Monday lunchtimes.
Q🕮🕮🍴🕮(Great Western St)♣P🚶🚪(311)

Wednesfield

Vine ★ Ⓛ

35 Lichfield Road, WV11 1TN
🕘 12-11 ☎ (01902) 733529
Black Country Bradley's Finest Golden, Pig on the Wall, Fireside; guest beers Ⓗ
A rare intact example of a simple inter-war working-class pub, built in 1938. Identified by CAMRA as one of Britain's Best Real Heritage Pubs and Grade II-listed, this true community local retains its bar, lounge and snug. Six changing guest beers, often including LocAles, complement the three regular beers. A covered smokers' shelter and a beer garden provide outdoor drinking areas. Excellent-value home-cooked food is served (no food Sun eve or Mon). 🏚Q🕮🍴♣P🚶🚪(59,89)

West Bromwich

Old Hop Pole

474 High Street, B70 9LD
🕘 12-3, 5-11; 12-1am Fri & Sat; 12-11 Sun
Wye Valley HPA; guest beers Ⓗ
A friendly local just outside the town centre. The central bar serves a busy front bar and a quieter rear room, dispensing up to three changing guest ales together with the regular Wye Valley HPA. Cards, darts and dominoes are played at a competitive level. Live music or a disco is staged most Saturday nights. The place gets extremely busy when West Bromwich Albion are at home. 🏚🛏🕮(Dartmouth St)♣🚶🚪(74,79)

Vine

152 Roebuck Street, B70 6RD
🕘 11.30-2, 5-11; 11.30-11 Fri & Sat; 12-10.30 Sun
☎ (0121) 553 2866 ⊕ thevine.co.uk
Beer range varies Ⓗ
From the street this appears to be a traditional corner pub, but be prepared for a surprise. The traditional area consists of three small rooms off the corridor. But continue further and the building opens up into a large dining area where an extensive range of Indian meals is available, together with more usual British fare and vegetarian options – all excellent value. Two guest ales are regularly on handpump. This popular establishment gets very busy, especially when West Bromwich Albion are at home.
🛏🕮🍴🚶🚪(Kenrick Park)🚪🚪(74)

Willenhall

County
7 Walsall Street, WV13 2ES
🕐 12-11 (midnight Fri & Sat); 11-11 Sun ☎ (01902) 608283
Wye Valley Butty Bach; guest beer Ⓗ
Situated on the main Walsall road out of town, the County is a large street-corner pub dating from 1834. The venue includes a very comfortable wooden-beamed lounge. The public bar is more basic, with pool table and darts. The two handpumps are found in the lounge. Home-cooked food is served in the lounge daily and the Sunday lunches are very popular. There is a beer garden at the rear. 🏠🌙🍴🏵️♿👶⁼🚇(529)

Falcon Ⓛ
77 Gomer Street West, WV13 2NR (off B4464, behind flats)
🕐 12-11 (10.30 Sun) ☎ (01902) 633378
Exmoor Gold; Hop Back Summer Lightning; Olde Swan Dark Swan, Bumble Hole Bitter; Salopian Oracle; guest beers Ⓗ
The Falcon has long been the flagship real ale pub in Willenhall, boasting seven keenly priced beers. This venue has been run by the same family for the past 29 years and has established a strong local following. It was built in 1936 and has two rooms – a lively front bar and a quieter lounge at the back. Q🏠🌙🍴♿👶⁼🛏️🚇(525,529)

Malthouse Ⓛ
The Dale, New Road, WV13 2BG
🕐 9am-midnight (1am Fri & Sat) ☎ (01902) 635273
Greene King Abbot; Ruddles Best Bitter Ⓗ**; guest beers** Ⓗ/Ⓖ
Located on the main road junction in the town centre, this pub began life as a malthouse, becoming the Dale Cinema, then a bingo hall. It consists of a large L-shaped single room with a rear patio area downstairs for the use of smokers. Cask ale sales have doubled in the past year and six guest beers are now the norm, with up to eight guests during beer festivals. At least two traditional ciders are also sold. 🏠🌙👶♿🐕⁼

Wollaston

Graham's Place Ⓛ
73 Bridgnorth Road, DY8 3PZ (on A458 towards Bridgnorth, just before Wollaston)
🕐 11-11 (11.30 Sun) ☎ (01384) 440315
🌐 grahams-place.co.uk
Salopian Shropshire Gold, Oracle, Hop Twister; guest beers Ⓗ
Single-room pub with a modern, clean decor and a variety of different feels within the bar area. Freshly prepared meals made from locally sourced ingredients are served in the conservatory to the rear (Mon-Fri eves only), with a more intimate, cosy drinking area to the front and a long bar between the two. Up to seven real ales are on handpull. There is a covered smoking area and a large garden, very pleasant in summer. Tuesday is quiz night. 🚶🏠🌙👶♿P⁼🚇(227,228,X96)

Unicorn Ⓛ
145 Bridgnorth Road, DY8 3NX (on A458 towards Bridgnorth)
🕐 12-11; 12-4, 7-10.30 Sun ☎ (01384) 394823
Bathams Mild Ale, Best Bitter Ⓗ
A former brewhouse purchased by Bathams, it has barely altered in appearance since the Billingham family sold up in the early 1990s. The brewhouse is still there but it is no longer in use. The Unicorn is renowned for serving one of the best pints in the area. A traditional two-bar drinking house with a small back room where children are welcome, the pub is popular with all age groups and conversation is the order of the day. Fresh cobs are available on request. 🚶Q🌙🏵️👶♿P⁼🚇(227,228,X96)

Wolverhampton

Chindit Ⓛ
113 Merridale Road, WV3 9SE
🕐 4 (12 Sat & Sun)-11 ☎ (01902) 425582 🌐 thechindit.co.uk
Broughs Bitter; Wye Valley HPA; guest beers Ⓗ
Street-corner local, built in the 1950s originally as an off-licence. It is thought to be the only pub in the country named after the Chindits, a special force who fought in Burma in World War II, whose history is displayed on the wall in the lounge. The bar is extensively decorated with music memorabilia and hosts live music every Friday evening. Cobs are usually on sale from behind the bar. 🏠🍴P⁼🚇(3,4)

Combermere Arms Ⓛ
90 Chapel Ash, WV3 0TY (on A41 Tettenhall Rd)
🕐 11-3, 5-11; 12-midnight Fri & Sat; 12-10.30 Sun
☎ (01902) 421880
Banks's Mild; guest beers Ⓗ
Famous for having a tree growing in the Gents', this quaint little terrace pub lies just a short distance from the city centre. Although small, it still has three separate rooms, plus a covered backyard where live music often takes place at the weekend. The small car park at the rear is accessed via Bath Road around the corner. Up to four guest beers are on handpump. Good-value weekday lunches are popular with the business folk. ♿🏠🍴P⁼🚇

Great Western Ⓛ
Sun Street, WV10 0DJ (via subway from high level station and city centre)
🕐 11-11 (10.30 Sun) ☎ (01902) 351090
Bathams Best Bitter; Holden's Black Country Mild, Black Country Bitter, Golden Glow, Special; guest beers Ⓗ
Former CAMRA National Pub of the Year with four distinct drinking areas, this historic listed pub gets its name from its location opposite the gates of the city's old GWR station, now redeveloped. Plenty of Wolverhampton Wanderers and old railway memorabilia are on display. The pub is just a short walk from Wolverhampton's bus and railway stations and is popular on Wolves match days. Good-value traditional pub food is speedily served at lunchtimes and sandwiches/baguettes are available until 9pm (kitchen closed Sun). 🚶🏵️🍴🚆🚇(St George's)♿P⁼🚇

Hog's Head 🍷 Ⓛ
186 Stafford Street, WV1 1NA
🕐 10-midnight (1am Fri & Sat); 12-midnight Sun
☎ (01902) 717955
Beer range varies Ⓗ
Large city-centre pub built in the late 19th century and featuring an excellent terracotta exterior. A stained glass window above the front door reveals its original name, the Vine. The single-roomed interior is split into many areas, featuring large-screen TVs showing sport and music videos. A range of up to nine ales is available, always

including beers from local microbreweries, and Thatchers cider, making this pub popular with all ages. CAMRA members get a 10 per cent discount on real ales. ✪❃◗▶♿⇌🚃(St George's)●'–🚃

Lych Gate Tavern Ⓛ

44 Queen Square, WV1 1TX
✪ 11-11 (midnight Fri & Sat) ☎ (01902) 399516
⊕ lychgatetavern.co.uk
Black Country Bradley's Finest Golden, Pig on the Wall, Fireside; guest beers Ⓗ
A real ale pub converted from offices by Black Country Traditional Inns and opened in 2012. One of the oldest buildings in the city centre, the Georgian frontage of this historic pub dates from 1726, while the timber-framed rear dates back to the 15th century. The two small bars are down a short flight of stairs from street level and there is a function room with a bar available to hire for free upstairs. Seven regularly changing guest beers are served. Q❃&⇌🚃(St George's)'–🚃

Moon Under Water Ⓛ

53-55 Lichfield Street, WV1 1EQ (opp Grand Theatre)
✪ 7am-midnight (1am Fri & Sat) ☎ (01902) 422447
Banks's Mild; Greene King Abbot; Ruddles Best Bitter; guest beers Ⓗ
Since opening in the former Co-op building in 1995, this Wetherspoon pub has thrived, attracting a varied clientele from around the area. Old pictures of Wolverhampton adorn the walls and there is stained glass decoration in the ceiling around one of the pillars. The pub is handy for the Grand Theatre and also near the bus and railway stations. A try-before-you-buy scheme is offered on real ales. Accompanied children are welcome until 8pm. ◗&⇌🚃(St George's)●🚃

Newhampton Ⓛ

19 Riches Street, Whitmore Reans, WV6 0DW
✪ 11-11 (midnight Fri & Sat); 12-11 Sun ☎ (01902) 746747
Caledonian Deuchars IPA; Courage Best Bitter; Enville Ale; Fuller's London Pride; Taylor Landlord; Wye Valley HPA Ⓗ
A true local with a pool room, smoke room and bar. The upstairs function room is part of the local folk scene. There is a large garden, including crown green bowling, and a children's play area. The Newhampton has eight handpumps offering seven real ales and a traditional cider. ♨❃◗&●'–🚃

Penn Bowling & Social Club Ⓛ

10 Manor Road, Penn, WV4 5PY
✪ 12-midnight (1am Fri & Sat); 12-11 Sun
☎ (01902) 342516 ⊕ pennbowlingclub.com
Banks's Mild, Bitter Ⓟ**; guest beers** Ⓗ
The hub of this well-used family-friendly community club is a large bar with a pool table, dartboard, gaming machines and TV screens overlooking the floodlit crown bowling green. A small, quiet lounge, the Red Room, is accessed from the main bar. There is also a large function room which is the venue for regular events and entertainment, including occasional beer festivals. The outdoor seating area is ideal for watching bowls matches during the season. ☎❃◗&♣P'–🚃(255,256)

Posada Ⓛ

48 Lichfield Street, WV1 1DG (opp art gallery)
✪ 12-11 (1am Fri & Sat); closed Sun
Beer range varies Ⓗ

A splendid Victorian Grade II-listed city-centre pub. It is much altered but retains some of its original features; a recent refurbishment has made it cosier. It attracts a varied customer base, and is quiet during the day, with background music on weekend evenings. It has a courtyard to the rear for summer drinking and a smoking area. CAMRA members receive a discount on real ales. Old Rosie cider is regularly served. ✪❃⇌🚃(St George's)●'–🚃

Royal Oak Ⓛ

70 Compton Road, WV3 9PH (on A454 300yds from Chapel Ash jct)
✪ 11.30-11 (midnight Fri & Sat) ☎ (01902) 422845
Banks's Mild, Bitter; guest beers Ⓗ
Historic local pub, a short walk from the city centre, with a lively and friendly atmosphere in its single-bar room. Winning an industry award for the quality of its ales, the three changing guest beers are from a Marston's-owned brewery. There is an open mic night every Wednesday and local music acts regularly feature on Saturday evenings. A large patio, covered at one end, provides ample shelter for smokers, and stages live music in the summer. Families and dogs are welcome. ☎❃◗&♣●P'–🚃(10,890)

Stile Inn Ⓛ

3 Harrow Street, Whitmore Reans, WV1 4PB (off Newhampton Rd East/Fawdry St)
✪ 11.30-11 (midnight Fri; 1am Sat) ☎ (01902) 425336
Banks's Mild, Bitter; guest beers Ⓗ
Late-Victorian street-corner pub built in 1900 replacing a previous pub on the site. It is a true community local with a sporting prominence: darts and dominoes feature inside and bowling on the unusual L-shaped bowling green outside. The public bar, smoke room and snug are popular with Wolverhampton Wanderers fans on match days – the football ground is a short distance away. Guest ales are from the Marston's range. Excellent-value food, including Polish dishes, is served all day, every day. ☎❃◗&♣'–🚃(5,6)

Swan (at Compton) Ⓛ

Bridgnorth Road, Compton, WV6 8AE (at Compton Island, A454)
✪ 12-11 (11.30 Thu; midnight Fri & Sat) ☎ (01902) 754736
Banks's Mild, Bitter; guest beers Ⓗ
A Grade II-listed inn on the main road and close to the Staffs and Worcester Canal. It has a basic charm with a warm, friendly atmosphere and an interior that has not been tampered with. The main bar has traditional beams and a cosy fire and contains a humorous collection of placards around the serving area. A function room is used by local groups for meetings. The beers come from Marston's group breweries. Dogs are welcome in the bar area. Q❃&♣P'–🚃(10,890)

Woodcross

Horse & Jockey Ⓛ

64 Robert Wynd, WV14 9SB
✪ 12-11 (11.30 Fri & Sat) ☎ (01902) 662268
⊕ horseandjockeywoodcross.co.uk
Greene King Abbot; Hobsons Town Crier; St Austell Tribute; Tetley Bitter; guest beers Ⓗ
Friendly community local, run by a landlord who is an ale enthusiast. Four regular and two guest ales are on every day. Food, including vegetarian options, is served daily until 8.30pm (4pm Sun). Under-18s are not allowed in the bar, but are

welcome in the stylish lounge while eating. Pub games are played regularly and there is a popular quiz night every Tuesday. The smoking area is at the front, with a large beer garden at the back. ▲☎☺◑ ⬒♣P⅃━🚆(81)

Woodsetton

Park Inn ⅃
George Street, DY1 4LW (on A457, 200yds from A4123)
✪ 12-11 (10.30 Sun) ☎ (01902) 661279
Holden's Black Country Mild, Black Country Bitter, Golden Glow, Special; guest beer ⊞
Vibrant suburban brewery tap, held by the Holden family since 1915. Radiating out from the spacious main bar are a small games room, a raised dining area and a separate conservatory. Functions are catered for and reasonably priced food is served 12-8pm (4.30pm Sun). There is a 10p discount per pint for CAMRA members. Note that the new

brewery centre is on the right of the car park. Holden's seasonal beers are often available. ▲☎☺◑♣P⅃━🚆(126)

Wordsley

New Inn ⅃
117 High Street, DY8 5QR (on A491)
✪ 12-11 (10.30 Sun) ☎ (01384) 295614
Bathams Mild Ale, Best Bitter ⊞
On the main Wolverhampton to Stourbridge road, the building has an imposing three-storey Victorian façade. One of the Bathams 11, it has become very popular and can be busy. An L-shaped bar serves a single room with a small annexe at one end, and a patio area outside. Children are not allowed inside but an outside play area is available in the summer. Cobs are sold. The pub largely caters for the surrounding community and has the feel of a proper local. ☎☺&♣P⅃━🚆(256,257)

Bartons Arms, Birmingham: Newtown (Photo: Katie Hunt)

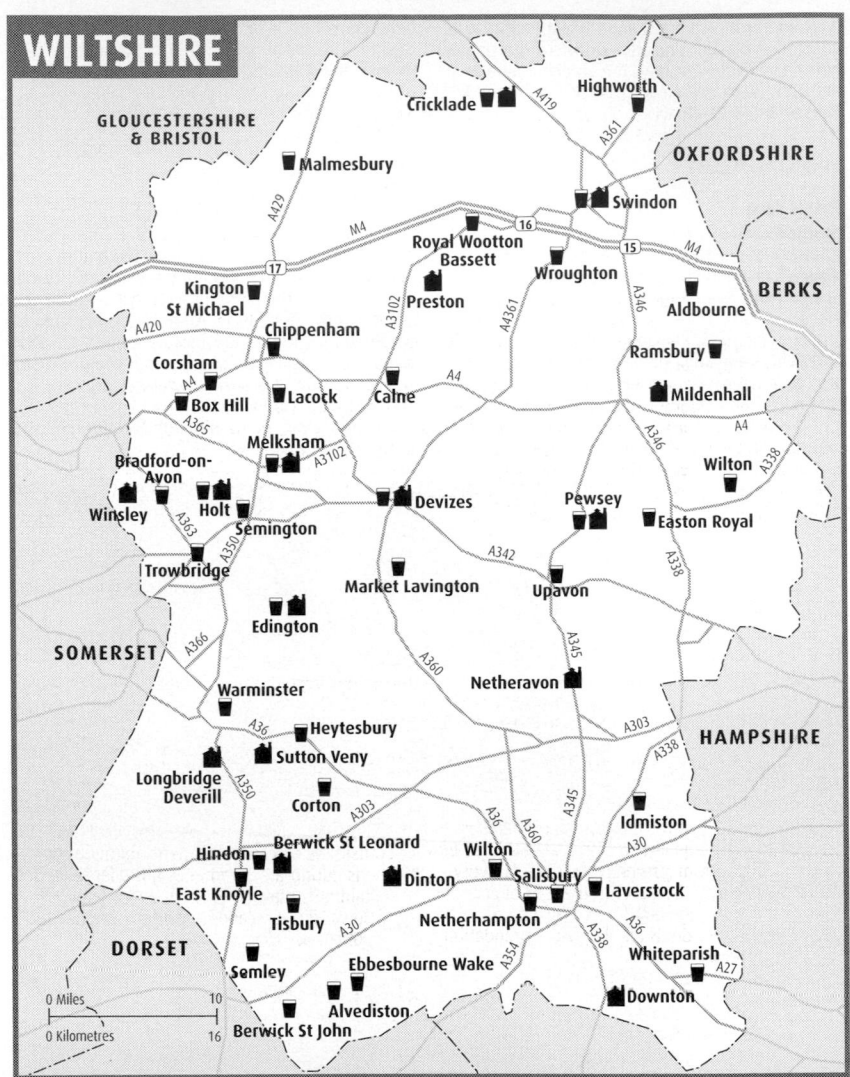

WILTSHIRE

GLOUCESTERSHIRE
& BRISTOL

Highworth

Cricklade

A419

A361

Malmesbury

A429

OXFORDSHIRE

Swindon

M4

Royal Wootton
Bassett

16

15

M4

A361

Wroughton

A346

BERKS

17

Kington
St Michael

A3102

Preston

Aldbourne

A420

Chippenham

Ramsbury

Corsham

A4

Box Hill

Lacock

Calne

A4

Mildenhall

A365

A346

A4

Melksham

Bradford-on-
Avon

A3102

Wilton

A338

Winsley

Holt

A363

Devizes

Pewsey

Easton Royal

Semington

A342

A338

Trowbridge

Market Lavington

Upavon

A350

Edington

A345

SOMERSET

A366

A360

Netheravon

Warminster

A36

Heytesbury

A303

HAMPSHIRE

Sutton Veny

A338

Longbridge
Deverill

A350

Corton

A303

A345

A36

A360

Idmiston

A30

Hindon

Berwick St Leonard

Wilton

Salisbury

Laverstock

East Knoyle

Dinton

A36

Tisbury

A30

Netherhampton

A338

DORSET

Whiteparish

A27

Semley

Ebbesbourne Wake

A354

Downton

0 Miles   10

0 Kilometres   16

Alvediston

Berwick St John

Aldbourne

Blue Boar 🛈
20 The Green, SN8 2EN
☼ 11.30-3, 5.30-11.30; 11.30-midnight Fri & Sat; 12-10.30
Sun ☎ (01672) 540237 ⊕ thepubonthegreen.com
Wadworth Henry's IPA, 6X; guest beer Ⓗ
Friendly and comfortable pub by the village green.
Food is home cooked and served in the bar or
dining room. Beer festivals are held twice a year in
April and October. A large collection of bottled
beers from around the country adorns the walls,
adding to the pleasant atmosphere. The pub
featured in a 1971 episode of Dr Who.
🏚Q🕸🐕◑🕭ᴭ🚃(46,48)

Crown Hotel
The Square, SN8 2DU
☼ 12-midnight (10.30 Sun) ☎ (01672) 540214
⊕ thecrownaldbourne.co.uk
**Sharp's Doom Bar; Shepherd Neame Spitfire; guest
beers** Ⓗ

Dating from the 18th century and probably a
former coaching inn, the Crown is set in the middle
of the village opposite the duck pond. The main bar
is stylishly refurbished and has a relaxed and
pleasant atmosphere, with a welcoming fire during
the colder seasons. The restaurant serves freshly
prepared food including daily specials until 10pm.
There is a conference room and four en-suite
bedrooms. Check the website for upcoming quiz
nights and live music. 🏚🕸🐕◑🕭🗨ᴭ♣

Alvediston

Crown Inn 🛈
The Street, SP5 5JY (off A30 near Donhead) ST977234
☼ 12-3, 5.30-11; 12-11 Sat; 12-9 Sun ☎ (01722) 780335
⊕ thecrown-inn-alvediston.co.uk
Beer range varies Ⓗ
Picturesque 15th-century thatched free house in
the heart of the Chalke Valley. The huge garden
offers outstanding views in summer and real log
fires make the pub cosy in winter. The four ales are

all local and normally include two from Sixpenny Brewery. West Country ciders are also kept. A sumptuous food menu offers locally sourced produce cooked to order. Occasional beer festivals are held. There is en-suite accommodation and a large car park. ⚫Q⚫⚫⚫⚫⚫P⚫⚫(29)

Berwick St John

Talbot

The Cross, SP7 0HA (S of A30, 5 miles E of Shaftesbury)
⚫ 12-2.30, 6-11; 12-4 Sun ☎ (01747) 828222
Draught Bass; Sixpenny IPA; Wadworth 6X; guest beers Ⓗ

Set in a small, rural, peaceful village, the Talbot opened as a beer house circa 1832 despite vehement opposition from the local parson's wife. The building is predominantly stone built, with a long, low bar with beams and an inglenook fireplace. One of the three regular beers is brewed by a local microbrewery. The more inquisitive visitor may find the cosy dining room behind the inglenook. The pub is popular with walkers from the local downs and cyclists on the 160-mile Wiltshire Cycleway. ⚫Q⚫⚫⚫⚫P⚫⚫(29)

Box Hill

Quarryman's Arms Ⓛ

SN13 8HN (S of A4 between Corsham and Box) ST834693
⚫ 11-11.30 ☎ (01225) 743569 ⊕ quarrymans-arms.co.uk
Butcombe Bitter; Moles Best Bitter; Wadworth 6X; guest beer Ⓗ

Tucked away off the main routes, the pub is a steep uphill walk from the nearest bus stop, but this 300-year-old miners' inn is well worth the effort. Offering a friendly welcome, the Quarryman's is renowned for high-quality food and ales, served in the bar, restaurant or garden. Quiz night is every second Wednesday, and county-themed beer festivals are held regularly (check website for details). Black Rat cider is on offer. Accommodation is available.
Q⚫⚫⚫⚫⚫⚫⚫P⚫⚫(X31,231,232)

Bradford-on-Avon

Castle Inn

10 Mount Pleasant, BA15 1SJ ST827612
⚫ 9-11; 10-10.30 Sun ☎ (01225) 865657
⊕ flatcappers.co.uk
Bath Ales Dark Side; Three Castles Barbury Castle, Vale Ale; guest beers Ⓗ

Acquired by pubco Flatcappers in 2006 and transformed by wholesale refurbishment, this quiet, cosy, relaxing pub caters for a wide clientele. The interior comprises a large bar with flagstone floor, lime-washed walls, open fireplace and magnificent reclaimed mahogany bar, and three smaller rooms with elm floorboards, exposed walls and worn club chairs. Food is served throughout the premises. The garden and terrace enjoy commanding views towards Salisbury Plain. The Vale Ale is badged as Flatcapper while three guests are sourced from local micros. Real cider is available in summer. ⚫Q⚫⚫⚫⚫⚫⚫P⚫⚫

Rising Sun

231 Winsley Road, BA15 1QS ST824613
⚫ 12 (4 Tue)-11; 12-10.30 Sun ☎ (01225) 862354
Beer range varies Ⓗ

Popular local at the top of a hill with two bars: a small, quiet lounge and a more spacious, livelier saloon with TV screens. At the back is a walled beer garden with patio. The pub is home to darts, quiz, crib, pool and football teams, and hosts regular live music including a Rhythm & Booze beer festival over the August bank holiday. The three beers change week by week and the cider is Thatchers Cheddar Valley. The pub's ancient spaniel is still there, ready to welcome you. ⚫⚫⚫⚫⚫⚫⚫⚫⚫

Calne

London Road Inn

85 London Road, SN11 0AD (500yds from town centre on A4)
⚫ 4-11; 3-1am Fri; 2-1am Sat; 2-11 Sun ☎ (01249) 813381
Bath Gem; guest beer Ⓗ

A community pub catering for all ages, serving two ales in the single-room bar. This pub also has a skittle alley and a popular secure beer garden. A variety of traditional pub games is available as well as sporting events on the television, and it is a local live music venue. In its recent past the pub has also been called Holly's Brewhouse. ⚫⚫⚫

Chippenham

Lysley Arrms

London Road, Pewsham, SN15 3RU
⚫ 11-11 (closed 3-5 winter) ☎ (01249) 652864
St Austell Tribute; Wickwar Bob; guest beer Ⓗ

This pub has been standing next to the London to Bath road since the 18th century but has been much extended in modern times. Although a food-led pub it has a large lounge bar area for drinkers. The guest beer comes from the Heavitree Brewery list. Outside is a semi-permanent marquee for functions during the summer. It has a large garden with children's play equipment, and a large car park. Bowood house and its gardens are nearby. ⚫⚫⚫⚫P⚫⚫

Old Road Tavern

Old Road, SN15 1JA (200yds N of railway station over footbridge)
⚫ 11-11.30 (12.30am Fri & Sat); 12-11.30 Sun
☎ (01249) 652094

INDEPENDENT BREWERIES

Arkells Swindon
Box Steam Holt
Braydon Preston
Downton Downton
Hop Back Downton
Hop Kettle Cricklade
Keystone Berwick St Leonard
Moles Melksham
Plain Sutton Veny
Ramsbury Mildenhall
Salisbury Dinton
Shed Ales Pewsey
Stonehenge Netheravon
Three Castles Pewsey
Three Daggers Edington (NEW)
Wadworth Devizes
Weighbridge Swindon
Wessex Longbridge Deverill
Willy Good Winsley
World's End Pewsey

Bath Gem; Hop Back Summer Lightning; Otter Bitter; Wye Valley HPA; guest beers Ⓗ
Grade II-listed, 140-year-old traditional community local. A diverse mix of regulars ensures lively and friendly conversation. Frequently changing guest beers come from local and distant breweries. Bar food is served Thursday, Friday and Saturday lunchtimes. The home of folk music in Chippenham, live bands play at the weekend and the pub is a venue for an annual folk festival held over the end of May bank holiday weekend. The large garden has plenty of seating and is popular in summer. ❀◐🖩🛇≷♣⌐➖🖩(55,231,232)

Three Crowns ♀ Ⓛ
18 Causeway, SN15 3DB
❋ 4.30-11; 12-midnight Fri & Sat; 12-11 Sun
☎ (01249) 449029 ∰ threecrownschippenham.co.uk
Beer range varies Ⓗ
This family-run traditional community local has been a pub since the 18th century and is a regular winner of local CAMRA awards. The free house offers a good choice of real ales including LocAles and at least two dark beers alongside three ciders and a perry. A CAMRA discount is available to members, so bring your card. The pub is a popular location for comedy, poetry and quiz nights, and hosts quarterly beer festivals. The railway station is half a mile away and there is a nearby bus stop. ♨Q🖩♣🍺P⛫🖩(33,55)

Corsham
Hare & Hounds
48 Pickwick, SN13 0HY
❋ 11-11 ☎ (01249) 701106
∰ hareandhoundscorsham.co.uk
Bath Ales Gem; Sharp's Cornish Coaster; guest beers Ⓗ
A large, busy, 17th-century coaching inn on the A4. Up to five ales are available including two changing guests. The occasional beer festival and a Tuesday evening quiz are held. A variety of good food is always on the menu. The pub has three drinking areas – the large lounge can be reserved for private functions. Outside is a covered, heated smoking area and lawned garden with seating and cider apple trees. Dogs are welcome. ♨Q🛇❀◐🖩P⛫🖩(X31,231,233)

Two Pigs
38 Pickwick, SN13 0HY
❋ 7-11; 12-2.30, 7-10.30 Sun ☎ (01249) 712515
∰ thetwopigs.co.uk
Stonehenge Pigswill, Danish Dynamite; guest beers Ⓗ
This classic free house is a gem of a pub. Several times local CAMRA Pub of the Year, it has featured in the Guide for many years. With flagstone floors and wood-panelled walls, the pub dates back to the 18th century and is Grade II-listed. Up to four ales are available, including two changing guests, usually locally sourced. Live music plays on Monday evening, often featuring local blues bands. The covered outdoor drinking area is known as The Sty. ❀🖩🖩(X31,231,232)

Corton
Dove Inn
BA12 0SZ

❋ 11-3, 6-11; 11-11 Sat & Sun ☎ (01985) 850109
∰ thedove.co.uk
Beer range varies Ⓗ
Following major restoration and redesign, the Dove has returned to what it does best – offering good beer in pleasant surroundings alongside flavoursome food and attractive accommodation. With more work still to be carried out, there will soon be even more places to enjoy a quiet pint including a new conservatory and landscaped garden. The three beers are mainly local. Situated on the Wiltshire cycleway and with horse-riding nearby, the pub caters well for the needs of locals and visitors alike. ♨Q🛇❀🚐◐🖩♣P⛫

Cricklade
Red Lion ♀ Ⓛ
74 High Street, SN6 6DD
❋ 12-11 (10.30 Sun) ☎ (01793) 750776
∰ theredlioncricklade.co.uk
Butcombe Bitter; Moles Best Bitter; Wadworth 6X; guest beers Ⓗ
Friendly, popular and comfortable inn, parts of which are quite ancient – the old town wall passes through the building. The pub is home to the Hop Kettle Brewing Co which started brewing in 2012. Ten real ales – three regular, three from Hop Kettle and four guests – are on handpump, plus real cider. Food is served lunchtimes and evenings Monday-Saturday, lunchtime only on Sunday. There is a large garden at the back. Five rooms are available for B&B. ♨Q❀🚐◐🖩♣P🖩(51,53)

Devizes
Bear Hotel
Market Place, SN10 1HS
❋ 8-11.30 (midnight Fri & Sat); 8.30-10.30 Sun
☎ (01380) 722444 ∰ thebearhotel.net
Wadworth Henry's IPA, 6X, seasonal beers Ⓗ
A smart but laid-back hotel bar with polite and well-turned-out staff serving well-kept Wadworth ales. Various seasonals are on offer such as Bishops Tipple, Old Timer and Farmers Glory. The large lounge area has plenty of wooden tables and chairs around the fireplace. Good food is served throughout the day, ranging from bar snacks to three-course meals. A good warm spot for a quiet ale or two. ♨🛇❀🚐◐🖩P⛫🖩

British Lion
9 Estcourt Street, SN10 1LQ (on A361 London road)
❋ 11-11 (midnight Fri & Sat); 12-11 Sun ☎ (01380) 720665
∰ britishliondevizes.co.uk
Beer range varies Ⓗ
The Lion is a real ale lover's dream – a no-nonsense, single-bar, wooden-floored pub with four handpumps delivering an ever-changing range of real ales, mainly from South-West microbreweries, with the occasional guest from up-country. The pub boasts a truly committed and professional landlord, an eclectic group of friendly locals and a warm and welcoming atmosphere. The best place in town and a must-visit if you are in Devizes. ❀♣🍺P⛫🖩(49)

Southgate Inn
Potterne Road, SN10 5BY
❋ 4 (12 Sun)-11; 12-midnight Fri & Sat ☎ (01380) 722872
Beer range varies Ⓗ

A regular in the Guide once more, the Southgate has been brought back to life by the landlord who took over the pub three years ago. It has a relaxed, laid-back feel with a choice of seating areas, background music and live gigs on some Saturdays. Ales from West Country breweries are regularly on offer alongside two changing beers from the Hop Back range. The pub hosts its own beer festival around Easter-time. Well worth the 10-minute walk from the town centre – a friendly welcome is assured. ⏃●P'–ᕱ(49)

East Knoyle

Fox & Hounds

The Green, SP3 6BN (signed from B3089 close to jct A303) ST87113135

✪ 11.30-3, 5.30-11; 11-3, 5.30-10 Sun ☎ (01747) 830573
⏀ foxandhounds-eastknoyle.co.uk

Beer range varies H

Attractive old thatched black and white pub situated high on a hillside with extensive panoramic rural views. Comfortable and cosy inside, the warm welcome is enhanced in winter by a blazing log fire In a huge inglenook fireplace. Three ales are always available, encompassing a wide range of strengths and varying continuously, with local beers given prominence. The real cider is Thatchers Cheddar Valley. Food is served at all sessions. An adjacent skittle alley doubles as a function room. ⏃Q⏃●⏀♣●P

Easton Royal

Bruce Arms ★ Ŀ

Easton Road, SN9 5LR

✪ 12-2.30 (not Mon-Thu), 6-midnight; 12-3, 7-midnight Sat; 12-3, 7-10.30 Sun ☎ (01672) 810216 ⏀ thebrucearms.net

Stonehenge Pigswill; Wadworth 6X; guest beer H

This mid-19th century local has been identified by CAMRA as one of Britain's Best Real Heritage Pubs. The small bar was fitted in 1934 and is furnished with tables and benches that probably go back to the 1850s. There is a small lounge on the left with easy chairs and a piano, reminiscent of a period living room. The large back room is used for dining. Vintage vehicle gatherings are held on the pub's caravan site. Bar snacks such as pies and rolls are available on Friday and Saturday. A guest beer is added during the busy season. ⏃Q⏃⏃⏃Å♣P

Ebbesbourne Wake

Horseshoe Inn

The Cross, SP5 5JF (just off A30) ST993239

✪ 12-3 (not Mon), 6.30-11; 12-4 Sun ☎ (01722) 780474

Bowman Swift One; Otter Bitter; Palmers Dorset Gold; guest beer G

Unspoilt 18th-century pub in a remote rural setting at the foot of an old ox drove. This friendly pub has two small bars that display an impressive collection of old farm implements, tools and lamps, a restaurant, conservatory and a pleasant garden. Good local food is available Tuesday to Sunday and five beers are served direct from casks stillaged behind the bar. The original serving hatch just inside the front door is still in use. Real cider is normally also available.
⏃Q⏃⏃●⏀♣●Pᕱ(29)

Edington

Three Daggers

Westbury Road, BA13 4PG

✪ 11-3, 5-11; 11-11 Sat; 11-10 (9 winter) Sun
☎ (01380) 830940 ⏀ threedaggers.co.uk

Wadworth Henry's IPA; guest beers H

A recently refurbished roadside pub in the middle of the village offering good locally sourced food and an interesting range of bar snacks (no food Sun eve). The main bar has three drinking areas, sofas and a small alcove. There is a dining area and stairs leading upstairs to accommodation and a small function room. The cider is from Thatchers and two guest beers are always available. Occasional sport is shown on TV screens hidden behind mirrors. Dogs are welcome, with free biscuits.
⏃⏃⏃●⏀♿♣●Pᕱ

Heytesbury

Red Lion

42A High Street, BA12 0EA

✪ 11-11 ☎ (01985) 840315 ⏀ redlionheytesbury.co.uk

Plain Ales Arty Farty; Ringwood Best Bitter; guest beer H

This popular pub is a proper village inn with a strong local following as well as an ideal base for visitors with its well-appointed guest rooms. The beers from Ringwood and Plain Ales are regulars alongside a guest ale. Traditional pub food ranges from sandwiches and snacks to more substantial main meals. The garden, running down to the River Wylye, has plenty of seating and a play area for children. Horses are welcome with their own 'parking' area at the rear of the pub.
⏃Q⏃⏃⏃●⏀♿Å♣P'–ᕱ

Highworth

Rose & Crown

19 The Green, SN6 7DB

✪ 12-midnight Mon; 12-3, 5-midnight Tue-Thu; 12-2am Fri; 12-1am Sat; 12-11.30 Sun ☎ (01793) 766287

Courage Best Bitter; Wadworth 6X; Wells Bombardier; guest beers H

One of the oldest pubs in Highworth. As well as the five real ales, the landlord also keeps a collection of around 70 malt whiskies and hosts tasting sessions on the last Sunday of the month. Good home-cooked food is available from Wednesday evening to Sunday lunchtime. Special events and parties can be catered for. Games such as darts, cards and chess are played and the back garden boasts a boules piste. ⏃⏃●⏀♿♣Pᕱ(7,64,74)

Saracen's Head Ŀ

High Street, SN6 7AG

✪ 11-11 (midnight Fri & Sat) ☎ (01793) 762284
⏀ saracenshead.co.uk

Arkells 2B, 3B, Moonlight, seasonal beer G

This former coaching inn is another of Highworth's oldest buildings – it was an inn in 1825 and the building is probably much older. It has a snug bar popular with locals, a lounge bar mainly used for dining, and comfortable outside seating. Occasional themed food nights are offered. Owned by Arkells, the ales – three regulars plus a seasonal – are on gravity dispense. The car park is in Brewery Street, with disabled access. Accommodation is in 12 en-suite bedrooms. ⏃⏃⏃●⏀⏃♿♣Pᕱ(7,64)

Hindon

Angel

High Street, SP3 6DJ ST90993287
✪ 11-11 ☎ (01747) 820696 ∰ angel-inn-at-hindon.co.uk
Otter Bitter; Sharp's Doom Bar; Taylor Landlord Ⓗ
A beautifully restored 18th-century coaching inn,
The Angel was originally known as the Grosvenor
Arms. Prior to its construction in 1750, a medieval
inn, The Angel, existed on the site. The pub has
retained many original features, with wooden
floors, beams and a huge stone fireplace. The bar is
warmed by open fires in winter, adding to the
welcoming ambience. A function room, discrete
dining areas and comfortable accommodation
complete the picture. ⚲Q↷❀⇔◑P'–♋(25)

Holt

Tollgate Inn

Ham Green, BA14 6PX (on B3105 between Bradford-on-
Avon and Melksham) ST858616
✪ closed Mon, 10-11; 11-3 Sun ☎ (01225) 782326
∰ tollgateholt.co.uk
Beer range varies Ⓗ
A real gem, this old village pub has an upmarket
atmosphere with a wood-burning stove, oak floors
and comfy sofas to relax in. The range of four or
five beers, which changes daily, includes a good
selection of local ales – often including a beer from
Box Steam in the village – alongside many from
smaller breweries further afield. A real cider is on
handpump in the summer months.
⚲❀⇔◑P'–♋(237)

Idmiston

Earl of Normanton Ⓛ

Tidworth Road, SP4 0AG (on A338) SU195382
✪ 12-2.30, 6-11; 12-3, 7.45-10.30 Sun ☎ (01980) 610251
∰ earlofnormanton.co.uk
**Exmoor Gold; Flowerpots Bitter; Hop Back Summer
Lightning; guest beers** Ⓗ
Popular roadside pub with a loyal village clientele
and a welcoming atmosphere enhanced by two
real fires in winter months. LocAle accredited, it
offers two guest ales mainly from local breweries.
Good-value home-cooked food is served (no
food Sun eve). There is a small, pleasant garden on
the steep hill behind the pub and a heated,
covered smoking area. B&B is available. A former
local CAMRA Pub of the Year.
⚲Q↷❀⇔◑P'–♋(66)

Kington St Michael

Jolly Huntsman Ⓛ

80 Kington St Michael, SN14 6JB (signed from A350,
between Chippenham and M4 jct 17)
✪ 11.30-2.30, 6-11 (midnight Fri & Sat); 12-2.30, 7-10.30 Sun
☎ (01249) 750305 ∰ jollyhuntsman.com
Moles Tap Bitter; Wadworth 6X; guest beers Ⓗ
Situated on the High Street, at the heart of the
village, this free house offers a friendly welcome to
all, with an open log fire in winter. A varying range
of real ales and ciders is always on offer. The
excellent food menu features regularly changing
chef's specials and themed evenings. Quiz night is
usually the first Monday of the month (check
website) and other entertainment includes live jazz
and blues. Accommodation is all en suite with free
Wi-Fi. ⚲Q⇔◑&♣♠P'–♋(99)

Lacock

Bell Inn

The Wharf, Bowden Hill, SN15 2PJ (½ mile E of Lacock)
✪ 11.30-2.30, 5-11; 11.30-11 Sat; 12-10.30 Sun
☎ (01249) 730308 ∰ thebellatlacock.co.uk
**Bath Ales Gem; GWB Maiden Voyage; Palmers Dorset
Gold; guest beers** Ⓗ
On the edge of the National Trust village of Lacock,
this free house has been run by the same family for
more than 10 years. Local CAMRA Pub of the Year
on many occasions, it has an excellent reputation
for quality food and ever-changing guest ales. An
annual winter beer festival is held in late January/
early February. Originally canal cottages, the pub
lies beside the National Cycle Route, with excellent
cycle tracks and walks between Chippenham and
Melksham. Q↷❀◑♣♠P'–

George Inn Ⓛ

West Street, SN15 2LH
✪ 11-11 (10.30 Sun) ☎ (01249) 730263
∰ georgeinnlacock.co.uk
Wadworth Henry's IPA, 6X, Bishops Tipple Ⓗ
Dating back to 1341, The George sits in the
National Trust village of Lacock. The pub retains an
olde-English character with exposed beams and
three separate seating areas, one with a large
inglenook fireplace which in times gone had a spit
driven by a breed of dog called a Turnspit. A range
of good-quality food is served. The Wadworth
Brewery range is often supplemented by a guest
ale. Real cider is available and often a perry can be
found. ⚲Q↷❀◑⊟P'–♋(234)

Laverstock

Duck Inn Ⓛ

Duck Lane, SP1 1PU (signed from village centre)
SU160303
✪ 12-midnight ☎ (01722) 327678
∰ theduckatlaverstock.com
**Hop Back GB, Crop Circle, Summer Lightning, seasonal
beer; guest beer** Ⓗ
Large open-plan pub with ample car parking. A full
menu is available lunchtimes and evenings, with a
popular Sunday roast and a regular barbecue. Live
music features at weekends with a weekly quiz on
Tuesdays. Music festivals and other events such as
themed dinner nights are held. Dogs are welcome
and there is full disabled access and facilities. Well
situated for walkers on the Clarendon Way. The
guest beer is from Downton.
⚲Q↷❀◑&♣P'–♋(R6,66)

Malmesbury

Whole Hog Ⓛ

8 Market Cross, SN16 9AS
✪ 11-11 (midnight Sat); 12-11 Sun ☎ (01666) 825845
**Stonehenge Pigswill; Wadworth 6X; Young's Bitter;
guest beers** Ⓗ
Located between the 15th-century Market Cross
and Abbey, this wooden-floored pub is popular
with locals and tourists. It offers five well-kept real
ales including two guests, frequently from nearby
breweries. Good, freshly prepared food is served in
the bar at lunchtime and in a separate dining room
in the evening (not Sun). The pub is unrivalled in
the area for local cask ale and cider, all served
efficiently in this friendly town-centre pub.
Q↷◑♠♋(91,92)

Market Lavington

Green Dragon L
26-28 High Street, SN10 4AG
🕔 9-midnight ☎ (01380) 813235
⊕ greendragonlavington.co.uk
Wadworth Henry's IPA, 6X, seasonal beers 🖽
A cracking village pub in the heart of the community, the Green Dragon has built up a deserved reputation for well-kept ales and an excellent food menu. Warm, cosy and welcoming, this is the ideal spot to while away an hour or two on a cold day. Children and dogs are welcome, and darts, pool and boules are available. The spacious interior is well furnished and the bar staff are polite and friendly. ♨🎝🏵🏮🌀🍴🅿🕭

Melksham

Bear
3 Bath Road, SN12 6LL
🕔 8-midnight (1am Fri & Sat) ☎ (01225) 792690
Greene King Abbot; Ruddles Best Bitter; Wadworth 6X; guest beers 🖽
A closed town pub purchased, renovated to a very high standard and reopened by Wetherspoon. Close to the town centre, buses stop outside. Various photographs and posters show the history of the pub and nearby Avon Tyres factory (note the tractor seat wall lights). Helpful and friendly staff serve numerous ales and an extensive food menu including weekly curry and steak nights. There is a large seating area in this family-friendly pub. Regular ale and cider festivals are held.
♨Q🎝🏵🌀🍴🚻➔(Melksham)🌀🕭🚃(234,272)

Netherhampton

Victoria & Albert
SP2 8PU (opp church) SU108298
🕔 11-3.30, 5.30-11; 12-3, 7-10.30 Sun ☎ (01722) 743174
Beer range varies 🖽
This welcoming classic thatched inn dates from 1540. Inside, a log fire welcomes customers in winter while outside a large garden and patio await on sunny days. Three handpulls dispense an ever-changing range of real ales from far and wide and Black Rat cider. Quality food is prepared in the pub, ranging from light snacks to full meals. Local CAMRA and Wessex Region Pub of the Year 2012. Quintessential England – a gem.
♨Q🎝🏵🌀🌂🕭🅿🕭

Pewsey

Coopers Arms L
37-39 Ball Road, SN9 5BL
🕔 5 (12 Sat)-11; 12-10.30 Sun ☎ (01672) 562495
Fuller's London Pride; Wadworth 6X; guest beers 🖽
Lively and friendly down-to-earth thatched pub on the eastern edge of Pewsey. Four real ales are served including two guest beers, one from the local Three Castles Brewery. A popular local, it runs a cricket team during the season and has connections with the local rugby team. Live music plays on Friday nights including bands from the US from time to time. Special entertainment is hosted at Christmas – this could be opera or an orchestra performing at the pub. Holiday cottages are available. ♨🏵🌀🍀🅿🚃(X5)

Crown Inn L
60 Wilcot Road, SN9 5EL
🕔 4 (12 Wed & Thu)-11; 12-11.30 Fri; 12-midnight Sat; 12-10.30 Sun ☎ (01672) 562653
⊕ thecrowninnpewsey.com
Wadworth 6X; guest beers 🖽
The Crown Inn is home to World's End Ales and always offers four of its own brews plus one each from Stonehenge and Hop Back. Two ciders are also available. This traditional village local has a small bar with pool and darts and a lounge with an attractive stone and brick fireplace in the centre. Chess and poetry nights feature regularly and live music twice a month. Food is served Friday evening and Sunday lunchtime only unless by prior arrangement. 🏵🌀🏮➔🍀🕭🚃(X5)

Ramsbury

Crown & Anchor L
1 Crowood Lane, SN8 2PT
🕔 closed Mon, 12-3, 6.30-11; 12-10.30 Sun
☎ (01672) 520335 ⊕ crownramsbury.co.uk
Ramsbury Kennet Valley, Gold; Wadworth Henry's IPA; guest beers 🖽
A quiet and welcoming 19th-century country pub with a small bar and three rooms, two with fireplaces. Interesting bric-a-brac adorns the low ceiling beams including 200-year-old blacksmith's fixings and a Victorian beer engine that was used behind the bar and is now on display. Thursday is acoustic music night and a quiz is held every Sunday evening. There is a garden area behind the pub. Two en-suite B&B rooms are available.
♨Q🎝🏵🌀🍴🅿🕭🚃(46,48)

Royal Wootton Bassett

Five Bells L
Wood Street, SN4 7BD
🕔 12-3, 5-11.30; 12-midnight Fri-Sun ☎ (01793) 849422
Black Sheep Best Bitter; Fuller's London Pride; guest beers 🖽
Dating back to around 1841, this characterful cosy local has a thatched roof and wood-beamed ceiling. The bar sports six handpumps for two regular and four guest beers, usually including a beer from Braydon Ales down the road. Westons Old Rosie cider is on another pump. Special events are celebrated throughout the year such as Burn's Night when a piper plays. Quiz night is the last Sunday of the month and there is a Tuesday book club and a summer beer festival. The pub has darts and crib teams. ♨🏵🌀🏮🍀🕭🚃(55)

Salisbury

Deacons L
118 Fisherton Street, SP2 7QT
🕔 5 (4 Fri; 12 Sat)-11; 12-10 Sun ☎ (01722) 504723
Hop Back GB, Summer Lightning; Sharp's Doom Bar 🖽
A welcoming no-frills town-centre locals' pub with a basic wooden-floored front bar and a larger back room with sofas and tables. Unusual artefacts abound on the walls and ceilings. A smoking area is available outside. This conveniently located pub is close to the railway station. Last entrance is 10.40pm Monday to Saturday. ➔🍀🕭🚃

Duke of York L
34 York Road, SP2 7AS
🕔 6 (2 Sat)-midnight; 2-11 Sun ☎ (01722) 503872

Beer range varies Ⓗ
Built in 1901 by Ushers and situated down a quiet side street, this small, single-bar pub reopened in 2011 after a long period of closure. A true free house, it offers five real ales from far and wide, usually including a selection of local beers. The two changing real ciders are from producers across the country. There is a strong community focus with regular quizzes and summer events, and conversation thrives. Beer festivals are held from time to time. Just a short walk from the station. ⚲☆⏬♣♿⊠(R1)

King's Head

Bridge Street, SP1 2ND
✪ 7am-midnight (1am Thu-Sat) ☎ (01722) 342050
Greene King Abbot; Ruddles Best Bitter; guest beers Ⓗ
This Wetherspoon Lloyds No.1 bar is arranged over two floors of a building that was rebuilt in the 1880s on a site where there has been a public house since 1470. Originally known as Bores Place, it became the King's Head around 1520 and the County Hotel when it was rebuilt. Now back to the King's Head, it offers four ever-changing guest ales include many from local breweries, and a large selection of bottled beers and ciders. The food is Wetherspoon's standard fare, and beer festivals are held twice a year. ⏬☆⚲⏸⑪♿⇄♦⊾⊠

Rai d'Or ⒧

69 Brown Street, SP1 2AS
✪ 5-11; closed Sun ☎ (01722) 327137
Beer range varies Ⓗ
Thirteenth-century characterful free house with a fascinating history. An inglenook fireplace and low ceilings make for an appealing ambience. Excellent, reasonably priced Thai food is complemented by two ever-changing, usually local, beers. It can be busy at food times, but drinkers are always welcome. There is a discount on food before 6.30pm and on beer for CAMRA members. Former local CAMRA Pub of the Year. ▶♣⊠

Village Freehouse ⒧

33 Wilton Road, SP2 7EF (on A36 near St Paul's roundabout)
✪ 11 (3 Mon-Thu)-11; 12-11 Sun ☎ (01722) 329707
Downton Quadhop; guest beers Ⓗ
Friendly city local close to the railway station with four changing guest beers. The focus is on local microbreweries and beers unusual for the area, with requests welcome. The only regular outlet in the city for dark beers, a dark ale, mild, porter or stout is always available. TV sport is screened and there is free Wi-Fi. This revitalised local is popular with rail users and features rail memorabilia and books. The pub sells fresh rolls but continues its bring-your-own-food policy. ⇄⊠

Winchester Gate ⓨ ⒧

113-117 Rampart Road, SP1 1JA
✪ 12 (2 Mon-Wed)-11 ☎ (01722) 322834
⊕ winchestergate.co.uk
Hop Back Crop Circle; guest beers Ⓗ
An inn since the 17th century, this free house once provided for travellers at the city's east tollgate. Four handpumps offer ales from across the UK, and a real cider is often alongside. Three beer festivals feature each year, and cider festivals in March and October. The garden has a pétanque terrain and boules are available. Live music plays every

weekend, with an open mic night on the third Wednesday of the month. Filled rolls are sold. LocAle accredited and local CAMRA Pub of the Year 2013. ☆♦P⊾⊠

Wyndham Arms ⒧

27 Estcourt Road, SP1 3AS
✪ 4.30 (12 Thu)-11.30; 12-midnight Fri & Sat; 12-11.30 Sun
☎ (01722) 331026
Hop Back Heracles, GB, Crop Circle, Summer Lightning, seasonal beers Ⓗ
The birthplace of Hop Back Brewery, the Wyndham celebrated 26 consecutive years in the Guide in 2013. A traditional ale house, it has a single bar with six handpumps serving a selection of Hop Back ales. A guest pump features Hop Back or Downton seasonal beers, or occasionally an ale from further afield. There is also a fine selection of bottled beers and wines. This is a pub for conversation, good-natured banter and fine ales. ⏬♣⊠(R2,R6,11)

Semington

Somerset Arms

High Street, BA14 6JR (N from roundabout on A361) ST898607
✪ 10-11 (10.30 Sun) ☎ (01380) 870067
⊕ somersetarmssemington.co.uk
Bath Ales Gem; guest beers Ⓗ
A coaching inn possibly dating back to the 16th century. It offers a regular beer and three guests from micros within 50 miles, while the highly regarded food is made from local ingredients. Close to the Kennet & Avon Canal, it is popular with boaters. Accommodation is in three luxury en-suite bedrooms. ⚲☆⚑⏸♿♦P⊾⊠(234)

Semley

Benett Arms

SP7 9AS (off A350, 4 miles N of Shaftesbury) ST891270
✪ 12-3, 5-11 ☎ (01747) 830221 ⊕ benettarms.co.uk
Ringwood Best Bitter; guest beers Ⓗ
A former Gibbs Mew country pub, this is now a genuine free house sitting by the village green and pond in a quiet village, with a single small bar and separate dining areas. The beer choice varies but there are usually three to choose from, either on handpump or direct from the cellar. Excellent home-cooked food is available at all sessions. A warm welcome is extended to all, including families and dogs, in an area popular with walkers. ⚲Q☆⚑⏸♿♣♦P⊾⊠(84,247)

Swindon

Glue Pot ⒧

5 Emlyn Square, SN1 5BP
✪ 12 (4 Mon)-11; 11.30-11 Fri & Sat; 12-10.30 Sun
☎ (01793) 325993
Hop Back Crop Circle, Summer Lightning; White Horse Bitter; guest beers Ⓗ
The Glue Pot is part of the historic sandstone Swindon Railway Village built in the 1840s. It offers six Hop Back or Downton ales including some seasonals, two guest ales and five real ciders. Food is served lunchtimes Wednesday to Friday. Although usually quiet, the pub can get busy on weekend evenings. Quiz night is Thursday. Well worth a visit. ☆⏸⇄♦⊠(8,14)

Hop Inn L

7 Devizes Road, SN1 4BJ
☼ 12-11 (midnight Fri & Sat); 12-10.30 Sun
☎ (01793) 976833 ⊕ hopinnswindon.co.uk
Beer range varies H

A converted former shop, this new venue has an unusually open aspect to the front, making it very inviting. Inside it is furnished in an eclectic style with bright plastic chairs and tables made from reclaimed wood. A genuine free house, it has five handpumps, one dispensing the house beer brewed by Ramsbury and the others offering an ever-changing variety of guest ales sourced from smaller breweries. There are also two real ciders in boxes. ♠🖿(11,12)

Weighbridge Brewhouse L

Penzance Drive, SN5 7JL
☼ 11 (12 Sun)-11 ☎ (01793) 881500
⊕ weighbridgebrewhouse.co.uk
Weighbridge English Ale, Best, Pooley's Golden, seasonal beers H

The former Archers Brewery reopened as an upmarket brew and gastro-pub in 2011. The focus is on dining, with a modern open-plan dining space serving freshly prepared quality food made with locally sourced ingredients. However, the long and shiny bar has five handpumps dispensing excellent beers crafted on the premises – five regulars plus seasonal brews. A taster trio of one-third pints can be ordered if you cannot make up your mind. Seating is limited in the bar area, with a terrace available for the milder season. ⌖◖▶P🖿(8,55)

Wheatsheaf L

32 Newport Street, SN1 3DP
☼ 12-3, 5-11; 12-midnight Fri & Sat; 12-11 Sun
☎ (01793) 496396
Wadworth Henry's IPA, Horizon, 6X, Bishops Tipple A; **guest beers** H

The pub underwent a major refurbishment in 2011 and is now more inviting with plenty of traditional features such as mirrors, wood fixtures and open brickwork. There are two rows of three wooden casks on new racking and six handpumps on the bar. These casks are decorative only – the beer is pumped up by air pressure from casks in the cellar. Two guest beers come from the Wadworth list. Both front and back bar are similar in appearance with comfortable seating. Wi-Fi is available. ⇞Q⌖⌖🖿(11,12)

Tisbury

Boot Inn L

High Street, SP3 6PS
☼ 12-2.30, 7 (5 Fri)-11; 12-4 Sun ☎ (01747) 870363
Beer range varies G

Fine village pub built of Chilmark stone, licensed since 1768, with a relaxed, friendly atmosphere appealing to locals and visitors alike. Run by the same landlord since 1976, it became a free house in 2009. It offers three or four ales sourced from local breweries, as well as from further afield, with a Sixpenny beer often available. Excellent food is served (pizzas only on Tue) and there is a spacious garden. A former local CAMRA Pub of the Year. ⇞⌖◖▶⇄♣P⌐🖿(25,26)

Trowbridge

King's Arms

5 Castle Street, BA14 8AN
☼ 11-11 (12 Thu; 1am Fri & Sat); 12-11 Sun
☎ (01225) 751310 ⊕ thekingsarmstrowbridge.co.uk
Bath Ales Gem; Sharp's Doom Bar; guest beers H

Following extensive refurbishment, this town-centre pub reopened in 2010 as a smart and welcoming free house. A single drinking area, served by a central bar, has partitions creating a number of separate snug-like areas. The patio behind the pub, with a listed tree, makes a pleasant spot for an alfresco drink. An interesting, varied food menu is offered. The beer range includes a guest, usually sourced from a local micro, sometimes Hop Back or Downton. Black Rat is the usual real cider. ⇞⌖◖▶⌖⇄♣⌐🖿

Upavon

Ship L

10 High Street, SN9 6EA
☼ 11-12.30am (1am Thu-Sat); 12-11 Sun ☎ (01980) 630313
⊕ theshipinnupavon.co.uk
Sharp's Doom Bar; Wadworth 6X; guest beers H

Parts of the Ship Inn date from the 15th century. Completely refurbished in recent years, it combines traditional wood beams with a light, open interior. The decor, including a huge model of the Cutty Sark in the dining room, has a nautical or local theme. Tuesday is fish and chips night and a wood-burning pizza oven at the back is fired up Thursday-Saturday. The four guest ales are usually local and three real ciders and 40 malt whiskies are available. Dog-friendly. ⇞⌖◖▶⌖♣🖿(X5)

Warminster

Fox & Hounds

6 Deverill Road, BA12 9QP ST870445
☼ 11-11 ☎ (01985) 216711 ⊕ pitcherpubs.co.uk
Wessex Foxy's Best, Warminster Warrior; guest beer H

This friendly two-bar pub was local CAMRA Pub of the Year 2012 and Community Pub of the Year in 2011. One bar is a cosy snug while the other has a pool table and TV at the back. A large skittle alley and function room opened in 2009. A regular outlet for Wessex Brewery, the guest beer is usually sourced from another local micro. At least six real ciders, including regulars from Rich's and Thatchers, are the pub's mainstay. Closing time may be later than 11pm.
⇞Q⌖⌖⌐⇄♣♣P⌐🖿(24,264,265)

Organ Inn

49 High Street, BA12 9AQ ST872451
☼ 4 (12 Sat)-midnight; 4-11 Sun ☎ (01985) 211777
⊕ theorganinn.co.uk
Beer range varies H

An inn until 1913, then shop premises, the building reopened as a pub in 2006. The welcoming interior comprises three rooms with a traditional feel, along with a snug, games room and skittle alley. Up to five ciders or perries – three from Westons and two guest – are served from a separate bar. The beer range includes Organ Bitter (a closely guarded secret) plus two guests, usually sourced from local breweries. An art gallery is upstairs. A beer festival is held each September.
⇞Q⌖⌖⌐⇄♣♣⌐🖿(24,264,265)

Whiteparish

Parish Lantern L

Romsey Road, SP5 2SA (on A27)

🌣 11.30-3, 5-11; 11.30-11 Fri & Sat; 12-10.30 Sun
☎ (01794) 884392 ⊕ theparishlantern.co.uk

Flack Manor Flack's Double Drop; Sharp's Doom Bar; guest beers Ⓗ

A welcoming pub run by the same couple since 1991. The single bar has a central fireplace and areas for dining, pool and darts. Guest beers are from Hop Back, Downton and other local breweries. There are family events on bank holidays and occasional beer festivals. Food is served lunchtimes and evenings, including regular themed nights. A spacious garden with play equipment for children and a chicken coop leads to a camping area with space for five caravans.
🏠🐕⊛◖🕭🅐♣P⚊➡(X7,34)

Wilton

Bear Inn

12 West Street, SP2 0DF (there are two Wiltons; this one is W of Salisbury; by Market Square)

🌣 11 (12 Sun)-11 ☎ (01722) 742468

Badger First Gold, Tanglefoot, seasonal beer Ⓗ

Dating back some 300 years, this traditional country-style pub is homely and welcoming with a woodburner adding warmth in winter. It has a heated, covered, smoking area and a peaceful walled garden offering both sun and shade. Parking is available in the nearby Market Square. A range of Badger bottled beers is available. Guinness, the pub dog, offers a friendly welcome to all who visit the pub. 🏠⊛◖♣⚊➡(R3,26)

Swan L

SN8 3SS (there are two Wiltons; this one is SE of Marlborough)

🌣 12-3, 6-11; 12-11 Sat; 12-10.30 Sun ☎ (01672) 870274
⊕ theswanwilton.co.uk

Beer range varies Ⓗ/Ⓖ

This is a pretty red-brick village pub near the Kennet & Avon Canal with an attractive interior. There is equal emphasis on good food and ale, with home-cooked meals including produce from nearby farms and a range of quality beers on stillage and gravity fed. The five varying guest ales are complemented by traditional draught ciders. The pub is ideally situated for inclusion in a circular walk starting at Great Bedwyn along the canal to the beam engines and the windmill at Wilton. It is also just off the Mid-Wilts Way.
🏠⊛◖🖙P➡(X5,22)

Wroughton

Carters Rest L

High Street, SN4 9JU

🌣 5-11 (midnight Fri); 12-midnight Sat; 12-11 Sun
☎ (01793) 812288

Bath Ales Gem; Cotswold Spring Stunner; Ramsbury Flint Knapper; Sharp's Doom Bar; guest beers Ⓗ

The Carters Rest opened as a beer house around 1866. The present large two-bar pub dates from 1904 and is a real ale mecca, with four regular and eight changing guest ales, plus ciders and perry. A quiz night is held on Thursday, a poker evening on Tuesday and a Christmas beer festival in December. The pub welcomes children until early evening and well-behaved pets. 🏠⊛🖭♣🖙P➡(54,71)

King's Arms, Trowbridge (Photo: sally m)

ENGLAND

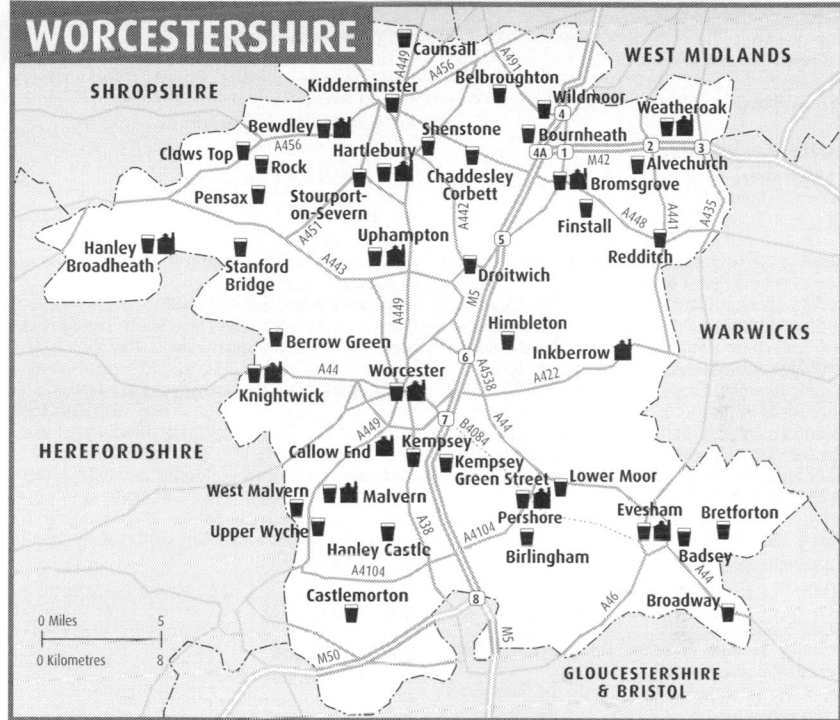

WORCESTERSHIRE

SHROPSHIRE

WEST MIDLANDS

Caunsall
Kidderminster Belbroughton
Wildmoor Weatheroak
Bewdley Shenstone Bournheath
Clows Top Hartlebury
Rock Chaddesley Alvechurch
Corbett Bromsgrove
Pensax Stourport-
on-Severn
Uphampton Finstall
Hanley Redditch
Broadheath Stanford Droitwich
Bridge
Himbleton WARWICKS
Berrow Green Inkberrow
Worcester
Knightwick
Callow End Kempsey
HEREFORDSHIRE Kempsey
Green Street Lower Moor
West Malvern Malvern Evesham Bretforton
Pershore
Upper Wyche Birlingham Badsey
Hanley Castle
Castlemorton Broadway

0 Miles 5
0 Kilometres 8

GLOUCESTERSHIRE
& BRISTOL

Alvechurch

Weighbridge ♀ Ⓛ
Scarfield Wharf, Scarfield Hill, B48 7SQ (follow signs to marina from village) SP022721
✪ 12-3, 7-11 (10.30 Sun) ☎ (0121) 445 5111
⊕ the-weighbridge.co.uk
Beer range varies Ⓗ
Adjacent to Alvechurch marina and near the rail station, this cosy canalside pub has two small lounges and a public bar adorned with many CAMRA awards. Popular beer festivals are held in spring and autumn. Value home-cooked food is served lunchtimes and evenings (not Tue or Wed) and excellent Sunday lunches. Ample outdoor seating includes a heated marquee which can be used for functions. The house beers are Weatheroak Tillerman's Tipple and Kinver Bargees Bitter, and three changing guest beers always include a mild. Real cider or perry is also on offer.
Q ☎ ❀ ◑ ▸ ⬛ ⬌ ⬤ P ⸺ ₪ (146)

Badsey

Round of Gras
47 Bretforton Road, WR11 7XQ (B4035/B4085 jct)
✪ 11-11 ☎ (01386) 830206 ⊕ roundofgras.co.uk
Flowers IPA; Uley Pigs Ear; guest beer Ⓗ
Open-plan roadside inn with a separate restaurant area, games area with pool table, comfortable bar and seating, and an attractive beer garden. The pub is uniquely named to celebrate the world-famous local asparagus that features prominently on the menu from March to July. The interior is decorated with photographs and old farming implements, including those used in asparagus cultivation. Food is served all day every day with a good-value carvery Tuesday to Thursday

lunchtimes. The ciders are Westons Old Rosie and a changing guest or a perry from Thatchers.
☎ ❀ ◑ ▸ ⬛ ♣ ⬤ P ⸺ ₪ (247)

Belbroughton

Belbroughton Club
5 High Street, DY9 9SY
✪ 6-11; 1-midnight Fri & Sat; 12-10.30 Sun
☎ (01562) 730490
Banks's Mild, Bitter Ⓟ; **Enville Ale** Ⓗ
This local club is Grade II-listed by English Heritage and dates back to the 17th century. The building's original timbers were salvaged from a ship named the Mermaid and can still be seen in some parts of the club today. There is bar-side seating for the locals and an open lounge as well as a separate pool table area and upstairs function room. The club was CAMRA branch Club of the Year in 2012 and is open to non-members. ❀ ♣ ⬤ ⸺ ₪ (318)

Berrow Green

Admiral Rodney Ⓛ
WR6 6PL
✪ 12-3 (not Mon), 5-11; 12-11 Sat; 12-10.30 Sun
☎ (01886) 821375 ⊕ admiral-rodney.co.uk
Wye Valley Bitter, HPA; guest beers Ⓗ
A light, airy country pub with three main bar areas and a restaurant serving freshly made and mainly locally produced food including excellent fish and chips (booking advised Fri and Sat eves). Guest ales are often from local microbreweries and real cider and perry are also on offer. The pub features a skittle alley, floodlit garden, covered and heated patio, disabled toilet and baby-changing facilities. Folk music is hosted on the third Wednesday of the month. En-suite accommodation is popular with

505

walkers on the Worcestershire Way. Well-behaved dogs are welcome in the locals bar.
ᴍQ🕸🚾◖◗🦽🏃♣☗P⚊⚊

Bewdley

Little Pack Horse 🅛
31 High Street, DY12 2DH (near Lax Lane 300yds from St Anne's Church)
❂ 12-3, 6-11; 12-3, 5-midnight Fri; 11-midnight Sat; 11-10.30 Sun ☎ (01299) 403762 ⊕ littlepackhorse.co.uk
Bewdley Worcestershire Way; Hobsons Town Crier; St Austell Tribute; guest beer ⊞
Tucked away at the narrow end of the High Street and dating from the 15th century, this welcoming pub has a reputation for good beer and great food. Four ales are available including one from the nearby Bewdley Brewery. The food menu specialises in pies from around the world such as Moroccan Chicken, Bombay Potato and Veg plus the famous Desperate Dan. Fish, vegetarian and daily specials are on the chalkboard.
ᴍ🏃🕸◖◗🍴≠(SVR)⚊⚊

Mug House 🅛
12 Severnside North, DY12 2EE (150yds from river bridge)
❂ 12-11 (11.30 Fri & Sat) ☎ (01299) 402543 ⊕ mughousebewdley.co.uk
Bewdley Worcestershire Way; Taylor Landlord; Wye Valley HPA; guest beer ⊞
Located on the side of the Severn, the Mug House is not to be missed – a friendly pub that welcomes locals and visitors alike. It serves three regular beers including one from Bewdley Brewery, plus a guest. The lounge bar has cosy settles and a log fire. To the rear is a sun terrace with a glass-covered patio in a lovely setting with grapevines and wisteria. Fine food is available in the restaurant and meals in the bar at lunchtime.
ᴍQ🏃🕸🚾◖◗♿≠(SVR)🏃⚊⚊

Waggon & Horses 🅛
91 Kidderminster Road, DY12 1DG (on Bewdley-Kidderminster road, Catchem's End)
❂ 12-11; 11.30-1am Fri & Sat ☎ (01299) 4031/0 ⊕ waggonbewdley.co.uk
Banks's Mild, Bitter; Bathams Best Bitter; guest beer ⊞
Popular with locals and visitors, this pub has a central bar that serves three distinct areas. The small wooden-floored snug has settles, tables and a dartboard; the larger room has a roll-down screen for major sporting events, bench seating and a TV. An old kitchen range in the dining area adds to the cottagey feel. Food is available Tuesday and Thursday evenings with a carvery on Sundays. The attractive terraced garden is on many levels. Guest ales come from local independents.
🕸◖◗🍴♿≠(SVR)♣🏃P⚊⚊

Woodcolliers Arms 🅛
76 Welch Gate, DY12 2AU (200yds from St Anne's Church up Welch Gate)
❂ 5-11 (midnight Tue & Thu); 4.30-midnight Fri; 12.30-midnight Sat; 12.30-11 Sun ☎ (01299) 400589 ⊕ woodcolliers.co.uk
Beer range varies ⊞
A short walk from Bewdley centre, this old pub offers a changing range of four guest beers. Tolly English Ale 2.8% is usually available plus three ciders. The Cordon Bleu chef offers a Russian and English menu freshly prepared seven days a week.

The Grade II-listed pub has beams and open fires, and no piped music. It stores bikes and fishing tackle for guests and provides a luggage service for Severn, Geopark and Worcestershire Way walkers – ring for details. Quiz night is Tuesday.
ᴍQ🕸🚾◖◗🍴≠(SVR)♣🏃P⚊⚊

Birlingham

Swan 🅛
Church Street, WR10 3AQ
❂ 12-3, 6.30-11 (10.30 Sun) ☎ (01386) 750485 ⊕ theswaninn.co.uk
Wye Valley Bitter; guest beers ⊞
Black and white thatched free house dating back over 500 years in a quiet village. The open bar/lounge boasts exposed beams and a wood-burning stove. More than 200 guest beers are served over the course of a year alongside two real ciders (one from Thatchers, the other Moles Black Rat). Two beer festivals are held in May and September. Traditional home-cooked food is available in the conservatory (not Sun eve). Crib, darts and dominoes are played in the bar. There is a large car park opposite and a pleasant south-facing garden.
ᴍ🕸◖◗♣🏃P⚊⚊(382)

Bournheath

Nailers Arms
62 Doctors Hill, B61 9JE
❂ 12-midnight (1am Fri & Sat); 12-11.30 Sun ☎ (01527) 873045 ⊕ thenailersarms.co.uk
Wadworth 6X; Wye Valley HPA; guest beer ⊞
Originally a 1780s nailmakers' workshop-cum-brewery, this whitewashed three-gabled building has a traditional quarry-tiled bar with a real fire. The bar has been recently refurbished. Two guest ales are usually available and occasionally a real cider. Regular beer festivals are held. The lounge/restaurant is accessible via a corridor or separate entrance. The restaurant closes occasionally for functions such as weddings. ᴍ🏃🕸◖◗🍴♣P⚊

Bretforton

Fleece Inn 🍺 ★ 🅛
The Cross, WR11 7JE (near church)
❂ 11-11.30 (10.30 Sun) summer; 11-3, 6-11; 11-11.30 Wed-Sat; 12-10.30 Sun winter ☎ (01386) 831173 ⊕ thefleeceinn.co.uk
Uley Pigs Ear; Wye Valley Bitter; guest beers ⊞
This renowned old National Trust village pub has been identified by CAMRA as one of Britain's Best

Real Heritage Pubs. It houses a world-famous collection of 17th-century pewter. Up to four ciders are available, including one produced at the Fleece using apples from various NT premises. The pub has its own orchard garden with children's play equipment. The good British pub food is highly recommended. Morris and music feature in the pub all year, with a folk session on Thursday and regular musical entertainment in the medieval barn. Pebworth Morris meet here.
🏚Q☺🏵🍴◑🎵👌🏃♣🐾⚂—🚃(554)

Broadway

Crown & Trumpet 🅛
14 Church Street, WR12 7AE (on road to Snowshill, just off Cotswolds Way)
✪ 11-2.30, 5-11; 11-11 Fri-Sun ☎ (01386) 853202
🌐 cotswoldholidays.co.uk
Cotswold Spring Codger; Stroud Tom Long; guest beers 🅗
Picturesque 17th-century Cotswold stone inn, popular with locals, tourists and walkers, complete with oak beams and log fires along with plenty of Flowers Brewery memorabilia. Stanway beers alternate throughout the seasons and other guest beers are sourced from Gloucestershire microbreweries. A regular mini beer festival is held over the Christmas period and Gwatkins cider is sold. The food menu offers specials featuring locally grown produce. The pub has an unusual range of pub games, and hosts entertainment including live music. 🏚☺🏵🍴◑👌♣🐾P⚂—🚃(559)

Bromsgrove

Golden Cross Hotel 🅛
20 High Street, B61 8HH (S end of High St)
✪ 8am-midnight (1am Fri & Sat) ☎ (01527) 870005
Greene King Abbot; Ruddles Best Bitter; guest beers 🅗
This Wetherspoon pub sits at the heart of Bromsgrove town centre – it was previously a hotel and coach house. Reasonably priced food is served from early morning breakfast to evening meals. Twelve handpumps dispense a range of beers, often including LocAles. Beer festivals are held monthly and CAMRA members receive a discount. There is a Pay & Display car park at the rear.
Q☺🏵◑👌🐾P⚂—🚃

Ladybird 🅛
2 Finstall Road, B60 2DZ (on B4184, adjacent to railway station) SO969695
✪ 11 (12 Mon & Tue)-11; 12-10.30 Sun ☎ (01527) 878014
🌐 ladybirdinn.co.uk
Bathams Best Bitter; Birds Amnesia; Wye Valley HPA 🅗
This popular local is situated adjacent to the town's railway station. The light, airy lounge, with polished wooden floor, has historic railway photographs and a dartboard in an alcove, in contrast to the busy bar. Pub grub is served every day, however if your taste is for Italian cuisine try the adjoining privately-run restaurant. Two function/meeting rooms of different sizes are available on the first floor. The attached 45-room Travelodge offers accommodation with breakfast available at the Ladybird.
🏵☺🏵◑👌🐾♣P⚂—🚃(140,141,143)

Castlemorton

Plume of Feathers
Gloucester Road, WR13 6JB (on B4208) SO788388
✪ 12-11 ☎ (01684) 833554
Thwaites Original; Wye Valley HPA, Butty Bach; guest beers 🅗
Classic country pub on the edge of Castlemorton Common with splendid views of the Malvern Hills. The location makes it an ideal starting point for walks across the common and on to the hills. The main bar has a wealth of beams and a real fire while a small side room has TV and darts. A separate room caters for diners. Occasional live music is hosted and a beer festival is held in midsummer. A local bus is available on Saturday, otherwise it is a pleasant walk over the common from nearby Welland. 🏚Q🐾☺◑◑🏵P🚃(379,380)

Caunsall

Anchor Inn 🅛
DY11 5YL (off A449 Kidderminster-Wolverhampton road)
✪ 11-4, 7-11; 11-3, 7-10.30 Sun ☎ (01562) 850254
🌐 theanchorinncaunsall.co.uk
Hobsons Best Bitter, Town Crier; Holden's Golden Glow; Wye Valley HPA, Butty Bach 🅗
Popular village pub run by the same family since 1927, this friendly traditional local is renowned for its six real ales, ciders and well-filled cobs. A central doorway leads to the little-changed bar with its original 1920s furniture and horse-racing memorabilia. The friendly staff welcome an impressive mix of customers and the pub gets very busy at lunchtimes. Easily reached from the nearby canal, this gem is well worth a visit. Local CAMRA Pub of the Year 2012. Q🐾☺◑◑👌♣🐾P⚂—🚃

Chaddesley Corbett

Swan 🅛
The Village, DY10 4SD SO892737
✪ 11-3.30, 6-11; 11-11 Sat; 12-3.30, 7-10.30 Sun
☎ (01562) 777302
Bathams Mild Ale, Best Bitter 🅗
Dating from 1606, this village pub has a large lounge, snug and public bar. Rolls and pork pies are available daily at lunchtime, the restaurant serves evening meals Thursday to Saturday. A jazz night is held every Thursday evening. The large garden with children's play area overlooks beautiful countryside. Bathams XXX is served seasonally and the regular cider is Westons Old Rosie. Dogs are welcome in the bar. The pub is well used by walkers and the Elizabethan Harvington Hall is a mile away. 🏚Q🐾☺◑👌♣🐾P⚂—

Clows Top

Colliers Farm Shop & Café 🅛
Tenbury Road, DY14 9HA (on main A456 Kidderminster-Tenbury road)
✪ 9am-6 (9 Fri) ☎ (01299) 832242 🌐 colliersfarmshop.co.uk
Hobsons Best Bitter 🅗
Local community farm shop and café with a bar serving a local real ale on draught and still cider from nearby producers. A steady stream of customers calls in to buy local produce, relax in the café or enjoy a beer. An extensive and unusual range of UK and foreign bottled beers is available in the shop. Food is served until 5.30pm (8.30pm Fri). ☺👌🐾P🚃

Droitwich

Hop Pole Ⓛ
40 Friar Street, WR9 8ED
✪ 12-11 (10.30 Sun) ☎ (01905) 770155 ⊕ thehoppole.com
Enville Ale; Malvern Hills Black Pear; Wye Valley HPA,
Butty Bach; guest beer Ⓗ
An 18th-century black and white timbered inn,
popular with locals and visitors alike. Guest beers
are mostly from local breweries. Good-value
home-cooked food is served at lunchtime. A
separate pool room adjoins the bar and there is a
heated patio area for smokers. Live music plays on
some weekends. Close by is the newly restored
Droitwich Barge Canal which offers secure
moorings. A warm welcome is assured at this
friendly pub. ⌂❄◖≠♣ᵉ⌐⊟

Ring o'Bells Ⓛ
The Holloway, WR9 8HD (off Hanbury Road)
✪ 1.30 (12 Sun)-11.30; 12-midnight Sat ☎ (01905) 770083
⊕ ringobells.webs.com
Holden's Black Country Bitter; Wye Valley HPA; guest
beers Ⓗ
Small pub just off the town centre and close to the
restored Droitwich Junction Canal. The modern
single bar has an area to the side with a TV. There is
a function room and a games bar to the rear with a
pool table, darts and fruit machine. Sport is keenly
followed by locals on Saturday. Bar snacks are
available at lunchtime. Up to three guest ales are
from local breweries such as Wye Valley and
Holdens. Live music plays occasionally.
♨⌂❄⊟♣♠P²⌐⊟

Evesham

Olde Red Horse
17 Vine Street, WR11 4RE
✪ 10-11 (midnight Fri & Sat); 12-11 Sun ☎ (01386) 442784
M&B Brew XI; Wells Bombardier; guest beer Ⓗ
A black and white 15th-century coaching inn with
award-winning floral displays and a courtyard
decorated with gargoyles and grotesques. This
popular and friendly two-room pub attracts old and
young alike. The public bar has a TV, dartboard and
jukebox. The lounge has an area set aside for
dining, with many features linked to the historic
Evesham Abbey. Traditional home-cooked food is
popular, especially the excellent-value steak night.
♨⌂❄◖◗◖⊟≠♣♠ᵉ⌐⊟(50)

Finstall

Cross Inn
34 Alcester Road, B60 1EW (on B4184)
✪ 12-11.30 (midnight Fri & Sat) ☎ (01527) 872911
Taylor Landlord; guest beers Ⓗ
Friendly village pub very popular with locals
offering a selection of guest beers, usually from
nearby breweries. Locally produced Tardebigge
Cider is sold from the tub. No hot food is available
but fresh cobs, pickled eggs and locally made
pickles, chutneys, jams and free range eggs are
sold at the bar. The beer garden at the rear of the
large car park has a shelter and is popular in
warmer weather. Two fundraising events are held
for the local hospice during the summer.
⌂❄≠(Bromsgrove)♣♠P⊟(143)

Hanley Broadheath

Fox Inn Ⓛ
WR15 8QS SO671652
✪ 5-midnight; 12-12.30am Fri & Sat; 12-10.30 Sun
☎ (01886) 853189
Bathams Best Bitter; Holden's Golden Glow; Joseph
Herbert Smith Foxy Lady; guest beer Ⓗ
Black and white timbered rural free house dating
from the 16th century. Three local real ales are
available including at least two from the pub's own
JHS brewery on site, plus occasional real cider in
summer. The friendly family-owned inn is warmed
by a welcoming wood-burning stove throughout
the winter. Meals are served Tuesday, Friday and
Saturday evenings and Sunday lunchtime, but
lunches can be ordered ahead on other days. Live
music plays occasionally and brewery trips are
arranged. Lawnmower racing is held in the
adjoining field in August. ♨Q⌂❄◖◗⊟⌂♣P²⌐

Hanley Castle

Three Kings ★ Ⓛ
Church End, WR8 0BL (signed off B4211) SO838420
✪ 12-3, 7-11 (10.30 Sun) ☎ (01684) 592686
Butcombe Bitter; Hobsons Best Bitter; guest beers Ⓗ
Identified by CAMRA as one of Britain's Best Real
Heritage Pubs, this unspoilt 15th-century country
inn on the village green near the church has been
run by the Roberts family since 1911. The three-
room interior comprises a small snug with large
inglenook, serving hatch and settle wall; a small
side room (no bar); and Nell's Lounge with another
inglenook, beams and its own entrance. Three
guest ales are on offer, often from local breweries,
and Westons Old Rosie cider. Live music sessions
feature regularly and a popular beer festival is held
in November. ♨Q⌂❄◖♣♠P⊟(363)

Hartlebury

Old Ticket Office Ⓛ
Station Road, DY11 7YJ
✪ 12-11 (midnight Fri & Sat); 12-10.30 Sun
☎ (01299) 253275 ⊕ oldticketoffice-hartlebury.co.uk
Attwood Farmers Dark Ale, Pale Ale, Nectar Bitter,
O'Ryan's Ⓗ
This interesting modern conversion of former
railway buildings is next to the platform of
Hartlebury station. The lounge bar has comfortable
bench seating reminiscent of former railway days,
and a large fireplace with woodburner and railway
signage. Outside, tables on the terrace overlook
the valley. Meals are served in the bar and in the
more formal oak-panelled restaurant. Beers are
from the Attwood Ales range brewed on-site and
the brewery also supplies other Katy O'Ryan's
outlets. ♨⌂❄◖◗ᵍ≠P⊟

White Hart
The Village, DY11 7TD (in old village near church)
✪ 12-11 (10.30 Mon & Sun; midnight Fri & Sat)
☎ (01299) 250286 ⊕ thewhitehartinhartlebury.co.uk
Beer range varies Ⓗ
Situated in the village opposite the church, this
attractive old pub has a comfortable lounge bar
with a log fire in winter and a restaurant with a
modern ambience. Meals are prepared on the
premises by experienced chefs. The regular beer is
usually Timothy Taylor Landlord, St Austell Tribute,
Sharp's Doom Bar or Wye Valley HPA, served
alongside up to two guest ales. ♨⌂❄◖◗⊟P²⌐⊟

Himbleton

Galton Arms 🅛
Harrow Lane, WR9 7LQ
❁ 12-2 (not Mon), 4.30-11; 11-11 Sun ☎ (01905) 391672
Banks's Bitter; Bathams Best Bitter; Wye Valley HPA; guest beer Ⓗ
A very comfortable and pleasant country pub with exposed beams and open fires, popular with locals and visitors alike. Good food is served at reasonable prices with themed food nights during the week. A separate dining area is available. The guest beer usually comes from a local brewer.
🅐🅠🗲🕸🕮🖒P🗝

Kempsey

Walter de Cantelupe 🅛
34 Main Road, WR5 3NA (on A38 next to Post Office)
❁ closed Mon; 12-2, 6-11; 12-3, 7-10.30 Sun
☎ (01905) 820572 ⊕ walterdecantelupe.co.uk
Cannon Royall Arrowhead Bitter; Mayfields Copper Fox; Taylor Landlord; guest beer Ⓗ
Named after a 13th-century Bishop of Worcester, the pub features a cosy drinking area, a large settle from the 1700s and an imposing inglenook fireplace. High-quality food uses local ingredients wherever possible. Events throughout the year include a paella party in June in the attractive walled garden. Local beers are served in lined glasses, with third-pint glasses available. Real cider is sometimes on offer in summer. CAMRA members receive a 10 per cent discount. The pub may stay open all day on summer weekends.
🅐🅠🗲🕸🖚🕮🖒🅐P🗝🖃(32,362)

Kempsey Green Street

Huntsman Inn
Green Street, WR5 3QB SO868490
❁ 5 (12 Sat)-11; 12-4, 7-11 Sun ☎ (01905) 820336
Bathams Best Bitter; Greene King IPA, Abbot Ⓗ
A former farmhouse dating back 300 years, this is now a cosy and friendly multi-roomed traditional local with exposed beams and a real fire. A separate restaurant serves reasonably priced home-cooked food. There is also a skittle alley with its own bar, an attractive garden and a large car park. The pub closes at lunchtimes during the week. Dogs are welcome in the bar and lounge.
🅐🗲🕸🕮🖚🖒🅟P

Kidderminster

Olde Seven Stars 🅛
13-14 Coventry Street, DY10 2BG
❁ 11-11 (11.30 Fri & Sat); 12-11 Sun ☎ (01562) 755777
⊕ yeoldesevenstars.co.uk
Beer range varies Ⓗ
With six ever-changing real ales and one draught cider, this traditional beer-and-banter pub is well worth visiting. It serves cobs and pork pies, and customers are also welcome to bring their own food (plenty of takeaways nearby) – tableware, serviettes and condiments provided. Live bands play monthly and a quiz is held on the second Wednesday. Families are welcome and there is a large rear garden with chickens. Winner of CAMRA Worcestershire Pub of the Year 2011 and local Pub of the Year 2013. 🗲🕸🖒🅐🖚🗝🖃

Swan 🅛
Vicar Street, DY10 1DE
❁ 10-11.30 (1am Fri & Sat); 12-6 Sun ☎ (01562) 823 0089
Castle Rock Harvest Pale; Holden's Golden Glow; Sharp's Doom Bar; Thwaites Wainwright; guest beers Ⓗ
This family-run one-room pub opposite the town hall, dating from 1865, is a worthy survivor of town-centre redevelopment. It serves six real ales including a couple from local breweries. Breakfast is available from 10am followed by bar food throughout the day (no food Sun). The pub is popular with shoppers, and in the evenings a small stage is used for live music on Thursdays once a month and regular DJs on Fridays and Saturdays. A beer festival is held in August. 🗲🕮🖒🖚🅐🖒🗝🖃

Knightwick

Talbot 🅛
WR6 5PH (on B4197, 400yds from A44 jct)
❁ 11-midnight; 12-10.30 Sun ☎ (01886) 821235
⊕ the-talbot.co.uk
Hobsons Best Bitter; Teme Valley T'Other, This, That Ⓗ
Dating back to the 14th century, this former coaching inn has been refurbished and extended. It has a tap room, lounge bar with real fire and an attractive conservatory for dining. Food is local and imaginative. Three or four beers from the Teme Valley Brewery behind the pub are usually available. There is a farmers' market on the second Sunday of the month and the very popular Green Hop Beer Festival in early October. Dog- and walker-friendly. 🅐🅠🗲🕸🖚🕮🖒🅐🅐🖚🗝P🖃(420)

Lower Moor

Old Chestnut Tree 🅛
Manor Road, WR10 2NZ
❁ 12-3 (not Mon & Tue), 5-11; 12-11 Fri-Sun
☎ (01386) 860380 ⊕ oldchestnuttreeinn.co.uk
Malvern Hills Black Pear; guest beers Ⓗ
Dating from the 16th century, the pub has an open bar and a snug with exposed beams. It retains many original features including an inglenook fireplace with stones scavenged from Pershore Abbey and a priest hole. Previously the Chestnut Club, it has the smallest designated ballroom in the country. Local guest beers and ciders supplement the regular ales. Beer festivals are held at Christmas, Easter and the August bank holiday, and a music festival in July. The pub also houses a post office and shop. 🅐🅠🗲🕮🖒🖚🅐🗝🖃(551)

Malvern

Great Malvern Hotel 🅛
Graham Road, WR14 2HN (by crossroads with Church St)
❁ 10-11; 11-10.30 Sun ☎ (01684) 563411
⊕ great-malvern-hotel.co.uk
Malvern Hills Black Pear; Tetley Bitter; guest beers Ⓗ
Popular hotel public bar a short walk from the Malvern theatres, ideal for pre- and post-performance refreshment. A beer from the nearby Malvern Hills Brewery is always on offer. Meals are served in the bar and in the adjoining brasserie including Sunday lunch. There is a comfortable lounge with lots of sofas, fresh coffee, daily newspapers and free Wi-Fi. Live music sessions are held throughout the week – check the website for details. On-site parking is limited but there is public parking nearby. 🗲🖚🕮🖚P🖃(42,43,44)

Morgan L

52 Clarence Road, WR14 3EQ
✪ 12-3.30, 5-11; 12-11 Fri & Sat; 12-10.30 Sun
☎ (01684) 578575
Wye Valley Bitter, HPA, Butty Bach; guest beer H
Wye Valley Brewery has created a real ale mecca here, named after the town's Morgan car factory. The open-plan interior is divided into a general drinking area, a slightly raised seating area with comfy settees to relax in, and an area for playing darts. The welcoming landscaped garden has plenty of seating, a fish pond and 'Them Organ' gates. Weekly activities include a book club, quizzes on Tuesday and an open-mic night on Wednesday. The guest beer is from the Wye Valley range. Q☎✿◑&⇙♣⌐₪(42,43,44)

Nag's Head

19-21 Bank Street, WR14 2JG
✪ 11-11.15 (11.30 Fri & Sat); 12-11 Sun ☎ (01684) 574373
⊕ nagsheadmalvern.co.uk
Banks's Bitter; Bathams Best Bitter; St George's Friar Tuck, Charger, Dragons Blood; Sharp's Doom Bar; guest beers H
A free house offering eight permanent beers including several from the owner's brewery, St George's, and up to six guests, plus two draught ciders, usually one local and one from Westons. Mismatched furniture and nooks and crannies provide a homely environment, although the pub does get busy most evenings and every weekend. Food is always popular. Outside is a large, covered, heated area to the front and a garden to the rear. A no swearing rule is enforced. The car park is small but there is ample parking on street.
₪✿◑♣♠P⌐₪(44,44A)

Pensax

Bell L

WR6 6AE (on B4202 Clows Top-Great Whitley road)
✪ 12-2.30 (not Mon), 5-11; 12-10.30 Sun ☎ (01299) 896677
⊕ thebellatpensax.co.uk
Bewdley Worcestershire Way; Exmoor Gold; Hobsons Best Bitter; Wye Valley HPA; guest beers H
Local CAMRA Pub of the Decade and previous West Midlands Pub of the Year, this family- and dog-friendly pub is not to be missed. Six constantly changing real ales are on offer, plus local cider and perry. There is a separate dining room and a snug where families are welcome. The menu offers good food made with local seasonal ingredients. Wooden floors, hanging hops, open fires and some pew seating give a true country feel. Well worth seeking out. ₪Q☎✿◑⑴⬤&♠P⌐

Pershore

Brandy Cask L

25 Bridge Street, WR10 1AJ
✪ 11.30-2.30, 7-11 (11.30 Thu); 11.30-3, 7-11.30 Fri & Sat; 12-3, 7-11 Sun ☎ (01386) 552602
Brandy Cask Whistling Joe, Brandy Snapper, John Baker's Original; guest beers H
At least three house ales are always available at this brewpub as well as a wide range of guest beers from around the country. Cheddar Valley cider is also normally stocked. Food is good and reasonably priced (no food Mon or Tue in winter). The beautifully kept rear garden runs down to the River Avon. This is a classic hostelry well worth a visit. ₪Q☎✿◑⬤₪

Redditch

Bramley Cottage L

Callow Hill Lane, Walkwood, B97 5QB (at jct of B4504 Windmill Drive and Callow Hill Lane)
✪ 11.30-midnight ☎ (01527) 542215
Purity Pure Ubu; Sharp's Doom Bar; Wye Valley Butty Bach; guest beers H
This comfortable modern pub is a popular meeting place for locals. The central L-shaped bar serves up to five real ales, and secluded dining and drinking areas have an intimate feel, with spacious seating and a real fire. Outside is a garden and patio area. Quiz nights on Sunday and Wednesday are well attended. Food is available until 10pm including a takeaway service. ₪Q☎✿◑⑴&P⌐₪(80)

Rock

Rock Cross Inn L

Rock Cross, DY14 9SD (follow signs from A456 to Rock)
✪ 5 (4 Fri; 12 Sat)-midnight; 12-11 Sun ☎ (01299) 832533
⊕ therockcrossinn.co.uk
Hobsons Best Bitter; Wye Valley HPA; guest beers H
Traditional village free house offering a public bar and lounge with a raised dining area. The beamed interior has a central serving area and is warmed by log fires in winter. The public bar has a pool table, dartboard and TV. A range of locally sourced food is available, with a curry night on Wednesday and steak night on Friday. Lunchtime meals are served Saturday and Sunday, evening meals Tuesday to Saturday. Walkers, children and dogs are all welcome in the bar. Outside is a small beer garden. ₪Q☎✿◑⑴⬤&♣♠P⌐₪(291)

Shenstone

Plough

DY10 4DL (off A450/A448) SO865735
✪ 12-3, 6-11; 12-3, 7-10.30 Sun ☎ (01562) 777340
Bathams Mild Ale, Best Bitter H
This traditional community pub has been at the heart of the village since 1840. The lounge and public areas are served by a long single bar and both have real fires. A large enclosed courtyard provides extra space in busy times. Cobs and pork pies are available at lunchtimes. Bathams XXX is added to the range in winter. Local morris teams dance during the summer months. Children are welcome in the courtyard. Harvington Hall is two miles down the road. ₪Q☎⬤&♣P⌐

Stanford Bridge

Bridge L

WR6 6RU (signed 100yds off B4203)
✪ 12-midnight; 11-1am Fri & Sat ☎ (01886) 812771
⊕ stanfordbridgepub.co.uk
Hobsons Mild, Twisted Spire; Otter Bright; Wye Valley HPA; guest beers H
The lively atmosphere of this pub near the River Teme is considerably heightened during quiz night on the last Wednesday of the month. Six real ales are served alongside Thatchers Heritage cider plus Westons perry. Traditional pub pastimes are played in the separate games room. Meals are served in the bar and an à la carte menu in the restaurant (no eve meals Sun). Beer festivals and charity fund-raisers are hosted. It's the home of the Teme Valley Cider Co-operative. There is a heated seating area outside and a large car park. ☎✿◑⬤♣♠P⌐

Stourport-on-Severn

Angel
14 Severn Side, DY13 9EW
✪ 11-11 ☎ (01299) 822661 ⊕ theangel-stourport.co.uk
Banks's Mild, Bitter; guest beer Ⓗ
This traditional pub is situated on the bank of the
River Severn, close to the canal basins, with public
moorings nearby. One changing guest beer from
the Marston's range is offered alongside the Bitter
and Mild from Banks's. Traditional pub games such
as crib, darts and dominoes are supported and a
pool table is available in a separate room. Home-
made food is a summer speciality served in the bar
and on the terrace overlooking the river.
🏚Q🕿🏵🚗🕪🖪🕭👗♣👕P⁵⁻🖳

Hollybush ♥ Ⓛ
Mitton Street, DY13 9AA (off Lion St down Gilgal)
✪ 12-11 (midnight Fri & Sat); 12-10.30 Sun
☎ (01299) 827435 ⊕ hollybushrealalespub.co.uk
**Black Country Bradley's Finest Golden, Pig on the
Wall, Fireside; guest beers** Ⓗ
This welcoming pub showcases beers from Black
Country Ales along with three ever-changing
guests from independent breweries. A single bar
serves a split-level lounge, a newly refurbished
function room and a beer garden. Weekly
entertainment includes live music, quizzes and
sport on TV. Beer festivals are held regularly
throughout the year. Winner of local CAMRA Pub of
the Year award in 2013 for its outstanding ales and
friendly community ambience. 🏚Q🕿🏵♣👕⁵⁻🖳

Uphampton

Fruiterer's Arms Ⓛ
Uphampton Lane, WR9 0JW (off A449 at Reindeer pub)
SO838648
✪ 12.30-3.30, 5-11.30; 12.30-midnight Fri; 12-midnight Sat;
12-11.30 Sun ☎ (01905) 620305
**Cannon Royall Fruiterer's Mild, King's Shilling,
Arrowhead Bitter; guest beers** Ⓗ
Located down a lane off the A449, the pub has
been in the same family for 162 years, with Ted
working here since 1951. The ales from the
independent Cannon Royall brewery behind the
pub are very reasonably priced in both the bar and
the comfortable lounge. The guest beers are
Cannon Royall seasonals and local perry and cider
are also served. Filled rolls are available Friday to
Sunday. Home-made pickles are sold at the bar.
Children under 14 are welcome until 9pm.
🏚Q🖪♣👕P⁵⁻🖳

Upper Wyche

Wyche Inn Ⓛ
Wyche Road, WR14 4EQ
✪ 12 (11 Sat)-11; 11-10.30 Sun ☎ (01684) 575396
⊕ thewycheinn.co.uk
Hobsons Best Bitter; Wye Valley HPA; guest beers Ⓗ
Set on the side of the Malvern Hills adjacent to the
Wyche Cutting, this free house has panoramic
views towards the Cotswolds. Ideally situated for
hill walkers, it offers two bars, one with traditional
games, a dining area and a patio. Tony and
Stephanie serve an ever-changing choice of ales –
check the website for current and upcoming beers.
Good home-cooked food is available with
occasional themed nights. Accommodation with
fantastic views over the Severn Vale is AA 4-star
rated. 🏵🚗🕪🖪♣P🖳

Weatheroak

Coach & Horses Ⓛ
Weatheroak Hill, B48 7EA (Alvechurch-Wythall road)
SP057740
✪ 11.30-11; 12-10.30 Sun ☎ (01564) 823386
⊕ coachandhorsesinn.co.uk
**Hobsons Mild, Best Bitter; Holden's Special;
Weatheroak Hill Icknield Pale Ale, Bitter; Wood
Shropshire Lad; guest beers** Ⓗ
This traditional free house has been run by the
same family for over 40 years. Up to 10 real ales
are available from breweries across the West
Midlands, including the on-site Weatheroak Hill
Brewery. The former coach house retains its
traditional bar with a real fire and quarry-tiled
floor, while food is served in a modern lounge bar
and restaurant lunchtimes and evenings (12-4pm
Sun). Fresh rolls are always available.
🏚Q🕿🏵🕪🖪🕭P⁵⁻

West Malvern

Brewers Arms Ⓛ
Lower Dingle, WR14 4BQ (down track by pub sign on
B4232)
✪ 12-3, 6-midnight; 12-midnight Fri-Sun ☎ (01684) 568147
**Malvern Hills Black Pear; Marston's Burton Bitter; Wye
Valley HPA; guest beers** Ⓗ
A comfy traditional pub, that is both the centre of
the village community and an ideal refreshment
stop for visitors to the Malvern Hills. Up to eight
real ales and a draught cider, usually Westons, are
available, and a beer festival is held in early
October. Home-cooked food is served lunchtimes
and evenings. The cosy bar can get busy, but extra
dining space is available in the function room or in
the garden with the 'best pub view in Britain' to
the Black Mountains beyond.
🏚Q🕿🏵🕪👕⁵⁻🖳(675)

Wildmoor

Wildmoor Oak Ⓛ
Top Road, B61 0RB SO963756
✪ 5-10.30 Mon; 12-11 (midnight Fri & Sat); 12-10.30 Sun
☎ (0121) 453 2696 ⊕ wildmooroak.com
Beer range varies Ⓗ
A rural inn that champions local cider and perry as
well as a changing range of ales, usually including
Wye Valley HPA. Located less than a mile from the
M5, the pub has a reputation locally for its
excellent Caribbean and British menu prepared by
award-winning chef Lorenzo. Monthly Caribbean
nights, music and quiz nights and an annual beer
and cider festival provide the entertainment at this
friendly community pub. CAMRA members receive
a 10 per cent discount on food and drink.
🏚🕪🖪♣👕P⁵⁻🖳

Worcester

Bell
35 St Johns, WR2 5AG (W side of the Severn off A44)
✪ 10-1am; 11-11.30 Sun ☎ (01905) 424570
**Fuller's London Pride; Thwaites Wainwright; guest
beers** Ⓗ
A community pub dating from the 17th century
with two small rooms on one side and the main
bar on the other, separated by a central corridor. At
the rear is a second bar used at busy times, and a
room available for functions. There is also a popular

skittle alley. Guest beers always include one from Hobsons and one or two from local independent brewers. Live music often plays at weekends. ⚒☺♣ᵔ🖳

Berkeley Arms
School Road, WR2 4HF
✪ 12-2 (not Tue-Thu), 5-midnight; 12-12.30am Fri & Sat; 12-3.30, 8-11.30 Sun ☎ (01905) 421427
Banks's Mild ⊞, Bitter ℗; guest beers ⊞
Family-run local with two main drinking areas served by a single bar. There is also a small adjacent room which can be used as a family room or for private functions, and an outside patio at the rear partially covered and heated for the benefit of smokers. Traditional pub games are popular. The draught cider is Thatchers Heritage.
Q☸☺♣ᵰℙᵔ🖳(44,44A)

Dragon Inn
51 The Tything, WR1 1JT (on A449, 300yds N of Foregate St station)
✪ 12-3 (not Mon & Tue), 4.30-11; 12-11 Fri & Sat; 1-4, 7-10.30 Sun ☎ (01905) 25845 ⊕ dragoninn-worcester.com
Beer range varies ⊞
This real ale-centric pub features six ever-changing beers from smaller independent brewers, usually including at least one from the co-owned Little Ale Cart brewery in Sheffield. A draught cider is also on handpull, usually Thatchers, and bottle-conditioned Belgian beers are kept. The pub owner is passionate about beer quality – but beware the list of banned conversation topics. A part-covered rear patio allows outdoor drinking in warmer weather. Good-value lunchtime meals are served on Friday and Saturday only. Well-behaved dogs welcome.
☸⊲≈(Foregate St)♣ᵰᵔ🖳

Firefly ⌷
54 Lowesmoor, WR1 2SE
✪ 4-midnight (1am Thu); 3-1am Fri; 1-2am Sat; 1-11 Sun ☎ (01905) 616996
Beer range varies ⊞
Offering period comfort in a regenerated part of the industrial city, the old vinegar works' manager's Georgian residence is now a delightful pub with its own on-site microbrewery. There are four handpulls for beer and two for cider. The interior is comfortable with soft furnishings and subtle lighting, warmed by an open fire. Downstairs is a cosy snug with bench sofas. The upstairs bar opens at weekends for live music.

Outside is a partially covered paved beer garden. Beer festivals are held throughout the year. ⚒☺▶≈(Foregate St)ᵰᵔ🖳

Plough ♈ ⌷
23 Fish Street, WR1 2HN (next to fire station)
✪ 12 (4.30 Thu)-11; 12-11.30 Fri & Sat; 12-10.30 Sun ☎ (01905) 21381 ⊕ theplough-worcester.com
Hobsons Best Bitter; Malvern Hills Black Pear; guest beers ⊞
This friendly and comfortable Grade II-listed pub is a must for any visitor to Worcester. Four ever-changing and well-kept guest ales come from breweries in Worcestershire and surrounding counties, and draught cider and perry are from local producers. A short flight of stairs leads to a bar flanked by two rooms, each with a gas fire and many original features. A small patio area provides views towards the Cathedral. Rolls are sometimes available. ☸☺⊲≈(Foregate St)♣ᵰᵔ

Postal Order
18 Foregate Street, WR1 1DN
✪ 8-midnight (1am Fri & Sat) ☎ (01905) 22373
Greene King Abbot; Ruddles Best Bitter; guest beers ⊞
This classic Wetherspoon pub was originally the old telephone exchange. It has one of the largest real ale turnovers in Wetherspoon's West Midlands region and a wide range of beers is served. Mini festivals showcasing beers from local breweries are a regular feature. Westons traditional cider is always available. Good value food is served daily 8am-10pm. The TV volume may be turned up for important games. Q☸⊲▶⚷≈(Foregate St)ᵰᵔ🖳

Wheatsheaf Inn ⌷
192 Henwick Road, WR2 5PF
✪ 12-midnight
Marston's Burton Bitter, Pedigree; St George's Friar Tuck; guest beers ⊞
A small Grade II-listed 18th-century terraced local attracting both young and old. A varied selection of guest ales is offered including at least one from St George's, and a draught cider. The rear balcony has views of the River Severn down to the Cathedral. A footpath from the riverside provides alternate access. The separate pool room is family-friendly. Sport on TV creates a lively atmosphere. Hot and cold pies and snacks are served all day. Newspapers and Wi-Fi are available and dogs are welcome. ⚒☸☺♣ᵰ🖳

Kitchen of an inn

In the evening we reached a village where I had determined to pass the night. As we drove into the great gateway of the inn, I saw on one side the light of a rousing kitchen fire beaming through a window. I entered, and admired for the hundredth time that picture of convenience, neatness, and broad honest enjoyment, the kitchen of an English inn. It was of spacious dimension, hung around by copper and tin vessels, highly polished, and decorated here and there with a Christmas green. Hams, tongues, and flitches of bacon were suspended from the ceiling; a smoke-jack made its ceaseless clanking behind the fireplace, and a clock ticked in one corner. A well-scoured deal table extended along one side of the kitchen, with a cold round of beef, and other hearty viands upon it, over which two foaming tankards of ale seemed mounting guard. Travellers of inferior order were preparing to attack this stout repast, while others sat smoking or gossiping over their ale, on two high-backed oaken settles beside the fire.
Washington Irving, Travelling at Christmas, 1884

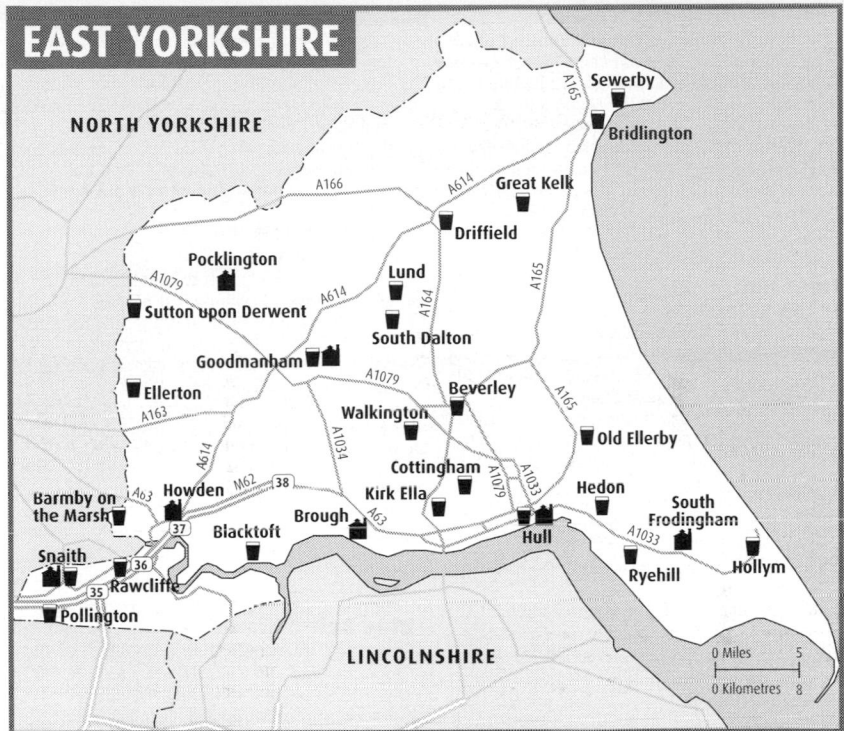

EAST YORKSHIRE

NORTH YORKSHIRE

Sewerby

Bridlington

A166

A614 Great Kelk

Driffield

Pocklington

Lund

A1079

Sutton upon Derwent

A614

A164

A165

South Dalton

Goodmanham

A1079

Ellerton

A163

Walkington

Beverley

A165

Old Ellerby

Cottingham

Barmby on the Marsh

Howden M62

38

Kirk Ella

Hedon

South Frodingham

Brough

Blacktoft

Hull

A1033

Snaith

36

37

Rawcliffe

35

Ryehill

Hollym

Pollington

LINCOLNSHIRE

0 Miles 5

0 Kilometres 8

ENGLAND

YORKSHIRE (EAST)

Barmby on the Marsh

King's Head 🄻
High Street, DN14 7HT (3 miles from Knedlington on B1228 near Howden on no through road) SE688286
🌑 12-2 (not Mon & Tue), 5-11; 12-midnight Sat; 12-11 Sun
☎ (01757) 630705 ⊕ thekingsheadbarmby.co.uk
Black Sheep Best Bitter; guest beers Ⓗ
Busy village pub that is well worth finding. Refurbished and extended in 2008, but dating back to the early 1800s, the pub is now a spacious and welcoming watering place and eatery. There is a bar with a stone-flagged floor for drinkers, a comfortable lounge, and a restaurant renowned for quality food featuring locally sourced ingredients. A function room is available for private parties. Four handpumps are in constant use, with three guests often from local breweries. ▨✿◑👭♣ℙ⧗

Beverley

Cornerhouse
2-4 Norwood, HU17 9EY
🌑 closed Mon; 5-midnight (1am Fri); 10-1am Sat; 10-11 Sun
☎ (01482) 882652
Abbeydale Deception; Black Sheep Best Bitter; Greene King IPA; Taylor Landlord; Tetley Bitter; guest beers Ⓗ
The Cornerhouse looks like a gastro-pub, but the customers are mainly here for the real ale on 12 handpumps, and the real cider on two handpumps. Yorkshire brewers feature prominently and there is a mild available sometimes. A coal fire warms the far end of the bar and there is unusual gallery seating off the bar. Curry night is Tuesday and quiz

night Wednesday. Food is served weekday evenings and all day weekends, plus full English breakfasts 10am-1pm. ▨✿◑👭♿●⧗➡

Dog & Duck
33 Ladygate, HU17 8BH
🌑 11-4, 7-midnight; 11-midnight Fri & Sat; 11.30-3, 7-11 Sun
☎ (01482) 862419 ⊕ bedandbreakfastbeverley.com
Black Sheep Best Bitter; Copper Dragon Golden Pippin; John Smith's Bitter; Taylor Golden Best; guest beers Ⓗ
Just off the main Saturday Market, next to the historic Picture Playhouse building (now Browns), the Dog & Duck was built in the 1930s and has been run by the same family for over 40 years. It comprises three areas: a bar with a period brick fireplace and bentwood seating, a front lounge, and a rear snug. The good-value, home-cooked lunches are popular. Lined glasses are used only for Black Sheep beer. Guest accommodation is in six purpose-built rooms to the rear. ▨➡◖●➡➡

Green Dragon 🏆
51 Saturday Market, HU17 8AA
🌑 11-11 (midnight Thu-Sat); 12-11 Sun ☎ (01482) 889801

INDEPENDENT BREWERIES

All Hallows Goodmanham (NEW)
Big River Brough
Bird Brain Howden
Brass Castle Pocklington
Great Newsome South Frodingham
Old Mill Snaith
Wellington Inn Hull
Whalebone Hull
Yorkshire Hull

Beer range varies Ⓗ
Historic Tudor-fronted inn renamed the Green Dragon in 1765. Up to seven beers from breweries throughout Yorkshire and the UK are featured, and beer festivals are held in the spring and at Halloween. Meals are served daily until 10pm, breakfast from 11am; Tuesday and Wednesday are quiz nights. The pub opens at 10am on race days. Outdoor seating is provided in a patio area with heating. Westons Old Rosie cider is sold. Local CAMRA Town Pub of the Year 2012. ❀❍▶👍🍴-♿

Tiger Inn
Lairgate, HU17 8JG
❀ 11 (12 Sun)-11 ☎ (01482) 869040
⊕ tiger-inn-beverley.co.uk
Black Sheep Best Bitter; WharfeBank Tether Blond; Wychwood Hobgoblin; guest beers Ⓗ
Attractive 18th-century building refronted in 1930s brewers' style by the now defunct Darley & Co, which once owned several pubs in Beverley. It has a multi-roomed interior with a public bar, snug, dining room/lounge and function room. Many local clubs and societies meet here and folk music sessions are held on Friday evening. The large car park to the rear was once stables and outbuildings. Meals are served lunchtimes and 5-8pm, with a Sunday carvery. Q❀❍▶🍺♣🍴P⅃-♿(X46,X47)

Woolpack Inn
37 Westwood Road, HU17 8EN (up Newbegin from Saturday Market)
❀ 4.30-10.30 Mon; 12-3, 4.30-11; 12-11 Sat & Sun
☎ (01482) 867095
Brakspear Oxford Gold; Jennings Bitter, Cocker Hoop, Sneck Lifter; Marston's EPA; Wychwood Hobgoblin Ⓗ
Located in a Victorian residential street west of the town centre, the Woolpack started life as pair of cottages and became a public house around 1831, later developing its own brewhouse and stables, and is now owned by Marston's. It retains a quarry-tiled snug from that period, with an open fire in the winter, but is extended to the rear. Meals are served at varying times, 12-7pm on Sunday. Quiz night is Thursday. ♨Q❀❍♣⅃

Blacktoft

Hope & Anchor
Main Street, DN14 7YW (3½ miles S of Gilberdyke railway station, follow signs to Blacktoft)
❀ 12 (4 Mon)-11; 12-10.30 Sun ☎ (01430) 440441
Greene King Abbot; Jennings Dark Mild; Marston's Pedigree; guest beers Ⓗ
Thriving village local in a superb location on the bank of the River Ouse. The RSPB's Blacktoft Sands bird sanctuary is visible on the far bank. Humour, past and present, is a feature of the old pub – look out for the Laurel and Hardy memorabilia. The conservatory offers river views and home-cooked meals – serving times are lunchtimes and evenings during the week, all day at weekends. Two guest beers change regularly. ➰❀❍👍♣♠P⅃

Bridlington

Marine Bar
North Marine Drive, YO15 2LS (1 mile NE of centre)
❀ 11-11 (11.30 Sat) ☎ (01262) 675347 ⊕ marinebar.net
John Smith's Bitter; Taylor Landlord; Wold Top Bitter; guest beers Ⓗ

Large open-plan bar, part of the Expanse Hotel, on the seafront with spectacular sea views from outdoor seating, attracting a good mix of regulars and welcoming to the influx of summer visitors. Home-cooked food, including vegetarian options, is served daily. Twice-weekly quizzes and live music nights are popular. Ample car parking is available on the Promenade. It is also on a land train route during the summer season. ❀❐❍▶👍♠♣⅃-♿

Telegraph Inn
110 Quay Road, YO16 4JB
❀ 12-midnight (1am Fri & Sat) ☎ (01262) 674592
Wold Top Angler's Reward; guest beers Ⓗ
Friendly free house away from the town centre, refurbished to create a pub that appeals to local drinkers and seasonal visitors alike. A wide range of ales is served, usually from Yorkshire breweries. A tranquil outdoor area, unusually with an open coal fire, allows for alfresco drinking. A jukebox plays '60s-'80s music, while live music can be enjoyed on Saturdays, folk on Tuesdays. Customers can use a retro tabletop games console. The pub is within a 10-minute walk of the railway station. ♨❀≒♣⅃-♿

Cottingham

Blue Bell
West Green, HU16 4BH
❀ closed Mon; 11-11 (midnight Fri & Sat); 12-10.30 Sun
☎ (01482) 847113 ⊕ bluebellinn-cottingham.co.uk
Brakspear Bitter; Ringwood Boondoggle; guest beers Ⓗ
In a picturesque setting overlooking the green near the village centre, this attractive building is split into a bar and restaurant. The restaurant has a log fire and enjoys a high reputation. The modern bar has deep armchairs and low-level music. To the rear there is a secluded beer garden with a covered smoking area and heaters. Open mic music night is Wednesday and live jazz plays on Sunday evening. Dogs are welcome in the bar. ♨❀❍👍P⅃-♿

King William IV
152 Hallgate, HU16 4DB
❀ 11-11 (midnight Fri & Sat); 12-11 Sun ☎ (01482) 875996
Jennings Cumberland Ale; Marston's Pedigree; guest beers Ⓗ
Village-centre pub with a traditional bar and lounge, both free of music. At the rear a former brewery has been converted into a function room offering live music and special events. The pub also hosts weekly quiz nights and an annual music festival. The rear beer garden and side courtyard have covered smoking areas. Excellent-value meals are served in large and small portions. Up to six guest beers are on handpump. Q❀❍🍺≒♣⅃-♿

Railway
11 Thwaite Street, HU16 4QT
❀ 12-midnight (12.30am Fri & Sat) ☎ (01482) 622980
Black Sheep Best Bitter; Taylor Landlord; Theakston Old Peculier; guest beers Ⓗ
This large detached pub has benefited from a tasteful refurbishment. There are deep leather seats in the comfortable lounge, where bands play at weekends. The separate bar has live sport on TV and is a base for darts, pool and football teams. This is a child-friendly pub and is popular with diners. Four guest beers and two ciders are usually on offer. ➰❀❍🍺≒♣♠⅃-♿

Driffield

Bell Hotel
46 Market Place, YO25 6AN
☼ 9.30am-11; 12-10.30 Sun ☎ (01377) 256661
Beer range varies Ⓗ
With a feeling of elegance, this inn features a long, wood-panelled bar and red leather seating, substantial fireplaces, antiques and prints. Two or three real ales are available, usually from local breweries, and more than 300 malt whiskies are stocked. A covered courtyard functions as a bistro, and there is a splendid lunchtime carvery buffet Monday to Saturday; Sunday lunch must be booked. Children are welcome until 7.30pm.
Q❀🕏🕪ⓓ&🕿P🖵(121)

Mariners Arms
47 Eastgate South, YO25 6LR
☼ 3 (12 Sat & Sun)-midnight ☎ (01377) 253708
Jennings Bitter; guest beers Ⓗ
A street-corner local that is well worth seeking out. The beer range is from the Marston's portfolio, as an alternative to the other breweries more commonly available in the town. Formerly part of the Hull Brewery estate, its four small rooms have now become two: a basic bar and a more comfortable lounge. Live sport is shown and the pub fields various sports teams. The long-standing licensees enjoy a loyal following among locals and offer a friendly welcome to all visitors.
🕏🕪🕿♣P🖵

Ellerton

Boot & Shoe
Main Street, YO42 4PB (just off B1228 Howden-York road) SE705398
☼ 5.30 (12 Sat & Sun)-midnight ☎ (01757) 288346
⊕ bootandshoeinn.co.uk
Dark Horse Old Boot, Tom Tate Ⓗ
A welcoming country village inn of character dating from the 17th century. The building wraps around a large tree and features low-beamed ceilings. There is a cosy bar area with exposed brick and an open fire, plus two intimate separate dining rooms. Four real ales are on offer in this free house, including Old Boot and Tom Tate especially brewed by the Dark Horse brewery. Food is served Friday and Saturday evenings and Sunday lunchtime (booking advisable). 🕏Qⓓ♣P

Goodmanham

Goodmanham Arms ♈
Main Street, YO43 3JA
☼ 11-midnight ☎ (01430) 873849
⊕ goodmanhamarms.co.uk
All Hallows Mischief Maker, Peg Fyfe Mild; Theakston Best Bitter, Old Peculier; Wold Top Bitter; guest beers Ⓗ
This pub is close to the Wolds Way footpath and is an ideal resting place for walkers. There is a small beer garden at the front and a small car park to the side. This traditional village pub serves up to seven real ales, usually including a mild. Old Peculier is served from the wood. A microbrewery on the site commenced brewing in 2012, producing All Hallows beers. Food is available lunchtimes and Friday evening. Local CAMRA Pub of the Year 2011-2013. 🕏Q🕏ⓓ🕪P🖵

Great Kelk

Chestnut Horse
Main Street, YO25 8HN
☼ closed Mon & Tue; 6 (5.30 Fri & Sat)-11; 12-10.30 Sun
☎ (01262) 488263 ⊕ chestnuthorsekelk.co.uk
Wold Top Bitter; guest beers Ⓗ
Built in 1793, this delightful Grade II-listed rural community pub nestles in the Yorkshire Wolds. A traditional inn, it features an open log fire in the winter and a walled beer garden for the summer. Local produce complements the special pie menu, served until 8.30pm (no meals 3-5pm Sun). Two guest beers are available alongside a selection of Belgian bottled beers, all served in their branded glasses. A games room doubles as a family room during the day. 🕏Q🕏ⓓ♣P🕪

Hedon

Haven Arms
Havenside, Sheriff's Highway, HU12 8HH (½ mile S of A1033 crossroads)
☼ 11-11 (midnight Fri & Sat); 12-11 Sun ☎ (01482) 897695
⊕ havenarms.co.uk
Black Sheep Best Bitter; Taylor Landlord; guest beers Ⓗ
Situated in the historic Haven area of town, once the largest port on the Humber. The bar is divided into different areas, and the concert and cabaret room serves as the focal point for the activities of a number of community clubs and teams. Reasonably priced pub food, freshly prepared from local ingredients, is served all day. Three guest beers are available, one usually from a local microbrewery. One real cider increases to two or three from April to September.
🕏🕏🕪ⓓ&🕏♣🕪P🕪🖵(75,76,77)

Hollym

Plough Inn
Northside Road, HU19 2RS
☼ 12 (5 Mon)-midnight summer; closed Mon, 12 (2 Tue-Thu)-midnight winter; 12-midnight (11 winter) Sun
☎ (01964) 612049 ⊕ theploughinnhollym.co.uk
Tetley Bitter; guest beers Ⓗ
Family-run, 200 year old free house of wattle and daub construction offering five real ales, often including Great Newsome and Bradfield beers. Primarily a locals' pub and a base for local sports clubs, but also a haven for discerning holidaymakers in the summer, with dogs welcome. It has two rooms warmed by open fires – one is also the dining room. Photographs of its role as a WWII ARP station decorate the walls. Three letting rooms are available.
🕏🕏🕪ⓓ🕏♣🕪🖵🖵(75,76,77)

Hull

Admiral of the Humber
1 Anlaby Road, HU1 2NT
☼ 8am-midnight ☎ (01483) 381850
Greene King Abbot; Ruddles Best Bitter; guest beers Ⓗ
A former paint and wallpaper shop, previously the site was well connected to Hull's seafaring past. Now a large single room pub and mostly on one level, the building is ideally suited to those who find steps or stairs a problem. A designated area is set aside exclusively for diners during the day –

food is served 8am-10pm throughout the week, with children welcome until 6pm. The pub is usually friendly to away football fans, but restrictions may apply at times. ⏰◐▮♿⇌🐾♿–▤

Hop & Vine

24 Albion Street, HU1 3TG (near Hull New Theatre)
✪ 11 (4 Tue)-11; closed Sun & Mon ☎ 07500 543199
Beer range varies Ⓗ
Atmospheric basement bar free house serving three changing guest beers from independent breweries, plus rare farmhouse ciders and a perry. Oversized lined glasses are used, and a wide range of continental bottled and draught beers is stocked. An interesting selection of freshly made snacks and hot drinks is served until 9pm. Shove-ha'penny and shut the box games are available. CAMRA Yorkshire Regional Cider Pub of the Year 2010-2012 and former National Cider Pub of the Year. Closed between Christmas and New Year. ◐⇌🐾🐶▤

Larkins

48-52 Newland Avenue, HU5 3AE
✪ 11-11 ☎ (01482) 440991 ⊕ larkinsbar.co.uk
Beer range varies Ⓗ
Named after poet Philip Larkin, this one-roomed café-bar was once two shops, and can be partitioned for functions. Changing beers are often from Great Newsome and Wold Top breweries, with a third often from Cottage Brewery. A selection of continental bottled beers is also available. Food is served noon-8.30pm (8pm Fri and Sat). There are outdoor drinking areas at the front and rear of the bar. ⏰▩◐♿–▤

Lion & Key

48 High Street, HU1 1QE
✪ 12-11 ☎ (01482) 225212
Beer range varies Ⓗ
There was first a pub at this address in 1817 and it has now reverted to its original name. Up to 11 real ales and three ciders are on handpump; the beer range is largely sourced from microbreweries, and sampling is encouraged to help you choose. Bottled beers from around the world complement the range. Delicious freshly cooked food featuring locally sourced ingredients, especially fresh fish, is served daily at lunchtimes and on weekday evenings to 7pm. A former local CAMRA Pub of the Year. ◐🐾

Olde Black Boy ★

150 High Street, HU1 1PS
✪ 12.30 (5.30 Mon & Tue)-11.30
⊕ yeoldeblackboy.weebly.com
Beer range varies Ⓗ
Historic pub, licensed since 1729 but which has also been, variously, a wine merchant and a tobacco dealer – traditionally represented by an Indian chief or black boy; note the carved boy's head above the fireplace. The first Monday of the month is for folk music – anyone is welcome to play. Guest beers vary widely and Westons Old Rosie cider is available. Bar snacks are now served at all times and an additional upstairs bar is open some weekends. Runner-up local CAMRA Pub of the Year 2012. ♨♣🐾

Olde White Harte ★

25 Silver Street, HU1 1JG
✪ 11 (12 Sun)-midnight ☎ (01482) 326363
⊕ yeoldewhiteharte.co.uk

Caledonian Deuchars IPA, Flying Scotsman, Golden XPA; Theakston Best Bitter, Lightfoot, Old Peculier; guest beer Ⓗ
Historic pub in a 17th-century merchant's house. The existing ground floor interior dates back to a major refurbishment in 1881, which was an idealised recreation of an old English inn, complete with massive inglenook fireplaces and stained glass windows. The first floor has restaurant facilities and the Plotting Parlour is available for meetings and functions. There is also a courtyard with heating providing an all-weather outdoor drinking area. The beer range now extends to a choice of six permanent beers plus a monthly changing guest. ❀◐🐾–▤

Pave

16-20 Princes Avenue, HU5 3QA
✪ 11-11.30 (midnight-Fri & Sat) ☎ (01482) 333181
⊕ pavebar.co.uk
Caledonian Deuchars IPA; Theakston Best Bitter, XB; guest beer Ⓗ
A continental-style café bar that attracts a diverse range of customers. As well as the regular real ales there is a guest ale, usually sourced locally, and a varied range of European draught and bottled beers. Food including vegetarian options is served every day. Complementary live entertainment is provided on Tuesday evenings and Sunday afternoons, but the bar closes to the general public when ticketed comedy nights and world music nights are held (details on the website). Westons cider is sold. ❀◐♿🐾–▤

Three John Scotts

Lowgate, HU1 1XW
✪ 8am-midnight (1am Fri & Sat) ☎ (01482) 381910
Greene King Abbot; Ruddles Best Bitter; guest beers Ⓗ
Originally an Edwardian post office, this open-plan Wetherspoon pub features modern decor and works of art. It is named after three past incumbents of the church opposite. The pub has established a broad customer base and appeals to a wide clientele. Wetherspoon's club meal offers are served Tuesday, Thursday and Sunday throughout the year. Up to 10 real ales and additional real ciders are available, and bi-annual Wetherspoon beer festivals are held. Children are welcome up to 7pm. ❀◐♿♣🐾–▤

Walters

21 Scale Lane, HU1 1LF
✪ 12-11 ☎ (01482) 224004 ⊕ waltersbar.co.uk
Beer range varies Ⓗ
The pub's name recalls an 1820s barber shop on the same premises. It is a free house under the same ownership as two other nearby pubs and attracts a broad cross-section of drinkers, offering up to 19 real ales and five real ciders. Many new microbreweries are given their Hull debut here, and established local breweries are also supported. No keg products using gas-assisted dispense are sold. An over-21s only door policy operates on Friday and Saturday evenings. 🐾

Wellington Inn ♈

55 Russell Street, HU2 9AB (just off Freetown Way)
✪ closed Mon; 6.30 (4 Tue)-11; 12-midnight Fri & Sat; 12-11 Sun ☎ (01482) 329486
Wellington 1st Duke; guest beers Ⓗ
Hidden free house gem that began brewing in 2011 and now serves up to seven real ales, with

three from its brewery. Real ciders and perry are also on sale, plus draught specialist European beers and many imported bottled beers. No food is served, but you can bring your own sandwiches. Quiz night is Wednesday, jazz plays on the last Thursday of the month and folk on the first and third Sunday afternoons. Local CAMRA Pub of the Year 2012 and joint Cider Pub of the Year.
❀≷♣♠P┵⬜

Whalebone
165 Wincolmlee, HU2 0PA (500yds N of North Bridge on W side of River Hull)
❀ 12-midnight ☎ (01482) 226648
Copper Dragon Best Bitter; Taylor Landlord; Tetley Bitter; Whalebone Neckoil Bitter, Diana Mild; guest beers Ⓗ
Built in 1796, the pub is situated in a former industrial area – look for the illuminated M&R Ales sign. The comfortable saloon bar is adorned with photos of bygone Hull pubs, CAMRA awards and the city's sporting heritage. The adjacent Whalebone Brewery opened in 2003 and its beers are exclusively available here. Broad Oak Kingston Black and Westons Old Rosie ciders are sold, together with European draught and bottled beers.
᠁♣♠

Wm Hawkes
32 Scale Lane, HU1 1LF
❀ 3 (12 Fri-Sun)-11 ☎ (01482) 225212 ⊕ wmhawkes.co.uk
Beer range varies Ⓗ
Named after a gunsmith who occupied the premises in the 19th century, this pub opened in the summer of 2012, yet it feels like it has been operating since Dickensian times. This is testament to the licensees' conversion of the building, using fittings reclaimed from other pubs and decorating with antiques and bric-a-brac to create an old-fashioned ambience. Nine real ales from a variety of national and local breweries and a changing real cider are available; there is no gas-assisted dispense. ♠

Kirk Ella

Beech Tree
Southella Way, HU10 7LY
❀ 11.30-11 (midnight Thu-Sat) ☎ (01482) 654350
Kirkstall Three Swords; Taylor Golden Best; Tetley Bitter; guest beers Ⓗ
Open-plan pub on the western outskirts of Hull, owned by a pub company committed to cask ale. Up to eight real ales are available, including at least one dark beer – try-before-you-buy is encouraged. Food is served 12-10pm every day, with table service after 5pm. Monday and Wednesday are quiz nights. Families with children are welcome throughout. Buses stop close to the pub until early evening, and later stop only a 10-minute walk away. ⬚❀❀◐♿P┵⬜(154,180)

Lund

Wellington Inn
19 The Green, YO25 9TE
❀ 12-3 (not Mon), 6.30-11 (11.30 Fri & Sat); 12-11 Sun
☎ (01377) 217294 ⊕ thewellingtoninn.co.uk
Taylor Landlord; Theakston Best Bitter; guest beers Ⓗ
Enjoying a prime location on the green in this award-winning Wolds village, most of the pub's trade comes from the local farming community.

Renovated by the present licensee, it features stone-flagged floors, beamed ceilings and three real fires. The multi-roomed interior includes a games room and a candlelit restaurant serving evening meals Tuesday-Saturday. Good food can also be enjoyed at lunchtime from the bar menu and specials board. Guest beers are usually sourced locally. ᠁❀◐♿♠P┵

Old Ellerby

Blue Bell
Crabtree Lane, HU11 5AJ
❀ closed Mon; 7-11.30; 12-4.30, 7-midnight Sat & Sun
☎ (01964) 562364
Tetley Bitter; guest beers Ⓗ
A 16th-century inn with an L-shaped bar and a single room divided into distinct areas, including a snug to the right and a rear pool area where children are welcome until 8.30pm. The pub has a strong community feel and is home to several darts and dominoes teams. Two guest beers in winter increase to three in summer. Outside is a fish pond and bowling green. Popular with walkers (wipe your boots please). ᠁Q❀▲♣P┵

Pollington

King's Head Ⓛ
Main Street, DN14 0DN (follow signs from A645)
❀ 5-11; 12-midnight Sat & Sun ☎ (01405) 861507
⊕ kingsheadpollington.co.uk
Old Mill Bitter; Tetley Bitter; guest beers Ⓗ
A real community pub popular with hikers and cyclists who use the nearby Trans-Pennine Trail. Behind the car park at the rear is the accommodation block for bed and breakfast customers. The single-room bar consists of two areas – a games area with pool and darts, plus a separate seating area for drinkers. Decorating the walls are pictures of the extinct 150 Squadron, RAF Snaith. Four real ales are kept in great condition by the enthusiastic landlord. ❀➘♿♣P┵

Rawcliffe

Jemmy Hirst at the Rose & Crown Ⓛ
26 Riverside, DN14 8RN (from village green turn N on Chapel Lane) SE683231
❀ 6 (5 Fri)-11; 12-11 Sat & Sun ☎ (01405) 831038
Taylor Landlord; guest beers Ⓗ
Outstanding village pub, well known in the region and winner of numerous local CAMRA branch awards, including Pub of the Year seven times and Yorkshire winner 2011. A warm welcome awaits you from the owners, locals and Bruno the dog. Book-lined walls and an open fire provide a haven on a cold winter's day. It is the perfect place to sample the four guest ales; a traditional cider can also be enjoyed. The patio or river bank beckon in warmer weather. ᠁Q❀♿♠P┵⬜(88,400)

Ryehill

Crooked Billet
Pitt Lane, HU12 9NN (off A1033 E of Thorngumbald)
❀ 4-midnight (1am Fri); 12-1am Sat & Sun
☎ (01964) 622303
Jennings Cumberland Ale; Marston's Burton Bitter; Wychwood Hobgoblin; guest beers Ⓗ
Sixteenth-century coaching inn with stone floors, upholstered bench seating and a rear dining area.

Customers can expect a warm welcome – and that is guaranteed in the colder months, with a real fire next to the entrance door. Five handpumps offer four Jenning's or Marston's beers, plus an occasional guest. Home-cooked food is served Thursday to Saturday evenings and Sunday lunchtimes. ⏸✿◐♣P⌐🖼(75,76)

Sewerby

Ship Inn
Cliff Road, YO15 1EW
✪ 11-11 (12.30am Fri & Sat) ☎ (01262) 672374
⊕ shipinnsewerby.co.uk
Banks's Bitter; guest beers Ⓗ
Village-centre pub, serving both locals and holidaymakers, comprising a wood-panelled bar with beamed ceiling, a separate dining room and a lounge. It is dog-friendly and has a beer garden with a children's play area. Food is available either as snacks or main meals; booking is recommended for the Sunday carvery (no food on Mon). Nearby is a model village and Sewerby Hall, with clifftop walks. A land train terminates close to the pub.
⏸🍴✿◐🚲👤♣P⌐🖼

Snaith

Brewers Arms Ⓛ
10 Pontefract Road, DN14 9JS (on A645)
✪ 11.30-11 (12.30am Fri & Sat) ☎ (01405) 862404
Old Mill Bitter, Blonde Bombshell, Red Goose, seasonal beer Ⓗ
Cartoon caricatures decorate the walls of the main bar of this fine example of a large village pub. As you enter the tree-lined car park you realise this is no ordinary pub. It is, in fact, the brewery tap for Old Mill, and its flagship establishment. There are stuffed animals and birds in the snug, three fires, a well (containing a skeleton) and fishing rods on display. Four real ales are always on, plus draught cider. ⏸Q🍴✿🚲◐👤🚆♣👜P⌐🖼(401)

South Dalton

Pipe & Glass
West End, HU17 7PN (follow signs from B1248)
✪ closed Mon; 12-11 (10.30 Sun) ☎ (01430) 810246
⊕ pipeandglass.co.uk
Black Sheep Best Bitter; guest beers Ⓗ
Delightful hostelry that stands at the site of the original gatehouse to Dalton Hall. It features exposed beams and custom-made furniture. The chef, who also runs the pub, holds a Michelin star for the third year running; meals are served lunchtimes and evenings. Three guest beers come from Yorkshire breweries, one from Wold Top, and the real cider is from Moorlands Cyder. Two double rooms are available to let, and walkers are made welcome. The pub closes for the first two weeks in January. ⏸✿🍴◐👤👜P⌐

Sutton upon Derwent

St Vincent Arms Ⓛ
Main Street, YO41 4BN (on B1228 S of Elvington)
✪ 11.30-3, 6-11; 12-3, 6.30-10.30 Sun ☎ (01904) 608349
⊕ stvincentarms.co.uk
Fuller's London Pride, ESB; Taylor Golden Best, Landlord; Wells Bombardier; York Yorkshire Terrier; guest beer Ⓗ

Winner of many local CAMRA awards over the years, this pretty white-painted village free house has been family-owned and well run for many years. A long-time supporter of Fuller's beers, it has a consistent but varied beer range, and serves excellent food in the restaurant every day, including many fish dishes. The bar is popular with locals. Another small bar with a serving hatch leads to the dining rooms. Occasionally a second guest is offered on handpump and the ESB is dispensed by gravity. Q✿◐🖼P

Walkington

Barrel Inn
35 East End, HU17 8RX (on main road through village)
✪ 4.30-midnight (1am Fri); 12-1am Sat; 12-midnight Sun ☎ 07550 078833
Thwaites Lancaster Bomber, Wainwright; guest beers Ⓗ
Friendly drinkers' local in a quiet three-pub village, and one of only two Thwaite's pubs in East Yorkshire. The cosy front bar features a log fire and beamed ceiling; a step up leads to a connecting lounge, also with a log fire. There is subtle piped music throughout and a TV for sport, particularly football, and occasional live music. Families are welcome. Between three and five real ales are sold, including one out of tie. A secluded cottage-style beer garden is at the rear. ⏸🍴✿◐♣⌐🖼

YORKSHIRE (NORTH)

Aldbrough St John

Stanwick Ⓛ
High Green, DL11 7SZ (1 mile from B6275)
✪ closed Mon Jan & Feb; 12-3, 5.30 (6.30 Sat)-11; 12-10.30 Sun ☎ (01325) 374258 ⊕ thestanwick.co.uk
Daleside Bitter; Jarrow Rivet Catcher; guest beers Ⓗ
In a picturesque village on one of the country's largest village greens, this welcoming 19th-century inn has two bars: one for drinkers and one for the two excellent restaurants where locally sourced food is served seven days a week. The Stanwick is the brewery tap for the village's Mithril Ales and one of its beers is always featured alongside two guest ales. You can stay at the pub and explore the Yorkshire Dales and Teesdale. Local cricket, quoits and football in the village are supported by the pub. ⏸Q✿🍴◐🚲♣P⌐🖼(29)

Appletreewick

Craven Arms Inn Ⓛ
BD23 6DA
✪ 11-11 (10.30 Sun) ☎ (01756) 720270
⊕ craven-cruckbarn.co.uk
Dark Horse Hetton Pale Ale; Thwaites Original; guest beers Ⓗ
Dating from 1548, this multi-roomed Dales free house has stone-flagged floors, oak beams and gas lighting. The main bar features an original Yorkshire range while the cosy taproom has ring the bull. A snug behind the bar leads to the cruck barn, added in 2006 and built using traditional techniques. The guest beers come from Lancashire and Yorkshire breweries and the house beer, Cruck Barn Bitter, is brewed by Dark Horse. Guest beers are served in summer.
⏸Q🍴✿◐👤👜♣👜P🖼(74)

New Inn 🅛

BD23 6DA
🌣 12-11 ☎ (01756) 720252
⊕ the-new-inn-appletreewick.com
Black Sheep Best Bitter; Daleside Blonde; Tetley Bitter; Theakston Old Peculier; guest beer 🅗
Friendly village local with good views of the Wharfe Valley from the seating area outside. All are welcome including walkers, horse riders, well-behaved dogs and cyclists (there is a nearby cycle livery). The main bar and newly refurbished dining room are both warmed by real fires. Black and white photographs of bygone Appletreewick adorn the walls. A fine range of bottled beers from around the world is always available.
🏚🌣🖼🕩🚻♣♥P🚉(74)

Askrigg

Crown Inn 🅛

Main Street, DL8 3HQ
🌣 12-11 ☎ (01969) 650387
Black Sheep Best Bitter; John Smith's Bitter; Theakston Best Bitter, Black Bull; guest beer 🅗
Three-roomed pub at the top of the main street of this village, which gained fame as the setting for the TV series All Creatures Great and Small. This busy, friendly Dales inn attracts a good mix of locals and visitors, and is particularly popular for its bar meals. The interior has been partly opened out but retains much of its traditional character, with a very impressive range in the snug. 🏚🕩P🚉(157)

Aysgarth

George & Dragon 🅛

DL8 3AD (on main A684 between Hawes and Leyburn)
🌣 8am-midnight ☎ (01969) 663358
⊕ georgeanddragonaysgarth.co.uk
Black Sheep Best Bitter; Theakston Best Bitter; Yorkshire Dales George & Dragon, seasonal beer; guest beers 🅗
Surrounded by beautiful Dales countryside and less than a mile from the spectacular Aysgarth Falls, this 17th-century coaching inn caters for drinkers and diners as well as offering en-suite accommodation. The cosy wood-panelled bar serves up to five real ales, usually including two from the local Yorkshire Dales brewery. There is a separate restaurant and an outside drinking area with thatched umbrellas and great views. Dogs are welcome.
🏚🌣🖼🕩🚻♣P⌐🚉(156)

Barkston Ash

Boot & Shoe 🅛

Main Street, LS24 9PR (100yds off A162 in village)
🌣 5-11 (midnight Fri & Sat); 12-10.30 Sun
☎ (01937) 557374 ⊕ bootandshoe.info
Brown Cow Boot & Shoe IPA; Leeds Pale; Tetley Bitter; Theakston Black Bull; guest beers 🅗
An 18th-century village pub free of tie, with two low-ceilinged rooms. It serves four regular cask beers, the house beer from Brown Cow and one guest, usually from a local brewery. Traditional good-value food is served evenings, Thursday to Saturday, and Sunday lunch. Pizzas to eat in or take out, and the pub also does takeaway beer cartons. An annual beer festival in the decked beer garden takes place on the second full weekend in July, with another in December.
🏚Q🌣🕩🚻🅑≈(Church Fenton)♣P⌐🚉(492,493)

Beck Hole

Birch Hall Inn

YO22 5LE (½ mile N of Goathland)
🌣 11-11 summer; 11-3, 7.30-11 (closed Mon eve & Tue) winter ☎ (01947) 896245
Birch Hall Beckwatter; Black Sheep Best Bitter; guest beers 🅗
An unspoilt, family-run rural gem, resting in the middle of a hamlet of nine cottages, run by the same licensee for 33 years. A frequent CAMRA award winner, it comprises one big and one small bar that uniquely sandwich a traditional sweet shop. Local rural scenes, painted by the licensee herself, adorn the walls. The house ale, Beckwatter, is organically brewed by North Yorkshire Brewing. Guest beers are sourced locally. Sandwiches, pies, beer cake and traditional sweets are always on offer. 🏚Q🌣🖤🅑♣

Bentham

Horse & Farrier

83 Main Street, LA2 7HR (½ mile from railway station)
🌣 12-2 (not Tue), 6-10.30; 12-midnight Fri & Sat; 12-10.30 Sun ☎ (01524) 261381 ⊕ horseandfarrierinn.co.uk
Copper Dragon Best Bitter; Thwaites Wainwright; guest beers 🅗

INDEPENDENT BREWERIES

Barkston Barkston Ash
Black Sheep Masham
Brown Cow Barlow
Captain Cook Stokesley
Conquest Whitby
Copper Dragon Skipton
Daleside Harrogate
Dark Horse Hetton
East Coast Filey
Four Thorns Heslington (NEW)
Great Heck Great Heck
Great Yorkshire Cropton
Hambleton Melmerby
Hop Studio Elvington
John Smith Tadcaster
Jolly Sailor Riccall (NEW)
Knaresborough Knaresborough (NEW)
Marston Moor Tockwith
Mithril Aldbrough St John
Naylor's Cross Hills
North Riding Scarborough
North Yorkshire Pinchinthorpe
Pennine Well
Redscar Redcar
Richmond Richmond
Rooster's Knaresborough
Rudgate Tockwith
Samuel Smith Tadcaster
Scarborough Scarborough
Settle Settle (NEW)
Theakston Masham
Three Peaks Settle
Treboom Shipton-by-Beningbrough
Truefitt Middlesbrough
Wainstones (Stokesley) Stokesley
Wall's Northallerton
Wensleydale Bellerby
Wold Top Wold Newton
York York
Yorkshire Dales Askrigg
Yorkshire Heart Nun Monkton

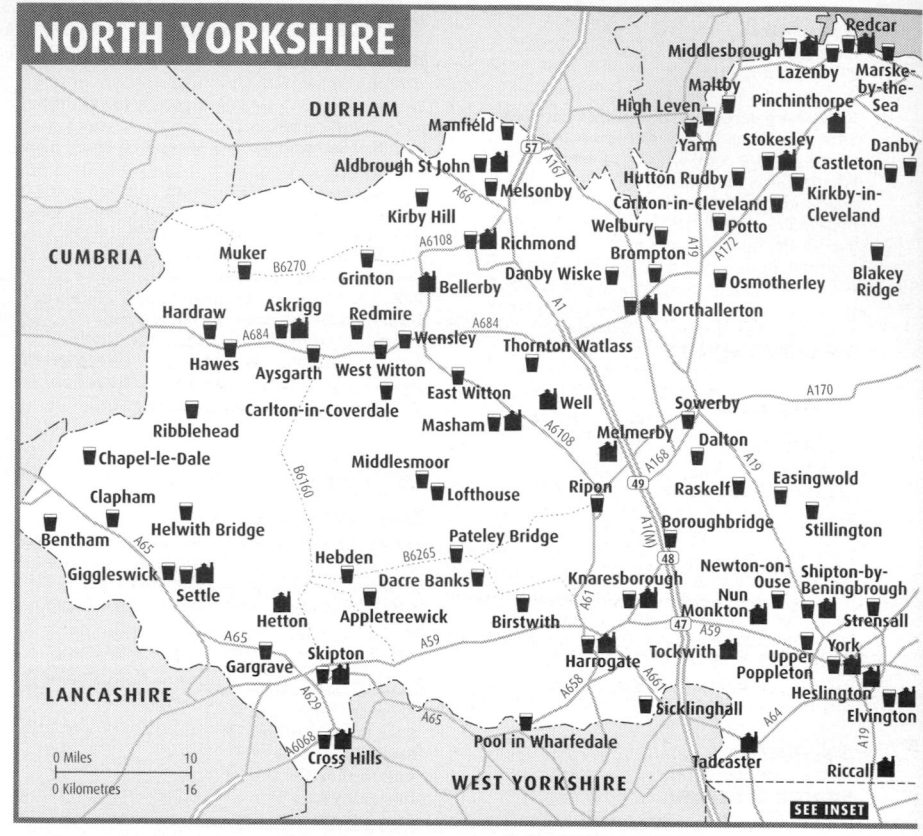

A 17th-century building at the western end of the village of High Bentham, now a low-beamed pub mainly used by locals. It has a patio area and a large garden for eating and drinking in warm weather, and log fires inside in winter. There is live music on Saturday nights, a quiz on Wednesdays, jam sessions on the first and third Thursdays of the month and, on Tuesdays in summer, Biker Bite Night. Pub food includes pizzas, which can be eaten in or taken away. ⚜️❀◑ ᛨ⚑Pᐟ⊟(80)

Birstwith

Station Hotel ⃝
Station Road, HG3 3AG
○ 11.30-11 (midnight Fri & Sat); 12-9 Sun
☎ (01423) 770254 ⊕ station-hotel.net
Tetley Bitter; guest beers ⊞
This former station hotel has undergone a high-quality refurbishment and is now a very popular village local. It has three public bar spaces and a separate large dining area. One room contains a library where locals can borrow books for a charity donation. There is a large beer garden at the back. Four rooms and a holiday cottage are available. The pub is noted for its locally sourced food, served all day. ⚜️⅄❀⚑◑ ⊞⅊♣Pᐟ⊟(24)

Blakey Ridge

Lion Inn
YO62 7LQ (from S, join A170, turn off at Hutton le Hole sign, follow road 6 miles past village) SE679997

○ 9am-11 ☎ (01751) 417320 ⊕ lionblakey.co.uk
Black Sheep Best Bitter; Copper Dragon Golden Pippin; Morland Old Speckled Hen; Theakston Best Bitter, XB, Old Peculier ⊞
In an isolated position above Rosedale and Farndale, this is the highest pub in the North Yorkshire Moors. The area is steeped in history, from ancient crosses to 19th-century iron workings. This historic inn has offered food, drink and shelter for well over 400 years. The heavily beamed and bare stone walled interior has several interconnected seating areas, and a separate restaurant with fires in winter. Weston's Old Rosie Scrumpy is also available. There is camping for walkers only. ⚜️Q⅄❀⚑◑ ⅊♣Pᐟ⊟

Boroughbridge

Black Bull Inn
6 St James Square, YO51 9AR
○ 11-midnight; 12-11 Sun ☎ (01423) 322413
⊕ blackbullboroughbridge.co.uk
John Smith's Bitter; Taylor Boltmaker ⊞
Nestling in the corner of the market square, this 13th-century pub, immaculately kept and comfortably furnished, is popular with locals and visiting tourists alike. A Grade II-listed gem, it has a resident ghost and is well worth a visit. Three drinking and dining areas include a small, cosy snug and a larger distinctive bar with open fires serving good-value beers. A wide range of bar meals is available and there is a discrete smart restaurant. ⚜️Q⚑◑ ⅊♣P⊟(142,143)

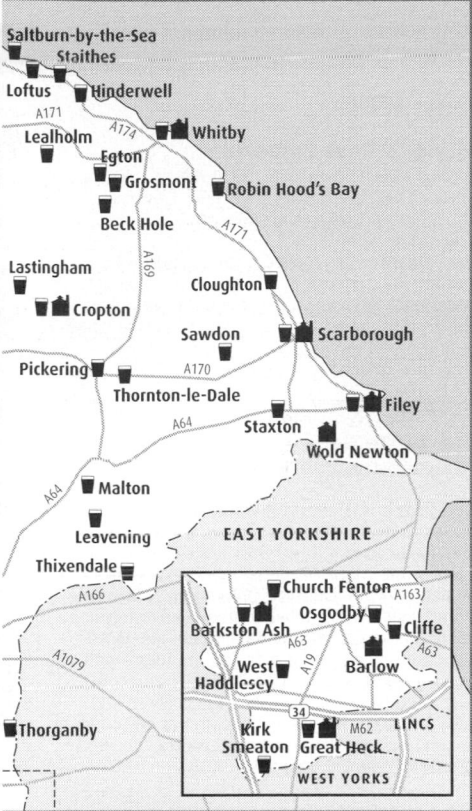

Saltburn-by-the-Sea
Staithes
Loftus
Hinderwell
A171
A174
Lealholm
Whitby
Egton
Grosmont
Robin Hood's Bay
Beck Hole
A171
Lastingham
A169
Cloughton
Cropton
Sawdon
Scarborough
Pickering
A170
Thornton-le-Dale
Filey
A64
Staxton
Wold Newton
A64
Malton
Leavening
EAST YORKSHIRE
Thixendale
A166
Church Fenton
A163
Osgodby
Barkston Ash
A63
Cliffe
A63
A1079
A19
West
Haddlesey
Barlow
34
Thorganby
Kirk
Smeaton
Great Heck
M62
LINCS
WEST YORKS

Carlton-in-Coverdale

Foresters Arms L

DL8 4BB
☼ 12-2, 6-11 (midnight Fri); 12-midnight Sat; 11-11 Sun
☎ (01969) 640272 ⊕ forestersarms-carlton.co.uk
Black Sheep Best Bitter; John Smith's Bitter; guest beers Ⓗ

Following a community buy-out and extensive refurbishment, the pub reopened in late 2011 as the Coverdale community pub. Beamed ceilings, open fires and wooden settles fashioned from old pews from the former village church give the 250-year-old building great character. Up to three guest ales from local and regional microbreweries are always on handpump, and lunchtime and evening meals using locally sourced produce are served daily. ﹩Q☼☎🚭◑ ⊟♿♣P⁵⊔

Castleton

Eskdale Inn

Station Road, YO21 2EU (next to railway station, 500yds N of village centre)
☼ 12-midnight (11 Sun) ☎ (01287) 660333
Black Sheep Best Bitter; Tetley Bitter; guest beer Ⓗ

Wedged between the Esk Valley railway station and the River Esk, this former station hotel offers a friendly welcome. The casks sit in a cool cellar directly beneath the handpumps and well away from the warming fire. The guest beer is often chosen by the locals themselves and is usually something interesting. A good-value menu, served all day every day, includes a specials board and a children's menu. The pub supports darts and pool teams. Two letting bedrooms are available. ﹩Q☼☎◑♿≢♣P⁵⊔⊟🚃

Brompton

Green Tree

Stokesley Road, DL6 2UA (on main A684)
☼ 12-2, 7-11 winter; 12-3, 6-11.30 summer; 12-midnight Sat; 12-10.30 Sun ☎ (01609) 780251
Copper Dragon Best Bitter; Theakston Lightfoot; guest beer Ⓗ

Small, traditional community free house located on the edge of the village and a short distance from Northallerton on the main A684 Osmotherley road. The single-room interior features a tiled bar with open fire and a separate area popular with diners. A sheltered beer garden – claimed to be sun-drenched – at the rear includes a quoits pitch. ﹩☎☼◑♣P⁵⊟(72,80,89)

Carlton-in-Cleveland

Blackwell Ox Inn

Main Street, TS9 7DJ (400yds E of A172)
☼ 11.30-11 ☎ (01642) 712287 ⊕ theblackwellox.co.uk
Beer range varies Ⓗ

In a beautiful area on the edge of the National Park, this impressive, multi-roomed village inn is renowned for its good-value Thai cuisine as well as its fine beers. Winter Monday evening Thai buffets can easily become habit-forming. Look out also for lunch and early doors year-round specials. But you do not have to eat, as drinkers are made most welcome. Four handpumps provide an eclectic range of varying beer styles. The garden has a children's play area. ﹩Q☼☎◑APⓇ(80)

Chapel-le-Dale

Hill Inn

LA6 3AR (on B6255)
☼ closed Mon; 12-3, 6-11; 12-11 Sat & Sun
☎ (01524) 241256 ⊕ oldhillinn.co.uk
Black Sheep Best Bitter; Dent Golden Fleece, Aviator; Theakston Best Bitter; guest beer Ⓗ

The inn dates from 1615 and is beloved of generations of hikers and potholers. Well-worn paths run from here to both Whernside (Yorkshire's highest peak) and Ingleborough (its best known). Lots of exposed wood and some stonework feature in the bar. Run by a family of chefs, the pub is popular with diners – puddings are a speciality (booking advisable for meals). There is a sugar sculpture exhibition in an adjoining room. ﹩Q☼☎◑P⁵🚃

Church Fenton

Fenton Flyer L

Main Street, LS24 9RF (E end of village in direction of airfield and Selby)
☼ 5-11 (midnight Fri); 12-midnight Sat; 12-10.30 Sun
☎ (01937) 558137 ⊕ thefentonflyer.com
John Smith's Bitter; Tetley Bitter; guest beers Ⓗ

Country village pub with historic connections to and memorabilia of the World War II airbase close by, hence the name. Three guest beers are chosen from the SIBA list, including two from local breweries. A weekly quiz night on Wednesday includes a Play Your Cards Right competition raising money for local charities. A monthly disco/karaoke night is staged on Saturday and live music on the first Friday. The rest of the time there is background music and TV sport. ♒Q♻☺❄⏖♣P⊱☷(492,493)

Clapham

New Inn
LA2 8HH
☼ 11-midnight ☎ (01524) 251203 ⊕ newinn-clapham.co.uk
Bowland Hen Harrier; Copper Dragon Best Bitter, Golden Pippin; Cross Bay Halo; guest beer ℍ
In a major tourist village, this spacious 18th-century coaching inn features two lounge bars. One includes oak panelling, the other has walls with photos and cartoons depicting caving, and is home to pub games. Children are welcome in the restaurant. The railway station is a mile away. ♒☺⊠⏖❄♣P⊱☷(581)

Cliffe

New Inn 𝕃
York Road, YO8 6NN SE661320
☼ 2-11; 12-midnight Fri & Sat; 12-10.30 Sun
☎ (01757) 633888
John Smith's Bitter; guest beers ℍ
Traditional two-room pub in the centre of the village and the focus for many local activities. Strongly engaged with the community, the pub is home to darts, dominoes and two football teams. An array of six handpumps offers predominantly Yorkshire beers, many sourced from the immediate area. It is a welcome addition to the growing number of fine ale establishments in the Selby area. ♒☺♿Å♣P⊱☷(4)

Cloughton

Bryherstones Inn
Newlands Road, YO13 0AR (about ½ mile up Newlands Rd off A171 at Cloughton)
☼ closed Mon & Tue; 12-3, 6-midnight; 12-11 Sun
☎ (01723) 870744 ⊕ bryherstones.info
Taylor Landlord; Wold Top Bryherstones Ale ℍ
A stone-built pub nestling between the North York moors and the coast, just outside the village of Cloughton. Now back in the hands of the Shipley family, it has been restored to its former glory. Its many rooms are full of features, and there is a separate games room. An extensive locally sourced menu is offered – booking is advised on an evening. The spacious beer garden has a children's play area, the pub is child and dog friendly, and there is a large car park. ♒Q♻☺⏖♨♣P⊱☷(115)

Cropton

New Inn 𝕃
Woolcroft, YO18 8HH (5 miles off the A170 Pickering-Kirkbymoorside road) SE755888
☼ 11-11 (midnight Fri & Sat) ☎ (01751) 417330
⊕ newinncropton.co.uk
Great Yorkshire Pale, Classic, Golden, Monkmans Slaughter, seasonal beer ℍ
The Great Yorkshire Brewery tap (formerly Cropton Brewery), this is a family-run pub on the edge of the North Yorkshire Moors National Park. An attractive stone building, it is a perfect base for walking and cycling, offering good food in the bars, conservatory or restaurant, and B&B or camping accommodation. With up to six of the well-regarded Great Yorkshire ales, it does not get more

LocAle than this. A legendary beer festival is held every November, plus a music festival in summer. Q♻☺⛽⏖Å♣P

Cross Hills

Naylor's Beer Emporium
Midland Mills, Station Road, BD20 7DT (in industrial estate on right over railway bridge from Cross Hills)
☼ 3.30-11 Fri only ⊕ naylorsbrewery.co.uk
Beer range varies ℍ
The Emporium has moved from its original tiny location in an industrial unit across to an all-new larger unit. However, the same basic principles apply – it continues to offer Naylor's beers, a range of British and foreign bottled beers, and the ambience of good company. Open on Friday only. ♿P⊱☷(66)

Old White Bear 𝕃
6 Keighley Road, BD20 7RN (on A6068, close to jct with A629)
☼ 11-11 ☎ (01535) 632115 ⊕ oldwhitebear.co.uk
Naylor's Pinnacle Mild, Cravenbrau, Bitter, Blonde, seasonal beers ℍ
Popular four-room village pub with exposed timbers said to have come from a ship of the same name. Built in 1735, it had a chequered history as a hotel, brothel, council meeting room and dance hall before becoming a pub. The top room, with stone-flagged floor, is used mainly as an eatery, with good-value meals dished up. Children and dogs are welcome. The back room has darts and ring the bull. A regular outlet for Naylor's Brewery. ♒☺⏖♣P⊱☷(66,66A)

Dacre Banks

Royal Oak Inn 𝕃
Oak Lane, HG3 4EN
☼ 11.30-11; 12-10.30 Sun ☎ (01423) 780200
⊕ the-royaloak-dacre.co.uk
Rudgate Viking ℍ
A family-run Grade II-listed pub dating from 1752 in the heart of Nidderdale. At the rear are views of the dale, while one of the front rooms has a real fire. Another front room is dedicated to games, with pool, darts and dominoes. Up to four real ales are on handpump, often from Rudgate. The pub majors on locally sourced food served in the bar and a separate restaurant. Outside is an attractive garden, and boules is played beside the car park. ♒Q♻☺⏖♣P⊱☷(24)

Dalton

Jolly Farmers Inn 𝕃
Brookside, YO7 3HY
☼ 7-11; 12.30-2.30, 6-11 Thu & Fri; 12-11 Sat & Sun
☎ (01845) 577359
Theakston Best Bitter; guest beers ℍ
A family-run village local at the heart of the community it serves, where there is always something going on. Local beers are sold regularly, with a changing range of guests from Yorkshire and beyond; in summer a second guest beer and a real cider are added. Freshly prepared home-made dishes using local produce are served from the kitchen (booking advisable for Sunday lunch). Three en-suite rooms provide an ideal base for exploring the dales and moors. ⛽⏖♣P⊱

Danby

Duke of Wellington

2 West Lane, YO21 2LY (200yds N of railway station)
☼ 12-3 (not Mon), 7-11; 12-11 Fri & Sat; 12-3, 7-10.30 Sun
☎ (01287) 660351 ⊕ dukeofwellingtondanby.co.uk
Copper Dragon Scotts 1816; Daleside Bitter; guest beer Ⓗ

An 18th-century inn that was 2012 local CAMRA Pub of the Year, set in idyllic National Park countryside, close to the visitor centre and Esk Valley railway station. It was used as a recruiting post during the Napoleonic Wars. A cast-iron plaque of the first Duke, unearthed during restorations, hangs above the fireplace. All the beers are sourced locally, as are the ingredients on the menu, offering traditional British home-cooked food at its best. Cider and perry are served Easter-October. ᴁQ✿✪⇔Ⅰ▶❀♣⌖🖵

Danby Wiske

White Swan Ⓛ

DL7 0NQ (approx 3 miles N of Northallerton off A167) SE 337986
☼ 12-10 (11 Thu-Sat) Apr-Oct; 7 (6 Fri)-11 (closed Tue); 12-3, 6-11 Sat Nov-Mar; 12-10 Apr-Oct (12-3, 7-10 Nov-Mar) Sun
☎ (01609) 775131 ⊕ thewhiteswandanbywiske.co.uk
Wall's Keeper's Gold, Gun Dog Bitter; guest beers Ⓗ

A welcome stopping-off point for Coast-to-Coast walkers, offering B&B and camping facilities. The opened-out interior features an attractive stone floor and wood-burning stoves. Locally sourced food includes meat from a mile or so away (ring first for winter availability). The CAMRA award-winning pub offers up to five changing beers and a cider depending on the time of year, and acts as the unofficial brewery tap for beers from Wall's of Northallerton. Local sword dancers meet here. ᴁQ✿✪⇔Ⅰ▶λ♣⌖P

Easingwold

George Hotel Ⓛ

Market Place, YO61 3AD
☼ 11-11 ☎ (01347) 821698 ⊕ the-george-hotel.co.uk
Black Sheep Best Bitter; Moorhouse's Pride of Pendle; guest beer Ⓗ

A traditional country hotel with food to match and the best range of beer in this town of half a dozen pubs. Seek out the bay window seats for a relaxing pause from the bustle of this fine example of a Georgian market town within easy reach of York and Thirsk. If Downton Abbey were real then the Earl of Grantham (or perhaps Mr Bates) would drink here. ᴁQ✿⇔Ⅰ(♣P⌖🖵

East Witton

Cover Bridge Inn Ⓛ

DL8 4SQ (½ mile N of village on A6108) SE144871
☼ 11-midnight; 12-11.30 Sun ☎ (01969) 623250
⊕ thecoverbridgeinn.co.uk
Black Sheep Best Bitter; John Smith's Bitter; Taylor Landlord; Theakston Best Bitter, Old Peculier; guest beers Ⓗ

The many CAMRA awards on display in this ancient inn tell their own story. Set near the confluence of the rivers Cover and Ure, the unspoilt public bar with a splendid hearth and open fire offers a warm welcome. A tiny lounge leads to an attractive garden with a riverside play area. The pub offers excellent home-cooked food, lunchtimes and evenings. Locally brewed beers, two real ciders and perry are on offer. The car park is across the road. ᴁQ✿✪⇔Ⅰ▶❀♣⌖P🖵🖵(159)

Egton

Wheatsheaf Inn

High Street, YO21 1TZ
☼ closed Mon; 11.30-2.30, 5.30-11; 11.30-11 Sat & Sun
☎ (01947) 895271 ⊕ wheatsheafegton.com
Black Sheep Best Bitter; Taylor Landlord; guest beer Ⓗ

Winner of many CAMRA awards, this Grade I-listed 19th-century pub is now in its 14th year in the Guide, and remains under the stewardship of a licensee who has had 27 years of continuous Guide recognition. Church pews, collectables from auctions and a roaring range add to the ambience. The menu features local meat, fish and game. The grassy area to the front and boules to the rear are ideal for summer. Six bedrooms and a holiday cottage are available. ᴁ✿⇔Ⅰ(▶❀♣≋♣P⌐🖵(99)

Elvington

Grey Horse

Main Street, YO41 4AG (on B1228 6 miles SE of York)
☼ 5 (3 Fri)-midnight; 12-midnight Sat & Sun
☎ (01904) 608335 ⊕ thegreyhorse.com
Copper Dragon Golden Pippin; Taylor Landlord; guest beers Ⓗ

Welcoming beamed country local opposite the village green, dating from the 17th century. The comfortable lounge area has a glass wall of bottled beers, a wooden propeller, an odd wooden hand seat and a collection of vintage radios. The central bar serves two regular and two to three guest beers, and is warmed by wood-burning stoves. Sunday lunch is a carvery only. There is a pleasant front garden with picnic tables and a covered, heated smoking area to the rear. ᴁ✿⇔Ⅰ▶♣⌐P⌐🖵(36)

Filey

Bonhomme's Bar

Royal Crescent Court, The Crescent, YO14 9JH
☼ 11 (12 winter)-midnight; 11-1am Fri & Sat; 12-midnight Sun ☎ (01723) 515325
East Coast Bonhomme Richard; guest beers Ⓗ

Just off the fine Victorian Royal Crescent Hotel complex, the bar's name celebrates John Paul Jones, father of the American Navy. His ship, the Bonhomme Richard, was involved in a battle off nearby Flamborough Head during the War of Independence. Five handpumps serve one East Coast beer plus four rotating guests. A fun quiz is held on Saturday, and the main quiz is on Sunday. Local CAMRA Rural Pub of the Year runner-up 2012 and 2013. ≋♣🖵

Gargrave

Masons Arms

Marton Road, BD23 3NL (on road over River Aire to railway station off A65)
☼ 12-midnight ☎ (01756) 749304
⊕ masonsarmsgargrave.co.uk
Taylor Boltmaker; Tetley Bitter; guest beers Ⓗ

In a quiet residential location opposite St Andrew's church, close to the railway station and the River Aire. This attractive, traditional village pub, with its low oak-beamed ceilings adorned with horse brasses, offers a comfortable and relaxing environment for both drinkers and diners. There are six en-suite rooms alongside the pub. Gargrave is on the main road and railway line between Skipton and Settle, and on the Leeds-Liverpool canal. ⋈Q❀♨◑&Å≈P⁵⊷⊟

Giggleswick

Hart's Head Hotel ⌊

Belle Hill, BD24 0BA (on B6480 ½ mile N of Settle)
✪ 12-2.30 (not Tue & Thu), 5.30-11; 12-11 Fri-Sun
☎ (01729) 822086 ⊕ hartsheadinn.co.uk
Caledonian 80; Kirkby Lonsdale Stanley's Pale Ale;
Tetley Bitter; guest beers ⊞
Open-plan 18th-century coaching inn where the bar separates the comfortable lounge from the area where pub games are played and sport is shown on TV. Freshly prepared meals from a varied menu are served in the adjacent dining room. The pleasant sloping beer garden at the rear is a great place to soak up the summer sun. Three changing guest beers are on offer from smaller Yorkshire, Lancashire and Cumbrian breweries such as Dent, Kirkby Lonsdale and Lancaster.
⋈❀♨◑&Å♣P⁵⊷⊟(580,581)

Great Heck

Bay Horse

Main Street, DN14 0BQ (follow signs to village from A19) SE594210
✪ closed Mon; 5-11 (midnight Thu); 12-midnight Fri & Sat; 12-10 Sun ☎ (01977) 661121
Old Mill Bitter, Blonde Bombshell; guest beers ⊞
Remote country pub that can be difficult to find, but is well worth the effort. The long, narrow building has parking at the front and also at the side. The lounge is divided into three separate areas by the central log-burning fireplace and the wall at the dining end. Meals are served by uniformed waitresses evenings and Sunday lunchtimes. Two regular Old Mill beers are available on handpulls. ⋈❀❀◑P⁵⊷

Grinton

Bridge Inn

DL11 6HH (on B6270, 1 mile E of Reeth) SE046984
✪ 12-midnight (11 Sun) ☎ (01748) 884224
⊕ bridgeinngrinton.co.uk
Jennings Cumberland Ale; guest beers ⊞
Close to the River Swale and the towering hills of Fremington Edge and Harkerside, this friendly, family-run country hotel lies in the heart of Swaledale and on the Coast-to-Coast and Inn Way walks, as well as on the Dales Cycle Way. It serves fresh, home-made food all day in the wood-panelled bar, lounge or two restaurant rooms. Grinton Beck runs between the pub and its car park. Heed the warnings – do not even think about using a mobile phone.
⋈Q❀❀♨◑⊟Å♣P⊟(30,36,831)

Grosmont

Crossing Club

Co-operative Building, Front Street, YO22 5QE (opp NYMR car park)
✪ 8am-11 ☎ 07766 197744
Beer range varies ⊞
Winner of the 2012 local CAMRA branch award, this venue is opposite the NYMR/Esk Valley railway stations in what was the village Co-operative store's delivery bay. Converted by dedicated volunteers into a railway-themed private members' club, a warm welcome is always extended to CAMRA members. For the railway enthusiast, both steam and diesel memorabilia adorn the walls. Four handpumps have served more than 800 different beers during the club's 14-year existence. Access is gained by ringing the door bell. Q≈♣⊟

Hardraw

Green Dragon ⌊

DL8 3LZ (about 1 mile N of Hawes, just off Buttertubs road) 868913
✪ 10-2am; 10-7 (2am Thu-Sat) Nov-Feb; 10-1am (7 Nov-Feb) Sun ☎ (01969) 667392 ⊕ greendragonhardraw.com
Taylor Landlord; Theakston Best Bitter ⊞, Old Peculier ⒼG; guest beers ⊞
Hardraw Force, England's highest single-drop waterfall, is located in the grounds of this old pub of character, and you can visit the spectacular attraction for a small fee. The bar has flagged floors, low beams and two impressive ranges, offering beers from local independent brewers and hosting regular live music events, including a folk weekend in July and a brass band competition in September. Meals are served all day. Real cider is only stocked in summer.
⋈Q❀❀♨◑⊟Å♣●P⁵⊷⊟(855)

Harrogate

Blues Bar

4 Montpellier Parade, HG1 2TJ
✪ 10-1am ☎ (01423) 566881 ⊕ bluesbar.co.uk
Beer range varies ⊞
A small, single-room live music bar modelled on an Amsterdam café bar. There is live music seven days a week, with two sessions on a Sunday. Very popular with music lovers, it can get busy. Four rotating guest beers are offered, sourced from far and wide. Food is served from 10am until early evening Monday to Saturday and until 2pm on Sunday. Children are allowed in until 7pm. Ⓓ

Coach & Horses ⌊

16 West Park, HG1 1BJ
✪ 11-11; 12-10.30 Sun ☎ (01423) 561802
⊕ thecoachandhorses.net
Daleside Bitter, Blonde; Taylor Landlord; Tetley Bitter ⊞
The central bar is surrounded by snugs and alcoves, creating a cosy atmosphere inside, and tables and chairs are provided outside for customers in summer, while window boxes create a quite spectacular display and add year-round colour. The guest beers usually include one from Roosters. Excellent meals are served at lunchtime, and there are frequent themed food evenings. Many of these, together with a Sunday night quiz, have raised over £250,000 for a local children's hospice. Q◑

Fat Badger 🅛

Cold Bath Road, HG2 0NF
🌣 11-midnight (11 Sun) ☎ (01423) 852788
⊕ thefatbadger.co.uk
Black Sheep Best Bitter; Copper Dragon Golden Pippin; Taylor Landlord; Tetley Bitter 🅗
A pub within the historic White Hart Hotel rather than a hotel bar, decorated in a Victorian style with raised areas to the sides. Six handpumps provide a choice of local favourites and two guests, usually from Ossett or York breweries. Outside is a large patio area, partly covered for year-round use. A beer club is convened once a month where quality food and real ales are paired, and bar meals are available until early evening. 🏠🍴🝙🍺

Hales Bar 🅛

1-3 Crescent Road, HG1 2RS
🌣 12-midnight (1am Thu-Sat); 12-11.30 Sun
☎ (01423) 725570 ⊕ halesbar.co.uk
Daleside Hales Ale, Old Legover; Draught Bass; Taylor Landlord 🅗
Harrogate's oldest pub it has a gas-lit Victorian interior; the pub was used in the filming of Chariots of Fire. There is also a separate snug. Two guest beers are served, usually including one from Black Sheep. It is a lively pub, with karaoke night on Thursday and occasional themed party nights at weekends and special dates. The pub prides itself on its floral displays in season. 🍴🍺🍺🝙

Old Bell Tavern 🅛

6 Royal Parade, HG1 2SZ
🌣 12-11 (11.30 Fri & Sat; 10.30 Sun) ☎ (01423) 507930
Black Sheep Best Bitter; Hawkshead Windermere Pale 🅗
Housed in the former Farrah's toffee shop, it became a pub in 1999 on the site of the Blue Bell Inn. There is a changing range of eight guest beers, usually including a Rooster's, a Taylor, one from owner Okell's of the Isle of Man, and a dark beer. A real cider and a range of UK and foreign bottled beers complete the choice. The side room has a collection of Farrah memorabilia and upstairs is a well-regarded restaurant. Q🍴🝙🍴

Swan on the Stray 🅛

17 Devonshire Place, HG1 4AA
🌣 11-11; 12-10.30 Sun ☎ (01423) 524587
Black Sheep Ale; Daleside Blonde; Ilkley Mary Jane; Taylor Landlord 🅗
A pub with a light, modern interior and a choice of regular and guest Yorkshire beers, plus occasional ones from further afield. A range of foreign beers is available on draught plus a real cider and an added selection in bottles. Allied to a good wine choice and excellent bar meals, the pub appeals to all age groups. There is a beer garden at the rear, well-behaved children are welcome until 8pm and dogs at any time. Q🏠🝙🍴🍴P🝙🚌(104,111)

Hawes

White Hart Country Inn 🅛

Main Street, DL8 3QL (on one-way system westbound)
🌣 11-11 ☎ (01969) 667214 ⊕ whitehartcountryinn.co.uk
Black Sheep Best Bitter; Theakston Best Bitter; guest beers 🅗
A traditional pub located on the short one-way system of this bustling little Dales town, frequented by walkers and other visitors. Extensively refurbished since becoming a free

house in 2011, the new management has successfully introduced guest beers, particularly from the local Wensleydale and Yorkshire Dales breweries. There is a separate dining room with food served daily 12-9pm, including beef and lamb from the family farm nearby.
🏠🍴🍺🍴🝙(156,157,855)

Hebden

Clarendon Hotel 🅛

BD23 5DE
🌣 10.30-3, 5.30-11; 10.30-11 Sat & Sun ☎ (01756) 752446
⊕ theclarendonhotel.co.uk
Taylor Boltmaker; Tetley Bitter; guest beers 🅗
Small family-owned hotel not far from Grassington, ideally situated for exploring the surrounding fells and dales (walkers with clean boots welcome). Handy bicycle storage is provided for cyclists on the Dales Way. There is a comfortable lounge bar and a separate dining room with a reputation for fine steaks. Guest beers include some from Thwaites and Black Sheep. Pride of the Dales bus 72 runs Monday-Saturday. 🏠🍴🍴🝙🍴P🝙(72)

Helwith Bridge

Helwith Bridge Inn 🅛

BD24 0EH (turn off B6479 at Helwith Bridge and cross river) SD810695
🌣 2.30 (12 Fri-Sun)-11 ☎ (01729) 860220
⊕ helwithbridgeinn.co.uk
John Smith's Bitter; Three Peaks Ingleborough Gold; guest beers 🅗
This independently owned pub changed hands in 2013, but retains its no-frills ethos, with walkers, cyclists and muddy dogs all welcome. Set in a fairly isolated location, it is adjacent to the River Ribble and Settle-Carlisle railway line, with a limited bus service. It offers its own basic camping facilities and a bunk barn. Guest ales are usually sourced from the Heineken UK list, mainly from northern breweries, and the house beer is from the local Three Peaks Brewery. Food is served Thursday to Sunday evenings and weekend lunchtimes. 🏠🍴🝙🝙🍴P🝙🚌(B10)

High Leven

Fox Covert

Low Lane, TS15 9JW (on A1044, 1 mile E of Yarm)
🌣 11.30-11 (midnight Fri & Sat); 12-11 Sun
☎ (01642) 760033 ⊕ thefoxcovert.com
Caledonian Deuchars IPA; Theakston Old Peculier 🅗
A previous local CAMRA award winner, this popular, long-established and uniquely named inn has been in the same family for more than 25 years. Originally a farmhouse, it was built in the traditional longhouse style, with whitewashed walls and a pantiled roof. Inside it is warm and cosy, with two open fires and two drinking areas offering superbly kept beers. The pub is noted for its food, served all day every day. Conference facilities are available. 🏠🍴🝙🍴P🝙(507)

Hinderwell

Brown Cow

55 High Street, TS13 5ET (on A174)
🌣 11 (12 Sun)-1am ☎ (01947) 840694
Beer range varies 🅗

Between the moors and the coast, this family-run pub has a strong local following as well as attracting visitors. Two busy handpumps serve weaker beers mid-week and stronger beers at weekends. The pub supports darts teams, charity nights, dominoes and whist drives, and has a separate pool room. Children and dogs are welcome, and smokers are also well provided for. There are snacks in addition to lunchtime and evening meals. Accommodation is in three bedrooms. The pub is a previous local CAMRA award winner. ▲☎☺️✿🌙◑🍴🕭💺♣P⅄—🚲(4,5)

Hutton Rudby

King's Head
36 North Side, TS15 0DA (W end of village)
🌣 12-11 (10.30 Sun) ☎ (01642) 700342
Camerons Strongarm; Jennings Cocker Hoop, Cumberland Ale; guest beer 🅗
Set in a beautiful village, this previous CAMRA branch award winner is a traditional locals' pub where a friendly welcome is assured. It comprises a main bar that is always busy and a snug where children are welcome. Four ales on handpump include a guest from the Marston's range. Real fires, a popular quiz night on Tuesday, steak nights on Wednesday and Friday, and live music on Saturday all add to the experience. Outside is a smokers' facility, complete with TV. Check winter opening hours before visiting. ▲☎☺️✿⅄—🚲(82)

Kirby Hill

Shoulder of Mutton
DL11 7JH (2½ miles from A66, 4 miles NW of Richmond)
🌣 12-3 (Sat & Sun only), 6-11.30 (11 Sun)
☎ (01748) 822772 ⊕ shoulderofmutton.net
Daleside Bitter; guest beers 🅗
Ivy-fronted country inn in a beautiful hillside setting overlooking Lower Teesdale and the ruins of Ravensworth Castle. The pub has an open front bar that links the lounge with a cosy restaurant to the rear. Three guest beers (four in summer) are chosen by the pub's regulars. On the edge of the Yorkshire Dales, this is a popular venue for walkers. There are five en-suite guest bedrooms. Excellent food is served Wednesday to Sunday, although the bar area remains for drinkers. ▲Q☺️🍴◑🍴♣P⅄—

Kirk Smeaton

Shoulder of Mutton
Main Street, WF8 3JY (follow signs from A1)
🌣 5-midnight (1am Fri & Sat); 11.30-midnight Sun
☎ (01977) 620348
Black Sheep Best Bitter; guest beer 🅗
A rural gem situated conveniently for the Went Valley and Brockadale Nature Reserve, popular with walkers and the local community. This award-winning pub comprises a large lounge with open fires and a cosy, dark-panelled snug. Friendly clientele assure a warm welcome and the beer is always in superb condition. The spacious beer garden has a covered and heated shelter for smokers and there is ample parking. Quiz night is Tuesday. ▲☺️♣P⅄—🚲(409)

Kirkby-in-Cleveland

Black Swan
Busby Lane, TS9 7AW (½ mile W of B1257)

🌣 12-midnight ☎ (01642) 712512
Black Sheep Best Bitter; Copper Dragon Golden Pippin; Taylor Landlord; guest beer 🅗
Nestling at the foot of the North York Moors, and at the crossroads of this ancient village, this warm and cosy free house, comprising a bar, lounge/restaurant and conservatory, affords a friendly and genuine welcome. Three regular beers and a guest beer, all usually sourced from Yorkshire, are served 365 days of the year – the pub shuts at 3pm on Christmas Day. Bar snacks and a full menu including daily specials represent good value. There is also a pool table. ▲Q☺️◑🍴♣P⅄—🚲(89)

Knaresborough

Blind Jack's 🅛
19 Market Place, HG5 8AL
🌣 4 (3 Fri; 12 Sat)-11; 12-10.30 Sun ☎ (01423) 869148
Black Sheep Best Bitter; Harviestoun Bitter & Twisted; Taylor Landlord 🅗
Multi award-winning ale house with bare brick walls, wooden floorboards and panelling that also houses a small brewery. Two small rooms on the ground floor are mirrored in two more up a steep staircase; the building was converted into a pub about 25 years ago. The beer range changes constantly and usually includes at least one beer brewed on the premises. A superb pub that has featured in this Guide for over 20 years. Q➹—🚲(1)

Cross Keys
Cheapside, HG5 8AX
🌣 4-11 Mon & Tue; 12-11 (midnight Fri & Sat); 12-10.30 Sun
☎ (01423) 863562
Fuller's London Pride; Ossett Yorkshire Blonde, Big Red, Silver King 🅗
Tucked away just off the marketplace, this is an Ossett brewery tied house that has been sympathetically refurbished, with a stone-flagged floor in front of the single bar and wooden floors to the sides. Due to links with Fuller's, a number of the London brewer's beers are available on the eight handpumps, as well as guests from microbreweries or other brewers within the Ossett Brewery group. A comfortable pub appealing to locals and tourists alike. ◑➹—🚲(1)

Half Moon
1 Abbey Road, HG5 8HY
🌣 5 (12 Sat)-11; 12-10.30 Sun ☎ (01423) 313461
Beer range varies 🅗
This free house has been carefully restored both inside and out by new independent owners, retaining many original features including much of the original brickwork and two open fires. The pub has a clean yet traditional feel, with a central bar and wood floor, and carpeted seating areas to the left and right. Four handpumps dispense a varying range of ales, mainly from local breweries such as Rooster's. There are plans to serve food in the near future. ▲Q☺️✿⅄—🚲(56,57)

Mitre Hotel 🅛
4 Station Road, HG5 9AA (opp railway station)
🌣 12-11 ☎ (01423) 868948 ⊕ mitre.squarespace.com
Black Sheep Ale; Copper Dragon Golden Pippin; Taylor Landlord; Thwaites Wainwright 🅗
Conveniently close to the railway station, the Mitre offers drinking and dining in smart modern surroundings within an old split-level building. The eight handpumps serve a choice of regular beers from Lancashire and Yorkshire, with a changing

range of guests often from Rooster's or Ilkley. Look out for the speciality bottled beer menu; some foreign beers are also available on draught. There is live acoustic music on Sunday evenings and dogs are welcome. No evening meals on Sunday.
Q🌜🏵🏠⊙🕇●🏠(1)

Lastingham

Blacksmiths Arms
Front Street, YO62 6TL (4 miles N of A170 between Helmsley and Pickering) SE728904
✪ 12-11.30 ☎ (01751) 417247
⊕ blacksmithslastingham.co.uk
Theakston Best Bitter; guest beers Ⓗ
Pretty stone inn in a conservation village opposite St Mary's Church, famous for its 11th-century crypt. The interior comprises a cosy bar with a York range lit in winter, a snug and two dining rooms. Excellent-quality food, including local game, is served alongside interesting changing guest beers, usually from independent breweries. A secluded beer garden is to the rear. This remote pub is popular with locals, walkers and shooting parties.
🏵Q🏵🏠⊙

Lazenby

Lazenby Social Club
High Street, TS6 8DX (in centre of village, off A174)
✪ 11.30-11; 12-10.30 Sun ☎ (01642) 453905
Brains The Rev James; guest beer Ⓗ
In a pleasant village, wedged between the remnants of Teesside's heavy industries and the Cleveland Hills, this private members' club extends a warm welcome to CAMRA members. A free house, it comprises a lounge, a large bar/games room, a concert room and a conservatory that houses a full-size snooker table. It was dry for years during Teesside's industrial heyday, but the club has now gained a deserved reputation for selling fine real ales. 🏵🍺🕇♣P�🏠(70,71)

Lealholm

Board Inn
Village Green, YO21 2AJ (by River Esk)
✪ 9am-midnight (2am Fri & Sat) ☎ (01947) 897279
Black Sheep Best Bitter; Camerons Strongarm; guest beers Ⓗ
Family-run 17th-century free house, alongside the River Esk, serving four beers, four real ciders and a huge selection of whiskies. It has a busy main bar, lounge and restaurant, and a riverside patio where a beer festival is held each Easter. The menu, which reflects the season, is virtually all sourced and traceable to within 500 yards of the pub. The licensees rear-cure their hams, keep hens, own a herd of prime beef, and also have local fishing rights. There are five letting bedrooms.
🏵Q🌜🏵🏠⊙🍺🕇▲≠♣●P�🏠(99)

Leavening

Jolly Farmers Ⓛ
Main Street, YO17 9SA SE785631
✪ 5.30-midnight; 5-1am Fri; 12-1am Sat; 12-midnight Sun ☎ (01653) 658276
Taylor Landlord; York Guzzler; guest beers Ⓗ
Seventeenth-century pub on the edge of the Yorkshire Wolds between York and Malton. The multi-room interior retains old world cosiness in

two small bars, a games/family room and a separate dining room. It is community focused, with cinema nights, meetings, charity events, darts and quiz leagues, occasional live music and beer festivals. Varied guest beers come from independent breweries. It offers an extensive menu of quality food dishes, including locally caught game in season. No food on Monday or Tuesday evenings. 🏵Q🌜🏵⊙🍺P�

Lofthouse

Crown Hotel
Thorpe Lane, HG3 5RZ
✪ 12-3, 7-11 ☎ (01423) 755206
Black Sheep Best Bitter; Theakston Best Bitter Ⓗ
Handsome stone building in almost the last village in beautiful Nidderdale. The unusual panelled entrance corridor leads to a traditionally furnished, comfortable bar with a dining room beyond. Local pictures, maps and lots of brassware decorate the walls. An open fire in winter warms your bones after exploring the surrounding area of outstanding natural beauty, and walking sticks are for sale if needed. There is no mobile phone coverage inside the pub and payment by card is not accepted.
🏵🏠⊙

Loftus

Station
Station Road, TS13 4QB (100yds S of A174)
✪ 3-midnight; 12-1.30am Sat & Sun ☎ (01287) 640373
Beer range varies Ⓗ
The Station hotel is now a free house, with the last passenger train having left in the 1960s – the platform is still there. The licensee, a keen musician and local independent councillor, has worked here for 22 years, and only serves best/premium bitters – anything under 4% ABV generally meeting with the locals' disapproval. The pub comprises a separate bar, a lounge and a function room where regular live music plays. Fans of eccentric railway memorabilia are particularly well catered for. 🏵🌜🏵🍺🕇♣P⊝🏠(4,5)

Maltby

Manor House
High Lane, TS8 0BN (at jct of A1044 and A1045, 2 miles E of Yarm and just W of A19)
✪ 11-11; 12-10.30 Sun ☎ (01642) 764153
Beer range varies Ⓗ
Situated on the western outskirts of this pretty village and adjacent to one of Europe's largest private housing estates. Now in its fifth year of operation following extensive renovations, this Sir John Fitzgerald house is a large, busy establishment with a welcoming cosiness and warmth to it. Food is served all day every day, and friendly, enthusiastic staff ensure that three, usually four, guest beers provide an interesting mix of different styles. Quiz night is Monday.
🏵⊙🍺P⊝🏠(507)

Malton

Crown Hotel (Suddaby's)
12 Wheelgate, YO17 7HP
✪ 11-11 (11.30 Fri & Sat); 12-11 Sun ☎ (01653) 692038
⊕ suddabys.co.uk

Brakspear Bitter; Suddaby's Double Chance, seasonal beers; guest beers 🄷
Grade II-listed market-town pub that has been in the same family for 134 years and in this Guide for over 25. Double Chance is brewed by Leeds Brewery, other Suddaby's beers by Brown Cow. Beer festivals are held at Easter, in summer and at Christmas. The on-site shop stocks more than 200 different beers, specialising in Belgian and local British microbreweries, plus wine and breweriana. A covered smoking patio is at the rear. Accommodation is available, with a discount for CAMRA members staying two nights or more.
⩩Q✿⊭≹♣P⅟–⊟

New Malton
2-4 Market Place, YO17 7LX
✪ 11.30-11; 12-10.30 Sun ☎ (01653) 693998
Beer range varies 🄷
Situated in the busy Market Place, this Grade II-listed building, formerly tea rooms, has been sensitively renovated. Although the pub is one large room it has three distinct drinking and dining areas. Three handpumps serve varying beers from Yorkshire breweries including Great Yorkshire, Partners and Acorn. Food is served from midday until 9pm every day. All food is locally sourced and prepared on site. There is a small area at the front for alfresco drinking; children and dogs are welcome. ⩩Q✿◐◑≹

Manfield

Crown Inn 🄻
Vicars Lane, DL2 2RF (500yds from B6275)
✪ 5 (12 Sat)-11.30; 12-11 Sun ☎ (01325) 374243
Village White Boar; guest beers 🄷
Voted local CAMRA Country Pub of the Year 11 times, and previously Yorkshire Pub of the Year, this attractive 18th-century inn sits in a quiet village. It has two bars, a games room, a large beer garden and a trellised heated smoking area. A mix of locals and visitors creates a friendly atmosphere. Seven guest beers come from microbreweries countrywide, along with up to two ciders or perries. Two beer festivals and a cider festival are held, and there is a monthly quiz on a Tuesday night. ⩩Q✿◐◑♣●P⅟–⊡⊟(29)

Marske-by-the-Sea

Clarendon
88-90 High Street, TS11 7BA
✪ 11-11 (11.30 Fri-Sun) ☎ (01642) 490005
Black Sheep Best Bitter; Camerons Strongarm; Copper Dragon Golden Pippin; Theakston Best Bitter, Old Peculier; guest beer 🄷
Known as the Middle House, this is a family-run, one-room locals' pub. It serves five regular beers plus a guest from an island bar, which is a rarity on Teesside. There is no TV or jukebox, no pool table, no children or teenagers – just the locals indulging in convivial conversation. There is no catering either, but tea and coffee are available, together with excellent home-made scones at lunchtimes, while a buffet is provided free of charge on Tuesday evenings. It has a south-facing outdoor drinking area. ✿♿≹P⅟–⊟(4,81)

Masham

White Bear 🄻
Wellgarth, HG4 4EN
✪ 11-midnight ☎ (01765) 689319
🌐 thewhitebearhotel.co.uk
Caledonian Deuchars IPA; Theakston Best Bitter, Black Bull Bitter, XB, Old Peculier 🄷
The de facto brewery tap for Theakston's but actually next door to the Black Sheep brewery and visitor centre. The White Bear offers food, drink, accommodation and conference facilities. There is a large dining area to one side and a small cosy taproom to the other serving almost the full range of Theakston beers. The pub was a victim of wartime bombing and derelict for many years before being renovated to a high standard.
⩩✿⊭◐◑⊡P⊟(159)

Melsonby

Black Bull
19 West Road, DL10 5ND (1 mile N of A66)
✪ 5-11 (midnight Fri); 4-midnight Sat; 12-11 Sun
☎ (01325) 718811
Beer range varies 🄷
Late 18th-century community inn with a warm and friendly welcome. This long single-roomed pub has seating at both ends of the central bar. Upstairs there is a function/pool room available for parties. Pub games include ring the bull. Up to three beers from national and local micros are on handpump, regularly from Jarrow and local Mithril Ales. Tasty Sunday lunches are served 12.30-6.30pm. Dominoes is played on Mondays, quizzes on alternate Tuesdays, there are men's and women's darts teams, and various clubs hold meetings here.
⩩✿◑♣⅟–⊟(29)

Middlesbrough

Swatter's Carr
228 Linthorpe Road, TS1 3QW (W side of University)
✪ 8am-midnight (1am Fri & Sat) ☎ (01642) 239060
Greene King Abbot; Ruddles Best Bitter; guest beers 🄷
Wetherspoon conversion of the Empire and now named after the original 17th-century farmstead. During the last 100 years the Empire has had a fascinating history as a hotel and an opera house, and Middlesbrough football and Yorkshire cricket games were once played here. Located in the heart of student land, and where Teesside University Real Ale Society meets, the pub is, not unsurprisingly, very popular. It has 10 handpulls and serves real cider. Meet the Brewer events, beer festivals and celebrations of saints' days all feature. ✿◐◑♿●⅟–⊟

Middlesmoor

Crown Hotel 🄻
Main Street, HG3 5ST (about 8 miles from Pateley Bridge at top of Nidderdale) SE092743
✪ closed Mon winter; 12-3, 6-11; 12-11 Sun
☎ (01423) 755204
Black Sheep Best Bitter 🄷
Unspoilt former shooting lodge, now a family-run hotel, high in Nidderdale, with glorious views down the dale. The availability of accommodation, home-cooked food Monday-Saturday, and log fires make it popular with walkers and sportsmen. It is

closed weekday lunchtimes in winter but it stays open longer in summer if busy. There are usually two or three guest ales and free snuff. No credit or debit cards are taken. There is a bus service from Pateley Bridge on summer Sundays. ⚄Q❀🚃◑❶🏠♿🕎♣P🅛

Muker

Farmers Arms 🅛

DL11 6QG
🌣 11-11 ☎ (01748) 886297 ⊕ farmersarmsmuker.co.uk
Black Sheep Best Bitter; Theakston Best Bitter, Old Peculier; Yorkshire Dales Muker Silver Ⓗ
Traditional Dales inn in a former lead-mining community in the heart of the splendid Swaledale walking country that is popular with walkers, cyclists and other visitors, whether tackling the nearby Coast-to-Coast and Pennine Way routes or just taking a stroll. Dogs are welcome and the stone-flagged bar offers local ales, good food and a warm welcome. A guest beer is added in summer. ⚄Q🐕❀🚃◑🏠♣P🅛(30)

Newton-on-Ouse

Dawnay Arms 🅛

YO30 2BR (on main street in village) SE510601
🌣 closed Mon; 12-2.30, 6-9.30; 12-6 Sun ☎ (01347) 848345
⊕ thedawnayatnewton.co.uk
Black Sheep Best Bitter; guest beers Ⓗ
Country pub in an 18th-century building with an emphasis on Yorkshire beer and locally sourced food; its modern British menu often includes local game. It is included on the Top Gastro Pubs list and booking is advisable. The interior is a mix of rustic wooden tables and comfortable upholstered chairs. Two open fires blaze in winter. The pleasant garden leads down to the River Ouse, where riverside mooring is available. The pub is handily placed for local walks and access to Beninbrough Hall (NT). ⚄Q❀◑♿P🅛🚃(29)

Northallerton

Standard

24 High Street, DL7 8EE (on A167, 500yds N of town centre opp Sainsbury's)
🌣 12-2.30, 5-11.30; 12-11.30 Fri-Sun ☎ (01609) 772719
⊕ thestandard-pub.co.uk
Copper Dragon Golden Pippin; Hambleton Stallion; Taylor Landlord; guest beer Ⓗ
In 1138 the English won a famous victory against the Scots just north of Northallerton at the Battle of the Standard, from which this pub takes its name. A community local and town-centre pub rolled into one, it serves good-value, wholesome meals lunchtimes Tuesday-Sunday and evenings Thursday-Saturday, with a beer festival over the spring bank holiday. Pop into the beer garden and a surprise awaits – an ex-RAF Jet Provost aircraft currently being restored. Q🐕❀◑♣🅛🚃

Tickle Toby 🅛

180 High Street, DL7 8JZ
🌣 11-11 (midnight Thu-Sat); 12-11 Sun ☎ (01609) 778760
Black Sheep Best Bitter; guest beers Ⓗ
Narrow single-bar town-centre pub named after a notorious local highwayman and pickpocket. It is popular with all age groups and offers a range of guest beers from local and regional breweries. Situated at the heart of the town's High Street, it is

busy at weekends and when the Wednesday and Saturday markets take place outside. Meals are served every lunchtime and Wednesday-Friday evenings. ◑🚃♿🏠🅛

Tithe Bar 🅛

2 Friarage Street, DL6 1DP (just off High St near hospital)
🌣 12-11 (midnight Fri & Sat) ☎ (01609) 778482
Ilkley Mary Jane; Okells MPA; guest beers Ⓗ
Just off the busy High Street on the road to the hospital, this cosmopolitan town-centre bar offers seven cask ales and a range of continental and speciality beers. The wooden floor and simple decor give a slightly spartan feel and the only noise comes from the buzz of conversation, with no music or other electronic entertainment. Bar meals are available lunchtimes and early evenings and a brasserie is open upstairs Tuesday-Saturday evenings. Children are welcome during the daytime. Q🐕◑♿🚃♣🅛

Osgodby

Wadkin Arms 🅛

Cliffe Road, YO8 5HU (just off A63 in village) SE641335
🌣 12-11 (midnight Fri & Sat) ☎ (01757) 702391
⊕ wadkinarms.co.uk
Brown Cow White Dragon; John Smith's Bitter; guest beers Ⓗ
Cosy old pub in the centre of the village, featuring real fires and wholesome food served at limited times – teatimes can be busy. Guest beers regularly come from nearby breweries such as Great Heck and Brown Cow, and a dark mild and a pale beer are usually on handpump. An annual beer festival is now established. The pub has a good local atmosphere and is frequented by Osgodby residents and nearby villagers alike. ⚄🐕❀♣P🅛🚃(4)

Osmotherley

Golden Lion

6 West End, DL6 3AA (in village centre, 1 mile E of A19)
🌣 12-2.30 (not Mon & Tue), 6-11; 12-midnight Sat; 12-10.30 Sun ☎ (01609) 883526 ⊕ goldenlionosmotherley.co.uk
Beer range varies Ⓗ
Popular with visitors to the North York Moors National Park, this village is at the start of the long-distance Lyke Wake Walk. Hikers and others can often be seen taking a well-earned rest at the tables outside. Inside, there is an emphasis on food, and the locally sourced fare has a fine reputation. However, there is also a warm welcome for drinkers, with regularly changing beers from local Yorkshire breweries and a beer festival each November. Dogs are welcome. ⚄Q🚃◑🏠🚃(80,89)

Pateley Bridge

Bridge Inn 🅛

Low Wath Road, HG3 5HL
🌣 12-11 ☎ (01423) 711484
Black Sheep Best Bitter; Theakston Best Bitter Ⓗ
A double-fronted old stone building extended to one side, situated about a mile distant from Pateley Bridge up the road heading north to the dalehead. It was at one time the manager's house for the neighbouring Foster Beck mill, which was driven by a huge waterwheel that still exists. Inside

are numerous rooms and spaces including a Sunday carvery area. Two guest beers are added in summer, a time when the patio gets popular with tourists and locals. ▲❀◑♣P╘

Pickering

Sun Inn
136 Westgate, YO18 8BB (on A170 400yds W of traffic lights in town centre)
✪ 4-11; 2.30-midnight Fri; 12-midnight Sat; 12-11 Sun
☎ (01751) 473661 ∰ thesuninn-pickering.co.uk
Leeds Best Bitter; Tetley Bitter; guest beers Ⓗ
Friendly local CAMRA Rural Pub of the Year, close to the Town & Steam railway. Five handpumps serve changing Yorkshire ales and one is dedicated to non-Yorkshire beers. A cosy bar with a real fire leads to a separate room, ideal for families and special events, which opens on to a large enclosed beer garden. Children, walkers and dogs (on leads) are welcome. Regular events for locals and visitors include a bi-weekly acoustic music session, community choir, a monthly charity quiz and a vinyl night every third Thursday.
▲❅❀♿≉♣♠╘❒(128)

Pool in Wharfedale

Hunters Inn
Harrogate Road, LS21 2PS
✪ 11-11; 12-10.30 Sun ☎ (0113) 284 1090
Black Sheep Best Bitter; Ossett Yorkshire Blonde; Thwaites Nutty Black Ⓗ
The inn is situated in lower Wharfedale, on the north side of the river, on the main Harrogate-Bradford road. The large single-room interior incorporates a raised area with a warming real fire during the colder months; the windowed front wall gives views across to the southern ridge of Wharfedale. The three-sided bar has handpumps all round so please check out the listing of up to 10 cask ales on the board on the right as you enter.
▲❀P╘❒(737,X52,X53)

Potto

Dog & Gun
2 Cooper Lane, DL6 3HQ
✪ 12-2.30 (not Mon), 5.30-midnight; 12-midnight Sat; 12-11 Sun ☎ (01642) 700232 ∰ thedogandgunpotto.com
Beer range varies Ⓗ
Country inn under the stewardship of an enthusiastic licensee who also runs the Captain Cook Brewery. Friendly staff ensure that a laid-back ambience prevails in this contemporary setting, which comprises a comfortable main bar, a classy restaurant, private dining areas, five luxury bedrooms and conference facilities. Alongside a selection of the various beers brewed by Captain Cook, a guest beer is sourced from a local microbrewery. Outside, open terraces are ideal for summer drinking. Live acoustic music plays on Friday. ▲❀♨◑♿P❒(89)

Raskelf

Old Black Bull Ⓛ
North End, YO61 3LF
✪ 7-11 Mon; 5 (12 Sat & Sun)-midnight ☎ (01347) 821431
∰ northyorkshotel.co.uk
Theakston Best Bitter, Old Peculier; guest beer Ⓗ

A free house, just west of Easingwold, which has been in the same hands and serving excellent ale for 20 years, yet this is its maiden entry in the Guide. It gives us faith that hidden gems really are still out there. Brisk trade means that the Theakston beers are always fresh, and a complementary guest is usually from the local area as well. It is a great place to spend the evening eating, drinking or trying the twice-monthly quiz; the locals are even friendly enough to let you win, sometimes. ▲❅♨◑♣P❒(30,30X)

Redcar

Turner's Mill
Greenstones Road, TS10 2RA (off B1269, ½ mile S of town)
✪ 11-midnight ☎ (01642) 496021
Durham White Gold; Marston's Pedigree; York Terrier; guest beers Ⓗ
Increasingly popular M&B Ember Inn situated on the edge of a new private housing estate and close to the town's racecourse. Though essentially a large, modern, one-room pub, it has a cosy, relaxing and welcoming ambience to it. The enthusiastic staff serve three regular beers, supplemented with five guests, one of which is usually a stout, porter or old ale. Reasonably priced food is served all day every day. Local CAMRA branch Pub of the Year 2013. ❀◑♿≉(East)P╘❒

Redmire

Bolton Arms Ⓛ
DL8 4EA
✪ 11-midnight ☎ (01969) 624336
∰ boltonarmsredmire.co.uk
Black Sheep Best Bitter; Theakston Best Bitter; Thwaites Original; guest beer Ⓗ
Redmire is an attractive village that marks the western terminus of the revived Wensleydale Railway, whose station is a 10-minute walk away – a good way to travel as parking is limited; buses also provide a vital link. This warm and friendly pub offers snacks all day, as well as lunchtime and evening meals, and there is a large dining area. A guest beer from a local or national brewer is sold during the summer. Easily accessible ground floor B&B accommodation is available.
▲❅♨◑Å≉P❒(157)

Ribblehead

Station
LA6 3AS (on B6255 nr B6479 jct)
✪ 11-11; 12-10.30 Sun ☎ (01524) 241274
∰ thestationinn.net
Black Sheep Best Bitter; Goose Eye Barm Pot Bitter, Chinook Blonde; Thwaites Wainwright; guest beer Ⓗ
The hostelry was built at the same time as the nearby viaduct, in 1874, and can be a welcome refuge in a bleak spot in the midst of superb walking country. A surprisingly large number of locals frequents the plainly furnished bar. There is a good train service – times are above the bar counter – but buses are rare. It has a bunk barn next door, and wild camping behind.
▲❀♨◑Å≉♣P╘❒(831)

Richmond

Bishop Blaize

40 Market Place, DL10 4QL

✪ 10-midnight (1am Fri & Sat) ☎ (01748) 518087
Taylor Landlord; guest beers Ⓗ

Close to the walls of Richmond's spectacular Norman fortress, this town-centre pub is located on the historic cobbled marketplace, near to the bus terminus. A strong commitment to cask ale has earned it CAMRA commendations. Home-cooked traditional pub food is available daily. Pool, live sport and music TV are popular features and there are also regular folk nights. ▲⑤☺☕◑≛☶

Ralph Fitz Randal Ⓛ

6 Queens Road, DL10 4AE (on edge of town centre on main Scotch Corner road)

✪ 9am-midnight (1am Fri & Sat) ☎ (01748) 828080
Greene King Abbot; Ruddles Bitter; guest beers Ⓗ

A large single-bar Wetherspoon house set on three levels in the town's former post office and telephone exchange, offering up to eight guest beers. A winner of numerous CAMRA awards, locally brewed ales are always on offer and there are themed monthly beer festivals, usually featuring a particular brewery or beer style. There is a large family dining area, and low-volume TVs cater for sports fans. It opens at 8am for breakfast. ☺◑♿♥≛☶

Ripon

Magdalens Ⓛ

26 Princess Road, HG4 1HW

✪ 4 (2 Tue & Wed; 1 Thu & Fri)-midnight; 12-midnight Sat & Sun ☎ (01765) 604746 ⊕ magdalensripon.co.uk
John Smith's Bitter; Taylor Landlord; Theakston Best Bitter Ⓗ

A friendly community pub with darts, dominoes, pool and football teams. The two (sometimes three) guest beers change on a regular basis. The landlord, a keen gardener, has created an award-winning beer garden, with a grassed play area for children at the rear. The venue is the recipient of many awards for its beer quality, as well as sporting and other prowess, as the walls and trophy cabinet testify. Sunday lunch must be pre-booked. ⑤☺◑♣P≛

One-Eyed Rat Ⓛ

51 Allhallowgate, HG4 1LQ

✪ 5 (12 Fri & Sat)-11; 12-10.30 Sun ☎ (01765) 607704
⊕ oneeyedrat.com
Beer range varies Ⓗ

A narrow-fronted building that goes back a long way both in time (200 years) and distance; inside is a cosy, traditional pub with a constantly changing range of seven guest beers. The immaculately kept beers come from Yorkshire and further afield; there is always a stout, porter or mild to complement the paler beers popular locally. Regular live music plays and the pub hosts two beer festivals a year, one with a German theme. ▲Q☺♥≛

Water Rat Ⓛ

24 Bondgate Green, HG4 1QW

✪ 11-11 (closed Mon winter) ☎ (01765) 602251
⊕ thewaterrat.co.uk
Black Sheep Best Bitter Ⓗ

Located by the side of the River Skell with a fine view of Ripon Cathedral from its sun-drenched conservatory and terrace, this is the city's only

riverside pub. An emphasis on affordable home-cooked traditional English pub food means it tends to get busy at times. There is a small snug at the front of the pub. The Black Sheep beer is supplemented by two other local ales, typically from Rudgate, Hambleton, Rooster's, Salamander or Copper Dragon. ⑤☺◑≛☶

Robin Hood's Bay

Dolphin

King Street, YO22 4SH (on steep pedestrian-only road, down towards the Bay, from top car park)

✪ 11 (12 Sun)-11 ☎ (01947) 880337
Caledonian Deuchars IPA; Theakston Best Bitter, Old Peculier; guest beer Ⓗ

Olde-worlde pub, full of memorabilia, popular with locals and visitors alike, where dogs and muddy boots are made equally welcome. It comprises a cosy public bar, where a real fire burns for most of the year, and a large family/dining room. Three regular beers and a guest are served. A quiz takes place on Sunday, R&B on Monday and a folk club on Friday. Access to this part of the village is not easy for the less able-bodied. ▲Q◑▲☶(56,93)

Victoria Hotel

Station Road, YO22 4RL (at top of cliff)

✪ 12-11.30 ☎ (01947) 880205 ⊕ thevictoriarhb.com
Camerons Best Bitter, Strongarm; Theakston Best Bitter; guest beers Ⓗ

A warm welcome awaits you at this 19th-century hotel, set in a superb location on the edge of the cliffs, overlooking the bay of this picturesque seaside resort and providing stunning views from the tea rooms and gardens. The busy and friendly bar serves six beers including three guests, usually from local Yorkshire breweries. A good-value, highly regarded menu, including daily specials, is served lunchtimes and evenings. A separate family room is available. There are 13 letting bedrooms. ▲Q⑤☺☕◑P♿☶(56,93)

Saltburn-by-the-Sea

Saltburn Cricket, Bowls & Tennis Club

Marske Mill Lane, TS12 1HJ (next to leisure centre)

✪ 8am-midnight (1am Fri & Sat); 11.30-3, 8-midnight Sun ☎ (01287) 622761
Beer range varies Ⓗ

Casual visitors are made welcome at this former local CAMRA branch award winner. A private sports club, well supported by the local community, it fields cricket, tennis and bowls teams, and is also the watering hole for the local diving club. The bar sits in a spacious, comfortable lounge, which can be divided for different functions and social events. The balcony, ideal for those lazy summer afternoons, overlooks the cricket field. Two changing beers are served. Open 2pm-midnight on Saturday match days. ☺♿≕♣P≛☶(X4,48)

Sawdon

Anvil Inn

Main Street, YO13 9DY (2 miles off A170)

✪ closed Mon & Tue; 12-2.30, 6-11; 12-3, 6-10.30 Sun ☎ (01723) 859896 ⊕ theanvilinnsawdon.co.uk
Daleside Bitter; guest beers Ⓗ

A heart-of-the-village pub, on the edge of the North York Moors National Park, Dalby Forest and

close to the coast, in excellent walking, cycling and mountain biking country. Formerly the village blacksmith's, it still retains the forge and, of course, the anvil. It has a cosy bar, with a separate lounge and dining area, and three handpumps dispensing beers from local independents. Food of the highest standard is served and booking is recommended. There are two well-appointed letting cottages.
🏚️🏵️⬤♣P

Scarborough

Angel
46 North Street, YO11 1DF
✪ 11 (12 Sun)-midnight ☎ (01723) 365504
Copper Dragon Golden Pippin; Black Sheep Best Bitter; Taylor Landlord; Tetley Bitter 🅗
Friendly town-centre local close to the main shopping area, with a single-room horseshoe bar displaying an excellent collection of saucy seaside postcards. An interest in sport and games is reflected in the impressive array of trophies won by various pub teams and the large-screen TVs for viewing sporting events. Occasional guest beers are added in summer. It has a surprisingly spacious and well-appointed patio garden at the rear.
🏵️🌿♣'—🚌

Cellars
35-37 Valley Road, YO11 2LX
✪ 12-midnight; 4-11 winter; 12-10.30 Sun
☎ (01723) 367158
Bradfield Farmers Blonde; Camerons Strongarm; Daleside Monkey Wrench; guest beers 🅗
A family-run pub converted from the cellars of a Victorian house, with 15 years in the Guide, this is Scarborough's longest consecutive entry. It has six handpumps dispensing guest beers from micros around the country. Excellent locally sourced, home-cooked food is served lunchtimes and evenings, with Sunday lunches particularly popular. Quiz night is Tuesday, open mic night is Wednesday, local acoustic acts appear on Thursday, and Saturday is live music night. The patio fronting the pub is popular in summer. Children and dogs are welcome and accommodation is available.
🏵️🛏️⬤🌿♣P🚌(4)

Indigo Alley
4 North Marine Road, YO12 7PD
✪ 3-11 (midnight Fri & Sat); 12-11 Sun ☎ (01723) 350599
Wychwood Hobgoblin; guest beers 🅗
Recently upgraded into a welcoming open-plan pub retaining a rustic feel and sporting a logburner, this venue has come back on the real ale and traditional cider trail after a few years in the wilderness. It is a true free house, with bare floorboards and the advantage of pool, darts, dominoes and chess. Locally brewed Indigo Ale and draught Thatchers cider complement specialist lagers. It is dog and child friendly, with live entertainment every Friday. Free Wi-Fi is available.
🏚️🛏️🌿♣⬤🚌

North Riding Brew Pub 🏆
161-163 North Marine Road, YO12 7HU
✪ 12-midnight (1am Fri & Sat) ☎ (01723) 370004
⊕ northridingbrewpub.com
Taylor Landlord; York Guzzler; guest beers 🅗
Scarborough's only brewpub and current local CAMRA Town Pub of the Year, it is on the North Bay, just down from the cricket ground. It has now served over 2,000 guest beers in addition to its

own North Riding beers. Two or more guests come from microbreweries from far and wide, and the place is a regular outlet for Elland, Thornbridge and Yorkshire Dales. The pub has a public bar, a quiet lounge and an upstairs dining room serving home-cooked food, all with real fires. Quiz night is Thursday. 🏚️Q🛏️⬤🍴♣⬤'—🚌(3A)

Scholars
Somerset Terrace, YO11 2PW
✪ 4.30 (12 Fri-Sun)-midnight ☎ (01723) 360084
Copper Dragon Golden Pippin; Hambleton Nightmare; York Yorkshire Terrier; guest beers 🅗
A warm, friendly atmosphere prevails at this town-centre pub at the rear of the main shopping centre. It has a large front bar and a games room. Seven handpumps serve a rotating range of beers from Ossett, Fernandes, Rat and other breweries throughout the Yorkshire region. Numerous screens show major sporting events. Twenty-eight pints are the prize at the Thursday quiz, and more free beer can be won rolling dice on Monday, Tuesday, Wednesday and Sunday nights. 🚻🌿♣🚌

Spa
45 Victoria Road, YO11 1SH
✪ 11-midnight; 12-11 Sun ☎ (01723) 350345
⊕ thespapub.co.uk
Tetley Bitter; guest beers 🅗
Recently refurbished locals' pub that now boasts up to five rotating guest beers with the occasional real cider. Fridays, Saturdays and Sundays host live music from the best of local talent. It has pool, darts and domino teams. A quiz is held on Thursday. With an enthusiastic landlord, this is a welcome addition to our real ale pubs portfolio.
🏚️🍴🚻🌿♣🚌

Valley
51 Valley Road, YO11 2LX
✪ 12-midnight (1am Thu-Sat) ☎ (01723) 372593
⊕ valleybar.co.uk
Dark Star Hophead; Scarborough Brewing Co Scarborough Stout; Theakston Best Bitter; guest beers 🅗
A cellar bar with six handpumps offering mainly microbrewery beers, usually including one or more from Scarborough Brewery. Up to eight real ciders and perries are also on handpump, together with over 100 bottles of Belgian beers including Cantillon. Further rooms provide additional seating upstairs, and can be used for meetings. There is also a pool table. Sandwiches are sold all day.
🏵️🛏️🌿♣⬤'—🖥️🚌

Settle

Talbot Arms ⓛ
High Street, BD24 9EX
✪ 11.30-11 ☎ (01729) 823924 ⊕ talbotsettle.co.uk
Theakston Best Bitter; guest beers 🅗
Recently extensively refurbished and re-energised, this is now a bright, welcoming place to drink. There is a large stone feature fireplace to the left of the main entrance and pool table, dartboard and dominoes tables. To the rear, the large terraced beer garden is a good place to soak up any summer sun. Look out for another pub feature – Dennis the cat. Guest beers tend to be from Cumbria, Lancashire and Yorkshire. Food is served 12-8pm all week. 🏚️🏵️⬤🌿♣⬤'—🚌

Thirteen ⃦

13 Duke Street, BD24 9DU (main road S of marketplace)
✪ 4-8 Mon; 11-8 Tue; 11-10 Wed-Thu; 11-11 Fri & Sat; closed Sun ☎ (01729) 824356 ⊕ thirteencafebar.co.uk
Dark Horse Best Bitter; Goose Eye Chinook Blonde; Three Peaks Ingleborough Gold Ⓗ
The owners are very hands-on at Thirteen, offering a friendly welcome to locals and tourists, creating a relaxed atmosphere. Situated on the main street near a pedestrian crossing, it is a narrow single-room café bar with a modern feel. Despite the smart wine bar ambience, walking boots are also welcome. The beers are all from local micros and the venue also sells a range of bottled Belgian beer. Themed dining evenings include steak nights and tapas. ◑ ⅃ ⅃ ⇌ ⊟ (580,581)

Shipton-by-Beningbrough

Dawnay Arms

Main Street, YO30 1AB (A19 NW from York, village after Skelton, SE from Thirsk past Easingwold, in centre of village)
✪ 12-2.30 (not Mon & Tue), 5.30 (Sat 6)-midnight; 12-11 Sun ☎ (01904) 470334 ⊕ thedawnayarms.co.uk
Tetley Bitter; guest beers Ⓗ
Built in 1730, this is a traditional country inn in the village centre. One of the three handpumps always serves a local ale. The wide-ranging pub food, cooked on the premises, includes gluten-free and vegetarian options. The pub has an open bar area with an open fire, a separate area for quieter dining, and a family room. Old pictures and items of local history are on display. Regular quiz nights and community charity events are hosted, including live music in the car park.
⚒ ⅀ ⊛◑ ⅃ P'⊟ (31,31X)

Sicklinghall

Scotts Arms

Main Street, LS22 4BD (3 miles W of Wetherby)
✪ 11-11 (10 Sun) ☎ (01937) 582100 ⊕ scottsarms.com
Black Sheep Best Bitter; Theakston Old Peculier Ⓗ
Welcoming village inn with an excellent reputation for food served in two large but intimate lounges. An upper level bar caters for drinkers while the lower level welcomes diners and drinkers. Guest beers tend to be from northern breweries. The garden area is popular with families and walkers in summer as this is good rambling territory. The pub also houses the village shop, with a visiting post office one day a week. ⚒ ⅀ ⊛◑ P'⇐

Skipton

Bistro des Amis ⃦

1 Jerry Croft, BD23 1DT (entrance is from Jerry Croft, next to town hall)
✪ 10-11; 11-10.30 Sun ☎ (01756) 797919 ⊕ lebistrodesamis.co.uk
Ilkley Mary Jane; Taylor Landlord Ⓗ
Comfortable, friendly and relaxed French-owned bar/bistro/café/restaurant, where the casual drinker is made very welcome. While the emphasis is on quality meals accompanied by fine wines, it is perfectly acceptable to order a pint and drink at the bar, or settle into one of the comfortable armchairs and enjoy waiter service while chilling out to the sounds of recorded chansons, jazz or blues. Lunchtime and evening meals are served all week. ◑ ⅃ ⇌ ⊟

Castle ⃦

2 Mill Bridge, BD23 1NJ
✪ 11-11 ☎ (01756) 796304 ⊕ castleinnskipton.co.uk
Theakston Best Bitter, Old Peculier; Thwaites Wainwright; guest beer Ⓗ
Imposing late-Georgian building adjacent to the medieval parish church and close to the eponymous castle. A single bar serves three distinct drinking areas including a cosy snug. The outside drinking area at the front is a magnet for people-watchers on a fine day. The enthusiastic young licensee has already won several awards. It is a regular outlet for Theakston's Old Peculier plus an occasional guest from the Heineken UK (formerly Scottish & Newcastle) range. Quiz night is Sunday, steak night Wednesday. ⊛◑ ⅃ ⇌ ♣ P⊟

Narrow Boat ⃦

38 Victoria Street, BD23 1JE (alleyway off Coach St near canal bridge)
✪ 12-11 ☎ (01756) 797922
Black Sheep Best Bitter; Ilkley Mary Jane; Taylor Landlord; guest beers Ⓗ
Civilised beer drinkers' emporium near the canal basin, furnished with old church pews and international breweriana. No piped music, jukebox or gaming machines disturb the conversation. Guest ales, usually including a dark beer, are mainly from northern independents, and there is a good range of continental bottled and draught beers plus up to four ciders or perries. A folk club is hosted on Monday evening and a quiz night on Wednesday. Well-behaved dogs are welcome, while children under 14 are only admitted when dining. Q ⊛◑ ⅃ ⇌ ♦ '⊟

Sowerby

Crown & Anchor ⃦

138 Front Street, YO7 1JN (½ mile from Thirsk)
✪ 12-midnight (1am Thu-Sat); 12-11 Sun ☎ (01845) 522448 ⊕ crownandanchorsowerby.co.uk
John Smith's Bitter; guest beers Ⓗ
A true community pub at the heart of this attractive village on the edge of Thirsk and winner of several CAMRA awards. Three guest ales are usually on offer, often from Black Sheep and Copper Dragon, while several annual beer or cider festivals use the outside bar. Inside there are several drinking areas with occasional live music and good, no-nonsense food all day ranging from bar snacks to Sunday lunches (booking advised). No food Monday lunchtimes. ⊛◑ ⅃ ♣ P'⊟ (146,148,149)

Staithes

Captain Cook Inn

60 Staithes Lane, TS13 5AD (off A174, by village car park)
✪ 11-midnight ☎ (01947) 840200
Beer range varies Ⓗ
Local CAMRA award-winning pub sitting high above this pretty coastal village and close to Boulby Cliffs, the highest in England. Six handpumps provide a mix of beer styles, now including the pub's own in-house brews. Five annual beer and pork pie/sausage festivals are held to celebrate St Patrick's Day, St George's Day, Lifeboat week, Halloween/Guy Fawkes and Winter Warmers week, between Christmas and New Year. Accommodation is in four bedrooms and a cottage. ⚒ Q ⊛ ⇌ ◑ ♣ P⊟ (5)

Staxton

Hare & Hounds
Main Street, YO12 4TA
✪ 12-11.30 ☎ (01944) 710243
Taylor Landlord; Theakston Old Peculier; guest
beers Ⓗ
Imposing former coaching inn on the A64 – an
excellent oasis when travelling to the east coast.
The bar and lounge/dining area feature low beams
and real fires. Guest beers are usually from the
Enterprise/SIBA scheme and often come from
Wold Top and Great Yorkshire breweries. The three
handpumps in winter rise to five in summer.
Home-cooked meals are on offer every day, with
seafood from Filey a speciality in summer. There
are large grassed drinking areas at the front and
rear of the pub. ♨Q✿❍❶⌷AP⅃–⊟(843)

Stillington

White Bear Inn Ⓛ
Main Street, YO61 1JU
✪ 12-2.30 (not Mon), 5.30-11; 12-midnight Sat; 12-11 Sun
☎ (01347) 810338
Marston's Burton Bitter; Samuel Smith's OBB; guest
beers Ⓗ
Many large towns would be envious of the choice
offered by this village alehouse – the three guests,
which regularly rotate, are usually from interesting
local breweries. The reasonably priced Yorkshire
fare does not impinge on the main occupation of
drinking and socialising or on the popular monthly
quiz; try the snowball if you dare. Easily reached by
bus from York or Easingwold, it is well worth the
trip. ⅏❶⌷❶♣P⅃–⊟(40)

Stokesley

Spread Eagle
39 High Street, TS9 5AD
✪ 11-1am; 12-12.30am Sun ☎ (01642) 710278
Camerons Strongarm; Marston's Pedigree; guest
beers Ⓗ
A fine welcome is assured at this small, unspoilt
market-town pub. Friendly regulars drink at one
end and an open fire welcomes diners at the other.
Excellent, good-value home-cooked food,
complete with details of where the produce has
come from, is served all day. Two interesting and
stronger guest beers are always available. Children
are welcome. A rear garden leads down to the
tranquil River Leven, where over-fed ducks amuse
children and adults alike. Tuesday is live music
night. ♨Q✿❍❶⌷A⅃–⊟(80,81)

White Swan
1 West End, TS9 5BL (at W end of town)
✪ 11.30 (12 Sun)-11 ☎ (01642) 710263
⊕ thewhiteswanstokesley.co.uk
Beer range varies Ⓗ
A local CAMRA branch award winner, this
traditional one-room 18th-century local is situated
in one of the prettiest areas of this market town.
Eight handpumps serve a selection of Captain Cook
and Trufitt beers, and a guest usually sourced from
a local microbrewery. The pub holds a quiz night on
Wednesday and music nights monthly. Beer
festivals take place at Easter and in October.
Ploughman's lunches are served Wednesday-
Saturday. Children are not allowed in the pub.
♨Q✿❍⌷⊟(29,81)

Strensall

Ship Inn
23 The Village, YO32 5XS
✪ 12-11 (11.30 Fri & Sat); 12-10.30 Sun ☎ (01904) 490302
⊕ theshipinn-strensall.co.uk
John Smith's Bitter; Taylor Landlord; guest beers Ⓗ
Approximately five miles north-east of York, this
quiet village local has built on its reputation, with a
dedicated bar and lounge and a separate
restaurant. Outside seating is provided, and there's
a children's play area. The bar has two permanent
cask beers and two handpumps for guest beers,
one mainly dedicated to microbreweries. The pub
also holds regular quiz and music nights supporting
local charities, and is popular with cyclists, ramblers
and caravanners in summer. The bus stop is
virtually outside the front door.
Q⅏✿❍⌷❶♣P⅃–⊟(5)

Thixendale

Cross Keys
YO17 9TG SE845611
✪ 12-3 (not Mon, or Tue-Thu winter), 6-11; 12-3, 7-10.30 Sun
☎ (01377) 288272
Tetley Bitter; guest beers Ⓗ
A single-room hostelry that first appeared on a
map dated 1851. At the heart of 16 dry valleys, it is
popular with walkers, including those on the Wolds
Way and, though remote, is well worth seeking
out. The two guest beers come from independent
breweries and are usually no more than 4% ABV.
Good-value, traditional food is served. Children are
welcome in the beer garden. Accommodation is in
the adjoining converted stable. Will open during
normally closed lunchtimes in winter by
arrangement. ♨Q✿✉❍❶♣

Thorganby

Ferry Boat Inn ♈ Ⓛ
Ferry Lane, YO19 6DD (1 mile NE of village, signed from
main road, by River Derwent) SE697427
✪ closed Mon; 7 (12 Sat)-11.30; 12-3, 7-11 Sun
☎ (01904) 448224
Brown Cow Best Bitter; guest beers Ⓗ
A warm, welcoming local in a beautiful and
secluded rural setting, run by the same family for
over 60 years. Free of tie, the landlord favours
beers from local micros and Yorkshire breweries,
served in oversized glasses. It has a cosy bar with a
real fire, a lounge with pub games, and a large
riverside garden where dogs are welcome. Caravan
hook-ups and fishing permits are available.
♨Q⅏✿✿❖AP⛟⊟(35)

Thornton Watless

Buck Inn Ⓛ
Village Green, HG4 4AH (off B6268 between Bedale and
Masham)
✪ 11-11 ☎ (01677) 422461 ⊕ buckwatlass.co.uk
Black Sheep Best Bitter; Theakston Best Bitter; guest
beers Ⓗ
Overlooking the village green, this traditional
country inn features a cosy bar room with a real
fire, a lounge/function room called the Long Room
and a separate dining area. Guest beers are usually
from northern micros. Food is home-cooked from
locally sourced ingredients and is served
lunchtimes and evenings. There is a tree-lined beer

garden at the rear and the pub hosts regular jazz sessions, usually on Sunday afternoons.
♨Q❀☕◑ ⬗P🖳(144)

Thornton-le-Dale

Buck
Chestnut Avenue, YO18 7RW
✪ 12-10 (4-10.30 winter) Mon; 12-midnight
☎ (01751) 474212
Tetley Bitter; guest beers Ⓗ
A welcoming, traditional pub with two guest beers (three in summer) coming from Yorkshire and beyond. Copper Dragon and Ossett ales are often available. Home-made pub food is served daily until 8.30pm (3pm Sun). Pool and darts matches and quizzes are held weekly. The beer garden is a suntrap in summer – the perfect place to relax after a day in Dalby Forest or on the moors, or just sit soaking up the beautiful village atmosphere.
♨⏚❀☕◑ ⬗♣Pˡ–🖳(128,840)

Upper Poppleton

Lord Collingwood
The Green, YO26 6DP (on village green)
✪ 12-3 (not Mon), 5-midnight; 12-midnight Fri-Sun
☎ (01904) 337537 ⊕ thelordcollingwood.co.uk
Beer range varies
Fine country pub on the village green in a lovely 17th-century Grade II-listed building, with friendly, welcoming staff. Up to seven ales from the Marston's list are on offer, including seasonals. Good honest food is served lunchtimes and evenings (no food Mon, lunch only Sun). The comfortable interior features a timber ceiling and pillars, real fires and a 19th-century carved oak bar. A fairy-lit beer garden, patio and children's play area are to the rear. Accessible from York by bus or rail. ♨❀◑⇌♣P🖳(10)

Welbury

Duke of Wellington
DL6 2SG (5 miles off A19)
✪ 12-3 (not Mon-Thu), 5-11; 12-11 Sun ☎ (01609) 882464
⊕ thedukeofwellingtonwelbury.com
Beer range varies Ⓗ
Little gem hidden in the picturesque village of Welbury. Through the front entrance you are welcomed by friendly staff behind a long bar, with open fires, offering up to five real ales, mainly sourced from local microbreweries. Off the bar area are several rooms dedicated to dining from a reasonably priced menu, many of the ingredients proudly sourced from local farmers and markets. Come and stay in one of five en-suite rooms. Well-known locally for its World Welly Wanging Championship. ♨Q⏚❀☕◑ ⬗♣Pˡ

Wensley

Three Horseshoes Ⓛ
DL8 4HJ (on A684)
✪ 11-3 (not Mon), 5.30-11; 11-11 Sat; 12-10.30 Sun
☎ (01969) 622327
Theakston Best Bitter; Wall's Gun Dog Bitter; Yorkshire Dales Three Horseshoes; guest beers Ⓗ
Traditional old country pub full of atmosphere, with a small bar and dining room both featuring low beams and real fires. The terraced beer garden to the rear offers glorious views across Wensleydale.

and is a suntrap on good days. Wholesome and very reasonably priced lunchtime and evening meals are served daily.
♨Q⏚❀☕◑ ⬗&♣P🖳(156,157)

West Haddlesey

George & Dragon Ⓛ
Main Street, YO8 8QA (1 mile W of A19, 5 miles S of Selby) SE565266
✪ 5-midnight (1am Fri); 2-1am Sat; 12-10.30 Sun
☎ (01757) 228198
Brown Cow White Dragon; guest beers Ⓗ
Privately owned free house with enthusiastic support for local microbreweries. It has low ceilings, a cosy bar with a real fire, a large-screen TV showing sporting events, a separate room for diners and an attractive outside decked area for summer days. Food is served evenings (not Sun and Mon) as well as Saturday and Sunday lunchtimes. A weekly quiz night, karaoke and frequent jazz nights are staged, and occasional beer festivals are held outdoors, including an annual April festival on the weekend closest to St George's Day. ♨Q❀☕◑ &♣Pˡ–🖳(405,407)

West Witton

Fox & Hounds ♈ Ⓛ
Main Street, DL8 4LP (on A684)
✪ 12-3, 6-midnight; 12-midnight Sat & Sun
☎ (01969) 623650 ⊕ foxwitton.com
Black Sheep Best Bitter; John Smith's Bitter; guest beers Ⓗ
Friendly, family-run free house full of character, with a down-to-earth bar and games room popular with locals and visitors alike. Good-value meals are served all week, with a roast on Sunday. Part of the pub was a rest house for monks from Jervaulx Abbey in the 1400s, and the dining room boasts an inglenook fireplace, complete with beehive oven. A pleasant patio at the rear leads onto the quoits pitch; beware the tight entry to the car park. Real cider is often served. ♨❀◑♣🍺Pˡ–🖳(156)

Whitby

Black Horse
91 Church Street, YO22 4BH (E side of bridge on approach to Abbey steps)
✪ 11-11; 12-10.30 Sun ☎ (01947) 602906
⊕ the-black-horse.com
Adnams Southwold Bitter; Black Dog Rhatas; Black Sheep Ale; guest beers Ⓗ
Dating from the 1600s, this previous local CAMRA branch award winner offers a warm welcome. The frontage, with its frosted glass windows, together with one of Europe's oldest public serving bars, were built in the 1880s and remain largely unchanged. Beer is dispensed from five handpumps, and hot meals are served during the winter months. Snuff, tapas, olives, Yorkshire cheeses and hot drinks are always available. The cider is Westons Traditional scrumpy. Accommodation is in four bedrooms.
Q☕◑ ⬗&Å⇌♣🍺🖳(93)

Endeavour
66 Church Street, YO22 4AS (on E side of river, 100yds S of swing bridge)
✪ 12-1am (11.30 Sun) ☎ (01947) 603557
John Smith's Bitter; guest beers Ⓗ

Named in celebration of James Cook's voyages to the South Seas, this cosy one-room town pub has an open fire that adds to the warm welcome from an enthusiastic licensee. Alongside the John Smith's, five handpumps serve approximately 140 different guest beers annually, which come from all parts of the country. A tremendous atmosphere prevails, enhanced during Whitby's various folk and Gothic celebrations. Regular folk and Irish music sessions are held on Friday and Saturday evenings and Sunday afternoons. Two bedrooms are available. ♨🛏🏕Å�''🚲(93)

Station Inn

New Quay Road, YO21 1DH (opp bus and railway stations)
✪ 10-midnight (11.30 Sun) ☎ (01947) 603937
⊕ stationinnwhitby.co.uk
Black Dog Whitby Abbey Ale; Camerons Strongarm; Copper Dragon Challenger IPA; Taylor Golden Best; guest beers Ⓗ
Next to the harbour and marina, a warm welcome awaits you at this popular multi-roomed pub and recent local CAMRA branch Pub of the Year. The enthusiastic licensees ensure that the eight beers always represent a superb range of varying styles, while Westons cider and a dozen fruit wines mean there is something for everyone. Opposite the bus station and the NYMR/Esk Valley railway terminus, the pub has become the discerning traveller's waiting room. Live entertainment features on Wednesday, Friday and Saturday evenings. ➪🚲(93)

Yarm

Black Bull

42 High Street, TS15 9BH (by town hall)
✪ 11-midnight (1am Fri & Sat) ☎ (01642) 791251
⊕ theblackbullyarm.co.uk
Draught Bass; York Terrier; guest beers Ⓗ
Situated in the centre of the town, and with the best beer garden/heated patio in the area, this popular M&B Nicholson's pub has been the favourite haunt, especially on Tuesdays, for Teesside's 30-somethings, and older, for decades. Much extended over the years, with two separate bars, the number of handpumps has now increased to five, which are very busy during the day, and extremely busy evenings/weekends. Good-value pub food is served all day every day. ♨💷🌙Å➪(Yarm/Eaglescliffe)🍴🚲(7,82)

York

Brigantes Bar & Brasserie Ⓛ

114 Micklegate, YO1 6JX (100yds from Micklegate Bar)
✪ 12-11 ☎ (01904) 675355
Beer range varies Ⓗ
Award-winning real ale haven, with 10 handpumps featuring Yorkshire beers, including two from York, one from Leeds, Black Sheep, Great Heck and Timothy Taylor, alongside four guests. It also stocks a selection of continental beers and a draught cider. It is a Market Town Taverns pub located just inside the bar walls. The ground-floor bar area leads to a lounge area, while upstairs is a period Georgian function/dining room. The menu features daily specials and a pie of the day. Q🌙Å➪🍴🚲

Maltings Ⓛ

Tanners Moat, Lendal, YO1 6HU
✪ 11-11; 12-10.30 Sun ☎ (01904) 655387 ⊕ maltings.co.uk
Black Sheep Best Bitter; Rooster's Yankee; York Guzzler; guest beers Ⓗ
A former CAMRA Yorkshire Pub of the Year, this place has a lovely atmosphere, a real-effect gas fire, a covered smoking area outside, live folk music every Tuesday and bags of character. There are reclaimed doors covering the ceiling and even a reclaimed toilet acting as a seat in one of the corners. A recent extension has provided more seating and a small outside area, while carefully maintaining the original character. Friendly, knowledgeable staff serve a wide and revolving range of local beers. Q♨🛏🌙➪🍴P🍴🚲

Minster Inn

24 Marygate, YO30 7BH
✪ 2-11; 11-midnight Fri & Sat; 12-10.30 Sun
☎ (01904) 624499
Jennings Sneck Lifter; Marston's Burton Bitter; guest beers Ⓗ
A traditional, unspoilt local pub that retains its multi-roomed layout. You can always find someone to talk to in the lively bar, meet with friends in one of the three rooms, or seek out a quiet spot. There are tabletop games to keep everyone busy (or frustrated) for hours. Although tied to Marston's, it makes the best of the range of beers available, always selecting the seasonal ones. ♨Q🌙🐾🌙➪🍴🚲

Old White Swan Ⓛ

80 Goodramgate, YO1 7LF
✪ 10-midnight (1am Fri & Sat) ☎ (01904) 540911
John Smith's Bitter; St Austell Nicholson's Pale Ale; Thornbridge Jaipur IPA; York Terrier; guest beers Ⓗ
A large three-roomed Nicholson's pub in the city centre. A seated courtyard area at the front leads to the Georgian dining room on the left, the Tudor bar straight ahead, and the Stagecoach bar to the right – which in turns opens onto an outdoor smoking area at the rear. Eight handpumps offer a variety of styles and strengths of beer from around the country, regularly including ales from local breweries. Good-quality pub food is served all day. 🌙💷🐶🍴

Phoenix

75 George Street, YO1 9PT
✪ 6-11; 4.30-11.30 Fri; 12.30-11.30 Sat; 2.30-11.30 Sun
☎ (01904) 656401 ⊕ thephoenixinnyork.co.uk
Copper Dragon Golden Pippin; Taylor Landlord; Wold Top Bitter; guest beers Ⓗ
Unspoilt, traditional and independently run pub, with preserved historic features from a major refurbishment a few years ago. Adjacent to the city walls, it is close to the tourist attractions of the Jorvik Viking Centre and Castle Museum. The pub has six real ales, mainly from northern breweries, and hosts beer festivals plus Meet the Brewer evenings. Live jazz nights, a quiz night and traditional pub games (bar billiards and shove-ha'penny) help create a convivial atmosphere. ♨Q🌙🐾🚲

Pivni

6 Patrick Pool, YO1 8BB
✪ 11.30-11.30 (11.45 Fri & Sat); 12-11.30 Sun
☎ (01904) 635464 ⊕ pivni.co.uk
Beer range varies Ⓗ

Part of the expanding group of Pivovar UK beer houses, featuring five cask ales from highly regarded breweries such as Thornbridge, Buxton, Hardknott, Marble, Dark Star and many more, changing regularly. There is also an extensive selection of bottled beers. Formerly a travel agents, the 12th-century timber-framed building dates back to 1190. Food is restricted to cold pies and cheeseboards. ⬤

Slip Inn 🄻
20 Clementhorpe, YO23 1AN
❂ 5-11.30; 4-midnight Fri; 12-midnight Sat; 12-11 Sun
☎ (01904) 621793 ⊕ theslipinnyork.co.uk
Leeds Pale; Rudgate Ruby Mild; Taylor Boltmaker; Wold Top Wold Gold; guest beer 🄷
An independent free house since 2010, this friendly, traditional community pub is situated just outside the city walls. Run by beer enthusiasts, permanent ales from four Yorkshire brewers feature plus a guest, and the range expands dramatically during events. Real cider is on offer too. The two bars and snug have been carefully updated. The paved outdoor area caters for smokers, and is also often used to host live music and food at events such as festivals and Battle of the Brewers. There are also TVs for sporting events. ⬤🌫🍴⬤🄻🄯(11)

Snickleway Inn 🄻
47 Goodramgate, YO1 7LS
❂ 12-11 (midnight Thu-Sat) ☎ (01904) 656138
⊕ thesnicklewayinn.co.uk
Bradfield Farmers Blonde; Jennings Cocker Hoop; Sneck Lifter; John Smith's Bitter; Moorhouse's Pendle Witches Brew; Rooster's Yankee 🄷
A cosy, friendly local in an unspoilt early 15th-century building, formerly the Royalists' powder magazine during the English Civil War. It has a galleried central bar with three seating areas, two with open fires. On Monday nights the York Philharmonic Male Voice Choir pop in for a thirst quencher and a few songs, and on the last Thursday of the month there is a reggae DJ offering new and old sounds to the mixed-age pubgoers. ⬤🄯🄻

Swan Inn ★ 🄻
16 Bishopgate Street, YO23 1JH
❂ 4-11 (11.30 Thu; midnight Fri); 12-midnight Sat; 12-10.30 Sun ☎ (01904) 634968
Saltaire Blonde; Taylor Landlord; Tetley Bitter; guest beers 🄷
Identified by CAMRA as one of Britain's Best Real Heritage Pubs and winner of numerous awards, this is definitely a York pub to visit. It is often busy, particularly on race days, but the rare West Riding lobby and two bar hatches means that you are never far from swift service. Be sure to ask about the three sister pubs in town which are all well worth a visit, one being eminently easy to slip into and the others not far away either.
🏛🌫🄯🍴⬤🄻🄯

Volunteer Arms 🄻
5 Watson Street, YO24 4BH
❂ 5-11 (midnight Fri); 12-midnight Sat; 12-11 Sun
☎ (01904) 541945 ⊕ volunteerarmsyork.co.uk
Brown Cow Thriller in Vanilla; Leeds Yorkshire Gold; Marston Moor Mongrel; Ossett Pale Gold; Treboom Yorkshire Sparkle; guest beers 🄷
An independent free house situated just off Holgate Road, close to the centre of York. The pub

has a real community feel, while being welcoming to all. It offers an excellent beer range for a suburban pub, with loyalties firmly with local breweries, emphasising the pub's commitment to LocAle. There are five permanent beers and two changing guests. Other features include live blues every Saturday night and a quiz every Sunday night. 🌫⬤🄻🄯(1,10,14)

Waggon & Horses 🄻
19 Lawrence Street, YO10 3BP (just outside Walmgate Bar)
❂ 3-11.30; 12-midnight Fri & Sat; 12-11.30 Sun
☎ (01904) 637478 ⊕ waggonandhorsesyork.co.uk
Batemans Yella Belly Gold; guest beers 🄷
Good all-round pub just outside the city walls, with several rooms including a lounge with sofas and a real fire, and a beer garden to the rear. At least one Bateman's beer is on handpump and up to eight guests from local microbreweries including Brass Castle, Great Heck and Ossett, as well as from the rest of the UK, plus two real ciders. Weekly quiz and music nights are held. Popular with visitors for its good-quality accommodation.
🏛Q🌫🍴⬤🄻🄯P🄻🄯(8,10)

York Tap
York Railway Station, YO24 1AB
❂ 9am-11 (midnight Wed-Sat); 10-11 Sun
☎ (01904) 659009 ⊕ yorktap.com
Beer range varies 🄷
Impressive conversion of former tea rooms on the station to a stunning pub with a circular wooden bar and stained glass in the ceiling domes and windows. There are 20 handpumps dispensing 18 cask beers plus two ciders or perries. The beers are chosen from some of Britain's finest breweries, with several usually from Thornbridge. All styles and strengths of beers are represented. 🌫⬤🄯

YORKSHIRE (SOUTH)

Arksey

Plough 🄻
2 High Street, DN5 0SF (behind church)
❂ 7 (6.30 Thu & Fri)-11; 12-2.30, 6.30-11 Sat; 12-3.30, 7-11 Sun ☎ (01302) 872472 ⊕ arkseyplough.co.uk
Beer range varies 🄷
A welcoming multi-roomed village pub with attractive hanging baskets in summer. The lounge has horse harnesses and brasses on display along with photographs of the village, some depicting floods of yesteryear. A log-burning fire keeps the room warm in winter. A free house, the beers are from local breweries, including Imperial and Old Mill, and there are guest ales. Reasonably priced bar meals are available and there's a popular Sunday lunch. Quiz nights are Thursday and Sunday. 🏛🌫🄯🄻🄯🍴🄻🄯(64,64a)

Auckley

Eagle & Child
24 Main Street, DN9 3HS (on B1396 in centre of village)
❂ 11-3, 5-11; 11.30-11.30 Fri & Sat; 12-10.30 Sun
☎ (01302) 770406 ⊕ eagleandchildauckley.co.uk
Black Sheep Best Bitter; John Smith's Bitter; guest beers 🄷
A gem of a village pub, recently refurbished while retaining its original character, with a long tradition of offering a range of quality ales; it has won

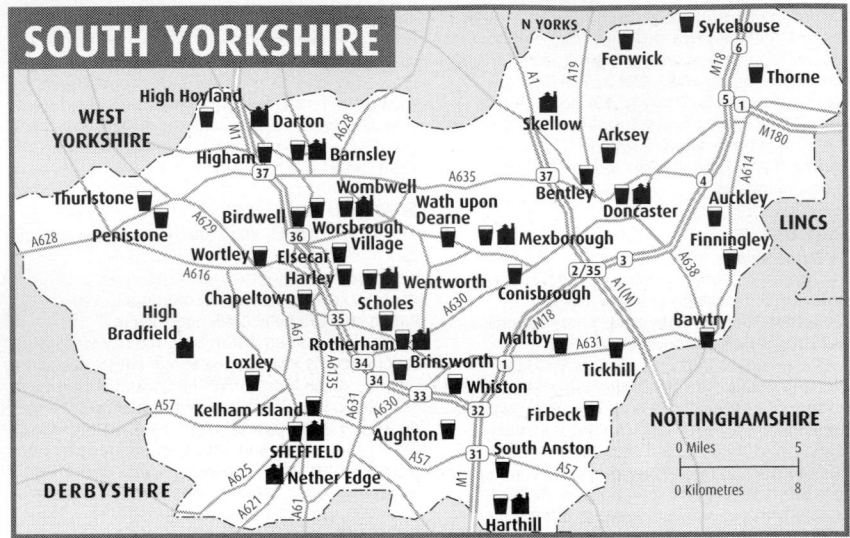

SOUTH YORKSHIRE

several CAMRA awards over the years. Family-friendly, it has a pleasant outdoor children's area to the rear of the car park. Five cask ales are always available. The pub offers a varied choice of freshly prepared meals at reasonable prices. Robin Hood Airport is nearby. Q❄☀🅰◐♣P⌐🖼(91,399)

Aughton

Robin Hood Inn 🅛
64 Main Street, S26 3XJ (2 miles from jctn 31 of M1)
✪ 12-11.30 (11 Sun) ☎ (01142) 871010
Beer range varies 🅷
Built in the 1600s as a farmhouse, this traditional pub has been known as the Robin Hood since 1865. Original features include low-beamed ceilings, an open fire and cosy seating areas. Five guest beers are always on offer, with at least three from local breweries, including Abbeydale. An attractive conservatory has proved popular with diners enjoying home-cooked food and excellent fish and chips. An outbuilding used in World War II by the Home Guard has been converted into accommodation. ⛨☀🅰◐♿♣P⌐🖼(25,49)

Barnsley

Commercial 🅛
74 Summer Lane, S70 2NN
✪ 4.30 (4 Fri)-11; 12-11 Sat & Sun ☎ (01226) 215277
Oakwell Barnsley Bitter; guest beers 🅷
Popular, lively, family-owned local on the edge of the town centre, catering for all. This free house offers three real ales, mostly from local microbreweries, which are served in lined glasses. The pale decor gives the interior a fresh feel while the urban garden to the rear is not just for smokers. There are large screens showing the latest sports events and the pub runs a popular pool team. Children are not allowed inside.
☀≈(Interchange)♣⌐🖳(14,43)

Old No.7 🍷 🅛
7 Market Hill, S70 2PX
✪ closed Mon; 12-midnight ☎ (01226) 244735
⊕ oldno7barnsley.co.uk

Acorn Barnsley Bitter, Yorkshire Pride; guest beers 🅷
The jewel in the crown of Barnsley town centre's burgeoning real ale scene. This Acorn Brewery-owned bar boasts seven real ales and one cider/perry, all on handpump. Two further ciders/perries are usually found behind the bar, plus an extensive range of quality foreign beers. The attentive staff and well-run bar attract a broad clientele including circuit drinkers, football fans and beer connoisseurs, who are all made equally welcome. Local CAMRA Pub of the Year 2012 and 2013 and Yorkshire Regional Cider Pub of the Year 2013.
Q≈(Interchange)●🖥

Silkstone Inn 🅛
64 Market Street, S70 1SN (160yds from Peel Square up Market St)
✪ 8am-midnight (1am Fri & Sat) ☎ (01226) 320860
Greene King Abbot; Ruddles Best Bitter; guest beers 🅷
Proudly displaying a photo montage showing this to be the 700th JD Wetherspoon pub, the Silkstone Inn goes from strength to strength, offering a

INDEPENDENT BREWERIES

Abbeydale Sheffield
Acorn Wombwell
Blue Bee Sheffield
Bradfield High Bradfield
Brew Company Sheffield
Chantry Rotherham (NEW)
Concertina Mexborough
Doncaster Doncaster (NEW)
Geeves Barnsley
Glentworth Skellow
Harthill Village Harthill (NEW)
Imperial Mexborough
Kelham Island Sheffield
Little Ale Cart Sheffield
On the Edge Nether Edge (NEW)
Sheffield Sheffield
Tapped Sheffield (NEW)
Toolmakers Sheffield (NEW)
Two Roses Darton
Wentworth Wentworth
Wood Street Sheffield

steady rotation of guest beers and a cider on handpump. Despite the open-plan layout it offers a cosy atmosphere, with several booths and screened tables around a central modern fireplace. The dark decor evokes the famous Silkstone coal seam that runs under much of Barnsley and beyond and gives the pub its name. Q❀❁◑❀☀≋(Interchange)☀≔

Bawtry

Ship
Gainsborough Road, DN10 6HT (on A631 near traffic lights)
❀ 12-11 (10.30 Sun) ☎ (01302) 710275
Beer range varies Ⓗ
One of the local CAMRA area's success stories. The current licensees took over this run-down roadside pub in 2007 and transformed it. Refurbished inside and out, the Ship offers good-quality meals at reasonable prices. Four cask ales from the Marston's range are always on handpump and the pub holds beer festivals twice a year. Quizzes and theme nights are popular. Local CAMRA District Pub of the Year in 2011 and Marston's Northern Region Food Pub of the Year in 2012. ❀❁◑❁❀♣P≔♞

Bentley

Three Horse Shoes Ⓛ
St Mary's Bridge, Town End, DN5 9AG (on roundabout where A638 meets new bridge on route N from Doncaster)
❀ 4-11; 12-midnight Fri & Sat; 12-10.30 Sun ☎ 07878 757474
Acorn Barnsley Bitter; guest beers Ⓗ
Friendly, traditional, multi-roomed pub, which features in CAMRA's Yorkshire's Real Heritage Pubs guide, only a five-minute walk from Doncaster centre over the old North Bridge. A beer garden overlooking the River Don and logburners in both the lounge and public bar are among the many improvements made by the owner of this free house, while still keeping its character. Note the unchanged pub frontage with leaded glass. ❀Q❀❁❀♣≔♞

Birdwell

Cock Inn Ⓛ
Pilley Hill, off The Walk, S70 5UD
❀ 12-11 (midnight Thu-Sat); 12-9 Sun ☎ (01226) 742155
Black Sheep Best Bitter; Courage Best Bitter; guest beers Ⓗ
Wonderful and welcoming stone-built village pub, with an open fire in the main room and Yorkshire stone and wood floors. The larger lounge area with plush leather seating and large windows looks out over a vast garden. There is a small snug room to the left on entry, often used for private functions. Five real ales are available – two regulars and three guests, one a local brew – plus a cider. Quality home-cooked food is very popular. Bookings are advised, especially for Sunday lunch. ❀Q❀❁Å❀P≔♞(7A,67A)

Brinsworth

Phoenix Ⓛ
Pavilion Lane, S60 5PA (off A631 Bawtry Rd, 1½ miles from M1 jct 33, look for sign)
❀ 10.30-11; 12-10.30 Sun ☎ (01709) 363788

Beer range varies Ⓗ
Members of the public are welcome at this multi award-winning club. Up to five changing guest beers are on offer, including a LocAle, and it is a rare local outlet for handpulled cider. Excellent food is served in the bar and Athel's restaurant. There is a popular family room, two full-sized snooker tables, sports TV and function rooms. Quiz nights, live music and dances are regularly held and facilities for a wide variety of sports are available. ❀❀❁◑❀P≔

Sidings
Whitehill Lane, S60 5HE
❀ 12-11 (11.30 Fri & Sat) ☎ (01709) 296024
⊕ thesidingspub.co.uk
Marston's Pedigree, seasonal beers; guest beers Ⓗ
A red-brick pub that has a friendly taproom with cosy alcoves and a large carpeted lounge with exposed roof beams and a real fire. Food here is as highly rated as the beer. The classic British menu, locally sourced and all freshly cooked from scratch, even down to the home-made sauces, is excellent value. Hand-made pies are a speciality, as is game when available, or try the hand-cut fish finger sandwich with real tartare sauce and mushy peas. ❀❀❁◑❀❁♣P♞(31,87)

Chapeltown

Commercial Ⓛ
107 Station Road, S35 2XF
❀ 12-11 (midnight Fri & Sat) ☎ (0114) 246 9066
Wentworth Imperial, WPA, Bumble Beer; guest beers Ⓗ
Built in 1890, this well-established free house is a regular outlet for Wentworth beers. As well as five guest ales, including a stout or porter, there is also a rotating cider. An island bar serves the lounge, games room and snug. Beer festivals are held at the end of May and November. Outdoor drinking facilities are to the side and rear, and there is an upstairs function room, which is home to regular live folk sessions. Children are welcome. No meals Sunday evening. ❀Q❀❁◑❀❁≋♣❀P♞(265)

Conisbrough

Hilltop Hotel Ⓛ
Sheffield Road, DN12 2AY (on A630 at jct of Sheffield Rd and Old Rd)
❀ closed Mon; 5-10 (midnight Wed & Thu); 3-midnight Fri; 12-midnight Sat & Sun ☎ (01709) 868811
⊕ thehilltophotel.co.uk
Beer range varies Ⓗ
Located on the outskirts of Conisbrough, the Hilltop is a traditional two-roomed free house with a relaxed, friendly atmosphere. The lounge/dining area is adorned with interesting photographs of old Conisbrough and the excellent food features locally sourced produce. Log fires provide a warm welcome in winter. The licensee is a strong supporter of local breweries, with up to four cask ales normally available. Wednesday is quiz night. ❀Q❀❀❁◑❀♣P≔♞(X78)

Doncaster

Cask Corner Ⓛ
3 Cleveland Street, DN1 3EH (opp Danum Hotel)
❀ 12-midnight (2am Fri & Sat) ☎ (01302) 366277
Beer range varies Ⓗ

Centrally located bar featuring 12 handpumps, including two real ciders. It also sells draught fruit beers and 100 bottled beers from around the world. The unusual, quirky decor includes pumpclips, old records and a cornucopia of useless bric-a-brac, some even suspended from the ceiling. Upstairs is a rear heated seating area. A classic jukebox provides unobtrusive background music, while live music takes place on Fridays and Saturdays. Customers are allowed to bring in food or takeaways. Local CAMRA Pub of the Year 2012. ⊛&≈⬢⌐🖵

Corner Pin
145 St Sepulchre Gate West, DN1 3AH (on W side of dual carriageway)
✪ 12-11.30 ☎ (01302) 340670
York Guzzler; guest beers 🅗
Convenient for the town centre and travel Interchange, this popular traditional pub offers changing guest beers in a variety of styles, sourced from small independent breweries. Beer festivals are held twice a year. The pub comprises a smart lounge area and public bar, with a decked area outside at the rear. Food is served from lunchtime onwards and booking is advised for the excellent Sunday lunches. ⊛◑≈⬢⌐🖵

Plough ★ 🕮
8 West Laith Gate, DN1 1SF (close to Frenchgate shopping centre)
✪ 11-11 (midnight Fri & Sat); 11-4, 7-11 Sun
☎ (01302) 738310 ⊕ thelittleplough.co.uk
Acorn Barnsley Bitter; guest beers 🅗
The Little Plough, as the locals know it, is a welcoming haven for those wishing to escape the town-centre bustle. CAMRA-friendly, the pub offers local guest ales and twice-yearly beer festivals. The interior dates from 1934 and the Plough has been identified by CAMRA as one of Britain's Best Real Heritage Pubs. The public bar has a locals' feel, while the comfortable lounge at the rear is decorated with old agricultural scenes. Winner of several CAMRA awards. Q⊞≈⌐🖵

Red Lion
37-38 Market Place, DN1 1NH (S corner of Market Place)
✪ 9am-11.30 (midnight Fri & Sat); 9am-11 Sun
☎ (01302) 732120
Greene King Abbot; Ruddles Best Bitter; guest beers 🅗
Now a Wetherspoon establishment but retaining a traditional feel, this large historic pub has stood on its marketplace site for over 200 years. It was here in 1778 that discussions took place to establish Doncaster's most famous horse race, the St Leger Stakes – an association commemorated by a wall display listing post-war winners. A lively front drinking area contrasts with a quieter haven towards the rear. The five changing guest ales are usually from microbreweries. Q◑&≈⬢⌐🖵

Salutation Hotel 🕮
14 South Parade, DN1 2DR (off South Parade, opp Regent Square)
✪ 12-11 (midnight Fri & Sat) ☎ (01302) 340705
⊕ thesalutationdoncaster.co.uk
Black Sheep Best Bitter; guest beers 🅗
Originally a coaching inn on the Great North Road, the Sal is a popular pub which was voted local CAMRA Pub of the Year and Best Real Pub by Doncaster Best Bar None for 2013. There are cosy

drinking areas downstairs and a large function room upstairs used by various local societies. A constantly changing range of guest beers is on offer plus a real cider. The pub often hosts events such as an evening with a brewer or live music. Sunday lunches are excellent. ⋒⊛◑≈⬢⬢⌐🖵

White Swan 🕮
34 Frenchgate, DN1 1QQ (close to Church Way and shopping centre)
✪ 10-11 (midnight Fri & Sat); 11-10.30 Sun
⊕ franciesirishbar-thewhiteswan.co.uk
Black Sheep Best Bitter; guest beers 🅗
Traditional town-centre pub with a small front tap leading past the raised bar into a long narrow lounge. The Irish-themed décor reflects the licensee's heritage and is complemented by interesting photos of old Doncaster. Very supportive of local micros, beers from Glentworth and Doncaster breweries are always available. Live music features on Thursday, Friday and Saturday evenings, occasionally on Sunday afternoons, and there is a popular jazz session on the first Saturday afternoon of the month. Good-value meals are served until 6pm Monday-Saturday. ⊛◑&≈⌐🖵

Elsecar

Crown Inn 🕮
Hill Street, S74 8EL (midway from railway station to Elsecar Heritage Centre)
✪ 12 (4 Mon)-11 ☎ (01226) 743823
Beer range varies 🅗
Stone-built roadside inn in the middle of a very real ale friendly village. The pub is two-roomed, with a single bar serving both the public bar and lounge. You will receive a typically warm welcome, not only from the licensee but also the local drinkers. The breadth of pub experience here ranges from the gentle quiet of the lounge to the football fervour of the public bar. Q⊛◑⊞≈⬢P⌐🖵(66)

Fitzwilliam Arms 🕮
42 Hill Street, S74 8EL
✪ 12-11 ☎ (01226) 740191
Old Mill Blonde Bombshell; guest beers 🅗
Friendly community pub right next to the rail station offering up to four cask beers. Families are made more than welcome, and the large beer garden, with its own big room and bar, and children's play area are great in the summer months. Inside, the central bar serves the lounge/dining area and the sloping games room (just look at the legs on the pool table). All the beers are from Yorkshire breweries and two are always LocAle. ⋩⊛◑≈⬢P⌐🖵(66)

Market Hotel 🕮
Wentworth Road, S74 8EP (on jct of Wentworth Rd and Wath Rd nr Elsecar Heritage Centre)
✪ 12-11; 11-1am Fri & Sat ☎ (01226) 742240
Acorn Barnsley Gold; guest beers 🅗
The pub is everything a local community pub should be. The traditional multi-roomed interior has plenty of character and characters. Fast-changing guest beers are sourced from local and national micros. A draught cider is also usually available. At the rear is a fantastic beer garden with seating and a large barbecue. The pub makes an ideal stop when visiting the nearby heritage centre or country park. Look for the Horse & Gig For Hire sign located above the front window. ⋒⋩⊛⊞≈⬢⌐🖵(66,227)

Milton Arms 🅛

Fitzwilliam Street, S74 8ES (2 mins' walk from Elsecar Heritage Centre)

🔵 12-3, 7 (6 Fri)-midnight; closed Wed; 12-5, 7-midnight Sun
☎ (01226) 742240

Beer range varies 🅗

Attractive, welcoming community pub with a long-standing landlord/chef who ensures a regular turnover of guest ales, mainly sourced from microbreweries, and who keenly supports the LocAle scheme. The three-roomed pub boasts a conservatory that leads to an award-winning garden and lovingly cared for aviary. At the hub of village life, the Milton is the focal point for the well-known Milton 6 road race, which attracts athletes from all over Yorkshire. One of Elsecar's many excellent pubs. ♨️🕸🌑➡♣P🗝-🖂🖵(66,227)

Fenwick

Baxter Arms

Fenwick Lane, DN6 0HA

🔵 5.30 (11.30 Sat & Sun)-midnight ☎ (01302) 702671

Theakston Best Bitter; guest beer 🅗

A lovely, welcoming pub converted from a farmhouse in 1973 and well worth seeking out. There are two rooms, both with open fires, the smaller having a snooker table. Bar food is served all day Saturday and Sunday, and evenings during the week. All dishes are cooked to order. Guest beers are sourced from small independent breweries. Wednesday is quiz night. Outside there is a sheltered garden with a small play area. ♨️Q🕸🌑🍴👶Å♣P🗝-

Finningley

Harvey Arms

Old Bawtry Road, DN9 3BH (follow B1396; pub in centre of village)

🔵 12-3, 5-11.30; 12-midnight Sat & Sun ☎ (01302) 770200

Beer range varies 🅗

Popular village pub set in an attractive location near the village green. Recently refurbished, the pub has gained an excellent reputation for its food as well as its beer. Four cask ales from a variety of breweries, local and national, are always on handpump. ♨️🌮🕸🌑P🗝-🖵(91,399)

Firbeck

Black Lion 🅛

9 New Road, S81 8JY (opp village hall) SK5688

🔵 closed Mon; 12-3, 5.30-11; 12-5 Sun ☎ (01709) 812575

John Smith's Bitter; guest beers 🅗

Traditional village pub and restaurant, now a free house. Excellent home-cooked food attracts diners, walkers and the local community. Four guest beers are offered, usually including one from a local microbrewer. Pictures of old Firbeck adorn the walls of the snug area. A quiz is held every Tuesday, with folk music every third Monday. There are two letting rooms. The famous St Leger horse race was first held in fields near the pub in 1776. Local CAMRA Pub of the Year 2012. ♨️Q🕸🍴🌑👶♣P🗝-

Harley

Horseshoe Inn 🅛

9 Harley Road, S62 7UD (off A6135 on B6090 1 mile from Wentworth)

🔵 4 (1 Sat)-11; 12-10.30 Sun ☎ (01226) 742204

Beer range varies 🅗

Street-corner local hosting regular events and home to football and pool teams. Guest beers change regularly, ensuring quality and variety, with ales often coming from local breweries. Sunday lunchtime is a carvery; book to avoid disappointment. The Horseshoe has been the hub of the local community for well over a century. 🕸🌑♣🖂(44)

Harthill

Beehive Inn 🍷 🅛

16 Union Street, S26 7YH (opp village church)

🔵 11.30-3 (not Mon), 6-11; 11-11 Sat & Sun
☎ (01909) 770205

Taylor Landlord; Tetley Bitter; guest beers 🅗

This has been a welcoming village inn since at least 1833, and it has an excellent reputation for quality food and real ales. Serving Tetley Bitter and up to nine real ales and ciders, this place has regular real ale and music festivals throughout the year. It is home to many local societies and the newly established Harthill Village Brewery. Local CAMRA Pub of the Year for 2013. Q🕸🌑🍴👶♣P🗝-🖂(25,49)

High Hoyland

Cherry Tree 🅛

Bank End Lane, S75 4BE (through village towards Clayton West, pub is on right)

🔵 12-3, 5.30-midnight; 12-midnight Sun ☎ (01226) 382541

Black Sheep Best Bitter; Elland Best Bitter; Taylor Landlord; guest beers 🅗

Near to Cannon Hall Country Park, the Cherry Tree has fantastic far-reaching views over Barnsley and open countryside. As well as the five real ales, the pub also offers good-value quality food (booking advised). It has a long central bar with dining areas to both sides. Outside, there is plenty of seating to enjoy the views. Walkers are welcome. The bus service to and from the pub is limited: daytime only and not Sunday. ♨️Q🕸🌑P🗝-🖂(96A)

Higham

Engineers Arms

Higham Common Road, S75 1PF

🔵 12-3, 7-11; 12-3.30, 7-10.30 Sun ☎ (01226) 384204

Samuel Smith OBB 🅗

A warm, welcoming community pub that hosts activities every night of the week. No TV or music – conversation is king. It is a sport-oriented pub, with three cricket teams whose playing field is just outside, with wonderful views. Inside, pool and darts dominate. The split-level bar serves the lounge that features original still photos from Last of the Summer Wine. The upper level is the public bar, where there is a Yorkshire doubles board. Prices here are very competitive. Q🕸🍴♣P🖂(92)

Loxley

Nag's Head 🅛

Stacey Bank, S6 6SJ SK906289

✪ 12-midnight ☎ (0114) 285 1202
Bradfield Farmers Blonde, Yorkshire Farmer, seasonal beers Ⓗ
A two-roomed country pub on the main road out of Loxley, the supposed birthplace of Robin Hood, towards High Bradfield. This is the nearby Bradfield Brewery's tap, with up to five beers from the range, including seasonal beers and specials. Good home-cooked food is available lunchtimes (no food Mon), as well as evenings Tuesday to Friday, and all day Saturday. Excellent views overlooking the Loxley Valley can be enjoyed from the outside drinking area. ᛘQ❀❍●⬗♣P'–⊟(61,62)

Maltby

Queens Hotel
Tickhill Road, S66 7NQ
✪ 8am-midnight (1am Thu-Sat)
Greene King Abbot; Ruddles Best Bitter; guest beers Ⓗ
The Queens Hotel has undergone an impressive refurbishment by Wetherspoon and was reopened in 2012. The spacious venue has an attractive family dining area and offers typical Wetherspoon's value for food and drink. Serving Greene King IPA, Abbot and up to four guest beers, the pub has brought real ales back to Maltby town centre and proved to be very popular. ❍❀❍●よ●P'–⊟(1)

Mexborough

Concertina Band Club Ⓛ
9A Dolcliffe Road, S64 9AZ (off Bank St, on left halfway up hill)
✪ 2-4; 12-5 Fri; 12-4, 7.45-11 Sat; 12-3, 7.45-10.30 Sun ☎ (01709) 580841
Concertina Club Bitter, Bengal Tiger, Dark Attic; John Smith's Bitter Ⓗ
Long-established and now unique club and brewery with an interesting history. Pictures and memorabilia of the Concertina Band who formed in 1887 decorate the main room. The Tina provides three regular ales, including the award-winning Bengal Tiger brewed in the cellar below the bar. An array of CAMRA and beer awards around the bar cover many years of dedicated achievements. CAMRA members are welcome – show a copy of this Guide or a CAMRA membership card for entry. ❀⇌♣'–⊟⊟(220,221,222)

Imperial Club & Brewery Ⓛ
Arcadia Hall, Cliff Street, S64 9HU (opp bus station off dual carriageway and near railway station)
✪ 4.30 (12 Sat & Sun)-midnight; closed Tue ☎ 07712 200382
Imperial Bitter, Bees Knees, Blonde, Stout; guest beer Ⓗ
A friendly club and brewery opposite the bus station. The club regularly provides five real ales – award-winning Blonde and Stout often feature – as well as a guest beer or an Imperial seasonal beer. A real cider is also served. Entertainment features throughout the week, with a buskers' night on Wednesday, Friday night prize bingo and a live singer on Saturday, while on Sunday there is a carvery at lunch and either live bands or a brass band concert in the evening. Families are welcome. ❍❀❍よ⇌♣●'–⊟

Penistone

Penistone Royal British Legion Club Ⓛ
St Mary's Street, S36 6DT
✪ 11-11 (11.30 Fri & Sat); 11.45-11 Sun ☎ (01226) 766911
Beer range varies Ⓗ
Comfortably appointed member's club near Penistone town centre. The lounge, concert room and separate large games and TV room provide a variety of diversions for drinkers. There are at least two constantly changing guest ales, usually locally sourced. Non-members must ask to be signed in. Please do so without concern; the committee is firm but friendly. ❀よ⇌♣P'–⊟(21,24,25)

Rotherham

Bluecoat Ⓛ
The Crofts, S60 2JD (behind town hall, off A618 Moorgate Rd)
✪ 8am-midnight (1am Fri & Sat) ☎ (01709) 580841
Greene King Abbot; Ruddles Best Bitter; guest beers Ⓗ
Originally a charity school opened in 1776, it became a pub called Ffeoffes in 1981 and then a Wetherspoon in 2001. The wide selection of beers on offer is listed on a screen at the end of the bar. Westons Old Rosie or Organic cider is served from a cask behind the bar. The pub frequently holds Meet the Brewer events, and has special curry and steak nights. Winner of local CAMRA Pub of the Year on five occasions. ❀❍よ⇌●P'–⊟

Bridge Inn Ⓛ
1 Greasbrough Road, S60 1RB (alongside Chantry Bridge, between bus and rail stations)
✪ 12-midnight (11 Sun) ☎ (01709) 836818
Old Mill Bitter, Yorkshire Porter, seasonal beers; guest beers Ⓗ
The original home of Rotherham CAMRA, this is an Old Mill tied house, built in 1930 using stone from the original Bridge Inn dating back to the 1700s. New management has revitalised the pub and guest beers now usually include a brew from the recently established Chantry Brewery, plus a changing real cider. Every Saturday evening there is live music, with folk and jazz once a month, and two function rooms upstairs are well used by local groups. CAMRA branch Town Pub of the Year 2013. よ⇌♣●⊟

Woodlands
Doncaster Road, S65 1NN (access from Ridge Road above)
✪ 7-11; 12-4, 7-midnight Fri; 2-midnight Sat; 12-11 Sun ☎ (01709) 382777 ⊕ thewoodlandsclub.co.uk
Beer range varies Ⓗ
Set in beautiful grounds, this club offers two excellent real ales from local breweries, served in oversized glasses at reasonable prices. The games room has two full-size snooker tables, the lounge has TV sport, and entertainment is provided every Thursday, Friday and Saturday evening. There is a monthly open mic session on Sunday from 4pm, and music festivals take place outside in summer. CAMRA members are welcome on production of a copy of this Guide or a CAMRA membership card. Q❍❀♣P'–⊟

Scholes

Bay Horse ⓛ
Scholes Lane, S61 2RQ (off A629, 1 mile from M1 jct 35)
✪ 5 (12 Sat & Sun)-11 ☎ (0114) 246 8085
Bradfield Farmers Blonde; Kelham Island Pale Rider; Taylor Landlord; guest beers Ⓗ
Traditional village pub by the cricket ground, on the Rotherham Round Walk and the TransPennine Trail. It serves home-cooked food including Dan's Cow Pie (certificate presented if you finish everything on the plate!), curries and Sunday lunches. A choir performs on Thursday and two quizzes are hosted. A regular local CAMRA award winner.
⋈Q✿ⓓ⪦P'–⊟(44)

Sheffield: Central

Bath Hotel ★
66 Victoria Street, S3 7QL
✪ 12-11; 5-10.30 Sun ☎ (0114) 249 5151
Thornbridge Wild Swan, Lord Marples; guest beers Ⓗ
A careful restoration of the 1930s interior gave this two-roomed pub a conservation award and acknowledgement by CAMRA as one of Britain's Best Real Heritage Pubs. The bar lies between the tiled lounge, a small corridor drinking area, and the cosy well-upholstered snug. There are usually three Thornbridge beers and three guests, plus a good choice of malt whiskies and continental beers. Live jazz/blues plays on a Sunday, a blues session on the first Wednesday of the month, and jazz on the second Wednesday. Q⊟⬛⊟

Devonshire Cat
49 Wellington Street, S1 4HG
✪ 11.30-11 (1am Fri & Sat); 12-10.30 Sun
☎ (0114) 279 6700 ⊕ devonshirecat.co.uk
Abbeydale Deception; Bradfield Farmers Blonde; Kelham Island Pale Rider; Oakwell Barnsley Bitter; Thornbridge Jaipur IPA; guest beers Ⓗ
With 12 handpumps adorning the bar – the house beer is brewed by the local Bradfield Brewery – and over 100 beers from around the world, the Dev Cat is a great place for the discerning drinker. The menu features light snacks through to hearty meals and is served all day to 8pm (6pm Sun). An essential calling point for anyone in search of an excellent range of the best beers. ⓓ⪦⊟♠⊟

Henry's ⓛ
38 Cambridge Street, S1 4HP
✪ 11-11 (1am Fri & Sat) ☎ (0114) 273 8742
Clarks Henry's Long Blonde; guest beers Ⓗ
Former café/bar reopened as a free house in 2010 after being derelict for a couple of years. Now thriving again, it offers one of the largest selections of cask ales in the city centre, with up to 11 guest beers. The ground floor is open plan, with seating at various levels around the long bar counter. Meals prepared from good locally sourced food are served daily 11-7pm in the main bar area. The in-house Aardvark Brewery is being established on site. ✿ⓓ⪯⊟♠'–⊟

Hop
Unit 14, West Street Plaza, Fitzwilliam Street, S1 4JB
✪ 12-12.30am ☎ (0114) 278 1000 ⊕ thehop-sheffield.com
Fuller's London Pride; Ossett Yorkshire Blonde, Big Red Bitter, Silver King, Excelsior; guest beers Ⓗ
Unusually, this is a pub conversion (by Ossett Brewery) from former supermarket premises in a modern bar/restaurant/shopping complex near the popular West Street district. From the entrance there is a small snug area, before you reach the main bar with 10 handpumps featuring up to four guest beers and a real cider. This leads to a larger room used for regular live music sessions, and is overlooked by a balcony seating area. Food is served all day to 7pm. ✿ⓓ⪦⊟♠'–⊟

Old House
113-117 Devonshire Street, S3 7SB
✪ 12-1am (2am Fri & Sat) ☎ (0114) 272 0569
⊕ theoldhousesheffield.com
True North First Blonde, First Porter; guest beers Ⓗ
Unlike many of the trendy bars that line Division Street and Devonshire Street, the Old House provides a homely atmosphere. There are seating areas either side of the entrance corridor leading into the main bar area, which is decorated with classic album covers and old photos, while the shelves are stacked with retro artefacts. Food ranging from snacks to hearty mains is home-cooked and available throughout the day. The True North beers are brewed at Welbeck Abbey and the guest beers are mostly local. ⋈ⓓ⪯⊟⊟

Red Deer ⓛ
18 Pitt Street, S1 4DD
✪ 12-midnight (11 Sun; 1am Fri & Sat) ☎ (0114) 272 2890
⊕ red-deer-sheffield.co.uk
Copper Dragon Golden Pippin; Kelham Island Easy Rider; Moorhouse's Pride of Pendle; Taylor Landlord; guest beers Ⓗ
A genuine, traditional local in the heart of the city. The small frontage of the original three-roomed pub hides an open-plan interior extended to the rear with a gallery seating area. As well as the impressive range of cask ales, including up to four guest beers, there is also a selection of continental bottled beers. Meals are served 12-3pm and 5-9pm daily. There is a function room upstairs which can be booked, and a pub quiz takes place every Tuesday. Q✿ⓓ⪯⊟♠'–⊟

Rutland Arms ⓛ
86 Brown Street, S1 2BS
✪ 12-11 (midnight Thu-Sat) ☎ (0114) 272 9003
⊕ rutlandmspeople.co.uk
Blue Bee Nectar Pale Ale, Bees Knees; guest beers Ⓗ
Occupying a corner spot in the Cultural Industries Quarter and near Sheffield's main railway station, this pub reopened as a free house in 2009. The comfortable interior provides ample seating either side of the central entrance, and the walls are decorated with changing displays of work from local artists, as well as photos of old Sheffield pubs. Most of the guest beers come from local breweries, and beer and cider festivals are held annually. Food is served throughout the day to 9pm (6pm Sun). ✿ⓓ⪯⊟♠'–⊟⊟

Sheffield Tap ⓛ
Platform 1b, Sheffield Station, Sheaf Street, S1 2BP
✪ 11-11; 10-midnight Fri & Sat ☎ (0114) 273 7558
⊕ sheffieldtap.com
Thornbridge Wild Swan, Jaipur IPA; guest beers Ⓗ
Opened in 2009, this was originally the first-class refreshment room for Sheffield Midland station, built in 1904. After years of neglect the main bar area has been the subject of an award-winning restoration and retains many original features. Further seating has been provided in the entrance corridor, and two more rooms have been opened up to the right of the bar. Beyond these in the

impressive former dining room is the new Tapped Brewery, which is separated by a glass screen from a small bar with more seating. Q🏠🚲🕭🚆🍴🚊

Sheffield: Kelham Island

Fat Cat 🅛
23 Alma Street, S3 8SA
✪ 12-11 (midnight Fri & Sat) ☎ (0114) 249 4801
Kelham Island Best Bitter, Pale Rider; Taylor Landlord; guest beers Ⓗ
Opened in 1981 and still ferociously independent, this is the pub that started the real ale revolution in the area. Beers from around the country are served alongside those from the adjacent Kelham Island brewery. Vegetarian and gluten-free dishes feature heavily on the menu (evening food to 8pm, not Sun). The walls are covered with the many awards presented to the pub and brewery. Beer festivals are held every August and at various other times. Monday is curry and quiz night.
🅐🅜Q🏠🍽️⬤♿🚆🕭🚊(11,12,57)

Harlequin 🅛
108 Nursery Street, S3 8GG
✪ 12-11 (11.30 Thu & Fri; midnight Sat) ☎ (0114) 275 8195
Brew Company Best Bitter, Blonde; guest beers Ⓗ
Operated by the Brew Company, the Harlequin (formerly the Manchester) takes its name from another former Ward's pub around the corner, now demolished. The large open-plan interior features a central bar, with seating on two levels. As well as the two regular beers, there are usually several other Brew Co beers as well as guests from far and wide, with an emphasis on microbreweries. A range of boutique bottled beers is also available. Wednesday is quiz night and there is live music at weekends. Q🏠🍽️🚆♣⬤🕭🚊(47,48,53)

Kelham Island Tavern 🅛
62 Russell Street, S3 8RW
✪ 12-midnight ☎ (0114) 272 2482
Abbeydale Deception; Acorn Barnsley Bitter; Bradfield Farmers Blonde; Pictish Brewers Gold; Thwaites Nutty Black; guest beers Ⓗ
Former CAMRA National Pub of the Year, this small gem was rescued from dereliction in 2002. Twelve handpumps dispense an impressive range of beers, always including a mild, a stout and a porter, so you are sure to find something to suit your palate. In the warmer months you can relax in the pub's multi award-winning beer garden. Regular folk music features on Sunday and quiz night is Monday; no meals Sunday.
Q🏠🍽️♿🚆⬤🕭🚊(11,12,57)

Riverside
1 Mowbray Street, S3 8EN
✪ 12-11 (midnight Fri & Sat) ☎ (0114) 281 3621
⊕ riversidesheffield.co.uk
Brew Company Kraken, Riverside Pale; guest beers Ⓗ
On the banks of the River Don, with a pleasant terrace that overlooks the river, the interior is largely open plan but with a separate room to the right of the main entrance. Furnishings comprise a mix of comfortable sofas and armchairs together with more spartan former school desks. The two house beers are complemented by a changing selection of guest ales, mostly from local breweries. Live music features at weekends.
🏠🍽️♿⬤🕭🚊(47,48,53)

Shakespeares 🍷 🅛
146-148 Gibraltar Street, S3 8UB
✪ 12-11.30 (1am Fri & Sat) ☎ (0114) 275 5959
⊕ shakespeares-sheffield.co.uk
Abbeydale Deception; guest beers Ⓗ
Originally built as a coaching inn in 1821, the pub reopened as a free house in the summer of 2011. The central bar serves two small rooms and the corridor, and there are two further rooms including a recent extension. Up to eight changing guest beers are available, together with real cider and a selection of over 100 whiskies. There is regular live music in the upstairs function room and a quiz is held on Thursdays. Several beer festivals take place each year. Q🏠♿🚆♣⬤🕭🚊(11,12,57)

Ship Inn 🅛
312 Shalesmoor, S3 8UL
✪ 12-3.30, 7.30-11.30 ☎ (0114) 281 2204
Abbeydale Moonshine; guest beers Ⓗ
Behind the impressive Tomlinson's frontage lies a friendly community local, with two lounge areas around the central L-shaped bar, and a small pool room to the rear. Although the pub is tied to Greene King, the three handpumps dispense beers from local independent breweries. Good-quality lunchtime meals are served. Most of the pictures and ornaments have a nautical theme in keeping with the pub's name. 🍽️🚆♣P🕭🚊(11,12,57)

Wellington 🅛
1 Henry Street, S3 7EQ
✪ 12-11; 12-3.30, 7-10.30 Sun ☎ (0114) 249 2295
Beer range varies Ⓗ
Popular street-corner pub, also known as the Bottom Wellie, which champions a varying range of beers from small independent brewers, with 10 handpumps always offering a stout or porter and a real cider, and a range of continental bottled beers is also stocked. The house brewery, which adjoins the secluded garden at the rear, recommenced brewing late in 2009. It now produces a wide range of brews, usually pale and hoppy, under the Little Ale Cart name, normally with three on sale.
🅐🅜Q🏠🚆⬤🕭🚊(11,12,57)

Sheffield: North

Blake Hotel
53 Blake Street, S6 3JQ
✪ 12-11.30 ☎ (0114) 233 9336
Acorn Blonde; guest beers Ⓗ
At the top of a steep hill, this community pub reopened as a free house in 2010 after seven years of closure. Extensively restored, it has many traditional Victorian features, original etched windows, and mirrors from bygone breweries. A large decked garden has been established to the rear. There are five guest beers, usually including a stout or porter, the majority from small independent breweries. The shelves behind the bar display possibly the most extensive range of whiskies in Sheffield. Q🏠⬤🕭🚊(31,95)

Gardeners Rest 🅛
105 Neepsend Lane, S3 8AT
✪ 3 (12 Thu)-11; 12-midnight Fri & Sat; 12-11 Sun ☎ (0114) 272 4978
Sheffield Crucible Best, Five Rivers, Porter, Seven Hills, seasonal beers; guest beers Ⓗ
The tap for the Sheffield Brewery, reopened in 2009 after refurbishment following severe flooding

in 2007. The clean, bright interior has retained the cosy lounge. The main bar features art exhibitions and live music on Friday and Saturday, and it contains the restored bar billiards table. To the rear is a conservatory leading to the beer garden overlooking the River Don. There are usually at least four Sheffield beers, together with six guests from other local and regional breweries. A quiz night is held on Sunday. Q✿✿&🖾♣♦²–🗗🖾(53)

Hillsborough L

54-58 Langsett Road, S6 2UB
✪ 12-11 (midnight Fri & Sat) ☎ (0114) 232 2100
Wood Street Pale Ale, Bitter, Honey Locust, Golden Larch, Ebony Stout, Yellow Wood IPA H

A privately owned hotel with six en-suite rooms, home-cooked meals are served throughout the day and a function room is available for all occasions. The Wood Street beers are from the house brewery in the cellar, with at least four from the range always available together with guest beers from local and other independent breweries. Brewery tours can be booked. Attractions include seasonal beer festivals, regular themed events, folk music on Sunday and a popular quiz night on Tuesday. Q✿✿🛏🅾&🖾♣²–🖾(11,12,57)

New Barrack Tavern L

601 Penistone Road, S6 2GA
✪ 5-11 Mon & Tue; 11-11 (midnight Fri & Sat); 12-11 Sun
☎ (0114) 234 9148
Acorn Barnsley Bitter; Bradfield Farmers Bitter; Castle Rock Harvest Pale, Screech Owl; guest beers H

Multi-roomed pub offering up to five guest beers including seasonal ales from Castle Rock. The home-cooked food is available daily, with a carvery on Sunday. The front bar has bar billiards, the main room features live music Friday and Saturday, and there is a comedy club on the first Sunday of the month. A wide choice of continental beers, single malts and a real cider is served. Outside is an award-winning heated, covered patio garden. ⋈Q✿🅾🖾♣²–🖾(53)

Sheffield: South

Broadfield Alehouse

452 Abbeydale Road, S7 1FR
✪ 11.30-midnight (1am Fri & Sat); 12-11 Sun
☎ (0114) 255 0200 ∰ thebroadfield.com
True North First Blonde, First Porter; guest beers H

Dating from 1896, the pub was acquired by the Forum Café Bars group in 2011. The large single room displays lots of solid wooden furniture around the central bar. An extensive menu is offered with much of the fare locally sourced. The eight real ales usually include two from the True North range brewed at the Welbeck Abbey plant, and many of the guest beers are local. There are also two rotating ciders and an extensive range of whiskies. Food is available all day to 10pm. ✿🅾&♦²–🖾(75,76,97)

Sheaf View

25 Gleadless Road, Heeley, S2 3AA
✪ 11.30-11.30 ☎ (0114) 249 6455
Acorn Blonde; Kelham Island Easy Rider; guest beers H

Significant renovation and conversion to a free house in 2000 changed the Sheaf's fortunes. Six rotating ales sourced both locally and nationally complement the regular beers. An extensive range of bottled continental beers is also available plus a

large selection of single malts. Add in the relaxed atmosphere and the competitive prices and it is no surprise that the Sheaf is very busy at most times. A popular quiz is held every Wednesday. Q✿&♣♦P²–🖾(20,20A,53)

White Lion L

615 London Road, S2 4HT
✪ 3-11 (11.30 Wed; midnight Thu; 1am Fri); 12-1am Sat; 12-11.30 Sun ☎ (0114) 255 1500 ∰ whitelionsheffield.co.uk
Abbeydale Moonshine; Tetley Bitter; Thornbridge Sequoia, Jaipur IPA; Wychwood Hobgoblin; guest beers H

Historic pub in Heeley Bottom, respectfully refurbished over the years. The many rooms display photographs and documents that relate the history of the pub and the surrounding area. A richly tiled central corridor connects the varied rooms, including two glazed snugs, to the former concert room at the rear. Jazz and folk feature on alternate Tuesdays, with live bands performing every Saturday. A superb traditional pub with real character and ambience. The guest ales are from the Punch list. ✿♣²–🖾(20,20A,53)

Sheffield: West

Cobden View L

40 Cobden View Road, Crookes, S10 1HQ
✪ 1-midnight; 12-1am Fri & Sat; 12-midnight Sun
☎ (0114) 266 1273 ∰ thecobdenview.co.uk
Black Sheep Best Bitter; Bradfield Farmers Blonde; Caledonian Deuchars IPA; Copper Dragon Best Bitter; Wychwood Hobgoblin H

Off the main Crookes thoroughfare, this busy community pub caters for a varied clientele, ranging from students to retired folk. The original room layout is still apparent, with the bar serving a snug at the front, a games area with pool and darts to the rear, and a lounge to the right of the front entrance. A quiz is held on Sunday evenings and there is live music most Thursdays and Saturdays. The well-kept rear garden hosts summer barbecues. ✿&♣♦²–🖾(52,95)

Greystones L

Greystones Road, S11 7BS
✪ 12-11 (11.30 Fri & Sat) ☎ (0114) 266 5599
∰ mygreystones.co.uk
Thornbridge Wild Swan, Brother Rabbit, Lord Marples, Kipling, Jaipur IPA H

A spacious yet homely family-friendly pub, serving as the flagship for Thornbridge Brewery. Nominated as best turnaround pub by the Morning Advertiser, it boasts eight handpulled real ales, mainly showcasing the Thornbridge range but occasionally featuring one or two guests. The Backroom hosts some of the finest in contemporary live folk/rock/blues and Americana in the country, along with comedy nights and community projects. Hot food is served up 12-6pm daily along with a range of locally sourced pies made using Thornbridge beer. ⋈Q🕭✿🅾&P²–🖾🖾(81)

Ranmoor Inn L

330 Fulwood Road, S10 3GD
✪ 11.30-11; 12-10.30 Sun ☎ (0114) 230 1325
Abbeydale Deception; Bradfield Farmers Bitter, Farmers Blonde; Taylor Landlord; guest beers H

Renovated Victorian local with original etched windows lying in the shadow of Ranmoor Church. Now open plan, the seating areas reflect the old room layout. A friendly, old-fashioned pub, it has a diverse clientele ranging from choir members to rugby and cricket teams. The piano by the bar is often played by regulars. Outside, there is a small front garden plus the former stable yard, which has been opened as a partly covered and heated drinking area. Lunches are available Tuesday to Saturday. Q✿❍❶–☷(120)

Rising Sun Ⓛ
471 Fulwood Road, S10 3QA
✪ 12-11 ☎ (0114) 230 3855 ⏣ risingsunsheffield.co.uk
Abbeydale Daily Bread, Brimstone, Moonshine, Absolution, seasonal beers; guest beers Ⓗ
Operated by local brewer Abbeydale, this is a large suburban roadhouse in the leafy western side of the city. The two rooms are comfortably furnished, and the main bar has a raised area to the rear. A range of Abbeydale beers is always served, with up to six guests, mainly from micros, dispensed from the impressive bank of 13 handpumps. Entertainment includes live music on Monday and quizzes on Sunday and Wednesday. An annual beer festival, Sunfest, is held in July.
Q✿❶❦♣P–☷(83a,120)

University Arms Ⓛ
197 Brook Hill, S3 7HG
✪ 12-11 (midnight Fri & Sat); closed Sun ☎ (0114) 222 8969
Acorn Thirst Degree; guest beers Ⓗ
Owned by the University of Sheffield, this former staff club became a pub in 2007. There is a bar with a small alcove seating area adjoining, and a main lounge area. A conservatory at the rear leads to the extensive beer garden. Up to six guest beers are available, many sourced locally. Entertainment includes a quiz on Tuesday night, live jazz or blues at weekends and regular beer festivals. No food on Saturday evening. Q✿❶❶☷–☷(51,52)

York Ⓛ
243-247 Fulwood Road, S10 3BA
✪ 11.30-11.30 (12.30am Fri & Sat) ☎ (0114) 266 4624
⏣ theyorksheffield.co.uk
Abbeydale Deception; Bradfield Farmers Blonde; guest beers Ⓗ
Occupying a prominent site in the centre of Broomhill, the York reopened as a free house in 2010 after a period of closure following its disposal by a pubco. Extensively refurbished, with parquet flooring and wood-panelled walls, it now offers high-quality dining complemented by a range of up to five – mainly local – guest ales and two real ciders. There is a wide range of cocktails, and beer and food events feature regularly throughout the year. Q✿❶❶♿♠–☷(52,120)

South Anston

Loyal Trooper Ⓛ
34 Sheffield Road, S25 5DT (off A57, 3 miles from M1 jct 31 heading for Worksop)
✪ 12-11 (midnight Fri & Sat) ☎ (01909) 562203
Adnams Southwold Bitter; Taylor Landlord; Tetley Bitter; guest beers Ⓗ
Friendly oak-beamed village local selling a range of real ales and good wholesome food at reasonable prices. Guest beers often come from local breweries. Largely unchanged since the 1960s, parts of the building date back to 1690. The interior comprises a public bar, snug, lounge and a function room upstairs used by many local groups, including a thriving folk club. Q✿❶❶♿♣P–☷(19,19B,29)

Sykehouse

Old George
Broad Lane, DN14 9AU
✪ 12-midnight ☎ (01405) 785635
Tetley Bitter; guest beers Ⓗ
A friendly pub, the Old George is housed in a 200-year-old building with several rooms including a lounge with an open fire, a restaurant and a games room. A free house, the two guest beers are from nationwide breweries, often unusual ones. Excellent food is served throughout, including OAP specials. The Sunday carvery is not to be missed. Outside there is a patio, where barbecues are held in summer, and a large playground that includes a bathing pool for children.
🏠➺✿❶❶♿▲♣P–☷(69)

Thorne

Windmill Ⓛ
19 Queen Street, DN8 5AA (close to Sainsbury's in town centre)
✪ 2-11 (midnight Fri & Sat); 12-midnight Sun
☎ (01405) 812866
Black Sheep Best Bitter; guest beers Ⓗ
Situated close to the town centre, this friendly pub is very popular with the local community and comprises a smart, cosy lounge linked by an archway to a larger public bar. There are big screens but they are unobtrusive; conversation and banter are the essential ingredients here. The guest beers come mainly from small independent breweries. Outside there is a large beer garden and ample parking. Sunday is quiz night.
✿➾(North)P–☷(87,88)

Thurlstone

Huntsman Ⓛ
136 Manchester Road, S36 9QW (on A628)
✪ 6 (5 Sat)-11; 12-10.30 Sun ☎ (01226) 764892
⏣ thehuntsmanthurlstone.co.uk
Black Sheep Best Bitter; Taylor Landlord; Tetley Bitter; guest beers Ⓗ
On the main east-west trans-Pennine route (A628), this oak-beamed, long and thin pub is a popular venue for discerning drinkers. Six or more real ales are always on handpump. The three guest ales are supplied from local small or microbreweries; with luck you will supply the conversation and bonhomie. The pub is the centre of village life, hosting and supporting many local groups. Dogs are very welcome. 🏠Q➺✿♣–☷(23,23A,25)

Tickhill

Scarbrough Arms
Sunderland Street, DN11 9QJ (on A631 near Buttercross)
✪ 12-11 (10.30 Sun) ☎ (01302) 742977
Greene King Abbot; John Smith's Bitter; Morland Old Speckled Hen; Shepherd Neame Spitfire; guest beers Ⓗ
A deserving Guide entry since 1990, this three-roomed stone-built pub has won several local CAMRA awards over the years. Originally a farmhouse, the building dates back to the 16th century. Although structural changes have taken place, the snug is a delight, with its barrel-shaped furniture and real fire, while bar billiards can be played in the bar. An outbuilding doubles as a

covered smoking area and an extension for beer festivals – held in spring and autumn. Real cider is sold in summer. ▲Q❀✿❦❧✦P↿–⊟(22,205)

Wath upon Dearne

Church House ⚲
Montgomery Square, S63 7RZ
❂ 9am-midnight ☎ (01709) 879518
Marston's Pedigree; Ruddles Best Bitter; guest beers ⊞
Large pub with an impressive frontage set in a pedestrian square in the town centre, with excellent access to local bus services. It was built in 1810, consecrated by the nearby church in 1912, became a pub in the 1980s, and then a Wetherspoon in 2000. It serves a wide variety of beers from both national and local brewers, including the nearby Acorn and Wentworth breweries. Westons ciders are on handpull.
▲❀✿❦❧✦P↿–⊟(22,220,229)

Wentworth

George & Dragon ⚲
85 Main Street, S62 7TN (stands back from road on B6090)
❂ 10-11 (10.30 Sun) ☎ (01226) 742440
⊕ georgeanddragonwentworth.co.uk
Taylor Landlord; guest beers ⊞
In a picturesque village, this free house offers up to five ales from local and national brewers, including Abbeydale and Wentworth. The pub has a car park and patio, and a grassed area at the rear with a children's adventure playground and a craft shop. Home-cooked food is popular here. This local is near to historic Wentworth Woodhouse and the Needles Eye, and has been licensed since 1804.
▲Q❀✿❦P↿–⊟(44,227)

Whiston

Chequers
Pleasley Road, S60 4HB (on A618, 1½ miles from M1 jct 33)
❂ 12 (4 Mon & Tue)-11; 12-11.30 Fri & Sat
☎ (01709) 829168
Tetley Bitter; guest beers ⊞
Next to the 13th-century thatched Manorial Barn, in the heart of Whiston, this friendly local replaced the original inn when the road was widened in 1933. One side of the bar acts as a taproom, with a split-level lounge to the right. The large garden features a barbecue area. The pub is a regular local CAMRA award winner. The food is freshly home-cooked. Features include quiz nights, discos, occasional live music and scooter club meets.
❀✿❦❧✦P↿–⊟(21,25,25A)

Hind
285 East Bawtry Road, S60 4ET (on A631 link road between M1 and M18)
❂ 12-11 (midnight Thu-Sat) ☎ (01709) 704351
Taylor Landlord; Tetley Bitter; guest beers ⊞
Large pub, built for Mappins Brewery of Rotherham in 1936 on the border of Whiston and Rotherham. Originally known as the King Edward VIII, it was renamed when the king abdicated. Since refurbishment the interior has been opened out, creating good disabled access. There are extensive gardens and a patio to the rear, with a snooker table upstairs (membership required to play).

Daytime, evening – and now takeaway – food is popular at this Ember Inn, and third-pint tasting racks are offered. ▲Q❀✿❦❧P↿–⊟(10,10A,19B)

Wombwell

Anglers Rest ⚲
66 Park Street, S73 0HS (5 mins' walk from town centre)
❂ 5-midnight; 12-1am Sat; 12-midnight Sun
☎ (01226) 345747
Beer range varies ⊞
A short walk from the town's shopping area, this popular community local is Geeves Brewery's tap. It is a multi-roomed local with a TV lounge, a meeting and games room as well as a bar area. A choice of classic games can be played, from chess to darts. The covered outside seating area has wood-burning stoves for those cold nights, but is a suntrap in the summer months. Beers can change daily; guest beers come from other breweries and the cider is usually local. Smokers are welcome.
Q❀❦❧✦P↿–⊟(22,222,226)

Worsbrough Village

Edmund's Arms
25 Worsbrough Road, S70 5LW (off A61 onto Worsbrough Rd)
❂ 11.45-3 (4 Sat), 6-11; 12-4, 7-10.30 Sun
☎ (01226) 206865
Samuel Smith OBB ⊞
Opposite the ancient church, this traditional cosy local has been a Samuel Smith's house for as long as anyone can remember, and has continued to sell its one real ale at an amazing price. A warm snug and public bar with open fires at the front lead to a lounge and restaurant at the rear; the back garden offers further space for drinkers and smokers alike. Only a short bus ride from Barnsley and well worth the trip.
▲Q❀✿❦❧⚘✦P↿–⊟(265,67,X10)

Wortley

Wortley Men's Club & Institute ⚲
Reading Room Lane, S35 7DB (directly behind the Wortley Arms on A629)
❂ 12-11 (11.30 Fri); 12-10.30 Sun ☎ (0114) 2882066
Taylor Landlord; guest beer ⊞
This pretty club with its traditional timber frame exterior and opulent interior is well worth a visit. Formerly the hall library, the club comprises a small bar area, a plush lounge with open fire and a large games room. To the outside is a small beer garden. The club holds regular community events and live entertainment. The guest ale is from a local brewery and a guest draught cider is always available. Show your CAMRA membership card or a copy of this Guide on entry.
▲Q❀❦❧✦P↿–⊟(23,29)

YORKSHIRE (WEST)

Addingham

Swan Inn ⚲
106 Main Street, LS29 0NS
❂ 5.30-11; 12-midnight Sat; 12-10.30 Sun
☎ (01943) 831999 ⊕ swan-addingham.co.uk
Copper Dragon Best Bitter; Ilkley Mary Jane; guest beers ⊞

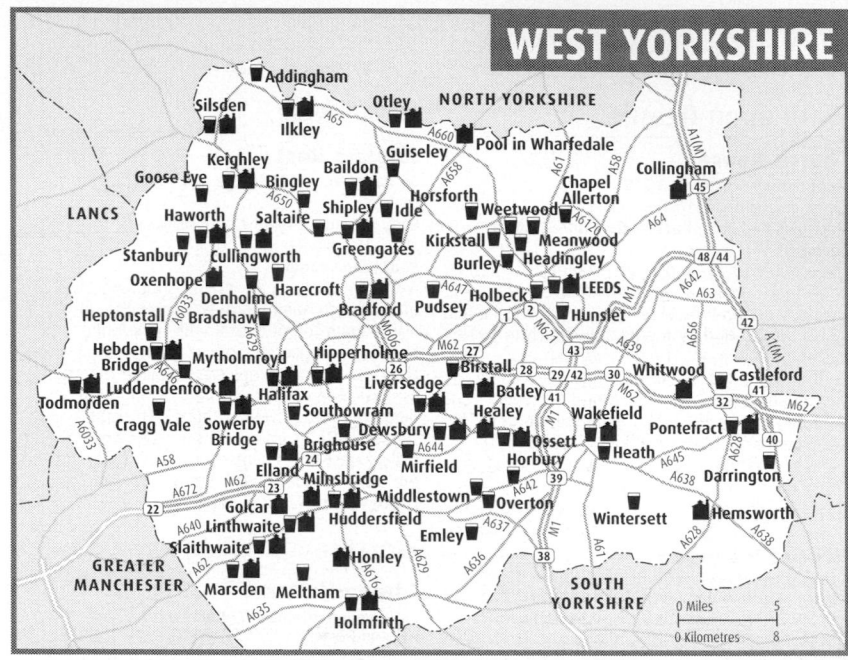

WEST YORKSHIRE

Addingham
Silsden
Otley
NORTH YORKSHIRE
Ilkley
Keighley
Guiseley
Pool in Wharfedale
Goose Eye
Bingley
Baildon
Chapel
Allerton
Collingham
LANCS
Haworth
Saltaire
Shipley
Idle
Horsforth
Weetwood
Stanbury
Cullingworth
Greengates
Kirkstall
Meanwood
Oxenhope
Denholme
Harecroft
Burley
Headingley
Heptonstall
Bradshaw
Bradford
Pudsey
Holbeck
LEEDS
Hebden
Bridge
Mytholmroyd
Hipperholme
Birstall
Whitwood
Castleford
Luddendenfoot
Halifax
Liversedge
Batley
Todmorden
Southowram
Healey
Wakefield
Cragg Vale
Sowerby
Bridge
Dewsbury
Ossett
Pontefract
Brighouse
Heath
Elland
Milnsbridge
Mirfield
Horbury
Darrington
Golcar
Middlestown
Overton
Wintersett
Hemsworth
Linthwaite
Huddersfield
Emley
Slaithwaite
Honley
GREATER
MANCHESTER
Marsden
Meltham
SOUTH
YORKSHIRE
Holmfirth

Friendly village local that retains a four-room layout around a central bar. The stone-flagged bar, snug and taproom are all warmed by real fires in winter. Live bands perform on Saturday evening, Monday is folk night and there is a quiz each Wednesday (see website for additional events). Food is served Wednesday, Friday and Saturday evenings and Saturday and Sunday lunchtimes. Guest beers come from the SIBA and Enterprise lists. Well-behaved dogs are welcome. ♨☆◗▶♣P☷(X84,762,765)

Baildon

Junction ⃝
1 Baildon Road, BD17 6AB (on Otley road)
✪ 12-midnight (1am Fri & Sat) ☎ (01274) 582009
Fuller's ESB; Oakham JHB; Saltaire Blonde; Tetley Bitter; guest beers ⓗ
Award-winning, friendly local with three rooms – bar, games and lounge. Three guest beers and four regulars are usually supplied. An additional beer often comes from the on-site brewery located in the cellar. Food is available weekday lunchtimes and at other times by arrangement. Sports events on TV are popular, a quiz night is held on Thursday, a jam session on Sunday and there are various pub games evenings. A regular beer festival takes place in late July. ☆◗≢(Shipley)♣♠⌐☷(656,658,737)

Batley

Taproom
4 Commercial Street, WF17 5HH
✪ 4-11; 3-midnight Fri; 12-midnight Sat; 12-11 Sun
☎ (01924) 473223 ⊕ taproombatley.co.uk
Ossett Yorkshire Blonde; Taylor Landlord; Theakston Old Peculier; guest beers ⓗ
The Wilton Arms reopened in 2012 as the Taproom, featuring real ales, fine wine and live music where quality rules over volume. Local musicians

entertain in the left-hand bar on Friday and Saturday nights, or you can relax on comfy sofas in the room on the right. Barstow's Snug function room celebrates local characters. Wednesday is quiz night. Three guest beers come mainly from Yorkshire and usually include a dark mild or a stout. A 20p per pint discount is given to CAMRA members. ♨☆≢♠P¹⌐☷

Bingley

Off the Tap ⃝
Burrage Street, BD16 1GH (off Chapel Lane)
✪ closed Mon; 12-11.30 ☎ (07960 995267)
⊕ offthetap.co.uk
Beer range varies ⓗ/ⓖ
Single room café-style pub opened in 2012. It is off Chapel Lane and close to the railway station. Up to six real ales are on offer covering a variety of beer styles, and many are from local breweries. The majority are served by gravity direct from the casks racked behind the bar, while two are served via handpull. At least one real cider is always available. Open mic nights are held every second and fourth Wednesday of the month, and live bands often play. &≢♠☷

Birstall

Horse & Jockey
97 Low Lane, WF17 9HB (200yds W of marketplace)
✪ 12 (4 Wed)-11.30; 12-midnight Thu; 12-1am Fri & Sat
☎ (01924) 472559
Copper Dragon Golden Pippin; John Smith's Bitter; Ossett Silver King; guest beers ⓗ
A country-style pub first licensed in the 1750s, west of the village centre, once a Kirkstall Brewery house. The open-plan bar, divided into four areas, has half-panelled walls and beamed ceilings. Darts, dominoes and pool are played, and sandwiches and burgers are served. One or two guest beers

come from SIBA breweries. Outside is a paved patio drinking and smoking area. Pub policy says no hats, no tracksuit bottoms. There is a 20p CAMRA discount on pints. ✿♣P'-🖵

Bradford

Castle Hotel 🅛
20 Grattan Road, BD1 2LU
✪ 12-11; 1-9 Sun ☎ 07967 144474
⊕ castle-hotel-bradford.co.uk
Jennings Cumberland Ale; guest beers Ⓗ
An established real ale pub in the city centre within easy reach of the transport network, this former Webster's house now stocks a changing range of beers. It supports local breweries, including Old Spot and Goose Eye, and also offers ales from further afield. A real cider is often on tap. The 19th-century building features a semicircular wraparound bar, forming two almost separate areas, with a dartboard and a TV at one end. Live folk music features on Fridays.
&≈(Forster Square/Interchange)♣♥🖵(662)

City Vaults 🅛
33 Hustlergate, BD1 1NS
✪ 10.30-11 (midnight Fri & Sat) ☎ (01274) 739697
Black Sheep Best Bitter; Saltaire Blonde; Tetley Bitter; guest beers Ⓗ
Bustling city-centre pub in former bank premises opposite the famous Wool Exchange. There are five ales on handpump, with local breweries such as Salamander, Bridgehouse and Phoenix strongly supported. Good-value home-cooked food is served all day (until 6pm Sat and Sun). The pub has a comfortable, traditional feel, with fine stained glass and a wrought-iron spiral staircase to the upper drinking area. Extracts from American newspapers on the walls make interesting reading. There is live music on Saturday, jazz every Sunday and a popular quiz on Wednesday.
✿◑&≈(Forster Square/Interchange)'-🖵

Corn Dolly 🅛
110 Bolton Road, BD1 4DE (5 mins walk from railway station, 10 mins from city centre)
✪ 11.30-11; 12-10.30 Sun ☎ (01274) 720219
Black Sheep Best Bitter; Everards Tiger; guest beers Ⓗ
This multi award-winning pub has been a Guide entry for many years. It used to be called the Wharf, as it was near the former Bradford canal, and it opened for the first time in 1834. An open-plan layout incorporates a separate games area. Good-value food is served weekday lunchtimes. A collection of over 1,000 pumpclips adorns the beams. The jukebox has a good collection of classic rock and '80s tunes.
🏠✿◑&≈(Forster Square/Interchange)
♣P'-🖵(611,640)

Fighting Cock ♥ 🅛
21-23 Preston Street, BD7 1JE (off Thornton Rd)
✪ 11.30-11; 12-10.30 Sun ☎ (01274) 726907
Copper Dragon Golden Pippin; Greene King Abbot; Taylor Boltmaker, Landlord; Theakston Old Peculier; guest beers Ⓗ
Popular, unassuming pub, just a short bus ride or a 20-minute walk from the city centre. Twelve real ales are usually on sale, including at least one dark beer. The guest beers are continually changing. Ciders, foreign bottled beers and fruit wines are also stocked. The pub attracts a wide variety of customers from near and afar. Lunches are served

Monday to Saturday. A regular award winner and local CAMRA Pub of the Year 2011 and 2013.
🏠◑&♥🖵(607,615,636)

Ginger Goose 🅛
Market Street, BD1 1LH
✪ 10-11 ☎ (01274) 390584
Saltaire Blonde; Tetley Bitter; guest beers Ⓗ
Large open-plan modern-style pub just a few minutes' walk from the bus and train interchange. It is friendly and welcoming with easy access throughout for all visitors. Up to six real ales are served, many from local breweries such as Ilkley, Naylor's and Salamander. There is a first-floor

INDEPENDENT BREWERIES

Barearts Todmorden
Barge & Barrel Elland
Barley Bottom Silsden
Bob's Healey
Bridestones Hebden Bridge
Bridgehouse Oxenhope
Briscoe's Otley
Burley Street Leeds
Cap House Batley
Clark's Wakefield
Collingham Collingham (NEW)
Elland Elland
Empire Slaithwaite
Fernandes Wakefield
Five Towns Wakefield
Golcar Golcar
Goose Eye Keighley
Halifax Steam Hipperholme
Hamelsworde Hemsworth (NEW)
Hand Drawn Monkey Huddersfield (NEW)
Haworth Steam Haworth
Ilkley Ilkley
James & Kirkman Pontefract
Junction Baildon (NEW)
Kirkstall Leeds
Landlord's Friend Luddendenfoot
Leeds Leeds
Linfit Linthwaite
Little Valley Hebden Bridge
Magic Rock Huddersfield
Mallinson's Huddersfield
Malthouse Ossett (NEW)
Milltown Milnsbridge
New Inn Liversedge (NEW)
Nook Holmfirth
Oates Halifax
Old Bear Keighley
Old Spot Cullingworth
Ossett Ossett
Owenshaw Mills Sowerby Bridge
Partners Dewsbury
Rat Huddersfield
Revolutions Whitwood
Ridgeside Leeds
Riverhead Marsden
Rodham's Otley
Salamander Bradford
Saltaire Shipley
Slightly Foxed Sowerby Bridge
Sportsman Huddersfield
Summer Wine Honley
Sunbeam Leeds (NEW)
Tigertops Wakefield
Timothy Taylor Keighley
WharfeBank Pool in Wharfedale
Wharfedale Ilkley (NEW)

function room but the only bar is on the ground floor. The impressive city hall and newly constructed city park are visible from the front of the pub. ◑&≠(Forster Square/Interchange)🚇

Haigy's 🅛

31 Lumb Lane, Manningham, BD8 7QU
◑ 5 (12 Sat)-2am; 2-11 Sun ☎ (01274) 731644
Tetley Mild, Bitter; guest beers 🅗
Friendly locals' pub and a former local CAMRA Pub of the Year, on the edge of the city centre. It offers up to four guest ales, often of the blonde and golden variety and mainly from local micros, with Westons Old Rosie cider. The comfortable lounge sports a fine collection of porcelain teapots and an extensive range of pictures. It has a heated smoking area and a large-screen TV, and is popular with Bradford City and away fans on match days.
≠(Forster Square/Interchange)
♣♠P⁵–🚇(620,621)

New Beehive Inn ★ 🅛

171 Westgate, BD1 3AA
◑ 12-11 (1am Fri & Sat); 6-11 Sun ☎ (01274) 721784
⊕ newbeehive.co.uk
Beer range varies 🅗
Gas-lit pub on the fringe of the city centre. Built in 1901, this imposing building is deservedly identified by CAMRA as one of Britain's Best Real Heritage Pubs for its multi-roomed interior. Note its external features too. Up to eight real ales are served, almost exclusively from local micros. A separate cellar bar offers weekend music, and folk and jazz can sometimes be experienced in the pub itself. See the splendid paintings in the back bar. No food is served Sunday. Three-star en-suite accommodation is available.
🏚🅟🏠◑🛏♣♠P⁵–🚇(617,618)

Sir Titus Salt 🅛

Unit B, Windsor Baths, Morley Street, BD7 1AQ (behind Alhambra Theatre)
◑ 9am-midnight (1am Fri & Sat) ☎ (01274) 732853
Greene King Abbot; Ruddles Best Bitter; guest beers 🅗
An excellent conversion of former public baths by Wetherspoon. It comprises a large open-plan main room with an additional ground floor to one side and an upper balcony area. Ten handpumps serve a wide range of real ales, and real cider is also available. Named in honour of a local industrialist, the pub's decor includes photographs and other artefacts relating to his life and times. Close to the National Media Museum.
Q🏠◑&≠(Forster Square/Interchange)♠🚇

Sparrow Bier Café 🅛

32 North Parade, BD1 3HZ
◑ 11-11 (8 Mon; midnight Fri & Sat); 12-6 Sun
☎ (01274) 270772 ⊕ thesparrowbradford.co.uk
Beer range varies 🅗
Opened in 2011 by local enthusiasts, this pub won the local CAMRA Pub of the Year in 2012. On two floors, it is simply furnished and features local art on the walls. Four rotating cask ales are from quality breweries such as Salamander, Kirkstall, Saltaire, Thornbridge and Magic Rock. There are always at least two real ciders on sale as well. An extensive range of international beers includes Bernard pilsner on tap. No meals are provided but deli sandwiches and platters are on offer.
&≠(Forster Square/Interchange)
♠🚇(622,662,680)

Bradshaw

Golden Fleece

1 Bradshaw Lane, HX2 9UR
◑ 4 (12 Sat & Sun)-11.30 ☎ (07522) 190990
Saltaire Blonde; guest beers 🅗
A friendly, busy community pub with a large car park and beer garden. Sports oriented, it has a ski club, a Sky TV dominoes team, a Sunday football team, a quiz league on Tuesday, and pool teams. There is a free workers' buffet on Friday and a pub quiz on Wednesday. Discos are on Saturdays (the landlord is a DJ). Although there are no meals for sale, there is often free food, and barbecues in summer. 🏚Q🏠&♣P⁵–🚇

Brighouse

Red Rooster

123 Elland Road, Brookfoot, HD6 2QR (on A6025 towards Elland)
◑ 4 (12 Fri & Sat)-11; 12-10.30 Sun
Abbeydale Moonshine; Marble Pint; Saltaire Blonde; Taylor Boltcutter, Landlord; guest beers 🅗
Half a mile from Brighouse town centre, it is well worth the walk to this excellent free house. Formerly known as the Wharf, the pub was purpose-built around 1900 to serve the adjacent coal wharf, which supplied much of West Yorkshire. Three wharfmen's cottages still stand alongside the pub. About 400 yards further on is the Cromwell Bottom nature reserve, from where it is possible to walk back to Brighouse along the canal. Dark beers are always available. 🏠♣P⁵–🚇(571,E8)

Richard Oastler

Bethell Street, HD6 1JN SE145227
◑ 8am-11 ☎ (01484) 401756
Greene King Abbot; Ruddles Best Bitter; guest beers 🅗
A Grade II-listed former Methodist chapel converted to a successful Wetherspoon pub, it has a magnificent but inaccessible upper floor with original chapel pews, and the impressive ceiling is retained. Eight guest ales are served, always including a dark beer, and local microbreweries are regularly featured. Two traditional ciders from the Weston's range are also on tap. The usual good-value Wetherspoon food menu is served all day.
🏠◑&≠♠⁵–🚇

Castleford

Junction 🍸 🅛

Carlton Street, WF10 1EE (in town centre)
◑ 2-8.30 (11 Wed & Thu); 12-11.30 Fri-Sun
☎ (01977) 278867
Beer range varies 🅗
Town-centre community pub just two minutes' walk from bus and train stations. Open fires and lively banter keep the large horseshoe-shaped bar warm and friendly. There is a separate stove-heated snug, which is also available for functions and meetings. Up to six guest ales, mainly from Yorkshire micros, including Ridgeside beers from the wood, are served, as well as a good selection of Sam Smith's bottled beers. Quiz night is Wednesday. Rare for the area is a bar billiards table. Dog- and child-friendly. 🏚≠♣🚇

Cragg Vale

Hinchliffe Arms

Church Bank Lane, HX7 5TA (300yds down hill off B6138, 2 miles S of Mytholmroyd) SD999232
☻ closed Mon; 12-3 (not Tue), 5-11; 12-11 Sat; 12-9 Sun
☎ (01422) 883256 ⊕ hinchliffearmscraggvale.co.uk
Ilkley Dinner Ale; guest beers Ⓗ
Food-based country pub near to the church. The new licensee has been keen to increase real ale sales, selling over 200 different beers in the first year. Attracting a mix of locals and visitors from further afield, food bookings are advisable, and probably essential at weekends. Dogs are welcome in the bar. The local area is ideal for walkers and cyclists. Cragg Vale is on the route of the 2014 Tour de France. Check Facebook for current beers.
🏚Q❀❀◖●P☵(900,901,C)

Cullingworth

George Hotel Ⓛ

Station Road, BD13 5HN
☻ 4 (12 Wed & Thu)-11; 12-midnight Fri & Sat; 12-11 Sun
☎ (01535) 275566 ⊕ thegeorgecullingworth.co.uk
Old Spot Light But Dark, Spot Light, OSD, Spot o' Bother; guest beer Ⓗ
A lovely old-fashioned village pub, rescued from oblivion by local brewery owners, in a pleasant setting by the church. Four distinct drinking areas, one primarily for dining, welcome the visitor. A fine range of local beer is on sale – the pub is effectively the brewery tap for Old Spot, located nearby. Children are welcome until 9pm. Food is served until 8.45pm every day and an extensive and imaginative food menu will impress. Steak night is every Wednesday. 🏚Q❀❀◖●P☵(697)

Darrington

Spread Eagle Ⓛ

Estcourt Road, WF8 3AP (on main road through village)
☻ closed Mon; 12-3, 5-11; 12-10.30 Sun ☎ (01977) 699698
Copper Dragon Golden Pippin Ⓗ
A friendly and welcoming community pub in the heart of the village. The landlady is particularly adventurous in her choice of three guest ales. Good-quality food is served both in the bar and in a small dining area (no food Sun eve or all day Mon). Monday is quiz night. It is said there have been sightings here of the ghost of a boy who was shot for horse rustling in 1685. Unusually, it is the meeting place for the local parish council.
Q❀◖●P☵(408,409)

Denholme

New Inn Ⓛ

Keighley Road, BD13 4JT
☻ 4-11; 2-midnight Sat; 2-11 Sun ☎ (01274) 833871
Old Spot Light But Dark; Tetley Bitter; guest beers Ⓗ
A warm welcome is assured at this lovely pub that supports local microbreweries and frequently offers guest ales from further away. Local beers from Saltaire, Salamander and Goose Eye are often found here and all beers are keenly priced. Tuesday night hosts a jam session while on Thursday free snacks are available from 6pm. Well-behaved children and dogs are welcomed. The pub sits high on the hillside with stunning views. For the energetic the Great Northern walking/cycling trail is nearby. 🏚❀❀♣P☵☵(696,697)

Dewsbury

Leggers Inn

Calder Valley Marina, Mill Street East, WF12 9BD (off B6409; follow brown signs to Canal Basin)
☻ 10.30-11 (midnight Fri & Sat); 11-10.30 Sun
☎ (01924) 502846
Abbeydale Moonshine; Everards Tiger; guest beers Ⓗ
Once the hayloft above stables by the canal basin, low beams, a powerful stove, deep seating and quirky items on display make for a unique atmosphere. The six beers listed on the school blackboard include ale from Rooster's, plus one rotating cider on handpump. Outside, a large decked area is excellent in summer. Sunday lunches are served; light meals can be had all day until 8pm and there is a pool table and a function room. Bus and rail stations are within a mile.
🏚❀◖♣●P☵

West Riding Licensed Refreshment Rooms Ⓛ

Railway Station, Wellington Road, WF13 1HF (platform 2 Dewsbury Station)
☻ 12-11 Mon; 11-11 Tue-Thu & Sun; 11-midnight Fri; 10 midnight Sat ☎ (01924) 459193 ⊕ imissedthetrain.com
Black Sheep Best Bitter; Taylor Landlord; guest beers Ⓗ
Multiple award-winning pub in a Grade II-listed Victorian building on the railway station, in the Guide since its establishment 20 years ago. It serves a broad range of six carefully selected guest ales, usually including a Sportsman Brewery beer, plus two real ciders or perries, often from local producer Pure North. Live music plays every weekend in summer. A large, decked, partially covered patio serves as a beer garden. Good-value, quality lunches are available daily, with early evening meals Tuesday to Thursday.
🏚❀◖♿≠●☵☵

Elland

Barge & Barrel

10-20 Park Road, HX5 9HP (on A6025 NE of town centre)
☻ 12-11.30 ☎ (01422) 371770
Abbeydale Moonshine; Black Sheep Best Bitter; Milltown Platinum Blonde; Phoenix Wobbly Bob; Taylor Landlord; guest beers Ⓗ
A large roadside pub built to serve the former Elland station. A three-sided bar supplies the comfortable lounge, with views over the canal and river to Elland town. Opposite, a games area and a snug with an open fire are separated from the bar by partitions of modern stained glass. Guest beers are mainly from microbreweries and the in-house brewery is due to restart any day. The smoking shelter is heated. Thursday is quiz night.
🏚❀◖♿♣P☵☵(537,E7,E8)

Drop Inn

12 Elland Lane, HX5 9DU (off link road from A629 to town centre)
☻ 4-11; 12-midnight Fri & Sat; 12-11 Sun ☎ (01422) 387484
Ossett Pale Gold, Yorkshire Blonde, Silver King; guest beer Ⓗ
Stone flags and floorboards, and a brick arch between rooms, exhibit the Ossett Brewery pub style. French Renaissance pictures add to the decor along with cigar containers, stone jars and tankards. A stove occupies a large cottage fireplace in the side room. Food is served Friday lunchtime

only. A quiz is held every Thursday. Guest beers are from Fuller's, other Ossett group breweries and microbreweries. Outside is a heated smoking shelter. Q❀❶♣⚓℠➡(278,503)

Emley

White Horse Ⓛ
2 Chapel Lane, HD8 9SP (on main road through village)
❀ 12 (4 Mon)-11; 12-11.30 Fri-Sat ☎ (01924) 849823
⊕ white-horse-emley.co.uk
Ossett Yorkshire Blonde, Emley Cross, Excelsior; guest beers Ⓗ
Friendly local that is Ossett Brewery's only tenanted pub, traditional in style, with a stone floor and range. A small flight of steps leads up to another room with a stove, which is used as a family room. The regular Ossett beers are complemented by five guests from small local and more distant breweries; there is always a mild, stout or porter on handpump as well as a real cider. Bar meals are served, as is Sunday lunch.
🏚🌄❀❶♣🌸P℠➡(232)

Goose Eye

Turkey Inn Ⓛ
BD22 0PD
❀ 12-11 (midnight Fri & Sat) ☎ (01535) 681339
⊕ theturkeyinn.com
Goose Eye Bronte Bitter, Chinook Blonde, seasonal beers; Taylor Golden Best, Landlord Ⓗ
Friendly, historic inn in a tiny hamlet approached by steep roads or a riverside footpath. It has three snugs, all with real fires to keep out the winter chill. The stained glass windows facing the road date from when it was an Aaron King pub. It has a pool table, a quiz night on Wednesday and live music. House beer Turkey Delight is from Goose Eye brewery. In summer the pub is a good base for walkers. 🏚❀❶♣P℠➡

Greengates

Albion Inn
25 New Line, BD10 9AS (on main Keighley-Leeds road)
❀ 12-11 (midnight Fri & Sat) ☎ (01274) 613211
Acorn Barnsley Bitter; Tetley Bitter; guest beers Ⓗ
Comfortable, traditional, neighbourhood pub with an L-shaped lounge and a separate public bar where pub games are played. Consistently good beer is served here by dedicated staff. The venue is popular with the local community and is home to a thriving social club. Visitors are also made welcome. ➍♣P℠➟➡(760)

Guiseley

Coopers Ⓛ
4-6 Otley Road, LS20 8AH (opp Morrisons on A65)
❀ 12-11 (midnight Fri & Sat) ☎ (01943) 878835
Black Sheep Golden Sheep; Rooster's Wild Mule; Taylor Golden Best; guest beers Ⓗ
Light, modern, airy bar/diner converted from a former Co-operative store. Eight ales are served, generally from Yorkshire or northern micros, with a dedicated dark beer pump and a large selection of continental bottled beers. A diverse range of meals is available until 9pm. The large upstairs function room has regular music events and a monthly comedy club, and this area also serves as extra dining space. ❀❶≈🌸℠➡(33,33A,97)

Guiseley Factory Workers Club Ⓛ
6 Town Street, LS20 9DT (in Towngate near St Oswald's Church)
❀ 1-11 (midnight Fri); 11.30-midnight Sat; 11-11 Sun
☎ (01943) 874793 ⊕ guiseleyfactoryworkersclub.co.uk
Tetley Bitter; guest beers Ⓗ
Founded over 100 years ago by the Yeadon & Guiseley Factory Workers Union, this is a friendly club serving three rapidly changing guest ales from micros and independents from anywhere in the UK; normally one will be a dark beer. It is three-roomed, with a small lounge, concert room and snooker room. The club hosts many other local clubs and organisations. An annual beer festival is held in April. CAMRA members are welcome – show a copy of this Guide or a membership card.
❀≈♣P℠➡(33A,97,737)

Halifax

Big Six
10 Horsfall Street, Saville Park, HX1 3HG (off A646 Skircoat Moor road at King Cross) SE081241
❀ 4 (3.30 Fri)-11; 12-midnight Sat & Sun ☎ (01422) 350169
Old Mill Bitter; guest beers Ⓗ
An unusual pub in the middle of a terrace of houses adjacent to the Free School Lane recreation ground. Dogs are always welcome at this busy and friendly venue. A through corridor separates the bar and games room from the two lounges. Memorabilia from the Big Six mineral water company, which operated from the premises a century ago, adorn the walls. Three changing guest beers from regional or microbreweries are sold. A quiz features every Monday. Dogs are welcome.
🏚Q❀♣➡(577,832)

Shears Inn
1 Paris Gates, HX3 9EZ (rear of flats by Shay Stadium, then head for the mill chimney) SE097241
❀ 11.30-midnight ☎ (01422) 362936
⊕ shearsinnparisgates.co.uk
Taylor Golden Best, Boltmaker, Landlord; guest beers Ⓗ
Family-run true free house between Shaw Lodge Mills (formerly Moquette) and Hebble Brook. It is now a single room but with two back-to-back fireplaces in the centre, and is a popular meeting place for many social and sports clubs. There are regular beers from Timothy Taylor, Moorhouse's and Thwaites, as well as a guest from a regional microbrewery. Food, including the home-made pie of the day, is available at all sessions except Sunday evening. There is an unheated smoking shelter. 🏚❀❶P℠➡(531,542,555)

Sportsman Inn
Bradford Old Road, Swalesmoor, HX3 6UG (off A647, 1 mile N of centre)
❀ 12-2.30 (not Mon), 6-11 (midnight Fri); 12-midnight Sat; 12-11 Sun ☎ (01422) 367000
Tetley Bitter; guest beers Ⓗ
Countryside pub with stunning views and a good base for walkers. The landlord is a real ale enthusiast and always offers seven guest beers, many from local microbreweries. There is free room hire for events. The pub has its own children's playground and is close to a dry ski slope and a children's adventure playground. A quiz night takes place every Friday.
🏚Q🌄❀❶♣P℠➡(576)

Three Pigeons ★

1 Sun Fold, South Parade, HX1 2LX
✪ 4 (12 Fri-Sun)-11.30 ☎ (01422) 347001
Ossett Pale Gold, Big Red, Excelsior; guest beers ⊞

A striking octagonal drinking lobby forms the hub from which several distinctive rooms radiate in this Art Deco pub, built in 1932 by Webster's Brewery. Sensitively refurbished and maintained by Ossett Brewery, the Three Pigeons attracts a variety of local groups and societies, together with football and Rugby League enthusiasts. Up to five guest beers are supplied by local and regional microbrewers, by Fuller's, and from Ossett's own stable of pub-based microbreweries.
🏚️🏵️🕸️♣️🌶️ᐟ🚬🖳

Harecroft

Station Hotel

Haworth Road, BD15 0BP
✪ 4 (12 Sun)-midnight ☎ (01535) 272430
Taylor Landlord; guest beers ⊞

Rural pub located in a small village on the road between Bradford and Haworth. It comprises two main rooms divided by a central bar, with an additional games room to the rear. The guest beers are often from a variety of local breweries, including Goose Eye, Ossett, Salamander and WharfeBank. A jazz/swing band plays on Monday nights and the pool team competes in the local league. 🏚️🏵️♣️P ᐟ🚬🖳

Haworth

Fleece Inn Ⓛ

67 Main Street, BD22 8DA
✪ 12-11 (11.30 Fri); 10-11.30 Sat; 10-10.30 Sun
☎ (01535) 642172 ⊕ fleece-inn.co.uk
Taylor Dark Mild, Golden Best, Boltmaker, Landlord, Ram Tam ⊞

Historic coaching inn on Haworth's famous cobbled Main Street and near the Keighley and Worth Valley Preserved Railway. The stone-flagged bar serves the full range of Timothy Taylor beers as well as an interesting selection of foreign bottled beers. Offering good pub food, accommodation and a beer garden three storeys up from the bar on the roof, the Fleece is popular with tourists and locals alike. 🏚️🏵️🛏️🕸️♿♠️🎡♣️🌶️ᐟ🖳(663,664,665)

Heath

King's Arms ★ Ⓛ

Heath Common, WF1 5SL (off A655 Wakefield-Normanton road)
✪ 12-11 (midnight Fri & Sat) ☎ (01924) 377527
Ossett Silver King, Yorkshire Blonde, seasonal beer; Tetley Bitter ⊞

A stone terraced house dating from the 1700s converted to a pub in 1841, the King's Arms has stone-flagged floors, gas lighting, oak settles and blazing fires in winter. At the rear is a conservatory overlooking a large beer garden. There is wheelchair access. A weekly quiz is held every Tuesday at 9.30pm. 🏚️Q🏵️🕸️🍴🛏️♿ᐟ🖳(188)

Hebden Bridge

Stubbing Wharf

King Street, HX7 6LU (on A646 ½ mile W of Hebden Bridge)
✪ 12-midnight (11 Sun) ☎ (01422) 844107
⊕ stubbingwharf.com
Black Sheep Best Bitter; Copper Dragon Golden Pippin; Taylor Landlord; guest beers ⊞

A favourite both with locals and tourists, the Stubbing Wharf has gained an excellent reputation for good home-cooked food. Six real ales are always on handpump from local brewers and further afield, alongside at least two real ciders. It has a lovely canalside location with plenty of outside seating. Drivers can take advantage of the large car park, and the train station is a short walk along the towpath. A canalside function room is available for larger groups.
🏚️🛏️🏵️🕸️🍴♿🎡🌶️ᐟ🖳(590,592)

Heptonstall

White Lion

58 Towngate, HX7 7NB
✪ 12-midnight summer; 12-10.30 (midnight Fri & Sat) winter
☎ (01422) 842027
Saltaire Pride; Thwaites Wainwright; guest beers ⊞

The publican is a lifelong and knowledgeable cask beer enthusiast. Five ales, three real ciders and an expanding range of single malts are served between two distinct areas featuring real fires. Situated in a historic cobbled village dating from the 15th century, fittingly there is no jukebox, bandit or pool table. Popular with walkers and dog lovers, the pub hosts a one-week Irish folk session (established for 22 years) and monthly quality live music. 🏚️Q🏵️🕸️🌶️P ᐟ🖳

Hipperholme

Cock o' the North

The Conclave, South Edge Works, Brighouse Road, HX3 8EF (on A644)
✪ 5 (4 Fri)-11; 12-11 Sat & Sun ☎ 07974 544980
⊕ halifax-steam.co.uk
Halifax Steam Aussie Kiss, Lily Fogg, Jamaican Ginger, Child Catcher, Cock o' the North; guest beer ⊞

The sectional building shared with the brewery, next to the imposing red-brick Vulcan works, belies a well-fitted-out single-roomed bar with polished floors and fittings, inspired by 1930s Art Deco ocean liners. The atmosphere is relaxed, with a friendly, varied clientele. Ten handpumps showcase Halifax Steam beers. The occasional guest is from a Yorkshire microbrewery. Wednesday is quiz night. Q🏵️♿AP ᐟ🖳(548,549)

Travellers Inn

53 Tanhouse Hill, HX3 8HN
✪ 12-midnight (11 Mon; 11.30 Tue & Wed); 12-11 Sun
☎ (01422) 202494
Ossett Pale Gold, Yorkshire Blonde, Excelsior; guest beers ⊞

Opposite the former railway station, this traditional 18th-century, stone-built local has taken in adjoining cottages to create a series of distinct spaces. Well-behaved children and dogs are welcome until 7pm. A covered yard with heating is provided for smokers. Guest beers are from Ossett group breweries, Fuller's and microbreweries, and always include a dark brew.
🏚️🛏️🏵️♣️🌶️ᐟ🖳(255,548,549)

Holmfirth

Brambles Bar & Café L

Towngate, HD9 1HA

✪ 10-midnight (1am Fri & Sat) ☎ (01484) 684166

⊕ bramblesholmfirth.co.uk

Empire Brambles Mild, Brambles Bitter; guest beers Ⓗ

Lively, vibrant, modern pub/bar serving traditional ales and cider. House beers are brewed locally by Empire, and the guest beers normally come from within a 100-mile radius. Milltown, Brew Co and Wentworth beers are often on the bar. Cider from Pure North is always sold. Restaurant-quality food is served in the bar, tea and coffee are always available, and there is an upstairs function room for 100 people. Marvel at the scantily clad giant statue. ⋔☎◑&●🖛(313,314,316)

Nook (Rose & Crown) L

7 Victoria Square, HD9 2DN (down alley off Hollowgate)

✪ 11.30 (12 Sun)-midnight ☎ (01484) 682373

⊕ thenookbrewhouse.co.uk

Nook Yorks, Baby Blond, Best, Blonde, Oat Stout; guest beers Ⓗ

The Nook (properly, the Rose & Crown) dates from 1754, has appeared more than 30 times in this Guide, and continues to evolve. It serves home-cooked food all day, and has been dispensing beers from its own Nook Brewhouse since 2009. One or two guest beers are also on the bar, as well as Pure North cider. There is a popular folk club every Sunday evening, and real ale festivals on the weekend before Easter and the August bank holiday weekend. ⋔☎❀☎◑&♣●½🖛(313,314,316)

Horbury

Cricketers Arms L

22 Cluntergate, WF4 5AG (on E edge of town)

✪ 4 (11 Fri & Sat)-11; 12-11 Sun ☎ (01924) 267032

Black Sheep Golden Sheep; Taylor Dark Mild, Landlord Ⓗ

Located on the edge of the town, this former Tetley's establishment has now reopened as a genuine free house. The pub has had a tasteful refurbishment and the length of the bar has been extended. Cheese and mezes boards are available at all times. There is a bus stop close by with a frequent service to Wakefield and Dewsbury. Local CAMRA Pub of the Year 2011. ⋔Q☎❀♣●P½🖛(126,127,231)

Huddersfield

Grove L

2 Spring Grove Street, HD1 4BP

✪ 12-11 (midnight Thu-Sat) ☎ (01484) 430113

Magic Rock Curious; Taylor Landlord; Thornbridge Jaipur IPA; guest beers Ⓗ

The Grove Inn has a phenomenal list of 18 ales on handpull, all year round, including a dedicated low-gravity pump serving a beer at around 3.8%. Nine rotating pumps dispense two beers from Thornbridge alongside Fuller's, Gadds', Durham, Marble, Buxton, Dark Star and a second from Magic Rock. The remaining six beers are selected randomly from across the country. Stout, porter and strong ales are regularly on handpump. In addition, there are over 250 foreign bottled beers from Europe, the US and the rest of the world. Q☎❀⊟≢●½🖫🖛

King's Head

St George's Square, HD1 1JF (in station buildings, on left when exiting station)

✪ 11.30-11; 12-10.30 Sun ☎ (01484) 511058

Bradfield Farmers Blonde; Taylor Landlord; guest beers Ⓗ

A popular fixture in Huddersfield's real ale scene and conveniently situated at the railway station. The pub's warm and friendly atmosphere makes it a necessary stop for the weary traveller. The 10 beers on handpump are all top quality and sold at competitive prices. There are always two dark ales, as well as a real cider on handpull. A mosaic-tiled floor dominates the main room, which hosts live bands on Sunday afternoons. It can get very busy at weekends, but is a real local gem to appreciate. ⋔&≢●½🖛

Rat & Ratchet L

40 Chapel Hill, HD1 3EB (on A616 below ring road)

✪ 3-midnight; 12-12.30am Fri & Sat; 12-11 Sun ☎ (01484) 542400

Ossett Pale Gold, Silver King, Excelsior; Rat White Rat, Black Rat; guest beers Ⓗ

The Rat has been part of Huddersfield's real ale scene for many years. This friendly pub offers Ossett, Fuller's and Mallinsons beers, as well as three rotating beers from the recently established on-site Rat Brewery. You will always find a mild and a stout/porter among its 13 handpumps. Pub games are played and regular beer festivals are held. A range of six ciders and two perries are also available at this local CAMRA Cider Pub of the Year 2012. ❀≢♣●P½🖛

Slubbers Arms L

1 Halifax Old Road, Hillhouse, HD1 6HW (off A641)

✪ 12-11 ☎ (01484) 429032

Taylor Boltcutter, Landlord; guest beers Ⓗ

An award-winning free house which prides itself on the quality of its ale. It is a former Timothy Taylor pub, with a heritage of over 150 years. The venue features a lounge with a horseshoe bar, a games room, a quiet room ideal for small private gatherings and a suntrap patio/smoking area. It offers good-value pub fare which is available at all times, and is particularly popular on match days, when the pub is busy. A cider and a perry always feature. ⋔❀◑&●½🖛(363)

Sportsman ♟ L

1 St John's Road, HD1 5AY

✪ 12-11; 11-midnight Fri & Sat ☎ 07766 131123

⊕ undertheviaduct.com

Taylor Landlord; guest beers Ⓗ

This restored 1930s pub has won a CAMRA English Heritage Conservation Pub Design award. With its on-site Sportsman Brewing Company, it regularly features at least three of its own beers among its eight handpumps; these include dedicated pumps for mild and stout/porter. Guest beers often come from local breweries Mallinsons and Summer Wine. Three ciders and a perry are also sold. This pub has established itself as a favourite of the Huddersfield drinking scene, and was local CAMRA Pub of the Year in 2012. ⋔❀◑≢●½🖛

Star Inn L

7 Albert Street, Folly Hall, HD1 3PJ (off A616)

✪ closed Mon; 5 (12 Sat)-11; 12-10.30 Sun

☎ (01484) 545443 ⊕ thestarinn.info

Pictish Brewers Gold; Taylor Boltcutter, Landlord; guest beers Ⓗ

Multi-award-winning back-street local featuring for over 10 years in this Guide. It is a showcase for new breweries, with the emphasis on varying guest ales sourced nationally and locally, supporting a dark beer and a dedicated Mallinson's pump. With no jukebox, pool table or games machine, there is always a great atmosphere, with lively conversation around the bar and a real fire during winter months. Three highly rated beer festivals are held annually in its marquee, with all beers on handpull. ＭＱ❀♿᛫–ᘖ

Vulcan ⃝

32 St Peter's Street, HD1 1RA
✪ 9am-2am ☎ (01484) 302040
Copper Dragon Golden Pippin; Thwaites Wainwright ⃝
A traditional town-centre pub with a long-standing licensee and generous opening hours. It has six handpumps, with four rotating guest beers most commonly from Yorkshire and Lancashire, with Mallinsons and Moorhouse's featuring regularly. Bargain-priced lunches are available every day, and free food is served for regulars Friday teatime. There is a daily happy hour extended on Wednesday evenings. The pub attracts all age groups, catering for enthusiasts of pool, karaoke and televised horse racing on Racing UK. Live bands are on stage every Sunday evening.
❀⃝♿≒♣᛫–ᘖ

White Cross Inn

2 Bradley Road, Bradley, HD2 1XD (on A62, 3 miles from town centre, at Leeds Rd/Bradley Rd crossroads)
✪ 11.45-11 (midnight Fri & Sat); 12-10.30 Sun
☎ (01484) 425728
Copper Dragon Golden Pippin; John Smith's Bitter; guest beers ⃝
At a busy crossroads and close to the canal, this award-winning local has featured for over 10 years in the Guide. Its historic roots date from 1806 and the pub still retains its Bentley's Yorkshire Breweries green-tiled entrance and windows. The dining area and lounge sit either side of the central bar, where two regular beers are supported by up to four varied guests. Home-cooked food is served lunchtimes except Saturday. A beer festival is held each February. ❀⃝♿♣P᛫–ᘖ(202,203,229)

Idle

Brewery Tap ⃝

51 Albion Road, BD10 9QE
✪ 4-11 (midnight Thu-Sat); 2-11 Sun ☎ (07515) 469441
Copper Dragon Golden Pippin; Ossett Yorkshire Blonde; Tetley Bitter; guest beers ⃝
Single-roomed pub with an island bar, behind which lies the cellar trap door and its vertiginous steps. This pub was part of the Trough Brewery estate until its demise. Locally famous for its regular live rock bands, it attracts talent and customers from afar. Look around you for pithy mottoes as well as evidence of the Trough era, and ask about the ashes in the niche. Two different ciders are always on sale. A beer festival is held in August. The garden area is well sheltered.
❀♣●ᘖ(640,641,760)

Symposium Ale & Wine Bar ⃝

7 Albion Road, BD10 9PY
✪ 12-2.30 (not Mon-Wed), 5.30-11; 12-11 Fri & Sat; 12-10.30 Sun ☎ (01274) 616587

Copper Dragon Golden Pippin; Thwaites Wainwright; guest beers ⃝
Easy to find in the heart of the village, this pub always has six real ales on. It is a popular bar/restaurant with a rolling beer festival, predominantly featuring northern breweries. Beers from many parts of the world are also on sale, draught and bottled, and the wine list is impressive. Excellent meals are served from an inventive menu with regular themes. The rear snug leads to an elevated terrace, popular in summer.
❀⃝◗᛫–ᘖ(610,611,612)

Ilkley

Bar T'at ⃝

7 Cuncliffe Road, LS29 9DZ
✪ 12-11 ☎ (01943) 608888
Black Sheep Best Bitter; Ilkley Mary Jane; Taylor Landlord; guest beers ⃝
Popular side-street pub, renowned for the quality of its beer and food. There are three regular beers plus five guest ales, usually of a variety of styles and focusing on smaller, independent, northern breweries. A wide range of good foreign beer is sold, bottled and draught. Home-cooked food is on the menu every day. This three-storey building has a music-free bar area, a cellar room used predominantly for dining, and a patio to the rear. It stands next to the town-centre car park.
Q❀⃝◗≒●᛫–ᘖ

Crescent Inn ⃝

Brook Street, LS29 8DG
✪ 12-11 (midnight Thu); 12-12.30am Fri & Sat
☎ (01943) 811250 ⊕ thecrescentinn.co.uk
Copper Dragon Best Bitter; Ilkley Gold; Leeds Pale; Saltaire Blonde; guest beers ⃝
Refurbished in 2011, this pub is located on the ground floor of a town-centre building that has been a hotel since 1861. Up to eight real ales are always on; four regulars plus others from local breweries. Up to 20 worldwide bottled beers are also stocked. The decor and furnishings are smart, with two unobtrusive TV screens for sport. Bar meals are available lunchtimes and evenings and the attached restaurant is part of the Le Bistro Pierre chain. Quizzes and themed food nights are regular events. Ｍ❀⌂◗≒᛫–ᘖ

Keighley

Boltmakers Arms ♥ ⃝

117 East Parade, BD21 5HX
✪ 11-midnight (11 Mon); 12-11 Sun ☎ (01535) 661936
Taylor Dark Mild, Golden Best, Boltmaker, Landlord, Ram Tam; guest beers ⃝
Unchanging classic Keighley town-centre pub, the de facto Taylor brewery tap; it was local CAMRA branch Pub of the Year 2012 and 2013. The licensee takes pride in the pub and it is always very welcoming. It has a tiny split-level layout with brewery, whisky and music memorabilia adorning the walls. The guest beers and handpulled cider are from various sources at the licensee's whim, and there is also a fine selection of single malts. It has a quiz every Tuesday night and occasional live music.
Ｍ❀≒♣●᛫–ᘖ

Brown Cow ⃝

5 Cross Leeds Street, BD21 2LQ (bottom of West Lane, corner of Oakworth Rd)

✿ 4-11; 12-10.30 Sun ⊕ browncowkeighley.co.uk
Taylor Golden Best, Bitter, Landlord; guest beers Ⓗ
After running the Brown Cow since 2003, Barry and
Carol purchased it from Timothy Taylor in January
2013. The ethos of this award-winning community
local remains the same, with quality, choice of ale
and the comfort of customers a priority. Up to four
guest beers come mainly from local micros. The
pub is adorned with local breweriana, and has a
no-bad-language policy. A discounted beer on
Super Saver Sunday is always popular. ⌚Q✿♣P⌐⊟

Cricketers Arms
Coney Lane, BD21 5JE
✿ 2 (11.30 Mon)-11; 11.30-midnight Fri & Sat; 12-11 Sun
☎ (01535) 669912 ⊕ cricketersarmskeighley.co.uk
Yates Bitter; guest beers Ⓗ
Serving four guest ales and a range of bottled
beers alongside the regular Yates Bitter, the guests
are from regionals and micros, often brews rarely
found in Keighley. Live bands play here, mainly at
weekends. The downstairs bar opens Friday and
Saturday from 7.30pm, selling two real ales.
Occasional beer festivals take place over both
upstairs and downstairs bars. It is seven minutes'
walk from the railway station and five minutes
from the bus station. ✿⇌⌐⊟

Leeds: Burley

Fox & Newt Ⓛ
9 Burley Street, LS3 1LD
✿ 12-11 (1am Fri; midnight Sat) ☎ (0113) 245 4527
Beer range varies Ⓗ
This great little pub, a Leeds institution, has been
through many incarnations, as has its brewery.
Some things have not changed, though, like the
wacky wedge shape, the cosy raised area, the
friendly, cosmopolitan atmosphere and the
willingness to serve an interesting range of beers.
Discerning drinkers visit to sample the brewpub's
own Burley Street ales which are sold alongside
imaginative guests. The bar food is a notch up from
the usual pub grub and live music attracts the local
students. ✿◖ᵴ♠⊟(49,50,50A)

Leeds: Chapel Allerton

Regent Ⓛ
15-17 Regent Street, off Harrogate Road, LS7 4PE
✿ 12-11 (midnight Thu-Sat); 11-11 Sun ☎ (0113) 293 9395
Kirkstall Three Swords; Leeds Pale; Tetley Bitter;
WharfeBank Tether Blond; guest beers Ⓗ
Long-established two-room pub in the heart of
Chapel Allerton with a history of serving quality
ales and good food. Guest ale turnover is usually
eight a week, making a visit a must for any drinker
wanting variety. Beers vary from milds to pale ales
and porters. It has regular quiz nights and TVs
showing sport, and a friendly welcome is assured.
Food is served from lunchtime until late. Draught
cider makes an occasional appearance.
✿◖♣P⌐⊟

Three Hulats Ⓛ
13 Harrogate Road, LS7 3NB
✿ 8am-midnight (1am Fri & Sat) ☎ (0113) 262 0524
Greene King Abbot; Ruddles Best Bitter; guest
beers Ⓗ
Large 1930s pub, formerly the Mexborough, with
three drinking areas. Two regular beers and six
guests come from all over the country; both

regional and microbreweries are represented. It is
home to the local knitting club and other groups,
giving the Hulats a genuine community feel. Meet
the Brewer nights and themed beer festivals are
occasionally held along with brewery visits.
Families are welcome until 9pm, food is served
until 10pm. The beer garden has a covered area for
smokers. ✿◖ᵴ♣P⌐⊟

Leeds: City Centre

Friends of Ham
4 New Station Street, LS1 5DL
✿ 12-11 (midnight Thu-Sat); 2-8 Sun ☎ (0113) 242 0275
⊕ friendsofham.com
Beer range varies Ⓗ
Cafe bar and charcuterie serving real ales. The bar
and food counter are at street level while
downstairs is a room with a long bench and comfy
chairs. A shuffleboard table and books are available
for entertainment. The three handpumps serve
beers mainly from microbreweries, and there is
also a range of bottled beers. The food counter
offers a variety of meats and cheeses. ◖⇌⊟

Hop Ⓛ
The Dark Arches, Granary Wharfe, Neville Street,
LS1 4BR
✿ 12-midnight ☎ (0113) 243 9854
Ossett Pale Gold, Yorkshire Blonde, Big Red, Silver
King, Excelsior; guest beers Ⓗ
Opened in 2010 directly under platform 17 of Leeds
railway station in the Dark Arches, this Ossett
Brewery pub has a varied programme of weekly
events ranging from a pub quiz to Sunday
gatherings of live bands. Ten handpumps dispense
the Ossett range along with guest ales, and it is a
rare Leeds outlet for perry. Biannual beer festivals
are a recent addition. It has disabled access to the
ground floor and a stage area on the first-floor
gallery. ✿⇌⊛⌐

Mr Foleys Cask Ale House Ⓛ
159 The Headrow, LS1 5RG
✿ 11-11 (1am Fri & Sat) ☎ (0113) 242 9674
⊕ mrfoleysleeds.wordpress.com
York Guzzler, Yorkshire Terrier; guest beers Ⓗ
Busy city-centre venue usually serving four beers
from York Brewery's range plus six guest ales. Also
available is a range of bottled beers from around
the world. The building is an impressive edifice
built of Portland stone and polished marble,
formerly owned by Pearl Assurance. The company
was founded by Patrick James Foley, hence the
name of the pub, and his statue is at the top of the
building. The interior is on several levels, with a
variety of seating. ◖ᵴ⇌⊟

North Ⓛ
24 New Briggate, LS1 6NU
✿ 12-2am (1am Mon & Tue); 12-midnight Sun
☎ (0113) 242 4540
Beer range varies Ⓗ
One of the great originals in the Leeds beer
drinking scene, North has seen more product
launches, beer firsts and exclusive beer deals than
just about anywhere else. With an enthusiastic and
knowledgeable team behind the pumps, the five
real ales are an agreeable mix of local and
innovative modern beers. Add to this the biggest
range of bottles any ale fan could hope to find, plus
quality continental draught beers, and you have a
pub that truly loves beer. ◖⇌⊟

Palace 🅛

Kirkgate, LS2 7DJ

☼ 10-11.30 (midnight Fri & Sat); 10-11 Sun

☎ (0113) 244 5882

Moorhouse's Pride of Pendle; Tetley Bitter; guest beers Ⓗ

In the shadow of Leeds Minster, this white-painted former Melbourne Brewery house is a supporter of local ales. It is common to find a Leeds Brewery ale, stout or porter and cider on sale, as well as choice ales from further afield. The long bar joins the two rooms of the pub together, making a large and spacious drinking area. A heated courtyard, bedecked with fairy lights, is provided for drinking outdoors. Food is served all day. 🏰🕩🚻♿🕿🚲☀✦–🚌

Scarbrough Hotel 🅛

Bishopgate Street, Leeds, LS1 5DY

☼ 11-midnight; 10-10.30 Sun ☎ (0113) 243 4590

Fuller's London Pride; Tetley Bitter; guest beers Ⓗ

Busy ale house, convenient for Leeds railway station. The building dates from 1765 and became a pub in 1826. It is named after Henry Scarbrough, the first owner of the pub, though it was then known as the King's Arms. At either end of the long bar are comfortable seating areas. The selection of guest ales is both from local breweries and further afield. A good range of pies is available. 🏰🕩♿🚉(City)✦–🚌

Ship 🅛

71a Briggate, LS1 6LH

☼ 11-11 (midnight Wed & Thu; 1am Fri & Sat); 12-10.30 Sun

☎ (0113) 246 8031 ● theshipleeds.co.uk

Greene King IPA; Tetley Bitter; guest beers Ⓗ

A two-level open-plan room served by a central bar, adorned with nautical memorabilia in keeping with its name, with brass fittings, period lighting and an impressive wall clock. It is often visited by thespians from the nearby Grand Theatre, so bring your autograph book. Live music features on Saturday from 8pm and an open mic night on Wednesday. Do not miss the Ship's special fish dish on Friday – a real treat. 🏰🕩🚉🚌

Stick or Twist 🅛

The Podium Suite, Merion Way, LS2 8PD

☼ 8am-midnight (1am Fri & Sat) ☎ (0113) 234 9748

Greene King Abbot; Ruddles County; guest beers Ⓗ

Large, open-plan bar underneath a Leeds casino – hence the name. It has an array of well-kept LocAle and is a welcome addition to this area of the city, with a large licensed seating area outside making a pleasant suntrap during the summer months. The pub's surroundings are very much a post-war development, however it is in close proximity to the new Leeds Arena. Food is served 8am-10pm. Q🚏🏰🕩♿🚉✦🚌

Templar 🅛

2 Templar Street, LS2 7NU

☼ 11-11; 12-10.30 Sun ☎ (0113) 243 0318

Tetley Bitter; guest beers Ⓗ

At the heart of the soon-to-be-developed Eastgate quarter, you are welcomed by the green and cream glazed Burmantofts tiles on the exterior of the building. The Bowing Courtier logo can be seen in the leaded window panes from when it was a Melbourne's pub. Adorned with wooden panelling and retaining the service bells, it has large-screen TVs throughout the pub showing a variety of sporting events. Guest beers range from local ales to those from further afield. 🕩🚉♣🚌

Veritas Ale & Wine Bar 🅛

43 Great George Street, LS1 3BB

☼ 11-11; 12-10.30 Sun ☎ (0113) 242 8094

Black Sheep Best Bitter; Ilkley Mary Jane; Taylor Landlord; Thwaites Wainwright; guest beers Ⓗ

Modern bar attracting a wide clientele, with an L-shaped open-plan room divided into four separate areas. It is well known for the quality of its food and the deli bar featuring local produce, which is available to eat in or take away. Guest beers are mainly from local microbreweries. A good range of wines is present along with draught and bottled foreign beers and real cider. Dogs are welcome. 🕩🐕♿🌿♣✦🚌

Victoria Family & Commercial 🅛

28 Great George Street, LS1 3DL (behind town hall)

☼ 11.30-11 (midnight Fri-Sat); 12-10 Sun ☎ (0113) 245 1386

St Austell Nicholson's Pale Ale; Tetley Bitter; guest beers Ⓗ

A real gem full of Victorian-style wood panelling and glass; the long main room is divided into separate drinking alcoves. Two smaller lounges off the entrance hallway can be hired for private functions. The row of nine handpumps carries a selection of ales from all over the country – one pump is reserved for a guest mild which changes every three months. A very popular jazz night is held each Thursday. 🕩🚉🚌

Whitelock's First City Luncheon Bar ★ 🅛

Turks Head Yard, off Briggate, LS1 6HB (near Marks & Spencer)

☼ 11-11 (midnight Fri & Sat); 12-midnight Sun

☎ (0113) 245 3950

Leeds Pale; Taylor Golden Best; Theakston Best Bitter; guest beers Ⓗ

Licensed since 1715, although the building predates this, with a Victorian interior dating back to 1895. The fine ceramic bar counter and brewery mirrors are of particular note, and CAMRA has identified this as one of Britain's Best Real Heritage Pubs. Inside the pub there has been little change since it was laid out by the Whitelock family in 1886. The sumptuous display of faience tiling is just one of the many items of historic interest at this must-visit hostelry. 🏛Q🏰🕩🚉🚌

Leeds: Headingley

Arcadia Ale & Wine Bar 🅛

34 Arndale Centre, Otley Road, LS6 2UE (corner of Alma Road)

☼ 12-11 ☎ (0113) 274 5599

Black Sheep Best Bitter; Taylor Landlord; guest beers Ⓗ

Cleverly converted former bank that is a well-established and multi-award-winning pub. The bar has ground floor rooms plus an upstairs mezzanine level, and is a dog-friendly environment. Eight beers are offered, often from Rooster's, Elland and Ilkley, plus guest beers from around the region. Draught and bottled foreign beers together with a range of wines also feature. Food is served Thursday to Sunday (all day Sat). A drinks waiter service is sometimes offered on busy nights. Children are not permitted. Q🕩♿🚌

Leeds: Holbeck

Grove Inn 🅛
Back Row, LS11 5PL
❂ 12-11 (midnight Fri & Sat) ☎ (0113) 243 9254
⊕ thegroveinn.com
Daleside Blonde; Moorhouse's Black Cat, Pride of Pendle; guest beers Ⓗ
Dwarfed by the surrounding modern buildings, the Grove is a traditional West Riding pub with four rooms off a corridor. To the front is a public bar and two small side rooms. Live music takes place in the concert room to the rear of the pub. The bar has eight handpumps serving both regular beers and guests, which are mostly from local breweries. Outside is a heated drinking area. Lunchtime food is served Monday to Friday. ▲Q❀❁❈⇄♣♠⚹—🖫

Midnight Bell 🅛
101 Water Lane, LS11 5QN
❂ 11.30-11 (midnight Fri & Sat); 12-11 Sun
☎ (0113) 244 5044 ⊕ midnightbell.co.uk
Leeds Pale, Best, Midnight Bell; guest beers Ⓗ
Located in Holbeck Urban Village and recently visited by Jamie Oliver, this contemporary Leeds Brewery pub caters for office workers during the day, with diners and drinkers taking over later on. On the ground floor there is chunky wooden furniture and a standing area by the bar for the drinkers, while upstairs is more food-oriented but still maintains a welcoming pub atmosphere. The fantastic courtyard beer garden, complete with serving hatch, provides the ultimate alfresco drinking experience. ▲❀❁❈⇄♠⚹—🖫

Leeds: Horsforth

Town Street Tavern 🅛
16-18 Town Street, LS18 4RJ
❂ 12-11 (10.30 Sun) ☎ (0113) 281 9996
Black Sheep Best Bitter; Copper Dragon Golden Pippin; Leeds Pale; Taylor Golden Best; guest beers Ⓗ
A relative newcomer to the Horsforth drinking scene and with a lot of attractions you would expect from a young pub – large clear windows, basic furnishings and an emphasis on food. The Town Street offers all this and more; the food is restaurant quality, the real ale range has a strong local focus, and the foreign beer selection is unequalled in the area. Dog-friendly, family-friendly and, in well, just attractive to all. Q❀❁❈⚹—🖫

Leeds: Hunslet

Garden Gate ★ 🅛
3 Whitfield Place, LS10 2QB (off Church St, to right of Penny Hill Centre)
❂ 12-3, 5-11 (midnight Fri & Sat); 12-9 Sun
☎ (0113) 277 7705 ⊕ gardengateleeds.co.uk
Leeds Pale, Best, Midnight Bell; guest beer Ⓗ
Gem of a pub quite rightly afforded Grade II*-listed status. Dating from 1903, the unaltered Edwardian pub was built and fitted by local firms. It was purchased by Leeds Brewery in 2010, who retained a tiled central corridor with serving hatch and full-length glass and wood screening. Four rooms are accessed from the corridor. Note the bar-back and rare curved ceramic bar counter. Lunchtime and evening meals are available daily (12-6pm on Sun). ▲Q❂❀❁❈♣🖫

Leeds: Kirkstall

West End House 🅛
26 Abbey Road, LS5 3HS
❂ 11.30-11 (midnight Thu-Sat); 12-11 Sun
☎ (0113) 228 9108 ⊕ westendleeds.co.uk
Beer range varies Ⓗ
Traditional, welcoming pub close to Kirkstall Abbey, with a central bar surrounded by comfortable seating and a dining area serving high-quality food. The main area provides a convivial atmosphere. Popular quiz nights take place Tuesday and Thursday. Constant rotation on four handpumps supplies beers from local breweries and further afield. There are also handpumps for cider and perry. Excellent food is served lunchtimes and evenings Monday-Saturday, 12-4pm on Sunday. ❀❁❈⇄(Headingley)♠⚹—🖫(33,33A,757)

Leeds: Meanwood

East of Arcadia 🅛
607 Meanwood Road, LS6 4HQ
❂ 10-11 (11.30 Fri & Sat) ☎ (0113) 275 5488
Black Sheep Best Bitter; Ilkley Mary Jane; Leeds Pale; guest beers Ⓗ
Newly built pub with one large curved room lit by huge windows and divided into two areas. The wood-floored drinking space features tables made from large wooden casks, and the carpeted area provides seating for drinkers and diners – with excellent food available. The beer range always includes a rotating ale from Ridgeside and Timothy Taylor. Guests concentrate mainly on northern microbreweries. Draught and bottled foreign beers also feature. Wednesday is quiz night. ❈♠🖫

Leeds: Weetwood

Victory Pub & Kitchen, Village Hotel 🅛
186 Otley Road, LS16 5PR
❂ 11-11 (midnight Fri & Sat); 12-11 Sun ☎ (0113) 278 1000
Marston's Pedigree; guest beers Ⓗ
The bar of the Village Hotel, open to the public, was constructed about 17 years ago, but the use of recycled barn timbers gives it an older appearance. Of the six handpumps, three dispense ales from the Marston's range, one is dedicated to Kirkstall Brewery, one to Ridgeside Brewery, while a changing guest completes the selection. Quizzes are hosted on Tuesday, Friday and Sunday. Large sport screens attract locals. Beer festivals are held in May and October. ⟵❀❁❈♠♣P⚹—🖫(1,6)

Linthwaite

Sair Inn 🅛
139 Lane Top, HD7 5SG (top of Hoyle Ing, off A62)
❂ 5 (12 Fri & Sat)-11; 12-10.30 Sun ☎ (01484) 842370
Linfit Bitter, Gold Medal, Swift, Special, Autumn Gold, Old Eli Ⓗ
High on the edge of the Colne Valley, the Sair Inn is home to the famous Linfit Brewery, which recently celebrated over 30 years of brewing. The brewpub, steeped in local history, is a traditional multi-roomed stone building with a central bar, real fires and a long-suffering landlord. The beer range is as LocAle as it gets, with eight beers unique to the pub, and real cider from Pure North. It is a welcome refuge for walkers, musicians and visitors alike. ▲Q❀♣♠🖫(181,183,184)

Liversedge

Black Bull 🅛

37 Halifax Road, WF15 6JR (on A649, near A62)
☼ 12-midnight (1.30am Fri & Sat) ☎ (01924) 403779
Fuller's London Pride; Ossett Pale Gold, Yorkshire
Blonde, Silver King, Excelsior; guest beers �🅗
In the Guide for the 10th year running, this is an
excellent, sociable, community local with a warm
welcome. The first of Ossett Brewery's chain of
lovingly restored pubs, it offers a blend of cosy
corners and open spaces where groups can mix,
including a former garage, now the chapel, with its
high roof, stained glass and woodwork. Nine
pumps dispense a range of beer styles including a
mild or dark ale. Quiz night on Tuesday is always
popular. Last admission 11.30pm.
🏚🕏🟫♣P⦡🖳(252,254)

New Inn 🍷 🅛

139 Roberttown Lane, Roberttown, WF15 7NP (near
Roberttown village centre)
☼ 3-11; 12-11.30 Thu-Sat; 12-10.30 Sun ☎ (01924) 402069
Abbeydale Moonshine; Leeds Best; Mallinson
Bobtown Blonde; guest beers �🅗
The social centre of the village, three rotating ales
usually include a dark beer and one from the
microbrewery in the cellar, where excellent,
exclusive beers of all styles are produced. Bobtown
Blonde is brewed for the pub by Mallinsons. There
is a snug with comfy chairs, a taproom, a sociable
lounge and a function room used for occasional live
music and events. The Wednesday quiz is
recommended. 🏚🕏🟫🀱♣P⦡🖳(229,253)

Shears

201 Halifax Road, Hightown, WF15 6NR
☼ 12-midnight (1am Fri); 1-1am Sat; 1-midnight Sun
Black Sheep Best Bitter; Tetley Bitter; guest beers �🅗
Rescued from pubco abandonment in 2010, this
well-loved historic pub features log fires and
stained-glass windows. Luddites used to hold
secret meetings upstairs as they planned their
attacks on local mills 200 years ago. There are fine
views from the garden. There is a Tuesday quiz, a
Sunday music quiz and occasional open mic
sessions. The popular taproom provides TV, pool
and traditional pub games. Luddites Ale is a
Moorhouse's house beer; the guest beers are
usually from renowned local and national
breweries. 🏚🕏🟫🀱♣P⦡🖳(220,254)

Marsden

Riverhead Brewery Tap 🅛

Argyle Street, HD7 6BR (overlooking River Colne in the
centre of Marsden)
☼ 12-midnight (1am Fri); 11-1am Sat ☎ (01484) 841270
Ossett Pale Gold, Silver King; Riverhead Sparth Mild,
Butterley Bitter, March Haigh; guest beers �🅗
Up to 10 beers are served at this Ossett Brewery
pub, usually six from Riverhead, two from Ossett,
London Pride and a guest. A pub since 1995 and
previously a Co-op store, it offers a friendly
welcome to all. The upstairs restaurant serves great
food and the microbrewery is visible from the bar.
As a popular stop on the real ale rail trail, it gets
very busy on Saturdays. Walkers and dogs are
welcome. It also has a riverside terrace for alfresco
drinking. Q🕏🀱🕏≈♣🖳(185)

Meltham

Wills o' Nats

Blackmoorfoot Road, HD9 5PS SE091121
☼ 11.45-3, 5-midnight; 12-midnight Sat & Sun
☎ (01484) 850078
Black Sheep Best Bitter; Greene King IPA; Taylor
Landlord; guest beers �🅗
In 1890, William, son of Nathaniel, became
landlord of the Spotted Cow. The name gradually
became Wills o' Nats. Today the pub is renowned
for its locally sourced home-cooked food and five
ales. Live music events are held on the last
Saturday of each month in the summer. It is in Last
of the Summer Wine country, close to the Peak
District, with stunning views, and is a welcome
stop for families, walkers and their dogs. It's a
regular in the Guide. 🏚🕏🀱🖧P⦡🖳(388)

Middlestown

Little Bull 🅛

72 New Road, WF4 4NR
☼ 12-11.30 (12.30am Thu-Sat) ☎ (01924) 726142
⊕ thelittlebull.co.uk
Bob's White Lion; guest beers �🅗
Established since 1830, a single bar services a
number of small rooms, with an open fire in colder
weather. Draught beers come from local and
regional breweries alongside a range of world
bottled beers plus real cider. All food is locally
sourced and home cooked – meals are available
lunchtimes and Wednesday evening. There is a
well-stocked games room, a car park and a large
grassed area to the rear. The pub is popular with
walkers and visitors to the nearby National Coal
Mining Museum. Families and animals are
welcome until 8.30pm.
🏚🕏🀱🖧🖧P⦡🖳(128,217,232)

Mirfield

Flowerpot 🅛

65 Calder Road, Lower Hopton, WF14 8NN (over river,
400yds S of railway station)
☼ 12-12.30am (1.30am Fri & Sat) ☎ (01924) 496939
Fuller's London Pride; Ossett Big Red, Excelsior, Silver
King, Yorkshire Blonde; guest beers ⅋🅗
An 1807 pub recently taken over by Ossett Brewery
and given a major refurbishment to an excellent
standard, with interesting features and three real
fires. It has three rooms and a central bar with an
impressive tiled flowerpot centrepiece, and the
garden enjoys riverside views. Eight ales come
from the likes of Ossett, Riverhead, Rat and
Fernandes, plus independent guests that change
on a daily basis, as well as a mild or stout. Haigh's
pie and peas are sold Monday to Friday lunchtimes.
Dog and family friendly. 🏚🕏≈♣P⦡🖳(262)

Navigation Tavern

6 Station Road, WF14 8NL (between rail station and
canal)
☼ 11.30 (12 Sun)-11 ☎ (01924) 492476
John Smith's Bitter; Theakston Best Bitter, Black Bull
Bitter, XB, Old Peculier; guest beers ⅋🅗
Popular canalside free house serving up to eight
regulars including Caledonian ales, plus up to four
guests at weekends. It is a registered ambassador
for Theakston beers at keen prices. Close to Mirfield
station, it features on the TransPennine Rail Ale
Trail. Renowned beer festivals are held late in
January, June and September. There is Saturday

night entertainment, active sports and pool teams, a large function room and en-suite B&B with a stairlift. At least two real cider/perry choices are offered. ✿🛏🍴🕭🌺🖤P⤴🚆🚃

Old Colonial Ⓛ

Dunbottle Lane, WF14 9JJ (off A644 up Church Lane, 1 mile NNE of station)
✿ 12-2.30, 4-1am; 12-1am Fri & Sat; 12-11 Sun
☎ (01924) 496920 ⊕ theoldcolonial.webplus.net
Copper Dragon Best Bitter; guest beers Ⓗ
National Pubs in Bloom winner, a former club with fascinating colonial memorabilia offering a cosy corner with sofas around the fire. There is a Royal British Legion memorial in the garden and local charities are well supported. The spacious conservatory is popular for meetings and functions. Up to six ales from the likes of Thwaites, Lees, Cottage and small brewers are on offer, often including one-off or commemorative brews. The excellent-value Sunday lunch is recommended. Evening meals are served Thursday to Saturday.
🏨🛏✿🕭🖤P🚆(202,205)

Mytholmroyd

Shoulder of Mutton

38 New Road, HX7 5DZ (on B6138, near station)
✿ 11.30-3 (not Tue), 7-11; 11.30-11 Sat; 12-10.30 Sun
☎ (01422) 883165
Black Sheep Best Bitter; Copper Dragon Golden Pippin; Taylor Landlord; Thwaites Wainwright; guest beers Ⓗ
A traditional village inn with a strong community feel and a warm welcome for walkers and other visitors. Excellent-value home-cooked food is served lunchtimes and evenings. Two guest beers are from the local SIBA list. Major sporting events are shown on a large-screen TV, but there is normally a quiet corner to be found. The bar displays memorabilia relating to the Cragg Vale Coiners, a gang of 18th-century forgers.
✿🕭🎠P⤴🚆🚃

Ossett

Brewers Pride Ⓛ

Low Mill Road, WF5 8ND (bottom of Healey Road, 1½ miles from town centre)
✿ 12-11 (10.30 Sun) ☎ (01924) 273865
⊕ brewers-pride.co.uk
Bob's White Lion; Rudgate Ruby Mild; guest beers Ⓗ
A genuine free house on the outskirts of Ossett, five minutes' walk from the Calder & Hebble Canal. Two resident beers plus seven guest ales from a wide range of microbreweries are served. The excellent-value menu (often themed) can be enjoyed lunchtimes and evenings. Monday is quiz night, and there is live music on the first Sunday of each month. Dogs and well-behaved children are welcome until 7pm. This venue puts on an annual August bank holiday beer festival.
🏨Q✿🕭🖤🌺⤴🚃(102)

Red Lion Ⓛ

73 Dewsbury Road, Flushdyke, WF5 9NQ (on old Dewsbury Rd on outskirts of town)
✿ 12-11 (10.30 Sun) ☎ (01924) 629530
Bob's White Lion Ⓗ
The Red Lion is the oldest pub in Ossett, a former coaching house with a large function room and a small snug. Live music is hosted every Saturday

night. Meals are only available at weekends. Very much a community pub, it raises money for charity through sponsored events. Q🕭🖤🌺🖤P⤴🚆🚃

Tap Ⓛ

2 The Green, WF5 8JS (from town centre turn left onto Queen St, which becomes The Green)
✿ 3 (12 Thu & Sun)-1am; 12-2am Fri & Sat
☎ (01924) 272215
Ossett Excelsior, Pale Gold, Silver King, Yorkshire Blonde, seasonal beer Ⓗ
On the edge of the town centre and formerly known as the Mason's Arms, the pub was bought by the Ossett Brewery and is now its brewery tap. Alongside the four regular Ossett beers there is usually a special or seasonal beer from the brewery and five guest ales – one from Fuller's and two each from Rat and Riverhead. A real wood fire and stone-flagged floors give the pub an old-fashioned feel. Disabled access is to the bar only.
🏨Q🎠✿🕭P🚆(117)

Otley

Bowling Green Ⓛ

18 Bondgate, LS21 3AB
✿ 8am-midnight (1am Fri & Sat; 11 Sun) ☎ (01943) 858980
Greene King Abbot; Ruddles Best Bitter; guest beers Ⓗ
This Wetherspoon pub is a conversion of a previous hostelry that had stood on this site since 1825. The Grade II-listed building itself has previously been a court, assembly rooms, and a place of worship, and was originally built in 1757. To the front is the main drinking area, and it has an atrium with original cobbles from the previous pub yard. At the back is the long bar with eight beers; some of them are from local microbreweries, including WharfeBank.
🏨Q✿🕭🖤🚆

Horse & Farrier Ⓛ

7 Bridge Street, LS21 1BQ
✿ 11-11 ☎ (01943) 468400
Black Sheep Best Bitter; Ilkley Mary Jane; guest beers Ⓗ
Open-plan pub with one large room divided into three wood-floored drinking areas and a carpeted area for diners. The rectangular bar has eight handpumps, mainly dispensing ales from northern breweries. Normally available are beers from Timothy Taylor and Rooster's breweries. A good selection of bottled foreign beers and a choice of wines is also stocked. Dogs are welcome and children may accompany diners until 8pm. Upstairs is a function room.
🏨Q✿🕭🖤🖤P⤴🚆(X84,940,965)

Junction Ⓛ

44 Bondgate, LS21 1AD
✿ 11-11 (11.30 Thu; midnight Fri & Sat); 12-10.30 Sun
☎ (01943) 463233
St Austell Tribute; Taylor Boltmaker, Landlord; Theakston Best Bitter, Old Peculier; guest beers Ⓗ
The Junction is on a prominent street-corner site on the approach from Leeds. Up to 11 ales from around the country are served, along with a real cider. There is a central fireplace, and a collection of leather harnesses and saddles hangs from the ceiling. Pictures of old Otley and some interesting metal beer advertisements and mirrors complete the decor. There is live music on Tuesdays, and a DJ on Sundays. Roadside tables allow for outdoor drinking. Dogs are welcome. 🏨✿🌺🖤⤴🚃

Old Cock ♈ L

11-13 Crossgate, LS21 1AA
✪ 11-11 ☎ (01943) 464424 ⊕ theoldcockotley.co.uk
Ilkley Mary Jane; Theakston Best Bitter; guest beers Ⓗ
A genuine free house which opened in 2010 after painstaking work to convert a former café into a compact and welcoming traditional pub. There are two rooms downstairs with stone-flagged floors and a further room upstairs. The guest ales are mostly from local breweries. At least two real ciders are also served plus a range of foreign beers. No admittance to under-18s. Local CAMRA Pub of the Year 2011 and 2012. ⚲Q৬🍴🕭🚃

Overton

Reindeer L

204 Old Road, WF4 4RL (turn left off A642 in Middlestown, continue for 1 mile, pub on right at end of village)
✪ 12 (4 Mon)-midnight; 12-11 Sun ☎ (01924) 848374
Beer range varies Ⓗ
A traditional free house, this is the tap for Cap House Brewery. Guest beers are mainly from local breweries and there is also real cider on handpull. Home-cooked food is served in the separate restaurant or conservatory, which leads to the beer garden overlooking the National Coal Mining Museum. A free quiz and supper are hosted on Wednesday night. The games room has a pool table, dartboard, dominoes and games machines. Outside is a covered smoking area, a children's play area and an aviary.
⚲Q🐕🌞🕭🌓🍴🕭P🚃(128,232)

Pontefract

Broken Bridge L

5 Horsefair, WF8 1PD (100yds uphill from bus station)
✪ 8am-midnight (1am Fri & Sat) ☎ (01997) 781640
Greene King Abbot; Moorhouse's Pontus Fractus; Ruddles Best Bitter Ⓗ
A Wetherspoon pub that was formerly a charity shop and is named after the Latin name for Pontefract. There are numerous pictures depicting the history of the town adorning the walls. Popular at weekends, the small entrance belies the large one-room interior, which features two open fires in winter. Food is served daily and the guest beers come from Moorhouse's, Saltaire, Wentworth and Clark's. There are regular monthly events such as Meet the Brewer evenings. A rear courtyard can be used by smokers.
⚲🐕🌞🕭৬≈(Monkhill/Baghill/Tanshelf)🕭🚃

Robin Hood

4 Wakefield Road, WF8 4HN (on jct of A639 and A645 at edge of town)
✪ 12-11 Mon; 5-midnight; 12-1am Fri & Sat; 12-midnight Sun ☎ (01977) 702231
Draught Bass; East Coast Little John Ⓗ
Busy pub near the notorious Town End traffic lights, known as Jenkins' Folly. There are four separate drinking areas including a public bar. Quizzes are held on Sunday and Tuesday evenings, and darts and dominoes teams play in the local charity leagues. An on-site brewery is now open.
⚲Q🌞৬≈(Tanshelf/Monkhill/Baghill)🍴🕭🚃

Pudsey

Fleece L

100 Fartown, LS28 8LU
✪ 12-11 (10.30 Sun) ☎ (0113) 236 2748
⊕ fleecefartown.co.uk
Copper Dragon Best Bitter; Taylor Golden Best, Landlord; Tetley Bitter; guest beer Ⓗ
On the western edge of Pudsey, this is a locals' hostelry with a friendly welcome for all. It is a big stone-built pub with a tiny traditional tap and, on the other side of the bar, a larger lounge. Here, surrounded by images of Hollywood stars, you can relax in comfort. Old-fashioned values rule – it is a clean, tidy establishment and service is always with a smile. The guest is usually a pale beer from a local brewery. ⚲🌞🍴🕭P🚃

Saltaire

Fanny's Ale & Cider House L

63 Saltaire Road, BD18 3JN (on A657 opp fire station)
✪ 5-11 Mon; 12-11 (midnight Fri & Sat) ☎ (01274) 591419
Ossett Treacle Stout; Taylor Golden Best, Landlord; guest beers Ⓗ
Near the World Heritage Site of Saltaire Village and the historic Salts Mill, this cosy pub was originally a beer shop. It is now a fully licensed free house stocking an excellent range of beers – three regulars and up to six guests – and serving a number of draught ciders. Extensions to the building have increased the seating capacity downstairs and added disabled access, while an upstairs room has comfortable seating. The gas lit lounge is adorned with breweriana. Real fires add nicely to the warm welcome.
⚲৬≈🍴🕭🚃(662,760)

Victoria L

192 Saltaire Road, BD18 3JF (5 mins' walk from railway station)
✪ 12-11.30 (12.30am Fri & Sat) ☎ (01274) 593725
Beer range varies Ⓗ
Traditional community pub close to the Saltaire World Heritage Site. It has a friendly atmosphere where children and dogs are welcome. There is a lounge with real fires and a separate public bar/games room with a pool table, jukebox and pinball machine. In the lounge, five real ales from a variety of breweries including Copper Dragon and WharfeBank are served alongside a real cider. The aerial photograph of Saltaire in the lounge is worth a look. A quiz is held on Wednesday nights.
⚲🌞🕭≈🍴🕭P🚃(662,760)

Shipley

Ring o' Bells L

3 Bradford Road, BD18 3PR (on A650)
✪ 11-midnight; 12-11 Sun ☎ (01274) 584386
Leeds Pale; Saltaire Blonde; Taylor Golden Best; Tetley Bitter; guest beers Ⓗ
Traditional broad-based local with a warm, homely feel showing all the up-to-date sports matches on several TV screens. Occasional bands perform and the pub takes part in popular poker games and weekly quizzes. A small Edwardian smoke room is where activity groups can meet including writers and anglers. The pub is near the historic village of Saltaire and is served by a frequent bus service.
🌞🕭৬≈(Saltaire)🍴P🚃(662)

Sir Norman Rae 🅛

Victoria House, Market Place, BD18 3QB (50yds from clock tower)
◐ 8-11 (midnight Fri & Sat) ☎ (01274) 535290
Greene King Abbot; Ruddles Best Bitter; guest beers Ⓗ

A typical conversion by Wetherspoon from a previous use. Formerly a Co-op department store, this example opened originally as a Lloyds No.1, but then converted to the standard format. There are 10 handpumps dispensing real ale, usually focusing on local breweries, with Greene King products also on the bar. Real cider is also served. Regular Meet the Brewer nights are held. The pub is situated at the edge of the bus interchange and five minutes' walk from Shipley railway station.
Q🏡🕔🍴♿🚲🚃🕮🚌

Silsden

King's Arms 🅛

Bolton Road, BD20 0JY
◐ 12-midnight ☎ (01535) 653216
Saltaire Blonde; Theakston Best Bitter; guest beers Ⓗ

Award-winning, spacious community hostelry with plenty going on. Music nights, quiz nights, a pool table and beer festivals combine to make it a great pub to visit. The beer range always has something for all tastes. Regular buses between Keighley, Addingham and Ilkley stop outside. Guest beers come from the Punch Finest Cask list, and this local is a regular outlet for Westons cider/perry. Dogs and well-behaved children are allowed.
🚶🕌🕔♣♿P🕮🚌(762,765,903)

Slaithwaite

Commercial 🅛

1 Carr Lane, HD7 5AN (village centre, off A62)
◐ 12-midnight (1am Fri & Sat) ☎ (01484) 846258
⊕ commercial-slaithwaite.co.uk
Empire Moonraker Mild, Commerciale; guest beers Ⓗ

Since reopening in 2009, this village-centre free house has enjoyed enviable success. Nine handpumps provide ample variety, with the keenly priced house beers (Commerciale and Moonraker Mild supplied by Empire Brewery), six rotating guests, and Cornish Orchards farmhouse cider permanently on tap. Very community-focused, it nonetheless has a varied clientele including locals, enthusiasts tackling the TransPennine Rail Ale Trail, ramblers and their dogs – the pub is dog-friendly. Light snacks and beverages are served Friday-Sunday. An upstairs function room is available free of charge. Q🕌🚃♣♿🕮🚌(181,335,339)

Southowram

Shoulder of Mutton

14 Cain Lane, HX3 9SB
◐ 2-11; 12-midnight Fri & Sat; 12-10.30 Sun ☎ (07707 358697)
Saltaire Blonde; guest beers Ⓗ

A popular local built in the 18th century in a hilltop village important for its stone quarries. It has won awards for the floral displays on its frontage, and for its strong community spirit. The L-shaped lounge includes exposed stonework behind the bar, and a separate room has a pool table. Regularly changing guest beers are sold. Activities include a Thursday evening quiz. Dogs are welcome. ♣🕮🚌(571,572)

Sowerby Bridge

Jubilee Refreshment Rooms

Station Road, HX6 3AB (at railway station)
◐ 12-10 (9 Sun) ☎ (01422) 648285
⊕ jubileerefreshmentrooms.co.uk
Beer range varies Ⓗ

Run by two real ale enthusiasts, the Jubilee is an award-winning café bar in converted railway buildings. The long, narrow room is lit by Art Deco lamps and displays railway and brewery memorabilia. Up to six beers are served from breweries in West Yorkshire and surrounding areas. Hot food is available 9-2pm Monday to Friday and 9.30-2pm Saturday. The website announces various events that often centre around railways and brewery history. Limited daytime parking.
🏚Q♿🚃P🕮

Puzzle Hall

21 Hollins Mill Lane, HX6 2RF (400yds from A58)
◐ 3-midnight (1am Fri); 1-1am Sat; 1-11.30 Sun
☎ (01422) 835547 ⊕ puzzlehall.com
Beer range varies Ⓗ

The Puzzle Hall can be found nestling between the canal and the river. The 17th-century building once included a brewery; it now provides a welcoming atmosphere, good beer and a venue for live music. Bands feature on Thursday and Saturday nights, and poetry recitals on the first Monday of the month. Thai food is served from Wednesday to Sunday 5-9pm. The six varying real ales are from microbreweries. 🏚🕌🚃♣🍴🕮🚌

Shepherd's Rest

125 Bolton Brow, HX6 2BD (on A58 towards Halifax)
◐ 3 (12 Fri-Sun)-11 ☎ (01422) 831937
Ossett Pale Gold, Shepherd's Rest, Excelsior; Taylor Landlord; guest beers Ⓗ

Built in 1877, this establishment took the name of a previous pub on the other side of the busy main road. It was purchased by Ossett Brewery in 2005 and the available space has been used to good effect. From the entrance steps a triangular area leads to the bar, which faces a cosy and compact lounge with a large brick-arched fireplace, comfortable seating and a flagged floor, which in turn leads to an enclosed outside area. Quiz night is Monday. 🏚Q🕌🚃♣🍴🕮🚌

Works 🅛

12 Hollins Mill Lane, HX6 2QG
◐ 12-11 (10.30 Sun) ☎ (01422) 834821
⊕ theworkssowerbybridge.co.uk
Taylor Golden Best, Best Bitter, Landlord; guest beers Ⓗ

Converted from a former joinery, the pub won CAMRA's Best Conversion to Pub Use award in 2006. This large open-plan local beside the Rochdale Canal on the western side of the town centre features exposed beams and floorboards. Nine real ales are served, including three from Timothy Taylor and six rotating guests. Food, made with love, is served both lunchtime and teatime. Entertainment includes jazz, folk or comedy. 🏚🕌🕔🚃P🕮🚌

Stanbury

Friendly 🅛

54 Main Street, BD22 0HB (on Colne Road between Haworth and Colne)
◐ 12-11 (10.30 Sun) ☎ (01535) 645528

Beer range varies Ⓗ
Popular village local that also attracts those walking the Pennine Way or visiting the ruined farmhouse that claims to be Wuthering Heights. This is a three-room pub with two lounges either side of a central bar plus a separate games room. Beers from Goose Eye often feature. Stanbury is only two miles from Haworth but a million miles from its tourist hustle and bustle.
❀♿♣P🚌(664,916,917)

Old Silent Inn 🄻
Hob Lane, BD22 0HW SE002371
⏲ 12-11 (midnight Sat; 10.30 Sun) ☎ (01535) 647437
🌐 old-silent-inn.co.uk
Taylor Landlord; Theakston Old Peculier; guest beers Ⓗ
A 400-year-old roadside inn at the west edge of the village, only five minutes' walk from the bus stop. With oak beams, flagged floors and open fires, it is a building with considerable charm. Drinkers are welcome and award-winning food is served. Walkers will find it close to the Pennine Way, Bronte Way and Millennium Way. Rotating guest beers are usually from local breweries within a 20-mile radius. 🔥🛏❀🛏◐◑♣P🚌(664,916,917)

Todmorden

Masons Arms 🏆
1 Bacup Road, OL14 7PN (on A681 near jct with A6033)
⏲ 3-11.30; 12-midnight Fri & Sat; 12-11.30 Sun
☎ (01706) 812180
Beer range varies Ⓗ
Located almost under a railway viaduct and close to the Rochdale Canal, this traditional local has a corridor entrance leading to the bar. There is seating and a pool table to the left and a small area with an open fire to the right. The fixed tables were formerly used for laying out bodies. Food is served until 6pm Tuesday to Sunday. Wednesday is quiz night. Guest beers are from independent breweries. 🔥Q🛏❀◐◑⇌(Walsden)⚐🚌(589,590)

Polished Knob
31 Burnley Road, OL14 7BU SD936242
⏲ 10-1am (2am Fri & Sat) ☎ (01706) 810480
Thwaites Wainwright, Nutty Black; guest beers Ⓗ
Situated in the centre of the town opposite the market and the town hall, this pub serves beers from local breweries. Friendly and efficient staff can provide a tasty and filling lunch. The pavement area tables catch the sun for eight months of the year. Very loud, quality live bands play here on Wednesdays and weekend nights from about 9pm.
🔥❀◐⇌⚐🚌

Staff of Life
550 Burnley Road, Lydgate, OL14 8JF SD916257
⏲ 12-3 (not Mon & Tue), 5.30-11; 12-11 Fri-Sun
☎ (01706) 819033 🌐 staffoflifeinn.org.uk
Taylor Boltmaker, Landlord; guest beers Ⓗ
A rural roadside pub in a deep valley, almost an unexpected delight. Two Taylor beers and an excellent choice of local bitters await the visitor. The pub has a reputation for the quality of its food, which is served to your table in one of the many nooks in the downstairs area, or on the balcony. The pub has a large parking area beside it (on the Yorkshire side). 🔥🛏❀🛏◐◑♣P🚌(589,592)

Wakefield

Alverthorpe WMC 🄻
111 Flanshaw Lane, Alverthorpe, WF2 9JG (between Dewsbury Rd and Batley Rd, 2 miles from city centre)
⏲ 2 (11.30 Fri & Sat)-11; 12-3.30, 7-11 Sun
☎ (01924) 374179
Bob's White Lion; Tetley Bitter; guest beers Ⓗ
Multi-roomed CIU-affiliated club, with a cosy interior with unusual stained glass features and an extensive collection of pot horses. A wide selection of guest ales is featured, mainly from local micros. The club is a regular winner of local CAMRA awards. Live entertainment takes place on Saturday and Sunday. Snooker and darts are among the traditional games, with a wide-screen TV for the armchair enthusiasts. It has sporting teams and also a floodlit bowling green.
❀🄶♿♣P⚐🚌(114,115)

Black Rock
19 Cross Square, WF1 1PQ (at top of Westgate near Bull Ring)
⏲ 11-11 (midnight Sat); 12-10.30 Sun ☎ (01924) 375550
Tetley Bitter; guest beers Ⓗ
An arched, tiled façade leads into this compact city-centre local, with a warm welcome and comfortable interior displaying photographs of old Wakefield. The Rock stands as one of the few proper pubs left in the middle of the clubs and bars of Westgate, and is popular with drinkers of all ages looking for a real pint. Customers are encouraged to suggest beers to try, with three different ales on offer. There is a free function room available. ⇌(Westgate/Kirkgate)🚌

Bull & Fairhouse 🄻
60 George Street, WF1 1DL (left out of Westgate station, right at the lights, left at the bottom of the hill and the pub is 200yds on the left)
⏲ 4-11; 12-midnight Fri & Sat; 12-11 Sun ☎ (01924) 362930
Bob's White Lion; Great Heck Golden Bull; guest beers Ⓗ
The tap for the Great Heck Brewery, the pub has reverted to an earlier name alluding to the cattle market and fairground in the area. The comfortable multi-roomed premises now enjoys a lighter feel, with a new lounge at the front and the toilets relocated to the rear, with limited disabled access via a passageway. A lively bingo quiz with meat raffle and hot supper is held on Thursdays, with live music at weekends. A changing real cider or perry is served on gravity.
🔥⇌(Westgate/Kirkgate)♣⚐🚌(443,444)

Fernandes Brewery Tap & Bier Keller 🄻
5 Avison Yard, Kirkgate, WF1 1UA (turn right 100yds S of George St/Kirkgate jct)
⏲ Pub: 4-11 (11.30 Thu); 12-midnight Fri & Sat; 12-11 Sun; Bier Keller: 4-midnight Fri & Sat ☎ (01924) 386348
Beer range varies Ⓗ
Owned by Ossett Brewery, although Fernandes Brewery still brews in the cellar, with a beer range that includes Ossett, Fernandes and Fuller's beers. The pub has 10 handpulls, one dedicated to a mild, stout or porter, as well as a draught cider. The Bier Keller has several premier foreign beers on draught, plus Ossett Yorkshire Blonde and a cider on handpump. There is live music on Sunday afternoons. Pets are welcome.
Q⇌(Westgate/Kirkgate)🍎⚐🚌

Harry's Bar 🄻

107B Westgate, WF1 1EL (out of Westgate Station, turn left and cross the road, then take 2nd alley on right)
☻ 5 (4 Sat)-1am; 12-midnight Sun ☎ (01924) 373773
Bob's White Lion; Leeds Pale; Ossett Silver King; guest beers Ⓗ

A previous winner of CAMRA branch Pub of the Year, this compact, one-roomed pub has a bare brick and wood interior complemented by a sun deck and a shady yard. Hidden away down a ginnel off Westgate, it is secluded from the fizz-and-yoof zone of the city centre, a thriving and friendly community local. Live music is staged on Wednesdays. There is a Pay & Display car park adjacent to the pub. A discount is offered to CAMRA members on Mondays.
🚸🏵️🜨(Westgate/Kirkgate)♣🐾⌐🚌

Henry Boons 🄻

130 Westgate, WF2 9SR (right out of Westgate Station; pub is 200yds under bridge)
☻ 11-11 (1am Fri & Sat); 12-10.30 Sun ☎ (01924) 378126
Clark's Classic Blonde, Westgate Gold; Taylor Landlord; guest beers Ⓗ

Quiet in the daytime, the pub gets very busy in the evenings as it is on what is known as the Westgate Run. It is the tap for Clark's Brewery which is behind the pub. Hogsheads are in use as tables and there many items of breweriana plus a thatched bar. This pub caters for drinkers of all ages and features live music. Two function rooms are available for hire. Most bus routes to the west of the city pass the door. 🜨(Westgate/Kirkgate)🚌

Hop 🄻

19 Bank Street, WF1 1EH (opp opera house)
☻ 4-midnight (2am Fri); 12-2am Sat ☎ (01924) 367111
🌐 thehop-wakefield.co.uk
Fuller's London Pride; Ossett Silver King, Excelsior, Yorkshire Blonde; guest beers Ⓗ

Converted into a venue for music, comedy and conversation, this Georgian building retains bare brick walls, fireplaces and other original features, along with new additions including a VW camper van converted into a bar. The main bar has nine handpumps, one reserved for a dark beer and one for a Fernandes or Rat Brewery beer; there is also a selection of bottled Belgian beers. Open mic night is on Monday, a quiz on Tuesday, and live music Thursday-Saturday. Rooms are available for private hire. 🚸Q🏵️🜨(Westgate/Kirkgate)⌐🚌

Inns of Court

22 King Street, WF1 2SR (behind town hall)
☻ 11-midnight (1 Fri & Sat) ☎ (01924) 375560
Jennings Bitter; Wychwood Hobgoblin; guest beers Ⓗ

Named after its proximity to the law courts, the pub is surrounded by offices and solicitors' practices. Along with a friendly atmosphere there is a varied clientele, depending on the time of visit. Popular with office staff and students during weekdays, on weekend evenings the jukebox normally plays heavy rock music. Two additional handpumps dispense guest ales from the Marston's range, with the landlord keen to feature as many specials as possible. 🏵️🜨(Westgate)⌐

Wakefield Labour Club (Red Shed) 🄻

18 Vicarage Street, WF1 1QX (at top of Kirkgate turn right, then first left onto Vicarage St)
☻ 11-4 Sat only, 7-11 ☎ (01924) 215626
🌐 theredshed.org.uk
Beer range varies Ⓗ

The Red Shed is an old army hut that has survived the redevelopment of the area. Home to many trade union, community and charity groups, quiz night is Wednesday and live music plays on the second and last Saturdays of the month. There are three rooms; two can be hired for functions. An extensive collection of union plates and badges is displayed over the bar, and CAMRA awards adorn the walls. The beers are usually from micros nationwide. Q🜨(Westgate/Kirkgate)♣🐾P⌐🚌

Wintersett

Angler's Retreat 🄻

Ferry Top Lane, WF4 2EB (centre of village) SE382157
☻ 12-3, 7-11 (not Tue); 12-11 Sat; 12-3.30, 7-10.30 Sun ☎ (01924) 862370
Acorn Barnsley Bitter; Samuel Smith OBB; guest beers Ⓗ

Rural ale house that is an increasingly rare example of an old-fashioned, no frills community pub. There is a loyal local clientele, with many old pitmen and many old tales to be told. Close to the Anglers Country Park, Haw Wood and the TransPennine Trail, it is also frequented by birdwatchers, walkers, cyclists and bikers. There are benches and a garden for fine-weather drinking, with a large car park opposite. Due to its isolated location it may close early if trade is slow.
🚸Q🏵️🍴♣P⌐🚌(194,195,196)

It warms in winter, in summer opes the pores,
'Twill make a Sovereign Salve 'gainst cuts and sores:
It ripens wit, exhillerates the mind,
Makes friends of foes, and foes of friends full kind;
It's physical for old men, warms their blood,
Its spirits makes the Coward's courage good:
The tatter'd Beggar being warmed with Ale,
Nor rain, hail, frost, nor snow can him assail,
He's a good man with him can then compare,
It makes a Prentise great as the Lord Mayor;
The Labouring man, that toiles all day full sore,
A pot of ale at night, doth him restore,
And makes him all his toil and paines forget,
And for another day's work, he's then fit.
GM Gent, The praise of Yorkshire ale, 1697

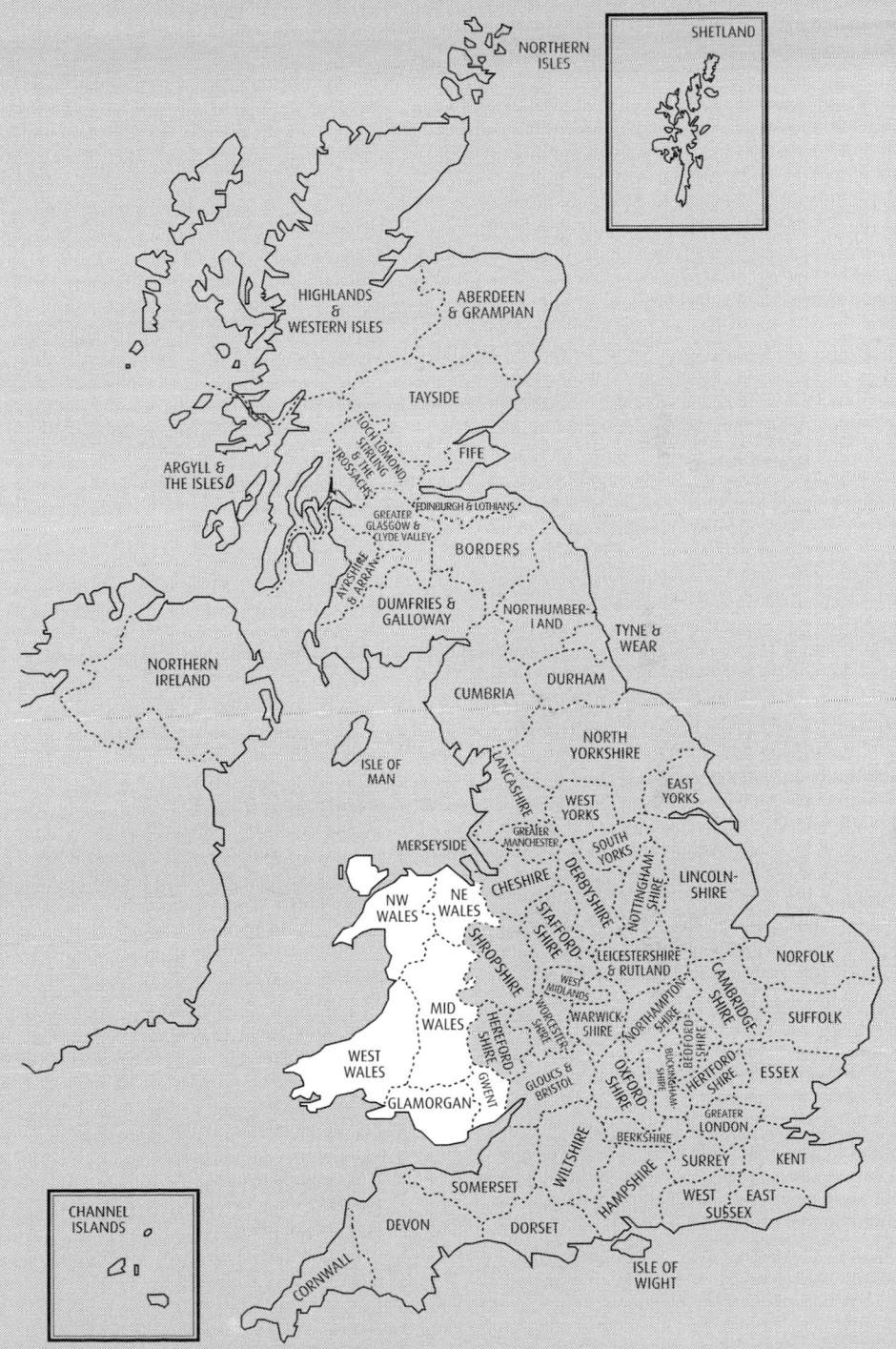

SHETLAND

NORTHERN
ISLES

HIGHLANDS
&
WESTERN ISLES

ABERDEEN
& GRAMPIAN

TAYSIDE

ARGYLL &
THE ISLES

LOCH LOMOND,
THE
TROSSACHS
& STIRLING

FIFE

EDINBURGH & LOTHIANS

GREATER
GLASGOW &
CLYDE VALLEY

BORDERS

AYRSHIRE
& ARRAN

DUMFRIES &
GALLOWAY

NORTHUMBER-
LAND

TYNE &
WEAR

NORTHERN
IRELAND

CUMBRIA

DURHAM

ISLE OF
MAN

NORTH
YORKSHIRE

LANCASHIRE

WEST
YORKS

EAST
YORKS

MERSEYSIDE

GREATER
MANCHESTER

SOUTH
YORKS

CHESHIRE

DERBYSHIRE

NOTTINGHAM-
SHIRE

LINCOLN-
SHIRE

NW
WALES

NE
WALES

SHROPSHIRE

STAFFORD-
SHIRE

LEICESTERSHIRE
& RUTLAND

NORFOLK

WEST
MIDLANDS

CAMBRIDGE-
SHIRE

SUFFOLK

MID
WALES

WORCESTER-
SHIRE

WARWICK-
SHIRE

NORTHAMPTON-
SHIRE

HEREFORD-
SHIRE

BEDFORD-
SHIRE

WEST
WALES

HEREFORD-
SHIRE

BUCKINGHAM-
SHIRE

HERTFORD-
SHIRE

ESSEX

GLAMORGAN

GWENT

GLOUCS &
BRISTOL

OXFORD-
SHIRE

GREATER
LONDON

BERKSHIRE

KENT

WILTSHIRE

SURREY

CHANNEL
ISLANDS

SOMERSET

HAMPSHIRE

WEST
SUSSEX

EAST
SUSSEX

DEVON

DORSET

ISLE OF
WIGHT

CORNWALL

Wales

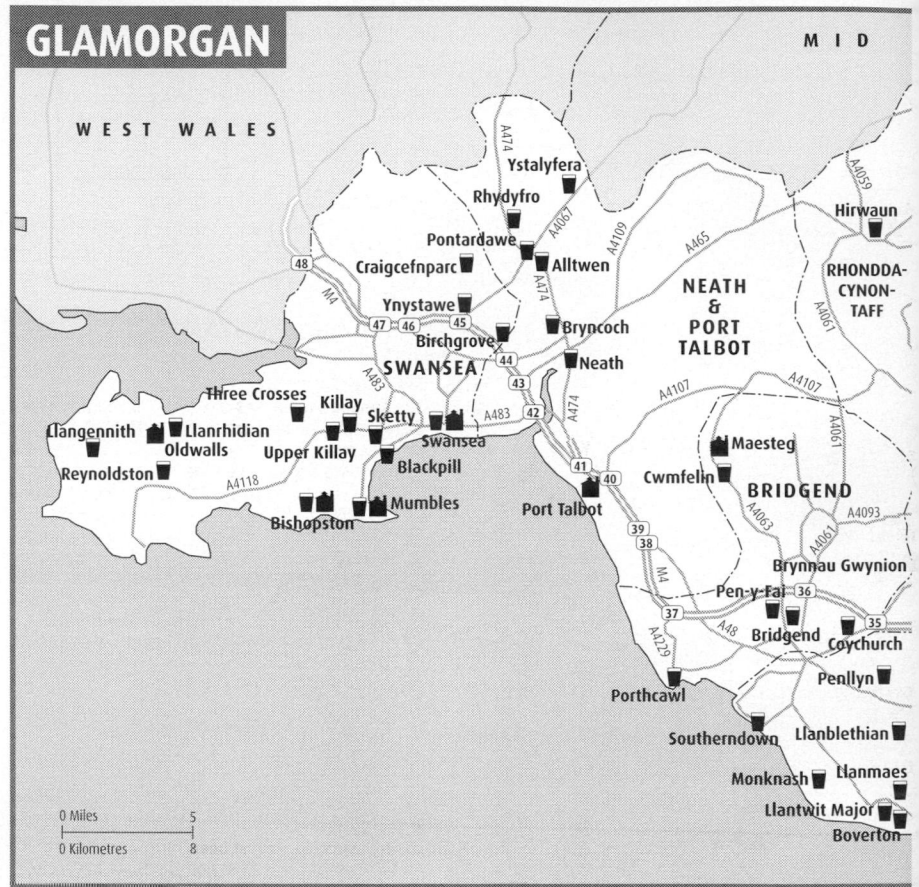

GLAMORGAN

M I D

WEST WALES

Ystalyfera
Rhydyfro
Hirwaun
Pontardawe
Craigcefnparc
Alltwen
RHONDDA-
CYNON-
TAFF
Ynystawe
NEATH
&
PORT
TALBOT
Bryncoch
Birchgrove
Neath
SWANSEA
Three Crosses
Killay
Llangennith
Llanrhidian
Sketty
Oldwalls
Upper Killay
Swansea
Maesteg
Reynoldston
Blackpill
Cwmfelin
BRIDGEND
Bishopston
Mumbles
Port Talbot
Brynnau Gwynion
Pen-y-Fai
Bridgend
Coychurch
Penllyn
Porthcawl
Southerndown
Llanblethian
Monknash
Llanmaes
Llantwit Major
Boverton

0 Miles 5
0 Kilometres 8

Authority areas covered: Bridgend UA, Caerphilly UA, Cardiff UA, Merthyr Tydfil UA, Neath & Port Talbot UA, Rhondda, Cynon & Taff UA, Swansea UA, Vale of Glamorgan UA

Aberdare

Whitcombe Inn
11 Whitcombe Street, CF44 7DA
🟠 12-11.15 ☎ (01685) 875106
Exmoor Gold; Felinfoel Double Dragon; Sharp's Doom Bar; guest beer 🅗
Bustling traditional local with a friendly atmosphere in a valleys terrace, just off the town centre. There is one large bar with a separate pool room. Real fires provide warmth at both ends of the bar. TV sport on several screens can sometimes dominate. Live music plays occasionally. ﹌🚱♣🖵

Alltwen

Butchers at Alltwen
Alltwen Hill, SA8 3BP (off A474)
🟠 12-2.30, 6-11; 12-midnight Fri & Sat; 12-11 Sun
☎ (01792) 863100 ⊕ thebutchersarmsalltwen.co.uk
Beer range varies 🅗
A free house offering a choice of two real ales from the Marston's guest range and occasionally from the Wye Valley Brewery and selected local breweries. The pub has been extensively refurbished to a high standard and offers restaurant-quality food. This is a diners' rather than a drinkers' pub but the ales are well kept, if a little

pricey for the area. The decking outside the pub makes the most of the location, giving a panoramic view of the Lower Swansea Valley.
﹌🚱🌣🌓🕭🚻🖵(122)

Barry

Sir Samuel Romilly 🄻
Romilly Buildings, Broad Street, CF62 7AU
🟠 8am-midnight (1am Fri & Sat) ☎ (01446) 724900
Greene King Abbot; Ruddles Best Bitter; guest beers 🅗
The building has had many incarnations over the years – including a bank, theatre, bingo hall and market hall – before its conversion to a Wetherspoon house in 2009. The spacious split-level venue has a range of comfortable seating inside, and the garden and smoking area is accessed via a door next to the bar. Vale of Glamorgan and Bullmastiff breweries are regularly represented among the beers, along with other Welsh ales. Q🚱🌣🌓🕭🚻♿🖵(94,97A)

Birchgrove

Bowens Arms 🄻
2 Birchgrove Road, SA7 9JR (just off M4 jct 44)
🟠 12-11 (midnight Fri & Sat) ☎ (01792) 324712

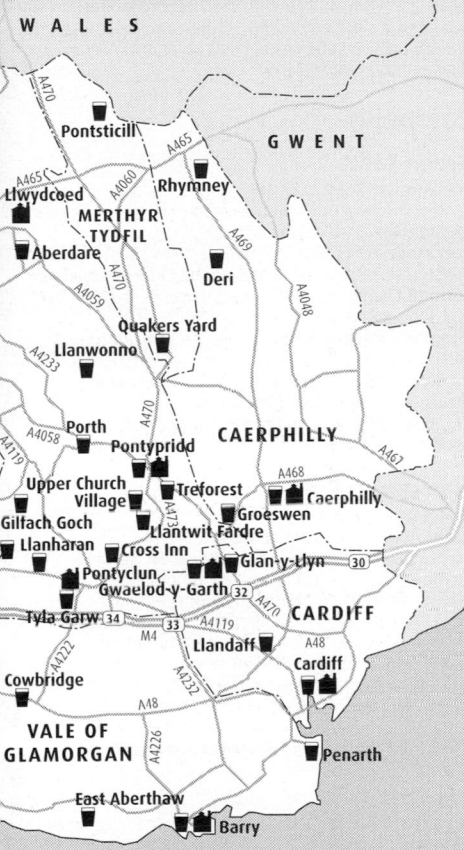

WALES

Pontsticill

GWENT

Llwydcoed Rhymney
MERTHYR
TYDFIL
Aberdare
Deri

Quakers Yard
Llanwonno

Porth
Pontypridd CAERPHILLY
Upper Church
Village Treforest Caerphilly
Gilfach Goch Groeswen
Llanharan Llantwit Fardre
Cross Inn
Pontyclun Glan-y-Llyn 30
Gwaelod-y-Garth 32
Tyla Garw 34 33 CARDIFF
Llandaff
Cardiff
Cowbridge

VALE OF
GLAMORGAN Penarth

East Aberthaw
Barry

Felinfoel Bitter, Double Dragon; guest beer Ⓗ
Comfortable, recently refurbished pub with a separate function room. Outside, there is a play area for children and extensive seating. A games room adjoins the main bar, with a pool table, dartboard and TV sport. Live music plays occasionally during holiday periods and some weekends. Popular with diners, meals are available lunchtimes and evenings Monday-Thursday, all day until 8pm Friday and Saturday, and lunchtimes until 4pm Sunday.
🏵🌑♿♣Pˡ🚲(30,59)

Bishopston

Joiners Arms Ⓛ
50 Bishopston Road, SA3 3EJ
🌑 11.30-11; 3-10.30 Mon-Fri winter; 12-10.30 Sun
☎ (01792) 232658
Courage Best Bitter; Swansea Bishopswood, Three Cliffs Gold, Original Wood; guest beers Ⓗ
Situated in the heart of the village, this 1860s free house is popular with locals and busy in both bars. Home of the Swansea Brewing Company, beer festivals and music events are held occasionally. Good-value food is served lunchtimes and evenings (not Mon and eve Sun). The pub has won several local CAMRA awards. There is a small car park. Opening hours vary in winter so check first.
🏰🏵🌑♿Pˡ🚲(14,114)

Valley
41 Bishopston Road, SA3 3EJ
🌑 12-11 ☎ (01792) 234820
Brains The Rev James; Courage Best Bitter; guest beers Ⓗ
Local CAMRA award-winning country pub set in the heart of the village of Bishopston. The traditional inn has a large porch area leading to a split-level bar and dining area, with exposed beams and a big open fire and hearth. A wide variety of home-cooked meals made using local ingredients is served daily lunchtimes and evenings (until 8pm Sun). 🏰🏵🌑♿♣Pˡ🚲(14)

Blackpill

Woodman
120 Mumbles Road, SA3 5AS (near turn off for B4436)
🌑 12-11; 11.30-10.30 Sun ☎ (01792) 402700
Beer range varies Ⓗ
Local scenes of yesteryear decorate the various rooms of this spacious pub situated between the seafront and the entrance to the beautiful Clyne Gardens. Popular with both families and diners, the pub is also welcoming to those wishing to forego the ubiquitous electronic sounds and screens. A constantly changing range of guest ales is offered. There are three outside seating areas including a small beer garden. Meals are served until 10pm (9.30pm Sun). 🏰Q🏵🌑♿Pˡ🚲(2,3,14)

Boverton

Boverton Castle
311 Eagleswell Road, CF61 1UH
🌑 12-11 (midnight Fri & Sat) ☎ (01446) 678114
⊕ bovertoncastle.co.uk
Sharp's Doom Bar; guest beers Ⓗ
A mile east of Llantwit Major, the Bovy has a large comfortable lounge, a traditional public bar with pool and darts and an upstairs function room. On the landing you can read the legend of the black lady of Boverton Castle. The pub has a reputation for mammoth Sunday lunches and an array of superb curries – food is locally sourced and excellent value. Two varying guest ales are available. Quiz nights are held regularly.
🏰🏵🌑♿🍴♿▲♣Pˡ

Bridgend

Cabo Roche
Five Bells Road, CF31 3HW

WALES

✪ 11 (12 Sat & Sun)-11.30
Sharp's Doom Bar; guest beer Ⓗ
This pub could also be classified as a wine bar, coffee shop and sports bar. Situated near the college, it was a bath and shower showroom until conversion in 2007. Real ales were introduced in 2011. The front has three distinct areas – a café, a bar and a lounge with a deep comfy settee and easy chairs. The clientele ranges from hen parties to ladies taking coffee to barflies, and everyone in between. Lunches are served Monday-Friday and a function room is available. ⏵❀◖&⇌♣Pⁱ–⊟

Coach
37 Cowbridge Road, CF31 3DH
✪ 11.30-11; 12-10.30 Sun ☎ (01656) 649231
Wye Valley Butty Bach Ⓗ; **guest beers** Ⓗ/Ⓖ
This single-bar pub close to Bridgend College continues to uphold the quality of its ever-changing beer list. As well as four beers on handpull, there are often two on stillage behind the bar. Real cider and a large selection of bottled beers from around the world add to the range. Beer festivals are held at Easter and in November, and brewery trips and theme nights are arranged. The unusual pub sign shows the front and rear views of a 1960s Cardiff to Neath coach. ⇌♣◖ⁱ–⊟

Wyndham Arms Ⓛ
Dunraven Place, CF31 1JE
✪ 7am-midnight (1am Fri & Sat) ☎ (01656) 673671
Greene King Abbot; Ruddles Best Bitter; guest beers Ⓗ
Beers from south Wales brewers feature strongly in this town-centre Wetherspoon pub which hosts regular Meet the Brewer nights to promote local cask ales. The building dates from 1792 and is divided into three distinct areas, including a dining space, with seating ranging from high stools to comfortable settees. Accommodation is available in 25 bedrooms. Q⏵⇦◖&⇌◖⊟

Bryncoch

Dyffryn Arms
Neath Road, SA10 7YF (on A474)
✪ 12-11 ☎ (01639) 636184 ⊕ thedyffrynarms.com
Taylor Landlord; Wadworth 6X Ⓗ
A pleasant, clean and well-presented pub. Modern furniture and decor give a light and airy feel. There is a real log fire in a central fireplace and historic photos of the local area displayed on the walls. Food is served until 9pm in the restaurant and bar area. The pub stands on its own in a rural environment but is on the main road to Neath and well served by local buses. ⋈Q❀◖&Pⁱ–⊟(122,132)

Brynnau Gwynion

Mountain Hare
Brynna Road, CF35 6PG (off A473 between Pencoed and Llanharan)
✪ 5-11; 12-10.30 Sun ☎ (01656) 860458
⊕ mountainhare.co.uk
Wickwar BOB, Rite Flanker; guest beer Ⓗ
Family-owned village pub, situated where the Vale of Glamorgan meets the former mining valleys. It has a large lounge bar, a traditional public bar and a pool room. The pub is the proud home of Brynna FC and is unashamedly sport-oriented, welcoming

locals and visitors alike with the friendly banter typical of a close community. It has a popular weekly quiz on Sunday and hosts an annual Ales of Wales festival. ⋈❀⊟&♣Pⁱ–⊟

Caerphilly

Green Lady
Pontygwindy Road, CF83 3HF
✪ 10-11 (midnight Fri); 9am-midnight Sat; 9am-11 Sun
☎ (029) 2085 1510
Beer range varies Ⓗ
Marston's pub situated alongside the old main road north of Caerphilly centre. The interior is modern and spacious, well laid out and comfortably furnished. Three changing beers are sourced from all corners of the Marston's group, complemented by occasional local beers. Lunches and evening meals are served daily (no food Sun eve). Live music features most Friday and Saturday evenings. ⏵❀◖&Pⁱ–⊟(26,50)

Malcolm Uphill
Cardiff Road, CF83 1FQ
✪ 8am (9am Sun)-midnight ☎ (029) 2076 0720
Greene King Abbot; Ruddles County; guest beers Ⓗ
Rhymney Valley's first Wetherspoon outlet celebrates a local motorbike racing champion. Close to the bus and rail interchange, this pub is also handy for the town centre and the renowned castle. One or two guest beers are usually on sale, often from local brewers. Keenly priced food and drink offers apply on certain days. An accessible entrance for wheelchair users is located a few yards from the main door. Q⏵◖&⇌◖ⁱ–⊟

Cardiff

Albany Ⓛ
105 Donald Street, CF24 4TL
✪ 12-11 (10.30 Sun) ☎ (029) 2031 1075
Brains Dark, Bitter, SA, SA Gold; guest beers Ⓗ
This award-winning pub occupies a street-corner plot. Although situated in an area with a large student population, it maintains the feel of a locals' pub, attracting a varied clientele, who come for the quality beer and friendly, lively atmosphere. In the public bar a television screen shows sporting events, while the lounge is quieter, providing the opportunity for conversation. There is an outside covered and heated smoking area, a beer garden and a well-used skittle alley. Q❀◖⊟♣◖ⁱ–⊟(57,58)

Andrew Buchan Ⓛ
Albany Road, Roath, CF24 3LH
✪ 11-10.30
Rhymney Best, Hobby Horse, Dark, Bevans Bitter, Bitter, Export Ale Ⓗ
Recently converted by Rhymney Brewery from a disused shop on a street corner, this is the only regular outlet in Cardiff for the full range of Rhymney beers. The premises features an open fireplace with the brewery moosehead hanging above. There is an upstairs meeting room available free of charge to groups. No food is served but the surrounding cosmopolitan district outside offers a diverse range. ⋈❀◖ⁱ–⊟

Birchgrove
1-3 Birchgrove Road, CF14 1RR
✪ 12-11 (midnight Thu-Sat) ☎ (029) 2031 1319

Brains Dark, Bitter, SA, The Rev James; St Austell Tribute; guest beers 🅷
Busy suburban community pub in a prominent position at a major crossroads. Built in Arts & Crafts style but modernised in recent years, it has retained original features including wood panelling in the public bar and two red-brick fireplaces. The full range of Brain's beers is served together with seasonals and guest ales from family and microbreweries. The pub has a traditional skittle alley, attracts local darts teams, and hosts a Sunday quiz.
🏵️🅓🅓&≈(Heath High/Low Level/Birchgrove)
♣●⁵⁻₩(21,23)

Chapter Arts Centre
Market Road, Canton, CF5 1QE
🕐 12-11 (12.30am Fri; midnight Sat); 12-10.30 Sun
☎ (029) 2030 4400 ⊕ chapter.org
Ringwood Best Bitter; guest beers 🅷
Lying to the west of the city, Chapter is an excellent contemporary café-bar. Up to five guest ales are on offer, some from the Marston's range and some from newer breweries, along with a guest real cider and an almost incomparable range of German and other continental beers. Food is reasonably priced and of good quality. For those who want more, Chapter includes a theatre, two cinemas, performance spaces and an art gallery.
🏵️🅓&Å≈(Ninian Park)●P⁵⁻₩(17,18)

City Arms ⚐ 🅛
Quay Street, CF10 1EA
🕐 11-11 (2am Fri & Sat); 12-10.30 Sun ☎ (029) 2064 1913
⊕ thecityarmscardiff.com
Brains Dark, Bitter, SA, The Rev James; guest beers 🅷
The inspiring range of real ales makes this a must-visit venue. A Brain's pub with a difference, the keen manager is free to order beers as he sees fit, often bringing in an unusual ale or two. A guest cider or perry is also available for those who fancy a change. Occasional festivals and live music nights are hosted. Regular visitors should apply for beer club membership to accrue discount points. A former local CAMRA Pub of the Year.
Q🏵️🅓&Å≈(Central)♣●₩

Cottage 🅛
25 St Mary Street, CF10 1AA
🕐 11-11 (midnight Fri & Sat) ☎ (029) 2033 7195
Brains Dark, Bitter, SA, The Rev James, SA Gold; guest beer 🅷
Built around 1750, the Cottage is one of the oldest inns in Cardiff. Behind an ornate wood and glass frontage, it has a long, narrow interior. Offering a warm welcome, this classic Brain's pub serves a full range of the brewery's ales and a guest beer, along with home-cooked food until mid-evening. Decorated with old photographs of the city, this is a convivial retreat on a main street where the nightlife can be hectic. Families are welcome.
🅓≈(Central)₩

Fire Island
17 Westgate Street, CF10 1DD
🕐 10-1.30am ☎ (029) 2023 6091 ⊕ fireislandcardiff.co.uk
Tiny Rebel Beat Box; guest beers 🅷
Fast growing in popularity, this city-centre bar opposite the Millennium Stadium was recently converted from a former social club. The ground floor is open plan and decorated in an industrial style with bare brick walls; the upper floor is quieter and has more luxurious furnishings. Up to

eight guest beers and a cider are served, with an emphasis on newly established craft breweries. The in-house beer is unique to the pub.
🅓&Å≈(Central)●

Goat Major 🅛
33 High Street, CF10 1PU
🕐 12-midnight (6 Sun) ☎ (029) 2033 7161
Brains Dark, Bitter 🅷, SA 🅖; guest beers 🅷
Situated opposite the entrance to Cardiff Castle, this pub is popular with visitors to the city. It is named after the keeper of the goat – the mascot of the Royal Regiment of Wales. A rare outlet for gravity-dispensed SA, the range of beers frequently includes brews from Brains. Home-made pies with imaginative tasty fillings are a speciality. There are tables and chairs outside on the pavement.
🏵️🅓≈(Central)₩

Half Way 🅛
247 Cathedral Road, Pontcanna, CF11 9PP
🕐 12-11.30 (midnight Fri); 10-midnight Sat; 12-11 Sun
☎ (029) 2066 7135
Brains Dark, Bitter, SA, The Rev James, SA Gold; guest beers 🅷
Managed by an enthusiastic licensee, this busy open-plan establishment has a large central bar and three drinking and dining areas to choose from. Real fires add warmth and character, and the pub has a genuine, comfortable feel to it. Popular with a mixed clientele, it has the added attraction of a full range of Brain's beers and guest ales, with a beer festival hosted in late summer. There is a traditional skittle alley. 🏚️🏵️🅓&Å♣⁵⁻₩

Mochyn Du
Sophia Close, Pontcanna, CF11 9HW
🕐 12-11 (midnight Fri & Sat); 12-10.30 Sun
☎ (029) 2037 1599 ⊕ ymochyndu.com
Vale of Glamorgan Cwrw'r Mochyn Du, Cwrw Cymru; guest beers 🅷
Located near Glamorgan County Cricket ground, this large, attractive free house is just a short walk from the city centre. It hosts regular Welsh-themed events and is frequented by a varied clientele including Welsh speakers. The conservatory provides a smart and comfortable atmosphere in which to enjoy the home-cooked food. The large decked areas outside offer pleasant surroundings in fine weather. 🏵️🅓&ÅP⁵⁻₩

Pen & Wig
1 Park Grove, CF10 3BT
🕐 11-midnight (1am Fri & Sat); 12-11.30 Sun
☎ (029) 2057 1217 ⊕ penandwigcardiff.co.uk
Beer range varies 🅷
A lively city-centre pub that attracts a mixed clientele of students and professionals – some of the latter, as the name suggests, are from local law firms. It offers a varied beer range which constantly changes, featuring brews from large, micro and local breweries. Free board games and Wi-Fi are available. An extensive garden and covered area for smokers are at the rear of the basically furnished bar.
🏵️🅓&≈(Cathays/Queen St)♣⁵⁻₩(27,35)

Queen's Vaults
Westgate Street, CF10 1EH
🕐 10-11 (midnight Sat); 11-11 Sun ☎ (029) 2022 7966
Brains The Rev James; Felinfoel Double Dragon; guest beers 🅷

Run by local pub company JW Bassett, the pub offers a warm and friendly welcome to all who walk in. As well as the two regular ales, two guest ales are available plus a choice of up to six ciders and perries. A popular place to relax after a day's work or shopping, the pub is usually quiet, although it can be lively when sporting events are shown on the large screen. A reasonably priced daytime carvery is on offer.
❍▷&Å≈(Central)♣●⊟

Rummer Tavern
14 Duke Street, CF10 1AY
✿ 11.30-11 (midnight Fri & Sat); 12-11 Sun
☎ (029) 2023 5091 ⊕ therummertaverncardiff.co.uk
Hancock's HB; Wye Valley HPA; guest beers Ⓗ
The Tavern is located opposite the castle. It features traditional dark wood panelling throughout. There are various seating areas, with a function room upstairs available to hire. The bar is to the rear and stocks three guest ales and a cider in addition to the two regular beers. Food is served until early evening from a traditional menu.
❍▷≈(Central)●⊟

Cowbridge

Vale of Glamorgan Inn
53 High Street, CF71 7AE
✿ 11.30-11 (midnight Fri & Sat); 12-11 Sun
☎ (01446) 772252
Greene King Abbot; Hancock's HB; Wye Valley HPA, Butty Bach; guest beer Ⓗ
Cosy, single-roomed pub in the vibrant main street of this small market town. The wooden-floored bar area is warmed by a real fire; venture in further and more seating can be found. A large beer garden is situated to the rear along a passageway and there is a separate heated smoking area. Lunchtime food Monday to Saturday is good value. A beer festival is held in October as part of the town's food and drink festival.
▲Q✿▷●ᶜ⊟(X2,E11)

Coychurch

White Horse
Church Terrace, CF35 5HD
✿ 12-11 (midnight Fri & Sat); 12-10.30 Sun
☎ (01656) 652583
Brains Bitter, SA, The Rev James; Morland Old Speckled Hen; guest beer Ⓗ
A friendly pub situated at the western end of Coychurch opposite the parish church of Saint Crallo. The pub serves five real ales alongside a popular all-day menu, and the single L-shaped interior maintains a homely feel. Outside there is a car park accessible by the road to the left of the pub, a garden and a smokers' area.
✿▷&♣●Pᶜ⊟

Craigcefnparc

Rock & Fountain Ⓛ
Rhyddwen Road, SA6 5RA
✿5 (3 Fri & Sat)-11; 12-11 Sun ☎ (01792) 843347
Felinfoel Double Dragon, Stout; guest beer Ⓗ
Friendly local situated on the side of a steep hill close to the RSPB Cwm Clydach bird sanctuary. There is an outside patio area with seating where you can enjoy the view across the valley. The pub has a comfortable lounge featuring pictures of local

interest and pub memorabilia, with a separate games bar for pool, darts, dominoes and sport on TV. One rotating guest beer is mainly from a Welsh brewery. ✿⊟♣Pᶜ⊟(121)

Cross Inn

Cross Inn Hotel
Main Road, CF72 8AZ
✿ 12-11 ☎ (01443) 223431
Hancock's HB; Sharp's Doom Bar; Wye Valley HPA; guest beer Ⓗ
This friendly, lively single-roomed pub has a strong local following and offers a warm welcome to visitors. The four handpumps serve three regular and one guest beer. Poker is played on Monday, and curry night is Wednesday. Sunday lunches are excellent value and very popular – booking is advised. ✿▷♣Pᶜ⊟

Cwmfelin

Cross Inn
Maesteg Road, CF34 9LB (on A4063)
✿ 11.45-midnight (1am Fri & Sat) ☎ (01656) 732476
⊕ cerddinbrewery.co.uk
Cerddin Solar, Cascade; Wye Valley Butty Bach; guest beers Ⓗ
In an area where good real ales are hard to find, this friendly multi-roomed pub with its own green-energy-run Cerddin Brewery is a breath of fresh air. Winner of the local CAMRA Pub of the Year 2013, the pub is situated between Maesteg and Bridgend, with good bus and rail links nearby. Five ales are on handpump, usually including a dark beer, and the brewery's own bottle-conditioned ales are also available at the bar.
Q✿⊟≈(Garth)♣●ᶜ⊟(32)

Deri

Old Club
93 Bailey Street, CF81 9HX
✿5 (12 Sat & Sun)-midnight ☎ (01443) 830278
Beer range varies Ⓗ
A proudly independent public house that makes a virtue of its freedom from tie. Two guest beers are always available, three at weekends. The vast collection of pumpclips on display records an eclectic beer range, with ales mainly from small independent brewers. Handy bus and taxi links can be found at Bargoed station, or it is a leisurely 45-minute stroll or cycle ride along the ex-railway Cwm Darran path. Nearby is Cwm Darran country park and hilltops popular with ramblers and paragliders. Å♣⊟(1)

East Aberthaw

Blue Anchor
CF62 3DD
✿ 11-11; 12-10.30 Sun ☎ (01446) 750329
⊕ blueanchoraberthaw.com
Brains SA; Theakston Old Peculier; Wadworth 6X; Wye Valley HPA; guest beer Ⓗ
A popular and picturesque thatched 14th-century pub run by the same family for over 70 years. A warren of rooms of all sizes with low doors and thick stone walls divides the interior, furnished with an eclectic range of old furniture. There is a highly regarded restaurant upstairs. The guest beer is usually a local brew. Plenty of parking is

available in a small car park to the front and a large car park across the road, and regular buses stop outside. ♨Q✿❀❐☕⊞❀P⁵⊟(X91,145)

Gilfach Goch

Griffin Inn
Hendreforgan, CF39 8YL (down lane off A4093) OS988875
☺ 7 (6 Fri)-11; 12-11 Sat & Sun ☎ (01443) 670379
Brains SA Ⓗ
Although there is usually just one cask ale on offer, this friendly village pub at the end of a country lane is well worth visiting and you can be sure of a warm welcome. It has been in the same family for over 50 years and features many interesting, highly polished artefacts and gleaming brasses. Listed in CAMRA's Real Heritage Pubs of Wales. ♨Q❧✿❀P⁵⊟(150,172)

Glan-y-Llyn

Fagin's Ale & Chop House Ⓛ
9 Cardiff Road, CF15 7QD
☺ 11-11 (midnight Thu & Fri); 12-midnight Sat; 12-10.30 Sun
☎ (029) 2081 1800
Dark Star Hophead Ⓗ; guest beers Ⓖ
Highly regarded free house at the northern end of Taffs Well, popular with all ages. The range of three gravity-dispensed guest ales changes continually, focusing on zesty hoppy brews. Two ciders from Gwynt y Ddraig are also on handpulls. The traditional flagstone floor and log fire are a delight on winter days. Good-value meals are served (no food Sun eve or Mon). Roadside tables form an outside drinking area. Close to the M4 jct 32, the pub is also well served by buses and trains. A regular local CAMRA Pub of the Year finalist. ♨✿❐☕●⁵⊟(26,132)

Groeswen

White Cross Inn
CF15 7UT (overlooking Groeswen Chapel)
☺ 4 (12 Fri)-11; 12-11 Sun ☎ (029) 2085 1332
∰ thewhitecrossinn.co.uk
Beer range varies Ⓗ
With commanding views over Caerphilly, this excellent stone-built pub shares its origins with the chapel next door dating from 1742. Three handpumps offer an ever-changing range, including a dark ale, at very good prices. A local cider is sometimes stocked. The pub hosts diverse events ranging from brewery visits to home-made curry contests. Frequent local buses stop a mile away, and road access is easiest via Nantgarw or Hendredenny, but all routes are narrow. Rhymney Valley Ridgeway Walk passes close by. ♨Q✿♣●P

Gwaelod-y-Garth

Gwaelod-y-Garth Inn ♈
Main Road, CF15 9HH
☺ 11-11 ☎ (029) 2081 0408 ∰ gwaelodinn.co.uk
Wye Valley Bitter; guest beers Ⓗ
Multi award-winning pub in the heart of an attractive village with superb views across the valley. A beer from the on-site Violet Cottage Brewery is usually available alongside up to five other guest ales and a cider. The interior has recently been expanded to utilise a former cellar,

with its own well. There is a very popular dining room upstairs but diners are equally welcome to eat in the bars. Local CAMRA Pub of the Year 2013. ♨Q✿❀❐☕⊞♣●P⁵⊟(26B)

Hirwaun

Glancynon Inn
Swansea Road, CF44 9PH
☺ 11-11; 12-10.30 Sun ☎ (01685) 811043
∰ glancynoninn.co.uk
Greene King IPA, Abbot; guest beer Ⓗ
Imposing pub that is a real ale oasis in the village. The main bar sprawls delightfully over two levels, leading to a well-kept garden. The spacious lounge is popular with diners, attracted by a quality menu offering good food made with local organic produce whenever possible. Lunches are served daily, evening meals Monday to Saturday. Demand is high at weekends (booking advisable). A little off the beaten track, the pub is nevertheless easy to find. ✿❐☕⊞❀P⁵⊟(9)

Killay

Village Inn Ⓛ
5-6 Swan Court, The Precinct, Gower Road, SA2 7BA
☺ 10.30-11.30; 12-11 Sun ☎ (01792) 203311
Evan Evans Warrior; Fuller's London Pride; Taylor Landlord; guest beer Ⓗ
Cosy pub with an L-shaped bar and wood panelling, situated in a small shopping precinct. Home-made food is served until 8pm daily from a wide-ranging, daily-changing menu, both in the bar and separate restaurant (booking advised). The pub offers Sky Sports, holds a quiz on Sunday and Tuesday evenings and hosts occasional chess tournaments and monthly gatherings of a Song Writers Guild. An annual beer festival is held over the Easter weekend. Local CAMRA Pub of the Year 2012. ❐☕❀P⁵⊟(20,21)

Llanblethian

Cross Inn
Church Road, CF71 7JF (on B4270)
☺ 11-11 ☎ (01446) 772995 ∰ crossinncowbridge.co.uk
Hancock's HB; Wye Valley Butty Bach; guest beer Ⓗ
Sixteenth-century pub with a strong local customer base, also popular with visitors. The cosy bar warmed by a log fire is welcoming for walkers; others enjoy the separate lounge/dining room. A recently introduced convenience store is handy for village residents. Guest ales, often locally brewed, vary according to customer preference – hoppy varieties are always in demand – and beer festivals are held. There is real cider in summer. Food, including vegetarian and children's dishes, is well regarded and made using locally sourced ingredients wherever possible. Free Wi-Fi available. ♨❧✿❐☕⊞❀●P⁵⊟(V1)

Llandaff

Butchers Arms
16 High Street, CF5 2DZ
☺ 12-11 (11.30 Fri & Sat) ☎ (029) 2055 1000
Draught Bass; Hancock's HB; Sharp's Doom Bar; Wye Valley Bitter Ⓗ
Originally a butcher's shop, from where it gets its name, this charming local is situated close to the historic Llandaff Cathedral. There are a number of

photographs which adorn the walls, detailing times gone by. Good-quality home cooked food is served during the day. This venue hosts quiz nights and occasional live music events. ⭐🐕🍴🅿🚆

Llangennith

King's Head 🅛
SA3 1HX
✪ 11-11; 12-10.30 Sun ☎ (01792) 386212
⊕ kingsheadgower.co.uk
Gower Brew One, Sampson Jack, Best Bitter, Gold, seasonal beers; guest beers 🅗
A row of three 16th-century stone-built cottages, the pub has been owned and run by the same family for many years. The full range of ales from nearby Gower Brewery is available plus a cask cider. An impressive variety of home-made food is served all day with dishes inspired by fresh local produce. Situated a short distance from the sandy stretches of Llangennith Beach, the pub offers quality 4-star accommodation.
🏨Q🛏🐕🍴🍽️🅿🚆(116)

Llanharan

Turberville Hotel
Chapel Road, CF72 9QA
✪ 12-11.30 (12.30am Fri & Sat) ☎ (01443) 222143
Felinfoel Double Dragon; guest beers 🅗
This two-roomed pub is within yards of the recently reopened Llanharan railway station, as well as several bus routes. Up to four real ales are available on handpumps, and gravity dispensed Draught Bass appears fortnightly. Three real ciders are also frequently on offer. TV sport features in the public bar. Meals are served in the lounge/dining room each evening and curry nights are popular.
Q🐕🍴🍽️🅿🚆(244)

Llanmaes

Blacksmiths Arms 🅛
CF61 2XR
✪ 12-11.30 (10.30 Sun) ☎ (01446) 795996
⊕ blacksmithsarmsllanmaes.co.uk
Brains The Rev James; Hancock's HB; guest beers 🅗
This deservedly popular pub opposite the green hosts a beer festival each summer as part of the village fair. Highly regarded food includes traditional Sunday roasts that change every week, and Tuesday night steaks. Charity quiz nights are held on Wednesday and Sunday. Free Wi-Fi, disabled access throughout and a heated and canopied smoking area help to make this pub a welcoming venue for all. Dog-friendly, too.
🏨Q🐕🍴🅿(V1)

Llanrhidian

Dolphin Inn
SA3 1EH (just off B4295 N Gower Road)
✪ 1 (4.30 Mon)-11 summer; 4.30 (1 Fri & Sat)-11 winter; 12-10.30 Sun ☎ (01792) 391069
Brains The Rev James; Fuller's London Pride; guest beers 🅗
Cosy village pub on the north side of Gower next to a 13th-century church, with stunning views of the estuary from the lovely beer gardens. The characterful single room, warmed by a solid fuel stove, has a welcoming ambience. There is a children's play area at the rear with a fenced area

for rabbits and poultry to roam. Cold snacks are available until 8pm. Check opening times before visiting. 🏨🐕🍴🅿🚆(115,116)

Greyhound Inn 🅛
Oldwalls, SA3 1HA (1 mile W of Llanrhidian on B4295)
✪ 11-11 ☎ (01792) 391027
⊕ thegreyhoundinnoldwalls.co.uk
Gower Brew One, Sampson Jack, Best Bitter, Gold, seasonal beers; guest beers 🅗
Traditional 19th-century inn with a friendly welcome, offering the full range of ales from the pub's on-site microbrewery. An extensive home-cooked bar menu is served until 9pm every day. There is a dartboard and pool table. Outside at the rear is a large beer garden with a children's play area and wonderful views over the Gower countryside. Home of the Halfpenny Folk Club every Sunday evening. Local CAMRA branch Pub of the Year 2013. 🏨🐕🍴🅿🚆(115,116)

Llantwit Fardre

Bush Inn
Main Road, CF38 2EP
✪ 4-midnight (1am Thu); 3-1am Fri; 12-1am Sat; 12-midnight Sun ☎ (01443) 203958
Worthington's Bitter; guest beers 🅗
A welcoming, busy village local offering one regular and up to three guest beers, which can be from any brewer, large or small, with up-and-coming ales noted at the bar. Entertainment includes popular quizzes on Tuesday and Wednesday, open mic sessions on Thursday and a live band on Saturday – all nights can be busy. Pool and darts are played in a separate area.
🐕🍴🅿🚆(100,400)

Crown Inn
Main Road, CF38 2HL
✪ 12-midnight ☎ (01443) 218277 ⊕ freewebs.com/crowninn
Beer range varies 🅗
Bright, friendly pub with a large bar, dining area and function room. At least two guest beers are available, plus a cider from Gwynt y Ddraig made nearby. The pub aims to keep beer costs down and offers a discount on cask ales to CAMRA members. Good food includes traditional and international choices. Live music plays on Friday and Saturday while Sunday is quiz night. A popular beer and cider festival is held in late August. The pub was recently awarded a national prize recognising its charity work. 🏨Q🐕🍴🅿🚆(100,400)

Llantwit Major

King's Head
East Street, CF61 1XY
✪ 11.30-11; 12-10.30 Sun ☎ (01446) 792697
Brains Bitter, SA; guest beers 🅗
A friendly establishment with a warm welcome for locals and visitors alike. Darts and pool teams are based here and sporting events are well supported in the large flagstoned public bar and separate comfortable lounge bar. The licensee is a second-generation tenant, having taken over the pub from his parents. A regular in this Guide for 15 years, the pub holds a number of mini beer festivals throughout the year. Parking is limited, but the town car park is just two minutes' walk away.
🐕🍴🅿🚆

Old Swan Inn

Church Street, CF61 1SB
✪ 12-11 (10.30 Sun) ☎ (01446) 792230 ⊕ oldswaninn.co.uk
Beer range varies Ⓗ
The oldest pub in the historic town of Llantwit Major. Within the 12th-century thick stone walls, a bar and dining room serving traditional pub food sit at the front of the building, while the public bar to the rear is a magnet for younger drinkers, with pool table and jukebox. At least two ales are usually available and four at the weekend, often local. One or two beer festivals are held every summer in the pleasant seating area outside.
🅐Q✿①Ⓖ≉⅄⊞

Old White Hart

Wine Street, CF61 1RZ
✪ 11.30-11 (midnight Fri & Sat); 12-10.30 Sun
☎ (01446) 772558 ⊕ old-white-hart.co.uk
Morland Old Speckled Hen; Wye Valley HPA; guest beer Ⓗ
A beautiful historic pub in the centre of this picturesque town, one of a number of old pubs surrounding the town square. Inside is a typical public bar with a big stone fireplace, while the lounge bar offers quieter surroundings. There is an extensive beer garden to the rear where children are most welcome, accessed through a long narrow passageway – a feature of the pub's original design. Parking outside is very limited but the town car park is nearby. 🅐➤✿➡①Ⓖ≉⊞

Llanwonno

Brynffynon Hotel

CF37 3PH (opp St Gwynnos Church) ST030955
✪ 12-11 (10.30 Sun) ☎ (01443) 790272
⊕ brynffynonhotel.com
Beer range varies Ⓗ
Perched on top of the mountain between the Cynon and Rhondda Fach valleys, this tranquil country inn is well worth the effort to seek out. The lounge has a timeless atmosphere with its relaxing leather couches and log-burning stove. The dining room serves food of an excellent standard (booking recommended). Two guest ales are available at the bar, and regular beer festivals are held throughout the year. A patio offers views of the forest and churchyard. 🅐✿➡①ÅP⅄

Monknash

Plough & Harrow

CF71 7QQ (off B4265 between Wick and Marcross)
SS918705
✪ 12-11 ☎ (01656) 890209 ⊕ ploughandharrow.org
Beer range varies Ⓗ/Ⓖ
Renowned 14th-century pub, originally a monastic farmhouse for Neath Abbey, with many original features remaining. Up to eight real ales are offered, four on handpump and the others direct from casks behind the bar, with local breweries well supported, along with real cider and perry. Good home-cooked food is served, and the large log fires add warmth in winter. The spacious garden is popular, and hosts beer festivals in summer. Local CAMRA Cider Pub of the Year 2013.
🅐Q✿①Ⓖ❀P⅄⊞(145)

Mumbles

Park Inn Ⓛ

23 Park Street, SA3 4AD
✪ 4 (12 Fri-Sun)-midnight ☎ (01792) 366738
Felinfoel Stout; guest beers Ⓗ
A regular local CAMRA Pub of the Year award winner, with five handpumps dispensing an ever-changing range of beers, with particular emphasis on independent breweries from Wales and the west of England. The convivial atmosphere in this small establishment attracts discerning drinkers of all ages, though the games room is particularly popular with younger people. Alongside a fine display of pumpclips are pictures of old Mumbles and its pioneering railway. 🅐Q♣⅄⊞(2,3)

Pilot

726 Mumbles Road, SA3 4EL (on seafront close to pier)
✪ 12-11 (midnight Fri & Sat) ☎ (01792) 369909
⊕ thepilotofmumbles.co.uk
Draught Bass; Taylor Landlord; guest beers Ⓗ
Welcoming and friendly local on the seafront at Mumbles with a good selection of ales on six handpumps. The licensees also plan to brew their own beers. A wide range of bottled ciders is available and hot drinks are also served. The historic pub, built in 1849, is next to the coastal path and popular with lifeboatmen, locals, real ale fans, walkers and cyclists. Dogs are welcome and free Wi-Fi is provided. Q⊞(2B)

Neath

Borough Arms

2 New Henry Street, SA11 1PH (off Briton Ferry road)
✪ 4-11 (8 Mon); 12-11 Sat; 12-8 Sun ☎ (01639) 644902
Draught Bass; guest beers Ⓗ
A traditional pub with a strong local following and a reputation for quality ales. A central bar serves two distinct areas, offering a constantly changing range of up to five beers sourced both locally and nationally. An annual beer festival is held every September. The pub gets very busy on days when Six Nations and Ospreys matches are televised. Local CAMRA Pub of the Year for three consecutive years and well worth the half mile walk from the town centre. Q✿♣≉♣⅄⊞

Smiths Arms Ⓛ

New Road, Neath Abbey, SA10 7DG (off A465 on A4320 to Skewen)
✪ 2 (12 Sun)-11 ☎ (01639) 641770
Neath Firebrick, Witch Hunter Ⓗ
Situated within walking distance of Neath Abbey ruins, the lounge has a convivial feel with an open fire and leather tub chairs while the large original back bar, typical of a Victorian pub, displays crystalware. Sunday is bingo and quiz night and the pub is home to two darts teams. The smoking area, although unheated, is clean and under cover. A regular bus serves the pub to and from the town centre. 🅐✿Ⓖ♣⅄⊞(158)

Pen-y-Fai

Pheasant

Heol Eglwys, CF31 4LY
✪ 11-11.30 (12.30am Fri & Sat) ☎ (01656) 653614
Brains Dark, Bitter, SA, The Rev James Ⓗ
Sitting opposite the village green, the Pheasant is a large converted farmhouse and a rare local outlet for Brains Dark. Very much food oriented but not to

WALES

the detriment of drinkers, there are two bars and a games room with a pool table and dartboard. The pub supports many charity events throughout the year and hosts a Sunday quiz night, Thursday grill night and regular live music. Q ⌂ ⊛ ⏃ ⊕ ⬩ ♣ P ⸌ ⌿

Penarth

Bear's Head
37-39 Windsor Road, CF64 1JD
⊛ 8am-11.30 ☎ (029) 2070 6424
Bullmastiff Son of a Bitch; Greene King Abbot;
Ruddles Best Bitter; guest beers ⊞
A Wetherspoon outlet in the town centre with an extensive open-plan interior including a smaller area upstairs comfortable for families. A clientele of all ages enjoys a variety of up to eight ales, with locally brewed Vale of Glamorgan, Bullmastiff, Celt and other Welsh beers making regular appearances. There is a steady trade most of the week, but it can get busy on Friday and Saturday evenings. The pub's name is a rough English translation of Penarth – pen meaning head and arth meaning bear. Q ⏃ ⬩ ≈ ♣ ⸌ ⌿ (89,92)

Golden Lion
69 Glebe Street, CF64 1EF
⊛ 11-11 (midnight Fri & Sat); 12-10.30 Sun
☎ (029) 2070 1574
Felinfoel Cambrian; guest beers ⊞
A lively JW Bassett community pub situated a short walk from the town centre. Large portions of good-value food are served, with a carvery on Sundays, along with up to three well-kept real ales, often from Vale of Glamorgan Brewery and nearly always from Welsh breweries. Sky Sports is available throughout, even in the small beer garden, and the jukebox has a seemingly infinite number of tracks – it can be noisy at times. The pub has a darts team. ⊛ ⏃ ⬩ ≈ ⸌

Windsor
93 Windsor Road, CF64 1JF
⊛ 9am-11.30 (11 Sun) ☎ (029) 2070 2821
Greene King Abbot; St Austell Tribute; Taylor
Landlord; guest beers ⊞
A large collection of pumpclips on the wall, along with a good range of up to five beers on handpump, are tribute to the landlord's commitment to real ale. The open-plan interior features Welsh rugby and nautical themes, and with background music kept low, the pub is comfortable for conversation. Regular activities include live jazz on Wednesday, unplugged music on Sunday and bingo on Monday in the adjoining function room, which also hosts live music and community events. ⊛ ⏃ ≈ (Dingle Rd) ⸌ ⌿ (92,93,94)

Penllyn

Red Fox
CF71 7RQ (half mile off A48) SS973763
⊛ 12-11 (10.30 Sun) ☎ (01446) 772352 ⊕ redfoxinn.co.uk
Hancock's HB; Tomos Watkins OSB; guest beers ⊞
Popular with the local community and visitors enjoying nearby walks, the Fox has a convivial atmosphere. The restaurant is particularly pleasant, with white linen tablecloths to complement the excellent food and drinks. The main room has a flagstone floor with nooks and crannies and a large log fire. Children are welcome, as are friendly dogs.

There is a large, attractive beer garden, play area and pretty front patio. Quiz and curry night is on the last Thursday of the month.
⌂ Q ⊛ ⏃ ⊕ ⬩ P ⸌ ⌿ (V3)

Pontardawe

Dillwyn Arms Hotel
The Cross, SA8 4EB
⊛ 12-midnight ☎ (01792) 863310 ⊕ dillwynshotel.com
Young's Special; guest beer ⊞
Traditional town-centre pub with 3-star en-suite accommodation. The central bar serves a comfortable lounge and separate restaurant with meal deals on weekdays. The rotating guest ale may be from a local or national brewery. Live music features on Friday and Sunday evenings. A terrace overlooking the river caters for smokers and alfresco drinkers. If quiet, the pub may close early on week nights. ⊛ ⇌ ⏃ ⬩ ♣ P ⸌ ⌿ (120,125)

Pontardawe Inn
123 Herbert Street, SA8 4ED
⊛ 12-midnight ☎ (01792) 447562 ⊕ pontardaweinn.co.uk
Beer range varies ⊞
This centuries-old inn has four separate rooms served by a central bar. A popular venue for musicians for decades, live bands can often be found and there are occasional jamming sessions Thursday to Saturday. An annual beer and music festival features in August plus a number of smaller events during the year. The pub, a vital community focal point, also serves walkers and cyclists from the adjacent national cycling route 43. No food on Sunday evening. Q ⌂ ⊛ ⏃ ⊕ ⬩ ♣ ⊛ P ⸌ ⌿ (120,125)

Pontsticill

Red Cow
CF48 2UN (follow signs for Brecon Mountain Railway)
⊛ 10.30-midnight ☎ (01685) 384828
Wye Valley Bitter; guest beers ⊞
Very welcoming pub where the staff know their beer. Set within the Brecon Beacons National Park, this is a traditional inn with a polished stone floor. It is popular with locals, walkers and visitors to the nearby picturesque Pontsticill reservoirs. The Brecon Mountain Railway is a modest but steep walk away. A few pints here may tempt you to join the unusual Snipers Club – ask at the bar for details. Lunches served until 4pm. ⌂ Q ⏃ ⊛ ⏃ ♣ P ⸌ ⌿ (24)

Pontypridd

Bunch of Grapes Ⓛ
Ynysangharad Road, CF37 4DA (off A4054)
⊛ 11-1am (midnight Sun) ☎ (01443) 402934
⊕ bunchofgrapes.org.uk
Otley O1 ⊞; guest beers ⊞/Ⓖ
Close to the town centre and bus station, this popular pub has distinct seating areas in an open-plan layout. Up to eight ales, usually four from Otley Brewery, are available, plus two ciders or perries. Guest ales are varied and wide ranging. A separate acclaimed restaurant serves locally sourced food with speciality themed nights a feature – booking recommended. There are numerous beer festivals, occasional Meet the Brewer evenings and other imaginative activities. Winner of many CAMRA awards. ⌂ ⊛ ⏃ ♣ ⊛ P ⸌ ⌿

WALES

Llanover Arms
Bridge Street, CF37 4PE (opp N entrance to Ynysangharad Park, off A470)
🌣 12-midnight (11 Sun) ☎ (01443) 403215
Brains Bitter; guest beer Ⓗ
Historic free house dating from the late 18th century, and run by the same family for over a century. Opposite is the war memorial park, and nearby the iconic old bridge and town museum. Internally, the three rooms and passageway each have their own ambience and regular clientele. Old mirrors, paintings and clocks feature throughout. The bus station is five minutes' walk away, and the Taff Trail passes by. ♨Q❀☻☺⇒♣P☒

Patriot Bar
25B Taff Street, CF37 4UA (at N end of main street opposite Iceland)
🌣 10 (12 Sun)-midnight ☎ (01443) 407915
Rhymney Hobby Horse, Dark, Bevans Bitter, Bitter, Export Ⓗ
Owned by Rhymney Brewery, this no-frills bar serves well kept and keenly priced beer to an appreciative and varied clientele. Formerly a shop and known locally as the Wonky Bar, it has a functional and basic interior, although there are plans for refurbishment. Gwynt y Ddraig cider is sometimes available. Convenient for the bus station and situated on the main shopping street, close to Muni Arts Centre, the bar offers a 'husband minding' service! ♿⇒☺☒

Porth

Rheola
Rheola Road, CF39 0LF
🌣 2-midnight; 1-1am Fri; 12-1am Sat; 12-midnight Sun
☎ (01443) 682633
Draught Bass; guest beer Ⓗ
Large, pristine, three-roomed free house situated where the Rhondda Valley divides, and easily accessible by bus or train. The bar can sometimes become loud, but the lounge offers a quiet haven. An extra guest beer is added at the weekend, and all beers are competitively priced. The outdoor smoking area is sheltered. ❀☻⇒♣P☺☒

Porthcawl

Lorelei Hotel
36-38 Esplanade Avenue, CF36 3YU
🌣 5 (12 Sat)-11; 12-10.30 Sun ☎ (01656) 788342
Draught Bass Ⓖ; **Rhymney Export** Ⓗ; **guest beers** Ⓗ
In 18 years of running the hotel, this is the owners' 15th consecutive year in the Guide. Four draught ales and five European keg beers are available, along with cider in the summer months. The hotel is situated just off the esplanade near the Grand Pavilion. The front bar features an old central fireplace and the smaller back bar leads to the garden. Q❀☺♣♦☺☒

Quakers Yard

Glantaff Inn
Cardiff Road, CF46 5AH
🌣 11-4, 6-1am; 11-1am Fri & Sat; 11-midnight Sun
☎ (01443) 410822
Beer range varies Ⓗ
Set above the river, this pub is popular with walkers and cyclists on the nearby Taff Trail. Its

comfortable bar has a collection of historic artefacts and early photographs of the area. Three handpumps serve a varying range, often including local ales. Good-value, good-quality food is available. ◑⇒☺(7,78)

Reynoldston

King Arthur Hotel Ⓛ
Higher Green, SA3 1AD (on village green)
🌣 11 (12 winter)-11; 12-10.30 Sun ☎ (01792) 390775
⊕ kingarthurhotel.co.uk
Kite Gorslas Ale; guest beers Ⓗ
Family-run hotel beside Cefn Bryn on the Gower Peninsula, popular with walkers and riders and a regular wedding venue. It has a cosy interior and a large outdoor drinking area. Food is home cooked using local produce, served lunchtimes and evenings, with bar snacks available until 3pm then from 6pm. Beers can be bought to take out. ♨⇖❀☻◑☺☺P☺☒(118)

Rhydyfro

Travellers Well
76 Commercial Road, SA8 4SL
🌣 3-11; 12-12.30am Fri & Sat; 12-11 Sun ☎ 07757 561568
⊕ thetravellerswell.info
Beer range varies Ⓗ
Recently refurbished and reopened, the Travs has a public bar, lounge and games area. Beers are from Celt/Newmans Brewery and the landlord is keen to introduce more ales from other Welsh micros. Hot and cold snacks, made to order, are available. The pub is situated between the Baran and Gwrhyd mountains and is an ideal base for exploring the area. Carn Llechart stone circle and the 1500 year old Llangiwg Church are worth visiting while in the vicinity. Q❀☻♣P☺

Rhymney

Farmers Arms
Old Brewery Lane, NP22 5EZ
🌣 12-11; 12-3.30, 7-11 Sun ☎ (01685) 840257
Beer range varies Ⓗ
Large, traditional pub and restaurant near the site of the original Rhymney Brewery, recalled in photographs and breweriana. Three rooms, full of individual character, surround a central serving area. Two guest beers from regional and national brewers are usually on. The bar is delightfully restful, with a flagstone floor and real fire. A large function room is available. The pub hosts the local Silurian Choir and a popular Thursday quiz night. No food on Sunday and Monday evenings. Rhymney railway station is nearby. ♨Q❀◑⇒♣P

Sketty

Vivian Arms
104 Gower Road, SA2 9BZ
🌣 12-11 (midnight Fri & Sat) ☎ (01792) 516194
Brains Bitter, SA, The Rev James; guest beers Ⓗ
Situated on the main crossroads in Sketty, this spacious pub attracts a wide range of customers young and old. It offers a mixture of seating areas with comfortable sofas and plenty of TV screens throughout showing live sport. Two changing guest beers, frequently from the Brain's craft range, are available alongside the brewery's standards. The pub has a small meeting room and is suitable for

family dining. Meals are served until 9pm (4pm Sun). A quiz is held on Sunday evening.
⊛❶&⅃~🖳(20,21)

Southerndown

Three Golden Cups
CF32 0RW
✪ 12-11 (1am Sat); 12-10.30 Sun ☎ (01656) 880432
⊕ tuskasurf.co.uk/threegoldencups
Sharp's Doom Bar; guest beer Ⓗ
Set half a mile from the Heritage Coast, the area is a popular spot for location filming by TV and film producers. The inn offers a wide range of meals and snacks including daily specials. Camping is now available on site, useful for those enjoying the pub's music festivals in June and September. There is a covered, heated smoking area. A favourite stop-off for walkers, the pub also welcomes dogs and families. Pool and darts are played in the bar, and there is a traditional lounge.
⋈Q⅄⊛❶⊟▲♣P⅃🖳(145)

Swansea

Bank Statement
57/58 Wind Street, SA1 1EP
✪ 8am-midnight (1am Wed & Thu; 1.30am Fri; 2am Sat)
☎ (01792) 455477
Greene King Abbot; Ruddles Best Bitter; guest beers Ⓗ
A former Midland Bank, sympathetically transformed by Wetherspoon while retaining its original ornate interior. Trading as a Lloyds No.1, the pub is at the heart of the city's popular bar quarter and has a large ground floor with plenty of seating. Popular with all ages, it is particularly busy at weekends. An increased commitment to real ale has resulted in the availability of four guest beers and a cask cider. ❶&~(High St)♥⅃

Brunswick Arms Ⓛ
3 Duke Street, SA1 4HS (between St Helens Rd and Walter Rd)
✪ 11.30-11; 12-10.30 Sun ☎ (01792) 465676
⊕ brunswickswansea.com
Caledonian Flying Scotsman; Courage Best Bitter; Greene King Abbot; Morland Old Speckled Hen Ⓗ; guest beer Ⓖ
Well-run side-street pub with the air of a country inn in the city. Wooden beams and comfortable seating create a traditional, relaxing atmosphere. The walls are adorned with ever-changing displays of artwork, with pictures for sale. Food is available until 7.30pm weekdays, 2.30pm at weekends. A quiz is held on Monday, live music on Sunday, Tuesday and Thursday, augmented by monthly open mic and poetry readings. The guest beer is gravity dispensed, often from a local microbrewery. Cask cider is also available.
⋈❶&♥

No Sign Bar
56 Wind Street, SA1 1EG
✪ 11-11 (1am Fri & Sat); 12-10.30 Sun ☎ (01792) 456300
⊕ nosignbar.co.uk
Brains The Rev James; guest beers Ⓗ
Historic narrow bar established in 1690, formerly known as Mundays Wine Bar and reputedly a regular haunt of Dylan Thomas. The premises has recently been extended, but fortunately the pub's charm has been retained and it continues to offer a

wonderful drinking experience. Quality food and wine are available and there are usually three cask ales on sale. Live acoustic music features on Sunday and local bands play in the extensive Vault basement on Friday and Saturday evenings.
⋈⊛❶&~(High St)⅃

Potters Wheel Ⓛ
85 The Kingsway, SA1 5JE
✪ 8am-midnight (1am Thu-Sat) ☎ (01792) 465113
Greene King Abbot; Ruddles Best Bitter Ⓗ; guest beers Ⓗ/Ⓖ
A city-centre Wetherspoon outlet named after the old pottery industry. The long sprawling bar area has various seating layouts and attracts customers of all ages and backgrounds. A strong connection to the local CAMRA branch is evident from the real ale information board. An interesting selection of guest beers and a commitment to local microbreweries, enhanced by the introduction of casks on back-bar stillage, has boosted the pub's sale of real ales. Cask cider is always available.
❶&~(High St)♥⅃

Queens Hotel Ⓛ
Gloucester Place, SA1 1TY (near Waterfront Museum)
✪ 11-11 (midnight Sat); 12-10.30 Sun ☎ (01792) 521531
Theakston Best Bitter, Old Peculier; guest beers Ⓗ
This vibrant free house is near the Dylan Thomas Arts Centre, City Museum, National Waterfront Museum and marina. The walls display photographs depicting Swansea's rich maritime heritage. The pub enjoys strong local support and home-cooked lunches are popular. Evening entertainment includes a Sunday quiz and live music on Saturday. This is a rare local outlet for Theakston Old Peculier in addition to a seasonal guest beer from a local microbrewery. Beware the bear! ⊛❶&♣⅃

Uplands Tavern
42 Uplands Crescent, Uplands, SA2 0PG
✪ 11-11 (midnight Fri & Sat) ☎ (01792) 458242
Greene King IPA, Abbot; Morland Old Speckled Hen; guest beer Ⓗ
In the heart of Swansea's student quarter, this large, single-room pub is currently enjoying something of a renaissance under its present management, attracting regulars from all walks of life. Another former haunt of Dylan Thomas, commemorated in a separate snug area, it now has a deserved reputation for the quality and variety of its live music. There is a large outdoor drinking area at the front. Quiz night is Wednesday, and major sporting events are screened on TV.
⊛&♣⅃🖳(20,21)

Westbourne
1 Brynymor Road, SA1 4JQ
✪ 11-11.30 (11 Mon; 12.30am Fri & Sat); 12-11 Sun
☎ (01792) 476637 ⊕ westbourneswansea.com
Greene King Abbot; guest beers Ⓗ
Located on the western fringe of the city centre, this street-corner single-bar pub has a refurbished interior. Renowned in the area, it is now the place to go for young and old alike. Four ales are always available – customers are able to request a particular beer on the pub's website. Other enterprising initiatives are the availability of schooner beer measures, takeaway beer containers and loyalty cards. Food is served until 6pm (4pm Sun). A quiz is held on Tuesday evening.
⊛❶&⅃🖳(2,3)

Three Crosses

Poundffald
Tir Mynydd Road, SA4 3PB
☼ 11-midnight ☎ (01792) 873428
Greene King Abbot; Sharp's Doom Bar; guest beer Ⓗ
Traditional village pub with open fires in both the bar and lounge. Dining is in the lounge but meals are also served in the bar lunchtimes and evenings. There is a convivial atmosphere in the bar which has a large quantity of old farming tools and harness items hanging from open wooden beams. Show your CAMRA membership card for a 10p a pint discount. ♨❀✪ ⬭P♿️−♘(21b)

Trefforest

Rickards Arms
61 Park Street, CF37 1SN (100yds N of railway station)
☼ 10-midnight (1am Fri & Sat); 12-midnight Sun
☎ (01443) 402305
Otley 01; guest beer Ⓗ
A firm favourite with students from the nearby university campus, and equally popular with locals. The cosy atmosphere is enhanced by separate drinking spaces including a vaulted cellar and upstairs dining area. Famed for its good-value bar food, the breakfasts are a notable feast. Regular quiz nights and music events are held. Two guest beers are often from the Otley Brewing range, and occasionally another Otley beer stands in for 01.
❀✪➤♣♿️−♘(100,244)

Treforest

Otley Arms
Forest Road, CF37 1SY (on gyratory system)
☼ 11-midnight (1am Sat); 12-midnight Sun
☎ (01443) 402033 ⊕ otleyltd.co.uk
Otley 01, 05 Gold; guest beers Ⓗ
The original Otley family pub, this end-of-terrace local has absorbed adjacent houses. The beer range gives equal prominence to Otley beers alongside two or three guests from micros and occasionally regional breweries. A bustling beer festival is held annually in October. Popular with university students and locals, this establishment is well served by public transport, and easily accessible from Cardiff and many valley towns. Inside, there are a number of drinking areas, and outside, a heated and covered smoking area.
✪➤♣♿️−♘(100,244)

Tyla Garw

Boar's Head ♈
Coedcae Lane, CF72 9EZ (600yds from A473 over level crossing) ST029815
☼ 4-10 Mon; 12-11; 12-10 Sun ☎ (01443) 225400
Beer range varies Ⓗ
Local CAMRA Pub of the Year 2013, with four rooms served by one bar, and up to eight beers on handpump. The range is ever changing, and staff and locals are happy to advise on choices. Two rooms are set aside for dining – book ahead for Sunday lunch. Tuesday steak and Wednesday curry nights are also popular. One or two beer festivals are held each year, with some beers on gravity. Pontyclun station is nearby along a footpath through a small industrial area.
Q❀✪ ⬭➤(Pontyclun)P♿️−

Upper Church Village

Farmers Arms
St Illtyd Road, CF38 1EB
☼ 3-11; 12-midnight Thu-Sat; 12-10.30 Sun
☎ (01443) 205766
Brains The Rev James; guest beer Ⓗ
Single bar village local with pleasant garden areas. A popular quiz is held on Tuesday, and a music night on Thursday. Beer and conversation are the main attractions at other times unless there is rugby on TV, or a choir or two at Christmas. Guest beers range from national brands to unusual choices for the area from independent breweries, often, but not always, including a bitter. No meals on Monday. ♨❀✪➤P♘(11,100)

Upper Killay

Railway Inn Ⓛ
553 Gower Road, SA2 7DS
☼ 12-11 (10.30 Sun) ☎ (01792) 203946
Swansea Deep Slade Dark Mild, Bishopswood Bitter, Three Cliffs Gold, Original Wood; guest beers Ⓗ
A classic multi-roomed locals' pub set in woodlands at the top end of Clyne Valley. The adjacent former railway line now forms part of route 4 of the National Cycle Network. In winter the real fire in the lounge provides welcome warmth and cheer. Traditional cider and at least one guest beer are kept alongside the Swansea Brewing Company beers. Hot pies are available daily. A large area outside hosts occasional barbecues and boules tournaments. ♨❀⬭♣🐾P♿️−♘(20,21)

Ynystawe

Millers Arms Ⓛ
634 Clydach Road, SA6 5AY (on B4603, ½ mile N of M4 jct 45)
☼ 11.30-2, 6 (5 Sat)-11; 12-3, 7-10.30 Sun
☎ (01792) 842614 ⊕ millers-arms.co.uk
Rhymney General Picton; Tomos Watkin OSB; guest beers Ⓗ
Friendly community pub with a highly decorative interior. Busy periods require bookings for meals, which are good value and home-cooked, served in the pub and separate restaurant. In spring a garden nesting box is on CCTV for the twitchers. Occasional brewery trips are run for locals. The pub is on the main bus routes to/from Swansea Valley and on cycle path 43. ❀✪♿️🐾♙P♿️−♘

Ystalyfera

Wern Fawr Ⓛ
47 Wern Road, SA9 2LX
☼ 2-5 (not Mon), 7-11; 6.30-11 Fri; 7-11 Sat; 12-11 Sun
☎ (01639) 843625
Bryncelyn Buddy Marvellous, Oh Boy, Sleeping Giant, seasonal beer Ⓗ
This rare unspoilt village pub is the brewery tap for the award-winning Bryncelyn Brewery whose beer was brewed on site until 2007. A central bar serves both public and lounge areas. An eclectic mix of old industrial mining and domestic artefacts is displayed in the bar together with an old stove nicknamed 'the nuclear reactor'. A popular venue for watching rugby internationals when the pub extends its opening hours. Live music features occasionally. ♨Q❀⬭♣−♘(125)

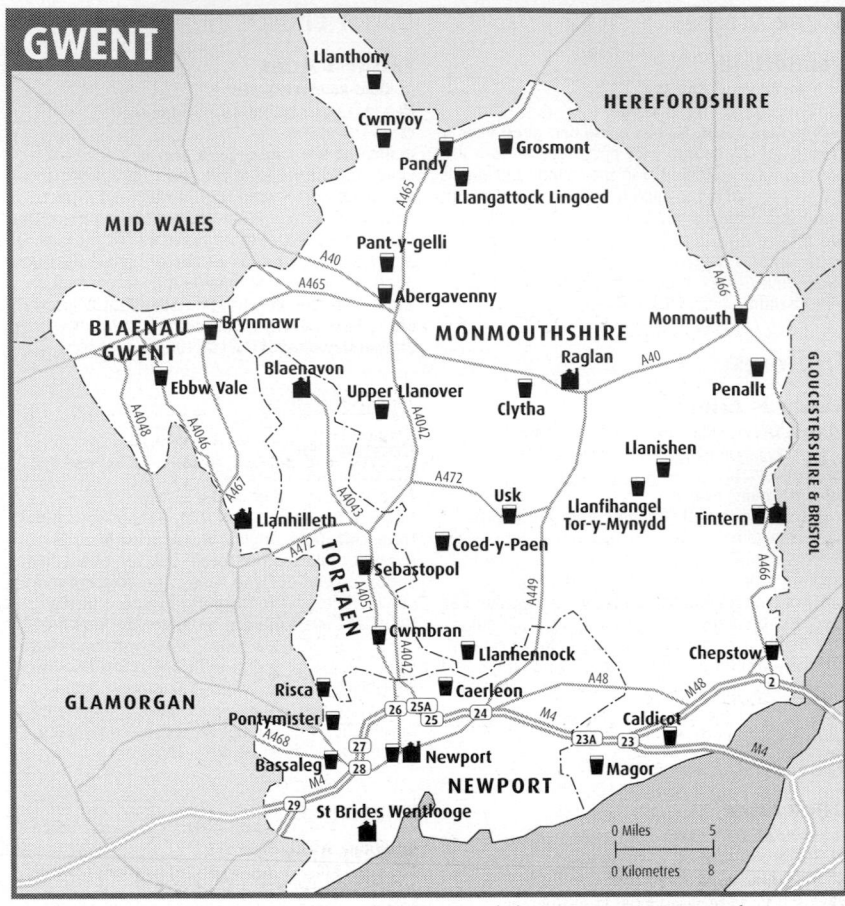

GWENT

Llanthony

HEREFORDSHIRE

Cwmyoy

Grosmont

Pandy

Llangattock Lingoed

MID WALES

Pant-y-gelli

Abergavenny

Monmouth

BLAENAU GWENT

Brynmawr

MONMOUTHSHIRE

Raglan

Penallt

Blaenavon

Ebbw Vale

Upper Llanover

Clytha

GLOUCESTERSHIRE & BRISTOL

Llanishen

Usk

Llanfihangel Tor-y-Mynydd

Tintern

Llanhilleth

Coed-y-Paen

TORFAEN

Sebastopol

Cwmbran

Chepstow

Llanhennock

Risca

Caerleon

Caldicot

Pontymister

GLAMORGAN

Bassaleg

Newport

Magor

NEWPORT

St Brides Wentlooge

0 Miles   5

0 Kilometres   8

Authority areas covered: Blaenau Gwent UA, Monmouthshire UA, Newport UA, Torfaen UA

Abergavenny

Angel Hotel
15 Cross Street, NP7 5EW
☼ 10-2.30, 6-11 (11.30 Fri & Sat); 12-2.30, 6-10.30 Sun
☎ (01873) 857121 ⊕ angelhotelabergavenny.com
Draught Bass; Rhymney Bitter; Wye Valley HPA Ⓗ
Popular and historic hotel with a commitment to cask ale as well as to high-quality food and comfortable accommodation. The bar has a mix of comfortable leather settees and large tables, with a fine log fire during the winter. Two other rooms are off the main bar, each with a distinct character that helps explain this establishment's high reputation. The pub plays a major role in the annual Abergavenny food and drink festival.
ᴁQ☕⊛⛱◑⊟♿⇌P▤(X3,X4)

Grofield Ⓛ
Baker Street, NP7 5BB
☼ 5-11 Mon; 11.30-11.30 ☎ (01873) 858939
Rhymney Bitter; Sharp's Doom Bar; guest beer Ⓗ
Welcoming side-street pub, just opposite the cinema and a short stroll from the main shopping precincts. The lounge bar is decorated with modern artwork, giving it an air of sophistication that distinguishes it from other pubs in town. There is comfortable seating on both sides of the central bar. The policy of trying local ales alongside well-

known brands seems to be reaping rewards, and good-quality bar meals are available. A beer garden is at the rear. Q☕⊛◑⇌♣⇌▤(X3,X4)

Hen & Chickens Ⓛ
7 Flannel Street, NP7 5EG
☼ 10.30-11 (midnight Fri & Sat); 12-10.30 Sun
☎ (01873) 853613
Brains Dark, Bitter, SA, The Rev James, SA Gold; guest beer Ⓗ
Popular pub acquired by SA Brain of Cardiff in 1996. The sale included the neighbouring property which was linked in to create more space. This was controversial but efforts were made to retain as much of the original character as possible. The bar now leads to an adjoining room but the cosy snug and Chicks Parlour remain much the same. The pub continues to sell plenty of real ale while food service has become a significant part of the business. ᴁ☕⊛◑⊟⇌♣P▤(X3,X4)

Station Hotel
37 Brecon Road, NP7 5UH
☼ 5 (2 Wed; 1 Thu)-11; 1-11.30 Fri; 12-11.30 Sat; 11.30-11
Sun ☎ (01875) 854759
Banks's Bitter; Butcombe Bitter; Draught Bass; Wye
Valley HPA; guest beer Ⓗ
One of the few pubs in town that still has a
separate bar and lounge. It retains an air of shabby-
chic – the walls are covered in railway memorabilia
although the line that gives the pub its name has
long gone. This pub has long been a stalwart of real
ale and as a classic town pub it features in CAMRA's
Real Heritage Pubs of Wales. The landlord is a well-
known jazz drummer in south Wales, and hosts
occasional live music. ⬗♣Pᴸ-🚋(X4,X43)

Bassaleg
Tredegar Arms
Caerphilly Road, NP10 8LE
☼ 11-11 (midnight Fri & Sat); 11-11.30 Sun
☎ (01633) 893247
Greene King IPA, Abbot; Morland Old Speckled Hen;
Ruddles Best Bitter Ⓗ; guest beers Ⓖ
This imposing building comprises three distinct
areas. Entering from the main road takes you
straight into the bar. No handpulls are on this side
of the bar – they are all in the lounge. Passing
through takes you past the rear entrance to a large
dining area/conservatory with French doors to the
garden and play area. The main lounge features a
good array of Greene King beers on handpull and
gravity. One or two guests are often available.
Q🏰⚜🍽️ ◗ ⬗♣Pᴸ-🚋(37,50)

Brynmawr
Hobby Horse
30 Greenland Road, NP23 4DT
☼ 12-3, 7-11; 11.30-midnight Sat; 11.30-10.30 Sun
☎ (01495) 310996 ⊕ freewebs.com/hobbyhorseinn/
home.htm
Beer range varies Ⓗ
This well-refurbished local is at the heart of the
community yet only minutes via back streets from
the bus station. Although limited in space, the pub
serves as a popular meeting place, a venue for live
sport on TV, and an eatery offering a good-value
menu. There is also a separate restaurant. Outside,
the west-facing patio is perfect for summer
evenings. Two constantly changing guest ales are
sourced from local breweries as well as from
farther afield. 🏰⚜🍽️ ◗ ⬗♣Pᴸ-🚋(X4,X15)

Caerleon
Bell
Bulmore Road, NP18 1QQ
☼ 12 (11 Sat)-11; 11-10.30 Sun ☎ (01633) 420613
⊕ thebellatcaerleon.co.uk
Beer range varies Ⓗ
Award-winning former coaching inn with low
beams, dating back 400 years. It comprises a
restaurant offering superb food, a cosy fireside bar-
cum-dining area, and a third area mainly for
drinkers. Three real ales rotate quickly, varying
between national and small brewery brands. The
pub is one of CAMRA's top cider outlets and offers
an impressive range of draught ciders and perries.
A pleasant suntrap garden can be found at the rear.
🏰⚜ ◗ ⬗♣Pᴸ-🚋(27,28,29)

Caldicot
Cross Inn
1 Newport Road, NP26 4BG
☼ 11-11 (12.30am Thu-Sat); 12-11 Sun ☎ (01291) 420692
Sharp's Doom Bar; guest beers Ⓗ
This popular pub is adjacent to the iconic Caldicot
Cross war memorial. It has a small bar with games
and a large open-plan room with a central fireplace
and two comfortable seating areas on different
levels. The main room accommodates live bands.
One guest ale is usually sourced from a brewery
from south Wales or the West Country, alongside a
traditional cider. Main bus stops, local shops and
takeaways are just outside.
🏰⚜⬗🍽️➼♣●P🚋(14,74)

Chepstow
Chepstow Athletic Club Ⓛ
Mathern Road, Bulwark, NP16 5JJ (off Bulwark Rd)
☼ 7-11 (11.30 Fri); 12.30-11.30 (12-midnight summer) Sat;
12-4.30, 7 11 Sun ☎ (01291) 622126
Brains SA; Flowers IPA; Rhymney Bitter; guest
beers Ⓗ
Five good-value ales slake the thirsts of customers
enjoying a broad range of sports active and
passive, with rugby to the fore. This is a popular
community venue too, so non-sporty folk (and
CAMRA members) are welcome. Many local
organisations embrace the Athy including
Chepstow Male Voice Choir. The main lounge leads
to a patio where fine-weather drinkers might just
catch some sun and even a well-hit cricket ball.
Upstairs, a large function room also serves real ale.
🏰⚜⬗➼♣Pᴸ-🚋(14,74)

Chepstow Castle Inn Ⓛ
12 Bridge Street, NP16 5EZ
☼ 12-11 ☎ (01291) 630956 ⊕ chepstowcastleinn.co.uk
Bath Gem; Otter Ale; guest beer Ⓗ
Within an arrow's throw of Chepstow's classic
castle, this pub fortifies the thirsty and the hungry
with consistently good beer and pies to delight –
including the popular home-cooked fish pie. A
three-level bar provides a variety of seating
including sofas from which to admire the passing
throng and enduring castle. Acoustic singers,
musicians and their audiences regularly embrace a
raised area towards the rear of the pub and a big
back garden makes for a perfect place for sunshine
times. 🏰🍽️ ◗ ➼♣🚋(14,74)

Coach & Horses 🍸 Ⓛ
Welsh Street, NP16 5LN
☼ 12-11 (10.30 Sun) ☎ (01291) 622626
Brains Bitter, SA, The Rev James; guest beers Ⓗ
This comfortable family-run town-centre pub with
its gently split-level bar focuses on distinctive ales,
particularly light-coloured beers from independent
breweries from all parts of the UK. In summer,
Westons cider complements the regular Brain's
ales. Four ale-based festivals each year embrace
various themes, including a real sausage fest.
Consecutive local CAMRA Town Pub of the Year
awards from 2011 to 2013 reflect the pub's quality
ale consistency. 🏰⚜🍽️➼●ᴸ-🚋(14,74)

Clytha
Clytha Arms Ⓛ
Groesonen Road, NP7 9BW (on B4598 old road
between Abergavenny and Raglan)

✪ closed Mon; 12-3, 6-midnight; 12-midnight Fri-Sun
☎ (01873) 840206 ⊕ clytha-arms.com
Rhymney Bitter; Wye Valley Bitter; guest beers Ⓗ
This former dower house has built an excellent
reputation for good, innovative food – booking is
advised. On the bar you can expect to find an
interesting choice of local beers plus some from
farther afield as well as a range of ciders and/or
perries. The interior perhaps epitomises many
people's vision of what a country inn should look
like. Accommodation is top class and there is a
large area outside with camping available for big
occasions. ♨Q✿☞✿⁂◑●🍴●P⌐♿(83)

Coed-y-Paen

Carpenters Arms

NP4 0TH (aim for Llandegfedd Reservoir, cross the dam,
the pub is about ½ mile on the left) SO986334
✪ closed Mon; 12-3, 6-11; 12-midnight Sat; 12-5 Sun
☎ (01291) 672621 ⊕ thecarpenterscoedypaen.co.uk
Draught Bass; Wye Valley Butty Bach; guest beer Ⓗ
Much extended village pub which retains a good
deal of its original character in the bar and lower
dining area, but now has an additional dining space
and upstairs function room. Food is a good part of
the pub's trade, but it remains popular with locals
and regulars enjoying the ales. A patio and
smoking area overlooks the car park in front of the
pub, with a beer garden and camping area
adjacent. A lovely location close to many outdoor
pursuits. ♨Q✿☿◑●🍴♿AP⌐

Cwmbran

Bush

Graig Road, Upper Cwmbran, NP44 5AN
✪ 4 (12 Thu-Sat)-11.30; 1-11 Sun ☎ (01633) 483764
⊕ thebushuppercwmbran.co.uk
Beer range varies Ⓗ
Charming hillside pub with excellent views over
Cwmbran and beyond. The split-level interior has a
cosy parlour with a coal fire and a gallery of old
pictures of the pub and its surrounds. The raised
area has comfy fireside sofas and games. A
highlight is the popular curry night on Wednesday –
booking advised. The owners' aim was to create 'a
proper pub suitable for all ages... there will be real
ale, real fire and real music'. They seem to have
succeeded. ♨✿◑●♿P⌐(1,8)

Mount Pleasant Ⓛ

Wesley Street, Old Cwmbran, NP44 3LX
✪ 12 (4 Mon)-11 (midnight Fri & Sat) ☎ (01633) 712176
⊕ mountpleasantcwmbran.co.uk
Beer range varies Ⓗ
Situated in old Cwmbran and already popular with
locals, this homely pub has stepped up a gear since
the arrival of innovative licensees who have
attracted people from farther afield. The
comfortable interior is open plan, with a raised
area in the left corner. With a chef at the helm in
the kitchen, you can now enjoy more adventurous
à la carte meals as well as standard pub grub. Two
ever-changing ales usually include one local brew.
✿✿◑●♿P⌐⌐(6,23)

Cwmyoy

Queen's Head

NP7 7NY (leave A465 at Llanfihangel Crucorney, take
lane signed Llanthony, pub is about a mile on right)
SO311221
✪ 11-2.30 (not Tue & Fri), 6-11; 11-3, 6-11 Sat; 12-3, 7-10.30
Sun ☎ (01873) 890241
Beer range varies Ⓗ
A couple of miles along the scenic Llanthony
Valley, the pub is situated in quiet, rolling
countryside much loved by walkers and trekkers,
especially in summer. This old stone-built inn has a
single, stone-flagged bar and beams that reflect its
antiquity. Beers vary but are generally from the
Newman range. Known locally as Billy's, in honour
of the landlord who has presided for over a third of
a century – the longest serving publican in the
county. ♨Q✿◑P

Ebbw Vale

King's Arms Ⓛ

Newchurch Road, Newtown, NP23 5BD
✪ 7 (5 Sat)-midnight; 12-11 Sun ☎ (01495) 352822
Brains The Rev James; guest beer Ⓗ
Comfortable and welcoming two-bar pub perched
above Eugene Cross Park, home of proud valleys
rugby club Ebbw Vale RFC. Opening hours may vary
if a match is on. The guest beer is usually
Wadworth 6X or Sharp's Doom Bar but others put in
an appearance occasionally. A function room is
popular with local societies, while comfortable en-
suite B&B accommodation is available, making this
a convenient place to stay for those visiting the
Brecon Beacons and other local places of interest.
Q✿✿☞✿◑●♿P⌐(X4,22)

Grosmont

Angel Inn

NP7 8EP (on B4347)
✪ 12 (6 Mon & winter Wed)-11 ☎ (01981) 240646
⊕ grosmont.org/group/the-angel-inn
Wye Valley Butty Bach; guest beers Ⓗ
Perched high up, almost on the border with
England, this pub really is the village hub, with lots
of activities taking place. The small bar is to the left
as you enter; the larger area to the right of the
central fireplace is mainly used for dining and
functions. Regular live music events are held,
particularly at summer weekends, and musical
instruments decorate one wall of the bar. Beer and
cider festivals take place in summer and autumn
respectively. ♨✿◑●♿◑●P

Llanfihangel Tor-y-Mynydd

Star Inn Ⓨ

Llansoy, NP15 1DT
✪ closed Mon; 12-3, 6 (5 Sat)-11; 12-4 Sun
☎ (01291) 650256 ⊕ thestarinn.org.uk
Butcombe Bitter; guest beers Ⓗ
This attractive country pub has a public bar styled
on traditional lines while the cosy snug has a
fabulous fireplace as its focal point. The restaurant
is stylish and extends into a conservatory, leading
to the garden and play area. Top-class food is
served, from traditional pub grub to gastro
delights. Tthe pub stays open all day on bank
holidays and during summer. Local CAMRA Pub of
the Year 2012 and 2013. ♨✿◑●♿●P⌐

Llangattock Lingoed

Hunters Moon Inn
NP7 8RR (2 miles off B4521 Abergavenny-Monmouth 'old road' at Llanvetherine at road bridge at end of village) SO363201
✪ closed Mon; 12-2.30 (not Tue-Fri), 6.30-11; 12-3, 7-11 Sun ☎ (01873) 821499 ⊕ hunters-moon-inn.co.uk
Wye Valley HPA Ⓗ, **Butty Bach; guest beer** Ⓖ
Charming, ancient pub lying very close to the long-distance Offa's Dyke Path and historic village church. Two outside drinking areas are the perfect place to enjoy the tranquility on warm days, when the pub attracts many walkers. Inside, within the thick, historic walls, the small bar has stone-flagged floors and beams – and a large screen used mainly on rugby international days. A woodburner provides extra warmth when needed. Ask the landlord about his recent novel.
🏚Q🛏☀🍴🍽🕙&♣P

Llanhennock

Wheatsheaf
Caerleon, NP18 1LT (turn right 1 mile along Usk Road heading N from Caerleon, then bear left at fork) ST353927
✪ 11-11; 12-4, 8-11 Sun ☎ (01633) 420468
⊕ thewheatsheafatllanhennock.webs.com
Fuller's London Pride; guest beers Ⓗ
One of only two pubs in the area to have appeared in the past 25 issues of the Guide, the Wheatsheaf is testament that country pubs can thrive without serving food in the evening. There are bars to the left and right on entering, both full of bric-a-brac, memorabilia and old photographs. The guest beers usually include one from a local brewery. Outside there is a play area and boules is played in the car park, which has fine views north and south.
🏚☀🍴♣P

Llanishen

Carpenters Arms
NP16 6QH
✪ closed Mon; 12-3 (not Tue), 5.30 (6 Tue & Wed; 6.30 Thu)-11; 12-3, 7-11 Sun ☎ (01600) 860812
Wadworth 6X; guest beer Ⓗ
Friendly, warm and welcoming country inn with two seating areas, one with a pool table, separated by a partition, plus a small side room for busier times. Good-value home-cooked meals made with locally sourced produce where possible include excellent curries and seafood. The guest ale is frequently from a south-east Wales brewery, often Kingstone. Two newly built self-catering flats nearby complement this four-centuries-old pub, providing comfortable accommodation for visitors to this wonderfully scenic corner of Gwent.
🛏☀🍴🕙♣P🚲(65)

Llanthony

Priory Hotel
NP7 7NN (turn off A465 Hereford Rd at Llanfihangel Crucorney, turn left next to Skirrid Mountain Inn, continue for about 6 miles) SO288279
✪ 11-3, 6-11 Mon-Fri summer; 11-11 (12-10.30 winter) Sat; 12-10 (4 winter) Sun ☎ (01873) 890487
⊕ llanthonyprioryhotel.co.uk
Felinfoel Double Dragon; guest beer Ⓗ
An extraordinary bar in the former abbot's cellars of what was once a 12th-century priory situated deep in the Black Mountains. Extensive lawned ruins surrounded by steep hillsides create an exquisite backdrop, making it extremely popular with walkers and trekkers, who outnumber locals in the tiny hamlet. Its location makes it a mobile-free zone. The bar is closed during the week in winter and it is advisable to check opening times, but a visit is always well worth the effort.
☀🍴🕙ÅP

Magor

Wheatsheaf Ⓛ
The Square, NP26 3HN
✪ 11-11 (midnight Fri & Sat); 12-11 Sun ☎ (01633) 880608
Beer range varies Ⓗ
Large pub standing at the heart of this attractive des-res area. If you like your pub traditional, with low beams, stonework and wooden floorboards, this is for you. The taproom has games while the lounge has a cosy lived-in feel to it, and a small snug leads to the popular restaurant. Despite beer tie restrictions the range is usually interesting – see the regularly updated list pinned on the wall with details of what's been, what's on and what's to come. 🛏☀🍴🍽&♣●P🚲(14,74)

Monmouth

King's Head Hotel
8 Agincourt Square, NP25 3DY
✪ 7am-midnight (1am Fri & Sat) ☎ (01600) 713417
Greene King Abbot; guest beers Ⓗ
Monmouth, the birthplace of Henry V and Charles Rolls (of Rolls Royce fame), has many historic buildings including this old hotel. Many original features have been incorporated into an excellent restoration that includes a family room with a Royal Stuart theme. The hotel retains the ambience of an old building with historic pictures, artwork and many books in a number of dining and drinking areas. A choice of ales is offered alongside one or two local ciders.
Q🛏☀🍴🍽&Å●🚲(60,416)

Newport

Godfrey Morgan Ⓛ
158 Chepstow Road, Maindee, NP19 8EG
✪ 8am-midnight (1am Fri & Sat) ☎ (01633) 221928
Greene King Abbot; Rhymney Best; guest beers Ⓗ
This pleasant Wetherspoon pub was a cinema in a former life, then a bingo hall, before it was transformed into a spacious hostelry. The main bar is reached through a lower entrance area, which opens up into a fairly typical Spoon's environment. As befits its history, there are many photos of former cinema idols on the walls. Outside, there is a patio/smoking area to one side and limited parking at the rear. Q🛏☀🍴&♣●P🚲(8,74)

Red Lion
47 Charles Street, NP20 1JW
✪ 12-11 (10.30 Sun) ☎ (01633) 264398
Beer range varies Ⓗ
Gwent CAMRA branch was founded at this pub 40 years ago in 1974. It is styled as a traditional ale house with wooden casks and beer engines on display, and has a sports theme with a variety of sporting memorabilia dotted around the walls. Two

ales chosen for their popularity among the regulars are selected from the Punch list, which now and again throws up a surprise rare visitor to the area. ▲⊛⊟⇆♣⌐–🖳(1,151)

St Julian Inn
Caerleon Road, NP18 1QA
❂ 11.30-11.30 (midnight Fri & Sat); 12-11 Sun
☎ (01633) 243548 ⊕ stjulian.co.uk
John Smith's Bitter; Wells Bombardier; Young's Bitter; guest beer Ⓗ
This very popular pub, on the fringe of Newport, enjoys a scenic location perched on the bank of the River Usk, giving views over countryside and historic Caerleon with its impressive Roman remains. A central bar serves several adjoining areas – a bar and games room, suntrap riverside balcony, and lounge with wood panelling and fireplace. There is also a downstairs function room-cum-skittles alley. Interesting guest ales are sourced mainly from Welsh and West Country brewers. ⌂⊛⊕◗⊟♣P⌐–🖳(27-29, 60)

Pandy

Rising Sun
Old Hereford Road, NP7 8DL (just off A465 at S end of village)
❂ closed Mon; 12-3 (not Tue-Fri), 7-11; 12-11 Sat & Sun summer ☎ (01873) 890254 ⊕ therisingsunpandy.com
Sharp's Doom Bar; Wye Valley Butty Bach; guest beers Ⓗ
Situated just off the A465, close to Offa's Dyke Path, and set among beautiful rolling fields, this pub has its own campsite (open March-October). There is wheelchair access via the front door or entry direct from the car park. A restaurant/dining area is down a level. The menu of popular dishes is supplemented by blackboard specials, and takeaway meals are also available. Popular ales are sold with periodic changes. The bar has pub games. There are plans for guest accommodation. ▲⌂⊛⊕◗&Å♣P⌐–🖳(X4)

Pant-y-gelli

Crown Inn Ⓛ
Old Hereford Road, NP7 7HR
❂ 12-2.30 (not Mon; 3 Sat), 6-11; 12-3, 6-10.30 Sun
☎ (01873) 853314 ⊕ thecrownatpantygelli.com
Draught Bass; Rhymney Best; Wye Valley HPA; guest beer Ⓗ
A monumental free house and gastro-pub with a wide reputation for the excellence of its beer and food. It features in CAMRA's publication Great British Pubs and has been the subject of several national articles on food and drink. Serving high-quality beer remains at the heart of what this pub is about – the guest beer changes weekly and is always from a Welsh microbrewery. On warm days the garden patio is extremely popular. ▲⌂⊛◗♣P

Penallt

Boat Inn
Lone Lane, NP25 4AJ
❂ 12-11 ☎ (01600) 712615 ⊕ theboatpenallt.co.uk
Wye Valley Butty Bach; guest beers Ⓖ
An attractive and popular riverside nook that exudes charm. Local river scenes adorn one wall including a picture of a steam locomotive hauling a

train across the old railway bridge that continues to overlook the pub. Off the main bar is a smaller room with a few books and table-top games. The appetising menu includes long-established favourite dishes. Up to three ales are served alongside a lip-smacking range of local ciders from both sides of the border. ▲⌂⊛⊕◗⊟♣♠P⌐–🖳(69)

Pontymister

Commercial
Commercial Street, NP11 6BA
❂ 11 (12 Sun)-11.30 ☎ (01633) 612608
⊕ thecommercialpontymister.com
Beer range varies Ⓗ
Busy roadside pub in a thriving valley village. The beers are sourced from an interesting range of breweries, frequently including Newport's newest brewery, Tiny Rebel. The front patio has a retractable awning for protection from the elements while, inside, the large bar is divided broadly into a dining section to the left, a central drinking area and a games area to the right. Several TVs dominate the bar, but are usually muted. There is also a high-quality jukebox. ⌂⊛◗&⇆(Risca & Pontymister)♣–🖳(X15/16,151)

Risca

Fox & Hounds
Park Road, NP11 6PW
❂ 12-midnight (10.30 Sun) ☎ (01633) 612937
Beer range varies Ⓗ
Friendly, old-fashioned village pub set back from the main street through Risca, with views across the park to the hillside beyond. It has just one bar, with a pool table to the right as you enter. A single ale is served, chosen from a wide range and always well kept. The pub is a venue for the local 'corks' team. Outside, there are extensive drinking and smoking areas, some covered. ⊛⇆♣♠P🖳(X15/16,151)

Sebastopol

Open Hearth
Wern Road, NP4 5DR
❂ 11.30-midnight; 12-11.30 Sun ☎ (01495) 763752
Wye Valley HPA; guest beers Ⓗ
Popular canalside pub run by a family who have been at the forefront of the CAMRA and industry-backed campaign to get a fairer deal from pub-owning companies. It has served as a cowman's cottage, wash house and a hotel before becoming the pub it is today. Diners enjoy tasty food in the lounge, washed down with ales carefully selected from a list of popular favourites. An extensive garden with a play area and seating beside the Monmouthshire & Brecon Canal towpath make this a great family-friendly venue in good weather. Last entry is 11pm. ⌂⊛◗⊟♣P⌐–🖳(X3,X24/24)

Sebastopol Social Club Ⓛ
Wern Road, NP4 5DU
❂ 12-11 (midnight Fri & Sat); 12-10.30 Sun
☎ (01495) 763808 ⊕ sebastopolsocial.org.uk
Wye Valley HPA; guest beers Ⓗ
UK CAMRA Club of the Year is just one of many accolades won by this well-run and welcoming club. Enjoy the comfort of the two main rooms and

savour the delights of an interesting range of keenly priced ales sourced from microbreweries UK-wide. Whether you are an active or passive sports person there is plenty of choice with darts, pool and skittles, and lots of sport on TV. There is a function room upstairs and a skittles alley downstairs. ✿❧♣♠P⁺⧠(X3,X24/24)

Tintern

Anchor Inn
NP16 6TE (off A466 at Tintern Abbey)
✪ 9-11; 12-10.30 Sun ☎ (01291) 689582
⊕ theanchortintern.com
Otter Ale; Wye Valley Bitter; guest beers Ⓗ
History flows here as powerfully as the River Wye alongside the pub, particularly in vigorous weather when the Cistercian abbey, just across the road, provides a shelter almost as welcoming as this family-run pub. The monks used the main bar as a cider mill and left behind their massive stone press, now right next to the bar. Four ales are available and one cider, usually Old Rosie. There is a separate restaurant and several seating areas include a capacious garden room.
♨✿❧⦿❧♣P⧠(69)

Wye Valley Hotel
Monmouth Road, NP16 6SQ
✪ 11-3, 6-11; 12-3, 6-10.30 Sun ☎ (01291) 689441
⊕ thewyevalleyhotel.co.uk
Wye Valley Bitter; guest beers Ⓗ
Travellers on water, foot, hoof and wheels from faraway places mingle happily with locals here at the northern end of the village. Outside, the Wye Valley scenery is majestic and competes with the internal view of special and commemorative bottled ales on shelves around this distinctive multi-angled 1930-built pub and hotel. Wye Valley beer is always here (one in winter, often two in summer) and a broad range of food is available in the main bar and adjoining restaurant.
♨✿❧⦿❧♣P⧠(69)

Upper Llanover

Goose & Cuckoo Ⓛ
NP7 9ER (turn off A4042 at sign to Upper Llanover at end of Llanover village, then follow hand-written signs)
SO292073
✪ closed Mon; 11.30-3, 7-11; 11.30-11 Fri & Sat; 12-10.30 Sun ☎ (01873) 880277 ⊕ gooseandcuckoo.com
Beer range varies Ⓗ
Originally the New Inn, Goose and Cuckoo were the nicknames of a couple who ran the pub in the 19th century. It once served workers at nearby lime kilns and charcoal-burning sites. Today you can enjoy a charming, unspoilt country pub where a real fire adds to the cosiness of a time-warp interior. An old piano in the corner of the room acts as a repository for tourist information and books. Occasional beer and cider festivals are held. ♨Q✿❧⦿❧♣P⁺

Usk

King's Head Hotel
18 Old Market Street, NP15 1AL
✪ 11-11 (10.30 Sun) ☎ (01291) 672963
Fuller's London Pride; Greene King Abbot; Taylor Landlord Ⓗ
A popular village pub with the main bar likely to be as full of diners enjoying the locally produced food as drinkers. There is another dining room as well as a large function room. The bar features a roaring fire in winter, and the walls are adorned with hunting and fishing memorabilia. A modestly sized car park is opposite. The pub was awarded a certificate in 2012 celebrating 25 unbroken years in the Guide. ♨Q❧⦿♣P⧠(60,63)

Reading the runes

There are terms and expressions used in the pub trade that need to be translated in to a language understood by consumers.

'Wet pub' doesn't mean the roof leaks but indicates that beer and other alcohols are the main feature, rather than food.

Stillage is a cradle or platform in the pub cellar where casks of beer are stored horizontally while a secondary fermentation takes place.

'Barrel behind the bar' is a widely-used description but usually inappropriate as a barrel is a large 36-gallon container, too big to store at bar level. The correct term for a container for real ale is cask and casks come in several sizes: 4 1/2 gallon pins; nine-gallon firkin; 18-gallon kilderkin; 36-gallon barrels; and 54-gallon hogshead. Hogsheads are rare, though Joseph Holt's brewery in Manchester still uses them. Most pubs use firkins and kilderkins these days. If a cask is used at bar level to serve a seasonal beer such as winter ale, it's likely to be a pin.

Beer 'served by gravity' means it comes straight from the cask and is not drawn by a beer engine and handpump.

'Tight sparkler' is a small device containing a mesh that s screwed to the nozzle of a beer engine operated by a handpump on the bar. The sparkler agitates the beer as it enters the glass and creates the tight, thick head of foam preferred by northern drinkers. If you don't like beer with a northern head, ask the bar staff to remove the sparkler.

'Cask breather' is a system used by a few brewers to prolong the life of cask beer – and it's not acceptable to CAMRA and the Good Beer Guide. Casks are connected to cylinders of carbon dioxide and a demand valve injects gas in to the cask as beer is drawn off. If the gas is absorbed in to the beer, it can become unnaturally gassy.

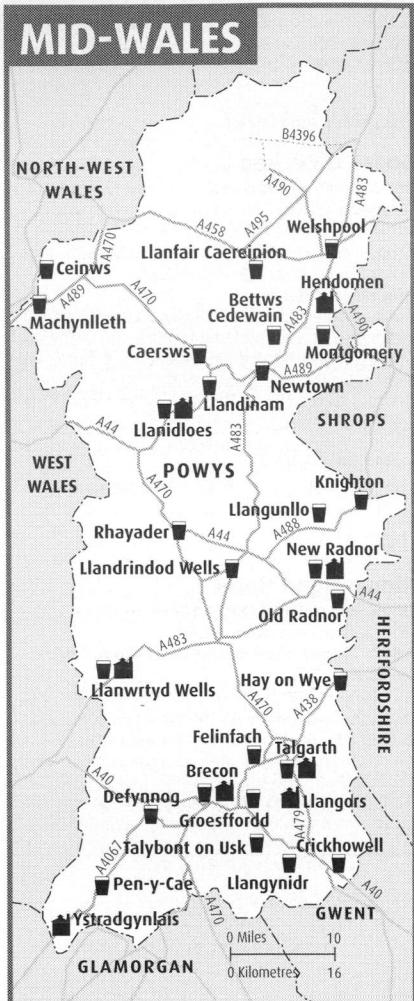

MID-WALES

NORTH-WEST WALES

Welshpool

Ceinws

Llanfair Caereinion

Hendomen

Bettws Cedewain

Machynlleth

Caersws

Montgomery

Newtown

Llandinam

SHROPS

Llanidloes

WEST WALES

POWYS

Knighton

Llangunllo

Rhayader

New Radnor

Llandrindod Wells

Old Radnor

Llanwrtyd Wells

Hay on Wye

Felinfach

Talgarth

Brecon

Defynnog

Llangors

Groesffordd

Talybont on Usk

Crickhowell

Pen-y-Cae

Llangynidr

Ystradgynlais

GWENT

GLAMORGAN

HEREFORDSHIRE

0 Miles 10
0 Kilometres 16

Authority area covered: Powys UA

Bettws Cedewain

Bull & Heifer

SY16 3DS (off B4389)
🌣 11-11.30 (12.30am Fri & Sat) ☎ (01686) 651210
🌐 bullandheifer.co.uk
Sharp's Doom Bar; Tetley Bitter; Wye Valley Butty Bach Ⓗ
A new pub converted from the old village shop to replace the centuries-old New Inn. The owner Bettws Hall has done a tremendous job in creating a pub that offers something for everyone. It has a flagstone floor and wooden beams throughout, with fires in both bars. The back bar has the New Inn's collection of water jugs hanging from the beams. Food is served in the well-presented restaurant. 🏚️🕮🕦🌣♣

Brecon

Brecon Rugby Football Club

63 The Watton, LD3 7EL
🌣 5-11 (midnight Fri); 11-midnight Sat; 11-11 Sun
☎ (01874) 624848 🌐 breconrfc.co.uk

Beer range varies Ⓗ
A founder member of the Welsh RFU, this friendly and welcoming club is open to all. A big main bar and separate lounge are to the front, and a large function room with a screen for sport are to the rear. Outside, the spacious patio garden is home to Brecon Pétanque Club's 16 pistes. Beers from Brecon Brewing and Wye Valley are frequently available plus bottled ciders from Gwynt y Ddraig. The club gets busy during the rugby season, particularly when Wales are playing. Local CAMRA Club of the Year 2013. 🕮🕦🕧🌣♣P꜀⁻🚻

Clarence

25 The Watton, LD3 7ED
🌣 12-midnight (2am Fri & Sat) ☎ (01874) 622810
Wye Valley Butty Bach, Bitter; guest beers Ⓗ
Two-roomed town-centre community pub with a contemporary, welcoming, relaxed atmosphere. The front bar tends to be frequented by locals, while the larger back bar is more popular with diners, and a large screen draws a crowd for big sporting events. The spacious, splendidly equipped garden is a major attraction, especially during the jazz festival. Guest beers are usually sourced from local breweries. 🏚️🕮🕦🕧🌣♣♦꜀⁻🚻♠

Caersws

Red Lion

Main Street, SY17 5EL (on B4569)
🌣 3-11 (midnight Fri, Sat & summer) ☎ (01686) 688023
Beer range varies Ⓗ
Wood-beamed village locals' pub with two bars, attracting a varied clientele of all ages. Early evenings can be busy and boisterous with many villagers calling in on their way home from work. A locally produced beer from Monty's and a local cider are always available plus occasional guests. Outside there is a drinking area and a large car park to the rear. A beer festival is usually held in the car park in summer. 🏚️🕮🕧🍴♣♦P🚻(X75,X85)

Ceinws

Tafarn Dwynant

SY20 9HA (off A487 3 miles N of Machynlleth) SH759059
🌣 5.30 (3 Sat & Sun)-11; closed Mon & winter Sun
☎ (01654) 761660 🌐 tafarndwynant.co.uk
Purple Moose Snowdonia Ale; guest beers Ⓗ
Situated in a quiet village, this friendly community free house is handy for attractions such as the Centre for Alternative Technology. The landlord's own artwork is on display. Occasional mini beer festivals are held and the front patio is used for alfresco drinking. Acoustic live music plays occasionally. The local 34 bus stops near the pub; longer-distance buses stop on the main road, just across the river from the village. 🏚️🕮🕧🛏️꜀⁻🚻(34)

Crickhowell

Bear Hotel
High Street, NP8 1BW
☼ 11-3, 6-11; 7-10.30 Sun ☎ (01873) 810408
⊕ bearhotel.co.uk
Draught Bass; Brains The Rev James; guest beer ⊞
Formerly a 15th-century coaching inn, this is now an award-winning hotel. The multi-roomed bar enjoys grand surroundings with exposed beams, wood panelling and fine settles, and an eclectic selection of furnishings and decorations. There are open fireplaces in both bar rooms and a side room. An excellent and varied food menu is offered, featuring much local produce, to complement the four ales on handpump. The hotel is an ideal base for exploring the Black Mountains and Brecon Beacons National Park. ▲Q❀⊨⍟●⊟&P≟⊒(X43)

Defynnog

Tanners Arms
LD3 8SF
☼ 5 (12 Sat & Sun)-midnight ☎ (01874) 638032
⊕ tannersarmspub.com
Beer range varies ⊞
Originally three separate workers' cottages for the nearby tannery, this is now a fabulous, award-winning, village-centre community pub. An ideal base for exploring the Brecon Beacons, it offers excellent B&B accommodation. The main bar boasts six handpumps, four dispensing an ever-changing range of beers – some local, some from farther afield – with Gwynt y Ddraig ciders on the other two. Excellent food is available to eat in or take away. The large suntrap garden is popular in summer. ▲❀⊨⍟●Å♣♠P⊒(X63)

Felinfach

Griffin ⓛ
LD3 0UB (just off A470 3 miles NE of Brecon)
☼ 12-11.30 ☎ (01874) 620111 ⊕ eatdrinksleep.ltd.uk
Brecon Three Beacons; Monty's Sunshine; Otley 01; Waen Festival Gold ⊞
The Griffin's ethos – the simple things in life done well – says it all. An award-winning country pub, restaurant and hotel, the multi-roomed layout offers discrete areas for drinking and dining. Warmth is provided by a huge fireplace between the bar and main dining area while a full-sized Aga lurks in a side room. The large garden affords superb views of the Brecon Beacons and Black Mountains. Regular beer-themed events are growing in popularity. Listed beers may give way to seasonal ales from the same breweries. ▲Q❀⊨⍟●&P≟⊒(T4,39)

Groesffordd

Three Horseshoes
LD3 7SN
☼ 12-3 (not Mon), 5-11; 12-11 Fri-Sun ☎ (01874) 665672
⊕ threehorseshoesgroesffordd.co.uk
St Austell Tribute ⊞
Busy village pub in the heart of the Brecon Beacons, boasting superb views from both the front and rear outdoor seating areas. The pub is just a 10-minute walk from the Brynich Lock on the Monmouthshire & Brecon Canal, and is a popular stopping off point for boaters and other visitors to the area. Excellent food, sourced locally, is on offer,

and quizzes and various events take place regularly. Brynich Caravan Site and the Brecon YHA are also close by. ▲❀⍟●&Å♣♠P≟⊨

Hay on Wye

Blue Boar
Oxford Road, HR3 5DF
☼ 9 (11 Sun)-11 ☎ (01497) 820884
Taylor Landlord; guest beers ⊞
Family owned and run, this is a comfortable and friendly town-centre pub with oak beams, exposed stonework, two open fires and a separate dining area. Locally sourced and freshly prepared food is available all day. Four handpumps are on the bar, supplying a range of beers from around the country. A great base for exploring the bibliophile's paradise of Hay, as well as for the Hay festivals. ▲Q➰●⊒(39)

Kilvert's ⓛ
The Bull Ring, HR3 5AG
☼ 11-11 (midnight Fri & Sat) ☎ (01497) 821042
⊕ kilverts.co.uk
Brecon Welsh Beacons; Wye Valley Butty Bach; guest beers ⊞
Popular with locals and visitors alike, this award-winning inn has a large beer garden and en-suite accommodation. The focus is on quality beer, with tutored tastings, food pairings, regular Meet the Brewer events and a beer festival. Five handpumps boast ales from near and far, alongside three pumps for ciders from Gwynt y Ddraig and a selection of world beers. Fresh home-made food includes local organic specialities. Tuesday is open mic night and jazz plays on the lawn throughout the summer. ▲❀⊨⍟●&Å♣♠P≟⊒(39)

Knighton

Horse & Jockey
Wylcwm Place, LD7 1AE
☼ 11-11 ☎ (01547) 520062 ⊕ thehorseandjockeyinn.co.uk
Hobsons Best Bitter; Morland Old Speckled Hen; Three Tuns XXX ⊞
Late medieval coaching inn, sprawling around a courtyard. First on the left is a cosy lounge bar, next is a larger public bar, which leads to a pool room. At the end of the courtyard lies an 80-seater restaurant, with letting bedrooms above. Courtyard seating is available for fine weather. The pub is ideally situated for exploring Offa's Dyke Path. The regular beers may be replaced by alternative ales from the same breweries. Book ahead for meals at weekends. ▲Q➰❀⊨⍟●⊟&⟅≟⊒(41,740)

Llandinam

Lion
SY17 5BY (on A470)
☼ closed Mon; 12-midnight (12-3, 6-midnight winter)
☎ (01686) 688233
Sharp's Doom Bar; Three Tuns XXX ⊞
Comfortable, relaxing village hotel with a bar dominated by a large wooden beam and an open stone fire. The hotel is now owned by an award-winning chef and has a large restaurant. The venue is popular and a large selection of bar meals is available (booking advised). There are wooden benches at the rear for outside drinking. The hotel aims to be the hub of the village and families are welcome. ▲❀⊨⍟●P⊒(X75)

WALES

Llandrindod Wells

Conservative Club
South Crescent, LD1 5DH
⊛ 11-2, 5.30-11; 11-11.30 Fri & Sat; 11-10.30 Sun
☎ (01597) 822126
Hancock's HB; Marston's Pedigree; guest beer ⊞
Located in the centre of the historic spa town of Llandrindod Wells, this club is a smart, clean and friendly destination for those wishing to enjoy a quiet drink. Visitors will find a large lounge, TV room, back bar with games room, and front patio. Two snooker tables and a pool table are in the basement. Book ahead for Sunday lunch. Live entertainment features occasionally in the evening. CAMRA members are welcome but non-members must be signed in. Radnorshire CAMRA meetings are held here. Q⊛◖&⇌♣🖵(104,461,462)

Llanfair Caereinion

Goat Hotel
High Street, SY21 0QS (off A458)
⊛ 11-11 (midnight Fri & Sat) ☎ (01938) 810428
Beer range varies ⊞
This excellent inn has a welcoming atmosphere and attracts both locals and tourists. The plush lounge, dominated by a large inglenook with an open fire, has comfortable leather armchairs and sofas, complemented by a dining room serving home-cooked food and a games room at the rear. The choice of three real ales always includes one from the Wood Brewery. ⋈⊛🖛◖♣P

Llangunllo

Greyhound
LD7 1SP (on B4356, off A488)
⊛ 4.30 (1 Sun)-11; 1-1am Sat ☎ (01547) 550400
Beer range varies ⊞
A lovely old-fashioned inn in a picturesque rural setting, this 16th-century cottage is the first pub stop on the Glyndwr's Way National Trail. The owners are bringing it back to life as a community pub. The beers are from Ironbridge, Six Bells and Radnorshire Ales, and ciders include Westons and 1st Quality. An open mic night is held on the first Saturday of the month. Opening times can vary, especially in winter - telephone in advance to check. Dog- and biker-friendly. ⋈⊛⇌♣🍷P¹⁄-🗄

Llangynidr

Red Lion
Duffryn Road, NP8 1NT (off B4558)
⊛ 11-11; 12-10.30 Sun ☎ (01874) 730223
⊕ theredlion1.vpweb.co.uk
Beer range varies ⊞
Popular village local with a warm welcome for walkers, boaters, families and dogs. The beer range changes regularly, sourced from local brewers, as well as from farther afield. Good-value home-cooked food is served in the bar. A separate games area, outside seating and children's play area make this a pub with something for everyone. Regular quiz nights are hosted as well as live music and food themed events. ⋈⊛⊛🖛◖🎺♣P🖵(43)

Llanidloes

Angel Hotel
High Street, SY18 6BY (off A470)
⊛ 11.30-2.30 (not Wed), 5-1am; 12-3, 7-midnight Sun
☎ (01686) 414365
Everards Tiger; Greene King Abbot; Shepherd Neame Bishops Finger; guest beer ⊞
Attractive and friendly edge-of-town pub with two comfortable bars. The larger of the two rooms has a big stone fireplace and old photographs on the wall. The smaller room has an interesting bar inlaid with old pennies. There is a restaurant at the rear that can seat 40 people. The building was built in 1748 and Chartists held meetings here between 1838 and 1839. Outside seating is available at the front of the pub. ⊛◖♣🖵(X47,X75,525)

Crown & Anchor Inn ★
41 Long Bridge Street, SY18 6EF (off A470)
⊛ 11-11; 12-10.30 Sun ☎ (01686) 412398
Brains The Rev James; Worthington's Bitter ⊞
Wonderful, unspoilt town-centre gem with a relaxed and friendly atmosphere, identified by CAMRA as one of Britain's Best Real Heritage Pubs. The landlady has been in charge since 1965 and throughout that time the pub has remained unchanged, retaining its public bar, lounge, snug and two further rooms, one with a pool table and games machine. Serving hatches connect the small end rooms to the bar and there is another hatch to pass drinks into the games room. ⊟♣🖵(X47,X75,525)

Stag
15 Great Oak Street, SY18 6BU (off A470)
⊛ 12 (11 Sat)-12.30am ☎ (01686) 414824
Shepherd Neame Bishops Finger; Snowdonia Purple Moose ⊞
Friendly town-centre pub offering three ales. The long premises is divided in two - the wooden-floored front space has wall seating and a wood-burning stove, the rear area through an archway has comfortable sofas, a pool table and a piano. There is an outside drinking area to the rear. The pub hosts live music on Fridays and Sundays. A real cider is usually on draught. Reasonably priced bar snacks are served and takeaway tea and coffee are available. Dogs welcome. ⋈⊛♣🍷¹⁄-🖵(X47,X75,525)

Llanwrtyd Wells

Neuadd Arms Hotel 🗍
The Square, LD5 4RB
⊛ 9.30am-midnight (1am Fri & Sat) ☎ (01591) 610236
⊕ neuaddarmshotel.co.uk
Heart of Wales Aur Cymreig, Bitter, Noble Eden, Welsh Black, Innstable, seasonal beers ⊞
Imposing Victorian hotel and Heart of Wales Brewery tap. The Bell Bar features a large fireplace and an eclectic mix of furniture. The bells that once summoned servants remain on one wall, along with winners' boards from some of the town's more unusual competitions. The lounge has deep carpets and sofas. The hotel is the centre for many of the town's events, and holds beer festivals in November and January. Nine handpumps dispense ales, with a 10th offering cider. Two or three - usually Welsh - ciders are served from behind the bar. ⋈Q⊛🖛◖⊟▲⇌♣🍷P

Stonecroft Inn
Dolecoed Road, LD5 4RA
✪ 5-midnight; 12-1am Fri-Sun ☎ (01591) 610332
⊕ stonecroft.co.uk
Brains The Rev James; guest beers 🅷
This warm and friendly community pub participates in the town's many and varied festivities – bog-snorkelling, beer and food festivals, real ale rambles and much more. The hostelry has three main areas for drinking, dining and games, plus a large riverside garden. Excellent food complements the fine range of beers. Lodge accommodation is popular with walkers and mountain bikers.
🏨🏮🅰🍴🅿🚃

Machynlleth

White Horse
42 Maengwyn Street, SY20 8DT
✪ 12-3 (not Mon & Tue), 7 (6 Fri)-11.30; 12-11.30 Sat & Sun
Beer range varies 🅷
Friendly locals' pub on the main street of this bustling market town, once the capital of Wales – just across the street, the site of Owain Glyndwr's Parliament House of 1404 now houses a visitor centre. Both bars have open log fires in winter, and there is a pool table. Two real ales are usually on offer, drawn from a wide range of family and microbrewers. The beer garden at the rear affords access for disabled customers. 🏨🕮🅿🚃

Montgomery

Crown Inn
Castle Street, SY15 6PW
✪ 11-11 ☎ (01686) 668533
Brains The Rev James; Wye Valley Butty Bach; guest beer 🅷
The Crown is the last traditional local in a town that once supported a multitude of hostelries. This community-based pub is home to many sports teams and the pub sponsors the town's football team. There is a large array of trophies in one of the rooms opposite the bar. Tall people beware as the beams are very low in the bar area. 🏨🕮🍴🚃

New Radnor

Radnor Arms
Broad Street, LD8 2SP (off A44, 6 miles W of Kington)
✪ 12-2.30 (not Wed), 5-10.30; 12-11 Sat; 12-10.30 Sun
☎ (01544) 350232
Beer range varies 🅷
Set in the Welsh Marches close to the English border, this cosy pub is an ideal base for an away-from-it-all break. The area offers excellent walking, trekking and cycling – Offa's Dyke Walk is nearby. Food is served every day with a popular carvery on Sunday. The beers change on rotation and are mainly from local breweries including Radnorshire Ales. Two Westons real ciders, Ralph's cider and a perry are also available.
🏨🅰🕮🏮🍴🅿🚃(461)

Newtown

Elephant & Castle
Broad Street, SY16 2BQ (off A483)
✪ 11-11 ☎ (01686) 626271 ⊕ elephantandcastlehotel.co.uk
Six Bells Big Nev's; guest beers 🅷

Open-plan town centre hotel next to the River Severn with a number of drinking areas off the main bar. Old photographs and prints adorn the walls, and several TVs show sporting events. There are three beers on offer, two local, usually from Monty's or Six Bells breweries. To the rear is a separate building used for functions. Outside, there is bench seating by the river wall. 🏨🏮🅰🍴🅿

Railway Tavern
Old Kerry Road, SY16 1BH (off A483)
✪ 12-2.30, 6-midnight Mon, Wed & Thu; 11-1am Tue, Fri & Sat; 12-11 Sun ☎ (01686) 626156
Worthington's Bitter; guest beers 🅷
Traditional locals' pub on the edge of the town centre and handy for the railway station. The friendly, welcoming atmosphere and devoted clientele are down to the long-serving landlord and landlady who have been in charge for more than 31 years. The pub is home to a successful darts team and match nights can get busy. Guest beers come from a wide range of independent breweries. Beware the cellar hatch which is right in front of the dartboard. 🏨🍴🚃

Sportsman 🍷 🅻
Severn Street, SY16 2BQ (off A483)
✪ closed Mon; 12-11 (10.30 Sun) ☎ (01686) 623978
Monty's Manjana, Pale Ale, Sunshine, Mischief; guest beers 🅷
This is Monty's brewery flagship pub. Five Monty's beers are usually available alongside a guest ale and two guest ciders, with further additions planned. There are three areas to drink in – the main bar with a brick fireplace and wood-burning stove, a quiet area with comfortable leather seating, and a rear space with slate-tiled floor, pool table and TV. The muted TV in the main bar shows classic children's cartoons and silent comedies. The walls of the bar display Monty's brewing awards. 🏨🕮🍴🏮

Old Radnor

Harp Inn
LD8 2RH (signed off main A44 Kington-Crossgates road)
✪ closed Mon; 12-3, 6-11 (10.30 Sun) ☎ (01544) 350655
⊕ harpinnradnor.co.uk
Beer range varies 🅷
This early 15th-century Welsh longhouse commands a fine view over the Radnor Valley. It was rescued and restored by the Landmark Trust in 1972 and then sold on in 1983. The interior is a tasteful mix of old and new, including a modern restaurant. Beers are sourced from Wales and Welsh Marches microbreweries, including Hobsons, Radnorshire Ales and Wye Valley. The pub holds occasional beer festivals. 🏨🆀🕮🍴🅿

Pen-y-Cae

Ancient Briton 🍷
Brecon Road, SA9 1YY (on A4067 between Ystradgynlais and Dan-yr-Ogof caves)
✪ 12-11 ☎ (01639) 730273 ⊕ ancientbriton.co.uk
Wye Valley Butty Bach; guest beers 🅷
Lovely country pub situated in the Brecon Beacons National Park and recently designated Fforest Fawr Geopark. On entering you are greeted by a welcoming array of 13 handpumps dispensing up to 10 ales, two ciders and a perry. There is an open-plan bar with a real fire and adjoining

restaurant. New facilities for camping and caravanning are available. The pub has won CAMRA local Pub of the Year for the last five years and was South & Mid Wales regional winner in 2011.
♨Q❀🌮◑◐👶♣🐕P⅃🖼(X63)

Rhayader

Cornhill Inn
West Street, LD6 5AB
✪ 4 (12 Sat & Sun)-midnight ☎ (01597) 810029
Marston's Pedigree; Wychwood Hobgoblin; Marston's seasonal beers 🅗
Sixteenth-century inn providing a pub experience sometimes lost in the modern world. A well-used community venue, there are two separate rooms either side of the entrance, one with a log fire in winter, and a beer garden and covered smoking area outside. For many years there was a blacksmith's forge at the rear – now converted into a self-contained holiday cottage. Seasonal beers are from the Marston's/Wychwood stable. The pub hosts occasional live music. ♨❀🌮👶⅃🖼(47,X47)

Talgarth

Tower Hotel 🅛
The Square, LD3 0BW
✪ 4-11; 12-midnight Fri-Sun ☎ (01874) 711253
⊕ towerhoteltalgarth.co.uk
Rotters Utter Rotter, Grounds for Divorce, seasonal beer 🅗
Now refurbished, this bright yet cosy modern establishment has two bars and a real log fire. The pub is the brewery tap for the on-site Rotters Brewery and its beers are offered next to an ever-changing range of guests. A spring beer festival is hosted alongside a bike festival. The large screen shows Sky Sports and is popular for major rugby and football matches. A range of real ciders is also available. ❀🌮◑◐🍴👶♣🐕P⅃🖼(39,39A)

Talybont on Usk

Star Inn ▼ 🅛
LD3 7YX (on B4558 between Brecon and Crickhowell)
SO114226
✪ 11-3, 5-11; 12-11 Sun ☎ (01874) 676635
⊕ starinntalybont.co.uk
Beer range varies 🅗
Large pub alongside the Brecon & Monmouthshire Canal with a spacious garden that is an attraction in summer. The five beers are always an interesting selection, drawn from local breweries and elsewhere. Real cider is also available. Live music evenings are held regularly, and quiz nights are well attended. The excellent food makes good use of local produce. Very popular beer festivals are held in June and October, with other events throughout the year. ♨❀🌮◑◐🍴👶♣🐕🖼(X43)

Welshpool

Royal Oak Hotel
The Cross, SY21 7DG (off A483)
✪ 11.30-11 ☎ (01938) 552217 ⊕ royaloakwelshpool.co.uk
Beer range varies 🅗
A former manor house of the Earls of Powis, the building is now a hotel in the centre of the town trading under the Best Western name. The Oak is most unusual for a three star hotel in that it offers a choice or real ales, albeit at hotel prices – be warned. Up to four beers are available, often from local producers. The hotel has two main drinking areas, a large function room and its own secure car park. ♨Q🌀🌮◑◐👶➡P⅃🖼(X75)

Food for thought

Ale is an enemy to idlenesse, it will worke and bee working in the braine as well as in the Barrel; if it be abused by any man, it will trip up his heeles, and give him either a faire or fowle fall, if hee bee the strongest, stowtest, and skilfullest Wrastler either in Cornwall or Christendome. But if Ale bee moderately, mildly, and friendly dealt withall it will appease, qualifie, mitigate, and quench all striffe and contention, it wil lay anger asleepe, and give a furious man or woman a gentle Nap, and therefore it was rightly called Nappy ALE, by our Learned and Reverend Fore-fathers.

Besides it is very medicinable, (as the best Physitians doe affirme) for Beere is seldom used or applyed to any inward or outward maladies, except sometimes it bee warmed with a little Butter to wash the galled feete, or toes of a weary Traveller; but you shall never knowe or heare of a usuall drinker of ALE, to bee troubled with the Hippocondra, with Hiopocondragacall obstructions or convulsions, nor are they vexed (as others are) with severall paines of sundry sorts of Gowts, such as are the Gonogra, Podegra, Chirocgra, and the lame Hop-halting Sciatica, or with the intollerable griefe of the Stone in the Reines, Kidneys, or Bladder.

Beere is a dutch Boorish Liquor, a thing not knowne in England, till of late dayes an Alien to our Nation, till such time as Hops and Heresies came amongst us, it is a fawcy intruder into this Land, and it s sold by usurpation; for the houses that doe sell Beere onely, are nickname Ale-houses; marke beloved, an Ale-house is never called a Beere-house, but a Beere-House would have but small custom, if it did not falsely carry the name of an Ale-house; also it is common to say a Stand of Ale, it is not onely a Stand, but it will make a man understand, or stand under; but Beere is often called a Hogshead, which all rational men doe knowe is but a swinish expression.

John Taylor (1580-1653), Ale ale-vated into the Ale-titude, 1651

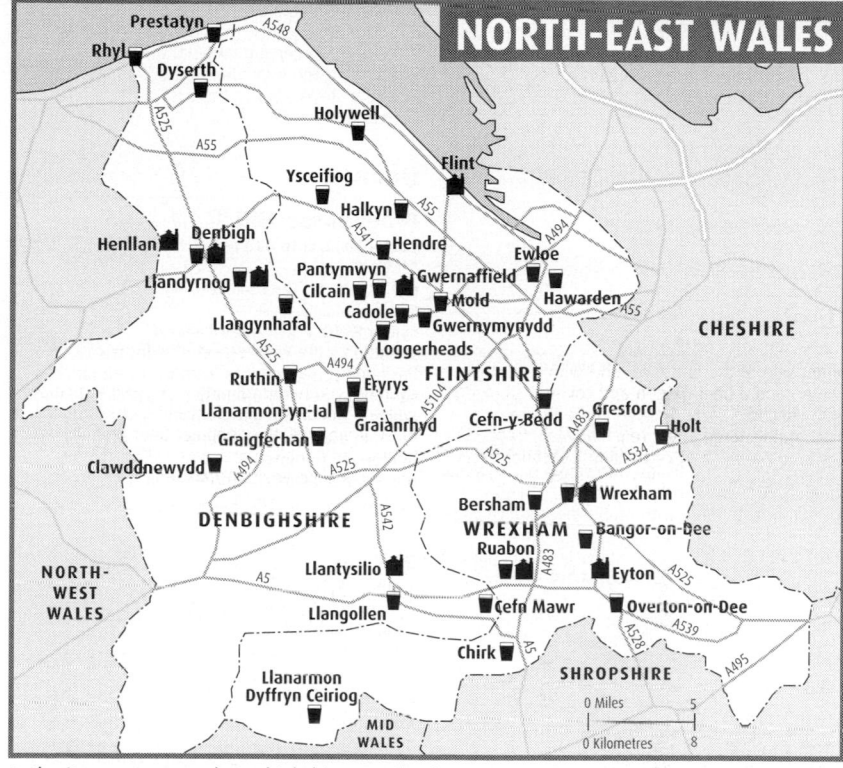

NORTH-EAST WALES

WALES

Authority areas covered: Denbighshire UA, Flintshire UA, Wrexham UA

Bangor-on-Dee

Buck House Hotel 🅛
High Street, LL13 0BU (opp church)
✪ 11.30 (12 Sun)-midnight ☎ (01978) 780336
⊕ buckhousehotel.co.uk
Tetley Mild; guest beers 🅗
This traditional family-run village inn is a hub for the community and local groups regularly meet here. It has a friendly atmosphere and a warm welcome for all. Reasonably priced food is available in the quiet lounge, which has a very large collection of teapots hanging from the ceiling. Unusually, the lobby is home to a red telephone box and an old well. The pub usually hosts two beer festivals a year. On race days the hotel minibus shuttles visitors to and from the racecourse. Q🌣🏵🚪🌗 🕭♣P½🚽

Bersham

Black Lion
Y Ddol, LL14 4HN (near Bersham Heritage Centre)
✪ 11.30-12.30am (1am Fri-Sun); 11.30-midnight Sun
☎ (01978) 365588
Hydes Original Bitter, seasonal beers 🅗
A pub with a real local feel to it – some of the regulars travel a considerable distance to get here. The wood-panelled bar serves two rooms, heated by coal fires in the winter. The pub has a very comfortable and homely feel, with a games room and a children's play area in the garden. Locally sourced but basic food is available all day. Beer and music festivals are usually held in July and October.
🏚🌣🏵🕭♣P½🚽

Cadole

Colomendy Arms
Village Road, CH7 5LL (off A494 Mold-Ruthin road)
✪ 7 (6 Thu; 4 Fri)-11; 2-11 Sat & Sun ☎ (01352) 810217
Beer range varies 🅗
Under the same ownership for over a quarter of a century and in the Guide for almost as the long, the Colly has remained virtually unchanged over the years and retains its unique atmosphere. Situated on the edge of Loggerheads Country Park, it offers an ever-changing selection of ales on six handpumps from both local and more distant independent breweries. Visitors to the Gents should look upwards for items of interest.
🏚Q🏵♣P🚽

Cefn Mawr

Mill 🅛
Mill Lane, LL14 3NL
✪ 12-midnight (1am Fri & Sat) ☎ (01978) 821799

589

Beer range varies Ⓗ
Small, basic, uncommercialised locals' free house within easy walking distance of Llangollen Canal, Trevor Basin and the world-famous Pontcysyllte Aqueduct. The pub is situated down a narrow one-way lane in the lower part of an old industrial village. The smoking area backs on to the original mill stream. Two beers are usually sourced from local micros. There is Wi-Fi and a large-screen TV for sport in the main bar. No food is served.
Q🌢Ⓓ🕭～🚲

Cefn-y-Bedd

Ffrwd
Minera Road, LL12 9TR
✪ closed Mon; 6.30 (12 Fri & Sat)-midnight; 12.30-10 Sun
☎ (01978) 757951
Beer range varies Ⓗ
Compact roadside pub set in a rural area on the edge of a small wooded area and alongside a picturesque stream. Inside, the single bar serves the bar room with an open fire, and a larger restaurant area, both with timber-beamed ceilings. Excellent home-cooked meals are available throughout the day (lunchtime only on Sunday). A TV in the bar area shows most sporting activities.
🚶🌢Ⓓ🕭⇌🍴P～🚲

Chirk

Hand Hotel Ⓛ
Church Street, LL14 5EY
✪ 10.30-11 (midnight Thu-Sat); 12-10.30 Sun
☎ (01691) 773472 ⊕ thehandhotelchirk.co.uk
Stonehouse Station Bitter; guest beer Ⓗ
This old coaching inn in the centre of Chirk is situated on the former Holyhead to London road. A large wooden sculpture of a Welsh dragon presides over the lounge bar. Meals are served in the bar and in the classically styled restaurant. The old brewery building behind the hotel is now converted for functions. An occasional guest beer is available alongside two Stonehouse beers. There is a caravan site nearby. 🚶Q🌢🌢🖂Ⓓ🕭🅿Ⓨ⇌P～🚲

Cilcain

White Horse
The Square, CH7 5NN (signed from A451 Mold-Denbigh road) SJ177651
✪ 12-3, 6-11; 12-11 Sat; 12-10.30 Sun ☎ (01352) 740142
Banks's Bitter; guest beer Ⓗ
Picturesque, whitewashed pub in an attractive village beside the Clwydian range, popular with walkers exploring the nearby Offa's Dyke and Moel Famau. It has a separate, quarry-tiled public bar where prices are lower and both walkers and dogs are welcome. The beers are from the Marston's list, with a regularly changing guest. Four log fires keep the pub warm in winter. Food is served lunchtimes and evenings throughout the week.
🚶Q🌢Ⓓ🕭🅿P～(14C)

Clawddnewydd

Glan Llŷn Ⓛ
LL15 2NA (on B5105) SJ083524
✪ 5-midnight (1am Sat); 12-11 Sun ☎ (01824) 750754
Facer's Flintshire Bitter; guest beers Ⓗ
In the centre of the village, this 16th-century multi-roomed pub acts as a hub for the local community,

and is a meeting place for local football, pool, darts and dominoes teams. The house beer is brewed by Facer's, with a varying range of guest ales. Exposed beams and stonework lend a traditional feel while a central stove adds to the cosy atmosphere.
🚶🌢🌢Ⓓ🕭♣🍴P～

Denbigh

Brookhouse Mill Ⓛ
Ruthin Road, LL16 4RD (off A525 S of Denbigh) SJ072658
✪ 12-3, 6-11.30; 12-11 Sun ☎ (01745) 813377
⊕ brookhousemill.co.uk
Conwy Welsh Pride; guest beers Ⓗ
Situated by the River Ystrad, this former water mill has been converted into a smart restaurant, with a central bar serving a number of satellite dining areas. Upstairs is a conservatory and separate function area. The old mill cogs and wheels can still be seen in the low-beamed interior. Two cask beers are available from local north Wales microbreweries. Q🌢Ⓓ🕭🅿P🚲

Railway
2 Ruthin Road, LL16 3EL SJ059664
✪ 12-midnight (1am Fri & Sat) ☎ (01745) 812376
Purple Moose Glaslyn Ale; guest beer Ⓗ
Named after the defunct Vale of Clwyd Rhyl-Corwen railway line, this unspoilt local is situated half a mile north-east of the town centre and its historic castle built by Edward I. It retains the original five small rooms but with screens showing TV sport throughout. Darts, dominoes and pool are played. A beer from Purple Moose brewery is always available plus one guest. Bus route 51 from Rhyl to Ruthin stops nearby. 🅿♣P～🚲(14,51,76)

Dyserth

New Inn
Waterfall Road, LL18 6ET (on B5119 close to Dyserth Waterfall) SJ054794
✪ 12-11 ☎ (01745) 570482 ⊕ thenewinndyserth.co.uk
Banks's Mild; Marston's Burton Bitter, Pedigree Ⓗ
In the charming village of Dyserth and close to Dyserth Waterfall, this 400-year-old pub, originally a pay house and hostelry for coal miners, now greatly modified, concentrates mainly on food, with seating for 80 diners. The beers are from the Marston's range, with a mild as a regular – rare in this area. There is a pleasant garden. Buses connect to Prestatyn and Rhyl. Q🌢🌢Ⓓ🕭P～🚲(19,35,36)

Eryrys

Sun Inn
Village Road, CH7 4BX
✪ 3.30-11; 1-10.30 Sun ☎ (01824) 780402
Theakston Best Bitter; guest beers Ⓗ
This country pub, close to the village church and located within the Clwydian Range, is also reputedly one of the highest pubs in Wales, set 1148ft above sea level. It has a separate area for diners, with meals served Tuesday to Saturday 5.30-9pm and Sunday lunchtime 1-4.30pm. One or two guest ales are available, usually sourced from local microbreweries. Accommodation is offered in a well-appointed two-bedroom apartment above the pub. 🚶🖂Ⓓ🍴P～

Ewloe

Crown & Liver
The Highway, CH5 3DN (on B5125 ½ mile from A494 intersection)
✪ 12-midnight (2am Fri & Sat) ☎ (01244) 531182
⊕ crownandliverhawarden.co.uk
Jennings Bitter; guest beers ⊞
Comfortable pub diner with a T-shaped bar, 1950s Hollywood theme and an unusual collection of musical instruments on one wall. Drinkers can choose from six handpumps dispensing beers from the Marston's group. A separate room off the main bar has a dartboard and a TV screen. The furnished terrace has a large water feature and smokers' area. Live bands play on Saturdays from 10pm. Beer festivals are held three or four times a year.
✪◑ ⊟⅄≈(Hawarden)♣P⁵⌐⊠

Graianrhyd

Rose & Crown
Llanarmon Road, CH7 4QW (on B5430, off A5104) SJ218560
✪ 4 (12 Fri & Sat)-11; 12-10.30 Sun ☎ (01824) 780727
⊕ theroseandcrownpub.co.uk
Black Sheep Best Bitter; guest beers ⊞
Traditional old rural pub in an area popular with walkers – somewhat isolated but welcoming to the local community and visitors alike. The cosy bar offers two guest ales, usually from local micros or well-established small breweries such as Phoenix and Salopian. Simple good-value food is available made with local produce (no eve meals Mon).
∰Q◑ ⊟♣P⁵⌐

Graigfechan

Three Pigeons Inn
LL15 2EU (on B5429 about 3 miles S of Ruthin) SJ145545
✪ 12-3 (not Mon); 5-11; 12-11 Sat; 12-10.30 Sun
☎ (01824) 703178 ⊕ threepigeonsinn.co.uk
Sharp's Doom Bar; guest beers ⊞
Multi-roomed pub with a spacious dining room and a games room with pool table and darts. The bar offers three changing guest beers, which can be served in earthenware tankards on request. A central lounge area features a well-stocked bookcase, interesting old pictures, posters, brasses, pottery and real fires. Rustic decoration, with oak beams and pew-style seating, adds to the relaxed atmosphere. There are stunning views of the Clwydian Range from the garden. The pub participates in the Route 76 beer festival each July.
∰⅄✪≈◑ ⊟⅄♣●P⁵⌐⊠(76)

Gresford

Griffin Inn
Church Green, LL12 8RG
✪ 4 (7.30 Wed)-11.30; 4-11 Sun ☎ (01978) 852231
Adnams Southwold Bitter; Courage Best Bitter; guest beer ⊞
Friendly community pub built on a site that was a hostelry for pilgrims in the 14th century. The irregularly shaped open-plan bar area has a variety of interesting pictures on the walls. Outside, the lawned area to the side is adjacent to the 15th-century All Saints Church, whose bells are one of the Seven Wonders of Wales. The landlady celebrated 40 years working behind the bar in February 2013. Q✿P⊠

Pant-yr-Ochain ⌷

Old Wrexham Road, LL12 8TY (off A5156, E from A483, follow signs to The Flash)
✪ 11.30-11; 12-10.30 Sun ☎ (01978) 853525
⊕ pantyrochain-griffin.co.uk
Brunning & Price Original Bitter; Flowers IPA; Purple Moose Snowdonia Ale; guest beers ⊞
This magnificent, converted 16th-century manor house is approached via a long sweeping driveway and sits within award-winning landscaped gardens with its own small lake. The pub is well known for its high-quality food, and a fine choice of beers and usually a draught cider is available from the central bar. In summer the lawn is ideal for alfresco dining or relaxing, while in winter you can sit beside the ancient inglenook fireplace or in the large garden room. ∰Q⅄✿✪◑⅄●P

Gwernymynydd

Owain Glyndwr
Glyndwr Road, CH7 5LP
✪ 5-11; 12-10 Sun ☎ (01352) 752913
Thwaites Wainwright; guest beer ⊞
Traditional single-room pub with commanding views over the local countryside. Named after a famous Welsh freedom fighter, an imposing portrait adorns one wall. Elsewhere, there are numerous old photographs depicting village life in times gone by. The small, central bar divides the room into a dining area with a Victorian fireplace on one side and a space with seating and a pool table on the other. Sunday lunch is served and evening meals 5-8pm Thursday to Saturday.
∰⅄✿✪◑⅄P⁵⌐

Halkyn

Blue Bell Inn ⌷
Rhosesmor Road, CH8 8DL (on B5123) SJ209703
✪ closed Tue; 5-11 (midnight Fri); 12-midnight Sat; 12-11 Sun
☎ (01352) 780309 ⊕ bluebell.uk.eu.org
Beer range varies ⊞
Situated on Halkyn Mountain with spectacular views across the Dee Estuary and local countryside, the pub is a winner of many awards, including CAMRA Regional Pub of the Year. The landlords are enthusiastic supporters of real ale and cider. Four beers, two ciders and a perry are available including two house regulars from local brewery Facer's plus ever-changing guests from Welsh micros. The pub is a focal point for the local community, with regular walks, music including Sunday jazz, and a class in conversational Welsh. CAMRA members receive a discount.
∰Q✿◑Å♣●P⁵⌐⊠(126)

Hawarden

Glynne Arms ⌷
3 Glynne Way, CH5 3NS
✪ 11-11 (midnight Fri & Sat) ☎ (01244) 569988
⊕ theglynnearms.co.uk
Beer range varies ⊞
This 200-year-old building owned by the Gladstone family has recently been completely refurbished inside and out. The unusual multi-roomed layout has a central bar serving two distinct rooms, plus a separate restaurant area and intimate side room. A large courtyard at the rear is a boon in warmer weather. Food and beers are sourced as locally as possible, with four rotating ales from local

breweries on offer at any time. Popular with visitors to Hawarden Estate, dogs are permitted in both bar areas. ⌂✿❀◐⚅◧⚏☞P⚌☐

Hendre

Dderwen (Oak) ⃝

Denbigh Road, CH7 5QE (on A541) SJ191677
✪ 7-midnight ☎ (01352) 741466 ⊕ ydderwen-theoak.com
Beer range varies Ⓗ
Roadside pub with a strong community focus. The central bar serves two rooms, each with an impressive pottery collection. Two cask ales are usually available, at least one from a local microbrewery, often a house beer from Hafod. The pub is a popular meeting point for ramblers and visitors to the surrounding countryside, and it hosts a range of social activities. Local CAMRA Pub of the Year 2012. ⚏Q✿❀⚅◧⚏AP⚌☐☐(14)

Holt

Peal o' Bells

12 Church Street, LL13 9JP (400yds S of Holt-Farndon bridge)
✪ 12-midnight (11 Sun) ☎ (01829) 270411
⊕ pealobells.co.uk
Sharp's Doom Bar; Thwaites Wainwright; guest beers Ⓗ
The new tenants of this family-friendly village pub adjacent to St Chad's Church have maintained the high standards set by the previous landlord. Two regular beers are usually supplemented by two changing guest ales, and good-value meals are now available. The bar serves two front rooms and a back room with a dartboard and pool table. The large fully enclosed garden with a small play area has excellent views of the Dee Valley and Peckforton Hills. ⚏⌂✿❀◐⚅❀P⚌☐

Holywell

Market Cross

9-11 High Street, CH8 7LA (on main walkway)
✪ 8-midnight ☎ (01352) 717800
Greene King Abbot; Ruddles Best Bitter; guest beers Ⓗ
Situated at the top of the main street, this town-centre Wetherspoon pub is a welcome conversion of a High Street store. It offers an improving range of real ales, with three regularly changing guests, including beers from Welsh and Wirral microbreweries. Internal decoration includes an interesting display commemorating Flintshire's industrial heritage. ⚏Q⌂⚅☐(X11,11)

Old Wine Vaults ⃝

Cross Street, CH8 7LP (at jct of High St & Cross St)
✪ 10-midnight (2am Fri & Sat) ☎ (01352) 714801
Theakston Best Bitter; guest beers Ⓗ
The open-plan bar has several TV screens showing sport channels; there is also a TV in the enclosed outdoor area. Three handpumps serve the Theakston beer and two Welsh bitters from a national and a microbrewery. The pub has close links with lead mining nearby and was used as a pay office – the safes are still visible. The landlady's family has long-standing connections with the local pub trade. Home to a Sunday League football team. A customer loyalty scheme is provided.
⚌⚌☐(X11,11)

Llanarmon Dyffryn Ceiriog

Hand at Llanarmon

LL20 7LD (end of B4500 from Chirk)
✪ 11-11 (12.30am Fri & Sat); 12-11 Sun ☎ (01691) 600666
⊕ thehandhotel.co.uk
Beer range varies Ⓗ
Family-run, cosy free house, situated in a scenic location at the head of the Ceiriog Valley. There is always one real ale, often from Weetwood, on offer, supplemented by a second from an independent brewery during busy periods. Food and accommodation are of a high standard – it is advisable to book meals at busy times. This dog-friendly pub is popular with walkers. The enthusiastic owners have published a book of local walks. ⚏Q⌂✿❀✿◐⚅◧A❀P⚌☐

Llanarmon-yn-Ial

Raven Inn ⃝

Ffordd-Rhew-Ial, CH7 4QE (signed 500yds W of B5430) SJ191562
✪ closed Mon; 5-10.30 (11 Fri); 12-11 Sat; 12-9 Sun
☎ (01824) 780833 ⊕ raveninn.co.uk
Beer range varies Ⓗ
The Raven has been a pub since 1772. It was rescued from housing developers by the village locals and is run almost entirely by them. Within, it has four drinking areas, one with a tiled floor where walkers and their dogs are welcome. The house beer is brewed by Purple Moose, with two local ales changing constantly; real local cider is also stocked. Local CAMRA Pub of the Year 2011.
⚏Q⌂✿❀◐⚅◧A❀P⚌

Llandyrnog

White Horse (Ceffyl Gwyn)

LL16 4HG (on B5429, adjacent to church) SJ108651
✪ closed Mon & Tue; 12-2 (not Wed-Fri), 5-11 Sat & Sun
☎ (01824) 790582 ⊕ whitehorsellandyrnog.co.uk
Beer range varies Ⓗ
Situated next to the village church in the picturesque village of Llandyrnog, this quiet pub enjoys an excellent reputation for its home-cooked food, with dining areas to the rear and left of the bar. A central bar serves all areas, with comfortable seating available next to the fireplace. The pub participates in the Route 76 inter-pub beer festival in July. ⚏✿❀◐A❀P⚌☐(76)

Llangollen

Abbey Grange Hotel ⃝

Horseshoe Pass Road, Llantisilio, LL20 8DD (1½ miles NW of Llangollen along A542)
✪ 12-11; 12-10 Sun ☎ (01978) 860753
⊕ abbey-grange-hotel.co.uk
Llangollen Bitter, seasonal beers Ⓗ
Hotel, bar and microbrewery complex which was once the home of a local slate quarry owner at the bottom of the Horseshoe Pass. Close by are the evocative ruins of the Cistercian Valle Crucis Abbey dating from the 13th century. Beers from their own brewery are always on sale (only one handpump is on during quiet winter periods) plus their own bottled range. A good selection of reasonably priced food is always for sale. Call to check winter times. ⌂✿❀◐⚅◧A❀P

Ponsonby Arms 🅛

Mill Street, LL20 8RY (near steam railway)
🌣 11-11 (midnight Fri & Sat); 10-11 Sun ☎ (01978) 447985
🌐 ponsonbyarms.com
Purple Moose Snowdonia Ale; Salopian Shropshire Gold; guest beers 🅗

After years of neglect, this Grade II-listed pub is now owned and run as a free house by the team from the nearby Sun. Planned improvements include evening meals and accommodation. Two regular beers and eight guests from microbreweries are on offer, alongside two ciders. Local bottle-conditioned and Belgian beers are stocked plus freshly squeezed orange juice. The extensive riverside garden can be reached by a footpath following the closed railway on the opposite side of the bridge from the restored station. Q⏴🌣◔▲♠P🔑–🕮🖳

Sun Inn

49 Regent Street, LL20 8HN (1 mile E of town centre on A5)
🌣 12 (5 winter)-1am; 12 (3 winter)-2am Fri & Sat; 12 (3 winter)-1am Sun ☎ (01978) 860079 🌐 sunllan.com
Purple Moose Snowdonia; Salopian Shropshire Gold; guest beers 🅗

A superb free house serving up to six changing real ales. The large front room has two small open fires, a games area and a stage. Live music is hosted Wednesday to Saturday evenings. A small snug room at the rear of the bar leads to a covered seating area with a large-screen TV. This characterful room has mirrored panels with an etched design. 🏚🌣♣♠🖳

Llangynhafal

Golden Lion Inn

LL16 4LN (at village crossroads) SJ131634
🌣 closed Mon; 6-11; 4-midnight Fri; 12-midnight Sat; 12-11 Sun ☎ (01824) 790451 🌐 thegoldenlioninn.com
Beer range varies 🅗

Welcoming inn at a village crossroads with an L-shaped counter serving a public bar with a pool table, lounge and dining area. The regularly changing guest beers are often from north Wales microbreweries. The licensees are enthusiastic supporters of the inter-pub Route 76 beer festival each July. The pub was twice voted local CAMRA Pub of the Year. 🏚Q⏴🌣◔🍴◔▲♣♠P🕮(76)

Loggerheads

We Three Loggerheads 🅛

Ruthin Road, CH7 5LH (on A494)
🌣 12-11 ☎ (01352) 810337 🌐 we-three-loggerheads.co.uk
Black Sheep Best Bitter; guest beers 🅗

Popular with Loggerheads Country Park visitors, this split-level pub has a comfortable front bar area and a large restaurant/dining area to the rear. The story behind its unusual name can be found inside and is depicted on a painting above the stairs. Bar meals and a full à la carte menu are available, prepared from produce sourced from local suppliers. The two guest beers usually include one form the local Hafod microbrewery.
Q⏴🌣◔🍴◔▲♠P🔑–🖳(1,2)

Mold

Glasfryn 🅛

Raikes Lane, CH7 6LR (off A5119 ½ mile N of Mold) SJ240649
🌣 11.30-11; 12-10 Sun ☎ (01352) 750500
🌐 glasfryn-mold.co.uk
Flowers Original; guest beers 🅗

Near to Theatre Clwyd and set in its own grounds, this large upmarket pub and restaurant was once the residence for circuit judges attending the nearby court. The house beer is brewed by Phoenix – a total of 12 handpumps supply national and local north Wales beers. Food is served all day.
🏚Q🌣◔🍴♠P🔑–🖳(28,X44)

Gold Cape

8-8A Wrexham Road, CH7 1ES (next to Market Square crossroads)
🌣 8am-midnight (1am Fri & Sat) ☎ (01352) 705920
Greene King Abbot; Ruddles Best Bitter; guest beers 🅗

This Wetherspoon free house, a converted shop in the town centre, is named after a 4,000-year-old gold peytrel found nearby – a copy can be seen in the pub. The managers and staff have a passion for cask beer and real cider. The pub can get busy on Wednesday to Saturday market days and serves a range of food with special deals and offers.
Q⏴🌣◔🍴♠–🖳

Overton-on-Dee

White Horse Inn

21 High Street, LL13 0DT
🌣 closed Mon; 5.30-10.30 Tue; 12-2.30, 5.30-midnight Wed-Fri; 12-midnight Sat; 12-11 Sun ☎ (01978) 710111
🌐 thewhitehorseoverton.co.uk
Joule's Blonde, Pale Ale, Slumbering Monk 🅗

Attractive red-brick mock-Tudor building situated in the heart of the village. This Joule's outlet is a CAMRA pub design winner, featuring frosted and latticed windows, pristine wood partitioning and restored fireplaces with wood-burning stoves. A former pantry, coal shed and washhouse to the rear have been converted into dining spaces. Food is served lunchtimes and evenings, with speciality carvery, steak and curry sessions. The pub hosts a number of local group meetings, some open to visitors. 🏚Q🌣◔🍴♠–🖳

Pantymwyn

Crown 🅛

Cilcain Road, CH7 5EH
🌣 12 (5 Mon)-11; 12-midnight Thu-Sat ☎ (01352) 740462
Facer's Splendid; Wychwood Hobgoblin; guest beers 🅗

A bright and airy roadside pub with three separate rooms served from a central bar. The bay windows overlook the front terrace and there is an extensive children's play area to the rear. Now a free house, four cask ales are available including a house beer from Facer's and a rotating guest. Meals are served daily – see the specials board in the dining area. Popular with walkers and golfers, and dog-friendly. Accommodation is in two en-suite rooms.
🏚⏴🌣◔🍴◔♣P🔑–🖳(6)

WALES

Prestatyn

Archie's ⓛ

151 High Street, LL19 9AS

✪ 5-11 Tue-Thu; 12-1.30am Fri & Sat; 12-11
Sun ☎ 07971 164222

Facer's Flintshire Bitter; guest beers Ⓗ

Archie's is a welcome newcomer to the Prestatyn real ale scene. Situated at the southern end of the High Street, the licensee is very keen on supporting real ale, and local breweries in particular. The single-room interior has an alcove and sport fans are well catered for, with six screens facing in every direction. Entertainment includes an impromptu blues night on Wednesday, karaoke on Thursday and a disco on Friday and Saturday. No food is served but tea and coffee are available. ❀≠(11,35,36)⌐₌

Halcyon Quest ⓛ

17 Gronant Road, LL19 9DT (on A547 just E of town centre) SJ069826

✪ 3-11.30 (12.30am Fri & Sat); 12-11.30 Sun
☎ (01745) 852442 ⊕ halcyonquest-hotel.com

Facer's Flintshire Bitter; guest beers Ⓗ

The Halcyon Quest, or HQ as it is known locally, is located on the southern edge of the town. The single bar has much sporting memorabilia and even a rowing boat hanging from the ceiling. Five beers are usually available, including one from local brewery Facer's. There is a pleasant garden at the rear. The northern end of Offa's Dyke is close by. Accommodation is in eight doubles and one single room. ☎❀❀Å≠♣♠P⌐₌(11,35,36)

Rhyl

Sussex

26 Sussex Street, LL18 1SG

✪ 8am-midnight (1am Fri & Sat); 8am-10.30 Sun
☎ (01745) 362910

Greene King Abbot; Ruddles Best Bitter; guest beers Ⓗ

Medium-sized Wetherspoon pub divided into three areas. Originally, the building was a Welsh Wesleyan chapel before becoming the Old Comrades Club. It was then converted to the Sussex in 1992 before its current owners took over in 2001. The walls feature pictures of Rhyl's past, including references to Laurel and Hardy's visit to the resort in 1953 and the pioneering hovercraft service from Rhyl to Wallasey in 1962. Guest ales are often from Welsh breweries. Q☎❀❀①&≠♠₌

Ruabon

Bridge End Inn ⓛ

5 Bridge Street, LL14 6DA

✪ 5 (4 Fri)-11; 12-11 Sat & Sun ☎ (01978) 810881
⊕ mcgivernales.co.uk

Beer range varies Ⓗ

This welcoming and cosy former coaching inn close to the station has won numerous awards since being taken over and completely revitalised by the McGivern family in 2009. The pub was deservedly awarded the ultimate accolade of CAMRA National Pub of the Year in 2011. Seven ever-changing cask ales are available with at least one from McGivern

Ales at the rear of the premises. Real cider is also served. Families and well-behaved dogs are welcome in the lounge. ❀Q☎❀❀❀♣♠P⌐♟₌

Ruthin

Castle Hotel

St Peter's Square, LL15 1AA

✪ 7-midnight (1am Fri & Sat) ☎ (01824) 709960

Greene King Abbot; Ruddles Best Bitter; guest beers Ⓗ

A Wetherspoon hotel on the town square with a spacious, multi-roomed interior decorated with items of local historical interest. The Stag Room features Owain Glyndwr, another room pays tribute to Darwin, while the lower Barrel Room has a display of old beer taps and other brewery-related items, in recognition that there was a brewery on site in long bygone days. Guest beers are usually from local Welsh micros such as Big Bog and Hafod. Car parking is for residents only.
❀☎❀❀♥①&♠P⌐₌

Wrexham

Elihu Yale

44-46 Regent Street, LL11 1RR

✪ 8am-midnight (1am Fri & Sat); 9am-midnight Sun
☎ (01978) 366646

Beer range varies Ⓗ

A popular Wetherspoon's pub in the town centre, close to bus and train stations. As well as the regular Wetherspoon beers, there are usually four guest beers, which generally include at least one from a north Wales brewery. The large single-room interior has various seating areas, including a quieter raised part in a corner at the front. Families are welcome until 9pm. Q☎①&≠♠₌

Royal Oak ♛

35 High Street, LL13 8HY

✪ 12-midnight ☎ (01978) 358547

Joule's Blonde, Pale Ale, Slumbering Monk; guest beer Ⓗ

A Grade II-listed building with a long and narrow interior. The real fire, wood panelling and etched brewery mirrors around the bar help to create a comfortable ambience. One guest beer is always on offer alongside the three Joule's beers. No food is available but crockery and cutlery can be provided if you want to bring your own. A small beer garden is open April to September.
❀❀&≠♣⌐₌

Ysceifiog

Fox ★

Village Road, CH8 8NJ (signed from B5121) SJ153714

✪ 4 (3 Fri; 1 Sat & Sun)-11 ☎ (01352) 720241

Thwaites Original, Lancaster Bomber; guest beers Ⓗ

Identified by CAMRA as one of Britain's Best Real Heritage Pubs, this classic village inn's four-roomed interior has remained intact since the 1930s. The tiny front bar, accessed via a sliding door, has bench seating attached to the front counter, which may be unique to the Fox. Guest beers usually come from Welsh breweries. No food on Wednesday. ❀Q❀①⊟

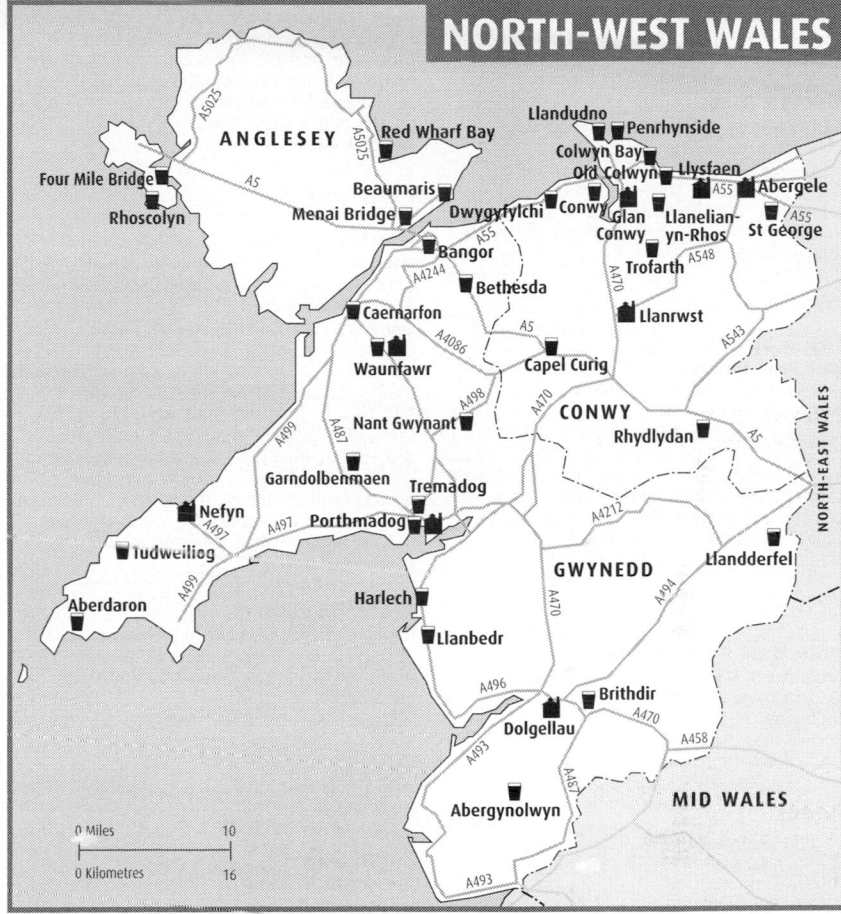

NORTH-WEST WALES

WALES

NORTH-EAST WALES

Authority areas covered: Anglesey UA, Conwy UA, Gwynedd UA

Aberdaron

Gwesty Ty Newydd ⃝L
Llŷn Peninsula, LL53 8BE
☼ 10.30-midnight ☎ (01758) 760207
⊕ gwesty-tynewydd.co.uk
Beer range varies Ⓗ
The hotel is situated at the centre of a picturesque and historic village on the Llŷn Peninsula. Beers are from local breweries Purple Moose and Cwrw Llŷn, and freshly caught Bardsey lobster and crab are on the menu, as well as afternoon teas. 11 en-suite bedrooms are available, with stunning sea views. The Wales coastal footpath passes through the village. Bus services run from Pwllheli.
Q❧❀⊅◑⊟♿▲⊠

Abergynolwyn

Railway Inn
LL36 9YN (on B4405)
☼ 12-midnight (11 Sun) ☎ (01654) 782279
Beer range varies Ⓗ
Hospitable community local in the centre of the village not far from the Talyllyn Railway. You can still see the remains of the old incline that brought goods traffic down from the railway to the village. Excellent food is served and, following a refit, the range of beers is set to increase. The pub has stunning views of the nearby hills and there is wonderful walking nearby. ♨Q❀✿◑⊟♿⇌

Bangor

Boatyard
Garth Road, LL57 2SF (off old A5, follow pier signs)
☼ 11 (12 Sun)-11 ☎ (01248) 362462
⊕ theboatyardinn.org.uk
Marston's Burton Bitter, Pedigree; guest beers Ⓗ
Formerly the Union Garth, this large multi-roomed pub is in lower Bangor. It has been refurbished and now has a well-appointed restaurant and pleasant seating areas. The garden area overlooks the sea

INDEPENDENT BREWERIES
Big Bog Waunfawr
Cader Dolgellau (NEW)
Conwy Llysfaen
Great Orme Glan Conwy
Llŷn Nefyn
Nant Llanrwst
North Wales Abergele
Purple Moose Porthmadog
Snowdonia Waunfawr

and Penrhyn Harbour. Guest beers are usually from the Marston's range. The Boatyard is popular with clubs, students and locals. ♨Q🏠🛏🌙🕽P↕–🖳

Mostyn Arms

27 Ambrose Street, LL57 1BH (off Beach Rd)
🌣 3 (1 Sat & Sun)-midnight ☎ (01248) 364572
Beer range varies Ⓗ
This small, friendly, back-street pub has been completely refurbished with a pool area, lounge space with TV sport, and a small bar. Beers are sourced locally, usually from Purple Moose and Great Orme breweries. No food is served. Note the limited opening hours.

Tap & Spile

Garth Road, LL57 2SW (off old A5, follow pier signs)
🌣 12-11 (11.30 Tue, Fri & Sat) ☎ (01248) 370835
Beer range varies Ⓗ
Busy pub attracting locals, students and visitors to Bangor, with a changing range of up to six real ales from different breweries. It enjoys excellent views of the magnificent pier, Menai Straits and over to Beaumaris. Good wholesome food including vegetarian options is served at sensible prices, and seven letting rooms are available. 🕽♣

Beaumaris

Olde Bull's Head Inn

Castle Street, LL58 8AA
🌣 11-11; 12-10.30 Sun ☎ (01248) 810329
⊕ bullsheadinn.co.uk
Draught Bass; Hancock's HB; guest beer Ⓗ
Grade II-listed building that was the original posting house of the borough. In 1645 General Mytton, a parliamentarian, commandeered the inn while his forces laid siege to the nearby castle. Dr Johnson and Charles Dickens were famous guests and each bedroom is named after a Dickens character. The beamed bar has a large open fire. Parking is limited. ♨Q🛏🕽P🖳

Bethesda

Douglas Arms Hotel ★

London Road, LL57 3AY
🌣 6-midnight, 3.30-midnight Sat; 1-4, 7-midnight Sun
☎ (01248) 600219 ⊕ douglas-arms-bethesda.com
Marston's Burton Bitter, Pedigree; guest beer Ⓗ
Built in 1820, this was an important coaching inn on the historic Telford post route from London to Holyhead. The Grade II-listed building has been identified by CAMRA as one of Britain's Best Real Heritage Pubs. The four-room interior has remained unchanged since the 1930s and includes a snug, lounges and a large tap room with a full-size snooker table. Bethesda is convenient for buses to the Ogwen Valley and the surrounding mountains. Check website for seasonal opening times.
Q🏵Å♣🖳

Brithdir

Cross Foxes Ⓛ

LL40 2SG (jct of A470 and A487)
🌣 10-midnight (2am Fri & Sat) ☎ (01341) 421001
⊕ crossfoxes.co.uk
Cader Idris Bitter; guest beers Ⓗ
A newly refurbished Grade II-listed building situated near the foot of Cader Idris mountain and four miles from the historic town of Dolgellau.

Beers are usually from Cader Ales and other local microbreweries. Breakfast is served from 8am and meals are available all day until 9pm. Dogs are welcome in the bar area. The hotel has Welsh Tourist Board 5 star grading. Bus service T2 passes by, but please check times.
♨Q🌣🏵🛏🕽♿ÅP↕–🖳

Caernarfon

Anglesey Arms

Slate Quay, LL55 1SG (on Menai Straits next to castle)
🌣 12-midnight (1am Fri & Sat) ☎ (01286) 672158
⊕ anglesey-arms.co.uk
Jennings Cumberland Ale; Marston's Bitter, Pedigree Ⓗ
An ancient pub in a superb location with amazing views across the Menai Straits to the Isle of Anglesey. Built against the town walls and next to Caernarfon Castle, and attracting a mix of locals and visitors, the Anglesey is a fabulous place to drink real ale and enjoy good seasonal food. Sitting outside on the sea wall, the views of birdlife and sunsets are breathtaking. The Welsh Highland Railway station is half a mile away.
♨🏵🛏🕽♿Å🚌

Black Boy Inn

Northgate Street, LL55 1RW (near marina)
🌣 11-11 (11.30 Fri & Sat); 12-10.30 Sun ☎ (01286) 673604
Brains The Rev James; Draught Bass; Hancock's HB; guest beer Ⓗ
The pub is set within the town walls between the marina and castle. This historic town, a World Heritage Site, is well worth a visit, ending with a welcome pint at the Black Boy. The public bar and small lounge are warmed by roaring fires. Good-value food is served and the guest beer usually comes from Purple Moose. A previous local CAMRA award winner. ♨🏵🛏🕽 🖳Å🚌P

Tafarn Y Porth

5-9 Eastgate Street, LL55 1AG (just off Bangor Rd near Barclays Bank)
🌣 9-midnight ☎ (01268) 662920
Big Bog Big Bog Bitter; Greene King Abbot; Ruddles Best Bitter Ⓗ
Friendly, welcoming Wetherspoon pub opposite the town walls and close to the castle. It has a large open-plan interior and a spacious partly covered courtyard outside with plenty of seating. The real ale range often includes a beer from the Big Bog Brewing Company in Waunfawr, just a few miles away. Good-value food is served all day. The pub's location is handy for the Welsh Highland Railway, which takes you to the heart of Snowdonia. Q🌣🏵🕽♿Å🚌♣♠P↕–🖳

Capel Curig

Plas y Brenin Ⓛ

LL24 0ET
🌣 12-2, 6-11 (10.30 Sun); 11-11 Sat ☎ (01690) 720214
Beer ranges varies Ⓗ
Plas y Brenin is an outdoor centre in a lovely rural area. The raised bar overlooks the two lakes of Llŷnnau Mymbyr, with spectacular views of Mount Snowdon in the distance. The interior is basic but modern with board floors and wooden tables and chairs. A good selection of hearty and reasonably priced meals is served. There is a large dining area and a TV. The three handpumps dispense local

beers from Nant, Purple Moose, Great Orme and Conwy breweries. An alfresco pint is the best way to enjoy the view. Q✪☞◗◖❀♠AP⌐⊟

Colwyn Bay

Pen-y-Bryn L
Pen-y-Bryn Road, LL29 6DD (top of King's Road) SH842782
☼ 11.30-11; 12-10.30 Sun ☎ (01492) 533360
⊕ penybryn-colwynbay.co.uk
Brunning & Price Original Bitter; Purple Moose Snowdonia Ale; guest beers H
Open-plan pub popular with all ages, with large bookcases and old furniture, and real fires in the winter months. Panoramic views of Colwyn Bay and the Great Orme can be admired from the terrace and garden. Imaginative bar food is served – the menu is updated daily. Four guest beers are mainly sourced from local and independent breweries, and there is an extensive choice of malt whiskies. Former local CAMRA Pub of the Year.
❀✪◗⅏♣P⊟

Picture House L
24-26 Princes Drive, LL29 8LA SH849791
☼ 9-midnight (1am Fri & Sat) ☎ (01492) 535286
Greene King Abbot; Ruddles Best Bitter; guest beers H
Wetherspoon pub in the former Princess cinema, now a Grade II-listed building. The walls of the three-level building, including an upper balcony, are adorned with theatre memorabilia. There are eight handpumps featuring at least one beer from a local brewery such as Conwy, plus guest ciders. Local beer festivals, in addition to Wetherspoon's national events, are held throughout the year. A former local CAMRA Pub of the Year.
Q◗⅏≒❀⊟(12,14,15)

Conwy

Albion Ale House ♟ ★ L
Uppergate Street, LL32 8RF
☼ 12-11; 11-midnight Fri & Sat ☎ (01492) 582484
⊕ albionalehouse.weebly.com
Beer range varies H
Multi-room heritage pub superbly refurbished by the current owners. The rooms all retain original 1920s features including some amazing fireplaces. There is no music, TV or fruit machines, just pleasant conversation. The pub is managed by four local brewers – Conwy, Great Orme, Nant and Purple Moose – and showcases their beers as well as guest ales. There are two guest Welsh ciders. An excellent wine list and a good selection of malt whiskies is also offered. Local CAMRA Pub of the Year 2013. ❀Q✪❀≒♣❀⌐☐⊟

Castle Hotel L
High Street, LL32 8DB
☼ 10.30-11.30 (11 Sun) ☎ (01492) 582800
⊕ castlewales.co.uk
Beer range varies H
An old coaching inn dating back to the 15th century, standing on the site of a Cistercian abbey. This privately owned hotel had a major refurbishment a few years ago and the public bar is now an upmarket meeting place. One of the partners is also head of the Welsh National Culinary Team, so it is no surprise that the excellent food menu, available in the bar and restaurant, features

the finest local produce. The beer is also local, coming from the nearby Conwy Brewery, and the cider is supplied by Gwynt y Ddraig.
Q✪☞◗⅏≒❀P⌐⊟

Old White House
Bangor Road, LL32 8DP (½ mile W of Conwy on old A55) SH770780
☼ 4 (12 summer)-11; 12-midnight Thu-Sun
☎ (01492) 573133 ⊕ oldwhitehouseconwy.com
Taylor Landlord; Tetley Bitter; guest beer H
This 17th-century building was once the coach house stable for a now-demolished hotel. The long central bar room, featuring a large log-burning stove and a high-beamed roof space, leads to an open-plan front lounge and a small rear dining area. The pub hosts a general knowledge quiz on Tuesday, a music quiz on Friday night and live entertainment on Saturday night. Food is available Tuesday to Sunday evening and all day every day in the summer. ❀✪◗⅏≒♣P⌐⊟(5,X5)

Dwygyfylchi

Gladstone L
Ysgubor Wen Road, LL34 6PS (off jct 16 A55) SH730772
☼ 12-11 (midnight Fri & Sat); closed Mon & Tue winter
☎ (01492) 623231 ⊕ thegladstone.co.uk
Beer range varies H
Renowned for its magnificent sea views, this recently refurbished pub retains many original features including alcoves and traditional decor with wood panelling and old photographs. Comfortable sofas surround a wood-burning stove, and a galleried balcony with tables and booths overlooks the bar. The restaurant offers imaginative food sourced locally. There is a function room, accommodation in six luxury rooms and the pub has a wedding licence. Live music plays on Saturday nights. ❀✪☞◗⅏AP⌐⊟

Penmaenmawr Golf Club
Conwy Old Road, LL34 6RD
☼ 11-11 (may close earlier in winter); 11.30-10.30 Sun
☎ (01492) 623330 ⊕ pengolf.co.uk
Beer range varies H
Plush one-roomed clubhouse with stunning sea and mountain views from the outdoor drinking area that overlooks the golf course. Inside, there is a pool table and a TV for sporting events, and regular entertainment is hosted in the evenings. Good-value hearty meals are served from the kitchen. Up to two guest beers are available from local and independent breweries. The club is local CAMRA Club of the Year and was runner-up in the 2012 Welsh Club of the Year competition.
✪◗P⌐⊟

Four Mile Bridge

Anchorage Hotel
LL65 2EZ (on B4545, just past bridge to Holy Island)
☼ 11 (12 Sun)-11 ☎ (01407) 740168
Draught Bass; Taylor Landlord; Theakston XB; guest beer H
Family-run hotel situated on Holy Island close to Trearddur Bay. It has a large, comfortable lounge bar and a dining area serving a wide selection of meals. The hotel is near some fine sandy beaches and coastal walks. Its proximity to the A55 makes it a useful stopping-off point for Holyhead Port.
Q✪☞◗ AP⌐⊟

Garndolbenmaen

Cross Foxes

LL51 9TX (between Caernarfon and Porthmadog off A487)
✪ 6-11; closed Mon & Tue winter; 12.30-2.30, 6.30-11 Sun
☎ (01766) 530246 ⊕ crossfoxesinn.co.uk
Beer range varies Ⓗ
Two-roomed village inn dating from the 19th century with a central bar. The pub is popular with locals and visitors for an ever-changing range of beer and good home-cooked food. Meals are served Sunday lunchtime and every evening. The dining area converts into a popular skittle alley in winter. The local bus stops close by, with regular services Monday to Saturday to Porthmadog and Caernarfon. ⁂⬤♣P🖭

Harlech

Branwen Hotel

Ffordd Newydd, LL46 2UB (on A462 below Harlech Castle) SH583312
✪ 11-11 ☎ (01766) 780477 ⊕ branwenhotel.co.uk
Beer range varies Ⓗ
Warm and welcoming family-run hotel and bar overlooked by Harlech Castle. The popular and stylish bar offers a wide range of cask ales as well as foreign beers. A large selection of wines and malt whiskies is also stocked. Ask for your favourite malt – they are sure to have it. A former local CAMRA award winner. ⁂🖾⬤&Å⇌♣P'-🖭

Llanbedr

Ty Mawr Hotel

LL45 2HH
✪ 11-11 ☎ (01341) 241440 ⊕ tymawrhotel.com
Beer range varies Ⓗ
Small country hotel set in its own grounds. The modern lounge bar has a slate-flagged floor and cosy wood-burning stove. Unusual flying memorabilia reflect connections with the local airfield. French windows open out onto a veranda and landscaped terrace with seating. A beer festival is held in a marquee on the lawn each year. Popular with locals and walkers, dogs and children are welcome. Meals are served all day.
⁂🖾⬤&Å⇌P

Llandderfel

Bryntirion Inn Ⓛ

LL23 7RA (on B4401 4 miles E of Bala) SJ986364
✪ 11 (12 Sun)-11 ☎ (01678) 530205 ⊕ bryntirioninn.co.uk
Purple Moose Snowdonia; guest beer Ⓗ
Overlooking the River Dee, this former hunting lodge and coaching inn is now a real ale pub with a small, intimate, dining area and a restaurant catering for 100 people, providing meals to suit all dietary needs. A medium-sized bar leads to a family/games room with unusual games including giant versions of Connect Four and Jenga. One of the beers is from Purple Moose Brewery. Two double and one single room provide good-value accommodation. Buses on Route X94 pass outside.
⁂⬅🖾⬤🖰♣P'-🖭(X94)

Llandudno

Albert

56 Madoc Street, **LL30 2TW**

✪ 11-11; 12-10.30 Sun ☎ (01492) 877188
⊕ albertllandudno.co.uk
Beer range varies Ⓗ
Just off the town centre and close to the railway station, this popular pub restaurant offers five handpulled ales from local and independent breweries and a range of tasty meals throughout the day. Current beers are clearly displayed on blackboards above and beside the L-shaped bar. The decor is modern, with a range of interesting photographs and pictures on display.
⁂⬤&⇌🖭'-🖭

Cottage Loaf Ⓛ

Market Street, LL30 2SR SH781824
✪ 11-11 (11.30 Fri & Sat) ☎ (01492) 870762
⊕ the-cottageloaf.co.uk
Conwy Welsh Pride; Courage Directors; guest beers Ⓗ
The pub was previously a bakery, hence the name. The building underwent major refurbishment including an extension early in 2013. The interior features stone-flagged floors, an impressive fireplace and a raised timber-floored area – much of the wood came from the Flying Foam, a schooner shipwrecked at Llandudno's West Shore. With great home-cooked food served daily, the Loaf is a popular meeting place for people of all ages. The guest cider comes from Gwynt y Ddraig.
⁂🖾⬤⇌'-🖭

Gresham Ⓛ

143 Upper Mostyn Street, LL30 2PE
✪ 12.30-10 (midnight Fri & Sat) ☎ (01492) 874004
Tetley Bitter; guest beers Ⓗ
Plush town-centre tapas bar with an alfresco pavement seating area. Three real ales are always on offer at very reasonable prices including at least one local beer from breweries such as Conwy or Purple Moose. The long narrow downstairs central bar with an intimate dining area is complemented by the large upstairs restaurant/function room with its own bar. Bright Mediterranean-style paintings adorn the walls. ⁂⬤&⇌'-🖭

Snowdon Ⓛ

11 Tudno Street, LL30 2HB
✪ 12-11 (11.30 Fri & Sat) ☎ (01492) 872166
⊕ the-snowdonhotel.co.uk
Draught Bass; guest beers Ⓗ
Recently refurbished building just off the town centre and near the tram station. The Snowdon is one of the oldest pubs in Llandudno, frequently referred to as the locals' local. Four real ales are usually available – with three thirds for the price of a pint an offer to consider if you can't make up your mind. The large main bar area has a small snug to the side. Look out for the Snowdon mirror above the fireplace. A drinking area by the road at the front of the pub has a fine view of the Great Orme and the goats if you are lucky. ⁂🖾⇌●'-🖭

Llanelian-yn-Rhos

White Lion

LL29 8YA (off B583) SH863764
✪ closed Mon; 11.30-3, 6-midnight; 12-11 Sun
☎ (01492) 515807 ⊕ whitelioninn.co.uk
Marston's Burton Bitter, Pedigree; guest beer Ⓗ
A regular in the Guide for more than 20 years, this 16th-century inn situated in the hills above Old Colwyn, next to St Elian's Church, offers a warm welcome. Gracing the entrance are two stone white lions, leading into the bar area with its slate-

flagged flooring and large comfortable chairs around the log fires. Decorative stained glass is mounted above the bar in the tiny snug. A spacious restaurant serves delicious home-cooked food, with a wide menu choice. Jazz night is Tuesday, quiz night Thursday. ⚱Q⟱☹❍◑⊟Å♣Pᵇ—

Menai Bridge

Liverpool Arms 🅛

St George's Road, LL59 5EY (100yds from village centre towards pier)
✪ 12-2, 5-11.30; 12-11.30 Fri-Sun ☎ (01248) 712453
⊕ thelivvy.co.uk
Draught Bass; Greene King Abbot; Purple Moose Dark Side of the Moose; guest beer 🅷
Recently refurbished to a high standard, the Livvy now has four cask ales on offer and serves good-quality home-cooked food. This nautically themed pub is frequented by locals, students in term time and the sailing fraternity. A short walk from the pub takes you beneath the famous suspension bridge. ⟱☹❍◑♣Å♣ᵇ—

Nant Gwynant

Pen-y-Gwryd 🅛

LL55 4NT (at jct of A486 and A4086)
✪ 11-11 (winter hours limited) ☎ (01286) 870211
⊕ pyg.co.uk
Purple Moose Madog's Ale, Glaslyn Ale 🅷
Built in 1810 and Grade II-listed, this famous hotel is situated in the heart of Snowdonia. It was used by the team who made the first ascent of Everest. The Everest room has famous signatures on the ceiling and there are two further small rooms plus a dining room. The hotel is featured in CAMRA's Real Heritage Pubs of Wales and Great British Pubs. Please note that winter opening is restricted but the bar does open for festivities over the New Year. ⚱Q☹❒◑⊟Å♣Pᵇ—▣

Old Colwyn

Red Lion

385 Abergele Road, LL29 9PL (on main Colwyn Bay to Abergele road) SH868783
✪ 5 (12 Sun)-11; 4-midnight Fri; 12-midnight Sat
☎ (01492) 515042
Holden's Black Country Mild; Marston's Burton Bitter; guest beers 🅷
Free house serving up to five guest ales from independent and local brewers. A winner of many awards, the popular local is a former CAMRA branch Pub of the Year. It has a cosy L-shaped lounge featuring a real coal fire, antique brewery mirrors and other memorabilia, and a traditional public bar with a pool table, darts and TVs. To the rear is a superb Victorian-style covered and heated smoking conservatory. The Real Ale Club every Thursday offers nine beers at reduced prices. Guest ciders are also available. ⚱Q☹⊟♣ᵇ—▣

Penrhynside

Cross Keys Inn 🅛

Pendre Road, LL30 3DD (off B5115) SH814815
✪ 5-midnight (11 Mon); 12-midnight Sat & Sun
☎ (01492) 547070 ⊕ crosskeys-inn.co.uk
Facer's Flintshire Bitter; guest beers 🅷
This family owned and run 19th-century free house is a winner of local CAMRA awards and offers a

warm and friendly welcome. It has a cosy front room with a central bar, rear pool room and side lounge boasting unrivalled views of the surrounding area towards Penrhyn Bay and Rhos-on-Sea. Occasional karaoke and live music nights are hosted. The guest cider comes from Gwynt y Ddraig. ⚱☹⊟Å♣●▣

Penrhyn Arms 🅛

Pendre Road, LL30 3BY (off B5115) SH814816
✪ 5.30 (4.30 Thu; 4 Fri)-midnight; 12-1am Sat; 12-11 Sun ☎ 07780 678927 ⊕ penrhynarms.com
Banks's Bitter; Marston's Pedigree; guest beers 🅷
A winner of many awards including local CAMRA Pub of the Year, plus regional, Welsh and national cider awards including National Cider Pub of the Year finalist. The welcoming local offers up to four guest beers including local ales. Ten or more guest ciders and perries include Rosie's Triple D and several from Gwynt y Ddraig. The spacious L-shaped bar has pool, darts and a wide-screen TV. Thursday is cheese night. Accommodation is available in a self-contained flatlet for up to eight people. ⚱☹❒Å♣●ᵇ—▣

Porthmadog

Ship Inn

14 Lombard Street, LL49 9AP
✪ 12-2.30, 5.30-11 (11.30 Thu-Sat) ☎ (01766) 512990
Beer range varies 🅷
A traditional pub set in a picturesque location behind the park in the centre of this harbour town. Friendly and efficient staff dispense frequently changing ales and serve quality food, including pub favourites steak and ale pie, lasagne and barbecue ribs. The pub has a separate bar and lounge, and a room available for private events, and is popular with locals and tourists. A quiz is hosted on Thursday night. Local CAMRA Pub of the Year 2011. ⚱Q☹◑≈P▣(1,3,X32)

Spooner's Bar

Harbour Station, LL49 9NF
✪ 10-11; 12-10.30 Sun ☎ (01766) 516032 ⊕ festrail.co.uk
Beer range varies 🅷
Spooner's has built its reputation on a changing range from small breweries, including the local Purple Moose. Situated in the terminus of the world-famous Ffestiniog Railway, steam trains are outside the door most of the year. Food is served every lunchtime, evening meals Tuesday to Saturday, but check first out of season. A former local CAMRA Pub of the Year award winner. Q☹☹◑&≈P▣

Station Inn

LL49 9HT (on mainline station platform)
✪ 11-11 (midnight Thu-Sat); 12-11 Sun ☎ (01766) 512629
Brains The Rev James; Purple Moose Snowdonia; guest beer 🅷
Situated on the Cambrian Coast railway platform, this pub is popular with locals and visitors alike. It has a large lounge and a smaller public bar, and can get busy at weekends and on nights when live football is shown on TV. A range of pies and sandwiches is available all day. ☹⊟&Å≈♣P▣

Red Wharf Bay

Ship Inn

LL75 8RJ (off A5025 between Pentraeth and Benllech)

WALES

✪ 11-11 (10.30 Sun) ☎ (01248) 852568
⊕ shipinnredwharfbay.co.uk
Adnams Southwold Bitter; Brains SA; guest beers Ⓗ
Red Wharf Bay was once a busy port exporting coal
and fertilisers in the 18th and 19th centuries.
Previously known as the Quay, the Ship enjoys an
excellent reputation for its bar and restaurant, with
meals served lunchtimes and evenings. It gets busy
with locals and visitors in the summer. The garden
has panoramic views across the bay to south-east
Anglesey. The resort town of Benllech is two miles
away and the coastal path passes the front door.
Beers can be expensive. ♨Q❄☎◑ⓏP≒

Rhoscolyn

White Eagle
LL65 2NJ (off B4545 signed Traeth Beach) SH271755
✪ 12-3, 6-11; 12-11 Sat; 12-10.30 Sun ☎ (01407) 860267
⊕ white-eagle.co.uk
**Marston's Burton Bitter, Pedigree; Weetwood
Eastgate Ale; guest beers** Ⓗ
Saved from closure by new owners, this pub has
been renovated and rebuilt with an airy, brasserie-
style ambience. It has a fine patio enjoying superb
views over Caernarfon Bay and the Lleyn Peninsula
to Bardsey Island. The nearby beach offers safe
swimming with a warden on duty in the summer
months. The pub is also close to the coastal
footpath. Excellent food is available lunchtimes and
evenings, all day during the school holidays.
♨Q❄◑Ⓩ♿ẠP

Rhydlydan

Giler Arms
LL24 0LL SH892508
✪ closed Mon; 12-3 (not Tue-Fri), 6 (7 winter)-11
☎ (01690) 770612 ⊕ giler.co.uk
Bathams Mild Ale, Best Bitter, XXX Ⓗ
Friendly country hotel set in six acres of grounds
with a one-acre lake, camping and caravan site
with recently refurbished facilities, and picturesque
gardens beside the small River Merddwr. It offers a
welcoming, comfortable lounge, a separate public
bar popular with locals, and a small pool room. The
restaurant has lovely views over the lake. Quiz
night is the middle Wednesday of the month. B&B
accommodation is in seven bedrooms and children
and dogs are welcome. ♨Q❄☎✉◑Ⓩ♿Ạ♣P≒▣

St George

Kinmel Arms Ⓛ
LL22 9BP SH974758
✪ closed Sun & Mon; 12-3, 6-11 (11.30 Fri & Sat)
☎ (01745) 832207 ⊕ thekinmelarms.co.uk
Facer's Flintshire Bitter; guest beers Ⓗ
A local CAMRA Pub of the Year winner, this 17th-
century former coaching inn is set on a hillside
overlooking the sea. A central bar serves a large
combined dining and drinking area with a real log
fire in one corner and a spacious conservatory at
the rear. Two guest beers come from independent
breweries, plus a Welsh cider or perry and a
selection of Belgian and continental beers. The pub
has a reputation for good food. Luxury
accommodation is available in four comfortable
suites. ♨Q❄✉◑♿P≒▣

Tremadog

Union Inn
7 Market Square, LL49 9RB
✪ 12-2, 5.30-12.30am (11 Sun) ☎ (01766) 512748
⊕ union-inn.com
**Big Bog Bog Standard Bitter; Great Orme Great Welsh
Bitter; Purple Moose Snowdonia Ale** Ⓗ
Friendly village local situated in the village square,
with two separate cosy bars and a restaurant at the
rear. The pub has a policy of using locally sourced
produce, and the ale range features mainly local
beers. Children are welcome and board games are
available. Excellent food is served in the bar and
restaurant. Frequent bus services pass the building.
♨Q❄◑Ⓩ♿⇌(Porthmadog)♣≒▣(1A,X32)

Trofarth

Holland Arms Ⓛ
Llanrwst Road, LL22 8BG SH840708
✪ 12-3, 7 (6 Fri & Sat)-11; closed Wed & Thu; 12-10.30 Sun
☎ (01492) 650777 ⊕ thehollandarms.co.uk
Beer range varies Ⓗ
Eighteenth-century coaching house set in a country
landscape within sight of Snowdonia. Family run
with a warm welcome for locals and visitors alike,
it has a pleasantly furnished bar, lounge and
restaurant areas. Excellent, value-for-money meals
are available daily, with a special themed menu on
Monday. Beers are all local from Conwy, Great
Orme, Purple Moose and Nant. Live music features
occasionally. The pub has picked up many local
CAMRA awards in recent years. ♨Q❄◑♣P

Tudweiliog

Lion Hotel
LL53 8ND (on B4417)
✪ 11-11 (12-2, 6-11 winter); 11.30-11 Sat; 11-10.30 (12-3
winter) Sun ☎ (01758) 770244
Beer range varies Ⓗ
The origins of this free house go back more than
300 years. A village inn set on the glorious, quiet
north coast of the Lleyn Peninsula, cliffs and
beaches are a mile away by footpath, a little
further by road. Up to three beers are served
depending on the season, with Purple Moose a
firm favourite. The pub is accessible by number 8
bus from Pwllheli during the day only. Closed
Monday lunchtimes in winter. A former local
CAMRA Pub of the Year. Q❄✉◑Ⓩ♿P▣

Waunfawr

Snowdonia Parc ♈ Ⓛ
Beddgelert Road, LL55 4AQ
✪ 11-11 (10.30 Sun) ☎ (01286) 650409
⊕ snowdonia-park.co.uk
Beer range varies Ⓗ
Home of the Snowdonia and Big Bog Breweries,
this is a popular pub for walkers, climbers and
families, with children's play areas inside and out.
Meals are served all day. The pub adjoins
Waunfawr station on the Welsh Highland Railway –
stop off here before continuing on one of the most
scenic sections of narrow gauge railway in Britain.
There is a large campsite adjacent on the riverside.
Local CAMRA Pub of the Year 2012 and 2013.
Q❄☎◑Ⓩ♿Ạ⇌♣P▣

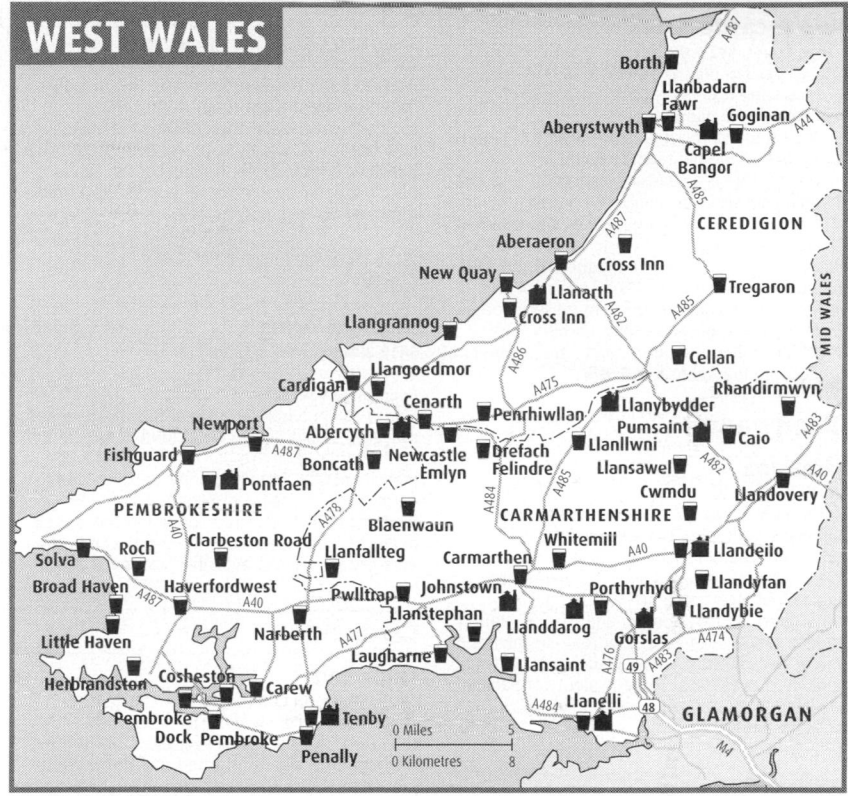

WEST WALES

Borth
Llanbadarn Fawr
Aberystwyth
Goginan
Capel Bangor
CEREDIGION
Aberaeron
New Quay
Cross Inn
Llanarth
Tregaron
Cross Inn
Llangrannog
Cellan
Llangoedmor
Cardigan
Rhandirmwyn
Cenarth
Penrhiwllan
Llanybydder
Newport
Pumsaint
Abercych
Caio
Fishguard
Boncath
Newcastle Emlyn
Drefach Felindre
Llanllwni
Llansawel
Pontfaen
Cwmdu
Llandovery
PEMBROKESHIRE
Blaenwaun
CARMARTHENSHIRE
Clarbeston Road
Whitemill
Roch
Llanfallteg
Llandeilo
Solva
Carmarthen
Broad Haven
Haverfordwest
Johnstown
Porthyrhyd
Llandyfan
Pwlltrap
Llanstephan
Llandybie
Little Haven
Narberth
Llanddarog
Gorslas
Laugharne
Lansaint
Herbrandston
Cosheston
Carew
Llanelli
GLAMORGAN
Pembroke Dock
Pembroke
Tenby
Penally

0 Miles 5
0 Kilometres 8

Authority areas covered: Carmarthenshire UA, Ceredigion UA, Pembrokeshire UA

Aberaeron

Cadwgan

10 Market Street, SA46 0AU (off A487 overlooking inner harbour)
☼ 12-11 (midnight Fri & Sat); 12-5 Sun ☎ (01545) 570149
Hancock's HB; guest beer Ⓗ
The pub takes its name from the last ship to be built in Aberaeron harbour. This old-fashioned one-room hostelry offers a friendly welcome, and lively conversation can be expected, with the TV largely reserved for rugby internationals. The guest beer is sourced from a wide range of generally smaller breweries. The outside drinking area overlooking the harbour (and free public car park) is a suntrap. Dogs are very welcome. ▲ᗒ☼Αᒪⴲ(40,50,550)

Harbourmaster

2 Quay Parade, SA46 0BT (off A487, overlooking harbour)
☼ 8am-11.30 ☎ (01545) 570755 ⊕ harbour-master.com
Purple Moose HM Best, Glaslyn Ale; guest beer Ⓗ
Occupying a former grain warehouse overlooking Aberaeron harbour, this light, modern bar offers a warm welcome from friendly, bilingual staff. Award-winning food is locally sourced. The guest beer, available Easter to October, comes from a Welsh brewery. While the bar is usually free of electronic entertainment, an exception is made for rugby internationals on TV. In the summer drinks can be enjoyed outside on the harbour wall. The boutique-style hotel accommodation has been widely praised – parking is for residents only.
Q ᗒ☼ⴲⴀ◖ΑPⴲ(40,50,550)

Abercych

Nag's Head

SA37 0HJ (on B4332 between Cenarth and Eglwyswrw)
☼ 11-3 (not Mon), 6-11; 12-10.30 Sun ☎ (01239) 841200
Beer range varies Ⓗ
Well-restored old smithy boasting a beamed bar and riverside garden. The bar area is furnished with collections of old medical instruments, railway memorabilia, beer bottles and timepieces showing the time around the world. Cych Valley beers come from brewery behind the pub, reopened in 2012 after a decade of inactivity. Abercych is a hamlet in the beautiful Cych Valley, which features in the Welsh tales of the Mabinogion. ▲ᗒ☼◖Ϟ⅄Pⴀ

Aberystwyth

Glengower Hotel

3 Victoria Terrace, SY23 2DH (N end of promenade)
☼ 12-11 ☎ (01970) 626191 ⊕ glengower.co.uk
Beer range varies Ⓗ
Traditionally a student haunt but welcoming to all, this seafront hotel enjoys excellent coastal views. Outside seating is on the front terrace, which catches the sun but can be bracing in winter. Two real ales are offered, three at busier times, from Wye Valley brewery and Wales and Marches micros. Well-behaved accompanied children are welcome until 9pm. Buses call nearby en route from university campus to town. Meals finish at 8pm weekdays, 6pm Sundays. The pub closes for a fortnight over the Christmas-New Year period.
☼ⴲ◖Αⴍ♣ᒪⴲ(2,3)

Ship & Castle

1 High Street, SY23 1JG
❂ 2-midnight (1am Fri); 12-1am Sat ☎ 07773 778785
⊕ shipandcastle.co.uk
Wye Valley HPA; guest beers Ⓗ

Its 2009 refurbishment wearing well, this street-corner pub in the old town remains the area's real ale mecca. HPA is a constant, flanked by four ever-changing guests from an increasingly eclectic range of mainly microbrewery beers; the cider is Gwynt y Ddraig Black Dragon. Beer festivals in spring and autumn are eagerly awaited highlights. While the interior is essentially one room, the pool area is well segregated and there is a more secluded area to the rear. The decor features an old OS map, a mural illustrating the pub's name, and a variety of nautical photographs. ▲⇌♣☻🖫

Blaenwaun

Lamb Inn

SA34 0JD SN236271
❂ 4.30-midnight (2am Fri & Sat) ☎ (01994) 448899
Batemans XXXB; Evan Evans Cwrw; Greene King Abbot; Morland Old Speckled Hen Ⓗ

The Lamb is set in an idyllic area and has an original old local ambience with a relaxing atmosphere and welcoming and friendly staff. It offers a range of three to four real ales alongside one or two ciders. A small, quaint pub, darts and pool are played here. There is plenty of parking available and a campsite half a mile away. ▲⊛◑♿▲☻ᐟ

Boncath

Boncath Inn

SA37 0JN (on B4332 between Cenarth and Eglwyswrw)
❂ 11-11; 12-8.30 Sun ☎ (01239) 841241
Worthington's Bitter; guest beers Ⓗ

This pub dates back to the 18th century and is the centre of life in this attractive village, which developed as a result of the opening of the now long-closed Whitland-Cardigan railway. The interior is divided into several seating areas, creating an intimate atmosphere, and the walls display items of local historic interest. Home-cooked meals are recommended. A beer festival is held each August bank holiday weekend. ▲⊛◑♿▲♣Pᐟ🖫(430)

Borth

Victoria Inn

High Street, SY24 5HZ
❂ 11-2am ☎ (01970) 871417
Sharp's Doom Bar; Wye Valley HPA; guest beer Ⓗ

This recently renovated family friendly beachside pub has two downstairs bars and a decking area outside. Upstairs, a bar/games room leads to a terrace with stunning sea views. Log fires give a cosy feel. Live music plays on some weekends. Home-cooked food is available all day, with barbecues in summer. There is a covered area for smokers. Buses from Aberystwyth stop outside, but few in evenings and none on Sundays – trains run until late all week. ▲⇌⊛◑⊟♿⇌♣ᐟ🖫(512)

Broad Haven

Galleon

35A Enfield Road, SA62 3JW (on seafront)

❂ 10-midnight (1am Fri & Sat) ☎ (01437) 781152
Brains Bitter, SA, The Rev James; guest beer Ⓗ

The Galleon's hospitable and welcoming landlady helps to bring a cosy ambience to this friendly pub. Converted from a tea room in the 1980s, with splendid views over St Brides Bay, the hostelry has now become a widely appreciated feature of the Havens community. With its delightful sandy beach, Broad Haven remains popular as a holiday resort for visitors. ▲Q⍾⊛◑♿▲♣☻ᐟ🖫(311)

Caio

Brunant Arms

SA19 8RD (off A482 near Pumsaint)
❂ 11-11 (1am Fri & Sat) ☎ (01558) 650483
Beer range varies Ⓗ

Family-run pub in the centre of the village near the Dolaucothi Gold Mines. Good food is served until 9pm every day. There are plenty of outdoor pursuits nearby including pony trekking, and a horse-tethering rail is provided at the pub. A legendary Welsh wizard is buried in the church opposite. Two beers from the local Evan Evans Brewery are usually available. ▲⊛⇌◑▲♣Pᐟ

Cardigan

Eagle Inn

Castle Street, SA43 3AA (S of town bridge)
❂ 10-11 ☎ (01239) 612046 ⊕ theeaglecardigan.co.uk
Evan Evans Warrior; guest beer Ⓗ

A sympathetically refurbished traditional Welsh pub on the outskirts of Cardigan town. Real ale and good food (available noon to late evening) are served by friendly and attentive staff. Live bands play regularly and open mic nights are hosted. Live sport is shown on TV. Quiz nights are popular and the pub has its own teams. Well worth venturing over the bridge for. ⊛◑♣ᐟ🖫

Grosvenor

Bridge Street, SA43 1HY (opp castle outer walls)
❂ 11 (12 Sun)-11 ☎ (01239) 613792
Greene King Abbot; Worthington's Bitter; guest beer Ⓗ

Situated on the edge of the town centre next to Cardigan Castle and the River Teifi, this large pub offers a good choice of ales, including a selection of bottled beers. The large open-plan bar/lounge provides various areas to relax, eat and drink, and there is an extra room upstairs for dining or functions. Good-value food is served lunchtimes and evenings every day. ⊛◑♿ᐟ🖫

INDEPENDENT BREWERIES

Coles Llanddarog
Cych Valley Abercych (NEW)
Evan Evans Llandeilo
Felinfoel Llanelli
Friends Arms Johnstown
Gwaun Valley Pontfaen
Gwynant Capel Bangor (Brewing suspended)
Jacobi Pumsaint
Kite Gorslas
Mercian Llanybydder (NEW)
Penlon Cottage Llanarth
Preseli Tenby

Carew

Carew Inn

SA70 8SL (off A477 before Pembroke Dock)
🌣 11-11 (11.30 Sun) ☎ (01646) 651267 ⊕ carewinn.co.uk
Evan Evans Cwrw; Brains The Rev James Ⓗ
Situated close to Carew's historic Celtic Cross, castle
and tidal mill, this former estate pub of the
Trollope-Bellew family makes an ideal stop-off
with its village location and many local attractions.
A pine-boarded bar features photographs of the
local area from the past. Outside there is a
marquee and a large grassed garden with a
children's play area. ⚠✿❍▶ⓐP⚊Ⓡ(361)

Carmarthen

Friends Arms

Old St Clears Road, Johnstown, SA31 3HH
🌣 11-11 (midnight Fri & Sat) ☎ (01267) 234073
⊕ thefriendsarms.co.uk
Evan Evans Cwrw; Friends Arms JPA; guest beer Ⓗ
Excellent local hostelry half a mile from
Carmarthen town centre, with a cosy and friendly
atmosphere and a warm welcome, enhanced by
two open fires. Popular with sports fans, it has Sky
Sports and ESPN, Wi-Fi, pool and darts. A quiz and
bingo are held on alternate Wednesdays. Three
real ales are usually offered including one from the
microbrewery on site, with a 10 per cent discount
for CAMRA members. Local CAMRA Pub of the Year
2011. ⚠Q✿⚊Ⓡ(222,322)

Hen Dderwen

47-48 King Street, SA31 1BH
🌣 9am-midnight (1am Sat); 9am-11 Sun ☎ (01267) 242050
**Greene King Abbot; Ruddles Best Bitter; guest
beers** Ⓗ
This Wetherspoon pub opened in 2000 and is
named after the Carmarthen legend of Merlin and
the Old Oak – the story is told in pictures and
plaques on the walls. The interior is divided into
two distinct spaces – the principal drinking area is
at the front while the area to the rear tends to be
mainly used by diners. A good selection of real ales
is offered. Food is available all day including the
chain's standard meal deals. ❍▶≈✦⚊Ⓡ

Queen's Hotel ⓨ

Queen Street, SA31 1JR
🌣 10-11 (midnight Sat); 11-8 Sun ☎ (01267) 231800
⊕ thequeenscarmarthen.co.uk
Beer range varies Ⓗ
Town-centre pub and long-standing Guide entry
near Carmarthenshire county hall, with a bar,
lounge and small function room. A coaching inn
dating back to the 19th century, it retains the
traditional wood-panelled walls. The public bar is
used by locals and has TV for sporting events. Three
beers are usually available, sometimes four, one
sourced locally. The patio nestles beneath the
castle walls and is a suntrap in the summer
months. Upstairs function rooms are available, and
the local CAMRA branch meets here. Dogs are
welcome. Local CAMRA Pub of the Year 2013.
✿≈⚊Ⓡ

Stag & Pheasant

34 Spilman Street, SA31 1LQ
🌣 12-11 (midnight Sat) ☎ (01267) 232040
Ringwood Fortyniner Ⓗ
A busy locals' pub with a warm and friendly
atmosphere on the main thoroughfare in

Carmarthen, making it a popular venue for tourists
and locals, including fishermen and golfers. The
pub boasts an excellent beer garden with outdoor
heaters at the rear. Fortyniner is joined by another
beer from the Marston's group during busy periods,
particularly when big matches are televised.
Historically, the building was a stable block serving
the hotel opposite. It is within walking distance of
bus and railway stations. ✿⚙≈✦⚊Ⓡ

Cellan

Fishers Arms

SA48 8HU (on B4343)
🌣 4.30-8 (11 Fri & Sat) ☎ (01570) 422895
**Evan Evans Cwrw, Warrior; Young's Special; guest
beers** Ⓗ
A hostelry since 1580, this is a family-friendly pub
where all ages are welcome and novice Welsh
speakers encouraged. Lively conversation includes
tales of fishing on the nearby Afon Teifi, and tips on
the many rural attractions. The garden has a
children's play area and a small restaurant serves
locals and visitors. Entertainment includes quiz and
gourmet nights, charity barbecues, pool and lively
TV rugby internationals. The pub's live music
tradition thrives with hymns, arias and folky sing-
songs throughout year. ⚠Q✿▶ⓐ✦P Ⓡ(585)

Cenarth

Three Horse Shoes

SA38 9JL (on A484 just E of river bridge)
🌣 11 (12 winter)-11 ☎ (01239) 710119
Evan Evans Best Bitter; guest beer Ⓗ
A gem of an inn in a popular tourist village in west
Wales. The interior has been modified in recent
years but retains an abundance of original features
including an inglenook fireplace that is big enough
to sit in and huge, exposed beams. The pub can be
touristy in high season but retains a local
atmosphere. Good food is available lunchtimes and
evenings. ⚠✿❍▶ⓐP⚊Ⓡ(460)

Clarbeston Road

Cross Inn

SA63 4UL (N of railway station) SN019211
🌣 12-midnight (1am Fri & Sat) ☎ (01437) 731506
**Courage Directors Bitter; Greene King Abbot; guest
beer** Ⓗ
Multi-roomed village inn, well worth seeking out,
with stone and wood floors and original oak beams
in abundance. The large bar area housing pool, a TV
for sport and jukebox is complemented by two
small snugs and a dining room where reasonably
priced home-cooked food from a largely grill-based
menu is served Thursday to Saturday evenings and
Sunday lunchtime. Outside there are more spacious
drinking areas. A beer festival is held in summer.
⚠✿ⓐ≈✦P⚊Ⓡ(313)

Cosheston

Brewery Inn

SA72 4UD
🌣 closed Mon; 12-3, 6-11; 12-4, 7-11 Sun ☎ (01646) 686678
Courage Best Bitter; guest beers Ⓗ
Set between Cosheston Pill and the Carew Estuary
just north-east of Pembroke, this light and airy
stone-built inn boasts a traditional slate floor and
bar, roof beams and comfortable seating with old

WALES

tables. Paintings and drawings by local artists adorn the walls. The outdoor smoking area is heated in winter. Despite the name, there has been no brewery here since 1889. Q☺☺◑❀P՞↩

Cross Inn (Llanon)

Rhos yr Hafod Inn
SY23 5NB (at B4337/B4577 crossroads)
✪ 5-11; closed Sun ☎ (01974) 272644
⊕ rhos-yr-hafod-inn.co.uk
Evan Evans BB; guest beer ⊞
Quiet, friendly pub in a small village offering a regularly changing guest beer, often from a Welsh brewery. Cosy drinking areas cluster around a small central bar; the back room has old photographs of local scenes. The roadside drinking area at the front captures the evening sun and there is a large, attractive garden at the rear. Easy to find at a prominent country crossroads, this pub is a haven for local real ale fans and visitors alike. Ample parking; dogs welcome. ㈱Q☺☺❀➊♣P՞↩

Cross Inn (New Quay)

Penrhiwgaled Arms
SA44 6LN (2 miles S of New Quay on A486)
✪ 12-11; 12-1am (2am Fri & Sat) summer
☎ (01545) 560238 ⊕ penrhiwgaled.moonfruit.com
Hancock's HB; guest beer ⊞
Sometimes quiet in winter, this large village pub attracts busy custom in summer from local campsites. The main room is flanked by a pool area and dining/function room. A guest beer, often from a smaller family brewery or a larger micro, is offered Easter to October, and an alternative beer sometimes replaces the HB. Activities include pool night Wednesday, Thursday quiz, alternate Sundays clay pigeon club, and occasional live music. The smoking shelter is heated, lit and covered. The car park is a licensed stopover for motorhomes. ㈱☺❀◑➊♣P՞↩(50,550)

Cwmdu

Tafarn Cwmdu
SA19 7DY (off B4302 at Halfway)
✪ 7-11; closed Sun-Tue ☎ (01558) 685088 ⊕ cwmdu.com
Beer range varies ⒢
Owned by the National Trust and run by the local community, this is one of CAMRA's Real Heritage Pubs of Wales. The pub is the centre of activities for the village alongside the local shop and post office, also run by the community. A folk night features on the first Friday of the month. The pub will open on request for a special occasion and can be hired for private parties. There is a sitting room upstairs with free access to a computer. ㈱Q❀♣P

Drefach Felindre

Tafarn John Y Gwas
SA44 5XG (just E of river bridge, near school and church) SN354383
✪ 5-11; 4-midnight Fri; 12-midnight Sat; 12-11 Sun
☎ (01559) 370469 ⊕ johnygwas.co.uk
Beer range varies ⊞
This early 19th-century village tavern with its striking yellow and black livery attracts locals and tourists alike with snugs, wood-burning stoves, quality beer and cider, and a warm welcome. At least two ales are generally offered, with a

nationally recognised name flanked by local and/or microbrewery beers. A wide variety of bottled beers and ciders is also available. Local attractions include many walks and the Welsh Wool Museum. A pub menu featuring local produce is available on Friday and Saturday evenings. ㈱◑⊞♣♣P՞↩(460)

Fishguard

Pendre Inn
High Street, SA65 9AT (on A487 300yds SW of market square)
✪ 11 (4 Mon)-midnight; 12-11.30 Sun ☎ (01348) 874128
Worthington's Bitter; guest beers ⊞
Friendly, traditional pub on the main road south out of town with a good local following and a growing reputation for its beer. Two guest beers change regularly and may come from anywhere in the UK – sometimes from the Gwaun Valley Brewery, a few miles away up the valley. Pool and darts are played in the big back bar. ㈱◑⊞P՞↩(412,413)

Goginan

Druid Inn �
High Street, SY23 3NT (on A44 6 miles E of Aberystwyth)
✪ 12-midnight (1am Fri & Sat) ☎ (01970) 880650
Wye Valley Bitter, Butty Bach, HPA; guest beer ⊞
Thriving community local with an L-shaped main bar flanked by a dining room and pool room. It continues to serve friendly regulars and many visitors with quality ales and excellent home-cooked food (no meals Tue lunch). The guest beer, available at most busy times, is typically from a micro in Wales or the Marches, often a Wye Valley monthly special. A second guest is occasionally also on offer. Real cider sometimes appears in summer. Live bands play at least monthly. Local CAMRA Pub of the Year 2013. ㈱☺❀◑♣P՞↩(X47,525)

Haverfordwest

Bristol Trader
Quay Street, SA61 1BE
✪ 11-11 (1am Sat); 12-10.30 Sun ☎ (01437) 762122
Worthington's Bitter; guest beers ⊞
Dating back to Haverfordwest's days as a port, this pub retains some character despite modernisation. A quiet venue in the daytime, it is popular for dining, with food served in a large dining area or outside tables overlooking the river. It gets lively in the evening. In the late '50s this was the first pub in town to have carpet on the floor. Two guest ales are served – beers can be dispensed without tight sparkler on request. ◑♣⇄P↩

Pembroke Yeoman
11 Hill Street, SA61 1QQ
✪ 11-11 ☎ (01437) 762500
Draught Bass; Flowers IPA; guest beers ⊞
A little off the beaten track, conversation rules at this local pub, though there is a well-stocked jukebox should it flag. Two guest ales come from small breweries and change often. Food is served in generous portions. Known as the Upper Three Crowns until the 1960s, the pub's name was changed to reflect the presence of the local yeomanry headquarters nearby. ㈱Q◑♣↩

WALES

William Owen
Quay Street, SA61 1BG
✪ 9-midnight (1am Fri & Sat) ☎ (01437) 771900
Greene King Abbot; Ruddles Best Bitter; guest
beers Ⓗ
Pembrokeshire's first and so far only Wetherspoon
pub occupies a handsome 19th-century building,
formerly a shop, hotel and restaurant, now with a
spacious extension to the rear. Beer from a
Pembrokeshire brewery is often available. The pub
offers the chain's customary menus, promotional
deals and policies (with 7am opening for hot drinks
and breakfast). ✪◖◗ᚹ✦ᚱ-🚆

Herbrandston
Taberna Inn ♛
SA73 3TD (3 miles W of Milford Haven)
✪ 12-11 ☎ (01646) 693498
Hop Back Summer Lightning; guest beers Ⓗ
Designed and built in 1963 by a local carpenter and
builder with an eye to the area's then rapidly
developing oil and petrochemical industry, this pub
has a pleasant atmosphere and welcoming locals.
Two guest beers are served alongside a cider from
Westons and Moles Black Rat, and the pub issues a
list of all guests sold throughout the year. Local
CAMRA Pub of the Year 2012 and 2013.
🏰Q✪ᚹ◖◗ᚹᚢ●P-

Laugharne
New Three Mariners
Market Street, SA33 4SA
✪ 12 (4 Mon-Fri winter)-11 ☎ (01994) 427426
⊕ newthreemarinersinn.co.uk
Greene King Abbot; Morland Old Speckled Hen; guest
beer Ⓗ
The building is located in the centre of the historic
township of Laugharne and only yards from its
early 11th-century castle. Dylan Thomas lived in
the town for a number of years and he and his wife
Caitlin are laid to rest in the graveyard of St
Martin's Church. The pub moved to its current site
when the original ale house opposite was
converted to a carpentry shop. Very popular with
locals, it hosts a weekly quiz night.
🏰✪ᚹ◖◗Åᚢ P-🚆(222)

Little Haven
Castle
1 Grove Place, SA62 3UG (opp beach)
✪ 10-11 (1am Fri) ☎ (01437) 781445
Jennings Cocker Hoop; Mansfield Cask Ale; Marston's
Pedigree; guest beer Ⓗ
The main bar of this tastefully modernised pub is
split into separate areas by pillars and low dividers.
A separate games area has darts and pool. Steeped
in local history, the Castle opened in 1871 and is
reputedly haunted – a phenomenon attributed by
some to its use in former times as a place to lay out
the bodies of drowned sailors, washed ashore on
the beach, to await burial. 🏰✪◖◗ᚢÅᚱ-

Saint Bride's Inn
St Brides Road, SA62 3UN
✪ 10.30-midnight summer; 11-3 winter ☎ (01437) 781266
⊕ saintbridesinn.co.uk
Banks's Bitter; Marston's Pedigree; guest beer Ⓗ
Formerly known as the New Inn, the pub acquired
its present name, taken from the bay in which the

village is set, in 1904, and is noted for the ancient
well in the cellar. The attractive interior includes a
separate dining area, and there are heaters on the
patio in the pretty suntrap garden. Live music is
performed occasionally. 🏰Q✪ᚹ◖◗-

Llanbadarn Fawr
Black Lion
SY23 3RA
✪ 12-midnight (11.30 Sun) ☎ (01970) 623448
Banks's Bitter; guest beers Ⓗ
Set in the village centre, a mile from the university
town of Aberystwyth, this modernised pub is
popular with locals and students alike. The spacious
main bar has seating at one end, darts and pool at
the other, while the rear function room can also be
used to enjoy home-cooked, locally sourced food
(lunches Tue-Sun, evening meals Thu-Sat). The
large rear beer garden, next to the village's ancient
church, has a delightful air of rural seclusion. Two
guest beers are from the Marston's list – customers
are consulted on the selection.
🚂✪◖◗Åᚢ P-🚆(1,2)

Llandeilo
Angel Hotel
62 Rhosmaen Street, SA19 6EN
✪ 11-3.30, 5.30-11; 11-midnight Sat; closed Sun
☎ (01558) 822765 ⊕ angelbistro.co.uk
Beer range varies Ⓗ
Ideally located in the centre of this picturesque
Tywi Valley town, the Angel ministers to all needs.
The main bar is a U-shaped room providing three
real ales, mainly from local breweries, and bar
meals. At the back is a bistro dating back to the
1700s, while the first floor offers a beer garden to
the rear and a function room boasting a
Michelangelo-inspired hand-painted mural.
Themed meal nights and music nights are held
regularly. Q🚂✪◖◗ᚹ✦🚆(X13,103,280)

Cottage Inn
Pentrefelin, SA19 6SD (on A40 2 miles W of town)
SN601237
✪ 10-midnight ☎ (01558) 824645 ⊕ cottageinnbandb.co.uk
Gower Gold; Sharp's Doom Bar; guest beer Ⓗ
A popular family-run local community pub. Dating
back to the 1850s, it was formerly a coaching inn
and a drovers' hostelry. Sky TV is available and the
pub gets busy when major sporting events are
screened. It has a separate restaurant/function
room area. At the rear is a large covered smoking
area and outside is a large car park with
caravanning and camping space.
🏰Q🚂✪ᚹ◖◗ᚹᚢÅ●P-🚆(280,281)

White Horse
Rhosmaen Street, SA19 6EN
✪ 11-11; 12-10.30 Sun ☎ (01558) 822424
Evan Evans Cwrw, seasonal beers; guest beers Ⓗ
Grade II-listed coaching inn dating from the 16th
century. The tap for the local Evan Evans Brewery,
this multi-roomed pub is popular with all ages.
There is a small outdoor drinking area to the front
and a large council car park to the rear with access
to the pub down a short flight of steps. The covered
area for smokers has its own TV showing sport.
✪✦♣-🚆(X13,103,280)

Llandovery

King's Head
1 Market Square, SA20 0AB
✪ 10-11 ☎ (01550) 720393 ⊕ kingsheadcoachinginn.co.uk
Tomos Watkin Best Bitter, OSB; guest beer Ⓗ
Former coaching inn dating from the 1700s in a
historic town on the edge of the Brecon Beacons.
Newly refurbished yet remaining traditional, it is a
popular base for many organisations including the
Rotary Club and cattle breeders. Good food ranges
from bar meals to à la carte. Once a noted droving
centre, Llandovery is still a working market town,
serving the local farming community with weekly
livestock auctions. Q⋈◑点Å≈P⊟(280,281)

Llandybie

Ivy Bush
Church Road, SA18 3HZ (100yds from church)
✪ 12-midnight (11 Mon); 11-midnight Sat & Sun
☎ (01269) 850272
Taylor Landlord; guest beer Ⓗ
The oldest pub in the village, this friendly local
dates back nearly 300 years. The single-bar room
has two comfortable seating areas. Pub games and
quizzes run weekly and a large-screen TV shows
sport. The guest beer changes regularly. The
railway station nearby is on the Heart of Wales line.
❀≈♣♠P'-⊟(X13,103)

Llandyfan

Square & Compass
SA18 2UD (between Ammanford and Trapp)
✪ 12 (1 Sat)-11 summer; 5-11 winter; 12-8 Sun
☎ (01269) 850402
Beer range varies Ⓗ
Originally the village blacksmith's, this 18th-
century building was converted into a pub in the
1960s. Nestling on the western edge of the Brecon
Beacons National Park, it offers magnificent local
views and plenty of walking opportunities. A
traditional family pub, it has a wonderful rustic
charm and a warm, friendly welcome. Usually two,
occasionally three, guest beers are kept, at least
one from a local brewery. Opening hours vary in
winter – ring first to check. Q▷点ÅP'-

Llanelli

Harry Watkins
2 Millfield Road, SA14 8HY (on A476)
✪ 12-11 (5 Mon) ☎ (01554) 776644
Banks's Bitter; guest beers Ⓗ
Renamed after a local rugby hero of yesteryear
who features on the pub walls, the pub was
originally called the Bear. The open-plan, split-
level, family-friendly hostelry has defined dining
spaces and a function room. Two guests are usually
available from the Marston's group. Outside, there
are both covered and open drinking areas. The pub
has no car park but there is usually ample room on
the road. National cycle and walking paths to the
Swiss Valley are nearby. ⋗❀◑'-⊟(128,196)

York Palace
51 Stepney Street, SA15 3YA (opp Town Hall Square
Gardens)
✪ 9am-11 (midnight Thu; 1am Fri & Sat) ☎ (01554) 758609
**Greene King Abbot; Ruddles Best Bitter; guest
beers** Ⓗ

This former cinema in the town centre is a typical
Wetherspoon conversion. The walls are adorned
with photographs of local industrial history
including Llanelli's famous tin plate industry. Guest
beers are often sourced locally and are discounted
on Wednesdays. The bus station is a short walk and
the railway station a 10-minute walk.
◑点≈♠'-⊟

Llanfallteg

Plash
SA34 0UN (off A40 at Llanddewi Velfrey)
✪ 5-11; 12-midnight Wed-Sun ☎ (01437) 563472
**Black Sheep Best Bitter; Wye Valley Butty Bach; guest
beer** Ⓗ
An inn for over 180 years, this terrace-style cottage
pub has had four different names in that time. The
Plash is the centre of village life, with a friendly
welcome from the locals. The guest beer is usually
from a small, independent brewery. Home-made
pizzas are a speciality, and a small selection of bar
snacks is also available. The disabled entrance is to
the rear. A cottage sleeping two is available to let.
Local CAMRA Pub of the Year 2012.
⌂Q❀⋈◑点♣P

Llangoedmor

Penllwyndu
SA43 2LY (on B4570, 4 miles E of Cardigan) SN241458
✪ 12-11 (midnight Sun) ☎ (01239) 682533
Brains Buckleys Best Bitter; guest beer Ⓗ
Old-fashioned ale house standing at an isolated
crossroads where Cardigan's evil-doers were once
hanged – the pub sign is worthy of close inspection.
The cheerful and welcoming public bar retains its
quaintness with a slate floor and inglenook with
wood-burning stove. Good home-cooked food
including traditional favourites is available all day
in the bar and separate restaurant. Free live music
plays on the third Thursday evening of the month.
⌂❀◑♣P'-

Llangrannog

Pentre
SA44 6SP (at seaward end of B4321/B4334)
✪ 12-midnight ☎ (01239) 654345 ⊕ pentrearms.co.uk
Gale's Seafarers Ale; St Austell Tribute; guest beer Ⓗ
Right on the shore in a former seafaring village,
this welcoming pub enjoys stunning sea views that
can also be enjoyed on the pub's website – a
webcam overlooks the beach. The main bar is
complemented by a games room offering darts
and pool. A guest beer, usually from a Welsh
brewer, is available in summer. Live music plays on
summer weekends. The Cardi Bach coastal tourist
bus now runs all year, and in high summer, when
the village's narrow lanes can get busy and parking
difficult, there is a park-and-ride link from the top
of the village. ⋈◑Å♣⊟(600)

Llanllwni

Talardd
SA39 9DX (on A485 near village shop)
✪ 12-3, 6-late ☎ (01559) 395633 ⊕ talardd.com
Beer range varies Ⓗ
There are records of this old drovers' inn dating
back to 1626 – drovers would stop for refreshments
for man and beast before driving their livestock

over Llanllwni Mountain on their way to markets over the border. Though modernised these days, Tafarn y Talardd still offers that old, warm and friendly welcome. Live music, quizzes and film nights are organised most Mondays. Two varying guest beers are available. ▲◑🚲♣P

Llansaint

King's Arms
13 Maes yr Eglwys, SA17 5JE
✪ closed Mon & Tue; 12-2.30 (Sat only), 6-11; 12-2.30, 6.30-10.30 Sun ☎ (01267) 267487
Young's Special; guest beers Ⓗ
A former local CAMRA Pub of the Year, this friendly village local has been a pub for more than 200 years. Situated near an 11th-century church, it is reputedly built from stone recovered from the lost village of St Ishmaels. Music and poetry nights are held on the third Friday of the month. Two well-chosen guest beers from smaller breweries are usually offered. Good-value home-cooked food is served. Carmarthen Bay Holiday Park is a few miles away. ▲Q🕷🚲◑▲♣P🖳(198)

Llansawel

Black Lion Hotel
SA19 7JQ
✪ 11-11; 12-10 Sun ☎ (01558) 685263
Beer range varies Ⓗ/Ⓖ
In years gone by the Black Lion was an old coaching inn. A popular and friendly pub set in the heart of the village, it is home to various clubs and the local rugby team. Home-made food is served all day every day. The beers are usually from Welsh breweries. Live music is hosted often and the local game of 'tip it' is played here. ▲◑&♣P⌐

Llanstephan

Castle Inn Ⓛ
The Square, SA33 5JG
✪ 11.30-11 (midnight Fri & Sat); 12-10.30 Sun
☎ (01267) 241225
Felinfoel Cambrian Bitter; guest beer Ⓗ
Guest beers are usually from local breweries including Evan Evans at this welcoming pub in the centre of a popular seaside village. The south-facing patio is favoured by visitors and villagers alike. Inside, there is a separate area for TV and a space away from the bar for families. The pub hosts the local cricket and football clubs and many village functions. The menu offers wholesome pub grub with some unusual twists – curries are a speciality with takeaways available. 🕷◑🖳(227)

Narberth

Angel Inn
43 High Street, SA67 7AS
✪ 11-3, 5.30-11; 7-10.30 Sun ☎ (01834) 860215
Brains The Rev James; guest beers Ⓗ
Long-established but modernised and extended former coaching inn in the town centre with a small public bar and larger lounge/dining area. It offers two guest beers and popular food. With a warm and friendly welcome, it can be busy at times. Outside is a good-sized beer garden for the summer months. Narberth Railway Station is a mile from the town. Q◑🚲▲⌐🖳(322,381,430)

New Quay

Sea Horse
Uplands Square, SA45 9QH (on B4342)
✪ 11-midnight (1am Fri & Sat) ☎ (01545) 560736
Beer range varies Ⓗ
This traditional one-room pub offers a warm welcome to locals and visitors. The cosy, beamed lounge has a pool table and nautical paraphernalia, and offers one real ale in winter, up to four in summer, often from local breweries. Filled rolls are available. Live music plays at weekends, quiz night is every Thursday, and a beer festival is held at the end of August. Dogs are welcomed with a titbit and fresh water. The seating area outside at the front is a suntrap. 🕿🕷▲♣🖳(50,550)

Newcastle Emlyn

Ivy Bush
Emlyn Square, SA38 9DG
✪ 10-11; 12-6 Sun ☎ (01239) 710542
Draught Bass; guest beer Ⓗ
Very much a local pub with a traditional separate bar area and plenty of small, intimate nooks. Located at the top end of the market town of Newcastle Emlyn, it has lots of local parking, shopping and public transport links. Pool and darts are available in an area to the rear of the pub. No food is served but there is a chip shop/cafe next door. ▲🚲&♣🖳(460)

Newport

Castle Hotel
Bridge Street, SA42 0TB
✪ 11-11; 12-10.30 Sun ☎ (01239) 820742
Morland Old Speckled Hen; Theakston Best Bitter, XB; guest beer Ⓗ
Friendly, popular local in a characterful small town halfway between Cardigan and Fishguard, with an attractive bar featuring some impressive wood panelling. Food is served at lunchtimes and in the evening in the extensive dining area. An off-street car park is situated behind the hotel. A wealth of prehistoric remains adds interest to the many local walks. ▲🕿🕷🚲◑▲P⌐🖳(412)

Golden Lion
East Street, SA42 0SY (on A487)
✪ 12-midnight (11 Sun) ☎ (01239) 820321
Brains The Rev James; Draught Bass; guest beers Ⓗ
Another of the town's sociable locals, this one is reputed to have its own resident ghost. A number of internal walls have been removed to form a spacious open-plan bar area, with distinct sections helping to retain a cosy atmosphere. Car parking space is available on the opposite side of the road. ▲Q◑▲P⌐🖳(412)

Pembroke

Royal Oak
138-140 Main Street, SA71 4HN
✪ 2 (12 Sat & Sun)-midnight ☎ (01646) 682537
Hancock's HB; guest beers Ⓗ
Situated at the east end of the town, this well-established pub with coach arch and stable yard – now used as a beer garden – offers a warm and friendly welcome from an enthusiastic licensee. The traditional interior features exposed oak beams in the bar. Pub games include shove-ha'penny.

Two guest beers are usually offered; one is either Sharp's Doom Bar or Brains Rev James.
曲❀&≠♣'-只(349,356)

Pembroke Dock

First & Last
London Road, Waterloo, SA72 6TX (on A477)
✪ 10-1am (1.30am Thu-Sat) ☎ (01646) 682687
Brains The Rev James; Worthington's Bitter; guest beer H
Small, friendly, single-bar local in the same family for the past 50 years. The walls display an eclectic mix of photos and prints. Food is standard pub fare. Formerly the Commercial, the pub acquired its current more distinctive name in 1991 to reflect its edge-of-town location. It is handy for the Cleddau Bridge, giving easy access to Haverfordwest and the beaches and other attractions of west and north Pembrokeshire. ❀❶≠♣P只(349,356)

Station Inn
Hawkestone Road, SA72 6HN (in station building)
✪ 7-11 Mon; 11-3, 6-midnight (12.30am Fri & Sat); 12-3, 7-10.30 Sun ☎ (01646) 621255
Beer range varies H
Housed in the town's railway station where trains still depart for Carmarthen and Swansea (and, on summer Saturdays, far-off Paddington), this town-centre pub is close to both the Irish Ferries terminal and the popular Pembrokeshire Coast Path. Meals are excellent value (no lunches Mon, evening meals Wed-Sat only). Three real ales are generally on sale, with Young's Bitter a frequent visitor and a new beer coming on every Tuesday. The June beer festival offers around 20 beers. Live music is played on Saturday evenings. 曲Q❀❺❶❶❹&≠P'-只

Penally

Cross Inn
SA70 7PU
✪ 12-11 (12.30am Fri & Sat); 12-midnight Sun
☎ (01834) 844665
Hancock's HB; guest beers H
Situated in a picturesque village with some well-preserved Georgian and Victorian houses, the pub has a wood and brick bar leading to the restaurant. Local pictures and shields of regiments stationed in a nearby barracks adorn the walls. The sporting prowess of the locals is evident from the cups and shields on the trophy shelf. A signed photo and a set of darts used by Phil 'The Power' Taylor is framed in an alcove. Food is sometimes available – ring to check first. ❀A≠'-只(349)

Penrhiwllan

Daffodil
SA44 5NG
✪ 11.30-3, 5.30-11 ☎ (01559) 370343 ⊕ daffodilinn.co.uk
Greene King Abbot; guest beers H
Formerly the Penrhiwllan Inn, the Daffodil is a pub and restaurant dating from 1750, in a country village 20 minutes from the popular coastal resort of New Quay. It has been modernised in an elegant style to provide separate, intimate dining areas and cosy drinking spaces catering for all, and has excellent disabled facilities. Two handpumps, three in the summer, dispense beers mostly from nationals, with guest ales from Welsh breweries.
曲Q❺❀❶❶❹&♣P'-

Pontfaen

Dyffryn Arms ★
SA65 9SE (off B4313)
✪ opening hours vary ☎ (01348) 881305
Draught Bass G
This much-loved pub, a reminder of how many country pubs must once have looked, is the hub of life in a secluded valley whose distinctive cultural traditions include a long history of farmhouse brewing. There is no bar counter – beer is still served by the jug through a sliding serving hatch. Conversation is the main form of entertainment, and the pub's relaxed atmosphere is captivating. The well-regarded Gwaun Valley Brewery is close, but the regulars are loyal to their Bass. A timeless gem to be treated with respect. 曲Q❀&A♣

Gwaun Valley Brewery
Kilkiffeth Farm, SA65 9TP (on B4313 to Maenclochog)
✪ 11-6; 11-6, 7-midnight Fri & Sat ☎ (01348) 881304
⊕ gwaunvalleybrewery.co.uk
Beer range varies H
Family-run brewery set in the North Pembrokeshire countryside, with views to the Gwaun Valley and the Preseli Hills. Half the converted farm building that houses the brewery is used as a tasting area, function room and bar, open daytime every day and Friday and Saturday evenings. Acoustic music sessions are held every Saturday night. The brewery's full range of draught and bottle-conditioned beers is normally on offer at this relaxed and welcoming venue. Q❺❀&AP

Porthyrhyd

Mansel Arms
Banc y Mansel, SA32 8BS (on B4310 between Porthyrhyd and Drefach)
✪ 5-11; 3-midnight Sat; 12-6 Sun ☎ (01267) 275305
Beer range varies H
Friendly 18th-century former coaching inn with wood-burning stoves in each room. The original limestone flags have been broken up and used in the fireplace, and low beams have been added to create atmosphere, with numerous jugs hanging from them in the bar. Pool and darts are played in a room to the rear, which was originally used for slaughtering pigs. Beers are varied, with the Young's range always popular as well as local ales. Food is served Friday and Saturday evenings and Sunday lunchtime. 曲Q❶A♣●只(129)

Pwlltrap

White Lion
SA33 4AT (off A40 W of St Clears)
✪ 11-11 (10.30 Sun) ☎ (01994) 230370
⊕ whitelion-pwlltrap.co.uk
Brains The Rev James; Worthington's Bitter; guest beer H
This roadside pub is warm and welcoming, with a real fire in winter months. It has an old-world charm with oak beams and panelled walls. A large annexe restaurant serves good food including a Sunday lunchtime carvery (booking advised). Pool and darts are available and a large-screen TV shows regular sporting fixtures. Polypins of cider are also on offer during summer months. There is on-street parking and buses from Carmarthen to Whitland and Haverfordwest serve the pub.
曲❀❶●P'-只(224,322)

Rhandirmwyn

Royal Oak

SA20 0NY

✪ 12-2, 6-11 (7-10.30 Sun) ☎ (01550) 760201

🌐 theroyaloakinn.co.uk

Beer range varies Ⓗ

Remote, stone-flagged inn with excellent views of the Tywi Valley and close to an RSPB bird sanctuary. Originally built as a hunting lodge for the local landowner, it is now a focal point for community activities and popular with fans of outdoor pursuits. Two or three guest beers are offered, a range of interesting bottled beers and whiskies is stocked, and the good wholesome food is recommended. There are panoramic views from the beer garden at the side of the pub. Four times local CAMRA Pub of the Year. ᴹ≜Q🌢🏚◀❤ A♣❤P

Roch

Victoria Inn

SA62 6AW (on A487)

✪ 12-2.30am (10.30 Sun) ☎ (01437) 710426

Beer range varies Ⓗ

A little gem with views across St Brides Bay, this locals' pub offers a warm welcome. The inn was established in 1851 although parts are older, and it has retained much of its olde-worlde charm, with beamed ceilings and low doorways. The menu features home-made Welsh dishes made with local produce where possible. Curry and a pint night is Friday. For those in a hurry there is a beer carry-out service. Live music plays occasionally. ᴹ≜Q🌢🌢🏚◀❶⬙♣P🏠(411)

Solva

Harbour Inn

SA62 6UU (on A487 next to harbour)

✪ 11-11 ☎ (01437) 720013

Brains Dark, SA; guest beers Ⓗ

Delightful seaside inn next to the tiny harbour, now the haunt of leisure sailors but once a port of embarkation for North America. It continues to showcase Brain's beers including seasonals and sometimes guests from other breweries. A community pub with a traditional atmosphere, it serves as a base for many village activities and is popular with locals who come to enjoy a quiet, relaxing pint. The nearby camping facilities cater for both caravans and tents. ᴹ≜Q🌢🏚◀⬙P⁵⁻🏠(411)

Tenby

Crown Inn

Lower Frog Street, SA70 7HU

✪ 12-11 (11.30 Sun) ☎ (01834) 842796

Brains The Rev James Ⓗ; guest beers Ⓗ/Ⓖ

Round the corner from the Five Arches, a defensive gatehouse in Tenby's medieval wall, this side-street pub offers, depending on the season, up to seven real ales. Brain's beers are flanked by guests mainly from national brewers, with gravity dispense sometimes used to augment choice. The large single room features a stage near the entrance for weekend live music. 🌢⬙ A🚄⁵⁻🏠

Tregaron

Talbot

The Square, SY25 6JL

✪ 11-11 (1am Fri & Sat) ☎ (01974) 298208 🌐 ytalbot.com

Beer range varies Ⓗ

Former drovers' inn at the heart of the town oozing character and heritage – the front snug is the perfect place to enjoy well-chosen guest beers from Wales and the borders. Ciders come from Gwynt y Ddraig. Excellent, good-value food is served lunchtimes and evenings. The back bar has a TV, elsewhere conversation rules. Outside is a beer garden and new, south-facing patio. Dogs and muddy-booted walkers are welcome. This much-improved pub is well worth seeking out. Local CAMRA Pub of the Year 2012. ᴹ≜Q🌢🌢🏚◀⬙⬙ A♣❤P⁵⁻🏠(585,588)

Whitemill

Whitemill Inn Ⓛ

SA32 7EN (300yds off A40 between Carmarthen and Nantgaredig)

✪ 12-3, 5-11; 12-11 Wed-Sun ☎ (01267) 290239

Beer range varies Ⓗ

Welcoming, traditional inn in a tiny hamlet just off the A40 around three miles from Carmarthen – there has been a pub here for several hundred years. The beer is generally from a Welsh brewery, with two on offer in the summer months. The pub has a good reputation for food, with bar meals, à la carte and specials available daily. Speciality nights such as a port and cheese evening feature occasionally. 🌢🌢◀⬙ A P⁵⁻🏠(279,280,281)

SIBA Direct Delivery Scheme

In 2003 the Society of Independent Brewers (SIBA) launched a Direct Delivery Scheme (DDS) that enables its members to deliver beer to individual pubs rather than to the warehouses of pub companies. Before the scheme came into operation, small craft brewers could only sell beer to the national pubcos if they delivered beer to their depots. In one case, a brewer in Sheffield was told by Punch Taverns that the pubco would only take his beer if he delivered it to a warehouse in Liverpool and then returned to pick up the empty casks. In the time between delivery and pick-up, some of the beer would have been delivered by Punch to...Sheffield.

Now SIBA has struck agreements with Admiral Taverns, Edinburgh Woollen Mills, Enterprise Inns, New Century Inns, Orchard Pubs, and Punch, as well as off-licence chains Asda and Thresher to deliver direct to their pubs or shops. The scheme has been such a success that DDS is now a separate but wholly-owned subsidiary of SIBA.

Edinburgh Pub Walks

Bob Steel

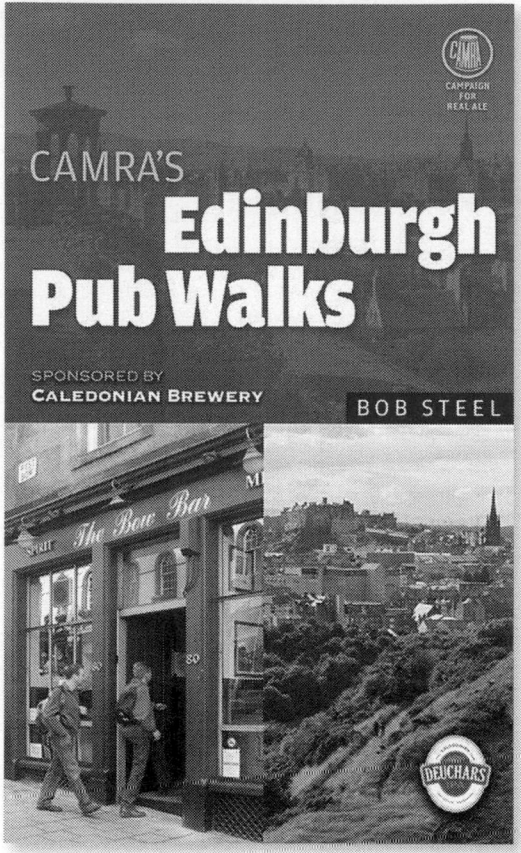

CAMRA's **Edinburgh Pub Walks** has everything you need to explore the many faces of Scotland's capital city, while never straying too far from a decent pint. A practical, pocket-sized guide to some of the best pubs in Edinburgh and the surrounding area, the book features 25 town, country and coastal walks, all accessible by public transport from the heart of the city. Fully illustrated throughout, street-level mapping helps you easily navigate and join up trails for longer walks.

£9.99 ISBN 978-1-85249-274-8 CAMRA members' price £7.99 160 pages

For this and other books on beer and pubs visit CAMRA's online bookshop at **www.camra.org.uk/books** or call **01727 867201**

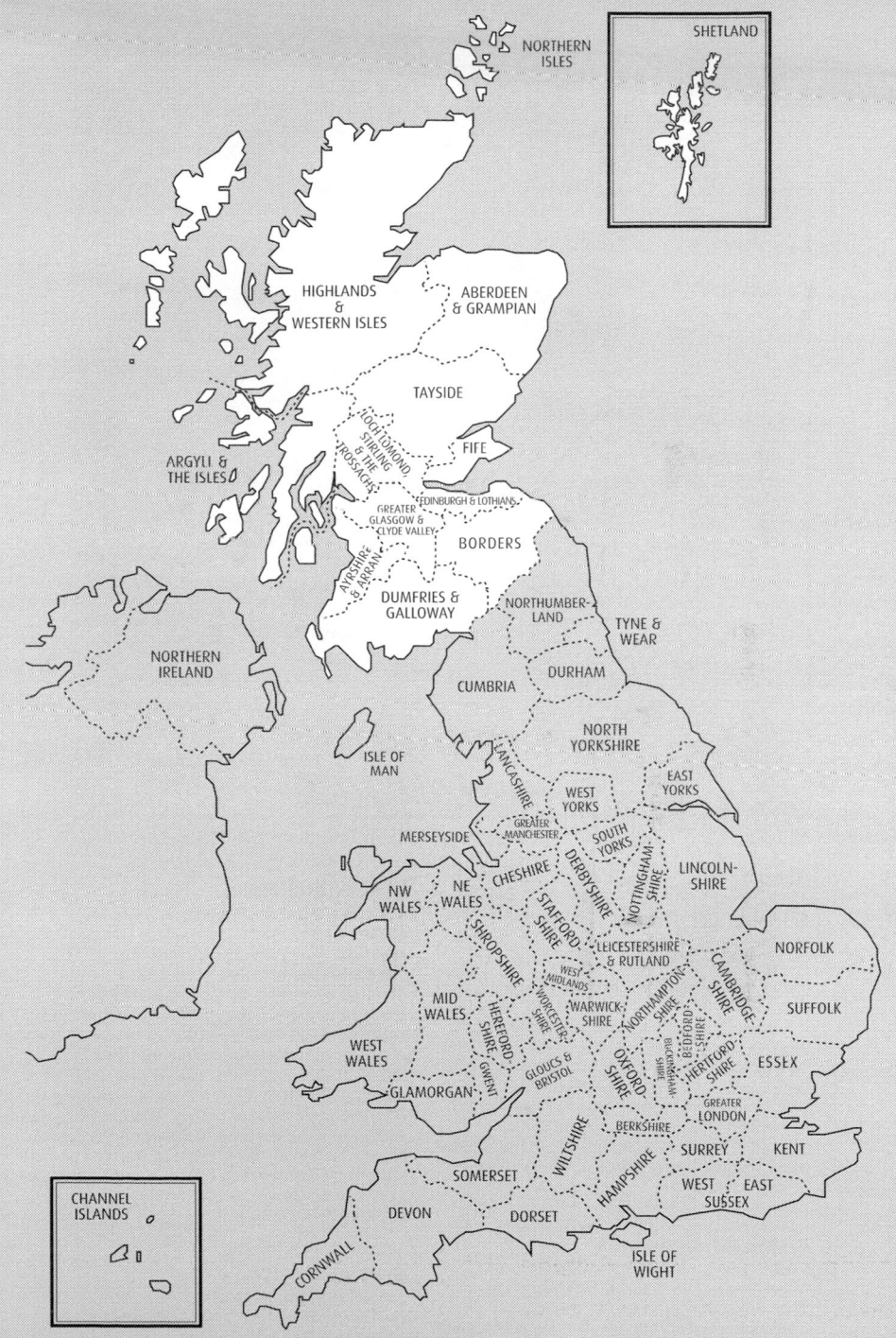

NORTHERN
ISLES

SHETLAND

HIGHLANDS
&
WESTERN ISLES

ABERDEEN
& GRAMPIAN

TAYSIDE

LOCH LOMOND
STIRLING
& THE
TROSSACHS

FIFE

ARGYLL &
THE ISLES

EDINBURGH & LOTHIANS

GREATER
GLASGOW &
CLYDE VALLEY

BORDERS

AYRSHIRE
& ARRAN

DUMFRIES &
GALLOWAY

NORTHUMBER-
LAND

TYNE &
WEAR

NORTHERN
IRELAND

CUMBRIA

DURHAM

ISLE OF
MAN

NORTH
YORKSHIRE

LANCASHIRE

EAST
YORKS

WEST
YORKS

MERSEYSIDE

GREATER
MANCHESTER

SOUTH
YORKS

LINCOLN-
SHIRE

CHESHIRE

DERBYSHIRE

NOTTINGHAM-
SHIRE

NW
WALES

NE
WALES

SHROPSHIRE

STAFFORD-
SHIRE

LEICESTERSHIRE
& RUTLAND

NORFOLK

CAMBRIDGE-
SHIRE

WEST
MIDLANDS

MID
WALES

HEREFORD-
SHIRE

WORCESTER-
SHIRE

WARWICK-
SHIRE

NORTHAMPTON-
SHIRE

SUFFOLK

WEST
WALES

GLOUCS &
BRISTOL

OXFORD-
SHIRE

BEDFORD-
SHIRE

BUCKING-
HAMSHIRE

HERTFORD-
SHIRE

ESSEX

GLAMORGAN

GWENT

BERKSHIRE

GREATER
LONDON

WILTSHIRE

SURREY

KENT

SOMERSET

HAMPSHIRE

WEST
SUSSEX

EAST
SUSSEX

CHANNEL
ISLANDS

DEVON

DORSET

CORNWALL

ISLE OF
WIGHT

Scotland

ABERDEEN & GRAMPIAN

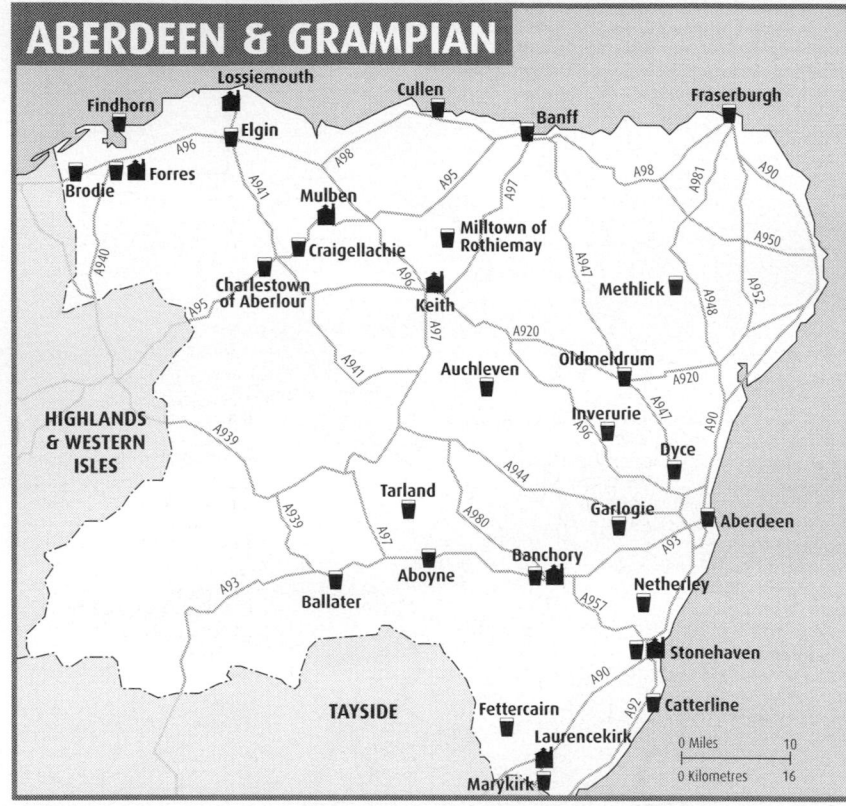

Authority areas covered: Aberdeenshire UA, City of Aberdeen UA, Moray UA

Aberdeen

Aitchies Ale House

10 Trinity Street, AB11 5LY
☼ 8am-10 (11 Fri & Sat); closed Sun ☎ (01224) 575972
Orkney Dark Island; guest beer Ⓗ
This small corner bar is the closest real ale outlet to the city rail/bus stations and the Union Square shopping complex. Renovated in 1994, it retains the flavour of an old-fashioned Scottish pub. Bar food is best described as traditional Scottish pub grub, including roast beef stovies. A good selection of whiskies includes Bell's special edition decanters. The friendly service here is second to none. The guest beer is frequently Caledonian Deuchars IPA. ♿≢🚃

Archibald Simpson's

5 Castle Street, AB11 5BQ (E end of Union St)
☼ 8am-midnight (1am Fri & Sat); 8-11 Sun
☎ (01224) 621365
Caledonian Deuchars IPA; Greene King Abbot; guest beers Ⓗ
A Wetherspoon pub in one of the monumental granite buildings in central Aberdeen designed by local architect Archibald Simpson. The former local headquarters of Clydesdale Bank, it retains many original architectural features. The main room is the high-ceilinged central hall, and there are additional seating areas to the side. The long bar features 12 handpumps offering a variety of beers, frequently from Scottish breweries, plus house beers from Houston and Isle of Skye. 🛏🍽♿≢🚃

Brentwood Hotel

101 Crown Street, AB11 6HH
☼ 11-2.30, 4.30-midnight; 11-midnight Fri & Sat; 5.30-11 Sun
☎ (01224) 595440 ⊕ brentwood-hotel.co.uk
Caledonian Deuchars IPA; guest beers Ⓗ
Mirrored downstairs bar in the basement of a modernised hotel, formerly known as Carriages, with lots of comfortable couches and seating areas. A winner of numerous local CAMRA awards, it offers 10 changing beers, usually sourced from a mix of nationals and Scottish micros including Houston, Highland and Orkney. Lunches are available in the bar, and the adjoining restaurant serves good food in the evening. Railway and bus stations are easily reached by descending the stairs from nearby Crown Terrace to Bridge Street. 🛏🍽≢P🍴🚃

Grill ★

213 Union Street, AB11 6BA
☼ 10-midnight (1am Fri & Sat); 12.30-midnight Sun
☎ (01224) 573530 ⊕ thegrillaberdeen.co.uk

INDEPENDENT BREWERIES

Brewmeister Keith
Burnside Laurencekirk
Deeside Banchory
Six° North Stonehaven (NEW)
Spey Valley Mulben
Speyside Craft Forres (NEW)
Windswept Lossiemouth (NEW)

Caledonian 80; Harviestoun Bitter & Twisted; guest beers Ⓗ
With an exquisite interior redesigned in 1926 and remaining largely unchanged since, this is the only pub identified by CAMRA as one of Britain's Best Real Heritage Pubs in the area. One of three men-only bars in the city until 1975, ladies' toilets were eventually provided in 1998. Situated across from the Music Hall, musicians often visit during concert breaks. Guest ales are frequently from Burnside, Fyne Ales or Orkney. A large selection of whiskies is stocked and bar snacks are available. CAMRA branch Pub of the Year 2012. ⇌🖳

Justice Mill
423 Union Street, AB11 6DR
🌣 8am-midnight (1am Fri & Sat); 9am-11 Sun
☎ (01224) 252410
Caledonian Deuchars IPA; Greene King Abbot; guest beers Ⓗ
Long, narrow, dark Wetherspoon Lloyds No.1 outlet with raised seating near the bar and booth seating at both the front and rear entrances. The quieter, family-friendly atmosphere changes to a loud maelstrom favoured by a younger clientele in the evening. The pub has two statement art pieces – a statue of an upside down man and a fire behind glass. ⬗◑&⇌●🖳

Moorings
2 Trinity Quay, AB11 5AA (opp quayside at bottom of Market St)
🌣 12-midnight; 1-3am Fri & Sat; 1-midnight Sun
☎ (01224) 587602
Beer range varies Ⓗ
Historic harbourside bar that changes character from friendly laid-back local to raucous rock bar on weekend evenings, when there may be a cover charge. The eclectic jukebox is in regular use by a varied clientele. Movies are screened on Sunday afternoons. A wide selection of guest beers comes mainly from Scottish micros, with a discount for CAMRA members. Real ales are now dispensed from 12 red-handled American-style fonts after the recent cellar refurbishments. A frequent winner of local CAMRA City Pub of the Year including 2013. ⇌♣●🖬🖳

Prince of Wales
7 St Nicholas Lane, AB10 1HF (lane opp Marks & Spencer)
🌣 10-midnight (1am Fri & Sat) ☎ (01224) 640597
Beer range varies Ⓗ
Listed in Scotland's True Heritage Pubs, the Prince of Wales has a friendly atmosphere and a large following of regulars. It offers a varied range of eight ales, including Scottish beers, favourites such as Theakston Old Peculier, Kelham Island Pale Rider or Hop Back Summer Lightning, and the usual Greene King/Belhaven brands. The two house beers are Prince of Wales from Inveralmond and Kenny's Bitter from Greene King. Sunday is folk night and Monday is quiz night. Good-value food is served daily until 9pm (6pm Sun). Complementary buffet on Fridays at 5pm. ◑⇌🖳

St Machar Bar
97 High Street, Old Aberdeen, AB24 3EN
🌣 11-11 (midnight Fri); 12.30-6 Sun ☎ (01224) 483079
⊕ themachar.com
Caledonian Deuchars IPA; guest beers Ⓗ
Located in the photogenic and historic Old Aberdeen conservation area amid the university buildings and close to Kings College, the pub is frequented by academia and locals alike. Up to three guest beers, frequently from Scottish microbreweries, are available alongside a comprehensive selection of whiskies. A splendid mirror from the long-gone Thomson Marshall Aulton Brewery just down the street adorns the wall inside the front door, and one from the Devanha Brewery is outside the toilets. CAMRA members, students and OAPs receive a discount. Open until midnight in term time. 🌣◑♣⌐🖳(20)

Under the Hammer
11 North Silver Street, AB10 1RJ (off Golden Square)
🌣 5-midnight (1am Thu); 4-1am Fri; 2-1am Sat; 6-11 Sun
☎ (01224) 640253
Caledonian Deuchars IPA; Inveralmond Ossian; guest beer Ⓗ
Just minutes off Union Street, this regular Guide entry is located in a basement next to the auction house – hence the name. Works by local artists displayed on the walls are for sale if they take your fancy. Convenient for the Music Hall and His Majesty's Theatre. Guest beers tend to contrast in style from the two regulars, with local Burnside beers frequent favourites plus Taylor Landlord. Unobtrusive background music plays. ⇌

Aboyne

Boat Inn
Charleston Road, AB34 5EL (N bank of River Dee next to Aboyne Bridge)
🌣 11-11 (midnight Fri & Sat) ☎ (01339) 886137
⊕ theboatinnaboyne.co.uk
Beer range varies Ⓗ
Popular riverside inn with a food oriented lounge featuring a spiral staircase leading to the upper dining area. Junior diners (and adults) may request to see the model train, complete with sound effects, traverse the entire pub at picture-rail height upon completion of their meal. Three ales are served, usually from local Scottish micros. The local Rotary Club regularly meets here. Self-catering accommodation is available – five en-suite twin rooms, a family room and a room with full disabled facilities. Q⬗⌐◑🖬&Å♣P

Auchleven

Hunter's Moon
3 The Belts, AB52 6QB (at crossroads at centre of hamlet)
🌣 closed Mon-Wed; 5-11 Thu; 4-1am Fri; 4-12.30am Sat; 11-11 Sun ☎ (01464) 820380
Beer range varies Ⓗ
A friendly welcome is assured at this smart village one-bar local, with green wood panelling all around. Pool and darts are at one end of the bar, while seating for food is at the other. An interesting, seasonal menu offering freshly cooked, locally sourced food is available (lunchtime only on Sunday). Children are permitted until 8pm. Quiz night is the first Thursday of the month, folk night the fourth Thursday. Ever-changing beers often come from Scottish microbreweries, chosen by customers. Occasional beer festivals are hosted. 🏨🌣◑&♣P

Ballater

Alexandra Hotel
12 Bridge Square, AB35 5QJ
✪ 11-2.30, 5-midnight; 11-midnight Fri-Sun
☎ (01339) 755376 ⊕ alexandrahotelballater.co.uk
Cairngorm Trade Winds; guest beers Ⓗ
Originally built as a private home in 1800 and becoming the Alexandra Hotel in 1915, the smart and recently refurbished lounge bar is popular with locals for bar suppers and regular bar drinkers too. Ales are supplied by Cairngorm, Inveralmond and Orkney. The location is handy for a stop-off on your way to Braemar for the Highland Games or for a visit with the royals at Balmoral. ⌫🚪🍴◑⅊⅄P⅄-🚻

Banchory

Douglas Arms Hotel
22 High Street, AB31 5SR
✪ 11-midnight (1am Fri & Sat); 11-11 Sun
☎ (01330) 822547 ⊕ douglasarms.co.uk
Caledonian Deuchars IPA; guest beers Ⓗ
Small hotel offering relatively inexpensive accommodation with three separate bars, rooms with plasma TVs and a function room. The public bar is a classic Scottish long bar with etched windows and vintage mirrors. A newly refurbished snug area is adjacent. The three-part lounge is divided by former exterior and internal walls and a fireplace, and is primarily used for dining. To the rear is a large outside decking area, ideal for fair-weather drinking. The public bar does not usually open until 3pm. ⅄Q⌫🏠🍴◑🚪⅊A♣⅄-🚻

Ravenswood Club (Royal British Legion)
25 Ramsay Road, AB31 5TS (up Mount St from A93, second right)
✪ 11-11 (midnight Fri & Sat) ☎ (01330) 822347
⊕ banchorylegion.com
Beer range varies Ⓗ
Large British Legion club with a comfortable lounge adjoining a pool and TV room, and a spacious function room well utilised by local clubs and societies. Darts and snooker are popular and played most evenings. The two handpumps offer a constantly changing choice of excellent value beers, with ales consistently the best quality in the village. An elevated terrace has fine views of the Deeside hills. Show a CAMRA membership card or copy of this Guide for entry. 🏠🍴◑🚪⅊A♣P

Banff

Ship Inn
8 Deveronside, AB45 1HP (on seafront near harbour)
✪ 12-midnight (1am Fri & Sat) ☎ (01261) 812620
⊕ theshipbanff.co.uk
Theakston XB; guest beer Ⓗ
The interior of this historic nautical-themed inn featured in the film Local Hero. It has a wood-panelled bar and lounge with sea views through the small windows. A blocked carriage arch hints at the earlier history of the building. Banff Marina, Duff House Gallery and Macduff Aquarium are close by, as are several golf courses. The pub has a fine view across the mouth of the Deveron to Macduff. Bar snacks are served all day. Karaoke and live music feature at weekends. One guest ale is selected by the regulars. ⅄🚪A♣⅄-🚻

Brodie

Old Mill Inn
IV36 2TD (on main A96 between Forres and Nairn)
✪ 11.30-11 ☎ (01309) 641605 ⊕ oldmillinnbrodie.com
Beer range varies Ⓗ
Spacious, family-friendly pub restaurant, with a cosy fireside area, smart restaurant and function room. The conservatory has a view of the old watermill and garden, including a bird table that attracts a pair of woodpeckers. Very good, freshly cooked food includes steak on Monday, fish on Friday and roasts on Sunday. Live Scottish/Irish instrumental music plays on Sunday evenings. A beer festival is held in June. Brodie Castle is nearby and the popular shopping destination Brodie Country Fare is opposite. ⅄Q⌫🏠🍴◑🚪⅊P⅄-🚻

Catterline

Creel Inn
AB39 2UL (on coast off A92, 5 miles S of Stonehaven)
✪ closed Mon & Tue; 12-2, 5-midnight (1am Fri & Sat); 12-midnight Sun ☎ (01569) 750254 ⊕ thecreelinn.co.uk
Beer range varies Ⓗ
Set in a scenic cliff-top location, the view from the rear of this small village inn is strongly recommended. Catterline is known as an artists' village, the most famous being Joan Eardley – one of her paintings is on display in the pub along with other local artists' work. The Creel is primarily a food venue but the bar area remains dedicated to drinking and serves as the village local. Up to four beers, usually from Scottish micros, are on offer. Crawton Bird Sanctuary, Todhead Lighthouse and Kinneff Old Church are all nearby. ⅄Q🏠◑⅊♣P⅄-🚻

Charlestown of Aberlour

Mash Tun
8 Broomfield Square, AB38 9QP (follow signs for Speyside Way Visitor Centre)
✪ 12-12.30am (1am Fri & Sat); 12.30-12.30am Sun
☎ (01340) 881771 ⊕ mashtun-aberlour.com
Beer range varies Ⓗ
Built in 1896 as the Station Bar, a pledge in the title deeds allowed a name change if the railway closed – but it must revert to the Station Bar if a train ever pulls up again outside. Patrons may now drink their ale on the former station platform and enjoy the view of the old railway line running past the door, now the Speyside Way. At least one beer comes from Cairngorm, with another local Scottish ale added in summer. The bar also offers more than 100 varieties of malt whisky. Q🏠🍴◑⅊A♣P⅄-🚻(314)

Craigellachie

Highlander Inn
10 Victoria Street, AB38 9SR (on A95, opp post office)
✪ 12-11 (12.30am Fri & Sat) ☎ (01340) 881446
⊕ whiskyinn.com
Cairngorm Trade Winds; guest beers Ⓗ
Picturesque whisky and cask ale bar on Speyside's Whisky Trail, close to the Speyside Way. It offers an excellent selection of malt whiskies and good-value tasting sessions, alongside a selection of ales from three handpumps (two in winter). CRAC (Craigellachie Real Ale Club) meets on the first Wednesday of each month, and its members,

whose etched glass tankards hang above the bar, help to choose the pub's guest ales, with the support of the owners and staff. The area is good for fishing and walking. Q 🍽️🐕🏠🍴◐ ♿♣P⚲⚲(336)

Cullen

Three Kings
17-21 North Castle Street, AB56 4SA
🟢 12-2, 5-11 (12.30am Thu-Sat) ☎ (01542) 840031
Beer range varies Ⓗ
Situated close to impressive but now defunct railway viaducts, this small, family-run pub was converted over 40 years ago from 150-year-old railway workers' cottages. A low-beamed roof and real fire help to create a cosy atmosphere on colder days. There is a separate restaurant to the rear and a large outdoor drinking area complete with pétanque courts. Three beers are served, mainly from Scottish micros including Windswept, Cairngorm and Orkney. 🏨🐕🏠◐P⚲⚲

Dyce

Granite City
Main Terminal, Aberdeen Airport, AB21 7DU
🟢 6am (8am Sat)-10; 8am-9 Sun ☎ (01224) 725711
Greene King Abbot; guest beers Ⓗ
In the main terminal of Aberdeen Airport, close to the entrance and luggage carousel, the pub was refurbished by Wetherspoon in 2010, and attracts airport staff, travellers and offshore workers. The walls display informative framed photographs of local personalities, including 'the Scottish Samurai' Thomas Blake Glover – one of the prime movers of Japan's industrialisation in the late 19th century. An extensive outdoor area features the Baby Boar, a sculpture carved from a one-ton boulder of local Kemnay granite. 🐕◐♿⚲⚲(727)

Elgin

Muckle Cross
34 High Street, IV30 1BU
🟢 11-midnight (1am Fri & Sat); 11-11.45 Sun
☎ (01343) 559030
Greene King Abbot; guest beers Ⓗ
A particularly good and deservedly popular small Wetherspoon establishment in a former bicycle repair shop, with friendly, efficient staff. The long, pleasant room has ample seating, including a family area. Eight handpumps offer a wide range of beers from national and Scottish micros. The pub also stocks a wide range of malt whiskies from more than 20 local distilleries. An extensive menu features healthy options as well as pub grub. Open from 8am (9am Sun) for coffee and breakfast. ◐♿≈🍴⚲

Sunninghill Hotel
Hay Street, IV30 1NH (500yds from railway station)
🟢 12-2.30, 5-11 (12.30am Fri & Sat) ☎ (01343) 547872
🌐 sunninghillhotel.com
Beer range varies Ⓗ
This long-established family hotel is a favourite for coffee, lunch and dinner, and the staff are friendly and efficient. Five different menus offer imaginative and good-quality food. There are a number of plush, comfortable seated areas, including two conservatories. Four handpumps dispense a variety of ales from Scottish

microbrewers, including the local Speyside Craft and Windswept breweries. The bar features a good selection of malt whiskies. Q 🍽️🐕🏠🍴◐♿≈P⚲⚲

Fettercairn

Ramsay Arms
Burnside Road, AB30 1XX
🟢 12-3, 5.30-11; 12-11.30 Fri & Sat; 12.30-11 Sun
☎ (01561) 340334 🌐 ramsayarmshotel.co.uk
Inveralmond Ossian, Thrappledouser Ⓗ
In the shadow of the Victoria Commemorative Arch, erected in recognition of the Queen's first trip to the north-east of Scotland when she spent the night at the hotel, the building's Victorian heritage lends itself to the traditional cuisine in the open, modern lounge. Close to Fasque Estate, residence of Sir William Gladstone, and near to the visitor centre at the Fettercairn distillery. 🏨🐕🏠◐♿P⚲

Findhorn

Kimberley Inn
94 Findhorn, IV36 3YG
🟢 12-midnight ☎ (01309) 690492
Beer range varies Ⓗ
A friendly welcome is assured at the Kimberley – self-styled as 'Moray's Seafood Pub' – situated on the shore of Findhorn Bay. The venue offers a well-stocked bar, family room and a snug with splendid views of Findhorn Bay, Forres and the hills across the Moray Firth. Two handpumps (one in winter) dispense a wide variety of beers, mainly from Scottish micros. The extensive menu features home-cooked food, especially local seafood, and even local ice cream. Popular with yachtsmen and holidaymakers as well as locals, Findhorn is a charming seaside village with a fine stretch of beach. 🏨Q🍽️🐕◐♿♣P⚲⚲

Forres

Mosset Tavern
Gordon Street, IV36 1DL
🟢 11-12.30am (1.30am Fri & Sat); 12-midnight Sun
☎ (01309) 672981 🌐 mossettavern.com
Cairngorm Trade Winds; Speyside Craft Moray IPA, Randolph's Leap; guest beer Ⓗ
Described as 'The country pub in the heart of Forres', this smart, extremely popular Scottish lounge bar/restaurant is situated next to the Mosset burn and pond, with swans and ducks. The friendly, efficient staff serve ale from a single handpump in the lounge and three in the public bar, where there are pool tables and large screens showing sport. A spacious function room is available and live music plays on Friday evenings. 🐕🏠◐🍷♿♣P⚲⚲

Fraserburgh

Elizabethan Bar & Lounge
36 Union Grove, AB43 9PH
🟢 9.30 (11 Sun)-1am ☎ (01346) 515148
Beer range varies Ⓗ
Set in the middle of a housing estate and near the local Academy, with a mock-Tudor exterior, the pub has a large bar and lounges in three distinct sections, with TV sport usually featuring in two of them. The Elizabethan has a formidable reputation for its variety of quality ales from throughout the country. Local CAMRA membership has increased

as a direct result of the landlord's avid promotion of real ale, and a CAMRA discount applies. The bar also features over 200 malts – the largest collection in the area. CAMRA Pub of the Year 2011.
ॐ⊞ᚕ♣P⌐-♿️⎚

Garlogie

Garlogie Inn
AB32 6RX
✪ 11-2.30, 5-10.30 (11.30 Fri & Sat); closed Mon eve winter; 12.30-9 Sun ☎ (01224) 743212 ⊕ garlogieinn.com
Beer range varies Ⓗ
This roadside inn dating from the early 19th century has been run by the Quinn family for nearly 30 years. Numerous extensions have been added to the original building, including a large restaurant area, and the pub has a reputation for excellent food (booking advised). Drinkers are welcome in the small bar area, with beers from Scottish breweries, frequently the Harviestoun range, and occasionally from English brewers including Black Sheep. Drum Castle and Cullerlie stone circle are close at hand. ᚕQ✿◑⅁P♿️

Inverurie

Gordon Highlander
West High Street, AB51 3QQ
✪ 8-11.30 (1am Fri; 12.30am Sat); 9-11 Sun
☎ (01462) 626780
Caledonian Deuchars IPA; Greene King Abbot; guest beers Ⓗ
A fairly new Wetherspoon outlet in a splendid Art Deco building that used to be the Victoria Cinema. The name refers to the famous local regiment, and also to a preserved steam engine named after the regiment, which was based at the now defunct Inverurie Locomotive Works nearby. Both historical references are documented in various displays. The books on the shelves are free to read and take home (and donations are welcome). There are at least three guest ales. ᚕॐ◑⅁⇄♿️

Marykirk

Marykirk Hotel
Main Street, AB30 1UT
✪ 12-2.30, 5-11; 12-midnight Sat & Sun ☎ (01674) 840239
⊕ marykirkhotel.co.uk
Inveralmond Thrappledouser Ⓗ
Built in the 18th century, this listed building is a former coaching inn in the village of Marykirk, which lies between Montrose and Laurencekirk. The area is popular for hunting and fishing, with the river North Esk, one of the top salmon rivers in Scotland, close by. Aficionados of old brewery mirrors will appreciate the examples here from Lochside Brewery in Montrose and Boroughlodge Brewery in Edinburgh. Bus services between Montrose and Laurencekirk stop in the village.
ᚕ✿⇆◑♣P⌐-♿️(8,9)

Methlick

Ythanview Hotel
Main Street, AB41 7DT
✪ 11-2.30, 5-11 (1am Fri); 11-12.30am Sat; 12-11 Sun
☎ (01651) 806235 ⊕ ythanviewhotel.co.uk
Beer range varies Ⓗ
Traditional inn in the village centre, home of the other MCC, Methlick Cricket Club. The small public bar at the rear is heavily sport themed. Log fires warm both the lounge and public bars. The pub is renowned for Jay's special curry with whole chillies – a challenge worth taking. Thursday is steak night. Bands play on some Saturdays. Beers are mainly from Scottish micros such as Inveralmond and Fyne Ales. Haddo House, Tolquhon Castle and Pitmedden Garden are nearby. ᚕ✿⇆◑⊞♣P⌐-♿️(290,291)

Milltown of Rothiemay

Forbes Arms Hotel
AB54 7LT
✪ 12-2.30 (not Mon & Tue), 5-11 ☎ (01466) 711248
⊕ forbesarms.co.uk
Beer range varies Ⓗ
Small, cosy, family-run hotel in a pleasant country location near the River Deveron, with fishing and shooting activities nearby. It has public and lounge bars and a separate dining area. The local folk club hosts a live session on the second Thursday of the month. Two beers are usually available, sourced mainly from Scottish micros and occasional Welsh breweries, including Brains. Over 60 malt whiskies are stocked. Accommodation is in six en-suite rooms. ✿⇆◑⊞⅁P⌐-

Netherley

Lairhillock Inn
AB39 3QS (signed off B979, 3 miles S of B9077)
✪ 11-11 (midnight Fri & Sat) ☎ (01569) 730001
⊕ lairhillock.co.uk
Caledonian Deuchars IPA; Taylor Landlord; guest beers Ⓗ
The 'INN' sign on the roof of this rambling building in attractive open countryside makes it easy to spot from the road. It has a traditional, wood-panelled bar warmed by a large log fire in winter, and a lounge with an open fireplace and a large conservatory area, popular for dining. A separate function room, the Crynoch, is also available. Two guest beers in summer and one in winter are frequently sourced from Scottish breweries. Convenient for the attractions of Stonehaven and Royal Deeside. ᚕQॐ✿◑⅁♣P⌐-

Oldmeldrum

Redgarth Hotel
Kirk Brae, AB51 0DJ (signed off A947)
✪ 11-3, 5-11 (midnight Fri & Sat); 12-3, 5-11 Sun
☎ (01651) 872353 ⊕ redgarth.com
Beer range varies Ⓗ/Ⓖ
This local hotel and pub has excellent views of the Grampian mountains to the west, and is a favourite haunt of crime writer Stuart MacBride. Beers on three handpumps plus occasional gravity ales are sourced from Scottish breweries including Inveralmond, Cairngorm, Kelburn, Orkney, Houston and Highland, and occasional Brewer in Residence evenings are held. Traditional bar meals are served at lunchtime throughout the week, with a more extensive menu and a separate restaurant area available in the evening. ॐ✿⇆◑ᚕ♣-

Stonehaven

Marine Hotel ♈
9-10 Shorehead, AB39 2JY (overlooking harbour)
✪ 11-midnight (1am Fri & Sat); 11-midnight (11 winter) Sun
☎ (01569) 762155 ⊕ marinehotelstonehaven.co.uk

Caledonian Deuchars IPA; Taylor Landlord; guest beers H

CAMRA branch Pub of the Year in 2013, this small harbourside hotel features a bar with simple wood panelling, a rustic lounge with an open fireplace, and a restaurant upstairs. Seating outside offers a splendid view of the harbour. Guest ales are mostly from local and regional breweries. Several Belgian beers are on draught and a massive choice of bottled Belgian beers is also available. A house brewery, Six° North, has recently started up. Historic Dunnottar Castle is one mile south.
♨✿⌂◑⌐🏠

Ship Inn

5 Shorehead, AB39 2JY (on harbour front)
✪ 11-midnight (1am Fri & Sat) ☎ (01569) 762617
⊕ shipinnstonehaven.com
Beer range varies H
Traditional harbour-front hotel with a maritime themed, wood-panelled bar and an outdoor seating area overlooking the water. In the bar, a mirror from the defunct Devanha Brewery is a prominent feature. Two beers are offered, one

from Inveralmond. An extensive range of malt whiskies is stocked. A modern restaurant, with panoramic harbour views, is adjacent to the bar, with food served all day at the weekend. Accommodation is available in 11 guest rooms.
♨✿⌂◑⌐🏠

Tarland

Aberdeen Arms

31 The Square, AB34 4TX (in village square)
✪ closed Mon winter; 12-2.30, 5-11 (1am Tue & Fri); 12-1am Sat; 12-11 Sun ☎ (01339) 881225
Beer range varies H
Part of a 300-year-old listed building in the village centre, this traditional inn has a wood-lined bar area, stripped wooden floors, low ceilings and a real fire. Live music features on Tuesday nights and the Cromar Folk Club meets on the last Friday of the month. Craigievar Castle, Grampian Transport Museum at Alford and the Queen's View beauty spot are close by. The bus service is infrequent.
♨✿♿⚲♣P🚌(210)

St Machar Bar, Aberdeen (Photo: Gordon M Robertson)

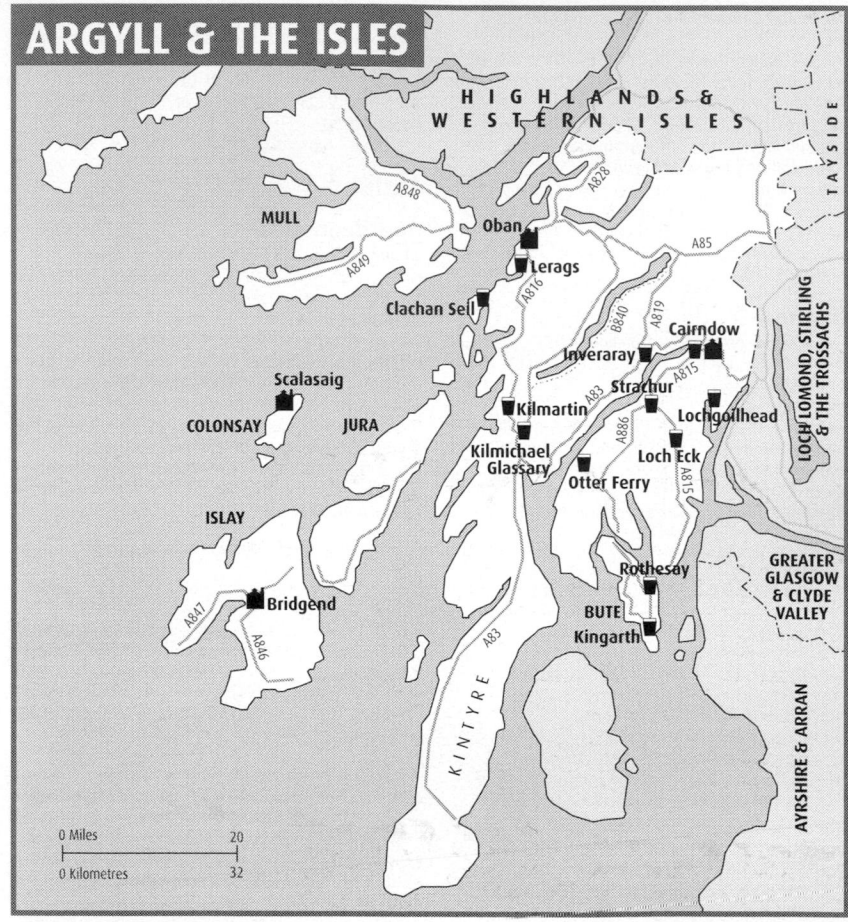

ARGYLL & THE ISLES

Authority area covered: Argyll & Bute UA

Cairndow

Fyne Ales Brewery Tap & Shop ⬡

Achnadunan, PA26 8BJ (down side road off A83 at head of Loch Fyne) NN198131

☼ 10-6 ☎ (01499) 600120 ⊕ fyneales.com

Beer range varies Ⓗ

Opened in 2012, this brewery tap and shop is housed in one of the original farm buildings alongside the brewery itself, set up in a redundant milking parlour. The bar front is made from local granite etched and polished by the owner's son and displays the beers produced, the ingredients and the names of the two founders. Five handpumps dispense a choice of the brewery's beers, although only three may be in use over the winter. Excellent hot pies and meat from the farm can be purchased to take away. Q⬡✿&P

Stagecoach Inn

PA26 8BN (near head of Loch Fyne) NN181109

☼ 11-11 (1am Fri & Sat); 11-midnight Sun

☎ (01499) 600286 ⊕ cairndowinn.com

Beer range varies Ⓗ

Down a loop road, once the main road and signed on the current A83 section, this former coaching inn offers a pleasant spot at which to break a long journey through Argyll. The bar has two handpumps dispensing beers, mainly from nearby Fyne Ales but occasionally from other Scottish breweries. Archways lead to the dining room and comfortable lounge with a log fire. In summer, attractive views over Loch Fyne can be enjoyed from the loch-side garden.

▲⬡✿🛏❍🅳&Å♣P🔑☐🚃(926,976)

Clachan Seil

Tigh an Truish ⬡

PA34 4QZ (on B844 5 miles W of A816 jct, by Clachan Bridge) NM784197

☼ 11-1.30am summer (11-2.30, 5-8 (1am Thu & Fri); 12-1am Sat winter); 11 (12 winter)-1am Sun ☎ (01852) 300242

⊕ tighantruish.co.uk

Beer range varies Ⓗ

Twice winner of local CAMRA Pub of the Year, this charming inn is worth veering off the A816 to visit. The rustic wooden interior has an L-shaped counter with an unusual high bench seat known as the Perch. Three handpumps serve Scottish ales with beers from Fyne and Orkney frequent guests. A stone fireplace houses a coal-burning iron stove with a Highland Games hammer above. There is a separate dining room. In summer the garden and patio are a delight. ⚅⚆✦◖P⇌▤(418)

Inveraray

George Hotel
Main Street East, PA32 8TT
✪ 11 (12 Sun)-midnight ☎ (01499) 302111
⊕ thegeorgehotel.co.uk
Beer range varies Ⓗ
Owned by the same family for six generations, the George sits in the centre of this 18th-century town built by the Duke of Argyll. Two beers are usually available, often from Fyne Ales. The food menu offers the best of quality local produce. Live music (blues, folk and rock) plays on Friday and Saturday evenings and music festivals are held in May and August. In September the hotel provides Fyne Ales beers for the Best of the West festival at Inverary Castle. ⚅Q⛵✦◖⛃✦▲P⇌▤(926,976)

Kilmartin

Kilmartin Hotel Ⓛ
PA31 8RQ (on A816 10 miles N of Lochgilphead)
NR835989
✪ 12 (5 Mon-Thu winter)-11; 12-midnight Fri; 12-1am Sat; 12-11 Sun ☎ (01546) 510250 ⊕ kilmartin-hotel.com
Beer range varies Ⓗ
A pleasant hotel set above Kilmartin Glen, one of Scotland's most important prehistoric sites. The bar serves at least two beers, usually from Fyne and Orkney breweries. Home-made food is served lunchtimes and evenings. Children are welcome if dining. Pub games are available. A museum, standing stones, and cairns dating from 5000 years ago are nearby. The bar is closed weekday lunchtimes in winter. ⛵✦◖⛃▲P⇌▤(423)

Kilmichael Glassary

Horseshoe Inn Ⓛ
Bridgend, PA31 8QA (off A816 3 miles N of Lochgilphead) NR852928
✪ 5-11; 12-midnight Sat & Sun ☎ (01546) 606369
⊕ horseshoeinn.biz
Fyne Jarl; guest beers Ⓗ
The hotel is situated to one side of a small glen, close to many historic sites, from stone barrows to the volcanic plug of Dunadd Fort where the ancient kings of Dalriada were crowned. The pub buildings were once part of an old farmhouse. Excellent meals are served in the stone-walled lounge and dining rooms all day at the weekend, evenings only during the week. The public bar displays pictures of local sights. Two handpumps dispense the beers – see the blackboards over the bar for what's on. ⚅Q⛵✦◖⛃P▤(423)

> There can't be a good living where there is not good drinking. **Benjamin Franklin**

Kingarth: Isle of Bute

Kingarth Hotel
PA20 9LU (on A844 at jct with road to Kilchattan Bay)
NS094563
✪ 12-midnight ☎ (01700) 831662 ⊕ kingarthhotel.co.uk
Beer range varies Ⓗ
A friendly welcome awaits you at this rare gem of a pub set in a secluded yet accessible location on the south of the Isle of Bute. Two handpumps supply an ever-changing range of beers from all over Britain. A very popular destination for drinkers and diners, it is the perfect place to return to after a stroll to Kilchattan Bay, for a few beers, a game of pool and an alfresco meal under cover on the veranda, or on the patio. ⚅✦✦◖⛃P⇌▤(490)

Lerags

Barn Ⓛ
Cologin, Lerags Glen, PA34 4SE (down minor road off A816) NM853260
✪ 11-1am (12-1am Sat & Sun only winter)
☎ (01631) 564618 ⊕ cologin.co.uk
Fyne Highlander Ⓗ
To get away from the usual routes, leave the A816 for Lerags Glen and then take the first right. Cologin is a set of 18 chalets, cottages and a farmhouse set amid attractive scenery, centred around the Barn bar restaurant. A guest beer, usually from Fyne Ales, may be offered in summer. Food is served all day from a varied menu. The venue is dog-friendly and there is a children's play park outside. Fishing is available and there are good walks nearby. Telephone to check opening hours in winter. ⚅✦✦◖P⇌

Loch Eck

Coylet Inn
PA23 8SG (on A815 near S end of Loch Eck) NS143885
✪ 12-1am ☎ (01369) 840426 ⊕ coyletinn.co.uk
Fyne Highlander; guest beers Ⓗ
Seventeenth-century coaching inn in scenic surroundings on the banks of Loch Eck. There is an attractive and inviting bar where you can relax around the open fire after a day's fishing, touring or walking in the hills. Fyne Ales are available from two handpumps. Varied food menus offer local game, seafood, traditional, modern and children's dishes, served in the bar and the more formal restaurant, which has views of the loch and mountains. ⚅✦✦◖▲P⇌▤(484,486)

Whistlefield Inn
PA23 8SG (jct of A815 and unclassified road to Ardentinny) NS144933
✪ 12 (5 Mon-Fri winter)-11 ☎ (01369) 860440
⊕ whistlefield.co.uk
Beer range varies Ⓗ
A traditional 17th-century Scottish drovers' inn refurbished to 21st-century standards. Two handpumps offer a range of beers from Kelburn, Arran and Skye breweries, with both dark and light ales usually available. The bar features several large and amusing ornaments, including a highland cow's head above the fire and a wooden Easter Island statue. The connecting lounge, dining room and suntrap front garden offer spectacular views over Loch Eck and the hills to the west. ⚅⛵✦◖P▤(484,486)

Lochgoilhead

Shore House Inn L

PA24 8AD (at head of Loch Goil) NN198014
☼ 12-11; closed Tue & winter Mon ☎ (01301) 703340
⊕ theshorehouse.net
Beer range varies H

The Shore House was built in the 1850s and sits in a commanding position at the head of Loch Goil. Access to the car park is off the B839 before entering the village. There is also a path next to a cottage by the loch. Two beers (one in winter) from Fyne Ales are offered. Pizzas cooked in a wood-fired oven are a speciality on the varied menu. The restaurant and beer garden enjoy views down the loch. The pub closes in January – phone ahead in winter. ❀❦◑⅃♣P⅃₋ᕟ(302,484)

Otter Ferry

Oystercatcher L

PA21 2DH (on B8000 on E coast of Loch Fyne) NR930844
☼ 11-11 summer (closed Mon-Thu; 5-11 Fri; 11-11 Sat winter); 12.30 (5 winter)-11 Sun ☎ (01700) 821229
⊕ theoystercatcher.co.uk
Fyne Highlander; guest beers H

Attractive pub near a former ferry dock, well worth the scenic trip down Loch Fyne on the single track B8000. Beers are from Fyne Ales with occasional guests from other breweries in the summer. Large windows in the bar and restaurant offer majestic views of Loch Fyne and the Kintyre Peninsula. The garden leads to a beach and a pontoon with 15 moorings. A varied menu specialises in locally sourced seafood, the perfect treat after a spell of boating or walking. ᕟ❀◑⅃♣P⅃₋

Rothesay: Isle of Bute

Black Bull Inn

3 West Princess Street, PA20 9AF (opp harbour)
☼ 11-11 (midnight Fri & Sat); 12.30-11 Sun
☎ (01700) 502366
Caledonian Deuchars IPA; Inveralmond Lia Fail H

Enjoy the pleasant train ride along the Clyde from Glasgow, embark the ferry from the splendour of Wemyss Bay station, and perhaps visit the Victorian toilets on Rothesay pier and look at the rare Victorian postbox by the Discovery Centre before sampling the beers in this two-bar pub. Food is served in a separate dining area. A visit to Mount Stuart House could be taken before a final beer and the ferry home. Popular with locals and yachtsmen. ◑ᕟᕟ

Strachur

Creggans Inn L

PA27 8BX (on A815, near A886 jct) NN087022
☼ 11 (12 Sun)-11 ☎ (01369) 860279 ⊕ creggans-inn.co.uk
Beer range varies H

The small bar with a cosy fire set in a stone wall has two handpumps offering a changing selection of beers from Fyne Ales. Drinks may be taken to other lounges, the pool room, restaurant or enjoyed in the garden overlooking the loch, with views to Inveraray. At the other end of the building there is a range of accommodation and a shop selling locally produced food and crafts. A convenient stopping place along Loch Fyne. The hotel holds a license for civil wedding ceremonies, and can host functions for up to 80 people. ᕟ❀❦◑P⅃₋ᕟ(484,486)

Stagecoach Inn, Cairndow (Photo: Tom Ord)

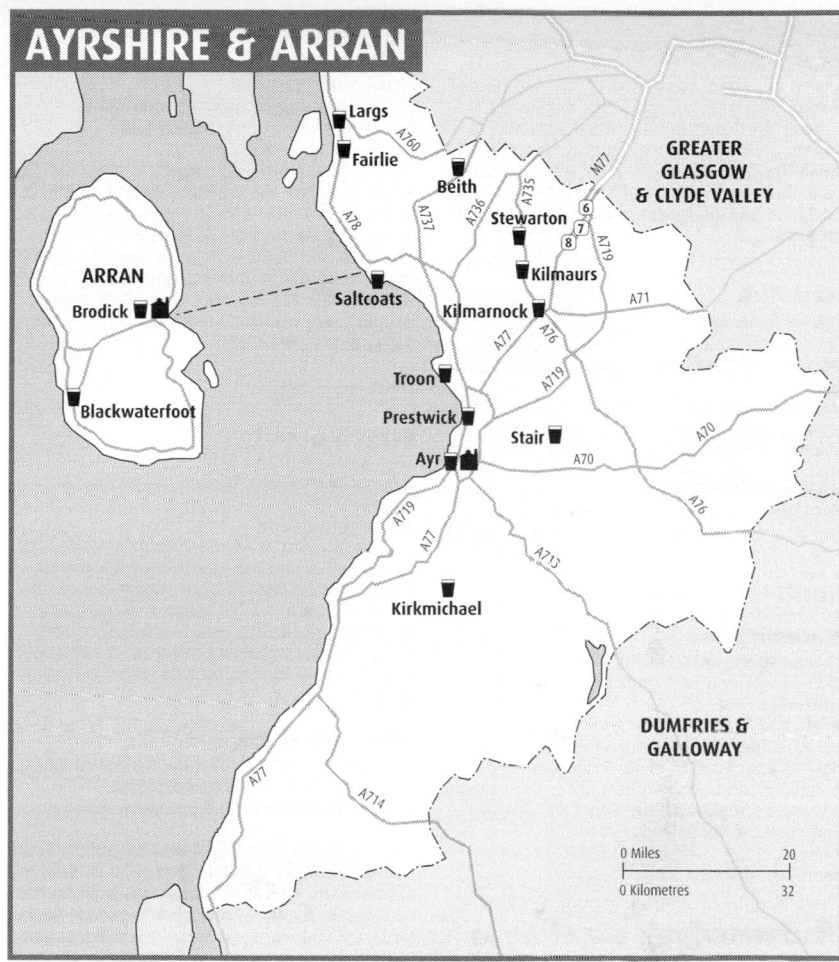

AYRSHIRE & ARRAN

Largs
Fairlie
Beith
Stewarton
Kilmaurs
ARRAN
Brodick
Saltcoats
Kilmarnock
GREATER GLASGOW & CLYDE VALLEY
Troon
Blackwaterfoot
Prestwick
Stair
Ayr
Kirkmichael
DUMFRIES & GALLOWAY

0 Miles 20
0 Kilometres 32

SCOTLAND

Authority areas covered: East Ayrshire UA, North Ayrshire UA, South Ayrshire UA

Ayr

Abbotsford Hotel

14 Corsehill Road, KA7 2ST
✪ 10-12.30am (midnight Sun) ☎ (01292) 261506
⊕ abbotsfordhotel.co.uk
Caledonian Deuchars IPA; Marston's Pedigree; guest beer Ⓗ
Family-run hotel convenient for local attractions. Three real ales are offered in the Copper Bar. Meals are served in both the bar and a separate restaurant area. There is also a pool/TV room and a function room/conservatory. The guest beer on handpump tends to be from a larger brewery – and is often a darker English beer.
▲☎🏨🛏️◑⬛🚻♣P♿🚃(57,361)

Chestnuts Hotel

52 Racecourse Road, KA7 2UZ (A719, 1 mile S of centre)
✪ 10-midnight (12.30am Sat) ☎ (01292) 264393
⊕ chestnutshotel.com
Beer range varies Ⓗ
Three changing real ales, from both local and larger regional breweries, are offered in The 19th Hole at this well-appointed, family-run hotel. The bar itself features discreet seating around a cosy log fire and

a vaulted ceiling. High-quality meals are served in the bar and separate restaurant. The spacious garden has plenty of seating. ▲☎🏨🛏️◑⬛♿P🚃(9)

Geordie's Byre

103 Main Street, KA8 8BU (N of centre, over river towards Prestwick)
✪ 11-11 (midnight Thu-Sat); 12.30-11 Sun
☎ (01292) 264925
Beer range varies Ⓐ
CAMRA award-winning, 18th-century pub, located in the Newton area of Ayr, serving up to four guest ales sourced from far and wide. This is one of just a few Scottish pubs using traditional Scottish tall founts. A wide selection of malt whiskies and rums is also available. Handy for several local buses. 🚌🚃

Wellingtons Bar

17 Wellington Square, KA7 1EZ
✪ 11-12.30am; 12-midnight Sun ☎ (01292) 262794
⊕ welliesbar.weebly.com

INDEPENDENT BREWERIES

Arran Brodick: Isle of Arran
Ayr Ayr

Beer range varies H
Close to the seafront, bus station and local
government offices, this basement bar attracts
tourists and office workers alike. The Wednesday
evening quiz is very popular and weekend music
features live bands or a DJ on Saturday and an
acoustic session on Sunday. The two changing ales
usually include at least one from either Kelburn or
Fyne Ales. Good-value food is served every
lunchtime and all day Thursday to Sunday.
ॐ◑≈❐

West Kirk L

58A Sandgate, KA7 1BX (close to bus station)
✪ 10-midnight (12.30am Fri & Sat) ☎ (01292) 880416
**Caledonian Deuchars IPA; Greene King Abbot; guest
beers** H
This Wetherspoon conversion of a former church
retains many original features – access to the
toilets is via the pulpit. Up to eight changing guest
ales are offered and local micros are usually well
represented. Meals are available all day, with
breakfast from 8am. Outside, the front drinking
area has a shelter for smokers. ॐ֍◑৬≈●ᐟ➖❐

Beith

Masonic Arms L

21 Main Street, KA15 2AD
✪ 11-midnight ☎ (01505) 502786
Beer range varies H
Small, traditional pub where well-behaved dogs
are welcome, situated on a narrow main street
close to bus routes heading north, south and west.
A friendly, sport-oriented hostelry, pool, darts and
dominoes are played here. Beers are normally
from local breweries and a large selection of malt
whiskies is also available. Children are not
permitted. ♣❐(X34,X36)

Blackwaterfoot: Isle of Arran

Kinloch Hotel

KA27 8ET
✪ 12-midnight ☎ (01770) 860444 ⊕ bw-kinlochhotel.co.uk
Caledonian Deuchars IPA; guest beer H
A hidden gem in a rural village on the west coast of
the Isle of Arran. Family owned and run, it has 37
bedrooms, a restaurant and three bars. Quality
food features fresh local produce including fish and
seafood. Facilities include a heated indoor
swimming pool, children's pool, squash court,
snooker room, fitness room and sauna.
ॐ֍⇦◑৬♣Åᐟ➖❐

Brodick: Isle of Arran

Ormidale Hotel

Knowe Road, KA27 8BY (off A841 at W end of village)
✪ 12.30-2.30 (summer only), 4.30-midnight; 12-midnight Sat
& Sun ☎ (01770) 302293 ⊕ arran-hotel.co.uk
Arran Ale, Blonde; guest beer A
Large red sandstone hotel with a small bar and
spacious conservatory set in seven acres of
grounds. Beers are served from traditional Scottish
tall founts on the boat-shaped bar. Home-cooked
meals are recommended. Discos and folk nights
are held and the attractive beer garden has views
across Brodick Bay. Accommodation is available in
the summer only. ᘯ֍⇦◑❸♣Pᐟ➖❐(324)

Fairlie

Village Inn ♥ L

46 Bay Street, KA29 0AL
✪ 11-midnight (1am Fri & Sat); 12.30-midnight Sun
☎ (01475) 568432 ⊕ villageinnfairlie.co.uk
Beer range varies H
Three regularly changing, usually Scottish, real ales
are served here. The pub reopened in 2010 after
two years of closure and the locals, determined not
to lose it again, support the Tuesday night quiz and
occasional live music nights. The pub has quickly
gained a reputation for excellent food and friendly
staff. Children are welcome until 10pm, although
the public bar is a child-free oasis.
ᘯQॐ֍◑❸Pᐟ➖❐(585)

Kilmarnock

Brass & Granite

53 Grange Street, KA1 2DD
✪ 11-midnight (12.30am Thu-Sat); 12.30-midnight Sun
☎ (01563) 523431
Beer range varies H
Open-plan pub near Kilmarnock town centre, close
to Rugby Park football ground. Guest beers are
usually sourced from local or Cumbrian brewers
and there is also a wide range of draught and
bottled Belgian beers. Food is available all day.
Several TVs in the pub show live sport, and quizzes
are held every Sunday, Monday and Wednesday.
◑৬♣Åᐟ➖❐

Wheatsheaf Inn

70 Portland Street, KA1 1JG (near bus and rail stations)
✪ 10-midnight (1am Fri) ☎ (01563) 572483
**Caledonian Deuchars IPA; Greene King Abbot; guest
beers** H
Sizeable town-centre Lloyds No.1 bar, originally the
historic Wheatsheaf Hotel, famous for its links to
Robert Burns, whose first book was published in
Kilmarnock. The bar is divided into various seating
areas, with booths, sofas and a raised dining space.
DJs entertain on a Friday and Saturday, with
karaoke early on Friday evening, but otherwise
conversation holds sway. Food is the standard
Wetherspoon fare and nine handpumps dispense a
range of ales plus real cider. Open from 8am for
breakfast. ॐ֍◑৬≈●ᐟ➖❐

Kilmaurs

Weston Tavern

27 Main Street, KA3 2RQ
✪ 11-midnight (1am Fri & Sat); 12.30-midnight Sun
☎ (01563) 538805 ⊕ westontavern.co.uk
Beer range varies H
Classic country pub and restaurant with a tiled
floor, stone walls and a wood-burning fire. It sits
beside the Jougs, a former jailhouse and tollbooth
(jougs were iron collars used to restrain miscreants
and a set still hangs from the walls today). A single
pump dispenses ale from a rotating list of local
breweries. Regular live music and quiz nights are
held. ᘯ֍◑❸৬≈P➖❐(1,13,337)

Kirkmichael

Kirkmichael Arms

3-5 Straiton Road, KA19 7PH
✪ 12-midnight (12.30am Fri & Sat) ☎ (01655) 750200
⊕ kirkmichaelarms.co.uk

Beer range varies ℍ
Newly reopened village local with a comfortable lounge bar/restaurant and a separate public bar with slate flooring, a wood-burning stove and fireplace. High-quality food is served all day – accredited by EatScotland, celebrating the best of Scottish food and drink. Two ales are usually available, one each from Ayr and Houston breweries. A welcome return of a good community pub after a gap of a few years. ᴹQ⌣ᴄⅅ◔⌂♣⊞(361)

Largs

Charlie Smith's
14 Gallowgate Street, KA30 8LX (on A78, opp pier)
✪ 10-midnight (1am Fri & Sat) ☎ (01475) 672250
Beer range varies ℍ
This friendly, one-roomed pub is situated on the seafront opposite the Cumbrae ferry terminal, close to the railway station. A child free establishment with a modern feel to it, good-quality pub food is served daily. There is one ever-changing ale, sometimes from a local brewery, but frequently from farther afield. Handy for the Waverley paddle steamer in summer. ⌣ⅅ◔⇌♣⊞

JG Sharps Bar
34-36 Nelson Street, KA30 8LW
✪ 11-midnight (1am Fri & Sat); 12.30-midnight Sun
☎ (01475) 675515 ⊕ jgsharps.co.uk
Caledonian Deuchars IPA ℍ
Set back from the seafront and main street on the corner of Nelson Street and Boyd Street, this is a large traditional pub with many different drinking areas. An open fire warms the bar area and there is space for smokers in the beer garden outside. Good-quality pub meals are served at lunchtime and Friday-Sunday evenings. Games and TV are in evidence and there is occasional live music. An additional guest beer may be available in summer. ᴹQ⌣⊛ⅅ◔♣⌐⊞

Prestwick

Prestwick Pioneer
87 Main Street, KA9 1JS
✪ 10-midnight (12.30am Fri & Sat) ☎ (01292) 473210
Caledonian Deuchars IPA; Greene King Abbot; guest beers ℍ
Modern Wetherspoon outlet named after the first Scottish Aviation Pioneer built nearby. It has an airy feel with light wood décor, and features photographs of early Open Golf Championships at Prestwick and of Elvis at the nearby airport – the only place in the UK on which he stepped foot. Ten handpumps serve local and national ales, and food is available all day. ᴹ⌣ⅅ◔⇌◔⊞

Saltcoats

Salt Cot 𝕃
7 Hamilton Street, KA21 5DS
✪ 10-11 (midnight Thu; 1am Fri & Sat) ☎ (01294) 465924
Greene King Abbot; Ruddles Best Bitter; guest beers ℍ
A good Wetherspoon conversion of a former cinema, the pub gets its name from the original cottages at the salt pans. It has an area where children are permitted and there is a family menu. At least one of the guest beers is locally sourced, often from Strathaven or Arran. Although there are

TVs in the bar area, the sound is only turned on a few times a year for rugby internationals. Opens at 8am for breakfast. Q⌣ⅅ◔⌂⇌◔⊞(11,585)

Stair

Stair Inn
KA5 5HW (on B730 7 miles E of Ayr)
✪ 12-11 (1am Fri & Sat) ☎ (01292) 591650 ⊕ stairinn.co.uk
Beer range varies ℍ
This family-run hotel, on the banks of the River Ayr, is not accessible by public transport but is well worth seeking out. The comfortable bar and adjacent restaurant feature bespoke handmade furniture and the bedrooms are furnished in a similar style. One or two real ales are available, usually from Houston Brewery. The food menu relies heavily on local produce and fish from the inn's own smokehouse is a speciality. Booking for meals at weekends is strongly recommended. ᴹQ⊛⌂ⅅ◔⌐

Stewarton

Millhouse Hotel
6-8 Dean Street, KA3 5EQ
✪ 11-midnight (1am Fri & Sat); 12-midnight Sun
☎ (01560) 482255 ⊕ millhousehotelayrshire.co.uk
Beer range varies ℍ
Real ale trade continues to flourish under the hotel's new owners, with the three handpumps serving weekly changing ales from local breweries Kelburn, Houston, Ayr, Arran or Strathaven, usually alongside a beer from farther afield. Recent refurbishment of the restaurant has led to increased food service and the hotel now offers accommodation after extensive upgrade of the bedrooms. ⌣⊛⌂ⅅ◔⌂⇌◔⌐⊞(1,337)

Troon

Bruce's Well
91 Portland Street, KA10 6QN
✪ 11-midnight (1am Fri & Sat); 12-midnight Sun
☎ (01292) 311429
Caledonian Deuchars IPA; guest beer ℍ
A friendly, spacious and comfortable lounge bar. A number of TVs around the bar area show football and other sports but the volume is usually low or off. The bar may open earlier than advertised if there is a big sporting event on TV. The guest ale comes from the Belhaven list and changes regularly. Unusually, the cellar is situated in a temperature-controlled room off the main bar area. ⇌◔⊞(10,14,110)

Fullartons
10 Portland Street, KA10 6EA
✪ 10-11.30 (12.30am Fri & Sat) ☎ (01292) 311212
⊕ fullartons.co.uk
Cairngorm Wildcat; Greene King IPA; guest beers ℍ
A smart, comfortable lounge bar decorated to a high standard close to Troon cross. Three guest ales are sourced from the Belhaven guest list. The gantry also hosts speciality malt whiskies, vodkas and rums. The bar is also very popular for its locally sourced food, which is prepared daily in its own kitchen. Regular live music sessions are held on a Saturday night. ⌣ⅅ◔⇌♣⌐⊞(14,10,110)

BORDERS

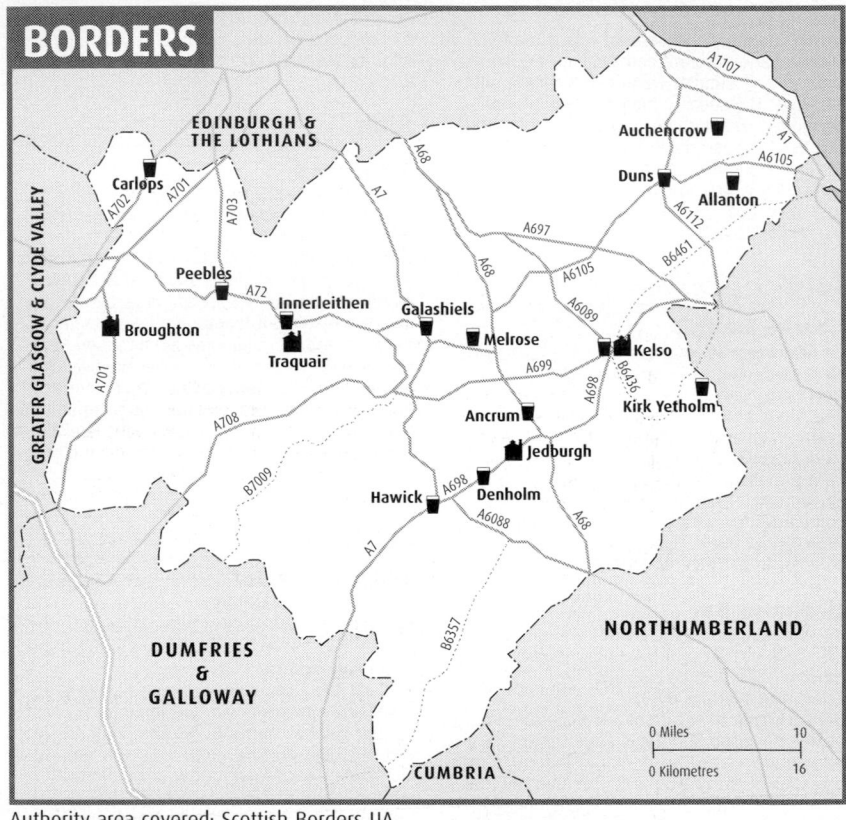

Authority area covered: Scottish Borders UA

Allanton

Allanton Inn
TD11 3JZ
✪ 12-11 ☎ (01890) 818260 ⊕ allantoninn.co.uk
Beer range varies Ⓗ
Dating back to the 18th century, this old coaching inn has a bright, airy feel. Quality food featuring local Borders produce is served in the front dining rooms, and the rear bar area, which overlooks the beer garden to the countryside beyond, is also used by diners at busy times. Two real ales are available, often from Scottish Borders Brewery and other Scottish micros such as Fyne. With six en-suite rooms, this is an ideal base for exploring Berwickshire and Northumbria. ⌂▭☆🍴◗♣P▤

Ancrum

Cross Keys Inn
The Green, TD8 6XH (on B6400, off A68)
✪ 11-11 (1am Fri & Sat); 12.30-11 Sun ☎ (01835) 830242
Scottish Borders Game Bird; guest beer Ⓗ
Perched on the Ale Water (yes really!), this friendly village local's front bar has remained largely untouched since 1906, retaining the pine-panelled gantry. Two larger rooms to the rear provide additional space. Recently bought by Scottish Borders Brewery, the pub is expected to specialise in food using locally sourced produce in line with the brewery's 'Plough to Pint' ethos. There are also plans for B&B accommodation. Dogs are welcome in the public bar. ⌂▭☆◗Ⓓ🍴å♣P⌂▤(25,68)

Auchencrow

Craw Inn
TD14 5LS (signed from A1)
✪ 12-2.30, 6-11 (midnight Fri); 12-midnight Sat; 12.30-11 Sun ☎ (01890) 761253 ⊕ thecrawinn.co.uk
Beer range varies Ⓗ
A friendly 18th-century inn situated in a tiny Borders village. The bar has a wood-burning stove and tables for both dining and drinking. Three real ales are usually sourced from smaller breweries, and the roof beams are festooned with many pumpclips as evidence. Excellent home-cooked food is served in both the bar and the well-appointed restaurant. Beer festivals are held in November and July. Accommodation includes B&B and a self-catering annexe. ⌂Q☆▭◗Ⓓå♣P▤

Carlops

Allan Ramsay Hotel
Main Street, EH26 9NF
✪ 12-11 (1am Fri & Sat); 12-midnight Sun ☎ (01968) 660258 ⊕ allanramsayhotel.com
Stewart Pentland IPA; guest beer Ⓗ

The hotel, dating from 1792, is set in a small village beside the Pentland Hills, and has a distinct Scottish feel to it. Several rooms have been knocked through to create a large single area, retaining many original features. One end is a restaurant, the bar area is in the middle. The bar is inlaid with pre-decimal pennies. Food is served all day. Dogs are admitted. Opening hours may vary in winter. ▲¿ڿ◑◔ُ◐♣P🖵

Denholm

Auld Cross Keys Inn
Main Street, TD9 8NU
✿ 12-11 (midnight Thu; 1am Fri & Sat); 12.30-midnight Sun
☎ (01450) 870305 ⊕ crosskeysdenholm.co.uk
Scottish Borders Game Bird; guest beer Ⓗ
This recently refurbished and extended village hotel is a venue for folk music sessions and concerts. The public bar tends to be favoured by drinkers while diners prefer the additional comfort of the lounge and function room. The guest beer is normally from Northumberland brewery. The hotel has recently received several accolades for its food (served lunchtimes and evenings, all day on Sunday). Dogs are allowed in the bar.
▲Q¿ڿ◑◔◐Ȼ♣P⁴┶🖵(20)

Fox & Hounds Inn
Main Street, TD9 8NU
✿ 11.30-3, 5-midnight Mon & Wed; 11.30-midnight (1am Fri & Sat); 12.30-midnight Sun ☎ (01450) 870247
Scottish Borders Game Bird; guest beer Ⓗ
A village local, built in 1728, overlooking the green. The small bar is half wood-panelled and a real fire adds a cosy feel in winter. Pictures and memorabilia decorate the walls. The rear lounge has a coffee-house feel and an upstairs dining room is used in the evening. A guest beer is served in summer. The courtyard provides space for smokers and a sheltered outdoor drinking area in warmer weather. Dogs are permitted.
▲¿ڿ◑◔◐Ȼ♣⁴┶🖵(20)

Duns

Black Bull Hotel
15 Black Bull Street, TD11 3AR
✿ 11-midnight (1am Fri & Sat); 12-midnight Sun
☎ (01361) 883379
Beer range varies Ⓗ
Family-run 200-year-old hotel situated just off the town square, offering real ales from both sides of the border. The cosy wood-panelled bar is popular with locals and the lounge area, with bench seating, is more suited to families. Fresh fish is the speciality in the restaurant, which has an intimate, relaxed, candlelit atmosphere. A secluded beer garden can be enjoyed during the summer. Letting rooms are all named after local historic figures. Dogs are welcome in the bar.
¿ڿ◑◔Ȼᛣ♣P⁴┶🖵

Galashiels

Ladhope Inn
33 High Buckholmside, TD1 2HR (A7, ⅓ mile N of centre)
✿ 4-11 (midnight Thu); 3-midnight Fri; 11-1am Sat; 12.30-11 Sun ☎ (01896) 752446
Caledonian Deuchars IPA; guest beer Ⓗ

Comfortable, friendly local with a vibrant Borders atmosphere. Originating circa 1792, it has been altered considerably inside. Now a single room, it is decorated with a large inked map of the Galashiels area and has a wee alcove with a golfing theme. Three flat-screen TVs ensure the pub is busy during sporting events. The guest beer is often from Scottish Border Brewery but changes regularly. Excellent home-made soup is served on Sundays. Live music plays frequently. Dogs are welcome, but children are not permitted.
✿▲♣🖵(95)

Salmon Inn
54 Bank Street, TD1 1EP (opp gardens)
✿ 11-11 (midnight Thu; 1am Fri & Sat); 12.30-midnight Sun
☎ (01896) 752577
Caledonian Deuchars IPA; guest beers Ⓗ
A comfortable, friendly, centrally situated pub that can be very lively when sporting events are screened on TV. The single L-shaped room is split into two areas and decorated with historic photographs of the Galashiels area. Guest beers are often from smaller Scottish and English breweries. Good home-cooked meals are popular (no food Sun). Families are welcome at lunchtime only. Dogs are also welcome. ¿✿◑ᛣ▲♣⁴┶🖵(62,95)

Hawick

Bourtree
22 Bourtree Place, TD9 9HL (NE edge of town centre)
✿ 11-midnight (1am Fri & Sat); 12.30-midnight Sun
☎ (01450) 360450
Beer range varies Ⓗ
Built as Hawick Conservative Club in 1897, this listed building has been stunningly transformed into a Wetherspoon pub. The former snooker hall forms the main area, while there are three further areas for quieter or private use. Images on the walls represent a history of Hawick life, including mills, railways, common riding and motorcycling. Regular cask ale and cider promotions and festivals are held. Opens at 8am for food, which is served all day. ▲Q¿ڿ◑◔◐ȻP⁴┶🖵(20,95)

Exchange Bar (Dalton's)
1 Silver Street, TD9 0AD (off SW end of High St)
✿ 11-11 (1am Fri & Sat); 12.30-11 Sun ☎ (01450) 376067
Beer range varies Ⓗ
Hidden away between the imposing St Mary's Parish Kirk with its winkie bells and the Hawick Heritage Hub, this local was once Hawick Corn Exchange. A previous owner was named Dalton and the name has stuck ever since. The building is a Victorian gem with dark wood panelling and ornate cornice work. The bar is popular with knowledgeable locals and there is a comfy lounge used for parties and Friday karaoke. Children are not admitted. Ȼ♣⁴┶🖵(20,95)

Innerleithen

Traquair Arms Hotel
Traquair Road, EH44 6PD (B709, off A72)
✿ 11-11 (midnight Fri & Sat); 12-11.30 Sun
☎ (01896) 830229 ⊕ traquairarmshotel.co.uk
Caledonian Deuchars IPA; Taylor Landlord; Traquair Stuart Ale Ⓗ
Elegant 18th-century hotel in the scenic Tweed Valley. The comfortable lounge bar features a welcoming real fire in winter and a relaxing

SCOTLAND

tropical fish tank. An Italian bistro area and separate restaurant provide plenty of room for diners. Food is served all day at weekends. One of the few outlets for draught ales from Traquair House. Dogs are permitted.
⚞⛵☺️🍴◑♿▲P⸵☗(62)

Kelso

Cobbles 🍸

7 Bowmont Street, TD5 7JH (off NE side of town square)
🕒 3-10 Mon; 11.30-11; 11-1am Fri & Sat; 12-10 Sun
☎ (01573) 223548 ⊕ thecobbleskelso.co.uk
Beer range varies Ⓗ

An award-winning gastro-pub offering an eclectic mix of British classics, Pacific Rim and modern European cuisine, using the finest locally sourced and seasonal ingredients. To the right of the main dining area is a lounge bar where beers from Tempest, the pub's own microbrewery, are featured. Though the focus is on food, drinkers are welcome here. Private functions are catered for upstairs. Local CAMRA Pub of the Year 2013.
⚞⛵☺️◑♿☗

Kirk Yetholm

Border Hotel

The Green, TD5 8PQ
🕒 11.30-midnight (1am Fri & Sat); 12-11 winter; 12-midnight Sun ☎ (01573) 420237 ⊕ theborderhotel.com
Beer range varies Ⓗ

An attractive 260-year-old coaching inn with bar areas and a conservatory restaurant. Popular with walkers, it is at the start of the new Scottish National Trail, on St Cuthbert's Way, and marks the official end of the Pennine Way. Those completing the Pennine Way are entitled to a free half pint, a tradition from Wainwright's time. The inn is noted for its hearty food and quality real ales from independent breweries on both sides of the border. Dogs are welcome in the bar.
⚞⛵☺️🍴◑▲♣P☗

Melrose

Burt's Hotel

Market Square, TD6 9PL
🕒 11-2, 5 (6 Sun)-11 ☎ (01896) 822285 ⊕ burtshotel.co.uk
Scottish Borders Game Bird; Taylor Landlord; guest beer Ⓗ

An elegant, family-run hotel in the main square, with colourful window boxes creating a cheerful frontage in summer. In the lounge bar, the décor reflects the countryside sporting interests of many of its clientele. The focus is unashamedly on food, and space may be at a premium for those who only wish to drink. But the food is very good, so go on,

treat yourself. Weather permitting, the beer garden is an option, but only at lunchtime. Dogs are welcome. ⚞Q☺️🍴◑♿▲♣P⸵☗(62,68)

King's Arms Hotel

High Street, TD6 9PB
🕒 11-11 (midnight Fri & Sat); 12-11 Sun ☎ (01896) 822143
Caledonian Deuchars IPA; guest beers Ⓗ

An old coaching inn dating from 1793, the bar has a wooden floor and church pew seating, and is decorated with rugby memorabilia and old local photographs. There is a large-screen TV for sports eventing. The quieter lounge is comfortably furnished and has a lovely old carved door set into the ceiling. There are also dining rooms upstairs. Food is served all day on Sunday. National Cycle Route 1 passes the door. Dogs are welcome.
⚞Q⛵🍴◑♿▲♣P⸵☗(62,68)

Peebles

Bridge Inn

Portbrae, EH45 8AW
🕒 11-midnight (1am Fri & Sat); 12-midnight Sun
☎ (01721) 720589
Caledonian Deuchars IPA; guest beers Ⓗ

Cheerful, welcoming, town-centre local, also known as the Trust. The mosaic entrance floor shows it was once the Tweedside Inn. The bright, comfortable single bar is decorated with jugs, bottles, memorabilia of outdoor pursuits and photos of old Peebles. A heated patio area overlooks the river. The Gents is superb, with well-maintained original Twyford Adamant urinals. Children are not admitted, but dogs are welcome. Local CAMRA Pub of the Year runner-up 2013.
☺️▲♣⸵☗

Neidpath Inn

27-29 Old Town, EH45 8JF (A/2 W of town centre)
🕒 11-midnight (1am Fri & Sat); 12.30-midnight Sun
☎ (01721) 724306 ⊕ neidpathinn.co.uk
Stewart Edinburgh Gold; guest beer Ⓗ

Traditional town pub providing a contrast for drinkers. At the front of the bar room is a cosy place to enjoy a relaxing drink, while the rear space has a pool table and jukebox. Wood, musical instruments and glasswork add to the atmosphere. A separate, comfortable lounge leads to a dining area which in summer spills out onto an outdoor decked area. Meals are served all day at weekends and families are welcome in the lounge until 7pm. Dogs are permitted in the bar. ⚞⛵☺️🍴◑♿▲♣⸵☗(62)

Learned drinker

He was a learned man, of immense reading, but is much blamed for his unfaithfull quotations. His manner of studie was thus, he wore a long quilt cap, which came two or rather three inches at least over his eies, which served him as an umbrella to defend his eies from the light. About every three houres his man was to bring him a roll and a pot of ale to refocillate (refresh) his wasted spirits so he studied, and dranke, and munched some bread and this maintained him till night, and then he made a good supper.
An Oxford man, William Prynne (1600-69), as described by **John Aubrey** in Brief Lives, ed. John Buchanan-Brown, 2000

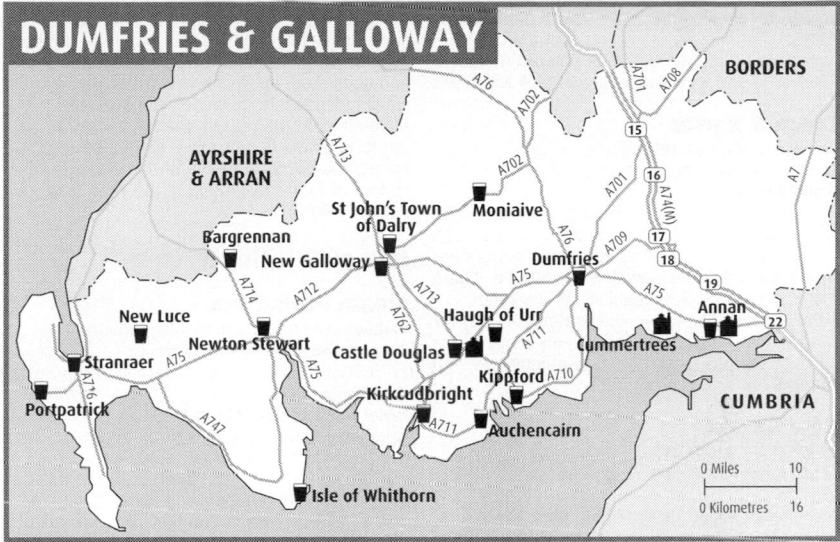

Authority area covered: Dumfries & Galloway UA

Annan

Blue Bell Inn
10 High Street, DG12 6AG
☼ 11-11 (midnight Thu-Sat); 12.30-11 Sun
☎ (01461) 202385
Caledonian Deuchars IPA; guest beers Ⓗ
A focus for cask ale enthusiasts in the Annan area for many years, this pub has won the local CAMRA Pub of the Year title on several occasions. A former coaching inn, the busy, friendly hostelry offers three or four ales from anywhere in the UK. The outside courtyard at the rear provides a pleasant seated area in summer. The pub retains traditional features from its time within the Gretna & District State Management Scheme, notably the wood-lined interior. ☺≢P⁵-⊟

Auchencairn

Old Smugglers Inn
11-13 Main Street, DG7 1QU
☼ 12 (5 Mon)-11; 12-midnight Fri & Sat ☎ (01556) 640331
⊕ solwaysmugglers.co.uk
Beer range varies Ⓗ
Situated in a quiet village on the Solway coast, this inn has been a popular pub with villagers and visitors over many years. Managed by a CAMRA member with experience in the brewing industry, two cask ales are available. The hotel serves good, freshly cooked, locally sourced food in the restaurant and in the welcoming public bar.
🏨Q☼☺🛏🌑◑🖳♣P⁵-⊟

Bargrennan

House O' Hill Hotel
DG8 6RN (just off A714 on Glentrool road)
☼ 12-11 (closed Mon Nov-Mar) ☎ (01671) 840243
⊕ houseohill.co.uk
Beer range varies Ⓗ
Close to the Southern Upland Way and situated within the Galloway Forest Park, this small hotel is popular with walkers, climbers, anglers and cyclists. Fully refurbished, it has an attractive

interior including a small function room. Two beers are offered, mainly from Scottish microbreweries, and three-day beer festivals with food and live music feature twice a year. The pub specialises in good-value home cooking featuring locally sourced supplies as well as home-grown produce. Regular music events featuring local artists are held throughout the year.
🏨☼☺🛏◑♿👤♣P⁵-⊟(359)

Castle Douglas

Sulwath Brewery Tap Room Ⓛ
The Sulwath Brewery, 209 King Street, DG7 1DT
☼ 10-6; closed Sun ☎ (01556) 504525
⊕ sulwathbrewers.co.uk
Beer range varies Ⓗ
The taproom and visitor centre for Dumfries & Galloway's principal brewery, the bar is popular with real ale lovers in Castle Douglas and surrounds. Six of the brewery's award-winning ales are offered, although not all are in cask-conditioned form, along with two draught ciders. Guest ales from other breweries are available on occasion. Mini festivals are held in May and June, the latter in conjunction with the Food Town celebrations. Q♿👤🌑⁵-⊟

Dumfries

Cavens Arms Ⓨ
20 Buccleuch Street, DG1 2AH (next to Barbours department store)
☼ 11-11 (midnight Thu-Sat); 12.30-11 Sun
☎ (01387) 252896
Beer range varies Ⓗ
Recently renovated and extended, this busy town-centre pub offers four house ales and four guest beers drawn from breweries north and south of the

border. Great-value meals are served until 9pm daily except Monday, and occasional themed nights are hosted. Local CAMRA Pub of the Year 2006-2011 and joint winner in 2012. ❶❺♿≠⬥—▥

Coach & Horses
66 Whitesands, DG1 2RS (on Whitesands)
❸ 11 (12.30 Sun)-11 ☎ (01387) 279754
Draught Bass ⊞
Former coaching inn featuring a pleasant bar area with a fabulous flagstone floor and warming open fire. The lunchtime food menu offers a variety of freshly cooked dishes, served in the upstairs dining room. Live music plays regularly at weekends, attracting real blues fans. The location is handy for nearby tourist attractions, with plenty of car parking. The pub may close early if quiet.
🅼❶≠♣P▥

New Bazaar
39 Whitesands, DG1 2RS (on Whitesands)
❸ 11-11 (midnight Thu-Sat); 12.30-11 Sun
☎ (01387) 268776
Greene King Abbot; Theakston XB; guest beers ⊞
Former coaching inn beside the River Nith with a pleasant airy bar featuring an impressive Victorian gantry and a warming coal fire in winter. Four cask ales are usually served – two regulars and two varying guests. The pub is a favourite with football supporters before and after matches at nearby Palmerston Park, and ideally situated for local tourist attractions. There is a good area outside for smokers. Closing time may vary depending on custom. 🅼❀❺≠♣P—▥

Ship Inn
97-99 St Michael Street, DG1 2PY (opp St Michael's churchyard)
❸ 11-11; 12.30-11 Sun ☎ (01387) 255189
Caledonian Deuchars IPA; Morland Old Speckled Hen; guest beers ⊞
A long-time favourite with real ale enthusiasts in the Dumfries area, this small, busy, traditional pub offers up to six beers on handpump. Welcoming to locals and visitors, it has a front bar and a small back lounge. The pub is opposite St Michael's churchyard where Robert Burns is buried and 200 yards from Burns House where he spent his final years. Q≠♣▥

Tam o' Shanter Ⓛ
114-117 Queensberry Street, DG1 1BH (off High Street near Burns statue)
❸ 11-11 (midnight Wed-Sat); 12.30-7.30 Sun ☎ 07855 473 933
Broughton Clipper; guest beers ⊞
Well positioned just off the High Street, this 17th-century coaching inn has been a feature of the Dumfries beer scene for many years. The cosy, traditional pub has a comfortable public bar and a couple of small, quiet rooms to the rear. A rotating range of five ales includes at least three from Broughton Brewery. Dogs are welcome. Q≠♣▥

Haugh of Urr

Laurie Arms Hotel
11-13 Main Street, DG7 3YA (on B794, 1 mile S of A75)
❸ 12 (12.30 Sun)-3, 5.30-midnight ☎ (01556) 660246
⊕ haugh-of-urr.com
Beer range varies ⊞
Welcoming family-run pub and restaurant on the main street in a charming, quiet location. It has a

genuine village inn atmosphere, enhanced on cold winter nights by the warming log fire in the bar. Popular with locals and visitors for its range of ales and good food, up to four cask beers, mainly from small independent breweries, are available depending on the season. The toilets feature an interesting selection of saucy seaside postcards. Former CAMRA Scottish Pub of the Year and joint winner of local CAMRA Pub of the Year 2012. 🅼Q❀❶♣P▥

Isle of Whithorn

Steam Packet Inn
Harbour Row, DG8 8LL (B7004 from Whithorn)
❸ 11-11 (1am Fri; 12.30am Sat) summer; 11-3, 6-11 Tue-Thu; 11-midnight (11 Mon) winter; 12-11 Sun ☎ (01988) 500334
⊕ steampacketinn.biz
Taylor Landlord; guest beers ⊞
Traditional and historic family-run hotel overlooking the harbour and surrounding area, welcoming to locals and visitors alike, including families and pets. The public bar has stone walls and a multi-fuel stove, and there are pictures of the village and maritime events throughout. Four guest ales from a wide variety of breweries are available in both bars. The extensive food menu features local produce – the Sunday hot buffet is a speciality and themed food nights are held regularly. Discounted B&B is available for CAMRA members. 🅼Q❧❀🛏❶🍴❺♣—▥(415)

Kippford

Anchor Hotel
DG5 4LN
❸ 11-3, 6-11 (midnight summer); 12.30-11 (midnight summer) Sun ☎ (01556) 620205 ⊕ anchorkippford.co.uk
Beer range varies ⊞
Popular sailing centre with fine views over the Urr estuary. Two cask ales are always available, with another added during the summer season, usually from the local Sulwath Brewery. This busy establishment has a dining area serving excellent food from a varied menu using local produce, with good vegetarian options (book ahead for the restaurant). Outside seating overlooking the Solway estuary is pleasant in summer.
🅼Q❀🛏❶❺♣P▥

Kirkcudbright

Selkirk Arms Ⓛ
High Street, DG6 4JQ
❸ 11 (12.30 Sun)-11 ☎ (01557) 330402
⊕ selkirkarmshotel.co.uk
Sulwath The Grace; guest beer ⊞
A traditional hotel with an excellent reputation for meals and accommodation. Two cask ales are available in the lounge and public bars. Outside is a large garden area with tables for the summer months. Kirkcudbright is notable for its artistic heritage and houses a number of interesting galleries and museums. Robert Burns is reputed to have written his famous Selkirk Grace while visiting the hotel, hence the name of the house ale.
Q❀🛏❶🍴❺♣P—▥

Moniaive

Craigdarroch Hotel
Main Street, DG3 4HN

☼ 12-midnight ☎ (01848) 200205 ⊕ craigdarrocharms.co.uk
Beer range varies Ⓗ
The Craigdarroch Hotel has been at the heart of
Moniaive's community for over a century. It attracts
many outdoor enthusiasts, including cyclists,
anglers and shooters. The hotel hosts regular music
festivals – with an amazing range of major artists
performing to audiences in its Marquee Club in the
garden. Normally two ales are served. It also holds
an annual beer festival. The restaurant serves
excellent, freshly prepared meals. Children are
welcome, the children's menu having been
recently reworked to make it healthier.
🏚Q👪🕮🍴◑🍽🌳P¹⌐🚌

New Galloway

Ken Bridge Hotel Ⓛ
DG7 3PR (next to river bridge at head of Loch Ken on
A713)
☼ 11 (12 Sun)-11 ☎ (01644) 420211
⊕ kenbridgehotel.co.uk
Beer range varies Ⓗ
The hotel sits on the bank of the River Ken at the
head of Loch Ken, both renowned for good fishing
and picturesque views. The owners of this family-
run establishment have local connections reaching
back through generations. Good freshly cooked
meals are served in the restaurant and bar, with
two or more cask ales available, usually at least
one from the local Sulwath Brewery. A superb
centre for water sports and outdoor pursuits or for
simply relaxing and taking in the spectacular
scenery. 🏚Q👪🕮◑🍽🌳ÅP¹⌐🚌

New Luce

Kenmuir Arms Hotel
31 Main Street, DG8 0AJ (8 miles N of Glenluce along
old military road)
☼ 11-midnight ☎ (01581) 600218
⊕ kenmuirarmsnewluce.com
Beer range varies Ⓗ
Situated in a beautiful village on the bank of the
River Luce, this picturesque hotel has well-kept
gardens by the river. The public bar offers one real
ale all year round, two in summer, sourced from all
over the UK. Home-cooked, freshly prepared food
is served at lunchtime and in the evening. This is a
popular stopping-off point for walkers on the
Southern Upland Way and the hotel offers a
luggage transfer service. Q👪🕮◑🍽🌳Å🌳P¹

Newton Stewart

Galloway Arms Hotel
54-56 Victoria Street, DG8 6DB
☼ 11-midnight (11 Sun) ☎ (01671) 402653
⊕ gallowayarmshotel.com
Belhaven IPA; guest beer Ⓗ
Old town-centre hotel dating back to 1750 and
built for the Earl of Galloway. The Earls Room
Lounge boasts over 120 whiskies in addition to the
real ale. The building has many original features

and welcoming log fires. One real ale is served in
both the bar and lounge, with a guest ale
sometimes available. The hotel caters for locals and
visitors alike and is used widely by fishermen,
golfers and walkers. It specialises in local produce,
particularly Angus beef and venison.
🏚Q👪🕮🍴◑🍽🌳P¹⌐🚌(X75,500)

Portpatrick

Crown Hotel
9 North Crescent, DG9 8SX (overlooking harbour)
☼ 11-midnight (1am Fri & Sat); 12-midnight Sun
☎ (01776) 810261 ⊕ crownportpatrick.com
Beer range varies Ⓗ
This hotel overlooks the picturesque and historic
Portpatrick harbour with views on a clear day
across to Ireland. The large, comfortable bar area is
at the front of the building and serves two
regularly changing ales from across the UK. The
interior is adorned with some fine pictures and
ornaments along with an open fire. Quality food is
served in the cosy lounge bar and outside on the
seafront terrace. There is regular live music on
Friday and Saturday nights, featuring both local and
visiting performers. 🏚👪🕮🍴◑🌳Å🌳¹⌐🚌(367)

St John's Town of Dalry

Clachan Inn
8-10 Main Street, DG7 3UW
☼ 11 (12 Sun)-11 ☎ (01644) 430241 ⊕ theclachaninn.co.uk
Beer range varies Ⓗ
In a picturesque village, this hotel has a reputation
for excellent food, cosy, well-appointed bedrooms
and a welcoming atmosphere. It features an
attractive, traditional main bar with a separate
restaurant. Two cask ales, usually from Scottish
breweries, are always available. A varied menu,
featuring local produce such as organic lamb and
venison, includes excellent daily specials. The
Clachan suits the needs of hunters, fishermen,
cyclists and all visitors who enjoy country life. A
handy stop for those walking the Southern Upland
Way. 🏚Q👪🕮◑🍽🌳ÅP¹⌐🚌

Stranraer

Grapes
4-6 Bridge Street, DG9 7HY
☼ 11-11.30 (midnight Thu-Sat); 12.30-11.30 Sun
☎ (01776) 703386 ⊕ thegrapesbar.co.uk
Beer range varies Ⓗ
The public bar in this popular, historic pub has an
impressive mirror and gantry, and has altered little
in over 50 years. There is also a separate
refurbished snug bar, an upstairs function room
with 1930s Art Deco gantry and counter, and a
small courtyard with tables and chairs. Regular live
music is hosted in the public bar on Friday
evenings, and occasional music nights in the
function room. Two handpumps serve ales sourced
from all over Britain, although there may only be
one ale in winter. 👪🕮🍴🍽🌳¹⌐🚌

> How easy can the barley-bree
> Cement the quarrel.
> It's aye the cheapest lawyer's fee
> To taste the barrel.
> **Robert Burns**

EDINBURGH & THE LOTHIANS

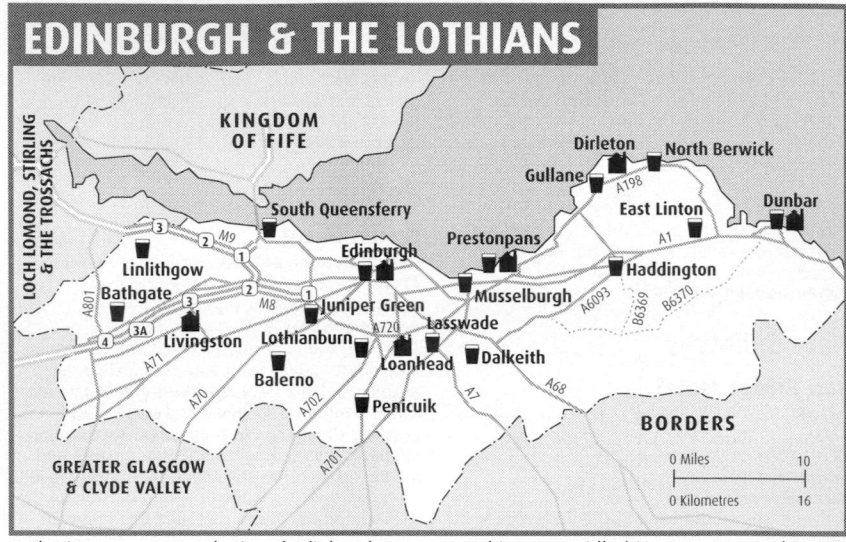

Authority areas covered: City of Edinburgh UA, East Lothian UA, Midlothian UA, West Lothian UA

Balerno

Grey Horse
20 Main Street, EH14 7EH (off A70, in pedestrian area)
🕙 10 (12.30 Sun)-1am ☎ (0131) 449 2888
⊕ greyhorsebalerno.com
Caledonian Deuchars IPA; guest beers Ⓗ
Traditional stone-built village-centre pub, dating back 200 years. The public bar retains some original features including wood panelling and a fine Bernard's mirror. The lounge has green banquette seating. The restaurant next door is part of the pub so you can have a beer with your meal in the evening. Families are welcome in the lounge and dogs are greeted with water and biscuits. CAMRA Lothian Pub of the Year runner-up 2013.
🏰Q🌜🏵🕕🍽♣🚲🚌(44)

Bathgate

James Young
36-40 Hopetoun Street, EH48 4EU NS975689
🕙 8am-11 (midnight Thu; 1am Fri & Sat) ☎ (01506) 651600
Caledonian Deuchars IPA; Greene King Abbot; guest beers Ⓗ
This Wetherpoon pub has an enthusiastic manager and a mixed clientele. The building, named after James 'Paraffin' Young, famous for extracting oil from coal and shale, is on two levels. TVs screen major live sports, at other times news with subtitles. Background music plays from 5pm, louder from 9pm. Guest beers tend to be dark and strong, and real cider is available. Families with children are welcome until 7pm. The pub serves breakfast from 8am, alcohol from 11am (12.30pm Sun). 🏵🕕&🚶🚲🍽♣🚲🚌(23,34)

Dalkeith

Blacksmith's Forge
Newmills Road, EH22 1DU
🕙 11-11 (1am Fri & Sat); 12.30-11 Sun ☎ (0131) 561 5100
Caledonian Deuchars IPA; Greene King Abbot; guest beers Ⓗ

Wetherspoon establishment with a mixture of differently styled seating areas. Dimmed lighting helps to create a soothing environment and the ambience is mostly quiet despite the two small TVs and gaming machine. Friday and Saturday evenings are more lively, with a DJ providing the entertainment, and the pub can get very busy. Meals are served all day from 8am. An outdoor drinking area is open until 10pm. 🚶🏵🕕&🚲🚌

Dunbar

Volunteer Arms
17 Victoria Street, EH42 1HP (near swimming pool)
🕙 12-11 (midnight Thu; 1am Fri & Sat); 12.30-midnight Sun
☎ (01368) 862278
Beer range varies Ⓗ
Close to Dunbar harbour, this is a friendly, traditional locals' pub. The cosy panelled bar is decorated with lots of fishing and lifeboat-oriented memorabilia. Two real ales are on offer, often from smaller breweries. Upstairs is a restaurant serving an excellent good-value menu with an emphasis on seafood. In summer, meals are available all day until 9.30pm. Dogs are permitted after 9pm.
🏵🕕🅰🚲♣🚲🚌

East Linton

Linton
3 Bridge End, EH40 3AF
🕙 12-11 (midnight Fri & Sat) ☎ (01620) 860202
⊕ thelintonhotel.co.uk
Beer range varies Ⓗ

INDEPENDENT BREWERIES

Alechemy Livingston
Barney's Edinburgh
Belhaven (Greene King) Dunbar
Caledonian Edinburgh
Knops Dirleton
Prestonpans Prestonpans (NEW)
Stewart Loanhead

Small, welcoming, traditional hotel by the historic brig over the Tyne in a pretty conservation village. There is a comfortably furnished, quiet public bar and a popular restaurant to the rear. Three real ales usually include at least one from a Scottish microbrewery. The restaurant features good-quality locally sourced Scottish cuisine. Stained glass windows and a roof top statue indicate the hotel's former name – the Red Lion. Dogs are welcome in the bar. ♨Q♿☕🚲◗🕩&♣🚆(X6,120)

Edinburgh

Abbotsford Bar & Restaurant ★
3-5 Rose Street, EH2 2PR (city centre)
☼ 11-11 (midnight Fri & Sat); 12.30-11 Sun
☎ (0131) 225 5276 ⊕ theabbotsford.com
Beer range varies Ⓗ/Ⓐ
A traditional Scottish bar identified by CAMRA as one of Britain's Best Real Heritage Pubs. The magnificent island bar and gantry in dark mahogany have been a fixture since 1902. The ornate plasterwork and corniced ceiling are outstanding and picked out by concealed lighting. The beers are normally from Scottish microbreweries. An extensive food menu is available, with meals served all day in the bar. There is also an upstairs restaurant where real ale from downstairs can be enjoyed.
Q♿◗🕩⇌(Waverley)🚆🚆

Athletic Arms (Diggers)
1-3 Angle Park Terrace, EH11 2JX (1 mile SW of centre)
☼ 11 (12.30 Sun)-1am ☎ (0131) 337 3822
Caledonian Deuchars IPA, Flying Scotsman; Stewart Diggers 80/- Ⓐ**; guest beers** Ⓗ
Situated between two graveyards, the name Diggers became synonymous with this Edinburgh pub legend, which opened in 1897. Banquette seating lines the walls and a compass drawing in the floor aids the geographically challenged. A smaller back room has a dartboard and further seating. Quieter now than in its heyday, though packed when Hearts are at home, it continues to extend a warm welcome to locals and visitors alike, along with their dogs. However, children are not admitted. ♣🚆

Auld Hoose
23/25 St Leonards Street, EH8 9QN (¾ mile S of centre)
☼ 12 (12.30 Sun)-12.45am ☎ (0131) 668 2934
⊕ theauldhoose.co.uk
Harviestoun Bitter & Twisted; Wychwood Hobgoblin; guest beer Ⓗ
Traditional pub dating back to the 1860s with a large central U-shaped bar and lots of pictures of old Edinburgh. This is a friendly pub with a broad clientele, including students. The jukebox features metal and punk. A pub quiz is held every Tuesday. Good food is served all day including vegetarian and vegan options (students receive a 10 per cent discount). The guest beer is usually from a smaller brewery. Dogs are welcome on a lead but children are not admitted. ◗🕩♣🚆

Blue Blazer
2 Spittal Street, EH3 9DX (SW side of centre)
☼ 11 (12.30 Sun)-1am ☎ (0131) 229 5030
Cairngorm Trade Winds; Caledonian Deuchars IPA Ⓐ**; Orkney Dark Island; Stewart 80/-; guest beers** Ⓗ
Wooden floors, high ceilings and old brewery window panels give this two-roomed pub a traditional feel, complemented by candles in front

of the handpumps in the evening. Named after a local school uniform, there is a blue blazer inlaid on the floor. The pub specialises in beers from Scottish micros. Toasties are available all day. Close to theatres and cinemas, closing time is later in August and December. Dogs are welcome but do not bring the children. 🚆

Bow Bar
80 West Bow, EH1 2HH (Old Town, off Grassmarket)
☼ 12-midnight; 12.30-11.30 Sun ☎ (0131) 226 7667
Broughton Coulsons EPA; Fyne Avalanche; Stewart Edinburgh No.3; guest beers Ⓐ
One of the first recreations of a classic Scottish one-roomed alehouse, dedicated to traditional Scottish air pressure dispense and upright drinking. The five guest beers can be from anywhere in the UK. The walls are festooned with original brewery mirrors and the superb gantry does justice to an award-winning selection of about 200 single malt whiskies and international bottled beers. Pies are available at lunchtime. Dogs are welcome but children are not admitted. Q⇌(Waverley)🚆🚆

Cafe Royal ★
19 West Register Street, EH2 2AA (off E end of Princes St)
☼ 11-11 (midnight Thu; 1am Fri & Sat); 12.30-11 Sun
☎ (0131) 556 1884
Caledonian Deuchars IPA; guest beers Ⓗ
One of the finest Victorian pub interiors in Scotland, dominated by an impressive oval island bar with ornate brass light fittings and magnificent ceramic tiled murals of innovators made by Doulton from pictures by John Eyre. The sporting windows of the Oyster Bar were made by the same firm that supplied windows for the House of Lords. Guest beers include ales from Scottish breweries such as Fyne, Harviestoun and Kelburn. Good food is served all day. ◗⇌(Waverley)🚆🚆

Caley Sample Room
56 Angle Park Terrace, EH11 2JR (1 mile W of city centre)
☼ 12-midnight (1am Fri); 11-1am Sat; 11-midnight Sun
☎ (0131) 337 7204 ⊕ thecaleysampleroom.co.uk
Caledonian Deuchars IPA; guest beers Ⓗ
Large one-roomed bar with iron pillars and brick walls, which resembles the sample cellar at the nearby Caledonian Brewery. The real ales are generally from micros and there is an interesting range of bottled beers. High-quality food is popular and available all day. The atmosphere is usually relaxed but hots up when Hearts are playing at home. Dogs are permitted outwith the food service area. ♿◗&🚆

Cask & Barrel (Southside)
24-26 West Preston Street, EH8 9PZ (1 mile S of centre)
☼ 12-midnight (1am Fri); 11-1am Sat; 12.30-midnight Sun
☎ (0131) 667 0856
Caledonian Deuchars IPA; Highland Orkney Best; Stewart 80/-; guest beers Ⓗ
Modern recreation of a Scottish city or tenement bar. The single room, with windows front and back, is divided by a horseshoe bar with a dark wood gantry adorned with decorative wooden casks. The walls support a fine range of old photos, framed advertisements and historic brewery and distillery mirrors. A good place to try beers from Scottish breweries, along with some from 'down south'. Children are not admitted. Local CAMRA Pub of the Year 2013. 🚆

SCOTLAND

Cloisters Bar
26 Brougham Street, EH3 9JH (SW edge of centre)
✪ 12-midnight (1am Fri & Sat); 12.30-midnight Sun
☎ (0131) 221 9997
Alechemy Cairnpapple IPA; Highland Scapa Special;
Stewart Pentland IPA, Holy Grale; guest beers Ⓗ
A former parsonage, this bare-boarded alehouse is
popular with a broad cross-section of drinkers. Old
pews give the interior a friendly feel. A fine
selection of brewery mirrors adorns the walls and
the wide range of single malt whiskies does justice
to the outstanding gantry. Bar meals are freshly
prepared from local ingredients (no food all day
Mon and Fri-Sun eves). Dogs are welcome but
children are not admitted. Q◑♣ℙ

Cumberland Bar
1-3 Cumberland Street, EH3 6RT (New Town)
✪ 11-midnight (1am Thu-Sat); 12.30-midnight Sun
☎ (0131) 558 3134 ⊕ cumberlandbar.co.uk
Caledonian Deuchars IPA; guest beers Ⓗ
Elegant, traditional New Town pub with half wood
panelling. The wood finish is enhanced by dark
green leather seating. Exquisite brewery mirrors
hang alongside framed, decorative and illustrative
posters. The corridor between the front drinking
area and the cosy area at the back is flanked by a
small snug and a further side room. There is usually
an interesting selection of guest beers available.
Meals are served all day Friday to Sunday. Quiz
night is Monday. Well-behaved dogs are welcome.
🏨Q☸◑☕ℙ♣ℙ

Dagda Bar
93-95 Buccleuch Street, EH8 9NG (¾ mile S of centre)
✪ 12 (1 Sun)-1am ☎ (0131) 667 9773 ⊕ dagda.co.uk
Beer range varies Ⓗ
A really cosy howff, situated in the heart of the
university area, attracting a wide-ranging clientele.
The small single room has a welcoming U-shaped
bar and banquette seating on three sides. The staff
are knowledgeable about their beers, which are
usually from local breweries, including their own
Dagda Ale of secret origin. There is also a good
range of whiskies and bottled beers. Dogs are
admitted but not children. An essential stop on any
Southside pub walk. ♣ℙ

Doctors
32 Forrest Road, EH1 2QN (½ mile S of centre)
✪ 10 (12.30 Sun)-1am ☎ (0131) 225 1819
Caledonian Deuchars IPA; Stewart 80/-; guest
beers Ⓗ
Corner hostelry facing the top of Middle Meadow
Walk, the old Infirmary and Medical School, hence
the name. Banquetted booths facilitate preparatory
consultations for future medicos. Black-painted
woodwork lends a certain gravitas to the otherwise
lounge-bar ambience. The real ales are sourced
from smaller breweries, often Scottish. Reasonably
priced meals are served all day. The pub can be
busy at weekends. No children or dogs are
permitted. ☸◑⇌(Waverley)ℙ

Guildford Arms
1 West Register Street, EH2 2AA (off E end of Princes
Street)
✪ 11-11 (midnight Fri & Sat); 12.30-11 Sun
☎ (0131) 556 4312 ⊕ guildfordarms.com
Caledonian Deuchars IPA; Fyne Jarl; Harviestoun Bitter
& Twisted; guest beers Ⓗ
This large venue was built in the golden age of
Victorian pub design. The high ceiling, cornices and

friezes are spectacular, as are the window arches
and screens. An unusual gallery above the main
bar, where the restaurant is located, is also
noteworthy. There is a large standing area around
the canopied bar plus seating areas to the rear. The
diverse beer range features various Scottish micros,
with specific breweries regularly showcased. Bar
snacks are available all day. ◑⇌(Waverley)ℙ♣ℙ

Halfway House
24 Fleshmarket Close, EH1 1BX (up steps opp station's
Market St entrance)
✪ 11-midnight (1am Fri & Sat); 12.30-midnight Sun
☎ (0131) 225 7101 ⊕ halfwayhouse-edinburgh.com
Beer range varies Ⓗ
Cosy, characterful bar hidden halfway down an Old
Town close. Railway memorabilia and current
timetables adorn the interior of this small, often
busy, establishment. Four interesting beers from
smaller Scottish breweries are usually available.
Food is served all day. The bar may stay open until
1am at busy times. Dogs are welcome. CAMRA
members receive a discount of 20p per pint.
☸◑⇌(Waverley)ℙ☕ℙ

Haymarket
11-14 West Maitland Street, EH12 5DS (W edge of
town)
✪ 10-midnight (1am Fri & Sat); 12.30-midnight Sun
☎ (0131) 228 2537
Caledonian Deuchars IPA; Harviestoun Natural
Blonde; St Austell Nicholson's Pale Ale; Stewart 80/-;
guest beers Ⓗ
Situated at the corner of Haymarket, this
Nicholson's pub has a smart black exterior and
comfortable interior decorated with historic prints
of the pub and the locality. An island bar with nine
handpumps overlooks a large central area with
arches leading to the restaurant. Food is served all
day. Several large TVs feature sport and the pub
can be very busy when matches are played at
Murrayfield or Tynecastle. ◑⇌(Haymarket)ℙℙ

Jolly Judge
7a James Court, High Street, EH1 2PB (Old Town – off
Lawnmarket)
✪ 12-11 (midnight Fri & Sat); 12.30-11 Sun
☎ (0131) 225 2669
Beer range varies Ⓗ
Cosy bar, hidden down an Old Town close just off
the Royal Mile, with an attractive painted ceiling.
Handy for those in need of liquid sustenance after a
hard day touring Edinburgh Castle, beers are often
from Scottish or Northumbrian micros. In summer,
literary tours stop off here. Occasional university
philosophy tutorials can also be seen – and heard.
Dogs are permitted after 3pm, but children are only
allowed at the outdoor tables. Cider festivals are
popular. ☸◑⇌(Waverley)ℙ♣●☕ℙ

Kilderkin
1 Browns Close, 65 Canongate, EH8 8BT (Old Town)
✪ 11-midnight (11 Mon; 1am Fri & Sat); 12.30-8 Sun
☎ (0131) 556 2101
Beer range varies Ⓗ
Vaulted, wood-panelled lounge bar at the foot of
the Royal Mile, very handy for the Scottish
Parliament, Holyrood Palace and other local
attractions. Real ales are often from Caledonian
and Scottish micros. Food is served all day and the
extraordinary evening menu features around 40
different wittily named pizzas. A separate
overflow/function/gig room hosts live music on

Saturday evenings. Dogs are welcome. Opening hours may be extended in summer.
��️⊙▶♿≈(Waverley)🚆

Lock 25

85-87 Fountainbridge, EH3 9PU (½ mile W of centre)
✪ 12-midnight (1am Fri & Sat); 12.30-10 Sun
☎ (0131) 228 8831 ⊕ lock25.co.uk
Caledonian Deuchars IPA; guest beers H
Remodelled pub that tries to create a traditional atmosphere with a modern edge to appeal to the wide clientele now living and working nearby. The interior is deceptively spacious with an L-shaped bar and seating ranging from high stools to comfortable armchairs. Guest beers are from Caledonian and local microbreweries. Home-made food is served all day including a steak and guest ale pie. 🌍⊙▶♿♥¹⁻🚆

Malt & Hops

45 The Shore, Leith, EH6 6QU (1½ miles N of centre)
✪ 12-11 (midnight Wed & Thu; 1am Fri & Sat); 12.30-11 Sun
☎ (0131) 555 0083 ⊕ maltandhopsleith.com
Caledonian Deuchars IPA; guest beers H
One-roomed public bar dating from 1749 in the heart of 'new' Leith's riverside restaurant district. Wood panelling gives an intimate feel, with numerous mirrors, artefacts and a large oil painting adding interest. The superb collection of pumpclips, many from now defunct breweries, reflects the ever-changing and interesting range of guest beers, often from Scottish breweries. Meals are only served on Friday. Families are welcome until 6pm. Dogs are permitted. 🖼🌀🌍⊙♣🚆

Old Chain Pier

32 Trinity Crescent, EH5 3ED (1½ miles N of centre)
✪ 12-11 (midnight Sat); 12.30-midnight Sun
☎ (0131) 552 4960 ⊕ old-chain-pier.co.uk
Caledonian Deuchars IPA; Harviestoun Bitter & Twisted; guest beers H
The only pub in Edinburgh directly on the seafront. Panoramic windows provide superb views across the Firth of Forth to Fife. The pub is situated in the 1821 booking office of a pier destroyed by a storm in 1898 and has had a colourful history. The conservatory and mezzanine are ideal for dining – traditional Scottish pub food is served all day. One guest beer is usually from Alechemy. Dogs are welcome. 🌀🌍⊙▶¹⁻🚆

Oxford Bar ★

8 Young Street, EH2 4JB (New Town, off Charlotte Sq)
✪ 11-midnight (1am Fri & Sat); 12.30-11 Sun
☎ (0131) 539 7119 ⊕ oxfordbar.co.uk
Caledonian Deuchars IPA; guest beers H
Small, basic, vibrant drinking shop unchanged since the late 19th century. The bar counter nearly fills the small front room but there is more space in the side room. A real taste of New Town past, the Ox is renowned as one of the favourite pubs of Inspector Rebus and his creator Ian Rankin, and a haunt of many other famous and infamous characters over the years, so you never know who you might bump into. Guest beers are normally from Scottish breweries. Dogs are welcome but children are not admitted. 🖼Q🚆♣¹⁻🚆

Stable Bar

Mortonhall Park, 30 Frogston Road East, EH16 6TJ (S edge of city by camp/caravan site)
✪ 11-11 (midnight summer); 12.30-11 Sun
☎ (0131) 664 0773

Belhaven IPA; Stewart Edinburgh Gold, 80/- H
A country pub in the city accessed via a cobbled courtyard. The main bar is dominated by a large fireplace and the walls are adorned with horse brasses and photographs of old Edinburgh. Little Miss Muffet would be at home here. Food is served all day in both the main bar and the dining room to the rear. The pub has a charity book exchange and a winter quiz is held every second Friday. Dogs are very welcome. 🖼🌀🌍⊙▶♿♣¹⁻🚆

Stockbridge Tap

2-4 Raeburn Place, Stockbridge, EH4 1HN (¾ mile N of centre)
✪ 12-midnight (1am Fri & Sat); 12.30-midnight Sun
☎ (0131) 343 3000
Alechemy Cairnpapple IPA; Stewart Pentland IPA, 80/-; guest beers H
Very much a specialist real ale house, the bar offers unusual and interesting beers from all over the UK, and beer festivals feature occasionally. The L-shaped room, with a bright bar area, boasts mirrors from lost breweries including Murray's and Campbell's. Plenty of seating is available as well as ample space for vertical drinking. The food menu is excellent (no food all day Monday and Fri-Sun eves). Children are not admitted but dogs are welcome. Local CAMRA Pub of the Year runner-up 2013. ⊙▶♿♣🚆

Teuchters Landing

1c Dock Place, Leith, EH6 6LU (1½ miles N of centre)
✪ 11 (12.30 Sun)-1am ☎ (0131) 554 7427
Caledonian Deuchars IPA; Fyne Jarl; Highland Sneaky Wee Orkney Stout; Inveralmond Ossian; guest beer H
A historic pub converted from the former waiting room for the Leith to Aberdeen ferry. To the front is a comfortable bar with a series of interesting Scottish place names listed around the top and a wood-panelled ceiling in the shape of an upturned boat. To the rear is a larger restaurant and bistro, with a conservatory extension that opens out on to a pontoon floating on the Water of Leith. Good-quality food is served all day. Dogs are permitted in the bar until 6pm. Q🌀⊙▶♿¹⁻🚆

Thomson's Bar

182-184 Morrison Street, EH3 8EB (W edge of centre)
✪ 12-11.30 (midnight Thu & Sat; 1am Fri); 4-11.30 Sun
☎ (0131) 228 5700 ⊕ thomsonsbaredinburgh.co.uk
Beer range varies H/A
Superb single-roomed bar modelled on the style of Glasgow architect Alexander 'Greek' Thomson. The hand-made gantry and room panelling are inlaid with scenes from Greek mythology, and the walls are adorned with rare mirrors, adverts and point of sale material from long-forgotten breweries. Six real ales are offered, often including hoppy beers from Scottish breweries. No food is served on Sunday and pies only on Saturday. Dogs are welcome but children are not admitted. Q🌀⊙▶≈(Haymarket)🚆♣¹⁻🚆

Gullane

Old Clubhouse

East Links Road, EH31 2AF (W end of village, off A198)
✪ 11-11 (midnight Thu-Sat); 12-11 Sun ☎ (01620) 842008
⊕ oldclubhouse.com
Caledonian Deuchars IPA; Taylor Landlord; guest beer P
There is a colonial touch to this pub, with views over the golf links to the Lammermuir Hills. The

half-panelled walls are adorned with historic memorabilia and stuffed animals. Caricature statuettes of the Marx Brothers and Laurel and Hardy look down from the gantry. Food features and is served all day – the extensive menu includes seafood, pasta, barbecue, curries, salads and burgers. Dogs are welcome. ♨☞❀❀❀♣⁻🖵(X24)

Haddington

Victoria Inn & Avenue Restaurant
9 Court Street, EH41 3JD
✪ 11-11 (midnight Fri & Sat) ☎ (01620) 823332
⊕ theavenuerestaurant.co.uk
Beer range varies Ⓗ
A stylish inn overlooking the town square. The focus is on quality food, with an all-day carvery popular on Sunday. However, drinkers are made most welcome – the cosy bar with its horseshoe counter has bar chairs and two tall tables backing the ground floor dining area. In summer the front of the inn is a popular suntrap – the perfect place to sit and watch the world go by. ♨Q☞❀❀❀❀Ⓓ&🖵

Juniper Green

Juniper Green Inn
542 Lanark Road, EH14 5EL
✪ 10-11 (midnight Wed-Sat); 12.30-11 Sun
☎ (0131) 458 5395
Caledonian Deuchars IPA; Taylor Landlord; guest beers Ⓗ
Well-appointed, single-roomed lounge bar in a late 1800s building. The decor is clean and attractive throughout, and a very strong community spirit is in evidence within the pub. The bar counter is mahogany and a more modern gantry is designed to match. Pictures of the old Balerno branch line provide interest. Food is freshly cooked to a high standard. A secluded patio and garden are popular in summer. Children are not admitted.
Q❀Ⓒ⁻🖵(44,45)

Lasswade

Laird & Dog Inn
5 High Street, EH18 1NA (A768, near river)
✪ 11-11 (midnight Thu; 1am Fri & Sat); 12.30-11 Sun
☎ (0131) 663 9219 ⊕ lairdanddoginn.co.uk
Caledonian Deuchars IPA; guest beers Ⓗ
Comfortable village local divided into several areas catering for all tastes, from those who enjoy a drink or meal to music-loving pool players. The two guests ales are usually from smaller breweries. Food is available all day including light bar snacks until 4pm. Old photographs decorate the bar areas. There is also a conservatory, an unusual bottle-shaped well and a real fire. Dogs and cats are welcome. ♨☞❀❀Ⓓ&♣P⁻🖵(31,141)

Linlithgow

Four Marys Ⓛ
65-67 High Street, EH49 7ED
✪ 12-11 (midnight Wed & Thu; 12.30am Fri & Sat); 12.30-11 Sun ☎ (01506) 842171 ⊕ thefourmarys.co.uk
Belhaven 80/-, St Andrews Ale; Caledonian Deuchars IPA; guest beers Ⓗ
A stone's throw from Linlithgow Palace, birthplace of Mary Queen of Scots, the building dates back to around 1500. The pub is named after the Queen's four ladies-in-waiting. Initially a dwelling house,

the building has had several changes of use over the years – at one time it was a chemist's run by the Waldie family whose most famous member, David, established the anaesthetic properties of chloroform in 1847. Beer festivals are held in May and October. Forth Valley South Pub of the Year 2013. ❀Ⓓ❀⇌⁻🖵

Platform 3 Ⓛ
1A High Street, EH49 7AB (just below railway station)
✪ 10.30-midnight (1am Fri & Sat); 12.30-midnight Sun
☎ (01506) 847405 ⊕ platform3.co.uk
Caledonian Deuchars IPA; guest beers Ⓗ
Small, friendly hostelry on the railway station approach, originally the public bar of the hotel next door. It was purchased and renovated in 1998 as a pub in its own right and is now closely involved with the local community. Look out for the train that journeys above the bar. One of the guest beers always comes from Stewart Brewing and the other from another Scottish brewery. Live music includes regular folk sessions. Dogs are welcome, with biscuits 'on tap'. ⇌♣🖵

Lothianburn

Steading
118-120 Biggar Road, EH10 7DU (A702, just S of bypass)
✪ 11-11 (midnight Fri & Sat); 12.30-11 Sun
☎ (0131) 445 1128
Caledonian Deuchars IPA; Taylor Landlord; guest beer Ⓗ
A pub originally created from a row of farm cottages, the bar here is split, with areas of comfy chairs and settees perfect for relaxing with a drink and higher tables more suitable for eating. The popular restaurant includes a large conservatory extension, and food is served all day. Outside, there are excellent views of the Pentland Hills – the pub is ideally placed for a relaxing pint after a walk in the hills or a visit to the nearby dry ski slope. Dogs are welcome. Closing time may be earlier if quiet. ♨☞❀❀ⓄP🖵

Musselburgh

David Macbeth Moir
Bridge Street, EH21 6AG
✪ 11-11 (midnight Fri & Sat); 12.30-11 Sun
☎ (0131) 653 1060
Caledonian Deuchars IPA; Greene King Abbot; Houston Peter's Well; guest beers Ⓗ
Wetherspoon outlet named after a local physician and writer, in a converted cinema dating back to 1935. The main door and original features have been beautifully restored, and the vast single-roomed bar is filled with cinema-themed Art Deco artefacts. The long bar has 10 handpumps featuring a good mix of guest beers. Reasonably priced food is served all day and there is a separate area for families. Free Wi-Fi is available. ♨☞❀Ⓓ&⁻🖵(26,44)

Levenhall Arms
10 Ravensheugh Road, EH21 7PP (B1348, 1 mile E of centre)
✪ 12-11 (midnight Thu; 1am Fri & Sat); 12.30-midnight Sun
☎ (0131) 665 3220
Inveralmond Ossian Ⓟ; guest beers Ⓗ
This three-roomed hostelry dates from 1830 and is popular with locals and racegoers. The lively,

cheerfully decorated public bar is half timber panelled and carpeted. A smaller area leads off, with a dartboard and pictures of old local industries. The lounge has been franchised as an Indian restaurant and has a hardwood floor and comfortable seating. Dogs are welcome in the bar. ⛄❀◑◗⬠Å⇌(Wallyford)♣P⁵⁻♿(26,44)

Volunteer Arms (Staggs)

81 North High Street, EH21 6JE (behind Brunton Hall)
✪ 12-11 (11.30 Thu; midnight Fri); 11-midnight Sat; 12.30-11 Sun ☎ (0131) 665 9654 ⊕ staggsbar.com
Beer range varies Ⓗ
Superb pub run by the same family since 1858. The bar and snug are traditional with a wooden floor, wood panelling and mirrors from defunct local breweries. The attractive gantry is topped with old casks. The more modern lounge opens at the weekend. Up to seven guest beers, mostly pale and hoppy but always one darker, change very regularly. Dogs are welcome in the bar. CAMRA Lothian Pub of the Year 2013. Many previous awards are on display in the bar.
❀◑♣⁵⁻♿(26,44)

North Berwick

Nether Abbey Hotel

20 Dirleton Avenue, EH39 4BQ (A198, ¾ mile W of centre)
✪ 11-11 (midnight Thu; 1am Fri & Sat) ☎ (01620) 892802
⊕ netherabbey.co.uk
Beer range varies Ⓟ
Busy, family-run hotel in a stone-built villa offering a bright, contemporary interior with open-plan, split-level rooms. The lower area is the Fly Half Bar and the upper a restaurant. The marble-topped bar counter has a row of modern chrome founts. The founts, with horizontally moving levers, dispense the real ales, often from the newer Scottish micros; sparklers can be removed on request. Food is served all day Friday-Sunday. Dogs are welcome.
⛄❀⛌◑◗♿Å⇌P⁵⁻♿(X24,124)

Ship

7-9 Quality Street, EH39 4HJ
✪ 11-11 (1am Thu-Sat) ☎ (01620) 890676
Beer range varies Ⓗ
Spacious, open-plan bar located beneath a tenement block at the leafy east end of town. The bar area has pine floorboards, a mahogany counter and a dark-stained wood gantry. A quieter carpeted area is to the rear. The various guest beers tend to have higher ABVs. The pub is popular for food, served all day until 8pm – the menu recommends a beer to complement each dish. Regular live music plays on weekend evenings. Dogs are welcome. ⛄❀◑◗ Å⇌⁵⁻♿(X24,120)

Penicuik

Navaar House Hotel

23 Bog Road, EH26 9BY
✪ 12-1am (midnight Sun) ☎ (01968) 672683
Beer range varies Ⓗ
A lively pub with a strong community spirit, situated in an old private house, built circa 1895. The large bar is open plan with a log/coal fire and TV screens for sport. The real ale is usually from Stewart, Fyne or another Scottish micro. The restaurant, with an extensive à la carte menu, serves meals all day. Snacks are available in the bar. A large patio and decked area is popular in summer. Dogs are welcome.
🏨❀⛌◑♣P⁵⁻♿(37)

Prestonpans

Prestoungrange Gothenburg ★

227 High Street, EH32 9BE
✪ closed Mon; 12-3, 5-11; 12-midnight Fri & Sat; 12.30-11 Sun ☎ (01875) 819922 ⊕ thegoth.co.uk
Beer range varies Ⓐ
Superb Gothenburg pub identified by CAMRA as one of Britain's Best Real Heritage Pubs, with a magnificent painted ceiling in the bar. The real ales may be from the in-house microbrewery, which can be viewed from the bar as you sample the ales. There is also a bistro and, upstairs, a lounge and function room with superb views over the Forth. The walls throughout are covered in murals and paintings depicting past local life. Meals, including gluten-free options, are served all day Friday to Sunday. 🏨⛄◑◗⛌⛌ÅP♿(26,44)

South Queensferry

Hawes Inn

7 Newhalls Road, EH30 9TA (under rail bridge)
✪ 11-11; 12.30-10.30 Sun ☎ (0131) 331 1990
Caledonian Deuchars IPA; guest beers Ⓗ
This old coaching inn beneath the mighty Forth Rail Bridge was modernised several years ago. It is now a multi-roomed establishment, with salvaged furniture and wooden beams creating an olde-worlde feel. Robert Louis Stevenson is said to have stayed here and his novel Kidnapped includes a passage about the Hawes Inn. Although very food-oriented, there is a drinking area to the rear. Guest beers tend to come from smaller breweries, UK-wide, and the menu has a good selection of country-pub food available all day.
🏨Q⛄❀⛌◑◗⛌⇌(Dalmeny)♣P⁵⁻♿(43)

The discreet barman

Over the mahogany, jar followed jorum, gargle, tincture and medium, tailor, scoop, snifter and ball of malt, in a breathless pint-to-pint. Discreet barman, Mr Sugrue thought, turning outside the door and walking in the direction of Stephen's Green. Never give anything away – part of the training. Is Mr so-and-so there, I'll go and see, strict instructions never to say yes in case it might be the wife. Curious now the way the tinge of wickedness hung around the pub, a relic of course of Victorianism, nothing to worry about as long as a man kept himself in hand.

Jack White, The Devil You Know, 1970

GREATER GLASGOW & CLYDE VALLEY

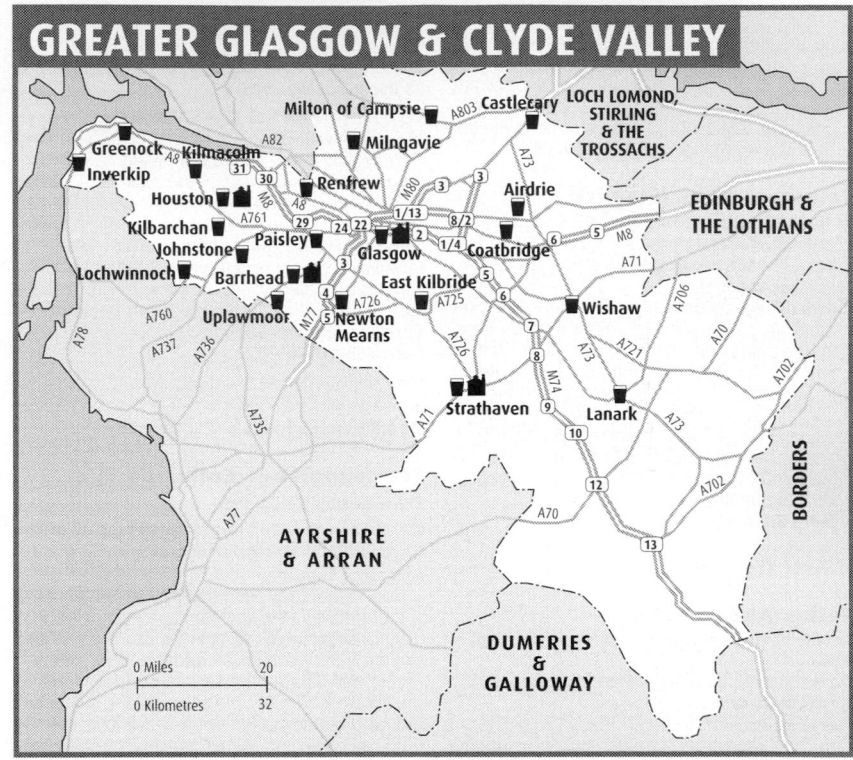

Authority areas covered: Argyll & Bute UA, Ayrshire UAs, City of Glasgow UA, Dunbartonshire UAs, Inverclyde UA, Lanarkshire UAs, Renfrewshire UAs

Airdrie

Robert Hamilton

12-14 Bank Street, ML6 6AF

✪ 11-11 (midnight Wed & Thu; 1am Fri & Sat)

☎ (01236) 771110

Beer range varies Ⓗ

A 2002 Wetherspoon conversion of an old bank building, named after the town's founder. The main bar is on the ground floor, there are more private seating areas on the middle floor, and a quiet lounge, complete with leather settees, is at the top. Five or six handpumps are usually in operation serving a wide range of ales, with dark beers particularly prevalent. Q❀❂◑♿⇌🌺≗

Barrhead

Cross Stobs Inn Ⓛ

2-6 Grahamston Road, G78 1NS (on B7712)

✪ 11-11 (midnight Thu & Sat; 1am Fri); 12.30-11 Sun

☎ (0141) 881 1581

Beer range varies Ⓗ

Eighteenth-century coaching inn on the road to Paisley. The public bar has a real coal fire and retains much of its original charm with antique furniture and service bells. The lounge is now a restaurant serving à la carte food. There is an enclosed garden to the rear. The bar leads to a pool room and a function suite. The beers are always from the nearby Kelburn Brewery. ♨⇲❀◑🍴♿⇌🚲🚆(51,101)

Waterside Inn Ⓛ

The Hurlet, Glasgow Road, G53 7TH (A736 near Hurlet, on edge of Barrhead)

✪ 11-11 (midnight Fri & Sat); 12.30-11 Sun

☎ (0141) 881 2822 ⊕ thewatersideinn.net

Beer range varies Ⓗ

Comfortable, welcoming and friendly pub on the outskirts of town. Food is the main focus here but there is a cosy area with a log fire for those just wanting to enjoy a drink. The decor is clean and traditional. Various theme nights are held regularly. There is also a spacious function suite to the rear of the building. The beer is always from the local Kelburn Brewing Company.
♨Q⇲◑♿P🚲🚆(103,X44B)

Castlecary

Castlecary House Hotel

Castlecary Road, G68 0HD (just off A80 near M80 jct 4)

✪ 11-11 (11.30 Fri & Sat); 12.30-11 Sun ☎ (01324) 840233

⊕ castlecaryhotel.com

Beer range varies Ⓗ

A large hotel in a small village within two miles of Cumbernauld and close to the site of a fort on the Roman Antonine Wall. Real ale can be enjoyed in

INDEPENDENT BREWERIES

Clockwork Glasgow
Houston Houston
Kelburn Barrhead
Strathaven Strathaven

three bars, with the handpumps situated in the Wee Bar. Up to four ales are available, mainly from Lanarkshire's Strathaven brewery, but other breweries also feature. Q🅰️🍴🌓🍺♿P⌐🚪(X37,X39)

Coatbridge

Vulcan
181 Main Street, ML5 3HH (jct with Dunbeth Rd)
✪ 11-midnight (1am Fri & Sat) ☎ (01236) 437972
Beer range varies Ⓗ
A rare example of an existing pub (formerly Brogan's) adopted by Wetherspoon, this welcome real ale outlet in North Lanarkshire continues to grow in popularity. It is named after the world's first iron-hulled boat, which sailed on the nearby Monkland Canal. The venue's small size helps to give it a traditional pub atmosphere. Caledonian Deuchars IPA and Greene King Abbot are frequently on offer, with up to three guest ales, often from Scottish breweries. Good-value food is served all day. 🍺♿🚋(Sunnyside)⌐🚪(62)

East Kilbride

Hudsons Bar Ⓛ
14-16 Cornwall Way, G74 1JR
✪ 11-midnight ☎ (01355) 581040 ⊕ hudsonsglasgow.co.uk
Beer range varies Ⓗ
Busy, handily placed town-centre pub facing the bus station, near the entrance to the shopping centre and cinema complex, and just half a mile from the rail station. It started serving real ale just two years ago and offers two beers from either nearby Strathaven Ales or Greene King. The long elliptical-shaped bar has seating round about and TV screens are strategically placed on the walls. Over-18s only. ♿🚋🚪

Glasgow

Babbity Bowster
16-18 Blackfriars Street, Merchant City, G1 1PE
✪ 11 (12.30 Sun)-midnight ☎ (0141) 552 5055
Caledonian Deuchars IPA; Fyne Jarl; guest beer Ⓐ
This pub/hotel/restaurant is simply and practically furnished with plain wooden tables and chairs alongside bench seating around the walls. There is more seating outside in the beer garden – a Glasgow city rarity. Three Scottish tall founts serve two regular beers plus a guest which is usually local but sometimes from further afield. A French chef prepares meals for the upstairs restaurant from Scottish produce including fish/seafood, game and other meats. Quality food including daily specials is also served in the bar. 🛏️Q🅰️🍴🍷🚋(High St/Argyle St/Queen St)🚪♣P⌐🚪

Blackfriars Ⓛ
36 Bell Street, Merchant City, G1 1LG
✪ 11 (12.30 Sun)-midnight ☎ (0141) 552 5924
⊕ blackfriarsglasgow.com
Beer range varies Ⓗ
Friendly pub in the middle of the cosmopolitan Merchant City area. Low lighting and candles create an intimate feel in the central bar, while a brighter café-style corner overlooks the streets; a quieter rear area is suited for dining. Five handpumps serve beers from all over the UK, with many Scottish and always one from the local Kelburn Brewing Co. A good selection of American and

European bottled beers is also stocked. Live music plays on Tuesday and Sunday nights.
🅰️🍷♿🚋(High St/Argyll St/Queen St)🚪🚪(18,62)

Bon Accord Ⓛ
153 North Street, G3 7DA
✪ 11 (12.30 Sun)-midnight ☎ (0141) 248 4427
⊕ bonaccordweb.co.uk
Caledonian Deuchars IPA; Marston's Pedigree; guest beers Ⓗ
Local CAMRA Cider Pub of the Year 2013 and a multiple Pub of the Year winner. Up to 10 real ales come from Scotland and all over the UK. The pub holds beer festivals several times a year, often themed or featuring a particular area – the 'Wars of the Roses' showcased ales from Lancashire and Yorkshire. Fast building a reputation for malt whiskies, more than 350 are available, and regular tasting nights are held. Food is served daily until 7.45pm. A live band plays on Saturday nights. 🅰️🍷♿🚋(Charing Cross/Anderston)●⌐🚪(9,62)

Camperdown Place
4-5 West George Street, G2 1DR
✪ 11-midnight ☎ (0141) 331 6600
Caledonian Deuchars IPA; Greene King Abbot; Kelburn Jaguar; guest beers Ⓗ
Situated below street level with a wheelchair lift, this is the smallest Glasgow city Wetherspoon. Upholstered furniture and Tiffany lamps create an attractive and comfortable setting. The outdoor area offers views of George Square. Its location at the entrance to Queen Street station guarantees a steady passing trade. However, it also attracts a regular clientele who enjoy the well-kept beers on eight handpumps, with ever-changing guests to accompany the permanent beers. A friendly, accessible pub in the heart of the city. 🅰️🍷♿🚋(Queen St)🚪●⌐🚪

Clockwork Beer Co Ⓛ
1153-1155 Cathcart Road, Mount Florida, G42 9HB (near rail bridge)
✪ 11-11 (midnight Thu-Sat); 12.30-11 Sun
☎ (0141) 649 0184 ⊕ clockworkbeercompany.co.uk
Caledonian Deuchars IPA; guest beers Ⓐ
Ideally located for events at Hampden Park sports stadium, good public transport links and a car park mean there is no excuse not to visit Glasgow's only real ale brewpub. Its strong ales are conventionally cask conditioned while others use a unique tank system, retaining CO2 from fermentation. In addition there is a selection of guest ales from local breweries and further afield. Food is very good value. Several TVs show sports. 🐕🅰️🍷♿🚋(Mount Florida/Cathcart)P⌐🚪(44 66)

Counting House
2 St Vincent Place, G1 2DH (on George Sq)
✪ 11 (12.30 Sun)-midnight ☎ (0141) 225 0160
Caledonian Deuchars IPA; Greene King Abbot; guest beers Ⓗ
A former bank building in the heart of the city, with fine views over George Square to City Chambers. This Wetherspoon pub has experienced a revival and gained a reputation for serving ales from the UK's most innovative breweries, some new to the west of Scotland. The opulent decor includes a glass ceiling dome and statues. With 18 continually changing beers and a commitment to quality, this pub is well worth a visit.
Q🍷♿🚋(Queen St/Central)🚪●🚪(20 66)

SCOTLAND

Curlers Rest

256-260 Byres Road, G12 8SH
✪ 12-midnight ☎ (0141) 341 0737
⊕ thecurlersrestglasgow.co.uk
Caledonian Deuchars IPA; Harviestoun Old Engine Oil; Stewart 80/-; guest beers Ⓗ
Taking its name from a curling pond, there has long been a pub on this site. The building is converted from 18th-century cottages but little remains of the original. This is now a large open-plan pub spread over two floors with a second upstairs bar and some more private seating areas. Five handpumps serve the real ales along with a range of world beers, and a good selection of meals is available. Families welcome until 8pm. ♨⛄ⓓ🖶🚻(89,90)

Drum & Monkey

91-93 St Vincent Street, G2 5TF (corner with Renfield St)
✪ 11-midnight; 12.30-11 Sun ☎ (0141) 221 6636
Beer range varies Ⓗ
A local CAMRA Pub of the Year, this corner pub, housed in a former bank, has an opulent marble and wood-panelled interior and ornate ceilings. Convenient for both main railway stations and numerous bus routes, it is usually busy and attracts a mixed clientele. Family groups are welcome when dining. The large U-shaped central bar features five handpulls offering a wide variety of different styles from local and national favourites to contemporary microbrews.
ⓓ♿🚻(Central/Queen St)🚇🚌

Esquire House

1487 Great Western Road, Anniesland, G12 0AU (opp Anniesland rail station)
✪ 11-11 (midnight Thu-Sat); 12.30-11 Sun
☎ (0141) 341 1130
Caledonian Deuchars IPA; Greene King Abbot; guest beers Ⓗ
The original Esquire House was established around 1962 but the present open-plan pub is completely new, bought by Wetherspoon 10 years ago. One of the smaller pubs in the chain, it has developed a good community and local atmosphere. Both local and national beers are served on 10 handpumps. Open from 8am for breakfast.
🅿ⓓ♿🚻(Anniesland)♠P🚇-🚌(20,66,118)

Granary

10 Kilmarnock Road, G41 3NH (Jct with Pollokshaws Rd)
✪ 12-11 (midnight Fri & Sat); 12.30-11 Sun
☎ (0141) 649 0594
St Austell Nicholson's Pale Ale; guest beer Ⓗ
An unusually shaped two-room Nicholson's pub on the south side. Two handpumps in the rear room dispense the house beer and a guest, which is predominantly Scottish and golden. Much of the seating in this room is reserved for diners. The front room is triangular, due to its location within the Y of a road junction, and opens at weekends and other times when required. Well served by rail and buses to the city.
ⓓ♿🚻(Crossmyloof/Shawlands)🚌(38,57)

Hengler's Circus

351-363 Sauchiehall Street, G2 3HU (corner with Holland St)
✪ 11-midnight ☎ (0141) 331 9810
Beer range varies Ⓗ
Demand has seen the number of handpumps rise to 14 in this Wetherspoon pub, with a wide range

of ales on offer from across the UK. The management are open to suggestions for forthcoming beers. Every two months a Battle of the Brewers generates much interest among real ale enthusiasts. Genial staff serve a broad spectrum of patrons from breakfast at 8am, including city regulars, shoppers, theatregoers and students. Easily accessed on a Glasgow ale tour by the 57 bus that terminates outside.
Q⛄ⓓ♿🚻(Charing Cross)♠🚌(9,44,57)

Horse Shoe Bar ★

17-19 Drury Street, G2 5AE (near Central Station)
✪ 11 (12.30 Sun)-midnight ☎ (0141) 248 6368
⊕ horseshoebar.co.uk
Caledonian Deuchars IPA Ⓗ; **Harviestoun Bitter & Twisted** Ⓐ; **guest beers** Ⓗ
Down a small side street near Central Station, the pub has been identified by CAMRA as one of Britain's Best Real Heritage Pubs. It has the longest continuous bar in Britain at 104ft 3in. The horseshoe theme is continued from the shape of the bar to the bespoke mirrors and other artefacts. Note the mosaic floor, carved wooden wall panelling, painted tiles and illuminated stained glass ceiling. Two guests from all over Britain augment the regular ales. Good-value food is served in the bar and upstairs lounge/diner.
ⓓ♿🚻(Central/Queen St)🚇🚌

Laurieston Bar ★ Ⅼ

58 Bridge Street, G5 9HU
✪ 11 (12.30 Sun)-11 ☎ (0141) 429 4528
⊕ thelauristonbar.com
Beer range varies Ⓗ
Characterful but unpretentious corner pub, owned by brothers whose family have been in the pub trade for generations. A rare survivor of authentic 1960s decor, it has been identified by CAMRA as one of Britain's Best Real Heritage Pubs. The traditional horseshoe bar is surrounded by small formica-topped tables. The walls are covered with vintage photographs, snapshots, mirrors, paintings and memorabilia. A smaller bar serves the lounge. The three beers are from Fyne Ales, often including Jarl. Situated opposite Bridge Street subway station and on many bus routes. 🚻(Central)🚇-🚌

Mulberry St

778 Pollokshaws Road, G41 2AE
✪ 11-11 (midnight Fri & Sat); 12.30-11 Sun
☎ (0141) 424 0858 ⊕ mulberrystbarbistro.com
Harviestoun Bitter & Twisted; guest beers Ⓗ
Well-established community pub on the south side near Queen's Park, Italian family run and named after a street in New York City's Little Italy. It serves at least two beers, usually three. Guest ales are all from Fyne Ales, with Jarl the favourite. A selection of foreign beers and West Brewery's St Mungo German-style lager are also available. Good food is served in the bar and bistro. Quiz night is Monday. Buses and the railway are nearby.
🅿ⓓ♿🚻(Queen's Park/Pollokshields West)'-🚌

Pot Still Ⅼ

154 Hope Street, G2 2TH
✪ 11 (12.30 Sun)-midnight ☎ (0141) 333 0980
⊕ thepotstill.co.uk
Caledonian Deuchars IPA; guest beers Ⓗ
Compact city pub near rail stations and major bus routes. The layout makes good use of the space, with a main central area, cosy alcove and a mezzanine corner that provides a retreat when

busy. Four handpumps serve the Deuchars alongside local/Scottish guest ales. The pub is renowned for its collection of around 300 malts, often rare, which draws whisky enthusiasts from afar, and it hosts popular whisky tasting evenings. Good-value pub food is available.
◑➡(Central/Queen St)🚇🚉

Society Room
151 West George Street, G2 2JJ
✪ 11 (12.30 Sun)-midnight ☎ (0141) 229 7560
Caledonian Deuchars IPA; Greene King Abbot; guest beers Ⓗ
Large Lloyds No.1 bar in the city centre attracting a diverse clientele. There are six handpumps dispensing two regular and up to four guest beers – often higher strength ales suiting the tastes of the daytime regulars. In addition to the biannual Wetherspoon beer festivals the pub holds mini festivals showcasing particular breweries and staff are receptive to beer suggestions. At night-time the pub is frequented by a younger crowd, accompanied by loud music.
◑&➡(Queen St/Central)🚇🚌🚉

State Bar 🍺 Ⓛ
148 Holland Street, G2 4NG
✪ 11 (12.30 Sun)-midnight ☎ (0141) 332 2159
Caledonian Deuchars IPA, 80; Houston Killellan; Stewart Edinburgh No.3; guest beers Ⓗ
Local CAMRA Pub of the Year in 2012, this popular and welcoming bar in the Charing Cross area is handy for restaurants and entertainment venues. As well as the four regular beers there are three guests, often from Scottish breweries including Fyne Ales and Williams Bros, but also from anywhere in Britain. Food is available at lunchtimes only. Live blues features in the public bar on a Tuesday night and comedy in the downstairs room on a Saturday. ◑➡(Charing Cross)🚇🚉(44,57)

Tennent's
191 Byres Road, G12 8TN
✪ 11-11; 12-midnight Thu-Sat ☎ (0141) 339 7203
🌐 thetennentsbarglasgow.co.uk
Brains The Rev James; Caledonian Deuchars IPA; Harviestoun Natural Blonde; Jennings Cumberland Ale; Marston's EPA; guest beers Ⓗ
One of Glasgow's oldest pubs, dating from 1884. Mitchells & Butlers decided to keep the bar unchanged after the regulars objected to plans for modernisation. Three guest beers usually supplement the regular range. Good-value food is served all day. Sport is shown on numerous TVs. A busy pub in the West End's heart near Glasgow University and the Western Infirmary.
◑&🚇🚉(44,89,90)

Three Judges
141 Dumbarton Road, G11 6PR
✪ 11-11 (midnight Thu-Sat); 12.30-11 Sun
☎ (0141) 337 3055 🌐 threejudges.co.uk
Caledonian Deuchars IPA; guest beers Ⓗ
A must-visit for ale enthusiasts, for more than 20 years this traditional corner pub has brought the best new real ales to Glasgow from all over Britain. Beers are available on eight handpumps with a ninth reserved for real cider. Numerous local CAMRA awards adorn the walls. No food is sold but customers may bring in their own. On Sunday afternoons the regulars make way for jazz fans.
🌟➡(Partick)🚇🚌🚉(9,62)

Greenock

James Watt
80-92 Cathcart Street, PA15 1DD
✪ 8-11 (midnight Thu; 1am Fri & Sat) ☎ (01475) 722640
Caledonian Deuchars IPA; Greene King Abbot; guest beers Ⓗ
Situated across the road from Greenock Central Station and 200 yards from the bus station, this large open-plan Wetherspoon, in a former post office, is named after one of Greenock's famous sons. The chain's standard value-for-money food is available all day and beer festivals are hosted at various times throughout the year. This pub is an oasis in a beer desert.
🌟◑&➡(Central)🚉(X7,X7A)

Houston

Fox & Hounds Ⓛ
South Street, PA6 7EN
✪ 11-midnight (12.30am Fri & Sat); 12.30-midnight Sun
☎ (01505) 612448 🌐 houston-brewing.co.uk
Houston Killellan, Peter's Well, Slainte, Warlock Stout, seasonal beer Ⓗ
Established in 1779 and home to the Houston Brewing Company. The Fox & Vixen lounge offers the full range of Houston's regular beers including Peter's Well, CAMRA Champion Best Bitter 2011, along with seasonal beers. A viewing window allows customers to see into the brewery and brewery trips are available on request (ask ahead). The Stables bar serves three Houston beers but is only open Friday to Sunday. Beer festivals are held twice yearly, usually in May and August. CAMRA Scotland and N Ireland Pub of the Year 2011.
🅿Q🐕◑🍴&P⌐🚉(X7,8)

Inverkip

Inverkip Hotel Ⓛ
Main Street, PA16 0AS
✪ 11 (12.30 Sun)-11.30 ☎ (01475) 521478 🌐 inverkip.co.uk
Arran Red Squirrel; guest beer Ⓗ
Small, family-run hotel just a short walk from the large Inverkip Marina, making it an ideal staging post for those just messing about on the river or passing through on the way to Largs and the Ayrshire coast. This is the only outlet in the area that regularly sells beer from the Isle of Arran Brewery, with a second beer usually from another local brewery. 🌟🛏◑🍴➡P⌐🚉(578,580)

Johnstone

Callum's 🍺 Ⓛ
26 High Street, PA5 8AH
✪ 11-11.30 (1am Fri & Sat); 12.30-11.30 Sun
☎ (01505) 322925 🌐 callums-bar.com
Caledonian Deuchars IPA; guest beers Ⓗ
Popular town-centre pub offering a friendly welcome and a comfortable atmosphere. A large but unobtrusive TV screen features major sporting events. The lounge has an area for formal dining with themed nights including Thursday curry and Friday steak. There is a function room for private parties. Quiz night is Thursday, live music plays on Saturday and open mic night is Sunday. Six real ales are available mainly from local Kelburn and Houston breweries. ◑🍴&➡🚉(36,38)

Kilbarchan

Glen Leven Inn
25 New Street, PA10 2LN
✪ 11.45-11 (midnight Thu; 1am Fri & Sat); 12.30-midnight
Sun ☎ (01505) 702481 ⊕ glenleveninn.co.uk
Beer range varies Ⓗ
Busy local pub within a conservation village and
100 yards from the famous Weaver's Cottage
owned by the National Trust. Ales are from the
Punch Taverns list. The pool table and TV screens
attract the locals. Look for 'Piper Habbie' above the
feature fireplace. Live music is hosted most
Saturday and Sunday nights plus a quiz on Tuesday
evenings. The beer garden is popular in summer.
Food is served in the separate Weavers Restaurant.
ᴹ❀◑よP🚌(36)

Trust Inn
8 Low Barholm, PA10 2ET
✪ 11.45-midnight (1am Fri & Sat); 12.30-midnight Sun
☎ (01505) 702401
Morland Old Speckled Hen; guest beers Ⓗ
This popular local pub in the centre of a
conservation village has been recently refurbished
with a bright modern interior and old village
photographs adorning the walls. Both guest beers
are from the Punch Taverns range. Live music plays
on Friday evening and a quiz is hosted on Tuesday
evening. Children are welcome until 8pm if dining.
Several TVs screen sporting events.
◑よ≑(Milliken Park)🚌(36)

Kilmacolm

Pullman Tavern
Elthinstone Court, Lochwinnoch Road, PA13 4LG
✪ 11-11 (midnight Wed; 1am Fri & Sat); 12.30-11 Sun
☎ (01505) 874501
Beer range varies Ⓗ
The only pub in this small conservation village, the
building was originally a railway station and the
Sustrans cycle path between Paisley and Gourock
passes close by. Seating outside is south facing and
a suntrap in summer months, attracting walkers,
cyclists and families. Beers are rotated from the
Mitchells & Butlers range, with Caledonian
Deuchars IPA or Harviestoun Bitter & Twisted often
available. ❀◑ᴖよP⅃🚌(1,X7)

Lanark

Clydesdale Inn
15 Bloomgate, ML11 9ET
✪ 11-11 (1am Fri; midnight Sat); 12.30-11 Sun
☎ (01555) 678740
Greene King Abbot; guest beers Ⓗ
CAMRA Lanarkshire Pub of the Year for 2012, this is
a Wetherspoon conversion of a former coaching inn
dating from the late 18th century. Today, the
three-room establishment is very popular with
locals and visitors to the nearby New Lanark Village
Heritage Site and the Falls of Clyde. Eight
handpumps in the main bar serve guest beers from
all over Britain, often featuring Scottish breweries
such as Strathaven, Houston and Kelburn. Opens at
8am for breakfast. Q❦❀◑よᴬ≑●P🚌

Lochwinnoch

Brown Bull
32 Main Street, PA12 4AH

✪ 12-11 (midnight Fri; 11.45 Sat); 12.30-11 Sun
☎ (01505) 843250
Caledonian Deuchars IPA; guest beers Ⓗ
This village pub, a family-run free house, is more
than 200 years old and popular with locals and
visitors alike. Quiz night is Tuesday and live music
features every second Sunday. An ever-changing
choice of three guest ales is offered. The
restaurant, situated upstairs, uses local produce
and bar meals are also available.
ᴹ❀◑よ≑●⅃🚌

Milngavie

Talbot Arms
30 Main Street, G62 6BU
✪ 11-midnight (1am Fri & Sat); 12.30-11.45 Sun
☎ (0141) 955 0981
Beer range varies Ⓗ
Named after the Talbot hunting dog, once bred on
a nearby estate, the pub is situated in a suburban
town a short train ride from Glasgow and a long
walk from Fort William on the West Highland Way.
The single-room bar plays host to locals who enjoy
playing board and card games and watching big
matches on the large-screen TVs. Three
handpumps serve beers from local brewers and
from farther afield, with the regulars selecting their
favourites. ❀よ≑♣🚌(10,119)

Milton of Campsie

Kincaid House Hotel
Birdston Road, G66 8BZ (signed on B757, just S of
village) NS650760
✪ 12-midnight (1am Fri); 12.30-midnight Sun
☎ (0141) 776 2226 ⊕ kincaidhouse.com
Beer range varies Ⓗ
Country house hotel at the end of a long drive, the
real ale is in the Stables Bar to the rear. There is a
bar area with a pool table and a dining/lounge
area with a fireplace. Guest beers, usually from
Taylor, Houston, Harviestoun or sometimes another
Scottish brewery, alternate between two
handpumps. The garden is a treat in summer and
the food is popular with locals and visitors. A TV
occasionally shows sports. ᴹ❀ᴖ◑よP⅃🚌(X85)

Newton Mearns

Osprey
Stewarton Road, G77 6NP
✪ 12-11; 12.30-10.30 Sun ☎ (0141) 639 7453
Caledonian Deuchars IPA; guest beer Ⓗ
Recently refurbished, this pub retains an olde-
worlde theme with oak beams and stone floors. It
has four rooms off a main bar area. Opposite the
bar, the snugs are adorned with various tiles and
artwork. An ideal refreshment stop for visitors to
the nearby Pollok House and Burrell Collection of
artworks. ᴹ❦❀◑よ≑(Patterton)♣P⅃🚌(44A)

Paisley

Bull Inn ★ Ⓛ
7 New Street, PA1 1XU
✪ 11-midnight (1am Fri & Sat); 12.30-midnight Sun
☎ (0141) 849 0472 ⊕ bullinnpaisley.co.uk
Caledonian Deuchars IPA; guest beers Ⓗ
Established in 1901 and identified by CAMRA as
one of Britain's Best Real Heritage Pubs, this is the
oldest inn in Paisley. The pub retains many original

features including stained-glass windows, three small snugs and a spirit cask gantry, and boasts the only original set of spirit cocks left in Scotland. Guest ales are usually Scottish with an emphasis on the local Houston and Kelburn breweries.
⚲◁⇌(Gilmour St)🚆(9,36)

Harvies Bar ℒ
86 Glasgow Road, PA1 3NU
✪ 11-midnight (1am Fri & Sat); 12.30-midnight Sun
☎ (0141) 889 0911
Theakston XB; guest beer Ⓗ
Popular tenement-style local situated on the main Paisley to Glasgow road. The spacious open-plan bar, with raised seating, has three large TV screens showing sport and music videos with the volume turned down low. The pub can get busy during major football matches. Sunday features a quiz night and Monday is poker night. Live music or a DJ play occasionally. The guest beer is from the local Kelburn Brewing. ◁▮ㅤ⇌(Hawkhead)🚆(9,36)

Last Post ℒ
2 County Square, PA1 1BN
✪ 8-midnight ☎ (0141) 849 6911
Caledonian Deuchars IPA; Greene King Abbot; Ruddles Best Bitter; guest beers Ⓗ
Large Wetherspoon pub converted from the town's main post office. Open plan in design, there is plenty of seating. The standard food menu is available and six guest ales are usually on offer. This was the first Wetherspoon pub to hold a Battle of the Brewers competition and it continues to run them regularly throughout the year. Next to Gilmour Street railway station and close to the bus station, it is handy for a pint between trains or buses. ◁▮ㅤ⇌(Gilmour St)🚆(9,36)

Wee Howff
53 High Street, PA1 2AN
✪ 11-midnight (1am Fri & Sat); 12.30-midnight Sun
☎ (0141) 889 2095
Beer range varies Ⓗ
The Wee Howff has appeared in the last 24 editions of the Guide and is a little piece of heaven in an otherwise crowded area of cheap drinking establishments. A traditional pub with a loyal clientele, the Howff offers up to three guest ales from all four corners of Britain. It has an open mic night on the first Monday of each month and a pub quiz every Thursday. The jukebox caters for even the most eclectic of tastes. ⇌(Gilmour St)🚆(9,36)

Renfrew

Lord of the Isles
Unit 21 Xscape, Kings Inch Road, PA4 8XQ
✪ 8-midnight (1am Fri & Sat) ☎ (0141) 886 8930
Greene King Abbot; guest beers Ⓗ
Large, purpose-built Wetherspoon establishment attached to the Xscape Leisure Complex and a short stroll from Yarrows Shipyard. Throughout the pub the walls display photographs depicting the history of industry on the River Clyde. The outside seating area is south facing and a real sunspot during warm summer days. Food is available all day and three ever-changing guest ales are on handpump.
✿◁▮ㅤ&P⁵-🚆

Sandpiper
Glasgow Airport, PA3 2SW
✪ 5-9.30 ☎ (0141) 842 7858
Greene King Abbot; guest beers Ⓗ
Positioned on the ground floor, in the public area of the airport, the Sandpiper is ideal if you are looking for an ale before heading through security, waiting for visitors arriving on an incoming flight, or just taking a break from plane spotting. With six handpumps serving ales you are spoiled for choice. Many TV screens show 24 hour news or major sporting events. ◁▮&🚆

Strathaven

Weavers ℒ
1-3 Green Street, ML10 6LT
✪ 11-midnight Mon; 4.45-midnight Tue-Thu; 11-1am Fri & Sat; 2-1am Sun ☎ 07749 332914
Beer range varies Ⓗ
Family-run pub in the centre of a small historic town with links to the 19th-century weaving industry. A local community hub where local groups and clubs meet, the single room has comfortable furnishings and is decorated with an assortment of black and white photographs of film stars. Three handpumps offer ales from an ever-changing range and the fourth is dedicated to beers from the nearby Strathaven Ales. A selection of imported bottled beers is also available. &🚆(13)

Uplawmoor

Uplawmoor Hotel ℒ
66 Neilston Road, G78 4AF (off A736)
✪ 11-11 (midnight Sat); 12.30-11 Sun ☎ (01505) 850565
⊕ uplawmoor.co.uk
Houston Killellan; Kelburn Red Smiddy Ⓗ
Situated in a tranquil village setting about 10 miles from Glasgow, the building dates back to the 18th century. It was originally a coaching inn used by travellers and customs officers chasing smugglers en-route between Glasgow and the south-west coast of Scotland. Today the hotel continues to offer travellers the opportunity to relax and explore. The interior is rustic and cosy, with a separate pool room. Bar meals are served until 9.30pm. ⚲Q✿♨◁▮ 🛏&P⁵-🚆(395,X44B)

Wishaw

Wishaw Malt
62-66 Kirk Road, ML2 7BL
✪ 11-midnight (1am Fri & Sat) ☎ (01698) 358806
Greene King Abbot; Ruddles Best Bitter; guest beers Ⓗ
Former furniture store converted into a pub a decade ago, taking the name of a Wishaw distillery of the 19th century. In many ways a typical small-town Wetherspoon pub, it buzzes with the sound of conversation, and TVs show racing in the background. Beers come from all over, with a preference for pale and blonde ales. To the side is a narrow patio beer garden. Breakfast is available from 8am every day, alcohol from 11am.
✿◁▮&⇌♦⁵-🚆(240,267)

Is there anywhere in this damned place where we can get a decent bottle of Bass?
Alfred, Lord Tennyson, during a public performance of one of his poems, 1862

SCOTLAND

HIGHLANDS & WESTERN ISLES

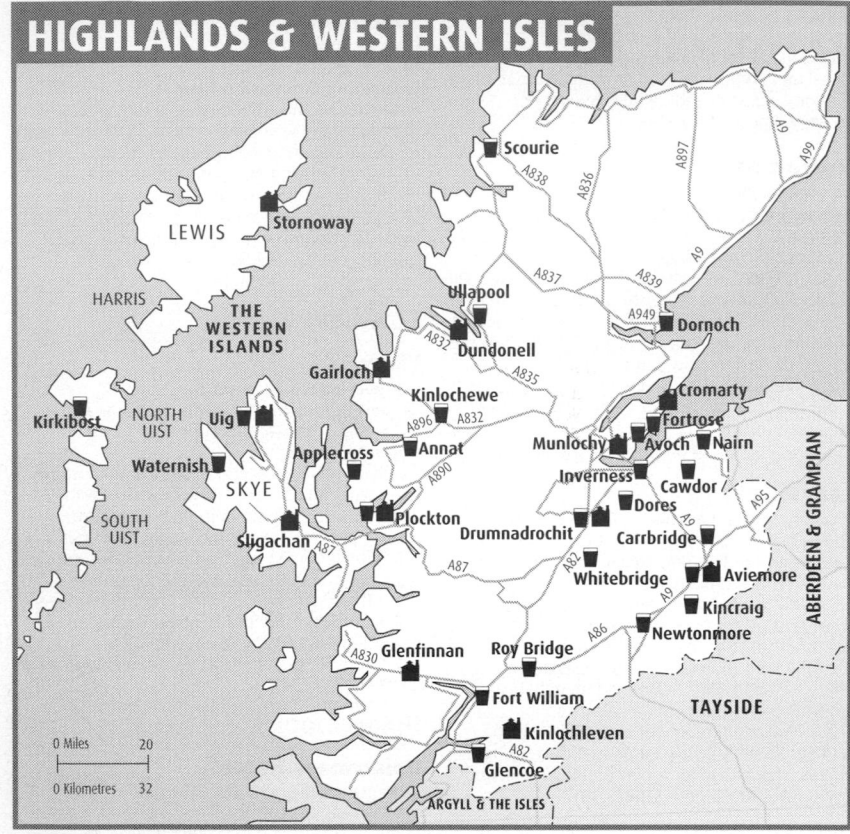

Authority areas covered: Highland UA, Western Isles UA

Annat

Torridon Inn L
IV22 2EY (close to Loch Torridon)
☼ 11-11 (closed Mon-Wed Nov-Mar); 12 (5 Nov-Mar)-11 Sun
☎ (01445) 791242 ⊕ thetorridon.com/inn
Beer range varies Ⓗ
One or two ales are served in winter and up to six
in summer, often from local An Teallach, Isle of
Skye and Cairngorm breweries. Real cider is also
sometimes available in summer. An excellent base
for outdoor enthusiasts and families alike, the pub
opens at 8am for breakfast and serves good food
all day in generous portions, made with locally
sourced ingredients. Traditional music features
weekly in the summer and there is a beer festival
in October. ♨❀⇄◖&🅰🐾P

Applecross

Applecross Inn
Shore Street, IV54 8LR NG710444
☼ 11-11.30 (midnight Fri); 12.30-11.30 Sun
☎ (01520) 74462 ⊕ applecross.uk.com/inn
Isle of Skye Red Cuillin; guest beers Ⓗ
On the shore of the Applecross Peninsula, enjoying
views of the Isle of Skye and Raasay, this inn is
reached by a single-track road over the highest
vehicular ascent in Britain, or by a longer scenic
coastal route, but is well worth finding. Isle of Skye
and An Teallach beers are served alongside a large
malt whisky selection. Accommodation is available

and local seafood is a speciality. Dogs are welcome
and there is a handy 24-hour petrol pump close by.
♨❀⇄◖&🅰P↝➡

Aviemore

Cairngorm Hotel L
Grampian Road, PH22 1PE (opp train station)
☼ 11-midnight (1am Fri & Sat); 11.30-midnight Sun
☎ (01479) 810233 ⊕ cairngorm.com
Cairngorm Stag, Gold Ⓗ
The lounge bar of this privately owned hotel,
though large, has a cosy feel. Although the trade is
mainly holidaymakers, the bar is also popular with
locals, and has a large-screen TV showing sport.
Decorated with tartan wall coverings, there is a
Scottish theme throughout the hotel and Scottish
entertainment features on many afternoons and
evenings. ❀⇄◖&🅰↝P↝➡

Old Bridge Inn L
Dalfaber Road, PH22 1PU
☼ 12-midnight (1am Fri & Sat); 12.30-midnight Sun
☎ (01479) 811137 ⊕ oldbridgeinn.co.uk
**Cairngorm Trade Winds; Caledonian Deuchars IPA;
guest beers** Ⓗ
Busy pub, popular with outdoor enthusiasts,
serving good-quality food made with locally
sourced ingredients. Originally a cottage and now
greatly enlarged, it lies on the road to the
Strathspey Steam Railway overlooking the River
Spey. The two guest handpumps dispense the

seasonal offering from the local Cairngorm Brewery plus another Scottish ale. Live music is hosted twice weekly, including traditional and modern Scottish music and bands. Children are welcome and there is a bunkhouse attached. ▨▧☖◑⟜Å⇌P⁴⊟(15,15X)

Avoch

Station Hotel Ⓛ
Bridge Street, IV9 8PP (on A832, 6 miles NE of Kessock Bridge)
✪ 11-1am (midnight Sat); 12.30-11.30 Sun
☎ (01381) 620246 ⊕ stationhotelavoch.co.uk
Beer range varies Ⓗ
This village inn was listed in the Guide in the '90s but stopped serving real ale for many years. Richard and Lorraine then bought it and gave it a refit before reopening in 2012. Now a well-run, busy pub, it offers an excellent selection of Scottish beers – sometimes with a Cromarty ale with a Cairngorm beer on the second pump. A third pump is used during the summer months. Generously sized meals are available at very reasonable prices (book at weekends). ▨Q➥☖◑⊟☖ÅP⊟(26)

Carrbridge

Cairn Hotel Ⓛ
PH23 3AS (on B9153)
✪ 11-midnight (1am Fri & Sat); 12.30-11 Sun
☎ (01479) 841212 ⊕ cairnhotel.co.uk
Beer range varies Ⓗ
Traditional Highland inn with seven guest rooms, set in the Cairngorm National Park and popular with both locals and visitors. Freshly cooked, seasonal bar meals are available alongside three real ales. Local beers from the Black Isle and Cairngorm breweries are favourites and the third pump features a different Scottish guest ale with every cask. ▨☖☖◑⇌♣⁴

Cawdor

Cawdor Tavern
The Lane, IV12 5XP
✪ 11-11 (3 winter); 11-midnight Fri & Sat; 12.30-11 Sun
☎ (01667) 404777 ⊕ cawdortavern.com
Beer range varies Ⓗ
Family-run pub at the heart of this conservation village, a short walk from the famous castle and within easy reach of local historic attractions. It has a spacious lounge and cosy public bar, both wood panelled with log fires, and a large restaurant. Up to five handpumps offer Orkney/Atlas ales – the family also owns the Orkney Brewery at Quoyloo. ▨Q➥☖◑⊟☖♣P⊟

Dores

Dores Inn
IV2 6TR (on B862 from Inverness at jct with B852)
✪ 11-11 (midnight Fri & Sat); 12.30-11 Sun
☎ (01463) 751203
Beer range varies Ⓗ
Situated on the south side of Loch Ness, just eight miles from Inverness, this inn enjoys spectacular views and is ideal for Nessie spotting. The cosy wood-finished bar serves up to four ales, nearly always from Scottish independent breweries such as Cairngorm, Highland and Fyne Ales, with an occasional English ale featured. The welcoming,

extended dining room serves good food made with locally sourced ingredients and can get busy at times. Home baking is available and the inn opens at 10am for coffee. ▨Q➥☖◑ÅP⊟(302,303)

Dornoch

Dornoch Castle Hotel Ⓛ
Castle Street, IV25 3SD
✪ 11-11 (1am Fri; 11.45 Sat); 12.30-11 Sun
☎ (01862) 810216 ⊕ dornochcastlehotel.com
Cromarty Happy Chappy; guest beer Ⓗ
Upmarket 500-year-old converted Scottish castle situated in the centre of town, close to the famous golf course and opposite a 13th-century cathedral. The hotel is a popular venue for weddings and so very occasionally closed to the public. Two handpumps are in use although during the winter season this can be reduced to one. Ales are sourced from Cromarty, Orkney and Cairngorm. Enthusiastic bar managers are more than willing to talk about the range of 150 fine malt whiskies. ▨Q➥☖➥◑☖ÅP⁴⊟(25X,X99)

Drumnadrochit

Benleva Hotel Ⓨ Ⓛ
Kilmore Road, IV63 6UH (signed, 800yds from A82)
✪ 12-midnight (1am Fri); 12.30-11 Sun ☎ (01456) 450080
⊕ benleva.co.uk
Beer range varies Ⓗ
Popular, friendly village inn near Loch Ness, catering for locals and visitors alike. A 400-year-old former manse, the sweet chestnut outside was once a hanging tree. Six handpumps dispense the hotel's own Loch Ness Brewery ales accompanied by other Scottish offerings and two real ciders. Lunches, evening meals and Sunday roasts are available. Entertainment includes occasional quiz nights and traditional music. Home of the famous Loch Ness Beer Festival in September and local CAMRA Pub of the Year 2013. ▨➥☖➥◑⊟Å♣♠P⁴⊟

Fort William

Ben Nevis Inn Ⓛ
Claggan, Achintee, PH33 6TE (at start of Ben Nevis footpath) NN125729
✪ 12-11 (closed Mon-Wed Nov-Mar) ☎ (01397) 701227
⊕ ben-nevis-inn.co.uk
Beer range varies Ⓗ
Popular with walkers, mountaineers and locals alike, this friendly bar and restaurant is in a unique location, housed in a traditional 200-year-old stone-built barn and warmed by a log-burning stove. There is usually a choice of three ales,

An Teallach Dundonell
Black Isle Munlochy
Cairngorm Aviemore
Cromarty Cromarty
Cuillin Sligachan: Isle of Skye
Glenfinnan Glenfinnan
Hebridean Stornoway: Isle of Lewis
Isle of Skye Uig: Isle of Skye
Loch Ness Drumnadrochit
Old Inn Gairloch
Plockton Plockton
River Leven Kinlochleven

SCOTLAND

mainly from Cairngorm, An Teallach and Isle of Skye breweries. The daily-changing food menu is a mix of fresh local produce and innovative international dishes. Live music is a regular feature. Bunkhouse accommodation sleeps up to 20 people. ᴹQ☕☎◑৬Å⇌Pˡ

Cobbs at Nevisport

Airds Crossing, High Street, PH33 6EU (beneath Nevisport shop) NN110742
❂ 11-midnight (1am Fri & Sat); 12.30-11 Sun
☎ (01397) 704790 ⊕ cobbs-at-nevisport.co.uk
Beer range varies ⊞
A warming open fire welcomes winter visitors to this large but cosy bar, located under the Nevisport outdoor shop. At the West Highland Way finish and Great Glen Way start, close to Glen Nevis, this is a favourite meeting place for outdoor enthusiasts. Bar meals are served all day including traditional Scottish breakfasts and home-baked cakes. Children are welcome in the upstairs restaurant. Regular music nights feature local bands. Beers are mostly Scottish, often from Orkney and Isle of Skye breweries. ᴹ➳◑৬Å⇌ˡ🖳

Grog & Gruel ⬡

66 High Street, PH33 6AE
❂ 12-11.30 (12.30am Thu-Sat); 12.30 (5 winter)-11.30 Sun
☎ (01397) 705078 ⊕ grogandgruel.co.uk
Beer range varies ⊞
This traditional ale house has featured in the Guide since 1994. It keeps up to six beers in summer, fewer in winter, usually Scottish and often including something from the local Glenfinnan and River Leven breweries. The bar is busy with locals, tourists and outdoor enthusiasts. Light meals and snacks are available all day in the bar and evening meals in the upstairs restaurant. Events include regular live music, open mic nights and beer festivals. ➳☸◑Å⇌●ˡ🖳

Fortrose

Anderson

Union Street, IV10 8TD (on A832)
❂ 4 (3 Sun)-11.30 ☎ (01381) 620236 ⊕ theanderson.co.uk
Beer range varies ⊞
The owners are an international beer writer and self-confessed beer geek, and his wife, a New Orleans-trained chef. Serving ale and cider from more than 250 breweries since 2003, this beer drinkers' mecca also offers more than 240 malts and 100 Belgian beers. Entertainment includes winter beer festivals, regular quizzes, music sessions and knitting nights. Food is reasonably priced, high-quality international cuisine. CAMRA members are offered a discount on accommodation in winter. The pub closes in November for an annual holiday.
ᴹ➳☸☎◑৬Å♣●Pˡ🖳(26)

Glencoe

Clachaig Inn ⬡

PH49 4HX (on slip road ½ mile off A82) NN128567
❂ 11-11 (midnight Fri; 11.30 Sat); 12.30-11 Sun
☎ (01855) 811 252 ⊕ clachaig.com
Beer range varies ⊞
Nestling among spectacular mountains, the Clachaig is frequented mainly by climbers, walkers and tourists who come for the stunning scenery. The main bar, furnished with wooden benches and upholstered seating around the walls, has up to 15 handpumps serving a selection of Scottish beers. A smaller selection of beers is available in the comfortable lounge – note the 'Monocle of the Glen', a fake stag's head wearing a monocle. There is a residents' lounge and dining area for those staying over. ᴹ➳☸☎◑ 🄳৬ÅPˡ🖳(916)

Inverness

Blackfriars ⬡

93-95 Academy Street, IV1 1LU
❂ 11-midnight (1am Fri; 12.30am Sat); 12.30-9 Sun
☎ (01463) 233881 ⊕ blackfriarshighlandpub.co.uk
Caledonian XPA; guest beers ⊞
This popular, traditional pub has a spacious single-room interior with a large standing area by the bar and ample seating in comfortable alcoves. The five handpumps deliver a combination of English and Scottish beers. The latter are often from Orkney and Highland, plus local ales from Loch Ness, Cairngorm and Cromarty. There is also a choice of Thistly Cross Scottish ciders. Good-value home-cooked Scottish fare is served, with daily specials including a home-made soup. A welcoming music-oriented venue, bands perform at weekends. ➳◑৬Å⇌🖳

Castle Tavern ⬡

1 View Place, IV2 4SA (top of Castle St)
❂ 11-1am (12.30am Sat); 12-midnight Sun
☎ (01463) 718178 ⊕ castletavern.net
Beer range varies ⊞
A 73-mile hike along the Great Glen Way or a five-minute stroll from the city centre bring you to this friendly hostelry in a listed building facing Inverness Castle and boasting fine views across the River Ness towards Inverness Cathedral. Six handpumps dispense a changing range of beers, regularly including Scottish independents and LocAle brews. Bar meals are served all day, and there is a restaurant on the first floor. A Victorian-style canopy covers the large beer patio.
➳☸◑Å⇌ˡ🖳(6,7,14)

Clachnaharry Inn

17-19 High Street, IV3 8RB (on A862 Beauly road)
❂ 11-11 (1am Thu-Sat); 12-11 Sun ☎ (01463) 239806
⊕ clachnaharryinn.co.uk
Beer range varies ⊞
Popular with locals and visitors, this friendly 17th-century coaching inn offers high-quality food made with locally sourced ingredients. Five handpumps (four in winter) dispense beers from Inveralmond, Orkney/Atlas and Cairngorm, as well as some from Greene King. The large patio area affords fine views over the Caledonian Canal sea lock and Beauly Firth toward the Munro Ben Wyvis. Families are welcome. ᴹQ➳☸◑ 🄳Å♣P🖳(28A)

King's Highway

72-74 Church Street, IV1 1EN
❂ 11-midnight (1am Thu & Fri); 12.30-midnight Sun
☎ (01463) 251800
Caledonian Deuchars IPA; Greene King Abbot; guest beers ⊞
This former hotel is now a Wetherspoon pub with a 27-room lodge attached. The vast single-roomed bar is broken up by several pillars and plenty of comfortable seating in alcoves. Up to 10 handpumps serve the regular ales alongside a good mix of guests, including beers from Houston, Cairngorm and An Teallach. Real cider is also available. Food is standard Wetherspoon, with

breakfast served from 7am. Customers are the typical eclectic mix and the pub gets busy at weekends. ⛄🏠🌒♿⚴🅰⇌⊛🖵

Number 27 🄻
27 Castle Street, IV2 3DU
✪ 11-11 (12.30am Fri & Sat); 12.30-11 Sun
☎ (01463) 241999 ⊕ number27inverness.co.uk
Beer range varies Ⓗ
Popular city-centre bar/restaurant with three handpumps and a large range of bottled beers including many continental brews. One ale from Cromarty is usually accompanied by another from a Scottish micro and one from England. There is also a good selection of malt whiskies. The venue has a reputation for excellent food – lunches range from sandwiches to light bites while the evening menu features traditional meals made with locally sourced ingredients including venison and steak.
⊘🅰⇌⊛🖵

Snowgoose
Stoneyfield, IV2 7PA (on A96 Aberdeen road)
✪ 12 (11 Sat Apr-Dec)-11; 12-10.30 Sun ☎ (01463) 701921
Caledonian Deuchars IPA; Harviestoun Natural Blonde; guest beer Ⓗ
Although close to two travel lodges, this traditional inn supports a popular, mostly local, bar trade, with an area reserved for drinkers. A converted 1788 coach house, the single large L-shaped room has alcoves and log fires to give it a more cosy and intimate feel. A wide variety of food is offered all day at reasonable prices. The guest handpump features an ever-changing ale from the Mitchells & Butlers Vintage Inn list. 🏔Q⛄🌒⊛⊘♿P⁵⁻🖵(110)

Kincraig

Suie Hotel 🄻
PH21 1NA (at head of Loch Insh on B9152)
✪ 5-11 (1am Fri & Sat) ☎ (01540) 651344 ⊕ suiehotel.com
Cairngorm Trade Winds; guest beers Ⓗ
This Victorian character hotel, located at the south end of the village, is run by only the second owner in 108 years. The wooden-floored bar features a large wood-burning stove plus a pool table and jukebox. Two guest pumps, plus a third in summer, dispense a selection of ales from the local Cairngorm Brewery. Close to the River Spey and Loch Insh, the bar is popular with locals, hillwalkers, skiers and cyclists. Traditional Scottish music features on Saturdays. Good food is served.
🏔🌒🏠♣P⁵⁻🖵(209)

Kinlochewe

Kinlochewe Hotel 🄻
IV22 2PA NH028619
✪ 11 (12.30 Sun)-midnight ☎ (01445) 760253
⊕ kinlochewehotel.co.uk
Beer range varies Ⓗ
The ambience in this refurbished bar is friendly and welcoming. Freshly cooked food uses the best of seasonal high-quality local produce, including seafood, game and beef, with an emphasis on simplicity and flavour. Set in the heart of the magnificent Torridon Mountains at the foot of Beinn Eighe, this is an ideal base for exploring the wild scenery of the North Western Highlands. Up to five handpumps serve ales from An Teallach and Orkney. 🏔Q🏠⊘♿🅰⊛P⁵⁻🖵

Kirkibost: North Uist

Westford Inn
Claddach, HS6 5EP (4 miles NW of A867/865 jct)
✪ 12-3, 6-10.30; winter hours vary ☎ (01876) 580653
⊕ j7mis.co.uk/westfordinn
Beer range varies Ⓗ
A Georgian listed building set in a remote area of the Outer Hebrides. Popular with walkers, shooting parties and tourists, this friendly pub has a traditional atmosphere – no fruit machines, jukebox or deep fat frier. Home-cooked pub food is available lunchtimes and evenings in summer and there are peat-fuelled fires. Dogs are welcome. Ales are from the Isle of Skye Brewery and a good range of bottled beers is stocked. Winter opening times depend on custom. 🏔Q⛄🌒🏠♿🅰♣P🖵

Nairn

Braeval Hotel 🄻
Crescent Road, IV12 4NB
✪ 12 (5 Mon & Tue Jan-Mar)-midnight; 12-12.30am Thu-Sat; 12.30 midnight Sun ☎ (01667) 452341 ⊕ braevalhotel.co.uk
Beer range varies Ⓗ
The award-winning Bandstand Bar is part of the Braeval Hotel, close to Nairn beach. Up to nine handpumps offer a wide selection of English and Scottish ales, featuring Cairngorm, Cromarty and Highland, as well as a real cider. An ale on gravity is also sometimes available in summer. The restaurant in this family-run hotel enjoys spectacular sea views overlooking the Moray Firth. The bar hosts a beer festival every spring featuring at least 60 ales. 🏔Q⊛🏠🌒⊘♿🅰♣⊛⁵⁻🖵(10)

Newtonmore

Glen Hotel 🄻
Main Street, PH20 1DD
✪ 11 (12.30 Sun)-midnight ☎ (01540) 673203
⊕ theglenhotel.co.uk
Caledonian Deuchars IPA; guest beers Ⓗ
Small, welcoming, family-run Edwardian hotel with the Monadhliath and Cairngorm mountain ranges on its doorstep. It has a good local trade and is also popular with outdoor enthusiasts and tourists. There is a large bar room and separate games and dining rooms, with regular quiz and games nights. Up to four handpumps dispense mainly Scottish beers, usually including one from the local Cairngorm Brewery, plus a Westons cider or perry. An extensive menu includes a good selection of vegetarian dishes. 🏔🌒🏠⊘♿🅰⇌⊛P⁵⁻🖵

Plockton

Plockton Hotel 🄻
41 Harbour Street, IV52 8TN
✪ 11-midnight; 12-30-11 Sun ☎ (01599) 544274
⊕ plocktonhotel.co.uk
Beer range varies Ⓗ
Sheltered by mountains and fanned by the warm air of the Gulf Stream, this hotel is at the edge of Loch Carron and boasts breathtaking views across the bay. Seafood is the speciality on an excellent menu that also features locally reared beef and Highland venison. The village has much to offer and is a regular haunt for outdoor enthusiasts. A beer from Loch Ness Brewery usually features along with brews from a variety of other Scottish micros. 🏔Q⛄🌒🏠⊘♿⇌P

Plockton Inn 🄻

Innes Street, IV52 8TW
✪ 11-1am (12.30am Sat); 11-11 Sun ☎ (01599) 544222
⊕ plocktoninn.co.uk
Beer range varies Ⓗ
Located in a picture postcard Highland village, this popular inn has been owned and run by a local family for many years. Locally caught fish and shellfish take pride of place on the menu – the seafood platter includes fish smoked on the premises. Every Tuesday and Thursday there are live music sessions in the public bar and all are welcome to join in. A regularly changing selection of real ales includes locally brewed Plockton Brewery beers. 🛏Q🌣🕸🍴◑&🛇🍽♣P'–

Roy Bridge

Stronlossit Inn 🄻

PH31 4AG
✪ 11-11.45 (1am Thu-Sat); 12.30-11.45 Sun
☎ (01397) 712253 ⊕ stronlossit.co.uk
Beer range varies Ⓗ
An ideal base for outdoor activities or touring the Highlands. Bar meals featuring local seasonal produce are available all day. The three handpumps dispense a selection of Scottish beers from Cairngorm and other Highlands and Islands breweries, and an occasional cider. Opening times may vary in December and January, depending on custom. Budget accommodation is available alongside standard rooms.
🛏🌣🕸🍴◑&🛇🍽♣P'–🚍

Scourie

Scourie Hotel 🄻

IV27 4SX (on A894 between Laxford Bridge and Kylesku)
✪ 11 (12 Sat)-2.30, 5-11 summer; 5-9.30 (10.30 Fri; 11 Sat) winter; 12.30-2.30, 6-10.30 Sun ☎ (01971) 502396
⊕ scourie-hotel.co.uk
Beer range varies Ⓗ
Converted 1640 coaching inn in the heart of the wonderland wilderness of north-west Sutherland. Close to the Handa Island ferry, and a short drive to the peaks of Arkle and Foinavon, this is an ideal base for exploring the remote landscape. It is popular with fishermen who can access around 300 lochs with 46 hotel-controlled beats. In addition to a fixed bar menu, the dining room offers high-quality meals featuring seafood. Up to four handpumps serve mainly Scottish beers, often including ales from Black Isle and/or Cairngorm, and a cider. Q🌣🍴◑&🛇♣P'–

Uig: Isle of Skye

Bakur Bar 🄻

The Pier, IV51 9XX
✪ 11.30-11 (midnight Thu; 1am Fri; 12.30am Sat); 12.30-11.30 Sun ☎ (01470) 542212
Isle of Skye Red Cuillin; guest beers Ⓗ
Traditional west-coast bar, conveniently located on the pier adjacent to the Western Isles ferry terminal and a stone's throw from the Isle of Skye Brewery which supplies all the ales. During the summer months up to four beers are available, with a more limited range in the quieter winter season. The Bakur has a pool table and is popular with the locals. 🌣◑&AP'–🚍

Ullapool

Argyll Hotel 🄻

18 Argyll Street, IV26 2UB
✪ 11-1am (midnight Sat); winter hours vary; 12.30-11.30 Sun ☎ (01854) 612422 ⊕ theargyllullapool.com
Beer range varies Ⓗ
Busy, small hotel offering breakfast, lunch and dinner, all made with locally sourced produce wherever possible. The beer range includes one from An Teallach and a changing English guest. Live music features on Monday, and regular live bands play on Tuesday and Saturday. A cider and blues music festival is now an autumn fixture. Weekly quiz and poker nights keep the lounge bar busy and there is a pool table and dartboard. Dogs are welcome. Hours may vary in winter depending on custom. 🛏🕸🍴◑&A♣🐾P'–

Morefield Motel 🄻

North Road, IV26 2TQ (off A835)
✪ 12 (12.30 Sun)-11 ☎ (01854) 612161
⊕ morefieldmotel.co.uk
Beer range varies Ⓗ
Locally caught seafood is the speciality on the menu at this friendly and welcoming hostelry. Three ales are predominantly from local Highland breweries and include at least one from Cairngorm. The annual Ullapool Beer Festival is held here in October. The Western Isles ferry terminal is a short distance away. Afternoon opening can be subject to seasonal variation. Q🕸🍴◑&A♣P'–

Waternish: Isle of Skye

Stein Inn

Stein, IV55 8GA (N of Dunvegan, on B886) NG263564
✪ 11-midnight (1am Fri; 12.30am Sat) summer; 12-11 (midnight Fri & Sat) winter; 11.30 (12.30 winter)-11 Sun ☎ (01470) 592362 ⊕ steininn.co.uk
Beer range varies Ⓗ
Dating back to the 18th century, this is the oldest inn on Skye, nestling among whitewashed cottages on the shores of Loch Bay, and owned and run by the same family for 20 years. A large stove warms the cosy low-beamed bar which has fine views over the sea loch to Rubha Maol. Locally caught seafood, landed at the nearby jetty, is available Easter to October in the bar and restaurant. Facilities for seafarers include council moorings, showers, food supplies and message-relay services. 🛏Q🌣🕸🍴◑&P'–

Whitebridge

Whitebridge Hotel 🄻

IV2 6UN
✪ 11-11 summer; 11-2.30, 5-11 winter; 11-11 Sat; 12.30-11 Sun ☎ (01456) 486226 ⊕ whitebridgehotel.co.uk
Beer range varies Ⓗ
Built in 1899 and situated on the quieter side of Loch Ness, this hotel has fishing rights on two local lochs. Inside, the attractive pitch pine-panelled bar, with a welcoming wood-burning stove, has an alcove with a pool table and a separate area used for dining. Most of the traditional pub food is home cooked. One or two ales are stocked, usually from Cairngorm or Cromarty. The hotel has a green tourism policy. 🛏Q🕸🍴◑&♣P🚍(301)

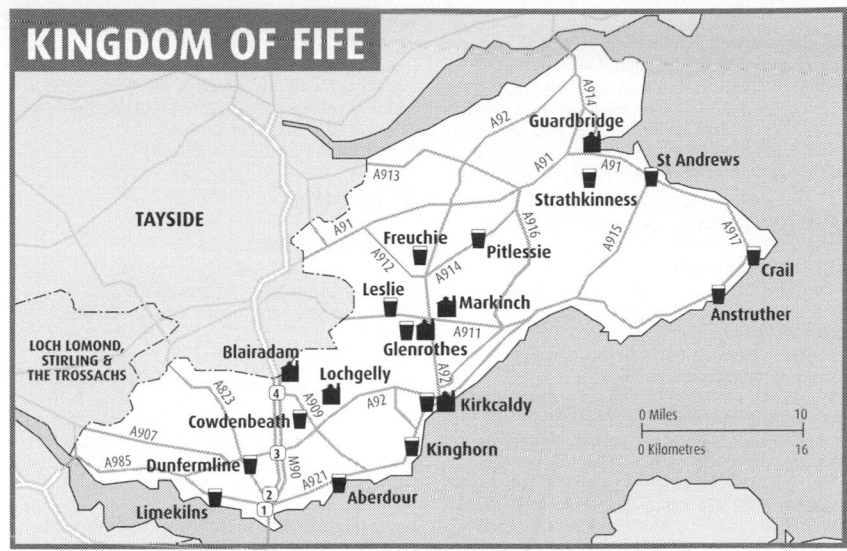

KINGDOM OF FIFE

Guardbridge
St Andrews
Strathkinness
TAYSIDE
Freuchie
Pitlessie
Crail
Leslie
Markinch
Anstruther
LOCH LOMOND,
STIRLING &
THE TROSSACHS
Blairadam
Glenrothes
Lochgelly
Cowdenbeath
Kirkcaldy
Kinghorn
Dunfermline
Limekilns
Aberdour

0 Miles 10
0 Kilometres 16

SCOTLAND

Authority area covered: Fife UA

Aberdour

Cedar Inn
20 Shore Road, KY3 0TR
⊕ 11 (12.30 Sun)-11.45 ☎ (01383) 860310
⊕ thecedarinn.co.uk
Caledonian Deuchars IPA; guest beers ⊞
Enter through the front door and to the right you will find a quiet bar with the real ale handpumps and a range of whiskies. To the left is a comfortable lounge bar with a Cotswold-stone fireplace. A conservatory is opposite. Carry on walking and you will come to another bar with a band area where live music plays every other Friday. On the wall is a lovely Alloa Brewery mirror as well as two TVs. Meals are served in the lounge and a separate restaurant, and bar snacks are available.
🏨🐕❄️⊘◑⊟➿P⁂–🚌(7,7A)

Foresters Arms
35 High Street, KY3 0SJ
⊕ 11 (12.30 Sun)-midnight ☎ (01383) 860544
⊕ forries.co.uk
Caledonian Deuchars IPA; guest beers ⊞
Situated in the centre of the village, the Foresters has a wood and tiled floor and a lovely oak gantry and bar front. There are stools around the bar and tables and chairs opposite. Warmed by a lovely coal fire, the public bar is a comfortable place to enjoy a good pub lunch (served Tue-Sun). Live music, quizzes and theme nights are held regularly. The Fife Coastal Path is right on the doorstep.
🏨❄️◑⊟♿➿♣⁂–🚌(7,7A)

Anstruther

Ship Tavern
49 Shore Street, KY10 3AQ (next to Scottish Fisheries Museum)
⊕ 11-midnight (1am Fri & Sat); 12.30-midnight Sun
☎ (01333) 310347
Beer range varies ⊞
This old, traditional pub on the harbour front is a popular meeting place for fishermen, locals and visitors to the museum. Next door to the famous

Anstruther Fish & Chip Restaurant, the main bar has a flagstone floor and a picture window overlooking the busy harbour. The room has a nautical theme with a mural of the harbour covering two walls, and features fishing memorabilia. A back room has a relaxing feel with comfortable sofas and tables and chairs. Ales from local microbreweries are among the range. ◑⊟⊞♿⚓P🚌(X60,95)

Cowdenbeath

Woodside Hotel
109 Broad Street, KY4 8JR
⊕ 11 (12.30 Sun)-midnight ☎ (01383) 511598
⊕ woodsidehotelcowdenbeath.co.uk
Beer range varies ⊞
Large single-roomed bar with two handpumps serving ales from local and north of England microbreweries in lined glasses. One side of the room has a pool table and dartboard, and four plasma screens show sport. A friendly atmosphere prevails, with live entertainment at the weekend. A separate lounge is available for functions. Outside, a covered, decked area with seating is a suntrap in summer. ❄️🛏️⊟♿➿♣P⁂–🚐🚌

Crail

Golf Hotel
4 High Street, KY10 3TD
⊕ 11-midnight (1am Thu-Sat) ☎ (01333) 450206
⊕ thegolfhotelcrail.com
Beer range varies ⊞
The Golf Hotel is a listed 16th-century coaching inn in a picturesque village in the East Neuk of Fife. The

historic bar dates back to 1721, making it one of the oldest in Scotland. The room retains the original low-beamed ceiling, wooden floor and a 16th-century fireplace with a marriage lintel over it bearing the initials of the original owners. Relax with a beer or two in the spacious beer garden or enjoy a meal in the restaurant after walking the coastal path. ♨✿✍⬧◐ ➤☗▲⬩➜➲(95)

Dunfermline

Commercial Inn
13 Douglas Street, KY12 7EB (opp post office)
✪ 11-11 (midnight Fri & Sat); 12.30-11 Sun
☎ (01383) 733876
Caledonian Deuchars IPA; Courage Directors; Theakston Old Peculier; guest beers 🅗
Well-known ale house in a building dating back to the 1820s. A cosy town-centre establishment, this is a place for conversation, with quiet background music. Good-quality food and friendly service attract an eclectic clientele. Seven ales are always available plus an occasional cider. An extensive food menu includes specials at lunchtime and evening meals Tuesday-Thursday and Saturday, with steak night on Tuesday and curry night on Wednesday. A former Fife CAMRA Pub of the Year and runner-up 2013. ◐➤➲

East Port Bar
7 East Port, KY12 7JG
✪ 11.30-11 (midnight Fri & Sat); 11-11 Sun
☎ (01383) 736678 ⊕ eastportbar.co.uk
Caledonian Deuchars IPA 🅗
Busy town-centre pub with welcoming staff and friendly service. The interior features wood panelling and a wood bar and gantry, alcove seating and comfortable sofas at the rear. An old Maclay mirror decorates the stairs leading to the beer garden. Two plasma screens show sport, and soft background music usually plays. Value-for-money bar food is served at lunchtime. The pub has received a Best Bar None award every year 2008-2012 from Fife Constabulary. ✿◐⬧➤➜➲

Freuchie

Albert Tavern
2 High Street, KY15 7EX
✪ 5 (12 Fri & Sat)-midnight; 12.30-midnight Sun
☎ (07876) 178863
Beer range varies 🅗
Friendly village local, reputedly a coaching inn when nearby Falkland Palace was a royal residence. Wainscot panelling and two old brewery mirrors adorn the walls of the bar. A TV in the lounge screens sport. Five handpumps offer weekly changing beers from the Flying Firkin range, usually including a dark mild. A multi-award winner, including Scotland & Northern Ireland CAMRA Pub of the Year, National CAMRA Pub of the Year finalist and local CAMRA Pub of the Year runner-up in 2013. ♨Q✿➤P➜➲(36,X54,64)

Lomond Hills Hotel
High Street, KY15 7EY
✪ 11-2, 5-midnight; 11-midnight Fri & Sat; 12.30-midnight Sun ☎ (01337) 857329 ⊕ lomondhillshotel.com
Beer range varies 🅗
Comfortable country hotel, originally a coaching inn established in 1733, with a marvellous view of the Lomond Hills and handy for visiting Falkland

Palace. The small, welcoming public bar sports a carved bar top and wood panelling on the walls. A plasma screen shows sport. Two beers are always available. Meals are served in the family lounge and in a separate dining room. Outside there is a smoking area and beer garden. ♨➤✿✍◐ ➤☗P➜➲(36,X54,64)

Glenrothes

Golden Acorn
1 North Street, KY7 5NA (next to bus station)
✪ 10-midnight; 12.30-11 Sun ☎ (01592) 755252
Caledonian Deuchars; Greene King Abbot; guest beers 🅗
Large Wetherspoon venue with its own accommodation. In the bar, scenes of the local area in days gone by decorate various pillars. Real ale on seven handpumps and a regular cider are on offer, as well as the usual Wetherspoon beer festivals and special deals. Breakfast is served from 7am (8am Sun). Plasma screens show sport and there is a smoking and seating area outside. The bus station is two minutes' walk from the pub. ♨➤✿✍◐➤▲⬩P➜➲

Kinghorn

Crown Tavern
55-57 High Street, KY3 9UW
✪ 11 (12.30 Sun)-11.45 ☎ (01592) 890430
Beer range varies 🅗
Bustling two-roomed local, also called the Middle Bar, situated to the west end of the High Street. Two ever-changing ales are dispensed by cheery bar staff. Attractive stained-glass panels adorn the windows and door and the high ceilings feature ornate plasterwork. Mainly a sports bar, two TVs and a large projector screen show games, and there is a pool table in a side room. Live bands play monthly. A collection of footballs autographed by Scottish Premier League players is on display in the bar. ➤♣⬩➲(7,7A)

Kirkcaldy

Feuars Arms ★
28 Bogies Wynd, KY1 2PH
✪ 11.30 (11 Sun)-11 ☎ (01592) 205577
Beer range varies 🅗
Identified by CAMRA as one of Britain's Best Real Heritage Pubs, the Edwardian interior features original fittings and displays of ceramics. A 59ft-long bar counter is fronted with brown Art Nouveau-style tiles. The large bar area has a mosaic floor, mahogany gantry and long-case clock. Other features include stained glass windows with the arms of Scotland, England and Ireland, lots of etched glass and two mosaic porch floors. The Gents is also worth a visit to view the original features. Beers are sourced from local micros. 🅗

Harbour Bar
471-475 High Street, KY1 2SN (opp harbour)
✪ 11-3, 5-midnight; 11-midnight Thu-Sat; 12.30-midnight Sun ☎ (01592) 264270
Beer range varies 🅗
Situated on the ground floor of a tenement building, this old pub has been described by regulars as a village local in the middle of town. It has a light and airy lounge with ornate cornices. Six handpumps sell up to 20 different beers each week

from micros all over Britain. Local CAMRA Pub of the Year on numerous occasions and a Scottish Pub of the Year finalist. Q⊕ᵇ–⊟

Robert Nairn
6 Kirk Wynd, KY1 1EH
🌑 11 (12.30 Sun)-midnight ☎ (01592) 205049
Caledonian Deuchars IPA; Greene King Abbot; guest beer Ⓗ
A Wetherspoon Lloyd's No.1 with a split-level lounge and pictures of old Kirkcaldy on the walls. Six handpumps dispense a variety of beers. There is also a good selection of bottled ciders. Beer festivals are held throughout the year plus regular Meet the Brewer evenings. The lively pub attracts a mixed clientele, young and old, who all enjoy the real ales. Breakfast is available from 8am and meals are served until 10pm. ᗡ🕸◖Ⓓᰠ◖ᵇ–⊟

Leslie

Burns Tavern
184 High Street, KY6 3DB
🌑 12 (11 Fri & Sat)-midnight; 12.30-midnight Sun
☎ (01592) 741345
Taylor Landlord; guest beers Ⓗ
Typical Scottish two-room, main-street local in a town once famous for papermaking. The public bar is on two levels, the lower lively and friendly with an open fire, the upper with a large-screen TV, pool table and football memorabilia on the walls. The lounge bar is quieter and more spacious. Competitions and quizzes are held weekly, and there's karaoke on Saturday. Leslie Folk Club plays here on a Sunday. ᗁ🕸⊕Å♣Pᵇ–⊟(X1,201)

Limekilns

Ship Inn
Halkett's Hall, KY11 3HJ (on promenade)
🌑 11-11 (midnight Fri & Sat); 12.30-11 Sun
☎ (01383) 872247
Beer range varies Ⓗ
Traditional white coastal building on the waterfront with seating outside providing superb views of the River Forth to watch the ships go by. There is always a friendly welcome here with fresh flowers, cosy alcoves and a maritime theme throughout. Three guest ales from micros are on handpump. Meals are served lunchtimes with fish and seafood the speciality. Qᗁ🕸ⒹPᵇ–⊟(76)

Pitlessie

Village Inn
Cupar Road, KY15 7SU
🌑 11.30-2.30, 5-midnight; 11.30-midnight Fri & Sat; 11.30-midnight Sun ☎ (01337) 830595
⊕ thevillageinnpitlessie.co.uk
Beer range varies Ⓗ
Old coaching inn decorated with pictures of the maltings that was once opposite. A lovely real fire helps create a cosy atmosphere in the wood-panelled, stone and plaster-walled interior. The room has a corner bar with bar stools and a separate seating area for bar meals or drinks. Two ever-changing ales are offered. There is also a large restaurant and separate pool room. High teas are served on Sunday afternoon.
🕮Qᗁ🕸ⒹⒹ⊕ᰠ♣Pᵇ–⊟(X24,X59)

St Andrews

Central Bar ♈
77-79 Market Street, KY16 9NU
🌑 11-11.45 (midnight Fri & Sat); 12.30-11.45 Sun
☎ (01334) 897684
Courage Directors; Fuller's London Pride; Inveralmond Lia Fail; Theakston Old Peculier Ⓗ
A good mix of students, locals, business folk and tourists makes this an interesting, bustling hostelry. It has a Victorian-style island bar, large windows and ornate mirrors creating a late 19th-century feel. There are tables outside on the pavement, weather permitting. Food is available until 9pm. The bar manager is dedicated to his ales and the staff are friendly. CAMRA members receive a discount on real ale. Local CAMRA Pub of the Year runner-up in 2011 and winner in 2012 and 2013.
🕸Ⓓᰠ◖Pᵇ–⊟

Criterion
99 South Street, KY16 9QW
🌑 11-midnight (1am Fri & Sat); 12.30-midnight Sun
☎ (01334) 474543
Caledonian Deuchars IPA; guest beers Ⓗ
Lovely local with outdoor seating on the pavement. It features a big picture window and oak-panelled walls adorned with photographs of St Andrews in days gone by. The pub is renowned for its home-made meals (served until 5pm). Background music plays and a plasma screen shows sport. Open music night on Monday is popular with local artists, and a regular quiz night is hosted during the week. 🕸ⒹPᵇ–⊟

Whey Pat Tavern
1 Bridge Street, KY16 9EX
🌑 11-11.30 (11.45 Fri & Sat); 11-midnight Sun
☎ (01334) 477740
Caledonian Deuchars IPA; Greene King IPA; guest beers Ⓗ
Town-centre pub on a busy road junction just outside the old West Port Gate. There has been a hostelry on this site for several centuries. The front bar is L-shaped with a dartboard and TV, and there is an airy lounge and meeting room to the rear. Seven beers are on handpump. Delicious bar snacks are served all day. A mixed clientele of all ages frequents this usually busy venue. Regular beer festivals are held throughout the year.
🕮Ⓓ⊕♣ᵇ–⊟

Strathkinness

Tavern
4 High Road, KY16 9RS (just off A91)
🌑 12-2, 5-11; 11-midnight Sat; 12-midnight Sun
☎ (01334) 850085 ⊕ strathkinnestavern.co.uk
Beer range varies Ⓗ
Public bar with seating and a comfortable lounge at one end. Two handpulls offer a choice of changing guest ales. There is a separate room with a dartboard, pool table and Sky TV. Quiz nights are the first and third Tuesday of each month, ceilidh evenings on a Monday. Lunches and evening meals are served in the bar and restaurant. There is a beer garden to the rear and lovely views over the river estuary to the front. Q🕸Ⓓ⊕Å♣Pᵇ–⊟(64,91,96)

LOCH LOMOND, STIRLING & THE TROSSACHS

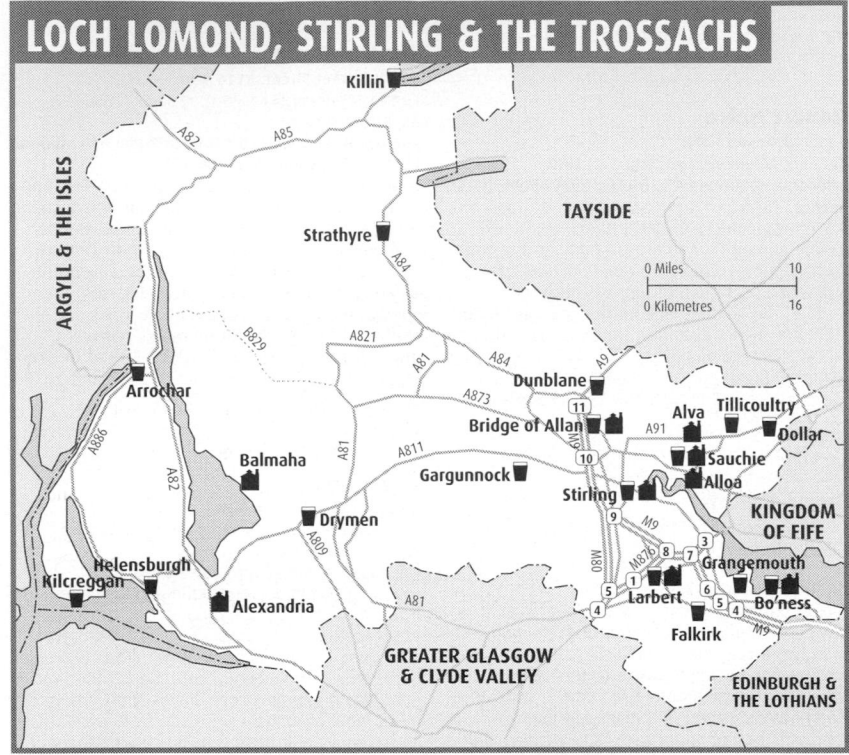

Authority areas covered: Argyll & Bute UA (part), Clackmannanshire UA, Falkirk UA, Stirling UA, West Dumbartonshire UA

Arrochar

Village Inn
Shore Road, G83 7AX (on A814) NN293034
🌣 11-midnight (1am Fri & Sat); 12-midnight Sun
☎ (01301) 702279 ⊕ villageinnarrochar.co.uk
Beer range varies Ⓗ
This picturesque inn offers views over Loch Long to the Arrochar Alps. The bar and restaurant are decorated in traditional Scottish country style. Five handpumps dispense ales from a variety of Scottish breweries. The clientele is a mixture of friendly locals and day trippers, hillwalkers and weekending tourists staying at the inn.
🏚Q🕏🌣🖾🕪🕭ΛP⁵⊐🖫(926,976)

Bo'ness

Corbie Inn
84 Corbiehall, EH51 0AS
🌣 12 (12.30 Sun)-11 ☎ (01506) 825307 ⊕ corbieinn.co.uk
Beer range varies Ⓗ
Six ales are normally to be found on handpump here, including one from the Kinneil Brew Hoose at the back of the premises. Third pint measures are available, enabling you to sample a range of ales. A beer garden provides extra seating on sunny days. An ideal place to stop off for refreshments following a visit to the Bo'ness and Kinneil Railway or the Bo'ness Motor Museum, and also very handy for the Hippodrome, Scotland's oldest purpose-built picture house. Very much a community pub involved in local charity projects. 🕭🕪

Bridge of Allan

Allanwater Brewhouse Ⓛ
Queens Lane, FK9 4NU (behind Adamo Hotel)
🌣 12-5 ☎ (01786) 834555
Tinpot Gold Pot 70/-, Pot of Gold; guest beers Ⓗ
The low lighting and candles here add to a warm, welcoming ambience. The single, barn-like, L-shaped room features hop pockets, breweriana, barrel seating, shelf after shelf of bottled ales for sale and a collection of decorative bottles. Ten handpumps dispense up to eight ales, all brewed on the premises. The pub attracts a cosmopolitan mix of students, walkers, cyclists and locals, and dogs and children are welcome. CAMRA members receive a 10 per cent discount. 🏚Q🕏⇄P🖫

Dollar

King's Seat
19-23 Bridge Street, FK14 7DE

INDEPENDENT BREWERIES
Balmaha Balmaha (NEW)
Devon Sauchie
Harviestoun Alva
Kinneil Bo'ness
Loch Lomond Alexandria
TinPot Bridge of Allan
Traditional Scottish Ales Stirling
Tryst Larbert
Williams Alloa

🕐 12-midnight (1am Fri & Sat); 12.30-midnight Sun
☎ (01259) 742515 ⊕ kingsseat.com
Harviestoun Bitter & Twisted; guest beers 🅷
Cosy, welcoming bar and restaurant situated in this quaint village. Up to six ales are offered, with a real cider in summer, along with bar snacks and restaurant food. Dogs and children are welcome and there are tables and chairs outside for warmer weather. Occasional barbecues and live folk music are hosted. Accommodation is available in a three bedroom apartment. 🏵️🛏️🕪🚶♿🅰️🌳🍴🚆(23,65)

Drymen

Clachan Inn
2 Main Street, Drymen Square, G63 0BL
🕐 11-midnight (1am Fri & Sat); 12.30-midnight Sun
☎ (01360) 660824 ⊕ clachaninndrymen.co.uk
Beer range varies 🅷
Run by the same family for more than 30 years, the free house was recently upgraded, retaining and incorporating original features that date back to 1734. A wood-burning stove in the bar adds atmosphere. Two handpumps supply an ever-changing range of excellent beer from mainly Scottish breweries, often local, to accompany traditional home-cooked fare. Very popular with locals, tourists, families, walkers and their dogs. 🏔️🛏️🕪🚆(8,309)

Dunblane

Dunblane Hotel
10 Stirling Road, FK15 9EP (opp station)
🕐 11-midnight (1am Fri & Sat) ☎ (01786) 822178
⊕ dunblanehotel.co.uk
Greene King IPA; Fuller's London Pride; guest beers 🅷
Traditional pub dating back to the 18th century, close to the cathedral, museum and famous Leighton Library, with views over Allan Water. There is also a pool room, restaurant and function room. Quizzes are held fortnightly and the pub has an active darts team. Guest ales are sourced from small Scottish breweries. High teas are served on Sunday afternoon. Accommodation includes three family rooms. 🏔️Q🚶🏵️🛏️🕪🍴♿🌳♣️P🌳🚆

Tappit Hen 🏆
Kirk Street, FK15 0AL (opp cathedral)
🕐 11-midnight (1am Fri & Sat) ☎ (01786) 825226
Belhaven IPA; guest beers 🅷
A varied range of five real ales is on offer at this friendly pub. The staff are knowledgeable and welcome locals and tourists alike. At least one beer festival is held, usually in May or October. Tuesday is folk night – all are encouraged to bring along an instrument and join in the fun. Local CAMRA Pub of the Year 2013 winner. 🌳♣️🚆

Falkirk

Behind the Wall
14 Melville Street, FK1 1HZ
🕐 5-9 (11 summer; 1am Fri & Sat); 12.30-midnight Sun
☎ (01324) 633338 ⊕ behindthewall.co.uk
Caledonian Deuchars IPA; guest beers 🅷
This spacious venue for drinking, dining and entertainment was once a bra factory. Popular for watching live sports events, it has plenty of seating and several wide screens in a large room that doubles as a live music and comedy venue with bands both local and from many parts of the UK.

Eglesbrech is the real ale and whisky bar upstairs, divided into two rooms with timber furnishings and a wood-burning stove. 🏔️🏵️🕪🛏️🌳(Grahamston)🚆

Carron Works 🅛
Bank Street, FK1 1NB (near rail and bus stations)
🕐 9.30am-11 (midnight Thu-Sat); 11-11 Sun
☎ (01324) 673020
Caledonian Deuchars IPA; Greene King Abbot; guest beers 🅷
Wetherspoon venue, centrally situated, with a spacious interior. The pub is keen to promote real ales and has frequent festivals. The standard Wetherspoon menu is available all day. 🚶🏵️🕪♿🌳(Grahamston)🍴🚆

Wheatsheaf Inn
16 Baxters Wynd, FK1 1PF
🕐 11-midnight (1am Fri & Sat); 12.30-midnight Sun
☎ (01324) 638282
Caledonian Deuchars IPA; guest beers 🅷
Dating from the late 18th century, this public house can be found off the High Street via one of the vennels opposite the Tron Steeple. The wood-panelled bar is furnished in traditional style and retains much of its original character. Guest beers come from microbreweries in Scotland and England, with two on offer midweek and three at the weekend. A must-visit venue, it was local CAMRA Pub of the Year for 2012. 🏵️🌳(Grahamston)🌳🚆

Gargunnock

Gargunnock Inn
Main Street, FK8 3BW
🕐 12-9; 12.30-11 Sun ☎ (01786) 860333
⊕ gargunnockinn.co.uk
Beer range varies 🅷
Dating from the 1700s, the pub has been extensively modernised and is now a roomy yet cosy pub/restaurant. The interior includes exposed original features and two wood-burning stoves. A single bar with two handpumps, offering at least one Scottish ale, serves the whole pub which has numerous restaurant rooms and seating areas. An extensive quality menu is served throughout. A beer festival is held on the second Sunday in August. Local walks abound. 🏵️🕪♿♣️P🚆(12)

Grangemouth

Earl of Zetland
Bo'ness Road, FK3 8AN
🕐 9-11 (1am Fri & Sat) ☎ (01324) 499940
Caledonian Deuchars IPA; Greene King Abbot; guest beers 🅷
Excellent Wetherspoon conversion of an old church in the town centre, retaining ecclesiastical features such as the organ pipes above the bar and stained glass windows. Ample seating at tables and in pew booths is provided. Two permanent beers are supplemented by two guests midweek and up to four at the weekend. TVs screen major sporting events with news channels on silent at other times. 🕪♿🍴🚆

Helensburgh

Commodore Hotel
112-117 West Clyde Street, G84 8ER (on seafront W of town)

✪ 11-11; 12.30-10.30 Sun ☎ (01436) 676924
Caledonian Deuchars IPA; guest beers Ⓗ
Just a short walk from the station, this bar offers a frequently changing range of beers from the Vintage Inns seasonal list via three handpumps. A wide selection of food is served in the informal restaurant. A regular jazz session is held on the first Thursday of the month. Enjoy sitting in the popular garden to the front of the hotel or joining in the game of 'spot a Trident sub' on a day trip up the Clyde. ᴹ❀⊠◑⅙P'–⊟(216)

Kilcreggan

Kilcreggan Hotel Ⓛ

Argyll Road, G84 0JP (off Shore Rd up Donaldsons brae) NS238805
✪ 12-midnight (1am Fri & Sat) ☎ (01436) 842243
⊕ kilcregganhotel.com
Beer range varies Ⓗ
Without doubt this hotel affords the best view of the Clyde from its lofty position on the Rosneath Peninsula. Set in verdant grounds, it can be approached via the ferry from Gourock or the bus from Helensburgh. Up to four pumps dispense a range of beers from Scottish micros plus surprises from throughout Britain – Bass is frequently on. Good food is available and the sun-catching patio garden is a pleasant place to relax.
ॐ❀⊠◑P'–⊟(316)

Killin

Falls of Dochart Inn

Gray Street, FK21 8SL
✪ 12-midnight ☎ (01567) 820270
⊕ falls-of-dochart-inn.co.uk
Fyne Pipers Gold; Harviestoun Bitter & Twisted; guest beer Ⓗ
The bar in this hostelry features a large open fireplace, a stone-tiled floor and three handpumps (not all in use in winter). Good-quality food is served lunchtimes and evenings in the bar and dining rooms. Children and dogs are very welcome. Rooms are available in the inn and in self-catering accommodation at the rear. Forth Valley Rural Stirlingshire Pub of the Year 2013. ᴹ❀⊠◑P

Larbert

Station Hotel

2 Foundry Loan, FK5 4AW (near station)
✪ 12-11 (midnight Thu; 1am Fri); 11-1am Sat; 12.30-11 Sun
☎ (01324) 557186 ⊕ thestationhotellarbert.co.uk
Caledonian Deuchars IPA; guest beers Ⓗ
Situated next to the railway station and on a regular bus route, this hotel is popular with visitors and locals and offers three or four cask ales. The traditional public bar is now adorned with chandeliers and there is an adjacent lounge bar and games room. A number of large-screen TVs show major sporting events. The hotel has 11 bedrooms and conference facilities. Local CAMRA Newcomer of the Year 2011.
❀⊠⊞⅙⇌P'–⊟(10,11)

Sauchie

Mansfield Arms

7 Main Street, FK10 3JR
✪ 11-11.30 (12.30am Fri & Sat); 12.30-11.30 Sun
☎ (01259) 722020 ⊕ devonales.com

Devon Original, Thick Black, Pride Ⓟ
The oldest operating microbrewery in the county, this pub brews three Devon ales which are dispensed via Scottish tall founts. Family owned and run, situated within an ex-mining community, the bar is popular with the locals, and families come to enjoy good-value meals served in the lounge. The pub is on the Stirling via Alloa circular bus route. ◑⊟⅙P⊠⊟(60,62)

Stirling

No. 2 Baker Street

2 Baker Street, FK8 1BJ
✪ 11-midnight (1am Fri & Sat) ☎ (01786) 448722
⊕ no2bakerstreet-stirling.co.uk
Belhaven 80/-; guest beers Ⓗ
With its red-brick walls and wooden floorboards, the cosy single-room interior has plenty of tables and seating. Entertainment includes music, poker and quiz nights on most evenings, and the pub gets especially lively when bands play. A Belhaven-managed venue, it has eight handpumps, four or five usually serving Belhaven, Greene King and Scottish micro ales. ❀◑⅙⇌

Portcullis Hotel

Castle Wynd, FK8 1EG
✪ 11.30-midnight (11 Sun-Tue) ☎ (01786) 472290
⊕ theportcullishotel.com
Beer range varies Ⓗ
Exposed stone walls and an open fireplace with an ornate surround provide traditional character at this venue. Frequented by tourists and supported by locals, the pub is renowned for its food and a regularly changing selection of Scottish ales from the far north and west. Always busy, diners are advised to reserve a table. ᴹQ❀⊠◑⇌P⊟

Strathyre

Inn & Bistro

Main Street, FK18 8NA (on A84)
✪ 12 (12.30 Sun)-11 ☎ (01877) 384224
⊕ innatstrathyre.com
Beer range varies Ⓗ
Cosy, popular pub serving meals in the bar or bistro, all made with local produce. The beer garden in a raised position enjoys panoramic views. Hill walking, fishing, golf and watersports are all close at hand. Stirling, Callander and the Trossachs are within easy travelling distance. Accommodation is available and dogs and children are permitted in the bar. The beers are mainly Scottish during the summer tourist season and from south of the border off season.
ᴹQ❀⊠◑⅙⚘⋇P'–⊟

Tillicoultry

Woolpack Inn

1 Glassford Square, FK13 6AU
✪ 11-midnight (1am Fri & Sat) ☎ 07870 246168
Beer range varies Ⓗ
Well used by friendly locals, it has a comfortable feel with a log fire and low ceilings, and without intrusive TV and music. Ales on four handpumps change regularly and there is a good selection of malt whiskies. Meals cooked on the premises are available Thursday to Monday. CAMRA Scotland & Northern Ireland Pub of the Year 2012.
ᴹQॐ◑⊟⚘⊟(62,63)

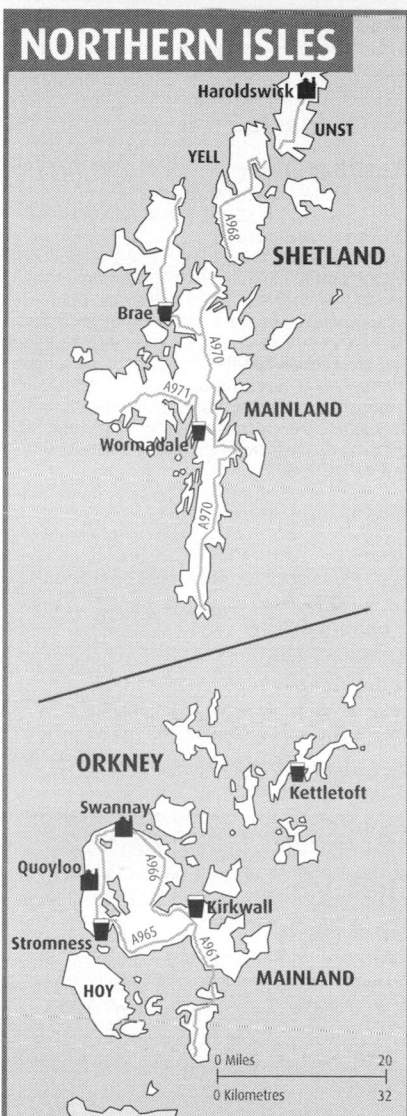

NORTHERN ISLES

Haroldswick

UNST

YELL

A968

SHETLAND

Brae

A970

A971

MAINLAND

Wormadale

A970

ORKNEY

Kettletoft

Swannay

Quoyloo

A966

Kirkwall

A965

Stromness

A96?

MAINLAND

HOY

0 Miles 20

0 Kilometres 32

Authority area covered: Highland UA

Brae: Shetland

Busta House Hotel
ZE2 9QN
☼ 12-midnight ☎ (01806) 522506 ⊕ bustahouse.com
Beer range varies Ⓗ
Rambling mansion house on many different levels converted to a friendly country house hotel. Dating from 1588 with numerous later additions, it is set in extensive grounds running down to the seashore. The beamed main bar area is lined with ship drawings. One beer, usually from Valhalla, is supplemented by an extensive range of over 150 malt whiskies. The hotel is near the centre of the Shetland mainland and Mavis Grind, where the Atlantic and the North Sea are separated only by the width of the road. Allegedly haunted by the ghost of Barbara Pitcairn. ☎⚅⇦◑P

Kettletoft: Orkney

Kettletoft Hotel
KW17 2BJ (7½ miles from ferry terminal)
☼ 12 (12.30 Sun)-midnight ☎ (01857) 600217
⊕ kettletofthotel.co.uk
Highland Dark Munro Ⓗ
Small, family-run hotel by the sea close to the local shops with direct access to one of the most beautiful beaches on the island, Backaskaill Bay. Watch the seals and wildlife from the comfort of the well-stocked bar. Good food is made with local produce wherever possible, including a wide selection of home-made puddings. Meals are served throughout the day, with fish and chips to take away on Wednesday and Saturday evenings. The beer is from the Highland Brewery but is usually only available in the summer months.
☎⚅⇦◑ ⊟⅚🅰

Kirkwall: Orkney

Bothy Bar (Albert Hotel)
Mounthoolie Lane, KW15 1HW (100yds from harbour)
☼ 11-11 (1am Thu-Sat); 12-1am Sun ☎ (01856) 876000
⊕ alberthotel.co.uk
Highland Scapa Special; Orkney Red MacGregor, Dark Island Ⓗ
After reconstruction following a fire a few years ago, the Bothy has maintained its position as a popular local. Sports fans are catered for and there are alcoves for more intimate gatherings. Handy for the bus station and situated not far from Kirkwall's main shopping area, its central location is also ideal for visiting tourist attractions including St Magnus Cathedral. A premium is paid for buying half pints. ♿⇦◑▶🅰⊟

Helgi's Bar
14 Harbour Street, KW15 1LE
☼ 11-11 (midnight Thu; 2am Sat); 12.30-11 Sun
☎ (01856) 879293 ⊕ helgis.co.uk
Highland Scapa Special, Orkney IPA; guest beer Ⓗ
Step into this harbourside bar, named in honour of the warrior Helgi who had a tavern on the harbour front, and friendly staff will welcome you with an excellent choice of beers. Small and traditional with a slate floor and wooden panelled walls, it buzzes with the sound of conversation or, on a Thursday night, the quizmaster's questions. The cosy upstairs room overlooks the harbour, so fill in time here before island hopping on the many ferries to the outlying parts. CAMRA Northern Isles Pub of the Year 2012. Gets a mention in Ellie Brooks' book, Mud, Sweat and Tears. Q◑⅚🅰⊟

Stromness: Orkney

Ferry Inn
John Street, KW16 3AA (opp ferry terminal)
☼ 9-midnight (1am Thu-Sat); 9.30-midnight Sun
☎ (01856) 850280 ⊕ ferryinn.com
Highland Scapa Special, Orkney IPA, St Magnus Ale; Orkney Red MacGregor, Corncrake, Dark Island; guest beer Ⓗ

SCOTLAND

Recently reopened after refurbishment in 2013, the Ferry takes centre stage for musical events in Stromness including blues, folk and jazz festivals held throughout the year, when a temporary outdoor bar is constructed. Pub customers include divers on Orkney to explore the sunken German fleet at Scapa Flow, and visitors to the various attractions nearby such as the Ring of Brodgar and Skara Brae village. ⊯◁❶ ⅄ᴸ⊟

Stromness Hotel

15 Victoria Street, KW16 3AA (opp pier head)
✪ 11-11 (1am Fri & Sat); 12-11 Sun ☎ (01856) 850298
⊕ stromnesshotel.com
Highland Scapa Special, Duke; Orkney Northern Light, Red MacGregor; guest beer Ⓗ
The main bar is the Hamnavoe lounge on the first floor with a commanding view of the harbour. To complement the beers, more than 100 whiskies are served in the adjoining whisky bar. Rock, jazz and blues festivals are hosted in the downstairs function room. The hotel usually closes in January and February, but a single ale is always available in the ground floor Flattie bar. ⚌⚘⊯◁❶▶⅄P⊟

Wormadale: Shetland

Westings Inn

ZE2 9LJ (8 miles N of Lerwick on A971)
✪ 12.30-2.30, 5.30 (6.30 Sun)-10.30 ☎ (01595) 840242
⊕ westings.shetland.co.uk
Beer range varies Ⓗ
White-painted inn in a stunning location on the side of Wormadale Hill, two miles west of Tingwall airstrip, with marvellous sea views of Whiteness Voe, Western Shetland and the outlying islands. One ale is usually available and up to two guests in summer. Evening meals are served 7-8pm by arrangement. The bar may stay open until midnight if busy. Caravans are welcome and camping is available in the pub grounds.
Q⚘⊯◁❶♿⅄♣P

Scottish beer

Just as monks call their Lenten beers 'liquid bread', it s tempting to call traditional Scottish ales 'liquid porridge'. They are beers brewed for a cold climate, a country in which beer vies with whisky (uisge breatha – water of life) for nourishment and sustenance.

Brewers blend not only darker malts such as black and chocolate with paler grains, but also add oats, that staple of many foodstuffs in the country. In common with the farmer-brewers of the Low Countries and French Flanders in earlier centuries, domestic brewers in Scotland tended to use whatever grains, herbs and plants were available to make beer. The intriguing use of heather in the Fraoch range of ales recalls brewing practice in Scotland from bygone times.

The Industrial Revolution arrived later in Scotland than in England, and industry tended to concentrate in the Lowland belt around Alloa, Edinburgh and Glasgow. As a result, brewing remained a largely domestic affair for much longer than it did south of the border and – as with early Irish ales – made little use of the hop, which could not grow in such inhospitable climes.

Brewing developed on a commercial scale in the Lowlands in the early 19th century at the same time as many French emigres, escaping the revolution, settled in the Scottish capital. They dubbed the rich, warming local ales 'Scottish Burgundy'. Real wine from France, always popular in Scotland as a result of the Auld Alliance, become scarce during the Napoleonic Wars, and commercial brewing grew rapidly to fill the gap and to fuel the needs of a growing class of thirsty industrial workers.

Traditionally, Scottish ales were brewed in a different manner to English ones. Before refrigeration, beer was fermented at ambient temperatures far lower than in England. As a result, not all the sugars turned to alcohol, producing rich, full-bodied ales. As hops had to be imported from England at considerable cost, they were used sparingly. The result was a style of beer markedly different to English ones: vinous, fruity, malty and with only a gentle hop bitterness.

Many of the new breed of ales produced by micro-brewers in Scotland tend to be paler and more bitter than used to be the norm. For the true taste of traditional Scottish ales you will have to sample the products of the likes of Belhaven, Broughton, Caledonian and Traquair.

The language of Scottish beers is different, too. The equivalent to English mild is called Light (even when it's dark in colour), standard bitter is called Heavy premium bitter Export, while strong old ales and barley wines (now rare) are called Wee Heavies.

To add to the complexities of the language differences, many traditional beers incorporate the word Shilling in their names. A Light may be dubbed 60 Shilling, a Heavy 70 Shilling, an Export 80 Shilling, and a Wee Heavy 90 Shilling. The designations stem from a pre-decimalisation method of invoicing beer in Victorian times. The stronger the beer, the higher the number of shillings.

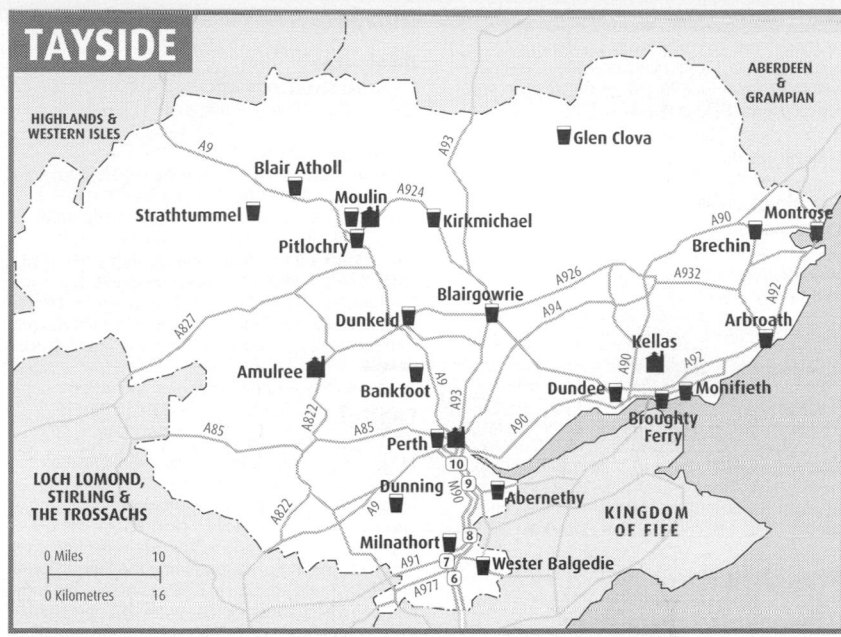

Authority areas covered: Angus UA, City of Dundee UA, Perth & Kinross UA

Abernethy

Crees Inn
Main Street, PH2 9LA
☼ 11-2, 5-11; 11-11 Sat & Sun ☎ (01738) 850714
⊕ creesinn.co.uk
Beer range varies Ⓗ
Comfortable former farmhouse, lying in the shadow of one of only two Pictish watchtowers in Scotland. A free house, it has timber panels and beams that display an impressive collection of pumpclips reflecting the varied beer range. Up to six ales are available, mostly from English breweries. A good selection of meals is served lunchtimes and evenings made with fresh local produce. Q✿✿♠◑Ⓓ♿P무(36)

Arbroath

Corn Exchange
Market Place, DD11 1HR
☼ 11-midnight (1am Fri & Sat) ☎ (01241) 432430
Caledonian Deuchars IPA; Greene King Abbot; guest beers Ⓗ
Just off the High Street, at this Wetherspoon two guest beers are usually offered in addition to the two regulars. Although largely open plan there are a number of booths providing some privacy. Food is served daily from 8am or you could try the famous Arbroath Smokies from one of the local producers. Boat trips offering fishing or a visit to the 200-year-old Bell Rock lighthouse can be found at the nearby harbour. ◑♿≑♣

Bankfoot

Bankfoot Inn Ⓛ
Main Street, PH1 4AB (just off A9)
☼ 5.30-11 (11.45 Thu; 12.30am Fri); 12-12.30am Sat; 12.30-11.30 Sun ☎ (01738) 787243 ⊕ bankfootinn.co.uk
Beer range varies Ⓗ
Traditional 18th-century coaching inn situated on the main street in the village. Extensively refurbished over the past few years, it has a small public bar, a lounge with a fine oak bar and an adjoining restaurant. Two real fires in winter make it a cosy howff. The owners are real ale enthusiasts and strongly committed to local breweries. Live music nights are held regularly. Catering for all interests – golf, fishing, shooting, hiking and cycling – dogs are also welcome. ♣✿♠◑Ⓓ⊟무(23)

Blair Atholl

Atholl Arms Hotel
PH18 5SG NN878654
☼ 12 (3 Nov-Feb)-11 (11.45 Fri & Sat), 12-11 Sun
☎ (01796) 481205 ⊕ athollarmshotel.co.uk
Moulin Light, Braveheart, Ale of Atholl, Old Remedial Ⓗ
There are few more imposing sights in the Scottish Highlands than the superb façade and grandeur of the Atholl Arms Hotel. The characterful Highland Bothy Bar is very inviting, offering four ales produced by the local Moulin Brewery and freshly cooked food served all day. Blair Atholl and the surrounding area are popular for walking, climbing, biking and sightseeing. ♣Q➲✿♠◑Ⓓ≑

Blairgowrie

Ericht Alehouse
13 Wellmeadow, PH10 6ND NO180452
☼ 1-11 (11.45 Thu; 12.30am Fri & Sat); 1-11.30 Sun
☎ (01250) 872469
Beer range varies Ⓗ
Classic town-centre pub with a friendly atmosphere. There are two seating areas separated by a well-stocked bar. An open log fire in the lounge adds to the warm welcome. Up to six handpumps serve a wide range of ever-changing ales and a cider. A range of bottled continental

beers is also available. No food is served but customers are welcome to bring their own. Occasional live music plays on Friday evenings. A winner of Local CAMRA Pub of the Year on several occasions. ♨Q✿❺♿Å♣❼♖(57,58)

Brechin

Caledonian Hotel
43-47 South Esk Street, DD9 6DZ
✪ 5-11 (midnight Fri); 3-1am Sat; 3-11 Sun
☎ (01356) 624345
Beer range varies Ⓗ
Taking its name from the privately run railway whose terminus is opposite, the Caledonian features a large bar and dining area. An extensive use of wood creates a warm and inviting appearance. Houston and Inveralmond provide the regular ales, and guest beers sourced by the landlord on trips to Hampshire are frequently available. A wide range of continental bottled beers is also offered. Live folk music on the last Friday of the month is popular. Check up on opening hours in summer. ♨Q✿❹◑♣'—♖(30)

Broughty Ferry

Fisherman's Tavern Hotel
10-16 Fort Street, DD5 2AD (by lifeboat station)
✪ 11-midnight (1am Fri & Sat); 12.30-midnight Sun
☎ (01382) 775941 ⊕ fishermanstavern-broughtyferry.co.uk
Beer range varies Ⓗ
Licensed since 1857, this is one of a row of fishermen's cottages, three of which have been converted into a small hotel. The bar is to the right of the entrance, a snug is on the left, leading to the dining room/lounge warmed by a real fire. The lounge to the rear has disabled access from Bell's Lane. Entertainment includes traditional music on a Thursday night, a monthly quiz and an annual beer festival in late May. At least four ales are offered from the Belhaven list. ♨Q✿❹◑❺♿≈♖(5,73)

Royal Arch Ⓛ
285 Brook Street, DD5 2DS
✪ 11 (12.30 Sun)-midnight ☎ (01382) 779741
⊕ royal-arch.co.uk
Caledonian Deuchars IPA; guest beers Ⓗ
A busy, popular local in the centre of 'the Ferry' near the rail station. There are three TVs in the public bar for the many sports fans, and meals are served in the Art Deco lounge. Pavement tables are popular in clement weather and with smokers. Ales from all over Britain are served through three handpulls, with local beers from Inveralmond regularly available. ✿◑❺≈'—♖(5,73)

Ship Inn
121 Fisher Street, DD5 2BR
✪ 11 (12.30 Sun)-midnight ☎ (01382) 779176
⊕ theshipinn-broughtyferry.co.uk
Caledonian Deuchars IPA; Taylor Landlord; guest beers Ⓗ
The Ship Inn is a traditional free house situated on the waterfront at Broughty Ferry, with amazing views over the Tay towards Fife. Dating back to 1847, this cosy retreat is atmospheric and interesting. The staff are friendly, hospitable and consistently provide a good choice of well-kept real ales. A range of tasty bar meals is on offer and there is also an excellent restaurant upstairs. ✿◑≈♖(5,73)

Dundee

Bank Bar
7-9 Union Street, DD1 4BN
✪ 11-midnight (10 Mon & Tue); 12.30-11 Sun
☎ (01382) 205037
Beer range varies Ⓗ
A former bank, now a no-nonsense ale house, with a bare-boards floor, wood furniture and a series of alcoves with tables in the tradition of older Scottish city pubs. The management is enthusiastic about supporting small brewers and, while beers from many parts are available, Inveralmond features regularly among the two or three ales on handpump. Food is served until 7pm. Live music plays on Friday and Saturday nights. ◑≈♖

Capitol
7-9 Seagate, DD1 2EG
✪ 11-midnight (2.30am Fri & Sat) ☎ (01382) 205950
Greene King Abbot; guest beers Ⓗ
A 1945 cinema, this was converted by Wetherspoon into a Lloyd's No.1 bar in 2003. A family area is in the foyer, with steps leading up to the main seating area containing the long bar with nine handpulls, and a staircase to access the large balcony. The pub is popular with shoppers during the day and lively on Friday and Saturday evenings. It is a great place to enjoy the annual Dundee Blues Bonanza when the balcony fills with younger drinkers. At least three guest beers are available, mostly from Scottish breweries including Houston, Strathaven, TSA and Williams Bros. ♿◑❺≈♖

Counting House
67-71 Reform Street, DD1 1SP
✪ 11-midnight ☎ (01382) 225251
Caledonian Deuchars IPA; Greene King Abbot; guest beers Ⓗ
This Wetherspoon conversion of a former bank in the heart of Dundee has become a popular local for many city ale drinkers. Halfway between the Overgate and Wellgate shopping centres, on the corner of Albert Square, it is a handy watering hole for visitors to the McManus Galleries. Thatchers cider is regularly available, with additions during beer festivals. Guest beers frequently include seasonal ales from Caledonian. Food is available 8am-10pm. ◑≈♣♖

Drouthy's
142 Perth Road, DD1 4NY
✪ 11-midnight ☎ (01382) 202187 ⊕ drouthysdundee.co.uk
Beer range varies Ⓟ
Situated directly opposite the Art College, this pub has an eclectic mix of customers. There are no handpulls on the wooden bar – ales are dispensed by four turn handles behind the bar. The bar area has comfy, neat seating that makes best use of the available space. A spiral staircase leads down to a basement bar with additional seating. Blackboards describe the food and ale on offer, with beers usually sourced from Eden, Inveralmond and Williams Bros breweries. Q◑♖

INDEPENDENT BREWERIES	
Inveralmond	Perth
MòR	Kellas
Moulin	Moulin
Strathbraan	Amulree

Phoenix 🏆
103 Nethergate, DD1 4DH
◯ 11-midnight ☎ (01382) 200014
Caledonian Deuchars IPA; Taylor Landlord; guest beers Ⓗ
This splendidly recreated traditional local – only the ceiling and pillars are original – has proved to be one of the city's most popular real ale outlets down the years. Eccentric in decor, it has sturdy wooden seats and tables and green leather benches, plus intimate nooks for a quiet drink. Look out for the Ballingall Brewery mirror, a rarity. One of the guest ales is from the local MòR Brewery. The atmosphere is always friendly and busy. ◖Ⅱ➤🖵

Speedwell (Mennies) ★
165-167 Perth Road, DD2 1AS
◯ 11 (12.30 Sun)-midnight ☎ (01382) 667783
⊕ mennies.co.uk
Caledonian Deuchars IPA; guest beers Ⓗ
One of the finest examples of an Edwardian pub interior in the country, built for James Speed in 1903, it features in CAMRA's Scotland's True Heritage Pubs. The L-shaped bar is divided by a part-glazed screen and features a magnificent mahogany gantry and counter, dado wall panelling and an anaglypta Jacobean ceiling. There are also two sitting rooms separated by a glass screen. Alongside the three real ale handpulls are over 20 fonts serving a range of lagers. Q🕮🖵

Dunkeld

Royal Dunkeld Hotel
Atholl Street, PH8 0AR (near cathedral)
◯ 11-11 (12.15am Fri & Sat); 12-11 Sun ☎ (01350) 727322
⊕ royaldunkeld.co.uk
Cairngorm Trade Winds; Stewart Pentland IPA; guest beer Ⓗ
This former coaching inn is now a comfortable hotel. It has a restaurant, lounge bar and public bar with an open fire. Three handpulls serve real ale. A pool room with dartboard is adjacent. Outside, the large beer garden is a suntrap in summer. Good food is served in the bar and restaurant. An ideal base for a variety of outdoor activities including walking, fishing and golf. 🏚🏡🕮◖Ⅱ🖵P♨🖵(23)

Dunning

Kirkstyle Inn
Kirkstyle Square, PH2 0RR NO019144
◯ 11-2.30 (not Mon winter), 5-11 (midnight Fri); 11-midnight Sat; 12.30-11 Sun ☎ (01764) 684248
⊕ kirkstyle-dunning.co.uk
Beer range varies Ⓗ
Traditional village inn dating from 1760 overshadowed by the impressive Norman steeple of St Serf's Church, which contains the ancient Dupplin Cross and other Pictish relics. Up to three ales in the small public bar come from a variety of Scottish independents, as well as English and Welsh regional breweries. A small snug area is next to the bar and there is a separate restaurant. Around a mile west of Dunning village stands a 20-foot-high stone cross, a memorial to Maggie Wall who was burned here as a witch in 1657. 🏚Q🕮◖Ⅱ🖵🖵(17)

Glen Clova

Glen Clova Hotel
DD8 4QS (on B955 15 miles N of Kirriemuir) NO327731
◯ 11-11 (1am Fri & Sat); 12-11 Sun ☎ (01575) 550350
⊕ clova.com
Beer range varies Ⓗ
Situated near the head of one of Scotland's most beautiful glens, this hotel's bar has been recently renovated, retaining a large log-fired stove and plenty of character. Popular with walkers after a day on the hills, the bar has two handpumps usually supplying ale from Scottish breweries. Local food, including lamb and venison, is served in the bar and restaurant. A summer beer festival is held in the field opposite. 🏚Q🕮🏡◖Ⅱ🖵🖵♨P♨

Kirkmichael

Strathardle Inn Ⓛ
PH10 7NS (on A924) NO082599
◯ 12-2 Tue-Sun summer (Sat & Sun only winter), 5-11 ☎ (01250) 881224 ⊕ strathardleinn.co.uk
Beer range varies Ⓗ
Small, friendly hotel, set in a peaceful area, with a bar room with a coal fire and horse brasses around the mantelpiece. Up to three ales are available from Scottish micros, and good food is served. This historic coaching inn, dating back to the late 1700s, has a 700-yard fishing beat on the River Ardle which flows in front of the inn. The Cateran Trail also passes by, and the Southern Highlands, Glenshee ski slopes, Deeside and Angus glens are within reach. 🏚Q🖎🕮🏡◖Ⅱ♨P

Milnathort

Village Inn
36 Westerloan, KY13 9YH
◯ 2-11 (midnight Fri); 12-midnight Sat; 12.30-11 Sun ☎ (01577) 863293
Beer range varies Ⓗ
This friendly local has a semi open-plan interior featuring classic brewery mirrors and local historic photographs. A comfortable lounge area is at one end with low ceilings, exposed joists and stone walls, and at the other end is the bar area with log fire. The games room at the rear has a pool table. This pub has been family owned since 1985 and serves various beers, often local. Milnathort links some great cycling routes through the Ochils, via Burleigh Castle, to the more leisurely Loch Leven Heritage Trail. 🏚🕮♨♨🖵(23,56)

Monifieth

Milton Inn
Grange Road, DD5 4LU NO484327
◯ closed Mon; 12-2.30, 5-11; 12-midnight Fri & Sat; 12-11 Sun ☎ (01382) 532620 ⊕ themiltoninn.co.uk
Caledonian Deuchars IPA; guest beers Ⓗ
Set back from the road with large gardens and a sunny deck area to the rear, this is a family-run inn. The interior is bright but cosy, and the decor is a refreshing combination of traditional and modern styles. Well-kept ales change frequently and two interesting session beers can usually be found alongside a seasonal one from Caledonian. These are complemented by excellent food and an impressive selection of single malt whiskies, all served by pleasant, enthusiastic and knowledgeable staff. Q🕮🏡◖Ⅱ♨P♨🖵(39A,73)

Montrose

Market Arms
95 High Street, DD10 8QY
✪ 11-midnight (1am Thu-Sat) ☎ (01674) 673384
Caledonian Deuchars IPA; guest beers Ⓗ
Stylishly renovated a few years ago, this busy town-centre pub provides a comfortable retreat for a wide mix of customers. Two handpulls are conveniently sited on a long bar in the main open area. Several TVs show live sporting events but there is a small snug at the front for those wishing to enjoy a quiet pint. Beers usually come from Scottish brewers. Visitors may want to visit the Montrose Air Station Heritage Centre at the first operational military airfield in the UK, set up in 1913. ♿⚞❄☞⚞(X7)

Moulin

Moulin Inn
11-13 Kirkmichael Road, PH16 5EH NN991642
✪ 11 (12 Nov-Apr)-11 (11.45 Fri & Sat); 12-11 Sun
☎ (01796) 472196 ⊕ moulininn.co.uk
Moulin Light, Braveheart, Ale of Atholl, Old Remedial Ⓗ
Situated in the shadow of Ben Vrackie, this delightful haven of Highland hospitality was founded in 1695. The interior of the cosy hostelry is divided into small alcoves warmed by two log fires. Its four ales are produced in the hotel's own brewery in the former coach house and stable behind the main building. A good choice of home-cooked fare is served all day. A popular destination for hill walkers and tourists visiting Pitlochry and the surrounding area. ⚞Q⚞☀☞⚞♣P

Perth

Capital Asset Ⓛ
26 Tay Street, PH1 5LQ
✪ 11-11.30 (12.30am Thu-Sat) ☎ (01738) 580457
Caledonian Deuchars IPA; Greene King Abbot; guest beers Ⓗ
The name of this Wetherspoon pub recalls the building's bank origins and Perth's status in medieval times as capital of Scotland. The high ceilings and ornate cornices have been retained and pictures of old Perth adorn the walls of the open-plan lounge which overlooks the River Tay. A variety of five ales is dispensed and food is available all day. Beer festivals twice a year are popular with local ale drinkers. Q⚞☀☞♿⚞☞⚞

Cherrybank Inn Ⓛ
210 Glasgow Road, PH2 0NA
✪ 11-11 (12.30am Thu-Sat); 12-midnight Sun
☎ (01738) 624349 ⊕ cherrybankinn.co.uk
Inveralmond Independence, Ossian; guest beers Ⓗ
Local CAMRA Pub of the Year 2011, this is a 250-year-old former drovers' inn. Five ales from Inveralmond and other Scottish independents are available from the multi-roomed public bar or in the larger L-shaped lounge with views up to a woodland walk. Good bar lunches and evening meals are served. The inn has seven well-appointed en-suite rooms and golf can be arranged for residents. Q⚞☞⚞AP☞⚞(7)

Greyfriars
15 South Street, PH2 8PG
✪ 11-11 (11.45 Fri & Sat); 3-11 Sun ☎ (01738) 633036
⊕ greyfriarsbar.com
Beer range varies Ⓗ
Small but friendly city-centre lounge bar serving up to four ales, often including an Inveralmond beer. Good-value lunches are available in the bar or in a small upstairs seating area. The pub takes its name from the former Greyfriars monastery, which was gutted by followers of John Knox in 1559. Ideally located on the edge of the shopping area, nearby attractions include a Victorian theatre, art gallery, museum and concert hall. ⚞⚞⚞

Pitlochry

Old Mill Inn
Mill Lane, PH16 5BH
✪ 12-11 (midnight Sat & Sun) ☎ (01796) 474020
⊕ theoldmillpitlochry.co.uk
Strathbraan Due South, Head East; guest beers Ⓗ
Built in the 19th century as a mill, with the original mill wheel still on view, this establishment in the town centre is run by the family who own it. It offers accommodation, a beer garden and a restaurant open all day, serving good food with the emphasis on fresh local produce. The bar, which has a real fire, offers a varied selection of guest ales usually from Scottish breweries. ⚞⚞☀☞⚞♿⚞P☞⚞

Strathtummel

Loch Tummel Inn Ⓛ
PH16 5RP (9 miles W of Pitlochry on B8019) NN819602
✪ 11-11 (closed Mon & Tue winter) ☎ (01882) 634272
⊕ lochtummelinn.co.uk
Beer range varies Ⓗ
Located on a hillside with spectacular views across Loch Tummel, this 200-year-old former coaching inn is an ideal place to stop off and enjoy warm and friendly Highland hospitality. The bar area comprises the former coach house and stables, with pews and a wood-burning stove adding to the traditional ambience. The outside drinking area overlooking the loch is a superb spot to linger on a summer's day. Two ales are usually available, often from Inveralmond, and good food is served daily. ⚞Q☀☞⚞♿P☞

Wester Balgedie

Balgedie Toll Tavern
KY13 9HE (jct of A911 and B919) NO164039
✪ 11-11 (11.30 Thu; 12.30am Fri & Sat); 12.30-11.30 Sun
☎ (01592) 840212
Harviestoun Bitter & Twisted; guest beer Ⓗ
Welcoming and comfortable rural tavern dating from 1534. Now much extended, the oldest part of the building (the toll house) is at the southern end. It has three seating areas plus a small bar with low ceilings, oak beams, horse brasses, wooden settles and works of art by a local painter. A good selection of meals and bar snacks is available. Guest beers are rotated, mainly from Scottish independent breweries. ☀☞P☞⚞(201,205)

What care I how time advances: I am drinking ale today. **Edgar Allan Poe**

NORTHERN ISLES

SHETLAND

HIGHLANDS
&
WESTERN ISLES

ABERDEEN
& GRAMPIAN

TAYSIDE

LOCH LOMOND,
STIRLING
&
THE
TROSSACHS

FIFE

ARGYLL &
THE ISLES

EDINBURGH & LOTHIANS

GREATER
GLASGOW &
CLYDE VALLEY

BORDERS

NORTHERN
IRELAND

AYRSHIRE
& ARRAN

DUMFRIES &
GALLOWAY

NORTHUMBER-
LAND

TYNE &
WEAR

DURHAM

ISLE OF
MAN

CUMBRIA

NORTH
YORKSHIRE

LANCASHIRE

WEST
YORKS

EAST
YORKS

MERSEYSIDE

GREATER
MANCHESTER

SOUTH
YORKS

LINCOLN-
SHIRE

NW
WALES

NE
WALES

CHESHIRE

DERBYSHIRE

NOTTINGHAM-
SHIRE

SHROPSHIRE

STAFFORD-
SHIRE

LEICESTERSHIRE
& RUTLAND

NORFOLK

MID
WALES

WEST
MIDLANDS

WORCESTER-
SHIRE

WARWICK-
SHIRE

NORTHAMPTON-
SHIRE

CAMBRIDGE-
SHIRE

SUFFOLK

WEST
WALES

HEREFORD-
SHIRE

BEDFORD-
SHIRE

HERTFORD-
SHIRE

ESSEX

GLAMORGAN

GWENT

GLOUCS &
BRISTOL

OXFORD-
SHIRE

BUCKINGHAMSHIRE

GREATER
LONDON

BERKSHIRE

SURREY

KENT

WILTSHIRE

HAMPSHIRE

WEST
SUSSEX

EAST
SUSSEX

SOMERSET

CHANNEL
ISLANDS

DEVON

DORSET

ISLE OF
WIGHT

CORNWALL

Northern Ireland
Channel Islands
Isle of Man

NORTHERN IRELAND

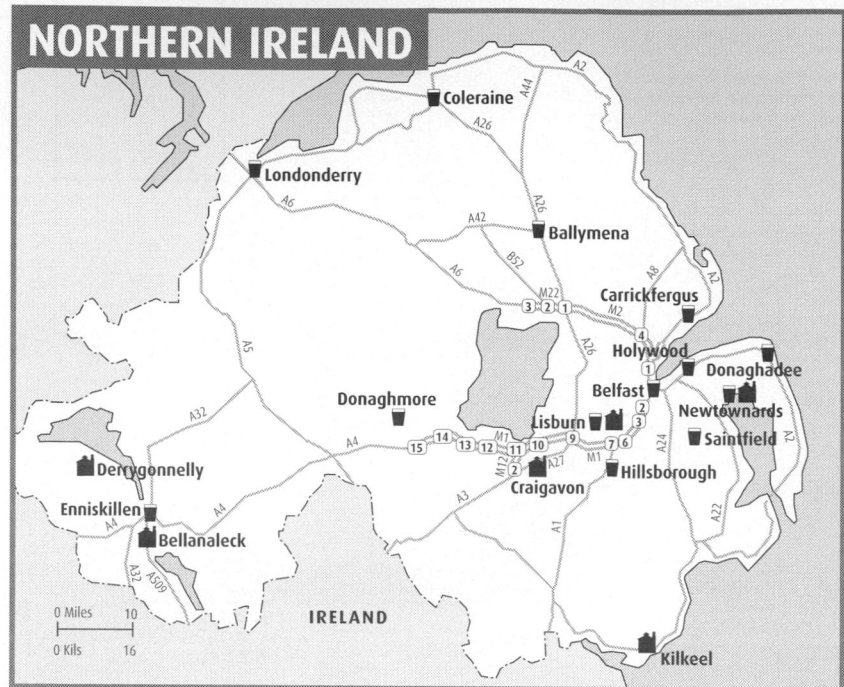

Ballymena

Spinning Mill
17-21 Broughshane Street, BT43 6EB
☼ 8am-11 (midnight Fri & Sat) ☎ (028) 2563 8985
Adnams Broadside; Greene King Abbot; guest beers ⊞
CAMRA Northern Ireland's Pub of the Year 2012 is a popular venue in the centre of the shopping district. The main bar downstairs has five handpumps and tends to be very busy – fortunately there is a smaller bar upstairs also serving real ale. Different in style from many Wetherspoon outlets, the pub has retained the character of a traditional local. Open for breakfast from 8am, alcohol served from 11.30am (12.30pm Sun). 🅰🌙⏺️♿🕯️♨️🚃

Belfast

Botanic Inn
23-27 Malone Road, BT9 6RU
☼ 11.30-1am; 12-midnight Sun ☎ (028) 9050 9740
⊕ thebotanicinn.com
Whitewater Belfast Ale ⊞
Large, popular destination in the university area, catering for all ages. The public bar retains a traditional aspect, the large bar is more modern, and there is a nightclub upstairs. Real ale is sold at a lower price in the public bar and very good food is also available. The pub can get busy, particularly when sporting events are on TV. ⏺️⏺️♿🕯️🚃(8B)

Bridge House
37-43 Bedford Street, BT2 7EJ
☼ 8am-midnight (1am Fri & Sat) ☎ (028) 9072 7890
Greene King Abbot; guest beers ⊞
The largest pub selling real ale in the Province, with eight handpumps all located in the downstairs bar. A good selection of guest ales has made the pub popular with CAMRA members who voted it local Pub of the Year in 2011. The bar tends to get

very busy, though there is a quieter family area upstairs. Open from 8am for breakfast, alcohol served from 11.30am (12.30pm Sun).
🐾⏺️♿🚃(Gt Victoria St)♨️🕯️🚃

Crown ♀ ★
46 Great Victoria Street, BT2 7BA (opp Europa Hotel and Great Victoria St station)
☼ 11.30-11 (midnight Thu-Sat); 12.30-10 Sun
☎ (028) 9024 3187 ⊕ crownbar.com
Hilden Ale; St Austell Nicholson's Pale Ale;
Whitewater Belfast Ale, guest ales ⊞
This is the place to visit if you want to see a proper Victorian pub. Owned by the National Trust but managed by Nicholson's, it is a joy to behold both inside and out. In the past year the availability of real ale has increased greatly. There are now five handpumps dispensing two local ales, Nicholson's house beer and two guests. The pub can be very busy, especially at weekends. Local CAMRA Pub of the Year 2013. ⏺️♿🚃(Gt Victoria St)🚃

John Hewitt
51 Donegal Street, BT1 2FH (100yds from St Anne's Cathedral)
☼ 11.30 (12 Sat)-1am; 7-midnight Sun ☎ (028) 9023 3768
⊕ thejohnhewitt.com
Hilden Ale; guest beer ⊞
Something of a rarity, this pub is not owned by an individual, a family or a pub chain. It is run by the Belfast Unemployed Resource Centre, and helps to

INDEPENDENT BREWERIES

Ards Newtonards
Clanconnel Craigavon
Hilden Lisburn
Inishmacsaint Derrygonnelly
Sheelin Bellanaleck (NEW)
Whitewater Kilkeel

fund the organisation's work. On the bar are two handpumps serving ales from Hilden Brewing, along with an occasional guest from other breweries. The pub is a major centre for live music and other events. Good food is available at lunchtime. Q♪&▤

King's Head
829 Lisburn Road, BT9 7GY (opp Kings Hall at Balmoral)
✪ 12-midnight (1am Thu-Sat) ☎ (028) 9050 9950
Whitewater Belfast Ale Ⓗ
Located some three miles outside the centre of Belfast, the King's Head is an appealing place to drink and dine in. It has a comfortable lounge, a large public bar, a music venue and an excellent restaurant upstairs. There is one handpump in the public bar, usually serving Whitewater Belfast Ale, although guest beers may be available in winter. Well worth a visit, it is on a bus route and beside a train halt. Q❀①❑&⇌(Balmoral)P⇐

Molly's Yard
1 College Green Mews, Botanic Avenue, BT7 1LN
✪ 12-9 (9.30am Fri & Sat); closed Sun ☎ (028) 9032 2600
⊕ mollysyard.co.uk
Hilden Ale; guest beers Ⓗ
Situated near the back of Queen's University, Molly's Yard restaurant is a quiet haven to dine in and has won awards for its food. There is a small bistro downstairs and a larger dining room upstairs. Two handpumps sell College Green and Hilden beers (all brewed at Hilden Brewing). Look for the headless dog mural. ❀①&⇌(Botanic)⇐▤(7A)

Ryan's
116-118 Lisburn Road, BT9 6AH
✪ 11.30 (12 Sat)-1am; 12-midnight Sun ☎ (028) 9050 9850
⊕ ryansbelfast.com
Whitewater Belfast Ale Ⓗ
Popular, busy pub belonging to the Botanic Inns chain. Downstairs, the bar divides the room into different drinking areas, while upstairs is a large restaurant. A single handpump usually dispenses Whitewater Belfast Ale. The building has undergone something of a renaissance recently with a large street art mural adorning one of the walls. The pub attracts a mixture of locals and students for live music, quizzes and sport on TV. It is easily accessible via a short bus journey from the city centre. ①&⇐▤

Carrickfergus

Central Bar
13-15 High Street, BT38 7AN
✪ 8am-11 (1am Fri & Sat) ☎ (028) 9335 7840
Adnams Broadside; Greene King Abbot; guest beers Ⓗ
Lively market town community local with a dedicated clientele. This Wetherspoon pub has a ground floor public bar of robust character and a quieter family-friendly first-floor loggia-style sitting room with exposed timber trusses, affording inspirational views from its many windows over Belfast Lough and the adjacent 12th-century castle. Handpumps on both levels serve two house beers and three guest ales usually from mainland micros and seasonal specials from various breweries. Alcohol is served from 11.30am (12.30pm Sun). Q➹①❑&⇌▤(563)

Coleraine

Old Courthouse
Castlerock Road, BT51 3HP
✪ 8am-11 (1am Fri & Sat) ☎ (028) 7032 5820
Adnams Broadside; Greene King Abbot; guest beers Ⓗ
A bright Wetherspoon conversion of an old county courthouse. On the right is a large staircase that leads to a balcony area overlooking the spacious downstairs bar area with its impressive black and white floor tiling. There are five handpumps on the bar serving the regular ales plus a range of guests. Open at 8am for breakfast, alcohol served from 11.30am (12.30pm Sun). ➹➹❀①&⇐

Donaghadee

Moat Inn
102 Moat Street, BT21 0ED
✪ 11.30-11.30; 12.30-10 Sun ☎ (028) 9188 3297
⊕ moatinn.co.uk
Beer range varies Ⓗ
Located on the edge of this seaside town, the Moat has friendly, welcoming staff and customers. There are two handpumps but usually only one is in use. The beer tends to be from Whitewater but the knowledgeable manager is keen to try guest ales from other breweries. Obliging staff are willing to serve ale in the restaurant upstairs or adjoining lounge. Lunches and evening meals are highly recommended. There is a pleasant beer garden to the rear. An oasis, this is the only pub in town serving real ale. ❀①❑&P⇐▤(7)

Donaghmore

Brewer's House
73 Castlecaulfield Road, BT70 3HB
✪ closed Mon & Tue; 12-8 (10 Sat) ☎ (028) 8776 1932
⊕ thebrewershouse.com
Whitewater Belfast Ale Ⓗ
The Brewer's House, located some four miles from Dungannon, is a new pub/restaurant selling real ale. Run by an enthusiastic brewer, this is the first real ale outlet in Tyrone. The building, which dates from the 18th century, houses a bar and a large restaurant serving high-quality food. The owner is currently establishing a new microbrewery on the premises. ①&

Enniskillen

Linen Hall
11-13 Townhall Street, BT74 7BD
✪ 8am-midnight (1am Wed & Sat) ☎ (028) 6634 0910
Adnams Broadside; Greene King Abbot; guest beers Ⓗ
The Linen Hall is perhaps Northern Ireland's most remote Wetherspoon pub. The only real ale outlet in County Fermanagh, it is located in a picturesque part of the Province. The bar features five handpumps with the regular beers supplemented by changing guests. The venue tends to be busy despite being in a street with a lot of pubs and eateries. Open at 8am for breakfast, alcohol served from 11.30am (12.30pm Sun). ➹❀①&♦⇐

Hillsborough

Hillside
21 Main Street, BT26 6AE
✪ 12-11.30 (1am Fri & Sat); 12-11 Sun ☎ (028) 9268 9233
⊕ hillsidehillsborough.co.uk

Hilden Ale, Twisted Hop; guest beer ⊞
A regular in the Guide, this pub has sold real ale for many years. It has two bars and a dining area. The ale is on the front bar and comes from Hilden Brewing, with occasional guests from other breweries. An enclosed beer garden is ideal for outdoor drinking. The Hillside holds a summer beer festival and puts on some additional ales during September's Oyster Festival. The express bus can get to Hillsborough in 20 minutes from Belfast.
🏰Q❀❶▶❒❦-🖳(38,238)

Holywood

Dirty Duck Ale House
3 Kinnegar Road, BT18 9JN (300yds from railway station)
✪ 11.30-11.30 (1am Thu-Sat); 12.30-11 Sun
☎ (028) 9059 6666 ⊕ thedirtyduckalehouse.co.uk
Beer range varies ⊞
A compact pub with a great location, yards from Belfast Lough. The Dirty Duck is a stalwart supporter of real ale and is always in the running for local CAMRA Pub of the Year. Three beers are usually available, often from Barney's, Inveralmond, Hilden or Shepherd Neame. The Dirty Duck Ale is brewed by Hilden. Great food is available in the bar downstairs and in the restaurant. The view is impressive and there is a corner celebrating local golfing hero Rory McIlroy.
🏰❀❶❦-🖳

Lisburn

Tap Room
Hilden Brewery, Hilden, BT27 4TY (5 mins walk from Hilden railway halt)
✪ closed Mon; 12-3, 5.30-9 (not Sun eve)
☎ (028) 9266 3863 ⊕ taproomhilden.com
Hilden Ale, Twisted Hop ⊞
The Tap Room forms part of Hilden Brewing and sits adjacent to the brewhouse in the courtyard of the Scullion's Georgian mansion. A licensed restaurant, it concentrates on its own Hilden beer and good locally sourced food. There are usually two ales available on handpump and brewery tours can be booked. Weddings and events are hosted throughout the year, including a three-day beer festival in August.
🏰Q❀❶❦=(Hilden)P-🖳(325H)

Tuesday Bell
4 Lisburn Square, BT28 1TS
✪ 8am-11 ☎ (028) 9262 7390
Adnams Broadside; Greene King Abbot; guest beers ⊞
A large, two-floor Wetherspoon pub, part of the Lisburn Square shopping precinct. Up to eight real ales are available, five downstairs and three

upstairs. Local ale from Hilden is regularly served alongside the house beers and guests. There are TV screens showing BBC news and occasional sporting events. Background music is on in the upstairs bar at the weekend. Open from 8am for breakfast, alcohol served from 11.30am (12.30pm Sun).
❶❦=❦-🖳

Londonderry

Diamond
23-24 The Diamond, BT48 6HP (centre of walled city)
✪ 8am-midnight (1am Fri & Sat) ☎ (028) 7127 2880
Adnams Broadside; Greene King Abbot; guest beers ⊞
One of the city's two Wetherspoon pubs, The Diamond occupies a corner site in the historic Diamond Square. This former department store is now a large pub affording some very good views from the upstairs bar. Real ale is available in both upstairs and downstairs bars and the 10 handpumps feature a variety of guests. As with other pubs in the chain, alcohol is served from 11.30am (12.30pm Sun). 🖙❶❦❦-🖳

Newtownards

Spirit Merchant
54-56 Regent Street, BT23 4LP (opp bus station)
✪ 8am-11 (midnight Fri & Sat) ☎ (028) 9182 4270
Adnams Broadside; Greene King Abbot; guest beers ⊞
A centrally located Wetherspoon bar on the main street into Newtownards. This single-floor pub features a long bar with five handpumps offering a variety of guest ales. The main bar area can be very busy but there is quieter seating space to the side. A large beer garden is a very appealing place to drink in good weather. Open from 8am, alcohol served from 11.30am (12.30pm Sun).
❀❶❦❦P-🖳(5,7,9)

Saintfield

White Horse
49-53 Main Street, BT24 7AB
✪ 11.30-1am; 12-10 Sun ☎ (028) 9751 1143
⊕ whitehorsesaintfield.com
Whitewater Copperhead Ale, Belfast Ale, Crown Glory; guest beers ⊞
This is the Whitewater Brewery tap and features three or four of its ales and occasional guests. Located about 10 miles from Belfast, it is very much a community pub, appealing to locals and visitors alike. A popular bistro and pub, it offers good food to accompany the ale. There are two screens for sporting events, regular live music in the bar and an annual beer festival. A former local CAMRA Pub of the Year. 🏰❀❶❦-🖳(15,215)

Choosing pubs

CAMRA members and branches choose the pubs listed in the Good Beer Guide. There is no payment for entry, and pubs are inspected on a regular basis by personal visits; publicans are not sent a questionnaire once a year, as is the case with some pub guides. CAMRA branches monitor all the pubs in their areas, and the choice of pubs for the guide is often the result of democratic vote at branch meetings. However, recommendations from readers are welcomed and will be passed on to the relevant branch: write to Good Beer Guide, CAMRA, 230 Hatfield Road, St Albans, Hertfordshire, AL1 4LW; or send an email to: **gbgeditor@camra.org.uk**

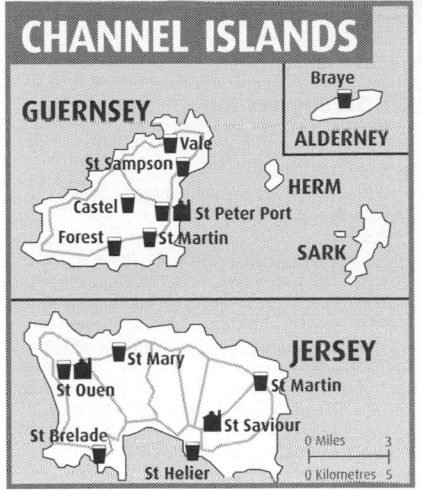

CHANNEL ISLANDS

GUERNSEY
Braye
Vale
St Sampson
ALDERNEY
HERM
Castel
St Peter Port
Forest
St Martin
SARK

St Mary
JERSEY
St Ouen
St Martin
St Brelade
St Saviour
St Helier

0 Miles 3
0 Kilometres 5

ALDERNEY

Braye

Rea's Bistro, Bar & Terrace
Braye Street, GY9 3XT
✪ 10-midnight ☎ (01481) 824944
Black Sheep Best Bitter; Randalls Ruby Tuesday Ⓗ;
guest beers Ⓗ/Ⓖ
Formerly known as the Coxswain (which was the
locals' name for the moorings), the bar is now in
new hands with a new name. Three beers can be
found on the handpumps and occasionally in casks
on the bar. The public bar, which is used during
quiet moments, acts as an overflow for dining
during the summer. The outdoor terrace is a
pleasant place to relax on sunny days and hosts
barbecues. There is disabled access, but no
disabled toilet. ♿🛏️🌳➊🍺👜♣♠

GUERNSEY

Castel

Fleur du Jardin
Kings Mills, GY5 7JT
✪ 10.30-11.45 ☎ (01481) 257996 ⊕ fleurdujardin.com
Fuller's London Pride; Sharp's Doom Bar; Shepherd
Neame Bishops Finger Ⓗ
A building of unique charm with two bars – one
traditional, small and cosy, attached to the
restaurant, the other recently renovated in a more
contemporary style to create a comfortable,
relaxing area to enjoy a beer. A door from this area
leads to a large covered patio and out to the
garden. Menus in both the bar and restaurant
feature fresh local produce. ♿Q🛏️🌳➊🍺👜P♠🚃

Forest

Deerhound
Le Bourg, GY8 0AN
✪ 11 (12 Sun)-11 ☎ (01481) 238585
Liberation Ambree Ⓗ
Modern pub on the main road to the airport. The
emphasis is on food, and a popular choice of meals
is served. Tables cannot be booked ahead and the
bar can get busy in the evenings. Outside, there is
a large, sunny, decked patio perfect for summer

dining, as well as benches dotted about on the
grass. The car park fills up quickly at peak times.
Stays open later if busy. 🌳➊👜P🚃

St Martin

Captain's Hotel
La Fosse, GY4 6EF
✪ 11-11 (midnight Fri & Sat); 12-4 Sun ☎ (01481) 238990
Fuller's London Pride; Greene King London Glory Ⓗ
In a secluded location down a country lane, this is a
popular locals' pub with a lively, friendly
atmosphere. It has a small, raised area in front of
the bar furnished with a sofa to make a comfy
zone. Good quality meals can be eaten in the bar or
bistro area, or you can take away a pizza. A meat
draw is held on Friday. The car park to the rear fills
up quickly. 🚲👜P♠🚃

Les Douvres Hotel
La Fosse, GY4 6ER
✪ 11-midnight ☎ (01481) 238731 ⊕ lesdouvreshotel.co.uk
Beer range varies Ⓗ
Former 18th-century manor house two and a half
miles from St Peter Port set in private gardens in St
Martin near the south coast, cliff walks and a tiny
fishing harbour. It offers a well-kept, changing
range of beers on two handpumps. Excellent meals
are served in the bar and separate restaurant. Live
music plays on Friday nights and occasional
Wednesdays. The bar is popular with locals and
visitors. ♿🚲➊🍺👜P♠🚃

St Peter Port

Cock & Bull
Lower Hauteville, GY1 1LL
✪ 11.30-12.45am; closed Sun ☎ (01481) 722660
Beer range varies Ⓗ
Popular pub, up the hill from the town church, with
five handpumps providing a changing range of
beer and cider. Randall's beer can be found here,
along with local cider when available. Live music
takes place throughout the week, with baroque or
jazz on Monday, open mic on Tuesday and Irish on
Thursday. A meat draw is held on Friday. Seating is
on three levels, with a pool table on the lower
level. Toasties are available. The pub opens on
Sunday for major sporting events. 👜♠

Cornerstone Café Bar ♈
La Tour Beauregard, GY1 1LQ (top of Cornet Street)
✪ 10 (8am Thu & Fri)-midnight; 12-6 Sun ☎ (01481) 713832
⊕ cornerstoneguernsey.co.uk
Beer range varies Ⓗ
Situated across the road from the States Archives,
this café has a small bar area to the front and
further seating to the rear. Regular quiz evenings
are held. The menu offers a wide range of good-
quality hot and cold meals, plus a daily specials
board (no food Sun). There is a large screen for
sporting events. Ales from Randalls and Liberation
are often among the range available on the four
handpumps – check the website for what's on and
what's up and coming. Local CAMRA Pub of the
Year 2012. ➊

Drunken Duck
La Charroterie, GY1 1EL (opp Charles Frossard House)
✪ 11 (12 Sun)-12.45am ☎ (01481) 726170
Shepherd Neame Amber Ale; Thwaites Big Ben Ⓗ

ISLANDS

Welcoming locals' hostelry with the bar divided into two areas. At the front, a comfortable drinking area has a couple of sofas alongside plenty of traditional pub seating. To the rear, there are bench seats around the walls and a dartboard. A variety of sports events is shown on big screens. Light bites such as baguettes and toasties are available. ⏱—

Ship & Crown

North Esplanade, GY1 2NB (opp Crown Pier car park)
✪ 10-12.15am ☎ (01481) 721368
⊕ crowsnestguernsey.com
Beer range varies Ⓗ

A busy free house in the centre of town, popular with locals and tourists alike. Situated opposite the harbour, it offers fantastic views of the castle and has an interesting collection of local maritime and occupation photographs. The beer range is constantly changing, with up to four ales of all styles and from many different breweries available, sourced through the Liberation group. ⓘ👍🖪

St Sampson

La Fontaine

Vale Rord, GY2 4DS
✪ 11 (10 Sat)-midnight; 12-6 Sun ☎ (01481) 247644
Randalls Patois Ⓗ

The pub is situated on the main road from the Halfway towards L'Ancresse Common and Pembroke Bay. There is a public bar facing the road and a large back bar with a serving hatch. Occasional live music and various social events are hosted, and euchre teams meet once a week. Traditional pub games, such as shove-ha'penny, bar billiards and darts are played. With a welcoming host, the pub is popular with the locals, particularly for the meat draw on Friday and early evening on Saturday. 🐾🍴♣P⏱—🖪

Pony Inn

Les Capelles, GY2 4GX (on main road between Guernsey Candles and Oatlands Centre)
✪ closed Mon; 11-10.30; 12-2.30 Sun ☎ (01481) 244374
Beer range varies Ⓗ

A convivial pub with well-maintained beer and generous portions of excellent food served in the main bar, conservatory area and separate family dining room (booking advisable, particularly at weekends). The public bar at the side shows televised sports and has a pool table. The staff are friendly and families are welcome. There is disabled access for wheelchair users. ♿🐾ⓘ🍴♣P⏱—🖪

Vale

Houmet Tavern

Rousse, GY6 8AR (between Vale Church and Rousse Tower)
✪ 10-12.45am (6 Sun) ☎ (01481) 242214
Wells Bombardier; Wychwood Hobgoblin Ⓗ

A popular pub, the Houmet has two bars – the Anchor Bar, which is the public bar at the rear with pool and darts, and the Front Bar (closed in the afternoon during the week) with picturesque views of the north of the island, where there is more of an emphasis on food. The same beers are available in both bars plus occasional guests. Meat and crab draws are held on Friday and Saturday. ⓘ🍴P⏱—🖪

JERSEY
St Brelade

Old Smugglers Inn

Le Mont du Ouaisne, JE3 8AW
✪ 11-11 (winter hours vary) ☎ (01534) 741510
⊕ oldsmugglersinn.com
Draught Bass Ⓗ; Greene King Abbot Ⓖ; Wells Bombardier; guest beers Ⓗ

Perched close to the beach on the edge of Ouaisne Bay, the Smugglers has been the jewel in the crown of the Jersey real ale scene for many years. Steeped in history, dating back to when pirates coming into the bay enjoyed an ale or two here, it is set within granite-built fishermen's cottages with foundations reputedly from the 13th century. Up to four real ales are usually available including one from Skinner's, and mini beer festivals are regularly held. The pub is well known for its good food and fresh daily specials. 🏠Qⓘ🖪(12)

St Helier

Dog & Sausage

9 Halkett Street, JE2 4WJ
✪ 10-11 ☎ (01534) 730982
Skinner's Ginger Tosser, Betty Stogs Ⓗ

Down a back lane near the central market, with a corner entrance and a small alfresco area, the Dog has a character all of its own. A local pub for local people, but welcoming to all, there is usually a choice of two well-looked-after Skinner's ales on offer. Lunchtime snacks are served and there is a jukebox but no TV. Probably the coldest toilet on the island. ⓘ

Forum Ⓛ

13 Grenville Street, JE2 4UF
✪ 11-11.30 ☎ (01534) 768105
Liberation Ale, seasonal beers; guest beers Ⓗ

Situated just on the outskirts of the town centre, the pub is named after the cinema that once occupied the site opposite. It has a modern interior but with a classic feel and includes a number of brass plaques that were taken from the old Royal Court building. This is not a quiet pub – live sport and background music often feature. Three real ales are always available, and a large range of real ciders. Food is served in the bar from the Indian restaurant above. Local CAMRA Pub of the Year 2011. ⓘ👍👍⏱—

Lamplighter 🍽 Ⓛ

9 Mulcaster Street, JE2 3NJ
✪ 11-11 ☎ (01534) 723119
Ringwood Best Bitter, Fortyniner; Wells Eagle IPA, Bombardier; guest beers Ⓗ

A traditional pub with a modern feel. The gas lamps that gave the pub its name remain, as does the original antique pewter bar top. An excellent range of up to eight real ales is available including one from Skinner's – recent refurbishment means all are now served direct from the cellar. A real cider is sometimes also on offer. Local CAMRA Pub of the Year 2012. ⓘ👍🖪(5)

Peirson 🅛

17 Royal Square, JE2 4WA

☼ 10 (11 Sun)-11 ☎ (01534) 722726

Draught Bass; Liberation Ale Ⓗ**; guest beer** Ⓖ

The pub is nestled in the corner of the Royal Square in the centre of St Helier. Named after Major Francis Peirson, it contains historical reminders of the Battle of Jersey in 1781. Two ales are always on handpump plus an occasional additional ale on gravity. Excellent food is served at lunchtime throughout the year, with evening meals also on offer in summer. The pub has a good reputation with locals and visitors alike. Outside seating is extremely popular in the summer months.
Q✿◑♿—

Post Horn 🅛

Hue Street, JE2 3RE

☼ 10 (11 Sun)-11 ☎ (01534) 872853

Liberation Ale, seasonal beer; guest beer Ⓗ

Busy, friendly pub adjacent to the precinct and five minutes' walk from the Royal Square. Popular at lunchtimes with its own nucleus of regulars, it offers up to four draught ales. The large L-shaped public bar extends into the lounge area where there is an open fire and TV showing sport. A good selection of freshly cooked food is served. There is a large function room on the first floor, a drinking area outside and a public car park nearby.
🏠✿◑♿—

St Helier Yacht Club 🅛

South Harbour, JE2 3NB (on harbour)

☼ 11-11 ☎ (01534) 732229 ⊕ shyc.je

Liberation Ale Ⓗ

Situated in a prominent position overlooking the busy port of St Helier, the Yacht Club, now in its second century, enjoys an unrivalled view of local boating activity. Open to members, signed guests and visiting yachtsmen, it is one of the largest yacht clubs in British waters – the clubhouse is always a hive of activity. Many social events are organised throughout the year, plus year-round sailing that includes coastal, offshore and inshore racing and rallies. ⟳✿◑♦P

St Martin

Rozel Bar & Restaurant

La Valle de Rozel, JE3 6AJ

☼ 10-11 ☎ (01534) 863478 ⊕ rozelbarandrestaurant.co.uk

Draught Bass; Liberation Ale; guest beer Ⓗ

A charming hostelry tucked away in the north-east corner of the island, under new management as a Liberation Group partner pub. It has a delightful beer garden and an excellent restaurant upstairs. Bar meals are served in the public bar and snug, where there is a real fire in the winter. Guest beers

from Skinner's and Ringwood are often available. Locals are friendly if sometimes a little rumbustious. 🏠⟳✿◑ ⊟♿P—🚌(3)

St Mary

St Mary's Country Inn 🅛

La Rue des Buttes, JE3 3DS

☼ 10 (11 Sun)-11 ☎ (01534) 482897

Liberation Ale; guest beers Ⓗ

An archetypal country inn from the outside, this 17th-century farmhouse is sited opposite the parish church which has a history dating back to Norman times. Following refurbishment in 2009, the interior is contemporary with a main bar and an extensive dining area. The four handpumps serve Liberation and three guest beers, and reasonably priced good food is available daily from an extensive menu. The inn has a comfortable and relaxed atmosphere with seating outside front and rear for when the sun shines. A reasonable walk from the north coast. 🏠⟳✿◑ ⊟♿P—🚌(25)

St Ouen

Farmers Inn 🅛

La Grande Route de St Ouen, JE3 2HY

☼ 10 (11 Sun)-11 ☎ (01534) 485311

Draught Bass; Liberation Ale, seasonal beers Ⓗ

Situated in the hub of St Ouen, the rustic Farmers Inn is a typical country pub offering up to three ales as well as a locally made cider when available (usually April-July). Traditional pub food is served in generous portions. Best described as a friendly community local, there is a good chance of hearing Jersey French (Jerriais) spoken at the bar. 🏠✿◑ ⊟♿▲♦P—🚌(8,9)

Moulin de Lecq

Le Mont de la Greve de Lecq, JE3 2DT

☼ 11-11 (winter hours vary) ☎ (01534) 482818

⊕ moulindelecq.com

Greene King Abbot Ⓖ**, seasonal beers; Morland Old Speckled Hen; Wells Bombardier; guest beers** Ⓗ

Another free house on the island offering a range of real ales, the Moulin is a converted 12th-century watermill situated in the valley above the beach at Greve de Lecq. The waterwheel is still in place and the turning mechanism can be seen behind the bar. A restaurant adjoins the mill. There is a children's play space and a barbecue area used extensively in the summer. 🏠Q✿◑♦P—🚌(9)

Publican – a posset, if you please

Anne Boleyn as a Maid of Honour had an allowance of two gallons of ale a day – perhaps to be shared with others? – but to make such ale interesting it was served in possets and caudles, the warmest sweet liquor mixed with honey, spices, roasted crabs or anything else which took the fancy. The weaker ales were relatively baby food. Elizabeth, when queen, issued repeated regulations in defence of weak ale and against strong beer; yet for herself, although she was abstemious, when she wished for a nip drank beer 'so strong that was no man durst touch it'.

Frank Morley, The Great North Road, 1961

ISLANDS

Good Bottled Beer Guide – 8th Edition

NEW TITLE

Jeff Evans

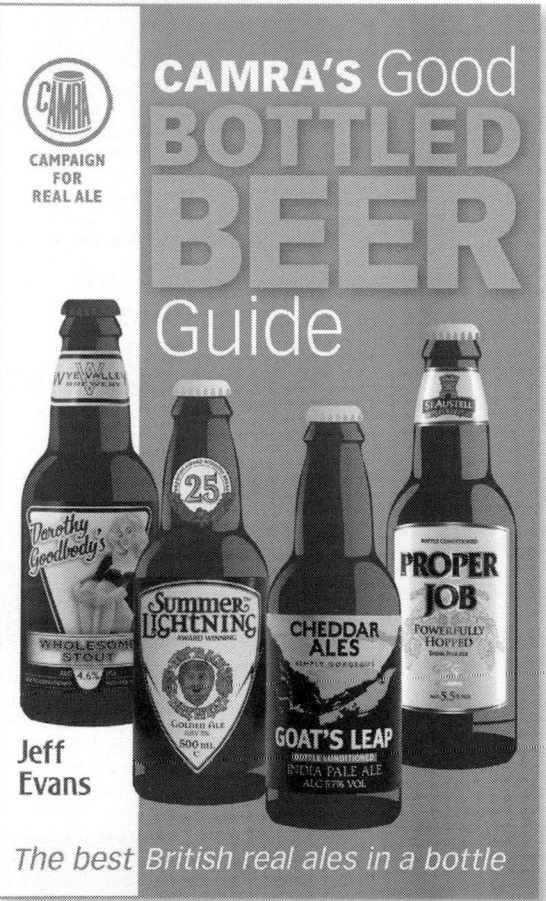

CAMRA'S Good **BOTTLED BEER** Guide

CAMPAIGN FOR REAL ALE

Jeff Evans

The best British real ales in a bottle

A pocket-sized guide for discerning drinkers looking to buy bottled real ales and enjoy a fresh glass of their favourite beers at home. The new 8th edition of the **Good Bottled Beer Guide** is completely revised, updated and redesigned to showcase the very best bottled British real ales now being produced, and detail where they can be bought. Everything you need to know about bottled beers; tasting notes, ingredients, brewery details, and a glossary to help the reader understand more about them.

£12.99   ISBN 978-1-85249-309-7   CAMRA members' price £10.99   440 pages

For this and other books on beer and pubs visit CAMRA's online bookshop at **www.camra.org.uk/books** or call **01727 867201**

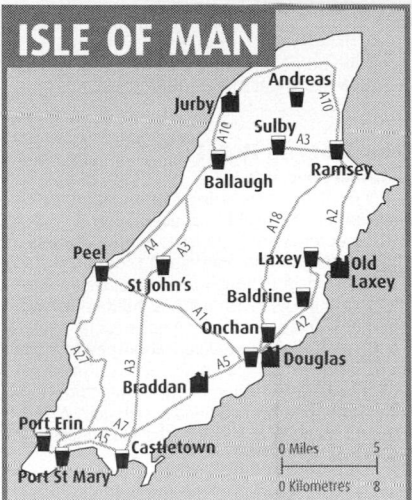

ISLE OF MAN

Jurby
Andreas
Sulby
Ballaugh
Ramsey
Peel
St John's
Laxey
Old Laxey
Baldrine
Onchan
Douglas
Braddan
Port Erin
Castletown
Port St Mary

0 Miles 5
0 Kilometres 8

Andreas

Grosvenor Hotel Ⓛ
Kirk Andreas, IM7 4HE
✪ 11-11 ☎ (01624) 888007 ⊕ grosvenor.im/location.php
Okells Bitter; guest beers Ⓗ
The Grosvenor is a popular destination for both drinking and dining, with a good choice of reasonably priced food. The Tap Room is a long-established favourite with locals and patrons from farther afield, from families to farmers. It is very much a traditional country bar with a real sense of period charm and character. Beers come from the island's largest brewery, Okells. Quiz night is Sunday – everyone is welcome. It's the Isle of Man's most northerly pub. Q✿❀⚫️◑⊟♣P⌨

Baldrine

Liverpool Arms Ⓛ
Main Road, IM4 6AE
✪ 12-11 (midnight Sat & Sun) ☎ (01624) 674787
Okells Bitter; guest beers Ⓗ
Standing midway between Onchan and Laxey, this former coaching house is the original halfway house and the road it stands on is universally referred to as 'The LA Straight'. Although a popular venue for dining, the landlord prides himself on taking as much care over the beer as the food. A pool table, dartboard and football on TV are available in the bar area. ⚏✿❀◑⊟♣P⌐⊟

Ballaugh

Raven Ⓛ
The Main Road, IM7 5EG
✪ 12-midnight ☎ (01624) 896128
Okells Bitter, Raven's Claw; guest beers Ⓗ
Village-centre hostelry on the TT course adjacent to Ballaugh Bridge. A family-friendly locals' pub with good quality food and ale, the house brew is Raven's Claw, brewed by Okells. It has a comfortable main bar with three areas, one mainly for dining, and a separate games room with pool and darts. The paved patio adjacent to the car park is ideal for watching the TT and Manx Grand Prix races. ⚏✿◑♿A♣P⌐⊟(5,6)

Castletown

Castle Arms (Glue Pot) Ⓛ
The Quay, IM9 1LD
✪ 12-11 (midnight Fri & Sat) ☎ (01624) 824673
Draught Bass; Okells Bitter; guest beers Ⓗ
Dating from the early 1750s, the Castle Arms – or the Glue Pot as it is known locally – has been serving pints to soldiers and fishermen for over 200 years, more recently even to film stars. Situated in the shadow of Castle Rushen, you can feel the history outside and in – the interior is decorated with nautical artefacts and pictures of past heroes riding their motorbikes in the Southern 100 races. On sunny days you can enjoy a drink on the harbour quayside. Q✿❀☰(IMR)♣♠'–⊟(1,2)

Sidings Ⓛ
Victoria Road, IM9 1EF (next to railway station)
✪ 11.30-11.30 (12.30am Fri & Sat) ☎ (01624) 823282
⊕ thesidings.im
Bushy's Ruby Mild, Bitter, Castletown Bitter; Okells Bitter; guest beers Ⓗ
Local CAMRA Pub of the Year 2012, the Sidings is a traditional pub situated next to the steam railway. Four local ales are always available alongside several ever-changing guests. A beer festival is held the first two weeks of July. A log fire, games room, live entertainment and a large beer garden make the pub popular with locals and visitors. It's conveniently situated 50 yards from the bus stop and the railway station platform.
⚏✿◑☰(IMR)♣P'–⊟

Douglas

Albert Hotel Ⓛ
3 Chapel Row, IM1 2BJ (next to bus station)
✪ 10-11 (11.45 Fri & Sat); 12-11 Sun ☎ (01624) 673632
Bushy's Castletown Bitter; Okells Bitter, Jough; guest beers Ⓗ
The Albert is an unspoilt local, popular with many regulars, featuring a traditionally laid-out central bar and dark wood panelling. It has a pool table in one room and interesting pictures of IOM Steam Packet boats in the other. Sport is screened on TV but never loud enough to spoil conversation. Drinks are reasonably priced, with house brew Jough from Okells now back as a seasonal beer.
◑☰(IMR)♣'–⊟

Cat With No Tail Ⓛ
Hailwood Court, Governors Hill, IM2 7EA
✪ 12-11 (midnight Fri & Sat) ☎ (01624) 616364
Okells Bitter, seasonal beers; guest beers Ⓗ
A modern pub serving Governors Hill, situated two miles from central Douglas. The Cat has a public bar with a large screen showing TV sport, a pool table and a dartboard. Karaoke is hosted on the last Friday of the month. The large lounge has a conservatory that leads to an outside seating area with a patio and children's play area. Food is served lunchtimes and evenings. The Okells Bitter is complemented by an Okells seasonal or guest beer. ✿◑⊟♿P'–⊟

INDEPENDENT BREWERIES
Bushy's Braddan
Doghouse Jurby
Okells Douglas
Old Laxey Old Laxey

ISLANDS

Old Market Inn ⃝L

Chapel Row, IM1 2BJ (near bus station)
✪ 9-midnight (11 Sun) ☎ 07624 381076
Bushy's Old Bushy Tail; guest beer Ⓗ
One of the island's smallest, friendliest and oldest pubs, the Old Market Inn has been owned by the same family for many decades. Very popular with locals, it could never be described as a quiet pub. The landlord is a keen TT and Manx Grand Prix supporter and the pub's walls are adorned with photographs of the races. A rare outlet for Old Bushy Tail outside the south of the island. If you are visiting downtown Douglas it is well worth calling in here. ⚒Ⓠ✿≈(IMR)♣≛–₪

Prospect Hotel ⃝L

Prospect Hill, IM1 1ET
✪ 12-11 (midnight Fri); 6-midnight Sat; closed Sun
☎ (01624) 616773
Okells Bitter; guest beers Ⓗ
Opened in 1857, the pub is situated in the finance sector of the island's capital. The law courts are in close proximity and the walls feature many pictures relating to the law profession. The bar is very busy and popular, especially among office workers. A library area is for those wanting a quiet drink. Several handpumps dispense the Okells regulars, seasonals and guest beers, often chosen by customers. Wednesday is quiz night. ◖≈(IMR)₪

Queen's Hotel ⃝L

Queen's Promenade, IM2 4NL (on seafront, N end of promenade)
✪ 12-11 (midnight Fri & Sat) ☎ (01624) 674438
Okells Bitter; guest beers Ⓗ
In an excellent location on Douglas promenade, the Queen's is popular with visitors and locals alike. Outside there is ample seating under heated awnings, offering great views of Douglas Bay, ferries and horse trams. The interior has three distinct areas, one with a pool table and the others with low-volume TVs screening sport. Up to three guest beers are on offer alongside the Okells. Pub grub is served seven days a week. Live music plays at the weekend and often on Tuesday too.
✿◖Ⓠ⑀♣≛–₪

Rovers Return ⃝L

11 Church Street, IM1 2AG (behind town hall)
✪ 12-11 (midnight Fri & Sat) ☎ (01624) 676459
Bushy's Ruby Mild, Bitter, seasonal beers; guest beers Ⓗ
The Rovers is a fascinating pub – there are brass handpumps fashioned from the ends of fire hoses, a real fire beneath the dartboard, Desperate Dan-sized food portions and a shrine in honour of Blackburn Rovers FC. Then there is the eclectic clientele. The pub's first highly acclaimed beer festival was held in 2010, now an annual event. The Rovers would be a famous landmark if it was not tucked away behind the town hall.
⚒✿◖≈(IMR)♣●≛–₪

Terminus Tavern ⃝L

Strathallan Crescent, IM2 4NR
✪ 12-11 (midnight Fri & Sat) ☎ (01624) 624312
Okells Bitter; guest beers Ⓗ
Located next to the starting point for the seasonal Manx Electric Railway and horse trams, the Terminus has a comfortable spacious front bar with alcoves around the large front windows. This friendly pub is popular for dining, and can get busy during peak times. It has a side bar for pool and

darts, and a large outside seating area with views across Douglas Bay. Okells Bitter is offered alongside numerous guest beers.
⚒Ⓠ✿◖⑀≈(MER)♣P≛–₪(25,26,27)

Woodbourne Hotel ⃝L

Alexander Drive, IM2 3QF
✪ 4 (3 Fri; 12 Sat & Sun)-midnight ☎ (01624) 676754
Okells Bitter, seasonal beers; guest beers Ⓗ
Striking gothic-style Victorian pub with a quirky three-bar layout and pool room. Some original features remain although the former Gents Only bar is now unisex. Each bar has a different feel, whether you are looking for a quiet corner to enjoy a book or prefer a more lively atmosphere. A good choice of ever-changing guest ales is offered as well as a large selection of wine. This true community pub hosts a Sunday pub quiz. A frequent local CAMRA Pub of the Year finalist.
Ⓠ⑀♣≛–₪

Laxey

Bridge Inn ⃝L

6 New Road, IM4 7BE
✪ 12-11 (midnight Fri & Sat) ☎ (01624) 862414
⊕ bridgeinn.im
Bushy's Ruby Mild, Bitter; guest beers Ⓗ
Popular and lively local pub in the centre of the village. The two-roomed Bridge has been refurbished but has lost none of its friendly ambience and continues to serve an excellent pint. It offers occasional live music, a wide-screen TV and a pool table. In 1897, after the Snaefell mining disaster in which 20 men perished, the cellar area was used as a temporary morgue. There are rumours of a resident ghost.
⚒Ⓠ✿⑀≈(MER)♣P≛–₪(3,3a)

Shore Hotel ⃝L

Old Laxey Hill, IM4 7DA (signed from main road)
✪ 12-midnight ☎ (01624) 861509 ⊕ theshorehotel.im
Old Laxey Bosun Bitter Ⓗ
The island's only brewpub offers a warm welcome to all. Well worth a detour from upper Laxey and there is always the chance of meeting the brewer. A comfy venue with a maritime theme, it also celebrates the success of local cycling hero Mark Cavendish. The annual blues festival and other events during the year make it a popular destination for visitors and locals alike.
⚒✿◖⑀Ⓐ♣P≛–

Onchan

Manx Arms ⃝L

Main Road, IM3 1BE
✪ 12-11 (midnight Fri-Sun) ☎ (01624) 675484
Okells Bitter, seasonal beers; guest beers Ⓗ
Traditional local situated on the main road with a lounge and bar with pub games including pool, darts, dominoes, and a large-screen TV for sports. Live music features most Saturday evenings and the occasional karaoke night is hosted. There is a heated patio at the front for smokers and another at the rear next to the large car park. The regular beer is from Okells with a seasonal or guest ale usually also served. An often lively and very friendly pub. ✿⑀♣P≛–₪(3,23)

Peel

Creek Inn 🄻

Station Place, IM5 1AT (overlooking Peel Marina)
✪ 10-midnight (12.30am Fri & Sat); 12-midnight Sun
☎ (01624) 842216 ⊕ thecreekinn.co.uk
Okells Bitter; guest beers Ⓗ
Traditional marina-side pub with a warm welcome, popular with locals and tourists. The main lounge bar is very busy especially at meal times. Seating areas have a nautical theme, with etched glass screens featuring sailing ships, and mirrors rescued from bygone Manx pubs. A good selection of ales – up to 15 at busy times – is on offer to complement the comprehensive food menu. Locally caught Manx queenies (queen scallops) and lobster are specialities. Live music features every weekend.
❀🄍🄴▲🌢ᵇᐟ–🍴(5,6)

Marine Hotel 🄻

Shore Road, IM5 1AH
✪ 12-midnight ☎ (01624) 842337 ⊕ marinehotelpeel.co.uk
Bushy's Bitter; Okells Bitter; guest beers Ⓗ
Popular with all ages, the Marine Hotel first opened in 1890 and overlooks the beautiful sandy beach and historic Peel Castle. It has two bars areas and a large restaurant accessed via a separate entrance, serving a wide variety of food seven days a week. Locally brewed Bushy's and Okells beers are offered including seasonal specials plus up to two guest ales. Free Wi-Fi is available.
🄼🄍🄴&▲🌢ᵇᐟ–🍴(5)

White House Hotel ⚲ 🄻

Tynwald Road, IM5 1LA (150yds from bus station)
✪ 11-midnight ☎ (01624) 842252
⊕ thewhitehousepeel.com
Bushy's Ruby Mild, Bitter; Moorhouse's Pride of Pendle; Okells Bitter; guest beers Ⓗ
This is a superb traditional establishment – cosy, friendly and welcoming – with real fires, exposed beams, snugs and a large room showing sport on TV and hosting live music at the weekend. The White House is one of the very few pubs on the island that sells real cider – usually Westons. It is also the only pub on the island to have won local CAMRA Pub of the Year three times in a row. A vast range of malt whiskies is available.
🄼Q❀🄴▲♣🌢P🍴(5,6)

Port Erin

Bay Hotel 🄻

Shore Road, IM9 6HL (far end of lower promenade)
✪ 12-midnight (4 winter); 12-1am Fri & Sat
☎ (01624) 832084 ⊕ bushys.com/the-bay
Bushy's Ruby Mild, Bitter, Castletown Bitter, Old Bushy Tail, seasonal beers; guest beers Ⓗ
Bushy's flagship pub occupies an idyllic seafront location, with concerts held on the beach in summer. The tastefully restored interior features two public bars, with major sporting events screened on TV and live music most weekends. There is an additional dining area open most lunchtimes and evenings. The full range of Bushy's beers is on offer – if you cannot make up your mind, you could try the taster tray offering third-pint glasses of different ales. A good choice of Belgian bottled beers is also available. The pub hosts an annual real ale festival.
🄼Q➲❀🄍🄴≈(IMR)♣🌢ᐟ

Falcon's Nest Hotel 🄻

Station Road, IM9 6AF (200yds from railway station)
✪ 11-midnight (1am Fri & Sat) ☎ (01624) 834077
⊕ falconsnesthotel.co.uk
Bushy's Bitter; Okells IPA; guest beers Ⓗ
Family-run seafront hotel with a conservatory running the length of the building, enjoying superb elevated panoramic views over the bay and sandy beach. Real ale is served only in the lounge bar due to the location of the cellar, with a range of local ales on offer. Food is available until 9pm in the restaurant, conservatory and lounge, including a popular carvery on Sunday lunchtime.
🄼Q➲🄍🄍🄴≈(IMR)♣ᐟ–🍴

Port St Mary

Albert Hotel 🄻

Athol Street, IM9 5DS (next to bus terminal)
✪ 11-midnight (1am Fri & Sat); 12-midnight Sun
☎ (01624) 832118
Bushy's Bitter, Old Bushy Tail; Okells Bitter; guest beer Ⓗ
Traditional pub in the heart of the town with impressive views over the harbour. The pub comprises three rooms including a large games room, warmed by real fires throughout the colder months. A third seating area is available in busier times. Well decorated and comfortably furnished, Manx Gaelic language quotations adorn the walls. An ideal pub to relax in following a sea fishing trip.
🄼Q❀🄍🄍🄴♣Pᐟ–🍴🍴

Shore Hotel 🄻

Shore Road, Gansey, IM9 5LZ
✪ 12-midnight (1am Fri & Sat) ☎ (01624) 832269
Bushy's Old Bushy Tail; Okells Bitter; guest beers Ⓗ
Friendly free house overlooking Gansey Bay, popular with locals and visitors alike. Regular and seasonal beers from the island's two larger breweries are available in both the recently refurbished main bar and separate dining room. Home-cooked food is offered with occasional themed evenings, such as curry night, and parties and functions are hosted. B&B accommodation is available in four en-suite rooms. Triumph MCC HQ for the TT and Manx Grand Prix. 🄼➲❀🄍🄍Pᐟ–🍴

Ramsey

Plough 🄻

40 Parliament Street, IM8 1AN
✪ 4-11.30 (12.30am Fri); 12-12.30am Sat; 12-11.30 Sun
☎ (01624) 813323
Okells Bitter; guest beer Ⓗ
A now rare traditional unspoilt pub on the high street. In the evenings a mixed clientele vie for space in two small bar areas. This free house has sold Okells Bitter for many years and in recent times has added an ever-changing guest beer. An interesting snack menu is available all day. The Plough is a proud sponsor of Shennaghys Jiu, a Manx music festival held in Ramsey at the end of March/beginning of April. 🄼🄍♣ᐟ

Trafalgar Hotel 🄻

West Quay, IM8 1DW (on quayside)
✪ 11.30-11 (12.15am Fri & Sat) ☎ (01624) 814601
Moorhouse's Black Cat; Okells Bitter; guest beers Ⓗ
Established in 1870, this cosy, friendly and popular pub is a traditional quayside free house, overlooking the harbour and a short walk from the

ISLANDS

shopping area. Close to the course, it is popular with bikers in TT week. A good and varied selection of local, seasonal and guest ales is always available. Beers are listed on a chalkboard for convenience. A frequent local CAMRA Pub of the Year finalist. Q♠♣♿(MER)♣☒(3,5,6)

St John's

Glen Helen Inn 🗓

Glen Helen, IM4 3NP (continue round TT course from St John's for 1 mile)
🕒 11-11 (11.45 Fri & Sat) ☎ (01624) 801294
⊕ glenheleninn.com
Bushy's Bitter; guest beers ⓗ
The inn nestles among trees in the heart of Glen Helen, on the famous TT motorcycle course. Now refurbished with a contemporary decor and a relaxed ambience, the main bar offers a mixture of tables and lounge-style seating areas. There are further dining areas and more seating outside overlooking the river. Popular for weddings and functions, the Glen Helen carries a surprisingly large cask ale range for its idyllic rural location.
♣☒❶♿♠P✝

Sulby

Ginger Hall Hotel 🗓

Ballamanagh Road, IM7 2HB

🕒 12-midnight (4 Mon) ☎ (01624) 897231
⊕ gingerhallhotel.com
Bushy's Castletown Bitter; Moorhouse's Black Cat; guest beers ⓗ
The Ginger Hall is instantly recognisable by its colour. Inside, the welcoming one-room bar is dominated by an impressive beer engine and warmed by a real fire in colder months. Try not to spill your beer while admiring the huge TT map on the ceiling. Each window features a black and white picture of a TT bike rider. The popular restaurant also offers reasonably priced takeaway food. Accommodation is available in eight rooms.
🛏☒❶♿♠P✝☒(5,6)

Sulby Glen Hotel 🗓

Main Road, IM7 2HR

🕒 12-midnight (1am Fri & Sat); 12-11 Sun
☎ (01624) 897240 ⊕ sulbyglen.net
Bushy's Bitter; Okells Bitter; guest beers ⓗ
Friendly, welcoming inn with 11 en-suite rooms, located in a picturesque setting on the Sulby Straight on the TT course. It is renowned for its home-cooked food, served in the lounges and a separate dining area. The motorcycle engine on the bar is a talking point, used to dispense keg beer and lager. This large rural pub hosts beer and cider festivals, and CAMRA members receive a discount on real ale. The bus stops outside.
🛏Q♿♣☒❶♿♠P✝☒(5,6)

Shore Hotel, Laxey (Photo: Tom Stainer)

Oakham Ales' Brewery Tap, Peterborough (p64, 812)

The
Breweries

A word from our sponsor: SIBA	**674**
How to use the Breweries section	**676**
The breweries	**677**
Republic of Ireland breweries	889
Closed & future breweries	**892**

The Power of One Voice

From individual potential...

Don't believe what you've read about a so-called 'real ale stereotype' – even if a glance at your reflection these days reveals that you might actually fit it better than your image squeezes into full view in the mirror (and take note: the beer's not to blame, it's the cheese on toast after the beer).

We are all individuals and life would be boring as hell if we were programmed to look the same, think the same and agree about everything. That's a scenario that from time to time has persisted as the dream of dreary brewery marketing executives, and if any of it were true the world would still be awash with Watney's Red.

The beauty of homo sapiens, however, extends beyond our unique individuality to our ability to communicate, find common cause and campaign for it. In 1971, four friends, bemoaning the bland homogeneity of said Red and its equally abysmal keg bedfellows, did just that with astounding success. From four to 150,000 CAMRA members in a little over forty years... these stereotypes breed like rabbits!

Similarly, twenty pioneering microbrewers met in a pub in Wootton Bassett in 1980 and founded the Small Independent Brewers' Association. The name subsequently changed but the acronym has stuck, and today SIBA is moving ever closer to 700 brewing members.

It is unlikely that any other organisation of supposedly like-minded individuals can contain a more cussed bunch of fiercely independent people. SIBA's chief executive, tasked with pulling together the trade association's operational activities into a coherent and cogent force, has been heard to comment that many of the members (who pay his wages) have to run businesses themselves because nobody else would employ them. It's like herding cats, he says.

But it is precisely this individualistic drive and independent sense of purpose that explain and give backbone to today's Great British Beer success story. These are characteristics that have massively enriched the brewing scene and translated into the wealth of choice and variety that drinkers now enjoy. They have given us the bursting-at-the-seams Breweries section that follows these pages and brought unprecedented imagination and innovation to beer making.

All the more reason, then, to celebrate when we manage to harness these qualities to promote and defend the interests of beer and pubs.

...to collective achievement

As *Good Beer Guide* sponsor last year, SIBA quoted Richard Boston, the late beer writer and early champion of the beer movement:

'The purpose of pub conversation is to find areas of agreement and common ground.'

Wise words, we said then... this time let's just call them prophetic. With the pub at the heart of its activities (how many branch meetings aren't

The great variety of beer now brewed in Britain was well represented at SIBA's 2013 BeerX in Sheffield

SIBA Chairman Keith Bott (3rd from left) along with CAMRA's Jonathan Mail (left), the BBPA's Brigid Simmonds (right) and MPs outside HM Treasury in February 2013, presenting a petition from MPs to scrap the Beer Duty Escalator

held in a pub?) CAMRA has done a brilliant and unequalled job of getting beer consumers to pull together. From its inaugural pub meeting, SIBA has worked from the smallest brewer up to build a strong voice for independent brewing that is greater than the sum of its parts. And the BBPA (British Beer & Pub Association) continues to be a potent lobbying force, principally representing larger brewers, family brewers and pub operators.

But it has taken an extra step, from these three (and other) individually united but essentially separate interest groups, to forge an over arching campaign that could bring us all together with one voice. Nothing has been more vital for the beer and pub industries than for us to see an end to the Beer Duty Escalator and, by delivering a collective, indivisible and unequivocal message, beer brewers, retailers and consumers – with the crucial support of our parliamentary allies – have achieved that aim and secured government acknowledgement that beer and pubs should be recognised and supported for their contribution to community life.

There might well remain areas on which we will continue to disagree, but we should never forget a year that reinforced a sense of positivity and restored confidence in our industry, and gave us a lesson in the power of unity.

SIBA Locals: Great local pubs... great local beer!

Pubs reflect the unique individuality of people. No two pubs are the same, and every pub is proud to be different. But they do share qualities and the overwhelming majority of them share a commitment to quality. And they too can unite to deliver a positive message about what they offer to punters, politicians, commentators and communities.

The **SIBA Locals** scheme is building a national network of on-trade local beer champions within the broader membership of SIBA, which encompasses not just brewers but their many and various supplier associates, representing the total supply-chain infrastructure of a vital British manufacturing industry.

Working alongside CAMRA's own excellent **'LocAle'** initiative, **SIBA Locals** strive to embody the ideals and ethics of local brewers, the dedication and enterprise of community publicans, and the commitment and campaigning zeal of discerning beer drinkers.

Could you be the next SIBA Local?

If you are in the pub trade and would like to know more, please go to **http://siba.co.uk** and click on the **SIBA Locals** link.

How to use the Breweries section

This section lists breweries operating in the British Isles: the United Kingdom, the Isle of Man, Channel Islands and the Irish Republic. Breweries are listed in alphabetical order. They include independent companies (regional, family, micro-brewers and brewpubs), national brewers and global groups. If a brewery owns more than one site, these are cross-referenced. Within each brewery entry, beers are listed in increasing order of strength. Websites should be consulted when breweries produce occasional or seasonal beers that are available for less than six months of the year. We mention when breweries produce bottle-conditioned beers but do not list or evaluate them: for further information, see the Guide's sister publication, the *Good Bottled Beer Guide*. The section ends with a list of independent breweries in the Irish Republic where choice for beer drinkers has improved dramatically in recent years.

KEY TO SYMBOLS

🛢 A brew-pub: a pub that brews beer on the premises.

👁 The brewery is affiliated with the Cyclops system for describing beers to consumers.

◆ CAMRA tasting notes, supplied by a trained CAMRA tasting panel. Beer descriptions that do not carry this symbol are based on more limited tastings or have been obtained from other sources.

🗍 A CAMRA Beer of the Year in 2012.

🎗 One of the 2013 CAMRA Beers of the Year: a finalist in the Champion Beer of Britain competition held during the Great British Beer Festival in London in August 2013, or the Champion Winter Beer of Britain competition held earlier in the year.

☺ The brewery's beers can be acceptably served through a 'tight sparkler' attached to the nozzle of the beer pump, designed to give a thick collar of foam on the beer.

⊗ The brewery's beers should NOT be served through a tight sparkler. CAMRA is opposed to the growing tendency to serve southern-brewed beers with the aid of sparklers, which aerate the beer and tend to drive hop aroma and flavour into the head, altering the balance of the beer achieved in the brewery. When neither symbol is used it means the brewery in question has not stated a preference.

ABBREVIATIONS

OG Stands for Original Gravity, the measure taken before fermentation of the level of 'fermentable material' (malt sugars and added sugars) in the brew. It is only a rough indication of strength and is no longer used for duty purposes.

ABV Stands for Alcohol by Volume, which is a more reliable measure of the percentage of alcohol in finished beer. Many breweries now only disclose ABVs but the Guide lists OGs where available. Often the OG and the ABV of a beer are identical, i.e. 1035 and 3.5 per cent. If the ABV is higher than the OG, i.e. OG 1035, ABV 3.8, this indicates that the beer has been 'well attenuated' with most of the malt sugars turned into alcohol. If the ABV is lower than the OG, this means residual sugars have been left in the beer for fullness of body and flavour: this is rare but can apply to some milds or strong old ales, barley wines and winter beers.

SIBA Indicates a member of the Society of Independent Brewers.

IFBB Indicates a member of the Independent Family Brewers of Britain.

NOTE: The Breweries section was correct at the time of going to press and every effort has been made to ensure that all regularly-available cask-conditioned beers are included.

The Breweries

The breweries listed in this section include micro, small, family, regional, national and global companies. Please use the Beer index (p905) to help locate beers.

1648 SIBA

☰ Old Stables Brewery, Mill Lane, East Hoathly, East Sussex, BN8 6QB
☎ (01825) 840830 ⊕ 1648brewing.co.uk
Tours by arrangement

⊠ The 1648 brewery, set up in the old stable block at the King's Head pub in 2003, derives its name from the year of the deposition of King Charles I. One pub is owned and more than 40 outlets are supplied. Seasonal beers: see website. Bottle-conditioned beers are also available.

Triple Champion (OG 1041, ABV 4%)
A chestnut-coloured traditional English ale, deeply flavoured and full-bodied.

Royal Britannia (OG 1041, ABV 4.1%)
Pale gold-coloured beer with a malty flavour. Lightly hopped with a citrus aroma.

Signature (OG 1044, ABV 4.4%)
Pale, crisply refreshing ale with a bitter aftertaste.

Laughing Frog (OG 1052, ABV 5.2%)
Gold-coloured, full-bodied French/Belgian style beer with a full, malty flavour.

3 Brewers (NEW)

The Potato Shed, Symonds Hyde Farm, Symonds Hyde Lane, Hatfield, Hertfordshire, AL10 9BB
☎ (01707) 271636 ⊕ 3brewers.co.uk

Launched in 2013, the brewery has one permanent beer and is seeking strong links with local Hertfordshire pubs. Seasonal beers are planned.

Classic English Ale (ABV 4.1%)
A light and hoppy amber-coloured beer with a smooth, full and refreshing flavour.

4Ts

Unit 15, EBL Centre, Picow Farm Road, Runcorn, Cheshire, WA7 4UA
☎ 07917 730184

Office: 72 Rydal Avenue, Warrington, Cheshire, WA4 6AT ⊕ 4tsbrewery.co.uk

4Ts began brewing in 2010 in Warrington but moved to larger premises in Runcorn using a five-barrel plant in 2012. Beers are usually available in the Tavern, Warrington. Many themed and special beers are also brewed.

Keep Calm (ABV 3.7%)
A pale, refreshing, smooth-tasting session beer.

Wise (ABV 4%)
A refreshing, bitter beer with grapefruit and citrus aromas.

Stack (ABV 4.2%)
A pale, hoppy, well-balanced beer.

Side (ABV 4.8%)
A tawny coloured bitter with a complex flavours from the malts, combining well with the hops, for a full body with a refreshing hoppy aftertaste.

Loaded (ABV 5%)

A pale beer with a strong hop finish. Tropical fruits, grapefruit and passion fruit aromas come through in the mouth.

Master (ABV 5.9%)
A well-balanced, easy-drinking strong ale.

8 Sail SIBA

Heckington Windmill, Hale Road, Heckington, Lincolnshire, NG34 9JW
☎ (01529) 469308 ☎ 07866 183479
⊕ 8sailbrewery.co.uk
Shop Thu-Sun 12-5pm

8 Sail Brewery was established in 2010 and operates on a six-barrel brew plant. The brewery nestles in the shadow of Heckington Windmill, Britain's only eight sailed windmill, from where the brewery takes its name. The brewery shop stocks Lincolnshire bottle-conditioned beers alongside local ciders. Plans are ongoing to install a Victorian bar and display of pub drinking vessels. All beers are also available bottle conditioned.

Millwright Mild (OG 1035, ABV 3.5%)
A rich, dark mild.

8 Sail Ale (OG 1038, ABV 3.8%)

Windmill Bitter (OG 1038, ABV 3.8%)
Dark and fruity session beer. Pleasant and easy-drinking.

Windy Miller (OG 1038, ABV 3.8%)

Blonde (OG 1040, ABV 4%)
A blonde beer, gently hopped to create a refreshing taste.

Merry Miller (OG 1041, ABV 4.1%)
A traditional bitter. Mid-brown in colour with a nutty, malty flavour.

Flour Power (OG 1042, ABV 4.2%)
Light, floral and hoppy.

Golden Ale (OG 1044, ABV 4.4%)
Pale beer with a good balance of hop flavour, aroma and bitterness.

Millstone (OG 1045, ABV 4.5%)
Traditional brown bitter with a good balance of malt flavours and hops.

Damson Porter (OG 1050, ABV 5%)
Fruit flavoured version of the Victorian Porter.

Sail Away (OG 1050, ABV 5%)
Brewed in the style of a German Kölsch beer with a good balance of malt and hops.

Victorian Porter (OG 1050, ABV 5%)
Brewed to a classic Victorian porter recipe. Slight bitterness at the end. Only lightly hopped. Full-bodied, dark and dominated by dark malt flavours.

Black Widow (OG 1055, ABV 5.5%)
A strong dark ruby mild. Dark malt and liquorice flavours dominate.

John Barleycorn IPA (OG 1055, ABV 5.5%)
A traditional English IPA. Light copper-coloured.

AB InBev

Porter Tun House, 500 Capability Green, Luton, Bedfordshire, LU1 3LS
☎ (01582) 391166 ⊕ inbev.com

The biggest merger in brewing history in 2008 created AB InBev, when InBev of Belgium and AmBev of Brazil bought American giant Anheuser-Busch, best-known for the world's biggest (but not best) beer brand, Budweiser. The giant is a major player in the European market with such lager brands as Stella Artois and Jupiler. It has a slight interest in ale brewing with the cask- and bottle-conditioned wheat beer, Hoegaarden, and the Abbey beer Leffe. It has a ruthless track record of closing plants and disposing of brands: it has already announced the closure of the historic Stag Brewery in Mortlake, London, formerly Watney's, where the British version of Budweiser is brewed. It's not known where the brand will be produced following the closure of the Mortlake plant but it's unlikely that many readers of the Good Beer Guide will care. In 2000 Interbrew, as it was then known, bought both Bass's and Whitbread's brewing operations, giving it a 32 per cent market share. The British government told Interbrew to dispose of parts of the Bass brewing group, which were bought by Coors, now Molson Coors (qv). Draught Bass has declined to around 37,000 barrels a year: it once sold close to one million barrels a year, but was sidelined by the Bass empire. It is now brewed under licence by Marston's (qv). Cask conditioned Boddingtons was brewed for AB InBev by Hydes but the contract expired in 2012 and the beer is currently not being brewed. AB InBev has put Draught Bass, Boddingtons and Flowers cask beers up for sale for £15 million.

Abbey SIBA ◉

Abbey Brewery, Camden Row, Bath, BA1 5LB
☎ (01225) 444437 ⊕ abbeyales.co.uk
Tours by arrangement

Founded in 1997, Abbey Ales was the first brewery in Bath for over 50 years. It supplies more than 80 regular outlets within a 20-mile radius of Bath, while selected wholesalers deliver beer nationally. It has four tied houses one of which, the Star Inn in Bath, is one of CAMRA's Real Heritage Pubs. Seasonal beers: see website.

Bellringer (OG 1042, ABV 4.2%) ◄
A notably hoppy ale, light to medium-bodied, clean-tasting, refreshingly dry, with a balancing sweetness. Citrus, pale malt aroma and dry, bitter finish.

Abbey Grange

See Llangollen

Abbeydale SIBA ◉

Unit 8, Aizlewood Road, Sheffield, South Yorkshire, S8 0YX
☎ (0114) 281 2712 ⊕ abbeydalebrewery.co.uk

Since starting in 1996, Abbeydale Brewery has grown steadily; it now produces upwards of 130 barrels a week, and recent investment has enabled further growth. The regular range is complemented by ever-changing seasonals – see website.

Matins (OG 1034.9, ABV 3.6%)
Pale and full flavoured; a hoppy session beer.

Brimstone (OG 1039, ABV 3.9%)
A russet-coloured bitter beer with a distinctive hop aroma.

Moonshine (OG 1041.2, ABV 4.3%)
A beautifully balanced pale ale with a full hop aroma. Pleasant grapefruit traces may be detected.

Absolution (OG 1050, ABV 5.3%)
A fruity pale ale, deceptively drinkable for its strength. Sweetish but not cloying.

Black Mass (OG 1065, ABV 6.7%)
A strong black stout with complex roast flavours and a lasting bitter finish.

Last Rites (OG 1097, ABV 11%) ⎙

Acorn SIBA ◉

Unit 3, Aldham Industrial Estate, Mitchell Road, Wombwell, Barnsley, South Yorkshire, S73 8HA
☎ (01226) 270734 ⊕ acorn-brewery.co.uk
Shop Mon-Fri 9am-5pm
Tours by arrangement

⊛Acorn was set up in 2003 with a 10-barrel plant expanding to 20-barrels when the brewery moved to larger premises and currently has a 160-barrel a week capacity. All beers are produced using the Barnsley Bitter yeast strain, dating back to the 1850s. Seasonal and bottle-conditioned beers – see website.

Yorkshire Pride (OG 1037, ABV 3.7%) ◄
A golden coloured bitter with hint of wheat and a clean bitter finish. Very drinkable session beer.

Barnsley Bitter (OG 1038, ABV 3.8%) ⎙ ▮ ◄
A smooth malty bitter with notes of chocolate and caramel. Fruity bitter finish.

Barnsley Gold (OG 1041.5, ABV 4%) ◄
Fruit in the aroma and taste. There is also a hoppy flavour throughout. A well-hopped, clean, dry finish.

Blonde (OG 1040.5, ABV 4%) ◄
A clean tasting hoppy beer with a refreshing bitter and fruity aftertaste.

Old Moor Porter (OG 1045, ABV 4.4%) ◄
A rich tasting porter, smooth throughout with a hint of chocolate. Leaves you wanting more.

Sovereign (OG 1044, ABV 4.4%) ◄
Malt and hop aroma, a roast nut and burnt bitterness and a hint of sulphur throughout.

Gorlovka Imperial Stout (OG 1058, ABV 6%) ⎙ ◄
Full of chocolate and liquorish flavours. Rich and smooth with a fruity creamy finish.

Adkin

Correspondence only: c/o 52 Adkin Way, Wantage, Oxfordshire, OX12 9HW
☎ 07709 86149 ⊕ adkinbrewery.co.uk
Tours by arrangement

Adkin was established on a 0.5-barrel plant in 2007. Eleven brews are produced by prior order. The beers are most easily found at regional beer festivals, but are starting to appear in the local free trade. Bottle-conditioned beers are available.

Adnams SIBA ⟨⊙⟩

Sole Bay Brewery, East Green, Southwold, Suffolk, IP18 6JW
☎ (01502) 727200 ⊕ adnams.co.uk
Shop 10am-6pm daily
Tours by arrangement

⊠ The company was founded by George and Ernest Adnams in 1872. About 70 pubs are owned and there is national distribution. Beers are from a new 300 barrel plant within the confines of the present site. Head brewer Fergus Fitzgerald was named Brewer of the Year by the Parliamentary Beer Club in 2013. Seasonal beers: see website.

Sole Star (OG 1032, ABV 2.7%)
A light bitter.

Lighthouse (OG 1037, ABV 3.4%) ◄
A quaffable beer with bitterness predominating.

Southwold Bitter (OG 1037, ABV 3.7%) ⬧ ◄
Aromas of toffee apple, caramel and sulphur. Taste is a complex mix of malt, toffee and roast bitterness with hops. Malty bitter and apple flavours linger into the aftertaste.

Gunhill (OG 1045, ABV 4%)

Old Ale (OG 1044, ABV 4.1%) ⬛ ◄
Aromas of malt and soft cheese, leading into malty and sweet flavours with fruit berries and vanilla. Caramel and roast finish.

Explorer (OG 1042, ABV 4.3%) ⬧ ◄
Fruity bitter taste with very delicate sweet aftertaste.

Ghost Ship (OG 1046, ABV 4.5%)

Broadside (OG 1049, ABV 4.7%) ◄
Rich, malty aroma with blackberries and dried fruit. Rich and full flavours of malt and fruit, with roast and caramel notes and subtle hops. Well-balanced, long-lasting aftertaste.

Adur

Brick Barn, Charlton Court, Mouse Lane, Steyning, West Sussex, BN44 3DG
☎ (01903) 867614

Office: 2 Sullington Way, Shoreham-by-Sea, West Sussex, BN43 6PJ ⊕ adurvalleycoop.com
Tours by arrangement

⊠ Adur Brewery was launched in 2008 on a 5.5-barrel plant, marking the return of brewing to the Adur Valley after an interval of nearly 100 years. A large part of the output is sold as bottle-conditioned beer. In summer 2013, the brewery was in the course of a transition to a co-op. See the website for the latest information.

Ropetackle Golden Ale (OG 1036, ABV 3.4%)
A light, golden ale with an initial sweetness and delicate aroma balanced by a dry finish.

Hop Token: Amarillo (OG 1040, ABV 4%)
An amber bitter, made with Amarillo hops, giving notes of peach and grapefruit in both aroma and taste, a good bitterness and a long, dry finish.

Hop Token: Summit (OG 1040, ABV 4%)

Velocity (OG 1044, ABV 4.4%)
Traditional best bitter with a hoppy aroma and a hint of marmalade in the taste.

Black William (OG 1055, ABV 5%)
A rich, black stout with dark chocolate aromas and roasted flavours.

Robbie's Red (OG 1050, ABV 5.2%)
A strong red-brown ale with an aroma of malt and hops. Slight initial sweetness leads into complex flavours including smoky orange peel.

Adventure (NEW)

Sutton, Surrey
☎ 07768 045674 ⊕ adventurebrewery.com

⊠ Adventure began brewing in 2012 on a 2.5-barrel plant in a converted garage in a residential property in Sutton. Seasonal and bottle-conditioned beers are also available.

North (ABV 4.5%)
Rich yet easy-drinking dark amber beer. Toasted malts with blackcurrant undertones.

South (ABV 5%)
A subtle bitter. Hints of lychee and passion fruit make this an easy-drinking session ale.

West (ABV 5.8%)
A rich, strong porter. Mocha and espresso flavours, followed by a smooth bitterness.

East (ABV 6.6%)
A big, bold IPA. Hints of gooseberries and a lingering dry but fruity finish.

Alcazar SIBA

⧮ Alcazar Brewery, Church Street, Old Basford, Nottingham, NG6 0GA
☎ (0115) 978 2282

Office: Turnstone Taverns, c/o Railway Tavern, 188 Station Road, Langley Mill, Nottinghamshire, NG16 4AE ⊕ turnstonetaverns.co.uk
Tours by arrangement

Alcazar was established in 1999 and is located behind its brewery tap, the Fox & Crown. The brewery is full mash with a 10-barrel brew length. Seasonal beers are available.

Sheriffs Gold (OG 1036, ABV 3.6%) ◄
Slightly sweet yellow session bitter made with First Gold and Goldings hops.

Alcazar Ale (OG 1040, ABV 4%) ◄
Flagship golden ale, full of citrus hops with a dry, bitter aftertaste.

New Dawn (OG 1045, ABV 4.5%) ◄
Full-bodied golden ale, brewed with Cascade hops.

Foxtail (OG 1049, ABV 4.9%) ◄
A strong malty and bitter brown ale. Named 'Brush Bitter' in the brewery tap.

Vixen's Vice (OG 1052, ABV 5.2%) ◄
A premium strength hoppy pale ale.

Ale Craft

See Verulam

Alechemy SIBA

Unit 2c, Young Square, Brucefield Industrial Estate, Livingston, West Lothian, EH54 9BX
☎ 07748 156973 ⊕ alechemybrewing.com

Dr James Davies, a keen brewer and chemist, started brewing on a 10-barrel plant in 2012.

Further beers are planned. Seasonal beers: see website.

Cairnpapple IPA (OG 1042, ABV 4.1%) ◆
Well-balanced golden ale. A strong hop character, balanced by malt and fruit with a long, dry finish.

Five Sisters (OG 1045, ABV 4.3%) ◆
A tawny beer with an excellent balance of malt, hops and fruit plus hints of roast and caramel. Lingering distinctive finish.

Cockleroy Black IPA (OG 1047, ABV 4.6%) ◆
A dark robust beer with substantial malt and significant hop character. Roast, caramel and fruit add to the complexity.

Ales of Scilly SIBA

2b Porthmellon Industrial Estate, St Mary's, Isles of Scilly, Cornwall, TR21 0JY
☎ (01720) 423233 ☎ 07810 816681
✉ mark@alesofscilly.co.uk
Shop by arrangement with the brewer – call first
Tours by arrangement

⊠ Opened in 2001, Ales of Scilly is the most south-westerly brewery in Britain. Nine local pubs are supplied, with regular exports to mainland pubs and beer festivals. Seasonal beers are available.

Scuppered (OG 1043, ABV 4.6%) ◆
Faint aroma of malt and apples giving sweet maltiness balanced by bitterness and fruit esters. Malt and sweet fruit finish.

Alfred's (NEW) SIBA

5B Scylla Industrial Estate, Winnall Valley Road, Winchester, Hampshire, SO23 0LD
☎ (01962) 859999 ☎ 07980 483124
⊕ alfredsbrewery.co.uk
Shop Fri 3-7pm; Sat 9.30am-12.30pm
Tours by arrangement

⊠ Alfred's is a four-barrel brewhouse opened by Steve and Isabelle Haigh in 2012. Steve previously brewed for three other renowned Hampshire breweries. Beers are distributed within 15 miles of Winchester.

Saxon Bronze (OG 1038, ABV 3.8%)
Three speciality malts combine to produce a distinct, bronze brew. Tangerine and citrus fruit from the hops lead to a clean finish.

All Hallows (NEW)

⊟ Goodmanham Arms, Main Street, Goodmanham, East Yorkshire, YO43 3JA
☎ (01430) 873849

⊕Abbie Logozzi started brewing in 2012 in outbuildings behind the Goodmanham Arms and is currently using both a one and a five-barrel plant. Beer is brewed for the pub but is supplied to beer festivals on request, and also to the free trade.

Peg Fyfe Dark Mild (OG 1036, ABV 3.6%)

Mischief Maker (OG 1040, ABV 4%)

Allendale SIBA ◉

Allen Mills, Allendale, Northumberland, NE47 9EQ
☎ (01434) 618686 ⊕ allendalebrewery.com
Shop Mon-Fri 9am-5pm
Tours by arrangement

⊕Brewing returned to Allendale in 2006 and the business now supplies over 300 pubs, shops and restaurants across the North of England from its 10 barrel plant. Seasonal beers: see website.

North Sheep (OG 1036, ABV 3.6%)
A light summery ale, golden amber in colour.

Wagtail Best Bitter (OG 1037, ABV 3.8%) ◆
Amber bitter with spicy aromas and a long, bitter finish.

Golden Plover (OG 1039, ABV 4%) ◆
Light, refreshing, easy-drinking blonde beer with a clean finish.

Pennine Pale (OG 1040, ABV 4%)
A light golden ale with a full citrus fruit flavour and a refreshing finish.

Swift (OG 1045, ABV 4.5%)
Golden Amber ale with a delicious grapefruit hop bite. Full bodied with a hoppy finish.

Adder Lager (OG 1050, ABV 5%)
Crisp, refreshing Pilsner style lager, slow fermented and traditionally lagered at 0 deg C for 8 weeks.

APA (OG 1056, ABV 5.5%)
A full bodied IPA with citrus and tropical aromas, full of flavour and refreshing bitterness.

Wolf (OG 1053, ABV 5.5%) ◆
Full-bodied red ale with bitterness in the taste giving way to a fruity finish.

AllGates SIBA ◉

The Old Brewery, Brewery Yard, off Wallgate, Wigan, WN1 1JU
☎ (01942) 234976 ⊕ allgatesbrewery.com
Tours by arrangement

⊕AllGates commenced brewing 2006 in a fully-restored Grade II-listed tower brewery at the rear of Wigan's General Post Office as a modern five-barrel plant. Beers are principally delivered to its own estate of eight pubs. Seasonal beers and monthly specials: see website.

All Black (OG 1036, ABV 3.6%) ◆
Dark brown beer with a malty, fruity aroma. Creamy and malty in taste, with blackberry fruits and a satisfying aftertaste.

Ostara (OG 1036, ABV 3.6%)

California (OG 1037, ABV 3.8%) ◆
A pale yellow beer with a restrained hoppy and fruity aroma. It is clean and fresh tasting, with hops and fruit in the mouth and a bitter hoppy finish.

Napoleon's Retreat (OG 1038, ABV 3.9%)
A deep golden/copper-coloured traditional bitter.

Pretoria (OG 1039, ABV 3.9%)

Citra (OG 1042, ABV 4.2%)

Allsaints

c/o Coastal Brewery, Unit 10B, Cardrew Industrial Estate, Redruth, Cornwall, TR15 1SS

Formerly known as Doghouse Brewery, which closed in 2007, Allsaints recommenced production in 2008 and currently use spare capacity at Coastal Brewery in Redruth. Four regular beers are produced (see Coastal for beer list) and changing seasonal beers.

Alnwick

See Hadrian & Border

Amber SIBA

Unit A, Asher Lane Business Park, Pentrich, Ripley, Derbyshire, DE5 3SW
☎ (01773) 512864 ⊕ amberales.co.uk
Tours by arrangement

Amber Ales began production in 2006 on a five-barrel plant. Five core beers are produced and a range of experimental and seasonal ales all available at the brewery tap, the Talbot Taphouse in Ripley. Around 50 outlets are supplied direct, further afield via distributors. Bottle-conditioned beers are available and are suitable for vegetarians and vegans.

Chocolate Orange Stout (OG 1040, ABV 4%)

Derbyshire Gold (OG 1039, ABV 4%)

Original Black Stout (OG 1040, ABV 4%)

Barnes Wallis (OG 1040, ABV 4.1%)

Revolution (OG 1047, ABV 4.5%)

Dambuster (OG 1051, ABV 5.5%)

Imperial IPA (OG 1058, ABV 6.5%)

Ambridge (NEW)

Unit 2a, Priory Piece Business Park, Priory Farm Lane, Inkberrow, Worcestershire, WR7 4HT
☎ (01386) 792233 ☎ 07964 630355
⊕ ambridgebrewery.co.uk

⊕Ambridge began brewing in 2013 initially for the family pub, the Bulls Head in Inkberrow. In April 2013 they acquired the Wyre Piddle Brewery, the beers from which continue to be brewed. Further beers including seasonals are planned.

IPB Mild (OG 1039, ABV 3.9%)
A typical Midlands county mild with a good balance of hops and a malty, roast flavour.

Just Jane (OG 1039, ABV 4%)
A refreshing golden session beer. Hops are balanced by malt throughout.

Bomber (OG 1040, ABV 4.2%)
A pale ale with flavours of tropical fruits, citrus and pine.

Red Zeppelin (OG 1040, ABV 4.2%)
A deep amber/red ale with a distinctive hop aroma and palate.

Shires Bitter (OG 1044, ABV 4.5%)
A premium bitter with a good balance of hops and malt. Hops carry on in the bittersweet finish.

Young Blonde (OG 1049, ABV 4.9%)
A blonde beer with a hoppy, dry finish.

Under the Wyre Piddle name:

Piddle in the Hole (OG 1039, ABV 3.9%)

Piddle in the Dark (OG 1045, ABV 4.5%)

Piddle in the Wind (OG 1045, ABV 4.5%)

An Teallach

Camusnagaul, Dundonnell, Garve, Ross-shire, IV23 2QT
☎ (01854) 633306 ✉ ataleco1@yahoo.co.uk

Tours by arrangement

An Teallach was formed in 2001 by husband and wife team David and Wilma Orr on Wilma's family croft on the shores of Little Loch Broom, Wester Ross. 60 pubs are supplied.

Beinn Dearg Ale (OG 1038, ABV 3.8%) ◗

Ale (OG 1042, ABV 4.2%) ◗
A classic pint in the Scottish 80/- tradition. Plenty of malt in the nicely-balanced bittersweet taste.

Crofters Pale Ale (OG 1042, ABV 4.2%) ◗
A good quaffing, lightly-flavoured golden ale. Citrus hops in the taste and with a slight astringency in the finish.

Suilven (OG 1043, ABV 4.3%) ◗
A refreshing yellow brew with plenty of citrus fruits and hops throughout.

Kildonan (OG 1044, ABV 4.4%) ◗
Plenty of fruit and a good smack of bitterness in this golden ale.

Anarchy SIBA

Unit 5, Whitehouse Farm Centre, Stannington, Northumberland, NE61 6AW
☎ (01670) 789755 ☎ 07702 810111
⊕ anarchybrewco.com
Shop 12-5.30pm first Sat of month
Tours by arrangement

⊕Formerly known as Brew Star, Anarchy began brewing in 2012 and sells a range of hand crafted ales and lagers to outlets nationwide, focusing on the North East. Seasonal and bottle-conditioned beer is also available.

Smoke Bomb (OG 1043, ABV 3.9%)
The smoked malt takes centre stage giving way to oranges, pine and lychees. Lasting bitterness.

Blonde Star (OG 1041, ABV 4.1%)

Citra Star (OG 1041, ABV 4.1%)
A blonde, refreshing session beer.

Rough Justice (OG 1046, ABV 4.5%)

Grin & Bare It (OG 1050, ABV 5%)

Crime Scene (OG 1056, ABV 5.5%)
Big tropical fruit flavours, smooth and creamy with a lasting bitterness. Tangerine, clementine and pineapple aromas.

Quiet Riot (OG 1063, ABV 6.6%)
Smooth and bitter profiles give way to huge fruit flavours. Passionfruit, mango, orange and guava on the nose.

Sublime Chaos (OG 1075, ABV 7%)
Stout infused with Ethiopian Guji coffee beans, with rich dark malt and oat flavours and a silky smooth finish.

Anchor Springs SIBA

Lineside Way, Wick, West Sussex, BN17 7EH
✉ debbie@jenkinslittlehampton.co.uk

Kevin Jenkins, owner of the Crown in Littlehampton, established the brewery in 2010 using the five-barrel plant previously used at the Dark Star brewery. The main outlets are its brewery tap, the Crown in Littlehampton, and the Spy Glass in Worthing.

LA Gold (OG 1039.5, ABV 3.7%)

A golden session ale; initial sweetness leads to a citrus kick and lingering crisp, clean finish.

Mild (OG 1045.5, ABV 3.8%)

IPA (OG 1042.5, ABV 4%)
A full-bodied, complex beer with a good mouthfeel and lingering hop finish. Light gold in colour, initial sweetness gives way to malt then a dry aftertaste.

Worthing Best (OG 1045, ABV 4%)
A sweet initial taste is followed by bitter sharpness. A good malty mouthfeel with more dark berry fruit leads to a lingering, rising bitter finish.

Riptide (OG 1045, ABV 4.1%)
Copper-coloured ale, lightly hopped with a malted caramel nose. Initial sweetness of milk chocolate leads to a complex palate and bitter finish.

Hornblower (OG 1045, ABV 4.5%)

Mothers Ruin (OG 1063, ABV 6%)
Copper red-coloured ale, very malty and with spices and orange zest, a very complex flavour with a balance of sweetness and bitter finish.

Andrews

1 Railway Cottages, Cummertrees, Dumfriesshire, DG12 5QG
☎ (01461) 700387
✉ aemmerson999@googlemail.com

Andrews Ales began brewing in 2011 using a one-barrel plant but soon expanded to three barrels. Regular and seasonal beers are supplied direct to local pubs.

Supus Lupus (OG 1036, ABV 3.6%)

Cummertrees Pale Ale (OG 1041, ABV 4%)

Tinfast (OG 1044, ABV 4.3%)

Andwell SIBA ◉

Andwell Lane, Andwell, Hampshire, RG27 9PA
☎ (01256) 761044 ⊕ andwells.com
Shop Mon-Fri 10am-6pm; Sat 10.30am-1pm
Tours by arrangement

⊗ Andwell Brewing Company commenced brewing in 2008 on a 10-barrel plant. The brewery relocated and expanded in 2011 to an idyllic riverside location with a new bespoke 20-barrel plant and now offers tours and direct sales from its brewery shop. Beer is distributed within a 40-mile radius of the brewery. More than 200 outlets are supplied. Seasonal beers are available.

Resolute Bitter (OG 1038, ABV 3.8%) ◀
An easy-drinking session bitter. A malty aroma leads into an initially malty flavour with some bitterness and a sweetish finish.

Gold Muddler (OG 1039, ABV 3.9%) ◀
Although light golden in colour, this is a standard bitter, with an aroma of hops and malt. These characteristics are carried into the flavour with a solid bitterness and a dry, biscuity finish.

King John (OG 1042, ABV 4.2%) ◀
Malty best bitter, low in hops with a short initial bitterness and a underlying sweetness, leading to some dryness in the finish.

Rudy Darter (OG 1047, ABV 4.6%)
A ruby chestnut-coloured ale with a hoppy, spicy aroma and a full-bodied and fruity taste with a dry finish.

Angel SIBA

62a Furlong Lane, Halesowen, West Midlands, B63 2TA
☎ 07847 300350 ⊕ angelales.co.uk

Angel Ales began brewing in 2011. The brewery building has been a Chapel of Rest, a coffin makers' workshop and a pattern makers before becoming a brewhouse. All beers are produced using organic ingredients and are vegan-friendly where possible. Seasonal beers: see website.

Ale (OG 1042, ABV 4.1%)
A pale beer with a citrus nose and a lingering bitter finish.

Animal

See XT

Appleford SIBA

Unit 14, Highlands Farm, High Road, Brightwell-cum-Sotwell, Wallingford, Oxfordshire, OX10 0QX
☎ (01235) 848055 ⊕ applefordbrewery.co.uk

Appleford Brewery opened in 2006 when two farm units were converted to house an eight-barrel plant. Deliveries are made to a number of local outlets as well as nationally, via the brewery or wholesalers. Occasional and bottle-conditioned beers are available.

Brightwell Gold (OG 1041, ABV 4%)

Power Station (OG 1043, ABV 4.2%)
A copper-coloured, slightly malty bitter.

Arbor SIBA ◉

Unit 4, Lawrence Hill Industrial Estate, Croydon Street, Bristol, BS5 0EB
☎ (0117) 329 2711 ⊕ arborales.co.uk

⊗ Arbor Ales opened in 2007 in the back of the Old Tavern pub. In 2012 it moved and expanded to a new 12-barrel plant. Two pubs are owned. A wide range of beers are brewed with particular pride taken in the darker ales due to the brewer's involvement with the Bristol & District Rare Ales Group (www.badrag.co.uk). Seasonal beers are available: see website. Around 200 outlets are supplied direct.

Hoptical Delusion (ABV 3.8%)

Brigstow Bitter (OG 1042, ABV 4.3%) ◀
Mid-brown best bitter in the Bristol style with plenty of malt and fruit on the tongue. Bitter balancing hop with a long and fruity finish.

Oyster Stout (OG 1046.5, ABV 4.6%) ◀
A rich stout with chocolate undertones. Real oysters are added in the copper. Fruity and roast flavours with a creamy mouthfeel.

Yakima Valley (ABV 7.3%)

Archerfield

See Knops

Archers

See Evan Evans

Ards

34B Carrowdore Road, Newtonards, Co Down,
BT22 2LX
☎ 07515 558406
✉ ardsbrewing@blackwood34.plus.com

Ards began brewing in 2011 using a 100 litre plant.

Pig Island Pale (ABV 4.9%)
Fruity pale ale with orangey notes.

Argyll SIBA

⊟ Cuan Mor, 60 George Street, Oban, Argyll, PA34 5DS
☎ (01631) 565078 ⊕ obanbaybrewery.co.uk
Tours by arrangement

Argyll Breweries was formed in 2010 following the merger of Oban Bay and Isle of Mull breweries, continuing to trade under those names. Cask production is only at the Oban site.

Kilt Lifter (OG 1039, ABV 3.9%)

Skinny Blonde (OG 1041, ABV 4.1%)

Ginger Jakey (OG 1042, ABV 4.2%)

Skelpt Lug (OG 1042, ABV 4.2%)

Fair Puggled (OG 1045, ABV 4.5%)

Arkell's SIBA IFBB ⊚

Kingsdown, Swindon, Wiltshire, SN2 7RU
☎ (01793) 823026 ⊕ arkells.com
Brewery merchandise can be purchased at reception
Tours by arrangement

Arkells Brewery was established in 1843 and is still run by the family. The brewery owns 99 pubs in Berkshire, Gloucestershire, Oxfordshire and Wiltshire. Seasonal beers: see website.

2B (OG 1035, ABV 3.2%) ◕
Light brown in colour, malty but with a smack of hops and an astringent aftertaste. It has good body for its strength.

3B (OG 1040, ABV 4%) ◕
A medium brown beer with a strong, sweetish malt/caramel flavour. The hops come through strongly in the aftertaste, which is lingering and dry.

Wiltshire Gold (OG 1040, ABV 4%)
A light golden-coloured ale with a sweet, malty flavour, a mellow floral hop aroma and distinctive hoppy taste.

Moonlight (OG 1045, ABV 4.5%)
A golden beer with a lingering taste, toasty aroma and citrus hoppiness.

Kingsdown Special Ale (OG 1050, ABV 5%) ◕
A rich, deep russet-coloured beer, a stronger version of 3B. The malty/fruity aroma continues in the taste, which has a hint of pears. Hops come through in the aftertaste.

Arkwright's

c/o The Real Ale Shop, 47 Lovat Road, Preston,
Lancashire, PR1 6DQ
☎ 07944 912326 ⊕ realaleshop.net

Arkwright's began brewing at the rear of the Real Ale Shop in 2010 using a 2.5-barrel plant.

Arran SIBA

Cladach, Brodick, Isle of Arran, North Ayrshire,
KA27 8DE
☎ (01770) 302353

Office: 100 Wellington Street, Glasgow, G2 6DH
⊕ arranbrewery.com
Shop summer Mon-Sat 10am-5pm, Sun 12.30-4.30pm; winter Tue-Sat 10.30am-4.30pm, Sun-Mon closed
Tours by arrangement

The brewery opened in 2000 using a 20-barrel plant. 300 outlets are supplied direct. Seasonal and bottle-conditioned beers are also available.

Guid Ale (OG 1038, ABV 3.8%)

Red Squirrel (OG 1038, ABV 3.9%)
Session beer with balanced malty, hop blend containing hint of liquorice and burnt toffee with a characteristic nutty aroma.

Dark (OG 1042, ABV 4.3%) ◕
A well-balanced malty beer with plenty of roast and hop in the taste and a dry, bitter finish.

Sunset (OG 1042, ABV 4.4%)
A mid-amber summer ale, light perfumed aroma, good balance of malt, fruit and hops with a pleasant dry finish.

Clyde Puffer (OG 1045, ABV 4.5%)
A stout with a deep dark colour. Sweet and mellow with a low hop taster.

Fireside (OG 1044, ABV 4.7%)
A smooth malty brew with a pleasant hop character. A bittersweet finish with a hint of ginger.

Blonde (OG 1048, ABV 5%) ◕
A hoppy beer with substantial fruit balance. The taste is balanced and the finish increasingly bitter. An aromatic strong bitter that drinks below its weight.

Brewery Dug (ABV 5.5%)
An American style IPA with a fine aroma. Dry hopped for extra flavour.

Arrow

⊟ c/o Wine Vaults, 37 High Street, Kington,
Herefordshire, HR5 3BJ
☎ (01544) 230685 ✉ deanewright@yahoo.co.uk

Brewer Deane Wright built this five-barrel brewery at the rear of the Wine Vaults and started brewing in 2005. The Wine Vaults is the only pub outlet for Arrow Bitter.

Bitter (OG 1041, ABV 4.2%)

Art Brew SIBA

Art Brew Barn, Northend Farm, off Venn Lane, North Chideock, Dorset, DT6 6JY
☎ 07881 783626 ⊕ artbrew.co.uk

⊠ Brewing started in 2008 on a five-barrel plant with its own water source near the Jurassic Coast. The brewery also produces the Hip Hop series of beers, one of which is always available, using a different single hop each time (ABV 4.3%). Around 120 outlets are supplied throughout the country. Bottle-conditioned beers are available. Seasonal beers: see website.

Art Nouveau (ABV 3.9%)
Golden and hoppy.

i Beer (ABV 4%)
Speciality vanilla beer.

Monkey IPA (OG 1058, ABV 6.4%)
Massively hopped proper IPA.

Orange IPA (ABV 6.4%)

Spanked Monkey IPA (ABV 6.4%)

Artisan

183a Kings Road, Cardiff, Glamorgan, CF11 9DF
☎ 07505 401939 ⊕ artisanbeer.co.uk
Tours by arrangement

Artisan was established in 2008. No real ale but all beers are unfiltered, without additives or preservatives and suitable for vegans.

Arundel SIBA ◉

Unit C7, Ford Airfield Industrial Estate, Ford, Arundel, West Sussex, BN18 0HY
☎ (01903) 733111 ⊕ arundelbrewery.co.uk
Off-sales available Mon-Fri 9am-4pm at brewery
Tours by arrangement (1st Sat of month, 11am & 2pm)

⊗ Founded in 1992, Arundel Brewery is the historic town's first brewery in more than 70 years. A range of occasional brands is available in selected months. Seasonal beers: see website.

Castle (OG 1038, ABV 3.8%) ◄
A pale tawny beer with fruit and malt noticeable in the aroma. The flavour has a good balance of malt, fruit and hops, with a dry, hoppy finish.

Sussex Gold (OG 1042, ABV 4.2%) ◄
A golden-coloured best bitter with a strong floral hop aroma. The ale is clean-tasting and bitter for its strength, with a tangy citrus flavour. The initial hop and fruit die to a dry and bitter finish.

Heritage IPA (OG 1045, ABV 4.5%)
Formerly known as ASB. A special bitter with a complex roast malt flavour leading to a fruity, hoppy, bittersweet finish.

Stronghold (OG 1047, ABV 4.7%) ◄
A smooth, full-flavoured premium bitter. A good balance of malt, fruit and hops comes through in this rich, chestnut-coloured beer.

Trident (OG 1050, ABV 5%)
An amber-coloured strong beer with a citrus, fruity aroma. The taste is clean and refreshing with a hoppy, fruity flavour and a dry, bitter finish.

Ascot SIBA ◉

Unit 5, Compton Place Business Centre, Surrey Avenue, Camberley, Surrey, GU15 3DX
☎ (01276) 686696 ⊕ ascot-ales.co.uk
Shop Mon-Fri 10am-3pm
Tours by arrangement

⊗ Ascot Ales began production in 2007 on a four-barrel plant. The addition of a fourth fermenter has given scope for more seasonal/one off brews including their single hop series. Bottle-conditioned beers are available and suitable for vegetarians and vegans.

Aureole Ale (OG 1032, ABV 3.3%)
Golden ale with a citrus flavour.

Alley Cat Ale (OG 1038, ABV 3.8%) ◄
A pale brown session bitter with citrus hop present throughout, but balanced by malt. Dry with a lasting bitter finish.

On the Rails (OG 1039, ABV 3.8%) ◄
Dark, fruity and roasty mild with a notable hop character throughout, bittersweet in the taste and aftertaste.

Posh Pooch (OG 1042, ABV 4.2%) ◄
A hoppy best bitter with balancing biscuity malt sweetness. The citrus fruitiness lasts throughout. Clean hoppy aftertaste.

Penguin Porter (OG 1045, ABV 4.5%)

Alligator Ale (OG 1047, ABV 4.6%) ◄
American hops provide grapefruit notes in this golden ale. Hop and bitterness dominate, but there is some balancing biscuit in the aroma and taste. A residual sweetness remains even in the sharp, dry finish.

Single Hop (OG 1045, ABV 4.6%)
Copper IPA brewed each month showcasing a single hop variety.

Anastasia's Exile Stout (OG 1049, ABV 5%) 🗂 ◄
Burnt coffee aromas lead to a roast malt flavour in this black beer. Notably fruity throughout. The presence of some hop feeds into the bittersweet aftertaste.

Red IPA (OG 1054, ABV 5.5%)
An intensely hopped red IPA, using several varieties of New World hops to give a citrus, grapefruit taste.

Ashley Down

15 Wathen Road, St Andrews, Bristol, BS6 5BY
☎ (0117) 983 6567
✉ ashleydownbrewery@gmail.com

⊗ Ashley Down began brewing in 2011. An 8.5-barrel plant is used in the owner's large garage.

Vanguard (OG 1042, ABV 3.9%) ◄
A dark mild style ale with strong roast on the nose. Fruit and malt on the tongue with a dry finish.

Landlord's Best (OG 1040, ABV 4.2%) ◄
Best bitter with hints of toffee and fruit. Malty aroma with a hint of sulphur. A well balanced flavour with an astringent aftertaste.

Pale Ale (OG 1040, ABV 4.3%) ◄
A good balance between malt and hoppy bitterness.

Ashover SIBA

🏠 1 Butts Road, Ashover, Chesterfield, Derbyshire, S45 0EW
☎ 07803 708526 ⊕ ashoverbrewery.com
Tours by arrangement

Ashover Brewery first brewed in 2007 on a 3.5-barrel plant in the garage of the cottage next to the Old Poets' Corner pub. The brewery caters mainly for this and its sister pub, the Poet and Castle in Codnor. Other local free houses and festivals are also supplied.

Light Rail (OG 1038, ABV 3.7%) ◄
Light in colour and taste, with initial sweet and malt flavours, leading to a bitter finish and aftertaste.

Poets Tipple (OG 1041, ABV 4%) ◄

Complex, tawny-coloured beer that drinks above its strength. Predominantly malty in flavour, with increasing bitterness towards the end.

Hydro (OG 1043, ABV 4.2%) 🍷 ◆
Easy-drinking golden beer with a predominantly hoppy aroma. Hop and fruit flavours and an initial sweetness lead to a dry, clean finish and aftertaste.

Rainbows End (OG 1045, ABV 4.5%) ◆
Slightly smooth, bitter golden beer with an initial sweetness. Grapefruit and lemon hop flavours come through strongly as the beer gets increasingly dry towards the finish, ending with a bitter, dry aftertaste.

Coffin Lane Stout (OG 1050, ABV 5%) ◆
Excellent example of the style, with a chocolate and coffee flavour, balanced by a little sweetness. Finish is long and quite dry.

Butts Pale Ale (OG 1055, ABV 5.5%) ◆
Pale and strong yet easy to drink golden bitter. Combination of bitter and sweet flavours mingle with an alcoholic kick, leading to a warming yet bitter finish and aftertaste.

Atlantic

Treisaac Farm, Treisaac, Newquay, Cornwall, TR8 4DX
☎ (01637) 880326 ⊕ atlanticbrewery.com

Atlantic is a specialist microbrewery producing organic and vegan ales. All ales are unfiltered and finings-free. There are nine core brews including four food-matched Dining Ales developed with Michelin chef Nathan Outlaw. Casks are supplied locally and to London, with bottles available nationally.

Ale (OG 1038, ABV 4%) ◆
A pale amber ale, with good body, sweet malt and hints of vanilla. Well-hopped yet balanced.

Gold (OG 1043, ABV 4.6%) ◆
Refreshing, crisp golden ale lightly spiced with zingy ginger. Finishing with the lingering light marmalade of First Gold hops.

Blue (OG 1045, ABV 4.8%) ◆
This dark ruby porter floods the palate with sweet malt, roast coffee, dark chocolate, a soft smokiness and orangey nose.

Red (OG 1047, ABV 5%) ◆
Full-bodied red ale with hints of caramel and nuttiness. The dryness of the big hop finish is balanced by sweet malt.

Fistral (OG 1048, ABV 5.2%) ◆
A creamy, crisp golden beer using extra pale and wheat malt. Refreshing citrus tangs and floral hop notes with sweetness.

Discovery – Easterly (OG 1050, ABV 5.5%) ◆
A golden pale ale with crisp distinct flavours of lime, chilli and ginger. Sweet malt balances the citrus aroma tones.

Discovery – Northerly (OG 1050, ABV 5.5%) ◆
Rich Cornish porter with blackcurrant and molasses. Full-bodied dark roasted malts, hints of chocolate, ripe blackcurrants and black cherries.

Discovery – Southerly (OG 1050, ABV 5.5%) ◆
Smooth blonde ale with elderflower and lemon. Gentle hops, sweet malt with a floral and citrus zest finish.

Discovery – Westerly (OG 1050, ABV 5.5%) ◆

Red Celtic ale with cinnamon and orange. Full-bodied bitter with gentle citrus marmalade and mild nutty spice flavours.

Atlas

See Orkney

Atomic

⧉ c/o Alexandra Arms, 72-73 St James Street, Rugby, Warwickshire, CV21 2SL
☎ (01788) 576194

Correspondence: 1 Lower Hillmorton Road, Rugby, Warwickshire, CV21 3ST ⊕ atomicbrewery.com
Tours by arrangement

Atomic Brewery started production in 2006 and is run by CAMRA members Keith Abbis and Nick Pugh. Two pubs are owned, the Victoria Inn and the Alexandra Arms in Rugby, the latter being where the brew plant resides.

Strike (OG 1039, ABV 3.7%)
A pale golden ale with a sharp, fruity aroma and a good sharp, bitter finish.

Fission (OG 1040, ABV 3.9%)
An amber-coloured session ale with a well-hopped, lasting bitter finish.

Power (OG 1050, ABV 4.8%)
A deep ruby-coloured ale with a sweet chocolate aroma and taste. Bitterness develops and gives way to a pleasant chocolate finish.

Half-Life (OG 1051, ABV 5%)
A pale, well-hopped ale with a sharp fresh citrus bitterness.

Bomb (OG 1054, ABV 5.2%)
A powerful deep golden ale with a full aromatic nose and a well-hopped increasingly bitter finish.

Attwood ⓈⒾⒷⒶ ◎

Hartlebury Brewery, Station Road, Hartlebury, Worcestershire, DY11 7YJ
☎ (01384) 220046 ⊕ attwoodales.com

◎Attwood was established in 2011 using a 10-barrel plant. It is housed in old railway buildings, a conversion of the Hartlebury railway station.

Farmers Dark Ale (OG 1038.8, ABV 3.7%)
A smooth, dark session ale; slightly smoky with a caramel finish.

Attwood's Pale Ale (APA) (OG 1039.8, ABV 4%)
A crisp, light and refreshing IPA with a clean bitterness and hoppy aroma.

Nectar Bitter (OG 1043.8, ABV 4.2%)
A light golden bitter, well-balanced with a gentle sweetness throughout.

O'Ryan's (OG 1049.8, ABV 5%)
A dark premium bitter with a bite.

Austendyke (NEW)

The Beeches, Austendyke Road, Weston Hills, Spalding, Lincolnshire, PE12 6BZ
☎ 07866 045778

Austendyke started brewing in 2012 on a seven-barrel plant. The brewery is operated on a part-time basis by brewer Charlie Rawlings and business partner Nathan Marshall.

Long Lane (OG 1039, ABV 4%)
A traditional copper-coloured bitter.

Holbeach High Street (OG 1045, ABV 4.5%)
An old fashioned dark best bitter.

Axholme SIBA

7H Lake Enterprise Park, Birkdale Road, Luddington, Lincolnshire, DN17 2AU
☎ 07551 910040

Office: 2 Garthorpe Road, Luddington, Lincolnshire, DN17 4QT ⊕ axholmebrewing.co.uk

Former Thorne brewer Mike Richards commissioned Scunthorpe's first-ever microbrewery in 2012 using a 2.5-barrel plant from Brupaks. Seasonal and one-off brews are also available.

Best Bitter (OG 1037.4, ABV 3.8%)

IPA (Isle Pale Ale) (OG 1039.8, ABV 4.1%)

Aylesbury

⊟ Hop Pole, 83 Bicester Road, Aylesbury, Buckinghamshire, HP19 9AZ
☎ (01844) 239237 ⊕ aylesburybrewhouse.co.uk
Shop Wed-Sat 12-6pm
Tours by arrangement

⊠ Established in 2011 at the Hop Pole as a sister brewery to Vale in Brill. Limited edition, one-off beers are brewed on a weekly basis.

Ayr SIBA

⊟ 5 Racecourse Road, Ayr, KA7 2DG
☎ (01292) 263891
✉ anthony.valenti@btinternet.com
Tours by arrangement

☺Ayr began brewing in 2009 on a five barrel plant and is located at the Glenpark Hotel. As well as the hotel, around 50 other outlets are supplied throughout Scotland and the north of England. Seasonal Beers are also available.

Leezie Lundie (OG 1037.5, ABV 3.8%) ◆
A pale golden session ale with hints of grapefruit and a dry lingering finish.

Jolly Beggars (OG 1041, ABV 4.2%) ◆
A complex best bitter with plenty of character and lingering malty after taste.

Rabbie's Porter (OG 1042.5, ABV 4.3%) ▮ ◆
A robust full-bodied porter with well-balanced toffee, fruity malt and a slightly smoky finish.

Towzie Tyke (OG 1044.5, ABV 4.6%)
An amber ale with a refreshingly dry, bitter finish.

B&T SIBA ◉

The Brewery, Shefford, Bedfordshire, SG17 5DZ
☎ (01462) 815080 ⊕ banksandtaylor.com
Tours by arrangement (CAMRA branches only)

⊠ Banks & Taylor – now just B&T – was founded in 1982. It produces an extensive range of beers, including monthly specials and occasional beers: see website for details. There are six tied houses, all sell B&T beers plus guest beers.

Two Brewers Bitter (OG 1036, ABV 3.6%) ◆
Bronze-coloured bitter with citrus hop aroma and taste and a dry finish.

Shefford Bitter (OG 1038, ABV 3.8%) ◆
A pale brown beer with a light hop aroma and a hoppy taste leading to a bitter finish.

Shefford Dark Mild (OG 1038, ABV 3.8%) ◆
A dark beer with a well-balanced taste. Sweetish, roast malt aftertaste.

Golden Fox (OG 1041, ABV 4.1%)
A golden, hoppy ale, dry tasting with a fruity aroma and citrus finish.

Fruit Bat (OG 1045, ABV 4.2%) ◆
A warming straw-coloured beer with a generous taste of raspberries and a bitter finish.

Black Dragon Mild (OG 1043, ABV 4.3%) ◆
Black in colour with a toffee and roast malt flavour and a smoky finish.

Dunstable Giant (OG 1044, ABV 4.4%)
Dark tawny bitter with a subtle blend of malt and hops.

Dragon Slayer (OG 1045, ABV 4.5%) ◆
A golden beer with a malt and hop flavour and a bitter finish. More malty and less hoppy than is usual for a beer of this style.

Edwin Taylor's Extra Stout (OG 1045, ABV 4.5%) ◆
A complex black beer with a bitter coffee and roast malt flavour and a dry, bitter finish.

Shefford Pale Ale (SPA) (OG 1045, ABV 4.5%) ◆
A well-balanced beer with hop, fruit and malt flavours. Dry, bitter aftertaste.

SOD (OG 1050, ABV 5%)
SOS with caramel added for colour.

SOS (OG 1050, ABV 5%) ◆
A rich mixture of fruit, hops and malt is present in the taste and aftertaste of this beer. Predominantly hoppy aroma.

Baby Ox

See Oxfordshire

Bacchus

⊟ Bacchus Hotel, 17 High Street, Sutton-on-Sea, Lincolnshire, LN12 2EY
☎ (01507) 441204 ⊕ bacchushotel.co.uk
Tours by arrangement

Bacchus began brewing in 2010 on a one-barrel plant supplying the Bacchus Hotel.

Bittermans (OG 1043, ABV 4%)

Best Bitter (OG 1043, ABV 4.3%)

Stingo (OG 1045, ABV 4.5%)

Backyard SIBA ◉

Unit 8a, Gatehouse Trading Estate, Lichfield Road, Brownhills, Walsall, West Midlands, WS8 6JZ
☎ 07591 923370 ⊕ thebackyardbrewhouse.com
Tours by arrangement

☺Backyard began brewing in 2008 and expanded in 2012 to a 12-barrel plant brewing up to 50 barrels a week. One pub is owned, the Fountain in

Walsall. Seasonal beers and monthly specials are available: see website.

Bitter (OG 1040, ABV 3.8%)
A blonde beer, slightly sweet with hints of tangerine and fruit salad.

The Hoard (OG 1040, ABV 3.9%)

Blonde (OG 1041, ABV 4.1%)

Badger

See Hall & Woodhouse

Baldy (NEW)

Unit 5b, The Old Sawyard, Parham House Estate, Greatham Lane, Pulborough, West Sussex, RH20 4HS
☎ 07718 641195

Office: 4 Winchester Court, Portchester Close, Southwater, West Sussex, RH13 9XU
⊕ thebaldybrewery.co.uk

Baldy began brewing in 2012 in Southwater, moving to new premises later that year on the Parham House Estate in Pulborough.

Kiln Dust (OG 1046, ABV 4.1%)
Silky and sweet to start with a balanced mouthfeel with hints of burnt sugar forged together with subtle hopping.

Shotgun (OG 1040, ABV 4.2%)
Smooth and complex in palate but not heavy. The roastness of the malts is complemented by large quantities of hops.

Southwater Gold (OG 1046, ABV 4.5%)
A golden amber ale with a sweet start and fresh floral hop notes. A balanced body complements a mildly bitter finish with a lasting mouthfeel.

Hops Save The Queen IPA (OG 1046, ABV 4.6%)
A steady bitterness is held throughout with moments of sweetness.

Blonde Bombshell (OG 1046, ABV 4.7%)
A hybrid of a lager and an ale combined with delicate hop additions.

Fiery Redhead (OG 1042, ABV 4.8%)
A clean and crisp ruby ale, rich in colour and not too heavy on the palate. A well-balanced body and character with a lively, lasting finish.

Sussex Superior XX (OG 1050, ABV 4.8%)
Sweet malts to the fore with a chocolate aroma, complemented by a fresh and tangy hop finish.

Ballard's ⟨SIBA⟩ ⟨◉⟩

The Old Sawmill, Nyewood, Petersfield, GU31 5HA
☎ (01730) 821362 ⊕ ballards-brewery.co.uk
Shop Mon-Fri 8am-4pm
Tours by arrangement

Launched in 1980 by Mike and Carola Brown at Cumbers Farm, Trotton, Ballard's has been trading at Nyewood since 1988 and now supplies 70-80 outlets. Seasonal beers: see website. Bottle-conditioned beers are also available.

Midhurst Mild (OG 1034, ABV 3.4%)
Traditional dark mild, well-balanced, refreshing, with a biscuity flavour.

Golden Bine (OG 1038, ABV 3.8%) ◄

Amber, clean-tasting bitter. A roast malt aroma leads to a fruity, slightly sweet taste and a dry finish.

Best Bitter (OG 1042, ABV 4.2%) ◄
A copper-coloured beer with a malty aroma. A good balance of fruit and malt in the flavour gives way to a dry, hoppy aftertaste.

Wild (ABV 4.7%)
A blend of Mild and Wassail.

Nyewood Gold (OG 1050, ABV 5%)

Wassail (OG 1060, ABV 6%) ◄
A strong, full-bodied, tawny-red, fruity beer with a predominance of malt throughout, but also an underlying hoppiness.

Balmaha (NEW)

⊟ Oak Tree Inn, Balmaha, G63 0JQ
⊕ oak-tree-inn.co.uk
Tours by arrangement (CAMRA members only, max 12)

Balmaha began brewing in 2012 using a one-barrel plant.

70/- (ABV 4%)

Lomond Hop (ABV 4%)

Best (ABV 4.5%)

Blonde (ABV 5%)

Firkin Point (ABV 5%)

Bank Top ⟨SIBA⟩ ⟨◉⟩

The Pavilion, Ashworth Lane, Bolton, Lancashire, BL1 8RA
☎ (01204) 595800 ⊕ banktopbrewery.com
Tours by arrangement

☺Bank Top was established in 1995. Since 2002 the brewery has occupied a Grade II-listed tennis pavilion. In 2007 the brewing capacity was doubled with the installation of a new 10-barrel plant and in 2008 David Sweeney became the sole proprietor.

Barley to Beer (OG 1036, ABV 3.6%)
A pale bitter with a citrus lemon and herbal finish.

Sweeneys (OG 1038, ABV 3.8%)
An amber bitter with a bold, crisp flavour and a delicate, slightly spicy aroma.

Bad to the Bone (OG 1040, ABV 4%)
A tan-coloured beer with floral qualities and delicate citrus notes.

Dark Mild (OG 1040, ABV 4%) ▢ ◄
Dark brown beer with a malt and roast aroma. Smooth mouthfeel, with malt, roast malt and hops prominent throughout.

Flat Cap (OG 1040, ABV 4%) ▢ ◄
Amber ale with a modest fruit aroma leading to a beer with citrus fruit, malt and hops. Good finish of fruit, malt and bitterness.

Gold Digger (OG 1040, ABV 4%) ◄
Golden coloured, with a citrus aroma, grapefruit and a touch of spiciness on the palate; a fresh, hoppy citrus finish.

Old Slapper (OG 1042, ABV 4%)

Pavilion Pale Ale (OG 1045, ABV 4%) ◄

A yellow beer with a citrus and hop aroma. Big fruity flavour with a peppery hoppiness; dry, bitter yet fruity finish.

Blonde (OG 1050, ABV 5%)
An extremely pale ale made with New Zealand hops resulting in a pleasant woody flavour and distinct berry aroma.

Port O Call (OG 1050, ABV 5%) ◀
Dark brown beer with a malty, fruity aroma. Malt, roast and dark fruits in the bittersweet taste and finish.

Leprechaun Stout (OG 1060, ABV 6%)

Banks's

Park Brewery, Wolverhampton, West Midlands, WV1 4NY
☎ (01922) 711811 ⊕ bankssbeer.co.uk
Shop Mon-Fri 10am-5pm; Sat 9.30am-12pm (excluding Bank Holidays)
Tours can be booked online or phone (01902) 329653

Banks's was formed in 1890 by the amalgamation of three local companies. Hanson's was acquired in 1943 but its Dudley brewery was closed in 1991. Hanson's beers are now brewed in Wolverhampton, though a few of its pubs retain the Hanson's livery. Banks's Mild is a fine example of West Midlands mild ale and in 2010 the group decided to return to the traditional name of Mild, rather than Original, to keep pace with growing demand for the style. Beers from the closed Mansfield Brewery are now brewed at Wolverhampton. Hanson's Mild has been discontinued. Part of Marston's PLC.

Mild (OG 1036, ABV 3.5%) ◀
An amber-coloured, well-balanced, refreshing session beer.

Bitter (OG 1038, ABV 3.8%) ◀
A pale brown bitter with a pleasant balance of hops and malt. Hops continue from the taste through to a bittersweet aftertaste.

Mansfield Cask Ale (OG 1038, ABV 3.9%)

Sunbeam (OG 1042, ABV 4.2%)
A zesty golden ale with citrus overtones. A vibrant hop aroma leads to a long finish.

Brewed for Carlsberg Tetley:

Tetley Mild (OG 1034, ABV 3.3%) ◀
A mid-brown beer with a light malt and caramel aroma. A well-balanced taste of malt and caramel follows, with good bitterness and a satisfying finish.

Tetley Bitter (OG 1035, ABV 3.7%) ◀
A smooth, creamy bitter with a hoppy nose. Hops are joined by a good dose of balancing malt until both give way to the long, bitter finish.

Barearts

Studio Bar & Gallery, 108-110 Rochdale Road, Todmorden, West Yorkshire, OL14 7LP
☎ (01706) 839305 ⊕ barearts.com
Shop Wed-Fri 4-9.45pm; Sat 12-9.45pm; Sun 12-8.45pm

A four-barrel brewery that began production in 2005 and is named after an art gallery dedicated to nude artwork. Beer is available only from the beer shop and studio bar or by mail order. All beers are sold in bottles or five-litre mini casks and are all conditioned by secondary fermentation.

Barge & Barrel

Barge & Barrel, 10-12 Park Road, Elland, West Yorkshire, HX5 9HP
☎ 07949 148476 ⊠ taggartkeith@yahoo.co.uk
Tours by arrangement

⊛The brewery was founded by John Eastwood at the Barge & Barrel pub. 50-70 outlets are supplied direct. Seasonal beers are also available.

Gold Award (OG 1044, ABV 4.4%) ◀
Complex copper-coloured beer with malt, roast and caramel flavours. It has a hoppy and bitter aftertaste.

Black Prince (OG 1050, ABV 5%)
A distinctive strong black porter with a blend of pale and chocolate malts and roasted barley.

Barkston

Orchard House, Saw Wells Court, Barkston Ash, North Yorkshire, LS24 9JU
☎ 07764 750959 ⊕ barkstonbrewery.com

Barkston began brewing in 2011. Three beers are produced on an on-demand basis: 3B (ABV 4%), Blonde (ABV 4%), and Belle (ABV 4.7%). New fermenting tanks and conditioning vessels were installed in 2012 and the brewery hopes to expand production.

Barley Bottom

Unit 1a, Howden Industrial Estate, Howden Road, Silsden, West Yorkshire, BD20 0HJ
☎ (01535) 656797 ☎ 07954 173473
⊕ barleytrading.co.uk

Based at the Homebrew supplies shop of the same name, Barley Bottom began brewing in 2012 using a one-barrel plant. Four regular ales and an occasional stout are brewed with other bespoke beers produced to order.

Cobbydale Bitter (ABV 4%)

Cobbydale Blonde (ABV 4%)

Cobbydale Gold (ABV 4%)

Golden Cascade (ABV 4%)

Barlick (NEW)

☰ 61 Manchester Road, Barnoldswick, Lancashire, BB18 5PW
☎ 07722 388155 ⊕ barlick-brewery.co.uk

⊛Barlick began brewing in 2012 at the Greyhound in Barnoldswick, where a beer is always available. Barlick is the colloquial name for the town.

Barlow SIBA

Units 5 & 6, Shippen Rural Business Centre, Church Farm, Barlow, Derbyshire, S18 7TR
☎ (0114) 289 1767 ⊕ barlowbrewery.co.uk
Ring for shop opening times

Brewing started in 2009 on a self-built 2.5-barrel plant. Beers are supplied to the Hare & Hounds in Barlow and other local outlets.

Heath Robinson (OG 1039, ABV 3.8%)

A traditional dark bitter with a malty background and a balanced, bitter finish.

Betty's Blonde (OG 1042, ABV 4%)
Brewed with a blend of pale malts to give a light golden colour, hopped for subtle citrus and passion fruit flavours with a clean, crisp finish.

Carnival Ale (OG 1042, ABV 4%)
A light, golden pale ale with a citrus finish.

Dark Horse (OG 1043, ABV 4.2%)
A dark bitter, brewed with English malts to give a dark colour and coffee aroma. English hopped for a well-balanced finish.

Three Valleys IPA (OG 1052, ABV 5%)
An American style IPA bursting with tropical fruit and citrus flavours with a clean, bitter finish.

Full Monty (OG 1067, ABV 6.5%)
A strong, full-flavoured IPA. Golden in colour with complex passion fruit, citrus and mandarin orange flavours with a warming alcoholic finish.

Anastasia (OG 1076, ABV 8%)
Strong, dark and smooth with complex malt flavours, chocolate, coffee and a hint of fruit.

Barnet (NEW)

≣ Black Horse, Wood Street, Barnet, EN5 4BW
☎ (020) 8449 2230 ⊕ blackhorsebarnet.co.uk

Brewing began in 2013. One beer is regularly available with additional different brews produced each week.

Palomino (ABV 4%)

Barney's SIBA

Summerhall Brewery, 1 Summerhall, Edinburgh, EH9 1PL ⊕ barneysbeer.com
Tours by arrangement

One of only two breweries in Edinburgh, Barney's Beer was founded in 2010 and is now brewed on the site of the original 1800s Summerhall brewery. Summerhall is Edinburgh's centre for the arts and science.

Good Ordinary Pale Ale (OG 1038, ABV 3.8%)
A gold-coloured, full-bodied pale ale with a subtle citrus and spicy hop finish.

Red Rye (OG 1044, ABV 4.5%)
Copper/dark amber in colour, with a clean, crisp, dry and fruity taste.

Volcano IPA (OG 1048, ABV 5%)
A straw-coloured beer with an assertive bitterness, erupting with US-style hop character.

Barngates SIBA ◉

Barngates, Ambleside, Cumbria, LA22 0NG
☎ (01539) 436575 ⊕ barngatesbrewery.co.uk
Tours by arrangement

◉Barngates was established in 1997 to supply only the Drunken Duck Inn. Expansion over the years means it now supplies over 150 outlets throughout Cumbria, Lancashire, Yorkshire and Northumberland. Occasional beers are produced.

Cat Nap (OG 1037, ABV 3.6%) 🍴 ◆
Pale beer unapologetically bitter with a dry, astringent finish.

Tenacious Ted (OG 1039, ABV 3.8%)

Amber-coloured ale with a vibrant hop character on the nose and palate. Bittersweet.

Cracker Ale (OG 1038, ABV 3.9%) ◆
A flavoursome malty bitter, fruity but not sweet. Dry in taste rather than finish.

Brathay Gold (OG 1042, ABV 4%)
Golden ale bursting with fresh hoppy intensity.

Pride of Westmorland (OG 1042, ABV 4.1%) ◆
Hoppy, bitter beer, with some malt undertones and fruit, which gives way to a bitter finish.

Westmorland Gold (OG 1043, ABV 4.2%) ◆
A golden ale with a good balance of malt and hops, perhaps not as intense as previously.

Tag Lag (OG 1044, ABV 4.4%) 🍴 ◆
A pale amber beer, smooth and sweetly malty to begin but a lasting, bitter finish.

Barnsley

See Wentworth

Barrowden

≣ c/o Exeter Arms, 28 Main Street, Barrowden, Rutland, LE15 8EQ
☎ (01572) 747247 ⊕ exeterarmsrutland.co.uk
Shop 12-2.30pm (3.30pm Sat), 6-11pm; 12-5pm Sun; closed Mon

⊠ The brewery was established in 1998. Martin Allsopp bought the pub and brewery in 2005, which is situated in a barn at the back of the Exeter Arms. Seasonal beers: see website.

Pilot (OG 1028, ABV 2.6%)

Seventy Lambs (OG 1038, ABV 3.6%)

Beech (OG 1040, ABV 3.8%)

Own Gear (OG 1040, ABV 4%)

Hop Gear (OG 1046, ABV 4.4%)

Bartrams

Rougham Estate, Ipswich Road (A14), Rougham, Suffolk, IP30 9LZ
☎ (01449) 737655 ☎ 07768 62581
⊕ bartramsbrewery.co.uk
Shop Tue & Sat 12-6pm
Tours by arrangement

⊠ The brewery was set up in 1999. In 2005 the plant was moved to a building on Rougham Airfield, the site of Bartram's Brewery between 1894 and 1902 run by Captain Bill Bartram. His image graces the pump clips. Beers are available in a selection of local pubs and there is a large amount of trade through local farmers' markets. Marld, Beltane Braces and all porters and stouts are suitable for vegetarians and vegans. Seasonal beers: see website.

Marld (OG 1033, ABV 3.4%)
A traditional mild. Spicy hops and malt with chocolate, slightly smoky with a light, roasted finish.

Premier Bitter (OG 1038, ABV 3.7%)
A traditional quaffing ale, full-flavoured but light, dry and hoppy.

Rougham Ready (OG 1038, ABV 3.8%)
A light, crisp bitter, surprisingly full bodied for its strength.

THE BREWERIES

Red Queen (OG 1039, ABV 3.9%)
Typical IPA style with chocolate malt in the foreground while the resiny hop flavour lingers.

Cat's Whiskers (OG 1040, ABV 4%)
A straw-coloured beer with ginger and lemons added; a unique flavour experience.

Grozet (OG 1040, ABV 4%)
Using Little Green Man as the base beer, gooseberries are added to give an appealing extra dimension.

Bee's Knees (OG 1042, ABV 4.2%)
An amber beer with a floral aroma; honey softness on the palate leads to a crisp, bitter finish.

Catherine Bartram's IPA (OG 1043, ABV 4.3%)
A full-bodied malty IPA style; tangy hops lead the malt throughout and dominate the dry, hoppy aftertaste.

Jester Quick One (OG 1044, ABV 4.4%)
A sweet reddish bitter using fruity American hops.

Beltane Braces (OG 1046, ABV 4.5%)

Stingo (OG 1045, ABV 4.5%)
A sweetish, fruity bitter with a hoppy nose. Light honey softens the bitter finish.

Beer Elsie Bub (OG 1048, ABV 4.8%)
Originally brewed for a Pagan wedding, this strong honey ale is now brewed all year round.

Captain Bill Bartram's Best Bitter (OG 1048, ABV 4.8%)
Modified from a 100-year old recipe, using full malt and traditional Kentish hops.

Captain's Stout (OG 1049, ABV 4.8%)
Biscuity dark malt leads to a lightly smoked aroma, plenty of roasted malt character, coffee notes and a whiff of smoke.

Cherry Stout (OG 1048, ABV 4.8%)
Sensuous hints of chocolate lead to a subtle suggestion of cherries.

Suffolk 'n' Strong (OG 1050, ABV 5%)
A smooth and dangerously potable strong bitter, well-balanced malt and hops with an easy finish.

Comrade Bill Bartram's Egalitarian Anti Imperialist Soviet Stout (OG 1070, ABV 6.9%) 🍷
A Russian stout by any other name, a luscious easy-drinking example of the style.

Barum SIBA

🍺 c/o Reform Inn, Pilton, Barnstaple, Devon, EX31 1PD
☎ (01271) 329994 ⊕ barumbrewery.co.uk
Tours by arrangement

Barum was formed in 1996 by Tim Webster and is housed in a conversion attached to the Reform Inn that acts as the brewery tap and main outlet. Distribution is exclusively within Devon. Seasonal beers are brewed.

Original (OG 1044, ABV 4.4%)

EPA (OG 1046, ABV 4.6%)

Breakfast (OG 1048, ABV 5%)

Baseline

Golding Barn Industrial Estate, Henfield Road, Small Dole, West Sussex, BN5 9XH
☎ (01903) 879111 ⊕ baselinebrewing.co.uk

⊗ Baseline began brewing in 2012 on a five-barrel plant. The beer is unfined and no Isinglass is used, meaning it is suitable for vegetarians.

Thunderbolt Bitter (ABV 4%)
A copper-coloured session bitter with a spicy, earthy and floral flavour.

Dark Matter (ABV 5.5%)
A dark, full bodied ale. The initial flavour is roasted malt with spicy hops and a fruity but dry bitter finish.

English Electric Lightning (ABV 6%)
A pleasant citrus/fruity and floral hop aroma. A rich biscuity malt flavour with hints of Seville orange, citrus and fruitcake.

Batch Brew

c/o 17 Sussex Street, Winchester, Hampshire, SO23 8TG
☎ 07917 035625 ⊕ batchbrew.com

Established in 2012, Batch Brew's bottle-conditioned beers are contract brewed by Oakleaf Brewery at present: Batch 9 (ABV 5%) – a black lager, Batch 16 (ABV 5%) – a wheat beer, Batch 18 (ABV 5%) – an American-style pale ale.

Batemans SIBA IFBB 👁

Salem Bridge Brewery, Mill Lane, Wainfleet, Lincolnshire, PE24 4JE
☎ (01754) 880317 ⊕ bateman.co.uk
Visitor Centre & Shop : 11.30am-4pm Wed-Sun and Bank Holiday Mon. Closed 25 Dec-31 Jan
Tours by arrangement

☺Bateman's Brewery is one of Britain's few remaining independent family-owned and managed brewers. Established in 1874 it has been brewing award-winning beers for four generations. All 62 tied houses serve cask-conditioned beer. See website for seasonal and speciality beers.

Dark Mild (OG 1030, ABV 3%) 🍺 🌾
Gentle roast fruity airs preface this red-brown, caramel-infused brew. Malt and a stewed plummy sweetness initially give depth. Caramel dominates the short simple finish.

XB (OG 1037, ABV 3.7%) 🌾
A well-rounded, smooth malty beer with a blackcurrant fruity background. Hops flourish initially before giving way to a bittersweet dryness that enhances the mellow malty ending.

Yella Belly Gold (OG 1039, ABV 3.9%)
A gold-coloured, refreshing beer with a citrus flavour and aroma, which is quite dry.

XXXB (OG 1048, ABV 4.5%)
A blend of malt, hops and fruit on the nose with a bitter bite over the top of a faintly banana maltiness that stays the course. A russet-tan brown classic.

Salem Porter (OG 1048, ABV 4.7%) 🍺 🌾
A black and complex mix of chocolate, liquorice and cough elixir.

Bath Ales SIBA 👁

Units 3-7, Caxton Business Park, Crown Way, Warmley, Bristol, BS30 8XJ
☎ (0117) 947 4794

Office: Hare House, Southway Drive, Warmley, Bristol, BS30 5LW ⊕ bathales.com
Shop Mon-Fri 9am-5pm; Sat 9am-12pm
Tours by arrangement

⊗ Brewing since 1995, new premises nearby include a head office and bottling plant. Around 400 outlets are supplied. Ten pubs are owned, all serving cask ale. Seasonal beers: see website. An ever-changing range of beer is also brewed under the Beerd Brewery name on a separate five-barrel plant.

Special Pale Ale (OG 1039, ABV 3.7%) ◆
Hoppy, pale golden session bitter. Light citrus aroma with bitter flavours, a hint of caramel and a bitter aftertaste.

Gem (OG 1042, ABV 4.1%) ◆
Pale brown best bitter with sweet fruit and caramel flavours. Hops make for a slight bitter aftertaste.

Barnsey (OG 1045, ABV 4.5%) ◆
Dark brown strong bitter with caramel on the nose. Caramel continues on the palate with a hint of bonfire toffee and a short finish.

Batham IFBB

Delph Brewery, Delph Road, Brierley Hill, West Midlands, DY5 2TN
☎ (01384) 77229 ⊕ bathams.com

☺A classic Black Country small brewery established in 1877. Tim and Matthew Batham represent the fifth generation to run the company. The Vine, one of the Black Country's most famous pubs, is also the site of the brewery. The company has 11 tied houses and supplies around 30 other outlets. Batham's Bitter is delivered in 54-gallon hogsheads to meet demand. Seasonal beer is also brewed.

Mild Ale (OG 1036.5, ABV 3.5%) ◆
A fruity, dark brown mild with malty sweetness and a roast malt finish.

Best Bitter (OG 1043.5, ABV 4.3%) ⬠ ▮ ◆
A pale yellow, fruity, sweetish bitter, with a dry, hoppy finish. A good, light, refreshing beer.

Battledown SIBA ◉

Keynsham Works, Keynsham Street, Cheltenham, Gloucestershire, GL52 6EJ
☎ (01242) 693409 ☎ 07734 834104
⊕ battledownbrewery.com
Shop open Wed-Sat am – see website for times
Tours by arrangement

⊗ Established in 2005 by Roland and Stephanie Elliott-Berry, and joined in 2006 by Ben Jennison-Phillips (ex-Whittingtons), Battledown operates an eight-barrel plant from an old engineering works and supplies more than 250 outlets. Visitors are always welcome. There is an online shop for mail order purposes. Seasonal beers are also brewed.

Sunbeam (OG 1037, ABV 3.8%)
A golden pale ale with a refreshing aroma and sharp but smooth taste, leaving a dry, hoppy aftertaste which lingers on the palate.

Natural Selection (OG 1041, ABV 4.2%)
A deep golden beer, the malt is evident but gives way to a spicy and slightly citrus finish.

Premium (OG 1046, ABV 4.6%)

A rich amber ale. A malty aroma and taste with a deep satisfying, full-bodied fruit and malt texture leaving a well-rounded mellow aftertaste.

Special (OG 1050, ABV 5.2%)
A well-balanced and crisp pale ale.

Battlefield

See Tunnel

Bays SIBA ◉

Aspen Way, Paignton, Devon, TQ4 7QR
☎ (01803) 555004 ⊕ baysbrewery.co.uk
Shop Mon-Fri 8am-5pm
Tours by arrangement

⊗ Bays Brewery opened in 2007 in an old steel fabrication unit in Paignton using a 20-barrel plant. The brewery delivers to many pubs, hotels and restaurants in the south-west and further afield. Seasonal beers: see website.

Topsail (OG 1040, ABV 4%)

Gold (OG 1042, ABV 4.3%)

Devon Dumpling (OG 1048, ABV 5.1%)

Beachy Head SIBA

Seven Sisters Sheep Centre, Birling Manor Farm, Gilberts Drive, East Dean, East Sussex, BN20 0AA
☎ (01323) 423313

Estates Office: The Green, East Dean, East Sussex, BN20 0BS ⊕ beachyhead.org.uk
Tours by arrangement

⊗ The 2.5-barrel brew plant was installed at the rear of the sheep centre in late 2006. Beachy Head Brewery produces both cask and bottle-conditioned ales, supplied regularly to around 25 outlets, three of which are local pubs. The full range of ales (including seasonals) can be sampled at the Tiger Inn in East Dean village, which is the brewery tap.

Parsons Darby Hole (OG 1040, ABV 4%)

Beachy Original (OG 1045, ABV 4.5%)

Legless Rambler (OG 1050, ABV 5%)

Bear Claw (NEW)

Unit 3, Meantime Workshops, Spittal, Berwick upon Tweed, Northumberland, TD15 1RG
☎ 07919 276715 ✉ enderkue@netscape.net

Bear Claw began brewing in 2012 on a two-barrel plant, producing a variety of mainly highly-hopped cask ales, including continental styles. Bottle-conditioned beers are available. Beers are reguarly available at the Barrels Alehouse in Berwick upon Tweed.

Beartown SIBA ◉

Bromley House, Spindle Street, Congleton, Cheshire, CW12 1QN
☎ (01260) 299964 ⊕ beartownbrewery.co.uk
Shop Mon-Fri 9am-5pm; Sat 9am-4pm
Tours by arrangement

☺Congleton's links with brewing can be traced back to 1272. Two of its most senior officers at the time were Ale Taster and Bear Warden, hence the name of the brewery. Both the brewery's Navigation in Stockport and the Beartown Tap have been named CAMRA regional pubs of the year. Beartown supplies 250 outlets and owns five pubs. Seasonal beers: see website.

Best Bitter (OG 1037, ABV 3.7%)
A copper-coloured session beer with a full palate of malt and crisp hops.

Bear Ass (OG 1040, ABV 4%)
Dark ruby-red, malty bitter with good hop nose and fruity flavour with dry, bitter, astringent aftertaste.

Ginger Bear (OG 1040, ABV 4%)
The flavours from the malt and hops blend with the added bite from the root ginger to produce a superbly quenching blonde ale.

Kodiak Gold (OG 1040, ABV 4%) ◕
Hops and fruit dominate the taste of this crisp yellow bitter and these follow through to the dryish aftertaste. Biscuity malt also comes through on the aroma and taste.

Bearskinful (OG 1042, ABV 4.2%) ◕
Biscuity malt dominates the flavour of this amber best bitter. There are hops and a hint of sulphur on the aroma. A balance of malt and bitterness follow through to the aftertaste.

Bearly Literate (OG 1045, ABV 4.5%)
Golden pale ale. Floral sented and packed with the flavours of summer fruits and lemon, ending with a smooth dryness.

Polar Eclipse (OG 1048, ABV 4.8%) ◫ ◕
Classic black, dry and bitter stout, with roast flavours to the fore. Good hop on the nose follow through the taste into a long dry finish.

Blackbear (OG 1050, ABV 5%)
Dark ruby-coloured strong mild ale. Subtle roast and malt flavours fill the taste, Complemented by a mellow sweetness.

Bruins Ruin (OG 1050, ABV 5%)
Deep copper-coloured premium ale. Full of malty character and a palate of sweet, smooth, fruity flavours.

Beavertown SIBA

Unit 4, Stour Road, Hackney Wick, London, E3 2NT
☎ (020) 3006 0794 ⊕ beavertownbrewery.com

⊗ Beavertown began brewing in 2012 using a four-barrel plant next door to its brewery tap, Duke's Brew & Que, N1. In 2013 the brewery relocated to bigger premises a stone's throw from the Lea Navigation Canal where they plan to have 'Beaver Bar and Beaver Food'. Only one regular cask-conditioned ale is produced but other beers in the range are sometimes available. Bottle-conditioned and special beers: see website.

Neck Oil (ABV 4.3%) ◕
Pale brown beer with a creamy mouthfeel. Hints of citrus and peach with a dry biscuity finish.

Beckstones

Upper Beckstones Mill, The Green, Millom, Cumbria, LA18 5HL
☎ (01229) 775294 ⊕ beckstonesbrewery.co.uk

⊗ Beckstones started brewing in 2003 on the site of an 18th-century mill with its own water supply.

It's a five-barrel, one-man operation. The beer names often have a connection to the long-closed Millom Iron Works or local characters. The brewer also designs the distinctive pump clips.

Barley Juice (OG 1033, ABV 3.4%) ◕
Full-flavoured, beautifully balanced, emphatically fruity, hoppy beer

Beer O'Clock (OG 1036, ABV 3.5%) ◕
A fascinating blend of flavours delivering ever-changing mouthfuls of sweet, fruity and hoppy bitterness.

**Black Gun Dog Freddy Mild
(OG 1038, ABV 3.8%)** ◕
A full-bodied, beautifully balanced ruby dark mild, replete with fruit and roast malt.

Iron Town (OG 1038, ABV 3.8%) ◕
Creamy sweet brown ale full of well-balanced fruit and hop.

Border Steeans (OG 1040, ABV 4.1%) ◕
An old-fashioned style tawny bitter with a sweet start, some bitter notes and plenty of aftertaste.

Rev Rob (OG 1044, ABV 4.6%) ◕
A golden beer with a pronounced grapefruit aroma and taste. The hoppy bitterness lasts through to the aftertaste.

Bedlam SIBA

Albourne Farm, Shaves Wood Lane, Albourne, West Sussex, BN6 9DX
☎ 07955 684041 ⊕ bedlambrewery.co.uk

Bedlam began brewing in 2012. Brewing takes place on part time basis in a converted barn at Albourne Manor House. Beer is supplied to outlets in Sussex and Surrey and local beer festivals.

Best Bitter (ABV 4%)

Hoppy Golden Ale (ABV 4.2%)
A traditional English session bitter with an inviting copper colour.

Beeches (NEW)

39 The Beeches, Lochgelly, KY5 9QB
☎ (01592) 782474
✉ thebeechesbrewery@gmail.com

⊗ Beeches began production in 2012 using a 10-gallon plant in a small outbuilding at the rear of the family home.

Amazing Ale (OG 1040, ABV 3.8%)
A blonde pale ale, with a sweetness on the palate with a floral aftertaste.

Cats Whiskers (OG 1042, ABV 3.9%)
A golden pale ale, light and crisp with a citrus aftertaste.

Meedies Mash (OG 1046, ABV 4.4%)
Amber-coloured, with a malty nose, bitter finish and a slightly spicy aftertaste.

Beer Engine SIBA

Newton St Cyres, EX5 5AX
☎ (01392) 851282 ⊕ thebeerengine.co.uk
Tours by arrangement

Beer Engine was developed in 1983 and is the oldest continuously-working microbrewery in Devon. The brewery is visible behind glass downstairs in the pub. Several outlets are supplied, as well as local beer festivals. Seasonal beer is also available.

Rail Ale (OG 1037, ABV 3.8%) ◣
A straw-coloured beer with a fruity aroma and a sweet, fruity finish.

Silver Bullet (OG 1040, ABV 4%)
A light, medium-strength summer beer with a bitter aftertaste.

Piston Bitter (OG 1043, ABV 4.3%) ◣
A mid-brown, sweet-tasting beer with a pleasant, bittersweet aftertaste.

Sleeper Heavy (OG 1052, ABV 5.4%) ◣
A red-coloured beer with a fruity, sweet taste and a bitter finish.

Beer Geek SIBA

Unit D3, Aston Seedbed Centre, Aston, Birmingham, B7 4NT
☎ 0844 772 7207 ⊕ beergeekbrewery.com

⊗ Beer Geek began brewing in 2012 using a 15-barrel plant built by the brewer in his spare time to produce recipes developed over the past few years.

Beer Studio

See Hydes

Beerd

See Bath

Bees

Plot 2, Coast Road, Walcott, Norwich, NR12 0LS
☎ 07971 577526 ✉ bees-brewery@hotmail.co.uk

Bees first brewed in 2008 and was initially based at Queniborough near Leicester. It relocated in 2009 and the five-barrel plant is now located in a static caravan overlooking the sea. Brewer Alec Brackenbury operates the brewery on a part-time basis and mainly supplies pubs within a 10-mile radius of Walcott.

Amber (OG 1038, ABV 3.8%)

Navigator (OG 1045, ABV 4.5%)

Stripey Jack (OG 1046, ABV 4.6%)

3B's (OG 1048, ABV 4.8%)

Wobble (OG 1050, ABV 5%)

Honey (OG 1052, ABV 5.2%)

Beeston SIBA

Fransham Road Farm, Beeston, Norfolk, PE32 2LZ
☎ (01328) 700844 ☎ 07768 742763
⊕ beestonbrewery.co.uk
Tours by arrangement

⊗ The brewery was established in 2006 in an old farm building using a five-barrel plant. Brewing water comes from a dedicated borehole and raw ingredients are sourced locally whenever possible. All beers are also available bottle conditioned and in 5-litre mini casks.

The Squirrels Nuts (OG 1035, ABV 3.5%)

Afternoon Delight (OG 1036, ABV 3.7%)
An easy-drinking blonde ale.

Bloomers (OG 1039, ABV 4%)

Worth the Wait (OG 1041, ABV 4.2%) ◣
Well-balanced and complex with a soft hoppy nose. An initial burst of passion fruit mingles with malt and hops in a delightful first taste. A long-lasting finish develops a bittersweet dryness.

Stirling (OG 1045, ABV 4.5%)
Rich malty red bitter with toffee notes.

The Dry Road (OG 1048, ABV 4.8%)

Village Life (OG 1047, ABV 4.8%)
Amber bitter with a an abundance of interesting hop character.

On the Huh (OG 1048, ABV 5%) ▉ ◣
Deceptively smooth bitter with a fruity raisin aroma. A bittersweet maltiness jousts with caramel and roast. A dry hoppiness gives depth to a strong finale.

Norfolk Black (OG 1060, ABV 6%)
A warming, full-bodied strong stout.

Old Stoatwobbler (OG 1065, ABV 6%)

For Brancaster Brewery:

Best (OG 1038, ABV 3.8%)

Malthouse Bitter (OG 1042, ABV 4.2%)

Sharpie K12 (ABV 4.3%)

Oyster Catcher (ABV 4.4%)

The Wreck (ABV 4.8%)

Belhaven

Spott Road, Dunbar, EH42 1RS
☎ (01368) 862734 ⊕ belhaven.co.uk
Shop open during tours
Tours by arrangement

⊕Belhaven brewery is one of the oldest brewing sites in Scotland. Established in Dunbar in 1719, it brews beers made with water from its own well and local Scottish barley. Part of Greene King PLC.

60/- Ale (OG 1030, ABV 2.9%) ◣
A fine but virtually unavailable example of a Scottish light. This bittersweet, reddish-brown beer is dominated by fruit and malt with a hint of roast and caramel, and increasing bitterness in the aftertaste.

IPA (OG 1038, ABV 3.8%)
A golden ale with refreshing floral and citrus tones produced by a well-balanced fusion of malt and hops giving a clean, crisp flavour.

80/- Ale (OG 1040, ABV 4.2%) ◣
One of the last remaining original Scottish 80 Shillings. Malt is the predominant flavour characteristic, though it is balanced by fruit and a little hop. A complex ale, true to the 80/- style.

Black (OG 1041, ABV 4.2%)
A roasty stout.

St Andrew's Ale (OG 1046, ABV 4.9%)
A bittersweet beer with lots of body. The malt, fruit and roast mingle with hints of hop and caramel.

Bell Street (NEW)

▉ 57-59 Bell Street, Henley-on-Thames, Oxfordshire, RG9 2BA

☎ (01491) 576554 ⊕ bellstreetbrewery.co.uk

Bell Street was established in 2013 using a 2.5-barrel plant. It is situated at the rear of Brakspear Pub Co's newly refurbished Bull on Bell St. The beers are sold at the pub and through the Brakspear Pub Co estate. Seasonal beers are available.

Brakspear Special (OG 1043, ABV 4.3%)
Tawny/amber beer with a well-balanced aroma and a hint of sweetness. Full bodied, the initial sweetness gives way to a dry hop bitterness.

Belleville (NEW) SIBA

Unit 36, Jaggard Way, Wandsworth Common, London, SW12 8SG
☎ 07712 298273 ⊕ bellevillebrewing.co.uk
Tours by arrangement

Belleville began brewing in 2012. It was formed by a group of 10 fathers who met in the playground of Belleville Primary School.

Northcote Blonde (ABV 4.2%)

Battersea Brownstone (ABV 4.8%)

Chestnut Porter (ABV 4.9%)

Commonside Pale Ale (ABV 5%)

Thames Surfer (ABV 5.7%)

Bellinger's SIBA

Station Road, Grove, Oxfordshire, OX12 0DH
☎ (01235) 772255 ⊕ bellingersbrewery.co.uk
Shop Mon-Sat 6am-9pm; Sun 7am-8pm
Tours by arrangement

⊗ The late Mike Bellinger established Bellingers Brewery as a family partnership in 2011. The five-barrel plant produces three core beers plus seasonals. As well as supplying beer in casks, they sell bottles and polypins in the garage shop.

Blenheim (OG 1037, ABV 3.9%)
Light, malty session bitter

Original Bitter (OG 1040, ABV 4.1%)
A light and refreshing, easy-drinking beer

Best Bitter (OG 1046, ABV 4.9%)
Rich tasting with a complex flavour.

Belvoir SIBA ◉

Crown Park, Station Road, Old Dalby, Leicestershire, LE14 3NQ
☎ (01664) 823455 ⊕ belvoirbrewery.co.uk
Tours by arrangement

Belvoir (pronounced 'beaver') Brewery was set up in 1995 by former Shipstone's and Theakston's brewer Colin Brown. Long-term expansion has seen the introduction of a 20-barrel plant that can produce 50 barrels a week. There is also a visitor centre incorporating brewery memorabilia, a bar, restaurant and shop (open seven days a week). Around 150 outlets are supplied direct. Seasonal and bottle-conditioned beers are also available.

Dark Horse (OG 1034, ABV 3.4%)

Whippling (OG 1037, ABV 3.6%)

Star Bitter (OG 1039, ABV 3.9%) ◄
Reminiscent of the long-extinct Shipstone's Bitter, this mid-brown bitter lives up to its name as it is bitter in taste but not unpleasantly so.

Gordon Bennett (OG 1041, ABV 4.1%)
Light chestnut-coloured beer with a biscuity character and a pleasant hop finish.

Beaver Bitter (OG 1043, ABV 4.3%) ◄
A light brown bitter that starts malty in both aroma and taste but soon develops a hoppy bitterness. Appreciably fruity.

Oatmeal Stout (OG 1044, ABV 4.3%)

Peacock's Glory (OG 1048, ABV 4.7%)
A premium, full-bodied golden ale.

Old Dalby (OG 1050, ABV 5.1%)
A rich, smooth ruby red strong ale with pleasant hop character.

Contract brewed for Hoskins Brothers, Leicester:

Hob Bitter (ABV 4%)

IPA (ABV 4%)

White Dolphin (ABV 4%)

Contract brewed for Steamin' Billy Brewing Co:

Tipsy Fisherman (OG 1036, ABV 3.6%)

Bitter (OG 1043, ABV 4.3%)

1485 (OG 1050, ABV 5%)

Skydiver (OG 1050, ABV 5%)

Beowulf SIBA ◉

Forest of Mercia, Chasewater Country Park, Pool Lane, Brownhills, Staffordshire, WS8 7NL
☎ (01543) 454067 ⊕ beowulfbrewery.co.uk
Tours by arrangement

Beowulf Brewing Company beers appear as guest ales predominantly in the central region but also across the country. Seasonal beers: see website. Bottle-conditioned beers are also available.

Beorma (OG 1038, ABV 3.9%) ◄
A perfectly balanced session ale with a malty hint of fruit giving way to a lingering bitterness. Background spice excites the palate.

Chasewater Bitter (OG 1043, ABV 4.4%) ◄
Golden bitter, hoppy throughout with citrus and hints of malt. Long mouth-watering, bitter finish.

Dark Raven (OG 1048, ABV 4.5%) 🍷 ◄
So dark with apple and bonfire in the aroma, so sweet and smooth like liquid toffee apples with a sudden bitter finish.

Swordsman (OG 1045, ABV 4.5%) ◄
Pale gold, light fruity aroma, tangy hoppy flavour. Faintly hoppy finish.

Folden Cross (OG 1045, ABV 4.6%)

Hurricane (OG 1041, ABV 4.6%)

Dragon Smoke Stout (OG 1048, ABV 4.7%) ◄
Black with a light brown creamy head. Tobacco, chocolate, liquorice and mixed fruity hints on the aroma. Bitterness fights through the sweet and roast flavours and eventually dominates. Hints of a good port emerge.

Finn's Hall Porter (OG 1049, ABV 4.7%) ◄
Dark chocolate aroma, after dinner mints, coffee and fresh tobacco. Good bitterness with woodland hints of autumn. Long, late bitterness with lip-drying character.

Mercian Shine (OG 1048, ABV 5%) ◄
Amber to pale gold with a good bitter and hoppy start. Plenty of caramel and hops with background

malt leading to a good bitter finish with caramel and hops lingering in the aftertaste.

Berrow

See Towles'

Bespoke SIBA

Unit 5, The Mews, Mitcheldean, Gloucestershire, GL17 0SL
☎ (01594) 546557 ⊕ bespokebrewery.co.uk
Shop Mon-Fri 9am-5pm
Tours by arrangement

Brewing commenced in 2012 on a 5.5-barrel plant located on the site of the old Wintles Brewery in Mitcheldean. The brewery includes a brewery tap which opens on Friday evenings. Local freehouses are supplied and bottled beers are available via farm shops and specialist outlets.

Leading Light (OG 1035, ABV 3.5%)
A light blonde ale with a refreshing citrus hop finish.

Saved by the Bell (OG 1038, ABV 3.8%)
A light, refreshing session bitter with a spicy hop bite and a light floral aroma from the late hop addition.

Running the Gauntlet (OG 1046, ABV 4.4%)
Full malty-flavoured bitter with rich roasted undertones balanced with good hop bitterness with spicy blackcurrant aromas from late hopping.

Going off Half-cocked (OG 1045, ABV 4.6%)
A spicily hopped golden pale ale.

Money for Old Rope (OG 1049, ABV 4.8%)
Classic stout with rich, dry flavours of malt and grain with deep hop bitterness.

Over a Barrel (OG 1052, ABV 5%)
Richly-coloured, fruity strong ale with a generous peppery finish of Goldings hops.

Betjeman

⧉ Shoulder of Mutton, 38 Wallingford Street, Wantage, Oxfordshire, OX12 8AX ⊕ themutton.co.uk

⊗ Betjeman Brewery, established in 2011 and associated with the Shoulder of Mutton in Wantage, continues brewing at other premises while plans to build a new brewery plant are continuing. Occasional strong beers supplement the regular range.

Wantage Bells (OG 1054, ABV 5%)
An easy-drinking, strong bitter with an initial malty flavour followed by a refreshing hoppy dryness.

Poetry In Motion (OG 1059, ABV 5.5%)
A robust and full-flavoured red IPA bursting with Pacific Jade and Cascade hops.

Bewdley SIBA

Unit 7, Bewdley Craft Centre, Lax Lane, Bewdley, Worcestershire, DY12 2DZ
☎ (01299) 405148 ⊕ bewdleybrewery.co.uk
Tours by arrangement

⊗ Bewdley began brewing in 2008 on a six-barrel plant in an old school. Brewing experience days are offered, ring for details. Beers are brewed with a railway theme for the nearby Severn Valley

Railway. Seasonal beers: see website. Bottle-conditioned beers are also available.

Worcestershire Way (OG 1036, ABV 3.6%)
A light beer with citrus notes.

Old School Bitter (OG 1038, ABV 3.8%)
A session bitter with a hoppy finish.

Worcestershire Sway (OG 1049, ABV 5%)
A stronger version of Worcestershire Way, slightly sweeter with more body.

William Mucklows Dark Mild (OG 1060, ABV 6%)

Bexar County (NEW)

8 Belgic Square, Padholme Road, Peterborough, Cambridgeshire, PE1 5XF
☎ 07934 722584 ⊕ bexarcountybrewery.com

Bexar was established in 2013, brewing American-style beers. There is no regular beer list, as the brewer is constantly innovating new recipes.

Big Bog

c/o Snowdonia Park Free House, Waunfawr, Gwynedd, LL55 4AQ
☎ 07769 110791 ⊕ bigbog.co.uk

Big Bog was established in 2011 by Paul Jefferies of Hydes Brewery. The brewery has undergone rapid expansion and now supplies 60 outlets direct. Seasonal beers are available.

Bog Standard Bitter (OG 1036, ABV 3.6%)

Welsh Pale Ale (OG 1041, ABV 4.2%)

Swampy (OG 1044, ABV 4.7%)

Quagmire (OG 1058, ABV 6%)

Bog Super IPA (OG 1068, ABV 7%)

Big Hand (NEW) SIBA

Unit A1, Abbey Close, Redwither Business Park, Wrexham, LL13 9XG
☎ (01978) 660709 ☎ 07946 514238
✉ dave@bighandbrewing.co.uk
Tours by arrangement

Big Hand began brewing in 2013 using a 10-barrel plant.

First Hand (ABV 4.2%)
An amber ale, biscuity and light.

Stout (ABV 4.2%)
A dark, dry, easy-drinking stout.

Melyn (ABV 4.6%)
An easy-drinking golden bitter with a caramel flavour.

Big Lamp

Grange Road, Newburn, Newcastle upon Tyne, NE15 8NL
☎ (0191) 267 1689 ⊕ biglampbrewers.co.uk
Tours by arrangement

☺Big Lamp started in 1982 and relocated in 1997 to a 55-barrel plant in a former water pumping station. It is the oldest microbrewery in the north-east of England. Around 160 outlets are supplied and two pubs are owned, one of which (the Keelman) is attached to the brewery. Seasonal and bottle-conditioned beers are available.

Sunny Daze (OG 1036, ABV 3.6%) ◈
Golden, hoppy session bitter with a clean taste and finish.

Bitter (OG 1039, ABV 3.9%)
Hazlenut-coloured, clean-tasting bitter, full of hops and malt. A hint of fruit with a good, hoppy finish giving a slightly dry aftertaste.

Lamplight (OG 1042, ABV 4.2%)
A crisp, light-coloured refreshing ale with a dry aftertaste.

Summerhill Stout (OG 1044, ABV 4.4%) ◈
A rich, tasty stout, dark in colour with a lasting rich roast character. Malty mouthfeel with a lingering finish.

Prince Bishop Ale (OG 1048, ABV 4.8%) ◈
A refreshing, easy-drinking bitter. Golden in colour, full of fruit and hops. Strong bitterness with a spicy, dry finish.

Premium (OG 1052, ABV 5.2%) ◈
Hoppy ale with a good bitter finish.

Keelman Brown (OG 1057, ABV 5.7%)
A full-bodied ruby ale with a hint of toffee.

For Newcastle Arms, Newcastle:

Golden Star (OG 1040, ABV 4%)
A full-tasting, golden, hoppy ale.

Big River SIBA

48 Grange Park, Brough, East Yorkshire, HU15 1AA
☎ 07737 820922 ⊕ bigriverbrewery.co.uk

Big River started brewing commercially in 2011 on a 2.5-barrel plant in a garage. Local free houses in Hull and East Yorkshire are supplied as well as CAMRA beer festivals. Its bottle-conditioned beers are available at farmers' markets. The Big River is the Humber. The beer AKA Kiwi is offically called Taumatawhakatangihangakoauauotamateaturipu kakapikimaungahoronukupokaiwhenuakitanatahu.

Halcyon Daze (ABV 3.4%)

Rope Walk (ABV 3.5%)

AKA Kiwi (ABV 3.6%)

Windjammer (ABV 4.7%)

Sailmakers Porter (ABV 5.2%)

The Deep (ABV 5.2%)

The Spurn (ABV 5.2%)

M*U*D (ABV 5.5%)

The Hindustan IPA (ABV 5.7%)

The Humber Bridge (ABV 5.7%)

Bingham's SIBA

Unit 10, Tavistock Industrial Estate, Ruscombe, Berkshire, RG10 9NJ
☎ (0118) 934 4376 ⊕ binghams.co.uk
Shop Mon-Thu 5-6pm; Fri 5-8pm; Sat 12-8pm
Tours by arrangement

⊗ Bingham's began brewing in 2010. Head brewer Chris Bingham is a member of the local branch of CAMRA and previously worked at Hog's Back Brewery.

Twyford Tipple (OG 1040, ABV 3.7%)
A tawny-coloured bitter with a malty flavour and citrus hop finish.

Brickworks Bitter (OG 1045, ABV 4.2%)
Chestnut-coloured with a slightly nutty hint. The hops balance the maltiness to provide a well-rounded best bitter.

Coffee Stout (OG 1052, ABV 5%)
A mellow beer with darks malts that complement the coffee flavour.

Doodle Stout (OG 1052, ABV 5%)
A blend of dark malts provide a complex character. Named after the brewery dog called Stout that happens to be a Labradoodle.

Ginger Doodle Stout (OG 1056, ABV 5%)
A dark stout with a subtle hint of ginger that rounds off the bitterness.

Hot Dog Chilli Stout (OG 1056, ABV 5%)
Doodle Stout with a hint of chilli to provide a warm glow on the aftertaste.

Space Hoppy IPA (OG 1050, ABV 5%)
A pale golden ale with a citrus flavour.

Vanilla Stout (OG 1052, ABV 5%)
Infused with vanilla pods that complement the dark malts to create a smooth-drinking, deliciously dark stout.

Bird Brain

30 Hailgate, Howden, East Yorkshire, DN14 7SL
☎ (01430) 432166 ☎ 07790 615915
✉ birdbrainbrewery@tiscali.co.uk

⊕ Bird Brain began brewing in 2009 on a two-barrel plant expanded to four-barrel capacity in 2012. Brewing twice a month, the brewery supplies local pubs and beer festivals. Seasonal beers are available.

Puffin Pale Ale (OG 1038, ABV 3.9%)

Shiny (OG 1038, ABV 3.9%)

Howden Bittern (OG 1039, ABV 4%)

Bird's SIBA ◉

Ladybird Barn, Old Burcot Lane, Bromsgrove, Worcestershire, B60 1PH
☎ (01527) 889870 ⊕ birdsbrewery.co.uk
Shop Mon-Wed & Fri 9am-5pm; Thu 9am-6.30pm; Sat 10am-4pm
Tours by arrangement

⊕ Bird's began brewing in 2009, supplying their beers to pubs across the West Midlands. Beers are produced for special events. Bottle-conditioned beer is available.

Thunderbird (OG 1038, ABV 3.8%)
A malty beer with a hint of sweetness and a distinctive nutty finish.

Natural Blonde? (OG 1040, ABV 4%)
A refreshing pale beer. Floral on the nose, plenty of fruit and hops in the mouth with just the right amount of malt to balance. A pleasantly hoppy aftertaste with a gently crisp bitter finish.

Amnesia (OG 1045, ABV 4.5%)
A pale straw-coloured ale with a fruity zest, a slight orange citrus undertone combining with a mixture of hops to provide a dryish hoppy finish.

Black Widow Stout (OG 1045, ABV 4.5%)
A traditional smooth, satisfying stout with a roasted malt flavour with a bitter edge and overtones of blackcurrant, raisins and liquorice.

Bishop Nick SIBA

33 East Street, Braintree, Essex, CM7 3JJ
☎ (01371) 822814

Correspondence: The Chestnuts, Chelmsford Road, Felsted, Essex, CM6 3ET ⊕ bishopnick.com

⊗ Bishop Nick was launched in 2011 by Neilion Ridley, a member of the family that ran Ridley's Brewery near Chelmsford. Beers were initially brewed using spare capacity at Felstar, but in 2013 the brewery moved to Braintree using a 20-barrel plant. Three regular beers are brewed and additional beers, including bottled beers, are planned.

Ridley's Rite (OG 1036, ABV 3.6%)

Heresy (OG 1040, ABV 4%)

1555 (OG 1043, ABV 4.3%)

Bishop's Stortford (NEW)

c/o The Cartshed, Parsonage Farm, Henham, Essex, CM22 6AN
☎ (01279) 850923 ☎ 07981 856404

Office: 24 Trinity Street, Bishop's Stortford, Hertfordshire, CM23 3TJ
✉ daz_lawrence@hotmail.co.uk

⊗ Established in 2012, the brewery rapidly encountered demand that exceeded capacity. Brewer Darren Lawrence has therefore contracted use of the plant of neighbouring Saffron Brewery, retaining his own techniques for the ales together with occasional seasonal beers. Around 20 local outlets are supplied.

Stortford Sunrise (ABV 4%)
A refreshing golden ale.

Stortford Sunset (ABV 4.2%)
A complex beer with a golden hue and a long, firm finish.

Black Cat SIBA

Eridge Road, Groombridge, Kent, TN3 9NJ
☎ 07948 387718 ⊕ blackcat-brewery.com
Tours by arrangement

⊗ Black Cat began brewing in 2011 on a 2.5-barrel brew plant; five local pubs are supplied. It is owned and run by an airline pilot. Seasonal and bottle-conditioned beers are also available.

Original (OG 1042, ABV 4.2%)
A hoppy, bitter, amber-coloured beer balanced with malt.

Black Country SIBA ⊙

⊟ Rear of Old Bulls Head, 1 Redhall Road, Lower Gornal, West Midlands, DY3 2NU
☎ (01384) 480156

Office: Unit 4, Tansey Green Road, Pensnett, West Midlands, DY5 4TL ⊕ blackcountryinns.co.uk
Tours by arrangement

Brewing started on the site in the 1830s and continued until 1934. Brewing recommenced in 2004. In 2012 much of the equipment was replaced or refurbished. Seasonal beers: see website. Beers are also brewed under the Thomas Guest Brewing Company name.

Bradley's Finest Golden (OG 1040, ABV 4.2%)

A straw-coloured quaffing beer with a bold citrus hop aroma, fruity balanced sweetness and a lingering, refreshing aftertaste.

Pig on the Wall (OG 1042, ABV 4.3%)
A refreshing chestnut brown beer with a complex flavour of light hops giving way to a bittersweet blend of roasted malt. Suggestions of chocolate and coffee undertones.

Fireside (OG 1047, ABV 5%)
A well-rounded premium bitter, amber in colour, clean in taste leading to a pleasant, dry finish.

Black Dog

See Hambleton

Black Hole SIBA

Unit 63, Ground Floor, Imex Business Park, Shobnall Road, Burton upon Trent, Staffordshire, DE14 2AU
☎ (01283) 619943 (technical & visit enquiries)

Office: Gladden Place, Gillibrands Industrial Estate, Skelmersdale, Lancashire, WN8 9SY ☎ (0845) 601 6669 (commercial enquiries & orders)
⊕ blackholebrewery.co.uk
Tours by arrangement

⊗ This 10-barrel brewery was established in 2007 in the former Ind Coope bottling stores. Around 400 outlets are supplied direct and many more via wholesalers. Seasonal beers are available and occasional beers are produced to mark special anniversaries and events.

Bitter (OG 1040, ABV 3.8%) ◆
Amber glow and malt and spicy hop aroma. Fresh, lively session beer hopped to give a clean, crisp finish of hoppy dryness and touch of astringency.

Cosmic (OG 1044, ABV 4.2%) ◆
Almost golden with an initial malt aroma. The complex balance of malt and English hops give lingering tastes of nuts, fruit and dry, hoppy bitterness.

Red Dwarf (OG 1045, ABV 4.4%) ◆
Red as named with a sweetshop start of sugary sweet fruits with citrus centres. Malt is elbowed aside by the hops which dominate the tongue-tickling bitter end.

Supernova (OG 1048, ABV 4.8%) ◆
Pure gold. Like marmalade made from Seville oranges and grapefruit, the aroma mimics the sweet start but gives into the hops which deliver a dry, lingering bitter finish.

Milky Way (OG 1059, ABV 6%) ◆
Honey and banana nose advises the sweet taste but not the sweet, dry spicy finish from this wheat beer.

Black Horse (NEW)

⊟ Black Horse, Mill Lane, Grainthorpe, Lincolnshire, LN11 7HU
☎ (01472) 388989 ☎ 07557 789060
⊕ blackhorsebrewing.co.uk

Brewing began in 2013 using a 0.5-barrel plant located in former stables at the Black Horse pub. The brewery is operated on a part-time basis by Tony Howkins.

Pleasant Blonde (OG 1042, ABV 4.2%)

Black Frog (OG 1044, ABV 4.6%)

Black Iris SIBA

⊟ Flowerpot, 23-25 King Street, Derby, DE1 3DZ
⊕ blackirisbrewery.co.uk

Black Iris began brewing in 2011 using a six-barrel plant behind the Flowerpot pub in Derby. Occasional and seasonal beers are brewed: see website.

American Blonde (OG 1036, ABV 3.6%)

Sunflower (OG 1041, ABV 4%)
Pale, hoppy bitter, only available at the Flowerpot.

White Fang (OG 1042, ABV 4.2%)
A pale, citrus best bitter.

Great Eastern Transatlantic Porter (OG 1047, ABV 4.6%)

Peregrine Pale (OG 1045, ABV 4.6%)

Krasny Red IPA (OG 1054, ABV 5.3%)
Red-coloured strong bitter with a malty/hoppy balance.

Iron Gate Stout (OG 1056, ABV 5.5%)
Stout with dry, roast coffee flavours.

Black Mountain Black IPA (OG 1059, ABV 5.9%)

Intergalactic IPA (OG 1057, ABV 6%)

West Coast IPA (OG 1060, ABV 6.2%)

Black Isle

Old Allengrange, Munlochy, Ross-shire, IV8 8NZ
☎ (01463) 811871 ⊕ blackislebrewery.com
Shop Mon-Sat 10am-6pm; Sun 11am-5pm (Apr-Sep)
Tours by arrangement

☺Black Isle Brewery was set up in 1998 in the heart of the Scottish Highlands. All beers are organic with Soil Association certification. Seasonal beer: see website.

Yellowhammer (OG 1038, ABV 3.9%) ⬗
A refreshing, hoppy golden ale with light hop and passion fruit throughout. A short, bitter finish.

Red Kite (OG 1042, ABV 4.2%) ⬗
Tawny ale with light malt on the nose and some fruit on the palate. Slight sweetness in the taste and a short, bitter finish.

Porter (OG 1046, ABV 4.6%) ⬗
A hint of liquorice and burnt chocolate on the nose and a creamy mix of malt and fruit in the taste.

Black Paw SIBA

Unit 4, Westgate Road, Bishop Auckland, County Durham, DL14 7AX
☎ (01388) 602144 ☎ 07557 020664
⊕ blackpawbrewery.co.uk

Black Paw began brewing in 2011 using a 12-barrel plant. Pubs are supplied across the North East of England. Seasonal beers: see website.

Bishop's Best (OG 1038, ABV 3.8%)
A classic session bitter, dark amber/ruby-coloured with a noticeable bitter taste and an underlying hint of chocolate.

Paw's Gold (OG 1040, ABV 4%)
A rich golden bitter with a complex composition of malt and an abundance of aroma hops.

Archbishop's Ale (ABV 4.1%)

Polar Paw (ABV 4.4%)

Dark Seam (OG 1050, ABV 5%)
Full-flavoured beer inspired by a traditional porter recipe. Overtones of chocolate mixed with a hint of coffee alongside a pleasing aroma of hops.

Black Sheep SIBA ◉

Wellgarth, Masham, Ripon, North Yorkshire, HG4 4EN
☎ (01765) 689227 ⊕ blacksheepbrewery.co.uk
Visitor Centre Bistro, bar and shop Sun-Wed 10am-5pm; Thu-Sat 10am-11pm
Tours by arrangement

☺Black Sheep was established 1992 by Paul Theakston, a member of Masham's famous brewing family, in the former Wellgarth Maltings using the traditional Yorkshire Square fermenting system. The company supplies a free trade of around 600 outlets with national exposure through pubcos and wholesale channels, but owns no pubs. The brewery specialises in cask ales (75% of production).

Best Bitter (OG 1038, ABV 3.8%) ⬗
A hoppy and fruity beer with strong bitter overtones, leading to a long, dry, bitter finish.

Golden Sheep (OG 1039, ABV 3.9%)
A balanced blonde beer with a dry and refreshing bitterness. Light golden in colour with fresh citrus fruit flavours and a clean, crisp finish.

Ale (OG 1044, ABV 4.4%)
A premium bitter with robust fruit, malt and hops.

Riggwelter (OG 1059, ABV 5.9%) ⬗
A fruity bitter, with complex underlying tastes and hints of liquorice and pear drops leading to a long, dry, bitter finish.

BlackBar

Unit B3, Button End Industrial Estate, Harston, Cambridgeshire, CB22 7GX
☎ (01223) 872131 ☎ 07811 499914
⊕ blackbar.co.uk

BlackBar Brewery was established in 2011. 10 outlets are supplied direct.

Bitter (OG 1036, ABV 3.6%)
A malty tawny bitter with a noble hop finish.

Blacklight (OG 1040, ABV 4%)
Golden coloured beer with a hoppy nose.

Black Economy (OG 1046, ABV 4.6%)

Blackbeck

⊟ Blackbeck Inn, Egremont, Cumbria, CA22 2NY
☎ (01946) 841661 ⊕ blackbeckbrewery.co.uk

Blackbeck was established in 2009 using a five-barrel plant. Owned by a father and daughter team, it uses a purpose-built steam system. Beers have fairground themed names and are available in bottles and mini casks.

Belle (OG 1038, ABV 3.8%) ⬗
Sweet, tasty dark mild.

Trial Run (OG 1037, ABV 3.8%) ⬗
A fresh and fruity yellow beer with a lasting hoppy finish.

Blackedge SIBA ⊚

Shuttle House, Hampson Street, Horwich, BL6 7JH
☎ (01204) 692976 ⊕ blackedgebrewery.co.uk

⊠ Blackedge, established in 2011, is a traditional brewery producing ale using only natural ingredients. In addition to the core range, occasional specials known as the 'World hop series' are brewed based on hops from around the world.

HoP (OG 1039, ABV 3.8%)
A clean, dry, refreshing and hoppy citrus, floral-flavoured session beer.

Black (OG 1047, ABV 4%)
A velvety stout with intense roasted barley flavours and rich undertones of chocolate and coffee with a liquorice finish.

Pike (OG 1042, ABV 4%)
A pale ale with plenty of sweet, citrus hop flavour.

American Pale Ale (OG 1043, ABV 4.2%)
Light, hoppy beer made using American hops giving intense citrus aromas.

BLONDe (OG 1046, ABV 4.5%)
Full-flavoured, full-bodied blonde ale, well-hopped to give clean, crisp fruity flavour and aroma.

IPA (OG 1047, ABV 4.7%)
A generously-hopped beer. Full-bodied, full-flavoured and well-balanced. Hoppy and intensely citrus with a grapefruit aroma.

Black Port (OG 1045, ABV 4.9%) ◆
Black beer with malty, fruity aroma. Rich with chocolate and dark fruits to taste with a slightly dry finish.

Blacker & Son (NEW)

3 Chester Street, Saltney, Cheshire, CH4 8BL
☎ (01244) 676765 ☎ 07985 282436
⊕ blacker-brewery.co.uk

Blacker & Son is located behind Chester Homebrew Shop in Saltney, just outside Chester. A 1.5-barrel plant is used, and brewing takes place once a week. Fortnightly brewing courses are also offered.

Eclipse (ABV 4.1%)
Light and quaffable, this pale blonde ale is easy-drinking with a crisp taste and lingering hop finish.

Chester Best (ABV 4.3%)
A best bitter, mid-brown in colour. A good session ale, smooth and satisfying.

Village Idiot (ABV 4.6%)
A Yorkshire-style bitter with complex malt flavours. Hops provide a subtle balance to the malty body.

Blackhill (NEW) SIBA

Unit 1A, Pontop Business Park, Harelaw Industrial Estate, Stanley, County Durham, DH9 8HW
☎ 07905 778286 ⊕ blackhillbrewery.com

Blackhill began brewing in 2012 using spare capacity at Geltsdale Brewery. In 2013 it moved to its own premises using a 10-barrel plant. Further beers including seasonals are planned: see website.

Top Busty (ABV 3.7%)

70 Fathom (ABV 4%)

Brass Thill (ABV 4.3%)

Blackjack (NEW) SIBA

36 Gould Street, Manchester, M4 4RN
☎ (0161) 819 2767 ⊕ blackjackbeersltd.co.uk

Blackjack started brewing in 2012, using a 4.5-barrel plant aquired from Marble brewery. Beers are named on a playing card theme, and are widely available in the local free trade as well as further afield. House beers and one-off specials are also available.

Shuffled Deck (OG 1039, ABV 3.9%)

New Deck (OG 1042, ABV 4.2%)

First Deal (OG 1044, ABV 4.4%)

Stout (OG 1050, ABV 5%)

Aces High (OG 1055, ABV 5.5%)

Blackmore

Trooper Inn, Golden Hill, Stourton Caundle, Dorset, DT10 2JW
☎ (01963) 362405 ✉ kevinstaunton@aol.com

This small 0.5-barrel brewpub began brewing in 2011. One beer is produced per week.

Ale (OG 1038, ABV 3.8%)

Pale (OG 1042, ABV 4.2%)

Blackwater

See Salopian

Blakemere SIBA ⊚

Blakemere Craft Centre, Chester Road, Sandiway, Northwich, Cheshire, CW8 2EB
☎ (01606) 301000 ☎ 07768 790300
⊕ norbrew.co.uk
Shop Mon-Fri 10am-4pm; Sat & Sun 12-4pm

⊚Formerly known as Northern, Blakemere first brewed in 2003 on a five-barrel plant located in Runcorn. It relocated to a larger unit at Blakemere Craft Centre in 2005. Bottle-conditioned beers are available from the on-site shop.

Casino (OG 1038, ABV 3.6%)

Freshly Squeezed (OG 1039, ABV 3.8%)

Navajo (OG 1039, ABV 3.9%)

Bronze (OG 1043, ABV 4.1%)

Brown Ale (OG 1046, ABV 4.4%)

Gold (OG 1044, ABV 4.5%)

Hit & Run (OG 1044, ABV 4.5%)

Jewel IPA (OG 1046, ABV 4.6%)

One-Der-Ful Wheat (OG 1046, ABV 4.7%)

Blindmans SIBA

Talbot Farm, Leighton, Frome, Somerset, BA11 4PN
☎ (01749) 880038 ⊕ blindmansbrewery.co.uk
Tours by arrangement

Established in 2002 in a converted milking parlour and purchased by its current owners in 2004, this five-barrel brewery has its own water spring. The range of ales is regularly on tap at the Cornerhouse in Frome. Seasonal beers: see website.

Buff (OG 1036, ABV 3.6%)

Amber-coloured, smooth session beer.

Golden Spring (OG 1040, ABV 4%)
Fresh and aromatic straw-coloured beer, brewed using selected lager malt.

Mine Beer (OG 1042, ABV 4.2%)
Full-bodied, copper-coloured, blended malt ale.

Icarus (OG 1045, ABV 4.5%)
Fruity, rich, mid-dark ruby ale.

Blue Anchor SIBA

▤ 50 Coinagehall Street, Helston, Cornwall, TR13 8EL
☎ (01326) 562821 ⊕ spingoales.com
Tours by arrangement

⊠ The Blue Anchor is a 15th-century thatched brewpub, the oldest continuously brewing plant in the country. It's home to the famous Spingo ales which are produced from the well water beneath the establishment. All regular brews are available bottle-conditioned.

Flora Daze/Spingo Original (OG 1040, ABV 4%)
A well-hopped bitter with a strong floral/citrus aroma from a late addition of hops. A good hop character with a smooth, delicate, dry finish.

Ben's Stout (OG 1048, ABV 4.8%)
A classic stout complemented by the brewery's sweet spring water.

Spingo Middle (OG 1050, ABV 5.1%) ◥
Tawny in appearance, aromatic malt and esters lead into a sweet, malty and bitter taste with hints of green apple and grapefruit. The finish is lingering malt and dry bitterness.

Spingo Special (OG 1066, ABV 6.7%) ▨
Darker than Middle with a pronounced earthy character on the nose balanced by rich fruit. Fruit and peppery hops dominate the mouth, followed by a long finish with malt, fruit and hops.

Blue Ball

Kash 22 Brew & Chew, 22 Church Street, Frodsham, Cheshire, WA6 6QW
☎ (01928) 733116 ⊕ blueballbrewery.com

☺Blue Ball originally started brewing as Bridgewater Brewery in 2010 behind a homebrew shop in Frodsham. The business relocated and expanded later the same year using a five-barrel plant. A bar and restaurant, Kash, opened in Chester in 2011.

Mild Mannered Mae (OG 1033, ABV 3.5%)
A black/brown mild with a sweet, malty fruity aroma. The sweet taste is kept in check by a light bitterness from the hops and the roasted malt.

Indie Girl (OG 1036, ABV 3.8%)
Malts provide body and structure and a pale gold hue, while hops deliver an aroma of citrus and tropical fruits. The finish is clean and dry with a long, hoppy aftertaste.

Laid Back Lucille (OG 1036, ABV 3.8%)
An auburn bitter with a light malt profile showing some caramel notes. Hops give a floral and citrus fruit aroma. The finish is bitter but not overpowering.

Gold Digger (OG 1038, ABV 4%)
A subtle malt profile makes way for a tropical fruit explosion from the hops. The nose is sweet and

fruity giving hints of passion fruit. The taste is crisp and bitter with a refreshing dry finish.

Zeppelin (OG 1053, ABV 5.5%)

Spank (Industrial IPA) (OG 1059, ABV 6%)
Sweetish strong ale.

Blue Bee SIBA

Unit 29-30, Hoyland Road Industrial Estate, Sheffield, South Yorkshire, S3 8AB
☎ 07791 662484 ⊕ bluebeebrewery.co.uk
Tours by arrangement

Blue Bee Brewery was set up in 2010 by award-winning brewer Richard Hough. The beers are available to the free trade across Yorkshire, the Midlands and north west England with the core range complemented by an eclectic mix of seasonal beers: see website.

Bees Knees Bitter (OG 1040, ABV 4%)
A dark bitter, deep chestnut in colour with a distinctive hop character leading to a bitter finish.

Nectar Pale (OG 1040, ABV 4%)
A refreshing pale ale.

Lustin for Stout (OG 1048, ABV 4.8%)
A rich, complex stout, full-bodied and black in colour. Plenty of roast malt flavours.

Tangled Up IPA (OG 1060, ABV 6%)
A pale IPA with a floral, hoppy aroma, hoppy middle with citrus flavours and a bitter finish.

Blue Bell

Cranesgate South, Whaplode St Catherine, Lincolnshire, PE12 6SN
☎ (01406) 701000 ☎ 07813 819746

Office: Sycamore House, Lapwater Lane, Holbeach St Marks, Lincolnshire, PE12 8EX
⊕ bluebellbrewery.co.uk
Tours by arrangement

☺The Blue Bell Brewery was founded in 1998 in a former potato shed located behind the Blue Bell pub, Whaplode St Catherine. The brewery operates as a separate business from the Blue Bell pub but the pub does act as the brewery tap. Bottle-conditioned beers are available.

Frightened Pheasant (OG 1037, ABV 3.7%)

Old Honesty (OG 1040, ABV 4.1%)

Ingledingle Ale (OG 1054, ABV 5.1%)

Blue Cow

▤ High Street, South Witham, Lincolnshire, NG33 5QB
☎ (01572) 768432 ⊕ bluecowinn.co.uk
Tours by arrangement

☺Owned by Simon Crathorn since 2005, Blue Cow is a traditional 13th-century pub with a brewery. The beer is only available in the pub or at CAMRA beer festivals.

Best Bitter (OG 1038, ABV 3.8%)

Blue Monkey SIBA

10 Pentrich Road, Giltbrook Industrial Park, Giltbrook, Nottinghamshire, NG16 2UZ
☎ 0800 028 0329 ⊕ bluemonkeybrewery.com
Shop Mon-Sat 9.30am-4.30pm

⊕Blue Monkey was established in 2008 as a 10-barrel plant but moved in 2010 to a bigger site to meet increasing demand. It now brews around 15,000 pints a week to supply over 200 local outlets and selected national distributors. The name stems from a nickname for the blue flames that used to rise from the chimneys of Stanton Ironworks, a prominent local foundry.

BG Sips (OG 1041, ABV 4%) ▯ ◆
Pale golden hoppy beer, brewed mainly with Brewers Gold hops. Very fruity and bitter.

99 Red Baboons (OG 1042, ABV 4.2%) ◆
Red in colour with a malty fruitiness. Not overly hoppy.

Guerrilla (OG 1052, ABV 4.9%) ◆
A creamy stout, full of roast malt flavour and a slightly sweet finish.

Ape Ale (OG 1052, ABV 5.4%)

Bluestone (NEW)

Unit 6, Daniel Street Industrial Estate, Whitworth, Lancashire, OL12 8BX
☎ 07802 792536 ⊕ bluestonebrewery.co.uk

Bluestone is a small one-barrel brewery using traditional methods including a two-storey 'double drop' fermenting system. Brewing only takes place at weekends, operating from the back of the owner's industrial unit. There are plans for relocation and expansion.

Quarrymans Stout (OG 1041, ABV 4%)
A double-dropped stout, black and full of traditional flavours.

EPA (English Pale Ale) (OG 1042, ABV 4.2%)
A traditional dry pale ale. Clear with strong malt and hop flavours.

AKA (Amber Kitchen Ale) (OG 1043, ABV 4.4%)
Based on an old recipe this is a mid-brown, lightly-hopped ale with a caramel and liquorice malty flavour.

Blythe SIBA

Blythe House Farm, Lichfield Road, Hamstall Ridware, Staffordshire, WS15 3QQ
☎ 07773 747724 ⊕ blythebrewery.co.uk
Tours by arrangement

⊗ Blythe began brewing in 2003 using a 2.5-barrel plant in a converted barn. As well as specials, seasonal beers are produced on a quarterly basis. 15 outlets are supplied. Bottle-conditioned beers are also available.

Ridware Pale (OG 1042, ABV 4.3%) ◆
Bright and golden with a bitter floral hop aroma and citrus taste. Good and hop-sharp, bitter and refreshing. Long, lingering bite with ripples of citrus across the tongue.

Chase Bitter (OG 1044, ABV 4.4%) ◆
Fresh fruity aroma touched by malt from this amber beer. Sweet biscuity start with caramel support and fruit hints. Hops emerge and intensify to give a satisfyingly bitter finish.

Staffie (OG 1044, ABV 4.4%) ◆
Hoppy and grassy aroma with hints of sweetness from this amber beer. A touch of malt at the start is soon overwhelmed by hops. A full hoppy, mouth-watering finish.

Palmers Poison (OG 1045, ABV 4.5%) ◆
Refreshing darkish beer. Tawny but light headed. Coffee truffle aroma, pleasingly sweet to start but with a good hop mouthfeel.

Johnsons (OG 1056, ABV 5.2%) ▯ ▯ ◆
Black with a thick head. Refreshingly hoppy and full bodied with lingering bitterness of chocolate, dates, coal smoke and liquorice.

Bob's SIBA

Healey Brewery, Brewers Pride, Low Mill Road, Healey, West Yorkshire, WF5 8ND
☎ 07789 693597
Tours by arrangement

⊕The brewery was founded in 2002 by Bob Hunter in outbuildings behind the Red Lion pub and moved to a new 10-barrel plant, part of the original Ossett brewhouse, in 2009. Production is up to 650 gallons a week and the beers appear regularly in more than 25 freehouses across West Yorkshire and in the West Midlands via wholesalers.

White Lion (OG 1043, ABV 4.3%)
Pale, flowery, lager-style beer.

Chardonnayle (OG 1051.5, ABV 5.1%)
Complex, strong pale ale with hints of lemongrass and fruits, aroma hops dominating the flavour.

Boggart Hole Clough SIBA

Building 7, Wilsons Park, Monsall Road, Newton Heath, Manchester, M40 8WN
☎ (0161) 277 9666 ⊕ boggart-brewery.co.uk

⊕Boggart Hole Clough has expanded steadily and is now an eight-barrel plant in its third home with its own distribution arm, working extensively with north-west breweries and outlets. Monthly specials and commissions are available: see website.

Cascade (OG 1040, ABV 4%)
A bitter, hoppy session ale.

Dark Mild (OG 1040, ABV 4%)

I Am Beer (OG 1042, ABV 4.2%)

Rum Porter (OG 1046, ABV 4.6%)
A classic porter with a smooth roast finish, enhanced by a sweet, spicy hop taste, complemented with a hint of dark rum.

Bollington SIBA

▤ Adlington Road, Bollington, Cheshire, SK10 5JT
☎ (01625) 575380 ⊕ bollingtonbrewing.co.uk
Tours by arrangement

⊗ Lee Wainwright bought the Vale Inn, a closed freehouse in Bollington, in 2005 and started brewing in 2008. The brewery is situated just 50 metres from the pub. Around 40 outlets are supplied direct. A second pub, the Park Tavern in Macclesfield, opened in 2011.

Light Nancy (OG 1035, ABV 3.4%)
A pale beer with grapefruit and lemon hop flavours.

Long Hop (OG 1039, ABV 3.9%)
Pale lager-style bitter with fruity, refreshing hops.

Nights (OG 1038, ABV 3.9%)
A smooth, traditional dark ale with a light flavour and aroma, but a definite bitterness.

Park Life (OG 1041, ABV 4.1%)
A light golden bitter with a slightly spicy aroma and hop aftertaste.

White Nancy (OG 1040, ABV 4.1%)
A pale bitter with good hoppiness and a light body.

Best (OG 1041, ABV 4.2%)
A delightfully hoppy bitter. Clean and crisp with a refreshing bitter aftertaste.

Dinner Ale (OG 1042, ABV 4.3%)
Deep copper-coloured beer with a fresh, slightly fruity nose, a traditional-style bitter with a dry, hoppy finish.

Oat Mill Stout (OG 1049, ABV 5%)
An oatmeal stout with a twist. A hoppy, bitter taste keeps the sweetness in check.

Eastern Nights (OG 1056, ABV 5.6%)
A modern IPA.

Goldenthal (OG 1068, ABV 7.4%)
A golden, hoppy barley wine.

Bootleg

⧉ Horse & Jockey, 9 The Green, Chorlton-cum-Hardy, M21 9HS
☎ (0161) 860 7794 ⊕ horseandjockeychorlton.com
Tours by arrangement

⊗ Situated in the Horse & Jockey Inn, the brewery is in a tiny space above the dining room. The regular beers are complemented by seasonal ales.

Chorlton Pale Ale (OG 1040, ABV 4%)
A refreshing blonde beer with a hint of citrus and a long, dry finish.

Black Widow (OG 1041.3, ABV 4.4%)
A smooth, easy-drinking stout with subtle hints of coffee and chocolate and a long, dry finish.

Contraband (OG 1037.2, ABV 4.5%)
A crisp, dry pale ale, very hoppy with a hint of grapefruit.

Lawless (OG 1042.6, ABV 4.7%)
A somewhat dry taste, this copper coloured ale has a hint of spice in the nose and a slight presence of caramel in the after taste.

Punctured Pipeline (OG 1047, ABV 4.7%)

Borough Arms

⧉ 33 Earle Street, Crewe, Cheshire, CW1 2BG
☎ (01270) 254999 ⊕ borougharmscrewe.co.uk
Tours by arrangement

☺A two-barrel brewery opened in 2005 to supply the pub. The beers are available at the pub and beer festivals. Brewing is currently carried out by consultant Iain Turnbull and local guest brewers. Seasonal and one-off brews are available.

Botanist SIBA

⧉ Convivial London Pubs, 3-5 Kew Green, Kew, TW9 3AA
☎ (020) 8948 4838 ⊕ thebotanistkew.com/brewery
Tours by arrangement

⊗ Botanist Brewery brews both for the Botanist pub, which is its home and main outlet, and other pubs within the Convivial group.

65 Mild (OG 1035, ABV 3.4%) ◄

Light drinking traditional dark ruby red mild with roasted malt notes throughout. The name comes from the nearby bus route.

Humulus Lupulus (OG 1038, ABV 3.8%) ◄
Fruity American hops are pronounced on the nose, palate and slightly dry finish. Bitterness grows on drinking this golden ale.

391 Brown Ale (OG 1040, ABV 4%) ◄
Sweet chocolate roast nose with faint fruit. Flavour is roast, biscuity with a little bitterness and fruit fading in the aftertaste.

OK (OG 1040, ABV 4.2%) ◄
Pale brown refreshing best bitter with malt and delicate fudge notes and a dry, mildly bitter finish.

Q Gold (OG 1044, ABV 4.5%) ◄
Easy drinking ale with a biscuity sweetness and low bitterness. There is a gentle lager hop character throughout.

Night Porter (OG 1048, ABV 5%) ◄
Dark brown porter with a creamy mouthfeel but easy drinking. Dark roast is present with some fruit. Slightly bitter finish.

Queen Charlotte (OG 1049, ABV 5.2%)
A Kolsch-style beer; pale straw-coloured and clear. The taste is delicate and refreshing, gently fruity and a little sweet, often with some biscuitiness.

Maximus (OG 1056, ABV 5.8%)
Crystal malt comes through with a crisp bite along with a big American hop flavour

Botley SIBA

Botley Mills, Mill Hill, Botley, Hampshire, SO30 2GB
☎ (01489) 784867 ⊕ botleybreweryltd.webs.com

Botley began brewing in 2010 using a five-barrel plant. Seasonal and bottle-conditioned beers are also available.

Mill (OG 1038, ABV 3.8%)

Best (OG 1042, ABV 4.2%)

Gringo's Gold (OG 1045, ABV 4.5%)

Bottle Brook

Church Street, Kilburn, Belper, Derbyshire, DE56 0LU
☎ (01332) 880051 ☎ 07971 189915

⊗ A sister brewery to Leadmill (qv), Bottle Brook was established in 2005 using a 2.5-barrel plant on a tower gravity system. New World hops are predominantly used. The core range of beers is supplemented by one-off brews.

Columbus (OG 1040, ABV 4%)

Heanor Pale Ale (OG 1041, ABV 4.2%)

Roadrunner (OG 1047, ABV 4.8%)

Mellow Yellow (OG 1054, ABV 5.7%)

Rapture (OG 1058, ABV 5.9%)

Sand in the Wind (OG 1060, ABV 6.1%)

Bowland SIBA

Bashall Town, Clitheroe, Lancashire, BB7 3LQ
☎ (01200) 443592 ☎ 07952 639465
⊕ bowlandbrewery.com
Shop Mon-Sun 10.30am-5pm
Tours by arrangement

☺Now at full capacity of 50 barrels per week, with 100 outlets, Bowland (formed 2003) is developing its range of beers, while increasing production of Artisan Gold, a premium bottle-conditioned beer. Seasonal beers: see website.

Pheasant Plucker (OG 1036, ABV 3.6%)

Sawley Tempted (OG 1038, ABV 3.7%)
A copper-coloured fruity session bitter with toffee in the mouth and a spicy finish.

Gold (OG 1039, ABV 3.8%)
A hoppy golden bitter with intense grapefruit flavours.

Hen Harrier (OG 1040, ABV 4%)
A pale gold bitter with soft citrus, peach and apricot flavours throughout.

Dragon (OG 1043, ABV 4.2%)
A golden bitter with rounded fruit in the mouth and a refreshing finish.

Admiral of the Blues (OG 1046, ABV 4.4%)

Bowman SIBA ⊙

Wallops Wood, Sheardley Lane, Droxford, Hampshire, SO32 3QY
☎ (01489) 878110 ⊕ bowman-ales.com
Tours by arrangement

⊠ Brewing started in 2006 on a 20-barrel brew plant housed in converted farm buildings. The brewery supplies more than 100 outlets. In addition to the standard beers a range of celebratory and seasonal brews are produced. Bottle-conditioned beers are also available.

Elderado (OG 1036, ABV 3.5%) 🍺 ◆
Straw-coloured beer flavoured with elderflower. A citrus aroma with a fruity, bitter taste. Good hoppiness and a background sweetness. A dry, bitter finish.

Swift One (OG 1038, ABV 3.8%) ◆
A golden ale characterised by hoppiness throughout, although malt characteristics have increased recently. Aroma of grapefruit leads to a pleasing bitterness and a background sweetness. A long, dry finish.

Wallops Wood (OG 1040, ABV 4%) ◆
Well-balanced bitter, with no particular flavour dominating this well-crafted beer. Malt flavours throughout are balanced by toffee notes and sweetness in the flavour and a slightly dry finish.

Quiver Bitter (OG 1043, ABV 4.5%) 🍺 🍺 ◆
A fruity best bitter, golden in colour with a hoppy aroma leading through to a balanced, bittersweet taste and a refreshing hoppy finish.

Warbler (OG 1046, ABV 4.8%)
A conker-coloured premium bitter with an initial sweetness giving way to a dry chestnut finish. Smooth, full-bodied and fragrant.

Bowness Bay

Green Lane, Winster, Cumbria, LA23 3NL
☎ 07768 116794 ⊕ bownessbaybrewing.co.uk

Bowness Bay began brewing in 2012 using a four-barrel plant from the closed Northcote Brewery in Norwich.

Teal Tipple (ABV 3.6%)

Mere Gold (ABV 3.8%)

Swan Blonde (ABV 4%)

Swift Bitter (ABV 4.5%)

Swan Black (ABV 4.6%)

Box Steam SIBA ⊙

The Midlands, Holt, Wiltshire, BA14 6RU
☎ (01225) 782700 ⊕ boxsteambrewery.com
Tours by arrangement

⊠ The brewery was founded in 2004 and boasts a Fulton steam-fired copper, hence the name. Two pubs are owned and more than 100 outlets supplied. Seasonal beers are brewed.

Golden Bolt (OG 1037.5, ABV 3.8%)
A straw-coloured bitter with a slightly dry, hoppy aftertaste.

Chuffin Ale (OG 1040, ABV 4%)
A full-flavoured bitter, chestnut brown in colour with a fruity aroma and a smooth, rich taste.

Tunnel Vision (OG 1040.5, ABV 4.2%)
A well-rounded light amber bitter. Clean tasting, with a slight bitterness on the finish.

Steam Porter (OG 1045, ABV 4.4%)
A smooth drinking, well-rounded porter with a slightly smoky aroma. Roasted malts give way to chocolate undertones on the palate.

Funnel Blower (OG 1045, ABV 4.5%)
Dark brown in colour, with a subtle vanilla aroma. Vanilla sweetness contrasts nicely with the slight bitterness from roasted barley and chocolate malts.

Piston Broke (OG 1045, ABV 4.5%)
A fine, full-bodied deep golden ale with a refreshing hoppy, citrus palate and a subtle fruit-hop aroma.

Derail Ale (OG 1049, ABV 5.2%)
A hoppy traditional India Pale Ale. Full-flavoured with an intense floral aroma, finished with well-balanced bitterness.

Bradfield SIBA ⊙

Watt House Farm, High Bradfield, Sheffield, South Yorkshire, S6 6LG
☎ (0114) 285 1118 ⊕ bradfieldbrewery.co.uk
Shop Mon-Sat 10am-4pm

☺Established in 2005, Bradfield is a family-run business, based on a working farm in the Peak District using pure Milstone Grit springwater. In 2009 the brewery bought its first brewery tap, the Nags Head in Loxley. Seasonal beers: see website. Bottle-conditioned beers and five-litre mini casks are also available.

Farmers Bitter (OG 1039, ABV 3.9%)
A traditional copper-coloured malt ale with a floral aroma.

Farmers Blonde (OG 1041, ABV 4%)
Pale, blonde beer with citrus and summer fruits aromas.

Farmers Stout (OG 1045, ABV 4.5%)
A dark stout with roasted malts and flaked oats and a subtle, bitter hop character.

Brains IFBB ⊙

Crawshay Street, Cardiff, CF10 1SP
☎ (029) 2040 2060 ⊕ sabrain.com

⊕Brains began trading at the Old Brewery in Cardiff in 1882 when Samuel Arthur Brain and his uncle Joseph Benjamin Brain purchased a site founded in 1713. The company has remained in family ownership ever since. The full range of Brain's ales is now produced at the company's Cardiff Brewery (formerly Hancock's), bought from Bass in 1999. The company owns more than 270 pubs, spread throughout Wales, the West Country and the Midlands. Brains is the official sponsor of the Wales Rugby Union team, the Football Association of Wales and Glamorgan County Cricket Club. Seasonal beers: see website.

Dark (OG 1035.5, ABV 3.5%) ◆
A tasty, classic dark brown mild, a mix of malt, roast, caramel with a background of hops. Bittersweet, mellow and with a lasting finish of malt and roast.

Bitter (OG 1036, ABV 3.7%) ◆
Amber coloured with a gentle aroma of malt and hops. Malt, hops and bitterness combine in an easy-drinking beer with a bitter finish.

SA (OG 1042, ABV 4.2%) ◆
A mellow, full-bodied beer. Gentle malt and hop aroma leads to a malty, hop and fruit mix with a balancing bitterness.

SA Gold (OG 1042, ABV 4.2%) ◆
A golden beer with a hoppy aroma. Well balanced with a zesty hop, malt, fruit and balancing bitterness; a similar satisfying finish.

Rev James (OG 1045.5, ABV 4.5%) ◆
A faint malt and fruit aroma with malt and fruit flavours in the taste, initially bittersweet. Bitterness balances the flavour and makes this an easy-drinking beer.

Contract brewed for Molson Coors:

Hancock's HB (OG 1038, ABV 3.3%) ◆
A pale brown, slightly malty beer whose initial sweetness is balanced by bitterness but lacks a noticeable finish. A consistent if inoffensive Welsh beer.

Worthington's Bitter (OG 1038, ABV 3.6%)
A pale brown bitter of thin and unremarkable character.

M&B Brew XI (OG 1039.5, ABV 3.8%)
A sweet, malty beer with a hoppy, bitter aftertaste.

Brakspear ◉

Eagle Maltings, The Crofts, Witney, Oxfordshire, OX28 4DP
☎ (01993) 890800 ⊕ brakspear-beers.co.uk
Merchandise available online or in Brewery store Mon-Sat 10am-5pm (excluding Bank Holidays)
Tours by arrangement

Brakspear beers have been brewed in Oxfordshire since 1779. They continue to be traditionally crafted at the Wychwood Brewery (qv) in the historic market town of Witney using the original Victorian square fermenters and the renowned 'double drop' fermenting system. Part of Marston's PLC.

Bitter (OG 1035, ABV 3.4%)
A classic copper-coloured pale ale with a big hop resins, juicy malt and orange fruit aroma, intense hop bitterness in the mouth and finish, and a firm maltiness and tangy fruitiness throughout.

Oxford Gold (OG 1040, ABV 4%)

English Target hops give this beer a remarkable aroma. Late hopping with Goldings and fermentation by the Brakspear yeast creates a remarkable zesty aroma, a full fruity flavour and a golden colour.

Brampton SIBA

Unit 5, Chatsworth Business Park, Chatsworth Road, Chesterfield, Derbyshire, S40 2AR
☎ (01246) 221680 ⊕ bramptonbrewery.co.uk
Tours by arrangement

⊕The original Brampton brewery closed in 1955. In 2007 a new brewery was established, and brewing commenced on an eight-barrel plant. Two tied houses are situated close to the brewery. Seasonal and bottle conditioned-beers are available.

Golden Bud (OG 1037, ABV 3.8%) ◆
Crisp and refreshing golden bitter with a pleasant balance of citrus, sweetness and bitter flavours. Light and easy to drink.

1302 (OG 1040, ABV 4%)

Griffin (OG 1041, ABV 4.1%)

Best (OG 1041, ABV 4.2%) ◆
Classic, drinkable bitter with a predominantly malty taste, balanced by caramel sweetness and a developing bitterness in the aftertaste.

Impy Dark (OG 1047, ABV 4.3%) ◆
Strong roasted coffee aroma and a rich flavour of vine fruit and chocolate combine to make this a tasty mild ale.

Jerusalem (OG 1046, ABV 4.6%)

Wasp Nest (OG 1049, ABV 5%) ◆
Strong and complex with malt and hop flavours and a caramel sweetness.

Brancaster

See Beeston

Brandon

76 High Street, Brandon, Suffolk, IP27 0AU
☎ (01842) 878496 ☎ 07876 234689
⊕ brandonbrewery.co.uk
Shop Mon-Sat 9am-5pm (please ring before visiting); closed Thu
Tours by arrangement

Brandon started brewing in 2005 on the site of an old dairy. Beers are based on traditional styles which include unique recipes and incorporate locally-sourced ingredients. All beers are also available bottle-conditioned.

Breckland Gold (OG 1038, ABV 3.8%)
A combination of Goldings and Fuggles hops give a delicate, smooth, slightly spicy taste and a dry, lingering, malty finish.

Old Rodney (OG 1040, ABV 4%) ◆
Damson jam aroma precedes a flavoursome balance of malt, fruit and hops in this tawny best bitter. Gently fading finish.

Paddys Pride (OG 1040, ABV 4%)
A dark ruby mild, smooth malt flavours ending with a little roast bitterness.

Saxon Gold (OG 1040, ABV 4%)

A pale, golden beer with a subtle aroma of hops. The taste is a clean, crisp mix of spice and bitter fruits with a dry, hoppy finish.

Strawberry Wheat (OG 1040, ABV 4%)
A pale ale, includes torrefied wheat and pulped strawberries.

Waxies Dargle (OG 1040, ABV 4%)
A copper coloured beer with rich malt flavours and a rich hoppiness.

Molly's Secret (OG 1041, ABV 4.1%)
A pale ale based on an old recipe.

Norfolk Poacher (OG 1041, ABV 4.1%) ◆
A rich malty roast aroma that follows through to flavours of malt, hops, fruit and sweetness. Upstanding sweetness in a long complex finish.

Royal Ginger (OG 1041, ABV 4.1%)
A refreshing summer ale with a distinctive mix of malt and hoppy spice, balanced with a gentle ginger flavour and finish.

Gun Flint (OG 1042, ABV 4.2%)
Roasted malts are used to produce a malty, chocolate flavour. This combines well with spicy hops to give a dry, bittersweet, roasted malt finish.

Wee Drop of Mischief (OG 1042, ABV 4.2%)
An amber-coloured premium bitter. Gentle malt flavours give way to a delightful hop character and a dry, increasingly bitter aftertaste.

Rusty Bucket (OG 1044, ABV 4.4%) ◆
Aromas of figs and malt with dried fruit, and flavours of malt and hops, leading to a bitter, biscuity aftertaste. A well-balanced traditional brown best bitter.

Grumpy Bastard (OG 1045, ABV 4.5%)

Slippery Jack (OG 1045, ABV 4.5%)
A dark brown stout. Complex but well-balanced flavours of roasted grain and hop bitterness. Dry with a lingering, pleasantly bitter finish.

'Old on to your 'at (OG 1047, ABV 4.7%)
Dark amber in colour, big malt flavours overlaid with a tangy fruit bitterness.

Nappertandy (OG 1050, ABV 5%)
A reddish amber beer, full-bodied with a malty aroma. Crisp and spicy with an underlying citrus flavour and a dry, malty, bitter fruit finish.

Brandy Cask

≣ 25 Bridge Street, Pershore, Worcestershire, WR10 1AJ
☎ (01386) 552602
Tours by arrangement

☺Brewing started in 1995 in a refurbished bottle store in the garden of the pub. Brewery and pub now operate under one umbrella, with brewing carried out by the owner/landlord.

Branscombe Vale SIBA ⊙

Branscombe, Devon, EX12 3DP
☎ (01297) 680511 ⊕ branscombevalebrewery.co.uk

⊗ The brewery was set up in 1992 by two former dairy workers in cowsheds owned by the National Trust. The two partners converted the sheds and dug their own well. In 2008 a new 25-barrel plant was shoehorned in through the roof. Occasional and bottle-conditioned beers are also available: see website.

Mild (OG 1036, ABV 3.7%)

Branoc (OG 1038, ABV 3.8%) ▯ ◆
Pale brown brew with a malt and fruit aroma and a hint of caramel. Malt and bitter taste with a dry, hoppy finish.

Draymans Best Bitter (OG 1042, ABV 4.2%)

BVB Best Bitter (OG 1045, ABV 4.6%) ◆
Reddy/brown-coloured beer with a fruity aroma and taste, and bitter/astringent finish.

Summa That (OG 1049, ABV 5%)
Light golden beer with a clean and refreshing taste and a long, hoppy finish.

Brass Castle SIBA

82 Market Street, Brass Castle Hill, Pocklington, East Yorkshire, YO42 2AB
☎ 07563 579723 ⊕ brasscastlebrewery.co.uk
Tours by arrangement

Brass Castle is a one-barrel brewery in the garage of a townhouse in the centre of Pocklington. Production is boosted by using spare capacity at the Earl of Halifax's Garrowby Estate four-barrel brewhouse. All beers are unfined and so are suitable for vegetarians and vegans.

Cliffhanger (OG 1040, ABV 3.8%)
A refreshing hop-laden golden ale infused with citrus notes.

Flying Man (ABV 3.8%)

Tail Gunner (OG 1042, ABV 4%)
A dry-hopped rye session ale with a reddish hue.

Best Bitter (OG 1046, ABV 4.5%)
A brass-coloured traditional special bitter, designed as a malt showcase and crammed with hops.

Bad Kitty (OG 1060, ABV 5.5%)
A chewy chocolate vanilla dream of a porter.

Sunshine (OG 1061, ABV 5.7%)
A US West Coast hop-dominated IPA. Bitterness is balanced by malt sweetness and dry hopping rounds out the aroma.

Burnout (OG 1062, ABV 5.8%)
A robust peat-smoked porter.

Braydon SIBA

The Brewhouse, Preston West Farm, Preston, Chippenham, Wiltshire, SN15 4DX
☎ (01249) 892900 ⊕ braydonales.co.uk
Tours by arrangement

⊠ In 2009 three friends bought the former Burford Brewery and relocated it to a farm building in Wiltshire. Brewing takes place on a five-barrel plant and pubs and clubs are supplied in the area. Direct sales are also available.

RWB (Royal Wootton Bassett) (OG 1041, ABV 4%)
Light copper-coloured ale with a gentle bitter taste.

Yer Tiz (OG 1042, ABV 4.1%)
Triple-hopped but well-balanced standard bitter.

Potwalloper (OG 1044, ABV 4.4%)
A malty, ruby-coloured ale.

Brecon SIBA

8a, Brecon Enterprise Park, Brecon, Powys, LD3 8BT
☎ (01874) 620800 ⊕ breconbrewing.co.uk
Shop Mon-Fri 9am-5pm

Brecon was established in 2011 by Buster Grant. Seasonal and special beers are also available including beers from the Genesis Project: see website.

Three Beacons (OG 1030, ABV 3%)
An American Pale Ale, gold-coloured, full-bodied and extensively hopped.

Welsh Beacons (OG 1037, ABV 3.7%)
A golden bitter brewed in the style of a Welsh pale ale with a gentle floral bitterness and a full flavour.

Twilight Beacons (OG 1040, ABV 4%)
A session ale with a distinct hoppy finish.

Gold Beacons (OG 1042, ABV 4.2%)
A deep golden ale with a soft bitterness balanced by the blend of malts.

Red Beacons (ABV 5%)
A red-hued, smooth premium ale, full-bodied with a generous balance of hops.

Breconshire SIBA

Ffrwdgrech Industrial Estate, Brecon, Powys, LD3 8LA
☎ (01874) 623731 ⊕ breconshirebrewery.com
Shop Mon-Fri 8.30am-4.30pm
Tours by arrangement

Breconshire was founded in 2002 as part of C H Marlow, a wholesaler and distributor of beers, wines and spirits in south Wales. The 10-barrel plant uses British malts blended with a range of British whole hops. Bottle-conditioned beers are available.

Brecon County Ale (OG 1037, ABV 3.7%) ◆
A traditional amber-coloured bitter. A clean hoppy flavour, background malt and fruit, with a good thirst-quenching bitterness.

Welsh Pale Ale (OG 1037, ABV 3.7%)
Pale golden, mildy hopped session ale. Brewed to an old Welsh style of pale ale.

Golden Valley (OG 1042, ABV 4.2%) ◆
Golden in colour with a welcoming aroma of hops, malt and fruit. A balanced mix of these flavours and moderate, building bitterness lead to a satisfying, rounded finish.

Pist n' Broke (OG 1043, ABV 4.3%)

Cribyn (OG 1045, ABV 4.5%)
A pale, straw-coloured aromatic best bitter.

Red Dragon (OG 1047, ABV 4.7%)
A red-hued premium ale brewed with a complex grist and a blend of hops for extra bite.

Ramblers Ruin (OG 1050, ABV 5%) ◆
Dark amber, full-bodied with rich biscuity malt and fruit flavours; background hops and bitterness round off the beer.

Brentwood SIBA ◉

Calcott Hall Farm, Ongar Road, Brentwood, Essex, CM14 5RE
☎ (01277) 375577 ⊕ brentwoodbrewing.co.uk
Shop Mon-Fri 9am-5pm
Tours by arrangement

⊠ Since its launch in 2006 Brentwood has steadily increased its capacity and distribution, relocating to a new purpose-built brewery unit in 2013 with a visitor centre. Seasonal and special beers are also available including more unusual beer styles under the Elephant School brand name.

BBC2 (OG 1030, ABV 2.5%)
A full-bodied, mid-brown bitter with dry, tropical citrus flavour.

IPA (OG 1039, ABV 3.7%)
A lightly-hopped, pale session beer.

Marvellous Maple Mild (OG 1038, ABV 3.7%)
Dark brown mild with a hint of maple syrup.

Best (OG 1042, ABV 4.2%)
A traditional, light-coloured best bitter with a well-rounded flavour and aroma.

Gold (OG 1043, ABV 4.3%)
A heavily-hopped golden beer with a fruity taste and bitter finish.

Chockwork Orange (OG 1067, ABV 6.5%)
A deep chocolate, malty beer brewed with oranges.

Brewed for Hewitt's Brewery Ltd:

Red Menis (ABV 3.8%)

Urbane Gorilla (ABV 4.3%)

'alf Wit (ABV 4.6%)

Un-Hung Hero (ABV 5%)

Brew By Numbers (NEW)

79 Enid Street, London, SE16 3RA
☎ (020) 7237 9794 ⊕ brewbynumbers.co.uk

Brew By Numbers began brewing in 2012 using a one-barrel plant. Mainly bottle-conditioned beers are produced.

Brew Company SIBA

Unit C, G4 Business Centre, Carlisle Street East, Sheffield, South Yorkshire, S4 7QN
☎ (0114) 270 9991 ⊠ thebrewcompany@gmail.com
Tours by arrangement

☺Brewer Pete Roberts set up this eight-barrel plant in part of a former factory in Sheffield's industrial east end in 2008. House beers are brewed for the nearby Harlequin and Riverside pubs along with regular seasonal brews.

Brewers Gold (OG 1038.8, ABV 4%)

Abyss Best Bitter (OG 1040.7, ABV 4.2%)
Dark walnut-coloured and full of malty bitter flavours.

Hop Ripper IPA (OG 1041.7, ABV 4.3%)
A pale IPA, bitter and hoppy.

Hop Monster (OG 1043.6, ABV 4.5%)

Eclipse Porter (OG 1045.5, ABV 4.7%)
A traditional, heavy-bodied, dark, malty porter with a thick mouthfeel, a dry palate and a delicate toasted coffee grain finish.

Frontier IPA (OG 1045.5, ABV 4.7%)
Straw-coloured, crisp and dry with a bitter aftertaste.

Brew On

Brockhampton Brewery, Oast House Barn, Whitbourne, Bromyard, Herefordshire, WR6 5SH
☎ (01584) 711031 ☎ 07974 685388
⊕ brew-on.co.uk

Brew On CIC is a six-barrel brewery located on the National Trust Brockhampton Estate. It's a social enterprise providing employment for disadvantaged adults. No cask beer is produced, but one-off casks for festivals are planned. Bottle-conditioned beers are produced for sale at National Trust properties. Ciders and fruit juices are also made, using fruits from National Trust Estates in Herefordshire.

Brew Star

See Anarchy

Brew Wharf

⚏ Brew Wharf Yard, Stoney Street, London, SE1 9AD
☎ (020) 7378 6601 ⊕ brewwharf.com

Brew Wharf opened in 2005 and has a bar plus a restaurant where dishes are matched with beer. Two changing special beers are brewed each month.

BrewDog

Balmacassie Drive, Balmacassie Commercial Park, Ellon, AB41 8BX
☎ (01346) 519009 ⊕ brewdog.com
Tours by arrangement

BrewDog was established in 2007 by James Watt and Martin Dickie. Seven bars are owned. Most of the production goes into bottles with some keg production. No cask beers are produced at the moment.

Brewmeister

Unit L, Isla Bank Mills, Keith, AB55 5DD
☎ 07827 333646 ⊕ brewmeister.co.uk

Brewmeister began brewing in 2012 at Kincardine O'Neil, Aberdeenshire, but moved in 2013 to an industrial unit in Keith in Moray. Beer is mainly available in bottles in selected specialist off-licenses although cask is becoming available in a few outlets.

Blonde (OG 1050, ABV 4%)
Light and refreshing with a light, hoppy profile.

Hopped to the Gates of Hell (OG 1051, ABV 4%)
An American-style pale ale loaded with hops.

Lochnagar Spray (OG 1040, ABV 4%)

Single Malt (OG 1051, ABV 5%)
Made by burning old whisky barrels to smoke the malt, giving the beer a smoked whisky hint.

The Black Cock (OG 1051, ABV 5%)
Stout made with chocolate and Muscovado sugar.

Ten (OG 1098, ABV 10.1%)
Slightly sweet with a fruity aroma.

Brewshed SIBA

Gusto Pronto Ltd, 1 Tayfen Road, Bury St Edmunds, Suffolk, IP32 6BH
☎ (01284) 848066 ⊕ brewshedbrewery.co.uk

⊠ Brewshed began brewing in 2011 with a five-barrel plant in buildings located behind the beerhouse of one of its pubs.

Pale (OG 1040, ABV 3.9%)

Best (OG 1044, ABV 4.3%)

Rioja Porter (OG 1048, ABV 4.8%)

American Blonde (OG 1055, ABV 5.5%)

Brewster's SIBA ◉

Unit 5, Burnside, Turnpike Close, Grantham, Lincolnshire, NG31 7XU
☎ (01476) 566000 ⊕ brewsters.co.uk
Tours by arrangement

⊠ Brewster is the old English term for a female brewer and Sara Barton is a modern example. Brewster's Brewery was set up in the heart of the Vale of Belvoir in 1998. Beer is supplied to around 250 outlets in central England and further afield via wholesalers. Seasonal beers: see website.

Hophead (OG 1036, ABV 3.6%) ◀
This amber beer has a floral/hoppy character; hops predominate throughout before finally yielding to grapefruit in a slightly astringent finish.

Marquis (OG 1038, ABV 3.8%) ◀
A well-balanced and refreshing session bitter with maltiness and a dry, hoppy finish.

Hop A Doodle Doo (OG 1043, ABV 4.3%)
A copper-coloured ale with a rich, full-bodied feel and fruity hop character.

Decadence (OG 1044, ABV 4.4%)
A golden ale with a hint of malt sweetness with passion fruit and grapefruit aromas on the nose. First taste gives a complex, zesty hop palate leading on to a fresh herbal finish.

Rutterkin (OG 1046, ABV 4.6%) ◀
A premium bitter with a golden appearance. A zesty hop flavour from American Mount Hood hops combines with a touch of malt sweetness to give a rich, full-bodied beer.

Stilton Porter (OG 1049, ABV 5%)
A rich, roasty porter balanced with spicy rich hop flavours.

Bridestones SIBA

Smithy Farm, Long Causeway, Blackshaw Head, Hebden Bridge, West Yorkshire, HX7 7JB
☎ (01422) 847104 ⊕ bridestonesbrewery.co.uk

☺Bridestones started brewing in 2006 and supplies more than 60 outlets. Its brewery tap is the New Delight Inn in Blackshaw. Seasonal and bottle-conditioned beers are available.

Indians Head (OG 1037, ABV 3.7%)
Light amber session bitter with a citrus hop finish.

Sandstone (OG 1039, ABV 3.9%)
A pale session ale with a smooth, clean taste.

Pennine Gold (OG 1043, ABV 4.3%) ◀
Good hop aroma and flavour; fruity, refreshing and easy to drink best bitter.

Dark Mild (OG 1045, ABV 4.5%) ◀
Dark brown strong mild with a complex nose of caramel and roasted malt. Good balance of sweetness and bitterness on the palate. Upfront bitterness in the finish.

American Pale Ale (OG 1050, ABV 5%)
A strong but easy-drinking pale ale.

Bridgehouse SIBA

Hawkcliffe Works, Hebden Road, Oxenhope, West Yorkshire, BD22 9SY
☎ (01535) 642893 ⊕ bridgehousebrewery.co.uk
Tours by arrangement

Bridgehouse began brewing in 2010 using a 10-barrel plant. The brewery moved to its present site early in 2011 to take advantage of the spring water available.

Blonde (OG 1040, ABV 4%)

Porter (OG 1045, ABV 4.5%)

Moorland Bitter (OG 1052, ABV 5.2%)

Bridgetown

▤ Albert Inn, Bridgetown Close, Totnes, Devon, TQ9 5AD
☎ (01803) 863214

Bridgetown started brewing in 2008 on a 2.5-barrel plant. Seasonal beers are available.

Albert Ale (OG 1036, ABV 3.8%)

Brightlingsea (NEW)

▤ Rosebud, 66-67 Hurst Green, Brightlingsea, Essex, CO7 0EH
☎ (01206) 304571 ⊕ rosebudpub.co.uk

Brightlingsea operates from a 3.5-barrel plant within the Rosebud pub. Head brewer Duncan Adkinson is the manager of the Rosebud's sister pub in Colchester. Six beers have been brewed so far, and the pub aims to have at least one on sale at any time.

Brighton Bier (NEW)

c/o Hand in Hand, 33 Upper St James's Street, Brighton, East Sussex, BN2 1JN
☎ 07967 681203 ⊕ brightonbier.com

Brighton Bier was established in 2013 and is based at the Hand In Hand pub in Brighton (Kemptown Brewery). Beers are available in the pub and at other outlets in the South East.

50 Ways (ABV 4%)

Red Rye (ABV 4.5%)

Maple Porter (ABV 5%)

Oatmeal Stout (ABV 6%)

Brightside SIBA

Unit 10, Dale Industrial Estate, Radcliffe, M26 1AD
☎ 07870 207442 ⊕ brightsidebrewing.co.uk

Brightside began commercial production in 2011 using a 2.5-barrel plant. It started life in the back room of the family's bakery but expanded into a dedicated industrial unit in 2013. Bottle-conditioned beers are also available.

Odin (OG 1041, ABV 3.8%)
A pale blonde session ale.

The Beast (OG 1039, ABV 3.8%)
A dark amber-coloured session bitter.

The Inn Crowd (OG 1040, ABV 3.8%)

Best Bitter (OG 1044, ABV 4.3%)

Underworld (OG 1044, ABV 4.4%)

Solstice Golden Ale (OG 1044, ABV 4.5%)

Darkside Stout (OG 1053, ABV 4.6%)

Manchester Skyline (OG 1047, ABV 4.6%)

Maverick IPA (OG 1047, ABV 4.8%)

For Robert Peel, Bury:

Bobby Dazzler (ABV 4.2%)

Bobby's Best Bitter (ABV 4.2%)

For Sedge Lynn, Chorlton:

Golden Break (ABV 4.2%)

Pot Black (ABV 4.2%)

For Wahlbar, Fallowfield:

Spinning Top (ABV 3.8%)

Brightwater (NEW) SIBA

9 Beaconsfield Road, Claygate, Surrey, KT10 0PN
☎ (01372) 462334/940295 ☎ 07775 902205
⊕ brightbrew.co.uk

⊠ Pharmacologist and zoologist Alex Coomes started producing beers commercially in 2013. The five-barrel plant is situated in a domestic residential area of Claygate in Surrey. Beers are available in polypins for domestic home occasions and can be found in several local outlets.

Little Nipper (ABV 3.3%)
A dark chestnut session bitter with a chocolate aftertaste.

Top Notch (ABV 3.5%)
A slightly sweet, dark bitter with a chocolaty and fruity hop aftertaste.

Daisy Gold (ABV 4%) ◔
A golden ale with a moderate tropical fruit hoppy character and some balancing malt leading to a bitter finish but with some sweetness.

Brigstock (NEW)

7 Park Walk, Brigstock, Kettering, Northamptonshire, NN14 3HH
☎ (01536) 373428 ⊕ brigstockbrewhouse.co.uk

Potter Philip Wilks began brewing in 2012 on a 52-litre plant using natural spring water from a local limestone aquifer. Six regular beers are brewed, and are also available bottle conditioned.

Autumn Harvest (OG 1049, ABV 4.2%)

Gold (OG 1049, ABV 4.2%)
A golden summer ale, with a zesty aroma and a refreshing citrus taste

Liberator (OG 1049, ABV 4.2%)
Refreshing ale with a wonderful bitterness, and subtle flavours of toffee, honey and mead.

Old Nick's Favourite (OG 1053, ABV 4.8%)
Dark, rich beer with flavours of liquorice and toffee.

Old Nick's Favourite (Cocoa Edition) (OG 1053, ABV 4.8%)

Potter's Ruin (OG 1053, ABV 4.8%)
The finest English malted barley and hops are used to create this beer, giving it a distinctive fruity taste, rounded with a toffee flavour and a nice hoppy finish.

Brimstage SIBA

Home Farm, Brimstage, CH63 6HY
☎ (0151) 342 1181 ☎ 07870 968323
⊕ brimstagebrewery.com
Tours by arrangement

Brewing started in 2006 on a 10-barrel plant in a redundant farm dairy in the heart of the Wirral countryside. This is Wirral's first brewery since the closure of the Birkenhead Brewery in the late 1960s. Around 60 outlets are supplied.

Sandpiper Light Ale (OG 1036.5, ABV 3.6%)
A well-balanced session beer, light and refreshing with tropical fruit flavours.

Trappers Hat Bitter (OG 1037.5, ABV 3.8%)
Gold-coloured with a complex bouquet. It provides a mouthful of fruit zest, with hints of orange and grapefruit. A refreshingly hoppy session brew.

Rhode Island Red Bitter (OG 1039, ABV 4%) ◀
Red, smooth and well-balanced malty beer with a good dry aftertaste. Some fruitiness in the taste.

Scarecrow Bitter (OG 1041, ABV 4.2%)
Orange marmalade in colour, this well-balanced session brew has a distinct citrus fruit bouquet and a bitter finish.

Briscoe's

16 Ash Grove, Otley, West Yorkshire, LS21 3EL
☎ (01943) 466515 ✉ briscoe.brewery@virgin.net

☺The brewery was launched in 1998 by microbiologist/chemist Dr Paul Briscoe in the cellar of his house with a one-barrel brew length. One brew per week is produced with several other beers produced on an irregular basis.

Chevin Light (OG 1039, ABV 3.8%)
A golden, hoppy bitter.

Lighter Shade of Pale (OG 1040, ABV 4%)

Burnsall Classic (OG 1041, ABV 4.1%)

Bristol Beer Factory SIBA

Unit A, The Old Brewery, Durnford Street, Ashton, Bristol, BS3 2AW
☎ (0117) 902 6317

Office: c/o Tobacco Factory, Raleigh Road, Southville, Bristol, BS3 1TF ⊕ bristolbeerfactory.co.uk
Shop Mon-Fri 9am-5pm
Tours by arrangement

⊗ A 30-barrel microbrewery in a part of the former Ashton Gate Brewing Co, which closed in 1933. 50 outlets are supplied and output and brewing capacity are steadily increasing. Seasonal beers are also available.

Acer (OG 1040, ABV 3.8%) ◀
Strongly-hopped low ABV amber bitter with a citrus aroma and flavour with malt and fruit to support it.

Seven (OG 1043, ABV 4.2%) ◀
Mid-brown best bitter with malty aroma. Balanced malt and hops with fruit flavours. Malt and bitter remain on the aftertaste.

Sunrise (OG 1044, ABV 4.4%) ◀
Refreshing golden ale with grassy hops giving bitter citrus fruit flavours leading to a bitter finish.

Bitter Californian (OG 1045, ABV 4.5%)

Dark-brown best bitter with a drying, spicy hop bitterness and a roast malt background. Bitter hops and roast barley lead the aftertaste.

Milk Stout (OG 1049, ABV 4.5%)

Independence (OG 1046, ABV 4.6%)

Britannia SIBA

⊜ Royal Standard of England, Forty Green, Buckinghamshire, HP9 1XS
☎ (01494) 673382 ⊕ rsoe.co.uk

⊗ Britannia began brewing in 2012. The brewery is located in one of the outbuildings at the Royal Standard of England pub in Forty Green, Buckinghamshire.

Pale Ale (OG 1042, ABV 4%)

Golden Ale (OG 1044, ABV 4.2%)

Brockley (NEW) SIBA

31 Harcourt Road, Brockley, London, SE4 2AJ
☎ 07814 584338 ⊕ brockleybrewery.co.uk

Brockley began brewing in 2013 using a five-barrel plant. It was set up in a disused builder's workshop by a group of locals passionate about real ale. Seasonal and bottle-conditioned beers are planned.

Golden Ale (ABV 3.8%)

Pale Ale (ABV 4.1%)

Brodie's SIBA

816a High Road, Leyton, London, E10 6AE
☎ 07828 498733 ⊕ brodiesbeers.com
Tours by arrangement

⊗ Siblings James and Lizzie began commercial brewing in 2008 on a five-barrel plant at the back of the William IV pub in East London. Beers are available at the William IV and their small chain of family-owned pubs as well as other local outlets. All cask ales are available bottle conditioned. Seasonal ales and festival specials are also brewed regularly: see website.

Citra (OG 1031, ABV 3.1%) ◀
Refreshing light golden ale. Citrus and tropical fruit in the aroma and flavour, which is dry and bitter but with a faint malty sweetness. The bitterness grows on drinking.

Bethnal Green Bitter (ABV 4%) ◀
A brown-coloured, refreshing but full-bodied bitter with a malty sweetness. Finish is dry with an increasing bitterness.

Old Street Pale Ale (ABV 5%) ◀
Hops and citrus fruit are balanced in this golden beer by the bitterness, a biscuity sweetness and a creamy mouthfeel.

California (OG 1053, ABV 5.3%) ◀
A smooth, yellow-coloured beer with citrus fruit on the nose. Sweet citrus fruit with a hint of honey is balanced with bitterness on the palate and aftertaste.

Broughs

Springfield Brewery, Grimstone Street, Wolverhampton, West Midlands, WV10 0JP
☎ 07814 158292

THE BREWERIES

Office: 192 Staveley Road, Wolverhampton, West Midlands, WV1 4RL ✉ broughsltd@yahoo.co.uk
Tours by arrangement

☻Broughs is a small family-run company. After using spare capacity at several breweries in the West Midlands region it now has its own premises on the site of the old Springfield Brewery in Wolverhampton, re-establishing brewing there in 2011 using a four-barrel plant. 30 outlets are supplied direct.

Springfield Bitter (OG 1040, ABV 4%)
A light golden, easy-drinking session ale with a subtle taste.

Bitter (OG 1043, ABV 4.3%)
A typical Black Country-style golden bitter, well-balanced with a sweet aftertaste.

Blonde (OG 1046, ABV 4.6%)
A contemporary hoppy and fruity pale yellow ale. Refreshing and easy drinking.

Pale Ale (OG 1048, ABV 4.8%)
A traditional strong pale ale bursting with a sweet, even-hopped flavour and a pleasant bitter finish.

Broughton SIBA

Broughton, ML12 6HQ
☎ (01899) 830345 ⊕ broughtonales.co.uk
Shop Mon-Fri 8am-4pm
Tours by arrangement

☻Founded in 1979, Broughton Ales was then one of the very first microbreweries. Broughton has developed since then and though more than 60% of production is bottled for sale in Britain and abroad, it retains a sizeable range of cask ales. Seasonal beers: see website. All beers are suitable for vegetarians.

The Reiver (OG 1038, ABV 3.6%)
A light-coloured session ale with a predominantly hoppy flavour and aroma on a background of fruity malt. The aftertaste is crisp and clean.

Willacade (OG 1036, ABV 3.6%)
A crisp and easy drinking session beer with floral and citrus on the nose.

Bramling Cross (OG 1041, ABV 4.2%)
A golden ale with a blend of malt and hop flavours followed by a hoppy aftertaste.

Clipper IPA (OG 1042, ABV 4.2%)
A light-coloured, crisp, hoppy beer with a clean aftertaste.

Merlin's Ale (OG 1042, ABV 4.2%) ◥
A well-hopped, fruity flavour is balanced by malt in the taste. The finish is bittersweet, light but dry.

Exciseman's 80/- (OG 1046, ABV 4.6%)
A traditional 80/- cask ale. A dark, malty brew. Full drinking with a good hop aftertaste.

Dark Dunter (OG 1050, ABV 5%)
Bursting with oatmeal and chocolate aromas complemented by dark roasted malts and a rich aftertaste.

Old Jock (OG 1070, ABV 6.7%)
Strong, sweetish and fruity in the finish.

Brown Cow

Brown Cow Road, Barlow, Selby, North Yorkshire, YO8 8EH
☎ (01757) 618947 ⊕ browncowbrewery.co.uk

☻Brewing since 1997, Keith and Sue Simpson are operating the six-barrel plant at its maximum capacity of 17 barrels per week. In addition to the five regular beers a range of seasonal, occasional and one-off brews is also available. Bottled beers are also brewed for Suddaby's.

Sessions (OG 1033, ABV 3.6%)
A very pale, hoppy session beer with a refreshing finish and citrus notes in the aftertaste.

Bitter (OG 1038, ABV 3.8%)
Copper-coloured classic bitter brewed with English hops. Round and full in flavour with a smooth finish.

White Dragon (OG 1039, ABV 4%)
A pale, aromatic beer with a good level of bitterness, citrus undertones and a clean finish.

Captain Oates Mild (OG 1044, ABV 4.5%) ▨
A dark mild with complex mix of malts and oats. Well-balanced with undertones of coffee and chocolate.

Mrs Simpsons Thriller in Vanilla (OG 1049, ABV 5.1%)
A rich porter brewed with fresh vanilla pods complementing the dark malts.

Broxbourne (NEW)

Unit 17, Hoddesdon Industrial Estate, Pindar Road, Hoddesdon, Hertfordshire, EN11 0DD
☎ (01438) 940937 ⊕ broxbournebrewery.co.uk

Broxbourne began brewing in 2013 using a two-barrel plant. Bottle-conditioned beers are also produced under the Fallen Angel Brewery name.

Cowgirl Gold (ABV 4.2%)

Angry Ox Bitter (ABV 4.8%)

Brunswick

▤ 1 Railway Terrace, Derby, DE1 2RU
☎ (01332) 290677
✉ thebrunswickinn@btconnect.com
Tours by arrangement

▧ The Brunswick is a purpose-built tower brewery that started brewing in 1991. A viewing area allows pub users to watch production. Bought by Everards in 2002, it is now a tenancy supplying beers to local outlets and the Everard's estate. Seasonal beers are also brewed.

Father Mike's Dark Rich Ruby (OG 1055, ABV 5.8%) ▤
A smooth, near black mild with a hint of red. Well-balanced and filled with sweet roast flavours that conceal its strength.

Black Sabbath (OG 1058, ABV 6%) ▤ ▨
A genuine mild with a voluptuous feast of coffee, chocolate and caramel flavours. High alcohol balanced with fine body.

Brüpond (NEW) SIBA

15 Argall Avenue, Leyton, London, E10 7QE
☎ (020) 8556 7438 ⊕ brupond.com

Established in 2012 by David Brassfield, Brüpond specialises in producing unusual beers. The brewery hosts regular open days: see website. All beers are suitable for vegans. Bottle-conditioned beers are available.

AiN'CHO MUM's Porter (OG 1042, ABV 4.2%)
A dark porter, infused with Ancho chillies, which bring a hint of spice and smoke to the taste buds.

Tip Top Hop (OG 1042, ABV 4.2%)
A well-hopped IPA.

Sweet Bee Honey'd Wheat (OG 1045, ABV 4.5%)
A delicate balance of hops, barley and wheat, with a light dose of honey.

Bryncelyn

Unit 303, Ystradgynlais Workshops, Trawsffordd Road, Ystradgynlais, SA9 1BS
☎ (01639) 841900 ⊕ bryncelynbrewery.org.uk
Tours by arrangement

☺Opened in 1999 the brewery relocated to its present premises in 2008 with a six-barrel plant acquired from Webbs Brewery of Ebbw Vale. As the beer names imply, the owner is fond of Buddy Holly. Seasonal beers: see website.

Holly Hop (OG 1039, ABV 3.9%) ⬚ ✎
Pale amber with a hoppy aroma. A refreshing hoppy, fruity flavour with balancing bitterness; a similar lasting finish. A beer full of flavour for its gravity.

Buddy Marvellous (OG 1040, ABV 4%) ✎
Dark brown with an inviting aroma of malt, roast and fruit. A gentle bitterness mixes roast with malt, hops and fruit, giving a complex, satisfying and lasting finish.

Sleeping Giant (ABV 4.3%)
Hoppy bitter with a balance of malt

Oh Boy (OG 1045, ABV 4.5%) ▥ ✎
An inviting aroma of hops, fruit and malt, and a golden colour. The tasty mix of hops, fruit, bitterness and background malt ends with a long, hoppy, bitter aftertaste. Full-bodied and drinkable.

Buckingham SIBA

Unit 3, Hillcrest Way, Buckingham Industrial Estate, Buckingham, MK18 1HJ
☎ (01280) 422830 ⊕ buckingham-brewery.co.uk

Buckingham began brewing in 2011 using a 2.5-barrel plant and is the only microbrewery in Buckingham; the first to brew in the historic market town since 1897. All beers are also available bottle conditioned.

Golden (ABV 3.8%)

Bitter (ABV 4%)

Mild (ABV 4%)

Old English Ale (ABV 6%)

Buffy's SIBA ◉

Rectory Road, Tivetshall St Mary, Norfolk, NR15 2DD
☎ (01379) 676523 ⊕ buffys.co.uk

⊠ Established in 1993, Buffy's brewing capacity is 20 barrels. Two pubs are owned, the Cherry Tree in Wicklewood and the White Hart in Foulden. Barley for all brewing is grown in Norfolk. Around 100 outlets are supplied. Seasonal and bottle-conditioned beers are also available.

Norwich Terrier (OG 1036, ABV 3.6%) ✎
A fragrant peach aroma introduces this refreshing, gold-coloured bitter. Strong bitter notes dominate

throughout as hops mingle with grapefruit to produce a long, increasingly dry finish.

Bitter (OG 1039, ABV 3.9%) ✎
A strong plummy aroma leads into a sweet malty beginning. Caramel notes add depth to a long fruity finish.

Mild (OG 1042, ABV 4.2%) ✎
A complex brew, deep red with a smooth but grainy feel. Caramel and blackcurrant bolster the heavy malt influence that is the main characteristic of this understated, deceptively strong mild.

Polly's Folly (OG 1043, ABV 4.3%) ✎
Complex and well-balanced with a definitive malty spine. An elderberry sweetness complements the malty character throughout as a bittersweet dryness defines the long finale.

Hopleaf (OG 1044.5, ABV 4.5%) ✎
Pale brown beer with a gentle hop nose. Strawberries mingle with the hops and malt, remaining as the malt gently subsides to leave a bittersweet, dry finish.

Mucky Duck (OG 1044, ABV 4.5%) ✎
Roasted malt with sweet fruitiness giving depth without becoming dominant. Chewy mouthfeel and lingering finish.

Norwegian Blue (OG 1049, ABV 4.9%) ✎
A nutty aroma with caramel and malt. A well balanced mix of malt and bitterness floats above a background of caramel, hops, and sweetness. A strong, increasingly bitter finish.

Ale (OG 1055, ABV 5.5%)

Bullmastiff SIBA

14 Bessemer Close, Leckwith, Cardiff, CF11 8DL
☎ (029) 2066 5292 ⊠ bob.bullmastiff@live.co.uk

An award-winning small brewery run by brothers Bob and Paul Jenkins since 1987. The name stems from their love of the bullmastiff breed. 50 outlets are supplied.

Jack the Lad (OG 1041, ABV 4.1%)

Welsh Red (OG 1048, ABV 4.8%)

Son of a Bitch (OG 1062, ABV 6%) ✎
A complex, warming amber ale with a tasty blend of hops, malt and fruit flavours, with increasing bitterness.

Bumpmill (NEW)

The Cottage, Hallfieldgate, Shirland, Derbyshire, DE55 6AG
☎ (01773) 830431 ⊕ bumpmillbrewery.co.uk

A four-barrel family brewery located in a converted building overlooking the beautiful Amber Valley. The name comes from the site of an old Bump Mill close by – bump was coarse cotton used to make wicks for candles.

Drops of Jupiter (OG 1040, ABV 4%)
A blonde pale ale with grapefruit notes leading to a slightly bitter finish.

Heart of Gold (OG 1042, ABV 4.2%)
A golden pale ale.

Thunder Road (OG 1044, ABV 4.4%)
A copper-coloured premium bitter. Full-bodied chocolate and roast malt with a smooth finish.

Glory Daze (OG 1045, ABV 4.5%)

A traditional amber bitter.

Buntingford SIBA

Royston Fine Ales Ltd, Greys Brewhouse, Therfield Road, Royston, Hertfordshire, SG8 9NW
☎ (01763) 250749 ☎ 07879 698541
⊕ buntingford-brewery.co.uk
Tours by arrangement

⊠ Brewing commenced on the current site in 2005 and has expanded to a capacity of around 60 barrels per week. The beers are brewed using water from an on-site well and all liquid waste is treated in a reed bed. The brewery is located on a conservation farm and there is a wide variety of bird life visible from the doors of the brewhouse, often including rare and endangered species. Seasonal and occasional beers are available as well as themed specials.

Highwayman (OG 1036, ABV 3.6%)

Twitchell (OG 1038, ABV 3.8%) 🍺

Polar Star (OG 1041, ABV 4%)

Burley Street SIBA

Fox & Newt, 7-9 Burley Street, Leeds, West Yorkshire, LS3 1LD
☎ (0113) 245 4505 ⊠ dawn@zigzaglighting.co.uk

☺Burley Street Brewhouse is in the cellar of the Fox & Newt pub where the first brewery was installed by Whitbread in the 1980s. The freehold was purchased by the current owners and brewing recommenced in 2010. 12 outlets are supplied direct.

The Brickyard (OG 1038.5, ABV 3.7%) ◆
Drinkable session bitter with a good mix of malt and hops, amber-coloured with an increasingly bitter finish.

SPA Francorchamps (OG 1039.5, ABV 3.8%) ◆
Light-coloured beer with a lemony, bittersweet citrus flavour, the strong bitterness from the hops is present throughout.

Laguna Seca (OG 1041, ABV 4%) ◆
A smooth, golden beer, the citrus fruit hop flavours are balanced by sweetness, particularly in the lingering aftertaste.

Burnside SIBA

Unit 3, Laurencekirk Business Park, Laurencekirk, Aberdeenshire, AB30 1EY
☎ (01561) 377316 ⊕ burnsidebrewery.co.uk

Burnside began brewing in 2010 using a 2.5-barrel plant, upgraded in 2012 to 10 barrels. Beer festivals and local outlets are supplied. Bottle-conditioned beers are available.

Black Katz (OG 1036, ABV 3.6%)
Nutty and malty dark mild with dark chocolate and espresso coffee flavours.

3-BULLZ (OG 1038, ABV 3.8%)
Medium-bodied bitter, with fruity hops and a good sweet and bitter balance.

Mad Dogz (OG 1038, ABV 3.8%)
Golden IPA with spicy hops and fruit.

Wild Rhino (OG 1045, ABV 4.5%)
Medium bodied blonde beer with a delicate citrus aroma, floral sweetness and a soft dry bitter finish.

M-PIRE (OG 1052, ABV 5.2%)
Amber-coloured premium ale with oranges in the aroma, spicy hops and a touch of chocolate.

Stealth (OG 1058, ABV 6%)
Full bodied dark bitter chocolate ale with a hint of liquorice and coffee, and blackcurrant to finish.

Burscough SIBA

c/o Hop Vine, Liverpool Road North, Burscough, Lancashire, L40 4BY
☎ (01704) 893799 ☎ 07831 225656
⊕ burscoughbrewery.co.uk

Burscough commenced brewing in 2010 in old stable buildings in the courtyard to the rear of the Hop Vine. Currently brewing on a four-barrel plant but plans are underway to relocate and expand. Seasonal beers are available.

Flat Rib Mild (OG 1036, ABV 3.6%)

Priory Gold (OG 1038, ABV 3.8%) ◆
A sweet and fruity, lightly bittered, easy-drinking session beer.

Duke of Lancaster (OG 1040, ABV 4%)
A traditional amber best bitter. Full-flavoured with a blackcurrant finish.

Mere Blonde (OG 1040, ABV 4%)

Ringtail (OG 1042, ABV 4.2%)

Black Canon Stout (OG 1045, ABV 4.5%)

Mug Billy (OG 1045, ABV 4.5%)

Thorougood (OG 1051, ABV 5.1%)

Sutler's IPA (OG 1055, ABV 5.5%)
A powerful amber-coloured, heavily-hopped ale.

Burton Bridge SIBA 👁

24 Bridge Street, Burton upon Trent, Staffordshire, DE14 1SY
☎ (01283) 510573 ⊕ burtonbridgebrewery.co.uk
Shop at Bridge Inn 12-2.15pm, 5-11pm daily
Tours by arrangement

☺The brewery was established in 1982 by Bruce Wilkinson and Geoff Mumford and they own six pubs in the local area, including its CAMRA award-winning brewery tap. More than 300 outlets are supplied direct. A changing range of monthly beers plus bottle-conditioned beers are available.

Golden Delicious (OG 1037, ABV 3.8%) ◆
A Burton classic with sulphurous aroma and well-balanced hops and fruit. An apple fruitiness, sharp and refreshing start leads to a lingering mouth-watering bitter finish with a hint of astringency. Light, crisp and refreshing.

Sovereign Gold (OG 1040, ABV 4%) ◆
Sweet caramel aroma with a grassy hop start with malt overtones. Fresh and fruity with a bitterness that emerges and continues to develop.

XL Bitter (OG 1039, ABV 4%) ◆
Another Burton classic with sulphurous aroma. Golden with fruit and hops and a characteristic lingering aftertaste hinting of toffee apple sweetness.

Bridge Bitter (OG 1041, ABV 4.2%) ◆
Gentle aroma of malt and fruit. Good balanced start finishing with a robust hop mouthfeel.

Burton Porter (OG 1044, ABV 4.5%) ◆

Chocolate aromas and smooth taste of smoky roasted grain and coffee.

Damson Porter (OG 1044, ABV 4.5%)

Stairway to Heaven (OG 1049, ABV 5%) ❧
Golden bitter. A perfectly balanced beer. The malty and hoppy start leads to a hoppy body with a mouthwatering finish.

**Top Dog Stout/Bramble Stout
(OG 1049, ABV 5%)** 🍷 ❧
Black and rich with a roast and malty start. Fruity and abundant hops give a fruity, bitter finish with a mouth-watering edge.

Festival Ale (OG 1054, ABV 5.5%) ❧
Caramel aroma with plenty of hop taste balanced by malty sweetness.

Burton Old Cottage

Unit 10, Eccleshall Business Park, Hawkins Lane, Burton upon Trent, Staffordshire, DE14 1PT
☎ 07909 931250 ⊕ oldcottagebeer.co.uk
Tours by arrangement

☺The brewery was originally installed in the old Heritage Brewery, once Everard's production plant in Burton. When the site was taken over, the brewery moved to a modern industrial unit.

Oak Ale (OG 1044, ABV 4%) ❧
Tawny, full-bodied bitter. A sweet start with balanced fruit gives way to a slight roast taste with some caramel for interest. A dry, hoppy finish satisfies the palate.

Chestnut (OG 1042, ABV 4.2%)
A dark session ale with a touch of bitterness and a pleasant, full aftertaste.

Stout (OG 1047, ABV 4.7%) ❧
Roast aroma with background fruit, roast tastes with gentle sweetness. Bitterness develops surprisingly from the sweet start to leave a sharp edged mouthfeel. Roast throughout with a malt background.

Pastiche (OG 1050, ABV 5.2%)
A smooth, balanced ale with a complex taste and aroma.

Halcyon Daze (OG 1050, ABV 5.3%) ❧
Tawny and creamy with touches of hop, fruit and malt aroma. Fruity taste and finish.

Burtonwood

Bold Lane, Burtonwood, Warrington, Cheshire, WA5 4TH
☎ (01925) 220022 ⊕ thomashardybrewery.co.uk

Thomas Hardys only brewery, run by Peter Ward as a contract operation mainly for Heineken/John Smiths. Currently producing no real ale.

Bushy's SIBA

Mount Murray Brewery, Mount Murray, Braddan, Isle of Man, IM4 1JE
☎ (01624) 661244 ⊕ bushys.com
Tours by arrangement

☺Launched in 1986 as a brewpub, Bushy's relocated in 1990 when demand outgrew capacity. Bushy's goes one step further than the Manx Pure Beer Law preferring the German Reinheitsgebot (Pure Beer Law) that excludes sugar. Seasonal

beers are numerous and include Oyster Stout (ABV 4.2%) – see website.

Castletown Bitter (OG 1035, ABV 3.5%)
A light, golden beer full of floral and citrus hints. A refreshing session beer.

Ruby (1874) Mild (OG 1035, ABV 3.5%) 🍷 ❧
Classic full-bodied malty ruby mild with sweet caramel flavours throughout, and well-balanced hops.

Bitter (OG 1038, ABV 3.8%) ❧
A traditional malty and hoppy beer with good balance. The fruit lasts through to the bitter finish.

Old Bushy Tail (OG 1045, ABV 4.5%)
A reddish-brown beer with a pronounced hop and malt aroma. Slightly sweet and malty on the palate with distinct orange tones. The full finish is malty and hoppy with a hint of toffee.

Butcombe SIBA ◉

Cox's Green, Wrington, BS40 5PA
☎ (01934) 863963 ⊕ butcombe.com
Shop Mon-Fri 9am-5pm; Sat 9am-12pm
Tours by arrangement

⊗ Established in 1978 by Simon Whitmore and sold to Guy Newell and friends in 2003, Butcombe moved to a new purpose-built brewery with a 150-barrel plant in 2005. It supplies about 500 outlets direct and similar numbers via wholesalers and pub companies. The brewery has an estate of 21 freehouses. Seasonal beers: see website.

Bitter (OG 1039, ABV 4%) 🍺 ❧
Notably bitter tawny ale. Malt with hops contributing to a well-balanced flavour. Long, refreshing aftertaste.

**Adam Henson's Rare Breed
(OG 1044, ABV 4.2%)** ❧
Full-flavoured, pale brown best bitter. Rich, fruity apple flavours with a bitter, slightly astringent aftertaste. Well-hopped on the nose and palate.

Gold (OG 1045, ABV 4.4%) ❧
An amber-coloured ale with a light aroma of malt and hops, leading to well-balanced flavours of malt, fruit and hops. Slight astringency leading to a sweetish finish.

Butts SIBA

Northfield Farm, Wantage Road, Great Shefford, Berkshire, RG17 7BY
☎ (01488) 648133 ⊕ buttsbrewery.com
Shop 10am-4pm daily

⊗ The brewery was set up in 1994. In 2002 the brewery took the decision to become dedicated to organic production; all the beers brewed use organic malted barley and organic hops. Occasional, seasonal and bottle-conditioned beers are available: see website.

Jester (OG 1036, ABV 3.5%) ❧
A pale brown session bitter with a hoppy aroma and a hint of fruit. The taste balances malt, hops, fruit and bitterness with a hoppy aftertaste.

Traditional (OG 1040, ABV 4%) ❧
A pale brown bitter that is quite soft on the tongue with hoppy citrus flavours accompanying a gentle bittersweetness. A long, dry aftertaste is dominated by fruity hops.

Barbus Barbus (OG 1046, ABV 4.6%) ❧
Golden ale with a fruity hoppy aroma and a hint of malt. Hops dominate taste and aftertaste, accompanied by fruitiness and bitterness, with a hint of balancing sweetness.

Buxton SIBA

Units 7D & E, Staden Business Park, Staden Lane, Buxton, Derbyshire, SK17 9RZ
☎ (01298) 244200 ⊕ buxtonrealale.co.uk

Buxton Brewery was set up in 2009 after acquiring the former Wild Walker plant and has recently expanded. Bottle-conditioned beers are available.

Moor Top (OG 1037, ABV 3.6%)
Dry-hopped blonde ale with a citrus flavour and aroma. It has a sweetness balanced with a bitter finish backed up with a late grapefruit hit.

Bitter (OG 1040, ABV 3.8%)
A classic English bitter, copper-coloured with light malty, caramel flavours complemented with a gentle, fruity hop character.

Kinder Stout (OG 1044, ABV 4.1%)
A black stout with a creamy head. Aromas of burnt coffee, molasses, prunes, and a hint of smoke. Gently sweet and sour, with a moderate bitterness.

Old Big 'ead (OG 1042, ABV 4.1%)

SPA (Special Pale Ale) (OG 1041, ABV 4.1%)
Light and refreshing, delicately hopped ale with a clean taste, a creamy mouthfeel and nutty notes.

American Rye (ABV 4.3%)
Hoppy amber ale, brewed with rye.

Best Bitter (OG 1045, ABV 4.3%)
A hoppy, amber, rye best bitter.

Kinder Downfall (OG 1043, ABV 4.3%)
A refreshing, full-flavoured, hoppy golden ale.

Blonde (OG 1046, ABV 4.6%)
A classic blonde – crisp and malty, mashed with a blend of barley and wheat for a fruity character.

English Pale Ale (OG 1049, ABV 4.9%)

Kinder Sunset (OG 1050, ABV 5%)
A ruby red bitter with a complex taste profile and malty richness, tempered by a bitter, citrus finish.

Gold (OG 1052, ABV 5.2%)

Black Rocks (OG 1055, ABV 5.5%)

Wild Boar (OG 1057, ABV 5.7%)

High Tor (OG 1062, ABV 6.3%)

Buzzard (NEW)

Speddyd Farm, Llandyrnog, Denbighshire, LL16 4LE
☎ 07972 202880 ✉ stu@buzzardbrewery.co.uk

Brewing commenced in 2013 on a 2.5-barrel plant housed in a former farm building. 15-20 pubs are supplied locally.

Best Bitter (OG 1039, ABV 3.9%)

Pale of Clwyd (OG 1042, ABV 4.2%)

Vale Ale (OG 1045, ABV 4.5%)

By the Horns SIBA

25 Summerstown, London, SW17 0BQ
☎ (020) 3417 7338 ⊕ bythehorns.co.uk
Shop Thu & Fri 5-10pm; Sat 12-6pm

Tours by arrangement

⊗ By the Horns began brewing in 2012 using a 5.5-barrel plant. It is located in industrial units near Wimbledon Stadium. The brewery has a licence for off sales and holds regular (monthly) open days. Seasonal and bottle-conditioned beers are available. Recent expansion has seen the addition of an on-site brewery tap.

Stiff Upper Lip (OG 1038, ABV 3.8%) ❧
A classic amber-coloured bitter, well-balanced with hops to the fore and a hint of citrus. Dry, bitter finish.

Mayor of Garratt (OG 1043, ABV 4.3%)
An English best bitter with a soft floral finish.

Bobby on the Wheat (OG 1045, ABV 4.7%) ❧
Citrus fruit is present throughout this wheat beer with some spice on the nose and banana on the palate.

Diamond Geezer (OG 1049, ABV 4.9%) ❧
Malty, hoppy red ale with blackcurrant, citrus and faint roast notes. Bitterness develops and builds in the aftertaste.

Lambeth Walk (OG 1058, ABV 5.1%)

Wolfie Smith (OG 1059, ABV 5.2%)
A hoppy amber ale.

Prince Albert (OG 1059, ABV 5.5%)

Byatt's SIBA

Unit 10, Lythalls Lane Industrial Estate, Lythalls Lane, Coventry, CV6 6FL
☎ (024) 7663 7996 ⊕ byattsbrewery.co.uk

Established in 2011 using a six-barrel plant in an industrial estate on the north side of Coventry, this was the first commercial brewery in the city for over 80 years. Coventry, Warwickshire and the Midlands are supplied. Bottle-conditioned beers are also available.

XK Dark (OG 1038, ABV 3.5%)

Coventry Bitter (OG 1038, ABV 3.8%)

Phoenix Gold (OG 1042, ABV 4.2%)

Urban Red (OG 1047, ABV 4.5%)

Regal Blond (OG 1053, ABV 5.2%)

C&C Wellpark

Wellpark Brewery, 161 Duke Street, Glasgow, G31 1JD
No real ale.

Cader (NEW) SIBA

Unit 4, Marian Mawr Enterprise Park, Dolgellau, Gwynedd, LL40 1UU
☎ 07931 734655 ⊕ caderales.com

Cader was founded in 2012 by a husband and wife team. Three beers are brewed.

Gold (ABV 3.8%)

Idris Bitter (ABV 4.1%)

Red Bandit (ABV 5%)

Cains SIBA ◉

Stanhope Street, Liverpool, L8 5XJ
☎ (0151) 709 8734 ⊕ cains.co.uk

Brewing ceased: some beers badged Cains may still be found but the company does not say who is producing them.

Cairngorm SIBA ◉

Unit 12, Dalfaber Industrial Estate, Aviemore, Highlands, PH22 1ST
☎ (01479) 812222 ⊕ cairngormbrewery.com
Shop Mon-Sat 10am-5.30pm
Tours by arrangement

☺Cairngorm produces six regular cask beers along with seasonal ales. Now with its own bottling line and a capacity of 140 barrels, the free trade is supplied as far as the central belt, nationally via wholesalers. Seasonal beers: see website.

Stag (OG 1040, ABV 4.1%) 🗂 ◈
A fine best bitter with plenty of roast and hop throughout. This tawny brew also has plenty of malt in the lingering bitter-sweet aftertaste.

Trade Winds (OG 1043, ABV 4.3%) 🍺 ◈
A multi-award winning beer. A massive citrus fruit, hop and elderflower nose leads to hints of grapefruit in the mouth. The exceptional bitter sweetness in the taste lasts through the long, lingering aftertaste.

Black Gold (OG 1044, ABV 4.4%) 🗂 ◈
Roast malt dominates throughout, slight smokyness in aroma leading to a liquorice and blackcurrant taste giving it a background sweetness. Very long, dry bitter finish.

Nessies Monster Mash (OG 1044, ABV 4.4%) ◈
A good traditional English-type bitter with plenty of bitterness and strong malt flavour and a fruity background. Lingering bitterness in the aftertaste with diminishing sweetness.

Gold/Sheepshaggers Gold (OG 1044, ABV 4.5%) ◈
Fruit and hops to the fore with a hint of caramel in this sweetish brew.

Wildcat (OG 1049.5, ABV 5.1%) ◈
A full-bodied warming strong bitter. Malt predominates but there is an underlying hop character through to the well-balanced aftertaste. Drinks dangerously less than its 5.1%.

Caledonian ◉

42 Slateford Road, Edinburgh, EH11 1PH
☎ (0131) 337 1286 ⊕ caledonian-brewery.co.uk
Tours by arrangement

☺The brewery was founded by Lorimer & Clark in 1869 and was sold to Vaux of Sunderland in 1919. In 1987 the brewery was saved from closure by a management buy-out and became independent. The brewery was purchased by S&N in 2004 and became part of Heineken in 2008. Monthly guest beers are produced which are sometimes of an unusual style, as well as a rolling programme of special beers covering each of the seasons.

Deuchars IPA (OG 1039.5, ABV 3.8%) ◈
Golden session ale with hop aroma and dry, bitter finish. Balanced, with malt adding body and fruit a balancing sweetness.

Flying Scotsman (OG 1045.5, ABV 4%) ◈
Well-balanced, malty beer with a bittersweet character. Similar to a Scottish 80/-, but dryer and with more hop bitterness.

80 (OG 1042.4, ABV 4.1%) ◈
A predominantly malty, brown beer with soft roast and caramel throughout. Fruit gives sweetness, typical of a Scottish 80/-.

Golden XPA (OG 1044, ABV 4.3%) ◈
Nicely balanced golden ale with malt and fruit throughout. Hops come to the fore in the increasingly dry, bitter aftertaste.

Calvors SIBA

Home Farm, Coddenham Green, Suffolk, IP6 9UN
☎ (01449) 711055 ⊕ calvors.co.uk

No real ale. Calvors Brewery was established in 2008 and brews four lagers, 3Point8 Lager (ABV 3.8%), Amber Lager (ABV 4%), Dark Lager (ABV 4.5%) and Premium (ABV 5%). All are available bottled and on draught and are suitable for vegans and vegetarians.

Cambridge Moonshine

Hill Farm, Shelford Road, Fulbourn, Cambridgeshire, CB21 5EQ
☎ (01223) 514366 ☎ 07906 066794

Office: 28 Radegund Road, Cambridge, CB1 3RS
⊕ moonshinebrewery.co.uk

⊠ Established in 2004, the brewery moved in 2010 to larger premises incorporating a five-barrel plant. Locally-produced ingredients are used including water from the brewery's own well. It mainly concentrates on supplying CAMRA beer festivals, with two outlets supplied direct. Bottle-conditioned beers are available.

Trumpington Tipple (OG 1038, ABV 3.6%)

Sparkling Moon (OG 1036, ABV 3.7%)

Shelford Crier (OG 1038, ABV 3.8%)

Harvest Moon Mild (OG 1040, ABV 3.9%)

Barton Bitter (OG 1040, ABV 4%) ◈
Pale brown with red and amber highlights, balanced malt and hops and a fruity backdrop on both nose and palate. A bittersweet flavour dries as fruit and sweetness diminish.

Heavenly Matter (OG 1039, ABV 4%)

Molten Amber (OG 1040, ABV 4.1%)

CB1 Best Bitter (OG 1041, ABV 4.2%)

Red Watch Blueberry Ale (OG 1040, ABV 4.2%)

Reel Ale (OG 1041, ABV 4.2%)

Budding Moon (OG 1043, ABV 4.5%)

Nightwatch Porter (OG 1043, ABV 4.5%)

Black Hole Stout (OG 1048, ABV 5%) 🗂

Chocolate Orange Stout (OG 1068, ABV 6.7%)

Ison (OG 1074, ABV 8%)

Cambrinus

See Liverpool Organic

Camden Town SIBA

55-59 Wilkin Street Mews, Kentish Town, London, NW5 3NN
☎ (020) 7485 1671 ⊕ camdentownbrewery.com
Tours by arrangement

No real ale.

Camerons ◉

Lion Brewery, Stranton, Hartlepool, County Durham, TS24 7QS
☎ (01429) 852000 ⊕ cameronsbrewery.com
Shop Mon-Sat 12-4pm
Tours by arrangement

⊙Founded in 1865, Camerons was bought in 2002 by Castle Eden, which moved production to Hartlepool. In 2003 the Lions Den, a 10-barrel microbrewery, was set up to produce and bottle small batches of guest ales and undertake contract brewing and bottling. 75 pubs are owned, with five selling real ale. Monthly guest beers: see website.

Best Bitter (OG 1036, ABV 3.6%) ◕
A light bitter, but well-balanced, with hops and malt.

Strongarm (OG 1041, ABV 4%) ◕
A well-rounded, ruby-red ale with a distinctive, tight creamy head; initially fruity, but with a good balance of malt, hops and moderate bitterness.

Trophy Special (ABV 4%)
An amber ale, slightly sweet and malty, fruity and hoppy.

For John Smith (Heineken Tadcaster):

Bitter (OG 1035.8, ABV 3.8%) ◕
A copper-coloured beer, well-balanced but with no dominating features. It has a short hoppy finish.

Cannon Royall SIBA IFBB

⫲ Fruiterer's Arms, Uphampton Lane, Uphampton, Worcestershire, WR9 0JW
☎ (01905) 621161 ⊕ cannonroyall.co.uk
Tours by arrangement

Cannon Royall's first brew was in 1993 in a converted cider house behind the Fruiterer's Arms. The brewery supplies a number of mainly local outlets. Seasonal beers are regularly produced. Bottle-conditioned beers are also available.

Fruiterers Mild (OG 1037, ABV 3.7%) ◕
This black-hued brew has rich malty aromas that lead to a fruity mix of bitter hops and sweetness, and a short balanced aftertaste.

King's Shilling (OG 1038, ABV 3.8%) ◕
A golden bitter that packs a citrus hoppy punch throughout.

Arrowhead Bitter (OG 1039, ABV 3.9%) ◕
A powerful punch of hops attacks the nose before the feast of bitterness. The memory of this golden brew fades too soon.

Arrowhead Extra (OG 1045, ABV 4.3%)

Blond Bombshell (OG 1043, ABV 4.3%)

Canterbury Ales SIBA

Unit 7, Stour Valley Business Park, Ashford Road, Chartham, Kent, CT4 7HF
☎ (01227) 732541 ☎ 07944 657978
⊕ canterbury-ales.co.uk
Tours by arrangement

Brewing commenced in 2010 using an eight-barrel plant. Over 25 outlets are supplied direct.

Wife of Bath (OG 1038, ABV 3.9%) ◕

A golden beer with strong bitterness and grapefruit hop character, leading to a long, dry finish.

The Reeve's Ale (OG 1040, ABV 4.1%)

The Miller's Ale (OG 1044, ABV 4.5%)

Canterbury Brewers SIBA ◉

Foundry Brew Pub, White Horse Lane, Canterbury, Kent, CT1 2RU
☎ (01227) 455899 ⊕ thefoundrycanterbury.co.uk

The Foundry is a brewery, restaurant and bar occupying an industrial two storey building, originally a Victorian foundry, tucked away in the heart of Canterbury.

Loco IPA (OG 1038, ABV 3.9%)
A hoppy, American-style IPA at session strength.

Foundryman's Gold (OG 1040, ABV 4%)
A golden ale with citrus and elderflower aromas.

GB (OG 1040, ABV 4.1%)

Foundry Torpedo (OG 1044, ABV 4.5%)
An amber ale with a crisp finish.

Foundry Red Rye (OG 1058, ABV 5.6%)
Big bold spice from the rye and huge American hop flavours.

Streetlight Porter (OG 1059, ABV 5.8%)
A strong porter with toffee chocolate flavours and a floral aroma.

Cap House

444-446 Bradford Road, Batley, West Yorkshire, WF17 5LW
☎ (01924) 479909 ☎ 07981 858270
⊕ caphousebrewery.co.uk

⊙Cap House began in 2011 using a 2.5-barrel brew plant as a joint venture between Peter Lister, who has a plastics business at the location, and Gary Wardman of the Reindeer Inn in Overton, which is the brewery tap. Seasonal/special beers: see website.

Miners A Pint (OG 1038, ABV 3.8%)
A tangy bitter. Smooth mouthfeel balanced by a toffee undertone and a deep, dry finish with lingering fruit notes. A real session ale.

Blonde & Beyond (ABV 4%)
A light, hoppy beer brewed to create a well-balanced fruity taste. Refreshing citrus and grapefruit flavours for a bittersweet finish.

Fox Hunter (ABV 4%)
A subtle balance of hoppy, fruity, bittersweet flavours of caramel and a hint of liquorice with a malty fruit aroma. Easy-drinking, full-bodied ale.

Miners A Light (ABV 4.2%)
A smooth, blonde ale; light, fruity notes with a hint of citrus.

Ruby (OG 1054, ABV 5.6%)
A rich ruby red ale with a smooth finish and a fruity nut/toffee aroma and tangy palate.

Captain Cook SIBA ◉

⫲ White Swan, 1 West End, Stokesley, North Yorkshire, TS9 5BL
☎ (01642) 710263 ⊕ captaincookbrewery.co.uk
Tours by arrangement

⊛The Captain Cook Brewery is located within the 18th-century White Swan pub. The brewery, which started in 1999, has a six barrel plant. Seasonal beers are available.

Resolution (OG 1037, ABV 3.7%)

Red Bay (OG 1040, ABV 4%)
An Irish-style hoppy ale.

Sunset (OG 1040, ABV 4%)
A smooth, light ale with a hint of citrus flavours.

Slipway (OG 1042, ABV 4.2%)
A light-coloured, hoppy ale with bitterness coming through from the Challenger hops. A full-flavoured ale with a smooth malt aftertaste.

Endeavour (OG 1043, ABV 4.3%)

Black Porter (OG 1044, ABV 4.4%)
Chocolate notes and dominant roast flavours lead to a dry, bitter finish.

Discovery (OG 1044, ABV 4.4%)
Mid brown malted ale with bitter finish.

Schooner Granville (OG 1047, ABV 4.7%)
A classic dry stout.

Castle SIBA

Unit 9a-7, Restormel Industrial Estate, Liddicoat Road, Lostwithiel, Cornwall, PL22 0HG
☎ (01726) 871133 ✉ castlebrewery@aol.com

Brewing started in 2008 on a two-barrel plant. Only bottle-conditioned ales are produced: Cornish Best (ABV 4.2%), Moat Mild (ABV 4.4%), Battle Stout (ABV 4.6%), Once A Knight (ABV 5%), Lostwithiale (ABV 7%), Kernow Kurb Kisser (ABV 7.4%), Hung, Drawn & Slaughtered (ABV 10%).

Castle Rock SIBA ◉

Queensbridge Road, Nottingham, NG2 1NB
☎ (0115) 985 1615 ⊕ castlerockbrewery.co.uk
Shop Mon-Thu 10.30am-6pm; Fri 10.30am-4pm; Sat 10.30am-2pm
Tours by arrangement

⊛Castle Rock was established in 1998 with capacity steadily increasing since then. Beers are distributed through its estate of 20 pubs and further afield via wholesalers. A different beer is brewed monthly to support the Nottinghamshire Wildlife Trust and a unique Nottinghamian Celebration beer is brewed quarterly. Seasonal beers: see website. Bottle-conditioned beers are also available.

Sheriff's Tipple (OG 1034, ABV 3.4%)
A tawny session bitter with a malty, bitter taste.

Black Gold (OG 1037, ABV 3.8%) 🍺 ✦
A dark ruby mild. Full-bodied and fairly bitter.

Harvest Pale (OG 1037, ABV 3.8%) ✦
Pale yellow beer, full of hop aroma and flavour. Refreshing with a mellowing aftertaste.

Preservation Fine Ale (OG 1044, ABV 4.4%) ✦
A traditional copper-coloured English best bitter with malt predominant. Fairly bitter with a residual sweetness.

Elsie Mo (OG 1045, ABV 4.7%) 🍺 ✦
A strong golden ale with floral hops evident in the aroma. Citrus hops are mellowed by a slight sweetness.

Midnight Owl (OG 1055, ABV 5.5%)

A rich, warming winter ale with a distinctive hop and caramel finish.

Screech Owl (OG 1055, ABV 5.5%) 🍺 ✦
A classic golden IPA with an intensely hoppy aroma and bitter taste with a little balancing sweetness.

Castor SIBA

30 Peterborough Road, Castor, Peterborough, Cambridgeshire, PE5 7AX
☎ (01733) 380337 ⊕ castorales.co.uk
Tours by arrangement

This three-barrel brewery, established in 2009, is located in a converted outhouse in the garden of the founder brewer. The Prince of Wales Feathers in Castor village features the beers, as well as the Ostrich and the Beehive in Peterborough.

Roman Gold (OG 1037, ABV 3.7%)
Gold-coloured session bitter.

Imperial Palace Ale (OG 1045, ABV 4.6%)

Old Scarlet (OG 1045, ABV 4.6%)

Cathedral Heights

Unit 12, Churchill Business Park, Bracebridge Heath, Lincoln, LN4 2HD
☎ 07545 090318 ⊕ chbrewery.co.uk

Cathedral Heights began brewing in 2011 and was established by Steve Marston after previous experience of brewing at Milestone and Cathedral Ales. The brewery relocated in 2013 after a year out of production.

Just Married (OG 1037, ABV 3.8%)
A light, refreshing pale ale with a hoppy finish.

Churchills Pride (OG 1038, ABV 3.9%)
A copper-coloured ale.

BBH Bitter (OG 1042, ABV 4.3%)
A golden, refreshing, hoppy bitter.

Devils Nightmare (OG 1042, ABV 4.3%)
A smooth, refreshing dark mild; sweet and malty.

Steep Hill (OG 1041, ABV 4.3%)
A dark copper-coloured ale with malty tones. Bitter with a fruity finish.

Castle Dungeon (OG 1050, ABV 5.4%)
A full-bodied oyster stout.

Caveman (NEW)

▤ The Cave (below George & Dragon), 1 London Road, Swanscombe, Kent, DA10 0LQ
☎ 07787 196450 ⊕ cavemanbrewery.co.uk

Caveman began brewing in 2012 and is situated in the cellars of the George & Dragon in Swanscombe. There are plans to produce a number of seasonal and bottle-conditioned beers.

Citra (OG 1040, ABV 4.1%)

Chinook (OG 1042, ABV 4.3%)

Caythorpe SIBA

c/o Black Horse, 29 Main Street, Caythorpe, Nottinghamshire, NG14 7ED
☎ (0115) 966 4933 ☎ 07807 583724
⊕ caythorpebrewery.co.uk
Tours by arrangement

Established in 1996 using a 2.5-barrel plant in a building at the rear of the Black Horse pub, the brewery upgraded to a six-barrel plant in 2010.

Dark Gem (OG 1033.3, ABV 3.5%)
A subtly-hopped dark mild with a hint of chocolate.

One Swallow (OG 1034, ABV 3.6%)
A golden session bitter, crisp and well hopped.

Bitter (OG 1034.7, ABV 3.7%)
Copper-coloured, light-flavoured bitter.

Dover Beck (OG 1037, ABV 4%) ◆
Pale brown well-balanced session bitter. Initial malt is offset by a slight hoppy bitterness.

Stout Fellow (OG 1040, ABV 4.2%)
A dark stout, brewed with roasted barley to give a roast character.

Classic (OG 1042, ABV 4.6%)
Traditional copper-coloured premium bitter, malty and well hopped.

Celt Experience SIBA ◉

Unit 2E, Pontygwindy Industrial Estate, Pontygwindy Road, Caerphilly, CF83 3HU
☎ (029) 2086 7707 ☎ 0870 803 3876
⊕ theceltexperience.co.uk
Shop Mon-Fri 10am-4.30pm
Tours by arrangement

Celt Experience was established in 2007 by Tom Newman. In 2012 selected beers from its sister brewery, Newmans, were integrated to form one brand. Beers are distributed widely.

Iron Age (OG 1035, ABV 3.5%)

Dark Age (OG 1040, ABV 4%)

Golden (OG 1045, ABV 4.2%)

Native Storm (OG 1044, ABV 4.4%)

Bronze (OG 1046, ABV 4.5%)

Silures (OG 1046, ABV 4.6%)

Castell Coch (OG 1047, ABV 4.7%)

Bleddyn (OG 1056, ABV 5.6%)

Cerddin SIBA

▤ c/o Cross Inn, Maesteg Road, Maesteg, CF34 9LB
☎ (01656) 732476 ⊕ cerddinbrewery.co.uk

Cerddin was established in 2010 using a 2.5-barrel brewery in a converted garage. Beer is available in the owner's pub, the Cross Inn in Maesteg. Bottle-conditioned beers are available.

Solar (OG 1040, ABV 4%)

Cascade (OG 1047, ABV 4.8%)

Chalk Hill

▤ Rosary Road, Norwich, NR1 4DA
☎ (01603) 477078 ⊠ chalkhillinns@ntlworld.com
Tours by arrangement

⊠ Chalk Hill began production in 1993 on a 15-barrel plant. It supplies local pubs and festivals.

Tap Bitter (OG 1036, ABV 3.6%) ◆
Easy-drinking, well-balanced bitter with a light, hoppy character in both aroma and taste. Initially malt provides some contrast but fades rapidly in a quick, increasingly dry and bitter finish.

CHB (OG 1042, ABV 4.2%) ◆
Malt comes to the fore as a fruity cooking apple beginning melds into the hoppy bittersweet background. A gentle malt aroma and sticky mouthfeel. Long finish.

Gold (OG 1043, ABV 4.3%) ◆
Light hoppy airs introduce this yellow-gold ale. Grapefruit, banana and hops mingle in a well balanced beginning. The finish develops a growing bitterness as it slowly subsides.

Dreadnought (OG 1049, ABV 4.9%) ◆
A rich, resinous aroma fittingly introduces a heavily malt-influenced brew. Raisin and plum vie with each other to match the sweet malty backbone. Malt remains in a decidedly singular and abrupt ending.

Flintknapper's Mild (OG 1052, ABV 5%) ⬠ ◆
Red hued with a creamy mouthfeel. Malt emerges from a well-balanced mix of flavours including roast, sweetness and dates. Eventually only a malty sweetness remains.

Chantry (NEW) SIBA

Unit 1, Callum Court, Gateway Industrial Estate, Parkgate, Rotherham, South Yorkshire, S62 6NR
☎ (01709) 711866 ⊕ chantrybrewery.co.uk

Brewing returned to Rotherham with the opening of Chantry in 2012 using the latest brewing technology in a 20-barrel state of the art plant. Seasonal and special beers are also brewed.

New York Pale (ABV 3.9%)
A pale session bitter with a refreshing citrus taste and a crisp, bitter finish.

Iron & Steel Bitter (ABV 4%)
Chestnut-coloured beer with complex spicy flavours of dark fruits with a clean finish. An easy-drinking session bitter.

Diamond Black Stout (ABV 4.5%)
Full-bodied dry stout with a bitter finish, spicy with hints of liquorice and dark berries.

Cheddar SIBA ◉

Winchester Farm, Draycott Road, Cheddar, Somerset, BS27 3RP
☎ (01934) 744193 ⊕ cheddarales.co.uk
Shop Mon-Fri 8am-4pm; Sat-Sun by appointment
Tours by arrangement

⊠ Established in 2006 in Cheddar by Jem Ham, this 80-barrel brewery has a production split of approximately 85% cask-conditioned beer with the remainder bottle conditioned. Around 450 outlets and 80 pubs are supplied. Seasonal beers: see website.

Bitter Bully (OG 1038.5, ABV 3.8%) ◆
Light, refreshing bitter with balanced fruit and hops from nose to aftertaste.

Gorge Best (OG 1040, ABV 4%) ◆
Initial light aroma which belies the complex flavours of malts and pale fruit. The faint sweetness progresses to a dry, bitter finish.

Potholer (OG 1043.5, ABV 4.3%) ◆
Pale bitter with fruity hop aroma. Fruity sweetness on the palate turns into a bitter finish.

Totty Pot (OG 1044.5, ABV 4.5%) ◆

Roast, coffee and malt flavours throughout with hints of caramel on the nose and palate. Roast flavours remain in the smooth aftertaste.

Goat's Leap (OG 1054.5, ABV 5.5%) ◗
A pale amber-coloured IPA with good hop character. Full-bodied with pale fruit flavours, apricot notes and a bittersweet finish.

Cheshire (NEW) SIBA

Unit 5, Daneside Business Park, Riverdane Road, Congleton, Cheshire, CW12 1UN
☎ 07830 304929 ⊕ cheshirebrewhouse.co.uk

Cheshire Brewhouse was established in 2012 using a five-barrel plant.

Gap (ABV 3.7%)

Engine Vein (ABV 4.2%)
A copper-coloured session bitter named after the Alderley Copper Mine.

Set (ABV 4.2%)
Chocolate stout made with 100% Venezulan cacao.

DBA (ABV 4.6%)
A Burton-style bitter.

Chiltern SIBA ⊙

Nash Lee Road, Terrick, Aylesbury, Buckinghamshire, HP17 0TQ
☎ (01296) 613647 ⊕ chilternbrewery.co.uk
Shop Mon-Thu & Sat 9am-5pm; Fri 9am-7pm
Tours by arrangement

⊠ Founded 1980, Chiltern is the oldest independent brewery in Buckinghamshire. Now run by the second generation of the Jenkinson family it supplies more than 80 outlets including its own brewery tap, the Farmers' Bar at the King's Head in Aylesbury. Seasonal and bottle-conditioned beers are available.

Ale (OG 1037, ABV 3.7%) ◗
An amber, refreshing beer with a slight fruit aroma, leading to a good malt/bitter balance in the mouth. The aftertaste is bitter and dry.

Beechwood Bitter (OG 1043, ABV 4.3%) ◗
This pale brown beer has a balanced butterscotch/toffee aroma, with a slight hop note. The taste balances bitterness and sweetness, leading to a long bitter finish.

Julian Church

≡ c/o Alexandra Arms, 39 Victoria Street, Kettering, Northamptonshire, NN16 0BU
☎ 07794 289559 ⊕ jchurchbrewery.co.uk
Tours by arrangement

Julian Church started brewing in 2009 on Nobby's old five-barrel plant when Nobby's expanded and moved to Guilsborough. The brewery is based beneath the renowned Alexandra Arms in Kettering, where at least one of the beers is always available. Parson's Nose is rebadged as Father Nip for the Alexandra Arms. Seasonal and one-off beers are produced.

More Tea Vicar (OG 1037, ABV 3.7%)
A straw-coloured light ale with a dry finish and a hint of blackcurrant.

Parson's Nose (OG 1037, ABV 3.9%)

Full bodied mahogany-coloured bitter, with nutty caramel flavours and a warm spicy finish.

Lion's Den (OG 1040, ABV 4%)

Martyr (OG 1040, ABV 4.1%)
An amber-coloured beer with a caramel flavour and a light, bitter finish.

Church End SIBA ⊙

≡ Ridge Lane, Nuneaton, Warwickshire, CV10 0RD
☎ (01827) 713080 ⊕ churchendbrewery.co.uk
Shop open during tap opening hours
Tours by arrangement

⊠ The brewery started in 1994 in an old coffin shop in Shustoke. It moved to its present site and upgraded to a 10-barrel plant in 2001 with further expansion to a 20-barrel plant in 2008. Bottle-conditioned beers are available. Many non-regular beers are produced as well as one-off specials.

Poachers Pocket (OG 1036, ABV 3.5%)

Cuthberts (OG 1038, ABV 3.8%) ◗
A refreshing, hoppy beer, with hints of malt, fruit and caramel taste. Lingering bitter aftertaste.

Goats Milk (OG 1038, ABV 3.8%)

Gravediggers Ale (OG 1038, ABV 3.8%)

What the Fox's Hat (OG 1044, ABV 4.2%) ◗
A beer with a malty aroma, and a hoppy and malty taste with some caramel flavour.

Vicar's Ruin (OG 1044, ABV 4.4%) ◗
A straw-coloured best bitter with an initially hoppy, bitter flavour, softening to a delicate malt finish.

Stout Coffin (OG 1046, ABV 4.6%)

Fallen Angel (OG 1050, ABV 5%)

Church Farm (NEW) SIBA

Church Farm, Budbrooke, Warwickshire, CV35 8QL
☎ (01926) 411569 ☎ 07980 012716
⊕ churchfarmbrewery.co.uk

Church Farm Brewery was established in 2012 in the farm's former dairy. The three-barrel plant was converted from the old milk processing equipment. Beers are brewed from local ingredients and the water comes from the farm's own well.

Old Pal (OG 1038, ABV 3.6%)
A pale, golden ale. Slight flowery hop aroma and mouthfeel with a smooth mellow taste and long-lasting finish.

Brown's Porter (OG 1042, ABV 4%)
A porter with a smooth coffee taste and a slightly cloying, creamy aftertaste.

Ren's Pride (OG 1044, ABV 4.2%)
An amber-coloured best bitter with a slightly sweet taste. The distinctive initial flavour comes from a complex array of malts.

Ciren (NEW)

≡ Twelve Bells, 12 Lewis Lane, Cirencester, Gloucestershire, GL7 1EA
☎ (01285) 652230 ☎ 07702 489589
⊕ twelvebellscirencester.com/
cirencester-ales-brewery.html
Tours by arrangement

Ciren Ales was established in 2012 and is situated at the rear of the Twelve Bells pub in Cirencester.

Bells Bitter (OG 1040, ABV 3.8%)
A light brown bitter with a hoppy taste.

Bellend Blonde (OG 1044, ABV 4.2%)
A light, citrus, fruity beer.

Bells Best Mate (OG 1044, ABV 4.2%)
A dark, full-flavoured beer.

City of Cambridge

See Wolf

Clanconnel

PO Box 316, Craigavon, Co Armagh, BT65 9AZ
☎ 07711 626770 ⊕ clanconnelbrewing.com

Clanconnel started producing bottled beer in 2008:
McGrath's Irish Black (ABV 4.3%), McGrath's Irish
Red (ABV 4.3%), McGrath's Pale (ABV 4.4%),
McGrath's Blonde (ABV 4.5%), McGrath's White
(ABV 4.9%). Cask ale is seen occasionally. Beers are
currently brewed by Hilden Brewing Co (qv).

Clarence & Fredericks (NEW) SIBA

35a Neville Road, Croydon, CR0 2DS
☎ 07725 437396 ⊕ cfbrewing.co.uk

⊗ Clarence & Fredericks was established in 2012
using a 10-barrel plant. Seasonal beers are
available.

Golden Ale (OG 1038, ABV 3.8%) ◆
Refreshing yellow beer with a citrus character.
Bitterness grows on drinking with hints of dryness
balanced by a little malt.

Best Bitter (OG 1041, ABV 4.1%) ◆
Traditional best bitter with marmalade, spiced hops
and a little dried apricot fading in the finish as the
bitterness develops.

Smoked Red (OG 1051, ABV 5.1%) ◆
Reddish brown beer with smoke on nose and
palate where roast and sweet malt develop and
linger in the aftertaste.

Clark's SIBA ⟨⊙⟩

Westgate Brewery, Wakefield, West Yorkshire,
WF2 9SW
☎ (01924) 373328 ☎ 07801 922473 ⊕ hbclark.co.uk
Tours by arrangement

☺Founded in 1906, Clark's ceased brewing during
the 1960s/70s but resumed cask ale production in
1982 and now delivers to around 220 outlets.
Monthly specials complement the regular beer
range and its three pubs all serve cask ale.

Traditional (OG 1038, ABV 3.8%)

Classic Blonde (OG 1039, ABV 3.9%)

Westgate Gold (OG 1042, ABV 4.2%)

Clearwater SIBA

Manteo Way, Bideford, Devon, EX39 4LQ
☎ 07976 742849 ⊕ clearwaterbrewery.co.uk
Tours by arrangement

⊗ Clearwater began brewing in 1999 on a 10-
barrel brewery. It regularly supplies more than 250
outlets in the South West and increasingly supplies
national wholesalers with its 'Devon's Own'

labelled beers. In 2013 the brewery moved from
Great Torrington to larger premises in Bideford.

True Delight (OG 1033, ABV 3.4%)

Real Smiler (OG 1037, ABV 3.7%)
Crisp, fresh cut apples and melon on the nose
accompanies a honeyed tone. A light biscuit taste,
with the most delicate of tannins.

Devon Dympsy (OG 1039, ABV 4%)

Proper Ansome (OG 1041, ABV 4.2%)
Fresh, immediate hoppy aromas and caramel
colour. Eddying honeyed sweetness and lightly
earthy scent reveals a herbal edge.

Devon Darter (OG 1043, ABV 4.5%)

Dark Night (OG 1050, ABV 5.2%)

Cliff Quay

Unit 1, Meadow Works, Kenton Road, Debenham,
Suffolk, IP14 6RP
☎ (01728) 684097 ⊕ cliffquay.co.uk
Shop Mon-Fri 10am-5pm; Sat 10am-1pm

Cliff Quay was established in 2008 by former
Wychwood brewer Jeremy Moss and John Bjornson
(owner of the Earl Soham Brewery) in part of the
historic Tolly Cobbold brewery in Ipswich. In 2012
the brewery relocated to Debenham, a small,
picturesque market town, due to redevelopment of
the former brewery site.

Classic Bitter (OG 1034, ABV 3.4%) ◆
Pleasantly drinkable, well-balanced malty sweet
bitter with a hint of caramel, followed by a sweet/
malty aftertaste. A good flavour for such a low
gravity beer.

Anchor Bitter (OG 1040, ABV 4%)

Black Jack Porter (OG 1042, ABV 4.2%) ◆
Unusual dark porter with a strong aniseed aroma
and rich liquorice and aniseed flavours, reminiscent
of old-fashioned sweets. The aftertaste is long and
increasingly sweet.

Tolly Roger (OG 1042, ABV 4.2%) ◆
Well-balanced, highly drinkable, mid-gold summer
beer with a bittersweet hoppiness, some biscuity
flavours and hints of summer fruit.

Tumblehome (OG 1047, ABV 4.7%)

Sea Dog (OG 1053, ABV 5.3%)
A sack full of malted wheat and a blend of fragrant
punchy hops. Bursting with the flavours of lemon
and grapefruit with a full maltiness in contrast.

Clockwork

Maclay Inns PLC, 1153-1155 Cathcart Road,
Glasgow, G42 9HB
☎ (0141) 649 0184 ⊕ maclay.com
Tours by arrangement

Established in 1997, Clockwork has been taken
over by Maclay Inns. The beers are stored in cellar
tanks where fermentation gases from the
conditioning vessel blanket the beers (but not
under pressure). A wide range of ales, lagers and
specials are produced. Most beers are naturally
gassed while the Original Lager and Hazy Daze
Ginger are pressurised. Some updated Maclay's
recipes have been introduced as guest ales.

Amber IPA (OG 1038, ABV 3.8%)

Red Alt (OG 1044, ABV 4.4%)

Lager (OG 1048, ABV 4.8%)

Seriously Ginger (OG 1050, ABV 5%)

Clun SIBA

White Horse Inn, The Square, Clun, Shropshire,
SY7 8JA
☎ (01588) 640305 ⊕ clunbrewery.co.uk

Formerly a tiny brewery, capacity was increased to 2.5 barrels in 2010. Established behind the White Horse in Clun, beers are produced for the pub and increasingly the local trade. Seasonal specials are available.

Loophole (OG 1035, ABV 3.5%)
A dry, hoppy, light-coloured beer with a crisp, hoppy flavour.

Pale (OG 1040, ABV 4.1%)
A pale, clean-tasting bitter beer.

Citadel (OG 1065, ABV 5.9%)
A strong ale, golden in colour with rich, fruity malt flavour, met head on by intense hop bitterness and aroma which give rise to a long-lasting, dry finish.

Coach House SIBA ◉

Wharf Street, Howley, Warrington, Cheshire,
WA1 2DQ
☎ (01925) 232800 ⊕ coach-house-brewing.co.uk

⊕Coach House started in 1991 following the closure of Greenall Whitley Brewery, which had a presence in Warrington since 1762. With a fermentation capacity of 240 barrels, the brewery produces permanent and seasonal brews plus a range of speciality beers.

Coachman's Best Bitter (OG 1037, ABV 3.7%) ⬥
A well-hopped, malty bitter, moderately fruity with a hint of sweetness and a peppery nose.

Gunpowder Mild (OG 1037, ABV 3.8%) ⬥
Biscuity dark mild with a blackcurrant sweetness. Bitterness and fruit dominate with some hints of caramel and a slightly stronger roast flavour.

Honeypot Bitter (OG 1037, ABV 3.8%)

Farrier's Best Bitter (OG 1038, ABV 3.9%)

Cromwells Best Bitter (OG 1040, ABV 4%)

Cheshire Gold (OG 1042, ABV 4.1%)

Dick Turpin (OG 1042, ABV 4.2%) ⬥
Malty, hoppy pale brown beer with some initial sweetish flavours leading to a short, bitter aftertaste. Sold under other names as a pub house beer.

Flintlock Pale Ale (OG 1044, ABV 4.4%)

Innkeeper's Special Reserve
(OG 1045, ABV 4.5%) ⬥
A darkish, full-flavoured bitter. Quite fruity, with a strong, bitter aftertaste.

Postlethwaite (OG 1045, ABV 4.6%) ⬥
Thin bitter with a short, dry aftertaste. Biscuity malt dominates.

Posthorn Premium (OG 1050, ABV 5%) ⬥
Dry golden bitter with a blackcurrant fruitiness and good hop flavours leading to a strong, dry finish. Well-balanced but slightly thin for its gravity.

Coastal SIBA

Unit 10B, Cardrew Industrial Estate, Redruth,
Cornwall, TR15 1SS
☎ (01209) 212613 ☎ 07875 405407
⊕ coastalbrewery.co.uk

Coastal was set up in 2006 on a five-barrel plant by the former brewer and owner of the Borough Arms in Crewe, Cheshire. Seasonal beers and two monthly specials are produced as well as bottle-conditioned beers. See website for full beer list.

Cornish Bronze (OG 1058, ABV 3.7%)

Hop Monster (OG 1038, ABV 3.7%)

Handliner (OG 1040, ABV 4%)

Merry Maidens Mild (OG 1040, ABV 4%) ⬥
Dark red mild with roast malt aroma. Sweet malt, toffee, hop bitterness and roast notes, finishing dry with bitter coffee.

Poseidon (OG 1040, ABV 4%)

Angelina (OG 1042, ABV 4.1%)

Golden Hinde (OG 1044, ABV 4.3%)

Pier Porter (ABV 4.3%)

Winnies Honey Heaven (OG 1044, ABV 4.4%)

Sea King (OG 1056, ABV 5.5%)

Golden Gorse (ABV 5.6%)

St Piran's Porter (OG 1060, ABV 6%)

Erosion (OG 1080, ABV 8%) ⬥
After an aroma promising roast caramel this powerful, warming dark old ale bursts with molasses and roast malt. Liquorice adds to the finish.

Kernow Imperial Stout (OG 1090, ABV 9%)

For Allsaints Brewery:

St Piran Cornish Best Bitter (OG 1040, ABV 4%)

St Arnold (OG 1046, ABV 4.6%)

Colchester SIBA

Viaduct Brewhouse, Unit 16, Wakes Hall Business Centre, Wakes Colne, Essex, CO6 2DY
☎ (01787) 829422 ⊕ colchesterbrewery.com
Shop Mon-Fri 9am-5pm
Tours by arrangement

⊠ Set up in 2012 by three friends, Tom Knox, Roger Clark and Andy Bone, using the 'double drop' process. Popular during the early 20th century this process requires additional brewing vessels in a two-tier system resulting in clean beer with pronounced flavours.

Diesel (OG 1037, ABV 3.6%)
An amber-coloured session bitter.

AK Pale (OG 1038, ABV 3.7%)
A fresh and fruity pale ale, mildly hopped.

Metropolis (OG 1039, ABV 3.9%)
A golden hoppy beer, with enormous depth of flavour and a long, spicy finish.

No. 1 (OG 1040, ABV 4.1%)
A classic copper-coloured English best bitter.

Red Diesel (OG 1042, ABV 4.2%)
A well-balanced best bitter with a long, rich finish.

Trinovantes Gold (OG 1044, ABV 4.3%)

Anne Downes (OG 1045, ABV 4.4%)

A dark brown bitter, full and fruity with a lingering hoppy finish.

Mild Ale (OG 1047, ABV 4.5%)
Dark, ruby mild. Sweet and fruity.

Double Brown Ale (OG 1047.5, ABV 4.6%)
A dark brown, malty beer. Sweetish and balanced.

Old King Coel London Porter (OG 1052.5, ABV 5%)
Brewed the original way with brown malt.

Coles

▤ White Hart Thatched Inn & Brewery, Llanddarog, Carmarthen, SA32 8NT
☎ (01267) 275395 ⊕ thebestpubinwales.co.uk

The brewery is based at the ancient White Hart Inn, built in 1371, which historically had a brewery on site. Brewing started again in 1999 on a nine-gallon plant. A one-barrel plant was fitted in 2000. In 2012 the brewery was opened to the public. Cider is also produced.

Merlins Stout (ABV 4%)

Llanddarog Ale (ABV 4.2%)

Swn Y Dail (ABV 4.2%)

Cwrw Blasus (ABV 4.4%)

Collingham (NEW) SIBA

Leeds Road, Collingham, Leeds, West Yorkshire, LS22 5AA
☎ (01937) 573096 ☎ 07538 431921
⊕ collinghamales.co.uk

Microbrewery based in the village of Collingham, brewing handcrafted ales for the local community. Owner Steve Barrett was formerly head brewer at Samuel Smith's.

Journeyman (ABV 3.9%) ◆
A good mix of hops and malt characterise this amber beer, hops have the upper hand in the pleasant bitter finish.

Artisan's Choice (ABV 4.4%) ◆
A well-balanced beer with sweetness and bitterness in unison throughout this fruity beer, plenty of hop character too.

Colonsay SIBA

The Brewery, Scalasaig, Isle of Colonsay, PA61 7YT
☎ (01951) 200190 ⊕ colonsaybrewery.co.uk

Colonsay began brewing in 2007 on a five-barrel plant. Beer is mainly bottled or brewery conditioned for the local trade: Lager (ABV 4.4%), 80/- Ale (ABV 4.2%), IPA (ABV 3.9%).

Compass SIBA

7 Clare Terrace, Carterton, Oxfordshire, OX18 3ES
☎ (01993) 846846 ⊕ compassbrewery.com

⊠ Compass began brewing in 2009 as a 'cuckoo' brewery but moved to its own plant in Carterton in 2012. It is run by Matthias Sjoberg, who takes brewing ideas from around the world to create experimental and interesting recipes.

Isis Pale Ale (ABV 4.1%)
Malty aromas on a backdrop of distinct Cascade hops. Sweet malt with some fruity esters and a gentle bitterness that lingers.

Baltic Night Stout (ABV 4.8%)
Well-balanced roasted bitterness with a hoppy, floral aroma. Roasted barley gives it a hint of coffee and a long, dry cocoa finish.

King's Shipment IPA (ABV 6%)
A strong IPA with hoppy bitterness balanced with malty sweetness. Dry hopped with oak chips. Based on East London Bow Brewery's IPA brewed in the 1790s for shipment to India.

Complete Pig

Red Lion Farm, Britwell Salome, Oxfordshire, OX49 5LG
☎ (01491) 612134 ⊕ thecompletepig.co.uk

⊠ Based on an Oxfordshire pig farm, the Complete Pig's main business is making free-range pork products. The brewery was started in 2010 to provide another product for the farmer's markets and so the livestock could be fed on the spent grain and yeast. Originally only bottle-conditioned beers were produced but they proved popular and are now also supplied in casks to an ever-increasing number of local pubs.

Perfecta Porcus (OG 1035, ABV 3.6%)
Copper-coloured session ale with a well-balanced flavour.

Red Lion Best (OG 1043, ABV 4.5%)
A bronze-coloured, full-bodied traditional English best bitter.

Concertina SIBA

▤ 9a Dolcliffe Road, Mexborough, South Yorkshire, S64 9AZ
☎ (01709) 580841 ⊠ concertina@btconnect.com
Tours by arrangement

Concertina started in 1992 in the cellar of a club once famous as the home of a long-gone concertina band. The plant produces up to eight barrels a week for the club and other occasional direct outlets and the wider trade via wholesalers. Seasonal beers and specials are available.

Club Bitter (OG 1038, ABV 3.8%)
A fruity session bitter with a good bitter flavour.

Old Dark Attic (OG 1038, ABV 3.9%)
A dark brown beer with a fairly sweet, fruity taste.

One Eyed Jack (OG 1039, ABV 4%)
Fairly pale in colour with plenty of hop bitterness. Brewed with the same malt and hop combination as Bengal Tiger, but more of a session beer. Also badged as Mexborough Bitter.

Bengal Tiger (OG 1043, ABV 4.6%) ◆
Light amber ale with an aromatic hoppy nose followed by a combination of fruit and bitterness.

Dictators (OG 1044, ABV 4.7%)

Extreme (OG 1047, ABV 5.1%)

Ariel Square Four (OG 1046, ABV 5.2%)

Concrete Cow SIBA

59 Alston Drive, Bradwell Abbey, Milton Keynes, Buckinghamshire, MK13 9HB
☎ (01908) 316794 ☎ 07889 665745
⊕ concretecowbrewery.co.uk
Shop Sat 12-2pm
Tours by arrangement

⊠ Concrete Cow opened in 2007 on a 5.5-barrel plant. The beers are named after aspects of local history. The brewery supplies pubs, farmers markets, local shops and restaurants. Seasonal and bottle-conditioned beers: see website.

Bit o' Bully (OG 1035, ABV 3.5%)
A golden bitter full of biscuit, malt, grain and toast flavours.

Pail Ale (OG 1036, ABV 3.7%)
A light-coloured ale brewed using lager malt.

Fenny Popper (OG 1039, ABV 4%)
A light-coloured, zesty ale.

Cock 'n' Bull Story (OG 1041, ABV 4.1%)
A dark amber malty beer.

Cloven Hoof (OG 1045, ABV 4.5%)
A dark vanilla stout flavoured with vanilla pods.

Coniston SIBA ⊙

Coppermines Road, Coniston, Cumbria, LA21 8HL
☎ (01539) 441133 ⊕ conistonbrewery.com
Shop (in Black Bull Inn) 11am-11pm
Tours by arrangement

☺A 10-barrel brewery set up in 1995 behind the Black Bull inn, Coniston, it now brews 40 barrels a week and supplies numerous outlets locally and nationally. One pub is owned. Some bottle-conditioned Coniston beers are brewed using Hepworth's Horsham plant, others are bottled on site.

Oliver's Light Ale (OG 1035, ABV 3.4%) ◥
A fruity, hoppy, straw-coloured bitter with plenty of flavour for its strength.

Bluebird Bitter (OG 1036, ABV 3.6%) ◥
A yellow-gold, predominantly hoppy and fruity beer, well-balanced with some sweetness and a rising bitter finish.

Bluebird Premium XB (OG 1040.5, ABV 4.2%) ◥
Well-balanced, hoppy and fruity golden bitter. Bittersweet in the mouth with dryness building.

Old Man Ale (OG 1040.5, ABV 4.2%) ◥
Delicious fruity, vinous beer with a complex, well-balanced richness.

Special Oatmeal Stout (OG 1045, ABV 4.5%) ◥
A well-balanced, easy-drinking stout, fruity with a balanced ratio of malt to hop bitterness. A good starting point for novice stout drinkers.

Thurstein Pilsner (OG 1044.5, ABV 4.8%)

Blacksmiths Ale (OG 1047.5, ABV 5%)
A well-balanced strong bitter with hints of Christmas pudding.

Infinity IPA (OG 1055, ABV 6%)
A highly hopped India Pale Ale.

No 9 Barley Wine (OG 1087.5, ABV 8.5%) ⌷ ◥
Hops and alcohol dominate with appropriate sweetness and fruit on the tongue. A full-bodied and beautifully balanced beer.

Conquest SIBA

Unit 2B, Larpool Lane Industrial Estate, Larpool Lane, Whitby, North Yorkshire, YO22 4LX
☎ 07790 502035

Conquest was established in 2012. The brew plant was built from scratch by a keen home brewer and supplies pubs in the local area.

Abbey Blonde (ABV 3.8%)

Whitby Whaler (ABV 4%)

Black Death (ABV 4.5%)

Consett Ale Works SIBA ⊙

⧓ Grey Horse Inn, 115 Sherburn Terrace, Consett, Co Durham, DH8 6NE
☎ (01207) 591540 ⊕ consettaleworks.co.uk
Tours by arrangement

The brewery opened in 2006 in the stables of a former coaching inn, the Grey Horse, Consett's oldest pub. The name commemorates the historic Consett Steel Works that closed in 1980. The brewery expanded in 2007 to cope with demand. Around 100 outlets are supplied direct.

Steel Town Bitter (OG 1039, ABV 3.8%)

White Hot (OG 1040, ABV 4%)

Cast Iron (OG 1040, ABV 4.1%)

Men of Steel (OG 1045, ABV 4.3%)

Stout (OG 1045, ABV 4.3%)

Red Dust (OG 1045, ABV 4.5%)

Conwy SIBA

Unit 2, Ty Mawr Enterprise Park, Tan y Graig Road, Llysfaen, LL29 8UE
☎ (01492) 514305 ⊕ conwybrewery.co.uk
Shop Mon-Fri 9am-5pm (please ring if making special trip)
Tours by arrangement

☺Conwy started brewing in 2003, relocating to its present address in 2013. Around 50 outlets are supplied. Seasonal beers: see website. Bottle-conditioned beers are also available.

Clogwyn Gold (OG 1038, ABV 3.6%)

Infusion (OG 1040, ABV 3.9%)
Light, refreshing pale ale with a long, hoppy finish.

Welsh Pride/Balchder Cymru (OG 1041, ABV 4%) ◥
A clean-tasting malty bitter. Fruit in aroma and taste with a crisp, grainy mouthfeel and a lingering hoppy bitter aftertaste.

Celebration Ale (OG 1043, ABV 4.2%) ◥
Sweetish best bitter with a fruity nose and palate, and a good hoppy finish.

Honey Fayre/Cwrw Mel (OG 1045, ABV 4.5%) ⬛ ◥
Amber best bitter with hints of honey sweetness in the taste balanced by an increasingly hoppy, bitter finish. Slightly watery mouthfeel for a beer of this strength.

Rampart (OG 1046, ABV 4.5%)

Telford Porter (OG 1056, ABV 5.6%) ⌷

Copper Dragon SIBA IFBB ⊙

Snaygill Industrial Estate, Keighley Road, Skipton, North Yorkshire, BD23 2QR
☎ (01756) 702130 ⊕ copperdragon.uk.com
Bistro/Bar/Shop: see website for opening times
Tours by arrangement

☺Copper Dragon began brewing in 2003. Commissioned in 2008, the purpose-built 'double 60' brewhouse is the centrepiece of an impressive and technologically advanced operation. The site also boasts a visitor centre, shop, conference facilities and a bar/bistro. Beer distribution is widespread across northern England. The main beers are supplemented by limited edition ales throughout the year.

IPA (OG 1036, ABV 3.6%)
Gold-coloured ale with a smooth, hoppy finish.

Black Gold (OG 1036, ABV 3.7%) ◆
This creamy dark ale has a malty, roast character throughout with coffee notes and a bitter roast finish.

Best Bitter (OG 1036, ABV 3.8%) ◆
A traditional Yorkshire bitter with a malty aroma, a hoppy bitter taste with hints of fruit and a bitter finish.

Golden Pippin (OG 1037, ABV 3.9%) ◆
This golden ale has a citrus aroma and flavour. The dry, bitter astringency increases in the aftertaste.

Silver Myst (OG 1040, ABV 4%)
A cask-conditioned Pilsner.

Scotts 1816 (OG 1041, ABV 4.1%) ◆
This best bitter is fruity and malty with a bitter finish. Look for hints of nuts, tropical fruits and vanilla in the aroma and taste.

Copper Kettle (NEW)

Bencroft Grange, Bedford Road, Rushden, Northamptonshire, NN10 0SE
☎ 07958 331340 ⊕ ckcb.webs.com

Established in 2012 by three soldiers turned brewers who set up a 3.5-barrel plant on a historic farm and former site of an alehouse.

UXB (OG 1037, ABV 3.6%)
A chestnut-coloured beer, full-bodied for its strength.

Cornucopia (OG 1041, ABV 4%)
A dark gold-coloured session ale.

Bencroft Best Bitter (OG 1042, ABV 4.1%)

VIP (OG 1042, ABV 4.2%)
A pale gold-coloured, slightly dry session ale.

Coppice Side

Unit 3, Heanor Small Business Centre, Adams Close, Heanor, Derbyshire, DE75 7SW
☎ 07790 305682 ✉ chris@coppicesidebrewery.com

A 5-barrel plant, Coppice Side was established in 2010. The site is shared with Leadmill Brewery (qv) although the two breweries are separate enterprises. Traditional English hops are used wherever possible and the range of beers brewed is dependent on hop availability. The brewery tap is the Butchers Arms in Langley.

Nottingham Blonde (OG 1040, ABV 4%)
Crisp and hoppy with a fruity aroma.

Owd Miner (OG 1040, ABV 4%)
A traditional copper-coloured ale with good hop characteristics.

Unit 3 IPA (OG 1041, ABV 4.2%)

XOB (OG 1043, ABV 4.4%)

Coppice Light (OG 1044, ABV 4.5%)

Ninkasi (OG 1045, ABV 4.6%)

Scary Crow (OG 1052, ABV 5%)

A pale ale with a full, mellow flavour with citrus and floral notes.

Copthorne

Majors Farm, Woodcotes Lane, Darlton, Nottinghamshire, NG22 0TL
☎ 07523 340989

Former Milestones brewer Dean Penney started production in 2010 in outbuildings at the Nags Head. The 3.5-barrel plant was previously installed at the former Cathedral Brewery in Lincoln. The brewery relocated to larger premises in 2011.

Gold (OG 1037, ABV 3.6%)
A hoppy golden ale with a bitter finish.

Classic (OG 1038.2, ABV 3.8%)
A light, hoppy session ale.

Comanchie (OG 1040, ABV 4%)
Copper-coloured with caramel overtones.

Cossack (OG 1042.6, ABV 4.3%)
A bronze-coloured ale with a hint of toffee.

Coquetdale (NEW)

Unit 4c, Station Road, Rothbury, Northumberland, NE65 7QJ
☎ (01669) 621411

Coquetdale brews on a five-barrel plant, originally from Geltsdale brewery, where the owner/brewer also received brewing training. The brewery has an expanding portfolio of locally named beers.

Snitter (ABV 3.8%)

Ale (ABV 4.1%)

Thrum (ABV 4.3%)

Corfe Castle

Bucknowle Farm, Corfe Castle, Dorset, BH20 5PQ
☎ (01929) 480730 ⊕ corfecastlebrewery.co.uk

Corfe Castle is a family-owned brewery established in 2012, brewing in the beautiful Corfe Valley in Dorset. The range of four cask ales is brewed in limited quantities, being supplied to local pubs and festivals in and around Dorset.

Castle Ale (ABV 4.2%)
A refreshing, golden, light ale. Well-balanced with a light malt taste and crisp, dry hop finish.

Raven (ABV 4.2%)
A smooth porter with a rich blend of roasted malts and traditional English hops.

Gloriette (ABV 4.5%)
A traditional English best bitter with a fine balance of malt and hops.

Sovereign (ABV 4.5%)
A full-flavoured golden ale with a dry finish.

Corinium (NEW)

Cirencester, Gloucestershire, GL7 2HB
☎ 07716 826467 ⊕ coriniumales.co.uk

⊠ Corinium Ales was launched in 2012. Brewing takes place on a 0.5-barrel plant in a converted garage. Beers are mainly available bottle-conditioned and make up the brewer's 'Roman Collection' but cask-conditioned production of the beers is increasing.

Gold (OG 1043, ABV 4.2%)
An easy-drinking fruity ale with a mellow blend of malt and hops and a soft bitter finish.

Centurion (OG 1051, ABV 4.7%)
A rich, malty stout with chocolate undertones. Lightly hopped leaving a well-rounded aftertaste.

Ale Caesar (OG 1050, ABV 5%)
A well-hopped IPA with a tropical fruit aroma balanced with a pleasing bitterness.

Cornish Chough SIBA

Trethvas Farm, Lizard, Cornwall, TR12 7AR
☎ (01326) 290908
Tours by arrangement

Cornish Chough, the most southerly brewery on the UK mainland, commenced brewing in 2011 at its present location on Trethvas Farm, Lizard village. The brewery has its own borehole and draws water from between two seams of serpentine rock.

Serpentine (ABV 4%)
A light ruby-coloured beer with a big, malty nose, a bittersweet palate and a finish balanced by rich malt and tangy hops.

Kynance Blonde (OG 1039, ABV 4.2%) ◆
Refreshing gold bitter with soft malt and fruit aroma. Bitterness strikes the tongue balanced by malt and citrus fruit. Finish is sharp and clean, becoming dry.

Fire Raven (ABV 4.7%)
A distinctive and full-bodied porter. Aromas are nutty with notes of heavily roasted malts, some dark fruits, cocoa and mineral hops.

Lizard Storm (OG 1048, ABV 4.8%)
A rich malt and hop aroma with an underlying spice and fruit flavour.

For the Witch Ball, Lizard:

Witch Ball Special (ABV 3.6%)

Cornish Crown SIBA

End Unit, Badger's Cross Farm, Badger's Cross, Penzance, Cornwall, TR20 8XE
☎ (01736) 449029 ☎ 07870 998986
⊕ cornishcrown.co.uk

⊠ Cornish Crown began brewing in 2012 on a six-barrel plant and is based on a farm high above Mounts Bay. Head brewer is Josh Dunkley, the landlord of the Crown Inn in Penzance, which acts as the brewery tap. Beer is available in local outlets and can be found as far away as the Southampton Arms in London.

Ale (OG 1039, ABV 3.9%)

St Michaels (OG 1040, ABV 4%)

Causeway (OG 1041, ABV 4.1%)

SPA (OG 1048, ABV 4.8%)

Corvedale SIBA ⊙

⧢ Sun Inn, Corfton, Craven Arms, Shropshire, SY7 9DF
☎ (01584) 861239 ⊕ corvedalebrewery.co.uk
Tours by arrangement

☺Brewing started in 1999 behind the pub. Landlord Norman Pearce is also the brewer and uses only British malt and hops, with water from a local borehole. Seasonal beers are also brewed.

Bottle-conditioned beers are suitable for vegetarians and vegans.

Dale Ale (OG 1040, ABV 4%)
A rich, bronze-coloured best bitter with smoky aromas of sweet dates and a fruity, nutty taste. Smooth finish.

Golden Dale (OG 1043, ABV 4.2%)
Gold-coloured with a floral, fruity nose and a subtly sweet, smooth taste of hops with a dry finish.

Norman's Pride (OG 1043, ABV 4.3%)
An auburn premium bitter with hoppy grapefruit aromas and a warming, soft, fruity taste.

Farmer Rays Ale (OG 1045, ABV 4.5%)
A clear, ruby bitter with a smooth malty taste. Customers are invited to guess the hop!

St George's Stout (OG 1045, ABV 4.5%)
Traditional smooth, rich stout with soft aromas of chocolate and roasted malt.

Dark & Delicious (OG 1045, ABV 4.6%)
Ruby red premium bitter with soft, malty aromas and a smooth taste hinting at sweet berry fruit.

Cotleigh SIBA ⊙

Ford Road, Wiveliscombe, Somerset, TA4 2RE
☎ (01984) 624086 ⊕ cotleighbrewery.co.uk
Shop Mon-Sat 10am-4pm
Tours by arrangement

Established in 1979, Cotleigh is based in the historic brewing town of Wiveliscombe. 300 pubs and 250 retail outlets are supplied; the beers are also widely available through select wholesalers. Seasonal and bottle-conditioned beers are available: see website.

Harrier (OG 1035, ABV 3.5%)
Golden beer with a delicate floral and fruity aroma and a refreshing, sweet and lightly hopped finish.

Tawny Owl (OG 1038, ABV 3.8%) ◆
Well-balanced, tawny-coloured bitter with plenty of malt and fruitiness on the nose, and malt to the fore in the taste, followed by hop fruit, developing to a satisfying bitter finish.

25 (OG 1040, ABV 4%)
A golden beer with a fresh aroma and fruit-filled finish.

Commando Hoofing (OG 1040, ABV 4%)
An explosion of fruit filled flavours from Cascade and Styrian hops. A pale golden beer, refreshing and slightly sparkling.

Golden Seahawk Premium Beer (OG 1042, ABV 4.2%) ◆
A gold, well-hopped premium bitter with a flowery hop aroma and fruity hop flavour, clean mouthfeel, leading to a dry, hoppy finish.

Barn Owl Premium Ale (OG 1045, ABV 4.5%) ◆
A pale to mid-brown beer with a good balance of malt and hops on the nose; a smooth, full-bodied taste where hops dominate, but balanced by malt, following through to the finish.

Honey Buzzard (OG 1045, ABV 4.5%)
Copper-coloured beer infused with local Wiveliscombe honey. A smooth creamy and chocolate palate, giving a subtle bittersweet finish.

Buzzard Dark Ale (OG 1048, ABV 4.8%)
A traditional dark ale, deep copper red in colour. The chocolate malt gives a dry, nutty flavour with

hints of amarone biscuit. The finish in the mouth is dry with a smoky but smooth finish.

Cotswold SIBA

College Farm, Stow Road, Bourton on the Water, Gloucestershire, GL54 2HN
☎ (01451) 824488 ☎ 07760 889100
⊕ cotswoldlager.com
Tours by arrangement

Cotswold Brewing Co is an independent producer of lager and speciality beers. The brewery was established in 2005 and moved to its current location in 2010. More than 60 outlets are supplied. Seasonal and bottle-conditioned beers are also available.

Cotswold (ABV 4%)
Copper-coloured, well-hopped, easy-drinking ale.

Cotswold Lion SIBA

Grain Store 5, Dowmans Farm, Coberley, Gloucestershire, GL53 9QY
☎ (01242) 870164 ⊕ cotswoldlionbrewery.co.uk

⊠ Brewing began in 2012 using a 10-barrel plant located in a grain store on a farm in the Cotswolds. It's a new venture for John Kemp, former head brewer of Nailsworth Brewery, and Andy Forbes, formerly of Festival Brewery.

Shepherd's Delight (ABV 3.6%)
A light session ale, crisp and full of citrus flavours.

Best in Show (ABV 4.2%)
Plenty of blackberry fruit with a hint of honey.

Golden Fleece (ABV 4.4%)
An IPA, filled with Jamaican fruit.

Cotswold Spring SIBA ◉

Dodington Spring, Dodington Ash, Chipping Sodbury, Gloucestershire, BS37 6RX
☎ (01454) 323088 ⊕ springbrewing.com
Shop Mon-Fri 9am-5pm, Sat 10am-1pm
Tours by arrangement

⊠ Cotswold Spring opened in 2005 with a 10-barrel plant. All the beers are produced using spring water sourced from a borehole on site. Seasonal beers: see website. Bottle-conditioned beers are also available.

Ambler (OG 1040, ABV 3.8%) ◆
Malty aromas and taste give way to dried fruit flavours. Hop flavours lead to an astringent finish.

Old Sodbury Mild (OG 1039, ABV 3.9%) ▮
Initially dry with a bitter sweetness, chocolate notes and a long finish.

Stunner (OG 1041, ABV 4%) ◆
Spicy biscuit aromas blend into hoppy and pale fruit flavours. Refreshing, hoppy and slightly astringent finish.

Codger (OG 1042, ABV 4.2%) ◆
Quite bitter with a slightly malty background. Hops throughout give lasting bitterness which complements the hints of fruit flavour.

Cottage SIBA ◉

The Old Cheese Dairy, Hornblotton Road, Lovington, Somerset, BA7 7PS

☎ (01963) 240551 ⊕ cottagebrewing.co.uk
Tours by arrangement

⊠ The brewery was established in 1993 with the beer names mostly following a transport theme. A visitor centre and bar are now open. Seasonal/special beers are available: see website.

Southern Bitter (OG 1039, ABV 3.7%)
Gold-coloured beer with malt and fruity hops on the nose. Malt and hops in the mouth with a long, fruity bitter finish.

Pacific (OG 1040, ABV 4%)
A gold-coloured ale with a vibrant hop aroma and finish.

Duchess (OG 1042, ABV 4.2%)
A tawny-coloured ale with a balanced bitter finish and distinctive spicy aroma.

Somerset & Dorset (S&D) (OG 1045, ABV 4.4%)
A traditional best bitter with a deep red colour. Well-hopped with a rich, malty flavour.

Golden Arrow (OG 1045, ABV 4.5%)
A hoppy golden bitter with a powerful floral bouquet, a fruity, full-bodied taste and a lingering dry, bitter finish.

Goldrush (OG 1051, ABV 5%)
A deep golden premium ale. Well-balanced with a distinctive and vibrant aroma.

Norman's Conquest MM (OG 1050, ABV 5%)
A dark, mature, smooth ale. Full-bodied with hints of chocolate, bitter orange and vine fruits.

Country Life SIBA

The Big Sheep, Abbotsham, Bideford, Devon, EX39 5AP
☎ (01237) 420808 ☎ 07971 267790
⊕ countrylifebrewery.co.uk
Shop 12-4pm daily
Tours by arrangement

Country Life is based at the Big Sheep tourist attraction. The brewery offers a beer show and free samples in the shop during the peak season (Apr-Oct). A 15.5-barrel plant was installed in 2005, making Country Life the biggest brewery in north Devon. Around 100 outlets are supplied. Seasonal and bottle-conditioned beers are available.

Devonshire Piglet (OG 1042, ABV 4.2%)

Golden Pig (OG 1046, ABV 4.7%)

Country Bumpkin (OG 1058, ABV 6%)

Contract brewed for Heddon Valley Ales:

Dr Heale (ABV 3.8%)

Miss Loosemore (ABV 4.5%)

Cox & Holbrook

Manor Farm, Brettenham Road, Buxhall, Suffolk, IP14 3DY
☎ (01449) 736323
Tours by arrangement

First opened in 1997, the brewery concentrates on producing a range of bitters, four of which are available at any one time, along with more specialised medium strength beers and milds. There is also a strong emphasis on the preservation and resurrection of rare and traditional styles. Bottle-conditioned versions of draught beers are available at varying times of the year.

Crown Dark Mild (OG 1037, ABV 3.6%) ◆
Thin tasting at first but plenty of malt, caramel and roast flavours burst through to give a thoroughly satisfying beer.

Shelley Dark (OG 1036, ABV 3.6%)
Full flavoured and satisfying.

Beyton Bitter (OG 1038, ABV 3.8%)
A traditional bitter, pale tawny in colour, malty with Fuggles and Goldings hops.

Old Mill Bitter (OG 1038, ABV 3.8%)
Pale, hoppy and thirst quenching.

Rattlesden Best Bitter (OG 1043, ABV 4%)
A full-bodied and malty best bitter.

Albion Pale Ale (OG 1042, ABV 4.2%)
Refreshingly clean, hoppy ale.

Remus (OG 1045, ABV 4.5%)
An amber ale, soft on the palate with full hop flavours but subdued bitterness.

Goodcock's Winner (OG 1050, ABV 5%)
An amber ale, rather malty yet not too heavy, with a sharp hop finish.

Ironoak Single Stout (OG 1051, ABV 5%)
Full-bodied with strong roast grain flavours and plenty of hop bitterness plus a distinct hint of oak.

Stormwatch (OG 1052, ABV 5%)
An unusual premium pale ale with a full, slightly fruity flavour.

Stowmarket Porter (OG 1056, ABV 5%) ◆
Strong caramel flavour and lingering caramel aftertaste, balanced by full malt and roast flavours. The overall impression is of a very sweet beer.

East Anglian Pale Ale (OG 1059, ABV 6%)
Well-matured pale beer with a strong Goldings hops character.

Craddock's SIBA

⊟ Duke William, 25 Coventry Street, Stourbridge, West Midlands, DY8 1EP
☎ (01384) 440202 ⊕ thedukewilliam.com

Craddock's began production in 2011 using a four-barrel plant at the Duke William in Stourbridge, originally to provide beer festivals and the other family owned pub, where the deliveries are made by dray horse. Bottle-conditioned beer is also available at the local farmers market.

Saxon Gold (OG 1038, ABV 4%)

Crest (OG 1042, ABV 4.4%)
A copper-coloured premium ale. Well-balanced and full-bodied. A smooth, easy-drinking beer.

Stout (OG 1043, ABV 4.5%)
An easy-drinking stout. Coffee, burnt toast and bitter fruits, edging towards a dry finish.

Troll (OG 1052, ABV 5.4%)
A deceptively strong, sophisticated golden ale, with a bittersweet taste, and dry hop finish.

Crafty Beers (NEW)

⊟ Carpenters Arms, 10 High Street, Great Wilbraham, Cambridgeshire, CB21 5JD
☎ (01223) 882093
⊕ carpentersarmsgastropub.co.uk

Brewing began in 2012 using a one-barrel plant.

Sixteen Strides (ABV 3.9%)

Carpenter's Cask (ABV 4.2%)

Sauvignon Blonde (ABV 4.4%)

Crate (NEW)

Unit 7, White Building, Queens Yard, Hackney Wick, London, E9 5EN
☎ 07834 275687 ⊕ cratebrewery.com

Crate is a brewery and pizzeria opened in 2012, situated in a canalside former print factory.

Golden Ale (ABV 3.8%)

Best Bitter (ABV 4.3%)

Stout (ABV 5.7%)

India Pale Ale (ABV 5.8%)

Cromarty

Davidston, Cromarty, IV11 8XD
☎ (01381) 600440 ⊕ cromartybrewing.co.uk

Cromarty began brewing in 2011 using a new Bavarian brewhouse. To meet demand, additional fermenters were installed in 2013.

Happy Chappy (OG 1040, ABV 4.1%) ◆
A golden ale with plenty of hop character. Floral citrus hop aroma with a good bitter taste which increases in the aftertaste.

Brewed Awakening (OG 1048, ABV 4.7%) ◆
A roasted malty brew with added coffee, making for a dry, bitter finish.

Red Rocker (OG 1048.5, ABV 5%) ◆
Red-coloured bitter using rye.

Cronx (NEW) SIBA

Unit 6, Vulcan Business Centre, Vulcan Way, New Addington, Croydon, CR0 9UG
☎ (01689) 809093 ⊕ thecronx.com

⊗ Cronx began brewing in 2012 and is the first commercial brewery in the area since 1954. Seasonal and one-off beers are also available.

Standard (ABV 3.8%) ◆
Easy-drinking brown bitter with sweetish fudge and spicy hoppiness notes throughout. A malty bitter finish with a dryness that remains.

Kotchin (ABV 3.9%) ◆
Grapefruity beer with pleasant hoppy notes. A little sweetness is balanced by a crisp, bitter finish that grows on drinking.

Entire (ABV 5.2%) ◆
Dark brown porter with chocolate roast notes in the aroma, flavour and finish. The fruit character is of caramelised raisins.

Cropton

See Great Yorkshire

Cross Bay SIBA ◉

Newgate Brewery, White Lund Industrial Estate, Morecambe, Lancashire, LA3 3PT
☎ (01524) 39481 ⊕ crossbaybrewery.co.uk
Shop Mon-Fri 9am-4pm; Sat 9.30am-11.30am; Sun 10-11am
Tours by arrangement

⊕Cross Bay commenced brewing in 2011 on a 28-barrel brew plant and has a brewing capacity of 168 barrels per week. An expansion is planned in the near future.

Halo (OG 1037, ABV 3.6%) ◆
Initial sweetness leads to a fruity, delicate hoppy bitterness, ending with a light finish.

Nightfall Pale Bitter (OG 1038, ABV 3.8%) ◆
A sweet, malty, gently hopped bitter with some fruit.

Dusk Ruby Ale (OG 1040, ABV 4%)
A ruby ale, kicking in with a strong fruity nose, bursting on to the palate with a roasted but fruity bitter body with hints of cocoa, following through with a floral/blackcurrant aroma.

Sunset Blonde Bitter (OG 1043, ABV 4.2%) ◆
Sweet and fruity bitter.

Zenith (OG 1050, ABV 5%)
A reasonably strong IPA. Light and refreshing in colour with a distinct tropical aroma, bursting onto the palate with a citrus/fruity body followed by a hefty kick from the triple blend of hops.

Crouch Vale SIBA ⊙

23 Haltwhistle Road, South Woodham Ferrers, Essex, CM3 5ZA
☎ (01245) 322744 ⊕ crouchvale.co.uk
Shop Mon-Fri 8.30am-5pm
Tours by arrangement

⊗ Founded in 1981 by two CAMRA enthusiasts, Crouch Vale is now well established as a major player in Essex brewing, having moved to larger premises in 2006. The company is also a major wholesaler of cask ale from other independent breweries, which it supplies to more than 100 outlets as well as beer festivals throughout the region. One tied house, the Queen's Head in Chelmsford, is owned. Seasonal beers: see website.

Blackwater Mild (OG 1037, ABV 3.7%) ◆
A dark bitter rather than a true mild. Roasty and very bitter towards the end.

Essex Boys Best Bitter (OG 1038, ABV 3.8%)

Brewers Gold (OG 1040, ABV 4%) ◆
Pale golden ale with a striking citrus nose. Sweet fruit and bitter hops are well matched throughout.

Yakima Gold (OG 1042, ABV 4.2%)

Amarillo (OG 1050, ABV 5%)
A strong golden ale with a spicy aroma, juicy malt mouthfeel and a long and bitter hop finish.

Crown

See Wood Street

Cuerden

c/o Smithy Farm, Long Causeway, Blackshaw Head, Hebden Bridge, West Yorkshire, HX7 7JB
☎ 07938 000530 ✉ cuerdenbrewing@gmail.com

Cuerden was established in 2010 using spare capacity at Bridestones Brewery. Specially designed beers for individual groups and outlets are also brewed.

Munich (ABV 3.7%)

A golden-coloured, well-balanced, clean beer.

Mild (ABV 3.9%)
A session beer, ruby in colour with plenty of body.

Gold (ABV 4%)
A pale, sunny beer. Clean, dry and hoppy with a smooth aftertaste.

Pale (ABV 4.2%)
A traditionally brewed bitter, not too dry and refreshingly sharp.

Cuillin

⊟ Sligachan Hotel, Sligachan, Carbost, Isle of Skye, IV47 8SW
☎ (01478) 650204 ☎ 07795 250808
⊕ cuillinbrewery.co.uk
Tours by arrangement

⊕The five-barrel brewery opened in 2004 and is situated in central Skye at the foot of the Cuillin mountains. The water from the Cuillins provides a distinctive colour and taste to the ales. Specials and seasonal ales are available throughout the year. The brewery is closed in winter.

Eagle Ale (OG 1038, ABV 3.8%)
Smooth tasting session ale with a light caramel and slightly hoppy taste.

Skye Ale (OG 1041, ABV 4.1%)
Golden brown in colour with a slightly nutty flavour and well rounded.

Black Face (OG 1043, ABV 4.3%) ◆
A good balance of blackcurrants and malts highlight this dark ruby red strong mild. Liquorice and roast are also evident in the creamy mouthfeel.

Pinnacle (OG 1047, ABV 4.7%) ◆
The hoppy and fruity nose leads to more hop and plenty of pale malt flavour in this very drinkable golden amber bitter.

Cullercoats SIBA ⊙

Westfield Court, Maurice Road Industrial Estate, Wallsend, Tyne & Wear, NE28 6BY
☎ (0191) 252 8765 ☎ 07895 692881

Office: 17 St Oswins Avenue, Cullercoats, NE30 4PH
⊕ cullercoatsbrewery.co.uk

⊕Ex-solicitor Bill Scantlebury established Cullercoats in 2011 and produces approximately 18 barrels per week.

Lovely Nelly (OG 1039, ABV 3.9%)
A full-bodied amber session beer with a biscuit malt flavour balanced with a smooth bitterness.

Jack the Devil (OG 1045, ABV 4.5%)
Rich, chestnut-coloured ale with a good balance of malty nuttiness and a fresh, hoppy aroma.

Cumberland

The Forge, Great Corby, Carlisle, Cumbria, CA4 8LR
☎ (01228) 560899 ☎ 07747 841671
⊕ cumberlandbreweries.co.uk

⊕Cumberland was established in 2009 with a bespoke 10-barrel brew plant and is situated in a building at the heart of the village, previously the farriers shop from 1833. An expansion is planned.

Corby Ale (OG 1038, ABV 3.8%) ◆

A fruity session beer with sweetness leading to gentle bitterness in the aftertaste.

Corby Blonde (OG 1042, ABV 4.2%) 🍺
Melon fruity hoppiness gives a light, refreshing drink

Cumbrian Legendary SIBA 👁

Old Hall Brewery, Esthwaite Water, Hawkshead, Cumbria, LA22 0QF
☎ (01539) 436436 🌐 cumbrianlegendaryales.com
Tours by arrangement

👁First established in 2003, the brewery is located in an idyllic position in a renovated barn on the shores of Esthwaite Water.

Esthwaite Bitter (OG 1038.5, ABV 3.8%) 🍺🍺
Amber session ale with sweetness, fruit and hoppiness in fine balance.

Langdale (OG 1040, ABV 4%) 🍺🍺
Fresh grapefruit aromas with hoppy, fruity flavours and crisp long hop finish make for a well-balanced beer.

Grasmoor Dark Ale (OG 1043, ABV 4.3%) 🍺
Dark fruity beer with complex character and roast nutty tones leading to a short, refreshing finish.

Loweswater Gold (OG 1041, ABV 4.3%) 🍺🍺
A dominant fruity body develops into a light bitter finish. A beer that belies its strength.

Cych Valley (NEW)

Abercych, Pembrokeshire, SA37 0HJ
✉ salescychvalleybrewery@

Brewing began in 2012 on a 5-barrel plant in a brewhouse on the same site as the Nag's Head Inn. Cariad, Celtic Red and Pembrokeshire Supreme are available bottle-conditioned.

Cariad (ABV 3.9%)

Pembrokeshire Pale Ale (ABV 4.2%)

Celtic Red (ABV 4.3%)

Pembrokeshire Supreme (ABV 4.5%)

Pembrokeshire SA (ABV 5%)

Daleside SIBA 👁

Camwal Road, Starbeck, Harrogate, North Yorkshire, HG1 4PT
☎ (01423) 880022 🌐 dalesidebrewery.com
Shop Mon-Fri 9am-4pm (Off sales only)

👁Opened in 1991 in Harrogate with a 20-barrel plant, the brewery delivers direct to a range of outlets including pubs, restaurants and farm shops from Newcastle to Chesterfield as well as nationally via wholesalers. Seasonal beers: see website.

Bitter (OG 1039, ABV 3.7%) 🍺
Pale brown in colour, this well-balanced, hoppy beer is complemented by fruity bitterness and a hint of sweetness, leading to a long, bitter finish.

Blonde (OG 1040, ABV 3.9%) 🍺
A pale golden beer with a predominantly hoppy aroma and taste, leading to a refreshing hoppy, bitter but short finish.

Old Leg Over (OG 1043, ABV 4.1%) 🍺
Well-balanced mid brown beer that leads to an equally well-balanced fruity, bitter aftertaste.

Special Bitter (OG 1043, ABV 4.1%)
A mid-amber beer with a malty nose and a hint of fruitiness. Hops and malt carry over to leave a clean, hoppy aftertaste.

Monkey Wrench (OG 1055, ABV 5.3%)

Morocco Ale (OG 1057, ABV 5.5%)
A rich, dark spiced ale.

Dancing Duck SIBA

1 John Cooper Buildings, Payne Street, Derby, DE22 3AZ
☎ (01332) 205582 ☎ 07581 122122
🌐 dancingduckbrewery.com

Dancing Duck was established in 2010 by Rachel Matthews using a 10-barrel brew plant. Its name comes from the local greeting 'aye up me duck'. The brewery operates two local pubs, the Exeter Arms and the New Zealand Arms in Derby.

Ay Up/Ey Up (OG 1040.5, ABV 3.9%)
A pale ale session bitter. Subtle malt and floral notes are matched with citrus hop, rounded off with a slightly dry finish.

Nice Weather (OG 1042, ABV 4.1%)
Copper-coloured, fruity beer packed full of flavour; blackberry, strawberry and floral notes in balance with just the right amount of malt character.

22 (OG 1044.1, ABV 4.3%)
A well-balanced best bitter with good malty flavour and dark fruit notes offset by a strong hop with a very clean finish.

DCUK (OG 1042, ABV 4.3%)
A pale ale with a fruity aroma. A juicy citrus flavour with hints of orange, mango, lemon and pine. A drinkable session beer.

Dark Drake (OG 1051, ABV 4.5%)
Malty caramel liquorice flavours combine in a smooth-drinking, velvety oatmeal stout with a freshly roasted coffee and tea finish.

Gold (OG 1046.5, ABV 4.7%)
A modern IPA with powerful hoppy bitterness and aroma balanced with strong malt notes. Hops give peppery, plum-like and orange zesty flavours.

Amberillo (OG 1047.2, ABV 4.8%)
An easy-drinking amber ale. Earthy, aromatic hops are balanced with biscuit malt flavours leading to a spicy, peppery finish.

Duck's Courage (OG 1048.8, ABV 5%)

Abduction (OG 1053, ABV 5.5%)
A myriad of tropical flavours in balance with an enjoyable level of hoppy bitterness, a good malt character and clean finish.

Dancing Man

🍺 Platform Tavern, Town Quay, Southampton, SO14 2NY
☎ (023) 8033 7232 🌐 dancingmanbrewery.com

Dancing Man began brewing in 2011 at the Platform Tavern. Regular and seasonal beers are produced on the one-barrel plant in the windowed brewing room, visible from the pub.

Pilgrim's Pale Ale (OG 1040, ABV 3.9%)
Pale golden ale with a tropical fruit aroma and taste, smooth bitterness and a clean, crisp finish.

Troubador (OG 1041, ABV 4.1%)

A well-balanced, copper-coloured session beer with floral notes and a soft, clean finish.

Fiddler's Jig (OG 1046, ABV 4.8%)
Big, rich malt body, with chocolate and coffee notes giving way to an assertive bitterness.

Big Casino (OG 1049, ABV 5%)
Pine and citrus fruit aroma with a warming malt body and smooth bitterness. Huge juicy hop flavour leads to a clean, crisp finish.

Dark Horse SIBA

Coonlands Laithe, Hetton, North Yorkshire, BD23 6LY
☎ (01756) 730555
Tours by arrangement

☺Formerly the Wharfedale Brewery, Dark Horse opened in 2008 with new owners. The brewery is based in an old hay barn within the Yorkshire Dales National Park. More than 15 outlets are supplied direct.

Best Bitter (OG 1038, ABV 3.8%) ◥
Well-balanced tawny bitter has biscuity malt and fruit on the nose, which continue into the taste. Bitterness increases in the finish.

Hetton Pale Ale (OG 1041, ABV 4.2%) ◥
Well-balanced, full-bodied golden pale ale with hoppy bitterness on the palate overlaying a malty base and a spicy citrus character.

Dark Star SIBA ◉

22 Star Road, Partridge Green, West Sussex, RH13 8AL
☎ (01403) 713085 ⊕ darkstarbrewing.co.uk
Shop Mon-Tue 12.30-5.30pm; Wed-Fri 9am-5.30pm; Sat 9am-4pm
Tours by arrangement

⊗ Dark Star started in the cellar of the Evening Star in Brighton and in 2010 moved to its current premises using a 45-barrel plant. Copies of classic European, American or old English beer styles are regularly produced. The range of beer is divided between permanent, seasonal and monthly specials: see website. Bottle-conditioned beer is also available.

The Art of Darkness (OG 1040, ABV 3.5%)
A low gravity beer with classic roast flavours along with a hint of sweetness. Fruit and spicy flavours in perfect balance.

Hophead (OG 1040, ABV 3.8%) ◥
A golden-coloured bitter with a fruity/hoppy aroma and a citrus/bitter taste and aftertaste. Flavours remain strong to the end.

Partridge Best Bitter (OG 1041, ABV 4%)
Traditional Sussex-style best bitter.

Espresso (OG 1043, ABV 4.2%)
Freshly ground Arabica coffee beans are added to the copper for a few minutes after the boil of this rich, black beer.

American Pale Ale (OG 1048, ABV 4.7%) ⎙ ▮
American-style pale ale full of the aroma of hops.

Festival (OG 1051, ABV 5%) ⎙
A chestnut, bronze-coloured bitter with a smooth mouthfeel and freshness; a classic style strong bitter brewed as a Dark Star version of Festive, a former great Sussex beer from King & Barnes.

Original (OG 1051, ABV 5%)

A dark, strong and bitter beer that defies classification.

Winter Meltdown (OG 1051, ABV 5%)
A deep bronze-coloured beer cask conditioned with Chinese stem ginger and other spices to produce an aromatic warmth.

Revelation (OG 1056, ABV 5.7%)
Strong, massively hopped golden ale that is also dry-hopped.

DarkTribe

⚲ Dog & Gun, High Street, East Butterwick, Lincolnshire, DN17 3AJ
☎ (01724) 782324 ⊕ darktribe.co.uk
Tours by arrangement

☺A small brewery was built during the summer of 1996 in a workshop at the bottom of his garden by Dave 'Dixie' Dean. In 2005 Dixie bought the Dog & Gun pub and moved the 2.5-barrel brewing equipment there. The beers generally follow a marine theme, recalling Dixie's days as an engineer in the Merchant Navy and his enthusiasm for sailing. Local outlets are supplied. Seasonal beers are also produced.

Dixie's Mild (OG 1034, ABV 3.6%)

Honey Mild (OG 1032, ABV 3.6%)

Three Point Six (OG 1033, ABV 3.6%)

Full Ahead (OG 1034, ABV 3.8%) ◥
A malty smoothness is backed by a slightly fruity hop that gives a good bitterness to this amber-brown bitter.

Captain Floyd (OG 1035, ABV 3.9%)

Ruddy L (OG 1035, ABV 3.9%)

Albacore (OG 1036, ABV 4%)

Sternwheeler (OG 1037, ABV 4.2%) ⎙

Old Gaffer (OG 1038, ABV 4.5%)

Dartmoor SIBA ◉

The Brewery, Station Road, Princetown, Devon, PL20 6QX
☎ (01822) 890789 ⊕ dartmoorbrewery.co.uk
Tours by arrangement

⊗ Established in 1994, it is the highest brewery in England at 1,400 feet above sea level. In 2012 the capacity was increased to 360 barrels per week by the addition of another 60-barrel fermenter. Formerly named Princetown Brewery. Bottle-conditioned beer is available.

IPA (OG 1039.5, ABV 4%) ◥
There is a flowery hop aroma and taste with a bitter aftertaste to this full-bodied, amber-coloured beer.

Dragon's Breath (OG 1044, ABV 4.4%)
A winter warmer flavoured with black treacle. Deep ruby brown, rich and full-bodied with an aftertaste of morello cherries.

Legend (OG 1043.5, ABV 4.4%)
A classic cask-conditioned beer, smooth, full-flavoured and balanced with a crispy malt fruit finish. Golden brown-coloured with an aroma of fresh baked bread with a hint of spice.

Jail Ale (OG 1047.5, ABV 4.8%) ◥

Hops and fruit predominate in the flavour of this mid-brown beer, which has a slightly sweet aftertaste.

Darwin SIBA

1 West Quay Court, Sunderland Enterprise Park, Sunderland, Tyne & Wear, SR5 2TE
☎ (0191) 549 9450 ⊕ darwinbrewery.com
Tours by arrangement

☺Established in 1994, Darwin Brewery is now based in purpose-built premises in Sunderland with a 3.5-barrel brew plant. The brewery supports students on Brewlab brewing courses, who produce many unique specialist and international beers, often available locally. A range of established Darwin beers are also produced, some based on historical analysis or student initiatives.

Ghost Ale (OG 1041, ABV 4.1%)

Killer Bee (OG 1065, ABV 6%)
A strong but light ale matured with honey.

Extinction Ale (OG 1084, ABV 8.3%) ◪

Dawkins SIBA

The Now Thus Brewery, Unit 7, Timsbury Workshop Estate, Hayeswood Road, Timsbury, Bath, BA2 0HQ
☎ (01761) 472242 ⊕ dawkins-ales.co.uk
Tours by arrangement

The established Dawkins Taverns group of independent Bristol pubs bought the former Matthews Brewery in 2009. The regular Matthews' recipes continue unchanged under the Dawkins' banner. Five pubs are owned and around 80 outlets are supplied direct. Seasonal beers: see website.

Brassknocker (OG 1037, ABV 3.8%) ◈
A pale gold beer with a full, hoppy, citrus flavour and a satisfying dry finish.

Green Barrel Organic (OG 1039, ABV 4%)
An amber, well-balanced best bitter with a distinctively refreshing, clean bitter finish.

Bob Wall (OG 1041, ABV 4.2%) ◈
Fruity best bitter; roast hints with intense forest fruit and rich malt flavour continuing to a good, balanced finish.

DB SIBA

Unit 2a, Sutton Quays Business Park, Clifton Road, Sutton Weaver, Runcorn, Cheshire, WA7 3EZ
☎ 07739 325742 ⊕ dbbrew.com
Tours by arrangement

DB started brewing in 2011 on a small industrial site in the Clifton area of Runcorn in Cheshire.

Transporter (ABV 4.1%)

Blonde (ABV 4.3%)

Deeply Vale (NEW)

Unit 24, Peel Industrial Estate, Chamberhall Street, Bury, BL9 0LU
☎ (0161) 761 7334 ☎ 07736 936973
⊕ deeplyvalebrewery.com

Deeply Vale is a family-run business established in 2012 using a 2.5-barrel plant. The brewery's name immortalises the Deeply Vale area near Bury, famed for the legendary 1970s music festivals.

Still Walking (OG 1036, ABV 3.8%)
A light, well-balanced, easy-drinking session ale, with a fruity aroma and a velvety smooth feel.

Golden Vale (OG 1041, ABV 4.2%)
A deep golden ale. The flavour is refreshing, robust and satisfyingly malty. A complex bitterness with a smooth, caramel finish.

DV8 (OG 1050, ABV 4.8%)
A breakfast stout, thick and creamy.

Deeside SIBA

The Steading, Lochton of Leys, Banchory, AB31 5QB
☎ (01339) 883777 ⊕ deesidebrewery.co.uk

Originally established as Hillside Brewery in 2005, it quickly expanded and was renamed Deeside Brewery in 2006. The company was sold in 2012 and moved to new premises in 2013. New recipes have been devised to complement the old favourites. Seasonal beers: see website. Bottle-conditioned beers are also available.

Macbeth (OG 1041, ABV 4.1%)

Nechtan (OG 1037, ABV 4.1%) ⌖

Talorcan (OG 1051, ABV 4.5%) ◪

Delavals ⊙

26 Windsor Gardens, Whitley Bay, NE26 3BG
☎ 0844 504 2214 ⊕ delavals.com

Delavals started brewing in 2010, reviving an 18th century ale for Seaton Delaval Hall in partnership with the National Trust. They continue to work closely to create a range of ales that help to promote and preserve regional landmarks. Currently brewing on a two-barrel plant and directly supplying 50 outlets.

Souter Lighthouse Best Bitter
(OG 1037.5, ABV 3.8%)
A traditional copper-coloured English bitter. Well-rounded, bittersweet with a little malt and rich, fruity aromas.

Lindisfarne Castle Dark Ale (OG 1039, ABV 4%)
An old Scottish ale with a twist, an amber/stout fusion. Light and easy drinking for a dark ale. Sweet and malty, made with hyssop to give a silky finish.

Seaton Delaval Hall Pale Ale
(OG 1040.6, ABV 4.2%)
A gold-coloured classic English pale ale, crisp and refreshing with a hoppy aroma and a dry finish.

Washington Old Hall Honey Beer
(OG 1045.4, ABV 4.6%)
A golden ale with honey, not sweet but with a tantalising blend of biscuity malt, light floral aromas and warming honey.

Denbigh

c/o Hope & Anchor Inn, 94 Vale Street, Denbigh, LL16 3BW
☎ (01745) 817021 ⊕ bragdydinbych.co.uk

Brewing commenced in 2012 at the rear of the Hope & Anchor pub. Beers are mainly supplied to the pub although the brewery is run as a separate operation.

John the Thumbs/Sion y Bodiau (ABV 3.6%)

Cock Pit/Cadlas Ceiliogod (ABV 4.5%)

Earls Folly/Ffoled yr Iarl (OG 1045, ABV 4.5%)

Black/Cwrw Du'nbych (ABV 5%)

No X/Dim Ecs (ABV 5%)

The Mental/Y Mental (ABV 7.2%)

Dent SIBA

Hollins, Cowgill, Dent, Cumbria, LA10 5TQ
☎ (01539) 625326 ⊕ dentbrewery.co.uk
Merchandise available from George & Dragon, Dent
Tours by arrangement

Dent was set up in 1990 in a converted barn next to a former farmhouse in the Yorkshire Dales National Park. In 2005 the brewery was completely refurbished and capacity expanded. One pub is owned. Over 150 outlets supplied direct.

Golden Fleece (OG 1035, ABV 3.7%) ◆
Light, hoppy, fruity easy-drinking summer bitter with lingering bitter aftertaste.

Station Porter (OG 1042, ABV 3.8%)
A dark traditional porter with delicate tones of five different malts, a rich, smooth head and lingering, light bitter aftertaste.

Aviator (OG 1039, ABV 4%) ◆
This medium-bodied amber ale is characterised by strong citrus and hoppy flavours that develop into a long, bitter finish.

Ramsbottom Strong Ale (OG 1042, ABV 4.5%) ◆
This complex, mid-brown beer has a warming, dry, bitter finish to follow its unusual combination of roast, bitter, fruity and sweet flavours.

Kamikaze (OG 1047, ABV 5%) ◆
Hops and fruit dominate this full-bodied, golden, strong bitter, with a dry bitterness growing in the aftertaste.

T'owd Tup (OG 1056, ABV 6%) ◆
A rich, full-flavoured, strong stout with a coffee aroma. The dominant roast character is balanced by a warming sweetness and a raisiny, fruitcake taste that linger on into the finish.

Derby SIBA ◉

Masons Place Business Park, Nottingham Road,
Derby, DE21 6AQ
☎ (01332) 242888 ☎ 07887 556788
⊕ derbybrewing.co.uk
Tours by arrangement

A family-run microbrewery, established in 2004 in the old Masons Paintworks Varnish Shed by head brewer Trevor Harris, founder and former brewer at the Brunswick Inn, Derby (qv). The business has grown over the years and three pubs are now owned around Derby. More than 400 outlets are supplied including major retailers. In addition to the core range there are at least four new beers each month including the bi-monthly 'Brewers Choice' range of beers.

Hop Till You Drop (OG 1039, ABV 3.9%)
A polished blonde brew with fruity overtones and a dry finish.

Triple Hop (OG 1041, ABV 4.1%)
A classic pale ale, well-balanced with a combination of triple hop varieties.

Business As Usual (OG 1044, ABV 4.4%)

An easy-drinking, flavoursome copper-coloured beer, well-balanced, smooth and malty with a satisfying finish.

Double Mash (OG 1046, ABV 4.6%)
A balanced ruby brew, crafted using the double mash brewing process.

Penny's Porter (OG 1046, ABV 4.6%) 🍴
A rich, dark, robust brew, with a fine hop balance.

Old Friend (OG 1047, ABV 4.7%)
A classic wel-rounded brew, balanced and full-bodied.

Dashingly Dark (OG 1048, ABV 4.8%)
A smooth, dark brew with complex flavours and a chocolate roasted finish.

Mercia IPA (OG 1050, ABV 5%)
An IPA created with a modern twist.

Old Intentional (OG 1050, ABV 5%)
A full-bodied, malty premium beer, chestnut-coloured and well-balanced with a delicate sweet aroma and a smooth finish.

Quintessential (OG 1058, ABV 5.8%)
Complex and well-rounded with fruit and citrus flavours.

Derventio SIBA

Long Mill, Darley Abbey Mills, Darley Abbey,
Derbyshire, DE22 1DZ
☎ (01332) 380199 ☎ 07525 689095
⊕ derventiobrewery.co.uk
Tours by arrangement

Derventio Brewery was established in 2005 and first brewed in 2006 at Trusley Brook Farm. In 2011 the six-barrel brewery relocated to the Grade I-listed Long Mill, which is part of the Derwent Valley Mills World Heritage Site. The brewery tap can be hired for private parties. A popular 'Day with the Brewer' is available, by prior arrangement, for up to three people on Saturday mornings. The brewery is involved in sponsorship of local cricket teams as well as numerous outside events and is one of the founding members of the Derbyshire Brewers Collective. Seasonal beers and monthly specials are also brewed.

Cleopatra (OG 1048.4, ABV 5%)
A complex beer rounded off with First Gold hops and a hint of apricot.

Derwent SIBA

Units 2a-2c, Station Road Industrial Estate, Silloth,
Cumbria, CA7 4AG
☎ (01697) 331522 ⊕ derwentbrewery.co.uk

◉Derwent was set up in 1996 in Cockermouth and moved to Silloth in 1998. A large range of ales is produced, available throughout the north of England.

Carlisle State Bitter (OG 1036, ABV 3.7%) ◆
A gold-coloured, malty, biscuity, hoppy beer.

W&M Mild (OG 1036, ABV 3.7%)

Parsons Pledge (OG 1039, ABV 4%) ◆
Amber ale with a biscuity tang and a slightly fruity finish.

Mutineer (OG 1043, ABV 4.4%)

W&M Pale Ale (OG 1042, ABV 4.4%) ◆
A sweet, fruity, hoppy beer with a bitter finish.

Deverell's

Unit 16, Globe Industrial Estate, Grays, Essex, RM17 6ST

☎ 07843 627791

Established in 2012 using a 2.5-barrel plant, Deverell's was the first commercial brewer in Thurrock since Charringtons acquired and closed Seabrooks Brewery more than 80 years ago. Seasonal beers are available.

Best Bitter (ABV 3.6%)
An easy-drinking quaffable beer.

Tall Hot Blonde (ABV 4%)
A refreshing blonde ale. Nutty and sweet with a gentle bitterness.

Redemption (ABV 4.5%)
Full-flavoured amber ale; sweet with caramel with a well-balanced hop profile.

Devil's Dyke

◙ Dyke's End, 8 Fair Green, Reach, Cambridgeshire, CB25 0JD

☎ (01638) 743816

Tours by arrangement

Devil's Dyke came on stream in 2007 using a plant bought from the Red Rose Brewery. It is situated in outbuildings to the rear of the Dyke's End pub, the freehold of which was bought by the village in the late 1990s to save it from being turned back into a private house. Several outlets are supplied in the area. Seasonal beer is also brewed.

Bitter (OG 1036.7, ABV 3.8%)

No. 7 Pale Ale (OG 1039.8, ABV 4.1%)

Victorian Amber Ale (OG 1044, ABV 4.7%)

London Porter (OG 1052, ABV 5.2%)

Devon

◙ Mansfield Arms, 7 Main Street, Sauchie, Clackmannanshire, FK10 3JR

☎ (01259) 722020 ⊕ devonales.com

Tours by arrangement

☺Established in 1992 to produce high quality cask ales for the Mansfield Arms, Sauchie, Devon is the oldest operating brewery in the county. A second pub, The Inn at Muckhart, was purchased in 1994 and the only beers sold there are from the Devon Ales brewery. The brewery is now selling beer to the open market.

Original (70/-) (OG 1038, ABV 3.8%)
A full-bodied session ale with a prominent malty flavour and distinct hoppiness.

Thick Black (OG 1042, ABV 4.2%)

Pride (OG 1046, ABV 4.8%)
A flavourful, full-bodied beer.

Devon Earth SIBA

Office: 7 Fernham Terrace, Torquay Road, Paignton, Devon, TQ3 2AQ

☎ (01803) 525778 ☎ 07927 397871

⊕ devonearthbrewery.co.uk

⊠ Devon Earth was launched in 2008 on a 2.5-barrel plant. Now located at a Paignton pub, it is run on a part-time basis, supplying beer to festivals and pubs mainly around the Torbay area. Seasonal special brews are occasionally produced.

Dickensian SIBA

Roden Nurseries, Roden Lane, Roden, Shropshire, TF6 6BP

☎ 07752 331633 ⊕ dickensianbrewery.co.uk

Originally based at the Dolphin Inn in Shrewsbury, Dickensian now brew on a purpose-built plant in Roden. The beers names are themed around Dickens' novels.

Ale of Two Cities (ABV 3.8%)

David Hopperfield (ABV 4%)

Digfield SIBA

Lilford Lodge Farm, Barnwell, PE8 5SA

☎ (01832) 273954 ⊕ digfield-ales.co.uk

⊠ Digfield Ales started brewing in 2005 on a five-barrel plant, which was later expanded to seven barrels. Increased demand led to a move to larger premises in 2012. A reed bed effluent system has been installed and brewing capacity increased to 15 barrels with new equipment. More than 40 free houses are supplied. Seasonal beers: see website.

Fools Nook (OG 1037, ABV 3.8%) ◕
The floral aroma, dominated by lavender and honey, belies the hoppy bitterness that comes through in the taste of this golden ale. A fruity balance lasts.

Barnwell Bitter (OG 1039, ABV 4%) ◕
A fruity, sulphurous aroma introduces a beer in which sharp bitterness is balanced by dry, biscuity malt.

Shacklebush (OG 1044, ABV 4.5%) ◕
This amber brew begins with a balance of malt and sulphury hop on the nose which develops on the palate, complemented by a mounting bitterness. Good dry finish with lingering malt notes.

Doghouse SIBA

Unit 7, The Paddocks, Jurby Industrial Estate, Jurby, Isle of Man, IM7 3BD

☎ (01624) 890039 ⊕ doghousebrewery.im

☺Doghouse began brewing in 2012 using equipment manufactured in Germany by Biering.

Bitter (OG 1036, ABV 3.7%)

Gold (OG 1038, ABV 3.8%)

IPA (OG 1039, ABV 4%)

Dominion (NEW)

Unit Z, New House Farm, Little Laver Road, Moreton, Essex, CM5 0JE

☎ (01277) 890580 ☎ 07931 120806

⊕ dominionbrewerycompany.com

Tours by arrangement

⊠ Dominion was established in 2012 by Andy Skene, renting the premises and Pitfield Brewery brand names from the founder of Pitfield, Martin Kemp.

Dark Mild (OG 1036, ABV 3.4%)

Pitfield Bitter (OG 1036, ABV 3.7%)

Session beer. Amber, malty and nutty with a dry, bitter finish.

Pitfield Lager (OG 1037, ABV 3.7%)

Pure Gold (OG 1039, ABV 3.9%)
Gold-coloured, initially malty with a complex bitter finish.

Chococino Dark Beer (OG 1038, ABV 4%)

Shoreditch Stout (OG 1040, ABV 4%) ◆
Chocolate and a raisin fruitiness on the nose lead to a fruity roast flavour and a sweetish finish with a little bitterness.

Eco Warrior (OG 1043, ABV 4.5%) ◆
Golden ale with a vivid, citrus hop aroma. The hop character is balanced with a delicate sweetness in the taste, followed by an increasingly bitter finish.

Red Ale (OG 1046, ABV 4.8%) ◆
Complex beer with a full, malty body and strong hop character.

1850 London Porter (OG 1048, ABV 5%) ◆
Big-tasting dark ale dominated by coffee and forest fruits. The finish is dry but not acrid.

N1 Wheat Beer (OG 1048, ABV 5%)

1837 India Pale Ale (OG 1065, ABV 7%)
A true IPA, strong in alcohol, with lots of hops, a light copper-coloured beer with a floral aroma.

Imperial Chocolate Stout (OG 1070, ABV 7.3%)
A traditional stout with overtones of chocolate.

Yukon Gold (OG 1090, ABV 9.7%)

For Epping Brewery:

Epping Forest Bitter (OG 1036, ABV 3.7%)
A traditional amber-coloured bitter.

Doncaster (NEW)

Unit 4a, Coopers Mill Business Park, Clay Lane West, Doncaster, South Yorkshire, DN2 4QR
☎ 07770 958394 ⊕ doncasterbrewery.co.uk

The brewery was launched in 2012 to promote all things Doncaster, with beer names commemorating Doncaster history. The 15-barrel plant was built from scratch by husband and wife team Ian and Alison Blaylock.

Sand House (ABV 3.8%)

Cheswold (ABV 4.2%)

Gold Cup (ABV 4.5%)

First Aviation (ABV 5%)

Donnington IFBB ◉

Upper Swell, Stow-on-the-Wold, Gloucestershire, GL54 1EP
☎ (01451) 830603 ⊕ donnington-brewery.com

Thomas Arkell bought a 13th-century watermill in 1827 and began brewing on the site in 1865; the waterwheel is still in use. Thomas's descendant Claude owned and ran the brewery until his death in 2007, supplying 20 outlets direct. It has now passed to Claude's cousin, James Arkell, also of Arkells Brewery, Swindon (qv). Bottle-conditioned beer is available.

BB (OG 1035, ABV 3.6%) ◆
A pleasant amber bitter with a slight hop aroma, a good balance of malt and hops in the mouth and a bitter aftertaste.

SBA (OG 1045, ABV 4.4%) ◆
Malt dominates over bitterness in the subtle flavour of this premium bitter, which has a hint of fruit and a dry, malty finish.

Dorking SIBA

Engine Shed, Dorking West Station Yard, Station Road, Dorking, Surrey, RH4 1HF
☎ (01306) 877988 ⊕ dorkingbrewery.com
Tours by arrangement

⊗ Dorking started brewing in 2008 and supplies an increasing number of local pubs and clubs. Seasonal beers are available.

Gold (OG 1042, ABV 3.8%)

DB Number One (OG 1045, ABV 4.2%) ◆
Hoppy best bitter with underlying orange fruit notes. Some balancing malt sweetness in the taste leads to a dry, bitter finish.

Red India Ale (OG 1051, ABV 5%)

Dorset (DBC) SIBA ◉

The Jurassic Brewhouse, Hybris Business Park, Warmwell Road, Crossways, Dorset, DT2 8BF
☎ (01305) 777515 ⊕ dbcales.com
Tours by arrangement

⊗ Founded in 1996, Dorset Brewing Company, a family-run brewery, relocated from Brewers Quay, Weymouth, once the old Devenish & Groves site, to new premises in 2010. In 2008 it took over the running of Dorchester's brewpub, Tom Brown's (Goldfinch Brewery). Beers are available in local pubs and selected outlets throughout the south-west. Monthly specials are brewed: see website.

Dorset Knob (OG 1039, ABV 3.9%) ◆
Complex bitter ale with strong malt and fruit flavours despite its light gravity.

Tom Brown's (OG 1041, ABV 4%)
Smooth, amber-coloured quaffing ale with caramel notes and a subtle, spiced, fruity aroma.

Jurassic (OG 1042, ABV 4.2%) ◆
Clean-tasting, easy-drinking bitter. Well balanced with lingering bitterness after moderate sweetness.

Flashmans Clout (OG 1045, ABV 4.5%)
Richly-flavoured copper ale with plum and burnt toffee notes and a citrus finish.

Yatchsman (OG 1047, ABV 4.7%)
Pacific-style pale ale bursting with complex fruity aromas and a lingering hoppiness.

Durdle Door (OG 1049, ABV 5%) ◆
A tawny hue and fruity aroma with a hint of pear drops and good malty undertone, joined by hops and a little roast malt in the taste. Lingering bittersweet finish.

Dorset Piddle

See Piddle

Double Top SIBA

Unit 4, Kilton Terrace, Worksop, Nottinghamshire, S80 2DQ
☎ 07973 521824

Office: The Mallard, Station Approach, Carlton Road, Worksop, Nottinghamshire, S81 7AG
Tours by arrangement

⊕Double Top began brewing in 2011 and now uses a 2.5-barrel brew plant. It caters for its brewery tap, the Mallard on Platform 1 of Worksop railway station, and for regional beer festivals and free houses.

Golden Arrow (OG 1038, ABV 3.9%)
A golden ale with citrus notes.

Shanghai Bitter (OG 1041, ABV 4.2%)

Treble 20 (OG 1043, ABV 4.5%)
Straw-coloured, hoppy and bitter.

Tungsten (OG 1044, ABV 4.5%)

Serendipity (OG 1046, ABV 4.6%)

Madhouse (OG 1055, ABV 5.2%)
A modern porter.

Dove Street

⬙ 82 St Helens Street, Ipswich, Suffolk, IP4 2LB
☎ (01473) 211270 ☎ 07880 707077
⊕ dovestreetbrewery.co.uk
Shop 12-10pm daily
Tours by arrangement

⊗ Dove Street began brewing in 2011 using a 2.5-barrel plant in a garage opposite the Dove Street Inn. The pub and beer festivals are supplied.

Underwood Mild (OG 1033, ABV 3.2%)
Dark, traditional, thirst quenching mild, packed with flavour and aroma, with freshness and spice.

Dove Street Bitter (DSB) (OG 1038, ABV 3.7%)
A traditional bitter with a dryish finish.

Incredible Taste Fantastic Clarity (ITFC) (OG 1041, ABV 4%)
Golden, hoppy session beer; clean, clear and crisp.

Dove Elder (OG 1042, ABV 4.1%)
Traditionally brewed speciality beer.

Ed Porter (OG 1047, ABV 4.5%)
A traditional porter with a hint of sweetness.

Thirsty Walker (OG 1047, ABV 4.6%)
A strong, well-balanced and thirst quenching beer.

Summer Light Evening (OG 1051, ABV 5%)
Light with a bitter finish and underlying flavour of caramel.

Old Ipswich Liquor (OIL) (OG 1055, ABV 5.5%)
Aged for deep complex flavours, chocolate and liquorice notes with an in-depth, long, well-rounded finish.

Dow Bridge SIBA ◉

2-3 Rugby Road, Catthorpe, Leicestershire, LE17 6DA
☎ (01788) 869121 ⊕ dowbridgebrewery.co.uk
Tours by arrangement

Dow Bridge commenced brewing in 2001 and takes its name from a local bridge where Watling Street spans the River Avon. The brewery uses English whole hops and malt with no adjuncts or additives. More than 50 outlets are supplied direct. Seasonal and bottle-conditioned beers are also available: see website.

Bonum Mild (OG 1035, ABV 3.5%) ◆
Complex dark brown, full-flavoured mild, with strong malt and roast flavours to the fore and continuing into the aftertaste, leading to a long, satisfying finish.

Acris (OG 1037, ABV 3.8%)
Classic session bitter, packed with flavour.

Centurion (OG 1039, ABV 4%)
Copper-coloured, well rounded best bitter. Good balance of malt and hops in the flavour.

Legion (OG 1041, ABV 4.1%)
Golden hoppy ale. A good balance of malt and fruity hop on the nose and palate.

Ratae'd (OG 1041, ABV 4.3%) ◆
Tawny coloured full-bodied beer with bitter hop flavours against a grainy background, leading to a long, bitter and dry aftertaste.

Dow Bridge Dark (DBD) (OG 1042, ABV 4.4%)
A strong, dark, full-bodied ale with roast malt giving hints of chocolate.

Gladiator (OG 1046, ABV 4.5%)
Ruby chestnut, well-balanced beer. Smooth and malty but with a bitter, dry finish. Some fruit aroma and a slight toffee sweetness.

Fosse Ale (OG 1046, ABV 4.8%)
Well-balanced, premium beer with caramel and burnt toffee flavours leading to a hoppy, dry finish.

Praetorian Porter (OG 1048, ABV 5%)
Dark, rich, full-bodied porter. Slightly sweet with hoppy undertones.

Onslaught (OG 1049, ABV 5.2%)
A deep ruby strong ale. A good balance of fruit and hops with rich flavours and aroma.

Downlands (NEW)

Unit Z (2a), Mackley Industrial Estate, Small Dole, West Sussex, BN5 9XE
☎ (01273) 495596 ⊕ downlandsbrewery.com

⊗ Previously known as SouthDowns Brewery, Downlands began brewing in 2012 using a 10-barrel brew plant. Beers are distributed along the south coast and to CAMRA beer festivals. Seasonal and special beers are available.

Truleigh Gold (OG 1036, ABV 3.7%)
Crisp, clean, refreshing golden ale with apricot, orange and citrus aromas and a dab of sweetness.

Ruskin's Ram (OG 1041, ABV 4%)
Traditional English ale with a sharp, clean, malty taste complemented by a subtle aroma with hints of vanilla and elderflower.

Devils Dyke Honey Porter (OG 1050, ABV 5%)

Devils Dyke Porter (OG 1050, ABV 5%)
Toffee, chocolate and smoky flavours are complemented by a subtle hint of marmalade.

Three Rings (OG 1051, ABV 5.2%)
A strong pale ale, full-flavoured with a fruity finish.

Downton SIBA

Unit 11, Batten Road, Downton Industrial Estate, Downton, Wiltshire, SP5 3HU
☎ (01725) 513313 ⊕ downtonbrewery.com
Shop Mon-Fri 9am-5pm

⊗ Downton was set up in 2003. The brewery has a 20-barrel brew length and produces around 1,500 barrels a year. Six regular beers are produced together with speciality and experimental beers.

THE BREWERIES

Around 100 outlets are supplied direct. Bottle-conditioned beers are also available.

New Forest Ale (OG 1037, ABV 3.8%)

Quadhop (OG 1038, ABV 3.9%)

Elderquad (OG 1039, ABV 4%)

Honey Blonde (OG 1041, ABV 4.3%)

Dark Delight (OG 1053, ABV 5.5%) 📖

IPA (OG 1063, ABV 6.8%)

Draycott

Low Farm, 30 Mill Road, Buckden, Cambridgeshire, PE19 5SS
☎ (01480) 812404 ☎ 07740 374710
⊕ draycottbrewery.co.uk

The brewery is located in an old farm complex and was set up by Jon and Jane Draycott in 2009. Only bottle-conditioned beers are produced, for sale in the local area and from a shop catering to holiday makers at Dunster Beach in Somerset.

Driftwood

🍺 Driftwood Spars Hotel, Trevaunance Cove, St Agnes, Cornwall, TR5 0RT
☎ (01872) 552428 ⊕ driftwoodspars.com
Tours by arrangement

⊠ Brewing since 2000, Driftwood produce 10 regular beers which continuously rotate through the range. They are available mainly at the Driftwood Spars Hotel, but are also supplied to other outlets. A full range of bottle-conditioned beers is also produced.

Blackheads Mild (OG 1037, ABV 3.8%) 🗃 ◆
Refreshing dark mild with roast malt aroma. Malt and sweet caramel follow a burst of damson and liquorice. Dry, bitter end.

Dek (OG 1038, ABV 3.8%) ◆
Fruity, grassy hops on the nose lead to bitter, resinous, citrus hops and pronounced dryness in the mouth all the way through. Amber beer in the golden ale style.

Trouble & Strife (OG 1037, ABV 3.8%) ◆
Light-drinking amber session bitter with aroma of hop fruit. Goldings and Fuggles hops provide a dominant bitter flavour balanced by gentle sweetness, hop fruit, malt and astringency.

Blue Hills Bitter (OG 1039, ABV 4%) ◆
Medium-bodied refreshing bitter with a hoppy aroma. Flowery, grassy hops dominate the flavour to the end with gentle biscuity malt.

Red Mission (OG 1040, ABV 4%) ◆
Tawny best bitter with fruity hops and light malt on the nose. Malt and hops create a balanced taste with bitterness running through to a dry, hoppy finish.

Montol (OG 1040, ABV 4.1%) ◆
Grapefruit from citrus hops plus vine fruit aroma. Pronounced hop bitterness and sweet malt flavour lasting into a long finish.

Badlands Bitter (OG 1047, ABV 4.8%) ◆
Red winter warmer, rich in sweet malt, figs and raisins balanced by hoppiness, finishing with fruit esters, bitterness and dryness.

Lou's Brew (OG 1049, ABV 5%) ◆

Apple/pear aroma, light in citrus. Moderate fruity and hoppy bitterness with some malt in this golden ale. Long, bitter finish.

Alfie's Revenge (OG 1060, ABV 6.5%) 🗃 ◆
Rich, smooth old ale. Smoky malt, coffee and fudge flavours with fruit esters and bitter hops through to the finish.

Dronfield (NEW)

c/o Wood Street Brewery, Hillsborough Hotel, 54-58 Langsett Road, Sheffield, South Yorkshire, S6 2UB
☎ 07966 143420 ⊠ dronfieldbrewery@gmail.com

Dronfield began brewing in 2013 using spare capacity at Wood Street Brewery (qv). Different beers are brewed each month. Local pubs and beer festivals are supplied.

DT

🍺 Royal Standard Inn, 700 Dorchester Road, Upwey, Dorset, DT3 5LA
☎ (01305) 812558 ⊕ theroyalstandardupwey.co.uk

DT Ales began brewing in 2010 to supply the pub using a one-barrel plant. No other outlets are supplied.

dt3 (ABV 3.5%)
Summery session ale with light, hoppy notes and a pale complexion.

dt4 (ABV 4.5%)
A robust, smoky and hoppy ale.

Dukeries (NEW) SIBA

Carlton Forest Distribution Centre, Unit 6, Blyth Road, Worksop, Nottinghamshire, S81 0TP
☎ 07584 305027
⊠ phil.owen@dukeriesbrewery.co.uk

☺Founded in 2012 and located in the heart of the Dukeries in Nottinghamshire this five-barrel plant produces six permanent ales and several seasonal beers throughout the year. The brewery tap is the Anchor Inn in Worksop.

Blonde (ABV 3.8%)
A strong amber session ale with a blend of tropical fruit flavours.

Baronet (ABV 3.9%)
Traditional chestnut-coloured bitter with good hops on the nose and bags of fruity flavours going on to the end with a dry, bitter finish.

De Lovetot (ABV 4.2%)
A golden pale ale. Well-balanced with citrus fruit and hops aroma, leading to a smooth, hoppy finish.

Lime Tree (ABV 4.4%)

Mining (ABV 4.5%)

IPA (ABV 4.9%)
A traditional English IPA, full of complex character.

Dunham Massey

100 Oldfield Lane, Dunham Massey, WA14 4PE
☎ (0161) 929 0663 ⊕ dunhammasseybrewing.co.uk
Shop Mon-Fri 10am-5pm; Sat-Sun 11am-4pm

☺Opened in 2007, Dunham Massey brew traditional north-western ales using only English ingredients. The beer range is also available bottle conditioned. Around 30 outlets are supplied direct, along with the brewery tap, Costello's Bar in Altrincham.

Little Bollington Bitter (OG 1037, ABV 3.7%)
A straw-coloured, light and easy-drinking beer with a bitter finish.

Chocolate Cherry Mild (OG 1040, ABV 3.8%) 🍺
Dark chocolate, coffee and liquorice-flavoured dark mild, blended with a dry, bittersweet cherry flavour.

Dunham Dark (OG 1040, ABV 3.8%)
A traditional north western dark mild. Smooth and easy drinking.

Dunham Light (OG 1040, ABV 3.8%)
A creamy, malty, easy drinking, light mild.

Big Tree Bitter (OG 1041, ABV 3.9%)
A session bitter, golden in colour, full-bodied, with a good balance of hops and malt.

Obelisk (OG 1040, ABV 3.9%)
Light and hoppy but not too bitter with hints of citrus and grapefruit.

Dunham Milk Stout (OG 1051, ABV 4%)
A classic, full-bodied, sweet stout with a creamy, roast malt character.

Landlady (OG 1040, ABV 4%)
A light, refreshing, dry ale, with a spicy hop finish.

Dunham Stout (OG 1046, ABV 4.2%)
A creamy, full-bodied English dry stout, with a classic bitter, burnt, dark roast flavour.

Stamford Bitter (OG 1045, ABV 4.2%)
A golden, full-bodied bitter with a complex blend of hops giving a slightly dry finish.

Deer Beer (OG 1047, ABV 4.5%)
A clean, full-bodied, malty English ale with a hint of toffee and a distinct hop finish.

Cheshire IPA (OG 1047, ABV 4.7%)
A medium strong, pale, hoppy and bitter beer.

Altrincham Pilsner (OG 1048, ABV 4.8%)
A real lager; light, refreshing and full of flavour.

Dunham Porter (OG 1056, ABV 5.2%)
A classic old-style English porter; creamy, full-bodied and packed with flavour.

East India Pale Ale (OG 1062, ABV 6%)
Light and hoppy.

Dunham Gold (OG 1070, ABV 7.2%)
A Belgian-style English ale. Strong, light and fruity with a hoppy finish.

Dunscar Bridge SIBA 👁

🏭 The Brewery, Dunscar Business Park, Blackburn Road, Bolton, BL7 9PQ
☎ (01204) 600713 ⊕ dunscarbridgebrewery.co.uk
Tours by arrangement

😀Dunscar Bridge began brewing in 2009 on a 4.3-barrel plant, visible to customers in the bar through a glazed screen. An additional 25-barrel plant was added in 2012.

Bombay IPA (OG 1038, ABV 3.7%)

Steeplejack (OG 1039, ABV 3.8%)

Rialto 47 (OG 1040, ABV 3.9%)
Golden, fruity ale with a full-bodied hoppy taste.

Lubelski Pils (OG 1040, ABV 4%)

Wicketkeeper (OG 1040, ABV 4%)

Well balanced amber best bitter.

DBB (Dunscar Best Bitter) (OG 1040, ABV 4.1%)
Double drop best bitter, dry hopped for intensity of flavour and wonderful aroma.

Porters Black (OG 1048, ABV 5%)
Silky smooth on the palate with plummy fruit flavours.

Durham SIBA

Unit 6a, Bowburn North Industrial Estate, Bowburn, Co Durham, DH6 5PF
☎ (0191) 377 1991 ⊕ durhambrewery.co.uk
Shop Mon-Fri 8am-4pm; Sat 10am-2pm
Tours by arrangement

😀Established in 1994, Durham has a portfolio of around 40 beers, some permanent, more on rotation with new beers appearing regularly. Five litre mini-casks can be purchased in the shop or online. Bottle-conditioned beers are available and suitable for vegans.

Magus (OG 1036, ABV 3.8%) 🌾
Pale malt gives this brew its straw colour but the hops define its character, with a fruity aroma, a clean bitter mouthfeel, and a lingering dry, citrus-like finish.

White Amarillo (ABV 4.1%)

Earl Soham SIBA

The Street, Earl Soham, Suffolk, IP13 7RT
☎ (01728) 684097 ⊕ earlsohambrewery.co.uk
Shop Mon-Thu 8.30am-5pm; Fri 8.30am-6pm; Sat 9am-4.30pm
Tours by arrangement

⊗ Earl Soham was set up behind the Victoria pub in 1984 and continued there until 2001 when the brewery moved 100 yards down the road. The Victoria and the Station in Framlingham both sell the beers on a regular basis, as does the Brewery Tap in Ipswich. When there is spare stock, beer is supplied to local free houses and as many beer festivals as possible. 30 outlets are supplied and three pubs are owned. Seasonal beer is also brewed. Most of the beers are bottle conditioned for the shop next door and other selected outlets.

Gannet Mild (OG 1034, ABV 3.3%) 🌾
A beautifully balanced mild, sweet and fruity flavour with a lingering, coffee aftertaste.

Victoria Bitter (OG 1037, ABV 3.6%) 🌾
A light, fruity, amber session beer with a clean taste and a long, lingering hoppy aftertaste.

Sir Roger's Porter (OG 1042, ABV 4.2%) 🌾
Roast/coffee aroma and berry fruit introduce a full-bodied porter with roast/coffee flavours. Dry roast finish.

Albert Ale (OG 1045, ABV 4.4%) 🌾
Hops dominate every aspect of this beer, but especially the finish. A fruity, astringent beer.

Brandeston Gold (OG 1045, ABV 4.5%) 🌾
Popular beer brewed with local ingredients. Lovely sharp clean flavour, malty/hoppy and heavily laden with citrus fruit. Malty finish.

Earls (NEW)

Earl of Essex, 25 Danbury Street, Islington, London, N1 8LE

☎ (020) 7424 5828 ⊕ earlofessex.net

Brewing began in 2013 using a four-barrel plant.

East Coast SIBA

3 Clay House Yard, Rear of Mitford Street, Filey, North Yorkshire, YO14 9DX
☎ (01723) 514865
⊕ eastcoastbrewingcompany.co.uk
Tours by arrangement

The brewery is housed in a converted stable and coach house. Six regular beers are produced plus at least one special per month. 20 outlets are supplied direct.

Bonhomme Richard (ABV 3.6%)

Mary Rose (ABV 3.8%)

Commodore (ABV 4.1%)

John Paul Jones (ABV 4.3%)

High Tide (ABV 5.2%)

Alfred Moodies Mild (ABV 6%)

Empress of India (ABV 6%)

East London SIBA

Unit 45, Fairways Business Centre, Lammas Road, London, E10 7QB
☎ 07900 288873 ⊕ eastlondonbrewing.com

⊠ The East London Brewing Company commenced brewing in 2011 using a 10-barrel plant and is run by a husband-and-wife team.

Orchid (ABV 3.6%)
A dark mild, spiced with vanilla.

ELB Pale Ale (OG 1042, ABV 4%) ◈
Dark gold beer with a fruity aroma and a slightly citrus marmalade character in the flavour. Lingering bitter finish.

Foundation Bitter (OG 1044, ABV 4.2%) ◈
A hoppy brown best bitter with pronounced bitterness. It is balanced by a little maltiness and a touch of blackcurrant.

Nightwatchman (OG 1046, ABV 4.5%) ◈
A dark beer with red hues. Chocolate and roast flavours are present but fade in the dryish finish. Fruit throughout.

Jamboree (OG 1048, ABV 4.8%) ◈
Citrus and berries coupled with some hops are on the nose, palate and finish in this golden-coloured beer.

Quadrant Oatmeal Stout (ABV 5.8%)
A smooth stout with a silky mouthfeel, rich dark fruit flavour and hints of coffee.

Eastwood

See Barge & Barrel

Eccleshall

See Slater's

Eden SIBA

Brougham Hall, Brougham, Cumbria, CA10 2DE

☎ (01768) 210565 ☎ 07729 677692
⊕ edenbrewery.com

Set up in 2011, Eden is run by Jason Hill and Stephen Mitchell. The five-barrel brewery is located in the Old Brewery at historic Brougham Hall and has the capacity to brew 45 barrels per week.

Best (OG 1039, ABV 3.8%)
A well-balanced traditional ale. Light chestnut-coloured with subtle character and flavour.

Fuggle (OG 1039, ABV 3.8%)
A pale ale with character.

Dark Knight (OG 1040, ABV 4%)
A dark chestnut-coloured session ale.

Gold (OG 1042, ABV 4.2%)
A light golden colour, with a distinctive hop character and a pleasant citrus aroma.

First Emperor (OG 1046, ABV 4.6%)
A full-bodied IPA.

Eden St Andrews (NEW) SIBA

Main Road, Guardbridge, KY16 0UU
☎ 07786 060013 ⊕ edenbrewerystandrews.com
Shop Mon-Fri 10am-9pm; Sat 10am-4pm
Tours by arrangement

☺Established in 2012 using a five-barrel plant in part of the former Guardbridge paper mills. Bottle-conditioned beer is available.

Blonde (OG 1040, ABV 3.8%)

19th (OG 1041, ABV 3.9%)

Clock Brew (OG 1045, ABV 4.3%)

1882 Lager (OG 1048, ABV 4.5%)

Seggie Porter (OG 1053, ABV 5.5%)

Elgood's SIBA IFBB ◉

North Brink Brewery, Wisbech, Cambridgeshire, PE13 1LW
☎ (01945) 583160 ⊕ elgoods-brewery.co.uk
Shop Tue-Thu 11.30am-4.30pm (May-Sep)
Tours by arrangement

⊠ The North Brink brewery was established in 1795. Owned by the Elgood family since 1878, the fifth generation are now involved in running the business. The brewery has approximately 35 tied pubs within a 50-mile radius of Wisbech. Seasonal beers: see website.

Black Dog (OG 1036.8, ABV 3.6%) ▨ ◈
Black/red mild with liquorice and chocolate. Dry roasty finish.

Cambridge Bitter (OG 1037.8, ABV 3.8%) ◈
Fruit and malt on the nose with increasing hops and balancing malt on the palate. Dry finish.

Golden Newt (OG 1041.5, ABV 4.1%) ◈
Golden ale with floral hops and sulphur aroma. Floral hops and a fruity presence on a bittersweet background lead to a short, muted hoppy and fruity finish.

EP (OG 1043.8, ABV 4.3%)
A premium ale with an aroma of hops and malt.

THE BREWERIES · E

Elixir (NEW)

c/o Alechemy Brewing Ltd, Unit 2c, Young Square, Brucefield Industrial Estate, Livingston, West Lothian, EH54 9BX
☎ 07760 330122 ⊕ elixirbrew.com

Elixir was founded as a collaboration between Barry Robertson, manager of Cloisters Bar in Edinburgh, and Ben Bullen, an experimental home brewer originally from Australia. Beers are brewed at Alechemy in Livingston. Seasonal and special beers are available: see website.

Benedictine Groove (ABV 5.3%)

Conviction IPA (ABV 5.5%)
A powerfully-hopped amber IPA.

Cuzzy Brew (ABV 5.5%)
A black IPA.

Elland SIBA ◉

Units 3-5, Heathfield Industrial Estate, Heathfield Street, Elland, West Yorkshire, HX5 9AE
☎ (01422) 377677 ⊕ ellandbrewery.co.uk
Tours by arrangement

◉Orginally formed in 2002 as Eastwood & Sanders by the amalgamation of the Barge & Barrel and West Yorkshire Breweries, the company was renamed Elland in 2006 to reinforce its links with the town. The brewery has a capacity of 50 barrels per week. Seasonal beers: see website.

Bargee (OG 1038, ABV 3.8%) ◥
Amber, creamy session bitter. Fruity, hoppy aroma and taste complemented by a bitter edge in the finish.

Best Bitter (OG 1041, ABV 4%) ◥
Creamy, yellow, hoppy ale with hints of citrus fruits. Pleasantly strong bitter aftertaste.

Beyond the Pale (OG 1042, ABV 4.2%) ◨ ◥
Gold-coloured, robust, creamy beer with ripe aromas of hops and fruit. Bitterness predominates in the mouth and leads to a dry, fruity and hoppy aftertaste.

Eden (OG 1042, ABV 4.2%) ◥
A yellow, fruity, hoppy, creamy bitter. Citrus fruit with assertively bitter taste to finish.

Nettlethrasher (OG 1044, ABV 4.4%) ◥
Grainy amber-coloured beer. A rounded nose with some fragrant hops notes followed by a mellow nutty and fruity taste and a dry finish.

1872 Porter (OG 1065, ABV 6.5%) ◫ ◨ ◥
Creamy, full-flavoured porter. Rich liquorice flavours with a hint of chocolate from roast malt. A soft but satisfying aftertaste of bittersweet roast and malt.

Ellenberg's (NEW)

Unit 5, Boston Business Park, Trumpers Way, Hanwell, London, W7 2QA
☎ (020) 3261 1089 ☎ 07842 296302
⊕ ellenbergsbrewery.co.uk

Brewing began in 2013 using a 10-barrel plant with two dedicated fermenters on an industrial estate in Hanwell shared with Weird Beard Brewing Co (qv). Bottle-conditioned beer only.

Elliswood (NEW)

Unit 3, Southways Industrial Estate, Coventry Road, Hinckley, Leicestershire, LE10 0NJ
☎ 07717 662139 ✉ tracy.ellis53@ntlworld.com

Flliswood began brewing in 2013 using a David Porter 5.5-barrel plant. Further beers are planned.

Just One More (OG 1040, ABV 4.1%)
A citrus beer with blackberry and grapefruit undertones.

Elmtree SIBA

Snetterton Brewery, Unit 10, Oakwood Industrial Estate, Harling Road, Snetterton, Norfolk, NR16 2JU
☎ (01953) 887065 ⊕ elmtreebeers.co.uk
Shop Mon-Wed & Sat 11am-4pm

Elmtree was established in 2007 using a five-barrel plant and moved in 2008 to new premises. 120 outlets are supplied direct. Bottle-conditioned beers are available and are suitable for vegetarians and vegans.

Burston's Cuckoo (OG 1038, ABV 3.8%)
A nasal feast of floral hops with a hint of citrus, rounding off into a refreshingly long, dry finish.

Bitter (OG 1041, ABV 4.2%)
A well-balanced, copper-coloured crisp beer, the early malt notes give way to a distinctively complex Goldings hop finish.

Dark Horse (OG 1048, ABV 5%) ◥
A roast, slightly salty aroma and matching initial taste introduce this coal black stout. The roast notes are aided by a fruity, prune-like background. Increasingly malty finish.

Golden Pale Ale (OG 1048, ABV 5%)
A pale ale in the traditional style that is initially malty and delicately bittered. The long, dry biscuit finish is enhanced by the subtle citrus aromas.

Elveden

The Courtyard, Elveden Estate, Elveden, Thetford, Norfolk, IP24 3TA
☎ (01842) 878922

Elveden is a five-barrel brewery based on the estate of Lord Iveagh, a member of the ennobled branch of the Guinness family. The brewery is run by Frances Moore, daughter of Brendan Moore at Iceni Brewery (qv) and produces three ales: Elveden Stout (ABV 5%) and Elveden Ale (ABV 5.2%), which are mainly bottled in stoneware bottles. The third is Charter Ale (ABV 10%) to mark the celebrations for the award of a Royal Charter for Harwich in 1604. The beer is available in cask and bottle-conditioned versions. The phone number listed is shared with Iceni. The majority of sales take place through the farm shop, adjacent to the brewery.

Empire SIBA

The Old Boiler House, Unit 33, Upper Mills, Slaithwaite, Huddersfield, West Yorkshire, HD7 5HA
☎ (01484) 847343 ☎ 07966 592276
⊕ empirebrewing.com
Tours by arrangement

◉Empire Brewing was set up 2006 in a mill on the bank of the scenic Huddersfield Narrow Canal, close to the centre of Slaithwaite. In 2011 the brewery upgraded from a five-barrel to a 10-barrel plant. Beers are supplied to local free houses and through independent specialist beer agencies and wholesalers. Seasonal and bottle-conditioned beers are also available.

Golden Warrior (OG 1039.5, ABV 3.8%)
Pale bitter, quite fruity with a sherbet aftertaste and moderate bitterness.

Moonraker Mild (ABV 3.8%)

Strikes Back (OG 1041, ABV 4%)
Pale golden bitter with a hoppy aroma and good hop and malt balance with a citrus flavour, very light on the palate.

Longbow (OG 1043, ABV 4.3%)

Imperium (OG 1050, ABV 5.1%)

Emsworth

rear of 16 West Street, Emsworth, Hampshire, PO10 7DY
☎ 07717 510294
✉ room101.emsworth@virginmedia.com

Michael and Hilary Bolt began brewing in 2012 on a 2.5-barrel plant in a shed behind an antiques shop in Emsworth. Seasonal beer is also available.

Slipper (OG 1039, ABV 3.9%)

Wayfarer (OG 1039, ABV 3.9%)

Fairfield (OG 1041, ABV 4.1%)

Ennerdale

Croasdale Farm Barn, Ennerdale, Cumbria, CA23 3AT
☎ (01946) 861755 ☎ 07918 626652
⊕ ennerdalebrewery.co.uk
Tours by arrangement

☺Ennerdale first brewed in 2010. The brewery is situated in a barn overlooking the Ennerdale Valley. All the beers are produced using the brewery's own source of spring water. Beers are distributed largely in West Cumbria but also into the Lake District.

Blonde (OG 1039, ABV 3.8%) ◈
A sweet, fruity, light-coloured beer with gentle bitterness.

Copper (OG 1039, ABV 3.8%)

Black Sail Bitter (ABV 3.9%)

Darkest (OG 1044, ABV 4.2%)

Enville SIBA

Coxgreen, Hollies Lane, Enville, DY7 5LG
☎ (01384) 873728 ⊕ envilleales.com
Tours by arrangement

⊠ Enville Brewery is sited on a picturesque Victorian, Grade II-listed farm complex, using natural well water, traditional steam brewing and a reed and willow effluent plant. Enville Ale is infused with honey and is from a 19th-century recipe for beekeeper's ale passed down from the former proprietor's great-great aunt. Seasonal beers: see website.

Kasitra (OG 1034, ABV 3.5%)
An American-style IPA with zesty notes of lemon, lime, grapefruit, papaya and guava.

LPA (Light Pale Ale) (OG 1039, ABV 4%)

Traditional session bitter; dry and golden with a mellow, hoppy flavour.

Nailmaker Mild (OG 1041, ABV 4%)
A well-defined hop aroma and underlying sweetness give way to a dry finish.

Simply Simpkiss (OG 1039, ABV 4%)

Cherry Blonde (OG 1042, ABV 4.2%)

Saaz (OG 1042, ABV 4.2%) ◈
Golden lager-style beer. Lager bite but with more taste and lasting bitterness. The malty aroma is late arriving but the bitter finish, balanced by fruit and hops, compensates.

White (OG 1041, ABV 4.2%) ◈
Yellow with a malt, hops and fruit aroma. Hoppy but sweet finish.

Ale (OG 1044, ABV 4.5%) ◈
Sweet malty aroma and taste, honey becomes apparent before bitterness finally dominates.

Old Porter (OG 1044, ABV 4.5%) ◈
Black with a creamy head and sulphurous aroma. Sweet and fruity start with touches of spice. Good balance between sweet and bitter, but hops dominate the finish.

Ginger Beer (OG 1045, ABV 4.6%) ◈
Golden bright with gently gingered tangs. A drinkable beer with no acute flavours but a satisfying aftertaste of sweet hoppiness.

Phoenix IPA (OG 1047, ABV 4.8%)

Epping

See Dominion

Evan Evans SIBA

The New Brewery, 1 Rhosmaen Street, Llandeilo, Carmarthenshire, SA19 6LU
☎ (01558) 824455 ⊕ evan-evans.com
Shop Mon-Fri 10am-4pm
Tours by arrangement

☺Evan Evans opened in 2004. Brewing capacity is now 8,000 barrels per annum. Eight pubs are owned. It is Wales' first Soil Association organic-approved brewery. In 2009 the brewery bought Archers Brewery of Swindon's brands and now brew all of Archer's regular and seasonal ales.

Brewery Bitter (OG 1036, ABV 3.6%)
A refreshing, light session bitter with delicious malt and fruit.

Cwrw (OG 1043, ABV 4.2%)
Rich malty flavour, with a distinct fruity palate.

Warrior (OG 1046, ABV 4.6%)
A classic premium ale, distinctive and full bodied. Malty and fruity with a dry hop finish.

Under Archers Brewery Name:

Gold (OG 1040, ABV 4%)
Golden with a floral hop nose and dry palate and a malty, dry-hop finish.

ASB (OG 1041, ABV 4.1%)
Malty with a dry, fruity palate and dry, bitter finish.

Steam Ale (OG 1045, ABV 4.5%)
A full-bodied premium bitter. Rich, plummy fruit lingers on the palate with a dry, bitter finish.

Under WH Buckley name:

Buckley's Best (ABV 4%)
A traditional best bitter with a malty, fruity, bitter taste.

Evening Star (NEW)

🛗 Olde England Pub, 113 Corporation Street, St Helens, Merseyside, WA10 1SX
☎ 07754 730589 ⊕ 1854pub.com

Set up in a room at the rear of the Olde England pub, the brewery is named after the last steam locomotive to be built for British Railways. Four core beers are brewed for the pub plus one changing 'novelty' beer.

Evening Star (ABV 3.7%)
A hoppy session bitter.

Sans Pareil (ABV 4.5%)
A blonde beer.

George Stephenson IPA (ABV 5.8%)

The Rocket (ABV 6.5%)

Everards SIBA IFBB ⬤

Castle Acres, Narborough, Leicestershire, LE19 1BY
☎ (0116) 201 4100 ⊕ everards.co.uk
Shop Mon-Fri 10am-5pm; Sat 10am-2pm
Tours by arrangement

Established by William Everard in 1849, Everards brewery remains an independent family-owned company. Four core ales are brewed as well as a range of seasonal beers – see website for more details. Everards owns a pub estate of more than 170 tenanted houses throughout the Midlands.

Beacon Bitter (OG 1036, ABV 3.8%) ◄
Light, refreshing, well-balanced pale amber bitter in the Burton style.

Sunchaser Blonde (OG 1038, ABV 4%) ◄
A golden brew with a sweet, lightly-hopped character. Some citrus notes to the fore in a quick finish that becomes increasingly bitter.

Tiger Best Bitter (OG 1041, ABV 4.2%) 🍴 ◄
A mid-brown, well-balanced best bitter crafted for broad appeal, benefiting from a long, bittersweet finish.

Original (OG 1050, ABV 5.2%) ◄
Full-bodied, mid-brown strong bitter with a pleasant rich, grainy mouthfeel. Well-balanced flavours, with malt slightly to the fore, merging into a long, satisfying finish.

Evesham (NEW) SIBA

17 Oat Street, Evesham, Worcestershire, WR11 4PJ
☎ (01386) 443628 ✉ eveshambrewery@aol.com

☺Evesham Brewery is located in the former Green Dragon pub. Beer is produced as required by demand from the brewery's own pub, and other pubs supplied, mainly locally.

Exe Valley SIBA ⬤

Land Farm, Silverton, Exeter, Devon, EX5 4HF
☎ (01392) 860406 ⊕ exevalleybrewery.co.uk

Exe Valley was established as Barron's Brewery in 1984. The brewery is located in a converted barn overlooking the Exe Valley and Dartmoor hills. Locally sourced malt and English hops are used,

along with the brewery's own spring water. Around 100 outlets are supplied within a 45-mile radius of the brewery. Beers are also available nationally via wholesalers. Seasonal beers: see website.

Bitter (OG 1036, ABV 3.7%) ◄
Mid-brown bitter, pleasantly fruity with underlying malt through the aroma, taste and finish.

Barron's Hopsit (OG 1040, ABV 4.1%) ◄
Straw-coloured beer with strong hop aroma, hop and fruit flavour and a bitter hop finish.

Dob's Best Bitter (OG 1040, ABV 4.1%) ◄
Light brown bitter. Malt and fruit predominate in the aroma and taste with a dry, bitter, fruity finish.

Devon Glory (OG 1046, ABV 4.7%)
Mid-brown, fruity-tasting beer with a sweet, fruity finish.

Mr Sheppard's Crook (OG 1046, ABV 4.7%) ◄
Smooth, full-bodied, mid-brown beer with a malty-fruit nose and a sweetish palate leading to a bitter, dry finish.

Exeter Old Bitter (OG 1046, ABV 4.8%) ◄
Mid-brown old ale with a rich, fruity taste and slightly earthy aroma and bitter finish.

Exeter SIBA

Unit 1, Cowley Bridge Road, Exeter, Devon, EX4 4NX
☎ (01392) 823013 ⊕ theexeterbrewery.co.uk

Exeter Brewery, formerly Topsham & Exminster, began brewing in 2003. In 2012 the brewery moved to a larger site in Exeter.

Lighterman (OG 1036, ABV 3.6%)

Avocet (OG 1038.5, ABV 3.9%)
An organic beer.

Fraid Not (OG 1040, ABV 4%)
A golden, hoppy beer.

Ferryman (OG 1041, ABV 4.2%)

County Best (OG 1045, ABV 4.6%)

Darkness (OG 1050, ABV 5.1%) 🍴

Exmoor SIBA ⬤

Golden Hill Brewery, Wiveliscombe, Somerset, TA4 2NY
☎ (01984) 623798 ⊕ exmoorales.co.uk
Tours by arrangement

Somerset's largest brewery was founded in 1980 in the old Hancock's brewery, which closed in 1959. Around 250 outlets in the South-west are supplied and others nationwide via wholesalers and pub chains. Seasonal beers: see website.

Ale (OG 1039, ABV 3.8%) ◄
A pale to mid-brown, medium-bodied session bitter. A mixture of malt and hops in the aroma and taste lead to a hoppy, bitter aftertaste.

Fox (OG 1043, ABV 4.2%)
A mid-brown beer; the slight maltiness on the tongue is followed by a burst of hops with a lingering bittersweet aftertaste.

Gold (OG 1045, ABV 4.5%) ◄
A yellow/golden best bitter with a good balance of malt and fruity hop on the nose and the palate. The sweetness follows through an ultimately more bitter finish.

Stag (OG 1050, ABV 5.2%) 🍴 ◄
A pale brown beer, with a malty taste and aroma, and a bitter finish.

Beast (OG 1066, ABV 6.6%)
A dark beer brewed with chocolate and crystal malts.

Facer's

A8-9, Ashmount Enterprise Park, Aber Road, Flint, Aber Road, CH6 5QT
☎ 07713 566370 ⊕ facers.co.uk
Tours by arrangement for CAMRA groups only

Facer's is the oldest brewery in Flintshire, having moved west from Salford in 2006. Ex-Boddington head brewer Dave Facer ran the brewery single-handed from its launch in 2003 until 2007, when the first employee was recruited. The brewery was expanded to twice the floor space in early 2008. Around 80 outlets are supplied.

Clwyd Gold (OG 1034, ABV 3.5%) ◄
Clean-tasting session bitter, mid-brown in colour with a full mouthfeel. The malty flavours are accompanied by increasing hoppiness in the bitter finish.

Flintshire Bitter (OG 1036, ABV 3.7%) ◄
Well-balanced session bitter with a full mouthfeel. Some fruitiness in aroma and taste with increasing hoppy bitterness in the dry finish.

North Star Porter (OG 1040, ABV 4%) ◄
Dark, smooth, porter-style beer with good roast notes and hints of coffee and chocolate. Some initial sweetness and caramel flavours followed by a hoppy bitter aftertaste.

Sunny Bitter (OG 1040, ABV 4.2%) ◄
An amber beer with a dry taste. The hop aroma continues into the taste where some faint fruit notes are also present. Lasting dry finish.

DHB (Dave's Hoppy Beer) (OG 1041, ABV 4.3%) ◄
A dry-hopped version of Splendid Ale with some sweet flavours also coming through in the mainly hoppy, bitter taste.

This Splendid Ale (OG 1041, ABV 4.3%) ◄
Refreshing tangy best bitter, yellow in colour with a sharp hoppy, bitter taste. Good citrus fruit undertones with hints of grapefruit throughout.

Landslide (OG 1047, ABV 4.9%) ◄
Full-flavoured, complex premium bitter with tangy orange marmalade fruitiness in aroma and taste. Long-lasting hoppy flavours throughout.

Fakir

c/o 30 Harford Street, Norwich, NR1 3AY
⊕ fakirbrewery.com

⊠ Fakir began brewing in 2010 using spare capacity at several breweries based in Norfolk. Cask-conditioned beer is supplied to local pubs and Indian restaurants, bottle-conditioned beer is also available. Further beers are planned.

Old Fakir's Gold (OG 1048, ABV 5.1%)
A golden ale with a delicate citrus grapefruit aroma without compromising the lasting bitterness needed for a dry, satisfying finish.

Fallen

See Traditional Scottish Ales

Fallen Angel

See Broxbourne

Falstaff

🍴 24 Society Place, Normanton, Derby, DE23 6UH
☎ 07947 242710 ⊕ falstaffbrewery.co.uk

⊠ Attached to the Falstaff freehouse, the brewery dates from 1999 but was refurbished and re-opened in 2003 under new management. Themed special beers are produced all year round, including exclusive specials for the Babington Arms in Derby.

3 Faze (OG 1040, ABV 3.8%)
Light gold-coloured with a malt and honey nose. Smooth malt flavours lead to a clean, balanced malt and hop finish.

Fist Full of Hops (OG 1044, ABV 4.5%)
An amber ale with lots of hop.

Phoenix (OG 1045, ABV 4.7%) ◄
A smooth, tawny ale with fruit and hop, joined by plenty of malt in the mouth. A subtle sweetness produces a drinkable ale.

Smiling Assassin (OG 1050, ABV 5.2%)
A copper-coloured beer with sweet malt flavours.

Faringdon

🍴 1 Park Road, Faringdon, Oxfordshire, SN7 7BP
☎ (01367) 241480 ⊠ swanfaringdon@yahoo.co.uk
Tours by arrangement

⊠ Opened in 2010, brewing on a larger-scale began in 2011. The beers are brewed by Stuart Bruton and supplied to the brewery tap, the Swan. Occasional and bottle-conditioned ales are also available.

Folly Ale (OG 1039.5, ABV 4%)
A traditional English bitter with a sweet aroma but no lingering aftertaste.

Farmer's SIBA

Stable Brewery, Silver Street, Maldon, Essex, CM9 4QE
☎ (01621) 851000 ⊕ maldonbrewing.co.uk
Shop Mon-Fri 9am-4pm; Sat 10am-2pm
Tours by arrangement

⊠ Established in 2002, this family-run brewery is tucked away behind the 14th-century Blue Boar Hotel, which serves as the brewery tap. Around 30 local outlets are supplied. Seasonal and bottle-conditioned beers are also available.

IPA (OG 1036, ABV 3.6%)
A crisp, traditional amber IPA.

Drop of Nelson's Blood (OG 1038, ABV 3.8%) ◄
Red-brown session bitter. Initially quite sweet and fruity, with a pleasing bite to the aftertaste.

Hotel Porter (OG 1041, ABV 4.1%) ◄
Roast grain dominates this oatmeal stout, but an unusual fresh hop character is evident.

Pucks Folly (OG 1038, ABV 4.2%) ◄

Pale golden ale with spicy notes and sweet fruit. Biscuity malt in the taste fades and the finish is dominated by bitterness.

Golden Boar (OG 1050, ABV 5%) ◆
Powerful, deep-golden ale. The hop character is initially full and citrus, but becomes more spicy in the aftertaste.

Dark Horse (OG 1064, ABV 6.6%)
A chestnut bitter with a smooth taste and long finish.

Farnham

⊟ Claverton Marketing Ltd t/a Ball & Wicket Public House, 102-104 Upper Hale Road, Upper Hale, Farnham, Surrey, GU9 0PB
☎ **(01252) 735278 ⊕ theballandwicket.co.uk**

⊠ Farnham opened in 2006 and is located at the rear of the Ball & Wicket pub, which is also the only outlet. Three ales are brewed regularly with occasional seasonal specials.

Bishop Sumner (OG 1040, ABV 3.8%)
Amber-coloured session bitter with rounded bitterness and sweet, dry finish.

William Cobbett (OG 1045, ABV 4.5%) ◆
Malt slightly dominates this fruity best bitter, but balancing hop leads to a bitter finish, with some residual sweetness.

Mike Hawthorn (OG 1055, ABV 5.3%) ◆
Fruity and sweet throughout, with some balancing hop bitterness.

Farriers Arms

⊟ The Forstal, Mersham, Kent, TN25 6NU
☎ **(01233) 720444 ⊕ thefarriersarms.com**
Tours by arrangement

Brewing commenced in 2010 in this brewpub owned by a consortium of villagers. Seasonal beers are also available.

Farriers 1606 (OG 1038, ABV 3.7%)

Fat Cat

⊟ Fat Cat Brewery Tap, 98-100 Lawson Road, Norwich, NR3 4LF
☎ **(01603) 788508 ☎ 07795 633368**

Office: Fat Cat Pub, 49 West End Street, Norwich, NR2 4NA ⊕ fatcatbrewery.co.uk
Tours by arrangement

⊠ Fat Cat Brewery was founded by the owner of the Fat Cat free house in Norwich. Brewing started in 2005 at the Fat Cat's sister pub, the Fat Cat Brewery Tap, under the supervision of former Woodforde's owner Ray Ashworth. Seasonal beers, bottle-conditioned beers and occasional one-off brews are also available.

Bitter (OG 1038, ABV 3.8%) ◆
Gold-coloured with a grapefruit and sulphur aroma. A well-balanced citrus and hop beginning underpinned by malt and then an increasingly dry bitterness.

Hell Cat (OG 1040, ABV 4.1%) ◆
Clementines and hops anchor this lively but full-bodied brew. A strong bittersweet but satisfying finale.

Top Cat (OG 1047, ABV 4.7%) ◆

Copper-coloured, a complex malt, caramel, and blackberry aroma leads into a similar creamy beginning. This winter pudding feel continues to a rich and satisfying finish.

Marmalade Cat (OG 1055, ABV 5.5%) ⬚ ◆
Rich and complex with malt and marmalade dominating every corner. Copper-coloured and grainy with a solid bitter finale.

Felinfoel SIBA ◉

Farmers Row, Felinfoel, Llanelli, Carmarthenshire, SA14 8LB
☎ **(01554) 773357 ⊕ felinfoel-brewery.com**
Shop 9am-4pm
Tours by arrangement

Founded in the 1830s, the company is still family-owned and is now the oldest brewery in Wales. The present buildings are Grade II*-listed and were built in the 1870s. It supplies cask ale to half its 84 houses, though some use top pressure dispense, and to approximately 350 free trade outlets.

Best Bitter (OG 1038, ABV 3.8%) ◆
A well-balanced beer, with a low aroma. Bittersweet initially with an increasing moderate bitterness.

Double Dragon (OG 1042, ABV 4.2%) ◆
This pale brown beer has a malty, fruity aroma. The taste is also malt and fruit with a background hop presence throughout. A malty and fruity finish.

Fell (NEW)

Unit 27, Moor Lane Business Park, Flookburgh, Cumbria, LA11 7NG
☎ **(01539) 558980 ☎ 07967 503689**
⊕ **fellbrewery.co.uk**

Fell Brewery was founded in 2012 by homebrewer Tim Bloomer and friend Andrew Carter, brewing beers inspired by their travels in the USA and Belgium.

Robust Porter (OG 1051, ABV 4.8%)
London porter brewed with chocolate malt.

Progressive Pale (OG 1051, ABV 5.1%)
New World pale ale. Relatively low in bitterness with an uncomplicated malt base.

Fellows

2 Leopold Walk, Cottenham, Cambridgeshire, CB24 8XS
☎ **(01954) 250262 ⊕ fellowsbrewery.co.uk**

⊠ Fellows began production in 2010 though brewer Mark Burton had been developing recipes for a year or so before. Five regular beers are available with plans for a series of special ales. Beers are increasingly visible in the local free trade.

Cambridge Fellow (OG 1038, ABV 3.8%)
A golden session ale; light and clean-tasting.

Gulping Fellow (OG 1042, ABV 4.2%)
A dry, bitter finish complements the spicy hop character of this well-balanced best bitter.

Burton Snatch (OG 1048, ABV 4.8%)
Blonde ale with a citrus aroma and refreshing mouthfeel. A hint of wet leather completes the finish.

Jolly Fellows (OG 1050, ABV 5%)

Full-bodied, clean-tasting premium bitter.

Clever Fellow (OG 1052, ABV 5.2%)
Malt loaf and toffee flavours combine with back of the tongue bitterness to achieve a balanced richness.

Felstar

Felsted Vineyards, Crix Green, Felsted, Essex, CM6 3JT
☎ (01245) 361504 ☎ 07546 096374
⊕ felstarbrewery.co.uk
Shop 10am-dusk daily
Tours by arrangement

⊗ Felstar Brewery opened in 2001 with a five-barrel plant based in the old bonded warehouse of the Felsted Vineyard. A small number of outlets are supplied. Seasonal and bottle-conditioned beers are also available.

Felstar (OG 1034, ABV 3.4%)

Best (OG 1040, ABV 4%)

Crix Forest (OG 1040, ABV 4%)

Sunburst (OG 1040, ABV 4%)

Good Knight (OG 1050, ABV 5%)

Hoppy Hen (OG 1050, ABV 5%)

Peckin' Order (OG 1050, ABV 5%)

Fernandes

🍴 5 Avison Yard, Kirkgate, Wakefield, West Yorkshire, WF1 1UA
☎ (01924) 291709 ⊕ ossett-brewery.co.uk
Tours by arrangement

☺Opened in 1997 housed in a 19th-century malthouse, Ossett Brewing Company purchased the brewery and tap in 2007 but independent brewing continues. The tap sells Fernandes and Ossett beers as well as guest ales; the former are more widely available through Ossett's supply chain.

Malt Shovel Mild (OG 1038, ABV 3.8%) 🍴
A dark, full-bodied, malty mild with roast malt and chocolate flavours, leading to a lingering, dry, malty finish.

Triple O (OG 1041, ABV 3.9%)
A light, refreshing, hoppy session beer with a lingering fruity finish.

Ale to the Tsar (OG 1042, ABV 4.1%)
A pale, smooth, well-balanced beer with some sweetness leading to a nutty, malty and satisfying aftertaste.

Centennial (OG 1043, ABV 4.1%)
Light-coloured extremely hoppy beer with a long, lingering aftertaste.

Great Northern (OG 1050, ABV 5.1%)
Pale, citrussy and extremely hoppy.

Double Six (OG 1062, ABV 6%)
A powerful, dark and rich strong beer with an array of malt, roast malt and chocolate flavours and a strong, lasting malty finish, with some hoppiness.

FILO SIBA

🍴 The Old Town Brewery, Torfield Cottage, 8 Old London Road, Hastings, East Sussex, TN34 3HA
☎ (01424) 420212 ⊕ filobrewing.co.uk
Tours by arrangement

⊗ The brewery at the First In Last Out public house was established in 1985, with the current owners taking over in 1988. In 2011 the brewery relocated two minutes' walk away, remaining in the Old Town. The First In Last Out is still supplied direct together with pubs throughout Sussex and Kent.

Mike's Mild (OG 1035, ABV 3.4%)

Crofters (OG 1037, ABV 3.8%)

Churches Pale Ale (OG 1042, ABV 4.2%)

Old Town Tom (OG 1044, ABV 4.5%)

Gold (OG 1050, ABV 4.8%)

Firebrick (NEW)

Unit 10, Blaydon Business Centre, Cowen Road, Blaydon, NE21 5TW

Firebrick began brewing in 2013 on a 2.5-barrel plant from the former Bull Lane Brewery in Sunderland. Expansion is planned to a 12-barrel plant. Beers are available at selected pubs in Newcastle and the surrounding area.

Blaydon Brick (OG 1038, ABV 3.8%)

Coalface (OG 1039, ABV 3.9%)

Tyne 9 (OG 1039, ABV 3.9%)

Elder Statesman (OG 1043, ABV 4.3%)

Firefly

🍴 Firefly, 54 Lowesmoor, Worcester, WR1 2SE
☎ (01905) 616996 ☎ 07525 445988
✉ thefirefly@hotmail.co.uk

⊗ Firefly Brewing was established in 2012 using a 0.5-barrel plant. At present only the pub is supplied.

Pale Ale (OG 1042, ABV 4.2%)
An American-style IPA.

Black Colt (OG 1062, ABV 6.5%)
A hoppy black ale with a citrus aroma and a lingering bitter finish with a hint of chocolate.

First Chop (NEW) SIBA

c/o First Chop Bar & Restaurant, 43 Bolton Street, Ramsbottom, Lancashire, BL0 9HU
☎ 07970 241398 ⊕ firstchopbrewingarm.com

First Chop began brewing in 2012 at at the Outstanding Brewery in Bury. The brewery intends to move production to its own brewery in Salford to supply the First Chop bar in Ramsbottom and other outlets.

AVA (OG 1034, ABV 3.5%)
Hoppy blonde beer brewed with extra pale malt.

MIA (OG 1035, ABV 3.5%)

DOC (OG 1038, ABV 4.1%)
Ultra pale ale with a pleasant lingering bitterness.

HOP (OG 1038, ABV 4.1%)
Thirst quenching session beer with massive hop flavours.

TEA (OG 1048, ABV 5%)
Full bodied pale ale made with three malts.

SIP (OG 1052, ABV 5.4%)

Fisher (NEW) SIBA

Lower Farm, Noke, Oxfordshire, OX3 9TX
☎ (01865) 246611

⊗ Brewing commenced in 2012 on five-barrel plant. Up to five beers are brewed for the James Street Tavern in Oxford with a limited amount available for beer festivals and other local outlets.

Vicar's Daughter (ABV 3.7%)
Light and hoppy session bitter.

Piper At The Gates Of Dawn (ABV 3.9%)
A light bitter with malty overtones.

Solicitors (ABV 4.2%)
Dark, full-bodied smoky bitter.

Confessor (ABV 4.4%)
A well-hopped spicy golden beer.

Five Points (NEW) SIBA

3 Institute Place, Hackney Downs, London, E8 1JE
☎ (020) 8533 7746 ⊕ fivepointsbrewing.co.uk

Five Points commenced brewing in 2013 on a 10-barrel plant in the heart of Hackney. Based in a railway arch under Hackney Downs Railway Station, the brewery takes its name from the five-way junction where Dalston Lane, Amhurst Road and Pembury Road meet, The Five Points. Beers are available unfiltered in bottles.

Pale (OG 1042, ABV 4.4%)

Railway Porter (ABV 4.8%)

Hook Island Red (OG 1059, ABV 6%)
Red rye ale.

Five Towns

651 Leeds Road, Outwood, Wakefield, West Yorkshire, WF1 2LU
☎ (01924) 781887
✉ malcolmbastow@googlemail.com

⊕Five Towns began production on a 2.5-barrel plant in 2008 and mostly supplies outlets in Yorkshire. Seasonal and bottle-conditioned beers are also available.

Outwood Bound (OG 1040, ABV 4.2%)
A chestnut beer with a toffee nose and strong, dry, bitter finish.

Callum's Best (OG 1041, ABV 4.6%)
A dark-coloured bitter with a full flavour and bitter finish.

Ponte Carlo Stout (OG 1048.7, ABV 4.6%)
Bitter chocolate and malt aromas, smooth malt and chocolate with a hint of liquorice in the mouth and a dry bittersweet finish.

Niamh's Nemesis (OG 1053, ABV 5.7%)
A full bodied IPA with hints of grapefruit before a dry finish.

Flack Manor SIBA

8 Romsey Industrial Estate, Greatbridge Road, Romsey, Hampshire, SO51 0HR
☎ (01794) 518520 ⊕ flackmanor.co.uk
Shop Mon-Fri 9.30am-5pm; Sat 9.30am-12pm
Tours by arrangement

⊗ Flack Manor commenced brewing in 2010 using a 20-barrel plant purchased from Canada. The brewery employs the 'double drop' method of brewing. Beers are supplied to local outlets within a 30-mile radius of Romsey. Seasonal beers are available.

Flack's Double Drop (OG 1037, ABV 3.7%) ◥
Brown-coloured session bitter with a full aroma leading to a malty taste. Hops and some bitterness are in the taste with more hoppiness and some malt in the long finish.

Romsey Gold (OG 1041, ABV 4%)
A crisp and refreshing pale golden ale with a soft mouthfeel. Balanced by Fuggles and the summer aromas and flavours of First Gold.

Flack Catcher (OG 1043, ABV 4.4%) ◥
Well-balanced best bitter with a malty nose and a hint of citrus. Hoppy taste is balanced with a fruity sweetness, which follows through to a lingering finish.

Flash

Moss Top Farm, Moss Top Lane, Flash, Staffordshire, SK17 0TA ✉ flashbrewery@hotmail.com

The brewery is located high in the Peak District and was founded by two friends who brew on a part-time basis. All natural ingredients are used including spring water and seaweed finings, which make the beer suitable for vegans. Due to the altitude a brick boiler was found and is used in the brewing process rather than electrical equipment. Three bottle-conditioned beers are produced and are sold at Leek market, which is the only sales outlet.

Flipside SIBA ◉

The Brewhouse, East Link Trade Estate, Private Road No. 2, Colwick, Nottinghamshire, NG4 2JR
☎ (0115) 987 7500 ☎ 07970 25863
⊕ flipsidebrewery.co.uk

Andrew Dunkin, with the help of his wife Maggie, established a six-barrel brewery in an industrial unit in Colwick in 2010. Production is now at full capacity. The brewery recently opened a shop called Flipping Good Beer Shop.

Sterling Pale (OG 1039, ABV 3.9%)
A fairly hoppy, pale session ale. Easy-drinking with a bitter, spicy hop flavour.

Dark Denomination (OG 1041, ABV 4%)
Well-rounded, mildly-hopped beer. Chocolate and caramel malt flavours combine delicately with blackcurrant flavours.

Copper Penny (OG 1043, ABV 4.2%)
An easy-drinking session bitter. Light brown, moderately bitter but with good hop flavours, ending with a hint of tangerine.

Golden Sovereign (OG 1043, ABV 4.2%)
A golden session ale. Refreshingly bitter with dry biscuit flavours, American hops are added to produce a pleasant citrus and grapefruit flavour in the finish.

Random Toss (OG 1044, ABV 4.4%)
A refreshing pale ale with lemon and lime tropical fruit flavours.

Flipping Best (OG 1045, ABV 4.6%)
A traditional dark brown-coloured best bitter. Strong malt flavours complemented with good bitterness and gentle hop flavours.

Clippings IPA (OG 1062, ABV 6.5%)
A traditional IPA, gold-coloured with crushed gooseberry and bitter hop flavours.

Florence

≣ Capital Pub Co PLC, 131-133 Dulwich Road, Herne Hill, London, SE24 0NG
☎ (020) 7326 4987 ☎ 07973 465081
⊕ florencehernehill.com

The Florence has been brewing since opening in 2007. Purchased by beer historian Peter Haydon from Greene King following the acquisition of Capital Pubs, the Florence brews for Capital Pub Co pubs and produces 'A Head in a Hat' beers, specialising in London beer recipes, for the London free trade.

Flowerpots SIBA

≣ Brandy Mount, Cheriton, Hampshire, SO24 0QQ
☎ (01962) 771534 ⊕ flowerpots-inn.co.uk

⊠ Flowerpots began production in 2006. Catherine Bate and David Mackie are the brewers, alongside the brewery owner, Paul Tickner. Many local outlets are supplied direct. Seasonal beers: see website.

Perridge Pale (OG 1035.5, ABV 3.6%) ◆
Very pale, easy-drinking session beer. Honey-scented with high hops and bitterness throughout. Some citrus notes; extremely tasty for its strength.

Bitter (OG 1038, ABV 3.8%) 🍺 ◆
Dry, earthy hop flavours balanced by malt. Good bitterness with some hop in the aroma and a sharp, bitter finish. A refreshing, easy-going bitter.

Goodens Gold (OG 1046, ABV 4.8%) ◆
A yellow-coloured, full-bodied golden ale. More complex than many of its style, but still bursting with hops and citrus fruit in the aroma and taste and a snatch of sweetness, leading to a long dry finish.

Fool Hardy (NEW)

≣ Hope Inn, 118 Wellington Road North, Heaton Norris, SK4 2LL ⊕ foolhardyales.co.uk

⊕Martin Wood and Samantha Halfyard bought the Hope Inn in 2012 and installed a 2.5-barrel brewery. The first beers went on sale in 2013. The brewery currently only supplies the pub but there are plans to expand distribution locally.

Rash Dash (OG 1038, ABV 3.8%)
A rich amber-coloured beer with a light floral aroma. Initial toffee flavour gives way to hops that linger for a long aftertaste.

Risky Blond (OG 1042, ABV 4.4%)
An easy-drinking golden ale with a good balance of hops, hints of citrus and a well-rounded finish.

Reckless Danger (OG 1054, ABV 5%)
A sweet tasting beer with some bitterness, a clean, hoppy finish and moderate aftertaste.

Forge SIBA

Ford Hill Forge, Hartland, Devon, EX39 6EE
☎ (01237) 440015 ⊕ forgebrewery.co.uk

Forge Brewery was established in 2008 using a five-barrel plant. Bottle-conditioned and seasonal beer is also available.

Ambrosia (OG 1036.5, ABV 3.6%)
A light brown full-bodied beer.

Discovery (OG 1039, ABV 3.8%)
A golden, hoppy ale.

Hartland Blonde (OG 1040, ABV 4%)
A light, hoppy beer with citrus notes.

Lite House (OG 1042, ABV 4.3%)
Gold-coloured beer with hints of elderflower and a citrus bite.

IPA (OG 1044, ABV 4.5%)
Light, hoppy beer with grapefruit and citrus notes.

Ascension (OG 1046, ABV 4.6%)
Amber-coloured beer with complex hops.

Dreckly (OG 1046, ABV 4.8%)
A warm, ruby-coloured strong premium ale fortified with gorse and heather, rich in malt with a spicy aroma and a malty aftertaste.

Handsome (OG 1048, ABV 5.1%)
A light brown-coloured, well balanced, hoppy beer.

Foundry

See Canterbury Brewers

Four Alls

Ovington, North Yorkshire, DL11 7BP
☎ (01833) 627302 ⊕ thefouralls-teesdale.co.uk
Tours by arrangement

⊕The one-barrel brewery was launched in 2003 by John Stroud, one of the founders of Ales of Kent, using that name. In 2004 it became Four Alls, named after the pub where it is based, the only outlet for the beers.

Four Thorns (NEW)

≣ Deramore Arms, Main Street, Heslington, York, North Yorkshire, YO10 5EA
☎ 07815 153376 ✉ fourthorns@mail.com

⊕Rob Franklin has been operating this one-barrel plant in an outbuilding at the back of the Deramore Arms since 2012. The beer range is supplied to the Deramore Arms and as guest beers to Whitelocks in Leeds.

Bitter (OG 1038, ABV 3.8%)
Traditional Yorkshire amber-coloured session bitter.

Pale (OG 1044, ABV 4.3%)
A fruity, well-balanced pale ale with hoppy tones in the finish.

Red Eye IPA (OG 1052, ABV 5.2%)
American-style IPA, ruby-coloured, well-hopped.

Fownes (NEW)

25 Clarence Street, Upper Gornal, West Midlands, DY3 1UL

Office: 42 The Ridgeway, Sedgley, West Midlands, DY3 3UR ⊕ fownesbrewing.co.uk

Fownes is situated to the rear of the Jolly Crispin in Upper Gornal. Beers are available in the pub.

Gunhild (OG 1041, ABV 4%)

Frost Hammer (OG 1047, ABV 4.6%)

Firebeard's Old Favourite No. 5 Ruby Ale
(OG 1051, ABV 5%)

King Korvak Porter (OG 1055, ABV 5.4%)

Fox

☰ 22 Station Road, Heacham, Norfolk, PE31 7EX
☎ (01485) 570345 ✉ info@foxbrewery.co.uk
Tours by arrangement

⊠ Based in an old cottage adjacent to the Fox &
Hounds pub. Fox Brewery was established in 2002
and now supplies around 50 outlets as well as the
pub. All the Branthill beers are brewed from barley
grown on Branthill Farm and malted at Crisps in
Great Ryburgh. A hop garden next to the brewery,
trialled during 2009, has been enlarged. Seasonal
and bottle-conditioned beers are also available.

All Black Pale Ale (OG 1039, ABV 3.8%)

Heacham Gold (OG 1037, ABV 3.9%) ◆
A gentle beer with light citrus airs. A low but
increasing bitterness is the major flavour as some
initial sweet hoppiness quickly declines.

Red Knocker (OG 1037, ABV 3.9%)
Copper coloured and malty.

LJB (OG 1040, ABV 4%) ◆
A well-balanced malty brew with a hoppy, bitter
background. The long finish holds up well, as a
sultana-like fruitiness develops. Mid-brown with a
slightly thin mouthfeel.

Warrior (OG 1043, ABV 4.4%)

Grizzly Beer (OG 1048, ABV 4.8%)
Honey wheat beer brewed from an American
recipe.

Nelson's Blood (OG 1049, ABV 5.1%)
A liquor of beers. Red, full-bodied; made with
Nelson's Blood Rum.

IPA (OG 1051, ABV 5.2%)
Based on a 19th-century recipe. Easy drinking for
its strength.

Foxfield SIBA

☰ Prince of Wales, Foxfield, Broughton in Furness,
Cumbria, LA20 6BX
☎ (01229) 716238 ⊕ princeofwalesfoxfield.co.uk
Tours by arrangement

☺Foxfield is a 4.5-barrel plant in old stables
attached to the Prince of Wales. Several other
outlets are supplied. Tiger Tops in Wakefield is also
owned. The beer range constantly changes with
many occasional and seasonal beers. Dark Mild is
suitable for vegans.

Dark Mild (OG 1040, ABV 3.7%)

Franklins SIBA

1066 Country Brewery, Pebsham Farm Industrial
Estate, Pebsham Lane, Bexhill-on-Sea, East Sussex,
TN40 2RZ
☎ (01424) 731066 ⊕ franklinsbrewery.co.uk
Tours by arrangement

⊠ Formerly White Brewery, in 2011 the Franklins
name was purchased from Sean Franklin of
Roosters, who originally set up the brewery in

1980. Steve Medniuk joined the brewery in 2012
as head brewer. There are plans for expansion.

English Garden (OG 1043, ABV 3.8%)

Mumma Knows Best (ABV 4.1%)

Pudding Stout (OG 1046, ABV 4.2%)

Grumpy Guvnor (OG 1046, ABV 4.5%)

Citra IPA (OG 1056, ABV 5.5%)

Freedom SIBA ⊙

1 Park Lodge House, Bagots Park, Abbots Bromley,
Staffordshire, WS15 3ES
☎ (01283) 840721 ⊕ freedomlager.com
Shop Mon-Fri 8.30am-5pm
Tours by arrangement

No real ale. Freedom specialises in producing handcrafted English lagers, all brewed in accordance
with the German Reinheitsgebot purity law. It is
situated on top of a natural underground lake of
Burton brewing water. Water is drawn from this
sustainable source and used in the brewing
process. Six beers are currently produced; Freedom
Four (ABV 4%), Freedom Stout (ABV 4%), Freedom
Pioneer (ABV 4.6%), Freedom Dark Lager (ABV
4.7%), Freedom Organic Lager (ABV 4.8%),
Freedom Pilsner (ABV 5%).

Freeminer SIBA

Whimsey Road, Steam Mills, Cinderford,
Gloucestershire, GL14 3JA
☎ (01594) 827989 ✉ sales@freeminer.co.uk

Founded by Don Burgess in 1992, Freeminer –
previously Freeminer Brewery – changed hands in
2006 but Don Burgess remained in post. Bottle-
conditioned beers are available (brewed for the Co-
op). Co-op beers are now brewed with barley
grown on Co-op farms and malted at Warminster.
Fairtrade and organic beers are also produced, with
limited edition cask versions available for Fairtrade
fortnight.

Slaughter Porter (OG 1047, ABV 4.8%)

Friday Beer (NEW)

Unit 20, Link Business Centre, Malvern,
Worcestershire, WR14 1UQ
☎ (01684) 438141 ⊕ thefridaybeer.com
Shop: call for details
Tours by arrangement

The Friday Beer Company was the brain-child of
three scientists from Malvern in Worcestershire.
Founded in 2011, it primarily produces bottle-
conditioned beers, which are sold across the Three
Counties. Beers are available in cask form in a
limited number of local pubs.

Friends Arms

☰ Old St Clears Road, Johnstown, Carmerthen,
SA31 3HH
☎ (01267) 234073 ⊕ thefriendsarms.co.uk

⊠ The Friends Arms brewery opened in 2011 on
the premises of the Friends Arms, a traditional local
community pub, which acts as the brewery tap.

Frodsham SIBA

Lady Heyes Craft Centre, Kingsley Road, Frodsham, Cheshire, WA6 6SU
☎ (01928) 787917 ☎ 07776 391196
⊕ frodshambrewery.co.uk
Shop 10am-4pm daily
Tours by arrangement

☺Frodsham has been brewing since 2005 (initially as Stationhouse Brewery in Ellesmere Port). Seasonal/occasional beers: see website. Most beers are also available bottle conditioned.

Flaxen Jade (ABV 3.7%)

1'st Lite (OG 1037.8, ABV 3.8%) ◆
Light, hoppy bitter with clean lemon/grapefruit hop flavours, bitterness and dry aftertaste. Clean and refreshing.

Maiden's Cross (OG 1036, ABV 3.8%)
A traditional bitter using Maris Otter malt and Northdown hops. Based on the original Walker's Bitter.

Devil's Garden (OG 1037, ABV 3.9%)
An amber beer with traditional biscuit flavour and raisin aftertaste.

Splash! (OG 1038, ABV 3.9%)
A blonde, refreshing summer beer. Crisp and citrus with hoppy flavours.

Danny (OG 1038, ABV 4%)
Golden, floral, hoppy ale.

Dark Ark Ale (OG 1039.6, ABV 4%)
A dark malty beer with rich raisin and fruit flavours, and a deep, dense and complex aftertaste.

Gold (OG 1037.9, ABV 4.1%)
Golden ale with rich hoppy flavours and a spicy tang.

Froda's Ale (OG 1040, ABV 4.2%)
A tawny bitter, with a hoppy and slight liquorice taste. Named after Froda, Saxon leader of Frodsham.

Buzzin' (OG 1042, ABV 4.3%) ◆
Golden fruity bitter dominated by a honey sweetness. Good hop flavours in initial taste and a long, lasting dry finish.

Iron Man (OG 1043, ABV 4.5%)
Chestnut-coloured ale, nutty with a full hop flavour.

800 Ale (OG 1045.5, ABV 4.7%)
Gold-coloured bitter. Floral with late wine flavours.

Aonach (OG 1049, ABV 4.9%)
A typical Scottish-style 80/- beer. Dark amber-coloured, late hopped with New Zealand hops.

Lammastide (OG 1052, ABV 5%)
A wheat beer with distinct elderflower aromas.

Frog Island SIBA

The Maltings, Westbridge, St James Road, Northampton, NN5 5HS
☎ (01604) 587772 ⊕ frogislandbrewery.co.uk
Tours by arrangement

Established in 1994, Frog Island specialises in beers with personalised bottle labels, available by mail order. Some 40 free trade outlets are supplied. The brewery changed hands in 2013 and is now run by husband and wife team Paul Burchell and Zoe Cushnie. They intend on brewing the current range of beers as well as introducing some new ones.

Seasonal and bottle-conditioned beers are available.

Best Bitter (OG 1038, ABV 3.8%) ◆
Blackcurrant and gooseberry enhance the full malty aroma with pineapple and papaya joining on the tongue. Bitterness develops in the fairly long finish.

Shoemaker (OG 1043, ABV 4.2%) ◆
An orangey aroma of fruity Cascade hops is balanced by malt. Citrus and hoppy bitterness last into a long, dry finish. Amber-coloured.

That Old Chestnut (OG 1044, ABV 4.4%)
A smooth, easy-drinking beer with subtle roasted notes. Cascade hops bring a sweet spiciness to the beer while Target hops contribute bitterness to the dry, malty finish.

Natterjack (OG 1048, ABV 4.8%) ◆
Deceptively robust, golden and smooth. Fruit and hop aromas fight for dominance before the grainy astringency and floral palate give way to a long, dry aftertaste.

Croak & Stagger (OG 1054, ABV 5.6%) ◆
The initial honey/fruit aroma is quickly overpowered by roast malt then bitter chocolate and pale malt sweetness on the tongue. Gentle, bittersweet finish.

Front Row SIBA

Unit 1, Hopkins Close, Greenfield Farm Industrial Estate, Congleton, Cheshire, CW12 4TR
☎ 07861 718673 ⊕ frontrowbrewing.co.uk

After starting operations on a 2.5-barrel plant in 2012, Front Row has steadily expanded the range of local outlets its beers are regularly seen at and is developing a range of occasional brews to complement the main range.

Crouch (ABV 3.8%)

Touch (ABV 4%)

Pause (ABV 4.5%)

Engage (ABV 4.8%)

Collapsed (ABV 5.6%)

Front Street SIBA

▤ 45 Front Street, Binham, Norfolk, NR21 0AL
☎ (01328) 830297 ⊕ binhamchequers.info
Tours by arrangement

Situated at the Chequers Inn, Front Street is possibly Britain's most compact four-barrel installation. Brewing started in 2005 and three regular cask beers are produced as well as seasonal and occasional brews: see website. Bottle-conditioned beers are also available.

Binham Cheer (OG 1039, ABV 3.9%)
A quaffable, straw-coloured beer, not over-hopped. Tending towards a light mild.

Callums Ale (OG 1043, ABV 4.3%)
A copper-coloured, well-balanced ale with a malty flavour.

Unity Strong (OG 1051, ABV 5%)
A deep mahogany-coloured old-style strong bitter, well-balanced with malty complexity.

Fry's SIBA

Trerice, Boyton, Cornwall, PL15 8NU

☎ (01566) 785840 ⊕ frysbrewery.co.uk

⊠ Fry's began brewing in 2011 on a 2.5-barrel plant previously used by Forgotten Corner Brewery. Further beers including seasonals may be available – contact brewery for further information.

Frydeal (OG 1037, ABV 3.7%)

Haven (OG 1043, ABV 4.3%)
A smooth, refreshing bitter.

Golden Chough (OG 1047, ABV 4.7%)

Fugelestou

See Fulstow

Fulflood Arms

28 Cheriton Road, Winchester, Hampshire, SO22 5EF
☎ (01962) 842996
✉ thefulfloodarms@hotmail.co.uk

The brewery was established in 2012 using a one-barrel plant and supplies the pub and other local outlets.

Bill's Boys Bitter (ABV 3.5%)

Fulflood Best (ABV 3.8%)

Accidental Porter (ABV 4.5%)

Full Mash SIBA

17 Lower Park Street, Stapleford, Nottinghamshire, NG9 8EW
☎ (0115) 949 9262 ⊕ fullmash.net

☺Full Mash started brewing in 2003 with a quarter-barrel plant. The brewery has grown steadily with an expansion in outlets and capacity, which is set to continue. The core range is complemented by seasonal and one-off brews.

ESP (OG 1039, ABV 3.8%)
Sweet and hoppy yellow-coloured beer with a little bitterness.

Horse & Jockey (OG 1039, ABV 3.8%)

Séance (OG 1041, ABV 4%) ❧
Predominantly hoppy golden beer, with a refreshing bitter finish.

Illuminati (OG 1043, ABV 4.2%)

Warlord (OG 1045, ABV 4.4%)
A rich-flavoured malty ale with an intense hop bite.

Apparition (OG 1046, ABV 4.5%) ❧
A pale hoppy bitter brewed with Brewers Gold hops.

Nevermore Stout (OG 1047, ABV 4.6%)

Manhaton Pale?? (OG 1053, ABV 5.2%)

Full Moon SIBA

Sharpes Farm, Henley Down, Catsfield, Battle, East Sussex, TN33 9BN
☎ 07832 220745 ⊕ fullmoonbrewery.co.uk

⊠ Full Moon was established in 2007 by James Pryke and Professor Philip Parsons, and were joined in 2012 by Roger Massey, an experienced brewer.

Hopdance (OG 1037, ABV 3.9%)
A dry golden ale with a fresh fruit and citrus aroma.

Celestial Blonde (OG 1039, ABV 4.3%)
Pale ale, light golden in colour, fairly dry and slightly bitter wth pine and lemon aroma and a crisp hop and peppery taste.

Pacific Red (ABV 4.7%)
A ruby ale with a tropical fruit aroma with spicy notes producing a smooth, strong beer without being too heavy or sweet.

Fuller's IFBB ◉

Griffin Brewery, Chiswick Lane South, London, W4 2QB
☎ (020) 8996 2000 ⊕ fullers.co.uk
Shop Mon-Fri 10am-8pm; Sat 10am-6pm
Tours by arrangement

⊠ Fuller, Smith & Turner's Griffin Brewery has stood on the same site in Chiswick for more than 350 years. The partnership from which the company now takes its name was formed in 1845 and members of the founding families are still involved in running the company today. Three different Fuller's beers have won the Champion Beer of Britain title, Chiswick Bitter, London Pride and ESB. At the end of 2005 Fuller's announced an agreed acquisition of Hampshire brewer George Gale. The company now operates 362 pubs and hotels. Fuller's stopped brewing at the Gale's Horndean site in 2006 and all the brands, including some seasonals, are now brewed at Chiswick. Seasonal beers: see website. Bottle-conditioned beers are also available.

Chiswick Bitter (OG 1034.5, ABV 3.5%) ❧
Refreshing pale brown bitter with some citrus notes on the palate fading in the aftertaste, which is hoppy and slightly dry. Aroma is of hops with a trace of biscuit.

Discovery (OG 1039.5, ABV 3.9%) ❧
Golden ale served cold, which results in a low aroma. Fruit throughout with a sweet malt that becomes more prominent as the beer warms. Finish has a trace of dryness.

London Pride (OG 1040.5, ABV 4.1%) ❧
Well-balanced, smooth best bitter with orange citrus fruit, malt and hops in aroma and flavour, which linger into a slightly bitter aftertaste. Honey and toffee develop as the beer matures.

Bengal Lancer (OG 1049.5, ABV 5%) ❧
Rich, creamy and well-balanced pale brown IPA with a gold hue. Hops with a dryish bitterness harmonise with the fruit and malty sweetness that linger into the aftertaste.

ESB (OG 1054, ABV 5.5%) ❧
Bitter orange marmalade with hops, creamy toffee and some raisins are all present in this multifaceted strong brown bitter. A satisfying long, bitter, dry finish balanced by a malty sweetness.

Under the Gale's brand name:

Seafarers Ale (OG 1036.8, ABV 3.6%) 🏳 ❧
A pale brown bitter, predominantly malty, with a refreshing balance of fruit and hops that lingers into the aftertaste where a dry bitterness unfolds.

HSB (OG 1050, ABV 4.8%) ❧
Dates and dried fruit with some spicy hops in the nose add to the caramelised orange and treacle in the flavour of this smooth brown beer. Malty throughout with a bittersweet finish.

Fulstow SIBA

☰ 13 Thames Street, Louth, Lincolnshire, LN11 7AD
☎ (01507) 608202 ⊕ fulstowbrewery.com
Shop 7-11pm (at brewery tap)
Tours by arrangement

Fulstow operates on a 2.5-barrel plant and started brewing in Fulstow in 2004. The brewery then moved to Louth in 2006. 'Fugelstou Ales' are distributed throughout Britain and one-off brews are produced on a regular basis. The brewery tap, the Gas Lamp Lounge, opened in Louth in 2010.

Common (OG 1038, ABV 3.8%) 🍷
A copper-coloured, medium-bodied beer with a strong hop character and malt in the taste.

Marsh Mild (OG 1039, ABV 3.8%)
Traditional mild with a malty aroma. Chocolate malt on the palate with toffee and caramel overtones.

Village Life (OG 1040, ABV 4%)
Ruby red ale with great depth of malt and hop balance.

Northway IPA (OG 1042, ABV 4.2%)
A clean, crisp ale with a citrus aroma; very hoppy with a dry finish.

Pride of Fulstow (OG 1045, ABV 4.5%)
Copper-coloured bitter with a ripe malt taste in the mouth and a good hop balance. A dry finish with blackcurrant fruit notes.

Sledgehammer Stout (OG 1077, ABV 8%) 🍺
A strong, dark stout with raisin and liquorice and roast barley notes balanced by a strong hop flavour

Funfair SIBA

☰ Chequers Inn, Toad Lane, Elston, Nottinghamshire, NG23 5NS
☎ 07971 540186 ⊕ funfairbrewingcompany.co.uk

Funfair was launched in 2004 in Holbrook and is now situated at the Chequers Inn in Elston, where a new 10-barrel plant is used. The Chequers also serves as the brewery tap. More than 40 outlets are supplied. Seasonal beers: see website. Bottle-conditioned beers are also available.

Gallopers (OG 1037, ABV 3.8%)

Teacups (OG 1040, ABV 4%)

Waltzer (OG 1044, ABV 4.5%)

Brandy Snap (OG 1046, ABV 4.7%)

Dive Bomber (OG 1047, ABV 4.7%)

Dodgem (OG 1047, ABV 4.7%)

Fuzzy Duck SIBA

18 Wood Street, Poulton Industrial Estate, Poulton-le-Fylde, Lancashire, FY6 8JY
☎ 07904 343729 ⊕ fuzzyduckbrewery.co.uk
Tours by arrangement

Fuzzy Duck was established on a half-barrel plant at the owner's home in 2006. It relocated to an industrial unit on the edge of Poulton-le-Fylde and expanded capacity to eight barrels. Bottled-conditioned beers are also available.

Golden Cascade (OG 1038, ABV 3.8%)

Mucky Duck (OG 1042, ABV 4%)

Cunning Stunt (OG 1044, ABV 4.3%)

Pheasant Plucker (OG 1044, ABV 4.3%)

Ruby Duck (OG 1053, ABV 5.3%)

Fyfe

☰ 469 High Street, Kirkcaldy, Fife, KY1 2SN
☎ (01592) 646211 ⊕ fyfebrewery.co.uk
Tours by arrangement

⊛Fyfe was established in an old sailmakers behind the Harbour Bar in 1995. It was the first new brewery in Fife for some 80 years. Most of the output is taken by the pub, the remainder being available at beer festivals and local outlets.

Auld Alliance (OG 1040, ABV 4%) 🍺
A bitter beer with a lingering, dry, hoppy finish. Malt and hop, with fruit, are present throughout, fading in the finish.

Lion Slayer (OG 1042, ABV 4.2%)

Weiss Squad (OG 1045, ABV 4.5%)
Hoppy, bitter wheat beer with bags of citrus in the taste and finish.

Fyre (OG 1048, ABV 4.8%)
Gold-coloured best bitter, full-bodied and balanced with malt, hops and fruit. Hoppy bitterness grows in an increasingly dry aftertaste.

Fyne SIBA 👁

Achadunan, Cairndow, Argyll, PA26 8BJ
☎ (01499) 600120 ⊕ fyneales.com
Shop Mon-Sat 10am-5pm; Sun 12.30-5pm
Tours by arrangement

⊛Fyne Ales has been brewing since 2001. The 10-barrel plant is situated in a redundant milking parlour on a farm in Argyll, set in a beautiful glen at the head of Loch Fyne. In 2012 an on-site brewery tap was added. Seasonal beers are available.

Jarl (OG 1038, ABV 3.8%) 🍺
A light, gold-coloured ale with strong citrus notes.

Piper's Gold (OG 1037.5, ABV 3.8%) 🍺 🍺
Fresh, golden session ale. Well bittered but balanced with fruit and malt. Long, dry, bitter finish.

Maverick (OG 1040.5, ABV 4.2%) 🍷 🍺 🍺
Full-bodied, roasty, tawny best bitter. It is balanced, fruity and well hopped.

Hurricane Jack (OG 1042.5, ABV 4.4%)
Smooth golden ale with deep citrus flavours that mellow to a lingering, citrus bitter finish.

Vital Spark (OG 1042.5, ABV 4.4%)
A rich, dark beer. The taste is clean and slightly sharp with a hint of blackcurrant.

Avalanche (OG 1043.5, ABV 4.5%) 🍺
This golden ale starts with stunning citrus hops on the nose. Well-balanced with good body and fruit balancing a refreshing, hoppy taste. It finishes with a long, bittersweet aftertaste.

Highlander (OG 1046, ABV 4.8%) 🍺
Full-bodied, bittersweet ale with a good dry hop finish. In the style of a Heavy although the malt is less pronounced and the sweetness ebbs away to leave a bitter, hoppy finish.

Black IPA (OG 1056, ABV 5.9%)

Sublime Stout (OG 1067, ABV 6.8%)
A stout with a hint of liquorice on the aftertaste.

THE BREWERIES · G

Superior IPA (OG 1070, ABV 7.1%)
The aroma of apricot and pine resin is present giving a dusty, hoppy bitterness with a dry, fruity and hoppy aftertaste.

Gadds

See Ramsgate

Gale's

See Fuller's

Gambling Man

61 Low Willington, Willington, County Durham, DL15 0BG
☎ 07977 154675 ⊕ gamblingmanbrewco.com

Gambling Man was established in 2011 by avid home brewers Paul Armstrong and Dave Walls. The brewery name was devised by the brewers during a game of five card draw and all of the regular ales have gambling/casino related names. Bi-monthly specials are also available.

Croupier (ABV 3.4%)
Session beer with aromas of pineapple and lychee. A gentle hoppiness cleans the palate, with a long, light bitterness in the aftertaste.

Pit Boss (ABV 4.4%)
US-style pale ale. Fruity grapefruit notes complement its balanced maltiness.

Jack O'Clubs (ABV 4.7%)
Dark ale with spicy undertones, with dark fruit and a little smokiness on the palate. Raisin and dark chocolate gives way to plum-like notes in the aftertaste.

Garage

c/o London Inn, 8 Church Road, Plympton St Maurice, Devon, PL7 1NH
☎ 07789 437021 ⊕ garagebrewery.co.uk
Tours by arrangement

Garage was established in 2011 by Russ Gibbs, a keen home brewer, in an outbuilding of the London Inn. It uses a one-barrel, self-constructed brew plant. The brewery is separate to the pub.

Stout Sam (OG 1040, ABV 3.9%)
Full-flavoured with a hint of toasted malt.

Firkin Folly (OG 1044, ABV 4.4%)
Amber-coloured, refreshing and clean to the palate with a dry, hoppy finish.

Radiator Spring (OG 1046, ABV 4.5%)
Ruby red-coloured with complex flavours and a long-lasting finish.

Young Bob (OG 1064, ABV 6.2%)
Strong tasting, malty and ruby red-coloured with a hoppy finish.

Gargoyles

See Isca

Gas Dog (NEW) SIBA

6 Main Street, Burrough on the Hill, Leicestershire, LE14 2JQ

☎ 07921 260063

Office: 9 Westview, Somerby, Melton Mowbray, Leicestershire, LE14 2QH ⊕ gasdogbrewery.co.uk

Gas Dog began brewing in 2013 at the same premises as Parish Brewery, but using a separate 0.5-barrel plant. Seasonal and special beers are available.

Bitter (OG 1040, ABV 4%)
Hoppy, golden ale.

Dark Ale (OG 1040, ABV 4%)
Chocolate, dark malty brew.

Gates Burton

7 Reservoir Road, Burton upon Trent, Staffordshire, DE14 2BP
☎ (01283) 532567
✉ gatesburtonbrewery@talktalk.net
Tours by arrangement

⊕The Gates Burton Brewery was established in 2011 using a one-barrel plant. Further beers are planned.

Reservoir Premium (OG 1046, ABV 4.6%)
Full-bodied, amber-coloured with a finely balanced malt and hop character giving a smooth finish.

Damn (OG 1050, ABV 5%)
Smooth drinking with chocolate malt tones and delicately hopped with a subtle, sweet finish.

Geeves SIBA

Unit 12, Grange Lane Industrial Estate, Carrwood Road, Stairfoot, Barnsley, South Yorkshire, S71 5AS
☎ 07859 039259 ⊕ geevesbrewery.co.uk
Tours by arrangement

Geeves began brewing in 2011 using a 5.5-barrel plant with recipes developed when the owners lived on a narrow boat where they had to use rather ingenious brewing methods. This unusual heritage is reflected in the names of the regular and seasonal beers.

No. 1 (OG 1038, ABV 3.8%)
Traditional bitter with a well-rounded malty base and a hoppy finish.

Bow Hauler (OG 1041, ABV 4.1%)
A dry, grainy body balanced by Goldings hops.

Red Diesel (OG 1042, ABV 4.1%)

Gunwale Dance (OG 1043, ABV 4.2%)
A pale ale with a dry, citrus bitterness coupled with a zingy aftertaste and aroma.

Smokey Joe Stout (OG 1050, ABV 5%)
A strong stout; rich and robust.

Fully Laden (OG 1060, ABV 6%)
A strong IPA with a juicy, citrus, sweet floral taste and aroma with a satisfying bitterness.

Geltsdale SIBA

Unit 1b, Townfoot Industrial Estate, Brampton, Cumbria, CA8 1SW
☎ (01697) 741541 ⊕ geltsdalebrewery.com
Shop Mon-Sat 9am-5pm
Tours by arrangement

⊕Geltsdale Brewery, established in 2006 by Fiona Deal, initially operated from a small unit in Bramptons Old Brewery which dated back to 1785.

751

In 2013 production moved to Townfoot Industrial Estate. Beers are named after local landmarks within Geltsdale.

Black Dub (OG 1036, ABV 3.6%)
Treacle toffee, dark toast and molasses on the palate with malt and sweet raisins. A soft, malty aroma.

King's Forest (OG 1039, ABV 3.8%)
Malty, brown bread, digestive biscuits and hazelnuts on the palate with a citrus aroma.

Aurora (OG 1039, ABV 3.9%)
A refreshingly bitter beer with a smooth and silky mouthfeel.

Cold Fell (OG 1038, ABV 3.9%)
Sharp, fresh beer with a grassy taste and a sweet, malty aftertaste. Zesty, hoppy aromas with a hint of pepper and pine.

Bewcastle Brown Ale (OG 1039, ABV 4%)
Warm and nutty beer, delicately bittered and full-bodied with an aroma of malty digestive biscuits.

Brampton Bitter (OG 1039, ABV 4%) ◆
Sweet, fruity, well-balanced, hoppy bitter with a clean, bitter aftertaste.

Tarn (OG 1039, ABV 4%)
A well-balanced beer, warm and smooth with subtle whisky notes and soft bitterness. An aroma of malt whisky and honey.

Hell Beck (OG 1042, ABV 4.2%)
A soft, smooth start with espresso, toast, chocolate, truffles and digestive biscuit on the palate. Faint hints of liquorice, coffee and toast on the nose.

George N Porter

See under Porter

George Wright

See under Wright

George's

See Hop Monster

Gertie Sweet

See New Plassey

Glastonbury SIBA

Unit 11, Wessex Park, Bancombe Road, Somerton, Somerset, TA11 6SB
☎ (01458) 272244 ⊕ glastonburyales.com
Shop Mon-Fri 10am-4pm; Sat 10am-12.30pm
Tours by arrangement

Glastonbury Ales was established in 2002 on a five-barrel plant. In 2006 the brewery changed ownership and has now expanded to a 20-barrel plant. A shop opened in late 2009. Seasonal beers: see website.

Mystery Tor (OG 1040, ABV 3.8%) ◆
A golden bitter with plenty of floral hop and fruit on the nose and palate, the sweetness giving way to a bitter hop finish. Full-bodied for a session bitter.

Lady of the Lake (OG 1042, ABV 4.2%) ◆

A full-bodied amber best bitter with plenty of hops to the fore balanced by a fruity malt flavour and a subtle hint of vanilla, leading to a clean, bitter hop aftertaste.

Love Monkey (OG 1042, ABV 4.2%)
A golden ale with zesty, fruity hops and a variety of malts. Refreshing fruity notes give way to a robust, full body.

Hedge Monkey (OG 1048, ABV 4.6%)
A well-rounded deep amber bitter. Malty, rich and very hoppy.

Golden Chalice (OG 1048, ABV 4.8%)
Light and golden best bitter with a robust malt character.

Glenfinnan

Sruth A Mhuilinn, Glenfinnan, PH37 4LT
☎ (01397) 704309 ☎ 07999 261010
⊕ glenfinnanbrewery.co.uk

⊛Glenfinnan opened in 2007 and operates on a four-barrel plant. It produces around 600 litres per week during the tourist season. Further expansion is planned. Seasonal beer is available.

Gold Ale (OG 1040, ABV 3.8%)

Standard Ale (OG 1044, ABV 4.2%)

Glentworth

Glentworth House, Crossfield Lane, Skellow, Doncaster, South Yorkshire, DN6 8PL
☎ (01302) 725555

⊛The brewery was founded in 1996 and is housed in former dairy buildings. The five-barrel plant supplies more than 80 pubs. Production is concentrated on mainly light-coloured, hoppy ales. Seasonal beers are available and brewed to order.

Globe

▤ 144 High Street West, Glossop, Derbyshire, SK13 8HJ
☎ (01457) 852417 ⊕ globemusic.org

Globe was established in 2006 on a 2.5-barrel plant in an old stable behind the Globe pub. The beers are mainly for the pub but special one-off brews are produced for beer festivals.

Amber (OG 1040, ABV 3.9%)

Blondie (OG 1039, ABV 3.9%)

Stout (OG 1040, ABV 3.9%)

Comet (OG 1043, ABV 4.3%)

Gloucester SIBA

Llanthony Warehouse, The Docks, Gloucester, GL1 2EH
☎ (01452) 690541 ☎ 07503 152749
⊕ gloucesterbrewery.co.uk
Tours by arrangement

⊗ Gloucester began brewing in 2011 in an old warehouse in the historic Gloucester Docks. All ales are also available bottle conditioned.

Gold (ABV 3.9%)
A crisp, hoppy, golden ale.

Mariner (ABV 4.2%)
A smooth, malty and hoppy, copper-coloured session ale.

Dockside Dark (ABV 5.2%)
A silky rich ale, warm and chocolaty with a subtle sweetness.

Goacher's

Unit 8, Tovil Green Business Park, Burial Ground Lane, Tovil, Maidstone, Kent, ME15 6TA
☎ (01622) 682112 ⊕ goachers.com
Tours by arrangement

A traditional brewery that uses only malt and Kentish hops for all its beers. Phil and Debbie Goacher have concentrated on brewing good wholesome beers without gimmicks. Two tied houses and around 30 free trade outlets in the mid-Kent area are supplied. Special is brewed for sale under house names. Seasonal beers are available.

Real Mild Ale (OG 1033, ABV 3.4%) ◀
A rich, flavourful mild with moderate roast barley and a generous helping of chocolate malt.

Fine Light Ale (OG 1036, ABV 3.7%) ◀
A pale, golden brown bitter with a strong, floral, hoppy aroma and aftertaste. A hoppy and moderately malty session beer.

Special/House Ale (OG 1037, ABV 3.8%)

Best Dark Ale (OG 1040, ABV 4.1%) ◀
Dark-coloured but light and quaffable in body, this ale features hints of caramel and chocolate malt throughout.

Crown Imperial Stout (OG 1044, ABV 4.5%) ◀
A good, well-balanced roasty stout, dark and bitter with just a hint of caramel and a lingering, creamy head.

Gold Star Strong Ale (OG 1050, ABV 5.1%) ◀
A strong pale ale.

Old 1066 (OG 1066, ABV 6.7%) ▱

Goddards SIBA ◉

Barnsley Farm, Bullen Road, Ryde, Isle of Wight, PO33 1QF
☎ (01983) 611011 ⊕ goddardsbrewery.com

Goddards was established in 1993 on a farmstead on the Isle of Wight. Originally occupying an 18th-century barn, expansion has meant that a new brewery was built in 2008. Seasonal beers: see website.

Ale of Wight (OG 1037, ABV 3.7%)
An aromatic, fresh and zesty pale beer.

Scrumdiggity (OG 1039, ABV 4%) ◀
Well-balanced session beer that maintains its flavour and bite with compelling drinkability.

Fuggle-Dee-Dum (OG 1047, ABV 4.8%) ◀
Brown-coloured strong ale with plenty of malt and hops.

Goff's SIBA

9 Isbourne Way, Winchcombe, Gloucestershire, GL54 5NS
☎ (01242) 603383 ⊕ goffsbrewery.com

⊠ Goff's is a family concern that has been brewing cask-conditioned ales since 1994. The ales are available regionally in more than 200 outlets and nationally through wholesalers. The addition of seasonal Ales of the Round Table provides a range

of 12 beers of which four or five are always available: see website for details.

Jouster (OG 1040, ABV 4%) ◀
A drinkable, tawny-coloured ale, with a light hoppiness in the aroma. It has a good balance of malt and bitterness in the mouth, underscored by fruitiness, with a clean, hoppy aftertaste.

Tournament (OG 1037, ABV 4%) ◀
Dark golden in colour, with a pleasant hop aroma. A clean, light and refreshing session bitter with a pleasant hop aftertaste.

White Knight (OG 1046, ABV 4.7%) ◀
A well-hopped bitter with a light colour and full-bodied taste. Bitterness predominates in the mouth and leads to a dry, hoppy aftertaste.

Black Knight (OG 1053, ABV 5.3%)

Golcar

60a Swallow Lane, Golcar, West Yorkshire, HD7 4NB
☎ (01484) 644241 ☎ 07970 267555
✉ golcarbrewery@btconnect.com
Tours by arrangement

☺Golcar started brewing in 2001 and production has increased from 2.5 barrels to five barrels a week. The brewery owns one pub, the Rose & Crown at Golcar, and supplies other outlets in the local area.

Dark Mild (OG 1034, ABV 3.4%) ◀
Dark mild with a light roasted malt and liquorice taste. Smooth and satisfying.

Bitter (ABV 3.9%)
Amber bitter with a hoppy citrus taste with fruity overtones and a bitter finish.

Pennine Gold (OG 1038, ABV 4%)
A hoppy and fruity session beer.

Guthlac's Porter (OG 1047, ABV 5%)
A robust, malty porter.

Golden Duck SIBA

Unit 2, Redhill Farm, Top Street, Appleby Magna, Leicestershire, DE12 7AH ⊕ goldenduckbrewery.com

Golden Duck began brewing in 2012 using a five-barrel plant. It is run by the father and son team of Andrew and Harry Lunn. Beers have a cricket-related theme.

LFB (Lunns First Brew) (OG 1043, ABV 4.3%)
A traditional, golden, hoppy session ale with citrus overtones.

Nosey Parker (OG 1050, ABV 5%)
Premium golden ale, hoppy with a hint of citrus.

Reverend Green (OG 1055, ABV 5.5%)
A strong IPA with deep hoppy and fruity flavours.

Golden Triangle SIBA

Unit 9, Watton Road, Norwich, NR9 4BG
☎ (01603) 757763 ☎ 07976 281132
⊕ goldentrianglebrewery.co.uk

⊠ Golden Triangle began brewing in 2011 using spare capacity at Ufford Brewery. The brewery soon expanded, purchasing Ufford's old 10-barrel plant when the latter relocated and installing it in new premises in Norwich in 2012. They continue to add new beers to their range.

City Gold (OG 1038, ABV 3.8%) ◆
A lemony hop aroma introduces a smoky mix of citrus, hop, and bitterness. The finish develops a dry artringency.

Citropolis (OG 1039, ABV 3.9%)
A golden blonde ale. Light, refreshing and zesty with citrus hop notes and a fruity aroma.

Bonny's Gold (OG 1040, ABV 4%)
A golden blonde ale with citrus hop notes and a fruity aroma.

City Pale Ale (OG 1042, ABV 4.2%)
A golden pale beer with grapefruit, lemon and marmalade hop aromas, and a sweet malty body with floral hints on the palate.

Red Square (OG 1046, ABV 4.6%)

Goldmark (NEW) SIBA

Unit 23, The Vinery, Arundel Road, Poling, West Sussex, BN18 9PY
☎ (01903) 297838 ☎ 07900 555415
⊕ goldmarks.co.uk

Home brewer Mark Lehmann began commercial brewing in 2012, and moved to purpose-built premises in 2013 using an 11-barrel plant. Beers are available in many outlets in West Sussex and beyond.

Amber Ale (ABV 4%)
A well-balanced session ale.

Best Bitter (ABV 4%)
A tawny-coloured bitter with subtle hints of toffee and caramel, ending with a smooth, bitter finish.

Liquid Gold (ABV 4%)
A refreshing golden ale with citrus and wild berries.

Ebony (ABV 5.2%)

Hercules IPA (ABV 7%)
A golden hoppy beer that is light and refreshing despite its strength.

Goodall's

⊟ **The Lodge, 88 Crewe Road, Alsager, Staffordshire, ST7 2JA**
☎ (01270) 873669
✉ goodalls.brewery@hotmail.co.uk
Tours by arrangement

Goodall's began brewing in 2010 at the Lodge in Alsager using a 2.5-barrel plant.

Goody SIBA

Bleangate Brewery, Braggs Lane, Herne, Kent, CT6 7NP
☎ (01227) 361555 ⊕ goodyales.co.uk

Goody began brewing in 2012 using a 10-barrel plant and local ingredients.

Genesis (OG 1035, ABV 3.5%)

Good Health (OG 1038, ABV 3.6%)
A honey-coloured golden ale with a fresh, hoppy finish and undertone of zesty orange.

Good Heavens (OG 1042, ABV 4.1%)
Amber-coloured, hoppy bitter.

Good Sheppard (OG 1045, ABV 4.5%)
Deep amber-coloured ale with a vanilla twist on the palate and a soft feel on the tongue.

Goose Eye SIBA

Ingrow Bridge, South Street, Keighley, West Yorkshire, BD21 5AX
☎ (01535) 605807 ⊕ goose-eye-brewery.co.uk
Tours by arrangement

☺Goose Eye is a family-run brewery supplying 60-70 regular outlets, mainly in Yorkshire and Lancashire. The beers are available through national wholesalers and pub chains. It produces monthly occasional and seasonal beers with entertaining names.

Barm Pot Bitter (OG 1038, ABV 3.8%) ◆
Bitter, hop and fruit flavours dominate this golden session bitter, over a malty base. Increasingly dry and bitter finish.

Bitter (OG 1038, ABV 3.9%) ◆
Traditional Yorkshire brown session bitter, well-balanced malt and hops with a pleasingly bitter finish.

Bronte Bitter (OG 1040, ABV 4%) ◆
A brown, malty and hoppy best bitter. Bitterness increases to give a lingering, dry finish.

No-Eye Deer (OG 1040, ABV 4%) ◆
A faint fruity and malty aroma. Strong hoppy flavours and an intense, bitter finish characterise this pale brown bitter.

Chinook Blonde (OG 1042, ABV 4.2%) ⬚ ◆
An increasingly tart, bitter finish follows assertive grapefruit hoppiness in the aroma and taste of this satisfying blonde brew.

Golden Goose (OG 1045, ABV 4.5%)
A straw-coloured beer light on the palate with a smooth and refreshing hoppy finish.

Over and Stout (OG 1052, ABV 5.2%) ◆
A full-bodied stout with roast and malt flavours mingling with hops, dark fruit and liquorice on the palate. Look also for tart fruit on the nose and a growing bitter finish.

Pommies Revenge (OG 1052, ABV 5.2%) ◆
Golden strong bitter combining grassy hops, a cocktail of fruit flavours, a peppery hint and a hoppy, bitter finish.

Goosnargh (NEW)

⊟ **Horns Inn, Goosnargh, Lancashire, PR3 2FJ**
☎ (01772) 864382 ⊕ yehornsinn.co.uk

Brewing began in 2013 using a five-barrel plant. Seasonal beers are available.

Truckle (ABV 3.7%)
A dark, malty beer giving a slightly nutty taste with a hint of sweetness.

Bit O' Blonde (ABV 4%)
A light, crisp, clean ale.

Gold (ABV 4%) ◆
A light, hoppy beer with a zesty finish.

RGB (Real Goosnargh Bitter) (ABV 4.3%)
A copper-coloured beer with an earthy, fruity flavour.

Gower SIBA ◉

Greyhound Inn, Oldwalls, Llanrhidian, SA3 1HA
☎ 07967 484356 ⊕ gowerbrewery.com

⊗ Gower began brewing in 2011 using a five-barrel plant. There are plans for expansion.

Brew 1 (OG 1039, ABV 3.8%)
Honey-coloured ale with a pronounced floral aroma.

Black Diamond (OG 1042, ABV 4.2%)

Sampson Jack (OG 1042, ABV 4.2%)
A traditional, copper-coloured ale.

Best Bitter (OG 1045, ABV 4.5%)
Honey-coloured ale with a full-bodied flavour and crisp, lingering bite of hop.

Gold (OG 1045, ABV 4.5%)
A golden ale with refreshing citrus flavours and a hoppy aroma.

Lighthouse (OG 1046, ABV 4.5%)
A continental-style lager.

Rumour (OG 1050, ABV 5%)
Ruby-coloured ale made with a chocolate/citrus taste.

Power (OG 1052, ABV 5.5%)
A traditional IPA with a full, hoppy flavour.

Grafters SIBA

⊟ Half Moon, 23 High Street, Willingham by Stow, Lincolnshire, DN21 5JZ
☎ (01427) 788340 ⊕ graftersbrewery.com
Tours by arrangement

☺Brewing started on a 2.5-barrel plant in 2007 in a converted garage adjacent to the owner's freehouse, the Half Moon. 2013 saw an upgrade to a 10-barrel plant. Seasonal and occasional beers are also produced.

Moonlight (OG 1038, ABV 3.6%)
A light, citrus beer.

Traditional Bitter (OG 1039, ABV 3.7%)
A pale brown bitter with a light, hoppy flavour.

Over The Moon (OG 1041.5, ABV 4%)
A traditional chestnut-coloured best bitter.

Darker Side of the Moon (OG 1043, ABV 4.2%)
A dark, red-hued strong mild with a smooth, smoky roasted flavour and chocolate overtones.

Luvly Jubblies (OG 1045, ABV 4.2%)
A refreshing golden brew with tropical hoppiness.

Howler (OG 1044, ABV 4.3%)
A bronze-coloured bitter with a deep and long-lasting, rounded, full malt in the mouth taste that stays on the palate for a long time.

Wobble Gob (OG 1048, ABV 4.9%)
A deep ruby-coloured beer. A blend of hops gives this beer a slightly floral and roasted taste.

Grafton SIBA ◉

Unit 5, Peppers Warehouse, Blyth Road, Worksop, Nottinghamshire, S81 0TP
☎ (01909) 476121 ☎ 07837 962688

Office: 8 Oak Close, Crabtree Park Estate, Worksop, Nottinghamshire, S80 1BH
✉ allbeers@oakclose.orangehome.co.uk
Tours by arrangement

☺Grafton began brewing in 2007 and moved into larger premises at the same location in 2013 with plans to double the size of the current five-barrel plant. Two pubs are owned; the Packet Inn in Retford, where the brewery was originally located, and the Grafton Hotel in Worksop, which is the current brewery tap.

Bananalicious (OG 1040, ABV 4%)
A mid brown-coloured ale with a banana and toffee aftertaste.

Black Abbots (OG 1040, ABV 4%)
A roast-flavoured beer, smooth and dark with a roast aftertaste.

Lasamboo (OG 1040, ABV 4%)
The addition of stem and fresh ginger into fermentation gives subtle ginger and lemon flavours.

Silhouette (OG 1040, ABV 4%)
A pale beer, the addition of vanilla pods into the fermentation gives a smoky flavour.

Lady Julia (OG 1042, ABV 4.3%)
A crisp golden ale with a floral hop aroma.

Lady Catherine (OG 1044, ABV 4.5%)
A golden ale, fruity on the nose with a pleasant bittersweet taste on the palate.

Blondie (OG 1046, ABV 4.8%)
A crisp pale beer with citrus flavours and a hoppy finish.

Grain SIBA

South Farm, Tunbeck Road, Alburgh, Harleston, Norfolk, IP20 0BS
☎ (01986) 788884 ⊕ grainbrewery.co.uk
Shop Mon-Fri 10am-4pm; Sat 11am-3pm
Tours by arrangement

⊗ Grain Brewery was launched in 2006 by Geoff Wright and Phil Halls in a converted dairy in the Waveney Valley. It upgraded to a 15-barrel plant in 2012. One pub is owned, the Plough in Norwich.

Oak (OG 1038, ABV 3.8%) ◀
A balanced mix of malt and hops with marmalade overtones. There's hint of molasses in the short sharp ending.

3.1.6. (ABV 3.9%)
A light beer, brewed with lager malt, with a hoppy nose and taste.

Blonde Ash Wheat Beer (OG 1040, ABV 4%) ◀
Banana notes flow through this sweet smoky brew. Yellow-coloured with a grainy mouthfeel and a quick, fruity finale.

Best Bitter (OG 1042, ABV 4.2%) ◀
A well-balanced, complex bitter. A mix of flavours with malt and hops ably supported by caramel and bitterness.

Redwood (OG 1049, ABV 4.8%) ◀
Heavy blackcurrant airs give way to a rich fruity bitterness with malt overtones. Copper-coloured, crisp and satisfying.

Blackwood Stout (OG 1050, ABV 5%) ◀
Based on a 1790 Whitbread recipe. It's black and brooding with roast dominating from the initial aroma to the long, lingering ending. A bittersweet chocolate undercurrent adds depth.

Porter (OG 1052, ABV 5%) ◀
A creamy dark chocolate and roast character prevades throughout. A bittersweet edge grows in intensity.

India Pale Ale (OG 1062, ABV 6.5%) ◀

Powerful, complex and rich throughout. Malt and hops vie with tropical fruit and bitterness for dominance.

Grainstore SIBA ⊙

▤ Station Approach, Oakham, Rutland, LE15 6RE
☎ (01572) 770065 ⊕ grainstorebrewery.com
Tours by arrangement

☺Grainstore, the smallest county's largest brewery, has been in production since 1995. It was founded by Tony Davis and Mike Davies. After 30 years in the industry Tony decided to set up his own business after finding a derelict Victorian railway grainstore building. 80 outlets are supplied.

Rutland Bitter (OG 1032, ABV 3.4%)
A well-balanced session beer, light in colour and taste. It is one of the few beers that are registered PGI (Protected Geographical Indication).

Rutland Panther (OG 1034, ABV 3.4%) ◆
This reddish-black mild punches above its weight with malt and roast flavours combining to deliver a brew that can match the average stout for intensity of flavour.

Cooking (OG 1036, ABV 3.6%) ◆
Tawny-coloured beer with malt and hops on the nose and a pleasant grainy mouthfeel. Hops and fruit flavours combine to give a bitterness that continues into a long finish.

Triple B (OG 1042, ABV 4.2%) ◆
Initially hops dominate over malt in both the aroma and taste, but fruit is there, too. All three linger in varying degrees in the sweetish aftertaste of this brown brew.

GB Best (OG 1043, ABV 4.3%)
A pronounced floral aroma and flavour.

Gold (OG 1045, ABV 4.5%)
A refreshing, light golden brew whose flavour is a complex combination of mellow malt sweetness finely balanced by a smooth bitterness and floral aromas.

Ten Fifty (OG 1050, ABV 5%) ◆
Pungent banana and malt notes on the nose. On the palate, rich malt and fruit are joined by subtle hop on a bittersweet base. Dry malt aftertaste with some fruit.

Rutland Beast (OG 1053, ABV 5.3%)
A unique strong mild ale, having a complex flavour made up of a combination of chocolate/coffee notes and those of raisins and autumn fruits.

Nip (OG 1073, ABV 7.3%)
A well-balanced blend of flavours, sweetness and hop bitterness that complement each other. A true barley wine, smooth and warming with raisins and winter fruit as the dominant flavor notes.

Contract brewed for Phipps NBC:

Red Star (OG 1038, ABV 3.8%)
A malty, sweet beer.

India Pale Ale (OG 1042, ABV 4.2%)
A pale amber-coloured beer with a residual malt sweetness which, coupled with grapefruit notes from the hops, gives a fine, fresh, crisp finish.

Great Gable

Unit 2G, Bridge End Industrial Estate, Egremont, Cumbria, CA22 2RD

☎ (01946) 823846 ⊕ greatgablebrewing.com
Tours by arrangement

Great Gable began brewing in 2002 using a five-barrel plant at the Wasdale Head Inn in Gosforth. It moved to its current location in 2010, which also saw the acquisition of its first pub, the Horse & Groom at Gosforth. Seasonal and bottle-conditioned beers are available.

Iron Awe (OG 1039.5, ABV 3.8%) ◆
Well-balanced, full-flavoured beer with a fruity, hoppy nose and a bitter finish.

Wastwater Gold (OG 1041, ABV 3.9%) ◆
Hoppy, fruity session beer with a dry, bitter finish.

Burnmoor Pale Ale (OG 1040, ABV 4.2%) ◆
A dry, hoppy bitter, refreshing and clean-tasting. Straw-coloured with a fruity taste and grapefruit overtones. Long, bitter finish.

Yewbarrow (OG 1054, ABV 5.5%) ◆
Strong, mild dark ale with robust roast flavours, rich and malty. Satisfying with hints of spice and fruit. Smooth chocolate and coffee aromas.

Great Heck SIBA

Rosebank Cottage, Main Street, Great Heck, North Yorkshire, DN14 0BQ
☎ (01977) 661430 ☎ 07723 381002
⊕ greatheckbrewery.co.uk
Tours by arrangement

☺Great Heck began production in 2008 in a converted slaughterhouse. The brewery moved across the road to a converted cottage in 2012 and now produces its regular beers on a 15-barrel plant with capacity for 45 barrels per week. Seasonal beers are also available.

Powermouse (OG 1035, ABV 3.6%)
Pale session beer brewed with a unique blend of hops.

Angel (OG 1037, ABV 3.9%)
A clean, dry, moderately bittered pale ale.

Dave (OG 1038, ABV 3.9%)
A dark session bitter with a satisfying roasty taste.

Blonde (OG 1043, ABV 4.3%)
A richly-balanced blonde beer with a zesty finish.

Voodoo Mild (OG 1043, ABV 4.3%)
Rich, black mild bursting with flavour from the roasted malts.

Yorkshire Pale Ale (OG 1043, ABV 4.3%)
A premium pale ale with a complex malt character and zesty finish.

Slaughterhouse Porter (OG 1045, ABV 4.5%)
A rich, dark, smooth-drinking porter with a tight, creamy white head.

Hopfweizen (OG 1045, ABV 4.7%)
Unusual, effervescent German-style wheat beer with American IPA-style flavour and aroma hops.

Powerhouse (OG 1048, ABV 5%)
Golden ale made with a blend of hops giving low bitterness and loads of fruity flavour and aroma.

Treason Stout (OG 1054, ABV 5.4%)
Unfined wheat stout fermented with German wheat beer yeast.

Yakima IPA (OG 1070, ABV 7.4%)
Deep gold-coloured and low in bitterness, the alcohol balances the fruity hop flavours and aromas.

Great Newsome SIBA ◁⊙▷

Great Newsome Farm, South Frodingham, East Yorkshire, HU12 0NR
☎ (01964) 612201 ☎ 07808 367386
⊕ greatnewsomebrewery.co.uk
Shop Mon-Fri 9am-4pm

⊛Nestled in the Holderness countryside, Great Newsome began brewing in 2007 on a 10-barrel plant, located in renovated farm buildings. Beer is distributed throughout Yorkshire as well as North Lincolnshire. Seasonal beers: see website.

Sleck Dust (OG 1037, ABV 3.8%)
Straw-coloured, refreshingly bitter session beer with a floral aroma and subtle dry finish.

Pricky Back Otchan (OG 1042, ABV 4.2%)
Hoppy golden bitter with a fresh citrus aroma.

Frothingham Best (OG 1042, ABV 4.3%)
Dark amber-coloured best bitter with a subtle dry finish.

Jem's Stout (OG 1044, ABV 4.3%)
Dark, smooth beer with smoky, roasted malt flavours and aroma.

Great Oakley SIBA ◁⊙▷

Ark Farm, High Street South, Tiffield, Northamptonshire, NN12 8AB
⊕ greatoakleybrewery.co.uk
Tours by arrangement

The brewery commenced production in 2005 in Great Oakley and relocated to Tiffield in 2012. It is run by husband and wife team Phil and Hazel Greenway. More than 60 outlets are supplied, including the George in Tiffield and the Malt Shovel Tavern in Northampton, which are the brewery taps. Seasonal beers: see website. Bottle-conditioned beers are also available.

Welland Valley Mild (OG 1037, ABV 3.6%)
A dark, traditional mild. Full of flavour.

Eleanor Cross (OG 1039, ABV 3.8%)

Wagtail (OG 1040, ABV 3.9%)
Light-coloured with a unique bitterness.

Wot's Occurring (OG 1040, ABV 3.9%) ⎅
A session bitter with a subtle hop finish.

Oakley Blonde (OG 1040, ABV 4%)
A blonde ale brewed with lager malt and German Hersbrucker hops.

Marching In (OG 1041, ABV 4.1%) ⎅
A golden, clean-tasting beer.

Harpers (OG 1044, ABV 4.3%)
Traditional mid-brown-coloured bitter with a malty taste and slight hints of chocolate and citrus in the finish.

Gobble (OG 1045, ABV 4.5%)
Straw-coloured with a pleasant hop aftertaste.

Delapre Dark (OG 1047, ABV 4.6%)
A dark, full-bodied ale made from five different malts.

Newport Delta (OG 1047, ABV 4.6%)

Abbey Stout (OG 1051, ABV 5%)

Tailshaker (OG 1051, ABV 5%)
A complex golden ale with a great depth of flavour.

Great Orme SIBA ◁⊙▷

Nant y Cywarch, Glan Conwy, LL28 5PP
☎ (01492) 580548 ⊕ greatormebrewery.co.uk

Great Orme is a five-barrel microbrewery situated on a hillside in the Conwy Valley between Llandudno and Betws-y-Coed, with views of the Conwy Estuary and the Great Orme. Established in 2005, it is housed in a number of converted farm buildings. Around 50 outlets are supplied.

Cambria (OG 1038, ABV 3.8%) ◀
A pale brown malty session bitter with a dry taste. Some hoppy flavours develop in the bitter aftertaste.

Welsh Black (OG 1042, ABV 4%) ▮ ◀
Smooth-tasting dark beer with roast coffee notes in aroma and taste. Sweetish in flavour and having some characteristics of a mild ale with hoppiness also present in the aftertaste.

Great Welsh (ABV 4.1%) ◀
Sweetish best bitter with a smooth taste and a juicy mouthfeel. Hoppy bitterness comes through in the finish.

Orme (OG 1043, ABV 4.2%) ◀
Malty best bitter with a dry finish. Faint hop and fruit notes in aroma and taste, but malt dominates throughout.

Celtica (OG 1045, ABV 4.5%) ◀
Yellow in colour with a zesty taste full of citrus fruit flavours. Some initial sweetness followed by peppery hops and a bitter finish.

Merlyn (OG 1051, ABV 5%) ◀
A strong ale with balanced hop bitterness and sweet malt.

Great Western SIBA

Stream Bakery, Bristol Road, Hambrook, Bristol, BS16 1RF
☎ (0117) 957 2842
⊕ greatwesternbrewingcompany.co.uk
Shop Mon, Wed-Thu 10am-5pm; Fri 10am-5pm; Sat 10am-2pm
Tours by arrangement

⊠ Great Western is a 12-barrel brewery set up in 2008 by Kevin Stone in a former bakery. The property has been renovated resulting in a bespoke showpiece brewery retaining many of the building's original features. 200 outlets are supplied and one pub is owned. Seasonal beers are also available.

HPA (OG 1040, ABV 3.9%) ◀
Hoppy yellow-coloured bitter with fresh fruit and pale malt aromas. Clean bitter citrus flavours with a lingering, astringent finish.

Maiden Voyage (OG 1040, ABV 4%) ◀
An amber bitter with a light aroma of malt and fruit. The complex taste is initially sweet and fruity (damson notes) and the slightly astringent finish is dry and biscuity.

Bees Knees (OG 1041, ABV 4.2%) ◀
A powerful aroma of honey with hints of malt and meadow flowers leads to a taste of honey and malt developing through a slightly astringent but finely balanced aftertaste.

The Shires (OG 1043, ABV 4.4%) ◀
Tawny best bitter with fruit on the nose. Well-balanced apple and malt flavours with hints of

biscuit and vanilla. Long astringency in the aftertaste.

Classic Gold (OG 1044, ABV 4.6%) ◆
Golden ale with subtle aromas of pale malt and fruits. Citrus fruits with balanced hop and malt character with a lingering bitter finish.

Old Higby (OG 1045, ABV 4.8%) ◆
Full-bodied malty bitter with roast notes on the nose. Hints of fruit flavour give way to a bitter hop finish with some astringency throughout.

Great Yorkshire SIBA

Cropton, North Yorkshire, YO18 8HH
☎ (01751) 417330
⊕ thegreatyorkshirebrewery.co.uk
Tours by arrangement

☺Great Yorkshire took over the Cropton Brewery in 2012 concentrating on the production of keg beers. The cask beer range is limited but includes seasonal and special beers: see website.

Yorkshire Pale (ABV 3.8%)

Yorkshire Classic (ABV 4%)

Yorkshire Golden (ABV 4.2%)

Green Dragon

▤ Green Dragon, 29 Broad Street, Bungay, Suffolk, NR35 1EF
☎ (01986) 892681
Tours by arrangement

The Green Dragon pub was purchased in 1991 and the buildings at the rear converted to a brewery. In 1994 the plant was expanded and moved into a converted barn. The doubling of capacity allowed the production of a larger range of ales, including seasonal and occasional brews. The beers are available at the pub and beer festivals.

Chaucer Ale (OG 1037, ABV 3.8%)

Gold (OG 1045, ABV 4.4%)

Bridge Street Bitter (OG 1045, ABV 4.5%)

Green Duck

Unit 13, Gainsborough Estate, Rufford Road, Stourbridge, West Midlands, DY9 7ND
⊕ greenduckbrewery.co.uk

Green Duck began brewing in 2012 via Grafton Brewery while acquiring equipment and premises. In 2013 brewing moved to Stourbridge with a tap room overlooking the brew plant. Monthly seasonal beers are available.

Drunkun Duck (ABV 3.9%)

Duck Blonde (ABV 4.2%)

Green Jack SIBA ◉

Argyle Place, Love Road, Lowestoft, Suffolk, NR32 2NZ
☎ (01502) 562863 ⊕ green-jack.com
Tours by arrangement

⊠ After 10 years at Oulton Broad, Green Jack moved to the Triangle Tavern in Lowestoft in 2003 and then to a nearby 35-barrel plant in 2009. Three pubs are owned and more than 150 outlets supplied. Bottle-conditioned beers: see website.

Golden Best (OG 1038, ABV 3.8%) ◆
Cut grass hop aroma deepens on the palate of this golden bitter. Initially bitter, the aftertaste is fairly short and hoppy.

Orange Wheat Beer (OG 1041, ABV 4.2%) ◆
Marmalade aroma with a hint of hops, leading to a well-balanced blend of sweetness, hops and citrus with a malt background. Mixed fruit flavours in the aftertaste.

Trawlerboys Best Bitter (OG 1045, ABV 4.6%) ⎁ ◆
Tawny beer with aroma of apple, sultana and malt plus hints of caramel and hops. Rich fig and plum base with malt and roast overtones. Strong finish with a sticky mouthfeel.

Lurcher Stout (OG 1046, ABV 4.8%) ◆
Pleasant malt, roast and fruit aromas. Blackberry, raisin and port flavours. Long, dry, bitter roast finish.

Rising Sun (OG 1048, ABV 5%)

Red Herring (OG 1048, ABV 5.1%)

Gone Fishing ESB (OG 1052, ABV 5.5%)

Mahseer IPA (ABV 5.8%)

Ripper Tripel (OG 1074, ABV 8.5%)

Baltic Trader Export Stout (OG 1092, ABV 10.5%)

Green Mill SIBA

Cask & Feather, 1 Oldham Road, Rochdale, OL16 1UA
☎ 07967 656887 ⊕ greenmillbrewery.co.uk

☺Green Mill started brewing in 2007 on a 2.5-barrel plant and moved in 2010 to the Cask & Feather public house, where fermenting capacity could be expanded. A number of occasional beers are brewed. Around 40 outlets are supplied.

Gold (OG 1035, ABV 3.6%)
A golden session bitter.

Stellar (OG 1037, ABV 4%)
A pale ale with floral and subtle spice notes.

Chief (OG 1041, ABV 4.2%)
A smooth pale bitter with American hop varieties.

Citrus Snap (OG 1040, ABV 4.2%)
A copper-coloured bitter with lots of citrus notes.

Old Git (OG 1040, ABV 4.2%)
A complex, well-hopped golden ale.

Talisman (OG 1040, ABV 4.2%)
A straw-coloured golden ale with tropical fruit notes.

Flavia (OG 1042, ABV 4.5%)
A blonde beer with a fresh hop aroma brewed with lager malt, leading to a clean, dry finish.

Northern Lights (OG 1045, ABV 4.5%)
A pale premium bitter.

Big Chief (OG 1052, ABV 5.5%)

Green Room

Office: St Stephen Road, Sticker, St Austell, Cornwall, PL26 7HA
☎ 07843 10950 ⊕ greenroomales.co.uk

Stephen Burton started brewing in 2009 on a 2.5-barrel plant at the listed address. Due to increased demand he started using spare capacity at Keltek Brewery (qv), along with its bottling facilities.

Production was relocated from early 2010, with the original plant subsequently moved to Keltek to increase flexibility. Cask beers are occasionally produced but most of the output is bottled, although at present none of the brews are bottle-conditioned.

Green Tye

Green Tye, Much Hadham, Hertfordshire, SG10 6JP
☎ (01279) 841041 ☎ 07770 766376
✉ info@gtbrewery.co.uk
Tours by arrangement

⊗ Established in 1999 near Much Hadham, on the edge of the Ash Valley. The local free trade and neighbouring counties are supplied, further afield via beer agencies and swaps with other micro-breweries. Bottle-conditioned beers are available.

Union Jack (OG 1036, ABV 3.6%)
A copper-coloured bitter, fruity with a citrus taste and a hoppy, citrus aroma, with a balanced, bitter finish.

Hadham Gold (OG 1040, ABV 4%)

Greene King ◉

Westgate Brewery, Westgate Street, Bury St Edmunds, Suffolk, IP33 1QT
☎ (01284) 763222 ⊕ greeneking.co.uk
Shop and Visitor Centre Mon-Fri 10.30am-4.30pm;
Sat 10.30am-5.30pm
Tours by arrangement

⊗ Greene King has been brewing in the market town of Bury St Edmunds since 1799. It brews its beers using water drawn from artesian chalk wells below its brew house as well as local East Anglian malt. Seasonal and bottle-conditioned beers are available. Part of Greene King PLC.

XX Mild (OG 1035, ABV 3%)
A dark mild with a sweet and roast flavour.

IPA (OG 1036, ABV 3.6%) ◄
Hop-infused fruit cake aromas. Complex flavours of malt, caramel and hop with both sweetness and bitterness. A lingering mellow aftertaste with blackberries.

London Glory (OG 1041.1, ABV 4%)
Rich, fruity and full of flavour, combining crystal malt with Challenger and Golding hops

IPA Gold (OG 1041, ABV 4.1%)
A deep golden ale brewed with Savinsjki Goldings hops which creates a blend of tropical fruits, mango and spicy notes.

Abbot Ale (OG 1049, ABV 5%) ◄
Strong malt, toffee and caramel aromas. Rich malty caramel flavours with vine fruit and a little hop bite. Heavy sweet finish with a subtle hint of bitterness in the aftertaste.

IPA Reserve (OG 1055.5, ABV 5.4%)
A full-bodied amber ale. Grapefruit and orange citrus tones combine with floral and herbal notes leading to a dry, bitter finish.

Brewed under the H&H brand:

H&H Bitter (OG 1038, ABV 3.9%)
A balance of sweetness and bitterness that combines with a subtle hop character. A distinctive beer with a full finish.

H&H Olde Trip (OG 1043, ABV 4.3%)

A rich toffee flavoured beer with a fruity character and a clean, bitter finish.

Brewed under the Morland brand:

Morland Original Bitter (OG 1039, ABV 4%)
A subtle malt and fruit character and a pronounced bitter finish.

Morland Old Golden Hen (OG 1038.6, ABV 4.1%)
Light golden beer with tropical fruit notes.

**Morland Old Speckled Hen
(OG 1045, ABV 4.5%)** ◄
Smooth, malty and fruity, with a short finish.

Brewed under the Ruddles brand:

Ruddles Best Bitter (OG 1037, ABV 3.7%) ◄
An amber/brown beer, strong on bitterness but with some initial sweetness, fruit and subtle, distinctive Bramling Cross hop. Dryness lingers in the aftertaste.

Ruddles County (OG 1043, ABV 4.3%) ◄
Sweet, malty and bitter, with a dry and bitter aftertaste.

Brewed under the Tolly Cobbold brand:

Tolly Cobbold English Ale (OG 1033.6, ABV 2.8%)
Amber-coloured ale brewed using a complex mix of hops to offer balanced bitterness with strong tropical notes.

Greenfield SIBA ◉

Unit 8, Waterside Mills, Greenfield, Saddleworth, OL3 7PF
☎ (01457) 879789 ⊕ greenfieldbrewery.co.uk
Shop 9am-5pm daily
Tours by arrangement

◉Greenfield was launched in 2002 and is situated in an old spinning mill next to the River Chew on the edge of the Peak District National Park. Spring water from the National Park is used for brewing. More than 200 outlets are supplied. Seasonal beers are available.

Black Five (OG 1040, ABV 4%) ◄
A dark brown-coloured beer in which malt, roast, toffee, fruit and chocolate can all be found in aroma and taste. Smooth, malty aftertaste.

Delph Donkey (OG 1041, ABV 4.1%)

Thirst Born (OG 1041, ABV 4.1%)

Dobcross Bitter (OG 1041, ABV 4.2%)

Summer Ice (OG 1042, ABV 4.2%)

Copper Caskade (OG 1042, ABV 4.3%)
Full-bodied, copper-coloured beer with a hoppy finish. The final flavours reveal citrus and fruit tones.

Icicle (OG 1044, ABV 4.4%)

Uppermill Ale (OG 1044, ABV 4.4%)

The Full Malty (OG 1046, ABV 4.5%)
A rich-flavoured beer with a silky body. Aromas of toffee and caramel arrive first, leading to a sweet, malty taste with hints of roasted barley.

Vanilla Stout (OG 1048, ABV 5.2%)
A black stout, initial flavours of both chocolate and coffee are revealed before the roasted malts give way to a natural vanilla finish, created by the use of real vanilla pods during the cask maturation stage.

Greenodd

🍺 Ship Inn, Main Street, Greenodd, Cumbria, LA12 7QZ
☎ 07782 655294 ✉ greenoddbrewery@yahoo.co.uk
Tours by arrangement

Greenodd was established in 2010 at the Ship Inn using a two-barrel plant. There is a viewing window from the street behind the pub. The majority of production goes to the Ship with the remainder going to local free trade.

Blonde (OG 1040, ABV 4%)

Best Bitter (OG 1041, ABV 4.1%)

Roundabout (OG 1043, ABV 4.3%)

Brunette (OG 1045, ABV 4.5%)

Grey Trees

🍺 Red Cow Inn, 6 Merthyr Road, Llwydcoed, CF44 0YE
☎ (01685) 873924

Grey Trees was established in 2011 and uses a one-barrel plant in a converted container at the Red Cow Inn.

Diggers Gold (OG 1040, ABV 4%)

Rechabites (OG 1038, ABV 4%)

Gribble

🍺 Gribble Inn, Oving, West Sussex, PO20 2BP
☎ (01243) 786893 ⊕ gribbleinn.co.uk

⊠ The Gribble Brewery, established in 1980, is an independent microbrewery owned by the publicans of the Gribble Inn on the same site. Around 20 outlets are also supplied. Seasonal beers are available.

CHI P A (ABV 3.8%)

Ale (ABV 4.1%)

Fuzzy Duck (ABV 4.3%)

Reg's Tipple (ABV 4.8%)
Reg's Tipple was named after a customer from the early days of the brewery. It has a smooth, nutty flavour with a pleasant afterbite.

Plucking Pheasant (ABV 5%)

Pig's Ear (ABV 6%)

Griffin

🍺 Church Road, Shustoke, Warwickshire, B46 2LB
☎ (01675) 481205
Tours by arrangement

☺Brewing started in 2008 in the old coffin shop premises adjacent to the Griffin Inn. The five-barrel plant supplies the free trade as well as the Griffin Inn. A number of seasonal and special ales are brewed throughout the year including experimental brews for sale in the pub.

Pain in the Arse (OG 1037, ABV 3.7%)
Classic bitter, well-hopped with a malty after taste.

Gold (OG 1042, ABV 4.2%)
A light golden ale. Soft but with a full-bodied taste and citrus aroma.

Yeti (OG 1047, ABV 4.7%)
A light-coloured pale ale with a grapefruit after taste.

Growler SIBA

The Street, Pentlow, Essex, CO10 7JJ
☎ (01787) 283220 ⊕ growlerbrewery.com

⊠ Originally named Nethergate and starting at Clare, Suffolk in 1986, the brewery moved to Pentlow, Essex in 2005 and rebranded in 2012 as the Growler Brewery. Seasonal beers are available.

IPA (OG 1036, ABV 3.5%) ◕
Bitter-tasting session beer with some fruit and malt balancing the predominate hop character. Dry aftertaste.

Priory Mild (OG 1036, ABV 3.5%) ◕
A 'black bitter' rather than a true mild. Strong roast and bitter tastes dominate throughout.

Umbel Ale (OG 1039, ABV 3.8%) ◕
Pleasant, easy-drinking bitter, infused with coriander, which dominates.

Growler Bitter (OG 1040, ABV 3.9%) ◕
Light tasting, sweetish and fruity session beer.

Lemon Head (OG 1041, ABV 4%)

Hound Dog (OG 1043, ABV 4.2%)
Light golden, gently-hopped beer, smooth and refreshing at the start with a well-rounded bitterness before the hop explosion leaves a slightly fruity taste at the end.

Essex Border (OG 1049, ABV 4.8%)
A pale golden summer ale, fruity and spicy with a pleasant malty finish; a very easy drinking beer.

Old Growler (OG 1051, ABV 5%) 🍺 ◖ ◕
Well-balanced porter in which roast grain is complemented by fruit and bubblegum.

Umbel Magna (OG 1051, ABV 5%) 🍺 ◖ ◕
Old Growler flavoured with coriander. The spice is less dominant than in Umbel Ale, with some of the weight and body of the beer coming through.

Essex Beast (OG 1063, ABV 6.2%)
Strong, dark, complex and robust ale with chocolate and rich toffee flavours. Brewed in memory of Essex CAMRA stalwart Andrew Clifton.

Gun Dog SIBA

Unit 5b, Great Central Way, Woodford Halse, Northamptonshire, NN11 3PZ
☎ (01327) 264095 ☎ 07834 374751
⊕ gundogales.co.uk
Shop Mon-Fri 9am-5pm; Sat 10am-1.30pm
Tours by arrangement

☺Gun Dog began brewing in 2012 using a six-barrel plant. All four core beers are available bottle conditioned. Special beers are also brewed.

Jack's Spaniels (ABV 3.8%)
A careful blend of malt and hops create this floral, refreshing blonde.

Booze Hound (ABV 4.2%)
Copper-coloured, malty ale. The hop blend creates a traditional, easy-drinking ale.

Lord Barker (ABV 4.2%)
Rich, dark, smooth and well-balanced, this stout has a chocolate nose, rounded taste in the mouth and a clean finish.

Bad to the Bone (ABV 4.5%)
A light brown bitter. Biscuit undertones are balanced with a fruity hop finish.

Gundog

Unit 2, 13R Castle Island Way, North Seaton, Northumberland, NE63 0XL
☎ 07707 703182 ⊕ gundogbrewery.co.uk

Brewing began in 2011 using a 10-barrel plant. Regular ales are produced on a rotating schedule, along with monthly ales and specials.

Fox (ABV 3.8%)

Magnificent Seven (ABV 3.8%)

HDA (ABV 3.9%)

Pale (ABV 3.9%)

Red Setter (ABV 3.9%)

Black Hunter (ABV 4%)

Golden Hunter (ABV 4%)

Game Keeper Gold (ABV 4.1%)

Golden Cocker (ABV 4.1%)

Duck Hunter (ABV 4.3%)

Pointer (ABV 4.3%)

The Flush (ABV 4.3%)

Gundog (ABV 4.5%)

Stag (ABV 4.9%)

Shotgun IPA (ABV 5%)

Top Dog (ABV 5.1%)

Gwaun Valley

Kilkiffeth Farm, Pontfaen, Fishguard, SA65 9TP
☎ (01348) 881304 ⊕ gwaunvalleybrewery.co.uk
Shop & Vistor Centre 10am-6pm daily
Tours by arrangement

Gwaun Valley began brewing in 2009 on a four-barrel plant in a converted granary. The brewery also has a camp site and pitches for five caravans.

Bitter (OG 1040, ABV 4%)

Dark (OG 1040, ABV 4%)

Farmhouse (OG 1040, ABV 4%)

Light (OG 1040, ABV 4%)

Pembrokeshire Best (OG 1045, ABV 4.5%)

Gwynant

▤ Tynllidiart Arms, Capel Bangor, Aberystwyth, Ceredigion, SY23 3LR
☎ (01970) 880248 ⊕ tynllidiartarms.com
Tours by arrangement

Brewing started in 2004 in a former men's toilet at the front of the Tynllidiart Arms. Its 9-gallon brew length is recognised as the world's smallest commercial brewery by the Guinness Book of Records. Brewing is currently suspended.

Cwrw Gwynant (OG 1045, ABV 4.5%)

Hackney SIBA

Arch 358, Laburnum Street, London, E2 8BB
☎ (020) 3489 9595 ⊕ hackneybrewery.co.uk

⊗ Having met eight years ago while working at the Eagle on Farringdon Road, home brewers and good friends Jon Swain and Peter Hills decided to turn their pastime in to a profession and brew beer in the heart of Hackney. They are committed to giving a penny from every pint sold to local community charities. Bottle-conditioned beers are also available.

Gold (OG 1041, ABV 4%) ◆
A light fruity ale with a malty biscuit quality. A touch of dryness and a pleasant bitterness in the finish.

American Pale Ale (OG 1045, ABV 4.5%) ◆
Copper brown-coloured beer with a sweet citrus aroma and full, smooth mouthfeel. Citrus and floral hops on the palate .

Best Bitter (OG 1044, ABV 4.5%) ◆
Malty sweetness is present with a trace of toffee. Hop notes and a fruit-cocktail flavour diminish in the dry aftertaste.

Hadrian Border SIBA

Unit 5, The Preserving Works, Newburn Industrial Estate, Shelley Road, Newburn, Newcastle upon Tyne, NE15 9RT
☎ (0191) 264 9000 ⊕ hadrian-border-brewery.co.uk
Tours by arrangement

Originally based at the Four Rivers site in Newcastle, the brewery relocated to Newburn in 2011 with a new 30-barrel brew plant to meet increased demand. The company's products are popular on Tyneside and its customer base extends through Northumberland to Edinburgh and Glasgow and down to Yorkshire. The brands are also available nationally via wholesalers. Seasonal beers: see website.

Tyneside Blonde (OG 1037, ABV 3.9%) ◆
Refreshing blonde ale with zesty notes and a clean, fruity finish.

Farne Island Pale Ale (OG 1038, ABV 4%) ◆
A copper-coloured bitter with a refreshing malt/hop balance.

Flotsam (OG 1038, ABV 4%)
Bronze-coloured with a citrus bitterness and a distinctive floral aroma.

Needles & Pins (OG 1041.5, ABV 4.2%)
Dark amber-coloured, beer, fruity and full-bodied.

Secret Kingdom (OG 1042, ABV 4.3%)
Dark, rich and full-bodied, slightly roasted with a malty palate ending with a pleasant bitterness.

Coast to Coast (OG 1041.5, ABV 4.4%)
Light amber-coloured, hoppy beer with a nice malt balance.

Reiver's IPA (OG 1042, ABV 4.4%)
Golden bitter with a clean citrus palate and aroma with subtle malt flavours breaking through at the end.

Jetsam (OG 1043, ABV 4.5%)

Northumbrian Gold (OG 1044, ABV 4.5%)

Grainger Ale (OG 1045, ABV 4.6%)
Pale in appearance with a well-balanced, refreshingly bitter finish.

Hafod SIBA

c/o Hafod Road, Pant Glas, Gwernaffield, Flintshire, CH7 5ES
☎ 07901 386638 ⊕ welshbeer.com

⊕Hafod began brewing in 2011 on a small scale supplying local outlets. In addition to the core range, a number of speciality beers using ingredients from the local upland areas and heathlands are also produced on a limited basis.

Taverns Tipple (OG 1035, ABV 3.5%)

Classic (OG 1038, ABV 3.8%) ◄
Copper coloured, smooth and full-bodied. Juicy malt taste with some initial toffee flavours and hops developing in the aftertaste.

Moel Famau Ale (OG 1041, ABV 4.1%) ◄
A speciality dark ale brewed using local heather giving a dry, roasty taste with underlying sweet malt flavours.

HE (OG 1043, ABV 4.3%)

Hopper (OG 1043, ABV 4.3%) ◄
A full-flavoured session bitter with a mouthwatering taste of peppery hops and a lasting dry finish.

Hafod Light (OG 1046, ABV 4.6%) ◄
Amber beer with a citrus fruit nose, sweetish taste with hints of vanilla, and a clean bittersweet finish.

Hammer (OG 1066, ABV 6.6%) ◄
A sweet strong bitter full of tropical fruits in aroma and taste, balanced by a powerful hoppy finish.

Halfpenny SIBA

≣ Crown Inn, High Street, Lechlade, Gloucestershire, GL7 3AE
☎ (01367) 252198 ☎ 07740 932933
⊕ halfpennybrewery.co.uk
Shop at pub
Tours by arrangement

⊠ Halfpenny was established in 2008 on a four-barrel plant at the Crown at Lechlade, visible in an outbuilding, and has since expanded to a third fermentation vessel. Around 20 local outlets are supplied direct. Bottle-conditioned beers are available.

Ha'penny Ale (OG 1039, ABV 4%)

Thames Tickler (OG 1040, ABV 4%)

Anniversary Ale (OG 1042, ABV 4.2%)

Four Seasons' Ale (OG 1042, ABV 4.3%)

Old Lech (OG 1045, ABV 4.5%)

Halifax Steam

≣ The Conclave, Southedge Works, Brighouse Road, Hipperholme, West Yorkshire, HX3 8EF
☎ 07974 544980 ⊕ halifax-steam.co.uk

⊕Halifax Steam was established in 2001 on a five-barrel plant and supplies only its brewery tap, the Cock o' the North, which is adjacent to the brewery. Approximately 150 different rotating beers are produced, three of which are permanent. 10-12 Halifax Steam beers are available at any one time, plus occasional guests on a fair trade basis.

Aussie Kiss (ABV 3.8%)

Uncle John (OG 1043, ABV 4.3%) ◄
Roast predominates in this creamy, dark brown stout. The finish is smooth with no harsh edges.

Child Catcher (OG 1048, ABV 4.8%)

Hall & Woodhouse (Badger) IFBB ◉

Blandford St Mary, Blandford Forum, Dorset, DT11 9LS
☎ (01258) 452141 ⊕ hall-woodhouse.co.uk
Shop Mon-Sat 9am-6pm; Sun 11am-3pm (Easter-Oct)
Tours by arrangement

⊠ Founded by Charles Hall in 1777, Hall & Woodhouse is a major independent family brewer, today run by the seventh generation of the founding family. The Badger logo was adopted in 1875. The company moved from Ansty to its present site in 1900 and a new brewery has been built on part of the existing site, which took over full production from the 1899 brewery in 2012. Cask beer is sold in all 220 pubs. Seasonal beers are available.

First Gold (OG 1041, ABV 4%) ◄
Good example of a best bitter with good, but not over-powering, hop aromas and flavours and a good bittersweet aftertaste.

Tanglefoot (OG 1047, ABV 4.9%) ◄
Relatively sweet-tasting and deceptive, given its strength. Pale malt provides caramel overtones and bittersweet finish.

Brewed under King & Barnes brand:

K&B Sussex Bitter (OG 1036, ABV 3.5%) ◄
Traditional, lightly-hopped, easy-drinking session bitter with hints of malt and caramel and the traditional Badger fruit flavour predominating in the lingering bitter aftertaste.

Hambleton SIBA ◉

Melmerby Green Road, Melmerby, North Yorkshire, HG4 5NB
☎ (01765) 640108 ⊕ hambletonales.co.uk
Tours by arrangement

⊕Hambleton Ales was established in 1991 on the banks of the River Swale in the heart of the Vale of York. Expansion over the years has resulted in relocation to larger premises on several occasions, the last being in 2007. Capacity in the custom-built brewery is 100 barrels a week with a bottling line also catering for other micros and larger brewers, handling more than 50 brands. Four core ales are brewed constantly along with a monthly special and are supplied to more than 100 outlets throughout Yorkshire and north-east England. The company also contract brews for the Village Brewer and Black Dog Brewery.

Bitter (OG 1038.5, ABV 3.8%)
A golden bitter with a good balance of malty and refreshing citrus notes leading to a mellow, tangy finish.

Stallion (OG 1041, ABV 4.2%) ◄
A premium bitter, moderately hoppy throughout and richly balanced in malt and fruit, developing a sound and robust bitterness, with earthy hops drying the aftertaste.

Stud (OG 1042.5, ABV 4.3%) ◄
A strongly bitter beer, with rich hop and fruit. It ends dry and spicy.

Nightmare (OG 1050, ABV 5%) ◄
This impressively flavoured beer satisfies all parts of the palate. Strong roast malts dominate, but hoppiness rears out of this complex blend.

Contract brewed for Black Dog Brewery, Whitby:

Whitby Abbey Ale (OG 1037.5, ABV 3.8%)

Schooner (OG 1041.5, ABV 4.2%)

Rhatas (OG 1045, ABV 4.6%)

Contract brewed for Village Brewer:

White Boar (OG 1037.5, ABV 3.8%) ◥
A light, flowery and fruity ale; crisp, clean and refreshing, with a dry-hopped, powerful but not aggressive bitter finish.

Bull (OG 1039, ABV 4%)

Hamelsworde (NEW)

16 Longworth Road, Hemsworth, West Yorkshire, WF9 4SZ
☎ 07530 669332 ⊕ hamelsworde.co.uk

The brainchild of enthusiastic home brewer Dan Jones, his beers were originally brewed using a 50-litre boiler in a converted garage. A one-barrel plant was installed in 2013.

Spanish Stout (ABV 4.2%)
A traditional stout with a strong roasted flavours and a sweet liquorice taste complemented by aniseed.

Haley's Comet (ABV 4.5%)
A fresh summery ale which is light and easily quaffed, with a citrus aroma and taste.

Jumping Pirate (ABV 4.9%)
A light golden ale in a Bavarian style, with floral, piney and citrus notes. A complex beer which is smooth on the finish.

Colin Brown Ale (ABV 5.2%)
A unique twist on a traditional English ale with a deep amber-red colour. A fruity hop aroma leads on to a malty, nutty bittersweet flavour with a long dry aftertaste.

Scalded Shoulder (ABV 5.2%)
A golden wheat beer, single hopped and finished with coriander and orange.

Cherokee America IPA (ABV 6%)
A copper coloured IPA with strong fruity hop aroma.

Hammerpot SIBA

Unit 30, The Vinery, Arundel Road, Poling, West Sussex, BN18 9PY
☎ (01903) 883338 ⊕ hammerpot-brewery.co.uk

⊗ Hammerpot started brewing in 2005 using a five-barrel plant, which was upgraded to a 10-barrel plant in 2011. The brewery supplies as far north as Berkshire and into London and from Eastbourne to Southampton. Seasonal, special and occasional beers: see website. Bottle-conditioned beers are also available.

Shooting Star (OG 1038, ABV 3.8%)

HPA (OG 1044, ABV 4.1%)
A light, golden tangy pale ale with a full, fresh hop flavour.

Red Hunter (OG 1046, ABV 4.3%)
A ruby red-coloured, smooth-drinking bitter with a full-bodied, rich character.

Woodcote (OG 1047, ABV 4.5%)
A tangy amber-coloured bitter with a pleasant, dry finish.

Bottle Wreck Porter (OG 1047, ABV 4.7%) ⬗ ▮

A traditional black porter with coffee, chocolate and rich roast malt flavours.

Madgwick Gold (OG 1050, ABV 5%)
A golden ale with a fresh citrus spice hop aroma. Very drinkable with a refreshing, thirst quenching finish.

Hand Drawn Monkey (NEW)

Plover Road Garage, Plover Road, Lindley, Huddersfield, West Yorkshire, HD3 3HS
☎ (01484) 655262 ☎ 07739 754816
✉ robarooallenn@gmail.com

Hand Drawn Monkey commenced cuckoo brewing on the Mallinson's Brewery plant during 2012 and took over the plant after Mallinson's moved premises.

Malpa (ABV 3.9%)

Pale Ale (ABV 4%)

Monkeys Love Hops (ABV 4.2%)

What Would Jephers Do? (ABV 4.5%)

Porter (ABV 4.8%)

IPA (ABV 5%)

Double Belgium (ABV 6%)

Handley's

▤ Two Drinks Ltd, Willow Tree, Front Street, Barnby in the Willows, Nottinghamshire, NG24 2SA
☎ (01636) 629003 ⊕ willowtreebarnby.co.uk/

Handley's began brewing in 2011 on a 0.5-barrel plant installed behind the Willow Tree pub by owner Brett Handley. Beer is mostly sold in the pub but can be found at beer festivals and in other outlets if stocks permit.

Ha'penny SIBA

Cuckoo Hall Brewery, Unit 8, Aldborough Hall Farm, Aldborough Hatch, Ilford, Essex, IG2 7TD
☎ (020) 8599 1338 ☎ 07961 161869
⊕ hapenny-brewing.co.uk
Tours by arrangement

⊗ Ha'penny was established in 2009 by two CAMRA members in a disused stable block that had a former life as a pub and beer house for the Aldborough Hall estate workers.

Happy Valley

8 Hazelhurst Drive, Bollington, Cheshire, SK10 5QT
☎ 07758 512080 ⊕ happyvalleybrewery.co.uk
Tours by arrangement

⊗ Happy Valley was established in 2010 by David and Nicola Hughes using a 2.5-barrel plant. Pubs are supplied in Cheshire, Derbyshire, Greater Manchester and Staffordshire.

Sworn Secret (OG 1038, ABV 3.8%)
Pale straw-coloured ale with a strong hop character. It has a very pleasant hoppy nose with a citrus aftertaste.

Little Rascal (OG 1039, ABV 3.9%)
A light, golden session ale. Well-balanced with a lingering citrus and grapefruit aftertaste.

Five Rings (OG 1040, ABV 4%)
Crisp, clean tasting ale.

Lazy Daze (OG 1042, ABV 4.2%)
Gold-coloured ale with a hoppy finish.

Black Magic (OG 1046, ABV 4.6%)
A full-bodied stout.

Tie the Knot (OG 1050, ABV 5%)
A straw-coloured strong bitter with malt tastes and big hop character. Very drinkable despite the strength.

Dangerously Dark (OG 1056, ABV 5.6%)
A black IPA-style beer.

Harbour SIBA

Trekillick Farm, Kirland, Bodmin, Cornwall, PL30 5BB
☎ (01208) 832131 ☎ 07870 305063
⊕ harbourbrewing.com

⊠ Harbour is an innovative 10-barrel brewery founded on the outskirts of Bodmin in 2011. Brewed using local spring water, the four regular beers are established in an increasing number of outlets.

Light (OG 1037, ABV 3.7%)
Pale ale with a light/medium body with lemon/grapefruit notes on the finish.

Amber (OG 1037.5, ABV 4%) ◆
Ripe fruit and malt in the aroma and taste with hints of toffee and ginger biscuit. Bitter and dry short finish.

IPA (OG 1048.5, ABV 5%) ◆
Bitterness dominates the taste with citrus hop flavour balanced by caramel maltiness and butterscotch. Citrus aroma and thin, dry finish.

Porter (OG 1055, ABV 5.5%)
Dark ruby-coloured beer with complex toasted, rich chocolate flavours. Based on beers from the 1800's.

Hardknott SIBA

Unit 10, Devonshire Road Industrial Estate, Millom, Cumbria, LA18 4JS
☎ (01229) 779309 ⊕ hardknott.com
Tours by arrangement

☺Hardknott began brewing in 2005 at the Woolpack Inn in Boot. The brewery relocated to Millom and expanded in 2010. It specialises in limited edition bottle-conditioned and regular cask-conditioned beers. All bottled beers are suitable for vegans.

Katalyst (OG 1040, ABV 3.8%) ◆
An assertively hoppy, bitter beer, with a sweet, fruity taste that diminishes in the finish.

Continuum (OG 1042, ABV 4%) ◆
An amber-coloured beer with pronounced hops and bitterness right through to the aftertaste. Some maltiness in the aroma and taste.

Cold Fusion (OG 1044, ABV 4.4%) ◆
A well-balanced, mild, sweet beer with ginger. The ginger bite builds in the finish.

Duality (OG 1044, ABV 4.5%)

Dark Energy (OG 1052, ABV 4.9%) ◆
A hoppy aroma leads to a dry, hoppy beer with plenty of roast.

Code Black (OG 1056, ABV 5.6%)

Azimuth (OG 1057, ABV 5.8%)

Infra Red (OG 1065, ABV 6.2%)
Hints of toffee and popcorn. Citrus fruits dominate.

Hardys & Hansons

See Greene King

Hart Family (NEW) SIBA

The 1833 Brewery, 21 Nene Court, The Embankment, Wellingborough, Northamptonshire, NN8 1LD
⊕ hartfamilybrewers.com
Shop Sat 9am-5pm. Other times by appt
Tours by arrangement

⊠ Hart Family Brewers was established in 2012 using an eight-barrel plant. It is owned and operated by Rob and Sarah Hart, who are indulging their passion after their a combined 25 years in the drinks industry. Seasonal and bottle-conditioned beers are also available: see website.

No. 1 (OG 1043, ABV 4.1%)
A tawny beer with fruity, malty aromas with grassy, citrus notes. Fresh and fruity on the palate with spicy bitterness.

No. 9 (OG 1044, ABV 4.3%)
Golden beer with honeyed malt flavours and bright, citrus aromas across a long, refreshing finish.

No. 3 (OG 1050, ABV 4.7%)
A fruity, ruby-coloured beer with malty, spicy aromas. Full-bodied with rich, malty flavours and a gentle spicy hoppiness.

No. 8 (OG 1055, ABV 5%)
A dark beer with toasted fruit aromas with hints of espresso. Full-bodied and warming with roasted fruit and molasses flavours balanced by bitter coffee and chocolate.

Hart of Preston SIBA

Unit 5, Oxhey Trading Estate, Greenbank Street, Preston, Lancashire, PR1 7PH
☎ (01772) 437651 ⊕ hartbreweryltd.co.uk
Tours by arrangement

☺Hart opened in 1995 behind the Cartford Hotel in Little Eccleston. In 2010 the brewery relocated to Preston. It supplies a number of local outlets and arranges exchanges with other microbreweries.

Lancashire Best Bitter (OG 1039, ABV 3.9%)

Ayson (OG 1042, ABV 4.2%)

Hart of Stebbing

🍺 White Hart, High Street, Stebbing, Essex, CM6 3SQ
☎ (01371) 856383 ⊕ hartofstebbingbrewery.co.uk

⊠ The brewery was established in 2007 by Bob Dovey and Nick Eldred, who is also the owner of the White Hart pub where the brewery is based. At present only the White Hart and local beer festivals are supplied. Occasional specials are also brewed.

Hart IPA (OG 1035, ABV 3.5%)

Harthill Village (NEW) SIBA

The Paddocks, 6 Union Street, Harthill, South Yorkshire, S26 7YH
☎ (01909) 774954 ⊕ harthillbrewery.co.uk

Brewing began in 2013 using a five-barrel plant. Seasonal beers are available.

Ace of Harts (ABV 3.9%)
A traditional, well-balanced amber bitter with a subtle malty sweetness and spicy, fruity aroma.

Hart Stopper (ABV 4%)
A hoppy blonde ale with a fresh aroma of citrus and berry fruits with hints of zest and spice.

Hart's Desire (ABV 4.4%)
An amber premium ale with a fresh aroma of citrus with floral and spicy notes balanced with biscuity, malty, sweet flavours.

Dark Hart (ABV 4.8%)
A rich, smooth, full-bodied dark ale with a toffee, malty sweetness and a dry, biscuity fullness complemented by the spicy, blackcurrant aroma.

Dark Hart Festival Reserve (ABV 6.5%)

Hartshorns

Unit 4, Tomlinsons Industrial Estate, Alfreton Road, Derby, DE21 4ED
☎ 07830 367125 ⊕ hartshornsbrewery.com

Hartshorns began brewing in 2012 using a six-barrel plant installed by brothers Darren and Lindsey Hartshorn.

Highgate (OG 1044, ABV 4.3%)
Smooth, easy-drinking pale copper-coloured ale. Well-balanced malt sweetness with fruity hop flavour and a well-rounded bitterness.

Stormin Auburn (OG 1045, ABV 4.5%)
A mild bitterness and crystal malt flavour characterise this amber-coloured ale, complemented by distinctive American hop flavour and aroma.

Floss the Boss (OG 1046, ABV 4.6%)
A thirst quenching pale golden ale with a distinct flavour balanced with a rich, malty sweetness.

Brooklyn Nights (OG 1052, ABV 5.4%)
A brown-coloured ale with a complex malt base, an assertive bitterness and a clean, dry finish.

Shakademus (OG 1052, ABV 5.4%)
Full-bodied with a citrus hop bite, a satisfying premium golden ale.

Apocalypse (OG 1055, ABV 6.2%)
Surprisingly easy-drinking golden ale with a clean, bitter finish. Refreshingly crisp and packed with hop character.

Harveys IFBB ⊚

Bridge Wharf Brewery, 6 Cliffe High Street, Lewes, East Sussex, BN7 2AH
☎ (01273) 480209 ⊕ harveys.org.uk
Shop Mon-Sat 9.30am-5.30pm
Tours by arrangement

⊠ Established in 1790, this independent family brewery operates from the banks of the River Ouse in Lewes. A major development in 1985 doubled the brewhouse capacity and subsequent additional fermenting capacity has seen production rise to more than 45,000 barrels a year. There is also a microbrewery on site used to brew special beers including replicating old Lewes Brewery recipes using the County Town Beers name. Harveys supplies real ale to all its 48 pubs and 450 free trade outlets in the south-east. Seasonal beers: see website. Bottle-conditioned beer is also available.

Sussex XX Mild Ale (OG 1030, ABV 3%) 🍴 ◆
A dark copper-brown colour. Roast malt dominates the aroma and palate leading to a sweet, caramel finish.

IPA (OG 1033, ABV 3.5%)

Sussex Wild Hop (ABV 3.7%)

Sussex Best Bitter (OG 1040, ABV 4%) ◆
Full-bodied brown bitter. A hoppy aroma leads to a good malt and hop balance, and a dry aftertaste.

Old Ale (OG 1043, ABV 4.3%)

Olympia (OG 1042, ABV 4.3%)

Armada Ale (OG 1045, ABV 4.5%) ◆
Hoppy amber-coloured best bitter. Well-balanced fruit and hops dominate throughout with a fruity palate.

Harviestoun SIBA ⊚

Alva Industrial Estate, Alva, Clackmannanshire, FK12 5DQ
☎ (01259) 769100 ⊕ harviestoun.com
Tours by arrangement

⊚Harviestoun started in a barn in the village of Dollar in 1985 with a five-barrel brew plant, but now operate on a state-of-the-art 60-barrel brewery in Alva. The brewery supplies local outlets direct and nationwide via wholesalers. It was bought by Caledonian Brewing Co in 2006 but is now independent following the takeover of Caledonian by Scottish & Newcastle in 2008. Further expansion is planned. Seasonal beers: see website.

Bitter & Twisted (OG 1036, ABV 3.8%) ◆
Refreshingly hoppy beer with fruit throughout. A bittersweet taste with a long bitter finish. A golden session beer.

Natural Blonde (OG 1040, ABV 4%)

Schiehallion (OG 1048, ABV 4.8%) ◆
A Scottish cask lager, brewed using a lager yeast and Hersbrucker hops. A hoppy aroma, with fruit and malt, leads to a malty, bitter taste with floral hoppiness and a bitter finish.

Harwich Town

Station Approach, Harwich, Essex, CO12 3NA
☎ (01255) 551155 ⊕ harwichtown.co.uk
Tours by arrangement

Brewing started in 2007 on a five-barrel plant next to Harwich Town railway station. The brewer is a CAMRA member and former customs officer. Beers are named after local landmarks, characters or events. 50 outlets are supplied. The brewery holds a beer festival in July and a festival special is brewed for the Harwich & Dovercourt Bay Winter Ale Festival in December. Seasonal and bottle-conditioned beers are also available.

Bay Bitter (OG 1036, ABV 3.6%)

Ha'Penny Mild (OG 1036, ABV 3.6%)

EPA 100 (OG 1038, ABV 3.8%)

Leading Lights (OG 1038, ABV 3.8%)

Ganges (OG 1040, ABV 4%)

Misleading Lights (OG 1040, ABV 4%)

Bathside Battery Bitter (OG 1042, ABV 4.2%)

Redoubt Stout (OG 1042, ABV 4.2%)

Parkeston Porter (OG 1045, ABV 4.5%)

Lighthouse Bitter (OG 1048, ABV 4.8%)

Phoenix APA (OG 1052, ABV 5%)

Hastings SIBA

Unit 12, Conqueror Industrial Estate, Moorhurst Road, St Leonards-on-Sea, East Sussex, TN38 9NB
☎ (01424) 850961 ☎ 07708 259342
⊕ hastingsbrewery.co.uk

⊗ Hastings is a small brewery established in 2010, exclusively producing unfined beers suitable for vegetarians and vegans. It currently operations on a five-barrel plant.

Blonde (OG 1040, ABV 3.9%)

Best (OG 1042, ABV 4.1%)

Porter (OG 1050.5, ABV 4.5%)

Havant SIBA ◉

Unit 25, The Tanneries, Brockhampton Lane, Havant, Hampshire, PO9 1JB
☎ (023) 9247 6067 ⊕ thehavantbrewery.co.uk
Shop Tue-Fri 2-5pm; Sat 11am-2pm
Tours by arrangement

⊗ Havant began brewing in 2009 on a one-barrel plant, upgraded in 2011 to a bespoke 3.5-barrel plant. Seasonal and special beers: see website.

Decided (OG 1038, ABV 3.8%)

Started (OG 1042, ABV 4%)

Finished (OG 1051, ABV 5%)

Hawkshead SIBA ◉

Mill Yard, Staveley, Cumbria, LA8 9LR
☎ (01539) 822644 ⊕ hawksheadbrewery.co.uk
Shop Mon 12-5pm; Tue-Thu 12-6pm; Fri & Sat 12-11pm; Sun 12-8pm
Tours by arrangement

⊚ Hawkshead brewery complex is a showcase for real ale. The brewery expanded in 2006, having outgrown its original site (opened in 2002) in a barn at Hawkshead. Further expansion in 2010 added a second bar to the Beer Hall, which is the visitor centre and brewery tap. A kitchen serves 'beer tapas' to complement the beer. Windows throughout look into the cellar, specialist beer shop, brew house and the new fermentation room, which is in the main bar. Pubs are supplied throughout the north west.

Windermere Pale (OG 1036, ABV 3.5%) 🍴 ◆
Crisp and fruity yellow beer with hints of melon and grapefruit and a strong, bitter aftertaste.

Bitter (OG 1037, ABV 3.7%) 🍴 ◆
Well-balanced, thirst-quenching beer with fruit and hops aroma, leading to a lasting bitter finish.

Red (OG 1042, ABV 4.2%) 🍴 ◆
An impressive colour for this richly flavoured beer; lots of fruitiness and good hop flavour with a lingering aftertaste.

Lakeland Gold (OG 1043, ABV 4.4%) ◆
Fresh, well-balanced fruity, hoppy beer with a clean, bitter aftertaste.

Drystone Stout (OG 1044, ABV 4.5%) ◆
Black, dry, bitter stout with an astringent, roast finish.

Brodie's Prime (OG 1048, ABV 4.9%) 🍴 🍴 ◆
Complex, dark brown beer with plenty of malt, fruit and roast taste. Satisfying full body with clean finish.

Cumbrian Five Hop (OG 1050, ABV 5%)
Highly hopped golden ale with an aroma of tropical fruit from a blend of English and American hops. Full flavour and long, dry finish.

Lakeland Lager (OG 1045, ABV 5%)
A cask-conditioned lager.

Haworth Steam SIBA

98 Main Street, Haworth, West Yorkshire, BD22 8DP
☎ (01535) 646059 ☎ 07974 483310
⊕ haworthsteambrewery.co.uk
Shop Mon-Thu & Sun 10am-6pm; Fri & Sat 10am-9pm

⊚ Haworth Steam was established in 2011 using a five-barrel plant, bringing brewing back to Haworth for the first time in over 70 years. The brewery now has online sales and a café, bar and bistro.

True Tyke (OG 1038, ABV 3.8%)
Amber-coloured Yorkshire bitter with creamy biscuit notes and a distinctive breadiness.

W D Austerity (OG 1038, ABV 3.8%)
A blonde ale with plenty of cereal and digestive biscuit on the nose. Creamy malt body gives a floral finish.

Ironclad 957 (OG 1043, ABV 4.3%)
Stout with caramel and raisin on the nose and a little drying smoke on the finish.

Fallwood XXXX (OG 1052, ABV 5.2%)
Full-bodied ale full of roasted barley and hops, giving a toffee apple red colour with a hint of cider.

Hay Rake (NEW)

Blackstone Edge Old Road, Littleborough, OL15 0JX
☎ (01706) 379689 ☎ 07775 792684
⊕ hayrakebrewery.info

Mark Wickham, the landlord of the Rake Tapas Restaurant, resurrected the Hay Rake microbrewery in 2013. The Rake brewed its own beer during the reign of Queen Victoria but stopped in 1901. Mark is keen to revive the tradition of locally-brewed ale.

Dawn's Hopping Mad (ABV 3.8%)

Dawn's Called Thyme (ABV 4%)

Early Dawn (ABV 4.1%)

Dawn's Dark Side (ABV 4.4%)

Dawn's Autumn Gold (ABV 4.5%)

Haywood Bad Ram SIBA

Callow Top Holiday Park, Buxton Road, Sandybrook, Ashbourne, Derbyshire, DE6 2AQ
☎ (01335) 344020 ☎ 07974 948427
⊕ callowtop.co.uk/callow-top-brewery
Shop 9am-5pm (seasonal)
Tours by arrangement

⊗ Established in 2003, the brewery was based in a converted barn but a new brewery and bottling plant became operational in 2012. One pub is owned (on site) and several other outlets are supplied. Bottle-conditioned beers are available.

Thoroughbred Bad Ram (ABV 3.8%)
A refreshing straw-coloured ale brewed using a combination of two malted barleys. Hops add spice and flowery notes.

Dr Samuel Johnson (OG 1044, ABV 4.5%)
Malt and hops combine to produce a slightly fruity and refined spicy flavour.

Callow Top Imperial IPA (OG 1050, ABV 5.2%)
A full bodied, rich ale with a fruity and slightly citrus after-taste.

Head in a Hat

See Florence

Healey's (NEW)

⬛ Wellington Inn, Main Street, Loppergarth, Cumbria, LA12 0JL
☎ (01229) 582388

Healey's began brewing in 2012 using a custom-made 2.5-barrel stainless steel plant, which can be viewed through full-length windows in the pub.

Golden (OG 1037, ABV 3.6%)

Dark Mild (OG 1038, ABV 3.7%)

Blonde (OG 1040, ABV 4%)

Best Bitter (OG 1042, ABV 4.2%)

Hearsall (NEW)

⬛ c/o Hearsall Inn, 45 Craven Street, Coventry, West Midlands, CV5 8DS
☎ (024) 7671 5729

Hearsall began brewing in 2012 using a one-barrel plant. Beer is produced for the pub.

Session Ale (ABV 3.4%)

Chapelfields Best (ABV 4%)

Heart of Wales

⬛ Stables Yard, Zion Street, Llanwrtyd Wells, Powys, LD5 4RD
☎ (01591) 610236 ⊕ heartofwalesbrewery.co.uk
Shop 10am-6pm daily
Tours by arrangement

☺The brewery was set up with a six-barrel plant in 2006 in old stables at the rear of the Neuadd Arms Hotel. Beers are brewed using water from the brewery's own borehole. Seasonal brews celebrate local events such as the World Bogsnorkelling Championships. Seasonal and bottle-conditioned beers are available. All bottle-conditioned beers are suitable for vegetarians and vegans. Cambrian Heart was commissioned by and is brewed for the Cambrian Mountains Initiative, inspired by the Prince of Wales, which aims to promote and support rural producers and communities in the region.

Irfon Valley Bitter (OG 1038, ABV 3.6%)

Aur Cymru (OG 1040, ABV 3.8%)

Bitter (OG 1042, ABV 4.1%)
A light chestnut-coloured, well-balanced bitter.

Welsh Black (OG 1045, ABV 4.4%) 🍶 🍺
A full-flavoured, complex and smooth stout.

Cambrian Heart Ale (OG 1045, ABV 4.5%)
Light golden brown beer with a refreshing fruity body and lots of hops in the finish.

Noble Eden Ale (OG 1046, ABV 4.6%)
A dark brown, full-bodied premium ale bursting with fruit and malt, with just a hint of chocolate.

Inn-stable (OG 1065, ABV 6.8%)
A powerful ale with a warming malty body and a smooth finish.

High as a Kite (OG 1095, ABV 10.5%) 🍶 🍺
Rich and warming flavours caress the palate; a rich old ale to be savoured slowly and in moderation.

Heavy Industry (NEW) SIBA

The Old Slaughterhouse, Denbigh Street, Henllan, LL16 5AR
☎ (01745) 816316 ✉ heavybrew@gmail.com

Established in 2012, Heavy Industry brews with a 10-barrel microbrewery.

Electric Mountain (ABV 3.8%)

High Voltage (ABV 4.5%)

Collaborator (ABV 5%)

Hebridean

18a Bells Road, Stornoway, Isle of Lewis, HS1 2RA
☎ (01851) 700123 ⊕ hebridean-brewery.co.uk
Shop open in summer months only

☺The company was set up in 2001 with a 14-barrel brew length. A shop is attached to the brewery. Seasonal beers are produced for Mods, Gaelic festivals that are the Scottish equivalent of the Welsh Eisteddfod.

Celtic Black Ale (OG 1036, ABV 3.9%)
A dark ale full of flavour, balancing an aromatic hop combined with a subtle bite and a pleasantly smooth caramel aftertaste.

Clansman Ale (OG 1036, ABV 3.9%)
A light Hebridean beer, brewed with Scottish malts and lightly hopped to give a subtle bittering.

Seaforth Ale (ABV 4.2%) 🍺
A light, quaffable beer with a delicate nose. A complex mixture of biscuity malt and fruit in the taste leads to a lasting, bittersweet finish.

Islander Strong Premium Ale (OG 1044, ABV 4.8%) 🍺
A malty, fruity strong bitter drinking dangerously below its ABV.

Berserker Export Pale Ale (OG 1068, ABV 7.5%) 🍺
This malty, fruity winter warmer is packed full of flavour, with toffee apple and caramel notes right through to the long, satisfying aftertaste.

Heddon Valley

See Country Life

Heineken Royal Trafford

Royal Brewery, 201 Denmark Road, Manchester, M15 6LD
☎ (0161) 220 4371

No real ale.

Hektor's

The Office, Henham Park, Southwold, Suffolk, NR34 8AN
☎ 07900 553426 ⊕ hektorsbrewery.com

Beers are brewed by the owner on the equipment of other breweries, including Green Jack and Oakham. However, there are plans to install a brewery in a converted barn at Henham Park in the future. Hektor's beers are provided to Henham Park's 65,000 annual visitors in addition to five other outlets and local events.

Pure (OG 1038, ABV 3.8%)

House (OG 1042, ABV 4.2%)

Scarecrow (OG 1050, ABV 5%)

Hellhound

6 Seager Court, Crockatt Road, Hadleigh, Suffolk, IP7 6RL
☎ 07850 076202 ⊕ hellhoundbrewery.co.uk

Hellhound began brewing in 2010 using a six-barrel plant. Seasonal beer is available.

Hen House

The Old Dairy, Walliscote Farm, High Street, Whitchurch-on-Thames, Oxfordshire, RG8 7EP
⊕ henhousebrewery.co.uk
Shop Sat 2-4pm

Hen House began brewing in 2012 on a 30-litre plant. Only bottle-conditioned beers are produced, available from the brewery shop. Seasonal and special beers: see website.

Henley (NEW)

Henley Brew House, 35 Market Place, Henley-on-Thames, Oxfordshire, RG9 2AH
☎ 07449 931657 ⊕ thehenleybrewingcompany.com

⊠ Henley began brewing in 2012 using a five-barrel plant. The brewery is situated in an old police station. The head brewer, James Godman, was previously the senior brewer at Hopback Brewery in Salisbury. Seasonal beers are available.

Jail House (ABV 3.9%)
A copper-coloured beer with a light, refreshing bitterness.

Temple Island (ABV 4.5%)
A hoppy pale ale.

Hensting

Hill View Farm, Hensting Lane, Owslebury, Hampshire, SO21 1LE
☎ 07775 601827 ⊠ rebecca@henstingbrewery.co.uk

⊠ Hensting Brewery was established in 2010 on the owner's farm using a 0.5-barrel plant. Beers are brewed using Maris Otter barley grown on the farm. Brewing is occasional while an upgrade to a six barrel plant is completed.

Hepworth SIBA

Beer Station, Railway Yard, Horsham, West Sussex, RH12 2NW
☎ (01403) 269696 ⊕ hepworthbrewery.co.uk
Sales 9am-6pm daily
Tours by arrangement

⊠ Hepworth's was established in 2001, initially bottling beer only. In 2003 draught beer brewing was started using Sussex malt and hops. Around 270 outlets are supplied direct. Seasonal beers are also available.

Traditional Sussex Bitter (OG 1035, ABV 3.6%) ◆
A fine, clean-tasting amber session beer. A bitter beer with a pleasant fruity and hoppy aroma that leads to a crisp, tangy taste. A long, dry finish.

Dark Horse (OG 1038, ABV 3.8%)

Summer Ale (OG 1038, ABV 3.8%)

Pullman First Class Ale (OG 1041, ABV 4.2%) ◆
A sweet, nutty maltiness and fruitiness are balanced by hops and bitterness in this easy-drinking, pale brown best bitter. A subtle bitter aftertaste.

Prospect Organic (OG 1045, ABV 4.5%)
A well-balanced and traditional brew.

Classic Old Ale (OG 1046, ABV 4.8%)
A traditional winter brew, rich with a variety of roasted malts balanced with sweetness and the bitterness of Admiral hops.

Iron Horse (OG 1048, ABV 4.8%) ◆
There's a fruity, toffee aroma to this light brown, full-bodied bitter. A citrus flavour balanced by caramel and malt leads to a clean, dry finish.

Hereford SIBA ◉

⊟ 88 St Owen Street, Hereford, HR1 2QD
☎ (01432) 342125 ⊠ jfkenyon@aol.com
Tours by arrangement

From its inception in 2000, the brewery has steadily increased production. In 2010 it's name changed from Spinning Dog to Hereford Brewery. Around 200 outlets are supplied. Seasonal and bottle-conditioned beers are also available.

Herefordshire Owd Bull (OG 1039, ABV 3.9%)
A session beer with an abundance of hops and bitterness. Dry, with a citrus aftertaste.

Dark (OG 1040, ABV 4%)
A dark, malty mild with a hint of bitterness and a touch of roast caramel. A smooth, drinkable ale.

Herefordshire Light Ale (HLA) (OG 1040, ABV 4%)
Light and refreshing.

Best Bitter (OG 1042, ABV 4.2%)
A full-bodied, amber-coloured best bitter, rich in malt undertones with a fresh, fruity aroma.

Gamekeepers Bitter (OG 1042, ABV 4.2%)

Celtic Gold (OG 1045, ABV 4.5%)
A bright gold best bitter full of fruit and blackcurrant flavours.

Mutleys Revenge (OG 1048, ABV 4.8%)
A strong, smooth, hoppy beer, amber-coloured and full-bodied with a dry citrus aftertaste.

Mutts Nutts (OG 1050, ABV 5%)
A dark, strong ale, full-bodied with a hint of chocolate aftertaste.

Hereward

50 Fleetwood, Ely, Cambridgeshire, CB6 1BH
☎ (01353) 666441
✉ michael.czarnobaj@ntlworld.com

A small home-based brewery launched in 2003 on a 10-gallon kit. The brewery mainly supplies beer festivals and also brews festival specials (brewed to order). Real cider is produced. Seasonal beers are also available.

Hesket Newmarket SIBA

Old Crown Barn, Back Green, Hesket Newmarket, Cumbria, CA7 8JG
☎ (01697) 478066 ⊕ hesketbrewery.co.uk
Shop Mon-Fri 8.30am-5pm; Sat 10am-2pm (summer)
Tours by arrangement

☺The brewery was established in 1988 and was bought by a co-operative of villagers in 1999, anxious to preserve a community resource. All the beers are named after local fells except for Doris's 90th Birthday Ale. Bottle-conditioned beers are available.

Blencathra Bitter (OG 1035, ABV 3.2%) ◀
A malty, tawny ale, mild and mellow for a bitter, with a dominant caramel flavour.

Haystacks (OG 1037, ABV 3.7%) ◀
Light, easy-drinking, thirst-quenching blond beer; very pleasant for its strength.

Skiddaw Special Bitter (OG 1037, ABV 3.7%)
An amber-coloured session beer, malty throughout. Well-balanced with a dryish finish.

Black Sail (OG 1042.1, ABV 4%) ◀
A sweet stout with roast flavours.

Helvellyn Gold (OG 1039, ABV 4%)
A smooth, golden bitter. Light in colour but full-flavoured.

High Pike (OG 1042, ABV 4.2%) ◀
A traditional style bitter; fruity with a dry finish.

Doris's 90th Birthday Ale (OG 1045, ABV 4.3%)
Fruity premium beer.

Scafell Blonde (OG 1043, ABV 4.4%) ◀
A hoppy, sweet, fruity, pale-coloured bitter.

Catbells Pale Ale (OG 1050, ABV 5%) ◀
Golden ale with a nice balance of fruity sweetness and bitterness, almost syrupy but with an unexpectedly dry finish.

Old Carrock Strong Ale (OG 1060, ABV 6%) 🍷 ◀
Reddy brown strong ale, vine-fruity in flavour with slightly astringent finish.

Hewitt's

See Brentwood

Hexhamshire SIBA ◉

Leafields, Ordley, Hexham, Northumberland, NE46 1SX
☎ (01434) 606577 ⊕ hexhamshire.co.uk

Hexhamshire was founded in 1993 and is run by one of the founding partners and his family. 30 outlets are supplied direct and many others through the SIBA direct delivery scheme.

Devil's Elbow (OG 1036, ABV 3.6%) ◀
Amber brew full of hops and fruit, leading to a bitter finish.

Shire Bitter (OG 1037, ABV 3.8%) ◀
A good balance of hops with fruity overtones, this amber beer makes an easy-drinking session bitter.

Blackhall English Stout (OG 1040, ABV 4%)
A pleasant bitter beer with a strong roast malt flavour.

Devil's Water (OG 1041, ABV 4.1%) ◀
Copper-coloured best bitter, well-balanced with a slightly fruity, hoppy finish.

Whapweasel (OG 1048, ABV 4.8%) ◀
An interesting smooth, hoppy beer with a fruity flavour. Amber in colour, the bitter finish brings out the fruit and hops.

Old Humbug (OG 1055, ABV 5.5%)

High House Farm SIBA

Matfen, Newcastle upon Tyne, NE20 0RG
☎ (01661) 886192/886769 (Sales line)
⊕ highhousefarmbrewery.co.uk
Shop Sun-Tue 10.30am-5pm; Thu-Sat 10.30am-9pm; closed Wed
Tours by arrangement

The brewery was founded in 2003 on a working farm with visitor centre, brewery shop and exhibition and function room. Over 350 outlets are supplied. Seasonal beers: see website.

Sundancer (OG 1036, ABV 3.6%)

Pullet Please (OG 1037, ABV 3.7%)
A pale gold-coloured refreshing ale with a delicate grapefruit nose and a crisp, dry finish. An easy-drinking bitter.

Auld Hemp (OG 1038, ABV 3.8%) 🍷 ◀
Tawny-coloured ale with hop, malt and fruit flavours and a good bitter finish.

Nel's Best (OG 1041, ABV 4.2%) ◀
Golden hoppy ale full of flavour with a clean, bitter finish.

Matfen Magic (OG 1046.5, ABV 4.8%) ◀
Well-hopped brown ale with a fruity aroma. Malt and chocolate overtones with a rich, bitter finish.

High Weald (NEW)

Unit 8, Bulrushes Business Park, Coombe Hill Road, East Grinstead, West Sussex, RH19 4LZ
☎ 07836 291430

Office: 23 Hermitage Road, East Grinstead, West Sussex, RH19 2BP ✉ andy@highwealdbrewery.co.uk
Tours by arrangement

Established by a keen home brewer, High Weald began brewing commercially in 2013. A limited number of local free houses, shops and festivals are supplied. Expansion of the beer range is planned. All beers are also available bottle-conditioned.

Best (OG 1038, ABV 3.8%)
A classic Sussex-style session bitter.

Greenstede Gold (OG 1040, ABV 4%)
Refreshing golden ale.

Wealden Pale Ale (OG 1041, ABV 4.1%)
A copper ale with good hop character and a long malty finish.

THE BREWERIES

Charcoal Burner (OG 1043, ABV 4.3%)
Traditional English stout. Roasted malts bring a rich flavour, combined with velvety smoothness from generous quantities of oats.

Highland SIBA

Swannay Brewery, Swannay by Evie, Birsay, Orkney, KW17 2NP
☎ (01856) 721700
⊕ highlandbrewingcompany.co.uk
Tours by arrangement

☺Brewing began in 2006 and bigger plant was installed a year later. A visitor centre, café and 20-barrel plant are planned. Around 300 outlets are supplied. Seasonal beers are also available.

Orkney Best (OG 1038, ABV 3.6%) 🗗 ◆
A refreshing, light-bodied, low gravity golden beer bursting with hop, peach and sweet malt flavours. The long, hoppy finish leaves a dry bitterness.

Island Hopping (OG 1039, ABV 3.9%) ◆
Fruity hoppiness with some caramel with a lasting bitter aftertaste.

Dark Munro (OG 1040, ABV 4%) 🗗 ◆
The nose presents an intense roast hit which is followed by summer fruits in the mouth. The strong roast malt continues into the aftertaste.

Scapa Special (OG 1042, ABV 4.2%) ◆
A good copy of a typical Lancashire bitter, full of bitterness and background hops, leaving your mouth tingling in the lingering aftertaste.

Orkney IPA (OG 1048, ABV 4.8%) 🗗 ◆
A traditional bitter, with light hop and fruit flavour throughout.

St Magnus Ale (OG 1049, ABV 5.2%) ▮ ◆
A complex, tawny bitter with a stunning balance of malt and hop and some soft roast. Full-bodied.

Orkney Blast (OG 1058, ABV 6%) ◆
Plenty of alcohol in this warming strong bitter/barley wine. A mushroom and woody aroma blossoms into a well-balanced smack of malt and hop in the taste.

Highwood

See Tom Wood (under W)

Highwood (Cann Do Beers) SIBA

Pool's Lane, Highwood, Essex, CM1 3QL
☎ (01245) 249300 ✉ canndobeers@btconnect.com
Brewing began in 2010 using a 10-barrel plant.

Essex IPA (ABV 3.6%)

Cannon's Gold (ABV 3.8%)

Hilden SIBA

Hilden House, Hilden, Lisburn, Co Antrim, BT27 4TY
☎ (028) 9266 0800 ⊕ hildenbrewery.co.uk
Shop Tue-Sun 12-2.30pm (3pm Sun) – Taproom restaurant
Tours by arrangement

☺Established in 1981, Hilden is Ireland's oldest independent brewery. Now in the second generation of family ownership, the beers are widely distributed across the UK. Occasional brews plus seasonals are also produced. Beers are regularly available in Wetherspoons in Northern Ireland.

Ale (OG 1038, ABV 4%) ◆
An amber-coloured beer with an aroma of malt, hops and fruit. The balanced taste is slightly slanted towards hops, and hops are also prominent in the full, malty finish.

Molly's Chocolate Stout (OG 1042, ABV 4.2%)
A dark chocolate-coloured beer with a full-bodied character.

Silver (OG 1042, ABV 4.2%)
A pale ale, light and refreshing on the palate but with a satisfying mellow hop character.

Headless Dog (OG 1042, ABV 4.3%)
A well-hopped bright amber-coloured ale.

Molly Malone (OG 1045, ABV 4.6%)
Dark ruby-red porter with complex flavours of hop bitterness and chocolate malt.

Scullion's Irish (OG 1045, ABV 4.6%)
A bright amber ale, initially smooth with a slight taste of honey that is balanced by a long, dry aftertaste that lingers on the palate.

Halt (OG 1058, ABV 6.1%)
A premium traditional Irish red ale with a malty, mild hop flavour. This special reserve derives its name from the local train stop, which was used to service the local linen mill.

Hill Island SIBA

Unit 7, Fowlers Yard, Back Silver Street, Durham, DH1 3RA
☎ 07740 932584 ⊕ myspace.com/hillisland
Shop Sat 10am-4pm
Tours by arrangement

☺Established in 2002, the brewery name is a literal translation of Dunholme from which Durham is derived. It is situated in the Fowlers Yard complex by the banks of the Wear in the heart of Durham City. Seasonal beers are available and brews can be crafted exclusively for individual pubs.

Peninsula Pint (OG 1036.5, ABV 3.7%)
Blonde and hoppy with a zesty aroma.

Bodkin's Bitter (OG 1038, ABV 3.8%)

Bitter (OG 1038, ABV 3.9%)
Red-gold in colour with pronounced caramel notes, balanced with grassy hop aromas.

Dun Cow Bitter (OG 1041, ABV 4.2%)
Golden ale with hints of caramel and citrus hop flavours.

Cathedral Ale (OG 1042, ABV 4.3%)
Ruby red ale with hints of roast malts and crisp bitterness.

Griffin's Irish Stout (OG 1045, ABV 4.5%)
Black and bitter. Traditional Irish-style stout.

Hobsons SIBA ◉

Newhouse Farm, Tenbury Road, Cleobury Mortimer, Shropshire, DY14 8RD
☎ (01299) 270837 ⊕ hobsons-brewery.co.uk
Shop Mon-Fri 9am-5pm
Tours by arrangement

Established in 1993 in a former sawmill, Hobsons relocated to a farm site with more space in 1995. A second brewery, bottling plant and a warehouse have been added along with significant expansion to the first brewery. Beers are supplied within a radius of 50 miles. The brewery has an onsite wind turbine and utilises environmental sustainable technologies where possible. Seasonal beer is also available.

Mild (OG 1034, ABV 3.2%) 🗂 ◆
A classic mild. Complex layers of taste come from roasted malts that predominate and give lots of flavour.

Twisted Spire (OG 1036, ABV 3.6%)
Blonde beer with a sweet floral aroma bringing bursts of refreshing flavour and a crisp, dry finish.

Best Bitter (OG 1038.5, ABV 3.8%) 🍴 ◆
A pale brown to amber-coloured, medium-bodied beer with strong hop character throughout. It is consequently bitter, but with malt discernible in the taste.

Town Crier (OG 1044, ABV 4.5%) 🗂
A full-flavoured, crisp golden ale, this straw-coloured bitter has a hint of sweetness complemented by subtle hop flavours, leading to a dry finish.

Hoggleys SIBA

Unit 12, Litchborough Industrial Estate, Northampton Road, Litchborough, Northamptonshire, NN12 8JB
☎ (01327) 831308 ⊕ hoggleys.co.uk
Tours by arrangement

Hoggleys was established in 2002 as a part-time brewery. It expanded to an eight-barrel plant in 2006, became full-time and moved to larger premises. Seasonal and bottle-conditioned beers are also available. Solstice Stout and Mill Lane Mild are suitable for vegans as are all bottle-conditioned beers.

Kislingbury Bitter (OG 1040, ABV 4%)

Mill Lane Mild (OG 1040, ABV 4%)

Northamptonshire Bitter (OG 1040, ABV 4%)

Brewery Tap Bitter (OG 1040, ABV 4.1%)

Reservoir Hogs (OG 1042, ABV 4.3%)
Gold-coloured, hoppy and refreshing.

Pump Fiction (OG 1045, ABV 4.5%)
Light copper-coloured, complex but easy drinking.

Indian Pale Ale (OG 1050, ABV 5%)

Solstice Stout (OG 1050, ABV 5%)

Hogs Back SIBA ◉

Manor Farm, The Street, Tongham, Surrey, GU10 1DE
☎ (01252) 783000 ⊕ hogsback.co.uk
Shop: see website
Tours by arrangement

This traditionally-styled brewery, established in 1992, boasts an extensive range of award-winning ales, brewed from the finest malted barley and whole English hops. The shop sells all the brewery's beers and related merchandise plus over 400 beers and ciders from around the world. Fully guided tours with tastings are available. Over half a million bottles are produced annually for home and export. Seasonal beers: see website.

HBB (Hogs Back Bitter) (OG 1039, ABV 3.7%) ◆

An aromatic session beer. Biscuity aroma with some hops and lemon notes. Well-balanced, plenty of hoppy impact in the mouth with a long-lasting dry hoppy bitter aftertaste.

TEA (Traditional English Ale) (OG 1044, ABV 4.2%) ◆
A tawny-coloured best bitter with more malt than hops present in the nose. These carry through into a well-rounded flavour with malt slightly dominant and more fruity sweetness than bitterness.

Hop Garden Gold (OG 1048, ABV 4.4%) ◆
Pale golden best bitter. Full-bodied and well-balanced with an aroma of malt, hops and fruit. Hoppy bitterness grows in an increasingly dry aftertaste with a hint of sweetness.

A Over T (Aromas Over Tongham) (OG 1094, ABV 9%) 🍴 ◆
A full-bodied, tawny-coloured barley wine. The malty aroma with hints of vanilla lead to a well-balanced taste where the hops cut through the underlying sweetness and dominate in the finish.

Hogswood SIBA

Higher Goshen, Mithian, St Agnes, Cornwall, TR5 0QE
☎ (01872) 554224 ☎ 07980 275897
⊕ hogswood.co.uk

⊠ Hogswood is a small family business set up in 2009 by Vaughan Haynes, a local CAMRA member. Currently with a production capacity of 2.5 barrels, on-site production of a bottle-conditioned range commenced in 2011.

Broken Piston (OG 1044, ABV 4.2%) ◆
Rich malt dominates this copper-coloured beer from start to finish. Sweet caramel is balanced by bitterness.

Black Boar (OG 1047, ABV 4.6%) ◆
Robust dark brown stout with aroma of roast malt. Rich flavour initially of grapes but turning to roast malt and sweetness. The finish is long, gaining caramel and nutty bitterness.

Holden's SIBA IFBB ◉

George Street, Woodsetton, Dudley, West Midlands, DY1 4LW
☎ (01902) 880051 ⊕ holdensbrewery.co.uk
Shop Mon-Fri 9am-5pm
Tours by arrangement

☺A family brewery spanning four generations, Holden's began life as a brew-pub in the 1920s. Continued expansion sees 20 tied pubs, a new brewhouse (completed in 2013) and a new shop. Seasonal beers: see website.

Black Country Mild (OG 1037, ABV 3.7%) 🍴 ◆
A good, red/brown mild; a refreshing, light blend of roast malt, hops and fruit, dominated by malt throughout.

Black Country Bitter (OG 1039, ABV 3.9%) ◆
A medium-bodied, golden ale; a light, well-balanced bitter with a subtle, dry, hoppy finish.

Golden Glow (OG 1045, ABV 4.4%) ◆
A pale golden beer with a subtle hop aroma plus gentle sweetness and a light hoppiness.

Special (OG 1052, ABV 5.1%) ◆
A sweet, malty, full-bodied amber ale with hops to balance in the taste and in the good, bittersweet finish.

THE BREWERIES

Holsworthy

Unit 5, Circuit Business Park, Clawton, Devon,
EX22 6RR
☎ (01566) 783678 ⊕ holsworthyales.co.uk
Shop open Sat afternoon
Tours by arrangement

Holsworthy began brewing in 2011 using a six-barrel plant, serving the surrounding rural community.

Tamar Sauce (OG 1041, ABV 4.1%)
A light refreshing pale ale with strong fruity notes balanced by hop bitterness.

Muck & Straw (OG 1044, ABV 4.4%)
A traditional English bitter with some delicate flavours in the finish.

Tamar Black (OG 1048, ABV 4.8%)
A rich, deep roasted stout, well-balanced beer with a pleasant finish.

Holt IFBB ◉

The Brewery, Empire Street, Cheetham, Manchester,
M3 1JD
☎ (0161) 834 3285 ⊕ joseph-holt.com
Shop Mon-Fri 9am-4pm

☺The brewery, established in 1849 by Joseph and Catherine Holt, is still a family-run business and is now in the hands of the great, great-grandson of the founder. It supplies approximately 130 outlets as well as its own estate of 130 tied pubs.

Mild (OG 1033, ABV 3.2%) ◆
A dark brown/red beer with a fruity, malty nose. Roast, malt, fruit and hops in the taste, with strong bitterness for a mild, and a dry malt and hops finish.

IPA (OG 1038, ABV 3.8%) ◆
Golden bitter with biscuity malt, hops and restrained lemon notes. Dry, bitter finish.

Bitter (OG 1040, ABV 4%) ◆
Copper-coloured beer with malt and hops in the aroma. Malt, hops and fruit in the taste with a bitter and hoppy finish.

Hook Norton SIBA IFBB ◉

The Brewery, Brewery Lane, Scotland End, Hook
Norton, Oxfordshire, OX15 5NY
☎ (01608) 737210 ⊕ hooky.co.uk
Visitor Centre & Shop Mon-Sat 9.30am-4.30pm
Tours by arrangement

⊠ Hook Norton was founded in 1849 by John Harris, a farmer and maltster. The current premises were built in 1900 and Hook Norton is one of the finest examples of a Victorian tower brewery. It is the oldest independent brewery in Oxfordshire, still housing much of the original machinery including a 25hp steam engine, which still operates occasionally. Seasonal beers: see website.

Hooky Mild (OG 1033, ABV 2.8%) ◆
A chestnut brown, easy-drinking mild. A complex malt and hop aroma give way to a well-balanced taste, leading to a long, hoppy finish that is unusual for a mild.

Hooky (OG 1036, ABV 3.5%) ◆
A classic golden session bitter. Hoppy and fruity aroma followed by a malt and hops taste and a continuing hoppy finish.

Lion (OG 1043, ABV 4%)
A complex fruity nose and bittersweet finish.

Old Hooky (OG 1048, ABV 4.6%) ◆
A strong. tawny-coloured bitter. A well-rounded fruity taste with a balanced bitter finish.

Double Stout (OG 1051, ABV 4.8%)

Hop Back SIBA ◉

Units 22-24, Batten Road Industrial Estate, Downton,
Salisbury, Wiltshire, SP5 3HU
☎ (01725) 510986 ⊕ hopback.co.uk
Tours by arrangement

Founded in 1987, Hop Back owns 10 pubs and distributes nationally. Monthly seasonal and bottle-conditioned beers are available. Entire Stout is suitable for vegans.

Heracles (OG 1028, ABV 2.8%)
Refreshing, slightly citrus beer with a clean, malty palate with plenty of aroma.

Golden Best (OG 1035, ABV 3.5%) ◆
A golden beer, with a light, clean quality that makes it an ideal session ale. A hoppy aroma and taste lead to a good, dry finish.

Redsells EKG (OG 1039, ABV 3.9%)
A classic English bitter. Burnished copper in colour with a strong malty flavour and a clean lemon and spice finish.

Crop Circle (OG 1041, ABV 4.2%) ◆
A refreshingly sharp and hoppy summer beer. Gold-coloured with a slight citrus taste. The crisp, dry aftertaste lingers.

Taiphoon (OG 1041, ABV 4.2%)
A light gold-coloured speciality beer flavoured with lemongrass.

Entire Stout (OG 1044, ABV 4.5%) ▣ ◆
A rich, dark stout with a strong roasted malt flavour and a long, sweet and malty aftertaste.

Summer Lightning (OG 1048, ABV 5%) ▣ ◆
A pleasurable pale bitter with a good, fresh, hoppy aroma and a malty, hoppy flavour. Finely balanced, it has an intense bitterness leading to a long, dry finish.

Hop Fuzz SIBA

Unit 8, Riverside Industrial Estate, West Hythe, Kent,
CT21 4NB
☎ (01303) 230304 ⊕ hopfuzz.co.uk

Hop Fuzz was started by two friends in 2011 and is situated on an industrial estate next to the Royal Military Canal (and a major cycle route) at West Hythe. The brewery is environmentally friendly, using solar power, recovering and reusing heat and supplying feed to the local animal park.

Martello (OG 1038, ABV 3.8%)

APA (OG 1040, ABV 4%)
Sweet and hoppy, with a citrus flavour.

English (OG 1040, ABV 4%)

Tomahawk (OG 1040, ABV 4%)
A light, refreshing ale, brewed using a single hop chosen for its delicate piney flavour.

Veteran (OG 1040, ABV 4%)

Steam Beer (OG 1044, ABV 4.4%)

Hop Kettle

▊ Red Lion, 74 High Street, Cricklade, Wiltshire, SN6 6DD

☎ (01793) 750776 ⊕ hopkettlebrewery.co.uk

Brewing began in 2012 using a four-barrel plant. The brewery is situated in a stone barn behind the Red Lion Inn in Cricklade. Many beer styles are brewed with some being barrel aged in whisky and rum casks on site.

Pond Skipper (ABV 3.8%)

Single Hop (ABV 4.1%)

North Wall (ABV 4.2%)

Snakes Head IPA (ABV 6.2%)

Flapjack Black (ABV 7.4%)

Hop Me Up

See Sleaford

Hop Monster SIBA

Common Road, Great Wakering, Essex, SS3 0AG

☎ 07771 871255 ⊕ hopmonster.co.uk

Tours by arrangement

⊠ Hop Monster and George's Brewery are owned by the same brewer, brewing on the same plant. George's concentrates on traditional styles and Hop Monster on the more unusual. Brewing began in 2011. Seasonal/special beers are available.

Freak Show (OG 1042.5, ABV 4.2%)
A copper-coloured beer full of malt and complex hop flavour. Permanent hop trial: different hops for each brew.

Banshee Porter (OG 1044, ABV 4.4%)
A complex porter made with 30% smoked malt.

Warlock Black IPA (OG 1044, ABV 4.4%)
Classic IPA flavour with a dark twist.

For the Trout Tavern, Southend:

Trout Ale (OG 1037.5, ABV 3.6%)

Under the George's Brewery name:

Wallasea Wench (OG 1037.5, ABV 3.6%)
Copper-coloured, easy-drinking beer with low bitterness and a smooth flavour.

Wakering Gold (OG 1039.5, ABV 3.8%)
Bursting with fresh hop aroma; a refreshing blend of English and American hops.

Best (OG 1041, ABV 4%)
Copper-coloured session bitter.

Broadsword (OG 1046, ABV 4.7%)
A ruby/copper-coloured ale with a malty, smooth start and a well-balanced dry finish.

Excalibur (OG 1051.5, ABV 5.4%)
Brewed in collaboration with Russ Barnes of Red Fox Brewery.

Merry Gentlemen (OG 1058, ABV 6%)
A warming winter ale. Dark chocolate, black cherries and old port flavours dominate this velvety old ale.

Excalibur Reserve (OG 1067, ABV 7.2%)
A citrus rush with fruit overtones and the warmth of an ancient Armagnac.

Hop & Stagger

▊ 3 West Castle Street, Bridgnorth, Shropshire, WV16 4AB

☎ (01746) 763962 ⊕ hopandstaggerbrewery.co.uk

Shop Sat & Sun 11am-4pm

Hop & Stagger began brewing in 2012 having set up a 2.5-barrel plant at the White Lion Inn in Bridgnorth. It brews a range of bitters and occasional seasonal ales exclusively for the pub.

Golden Wander (OG 1044, ABV 4.1%)
A crisp, pale golden ale with fruity notes and a light hopped finish.

High Town Ale (OG 1045, ABV 4.5%)
A sharp, pale golden ale with a good head and an extreme hoppy taste.

Hop Studio SIBA

3 Handley Park, Elvington Industrial Estate, York Road, Elvington, North Yorkshire, YO41 4AR

☎ (01904) 608029 ⊕ thehopstudio.co.uk

Brewing began in 2012 using a 10-barrel plant. Seasonal and occasional ales are also brewed. Free houses in Yorkshire and Humberside are supplied direct and the beers are available further afield by arrangement or via wholesalers.

XL (ABV 3%)

Blonde (ABV 3.5%)
A light crisp session bitter.

Pilsner (ABV 4%)
Clean, crisp-tasting Pilsner, with strong herbal aromas and a dry hop finish.

XP (ABV 4%)
Extra pale ale, full of hops with a dry bitter finish.

Gold (ABV 4.5%)
A full-flavoured, easy-drinking contemporary ale.

Obsidian (ABV 5%)

XS (ABV 5.5%)
Strong, malty and complex ale.

Vindhya (ABV 6%)

Hopcraft

See Pixie Spring

Hopdaemon SIBA

Unit 1, Parsonage Farm, Seed Road, Newnham, Kent, ME9 0NA

☎ (01795) 892078 ⊕ hopdaemon.com

Tours by arrangement

Hopdaemon began brewing on the edge of the historic city of Canterbury in 2000 and moved to the heart of the hop gardens of East Kent at Newnham in 2005. The brewery currently supplies more than 100 outlets and is working at full capacity.

Golden Braid (OG 1039, ABV 3.7%) ◥
A refreshing golden session bitter with a good blend of bittering and aroma hops underpinned by pale malt.

Incubus (OG 1041, ABV 4%) ◥
A well-balanced, copper-hued best bitter. Pale malt and a hint of crystal malt are blended with

THE BREWERIES

bitter and slightly floral hops to give a lingering hoppy finish.

Skrimshander IPA (OG 1045, ABV 4.5%)
An aromatic, copper-coloured pale ale with a refreshing taste and fruity finish.

Green Daemon (OG 1048, ABV 5%)
A golden beer with tropical fruit aromas and a crisp, clean finish. Brewed in the style of a Bavarian Helles (light lager).

Leviathan (OG 1057, ABV 6%)
A strong ruby ale with spicy hop aromas and a rich, malty finish.

Hope Valley

Castleton Youth Hostel, Castle Street, Castleton, Derbyshire, S33 8WG

Brewing started in 2009. The location is a brewing school and it does not produce beer commercially. However beers sometimes appear at beer festivals. The two-barrel plant was formerly used by Edale.

Hopping Mad SIBA

42 Yardley Road, Olney, Buckinghamshire, MK46 5ED
☎ (01234) 240880 ⊕ hoppingmad.com
Tours by arrangement

☺Hopping Mad began brewing in 2010 using an 11-barrel plant. Six regular beers are brewed as well as seasonal specials.

Hopnotch (OG 1034, ABV 3.6%)
A malty amber-coloured ale with a spicy and fruity hop finish.

Hoppiness (OG 1034, ABV 3.7%)
Traditionally-hopped, well-balanced English ale.

Balmy Days (OG 1036, ABV 3.9%)
A zesty, crisp and dry pale ale with hop aromas and a dry finish.

Brainstorm (OG 1040, ABV 4.3%)
A full-bodied yet crisp, drinkable traditional best bitter with a hoppy finish.

Fruitcase (OG 1041, ABV 4.5%)
A refreshing, well-balanced, golden ale with a fruity, citrus hoppiness.

Patriot (OG 1048, ABV 5%)
Triple hopped, full-bodied pale ale.

Hoppy Collie (NEW) SIBA

106 Fulham Palace Road, Fulham, London, W6 9PL
⊕ hoppycollie.com

No real ale.

Hopshackle SIBA

Unit F, Bentley Business Park, Blenheim Way, Northfields Industrial Estate, Market Deeping, Lincolnshire, PE6 8LD
☎ (01778) 348542 ⊕ hopshacklebrewery.co.uk
Tours by arrangement

☺Hopshackle was established in 2006 using a five-barrel plant. Monthly seasonals are brewed providing variety in styles and ABVs. More than 40 outlets are supplied direct. Bottle-conditioned beers are also available.

Simarillo (OG 1037, ABV 3.8%)

Gold-coloured beer with an aroma of citrus and soft fruits. The taste is tangy fruit with blackberry, plum and pineapple.

Hopstar SIBA

Unit 9, Rinus Business Park, Grimshaw Street, Darwen, Lancashire, BB3 2QX
☎ 07933 590159 ⊕ hopstarbrewery.co.uk
Tours by arrangement

☺Hopstar first brewed in 2004 on a 2.5-barrel kit and expanded in 2010 to a new unit with a six-barrel plant. More than 100 outlets are supplied around Lancashire and the Greater Manchester area. A brewery tap recently opened, Number 39 in Darwen.

Chilli (OG 1039, ABV 3.8%)

Dizzy Danny Ale (OG 1039, ABV 3.8%)

Dark Knight (OG 1041, ABV 4%)

JC (OG 1041, ABV 4%)

Lancashire Gold (OG 1041, ABV 4%)

Lush (OG 1041, ABV 4%)

Smokey Joe's Black Beer (OG 1041, ABV 4%)

For Jubilee Tower Brewing Co:

Paper Chain (ABV 3.8%)
Copper-coloured session beer.

Hornbeam SIBA

1-1c Grey Street, Denton, Manchester, M34 3RU
☎ (0161) 320 5627 ☎ 07984 443383
⊕ hornbeambrewery.com
Tours by arrangement

☺Hornbeam began brewing in 2007 on an eight-barrel plant. Regular monthly special beers are brewed. Seasonal beers: see website. Bottle-conditioned beers are also available.

Lemon Blossom (OG 1037, ABV 3.7%)
Golden, citrussy and light in colour.

Mary Rose (OG 1037, ABV 3.8%)
Chestnut-coloured bitter with an initial citrus taste, with floral and grassy notes in the finish.

Top Hop Best Bitter (OG 1041, ABV 4.2%)
Full-bodied with malt appeal and ample bitterness.

Black Coral Stout (OG 1043, ABV 4.5%)
A smooth, dry roast malt. Dark and full-bodied with a rich, creamy head. Satisfying with a subtle bitterness.

Hoskins Brothers

See Belvoir

Houston SIBA ◉

≣ South Street, Houston, Renfrewshire, PA6 7EN
☎ (01505) 612620 ⊕ houston-brewing.co.uk
Shop open pub hours, daily
Tours by arrangement

Established by Carl Wengel in 1997, the brewery is attached to the Fox & Hounds pub and restaurant. Houston deliver throughout Britain either direct or via a network of distributors. Seasonal and monthly beers: see website.

Killellan Bitter (OG 1037, ABV 3.7%) ◄
A light session ale, with a floral hop and fruity taste. The finish of this amber beer is dry and quenching.

APA (American Pale Ale) (OG 1039, ABV 3.9%)
A pale, refreshing citrus ale. Zingy and packed full of hop aroma with an intense fruit taste.

Blonde Bombshell (OG 1040, ABV 4%)
A gold-coloured ale with a fresh hop aroma and rounded maltiness.

Peter's Well (OG 1042, ABV 4.2%) ◄
Well-balanced fruity taste with sweet hop, leading to an increasingly bittersweet finish.

Slainte (OG 1043, ABV 4.3%)
Hops explode on the nose leaving an aroma of malt and hops. The taste is long and deep with mature fruit notes that linger.

Tartan Terror (OG 1045, ABV 4.5%)

Howard Town SIBA

Hawkshead Mill, Hope Street, Glossop, Derbyshire, SK13 7SS
☎ (01457) 869800 ⊕ howardtownbrewery.co.uk
Tours by arrangement

Howard Town was established in 2005 and is the Midlands most northerly brewery. More than 100 outlets are supplied – mainly as guest beers in the free trade. Seasonal and bottle-conditioned beers are available.

Mill Town (OG 1038, ABV 3.5%)
A dark mild, slightly sweet with a hint of liquorice.

Bleaklow (OG 1038, ABV 3.8%)
A session beer with a light citrus flavour.

Longdendale Lights (OG 1039, ABV 3.9%)
A pale, light, easy-drinking beer.

Monk's Gold (OG 1040, ABV 4%)
Light and hoppy.

Wren's Nest (OG 1042, ABV 4.2%)
A light, hoppy beer.

Dinting Arches (OG 1045, ABV 4.5%)
A copper-coloured beer, quite hoppy with a malty flavour with a hint of blackcurrant.

Glott's Hop (OG 1049, ABV 5%)
A strong, hoppy, full-flavoured bitter.

Dark Peak (OG 1062, ABV 6.4%)
A strong dark porter.

Howling Hops (NEW)

⊟ Cock Tavern, 315 Mare Street, Hackney, London, E8 1EJ ⊕ howlinghops.co.uk

⊗ Brewing began in 2012. A wide range of cask and bottle-conditioned beers are available with one-off speciality beers also produced using new hop varieties.

Mild (ABV 3.3%)

Pale Ale (ABV 3.8%)

Light Ale (ABV 4.2%)

Pale XX (ABV 5%)

Ruby Red (ABV 5%)

Smoked Porter (ABV 5.2%)

IPA (ABV 6%)

Old London Stout (ABV 6%)

Sarah Hughes

⊟ Beacon Hotel, 129 Bilston Street, Sedgley, Dudley, West Midlands, DY3 1JE
☎ (01902) 883381 ⊕ sarahhughesbrewery.co.uk
Tours by arrangement

Traditional Black Country Victorian tower brewery, taken over by Sarah Hughes in 1921. Brewing ceased in the 1950s and recommenced in 1987. The original grist case and rare open-topped copper give a unique character to the brews. The Beacon Hotel is the brewery tap. A seasonal winter beer is also brewed.

Pale Amber (OG 1038, ABV 4%)
A well-balanced beer, initially slightly sweet but with hops close behind.

Sedgley Surprise (OG 1048, ABV 5%) ◄
A bittersweet, medium-bodied, hoppy ale with some malt.

Dark Ruby Mild (OG 1058, ABV 6%) ◄
A dark ruby strong ale with a good balance of fruit and hops, leading to a pleasant, lingering hops and malt finish.

Humpty Dumpty SIBA

Church Road, Reedham, Norfolk, NR13 3TZ
☎ (01493) 701818 ☎ 07843 248865
⊕ humptydumptybrewery.co.uk
Shop 12-5 daily (Easter-end Oct); Sat 12.30-4pm (Nov-Xmas); closed Jan-Easter
Tours by arrangement

Established in 1998, this 11-barrel, award-winning brewery continues to grow and expand its range of beers. The on-site shop sells bottled beer from the brewery and local cider. Seasonal beers: see website.

Nord Atlantic (OG 1039, ABV 3.7%) ▣ ◄
Copper coloured, full bodied, with a grainy character this lively mix of malt, caramel and apple fruitiness provides something for all. Hops and a liquorice bitterness appear at the end.

Little Sharpie (OG 1040, ABV 3.8%) ◄
Pronounced malty aroma gives way to a swirling biscuity mix of malt and hop. Growing bitterness in a long finish.

Lemon and Ginger (OG 1041, ABV 4%)
An amber, crisp ale with a ginger and lemon tang.

Swallowtail (OG 1041, ABV 4%) ◄
Easy drinking with a malty bittersweet character following from a strong hop aroma. An amber hued crisp finishing beer.

Ale (OG 1043, ABV 4.1%) ◄
A hoppy vanilla fudge bouquet develops through the initial taste to become the signature flavour. Malt provides balance as a gentle bitterness quickly recedes. Long, sweet, sticky finish.

Broadland Sunrise (OG 1044, ABV 4.2%) ◄
Hoppy throughout with a strong malt and bitter background. A grainy mouthfeel, hoppy aroma and long strong finale.

Reedcutter (OG 1045, ABV 4.4%) ◄
A sweet, malty beer, golden hued with a gentle malt background. Smooth and full-bodied with a quick, gentle finish.

Cheltenham Flyer (OG 1048, ABV 4.6%) ◣
A full-flavoured golden, earthy bitter with a long, grainy finish. A strong hop bitterness dominates throughout. Little evidence of malt.

East Anglian Pale Ale (OG 1046, ABV 4.6%) ◣
A heavy sulphurous nose is lightened by hints of rhubarb. This carries into the flavour where a fruity sweetness contrasts with a grainy hoppiness. A long finish.

Norfolk Nectar (OG 1048, ABV 4.6%) ◣
A sweet honeyed note wraps around other flavours and aromas. Hops and caramel maintain a presence throughout to give a counterpoint to the rich, sweet base.

Hunsbury Craft

23 Limefields Way, East Hunsbury, Northampton, NN4 0SA
☎ (01604) 766228 ☎ 07798 907242
✉ johngeorgemargetts@tiscali.co.uk

Hunsbury Craft was established in 2010 using a 0.5-barrel plant, increasing to 2.25-barrels to meet demand.

Copper (OG 1041, ABV 4.2%)

JD's Robust Porter (OG 1051, ABV 5.4%)

Mel's Mild (OG 1054, ABV 5.4%)

Young Chick (OG 1060, ABV 6%)

Hunter's SIBA

Bulleigh Barton Farm, Ipplepen, Devon, TQ12 5UE
☎ (01803) 814399 ☎ 07540 657115
⊕ thehuntersbrewery.co.uk

Hunters began brewing in 2008 on a five-barrel brew plant. Expansion means the brewery now has six fermenters and is capable of a 60-barrel brew length. Seasonal and bottle-conditioned beers are also available.

Crack Shot (OG 1038, ABV 3.8%)

Half Bore (OG 1040, ABV 4%)

Denbury Dreamer (OG 1042, ABV 4.2%)

Pheasant Plucker (OG 1043, ABV 4.3%)

Hurns

See Tomos Watkin (under W)

Hurst (NEW) SIBA

Western Road, Hurstpierpoint, West Sussex, BN6 9SP
☎ 07866 438953 ✉ hurstbrewery@hotmail.co.uk
Tours by arrangement

Hurst began brewing in 2013 using a four-barrel plant. Seasonal beer is also available.

Founders Bitter (ABV 4.2%)

Hydes IFBB ◉

The Beer Studio, 30 Kansas Avenue, Salford, M50 2GL
☎ (0161) 226 1317 ⊕ hydesbrewery.com

◉Hydes is a family-owned brewery dating from 1863. It had been on the same site for more than 120 years but moved to a new site in Salford in 2012. The brewery currently focuses entirely on the production of cask ales to be supplied to its own tied estate of more than 70 pubs and the wholesale market. Hydes also produce a range of cask-conditioned beers using rare hops and malts separately marketed as The Beer Studio.

Light Mild/1863 (OG 1033.5, ABV 3.5%) ◣
Lightly hopped, pale brown session beer with some hops, malt and fruit in the taste and a short, dry finish.

Owd Oak (OG 1033.5, ABV 3.5%) ◣
Dark brown/red in colour, with a fruit and malt nose. Taste includes biscuity malt and green fruits, with a satisfying aftertaste.

Original Bitter (OG 1036.5, ABV 3.8%) ◣
Pale brown beer with a malty nose, malt and an earthy hoppiness in the taste, and a good bitterness through to the finish.

Hyde's Finest (OG 1044, ABV 4.5%)
Full-bodied and slightly sweet.

Iceni SIBA

Foulden Road, Ickburgh, Norfolk, IP26 5HB
☎ (01842) 878922 ⊕ icenibrewery.co.uk
Shop Mon-Fri 8.30am-5pm; Sat 9am-3pm
Tours by arrangement

Iceni was launched in 1995 by Brendan Moore. The brewery is also the headquarters of the East Anglian Brewers Co-op (EAB).

Fine Soft Day (OG 1038, ABV 4%) ◣
Toffee tickles both the nostrils and tastebuds as it hovers over a creamy, lightly-hopped backdrop in this golden brew. A gentle mix of flavours softly sinks into a pleasant sweetness.

Idle SIBA

⊞ White Hart Inn, Main Street, West Stockwith, South Yorkshire, DN10 4EY
☎ (01427) 753226 ☎ 07949 137174
✉ theidlebrewery@btinternet.com
Tours by arrangement

⊕The brewery began production in 2007 and is situated in a converted stable at the back of the White Hart Inn alongside the River Idle. Seasonal beers are also available.

Golden Crown (OG 1038, ABV 3.8%)

Dog (OG 1041, ABV 4.2%)
A copper-coloured ale, moderately hoppy with a good balance of malt and hops leading to a bitter finish.

Sod (OG 1041, ABV 4.2%)

Tongue (OG 1041, ABV 4.2%)

Black & Tan (OG 1042, ABV 4.3%)

Black Abbot (OG 1044, ABV 4.6%)

Idle Landlord (OG 1044, ABV 4.6%)
A dark brown ale with plenty of body, a malty flavour and a caramel/coffee finish.

Ilkley SIBA ◉

The New Brewery, Ashlands Road, Ilkley, West Yorkshire, LS29 8JT
☎ (01943) 604604 ⊕ ilkleybrewery.co.uk
Tours by arrangement

Ilkley began brewing in 2009 on an eight-barrel plant, bringing brewing back to the town after a gap of some 80 years. In 2011 the brewery moved to larger premises and upgraded to a 20-barrel plant with plans for further expansion. Seasonal and bottle-conditioned beers: see website.

Mary Jane (OG 1037, ABV 3.5%)
A refreshing and satisfying pale ale.

Black (OG 1040, ABV 3.7%)
A dark beer, mellow with a hint of liquorice in the finish and berry fruits and coffee on the nose.

Joshua Jane (ABV 3.7%)
A rich, nut-brown Yorkshire ale with a light caramel sweetness, modest salt and a keen, lasting bitterness.

Gold (OG 1040, ABV 3.9%) ◈
An easy drinking, golden-coloured ale with a light floral aroma leading to a soft citrus fruit flavour and a gentle bitter aftertaste.

Best (OG 1041, ABV 4%) ▣
A highly hopped golden ale with a strong, bitter finish.

Pale (OG 1042, ABV 4.2%)
A dry, crisp pale ale heavily hopped to give a strong but mellow floral finish.

Lotus IPA (OG 1055, ABV 5.6%)
Golden-coloured IPA with strong aromas and flavours of mango and grapefruit. Warming and smooth with a powerful, dry bitter finish.

Imperial

▤ Arcadia Hall, Cliff Street, Mexborough, South Yorkshire, S64 9HU
☎ 07428 422703
✉ imperial.brewery@btinternet.com

Five regular beers are produced on a six-barrel tower brewery system located in the basement of the Imperial Club, Mexborough. The brewery provides beers for the club as well as other local outlets.

Best Bitter (OG 1040, ABV 3.9%)

Blonde (OG 1042, ABV 4%)

Bees Knees (ABV 4.2%)

Darkness (OG 1042, ABV 4.2%)

Stout (OG 1047, ABV 4.6%)

Independent Lakeland

See Strands

Indian Summer SIBA

Unit 3, Ashdon Road Commercial Centre, Saffron Walden, Essex, CB10 2NH
☎ 07986 637826 ∰ bombayblonde.co.uk

⊗ Indian Summer began brewing in 2012. Beers are branded as the Hop & Soul range. A bottled ale is also produced for Indian restaurants.

Hop & Soul Mild (OG 1038, ABV 3.7%)

Hop & Soul Amber (OG 1038, ABV 3.8%)
Light amber-coloured with gentle bitterness and a warm, nutty finish.

Hop & Soul Blonde (OG 1045, ABV 4.5%)

Well-balanced, light and refreshing with a pleasant mouthfeel.

Hop & Soul Porter (OG 1047, ABV 4.6%)

Inishmacsaint

7 Drumadown Road, Drumskimly, Derrygonnelly, County Fermanagh, BT93 6DN
☎ (028) 6864 1031 ✉ gordyfallis@hotmail.com

Inishmacsaint is a small-scale brewery that has been in production since 2009 brewing mainly bottle-conditioned beers. A larger brew plant has now come on stream.

Innis & Gunn

Canning Street, Edinburgh, EH3 8EG
☎ (0131) 272 2782 ∰ innisandgunn.com

Innis & Gunn does not brew but Tennents produces one regular bottled (not bottle-conditioned) beer for the company, Oak Aged Beer (ABV 6.6%). There are three further beers in the permanent range: Original (ABV 6.6%), Blonde (ABV 6%) and Rum Cask (ABV 7.4%). A range of limited edition beers is also produced each year.

Interbrew Magor

Magor Brewery, Magor, NP26 3DA

UK subsidiary of AB InBev. No real ale.

Interbrew Samlesbury

Cuerdale Lane, Samlesbury, Lancashire, PR5 0XD

UK subsidiary of AB InBev. No real ale.

Inveralmond SIBA ◉

22 Inveralmond Place, Inveralmond, Perth, PH1 3TS
☎ (01738) 449448 ∰ inveralmond-brewery.co.uk
Shop Mon-Fri 10am-5pm
Tours by arrangement

Established in 1997, Inveralmond was the first brewery in Perth for more than 30 years. The brewery has expanded from a 10-barrel to a 30-barrel plant and there are plans for further growth. Around 250 outlets are supplied. Seasonal beers: see website.

Independence (OG 1040, ABV 3.8%) ◈
A well-balanced Scottish ale with fruit and malt tones. Hop provides an increasing bitterness in the finish.

Ossian (OG 1042, ABV 4.1%) ◈
Well-balanced best bitter with a dry finish. This full-bodied amber ale is dominated by fruit and hop with a bittersweet character although excessive caramel can distract from this.

Thrappledouser (OG 1043, ABV 4.3%) ◈
A refreshing amber beer with reddish hues. The crisp, hoppy aroma is finely balanced with a tangy but quenching taste.

Lia Fail (OG 1048, ABV 4.7%) ◈
The Gaelic name means Stone of Destiny. A dark, robust, full-bodied beer with a deep malty taste. Smooth texture and balanced finish.

Sunburst Pilsner (OG 1045, ABV 4.8%)

Ironbridge

Unit 7, Merrythought, The Wharfage, Ironbridge,
Telford, Shropshire, TF8 7NJ
☎ (01952) 433910 ⊕ ironbridgebrewery.co.uk
Shop & Bar Thu Sat 12-6pm
Tours by arrangement

☺Ironbridge was established in 2008 and operates
on a 12-barrel brewery in an old Victorian
warehouse alongside the River Severn in the heart
of the Ironbridge Gorge. A visitor centre and shop
were opened in 2009. Wenlock Stout is on limited
supply and is stored for four weeks and supplied in
oak casks.

Blond (OG 1037, ABV 3.6%)

IPA (Ironbridge Pale Ale) (OG 1040, ABV 4%)

Gold (OG 1045, ABV 4.4%)

Stout (OG 1052, ABV 5.1%)

Irving SIBA ◉

Unit G1, Railway Triangle, Walton Road, Portsmouth,
Hampshire, PO6 1TQ
☎ (023) 9238 9988 ⊕ irvingbrewers.co.uk
Shop Thu & Fri 3-6pm
Tours by arrangement

⊗ Irving's was set up by former Gale's brewer
Malcolm Irving and a small team of ex-Gale's
employees using a 15-barrel plant. Around 60
outlets are supplied direct. Seasonal beers: see
website.

Frigate (OG 1039, ABV 3.8%)
Golden bitter with citrus hop flavour
complemented by a background sweetness.

Type 42 (OG 1042, ABV 4.2%)
A robust best bitter with a deep ruby red hue
balancing sweet hedgerow berry notes with a
long, roasted malt finish and a deep bitterness.

Admiral Stout (OG 1042.5, ABV 4.3%)
A classic dark oatmeal stout, deep black in colour
with a smooth, rounded malt flavour balanced with
a strong bitterness.

Invincible (OG 1048, ABV 4.6%) ◆
A tawny-coloured strong bitter. Sweet and fruity
with an underlying maltiness throughout and a
dryness that increases gradually, contrasting well
with the sweetness of the finish.

Irwell Works SIBA

Irwell Street, Ramsbottom, Lancashire, BL0 9YQ
☎ (01706) 825019 ⊕ irwellworksbrewery.co.uk
Tours by arrangement

☺Irwell Works started brewing in 2010 in a
building dating from 1888 that once housed the
Irwell Works Steam, Tin, Copper & Iron Works. It
now houses a six-barrel plant. A bar opened on the
first floor in 2011.

Lightweights & Gentlemen (ABV 3.2%)
Refreshing, light session ale.

Tin Plate (ABV 3.6%)
A rich, roasted dark mild.

Copper Plate (OG 1037, ABV 3.8%)
Traditional copper-coloured bitter. Complex
bitterness with a strong hop character.

Richard Mason 1888 (OG 1039, ABV 4%)

Refreshing light-coloured pale ale.

Steam Plate (ABV 4.3%)
Traditional golden-coloured best bitter. Mild
bitterness and a refreshing citrus hop aroma.

Iron Plate (OG 1042, ABV 4.4%)
Lancashire Stout. Sweet stout with roasted barley
aromas and a dark chocolate aftertaste.

Mad Dogs & Englishmen (ABV 5.5%)
An easy-drinking IPA.

Isca SIBA

The Brewery, Court Farm, Holcombe Village, Dawlish,
Devon, EX7 0JT
☎ 07773 444501 ✉ iscaales@yahoo.co.uk

Two CAMRA members took over Gargoyles
Brewery in 2009 under the name Isca Ales. 10
outlets are supplied. Bottle-conditioned beers are
available.

Citra (ABV 3.8%)

Golden Ale (OG 1038, ABV 3.8%)

Dawlish Bitter (OG 1042, ABV 4.2%)
An amber-coloured beer with a fresh, hoppy
aftertaste.

Glorious Devon (ABV 4.4%)

Falcon Gold (ABV 4.5%)

Dawlish Pale (ABV 5%)

Achilles (ABV 5.4%)

Isfield SIBA ◉

Unit 16, New Place Farm, Framfield, East Sussex,
TN22 5RH
☎ (01825) 750633 ☎ 07803 716758

Office: Imperial Cottage, Station Road, Isfield, East
Sussex, TN22 5UJ ✉ enquiries@isfieldbrewing.co.uk

⊗ Isfield began brewing in 2012 using a five-barrel
plant. Seasonal beer is also available.

Straw Blond (OG 1042, ABV 4.1%)

Imperial Pale Ale (OG 1043, ABV 4.2%)

Toad in the Ale (OG 1050, ABV 4.8%)

Island SIBA

Dinglers Farm, Yarmouth Road, Newport, Isle of
Wight, PO30 4LZ
☎ (01983) 821731 ⊕ isleofwightbrewery.com
Tours by arrangement

⊗ Island Brewery is the realisation of Tom
Minshull's ambition to brew real ales to
complement the existing family-owned drinks
distribution business. Brewing commenced in 2010
using a 12-barrel brewery. 45 outlets are supplied
direct.

Nipper Bitter (OG 1038, ABV 3.8%)
Straw-coloured, light and refreshing with a good
balance of malt and hops and a satisfying afterbite.

Wight Gold (OG 1040, ABV 4%)
Golden brown in colour with rounded malt and
hops throughout.

Yachtsmans Ale (OG 1042, ABV 4.2%)
Chestnut-coloured ale with a rich, malty mouthfeel
and hop aroma.

Wight Diamond (OG 1046, ABV 4.4%)
Wight Knight (OG 1045, ABV 4.5%)
Strong, full-bodied beer.

Vectis Venom (OG 1048, ABV 4.8%)
Easy-drinking with an underlying smoothness.

Earls RDA (OG 1052, ABV 5%)
Rich yet understated stout, with strong espresso aftertaste.

Islay SIBA

The Brewery, Islay House Square, Bridgend, Isle of Islay, PA44 7NZ
☎ (01496) 810014 ⊕ islayales.com
Shop Mon-Sat 10.30am-5pm
Tours by arrangement

☺Brewing started on a four-barrel plant in a converted tractor shed in 2004. The brewery shop is next door. The island is more famous for its whisky, but the brewery has established itself as a must-see place for those visiting the eight working distilleries. Bottle-conditioned beers are available. Special beers are also brewed.

Finlaggan Ale (OG 1039, ABV 3.7%)
A mid brown beer with a gentle, rounded bitterness and a fresh, fruity and hoppy flavour.

Black Rock Ale (OG 1040, ABV 4.2%)
A reddish beer with a soft, nutty flavour, a robust body and a floral, grassy and herbal nose.

Dun Hogs Head Ale (OG 1044, ABV 4.4%)
A dark, dry stout with a fruity edge and dry bitterness.

Saligo Ale (OG 1044, ABV 4.4%)
A golden ale with a rounded bitterness and a refreshing citrussy, lemon and grapefruit nose and taste.

Angus Og Ale (OG 1045, ABV 4.5%)

Ardnave Ale (OG 1048, ABV 4.6%)
A dry, thirst-quenching, hoppy bitter.

Nerabus Ale (OG 1046, ABV 4.8%)
A deep ruby-coloured brew with a black treacle, spicy flavour balanced by the use of spicy and citrussy hops.

Single Malt Ale (OG 1050, ABV 5%)
A pale beer with a sweet edge and a long, bitter finish.

Isle of Avalon

See Wessex

Isle of Mull

See Argyll

Isle of Purbeck SIBA

⊟ Manor Road, Studland, Dorset, BH19 3AU
☎ (01929) 450227 ⊕ isleofpurbeckbrewery.com
Tours by arrangement

⊠ Founded in 2003, the brewery is situated in the grounds of the Bankes Arms Hotel, overlooking Studland Bay on the Jurassic Coast. Expansion has converted the brewery from a 10-barrel to a 20-barrel plant. The beers can be found all over Dorset and nationally due to swaps with other microbreweries. Seasonal and bottle-conditioned beers are available.

Best Bitter (OG 1036, ABV 3.6%) ◣
A classic malty best bitter with rich malt aroma and taste and smooth malty bitter finish.

Fossil Fuel (OG 1040, ABV 4.1%) ◣
Amber bitter with complex aroma with a hint of pepper; rich malt dominates the taste, leading to a smooth dry finish.

Studland Bay Wrecked (OG 1044, ABV 4.5%) ◣
Deep red ale with slightly sweet aroma reflecting a mixture of caramel, malt and hops that lead to a dry, malty finish.

Isle of Purbeck Ale (IPA) (OG 1047, ABV 4.8%) ◣
A novel twist on an old style of ale; golden-amber with a spicy hop aroma and well-balanced taste and aroma, leading to a dry bitter, hoppy finish.

Isle of Skye

The Pier, Uig, Isle of Skye, IV51 9XP
☎ (01470) 542471 ⊕ skyebrewery.co.uk
Shop Mon-Sat 10am-6pm; Sun 12.30-4.30pm (Apr-Oct)

☺The Isle of Skye Brewery was established in 1995. Originally a 10-barrel plant, it was upgraded to 20-barrels in 2004. Fermenting capacity stands at 80 barrels, with further plans to increase this and upgrade bottling facilities. Seasonal beers: see website.

Tarasgeir (OG 1040, ABV 4%) ◣
The peat roasted barley dominates giving a mellow peaty whisky taste.

Young Pretender (OG 1039, ABV 4%) ◣
A fruity, full-bodied golden ale, predominantly hoppy and fruity. The bitterness in the mouth is also balanced by summer fruits and hops, continuing into the lingering bitter finish.

Red Cuillin (OG 1041, ABV 4.2%) ▊ ◣
A light, fruity nose with a hint of caramel leads to a hoppy, malty, fruity flavour and a dry, bittersweet finish.

Hebridean Gold (OG 1041.5, ABV 4.3%) ◣
Porridge oats are used to produce this delicious speciality beer. Nicely balanced. it has a refreshingly soft fruity, bitter flavour with an oaty background.

Black Cuillin (OG 1044, ABV 4.5%) ⬒ ◣
A complex, tasty brew worthy of its many awards. Full-bodied with a malty richness. Malt holds sway but there are plenty of hops and fruit to be discovered in its varied character. A delicious Scottish old ale.

Blaven (OG 1047, ABV 5%) ◣
A well-balanced strong amber bitter with kiwi fruit and caramel in the nose and a lingering sharp bitterness.

Cuillin Beast (OG 1066, ABV 7%) ⬒ ▊ ◣
A winter warmer; sweet and fruity, and much more drinkable than the strength would suggest. Plenty of caramel throughout with a variety of fruit on the nose.

Itchen Valley SIBA ◉

Unit 4, Prospect Commercial Park, Prospect Road, New Alresford, Hampshire, SO24 9QF
☎ (01962) 735111/736429 ⊕ itchenvalley.com

THE BREWERIES

Shop Mon-Fri 9am-5pm
Tours by arrangement

⊠ Established in 1997, Itchen Valley moved to new premises in 2006 with a 20-barrel plant. The brewery has a gift shop and offers brewery tours and mini conferencing facilities. More than 350 pubs are supplied, with wholesalers used for further distribution. Seasonal and bottle-conditioned beers as well as monthly specials are available.

Godfathers (OG 1038, ABV 3.8%) ◆
A pale brown bitter, with a malty aroma and taste and a light body, leading to a bittersweet finish.

Fagin's (OG 1041, ABV 4.1%) ◆
Enjoyable copper-coloured best bitter with a hint of crystal malt and a pleasant bitter aftertaste.

Hampshire Rose (OG 1042, ABV 4.2%)
A golden amber ale. Fruit and hops dominate the taste throughout, with a good mouthfeel.

Winchester Ale (OG 1042, ABV 4.5%)
Traditional English bitter, nut brown with a sweet, malty flavour and a good hoppy nose.

Pure Gold (OG 1046, ABV 4.8%) ◆
An aromatic hoppy, strong bitter. Golden in colour, with initial maltiness and grapefruit flavours counter-balanced with some sweetness, leading to a dry finish.

Jacobi

Penlanwen Farm, Pumsaint, Carmarthenshire, SA19 8RR
☎ (01558) 650605 ⊕ jacobibrewery.co.uk

Brewing started in 2006 in a converted barn. Brewer Justin Jacobi is also the owner of the Brunant Arms in Caio, which is a regular outlet for the beers. A visitor centre and bottling line are planned.

Light Ale (OG 1038, ABV 3.8%)

Red Squirrel (OG 1040, ABV 4%)
Auburn coloured beer with fruit undertones and a dry bitter finish.

Dark Ale (OG 1052, ABV 5%)

James & Kirkman

▤ rear of Robin Hood, 4 Wakefield Road, Pontefract, West Yorkshire, WF8 4HN
☎ (01977) 702231
✉ eastcoastbrewing@hotmail.co.uk

Brewing began in 2013 behind the Robin Hood pub using a 2.5-barrel plant. Beers were previously brewed at East Coast Brewing (qv), owned by the same brewers. Pubs and festivals in the local area are supplied. Special beers are planned.

Star Light (OG 1032, ABV 3.2%)
A light, fruity bitter.

Jarrow SIBA ◉

▤ The Maltings, 9 Claypath Lane, South Shields, Tyne & Wear, NE33 4PG
☎ (0191) 483 6792 ⊕ jarrowbrewery.co.uk
Tours by arrangement

◉Real ale enthusiasts Jess and Alison McConnell commenced brewing at the Robin Hood, Jarrow, in 2002. In 2008 all brewing was transferred to the Maltings in South Shields. Seasonal and bottle-conditioned beers are also available.

Jarrow Bitter (OG 1037.5, ABV 3.8%)

Rivet Catcher (OG 1039, ABV 4%) ◆
A light, smooth, satisfying gold bitter. Subtle fruity hops give the taste profile on the tongue and nose.

Joblings Swinging Gibbet (OG 1041, ABV 4.1%)
A copper-coloured, well-balanced beer with a good hop aroma and a fruity finish.

Red Ellen (OG 1042.5, ABV 4.4%)
A rich ruby red, full-bodied ale with a citrus hop aroma.

McConnells Irish Stout (OG 1045, ABV 4.6%) ▣ ◆
A rich, creamy stout with a long, lingering liquorice and pale chocolate finish.

Westoe IPA (OG 1044.5, ABV 4.6%)
A pale, easy-drinking gold ale with a soft malt character and complex hop aroma.

Isis (OG 1049, ABV 5%)
A well-balanced golden premium ale with a full hop aroma and grapefruit presence on the palate.

Jennings ◉

Castle Brewery, Cockermouth, Cumbria, CA13 9NE
☎ 0845 129 7185 ⊕ jenningsbrewery.co.uk
Shop Mon-Sat 10am-4pm
Tours by arrangement

◉Jennings Brewery was established as a family concern in 1828 in the village of Lorton. The company moved to its present location in 1874. Pure Lakeland water is still used for brewing, drawn from the brewery's own well. Monthly seasonal beers are available. Part of Marston's PLC.

Dark Mild (OG 1031, ABV 3.1%) ◆
A well-balanced, dark brown mild with a malty aroma, strong roast taste, not over-sweet, with some hops and a slightly bitter finish.

Bitter (OG 1035, ABV 3.5%) ◆
A malty beer with a good mouthfeel that combines with roast flavour and a hoppy finish.

Nuture Lakeland Ale (ABV 3.8%)
5p from every pint sold is donated to Nuture Cumbria who are involved in restoring the fells.

Cumberland Ale (OG 1039, ABV 4%) ◆
A light, creamy, hoppy beer with a dry aftertaste.

Cocker Hoop (OG 1044, ABV 4.6%)
A rich, creamy, copper-coloured beer with raisiny maltiness balanced with a resiny hoppiness, with a developing bitterness towards the end.

Sneck Lifter (OG 1051, ABV 5.1%) ▣ ◆
A strong, dark brown ale with a complex balance of fruit, malt and roast flavours through to the finish.

Jo C's (NEW) SIBA

The Old Store, Walsingham Road, West Barsham, Norfolk, NR21 9NP
☎ (01328) 863854 ⊕ jocsnorfolkale.co.uk

Starting in 2010, Jo Coubrough (the county's only brewster) established a 10-barrel brewery in a former farm building in Norfolk. The beers are available in Flying Kiwi Inns and other free trade outlets.

Norfolk Kiwi (ABV 3.8%)
An easy-drinking, straw-coloured bitter.

Bitter Old Bustard (ABV 4.3%)
A russet-coloured ale with warm, nutty biscuit flavours coming through a smooth malt body.

Knot Just Another IPA (ABV 5%)
Amber-coloured strong bitter with plenty of hop character and balancing bitterness. Often develops fruity notes.

Jolly Sailor (NEW) SIBA

Unit 2, Riccall Business Park, Riccall, York, North Yorkshire, YO19 6QR
☎ (01757) 268918 ☎ 07923 635755
✉ dr_david_welsh@yahoo.co.uk

Jolly Sailor began brewing in 2012 at a former mine site near York, now Ricall Business Park. Beers are produced mainly for the Jolly Sailor in Cawood but can also be found in other local outlets.

Bullseye Bitter (ABV 3.8%)

Jolly Blonde (ABV 3.8%)

Jolly Scotsman's Bitter (ABV 3.8%)
A fruity amber ale with citrus notes.

Yellow Jersey (ABV 3.8%)
A pale ale brewed with English hops.

Cue Brew (ABV 4%)

Jollyboat SIBA

The Coach House, Buttgarden Street, Bideford, Devon, EX39 2AU
☎ (01237) 424343
Tours by arrangement

⊠ Established in 1995, the brewery is named after a sailor's leave vessel and all the beers have a nautical theme. Most outlets supplied are in Devon.

Plunder (OG 1047, ABV 4.8%)
Red/brown beer with an aromatic nose, a good balance of malt, hops and fruit present throughout, leading to a bitter finish.

Contraband (OG 1056, ABV 5.8%)
Dark brown in colour with chocolate, roasted malts, raisins and some spiciness in the aroma. Cinnamon and nutmeg spiciness melds with chocolate and fruity flavours with strong roasty bitterness in the finish.

Joule's SIBA

The Brewery, Great Hales Street, Market Drayton, Shropshire, TF9 1JP
☎ (01630) 654400 ⊕ joulesbrewery.co.uk
Tours by arrangement

The brewery opened in 2010 after a break of 40 years. It is situated in Market Drayton in order to source the purest mineral water which, as before, is the essential foundation for its ales.

Blonde (OG 1038, ABV 3.8%)
A well-balanced, light and refreshing blonde beer with a citrus and hoppy aroma.

Pale Ale (OG 1042, ABV 4.1%)
A crisp, fresh beer with initial impact giving way to a pleasant bitter finish.

Slumbering Monk (OG 1045, ABV 4.5%)
Full-bodied with a deep, malty and nutty fullness. Hints of caramel give a round, soft, satisfying

smoothness to this bright copper-coloured ale, cut with light bitterness.

Jubilee Tower (NEW)

Correspondence: 4 Moor Close, Darwen, Lancashire, BB3 3LG

Brewing began in 2012 using spare capacity at Hopstar Brewery; Hopstar distributes the beer through its business.

Paper Chain (ABV 3.8%)
A copper-coloured session beer.

Junction (NEW)

🏠 1 Baildon Road, Baildon, Shipley, West Yorkshire, BD17 6AB
☎ (01274) 582009

Junction is a small microbrewery established in 2012 in the cellar of the Junction pub in Baildon, brewing about 300 gallons a week. Beer is sold in the pub and other local outlets. Bottle-conditioned beer is also available.

Tommy's Tipple (ABV 3.7%)
A chestnut session bitter; smooth tasting with a hoppy finish.

Blonde (ABV 4%)
A blonde session bitter, offering a big flavour and a dry finish.

Dark Thoughts (ABV 4.6%)
A porter with roasted, nutty flavours and hops which give a bitter edge.

Just A Minute

c/o Deerness Rubber Co Ltd, Coulson Street, Spennymoor, County Durham, DL16 7RS
☎ 07586 896091
⊠ justaminutebrew@btinternet.com

Just A Minute was established by two friends in 2010, initially with experimental brews for local festivals and pubs. A 2.5-barrel plant came into operation in 2011. Seasonal beers are also available.

Ruby Tuesday (OG 1039, ABV 3.9%)

Tyme Tunnel (OG 1041, ABV 4.1%)

Golden Dawn (OG 1043, ABV 4.3%)

IPA (OG 1046, ABV 4.6%)

Time 'n' 'Arf (OG 1050, ABV 5%)

Justice (NEW)

15 Heron Way, Mansfield, Nottinghamshire, NG19 6EQ
☎ 07954 989594
⊠ matthew.hartshorn@talktalk.net
Brewing began in 2012 using a 0.5-barrel plant.

Gold Digger (ABV 4.2%)

Gavel Bitter (ABV 4.6%)

Kelburn SIBA 👁

10 Muriel Lane, Barrhead, East Renfrewshire, G78 1QB
☎ (0141) 881 2138 ⊕ kelburnbrewery.com
Tours by arrangement

⊠ Kelburn is an award-winning family business established in 2002. Beers are available bottled and in take-away polypins. Seasonal beers: see website.

Goldihops (OG 1038, ABV 3.8%) ◆
Well-hopped session ale with a fruity taste and a bitter finish.

Pivo Estivo (OG 1038, ABV 3.9%)

Misty Law (OG 1040, ABV 4%)
A dry, hoppy amber ale with a long-lasting bitter finish.

Red Smiddy (OG 1040, ABV 4.1%) ◆
This bittersweet ale predominantly features an intense citrus hop character that assaults the nose and continues into the flavour, balanced perfectly with fruity malt.

Dark Moor (OG 1044, ABV 4.5%) ▣
A dark, fruity ale with undertones of liquorice and blackcurrant.

Jaguar (OG 1043, ABV 4.5%)

Cart Noir (OG 1046, ABV 4.8%)

Cart Blanche (OG 1048, ABV 5%) ◆
A golden, full-bodied ale. The assault of fruit and hop camouflages the strength of this easy-drinking ale.

Kelham Island SIBA

23 Alma Street, Sheffield, South Yorkshire, S3 8SA
☎ (0114) 249 4804

Office: Prospect House, 17 Alma Street, Sheffield, South Yorkshire, S3 8RY ⊕ kelhambrewery.co.uk
Shop Mon-Fri 9am-4pm (some weekends)
Tours by arrangement

⊚Established in 1990 behind the Fat Cat pub, the brewery moved to new purpose-built premises in 1999. The old building is used as a visitor centre. A brewery shop opened recently together with new offices in nearby Prospect House. Monthly specials and bottle-conditioned beers are available.

Best Bitter (OG 1038, ABV 3.8%)

Pride of Sheffield (OG 1040.5, ABV 4%) ⌕
A full-flavoured, amber-coloured bitter.

Easy Rider (OG 1041.8, ABV 4.3%) ◆
A pale, straw-coloured beer with a sweetish flavour and delicate hints of citrus fruits. A beer with hints of flavour rather than full-bodied.

Riders on the Storm (OG 1045, ABV 4.5%)
A robust golden pale ale with berry notes and slight roasted notes.

Pale Rider (OG 1050, ABV 5.2%) ◆
A full-bodied, straw-coloured pale ale, with a good fruity aroma and a strong fruit and hop taste. Its well-balanced sweetness and bitterness continue in the finish.

Keltek SIBA

Candela House, Cardrew Way, Redruth, Cornwall, TR15 1SS
☎ (01209) 313620 ⊕ keltekbrewery.co.uk
Shop Mon-Fri 9am-5pm

⊠ Keltek has undergone a number of expansions in recent years and is now a major force in Cornwall and further afield. Bottle-conditioned

beer is available and bottling is carried out for several other Cornish breweries.

Even Keel (OG 1034, ABV 3.4%)

Golden Lance (OG 1038, ABV 4%) ◆
Golden bitter promising fruit and hops. Refreshing citrus and sweetness fills the mouth with bitterness coming through in the finish.

Magik (OG 1040, ABV 4.2%) ◆
Tawny best bitter with malt and complex fruit on the nose. On the tongue there is perfumed malt, sweetness and bitterness, followed by a long, bitter finish becoming dry.

King (OG 1049, ABV 5.1%)

Contract brewed for St Ives Brewery:

Boilers Golden Cornish Ale (ABV 4%)
Light golden with a citrus aroma.

Knill by Mouth (ABV 5%)
Full-bodied and hoppy.

Kemptown

🍺 **Hand in Hand, 33 Upper St James's Street, Kemptown, Brighton, East Sussex, BN2 1JN**
☎ 07967 681203
Tours by arrangement

⊚Kemptown was established in 1989 and built in the tower tradition behind the Hand in Hand, which is possibly the smallest brewpub in England. It takes its name and logo from the former Charrington's Kemptown Brewery, which closed in 1964. In 2011 work was undertaken to restore the brewery and upgrade all facilities. Beer is only available at the Hand in Hand. Quarterly seasonal beers are also brewed.

Gold (ABV 4%)

Cascadian (ABV 4.5%)

Red (ABV 4.5%)

IPA (ABV 6%)

Kendal

🍺 **Brewhouse at Burgundy's, 19 Lowther Street, Kendal, Cumbria, LA9 4DH**
☎ (01539) 733803 ⊕ burgundyswinebar.co.uk
Tours by arrangement

⊚Kendal began brewing in 2011. Beer is now produced every week and the brewery is at full production.

Beast Banks Bitter (OG 1037, ABV 3.7%)
A light, refreshing ale with hoppy bitterness that lingers to a citrus finish.

Helga's Dunkel Bier (OG 1037, ABV 3.7%)
Brewed to the style of a traditional German dunkel bier (dark lager) with a smooth and malty taste.

Frankies Gold (OG 1039, ABV 3.9%)

Pale Ale (OG 1042, ABV 4.2%)

Silver Tanner (OG 1044, ABV 4.4%)
Tan-coloured ale with malt flavour, citrus aroma and crisp hop bitterness.

Grisley Mires (OG 1048, ABV 4.8%)

Kent SIBA ⊙

The Long Barn, Birling Place Farm, Stangate Road, Birling, Kent, ME19 5JN
☎ (01634) 780037 ⊕ kentbrewery.com

Kent Brewery was founded in 2010 by Toby Simmonds (ex-brewer from Dark Star) and Paul Herbert. Originally brewed at Larkins, a 10-barrel plant is now used at the Birling site. More than 150 outlets are supplied direct, mainly throughout Kent and London. Seasonal and bottle-conditioned beers are also available.

Black Gold (OG 1040, ABV 4%)

Pale (OG 1040, ABV 4%)

Cobnut (OG 1041, ABV 4.1%)

KGB (Kent Golding Bitter) (OG 1041, ABV 4.1%)

Zingiber (OG 1041, ABV 4.1%)

Beyond The Pale (OG 1054, ABV 5.4%)

Enigma (OG 1055, ABV 5.5%)

Kernel SIBA

Arch 11, Dockley Road Industrial Estate, London, SE16 3SF
☎ (020) 7231 4516 ☎ 07757 552636

Office: 01 Spa Terminus, Spa Road, London, SE16 4QT
⊕ thekernelbrewery.com
Shop Sat 9am-3pm

Kernel was established in 2010 by Evin O'Riordain and moved to larger premises in 2012 to keep up with demand. The brewery produces bottle-conditioned beers, as well as the occasional cask, and has won many awards for its wide, ever-changing range of pale and dark beers.

Table Beer (ABV 3%)

Keswick SIBA

The Old Brewery, Brewery Lane, Keswick, Cumbria, CA12 5BY
☎ (01768) 780700 ⊕ keswickbrewery.co.uk
Shop – call for details (usually Mon-Fri 9am-5pm)
Tours by arrangement

Keswick began brewing in 2006 using a 10-barrel plant. It is located on the site of a brewery that closed in 1897. The beer is always available in the Queen's Head Hotel and the Dog & Gun in Keswick with many other Lakeland pubs supplied. Seasonal beers: see website.

Thirst Gold (OG 1035, ABV 3.6%)
Golden in colour and full-flavoured.

Keystone SIBA

Old Carpenters Workshop, Berwick St Leonard, Wiltshire, SP3 5SN
☎ (01747) 820426 ⊕ keystonebrewery.co.uk
Shop Mon, Tue & Fri 10am-5pm
Tours by arrangement

⊠ Keystone Brewery was set up in 2006 using a 10-barrel plant. The beers have low food miles to help support a sustainable local community. The brewery also use an award-winning solar heating system, which reduces carbon emissions. Around 150 outlets are supplied. Seasonal beers: see website.

Bedrock (OG 1035, ABV 3.6%)
Well-balanced beer with sweet citrus flavours.

Gold Hill (OG 1039, ABV 4%)
A golden ale full of citrus and floral aromas.

Gold Spice (OG 1039, ABV 4%)
Light-coloured beer, well-hopped with stem ginger added to the cask.

Large One (OG 1041, ABV 4.2%)
Distinct malty flavour and a delicate addition of bittering hops with hints of fruit and spice in the aftertaste.

Very Pale Ale (OG 1045, ABV 4.6%)
Pale in colour with subtle malt flavours and medium bitterness leading to crisp hop flavours and aromas.

Cornerstone (OG 1047, ABV 4.8%)
A dark, strong beer with plenty of hops, well-balanced with a long, satisfying finish.

King SIBA ⊙

3-5 Jubilee Estate, Foundry Lane, Horsham, West Sussex, RH13 5UE
☎ (01403) 272102 ⊕ kingbeer.co.uk
Shop Mon-Fri 9am-5pm; Sat 10am-2pm
Tours by arrangement

⊠ Launched in 2001, the brewery had expanded to a capacity of 50 barrels a week by 2004, and continues to expand. The brewery was purchased by Ian Burgess and Nigel Lambe in 2010, with Nigel then selling to Nikki and Justin Deighton in 2013. Seasonal beers: see website.

Horsham Best Bitter (OG 1038, ABV 3.8%) ❧
A predominantly malty best bitter, brown in colour. The nutty flavours have some sweetness with a little bitterness that grows in the aftertaste.

Brighton Blonde (OG 1039, ABV 3.9%)
A crisp, refreshing, hoppy beer with a distinctive hoppy aroma. The taste is sharply hoppy with a hint of malt. The aftertaste develops the hops further with an increasing dryness and straw bitterness to finish.

Brighton Best (OG 1040, ABV 4%)
Golden beer with a complex blend of floral hop on the aroma. The mouth feels clean and well-balanced with a lingering aftertaste. The subtle fresh hop remains into the finish.

Festive (OG 1047, ABV 4.7%)

Kings Clipstone (NEW)

Keepers Bothy, Kings Clipstone, Nottinghamshire, NG21 9BT
☎ (01623) 823589 ☎ 07790 190020
⊕ kingsclipstonebrewery.co.uk

Located in the heart of Sherwood Forest, Kings Clipstone began brewing in 2012 using a five-barrel plant. Further beers including seasonals are planned.

Hop On (OG 1039, ABV 3.8%)
A pale and refreshing session beer with a fruity aroma.

Sire (OG 1043, ABV 4.2%)
A well-rounded beer with a clean, bitter finish.

THE BREWERIES

Kings Head

Kings Head, 132 High Street, Bildeston, Ipswich, Suffolk, IP7 7ED
☎ (01449) 741434 ⊕ bildestonkingshead.co.uk
Tours by arrangement

⊗ Kings Head has been brewing since 1996 in an old cart lodge at the back of the pub. Under new ownership since 2008, the three-barrel plant brews fortnightly. Seasonal beers are also available.

Bildeston Best (OG 1036, ABV 3.6%)
A traditional best bitter, well-hopped with a malty sweetness and dry finish.

Brettvale Gold (ABV 3.6%)

Kingstone SIBA

Meadow Farm, Tintern, Monmouthshire, NP16 7NX
☎ (01291) 680111/680101
⊕ kingstonebrewery.co.uk

Kingstone Brewery is located in the Wye Valley where brewing began on a four-barrel plant in 2005. All cask ales are also available bottle conditioned. Seasonal beers are marketed under the Hapax Brewing Co label.

Tewdric's Tipple (OG 1038, ABV 3.8%)
An ale with a dry, bitter character and tangy core.

Challenger (OG 1040, ABV 4%)
A smooth, richly-hopped, well-balanced ale with a malted nose and toffee undertones.

Gold (OG 1040, ABV 4%)
A straw-coloured, smooth ale with citrus notes and a balanced, hoppy finish.

Premium Stout (OG 1044, ABV 4.4%)
A smooth, rich stout with a bitter finish.

Classic Bitter (OG 1045, ABV 4.5%)
A balanced, distinctively hoppy, dry ale with a floral nose and smooth, well-balanced finish.

1503 (OG 1048, ABV 4.8%)
A deep chestnut red, lightly-hopped ale bursting with complex rich flavours.

Abbey Ale (OG 1051, ABV 5.1%)
An amber-coloured, full-flavoured ale. The hoppy edge is balanced by a smooth, malty richness.

Humpty's Fuddle (OG 1058, ABV 5.8%)
An IPA with a slightly sweet, floral nose, a balanced level of malt supporting the hops and finally a subtle but slightly citrus finish.

Kinneil

Corbie Inn, 84 Corbiehall, Bo'ness, West Lothian, EH51 0AS
☎ (01506) 824574 ⊕ kinneilbrew.co.uk

Kinneil began brewing in 2011 using a 2.5-barrel plant. The brewery is adjacent to the Corbie Inn but separately owned.

Kinver SIBA ⊚

Unit 1, Britch Farm, Rocky Wall, Kinver, Staffordshire, DY7 5NW
☎ 07906 146777 ⊕ kinverbrewery.co.uk
Tours by arrangement

⊚Established in 2004, Kinver produces a wide range of different beer styles including one-off specials. The brewery relocated in 2012 using a new eight-barrel plant. Around 30 outlets are supplied direct.

Light Railway (OG 1038, ABV 3.8%) ⬛ ◀
Straw-coloured session beer. A malty start quickly gives way to well-hopped bitterness and lingering hoppy aftertaste.

Edge (OG 1041, ABV 4.2%) ◀
Amber with a malty aroma. Sweet fruity start with a hint of citrus marmalade in the spicy-edged malt; lasting hoppy finish that is satisfyingly bitter.

Noble 600 (OG 1045, ABV 4.3%) ◀
Fruity hop aroma. Very fruity start then the grassy hops give a sharp bitter finish with malt support.

Half Centurion (OG 1048, ABV 5%) ◀
A golden best bitter; malty before the American Chinook hop takes command to give a balanced hoppy finish and provide the aftertaste.

Khyber (OG 1054, ABV 5.8%) ◀
Golden strong bitter with a Centennial hop bite that overwhelms the fleeting malty sweetness and drives through to the long, dry finish.

Over the Edge (OG 1074, ABV 6.8%) ⬡ ⬛

Kirkby Lonsdale SIBA

Unit 2F, Old Station Yard, Kirkby Lonsdale, Lancashire, LA6 2HP
☎ (01524) 272221 ☎ 07793 149999
⊕ kirkbylonsdalebrewery.com

⊚Kirkby Lonsdale is a family-run business established in 2009 on a six-barrel plant. Seasonal beers are also available.

Tiffin Gold (OG 1036, ABV 3.6%) ◀
A full-flavoured, grapefruit, hoppy and bitter beer with a dry finish.

Stanleys Pale Ale (OG 1038, ABV 3.8%)
A pale ale with a delicate bitter start with hints of malt joined by lemon and a flowery aroma.

Ruskins Bitter (OG 1039, ABV 3.9%) ◀
A tawny bitter with a distinctive aroma of fruit and malt. The clean, hoppy flavour is well-balanced with fruity sweetness leading to a sustained bittersweet finish.

Radical Red (OG 1042, ABV 4.2%) ◀
Malty beer with a caramel sweetness that is balanced by a bitter finish.

Monumental Blonde (OG 1045, ABV 4.5%) ◀
Distinctly hoppy; a fruity, sweet, pale-coloured, full-bodied bitter.

Jubilee Stout (OG 1055, ABV 5.5%) ◀
Rich, well-balanced stout with a strong malt character. A long aftertaste retains this complexity and is surprisingly refreshing.

Kirkstall SIBA

Unit 6, Canal Wharf, Wyther Lane, Kirkstall, Leeds, West Yorkshire, LS5 3BT
☎ (0113) 345 8835 ⊕ kirkstallbrewerycompany.com
Tours by arrangement

⊚Kirkstall began brewing in 2011 and is located within yards of the original Kirstall Brewery. Many of the beer names are derived from the local area or have links with Yorkshire breweries of old. Occasional special one-off brews are created.

Pale Ale (OG 1040, ABV 4%) ◀

Golden-coloured with a feast of hop and grapefruit flavours, the tangy bitterness throughout defines this well balanced beer.

Three Swords (OG 1045, ABV 4.5%) ♦
Golden-yellow beer with good quantities of hops and juicy fruit, a bittersweet taste and an almost marmalade finish.

Dissolution IPA (OG 1050, ABV 5%) 🍴 ♦
Hops define this amber beer in the massive aroma, through the citrus fruit taste and right to the end which is lingering and satisfyingly bitter.

Black Band Porter (OG 1055, ABV 5.5%) ♦
Dark, smooth and rich with a full aroma and even bigger flavour. A generous fruity/roasty taste with a liquorice finish.

Kissingate

Church Lane Farm Estate, Church Lane, Lower Beeding, West Sussex, RH13 6LU
☎ (01293) 891335 ⊕ kissingate.co.uk
Tours by arrangement

⊠ Kissingate was founded in 2010 by husband and wife team Gary and Bunny Lucas. In 2012 the brewery moved into a new purpose-built barn conversion. Local outlets and beer festivals are supplied.

Storyteller (OG 1035, ABV 3.5%)

Best (OG 1040, ABV 4%)

Old Tale Porter (OG 1052, ABV 4.5%)
A classic, full-flavoured London porter.

Moon (OG 1050, ABV 4.8%)
Golden beer with a taste of lightly roasted malts, late autumn apples and a lingering bitterness.

Chennai (OG 1050, ABV 5%)

Smelter's Stout (OG 1052, ABV 5.2%)

Mary's Ruby Mild (OG 1072, ABV 6.5%)
Deep ruby in colour with gentle aromas of well-aged port. Intense and rounded malt flavours with a light and floral hop aftertaste.

Kitchen Garden

Old Walled Garden, Sheffield Park, East Sussex, TN22 3QX
☎ (01825) 790775
✉ admin@kitchengardenbrewery.co.uk
Shop Mon 1-5pm; Tue-Sun 10am-5pm

Kitchen Garden is a small one-barrel plant producing only bottle-conditioned ales, all suitable for vegetarians. It is situated in a Victorian walled kitchen garden at Sheffield Park. Occasional seasonal beers are produced. The beers are available from the brewery shop and at several outlets in Sussex including Middle Farm at Firle.

Orange Hefeweizen (ABV 4.3%)
Sweet, orange marmalade-flavoured wheat beer with light hoppiness.

Kite SIBA

Cwmcerrig Farm, Gorslas, Carmarthenshire, SA14 7HU
☎ (01269) 842300

Office: Unit B, Llantrisant Business Park, Rhondda Cynon Taff, Llantrisant, CF72 8LF
⊕ thekitebrewery.com

Tours by arrangement

Kite brewery was established in 2011 on a 20-barrel plant at Cwmcerrig Farm. Head brewer Iain Masson, formerly of Greene King, brews three core beers. Seasonal beers are available: see website.

Cwrw Gorslas (OG 1041, ABV 4%)
A spicy resinous hop aroma. The bitterness remains into the finish with dry fruit notes.

CPA/Carmarthen Pale Ale (OG 1042, ABV 4.1%)
A traditionally crafted light golden ale with a clean crisp palate balanced by a fruity citrus hop character.

Thunderbird (OG 1046, ABV 4.5%)
A predominantly hoppy ale, mid brown in colour, malty with a slight touch of sweet fruit aromas.

Knaresborough (NEW)

🍴 19 Market Place, Knaresborough, North Yorkshire, HG5 8AL
☎ (01423) 869148

Established in 2012 above Blind Jacks in Knaresborough using a one-barrel plant, mainly supplying the pub. The brewery specialises in stronger, sometimes experimental beers inspired by US craft brewing.

TY PA (OG 1038, ABV 3.5%)

American Style Milk Stout (OG 1074, ABV 6.9%)

Mea Culpa Pale Ale (OG 1072, ABV 6.9%)

Knops

The Walled Garden, Archerfield Estate, Dirleton, North Berwick, EH39 5HQ
☎ 07949 879147 ⊕ knopsbeer.co.uk
Tours by arrangement

☺Knops began brewing under contract in 2010. In 2013 it moved to an 11-barrel plant on the Archerfield Estate at Dirleton. Beers are modern interpretations of traditional styles, and are bottled in-house.

Musselburgh Broke (OG 1045, ABV 4.5%)

California Common (OG 1048, ABV 4.6%)

India Pale Ale (OG 1047, ABV 5%)

Black Cork (ABV 6.5%)

Contract brewed for Archerfield Fine Ales:

Golden Ale (OG 1039, ABV 3.8%)

Dark Ale (ABV 4.7%)

India Pale Ale (OG 1047, ABV 5%)

Kubla (NEW)

The Source Building, Tower Farm, Dean's Cross, Lydeard St Lawrence, Somerset, TA4 3QN
☎ 07855 342208 ⊕ kubla.co.uk

Kubla began brewing in 2012 using a one-barrel plant on Tower Farm in the Brendon Hills, Exmoor. Three bottle-conditioned beers are produced; Rise: Pale Ale (ABV 4.2%), Rock: Saison (ABV 4.2%), Paradise: Stout (ABV 4.8%).

Lacons (NEW) SIBA

The Courtyard, Main Cross Road, Great Yarmouth, Norfolk, NR30 3NZ
☎ (01493) 850578 ⊕ lacons.co.uk
Shop Wed & Thu 12-2.30pm
Tours by arrangement: 12 & 2pm alternate Sat in summer. Booking required

Lacons is a famous Yarmouth brewery, axed by Whitbread in 1968, and brought back in 2013 with a 20-barrel plant, using the original yeast culture. Further beers are planned.

Encore (ABV 3.8%)

Legacy (ABV 4.4%)

Affinity (ABV 4.8%)

Lamb (NEW)

9 Barley Mow Passage, Chiswick, London, W4 4PH
☎ (020) 8994 1880 ⊕ thelambbrewery.com

Lamb Brewery uses a 1,000-litre brew plant which brews up to four times a week and is able to produce nearly 4,400 pints of ale per week. The brewery follows traditional brewing techniques and uses only the finest British malt and hops from all over the globe.

Dark (ABV 3.8%)

One in the Bush (ABV 4.2%)

Lancaster SIBA ◉

Heartwick Brewery, Lancaster Leisure Park, Wyresdale Road, Lancaster, LA1 3LA
☎ (01524) 848537 ⊕ lancasterbrewery.co.uk
Shop 10am-5pm daily
Tours by arrangement

☺Lancaster began brewing in 2005. The brewery moved to new premises in Lancaster in 2010 and installed a larger brewing plant. Production now stands at over 200 barrels per week. Seasonal beers are also available.

Straw (OG 1035, ABV 3.5%)

Amber (OG 1038, ABV 3.7%)
Dark gold session beer with a hoppy bouquet and subtle floral and citrus aromas.

Blonde (OG 1042, ABV 4.1%) ◣
A crisp, hoppy flavour with a touch of caramel and a hint of citrus. Golden hued with a smooth, easy-drinking feel. Hops follow through to dominate in the aftertaste.

Black (OG 1046, ABV 4.6%) ◣
A satisfying roast bitter beer.

Red (OG 1048, ABV 4.9%)
Robust ale with a malt dominated body.

Landlord's Friend

▤ Kershaw House Inn, Luddenden Lane, Luddendenfoot, West Yorkshire, HX2 6NW
☎ (01422) 882222 ✉ landfriendbeers@aol.co.uk

Landlord's Friend began brewing in 2010 using a 2.5-barrel plant. Around 30 outlets are supplied direct. Seasonal and one-off brews are also available. A change of name is under consideration, possibly to Luddendenfoot Brewery.

Mr Smith (ABV 3.7%)

Project Douglas (ABV 4.1%)

Langham SIBA

Old Granary, Langham Lane, Lodsworth, West Sussex, GU28 9BU
☎ (01798) 860861 ⊕ langhambrewery.co.uk
Shop Tue & Sat 9am-5pm
Tours by arrangement

Langham was established in 2006 in an 18th-century granary barn and is set in the heart of West Sussex with fine views to the rolling South Downs. It is owned by Steve Mansley, Lesley Foulkes and James Berrow who all brew and run the business. The brewery is a 10-barrel steam heated plant and more than 100 outlets are supplied.

Halfway to Heaven (OG 1035, ABV 3.5%)
A chestnut-coloured beer with a balanced biscuit maltiness and citrus and fruit hop character with a hint of spice.

Hip Hop (OG 1040, ABV 4%)
A blonde beer – clean and crisp. The nose is loaded with floral hop aroma while the pale malt flavour is overtaken by a dry and bitter finish.

Best (OG 1042, ABV 4.2%)
A tawny-coloured classic best with well-balanced malt flavours and bitterness.

Sundowner (OG 1042, ABV 4.2%)
A deep golden beer. The nose has tropical fruit, pineapple and citrus notes with a smooth maltiness in the background. There is a balanced dry and bitter finish with floral hop aroma.

LSD (Langham Special Draught)
(OG 1049, ABV 5.2%)
An auburn beer with rich, complex flavours and a deep red glow. The sweet maltiness is balanced with spicy hop aromas and a dry finish.

Langton SIBA ◉

Grange Farm, Welham Road, Thorpe Langton, Leicestershire, LE16 7TU
☎ (01858) 540116 ☎ 07840 532826
⊕ langtonbrewery.co.uk
Tours by arrangement

Established in 1999 in outbuildings behind the Bell Inn, East Langton, the brewery relocated in 2005 to a converted barn at Thorpe Langton, where a four-barrel plant was installed. Further expansion in 2010 significantly increased capacity. Seasonal beers are available.

Caudle Bitter (OG 1039, ABV 3.9%) ◣
Copper-coloured session bitter that is close to pale ale in style. Flavours are relatively well-balanced throughout with hops slightly to the fore.

Inclined Plane Bitter (OG 1042, ABV 4.2%)
A straw-coloured bitter with a citrus nose and long, hoppy finish.

Hop On (OG 1044, ABV 4.4%)
A premium bitter, deep chestnut-coloured with a good balance of flavours and aroma.

Scarecrow (OG 1044, ABV 4.4%)
Smooth, well-balanced, slightly fruity and sweet.

Bowler Strong Ale (OG 1048, ABV 4.8%)
A strong traditional ale with a deep red colour and a hoppy nose.

Bullseye (OG 1050, ABV 4.8%)

Intensely dark stout with flavours of liquorice and chocolate.

Larkins SIBA

Larkins Farm, Hampkins Hill Road, Chiddingstone, Kent, TN8 7BB
☎ (01892) 870328
Tours by arrangement

⊠ It's been over 25 years since the farming and hop growing Dockerty family bought the original Royal Tunbridge Wells Brewery and moved it to Larkins Farm where Bob Dockerty started brewing in 1987. Production of its three main brews and two seasonal ales has steadily increased. All beers now include hops grown on Larkins Farm itself. Ales are delivered direct to around 70 free houses within a radius of 20 miles.

Traditional Ale (OG 1035, ABV 3.4%)
Tawny-coloured, a full-tasting hoppy ale with plenty of character for its strength.

Chiddingstone (OG 1040, ABV 4%)
A mid-strength, hoppy, fruity ale with a long, bittersweet aftertaste.

Best (OG 1045, ABV 4.4%) ◆
Full-bodied, slightly fruity and unusually bitter for its gravity.

Late Knights (NEW) SIBA

21 Southey Street, Penge, London, SE20 7JD
⊕ lateknightsbrewery.co.uk

Originally using spare capacity at Truefitt Brewery in Middlesbrough in 2012, Late Knights began brewing using a six-barrel plant in London in 2013. Seasonal and special beers are also available.

Crack of Dawn Pale Ale (ABV 3.9%)

Hop o' The Morning Stout (ABV 4.2%)

Morning Glory Bitter (ABV 4.5%)

Old Red Eyes Red Ale (ABV 4.5%)

Worm Catcher IPA (ABV 5%)

Latimer (NEW) SIBA

13 South Folds Road, Oakley Hay, Northamptonshire, NN18 9EU
☎ 07812 450988

Office: 11 Meadway Close, Kettering, Northamptonshire, NN15 6QG ⊕ latimerales.com

Latimer is a small two-barrel brewery specialising in styles from all around the world as well as classic English beers. Brewer James Trent built the brewery himself over an 18 month period and commenced brewing in 2012. Bottle-conditioned ales are also available.

Midland Mild (OG 1038, ABV 3.5%)
A light-bodied, deep auburn-coloured English ale with rich flavours of coffee and toasted malt with a slightly sweet finish.

William George IPA (OG 1045, ABV 4.4%)
A refreshing, bright golden-coloured IPA with a medium body, balanced hop bitterness and dry finish.

Burton Best (OG 1046, ABV 4.5%)
A chestnut-coloured, medium-bodied best bitter.

Amber Wrangler (OG 1047, ABV 4.6%)

A full-bodied, amber-coloured American-style ale with a good balance of malt and hops and rich caramel flavours.

Uncle Sam's Pale Ale (OG 1050, ABV 5%)
A light-bodied, clear and pale ale with a crisp and fresh-tasting flavour with citrus notes and a dry finish.

Leadmill

Unit 3, Heanor Small Business Centre, Adams Close, Heanor, Derbyshire, DE75 7SW
☎ 07971 189915 ⊠ leadmill@fsmail.net

⊠ Set up in Selston in 1999, Leadmill moved to Denby in 2001 and again in 2010 to Heanor where it shares a site with Coppice Side Brewery (qv). A sister brewery to Bottle Brook (qv), the brewery tap is the Old Oak in Horsley Woodhouse.

Langley Best (OG 1036, ABV 3.6%)

Mash Tun Bitter (OG 1036, ABV 3.6%)

Old Oak Bitter (OG 1037, ABV 3.7%)

B52 (OG 1050, ABV 5.2%)

Slumdog (OG 1058, ABV 5.9%)

Leamside

Three Horseshoes, Pit House Lane, Leamside, County Durham, DH4 6QQ
☎ (0191) 584 2394
⊕ threehorseshoesleamside.co.uk

Brewing began in 2012 using a 2.5-barrel plant. Beers are available at the Three Horseshoes as well as its two sister pubs, the Kings Arms in Sunderland and the Courtyard in Washington.

Adventure (OG 1038, ABV 3.8%)
A deep golden-coloured session bitter. Soft fruit flavours and well-balanced medium bitterness.

Alexandrina (OG 1041, ABV 4.2%)
Light gold in colour. Initial bitterness gives way to citrus fruit flavours.

Brockwell (OG 1042, ABV 4.2%)
A straw-coloured pale ale with tropical fruit flavours.

Five Quarter (OG 1052, ABV 4.5%)
A silky smooth mouthfeel with berry fruit flavours and hints of coffee and chocolate.

Resolution (OG 1052, ABV 4.5%)
Premium pale ale brewed with a blend of American hops. Well-balanced bitterness and subtle fruit flavours.

Leatherbritches

Tap House, Annwell Lane, Smisby, Derbyshire, LE65 2TA
☎ 07976 279253 ⊠ leatherbritches@btconnect.com
Tours by arrangement

☺The brewery, founded in 1993 in Fenny Bentley, has relocated and expanded over the years, moving to its current address in 2011. Both the Tap House Brewery (qv) and Leatherbritches brew on the same plant but the two businesses are separate. Seasonal and bottle-conditioned beers are also available.

Goldings (OG 1036, ABV 3.6%)

A light golden beer with a flowery hoppy aroma and a bitter finish.

Lemongrass & Ginger (OG 1036, ABV 3.8%)

Ashbourne Ale (OG 1040, ABV 4%)
A pale bitter with a crisp, lasting taste.

Doctor Johnsons (OG 1040, ABV 4%)
A mid-brown ale, not heavily hopped but full-bodied with some caramel flavour.

Scoundrel (OG 1040, ABV 4.1%)

Dovedale (OG 1044, ABV 4.4%)
A copper-coloured bitter with a crisp finish.

Ginger Helmet (OG 1047, ABV 4.7%)
As for Hairy Helmet but with a hint of China's most astringent herb.

Hairy Helmet (OG 1047, ABV 4.7%)
Pale bitter, well-hopped but with a sweet finish.

Bespoke (OG 1050, ABV 5%)
Full-bodied, well-rounded premium bitter.

Porter (OG 1055, ABV 5.5%)

Scary Hairy (ABV 5.9%)

Ledbury (NEW) SIBA

Gazerdine House, Hereford Road, Ledbury, Herefordshire, HR8 2PZ
☎ (01531) 671184 ☎ 07957 428070
⊕ ledburyrealales.co.uk
Tours by arrangement

☺Brewing began in 2012. Three regular beers are produced using locally-sourced ingredients whenever possible. Distribution is generally within a 15-mile radius of the brewery.

Bitter (ABV 3.8%)

Dark (ABV 3.9%)

Gold (ABV 4%)

Leeds SIBA IFBB ‹⊙›

▤ 3 Sydenham Road, Leeds, West Yorkshire, LS11 9RU
☎ (0113) 244 5866 ⊕ leedsbrewery.co.uk

☺Production began in 2007 using a 20-barrel plant. The largest independent brewer in the city, it uses a unique strain of yeast originally used by a defunct West Yorkshire brewery. Five pubs are owned and around 300 outlets are supplied direct. Seasonal beers: see website. A 2.5-barrel plant is also used at the Brewery Tap pub in Leeds producing seasonal beers for the pub.

Pale (OG 1037.5, ABV 3.8%) ✎
Well-balanced with citrus in both aroma and flavour.

Yorkshire Gold (ABV 4%) ✎
Zesty, citrus flavours dominate with hops and bitterness supporting, the long lasting bitter finish makes this a refreshing beer.

Best (OG 1041, ABV 4.3%) ✎
Full-flavoured, smooth amber beer with a pleasing mix of malt and hops, a drinkable bittersweet beer.

Midnight Bell (OG 1047.5, ABV 4.8%) ✎
A full-bodied strong mild, deep red/brown in colour. The malty caramel character can lead to a hint of chocolate.

Leek

See Staffordshire

Lees IFBB ‹⊙›

Greengate Brewery, Middleton Junction, Manchester, M24 2AX
☎ (0161) 643 2487 ⊕ jwlees.co.uk
Tours by arrangement

☺Family owned since its foundation by John Lees in 1828, the brewery has a tied estate of around 170 pubs, mostly in north Manchester, Cheshire, Lancashire and North Wales. The vast majority serve cask beer. The current head brewer is a family member.

Brewer's Dark (OG 1032, ABV 3.5%) ✎
Formerly GB Mild, this is a dark brown beer with a malt and caramel aroma. Creamy mouthfeel with malt, caramel and fruit flavours and a malty finish. Becoming rare.

Manchester Pale Ale (MPA) (OG 1036, ABV 3.7%)
Golden yellow in colour with floral aromas with citrus and malt. Medium-bodied and well-rounded, with light fruits, citrus and malt to taste. A refreshing, rather bitter finish.

The Governor (OG 1038, ABV 3.8%)
Malty auburn/amber-coloured beer with floral and citrus notes and a clean, dry finish.

Bitter (OG 1037, ABV 4%) ✎
Copper-coloured beer with malt and fruit in aroma, taste and finish.

John Willie's (OG 1041, ABV 4.5%)
A well-balanced, full-bodied premium bitter.

Moonraker (OG 1070, ABV 6.5%) ✎
A reddish-brown beer with a strong, malty, fruity aroma. The flavour is rich and sweet, with roast malt, and the finish is fruity yet dry. Available only in a handful of outlets.

Brewed for Carlsberg:

Draught Burton Ale (OG 1047, ABV 4.8%) ✎
A beer with hops, fruit and malt present throughout, and a lingering complex aftertaste, but lacking some hoppiness compared to its Burton original.

Leila Cottage SIBA

▤ Countryman, Chapel Road, Ingoldmells, Skegness, Lincolnshire, PE25 1ND
☎ (01754) 872268 ⊕ countryman-ingoldmells.co.uk
Tours by arrangement

Leila Cottage started brewing in 2007 using a 0.5-barrel plant, which was upgraded in 2009 to a 2.5-barrel one. The brewery is situated at the Countryman pub – Leila Cottage was the original name of the building before it became a licensed club and more recently a pub. The brewery now owns its own bottling line meaning that all beers are also available bottle conditioned, including seasonals.

Leila's Lazy Days (OG 1040, ABV 3.6%)

Ace Ale (OG 1040, ABV 3.8%)

Lincolnshire Life (OG 1040, ABV 4.2%)

Leila's One Off (OG 1045, ABV 5.1%)

Leith Hill

▤ c/o Plough Inn, Coldharbour Lane, Coldharbour, Surrey, RH5 6HD
☎ (01306) 711793 ⊕ ploughinn.com
Tours by arrangement

Leith Hill was established in 1996 at the Plough Inn using home-made equipment and was moved to converted storerooms at the rear in 2001, increasing capacity to 2.5-barrels in 2005. All beers brewed are sold only on the premises.

Beautiful South (OG 1036, ABV 3.6%)
Yellowish in colour, a hoppy session beer with a little malt character.

Crooked Furrow (OG 1040, ABV 4%) ◀
A malty beer, with some balancing hop bitterness. Pale brown in colour with an earthy malty aroma and a long, dry and bittersweet aftertaste. Some fruit is also present throughout.

Tallywhacker (OG 1048, ABV 4.8%) ◀
Dark, sweet and fruity old ale with good roast malt character.

Leyden SIBA

▤ Lord Raglan, Walmersley Old Road, Nangreaves, BL9 6SP
☎ (0161) 764 6680 ⊕ lordraglannangreaves.co.uk
Tours by arrangement

☺Leyden was established in 1999. In addition to the permanent range a number of seasonal and occasional beers are brewed.

Black Pudding (OG 1040, ABV 3.8%)
A dark brown, creamy mild with a malty flavour, followed by a balanced finish.

Nanny Flyer (OG 1040, ABV 3.8%)
A drinkable session bitter with an initial dryness and a hint of citrus, followed by a strong, malty finish.

Balaclava (OG 1040, ABV 4.2%)
A brown-coloured session bitter with malty and hoppy flavours.

Rammy Rocket (OG 1042, ABV 4.2%)
A smooth, straw-coloured ale.

Forever Bury (OG 1047, ABV 4.5%)
This dark brown bitter has a distinct fruity aroma with a smooth malty finish.

Light Brigade (OG 1047, ABV 4.6%) ◀
Copper in colour with a citrus aroma. The flavour is a balance of malt, hops and fruit, with a bitter finish.

Raglan Sleeve (OG 1047, ABV 4.6%) ◀
Dark red/brown beer with a hoppy aroma and a dry, roasty, hoppy taste and finish.

Crowning Glory (OG 1068, ABV 6.8%)
A smooth-tasting beer for its strength.

Liberation SIBA ◉

Tregear House, Longueville Road, St Saviour, Jersey, JE2 7WF
☎ (01534) 764089 ⊕ liberationgroup.com
Tours by arrangement

Following the closure of the original brewery in Ann Street in 2004, the brewery is now located in an old soft drinks factory using a 40-barrel plant. Formerly known as the Jersey Brewery it was renamed in 2010 as the Liberation Brewery following its sale to the Liberation Group. Its flagship beer, Liberation Ale, is now regularly seen on the mainland. 66 pubs are owned with around two-thirds of these serving cask ale. Seasonal beers are brewed on the five-barrel plant formerly known as the Tipsy Toad Brewery.

Ale (OG 1039, ABV 4%)
Golden beer with a hint of citrus on the nose.

Lincoln Green SIBA ◉

Unit 5, Enterprise Park, Wigwam Lane, Hucknall, Nottinghamshire, NG15 7SZ
☎ (0115) 963 4233 ☎ 07748 111457
⊕ lincolngreenbrewing.co.uk

Anthony Hughes established the Lincoln Green Brewing Company in 2012 using a 10-barrel plant. Locally-sourced ingredients are used to create five regular beers and, in addition, seasonal and special brews are available that link to local and national events. The brewery takes its name from the colour of dyed woollen cloth associated with the legend of Robin Hood.

Marion (OG 1038, ABV 3.8%)
Full-bodied pale ale packed with citrus hop and a hint of grapefruit.

Hood (OG 1042, ABV 4.2%)
Best bitter in a classic English style, giving a full-rounded bitterness with a gentle floral aroma.

Sherwood (OG 1044, ABV 4.4%)
A pale ale with orange citrus aroma and biscuit malt.

Tuck (OG 1047, ABV 4.7%)
A well-rounded porter with a hint of dark chocolate and blackcurrant aroma.

Sheriff (OG 1055, ABV 5.5%)
An English pale ale with strong bitterness and orange citrus hop.

Linfit

▤ Sair Inn, 139 Lane Top, Linthwaite, Huddersfield, West Yorkshire, HD7 5SG
☎ (01484) 842370

☺A 19th-century brew-pub that started brewing again in 1982. The beer is only available at the Sair Inn.

Bitter (ABV 3.7%) ◀
A refreshing session beer. A dry-hopped aroma leads to a clean-tasting, hoppy bitterness, then a long, bitter finish with a hint of malt.

Gold Medal (ABV 4.2%)
Pale and hoppy with an aromatic and fruity character.

Special (ABV 4.3%) ◀
Dry-hopping provides the aroma for this rich and mellow bitter, which has a very soft profile and character: it fills the mouth with texture rather than taste. Clean, rounded finish.

Swift (ABV 4.3%)

Autumn Gold (ABV 4.7%) ◀
Straw-coloured best bitter with hop and fruit aromas, then the bittersweetness of autumn fruit in the taste and the finish.

Old Eli (ABV 5.3%)

A well-balanced premium bitter with a dry-hop aroma and a fruity, bitter finish.

Leadboiler (ABV 6.6%)

Lion's Tale SIBA

🍺 Red Lion, High Street, Cheswardine, Shropshire, TF9 2RS

☎ (01630) 661234 ✉ cheslion96@yahoo.co.uk

The building that houses the brewery was purpose-built in 2005 and houses a 2.5-barrel plant. Jon Morris and his wife Sheila have owned the Red Lion pub since 1996. Seasonal beer is available.

Blooming Blonde (OG 1041, ABV 4.1%)

Lionbru (OG 1041, ABV 4.1%)

Chesbrewnette (OG 1045, ABV 4.5%)

Little Ale Cart

🍺 c/o Wellington, 1 Henry Street, Sheffield, South Yorkshire, S3 7EQ

☎ (0114) 249 2295

Brewing started in 2001, as Port Mahon, in a purpose-built brewery behind the Cask & Cutler. In 2007 the brewery and pub were taken over and the names of both changed to Little Ale Cart Brewing and the Wellington. Beer is only brewed for the Wellington and the Dragon pub in Worcester. The beer range varies as the brewer trials new recipes, but tends to include a 4%, 4.3% and a 5% ABV beer.

Little Beer (NEW)

Unit 16, Enterprise Units, Moorfield Road, Slyfield Industrial Estate, Guildford, Surrey, GU1 1RB
⊕ littlebeer.co.uk

Jim Taylor is brewing beers on a small scale and selling to a closed customer base. See website for details.

Little Brew

43 Carol Street, Camden, London, NW1 0HT
⊕ littlebrew.co.uk

Brewing began in 2012 using a one-barrel plant. At present only bottle-conditioned ales are produced plus one-off bespoke brews for special events. Little Brew concentrate on supplying outlets in the Camden area and delivers the beer in a handcart.

Little Valley SIBA

Unit 3, Turkey Lodge Farm, New Road, Cragg Vale, Hebden Bridge, West Yorkshire, HX7 5TT
☎ (01422) 883888 ⊕ littlevalleybrewery.co.uk
Shop Mon-Fri 9am-5pm
Tours by arrangement

Little Valley Brewery began brewing in 2005 on a 10-barrel plant. All beers are organic and vegan, and Ginger Pale Ale uses Fairtrade ingredients. Around 100 outlets are supplied. Several beers are contract brewed for Suma Wholefoods and in 2012 the brewery was contracted by the Benedictine Order of Ampleforth Abbey to brew and bottle their Ampleforth Abbey Beer (ABV 7%). Bottle-conditioned and monthly special beers are also available.

Ginger Pale Ale (OG 1037, ABV 4%) ◆
Full-bodied speciality ale. Ginger predominates in the aroma and taste. It has a pleasantly powerful, fiery and spicy finish.

Cragg Vale Bitter (OG 1039, ABV 4.2%) ◆
Grainy, pale brown session bitter, light on the palate with a delicate flavour of malt and fruit and a bitter finish.

Hebden's Wheat (OG 1043, ABV 4.5%) 🍴 ◆
A pale yellow, creamy wheat beer with a good balance of bitterness and fruit, a hint of sweetness but with a lasting, dry finish.

Stoodley Stout (OG 1044, ABV 4.8%) ◆
Dark brown creamy stout with a rich roast aroma and luscious fruity, chocolate, roast flavours. Well-balanced with a clean bitter finish.

Tod's Blonde (OG 1045, ABV 5%) ◆
Bright yellow, grainy, speciality beer with a citrus hop start and a dry finish. Fruity, with a hint of spice. Similar in style to a Belgian blonde beer.

Python IPA (OG 1055, ABV 6%) ◆
Amber coloured grainy beer with a complex bitter fruit palate subtly balance by a malty sweetness, leading to a strongly lingering bitter afterftaste.

Liverpool Craft SIBA

10 Love Lane, The Railway Arches, Liverpool, L3 7DD
☎ (0151) 236 9400 ⊕ liverpoolcraftbeer.com

☺Liverpool Craft began brewing in 2011 using a 10-barrel plant. Beers are widely available across the north-west. Seasonal, speciality and bottle-conditioned beers are available.

Icon (OG 1037, ABV 3.8%)
A pale ale with a long dry finish with citrus undertones.

Hop Beast (OG 1039, ABV 4%)
A strong hop flavour and bitterness.

Viking Bitter (OG 1041, ABV 4.2%)
A refreshing, light-coloured bitter with some fruity tones.

Icon Dark (OG 1047, ABV 4.8%)
A traditional rich and warming porter.

American Red (OG 1047, ABV 5%)
An American ale packed with hop flavour balanced with a subtle sweetness.

IPA (OG 1047, ABV 5%)
An IPA with a strong, hoppy finish.

Liverpool One

82-84 Vauxhall Road, Liverpool, L3 6DL
☎ 07974 140023 ⊕ liverpoolonebrewery.co.uk
Tours by arrangement

☺Liverpool One started brewing in 2010 using a five-barrel plant. Expansion took place in 2012 to cope with increased demand. Its own pub, Liverpool 1 in Bridewell, opened in 2011. Seasonal, occasional and bottle-conditioned beers are also available.

Kings Regiment (OG 1038, ABV 3.8%)
A traditional, dark-coloured malty best bitter, smooth and rich.

Mersey Mist (OG 1040, ABV 4%)

A cloudy wheat beer brewed to the Belgian style, flavoured with fresh oranges and lemons with a touch of coriander.

Light (OG 1041, ABV 4.1%)
Light, hoppy and fruity.

Three Graces (OG 1042, ABV 4.2%)
Straw-coloured beer with an intense bitter bite.

Dark (OG 1050, ABV 5%)
A full-flavoured classic porter. Roasted and toasted flavours with a smoky finish.

Maharaja IPA (OG 1053, ABV 5.3%)
A classic IPA, deep golden in colour and packed full of bitterness.

Liverpool Organic SIBA

39 Brasenose Road, Liverpool, L20 8HL
☎ (0151) 933 9660 ⊕ liverpoolorganicbrewery.com
Tours by arrangement

⊠ Liverpool Organic started brewing in 2009. Outlets are supplied around the extended Merseyside area with its cask range and bespoke food outlets with its bottle-conditioned beers. Seasonal beers are also available. Beers are also brewed under the name of the now defunct Cambrinus brewery.

Cascade (OG 1038, ABV 3.8%)

Iron Men (OG 1040, ABV 4%)

Joseph Williamson (OG 1039, ABV 4%)

Liverpool Pale Ale (OG 1039, ABV 4%)

Bier Head (OG 1040, ABV 4.1%)

24 Carat (OG 1041, ABV 4.2%)

Best Bitter (OG 1042, ABV 4.2%)

Liverpool Stout (OG 1048, ABV 4.3%)

Jade (OG 1047, ABV 4.4%)

Honey Blond (OG 1043, ABV 4.5%)

Josephine Butler (OG 1043, ABV 4.5%)

Kitty Wilkinson Chocolate & Vanilla Stout (OG 1047, ABV 4.5%)

Liverpool Pilsner (OG 1047, ABV 4.5%)

Simcoe (OG 1047, ABV 4.7%)

Stella Gold (OG 1046, ABV 4.8%)

Empire (OG 1056, ABV 5.3%)

Shipwreck IPA (OG 1059, ABV 6.5%)

Under the Cambrinus Brewery name:

Deliverance (OG 1042, ABV 4.2%)

Endurance (OG 1044, ABV 4.3%)

St Antonys (OG 1048, ABV 5.2%)

Lizard

The Old Nuclear Bunker, Pednavounder, Cornwall, TR12 6SE
☎ (01326) 281135 ⊕ lizardales.co.uk
Tours by arrangement

Launched in 2004, Lizard Ales is now based in the former RAF Treleaver, a massive disused nuclear bunker in the countryside near Coverack on the Lizard Peninsula. Specialising in bottle-conditioned ales, it mainly supplies west Cornwall.

Kernow Gold (OG 1037, ABV 3.7%)

Bitter (OG 1041, ABV 4.2%)

Frenchman's Creek (OG 1042, ABV 4.8%)

An Gof (OG 1049, ABV 5.2%) ◄
Robust and smooth tawny ale dominated by malt in the mouth with a hint of smoke. Fruity hops follow on into the bitter finish.

Llangollen SIBA

⊟ Abbey Grange Brewing Ltd, Abbey Grange Hotel, Horseshoe Pass Road, Llantysilio, Llangollen, LL20 8DD
☎ (01978) 861916 ⊕ llangollenbrewery.com
Shop open daily in summer; the hotel sells bottles throughout the year
Tours by arrangement

The brewery began brewing in 2010 using a 2.5-barrel plant. All beers are also available bottle conditioned.

Grange No. 1 (OG 1032, ABV 3.2%)
A light brown beer with a fruity aroma and a slight hoppy finish.

Wrexham Borders Bitter (OG 1039, ABV 3.9%)
A pale ale with fruity notes, haylike and distinctively hoppy.

Bitter (OG 1042, ABV 4.2%)
A best bitter with a fruity aroma and a distinctive hoppy finish.

Welsh Black (OG 1055, ABV 5.5%)
A black beer with chocolate and toffee notes and a hoppy finish.

Llangorse

Red Lion, Llangors, Powys, LD3 7TY
☎ (01874) 658825 ⊕ llangorsebrewery.co.uk

Llangorse began brewing in 2012 and is owned by Howard Marlow who also owns the Breconshire Brewery.

Maid in Llangorse (OG 1042, ABV 4.2%)
A red-coloured beer with a smooth, hoppy finish.

Maid for Horsin' Around (OG 1044, ABV 4.4%)
A light yellow premium ale with a refreshing flavour. A full-bodied, crisp, Welsh-style hoppy bitter.

Maid for the High Life (OG 1048, ABV 4.8%)
A smooth, well-balanced, traditional old-style Welsh ale.

Llŷn SIBA

Unit 6, Ffordd Dewi Sant, Nefyn, Gwynedd, LL53 6EG
☎ 07792 050134 ⊕ cwrwllyn.com

The brewery is a co-operative of 12 friends that began brewing in 2011 producing 44 barrels per week.

Brenin Enlli (ABV 4%)

Seithenyn (ABV 4.2%)

Cochyn (ABV 4.5%)

Loch Leven

Criochan House, Maryburgh, Blairadam, KY4 0JE
☎ (01383) 831751 ☎ 07592 575329
⊕ lochlevenbrewery.com

THE BREWERIES

Loch Leven was established in 2009 on a four-barrel brewery. It supplies beer to most Scottish beer festivals and trades mostly with pubs in Fife and Perthshire. Seasonal beers are also available.

Golden Goose (OG 1037, ABV 3.7%)
Golden ale; light, crisp and well-hopped with a dry aftertaste.

Cock Robin (OG 1041, ABV 4.1%)
A Scottish style ale, full-bodied with a malty aftertaste.

Nightjar (OG 1042, ABV 4.2%)
A malty ale with a taste of chocolate, lightly hopped with a floral finish.

Falcon Hell (OG 1056, ABV 5.6%)

Loch Lomond SIBA

Block 1, Unit 5, Lomond Industrial Estate, Alexandria, G83 0TL ⊕ lochlomondbrewery.com
Shop 10am-5pm daily except Wed & Sun closed
Tours by arrangement

Loch Lomond was established in 2011 by Fiona and Euan MacEachern and is the only brewery in the Loch Lomond area.

Bonnie n' Bitter (OG 1036, ABV 3.6%)
A blonde, easy-drinking bitter with citrus flavours and a full, rounded bitterness.

The West Highland Way (OG 1038, ABV 3.8%)
A light ale with fruity flavours.

Bonnie n' Blonde (OG 1040, ABV 4%)
A light, refreshing ale with a well-rounded citrus flavour.

The Ale of Leven (OG 1045, ABV 4.5%)
An amber-coloured, easy-drinking beer with a slight sweetness and a spicy bitterness.

Silkie Stout (OG 1050, ABV 5%)
A black stout with chocolate orange spicy notes.

Kessog Dark Ale (OG 1052, ABV 5.2%)
Dark with warm, spicy flavours.

Loch Ness SIBA

🏠 Blarmor, Drumnadrochit, IV63 6UG
☎ (01456) 450080 ⊕ lochnessbrewery.com
Tours by arrangement

☺Loch Ness began brewing in 2011 using a two-barrel plant in the grounds of the Benleva Hotel. The brewery moved in 2012 to nearby premises using an eight-barrel plant. Beers are available in the local area and central Scotland. Bottle-conditioned beers are available.

Light Ness (OG 1040, ABV 3.9%) ◣
Golden, refreshing, hoppy bitter with a hint of peaches.

Wilder Ness (OG 1040, ABV 3.9%) ◣
Fruity, hoppy brew with a slight malt background. Bittersweet turning to a more bitter finish.

Red Ness (OG 1042, ABV 4.2%) ◣
Reddy brown colour with a good mix of malt and hops with a raspberry background in this sweetish brew.

Loch Ness (OG 1044, ABV 4.4%) ◣
A malty, fruity, sweetish brew in the 80/- style. Hints of chocolate and blackcurrant.

Dark Ness (OG 1052, ABV 4.5%) ◣

Roasted chocolate malt with a slight blackcurrant background. Thick brown head all the way to the bottom.

Hoppy Ness (OG 1050, ABV 5%) ◣
Golden, smooth, citrus, hoppy brew. The initial sweetness turns to a bitter finish. Does not drink its strength.

Loddon SIBA 👁

Dunsden Green Farm, Church Lane, Dunsden, Oxfordshire, RG4 9QD
☎ (0118) 948 1111 ⊕ loddonbrewery.com
Shop Mon-Fri 9am-5pm; Sat 9.30am-3pm
Tours by arrangement

⊠ Loddon, established 2002 in a brick and flint barn housing a 17-barrel brewery, can produce 120 barrels a week. Over 500 outlets are supplied. 2012 saw a comprehensive re-branding across the board. Seasonal beers and monthly specials: see website.

Hoppit (OG 1036.2, ABV 3.5%) ◣
Hops dominate the aroma of this drinkable, light-coloured session beer. Malt and hops create a balanced taste and a pleasant bitterness carries through to the aftertaste.

Hullabaloo (OG 1043.8, ABV 4.2%) ◣
A hint of fruit in the initial taste develops into a balance of hops and malt in this well-rounded, medium-bodied bitter with a bitter aftertaste.

Ferryman's Gold (OG 1045.8, ABV 4.4%) ◣
Golden-coloured with a strong hoppy character throughout, accompanied by fruit in the taste and aftertaste.

Bamboozle (OG 1049.5, ABV 4.8%) ◣
Full-bodied and well balanced. Distinctive bittersweet flavour with hop and caramel to accompany.

Forbury Lion (OG 1056.5, ABV 5.5%)
A malty IPA with a strong, complex hop finish.

London Brewing

Bull 13 North Hill, Highgate, London, N6 4AB
☎ (020) 8341 0510 ⊕ londonbrewing.com

⊠ London Brewing Co began brewing in 2011 at the Bull in Highgate using a 2.5-barrel plant. Seasonal and special beers are also available.

Highrise (ABV 3.9%) ◣
A golden ale with lemon citrus notes from American hops and a touch of green grass on the finish.

Beer Street (ABV 4%) ◣
Well balanced copper brown best bitter with the hoppy bitterness underpinned by a biscuity malt character. A trace of citrus.

Vista (ABV 4.4%) ◣
A copper coloured smooth best bitter with a fudge flavour and some roast notes balanced by citrus fruit.

London Fields SIBA

365-366 Warburton Street, Hackney, London, E8 3RR
☎ (020) 7254 7174 ☎ 07982 367051
⊕ londonfieldsbrewery.co.uk
Tours by arrangement

⊗ London Fields was first established in 2011, operating from a railway arch beneath London Fields Railway Station. 2012 saw considerable expansion of brewing capacity at a site nearby. London pubs are supplied, as well as events at the brewery itself.

Pale Ale (ABV 3.7%) ◄
A quaffable, hoppy, yellow-coloured bitter with some citrus and apple fruitiness.

Hackney Hopster (OG 1042, ABV 4.2%) ◄
Amber beer that is malty sweet with traces of honey but is balanced by mixed fruits and a bitter dryness.

Love not War (OG 1044, ABV 4.2%) ◄
Peppery hop character and some citrus is present throughout this copper-coloured beer with a dry finish and increasing bitterness.

Long Itch (NEW) SIBA

c/o Manor Farm, Hunningham Lane, Offchurch, Warwickshire, CV33 9AG
☎ 07780 900699

Office: Walnut House, Leamington Road, Long Itchington, Warwickshire, CV47 9PL
⊕ longitchbrewery.co.uk

Long Itch Brewery commenced brewing in 2013 on a 5.5-barrel plant housed in a converted barn among the outbuildings of Manor Farm just outside Offchurch. Local freehouses and beer festivals are supplied.

Light Relief (OG 1037, ABV 3.8%)

Honey Trap (OG 1039, ABV 4.1%)

Backscratcher (OG 1044, ABV 4.5%)

Dubbel Trubbel (OG 1057, ABV 5.9%)

Long Lane

Matchless Home Brewing, 48 Belvoir Road, Coalville, Leicestershire, LE67 3PP
☎ (01530) 813800 ⊕ matchlesshomebrewing.co.uk

This small 100-litre brewery was established in 2010 and is based in the Matchless Homebrew shop. Beers are mostly bottle-conditioned but cask beers can be produced to order.

Long Man SIBA ◉

Church Farm, Litlington, East Sussex, BN26 5RA
☎ (01323) 871850 ☎ 07976 777992
⊕ longmanbrewery.com
Tours by arrangement

⊗ Long Man began brewing in 2012 using a 20-barrel plant. Hops and grain are sourced locally with a view to using barley currently being grown on the farm as well as a traditional strain of Sussex yeast.

Long Blonde (OG 1037, ABV 3.8%)
A light-coloured golden ale with a distinctive hoppy aroma and crisp, clean bitterness on the finish. Smooth, light and refreshing.

Best Bitter (OG 1040, ABV 4%)
Well-balanced with a complex bittersweet malty taste, fragrant hops and a characteristic long deep finish. A traditional Sussex-style best bitter.

Old Man (OG 1048, ABV 4.3%)

Dark beer with soft malt notes of coffee and chocolate combined with a pleasant light hoppiness creating a rich, full tasting old ale.

Sussex Pride (OG 1045, ABV 4.5%)
A classic strong pale ale. Bronze-coloured with a fruity nose and full round flavours. A perfect balance between malt and hops

American Pale Ale (OG 1046, ABV 4.8%)
Made using only the choicest US hops, this triple-hopped APA has a pleasant citrus fruit aroma and characteristic robust bitterness.

Longdog SIBA

Unit A1, Moniton Trading Estate, West Ham Lane, Worting, Basingstoke, Hampshire, RG22 6NQ
☎ (01256) 324286 ☎ 07827 618733
⊕ longdogbrewery.co.uk
Tours by arrangement

⊗ Longdog was established in 2011 using a six-barrel plant. The name is inspired by the owner's greyhound. Seasonal beers are available.

Bunny Chaser (OG 1036, ABV 3.6%)
A dark copper-coloured session bitter with plenty of malt in the mouth and a good whack of bitterness.

Golden Poacher (OG 1038, ABV 3.9%)
A very hoppy beer with a crisp, citrus aroma.

Brindle Bitter (OG 1041, ABV 4.2%) ◄
A well-crafted best bitter. Malt nose with hints of caramel and berry fruits. An initial balanced maltiness leads into a moderate hop flavour with bitterness building on the aftertaste.

Lamplight Porter (OG 1048, ABV 5%) ◄
Smoky and drier than many porters, with strong roast flavours giving way to blackberry in the taste and a slightly vinous finish.

Longhill

Longhill Cottage, Whitstone, Cornwall, EX22 6UG
☎ (01288) 341466

⊗ Longhill began brewing in 2011 using a 0.5-barrel plant, upgraded in 2012 to a four-barrel plant to meet demand. The beers are named with a wind theme. Eight outlets are supplied direct. Seasonal beers are available.

Whistler (OG 1038, ABV 3.8%)

Westerly (OG 1040, ABV 4%)

Gale Force (OG 1048, ABV 4.8%)

Hurricane (OG 1048, ABV 4.8%)

Loose Cannon SIBA

Unit 6, Suffolk Way, Abingdon, Oxfordshire, OX14 5JX
☎ (01235) 531141 ⊕ lcbeers.co.uk
Shop Mon-Sat 9am-5pm
Tours by arrangement

Loose Cannon began production in 2010 using a 15-barrel brew plant, reviving Abingdon's brewing history after the Morland Brewery closed in 2000. Beers can be found in an increasing number of local pubs. Seasonal beers are available.

Gunners Gold (OG 1034.5, ABV 3.5%)
Golden, easy-drinking session ale with a subtle peach flavour.

Abingdon Bridge (OG 1041, ABV 4.1%)
Full-flavoured and smooth, with well-rounded bitterness and a light citrus and floral finish.

Bandwagon (OG 1041.5, ABV 4.2%)
Full-flavoured, copper-coloured bitter with a rounded malty body and mixed berry finish.

Dark Horse (OG 1042, ABV 4.3%)
A dark beer with a fruity hop aroma.

Lord Conrad's

Unit 21, Dry Drayton Industrial Estate, Scotland Road, Dry Drayton, Cambridgeshire, CB23 8AT
☎ 07736 739700 ⊕ lordconradsbrewery.co.uk

⊠ Lord Conrad's began commercial brewing in 2011 using a 2.5-barrel plant. One permanent outlet is supplied, the Pavilion in Longstanton, along with other local free houses and beer festivals. Seasonal/special beers: see website.

Lickety Split (OG 1038, ABV 3.8%)
Sweet, malty brown ale, light but not overly hoppy.

Conkerwood (OG 1044, ABV 4%)
A dark porter with hints of liquorice.

Gubbins (OG 1040, ABV 4%)
A medley of flavours; light, spicy notes and warm, sweet tones.

Slap N' Tickle (OG 1042, ABV 4.3%)
A summer blonde with huge hit of bitterness and a tickle of hops.

Hedgerow Hop (OG 1039, ABV 4.5%)
An amber-coloured ale made with locally picked hops and supporting the RSPB.

Zulu (OG 1047, ABV 4.5%)
A strong black bitter made with hibiscus extract. Tastes sweet and burnt like coffee and tobacco.

Pheasant's Rise (OG 1050, ABV 5%)
A smoky, woody, traditional strong ale.

Stubble Burner (OG 1050, ABV 5%)
A straw-like beer with a good earthy nose and a well-balanced fruity bitterness.

Lovibonds

rear of 19-21 Market Place, Henley-on-Thames, Oxfordshire, RG9 2AA
☎ (01491) 576596 ⊕ lovibonds.com
Shop Fri 4-9pm; Sat 11am-7pm; Sun & Bank Hols 12-5pm
Tours by arrangement

Lovibonds Brewery was founded by Jeff Rosenmeier in 2005 and is named after Joseph William Lovibond, who invented the Tintometer to measure beer colour. No real ale.

Luckie

Haig Business Park, Balgonie Road, Markinch, KY7 6AQ
☎ (01333) 352801 ⊕ luckie-ales.com

Luckie Ales was established by Stuart McLuckie in 2009. Brewing moved to Haigs Business Park in 2012 using a one-barrel plant. The brewery specialises in handcrafted Scottish beers and historic British ales. Beers are brewed on demand.

Ludlow SIBA ◉

The Railway Shed, Station Drive, Ludlow, Shropshire, SY8 2PQ
☎ (01584) 873291
⊕ theludlowbrewingcompany.co.uk
Shop Mon-Fri 10am-5pm; Sat 10am-1pm
Tours by arrangement

Established in 2006, the brewery operates from a converted railway sidings shed utilising a 20-barrel brew plant. The premises also functions as a brewery tap, visitor centre and events area.

Best (OG 1037, ABV 3.7%)

Gold (OG 1041, ABV 4.2%)

Black Knight (OG 1045, ABV 4.5%)

Boiling Well (OG 1045.5, ABV 4.7%)

Stairway (OG 1047, ABV 5%)

Lymestone SIBA ◉

The Old Brewery, Mount Road, Stone, Staffordshire, ST15 8LL
☎ (01785) 817796 ☎ 07891 782652
⊕ lymestonebrewery.co.uk
Shop Mon-Fri 8am-5pm; Sat & Sun by arrangement
Tours by arrangement

☺Lymestone commenced brewing in 2008. Rapid growth has seen the beers supplied direct to 300 outlets, with beer also being available via wholesalers. The brewery opened its first pub in 2012, the Lymestone Vaults in Newcastle-under-Lyme.

Stone Cutter (OG 1037, ABV 3.7%) ◄
Sulphurous aroma gives way to a caramel sweet start and pleasing hop and fruit balance. The mouth-watering hoppy promise is fulfilled in to the finish.

Stone Faced (OG 1040, ABV 4%)
Subtle citrus and toffee flavours balanced by a hoppy aroma and bitter finish.

Foundation Stone (OG 1047, ABV 4.5%) ◄
An IPA-style beer with pale and crystal malts. Faint biscuit and chewy, juicy fruits burst on to the palate then the spicy Boadicea and Pilot hops pepper the taste buds to leave a dry, bitter finish.

Ein Stein (OG 1052, ABV 5%)
A very pale, citrus, hoppy ale.

Stone the Crows (OG 1056, ABV 5.4%) ◄
A rich dark beer from chocolate malts. Fruit, roasts and hops abound to leave a deep lingering bitterness from the Styrian Goldings and Millennium hop mix.

Lytham SIBA

8 Campbell's Court, Lord Street, St Annes, Lancashire, FY8 2DF
☎ (01253) 725440 ⊕ lythambrewery.co.uk
Tours by arrangement

☺Lytham started brewing in 2008, upgrading from a 2.5-barrel to a 10-barrel plant in 2010 to cope with increased demand. Seasonal beers are available.

Amber (OG 1037, ABV 3.6%)
A traditional malty beer using English hops.

Blonde (OG 1038, ABV 3.8%)

A pale golden beer with a subtle hop aroma and a smooth, dry finish.

Gold (OG 1042, ABV 4.2%)
A golden beer with a fruity aroma and lasting bitter finish.

Royal (OG 1044, ABV 4.4%)
A full-bodied English ale with a crisp fruity aroma and a smooth, dry finish.

Dark (OG 1047, ABV 5%)
Dark chocolate malt with a hint of vanilla and a smooth, dry finish.

IPA (OG 1054, ABV 5.6%)
A pale bitter with a fresh, sweet, hoppy flavour leading to a long, dry finish.

McGivern

c/o Bridge End Inn, 5 Bridge Street, Ruabon, LL14 6DA
☎ (01978) 810881 ☎ 07891 676614
⊕ mcgivernales.co.uk

☺The brewery was established in 2008 and was originally based at the brewer's home in Wrexham but moved in 2011 to the Bridge End Inn in Ruabon using a 2.5-barrel plant.

Bridge Pale (OG 1039, ABV 3.9%)

McMullen SIBA IFBB ⊙

26 Old Cross, Hertford, SG14 1RD
☎ (01992) 584911 ⊕ mcmullens.co.uk
Tours by arrangement

⊗ McMullen, Hertfordshire's oldest independent brewery, was founded in 1827. A new brewhouse opened in 2006, giving the company flexibility to produce its regular cask beers and up to eight seasonal beers a year. Cask beer is served in all its 140 pubs.

AK (OG 1035, ABV 3.7%) ⬦
A pleasant mix of malt and hops leads to a distinctive, dry aftertaste that isn't always as pronounced as it used to be.

Cask Ale (OG 1039, ABV 3.8%)
A light and refreshing, well-balanced beer with a subtle biscuity flavour.

Country Bitter (OG 1042, ABV 4.3%) ⬦
A full-bodied beer with a well-balanced mix of malt, hops and fruit throughout.

IPA (OG 1047, ABV 4.8%)
A strong bitter with deep, rich flavours.

Mad Cat (NEW) SIBA

Brogdale Farm, Brogdale Road, Faversham, Kent, ME13 8XU
☎ (01795) 597743 ☎ 07960 263615
⊕ madcatbrewery.co.uk
Shop Sat & Sun 10am-2pm

Mad Cat was established in 2012 by Peter Meaney in a refurbished cold store using an eight-barrel plant.

Auburn Copper Ale (ABV 4.2%)

Golden IPA (ABV 4.2%)

Platinum Blonde (ABV 4.2%)

Mad Hatter (NEW)

Unit D22, Ayrton House, Commerce Way, Liverpool, L8 7BA
☎ (0151) 739 1702 ☎ 07871 645864
⊕ madhatterbrewing.co.uk

Mad Hatter began brewing in 2013 combining traditional techniques with new flavours and approaches to brewing. Bottle-conditioned beers are also available: see website.

Mad Hat Mild (ABV 4.5%)

Unhinged (ABV 5%)

Crazy Cascade (ABV 5.5%)

American Psycho (ABV 6%)

IPA (Insane Pale Ale) (ABV 6.5%)

REDRUM (ABV 7%)

Madcap SIBA

Office: Greenknowe Avenue, Annan, DG12 6ER
☎ (01461) 203495 ☎ 07801 699161
⊕ madcapbrewery.com

Madcap began brewing in 2009. It concentrates on the production of bottle-conditioned beers. Seasonal beers are available.

Magic Rock

Unit 1, Quarmby Mills, Tanyard Road, Oakes, Huddersfield, West Yorkshire, HD3 4YP
☎ (01484) 649823 ⊕ magicrockbrewing.com

Magic Rock began brewing in 2011 in the Old Bed Factory attached to the Rockshop Wholesale Company in Huddersfield. Bottle-conditioned and special beers are available.

Curious (OG 1038, ABV 3.9%)
Pale ale with a floral/grassy aroma and citrus hops.

Rapture (OG 1044.5, ABV 4.6%)
Full-bodied red ale with grapefruit and pine aromas, pithy orange and a rich, malty body.

High Wire (OG 1051, ABV 5.5%)
West Coast-style pale ale with mango, lychee and grapefruit flavours.

Dark Arts (OG 1057, ABV 6%)
Chocolate, liquorice, blackberry and fig flavours with a long roasted bitter finish.

Magpie SIBA ⊙

Unit 4, Ashling Court, Ashling Street, Nottingham, NG2 3JA
☎ 07738 762897 ⊕ magpiebrewery.com

☺Magpie is a six-barrel brewery launched in 2006. It is located a few feet from the perimeter of the Meadow Lane Stadium, home of Notts County FC (the Magpies) from which the brewery name naturally derived. Seasonal and occasional beers: see website. Bottle-conditioned beers are also available.

Hoppily Ever After (OG 1035, ABV 3.8%)
Blonde, refreshing beer with a distinct hop flavour.

Best (OG 1040.7, ABV 4.2%) ⬦
A malty traditional pale brown best bitter with balancing hops giving a bitter finish.

Blonde (OG 1039.9, ABV 4.2%)

Blonde, light and refreshing summer ale. Lightly-hopped giving floral and fruity hints.

Raven Stout (OG 1044, ABV 4.4%)
Rich and full-bodied, roast and smoky-flavoured smooth, dark stout.

Thieving Rogue (OG 1042, ABV 4.5%) ◆
A hoppy golden ale with a long-lasting, bitter finish.

Midnight Porter (OG 1049.4, ABV 5%)
Rich and creamy dark porter with coffee, raisins and chocolate flavours.

For Home Bar, Arnold:

Home IPA (OG 1047.5, ABV 5.2%)

Maldon

See Farmer's Ales

Mallard SIBA

Unit A, Maythorne, Nottinghamshire, NG25 0RS
☎ 07811 193930
Tours by arrangement

Phil Mallard built and installed a two-barrel plant in a shed at his home and started brewing in 1995. The brewery was taken over in 2010 and moved to its current address. There are plans to expand the plant, increase the range of beers and introduce bottle-conditioned ales.

Duck 'n' Dive (OG 1039, ABV 3.7%) ◆
A bitter, pale golden beer, with a dry finish. Brewed with First Gold hops.

Hearty Good Feather (OG 1039, ABV 3.9%)

Puddle Duck (OG 1040, ABV 4%)

Quacker Jack (OG 1040, ABV 4%)

Feather Light (OG 1040, ABV 4.1%) ◆
A straw-coloured lager style beer with a hoppy taste and aroma.

Duckling (OG 1041, ABV 4.2%) ◆
A dry-hopped, golden ale. Very bitter; hops dominate in the aroma and aftertaste.

Decoy (OG 1045, ABV 4.5%)

Mallinson's

Unit 1, Waterhouse Mill, 65-71 Lockwood Road, Huddersfield, West Yorkshire, HD1 3QU
☎ (01484) 654301 ☎ 07850 446571
⊕ drinkmallinsons.co.uk
Tours by arrangement

⊛The brewery was originally set up in 2008 on a six-barrel plant by CAMRA members Tara Mallinson and Elaine Yendall. The company moved to new premises in 2012 after trial brewing its core beers on a new 15-barrel plant for several weeks. For beer range including seasonal and special beers: see website.

Emley Moor Mild (ABV 3.4%)
Black with a ruby hint. A full-bodied mild with a nutty taste and slightly bitter finish.

Stadium Bitter (ABV 3.8%)
Straw-coloured with a clean, bitter taste and dry, fruity finish.

Station Best Bitter (ABV 4.2%)

An amber-coloured best bitter with a balance of malt and fruity hops.

Castle Hill Premium (ABV 4.6%)
A golden-coloured premium bitter, hoppy with citrus tones.

Malt (NEW) SIBA

Collings Hanger Farm, 100 Wycombe Road, Prestwood, Buckinghamshire, HP16 0HP
☎ (01494) 865063 ☎ 07815 187113
⊕ maltthebrewery.co.uk
Shop Fri 12-6pm; Sat 10am-6pm
Tours by arrangement

⊗ Opened in 2012 in a converted dairy, the 10-barrel brewery has conservation at its heart; from the use of local ingredients to spent grain sent to the local farm. The ales are also used in pies and fish batter.

Golden Ale (OG 1038, ABV 3.9%)
Mellow, malty and a little bit fruity.

Malt Dark Ale (OG 1038, ABV 3.9%)
Smooth and decidedly drinkable. Full of deep malt tones.

Best Bitter (OG 1043, ABV 4.4%)
Full-flavoured with a refreshing finish.

IPA (OG 1048, ABV 5%)
Aromatic with a bitter finish.

Malthouse (NEW) SIBA

Unit 4, Parkway House, Ashley Industrial Estate, Wakefield Road, Ossett, West Yorkshire, WF5 9JD
☎ 07980 386361 ⊕ themalthousebrewery.co.uk

Malthouse began brewing in 2013 using a four-barrel plant. Seasonal and speciality beers are also available: see website.

Challenge 2.5 (ABV 2.5%)
A light beer with tones of biscuit and nut.

Horbury Blonde (ABV 3.8%)
A light beer with a sweet, refreshing finish.

Insomniac Stout (ABV 4%)
A rich, smooth stout packed with roasted coffee flavour.

House Brown (ABV 4.4%)
A copper-coloured best bitter with toffee overtones.

Malvern Hills SIBA

15 West Malvern Road, Malvern, Worcestershire, WR14 4ND
☎ (01684) 560165 ⊕ malvernhillsbrewery.co.uk
Tours by arrangement

Founded in 1998 in an old quarrying dynamite store and now an established presence in the Three Counties, Birmingham and the Black Country. The core brews are supplemented by a rolling programme of monthly specials.

Feelgood (OG 1037, ABV 3.8%)

Cyneweard (OG 1038, ABV 3.9%)
Pale blonde and hoppy.

Swedish Nightingale (OG 1039, ABV 4%)

Priessnitz Plzen (OG 1040, ABV 4.3%) ◆

A mix of soft fruit and citrus give this straw-coloured brew its quaffability, making it ideal for quenching summer thirsts.

Black Pear (OG 1042, ABV 4.4%) 🍽 ◆
A sharp citrus hoppiness is the main constituent of this golden brew that has a long, dry aftertaste.

Marble SIBA

41 Williamson Street, Manchester, M4 4JS
☎ (0161) 819 2694 ⊕ marblebeers.com
Tours by arrangement

☺Marble began brewing in 1997 at the Marble Arch Inn in Manchester but now brew at a larger 12-barrel plant in a nearby unit, producing organic and vegan beers plus some non-organic ales. It supplies its own three pubs and more than 70 other outlets. Bottle-conditioned and regular seasonal beers are available.

Draft (OG 1039, ABV 3.9%) ◆
Yellow beer with a hoppy, fruity aroma. Grapefruit and a bitter hoppiness dominate throughout.

Pint (OG 1038.5, ABV 3.9%)
A dry session bitter with notes of citrus and grapefruit.

Manchester Bitter (OG 1041.7, ABV 4.2%) ◆
Yellow beer with a fruity and hoppy aroma. Hops, fruit and bitterness on the palate and in the finish.

Ginger (OG 1046, ABV 4.5%) 🍽
Full-bodied, copper-coloured ale with a delicate blend of cloves, coriander and heaps of fiery ginger.

Stouter Stout (OG 1046.5, ABV 4.7%) 🍽 ◆
Black in colour, with roast malt dominating the aroma. Roast malt and hops in the mouth, with a little fruit. Pleasant, dry, bitter aftertaste.

Lagonda IPA (OG 1048, ABV 5%) ◆
Golden yellow beer with a spicy, fruity nose. Fruit, hops and malt in the mouth, with a dry fruitiness continuing into the bitter aftertaste.

Chocolate Marble (OG 1054.5, ABV 5.5%)
A strong, stout-like ale.

Dobber (OG 1055.5, ABV 5.9%) 🍽

Marlpool

5 Breach Road, Marlpool, Heanor, Derbyshire, DE75 7NJ
☎ (01773) 711285 ⊕ marlpoolbrewing.co.uk
Shop Fri 3-9pm; Sat & Sun 12-9pm
Tours by arrangement

Marlpool was set up by brothers Andy and Chris McAuley in 2010 using a 2.5-barrel plant situated in an old slaughterhouse. The majority of the beer is sold through its own ale house, attached to the brewery. The remainder is supplied to pubs within a 10-mile radius.

Blind Boris (OG 1038, ABV 3.5%)
Traditional dark mild.

Otters Pocket (OG 1040, ABV 4%)
Easy-drinking, smooth amber ale.

Scratty Ratty (OG 1044, ABV 4.4%)
Pale ale, lightly hopped with a bitter, dry finish.

Marston Moor

PO Box 9, York, North Yorkshire, YO26 7XW
☎ (01423) 359641 ⊕ rudgatebrewery.co.uk

☺Established in 1983 in Kirk Hammerton, the brewery had a re-investment programme in 2005, moving brewing operations to nearby Tockwith, where it shares the site with Rudgate Brewery (qv). Two special beers are available each month. Around 250 outlets are supplied.

Matchlock Mild (OG 1038, ABV 4%)
Traditional, full-flavoured dark mild.

Mongrel (OG 1038, ABV 4%)
A balanced bitter with plenty of fruit character.

Fairfax Special (OG 1039, ABV 4.2%)
A full-bodied premium bitter, pale in colour with a well-balanced slightly citrus aroma.

Merriemaker (OG 1042, ABV 4.5%)
A premium straw-coloured ale with a typical Yorkshire taste.

Brewers Droop (OG 1045.5, ABV 5%)
A powerful golden ale with a sweet taste.

Marston's ⊙

Marston's Brewery, Shobnall Road, Burton upon Trent, DE14 2BW
☎ (01283) 531131 ⊕ marstons.co.uk
Shop Mon-Fri 10am-5pm; Sat 9.30am-12pm (excluding Bank Holidays)
Tours by arrangement

Marston's has been brewing cask beer in Burton since 1834 and the current site is the home of the only working Burton Union fermenters, housed in rooms known as the Cathedral of Brewing. Burton Unions were developed in the 19th century to cleanse the new style of pale ale of yeast. Only Pedigree is fermented in the unions but yeast from the system is used to ferment the other beers. Pedigree celebrated its 60th anniversary in 2012. Part of Marston's PLC.

EPA (OG 1036, ABV 3.6%)

Burton Bitter (OG 1037, ABV 3.8%) ◆
Overwhelming sulphurous aroma supports a scattering of hops and fruit with an easy-drinking sweetness. The taste develops from the sweet middle to a satisfyingly hoppy finish.

Pedigree (OG 1043, ABV 4.5%) ◆
Pale brown with a sweet, hoppy aroma. Malt with a dash of hop flavours give a satisfying tasty finish.

Old Empire (OG 1057, ABV 5.7%) ◆
Sulphur dominates the gentle malt aroma. Malty fruit and sweet to start but developing bitterness with fruit and a touch of sweetness. A balanced aftertaste of hops and fruit leads to a lingering bitterness.

For AB InBev:

Draught Bass (OG 1043, ABV 4.4%) ◆
Hints of caramel aroma and taste, lightly hopped for a short, bitter finish.

Masters

8 Greenham Business Park, Greenham, Somerset, TA21 0LR
☎ (01823) 674444 ⊕ mastersbrewery.co.uk
Tours by arrangement

The brewery first started in 2006 but had to close in 2009. In 2011 it was reopened using a 2.5-barrel plant.

Devon's Pride (OG 1043, ABV 3.8%)

Spypost Bitter (OG 1040, ABV 4%)

Whiteball (OG 1038, ABV 4%)

Immenstadt Weiss Bier (OG 1043, ABV 4.3%)

Thunderbridge Ale (OG 1047, ABV 4.7%)

Mauldons SIBA ⊙

Black Adder Brewery, 13 Church Field Road, Sudbury, Suffolk, CO10 2YA
☎ (01787) 311055 ∰ mauldons.co.uk
Shop Mon-Fri 9.30am-4pm
Tours by arrangement

The Mauldon family started brewing in Sudbury in 1795. The brewery with 26 pubs was bought by Greene King in the 1960s. The current business, established in 1982, was bought by Steve and Alison Sims in 2000. They relocated to a new brewery in 2005, with a 30-barrel plant that has doubled production. Two pubs are owned and around 150 outlets are supplied. There is a rolling programme of seasonal beers: see website.

Micawber's Mild (OG 1035, ABV 3.5%) ◆
Fruit and roast flavours dominate the nose, with vine fruit and caramel on the tongue and a short, dry, coffeeish aftertaste. Full-bodied and satisfying.

Moletrap Bitter (OG 1038, ABV 3.8%) ◆
Easy-drinking session bitter. Crisp and refreshing, hoppy and fruity throughout.

Silver Adder (OG 1042, ABV 4.2%)
A light-coloured bitter with five hop and malt combinations giving a refreshing, crisp finish.

Suffolk Punch (OG 1048, ABV 4.8%)

Black Adder (OG 1053, ABV 5.3%) ◆
Superbly balanced dark, sweet ale, but with rich vine fruit throughout. The brewery's flagship beer.

Maxim SIBA ⊙

1 Gadwall Road, Rainton Bridge South, Houghton le Spring, County Durham, DH4 5NL
☎ (0191) 584 8844 ∰ maximbrewery.co.uk
Tours by arrangement

⊛Rising from the ashes of Sunderland brewer Vaux, Maxim was set up with a 20-barrel plant in Houghton le Spring in 2007. In 2010 two former brewers from the Federation Brewery joined the team. More than 100 outlets are supplied direct and four pubs are owned. Seasonal beers are also available.

Samson (OG 1040, ABV 4%)
A distinctive, well-balanced beer with a lingering, smooth flavour.

Swedish Blonde (OG 1042, ABV 4.2%)
Light-coloured beer with a refreshing hoppy and grapefruit flavour on the palate.

May Hill SIBA ⊙

Holly Bush Farm, Ross Road, Longhope, Gloucestershire, GL17 0NG
☎ (01452) 830222 ∰ mayhillbrewery.com

Shop Mon, Wed, Fri & Sat 9am-2pm; other times by arrangement
Tours by arrangement

Brewing commenced in 2011 using a six-barrel plant housed in a reconstructed farm dairy. A 200-foot bore hole gives the brewery its water supply. Local freehouses are supplied and bottle-conditioned beer is also available via farm shops and specialist outlets. Seasonal beers are also available.

Admiral May (OG 1036, ABV 3.8%)
A full-flavoured light bitter.

Legend (OG 1040, ABV 4.5%)
A rich pale ale with a strong hop finish.

Legless Cow (OG 1044, ABV 4.8%)
A distinctive fruity ale with a palate cleansing hop finish.

Summit (OG 1045, ABV 4.9%)
A full-flavoured beer with a malty aroma with subtle bitter aftertaste.

Mayfields SIBA ⊙

No. 8 Croft Business Park, Leominster, Herefordshire, HR6 0QF
☎ (01568) 611197 ∰ mayfieldsbrewery.co.uk
Shop Wed-Fri 10am-4pm (other times by appt)
Tours by arrangement

This small family brewery was established in 2005 at Mayfields Farm near Bishops Frome, a major hop growing region. 2008 saw a move to a business park in Leominster. Seasonal beers are brewed on a monthly basis: see website.

Copper Fox (OG 1037, ABV 3.8%)
A copper-coloured ale with fruity, hoppy flavours and a bitter malt finish.

Priory Pale Ale (OG 1039, ABV 4%)
A light golden ale with a refreshing malt body and plenty of hops in the aroma leading to a gentle bitter finish.

Ducking Stool (OG 1041, ABV 4.2%)

Marches Gold (OG 1043, ABV 4.3%)

Aunty Myrtle's (OG 1044, ABV 4.5%)
A dark copper-coloured ale with gentle malt flavours and a strong hop finish.

Maypole

North Laithes Farm, Wellow Road, Eakring, Newark, Nottinghamshire, NG22 0AN
☎ 07971 277598 ∰ maypolebrewery.co.uk

⊛The brewery opened in 1995 in a converted 18th-century farm building. After changing hands in 2001 it was bought by the former head brewer, Rob Neil, in 2005. Seasonal beers can be ordered at any time for beer festivals: see website for details and list.

Midge (OG 1035, ABV 3.5%)
A pale beer with a lasting bitter finish.

Little Weed (OG 1037, ABV 3.8%)
Deep golden in colour with subtle bitterness.

Celebration (OG 1038, ABV 4%)
Amber-coloured traditional English ale with slightly nutty overtones.

Gate Hopper (OG 1040, ABV 4%)

Golden ale with a floral aroma and lingering hoppy bitterness.

Major Oak (OG 1042, ABV 4.4%)
A well-balanced red/brown, full-bodied bitter with hints of fruit and burnt malt.

Wellow Gold (OG 1044, ABV 4.6%)
A refreshing blonde ale with citrus flavours on the nose and aftertaste.

Meantime SIBA ⊙

Units 4 & 5, Lawrence Trading Estate, Blackwall Lane, London, SE10 0AR
☎ (020) 8293 1111

Head Office: Norman House, 110-114 Norman Road, London, SE10 9EH ⊕ meantimebrewing.com
Tours by arrangement

⊗ Founded in 2000, Meantime brews a wide range of continental style beer and traditional English bottle-conditioned ales. Two pubs are owned. In 2010 the brewery relocated to larger premises in Greenwich. Bottle-conditioned beers are produced, all suitable for vegetarians and vegans. A six-barrel brewery is also owned at the Old Brewery, the Old Royal Naval College in Greenwich and is used to brew limited edition beers.

London Pale Ale (OG 1043, ABV 4.3%) ◁
Amber-coloured best bitter with a citrus hop aroma. The malty sweetness is balanced by strong bitter hops on the palate that fade in the slightly dry finish.

Medieval

Home Farm, New Road, Colston Bassett, Nottinghamshire, NG12 3FQ
☎ 07552 798027 ⊕ medievalbeers.co.uk

⊗ Medieval started production in 2012 in Nottingham and moved to its current brewery site at Colston Bassett later that year. The 10-barrel plant is used to produce 45 casks a week. Seasonal/special beers are available.

Chivalry (ABV 3.8%)
Pale session ale with a balanced combination of malt and hop.

Knight Hood (ABV 4.2%)
An amber ale with a deep hoppy taste.

Excalibur (ABV 4.3%)
A pale ale infused with oak chippings.

Crusader (ABV 4.4%)
A pale ale, slightly sweet with a refreshing citrus finish.

Melbourn

All Saints Brewery, All Saints Street, Stamford, Lincolnshire, PE9 2PA
☎ (01780) 752186
Tours by arrangement

A famous Stamford brewery that opened in 1825 and closed in 1974. It reopened in 1994 and is owned by Samuel Smith of Tadcaster (qv). Melbourn brews four handcrafted, organic fruit beers (Cherry, Strawberry, Apricot and Raspberry) using antique steam-driven brewing equipment. The beers are all suitable for vegans and are organic. Sold in bottles only, they are not bottle-conditioned.

Melwood (NEW)

7 Stanley Grange, Knowsley Park, Merseyside, L34 4AR
☎ (0151) 214 3340 ☎ 07545 265283
⊕ themelwoodbeercompany.co.uk

Melwood began brewing in 2013 using a five-barrel plant. Seasonal beers are available as well as monthly specials in the Icons of Rock series.

Love Light (ABV 3.8%)

Equinox (ABV 4%)

Deadhead (ABV 4.1%)

Citradelic (ABV 5.1%)

Mercian (NEW)

Tyr Add, Station Terrace, Llanybydder, Carmarthenshire, SA40 9XX
☎ (01570) 481280 ⊕ mercianbreweryltd.co.uk

Brewer Andy Abram decided to combine his profession as a medieval historian and enthusiast for traditional, characterful beers by setting up a small, locally-based brewery in 2013. Beers are available at beer festivals and food fairs.

Warrior King (OG 1040, ABV 4%)
Pale ale, fruity with a light hoppy finish.

Hergest Ridge (OG 1046, ABV 4.6%)
Characterful ale with malty and sweet aroma, balanced by dry citrus flavours.

Leofric (OG 1048, ABV 4.6%)
Dark, smooth beer with a distinctive roasted malt flavour and rich hop aroma.

Merlin SIBA

3 Spring Bank Farm, Congleton Road, Arclid, Cheshire, CW11 2UD
☎ (01477) 500893 ☎ 07812 352590
⊕ merlinbrewing.co.uk
Tours by arrangement

Merlin was established in 2010 using an eight-barrel plant in a farm unit just outside Sandbach. Beers are principally supplied to outlets within a 30-mile radius. Bottle-conditioned beers are available.

King's Ale (OG 1036, ABV 3.6%)
A light brown easy-drinking bitter with a slightly floral and spicy aroma.

Merlin's Gold (OG 1038, ABV 3.8%)
Light golden ale with rounded floral citrus flavours.

Excalibur (OG 1039, ABV 3.9%)

Spellbound (OG 1040, ABV 4%)
A full-flavoured bitter, light chestnut in colour with a dry finish.

The Wizard (OG 1042, ABV 4.2%)
A hoppy, bitter, golden-coloured ale with generous hints of grapefruit flavour.

Dragonslayer (OG 1056, ABV 5.6%)
A dark brew with complex flavours.

Merry Miner

Unit 20-21, Grendon House Farm, Grendon, Warwickshire, CV9 3DT ⊕ merryminerbrewery.com
Tours by arrangement

THE BREWERIES

⊛Merry Miner commenced brewing in 2010. The brewery is based in farm buildings on the outskirts of the village of Grendon, near Atherstone. The brewer is a former coal miner and played for the Merry Miner football team, hence the name. Seasonal beers are also available.

Warwickshire's Finest (OG 1036, ABV 3.8%)
Light amber-coloured session bitter.

Davy's Lamp (OG 1038, ABV 4%)
Pale, full-flavoured bitter.

Cap Lamp (OG 1039, ABV 4.2%)
Gold-coloured beer with a refreshing crisp bitterness.

Deputy Drop (OG 1040, ABV 4.3%)

Going Underground (OG 1041, ABV 4.4%)
A refreshing amber-coloured beer.

Pit Pony (OG 1041, ABV 4.5%)
Deep golden-coloured smooth bitter.

Methane (OG 1045, ABV 5%)
A light golden bitter with a citrus bitter finish.

Mersea Island

Rewsalls Lane, East Mersea, Essex, CO5 8SX
☎ (01206) 385900 ⊕ merseabrewery.co.uk
Shop & Café Wed-Sun 10.30am-4pm; closed Mon & Tue

⊠ The brewery was established at Mersea Island Vineyard in 2005, producing cask and bottle-conditioned beers. The brewery supplies several local pubs on a guest beer basis as well as most local beer festivals. The brewery holds its own festival of Essex-produced ales over the four-day Easter weekend.

Mersea Mud (OG 1036, ABV 3.8%)
An easy-drinking mild with a malty flavour.

Yo Boy! (OG 1038, ABV 3.8%)
A session bitter with a long-lasting bitterness on the finish.

Lion Bitter (OG 1038, ABV 3.9%)
A pale amber bitter with nutty and caramel flavours and a smooth finish on the taste.

Gold (OG 1043, ABV 4.4%)

Skippers (OG 1047, ABV 4.8%)
Dark amber-coloured best bitter with a good malty flavour and a smooth bitterness.

Oyster Stout (OG 1048, ABV 5%)

Middle Earth

Rowditch Inn, 246 Uttoxeter Road, Derby, DE22 3LL
☎ 07504 304564

Office: 53 Springfield Road, Etwall, Derbyshire, DE65 6JZ ⊕ mebrewco.com

Set up in 2011, Middle Earth uses the four-barrel plant based at the Rowditch Inn in Derby (also used by the Rowditch Brewery). Steve Twells (the Rowditch brewer) established Middle Earth as a separate venture to utilise spare plant capacity to produce different brews for free trade sale.

Rivendale (OG 1041, ABV 4%)
A well-balanced golden bitter.

Honey Dragon (OG 1041, ABV 4.2%)
A balanced golden bitter with subtle honey notes.

Black Rose (OG 1048, ABV 4.6%)

Complex malt flavours, chocolate predominates, combined with subtle ginger.

Fellowship (OG 1050, ABV 5%)
Triple-hopped English golden ale.

IPA (OG 1058, ABV 5.9%)
A balanced IPA, smooth on the palate with some dark malt flavours.

Mighty Hop SIBA

Silverdale, Woodmead Road, Lyme Regis, Dorset, DT7 3AD
☎ (01297) 445358 ⊕ mightyhopbrewery.co.uk

Mighty Hop began brewing in 2010 using a one-barrel plant, upgrading to a 2.5-barrel plant in 2012. It features one of the few brewsters in the south west. Seasonal and bottle-conditioned beers are available.

Summit Pale Ale (ABV 3.3%)

Festival Special Bitter (ABV 3.8%)

Mighty Red IPA (ABV 3.8%)

What-Ho Ginger! (ABV 3.9%)

Golden Cap Bitter (ABV 4%)

Nut Brown Ale (ABV 4%)

Black Pearl Porter (ABV 4.4%)

Mighty Blonde (ABV 4.4%)

Lymebrau (ABV 5%)

Vallance's Stout (ABV 5%)

Mighty Oak

14b West Station Yard, Spital Road, Maldon, Essex, CM9 6TW
☎ (01621) 843713 ⊕ mightyoakbrewing.co.uk
Tours by arrangement

⊠ Mighty Oak was formed in 1996 and has expanded considerably following a move to Maldon in 2001. 350 outlets are supplied. Twelve monthly ales are brewed based on a theme, which for 2014 is Cockney rhyming slang.

IPA (OG 1031.5, ABV 3.5%) ◆
Light-bodied, pale session bitter, hop notes are initially suppressed by a delicate sweetness but the aftertaste is more assertive.

Oscar Wilde (OG 1039.5, ABV 3.7%) ◆
Roasty dark mild with suggestions of forest fruits and dark chocolate. A sweet taste yields to a more bitter finish.

Captain Bob (OG 1039.5, ABV 3.8%)
A traditional deep amber bitter with a fruity and hoppy aroma. There is a slight sweet maltiness that balances an easy going bitterness, followed by hints of gooseberry, elderflower and grape in the finish.

Maldon Gold (OG 1039.5, ABV 3.8%) ◆
Pale golden ale with a sharp citrus note moderated by honey and biscuity malt.

Kings (OG 1042.6, ABV 4.2%)
A deep golden beer bursting with hoppy fruitiness. The orange, nectarine and passion fruit flavours last long into the finish.

English Oak (OG 1047.9, ABV 4.8%) ◆

Strong tawny, fruity bitter with caramel, butterscotch and vanilla. A gentle hop character is present throughout.

Mile Tree (NEW) SIBA

Secret Garden Touring Park, Mile Tree Lane, Wisbech, Cambridgeshire, PE13 4TR
☎ 07858 930363 ⊕ miletreebrewery.co.uk
Shop (at campsite) 9am-5pm daily

Mile Tree began brewing in 2012 using a five-barrel plant. Special and bottle-conditioned beers are available. Local outlets and beer festivals are supplied.

Appolds Dark (ABV 3.8%)

Adventurer (ABV 4%)

Wellstream (ABV 4.9%)

Milestone SIBA ◉

Great North Road, Cromwell, Newark, Nottinghamshire, NG23 6JE
☎ (01636) 822255 ⊕ milestonebrewery.co.uk
Shop Mon-Fri 8am-5pm; Sat 9am-3pm
Tours by arrangement

◉The brewery has been in production since 2005 using a 12-barrel plant. More than 150 outlets are supplied. Seasonal and bottle-conditioned beers are also available.

Lion's Pride (OG 1038, ABV 3.8%)

Shine On (OG 1039, ABV 4%)

Loxley Ale (OG 1042, ABV 4.2%)

Black Pearl (OG 1043, ABV 4.3%)

Crusader (OG 1044, ABV 4.4%)

Rich Ruby (OG 1044, ABV 4.5%)

Olde English (OG 1049, ABV 4.9%)

Game Keeper (OG 1052, ABV 5.2%)

Raspberry Wheat Beer (OG 1055, ABV 5.6%) 🍷 🍴

Milk Street SIBA ◉

🍺 Griffin, 25 Milk Street, Frome, Somerset, BA11 3DB
☎ (01373) 467766 ⊕ milkstreetbrewery.co.uk
Tours by arrangement

⊠ Milk Street was established in 1999 in a former porn cinema situated behind the pub. The cinema is long gone and now houses the brewery, which expanded in 2005 and is now capable of producing 30 barrels per week. It mainly produces for its own estate of three outlets with direct delivery to pubs in a 30-mile radius. Wholesalers are used to distribute the beers further afield.

Mermaid (OG 1041, ABV 3.8%)
Amber-coloured ale with a rich hop character on the nose, plenty of citrus fruit on the palate and a lasting bitter and hoppy finish.

Funky Monkey (OG 1040, ABV 4%) 🍷
Copper-coloured summer ale with fruity flavours and aromas. A dry finish with developing bitterness and an undertone of citrus fruit.

The Usual (OG 1045, ABV 4.4%)

Zig-Zag Stout (OG 1046, ABV 4.5%)

A dark ruby stout with characteristic roastiness and dryness with bitter chocolate and citrus fruit in the background.

Beer (OG 1049, ABV 5%)
A blonde beer with musky hoppiness and citrus fruit on the nose, while more fruit surges through on the palate before the bittersweet finish.

Mill Green SIBA

🍺 White Horse, Edwardstone, Sudbury, Suffolk, CO10 5PX
☎ (01787) 211118 ⊕ millgreenbrewery.co.uk

⊠ Mill Green started brewing in 2008 in a new complex behind the White Horse pub in Edwardstone. It has won awards for environmental innovation. Brewing liquor is heated by solar panels and a wood-fired boiler while a wind turbine supplements power on site. A 10-barrel fermentation run is used to produce a number of seasonal and one-off brews in addition to the regular beers.

Mawkin Mild (OG 1028, ABV 2.9%) ◖
A complex mild, with a strong aroma and flavour for such a low gravity beer. Bitter coffee notes in the taste and aftertaste.

White Horse Bitter (OG 1036, ABV 3.6%)
A traditional session bitter with a spicy, bitter, lasting finish.

Loveleys Fair (OG 1040, ABV 4%)
A modern-style pale ale, golden in colour and heavily hopped with a tangy, citrus bite.

Tornado Smith (OG 1042, ABV 4.3%)
Fruity pale ale, strong on hop.

Good Ship Arbella (OG 1054, ABV 5.4%)
An American-style pale ale, strong on hop.

Millis

St Margaret's Farm, St Margaret's Road, South Darenth, Dartford, Kent, DA4 9LB
☎ (01322) 866233 ⊕ millisbrewing.com

◉John and Miriam Millis started with a 0.5-barrel plant at their home in Gravesend. Demand outstripped the facility and Millis moved in 2003 to its current location – a former farm cold store – using a 10-barrel plant. They now supply around 40 outlets within a 50-mile radius. Wetherspoon's pubs are supplied within a 30-mile radius with Kentish Gold (ABV 4.8%). Seasonal and bottle-conditioned beers are also available.

Gravesend Guzzler (OG 1037, ABV 3.7%)
Pale, easy-drinking, fruity session beer.

Dartford Wobbler (OG 1043, ABV 4.3%)
A tawny-coloured, full-bodied best bitter with complex malt and hop flavours and a long, clean, slightly roasted finish.

Millstone SIBA ◉

Unit 4, Vale Mill, Micklehurst Road, Mossley, nr Oldham, OL5 9JL
☎ (01457) 835835 ⊕ millstonebrewery.co.uk

Established in 2003 by Nick Broughton and Jon Hunt, the brewery is located in an 18th-century textile mill. The eight-barrel plant produces a range of pale, hoppy beers and a traditional stout. More than 40 regular outlets are supplied.

Vale Mill (OG 1039, ABV 3.9%)
A pale gold session bitter with a floral and spicy aroma building upon a crisp and refreshing taste.

Three Shires Bitter (OG 1040, ABV 4%) ◆
Yellow beer with hop and fruit aroma. Fresh citrus fruit, hops and bitterness in the taste and aftertaste.

Tiger Rut (OG 1040, ABV 4%)
A pale, hoppy ale with a distinctive citrus/ grapefruit aroma.

Stout (OG 1049, ABV 4.5%)
A traditional dry stout; pale chocolate malt, roasted barley, and hint of sweetness to the aroma.

True Grit (OG 1040, ABV 5%)
A well-hopped strong ale with a mellow bitterness and a citrus/grapefruit aroma.

Milltown SIBA

The Brewery, The Old Railway Goods Yard, Scar Lane, Milnsbridge, Huddersfield, West Yorkshire, HD3 4PE
☎ 07946 589645 ⊕ milltownbrewing.co.uk
Tours by arrangement

⊛Milltown began brewing in 2011 using a four-barrel plant. Seasonal and special beers are brewed.

Golden Hop (OG 1037, ABV 3.8%)
Easy-drinking golden session bitter with a good malt and hop balance.

Platinum Blonde (ABV 4%)
Pale, hoppy, bitter, easy-drinking session beer.

Slubbers Gold (OG 1040, ABV 4.2%)
A pale golden bitter with a good balance of malt and hops and a lingering, hoppy finish.

Maltissimo (ABV 5.3%)

Milton SIBA

Pegasus House, Pembroke Avenue, Waterbeach, Cambridgeshire, CB25 9PY
☎ (01223) 862067 ⊕ miltonbrewery.co.uk

⊠ The brewery has grown steadily since it was founded in 1999 and now operates pubs in Cambridge, London, Peterborough and Norwich through a sister company. In 2012 the brewery moved to larger premises in the village of Waterbeach. Seasonal/special beers: see website.

Minotaur (OG 1035, ABV 3.3%) ◆
A dark ruby mild with liquorice and raisin fruit throughout. Light, dry finish.

Dionysus (OG 1037, ABV 3.6%) ◆
Yellow bitter with good balance of biscuity malt and citrus hop. Some malt and hops linger on long, dry aftertaste.

Tiki (ABV 3.8%) ◆
Straw-coloured golden ale with passion fruit, grapefruit and lemon hop character. Dry, slightly astringent aftertaste.

Justinian (OG 1039, ABV 3.9%) ◆
Straw-coloured bitter with pink grapefruit hop character and light malt softness. Very dry finish.

Pegasus (OG 1043, ABV 4.1%) 🍴 🍺 ◆
Malty, amber, medium-bodied bitter with faint hops. Bittersweet aftertaste.

Sparta (OG 1043, ABV 4.3%) ◆

A yellow/gold best bitter with floral hops, kiwi fruit and balancing malt softness which fades to leave a long, dry finish.

Nero (OG 1050, ABV 5%) ◆
A creamy, mouth filling black beer with a rich blend of milk chocolate, raisins and liquorice flavours. Aftertaste is full of roast malt bitterness and fruity sweetness.

Cyclops (OG 1055, ABV 5.3%)
Deep copper-coloured ale, with a rich hoppy aroma and full body; fruit and malt notes develop in the finish.

Marcus Aurelius (OG 1075, ABV 7.4%)
Imperial Roman Stout – an enormous, velvety stout. Bursting with dark roasty flavour with an underlying vanilla richness.

Mitchell Krause

The Tractor Shed, Calva Brow, Workington, Cumbria, CA14 1DB
☎ 07825 580694 ⊕ mkbrewing.co.uk

Mitchell Krause was set up in 2009, originally having its beers contract brewed. A new brewery opened in 2013 in an old tractor shed on the family farm. The brewery focuses on bottled continental-style beers although Hefe Weiss (ABV 5%) is also available bottle-conditioned.

Mithril

Mithril, Aldbrough St John, Richmond, North Yorkshire, DL11 7TL
☎ (01325) 374817 ☎ 07889 167128
⊕ mithrilales.co.uk

⊛Mithril started brewing in 2010 in an old stables opposite the brewer's house on a 2.5-barrel plant. Owner/brewer Pete Fenwick brews twice a week to supply the local area of Darlington and Richmond. Weekly specials are available.

Route A66 (OG 1041, ABV 4%)
A crisp, refreshing, satisfying golden beer. A dry bitterness, with a lingering citrus and spicy hop taste and aroma.

Mobberley SIBA

Dairy Farm, Church Lane, Mobberley, Cheshire, WA16 7RA
☎ 07879 771209 ⊕ mobberleyfineales.co.uk

⊠ Mobberley began brewing in 2011 in an old milking parlour on a working farm in the heart of the Cheshire countryside.

HedgeHopper (OG 1039, ABV 3.8%)
A golden refreshing fine ale, light and aromatic.

RoadRunner (OG 1039, ABV 3.8%)
A light-coloured pale ale; refreshing with a delicate, lightly spicy finish. Rich in flavours, sweet to the taste and smooth with a sweet, delicate, refreshing hop aroma.

WhirlyBird (OG 1040, ABV 4%)
Pale ale, sweet yet full-bodied, light yet complex with a smooth, subtle, zesty finish.

BarnBuster (OG 1042, ABV 4.2%)
A rich amber-coloured ale, full-bodied, rich in colour and taste, mildly bitter with a hint of spice and with a malty, mildly bitter yet slightly spicy/ citrus finish.

Moles SIBA ◎

5 Merlin Way, Bowerhill, Melksham, Wiltshire, SN12 6TJ
☎ (01225) 708842 ⊕ molesbrewery.com
Shop Mon-Fri 9am-5pm; Sat 9am-12pm
Tours by arrangement

Moles was established in 1982 by Roger Catte, a former Ushers brewer, using his nickname to name the brewery. 10 pubs are owned, all serving cask beer. Over 200 outlets are supplied direct. Seasonal beers: see website.

Tap Bitter (OG 1035, ABV 3.5%)
A session bitter with a smooth, malty flavour and clean, bitter finish.

Best Bitter (OG 1040, ABV 4%)
A well-balanced, amber-coloured bitter, clean, dry and malty with some bitterness, and delicate floral hop flavour.

Elmo's Fire (OG 1044, ABV 4.4%)
Medium-bodied pale ale. Refreshingly bitter with a fruity spicy aroma leaving a long, bitter finish.

Landlords Choice (OG 1045, ABV 4.5%)
A dark, strong, smooth porter, with a rich fruity palate and malty finish.

Rucking Mole (OG 1045, ABV 4.5%)
A chestnut-coloured premium ale, fruity and malty with a smooth bitter finish.

Mole Catcher (OG 1050, ABV 5%)
A copper-coloured ale with a spicy hop aroma and taste, and a long, bitter finish.

Molson Coors ◎

Molson Coors (Burton): 137 High Street, Burton upon Trent, Staffordshire, DE14 1JZ
☎ (01283) 511000

Molson Coors (Alton): Manor Park Brewery, Alton, Hampshire, GU34 2PS

Molson Coors (Tadcaster): Tower Brewery, Wetherby Road, Tadcaster, North Yorkshire, LS24 9SD
⊕ molsoncoorsbrewers.com

Molson Coors is the result of a merger between Molson of Canada and Coors of Colorado, US Coors established itself in Europe in 2002 by buying part of the former Bass brewing empire, when Interbrew (now AB InBev) was instructed by the British government to divest itself of some of its interests in Bass. Coors owns several cask ale brands. It brews 110,000 barrels of cask beer a year (under licensing arrangements with other brewers) and also provides a further 50,000 barrels of cask beer from other breweries. In 2011 Molson Coors bought Sharp's brewery in Cornwall in a bid to increase its stake in the cask beer sector. No real ale is brewed at Alton or Tadcaster.

Moncada SIBA

Unit 1, Buspace Studios, Conlan Street, London, W10 5AP
☎ (020) 8964 0829 ☎ 07795 511505
⊕ moncadabrewery.co.uk

⊗ Moncada began brewing in 2011 using a six-barrel plant. Bottle-conditioned and seasonal beers are also available.

Notting Hill Bitter (ABV 3.8%)

A traditional British bitter with a good balance of hop flavour and underlying sweet notes. Soft on the palate leaving a pleasant aftertaste.

Notting Hill Blonde (ABV 4.2%)
A continental-style yellow beer with a mix of hops, bitterness and sweetness. Fruity hops on the nose and palate fade in the aftertaste, leaving a dry, bitter character with a little spiciness.

Notting Hill Amber (ABV 4.7%)
A full-bodied, creamy, amber-coloured beer with a citrus aroma and flavour, well-balanced by the sweet, slightly toffee maltiness and a bitter dryness that lingers. There is a little flowery hop throughout.

Notting Hill Ruby Rye (ABV 5.2%)
A robust ruby ale made with rye complemented by a fruity hop aroma.

Monty's SIBA

Unit 1, Castle Works, Hendomen, Montgomery, Powys, SY15 6HA
☎ (01686) 668933 ⊕ montysbrewery.co.uk

Monty's began brewing in 2009 and was the first brewery in Montgomeryshire since the Eagle brewery in Newtown closed in 1990. Three pubs are owned by the brewery's sister company, Hophouse Inns; the Sportsman in Newtown, the Red Lion in Caersws and the Abermule in Abermule. Seasonal and bottle-conditioned beers are available.

Manjana (OG 1039.5, ABV 3.9%)

Midnight (OG 1040, ABV 4%)
A dark, smooth, creamy stout.

Moonrise (OG 1040, ABV 4%)
A copper-coloured, gently malty, well-balanced traditional brew.

MPA (OG 1040.5, ABV 4%)

Sunshine (OG 1041, ABV 4.2%)
A golden, hoppy, floral/citrus ale with a pleasantly dry finish.

Mischief (OG 1050, ABV 5%)
Strong golden ale with a good balance of malt and hop bitterness.

Moonstone

⊟ Ministry of Ale, 9 Trafalgar Street, Burnley, Lancashire, BB11 1TQ
☎ (01282) 830909 ⊕ moonstonebrewery.co.uk
Tours by arrangement

◎A small, three-barrel brewery, based in the front room of the Ministry of Ale pub. Brewing started in 2001 and beer is only available in the pub.

Black Star (OG 1037, ABV 3.4%)

Moorhouse's SIBA ◎

The Brewery, Moorhouse Street, Accrington Road, Burnley, Lancashire, BB11 5EN
☎ (01282) 422864 ⊕ moorhouses.co.uk
Tours by arrangement

Established in 1865 as a drinks manufacturer, the brewery started producing cask-conditioned ale in 1978. A new 40,000-barrel brewhouse and visitor centre opened in 2012. The company owns six pubs, all serving cask-conditioned beer. Monthly special beers: see website.

Black Cat (OG 1036, ABV 3.4%) ◆
A dark mild-style beer with delicate chocolate and coffee roast flavours and a crisp, bitter finish.

Premier Bitter (OG 1036, ABV 3.7%) ◆
A clean and satisfying bitter aftertaste rounds off this well-balanced, hoppy, amber session bitter.

Pride of Pendle (OG 1040, ABV 4.1%) ◆
Well-balanced amber best bitter with a fresh initial hoppiness and a mellow, malt-driven body.

Blond Witch (OG 1045, ABV 4.5%) ◆
Light ale, fruity with a lasting finish.

Pendle Witches Brew (OG 1050, ABV 5.1%) ☐ ◆
Well-balanced, full-bodied, malty beer with a long, complex finish.

Moor SIBA ◎

c/o Chapel Court, Pitney, Somerset, TA10 9AE
☎ 07887 556521 ⊕ moorbeer.co.uk
Tours by arrangement

⊗ Moor Beer was founded in 1996. The brewery's capacity was quadrupled in 2011 to meet demand. All beers are produced without isinglass finings. Special and bottle-conditioned beers are also available. The brewery is situated at Long Sutton.

Revival (OG 1038, ABV 3.8%) ▣
An immensely hoppy and refreshing pale ale.

Nor'Hop (OG 1041, ABV 4.1%)
Pale, hoppy, modern ale showcasing northern hemisphere hops.

So'Hop (OG 1041, ABV 4.1%)
Pale, hoppy, modern ale showcasing southern hemisphere hops.

Raw (OG 1043, ABV 4.3%) ◆
Dark amber-coloured, complex, full-bodied beer, with fruity notes.

Amoor (OG 1045, ABV 4.5%) ◆
Dark brown/black beer with an initially fruity taste leading to roast malt with a little bitterness. A slightly sweet malty finish.

Dark Alliance (OG 1045, ABV 4.5%)
Hoppy coffee stout.

Illusion (OG 1045, ABV 4.5%)
Session strength version of a Black IPA, powerfully hopped on the dark side.

Ported Amoor (OG 1047, ABV 4.7%)
Amoor with added Reserve Port.

Somerland Gold (OG 1050, ABV 5%)
Hoppy blonde ale with hints of honey and a long, hoppy finish.

Hoppiness (OG 1065, ABV 6.5%)
All the rich malt and fruit flavours of a barley wine combined with the hoppy crispness of a pale ale.

Old Freddy Walker (OG 1073, ABV 7.3%) ☐ ◆
Rich, dark, strong ale with a fruity complex taste, leaving a fruitcake finish.

JJJ IPA (OG 1085, ABV 9%)
Copper-coloured, new world triple IPA. Immensely hoppy and malty.

MòR SIBA

Old Mill, Kellas, DD5 3PD

☎ 07593 245000 ⊕ morbrewing.co.uk
Tours by arrangement

Retired lifeboat coxswain Jim Hughan teamed up with CAMRA enthusiast Ross Niven to establish this 2.5-barrel brewery in 2012. More than 10 outlets are supplied, mainly in Tayside. Seasonal, special and bottle-conditioned ales are also available.

MòR Tea, Vicar? (OG 1038, ABV 3.8%)
A pale amber bitter with a malty, fruity aroma and a pronounced bitter finish. A well-balanced, refreshing session ale.

MòR-bidly Dark! (OG 1039, ABV 3.9%)
A dark, chocolate, malty mild, lightly hopped with an aromatic, coffee/vanilla aftertaste.

MòR-ish! (OG 1042, ABV 4.2%)
A bright amber ale with a malty, fruity aroma and a well-balanced and controlled bitter finish.

MòR Please! (OG 1045, ABV 4.5%)
This clean-tasting, full-bodied golden bitter is bursting with malt and hops. There's a hint of honey with a good hoppy finish.

Mordue SIBA ◎

Units D1 & D2, Narvic Way, Tyne Tunnel Estate, North Shields, Tyne & Wear, NE29 7XJ
☎ (0191) 296 1879 ⊕ morduebrewery.com
Shop: see website for opening times
Tours by arrangement

◎In 1995 the Fawson brothers revived the Mordue Brewery name (the original closed in 1879). High demand required moves to larger premises and replacing the original five-barrel plant with a 20-barrel one. The beers are distributed nationally and 300 outlets are supplied direct. Seasonal beers: see website.

Five Bridge Bitter (OG 1038, ABV 3.8%) ◆
Crisp, golden beer with a good hint of hops, the bitterness carries on in the finish. A good session bitter.

Northumbrian Blonde (OG 1040, ABV 4%) ◆
A blonde beer with a citrus aroma and hoppy finish.

Geordie Pride (OG 1042, ABV 4.2%) ◆
Well-balanced and hoppy copper-coloured brew with a long, bitter finish.

Workie Ticket (OG 1045, ABV 4.5%) ▣ ◆
Complex bitter with plenty of malt and hops and a long, satisfying bitter finish.

Radgie Gadgie (OG 1048, ABV 4.8%) ☐ ◆
Strong, easy-drinking bitter with plenty of fruit and hops.

IPA (OG 1051, ABV 5.1%) ◆
Easy-drinking golden ale with plenty of hops, the bitterness carries on in the finish.

Morland

See Greene King

Morton

Unit 10, Essington Light Industrial Estate, Essington, Staffordshire, WV11 2BH
☎ 07988 69647

Office: 96 Brewood Road, Coven, Staffordshire, WV9 5EF ⊕ mortonbrewery.co.uk
Tours by arrangement

Morton was established in 2007 on a three-barrel plant. The brewery moved to Essington in 2008 to increase production. Essington Ale was introduced to celebrate the move and became so popular with the locals that a full range of Essington beers is brewed regularly. 30 outlets are supplied direct plus various beer festivals. Seasonal, special and bottle-conditoned beers are available: see website.

Essington Bitter (OG 1037, ABV 3.8%)
Fruity, hoppy session ale.

Merry Mount (OG 1037, ABV 3.8%)
A traditional bitter.

Essington Blonde (OG 1039, ABV 4%)
A thirst quenching pale ale made with American hops.

Essington Ale (OG 1041, ABV 4.2%)
A refreshing golden session ale.

Jelly Roll (OG 1041, ABV 4.2%)
A dry-hopped best bitter.

Essington Gold (OG 1044, ABV 4.4%)
A dry-hopped golden ale.

Scottish Maiden (OG 1045, ABV 4.6%)
A malty premium bitter.

Essington IPA (OG 1047, ABV 4.8%)
A pale, hoppy IPA.

Moulin

⊟ 2 Baledmund Road, Moulin, Pitlochry, Perthshire, PH16 5EL
☎ (01796) 472196

Office: Moulin Hotel, 11-13 Kirkmicheal Road, Moulin, Pitlochry, PH16 5EH ⊕ moulinhotel.co.uk
Tours by arrangement

☺The brewery opened in 1995 to celebrate the Moulin Hotel's 300th anniversary. Two pubs are owned and four outlets are supplied. Bottle-conditioned beer is available.

Light (OG 1036, ABV 3.7%) ◄
Thirst-quenching, straw-coloured session beer, with a light, hoppy, fruity balance, ending with a gentle, hoppy sweetness.

Braveheart (OG 1039, ABV 4%) ◄
An amber bitter, with a delicate balance of malt and fruit and a Scottish-style sweetness.

Ale of Atholl (OG 1043.5, ABV 4.5%) ◄
A reddish, quaffable, malty ale, with a solid body and a mellow finish.

Old Remedial (OG 1050.5, ABV 5.2%) ◄
A distinctive and satisfying dark brown old ale, with roast malt to the fore and tannin in a robust taste.

Mouselow Farm (NEW)

3 Mouselow Farm, Dinting, Derbyshire, SK13 7QQ
☎ 07920 048252
✉ mouselowfarmbrewery@gmail.com

Mouselow Farm began brewing in 2013 using a three-barrel plant housed in a converted barn. Further regular beers are planned along with seasonals and specials.

Bankswood Bitter (ABV 4.2%)

Golden Goose (ABV 4.3%)

Mr Grundy's SIBA

⊟ Georgian House Hotel, 34 Ashbourne Road, Derby, DE22 3AD
☎ (01332) 349806 ⊕ mrgrundysbrewery.co.uk

The brewery opened in 2010 using a four-barrel plant constructed from made to measure vessels to fit into a converted bedroom. Beers are produced for the company's own tavern (Mr Grundy's) and hotels.

Trench Foot (ABV 3.8%)
Dark-coloured beer with strong malt flavours.

Passchendaele (ABV 3.9%)
A straw-coloured bitter with citrus overtones.

Over the Top (ABV 4.1%)
A pale, hoppy bitter.

No Man's Land (ABV 4.5%)
Dark-coloured yet hoppy beer retaining the soft, malty flavours of a traditional bitter.

Coffin Nail (ABV 5%)

Muirhouse

Unit 1, Enterprise Court, Manners Avenue, Manners Industrial Estate, Ilkeston, Derbyshire, DE7 8EW
☎ 07916 590525 ⊕ muirhousebrewery.co.uk
Tours by arrangement

Muirhouse was established in 2009 in a domestic garage in Long Eaton, it expanded in 2011 to an industrial unit in Ilkeston where brewing takes place up to four times a week. Bottle-conditioned beers are available.

Shunters Pole (OG 1040, ABV 3.8%)
A pale, refreshing, hoppy beer bitter.

Ruby Jewel (OG 1040, ABV 3.9%)
A ruby-coloured malty beer with tastes of toffee.

Shopping for Hops (OG 1040, ABV 3.9%)
Pale session beer with a citrus bitterness.

Fully Fitted Freight (OG 1041, ABV 4%)
A premium bitter with a fine blend of malt and hops and a distinctive finish.

Magnum Mild (OG 1045, ABV 4.5%)
Dark, smooth, strong mild.

Pirate's Gold (OG 1045, ABV 4.5%)
Pale golden beer with hint of caramel.

Smoked Porter (OG 1045, ABV 4.5%)
Rich porter with a light smoked finish.

Belly's Beverage (OG 1048, ABV 5%)
Pale and hoppy beer using New Zealand and American hops.

Coffee Porter (OG 1048, ABV 5%)
A dark porter with a hint of coffee.

Lurch's Liquor (OG 1050, ABV 5%)
Sweet, smooth stout packed with dark malts.

Foundries IPA (OG 1052, ABV 5.2%)
Deceptive in strength, a blend of English and American hops.

Hat Trick IPA (OG 1052, ABV 5.2%)

Stumbling Around (OG 1050, ABV 5.2%)
Dark red strong malty beer.

THE BREWERIES

Mulberry Duck (NEW)

Elan Portway, Burghill, Herefordshire, HR4 8NF
☎ 07740 468675 ⊕ mulberryduck.co.uk

Mulberry Duck opened in 2012 in a former dairy using a 3.75-barrel plant.

Golden Sparkle (ABV 3.8%)

The Wildfowler (ABV 4%)

Amber Sparkle (ABV 4.1%)

Mumbles (NEW) SIBA

⧓ 726 Mumbles Road, Mumbles, Swansea, SA3 4EL
☎ 07897 895511 ⊕ mumblesbrewery.co.uk
Shop at pub Mon-Thu & Sun 12-11pm; Fri & Sat 12-midnight
Tours by arrangement

⊚Mumbles began brewing in 2013 and is situated in the back of the Pilot pub. Owners Richard and Rob supply the Pilot and have plans to supply other local outlets. Seasonal beers are available.

Mile (OG 1039, ABV 3.8%)

Gold (OG 1043, ABV 4.3%)

Lifesaver (OG 1051, ABV 5.1%)

Nailsworth SIBA

⧓ Village Inn, The Cross, Nailsworth, Gloucestershire, GL6 0HH
☎ 07963 200768 ⊕ nailsworth-brewery.co.uk
Tours by arrangement

After 96 years' commercial brewing returned to Nailsworth in 2004 in the form of a six-barrel microbrewery. Beers are mainly sold at the Village Inn above the brewery. Seasonal and bottle-conditioned beers are also available.

Alestock (OG 1036, ABV 3.6%)
A light-coloured ale full of elderflower notes.

Mayor's Bitter (OG 1042, ABV 4.3%)
A best bitter with malt textures complemented by a long-lasting taste of blackcurrant.

Old Rocky (OG 1044, ABV 4.4%)
Light IPA style with loads of grapefruit flavour.

Town Crier (OG 1046, ABV 4.5%)
A premium ale with delicate grassy and floral overtones.

Red October (OG 1049, ABV 4.9%)
A ruby, rich and malty, well-balanced strong bitter.

Naked

⧓ Corner Pin, Palmerston Street, Westwood, Nottinghamshire, NG16 5HY
☎ 07908 531901
✉ cornerpinwestwood@hotmail.co.uk
Tours by arrangement

The brewery was set up in 2010 in a skittle alley behind the Corner Pin pub and can be viewed from the function room. Beer is mainly brewed for the pub but is occasionally supplied to beer festivals and other local pubs. Due to demand the skittle alley may need to be moved to allow for increased production.

Hopsession (OG 1038, ABV 3.8%)

A light amber bitter retaining a smooth creamy head, with a malty/straw-like aroma and crisp bitter finish.

Blush (OG 1045, ABV 4.5%)
A dark ruby bitter with caramel undertones and a mid bitter finish.

Palindrome (OG 1048, ABV 4.7%)

Nant SIBA

The Outbuildings, Penrhwylfa, Maenan, Llanrwst, Conwy, LL26 0UF
☎ 07723 36862 ⊕ bragdynant.co.uk

⊗ Nant commenced brewing in 2007 with a plant purchased from the Yorkshire Dales Brewery. Capacity is currently 10-15 nine gallon firkins a week. Seasonal and one-off beers are also produced.

Brenin Bootliquor (OG 1038, ABV 3.8%)
A light golden session ale with balanced hops and malt.

Cwrw Coryn (OG 1042, ABV 4.2%)
Traditional amber-coloured bitter. Slightly malty with good bitter overtones.

Chawden Aur (OG 1043, ABV 4.3%)
Golden orange-coloured ale with a citrus aroma and full mouthfeel. Grapefruit and lemon citrus taste balance with biscuity malt for a long fruity finish.

Mwnci Nel (OG 1055, ABV 5.5%) ⊡

Navigation SIBA

⧓ Trent Navigation Inn, 17 Meadow Lane, Nottingham, NG2 3HS
☎ (0115) 986 9877 ⊕ navigationbrewery.com
Tours by arrangement

Brewing began in 2012 in the old stable block of the Trent Navigation Inn. The brewery is owned by sister company Great Northern Inns and supplies cask beers to the pubs in its estate with guest beers being provided by brewery swaps.

Traditional (OG 1038, ABV 3.8%)
Traditional style, amber-coloured, smooth, malty beer, well-balanced giving a mellow finish.

Pale Ale (OG 1039, ABV 3.9%)
Pale straw-coloured beer with a distinctive fruity nose, well-hopped leading to a refreshing sharp finish.

Golden (OG 1041.5, ABV 4.3%)
Medium-bodied and clean-tasting, refreshing ale, fruit and malt on the nose, satisfying biscuit flavours with a lasting malty aftertaste.

Stout (OG 1043.5, ABV 4.4%)
Traditional, robust stout with liquorice, roast almonds and chocolate flavours perfectly balanced with a tight creamy head.

Classic IPA (OG 1050, ABV 5.2%)
Straw-coloured with powerful citrus fruit balanced with malty sweetness and robust bitter flavours.

Naylor's SIBA ⊚

Midland Mills, Station Road, Cross Hills, North Yorkshire, BD20 7DT
☎ (01535) 637451 ⊕ naylorsbrewery.co.uk
Shop Mon-Fri 10am-5pm; Sat 10am-3pm

Tours by arrangement

⊕Naylors started brewing in 2005 at the Old White Bear pub in Cross Hills. Expansion required a move to the current site in 2006 and included a rebranding of the beers. Further expansion in 2013 gave bigger facilities for brewing as well as a shop and extended bar. Around 200 outlets are supplied. Bottle-conditioned ales are also produced, suitable for vegetarians.

Velvet (OG 1039, ABV 3.9%) ◆
Chocolate and roast aromas and flavours predominate in this dark brown mild which has an increasingly roast bitter finish.

Neath

Endeavour Close, Port Talbot, SA12 7PT
☎ 07772 468436 ⊕ neathales.co.uk

Neath Ales was established in 2009 and produces a range of single hop variety cask and bottle-conditioned beers. The brewery also releases small batches of strong, heavily-hopped beers under the Black Falls – Beers for Aficionados brand, available to order online. One-off monthly specials are also available.

Firebrick (OG 1042, ABV 4.2%)
Amber-coloured best bitter with refreshing citrus hop flavour and aroma.

Witch Hunter (OG 1042, ABV 4.2%)
Well-balanced ruby ale with roasted malt and hop fruit flavours.

Gold (OG 1050, ABV 5%)
Citrus/grapefruit hop aroma and flavour dominate this golden ale.

Black (OG 1055, ABV 5.5%)
Foreboding dark malt flavours are balanced by aggressive hopping rates making this strong black ale dangerously drinkable.

Nelson SIBA

Unit 2, Building 64, The Historic Dockyard, Chatham, Kent, ME4 4TE
☎ (01634) 832828 ⊕ nelsonbrewery.co.uk
Shop Mon-Fri 11am-4pm
Tours by arrangement

⊕Nelson brewery is based in Chatham's historic dockyard and has been in its current ownership since 2006 supplying direct to more than 250 outlets. Most cask beers are also available bottle conditioned. Seasonal and occasional beers: see website.

Admiral IPA (OG 1040, ABV 4%)
A traditional IPA with a combination of citrus flavours on the palate.

Midshipman Dark Mild (OG 1040, ABV 4%)
A dark mild leaving a roasted aftertaste on the palate.

Powder Monkey (OG 1043, ABV 4.3%)
A golden ale with a smooth aftertaste which leaves a sweetness on the palate.

Core Commander (OG 1045, ABV 4.4%)
A golden-coloured ale, brewed with Kentish hops and Bramley apples to give a unique combination of flavours.

Dogwatch Stout (OG 1044, ABV 4.5%)
A smooth, creamy stout that has a strong hop taste, leaving a smoky chocolate aftertaste.

Friggin' in the Riggin' (OG 1046, ABV 4.5%)
Premium bitter with smooth malt flavour and bittersweet aftertaste.

Pursers Pussy Porter (OG 1051, ABV 4.8%)
A traditional porter brewed with amber malt.

Nelson's Blood (OG 1062, ABV 6%)
A strong, malty ale with mellow roast tones, slightly nutty and fruity with a warm aftertaste.

Nene Valley SIBA

Oundle Wharf, Station Road, Oundle, Northamptonshire, PE8 4DE
☎ (01832) 272776 ⊕ nenevalleybrewery.com
Shop Fri 4-7pm; Sat 10am-6pm
Tours by arrangement

⊗ Nene Valley began brewing in 2011. As sales quickly outstripped supply, larger premises and new vessels were bought to increase capacity and the brewery moved to Oundle Wharf using a 15-barrel plant. There are plans for a restaurant and brewery tap on site.

SPA (Simple Pleasures Ale) (OG 1036, ABV 3.6%)
A light, clean and refreshing beer with a pleasing citrus hop aroma and flavour.

BSA (Blonde Session Ale) (OG 1038, ABV 3.8%)

NVB (Nene Valley Bitter) (OG 1040, ABV 4.1%)

DXB (Special Bitter) (OG 1044, ABV 4.6%)
Chestnut in colour with plenty of maltiness. Balanced with late-hopped spicy character.

JIP (Jim Irving Pale) (OG 1053, ABV 5.6%)
Full-bodied with a big malty taste backed with zesty hop flavour.

Nethergate

See Growler

New Inn (NEW)

⊟ New Inn, 112 Roberttown Lane, Roberttown, Liversedge, West Yorkshire, WF15 7NP
☎ (01924) 402069

Brewing commenced in 2012 using a 0.5-barrel plant in the cellar of the New Inn, Liversedge. The beer is produced in wood-clad vessels by Joe Kenyon, the ex-brewer at Riverhead Brewery. Seasonal beers are available.

Pale Bob (ABV 3.8%)
Slightly flowery pale ale with hints of fruit and a pleasant bitter aftertaste. A good session beer.

Golden Bob (ABV 4%)
A golden beer with a refreshing aftertaste.

Rusty Bob (ABV 4.5%)
A smooth, malty, traditional Yorkshire bitter with a slightly bitter aftertaste.

Bobmeister (ABV 4.9%)
A German lager-style pale beer.

Bombay Bob (ABV 6%)
A strong, pale beer full of flavours with ginger, mint and cardamom to the fore.

New Plassey SIBA

Eyton, Nr Wrexham, LL13 0SP
☎ 07769 155874 ⊕ plassey.com/brewery.php

Plassey brewery was founded in 1985 on the 250-acre Plassey Estate. Following the merger of Plassey and the Gertie Sweet Brewery in 2012, the New Plassey Brewery was formed. The new facility includes a visitors' viewing gallery, and brewery shop.

New World Pale (OG 1039, ABV 3.9%)
A pale beer. Well-balanced with a hoppy bite.

Plassey Bitter (OG 1040, ABV 4%) ◆
Smooth and malty best bitter, reddish brown in colour, with a good hop and fruit balance and a dry finish.

Midnight Mild (OG 1042, ABV 4.2%)
A medium strength mild with a fullness of character and flavour. Dark and subtle.

Offa's Dyke (OG 1043, ABV 4.3%)
A pale, crisp and refreshing bitter.

Dusky Maiden Stout (OG 1044, ABV 4.4%)
A dark, complex flavoured stout.

Deep Porter (OG 1045, ABV 4.5%)
A smooth, deep brown, well-balanced porter.

Cherry Diva (OG 1047, ABV 4.7%)
A pale beer with a subtle flavour of Maraschino cherry.

Cwrw Tudno (OG 1050, ABV 5%)
A pale strong bitter.

Dragons Breath (OG 1060, ABV 6%) ◆
Well-balanced strong bitter. Plum fruit in aroma with the initial sweetness followed by a powerful smack of hops and fruit.

Newark (NEW)

77 William Street, Newark, Nottinghamshire, NG24 1QU
☎ 07879 885000 ⊕ newarkbrewery.co.uk

Newark Brewery was established in 2012 on the site of a former maltings using an eight-barrel plant.

Best (OG 1039, ABV 3.7%)
A ruby-coloured, well-balanced session bitter.

Pride (OG 1039, ABV 3.7%)
A light, hoppy brew.

Newby Wyke SIBA

Unit 24, Limesquare Business Park, Alma Park Road, Grantham, Lincolnshire, NG31 9SN
☎ (01476) 565682 ⊕ newbywyke.co.uk
Tours by arrangement

⊠ The brewery is named after a Hull trawler skippered by brewer Rob March's grandfather. It started life in 1998 as a 2.5-barrel plant in a converted garage then moved to premises behind the Willoughby Arms at Little Bytham. In 2009 it moved back to Grantham with a brew length of 10 barrels. Seasonal beers: see website.

Banquo (OG 1036, ABV 3.8%)

Kingston Topaz (OG 1039, ABV 4.2%)
A single-hopped ale with floral undertones.

Bear Island (OG 1043, ABV 4.6%)

A blonde beer with a hoppy aroma and a crisp, dry finish.

White Squall (OG 1044, ABV 4.8%) ◆
Amber-hued with a hoppy aroma. Generous amounts of hop are well-supported by a solid malty undercurrent. An increasingly bittersweet tang makes itself known towards the finish.

Newmans

See Celt Experience

Nine Standards

See Settle

Nobby's SIBA

c/o Ward Arms, High Street, Guilsborough, Northamptonshire, NN6 8PY
☎ (01604) 740785 ⊕ nobbysbrewery.co.uk
Shop Mon-Fri 9am-5pm
Tours by arrangement

Paul 'Nobby' Mulliner stated commercial brewing in 2004 on a 2.5-barrel plant at the rear of the Alexandra Arms in Kettering, which also served as the brewery tap. In 2007 a 14-barrel plant was installed at the rear of the Ward Arms at Guilsborough, to where Nobby's Brewery moved. In 2011 the brewery was expanded with an additional fermenter and bottling line with further expansion planned.

Claridges Crystal (OG 1036, ABV 3.6%)
A pale summer ale, crisp and fresh with a slightly citrus hop finish.

Guilsborough Guzzler (OG 1036, ABV 3.6%)
An easy-drinking malty auburn-coloured ale with a gentle hop finish.

Best (OG 1037, ABV 3.8%)
A fine session ale with an excellent hop finish.

Guilsborough Gold (OG 1041, ABV 4%)
Well-balanced golden ale with a full-bodied traditional hop finish.

Wild West (OG 1046, ABV 4.6%)
Mahogany-coloured beer, full and flavoursome.

Tow'd Navigation (OG 1067, ABV 6.1%)
A dark, strong ale. Rich malt and hops and wonderfully warming.

Nomad (NEW)

Unit 1, Beggarlee Park, Engine Lane, Newthorpe, NG16 3RN ⊕ nomadbrewery.co.uk

Nomad began brewing on a one-barrel plant in 2013. Four regular beers are produced. At present beers are only available bottle-conditioned and in mini-pins.

Nook SIBA

▤ Riverside, 7b Victoria Square, Holmfirth, West Yorkshire, HD9 2DN
☎ (01484) 682373 ⊕ thenookbrewhouse.co.uk
Tours by arrangement

⊕The Nook Brewhouse is built on the foundations of a previous brewhouse dating back to 1752, next to the River Ribble, behind the Nook pub. Brewing commenced in 2009 and two brewery taps are supplied. A history room with renovated archives dating back to the 1700s and a brewery shop are planned.

Yorks (OG 1037, ABV 3.7%) ◈
A well-balanced bitter with light malt and hop aroma and hop and fruit in the taste, developing in strength. A good session beer.

Baby Blond (ABV 3.8%)

Spring into Spring (ABV 3.8%)

Bee's Knees (ABV 3.9%)

Best (OG 1040.5, ABV 4.2%) ◈
An easy-drinking best bitter with hints of malt and floral hops in the aroma. The taste has an abundance of hops and fruit and a pleasant, crisp malty aftertaste.

Blond (OG 1042.5, ABV 4.5%) ◈
A golden ale with intense fruit and hop tastes, which lessen in the aftertaste.

Red (OG 1044, ABV 4.5%) ◈
Complex tastes of fruit and roasted malt throughout, enhanced by a strong, fruity aroma.

Nook'y Brown Ale (ABV 4.9%)

Oat Stout (ABV 5.2%)

Norfolk SIBA

Moon Gazer Barn, Harvest Lane, Hindringham, Norfolk, NR21 0PW
☎ (01328) 878495 ⊕ norfolkbrewhouse.co.uk
Tours by arrangement

Brewing began in 2012 using a 10-barrel plant. The brewery is owned and run by Rachel and David Holliday. Chalk-filtered water is used from the brewery's own well.

Dewhopper Lager (ABV 3.8%)

Moongazer Amber (ABV 4%)
This amber ale combines a full-bodied bitterness with fruity overtones creating an impressive flavour and a smooth, lasting finish.

Moongazer Golden (ABV 4%)
This golden ale has a fresh, citrus aroma and a well-hopped character with fruit and hop flavour carrying through to the refreshing, crisp, dry finish.

Moongazer Ruby (ABV 4%)
A ruby-coloured bitter with a rich, spicy, roasted aroma and a full malty body, resulting in a full-bodied mouthfeel.

Stubblestag Lager (ABV 5%)

Norfolk Square

Japonica House, Mill Road, Stokesby, Norfolk, NR29 3AL
☎ (01493) 751975 ⊕ norfolksquarebrewery.co.uk

⊠ Norfolk Square began brewing in 2008 and is located in the Broadland village of Stokesby. It specialises in bottle-conditioned beers. Cask-conditioned beer is available locally.

Square Miled (OG 1038, ABV 4%)
A traditional mild ale with a sweet, malty flavour. The beer is not aged so it has a fresh spring taste.

Scroby (OG 1040, ABV 4.2%)
A refreshing pale ale with a hoppy, floral and spicy aroma.

Sunshiny (OG 1042, ABV 4.5%)
A refreshing golden ale with a honey twist and a rich, full-bodied, smooth flavour.

B52 (OG 1044, ABV 4.8%)
A creamy russet-coloured best bitter with a blackcurrant undertone. Smooth on the palate with a light, hoppy aroma.

Winklepicker (OG 1046, ABV 5%)

Lunatik IPA – Maverik (OG 1077, ABV 7%)
A sweet, hoppy beer with a peachy hop aroma.

Crazy Horse American IPA – Maverik (OG 1080, ABV 8%)
A smooth, sweet, caramelised flavour with a hint of bitterness with a tangerine, hoppy aroma.

Black Widow – Maverik (OG 1092, ABV 9%)
A full-bodied beer with loads of coffee, cocoa and subtle port notes with a sweet yet spicy background.

North Cotswold SIBA

Unit 3, Ditchford Farm, Stretton-on-Fosse, Warwickshire, GL56 9RD
☎ (01608) 663947 ⊕ northcotswoldbrewery.co.uk
Shop Mon-Fri 10am-4pm; Sat 10am-1pm

⊛North Cotswold started in 1999 as a 2.5-barrel plant, which was upgraded in 2000 to 10 barrels. Seasonal beers are available.

Windrush Ale (OG 1036, ABV 3.6%)
A thirst quenching amber-coloured session bitter with a malty, slightly sweet palate.

Cotswold Best (OG 1040, ABV 4%)
An easy-drinking, straw-coloured best bitter.

Shagweaver (OG 1045, ABV 4.5%)
A pale, hoppy bitter.

North Curry SIBA

The Old Coach House, Gwyon House, Church Road, North Curry, Somerset, TA3 6LH
☎ 07928 815053 ⊕ thenorthcurrybrewerycouk.com

⊠ The brewery opened in 2006 and is attached to one of the oldest properties in North Curry where brewing last took place in the village in the 1920s. Beers are available at farmers markets in Taunton and Minehead and in local shops. All beers are also available bottle conditioned. Seasonal beer: see website.

Howzat (OG 1036, ABV 3.7%)
A golden-coloured ale with fruity hops and a smooth aftertaste.

Gold (OG 1038, ABV 3.9%)
A golden ale inspired by a classic beer recipe from Somerset with a fruity aroma and smooth sweetness in contrast with the bitter hops.

Red Heron (OG 1041, ABV 4.3%)
A full-bodied, malty-flavoured ale, balanced by the bitterness of Golding hops.

Jubeelee (OG 1042, ABV 4.6%)
A golden, refreshing honey beer.

The Withyman (OG 1042, ABV 4.6%)
The malty flavour has a bitterness and punch from the fruity hops.

Level Headed (OG 1043, ABV 4.7%)
A traditional old English ale; dark ruby-coloured, rich and full of flavour.

Alfred's Stout (OG 1047, ABV 5.1%)
A black, dry stout with a good, robust flavour. A rounded body is balanced by the bitterness of roasted barley and Northern Brewer hops.

North Laine (NEW)

⊟ North Laine Bar & Brewhouse, 27 Gloucester Place, Brighton, East Sussex, BN1 4AA
☎ (01273) 683666
✉ northlainepub@drinkinbrighton.co.uk

North Laine Brewery was established in 2012 using a five-barrel plant, based within the North Laine pub in Brighton. The brewing equipment and process can be viewed from the bar. Seasonal beers are also available.

Black Rock (OG 1045, ABV 4.5%)

IPA (OG 1050, ABV 5%)

North Riding

⊟ North Riding Brewpub, North Marine Road, Scarborough, North Yorkshire, YO12 7HU
☎ (01723) 370004 ⊕ northridingbrewpub.com

Brewing commenced in 2011 using a two-barrel plant situated in the cellar of the pub. A new beer is brewed every week. Seasonal and bottle-conditioned beers are available.

PPA (Peasholm Pale Ale) (OG 1042, ABV 4.3%)
A pale and hoppy beer with a citrus bitterness and a long, smooth finish.

North Star SIBA

Unit 6, Gallows Industrial Park, off Furnace Road, Ilkeston, Derbyshire, DE7 5EP ⊕ northstarbeers.co.uk
Tours by arrangement

☺North Star is a family-run brewery established in 2012 using a 10-barrel plant.

Sentinel (OG 1039, ABV 3.8%)
A pale, fully-hopped American-style ale with citrus undertones.

Helmsman (OG 1041, ABV 4.2%)
A pale ale with a full malt flavour and a delicate hop balance with a satisfying fruit finish.

Pathfinder (OG 1045, ABV 4.5%)
A special bitter with full roast malt and rich orange peel overtones. The malt is balanced by four hop varieties.

Astronomer (OG 1048, ABV 4.8%)
A stout with rich roast malt flavour and dark chocolate overtones which lead to a dry biscuit finish.

Polaris (OG 1049, ABV 5%)
A dark ruby porter with chocolate, liquorice and coffee aromas. The flavours lead to a hoppy, bitter finish.

Endeavour (OG 1053, ABV 5.4%)
A dark beer with complex fruit flavours and notes of pepper, culminating in a full malt flavouring and a toffee and wine-like finish.

North Wales

Ty Tan-y-Mynydd, Moelfre, Abergele, Conwy, LL22 9RF

☎ (0800) 083 4100 ☎ 07710 042499
⊕ northwalesbrewery.net

John Wood established his brewery in 2007. In 2012 a bore hole was drilled to supply water for brewing. Bottle-conditioned beers are also available, and mead and soft drinks are produced.

Bodelwyddan Bitter (OG 1038, ABV 3.8%)

Abergele Ale (OG 1050, ABV 5%)

North Yorkshire SIBA

Pinchinthorpe Hall, Pinchinthorpe, North Yorkshire, TS14 8HG
☎ (01287) 630200 ⊕ nybrewery.co.uk
Shop Mon-Fri 9am-5pm
Tours by arrangement

☺Founded in Middlesbrough in 1989 the brewery moved to Pinchinthorpe Hall, a moated, listed medieval estate near Guisborough in 1998. Its own spring water produces a distinctive flavour. More than 100 trade outlets are supplied. Most cask beers are organic with some occasional beers not so. Bottle-conditioned beers are available.

Best (OG 1036, ABV 3.6%)
A clean-tasting, well-hopped, copper-coloured session beer.

Golden Ginseng (OG 1036, ABV 3.6%)
Clean tasting, well hopped traditional beer with gingseng.

Prior's Ale (OG 1036, ABV 3.6%) ◕
Light, refreshing and surprisingly full-flavoured for a pale, low gravity beer, with a complex, bittersweet mixture of malt, hops and fruit carrying through into the aftertaste.

Temptation (OG 1038, ABV 3.8%)
A refreshing beer with a citrus and grapefruit nose.

Archbishop Lee's Ruby Ale (OG 1040, ABV 4%)
Maltiness is predominant with some hops in the taste.

Boro Best (OG 1040, ABV 4%)
Mid brown with a malty aroma. A full bodied beer.

Crystal Tips (OG 1040, ABV 4%)
A full-bodied, malty ruby bitter.

Love Muscle (OG 1040, ABV 4%)

Honey Bunny (OG 1042, ABV 4.2%)
Golden bitter with a hoppy finish and a hint of honey.

Mayhem (OG 1043, ABV 4.3%)
Refreshing, clean tasting, well hopped pale ale.

Cereal Killer (OG 1045, ABV 4.5%)
Light-coloured unclouded wheat bitter with a distinctive hop nose.

Fools Gold (OG 1046, ABV 4.6%)
Pale, refreshingly complex golden ale. Fruity aroma with a bittersweet flavour.

Golden Ale (OG 1046, ABV 4.6%) ◕
A well-hopped, lightly-malted, golden premium bitter, using Styrian Goldings and Goldings hops.

Flying Herbert (OG 1047, ABV 4.7%)
Smooth, full flavoured premium bitter with a malty, fruity and dry finish.

Lord Lee's (OG 1047, ABV 4.7%) ◕
A refreshing, red/brown beer with a hoppy aroma. The flavour is a pleasant balance of roast malt and

sweetness that predominates over hops. The malty, bitter finish develops slowly.

White Lady (OG 1047, ABV 4.7%)
A hoppy, strong, pale coloured beer.

Dizzy Dick (OG 1048, ABV 4.8%)
Strong, smooth, dark ale with plenty of hops.

Rocket Fuel (OG 1050, ABV 5%)
A strong golden ale.

Valhalla (OG 1055, ABV 5.5%)
Very strong traditional bitter with plenty of hops and a subtle hint of malt.

Se7en (OG 1070, ABV 7%)
A strong golden ale with a grapefruit aroma.

Northern

See Blakemere

Northern FC (NEW)

McCracken Park, Great North Road, Gosforth, Newcastle upon Tyne, NE3 2DT
⊕ northernfootballclub.co.uk

Established in 2012 to supply the clubhouse for the Northern RUFC, the range is developing but brews are popular.

Northumberland SIBA ◉

Accessory House, Barrington Road, Bedlington, Northumberland, NE22 7AP
☎ (01670) 822112 ⊕ northumberlandbrewery.co.uk
Tours by arrangement

☺Brewing began in 1996 in Ashington using a five-barrel plant. Relocation and expansion mean that the brewery now use a 10-barrel plant and has an on-site brewery tap, Fuggles. 30-40 barrels are brewed per week of a wide range of ales including seasonals: see website.

Pit Pony (OG 1039, ABV 3.8%)

St James' Park Bitter (OG 1039, ABV 4%)

Fog on the Tyne (OG 1040.5, ABV 4.1%)

Norton

Norton Priory, Tudor Road, Manor Park, Runcorn, Cheshire, WA7 1SX

Norton Brewing was created in 2009 by Halton Borough Council as a social enterprise to provide employment opportunities for people with learning disabilities, autism and other disabilites. It is situated in the grounds of Norton Priory.

Priory Ale (ABV 4.5%)

Norwich Bear

Ketts Tavern, 29 Ketts Hill, Norwich, Norfolk, NR1 4EX
☎ (01603) 449654 ⊕ norwichbear.co.uk

⊠ Norwich Bear was launched in 2010. It brews bespoke ales exclusively for the Ketts Tavern and the Rose in Norwich. Seasonal beers are available.

Teddy Bear (OG 1037, ABV 3.7%) ◄
Rolling malt and hop aroma introduces similar flavours with an added hint of strawberries. A gently tapering finish turns woody.

Classic (OG 1038, ABV 3.8%) ◄
A crisp hoppy backbone is heightened by a tangy grapefruit edge. A short, noticeably drier finale.

Pooh (OG 1042, ABV 4.2%)
Amber-gold, a grassy citrus aroma flows into an easy drinking mix of malt, caramel, hop and grapefruit. Well-rounded with a lingering fruity ending.

Legend (OG 1044, ABV 4.3%) ◄
Tawny hued, grainy mouthfeel with a swirling malty and hop nose. Initial chocolate orange explosion fades into a bittersweet dryness.

Boudicca (OG 1045, ABV 4.5%) ◄
Caramel is dominant in aroma and taste. Malt, vine fruit and marmalade add to the complex intermingling of flavours.

NPA (Norwich Pale Ale) (OG 1047, ABV 4.7%) ◄
Golden-coloured with a grassy, hoppy nose. Easy drinking mix with hops flowing over a bittersweet citrus base.

Platinum Blonde (OG 1050, ABV 5%) ◄
Light, crisp, and refreshing with a miasma of interlinked flavours. Elderflower, grapefruit and hops mix well against a gentle, sweet, malty background. Fragrant aroma.

Noss Beer Works (NEW) SIBA

Unit 6, Ash Court, Pennant Way, Lee Mill, Devon, PL21 9GE ⊕ nossbeerworks.co.uk
Tours by arrangement

⊠ Brewing began in 2012 using a six-barrel plant.

Church Ledge (OG 1040, ABV 4%)
A late-hopped blonde IPA; light, hoppy and zesty.

Mew Stone (OG 1043, ABV 4.3%)
A copper-coloured, well-balanced and refreshing beer.

Ebb Rock (OG 1049, ABV 4.9%)
Dark copper-coloured and full-bodied.

Nottingham SIBA ◉

Plough Inn, 17 St Peter's Street, Radford, Nottingham, NG7 3EN
☎ (0115) 942 2649 ☎ 07815 73447
⊕ nottinghambrewery.com
Tours by arrangement

The former owners of the Bramcote and Castle Rock Breweries re-established the Nottingham Brewery in 2000 in a purpose-built brewhouse behind the Plough Inn. Philip Darby and Niven Balfour set out to revive the brands of the original Nottingham Brewery, closed by Whitbread in the 1950s, with a view to supplying local outlets within the LocAle ethos.

Rock Ale Bitter Beer (OG 1038, ABV 3.8%) ◄
A pale and bitter, thirst-quenching hoppy beer with a dry finish.

Rock Ale Mild Beer (OG 1038, ABV 3.8%) ◄
A reddish-black malty mild with some refreshing bitterness in the finish.

Trent Bridge Inn Ale (OG 1038, ABV 3.8%)

Legend (OG 1040, ABV 4%) ◄
A fruity and malty pale brown bitter with a touch of sweetness and bitterness.

Extra Pale Ale (OG 1042, ABV 4.2%) ◄

A hoppy and fruity golden ale with a hint of sweetness and a long-lasting bitter finish.

Broadway Reel Ale (OG 1044, ABV 4.4%)

Dreadnought (OG 1045, ABV 4.5%) ◆
Well-balanced best bitter. Blend of malt and hops give a rounded fruity finish.

Bullion (OG 1047, ABV 4.7%) ◆
A refreshing premium golden ale. Brewed with a single malt variety, it is triple-hopped and exceptionally bitter.

Supreme (OG 1052, ABV 5.2%) ◆
A strong, amber, fruity ale. A touch of malt in the taste is followed by a sweet and slightly hoppy finish.

Nutbrook SIBA ◉

6 Hallam Way, West Hallam, Derbyshire, DE7 6LA
☎ 0800 458 2460 ⊕ nutbrookbrewery.com
Shop Mon-Fri 10am-6pm (by invite only); Sat 9am-5pm at Oakfield Farm (open to all)
Tours by arrangement

Nutbrook was established in 2007 on a one-barrel brewery in the owners' garage. This was supplemented in 2010 with a six-barrel plant at Oakfield Farm, Stanley Common. Beers are brewed to order for domestic and corporate clients, and customers can design their own recipes. All beers are available bottle conditioned.

Or8 (OG 1041.4, ABV 3.8%)

Bitlyke (OG 1040.6, ABV 4.2%)

Banter (OG 1040.8, ABV 4.5%)

Midnight (OG 1048.4, ABV 4.5%)

Mongrel (OG 1046.9, ABV 4.5%)

O'Hanlon's SIBA ◉

Great Barton Farm, Whimple, Devon, EX5 2NY
☎ (01404) 822412 ✉ liz@ohanlonsbrewery.com

Since moving to Whimple in 2000, the brewery has continued to expand to cope with increasing demand. More than 100 outlets are regularly supplied, with wholesalers distributing nationwide. Seasonal and bottle-conditioned beers are also available.

Yellowhammer (OG 1041, ABV 4%) ◆
A well-balanced, smooth pale yellow beer with a predominant hop and fruit nose and taste, leading to a dry, bitter finish.

Dry Stout (OG 1043, ABV 4.2%) ◆
A dark malty, well-balanced stout with a dry, bitter finish and plenty of roast and fruit flavours up front.

Flagship IPA (OG 1044, ABV 4.2%)
Dark chestnut-coloured IPA with subtle malty undertones and a fresh grapefruit-like bitterness.

Red Ale (OG 1044, ABV 4.5%)

Port Stout (OG 1041, ABV 4.8%) 🗒 ◆
A black beer with roast malt in the aroma that remains in the taste but gives way to hoppy bitterness in the aftertaste.

Stormstay (OG 1048, ABV 5%) 🗒
A ruby-coloured complex ale with a toffee and floral hop aroma and a surprisingly clean finish after the malt toffee and biscuit flavours.

Oakham SIBA ◉

🏠 2 Maxwell Road, Woodston, Peterborough, Cambridgeshire, PE2 7JB
☎ (01733) 370500 ⊕ oakhamales.com
Shop Mon-Fri 9am-5pm
Tours by arrangement

⊗ The brewery started in 1993 in Oakham, Rutland and moved to Peterborough in 1998. The brewery's main production site is a 75-barrel plant. An additional six-barrel plant is located at its city-centre brewpub, which makes special and one-off brews. Around 350 outlets are supplied and three pubs are owned. Seasonal beers: see website.

Jeffrey Hudson Bitter/JHB (OG 1038, ABV 3.8%) ◆
Straw-coloured golden ale dominated by citrus hop character throughout. Long, dry, slightly astringent finish.

Inferno (OG 1039, ABV 4%) ◆
The citrus hop character of this straw-coloured brew begins on the nose and builds in intensity on the palate. Clean dry citrus finish.

Citra (OG 1042, ABV 4.2%) ◆
Refreshing grapefruit and peach aroma and flavour characterise this golden ale. Bittersweet palate gives way to a long dry aftertaste.

Scarlet Macaw (OG 1043, ABV 4.4%)

Bishops Farewell (OG 1046, ABV 4.6%) ◆
Powerfully citrusy, the hops and fruit on the aroma of this golden/yellow beer become bittersweet on the palate. Zesty citrus aftertaste.

Oakleaf SIBA ◉

Unit 7, Clarence Wharf Industrial Estate, Mumby Road, Gosport, Hampshire, PO12 1AJ
☎ (023) 9251 3222 ⊕ oakleafbrewing.co.uk
Shop (Brewpot in Gosport) Tue-Thu 11am-5pm; Fri & Sat 11am-6pm
Tours by arrangement

⊗ Ed Anderson set up Oakleaf with his father-in-law, Dave Pickersgill, in 2000. The brewery stands on the side of Portsmouth Harbour. Some 350 outlets are supplied direct with national deliveries via wholesalers. Seasonal beers: see website. Bottle-conditioned beers are also available.

Some Are Drinking (OG 1039, ABV 3.9%)
An easy-drinking light ale. Pale and refreshing with a zesty hop finish.

Quercus Folium (OG 1040, ABV 4%)
A traditional mid-brown bitter with an initial malty flavour leading to a long hoppy finish.

Nuptu'ale (OG 1042, ABV 4.2%) ◆
A full-bodied pale ale, strongly hopped with an uncompromising bitterness. An intense hoppy, spicy, floral aroma leads to a complex hoppy taste. Well-balanced with malt and citrus flavours and a hint of sweetness making for a refreshing bitter.

Pompey Royal (OG 1046, ABV 4.5%)
A traditional mid-brown malty ale with a delicate hop balance.

Hole Hearted (OG 1048, ABV 4.7%) ◆
An amber-coloured strong bitter with strong floral hop and citrus notes in the aroma. These continue in the flavour, with some malt coming through, leading to a long, bittersweet finish.

I Can't Believe It's Not Bitter
(OG 1048, ABV 4.9%)
Clean and crisp with a fruity aftertaste and a citrus finish that lingers on.

India Pale Ale (OG 1053, ABV 5.5%)
Initially dry and bitter, full-flavoured and complex marmalade/aniseed notes follow, which leave a lingering bitterness on the palate.

Brewed for Suthwyk Ales:

Old Dick (OG 1038, ABV 3.8%) ◀
Formerly known as Bloomfield Bitter, this is a pleasant, clean-tasting pale brown bitter. Easy-drinking and well-balanced. Beer is brewed by Oakleaf for Suthwyk using ingredients grown on the farm.

Liberation (OG 1042, ABV 4.2%)
Light-coloured ale with a soft, berry fruit flavour.

Skew Sunshine Ale (OG 1046, ABV 4.6%) ◀
An amber-coloured beer. Initial hoppiness leads to a fruity taste and finish. A slightly cloying mouthfeel. The beer is brewed by Oakleaf for Suthwyk using ingredients grown on the farm.

Palmerston's Folly (OG 1050, ABV 5%)

Oates SIBA

4C Ladyship Business Park, Mill Lane, Halifax, West Yorkshire, HX3 6TA
☎ (01422) 320100 ☎ 07770 572055
⊕ oatesbrewing.co.uk

Oates was founded in 2011 by former landlord Mark Oates and Master Brewer Richard Munro. Three core beers are produced on a six-barrel plant.

O.M.T. (ABV 3.8%)
A light, straw-coloured beer with a floral and hoppy aroma and delicate hints of lemon and pineapple in taste.

Golden Oates (ABV 4.1%)
A golden, honey coloured beer which oozes caramels and honey on the nose, with a long bitter finish.

Wild Oates (ABV 4.3%)
A full bodied amber-coloured beer. Well balanced with a rich floral fragrance and lingering bitterness to the finish.

Oban Bay

See Argyll

Odcombe

▤ Masons Arms, 41 Lower Odcombe, Lower Odcombe, Somerset, BA22 8TX
☎ (01935) 862591 ⊕ masonsarmsodcombe.co.uk
Tours by arrangement

Odcombe opened in 2000 and closed a few years later. It re-opened in 2005 with assistance from Shepherd Neame (qv). Brewing takes place once a week and beers are only available at the pub. Seasonal beers are also available.

No. 1 (OG 1040, ABV 4%)

Spring (OG 1042, ABV 4.1%)

Roly Poly (OG 1042, ABV 4.2%)

Offa's Dyke SIBA

▤ Chapel Lane, Trefonen, Shropshire, SY10 9DX
☎ (01691) 656889 ⊕ offasdykebrewery.com
Shop Mon-Fri 5-11pm; Sat & Sun 12pm-midnight
Tours by arrangement

Offa's Dyke was established in 2007. The brewery and adjoining pub straddle the old England/Wales border, Offa's Dyke. The owner has small-scale hop cultivation. The Olde Vaults in Oswestry serves as a second brewery tap.

Barley Gold (OG 1038, ABV 3.6%)
A light amber session beer with lingering bitterness.

Offa's Pride (OG 1040, ABV 3.8%)
An amber bitter with a balanced fruity finish.

Thirst Brew (OG 1042, ABV 4%)
A full-bodied premium bitter. Mid brown in colour, maltiness predominant throughout with bitterness coming through at the finish.

Grim Reaper (OG 1050, ABV 5%)
Dark and smooth with a rich flavour. Roast and chocolate dominate in the aroma. Not too sweet for its gravity.

Offbeat SIBA

Unit 6, Thomas Street, Crewe, Cheshire, CW1 2BD
☎ 07502 096438 ⊕ offbeatbrewery.com
Tours by arrangement

☺Offbeat began brewing in 2010, quickly expanding to a six-barrel plant. Brewery open nights (usually first Friday of the month) are a regular occurrence. The beers are available at local outlets around the North West. Monthly specials and bottle-conditioned beers are also available.

Wild Blackberry Mild (OG 1036.8, ABV 3.8%)

Outlandish Pale (OG 1037.8, ABV 3.9%)
Pale ale with a fresh burst of lemon hoppiness.

Odd Ball Red (OG 1040.4, ABV 4.2%)
Bold and fruity ruby red ale with a spicy flavour and finish.

Out of Step IPA (OG 1055.3, ABV 5.8%)
American-style India Pale Ale. Generously hopped with abundant citrus flavours leading to a dry, bitter finish.

Okells SIBA ◉

Kewaigue, Douglas, Isle of Man, IM2 1QG
☎ (01624) 699400 ⊕ okells.co.uk
Tours by arrangement

☺Founded in 1874 by Dr Okell, this is the main brewery on the island and moved in 1994 to a new, purpose-built plant at Kewaigue. All the beers are produced under the Manx Brewers' Act 1874 which permits only water, malt, sugar and hops to be used in brewing, but was amended in 1998 to allow the brewing of wheat and fruit beers. Seasonal beers: see website.

Bitter (OG 1035, ABV 3.7%) ◀
A golden beer, malty and hoppy in aroma, with a hint of honey. Rich and malty on the tongue, it has a dry, malt and hop finish. A complex but rewarding beer.

Olaf (OG 1040, ABV 3.9%)

Very deep black in colour with aromas of coffee and liquorice

Dr Okell's IPA (OG 1044, ABV 4.5%)
A light-coloured beer with a full-bodied taste. The sweetness is offset by strong hopping that gives the beer an overall roundness with spicy lemon notes and a fine dry finish.

Jiarg (OG 1047, ABV 4.7%)
A rich ruby red-coloured beer with a spicy citrus hop aroma.

Alt (OG 1050, ABV 4.9%)
A copper-coloured Altbier with a crisp flavour, with hints of gooseberry and citrus: production involves a cooler fermentation and two weeks cold storage.

Old Bear SIBA

Unit 1, Aireworth Mills, Aireworth Road, Keighley, West Yorkshire, BD21 4DH
☎ (01535) 601222 ⊕ oldbearbrewery.co.uk
Shop Mon-Fri 9am-4pm
Tours by arrangement

☺Old Bear is a family business founded in 1993 using a 10-barrel brewery in a 19th-century textile mill. The cask range is available nationally and also bottle-conditioned using bottles from sister company Bottle Rescue. The brewery offers placements in bottling and recycling for people in the community with learning disabilities.

Estivator (OG 1037, ABV 3.8%) ◆
This straw-coloured bitter has a grassy hop character in the aroma and taste with marmalade fruitiness. The finish is dry and bitter.

Great Bear (OG 1039, ABV 3.9%)

Black Mari'a (OG 1043, ABV 4.2%)
A black stout, smooth on the palate with a strong roast malt flavour and fruity finish.

Honeypot (OG 1044, ABV 4.4%)
Straw-coloured beer enhanced with honey.

Goldilocks (OG 1047, ABV 4.5%) ◆
A fruity, straw-coloured golden ale, well-hopped and assertively bitter through to the finish.

Hibernator (OG 1055, ABV 5%) ◆
A complex rich dark ale dominated by roast and bitter flavours against a background sweetness. Look for roast coffee, hints of caramel and dark vine fruit on the nose. The finish is distinctly bitter and quite astringent.

Old Bog

⊟ Masons Arms, 2 Quarry School Place, Oxford, OX3 8LH
☎ (01865) 764579 ✉ theoldbog@hotmail.co.uk

Brewing started in 2005 on a one-barrel plant behind the Masons Arms that only brews at weekends. Beers, when available, are sold at the pub and occasionally at local beer festivals. A number of one-off brews appear throughout the year.

Quarry Gold (OG 1041, ABV 4.1%)
Clean-tasting golden bitter with well balanced sweet and bitter characteristics.

Half Wit (ABV 4.5%)
A malty dark-amber wheat beer.

Quarry Goldish (ABV 4.6%)
Golden ale with mild fruit notes and a sweet finish.

Wheat Beer (ABV 5%)
Pale gold in colour, with a light citrus hoppiness.

Monstrous Mild (ABV 5.6%)
Strong, smooth, dark mild with fruity and malty tastes.

Old Brewery

See Meantime

Old Cannon SIBA

⊟ 86 Cannon Street, Bury St Edmunds, Suffolk, IP33 1JR
☎ (01284) 768769 ⊕ oldcannonbrewery.co.uk
Tours by arrangement

⊗ The St Edmunds Head pub opened in 1845 with its own brewery. Brewing ceased in 1917, and Greene King closed the pub in 1995. It re-opened in 1999 as the Old Cannon brewery complete with a unique state-of-the-art brewery housed in the bar area. A growing number of local outlets are supplied. Seasonal beers are also available.

Best Bitter (OG 1037, ABV 3.8%) ◆
Traditional East Anglian bitter. Rich hoppy aroma and bitterness dominate throughout with just a hint of sweetness in the aftertaste.

Hornblower (OG 1038, ABV 4%)
Very light in colour with an IPA hoppiness.

Gunner's Daughter (OG 1052, ABV 5.5%) ◆
A well-balanced strong ale with a complexity of hop, fruit, sweetness and bitterness in the flavour, and a lingering hoppy, bitter aftertaste.

Old Chimneys

Hopton End Farm, Church Road, Market Weston, Diss, Suffolk, IP22 2NX
☎ (01359) 221411/221013
⊕ oldchimneysbrewery.com
Shop Fri 2-7pm; Sat 11am-2pm
Tours by arrangement

Old Chimneys opened in 1995, moving to a converted farm building in 2001. Most of the beers are named after rare species of wildlife found nearby. Seasonal, special and bottle-conditioned beers are also available, along with a small quantity of cider.

Military Mild (OG 1035, ABV 3.3%) ◆
A rich, dark mild with good body for its gravity. Sweetish toffee and light roast bitterness dominate, leading to a dry aftertaste.

Ragged Robin (ABV 3.5%)

Great Raft Bitter (OG 1040, ABV 4%)
Pale copper bitter bursting with fruit. Malt and hops add to the sweetish fruity flavour, which is rounded off with hoppy bitterness in the aftertaste.

Black Rat Stout (OG 1048, ABV 4.4%)
Milk stout with roast malt and coffee flavours, and body and sweetness from added lactose.

Golden Pheasant (OG 1044, ABV 4.5%)
Pale, dry bitter with citrus, apple and malt, balanced with robust hop bitterness.

Barbastelle (ABV 6.2%)

Old Cross

▤ Old Cross Tavern, 8 St Andrew Street, Hertford, SG14 1JA
☎ (01992) 583133

⊠ The microbrewery was set up in 2008 and is located within the pub. Owner Nigel Beviss brews solely for the Old Cross Tavern. There are two regularly-available beers plus special single-hop brewed ales, with one always available at the bar.

Laugh & Titter (OG 1037, ABV 3.7%)

Gertcha! (OG 1039, ABV 3.9%)

Old Dairy ⌧ⒷⒶ ◉

The Old Parlour, Rawlinson Farm, Rolvenden, Kent, TN17 4JD
☎ (01580) 243185 ⊕ olddairybrewery.com
Tours by arrangement

Old Dairy was founded in 2009. Sales expanded rapidly across pubs in Kent and new staff were taken on after only three months to help cope with the demand. 50 outlets are supplied direct. Bottle-conditioned beers are available.

Red Top (OG 1038, ABV 3.8%) ◗
A sweetish copper-coloured bitter with hints of caramel and a subtle hop character.

Copper Top (OG 1041, ABV 4.1%)
Dark full-flavoured best bitter using chocolate malt.

Gold Top (OG 1043, ABV 4.3%) ◗
A well balanced golden ale with a good blend of malt and hops followed by a long, bittersweet finish.

Silver Top (OG 1046, ABV 4.5%) ◗
A well crafted complex stout with a good balance of dark malts, roast barley and caramel, and a long finish.

Blue Top (OG 1048, ABV 4.8%) ◗
Rich and full bodied, this pale brown ale has a long bittersweet finish and a hint of aroma hop.

Old Forge

▤ Radnor Arms, Coleshill, Oxfordshire, SN6 7PR
☎ (01793) 873915 ☎ 07771 613556
⊕ oldforgebrewery.co.uk
Tours by arrangement

Old Forge began brewing at the Radnor Arms in 2010 using a four-barrel plant. Alan Watkins (owner/brewer at the Halfpenny Brewery) is head brewer. Visitors can view the plant through several glass windows opposite the entrance to the pub.

Anvil Ale (OG 1037, ABV 3.8%)
Light session ale, amber-coloured with traditional bitterness.

Blacksmiths Gold (OG 1042, ABV 4%)
Refreshing straw-coloured ale with citrus notes and a hoppy floral finish.

Hammer & Tongs (OG 1043, ABV 4.2%)
Ruby chestnut in colour, bitter yet mellow in taste.

Sledgehammer (OG 1048, ABV 5%)
Deep red, full-bodied premium ale with hints of chocolate and caramel.

Old Inn

▤ Old Inn, Flowerdale Glen, Gairloch, IV21 2BD

☎ (01445) 712006 ⊕ theoldinn.net

Brewing began in 2010 using a 150-litre plant. Seasonal beers are also available.

Erradale IPA (OG 1041, ABV 4.2%)

The Blind Piper (ABV 4.6%)

Old Laxey

▤ Shore Hotel Brew Pub, Old Laxey, Isle of Man, IM4 7DA
☎ (01624) 863214 ⊕ shorehotel.im
Tours by arrangement

Beer brewed on the Isle of Man is brewed to a strict Beer Purity Act. Additives are not permitted to extend shelf life, nor are chemicals allowed to assist with head retention. Old Laxey's beer is mostly sold through the adjacent Shore Hotel.

Bosun Bitter (OG 1038, ABV 3.8%)
Crisp and fresh with a hoppy aftertaste.

Old Luxters

Chiltern Valley Vineyard, Hambleden, Henley-on-Thames, Oxfordshire, RG9 6JW
☎ (01491) 638330 ⊕ chilternvalley.co.uk
Shop Mon-Fri 9am-6pm; Sat-Sun 11am-6pm (5pm winter)
Tours by arrangement

Situated in a 17th-century barn beside the Chiltern Valley Vineyard, Old Luxters is a traditional brewery established in 1990 and was awarded a Royal Warrant of Appointment in 2007. There is some cask production, but beers are mostly bottle-conditioned.

Old Mill ⌧ⒷⒶ ◉

Mill Street, Snaith, East Yorkshire, DN14 9HU
☎ (01405) 861813 ⊕ oldmillbrewery.co.uk
Tours by arrangement

☺Opened in 1983 in a 200-year-old former malt kiln and corn mill, the brew-length is 60 barrels. The brewery is building a tied estate, now standing at 19 houses. Beers can be found nationwide through wholesalers and around 80 free trade outlets are supplied direct. Seasonal beers and monthly specials are brewed: see website.

Traditional Mild (OG 1034, ABV 3.4%) ◗
A satisfying roast malt flavour dominates this easy-drinking, quality dark mild.

Traditional Bitter (OG 1038.5, ABV 3.8%) ◗
A malty nose is carried through to the initial flavour. Bitterness runs throughout.

Blonde Bombshell (OG 1042, ABV 4%)
A straw-coloured beer, easy drinking with delicate fruity flavours.

Red Goose (OG 1042, ABV 4.2%)
A rich, ruby, malty beer.

Yorkshire Porter (OG 1044, ABV 4.4%)
Mahogany-coloured porter with sweet, roasted and chocolate flavours, and a pleasant hop aroma.

Bullion (OG 1047.5, ABV 4.7%) ◗
The malty and hoppy aroma is followed by a neat mix of hop and fruit tastes within an enveloping maltiness. Dark brown/amber in colour.

Old Pie Factory SIBA

Montague Road, Warwick, CV34 5LW
☎ (01926) 402100 ⊕ oldpiefactorybrewery.co.uk

😊Old Pie Factory began brewing in 2011 using a
5.5-barrel plant. The brewery is located at
Underwood Wines and is a joint venture between
Underwood Wines, the Old Fourpenny Shop Hotel
in Warwick and the Case is Altered in nearby Five
Ways.

Bitter (OG 1038.5, ABV 3.9%)
Classic session bitter brewed with only English
ingredients.

Pale (OG 1040, ABV 4.1%)
Light and refreshing straw-coloured ale with
pleasing hoppy notes.

Old Sawley (NEW)

▤ White Lion, 352 Tamworth Road, Sawley,
Derbyshire, NG10 3AT
☎ 07722 311209
✉ oldsawleybrewingcompany@gmail.com

Old Sawley Brewing Company was established in
2013. Brewing currently takes place upstairs at the
White Lion pub in Sawley, while a microbrewery is
installed at the rear of the pub.

Toll Bridge Porter (ABV 4.5%)

Old School (NEW) SIBA

Holly Bank Barn, Crag Road, Warton, Lancashire,
LA5 9PL
☎ (01524) 735005 ⊕ oldschoolbrewery.co.uk
Tours by arrangement

😊A 12-barrel brewery, founded in 2012, located in
a renovated 400-year-old former school
outbuilding overlooking the picturesque village of
Warton. Beer is mainly sold to local freehouses.
Regular brewery open nights are held.

Blackboard (OG 1037, ABV 3.7%) ◕
Dominant malts and a short finish characterise this
lightly-hopped, dark mild.

Hopscotch (OG 1037, ABV 3.7%)
A sunshine coloured pale ale. It balances a crisp
taste with a delicate lasting hoppiness of citrus
fruits.

Detention (OG 1041, ABV 4.1%) ◕
Light, malty bitter, sweetish middle with a gentle
hoppy bitter finish.

Headmaster (OG 1045, ABV 4.5%)
A dark, strong best bitter. It mixes a complex malty
flavour with a blackcurrant aroma, leaving a subtle
sweet nutty aftertaste.

Old Spot

Manor Farm, Station Road, Cullingworth, Bradford,
West Yorkshire, BD13 5HN
☎ (01535) 691144 ⊕ oldspotbrewery.co.uk
Tours by arrangement

😊Old Spot, named after the owner's sheepdog,
started brewing in 2005. Five beers are available
complemented by seasonal and one-off brews. The
beers are available locally with the George Hotel in
Cullingworth being the main outlet and de facto
brewery tap.

Light But Dark (OG 1043, ABV 4%)
Chestnut-coloured bitter with a slight malty taste
and pleasant bitter finish. An ideal session beer.

Spot Light (OG 1040, ABV 4.2%) ◕
This smooth-drinking golden ale has a slightly
fruity, hoppy aroma leading to a well balanced
fruit, hop flavour with hints of pineapple and a long
bittersweet finish.

Inn-Spired (OG 1043, ABV 4.3%)
Light-coloured bitter with a light, hoppy taste and a
slight, fruity finish.

OSB (OG 1042, ABV 4.5%)
A golden-coloured, full-bodied bitter.

Spot O'Bother (OG 1060, ABV 5.5%)
Porter with a chocolate ice cream taste and slight
liquorice bitterness to finish. A very complex brew.

Olde Swan

▤ 89 Halesowen Road, Netherton, Dudley, West
Midlands, DY2 9PY
☎ (01384) 253075
Tours by arrangement

😊A famous brew-pub best known as Ma Pardoe's
after the matriarch who ruled it for years. The pub
has been licensed since 1835 and the present
brewery and pub were built in 1863. Brewing
continued until 1988 and restarted in 2001. The
plant brews primarily for the on-site pub with
some beer available to the trade. Seasonal and
special beers are available.

Original (OG 1034, ABV 3.5%) ◕
Straw-coloured light mild, smooth but tangy, and
sweetly refreshing with a faint hoppiness.

Dark Swan (OG 1041, ABV 4.2%) ◕
Smooth, sweet dark mild with late roast malt in the
finish.

Entire (OG 1043, ABV 4.4%) ◕
Faintly hoppy, amber premium bitter with
sweetness persistent throughout.

Bumble Hole Bitter (OG 1052, ABV 5.2%) ◕
Sweet, smooth amber ale with hints of astringency
in the finish.

Oldershaw SIBA ◉

Heath Lane, Barkston Heath, Grantham, Lincolnshire,
NG32 2DE
☎ (01476) 572135 ⊕ oldershawbrewery.com
Shop Mon-Fri 10am-4pm
Tours by arrangement

⊠Established in 1997, and under new ownership
since 2010, demand has continued to grow for
Oldershaw's products. Many new beers have been
introduced, including those which are part of
Project Venus – a collaboration of brewsters to raise
the profile of women in the brewing industry.
Seasonal and bottle-conditioned beers are
available.

Mowbray's Mash (OG 1037, ABV 3.7%)
A golden amber, hoppy, session beer. Fruity and
flavoursome.

Heavenly Blonde (OG 1038, ABV 3.8%)
A pale blonde beer, packed with zesty tropical
fruits, with a crisp, dry finish.

Newton's Drop (OG 1041, ABV 4.1%) ◕

2065# THE BREWERIES · O

Balanced malt and hops but with a strong bitter, lingering taste in this mid-brown beer.

Caskade (OG 1042, ABV 4.2%) ◄
A gentle blend of flavours combine into a smooth pint. Malt vies with a hoppy bitterness for initial recognition. Traces of caramel and sulphur appear before the short, sharp finish.

Great Expectations (OG 1040, ABV 4.2%)
A pale gold beer with citrus rich hops.

Posh Blonde (OG 1041, ABV 4.2%)
Crisp lager-style beer, enhanced by fruity floral and citrus-infused notes.

Best Bitter (OG 1043, ABV 4.3%)
A well-hopped, traditional-style best bitter, chestnut brown in colour.

Grantham Stout (OG 1043, ABV 4.3%)
Dark brown and smooth with rich roast malt flavour, supported by some fruit and bitterness. A long, moderately dry finish.

Regal Blonde (OG 1042, ABV 4.4%) ◄
Straw-coloured, lager-style beer with a good malt/hop balance throughout; strong bitterness on the taste lingers.

Old Boy (OG 1047, ABV 4.8%) ◄
A full-bodied amber ale, fruity and bitter with a hop/fruit aroma. The malt that backs the taste dies in the long finish.

Blonde Volupta (OG 1050, ABV 5%)
Straw gold zesty beer, packed with complexity and intense tropical fruit flavours leading to a crisp dry finish.

Alchemy (OG 1052, ABV 5.3%)
A premium golden bitter, easy drinking with good hop aroma.

Ole Slewfoot SIBA

Unit 1b, Gaymers Way, North Walsham, Norfolk, NR28 0AN
☎ (01603) 279927 ☎ 07909 636966
⊕ oleslewfootbrewery.co.uk
Shop 12pm-5pm (please phone ahead)
Tours by arrangement

Ole Slewfoot was established in 2009. Five outlets are supplied direct.

Cabarrus Gold (OG 1036, ABV 3.6%) ◄
Citrus and hop flavours follow an elderflower aroma. Increasingly bitter finish.

January 8th (OG 1040, ABV 4.2%)

Orange Blossom Special (OG 1042, ABV 4.4%)

Fox on the Run (OG 1046, ABV 4.8%)

Devils Dream (OG 1048, ABV 5%)

Friend of the Devil (OG 1070, ABV 7.7%) 🍺

On the Edge (NEW)

Wath Road, Nether Edge, South Yorkshire, S7 1HE
☎ 07854 983197 ✉ ontheedgebrew@gmail.com

On the Edge started brewing commercially in 2012 using a 0.5-barrel plant in the brewer's home. Brewing takes place once a week. Three local pubs are supplied as well as beer festivals. There is no regular beer list as new brews are constantly being tried.

Opa Hay's

Glencot, Wood Lane, Aldeby, Norfolk, NR34 0DA
☎ (01502) 679144 ☎ 07916 282729
⊕ engelfineales.com

Opa Hay's began brewing in 2008. It is a small, family-run microbrewery, taking its name from the brewer's great grandfather. Seasonal beers are available.

Engel's Fruity Little Number (ABV 3.6%) ◄
Powerful citrus/grapefruit aroma with malt and hops. Smoky sweetish flavours with fruit notes, and a fruity, hoppy aftertaste.

Engel's Best Bitter (ABV 4%)
A triple hopped aromatic beer, a very old fashioned traditional ale.

Matilda's Revenge (ABV 4.3%)
Golden ale originally brewed to commemorate the resident ghost that haunts the Kings's Head Hotel.

Samuel Engel's Meister Pils (SEMP) (ABV 4.8%)
A Pilsner-style beer, light in colour with a hoppy aroma.

Liquid Bread (ABV 5.2%)
Bavarian-style wheat beer, naturally cloudy with a distinct aroma of cloves and banana.

Ordnance City (NEW) SIBA

The Old Brewery, Whitley Farm, Ashcott, Somerset, TA7 9QW
☎ (01458) 210050 ☎ 07849 005811
⊕ ordnancecitybrewery.co.uk

Established in 2012 by Arthur Frampton and Charlie Adcock, the latter of Events Horizon, an explosive technician's organisation, hence the name. Brewing takes place on a five-barrel plant on the old Moor Beer site, supplying local freehouses and beer festivals.

Detonator (OG 1039, ABV 3.8%)

Mark III (OG 1043, ABV 4.3%)

Claymore (OG 1046, ABV 4.5%)

J-Dam (OG 1051, ABV 5%)

Orkney SIBA 👁

Quoyloo, Stromness, Orkney, KW16 3LT
☎ (01667) 404555

Sinclair Breweries Ltd, Cawdor, Nairn, IV12 5XP
⊕ sinclairbreweries.co.uk
Shop and visitor centre (please call for opening hours)
Tours by arrangement

👁Orkney was established in 1988 in an old village school building. Having incorporated sister brewery Atlas (qv) it moved next door in 2010 to enable an increase in capacity and the completion of an award-winning visitor centre in 2012. Seasonal beers are available.

Raven (OG 1038, ABV 3.8%) 🍺 ◄
A well-balanced quaffable bitter. Malty fruitiness and bitter hops last through to the long, dry aftertaste.

Dragonhead (OG 1040, ABV 4%) ◄
A strong, dark malt aroma flows into the taste in this superb Scottish stout. The roast malt continues to dominate the aftertaste, and blends with chocolate to develop a strong, dry finish.

817

Northern Light (OG 1040, ABV 4%) ◄
A well-balanced golden ale with a real smack of fruit and hops in the taste and an increasing bitter aftertaste.

Red MacGregor (OG 1040, ABV 4%) ◄
This tawny red ale has a powerful smack of fruit and a clean, fresh mouthfeel. Generally a well balanced bitter.

Corncrake (OG 1042, ABV 4.1%) ◄
A straw coloured beer with soft citrus fruits and a floral aroma.

Dark Island (OG 1045, ABV 4.6%) ◄
The roast malt and chocolate character varies, making the beer hard to categorise as a stout or an old ale. A sweetish roast malt taste leads to a long-lasting roasted, slightly bitter, dry finish. Winner of many awards.

Skull Splitter (OG 1080, ABV 8.5%) ◄
An intense velvet malt nose with hints of apple, prune and plum. The hoppy taste is balanced by satiny smooth malt with fruity spicy edges, leading to a long, dry finish with a hint of nut.

For Atlas Brewery

Latitude (OG 1036, ABV 3.6%) ◄
This straw coloured ale has a light citrus taste with a smack of hops and grapefruit in the light bitter finish.

Three Sisters (OG 1043, ABV 4.2%) ◄
Malt, summer fruits and caramel in the nose and blackcurrant in the taste, followed by a short, hoppy, bitter finish.

Wayfarer (OG 1044, ABV 4.4%) ⊓

Nimbus (OG 1050, ABV 5%) ◄
A full-bodied golden beer using some wheat malt and three types of hops. Sweet and fruity at the front, it becomes slightly astringent with lasting fruit and a pleasant, dry finish.

Ossett SIBA ◉

Kings Yard, Low Mill Road, Ossett, West Yorkshire, WF5 8ND
☎ (01924) 261333 ⊕ ossett-brewery.co.uk
Shop Mon-Fri 9am-4.30pm
Tours by arrangement

◉Osset began brewing in 1998, moving to a new site in 2005 and adding a cold store in 2008; capacity is now 200 barrels per week. The brewery owns 18 pubs, three with microbreweries. The Riverhead (qv) was purchased in 2006, Fernandes (qv) in 2007 and brewing commenced at the Rat Brewery (qv) in 2011. See website for seasonal and one-off special beers.

Pale Gold (OG 1038, ABV 3.8%)
A light, refreshing pale ale with a light, hoppy aroma.

Yorkshire Blonde (OG 1040, ABV 3.9%)
A very pale, full-bodied and well-rounded ale. Slightly sweet on the palate, with a generous late addition of Mount Hood hops for aroma.

Big Red Bitter (OG 1042, ABV 4%)
Deep red, malty Yorkshire bitter.

Silver King (OG 1041, ABV 4.3%)
A lager-style beer with a crisp, dry flavour and citrus fruity aroma.

Excelsior (OG 1051, ABV 5.2%)

A strong pale ale with a full, mellow flavour and a fresh, hoppy aroma with citrus/floral characteristics.

Otley SIBA IFBB ◉

Unit 39, Albion Industrial Estate, Pontypridd, Mid Glamorgan, CF37 4NX
☎ (01443) 480555 ⊕ otleybrewing.co.uk
Tours by arrangement

◉Otley Brewing was established in 2005 and since then the brewery has almost tripled in size. Seasonal beers: see website. Bottle-conditioned beers are also available.

O1 (OG 1038, ABV 4%) ◄
A pale golden beer with a hoppy aroma. The taste has hops, malt, fruit and a thirst-quenching bitterness. A satisfying finish completes this beer.

O2 Croeso (OG 1040, ABV 4%) ▨
Light golden ale full of citrus hop aromas. Dry hopped with American hops.

O4 Colombo (OG 1040, ABV 4%) ⊓
Pale golden ale with high bitterness, and aromas of green grass and herbs.

O3 Boss (OG 1042, ABV 4.4%)
Chestnut red bitter using American hops for bitterness and aroma.

O9 Blonde (OG 1046.5, ABV 4.8%) ⊓

O5 Gold (OG 1050, ABV 5%)
Light bodied golden ale brewed using lager malt.

Oxymoron (OG 1055, ABV 5.5%)
Dry hopped black IPA-style bitter.

Motley Brew (OG 1070, ABV 7.5%)
American-style double IPA with big hop aromas and high bitterness giving a classic IPA mouthfeel.

Otter SIBA ◉

Mathayes, Luppitt, Honiton, Devon, EX14 4SA
☎ (01404) 891285 ⊕ otterbrewery.com
Tours by arrangement

▣ Otter Brewery is a family-run brewery (five generations of brewers) set high up in the Blackdown Hills. Environmental responsibility lies at the heart of the brewery's ethos. Otter's eco cellar has been built underground and is naturally chilled. The beers are made from the brewery's own springs and locally-sourced ingredients.

Bitter (OG 1036, ABV 3.6%) ◄
Well-balanced amber session bitter with a fruity nose and bitter taste and aftertaste.

Amber (OG 1038.5, ABV 4%) ⊓
A finely balanced bitter with hints of tropical fruit and spice.

Bright (OG 1039, ABV 4.3%) ◄
Pale yellow/golden ale with a strong fruit aroma, sweet fruity taste and a bittersweet finish.

Ale (OG 1043, ABV 4.5%) ◄
A full-bodied best bitter. A malty aroma predominates with a fruity taste and finish.

Head (OG 1054, ABV 5.8%)
Fruity aroma and taste, with a pleasant bitter finish. Dark brown and full-bodied.

Ouseburn Valley

c/o The Brandling Villa, Haddricks Mill Road, South Gosforth, Tyne & Wear, NE3 1QL
☎ 07932 677899 ⊕ ouseburnvalleybrewery.co.uk

Ouseburn Valley started in the owner's garage in 2010, and in 2011 the plant was moved to the cellar of the Brandling Villa pub where both capacity and beer range were increased. After a flood in 2012, brewing is back in the owner's garage.

Armstrong Bitter (OG 1042, ABV 4.1%)
Rich yellow beer with a light spicy aroma with soft caramel overtones, and a long bitter finish.

Golden Ale (OG 1044, ABV 4.4%)
Dark gold in colour with light hop aroma, sweet malty taste with a smooth finish.

India Pale Ale (OG 1047, ABV 4.7%)
Pale gold in colour with a strong hop aroma and a long dry finish.

Milk Stout (OG 1047, ABV 4.7%)
Traditionally dark in colour with a liquorice aroma, sweet liquorice and slighly coffee taste.

Out There (NEW) SIBA

Unit 4, Foundry Lane Industrial Estate, Newcastle upon Tyne, NE6 1LH
☎ 07946 579534 ⊕ outtherebrewing.com

Out There was established in 2012. Branding and beer names are themed around the 1950s space race.

Space is the Place (OG 1034, ABV 3.5%)

Laika (OG 1049, ABV 4.8%)

Celestial Love (OG 1051, ABV 5.1%)

Outlaw

See Roosters

Outstanding SIBA

Britannia Mill, Cobden Street, Bury, Lancashire, BL9 6AW
☎ (0161) 764 7723 ⊕ outstandingbeers.com

The brewery was set up in 2008 as a collaboration between Paul Sandiford, Glen Woodcock, David Porter and Alex Lord. It operates a dual system, brewing on a 15-barrel plant and utilising a 2.5-barrel plant for special and experimental brews. Selective free trade accounts are supplied nationally.

3.9 (OG 1036, ABV 3.9%)
Extra pale, light, hoppy ale.

Selling Out (OG 1037, ABV 3.9%)
Pale, smooth and fruity beer.

Red (OG 1042, ABV 4.4%)
Copper-coloured, mellow and biscuity ale.

Blond (OG 1044, ABV 4.5%)
Pale-coloured, citrus refreshing beer.

IPA (OG 1053, ABV 5.5%)
Golden, dry, bitter ale.

Stout (OG 1057, ABV 5.5%)
Jet black, roasty, liquorice stout.

Pushing Out (OG 1065, ABV 7.4%) 🍾

Highly-hopped strong golden ale.

Owenshaw Mill

Owenshaw Works, Old Cawsey, Sowerby Bridge, West Yorkshire, HX6 2AJ
☎ (01422) 839010 ⊕ owenshawmillbrewery.co.uk

Owenshaw Mill began production in 2011 using an eight-barrel plant. Beers are available in pubs and clubs around Halifax and Huddersfield, and at beer festivals.

Katy's Blonde (ABV 3.6%)
A fruity and full bodied blonde beer.

Skinny Duck (ABV 3.7%)

Salt Road Blonde (ABV 3.9%)

Gollum's Revenge (ABV 4%)

Oxfordshire Ales SIBA ◉

12 Pear Tree Farm Industrial Units, Bicester Road, Marsh Gibbon, Bicester, Oxfordshire, OX27 0GB
☎ (01869) 278765 ⊕ oxfordshireales.co.uk
Tours by arrangement

The company first brewed in 2005 and now supplies over 100 outlets as well as several wholesalers. Seasonal beers are produced on the 15-barrel plant. There is a bottling line onsite. The Baby Ox Brewery produces interesting one-off ales.

Triple B (OG 1037, ABV 3.7%) 🍂
This pale amber beer has a huge caramel aroma. The caramel diminishes in the initial taste, which changes to a fruit/bitter balance. This in turn leads to a long, refreshing, bitter aftertaste.

Pride of Oxford (OG 1042, ABV 4.1%) 🍂
An amber beer, the aroma is butterscotch/caramel, which carries on into the initial taste. The taste then becomes bitter with sweetish/malty overtones. There is a long, dry, bitter finish.

Blenheim (OG 1042, ABV 4.2%)
A golden ale with a fresh zesty, spicy hop aroma, biscuity malt taste and pleasant dry finish.

Churchill IPA (OG 1045, ABV 4.5%)
A full-bodied beer with a balance of malt, hops and fruit undertones. Dry, fruity bitter aftertaste.

Marshmellow (OG 1047, ABV 4.7%) 🍂
The slightly fruity aroma in this golden-amber beer leads to a hoppy but thin taste, with slight caramel notes. The aftertaste is short and bitter.

Padstow (NEW)

The Brewery, Padstow, Cornwall, PL28 8RW
☎ (01841) 532169 ☎ 07834 924312
⊕ padstowbrewing.co.uk

Established in 2013, this small brewery is run by a husband and wife team, Des and Caron Archer, Caron being the brewster. Expansion to a 10-barrel plant is planned.

Pale Ale (OG 1036, ABV 3.6%)

Pilot (OG 1040, ABV 4%)

Pride (OG 1045, ABV 4.5%)

IPA (OG 1048, ABV 4.8%)

Palmers SIBA IFBB ⬤

The Old Brewery, West Bay Road, Bridport, Dorset,
DT6 4JA
☎ (01308) 422396 ⊕ palmersbrewery.com
Shop Mon-Sat 9am-6pm
Tours by arrangement

⊗ Palmers is Britain's only thatched brewery and
dates from 1794. It is situated in Bridport, the heart
of the Jurassic Coast in south-west Dorset. The
company continues to make substantial
investment in its 53 tenanted pubs, all serving cask
ale. Around 400 outlets are supplied.

Copper Ale (OG 1036, ABV 3.7%) ◆
Beautifully balanced, copper-coloured light bitter
with a hoppy aroma.

Best Bitter (OG 1040, ABV 4.2%) ◆
Hop aroma and bitterness stay in the background in
this predominately malty best bitter, with some
fruit on the aroma.

Dorset Gold (OG 1046, ABV 4.5%) ◆
More complex than many golden ales thanks to a
pleasant banana and mango fruitiness on the
aroma that carries on into the taste and aftertaste.

200 (OG 1052, ABV 5%) ◆
This is a big beer with a touch of caramel
sweetness adding to a complex hoppy, fruit taste
that lasts from the aroma well into the aftertaste.

Tally Ho! (OG 1057, ABV 5.5%) ⬚ ◆
A complex dark old ale. Roast malts and treacle
toffee on the palate lead to a long, lingering finish
with more than a hint of coffee.

Panther

Unit 1, Collers Way, Reepham, Norfolk, NR10 4SW
☎ 07766 558215 ⊕ pantherbrewery.co.uk
Shop Mon-Fri 9am 6pm; Sat 10am-3pm
Tours by arrangement

⊗ Panther brewery began brewing in 2010 on an
industrial estate near the old railway station,
formerly the home of Reepham Brewery. Beer and
other merchandise can be purchased direct from
the brewery or online from the brewery website.

Cub Panther (OG 1036, ABV 2.5%)
An amber-coloured beer with a floral note.
Deceptively strong body and flavour for its ABV.

Ginger Panther (OG 1037, ABV 3.7%)
A ginger wheat beer with a fiery ginger flavour and
subtle lemon notes.

Golden Panther (OG 1037, ABV 3.7%)
A golden ale with a citrus flavour and a floral
aroma.

Pink Panther (OG 1039, ABV 4%)
A balanced wheat beer with a bittersweet fruity
finish.

Red Panther (OG 1041, ABV 4.1%) ◆
A nutty full-flavoured brew. Plenty of roasted malt
in both aroma and taste. Hops, and a residual
sweetness, provide balance.

Black Panther (OG 1047, ABV 4.5%)
A dark rich smooth ale with a complex full flavour
and a bittersweet balance which leads to a dry
finish.

Paradise

⊜ Bird in Hand, Trelissick Road, Hayle, Cornwall,
TR27 4HY
☎ (01736) 753974
✉ birdinhand@paradisepark.org.uk
Tours by arrangement

⊗ Brewing first started in 1981 under the name
Paradise Brewery, named after its location, the
Paradise Bird Park. The name was changed to
Wheal Ale in 1995. Brewing ceased in 2004 but re-
started in 2009 under the original Paradise name.

Bitter (OG 1043, ABV 4.3%) ◆
Gentle malt and fruit on the nose, followed by a
dominantly bitter flavour balanced by sweet malt
and fruity hop. The finish is bitter.

Artist (OG 1055, ABV 5.2%) ◆
Full-bodied tawny ale with faint aroma of malt.
Heavy sweet malt and bubblegum esters in the
mouth with a balance of hops. Dryness and
bitterness in the finish.

Parish

⊜ 6 Main Street, Burrough on the Hill, Leicestershire,
LE14 2JQ
☎ (01664) 454801 ☎ 07715 369410
✉ trudygrants@yahoo.co.uk
Tours by arrangement

Parish began in 1983 and now operates on a 32-
barrel plant located in a 400-year-old building next
to Grants Freehouse, which stocks the full range of
beers. Other local outlets are also supplied and
one-off brews are produced for beer festivals. Baz's
Bonce Blower is also available bottle conditioned.

PSB (OG 1038, ABV 3.8%)
Hoppy session beer with malty aftertaste.

Farm Gold (OG 1042, ABV 4.2%)
Light-coloured beer with distinctive hoppy taste
and powerful aroma.

Burrough Bitter (OG 1047, ABV 4.8%)
Darker version of PSB with good balance of malt
and hops.

Poachers Ale (OG 1060, ABV 6%)
Deep ruby red full-bodied malty blended beer
comprising one part Baz's Bonce Blower and two
parts PSB.

Baz's Bonce Blower (OG 1120, ABV 12%) ⬚
Strong, very dark beer with a rich, malty character.

Partizan (NEW)

8 Almond Road, South Bermondsey, London,
SE16 3LR
☎ (020) 8127 5053 ☎ 07708 263931
⊕ partizanbrewing.co.uk

Partizan began brewing in 2012. Only bottle-
conditioned beers are produced. Each brew is
different, but they are based on a variety of
international styles and all are vegan-friendly and
bottled by hand on site.

Partners SIBA ⬤

Unit 12, Saville Bridge Mill, Mill Street East,
Dewsbury, Mill Street East, WF12 9AG
☎ (01924) 457772 ☎ 07944 523429
⊕ partnersbrewery.co.uk

Tours by arrangement

⊕Partners brewery, formerly called Anglo Dutch, was bought in 2011 by landlord Paul Horne and partner Richard Sharp. Significant investment saw capacity doubled. It is based in an old dye house of the former Mungo & Shoddy Mill in Dewsbury.

Pure Gold (OG 1035, ABV 3.5%)
An easy-drinking session beer with a complex character, brewed using four different malts.

Blond (OG 1039, ABV 3.9%)
A blonde crisp aromatic session beer.

Triple Hop (ABV 4.2%)
A triple hopped American pale ale with excellent bitterness and a hoppy aftertaste.

Ghost (OG 1043, ABV 4.5%)
A pale, full-bodied bitter with a fresh gentle nose, taken over by a smooth hop and citrus finish.

Tabatha (OG 1054, ABV 6%) ◆
Golden Belgian-style Tripel with a strong fruity, hoppy and bitter character. Powerful and warming, slightly thinnish, with a bitter, dry finish.

Patriot

Norman Knight, Whichford, Shipston-on-Stour, Warwickshire, CV36 5PE
☎ (01608) 684621 ∰ thepatriotbrewery.co.uk
Tours by arrangement

⊠ Patriot began in 2010 using a four-barrel brew plant. It is located next to the Norman Knight pub, where the beers are regularly available. Seasonal specials are produced, including an oak cask-conditioned beer.

Morris (OG 1038, ABV 3.8%)

Kiwi (OG 1041, ABV 4.1%)

Pug IPA (OG 1057, ABV 5.6%)

Peak Ales SIBA

Barn Brewery, Cunnery Barn, Chatsworth, Derbyshire, DE45 1EX
☎ (01246) 583737 ∰ peakales.co.uk
Tours by arrangement

⊕Peak Ales opened in 2005 in former derelict farm buildings on the Chatsworth estate aided by a DEFRA Rural Enterprise Scheme grant and support from trustees of Chatsworth Settlement. The brewery supplies numerous local outlets. Seasonal beers: see website.

Swift Nick (OG 1038, ABV 3.8%) ◆
Easy-drinking, copper-coloured bitter with balanced malt and hops and a gentle hoppy bitter finish.

Bakewell Best Bitter (OG 1041, ABV 4.2%) ◆
Full-bodied tawny bitter with a hoppy bitterness against a malty background, leading to a hoppy dry aftertaste.

Chatsworth Gold (OG 1045, ABV 4.6%) ◆
Speciality beer made with honey, which gives a pleasant sweetness leading to a hop and malt finish.

DPA (OG 1045, ABV 4.6%) ◆
Subtle pale ale that is deceptively strong. Flavours of fruit, hops and malt build slowly towards a well-balanced bittersweet finish.

Peakstones Rock SIBA ⊙

Peakstones Farm, Cheadle Road, Alton, Staffordshire, ST10 4DH
☎ 07891 350908 ∰ peakstonesrock.co.uk
Tours by arrangement

⊠ Peakstones Rock was established in 2005 with a five-barrel brewery located on a farm in the Peak District National Park. The plant was expanded to 10-barrel capacity in 2009. The brewery supplies an expanding free trade market in the North Midlands and surrounding areas.

Nemesis (OG 1042, ABV 3.8%) ◆
Gentle caramel and hop aroma from the pale brown body; sweet start then hops and a touch of roast. Gentle finish.

Chained Oak (OG 1045, ABV 4.2%)
A copper-coloured beer with a bitter finish and hop aroma.

Alton Abbey (OG 1051, ABV 4.5%)

Black Hole (OG 1048, ABV 4.8%) ▌

Oblivion (OG 1055, ABV 5.5%)

Peerless SIBA ⊙

The Brewery, 8 Pool Street, Birkenhead, Merseyside, CH41 3NL
☎ (0151) 647 7688 ∰ peerlessbrewing.co.uk
Tours by arrangement

Peerless began brewing in 2009 and is under the directorship of Steve Briscoe. Beers are sold through festivals, local pubs and the free trade. Seasonal beers are available.

Pale (OG 1036, ABV 3.8%)

Jinja Ninja (OG 1040, ABV 4%)

Triple Blonde (OG 1040, ABV 4.1%)

Viking Gold (OG 1044, ABV 4.6%)

Storr Lager (OG 1042, ABV 4.8%)
A pale and hoppy cask lager.

Oatmeal Stout (OG 1050, ABV 5%)

Red Rocks (OG 1047, ABV 5%)
A strong ruby ale.

Full Whack (OG 1054, ABV 6%)
A strong pale ale with a fruity hop finish.

Penlon Cottage

Penlon Farm, Pencae, Llanarth, SA47 0QN
☎ (01545) 580022 ∰ penlon.biz

Penlon opened in 2004 on a smallholding with a strong focus on sustainability and self-sufficiency. Only bottle-conditioned beers are produced and are suitable for vegetarians and vegans.

Pennine SIBA

Well Hall Farm, Bedale Road, Well, North Yorkshire, DL8 2PX
☎ (01677) 470111 ∰ pennine-brewery.co.uk
Tours by arrangement

⊕Brewing began in Batley in 2012 using an 18-barrel plant and transferred to Well, near Bedale, in 2013. Seasonal beers: see website.

Amber Necker (OG 1035, ABV 3.5%)

Session beer with a smooth and creamy texture and a hoppy aftertaste.

Real Blonde (OG 1040, ABV 4%)
Finely-balanced blonde ale with a mouth-watering fruity aftertaste.

Natural Gold (OG 1042, ABV 4.2%)

Penpont SIBA

Inner Trenarrett, Altarnun, Launceston, Cornwall, PL15 7SY
☎ (01566) 86069 ⊕ penpontbrewery.co.uk
Shop at brewery (please ring first)
Tours by arrangement

⊠ Penpont opened in 2008 and has steadily increased the range and production since then. The brewery has also wona number of awards. Its beers are available in pubs across Cornwall. Seasonal and bottle-conditioned beers are brewed: see website.

St Nonna's (OG 1037, ABV 3.7%) ◆
Malt and apple fruitiness dominate the initial aroma of this brown beer. Hop bitterness is quickly apparent in the taste and lingers in the long aftertaste.

Cornish Arvor (OG 1040, ABV 4%)
Golden red ale, not overly floral, with distinctive hop notes and some malt complexity.

Shipwreck Coast (OG 1044, ABV 4.4%) ◆
Light aroma of orange citrus. Hops dominate with marmalade and tropical fruits. Malt emerges with a bitter and dry finish.

Roughtor (OG 1047, ABV 4.7%) ◆
Malt dominates aroma and taste balanced by sweetness and rising hop bitterness. Strong flavour slowly fades in the dry finish.

Penzance

⊟ Star Inn, Crowlas, Penzance, Cornwall, TR20 8DX
☎ (01736) 740375
Tours by arrangement

⊠ Brewing began in 2008 on a five-barrrel plant in the yard of the Star Inn. Owner Peter Elvin recently expanded the fermentation capacity, allowing an increase in the volume as well as range of beers brewed. Besides the pub, selected outlets and beer festivals are supplied.

Crowlas Bitter (OG 1037, ABV 3.8%) ◆
Perfectly balanced session bitter with malt, hops, bitterness and a hint of fruit and biscuit. Lingering finish of malty bitterness.

Jolly Farmer (OG 1036, ABV 3.9%)
Hoppy golden ale with citrus finish.

Potion No 9 (OG 1039, ABV 4%) ◆
Floral and grapefruit hops dominate the nose and taste. Bitterness rises and dominates the finish, balanced by sweetness and astringency.

Brisons Bitter (OG 1043, ABV 4.5%) ◆
Dominant malt in aroma and taste, balanced by fruity hops, sweetness and bitterness. Long malty finish becoming dry and bitter.

Trink (OG 1048, ABV 5.2%)
Well-balanced golden ale, with tropical fruit flavour and a citrus bite finish.

Mellow (OG 1050, ABV 5.5%) ◆

Powerful citrus hop and malt in aroma and taste leading to a very astringent finish balanced by subtle lemon fruitiness.

IPA (OG 1058, ABV 6%)
A strong traditional-style IPA.

Scilly Stout (OG 1067, ABV 7%)
Strong stout with a hint of chocolate.

Pheasantry SIBA ◉

High Brecks Farm, Lincoln Road, East Markham, Nottinghamshire, NG22 0SN
☎ (01777) 872728 ☎ 07948 976749
⊕ pheasantrybrewery.co.uk
Shop Tue-Sun 10am-6pm
Tours by arrangement

☺Pheasantry began brewing in 2012 using a 10-barrel plant. Situated in a listed barn on a farm, the brewery and visitor centre incorporates a restaurant, tearooms and bar with the brewery visible through glass partitions.

Best Bitter (ABV 3.8%)
Smooth tasting copper-coloured beer with medium bitterness and low to medium sweetness. It has a light, spicy aroma.

Pale Ale (ABV 4%)
A pale-coloured, smooth-tasting beer with floral and citrus notes and a dry finish.

Dark Ale (ABV 4.2%)
A smooth, soft, satisfying dark ale with malty flavours, balanced bitterness and a velvety texture.

Phipps

See Grainstore

Phoenix SIBA ◉

Green Lane, Heywood, Lancashire, OL10 2EP
☎ (01706) 627009 ✉ tony@phoenixbrewery.co.uk

☺Established in Ellesmere Port in 1982, Oak Brewery moved to the old Phoenix Brewery in Heywood and adopted the name in 1991. It now supplies 400-500 outlets plus wholesalers. Many seasonal beers are produced throughout the year. Restoration of the old brewery, built in 1897, is ongoing.

Hopsack (OG 1038, ABV 3.8%)
A light-drinking, hoppy session beer.

Navvy (OG 1039, ABV 3.8%) ◆
Amber beer with a citrus fruit and malt nose. Good balance of citrus fruit, malt and hops with bitterness coming through in the aftertaste.

Monkeytown Mild (OG 1039, ABV 3.9%)

Arizona (OG 1040, ABV 4.1%) ◆
Yellow in colour with a fruity and hoppy aroma. A refreshing beer with citrus, hops and good bitterness, and a shortish dry aftertaste.

Spotland Gold (OG 1041, ABV 4.1%)
A pale, hoppy beer with a lingering bitter finish.

Pale Moonlight (OG 1042, ABV 4.2%)

Black Bee (OG 1045, ABV 4.5%)

White Monk (OG 1045, ABV 4.5%) ◆
Yellow beer with a citrus fruit aroma, plenty of fruit, hops and bitterness in the taste, and a hoppy, bitter finish.

Thirsty Moon (OG 1046, ABV 4.6%) ◄
Tawny beer with a fresh citrus aroma. Hoppy, fruity and malty with a dry, hoppy finish.

West Coast IPA (OG 1046, ABV 4.6%) ◄
Golden in colour with a hoppy, fruity nose. Strong hoppy and fruity taste and aftertaste with good bitterness throughout.

Double Gold (OG 1050, ABV 5%)

Wobbly Bob (OG 1060, ABV 6%) ◄
A red/brown beer with malty, fruity aroma and creamy mouthfeel. Strongly malty and fruity in flavour, with hops and a hint of herbs. Both sweetness and bitterness are evident throughout.

For Brunning & Price Pub Co:

Original Bitter (ABV 3.8%)

Pictish

Unit 9, Canalside Industrial Estate, Rochdale, Greater Manchester, OL16 5LB
☎ (01706) 522227 ⊕ pictish-brewing.co.uk

☺The brewery was established in 2000 by Richard Sutton and supplies 60 free trade outlets in the north-west and West Yorkshire. Seasonal beers: see website.

Brewers Gold (OG 1038, ABV 3.8%) ◄
Yellow in colour, with a hoppy, fruity nose. Soft maltiness and a strong hop/citrus flavour lead to a dry, bitter finish.

Alchemists Ale (OG 1043, ABV 4.3%) ◄
Yellow beer with generous hop and fruit on the nose and palate. Good bitter hop finish.

Piddle SIBA

Unit 7, Enterprise Park, Piddlehinton, Dorset, DT2 7UA
☎ (01305) 849336 ⊕ piddlebrewery.co.uk

Piddle began brewing in 2007 on an eight-barrel plant. In 2011 the brewery moved to larger adjacent premises. It currently brews on an eight-barrel plant with plans to expand further. Seasonal beers are also available.

Jimmy Riddle (OG 1040, ABV 3.7%) ◄
Pale brown session beer with a good depth of malty flavours for its strength.

Piddle (OG 1042, ABV 4.1%) ◄
An enjoyable, well-balanced bitter with a lingering bitter finish.

Yogi Beer (OG 1052, ABV 4.9%)
Smooth with a hint of red, an easy drinking beer of character with a rounded fruitiness giving way to a hint of blackcurrant, liquorice and toffee.

Silent Slasher (OG 1051, ABV 5.1%)
Blonde, lager-style beer; light with hops chosen for their floral aroma and flavour. Sweet with a refreshing, dry bitter finish.

Pied Bull

⧈ Pied Bull Hotel, 57 Northgate Street, Chester, CH1 2HQ
☎ (01244) 325829 ⊕ piedbull.co.uk

☺Pied Bull began brewing in 2011 using a one-barrel plant. Beer is mainly for in-house consumption but local beer festivals are supplied

and occasional brewery swaps occur. Seasonal and special ales are also available.

Pied Eyed (OG 1040, ABV 4%)

Bulls Hit (OG 1055, ABV 4.3%)

Matador (OG 1049, ABV 5%)

Black Bull Porter (OG 1060, ABV 5.2%)

Pig Pub (NEW)

⧈ Pig in Muck, 1-3 Manor Road, Claybrooke Magna, Leicestershire, LE17 5AY
☎ (01455) 202859 ⊕ piginmuck.com

Brewing began in 2013 using a two-barrel plant. Beers are available in the Pig in Muck and the Criterion in Leicester. Special beers are brewed for the pub by customers.

Weiner Bitter (ABV 3.8%)
A straw-coloured session bitter. Hoppy and fruity throughout with a dry finish.

Pig Out (ABV 3.9%)
Dark amber-coloured beer, pleasantly bitter with a fruity, citrus finish.

Claybrooke Bitter (ABV 4.2%)
Full-bodied beer with a malty aroma. Bitter at the start with a hint of fruit on the palate and a soft hop finish.

Pigs Best Bitter (ABV 4.2%)
A golden brown best bitter with a hint of citrus. Fresh hoppiness comes through at the end with a malt finish.

Pilgrim SIBA

11 West Street, Reigate, Surrey, RH2 9BL
☎ (01737) 222651 ⊕ pilgrim.co.uk
Tours by arrangement

⊠ Pilgrim was set up in 1982 in Woldingham, Surrey, and moved to Reigate in 1985. The original owner, Dave Roberts, is still in charge. Beers are sold to around 40 outlets. Seasonal beers: see website.

Quench (OG 1037, ABV 3.6%)

Surrey Bitter (OG 1038, ABV 3.7%) ◄
Pineapple, grapefruit and spicy aromas in this quaffing beer. Biscuity maltiness with a hint of vanilla is balanced by a hoppy bitterness that becomes more pronounced in a refreshing bittersweet finish.

Progress (OG 1041.5, ABV 4%) ◄
A well-rounded tawny-coloured bitter. Predominantly sweet and malty with an underlying fruitiness and a hint of toffee. The flavour is balanced overall with a subdued bitterness. Little aroma and the aftertaste dissipates quickly.

Quest (OG 1043, ABV 4.3%)

Pin-Up SIBA

Unit 2, Rocks Farm Business Centre, Burnt Oat Road, Stone Cross, Crowborough, East Sussex, TN6 3SJ
☎ (01892) 611411 ⊕ pinupbeers.com

⊠ Brewing began in 2011. Beers were initially contract brewed at an unnamed Essex brewer, but Pin-Up began brewing on its own premises in 2012 using a five-barrel plant.

Natural Blonde (OG 1038, ABV 3.8%)

Honey Brown (OG 1039, ABV 4%)

Red Head (OG 1041, ABV 4.2%)

Milk Stout (OG 1044, ABV 4.5%)

Pitfield

See Dominion

Pixie Spring (NEW)

Unit C1, Cefn Coed Lane Industrial Estate, Pontyclun, CF72 9HG

☎ 07814 255943 ⊕ pixiespring.com

Pixie Spring began brewing in 2011 from the cellar of the Wheatsheaf in Llantrisant. In 2012 it moved to its own premises in Pontyclun using a 12-barrel plant. Seasonal and special beers are available, bottle-conditioned beers are planned. A range of experimental beers are also brewed under the Hopcraft Brewing name.

Golden Pixie (ABV 3.8%)

Black Army Stout (ABV 4.2%)

Deliverance APA (ABV 4.5%)

Prince of Bengal IPA (ABV 5.5%)

Under the Hopcraft Brewing name:

Paradox (ABV 4.7%)

Spanish Main (ABV 5.5%)

Plain Ales SIBA

17 Deverill Road Trading Estate, Sutton Veny, Wiltshire, BA12 7BZ

☎ (01985) 841481 ⊕ plainales.co.uk

Tours by arrangement

Plain Ales started production in 2008 on a 2.5-barrel plant in a garage, and expanded to a 20-barrel plant in 2011.

Sheep Dip (OG 1040, ABV 3.8%)

Session beer with zesty start tending to a dry hoppy finish.

The Wife's Bitter (OG 1041, ABV 3.8%)

A red ale with summer fruits and hints of tartness.

Arty Farty (OG 1039, ABV 3.9%)

Session beer with bursts of tropical fruit.

Innocence (OG 1042, ABV 4%)

A straw-coloured, fragrant bitter.

Innspiration (OG 1042, ABV 4%)

A traditional, copper-coloured, easy-drinking bitter.

Inntrigue (OG 1044, ABV 4.2%)

Ruby ale with succulent woodland berries and dark chocolate flavours.

Inndulgence (OG 1055, ABV 4.5%)

A dark ruby porter with coffee, chocolate and a hint of smoke.

Inncognito (OG 1053, ABV 4.8%)

Full-bodied stout with flavours of sweet roasted malt, aged port and robustly mature fruits of the vine.

Plassey

See New Plassey

Platform 5 (NEW)

Railway Inn, 197 Queen Street, Newton Abbot, Devon, TQ12 2BS

☎ (01626) 354166 ⊕ platform5brewing.co.uk

Platform 5 began brewing in 2006 using a six-barrel plant. The Railway Inn is supplied along with Molloys in Teignmouth and St Marychurch. The brewery is situated in part of an enclosed alley under the disused Platform 5 of Newton Abbot station, with the other part housing the pub's skittle alley.

Wheeltappers Bitter (ABV 4%)

Gold (ABV 4.8%)

Plockton

5 Bank Street, Plockton, Ross-shire, IV52 8TP

☎ (01599) 544276 ⊕ theplocktonbrewery.com

Tours by arrangement

The brewery started trading in 2007 and expanded to a 2.5-barrel plant in 2009. Bottle-conditioned beers are available and are suitable for vegetarians.

Ciste Dhubh (OG 1040, ABV 3.9%) ◆

Excellent mix of malts and hops in this dark brew. Initial bitter turning bittersweet.

Fiddlers Fancy (ABV 4.6%) ◆

Refreshing grapefruit aroma and taste turning to a more malty finish.

Plockton Bay (OG 1047, ABV 4.6%) ◆

A well-balanced, tawny coloured best bitter with plenty of hops and malt which give a bittersweet fruity flavour.

Plymouth SIBA

HQ Business Centre, 237 Union Street, Stonehouse, Plymouth, Devon, PL1 5QG

☎ (01752) 660837 ☎ 07899 730036

⊕ plymouthbeercompany.com

⊗ Plymouth was set up in the old Point's West Brewery at City College by Millfields Trust as a community brewery. The concept is to put the profits back into local youth projects in Stonehouse. The five-barrel plant was bought by college lecturer Roger Pengelly from the Bitter End Brewery in Cockermouth, Cumbria.

Fresher Ale (OG 1044, ABV 4.2%)

Bright copper-coloured bitter with wheat malt in the grist.

Mayflower (OG 1044, ABV 4.2%)

Pilgrim Ale (OG 1046, ABV 4.4%)

Traditional dark ruby-coloured bitter with a hint of rye malt in the grist.

Poachers SIBA

439 Newark Road, North Hykeham, Lincolnshire, LN6 9SP

☎ (01522) 807404 ☎ 07954 131972

⊕ poachersbrewery.co.uk

Tours by arrangement

⊛ Brewing started in 2001 on a five-barrel plant. In 2006 it was downsized to 2.5-barrel and relocated to outbuildings at the rear of the brewer's home. 2011 saw capacity returned to five barrels. Regular outlets in Lincolnshire and surrounding counties are supplied direct; outlets further afield via wholesalers. All beers are also available bottle-conditioned.

Trembling Rabbit Mild (OG 1034, ABV 3.4%)
Rich, dark mild, brewed with local honey, with a smooth malty flavour and a slightly bitter finish.

Shy Talk Bitter (OG 1037, ABV 3.7%)
A pale golden session beer with citrus overtones.

Rock Ape (OG 1038, ABV 3.8%)

Pride (OG 1040, ABV 4%)
Amber bitter with fine hop flavour and an aroma that lingers.

Bog Trotter (OG 1042, ABV 4.2%)
An amber, full-flavoured, malty beer with a bitter aftertaste.

Lincoln Best (OG 1042, ABV 4.2%)
A flowery hop-nosed, brown beer with a well-balanced but bitter taste that stays with the malt, becoming more apparent in the drying finish.

Billy Boy (OG 1044, ABV 4.4%)
A rich full-flavoured brown beer.

Imp Ale (OG 1044, ABV 4.4%)

Black Crow Stout (OG 1045, ABV 4.5%)
A full-bodied stout with burnt toffee and caramel flavours.

Hykeham Gold (OG 1045, ABV 4.5%)
A cask-conditioned lager.

Monkey Hanger (OG 1045, ABV 4.5%)
A ruby-red bitter with a smooth fruity flavour.

Jock's Trap (OG 1050, ARV 5%)
A strong, pale brown bitter with a slightly dry fruit finish.

Trout Tickler (OG 1055, ABV 5.5%)
A strong ruby bitter with sweet undertones with a hint of chocolate. A rich, malty beer.

Pocket

La Croix Farm, La Rue de la Croix, St Ouen, Jersey, JE3 2HA
☎ 07797 771931 ✉ jerseybeer@jerseymail.co.uk

Pocket began brewing in 2011 on a small scale. Bottle-conditioned beer is available. Most of the production is bottled, but casks are available at local freehouses and beer festivals.

Black Marion (ABV 3.9%)

Bracken (ABV 4%)

Fee de Bretagne (ABV 4%)

Lady Hamilton IPA (ABV 4.6%)

St Ouen Strong Stout (ABV 6.6%)

Pope's (NEW) SIBA

73a Blackpole Trading Estate West, Worcester, WR3 8TJ
☎ (01905) 755016 ✉ popesbrew@btconnect.com
Tours by arrangement

Pope's is a family-run brewery established in 2012 using a 4.5-barrel plant. Brewing takes place twice a week. Beer names are influenced by the local area. Bottle-conditioned beers are available and seasonal beers are planned.

Hop Market (OG 1038, ABV 3.8%)

A light and hoppy session bitter with lemon citrus and pine aromas.

Worcester Gold (OG 1040, ABV 4%)
A fruity and refreshing pale ale with tropical notes and a rounded malt finish.

Hope & Glory (OG 1046, ABV 4.6%)
A best bitter using four malts and English hops for a rounded flavour.

Pope's Yard (NEW)

Unit 12, Riverside Road, Watford, Hertfordshire, WD19 4HY
☎ (01923) 224182 ⊕ popesyard.co.uk

Pope's Yard began commercial brewing in 2012 using a one-barrel plant. Cask and bottle-conditioned beers are available but no regular beers are produced.

Poppyland (NEW)

46 West Street, Cromer, Norfolk, NR27 9DS
☎ (01263) 389804 ☎ 07887 389804
⊕ poppylandbeer.com

Established in 2012 by museum curator and geologist Martin Warren as a working retirement project, Poppyland brews and bottle-conditions small batches of beer, with no fixed range.

George N Porter (NEW)

Whitley Bay, NE26 1AP

George N Porter is a microbrewery established in 2012. Three beers are brewed.

The Twitcher (ABV 3.8%)

The Horn (ABV 4.3%)

The Full Wood (ABV 5.2%)

Portobello (NEW) SIBA

Unit 6, Mitre Bridge Industrial Estate, Mitre Way, Kensington, London, W10 6AU
☎ (020) 8969 2269 ☎ 07794 715913
⊕ portobellobrewing.com

⊠ Portobello began brewing in 2012 using a 10-barrel plant. Seasonal beers are also available.

Pale (ABV 4%)

Pilsner (ABV 4%)

VPA (ABV 4%)

Star (ABV 4.3%) ◆
Pale brown malty best bitter with a sweetish nose and a strong bitter finish. Hints of nut on the palate.

Market Porter (ABV 4.6%)

American Pale Ale (ABV 5%)

Potbelly SIBA ◉

25-31 Durban Road, Kettering, Northamptonshire, NN16 0JA
☎ (01536) 410818 ☎ 07834 867825
⊕ potbelly-brewery.co.uk
Tours by arrangement

Potbelly started brewing in 2005 on a 10-barrel plant and supplies some 200 outlets. The brewery has won more than 30 awards for its beers in only

six years of brewing. Seasonal beers: see website.
Bottle-conditioned beers are also available.

Potbelly Best (OG 1036.9, ABV 3.8%)
Traditional chestnut-coloured bitter, brewed using
a mixture of four different malts.

Aisling (OG 1038.5, ABV 4.4%)
A smooth pale bitter with an excellent balance of
hops and malt.

Pigs Do Fly (OG 1041, ABV 4.4%)
A light and golden single-hopped ale.

Bellowhead (OG 1045, ABV 4.5%)
A light-coloured bitter with a hoppy citrus finish.

Crazy Daze (OG 1050, ABV 5.5%)
A very light golden bitter with hidden strength.

Potton SIBA ◉

10 Shannon Place, Potton, Bedfordshire, SG19 2SP
☎ (01767) 261042 ∰ potton-brewery.co.uk
Shop: phone for opening hours
Tours by arrangement

◉Potton was established in 1998. It is now owned
by Garry Doel of Franklins Brewery but run
separately under manager Colin Morris. Production
averages at 50 barrels per week and around 250
outlets are supplied. Seasonal and bottle-
conditioned beers are available.

Shannon IPA (OG 1034, ABV 3.6%)
A well-balanced session bitter with good bitterness
and fruity late-hop character.

Penny Bitter (OG 1040, ABV 4%)
A quaffable session bitter with reddish hues. Malty
and smooth.

Gold (OG 1041, ABV 4.1%)
Deep golden in colour, not overly hopped.

Village Bike (OG 1043, ABV 4.3%) ◆
Classic English premium bitter, amber in colour,
heavily late-hopped.

Lion Pale Ale (OG 1044, ABV 4.4%)
A pale blonde, hoppy beer.

Porter (OG 1045, ABV 4.5%)
An old London recipe, smooth and quaffable.

Raker (OG 1052, ABV 5.2%)
A classic premium bitter.

Prescott SIBA

Unit 1, The Bramery Business Park, Alstone Lane,
Cheltenham, Gloucestershire, GL51 8HE
☎ 07526 934866 ∰ prescottales.co.uk
Tours by arrangement

Prescott Ales was established in 2008, and brews
on a 10-barrel plant. The bulk of its brewing
ingredients are sourced from within a 50 mile
radius of Cheltenham. Beer names are inspired by
the golden age of motoring. Seasonal beers are
available: see website.

Hill Climb (OG 1039.5, ABV 3.8%)
A fruity and refreshing IPA.

Track Record (OG 1044, ABV 4.4%)
Fruity best bitter brewed with a hint of local honey.

Grand Prix (OG 1050, ABV 5.2%)
A rich and smooth strong ale.

Preseli

Unit 15, The Salterns, Tenby, Pembrokeshire,
SA70 8EQ
☎ 07824 512103 ∰ preseli-brewery.co.uk

Preseli began brewing in 2009 on a six-barrel
plant. Seasonal beers are also available.

Even Keel (OG 1038, ABV 3.8%)

Old Mariners (OG 1040, ABV 4%)

Rocky Bottom (OG 1040, ABV 4%)

Pressure Drop (NEW)

Unit 19, Bohemia Place, Hackney, London, E8 1DU
☎ (020) 8533 0614 ∰ pressuredropbrewing.co.uk

Pressure Drop is run by three partners who were
home brewers but began commercial brewing in
2013 using a five-barrel plant. Beers are mainly
available bottle conditioned with cask-conditioned
beers supplied locally on request. Seasonal and
one-off beers are also brewed.

Prestonpans (NEW)

🏠 227-229 High Street, Prestonpans, East Lothian,
EH32 9BE
☎ (01875) 819922 ∰ thegoth.co.uk

A microbrewery was installed at the award-
winning pub, the Prestoungrange Gothenburg in
2004. Originally trading as Fowler's Ales, the
brewery is now under new management and beers
are brewed by guest brewer George Thompson.

Fowler's 80/- (ABV 4.2%)

Gothenburg Porter (ABV 4.4%)

Prior's Well

The Old Kennels, Clumber Park, Hardwick Village,
Nottinghamshire, S80 3PB
☎ 07971 277598 ∰ priorswell.co.uk

Prior's Well was established in a National Trust
building in Hardwick Village on the Clumber Park
Estate by Rob Neal of Maypole Brewery. The five-
barrel plant was previously used at Tydd Steam and
before that Oldershaws Brewery. Natural clumber
water from the estate is used in the brewing
process.

Gardener's Tap (OG 1038, ABV 3.8%)

Silver Chalice (OG 1040, ABV 4.1%)

Father Hawkins (OG 1044, ABV 4.5%)

Prior's Gold (OG 1045, ABV 4.7%)

Private Brewery of Bob (NEW)

c/o Farmers Boy, 134 London Road, St Albans,
Hertfordshire, AL1 1PQ
☎ 07880 743357 ∰ hmcm.co.uk/bob

The Private Brewery of Bob is run by Martin
Slaughter who produces a range of bottle-
conditioned beers for the off-trade and some local
pubs using the kit at the Verulam Brewery (qv).
Four regular beers are brewed, as well as several
seasonals and specials.

Privateer (NEW)

80 Temperance Street, Manchester, M12 6HU
☎ (0161) 273 7077 ☎ 07969 771102

Privateer began brewing in 2012 using a 6.5-barrel plant. Only American hops are used and all beers are brewed under 5% ABV. Seasonal beers are also available.

Roebuck (ABV 3.8%)

Dainty Blonde (ABV 4.2%)

Dark Revenge (ABV 4.5%)

Red Duke (ABV 4.8%)

Prospect SIBA ⟨◉⟩

Unit 11, Bradley Hall Trading Estate, Bradley Lane, Standish, Wigan, Lancashire, WN6 0XQ
☎ (01257) 421329 ⊕ prospectbrewery.org.uk
Tours by arrangement (Thu eve, max 30 people)

☺Prospect brewery was founded in 2007. A 12-barrel plant is used and the premises feature a brewery bar. One pub is jointly owned with Daniel Thwaites, the Silver Tally in Standish.

Silver Tally (OG 1037, ABV 3.7%)
A pale golden bitter with citrus aromas, and a full hop flavour with a dry bitter finish.

Whatever! (OG 1040, ABV 3.8%)
Pale bitter packed with hop flavour and aroma.

Nutty Slack (OG 1039, ABV 3.9%) ◈
Dark brown mild ale with malt and fruit in the aroma. Creamy and chocolaty on the palate, with both malt and fruit in evidence. Malty and moderately bitter finish.

Hopper (OG 1040, ABV 4%)
A pale golden beer with citrus hops and a satisfying sweet balance.

One Twenty (OG 1039, ABV 4%)
A yellow/gold beer with zesty citrus notes; clean tasting and refreshing.

One Twenty (OG 1039, ABV 4%)
A yellow/gold beer with zesty citrus notes.

Pioneer (OG 1040, ABV 4%)
A light bodied amber beer with aromas of dry pale malt and earthy hops.

Blinding Light (OG 1042, ABV 4.2%)
A pale, refreshing beer with citrus and spicy notes.

Gold Rush (OG 1045, ABV 4.5%)
A deep golden ale with hoppy and bitter flavours, light fruity notes and a grassy floral finish.

Big John (OG 1047, ABV 4.8%)
A dark stout bursting with smoky liquorice flavour with a satisfying bitter aftertaste.

Publisher (NEW)

Office: Hillkroft, Bromfield Road, Ludlow, Shropshire, SY8 1DW
☎ 07795 244060 ⊕ publisherales.co.uk

Publisher Ales is the brewing arm of Doghouse magazine, a quarterly about the British pub. Established in 2013 it uses spare capacity at several breweries in the Herefordshire, Shropshire and Worcestershire area supplying pubs and beer festivals in those counties.

Doghouse (ABV 3.8%)

A golden-coloured session ale with a crisp, refreshing taste and a lasting, hoppy, fruity finish.

Legend (ABV 4.4%)
A zesty, straw-coloured bitter with a fruity, hoppy aroma.

Purity SIBA ⟨◉⟩

The Brewery, Upper Spernal Farm, Spernal Lane, Great Alne, Warwickshire, B49 6JF
☎ (01789) 488007 ⊕ puritybrewing.com
Shop Mon-Fri 8am-5pm; Sat 10am-1pm
Tours by arrangement

☺Brewing began in 2005 in a purpose-designed plant housed in converted barns. The brewery incorporates an environmentally friendly effluent treatment system. It supplies the free trade within a 70 mile radius and delivers to more than 500 outlets.

Pure Gold (OG 1039.5, ABV 3.8%) ⬚
An easy-drinking beer with a dry and bitter finish.

Mad Goose (OG 1042.5, ABV 4.2%)
Light copper in colour with a zesty hop character with citrus overtone.

Pure Ubu (OG 1044.8, ABV 4.5%)
A full-flavoured premium amber-coloured beer.

Purple Moose SIBA ⟨◉⟩

Madoc Street, Porthmadog, Gwynedd, LL49 9DB
☎ (01766) 515571 ⊕ purplemoose.co.uk
Shop Mon-Fri 9am-5pm
Tours by arrangement

A 10-barrel plant opened in 2005 by Lawrence Washington in a former saw mill and farmers' warehouse in the coastal town of Porthmadog. The names of the beers reflect local history and geography. Seasonal beers are available: see website.

Cwrw Eryri/Snowdonia Ale
(OG 1035.3, ABV 3.6%) ⬚ ▮ ◈
Golden, refreshing bitter with citrus fruit hoppiness in aroma and taste. The full mouthfeel leads to a long-lasting, dry, bitter finish.

Cwrw Madog/Madog's Ale
(OG 1037, ABV 3.7%) ◈
Full-bodied session bitter. Malty nose and an initial nutty flavour but bitterness dominates. Well balanced and refreshing with a dry roastiness on the taste and a good dry finish.

Cwrw Glaslyn/Glaslyn Ale
(OG 1040.5, ABV 4.2%) ⬚ ▮ ◈
Refreshing light and malty amber-coloured ale. Plenty of hop in the aroma and taste. Good smooth mouthfeel leading to a slightly chewy finish.

Ochr Tywyll y Mws/Dark Side of the Moose
(OG 1045, ABV 4.6%) ▮
A delicious dark ale with a deep malt flavour and a fruity bitterness.

Quantock SIBA ⟨◉⟩

Unit E, Monument View, Summerfield Avenue, Chelston Business Park, Wellington, Somerset, TA21 9ND
☎ (01823) 662669 ⊕ quantockbrewery.co.uk

Quantock is a family-run brewery that began brewing in 2008 on an eight-barrel plant. The brewery supplies beers to outlets throughout the South West and further afield via wholesalers. Beers are available to the public direct from the brewery and via online sales from the website. Bottle-conditioned beers are available.

Quantock Ale (OG 1036, ABV 3.8%)
An amber coloured beer with a delicate spicy aroma, fruity, full-bodied flavour and a dry finish to the palate.

Ginger Cockney (OG 1037, ABV 4%)
A copper-coloured ale, generously hopped, with a hint of fresh ginger.

Rorke's Drift (OG 1039, ABV 4.2%)
A light, lager-style beer, a fruit filled experience with a delicate citrus aroma.

Sunraker (OG 1039, ABV 4.2%)
A pale straw-coloured beer with a delicate, clean grassy hop finish.

Wills Neck (OG 1040, ABV 4.3%)
A bright golden ale with a rich malty flavour, hints of grapefruit and cherries in the aroma, and a lasting bitterness on the palate.

Quantock Stout (OG 1044, ABV 4.5%)
A full-bodied traditional dry stout, dark ebony in colour, with an aroma of liquorice and citrus fruits.

White Hind (OG 1042, ABV 4.5%)
A chestnut-coloured best bitter with a full-bodied, malty flavour and a dry finish. A blend of English hops produce a spicy aroma.

Royal Stag IPA (OG 1056, ABV 6%)
A copper-coloured beer with a malty and fruity flavour, and a smoky aroma with hints of banana and toffee.

UXB (OG 1088, ABV 9%)
A strong beer, slightly sweet with a full malty flavour.

Quantum

Unit 4, Victoria Works, Hempshaw Lane, Stockport, Greater Manchester, SK1 4LG
☎ 07976 032465 ⊕ quantumbrewingcompany.co.uk
Tours by arrangement

☺The brewery was established in 2011 using a five-barrel plant on the site of the former Shaws Brewery. A number of seasonal beers, one-offs and specials are brewed: see website. Bottle-conditioned beers are also available.

American Light (OG 1033, ABV 3.6%)

Beagle Best (OG 1037, ABV 3.8%)

Bitter (OG 1038, ABV 3.8%)
A dry-hopped amber session bitter with hop bitterness and biscuit malt flavour.

Golden Globe (OG 1040, ABV 4.1%) ◆
Yellow beer with a modest hoppy/fruity aroma. Biscuity malt and tart fruits on the palate and in the bitter aftertaste.

Pale Ale (OG 1045, ABV 4.5%)
Hoppy beer, with the individual blend of hops being chosen by the brewery's Twitter followers each time it's brewed.

Stout (OG 1050, ABV 4.8%)
A dark rich stout, made with six malts and English hops.

Antipodean Amber Ale (OG 1052, ABV 5.3%)

Quartz SIBA ⊚

Archers, Alrewas Road, Kings Bromley, Staffordshire, DE13 7HW
☎ (01543) 473965 ⊕ quartzbrewing.co.uk
Shop Mon, Wed & Fri 9.30am-4.30pm (3.30pm in winter); Sat 10am-1.30pm
Tours by arrangement

☺Quartz was established in 2005 by Scott and Julia Barnett. There are five regular beers produced in cask, bottle and mini-cask, supplemented with seasonal specials. Around 50 outlets are supplied direct.

Blonde (OG 1038, ABV 3.8%) ◆
Little aroma, gentle hop and background malt. Sweet with unsophisticated sweetshop tastes.

Crystal (OG 1040, ABV 4.2%) ◆
Sweet aroma with some fruit and yeasty Marmite hints. Hoppiness begins but dwindles to a bittersweet finish.

Extra Blonde (OG 1042, ABV 4.4%) ◆
Sweet malty aroma with a touch of fruit. Sweet start, smooth with a hint of hops in the sugary finish.

Heart (OG 1045, ABV 4.6%) ◆
Pale brown with some aroma of fruit and malt. Gentle tastes of fruit and hops eventually appear to leave a bitter finish.

Cracker (OG 1050, ABV 5%)
Chestnut in colour with a slight roasted aroma, smooth fruit notes leaving a dry hop finish.

Quercus SIBA

Unit 2M, South Hams Business Park, Churchstow, Kingsbridge, Devon, TQ7 3QH
☎ (01548) 854888 ⊕ quercusdevonales.com
Shop Mon-Fri 10am-4pm (please call on Sat)

Quercus began trading in 2007 using an eight-barrel brew plant. The brewery was sold in 2007 by the founder Peter Walker to local residents John Tiner and Mike George. Beers are available in local pubs and shops.

Best Bitter (OG 1040, ABV 4%)
An amber bitter with balanced malt and bitterness.

Prospect (OG 1040, ABV 4%)
Subtle bitterness and sweet malt flavour with a rich aroma and colour.

Shingle Bay (OG 1042, ABV 4.2%)
A light, golden, easy-drinking ale with fruity citrus aroma and taste giving a subtle, crisp bite to refresh the palate.

Harry's (OG 1046, ABV 4.6%)
A rich, dark ale, with sweet malty chocolate aromas leading on to a complex finish of sweet malt and lingering hops.

Radnorshire (NEW) SIBA

Timberworks, Brookside Farm, New Radnor, LD8 2SU
☎ (01544) 350456 ☎ 07789 909748
⊕ radnorhillsholidaycottages.com
Tours by arrangement

Radnorshire is a microbrewery set up in 2012 in the grounds of a farm offering holiday cottage accommodation.

Whimble Gold (OG 1038, ABV 3.8%)

Light and hoppy golden ale.

Four Stones (OG 1040, ABV 4%)
A light amber ale with a subtle maltiness.

Smatcher Tawney (OG 1042, ABV 4.2%)
Mellow, tawny-coloured best bitter.

Rail Ale (NEW)

The Schooner, South Shore Road, Gateshead, Tyne &
Wear, NE8 3AF
☎ (0191) 477 7404 ☎ 07758 653510
⊕ railalebrewing@yahoo.com

Established in 2013, and based at the Schooner
pub, Rail Ale is the first microbrewery in
Gateshead. Beers are available at the Schooner and
other local outlets, and are named with a railway
theme.

Amber Aspect (OG 1039, ABV 3.8%)

Railway Tavern

📧 58 Station Road, Brightlingsea, Essex, CO7 0DT
Tours by arrangement

The brewery started life as a kitchen-sink affair in
1998. In 2012 the brewery was completely
refurbished; a two-barrel plant is used to create a
selection of dark beers suitable for vegetarians.

Crab & Winkle Mild (OG 1036, ABV 3.6%) 🍂
Thin-bodied mild with a pear drop aroma and a
rather roasty taste. The aftertaste is slightly ash-like
with suggestions of bitter chocolate.

Bladderwrack Stout (OG 1047, ABV 4.7%) 🍂
Full-bodied stout with an intense roast grain
character that is initially underpinned by subtle
sweetness, which subsides to leave a drier finish.

Rainbow (NEW)

74 Birmingham Road, Allesley, Coventry, CV5 6GT
☎ 07885 096125 ✉ rainbowbrewery@talktalk.net
Tours by arrangement

Rainbow Brewery reopened in 2013 at the rear of
the Rainbow pub under new ownership following
several years of closure.

Klondike Gold (ABV 4.1%)

Spectrum Bitter (ABV 4.5%)

Ramsbottom (NEW) SIBA

1 Heapworth Avenue, Ramsbottom, BL0 9EH
☎ 07976 263344 ⊕ ramsbottombrewery.com

Matt Holmes started brewing in 2011 in the garage
at his house using a 2.5-barrel plant; he produces
one brew a week and supplies five local pubs on a
regular basis plus other outlets further afield.
Bottle-conditioned beers are available: see
website.

Ramsbury SIBA

Mildenhall, Wiltshire, SN8 2NN
☎ (01672) 541407

Office: Priory Farm, Axford, Wiltshire, SN8 2HA
☎ (01672) 520647 ⊕ ramsburybrewery.com
Tours by arrangement

Ramsbury started brewing in 2004 and is situated
high on the Marlborough Downs in Wiltshire. The
brewery uses home-grown barley from the
Ramsbury Estate. At present a 10-barrel plant is
used but there are plans to increase capacity and
build a visitor centre and distillery.

Bitter (OG 1036, ABV 3.6%)
Amber-coloured beer with a smooth, delicate
aroma and flavour.

Deerstalker (OG 1040, ABV 4%)

Kennet Valley (OG 1041, ABV 4.1%)
A light amber, hoppy bitter with a long, dry finish.

Flint Knapper (OG 1042, ABV 4.2%)
Rich amber in colour with a malty taste.

Gold (OG 1045, ABV 4.5%)
A rich golden-coloured beer with a light hoppy
aroma and taste.

Ramsgate SIBA 👁

1 Hornet Close, Pyson's Road Industrial Estate,
Broadstairs, Kent, CT10 2YD
☎ (01843) 868453 ⊕ ramsgatebrewery.co.uk
Shop Mon-Fri 10am-5pm; Sat 10am-1pm
Tours by arrangement

Ramsgate was established in 2002 at the back of a
Ramsgate pub. In 2006 the brewery moved to its
current location, allowing for increased capacity
and bottling. Bottle-conditioned beers are
available. Seasonal and monthly specials: see
website.

Gadds' No. 7 (OG 1037, ABV 3.8%)
Pale bitter ale.

Gadds' Seasider (OG 1042, ABV 4.3%)
Amber ale with a malty body and balancing sweet
hop flavour.

Gadds' No. 5 (OG 1043, ABV 4.4%)
Traditional best bitter with a toffee malt and fresh
green hop aroma, a full body and a lingering bitter
finish.

Gadds' No. 3 (OG 1047, ABV 5%)
Premium pale ale.

Gadds Faithful DogBolter (OG 1054, ABV 5.6%)
Dark porter with a satisfying, rich, malty body full
of roast chocolaty flavours, balanced by a deep and
lasting hop bitterness.

Randalls SIBA

La Piette Brewery, St Georges Esplanade, St Peter
Port, Guernsey, GY1 2BH
☎ (01481) 720134 ⊕ randallsbrewery.co.uk
Tours by arrangement

Randalls has been brewing since 1868 and is the
only brewery operating in the Bailiwick of
Guernsey. A new 36-barrel brewhouse was
installed in 2008. 18 pubs are owned and a further
50 outlets are supplied.

Patois (OG 1045, ABV 4.5%)
Chestnut brown best bitter with a subtle hop aroma
and balanced bitterness.

Rat

📧 40 Chapel Hill, Huddersfield, West Yorkshire,
HD1 3EB

☎ (01484) 542400 ☎ 07906 279038
⊕ ossett-brewery.co.uk

⊛The Rat & Ratchet was originally established as a brewpub in 1994. Brewing ceased and it was purchased by Ossett (qv) in 2004. Brewing re-started in 2011 with a capacity of 18 barrels per week, producing seven regular beers with rat-themed names.

Dirty Rat (OG 1038, ABV 3.5%)
A velvety dark brown mild with low bitterness and a sweet malty finish. The delicate hop aroma is not overpowering.

Brown Rat (OG 1040, ABV 3.8%)
A medium-brown traditional malty ale. Bitterness is moderate and English hops give a fruity/spicy hop aroma.

Golden Rat (OG 1038, ABV 3.8%)
Golden, easy-drinking session bitter with a slightly sweet maltiness. Bitterness and spicy hop aromas dominate.

White Rat (OG 1040, ABV 4%)
Very pale hoppy ale with an intensely aromatic and resinous finish.

Cheating Rat (OG 1043, ABV 4.1%)
A pale hoppy bitter.

Rattus Rattus (OG 1045, ABV 4.3%)
Hazy wheat beer with flavours of banana and cloves. Fresh coriander gives a herbal, spicy aroma.

King Rat (OG 1050, ABV 5%)
Hoppy beer with a unique white wine aroma. Bitterness is high, but balanced by a residual malty sweetness.

Raw SIBA

Units 3 & 4, Silver House, Adelphi Way, Staveley, Derbyshire, S43 3LJ
☎ (01246) 475445 ⊕ rawbrew.com
Tours by arrangement

Raw began brewing in 2010 using a five-barrel plant from Prospect Brewery of Wigan. Six core beers and a seasonal special are always available.

Blonde Pale (OG 1039, ABV 3.9%)

JR Best (OG 1042, ABV 4.2%)

Dark Peak (OG 1045, ABV 4.5%)

Edge Pale (OG 1045, ABV 4.5%)

Anubis (OG 1051, ABV 5.2%)

Grey Ghost (OG 1056, ABV 5.9%)

RCH SIBA ◉

West Hewish, Somerset, BS24 6RR
☎ (01934) 834447 ⊕ rchbrewery.com
Shop: phone for opening hours

⊠ The brewery was originally installed in the early 1980s behind the Royal Clarence Hotel at Burnham-on-Sea. Since 1993 brewing has taken place in a former cider mill at West Hewish. A 30-barrel plant was installed in 2000. RCH supplies 150 outlets and the award-winning beers are available nationwide through its own wholesaling company, which also distributes beers from other small independent breweries. Seasonal and bottle-conditioned beers are also available.

Hewish IPA (OG 1036, ABV 3.6%) ◆

Session bitter with apple, malt and caramel flavours. Astringent finish comes after aromas of malt, fruit and hops.

Hewish Mild (OG 1036, ABV 3.6%)

PG Steam (OG 1039, ABV 3.9%) ◆
A tawny beer with apple-fruit flavours. Some malt flavours with bitterness and astringency throughout.

Pitchfork (OG 1043, ABV 4.3%) ◆
Fragrant citrus aromas are followed by a very bitter, hoppy taste. Finished with an astringent and bitter aftertaste.

Old Slug Porter (OG 1046, ABV 4.5%) ▆ ◆
Powerful aroma of roast and dark fruit which continues into the roast malt flavours. Bitter, slightly astringent finish.

East Street Cream (OG 1050, ABV 5%) ◆
Full bodied malty ale with strong malt and hops on the nose. Fruity flavours mellow into a smooth bitter-sweet finish.

Double Header (OG 1053, ABV 5.3%) ◆
A strong, full-bodied golden bitter with a citrus taste and fruity hop nose. It has a bitter, astringent finish.

Firebox (OG 1060, ABV 6%) ◆
Light, hoppy bitter with some malt and fruit, though slightly less fruit in the finish. Floral citrus hop aroma; pale brown/amber colour.

Santa Fe (OG 1075, ABV 7.3%) ▆

Reality

127 High Road, Chilwell, Nottingham, NG9 4AT
☎ 07801 539523
✉ alandenismonaghan@hotmail.com

Reality began brewing in 2010 in the unused space of an IT business, hence the pun on Real-ITy. It moved to larger premises in 2011 to allow for expansion. Beers are themed around the brewery name and are available in select local outlets and nationally at beer festivals.

Virtuale Reality (OG 1039, ABV 3.8%)
A pale session brew.

No Escape (OG 1043, ABV 4.2%)
Pale ale with Maris Otter malt and Cascade hops.

Bitter Reality (OG 1044, ABV 4.3%)
A copper coloured bitter made with pale and crystal malts.

Stark Reality (OG 1046, ABV 4.5%)
Amber bitter with a hint of rum.

Reality Czech (OG 1047, ABV 4.6%)
Pale beer with Czech hops and pilsner malt.

Rebel SIBA

Century House, Kernick Industrial Estate, Penryn, Cornwall, TR10 9EP
☎ (01326) 378517 ⊕ rebelbrewing.co.uk
Tours by arrangement

⊠ Rebel began brewing in 2011. In 2012 it expanded to a 15-barrel plant with visitor centre, shop and museum. The beers are available in pubs in Penryn and Falmouth. Bottle-conditioned beers are available.

Bal Maiden (OG 1041, ABV 4%)

Cornish Sunset (OG 1041, ABV 4%)

Penryn Pale Ale (OG 1043, ABV 4.3%)

Black Rock Bitter (OG 1049, ABV 4.8%)

80/- Scotch Ale (OG 1051, ABV 5%) ◆
Roast notes in aroma and little malt. Balance of roast and malt with gentle bitterness and rich berry fruit sweetness.

Rebellion SIBA

Marlow Brewery, Bencombe Farm, Marlow Bottom, Buckinghamshire, SL7 3LT
☎ (01628) 476594 ⊕ rebellionbeer.co.uk
Shop Mon-Fri 8am-6pm; Sat 9am-6pm
Tours by arrangement

⊠ Established in 1993, Rebellion filled the void left when Wethereds ceased brewing in 1987 in Marlow. The brewery has grown steadily, with one site move and several expansion projects. It currently supplies around 400 local outlets. Seasonal beers: see website. Bottle-conditioned beer is also available.

IPA (OG 1039, ABV 3.7%) ◆
Copper-coloured bitter, sweet and malty, with resinous and red apple flavours. Caramel and fruit decline to leave a dry, bitter and malty finish.

Smuggler (OG 1042, ABV 4.1%) ◆
A red-brown beer, well-bodied and bitter with an uncompromisingly dry, bitter finish.

Mutiny (OG 1046, ABV 4.5%) ◆
Tawny in colour, this full-bodied best bitter is predominantly fruity and moderately bitter with crystal malt continuing to a dry finish.

Rectory SIBA

Streat Hill Farm, Streat Hill, Streat, Hassocks, East Sussex, BN6 8RP
☎ (01273) 890570 ⊠ rectoryales@hotmail.com
Tours by arrangement

⊠ Rectory was founded in 1995 by the Rev Godfrey Broster to generate funds for the maintenance of his three parish churches. 107 parishioners are shareholders. Production is split between the Streat Hill Farm, where seasonal and specials beers are brewed, and Harvey's brewery (qv) micro-plant.

All Saints Tipple (OG 1045, ABV 4.5%)
A well-balanced, traditional-style mid-brown best bitter.

The Rector's Revenge (OG 1050, ABV 5%)
Traditional strong bitter with a long bitter finish.

Red SIBA

Unit 1, The Orchard, Garden Farm, The Town, Great Staughton, Cambridgeshire, PE19 5BE
☎ 07827 294229 ⊕ redbrewery.com

Red brewery was established in 2012 on a four-barrel plant in a converted farm building in the village of Great Staughton. A selection of seven beers is currently available.

Georgie's Pebble (OG 1035, ABV 3.5%)
A dark mild with light hop, blackcurrant and chocolate notes.

Staughton Bitter (OG 1040, ABV 4.1%)
Copper-coloured hoppy bitter.

Sundial Gold (OG 1041, ABV 4.1%)
A golden ale; citrus notes with a light hop finish.

Pathfinder (OG 1046, ABV 4.6%)
Amber-coloured ale with orange and grapefruit citrus notes.

All Saints Porter (OG 1051, ABV 5.2%)
Smooth, dark porter with a hint of chocolate and blackcurrant.

Valhalla (OG 1053, ABV 5.5%)
Bronze-coloured strong beer.

Juggernaut (OG 1063, ABV 6.7%)
Garnet-coloured winter ale. Floral and slightly sweet.

Red Fox SIBA

The Chicken Sheds, Upp Hall Farm, Salmons Lane, Coggeshall, Essex, CO6 1RY
☎ (01376) 563123 ⊕ redfoxbrewery.co.uk
Tours by arrangement

Red Fox began brewing in 2008 using a five-barrel plant and has continued to grow in line with increasing demand. Around 35 outlets are supplied direct. Bottle-conditioned beer is available as are seasonal and one-off beers. Mini pins and pins are available from the brewery.

Mild (OG 1037, ABV 3.6%)
A classic dark, full-flavoured mild with hints of chocolate and a deep roast barley flavour.

IPA (OG 1038, ABV 3.7%)
An East Anglian-style copper-coloured beer with a delicate flavour.

Bitter (OG 1039, ABV 3.8%)
A traditional-style bitter with balanced malt and fruit flavours.

Hunter's Gold (OG 1040, ABV 3.9%)
A golden beer with a delicate citrus aroma.

Best Bitter (OG 1041, ABV 4%)
A light brown bitter with a full flavour and a malty backbone.

Coggeshall Gold (OG 1044, ABV 4%)
Aromatic golden beer, with citrus and exotic fruit flavours. Unusually for a beer of this style it does not have a bitter finish.

Surrex Gold (OG 1040, ABV 4.1%)
Well-hopped, aromatic beer. Pink grapefruit and peach aromas abound, leading to a slightly bitter finish.

Black Fox Porter (OG 1046, ABV 4.8%)
A rich-flavoured black beer packed with malty flavour and undertones of chocolate.

Wily Ol' Fox (OG 1050, ABV 5.2%)
Aromatic amber ale made from English hops and malt, with a soft, fruity palate.

Red Rock SIBA

Higher Humber Farm, Bishopsteignton, Devon, TQ14 9TD
☎ (01626) 879738 ☎ 07894 35094
⊕ redrockbrewery.co.uk
Shop Mon-Fri 9am-4pm (phone for weekend hours)
Tours by arrangement

Red Rock first started brewing in 2006 with a four-barrel plant and upgraded in 2011 to a 7.5-barrel one. It is based in a converted barn on a working farm using locally-sourced malt, fresh hops and the farm's own spring water. It has a bar and can accommodate private functions. Bottle-conditioned and seasonal beers also available.

Red Rock (OG 1041, ABV 4.2%)
Well-balanced best bitter.

Red Shoot

Toms Lane, Linwood, Ringwood, Hampshire, BH24 3QT
☎ (01425) 475792 ⊕ redshoot.co.uk

The 2.5-barrel brewery was commissioned in 1998. In summer the brewery works to capacity, half the output going to the Red Shoot pub and half to other local outlets, being distributed by Wadworth (qv) who also direct and monitor the whole brewing process.

New Forest Gold (ABV 3.8%)
A refreshing golden ale, with a light floral citrus taste and a burnt toffee finish.

Red White & Brew (ABV 4%)
A hoppy, fresh golden ale, with increasing bitterness.

Muddy Boot (ABV 4.2%)
A dark chocolaty mild, brewed using molasses and chocolate malt.

Tom's Tipple (ABV 4.8%)
A copper-coloured strong malty bitter: hops give some citrus balance to the toffee and malt flavours.

Red Squirrel SIBA

Unit 24, Boxted Farm, Berkhamsted Road, Potten End, Hertfordshire, HP1 2SQ
☎ (01442) 256970 ⊕ redsquirrelbrewery.co.uk
Tours by arrangement

Red Squirrel started brewing in Hertford in 2004 using a 10 barrel plant. In 2011, it moved to Boxmoor near Hemel Hempstead. Seasonal and occasional beers are available.

Red Dawn Mild (OG 1037.7, ABV 3.7%)
Dark red in colour, drinkable and satisfying with mellow and nutty overtones and a smooth and rounded palate.

Hopfest (OG 1037, ABV 3.8%)
Pale, golden ale with a floral/citrus aroma and elderflower notes.

RSX (OG 1037, ABV 3.8%)
A chestnut brown-coloured ale with dried fruit and hoppy aromas.

Legally Blonde (OG 1040, ABV 4%)
Hops give a fresh, citrus flavour, with herbal, floral and buttery notes.

Conservation Bitter (OG 1040, ABV 4.1%)
A chestnut brown traditional bitter with a hoppy, fruity bitterness, and biscuit flavours with hints of spice and chocolate.

Mr Squirrel (OG 1042.9, ABV 4.3%)
A chestnut red premium bitter, lightly hopped with a creamy texture. Hints of caramel and vanilla complement the slightly hoppy and malty overtones.

Jack Black (OG 1047.7, ABV 4.8%)
A black IPA featuring the hop profile of an IPA with the dark colour of a porter.

London Porter (OG 1048, ABV 5%)
Dark brown/black porter with a good balance of chocolate and roasted barley. Full bodied on the palate with bittersweet liquorice and rich chocolate flavours and a creamy finish.

Redwood American IPA (OG 1051, ABV 5.4%)
Based on a secret Michigan recipe, golden orange in colour, with complex hoppy aromas, floral/citrus tones and a long lingering finish.

Redchurch SIBA

275-276 Poyser Street, Bethnal Green, London, E2 9RF
☎ 07968 173097 ⊕ theredchurchbrewery.com

Redchurch was established in 2011 by Gary Ward using an eight-barrel plant and is situated in a unit under the railway arches in Bethnal Green. The brewery produces five beers at present, primarily in key casks and bottles but with occasional casks for festivals: Shoreditch Blonde (ABV 4.5%), Bethnal Pale Ale (ABV 5.5%), Hackney Gold (ABV 5.5%), Hoxton Stout (ABV 6%), Great Eastern IPA (ABV 7.4%). A variety of specials is also brewed: see website.

Redemption SIBA

Unit 2, Compass West Industrial Estate, 33 West Road, Tottenham, London, N17 0XL
☎ (020) 8885 5227 ⊕ redemptionbrewing.co.uk
Tours by arrangement

Redemption began brewing in 2010 on a 12-barrel plant. Six beers are brewed regularly, with occasional festival specials. Most of the beer is supplied in casks to pubs in north and central London.

Trinity (OG 1030, ABV 3%)
Refreshing golden beer with strong citrus notes throughout. The strong bitterness is softened by a little sweet malt character that is also present in the aftertaste with a lingering dryness.

Pale Ale (OG 1037.5, ABV 3.8%)
A well-balanced amber bitter with hops and citrus orange throughout. The sweet maltiness fades in the aftertaste leaving a slightly dry, bitter finish. Orange and peach on the nose.

Hopspur (OG 1044.5, ABV 4.5%)
Hoppy bitter notes are present in this tawny brown best bitter which has a hint of coffee roast throughout and some caramelised citrus notes.

Urban Dusk (OG 1044, ABV 4.6%)
Full-bodied brown best bitter; chocolate and some toffee in the aroma. Citrus, creamy fudge and dark roast chocolate on the palate, drying to leave a slightly dry, bitter finish.

Friendship Porter (OG 1052.5, ABV 5.1%)
Sweetish smooth porter with a mix of liquorice, caramel and roast notes. A pleasant burnt roast gives dry, bitter overtones.

Big Chief (OG 1052.5, ABV 5.5%)
Golden ale with a creamy mouthfeel and a strong fruity aroma, flavour and finish, which is also dry and bitter.

Redscar SIBA

c/o The Cleveland Hotel, 9-11 High Street West, Redcar, North Yorkshire, TS10 1SQ

☎ 07828 855146 ⊕ redscar-brewery.co.uk
Tours by arrangement

😊Redscar first brewed in 2008 on a 2.5-barrel plant. The brewery supplies the hotel, local pubs and beer festivals. Occasional specials and seasonal beers are also brewed.

Jazz (OG 1040, ABV 3.8%)
A delicately-hopped, light session beer.

Sands (OG 1040, ABV 3.8%)
A refreshing golden ale.

Poison (OG 1042, ABV 4%)
A dark, medium-bodied ale with smooth, malty flavours.

Rocks (OG 1042, ABV 4%)
A medium-bodied red ale with rich, malty flavours and a subtle hop finish.

Pier (OG 1045, ABV 4.5%)
A dark, full-bodied ale with rich, fruity flavours and a satisfying warmth.

Beach (OG 1050, ABV 5%)
A strong, smooth, amber-coloured premium ale.

Redstone (NEW)

Tynwllyd Farm, Llangors, Powys, LD3 7UA
☎ 07581 878604 ⊕ redstone-brewery.com
Shop (phone for opening hours)
Tours by arrangement

❌ Redstone started brewing in 2013 using the remnants of the Tudor Brewery, formally based in Abergavenny. A four-barrel has been installed in a converted Edwardian granary to supply both cask and bottled beer to the local area.

Clipper (OG 1040, ABV 4%)

Gorsey (OG 1045, ABV 4.2%)
Light blonde pale ale. A vigorous grapefruit flavour delivers a medium bitterness with very little aftertaste.

Indy Amber Ale (OG 1042, ABV 4.5%)

Exile (ABV 4.8%)
An initial dry caramel flavour gives way to a hint of apple and a medium to light bitterness.

RedWillow SIBA

Sutton Mill, Gunco Lane, Macclesfield, Cheshire, SK11 7JL
☎ (01625) 502315 ⊕ redwillowbrewery.com

😊RedWillow began brewing in 2010 from a unit within Sutton Mill. The award-winning beers are distributed across the North West and into Yorkshire and are available in cask and bottle-conditioned form. Seasonal beers are brewed, and experimental brews are branded under the Faithless label: see website.

Headless (OG 1038, ABV 3.9%)
Light and hoppy pale ale.

Feckless (OG 1041, ABV 4.1%)
A classic English bitter.

Directionless (OG 1041, ABV 4.2%)
Pale ale with hop and malt flavours.

Wreckless (OG 1046, ABV 4.8%)
Fruity pale ale blending hops and malt.

Smokeless (OG 1055, ABV 5.7%)
Smoked porter infused with smoked chipotle chilli.

Ageless (OG 1067, ABV 7.2%)
A hoppy IPA.

Reedley Hallows SIBA

Unit 12, Farrington Court, Burnley, Lancashire, BB11 5SS
☎ 07749 414513 ⊕ reedley-hallows-brewery.co.uk

Brewing started on this four-barrel plant in 2012, with ex-Moorhouse brewer Peter Gouldsbrough. Beers are supplied to to wholesalers and pubs within a 50 mile radius of the brewery.

Old Laund Bitter (OG 1038, ABV 3.6%)
Smooth and creamy session beer with a distinctive hoppy aftertaste.

Filly Close Blonde (OG 1040, ABV 3.9%)
Well-balanced bitter and spicy ale with a fruity finish.

Monkholme Premium (OG 1042, ABV 4.2%)
Premium golden ale with a hoppy taste throughout.

New Laund Dark (OG 1044, ABV 4.4%)
A dark stout. Sweet at first, with a smoky, bitter finish.

Revolutions SIBA

Unit B7, Whitwood Enterprise Park, Speedwell Road, Whitwood, Castleford, West Yorkshire, WF10 5PX
☎ (01977) 552649 ☎ 07801 701089
⊕ revolutionsbrewing.co.uk
Tours by arrangement

Revolutions began brewing in 2010. Beers are inspired by and pay homage to music from the analogue era and are typically brewed to 3.3%, 3.9%, 4.5% and 6%, to reflect the speeds at which music used to revolve (33rpm, EP, 45rpm and C60). The Rewind 33 series of monthly specials references music from 33 years ago.

EP Session Pale (OG 1040, ABV 3.9%)
A pale ale with balanced levels of sweetness and bitterness, and a crisp lemon hop finish.

Atomic Blonde (OG 1045, ABV 4.5%)
Light-coloured, medium-bodied ale. Moderate levels of bitterness give way to a big hop finish full of soft fruit and berries.

Clash London Porter (OG 1045, ABV 4.5%)
A complex dark malty beer rounded off with a smooth hop finish.

Devolution Amber Ale (OG 1044, ABV 4.5%)
A classic American-style amber ale.

Rhymney SIBA

Gilchrist Thomas Industrial Estate, Blaenavon, Torfaen, NP4 9RL
☎ (01685) 722253 ⊕ rhymneybreweryltd.com
Visitor centre & shop 11.30am-5.30pm daily
Tours by arrangement

😊Rhymney first brewed in 2005. The 75-hl plant was sourced from Canada. Around 220 outlets are supplied. In 2012 the brewery relocated to Blaenavon with a new brewing centre and visitor facility.

Hobby Horse (OG 1038, ABV 3.8%) ◼

Dark (OG 1040, ABV 4%) ◻

Bevans Bitter (OG 1042, ABV 4.2%)
A traditional bitter with a smooth character and rounded aftertaste.

Bitter (OG 1043, ABV 4.3%)

Export Ale (OG 1050, ABV 5%) ⬚ ▮

Richmond SIBA

The Station Brewery, Station Yard, Richmond, North Yorkshire, DL10 4LD
☎ (01748) 828266 ⊕ richmondbrewing.co.uk
Shop Tue-Sun 12-4pm (may be open outside these hours)
Tours by arrangement

⊛Richmond opened in 2008 in the Victorian station complex beside the River Swale. The brewery concentrates mainly on bottled ales with around 20% of output being cask-conditioned and available in the local area, often in the Ralph Fitz Randal in Richmond.

SwAle (OG 1035, ABV 3.7%)
Dark mild brewed using chocolate malt with slightly more bitterness than a traditional mild.

Station Ale (OG 1039, ABV 4%)
Light golden bitter brewed using hedegrow hops.

Happiness (OG 1039, ABV 4.2%)
Tawny best bitter.

Pale Ale (OG 1044, ABV 4.6%)

Ridgeside SIBA

Unit 24, Penraevon 2 Industrial Estate, Meanwood, Leeds, West Yorkshire, LS7 2AW
☎ 07595 380568 ⊕ ridgesidebrewery.co.uk

⊛Ridgeside began brewing in 2010 using a four-barrel plant, and expansion is planned. Special brews are produced monthly alongside an extensive core range. Regular outlets are supplied around Leeds, and the Junction in Castleford serves Ridgeside beers from oak casks.

Jailbreak (OG 1038, ABV 3.8%) ⬦
A refreshing beer featuring large amounts of hops and citrus bitterness, this golden ale has a full and lasting finish.

Cascade (OG 1041, ABV 4.1%) ⬦
Strong grapefruit flavours define this beer with a liberal dose of hops and bitterness throughout.

Templar (OG 1042, ABV 4.2%)

Rushmore (OG 1043, ABV 4.3%) ⬦
Generous hops and citrus fruit take this smooth, golden ale right through from initial aroma to the lingering bitter finish.

Desert Aire (OG 1048, ABV 4.8%) ⬦
This gold-coloured beer is hoppy, bitter and dry, the orangy citrus hops dominate but there is some sweetness.

Stargazer (OG 1049, ABV 4.9%)

Black Night (OG 1050, ABV 5%) ⬦
Smooth black beer with an intriguing smoked malt, bitter coffee flavour, the roastiness balances well with the strong bitterness.

Long Way From Home (OG 1050, ABV 5%)

Eliminator (OG 1060, ABV 6%)

Ridgeway

Beer Counter Ltd, South Stoke, Oxfordshire, RG8 0JW
☎ (01491) 873474
✉ peter.scholey@beercounter.co.uk

Set up by ex-Brakspear head brewer Peter Scholey, Ridgeway specialises in bottle-conditioned beers, although cask beers are occasionally offered. At present the beers are brewed by Peter using his own ingredients on plants at Hepworth's brewery (qv) and Cotswold brewery (qv).

Bitter (OG 1040, ABV 4%)

Organic Beer/ROB (OG 1043, ABV 4.3%)

Blue (OG 1050, ABV 5%)

Ivanhoe (OG 1050, ABV 5.2%)

IPA (OG 1055, ABV 5.5%)
Golden ale with a citrus aroma, a bitter hoppy flavour and a long bitter aftertaste.

Ringway (NEW) SIBA

16 Station Road Industrial Estate, Reddish, Stockport, SK5 6ND
☎ (0161) 443 1818 ☎ 07960 855800
⊕ ringwaybrewery.co.uk

⊛Ringway started brewing in 2012 in a modern industrial estate unit, using a six-barrel kit. Brewing takes place twice a week, supplying the local trade. Extensive use is made of English hops in all beers. Beers are available in firkins and pins.

Session (OG 1038, ABV 3.8%)
A light, hoppy pale ale packed with hops to give a citrus punch.

Best Bitter (OG 1041, ABV 4.2%)
A classic English bitter with a delicate aroma.

Ringwood ⬬

Christchurch Road, Ringwood, Hampshire, BH24 3AP
☎ (01425) 471177 ⊕ ringwoodbrewery.co.uk
Shop Mon-Sat 9.30am-5pm
Tours by arrangement

⊗ Ringwood was bought in 2007 by Marstons for £19 million. The group plans to increase production to 50,000 barrels a year. Some 750 outlets are supplied and seven pubs are owned. Seasonal beers are available. Part of Marston's PLC.

Best Bitter (OG 1038, ABV 3.8%) ⬦
A malty session bitter with strong toffee notes in the aroma, leading to a short, bittersweet finish. Malt tends to dominate throughout.

Fortyniner (OG 1049, ABV 4.9%) ⬦
Robust bitter; a caramel, biscuity aroma, with hints of damson, lead to a sweet but well-balanced taste with malt, fruit and hop flavours all present. The finish is bittersweet with some fruit.

Old Thumper (ABV 5.1%)

Ripple Steam SIBA

Parsonage Farm, Vale Road, Sutton, Kent, CT15 5DH
☎ 07917 037611 ⊕ ripplesteambrewery.co.uk

Ripple Steam began brewing commercially on a farm in Kent in 2012. Seasonal beers are also available.

Best Bitter (ABV 4.1%)

Classic IPA (ABV 4.5%)

River Leven

Lab Road, Kinlochleven, PH50 4SG
☎ (01855) 831519 ☎ 07901 873273
⊕ riverlevenales.co.uk

River Leven was established 2011 in a former aluminium factory building in Kinlochleven. Only pure malt cask-conditioned ale is produced.

Blonde (OG 1040, ABV 4%)
Clean-tasting, pale golden beer.

Dark (OG 1040, ABV 4%)
All the smooth, malty flavour of traditional Scottish dark ale, but brewed to give a drier finish and a little more hop flavour.

Traditional IPA (OG 1014, ABV 4%)
Traditional British bittering hops combine with the nutty flavour of the crystal malt to produce this amber-coloured classic British ale.

Riverhead

⧉ 2 Peel Street, Marsden, Huddersfield, West Yorkshire, HD7 6BR
☎ (01484) 841270 (Pub) ⊕ ossett-brewery.co.uk
Tours by arrangement (through Ossett Brewing Co)

☺Riverhead is a brew-pub that opened in 1995. Ossett Brewing Co purchased the site in 2006 but runs it as a separate brewery. It has since opened the Dining Room on the first floor, which uses Riverhead beers in its dishes. There are many rotating beers produced as well as seasonals.

Sparth Mild (ABV 3.6%)

Butterley Bitter (ABV 3.8%) ◖
A dry, amber-coloured, hoppy session beer.

Wessenden Wheat (ABV 4%)

White Cloud (ABV 4.5%)

March Haigh (ABV 4.6%)
A golden-brown premium bitter. Malty and full-bodied with moderate bitterness.

Redbrook Premium (ABV 5.5%)

Riverside

Bee's Farm, Wainfleet, Lincolnshire, PE24 4LX
☎ (01754) 881288 ☎ 07779 280996
Tours by arrangement

⊗Riverside started brewing in 2003 on a five-barrel plant, moving to its present site in 2008. It supplies 15-20 regular local outlets and beers are also available in Hertfordshire and the West Midlands. Seasonal beers are available.

Dixon's Major (OG 1038, ABV 3.9%)

Life Saver (OG 1039, ABV 4%)

Robin Hood (NEW)

Unit 3, Northgate Place, High Church Street, New Basford, Nottingham, NG7 7JT
☎ 07804 499462
✉ brewery@robinhoodbrewery.com

Robin Hood began brewing in 2012, originally using spare capacity at another brewery. It moved to its own premises in 2013 using a 5.5-barrel plant producing the Robin Hood and His Outlaws range of beers. Seasonal and special beers are also available.

Maid Marian Extra Pale (OG 1039, ABV 3.9%)
A pale straw-coloured ale with overtones of honey, balanced with a hint of hop aroma and bitterness.

Robin Hood (OG 1040, ABV 4%)
A traditional English ale, light brown in colour with a smooth, dry finish.

Will Scarlet (OG 1042, ABV 4.2%)
Red-coloured ale with spicy hop overtones and port-like flavours.

Friar Tuck Stout (OG 1044, ABV 4.4%)
Dark, malty beer with coffee and chocolate flavours balanced with a hint of hop in the background.

Outlaw (OG 1044, ABV 4.4%)
Golden ale with floral citrus hop aroma and a crisp hop finish.

The Sheriff of Nottingham (OG 1046, ABV 4.6%)
A tawny-coloured special ale. An initial fruity hop flavour develops into a satisfying bitterness to finish.

Little John Strong (OG 1050, ABV 5%)
Deep gold-coloured strong ale. Full-bodied with an aroma and taste of barley wine to start then developing a bitter, hoppy but balanced finish.

Robinsons SIBA IFBB ◉

Unicorn Brewery, Lower Hillgate, Stockport, Cheshire, SK1 1JJ
☎ (0161) 612 4061 ⊕ robinsonsbrewery.com
Visitor centre & shop Tue-Sat 10.30am-6pm; Sun 12pm-4pm
Tours by arrangement

☺Robinsons has been brewing since 1838 and the business is still owned and run by the family. It has an estate of 370 pubs stretching from Cheshire to Cumbria and out to North Wales. A new brewhouse came on stream in 2012, which enables it to produce a wider range of seasonal and one-off beers, and the brewery added a visitor centre in 2013. Seasonal beers: see website.

1892 (OG 1032, ABV 3.3%)
Nut brown Cheshire ale with a dry roasted nutty malt palate and a delicate hop aroma.

1892 Dark (OG 1032, ABV 3.3%)

Dizzy Blonde (OG 1037, ABV 3.8%)
A straw-coloured summer ale with a distinctive hop aroma. A light, refreshing beer with a clean, zesty, hop-dominated palate complemented by a crisp, dry finish.

Hartleys XB (OG 1040, ABV 4%) ◖
An overly sweet and malty bitter with a bitter citrus peel fruitiness and a hint of liquorice in the finish.

Cumbria Way (OG 1040, ABV 4.1%)
A pronounced malt aroma with rich fruit notes. Rounded malt and hops in the mouth, long, dry finish with citrus fruit notes.

Cwrw'r Ddraig Aur (OG 1041, ABV 4.1%)
Full-bodied bitter beer with rich malt and hops complemented by complex aromas of spicy hop, malt and tart fruit. Long dry finish with citrus fruit notes.

Unicorn (OG 1041, ABV 4.2%) ◖
Amber beer with a fruity aroma. Malt, hops and fruit in the taste with a bitter, malty finish.

Double Hop (OG 1050, ABV 5%) ◆
Pale brown beer with malt and fruit on the nose.
Full hoppy taste with malt and fruit, leading to a
hoppy, bitter finish.

Old Tom (OG 1079, ABV 8.5%) ◆
A full-bodied, dark beer with malt, fruit and
chocolate on the aroma. A complex range of
flavours includes dark chocolate, full maltiness,
port and fruits and lead to a long, bittersweet
aftertaste.

Rock & Roll SIBA

🍴 Lamp Tavern, 157 Barford Street, Birmingham,
B5 6AH
☎ (0121) 688 1220 ☎ 07922 554181
✉ markwshepherd@btinternet.com
Tours by arrangement

The Rock & Roll Brewhouse started brewing in
2011 using a 2.5-barrel plant on the roof of the
Lamp Tavern. Dave Shepherd and Dave Bennett,
ex-brewers at Wetheroak Hill, brew three regular
beers, mainly for the pub, and a monthly special,
often available locally.

Lamplight (ABV 3.9%)

Instant Calmer (ABV 4%)

Brew Springsteen (ABV 4.2%)
Pale ale brewed with honey.

Rocket Science (NEW)

73 Firgrove Crescent, Yate, BS37 7AJ
⊕ rocketscienceales.co.uk

Rocket Science is a nanobrewery which
commenced brewing in 2013. Beer is currently
only available in bottles.

Rockin' Robin

6 Pickering Street, Maidstone, Kent, ME15 9RS
☎ 07779 986087

Brewing began in 2011 using a one-barrel plant.
Local outlets are supplied.

Hoppin Robin (ABV 3.7%)
Complex chestnut-coloured ale with malt and fruit
in the mouth and hops on the tongue.

Mildly Rockin (ABV 3.7%)
Dark ruby ale with a rounded bitterness and fine
bouquet.

Reliant Robin (ABV 4.2%)
An auburn-coloured best bitter brewed using four
malts, with hop notes on the palate and a fresh
spicy finish.

Reckless Robin (ABV 4.5%)
A strong bitter that delivers a fresh hoppy punch,
well-balanced with soft fruit malt.

Really Rockin (ABV 5%)
An English pale ale, dry hopped to enhance
bouquet.

Rockingham SIBA

c/o 25 Wansford Road, Blatherwycke, PE8 6RZ
280722 ⊕ rockinghamales.co.uk

⊗ A part-time brewery established in 1997 that
operates from a converted farm building with a
two-barrel plant producing a prolific range of beers

and supplies several local outlets. Seasonal beers
are available.

Rocky Head (NEW)

Unit 16, Glenville Mews, Kimber Road, Southfields,
London, SW18 4NJ
☎ (020) 8875 9917 ⊕ sites.google.com/site/
rockyheadbrewery

Rocky Head is a microbrewery set up in 2012 by a
group of friends inspired by the American craft
brewing scene. A range of vegan-friendly bottle-
conditioned beers is brewed on a five-barrel plant.

Rodham's

74 Albion Street, Otley, West Yorkshire, LS21 1BZ
☎ (01943) 464530

Michael Rodham began brewing in 2005 on a one-
barrel plant in the cellar of his house. Capacity has
gradually increased and is now 2.5 barrels. Relish is
the main beer brewed, with other beers produced
on a rolling basis. All beers produced are malt-only,
using whole hops. Occasional seasonal and bottle-
conditioned beers are available.

Relish (OG 1035, ABV 3.7%)
A pale ale with creamy malt and citrus fruit flavours
and a lasting hoppy bitterness.

Rooster's SIBA ◉

Unit 3, Grimbald Park, Wetherby Road,
Knaresborough, North Yorkshire, HG5 8LJ
☎ (01423) 865959 ⊕ roosters.co.uk
Tours by arrangement

⊙ Rooster's was founded in 1993 by Sean and
Alison Franklin. The brewery was acquired by the
Fozard family in 2011 when Sean and Alison
retired. One-off and occasional experimental brews
are also brewed under the Outlaw Brewing Co
name.

Buckeye (OG 1035.5, ABV 3.5%)
An easy-drinking, well-hopped pale ale, with an
orange, citrus fruit aroma.

Wild Mule (OG 1037, ABV 3.9%)
A New World, session-strength, pale ale with a
lasting grapefruit bitterness.

YPA (Yorkshire Pale Ale) (OG 1039.5, ABV 4.1%)
A pale, aromatic summer ale that offers up delicate
peachy and berry fruit flavours.

Yankee (OG 1041, ABV 4.3%) ◆
A straw-coloured beer with a delicate, fruity aroma
leading to a well-balanced taste of malt and hops
with a slight evidence of sweetness, followed by a
refreshing, fruity/bitter finish.

Roseland

🍴 c/o Roseland Inn, Philleigh, nr St Mawes, Truro,
Cornwall, TR2 5NB
☎ (01872) 580254 ☎ 07977 472484

⊗ Roseland was established in 2009 by Phil Heslip
at his pub, the Roseland Inn. The beers are mostly
named after local birds and are generally only
available in the pub or Victory Inn, St Mawes, and
occasionally at local beer festivals. Bottle-
conditioned beers are also available.

Cornish Shag (OG 1037, ABV 3.8%)

A copper-coloured session bitter.

Rossendale SIBA

🍺 Griffin Inn, 84 Hud Rake, Haslingden, Lancashire, BB4 5AF
☎ (01706) 214021 ⊕ rossendalebrewery.co.uk

⊚Formerly known as Pennine Ales, the brewery acquired the brew plant previously used by Porter Brewing Co in 2007 and is based in the cellar of the Griffin Inn in Haslingden. It produces seven regular cask ales.

Floral Dance (OG 1040, ABV 3.8%)
A pale and fruity session beer.

Hameldon Bitter (OG 1040, ABV 3.8%)
A dark traditional bitter with a dry and assertive character that develops in the finish.

Glen Top (OG 1040.5, ABV 4%)

Rossendale Ale (OG 1045, ABV 4%)

Halo Pail (OG 1045, ABV 4.5%)

Pitch Porter (OG 1050, ABV 5%)
A full-bodied, rich beer with a slightly sweet, malty start, counter balanced with sharp bitterness and a roast barley dominance.

Sunshine (OG 1055, ABV 5.3%)
A hoppy and bitter golden beer with a citrus character. The lingering finish is dry and spicy.

Rother Valley SIBA

Gate Court Farm, Station Road, Northiam, East Sussex, TN31 6QT
☎ (01797) 252922 ☎ 07798 877551
Tours by arrangement

⊠ Rother Valley began brewing in Northiam in 1993. Established and new hop varieties are grown on the farm and also sourced locally. Brewing is split between cask and an ever-increasing range of filtered bottled beers. Around 100 outlets are supplied direct and through wholesalers. A monthly seasonal ale is available.

Honeyfuzz (OG 1038, ABV 3.8%)
A pale bitter flavoured with Sussex honey, subtle but not sweet with a citrus twang on the finish.

Smild (OG 1038, ABV 3.8%)
A full-bodied, dark, creamy mild with hints of chocolate.

Level Best (OG 1040, ABV 4%) 🍺
Full-bodied tawny session bitter with a malt and fruit aroma, malty taste and a dry, hoppy finish.

Hoppers Ale (OG 1044, ABV 4.4%)
A copper-coloured ale. The initial burst of hop is followed by a pleasant caramel taste.

Boadicea (OG 1045, ABV 4.5%)
A straw-coloured beer with a delicate, fruity flavour.

Rotters

Tower Hotel, Talgarth, Powys, LD3 0BW
☎ (01874) 711253 ⊕ rottersbrewery.co.uk
Tours by arrangement

⊚Rotters brewery opened in 2010. Seasonal beers are also available: see website.

Utter Rotter (OG 1040, ABV 3.9%)

Copper-coloured session ale.

Grounds for Divorce (OG 1048, ABV 4.7%)
A dark, strong bitter with spicy bitterness and a butterscotch finish.

Round Tower (NEW)

Unit 11a, Robjohns House, Navigation Road, Chelmsford, Essex, CM2 6ND
☎ (01245) 807343 ☎ 07905 255909
⊕ roundtowerbrewery.co.uk

Round Tower began brewing in 2013, the first brewery in Chelmsford since Grays & Sons ceased brewing in 1974. Although very much a picobrewery at the moment there are plans for expansion. No regular beers are brewed at present but a regular portfolio is planned.

Rowditch

🍺 Rowditch Inn, 246 Uttoxeter New Road, Derby, DE22 3LL
☎ (01332) 343123

Rowditch began brewing in 2010 using a three-barrel plant on the premises of the Rowditch pub.

St Stephen's (OG 1038, ABV 3.6%)
A citrus flavoured, golden, bitter ale.

St Andrew's (OG 1042, ABV 3.9%)
A citrus flavoured golden bitter. St Stephen's stronger sister with less bitterness.

RPA (OG 1047, ABV 4.7%)
A well-balanced golden bitter.

Rowton SIBA

Stone House, Rowton, Telford, Shropshire, TF6 6QX
☎ 07746 290995 ⊕ rowtonbrewery.com

Rowton was established in 2008 on a four-barrel plant in a converted Victorian cow shed on the owner's farm. Barley grown on the farm is sent for malting and returned for use in the brews and water is from a borehole on site.

Bitter (OG 1040, ABV 3.9%)
A pale ale with a crisp, hoppy flavour.

Galaxy (OG 1044, ABV 4.3%)
A golden ale with a distinctive citrus taste.

Dark Side Stout (OG 1045, ABV 4.5%)

Ruddles

See Greene King

Rudgate SIBA ⊙

2 Centre Park, Marston Moor Business Park, Tockwith, York, North Yorkshire, YO26 7QF
☎ (01423) 358382 ⊕ rudgatebrewery.co.uk

⊚Rudgate began brewing in 1992 on a disused WWII airfield that was chosen because of its water suitability. Traditional methods are followed using a full mash infusion system and fermentation is achieved using its own strain of Yorkshire brewing yeast. Seasonal beers are available.

Jorvik Blonde (OG 1036, ABV 3.8%)
Blonde ale with a balanced hoppy bitterness and a crisp, fruity finish.

Viking (OG 1036, ABV 3.8%) ❧
An initially warming and malty, full-bodied beer, with hops and fruit lingering into the aftertaste.

Battleaxe (OG 1040, ABV 4.2%) ❧
A well-hopped bitter with slightly sweet initial taste and light bitterness. Complex fruit character gives a memorable aftertaste.

Ruby Mild (OG 1041, ABV 4.4%) ⏷ ❧
Nutty, rich ruby ale, stronger than usual for a mild.

Volsung (OG 1046, ABV 5%)
A premium bitter, golden-coloured with distinctive lemon on the nose.

IPA (OG 1053, ABV 5.2%)
Moderately bitter leading to a citrus, hoppy finish.

Saddleworth

🍴 **Church Inn, Church Lane, Uppermill, Oldham, Greater Manchester, OL3 6LW**
☎ (01457) 820902/872415
Tours by arrangement

☺Saddleworth started brewing in 1997 in a 120-year old brewhouse at the Church Inn. Brewery and inn are set above a valley overlooking Saddleworth Moor. Brewing capacity was significantly expanded in 2011 with a new 13-barrel plant. Seasonal beers are also available.

Mild (OG 1038, ABV 3.6%)

More (OG 1038, ABV 3.8%)

St George's Bitter (OG 1038, ABV 3.8%)

Blue Tree Bitter (OG 1040, ABV 4%)

Honey Smacker (OG 1042, ABV 4.1%)

Hop Smacker (OG 1042, ABV 4.1%)

Slap & Tickle (OG 1045, ABV 4.3%)

Shaftbender (OG 1060, ABV 5.4%)

Sadler's SIBA ◉

7 Stourbridge Road, Lye, Stourbridge, West Midlands, DY9 7DG
☎ (01384) 895230 ⊕ sadlersales.co.uk
Shop 12-11pm
Tours by arrangement

☺Third and fourth generation brewers John and Chris Sadler re-opened this historic brewery in its current location in 2004. The brewery tap house, the Windsor Castle, was built and opened next to the brewery in 2006. Around 250 outlets are supplied.

JPA (OG 1038, ABV 3.8%)
A very pale, hoppy bitter with a crisp and zesty lemon undertone.

Red House Mild (OG 1040, ABV 4%)
A Black Country dark mild with hints of chocolate and a dry finish.

Mellow Yellow (OG 1041, ABV 4.1%)
A pale ale brewed with plenty of hop and honey.

Worcester Sorcerer (OG 1043, ABV 4.3%)
Brewed with English hops and barley with hints of mint and lemon, creating a floral aroma and crisp bitterness.

Thin Ice (OG 1045, ABV 4.5%)
A pale ale. Bitter but with an orange and lemon finish.

Hop Bomb (OG 1050, ABV 5%)
A powerful India Pale Ale. Balanced malt sweetness supports the hop aroma and flavour.

Red IPA (OG 1057, ABV 5.7%)

Mud City Stout (OG 1066, ABV 6.6%)
Rich, full-bodied strong stout brewed with raw cocoa, fresh vanilla pods, oats, wheat and dark malts.

Saffron SIBA

The Cartshed, Parsonage Farm, Henham, Essex, CM22 6AN
☎ (01279) 850923 ☎ 07980 972067
⊕ saffronbrewery.co.uk
Tours by arrangement

Founded in 2005, the brewery was upgraded to a 15-barrel plant in early 2008 and re-located to a converted barn at Parsonage Farm, with a purpose-built reed bed for environmentally friendly disposal of waste products. 40 outlets are supplied direct. Seasonal and bottle-conditioned beers are also available.

Muntjac (OG 1037, ABV 3.7%)

Pledgdon Ale (OG 1037, ABV 3.7%)

Essex Pale Ale (OG 1039, ABV 3.9%)

Ramblers Tipple (OG 1040, ABV 3.9%)
A rich, copper-coloured bitter with toffee and caramel flavours.

Brewhouse Bell (OG 1041, ABV 4%)
Golden amber in colour with citrus and hop flavours balancing well for a clean, fresh finish.

Blonde (OG 1044, ABV 4.3%)
A light golden ale with a delicate balance of citrus and malty flavours, and a crisp finish.

Squires Gamble (OG 1044, ABV 4.4%)
Traditional-style copper ale, full-flavoured and hoppy with citrus and biscuit hints.

Tiddly Vicar (OG 1051, ABV 5%)
Dark copper-coloured nutty beer with a light, spicy finish.

St Andrews

Unit 4, Food Resource Base, Faraday Road, Glenrothes, KY6 2RU
☎ 07879 399441 ⊕ standrewsbrewingcompany.com

Established in 2012, St Andrews produces bottle-conditioned beers that are available across Fife and further afeld. Beers are brewed in small batches of just 750 bottles, concentrating on quality ingredients and full flavours. Seven regular beers are supplemented with monthly guest ales.

St Austell SIBA IFBB ◉

63 Trevarthian Road, St Austell, Cornwall, PL25 4BY
☎ (01726) 74444 ⊕ staustellbrewery.co.uk
Shop & Visitor Centre Mon-Fri 9am-5pm; Sat 10am-4pm
Tours by arrangement

⊗ Founded by Walter Hicks in 1851, St Austell Brewery remains family owned. Its cask beers are available in all its 170 pubs as well as in the free trade and throughout the UK. Seasonal and bottle-conditioned beers are also available: see website.

Dartmoor Best Bitter (OG 1035, ABV 3.5%) ◆
Easy-drinking, copper-coloured, light session bitter.
Smooth sweet malt, fruit and spicy hop bitterness
with some astringency flavours throughout.

Trelawny (OG 1039, ABV 3.8%) ◆
Refreshing bitter with aroma of stone fruits and
malt. Hop bitterness and some citrus develops into
caramel-malt sweetness. Bitter, dry finish.

Tribute (OG 1043, ABV 4.2%) ◆
Fruity aroma with trace of tangy ester. Dominant
citrus hop bitterness with elderflower notes but
little malt, ending refreshingly bitter.

Proper Job (OG 1046, ABV 4.5%) 🍾 ◆
Resinous hop aroma golden ale. Copious citrus
fruits with bitterness leading to crisp hop bitter and
fruity finish, becoming dry.

**Hicks Special Draught (HSD)
(OG 1052, ABV 5%)** ◆
Rich malt and ripe fruit aroma of this tawny
premium ale lead into an intense malt flavour
balanced by sweetness and bitterness which last
into the long finish.

St George's SIBA

**The Old Bakery, Bush Lane, Callow End,
Worcestershire, WR2 4TF**
☎ (01905) 831316 ⊕ stgeorgesbrewery.co.uk
Tours by arrangement

The brewery was established in 1998 in old village
bakery premises and acquired in 2006 by Duncan
Ironmonger. The brewery supplies local freehouses
and wholesalers for a wider distribution. At least
two monthly specials are usually available.

Crusade (OG 1038, ABV 3.8%)
Straw-coloured and noticeably hoppy, a crisp and
refreshing pale ale.

Friar Tuck (OG 1040, ABV 4%)
A golden bitter with a citrus character.

Roundel (OG 1042, ABV 4.2%)
Traditional chestnut ale with a smooth fruity start
giving way to a resinous hop finish.

Charger (OG 1046, ABV 4.6%)
A light golden beer with hops creating a citrus blast
and a hint of grapefruit.

Dragons Blood (OG 1048, ABV 4.8%)
Ruby red-coloured beer with a hint of chocolate.
Hops give an earthy and slightly spicy aroma.

St Ives

See Keltek

St Peter's SIBA 👁

**St Peter's Hall, St Peter South Elmham, Suffolk,
NR35 1NQ**
☎ (01986) 782322 ⊕ stpetersbrewery.co.uk
Shop Mon-Fri 9am-5pm; Sat & Sun 11am-4pm
(may close at weekends)
Tours by arrangement

⊠ St Peter's brewery is based adjacent to a
moated medieval hall near Bungay, Suffolk.
Established in 1996 it concentrates in the main on
bottled beer/keg (85% of capacity) but has a
rapidly increasing cask market. Two pubs are
owned. 45% of production is exported to 32
countries worldwide. Seasonal beers are also
available.

Best Bitter (OG 1038, ABV 3.7%) ◆
A complex but well-balanced hoppy brew. A gentle
hop nose introduces a singular hoppiness with
supporting malt notes and underlying bitterness.
Other flavours fade to leave a long, dry, hoppy
finish.

Mild (OG 1037, ABV 3.7%) ◆
Heady aroma of caramelised blackberries and black
toffee. Excellent complex flavours with caramel,
blackberries, hops and an astringent bitterness.
Long, sustained finish with a roast coffee
bitterness; increasingly dry.

Organic Best (OG 1041, ABV 4.1%) ◆
A very dry and bitter beer with a growing
astringency. Pale brown in colour, it has a gentle
hop aroma which makes the definitive bitterness
surprising. One for the committed.

Ruby Red (OG 1043, ABV 4.3%)
A tawny red ale with subtle malt undertones and a
distinctive spicy hop aroma.

Organic Ale (OG 1045, ABV 4.5%) ◆
A rich toffee apple aroma and a smooth grainy feel.
Malt and caramel initially match the dry hoppy
bitterness. As the flavours mature, liquorice
dryness develops. Full-bodied.

Golden Ale (OG 1047, ABV 4.7%) ◆
Amber-coloured, full-bodied, robust ale. A strong
hop bouquet leads to a mix of malt and hops
combined with a dry, fruity hoppiness. The malt
quickly subsides, leaving creamy bitterness.

Grapefruit Beer (OG 1047, ABV 4.7%) ◆
With a very strong aroma and taste of grapefruit,
this refreshing beer is exactly what it says on the
tin. A superb example of a fruit beer.

IPA (OG 1055, ABV 5.5%)
A full-bodied, highly-hopped pale ale with a zesty
character.

Salamander SIBA

**22 Harry Street, Dudley Hill, Bradford, West Yorkshire,
BD4 9PH**
☎ (01274) 652323 ⊕ salamanderbrewing.co.uk
Tours by arrangement

⊠ Salamander first brewed in 2000 in a former
pork pie factory. An expansion in 2004 increased
capacity to 40 barrels per week. Direct deliveries
are made to about 100 outlets in Cumbria,
Lancashire, North and East Yorkshire, Manchester
and Derbyshire.

Axolotl (OG 1038, ABV 3.9%)

Mudpuppy (OG 1042, ABV 4.2%) ◆
A well-balanced, copper-coloured best bitter with a
fruity, hoppy nose and a bitter finish.

Golden Salamander (OG 1045, ABV 4.5%) ◆
Citrus hops characterise the aroma and taste of this
golden premium bitter, which has malt undertones
throughout. The aftertaste is dry, hoppy and bitter.

Salisbury SIBA

**Unit 1, Oakley Business Park, Wylye Valley, Dinton,
Salisbury, Wiltshire, SP3 5EU**
☎ (01722) 716440 ⊕ salisburybrewery.com

THE BREWERIES

Salisbury Brewery was established in late 2010 at Dinton in the ancient Wylye Valley near Salisbury, to supply the free trade with traditional cask and bottled beer. The company brew using local malt and water.

Somer (ABV 3.9%)
A light golden, fruity beer, complemented by a citrus hop note and smooth finish.

English Ale (ABV 4.1%)
A traditional best bitter with malt notes and a subtle depth of hop character.

Salopian SIBA ⟨◉⟩

67 Mytton Oak Road, Shrewsbury, Shropshire, SY3 8UQ
☎ (01743) 248414 ⊕ salopianbrewery.co.uk
Shop Mon-Fri 9am-4pm
Tours by arrangement

⊚The brewery was established in 1995 in an old dairy on the outskirts of Shrewsbury and, having grown steadily, now produces more than 145 barrels a week. Salopian also brews under the Blackwater Brewery name: see website.

Shropshire Gold (OG 1037, ABV 3.8%) ⬚
A light, copper-coloured ale with an unusual blend of body and dryness.

Oracle (OG 1040, ABV 4%) ▮
A crisp golden ale with a striking hop profile. Dry and refreshing with a long-balanced aromatic finish.

Darwin's Origin (OG 1042, ABV 4.3%)
A light copper ale with a striking hop profile which is balanced by a refined malt finish.

Hop Twister (OG 1044, ABV 4.5%) ⬚
A premium bitter with a citrus flavour and complex hop finish. Refreshing and crisp.

Golden Thread (OG 1048, ABV 5%) ⬚ ▮
A bright gold ale. Strong and quite bitter but well-balanced.

Saltaire SIBA ⟨◉⟩

Unit 6, County Works, Dockfield Road, Shipley, West Yorkshire, BD17 7AR
☎ (01274) 594959 ⊕ saltairebrewery.co.uk
Tours by arrangement

⊚Launched in 2006, Saltaire is an award-winning brewery based in a former Victorian power station. A mezzanine bar gives visitors views of the brewing plant and the chance to taste the beers. More than 300 pubs are supplied across West Yorkshire and the north of England.

Blonde (OG 1040, ABV 4%) ◥
Thirst quenching and quaffable, this straw-coloured beer is slightly sweet and well rounded with fruit, malt and hops in the taste and a fruity hoppy finish.

Elderflower Blonde (OG 1040, ABV 4%) ◥
An easy drinking, smooth, golden-coloured ale with a subtle elderflower aroma leading to a pleasant elderflower fruit taste and a long refreshing finish.

Raspberry Blonde (OG 1040, ABV 4%)
Blonde ale infused with a hint of raspberries.

Cascade Pale Ale (OG 1047, ABV 4.8%) ◥

A well balanced golden bitter with smooth mouth feel, floral hop aromas and pronounced bitterness, culminating in a long dry finish and dry aftertaste.

Triple Chocoholic (OG 1048, ABV 4.8%) ▮ ◥
A creamy, dark brown, roast, chocolate stout with a dry bitter finish and a rich chocolate aroma.

Sambrook's SIBA ⟨◉⟩

Units 1-3, Yelverton Road, Battersea, London, SW11 3QG
☎ (020) 7228 0598 ⊕ sambrooksbrewery.co.uk
Shop Mon-Fri 10am-6pm; Sat 10am-1pm
Tours by arrangement

⊠ Sambrook's was founded by Duncan Sambrook and David Welsh in 2008, supplying its award-winning ales throughout London. The brewery bar hosts regular events and is open for members on the first Friday of every month. Seasonal beers are also available.

Wandle (OG 1038, ABV 3.8%) ◥
A touch of dryness balances the rounded sweetish malt flavour of this fruity, quaffable pale brown bitter. Some peach and citrus notes and hops are noticeable when fresh.

Pumphouse Pale Ale (OG 1041, ABV 4.2%) ◥
A refreshing golden beer with a mellow hint of citrus on the nose becoming more pronounced on the palate and lingering into the finish with a bitterness that develops on drinking.

Junction (OG 1045, ABV 4.5%) ◥
Soft fruit and figs on the nose of this well balanced best bitter. The fruit on the palate is a little more citrusy plus creamy toffee. Sweetish dry aftertaste.

Powerhouse Porter (OG 1050, ABV 4.9%) ◥
Dark brown porter with a pleasant roasted malt nose with some sultana and blackcurrant character. The flavour is of caramelised fruit, treacle and a hint of citrus. Dry roasted finish.

Sandstone SIBA

Unit 5, Wrexham Enterprise Park, Preston Road, off Ash Road, North Wrexham Industrial Estate, Wrexham, LL13 9JT
☎ 07851 001118 ⊕ sandstonebrewery.co.uk
Tours by arrangement

⊚Sandstone Brewery was established in 2008 using a four-barrel plant. More than 60 outlets in North Wales and North West England are supplied. In 2012 a new head brewer saw the ale portfolio expanded.

Edge (OG 1039, ABV 3.8%) ◥
A satisfying session ale, this pale, dry, bitter beer has a full mouthfeel and a lingering hoppy finish that belies its modest strength.

Onyx (OG 1040, ABV 4%)

Post Mistress (OG 1046, ABV 4.4%) ⬚ ◥
A full-bodied, smooth premium bitter, ruby-red in colour, with a rich, mellow taste. A good combination of malt, hops and fruit in aroma and initial taste leading to a lasting satisfying finish.

Sawbridgeworth SIBA

▤ **81 London Road, Sawbridgeworth, Hertfordshire, CM21 9JJ**
☎ (01279) 722313 ⊕ thegatepub.net

Tours by arrangement

☒ Set up in 2000 by owners Tom and Gary Barnett, the brewery is situated behind the Gate Inn. Tom is a former professional footballer whose clubs included Crystal Palace. Brewing is carried out by ex-Nethergate brewer Bob Renvoise. Special or one-off beers are regularly brewed.

Manor Mild (OG 1034, ABV 3.4%)

IPA (OG 1038, ABV 3.8%)

Selhurst Park Flyer (OG 1038, ABV 3.8%)

Gold (OG 1040, ABV 4%)

Is It Yourself (OG 1042, ABV 4.2%)

Dragon's Blood (OG 1043, ABV 4.3%)

Malt Shovel Porter (OG 1060, ABV 6%)

Saxon City

Glebe Farm Industrial Estate, Stoke Edith, Hereford, HR1 4HG
☎ (01432) 890688 ⊕ herefordcasks.co.uk

☺Chris Strange diversified into brewing in 2010 on a 6-barrel plant installed in a vacant unit adjoining his cask factory. Brewing is currently suspended.

Scarborough SIBA

Unit 1b, Stadium Works, Barry's Lane, Scarborough, North Yorkshire, YO12 4HA
☎ (01723) 367506 ☎ 07905 241495
⊕ scarboroughbrewery.co.uk

Scarborough Brewery was established in 2010 using a one-barrel plant. In 2011 commercial brewing began using a 10-barrel plant from Wold Top Brewery. Beers can be found at its brewery tap, Valley Bar in Scarborough, and nationwide via wholesalers. One-off and seasonal beers are also available.

Cascades (ABV 4.1%)

Blonde (ABV 4.2%)

IPA (ABV 4.4%)

Stout (ABV 4.6%)

Strong Gold (ABV 5.8%)

Scottish Borders SIBA

Lanton Mill, Jedburgh, TD8 6ST
☎ (01835) 830673 ⊕ scottishbordersbrewery.com

Scottish Borders is Scotland's only plough-to-pint brewery, and started brewing in 2011 using barley from its own farm estate.

Wee Beastie (OG 1037, ABV 3.6%)
A hint of dark malt and an unusual mash technique create an extremely light session ale with real body and a surprisingly rich taste.

Foxy Blonde (OG 1037.5, ABV 3.8%)
Golden ale bursting with citrus and floral flavours.

Game Bird (OG 1039.5, ABV 4%)
An amber ale with a balance of malty sweetness and late summer fruit, and a long, easy finish.

Holy Cow (OG 1041, ABV 4.2%)
Hints of dark malt combine with a long, floral finish.

Dark Horse (OG 1044, ABV 4.5%)
A classic dark ale that has overtones of coffee and chocolate, with a spicy finish.

Settle (NEW)

Unit 8a, The Sidings, Settle, North Yorkshire, BD24 9RP
☎ (01729) 824936 ⊕ settlebrewery.co.uk
Tours by arrangement

Settle Brewery is located in a small industrial unit adjacent to Settle railway station. Brewing started in 2013 using a new 12-barrel Johnsons kit. Brewer Ian Simkins originally brewed at Nine Standards Brewery in Kirkby Stephen. Outlets across Cumbria, Yorkshire and Lancashire are supplied.

Signal Light (OG 1035, ABV 3.4%)
A delicate straw-coloured beer with a subtle blend of fruit and spice flavours and citrus overtones.

Signal Main Line (OG 1036, ABV 3.6%)
A refreshing, delicately fruity golden IPA style beer with a little bit of sweetness.

Contract brewed for Nine Standards Brewery:

Original Standard (OG 1037, ABV 3.7%)
A dark amber bitter with a fruity, spicy nose.

Gold Standard (OG 1040, ABV 4.1%)
A flavoursome golden ale with a hint of blackcurrant.

Silver Standard (OG 1042, ABV 4.3%)
A classic pale ale with a strong, hoppy aroma.

Double Standard (OG 1048, ABV 4.7%)
A robust porter with caramel and coffee notes and smoky undertones.

Royal Standard (OG 1052, ABV 5.5%)
A fruity golden ale flavoured with five different hop varieties.

Severn Vale SIBA ◉

Woodend Lane, Cam, Dursley, Gloucestershire, GL11 5HS
☎ (01453) 547550 ☎ 07971 640244
⊕ severnvalebrewing.co.uk
Shop: Please ring first
Tours by arrangement

☒ Severn Vale started brewing in 2005 in an old milking parlour using a new five-barrel plant. Warminster malted barley is used and mainly Herefordshire hops. Around 50 outlets are supplied. Seasonal beers are also available.

Session (OG 1035, ABV 3.4%)
A classic bitter with a full-bodied malty flavour and a bitter, hoppy finish that lingers on the palate.

Vale Ale (OG 1039, ABV 3.8%)
A rich amber beer with full-bodied malt flavours and complex nose and taste.

Dursley Steam Bitter (OG 1043, ABV 4.2%)
Golden ale full of flowery hop flavours.

Luverley Jub'lee (OG 1043, ABV 4.2%)
A well-balanced golden best bitter with bold fruity hops in the finish.

Severn Sins (OG 1053, ABV 5.2%)
A jet-black stout with a dry roast malt flavour and hints of chocolate and liquorice.

Shalford SIBA

c/o PO Box 10411, Braintree, Essex, CM7 5WP
☎ (01371) 850925 ☎ 07749 658512
⊕ shalfordbrewery.co.uk

Shalford began brewing in 2007 on a five-barrel plant at Hyde Farm in the Pant Valley in Essex. More than 50 outlets are supplied direct. Bottle-conditioned beers are available.

1319 Mild (OG 1037, ABV 3.7%)
Roast malt and chocolate sweetness with a slight bitter finish.

Barnfield Bitter (OG 1038, ABV 3.8%) ◆
Pale-coloured but full-flavoured, this is a traditional, hoppy bitter rather than a golden ale. Malt persists throughout, with bitterness becoming more dominant towards the end.

Braintree Market Ale (OG 1040, ABV 4%)
Traditional, easy-drinking session ale with a hoppy, lingering, dry finish.

Levelly Gold (OG 1040, ABV 4%)
Golden, summery bitter with a pleasant finish.

Stoneley Bitter (OG 1042, ABV 4.2%) ◆
Dark amber session beer whose vivid hop character is supported by a juicy, malty body. A dry finish makes this beer very drinkable.

Hyde Bitter (OG 1047, ABV 4.7%) ◆
Stronger version of Barnfield, with a similar but more assertive character.

Rotten End (OG 1065, ABV 6.5%)
Strong beer with slightly sweet, nutty undertones and a bitter edge to finish.

Shamblemoose (NEW)

c/o 21 Southey Street, Penge, London, SE20 7JD
☎ (01428) 652765 ⊕ shamblemoose.co.uk

Shamblemoose began brewing in 2013 using spare capacity at Late Knights Brewery (qv). It was set up by husband and wife team Lera and Matthew O'Sullivan. Seasonal beers are also available.

Wyoming #7 Pale Ale (ARV 4%)

#10 Smoked Porter (ABV 5.2%)

#4 American Brown Ale (ABV 5.3%)

Shardlow

The Old Brewery Stables, British Waterways Yard, Cavendish Bridge, Leicestershire, DE72 2HL
☎ (01332) 799188 ✉ nev@shardlowbrewery.co.uk
Tours by arrangement

☺On a site associated with brewing since 1819, Shardlow delivers to more than 100 outlets throughout the East Midlands and is also one of the largest UK cider distributors. Reverend Eaton is named after a scion of the Eaton brewing family, Rector of Shardlow for 40 years. The brewery tap is the Blue Bell Inn at Melbourne, Derbyshire. Seasonal, bottle-conditioned beers and cask-conditioned five-litre canned beer are also available. Prolific supplier of beers to local beer festivals.

Chancellors Revenge (OG 1036, ABV 3.6%)
A light-coloured, refreshing, full-flavoured and well-hopped session bitter.

Cavendish Dark (OG 1037, ABV 3.7%)
A mild, well-balanced beer with a hoppy aftertaste.

Golden Hop (OG 1041, ABV 4.1%)
A golden, sweet tasting beer.

Kiln House (OG 1041, ABV 4.1%)
A refreshing golden ale with a lingering bitter finish.

Narrow Boat (OG 1043, ABV 4.3%)
A pale amber bitter, with a short, crisp hoppy aftertaste.

Cavendish Bridge (OG 1045, ABV 4.5%)
Pale amber premium bitter. Refreshing, clean and fruity with a pleasing bitter finish.

Cavendish Gold (OG 1045, ABV 4.5%)
Pale gold, bright and clean tasting. A full-bodied ale with pronounced bitterness and complexity.

Reverend Eaton (OG 1045, ABV 4.5%)
A smooth, medium-strong bitter, full of malt and hop flavours with a sweet aftertaste.

Mayfly (OG 1048, ABV 4.8%)
Fruit notes predominate together with a pronounced malty aroma. Easy-drinking but strong.

Five Bells (OG 1050, ABV 5%)
Dark rich ruby coloured ale, powerful and bittersweet to the palate. Coffee notes complete the profile.

Whistlestop (OG 1050, ABV 5%)
A smooth and surprisingly strong pale beer.

Sharp's ◉

Pityme Business Centre, Rock, Cornwall, PL27 6NU
☎ (01208) 862121 ⊕ sharpsbrewery.co.uk
Shop Mon-Fri 9am-5pm

⊠ Part of Molson Coors. Sharp's was bought by Molson Coors in 2011. The brewery was founded in 1994 and within 15 years had grown from producing 1,500 barrels a year to 60,000. Investment from Molson Coors has brought capacity up to 200,000 barrels per year. The company delivers beer to more than 1,200 outlets across the south of England. Molson Coors has stressed that it will maintain production in Cornwall. Seasonal beer: see website. Bottle-conditioned beer is also available.

Cornish Coaster (OG 1035.2, ABV 3.6%) ◆
Refreshing light session bitter with delicate fruit aroma. Gentle balance of hops, fruit, malt and bitterness in the mouth. Fruit persists in the finish with a little bitterness and dryness.

Doom Bar (OG 1038.5, ABV 4%) ◆
Faint aroma of resinous hops. Refreshing fruity bitterness perfectly balanced by sweet malt throughout to a peppery, dry finish.

Own (OG 1042.5, ABV 4.4%) ◆
Rich, tawny ale presenting gentle malt and fruit to the nose. The flavour develops from dominant sweet malt through to hoppy bitterness, both of which linger on in the finish.

Special (OG 1048.5, ABV 5%) ◆
Deep golden brown with a fresh hop aroma. Dry malt and hops in the mouth; the finish is malty but becomes dry and hoppy.

Shed (NEW)

2218 Stratford Road, Hockley Heath, Solihull, West Midlands, B94 6NU

☎ 07910 004041 ✉ perryclarke@aol.com

Shed began brewing in 2011 mainly producing bottle-conditioned beers (around 200 bottles per week). Cask-conditioned beer is produced for specific outlets. Bottled beers are suitable for vegetarians and vegans.

Session Bitter (OG 1039, ABV 3.8%)
A copper-coloured session bitter with a long, hoppy taste.

Gold (OG 1048, ABV 5%)
A golden beer with a smooth, easy taste.

Shed Ales

Broadfields, Pewsey, Wiltshire, SN9 5DT
☎ (01672) 564533 ☎ 07769 812643
⊕ shed-ales.com

Shed Ales was launched in 2012 operating using a one-barrel plant in a fully converted garden shed. The brewery currently produces two core ales along with several seasonal and bespoke ales, available at selected local outlets and beer festivals.

Shed Some Light (OG 1041, ABV 3.8%)
A refreshing blonde beer with a light, earthy hop aroma and flavour.

Forkin' Best (OG 1042, ABV 4.1%)
A dark amber traditional English ale, with a toffee and spicy orange aroma, and a clean bittersweet taste.

Pail Ale (OG 1045, ABV 4.3%)
An Anglo-American pale ale with a floral aroma. A good balance of lightly roasted malt and hops make it easy-drinking with a pleasantly dry finish.

Sheelin (NEW)

178 Derrylin Road, Bellanaleck, Co Fermanagh, BT92 2BA
☎ 07730 432232 ⊕ sheelin.com

Sheelin was established by brewer and chemist Dr George Cathcart in 2013. Beer is mainly available in bottles.

Sheffield SIBA

Unit 111, JC Albyn Complex, Burton Road, Sheffield, South Yorkshire, S3 8BT
☎ (0114) 272 7256 ⊕ sheffieldbrewery.com
Tours by arrangement

☺Sheffield began brewing in 2007 in the former Blanco polish works using a 10-barrel plant. The brewery operates on the tower principal in premises which are also used as a venue for corporate or social gatherings. More than 50 outlets are supplied direct.

Crucible Best (OG 1038, ABV 3.8%)
A complex traditional bitter.

Five Rivers (OG 1038, ABV 3.8%)
An easy-drinking, straw-coloured session ale with a hoppy aroma.

Blanco Blonde (OG 1042, ABV 4.2%)
A continental lager-style beer.

Seven Hills (OG 1041, ABV 4.2%)
A premium bitter.

Porter (OG 1045, ABV 4.4%)
A rich, chocolaty, malty porter with caramel flavours.

Shepherd Neame IFBB ◉

17 Court Street, Faversham, Kent, ME13 7AX
☎ (01795) 532106 ⊕ shepherd-neame.co.uk
Shop Mon-Sat 10.30am-4.30pm (Sun Apr-Oct 10.30am-1pm)
Regular tours, booking recommended

⊗ Shepherd Neame traces its history back to 1698, making it the oldest continuous brewer in the country, though brewing probably began even earlier. The same water source is still used today and 1914 oak mash tuns are still operational. The company has 345 tied houses in the South East, nearly all selling cask ale. More than 2,000 other outlets are also supplied. The cask beers are made with Kentish barley and water from their own artesian well. In 2007 a pilot brewery was installed within the brewery to brew speciality ales in small quantities. Over 15 seasonal beers are brewed annually and a bottle-conditioned beer is available.

Master Brew Bitter (OG 1032, ABV 3.7%) ◗
A distinctive bitter, mid-brown in colour, with a hoppy aroma. Well-balanced, with a nicely aggressive bitter taste from its hops, it leaves a hoppy/bitter finish, tinged with sweetness.

Whitstable Bay Pale Ale (OG 1038, ABV 3.9%)
Pale gold in colour with a malty sweetness balanced by pine and citrus.

Kent's Best (OG 1036, ABV 4.1%)
A mellow bitter which merges the biscuity sweetness of English malt with the fruity, floral bitterness of locally-grown hops.

Spitfire Premium Ale (OG 1036, ABV 4.2%)
Well-balanced bitter with hints of marmalade, red grapes and pepper alongside warm, mellow malts, with a fruity finish.

Bishops Finger (OG 1046, ABV 5%)
A strong ale with a complex hop aroma reminiscent of lemons, oranges and bananas, combined with malt, molasses and toffee.

Sherborne

▤ 257 Westbury, Sherborne, Dorset, DT9 3EH
☎ (01935) 812094 ⊕ sherbornebrewery.co.uk

☺Sherborne Brewery started in 2005 on a 2.5-barrel plant. It moved in 2006 to new premises at the rear of the brewery's pub, Docherty's Bar. The majority of the beer is bottled and there are plans to sell beer online.

257 (OG 1039, ABV 3.9%) ◗
Light coloured best bitter with fruit-hop aromas and flavour with burnt astringent undertones.

Cheap Street (OG 1044, ABV 4.4%)
Light coloured best bitter with fruit-hop aromas and flavour with astringent undertones.

Sherfield Village SIBA

Goddards Farm, Goddards Lane, Sherfield on Loddon, Hampshire, RG27 0EL
☎ 07906 060429 ⊕ sherfieldvillagebrewery.co.uk

Sherfield Village started brewing in 2011 using a five-barrel plant. It makes extensive use of New World hops, particularly those from New Zealand.

Dry-hopped versions of single-hop beers are usually available.

Threesome (OG 1030, ABV 3%)

SOLO Single Hop (OG 1042, ABV 4.3%)

SOLO Quintessential (OG 1043, ABV 4.4%)

Pioneer Stout (OG 1050, ABV 5%)

SOLO IPA (OG 1051, ABV 5.5%)

Shiny (NEW) SIBA

≣ Furnace Inn, 9 Duke Street, Derby, DE1 3BX
☎ (01332) 385981

After being made redundant, brewer Pedro Menon bought the Furnace Inn and installed a purpose-built 5.5-barrel brewery at the rear. Brewing began in 2012. Beers are available at the Furnace Inn, but wider distribution is planned.

New World (OG 1037, ABV 3.7%)
Light and hoppy, this beer punches above its strength.

Launch Pad (OG 1038, ABV 3.8%)

Obsidian (OG 1040, ABV 4%)
A dark mild with a sweet malt character and hints of treacle and coffee.

Golden Man (OG 1041, ABV 4.1%)
Golden ale with a delicate floral aroma.

4 Wood (OG 1045, ABV 4.5%)
Traditional, well-balanced, light chestnut ale with a delicate hop finish.

Reflection IPA (OG 1051, ABV 5.1%)
A strong, well-hopped, citrus IPA.

Ship Inn

≣ Ship Inn, Newton Square, Low Newton by the Sea, Northumberland, NE66 3EL
☎ (01665) 576262 ⊕ shipinnnewton.co.uk

Brewing commenced in 2008 on a 2.5-barrel plant, and the brewery now produces 7.5 barrels per week. All regular beers are brewed in constant rotation but are only available on the premises. Seasonal and bottle-conditioned beers are also available. A special beer (4.2% ABV) is brewed for every 100 brews.

Sandcastles at Dawn (ABV 3.8%)
A pale session beer, light and crisp with a delicate floral finish.

Sea Coal (ABV 4%)
A dark wheat beer with mild coffee and bittersweet chocolate flavours and a berry fruit finish.

Sea Wheat (ABV 4%)
A pale, crisp, sharp English-style wheat beer with a citrus burst and strong grapefruit flavours.

Ship Hop Ale (ABV 4.2%)
A light copper-coloured ale; dry with hints of orange and marmalade. Well-balanced and rounded.

Dolly Daydream (ABV 4.3%)
A classic premium bitter with a slight toffee edge and subtle vine fruit finish.

Shires

≣ All Nations Brewhouse, 20 Coalport Road, Madeley, Shropshire, TF7 5DP
☎ 07977 900212 ⊕ shiresbrewery.co.uk

Shires Brewery was launched in 2009 and is based at the historic All Nations Brewhouse in Madeley near Telford. Mike Handley supervises the 10-barrel plant that supplies the All Nations tap house next door as well as other trade outlets. Seasonal beers: see website.

Coalport Mild (OG 1034, ABV 3.5%)
Traditional dark mild, full of nutty flavour from dark malts, and full-bodied for its strength.

Best Bitter (OG 1039, ABV 3.8%)
Pale in colour with fruity undertones and a hint of citrus. Sold in the All Nations as Dabley Ale.

Ginger Cob (OG 1043, ABV 4.2%)
Straw-coloured single-hop bitter with a hint of fresh ginger.

OBJ (Oh Be Joyful!) (OG 1043, ABV 4.2%) ◣
A light and sweet bitter; delicate flavour belies the strength.

Shropshire Pride (OG 1045, ABV 4.5%)
A mid-coloured bitter, very full-bodied and malty with a pleasant bittersweet balance.

SPA (OG 1045, ABV 4.6%)
IPA-style beer with a hoppy bitter finish.

Severn Gorgeous (OG 1048, ABV 4.8%)
A light-bodied ale with full hop bitterness accompanying pine and citrus aromas.

Dabley Gold (OG 1050, ABV 5%)
The big brother of Dabley Ale, produced from the same recipe but brewed to a higher gravity giving a sweeter, fuller flavour.

Shoes SIBA

≣ Three Horseshoes Inn, Norton Canon, Hereford, HR4 7BH
☎ (01544) 318375
Tours by arrangement

Landlord Frank Goodwin was a keen home brewer who decided in 1994 to brew on a commercial basis for his pub. The beers are brewed from malt extract and are normally only available at the Three Horseshoes. Each September Canon Bitter is brewed with green hops fresh from the harvest. All beers are available bottle-conditioned.

Norton Ale (OG 1038, ABV 3.6%)

Canon Bitter (OG 1040, ABV 4.1%)

Peploe's Tipple (OG 1060, ABV 6%)

Farrier's Ale (OG 1114, ABV 15%)

Shortts Farm (NEW) SIBA

Shortts Farm, Thorndon, Suffolk, IP23 7LS
☎ 07900 268100 ⊕ shorttsfarmbrewery.com

Shortts Farm began brewing in 2012 using a five-barrel plant.

Strummer (ABV 3.8%)
An amber-coloured session bitter. Light, hoppy and easy-drinking with a rich malt character and mellow hints of citrus to finish.

Skiffle (ABV 4.5%)

A full-flavoured premium ale, full-bodied with complex, rich, malty flavours and a clean, dry bitter finish.

Shotover SIBA

Coopers Yard, Manor Farm Road, Horspath, Oxfordshire, UX33 1SD
☎ (01865) 876770 ☎ 07801 570444
⊕ shotoverbrewing.com
Shop: please ring or email first
Tours by arrangement

A family-owned and -run brewery four miles from Oxford city centre. It began brewing in 2009 and now supplies 18 outlets direct. Bottle-conditioned beers are available, suitable for vegetarians and vegans. Cask ale suitable for vegetarians can also be supplied.

Prospect (OG 1040, ABV 3.7%)
A pale copper, hoppy session bitter with a big mouthfeel and striking dry hoppiness.

Scholar (OG 1046, ABV 4.5%)
A copper-coloured bitter combining a silky malt base with a mixture of oranges, grapefruit and spiciness. It delivers a satisfying bitter finish.

Shottle Farm SIBA

School House Farm, Lodge Lane, Shottle, Derbyshire, DE56 2DS
☎ (01773) 550056 ⊕ shottlefarmbrewery.co.uk

Based on a farm in Shottle, which is part of the Chatsworth Estate, Shottle Farm brewery has brewed cask ales and bottle-conditioned beers since 2011 using its own natural spring water and local honey. The brewery taps are the Bulls Head, Belper Lane End and the George & Dragon, Belper.

Shottlecock (OG 1034.9, ABV 3.6%)
A single malt beer brewed with local honey. Created from an old Victorian recipe for breakfast beer, in the summer the honey is replaced with elderflower syrup.

Black Peggy (OG 1037.8, ABV 3.9%)
An oatmeal stout brewed using chocolate malt and oatmeal, with pleasant hints of liquorice.

Shottle Pale Ale (SPA) (OG 1037.8, ABV 4%)
Mid-bodied pale ale with a soft hoppy hit and a little taste of citrus tangerine.

8/- (OG 1038.8, ABV 4.1%)
Rich and malty dark beer. Full-bodied aftertaste with undertones of treacle and caramel.

Shottle Gold (OG 1041.7, ABV 4.3%)
Floral aroma with a hint of lemon and a crisp and a clean white head.

Dilks (OG 1048.4, ABV 5%)
Slightly sweet, smooth, mature beer with a hint of citrus.

Shugborough SIBA

Shugborough Estate, Milford, Staffordshire, ST17 0XB
☎ (01782) 823447 ⊕ shugborough.org.uk
Tours by arrangement

Brewing in the original brewhouse at Shugborough, home of the Earls of Lichfield, restarted in 1990 but a lack of expertise led to the brewery being a static museum piece until Titanic

Brewery of Stoke-on-Trent (qv) began helping in 1996.

Miladys Fancy (OG 1048, ABV 4.6%)

Lordships Own (OG 1052, ABV 5%)

Silhill SIBA

Office: 3 Bramshall Drive, Dorridge, West Midlands, B93 8TG
☎ 07977 444564 ⊕ silhillbrewery.co.uk

Silhill began brewing in 2010. Beers are contract brewed elsewhere by an unnamed brewery while premises are sought in Solihull. Seasonal beers are also available.

Gold Star (OG 1039, ABV 3.9%)

Yankee Flag (OG 1039, ABV 3.9%)

Silverstone

Kingshill Farm, Syresham, nr Silverstone, Northamptonshire, NN13 5TH
☎ (01280) 850629
⊕ silverstonebrewingcompany.com
Tours by arrangement

The brewery, which is located near the celebrated motor racing circuit, opened in 2008. In keeping with its motor racing theme, the brewery is the proud sponsor of Formula V10. 60 outlets are supplied direct. Seasonal and bottle-conditioned beers are also available.

Pitstop Bitter (OG 1038, ABV 3.8%)

Pole Position (ABV 4.1%)

Chequered Flag (OG 1043, ABV 4.5%)

Simpsons (NEW)

White Swan, Eardisland, Herefordshire, HR6 9BD
☎ (01544) 388123

Tim Simpson acquired the White Swan in 2011 and set up the brewery at the rear of the pub in 2013. His son Doug is training as the brewer. Beers are currently served in the White Swan, and locally to the free trade.

Golden Cockerel (OG 1037, ABV 3.7%)
A golden session ale.

Red Leg (OG 1043, ABV 4.3%)
A ruby-coloured premium bitter.

Black Grouse (OG 1046, ABV 4.6%)
An oatmeal stout.

Sinclair

See Orkney

Siren Craft (NEW)

Unit 1, Hogwood Industrial Estate, Weller Drive, Finchampstead, Berkshire, RG40 4QZ
☎ (0118) 973 0929 ⊕ sirencraftbrew.com

Siren is a 40-barrel brewery, established in 2013. Four American-style beers are produced regularly, with seasonal beers planned. The brewery is equipped with an external wort boiler and five 70hl fermenters.

**Undercurrent Oatmeal Pale Ale
(OG 1042, ABV 4.5%)**
A pale ale with spicy, grassy aromas and a taste of grapefruit and apricot.

Soundwave IPA (OG 1056, ABV 5.6%)
A west coast-style American IPA: golden, immensely hoppy and with grapefruit, peach and mango flavours.

Liquid Mistress Red IPA (OG 1061, ABV 5.8%)
A west coast-style American red ale: burnt raisins and crackers are balanced by a citrus grapefruit and peach spark.

**Broken Dream Breakfast Stout
(OG 1072, ABV 6.5%)**
A breakfast stout with a gentle touch of smoke, coffee and chocolate. Deep and complex.

Six Bells SIBA

 Church Street, Bishop's Castle, SY9 5AA
☎ (01588) 638930 ⊕ sixbellsbrewery.co.uk
Tours by arrangement

The Six Bells brewery started in 1997 with a five-barrel plant. It supplies customers both within Shropshire and over the border in Wales. A new 12-barrel plant opened in 2010. In addition to the three core beers, an ale of the month is also brewed.

Big Nev's (OG 1037, ABV 3.8%)
A pale, fairly hoppy bitter.

Ow Do! (OG 1040, ABV 4%)
A refreshing, easy-drinking ale with a spicy, fruity character.

Cloud Nine (OG 1043, ABV 4.2%)
Pale amber-coloured ale with a slight citrus finish.

Six° North (NEW)

Cowgate, Stonehaven, AB39 2LD
☎ 07840 678243 ✉ brewbob@icloud.com

Six° North began brewing in 2013 using a 20-hectolitre plant, brewing Belgian-style beers. An own-branded Belgian beer bar is situated in Aberdeen.

Prototype (ABV 4.2%)

Meas (ABV 4.6%)

66 IBU (ABV 6.6%)

Sixpenny SIBA

The Dairy Building, Manor Farm, Sixpenny Handley, Dorset, SP5 5NU
☎ (01725) 762006 ☎ 07956 531618
⊕ sixpennybrewery.co.uk
Shop Wed & Thu 4.30-6pm; Fri 4-6.30pm; Sat 11.30am-1pm
Tours by arrangement

Established in 2007, Sixpenny relocated to Dorset from Surrey in 2009 and now operates from a 20-barrel brewery close to the village of Sixpenny Handley, with its own retail outlet the Sixpenny Tap adjacent. Seasonal beers: see website.

6D Best Bitter (OG 1042, ABV 3.8%)
A well-balanced ale with a rounded malt flavour that leads to a pleasantly bitter and hoppy finish.

106 Jack FM Ale (OG 1042, ABV 4%)

An IPA-style refreshing golden ale. Rounded malt matched with a delicate citrus and spicy hop edge, good bitterness which finishes on gentle notes of lemon and elderflower.

Addlestone Ale (OG 1044, ABV 4.2%)
Copper-coloured premium best bitter with good balance of malt and hops.

Gold (OG 1044, ABV 4.2%)
A golden ale, slightly citrus flavoured with a distinct hoppy, floral aroma.

IPA (OG 1053, ABV 5.2%)
Traditional IPA with a powerful hop character and a long rounded malt finish.

Skinner's SIBA ⊚

Riverside, Newham Road, Truro, Cornwall, TR1 2SU
☎ (01872) 271885 ⊕ skinnersbrewery.com
Shop Mon-Sat 10am-5pm
Tours by arrangement

⊗ Award-winning brewery established in 1997. The brewery moved to bigger premises in 2003, opening a shop and visitor centre. Beers and merchandise are available to purchase online. Brewery tours are scheduled daily, plus additional tours by arrangement. Seasonal beers: see website.

Ginger Tosser (OG 1038, ABV 3.8%)
Hoppy golden ale fused with Cornish honey. The rounded finish has a hint of ginger.

Spriggan Ale (OG 1038, ABV 3.8%)
A light golden, hoppy bitter. Well-balanced with a smooth, bitter finish.

Betty Stogs (OG 1040, ABV 4%)
Refreshing copper ale with balance of bitter hops, apple fruit and malt, finishing bitter. Faint aroma of malt and hops.

Heligan Honey (OG 1040, ABV 4%)
Added honey detectable in the aroma and taste. Sweet taste balanced by bitterness and hops. Lingering bittersweet and dry aftertaste.

Cornish Knocker Ale (OG 1044, ABV 4.5%)
Refreshing golden ale with citrus hops all the way through. Spice and fruit in the mouth balanced by bitter and faint malt undertones, with a clean and lasting bitter finish.

Figgy's Brew (OG 1044, ABV 4.5%)
With subdued fruit and malt on the nose, a pale brown beer that is gently malty and sweet in the mouth, leading to bitterness that becomes dry in the finish.

Hunny Bunny (OG 1045, ABV 4.5%)
Premium strength golden ale brewed with Cornish honey. Clean-tasting with a hoppy aroma.

Pennycomequick (OG 1046, ABV 4.5%)
Traditional, dark, full-bodied stout. Smooth on the palate with a light, crisp finish.

Porthleven (OG 1048, ABV 4.8%)
Zingy golden citrus ale with bite. Very refreshing and smooth with bitter grapefruit and gooseberry and a hoppy, bitter aftertaste.

Slater's SIBA IFBB ⊚

Slater's Brewery, St Albans Road, Common Road Industrial Estate, Stafford, ST16 3DR
☎ (01785) 257976 ⊕ slatersales.co.uk

Shop Mon-Fri 9am-5pm; Sat 10am-12pm
Tours by arrangement

☺The brewery was opened in 1995 and in 2006 moved to new, larger premises. It has won numerous awards from CAMRA and SIBA and supplies a large number of outlets. One pub is owned, the George at Eccleshall, which serves as the brewery tap.

Bitter (OG 1035.5, ABV 3.6%)
Pale bitter with an earthy spicy hop character allied to juicy malt and tart fruit.

Original (OG 1040, ABV 4%) 🍺
Amber bitter. Malty aroma with caramel notes, hoppy taste develops into a dry hoppy finish with a touch of sweetness.

Top Totty (OG 1040, ABV 4%) 🍺
Great yellow colour with a fruit and hop nose. Hop and fruit balanced taste leads to citrus hints with mouth-watering edges. Dry finish with tangs of lemon.

Queen Bee (OG 1042, ABV 4.2%) 🍺
Golden with a sweet and spicy aroma and hop background. Honey sweet taste followed by a gentle bitter finish on the tongue.

Premium (OG 1044, ABV 4.4%) 🍺
Pale brown bitter with malt and caramel aroma. Malt and caramel taste supported by hops and some fruit provide a warming descent and satisfyingly bitter mouthfeel.

Slaughterhouse SIBA

🏠 Bridge Street, Warwick, CV34 5PD
☎ (01926) 490986 ⊕ slaughterhousebrewery.com
Tours by arrangement

Production began in 2003 on a four-barrel plant in a former slaughterhouse. Around 30 outlets are supplied. The brewery premises are licensed for off-sales direct to the public. In 2010 Slaughterhouse opened its first pub, the Wild Boar in Warwick.

Saddleback Best Bitter (OG 1038, ABV 3.8%)
Amber-coloured session bitter with a distinctive hop flavour.

Pale Ale (OG 1041, ABV 4.1%)
A classic English pale ale with a dry quenching balance of malt and hops, and a long finish with light fruit hints.

Extra Stout Snout (OG 1044, ABV 4.4%)

Boar D'eau (OG 1045, ABV 4.5%)

Wild Boar (OG 1052, ABV 5.2%)
A robust dark beer produced using both dark crystal and chocolate malts

Sleaford SIBA

21 Pride Court, Enterprise Park, Sleaford, Lincolnshire, NG34 8GL
☎ 07530 559322 ⊕ sleafordbrewery.co.uk
Shop hours vary – please ring in advance

Sleaford brewery was established in 2010 and produces a large range of bottle-conditioned and filtered bottled beers and ciders. Casks are available by pre-order. The bottles are available at farmers markets, the brewery shop and other retail outlets.

Royal Ruby Mild (ABV 3.5%)

Cats Eyes IPA (ABV 3.7%)

Partridge Pale (OG 1039, ABV 3.9%)

Hedgerow Silver (OG 1041, ABV 4%)

Crazy Kiwi (ABV 4.1%)

Go West (ABV 4.1%)

Pleasant Pheasant (ABV 4.2%)

Sleaford Stout (OG 1044, ABV 4.2%)

Hedgerow Gold (OG 1046, ABV 4.4%)

Golden Wheat (ABV 4.5%)

Old Albert (ABV 5%)

Midnight Runner (OG 1055, ABV 5.2%)

Route 17 (OG 1056, ABV 5.3%)

6066 (ABV 6%)

Slightly Foxed SIBA

Unit 25, Asquith Bottom Mill, Sowerby Bridge, West Yorkshire, HX6 3BS
☎ 07412 008221 ⊕ slightlyfoxedbrewery.co.uk

Slightly Foxed launched in 2011 as a venture between an award-winning landlord and a local businessman. Originally using spare capacity at Brass Monkey Brewery, Slightly Foxed bought the brewery in 2012. Seasonal and special beers are also available.

Howling Fox (ABV 3.5%)
Exceptionally pale with hoppy notes and a clean dry flavour with full hop aromas.

Slightly Foxed (ABV 3.8%)
Light and refreshing on the palate and pale golden in colour with a clean, spicy, grapefruit flavour, a light, fruity floral aroma and a clean, dry finish.

Fox Glove (ABV 4.3%)
A golden coloured premium best bitter with a full-bodied, fruity flavour.

Urban Fox (ABV 4.8%)
London Porter with layered bittersweet malt flavours of chocolate, treacle and toffee, and hits of citrus and orange notes.

Bengal Fox (ABV 5.2%)

Prarie Fox (ABV 5.2%)
American pale ale with a mildly spicy, fruity and predominantly citrus palate, and a dry finish.

Small Paul's

27 Briar Close, Gillingham, Dorset, SP8 4SS
☎ (01747) 823574 ✉ smallbrewer@aol.com
Tours by arrangement

⊗ Launched in 2006, this half-barrel brewery is located in the owner's garage. There are usually two brews a month but consideration is being given to increasing capacity following success at beer festivals. A small number of local pubs and clubs are supplied direct and beers can be designed and brewed to order. Seasonal beers are also available.

Gylla's Gold (OG 1039, ABV 3.8%) 🍺
Drinkable session ale. Mild fruit hop aromas lead to bitter hop flavours and a lingering dry hop aftertaste.

Challenger II (OG 1045, ABV 4.3%)
A copper-coloured malty bitter.

Wyvern (OG 1044, ABV 4.4%) ◆
Red-brown, well-balanced best bitter with malt and caramel flavours and a short, bittersweet finish.

Gillingham Pale (OG 1045, ABV 4.5%) ◆
Fruity, caramel aromas lead to complex bitter flavours and short, dry finish.

Joseph Herbert Smith

Fox Inn, Hanley Broadheath, nr Tenbury Wells, Worcestershire, WR15 8QS
☎ (01886) 853189 ☎ 07527 066474
✉ jhsbrewery@yahoo.co.uk
Tours by arrangement

☺The brewery was established in Staffordshire in 2007 by Jonathan Smith. In 2008 it relocated to barns adjacent to the Fox Inn. Now a four-barrel plant with a 12-barrel capacity, all equipment is gas fired and ingredients are sourced locally where possible. Seasonal and monthly beers are available.

Amy's Rose (OG 1040, ABV 4%)
A traditionally-brewed mild.

Snooty Fox (OG 1042, ABV 4.1%)
A copper-coloured English-style best bitter.

Foxy Lady (OG 1043, ABV 4.3%)
A premium light bitter.

Teddy's Tipple (OG 1044, ABV 4.4%)
Medium-coloured sweetish bitter.

Samuel Smith

High Street, Tadcaster, North Yorkshire, LS24 9SB
☎ (01937) 832225 ⊕ samuelsmithsbrewery.co.uk

☺Fiercely independent, family-owned company. Tradition, quality and value are important, resulting in brewing without any artificial additives. All real ale is supplied in wooden casks. Around 200 pubs are owned. A bottle-conditioned beer (Yorkshire Stingo, ABV 8%) is only available in specialist off-licences.

Old Brewery Bitter (OBB) (OG 1040, ABV 4%) ◆
Malt dominates the aroma, with an initial burst of malt, hops and fruit in the taste, which is sustained in the aftertaste.

Tom Smith (NEW)

15 Lindsay Street, Kettering, Northamptonshire, NN16 8RG
☎ (01536) 399859 ☎ 07956 051922
⊕ pigsandbeer.co.uk

Mobile catering company owner Mark Smith set up Tom Smith brewery in 2012 in a industrial unit in the back streets of Kettering. Four different ales are brewed.

Tom's Tipple (OG 1036, ABV 3.5%)
A medium dark mild, quite sweet but well-balanced with bittering hops.

Goat Sanctuary (OG 1040, ABV 4%)
A dry and hoppy bitter, crystal clear and pale straw-coloured.

Jamaican Tom (OG 1044, ABV 4.4%)
Delicately spiced ginger beer, dark amber in colour, with subtle ginger, chilli and orange flavours.

Golden Tom (OG 1047, ABV 5.2%)

Dark golden strong bitter.

John Smith's

The Brewery, Tadcaster, North Yorkshire, LS24 9SA
☎ (01937) 832091 ⊕ heineken.com

The brewery was built in 1879 by a relative of Samuel Smith (qv). John Smith's became part of the Courage group in 1970 before being taken over by S&N and now Heineken UK. Major expansion has taken place, with 11 new fermenting vessels installed. Traditional Yorkshire Square fermenters have been replaced by conical vessels. John Smith's cask Magnet has been discontinued. John Smith's Bitter is brewed under contract by Cameron's (qv) in Hartlepool.

Snowdonia

⊟ Snowdonia Parc Brewpub & Campsite, Waunfawr, Caernarfon, Gwynedd, LL55 4AQ
☎ (01286) 650409 ⊕ snowdonia-park.co.uk

Snowdonia started brewing in 1998 in a two-barrel brewhouse. The brewing is now carried out by the owner, Carmen Pierce. The beer is brewed solely for the Snowdonia Park pub and campsite.

Gwyrfai (OG 1037.4, ABV 3.8%)

Gold (OG 1040, ABV 4%)

Theodore Stout (OG 1040.7, ABV 4.1%)

Carmen Sutra (OG 1043, ABV 4.4%)

Cais (OG 1045.2, ABV 4.8%)

Dark & Delicious (OG 1046.7, ABV 5%)

Welsh Highland Bitter (OG 1048, ABV 5.2%)

Son of Sid

⊟ Chequers, 71 Main Road, Little Gransden, Bedfordshire, SG19 3DW
☎ (01767) 677348 ⊕ sonofsid.co.uk
Shop Mon-Thu 12pm-2pm, 7pm-11pm; Fri & Sat 12pm-11pm; Sun 12pm-6pm, 7pm-10.30pm
Tours by arrangement

⊠ Son of Sid was established in 2007 on a 2.5-barrel plant in a separate room of the pub. The brewery can be viewed from the lounge bar. It is named after the father of the current landlord, who ran the pub for 42 years. His son has carried the business on for the past 19 years as a family-run enterprise. Beer is sold in the pub and at local beer festivals.

English Ale (OG 1035, ABV 3.5%)
Traditional English ale with a clean, malty taste and a good hop character.

Muck Cart Mild (OG 1035, ABV 3.5%) ▢ ◆
Black mild with a resounding roast malt presence and a caramel background in aroma and taste. There is some sweetness but the balance is predominantly dry and bitter, with increasing bitterness in the aftertaste.

Golden Shower (OG 1039, ABV 3.9%)
Full-bodied golden beer with a light hop character and a defined maltiness.

Sonnet 43 (NEW) SIBA

Durham Road, Coxhoe, County Durham, DH6 4HX
☎ (0191) 377 3039 ⊕ sonnet43.com

Shop Mon-Fri 9am-5pm

☺Sonnet 43 was opened in 2012. The name and brewing ethos is inspired by the most famous work of the poet Elizabeth Barratt Browning. The Lambton Worm pub in Chester le Street is the brewery tap with a further two planned including the adjoining pub, the Kicking Cuddy. Six core beers are available with an ever-changing, cask-conditioned limited edition range.

Steam Beer (OG 1038, ABV 3.8%)
An amber ale with aromas of malt and hops and a sourdough and nut note.

Blonde Beer (OG 1041, ABV 4.1%)
A golden-straw coloured wheat-style beer with a sweet, delicate, floral aroma.

Bourbon Milk Stout (OG 1046, ABV 4.3%)
Dark beer brewed with bourbon, cocoa and oats for a rich, full-bodied, chocolaty bitterness.

IPA (OG 1044, ABV 4.4%)
Classic strong pale ale with a light gold appearance and a creamy white head.

Brown Ale (OG 1046, ABV 4.7%)
Rosy brown beer with flavours of malt and toffee blending well with a pleasant light bitterness.

American Pale Ale (OG 1055, ABV 5.4%)
Bronze-coloured pale ale with a spicy and peppery aroma.

South Hams SIBA

Stokeley Barton, Stokenham, Kingsbridge, Devon, TQ7 2SE
☎ (01548) 581151 ⊕ southhamsbrewery.co.uk
Tours by arrangement

The brewery moved to its present site, a milking parlour, in 2003, with a 10-barrel plant and plenty of room to expand. It supplies more than 60 outlets in Plymouth and South Devon. Wholesalers are used to distribute to other areas. Three pubs are owned. Seasonal beers: see website. Bottle-conditioned beers are also available.

Devon Pride (OG 1039, ABV 3.8%)

XSB (OG 1043, ABV 4.2%) ◆

Amber nectar with a fruity nose and a bitter finish.

Wild Blonde (OG 1044, ABV 4.4%)

Eddystone (OG 1050, ABV 4.8%)

SouthDowns

See Downlands

Southport SIBA

Unit 3, Enterprise Business Park, Russell Road, Southport, Merseyside, PR9 7RF
☎ 07748 387652 ⊕ southportbrewery.co.uk

☺The Southport brewery opened in 2004 as a 2.5-barrel plant but moved to a five-barrel plant due to demand. Seasonal beers: see website.

Cyclone (OG 1039.5, ABV 3.8%)
A bronze coloured bitter with a fruity blackcurrant aftertaste.

Sandgrounder Bitter (OG 1039.5, ABV 3.8%)
Pale, hoppy session bitter with a floral character.

Dark Night (OG 1040.5, ABV 3.9%)
A dark traditional mild.

Carousel (OG 1041.5, ABV 4%)
A refreshing, floral, hoppy best bitter.

Golden Sands (OG 1041.5, ABV 4%)
A golden-coloured, triple hopped bitter with citrus flavour.

Natterjack (OG 1043.5, ABV 4.3%)
A premium bitter with fruit notes and a hint of coffee.

Spencer's (NEW) SIBA

Unit 5, Ashford Works, Brunswick Road, Cobbs Wood, Ashford, Kent, TN23 1EH
☎ (01233) 610215 ☎ 07772 080777
⊕ spencersbrewery.co.uk

Spencer's is a family-run microbrewery which started production in 2012 on an eight-barrel plant. Three regular beers are produced.

Blonde (ABV 4.2%)

Bitter (ABV 4.4%)

Galaxy (ABV 4.7%)

Sperrin

Lord Nelson Inn, Birmingham Road, Ansley, Warwickshire, CV10 9PQ
☎ (024) 7639 2305 ☎ 07917 772208
✉ treeve2k@btinternet.com
Tours by arrangement

Sperrin began brewing in 2012 using a six-barrel plant by the side of the Lord Nelson Inn. The brewery is owned and run by three brothers, Craig, Warren and Treeve Sperrin.

Head Hunter (ABV 3.8%)

Band of Brothers (ABV 4.2%)

Third Party (ABV 4.8%)

Thick as Thieves (ABV 6.8%)

Spey Valley

Mains of Mulben, Mulben, Keith, AB55 6YH
⊕ speyvalleybrewery.co.uk

Spey Valley began brewing in 2007 making 13.5-18 gallons per brew and operates on a part-time basis around brewer David MacDonald's full-time job of whisky making. Four regular beers are brewed, as well as special editions. Most of the beer goes to the Mash Tun in Aberlour, the Craigellachie Hotel and beer festivals.

David's Not So Bitter (ABV 4.4%)
A simple well-balanced light brown ale with a good body and plenty of hoppy aroma.

Roystons Hoppy Handful (ABV 4.6%)
Bright, citrus and hoppy.

Stillmans IPA (ABV 4.6%)
Light bitter ale, easy on the palate with a floral aroma and long finish.

Spey Stout (ABV 5.4%)
Subtly bitter, lightly floral, sweet chocolaty stout.

Speyside Craft (NEW) SIBA

2 Greshop Road, Forres, IV36 2GU

☎ (01309) 358082 ☎ 07854 053277
⊕ speysidecraftbrewery.com
Shop Sat 11am-4pm

Based in a traditional whisky-producing area, Speyside brewery uses the same water that goes into the production of Scottish whiskies. Bottled beers are available in the shop and online. A number of local outlets are supplied. A donation from sales of Bottlenose Bitter goes to help support the work of the Whale and Dolphin Conservation Society.

Bottlenose Bitter (ABV 4.1%)

Randolph's Leap (ABV 4.9%)

Moray IPA (ABV 5.5%)

Spire SIBA

Unit 4, Deepdale Close, Hartington Industrial Estate, Staveley, Derbyshire, S43 3YF
☎ (01246) 476005 ☎ 07904 638550
⊕ spirebrewery.co.uk
Shop Mon-Fri 9.30am-4.30pm
Tours by arrangement

☺The brewery was set up by ex-Scots Guards musician and teacher David McLaren in 2006 and moved to larger premises in 2012. More than 100 outlets are supplied direct, including the Three Tuns in Dronfield. Seasonal beers: see website.

Brassed Off (OG 1036, ABV 3.7%)
Easy-drinking session bitter combining malt and fruit flavours, balanced by a long, bitter finish.

Whiter Shade of Pale (OG 1039, ABV 4%)
Pale straw-coloured session bitter with a subtle lemon hop finish. Smooth with a well balanced malt flavour.

Dark Side of the Moon (OG 1042, ABV 4.3%) ◆
Complex and satisfying ruby mild with coffee aroma and toffee flavours. Dark and sweet but not too strong.

Chesterfield Best Bitter (OG 1043, ABV 4.5%) ◆
Classic brown strong bitter with malt and fruit flavours and a hint of caramel and chocolate in the finish. There is a little bitterness in the aftertaste.

Coal Porter (OG 1045, ABV 4.5%)
A smooth dark beer combining coffee and bitter chocolate, becoming increasingly dry, leading to a bitter finish and aftertaste.

Land of Hop & Glory (OG 1044, ABV 4.5%) ◆
An excellent example of a clean, crisp-tasting golden ale. Easy to drink with grapefruit and lemon flavours developing. These complex citrus hop flavours lead to a bitter, dry aftertaste.

Twist & Stout (OG 1044, ABV 4.5%) ◆
Creamy and dark with flavours of bitter chocolate and coffee. Easy drinking.

Sovereigns Escort IPA (OG 1051, ABV 5.2%)
Strong amber coloured IPA, with a delicate orange flavour, leading to a bitter finish. Full bodied and easy to drink despite its strength.

Sgt Pepper Stout (OG 1053, ABV 5.5%) ◆
Unique full-flavoured stout brewed with ground black pepper. Liquorice and pepper flavours dominate on both aroma and taste in this original, complex dark and delicious beer.

Enigma (OG 1061, ABV 6.4%) ◆

Strong, complex beer to be savoured and appreciated. Full bodied, with hints of marmalade tartness and fruit, leading to a dry, slightly bitter finish.

Spitting Feathers SIBA ◉

Common Farm, Waverton, Chester, CH3 7QT
☎ (01244) 332052 ☎ 07974 348325
⊕ spittingfeathers.org
Tours by arrangement

☺Spitting Feathers was established in 2005. The brewery and visitors' bar are in traditional sandstone buildings around a cobbled yard. About 200 local outlets are supplied. A range of seasonal and special beers are produced, including those sold under the Heritage Ales and Ministry of Beer brands: see website.

Farmhouse Ale (OG 1035, ABV 3.6%)
A golden session bitter.

Thirstquencher (OG 1038, ABV 3.9%) ◆
Powerful hop aroma leads into the taste. Bitterness and a fruity citrus hop flavour fight for attention. A sharp, clean golden beer with a long, dry, bitter aftertaste.

Special Ale (OG 1041, ABV 4.2%) ◆
Complex tawny-coloured beer with a sharp, grainy mouthfeel. Malty with good hop coming through in the aroma and taste. Hints of nuttiness and a touch of acidity. Dry, astringent finish.

Old Wavertonian (OG 1043, ABV 4.4%) ◆
Creamy and smooth stout. Full-flavoured with coffee notes in aroma and taste. Roast and nut flavours throughout, leading to a hoppy, bitter finish.

Basket Case (OG 1046, ABV 4.8%) ◆
Reddish, complex beer. Sweetness and fruit dominate the taste, offset by hops and bitterness that follow through into the aftertaste.

Sportsman

⊟ 1-3 St John's Road, Huddersfield, West Yorkshire, HD1 5AY
☎ 07903 040873
⊕ sportsmanbrewingcompany.co.uk

☺The brewery opened in 2011 and the beers are brewed in the cellars of the Sportsman pub on a two-barrel plant. The beers are also available in the West Riding Refreshment Rooms, Dewsbury and the Cricketers Arms, Horbury.

Town Mild (OG 1033, ABV 3.5%)
A light pleasant-drinking dark mild with a chocolate start and a biscuit finish.

Hops Cotch (OG 1036, ABV 3.9%)
A pale golden beer, with slightly sweetish malt flavours developing a dryness with a lemon hint.

Sup Porter (OG 1040, ABV 4.3%)
Very dark, gently-hopped session porter.

Pigeon Bridge Porter (OG 1050, ABV 4.7%)
A liquorice-tasting porter, with a luscious blackberry finish.

Deco IPA (OG 1046, ABV 5%)
An easy-drinking IPA with blackberry notes to begin with, and a citrus strawberry hop to finish.

Springhead SIBA ◉

Robin Hood Site, Main Street, Laneham,
Nottinghamshire, DN22 0NA
☎ (01777) 228080 ☎ 07720 461655
⊕ springhead.co.uk
Shop open daily 9am-6pm
Tours by arrangement

☺Springhead Brewery opened in 1990, and relocated to its current address in 2011. Around 500 outlets are supplied direct and the brewery owns three pubs. Six beers are brewed all year round and bi-monthly seasonals are brewed. Drop of the Black Stuff is suitable for vegans. Springhead's latest pub, the Bees Knees, is adjacent to the brewery, where the core beers plus the current seasonal brew are always available.

The Bees Knees (OG 1036, ABV 3.9%)
A light golden beer made with local wildflower honey. Refreshing and mellow but not sweet.

Drop of the Black Stuff (OG 1041, ABV 4%)

Robin Hood (OG 1041, ABV 4%)
A dark traditional bitter with a good head and plenty of hops.

Maid Marian (OG 1045, ABV 4.5%)
A pale golden beer with a fruity orange aroma and a dry finish.

Leveller (OG 1047, ABV 4.8%)
Brewed in the style of Belgian Trappist ale, with a dark, smoky intense flavour and a toffee finish.

Roaring Meg (OG 1052, ABV 5.5%)
Smooth with a sweet, citrus honey aroma and a dry finish.

Stables

❚ Beamish Hall Country House Hotel, Beamish, County Durham, DH9 0YB
☎ (01207) 288750 ⊕ beamish-hall.co.uk/stables
Tours by arrangement

☺Stables was established as part of a £1 million development of an old stable block, converting a disused building to a pub and eight-barrel microbrewery. Seven regular beers are produced. Seasonal and special beers are also available.

Beamish Hall Best Bitter (OG 1038, ABV 3.8%)

Old Miner Tommy (OG 1037, ABV 3.8%)

Bobby Dazzler (OG 1042, ABV 4.2%)

Coppy Lane (OG 1043, ABV 4.2%)

Silver Buckles (OG 1044, ABV 4.4%)

Beamish Burn (OG 1045, ABV 4.5%)

Bell Tower (OG 1052, ABV 5%)

Staffordshire SIBA

12 Churnet Court, Cheddleton, Staffordshire, ST13 7EF
☎ (01538) 361919 ☎ 07971 808370
⊕ staffordshirebrewery.co.uk
Tours by arrangement

Brewing started in 2002 and the brewery has steadily increased in capacity since. A 20-barrel brew plant was completed in 2011. In recent years the brewery concentrated on producing bottle-conditioned beers but now produces filtered, pasteurised bottled beers with cask-conditioned beers to special order only.

Contract brewed for Wicked Hathern Brewery Ltd:

Albion Special (OG 1041, ABV 4%)

Cockfighter (OG 1043, ABV 4.2%)

Hawthorn Gold (OG 1045, ABV 4.5%)

Stamps (NEW)

The Basement, 17 Boundary Street, Everton, Liverpool, L5 9UB
☎ 07779 000094 ⊕ stampsbrewery.co.uk
Tours by arrangement

☺Stamps began brewing in 2012 on an environmentally-friendly brewplant: power for brewing comes from 52 solar panels and a biomass boiler, and used grain is sent to a local city farm for animal feed. The beers are named after famous world postage stamps. Beers and merchandise are available at Stamps Bar in Crosby.

Flying Cloud (OG 1037, ABV 3.7%)
A straw-coloured ale with an oaty flavour and a dry, hoppy finish.

The Russian (OG 1040, ABV 4.2%)
A copper ale with a hoppy finish.

Inverted Jenny (OG 1046, ABV 4.6%)
A light golden-coloured ale.

Stanway

Stanway House, Stanway, Cheltenham, Gloucestershire, GL54 5PQ
☎ (01386) 584320 ⊕ stanwaybrewery.co.uk

☺Stanway is a small brewery founded in 1993 with a five-barrel plant that confines its sales to the Cotswolds area (15 to 20 outlets). The brewery is the only known plant in the country to use wood-fired coppers for all its production. Seasonal beers: see website.

Stanney Bitter (OG 1042, ABV 4.5%) ◤
A light, refreshing, amber-coloured beer, dominated by hops in the aroma, with a bitter taste and a hoppy, bitter finish.

Star Inn

❚ Star Inn, Starcliff Ltd, 2 Back Hope Street, The Cliff, Higher Broughton, Greater Manchester, M7 2PD
☎ 07789 175219. ⊕ starinnbrewery.wix.com/brewery

☺A small on-site brewhouse was built in 2010 by the cooperative that owns the Star Inn. Former Bazens' brewers, Richard and Jude Bazen, produce four barrels a week and seasonal beers are also available.

Golden Crown (OG 1039, ABV 3.8%)

Starry Night (OG 1040, ABV 4%)
Pale amber bitter with moderate and distinctive floral and citrus hop flavours

Steamin' Billy

See Belvoir

Steel City

c/o The Wellington, 1 Henry Street, Sheffield, South Yorkshire, S3 7EQ ⊕ steelcitybrewing.co.uk

⊗ Steel City was established in 2009 and uses the brewing equipment at the Little Ale Cart in Sheffield. Beer is brewed once a month to a different recipe each time. A nine-gallon mini-plant is used to brew one-off, often extreme beers with an emphasis on pale and hoppy brews.

Stewart SIBA

26a Dryden Road, Bilston Glen Industrial Estate, Loanhead, Midlothian, EH20 9LZ
☎ (0131) 440 2442 ⊕ stewartbrewing.co.uk
Shop Mon-Thu 10am-5pm; Fri 10am-6pm; Sat 10am-4pm
Tours by arrangement

☺Established in 2004 by Steve Stewart, a qualified master brewer, and specialising in high-quality cask ales, made from natural ingredients. The brewery moved to a larger custom built plant in 2013. Seasonal and bottled-conditioned beers supplement the regular range.

Zymic (OG 1039, ABV 3.8%)
Straw-coloured hoppy golden ale.

Pentland IPA (OG 1040, ABV 3.9%) ◄
A pleasing, hoppy, golden session ale. The dry bitter taste is well balanced by sweetness from the malt, and fruit flavours. The aftertaste is dry with a lingering bitterness.

Copper Cascade (OG 1041, ABV 4.1%) ◄
This tawny-coloured beer is born from American hops and Scottish malt. The hop character overlays a solid malt base. Hints of roast and substantial fruitiness give a complex character. A bittersweet taste leads to a dry bitter finish.

Edinburgh No.3 Premium Scotch Ale (OG 1043, ABV 4.3%) ◄
An excellent example of a Scottish heavy ale. Full-bodied and dark with a predominantly malt character, fruit notes and a gentle infusion of hop. A bittersweet beer with a dry, moreish finish.

80/- (OG 1044, ABV 4.4%) ◄
Superb traditional Scottish heavy. The complex profile is dominated by malt with fruit flavours giving the sweetish character typical of this beer style. Hops provide a gentle balancing bitterness that intensifies in the dry finish.

Edinburgh Gold (OG 1048, ABV 4.8%) ◄
A full-bodied but easy-drinking Continental-style golden ale. Bitterness from the hop character is strong in the finish and complemented in the taste by a little sweetness from malt, and fruit flavours.

Sticklegs

Unit 7, Old Forge Court, Colchester Road, Elmstead Market, Essex, CO7 7EA
☎ 07962 12906 ⊕ sticklegs.co.uk
Shop Mon-Sat 9.30am-4.30pm; closed Sun
Tours by arrangement

⊗ Sticklegs was established in 2008 at the Cross Inn, Great Bromley. It has since moved and expanded and is now based on a two-barrel and six-barrel plant in Elmstead.

Malt Shovel Mild (OG 1032, ABV 3.4%)

Old Forge Bitter (OG 1038, ABV 3.8%)

Stour Gold (OG 1040, ABV 3.8%)

Tendring 100 (OG 1041, ABV 4%)

Elmstead Stout (OG 1046, ABV 4.8%)

Nemesis (OG 1048, ABV 5%)

Stocklinch (NEW) SIBA

Unit 3, Manor Farm, Stocklinch, Somerset, TA19 9JG
☎ 07711 479917 ⊕ stocklinchales.co.uk
Shop Fri 7-11pm; Sun 2-3pm
Tours by arrangement

⊗ Established in 2012 in a converted farm building, Stocklinch uses a five-barrel plant. A number of local outlets are supplied and beer is available in polypins to take away. There is a tap room which is open for a few days each month, and compensates for the lack of a village pub.

Ramblers Gold (OG 1038, ABV 3.8%)
Light golden beer with a slight aftertaste of grapefruit.

Rusty Boiler (OG 1045, ABV 4.5%)
Mid-brown best bitter, with strong fruity flavours and a hint of caramel.

Gunner Boyce (OG 1048, ABV 4.8%)

Black Smock (OG 1050, ABV 5%)
Dark beer with a strong rich taste of chocolate liquorish and coffee, with a hint of blackcurrant.

Stonehenge SIBA ◉

The Old Mill, Mill Road, Netheravon, Salisbury, Wiltshire, SP4 9QB
☎ (01980) 670631 ⊕ stonehengeales.co.uk
Tours by arrangement

The beer is brewed in a mill built in 1914 to generate electricity. The site was converted to a gravity-fed brewery in 1984 (Bunce's Brewery) and in 1994 the company was bought by Danish master brewer Stig Anker Andersen. More than 300 outlets and several wholesalers are supplied. Seasonal beers: see website.

Spire Ale (OG 1037, ABV 3.8%)
A light, golden, hoppy bitter.

Pigswill (OG 1039, ABV 4%)
A full-bodied beer, rich in hop aroma, with a warm amber colour.

Heel Stone (OG 1042, ABV 4.3%)
A crisp, clean, refreshing bitter, deep amber in colour, well balanced with a fruity blackcurrent nose.

Great Bustard (OG 1046, ABV 4.8%)
A strong, fruity, malty bitter.

Danish Dynamite (OG 1048, ABV 5%)
A strong, dry ale, slightly fruity with a well-balanced, bitter hop flavour.

Stonehouse SIBA

Stonehouse, Weston, Oswestry, Shropshire, SY10 9ES
☎ (01691) 676457 ⊕ stonehousebrewery.co.uk
Shop Mon-Fri 9am-5pm; Sat 10am-2pm
Tours by arrangement

Stonehouse was established in 2007. The brewery was housed in former chicken sheds next to the old Cambrian railway line. This is now the cellar of the new, expanded brewery, which includes a visitor centre and uses an 18-barrel plant. More than 200 outlets are supplied direct.

Sunlander (OG 1037, ABV 3.7%)

Station Bitter (OG 1041, ABV 3.9%)

Cambrian Gold (OG 1042, ABV 4.2%)

Wheeltapper's Wheatbeer (OG 1043, ABV 4.5%)

KPA (OG 1047, ABV 4.6%)

Off the Rails (OG 1048, ABV 4.8%)

Storm SIBA

2 Waterside, Macclesfield, Cheshire, SK11 7HJ
☎ (01625) 431234 ⊕ stormbrewing.co.uk

Storm Brewing was founded in 1998 operating from an old ICI boiler room. In 2001 it moved to its current location which, until 1937, was a pub called the Mechanics Arms. More than 60 outlets supplied. Seasonal and bottle-conditioned beers are also available.

Ale Force (OG 1042, ABV 4.2%) ◆
Amber, smooth-tasting, complex beer that balances malt, hop and fruit on the taste, leading to a roasty, slightly sweet aftertaste.

PGA (OG 1044, ABV 4.4%) ◆
Light, crisp, lager-style beer with a balance of malt, hops and fruit. Moderately bitter with a slight dry aftertaste.

Stowey

Old Cider House, 25 Castle Street, Nether Stowey, Somerset, TA5 1LN
☎ (01278) 732228 ⊕ stoweybrewery.co.uk
Tours by arrangement

Stowey was established in 2006, primarily to supply the owners' guesthouse and to provide beer to participants on 'real ale walks' run from the accommodation. The brewery also runs brewery workshop courses and supplies seasonal brews to the village pubs on a guest beer basis.

Strands

▤ Strands Inn, Nether Wasdale, Cumbria, CA20 1ET
☎ (01946) 26237 ⊕ strandshotel.com
Tours by arrangement

⊕Strands Brewery is a six-barrel plant with a 30-barrel fermentation capacity. The majority of beers are available bottle conditioned, and the brewery plans to sell them online. Six of the beers are available on the bar of the Strands Inn at all times.

Pied Piper (OG 1030, ABV 2.7%)
A dark mild full of roasted malts, with a hint of dandelion and burdock.

Green Bullet (OG 1037, ABV 3.5%)
A heavily hopped light and creamy wheat beer.

Responsibly (OG 1038, ABV 3.7%)
Heavily hopped and lightly smoked beer.

Brown Bitter (OG 1039, ABV 3.8%) ◆
A complex-tasting brown beer with a lingering bitter aftertaste.

Errmmm... (OG 1039, ABV 3.8%) ◆
A complex, traditional bitter.

Low Flyer (OG 1044, ABV 4.3%)
Autumnal seasonal beer with a dark biscuity malt flavour with a touch of whisky on the finish.

Red Screes (OG 1047, ABV 4.5%) ◆

An interesting, rich-tasting, smooth, strong bitter; full-flavoured with plenty of roast and malt tastes.

T'errmmm-inator (OG 1050, ABV 5%) ◆
A smooth, dark brown, roast-led beer. Full-bodied and well-balanced.

For Independent Lakeland Breweries:

Gold Wing (OG 1040, ABV 4%)
A clean, crisp golden ale with delicate citrus aromas and a refreshing finish.

Dark Knight (OG 1050, ABV 5%)
Deep, dark, well-balanced ale.

Strathaven SIBA ◉

Craigmill Brewery, Strathaven, ML10 6PB
☎ (01357) 520419 ⊕ strathavenales.co.uk
Shop Mon-Fri 9am-5pm (phone at weekend)
Tours by arrangement

Strathaven Ales is a 10-barrel brewery on the River Avon close to Strathaven and was converted from the remains of a 16th-century mill. The range is distributed throughout Scotland and the north of England. Seasonal beers: see website.

Clydesdale (OG 1038, ABV 3.8%)

Avondale (OG 1048, ABV 4%)

Old Mortality (OG 1046, ABV 4.2%)

Claverhouse (OG 1046, ABV 4.5%)

Strathbraan SIBA

Deanshaugh, Amulree, PH8 0EB
☎ (01350) 725264 ☎ 07747 857908
✉ strathbraan.bry@btinternet.com

Straathbraan began brewing in 2012 using a 10-barrel plant. Two beers are brewed.

Due South (OG 1038, ABV 3.8%)

Head East (OG 1042, ABV 4.2%)

Stringers SIBA

Unit 3, Low Mill Business Park, Ulverston, Cumbria, LA12 9EE
☎ (01229) 581387 ⊕ stringersbeer.co.uk

Stringers is a small family-run brewery. Brewing started in 2008 on a five-barrel plant run on 100% renewable energy. A small number of seasonal beers are produced. No. 2 Stout and Dark Country are suitable for vegans. Plan B is gluten free.

Plan B (OG 1036, ABV 3.7%) ◆
An easy-drinking, zingy, pale thirst-quencher.

No. 2 Stout (OG 1042, ABV 4%) ◆
A robust drying stout full of roast and hop bitterness.

Yellow Lorry (OG 1039, ABV 4%)
Golden ale with citrus aroma and firm, clean bitterness.

Best Bitter (OG 1041, ABV 4.2%) ◆
Well-crafted and well-balanced with a clean hoppy bitterness.

West Coast Blond (OG 1042, ABV 4.4%) ◆
A golden beer with a hoppy fruity aroma and taste that fades to a bitter, slightly astringent aftertaste.

Victoria IPA (OG 1053, ABV 5.5%)

An IPA with spicy, tropical fruit, then some bitter marmalade, with a definite bitter finish.

Stroud SIBA ◉

Unit 11, Phoenix Works, London Road, Thrupp, Stroud, Gloucestershire, GL5 2BU
☎ (01453) 887122 ☎ 07891 995878
⊕ stroudbrewery.co.uk
Shop Mon-Thu 9am-3pm; Fri 9am-5pm. Bar Fri 3pm-11pm
Tours by arrangement

⊗ Established in 2006, Stroud brews on a 20-barrel plant, and supports the local economy by not selling its organic bottled beers through supermarkets. Stroud ales are sold in 40-50 pubs, independent retailers and the brewery shop. Seasonal and bottle-conditioned beers are also available.

Tom Long (OG 1039, ABV 3.8%)
Amber session beer with a spicy citrus aroma and good body.

Organic Ale (OG 1041, ABV 4%)
A refreshing, golden organic ale with a delicate apple aroma.

Budding (OG 1045, ABV 4.5%)
Pale ale with a grassy bitterness, sweet malt and luscious floral aroma.

Stumptail (NEW)

North Street, Great Dunham, Norfolk, PE32 2LR
☎ (01328) 701042

Stumptail began commercial home-brewing in 2011 using a 100-litre plant. Bottle-conditioned beers are produced with cask-conditioned versions brewed to order. Only the west Norfolk area is supplied.

Stumpy's

See Yates'

Suddaby's

See Brown Cow

Sulwath SIBA

⊟ The Brewery, 209 King Street, Castle Douglas, Dumfries & Galloway, DG7 1DT
☎ (01556) 504525 ⊕ sulwathbrewers.co.uk
Shop Mon-Sat 10am-6pm
Tours by arrangement

⊚Sulwath started brewing in 1995. The beers are supplied to markets as far away as Devon in the south and Aberdeen in the north. The brewery has a fully licensed brewery tap. Cask ales are sold to around 100 outlets and four wholesalers. Seasonal and occasional beers are also available.

Cuil Hill (OG 1039, ABV 3.6%) ◆
Distinctively fruity session ale with malt and hop undertones. The taste is bittersweet with a long-lasting dry finish.

The Grace (OG 1044, ABV 4.3%)
A refreshing, rich ale with a full-bodied flavour that balances the caramel undertones.

Black Galloway (OG 1046, ABV 4.4%) ⊓
A robust porter/stout.

Criffel (OG 1044, ABV 4.6%) ◆
Full-bodied beer with a distinctive bitterness. Fruit is to the fore of the taste with hops becoming increasingly dominant in the taste and finish.

Galloway Gold (OG 1049, ABV 5%) ◆
A cask-conditioned lager that will be too sweet for many despite being heavily hopped.

Knockendoch (OG 1047, ABV 5%) ◆
Dark, copper-coloured, reflecting a roast malt content, with bitterness from Challenger hops.

Solway Mist (OG 1052, ABV 5.5%)
A naturally cloudy wheat beer. Sweet and fruity.

Summer Wine

The Old Furnace, Unit 15, Crossley Mills, New Mill Road, Honley, Holmfirth, West Yorkshire, HD9 6QB
☎ (01484) 665466 ⊕ summerwinebrewery.co.uk

⊚Brewing commenced in 2006 on a 10-gallon kit with an emphasis on bottle-conditioned beer. A 2007 upgrade saw a 0.5-barrel plant installed and in 2008 the brewery expanded to a six barrel plant. Over 500 outlets are supplied direct. Two differing specials are available each month.

Resistance (OG 1037, ABV 3.7%)

Zenith (OG 1040, ABV 4%)

Gambit (OG 1042, ABV 4.2%)

Barista (OG 1048, ABV 4.8%)

Rouge Hop (OG 1050, ABV 5%)

Teleporter (OG 1050, ABV 5%)

Diablo (OG 1060, ABV 6%)

Summerskills SIBA ◉

15 Pomphlett Farm Industrial Estate, Broxton Drive, Billacombe, Plymouth, Devon, PL9 7BG
☎ (01752) 481283 ⊕ summerskills.co.uk

Established in a vineyard in 1983 at Bigbury-on-Sea, Summerskills moved to its present site in 1985. Production has expanded to meet demand from wholesalers, who perform nationwide distribution, and national pub companies. Seasonal and bottle-conditioned beers are also available.

Start Point (OG 1036, ABV 3.7%)

Westward Ho! (OG 1040, ABV 4.1%)

Best Bitter (OG 1043, ABV 4.3%) ◆
A mid-brown beer, with plenty of malt and hops through the aroma, taste and finish. A good session beer.

Tamar (OG 1043, ABV 4.3%)
A tawny-coloured bitter with a fruity aroma and a hop taste and finish.

Devon Dew (OG 1045, ABV 4.5%)

Bolt Head (OG 1046, ABV 4.7%)

Sunbeam (NEW)

Leeds, West Yorkshire, LS11 6EW
☎ 07772 002437 ⊕ sunbeamales.co.uk

Sunbeam ales was established in a back-to-back house in Leeds in 2009. Brewing began commercially in 2011, and a range of six bottled (not bottle-conditioned) beers is brewed, with a small amount going into casks. Beers are available from local outlets, including Beer Ritz in Leeds.

Sunny Republic SIBA ⊚

The Old Grain Barn, North West Farm, West Street, Winterborne Kingston, Dorset, DT11 9AT
☎ (01929) 471600 ⊕ sunnyrepublic.com
Shop Wed 4.30pm-6pm; Fri 5pm-7pm
Tours by arrangement

⊗ Sunny Republic began brewing in 2012 using a 30-barrel plant. Located in two restored Georgian grain barns in Winterborne Kingston, the beers are now available nationally and exported to six countries.

Beach Blonde (OG 1035.5, ABV 3.7%)
Straw blonde ale with tropical aroma of mango, grapefruit and lychee. Upfront bitterness yields to a light malt body.

Dolphin Amber (OG 1041.5, ABV 4.2%)
Traditional copper-coloured best bitter based on a 1920s recipe from the Dolphin Brewery in Poole.

Huna Red (OG 1041, ABV 4.2%)
Red-hued ale with fruit and berry aromas, brewed with hibiscus flowers.

Dorset Cross (OG 1050, ABV 5%)
Copper red ale with a sweet body and a balanced bitterness. Complex malt tastes, with hints of roasted hazelnut, toffee and caramel.

Hop Dog IPA (OG 1053.5, ABV 5.5%)
Citrus-dominated IPA with an enduring bitter finish.

Surrey Hills SIBA

Denbies Wine Estate, London Road, Dorking, Surrey, RH5 6AA
☎ (01306) 883603 ⊕ surreyhills.co.uk
Shop Mon-Wed 10am-3pm; Thu-Sat 10am-5pm
Tours by arrangement

⊗ Surrey Hills began brewing in 2005 near Shere, moving to Dorking in 2011. Nearly 95% of production is sold within 15 miles of the brewery. Seasonal beers: see website.

Ranmore Ale (OG 1039, ABV 3.8%) ▦ ◈
A light session beer with plenty of flavour. An earthy hoppy nose leads into a grapefruit and hoppy taste and a clean, bitter finish.

Shere Drop (OG 1043, ABV 4.2%) ⬠ ▦ ◈
A golden amber ale, hoppy with some balancing malt. There is a pleasant citrus aroma and a noticeable fruitiness in the taste, with some sweetness also present. The finish is dry, hoppy and bitter.

Gilt Complex (OG 1047, ABV 4.6%)
Golden ale with a hint of spice in the fruity flavour, and a long finish.

Greensand IPA (OG 1047, ABV 4.6%)

Suthwyk

See Oakleaf

Swan

⧢ Swan on the Green, West Peckham, Maidstone, Kent, ME18 5JW

☎ (01622) 812271 ⊕ swan-on-the-green.co.uk
Tours by arrangement

The brewery was established in 2000 in an old coal shed behind the Swan on the Green pub using a two-barrel plant.

Fuggles Pale (OG 1037, ABV 3.6%)

Trumpeter Best (OG 1041, ABV 4%)

Cygnet (OG 1048, ABV 4.2%)

Bewick (OG 1052, ABV 5.3%)

Swansea SIBA

⧢ Joiners Arms, 50 Bishopston Road, Bishopston, Swansea, SA3 3EJ
☎ (01792) 232658/290197 (Office)
✉ rory@swansea_brewing.co.uk
Tours by arrangement

☺ Opened in 1996, Swansea Brewing Co was the first commercial brewery in the area for almost 30 years. Two regular outlets are supplied along with other pubs in the South Wales area. Seasonal beers are also available.

Deep Slade Dark (OG 1034, ABV 4%)
A dark brown-coloured beer with a reddish hue with a nutty, malty taste. The aroma is malty with a little roast.

Bishopswood Bitter (OG 1043, ABV 4.3%) ◈
A delicate aroma of hops and malt in this pale brown colour. The taste is a balanced mix of hops and malt with a growing hoppy bitterness ending in a lasting bitter finish.

Three Cliffs Gold (OG 1042, ABV 4.7%) ◈
A golden beer with a hoppy and fruity aroma, a hoppy taste with fruit and malt, and a quenching bitterness. The pleasant finish has a good hop flavour and bitterness.

Original Wood (OG 1046, ABV 5.2%) ◈
A full-bodied, pale brown beer with an aroma of hops, fruit and malt. A complex blend of these flavours with a firm bitterness increasing towards the end.

Taddington

Blackwell Hall, Blackwell, Buxton, Derbyshire, SK17 9TQ
☎ (01298) 85734

No real ale. Taddington started brewing in 2007, and brews one Czech-style unpasteurised lager in two different strengths: Moravka (ABV 4.4% and 5%), which is available on draught. Taddington also brews an unfiltered version of Moravka called Moravka Kvasnicove.

Talke O' Th' Hill (NEW)

Merelake Road, Talke, Staffordshire, ST7 1UE
☎ 07875 951399 ⊕ talkeothhill.co.uk

Talke O' Th' Hill began brewing in 2011 using a two-barrel plant on a family farm on the Staffordshire border. The brewery is based on two floors in old farm buildings. Local pubs and beer festivals are supplied. Many different beers are produced.

Citrade (ABV 4.4%)
A pale, hoppy ale with strong citrus notes.

Tap East

⬛ 7 International Square, Montfichet Road, Westfield Stratford City, Stratford, E20 1EE
☎ (020) 8555 4467 ⊕ tapeast.co.uk
Shop Mon-Sat 11am-11pm; 12-11pm Sun

⊗ Tap East began brewing in 2011 and is located in the Westfield shopping centre next to the Olympic Park.

Tonic Ale (OG 1032, ABV 3%) ◆
A refreshing golden ale with strong citrus throughout. Faint biscuit notes and a bitter dry aftertaste.

East End Mild (OG 1037, ABV 3.5%)
Mild with a dark toasty malt flavour and light hop notes.

Jim Wilson Bitter (JWB) (OG 1040, ABV 3.8%)
Bitter with malty backbone and a good dose of hops.

APA (OG 1046, ABV 4.4%)
An American-style pale ale with a grapefruit aroma and underlying notes of pine resin and spice.

Coffee in the Morning (OG 1059, ABV 5.3%)
Brewed with freshly-brewed coffee roasted in Greenwich.

IPA (OG 1054, ABV 5.3%)
A different hop is used for each brew.

Tap House

⬛ Tap House, Annwell Lane, Smisby, Derbyshire, LE65 2TA
☎ (01530) 413604 ☎ 07596 486673
⊕ taphouse-smisby.co.uk

⊗ Established in 2010, this purpose built brewery was recently upgraded to a 20-barrel plant. The brewery supplies beers to its two pubs; the Tap House, Smisby, and the Kings Arms, Coleorton, as well as pubs across Derbyshire and Leicestershire. Tap House and Leatherbritches share the same brewery plant and brewer, but the two businesses are run independently.

Ashby Pride (OG 1038, ABV 3.8%)
A light, quaffable, session beer.

Tap House Gold (OG 1042, ABV 4%)
A light, hoppy, golden ale.

Kingdom (OG 1046, ABV 4.5%)
A chestnut-coloured beer with a hint of caramel.

Malt Teaser (OG 1046, ABV 4.6%)
A rich crimson beer full of malt flavours with a light toffee aftertaste.

Dark & Dangerous (OG 1048, ABV 5%)
A dark and complex porter with subtle chocolate flavours.

Tapped (NEW)

⬛ Sheffield Tap, Platform 1b, Sheffield Station, Sheaf Street, Sheffield, South Yorkshire, S1 2BP
☎ (0114) 273 7558 ⊕ sheffieldtap.com

Brewing began in 2013 after the old Edwardian dining rooms were converted into an onsite brewery with a viewing gallery at the Sheffield Tap pub. The beer is also supplied to the Euston Tap, York Tap and Pivni, York.

Tatton SIBA

Unit 7, Longridge Trading Estate, Knutsford, Cheshire, WA16 8PR
☎ (01565) 750747 ☎ 07738 150898
⊕ tattonbrewery.co.uk
Shop Mon-Fri 9am-4pm (other times by arrangement)
Tours by arrangement

⊛ Tatton is a family-run business based in the heart of Cheshire. Brewing commenced in 2010 using a steam-fired, custom-built 15-barrel brewhouse. Seasonal and occasional beers are also available. It supplies pubs throughout Cheshire and the north-west.

Ale (OG 1036, ABV 3.7%)
An easy-drinking session ale with a rich copper colour. It has a full malty/toffee flavour balanced by a soft bitterness and hoppy, fruity taste and aroma.

Blonde (OG 1039, ABV 4%)
A clean tasting, smooth pale ale with a fine hop aroma.

Best (OG 1040.5, ABV 4.2%)
A classic light amber-coloured best bitter with a clean malt flavour and fine hop character derived from a blend of aroma hops.

Gold (OG 1046, ABV 4.8%)
A golden special ale with a maltiness backed by a robust hop character.

Tavy (NEW) SIBA ◉

Unit 9, Porsham Close, Beliver Industrial Estate, Plymouth, PL6 7DB
☎ 07966 522266

Office: Jasmine Cottage, Peter Tavy, Tavistock, Devon, PL19 9NN ⊕ tavyales.co.uk
Tours by arrangement

⊗ Tavy Ales is a family-run microbrewery, started in 2012, brewing on a six-barrel plant on the outskirts of Plymouth. To keep things local its spent barley goes to feed local cattle, pigs and brewery partner's chickens.

Best Bitter (OG 1043, ABV 4.3%)
A full-bodied chestnut brown beer with a well-rounded complex malt flavour and early bitterness.

Ideal Pale Ale (OG 1048, ABV 4.8%)
A well-balanced pale golden beer loaded with citrus flavour, with a strong floral, hoppy aroma.

Porter (OG 1052, ABV 5.2%)
A dark stout with a roasted, bittersweet flavour and an intense chocolate finish.

Timothy Taylor SIBA IFBB ◉

Knowle Spring Brewery, Keighley, West Yorkshire, BD21 1AW
☎ (01535) 603139 ⊕ timothy-taylor.co.uk

⊛ An independent, family-owned company established in 1858, Timothy Taylor has occupied the Knowle Spring site since 1863. Pennine spring water is used to brew its award-winning ales that are served in 26 tied pubs as well as more than 300 directly delivered outlets. Expanded brewing facilities opened on the main site in 2011.

Dark Mild (OG 1034, ABV 3.5%) ◆

Malt and caramel dominate throughout in this sweetish beer with background hop and fruit notes.

Golden Best (OG 1033, ABV 3.5%) ◈
Refreshing, amber-coloured traditional Pennine light mild. Malty throughout. Fruit in the nose increases to complement the delicate hoppy taste.

Boltmaker (OG 1038, ABV 4%) 🍺 ◈
Tawny bitter combining hops, fruit and nutty malt. Lingering, increasingly bitter aftertaste. Formerly and sometimes still sold as Best Bitter.

Landlord (OG 1042, ABV 4.3%) ◈
A hoppy, increasingly bitter finish complements the background malt and citrus character of this full-flavoured and well-balanced amber beer.

Ram Tam (OG 1043, ABV 4.3%) ◈
A black beer with red highlights topped by a coffee coloured head. Roast coffee bitterness is balanced by fruit and malt with burnt caramel coming through in the dry and bitter finish.

Teignworthy SIBA

The Maltings, Teign Road, Teignworthy, Newton Abbot, Devon, TQ12 4AA
☎ (01626) 332066 ⊕ teignworthybrewery.com
Shop Mon-Fri 10am-5pm at Tuckers Maltings
Tours by arrangement

Teignworthy brewery opened in 1994 within the historic Tuckers Maltings building. The 20-barrel plant produces 100 barrels a week using malt from Tuckers and supplies around 300 outlets in Devon and Somerset. A large range of seasonal ales is available: see website. Bottle-conditioned beers are also produced.

Neap Tide (OG 1038, ABV 3.8%)
A pale fruity bitter.

Reel Ale (OG 1039.5, ABV 4%) ◈
Clean, sharp-tasting bitter with lasting hoppiness; predominantly malty aroma.

Gun Dog (OG 1043.5, ABV 4.3%)
A light bronze-coloured ale with a flowery, fruity aromatic finish.

Spring Tide (OG 1043.5, ABV 4.3%) ◈
An excellent, full and well-rounded, mid-brown beer with a dry, bitter taste and aftertaste.

Old Moggie (OG 1044.5, ABV 4.4%)
A golden, hoppy and fruity ale.

Beachcomber (OG 1045.5, ABV 4.5%) ◈
A pale brown beer with a light, refreshing fruit and hop nose, grapefruit taste and a dry, hoppy finish.

Teme Valley SIBA

🍴 **The Talbot, Bromyard Road, Knightwick, Worcestershire, WR6 5PH**
☎ (01886) 821235 ⊕ temevalleybrewery.co.uk
Tours by arrangement

☺Teme Valley Brewery opened in 1997. In 2005, new investment enabled the brewery to expand to a 15-barrel brew-length. It maintains strong ties with local hop farming, using only Worcestershire-grown hops. Some 30 outlets are supplied. Seasonal beers: see website.

T'Other (OG 1035, ABV 3.5%) ◈

Refreshing amber beer offering an abundance of flavour in the fruity aroma, followed by a short, dry bitterness.

This (OG 1037, ABV 3.7%) ◈
Dark gold brew with a mellow array of flavours in a malty balance.

That (OG 1041, ABV 4.1%) ◈
A rich, fruity nose and a wide range of hoppy and malty flavours in this copper-coloured best bitter.

Talbot Blonde (OG 1044, ABV 4.4%)
A smooth, rich, well-hopped pale beer.

Tempest

Winchester Row, Kelso, TD5 7DT
☎ (01573) 229664 ⊕ tempestbrewingco.com
Tours by arrangement

Tempest was set up in 2010 by Gavin Meiklejohn, brewer and co-proprietor of the Cobbles in Kelso, which is the brewery tap. Gavin's focus is on using bold flavours and ingredients to produce interesting styles based on classic and New World beers. Seasonal and bottle-conditioned beers: see website.

Cascadian Blonde (OG 1041, ABV 4.1%)
Light body with floral, grapefruit and lychee notes.

Cresta (OG 1045, ABV 4.1%)
Full-bodied black ale with chocolate, spice, blackcurrant and floral notes.

Pale Ale (OG 1045, ABV 4.5%)
Full-bodied beer with blackcurrant, citrus and spicy notes.

Long White Cloud (OG 1054, ABV 5.6%)
A refreshing pale ale with tropical fruit and spice, vinous in hop character.

Temptation (NEW)

Unit 18D, Cherry Way, Dubmire Industrial Estate, Houghton le Spring, Tyne & Wear, DH4 5RJ
☎ 07932 774745
⊕ temptationbrewingcompany.co.uk

Temptation began brewing in 2011 using a 2.5-barrel plant upgrading to a six barrels in 2013. Local outlets are supplied in a 20-mile radius of the brewery. The beer range is subject to change.

Terrace (NEW)

Sandford Terrace, Aylburton, Gloucestershire, GL15 6DW
☎ (01594) 840100 ☎ 07942 205947
⊕ terracebrewery.co.uk

Terrace began brewing in 2012 using a 0.5-barrel plant situated in a shed in the brewer's garden. Only bottle-conditioned beers are produced. Beers are available in local farm shops. See website for details.

Thame

🍴 **1 East Street, Thame, OX9 3JS**
☎ (01844) 218202
✉ thamebrewery@btinternet.com
Tours by arrangement

⊗ This one-barrel brewery was set up in 2009 by Peter Lambert and Oak Taverns in the old stables at the Cross Keys. Beer is produced for the Cross Keys and beer festivals, and many one-off brews are produced.

Mr Splodge's Mild (OG 1040, ABV 4%)
A dark mild named after the pub cat.

Hoppiness (OG 1042, ABV 4.2%)
A golden ale.

That Little Brewery (NEW)

c/o Farmers Boy, 134 London Road, St Albans, Hertfordshire, AL1 1PQ

Correspondence: 5 Station Road, Harpenden, Hertfordshire, AL5 4SN

That Little Brewery is run by Alec Goodhand who produces two bottle-conditioned beers for his restaurant That Little Place. Cask-conditioned beer is occasionally available on request.

Theakston ⊙

The Brewery, Masham, North Yorkshire, HG4 4YD
☎ (01765) 680000 ⊕ theakstons.co.uk
Tours by arrangement

☺After several years under the control of other companies, Theakston is now owned by four brothers, grandsons of Thomas Theakston, the son of the company's founder, who built the brewery in 1875. A new fermentation room was built in 2004 to provide additional flexibility and capacity, and further capacity was added in 2006. Seasonal beers: see website.

Best Bitter (OG 1038, ABV 3.8%)
A golden-coloured beer with a full flavour. With a good bitter/sweet balance, this beer has a robust hop character, citrus and spicy.

Black Bull Bitter (OG 1037, ABV 3.9%) ◆
A distinctively hoppy aroma leads to a bitter, hoppy taste with some fruitiness and a short bitter finish.

Lightfoot (OG 1041, ABV 4.1%)

XB (OG 1044, ABV 4.5%)
A sweet-tasting bitter with background fruit and spicy hop. Some caramel character gives this ale a malty dominance.

Old Peculier (OG 1057, ABV 5.6%) ☐ ◆
A full-bodied, dark brown, strong ale. Slightly malty but with hints of roast coffee and liquorice. A smooth caramel overlay and a complex fruitiness leads to a bitter chocolate finish.

Thomas Guest

See Black Country

Abraham Thompson

Flass Lane, Barrow-in-Furness, Cumbria, LA13 0AD
☎ 07708 191437
✉ abraham.thompson@btinternet.com

☺The half-barrel plant was set up in 2005 to return Barrow-brewed beers to local pubs. Distribution is limited to a few outlets in the Low Furness area but can usually be found at Ulverston Beer Festival.

John Thompson

⊟ Ingleby, Melbourne, Derbyshire, DE73 7HW
☎ (01332) 862469 ⊕ johnthompsoninn.com

Tours by arrangement

⊗John Thompson set up the brewery in 1977. The pub and brewery are now run by his son, Nick. Seasonal beers are also available.

JTS XXX (OG 1041, ABV 4.1%)

Gold (OG 1045, ABV 4.5%)

Thornbridge SIBA ⊙

Riverside Business Park, Buxton Road, Bakewell, Derbyshire, DE45 1GS
☎ (01629) 641000 ⊕ thornbridgebrewery.co.uk
Shop Mon-Fri 9am-5pm
Tours by arrangement

☺The first Thornbridge beers were produced in 2005 using a 10-barrel brewery, housed in the grounds of Thornbridge Hall. The beers have had considerable success with over 300 consumer and industry awards being won. A 30-barrel brewery opened in Bakewell in 2009. The original site continues to develop new, seasonal and speciality beers. 200 outlets are supplied direct. 12 pubs are managed and owned. Unfiltered and bottle-conditioned beers are available.

Wild Swan (OG 1035, ABV 3.5%) ◨ ◆
Extremely pale yet flavoursome and refreshing beer. Plenty of lemon citrus hop flavour, becoming increasingly dry and bitter in the finish and aftertaste.

Brother Rabbit (OG 1035, ABV 4%)
Lemon zest in colour with a clean, hoppy aroma, a resinous finish and some bitterness.

Lord Marples (OG 1041, ABV 4%) ◆
Smooth, traditional, easy-drinking bitter. Caramel, malt and coffee flavours fall away to leave a long, bitter finish.

Ashford (OG 1043, ABV 4.2%)
A brown ale with a floral hoppiness, a smooth, malty kick and a delicate coffee finish.

Kipling (OG 1050, ABV 5.2%) ◆
Golden pale bitter with aromas of grapefruit and passion fruit. Intense fruit flavours continue throughout, leading to a long bitter aftertaste.

Jaipur IPA (OG 1055, ABV 5.9%) ◨ ◆
Flavoursome IPA packed with citrus hoppiness that's nicely counterbalanced by malt and underlying sweetness and robust fruit flavours.

Saint Petersburg (OG 1073, ABV 7.7%) ◆
Good example of an imperial stout. Smooth and easy to drink with raisins, bitter chocolate and hops throughout, leading to a lingering coffee and chocolate aftertaste.

Three B's SIBA ⊙

⊟ Black Bull, Brokenstone Road, Tockholes, Blackburn, Lancashire, BB3 0LL
☎ (01254) 581381 ⊕ threebsbrewery.co.uk
Tours by arrangement

Robert Bell acquired the Black Bull pub in Tockholes in 2011 and relocated his 2-barrel brewery there. This brewpub now supplies 50 outlets. A bottling plant has been installed and bottle-conditioned beers are available in local supermarkets.

Bee Thrifty (OG 1036, ABV 3.4%)
A light and refreshing amber-coloured beer.

Stoker's Slake (OG 1038, ABV 3.6%) ◆

Lightly roasted coffee flavours are in the aroma and the initial taste. A well-rounded, dark brown mild with dried fruit flavours in the long finish.

Honey Bee (OG 1039, ABV 3.7%)
A golden honey beer with honey apparent in both aroma and taste.

Bobbin's Bitter (OG 1038, ABV 3.8%)
A golden bitter with warm aromas of nutty grain and a full, fruity flavour with a light, dry finish.

Bee Blonde (OG 1041, ABV 4%)
A distinctive, pale bitter with a light, dry balance of grain and hops, and a delicate finish with citrus fruits.

Tackler's Tipple (OG 1044, ABV 4.3%)
A dark best bitter with full hop flavour, biscuit tones on the tongue and a deep, dry finish.

Doff Cocker (OG 1045, ABV 4.5%) ◥
Yellow with a hoppy aroma and initial taste giving way to subtle malt notes and orchard fruit flavours. Crisp, dry finish.

Pinch Noggin (OG 1046, ABV 4.6%)
A dark, strong best bitter with full hop flavour and a long aftertaste.

Knocker Up (OG 1047, ABV 4.8%) ◥
A smooth, rich, creamy porter. The roast flavour is foremost without dominating and is balanced by fruit and hop notes.

Shuttle Ale (OG 1050, ABV 5.2%)
A traditional strong pale ale.

For Black Bull, Tockholes:

Black Bull (OG 1042, ABV 4%)
Dark ruby-red bitter with a rich character and a hint of chocolate.

Three Castles SIBA

Unit 12, Salisbury Road Business Park, Pewsey, Wiltshire, SN9 5PZ
☎ (01672) 564433 ☎ 07725 148671
⊕ threecastlesbrewery.co.uk
Shop Mon-Fri 9am-4pm; Sat 9am-1pm
Tours by arrangement

Three Castles is an independent, family-run brewery, established in 2006. Seasonal beers: see website. Bottle-conditioned beers are available.

Barbury Castle (OG 1039, ABV 3.9%)
A balanced, easy-drinking pale ale with a hoppy, spicy palate.

Saxon Archer (OG 1040, ABV 4%)

Heritage (OG 1042, ABV 4.2%)

Vale Ale (OG 1043, ABV 4.3%)
Golden-coloured with a fruity palate and strong floral aroma.

Corn Dolly (OG 1047, ABV 4.7%)

Three Daggers (NEW)

Westbury Road, Edington, Wiltshire, BA13 4PG
☎ (01380) 830940 ⊕ threedaggersbrewery.com

Three Daggers was established in 2013 using a 2.5-barrel plant in a farm shop adjacent to the Three Daggers pub. Malt is sourced locally from Warminster Maltings and hops from Charles Faram in Worcestershire. Beer is available in the pub and

other local outlets. Bottled beers are available in the farm shop.

Daggers Ale (OG 1042, ABV 4.1%)
A malty, refreshing ale with a dry, hoppy finish.

Three Kings SIBA

14 Prospect Terrace, North Shields, Tyne & Wear, NE30 1DX
☎ 07580 004565 ⊕ threekingsbrewery.co.uk

Three Kings began in 2012 using a 2.5-barrel plant. An upgrade to a five-barrel plant is planned. Previously-brewed beers can be brewed again on request.

Gallowgate Raw (OG 1045, ABV 4.4%)

Highgate Sworn (OG 1047, ABV 4.4%)

Ring of Fire (OG 1048, ABV 4.5%)

Ha'penny Dodger (OG 1052, ABV 4.9%)

Pigge's Hede (OG 1050, ABV 4.9%)

Soleil D'or (OG 1048, ABV 4.9%)

Silver Darling (OG 1054, ABV 5.6%)

Three Peaks

Scar Top Brewery, Buck Haw Brow, Settle, North Yorkshire, BD24 0DJ
☎ (01729) 822939

Office: 7 Craven Terrace, Settle, North Yorkshire, BD24 9DB ⊕ threepeaksbrewery.co.uk

⊗ Established in 2006, Three Peaks is run by husband and wife team Colin and Susan Ashwell. Two beers are brewed at present on their five-barrel plant and a third is planned.

Pen-y-Ghent Bitter (OG 1040, ABV 3.8%) ◥
The malty character of this mid-brown session bitter is balanced by fruit in the aroma and taste. The finish is malty and hoppy.

Ingleborough Gold (OG 1041, ABV 4%) ◥
This golden coloured best bitter is hoppy throughout with fruit in the aroma and taste and a hoppy bitter finish.

Three Tuns SIBA ◉

16 Market Square, Bishop's Castle, Shropshire, SY9 5BN
☎ (01588) 638392 ⊕ threetunsbrewery.co.uk
Shop Mon-Fri 9am-5pm
Tours by arrangement

Brewing on this site started in the 16th century. The brewery was licensed in 1642 and is the oldest licensed brewery in the country. A small scale tower brewery from the late 19th century survives as well as parts of an earlier brewhouse dating from the 17th century. Seasonal beers: see website.

1642 Bitter (OG 1042, ABV 3.8%)
A golden ale with a light, nutty maltiness and spicy bitterness.

XXX (OG 1046, ABV 4.3%) ◥
A pale, sweetish bitter with a light hop aftertaste that has a honey finish.

Stout (OG 1048, ABV 4.4%)
Old fashioned-style stout.

Cleric's Cure (OG 1059, ABV 5%)

A light tan-coloured ale with a malty sweetness. Strong and spicy with a floral bitterness.

Old Scooge (OG 1065, ABV 6%)

Thurstons (NEW) SIBA

Crown, 104 High Street, Horsell, Surrey, GU21 4ST
☎ (01483) 771719 ☎ 07789 936784
⊕ thurstonsbrewery.com

⊠ Thurstons opened in 2012. The brewery currently produces about four firkins a week, mostly sold at the Crown. There are plans to expand the brew-plant and to brew more frequently.

Malt Way (OG 1042, ABV 4%)
A chestnut-coloured beer with malt notes, and a late hop finish.

Stedmans Ale (OG 1042, ABV 4.1%)
A balanced, golden ale with a crisp citrus taste.

McGintys Stout (OG 1055, ABV 4.5%)
A traditional milk stout: dark, creamy, and full-bodied, with chocolate and coffee notes.

Thwaites IFBB ◉

Star Brewery, PO Box 50, Blackburn, Lancashire, BB1 5BU
☎ (01254) 686868 ⊕ danielthwaites.com
Tours by arrangement

☺Established in 1807, Thwaites is still controlled by the Yerburgh family, descendants of the founder, Daniel Thwaites. The company owns around 350 pubs, with over two thirds selling real ale. Monthly and quarterly cask beers and three bottle-conditioned beers are produced. In 2011 a 20-barrel microbrewery was added.

Nutty Black (OG 1036, ABV 3.3%)
A tasty traditional dark mild presenting a malty flavour with caramel notes and a slightly bitter finish.

Original (OG 1036, ABV 3.6%)
Hop driven, yet well-balanced amber session bitter. Hops continue through to the long finish.

Wainwright (OG 1042, ABV 4.1%)
A straw-coloured bitter with soft fruit flavours and a hint of malty sweetness.

Lancaster Bomber (OG 1044, ABV 4.4%) ⌖
Well-balanced, copper-coloured best bitter with firm malt flavours, a fruity background and a long, dry finish.

Tigertops

22 Oakes Street, Flanshaw, Wakefield, West Yorkshire, WF2 9LN
☎ (01229) 716238 ☎ 07951 812986
✉ tigertopsbrewery@hotmail.com

☺Tigertops was established in 1995 by Stuart Johnson and his wife Lynda who, as well as owning the brewery, run the Foxfield brewpub in Cumbria (qv). The brewery is run on their behalf by Barry Smith, supplying five regular outlets. Seasonal and experimental beers are also brewed.

Dark Wheat Mild (OG 1036, ABV 3.6%)
An unusual mild made primarily with wheat malt.

Tom Tom Mild (ABV 3.7%)
Dark rye mild.

Off the Wall (ABV 4.1%)

Black Art (ABV 4.4%)

Palate Wrecker (ABV 4.4%)

Blanche de Newland (OG 1044, ABV 4.5%)
A cloudy Belgian-style wheat beer.

Ginger Fix (OG 1044, ABV 4.6%)
A mid-amber ginger beer.

White Max (OG 1044, ABV 4.6%)
A light, German-style wheat beer.

Dunkelweiss (OG 1046, ABV 4.8%)
A dark, German-style wheat beer.

Big Ginger (OG 1058, ABV 6%)
A strong, amber ginger beer.

Tillingbourne SIBA

Old Scotland Farm, Staple Lane, Shere, Surrey, GU5 9TE
☎ (01483) 222228 ⊕ tillybeer.co.uk
Shop Fri 1-6.30pm; Sat 10am-3.30pm (other times by arrangement)
Tours by arrangement

⊠ Tillingbourne began brewing in 2011 on a farm site previously used by Surrey Hills Brewery using its old 17-barrel plant. Around 25 local outlets are supplied. Seasonal beers: see website.

The Source (OG 1033, ABV 3.3%)
A light golden beer with a refreshing floral taste.

Black Troll (OG 1035, ABV 3.7%) ◆
A black bitter in which initial roast notes are eventually overpowered by citrus hop through to the finish.

AONB (OG 1036, ABV 4%) ◆
Golden ale in which citrus hop dominates throughout. Some balancing malt in the aroma and taste, however.

Falls Gold (OG 1037, ABV 4.2%) ◆
While hops dominate, balancing malt is evident throughout. Hints of grapefruit in the aroma and taste lead to a dry finish.

Hop Troll (OG 1045, ABV 4.8%)
An American-style IPA with plenty of hops.

TinPot

⊟ Allanwater Brewhouse, Queens Lane, Bridge of Allan, Stirlingshire, FK9 4NY
☎ (01786) 834555 ⊕ bridgeofallan.co.uk
Shop 12-5pm daily
Tours by arrangement

☺Tinpot opened in 2009 using a one-barrel plant designed to brew speciality beers and started supplying CAMRA Beer Festivals in 2010. Bottle-conditioned beers are available. The beer range varies depending on season and demand.

Gold Pot 70/- (OG 1040, ABV 3.9%)
A refreshing session beer with a taste of grapefruit.

Choc Pot 80/- (OG 1046, ABV 4.5%)

Pot Black (OG 1052, ABV 5%)

Procrastination (OG 1060, ABV 6%)

Tintagel SIBA

Condolden Farm, Tintagel, Cornwall, PL34 0HJ
☎ (01840) 213371 ⊕ tintagelbrewery.co.uk

Shop 9am-5pm (phone ahead to confirm)

⊗ This 7.5-barrel brewery was established in 2009 in a redundant milking parlour on the highest farm in Cornwall. Some 80 outlets are now supplied direct. Bottle-conditioned and seasonal beers are also available.

Black Knight (OG 1040, ABV 3.8%)

Castle Gold (OG 1038, ABV 3.8%) ⊓

Cornwall's Pride (OG 1040, ABV 4%) ◆
Ripe fruit with toffee on the nose. Full-bodied, copper-coloured and clean-tasting malty ale balanced by bitterness and sweetness, finishing dry.

Castle Gold Extra (OG 1042, ABV 4.2%) ◆
Medium-bodied golden ale with light fruity aroma. Powerful hoppy bitterness on the tongue balanced by fruit sweetness. Long, bitter and dry finish with some citrus hop fruit.

Gull Rock (OG 1042.6, ABV 4.2%) ◆
Tawny-coloured best bitter. Malt aroma with some berry fruit. The taste is malt sweetness with traces of hop bitterness and caramel, finishing the same but with a little dryness.

Harbour Special (OG 1048.9, ABV 4.8%) ◆
Tawny ale with ripe fruity, malty aroma. Rich malt, stone fruits and esters in the mouth finishing bitter and dry.

Tiny Rebel SIBA

Unit 12a, Maes Glas Industrial Estate, Greenwich Road, Newport, NP20 2NN
☎ (01633) 547378 ☎ 07980 798268
⊕ tinyrebel.co.uk
Shop Mon-Fri 8am-5pm
Tours by arrangement

☺Tiny Rebel was set up in 2012 by two enthusiastic home brewers. The brewery operates on a 12-barrel plant with 3 fermentation tanks and 4 conditioning tanks. Bottled beers are available.

Fubar (OG 1042, ABV 4.4%)

Billabong (OG 1044, ABV 4.6%)
Australian-style pale ale.

Cwtch (OG 1044, ABV 4.6%)
Welsh red ale.

The Full Nelson (OG 1046, ABV 4.8%)
Strong grape flavours are complemented by the sweet malt, making this beer crisp and refreshing.

Dirty Stopout (OG 1048, ABV 5%)
Smoked oak stout.

Urban IPA (OG 1054, ABV 5.5%)

Chocoholic (OG 1065, ABV 6.8%)

Hadouken (OG 1071, ABV 7.4%)

Tipples SIBA

Units 5 & 6, Damgate Lane Industrial Estate, Acle, Norfolk, NR13 3DJ
☎ (01493) 741007 ⊕ tipplesbrewery.com

⊗ Tipples was established by Jason Tipple in 2004 on a six-barrel brew plant and produces both cask and bottle-conditioned ales. An extensive range of bottled beers is produced, which can be found in some farmers markets and local supermarkets.

Hanged Monk (OG 1038, ABV 3.8%) ◆

Strong roast and malt notes dominate the aroma and follow through to the taste. A slightly grainy mouthfeel is softened by a hint of caramel and a growing vinous finish.

Sundown (OG 1040, ABV 3.9%) ◆
A barrage of berries and malt introduce this smooth creamy bitter. A muted bitterness gives depth to the fruity malt core as it slowly sweetens.

Redhead (OG 1042, ABV 4.2%) ◆
Malt and hops are well matched in both nose and palate. Toffee in the nose and initial taste soon gives way to an increasing bitterness. A fine finale retains the mix of flavours.

Brewers Progress (OG 1046, ABV 4.6%) ◆
A solid malty, tawny beer with strong caramel and vanilla support. The smooth creamy character is given added depth by a blackcurrant fruitiness. Some bitterness in the finish.

Moonrocket (OG 1050, ABV 5%) ◆
A complex golden brew with an earthy aroma. Malt hop bitterness and a fruity sweetness swirl round in an ever-changing kaleidoscope of flavours. A satisfying finish with hops finally emerging on top.

Tipsy Angel

≡ Lower Angel, 27 Buttermarket Street, Warrington, Cheshire, WA1 2LY
☎ (01925) 653326 ☎ 07775 946167
⊕ lowerangel.co.uk
Tours by arrangement

☺Tipsy Angel began brewing in 2011 using a one-barrel plant. The brewery was founded to recreate the brews from the original recipes of Walkers of Warrington. Beers are mainly produced for the Lower Angel pub, but are also occasionally available at beer festivals.

Angelic Mild (OG 1037, ABV 3.6%)

Angelic Blonde (OG 1044, ABV 4.4%)

Angel's Folly (OG 1052, ABV 5.2%)

Tír Dhá Ghlas

Cullins Yard, 11 Cambridge Road, Dover, Kent, CT17 9BY
☎ (01304) 211666 ⊕ cullinsyard.co.uk

⊗ Brewing began in 2012 using a two-barrel plant. Beers are available in the bar/restaurant, frequently at the Pier Three pub in Dover and occasionally at the nearby Royal Cinque Ports Yacht Club, particularly when they are holding festivals.

Jolly Roger (ABV 3.7%)

Pig's Ear (ABV 3.7%)

Jimmy's Riddle (ABV 4.7%)

Tirril SIBA

Red House, Long Marton, Appleby-in-Westmorland, Cumbria, CA16 6BN
☎ (01768) 361846 ⊕ tirrilales.co.uk
Tours by arrangement

☺Established in 1999, Tirril brewery has twice outgrown its premises and is now based at the Red House Barn in Long Marton beneath the Pennines. Capacity has grown to 60 barrels. It has over 100 outlets, 30 of which regularly stock the beer. One pub is owned.

Bewshers Bitter (OG 1038.5, ABV 3.8%)
A lightly-hopped, golden brown session beer.

Nameless Ale (OG 1038.5, ABV 3.8%)
A golden, easy-drinking session beer.

Brougham Ale (OG 1039, ABV 3.9%)
A gently hopped, amber bitter.

Eden Valley Pale Ale (OG 1040, ABV 4%)
Pale session bitter with a fresh hoppy taste.

Old Faithful (OG 1040, ABV 4%) ◆
Initially bitter, gold-coloured ale with an astringent finish.

1823 (OG 1041, ABV 4.1%)
A full-bodied session bitter with a gentle bitterness.

Academy Ale (OG 1041.5, ABV 4.2%)
A dark, full-bodied, traditional rich and malty ale.

Titanic SIBA ◉

Unit 5, Callender Place, Burslem, Stoke-on-Trent, Staffordshire, ST6 1JL
☎ (01782) 823447 ⊕ titanicbrewery.co.uk
Tours by arrangement

⊕Founded in 1985 and named after Captain Smith: a Potteries man and the captain of the Titanic. The brewery supplies more than 300 free trade outlets and has a small, constantly expanding tied house estate. Monthly seasonal and bottle-conditioned beers are available.

Mild (OG 1036, ABV 3.5%) ◆
Fresh fruity hop aroma leads to a caramel start then a rush of bitter hoppiness ending with a lingering dry finish.

Steerage (OG 1036, ABV 3.5%) ◆
Pale yellow bitter. Flavours start with hops and fruit but become zesty and refreshing in this light session beer with a long, dry finish.

Lifeboat (OG 1040, ABV 4%) ◆
Dark brown with fruit, malt and caramel aromas. Sweet start, malty and caramel middle with hoppiness developing into a fruity and dry lingering finish.

Anchor Bitter (OG 1042, ABV 4.1%) ◆
Amber beer with a spicy hint to the fruity start followed by a rush of hops that leads to a dry bitter finish.

Iceberg (OG 1042, ABV 4.1%) ◆
Yellow gold sparkling wheat beer with a flowery start leading to a massively hoppy, zesty finish.

Chocolate & Vanilla Stout (OG 1047, ABV 4.5%) ▣ ◆
Chocoholic paradise with real coffee and vanilla support. Cocoa, sherry and almonds lend depth to this creamy, drinkable stout.

Stout (OG 1046, ABV 4.5%) ⬠ ▣ ◆
Roasty, toasty with tobacco, autumn bonfires, chocolate and hints of liquorice; perfectly balanced with a bitter, dry finish reminiscent of real coffee.

White Star (OG 1050, ABV 4.8%) ◆
Hints of cinnamon apple pie are found before the hops take over to give a bitter edge to this well balanced refreshing fruity beer.

Plum Porter (OG 1051, ABV 4.9%) ◆

Dark brown with a powerful fruity aroma. A sweet plum fruitiness gives way to a gentle bitter finish.

Captain Smith's Strong Ale (OG 1054, ABV 5.2%) ◆
Red brown and full bodied, lots of malt and roast with a hint of honey but a strong bittersweet finish.

Toll End

⊟ c/o Waggon and Horses, 131 Toll End Road, Tipton, West Midlands, DY4 0ET
☎ 07903 725574
Tours by arrangement

The four-barrel brewery opened in 2004. With the exception of Phoebe's Ale (ABV 4.4%), named after the brewer's daughter, all brews commemorate local landmarks, events and people. Seasonal beers are brewed throughout the year.

Lil Devil Stout (ABV 5.4%)

Tollgate SIBA ◉

Unit 1, Southwood House Farm, Calke, Ashby-de-la-Zouch, Leicestershire, LE65 1RG
☎ (01283) 229194 ⊕ tollgatebrewery.com
Tours by arrangement

⊠ This six-barrel brewery was founded in 2005 on the site of the old Brunt & Bucknall Brewery in Woodville but relocated to new premises on the National Trust's Calke Park estate nearby in 2012. Seasonal, occasional specials and bottle-conditioned beers are also available.

Stand & Deliver (OG 1036, ABV 3.8%)
Traditional session bitter with malt flavour and a smooth finish.

Tollgate Bitter (TGB) (OG 1041, ABV 4.3%)
A smooth easy-drinking bitter.

Ashby Pale (OG 1043, ABV 4.5%)
A light, refreshing beer with a citrus finish.

Red Star IPA (OG 1043, ABV 4.5%)
A classic hoppy India Pale Ale.

Billy's Best Bitter (OG 1044, ABV 4.6%)
Dark amber best bitter.

Kalika IPA (OG 1046, ABV 4.8%)
Copper-coloured beer with four hops for real depth of flavour.

Red McAdy (OG 1048, ABV 5%)
Whisky-conditioned northern ale.

For Harrington Arms, Thulston:

Earl's Ale (OG 1042, ABV 4%)

Tolly Cobbold

See Greene King

Tonbridge SIBA

Unit 19, Branbridges Industrial Estate, East Peckham, Kent, TN12 5HF
☎ 07962 016286 ⊕ tonbridgebrewery.co.uk
Tours by arrangement

Tonbridge Brewery was launched in 2010 using a four-barrel plant and is run by Paul and Lynne Bournazian. It produces cask-conditioned ales using only Kent-grown hops and supplies pubs within a 25-mile radius of Tonbridge.

Golden Braun (OG 1034, ABV 3%)

Traditional (OG 1038, ABV 3.6%)

Copper Nob (OG 1040, ABV 3.8%)
Fairly dry summer ale with light maltiness, delicate bitterness and fruity taste.

Rustic (OG 1042, ABV 4%)
Deep bronze-coloured, rich-tasting country ale. Lightly hopped with the scarce, Kent-grown Epic variety, giving a delicate spicy taste and aroma.

Blonde Ambition (OG 1041, ABV 4.2%)
A crisp, clean blonde ale with a refreshing bitterness and slightly spicy aroma.

Ebony Moon (OG 1043, ABV 4.2%)
A rich porter with pronounced maltiness balanced by a mild bitterness.

Toolmakers (NEW) SIBA

6-8 Botsford Street, Sheffield, South Yorkshire, S3 9PF
☎ (0114) 245 4374 ☎ 07956 235332
⊕ toolmakersbrewery.co.uk

Toolmakers is a family-run brewery established in 2012. Beers are brewed on a five-barrel plant and available in local pubs. The beer list is still being developed.

Topsham SIBA

Globe Hotel, Fore Street, Topsham, Devon, EX3 0DP
☎ (01392) 873471 ⊕ topsham-ales.co.uk
Tours by arrangement

Topsham Ales has operated since 2010. It is run solely by volunteers as a community project, one of only a handful of co-operatively owned breweries in the UK. The beer is sold locally in Exeter and East Devon.

Trucklebed Alley (ABV 4.2%)

Tower SIBA

Old Water Tower, Walsitch Maltings, Glensyl Way, Burton upon Trent, Staffordshire, DE14 1PZ
☎ (01283) 562888 ⊕ towerbrewery.co.uk
Shop Mon-Thu 9am-5pm; Fri 9am-11.30pm
Tours by arrangement

⊚Tower was established in 2001 by John Mills in a converted derelict water tower of Thomas Salt's Brewery. The conversion was given a Civic Society award for the restoration of a historic building in 2001. Tower has 20 regular outlets. Seasonal beers are also available.

Thomas Salt's Burton Ale (OG 1035, ABV 3.5%)

Bitter (OG 1042, ABV 4.2%) ◄
Gold coloured with a malty, caramel and hoppy aroma. A full hop and fruit taste with the fruit lingering. A bitter and astringent finish.

Malty Towers (OG 1044, ABV 4.4%)

Gone for a Burton (OG 1046, ABV 4.6%)

Imperial Pale Ale (OG 1050, ABV 5%)

Towles' SIBA

Unit 11, Circuit 32, Easton Road, Easton, Bristol, BS5 0DB
☎ (0117) 321 3188 ⊕ towlesfineales.co.uk

Shop Mon-Fri 9.30am-2pm (other times by arrangement)
Tours by arrangement

⊠ Towles' is a 10-barrel brewery built in the tower style and run by Andrew and Anna Towle. Berrow Brewery was purchased in 2011 and brewing commenced on the site in Easton in 2012. The Berrow beers will continue to be brewed. The brewery includes a shop and tasting room. Bottle-conditioned beers are also available.

Berrow 4B (OG 1038, ABV 3.9%) ◄
A pale brown session beer with a fruity flavour and bitterness on the palate and finish.

Old Smiler (OG 1041, ABV 4.1%) ◄
Traditional malty best bitter. Malt and roast flavours continue into the complex aftertaste which includes subtle English hops.

Berrow Topsy Turvy (OG 1055, ABV 5.9%) ◄
Complex aromas of malt, hops and fruit in this golden ale. Sweet malt and zingy hop flavours with an astringent finish.

Town Mill SIBA

Mill Lane, Lyme Regis, Dorset, DT7 3PU
☎ (01297) 444354 ⊕ townmillbrewery.com
Shop & outside drinking area Mon-Fri 10am-5pm; Sat & Sun 11am-5pm

⊠ Town Mill began brewing in 2010 using a four-barrel plant in a part of the town mill that at one time had been the home of Lyme Regis' electricity generator, although historic use of the building was as a brewer's malthouse. There are plans to expand to a 10-barrel plant. Seasonal and bottle-conditioned beers are also available.

Cobb (OG 1041, ABV 3.9%)
An amber/brown bitter with a full flavour and traditional-tasting fruity hop finish.

Lyme Gold (OG 1042, ABV 4.2%)
A pale summer ale, easy drinking with a refreshing citrus aroma.

Best (OG 1045, ABV 4.5%)
A reddish brown bitter with a fruit and nut flavour.

Black Ven (OG 1050, ABV 5%)
A dark brown porter with a pronounced depth of flavour, enhanced by the blackcurrant fruitiness of the hops.

Townes

▤ Speedwell Inn, Lowgates, Staveley, Derbyshire, S43 3TT
☎ (01246) 472252
✉ curly@townes48.wanadoo.co.uk

Townes started in 1994 in an old bakery on the outskirts of Chesterfield using a five-barrel plant. It was the first brewery in the town for more than 40 years. In 1997 the Speedwell Inn at Staveley was bought and the plant was moved to the rear of the pub, becoming the first brew-pub in north Derbyshire in the 20th century. Seasonal beers are occasionally available.

Speedwell Bitter (OG 1039, ABV 3.9%) ◄
Straw-coloured session bitter with little aroma. Initially quite sweet leading to a bitterness developing in the long, slightly astringent aftertaste.

Staveley Cross (OG 1043, ABV 4.3%) ◆
Amber gold best bitter with a faint banana aroma. Hoppy with bitterness present throughout, culminating in a short, dry, slightly astringent aftertaste.

Pynot Porter (OG 1045, ABV 4.5%) ◆
Red-brown porter with a faint malt and roast coffee aroma. Roast malt flavours combine with vine fruit, becoming increasingly bitter towards the finish.

Townhouse

Units 1-4, Townhouse Studios, Townhouse Farm, Alsager Road, Audley, Staffordshire, ST7 8JQ
☎ 07976 209437/07812 035143
✉ nixon@njane2.orangehome.co.uk
Tours by arrangement

Townhouse was set up in 2002 with a 2.5-barrel plant. In 2004 the brewery scaled up to five barrels. Demand is growing rapidly and in early 2006 two additional fermenting vessels were added. Bottling is planned.

Traditional Scottish Ales SIBA ⊙

Unit 7c, Bandeath Industrial Estate, Throsk, Stirling, FK7 7NP
☎ (01786) 817000 ⊕ tsabrewingco.co.uk

☺Established in 2005, and now owned by VC2 Brands, the brewery is located in a former torpedo factory on the shores of the River Forth. A large range of award-winning cask and bottled beers are available, including many seasonal beers.

Ben Nevis (OG 1041, ABV 4%) ◆
A traditional Scottish 80/-, with a distinctive roast and caramel character. Bittersweet fruit throughout provides the sweetness typical of a Scottish Heavy.

Sporran Warmer Blonde (OG 1044, ABV 4%)
Classic pale golden ale with a hoppy aftertaste.

Stirling Silver (OG 1042, ABV 4%)

Bannockburn Ale (OG 1044, ABV 4.2%)
Pale golden ale with a thick tight head and complex hoppy and fruity aroma.

Caber Tosser (ABV 4.5%)

Glencoe Wild Oat Stout (OG 1050, ABV 4.5%) ◆
A sweetish stout, surprisingly not dark in colour. Plenty of malt and roast balanced by fruit and finished with a hint of hop.

Golden Thistle (OG 1048, ABV 4.5%)
Sharp-tasting golden ale with a hoppy aftertaste.

Sheriffmuir Ruby Red IPA (OG 1041, ABV 4.5%)
Ruby-coloured beer with a rich malty flavour and lightly-hopped aftertaste.

William Wallace (OG 1048, ABV 4.5%)
Classic ruby strong ale with hoppy fruit and a hint of treacle.

Lomond (OG 1052, ABV 5%) ◆
A malty, bittersweet golden ale with plenty of fruity hop character.

Contract brewed for Fallen Brewing Co:

1703 (ABV 3.9%)

Odyssey (ABV 4.1%)

Dragonfly (ABV 4.6%)

Blackhouse (ABV 5%)

For Trossach's Craft Brewery:

Waylade (OG 1040, ABV 3.9%)

LadeBack (OG 1048, ABV 4.5%)

LadeOut (OG 1055, ABV 5.1%)

Traquair House SIBA

Traquair House, Innerleithen, Peeblesshire, EH44 6PW
☎ (01896) 830323 ⊕ traquair.co.uk/brewery
Shop Easter-Oct 12-5pm daily (Jun-Aug 10.30am-5pm)
Tours by arrangement

The 18th-century brewhouse is based in one wing of the 1,000 year old Traquair House, Scotland's oldest inhabited building. The brewhouse was rediscovered in 1965 by the 20th Laird who began brewing again using all the original equipment, which remained intact, despite having lain idle for more than 100 years. All the beers are oak-fermented and 60 per cent of production is exported. Seasonal and occasional beers are also available.

Bear Ale (OG 1050, ABV 5%)

Treeboom SIBA

Millstone Yard, Main Street, Shipton-by-Beningbrough, North Yorkshire, YO30 1AA
☎ (01904) 471569 ☎ 07761 608662
Office: c/o Nova Scotia Cottage, Acaster Malbis, York, North Yorkshire, YO23 2PY ⊕ treeboom.co.uk

Treeboom began in 2011 using a 10-barrel plant with production going mainly to pubs within a 50-mile radius.

Drum Beat (OG 1038, ABV 3.8%)
A copper-coloured session bitter, easy drinking with a balance of malt and hops.

Yorkshire Sparkle (OG 1039, ABV 4%)
A pale ale with a fresh citrus taste.

Kettle Drum (OG 1042, ABV 4.3%)
A copper-coloured ale with distinct fruitiness, and robust hop flavours leading to a clean finish.

Hop Britannia (OG 1050, ABV 5%)
A hoppy, strong pale ale. Honey-coloured with intense citrus fruit and spice notes.

Baron Saturday (OG 1049, ABV 5.2%)
A strong, dark porter with flavours of coffee and liquorice.

Tring SIBA

Dunsley Farm, London Road, Tring, Hertfordshire, HP23 6HA
☎ (01442) 890721 ⊕ tringbrewery.co.uk
Shop Closed Sun; Mon-Tue 11am-5pm; Wed-Thu 9am-6pm; Fri 9am-7.30pm; Sat 9am-5pm
Tours by arrangement

Founded in 1992, Tring brewery produces a core range augmented by monthly and seasonal specials. The brewery champions the English hop industry through the inclusion of established and experimental varieties in its monthly beers.

Side Pocket for a Toad (OG 1035, ABV 3.6%)
A straw-coloured ale with citrus notes and floral aroma with a crisp dry finish.

Brock Bitter (OG 1036, ABV 3.7%)

A mid-brown quaffing ale with a hint of sweetness and caramel.

Mansion Mild (OG 1036, ABV 3.7%)
Smooth and creamy dark ruby mild with a fruity palate and gentle late hop.

Blonde (OG 1039, ABV 4%)
A refreshing blonde beer with a fruity palate, balanced with a lingering hop aroma.

Ridgeway (OG 1039, ABV 4%)
Balanced malt and hop flavours with a dry, flowery hop aftertaste.

Moongazer (OG 1042, ABV 4.3%)
Red-hued amber ale with a rounded bitterness and a hoppy aftertaste.

Tea Kettle Stout (OG 1047, ABV 4.7%)
Rich and complex traditional stout with a hint of liquorice and moderate bitterness.

Colley's Dog (OG 1051, ABV 5.2%)
Dark but not over-rich, strong yet drinkable, this premium ale has a long dry finish with overtones of malt and walnuts.

Death or Glory (OG 1074, ABV 7.2%)
A strong, dark, aromatic barley wine.

Trinity

Church Road, Gisleham, Suffolk, NR33 8DS
☎ (01502) 743121 ⊕ trinityales.co.uk

⊠ Trinity Ales was launched in 2009 using a four-barrel plant. Pure spring water is used from an ancient well along with Suffolk hops and barley from local farms. Outlets are supplied within a 30-mile radius of the brewery. Bottle-conditioned beers are also available.

Wishing Well (OG 1039, ABV 3.8%)

High Light (OG 1040, ABV 4%)

Black Street Smithy (OG 1045, ABV 4.5%)

Gisleham Gold (OG 1045, ABV 4.5%)

Triple fff SIBA ◉

Magpie Works, Station Approach, Four Marks, Alton, Hampshire, GU34 5HN
☎ (01420) 561422 ⊕ triplefff.com
Shop Mon-Thu 9am-5pm; Fri 9am-6pm; Sat 10am-4pm
Tours by arrangement

⊠ The brewery was established in 1997 with a five-barrel plant, and after various expansions, now brews on a 50-barrel plant. Quarterly seasonals and monthly specials are brewed, and bottle-conditioned beers are available. Two pubs are owned: the Railway Arms, Alton and the White Lion, Aldershot.

Alton's Pride (OG 1039, ABV 3.8%) 🍴 ◆
An excellent, clean-tasting brown session beer. Full-bodied for its strength with a glorious aroma of lemony hops. An initially malty flavour fades as citrus notes and hoppiness take over, leading to a lasting hoppy/bitter finish.

**Pressed Rat & Warthog
(OG 1039, ABV 3.8%)** 🍴 ◆
Complex hoppy and bitter mild, not in the classic style but nevertheless delicious. Ruby in colour, a toffee aroma with hints of blackcurrant and chocolate lead to a well-balanced flavour with

roast, fruit and malt vying with the hoppy bitterness and a dry bitter finish.

Moondance (OG 1045, ABV 4.2%) ◆
A golden ale, well-hopped, with an aromatic citrus hop nose, balanced by bitterness and a noticeable sweetness in the mouth. Bitterness increases in the finish as the fruit declines, leading to a bittersweet finish.

Trossach's Craft

See Traditional Scottish Ales

Truefitt

3 Carcut Road, Lawson Industrial Estate, Middlesbrough, TS3 6QL
☎ 07883 072389 ⊕ truefittbrewing.co.uk

◉ Truefitt began brewing in 2012 using a four-barrel plant, and now produces up to 16 barrels a week. Beers suitable for vegans are available to order. Seasonal and bottle-conditioned beers are available.

Erimus Pale Ale (OG 1041, ABV 3.9%)

North Riding Bitter (OG 1043, ABV 4%)
A traditional bitter loaded with hops.

Ironopolis Stout (OG 1051, ABV 4.7%)

Mydilsburgh IPA (OG 1052, ABV 5%)

Truman's

The Eyrie, 2 & 3 Stour Road, London, E2 2NT
☎ (020) 8533 3575 ⊕ trumansbeer.co.uk

Truman's opened in 2013 in Hackney Wick, reviving a great name in London brewing. The new company has won the right to use the title and logos of the former brewery in Whitechapel that closed in 1989. A porter is planned. The original Truman's yeast cultures are used.

Swift (ABV 3.9%)

Runner (ABV 4%)

Eyrie (ABV 4.6%)

Tryst SIBA

Lorne Road, Larbert, Stirlingshire, FK5 4AT
☎ (01324) 554000 ⊕ trystbrewery.co.uk
Tours by arrangement

Tryst started production in 2003. A large range of beers is produced, all available in cask and bottles.

Brockville Dark (OG 1039, ABV 3.8%)
A full-tasting session ale with hints of liquorice and roasted grains.

Brockville Pale (OG 1039, ABV 3.9%)
A pale golden session ale, smooth on the palate.

Hop Trial (OG 1040, ABV 3.9%)

Bla'than (OG 1041, ABV 4%)
A strong floral nose and refreshing taste, enhanced with elderflower and pale malts.

Drovers 80/- (OG 1041, ABV 4%)
A traditional, well-malted 80/- with an element of sweetness. A gentle nose complements a smooth finish.

Carronade Pale Ale (OG 1043, ABV 4.2%)

A pale ale bursting with citrus flavours.

Sherpa Porter (OG 1044, ABV 4.4%)

German Hops Pils (OG 1045, ABV 4.5%)

V.I.P (OG 1046, ABV 4.5%)
Light brown best bitter with a deep hop taste and floral nose.

Zetland Wheatbier (OG 1046, ABV 4.5%)
Continental-style cloudy wheat beer with a distinctive banana nose.

Raj IPA (OG 1055, ABV 5.5%)
English hopped IPA with balanced flavours and a hoppy aroma and palate.

Tudor SIBA

Unit 1, Llanhilleth Industrial Estate, Llanhilleth, NP13 2RX
☎ (01873) 851696 ⊕ tudor-brewery.co.uk
Tours by arrangement

☺Family-run brewery purchased in 2012 by a mother and son team brewing in memory of their late husband/father. Four beers are currently brewed and bottled on the four-barrel plant, with one pub supplied locally.

Blorenge (OG 1038, ABV 3.8%)
A light, pale ale with a fresh citrus undertone.

Skirrid (OG 1042, ABV 4.2%)
A full-flavoured dark beer.

Sugarloaf (OG 1047, ABV 4.7%)
A rounded, full-bodied ale with smooth caramelised undertones.

Black Rock (OG 1056, ABV 5.6%)
A rich dark beer, with undertones of toffee and coffee.

Tunnel SIBA ◉

Old Stable Block, Red House Farm, Nuneaton Road, Ansley, Warwickshire, CV10 0QU
☎ (024) 7639 4386 ⊕ tunnelbrewery.co.uk
Shop Mon-Fri 9am-3pm
Tours by arrangement

This five-barrel brewery, established in 2005 at the Lord Nelson Inn, relocated to the picturesque stable block at Red House Farm in 2011. Bottle-conditioned beers are also available and are suitable for vegans. Battlefield Brewery beers are produced for a visitor centre in Bosworth.

Percheron (OG 1037, ABV 3.7%)
Pale golden ale with a citrus notes.

East India Pale Ale (OG 1058, ABV 5.9%)
A true robust IPA.

Tunnfield (NEW) SIBA

Hope Valley, Minsterley, Shropshire, SY5 0JB
☎ 07828 053065 ⊕ tunnfieldbrewery.co.uk

Tunnfield began brewing in 2012 using a four-barrel plant.

Stiperstones (ABV 3.7%)
A smooth session ale, light and refreshing with grapefruit aromas and a crisp bitterness.

Devils Chair (ABV 4%)
A traditional ruby bitter with a full-bodied malt flavour.

Cannon Rock (ABV 4.2%)
An IPA-style beer, golden-coloured with a crisp finish.

Turners SIBA ◉

Highfield Farm, The Broyle, Ringmer, East Sussex, BN8 5AR
☎ (08456) 892689 ☎ 07896 598172
⊕ turnersbrewery.com

⊗ Turners began brewing in 2012, initially as a guest at a brewery in Hampshire, but moving to its own premises in Ringmer in 2013. Further beers are planned.

Golden Ale (ABV 3.5%)
A full-bodied, floral, fruity, hoppy beer with a pleasant aftertaste.

East Sussex Bitter (ABV 3.9%)
A light, refreshing beer with a floral nose, a fruity, hoppy palate and thirst quenching finish.

Best (ABV 4.1%)
An easy-drinking traditional best bitter.

Ruby Mild (ABV 4.6%)
A mild with a fruity body and smooth, subtle chocolatey finish.

Twickenham SIBA ◉

Unit 6, Mereway Road, Twickenham, TW2 6RG
☎ (020) 8241 1825 ⊕ twickenham-fine-ales.co.uk
Tours by arrangement

The brewery was set up in 2004 using a 10-barrel brew plant and was the first brewery in Twickenham since the 1920s. It expanded to a 25-barrel plant in larger premises in 2012. Pubs and clubs are supplied within 25 miles of the brewery, including central London. Seasonal beers: see website.

Sundancer (OG 1037, ABV 3.7%) ◕
A light zesty golden ale with citrus notes dominating from beginning to end. The finish is bitter but balanced by biscuity sweetness that stops the aftertaste being too intense.

Grandstand Bitter (OG 1037, ABV 3.8%) ◕
Pale brown beer with peach, citrus and some malt on the palate fading in the finish, which is bitter and slightly hoppy. Passionfruit, malt and honey aroma.

Vanguard (OG 1040, ABV 4.1%) ◕
A malty honey sweetness is balanced by hops and fruit throughout this pale brown best bitter with a creamy mouthfeel. Dryish, slightly bitter aftertaste.

Naked Ladies (OG 1044, ABV 4.4%) ◕
Dark golden ale with a perfumed nose and a touch of spicy hop, which is in the initial flavour but fruit dominates. There is a lasting bitterness with some dryness.

Twisted Oak (NEW) SIBA

Yeowood Farm, Iwood Lane, Wrington, Somerset, BS40 5NU
☎ 07917 457797 ⊕ twistedoakbrewery.co.uk

Twisted Oak began brewing in 2012 using a five-barrel plant. Seasonal and bottle-conditioned beers are also available.

Fallen Tree (ABV 3.8%)

An amber-coloured session ale, clean-tasting with light fruit notes and a bitter finish.

Old Barn (ABV 4.5%)
A traditional ruby-coloured ale with a distinctive fruit and spice flavour.

Spun Gold (ABV 4.5%)
A golden ale, well-balanced with medium bitterness and a floral, fruity finish.

Two Bridges

Fox & Hounds, 51 Gosbrook Road, Caversham, Reading, Berkshire, RG4 8BN
☎ (0118) 375 9205 ☎ 07915 540926
⊕ twobridgesbrewery.co.uk

Two Bridges was founded in 2009 by husband and wife Kevin and Kerri Durkan. It's named after the bridges spanning the Thames between Caversham and Reading. The 2.5-barrel plant is currently located in the brewer's garage. Local outlets are supplied direct; polypins are available.

Blond Berkshire Bevy (OG 1039, ABV 3.9%)
Light blonde ale brewed with three very different hops to give a crisp, hoppy and refreshing finish.

Ugly Duckling (ABV 4%)
Balanced session bitter.

Midnight Swan (ABV 4.4%)

Stormy Weather (ABV 4.6%)
India Pale Ale-style beer.

Golden Cygnet (OG 1045, ABV 4.8%)
Premium golden ale.

Across the Pond APA (OG 1049, ABV 5%)
Amber-coloured American-style IPA.

Two Cocks SIBA

Church Lane, Enborne, Newbury, Berkshire, RG20 0HB
☎ (01635) 47351 ☎ 07876 594501
⊕ twococksbrewery.com

⊗ The brewery was established in 2011 at Christmas Farm after wild hops were found growing in the farm's hedgerows. A 180-feet deep borehole supplies water for the brewery. Several local and regional outlets are regularly supplied.

Diamond Lil (OG 1035, ABV 3.2%)
A light and fruity golden ale developed for the Queen's Diamond Jubilee.

1643 Musket Mild (OG 1038, ABV 3.5%)
A dark and lightly bittered mild with a full depth of flavour.

1643 Cavalier (OG 1039, ABV 3.8%)
A light, refreshing, thirst-quenching golden ale with a combination of hops.

1643 Leveller (OG 1040, ABV 3.8%)
A malty session bitter brewed with a single variety of old English hop.

1643 Roundhead (OG 1042, ABV 4.2%)
A full-bodied, smooth best bitter.

1643 Puritan (OG 1049, ABV 4.5%)
A dark stout with notes of caramel and chocolate.

Two Rivers (NEW) SIBA

2 Sluice Bank, Denver, Downham Market, Norfolk, PE38 0EQ
☎ 07518 099868 ✉ denverbrewco@hotmail.com

The two Rivers' brewer has a background in pharmacology and fermentation technology. All the beers are currently bottle-conditioned, expansion into cask production is planned.

Two Roses SIBA

Unit 9, Darton Business Park, Barnsley Road, Darton, South Yorkshire, S75 5QX
☎ 07780 701254 ⊕ tworosesbrewery.co.uk
Tours by arrangement

⊗ Two Roses started brewing in 2011 using an eight-barrel plant installed in a former carpet factory. Four core beers are brewed, supplemented during the year with special brews.

Full Nelson (OG 1040, ABV 3.8%)

Galaxy (OG 1040, ABV 4%)

Heron Porter (OG 1040, ABV 4.2%)

Black Beauty (ABV 5%)

Two Towers SIBA

Unit 1, Mott Street Industrial Estate, 51 Mott Street, Hockley, Birmingham, West Midlands, B19 3HE
☎ (0121) 439 7253 ☎ 07540 574032
⊕ twotowersbrewery.co.uk
Tours by arrangement

Established in 2010, the brewery is based in the heart of Birmingham and produces ales largely in a traditional spirit, but has recently extended and broadened its portfolio. Beers draw heavily on the heritage, historic characters and features of Birmingham.

Baskerville Bitter (OG 1038, ABV 3.8%)
Full-bodied bitter with a blend of four hops, providing a complex but beautifully balanced ale.

Chamberlain Pale Ale (OG 1042, ABV 4.5%)
A crisp light ale loaded with grapefruit flavours, with a long hoppy finish.

Jewellery Porter (OG 1049, ABV 5%)
A full-bodied wholesome stout with a thick and slightly chocolate texture underlined with long, fulfilling English hops.

Birmingham Special Ale (OG 1043, ABV 5.4%)
Maltly strong bitter with a full body, reflecting the flavours and characteristics of traditional English ales.

Tydd Steam SIBA

Manor Barn, Kirkgate, Tydd Saint Giles, Cambridgeshire, PE13 5NE
☎ (01945) 871020 ☎ 07932 726552
⊕ tyddsteam.co.uk
Tours by arrangement

⊗ Tydd Steam Brewery opened in 2007 in a converted agricultural barn using a 5.5-barrel plant. A new 15-barrel plant was installed in 1999. The brewery is named after two farm steam engines. Around 70 outlets are supplied direct. Seasonal/occasional beers are brewed and bottle-conditioned beers are available on an occasional basis.

Barn Ale (OG 1038, ABV 3.9%) ◖
A golden bitter that has good biscuity malt aroma and flavour, balanced by spicy hops. Long, dry, fairly astringent finish.

Golden Kiwi (OG 1040, ABV 4.1%)

Piston Bob (OG 1044, ABV 4.6%) ◥
Malt and faint hops on the aroma progress through to a malty flavour complemented by a balance of hops and fruit. A long, dry finish rounds off this amber strong bitter.

Tyne Bank SIBA

Unit 11, Hawick Crescent Industrial Estate, St Lawrence Road, Newcastle upon Tyne, NE6 1AS
☎ (0191) 265 2828 ☎ 07989 426 604
⊕ tynebankbrewery.co.uk
Shop Tue-Thu 9am-5pm; Fri 9am-4.30pm
Tours by arrangement

⊗ Tyne Bank began brewing in 2011. It has three fermenters and seven conditioning tanks, meaning that it can produce 20 barrels per brew and attain 60 barrels or 17,000 pints per week. Monthly special beers are also available.

Single Blonde (OG 1037, ABV 3.5%)
A light ale with a slightly dry bitterness. Vanilla and herbal flavours complement the delicate floral fruit aroma.

Pacifica Pale Ale (ABV 4%)
A pale ale with mellow bitterness and a citrus twist.

Monument Bitter (OG 1042, ABV 4.1%)
Smooth, balanced bitter with a berry and fruit character.

Silver Dollar (OG 1051, ABV 4.9%)
Hoppy American-style ale with lasting bitterness and a kick of citrus.

Southern Star (OG 1051, ABV 5%)
A New Zealand-style IPA with a fruity aroma and crushed grapefruit flavour.

Uffa

☗ **White Lion, Lower Street, Lower Ufford, Suffolk, IP13 6DW**
☎ (01394) 460770 ⊕ uffordwhitelion.co.uk
Tours by arrangement

Uffa began brewing in 2010 using a 2.5-barrel plant. It is situated next to the White Lion pub in a converted coach house. Seasonal beers are available.

Tipple (ABV 3.5%)

Fox (ABV 3.7%)

Gold (ABV 3.7%)

Uley

The Old Brewery, 31 The Street, Uley, Gloucestershire, GL11 5TB
☎ (01453) 860120 ⊕ uleybrewery.com

⊗ Brewing at Uley began in 1833 as Price's Brewery. After a long gap, the premises were restored and Uley Brewery opened in 1985. It has its own spring water, which is used to mash Tucker's Maris Otter malt and boiled with Herefordshire hops. Uley serves 40-50 free trade outlets in the Cotswold area and is brewing to capacity. Seasonal beers are also available.

Hogshead Cotswold Pale Ale (OG 1035, ABV 3.5%) ◥

A pale-coloured, hoppy session bitter with a good hop aroma and a full flavour for its strength, ending in a bittersweet aftertaste.

Bitter (OG 1040, ABV 4%) ▨ ◥
A copper-coloured beer with hops and fruit in the aroma and a malty, fruity taste, underscored by a hoppy bitterness. The finish is dry, with a balance of hops and malt.

Laurie Lee's Bitter (OG 1045, ABV 4.5%)
A copper-coloured, full-flavoured, hoppy bitter with some fruitiness and a smooth, long, balanced finish.

Old Ric (OG 1045, ABV 4.5%) ◥
A full-flavoured, hoppy bitter with some fruitiness and a smooth, balanced finish. Distinctively copper-coloured, this is the house beer for the Old Spot Inn, Dursley.

Old Spot Prize Strong Ale (OG 1050, ABV 5%) ◥
A distinctive full-bodied, red/brown ale with a fruity aroma, a malty, fruity taste, with a hoppy bitterness, and a strong, balanced aftertaste.

Pig's Ear Strong Beer (OG 1050, ABV 5%) ◥
A pale-coloured beer, deceptively strong. Notably bitter in flavour, with a hoppy, fruity aroma and a bitter finish.

Ulverston

Lightburn Road, Ulverston, Cumbria, LA12 0AU
☎ (01229) 586870 ☎ 07840 192022
⊕ ulverstonbrewingcompany.co.uk
Shop Mon-Sat 11am-3pm (ring for winter opening times)
Tours by arrangement

☺The brewery was established in 2006, and in 2010 moved to new premises with a bespoke 12-barrel plant occupying the octagonal bull ring of the old livestock market on the outskirts of Ulverston. There is a shop on site selling local products and craftwork, and a bar that overlooks the brew plant. Seasonal beers are also available. Many of the beers have a Laurel and Hardy theme; Stan Laurel came from Ulverston.

Flying Elephants (OG 1037, ABV 3.7%) ◥
Clean, refreshing yellow bitter, sweet and fruity with a dry citrus finish.

Celebration Ale (OG 1039, ABV 3.9%) ◥
Yellow fruity bitter with hints of tangerine and a notably sustained dry finish.

Harvest Moon (OG 1039, ABV 3.9%)

Another Fine Mess (OG 1040, ABV 4%) ◥
A refreshing gold-coloured bitter. Initially fruity but with a rising bitterness.

Laughing Gravy (OG 1040, ABV 4%) ◥
Smooth and grainy brown bitter with a good mix of flavours.

Lonesome Pine (OG 1042, ABV 4.2%) ◥
A fresh and fruity pale gold beer; honeyed, lemony and resiny with an increasingly bitter finish.

Fra Diavolo (OG 1043, ABV 4.3%)

Royal Reserve (OG 1059, ABV 6%)

Uncle Stuarts

The Leisure Village, 58 Yarmouth Road, Blofield, Norwich, NR13 4LQ

☎ (01603) 713261
✉ unclestuartsbrewery@btconnect.com
Shop Mon-Sat 9.30am-4.30pm; Sun 10am-4pm

⊠ The brewery started in 2002. In 2009 it moved to Wroxham Barns Craft Centre and in 2013 relocated again to Norwich Camping & Leisure Village. Beers are available in nine gallon casks as well as bottle-conditioned from the brewery shop and other selected outlets.

North Norfolk Beauty (OG 1039, ABV 3.8%)

Pack Lane Mild (OG 1042, ABV 4%)

Broadland Bitter (ABV 4.1%)

Nut Brown Ale (ABV 4.1%)

Stout (ABV 4.4%)

Excelsior (OG 1044, ABV 4.5%)

Local Hero (OG 1047, ABV 4.7%)

Wroxham Barns Bitter (OG 1044, ABV 4.8%)

Ginger (OG 1048, ABV 5%)

Norwich Castle (OG 1048, ABV 5%)

Porter (OG 1053, ABV 5%)

Buckenham Woods (OG 1054, ABV 5.6%) ◈
Spicy, richly-flavoured ale with more than a hint of raisin and sultana and a light and creamy mouthfeel.

Strumpshaw Fen (OG 1057, ABV 5.7%)

Norwich Cathedral (OG 1059, ABV 6.5%)

Winter Ale (OG 1060, ABV 7%)
Dark, strong winter warmer.

Unsworth's Yard (NEW) SIBA

4 Unsworth's Yard, Cartmel, Cumbria, LA11 6PN
☎ 07810 461313 ⊕ unsworthsyardbrewery.co.uk
Shop & tasting room 10am-5pm

Opened in 2011, the 2.5-barrel plant produces beers named after Cartmel personalities and landmarks. Beers are available in Cartmel pubs and other local outlets. Bottle-conditioned beer is also available.

J.C.Dickinson's Land of Cartmel
(OG 1038, ABV 3.7%)
Light but hoppy beer with grapefruit notes and a zesty bitter finish.

Cartmel Peninsula (OG 1039, ABV 3.8%)

The Cromwell Door Pride of Cartmel 1643
(OG 1038, ABV 3.9%)
A mildly bitter but full-flavoured amber ale.

Sir William Marshal's Crusader Gold
(OG 1041, ABV 4.1%)
A crisp and refreshing golden ale.

Sir Edgar Harrington's Last Wolf
(OG 1045, ABV 4.5%)
Deep red, mellow but bitter beer with blackcurrant and raisin flavours.

Untapped

Unit 6, Little Castle Farm Business Park, Raglan, Monmouthshire, NP15 2BX
☎ 07988 199794 ⊕ untappedbrew.com

Untapped Brewing Company was established in 2009 and is owned and run by Owen Davies and Martyn Darby. Beers were intitally brewed at

Whittingtons Brewery in Newent, Gloucestershire, but in 2013 they moved to their own plant in Raglan. Bottle-conditioned beers are also available.

Border (ABV 3.8%)

Sundown (ABV 4%)
Golden ale with a subtle distinct flavour. Sweet aroma with a hint of spice, followed by a defined, dry yet mellow finish.

Eclipse (ABV 4.4%)
Traditional-style dark ale with darkly red hue and rich roasted flavours.

U.P.A. (ABV 4.5%)
Straw-coloured IPA-style beer with citrus fruit-driven flavours. Distinctly hoppy, with wonderful hop aromas.

Upham SIBA

Stakes Farm, Cross Lane, Upham, Hampshire, SO32 1FL
☎ (01489) 861383 ⊕ uphambrewery.co.uk
Shop Mon-Fri 9am-3pm
Tours by arrangement

⊠ Upham began brewing in 2009 using a 3.5-barrel plant and has recently expanded to a 30-barrel plant. It owns three pubs and supplies more than 70 other outlets. Bottled beers, beer boxes and casks are available from the brewery shop.

Tipster (OG 1035, ABV 3.6%) ◈
An easy drinking and light golden ale. Initial hoppiness and fruit is balanced by a maltiness that lasts into the finish.

Punter (OG 1039, ABV 4%)
Rich ochre in colour. Delicate yet structured with hints of syrup and toasted grain. The earthy richness on the palate brings with it a hoppy, dry finish.

Stakes (OG 1045, ABV 4.8%)
Strong, rich and smoky flavour with aromas of caramel.

Vale SIBA ◉

Tramway Business Park, Ludgershall Road, Brill, Buckinghamshire, HP18 9TY
☎ (01844) 239237 ⊕ valebrewery.co.uk
Shop Mon-Fri 9am-5pm; Sat 9.30-11.30am; Closed Sun & bank hols
Tours by arrangement

⊠ Established in 1994 and initially based in Haddenham, Vale moved to Brill in 2007. In 2010 it expanded to 20-barrel brew plant. Four pubs are owned, including the Hop Pole where sister brewery the Aylesbury Brewhouse (qv) opened in 2011. Bottle-conditioned beers are produced. Monthly specials and occasional beers are available: see website.

Best Bitter (OG 1036, ABV 3.7%) ◈
This pale amber beer starts with a slight fruit aroma. This leads to a clean, bitter taste where hops and fruit dominate. The finish is long and bitter with a slight hop note.

Black Swan Mild (OG 1038, ABV 3.9%)
Dark and smooth with hints of chocolate and coffee on the nose and a malty, dry finish.

Wychert Ale (OG 1038, ABV 3.9%)

A traditional Thames Valley beer. Woody flavours are notable in this malty beer with a finish of port and berries on the nose.

Red Kite (OG 1040, ABV 4%)
Refreshing, chestnut beer with a bitter finish.

VPA/Vale Pale Ale (OG 1042, ABV 4.2%)
An assertive, dry, hoppy ale with a citrus nose, combined with a pronounced malt background.

Special (OG 1046, ABV 4.5%)
Premium ale with a rich, complex and satisfying finish.

Grumpling Premium Ale (OG 1046, ABV 4.6%)
A rich, warming ruby brown traditional English bitter with mellow fruity malt flavours accompanied by a subtle dry, hoppy finish.

Gravitas (OG 1047, ABV 4.8%)
A strong pale ale packed with hop and citrus flavours, rounded off by a dry, malty, biscuit finish. A pronounced hop aroma throughout.

Vale of Glamorgan SIBA

Unit 8a, Atlantic Trading Estate, Barry, Vale of Glamorgan, CF63 3RF
☎ (01446) 730757 ⊕ vogbrewery.co.uk
Tours by arrangement

☺Founded in 2005 using a 10 barrel plant, Vale of Glamorgan has developed a reputation locally for its range of high quality beers. Local pubs and clubs are supplied, and the beers are available nationwide via swap deals with other brewers. Bottle-conditioned beers are available.

Light Headed (OG 1040, ABV 4%)
A light easy-drinking ale.

Cwrw Haf (OG 1042, ABV 4.2%)

Original No. 1 (OG 1042, ABV 4.2%)
Classic-style best bitter.

Bitter Than Ever (OG 1043, ABV 4.3%)
Traditional tawny best bitter, early and late hopped for a bitter aroma and flavour.

Choc's Away (OG 1045, ADV 4.5%)
Mahogany-coloured best bitter, full-bodied with chocolate flavour balanced by a satisfying bitter aftertaste.

Rorke's Draught (OG 1046, ABV 4.6%)
Well-bittered pale ale.

Cwrw Dewi (OG 1050, ABV 5%)
Rich dark malty best bitter.

Valhalla

Shetland Refreshments Ltd, Haroldswick, Unst, Shetland, ZE2 9TJ
☎ (01957) 711658 ⊕ valhallabrewery.co.uk
Tours by arrangement

The brewery started production in 1997, set up by husband and wife team Sonny and Sylvia Priest. A bottling plant was installed in 1999. A new brewery building was opened in 2012, converted from part of the former RAF SaxaVoord camp at Haroldswick.

Sjolmet Stout (OG 1048, ABV 5%) ◥
Full of malt and roast barley, especially in the taste. Smooth, creamy, fruity finish, not as dry as some stouts.

Vens

Unit 3, Clovelly Works, Chelmsford Road, Rawreth, Essex, SS11 8SY
☎ (01268) 574477 ☎ 07715 410489

Office: 28 Main Road, Hockley, Essex, SS5 4QS
☎ (01702) 205005 ⊕ vensbrewing.co.uk

Vens began brewing in 2010 with production of 15 barrels per week. Five regular beers are produced and the brewery now supplies 50 pubs in Essex. Bottle-conditioned beers also available via the brewery shop.

Mild (OG 1038, ABV 3.8%)
A smooth, malty dark mild with plenty of roasted flavours.

Gold (OG 1040, ABV 4%)
A pale golden beer with a well-balanced hop aroma.

Best (OG 1042, ABV 4.2%)
A classic best bitter with well-balanced malt flavours and bitterness.

Suze V (OG 1042, ABV 4.2%)

V4 (OG 1044, ABV 4.4%)

Verulam

⧩ Farmers Boy, 134 London Road, St Albans, Hertfordshire, AL1 1PQ
☎ (01727) 860535 ☎ 07799 137395
⊕ farmersboy.co.uk
Tours by arrangement

⊗ Established in 1997, Verulam is situated at the rear of the Farmer's Boy and produces beers for the pub. It also brews for the free trade under the Ale Craft name. The brewery is home to two 'cuckoo' breweries: the Private Brewery of Bob and That Little Brewery (qv).

Farmer's Delight (OG 1036, ABV 3.9%)
Straw-coloured beer with a distinct hop aroma and flavour.

Farmer's Joy (OG 1043, ABV 4.5%)
Ruby, almost black beer, with a lovely combination of dark malt roast and citrus hop flavours.

Citra (OG 1046, ABV 4.6%)
Award-winning pale ale with hop character throughout.

Vibrant Forest SIBA

Moonscross Bungalow, Jacobs Gutter Lane, Totton, Hampshire, SO40 9FR
☎ (023) 8066 9204 ⊕ vibrantforest.co.uk

⊗ Vibrant Forest is a small award-winning microbrewery located on the edge of the New Forest. It began brewing commercially in 2011 having brewed ales on a non-commercial basis for many years.

Vibrant Ale (OG 1040, ABV 4%)
A refreshing light amber English bitter. There is a pleasant balance of malt and fruity hops and the finish is dry and hoppy.

Flying Saucer (OG 1042, ABV 4.3%)
A full-flavoured golden ale with fruity, floral and citrus-like flavours. Fresh and very hoppy with a long bitter finish.

Wheatwave (OG 1048, ABV 4.8%)

A hazy blond wheat beer in the style of German weizen, with a pronounced banana and clove character.

Black Forest Porter (OG 1050, ABV 4.9%)
A flavoursome porter with notes of coffee and chocolate. Full-bodied on the palate with a good balance of roasted bitterness.

Village Brewer

See Hambleton

Violet Cottage

⊟ Gwaelod-y-Garth Inn, Main Road, Gwaelod-y-Garth, CF15 9HH
☎ (02920) 810408

⊗ Violet Cottage began brewing in 2012 on a two-barrel plant in a converted outbuilding at the rear of the Gwaelod-y-Garth Inn, within the grounds of the licensee's private house. Most of the beer produced is sold within the pub.

VIP SIBA

Unit E, Hawkshill Business Park, Lesbury, Alnwick, Northumberland, NE66 3PG
☎ 07545 885352 ⊕ thevillageinnpub.co.uk

Brewing began in 2012 using a five-barrel plant to serve the owner's pub, the Village Inn in Longframlington, and the local free trade. About 150 outlets are supplied. Further beers are planned.

Village Bike (ABV 4%)
A clean golden ale with a sweet tone and a mild bitter aftertaste.

Village Lite (ABV 4%)
Smooth session ale with a citrus afterkick.

Village Copper (ABV 4.2%)
Well-balanced ruby bitter with a subtle hint of ginger.

Village Ghost (ABV 4.5%)
Well-balanced stout with roasted dark malts. Sweet but bitter, with a caramel and liquorice aftertaste.

Wadworth SIBA IFBB ◉

Northgate Brewery, Devizes, Wiltshire, SN10 1JW
☎ (01380) 723361 ⊕ wadworth.co.uk
Shop Mon-Fri 10am-5.30pm (4.30pm winter); Sat 10am-4pm
Tours by arrangement

Established in 1885 by Henry Wadworth, this impressive market town brewery is one of few remaining producers to sell beer locally in oak casks. Traditional horse powered drays delivery beer daily around Devizes. It has 250 pubs throughout southern England. Seasonal beers: see website. Bottle-conditioned beer is also available.

Henry's IPA (OG 1035, ABV 3.6%)
A classic session beer with malt-led flavours.

Horizon (OG 1039, ABV 4%)
A pale gold beer with zesty citrus and hop aromas and a crisp, tangy finish on the palate.

6X (OG 1041, ABV 4.3%) ◄
Copper-coloured ale with a malty and fruity nose, and some balancing hop character. The flavour is

similar, with some bitterness and a lingering malty, but bitter finish.

Bishops Tipple (OG 1048, ABV 5%)
A golden brew giving well-balanced hop bitterness and a clean finish.

Swordfish (OG 1049, ABV 5%)
A full-bodied, deep copper coloured ale flavoured with Pussers Rum.

Waen SIBA

Unit 7, Maesyllan Industrial Estate, Llanidloes, Powys, SY18 6YU
☎ (01686) 627042 ⊕ thewaenbrewery.co.uk
Shop Fri-Sat 10am-5pm
Tours by arrangement

☺Waen began brewing in 2009 on a five-barrel plant in Penstrowed. Increased demand saw the brewery move to its current address. 100 outlets are supplied direct. Seasonal beers are also available.

TWA (OG 1036, ABV 3.7%)
Pale ale in the traditional Welsh style. Crisp and refreshing.

Janner's Pride (OG 1043, ABV 4%)
Malty best bitter with hints of ginger and whisky.

Wagtail

New Barn Farm, Wilby Warrens, Old Buckenham, Norfolk, NR17 1PF
☎ (01953) 887133 ⊕ wagtailbrewery.com

Wagtail Brewery went into full-time production in 2006. All beers are now only available bottle conditioned and all are suitable for vegetarians and vegans: see website for full range.

Wainstones SIBA

Unit 9, Terry Dicken Industrial Estate, Station Road, Stokesley, North Yorkshire, TS9 7AE
☎ 07885 240226 ⊕ stokesleybrewing.co.uk

Wainstones began brewing in 2010 using a 2.5-barrel plant set up in a small industrial unit in Stokesley, trading as the Stokesley Brewing Company.

Amber (OG 1038, ABV 3.8%)
Distinctive light golden ale with moderate bitterness and a pleasant floral nose.

Sandstone (OG 1040, ABV 4%)
Traditional brown-coloured ale with moderate bitterness and a pleasant aftertaste.

Ironstone (OG 1042, ABV 4.2%)
A classic rich ale made with a smooth aftertaste.

Copper (OG 1043, ABV 4.3%)
A copper-coloured ale.

Steel River (OG 1043, ABV 4.3%)
Traditional chestnut-coloured ale with medium bitterness.

Jet (OG 1045, ABV 4.5%)
An unusual black ale, full of flavour, with an excellent hoppy aftertaste.

Transporter (OG 1045, ABV 4.5%)
A dark porter with a creamy head and a deep malty taste.

Wall's

1 Binks Close, Standard Way Business Park,
Northallerton, North Yorkshire, DL6 2YB
☎ (01609) 258226 ☎ 07810 123084
⊕ wallsbrewery.co.uk

Brewing began in 2011 on a 5.5-barrel plant. Beers can be found in more than 100 local outlets along with a range of bottle-conditioned ales. Seasonal beers: see website.

County Best (OG 1034, ABV 3.2%)
Light amber-coloured session beer, with a blackcurrant and herbal aroma.

Mild & Easy (OG 1034, ABV 3.2%)

Summer Gold (OG 1036, ABV 3.6%)
Refreshing golden ale, with citrus flavours.

Gun Dog Bitter (OG 1039, ABV 3.8%)
Traditional amber-coloured bitter with a full hoppy flavour.

Keepers Gold (OG 1039, ABV 3.9%)

Brewers Gold (OG 1039, ABV 4%)
Malty flavoured session beer.

Northallerton Dark (OG 1040, ABV 4.4%)
Dark ale with an orangy aroma and taste.

The Darkside (OG 1040, ABV 4.4%)
Creamy milk stout, with a soft sweet taste followed by a light bitterness

Beaters Choice (OG 1050, ABV 4.6%)
Lightly roasted porter with a deep amber colour.

Explorer IPA (OG 1050, ABV 4.7%)
A traditional style IPA, darker in colour than its modern counterparts.

Wantsum SIBA

Units 22 & 23, Sparrow Way, Lakesview International Business Park, Hersden, Kent, CT3 4AL
☎ (0845) 040 5980 ⊕ wantsumbrewery.co.uk
Tours by arrangement

⊗ Wantsum Brewery was established in 2009 and takes its name from the nearby Wantsum Channel. In 2012 a new plant was installed which increased brewing capacity to 12 barrels. Around 60 outlets are supplied. Seasonal and bottle-conditioned beers: see website.

More's Head (OG 1033.5, ABV 3.5%)
A chestnut-coloured bitter with malt and roasted grains balanced against fruit and floral hops with a hint of citrus.

1381 (OG 1035, ABV 3.8%)
A light amber-coloured bitter with delicate citrus and herbal aromas.

Black Prince (OG 1036.5, ABV 3.9%)
A rich, full-bodied mild, smooth on the palate with subtle hop notes.

Miller's Mirth (OG 1042, ABV 3.9%)
A copper-coloured floral and spicy best bitter.

Imperium (OG 1037, ABV 4%)
A deep amber best bitter; smooth biscuit malts and rich hoppy nose balance this beer perfectly.

Fortitude (OG 1039, ABV 4.2%)
This bitter combines four types of malt to give depth of body, with English and American hops for a pronounced hop finish.

Turbulent Priest (OG 1038, ABV 4.4%)

A full-bodied best bitter offering chocolate and coffee notes on top of a sweet malt base.

One Hop (OG 1042, ABV 4.5%)
A single-hop beer; the hop used is changed every couple of months.

Dynamo (OG 1040, ABV 4.6%)
A crisp, light, golden ale, fruity and floral with an orange citrus twist.

Hengist (OG 1045, ABV 5%)
A golden pale ale with flavours of biscuit malt balancing a long, deep, mellow, fruity nose.

Ravening Wolf (OG 1052, ABV 5.9%)
A light amber strong pale ale; toasted biscuit and rye malt flavours support a pine lemon hop crispness with a hint of vanilla.

Wapping

▤ Baltic Fleet, 33a Wapping, Liverpool, Merseyside, L1 8DQ
☎ (0151) 709 3116 ⊕ wappingbeers.co.uk / balticfleet.co.uk
Tours by arrangement

☺Wapping brewery was established in 2002 in the cellars of the pub on the waterfront in Liverpool using the old Passageway Brewery plant. Around half a dozen house beers are produced with specials and seasonal brews appearing throughout the year.

Bitter (OG 1036, ABV 3.6%)

Baltic Gold (OG 1039, ABV 3.9%) ◣
Hoppy golden ale with plenty of citrus hop flavour. Refreshing with good body and mouthfeel.

Warcop

c/o 9 Nellive Park, St Brides Wentlooge, Gwent, NP10 8SE
☎ (01633) 680058 ☎ 07915 352542
⊕ warcopales.com
Tours by arrangement

A small brewery based in a converted milking parlour. Beers are also available bottle conditioned. The brewery has a portfolio of 28 beers that are made on a cyclical basis, with two to four beers normally in stock at any one time. Brewing is currently suspended.

Warwickshire SIBA

The Bakehouse Brewery, Queen Street, Cubbington, Warwickshire, CV32 7NA
☎ (01926) 450747 ⊕ warwickshirebeer.co.uk
Shop open most days inc Sat am (please ring first)

A six-barrel brewery in a former village bakery that has been in operation since 1998. Beers are available in more than 100 outlets and the brewery's four pubs. Bottle-conditioned beers are available at the brewery as well as local stockists.

Castle Mild (OG 1034, ABV 3.4%)
Dark mild with fruity overtones and a hoppy finish.

Shakespeare's County (OG 1034, ABV 3.4%)
A refreshing lower gravity golden ale.

Best Bitter (OG 1039, ABV 3.9%)
Easy-drinking golden brown session beer, with a malty flavour and a gentle bitterness which becomes more assertive in the aftertaste.

Darling Buds (OG 1041, ABV 4%)
Blonde bitter brewed with wheat and lager malt.

Golden Bear (OG 1049, ABV 4.9%)
Golden brown beer with a long-lasting slightly resiny bitterness. The finish is fruity and warming with hints of spice and orange.

Kingmaker (OG 1055, ABV 5.5%)
Rich, fruity beer. A grainy, spirit-like aroma leads on to a palate with overtones of whisky, orange and dark chocolate, and a warming alcoholic finish.

Watermill SIBA

Ings, Cumbria, LA8 9PY
☎ (01539) 821309 ☎ 07831 873300
⊕ lakelandpub.co.uk
Tours by arrangement

⊛Watermill was established in 2006 in a purpose-built extension to the inn, and extended in 2008. The beers brewed on the five-barrel plant have a doggie theme, dogs being very welcome in the pub. A new brewery is planned within the grounds of the pub, which will double production.

Collie Wobbles (OG 1037.5, ABV 3.7%)
A pale gold bitter with a slight citrus taste. A good hop and malt balance gives way to a dry finish.

Black Beard (OG 1038, ABV 3.8%)
A dark mild with bags of fruit and malt flavours.

A Bit'er Ruff (OG 1041.5, ABV 4.1%) ◄
Copper-coloured, balanced fruity beer with a lingering, bitter aftertaste.

Ruff Justice (OG 1041, ABV 4.2%)
A malty golden ale, well-balanced with caramel, light floral hops and a fresh, dry finish.

Windermere Blonde (OG 1041.5, ABV 4.2%)

Isle of Dogs (OG 1044, ABV 4.5%)
A golden bitter with a fresh, malty aroma and a distinctive citrus fruity flavour with an intense, dry aftertaste.

Wruff Night (OG 1047.5, ABV 5%) ◄
Straw-coloured, sweet and fruity, uncomplicated beer with bitterness in a short-lived aftertaste.

Dogth Vader (OG 1050, ABV 5.1%)
A dark, hoppy ale with a refreshing, dry finish.

Tomos Watkin SIBA

Unit 3, Alberto Road, Century Park, Valley Way, Swansea Enterprise Park, Swansea, SA6 8RP
☎ (01792) 797300 ⊕ tomoswatkin.com
Shop Mon-Fri 9am-5pm
Tours by arrangement

⊛Brewing started in 1995 in converted garages in Llandeilo using a 10-barrel plant. The brewery moved to bigger premises in Swansea in 2000 and the plant increased to a 50-barrel capacity. Over 60% of production is bottled beers (not bottle conditioned). More than 600 outlets are currently supplied.

Cwrw Braf (OG 1038, ABV 3.7%)
A clean-drinking, amber-coloured ale with a light bitterness and gentle hop aroma.

Blodwens Beer (OG 1045, ABV 4.5%)
Light blonde beer with a delicate creamy finish with a hint of citrus.

Old Style Bitter/OSB (OG 1045, ABV 4.5%) ◄

Amber-coloured with an inviting aroma of hops and malt. Full bodied; hops, fruit, malt and bitterness combine to give a balanced flavour continuing into the finish.

Waveney

⬟ Queen's Head, Station Road, Earsham, Norfolk, NR35 2TS
☎ (01986) 892623 ✉ lyndahamps@aol.com

⊠ Established at the Queen's Head in 2004, the five-barrel brewery produces three beers, regularly available at the pub along with other free trade outlets. Occasional and seasonal beers are also brewed.

East Coast Mild (OG 1037, ABV 3.8%) ◄
A traditional mild with distinctive roast malt aroma and red-brown colouring. A sweet, plummy malt start quickly fades as a dry roasted bitterness begins to make its presence felt.

Lightweight (OG 1039, ABV 3.9%) ◄
A gentle beer with a light but well-balanced hop and malt character. A light body is reflected in the quick, bitter finish. Golden hued with a distinctive strawberry and cream nose.

Welterweight (OG 1042, ABV 4.2%)

Weard'ALE

⬟ Hare & Hounds, 24 Front Street, Westgate, County Durham, DL13 1RX
☎ (01388) 517212

Brewing commenced in the Hare & Hounds in 2010. The beers are mainly sold on the premises but some has found its way to nearby beer festivals and other local pubs.

Weatheroak SIBA

Unit 7, Victoria Works, Birmingham Road, Studley, Warwickshire, B80 7AP
☎ (0121) 445 4411 (eve) ☎ 07798 773894 (day)

Office: Victoria Works, 33 Redditch Road, Studley, B80 7AU ⊕ weatheroakales.co.uk

⊠ The brewery was set up in 1997 in an outhouse at the Coach & Horses, Weatheroak Hill. It is now in a spacious factory unit in Studley. Weatheroak supplies 40 outlets. Seasonal beers are brewed on a regular basis. Its brewery tap is the nearby Victoria Works pub.

St Udley Mild (OG 1034, ABV 3.4%)

Light Oak (OG 1036, ABV 3.6%) ◄
This straw-coloured quaffing ale has lots of hoppy notes on the tongue and nose, and a fleetingly sweet aftertaste.

Weatheroak (OG 1041, ABV 4.1%) ◄
The aroma is dominated by hops in this golden-coloured brew. Hops also feature in the mouth and there is a rapidly fading dry aftertaste.

Victoria Works (OG 1043, ABV 4.3%)
A pale hoppy bitter with a citrus finish.

Redwood (OG 1047, ABV 4.7%)
A rich tawny strong but mellow beer with a short-lived sweet fruit and malt balance.

Keystone Hops (OG 1050, ABV 5%) ◄
A golden yellow beer that is surprisingly easy to quaff given the strength. Fruity hops are the

dominant flavour without the commonly associated astringency.

For Weighbridge, Alvechurch:

Tillerman's Tipple (OG 1039, ABV 3.9%)

Weatheroak Hill SIBA

🍺 Coach & Horses, Weatheroak Hill, Warwickshire, B48 7EA
☎ (01564) 823386 (pub)
Tours by arrangement

Weatheroak Hill started brewing on site in 2008 and supplies the pub and local beer festivals only. Beers are brewed on-site by an independent contract brewer who in 2012 added a summer and a winter seasonal beer to the core range.

Gold (OG 1035, ABV 3.5%)

Icknield Pale Ale (OG 1038, ABV 3.8%)

Bitter/WHB (OG 1042, ABV 4.2%)

Weetwood SIBA

The Brewery, Common Lane, Kelsall, Cheshire, CW6 0PY
☎ (01829) 752377 ⊕ weetwoodales.co.uk

☺One of the original Cheshire microbreweries set up at an equestrian centre in 1993. In 2011 a new 30-barrel brewery was built on a site around the corner and brewing commenced in 2012. More than 300 outlets are supplied regularly.

Best Bitter (OG 1038.5, ABV 3.8%) 🍺
Pale brown beer with an assertive bitterness and a lingering dry finish. Despite initial sweetness, peppery hops dominate throughout.

Mad Hatter (OG 1038.5, ABV 3.9%)
A red-brown beer with fruity and malty flavours throughout. Brewed with American Amarillo hops to give spicy and floral notes.

Cheshire Cat (OG 1040, ABV 4%) 🍺
Pale, dry bitter with a spritzy lemon zest and a grapey aroma. Hoppy aroma leads through to the initial taste before fruitiness takes over. Smooth creamy mouthfeel and a short, dry finish.

Eastgate Ale (OG 1043.5, ABV 4.2%) 🍺
Well-balanced and refreshing clean amber beer. Citrus fruit flavours predominate in the taste and there is a short, dry aftertaste.

Old Dog Bitter (OG 1045, ABV 4.5%) 🍺
Robust, well-balanced amber beer with a slightly fruity aroma. Rich malt and fruit flavours are balanced by bitterness. Some sweetness and a hint of sulphur on nose and taste.

Ambush Ale (OG 1047.5, ABV 4.8%) 🍺
Full-bodied malty, premium bitter with initial sweetness balanced by bitterness and leading to a long-lasting dry finish. Blackberries and bitterness predominate alongside the hops.

Oasthouse Gold (OG 1050, ABV 5%) 🍺
Straw-coloured, crisp, full-bodied and fruity golden ale with a good dry finish.

Weighbridge SIBA

🍺 Penzance Drive, Swindon, Wiltshire, SN5 7JL
☎ (01793) 881500 ⊕ weighbridgebrewhouse.co.uk

⊠ The Weighbridge Brewery forms part of the Weighbridge Brewhouse restaurant and bar, based in the former home of Archer's brewery. Opened in 2011, the brewery has gone from strength to strength under the stewardship of Mark Wallington.

English Ale (OG 1040, ABV 3.9%)
Rounded refreshing pale ale brewed only with English malt and hops. Delicate, slightly fruity aroma on the finish.

Best (OG 1044, ABV 4.3%)
A good bitter ale with a full palate, spicy aroma and a malty aftertaste.

Pooley's Golden (OG 1048, ABV 4.7%)
A robust golden ale, full bodied with plenty of bitterness and with an unusual gooseberry aroma. The aftertaste is an excellent balance of the malt and hop.

Weird Beard (NEW)

Unit 5, Boston Business Park, Trumpers Way, Hanwell, London, W7 2QA
☎ (020) 3645 2711 ⊕ weirdbeardbrewco.com

Brewing began in 2013 using a 10-barrel plant with two dedicated fermenters on an industrial estate in Hanwell. Premises are shared with Ellenberg's Brewery (qv). Beer is mostly bottled, but some is available cask conditioned.

Mariana Trench (OG 1049.3, ABV 5.3%)
A well-balanced, refreshing beer with passion fruit, mango and some sharp citrus on the nose and palate.

Hit the Lights (OG 1058.8, ABV 5.8%)
A clean, bitter IPA with loads of fruity hop character.

Fade to Black (OG 1064.5, ABV 6.3%)
A black IPA with fruity hops and dark toasted notes.

Welbeck Abbey SIBA

Lower Motor Yard, Welbeck, Nottinghamshire, S80 3LT
☎ (01909) 512539 ☎ 07921 066274
⊕ welbeckabbeybrewery.co.uk
Tours by arrangement

The microbrewery is housed in a listed barn at the centre of the Welbeck Estate – the brew plant was previously used at Kelham Island. The brewery, which opened in 2011, produces a range of different styles of beers. Head brewer Claire Monk trained at the Kelham Island Brewery after studying microbiology at Sheffield University.

Henrietta (OG 1035, ABV 3.6%)
Low-strength beer but crammed full of hop character.

Red Feather (OG 1040, ABV 3.9%)
A traditional dark amber ale with subtle notes of caramel and toffee.

Portland Black (OG 1043, ABV 4.5%)
A rich and smooth black beer with smoke, liquorice and burnt toffee flavours and a distinctly vanilla nose.

Cavendish (OG 1046, ABV 5%)
Blonde beer laced with zesty notes of grapefruit.

Wellington Inn

目 55 Russell Street, Hull, HU2 9AB
☎ (01482) 329486
⊕ thewellingtoninnbreweryhull.blogspot.com

☺Brewing began in an out-building at the Wellington Inn in 2011. The beers are produced primarily for sale on site although a small quantity are sent to beer festivals.

1st Duke (OG 1037, ABV 3.7%)
Soft copper-coloured bitter, with a fruity aroma and typically English malty taste, combined with a dry hop bitter finish.

Beau Douro (OG 1043, ABV 4.3%)
Very pale and hoppy.

Wells & Young's IFBB ◉

Bedford Brewery, Havelock Street, Bedford, MK40 4LU
☎ (01234) 272766 ⊕ wellsandyoungs.co.uk
Tours by arrangement

☺Wells & Young's was created following the merger of the brewing and brands divisions of Charles Wells of Bedford and Young & Co of Wandsworth in 2006, creating Britain's largest private brewery. Brewing has been synonymous with Bedford since 1876 when the founder, Charles Wells, established a brewery on the banks of the Great Ouse River. Since then the company has thrived, to become a major force in the brewing industry. Wells and Young's run separate pub estates. In 2007, Wells & Young's acquired the Courage brands from Scottish & Newcastle (now Heineken UK). Seasonal beers include Wells Waggle Dance. Bottle-conditioned beers are also available.

Wells Eagle (OG 1035, ABV 3.6%) ◄
A refreshing, amber session bitter with pronounced citrus hop aroma and palate, faint malt in the mouth, and a lasting dry, bitter finish.

Young's Bitter (OG 1036, ABV 3.7%) ◄
This light drinking amber bitter has citrus initially on the palate with sweet malt and a hint of hops that linger into a slightly dry and bitter finish.

Courage Best Bitter (OG 1038.3, ABV 4%)
Malt and hops on the nose, with a full palate of malt, fruit and hops, and a dry and bitter finish.

Wells Bombardier (OG 1042, ABV 4.1%) ◄
A heavy aroma of malt and raspberry jam. Traces of hops and bitterness are quickly submerged under a smooth, malty sweetness. A solid, rich finish.

Young's London Gold (ABV 4.5%) ◄
A dark gold beer with a smooth mouthfeel. Citrus and malt in the low aroma, coming through more strongly on the palate and aftertaste with a little peach. Dry finish.

Young's Special (OG 1044, ABV 4.5%) ◄
Pale brown in colour, this rounded best bitter has citrus throughout plus some slight creamy toffee, which balances the bitterness that grows in the aftertaste.

Courage Directors (OG 1045.5, ABV 4.8%)
A rich, fruity and full-bodied chestnut-coloured classic ale.

Weltons SIBA

1 Mulberry Trading Estate, Foundry Lane, Horsham, West Sussex, RH13 5PX
☎ (01403) 242901/251873 ⊕ weltonsbeer.co.uk
Tours by arrangement

☒ Ray Welton moved the brewery into this factory unit in 2003. Over 70 different beers are brewed every year. Pubs throughout the South East and London are supplied. Bottle-conditioned beers are available and are suitable for vegetarians and vegans.

Pridenjoy (ABV 2.8%) ◄
A light brown bitter with a slight malty and hoppy aroma. Fruity with a pleasant hoppiness and some sweetness in the flavour, leading to a short malty finish.

Horsham Bitter (ABV 3.8%)
Amber-coloured bitter with a huge aroma.

Sussex Pride (ABV 4%)

Old Cocky (ABV 4.3%)

Horsham Old (ABV 4.5%) ◄
Roast and toffee flavours predominate with some bitterness in this traditional old ale. Bittersweet with plenty of caramel and roast in a rather short finish.

Export Stout (ABV 4.7%)
Hints of burnt toast balanced by good levels of hops, with a long finish.

Old Harry (ABV 5.2%)

Headless Horseman (ABV 6%)

Wensleydale SIBA

Unit F, Manor Road, Bellerby, North Yorkshire, DL8 5QH
☎ (01969) 622463 ☎ 07765 596666
⊕ wensleydalebrewery.co.uk
Shop Mon-Fri 9am-5pm
Tours by arrangement

Wensleydale Brewery was set up in 2003 and currently operates on a 4.5 barrel plant. Most beers are also available in bottles. Around 100 outlets are supplied. Seasonal beers are also available: see website.

Lidstone's Rowley Mild (OG 1032, ABV 3.2%) ◄
Chocolate and toffee aromas lead into what, for its strength, is an impressively rich and flavoursome taste. The finish is pleasantly bittersweet.

Bitter (OG 1036, ABV 3.7%) ◄
Intensely aromatic, straw-coloured ale offering a superb balance of malt and hops on the tongue.

Falconer Session Bitter (OG 1038, ABV 3.9%)
A fruity, malt-based session ale, copper in colour, with a long, bitter, dry finish.

Semerwater Summer Ale (OG 1040, ABV 4.1%)
Pale best bitter with citrus aromas. The clean, hoppy nose is balanced by a light, malty sweetness.

Stuka (OG 1045, ABV 4.2%)
Amber-coloured ale made with Munich and lager malts.

Coverdale Gamekeeper (OG 1042, ABV 4.3%)
Copper-coloured best bitter, with spicy hop notes and a juicy malt flavour.

Black Dub Oat Stout (OG 1043, ABV 4.4%)

THE BREWERIES

Black and silky with a rich concentration of four different malts and oats. Enriched with roast barley, chocolate malt and malted oats.

Gold (OG 1044, ABV 4.5%)
Aromatic and spicy hop flavours combine with the lightest of kilned malts to make this light golden best bitter.

Coverdale Poacher IPA (OG 1048, ABV 5%) ◆
Citrus flavours dominate both aroma and taste in this pale, smooth, refreshing beer; the aftertaste is quite dry.

Wentwell

15 Wingfield Drive, Derby, DE21 4PW
☎ 07900 475755 ⊕ wentwellbrewery.com

Wentwell Brewery is a three-barrel plant established in 2011. Six regular beers are produced, with occasional seasonals. Several local outlets are supplied, with beers regularly available at the Little Chester Ale House. All beers are available bottle conditioned.

Jeremiah Mild (OG 1035, ABV 3.3%)
Smooth, dark and malty, with a lot of body.

Derby Pale Ale (OG 1039, ABV 3.8%)
A very pale straw coloured hoppy bitter.

Derbyshire Gold (OG 1039, ABV 3.9%)
A light, refreshingly hoppy and zesty session beer.

Little Tick (OG 1040, ABV 4%)
Straw coloured bitter, triple hopped for a fuller flavour.

Farm Hands' Bitter (OG 1042, ABV 4.1%)
A rich copper-coloured best bitter with a smooth rounded flavour and nicely balanced bitterness.

Barrel Organ Blues (OG 1046, ABV 4.5%)
Golden brown, full-bodied premium bitter with a rich malty flavour and aroma.

Wentworth SIBA

Power House, Gun Park, Wentworth, South Yorkshire, S62 7TF
☎ (01226) 747070 ⊕ wentworthbrewery.co.uk
Tours by arrangement

☺Founded in 1999 in the power house in the grounds of Wentworth Woodhouse, a custom-built 30-barrel brewery was commissioned in 2006. Bottled beers are brewed under the Wentworth and Barnsley Beer Company brands in addition to the seasonal cask range and two monthly specials: see website.

WPA (OG 1039.5, ABV 4%) ◆
An extremely well hopped IPA-style beer that leads to some astringency. A very bitter beer.

Wessex

Rye Hill Farm, Longbridge Deverill, Wiltshire, BA12 7DE
☎ (01985) 844532
✉ wessexbrewery@tinyworld.co.uk

▨ The brewery went into production in 2001 and moved to its current location in 2004. 15 local outlets are supplied. Beers are also available through selected wholesalers. Seasonal beers are also produced. Beers are occasionally contract brewed for the Isle of Avalon brewery.

Potter's Ale (OG 1038, ABV 3.8%)

Mild (OG 1038, ABV 3.9%)
Traditional sweetish dark mild.

Longleat Pride (OG 1040, ABV 4%)
A pale, hoppy bitter.

Crockerton Classic (OG 1041, ABV 4.1%)
A full-bodied, tawny, full-flavoured bitter; fruity and malty.

Merrie Mink (OG 1041, ABV 4.2%)
A full-flavoured best with a strong hop aroma.

Deverill's Advocate (OG 1046, ABV 4.5%)
A well-balanced golden premium ale.

Warminster Warrior (OG 1045, ABV 4.5%)
Full-flavoured premium bitter.

Golden Apostle (OG 1048, ABV 4.8%)

Russian Stoat (OG 1080, ABV 9%) ⬚

For Red Lion, Kilmington:

Whitesheet Wallop (OG 1042, ABV 4.2%)

West SIBA

⊟ Binnie Place, Glasgow Green, Glasgow, G40 1AW
☎ (0141) 550 0135 ⊕ westbeer.com
Tours by arrangement

No real ale. Brewery-bar and restaurant, producing German-style beer to the Bavarian Purity Law. Beers are usually served under pressure, but not pasteurised. Four regular beers are produced along with seasonals and Wild West, an unfiltered version of St Mungo. Beers: WEST (ABV 4%), Dunkel (winter, ABV 4.9%), Munich Red (ABV 4.9%), St Mungo (ABV 4.9%), Hefeweizen (ABV 5.2%).

West Berkshire SIBA

The Flour Barn, Frilsham Home Farm Units, Yattendon, Berkshire, RG18 0XT
☎ (01635) 202968 ⊕ wbbrew.com
Mon-Fri 10am-4pm; Sat 10am-1pm
Tours by arrangement

▨ The brewery was established in 1995 at the Potkiln pub in Frilsham. It is now based on the edge of Yattendon, having moved to a new 50-barrel brewhouse, with office and shop, in 2011. Around 150 outlets in London and the South are supplied.

Old Father Thames (OG 1038, ABV 3.4%)
A traditional pale ale with a full flavour despite its low strength.

Mr Chubb's Lunchtime Bitter (OG 1040, ABV 3.7%) ◆
A drinkable, balanced, session bitter. A malty caramel note dominates aroma and taste and is accompanied by a nutty bittersweetness and a hoppy aftertaste.

Maggs' Magnificent Mild (OG 1041, ABV 3.8%) ◆
Silky, full-bodied, dark mild with a creamy head. Roast malt aroma is joined in the taste by caramel, sweetness and mild, fruity hoppiness. Aftertaste of roast malt with balancing bitterness.

Good Old Boy (OG 1043, ABV 4%) ◆
Well-rounded, tawny bitter with malt and hops dominating throughout. A balancing bitterness accompanies the taste and aftertaste.

Dr Hexter's Wedding Ale (OG 1044, ABV 4.1%) ◆

Fruit and hops dominate the aroma and are joined in the taste by a hint of malt. The aftertaste has a pleasant bitter hoppiness.

Full Circle (OG 1047, ABV 4.5%) ◆
A golden ale with a pleasing aroma and taste of bitter hops with a hint of malt. The aftertaste is hoppy and bitter with a rounding note of malt.

Dr Hexter's Healer (OG 1052, ABV 5%) ◆
An amber strong bitter with malt, caramel and hops in the aroma. Taste is a balance of malt, caramel, fruit, hops and bittersweetness. Caramel, fruit and bittersweetness dominate the aftertaste.

Westerham SIBA ◉

Grange Farm, Pootings Road, Crockham Hill, Kent, TN8 6SA
☎ (01732) 864427 ⊕ westerhambrewery.co.uk
Shop Mon-Fri 10am-5pm
Tours by arrangement (min 30 people, charge made)

The brewery was established in 2004 at the National Trust's Grange Farm, and is housed in a former dairy. Around 200 outlets are supplied in Kent, Surrey, Sussex and south London. Monthly specials: see website. Bottle-conditioned beers are also available.

Finchcocks Original (OG 1036.2, ABV 3.5%)
Mid-gold session beer. Citrus notes on the palate with a hint of biscuit and resiny hoppiness.

Grasshopper Kentish Bitter (OG 1039, ABV 3.8%)
A dark, malty bitter with nutty, roasted notes from the chocolate malt.

Spirit of Kent (OG 1039.5, ABV 4%)
Crisp golden ale with floral and fruity notes. Complex tropical fruit and citrus flavours blend with the sweet malt. Assertive dry hop notes on the finish.

William Wilberforce Freedom Ale (OG 1040, ABV 4%)
Deep golden ale with a mellow bitterness and long, hoppy finish.

British Bulldog (OG 1043.5, ABV 4.3%)
A rich, full-bodied best bitter with a massive aroma and palate of jammy fruit, biscuity malt and bitter hop resins.

1965 Special Bitter Ale (OG 1047.5, ABV 4.8%)
A clean, refreshing bitter with a full-bodied flavour.

Audit Ale (OG 1061, ABV 6.2%)
Wonderful, hoppy, strong and bitter.

Whale (NEW) SIBA

Unit 5b, Brailes Industrial Estate, Brailes, Warwickshire, OX15 5JW
☎ (01608) 686974 ⊕ whaleale.co.uk

Whale Ale started brewing in 2013 using 100% British ingredients with no artificial additives.

Pale Whale (ABV 3.6%)
A grapefruit, zesty blonde ale with honey, citrus and tropical fruit aroma.

Ruby Moby (ABV 4%)
A nutty, sweet session ale with a malty, fruity aroma.

Whalebone

🏠 163 Wincolmlee, Hull, East Yorkshire, HU2 0PA
☎ (01482) 226648

☺The Whalebone pub, which dates from 1796, was bought by Hull CAMRA founding member Alex Craig in 2002. He opened the brewery the following year and his beers have names connected with the former whaling industry on the adjoining River Hull. Two or three outlets are supplied as well as the pub.

Diana Mild (OG 1037, ABV 3.5%)

Neckoil Bitter (OG 1039, ABV 3.9%)

WharfeBank SIBA ◉

Unit 4, Pool Business Park, Pool Road, Pool in Wharfedale, West Yorkshire, LS21 1FD
☎ (0113) 284 2392 ⊕ wharfebankbrewery.co.uk
Tours by arrangement

☺WharfeBank commenced brewing in 2010 using a 20-barrel plant in a converted paper mill on the banks of the River Wharfe. Beers are available across the north, with flagship brand Tether Blond available regionally through Enterprise and Punch.

VPA (Verbeia Pale Ale) (OG 1035, ABV 3.6%) ◆
Very light, easy-drinking beer, with a floral nose and a soft aftertaste.

Best Bitter (OG 1036, ABV 3.7%) ◆
A balance of malt and hop flavours along with bitterness is present throughout this subtle copper-coloured beer.

Slingers Gold (OG 1038, ABV 3.9%)
Golden-coloured session ale with fruit and hops carrying some bitterness to the finish.

Tether Blond (OG 1041, ABV 4.1%) ◆
A moderately-hopped light ale with some sweetness, smooth and easy-drinking, the fruit flavours continue to the gentle finish.

CamFell Flame (OG 1044, ABV 4.4%) ◆
Ruby red, sweetish malty ale with a smooth mouthfeel. Some caramel roastiness is present throughout.

WISPA (WharfeBank India Strong Pale Ale) (OG 1050, ABV 5.1%)

Wharfedale (NEW)

🏠 Back Barn, 16 Church Street, Ilkley, West Yorkshire, LS29 9DS
☎ (01943) 609587 ☎ 07721 880108
⊕ wharfedalebrewery.com

Wharfedale began brewing in 2012 using spare capacity at Five Towns Brewery in Wakefield. Brewing moved to Ilkley in 2013 using a 2.5-barrel plant. Further beers are planned.

Blonde (ABV 3.9%)

Best (ABV 4%)

Whim SIBA

Whim Farm, Hartington, Derbyshire, SK17 0AX
☎ (01298) 84991 ✉ info@whimales.co.uk

The brewery opened in 1993 in outbuildings at Whim Farm. The beers are available in 50-70 outlets and the brewery's tied house, the Wilkes

Head in Leek, Staffordshire. Occasional/seasonal beers are available.

Arbor Light (OG 1035, ABV 3.6%)
Light-coloured bitter, sharp and clean with lots of hop character and a delicate light aroma.

Hartington Bitter (OG 1039, ABV 4%) ▤
A light, golden-coloured, well-hopped session beer. A dry finish with a spicy, floral aroma.

Hartington IPA (OG 1045, ABV 4.5%)
Pale and light-coloured, smooth on the palate allowing malt to predominate. Slightly sweet finish combined with distinctive light hop bitterness.

Flower Power (OG 1053, ABV 5.3%)
Light, golden coloured beer with a flowery hop aroma, citrus with mild spice on the palate and a dry, bitter finish.

Whistling Kite (NEW) SIBA

35a Buccleuch Street, Kettering, Northamptonshire, NN16 9EE
☎ 07891 956055

Office: 23 New Road, Geddington, Northamptonshire, NN14 1AT ✉ phillipsjez@aol.com

Whistling Kite was established in 2013 using a six-barrel plant.

Wet Your Whistle (OG 1040, ABV 3.8%)
Flavoursome, mahogany-coloured session bitter.

Eleanor's Ise (OG 1041, ABV 4.2%)
Pale golden ale brewed with lager hops.

White Dog (NEW)

Unit 9, Sycamore House, Moorgreen Industrial Park, Eastwood, Nottinghamshire, NG16 3QU
☎ 07984 935700 ⊕ whitedogbrewery.co.uk
Tours by arrangement

⊠ White Dog was established in 2012 using a seven-barrel plant. It brews around 12,000 pints per month. The name comes from the brewer's dog – a white German shepherd.

Golden Retriever (OG 1039, ABV 3.8%)
A well-hopped golden bitter.

Growler (OG 1043, ABV 4.2%)

Scooby Brew (OG 1043, ABV 4.2%)

The Dark Un (OG 1046, ABV 4.5%)

White Horse SIBA ◉

3 Ware Road, White Horse Business Park, Stanford-in-the-Vale, Oxfordshire, SN7 8NY
☎ (01367) 718700 ⊕ breweryoxfordshire.co.uk
Shop Mon-Fri 9am-5pm; Sat 8am-12pm

⊠ White Horse was founded in 2004. The brewing plant uses the continental method of brewing with a lauter tun rather than an infusion mash tun. The brewery now has its own pubs in Oxford and Banbury as well as supplying more than 150 outlets. Four seasonal beers are brewed: see website.

White Horse Bitter (OG 1038.7, ABV 3.7%)
Golden bitter, well-hopped with a clean, fruity finish.

Village Idiot (OG 1041.8, ABV 4.1%)
A blonde ale with a complex hop aroma and taste.

Wayland Smithy (OG 1047.1, ABV 4.4%)
A red-brown ale with a nice biscuit flavour that is balanced with a spicy hop finish.

White Park SIBA

Perry Hill Farm, Bourne End Road, Cranfield, Bedfordshire, MK43 0BA
☎ (01223) 911357 ⊕ whiteparkbrewery.co.uk

⊠ White Park is a family business established in 2007 on a five-barrel plant. Spent malt is recycled as feed for rare breed cattle. 60 outlets are supplied direct. In 2009 the brewery began bottling and supplies pubs and local stores including Budgens. Seasonal beers: see website.

First Flight (OG 1036, ABV 3.7%)

White Rose SIBA

c/o 119 Chapel Road, Burncross, Chapeltown, Sheffield, South Yorkshire, S35 1QL
☎ (0114) 297 6150
✉ whiterose.brewery@btinternet.com
Tours by arrangement

☺Gary Sheriff, former head brewer at Wentworth brewery, set up White Rose in 2007. It shares the Little Ale Cart brewery's premises behind the Wellington in Sheffield. Some equipment is used jointly but White Rose uses its own fermenters.

Original Blonde (OG 1040, ABV 4%)

Stairway to Heaven (OG 1044, ABV 4.3%)

Raven (ABV 4.6%)

Whitewater

40 Tullyframe Road, Kilkeel, Co Down, Northern Ireland, BT34 4RZ
☎ (028) 4176 9449 ⊕ whitewaterbrewing.co.uk
Tours by arrangement

Set up in 1996, Whitewater is now the biggest brewery in Northern Ireland. One pub is owned, the White Horse in Saintfield, Co. Down. An expanding range of occasional and seasonal beers is also available.

Copperhead (OG 1037, ABV 3.7%)

Crown & Glory (OG 1038, ABV 3.8%)

Belfast Black (OG 1042, ABV 4.2%)

Belfast Ale (OG 1046, ABV 4.5%)

Clotworthy Dobbin (OG 1050, ABV 5%)

Hoppelhammer (ABV 6%)
A well-hopped IPA.

Whitstable SIBA

Little Telpits Farm, Woodcock Lane, Grafty Green, Kent, ME17 2AY
☎ (01622) 851007 ⊕ whitstablebrewery.info

Whitstable launched 2003 when the Green family purchased the Swale and North Weald Brewery to supply their own Whitstable outlets (a hotel and three restaurants). In 2006 they opened a bar in East Quay. The brewery supplies more than 75 outlets in Kent, Surrey and London.

Native Bitter (OG 1036, ABV 3.7%) ◗
A classic copper-coloured Kentish session bitter with hoppy aroma and a long, dry bitter hop finish.

Renaissance Ruby Mild (OG 1038, ABV 3.8%)
Traditional black mild.

East India Pale Ale (OG 1040, ABV 4.1%) ◈
A well hopped golden IPA with good grapefruit aroma hop character and lingering bitter finish.

Oyster Stout (OG 1045, ABV 4.5%)
Rich, dry stout with deep chocolate and mocha flavours.

Pearl of Kent (OG 1043, ABV 4.5%)
A light-coloured, well-rounded premium beer with tropical fruit flavours.

Winkle Picker (OG 1042, ABV 4.5%)
Amber-coloured slightly cereally best bitter, with a lasting beige head and some fruit on finish.

Kentish Reserve (OG 1047, ABV 5%)
A copper ale with warm plum pudding flavours and a ruby port finish.

Whittingtons SIBA ◉

Three Choirs Vineyards Ltd, Newent, Gloucestershire, GL18 1LS
☎ (01531) 890555 ✉ brewery@threechoirs.com
Shop 9am-5pm daily (later during summer)
Tours by arrangement (for a charge)

⊗ Whittingtons Brewery started in 2003, using a purpose-built, five-barrel plant producing 20 barrels a week. The legendary Dick Whittington came from nearby Pauntley, hence the name and feline theme. The beers are available in Party 9s and as bottle-conditioned ales, from the onsite shop, online and from local outlets. Seasonal beers are available.

Whittlebury SIBA

Stable Store, Home Farm Business Park, Whittlebury, Northamptonshire, NN12 8XS
☎ 07812 366369 ⊕ whittleburybrewery.com

⊗ Established in 2010 using a 5.5-barrel plant in an old dairy. The full range of beers are to be found throughout Northamptonshire and surrounding counties and are also available via the online shop.

Golden Vale (OG 1039, ABV 3.7%)

Northdown (OG 1040, ABV 3.9%)

Blue Eyed Dragon (OG 1040, ABV 4%)

Old Tun (OG 1042, ABV 4.1%)
Chestnut bitter with a crisp straw like finish.

Green Dragon (OG 1045, ABV 4.4%)
Traditional amber bitter with a crisp straw-like finish.

Whitworth SIBA

c/o 34 Dunard Road, Shirley, West Midlands, B90 2HR
☎ (0121) 347 6450 ⊕ whitworthbrewing.co.uk

⊗ Whitworth is a family-run brewery that started as a hobby 15 years ago but which, in 2012, began brewing commercially using a five-barrel plant. The brewery was inspired by CAMRA's LocAle scheme. Brewing takes place twice a week with local outlets and beer festivals supplied.

Sobriety Blonde (OG 1037, ABV 3.6%)
Quaffable ale with fruity tangerine notes.

Sobriety MPH (OG 1037, ABV 3.7%)

Mid- to dark-brown mild with refreshing roast malt notes.

Crooked Elbow (OG 1039, ABV 3.9%)
Roasted chestnut brown beer with warm roasted malt notes.

Sobriety (OG 1040, ABV 4%)
Well-balanced golden, mildly hoppy ale.

Why Not

27 Redfern Road, Norwich, NR7 9RB
☎ (01603) 300786 ⊕ thewhynotbrewery.co.uk

Why Not opened in 2006 with equipment located in a custom-built wooden unit. The brewery can produce up to two barrels per brew. All beers are available in bottle-conditioned form and are occasionally put into casks to order.

Wally's Revenge (OG 1040, ABV 4%) ◈
An overtly bitter beer with a hoppy background. The bitterness holds on to the end as an increasing astringent dryness develops.

Roundhead Porter (OG 1045, ABV 4.5%)
A traditional old-style London porter.

Cavalier Red (OG 1047, ABV 4.7%) ◈
Explosive fruity nose belies the gentleness of the taste. The summer fruit aroma dominates this red-gold brew. A sweet, fruity start disappears under a quick, bitter ending.

Norfolk Honey Ale (OG 1050, ABV 5%)
A golden beer with a honey nose. A definite hop edge leaves a honey aftertaste.

Chocolate Nutter (OG 1056, ABV 5.5%)

Wibblers SIBA

Joyces Farm, Southminster Road, Mayland, Essex, CM3 6EB
☎ (01621) 772044 ⊕ wibblers.com
Shop Mon-Fri 9am-4pm
Tours by arrangement

⊗ Wibblers was established in 2007 and expanded to a 20-barrel plant in 2009. Production is currently 45 barrels per week. More than 100 outlets are supplied. Seasonal and special beers: see website. Bottle-conditioned beers are also available.

Dengie IPA (OG 1037, ABV 3.6%)

Dengie Dark (OG 1038, ABV 3.8%)

Apprentice (OG 1039, ABV 3.9%)

Dengie Gold (OG 1040, ABV 4%)

Dengie Best (OG 1042, ABV 4.1%)

Crafty Stoat (OG 1056, ABV 5.3%)

Wicked Hathern

See Staffordshire

Wickwar SIBA ◉

Old Brewery, Station Road, Wickwar, Gloucestershire, GL12 8NB
☎ (01454) 292000 ⊕ wickwarbrewing.com
Shop Tue-Fri 10am-6pm; Sat 10am-4pm (Tel 01454 299592)
Tours by arrangement

THE BREWERIES

879

Wickwar was established as a 10-barrel brewery in 1990. In 2004 it expanded to 50 barrels. 350 outlets are supplied on a regular basis and the beers are available nationally through most distributors and SIBA. Seasonal beers are brewed.

Coopers WPA (OG 1036, ABV 3.5%) ◀
Golden-coloured, this well-balanced beer is light and refreshing, with hops, citrus fruit, apple/pear flavour and notable pale malt character. Bitter, dry finish.

Bankers Draft (OG 1040, ABV 4%)
An amber-coloured beer with a fruity citrus aroma. A biscuit malt flavour leads to a floral, crisp and clean finish.

BOB/Brand Oak Bitter (OG 1040, ABV 4%) ◀
Amber-coloured, this has a distinctive blend of hop, malt and apple/pear citrus fruits. The slightly sweet taste turns into a fine, dry bitterness, with a similar malty-lasting finish.

Cotswold Way (OG 1042, ABV 4.2%) ◀
Amber-coloured, it has a pleasant aroma of pale malt, hop and fruit. Good dry bitterness in the taste with some sweetness. Similar though less sweet in the finish, with good hop content.

Rite Flanker (OG 1043, ABV 4.3%)
A powerful fruity body is supported by a hoppy nose.

Station Porter (OG 1062, ABV 6.1%) 🍺 ◀
This is a rich, smooth, dark ruby-brown ale. Starts with roast malt; coffee, chocolate and dark fruit then develops a complex, spicy, bittersweet taste and a long roast finish.

Wild Card (NEW)

c/o 76 McCullum Road, Bow, London, E3 5JB
☎ 07982 402650 ⊕ wildcardbrewery.co.uk

Wild Card began brewing in 2013 using spare capacity at several breweries in and around London. Bottle-conditioned beer is also available.

Jack of Clubs (ABV 4.5%)

Wild Weather (NEW) SIBA

Unit 19, Easter Park, Benyon Road, Silchester, Hampshire, RG7 2PQ
☎ (0118) 970 1837 ⊕ wildweatherales.com

Wild Weather was established in 2013. American and New World hops are used to create distinctive ales. Bottle-conditioned beers are available.

Sundowner (ABV 3.4%)
A golden summer ale.

Big Muddy (ABV 3.8%)
A tawny-coloured session ale.

Little Wind (ABV 4.2%)
A deep amber ale with a touch of copper.

Stormbringer (ABV 4.5%)
Malty and hoppy.

Williams SIBA ◉

New Alloa Brewery, Kelliebank, Alloa, FK10 1NT
☎ (01259) 725511 ☎ 07739 323962
⊕ Williamsbrosbrew.com
Tours by arrangement

⊕Brothers Bruce and Scott Williams started brewing Heather Ale in 1993. A range of indigenous, historic ales were added over the following 10 years before the brothers invested in a 40-barrel brewery and bottling line in 2003. Hundreds of cask ale outlets are supplied worldwide. Seasonal beers: see website.

Gold (OG 1040, ABV 3.9%)
Golden session beer with a crisp mouthfeel and lemon, grapefruit and orange hop aromas.

Harvest Sun (OG 1041, ABV 3.9%)
Straw gold ale with a citrus aroma that gives way to a balanced and satisfyingly bitter finish.

Fraoch Heather Ale (OG 1041, ABV 4.1%) ◀
The unique taste of heather flowers is noticeable in this beer. A fine floral aroma and spicy taste give character to this drinkable speciality beer.

80/- (OG 1046, ABV 4.2%)
A rich mahogany ale, with malt and butter aroma, biscuit texture, orange peel infusion, and a clean, satisfyingly sweet finish.

Black (OG 1042, ABV 4.2%) 🍺
A light-bodied ale in the style of Czech dark lagers. Aromatic and full-flavoured with coffee and chocolate undertones and a blackcurrant aroma.

Roisin-Tayberry (OG 1040, ABV 4.2%)
A sweetish fruity beer, light pink from the tayberries which are used, giving a distinct soft fruity aroma and flavour.

Birds & Bees (OG 1044, ABV 4.3%)
Bright, golden ale brewed with fresh elderflowers and lemon zest. Fruity, aromatic and refreshing.

Cock O' the Walk (OG 1042, ABV 4.3%)
A classic red ale brewed with an eclectic blend of hops from around the globe.

Kelpie (OG 1045, ABV 4.4%)
A rich dark chocolate ale, with a distinctive malty texture. Fresh seaweed is included in the mash tun.

Red (OG 1045, ABV 4.5%)
Rich ruby red beer with toffee flavours and citrus hop aromas.

Good Times (OG 1050, ABV 5%)
This sparkling ale pours golden yellow with a refreshing botanical aroma.

Grozet (OG 1050, ABV 5%)
Lagered gooseberry beer. Crisp, fresh and clean tasting.

Joker IPA (OG 1050, ABV 5%)
Well-balanced IPA, golden in the glass, fruity on the nose with hints of cedar.

Seven Giraffes (OG 1051, ABV 5.1%)
Classic IPA with late infusion of elderflower and lemon. It pours a deep gold with aromas of elderflower and citrus, followed by sweet caramel.

Impale IPA (OG 1054, ABV 5.5%)
Hoppy IPA with biting bitterness and huge tropical fruit aromas.

Midnight Sun (OG 1058, ABV 5.6%)
A rich, black, smooth porter with an afterbite of fresh root ginger.

Ebulum (OG 1062, ABV 6.5%)
Rich, dark beer brewed with hops and bog myrtle then cold conditioned with fresh elderberrys. Adapted from a 16th century Scottish recipe.

Profanity Stout (OG 1068, ABV 7%)

Black stout with full, floral, fruity aromas and a huge roasted malt character that gives way to a profanely dry hopped finish.

Alba Scots Pine Ale (OG 1075, ABV 7.5%)
Triple-style ale spiced with spruce and pine. Brewed to a traditional recipe, popular in Northern Scotland until the end of the 19th century.

Willy Good

The Old Forge, Hartleys Farm, Winsley, Wiltshire, BA15 2JB
☎ 07711 364202 ⊕ willygoodale.com

Willy Good Ale opened in 2010, producing bottles and casks and supplying local public houses, a farm shop, off-license and restaurant. The brewery sources its malted barley from the Wiltshire area, but aims to have it grown at the farm and malted in Warminster in future.

Beerier Beer (ABV 4.2%)
Single-hop amber ale with a medium body and vanilla overtones.

Willy Hop (ABV 4.2%)
Full-flavoured dry-hopped pale ale.

High Fives (ABV 5%)
A light, but hoppy pale ale, with hints of grapefruit.

Wheat a Second (ABV 5%)
Wheat beer with a hint of orange and coriander.

Willy Brown (ABV 5%)
Rich, malty nut brown ale.

Willy's

▤ 17 High Cliff Road, Cleethorpes, Lincolnshire, DN35 8RQ
☎ (01472) 602145
Tours by arrangement

The brewery opened in 1989 to provide beer mainly for its in-house pub in Cleethorpes, although some beer is sold in the free trade. It has a five-barrel plant with a maximum capacity of 15 barrels a week. The brewery can be viewed at any time from the pub or street.

Original (OG 1039, ABV 3.9%) ◆
A light brown 'sea air' beer with a fruity, tangy hop on the nose and taste, giving a strong bitterness tempered by the underlying malt.

Wilson Potter SIBA

Unit E2, Hanson Close, Middleton, M24 2QZ
☎ (0161) 654 6446 ⊕ wilsonpotterbrewery.co.uk

☺Wilson Potter began brewing in 2011 using a six-barrel plant and was established by two former home brewers, Kathryn Harrison and Amanda Seddon. The brewery is named after their respective grandmothers. A full range of bottle-conditioned beers is also available.

Cascale (OG 1038, ABV 3.7%)
A pale, golden beer with a citrus aroma and a full-balanced bitterness with a clean, tangy finish.

Tandle Hill (OG 1040, ABV 3.9%)
A golden blonde beer with strong citrus flavours and aroma created using a blend of three hops.

Bon Don Doon (OG 1042, ABV 4.2%)
A refreshing pale blonde beer.

In the Black (OG 1048, ABV 4.2%)
A rich, dark stout with a fruity, roasted malt aroma and taste, with a liquorice finish.

Ruby Red (OG 1047, ABV 4.4%)
An easy-drinking rich ruby ale with a full-bodied malty berry taste and a floral hop finish.

Natural Progression (OG 1048, ABV 4.8%)
A fruity amber beer with a bitter hop flavour and a delicate aroma.

Wincle SIBA

Tolls Farm Barn, Dane Bridge, Wincle, Cheshire, SK11 0QE
☎ (01260) 227777 ⊕ winclebeer.co.uk
Shop 10am-4pm daily
Tours by arrangement

☺Wincle was set up in 2008 on a working farm in the Peak District National Park. In 2011 they relocated to a new 15-barrel plant in Wincle. Bottle-conditioned and seasonal beers are also available: see website.

Waller (OG 1038, ABV 3.8%)
A pale and refreshing beer with a distinctive hop character.

Life of Riley (OG 1043, ABV 4.2%)

Sir Phillip (OG 1041, ABV 4.2%)
Amber-coloured premium bitter with a light malty overtone balanced by hops.

Under Taker (OG 1044, ABV 4.5%)
Dark-coloured bitter with complex, nutty and fruit undertones.

Windsor & Eton SIBA ◉

Unit 1, Vansittart Estate, Duke Street, Windsor, Berkshire, SL4 1SE
☎ (01753) 854075 ⊕ webrew.co.uk
Shop Mon-Fri 8am-6pm; Sat 10am-2pm (often later, check website)
Tours by arrangement

⊗ Windsor & Eton Brewery was established in 2010 on an 18-barrel plant and has grown rapidly in volume. 250 outlets in London and the Thames Valley are supplied direct. Seasonal and special beers: see website.

Knight of the Garter (OG 1036.5, ABV 3.8%)
A straw-coloured golden ale with a distinctive fresh citrus hop aroma.

Windsor Knot (OG 1039, ABV 4%)
Amber ale with a grapefruit aroma. An initially sweet malt and fruit taste is followed by a mild, bittering finish.

Guardsman (OG 1041, ABV 4.2%)
A tangy best bitter, tawny in colour, with a fresh hoppy finish mellowed with the use of oak during conditioning.

Conqueror (OG 1049, ABV 5%) ⌂
A complex black IPA, with a full roasted taste and intense hop aroma and flavour.

Windswept (NEW) SIBA

Unit B, 13 Coulardbank Industrial Estate, Lossiemouth Moray, Lossiemouth, IV31 6NG
☎ (01343) 814310 ☎ 07896 897944
⊕ windsweptbrewing.co.uk

Tours by arrangement

Windswept began brewing in 2012 using a 10-barrel plant. It is situated near the gates of RAF Lossiemouth and run by two former Tornado pilots who are CAMRA members.

Blonde (OG 1039, ABV 4%)
A refreshing session beer with citrus hops and smooth malts.

APA (OG 1046, ABV 5%)
Well-balanced maltiness leads to a long, tangy finish.

Wolf (OG 1064, ABV 6%)
A strong, dark Scottish ale named after the Wolf of Badenoch. Sweet malts balanced with smooth chocolate bitterness.

Windy SIBA

☰ Volunteer Inn, New Road, Seavington St Michael, Somerset, TA19 0QE
☎ (01460) 240126 ⊕ thevolly.co.uk

Windy Brewery was established in 2011. The name of the brewery stems from the time when alterations were carried out to the back of the pub and the workmen suffered extremes of varying weather conditions.

Tornado (OG 1039, ABV 3.9%)
Traditional brown bitter.

Southerly (OG 1042, ABV 4%)

Flurry (OG 1042, ABV 4.1%)
A golden beer.

Fresh Breeze (OG 1043, ABV 4.1%)

Hurricane (OG 1043, ABV 4.2%)
American-style IPA.

Northerly (OG 1050, ABV 4.8%)

Winster Valley SIBA

☰ Brown Horse Inn, Winster, Cumbria, LA23 3NR
☎ (01539) 443443 ⊕ winstervalleybrewery.co.uk
Tours by arrangement

⊛Winster Valley was established in 2009 using a 2.5-barrel plant at the Brown Horse Inn in Winster.

Best Bitter (OG 1036, ABV 3.7%)

Old School (OG 1037, ABV 3.9%)

Winter's

8 Keelan Close, Norwich, NR6 6QZ
☎ (01603) 787820 ⊕ wintersbrewery.com

Winter's was established in 2001 by David Winter, who had previous award-winning success as brewer for both Woodforde's and Chalk Hill breweries. Winter's ales have won many awards with David now passing his brewing knowledge to his son, Mark, an award-winning brewer in his own right. Seasonal beer is also available.

Mild (OG 1036.5, ABV 3.6%) ◆
Classic dark mild, red-brown with a nutty roast character. A good balance of malt caramel and roast abetted by both sweetness and a light, hoppy bitterness. Lingering finish develops a plummy feel.

Cloudburst (OG 1037, ABV 3.7%) ◆

Tawny coloured with a malty nose. Initial balance of malt and hops tinged with bitterness drops off to a long dry bitter ending.

Bitter (OG 1039.5, ABV 3.8%) ◆
A well-balanced amber bitter. Hops and malt are balanced by a crisp citrus fruitiness. A pleasant hoppy nose with a hint of grapefruit. Long, sustained, dry, grapefruit finish.

Genius (OG 1040, ABV 4.1%) ◆
A dark brown stout that has a smooth mouthfeel with a grainy edge. Roast dominates throughout but is balanced by a mix of malt, a bittersweet fruitiness and an increasingly nutty finish.

Golden (OG 1041, ABV 4.1%) ◆
Just a hint of hops in the aroma. The initial taste combines a dry bitterness with a fruity apple buttress. The finish slowly subsides into a long, dry bitterness.

Revenge (OG 1047, ABV 4.7%) ◆
Blackcurrant notes give depth to the inherent maltiness of this pale brown beer. A bittersweet background becomes more pronounced as the fruitiness gently wanes.

Storm Force (OG 1053, ABV 5.3%) ◆
A well-defined, sweetish brew. Hops and vine fruit give depth to the malty backbone of this pale brown strong beer. All flavours hold up well as the finish develops a warming softness.

Wirksworth SIBA

25 St John Street, Wirksworth, Derbyshire, DE4 4DR
☎ (01629) 824011 ⊕ wirksworthbrewery.co.uk
Off sales: Fri 11am-5pm; Sat 9am-4pm

⊛Jeff Green started brewing in 2007 with a 2.5-barrel plant in a converted stone workshop. Wirksworth supplies Derbyshire pubs with six core beers and supplements these with at least one seasonal offering. Every September there is a brew house open weekend giving visitors the opportunity to gain an insight into the brewing process and taste the real ales.

Sunbeam (OG 1039, ABV 4%)
An easy-drinking, straw-coloured beer with a dry hoppy finish.

First Brew (OG 1041, ABV 4.2%)
Pale bitter with a rich hoppy aroma and light amber colour.

T'owd Man (OG 1048, ABV 4.9%)
A classic bitter, amber in colour with a well-hopped dry finish.

Snowfield (OG 1049, ABV 5%)
An easy-drinking, straw-coloured beer with a dry, hoppy finish.

Wissey Valley

1 High Street, Downham Market, PE38 9DA
☎ (01366) 386658 ⊕ norfolkfoodanddrink.co.uk
Shop Wed-Sun 9am-5pm
Tours by arrangement

After several moves since starting up in 2002 (as Captain Grumpy's), the brewery is now located at the rear of the local produce store, tea room and restaurant, the Hop & Hog.

Captain Grumpy's Best Bitter (OG 1039, ABV 3.9%)

Khaki Sargeant Strong Stout (OG 1059, ABV 6%)

Wizard SIBA

Unit 4, Lundy View, Mullacott Cross Industrial Estate, Ilfracombe, Devon, EX34 8PY
☎ (01271) 865350 ⊕ wizardales.co.uk
Tours by arrangement

Brewing started in 2003 on a 1.25-barrel plant, since upgraded to five barrels. The brewery moved from Warwickshire to Devon in 2007. Around 20 local outlets are supplied. Bottle-conditioned beers are also available.

Apprentice (OG 1038, ABV 3.6%)

Lundy Gold (OG 1042, ABV 4.1%)

Old Combe (OG 1043, ABV 4.2%)

Druid's Fluid (OG 1048, ABV 5%)

Wobbly (NEW)

Unit 22C, Beech Business Park, Tillington Road, Hereford, HR4 9QJ
☎ (01432) 278345 ⊕ wobblybrewing.co.uk

Wobbly began brewing in 2013 using a 2.5-barrel plant. Further beers are planned including seasonals.

Welder (ABV 4.8%)

Wold Top SIBA ⊚

Hunmanby Grange, Wold Newton, Driffield, East Yorkshire, YO25 3HS
☎ (01723) 892222 ⊕ woldtopbrewery.co.uk

⊛An integral part of Hunmanby Grange, a family farm, Wold Top brewed its first ale in 2003. The year-round range includes special edition cask and bottled beers plus two gluten-free beers, Against the Grain (ABV 4.5%) and Scarborough Fair IPA (ABV 6%). The brewery installed a bottling line in 2008 and contract bottles for other breweries. Seasonal beers: see website.

Bitter (OG 1036, ABV 3.7%)
A crisp, clean, aromatic session bitter. Full-flavoured with a long, hoppy finish.

Anglers Reward (OG 1039, ABV 4%)
A refreshing golden pale ale with a fruity bitterness and lingering aftertaste.

Headland Red (OG 1042, ABV 4.3%)
A red beer with a mellow malty flavour.

Wold Gold (OG 1046, ABV 4.8%)
A light-coloured summer beer with a soft, fruity flavour with a hint of spice.

Wolf SIBA ⊚

Decoy Farm, Old Norwich Road, Besthorpe, Attleborough, Norfolk, NR17 2LA
☎ (01953) 457775 ⊕ wolfbrewery.com
Shop Mon-Fri 9am-5pm

⊠ The brewery was founded in 1996 on a 20-barrel plant, which was upgraded to a 25-barrel one in 2006. The brewery also has a bottling plant. More than 300 outlets are supplied. Seasonal beers: see website.

Edith Cavell (OG 1037, ABV 3.7%)
A hoppy thirst-quenching beer with a fruity finish.

Golden Jackal (OG 1039, ABV 3.7%) ◄
A hoppy, citrus nose carries through to the initial taste. The citrus notes remain right to the end as the initial hoppiness is replaced by a dry bitterness.

Lavender Honey (OG 1037, ABV 3.7%)
Lavender honey is added during the brewing process to give this beer a delicate flavour.

Wolf in Sheep's Clothing (OG 1039, ABV 3.7%) ◄
A malty aroma with fruity undertones introduce this reddish-hued mild. Malt, with a bitter background that remains throughout, is the dominant flavour of this clean-tasting beer.

Ale (ABV 3.9%)
A copper-coloured, full-bodied ale.

RAF Collection Battle of Britain
(OG 1039, ABV 3.9%)
Copper-coloured, full-bodied ale brewed to commemorate The Few. A donation is made to the RAF Association Wings Appeal for every pint sold.

Flanders Ale (OG 1042, ABV 4.2%)
Pale golden ale infused with honey and fruity hops to give a delicate flavour.

Lupus Lupus (OG 1042, ABV 4.2%)
Unique flavoured blonde ale using fruity hops.

Coyote Bitter (OG 1044, ABV 4.3%) ◄
A well-balanced golden brew with a hop and citrus aroma. The dominant hoppy bitterness is countered by a malty, slightly sweet backdrop. Complex flavours continue to mix as the dry, bitter ending slowly fades.

At The Door (ABV 4.4%)
A maple-flavoured light beer.

Sirius Dog Star (OG 1044, ABV 4.4%)
Lightly hopped red ale with a soft fruity finish.

Straw Dog (OG 1045, ABV 4.5%) ◄
A delicately flavoured brew with a fruity nuance. An aroma reminiscent of redcurrants gives way to a low key marmalade and hop beginning. A stronger finish with increasing bitterness.

Mad Wolf (ABV 4.7%)
A smooth, malty, dark ale.

Granny Wouldn't Like It (OG 1049, ABV 4.8%) ◄
Red-brown with a pronounced malty bouquet. Bitterness increases throughout but is softened by a smoky malt background. Some roast notes and a gentle, fruity sweetness add depth.

Woild Moild (OG 1048, ABV 4.8%)
A rich and fruity traditional Norfolk mild. Good balance of malt with liquorice bitterness and lots of chocolate malt. Dark ruby-red mild with a long lasting finish.

For City of Cambridge Brewery:

Boathouse (OG 1037, ABV 3.7%)
A light copper-coloured session bitter with a pleasant aroma from the unique blend of hops and malt.

Hobson's Choice (OG 1041, ABV 4.2%) ◄
This golden ale has a predominantly spicy hop aroma. Bittersweet on the palate with plenty of hops leading through to a dry, hoppy finish.

Atom Splitter (OG 1045, ABV 4.5%) ◄
Robust, copper-coloured strong bitter with a hop aroma and taste, and a distinct sulphury edge.

Parkers Piece (OG 1050, ABV 5%) ◄

Impressive reddish brew with a defined roast character throughout, and a short, fruity, bittersweet palate.

Wollaton (NEW)

Wilkinson Street, Basford, Nottingham, NG7 5HD
☎ 07879 664702

Office: Lenton Business Centre, Nottingham, NG7 2BY
⊕ thewollatonbreweryco.co.uk

Wollatton is a 1,000 litre brewery that started production in 2013 initially producing just bottled beers, although cask-conditioned beers are being considered.

Wood SIBA ◉

Wistanstow, Craven Arms, Shropshire, SY7 8DG
☎ (01588) 672523 ⊕ woodbrewery.co.uk
Tours by arrangement

The brewery opened in 1980 in buildings next to the Plough Inn, still the brewery's only tied house. Steady growth over the years included the acquisition of the Sam Powell Brewery and its beers in 1991. Around 200 outlets are supplied. Seasonal beers: see website.

Parish Bitter (OG 1040, ABV 4%) ◆
A blend of malt and hops with a bitter aftertaste. Pale brown in colour.

Shropshire Lass (OG 1041, ABV 4.1%)
A golden ale with a zesty bitterness.

Special Bitter (OG 1042, ABV 4.2%) ◆
A tawny brown bitter with malt, hops and some fruitiness.

Shropshire Lad (OG 1045, ABV 4.5%)
A strong, well-rounded bitter.

Tom Wood's SIBA ◉

Melton High Wood Farm, Melton High Wood, Melton Ross, Lincolnshire, DN38 6AA
☎ (01652) 680001 ⊕ tom-wood.com

The Tom Wood range of beers is brewed in the 60-barrel Highwood plant, which the brewery took over in 2011. Tom Wood initially started in a converted Victorian granary on a family farm in 1995. Quarterly seasonal beers are available: see website.

Best Bitter (OG 1035.5, ABV 3.5%) ◆
A good citrus, passion fruit hop dominates the nose and taste, with background malt. A lingering hoppy and bitter finish.

Lincoln Gold (OG 1041, ABV 4%)
A pale bitter with a fruity aroma and slightly zesty flavour but retaining malt characteristics.

Bomber County (OG 1046, ABV 4.8%) ◆
An earthy malt aroma but with a complex underlying mix of coffee, hops, caramel and apple fruit. The beer starts bitter and intensifies to the end.

Wood Farm SIBA

Coalpit Lane, Willey, Warwickshire, CV23 0SL
☎ (01788) 833469 ☎ 07912 481250
⊕ woodfarmbrewery.co.uk
Tours by arrangement

◉Wood Farm was established in 2011. The brewery can be viewed from the bar of the visitor centre. Outside there is a patio area with tables set in 36 acres of Warwickshire countryside.

1823 Mild (OG 1035, ABV 3.5%)

Twickers (OG 1037, ABV 3.7%)

Webb Ellis (OG 1038, ABV 3.8%)

Best Bitter (OG 1042, ABV 4.2%)

Victorious (OG 1042, ABV 4.2%)

Union (OG 1046, ABV 4.6%)

No 8 (OG 1050, ABV 5%)

Wood Street SIBA

≣ Hillsborough Hotel, 54-58 Langsett Road, Sheffield, South Yorkshire, S6 2UB
☎ (0114) 2348307 ⊕ hillsborough-hotel.co.uk/woodstreet-brewery
Tours by arrangement

Formally the Crown Brewery, Wood Street opened in 2012 under new ownership at the re-named Hillsborough Hotel in Sheffield. Monthly specials are also brewed.

Pale Ale (OG 1038, ABV 3.9%)
A session beer with citrus notes and a fresh hoppy taste with a crisp, refreshing aftertaste.

Bitter (OG 1039, ABV 4%)
A traditional amber-coloured bitter, very smooth on the palate.

Golden Larch (OG 1043, ABV 4.5%)
A full-bodied well-rounded golden ale with a crisp fruitiness.

Honey Locust (ABV 4.6%)
A golden mild honey beer with local honey added to give a well-balanced ale with a touch of sweetness.

Ebony Stout (OG 1050, ABV 5%)
Dark stout with a ruby edge, with coffee and chocolate undertones and a big deep aroma.

Yellow Wood IPA (OG 1049, ABV 5.1%)
A well-balanced strong pale bitter, smooth tasting, with a distinct hoppy flavour and a long refreshing finish.

Wooden Hand SIBA ◉

Unit 3, Grampound Road Industrial Estate, Grampound Road, Truro, Cornwall, TR2 4TB
☎ (01726) 884596 ⊕ woodenhand.co.uk

Wooden Hand was founded in 2004, and now supplies around 50 outlets with a high percentage of production being sold further afield via wholesalers. A bottling line was installed in 2005, which also contract-bottles for other breweries.

Pirates Gold (OG 1040.6, ABV 4%)
A slightly tart pale session bitter with hop aroma, light fruit yet malty underlying flavour and tangy fruit finish.

Cornish Gribben (OG 1041.6, ABV 4.1%)
A well-hopped beer, with citrus and fruit notes. Well balanced bittersweet finish.

Cornish Buccaneer (OG 1043.6, ABV 4.3%)
A golden beer with full flavour hop character, good fruit and hop balance and a long, dry finish.

Black Pearl (OG 1050.6, ABV 4.5%)

A rich, nutty stout with good hop balance and dry chocolate finish.

Cornish Mutiny (OG 1048.6, ABV 4.8%)
Rich, full-bodied strong ale with distinctive full hop character. Biscuity and complex flavour with a full finish.

Woodforde's SIBA ⦿

Broadland Brewery, Woodbastwick, Norwich, NR13 6SW
☎ (01603) 720353 ⊕ woodfordes.co.uk
Shop Mon-Fri 10.30am-4.30pm; Sat & Sun 11.30am-4.30pm (01603 722218)
Tours by arrangement

⊗ Founded in 1981 in Drayton, Woodforde's moved to Erpingham in 1982, and then to a converted farm complex in Woodbastwick, with greatly increased production capacity, in 1989. Major expansion in 2001 saw a further increase in fermentation capacity and a new brewery shop and visitor centre. In 2008 a new Brigg's brewhouse, complete with hopback, was added. Woodforde's runs two tied houses, with around 600 outlets supplied on a regular basis.

Mardler's (OG 1036, ABV 3.5%) ◆
Chocolate and roast aromas introduce this well-balanced dark mild. Swathes of vanilla, caramel and malt boost the dominant roast and chocolate flavours. A fine, flavoursome finish.

Wherry (OG 1037.5, ABV 3.8%) ◆
Amber-coloured with an orange citrus nose. Complex, well-balanced but easy-drinking, the swirling mix of malt, hops, citrus and bitterness combine into a tangy marmalade dryness.

Once Bittern (OG 1040, ABV 4%) ◆
A light malty nose with a hint of sulphur. A dark marmalade tang gives an edge to the dominant malt character. Complex, grainy, but easily drinkable with a bittersweet ending.

Sundew (OG 1039, ABV 4.1%) ◆
Hops emerge from a competing fusion of malt, fruit and bitterness to provide a cutting edge to both taste and aroma. Smooth-drinking with a long ending.

Bure Gold (OG 1043, ABV 4.3%)
Golden ale with distinctive citrus aroma and a refreshing palate combining light malt and exotic fruit. The finish is satisfyingly dry.

Nelson's Revenge (OG 1045, ABV 4.5%) 🍴 ◆
An infusion of vine fruit, malt and hops provide a rich, rewarding experience. The aromas and flavours bounce merrily along to a sweet, Madeira-like finale.

Woodlands SIBA

Unit 3, Meadow Lane Farm, London Road, Stapeley, Cheshire, CW5 7JU
☎ (01270) 841511 ⊕ woodlandsbrewery.co.uk
Shop Mon-Fri 9am-4.30pm
Tours by arrangement

⊙The brewery opened in 2004 and moved to larger premises in 2008. An extension in 2010 allowed for increased production. The beers are brewed using water from a spring that surfaces on a nearby peat field at Woodlands Farm. More than 100 outlets are supplied including the brewery's

tied houses. Bottle-conditioned beers are also available.

Mild (OG 1035, ABV 3.5%)
A dark mild ale.

Old Faithful (OG 1036, ABV 3.6%)
A pale session bitter.

Red Squirrel (OG 1038, ABV 3.8%)
Session bitter with a hint of blackcurrant.

Oak Beauty (OG 1042, ABV 4.2%) ◆
Malty, sweetish, copper-coloured bitter with toffee and caramel flavours. Long-lasting and satisfying bitter finish.

Bitter (OG 1044, ABV 4.4%)

Midnight Stout (OG 1044, ABV 4.4%) ◆
Classic creamy dry stout with roast flavours to the fore. Well-balanced with bitterness and good hops on the taste and a good dry, roasty aftertaste. Some sweetness.

Redwood (OG 1049, ABV 4.9%)
A dark bitter with a sharp aftertaste.

General's Tipple (OG 1055, ABV 5.5%)
A refreshing, medium-hopped IPA.

World's End

🍴 **Crown Inn, 60 Wilcot Road, Pewsey, Wiltshire, SN9 5EL**
☎ (01672) 562653 ⊕ thecrowninnpewsey.com
Tours by arrangement

⊗ World's End Ales was established in 2009 on a one-barrel plant at the rear of the Crown Inn in Pewsey. World's End is the 18th-century name for the area in which the brewery is located.

Barbed & Tangled (ABV 4.5%)

Worsthorne SIBA

Unit 4, Oxford Mill, Burnley Road, Briercliffe, Burnley, Lancashire, BB10 2HQ
☎ 07815 708289
⊕ worsthornebrewingcompany.co.uk

Worsthorne began brewing in 2011 using a 5.5-barrel plant. 20 outlets are supplied direct. Seasonal beers are planned.

Chestnut Mare (OG 1038, ABV 3.5%)
Chestnut-coloured mild with liquorice undertones and dry blackcurrant finish.

Gold (OG 1036, ABV 3.6%)
Lightly-bittered golden ale with a spicy aroma.

Packhorse (OG 1039, ABV 3.7%)
Pale amber ale with subtle earthy bitterness and floral spicy finish.

Foxstones (OG 1041, ABV 3.9%)
Traditional-style amber bitter with a well-balanced hoppy aroma and lingering floral aftertaste.

Some Like It Blond (OG 1041, ABV 3.9%)
A blond beer with a lingering dry aftertaste.

Old Trout (OG 1047, ABV 4.5%)
A well-flavoured red/brown ale.

Worth SIBA

🍴 **Royal British Legion Club, George's Road West, Poynton, Cheshire, SK12 1JY**

☎ (01625) 873120/878526
⊕ poyntonlegionclub.co.uk
Tours by arrangement

Based alongside the Royal British Legion Club, Worth brews traditional English session beers for sale at the club and throughout Cheshire. The beer names celebrate Poynton's history and the pump clips are painted by a local artist.

Coppice (ABV 3.5%)
A true black mild beer, quite nostalgic in style, with a surprising depth of flavour.

Shared Space (ABV 3.6%)
A full-flavoured light session ale.

Nimrod (ABV 3.7%)
A bright copper-coloured session beer.

Blythe's Spirit (ABV 3.8%)
A traditionally hopped beer with a hint of sweetness and a bright golden colour.

Anson (ABV 4%)
A pale, hoppy, blonde bitter with a very clean palate and a lingering bitter finish.

Redacre (ABV 4%)
A rich ruby-red beer with a smooth clean head, malty in style, with hints of fruit and a smooth finish.

Seam Cutter (ABV 4.2%)
A rich dark beer, full-flavoured with a creamy tan head, smoky and chocolate overtones and a nice clean finish.

Worthington's

National Brewery Centre, Horninglow Street, Burton upon Trent, Staffordshire, DE14 1NG
☎ (01283) 511000 ⊕ nationalbrewerycentre.co.uk
Tours by arrangement

Molson Coors invested £1 million on this brewing plant in 2011, set within the brewery centre; the brewery is named after one of the famous Burton brewers from the 18th and 19th centuries who developed the pale ale style that transformed brewing in Britain. Based on possibly Britain's oldest microbrewery, this new brewing plant and its predecessor can be seen by visitors to the National Brewery Centre. In addition to regular beers seasonal beers are produced. Part of Molson Coors.

M&B Mild (OG 1033, ABV 2.8%)
A traditional Midland mild ale with a dark brown colour and ceamy head, the fruity yeast notes are balanced by the burnt roast flavour derived from dark malts.

Red Shield (OG 1040, ABV 4.2%) ◆
Hay and straw bales aroma. Old corner sweetshop taste with malt, too. Sweet aftertaste with hints of fruit and hop bitterness for a perfect balance.

E (OG 1044, ABV 4.8%) ◆
Grassy hop start with a bittersweet touch to follow. Bitterness grows with a dry edge and good hoppy finish.

White Shield (OG 1049, ABV 5.6%) ◆
Sweet aroma and woody tastes with angelica, nettles and sharp apples. Ever-changing tastes but a long, hoppy finish. Only available cask-conditioned at the National Brewery Centre.

Wrexham Lager (NEW)

Office: Park Lodge, Rhosddu Road, Wrexham, LL11 1NF
☎ (01978) 266222 ⊕ wrexhamlager.co.uk
No real ale.

George Wright SIBA

Unit 11, Diamond Business Park, Sandwash Close, Rainford, Merseyside, WA11 8LY
☎ (01744) 886686 ⊕ georgewrightbrewing.co.uk
Shop Tue-Fri 10am-4pm
Tours by arrangement

George Wright started production in 2003. The original 2.5-barrel plant was replaced by a five-barrel one, which has since been upgraded again to 25 barrels with production of 200 casks a week.

Black Swan (OG 1039, ABV 3.8%)
A dark, distinctive ale, creamy with a hint of fruit.

Drunken Duck (OG 1040, ABV 3.9%) ◆
Fruity, gold-coloured bitter beer with good hop and a dry aftertaste. Some acidity.

Long Boat (OG 1040, ABV 3.9%) ◆
Good hoppy bitter with grapefruit and an almost tart bitterness throughout. Some astringency in the aftertaste. Well-balanced, light and refreshing with a good mouthfeel and long, dry finish.

Blonde Moment (ABV 4%)
A premium blonde beer with a herbal nose and a sweet aftertaste.

Pipe Dream (OG 1044, ABV 4.3%) ◆
Refreshing hoppy best bitter with a fruity nose and grapefruit to the fore in the taste. Lasting dry, bitter finish.

Pure Blonde (OG 1045, ABV 4.6%)
A premium blonde ale, light and hoppy with an earthy hop flavour.

Cheeky Pheasant (OG 1047, ABV 4.7%)
Light amber-coloured, distinctive fruit, malty taste with a sweet aftertaste.

Roman Black (OG 1047, ABV 4.8%)
A dark premium ale, smooth and creamy leaving a long, malty, sweet taste.

Blue Moon (OG 1048, ABV 5%) ◆
Easy-drinking, strong, gold-coloured beer. Good malt/bitter balance and well hopped.

Mocne Piwo (ABV 5.1%)
Strong ale, light amber-coloured with a moreish hoppy aftertaste.

Northern Lights (OG 1049, ABV 5.1%)
Strong ale, amber-coloured with a strong citrus taste balanced by bitter hop.

Wychwood 👁

Eagle Maltings, The Crofts, Witney, Oxfordshire, OX28 4DP
☎ (01993) 890800 ⊕ wychwood.co.uk
Shop Mon-Sat 10am-5pm
Tours by arrangement

Wychwood brewery is located in the Cotswold market town of Witney. The brewers take inspiration from the myths and legends associated with the ancient medieval Wychwood forest to create a range of award-winning, characterful ales. Monthly seasonal beers are produced and bottle-conditioned beers are available. Part of Marston's PLC.

Hobgoblin (OG 1045, ABV 4.5%)
A full-bodied ruby beer, with chocolate toffee malt flavour balanced by a rounded moderate bitterness and overall fruity character.

Wye Valley SIBA ◉

Stoke Lacy, Herefordshire, HR7 4HG
☎ (01885) 490505 ⊕ wyevalleybrewery.co.uk
Shop Mon-Fri 9am-4.30pm
Tours by arrangement

⊠ Founded in 1985 in Canon Pyon, the brewery is now situated in Stoke Lacy. Regarded as a successful regional brewery a new brewhouse was completed in 2013. Bottle-conditioned beers are available and are bottled on site.

Bitter (OG 1037, ABV 3.7%) ◆
A beer whose aroma gives little hint of the bitter hoppiness that follows right through to the aftertaste.

HPA (OG 1040, ABV 4%) ◆
A pale, hoppy, malty brew with a hint of sweetness before a dry finish.

Dorothy Goodbody's Golden Ale (OG 1042, ABV 4.2%)
A light, gold-coloured ale with a good hop character throughout.

Butty Bach (OG 1046, ABV 4.5%)
A burnished gold, full-bodied premium ale.

Dorothy Goodbody's Wholesome Stout (OG 1046, ABV 4.6%) ◆
A smooth and satisfying stout with a bitter edge to its roast flavours. The finish combines roast grain and malt.

Wylam SIBA

South Houghton Farm, Heddon on the Wall, Northumberland, NE15 0EZ
☎ (01661) 853377 ⊕ wylambrewery.co.uk
Shop Mon-Fri 9am-5pm; Sat 11am-3pm
Tours by arrangement

☺Wylam started in 2000 on a 4.5-barrel plant. New premises and a 20-barrel plant were built on the same site in 2006 which now has a visitor area and shop, with further expansion planned. The brewery delivers to more than 200 local outlets. Seasonal beers: see website.

Bitter (OG 1039, ABV 3.8%) ◆
A refreshing, copper-coloured, hoppy bitter with a clean, bitter finish.

Gold Tankard (OG 1040, ABV 4%) ◆
Fresh clean flavour, full of hops. This golden ale has a hint of citrus in the finish.

Collingwood Festival Ale (OG 1041, ABV 4.1%)
A honey-coloured ale with a sweet tangerine aroma, citrus and pinewood flavour and a dry and bitter finish.

Angel (OG 1044, ABV 4.3%)
A well-balanced pale copper ale with citrus character in the aroma and finish.

Northern Kite (OG 1046.5, ABV 4.5%)
A ruby ale in the style of a traditional Scotch with a subtle hop character and a rich palate.

Locomotion No. 1 (OG 1050, ABV 5%)

Continental-style beer traditionally lagered for three weeks to give a distinctive lager style with classic flavour hop.

Wyre Piddle

See Ambridge

XT SIBA

Notley Farm, Chearsley Road, Long Crendon, Buckinghamshire, HP18 9ER
☎ (01844) 208310 ⊕ xtbrewing.com
Shop Sat 9.30am-12pm; Mon-Fri please ring first
Tours by arrangement

⊠ XT started brewing in 2011 with a British-built 18-barrel plant. It supplies direct to pubs in Buckinghamshire, Oxfordshire and the Midlands. The brewery shop sells its bottle-conditioned beers and locally-made cider. Seasonal beers: see website. The brewery also produces a range of limited edition, one-off brews under the Animal Brewing Co name.

Four (OG 1038, ABV 3.8%)
An amber beer brewed with a special Belgian malt.

Three (OG 1041, ABV 4.2%)

Two (OG 1041, ABV 4.2%)
A refreshing golden ale.

Six (OG 1044, ABV 4.5%)
Ruby red beer, malty and smooth with a hop finish.

Yard of Ale SIBA

▤ Surtees Arms, Chilton Lane, Ferryhill, County Durham, DL17 0DH
☎ (01740) 655724 ☎ 07540 733513
⊕ thesurteesarms.co.uk
Tours by arrangement

Established in 2008, the 2.5-barrel microbrewery supplies ales to its brewery tap, the Surtees Arms, beer festivals and to a growing number of pubs from North Tyne to South Tees. Seasonal specials are available as are bottle-conditioned beers.

One Foot In The Yard (OG 1044, ABV 4.5%)
Premium golden ale. Fruity on the nose and palate with a sweet finish.

Yates SIBA

Ghyll Farm, Westnewton, Cumbria, CA7 3NX
☎ (01697) 321081 ⊕ yatesbrewery.co.uk
Tours by arrangement

☺The first of Cumbria's new generation of breweries, established in 1986 and bought by Graeme and Caroline Baxter in 1998. It brews using a 20-barrel brewhouse and reed bed effluent system, and utilises a limited number of site-grown hops in its beers. Seasonal beers: see website.

Bitter (OG 1036, ABV 3.7%) ◆
A well-balanced, full-bodied bitter, golden in colour with complex hop bitterness. Good aroma and distinctive flavour.

Golden Ale (OG 1038, ABV 3.9%) ◆
Skilful use of lager malt and hops results in a pale beer with a light bitterness; melon fruit and a clean, refreshing finish.

Sun Goddess (OG 1041, ABV 4.2%) ◆

THE BREWERIES

A complex, full-bodied beer, packed with tropical fruit.

Yates' SIBA

Unit 4C, Langbridge Business Centre, Newchurch, Isle of Wight, PO36 0NP
☎ (01983) 867878 ⊕ yates-brewery.co.uk
Tours by arrangement

Brewing started in 2000 on a five-barrel plant at the Inn at St Lawrence. In 2009 the brewery moved to Newchurch and upgraded to a 10-barrel plant. Stumpy's Brewery was bought out by Yates' in 2009 and Old Stumpy (ABV 4.5%) and Tumbledown (ABV 5%) are now produced by Yates' on request. Seasonal and bottle-conditioned beers are also available.

Best Bitter (OG 1039, ABV 3.8%)

Golden Bitter (OG 1040, ABV 4%)
A light, refreshing ale with a bittersweet malt and hop taste with a dry, lemon edge that dominates the bitter finish.

Undercliff Experience (OG 1040, ABV 4.1%)
An amber ale with a bittersweet malt and hop taste with a dry, lemon edge that dominates the bitter finish.

Blonde Ale (OG 1045, ABV 4.5%)

Holy Joe (OG 1050, ABV 4.9%) ◄
Strongly bittered golden ale with pronounced spice and citrus character, and underlying light hint of malt.

Special Draught/YSD (OG 1056, ABV 5.5%)
Easy-drinking strong, amber ale with pronounced tart bitterness and a refreshing bite in the aftertaste.

Yule Be Sorry (OG 1072, ABV 7.2%)
A rich dark-coloured ale. Three different hops are used to give a rich full bodied beer.

Yeovil SIBA ⊙

Unit 5, Bofors Park, Artillery Road, Lufton Trading Estate, Yeovil, Somerset, BA22 8YH
☎ (01935) 414888 ⊕ yeovilales.com
Shop Fri 12-5.30pm
Tours by arrangement

Yeovil Ales was established in 2006 using an 18-barrel plant. Seasonal beers: see website. Bottle-conditioned beers are also available.

Glory (OG 1039, ABV 3.8%)
A well-balanced bitter with citrus hop notes.

Star Gazer (OG 1042, ABV 4%)
Dark copper bitter with late-hopped floral bouquet.

Summerset (OG 1042, ABV 4.1%)
Blonde ale with a fruity hop finish.

Lynx Wildcat (OG 1045, ABV 4.3%)

Stout Hearted (OG 1045, ABV 4.3%)

POSH IPA (OG 1054, ABV 5.4%)
A strong IPA with a fruity body and hoppy finish.

Yetman's

Bayfield Farm Barns, Bayfield Brecks Farm, Bayfield, Norfolk, NR25 7DZ
☎ 07774 809016 ⊕ yetmans.net

A 2.5-barrel plant built by Moss Brew was installed in restored medieval barns in 2005. The brewery supplies local free trade outlets. Bottle-conditioned beers are available.

Yellow (OG 1035, ABV 3.5%)

Red (OG 1036, ABV 3.8%)

Orange (OG 1040, ABV 4.2%) ◄
Well-balanced and smooth-drinking. A light fruity aroma leads into a stirring mix of malt and hops supported by a bittersweet background. A big finish combines malt and a vinous fruitiness.

Green (OG 1044, ABV 4.8%)

York SIBA ⊙

12 Toft Green, York, North Yorkshire, YO1 6JT
☎ (01904) 621162 ⊕ york-brewery.co.uk
Shop Mon-Sat 12-9pm
Tours by arrangement

York started production in 1996, it was the first brewery in the city for 40 years. It was acquired by Mitchell's of Lancaster in 2008. Five pubs are owned in York and Leeds. The brewery is open for guided tours, the 20-barrel plant has a viewing platform overlooking the conditioning and fermenting rooms. Seasonal beers: see website.

Guzzler (OG 1036, ABV 3.6%) ◄
Refreshing golden ale with dominant hop and fruit flavours developing throughout.

Yorkshire Terrier (OG 1041, ABV 4.2%) ◄
Refreshing and distinctive amber/gold brew where fruit and hops dominate the aroma and taste. Hoppy bitterness remains assertive in the aftertaste.

Centurion's Ghost Ale (OG 1051, ABV 5.4%) ◄
Dark ruby in colour, full-tasting with mellow roast malt character balanced by light bitterness and autumn fruit flavours that linger into the aftertaste.

Yorkshire

70 Humber Street, Kingston upon Hull, HU1 1TU
☎ (01482) 329999 ☎ 07850 494990
✉ info@yorkshirebrewing.co.uk
Tours by arrangement

Brewing started in 2012 in the Old Fruit Market using a six-barrel plant. Five beers are produced.

Tyger Tyger (OG 1036, ABV 3.6%)
A light, refreshing session bitter with a fruit twist aftertaste.

Supernatural Blonde (OG 1041, ABV 4.1%)
A refreshing blonde ale with a citrus taste and a lasting flavour.

True North (OG 1041, ABV 4.1%)
A classic Yorkshire bitter.

Yorkshire Dales

Seata Barn, Elm Hill, Askrigg, North Yorkshire, DL8 3HG
☎ (01969) 622027 ☎ 07818 035592
⊕ yorkshiredalesbrewery.com

⊛Situated in the heart of the Yorkshire Dales, brewing started in a converted milking parlour in 2005. Installation of a five-barrel plant increased capacity to 20 barrels a week. More than 150 pubs are supplied throughout the North of England. Four monthly specials and bottle-conditioned beers are available: see website.

Butter Tubs (OG 1037, ABV 3.7%)
A pale golden beer with a dry bitterness complemented by strong citrus flavours and aroma.

Leyburn Shawl (OG 1038, ABV 3.8%)
A crisp, dry, pale ale with an underlying sharpness.

Buckden Pike (OG 1040, ABV 3.9%)
A refreshing blonde beer with a crisp, fruity finish.

Nappa Scarr (OG 1041, ABV 4%)
A golden ale brewed with a trio of American hops for citrus and peach flavours throughout.

Muker Silver (OG 1041, ABV 4.1%)
A blonde lager-style ale, very crisp with a sharp, hoppy finish.

Askrigg Ale (OG 1043, ABV 4.3%)
A pale golden ale with intense aroma that generates a crisp, dry flavour with a long, bitter finish.

Garsdale Smokebox (OG 1057, ABV 5.6%)
A complex ale created by smoked and dark malts. Deep, rich chocolate and coffee flavours are complimented by the smokiness.

Yorkshire Heart SIBA

The Vineyard, Pool Lane, Nun Monkton, YO26 8EL
☎ (01423) 330716 ⊕ yorkshireheart.com
Tours by arrangement

⊠ Yorkshire Heart began brewing in 2011 and is situated adjacent to the Yorkshire Heart Vineyard and winery, not far from York. Six regular ales are produced all year and a new, larger brewhouse has been commissioned.

Lightheart (OG 1033, ABV 3.3%)
A pale ale full of fresh citrus flavours.

Hearty Mild (OG 1036, ABV 3.5%)
A mild made to a traditional recipe.

Hearty Bitter (OG 1037, ABV 3.7%)
A traditional chestnut brown bitter.

Silver Heart IPA (OG 1040, ABV 4%)

JRT Best Bitter (OG 1041, ABV 4.2%)
A golden ale with a refreshing taste.

Blackheart Stout (OG 1047, ABV 4.8%)

Young's

See Wells & Young's

Zerodegrees

⧮ Blackheath: 29-31 Montpelier Vale, Blackheath, London, SE3 0TJ
☎ (020) 8852 5619

Bristol: 53 Colston Street, Bristol, BS1 5BA ☎ (0117) 925 2706

Cardiff: 27 Westgate Street, Cardiff, CF10 1DD
☎ (029) 2022 9494

Reading: 9 Bridge Street, Reading, Berkshire, RG1 2LR ☎ (0118) 959 7959 ⊕ zerodegrees.co.uk
Tours by arrangement

⊠ Brewing started in 2000 in Greenwich, London and incorporates a state-of-the-art, computer-controlled German plant, producing unfiltered and unfined ales and lagers, served from tanks using air pressure (not CO2). Four pubs are owned. All beers are suitable for vegetarians. All branches of Zerodegrees follow the same concept of beers with natural ingredients. There are regular seasonal specials including fruit beers.

Mango Wheat Ale (OG 1040, ABV 4%) ⬥
Hazy yellow fruit beer with some wheat malt and a long sweet finish.

Wheat Ale (OG 1045, ABV 4.2%) ⬥
Powerful wheat aromas and flavour. Hints of coriander, clove and lemon on the nose. Fruity sweetness follows with a short citrussy aftertaste.

Black Lager (OG 1048, ABV 4.6%) ⬥
Czech-style beer with roast malt aromas and flavours and a long bittersweet aftertaste.

Pale Ale (OG 1046, ABV 4.6%) ⬥
American-style ale with hops, malt and a hint of caramel on the nose. Sweet malty taste with a peppery finish.

Pilsner (OG 1048, ABV 4.8%) ⬥
Clean refreshing lager in the European style with hints of sweetness. Short bitter finish.

REPUBLIC OF IRELAND BREWERIES

Beoir Chorca Dhuibhne/West Kerry

Tig Bhric, nr Ballyferriter, Co Kerry
☎ 00353 66 915 6325 ⊕ tigbhric.com/grudlann.html

Beer is brewed on a 400-litre plant in a remote area where Irish is the main language. The beers are available on draught in two pubs: Tig Bhric (adjacent to the brewery) and Tig Uí Chatháin in nearby Ballyferriter village. Bottle-conditioned versions are also produced.

Beal Bán (ABV 4.1%)

Cúl Dorcha (ABV 4.1%)

Carraig Dubh (ABV 6%)

Bo Bristle

Unit 5, Enterprise Centre, Banagher, Co Offaly
☎ 00353 86 125 0283 ⊕ bobristle.com

Established in 2011 as Brew-Eyed, rebranded the following year as Bo Bristle and based in Banagher in County Offaly. Also brews Carrig brand beers under contract.

IPA (ABV 5%)

Burren

Roadside Tavern, Kincora Road, Lisdoonvarna, Co Clare
☎ 00353 65 707 4084 ✉ roadsidetavern@gmail.com

Brewpub run by the owners of the Burren Smokehouse, specialising in local food, drink and music. The in-house brewery produces three keg beers for day-to-day sale, but cask editions are also available at the pub several times a year during festivals.

Carlow

Muine Bhaeg Business Park, Royal Oak Road, Carlow, Co Carlow
☎ 00353 59 972 0509 ⊕ carlowbrewing.com

One of the bigger Irish independents with a good range of cask beers. Operates the Brewery Corner pub in Kilkenny City as its tap.

O'Hara's Irish Stout (ABV 4.3%)

O'Hara's Red Ale (ABV 4.3%)

Curim Gold Wheat Beer (ABV 4.7%)

O'Hara's Pale Ale (ABV 5.2%)

Leann Folláin Stout (ABV 6%)

O'Hara's Double Irish Pale Ale (ABV 7.5%)

Donegal (NEW)

Market Street, Ballyshannon, Co Donegal
☎ 00353 71 985 1371
⊕ donegalbrewingcompany.com

A microbrewery based in the north-west, it first brewed in 2012.

Blonde (ABV 4.2%)

Dungarvan

Westgate Business Park, Dungarvan, Co Waterford
☎ 00353 58 24000
⊕ dungarvanbrewingcompany.com

Established in 2010 and producing three beers and several seasonals in bottle-conditioned format, increasingly available cask-conditioned.

Comeragh Challenger (ABV 3.8%)

Black Rock (ABV 4.3%)

Coffee & Oatmeal Stout (ABV 4.3%)

Copper Coast (ABV 4.3%)

Helvick Gold (ABV 4.9%)

Mahon Falls (ABV 5.1%)

Eight Degrees

Unit 3, Coolnanave, Dublin Road, Mitchelstown, Co Cork
☎ 00353 86 159 4855 ⊕ eightdegrees.ie

Founded by two Antipodean entrepreneurs, the brewery primarily produces bottled beers, though cask and unpasteurised keg versions are also available.

Barefoot Bohemian (ABV 4%)

Howling Gale (ABV 5%)

Knockmealdown Porter (ABV 5%)

Sunburnt (ABV 5%)

Kindred Spirit (ABV 7%)

Franciscan Well

14 North Mall, Cork City, Co Cork
☎ 00353 59 913 4356 ⊕ franciscanwellbrewery.com

Stalwart brewpub founded in 1998 and acquired by Molson Coors in 2012. A 70,000hl brewery was built in 2013 while small-scale brewing continues at the pub. Cask-conditioned versions of its range regularly appear on guest pumps around the country, while a series of special edition bottle-conditioned beers was launched in 2011.

Blarney Blonde (ABV 4.2%)

Shandon Stout (ABV 4.2%)

Rebel Red (ABV 4.3%)

Purgatory Pale Ale (ABV 4.5%)

Friar Weisse (ABV 4.7%)

Jameson Stout (ABV 7.8%)

Galway Bay

Oslo, Upper Salthill Road, Salthill, Co Galway
☎ 00353 91 448390 ⊕ galwaybaybrewery.com

Based at the Oslo Bar & Restaurant in Salthill, just outside Galway City, Galway Bay produces two ales and a porter.

Bay Ale (ABV 4.2%)

Full Sail (ABV 4.2%)

Buried At Sea (ABV 4.3%)

Galway Hooker

Roscommon Business Park, Racecourse Road, Roscommon, Co Roscommon
☎ 00353 87 77 62823 ⊕ galwayhooker.ie

Galway Hooker brews unpasteurised keg beer for the Irish market but also produces occasional casks for festivals in both Britain and Ireland.

Irish Pale Ale (ABV 4.4%)

Opus II (ABV 4.5%)

Stout (ABV 4.5%)

JW Sweetman

1-2 Burgh Quay, Dublin 2
☎ 00353 1 670 5777 ⊕ jwsweetman.com

Pub, brewery and restaurant in the historic O'Connell Bridge area of Dublin on the site of the former Messrs Maguire brewpub. Most beers are available cask-conditioned in rotation.

Golden Ale (ABV 4%)

The closed brewery

To be sure, it was a deserted place, down to the pigeon-house in the brewery-yard, which had been blown crooked on its pole by some high wind, and would have made the pigeons think themselves at sea, if there had been any pigeons there to be rocked by it. But, there were no pigeons in the dove-cot, no horses in the stable, no pigs in the sty, no malt in the store-house, no smells of grains and beer in the copper or the vat. All the uses and scents of the brewery might have evaporated with its last reek of smoke. In a by-yard, there was a wilderness of empty casks, which had a certain sour remembrance of better days lingering about them; but it was too sour to be accepted as a sample of the beer that was gone. **Charles Dickens**, Great Expectations

Red (ABV 4.3%)

Pale Ale (ABV 4.5%)

Porter (ABV 4.8%)

Weiss (ABV 5%)

Kinnegar

Aughavennon, Rathmullan, Co Donegal
⊕ kinnegarbrewing.com

A microbrewery situated in Donegal. Four bottle-conditioned ales are brewed, occasionally available cask-conditioned.

Devil's Backbone (ABV 4.5%)

Lime Burner (ABV 4.5%)

Rustbucket (ABV 5.1%)

Scraggy Bay (ABV 5.3%)

Kinsale (NEW)

Kinsale, Co Cork ⊕ kinsalecraftbrewery.com

A new arrival on the West Cork brewing scene, founded in 2013. Initial plans are for bottled and kegged beers, with cask to follow.

Metalman

14 Tycor Business Park, Tycor, Co Waterford
⊕ metalmanbrewing.com

Award winning Waterford microbrewery, known for its hop-dominated ales. Occasional casks are produced for festivals and pubs with real ale taps.

Pale Ale (ABV 4.3%)

Windjammer (ABV 4.8%)

Mountain Man (NEW)

Rananirree, Macroom, Co Cork
⊕ mountainmanbrewing.com

Brewing began in 2013 in rural County Cork.

Green Bullet (ABV 4%)

Hairy Goat (ABV 4.5%)

Porterhouse

Unit 6D, Rosemount, Park Road, Ballycoolin, Blanchardstown, Dublin 15

☎ 00353 1 822 7417 ⊕ theporterhouse.ie

Porterhouse has three pubs in Dublin plus one in Co Wicklow. There are also branches in Covent Garden, London and New York City. One permanent cask ale is produced, but a number of other beers are produced regularly in cask form for sale in the Temple Bar flagship and as guest ales in other pubs.

TSB (ABV 3.7%)

Plain Porter (ABV 4.3%)

Porterhouse Red (ABV 4.4%)

Oyster Stout (ABV 4.8%)

Hophead (ABV 5%)

Wrassler's XXXX (ABV 5%)

Brainblásta (ABV 7%)

Celebration (ABV 7%)

Trouble

Old Mill Industrial Estate, Kill, Co Kildare
☎ 00353 87 908 6658 ⊕ troublebrewing.ie

Small brewery producing three regular beers.

Ór (ABV 4.3%)
A golden ale.

Dark Arts (ABV 4.4%)

Sabotage (ABV 5%)

White Gypsy

Railway Road, Templemore, Co Tipperary
☎ 00353 86 17 24520 ⊕ whitegypsy.ie

Produces a wide range of cask ales, plus a range of bottle-conditioned strong beers. The brewery features Ireland's only commercial hop garden and produces the only beer made from 100% Irish ingredients. Distribution is mostly in the north Munster region.

Ruby (ABV 4.6%)

Emerald IPA (ABV 5%)

Doppelbock (ABV 7.5%)

Imperial Stout (ABV 7.5%)

India Pale Ale (ABV 7.5%)

Brewery organisations

There are two organisations mentioned in the Breweries section to which breweries can belong.

The Independent Families Brewers of Britain (IFBB) represents around 35 regional companies still owned by families. As many regional breweries closed in the 1990s, the IFBB represents the interests of the survivors, staging events such as the annual Cask Ale Week to emphasise the important role played by the independent sector.

The Society of Independent Brewers (SIBA) represents the growing number of small craft or micro brewers: some smaller regionals are also members. SIBA is an effective lobbying organisation and played a leading role in persuading the government to introduce Progressive Beer Duty. It has also campaigned to get large pub companies to take beers from smaller breweries and has had considerable success with Enterprise Inns, the biggest pubco.

R.I.P.

The following breweries have closed, gone out of business or suspended operations since the 2013 Guide was published:

ABC, Birmingham, West Midlands
Abigale, Ashford, Kent
Angus, Carnoustie, Tayside
Blackawton, Ilsington, Devon
Blue Buzzard, Darwen, Lancashire
Brass Monkey, Sowerby Bridge, W Yorkshire
Bull Lane, Sunderland, Tyne & Wear
DemonBrew, Prestonpans, Edinburgh & the Lothians
Devilfish, Hemington, Somerset
Devon, Yelland, Devon

Fallen Angel, East Hoathly, E Sussex
Fallons, Darwen, Lancashire
Garthela, Blackburn, Lancashire
Gidleys, Christow, Devon
Golden Valley, Peterchurch, Herefordshire
Holland, Kimberley, Nottinghamshire
Innocente, Livingstone, Edinburgh & the Lothians
Litton, Litton, N Yorkshire
Mayflower, Orrell, Lancashire
Minster, Kidderminster, Worcestershire
Moodley's, Penshurst, Kent

Morrissey Fox, Beverley, E Yorkshire
Oakwell, Barnsley, S Yorkshire
Red Rat, Denham, Suffolk
Ringmore, Teignmouth, Devon
Royal Tunbridge Wells, Royal Tunbridge Wells, Kent
Six Trees, Taunton, Somerset
Staithes, Staithes, N Yorkshire
Swaton, Swaton, Lincolnshire
Toft, Cheadle, Staffordshire
Union, South Brent, Devon
Urban, York, N Yorkshire

FUTURE

The following new breweries have been notified to the Guide and will start to produce beer during 2013/2014. In a few cases, they were in production during the summer of 2013 but were too late for a full listing:

Aardvark, Sheffield, S Yorkshire
Against the Grain, London, Greater London
Anspach & Hobday, London, Greater London
Bad Seed, Malton, N Yorkshire
Black Flag, Goonhavern, Cornwall
Black Tor, Christow, Devon
Borough, Lancaster, Lancashire
Bosun's, Horbury Bridge, W Yorkshire
Bournemouth, Poole, Dorset
Bow Wave, Bowness-on-Windermere, Cumbria
Briarbank, Ipswich, Suffolk
Brick, London, Greater London
Bridgnorth, Bridgnorth, Shropshire
Brixton, London, Greater London
Brown, Southwell, Nottinghamshire
Caffle, Llawhaden, W Wales
Carlisle, Carlisle, Cumbria

Fat Pig, Exeter, Devon
Fleetwood, Fleetwood, Lancashire
Fourpure, London, Greater London
Frothblowers, Erdington, West Midlands
Halfway, Salisbury, Wiltshire
Harrogate, Harrogate, N Yorkshire
Instant Karma, Chesterfield, Derbyshire
Jones the Brewer, Brilley, Herefordshire
Kettledrum, Rochester, Kent
Lion & Key, Hull, E Yorkshire
Littondale, Litton, N Yorkshire
Lymm, Lymm, Cheshire
MASH, East Stratton, Hampshire
Mulligans, London, Greater London
Mountain Hare, Brynnau Gwynion, Glamorgan
Oast House, Llanbadarn Fawr, W Wales
Pilot, Leith, Edinburgh & the Lothians

Pokertree, Carrickmore, Northern Ireland
Problem Child, Parbold, Lancashire
Queen Inn, Winchester, Hampshire
Red Hand, Donaghmore, Northern Ireland
Snaggletooth, Darwen, Lancashire
Stanley, Portslade, E Sussex
Star, Peterborough, Cambridgeshire
Strawman, London, Greater London
Thatched House, Poulton-le-Fylde, Lancashire
Thirstin, Honley, W Yorkshire
Tickenham Farm, Tickenham, Somerset
Titan, Derby, Derbyshire
Two Beach, Shaldon, Devon
Whaley Bridge, Whaley Bridge, Derbyshire
Wild Boar, Bowness-on-Windermere, Cumbria
Worcester, Worcester, Worcestershire

Indexes & Further Information

Places index	894
Beers index	905
Award winning pubs	933
Readers' recommendations	935
Have your say	936
National Brewing Centre	937
CAMRA books & products	939
Join CAMRA	944

Places index

A

Abbots Bromley 416
Abbotskerswell 114
Abbotts Ann 181
Aberaeron 601
Abercych 601
Aberdare 566
Aberdaron 595
Aberdeen 612
Aberdour 647
Abergavenny 578
Abergynolwyn 595
Abernethy 655
Aberystwyth 601
Abingdon 384
Abinger Common 438
Abington Pigotts 59
Aboyne 613
Abthorpe 361
Aby 260
Accrington 234
Acton 310
Adderbury 384
Addingham 547
Addiscombe 298
Adlington 235
Agden Wharf 68
Airdrie 636
Albury Heath 438
Alby 346
Alcester 473
Alcombe 402
Aldbourne 496
Aldbrough St John 518
Aldbury 201
Aldeburgh 428
Alderley Edge 68
Aldershot 181
Aldford 68
Aldgate 282
Aldridge 480
Aldworth 44
Alfold Bars 456
Allanton 624
Allendale Town 368
Allenheads 368
Allens Green 201
Allington 260
Allithwaite 88
Alltwen 566
Alnmouth 369
Alnwick 369
Alpraham 69
Alresford 181
Alrewas 416
Alsager 69
Alsagers Bank 417
Alston 88
Altarnun 78
Alton 182
Altrincham 316
Alvanley 69
Alvechurch 505
Alvediston 496
Amberley 167
Amblecote 480
Ambleside 89
Amington 417
Ampthill 36
Amwell 201

Ancaster 260
Ancrum 624
Andover 182
Andreas 667
Anick 369
Annan 627
Annat 642
Ansley 474
Anstey 201
Anstruther 647
Appleby-in-
  Westmorland 89
Applecross 642
Appleton Thorn 69
Appletreewick 518
Appley Bridge 316
Arbroath 655
Archway 290
Ardeley 202
Arksey 537
Arlesey 36
Arreton 210
Arrochar 650
Arthingworth 361
Arundel 456
Asfordby 250
Ash 402
Ashbourne 100
Ashburton 114
Ashcott 402
Ashford 438
Ashleworth 167
Ashover 100
Ashton 361
Ashton-in-Makerfield
  317
Ashton-under-Lyne 317
Ashurst 182
Ashwellthorpe 346
Askerswell 132
Askrigg 519
Aspull 317
Astley 318
Aston Abbotts 51
Aston 69
Atherstone 474
Atherton 318
Attleborough 346
Auchencairn 627
Auchencrow 624
Auchleven 613
Auckley 537
Audlem 69
Aughton Park 235
Aughton
  Lancashire 235
  Yorkshire (South) 538
Aviemore 642
Avoch 643
Avon 182
Awliscombe 115
Awsworth 374
Axbridge 403
Aycliffe Village 141
Aylesbury 51
Ayr 621
Aysgarth 519
Aythorpe Roding 152

B

Badsey 505
Baildon 548
Baldock 202
Baldrine 667
Balerno 630
Balham 304
Ballards Gore
  (Stambridge) 152
Ballater 614
Ballaugh 667
Ballymena 660
Balsall Heath,
  Birmingham 481
Balscote 385
Bamber Bridge 235
Bampton
  Devon 115
  Oxfordshire 385
Banbury 385
Banchory 614
Banff 614
Bangor 595
Bangor-on-Dee 589
Bank 182
Bankfoot 655
Banningham 346
Banstead 438
Barcombe 448
Bardwell 428
Barford St Michael 385
Bargrennan 627
Barholm 261
Barkby 250
Barking 286
Barkston Ash 519
Barlow 101
Barmby on the Marsh
  513
Barnard Castle 141
Barnes 304
Barngates 89
Barnham 456
Barnoldswick 235
Barnsley 538
Barnstaple 115
Barnston 336
Barnton 70
Barnwell 361
Barrhead 636
Barrow Haven 261
Barrow upon Soar 250
Barrow-in-Furness 89
Barrowby 261
Barrowden 250
Barry 566
Barton Bendish 347
Barton 236
Barton-under-
  Needwood 417
Barton-upon-Humber
  261
Baschurch 394
Basingstoke 183
Bassaleg 579
Bassenthwaite Lake 89
Batcombe 403
Bath 403
Bathgate 630
Batley 548

Battersea 304
Bawtry 539
Baxterley 474
Beamish 141
Beaumaris 596
Beccles 428
Beck Hole 519
Beckenham 298
Beckley 448
Bedford 36
Beenham 44
Beeston 374
Beith 622
Belbroughton 505
Belchamp Otten 152
Belchamp St Paul 153
Belfast 660
Belgravia 301
Belmesthorpe 251
Belton 261
Bembridge 210
Benenden 214
Benington 202
Bentham 519
Bentley 539
Benton, Newcastle 466
Bentworth 183
Bere Ferrers 116
Berkhamsted 202
Bermondsey 293
Berrow Green 505
Bersham 589
Berwick St John 497
Berwick upon Tweed
  369
Berwick 448
Bethesda 596
Bethnal Green 283
Bettws Cedewain 584
Beverley 513
Bewdley 506
Bexhill-on-Sea 448
Bexley 298
Bexleyheath 298
Beyton 428
Bicester 385
Biggleswade 37
Bignall End 417
Bildeston 428
Billericay 153
Billingborough 261
Billinge 318
Billingford 347
Billingham 141
Billinghay 261
Bilston 481
Binfield 44
Bingham 375
Bingley 548
Binham 347
Birchgrove 566
Birdwell 539
Birkenhead 336
Birling 214
Birlingham 506
Birmingham, City
  Centre 481
Birstall 548
Birstwith 520
Birtley 142

Bishop Auckland *142*
Bishop Middleham *142*
Bishop's Castle *394*
Bishops Lydeard *405*
Bishopsbourne *214*
Bishopsgate *780*
Bishopston *567*
Bishop's Stortford *202*
Bishop's Sutton *183*
Bishopswood *405*
Bispham, Blackpool *236*
Bispham Green *236*
Bittaford *116*
Black Lane Ends *236*
Black Torrington *116*
Blackburn *236*
Blackfen *298*
Blackheath *294*
Blackmore *153*
Blacko *236*
Blackpill *567*
Blackpool, Town Centre *236*
Blackrod *318*
Blacktoft *514*
Blackwater *183*
Blackwaterfoot, Isle of Arran *622*
Blaenwaun *602*
Blagdon Hill *405*
Blair Atholl *655*
Blairgowrie *655*
Blaisdon *167*
Blakeney *348*
Blakey Ridge *520*
Blandford *132*
Blaxhall *429*
Blaydon *465*
Bleadon *405*
Bleasby *375*
Bledington *167*
Blisland *78*
Bloomsbury *281*
Bloxham *386*
Bloxwich *484*
Blyth
  Northumberland *369*
  Nottinghamshire *375*
Blythe Bridge *417*
Bo'ness *650*
Bodmin *79*
Boldmere *484*
Bolingey *79*
Bollington *70*
Bolnhurst *38*
Bolsover *101*
Bolton *318*
Boncath *602*
Boot *90*
Bootle *336*
Boreham Street *448*
Borough *293*
Boroughbridge *520*
Borrowdale *90*
Borth *602*
Bosbury *197*
Boscastle *79*
Bosham *456*
Boston *262*
Botallack *80*
Boughton Monchelsea *215*
Boundstone *439*
Bourne *262*

Bournemouth *132*
Bournheath *506*
Bournmoor *142*
Bourton *133*
Bourton-on-the-Hill *168*
Bourton-on-the-Water *168*
Boverton *567*
Bovey Tracey *116*
Bow *283*
Bowes *142*
Bowness-on-Solway *90*
Box Hill *497*
Bracknell *44*
Bradford *549*
Bradford-on-Avon *497*
Brading *210*
Bradshaw *550*
Bradwell Village, Milton Keynes *56*
Brae, Shetland *653*
Braintree *153*
Braishfield *183*
Braithwaite *90*
Bramley *439*
Bramling *215*
Bramshall *417*
Brancaster Staithe *348*
Branston *251*
Brassington *101*
Bratton Clovelly *116*
Braughing *203*
Braye *663*
Brechin *656*
Brecon *584*
Brenchley *215*
Brendon *116*
Brent Eleigh *429*
Brentford *312*
Brentwood *154*
Bretforton *506*
Brewood *418*
Briden's Camp *203*
Bridge of Allan *650*
Bridgend *567*
Bridgnorth *395*
Bridgwater *405*
Bridlington *514*
Bridport *133*
Brierley Hill *484*
Brigg *262*
Brighouse *550*
Brightlingsea *154*
Brighton *449*
Brill *52*
Bringsty Common *197*
Brinsworth *539*
Bristol, Central *168*
Bristol, East *170*
Bristol, North *171*
Bristol, South *171*
Bristol, West *171*
Brithdir *596*
Brixham *116*
Brixton
  Devon *117*
  Greater London *303*
Broad Haven *602*
Broadheath *319*
Broads Green *154*
Broadway *507*
Broadwell *172*
Brockhampton *172*
Brockley *294*

Brodick, Isle of Arran *622*
Brodie *614*
Bromley *298*
Brompton
  Kent *215*
  Yorkshire (North) *521*
Bromsgrove *507*
Bromyard *197*
Broome *348*
Broughton *362*
Broughton-in-Furness *90*
Broughty Ferry *656*
Brownhills *485*
Broxted *154*
Broxton *70*
Bryncoch *568*
Brynmawr *579*
Brynnau Gwynion *568*
Bubbenhall *474*
Buckhorn Weston *133*
Buckingham *52*
Buckland Dinham *405*
Buckland Monachorum *117*
Budleigh Salterton *117*
Bugle *80*
Bulbourne *203*
Bulwick *362*
Bungay *429*
Buntingford *203*
Burbage *251*
Burgess Hill *456*
Burley, Leeds *556*
Burnham-on-Crouch *154*
Burnley *237*
Burntwood *418*
Burrington *117*
Burrough on the Hill *251*
Burrowbridge *405*
Burscough *237*
Burslem, Stoke-on-Trent *425*
Burton upon Trent *418*
Burtonwood *70*
Bury St Edmunds *429*
Bury *319*
Bushey *203*
Butleigh *406*
Butterleigh *117*
Buttermere *90*
Buxton *101*
Byker, Newcastle *466*
Byworth *457*

C
Cadole *589*
Caerleon *579*
Caernarfon *596*
Caerphilly *568*
Caersws *584*
Caio *602*
Cairndow *618*
Caldicot *579*
Calne *497*
Calverleigh *117*
Camberwell *294*
Cambridge *59*
Camden Town *291*
Camelford *80*
Cannock Wood *419*

Cannock *419*
Canon Pyon *198*
Canonbury *288*
Canterbury *216*
Cantley *348*
Capel Curig *596*
Capel *217*
Car Colston *375*
Cardiff *568*
Cardigan *602*
Cardington *396*
Carew *603*
Carey *198*
Cark-in-Cartmel *90*
Carlisle *91*
Carlops *624*
Carlton in Lindrick *376*
Carlton
  Bedfordshire *38*
  Durham *143*
Carlton-in-Cleveland *521*
Carlton-in-Coverdale *521*
Carmarthen *603*
Carnforth *238*
Carrbridge *643*
Carrickfergus *661*
Carshalton *306*
Carterway Heads *369*
Castel *663*
Castle Bytham *262*
Castle Carrock *91*
Castle Cary *406*
Castle Douglas *627*
Castle Hedingham *154*
Castlecary *636*
Castleford *550*
Castlemorton *507*
Castleton *521*
Castletown *667*
Castor *61*
Caterham *439*
Catfield *348*
Catford *295*
Catterline *614*
Catthorpe *251*
Caulcott *386*
Caunsall *507*
Caversham *45*
Cawdor *643*
Cefn Mawr *589*
Cefn-y-Bedd *590*
Ceinws *584*
Cellan *603*
Cenarth *603*
Cerne Abbas *133*
Chacombe *362*
Chadderton *320*
Chaddesley Corbett *507*
Chadlington *386*
Chadwell Heath *286*
Chagford *117*
Chalgrove *386*
Chance's Pitch *198*
Chancery Lane *281*
Chapel Allerton, Leeds *556*
Chapel-le-Dale *521*
Chapeltown *539*
Charing Cross *281*
Charing *217*
Charlbury *386*
Charlestown of Aberlour *614*

Charlestown 80
Charter Alley 183
Chasetown 419
Cheadle Hulme 321
Cheadle
  Greater Manchester 320
  Staffordshire 419
Cheam 306
Chearsley 52
Chelford 70
Chelmorton 102
Chelmsford 155
Chelsfield 299
Cheltenham 173
Chenies 52
Chepstow 579
Cheriton 184
Cherry Tree 238
Chertsey 439
Chesham 52
Chester 71
Chester-le-Street 143
Chesterfield 102
Cheswardine 396
Chetwynd Aston 396
Chevington 430
Chichester 457
Chiddingfold 439
Chiddingstone Hoath 217
Chiddingstone 217
Chideock 133
Child Okeford 134
Childer Thornton 72
Childwall 337
Chingford 284
Chinnor 386
Chippenham 497
Chipping Norton 386
Chipping Sodbury 173
Chipping
  Hertfordshire 203
  Lancashire 238
Chipstead 217
Chirk 590
Chiselhampton 387
Chiswick 310
Chittlehampton 118
Chorley 238
Chorleywood 203
Chorlton-cum-Hardy 321
Chudleigh Knighton 118
Chulmleigh 118
Church Crookham 184
Church Eaton 420
Church Enstone 387
Church Fenton 521
Churchill 406
Churt 439
Cilcain 590
Cirencester 173
Clachan Seil 618
Clacton-on-Sea 155
Clapham
  Greater London 303
  Yorkshire (North) 522
Clapton in Gordano 406
Clapton 284
Clarbeston Road 603
Clawddnewydd 590
Clayhidon 118
Claypole 263

Clayton le Moors 239
Clearwell 174
Cleator 91
Cleethorpes 263
Clenchwarton 348
Cleobury Mortimer 396
Clerkenwell 278
Clevedon 406
Cleveleys 239
Cliffe 522
Clifton
  Cumbria 91
  Oxfordshire 387
Cliviger 239
Clophill 38
Cloughton 522
Clowne 103
Clows Top 507
Clunton 396
Clutton Hill 406
Clytha 579
Coatbridge 637
Coatham Mundeville 143
Cockermouth 92
Cockfield 143
Cockfosters 290
Cockwood 118
Codsall 420
Coed-y-Paen 580
Coggeshall 156
Colchester 156
Cold Ash 45
Cold Norton 157
Coldred 217
Coleford 406
Colemans Hatch 450
Coleorton 251
Coleraine 661
Coleshill
  Oxfordshire 387
  Warwickshire 474
Collier Row 286
Colne Engaine 157
Colne
  Cambridgeshire 61
  Lancashire 239
Culney Heath 204
Colton 348
Colwyn Bay 597
Colyton 118
Combe Florey 406
Combe St Nicholas 407
Combeinteignhead 118
Compton 458
Congleton 72
Congresbury 407
Conisbrough 539
Coniston 92
Consall Forge 420
Consett 143
Constantine 80
Conwy 597
Conyer 217
Cookham Dean 45
Cookham 45
Cooling 217
Copford 157
Cople 38
Coppull 239
Corbridge 369
Corfe Castle 134
Corfe Mullen 134
Corley Moor 474
Cornish Hall End 157

Corsham 498
Corton Denham 407
Corton 498
Coseley 485
Cosheston 603
Cotebrook 72
Cotherstone 144
Coton-in-the-Elms 103
Cottingham 514
Countisbury 119
Covent Garden 282
Coventry 485
Cowbridge 570
Cowdenbeath 647
Cowes 210
Cowfold 458
Coxtie Green 157
Coychurch 570
Cragg Vale 551
Craigcefnparc 570
Craigellachie 614
Crail 647
Cramlington 370
Cratfield 430
Crawley 458
Crediton 119
Crewe 72
Crewkerne 407
Crich 103
Crick 362
Crickhowell 585
Cricklade 498
Croft 72
Cromer 349
Cromhall 174
Crooke 321
Cropton 522
Crosby 337
Croscombe 407
Cross Hills 522
Cross Inn (Llanon) 604
Cross Inn (New Quay) 604
Cross Inn 570
Cross 407
Croston 239
Crowborough 450
Crowlas 80
Crowntown 81
Crowton 73
Croxley Green 204
Croydon 299
Crystal Palace 296
Cublington 53
Cuckfield 458
Cullen 615
Cullingworth 551
Cullompton 119
Culmstock 119
Cumwhitton 92
Curthwaite 92
Cwmbran 580
Cwmdu 604
Cwmfelin 570
Cwmyoy 580

D
Dacre Banks 522
Dadlington 251
Dalham 430
Dalkeith 630
Dalton 522
Danby Wiske 523
Danby 523

Danehill 450
Darlington 144
Darrington 551
Dartford 218
Darwen 240
Dawley, Telford 399
Deal 218
Deddington 387
Defynnog 585
Delph 322
Denbigh 590
Denholm 625
Denholme 551
Denmark Hill 295
Dent 92
Denton 322
Deptford 295
Derby 103
Deri 570
Dersingham 349
Devizes 498
Dewlish 134
Dewsbury 551
Dial Post 458
Didcot 387
Didsbury 322
Digbeth, Birmingham 482
Dinnington 407
Dipton Mill 370
Diseworth 251
Disley 73
Diss 349
Dobcross 322
Docking 349
Dollar 650
Dolphinholme 240
Donaghadee 661
Donaghmore 661
Doncaster 539
Donisthorpe 252
Dorchester 134
Dorchester-on-Thames 387
Dores 643
Dorking 440
Dorney 53
Dornoch 643
Dorridge 486
Douglas 667
Dousland 119
Dover 219
Downe 300
Downham Market 349
Downley 53
Drayton 387
Drefach Felindre 604
Driffield 515
Droitwich 508
Dronfield 105
Droylsden 322
Drumnadrochit 643
Drymen 651
Dudley 487
Duffield 105
Dullingham 61
Dulverton 407
Dumfries 627
Dummer 184
Dunbar 630
Dunblane 651
Duncton 458
Dundee 656
Dundridge 184
Dunfermline 648

Dunkeld 657
Dunk's Green 219
Dunning 657
Duns 625
Dunstable 38
Dunton 39
Durham 144
Dursley 174
Duton Hill 158
Dutton 73
Dwygyfylchi 597
Dyce 615
Dyserth 590

E
Eaglescliffe 146
Ealing 310
Eardisley 198
Earl Soham 430
Earl Sterndale 105
Earl's Court 303
Earley 46
Earsham 349
Easingwold 523
East Aberthaw 570
East Ashling 459
East Boldon 465
East Boldre 184
East Brabourne 219
East Budleigh 119
East Butterwick 263
East Dean 450
East Dulwich 297
East Finchley 288
East Greenwich 295
East Grinstead 459
East Hoathly 451
East Kilbride 637
East Knoyle 499
East Linton 630
East Malling 219
East Markham 376
East Molesey 440
East Prawle 119
East Stour 134
East Stratton 184
East Wittering 459
East Witton 523
Eastbourne 451
Eastbridge 430
Eastergate 459
Eastoft 263
Easton Royal 499
Eastry 219
Eaton Ford 61
Eaton Socon 62
Ebbesbourne Wake 499
Ebbw Vale 580
Ebrington 174
Eccles 323
Eccleshall 420
Eccleston 240
Edenbridge 219
Edgeley, Stockport 333
Edgworth 240
Edinburgh 631
Edington 499
Edmonton 81
Edwardstone 430
Edwinstowe 376
Egglescliffe 146
Egham 440
Eglingham 370
Egton 523

Elford 421
Elgin 615
Elham 220
Elland 551
Ellerdine Heath 396
Ellerton 515
Elsecar 540
Elsing 349
Elsted 459
Elterwater 92
Eltham 295
Elton 62
Elvington 523
Elwick 146
Ely 62
Embleton 370
Emborough 408
Emley 552
Emmer Green 46
Emsworth 185
Enderby 252
Enfield 290
Englefield Green 440
Enniskillen 661
Enslow Bridge 388
Enville 421
Epping 158
Epsom 441
Erpingham 350
Eryrys 590
Eskdale 93
Essendon 204
Eton 46
Etruria, Stoke-on-Trent 425
Euston 291
Euxton 240
Eversholt 39
Evershot 135
Eversley Cross 185
Eversley
   Berkshire 46
   Hampshire 185
Everton 39
Evesham 508
Ewloe 591
Exbourne 120
Exeter 121
Exmouth 120
Exning 430
Eynsford 220

F
Fairlie 622
Fairseat 220
Fakenham 350
Falkirk 651
Fallowfield 323
Falmer 452
Falmouth 81
Fareham 185
Faringdon 388
Farnborough
   Greater London 300
   Hampshire 185
Farnham Common 53
Farnham Royal 53
Farnham
   Dorset 135
   Surrey 441
Farningham 220
Farthingstone 362
Faulkland 408
Faversham 220

Fazeley 421
Felinfach 585
Felixstowe 431
Felling 465
Feltham 312
Fence 240
Fenny Stratford, Milton Keynes 56
Fenton, Stoke-on-Trent 425
Fenwick 541
Ferryhill 146
Fettercairn 615
Fewcott 388
Filey 523
Findhorn 615
Findon 459
Finglesham 221
Finningley 541
Finsbury 279
Finstall 508
Finstock 388
Firbeck 541
Fishguard 604
Fleckney 252
Fleet Hargate 263
Fleet Street 280
Fleet 185
Fleetwood 240
Fleggburgh 350
Flitton 39
Folkestone 221
Forches Corner 408
Fordham 158
Fordwich 221
Forest Hill 297
Forest in Teesdale 146
Forest 663
Formby 337
Forres 615
Fort William 643
Forthampton 174
Fortrose 644
Forty Green 53
Fosdyke 263
Fossebridge 175
Four Mile Bridge 597
Four Oaks 487
Fowey 81
Fownhope 198
Foxfield 93
Framlingham 431
Frampton Cotterell 174
Frampton Mansell 175
Frampton-on-Severn 175
Framwellgate Moor 146
Fraserburgh 615
Freshwater 211
Freuchie 648
Frilsham 46
Fritham 186
Frittenden 222
Frodsham 73
Frognall 264
Frome 408
Frosterley 147
Fulbourn 62
Fulking 459
Fuller Street 158

G
Gainford 147
Gainsborough 264

Galashiels 625
Gargrave 523
Gargunnock 651
Garlogie 616
Garndolbenmaen 598
Garway 198
Gateshead 465
Gatley 323
Gayton 350
Gedney 264
Geldeston 350
Giggleswick 524
Gilfach Goch 571
Gillingham
   Dorset 135
   Kent 222
Gilmorton 252
Glan-y-Llyn 571
Glasgow 637
Glasson 93
Glemsford 431
Glen Clova 657
Glencoe 644
Glenfield 252
Glenrothes 648
Glossop 105
Gloucester Road 303
Gloucester 175
Godalming 442
Goginan 604
Goldhanger 158
Gomshall 442
Goodmanham 515
Goose Eye 552
Goosnargh 241
Gorleston-on-Sea 350
Gorton 323
Gosberton Risegate 264
Gosforth, Newcastle 468
Gosforth 93
Gosport 186
Gosta Green, Birmingham 482
Gotham 376
Graffham 460
Graianrhyd 591
Graigfechan 591
Granby 376
Grandborough 474
Grangemouth 651
Grantchester 62
Grantham 264
Grasmere 93
Gravesend 222
Grays 158
Greasby 337
Great Barford 39
Great Bircham 350
Great Brington 362
Great Corby 93
Great Cressingham 351
Great Dunmow 158
Great Easton 159
Great Eccleston 241
Great Gransden 62
Great Harwood 241
Great Haseley 388
Great Haywood 421
Great Heck 524
Great Kelk 515
Great Kimble 53
Great Langdale 93
Great Massingham 351
Great Salkeld 94

Great Torrington 121
Great Wratting 431
Great Yarmouth 351
Greatworth 362
Green Ore 408
Greenfield 323
Greenford 312
Greengates 552
Greenhead 370
Greenock 639
Greenodd 94
Gresford 591
Gretton 176
Greywell 186
Grimsby 265
Grimston 252
Grinton 524
Groesffordd 585
Groeswen 571
Grosmont
    Gwent 580
    Yorkshire (North) 524
Grundisburgh 431
Guildford 442
Guilsborough 363
Guiseley 552
Gullane 633
Gwaelod-y-Garth 571
Gwernymynydd 591
Gwithian 81

H
Habberley 396
Hackney Wick 284
Hackney 284
Haddenham
    Buckinghamshire 54
    Cambridgeshire 63
Haddington 634
Hadlow 222
Haggerston 283
Hailsham 452
Halesowen 487
Halifax 552
Halkyn 591
Hallatrow 408
Hallbankgate 94
Haltwhistle 370
Ham 176
Hambledon 443
Hammersmith 311
Hampstead 291
Hampton Hill 313
Hampton in Arden 488
Hampton Lucy 475
Hampton 312
Hamsterley 147
Hanley Broadheath 508
Hanley Castle 508
Hanley, Stoke-on-Trent 425
Hanslope 54
Hanwell 311
Harborne, Birmingham 482
Harbury 475
Hardraw 524
Hardstoft 106
Harecroft 553
Harefield 292
Harlech 598
Harley 541

Harlington
    Bedfordshire 39
    Greater London 313
Harmston 265
Harpenden 204
Harpley 351
Harriseahead 421
Harrogate 524
Harrow 292
Hartfield 452
Hartford 63
Harthill 541
Hartlebury 508
Hartlepool 147
Hartley Wintney 186
Hartshill, Stoke-on-Trent 426
Hartshorne 106
Harwich 159
Haskayne 241
Haslingden 241
Hastingleigh 222
Hastings 452
Hatfield Broad Oak 159
Hatfield 204
Hatherleigh 121
Hatton Garden 279
Haugh of Urr 628
Haughton 421
Havant 186
Haverfordwest 604
Haverhill 431
Hawarden 591
Hawes 525
Hawick 625
Hawkedon 431
Hawkesbury Upton 176
Hawkley 186
Hawkshead 94
Haworth 553
Hay on Wye 585
Hayes End 313
Hayes 313
Hayfield 106
Hayton 94
Hazel Grove 323
Headingley, Leeds 557
Heanor 106
Heath & Reach 39
Heath 553
Heaton, Newcastle 468
Heaton Norris, Stockport 333
Heavitree 121
Hebden Bridge 553
Hebden 525
Heddon Valley 121
Hedgerley 54
Hedley on the Hill 370
Hednesford 421
Hedon 515
Heighington
    Durham 148
    Lincolnshire 265
Helensburgh 651
Helpston 63
Helston 82
Helwith Bridge 525
Hemingby 265
Hemingford Grey 63
Hempstead 159
Hempton 351
Hendon 292
Hendre 592
Henham 159

Henley 460
Henley-on-Thames 388
Henlow 40
Henstridge 409
Heptonstall 553
Herbrandston 605
Hereford 198
Herne Bay 223
Herne Hill 297
Herne 223
Herongate Tye 159
Heronsgate 204
Herriard 187
Hertford 204
Hesket Newmarket 94
Heswall 337
Heydon 351
Heysham 241
Heytesbury 499
Heywood 324
High Barnet 290
High Hesleden 148
High Horton 371
High Hoyland 541
High Lane 324
High Leven 525
High Newton-by-the-Sea 371
High Offley 421
High Shincliffe 148
High Wych 205
High Wycombe 54
Higham
    Kent 223
    Yorkshire (South) 541
Higher Burwardsley 73
Higher Wheelton 241
Highgate, Birmingham 483
Highgate 288
Highworth 499
Hilborough 352
Hildenborough 223
Hill Head 187
Hillesley 176
Hillsborough 661
Himbleton 509
Hinckley 252
Hinderwell 525
Hindon 500
Hinton Blewitt 409
Hinton in the Hedges 363
Hipperholme 553
Hirwaun 571
Histon 63
Hitchin 205
Hockering 352
Hockley, Birmingham 483
Hockley 159
Holbeck, Leeds 558
Holborn 281
Holcombe Brook 324
Holcombe Rogus 121
Holcombe
    Devon 121
    Somerset 409
Hollins Green 73
Holloway 288
Hollym 515
Holmbury St Mary 443
Holme 63
Holmesfield 106
Holmfirth 554

Holsworthy 122
Holt
    North-East Wales 592
    Wiltshire 500
Holwick 148
Holybourne 187
Holywell 592
Holywood 662
Honiton 122
Hook Common 187
Hook 187
Hoole 73
Hope 106
Horbling 266
Horbury 554
Horncastle 266
Hornchurch 286
Horncliffe 371
Horndon-on-the-Hill 160
Hornsey 289
Horsell 443
Horsforth, Leeds 558
Horsham 460
Horsley Woodhouse 106
Horton 135
Horwich 324
Hose 253
Houghton Green 73
Houghton le Spring 466
Hounslow 313
Houston 639
Hove 453
Hoveringham 376
Hoxne 432
Hoxton 287
Hoylake 337
Hubberts Bridge 266
Hucknall 376
Huddersfield 554
Huish Episcopi 409
Hull 515
Hungerford 46
Hunslet, Leeds 558
Hurst 46
Hutton Rudby 526
Hutton 409
Hyde Lea 422
Hyde 324
Hythe
    Hampshire 187
    Kent 223

I
Ickford 54
Icklesham 453
Iddesleigh 122
Ideford 122
Iden Green 223
Idle 555
Idmiston 500
Ightham Common 223
Ilfracombe 122
Ilkeston 106
Ilkley 555
Illston on the Hill 253
Ingoldmells 266
Ings 94
Inkpen 46
Innerleithen 625
Inveraray 619
Inverkip 639
Inverness 644

Inverurie 616
Ipswich 432
Irby 338
Isham 363
Isle of Whithorn 628
Isleworth 313
Islington 287
Ivychurch 224
Ixworth 433

J

Jarrow 466
Johnstone 639
Juniper Green 634

K

Keelby 266
Kegworth 253
Keighley 555
Kelham Island, Sheffield 544
Kelso 626
Kelston 409
Kempsey Green Street 509
Kempsey 509
Kendal 94
Kenilworth 475
Kensworth 40
Kentchurch 199
Kentish Town 292
Kenton Bank Foot, Newcastle 469
Keswick 95
Kettering 363
Kettleshulme 74
Kettletoft, Orkney 653
Kew 306
Keynsham 409
Keyston 63
Kidderminster 509
Kidsgrove 422
Kilbarchan 640
Kilburn 107
Kilcreggan 652
Killay 571
Killin 652
Kilmacolm 640
Kilmarnock 622
Kilmartin 619
Kilmaurs 622
Kilmichael Glassary 619
Kilmington 122
Kilsby 363
Kilve 409
Kimberley 377
Kimbolton 199
Kincraig 645
Kingarth, Isle of Bute 619
King's Cross 287
King's Heath, Birmingham 483
Kinghorn 648
King's Lynn 352
Kings Nympton 123
Kingsbury Episcopi 410
Kingsclere 187
Kingsland 288
Kingston upon Thames 306
Kingston
    Devon 123
    Dorset 135

Kingswear 123
Kingswinford 488
Kington St Michael 500
Kington 199
Kinlochewe 645
Kinver 472
Kippford 628
Kirby Hill 526
Kirk Ella 517
Kirk Ireton 107
Kirk Smeaton 526
Kirk Yetholm 626
Kirkby on Bain 266
Kirkby Lonsdale 95
Kirkby-in-Ashfield 377
Kirkby-in-Cleveland 526
Kirkcaldy 648
Kirkcudbright 628
Kirkdale 338
Kirkibost, North Uist 645
Kirkmichael
    Ayrshire & Arran 622
    Tayside 657
Kirkoswald 95
Kirkstall, Leeds 558
Kirkwall, Orkney 653
Knaresborough 526
Knighton
    Mid-Wales 585
    Staffordshire 422
Knightwick 509
Knipton 253
Knowl Hill 47
Knowle 488
Knutsford 74

L

Lacey Green 54
Lach Dennis 74
Lacock 500
Laddingford 224
Lake 123
Lamarsh 160
Lambley 377
Lambs Green 460
Lanark 640
Lancaster University 242
Lancaster 242
Lancing 460
Langley 371
Langton Matravers 135
Larbert 652
Largs 623
Larling 352
Lasswade 634
Lastingham 527
Laugharne 605
Laverstock 500
Laxey 668
Laxfield 433
Layer Breton 160
Layer-de-la-Haye 160
Lazenby 527
Lea Town 242
Lealholm 527
Leamington Spa 475
Leamside 148
Leatherhead 443
Leavening 527
Lechlade 176
Ledbury 199

Lee-on-the-Solent 187
Leeds, City Centre 556
Leek 422
Leicester 253
Leigh 325
Leigh-on-Sea 160
Leighton Buzzard 40
Leintwardine 199
Lelant Downs 82
Leominster 200
Lerags 619
Leslie 649
Lessingham 352
Letchworth Garden City 205
Lewes 453
Lewisham 296
Lewknor 388
Ley Hill 55
Leyland 242
Leyton 285
Leytonstone 285
Lichfield 423
Limekilns 649
Limpsfield Chart 443
Lincoln 266
Lindal-in-Furness 95
Lingen 200
Linlithgow 634
Linthwaite 558
Linton
    Cambridgeshire 63
    Herefordshire 200
Lisburn 662
Litchborough 363
Litlington 454
Little Bollington 74
Little Bromley 160
Little Cawthorpe 267
Little Clacton 161
Little Downham 64
Little Eaton 107
Little Gransden 64
Little Haven 605
Little Hayfield 107
Little London 188
Little Longstone 107
Little Milton 389
Little Missenden 55
Little Stretton 396
Little Thurrock 161
Little Walden 161
Littleborough 325
Littleworth Common 55
Littleworth 389
Littley Green 161
Litton 107
Liverpool, City Centre 338
Liversedge 559
Lizard 82
Llanarmon Dyffryn Ceiriog 592
Llanarmon-yn-Ial 592
Llanbadarn Fawr 605
Llanbedr 598
Llanblethian 571
Llandaff 571
Llandderfel 598
Llandeilo 605
Llandinam 585
Llandovery 606
Llandrindod Wells 586
Llandudno 598
Llandybie 606

Llandyfan 606
Llandyrnog 592
Llanelian-yn-Rhos 598
Llanelli 606
Llanfair Caereinion 586
Llanfallteg 606
Llanfihangel Tor-y-Mynydd 580
Llangattock Lingoed 581
Llangennith 572
Llangoedmor 606
Llangollen 592
Llangrannog 606
Llangunllo 586
Llangynhafal 593
Llangynidr 586
Llanharan 572
Llanhennock 581
Llanidloes 586
Llanishen 581
Llanllwni 606
Llanmaes 572
Llanrhidian 572
Llansaint 607
Llansawel 607
Llanstephan 607
Llanthony 581
Llantwit Fardre 572
Llantwit Major 572
Llanwonno 573
Llanwrtyd Wells 586
Loch Eck 619
Lochgoilhead 620
Lochwinnoch 640
Loddington 364
Lofthouse 527
Loftus 527
Loggerheads 593
London Bridge 294
London Colney 205
Londonderry 662
Long Crendon 55
Long Eaton 108
Long Itchington 476
Long Marston 206
Long Melford 433
Long Newton 148
Long Stratton 352
Long Sutton
    Hampshire 188
    Somerset 410
Long Whatton 254
Longridge 243
Longshaw 108
Longton, Stoke-on-Trent 426
Loppergarth 95
Lostock Hall 243
Lostwithiel 82
Lothianburn 634
Loughborough 255
Loughton 161
Louth 268
Low Newton-by-the-Sea 371
Lower Edmonton 289
Lower Farringdon 188
Lower Gornal 488
Lower Halstow 224
Lower Heyford 389
Lower Moor 509
Lower Odcombe 410
Lower Ufford 433
Lower Weare 410

Lower Wield 188
Lowestoft 433
Loweswater 95
Loxley 541
Luddesdown 224
Ludford 268
Ludlow 397
Lullington 108
Lund 517
Luton 40
Lutterworth 255
Luxulyan 82
Lye 489
Lyme Regis 135
Lymington 188
Lynsted 224
Lytchett Matravers 136
Lytham 243

M
Macclesfield 74
Machynlleth 587
Madeley, Telford 399
Maghull 341
Magor 581
Maida Hill 311
Maidenhead 47
Maidstone 224
Makeney 108
Maldon 161
Malmesbury 500
Maltby
  Yorkshire (North) 527
  Yorkshire (South) 542
Malton 527
Malvern 509
Manaton 123
Manchester, City
  Centre 325
Manfield 528
Mansfield Woodhouse
  378
Mansfield 377
Manton 255
Maplehurst 461
March 64
Marchington 123
Marden 225
Marehay 108
Margaretting Tye 161
Margate 225
Market Deeping 268
Market Drayton 397
Market Harborough
  256
Market Lavington 501
Market Rasen 268
Market Weston 434
Marlow 55
Marple Bridge 328
Marple 327
Marsden 559
Marshchapel 269
Marshfield 176
Marshwood 136
Marske-by-the-Sea 528
Marsworth 55
Martock 410
Mary Tavy 123
Marykirk 616
Marylebone 308
Maryport 96
Masham 528
Matfen 371

Matlock Bath 109
Matlock 108
Mawdesley 243
Mawgan Porth 82
Maxey 64
Mayfair 308
Mayshill 176
Meanwood, Leeds 558
Meavy 123
Melbourne 109
Melksham 501
Melling 341
Mellor 328
Melmerby 96
Melrose 626
Melsonby 528
Meltham 559
Melton Mowbray 256
Menai Bridge 599
Mersham 226
Messingham 269
Metal Bridge 148
Methlick 616
Mevagissey 82
Mexborough 542
Middle Assendon 389
Middlesbrough 528
Middlesmoor 528
Middlestone Village
  149
Middlestown 559
Middleton in Teesdale
  149
Middleton
  Derbyshire 109
  Greater Manchester
  328
Middlezoy 410
Midhurst 461
Milfield 371
Milford 109
Milland 461
Miller's Dale 109
Milltown of Rothiemay
  616
Milnathort 657
Milngavie 640
Milnrow 328
Milton Combe 123
Milton Keynes 56
Milton Malsor 364
Milton of Campsie 640
Milton Regis 226
Milton 109
Milwich 423
Minchinhampton 177
Minehead 410
Minster-in-Thanet 226
Mirfield 559
Misson 378
Misterton 378
Mobberley 75
Mogador 443
Mold 593
Moneyrow Green 47
Moniaive 628
Monifieth 657
Monk Street 162
Monknash 573
Monmouth 581
Montgomery 587
Monton 328
Montrose 658
Morecambe 244
Moreton in Marsh 177

Moretonhampstead
  124
Morpeth 371
Moseley, Birmingham
  484
Mossley Hill 341
Mossley 328
Moulin 658
Mount Bures 162
Mountsorrel 256
Mudford 411
Mugswell 444
Muker 529
Mullion 83
Mumbles 573
Murcott 389
Musselburgh 634
Muswell Hill 289
Mylor Bridge 83
Mytholmroyd 560

N
Nairn 645
Nant Gwynant 599
Nantwich 75
Naphill 56
Narberth 607
Naseby 364
Naughton 434
Navenby 269
Near Sawrey 96
Neath 573
Nelson 244
Nether Wasdale 96
Nether Whitacre 476
Netherhampton 501
Netherley 616
Netherton 489
Nettleton Bottom 177
New Barnet 291
New Brighton 341
New Cross 296
New Ferry 342
New Galloway 629
New Luce 629
New Malden 307
New Quay 607
New Radnor 587
Newark 378
Newbiggin by the Sea
  372
Newbourne 434
Newbrough 372
Newburn 466
Newbury 47
Newcastle, City Centre
  467
Newcastle Emlyn 607
Newcastle-under-Lyme
  423
Newchurch 211
Newdigate 444
Newenden 226
Newland 177
Newport Pagnell 56
Newport
  Gwent 581
  West Wales 607
Newton Abbot 124
Newton Mearns 640
Newton St Cyres 124
Newton Solney 109
Newton Stewart 629
Newton 64

Newton-on-Ouse 529
Newtonmore 645
Newtown, Birmingham
  484
Newtown 587
Newtownards 662
Niton 211
No Place 149
Normanton on Trent
  379
North Berwick 635
North Cerney 177
North Creake 353
North Elmham 353
North Finchley 289
North Greenwich 295
North Hill 83
North Hykeham 269
North Kelsey 269
North Lopham 353
North Moreton 389
North Shields 469
North Tawton 124
North Waltham 188
North Warnborough
  188
North Wootton 136
Northallerton 529
Northampton 364
Northfield,
  Birmingham 484
Northfleet 226
Northwich 75
Northwood 211
Norton Bridge 424
Norton Disney 269
Norton Fitzwarren 411
Norton 149
Norwich 353
Norwood Green 313
Notting Hill Gate 311
Notting Hill 312
Nottingham, Central
  379
Nottingham, North 380
Nottingham, South 380
Nottingham, West 381
Nuneaton 476
Nuthampstead 206

O
Oad Street 226
Oadby 256
Oakengates, Telford
  399
Oakham 256
Oakhill 411
Ockbrook 109
Offham 226
Okehampton 124
Old Bolingbroke 269
Old Colwyn 599
Old Costessey 355
Old Dalby 257
Old Down 177
Old Ellerby 517
Old Harlow 162
Old Hartley 372
Old Hunstanton 355
Old Knebworth 206
Old Langho 244
Old Radnor 587
Old Street 279
Oldbury 489

Oldham 329
Oldmeldrum 616
Onchan 668
Onecote 424
Ongar 162
Openwoodgate 110
Orford 434
Orleton 200
Ormskirk 244
Orpington 300
Osgodby 529
Osmotherley 529
Ossett 560
Oswestry 397
Otford 227
Otley 560
Otter Ferry 620
Ottershaw 444
Ottery St Mary 124
Oulton 424
Overstrand 355
Overton
  Hampshire 189
  Yorkshire (West) 561
Overton-on-Dee 593
Oving 461
Ovingham 372
Ovington 149
Oxenholme 96
Oxford 389
Oxhey 206
Oxton 342

P

Padbury 56
Paddington 309
Padstow 83
Paglesham 162
Paignton 124
Paisley 640
Pakefield 434
Pamphill 136
Pandy 582
Pant-y-gelli 582
Pantymwyn 593
Parbold 244
Park Gate 189
Parkham 125
Parkside 96
Parsons Green 303
Partridge Green 461
Parwich 110
Pateley Bridge 529
Patricroft 329
Peasehill 110
Peaslake 444
Peckham 296
Peebles 626
Peel 669
Pelynt 83
Pembroke Dock 608
Pembroke 607
Pembury 227
Pen-y-Cae 587
Pen-y-Fai 573
Penallt 582
Penally 608
Penarth 574
Pendleton 244
Pendoggett 83
Penge 297
Penicuik 635
Penistone 542
Penketh 75

Penllyn 574
Penn Common 424
Penn 56
Penrhiwllan 608
Penrhynside 599
Penrith 96
Penryn 83
Pensax 510
Penshurst 227
Pensnett 489
Penwortham 245
Penzance 83
Perry Wood 227
Pershore 510
Perth 658
Peter Tavy 125
Peterborough 64
Peterlee 149
Petersfield 189
Petham 227
Pett 454
Petteridge 277
Petts Wood 300
Petworth 461
Pewsey 501
Phillack 84
Pickering 530
Piddlehinton 136
Piddletrenthide 136
Piece 84
Pimlico 301
Pinchbeck 270
Pinkneys Green 47
Pishill 390
Pitlessie 649
Pitlochry 658
Pitney 411
Pitsford 365
Plaistow 285
Playhatch 390
Plockton 645
Plumstead 296
Plungar 257
Plush 136
Plymouth 125
Plympton 126
Plymtree 126
Polebrook 365
Polesworth 477
Polkerris 84
Pollington 517
Polperro 84
Ponders End 291
Pontardawe 574
Pontefract 561
Pontfaen 608
Pontsticill 574
Pontymister 582
Pontypridd 574
Pool in Wharfedale 530
Pool 84
Poole 136
Poringland 355
Porlock Weir 411
Porlock 411
Port Erin 669
Port St Mary 669
Porth 575
Porthcawl 575
Porthmadog 599
Porthyrhyd 608
Portishead 411
Portland 137
Portpatrick 629
Portslade 454

Portsmouth 189
Portwood, Stockport 333
Postbridge 126
Potters Crouch 206
Potto 530
Potton 41
Poulton-le-Fylde 245
Poynton 75
Prescot 342
Prestatyn 594
Preston
  Dorset 137
  Hertfordshire 206
  Lancashire 245
Preston-le-Skerne 149
Prestonpans 635
Prestwick 623
Prestwood 57
Priddy 412
Princetown 127
Pudsey 561
Puriton 412
Purleigh 162
Putney 304
Puttenham 444
Pwlltrap 608
Pymore 138

Q

Quadring 270
Quainton 57
Quakers Yard 575
Quedgeley 177
Quenington 177
Quorn 257

R

Raby 342
Rackheath 355
Radcliffe-on-Trent 381
Radstock 412
Rainford 342
Rainham
  Greater London 286
  Kent 227
Rainhill 342
Rainow 75
Rampton 65
Ramsbottom 329
Ramsbury 501
Ramsey
  Cambridgeshire 65
  Isle of Man 669
Ramsgate 228
Raskelf 530
Rattlesden 434
Ravensthorpe 365
Rawcliffe 517
Rawtenstall 246
Rayleigh 162
Rayners Lane 293
Reading 47
Red Wharf Bay 599
Redbourn 206
Redcar 530
Redditch 510
Redhill 444
Redmire 530
Reepham 356
Renfrew 641
Renhold 41
Rennington 372
Retford 381

Reynoldston 575
Rhandirmwyn 609
Rhayader 588
Rhoscolyn 600
Rhydlydan 600
Rhydyfro 575
Rhyl 594
Rhymney 575
Ribblehead 530
Richmond
  Greater London 307
  Yorkshire (North) 531
Rickford 412
Rickinghall 434
Rickmansworth 206
Ridge Lane 477
Ridgewell 163
Ringmer 454
Ringwood 191
Ripley 110
Ripon 531
Risby 435
Risca 582
Robin Hood's Bay 531
Roch 609
Rochdale 330
Rochester 228
Rochford 163
Rock 510
Rockbourne 191
Rogate 461
Romford 286
Romiley 330
Romsey 192
Rookhope 149
Rosudgeon 85
Rothbury 372
Rotherham 542
Rotherhithe 296
Rothesay, Isle of Bute 620
Rothwell 365
Rottingdean 455
Rowberrow 412
Rowhedge 163
Rowington 477
Roy Bridge 646
Royal Wootton Bassett 501
Roydon 356
Royton 331
Ruabon 594
Rufford 246
Rugby 477
Ruislip Common 293
Ruislip Manor 293
Rumburgh 435
Runcorn 76
Rushden 365
Rusholme 331
Ruskington 270
Rusper 462
Ruthin 594
Rydal 96
Ryde 211
Ryehill 517

S

Saffron Walden 163
Saham Toney 356
St Agnes, Isles of Scilly 85
St Albans 207
St Andrews 649

St Annes on the Sea 247
St Austell 85
St Bees 97
St Brelade 664
St George's, Telford 400
St George 600
St Helens 342
St Helier 664
St Ives 65
St James's 302
St John's Chapel 150
St John's Town of Dalry 629
St John's Wood 292
St John's 670
St Just 85
St Leonards-on-Sea 455
St Martin 663
St Mary in the Marsh 229
St Mary's, Isles of Scilly 85
St Mary 665
St Mawgan 85
St Neots 66
St Newlyn East 85
St Nicholas Hurst 48
St Ouen 665
St Pancras 281
St Paul's Walden 207
St Peter Port 663
St Sampson 664
Saintfield 662
Sale 331
Salehurst 455
Salford
    Bedfordshire 41
    Greater Manchester 331
Salisbury 501
Salt 424
Saltaire 561
Saltburn-by-the-Sea 531
Saltcoats 623
Salwick 247
Sambrook 397
Samlesbury 247
Sampford Courtenay 127
Sampford Peverell 127
Sandbach 76
Sandford 127
Sandgate 229
Sandhurst 48
Sandown 212
Sandridge 208
Sandtoft 270
Sandwich 229
Sandy 41
Sarn 76
Sauchie 652
Sawbridgeworth 208
Sawdon 531
Sawley 110
Saxilby 270
Scampton 270
Scarborough 532
Scarcliffe 110
Scaynes Hill 462
Scholar Green 76
Scholes 543
Scorriton 127

Scourie 646
Scunthorpe 270
Seaford 455
Seahouses 372
Seathwaite 97
Seaton Sluice 372
Sebastopol 582
Sedbergh 97
Sedgefield 150
Sedgeford 356
Sedgley 489
Selattyn 398
Selborne 192
Selsey 462
Selston 381
Semington 502
Semley 502
Settle 532
Sevenoaks Weald 230
Sevenoaks 230
Sewerby 518
Sewstern 257
Shackerstone 257
Shadingfield 435
Shaftesbury 138
Shaldon 127
Shalford 163
Shamley Green 445
Shanklin 212
Shaw 332
Shearsby 257
Shebbear 127
Shedfield 192
Sheepscombe 178
Sheerness 230
Sheffield, Central 543
Sheffield, North 544
Sheffield, South 545
Sheffield, West 545
Shefford 41
Shenstone
    Staffordshire 424
    Worcestershire 510
Shepherd's Bush 312
Shepperton 445
Shepshed 257
Shepton Beauchamp 412
Shepton Mallet 412
Sherborne 138
Sheringham 356
Shevington 332
Shifnal 398
Shiplake 391
Shipley 561
Shippon 391
Shipston-on-Stour 478
Shipton Moyne 178
Shipton-by-Beningbrough 533
Shirland 111
Shirley 490
Shoreham-by-Sea 462
Short Heath 490
Shortstanding 178
Shorwell 212
Shottisham 435
Shrewsbury 398
Shustoke 478
Shutford 391
Sicklinghall 533
Sidcup 300
Sidlow Bridge 445
Sidmouth 128
Sileby 258

Silsden 562
Silverdale 247
Silverton 128
Sixpenny Handley 138
Skendleby 271
Sketty 575
Skillington 271
Skipton 533
Slad 178
Slaidburn 247
Slaithwaite 562
Slaley 373
Slapton 128
Sleaford 271
Slimbridge 178
Slipton 366
Slough 48
Smallburgh 356
Smithfield 279
Snaith 518
Snargate 230
Snettisham 357
Snitterby 271
Soho 309
Solva 609
Somerby 258
Sompting 462
Souldern 391
Souldrop 41
South Anston 546
South Brent 128
South Chailey 455
South Dalton 518
South Ferriby 271
South Gosforth, Newcastle 469
South Hackney 284
South Kenton 293
South Lambeth 303
South Molton 128
South Normanton 111
South Petherton 413
South Queensferry 635
South Rauceby 271
South Shields 469
South Wimbledon 305
Southall 314
Southampton 192
Southend-on-Sea 164
Southerndown 576
Southgate 289
Southminster 164
Southowram 562
Southport 343
Southrepps 357
Southwark 294
Southwell 381
Southwick 366
Southwold 435
Sowerby Bridge 562
Sowerby 533
Spalding 272
Spaldwick 66
Sparkwell 128
Spennymoor 150
Spetisbury 138
Spitalfields 283
Spreyton 128
Spurstow 76
Staffhurst Wood 445
Stafford 424
Staines 445
Stair 623
Staithes 533
Stalisfield Green 230

Stalybridge 332
Stamford 272
Stanbury 562
Standlake 391
Stanford Bridge 510
Stanford-le-Hope 164
Stanningfield 435
Stansted Mountfitchet 164
Stansted 230
Stanton in Peak 111
Staplefield 462
Stapleford Tawney 164
Stapleford 382
Staplehurst 231
Staplow 200
Staunton in the Vale 382
Staunton 178
Staveley
    Cumbria 97
    Derbyshire 111
Staverton 366
Staxton 534
Stebbing 164
Steeple Bumpstead 165
Stevenage 208
Steventon 391
Stevington 41
Stewarton 623
Steyning 462
Stibbard 357
Stickford 272
Sticklepath 129
Stillington 534
Stirling 652
Stock 165
Stockcross 48
Stockport, Central 332
Stockton-on-Tees 150
Stogumber 413
Stoke Bruerne 366
Stoke Golding 258
Stoke Goldington 57
Stoke Lyne 391
Stoke Mandeville 57
Stoke Newington 289
Stoke, Stoke-on-Trent 426
Stokesley 534
Stone in Oxney 231
Stone 426
Stonehaven 616
Stottesdon 399
Stoughton 463
Stourbridge 490
Stourmouth 231
Stourport-on-Severn 511
Stourton Caundle 138
Stow Maries 165
Stow-cum-Quy 66
Stowmarket 435
Stowting 231
Strachur 620
Stranraer 629
Stratford-upon-Avon 478
Strathaven 641
Strathkinness 649
Strathtummel 658
Strathyre 652
Stratton
    Cornwall 85
    Dorset 138

Strawberry Bank 97
Streatham Hill 303
Streatham 305
Street 413
Strensall 534
Stretham 66
Strines 333
Stromness, Orkney 653
Stroud Green 288
Stroud 178
Strumpshaw 357
Studham 42
Studley 478
Sudbury 436
Sulby 670
Sunderland 470
Surbiton 308
Sutterton 272
Sutton Bridge 272
Sutton Coldfield 490
Sutton cum
   Duckmanton 111
Sutton upon Derwent
   518
Sutton
   Cheshire 77
   Greater London 308
Sutton-in-Ashfield 382
Sutton-on-Sea 273
Swalwell 471
Swanage 138
Swanscombe 231
Swansea 576
Swanton Abbott 357
Swanton Morley 357
Swavesey 66
Sweffling 436
Swindon 502
Swineshead 273
Swinford 258
Swinhope 273
Swinley 333
Swinton 334
Swithland 258
Sydenham 392
Sykehouse 546
Syston 258

T

Tacolneston 357
Talgarth 588
Talkin 97
Tallentire 97
Talybont on Usk 588
Tamworth 426
Tangley 193
Taplow 57
Tarland 617
Tattingstone 436
Taunton 413
Tebworth 42
Teddington 314
Teignmouth 129
Temple 282
Tenby 609
Tewkesbury 179
Teynham 231
Thakeham 463
Thame 392
Thames Ditton 446
Thetford 357
Thixendale 534
Thompson 358
Thorganby 534

Thornborough 57
Thornbury 179
Thornby 366
Thorndon 436
Thorne 546
Thornford 139
Thornsett 111
Thornton Watless 534
Thornton-le-Dale 535
Thorpe Mandeville 366
Thorpe Market 358
Three Crosses 577
Three Mile Cross 49
Threekingham 273
Thrussington 258
Thurlaston 259
Thurlstone 546
Thurlton 358
Thurston 436
Tibenham 358
Tichborne 194
Tickhill 546
Tiffield 366
Tilbrook 67
Tilehurst 49
Tillicoultry 652
Tintagel 86
Tintern 583
Tipton 490
Tisbury 503
Titchfield 194
Tockholes 247
Toddington
   Bedfordshire 42
   Gloucestershire &
   Bristol 179
Todmorden 563
Tonbridge 231
Tongham 446
Tontine 247
Tooting 305
Topsham 129
Torquay 129
Torver 98
Totnes 129
Totternhoe 42
Towan Cross 86
Towcester 366
Tower Hill 280
Trebellan 86
Treen (Zennor) 86
Trefforest 577
Treforest 577
Tregaron 609
Treleigh 86
Tremadog 600
Trevaunance Cove 86
Trewellard 87
Tring 208
Trofarth 600
Troon 623
Trowbridge 503
Trowse 358
Trull 413
Trunch 358
Truro 87
Trysull 427
Tudweiliog 600
Tunbridge Wells 232
Turnchapel 129
Turners Hill 463
Tushingham 77
Twice Brewed 373
Twickenham 314
Twyford 194

Tyla Garw 577
Tynemouth 471
Tywardreath 87

U

Uckfield 456
Ufford 67
Ufton 479
Uig, Isle of Skye 646
Uley 179
Ullapool 646
Ulverston 98
Underbarrow 98
Upavon 503
Uphampton 511
Uplawmoor 641
Upper Basildon 49
Upper Belvedere 301
Upper Church Village
   577
Upper Farringdon 194
Upper Gornal 490
Upper Hale 446
Upper Heyford 392
Upper Killay 577
Upper Llanover 583
Upper Longdon 427
Upper Oddington 180
Upper Poppleton 535
Upper Upnor 232
Upper Walthamstow
   285
Upper Wyche 511
Uppermill 334
Uppingham 259
Upwey 139
Urmston 334
Usk 583
Uxbridge 314

V

Vale 664
Ventnor 212
Victoria 302
Vogue 87

W

Waberthwaite 98
Waddington
   Lancashire 248
   Lincolnshire 273
Wainfleet 273
Waingroves 111
Wakefield 563
Walberswick 436
Walcott 359
Walgrave 367
Walhampton 194
Walkden 334
Walkington 518
Wall Heath 491
Wallasey 344
Wallingford 392
Wallington 308
Walmer Bridge 248
Walmer 232
Walsall 491
Waltham Abbey 165
Waltham St Lawrence
   49
Waltham 273
Walthamstow 285
Walton on Thames 446

Walton on the Wolds
   259
Walton 344
Walton-on-the-Naze
   165
Wandsworth 305
Wanstrow 413
Wantage 392
Wardley 334
Wardlow Mires 112
Ware 209
Wareham 139
Wareside 209
Wargrave 49
Warham All Saints 359
Wark 373
Warley 165
Warminster 503
Warnham 463
Warrington 77
Warwick 479
Wasdale Head 99
Washford 414
Washington 471
Watchet 414
Waterbeach 67
Waterfoot 248
Waterley Bottom 180
Waterloo
   Greater London 294
   Merseyside 344
Waternish, Isle of Skye
   646
Watford 209
Wath upon Dearne 547
Watnall 382
Watton 359
Waunfawr 600
Wavertree 345
Waytown 139
Weatheroak 511
Wedmore 414
Wednesbury 492
Wednesfield 492
Weeley 165
Weetwood, Leeds 558
Welbury 535
Welcombe 130
Welford 367
Welling 301
Wellingborough 367
Wellington, Telford 400
Wellow 382
Wells 414
Wells-next-the-Sea 359
Welshpool 588
Wembury 130
Wendens Ambo 165
Wendover 57
Wendron 87
Wennington 248
Wensley 535
Wentworth 547
West Acre 359
West Boldon 471
West Bridgford 382
West Bromwich 492
West Chiltington 463
West Chinnock 414
West Ealing 312
West End 194
West Haddlesey 535
West Herrington 472
West Huntspill 414
West Itchenor 463

West Kirby 345
West Lulworth 139
West Malling 232
West Malvern 511
West Monkseaton 472
West Norwood 298
West Parley 139
West Stockwith 383
West Stour 139
West Tytherley 195
West Wickham 301
West Witton 535
West Wratting 67
Westbourne 464
Westcliff-on-Sea 166
Wester Balgedie 658
Westfield Stratford City 286
Westgate 150
Westgate-on-Sea 233
Westhoughton 334
Westminster 302
Weston by Welland 367
Weston 427
Weston-super-Mare 414
Westwoodside 274
Wetheral 99
Weybridge 446
Weymouth 140
Whaley Bridge 112
Whalley Range 334
Whalley 248
Wheelton 248
Wherwell 195
Whichford 479
Whimple 130
Whipsnade 42
Whiston
    Staffordshire 427
    Yorkshire (South) 547
Whitby 535
Whitchurch
    Hampshire 195
    Shropshire 400
White Notley 166
Whitebridge 646
Whitehall 302
Whitehaven 99
Whitehough 112
Whitemill 609
Whiteparish 504
Whiteshill 180
Whitley Bay 472
Whitstable 233
Whittlesey 67
Whitton 314
Whitwick 259
Whitworth 248
Wickham 49
Wickwar 180
Widdington 166
Widecombe in the Moor 130
Widnes 77
Wigan 334
Wigston 259
Wildhill 209
Wildmoor 511
Willaston 77
Willen, Milton Keynes 56
Willenhall 493
Willey 479

Willingham by Stow 274
Willington
    Derbyshire 112
    Durham 150
Williton 415
Willoughton 274
Wilmington 456
Wilpshire 249
Wilton 504
Wimbledon 306
Wimborne 140
Wincanton 415
Winchester 195
Winchfield 196
Winchmore Hill 290
Windermere 99
Windsor 49
Wing 58
Wingfield
    Bedfordshire 42
    Suffolk 436
Winkfield 50
Winmarleigh 249
Winsford 77
Winslow 58
Winsor 196
Winster 99
Wintersett 564
Winterton 274
Winterton-on-Sea 359
Wirksworth 112
Wisbech 67
Wishaw 641
Witham 166
Withersfield 437
Withington 200
Witney 393
Witton Gilbert 150
Witton le Wear 151
Wiveliscombe 415
Wivelsfield Green 456
Woking 447
Wokingham 50
Wollaston 493
Wolseley Bridge 427
Wolsingham 151
Wolverhampton 493
Wombourne 427
Wombwell 547
Wooburn Common 58
Wood End 479
Woodbastwick 359
Woodbridge 437
Woodchester 180
Woodchurch 233
Woodcross 494
Woodford Green 286
Woodford
    Greater Manchester 335
    Northamptonshire 367
Woodham Mortimer 166
Woodsetton 495
Woodstock 393
Woodthorpe 112
Woolaston Common 180
Woolhampton 50
Woolhope 200
Woolmer Green 209
Woolwich 296
Wootton 42

Worcester 511
Wordsley 495
Worksop 383
Wormadale, Shetland 654
Worsbrough Village 547
Worsley 335
Worsthorne 249
Worth Matravers 140
Worth 233
Worthing 464
Worthington 335
Wortley 547
Wortwell 360
Wotton-under-Edge 180
Wray 249
Wreay 99
Wreningham 360
Wrexham 594
Wrightington 249
Writtle 166
Wrotham 233
Wroughton 504
Wroxall 212
Wroxton 393
Wycombe Marsh 58
Wylam 373
Wymeswold 259
Wymondham 360
Wysall 383

Y

Yanwath 99
Yapton 464
Yardley Hastings 367
Yarm 536
Yaxley 437
Yelverton 130
Yeovil 415
Ynystawe 577
York 536
Yoxall 427
Ysceifiog 594
Ystalyfera 577

Beers index

These beers refer to those in bold type in the breweries section (beers in regular production) and so therefore do not include seasonal, special or occasional beers that may be mentioned elsewhere in the text.

#10 Smoked Porter
 Shamblemoose *842*
#4 American Brown Ale
 Shamblemoose *842*
Ór Trouble *891*
'alf Wit Hewitt's (Brentwood) *706*
'Old on to your 'at Brandon *705*
1st Duke Wellington Inn *875*
1'st Lite Frodsham *748*
106 Jack FM Ale Sixpenny *846*
1302 Brampton *704*
1319 Mild Shalford *842*
1381 Wantsum *872*
1485 Steamin' Billy (Belvoir) *694*
1503 Kingstone *784*
1555 Bishop Nick *697*
1642 Bitter Three Tuns *859*
1643 Cavalier Two Cocks *867*
1643 Leveller Two Cocks *867*
1643 Musket Mild Two Cocks *867*
1643 Puritan Two Cocks *867*
1643 Roundhead Two Cocks *867*
1703 Fallen (Traditional Scottish Ales) *864*
1823 Mild Wood Farm *884*
1823 Tirril *862*
1837 India Pale Ale Dominion *734*
1850 London Porter Dominion *734*
1872 Porter Elland *739*
1882 Lager Eden St Andrews *738*
1892 Dark Robinsons *835*
1892 Robinsons *835*
19th Eden St Andrews *738*
1965 Special Bitter Ale Westerham *877*
200 Palmers *820*
22 Dancing Duck *729*
24 Carat Liverpool Organic *791*
25 Cotleigh *725*
257 Sherborne *843*
2B Arkell's *683*
3.1.6. Grain *755*
3.9 Outstanding *819*
3 Faze Falstaff *742*
3-BULLZ Burnside *712*
391 Brown Ale Botanist *702*
3B Arkell's *683*
3B's Bees *693*
4 Wood Shiny *844*
50 Ways Brighton Bier *708*
60/- Ale Belhaven *693*
6066 Sleaford *847*
65 Mild Botanist *702*
66 IBU Six° North *846*
6D Best Bitter Sixpenny *846*
6X Wadworth *871*
70 Fathom Blackhill *699*
70/- Balmaha *687*
8 Sail Ale 8 Sail *677*
8/- Shottle Farm *845*
80 Caledonian *715*
80/- Ale Belhaven *693*
80/- Scotch Ale Rebel *831*

80/- Stewart *852*
 Williams *880*
800 Ale Frodsham *748*
99 Red Baboons Blue Monkey *701*

A

A Bit'er Ruff Watermill *873*
A Over T (Aromas Over Tongham) Hogs Back *771*
Abbey Ale Kingstone *784*
Abbey Blonde Conquest *723*
Abbey Stout Great Oakley *757*
Abbot Ale Greene King *759*
Abduction Dancing Duck *729*
Abergele Ale North Wales *810*
Abingdon Bridge Loose Cannon *794*
Absolution Abbeydale *678*
Abyss Best Bitter Brew Company *706*
Academy Ale Tirril *862*
Accidental Porter Fulflood Arms *749*
Ace Ale Leila Cottage *788*
Ace of Harts Harthill Village *765*
Acer Bristol Beer Factory *709*
Aces High Blackjack *699*
Achilles Isca *778*
Acris Dow Bridge *735*
Across the Pond APA Two Bridges *867*
Adam Henson's Rare Breed Butcombe *713*
Adder Lager Allendale *680*
Addlestone Ale Sixpenny *846*
Admiral IPA Nelson *807*
Admiral May May Hill *798*
Admiral of the Blues Bowland *703*
Admiral Stout Irving *778*
Adventure Leamside *787*
Adventurer Mile Tree *801*
Affinity Lacons *786*
Afternoon Delight Beeston *693*
Ageless RedWillow *833*
AiN'CHO MUM's Porter Brüpond *711*
Aisling Potbelly *826*
AK Pale Colchester *721*
AK McMullen *795*
AKA (Amber Kitchen Ale) Bluestone *701*
AKA Kiwi Big River *696*
Alba Scots Pine Ale Williams *881*
Albacore DarkTribe *730*
Albert Ale Bridgetown *708*
 Earl Soham *737*
Albion Pale Ale Cox & Holbrook *727*
Albion Special Wicked Hathern (Staffordshire) *851*
Alcazar Ale Alcazar *679*
Alchemists Ale Pictish *823*
Alchemy Oldershaw *817*
Ale Caesar Corinium *725*

Ale Force Storm *853*
Ale of Atholl Moulin *805*
The Ale of Leven Loch Lomond *792*
Ale of Two Cities Dickensian *733*
Ale of Wight Goddards *753*
Ale to the Tsar Fernandes *744*
Ale An Teallach *681*
 Angel *682*
 Atlantic *685*
 Black Sheep *698*
 Blackmore *699*
 Buffy's *711*
 Chiltern *719*
 Coquetdale *724*
 Cornish Crown *725*
 Enville *740*
 Exmoor *741*
 Gribble *760*
 Hilden *770*
 Humpty Dumpty *775*
 Liberation *789*
 Otter *818*
 Tatton *856*
 Wolf *883*
Alestock Nailsworth *806*
Alexandrina Leamside *787*
Alfie's Revenge Driftwood *736*
Alfred Moodies Mild East Coast *738*
Alfred's Stout North Curry *810*
All Black Pale Ale Fox *747*
All Black AllGates *680*
All Saints Porter Red *831*
All Saints Tipple Rectory *831*
Alley Cat Ale Ascot *684*
Alligator Ale Ascot *684*
Alt Okells *814*
Alton Abbey Peakstones Rock *821*
Alton's Pride Triple fff *865*
Altrincham Pilsner Dunham Massey *737*
Amarillo Crouch Vale *728*
Amazing Ale Beeches *692*
Amber Ale Goldmark *754*
Amber Aspect Rail Ale *829*
Amber IPA Clockwork *720*
Amber Necker Pennine *821*
Amber Sparkle Mulberry Duck *806*
Amber Wrangler Latimer *787*
Amber Bees *693*
 Globe *752*
 Harbour *764*
 Lancaster *786*
 Lytham *794*
 Otter *818*
 Wainstones *871*
Amberillo Dancing Duck *729*
Ambler Cotswold Spring *726*
Ambrosia Forge *746*
Ambush Ale Weetwood *874*
American Blonde Black Iris *698*
 Brewshed *707*
American Light Quantum *828*

American Pale Ale
Blackedge 699
Bridestones 707
Dark Star 730
Hackney 761
Long Man 793
Portobello 825
Sonnet 43 849
American Psycho Mad Hatter 795
American Red Liverpool Craft 790
American Rye Buxton 714
American Style Milk Stout
Knaresborough 785
Amnesia Bird's 696
Amoor Moor 804
Amy's Rose Joseph Herbert
Smith 848
Anastasia Barlow 689
Anastasia's Exile Stout Ascot 684
Anchor Bitter Cliff Quay 720
Titanic 862
Angel Great Heck 756
Wylam 887
Angel's Folly Tipsy Angel 861
Angelic Blonde Tipsy Angel 861
Angelic Mild Tipsy Angel 861
Angelina Coastal 721
Anglers Reward Wold Top 883
Angry Ox Bitter Broxbourne 710
Angus Og Ale Islay 779
Anne Downes Colchester 721
Anniversary Ale Halfpenny 762
Another Fine Mess Ulverston 868
Anson Worth 886
Antipodean Amber Ale
Quantum 828
Anubis Raw 830
Anvil Ale Old Forge 815
Aonach Frodsham 748
AONB Tillingbourne 860
APA (American Pale Ale)
Houston 775
APA Allendale 680
Hop Fuzz 777
Tap East 856
Windswept 882
Ape Ale Blue Monkey 701
Apocalypse Hartshorns 765
Apparition Full Mash 749
Appolds Dark Mile Tree 801
Apprentice Wibblers 879
Wizard 883
Arbor Light Whim 878
Archbishop Lee's Ruby Ale North
Yorkshire 810
Archbishop's Ale Black Paw 698
Ardnave Ale Islay 779
Ariel Square Four Concertina 722
Arizona Phoenix 822
Armada Ale Harveys 765
Armstrong Bitter Ouseburn
Valley 819
Arrowhead Bitter Cannon
Royall 716
Arrowhead Extra Cannon
Royall 716
Art Nouveau Art Brew 683
The Art of Darkness Dark Star 730
Artisan's Choice Collingham 722
Artist Paradise 820
Arty Farty Plain Ales 824
ASB Archers (Evan Evans) 740
Ascension Forge 746
Ashbourne Ale
Leatherbritches 788

Ashby Pale Tollgate 862
Ashby Pride Tap House 856
Ashford Thornbridge 858
Askrigg Ale Yorkshire Dales 889
Astronomer North Star 810
At The Door Wolf 883
Atom Splitter City of Cambridge
(Wolf) 883
Atomic Blonde Revolutions 833
Attwood's Pale Ale (APA)
Attwood 685
Auburn Copper Ale Mad Cat 795
Audit Ale Westerham 877
Auld Alliance Fyfe 750
Auld Hemp High House Farm 769
Aunty Myrtle's Mayfields 798
Aur Cymru Heart of Wales 767
Aureole Ale Ascot 684
Aurora Geltsdale 752
Aussie Kiss Halifax Steam 762
Autumn Gold Linfit 789
Autumn Harvest Brigstock 708
AVA First Chop 744
Avalanche Fyne 750
Aviator Dent 732
Avocet Exeter 741
Avondale Strathaven 853
Axolotl Salamander 839
Ay Up/Ey Up Dancing Duck 729
Ayson Hart of Preston 764
Azimuth Hardknott 764

B

B52 Leadmill 787
Norfolk Square 809
Baby Blond Nook 809
Backscratcher Long Itch 793
Bad to the Bone Bank Top 687
Gun Dog 760
Bad Kitty Brass Castle 705
Badlands Bitter Driftwood 736
Bakewell Best Bitter Peak
Ales 821
Bal Maiden Rebel 830
Balaclava Leyden 789
Balmy Days Hopping Mad 774
Baltic Gold Wapping 872
Baltic Night Stout Compass 722
Baltic Trader Export Stout Green
Jack 758
Bamboozle Loddon 792
Bananalicious Grafton 755
Band of Brothers Sperrin 849
Bandwagon Loose Cannon 794
Bankers Draft Wickwar 880
Bankswood Bitter Mouselow
Farm 805
Bannockburn Ale Traditional
Scottish Ales 864
Banquo Newby Wyke 808
Banshee Porter Hop Monster 773
Banter Nutbrook 812
Barbastelle Old Chimneys 814
Barbed & Tangled World's
End 885
Barbury Castle Three Castles 859
Barbus Barbus Butts 714
Barefoot Bohemian Eight
Degrees 890
Bargee Elland 739
Barista Summer Wine 854
Barley to Beer Bank Top 687
Barley Gold Offa's Dyke 813
Barley Juice Beckstones 692

Barm Pot Bitter Goose Eye 754
Barn Ale Tydd Steam 867
Barn Owl Premium Ale
Cotleigh 725
BarnBuster Mobberley 802
Barnes Wallis Amber 681
Barnfield Bitter Shalford 842
Barnsey Bath Ales 691
Barnsley Bitter Acorn 678
Barnsley Gold Acorn 678
Barnwell Bitter Digfield 733
Baron Saturday Treboom 864
Baronet Dukeries 736
Barrel Organ Blues Wentwell 876
Barron's Hopsit Exe Valley 741
Barton Bitter Cambridge
Moonshine 715
Baskerville Bitter Two
Towers 867
Basket Case Spitting Feathers 850
Bathside Battery Bitter Harwich
Town 766
Battersea Brownstone
Belleville 694
Battleaxe Rudgate 838
Bay Ale Galway Bay 890
Bay Bitter Harwich Town 765
Baz's Bonce Blower Parish 820
BB Donnington 734
BBC2 Brentwood 706
BBH Bitter Cathedral Heights 717
Beach Blonde Sunny
Republic 855
Beach Redscar 833
Beachcomber Teignworthy 857
Beachy Original Beachy
Head 691
Beacon Bitter Everards 741
Beagle Best Quantum 828
Beal Bán Beoir Chorca Dhuibhne/
West Kerry 889
Beamish Burn Stables 851
Beamish Hall Best Bitter
Stables 851
Bear Ale Traquair House 864
Bear Ass Beartown 692
Bear Island Newby Wyke 808
Bearly Literate Beartown 692
Bearskinful Beartown 692
Beast Banks Bitter Kendal 782
The Beast Brightside 708
Beast Exmoor 742
Beaters Choice Wall's 872
Beau Douro Wellington Inn 875
Beautiful South Hill 789
Beaver Bitter Belvoir 694
Bedrock Keystone 783
Bee Blonde Three B's 859
Bee Thrifty Three B's 858
Beech Barrowden 689
Beechwood Bitter Chiltern 719
Bee's Knees Bartrams 690
Nook 809
Beer Elsie Bub Bartrams 690
Beer O'Clock Beckstones 692
Beer Street London Brewing 792
Beer Milk Street 801
Beerier Beer Willy Good 881
Bees Knees Bitter Blue Bee 700
Bees Knees Great Western 757
Imperial 777
The Bees Knees Springhead 851
Beinn Dearg Ale An Teallach 681
Belfast Ale Whitewater 878
Belfast Black Whitewater 878

Bell Tower Stables *851*
Belle Blackbeck *698*
Bellend Blonde Ciren *720*
Bellowhead Potbelly *826*
Bellringer Abbey *678*
Bells Best Mate Ciren *720*
Bells Bitter Ciren *720*
Belly's Beverage Muirhouse *805*
Beltane Braces Bartrams *690*
Ben Nevis Traditional Scottish
 Ales *864*
Bencroft Best Bitter Copper
 Kettle *724*
Benedictine Groove Elixir *739*
Bengal Fox Slightly Foxed *847*
Bengal Lancer Fuller's *749*
Bengal Tiger Concertina *722*
Ben's Stout Blue Anchor *700*
Beorma Beowulf *694*
Berrow 4B Towles' *863*
Berrow Topsy Turvy Towles' *863*
Berserker Export Pale Ale
 Hebridean *767*
Bespoke Leatherbritches *788*
Best Bitter Axholme *686*
 Bacchus *686*
 Ballard's *687*
 Batham *691*
 Beartown *692*
 Bedlam *692*
 Bellinger's *694*
 Black Sheep *698*
 Blue Cow *700*
 Brass Castle *705*
 Brightside *708*
 Buxton *714*
 Buzzard *714*
 Camerons *716*
 Clarence & Fredericks *720*
 Copper Dragon *724*
 Crate *727*
 Dark Horse *730*
 Deverell's *733*
 Elland *739*
 Felinfoel *743*
 Frog Island *748*
 Goldmark *754*
 Gower *755*
 Grain *755*
 Greenodd *760*
 Hackney *761*
 Healey's *767*
 Hereford *768*
 Hobsons *771*
 Imperial *777*
 Isle of Purbeck *779*
 Kelham Island *782*
 Liverpool Organic *791*
 Long Man *793*
 Malt *796*
 Moles *803*
 Old Cannon *814*
 Oldershaw *817*
 Palmers *820*
 Pheasantry *822*
 Quercus *828*
 Red Fox *831*
 Ringway *834*
 Ringwood *834*
 Ripple Steam *834*
 Shires *844*
 St Peter's *839*
 Stringers *853*
 Summerskills *854*
 Tavy *856*

 Theakston *858*
 Tom Wood's *884*
 Vale *869*
 Warwickshire *872*
 Weetwood *874*
 WharfeBank *877*
 Winster Valley *882*
 Wood Farm *884*
 Yates' *888*
Best Dark Ale Goacher's *753*
Best in Show Cotswold Lion *726*
Best Balmaha *687*
 Bollington *702*
 Botley *702*
 Brampton *704*
 Brancaster (Beeston) *693*
 Brentwood *706*
 Brewshed *707*
 Eden *738*
 Felstar *744*
 George's (Hop Monster) *773*
 Hastings *766*
 High Weald *769*
 Ilkley *777*
 Kissingate *785*
 Langham *786*
 Larkins *787*
 Leeds *788*
 Ludlow *794*
 Magpie *795*
 Newark *808*
 Nobby's *808*
 Nook *809*
 North Yorkshire *810*
 Tatton *856*
 Town Mill *863*
 Turners *866*
 Vens *870*
 Weighbridge *874*
 Wharfedale *877*
Bethnal Green Bitter
 Brodie's *709*
Betty Stogs Skinner's *846*
Betty's Blonde Barlow *689*
Bevans Bitter Rhymney *834*
Bewcastle Brown Ale
 Geltsdale *752*
Bewick Swan *855*
Bewshers Bitter Tirril *862*
Beyond the Pale Elland *739*
Beyond The Pale Kent *783*
Beyton Bitter Cox & Holbrook *727*
BG Sips Blue Monkey *701*
Bier Head Liverpool Organic *791*
Big Casino Dancing Man *730*
Big Chief Green Mill *758*
 Redemption *832*
Big Ginger Tigertops *860*
Big John Prospect *827*
Big Muddy Wild Weather *880*
Big Nev's Six Bells *846*
Big Red Bitter Ossett *818*
Big Tree Bitter Dunham
 Massey *737*
Bildeston Best Kings Head *784*
Billabong Tiny Rebel *861*
Bill's Boys Bitter Fulflood
 Arms *749*
Billy Boy Poachers *825*
Billy's Best Bitter Tollgate *862*
Binham Cheer Front Street *748*
Birds & Bees Williams *880*
Birmingham Special Ale Two
 Towers *867*
Bishop Sumner Farnham *743*

Bishop's Best Black Paw *698*
Bishops Farewell Oakham *812*
Bishops Finger Shepherd
 Neame *843*
Bishops Tipple Wadworth *871*
Bishopswood Bitter
 Swansea *855*
Bit O' Blonde Goosnargh *754*
Bit o' Bully Concrete Cow *723*
Bitlyke Nutbrook *812*
Bitter Bully Cheddar *718*
Bitter Californian Bristol Beer
 Factory *709*
Bitter Old Bustard Jo C's *781*
Bitter Reality Reality *830*
Bitter Than Ever Vale of
 Glamorgan *870*
Bitter & Twisted Harviestoun *765*
Bitter Arrow *683*
 Backyard *687*
 Banks's *688*
 Big Lamp *696*
 Black Hole *697*
 BlackBar *698*
 Brains *704*
 Brakspear *704*
 Broughs *710*
 Brown Cow *710*
 Buckingham *711*
 Buffy's *711*
 Bushy's *713*
 Butcombe *713*
 Buxton *714*
 Caythorpe *718*
 Daleside *729*
 Devil's Dyke *733*
 Doghouse *733*
 Elmtree *739*
 Exe Valley *741*
 Fat Cat *743*
 Flowerpots *746*
 Four Thorns *746*
 Gas Dog *751*
 Golcar *753*
 Goose Eye *754*
 Gwaun Valley *761*
 Hambleton *762*
 Hawkshead *766*
 Heart of Wales *767*
 Hill Island *770*
 Holt *772*
 Jennings *780*
 John Smith's (Camerons) *716*
 Ledbury *788*
 Lees *788*
 Linfit *789*
 Lizard *791*
 Llangollen *791*
 Okells *813*
 Old Pie Factory *816*
 Otter *818*
 Paradise *820*
 Quantum *828*
 Ramsbury *829*
 Red Fox *831*
 Rhymney *834*
 Ridgeway *834*
 Rowton *837*
 Slater's *847*
 Spencer's *849*
 Steamin' Billy (Belvoir) *694*
 Tower *863*
 Uley *868*
 Wapping *872*
 Wensleydale *875*

Winter's 882
Wold Top 883
Wood Street 884
Woodlands 885
Wye Valley 887
Wylam 887
Yates 887
Bitter/WHB Weatheroak Hill 874
Bittermans Bacchus 686
Bla'than Tryst 865
Black Abbot Idle 776
Black Abbots Grafton 755
Black Adder Mauldons 798
Black Army Stout Pixie
    Spring 824
Black Art Tigertops 860
Black Band Porter Kirkstall 785
Black Beard Watermill 873
Black Beauty Two Roses 867
Black Bee Phoenix 822
Black Boar Hogswood 771
Black Bull Bitter Theakston 858
Black Bull Porter Pied Bull 823
Black Bull Three B's 859
Black Canon Stout Burscough 712
Black Cat Moorhouse's 804
The Black Cock Brewmeister 707
Black Colt Firefly 744
Black Coral Stout Hornbeam 774
Black Cork Knops 785
Black Country Bitter
    Holden's 771
Black Country Mild Holden's 771
Black Crow Stout Poachers 825
Black Cuillin Isle of Skye 779
Black Death Conquest 723
Black Diamond Gower 755
Black Dog Elgood's 738
Black Dragon Mild B&T 686
Black Dub Oat Stout
    Wensleydale 875
Black Dub Geltsdale 752
Black Economy BlackBar 698
Black Face Cuillin 728
Black Five Greenfield 759
Black Forest Porter Vibrant
    Forest 871
Black Fox Porter Red Fox 831
Black Frog Black Horse 698
Black Galloway Sulwath 854
Black Gold Cairngorm 715
    Castle Rock 717
    Copper Dragon 724
    Kent 783
Black Grouse Simpsons 845
Black Gun Dog Freddy Mild
    Beckstones 692
Black Hole Stout Cambridge
    Moonshine 715
Black Hole Peakstones Rock 821
Black Hunter Gundog 761
Black IPA Fyne 750
Black Jack Porter Cliff Quay 720
Black Katz Burnside 712
Black Knight Goff's 753
    Ludlow 794
    Tintagel 861
Black Lager Zerodegrees 889
Black Magic Happy Valley 764
Black Mari'a Old Bear 814
Black Marion Pocket 825
Black Mass Abbeydale 678
Black Mountain Black IPA Black
    Iris 698
Black Night Ridgeside 834

Black Panther Panther 820
Black Pear Malvern Hills 797
Black Pearl Porter Mighty
    Hop 800
Black Pearl Milestone 801
    Wooden Hand 884
Black Peggy Shottle Farm 845
Black Port Blackedge 699
Black Porter Captain Cook 717
Black Prince Barge & Barrel 688
    Wantsum 872
Black Pudding Leyden 789
Black Rat Stout Old
    Chimneys 814
Black Rock Ale Islay 779
Black Rock Bitter Rebel 831
Black Rock Dungarvan 890
    North Laine 810
    Tudor 866
Black Rocks Buxton 714
Black Rose Middle Earth 800
Black Sabbath Brunswick 710
Black Sail Bitter Ennerdale 740
Black Sail Hesket Newmarket 769
Black Smock Stocklinch 852
Black Star Moonstone 803
Black Street Smithy Trinity 865
Black Swan Mild Vale 869
Black Swan George Wright 886
Black & Tan Idle 776
Black Troll Tillingbourne 860
Black Ven Town Mill 863
Black Widow – Maverik Norfolk
    Square 809
Black Widow Stout Bird's 696
Black Widow 8 Sail 677
    Bootleg 702
Black William Adur 679
Black Belhaven 693
    Blackedge 699
    Ilkley 777
    Lancaster 786
    Neath 807
    Williams 880
Black/Cwrw Du'nbych
    Denbigh 732
Blackbear Beartown 692
Blackboard Old School 816
Blackhall English Stout
    Hexhamshire 769
Blackheads Mild Driftwood 736
Blackheart Stout Yorkshire
    Heart 889
Blackhouse Fallen (Traditional
    Scottish Ales) 864
Blacklight BlackBar 698
Blacksmiths Ale Coniston 723
Blacksmiths Gold Old Forge 815
Blackwater Mild Crouch Vale 728
Blackwood Stout Grain 755
Bladderwrack Stout Railway
    Tavern 829
Blanche de Newland
    Tigertops 860
Blanco Blonde Sheffield 843
Blarney Blonde Franciscan
    Well 890
Blaven Isle of Skye 779
Blaydon Brick Firebrick 744
Bleaklow Howard Town 775
Bleddyn Celt Experience 718
Blencathra Bitter Hesket
    Newmarket 769
Blenheim Bellinger's 694
    Oxfordshire Ales 819

Blind Boris Marlpool 797
The Blind Piper Old Inn 815
Blinding Light Prospect 827
Blodwens Beer Tomos
    Watkin 873
Blond Berkshire Bevy Two
    Bridges 867
Blond Bombshell Cannon
    Royall 716
Blond Witch Moorhouse's 804
Blond Ironbridge 778
    Nook 809
    Outstanding 819
    Partners 821
Blonde Ale Yates' 888
Blonde Ambition Tonbridge 863
Blonde Ash Wheat Beer
    Grain 755
Blonde Beer Sonnet 43 849
Blonde & Beyond Cap House 716
Blonde Bombshell Baldy 687
    Houston 775
    Old Mill 815
Blonde Moment George
    Wright 886
Blonde Pale Raw 830
Blonde Star Anarchy 681
Blonde Volupta Oldershaw 817
Blonde 8 Sail 677
    Acorn 678
    Arran 683
    Backyard 687
    Balmaha 687
    Bank Top 688
BLONDe Blackedge 699
BLONDe Brewmeister 707
    Bridgehouse 708
    Broughs 710
    Buxton 714
    Daleside 729
    DB 731
    Donegal 890
    Dukeries 736
    Eden St Andrews 738
    Ennerdale 740
    Great Heck 756
    Greenodd 760
    Hastings 766
    Healey's 767
    Hop Studio 773
    Imperial 777
    Joule's 781
    Junction 781
    Lancaster 786
    Lytham 794
    Magpie 795
    Quartz 828
    River Leven 835
    Saffron 838
    Saltaire 840
    Scarborough 841
    Spencer's 849
    Tatton 856
    Tring 865
    Wharfedale 877
    Windswept 882
Blondie Globe 752
    Grafton 755
Bloomers Beeston 693
Blooming Blonde Lion's Tale 790
Blorenge Tudor 866
Blue Eyed Dragon
    Whittlebury 879
Blue Hills Bitter Driftwood 736
Blue Moon George Wright 886

Blue Top Old Dairy *815*
Blue Tree Bitter Saddleworth *838*
Blue Atlantic *685*
  Ridgeway *834*
Bluebird Bitter Coniston *723*
Bluebird Premium XB
  Coniston *723*
Blush Naked *806*
Blythe's Spirit Worth *886*
Boadicea Rother Valley *837*
Boar D'eau Slaughterhouse *847*
Boathouse City of Cambridge
  (Wolf) *883*
Bob Wall Dawkins *731*
BOB/Brand Oak Bitter
  Wickwar *880*
Bobbin's Bitter Three B's *859*
Bobby Dazzler Brightside *708*
  Stables *851*
Bobby on the Wheat By the
  Horns *714*
Bobby's Best Bitter
  Brightside *708*
Bobmeister New Inn *807*
Bodelwyddan Bitter North
  Wales *810*
Bodkin's Bitter Hill Island *770*
Bog Standard Bitter Big Bog *695*
Bog Super IPA Big Bog *695*
Bog Trotter Poachers *825*
Boilers Golden Cornish Ale St
  Ives (Keltek) *782*
Boiling Well Ludlow *794*
Bolt Head Summerskills *854*
Bultmaker Timothy Taylor *857*
Bomb Atomic *685*
Bombay Bob New Inn *807*
Bombay IPA Dunscar Bridge *737*
Bomber County Tom Wood's *884*
Bomber Ambridge *681*
Bon Don Doon Wilson Potter *881*
Bonhomme Richard East
  Coast *738*
Bonnie n' Bitter Loch
  Lomond *792*
Bonnie n' Blonde Loch
  Lomond *792*
Bonny's Gold Golden Triangle *754*
Bonum Mild Dow Bridge *735*
Booze Hound Gun Dog *760*
Border Steeans Beckstones *692*
Border Untapped *869*
Boro Best North Yorkshire *810*
Bosun Bitter Old Laxey *815*
Bottle Wreck Porter
  Hammerpot *763*
Bottlenose Bitter Speyside
  Craft *850*
Boudicca Norwich Bear *811*
Bourbon Milk Stout Sonnet
  43 *849*
Bow Hauler Geeves *751*
Bowler Strong Ale Langton *786*
Bracken Pocket *825*
Bradley's Finest Golden Black
  Country *697*
Brainblásta Porterhouse *891*
Brainstorm Hopping Mad *774*
Braintree Market Ale
  Shalford *842*
Brakspear Special Bell Street *694*
Bramling Cross Broughton *710*
Brampton Bitter Geltsdale *752*
Brandeston Gold Earl Soham *737*
Brandy Snap Funfair *750*

Branoc Branscombe Vale *705*
Brass Thill Blackhill *699*
Brassed Off Spire *850*
Brassknocker Dawkins *731*
Brathay Gold Barngates *689*
Braveheart Moulin *805*
Breakfast Barum *690*
Breckland Gold Brandon *704*
Brecon County Ale
  Breconshire *706*
Brenin Bootliquor Nant *806*
Brenin Enlli Llŷn *791*
Brettvale Gold Kings Head *784*
Brew 1 Gower *755*
Brew Springsteen Rock &
  Roll *836*
Brewed Awakening
  Cromarty *727*
Brewer's Dark Lees *788*
Brewers Droop Marston
  Moor *797*
Brewers Gold Brew Company *706*
  Crouch Vale *728*
  Pictish *823*
  Wall's *872*
Brewers Progress Tipples *861*
Brewery Bitter Evan Evans *740*
Brewery Dug Arran *683*
Brewery Tap Bitter Hoggleys *771*
Brewhouse Bell Saffron *838*
Brickworks Bitter Bingham's *696*
The Brickyard Burley Street *712*
Bridge Bitter Burton Bridge *712*
Bridge Pale McGivern *795*
Bridge Street Bitter Green
  Dragon *758*
Bright Otter *818*
Brighton Best King *783*
Brighton Blonde King *783*
Brightwell Gold Appleford *682*
Brigstow Bitter Arbor *682*
Brimstone Abbeydale *678*
Brindle Bitter Longdog *793*
Brisons Bitter Penzance *822*
British Bulldog Westerham *877*
Broadland Bitter Uncle
  Stuarts *869*
Broadland Sunrise Humpty
  Dumpty *775*
Broadside Adnams *679*
Broadsword George's (Hop
  Monster) *773*
Broadway Reel Ale
  Nottingham *812*
Brock Bitter Tring *864*
Brockville Dark Tryst *865*
Brockville Pale Tryst *865*
Brockwell Leamside *787*
Brodie's Prime Hawkshead *766*
Broken Dream Breakfast Stout
  Siren Craft *846*
Broken Piston Hogswood *771*
Bronte Bitter Goose Eye *754*
Bronze Blakemere *699*
  Celt Experience *718*
Brooklyn Nights Hartshorns *765*
Brother Rabbit Thornbridge *858*
Brougham Ale Tirril *862*
Brown Ale Blakemere *699*
  Sonnet 43 *849*
Brown Bitter Strands *853*
Brown Rat Rat *830*
Brown's Porter Church Farm *719*
Bruins Ruin Beartown *692*
Brunette Greenodd *760*

BSA (Blonde Session Ale) Nene
  Valley *807*
Buckden Pike Yorkshire
  Dales *889*
Buckenham Woods Uncle
  Stuarts *869*
Buckeye Rooster's *836*
Buckley's Best WH Buckley (Evan
  Evans) *741*
Budding Moon Cambridge
  Moonshine *715*
Budding Stroud *854*
Buddy Marvellous Bryncelyn *711*
Buff Blindmans *699*
Bull Village (Hambleton) *763*
Bullion Nottingham *812*
  Old Mill *815*
Bulls Hit Pied Bull *823*
Bullseye Bitter Jolly Sailor *781*
Bullseye Langton *786*
Bumble Hole Bitter Olde
  Swan *816*
Bunny Chaser Longdog *793*
Bure Gold Woodforde's *885*
Buried At Sea Galway Bay *890*
Burnmoor Pale Ale Great
  Gable *756*
Burnout Brass Castle *705*
Burnsall Classic Briscoe's *709*
Burrough Bitter Parish *820*
Burston's Cuckoo Elmtree *739*
Burton Best Latimer *787*
Burton Bitter Marston's *797*
Burton Porter Burton Bridge *712*
Burton Snatch Fellows *743*
Business As Usual Derby *732*
Butter Tubs Yorkshire Dales *889*
Butterley Bitter Riverhead *835*
Butts Pale Ale Ashover *685*
Butty Bach Wye Valley *887*
Buzzard Dark Ale Cotleigh *725*
Buzzin' Frodsham *748*
BVB Best Bitter Branscombe
  Vale *705*

C

Cúl Dorcha Beoir Chorca
  Dhuibhne/West Kerry *889*
Cabarrus Gold Ole Slewfoot *817*
Caber Tosser Traditional Scottish
  Ales *864*
Cairnpapple IPA Alechemy *680*
Cais Snowdonia *848*
California Common Knops *785*
California AllGates *680*
  Brodie's *709*
Callow Top Imperial IPA
  Haywood Bad Ram *767*
Callum's Best Five Towns *745*
Callums Ale Front Street *748*
Cambria Great Orme *757*
Cambrian Gold Stonehouse *853*
Cambrian Heart Ale Heart of
  Wales *767*
Cambridge Bitter Elgood's *738*
Cambridge Fellow Fellows *743*
CamFell Flame WharfeBank *877*
Cannon Rock Tunnfield *866*
Cannon's Gold Highwood (Cann
  Do Beers) *770*
Canon Bitter Shoes *844*
Cap Lamp Merry Miner *800*
**Captain Bill Bartram's Best
  Bitter** Bartrams *690*

Captain Bob Mighty Oak 800
Captain Floyd DarkTribe 730
Captain Grumpy's Best Bitter
Wissey Valley 882
Captain Oates Mild Brown
Cow 710
Captain Smith's Strong Ale
Titanic 862
Captain's Stout Bartrams 690
Cariad Cych Valley 729
Carlisle State Bitter Derwent 732
Carmen Sutra Snowdonia 848
Carnival Ale Barlow 689
Carousel Southport 849
Carpenter's Cask Crafty Beers 727
Carraig Dubh Beoir Chorca
Dhuibhne/West Kerry 889
Carronade Pale Ale Tryst 865
Cart Blanche Kelburn 782
Cart Noir Kelburn 782
Cartmel Peninsula Unsworth's
Yard 869
Cascade Pale Ale Saltaire 840
Cascade Boggart Hole Clough 701
Cerddin 718
Liverpool Organic 791
Ridgeside 834
Cascades Scarborough 841
Cascadian Blonde Tempest 857
Cascadian Kemptown 782
Cascale Wilson Potter 881
Casino Blakemere 699
Cask Ale McMullen 795
Caskade Oldershaw 817
Cast Iron Consett Ale Works 723
Castell Coch Celt Experience 718
Castle Ale Corfe Castle 724
Castle Dungeon Cathedral
Heights 717
Castle Gold Extra Tintagel 861
Castle Gold Tintagel 861
Castle Hill Premium
Mallinson's 796
Castle Mild Warwickshire 872
Castle Arundel 684
Castletown Bitter Bushy's 713
Cat Nap Barngates 689
Catbells Pale Ale Hesket
Newmarket 769
Cathedral Ale Hill Island 770
Catherine Bartram's IPA
Bartrams 690
Cats Eyes IPA Sleaford 847
Cats Whiskers Beeches 692
Cat's Whiskers Bartrams 690
Caudle Bitter Langton 786
Causeway Cornish Crown 725
Cavalier Red Why Not 879
Cavendish Bridge Shardlow 842
Cavendish Dark Shardlow 842
Cavendish Gold Shardlow 842
Cavendish Welbeck Abbey 874
CB1 Best Bitter Cambridge
Moonshine 715
Celebration Ale Conwy 723
Ulverston 868
Celebration Maypole 798
Porterhouse 891
Celestial Blonde Full Moon 749
Celestial Love Out There 819
Celtic Black Ale Hebridean 767
Celtic Gold Hereford 768
Celtic Red Cych Valley 729
Celtica Great Orme 757
Centennial Fernandes 744

Centurion Corinium 725
Dow Bridge 735
Centurion's Ghost Ale York 888
Cereal Killer North Yorkshire 810
Chained Oak Peakstones
Rock 821
Challenge 2.5 Malthouse 796
Challenger II Small Paul's 847
Challenger Kingstone 784
Chamberlain Pale Ale Two
Towers 867
Chancellors Revenge
Shardlow 842
Chapelfields Best Hearsall 767
Charcoal Burner High Weald 770
Chardonnayle Bob's 701
Charger St George's 839
Chase Bitter Blythe 701
Chasewater Bitter Beowulf 694
Chatsworth Gold Peak Ales 821
Chaucer Ale Green Dragon 758
Chawden Aur Nant 806
CHB Chalk Hill 718
Cheap Street Sherborne 843
Cheating Rat Rat 830
Cheeky Pheasant George
Wright 886
Cheltenham Flyer Humpty
Dumpty 776
Chennai Kissingate 785
Chequered Flag Silverstone 845
Cherokee America IPA
Hamelsworde 763
Cherry Blonde Enville 740
Cherry Diva New Plassey 808
Cherry Stout Bartrams 690
Chesbrewnette Lion's Tale 790
Cheshire Cat Weetwood 874
Cheshire Gold Coach House 721
Cheshire IPA Dunham
Massey 737
Chester Best Blacker & Son 699
Chesterfield Best Bitter Spire 850
Chestnut Mare Worsthorne 885
Chestnut Porter Belleville 694
Chestnut Burton Old Cottage 713
Cheswold Doncaster 734
Chevin Light Briscoe's 709
CHI P A Gribble 760
Chiddingstone Larkins 787
Chief Green Mill 758
Child Catcher Halifax Steam 762
Chilli Hopstar 774
Chinook Blonde Goose Eye 754
Chinook Caveman 717
Chiswick Bitter Fuller's 749
Chivalry Medieval 799
Choc Pot 80/- TinPot 860
Choc's Away Vale of
Glamorgan 870
Chockwork Orange
Brentwood 706
Chococino Dark Beer
Dominion 734
Chocoholic Tiny Rebel 861
Chocolate Cherry Mild Dunham
Massey 737
Chocolate Marble Marble 797
Chocolate Nutter Why Not 879
Chocolate Orange Stout
Amber 681
Cambridge Moonshine 715
Chocolate & Vanilla Stout
Titanic 862
Chorlton Pale Ale Bootleg 702

Chuffin Ale Box Steam 703
Church Ledge Noss Beer
Works 811
Churches Pale Ale FILO 744
Churchill IPA Oxfordshire
Ales 819
Churchills Pride Cathedral
Heights 717
Ciste Dhubh Plockton 824
Citadel Clun 721
Citra IPA Franklins 747
Citra Star Anarchy 681
Citra AllGates 680
Brodie's 709
Caveman 717
Isca 778
Oakham 812
Verulam 870
Citrade Talke O' Th' Hill 855
Citradelic Melwood 799
Citropolis Golden Triangle 754
Citrus Snap Green Mill 758
City Gold Golden Triangle 754
City Pale Ale Golden Triangle 754
Clansman Ale Hebridean 767
Claridges Crystal Nobby's 808
Clash London Porter
Revolutions 833
Classic Bitter Cliff Quay 720
Kingstone 784
Classic Blonde Clark's 720
Classic English Ale 3 Brewers 677
Classic Gold Great Western 758
Classic IPA Navigation 806
Ripple Steam 835
Classic Old Ale Hepworth 768
Classic Caythorpe 718
Copthorne 724
Hafod 762
Norwich Bear 811
Claverhouse Strathaven 853
Claybrooke Bitter Pig Pub 823
Claymore Ordnance City 817
Cleopatra Derventio 732
Cleric's Cure Three Tuns 859
Clever Fellow Fellows 744
Cliffhanger Brass Castle 705
Clipper IPA Broughton 710
Clipper Redstone 833
Clippings IPA Flipside 746
Clock Brew Eden St Andrews 738
Clogwyn Gold Conwy 723
Clotworthy Dobbin
Whitewater 878
Cloud Nine Six Bells 846
Cloudburst Winter's 882
Cloven Hoof Concrete Cow 723
Club Bitter Concertina 722
Clwyd Gold Facer's 742
Clyde Puffer Arran 683
Clydesdale Strathaven 853
Coachman's Best Bitter Coach
House 721
Coal Porter Spire 850
Coalface Firebrick 744
Coalport Mild Shires 844
Coast to Coast Hadrian
Border 761
Cobb Town Mill 863
Cobbydale Bitter Barley
Bottom 688
Cobbydale Blonde Barley
Bottom 688
Cobbydale Gold Barley
Bottom 688

Cobnut Kent 783
Cochyn Llŷn 791
Cock 'n' Bull Story Concrete Cow 723
Cock O' the Walk Williams 880
Cock Pit/Cadlas Ceiliogod Denbigh 731
Cock Robin Loch Leven 792
Cocker Hoop Jennings 780
Cockfighter Wicked Hathern (Staffordshire) 851
Cockleroy Black IPA Alechemy 680
Code Black Hardknott 764
Codger Cotswold Spring 726
Coffee in the Morning Tap East 856
Coffee & Oatmeal Stout Dungarvan 890
Coffee Porter Muirhouse 805
Coffee Stout Bingham's 696
Coffin Lane Stout Ashover 685
Coffin Nail Mr Grundy's 805
Coggeshall Gold Red Fox 831
Cold Fell Geltsdale 752
Cold Fusion Hardknott 764
Colin Brown Ale Hamelsworde 763
Collaborator Heavy Industry 767
Collapsed Front Row 748
Colley's Dog Tring 865
Collie Wobbles Watermill 873
Collingwood Festival Ale Wylam 887
Columbus Bottle Brook 702
Comanchie Copthorne 724
Comeragh Challenger Dungarvan 890
Comet Globe 752
Commando Hoofing Cotleigh 725
Commodore East Coast 738
Common Fulstow 750
Commonside Pale Ale Belleville 694
Comrade Bill Bartram's Egalitarian Anti Imperialist Soviet Stout Bartrams 690
Confessor Fisher 745
Conkerwood Lord Conrad's 794
Conqueror Windsor & Eton 881
Conservation Bitter Red Squirrel 832
Continuum Hardknott 764
Contraband Bootleg 702 Jollyboat 781
Conviction IPA Elixir 739
Cooking Grainstore 756
Coopers WPA Wickwar 880
Copper Ale Palmers 820
Copper Cascade Stewart 852
Copper Caskade Greenfield 759
Copper Coast Dungarvan 890
Copper Fox Mayfields 798
Copper Nob Tonbridge 863
Copper Penny Flipside 745
Copper Plate Irwell Works 778
Copper Top Old Dairy 815
Copper Ennerdale 740 Hunsbury Craft 776 Wainstones 871
Copperhead Whitewater 878
Coppice Light Coppice Side 724
Coppice Worth 886
Coppy Lane Stables 851
Corby Ale Cumberland 728

Corby Blonde Cumberland 729
Core Commander Nelson 807
Corn Dolly Three Castles 859
Corncrake Orkney 818
Cornerstone Keystone 783
Cornish Arvor Penpont 822
Cornish Bronze Coastal 721
Cornish Buccaneer Wooden Hand 884
Cornish Coaster Sharp's 842
Cornish Gribben Wooden Hand 884
Cornish Knocker Ale Skinner's 846
Cornish Mutiny Wooden Hand 885
Cornish Shag Roseland 836
Cornish Sunset Rebel 831
Cornucopia Copper Kettle 724
Cornwall's Pride Tintagel 861
Cosmic Black Hole 697
Cossack Copthorne 724
Cotswold Best North Cotswold 809
Cotswold Way Wickwar 880
Cotswold Cotswold 726
Country Bitter McMullen 795
Country Bumpkin Country Life 726
County Best Exeter 741 Wall's 872
Courage Best Bitter Wells & Young's 875
Courage Directors Wells & Young's 875
Coventry Bitter Byatt's 714
Coverdale Gamekeeper Wensleydale 875
Coverdale Poacher IPA Wensleydale 876
Cowgirl Gold Broxbourne 710
Coyote Bitter Wolf 883
CPA/Carmarthen Pale Ale Kite 785
Crab & Winkle Mild Railway Tavern 829
Crack of Dawn Pale Ale Late Knights 787
Crack Shot Hunter's 776
Cracker Ale Barngates 689
Cracker Quartz 828
Crafty Stoat Wibblers 879
Cragg Vale Bitter Little Valley 790
Crazy Cascade Mad Hatter 795
Crazy Daze Potbelly 826
Crazy Horse American IPA – Maverik Norfolk Square 809
Crazy Kiwi Sleaford 847
Crest Craddock's 727
Cresta Tempest 857
Cribyn Breconshire 706
Criffel Sulwath 854
Crime Scene Anarchy 681
Crix Forest Felstar 744
Croak & Stagger Frog Island 748
Crockerton Classic Wessex 876
Crofters Pale Ale An Teallach 681
Crofters FILO 744
The Cromwell Door Pride of Cartmel 1643 Unsworth's Yard 869
Cromwells Best Bitter Coach House 721
Crooked Elbow Whitworth 879
Crooked Furrow Leith Hill 789

Crop Circle Hop Back 772
Crouch Front Row 748
Croupier Gambling Man 751
Crowlas Bitter Penzance 822
Crown Dark Mild Cox & Holbrook 727
Crown & Glory Whitewater 878
Crown Imperial Stout Goacher's 753
Crowning Glory Leyden 789
Crucible Best Sheffield 843
Crusade St George's 839
Crusader Medieval 799 Milestone 801
Crystal Tips North Yorkshire 810
Crystal Quartz 828
Cub Panther Panther 820
Cue Brew Jolly Sailor 781
Cuil Hill Sulwath 854
Cuillin Beast Isle of Skye 779
Cumberland Ale Jennings 780
Cumbria Way Robinsons 835
Cumbrian Five Hop Hawkshead 766
Cummertrees Pale Ale Andrews 682
Cunning Stunt Fuzzy Duck 750
Curim Gold Wheat Beer Carlow 890
Curious Magic Rock 795
Cuthberts Church End 719
Cuzzy Brew Elixir 739
Cwrw Blasus Coles 722
Cwrw Braf Tomos Watkin 873
Cwrw Coryn Nant 806
Cwrw Dewi Vale of Glamorgan 870
Cwrw Eryri/Snowdonia Ale Purple Moose 827
Cwrw Glaslyn/Glaslyn Ale Purple Moose 827
Cwrw Gorslas Kite 785
Cwrw Gwynant Gwynant 761
Cwrw Haf Vale of Glamorgan 870
Cwrw Madog/Madog's Ale Purple Moose 827
Cwrw Tudno New Plassey 808
Cwrw Evan Evans 740
Cwrw'r Ddraig Aur Robinsons 835
Cwtch Tiny Rebel 861
Cyclone Southport 849
Cyclops Milton 802
Cygnet Swan 855
Cyneweard Malvern Hills 796

D

Dabley Gold Shires 844
Daggers Ale Three Daggers 859
Dainty Blonde Privateer 827
Daisy Gold Brightwater 708
Dale Ale Corvedale 725
Dambuster Amber 681
Damn Gates Burton 751
Damson Porter 8 Sail 677 Burton Bridge 713
Dangerously Dark Happy Valley 764
Danish Dynamite Stonehenge 852
Danny Frodsham 748
Dark Age Celt Experience 718
Dark Ale Archerfield (Knops) 785 Gas Dog 751

BEERS INDEX

Jacobi 780
Pheasantry 822
Dark Alliance Moor 804
Dark Ark Ale Frodsham 748
Dark Arts Magic Rock 795
Trouble 891
Dark & Dangerous Tap House 856
Dark & Delicious Corvedale 725
Snowdonia 848
Dark Delight Downton 736
Dark Denomination Flipside 745
Dark Drake Dancing Duck 729
Dark Dunter Broughton 710
Dark Energy Hardknott 764
Dark Gem Caythorpe 718
Dark Hart Festival Reserve
Harthill Village 765
Dark Hart Harthill Village 765
Dark Horse Barlow 689
Belvoir 694
Elmtree 739
Farmer's 743
Hepworth 768
Loose Cannon 794
Scottish Borders 841
Dark Island Orkney 818
Dark Knight Eden 738
Hopstar 774
Independent Lakeland
(Strands) 853
Dark Matter Baseline 690
Dark Mild Bank Top 687
Batemans 690
Boggart Hole Clough 701
Bridestones 707
Dominion 733
Foxfield 747
Golcar 753
Healey's 767
Jennings 780
Timothy Taylor 856
Dark Moor Kelburn 782
Dark Munro Highland 770
Dark Ness Loch Ness 792
Dark Night Clearwater 720
Southport 849
Dark Peak Howard Town 775
Raw 830
Dark Raven Beowulf 694
Dark Revenge Privateer 827
Dark Ruby Mild Sarah
Hughes 775
Dark Seam Black Paw 698
Dark Side of the Moon Spire 850
Dark Side Stout Rowton 837
Dark Swan Olde Swan 816
Dark Thoughts Junction 781
The Dark Un White Dog 878
Dark Wheat Mild Tigertops 860
Dark Arran 683
Brains 704
Gwaun Valley 761
Hereford 768
Lamb 786
Ledbury 788
Liverpool One 791
Lytham 795
Rhymney 833
River Leven 835
Darker Side of the Moon
Grafters 755
Darkest Ennerdale 740
Darkness Exeter 741
Imperial 777
Darkside Stout Brightside 708

The Darkside Wall's 872
Darling Buds Warwickshire 873
Dartford Wobbler Millis 801
Dartmoor Best Bitter St
Austell 839
Darwin's Origin Salopian 840
Dashingly Dark Derby 732
Dave Great Heck 756
David Hopperfield
Dickensian 733
David's Not So Bitter Spey
Valley 849
Davy's Lamp Merry Miner 800
Dawlish Bitter Isca 778
Dawlish Pale Isca 778
Dawn's Autumn Gold Hay
Rake 766
Dawn's Called Thyme Hay
Rake 766
Dawn's Dark Side Hay Rake 766
Dawn's Hopping Mad Hay
Rake 766
DB Number One Dorking 734
DBA Cheshire 719
DBB (Dunscar Best Bitter)
Dunscar Bridge 737
DCUK Dancing Duck 729
De Lovetot Dukeries 736
Deadhead Melwood 799
Death or Glory Tring 865
Decadence Brewster's 707
Decided Havant 766
Deco IPA Sportsman 850
Decoy Mallard 796
Deep Porter New Plassey 808
Deep Slade Dark Swansea 855
The Deep Big River 696
Deer Beer Dunham Massey 737
Deerstalker Ramsbury 829
Dek Driftwood 736
Delapre Dark Great Oakley 757
Deliverance APA Pixie Spring 824
Deliverance Cambrinus (Liverpool
Organic) 791
Delph Donkey Greenfield 759
Denbury Dreamer Hunter's 776
Dengie Best Wibblers 879
Dengie Dark Wibblers 879
Dengie Gold Wibblers 879
Dengie IPA Wibblers 879
Deputy Drop Merry Miner 800
Derail Ale Box Steam 703
Derby Pale Ale Wentwell 876
Derbyshire Gold Amber 681
Wentwell 876
Desert Aire Ridgeside 834
Detention Old School 816
Detonator Ordnance City 817
Deuchars IPA Caledonian 715
Deverill's Advocate Wessex 876
Devil's Backbone Kinnegar 891
Devil's Elbow Hexhamshire 769
Devil's Garden Frodsham 748
Devils Chair Tunnfield 866
Devils Dream Ole Slewfoot 817
Devils Dyke Honey Porter
Downlands 735
Devils Dyke Porter
Downlands 735
Devils Nightmare Cathedral
Heights 717
Devil's Water Hexhamshire 769
Devolution Amber Ale
Revolutions 833
Devon Darter Clearwater 720

Devon Dew Summerskills 854
Devon Dumpling Bays 691
Devon Dympsy Clearwater 720
Devon Glory Exe Valley 741
Devon Pride South Hams 849
Devon's Pride Masters 798
Devonshire Piglet Country
Life 726
Dewhopper Lager Norfolk 809
DHB (Dave's Hoppy Beer)
Facer's 742
Diablo Summer Wine 854
Diamond Black Stout
Chantry 718
Diamond Geezer By the
Horns 714
Diamond Lil Two Cocks 867
Diana Mild Whalebone 877
Dick Turpin Coach House 721
Dictators Concertina 722
Diesel Colchester 721
Diggers Gold Grey Trees 760
Dilks Shottle Farm 845
Dinner Ale Bollington 702
Dinting Arches Howard Town 775
Dionysus Milton 802
Directionless RedWillow 833
Dirty Rat Rat 830
Dirty Stopout Tiny Rebel 861
Discovery – Easterly Atlantic 685
Discovery – Northerly
Atlantic 685
Discovery – Southerly
Atlantic 685
Discovery – Westerly Atlantic 685
Discovery Captain Cook 717
Forge 746
Fuller's 749
Dissolution IPA Kirkstall 785
Dive Bomber Funfair 750
Dixie's Mild DarkTribe 730
Dixon's Major Riverside 835
Dizzy Blonde Robinsons 835
Dizzy Danny Ale Hopstar 774
Dizzy Dick North Yorkshire 811
Dobber Marble 797
Dob's Best Bitter Exe Valley 741
Dobcross Bitter Greenfield 759
DOC First Chop 744
Dockside Dark Gloucester 753
Doctor Johnsons
Leatherbritches 788
Dodgem Funfair 750
Doff Cocker Three B's 859
Dog Idle 776
Doghouse Publisher 827
Dogth Vader Watermill 873
Dogwatch Stout Nelson 807
Dolly Daydream Ship Inn 844
Dolphin Amber Sunny
Republic 855
Doodle Stout Bingham's 696
Doom Bar Sharp's 842
Doppelbock White Gypsy 891
Doris's 90th Birthday Ale Hesket
Newmarket 769
Dorothy Goodbody's Golden Ale
Wye Valley 887
Dorothy Goodbody's
Wholesome Stout Wye
Valley 887
Dorset Cross Sunny Republic 855
Dorset Gold Palmers 820
Dorset Knob Dorset (DBC) 734

Double Belgium Hand Drawn Monkey 763
Double Brown Ale Colchester 722
Double Dragon Felinfoel 743
Double Gold Phoenix 823
Double Header RCH 830
Double Hop Robinsons 836
Double Mash Derby 732
Double Six Fernandes 744
Double Standard Nine Standards (Settle) 841
Double Stout Hook Norton 772
Dove Elder Dove Street 735
Dove Street Bitter (DSB) Dove Street 735
Dovedale Leatherbritches 788
Dover Beck Caythorpe 718
Dow Bridge Dark (DBD) Dow Bridge 735
DPA Peak Ales 821
Dr Heale Heddon Valley (Country Life) 726
Dr Hexter's Healer West Berkshire 877
Dr Hexter's Wedding Ale West Berkshire 876
Dr Okell's IPA Okells 814
Dr Samuel Johnson Haywood Bad Ram 767
Draft Marble 797
Dragon Slayer B&T 686
Dragon Smoke Stout Beowulf 694
Dragon Bowland 703
Dragon's Blood Sawbridgeworth 841
Dragon's Breath Dartmoor 730
Dragonfly Fallen (Traditional Scottish Ales) 864
Dragonhead Orkney 817
Dragons Blood St George's 839
Dragons Breath New Plassey 808
Dragonslayer Merlin 799
Draught Bass AB InBev (Marston's) 797
Draught Burton Ale Carlsberg (Lees) 788
Draymans Best Bitter Branscombe Vale 705
Dreadnought Chalk Hill 718
Nottingham 812
Dreckly Forge 746
Drop of the Black Stuff Springhead 851
Drop of Nelson's Blood Farmer's 742
Drops of Jupiter Bumpmill 711
Drovers 80/- Tryst 865
Druid's Fluid Wizard 883
Drum Beat Treboom 864
Drunken Duck George Wright 886
Drunkun Duck Green Duck 758
The Dry Road Beeston 693
Dry Stout O'Hanlon's 812
Drystone Stout Hawkshead 766
dt3 DT 736
dt4 DT 736
Duality Hardknott 764
Dubbel Trubbel Long Itch 793
Duchess Cottage 726
Duck 'n' Dive Mallard 796
Duck Blonde Green Duck 758
Duck Hunter Gundog 761
Duck's Courage Dancing Duck 729

Ducking Stool Mayfields 798
Duckling Mallard 796
Due South Strathbraan 853
Duke of Lancaster Burscough 712
Dun Cow Bitter Hill Island 770
Dun Hogs Head Ale Islay 779
Dunham Dark Dunham Massey 737
Dunham Gold Dunham Massey 737
Dunham Light Dunham Massey 737
Dunham Milk Stout Dunham Massey 737
Dunham Porter Dunham Massey 737
Dunham Stout Dunham Massey 737
Dunkelweiss Tigertops 860
Dunstable Giant B&T 686
Durdle Door Dorset (DBC) 734
Dursley Steam Bitter Severn Vale 841
Dusk Ruby Ale Cross Bay 728
Dusky Maiden Stout New Plassey 808
DV8 Deeply Vale 731
DXB (Special Bitter) Nene Valley 807
Dynamo Wantsum 872

E

E Worthington's 886
Eagle Ale Cuillin 728
Earl's Ale Tollgate 862
Earls Folly/Ffoled yr Iarl Denbigh 732
Earls RDA Island 779
Early Dawn Hay Rake 766
East Anglian Pale Ale Cox & Holbrook 727
Humpty Dumpty 776
East Coast Mild Waveney 873
East End Mild Tap East 856
East India Pale Ale Dunham Massey 737
Tunnel 866
Whitstable 879
East Street Cream RCH 830
East Sussex Bitter Turners 866
East Adventure 679
Eastern Nights Bollington 702
Eastgate Ale Weetwood 874
Easy Rider Kelham Island 782
Ebb Rock Noss Beer Works 811
Ebony Moon Tonbridge 863
Ebony Stout Wood Street 884
Ebony Goldmark 754
Ebulum Williams 880
Eclipse Porter Brew Company 706
Eclipse Blacker & Son 699
Untapped 869
Eco Warrior Dominion 734
Ed Porter Dove Street 735
Eddystone South Hams 849
Eden Valley Pale Ale Tirril 862
Eden Elland 739
Edge Pale Raw 830
Edge Kinver 783
Sandstone 840
Edinburgh Gold Stewart 852
Edinburgh No.3 Premium Scotch Ale Stewart 852
Edith Cavell Wolf 883

Edwin Taylor's Extra Stout B&T 686
Ein Stein Lymestone 794
ELB Pale Ale East London 738
Elder Statesman Firebrick 744
Elderado Bowman 703
Elderflower Blonde Saltaire 840
Elderquad Downton 736
Eleanor Cross Great Oakley 757
Eleanor's Ise Whistling Kite 878
Electric Mountain Heavy Industry 767
Eliminator Ridgeside 834
Elmo's Fire Moles 803
Elmstead Stout Sticklegs 852
Elsie Mo Castle Rock 717
Emerald IPA White Gypsy 891
Emley Moor Mild Mallinson's 796
Empire Liverpool Organic 791
Empress of India East Coast 738
Encore Lacons 786
Endeavour Captain Cook 717
North Star 810
Endurance Cambrinus (Liverpool Organic) 791
Engage Front Row 748
Engel's Best Bitter Opa Hay's 817
Engel's Fruity Little Number Opa Hay's 817
Engine Vein Cheshire 719
English Ale Salisbury 840
Son of Sid 848
Weighbridge 874
English Electric Lightning Baseline 690
English Garden Franklins 747
English Oak Mighty Oak 800
English Pale Ale Buxton 714
English Hop Fuzz 772
Enigma Kent 783
Spire 850
Entire Stout Hop Back 772
Entire Cronx 727
Olde Swan 816
EP Session Pale Revolutions 833
EP Elgood's 738
EPA (English Pale Ale) Bluestone 701
EPA 100 Harwich Town 765
EPA Barum 690
Marston's 797
Epping Forest Bitter Epping (Dominion) 734
Equinox Melwood 799
Erimus Pale Ale Truefitt 865
Erosion Coastal 721
Erradale IPA Old Inn 815
Errmmm... Strands 853
ESB Fuller's 749
ESP Full Mash 749
Espresso Dark Star 730
Essex Beast Growler 760
Essex Border Growler 760
Essex Boys Best Bitter Crouch Vale 728
Essex IPA Highwood (Cann Do Beers) 770
Essex Pale Ale Saffron 838
Essington Ale Morton 805
Essington Bitter Morton 805
Essington Blonde Morton 805
Essington Gold Morton 805
Essington IPA Morton 805
Esthwaite Bitter Cumbrian Legendary 729

Estivator Old Bear *814*
Even Keel Keltek *782*
 Preseli *826*
Evening Star Evening Star *741*
Excalibur Reserve George's (Hop
 Monster) *773*
Excalibur George's (Hop
 Monster) *773*
 Medieval *799*
 Merlin *799*
Excelsior Ossett *818*
 Uncle Stuarts *869*
Exciseman's 80/- Broughton *710*
Exeter Old Bitter Exe Valley *741*
Exile Redstone *833*
Explorer IPA Wall's *872*
Explorer Adnams *679*
Export Ale Rhymney *834*
Export Stout Weltons *875*
Extinction Ale Darwin *731*
Extra Blonde Quartz *828*
Extra Pale Ale Nottingham *811*
Extra Stout Snout
 Slaughterhouse *847*
Extreme Concertina *722*
Eyrie Truman's *865*

F

Fade to Black Weird Beard *874*
Fagin's Itchen Valley *780*
Fair Puggled Argyll *683*
Fairfax Special Marston Moor *797*
Fairfield Emsworth *740*
Falcon Gold Isca *778*
Falcon Hell Loch Leven *792*
Falconer Session Bitter
 Wensleydale *875*
Fallen Angel Church End *719*
Fallen Tree Twisted Oak *866*
Falls Gold Tillingbourne *860*
Fallwood XXXX Haworth
 Steam *766*
Farm Gold Parish *820*
Farm Hands' Bitter Wentwell *876*
Farmer Rays Ale Corvedale *725*
Farmer's Delight Verulam *870*
Farmer's Joy Verulam *870*
Farmers Bitter Bradfield *703*
Farmers Blonde Bradfield *703*
Farmers Dark Ale Attwood *685*
Farmers Stout Bradfield *703*
Farmhouse Ale Spitting
 Feathers *850*
Farmhouse Gwaun Valley *761*
Farne Island Pale Ale Hadrian
 Border *761*
Farrier's Ale Shoes *844*
Farrier's Best Bitter Coach
 House *721*
Farriers 1606 Farriers Arms *743*
Father Hawkins Prior's Well *826*
Father Mike's Dark Rich Ruby
 Brunswick *710*
Feather Light Mallard *796*
Feckless RedWillow *833*
Fee de Bretagne Pocket *825*
Feelgood Malvern Hills *796*
Fellowship Middle Earth *800*
Felstar Felstar *744*
Fenny Popper Concrete Cow *723*
Ferryman Exeter *741*
Ferryman's Gold Loddon *792*
Festival Ale Burton Bridge *713*

Festival Special Bitter Mighty
 Hop *800*
Festival Dark Star *730*
Festive King *783*
Fiddler's Jig Dancing Man *730*
Fiddlers Fancy Plockton *824*
Fiery Redhead Baldy *687*
Figgy's Brew Skinner's *846*
Filly Close Blonde Reedley
 Hallows *833*
Finchcocks Original
 Westerham *877*
Fine Light Ale Goacher's *753*
Fine Soft Day Iceni *776*
Finished Havant *766*
Finlaggan Ale Islay *779*
Finn's Hall Porter Beowulf *694*
Fire Raven Cornish Chough *725*
Firebeard's Old Favourite No. 5
 Ruby Ale Fownes *747*
Firebox RCH *830*
Firebrick Neath *807*
Fireside Arran *683*
 Black Country *697*
Firkin Folly Garage *751*
Firkin Point Balmaha *687*
First Aviation Doncaster *734*
First Brew Wirksworth *882*
First Deal Blackjack *699*
First Emperor Eden *738*
First Flight White Park *878*
First Gold Hall & Woodhouse
 (Badger) *762*
First Hand Big Hand *695*
Fission Atomic *685*
Fist Full of Hops Falstaff *742*
Fistral Atlantic *685*
Five Bells Shardlow *842*
Five Bridge Bitter Mordue *804*
Five Quarter Leamside *787*
Five Rings Happy Valley *763*
Five Rivers Sheffield *843*
Five Sisters Alechemy *680*
Flack Catcher Flack Manor *745*
Flack's Double Drop Flack
 Manor *745*
Flagship IPA O'Hanlon's *812*
Flanders Ale Wolf *883*
Flapjack Black Hop Kettle *773*
Flashmans Clout Dorset
 (DBC) *734*
Flat Cap Bank Top *687*
Flat Rib Mild Burscough *712*
Flavia Green Mill *758*
Flaxen Jade Frodsham *748*
Flint Knapper Ramsbury *829*
Flintknapper's Mild Chalk Hill *718*
Flintlock Pale Ale Coach
 House *721*
Flintshire Bitter Facer's *742*
Flipping Best Flipside *745*
Flora Daze/Spingo Original Blue
 Anchor *700*
Floral Dance Rossendale *837*
Floss the Boss Hartshorns *765*
Flotsam Hadrian Border *761*
Flour Power 8 Sail *677*
Flower Power Whim *878*
Flurry Windy *882*
The Flush Gundog *761*
Flying Cloud Stamps *851*
Flying Elephants Ulverston *868*
Flying Herbert North
 Yorkshire *810*
Flying Man Brass Castle *705*

Flying Saucer Vibrant Forest *870*
Flying Scotsman Caledonian *715*
Fog on the Tyne
 Northumberland *811*
Folden Cross Beowulf *694*
Folly Ale Faringdon *742*
Fools Gold North Yorkshire *810*
Fools Nook Digfield *733*
Forbury Lion Loddon *792*
Forever Bury Leyden *789*
Forkin' Best Shed Ales *843*
Fortitude Wantsum *872*
Fortyniner Ringwood *834*
Fosse Ale Dow Bridge *735*
Fossil Fuel Isle of Purbeck *779*
Foundation Bitter East
 London *738*
Foundation Stone
 Lymestone *794*
Founders Bitter Hurst *776*
Foundries IPA Muirhouse *805*
Foundry Red Rye Canterbury
 Brewers *716*
Foundry Torpedo Canterbury
 Brewers *716*
Foundryman's Gold Canterbury
 Brewers *716*
Four Seasons' Ale Halfpenny *762*
Four Stones Radnorshire *829*
Four XT *887*
Fowler's 80/- Prestonpans *826*
Fox Glove Slightly Foxed *847*
Fox Hunter Cap House *716*
Fox on the Run Ole Slewfoot *817*
Fox Exmoor *741*
 Gundog *761*
 Uffa *868*
Foxstones Worsthorne *885*
Foxtail Alcazar *679*
Foxy Blonde Scottish Borders *841*
Foxy Lady Joseph Herbert
 Smith *848*
Fra Diavolo Ulverston *868*
Fraid Not Exeter *741*
Frankies Gold Kendal *782*
Fraoch Heather Ale Williams *880*
Freak Show Hop Monster *773*
Frenchman's Creek Lizard *791*
Fresh Breeze Windy *882*
Fresher Ale Plymouth *824*
Freshly Squeezed Blakemere *699*
Friar Tuck Stout Robin Hood *835*
Friar Tuck St George's *839*
Friar Weisse Franciscan Well *890*
Friend of the Devil Ole
 Slewfoot *817*
Friendship Porter
 Redemption *832*
Frigate Irving *778*
Friggin' in the Riggin'
 Nelson *807*
Frightened Pheasant Blue
 Bell *700*
Froda's Ale Frodsham *748*
Frontier IPA Brew Company *706*
Frost Hammer Fownes *747*
Frothingham Best Great
 Newsome *757*
Fruit Bat B&T *686*
Fruitcase Hopping Mad *774*
Fruiterers Mild Cannon Royall *716*
Frydeal Fry's *749*
Fubar Tiny Rebel *861*
Fuggle Eden *738*
Fuggle-Dee-Dum Goddards *753*

Fuggles Pale Swan 855
Fulflood Best Fulflood Arms 749
Full Ahead DarkTribe 730
Full Circle West Berkshire 877
The Full Malty Greenfield 759
Full Monty Barlow 689
The Full Nelson Tiny Rebel 861
Full Nelson Two Roses 867
Full Sail Galway Bay 890
Full Whack Peerless 821
The Full Wood George N
  Porter 825
Fully Fitted Freight
  Muirhouse 805
Fully Laden Geeves 751
Funky Monkey Milk Street 801
Funnel Blower Box Steam 703
Fuzzy Duck Gribble 760
Fyre Fyfe 750

G

Gadds Faithful DogBolter
  Ramsgate 829
Gadds' No. 3 Ramsgate 829
Gadds' No. 5 Ramsgate 829
Gadds' No. 7 Ramsgate 829
Gadds' Seasider Ramsgate 829
Galaxy Rowton 837
  Spencer's 849
  Two Roses 867
Gale Force Longhill 793
Gallopers Funfair 750
Galloway Gold Sulwath 854
Gallowgate Raw Three Kings 859
Gambit Summer Wine 854
Game Bird Scottish Borders 841
Game Keeper Gold Gundog 761
Game Keeper Milestone 801
Gamekeepers Bitter
  Hereford 768
Ganges Harwich Town 765
Gannet Mild Earl Soham 737
Gap Cheshire 719
Gardener's Tap Prior's Well 826
Garsdale Smokebox Yorkshire
  Dales 889
Gate Hopper Maypole 798
Gavel Bitter Justice 781
GB Best Grainstore 756
GB Canterbury Brewers 716
Gem Bath Ales 691
General's Tipple Woodlands 885
Genesis Goody 754
Genius Winter's 882
Geordie Pride Mordue 804
George Stephenson IPA Evening
  Star 741
Georgie's Pebble Red 831
German Hops Pils Tryst 866
Gertcha! Old Cross 815
Ghost Ale Darwin 731
Ghost Ship Adnams 679
Ghost Partners 821
Gillingham Pale Small Paul's 848
Gilt Complex Surrey Hills 855
Ginger Bear Beartown 692
Ginger Beer Enville 740
Ginger Cob Shires 844
Ginger Cockney Quantock 828
Ginger Doodle Stout
  Bingham's 696
Ginger Fix Tigertops 860
Ginger Helmet
  Leatherbritches 788

Ginger Jakey Argyll 683
Ginger Pale Ale Little Valley 790
Ginger Panther Panther 820
Ginger Tosser Skinner's 846
Ginger Marble 797
  Uncle Stuarts 869
Gisleham Gold Trinity 865
Gladiator Dow Bridge 735
Glen Top Rossendale 837
Glencoe Wild Oat Stout
  Traditional Scottish Ales 864
Gloriette Corfe Castle 724
Glorious Devon Isca 778
Glory Daze Bumpmill 711
Glory Yeovil 888
Glott's Hop Howard Town 775
Go West Sleaford 847
Goat Sanctuary Tom Smith 848
Goat's Leap Cheddar 719
Goats Milk Church End 719
Gobble Great Oakley 757
Godfathers Itchen Valley 780
An Gof Lizard 791
Going off Half-cocked
  Bespoke 695
Going Underground Merry
  Miner 800
Gold Ale Glenfinnan 752
Gold Award Barge & Barrel 688
Gold Beacons Brecon 706
Gold Cup Doncaster 734
Gold Digger Bank Top 687
  Blue Ball 700
  Justice 781
Gold Hill Keystone 783
Gold Medal Linfit 789
Gold Muddler Andwell 682
Gold Pot 70/- TinPot 860
Gold Rush Prospect 827
Gold Spice Keystone 783
Gold Standard Nine Standards
  (Settle) 841
Gold Star Strong Ale
  Goacher's 753
Gold Star Silhill 845
Gold Tankard Wylam 887
Gold Top Old Dairy 815
Gold Wing Independent Lakeland
  (Strands) 853
Gold Archers (Evan Evans) 740
  Atlantic 685
  Bays 691
  Blakemere 699
  Bowland 703
  Brentwood 706
  Brigstock 708
  Butcombe 713
  Buxton 714
  Cader 714
  Chalk Hill 718
  Copthorne 724
  Corinium 725
  Cuerden 728
  Dancing Duck 729
  Doghouse 733
  Dorking 734
  Eden 738
  Exmoor 741
  FILO 744
  Frodsham 748
  Gloucester 752
  Goosnargh 754
  Gower 755
  Grainstore 756
  Green Dragon 758

Green Mill 758
Griffin 760
Hackney 761
Hop Studio 773
Ilkley 777
Ironbridge 778
John Thompson 858
Kemptown 782
Kingstone 784
Ledbury 788
Ludlow 794
Lytham 795
Mersea Island 800
Mumbles 806
Neath 807
North Curry 809
Platform 5 824
Potton 826
Ramsbury 829
Sawbridgeworth 841
Shed 843
Sixpenny 846
Snowdonia 848
Tatton 856
Uffa 868
Vens 870
Weatheroak Hill 874
Wensleydale 876
Williams 880
Worsthorne 885
Gold/Sheepshaggers Gold
  Cairngorm 715
Golden Ale 8 Sail 677
  Archerfield (Knops) 785
  Britannia 709
  Brockley 709
  Clarence & Fredericks 720
  Crate 727
  Isca 778
  JW Sweetman 890
  Malt 796
  North Yorkshire 810
  Ouseburn Valley 819
  St Peter's 839
  Turners 866
  Yates 887
Golden Apostle Wessex 876
Golden Arrow Cottage 726
  Double Top 735
Golden Bear Warwickshire 873
Golden Best Green Jack 758
  Hop Back 772
  Timothy Taylor 857
Golden Bine Ballard's 687
Golden Bitter Yates' 888
Golden Boar Farmer's 743
Golden Bob New Inn 807
Golden Bolt Box Steam 703
Golden Braid Hopdaemon 773
Golden Braun Tonbridge 863
Golden Break Brightside 708
Golden Bud Brampton 704
Golden Cap Bitter Mighty
  Hop 800
Golden Cascade Barley
  Bottom 688
  Fuzzy Duck 750
Golden Chalice Glastonbury 752
Golden Chough Fry's 749
Golden Cocker Gundog 761
Golden Cockerel Simpsons 845
Golden Crown Idle 776
  Star Inn 851
Golden Cygnet Two Bridges 867
Golden Dale Corvedale 725

Golden Dawn Just A Minute 781
Golden Delicious Burton
  Bridge 712
Golden Fleece Cotswold Lion 726
  Dent 732
Golden Fox B&T 686
Golden Ginseng North
  Yorkshire 810
Golden Globe Quantum 828
Golden Glow Holden's 771
Golden Goose Goose Eye 754
  Loch Leven 792
  Mouselow Farm 805
Golden Gorse Coastal 721
Golden Hinde Coastal 721
Golden Hop Milltown 802
  Shardlow 842
Golden Hunter Gundog 761
Golden IPA Mad Cat 795
Golden Jackal Wolf 883
Golden Kiwi Tydd Steam 868
Golden Lance Keltek 782
Golden Larch Wood Street 884
Golden Man Shiny 844
Golden Newt Elgood's 738
Golden Oates Oates 813
Golden Pale Ale Elmtree 739
Golden Panther Panther 820
Golden Pheasant Old
  Chimneys 814
Golden Pig Country Life 726
Golden Pippin Copper
  Dragon 724
Golden Pixie Pixie Spring 824
Golden Plover Allendale 680
Golden Poacher Longdog 793
Golden Rat Rat 830
Golden Retriever White Dog 878
Golden Salamander
  Salamander 839
Golden Sands Southport 849
Golden Seahawk Premium Beer
  Cotleigh 725
Golden Sheep Black Sheep 698
Golden Shower Son of Sid 848
Golden Sovereign Flipside 745
Golden Sparkle Mulberry
  Duck 806
Golden Spring Blindmans 700
Golden Star Big Lamp 696
Golden Thistle Traditional Scottish
  Ales 864
Golden Thread Salopian 840
Golden Tom Tom Smith 848
Golden Vale Deeply Vale 731
  Whittlebury 879
Golden Valley Breconshire 706
Golden Wander Hop &
  Stagger 773
Golden Warrior Empire 740
Golden Wheat Sleaford 847
Golden XPA Caledonian 715
Golden Buckingham 711
  Celt Experience 718
  Healey's 767
  Navigation 806
  Winter's 882
Goldenthal Bollington 702
Goldihops Kelburn 782
Goldilocks Old Bear 814
Goldings Leatherbritches 787
Goldrush Cottage 726
Gollum's Revenge Owenshaw
  Mill 819
Gone Fishing ESB Green Jack 758

Gone for a Burton Tower 863
Good Health Goody 754
Good Heavens Goody 754
Good Knight Felstar 744
Good Old Boy West Berkshire 876
Good Ordinary Pale Ale
  Barney's 689
Good Sheppard Goody 754
Good Ship Arbella Mill Green 801
Good Times Williams 880
Goodcock's Winner Cox &
  Holbrook 727
Goodens Gold Flowerpots 746
Gordon Bennett Belvoir 694
Gorge Best Cheddar 718
Gorlovka Imperial Stout
  Acorn 678
Gorsey Redstone 833
Gothenburg Porter
  Prestonpans 826
The Governor Lees 788
The Grace Sulwath 854
Grainger Ale Hadrian Border 761
Grand Prix Prescott 826
Grandstand Bitter
  Twickenham 866
Grange No. 1 Llangollen 791
Granny Wouldn't Like It Wolf 883
Grantham Stout Oldershaw 817
Grapefruit Beer St Peter's 839
Grasmoor Dark Ale Cumbrian
  Legendary 729
Grasshopper Kentish Bitter
  Westerham 877
Gravediggers Ale Church End 719
Gravesend Guzzler Millis 801
Gravitas Vale 870
Great Bear Old Bear 814
Great Bustard Stonehenge 852
Great Eastern Transatlantic
  Porter Black Iris 698
Great Expectations
  Oldershaw 817
Great Northern Fernandes 744
Great Raft Bitter Old
  Chimneys 814
Great Welsh Great Orme 757
Green Barrel Organic
  Dawkins 731
Green Bullet Mountain Man 891
  Strands 853
Green Daemon Hopdaemon 774
Green Dragon Whittlebury 879
Green Yetman's 888
Greensand IPA Surrey Hills 855
Greenstede Gold High Weald 769
Grey Ghost Raw 830
Griffin Brampton 704
Griffin's Irish Stout Hill Island 770
Grim Reaper Offa's Dyke 813
Grin & Bare It Anarchy 681
Gringo's Gold Botley 702
Grisley Mires Kendal 782
Grizzly Beer Fox 747
Grounds for Divorce Rotters 837
Growler Bitter Growler 760
Growler White Dog 878
Grozet Bartrams 690
  Williams 880
Grumpling Premium Ale
  Vale 870
Grumpy Bastard Brandon 705
Grumpy Guvnor Franklins 747
Guardsman Windsor & Eton 881
Gubbins Lord Conrad's 794

Guerrilla Blue Monkey 701
Guid Ale Arran 683
Guilsborough Gold Nobby's 808
Guilsborough Guzzler
  Nobby's 808
Gull Rock Tintagel 861
Gulping Fellow Fellows 743
Gun Dog Bitter Wall's 872
Gun Dog Teignworthy 857
Gun Flint Brandon 705
Gundog Gundog 761
Gunhild Fownes 746
Gunhill Adnams 679
Gunner Boyce Stocklinch 852
Gunner's Daughter Old
  Cannon 814
Gunners Gold Loose Cannon 793
Gunpowder Mild Coach
  House 721
Gunwale Dance Geeves 751
Guthlac's Porter Golcar 753
Guzzler York 888
Gwyrfai Snowdonia 848
Gylla's Gold Small Paul's 847

H

H&H Bitter Greene King 759
H&H Olde Trip Greene King 759
Ha'penny Ale Halfpenny 762
Ha'penny Dodger Three
  Kings 859
Ha'Penny Mild Harwich
  Town 765
Hackney Hopster London
  Fields 793
Hadham Gold Green Tye 759
Hadouken Tiny Rebel 861
Hafod Light Hafod 762
Hairy Goat Mountain Man 891
Hairy Helmet Leatherbritches 788
Halcyon Daze Big River 696
  Burton Old Cottage 713
Haley's Comet Hamelsworde 763
Half Bore Hunter's 776
Half Centurion Kinver 784
Half Wit Old Bog 814
Half-Life Atomic 685
Halfway to Heaven Langham 786
Halo Pail Rossendale 837
Halo Cross Bay 728
Halt Hilden 770
Hameldon Bitter Rossendale 837
Hammer & Tongs Old Forge 815
Hammer Hafod 762
Hampshire Rose Itchen
  Valley 780
Hancock's HB Molson Coors
  (Brains) 704
Handliner Coastal 721
Handsome Forge 746
Hanged Monk Tipples 861
Happiness Richmond 834
Happy Chappy Cromarty 727
Harbour Special Tintagel 861
Harpers Great Oakley 757
Harrier Cotleigh 725
Harry's Quercus 828
Hart IPA Hart of Stebbing 764
Hart Stopper Harthill Village 765
Hart's Desire Harthill Village 765
Hartington Bitter Whim 878
Hartington IPA Whim 878
Hartland Blonde Forge 746
Hartleys XB Robinsons 835

Harvest Moon Mild Cambridge Moonshine 715
Harvest Moon Ulverston 868
Harvest Pale Castle Rock 717
Harvest Sun Williams 880
Hat Trick IPA Muirhouse 805
Haven Fry's 749
Hawthorn Gold Wicked Hathern (Staffordshire) 851
Haystacks Hesket Newmarket 769
HBB (Hogs Back Bitter) Hogs Back 771
HDA Gundog 761
HE Hafod 762
Heacham Gold Fox 747
Head East Strathbraan 853
Head Hunter Sperrin 849
Head Otter 818
Headland Red Wold Top 883
Headless Dog Hilden 770
Headless Horseman Weltons 875
Headless RedWillow 833
Headmaster Old School 816
Heanor Pale Ale Bottle Brook 702
Heart of Gold Bumpmill 711
Heart Quartz 828
Hearty Bitter Yorkshire Heart 889
Hearty Good Feather Mallard 796
Hearty Mild Yorkshire Heart 889
Heath Robinson Barlow 688
Heavenly Blonde Oldershaw 816
Heavenly Matter Cambridge Moonshine 715
Hebden's Wheat Little Valley 790
Hebridean Gold Isle of Skye 779
Hedge Monkey Glastonbury 752
HedgeHopper Mobberley 802
Hedgerow Gold Sleaford 847
Hedgerow Hop Lord Conrad's 794
Hedgerow Silver Sleaford 847
Heel Stone Stonehenge 852
Helga's Dunkel Bier Kendal 782
Heligan Honey Skinner's 846
Hell Beck Geltsdale 752
Hell Cat Fat Cat 743
Helmsman North Star 810
Helvellyn Gold Hesket Newmarket 769
Helvick Gold Dungarvan 890
Hen Harrier Bowland 703
Hengist Wantsum 872
Henrietta Welbeck Abbey 874
Henry's IPA Wadworth 871
Heracles Hop Back 772
Hercules IPA Goldmark 754
Herefordshire Light Ale (HLA) Hereford 768
Herefordshire Owd Bull Hereford 768
Heresy Bishop Nick 697
Hergest Ridge Mercian 799
Heritage IPA Arundel 684
Heritage Three Castles 859
Heron Porter Two Roses 867
Hetton Pale Ale Dark Horse 730
Hewish IPA RCH 830
Hewish Mild RCH 830
Hibernator Old Bear 814
Hicks Special Draught (HSD) St Austell 839
High as a Kite Heart of Wales 767
High Fives Willy Good 881
High Light Trinity 865
High Pike Hesket Newmarket 769

High Tide East Coast 738
High Tor Buxton 714
High Town Ale Hop & Stagger 773
High Voltage Heavy Industry 767
High Wire Magic Rock 795
Highgate Sworn Three Kings 859
Highgate Hartshorns 765
Highlander Fyne 750
Highrise London Brewing 792
Highwayman Buntingford 712
Hill Climb Prescott 826
The Hindustan IPA Big River 696
Hip Hop Langham 786
Hit the Lights Weird Beard 874
Hit & Run Blakemere 699
The Hoard Backyard 687
Hob Bitter Hoskins Brothers (Belvoir) 694
Hobby Horse Rhymney 833
Hobgoblin Wychwood 887
Hobson's Choice City of Cambridge (Wolf) 883
Hogshead Cotswold Pale Ale Uley 868
Holbeach High Street Austendyke 686
Hole Hearted Oakleaf 812
Holly Hop Bryncelyn 711
Holy Cow Scottish Borders 841
Holy Joe Yates' 888
Home IPA Magpie 796
Honey Bee Three B's 859
Honey Blond Liverpool Organic 791
Honey Blonde Downton 736
Honey Brown Pin-Up 824
Honey Bunny North Yorkshire 810
Honey Buzzard Cotleigh 725
Honey Dragon Middle Earth 800
Honey Fayre/Cwrw Mel Conwy 723
Honey Locust Wood Street 884
Honey Mild DarkTribe 730
Honey Smacker Saddleworth 838
Honey Trap Long Itch 793
Honey Bees 693
Honeyfuzz Rother Valley 837
Honeypot Bitter Coach House 721
Honeypot Old Bear 814
Hood Lincoln Green 789
Hook Island Red Five Points 745
Hooky Mild Hook Norton 772
Hooky Hook Norton 772
Hop A Doodle Doo Brewster's 707
Hop Beast Liverpool Craft 790
Hop Bomb Sadler's 838
Hop Britannia Treboom 864
Hop Dog IPA Sunny Republic 855
Hop Garden Gold Hogs Back 771
Hop Gear Barrowden 689
Hop Market Pope's 825
Hop Monster Brew Company 706
Hop o' The Morning Stout Late Knights 787
Hop Ripper IPA Brew Company 706
Hop Smacker Saddleworth 838
Hop & Soul Amber Indian Summer 777
Hop & Soul Blonde Indian Summer 777

Hop & Soul Mild Indian Summer 777
Hop & Soul Porter Indian Summer 777
Hop Till You Drop Derby 732
Hop Token: Amarillo Adur 679
Hop Token: Summit Adur 679
Hop Trial Tryst 865
Hop Troll Tillingbourne 860
Hop Twister Salopian 840
HoP Blackedge 699
HOP First Chop 744
Hop On Kings Clipstone 783
Langton 786
Hopdance Full Moon 749
Hope & Glory Pope's 825
Hopfest Red Squirrel 832
Hopfweizen Great Heck 756
Hophead Brewster's 707
Dark Star 730
Porterhouse 891
Hopleaf Buffy's 711
Hopnotch Hopping Mad 774
Hopped to the Gates of Hell Brewmeister 707
Hoppelhammer Whitewater 878
Hopper Hafod 762
Prospect 827
Hoppers Ale Rother Valley 837
Hoppily Ever After Magpie 795
Hoppin Robin Rockin' Robin 836
Hoppiness Hopping Mad 774
Moor 804
Thame 858
Hoppit Loddon 792
Hoppy Golden Ale Bedlam 692
Hoppy Hen Felstar 744
Hoppy Ness Loch Ness 792
Hops Cotch Sportsman 850
Hops Save The Queen IPA Baldy 687
Hopsack Phoenix 822
Hopscotch Old School 816
Hopsession Naked 806
Hopspur Redemption 832
Hoptical Delusion Arbor 682
Horbury Blonde Malthouse 796
Horizon Wadworth 871
The Horn George N Porter 825
Hornblower Anchor Springs 682
Old Cannon 814
Horse & Jockey Full Mash 749
Horsham Best Bitter King 783
Horsham Bitter Weltons 875
Horsham Old Weltons 875
Hot Dog Chilli Stout Bingham's 696
Hotel Porter Farmer's 742
Hound Dog Growler 760
House Brown Malthouse 796
House Hektor's 768
Howden Bittern Bird Brain 696
Howler Grafters 755
Howling Fox Slightly Foxed 847
Howling Gale Eight Degrees 890
Howzat North Curry 809
HPA Great Western 757
Hammerpot 763
Wye Valley 887
HSB Gale's (Fuller's) 749
On the Huh Beeston 693
Hullabaloo Loddon 792
The Humber Bridge Big River 696
Humpty's Fuddle Kingstone 784
Humulus Lupulus Botanist 702

Huna Red Sunny Republic 855
Hunny Bunny Skinner's 846
Hunter's Gold Red Fox 831
Hurricane Jack Fyne 750
Hurricane Beowulf 694
Longhill 793
Windy 882
Hyde Bitter Shalford 842
Hyde's Finest Hydes 776
Hydro Ashover 685
Hykeham Gold Poachers 825

I

I Am Beer Boggart Hole
Clough 701
i Beer Art Brew 684
I Can't Believe It's Not Bitter
Oakleaf 813
Icarus Blindmans 700
Iceberg Titanic 862
Icicle Greenfield 759
Icknield Pale Ale Weatheroak
Hill 874
Icon Dark Liverpool Craft 790
Icon Liverpool Craft 790
Ideal Pale Ale Tavy 856
Idle Landlord Idle 776
Idris Bitter Cader 714
Illuminati Full Mash 749
Illusion Moor 804
Immenstadt Weiss Bier
Masters 798
Imp Ale Poachers 825
Impale IPA Williams 880
Imperial Chocolate Stout
Dominion 734
Imperial IPA Amber 681
Imperial Palace Ale Castor 717
Imperial Pale Ale Isfield 778
Tower 863
Imperial Stout White Gypsy 891
Imperium Empire 740
Wantsum 872
Impy Dark Brampton 704
In the Black Wilson Potter 881
Inclined Plane Bitter
Langton 786
Incredible Taste Fantastic Clarity
(ITFC) Dove Street 735
Incubus Hopdaemon 773
Independence Bristol Beer
Factory 709
Inveralmond 777
India Pale Ale Archerfield
(Knops) 785
Crate 727
Grain 755
Knops 785
Oakleaf 813
Ouseburn Valley 819
Phipps (Grainstore) 756
White Gypsy 891
Indian Pale Ale Hoggleys 771
Indians Head Bridestones 707
Indie Girl Blue Ball 700
Indy Amber Ale Redstone 833
Inferno Oakham 812
Infinity IPA Coniston 723
Infra Red Hardknott 764
Infusion Conwy 723
Ingleborough Gold Three
Peaks 859
Ingledingle Ale Blue Bell 700
The Inn Crowd Brightside 708

Inn-Spired Old Spot 816
Inn-stable Heart of Wales 767
Inncognito Plain Ales 824
Inndulgence Plain Ales 824
Innkeeper's Special Reserve
Coach House 721
Innocence Plain Ales 824
Innspiration Plain Ales 824
Inntrigue Plain Ales 824
Insomniac Stout Malthouse 796
Instant Calmer Rock & Roll 836
Intergalactic IPA Black Iris 698
Inverted Jenny Stamps 851
Invincible Irving 778
IPA (Insane Pale Ale) Mad
Hatter 795
IPA (Ironbridge Pale Ale)
Ironbridge 778
IPA (Isle Pale Ale) Axholme 686
IPA Gold Greene King 759
IPA Reserve Greene King 759
IPA Anchor Springs 682
Belhaven 693
Blackedge 699
Bo Bristle 889
Brentwood 706
Copper Dragon 724
Dartmoor 730
Doghouse 733
Downton 736
Dukeries 736
Farmer's 742
Forge 746
Fox 747
Greene King 759
Growler 760
Hand Drawn Monkey 763
Harbour 764
Harveys 765
Holt 772
Hoskins Brothers (Belvoir) 694
Howling Hops 775
Just A Minute 781
Kemptown 782
Liverpool Craft 790
Lytham 795
Malt 796
McMullen 795
Middle Earth 800
Mighty Oak 800
Mordue 804
North Laine 810
Outstanding 819
Padstow 819
Penzance 822
Rebellion 831
Red Fox 831
Ridgeway 834
Rudgate 838
Sawbridgeworth 841
Scarborough 841
Sixpenny 846
Sonnet 43 849
St Peter's 839
Tap East 856
IPB Mild Ambridge 681
Irfon Valley Bitter Heart of
Wales 767
Irish Pale Ale Galway Hooker 890
Iron Age Celt Experience 718
Iron Awe Great Gable 756
Iron Gate Stout Black Iris 698
Iron Horse Hepworth 768
Iron Man Frodsham 748
Iron Men Liverpool Organic 791

Iron Plate Irwell Works 778
Iron & Steel Bitter Chantry 718
Iron Town Beckstones 692
Ironclad 957 Haworth Steam 766
Ironoak Single Stout Cox &
Holbrook 727
Ironopolis Stout Truefitt 865
Ironstone Wainstones 871
Is It Yourself
Sawbridgeworth 841
Isis Pale Ale Compass 722
Isis Jarrow 780
Island Hopping Highland 770
Islander Strong Premium Ale
Hebridean 767
Isle of Dogs Watermill 873
Isle of Purbeck Ale (IPA) Isle of
Purbeck 779
Ison Cambridge Moonshine 715
Ivanhoe Ridgeway 834

J

J.C.Dickinson's Land of Cartmel
Unsworth's Yard 869
J-Dam Ordnance City 817
Jack Black Red Squirrel 832
Jack the Devil Cullercoats 728
Jack the Lad Bullmastiff 711
Jack O'Clubs Gambling Man 751
Jack of Clubs Wild Card 880
Jack's Spaniels Gun Dog 760
Jade Liverpool Organic 791
Jaguar Kelburn 782
Jail Ale Dartmoor 730
Jail House Henley 768
Jailbreak Ridgeside 834
Jaipur IPA Thornbridge 858
Jamaican Tom Tom Smith 848
Jamboree East London 738
Jameson Stout Franciscan
Well 890
Janner's Pride Waen 871
January 8th Ole Slewfoot 817
Jarl Fyne 750
Jarrow Bitter Jarrow 780
Jazz Redscar 833
JC Hopstar 774
JD's Robust Porter Hunsbury
Craft 776
Jeffrey Hudson Bitter/JHB
Oakham 812
Jelly Roll Morton 805
Jem's Stout Great Newsome 757
Jeremiah Mild Wentwell 876
Jerusalem Brampton 704
Jester Quick One Bartrams 690
Jester Butts 713
Jet Wainstones 871
Jetsam Hadrian Border 761
Jewel IPA Blakemere 699
Jewellery Porter Two Towers 867
Jiarg Okells 814
Jim Wilson Bitter (JWB) Tap
East 856
Jimmy Riddle Piddle 823
Jimmy's Riddle Tír Dhá Ghlas 861
Jinja Ninja Peerless 821
JIP (Jim Irving Pale) Nene
Valley 807
JJJ IPA Moor 804
Joblings Swinging Gibbet
Jarrow 780
Jock's Trap Poachers 825
John Barleycorn IPA 8 Sail 677

John Paul Jones East Coast 738
John the Thumbs/Sion y Bodiau
  Denbigh 731
John Willie's Lees 788
Johnsons Blythe 701
Joker IPA Williams 880
Jolly Beggars Ayr 686
Jolly Blonde Jolly Sailor 781
Jolly Farmer Penzance 822
Jolly Fellows Fellows 743
Jolly Roger Tír Dhá Ghlas 861
Jolly Scotsman's Bitter Jolly
  Sailor 781
Jorvik Blonde Rudgate 837
Joseph Williamson Liverpool
  Organic 791
Josephine Butler Liverpool
  Organic 791
Joshua Jane Ilkley 777
Journeyman Collingham 722
Jouster Goff's 753
JPA Sadler's 838
JR Best Raw 830
JRT Best Bitter Yorkshire
  Heart 889
JTS XXX John Thompson 858
Jubeelee North Curry 809
Jubilee Stout Kirkby Lonsdale 784
Juggernaut Red 831
Jumping Pirate
  Hamelsworde 763
Junction Sambrook's 840
Jurassic Dorset (DBC) 734
Just Jane Ambridge 681
Just Married Cathedral
  Heights 717
Just One More Elliswood 739
Justinian Milton 802

K
K&B Sussex Bitter Badger (Hall &
  Woodhouse (Badger)) 762
Kalika IPA Tollgate 862
Kamikaze Dent 732
Kasitra Enville 740
Katalyst Hardknott 764
Katy's Blonde Owenshaw
  Mill 819
Keelman Brown Big Lamp 696
Keep Calm 4Ts 677
Keepers Gold Wall's 872
Kelpie Williams 880
Kennet Valley Ramsbury 829
Kent's Best Shepherd Neame 843
Kentish Reserve Whitstable 879
Kernow Gold Lizard 791
Kernow Imperial Stout
  Coastal 721
Kessog Dark Ale Loch
  Lomond 792
Kettle Drum Treboom 864
Keystone Hops Weatheroak 873
KGB (Kent Golding Bitter)
  Kent 783
Khaki Sargeant Strong Stout
  Wissey Valley 883
Khyber Kinver 784
Kildonan An Teallach 681
Killellan Bitter Houston 775
Killer Bee Darwin 731
Kiln Dust Baldy 687
Kiln House Shardlow 842
Kilt Lifter Argyll 683
Kinder Downfall Buxton 714

Kinder Stout Buxton 714
Kinder Sunset Buxton 714
Kindred Spirit Eight Degrees 890
King John Andwell 682
King Korvak Porter Fownes 747
King Rat Rat 830
King Keltek 782
King's Ale Merlin 799
Kingdom Tap House 856
King's Forest Geltsdale 752
Kingmaker Warwickshire 873
Kings Regiment Liverpool
  One 790
Kings Mighty Oak 800
Kingsdown Special Ale
  Arkell's 683
King's Shilling Cannon Royall 716
King's Shipment IPA
  Compass 722
Kingston Topaz Newby Wyke 808
Kipling Thornbridge 858
Kislingbury Bitter Hoggleys 771
Kitty Wilkinson Chocolate &
  Vanilla Stout Liverpool
  Organic 791
Kiwi Patriot 821
Klondike Gold Rainbow 829
Knight Hood Medieval 799
Knight of the Garter Windsor &
  Eton 881
Knill by Mouth St Ives
  (Keltek) 782
Knockendoch Sulwath 854
Knocker Up Three B's 859
Knockmealdown Porter Eight
  Degrees 890
Knot Just Another IPA Jo C's 781
Kodiak Gold Beartown 692
Kotchin Cronx 727
KPA Stonehouse 853
Krasny Red IPA Black Iris 698
Kynance Blonde Cornish
  Chough 725

L
LA Gold Anchor Springs 681
LadeBack Trossach's (Traditional
  Scottish Ales) 864
LadeOut Trossach's (Traditional
  Scottish Ales) 864
Lady Catherine Grafton 755
Lady Hamilton IPA Pocket 825
Lady Julia Grafton 755
Lady of the Lake Glastonbury 752
Lager Clockwork 721
Lagonda IPA Marble 797
Laguna Seca Burley Street 712
Laid Back Lucille Blue Ball 700
Laika Out There 819
Lakeland Gold Hawkshead 766
Lakeland Lager Hawkshead 766
Lambeth Walk By the Horns 714
Lammastide Frodsham 748
Lamplight Porter Longdog 793
Lamplight Big Lamp 696
  Rock & Roll 836
Lancashire Best Bitter Hart of
  Preston 764
Lancashire Gold Hopstar 774
Lancaster Bomber Thwaites 860
Land of Hop & Glory Spire 850
Landlady Dunham Massey 737
Landlord Timothy Taylor 857
Landlord's Best Ashley Down 684

Landlords Choice Moles 803
Landslide Facer's 742
Langdale Cumbrian
  Legendary 729
Langley Best Leadmill 787
Large One Keystone 783
Lasamboo Grafton 755
Last Rites Abbeydale 678
Latitude Atlas (Orkney) 818
Laugh & Titter Old Cross 815
Laughing Frog 1648 677
Laughing Gravy Ulverston 868
Launch Pad Shiny 844
Laurie Lee's Bitter Uley 868
Lavender Honey Wolf 883
Lawless Bootleg 702
Lazy Daze Happy Valley 764
Leadboiler Linfit 790
Leading Light Bespoke 695
Leading Lights Harwich Town 765
Leann Folláin Stout Carlow 890
Leezie Lundie Ayr 686
Legacy Lacons 786
Legally Blonde Red Squirrel 832
Legend Dartmoor 730
  May Hill 798
  Norwich Bear 811
  Nottingham 811
  Publisher 827
Legion Dow Bridge 735
Legless Cow May Hill 798
Legless Rambler Beachy
  Head 691
Leila's Lazy Days Leila
  Cottage 788
Leila's One Off Leila Cottage 788
Lemon Blossom Hornbeam 774
Lemon and Ginger Humpty
  Dumpty 775
Lemon Head Growler 760
Lemongrass & Ginger
  Leatherbritches 788
Leofric Mercian 799
Leprechaun Stout Bank Top 688
Level Best Rother Valley 837
Level Headed North Curry 809
Leveller Springhead 851
Levelly Gold Shalford 842
Leviathan Hopdaemon 774
Leyburn Shawl Yorkshire
  Dales 889
LFB (Lunns First Brew) Golden
  Duck 753
Lia Fail Inveralmond 777
Liberation Suthwyk (Oakleaf) 813
Liberator Brigstock 708
Lickety Split Lord Conrad's 794
Lidstone's Rowley Mild
  Wensleydale 875
Life of Riley Wincle 881
Life Saver Riverside 835
Lifeboat Titanic 862
Lifesaver Mumbles 806
Light Ale Howling Hops 775
  Jacobi 780
Light Brigade Leyden 789
Light But Dark Old Spot 816
Light Headed Vale of
  Glamorgan 870
Light Mild/1863 Hydes 776
Light Nancy Bollington 701
Light Ness Loch Ness 792
Light Oak Weatheroak 873
Light Rail Ashover 684
Light Railway Kinver 784

Light Relief Long Itch 793
Light Gwaun Valley 761
Harbour 764
Liverpool One 791
Moulin 805
Lighter Shade of Pale
Briscoe's 709
Lighterman Exeter 741
Lightfoot Theakston 858
Lightheart Yorkshire Heart 889
Lighthouse Bitter Harwich
Town 766
Lighthouse Adnams 679
Gower 755
Lightweight Waveney 873
Lightweights & Gentlemen
Irwell Works 778
Lil Devil Stout Toll End 862
Lime Burner Kinnegar 891
Lime Tree Dukeries 736
Lincoln Best Poachers 825
Lincoln Gold Tom Wood's 884
Lincolnshire Life Leila
Cottage 788
Lindisfarne Castle Dark Ale
Delavals 731
Lion Bitter Mersea Island 800
Lion Pale Ale Potton 826
Lion Slayer Fyfe 750
Lion Hook Norton 772
Lionbru Lion's Tale 790
Lion's Den Julian Church 719
Lion's Pride Milestone 801
Liquid Bread Opa Hay's 817
Liquid Gold Goldmark 754
Liquid Mistress Red IPA Siren
Craft 846
Lite House Forge 746
Little Bollington Bitter Dunham
Massey 737
Little John Strong Robin
Hood 835
Little Nipper Brightwater 708
Little Rascal Happy Valley 763
Little Sharpie Humpty
Dumpty 775
Little Tick Wentwell 876
Little Weed Maypole 798
Little Wind Wild Weather 880
Liverpool Pale Ale Liverpool
Organic 791
Liverpool Pilsner Liverpool
Organic 791
Liverpool Stout Liverpool
Organic 791
Lizard Storm Cornish Chough 725
LJB Fox 747
Llanddarog Ale Coles 722
Loaded 4Ts 677
Local Hero Uncle Stuarts 869
Loch Ness Loch Ness 792
Lochnagar Spray
Brewmeister 707
Loco IPA Canterbury Brewers 716
Locomotion No. 1 Wylam 887
Lomond Hop Balmaha 687
Lomond Traditional Scottish
Ales 864
London Glory Greene King 759
London Pale Ale Meantime 799
London Porter Devil's Dyke 733
Red Squirrel 832
London Pride Fuller's 749
Lonesome Pine Ulverston 868
Long Blonde Long Man 793

Long Boat George Wright 886
Long Hop Bollington 701
Long Lane Austendyke 686
Long Way From Home
Ridgeside 834
Long White Cloud Tempest 857
Longbow Empire 740
Longdendale Lights Howard
Town 775
Longleat Pride Wessex 876
Loophole Clun 721
Lord Barker Gun Dog 760
Lord Lee's North Yorkshire 810
Lord Marples Thornbridge 858
Lordships Own Shugborough 845
Lotus IPA Ilkley 777
Lou's Brew Driftwood 736
Love Light Melwood 799
Love Monkey Glastonbury 752
Love Muscle North Yorkshire 810
Love not War London Fields 793
Loveleys Fair Mill Green 801
Lovely Nelly Cullercoats 728
Low Flyer Strands 853
Loweswater Gold Cumbrian
Legendary 729
Loxley Ale Milestone 801
LPA (Light Pale Ale) Enville 740
LSD (Langham Special Draught)
Langham 786
Lubelski Pils Dunscar Bridge 737
Lunatik IPA – Maverik Norfolk
Square 809
Lundy Gold Wizard 883
Lupus Lupus Wolf 883
Lurcher Stout Green Jack 758
Lurch's Liquor Muirhouse 805
Lush Hopstar 774
Lustin for Stout Blue Bee 700
Luverley Jub'lee Severn Vale 841
Luvly Jubblies Grafters 755
Lyme Gold Town Mill 863
Lymebrau Mighty Hop 800
Lynx Wildcat Yeovil 888

M

M&B Brew XI Molson Coors
(Brains) 704
M&B Mild Worthington's 886
O.M.T. Oates 813
MÒR Please! MÒR 804
MÒR Tea, Vicar? MÒR 804
MÒR-bidly Dark! MÒR 804
MÒR-ish! MÒR 804
M*U*D Big River 696
M-PIRE Burnside 712
Macbeth Deeside 731
Mad Dogs & Englishmen Irwell
Works 778
Mad Dogz Burnside 712
Mad Goose Purity 827
Mad Hat Mild Mad Hatter 795
Mad Hatter Weetwood 874
Mad Wolf Wolf 883
Madgwick Gold Hammerpot 763
Madhouse Double Top 735
Maggs' Magnificent Mild West
Berkshire 876
Magik Keltek 782
Magnificent Seven Gundog 761
Magnum Mild Muirhouse 805
Magus Durham 737
Maharaja IPA Liverpool One 791
Mahon Falls Dungarvan 890

Mahseer IPA Green Jack 758
Maid for the High Life
Llangorse 791
Maid for Horsin' Around
Llangorse 791
Maid in Llangorse Llangorse 791
Maid Marian Extra Pale Robin
Hood 835
Maid Marian Springhead 851
Maiden Voyage Great
Western 757
Maiden's Cross Frodsham 748
Major Oak Maypole 799
Maldon Gold Mighty Oak 800
Malpa Hand Drawn Monkey 763
Malt Dark Ale Malt 796
Malt Shovel Mild Fernandes 744
Sticklegs 852
Malt Shovel Porter
Sawbridgeworth 841
Malt Teaser Tap House 856
Malt Way Thurstons 860
Malthouse Bitter Brancaster
(Beeston) 693
Maltissimo Milltown 802
Malty Towers Tower 863
Manchester Bitter Marble 797
Manchester Pale Ale (MPA)
Lees 788
Manchester Skyline
Brightside 708
Mango Wheat Ale
Zerodegrees 889
Manhaton Pale?? Full Mash 749
Manjana Monty's 803
Manor Mild Sawbridgeworth 841
Mansfield Cask Ale Banks's 688
Mansion Mild Tring 865
Maple Porter Brighton Bier 708
March Haigh Riverhead 835
Marches Gold Mayfields 798
Marching In Great Oakley 757
Marcus Aurelius Milton 802
Mardler's Woodforde's 885
Mariana Trench Weird Beard 874
Mariner Gloucester 752
Marion Lincoln Green 789
Mark III Ordnance City 817
Market Porter Portobello 825
Marld Bartrams 689
Marmalade Cat Fat Cat 743
Marquis Brewster's 707
Marsh Mild Fulstow 750
Marshmellow Oxfordshire
Ales 819
Martello Hop Fuzz 772
Martyr Julian Church 719
Marvellous Maple Mild
Brentwood 706
Mary Jane Ilkley 777
Mary Rose East Coast 738
Hornbeam 774
Mary's Ruby Mild Kissingate 785
Mash Tun Bitter Leadmill 787
Master Brew Bitter Shepherd
Neame 843
Master 4Ts 677
Matador Pied Bull 823
Matchlock Mild Marston
Moor 797
Matfen Magic High House
Farm 769
Matilda's Revenge Opa
Hay's 817
Matins Abbeydale 678

Maverick IPA Brightside 708
Maverick Fyne 750
Mawkin Mild Mill Green 801
Maximus Botanist 702
Mayflower Plymouth 824
Mayfly Shardlow 842
Mayhem North Yorkshire 810
Mayor of Garratt By the
  Horns 714
Mayor's Bitter Nailsworth 806
McConnells Irish Stout
  Jarrow 780
McGintys Stout Thurstons 860
Mea Culpa Pale Ale
  Knaresborough 785
Meas Six° North 846
Meedies Mash Beeches 692
Mellow Yellow Bottle Brook 702
  Sadler's 838
Mellow Penzance 822
Mel's Mild Hunsbury Craft 776
Melyn Big Hand 695
Men of Steel Consett Ale
  Works 723
The Mental/Y Mental
  Denbigh 732
Mercia IPA Derby 732
Mercian Shine Beowulf 694
Mere Blonde Burscough 712
Mere Gold Bowness Bay 703
Merlin's Ale Broughton 710
Merlin's Gold Merlin 799
Merlins Stout Coles 722
Merlyn Great Orme 757
Mermaid Milk Street 801
Merrie Mink Wessex 876
Merriemaker Marston Moor 797
Merry Gentlemen George's (Hop
  Monster) 773
Merry Maidens Mild Coastal 721
Merry Miller 8 Sail 677
Merry Mount Morton 805
Mersea Mud Mersea Island 800
Mersey Mist Liverpool One 790
Methane Merry Miner 800
Metropolis Colchester 721
Mew Stone Noss Beer Works 811
MIA First Chop 744
Micawber's Mild Mauldons 798
Midge Maypole 798
Midhurst Mild Ballard's 687
Midland Mild Latimer 787
Midnight Bell Leeds 788
Midnight Mild New Plassey 808
Midnight Owl Castle Rock 717
Midnight Porter Magpie 796
Midnight Runner Sleaford 847
Midnight Stout Woodlands 885
Midnight Sun Williams 880
Midnight Swan Two Bridges 867
Midnight Monty's 803
  Nutbrook 812
Midshipman Dark Mild
  Nelson 807
Mighty Blonde Mighty Hop 800
Mighty Red IPA Mighty Hop 800
Mike Hawthorn Farnham 743
Mike's Mild FILO 744
Miladys Fancy Shugborough 845
Mild Ale Batham 691
  Colchester 722
Mild & Easy Wall's 872
Mild Mannered Mae Blue
  Ball 700

Mild Anchor Springs 682
  Banks's 688
  Branscombe Vale 705
  Buckingham 711
  Buffy's 711
  Cuerden 728
  Hobsons 771
  Holt 772
  Howling Hops 775
  Red Fox 831
  Saddleworth 838
  St Peter's 839
  Titanic 862
  Vens 870
  Wessex 876
  Winter's 882
  Woodlands 885
Mildly Rockin Rockin' Robin 836
Mile Mumbles 806
Military Mild Old Chimneys 814
Milk Stout Bristol Beer
  Factory 709
  Ouseburn Valley 819
  Pin-Up 824
Milky Way Black Hole 697
Mill Lane Mild Hoggleys 771
Mill Town Howard Town 775
Mill Botley 702
The Miller's Ale Canterbury
  Ales 716
Miller's Mirth Wantsum 872
Millstone 8 Sail 677
Millwright Mild 8 Sail 677
Mine Beer Blindmans 700
Miners A Light Cap House 716
Miners A Pint Cap House 716
Mining Dukeries 736
Minotaur Milton 802
Mischief Maker All Hallows 680
Mischief Monty's 803
Misleading Lights Harwich
  Town 765
Miss Loosemore Heddon Valley
  (Country Life) 726
Misty Law Kelburn 782
Mocne Piwo George Wright 886
Moel Famau Ale Hafod 762
Mole Catcher Moles 803
Moletrap Bitter Mauldons 798
Molly Malone Hilden 770
Molly's Chocolate Stout
  Hilden 770
Molly's Secret Brandon 705
Molten Amber Cambridge
  Moonshine 715
Money for Old Rope Bespoke 695
Mongrel Marston Moor 797
  Nutbrook 812
Monkey Hanger Poachers 825
Monkey IPA Art Brew 684
Monkey Wrench Daleside 729
Monkeys Love Hops Hand Drawn
  Monkey 763
Monkeytown Mild Phoenix 822
Monk's Gold Howard Town 775
Monkholme Premium Reedley
  Hallows 833
Monstrous Mild Old Bog 814
Montol Driftwood 736
Monument Bitter Tyne Bank 868
Monumental Blonde Kirkby
  Lonsdale 784
Moon Kissingate 785
Moondance Triple fff 865
Moongazer Amber Norfolk 809

Moongazer Golden Norfolk 809
Moongazer Ruby Norfolk 809
Moongazer Tring 865
Moonlight Arkell's 683
  Grafters 755
Moonraker Mild Empire 740
Moonraker Lees 788
Moonrise Monty's 803
Moonrocket Tipples 861
Moonshine Abbeydale 678
Moor Top Buxton 714
Moorland Bitter Bridgehouse 708
Moray IPA Speyside Craft 850
More Tea Vicar Julian Church 719
More Saddleworth 838
More's Head Wantsum 872
Morland Old Golden Hen Greene
  King 759
Morland Old Speckled Hen
  Greene King 759
Morland Original Bitter Greene
  King 759
Morning Glory Bitter Late
  Knights 787
Morocco Ale Daleside 729
Morris Patriot 821
Mothers Ruin Anchor Springs 682
Motley Brew Otley 818
Mowbray's Mash Oldershaw 816
MPA Monty's 803
Mr Chubb's Lunchtime Bitter
  West Berkshire 876
Mr Sheppard's Crook Exe
  Valley 741
Mr Smith Landlord's Friend 786
Mr Splodge's Mild Thame 858
Mr Squirrel Red Squirrel 832
Mrs Simpsons Thriller in Vanilla
  Brown Cow 710
Muck Cart Mild Son of Sid 848
Muck & Straw Holsworthy 772
Mucky Duck Buffy's 711
  Fuzzy Duck 750
Mud City Stout Sadler's 838
Muddy Boot Red Shoot 832
Mudpuppy Salamander 839
Mug Billy Burscough 712
Muker Silver Yorkshire Dales 889
Mumma Knows Best
  Franklins 747
Munich Cuerden 728
Muntjac Saffron 838
Musselburgh Broke Knops 785
Mutineer Derwent 732
Mutiny Rebellion 831
Mutleys Revenge Hereford 768
Mutts Nutts Hereford 768
Mwnci Nel Nant 806
Mydilsburgh IPA Truefitt 865
Mystery Tor Glastonbury 752

N
N1 Wheat Beer Dominion 734
Nailmaker Mild Enville 740
Naked Ladies Twickenham 866
Nameless Ale Tirril 862
Nanny Flyer Leyden 789
Napoleon's Retreat AllGates 680
Nappa Scarr Yorkshire Dales 889
Nappertandy Brandon 705
Narrow Boat Shardlow 842
Native Bitter Whitstable 878
Native Storm Celt Experience 718

Natterjack Frog Island 748
Southport 849
Natural Blonde Harviestoun 765
Pin-Up 823
Natural Blonde? Bird's 696
Natural Gold Pennine 822
Natural Progression Wilson
Potter 881
Natural Selection
Battledown 691
Navajo Blakemere 699
Navigator Bees 693
Navvy Phoenix 822
Neap Tide Teignworthy 857
Nechtan Deeside 731
Neck Oil Beavertown 692
Neckoil Bitter Whalebone 877
Nectar Bitter Attwood 685
Nectar Pale Blue Bee 700
Needles & Pins Hadrian
Border 761
Nel's Best High House Farm 769
Nelson's Blood Fox 747
Nelson 807
Nelson's Revenge
Woodforde's 885
Nemesis Peakstones Rock 821
Sticklegs 852
Nerabus Ale Islay 779
Nero Milton 802
Nessies Monster Mash
Cairngorm 715
Nettlethrasher Elland 739
Nevermore Stout Full Mash 749
New Dawn Alcazar 679
New Deck Blackjack 699
New Forest Ale Downton 736
New Forest Gold Red Shoot 832
New Laund Dark Reedley
Hallows 833
New World Pale New Plassey 808
New World Shiny 844
New York Pale Chantry 718
Newport Delta Great Oakley 757
Newton's Drop Oldershaw 816
Niamh's Nemesis Five Towns 745
Nice Weather Dancing Duck 779
Night Porter Botanist 702
Nightfall Pale Bitter Cross
Bay 728
Nightjar Loch Leven 792
Nightmare Hambleton 762
Nights Bollington 701
Nightwatch Porter Cambridge
Moonshine 715
Nightwatchman East London 738
Nimbus Atlas (Orkney) 818
Nimrod Worth 886
Ninkasi Coppice Side 724
Nip Grainstore 756
Nipper Bitter Island 778
No. 1 Colchester 721
Geeves 751
Hart Family 764
Odcombe 813
No. 2 Stout Stringers 853
No. 3 Hart Family 764
No. 7 Pale Ale Devil's Dyke 733
No. 8 Hart Family 764
No 8 Wood Farm 884
No 9 Barley Wine Coniston 723
No. 9 Hart Family 764
No Escape Reality 830
No Man's Land Mr Grundy's 805
No X/Dim Ecs Denbigh 732

No-Eye Deer Goose Eye 754
Noble 600 Kinver 784
Noble Eden Ale Heart of
Wales 767
Nook'y Brown Ale Nook 809
Nord Atlantic Humpty
Dumpty 775
Norfolk Black Beeston 693
Norfolk Honey Ale Why Not 879
Norfolk Kiwi Jo C's 780
Norfolk Nectar Humpty
Dumpty 776
Norfolk Poacher Brandon 705
Norman's Conquest MM
Cottage 726
Norman's Pride Corvedale 725
North Norfolk Beauty Uncle
Stuarts 869
North Riding Bitter Truefitt 865
North Sheep Allendale 680
North Star Porter Facer's 742
North Wall Hop Kettle 773
North Adventure 679
Northallerton Dark Wall's 872
Northamptonshire Bitter
Hoggleys 771
Northcote Blonde Belleville 694
Northdown Whittlebury 879
Northerly Windy 882
Northern Kite Wylam 887
Northern Light Orkney 818
Northern Lights George
Wright 886
Green Mill 758
Northumbrian Blonde
Mordue 804
Northumbrian Gold Hadrian
Border 761
Northway IPA Fulstow 750
Norton Ale Shoes 844
Norwegian Blue Buffy's 711
Norwich Castle Uncle Stuarts 869
Norwich Cathedral Uncle
Stuarts 869
Norwich Terrier Buffy's 711
Nor'Hop Moor 804
Nosey Parker Golden Duck 753
Notting Hill Amber Moncada 803
Notting Hill Bitter Moncada 803
Notting Hill Blonde Moncada 803
Notting Hill Ruby Rye
Moncada 803
Nottingham Blonde Coppice
Side 724
NPA (Norwich Pale Ale) Norwich
Bear 811
Nuptu'ale Oakleaf 812
Nut Brown Ale Mighty Hop 800
Uncle Stuarts 869
Nutty Black Thwaites 860
Nutty Slack Prospect 827
Nuture Lakeland Ale
Jennings 780
NVB (Nene Valley Bitter) Nene
Valley 807
Nyewood Gold Ballard's 687

O

O'Hara's Double Irish Pale Ale
Carlow 890
O'Hara's Irish Stout Carlow 890
O'Hara's Pale Ale Carlow 890
O'Hara's Red Ale Carlow 890
O'Ryan's Attwood 685

01 Otley 818
02 Croeso Otley 818
03 Boss Otley 818
04 Colombo Otley 818
05 Gold Otley 818
09 Blonde Otley 818
Oak Ale Burton Old Cottage 713
Oak Beauty Woodlands 885
Oak Grain 755
Oakley Blonde Great Oakley 757
Oasthouse Gold Weetwood 874
Oat Mill Stout Bollington 702
Oat Stout Nook 809
Oatmeal Stout Belvoir 694
Brighton Bier 708
Peerless 821
Obelisk Dunham Massey 737
OBJ (Oh Be Joyful!) Shires 844
Oblivion Peakstones Rock 821
Obsidian Hop Studio 773
Shiny 844
**Ochr Tywyll y Mws/Dark Side of
the Moose** Purple Moose 827
Odd Ball Red Offbeat 813
Odin Brightside 708
Odyssey Fallen (Traditional
Scottish Ales) 864
Off the Rails Stonehouse 853
Off the Wall Tigertops 860
Offa's Dyke New Plassey 808
Offa's Pride Offa's Dyke 813
Oh Boy Bryncelyn 711
OK Botanist 702
Olaf Okells 813
Old 1066 Goacher's 753
Old Albert Sleaford 847
Old Ale Adnams 679
Harveys 765
Old Barn Twisted Oak 867
Old Big 'ead Buxton 714
Old Boy Oldershaw 817
Old Brewery Bitter (OBB)
Samuel Smith 848
Old Bushy Tail Bushy's 713
Old Carrock Strong Ale Hesket
Newmarket 769
Old Cocky Weltons 875
Old Combe Wizard 883
Old Dalby Belvoir 694
Old Dark Attic Concertina 722
Old Dick Suthwyk (Oakleaf) 813
Old Dog Bitter Weetwood 874
Old Eli Linfit 789
Old Empire Marston's 797
Old English Ale Buckingham 711
Old Faithful Tirril 859
Woodlands 885
Old Fakir's Gold Fakir 742
Old Father Thames West
Berkshire 876
Old Forge Bitter Sticklegs 852
Old Freddy Walker Moor 804
Old Friend Derby 732
Old Gaffer DarkTribe 730
Old Git Green Mill 758
Old Growler Growler 760
Old Harry Weltons 875
Old Higby Great Western 758
Old Honesty Blue Bell 700
Old Hooky Hook Norton 772
Old Humbug Hexhamshire 769
Old Intentional Derby 732
Old Ipswich Liquor (OIL) Dove
Street 735
Old Jock Broughton 710

Old King Coel London Porter Colchester 722
Old Laund Bitter Reedley Hallows 833
Old Lech Halfpenny 762
Old Leg Over Daleside 729
Old London Stout Howling Hops 775
Old Man Ale Coniston 723
Old Man Long Man 793
Old Mariners Preseli 826
Old Mill Bitter Cox & Holbrook 727
Old Miner Tommy Stables 851
Old Moggie Teignworthy 857
Old Moor Porter Acorn 678
Old Mortality Strathaven 853
Old Nick's Favourite (Cocoa Edition) Brigstock 708
Old Nick's Favourite Brigstock 708
Old Oak Bitter Leadmill 787
Old Pal Church Farm 719
Old Peculier Theakston 858
Old Porter Enville 740
Old Red Eyes Red Ale Late Knights 787
Old Remedial Moulin 805
Old Ric Uley 868
Old Rocky Nailsworth 806
Old Rodney Brandon 704
Old Scarlet Castor 717
Old School Bitter Bewdley 695
Old School Winster Valley 882
Old Scooge Three Tuns 860
Old Slapper Bank Top 687
Old Slug Porter RCH 830
Old Smiler Towles' 863
Old Sodbury Mild Cotswold Spring 726
Old Spot Prize Strong Ale Uley 868
Old Stoatwobbler Beeston 693
Old Street Pale Ale Brodie's 709
Old Style Bitter/OSB Tomos Watkin 873
Old Tale Porter Kissingate 785
Old Thumper Ringwood 834
Old Tom Robinsons 836
Old Town Tom FILO 744
Old Trout Worsthorne 885
Old Tun Whittlebury 879
Old Wavertonian Spitting Feathers 850
Olde English Milestone 801
Oliver's Light Ale Coniston 723
Olympia Harveys 765
Once Bittern Woodforde's 885
One Eyed Jack Concertina 722
One Foot In The Yard Yard of Ale 887
One Hop Wantsum 872
One in the Bush Lamb 786
One Swallow Caythorpe 718
One Twenty Prospect 827
One-Der-Ful Wheat Blakemere 699
Onslaught Dow Bridge 735
Onyx Sandstone 840
Opus II Galway Hooker 890
Or8 Nutbrook 812
Oracle Salopian 840
Orange Blossom Special Ole Slewfoot 817

Orange Hefeweizen Kitchen Garden 785
Orange IPA Art Brew 684
Orange Wheat Beer Green Jack 758
Orange Yetman's 888
Orchid East London 738
Organic Ale St Peter's 839 Stroud 854
Organic Beer/ROB Ridgeway 834
Organic Best St Peter's 839
Original (70/-) Devon 733
Original Bitter Bellinger's 694 Brunning & Price (Phoenix) 823 Hydes 776
Original Black Stout Amber 681
Original Blonde White Rose 878
Original No. 1 Vale of Glamorgan 870
Original Standard Nine Standards (Settle) 841
Original Wood Swansea 855
Original Barum 690 Black Cat 697 Dark Star 730 Everards 741 Olde Swan 816 Slater's 847 Thwaites 860 Willy's 881
Orkney Best Highland 770
Orkney Blast Highland 770
Orkney IPA Highland 770
Orme Great Orme 757
OSB Old Spot 816
Oscar Wilde Mighty Oak 800
Ossian Inveralmond 777
Ostara AllGates 680
Otters Pocket Marlpool 797
Out of Step IPA Offbeat 813
Outlandish Pale Offbeat 813
Outlaw Robin Hood 835
Outwood Bound Five Towns 745
Over a Barrel Bespoke 695
Over the Edge Kinver 784
Over The Moon Grafters 755
Over and Stout Goose Eye 754
Over the Top Mr Grundy's 805
Ow Do! Six Bells 846
Owd Miner Coppice Side 724
Owd Oak Hydes 776
Own Gear Barrowden 689
Own Sharp's 842
Oxford Gold Brakspear 704
Oxymoron Otley 818
Oyster Catcher Brancaster (Beeston) 693
Oyster Stout Arbor 682 Mersea Island 800 Porterhouse 891 Whitstable 879

P
Pacific Red Full Moon 749
Pacific Cottage 726
Pacifica Pale Ale Tyne Bank 868
Pack Lane Mild Uncle Stuarts 869
Packhorse Worsthorne 885
Paddys Pride Brandon 704
Pail Ale Concrete Cow 723 Shed Ales 843
Pain in the Arse Griffin 760
Palate Wrecker Tigertops 860

Pale Ale Ashley Down 684 Britannia 709 Brockley 709 Broughs 710 Firefly 744 Hand Drawn Monkey 763 Howling Hops 775 Joule's 781 JW Sweetman 891 Kendal 782 Kirkstall 784 London Fields 793 Metalman 891 Navigation 806 Padstow 819 Pheasantry 822 Quantum 828 Redemption 832 Richmond 834 Slaughterhouse 847 Tempest 857 Wood Street 884 Zerodegrees 889
Pale Amber Sarah Hughes 775
Pale Bob New Inn 807
Pale Gold Ossett 818
Pale Moonlight Phoenix 822
Pale of Clwyd Buzzard 714
Pale Rider Kelham Island 782
Pale Whale Whale 877
Pale XX Howling Hops 775
Pale Blackmore 699 Brewshed 707 Clun 721 Cuerden 728 Five Points 745 Four Thorns 746 Gundog 761 Ilkley 777 Kent 783 Leeds 788 Old Pie Factory 816 Peerless 821 Portobello 825
Palindrome Naked 806
Palmers Poison Blythe 701
Palmerston's Folly Suthwyk (Oakleaf) 813
Palomino Barnet 689
Paper Chain Jubilee Tower (Hopstar) 774 Jubilee Tower 781
Paradox Hopcraft (Pixie Spring) 824
Parish Bitter Wood 884
Park Life Bollington 702
Parkers Piece City of Cambridge (Wolf) 883
Parkeston Porter Harwich Town 766
Parson's Nose Julian Church 719
Parsons Darby Hole Beachy Head 691
Parsons Pledge Derwent 732
Partridge Best Bitter Dark Star 730
Partridge Pale Sleaford 847
Passchendaele Mr Grundy's 805
Pastiche Burton Old Cottage 713
Pathfinder North Star 810 Red 831
Patois Randalls 829
Patriot Hopping Mad 774
Pause Front Row 748
Pavilion Pale Ale Bank Top 687

Paw's Gold Black Paw *698*
Peacock's Glory Belvoir *694*
Pearl of Kent Whitstable *879*
Peckin' Order Felstar *744*
Pedigree Marston's *797*
Peg Fyfe Dark Mild All
    Hallows *680*
Pegasus Milton *802*
Pembrokeshire Best Gwaun
    Valley *761*
Pembrokeshire Pale Ale Cych
    Valley *729*
Pembrokeshire SA Cych
    Valley *729*
Pembrokeshire Supreme Cych
    Valley *729*
Pen-y-Ghent Bitter Three
    Peaks *859*
Pendle Witches Brew
    Moorhouse's *804*
Penguin Porter Ascot *684*
Peninsula Pint Hill Island *770*
Pennine Gold Bridestones *707*
    Golcar *753*
Pennine Pale Allendale *680*
Penny Bitter Potton *826*
Pennycomequick Skinner's *846*
Penny's Porter Derby *732*
Penryn Pale Ale Rebel *831*
Pentland IPA Stewart *852*
Peploe's Tipple Shoes *844*
Percheron Tunnel *866*
Peregrine Pale Black Iris *698*
Perfecta Porcus Complete
    Pig *722*
Perridge Pale Flowerpots *746*
Peter's Well Houston *775*
PG Steam RCH *830*
PGA Storm *853*
Pheasant Plucker Bowland *703*
    Fuzzy Duck *750*
    Hunter's *776*
Pheasant's Rise Lord
    Conrad's *794*
Phoenix APA Harwich Town *766*
Phoenix Gold Byatt's *714*
Phoenix IPA Enville *740*
Phoenix Falstaff *742*
Piddle in the Dark Wyre Piddle
    (Ambridge) *681*
Piddle in the Hole Wyre Piddle
    (Ambridge) *681*
Piddle in the Wind Wyre Piddle
    (Ambridge) *681*
Piddle Piddle *823*
Pied Eyed Pied Bull *823*
Pied Piper Strands *853*
Pier Porter Coastal *721*
Pier Redscar *833*
Pig Island Pale Ards *683*
Pig Out Pig Pub *823*
Pig on the Wall Black Country *697*
Pig's Ear Strong Beer Uley *868*
Pig's Ear Gribble *760*
    Tír Dhá Ghlas *861*
Pigeon Bridge Porter
    Sportsman *850*
Pigge's Hede Three Kings *859*
Pigs Best Bitter Pig Pub *823*
Pigs Do Fly Potbelly *826*
Pigswill Stonehenge *852*
Pike Blackedge *699*
Pilgrim Ale Plymouth *824*
Pilgrim's Pale Ale Dancing
    Man *729*

Pilot Barrowden *689*
    Padstow *819*
Pilsner Hop Studio *773*
    Portobello *825*
    Zerodegrees *889*
Pinch Noggin Three B's *859*
Pink Panther Panther *820*
Pinnacle Cuillin *728*
Pint Marble *797*
Pioneer Stout Sherfield
    Village *844*
Pioneer Prospect *827*
Pipe Dream George Wright *886*
Piper At The Gates Of Dawn
    Fisher *745*
Piper's Gold Fyne *750*
Pirate's Gold Muirhouse *805*
Pirates Gold Wooden Hand *884*
Pist n' Broke Breconshire *706*
Piston Bitter Beer Engine *693*
Piston Bob Tydd Steam *868*
Piston Broke Box Steam *703*
Pit Boss Gambling Man *751*
Pit Pony Merry Miner *800*
    Northumberland *811*
Pitch Porter Rossendale *837*
Pitchfork RCH *830*
Pitfield Bitter Dominion *733*
Pitfield Lager Dominion *734*
Pitstop Bitter Silverstone *845*
Pivo Estivo Kelburn *782*
Plain Porter Porterhouse *891*
Plan B Stringers *853*
Plassey Bitter New Plassey *808*
Platinum Blonde Mad Cat *795*
    Milltown *802*
    Norwich Bear *811*
Pleasant Blonde Black Horse *697*
Pleasant Pheasant Sleaford *847*
Pledgdon Ale Saffron *838*
Plockton Bay Plockton *824*
Plucking Pheasant Gribble *760*
Plum Porter Titanic *862*
Plunder Jollyboat *781*
Poachers Ale Parish *820*
Poachers Pocket Church End *719*
Poetry In Motion Betjeman *695*
Poets Tipple Ashover *684*
Pointer Gundog *761*
Poison Redscar *833*
Polar Eclipse Beartown *692*
Polar Paw Black Paw *698*
Polar Star Buntingford *712*
Polaris North Star *810*
Pole Position Silverstone *845*
Polly's Folly Buffy's *711*
Pommies Revenge Goose
    Eye *754*
Pompey Royal Oakleaf *812*
Pond Skipper Hop Kettle *773*
Ponte Carlo Stout Five Towns *745*
Pooh Norwich Bear *811*
Pooley's Golden
    Weighbridge *874*
Port O Call Bank Top *688*
Port Stout O'Hanlon's *812*
Ported Amoor Moor *804*
Porter Black Isle *698*
    Bridgehouse *708*
    Grain *755*
    Hand Drawn Monkey *763*
    Harbour *764*
    Hastings *766*
    JW Sweetman *891*
    Leatherbritches *788*

Potton *826*
    Sheffield *843*
    Tavy *856*
    Uncle Stuarts *869*
Porterhouse Red
    Porterhouse *891*
Porters Black Dunscar Bridge *737*
Porthleven Skinner's *846*
Portland Black Welbeck
    Abbey *874*
Poseidon Coastal *721*
Posh Blonde Oldershaw *817*
POSH IPA Yeovil *888*
Posh Pooch Ascot *684*
Post Mistress Sandstone *840*
Posthorn Premium Coach
    House *721*
Postlethwaite Coach House *721*
Pot Black Brightside *708*
    TinPot *860*
Potbelly Best Potbelly *826*
Potholer Cheddar *718*
Potion No 9 Penzance *822*
Potter's Ale Wessex *876*
Potter's Ruin Brigstock *708*
Potwalloper Braydon *705*
Powder Monkey Nelson *807*
Power Station Appleford *682*
Power Atomic *685*
    Gower *755*
Powerhouse Porter
    Sambrook's *840*
Powerhouse Great Heck *756*
Powermouse Great Heck *756*
PPA (Peasholm Pale Ale) North
    Riding *810*
Praetorian Porter Dow
    Bridge *735*
Prarie Fox Slightly Foxed *847*
Premier Bitter Bartrams *689*
    Moorhouse's *804*
Premium Stout Kingstone *784*
Premium Battledown *691*
    Big Lamp *696*
    Slater's *847*
Preservation Fine Ale Castle
    Rock *717*
Pressed Rat & Warthog Triple
    fff *865*
Pretoria AllGates *680*
Pricky Back Otchan Great
    Newsome *757*
Pride of Fulstow Fulstow *750*
Pride of Oxford Oxfordshire
    Ales *819*
Pride of Pendle Moorhouse's *804*
Pride of Sheffield Kelham
    Island *782*
Pride of Westmorland
    Barngates *689*
Pride Devon *733*
    Newark *808*
    Padstow *819*
    Poachers *825*
Pridenjoy Weltons *875*
Priessnitz Plzen Malvern Hills *796*
Prince Albert By the Horns *714*
Prince Bishop Ale Big Lamp *696*
Prince of Bengal IPA Pixie
    Spring *824*
Prior's Ale North Yorkshire *810*
Prior's Gold Prior's Well *826*
Priory Ale Norton *811*
Priory Gold Burscough *712*
Priory Mild Growler *760*

Priory Pale Ale Mayfields 798
Procrastination TinPot 860
Profanity Stout Williams 880
Progress Pilgrim 823
Progressive Pale Fell 743
Project Douglas Landlord's
  Friend 786
Proper Ansome Clearwater 720
Proper Job St Austell 839
Prospect Organic Hepworth 768
Prospect Quercus 828
  Shotover 845
Prototype Six° North 846
PSB Parish 820
Pucks Folly Farmer's 742
Pudding Stout Franklins 747
Puddle Duck Mallard 796
Puffin Pale Ale Bird Brain 696
Pug IPA Patriot 821
Pullet Please High House
  Farm 769
Pullman First Class Ale
  Hepworth 768
Pump Fiction Hoggleys 771
Pumphouse Pale Ale
  Sambrook's 840
Punctured Pipeline Bootleg 702
Punter Upham 869
Pure Blonde George Wright 886
Pure Gold Dominion 734
  Itchen Valley 780
  Partners 821
  Purity 827
Pure Ubu Purity 827
Pure Hektor's 768
Purgatory Pale Ale Franciscan
  Well 890
Pursers Pussy Porter Nelson 807
Pushing Out Outstanding 819
Pynot Porter Townes 864
Python IPA Little Valley 790

Q
Q Gold Botanist 702
Quacker Jack Mallard 796
Quadhop Downton 736
Quadrant Oatmeal Stout East
  London 738
Quagmire Big Bog 695
Quantock Ale Quantock 828
Quantock Stout Quantock 828
Quarry Gold Old Bog 814
Quarry Goldish Old Bog 814
Quarrymans Stout Bluestone 701
Queen Bee Slater's 847
Queen Charlotte Botanist 702
Quench Pilgrim 823
Quercus Folium Oakleaf 812
Quest Pilgrim 823
Quiet Riot Anarchy 681
Quintessential Derby 732
Quiver Bitter Bowman 703

R
Rabbie's Porter Ayr 686
Radgie Gadgie Mordue 804
Radiator Spring Garage 751
Radical Red Kirkby Lonsdale 784
RAF Collection Battle of Britain
  Wolf 883
Ragged Robin Old Chimneys 814
Raglan Sleeve Leyden 789
Rail Ale Beer Engine 693
On the Rails Ascot 684

Railway Porter Five Points 745
Rainbows End Ashover 685
Raj IPA Tryst 866
Raker Potton 826
Ram Tam Timothy Taylor 857
Ramblers Gold Stocklinch 852
Ramblers Ruin Breconshire 706
Ramblers Tipple Saffron 838
Rammy Rocket Leyden 789
Rampart Conwy 723
Ramsbottom Strong Ale
  Dent 732
Randolph's Leap Speyside
  Craft 850
Random Toss Flipside 745
Ranmore Ale Surrey Hills 855
Rapture Bottle Brook 702
  Magic Rock 795
Rash Dash Fool Hardy 746
Raspberry Blonde Saltaire 840
Raspberry Wheat Beer
  Milestone 801
Ratae'd Dow Bridge 735
Rattlesden Best Bitter Cox &
  Holbrook 727
Rattus Rattus Rat 830
Raven Stout Magpie 796
Raven Corfe Castle 724
  Orkney 817
  White Rose 878
Ravening Wolf Wantsum 872
Raw Moor 804
Real Blonde Pennine 822
Real Mild Ale Goacher's 753
Real Smiler Clearwater 720
Reality Czech Reality 830
Really Rockin Rockin' Robin 836
Rebel Red Franciscan Well 890
Rechabites Grey Trees 760
Reckless Danger Fool Hardy 746
Reckless Robin Rockin' Robin 836
The Rector's Revenge
  Rectory 831
Red Ale Dominion 734
  O'Hanlon's 812
Red Alt Clockwork 720
Red Bandit Cader 714
Red Bay Captain Cook 717
Red Beacons Brecon 706
Red Cuillin Isle of Skye 779
Red Dawn Red Squirrel 832
Red Diesel Colchester 721
  Geeves 751
Red Dragon Breconshire 706
Red Duke Privateer 827
Red Dust Consett Ale Works 723
Red Dwarf Black Hole 697
Red Ellen Jarrow 780
Red Eye IPA Four Thorns 746
Red Feather Welbeck Abbey 874
Red Goose Old Mill 815
Red Head Pin-Up 824
Red Heron North Curry 809
Red Herring Green Jack 758
Red House Mild Sadler's 838
Red Hunter Hammerpot 763
Red India Ale Dorking 734
Red IPA Ascot 684
  Sadler's 838
Red Kite Black Isle 698
  Vale 870
Red Knocker Fox 747
Red Leg Simpsons 845
Red Lion Best Complete Pig 722
Red MacGregor Orkney 818

Red McAdy Tollgate 862
Red Menis Hewitt's
  (Brentwood) 706
Red Mission Driftwood 736
Red Ness Loch Ness 792
Red October Nailsworth 806
Red Panther Panther 820
Red Queen Bartrams 690
Red Rock Red Rock 832
Red Rocker Cromarty 727
Red Rocks Peerless 821
Red Rye Barney's 689
  Brighton Bier 708
Red Screes Strands 853
Red Setter Gundog 761
Red Shield Worthington's 886
Red Smiddy Kelburn 782
Red Square Golden Triangle 754
Red Squirrel Arran 683
  Jacobi 780
  Woodlands 885
Red Star IPA Tollgate 862
Red Star Phipps (Grainstore) 756
Red Top Old Dairy 815
Red Watch Blueberry Ale
  Cambridge Moonshine 715
Red White & Brew Red Shoot 832
Red Zeppelin Ambridge 681
Red Atlantic 685
  Hawkshead 766
  JW Sweetman 891
  Kemptown 782
  Lancaster 786
  Nook 809
  Outstanding 819
  Williams 880
  Yetman's 888
Redacre Worth 886
Redbrook Premium
  Riverhead 835
Redemption Deverell's 733
Redhead Tipples 861
Redoubt Stout Harwich Town 766
REDRUM Mad Hatter 795
Redsells EKG Hop Back 772
Redwood American IPA Red
  Squirrel 832
Redwood Grain 755
  Weatheroak 873
  Woodlands 885
Reedcutter Humpty Dumpty 775
Reel Ale Cambridge
  Moonshine 715
  Teignworthy 857
The Reeve's Ale Canterbury
  Ales 716
Reflection IPA Shiny 844
Regal Blond Byatt's 714
Regal Blonde Oldershaw 817
Reg's Tipple Gribble 760
The Reiver Broughton 710
Reiver's IPA Hadrian Border 761
Reliant Robin Rockin' Robin 836
Relish Rodham's 836
Remus Cox & Holbrook 727
Renaissance Ruby Mild
  Whitstable 879
Ren's Pride Church Farm 719
Reservoir Hogs Hoggleys 771
Reservoir Premium Gates
  Burton 751
Resistance Summer Wine 854
Resolute Bitter Andwell 682
Resolution Captain Cook 717
  Leamside 787

BEERS
INDEX

Responsibly Strands 853
Rev James Brains 704
Rev Rob Beckstones 692
Revelation Dark Star 730
Revenge Winter's 882
Reverend Eaton Shardlow 842
Reverend Green Golden
  Duck 753
Revival Moor 804
Revolution Amber 681
RGB (Real Goosnargh Bitter)
  Goosnargh 754
Rhatas Black Dog
  (Hambleton) 763
Rhode Island Red Bitter
  Brimstage 709
Rialto 47 Dunscar Bridge 737
Rich Ruby Milestone 801
Richard Mason 1888 Irwell
  Works 778
Riders on the Storm Kelham
  Island 782
Ridgeway Tring 865
Ridley's Rite Bishop Nick 697
Ridware Pale Blythe 701
Riggwelter Black Sheep 698
Ring of Fire Three Kings 859
Ringtail Burscough 712
Rioja Porter Brewshed 707
Ripper Tripel Green Jack 758
Riptide Anchor Springs 682
Rising Sun Green Jack 758
Risky Blond Fool Hardy 746
Rite Flanker Wickwar 880
Rivendale Middle Earth 800
Rivet Catcher Jarrow 780
Roadrunner Bottle Brook 702
RoadRunner Mobberley 802
Roaring Meg Springhead 851
Robbie's Red Adur 679
Robin Hood Robin Hood 835
  Springhead 851
Robust Porter Fell 743
Rock Ale Bitter Beer
  Nottingham 811
Rock Ale Mild Beer
  Nottingham 811
Rock Apc Poachers 825
Rocket Fuel North Yorkshire 811
The Rocket Evening Star 741
Rocks Redscar 833
Rocky Bottom Preseli 826
Roebuck Privateer 827
Roisin-Tayberry Williams 880
Roly Poly Odcombe 813
Roman Black George Wright 886
Roman Gold Castor 717
Romsey Gold Flack Manor 745
Rope Walk Big River 696
Ropetackle Golden Ale Adur 679
Rorke's Draught Vale of
  Glamorgan 870
Rorke's Drift Quantock 828
Rossendale Ale Rossendale 837
Rotten End Shalford 842
Rouge Hop Summer Wine 854
Rough Justice Anarchy 681
Rougham Ready Bartrams 689
Roughtor Penpont 822
Roundabout Greenodd 760
Roundel St George's 839
Roundhead Porter Why Not 879
Route 17 Sleaford 847
Route A66 Mithril 802
Royal Britannia 1648 677

Royal Ginger Brandon 705
Royal Reserve Ulverston 868
Royal Ruby Mild Sleaford 847
Royal Stag IPA Quantock 828
Royal Standard Nine Standards
  (Settle) 841
Royal Lytham 795
Roystons Hoppy Handful Spey
  Valley 849
RPA Rowditch 837
RSX Red Squirrel 832
Ruby (1874) Mild Bushy's 713
Ruby Duck Fuzzy Duck 750
Ruby Jewel Muirhouse 805
Ruby Mild Rudgate 838
  Turners 866
Ruby Moby Whale 877
Ruby Red Howling Hops 775
  St Peter's 839
  Wilson Potter 881
Ruby Tuesday Just A Minute 781
Ruby Cap House 716
  White Gypsy 891
Rucking Mole Moles 803
Ruddles Best Bitter Greene
  King 759
Ruddles County Greene King 759
Ruddy L DarkTribe 730
Rudy Darter Andwell 682
Ruff Justice Watermill 873
Rum Porter Boggart Hole
  Clough 701
Rumour Gower 755
Runner Truman's 865
Running the Gauntlet
  Bespoke 695
Rushmore Ridgeside 834
Ruskin's Ram Downlands 735
Ruskins Bitter Kirkby
  Lonsdale 784
Russian Stoat Wessex 876
The Russian Stamps 851
Rustbucket Kinnegar 891
Rustic Tonbridge 863
Rusty Bob New Inn 807
Rusty Boiler Stocklinch 852
Rusty Bucket Brandon 705
Rutland Beast Grainstore 756
Rutland Bitter Grainstore 756
Rutland Panther Grainstore 756
Rutterkin Brewster's 707
RWB (Royal Wootton Bassett)
  Braydon 705

S

SA Gold Brains 704
SA Brains 704
Saaz Enville 740
Sabotage Trouble 891
Saddleback Best Bitter
  Slaughterhouse 847
Sail Away 8 Sail 677
Sailmakers Porter Big River 696
St Andrew's Ale Belhaven 693
St Andrew's Rowditch 837
St Antonys Cambrinus (Liverpool
  Organic) 791
St Arnold Allsaints (Coastal) 721
St George's Bitter
  Saddleworth 838
St George's Stout Corvedale 725
St James' Park Bitter
  Northumberland 811
St Magnus Ale Highland 770

St Michaels Cornish Crown 725
St Nonna's Penpont 822
St Ouen Strong Stout Pocket 825
Saint Petersburg
  Thornbridge 858
St Piran Cornish Best Bitter
  Allsaints (Coastal) 721
St Piran's Porter Coastal 721
St Stephen's Rowditch 837
St Udley Mild Weatheroak 873
Salem Porter Batemans 690
Saligo Ale Islay 779
Salt Road Blonde Owenshaw
  Mill 819
Sampson Jack Gower 755
Samson Maxim 798
**Samuel Engel's Meister Pils
  (SEMP)** Opa Hay's 817
Sand House Doncaster 734
Sand in the Wind Bottle
  Brook 702
Sandcastles at Dawn Ship
  Inn 844
Sandgrounder Bitter
  Southport 849
Sandpiper Light Ale
  Brimstage 709
Sands Redscar 833
Sandstone Bridestones 707
  Wainstones 871
Sans Pareil Evening Star 741
Santa Fe RCH 830
Sauvignon Blonde Crafty
  Beers 727
Saved by the Bell Bespoke 695
Sawley Tempted Bowland 703
Saxon Archer Three Castles 859
Saxon Bronze Alfred's 680
Saxon Gold Brandon 704
  Craddock's 727
SBA Donnington 734
Scafell Blonde Hesket
  Newmarket 769
Scalded Shoulder
  Hamelsworde 763
Scapa Special Highland 770
Scarecrow Bitter Brimstage 709
Scarecrow Hektor's 768
  Langton 786
Scarlet Macaw Oakham 812
Scary Crow Coppice Side 724
Scary Hairy Leatherbritches 788
Schiehallion Harviestoun 765
Scholar Shotover 845
Schooner Granville Captain
  Cook 717
Schooner Black Dog
  (Hambleton) 763
Scilly Stout Penzance 822
Scooby Brew White Dog 878
Scottish Maiden Morton 805
Scotts 1816 Copper Dragon 724
Scoundrel Leatherbritches 788
Scraggy Bay Kinnegar 891
Scratty Ratty Marlpool 797
Screech Owl Castle Rock 717
Scroby Norfolk Square 809
Scrumdiggity Goddards 753
Scullion's Irish Hilden 770
Scuppered Ales of Scilly 680
Se7en North Yorkshire 811
Sea Coal Ship Inn 844
Sea Dog Cliff Quay 720
Sea King Coastal 721
Sea Wheat Ship Inn 844

Seafarers Ale Gale's (Fuller's) 749
Seaforth Ale Hebridean 767
Seam Cutter Worth 886
Séance Full Mash 749
Seaton Delaval Hall Pale Ale Delavals 731
Secret Kingdom Hadrian Border 761
Sedgley Surprise Sarah Hughes 775
Seggie Porter Eden St Andrews 738
Seithenyn Llŷn 791
Selhurst Park Flyer Sawbridgeworth 841
Selling Out Outstanding 819
Semerwater Summer Ale Wensleydale 875
Sentinel North Star 810
Serendipity Double Top 735
Seriously Ginger Clockwork 721
Serpentine Cornish Chough 725
Session Ale Hearsall 767
Session Bitter Shed 843
Session Ringway 834
Severn Vale 841
Sessions Brown Cow 710
Set Cheshire 719
Seven Giraffes Williams 880
Seven Hills Sheffield 843
Seven Bristol Beer Factory 709
Seventy Lambs Barrowden 689
Severn Gorgeous Shires 844
Severn Sins Severn Vale 841
Sgt Pepper Stout Spire 850
Shacklebush Digfield 733
Shaftbender Saddleworth 838
Shagweaver North Cotswold 809
Shakademus Hartshorns 765
Shakespeare's County Warwickshire 872
Shandon Stout Franciscan Well 890
Shanghai Bitter Double Top 735
Shannon IPA Potton 826
Shared Space Worth 886
Sharpie K12 Brancaster (Beeston) 693
Shed Some Light Shed Ales 843
Sheep Dip Plain Ales 824
Shefford Bitter B&T 686
Shefford Dark Mild B&T 686
Shefford Pale Ale (SPA) B&T 686
Shelford Crier Cambridge Moonshine 715
Shelley Dark Cox & Holbrook 727
Shepherd's Delight Cotswold Lion 726
Shere Drop Surrey Hills 855
The Sheriff of Nottingham Robin Hood 835
Sheriff Lincoln Green 789
Sheriffmuir Ruby Red IPA Traditional Scottish Ales 864
Sheriffs Gold Alcazar 679
Sheriff's Tipple Castle Rock 717
Sherpa Porter Tryst 866
Sherwood Lincoln Green 789
Shine On Milestone 801
Shingle Bay Quercus 828
Shiny Bird Brain 696
Ship Hop Ale Ship Inn 844
Shipwreck Coast Penpont 822
Shipwreck IPA Liverpool Organic 791

Shire Bitter Hexhamshire 769
Shires Bitter Ambridge 681
The Shires Great Western 757
Shoemaker Frog Island 748
Shooting Star Hammerpot 763
Shopping for Hops Muirhouse 805
Shoreditch Stout Dominion 734
Shotgun IPA Gundog 761
Shotgun Baldy 687
Shottle Gold Shottle Farm 845
Shottle Pale Ale (SPA) Shottle Farm 845
Shottlecock Shottle Farm 845
Shropshire Gold Salopian 840
Shropshire Lad Wood 884
Shropshire Lass Wood 884
Shropshire Pride Shires 844
Shuffled Deck Blackjack 699
Shunters Pole Muirhouse 805
Shuttle Ale Three B's 859
Shy Talk Bitter Poachers 825
Side Pocket for a Toad Tring 864
Side 4Ts 677
Signal Light Settle 841
Signal Main Line Settle 841
Signature 1648 677
Silent Slasher Piddle 823
Silhouette Grafton 755
Silkie Stout Loch Lomond 792
Silures Celt Experience 718
Silver Adder Mauldons 798
Silver Buckles Stables 851
Silver Bullet Beer Engine 693
Silver Chalice Prior's Well 826
Silver Darling Three Kings 859
Silver Dollar Tyne Bank 868
Silver Heart IPA Yorkshire Heart 889
Silver King Ossett 818
Silver Myst Copper Dragon 724
Silver Standard Nine Standards (Settle) 841
Silver Tally Prospect 827
Silver Tanner Kendal 782
Silver Top Old Dairy 815
Silver Hilden 770
Simarillo Hopshackle 774
Simcoe Liverpool Organic 791
Simply Simpkiss Enville 740
Single Blonde Tyne Bank 868
Single Hop Ascot 684
Hop Kettle 773
Single Malt Ale Islay 779
Single Malt Brewmeister 707
SIP First Chop 744
Sir Edgar Harrington's Last Wolf Unsworth's Yard 869
Sir Phillip Wincle 881
Sir Roger's Porter Earl Soham 737
Sir William Marshal's Crusader Gold Unsworth's Yard 869
Sire Kings Clipstone 783
Sirius Dog Star Wolf 883
Six XT 887
Sixteen Strides Crafty Beers 727
Sjolmet Stout Valhalla 870
Skelpt Lug Argyll 683
Skew Sunshine Ale Suthwyk (Oakleaf) 813
Skiddaw Special Bitter Hesket Newmarket 769
Skiffle Shortts Farm 844
Skinny Blonde Argyll 683
Skinny Duck Owenshaw Mill 819

Skippers Mersea Island 800
Skirrid Tudor 866
Skrimshander IPA Hopdaemon 774
Skull Splitter Orkney 818
Skydiver Steamin' Billy (Belvoir) 694
Skye Ale Cuillin 728
Slainte Houston 775
Slap N' Tickle Lord Conrad's 794
Slap & Tickle Saddleworth 838
Slaughter Porter Freeminer 747
Slaughterhouse Porter Great Heck 756
Sleaford Stout Sleaford 847
Sleck Dust Great Newsome 757
Sledgehammer Stout Fulstow 750
Sledgehammer Old Forge 815
Sleeper Heavy Beer Engine 693
Sleeping Giant Bryncelyn 711
Slightly Foxed Slightly Foxed 847
Slingers Gold WharfeBank 877
Slipper Emsworth 740
Slippery Jack Brandon 705
Slipway Captain Cook 717
Slubbers Gold Milltown 802
Slumbering Monk Joule's 781
Slumdog Leadmill 787
Smatcher Tawney Radnorshire 829
Smelter's Stout Kissingate 785
Smild Rother Valley 837
Smiling Assassin Falstaff 742
Smoke Bomb Anarchy 681
Smoked Porter Howling Hops 775
Muirhouse 805
Smoked Red Clarence & Fredericks 720
Smokeless RedWillow 833
Smokey Joe Stout Geeves 751
Smokey Joe's Black Beer Hopstar 774
Smuggler Rebellion 831
Snakes Head IPA Hop Kettle 773
Sneck Lifter Jennings 780
Snitter Coquetdale 724
Snooty Fox Joseph Herbert Smith 848
Snowfield Wirksworth 882
Sobriety Blonde Whitworth 879
Sobriety MPH Whitworth 879
Sobriety Whitworth 879
SOD B&T 686
Sod Idle 776
Solar Cerddin 718
Sole Star Adnams 679
Soleil D'or Three Kings 859
Solicitors Fisher 745
SOLO IPA Sherfield Village 844
SOLO Quintessential Sherfield Village 844
SOLO Single Hop Sherfield Village 844
Solstice Golden Ale Brightside 708
Solstice Stout Hoggleys 771
Solway Mist Sulwath 854
Some Are Drinking Oakleaf 812
Some Like It Blond Worsthorne 885
Somer Salisbury 840
Somerland Gold Moor 804

Somerset & Dorset (S&D) Cottage 726
Son of a Bitch Bullmastiff 711
SOS B&T 686
Soundwave IPA Siren Craft 846
The Source Tillingbourne 860
Souter Lighthouse Best Bitter Delavals 731
South Adventure 679
Southerly Windy 882
Southern Bitter Cottage 726
Southern Star Tyne Bank 868
Southwater Gold Baldy 687
Southwold Bitter Adnams 679
Sovereign Gold Burton Bridge 712
Sovereign Acorn 678
Corfe Castle 724
Sovereigns Escort IPA Spire 850
So'Hop Moor 804
SPA (Simple Pleasures Ale) Nene Valley 807
SPA (Special Pale Ale) Buxton 714
SPA Francorchamps Burley Street 712
SPA Cornish Crown 725
Shires 844
Space Hoppy IPA Bingham's 696
Space is the Place Out There 819
Spanish Main Hopcraft (Pixie Spring) 824
Spanish Stout Hamelsworde 763
Spank (Industrial IPA) Blue Ball 700
Spanked Monkey IPA Art Brew 684
Sparkling Moon Cambridge Moonshine 715
Sparta Milton 802
Sparth Mild Riverhead 835
Special Ale Spitting Feathers 850
Wood 884
Special Draught/YSD Yates' 888
Special Oatmeal Stout Coniston 723
Special Pale Ale Bath Ales 691
Special Battledown 691
Holden's 771
Linfit 789
Sharp's 842
Vale 870
Special/House Ale Goacher's 753
Spectrum Bitter Rainbow 829
Speedwell Bitter Townes 863
Spellbound Merlin 799
Spey Stout Spey Valley 849
Spingo Middle Blue Anchor 700
Spingo Special Blue Anchor 700
Spinning Top Brightside 708
Spire Ale Stonehenge 852
Spirit of Kent Westerham 877
Spitfire Premium Ale Shepherd Neame 843
Splash! Frodsham 748
Sporran Warmer Blonde Traditional Scottish Ales 864
Spot Light Old Spot 816
Spot O'Bother Old Spot 816
Spotland Gold Phoenix 822
Spriggan Ale Skinner's 846
Spring into Spring Nook 809
Spring Tide Teignworthy 857
Spring Odcombe 813

Springfield Bitter Broughs 710
Spun Gold Twisted Oak 867
The Spurn Big River 696
Spypost Bitter Masters 798
Square Miled Norfolk Square 809
Squires Gamble Saffron 838
The Squirrels Nuts Beeston 693
Stack 4Ts 677
Stadium Bitter Mallinson's 796
Staffie Blythe 701
Stag Cairngorm 715
Exmoor 742
Gundog 761
Stairway to Heaven Burton Bridge 713
White Rose 878
Stairway Ludlow 794
Stakes Upham 869
Stallion Hambleton 762
Stamford Bitter Dunham Massey 737
Stand & Deliver Tollgate 862
Standard Ale Glenfinnan 752
Standard Cronx 727
Stanleys Pale Ale Kirkby Lonsdale 784
Stanney Bitter Stanway 851
Star Bitter Belvoir 694
Star Gazer Yeovil 888
Star Light James & Kirkman 780
Star Portobello 825
Stargazer Ridgeside 834
Stark Reality Reality 830
Starry Night Star Inn 851
Start Point Summerskills 854
Started Havant 766
Station Ale Richmond 834
Station Best Bitter Mallinson's 796
Station Bitter Stonehouse 853
Station Porter Dent 732
Wickwar 880
Staughton Bitter Red 831
Staveley Cross Townes 864
Stealth Burnside 712
Steam Ale Archers (Evan Evans) 740
Steam Beer Hop Fuzz 772
Sonnet 43 849
Steam Plate Irwell Works 778
Steam Porter Box Steam 703
Stedmans Ale Thurstons 860
Steel River Wainstones 871
Steel Town Bitter Consett Ale Works 723
Steep Hill Cathedral Heights 717
Steeplejack Dunscar Bridge 737
Steerage Titanic 862
Stella Gold Liverpool Organic 791
Stellar Green Mill 758
Sterling Pale Flipside 745
Sternwheeler DarkTribe 730
Stiff Upper Lip By the Horns 714
Still Walking Deeply Vale 731
Stillmans IPA Spey Valley 849
Stilton Porter Brewster's 707
Stingo Bacchus 686
Bartrams 690
Stiperstones Tunnfield 866
Stirling Silver Traditional Scottish Ales 864
Stirling Beeston 693
Stoker's Slake Three B's 858
Stone the Crows Lymestone 794
Stone Cutter Lymestone 794

Stone Faced Lymestone 794
Stoneley Bitter Shalford 842
Stoodley Stout Little Valley 790
Storm Force Winter's 882
Stormbringer Wild Weather 880
Stormin Auburn Hartshorns 765
Stormstay O'Hanlon's 812
Stormwatch Cox & Holbrook 727
Stormy Weather Two Bridges 867
Storr Lager Peerless 821
Stortford Sunrise Bishop's Stortford 697
Stortford Sunset Bishop's Stortford 697
Storyteller Kissingate 785
Stour Gold Sticklegs 852
Stout Coffin Church End 719
Stout Fellow Caythorpe 718
Stout Hearted Yeovil 888
Stout Sam Garage 751
Stout Big Hand 695
Blackjack 699
Burton Old Cottage 713
Consett Ale Works 723
Craddock's 727
Crate 727
Galway Hooker 890
Globe 752
Imperial 777
Ironbridge 778
Millstone 802
Navigation 806
Outstanding 819
Quantum 828
Scarborough 841
Three Tuns 859
Titanic 862
Uncle Stuarts 869
Stouter Stout Marble 797
Stowmarket Porter Cox & Holbrook 727
Straw Blond Isfield 778
Straw Dog Wolf 883
Straw Lancaster 786
Strawberry Wheat Brandon 705
Streetlight Porter Canterbury Brewers 716
Strike Atomic 685
Strikes Back Empire 740
Stripey Jack Bees 693
Strong Gold Scarborough 841
Strongarm Camerons 716
Stronghold Arundel 684
Strummer Shortts Farm 844
Strumpshaw Fen Uncle Stuarts 869
Stubble Burner Lord Conrad's 794
Stubblestag Lager Norfolk 809
Stud Hambleton 762
Studland Bay Wrecked Isle of Purbeck 779
Stuka Wensleydale 875
Stumbling Around Muirhouse 805
Stunner Cotswold Spring 726
Sublime Chaos Anarchy 681
Sublime Stout Fyne 750
Suffolk 'n' Strong Bartrams 690
Suffolk Punch Mauldons 798
Sugarloaf Tudor 866
Suilven An Teallach 681
Summa That Branscombe Vale 705
Summer Ale Hepworth 768
Summer Gold Wall's 872

Summer Ice Greenfield 759
Summer Light Evening Dove
   Street 735
Summer Lightning Hop Back 772
Summerhill Stout Big Lamp 696
Summerset Yeovil 888
Summit Pale Ale Mighty Hop 800
Summit May Hill 798
Sun Goddess Yates 887
Sunbeam Banks's 688
   Battledown 691
   Wirksworth 882
Sunburnt Eight Degrees 890
Sunburst Pilsner
   Inveralmond 777
Sunburst Felstar 744
Sunchaser Blonde Everards 741
Sundancer High House Farm 769
   Twickenham 866
Sundew Woodforde's 885
Sundial Gold Red 831
Sundown Tipples 861
   Untapped 869
Sundowner Langham 786
   Wild Weather 880
Sunflower Black Iris 698
Sunlander Stonehouse 853
Sunny Bitter Facer's 742
Sunny Daze Big Lamp 696
Sunraker Quantock 828
Sunrise Bristol Beer Factory 709
Sunset Blonde Bitter Cross
   Bay 728
Sunset Arran 683
   Captain Cook 717
Sunshine Brass Castle 705
   Monty's 803
   Rossendale 837
Sunshiny Norfolk Square 809
Sup Porter Sportsman 850
Superior IPA Fyne 751
Supernatural Blonde
   Yorkshire 888
Supernova Black Hole 697
Supreme Nottingham 812
Supus Lupus Andrews 682
Surrex Gold Red Fox 831
Surrey Bitter Pilgrim 823
Sussex Best Bitter Harveys 765
Sussex Gold Arundel 684
Sussex Pride Long Man 793
   Weltons 875
Sussex Superior XX Baldy 687
Sussex Wild Hop Harveys 765
Sussex XX Mild Ale Harveys 765
Sutler's IPA Burscough 712
Suze V Vens 870
SwAle Richmond 834
Swallowtail Humpty Dumpty 775
Swampy Big Bog 695
Swan Black Bowness Bay 703
Swan Blonde Bowness Bay 703
Swedish Blonde Maxim 798
Swedish Nightingale Malvern
   Hills 796
Sweeneys Bank Top 687
Sweet Bee Honey'd Wheat
   Brüpond 711
Swift Bitter Bowness Bay 703
Swift Nick Peak Ales 821
Swift One Bowman 703
Swift Allendale 680
   Linfit 789
   Truman's 865
Swn Y Dail Coles 722

Swordfish Wadworth 871
Swordsman Beowulf 694
Sworn Secret Happy Valley 763

T

T'errmmm-inator Strands 853
T'Other Teme Valley 857
T'owd Man Wirksworth 882
T'owd Tup Dent 732
Tabatha Partners 821
Table Beer Kernel 783
Tackler's Tipple Three B's 859
Tag Lag Barngates 689
Tail Gunner Brass Castle 705
Tailshaker Great Oakley 757
Taiphoon Hop Back 772
Talbot Blonde Teme Valley 857
Talisman Green Mill 758
Tall Hot Blonde Deverell's 733
Tally Ho! Palmers 820
Tallywhacker Leith Hill 789
Talorcan Deeside 731
Tamar Black Holsworthy 772
Tamar Sauce Holsworthy 772
Tamar Summerskills 854
Tandle Hill Wilson Potter 881
Tangled Up IPA Blue Bee 700
Tanglefoot Hall & Woodhouse
   (Badger) 762
Tap Bitter Chalk Hill 718
   Moles 803
Tap House Gold Tap House 856
Tarasgeir Isle of Skye 779
Tarn Geltsdale 752
Tartan Terror Houston 775
Taverns Tipple Hafod 762
Tawny Owl Cotleigh 725
TEA (Traditional English Ale)
   Hogs Back 771
Tea Kettle Stout Tring 865
TEA First Chop 744
Teacups Funfair 750
Teal Tipple Bowness Bay 703
Teddy Bear Norwich Bear 811
Teddy's Tipple Joseph Herbert
   Smith 848
Teleporter Summer Wine 854
Telford Porter Conwy 723
Templar Ridgeside 834
Temple Island Henley 768
Temptation North Yorkshire 810
Ten Fifty Grainstore 756
Ten Brewmeister 707
Tenacious Ted Barngates 689
Tendring 100 Sticklegs 852
Tether Blond WharfeBank 877
Tetley Bitter Carlsberg Tetley
   (Banks's) 688
Tetley Mild Carlsberg Tetley
   (Banks's) 688
Tewdric's Tipple Kingstone 784
Thames Surfer Belleville 694
Thames Tickler Halfpenny 762
That Old Chestnut Frog Island 748
That Teme Valley 857
Theodore Stout Snowdonia 848
Thick as Thieves Sperrin 849˙
Thick Black Devon 733
Thieving Rogue Magpie 796
Thin Ice Sadler's 838
Third Party Sperrin 849
Thirst Born Greenfield 759
Thirst Brew Offa's Dyke 813
Thirst Gold Keswick 783

Thirstquencher Spitting
   Feathers 850
Thirsty Moon Phoenix 823
Thirsty Walker Dove Street 735
This Splendid Ale Facer's 742
This Teme Valley 857
Thomas Salt's Burton Ale
   Tower 863
Thoroughbred Bad Ram
   Haywood Bad Ram 767
Thorougood Burscough 712
Thrappledouser Inveralmond 777
Three Beacons Brecon 706
Three Cliffs Gold Swansea 855
Three Graces Liverpool One 791
Three Point Six DarkTribe 730
Three Rings Downlands 735
Three Shires Bitter Millstone 802
Three Sisters Atlas (Orkney) 818
Three Swords Kirkstall 785
Three Valleys IPA Barlow 689
Three XT 887
Threesome Sherfield Village 844
Thrum Coquetdale 724
Thunder Road Bumpmill 711
Thunderbird Bird's 696
   Kite 785
Thunderbolt Bitter Baseline 690
Thunderbridge Ale Masters 798
Thurstein Pilsner Coniston 723
Tiddly Vicar Saffron 838
Tie the Knot Happy Valley 764
Tiffin Gold Kirkby Lonsdale 784
Tiger Best Bitter Everards 741
Tiger Rut Millstone 802
Tiki Milton 802
Tillerman's Tipple
   Weatheroak 874
Time 'n' 'Arf Just A Minute 781
Tin Plate Irwell Works 778
Tinfast Andrews 682
Tip Top Hop Brüpond 711
Tipple Uffa 868
Tipster Upham 869
Tipsy Fisherman Steamin' Billy
   (Belvoir) 694
Toad in the Ale Isfield 778
Tod's Blonde Little Valley 790
Toll Bridge Porter Old
   Sawley 816
Tollgate Bitter (TGB)
   Tollgate 862
Tolly Cobbold English Ale Greene
   King 759
Tolly Roger Cliff Quay 720
Tom Brown's Dorset (DBC) 734
Tom Long Stroud 854
Tom Tom Mild Tigertops 860
Tomahawk Hop Fuzz 772
Tommy's Tipple Junction 781
Tom's Tipple Red Shoot 832
   Tom Smith 848
Tongue Idle 776
Tonic Ale Tap East 856
Top Busty Blackhill 699
Top Cat Fat Cat 743
Top Dog Stout/Bramble Stout
   Burton Bridge 713
Top Dog Gundog 761
Top Hop Best Bitter
   Hornbeam 774
Top Notch Brightwater 708
Top Totty Slater's 847
Topsail Bays 691
Tornado Smith Mill Green 801

Tornado Windy 882
Totty Pot Cheddar 718
Touch Front Row 748
Tournament Goff's 753
Tow'd Navigation Nobby's 808
Town Crier Hobsons 771
  Nailsworth 806
Town Mild Sportsman 850
Towzie Tyke Ayr 686
Track Record Prescott 826
Trade Winds Cairngorm 715
Traditional Ale Larkins 787
Traditional Bitter Grafters 755
  Old Mill 815
Traditional IPA River Leven 835
Traditional Mild Old Mill 815
Traditional Sussex Bitter
  Hepworth 768
Traditional Butts 713
  Clark's 720
  Navigation 806
  Tonbridge 863
Transporter DB 731
  Wainstones 871
Trappers Hat Bitter
  Brimstage 709
Trawlerboys Best Bitter Green
  Jack 758
Treason Stout Great Heck 756
Treble 20 Double Top 735
Trelawny St Austell 839
Trembling Rabbit Mild
  Poachers 825
Trench Foot Mr Grundy's 805
Trent Bridge Inn Ale
  Nottingham 811
Trial Run Blackbeck 698
Tribute St Austell 839
Trident Arundel 684
Trinity Redemption 832
Trink Penzance 822
Trinovantes Gold Colchester 721
Triple B Grainstore 756
  Oxfordshire Ales 819
Triple Blonde Peerless 821
Triple Champion 1648 677
Triple Chocoholic Saltaire 840
Triple Hop Derby 732
  Partners 821
Triple O Fernandes 744
Troll Craddock's 727
Trophy Special Camerons 716
Troubador Dancing Man 729
Trouble & Strife Driftwood 736
Trout Ale Hop Monster 773
Trout Tickler Poachers 825
Truckle Goosnargh 754
Trucklebed Alley Topsham 863
True Delight Clearwater 720
True Grit Millstone 802
True North Yorkshire 888
True Tyke Haworth Steam 766
Truleigh Gold Downlands 735
Trumpeter Best Swan 855
Trumpington Tipple Cambridge
  Moonshine 715
TSB Porterhouse 891
Tuck Lincoln Green 789
Tumblehome Cliff Quay 720
Tungsten Double Top 735
Tunnel Vision Box Steam 703
Turbulent Priest Wantsum 872
TWA Waen 871
Twickers Wood Farm 884
Twilight Beacons Brecon 706

Twist & Stout Spire 850
Twisted Spire Hobsons 771
Twitchell Buntingford 712
The Twitcher George N Porter 825
Two Brewers Bitter B&T 686
Two XT 887
Twyford Tipple Bingham's 696
TY PA Knaresborough 785
Tyger Tyger Yorkshire 888
Tyme Tunnel Just A Minute 781
Tyne 9 Firebrick 744
Tyneside Blonde Hadrian
  Border 761
Type 42 Irving 778

U

U.P.A. Untapped 869
Ugly Duckling Two Bridges 867
Umbel Ale Growler 760
Umbel Magna Growler 760
Un-Hung Hero Hewitt's
  (Brentwood) 706
Uncle John Halifax Steam 762
Uncle Sam's Pale Ale Latimer 787
Under Taker Wincle 881
Undercliff Experience Yates' 888
Undercurrent Oatmeal Pale Ale
  Siren Craft 846
Underwood Mild Dove Street 735
Underworld Brightside 708
Unhinged Mad Hatter 795
Unicorn Robinsons 835
Union Jack Green Tye 759
Union Wood Farm 884
Unit 3 IPA Coppice Side 724
Unity Strong Front Street 748
Uppermill Ale Greenfield 759
Urban Dusk Redemption 832
Urban Fox Slightly Foxed 847
Urban IPA Tiny Rebel 861
Urban Red Byatt's 714
Urbane Gorilla Hewitt's
  (Brentwood) 706
The Usual Milk Street 801
Utter Rotter Rotters 837
UXB Copper Kettle 724
  Quantock 828

V

V.I.P Tryst 866
V4 Vens 870
Vale Ale Buzzard 714
  Severn Vale 841
  Three Castles 859
Vale Mill Millstone 802
Valhalla North Yorkshire 811
  Red 831
Vallance's Stout Mighty Hop 800
Vanguard Ashley Down 684
  Twickenham 866
Vanilla Stout Bingham's 696
  Greenfield 759
Vectis Venom Island 779
Velocity Adur 679
Velvet Naylor's 807
Very Pale Ale Keystone 783
Veteran Hop Fuzz 772
Vibrant Ale Vibrant Forest 870
Vicar's Ruin Church End 719
Vicar's Daughter Fisher 745
Victoria Bitter Earl Soham 737
Victoria IPA Stringers 853
Victoria Works Weatheroak 873

Victorian Amber Ale Devil's
  Dyke 733
Victorian Porter 8 Sail 677
Victorious Wood Farm 884
Viking Bitter Liverpool Craft 790
Viking Gold Peerless 821
Viking Rudgate 838
Village Bike Potton 826
  VIP 871
Village Copper VIP 871
Village Ghost VIP 871
Village Idiot Blacker & Son 699
  White Horse 878
Village Life Beeston 693
  Fulstow 750
Village Lite VIP 871
Vindhya Hop Studio 773
VIP Copper Kettle 724
Virtuale Reality Reality 830
Vista London Brewing 792
Vital Spark Fyne 750
Vixen's Vice Alcazar 679
Volcano IPA Barney's 689
Volsung Rudgate 838
Voodoo Mild Great Heck 756
VPA (Verbeia Pale Ale)
  WharfeBank 877
VPA Portobello 825
VPA/Vale Pale Ale Vale 870

W

W&M Mild Derwent 732
W&M Pale Ale Derwent 732
W D Austerity Haworth
  Steam 766
Wagtail Best Bitter Allendale 680
Wagtail Great Oakley 757
Wainwright Thwaites 860
Wakering Gold George's (Hop
  Monster) 773
Wallasea Wench George's (Hop
  Monster) 773
Waller Wincle 881
Wallops Wood Bowman 703
Wally's Revenge Why Not 879
Waltzer Funfair 750
Wandle Sambrook's 840
Wantage Bells Betjeman 695
Warbler Bowman 703
Warlock Black IPA Hop
  Monster 773
Warlord Full Mash 749
Warminster Warrior Wessex 876
Warrior King Mercian 799
Warrior Evan Evans 740
  Fox 747
Warwickshire's Finest Merry
  Miner 800
Washington Old Hall Honey Beer
  Delavals 731
Wasp Nest Brampton 704
Wassail Ballard's 687
Wastwater Gold Great Gable 756
Waxies Dargle Brandon 705
Wayfarer Atlas (Orkney) 818
  Emsworth 740
Waylade Trossach's (Traditional
  Scottish Ales) 864
Wayland Smithy White Horse 878
Wealden Pale Ale High
  Weald 769
Weatheroak Weatheroak 873
Webb Ellis Wood Farm 884
Wee Beastie Scottish Borders 841

Wee Drop of Mischief Brandon 705
Weiner Bitter Pig Pub 823
Weiss Squad Fyfe 750
Weiss JW Sweetman 891
Welder Wobbly 883
Welland Valley Mild Great Oakley 757
Wellow Gold Maypole 799
Wells Bombardier Wells & Young's 875
Wells Eagle Wells & Young's 875
Wellstream Mile Tree 801
Welsh Beacons Brecon 706
Welsh Black Great Orme 757
Heart of Wales 767
Llangollen 791
Welsh Highland Bitter Snowdonia 848
Welsh Pale Ale Big Bog 695
Breconshire 706
Welsh Pride/Balchder Cymru Conwy 723
Welsh Red Bullmastiff 711
Welterweight Waveney 873
Wessenden Wheat Riverhead 835
West Coast Blond Stringers 853
West Coast IPA Black Iris 698
Phoenix 823
The West Highland Way Loch Lomond 792
West Adventure 679
Westerly Longhill 793
Westgate Gold Clark's 720
Westmorland Gold Barngates 689
Westoe IPA Jarrow 780
Westward Ho! Summerskills 854
Wet Your Whistle Whistling Kite 878
Whapweasel Hexhamshire 769
What the Fox's Hat Church End 719
What Would Jephers Do? Hand Drawn Monkey 763
What-Ho Ginger! Mighty Hop 800
Whatever! Prospect 827
Wheat a Second Willy Good 881
Wheat Ale Zerodegrees 889
Wheat Beer Old Bog 814
Wheatwave Vibrant Forest 870
Wheeltappers Bitter Platform 5 824
Wheeltapper's Wheatbeer Stonehouse 853
Wherry Woodforde's 885
Whimble Gold Radnorshire 828
Whippling Belvoir 694
WhirlyBird Mobberley 802
Whistler Longhill 793
Whistlestop Shardlow 842
Whitby Abbey Ale Black Dog (Hambleton) 763
Whitby Whaler Conquest 723
White Amarillo Durham 737
White Boar Village (Hambleton) 763
White Cloud Riverhead 835
White Dolphin Hoskins Brothers (Belvoir) 694
White Dragon Brown Cow 710
White Fang Black Iris 698
White Hind Quantock 828

White Horse Bitter Mill Green 801
White Horse 878
White Hot Consett Ale Works 723
White Knight Goff's 753
White Lady North Yorkshire 811
White Lion Bob's 701
White Max Tigertops 860
White Monk Phoenix 822
White Nancy Bollington 702
White Rat Rat 830
White Shield Worthington's 886
White Squall Newby Wyke 808
White Star Titanic 862
White Enville 740
Whiteball Masters 798
Whiter Shade of Pale Spire 850
Whitesheet Wallop Wessex 876
Whitstable Bay Pale Ale Shepherd Neame 843
Wicketkeeper Dunscar Bridge 737
Wife of Bath Canterbury Ales 716
The Wife's Bitter Plain Ales 824
Wight Diamond Island 779
Wight Gold Island 778
Wight Knight Island 779
Wild Blackberry Mild Offbeat 813
Wild Blonde South Hams 849
Wild Boar Buxton 714
Slaughterhouse 847
Wild Mule Rooster's 836
Wild Oates Oates 813
Wild Rhino Burnside 712
Wild Swan Thornbridge 858
Wild West Nobby's 808
Wild Ballard's 687
Wildcat Cairngorm 715
Wilder Ness Loch Ness 792
The Wildfowler Mulberry Duck 806
Will Scarlet Robin Hood 835
Willacade Broughton 710
William Cobbett Farnham 743
William George IPA Latimer 787
William Mucklows Dark Mild Bewdley 695
William Wallace Traditional Scottish Ales 864
William Wilberforce Freedom Ale Westerham 877
Wills Neck Quantock 828
Willy Brown Willy Good 881
Willy Hop Willy Good 881
Wiltshire Gold Arkell's 683
Wily Ol' Fox Red Fox 831
Winchester Ale Itchen Valley 780
Windermere Blonde Watermill 873
Windermere Pale Hawkshead 766
Windjammer Big River 696
Metalman 891
Windmill Bitter 8 Sail 677
Windrush Ale North Cotswold 809
Windsor Knot Windsor & Eton 881
Windy Miller 8 Sail 677
Winkle Picker Whitstable 879
Winklepicker Norfolk Square 809
Winnies Honey Heaven Coastal 721
Winter Ale Uncle Stuarts 869
Winter Meltdown Dark Star 730
Wise 4Ts 677
Wishing Well Trinity 865

WISPA (WharfeBank India Strong Pale Ale) WharfeBank 877
Witch Ball Special Cornish Chough (Cornish Chough) 725
Witch Hunter Neath 807
The Withyman North Curry 809
The Wizard Merlin 799
Wobble Gob Grafters 755
Wobble Bees 693
Wobbly Bob Phoenix 823
Woild Moild Wolf 883
Wold Gold Wold Top 883
Wolf in Sheep's Clothing Wolf 883
Wolf Allendale 680
Windswept 882
Wolfie Smith By the Horns 714
Woodcote Hammerpot 763
Worcester Gold Pope's 825
Worcester Sorcerer Sadler's 838
Worcestershire Sway Bewdley 695
Worcestershire Way Bewdley 695
Workie Ticket Mordue 804
Worm Catcher IPA Late Knights 787
Worth the Wait Beeston 693
Worthing Best Anchor Springs 682
Worthington's Bitter Molson Coors (Brains) 704
Wot's Occurring Great Oakley 757
WPA Wentworth 876
Wrassler's XXXX Porterhouse 891
The Wreck Brancaster (Beeston) 693
Wreckless RedWillow 833
Wren's Nest Howard Town 775
Wrexham Borders Bitter Llangollen 791
Wroxham Barns Bitter Uncle Stuarts 869
Wruff Night Watermill 873
Wychert Ale Vale 869
Wyoming #7 Pale Ale Shamblemoose 842
Wyvern Small Paul's 848

X

XB Batemans 690
Theakston 858
XK Dark Byatt's 714
XL Bitter Burton Bridge 712
XL Hop Studio 773
XOB Coppice Side 724
XP Hop Studio 773
XS Hop Studio 773
XSB South Hams 849
XX Mild Greene King 759
XXX Three Tuns 859
XXXB Batemans 690

Y

Yachtsmans Ale Island 778
Yakima Gold Crouch Vale 728
Yakima IPA Great Heck 756
Yakima Valley Arbor 682
Yankee Flag Silhill 845
Yankee Rooster's 836
Yatchsman Dorset (DBC) 734
Yella Belly Gold Batemans 690
Yellow Jersey Jolly Sailor 781

Yellow Lorry Stringers *853*
Yellow Wood IPA Wood
    Street *884*
Yellow Yetman's *888*
Yellowhammer Black Isle *698*
    O'Hanlon's *812*
Yer Tiz Braydon *705*
Yeti Griffin *760*
Yewbarrow Great Gable *756*
Yo Boy! Mersea Island *800*
Yogi Beer Piddle *823*
Yorks Nook *809*
Yorkshire Blonde Ossett *818*
Yorkshire Classic Great
    Yorkshire *758*
Yorkshire Gold Leeds *788*
Yorkshire Golden Great
    Yorkshire *758*
Yorkshire Pale Ale Great
    Heck *756*
Yorkshire Pale Great
    Yorkshire *758*
Yorkshire Porter Old Mill *815*
Yorkshire Pride Acorn *678*
Yorkshire Sparkle Treboom *864*
Yorkshire Terrier York *888*
Young Blonde Ambridge *681*
Young Bob Garage *751*
Young Chick Hunsbury Craft *776*
Young Pretender Isle of Skye *779*
Young's Bitter Wells &
    Young's *875*
Young's London Gold Wells &
    Young's *875*
Young's Special Wells &
    Young's *875*
YPA (Yorkshire Pale Ale)
    Rooster's *836*
Yukon Gold Dominion *734*
Yule Be Sorry Yates' *888*

Z

Zenith Cross Bay *728*
    Summer Wine *854*
Zeppelin Blue Ball *700*
Zetland Wheatbier Tryst *866*
Zig-Zag Stout Milk Street *801*
Zingiber Kent *783*
Zulu Lord Conrad's *794*
Zymic Stewart *852*

Award winning pubs

Local CAMRA Pubs of the Year

The Pub of the Year competition is judged by CAMRA members. Each of the CAMRA branches votes for its favourite pub: criteria include the quality and choice of real ale, atmosphere, customer service and value. The pubs listed below are current winners of the title; look out for the 🏆 symbol next to the entries in the Guide.

England

🏆 Bedfordshire
Albion, Ampthill
Devonshire Arms, Bedford
March Hare, Dunton

🏆 Berkshire
Bell Inn, Aldworth
Jack o' Newbury, Binfield
Nag's Head, Reading
Carpenters Arms, Windsor

🏆 Buckinghamshire
Farmers' Bar at The King's Head, Aylesbury
Red Lion, Marsworth
Lamb, Stoke Goldington

🏆 Cambridgeshire
Flying Pig, Cambridge
Townhouse Pub, Ely
Olde Sun, St Neots

🏆 Cheshire
Brewery Tap, Chester
Borough Arms, Crewe
Helter Skelter, Frodsham
Wharf, Macclesfield
Prospect, Runcorn

🏆 Cornwall
Star Inn, Crowlas

🏆 Cumbria
Midland Hotel, Appleby-in-Westmorland
Middle Ruddings Country Inn, Braithwaite
Manor Arms, Broughton-in-Furness
Agricultural Hotel, Penrith

🏆 Derbyshire
Smith's Tavern, Ashbourne
Old Poets' Corner, Ashover
Exeter Arms, Derby
Three Tuns, Dronfield
Rutland Arms, Holmesfield
Dewdrop Inn, Ilkeston
MoCa, Matlock
Royal Oak, Ockbrook
Black Bull's Head, Openwoodgate
Devonshire Arms, South Normanton

🏆 Devon
Butterleigh Inn, Butterleigh
Pig's Nose Inn, East Prawle
Ship & Pilot, Ilfracombe
Fortescue Hotel, Plymouth

🏆 Dorset
Three Elms Inn, North Wootton
Woodpecker, Spetisbury
Trooper Inn, Stourton Caundle

🏆 Durham
Quakerhouse, Darlington
Tap & Spile, Framwellgate Moor
Rat Race Ale House, Hartlepool

🏆 Essex
Old Lifeboat House, Clacton-on-Sea
Victoria Inn, Colchester
Compasses, Littley Green
Olde Trout Tavern, Southend-on-Sea
Rising Sun, Stanford-le-Hope
Prince of Wales, Stow Maries
Bell, Wendens Ambo

🏆 Gloucestershire & Bristol
Old Spot, Dursley
Horse & Groom, Upper Oddington

🏆 Hampshire
Prince of Wales, Farnborough
Waggon & Horses, Hartley Wintney
Hole in the Wall, Portsmouth
Black Horse, West Tytherley

🏆 Herefordshire
Barrels, Hereford

🏆 Hertfordshire
Orange Tree, Baldock
Sportsman, Croxley Green
Rising Sun, High Wych
Woodman, Wildhill

🏆 Isle of Wight
Old Village Inn, Bembridge

🏆 Kent
Halfway House, Brenchley
Foundry Brew Pub, Canterbury
Bell Inn, Ivychurch
Flower Pot, Maidstone
Three Hats, Milton Regis
Montefiore Arms, Ramsgate
George & Dragon, Swanscombe
Berry, Walmer

🏆 Lancashire
Hop Vine, Burscough
Snug, Carnforth
Strawberry Gardens, Fleetwood
Leyland Lion, Leyland

🏆 Leicestershire & Rutland
Blue Bell, Belmesthorpe
Queen's Head Inn, Hinckley
Rose & Crown, Hose
Salmon, Leicester
Organ Grinder, Loughborough
Boat, Melton Mowbray
Chandlers Arms, Shearsby

🏆 Lincolnshire
Five Bells, Claypole
Yarborough Hotel, Grimsby
Jolly Brewer, Lincoln
Gas Lamp Lounge, Louth
Royal Oak, Snitterby
Half Moon, Willingham by Stow

🏆 Greater London
Eagle Ale House, Battersea
Robin Hood & Little John, Bexleyheath
Tapping the Admiral, Camden Town
Hope, Carshalton
Catford Bridge Tavern, Catford
Eva Hart, Chadwell Heath
Grape & Grain, Crystal Palace
Fox, Hanwell
Olde Mitre Inne, High Barnet
Willoughby Arms, Kingston upon Thames
Churchill Arms, Notting Hill Gate
Old Fountain, Old Street
Sussex Arms, Twickenham

🏆 Greater Manchester
Costello's Bar, Altrincham
Jolly Nailor, Atherton
Victoria & Albert, Horwich
Park Hotel, Monton
Baum, Rochdale
Stalybridge Station Refreshment Rooms (Buffet Bar), Stalybridge
Berkeley, Wigan

☞ Merseyside
Gallaghers Pub & Barber's,
 Birkenhead
Freshfield Hotel, Formby
Clock Face, Prescot
Stamps Too, Waterloo
☞ Norfolk
Locks Inn, Geldeston
Angel Inn, Larling
☞ Northamptonshire
Queen's Head, Bulwick
Wig & Pen, Northampton
☞ Northumberland
Boathouse Inn, Wylam
☞ Nottinghamshire
Forest Lodge Hotel,
 Edwinstowe
Just Beer Micropub, Newark
Horse & Jockey, Stapleford
Staunton Arms, Staunton
 in the Vale
White Hart, West Stockwith
☞ Oxfordshire
Brewery Tap, Abingdon
Chequers, Chipping Norton
Bear at Home, North Moreton
Shoulder of Mutton,
 Wantage
☞ Shropshire
Cross Keys, Selattyn
Fighting Cocks, Stottesdon
Old Fighting Cocks, Telford:
 Oakengates
☞ Somerset
Raven, Bath
Plough, Congresbury
Crossways Inn, West Huntspill
☞ Staffordshire
Royal Oak, Barton-under-
 Needwood
Codsall Station, Codsall
Crown Inn, Elford
Cat Inn, Enville
Cross Keys Hotel, Hednesford
Holy Inadequate, Stoke-on-
 Trent: Etruria
Royal Exchange, Stone
☞ Suffolk
Dove, Bury St Edmunds
Fat Cat, Ipswich
Oddfellows, Pakefield
Cherry Tree, Yaxley
☞ Surrey
Happy Man, Englefield Green
Running Horse, Leatherhead
Surrey Oaks, Newdigate
☞ East Sussex
Dolphin, Hastings
Brewers Arms, Lewes
934

☞ West Sussex
Wilkes' Head, Eastergate
Gardeners Arms, Sompting
Jolly Tanners, Staplefield
☞ Tyne & Wear
Free Trade Inn, Newcastle:
 Byker
Isis, Sunderland
☞ Warwickshire
Royal Oak, Kenilworth
Seven Stars, Rugby
Griffin Inn, Shustoke
Bear at the Swan's Nest Hotel,
 Stratford-upon-Avon
Wild Boar, Warwick
☞ West Midlands
Starving Rascal, Amblecote
Wellington, Birmingham:
 City Centre
Bishop Vesey, Boldmere
Greyhound Inn, Coventry
Vaults, Knowle
Red Cow, Lower Gornal
Duke of Cambridge,
 Short Heath
Hog's Head, Wolverhampton
☞ Wiltshire
Three Crowns, Chippenham
Red Lion, Cricklade
Winchester Gate, Salisbury
☞ Worcestershire
Weighbridge, Alvechurch
Fleece Inn, Bretforton
Hollybush, Stourport-on-Severn
Plough, Worcester
☞ East Yorkshire
Green Dragon, Beverley
Goodmanham Arms,
 Goodmanham
Wellington Inn, Hull
☞ North Yorkshire
North Riding Brew Pub,
 Scarborough
Ferry Boat Inn, Thorganby
Fox & Hounds, West Witton
☞ South Yorkshire
Old No. 7, Barnsley
Salutation Hotel, Doncaster
Beehive Inn, Harthill
Shakespeare's, Sheffield:
 Kelham Island
☞ West Yorkshire
Fighting Cock, Bradford
Junction, Castleford
Sportsman, Huddersfield
Boltmakers Arms, Keighley
New Inn, Liversedge
Old Cock, Otley
Masons Arms, Todmorden

Wales

☞ Glamorgan
City Arms, Cardiff
Gwaelod-y-Garth Inn,
 Gwaelod-y-Garth
Boar's Head, Tyla Garw
☞ Gwent
Coach & Horses, Chepstow
Star Inn, Llanfihangel
 Tor-y-Mynydd
☞ Mid-Wales
Sportsman, Newtown
Ancient Briton, Pen-y-Cae
Star Inn, Talybont on Usk
☞ North-East Wales
Royal Oak, Wrexham
☞ North-West Wales
Albion Ale House, Conwy
Snowdonia Parc, Waunfawr
☞ West Wales
Queen's Hotel, Carmarthen
Druid Inn, Goginan
Taberna Inn, Herbrandston

Scotland

☞ Aberdeen & Grampian
Marine Hotel, Stonehaven
☞ Ayrshire & Arran
Village Inn, Fairlie
☞ Borders
Cobbles, Kelso
☞ Dumfries & Galloway
Cavens Arms, Dumfries
☞ Greater Glasgow
 & Clyde Valley
State Bar, Glasgow
Callum's, Johnstone
☞ Highlands & Western Isles
Benleva Hotel, Drumnadrochit
☞ Kingdom of Fife
Central Bar, St Andrews
☞ Loch Lomond, Stirling
 & The Trossachs
Tappit Hen, Dunblane
☞ Tayside
Phoenix, Dundee

Northern Ireland

☞ Crown, Belfast

Channel Islands

☞ Guernsey
Cornerstone Café Bar,
 St Peter Port
☞ Jersey
Lamplighter, St Helier

Isle of Man

☞ White House Hotel, Peel

Readers' recommendations

Suggestions for pubs to be included or excluded

All pubs are regularly surveyed by local branches of the Campaign for Real Ale to ensure they meet the standards required by the *Good Beer Guide*. If you would like to comment on a pub already featured, or on any you think should be featured, please fill in the form below (or a copy of it), and send it to the address indicated. Alternatively, email **gbgeditor@camra.org.uk**. Your views will be passed on to the branch concerned. Please mark your envelope/email with the county where the pub is, which will help us to direct your comments efficiently.

Pub name:

Address:

Reason for recommendation/criticism:

Pub name:

Address:

Reason for recommendation/criticism:

Pub name:

Address:

Reason for recommendation/criticism:

Your name and address:

Please send to: [Name of county] Section, Good Beer Guide,
230 Hatfield Road, St Albans, Hertfordshire AL1 4LW

Have your say

Feedback on the Good Beer Guide

We are always trying to improve the *Good Beer Guide* for our readers and we welcome your feedback. If you have any suggestions for how the *Good Beer Guide*, Good Beer Guide Mobile Edition or sat-nav POI could be improved, please let us know. Simply fill out the form below (or a copy of it) and send it to the address indicated, or make your comments on our website at: **www.camra.org.uk/gbgfeedback**. Thank you.

Colour sections:

Pubs section:

Brewery section:

Good Beer Guide e-book:

Good Beer Guide Mobile:

Good Beer Guide sat-nav POI:

What other suggestions do you have?

Please send to: Good Beer Guide – Have your say,
230 Hatfield Road, St Albans, Hertfordshire AL1 4LW

National Brewery Centre

Britain's proud brewing heritage and the crucial role played by Burton upon Trent are celebrated at the National Brewery Centre in the town. And beer lovers can support the role of the centre and help to protect the valuable collection of archives and artefacts held at Burton by becoming members of the National Brewery Heritage Trust.

For centuries, Burton has been an important brewing centre, due to the remarkable quality of the water drawn from wells and springs in the Trent Valley. The water is rich in gypsum and magnesium that act as flavour enhancers, drawing out the full flavours of malt and hops.

In the 18th century, Burton's reputation grew due to the success of a rich, strong, copper-coloured beer known as Burton Ale. As Britain's waterways developed, it was possible to export Burton Ale to London and other centres – and also to Europe, Russia and the Baltic States.

In the 19th century, Burton's fame grew as a result of a new style of beer brewed in the town: India Pale Ale. The powerful East India Company, which controlled trade in the sub-continent, encouraged the Burton brewers to develop a beer suitable for 'the Raj' and the large number of civil servants and troops based in India.

The leading Burton brewers harnessed the new technologies of the Industrial Revolution to use pale malt in their breweries. Previously, malt had been cured over wood fires, which produced brown malt and brown beer. The invention of coke made it possible for the first time to brew a genuinely pale beer. The result was India Pale Ale – IPA for short – that was exported in large quantities at first to India and later to Australia, New Zealand and the United States.

By 1881, 31 breweries in the town produced more than one million barrels of beer a year. At the turn of the 19th century, Bass alone was producing a million barrels of beer a year from three breweries in Burton and for a time was the biggest brewer in the world. The town's success was built on IPA and also lower-strength pale ale developed for the British market.

The key role of Burton in British brewing was commemorated in 1977 by the opening of the Bass Museum in part of the brewery's buildings. The museum traced the history of brewing in the town, the development of Burton Ale and IPA, and the role of scientists in improving the quality of beer in the 19th century. It also highlighted the social history of the town, showing the skills and the lives of the thousands of workers involved in malting, brewing and coopering. The site is also a repository of an invaluable archive of brewing records, artefacts and books.

When Bass left brewing in 2000, Coors – later Molson Coors – took over the museum and renamed it the Coors Visitor Centre. At its peak the museum attracted 12,000 visitors annually but, under-promoted, numbers declined and Molson Coors said it was losing £1 million a year.

Old brewing vessels form some of many artefacts at the brewery centre

It closed the museum in 2008 and created uproar among beer lovers throughout the country. The local MP, Janet Dean, called a meeting in the town that set up a task group to investigate ways to save the museum.

Just two years later, in 2010, the museum reopened, renamed the National Brewery Centre. As a result of protracted talks with the task group, Molson Coors handed over the running of the site to Planning Solutions, an experienced organiser of such visitor attractions. The centre features interactive displays and widens the scope of the centre to include the history of brewing throughout the country, including archive material from the now-closed Tetley Brewery in Leeds. Dray horses are stabled on site and old locomotives are on display to stress the importance of the rail system to Burton in the 19th and early 20th centuries.

A new micro-plant, William Worthington's Brewery, was installed by Molson Coors at a cost of £1 million. This enables visitors to watch the brewing process and then taste the end products in a bar on the site, part of a restaurant that serves highly-regarded food. SIBA, the Society of Independent Brewers, has moved its offices to the centre, while CAMRA has held its annual awards lunch there for the past three years.

Visitor numbers at the centre were small to begin with but they have gradually built up and it has now become a popular and well-attended site. It really is an excellent and engaging attraction with interest not just for beer lovers but the whole family. So if you are near Burton, do make a visit.

The role of the centre has been underscored by the creation of the National Brewery Heritage Trust, a voluntary and independent body that supports the centre. The trust's aims are:

- The protection, preservation and making available to the public the collection of archives and artefacts of brewing held at the NBC;
- The maintenance and expansion of the collection and ensuring it remains intact in perpetuity;

Beers can be bought from the museum shop

- Supporting educational displays and events that demonstrate the impact of brewing on social and economic development, not just in the UK but world-wide;
- Promoting a greater understanding of the history of brewing.

The trust is registered as a charity and was due to be officially launched at the centre in October 2013. CAMRA, among others, is heavily involved in the work of the trust. The treasurer is John Arguile of the Campaign's Derby branch and one of the directors is Nik Antona, a member of CAMRA's National Executive. Other directors include former MP Janet Dean and current MP Andrew Griffiths.

Membership of the trust costs £25 a year. Benefits include a 20 per cent discount on entrance fees at the NBC, NBC events, items purchased in the shop and meals in the restaurant. Members receive a newsletter and other trust publications. Corporate membership is also available at £100 a year.

For information on how to become a member of the trust, visit the trust's website: **www.nationalbreweryheritagetrust.co.uk**.

The National Brewery Centre is at Horninglow Street, Burton upon Trent, Staffs, DE14 1NG. For information about opening hours and events, see: **www.nationalbrewerycentre.co.uk**.

Early 20th-century vehicles, including the White Shield car, are on display at Burton

Books for beer lovers

300 More Beers to Try Before You Die!
Roger Protz

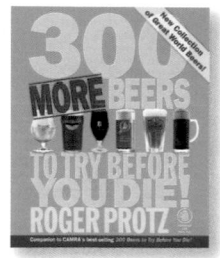

300 More Beers to Try Before You Die! takes beer lovers on an exciting new odyssey through 300 of the best beers from around the world. A companion volume to the best-selling *300 Beers to Try Before You Die!*, award-winning beer writer Roger Protz selects 300 more beers that represent the most interesting products of the brewer's art available today. The book charts the world-wide beer revival and features new ales from America, rediscovered classics like English abbey beer and inventive new twists on age-old recipes from experimental brewers in Europe and beyond, plus much, much more.

£14.99 ISBN 978-1-85249-295-3   CAMRA members' price £12.99

Good Bottled Beer Guide
Jeff Evans

A pocket-sized guide for discerning drinkers looking to buy bottled real ales and enjoy a fresh glass of their favourite beers at home. The new eighth edition of the *Good Bottled Beer Guide* is completely revised, updated and redesigned to showcase the very best bottled British real ales now being produced, and detail where they can be bought. Everything you need to know about bottled beers; tasting notes, ingredients, brewery details, and a glossary to help the reader understand more about them.

£12.99 ISBN 978-1-85249-309-7   CAMRA members' price £10.99

London Pub Walks
Bob Steel

CAMRA's pocket-size walking guide to London is back. This fantastic second edition is packed with interesting new routes, fully updated classic routes from the first edition, new pubs and a special selection of routes that take full advantage of London's public transport network. With 30 walks around more than 190 pubs, CAMRA's *London Pub Walks* enables you to explore the entire city while never being far from a decent pint.

£9.99 ISBN 978-1-85249-310-3   CAMRA members' price £7.99

Great British Pubs
Adrian Tierney-Jones

Great British Pubs is a practical guide that takes you around the very best public houses in Britain and celebrates the pub as a national institution. Every kind of pub is represented in these pages with categorised listings featuring full-colour photography illustrating a host of excellent pubs from the seaside to the city and from the historic to the ultra-modern. Articles on beer brewing, cider making, classic pub food recipes and traditional pub games are included to help the reader fully understand what makes a pub 'Great'.

£14.99 ISBN 987-1-85249-265-6   CAMRA members' price £12.99

Britain's Best Real Heritage Pubs
Geoff Brandwood

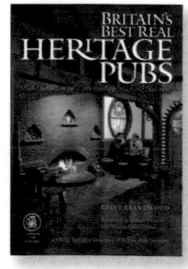

This new full-colour guide lists 270 pubs throughout the UK that have interiors of real historic significance – some over a century old. Illustrated with high quality photography, the book's extensive listings are the product of years of surveying and research by CAMRA's Pub Heritage Group, which is dedicated to preserving and protecting our rich pub heritage. The book features a forward by Simon Thurley, Chief Executive of English Heritage.

£9.99 ISBN 978-1-85249-304-2   CAMRA members' price £7.99

300 Beers to Try Before You Die!
Roger Protz

300 beers from around the world, handpicked by award-winning journalist and author Roger Protz for you to try before you die! This revised edition presents a comprehensive portfolio of top beers from the smallest micro-breweries in the U.S. through family-run British breweries to the world's largest brands. This book is indispensible for both beer novices and aficionados.

£12.99 ISBN 978-1-85249-273-1   CAMRA members' price £10.99

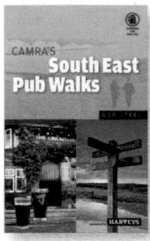

South East Pub Walks
Bob Steel

South East Pub Walks is a pocket-sized guide to some of the best walking and best pubs in South East England. It features 30 walks of varying lengths, all accessible by public transport and aimed at both the casual walker and more serious hiker. Each route has been selected for its unique and varied landscape, and its beer, with the walks taking you on a tour of the best real ale pubs the area has to offer. The essential guide for anyone wanting to see and taste the best of South East England.

£9.99 ISBN 978-1-85249-287-8   CAMRA members' price £7.99

101 Beers Days Out
Tim Hampson

101 Beer Days Out is the perfect handbook for the beer tourist wanting to explore beer and brewing culture in their local area and around the UK. From historic city pubs to beer festivals; idyllic country pub walks to rail ale trails; tourist brewery tours to serious brewing courses – Britain has beer and brewing experiences to rival any in the world. *101 Beer Days Out* brings together for the first time the best of these experiences, ordered geographically and with full visitor information, maps and colour photography – the best way to celebrate Britain's national drink.

£12.99 ISBN 978-1-85249-288-5   CAMRA members' price £10.99

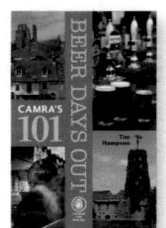

London's Best Beer, Pubs & Bars
Des de Moor

London's Best Beer, Pubs & Bars is the essential guide to beer drinking in London. This practical book is packed with detailed maps and easy-to-use listings to help you find the best places to enjoy perfect pints in the capital. Laid out by area, find the best pubs serving the best British and international beers wherever you are. Features tell you more about London's rich history of brewing and the city's vibrant modern brewing scene. The venue listings include a variety of real ale pubs, bars and other outlets with detailed information on opening hours, local landmarks, and public transport links to make planning any excursion quick and easy.

£12.99 ISBN 978-1-85249-285-4   CAMRA members' price £10.99

CAMRA's Book of Beer Knowledge
Jeff Evans

This absorbing, pocket-sized book is packed with beer facts, feats, records, stats and anecdotes so you'll never be lost for words at the pub again. More than 200 entries cover the serious, the silly and the downright bizarre from the world of beer. Inside this pint-sized compendium you'll find everything from the biggest brewer in the world to the beers with the daftest names. A quick skim before a night out and you'll always have enough beery wisdom to impress your friends.

£7.99 ISBN 978-1-85249-292-2   CAMRA members' price £6.99

Order these and other CAMRA books online at **www.camra.org.uk/books**, ask your local bookstore, or contact: CAMRA, 230 Hatfield Road, St Albans, AL1 4LW. Telephone 01727 867201.